"E. J. W. GIBB MEMORIAL"
SERIES

NEW SERIES, XX

SANGLAX

A Persian Guide to the Turkish Language

by

MUHAMMAD MAHDĪ XĀN

Facsimile Text

with an Introduction and Indices

by SIR GERARD CLAUSON

PRINTED FOR
THE TRUSTEES OF THE "E. J. W. GIBB MEMORIAL"
AND PUBLISHED BY MESSRS. LUZAC AND COMPANY LTD.
46 GREAT RUSSELL STREET, LONDON, W.C.1
1960

PRINTED IN GREAT BRITAIN BY HEADLEY BROTHERS LTD
109 KINGSWAY LONDON WC2 AND ASHFORD KENT

THIS VOLUME
IS ONE OF A SERIES
PUBLISHED BY THE TRUSTEES OF
"THE E. J. W. GIBB MEMORIAL"

The funds of this Memorial are derived from the Interest accruing from a Sum of money given by the late MRS. GIBB *of Glasgow, to perpetuate the Memory of her beloved Son*

ELIAS JOHN WILKINSON GIBB

and to promote those researches into the History, Literature, Philosophy and Religion of the Turks, Persians and Arabs, to which, from his Youth upwards, until his premature and deeply lamented Death in his forty-fifth year, on December 5, 1901, his life was devoted.

تِلْكَ آثارُنا تَدُلُّ عَلَيْنا . * فَانْظُرُوا بَعْدَنا إِلَى ٱلآثارِ

"*These are our works, these works our souls display;*
Behold our works when we have passed away."

PUBLISHER FOR THE TRUSTEES

MESSRS. LUZAC AND CO., LTD.,
46 GREAT RUSSELL STREET, LONDON, W.C.1.

TABLE OF CONTENTS

INTRODUCTION

TRANSCRIPTION

1. No generally accepted system of "Latin" transcription of the Turkish languages at present exists. The official alphabet of the Turkish Republic, used for writing Republican Turkish is, however, now widely used in scientific work on other Turkish languages and has been adopted for use in this book with four additions to represent sounds not separately represented in that alphabet, and one convention which departs from the conventions of that alphabet when used for writing Republican Turkish. The additions are (a) **é** to represent the closed *e* (as in French "été") described in the Sanglax as *kasra bilā işbā*ᶜ (see para. 61 (5)); (b) **w,** the labial semi-vowel (as in English "water") to represent consonantal *wāw,* since that is the likeliest pronunciation of that letter in Çağatay, and since **w,** which in many languages is pronounced as a voiced labial spirant, is less misleading than **v,** which is nowhere pronounced as a labial semi-vowel; (c) **x** to represent the unvoiced back guttural fricative (as in German "buch", or Scottish "loch"); (d) **ŋ** to represent the guttural nasal (as in English "sing") described in the Sanglax as *(nūn wa) kāf ma*ᶜ*a'l-imāla.* The convention is that with back vowels only **ğ,** and never **g,** is used and with front vowels only **g** and never **ğ.**

2. To avoid confusion, the same alphabet is used to transcribe words in Arabic, Persian and Mongolian (but not other languages), whether they are unassimilated loan-words in Turkish or words directly quoted from those languages, with one alteration and various additions. The alteration is that *qāf* is transcribed **q,** and not **k** as it is in Turkish transcriptions. The additions are (a) the marking of long vowels with a superimposed stroke—**ā, ī, ū**; (b) **ṯ** and **ḏ** for the unvoiced and voiced dental spirants* (as in English "think" and "that"); (c) **ḥ, ṣ, ḍ, ṭ** and **ẓ** to represent the Arabic "hard" letters usually so represented; (d)ᶜ for Arabic ᶜ*ayn*; and (e)ᵓ for medial, but not initial, Arabic *hamza* and the intervocalic hiatus in Mongolian. Neither of the last two signs is regarded as having an independent alphabetical position.

3. The actual transcriptions of Turkish words in this book are, in a sense, subjective, since the author of the Sanglax had perforce to use a very unsatisfactory alphabet, and his intentions are often uncertain; he tried by the use of certain technical terms (see para. 61) to make it more precise, but they were insufficient and he used them less fully than he might have. In particular, he had no means of distinguishing between back and front vowels, except in the case of verbs. Thus my transcriptions represent what I believe to have been the author's pronunciation of the words concerned (it will be noted that his "Rūmī"

---

* The voiced dental spirant existed in some Turkish languages until the 13th or 14th Century and sporadically a little later; it occurs twice in the Sanglax, in **çoḏın** "iron", mentioned (215v. 11) as the original form of **çoyın,** and in the (Sogdian) loan-word **ıxşıḏ.**

pronunciations do not always conform to the contemporary Osmanli pronunciation), and in cases of doubt I have added an asterisk.*

4. For Arabic a normal standard transcription is used, *mutatis mutandis*; similarly for Persian a standard system, including the conventional **a, i, u** for *fatḥa*, *kasra* and *ḍamma*; although the author's terminology (see para. 61 (5)) points rather towards **a, é** and **o,** the latter would look unusual and might be misleading.* For Mongolian, where the four authorities which I have used (see para. 46) have widely differing systems of transcription, a normalized system has been devised which is at any rate intelligible, though no doubt inaccurate in points of detail when applied to spoken Mongolian of any period.

5. The complete transcription alphabet employed (letters not normally used in Turkish transcriptions being bracketed) is, therefore:—

(ᶜ, ᵓ), **a, b, c, ç, d, ḏ,** (**ḍ**), **e, é, f, g, ğ, h,** (**ḥ**), **ı, i, j, k, l, m, n, ŋ, o, ö, p,** (**q**), **r, s,** (**ṣ**), **ş, t,** (**ṯ, ṭ**), **u, ü, w, x, y, z,** (**ẓ**).

ALPHABETICAL ORDER

6. It would not, however, be sensible to compile lists of Turkish words, particularly words belonging to several different Turkish languages, in the rigid order of this expanded alphabet, since the result would be that different forms of the same word, e.g. **epri-, ipre-, ofra-, öpre-; cercer, cércer; çérge, cérke; dapkur, tapkur** (all of which occur in the Sanglax) would appear in quite different places in the list and might never be linked together.

7. What had, therefore, to be devised for nearly all the Indices in this book† was a *quasi-alphabetical* arrangement, which would, so far as possible, bring different forms of the same word together, and so make it possible to discover rapidly whether a particular word occurs in the Sanglax, irrespective of the exact quality of the vowels and consonants of the form or forms listed therein.

8. As a foundation for such a quasi-alphabetical arrangement the letters of the expanded alphabet were arranged in the following fourteen groups, each containing letters which may interchange with one another in the various Turkish languages:—

1. (vowels) **a, e, é, ı, i, o, u, ö, ü,** prefixed ᶜ being disregarded.
2. (labials) **b, p, f, w.**
3. (affricates) **c, ç, j.**‡

* The fact that only (back) **a** and **u** are used in Persian transcriptions creates one minor difficulty, in the case of words containing *kāf*. Among the transcribed Persian loan-words which do not seem to have become fully assimilated in Turkish will be found such words as **kal** (300v. 25), in which, at first sight, a *qāf* might be implied; in case of doubt a reference to Index I (if the **k** is initial) or to the original text will show which letter is involved.

† The point did not arise on Index I, which is merely a list of all the words in the Sanglax in the order in which they occur, those which do not occur as main entries being inserted (indented) in the appropriate places according to their forms in Arabic script. Nor did it arise on Index X, a series of short lists of authorities arranged in their ordinary alphabetical order, titles like "Mīrzā" being disregarded.

‡ **J** is, of course, neither an affricate nor a basic Turkish sound, it occurs only in loan-words and secondary forms; in such cases it usually replaces, or is replaced by, **c** and it is accordingly placed here, although in some Turkish languages it is a secondary form of **ş.**

4. (dentals) **d, ḏ, (ḍ), t (ṯ, ṭ).**
5. (back gutturals) **ğ, k, x, (ḥ, h).***
6. (front gutturals) **g, k, (h).***
7. **l**; 8. **m**; 9. **n, ŋ**; 10. **r**; 11. **s, (ṣ)**; 12. **ş**; 13. **y**; 14. **z, (ẓ).**

9. The simple conception of treating letters in groups and not individually, however, still left various points of arrangement to be decided, for example the relative priorities of **cida-** (verb) and **cida** (noun); **telim** and **dilim; diblik** and **dibelik.** As a result of trial and error the following rules were found to lead to the simplest and most logical arrangement:—

(1) Verbs precede nouns with the same phonetic make-up, i.e. **cida-** precedes **cida,** and **bön**– precedes **biŋ.**

(2) Since the quality of the vowels in Turkish words is usually more stable than that of certain consonants (in particular voiced and unvoiced consonants alternate in the most confusing fashion in various Turkish languages), more regard is had to vowels than consonants in determining the order of words of the same general phonetic make-up, i.e. **telim** precedes **dilim.**

(3) Shorter words precede longer ones of the same general phonetic make-up, i.e. **tart-** precedes **tarat-** and **diblik dibelik.**

10. The application of the system, so far as it applies to the beginnings of words considered in isolation (in specific cases it might be varied by the phonetic make-up of the later parts of words), is exemplified in Index II, and its application to a mass of over a thousand words in Index III. Although it may seem confusing at first that **w** precedes **c** and that **t** immediately follows **d,** it will be found that, once the system is mastered, it is much easier to discover whether a word, or one synonymous with it but with a somewhat different phonetic make-up, exists in the Sanglax, then it would be by any other system hitherto used in Turkish dictionaries. Anyone who has tried to find a few words in Radloff's great Wörterbuch will readily appreciate the truth of this statement, since in that book, for example, **çöşkur-** and **çüşkür-,** both transcriptions of the same Çağatay verb, will be found on different pages (see the footnote to para. 38). **Çıban** (see para. 75) is another example of a word of which the various authentic and spurious forms are widely separated.

THE ARRANGEMENT OF THE SANGLAX

11. The Sanglax is a hand-book (grammar and vocabulary) in Persian of the Turkish language, and more specifically the variety known as Çağatay Turkish, written in the middle of the 18th Century. It is made up of four unequal parts.

12. Part I, extending from the beginning of the book to 26r. 29†, is the author's introduction and a treatise on Çağatay grammar, with references to some other Turkish languages, especially "Rūmī", which means, broadly speaking, but not quite precisely, Osmanli (see para. 41). The author explains (2r. 4) that he gave the whole work the name

* It should be noted that **k** and **h** with back vowels are in a different group from **k** and **h** with front vowels.

† All references like this are to the folio, its front (r.) or back (v.) and the line thereon, of the MS. reproduced herein.

Sanglax, "a stony place", because, as he remarks discouragingly, of the hardness of the language, and (2v. 4) that he gave to this part the separate name **Mabānī'l-luğat,** "the foundations of the language".

13. This is the only part of the whole work which has so far been printed. It was published by the late Sir Denison Ross under the title "*The Mabānī'l-Lughat, being a Grammar of the Turki Language in Persian by Mirzā Mehdi Khān*"; Bibliotheca Indica, New Series No. 1225, Calcutta, 1910. The text was printed from the MS. reproduced herein, without collation with other MSS., and is reasonably accurate. It is preceded by an Introduction (hereafter quoted as "*Ross's Introduction*") containing a detailed "Analysis of Contents" which is a great help to readers trying to find a path through the matted jungle of the author's grammatical exposition. It was this edition that was recently used by Dr. J. Eckmann in his article "*Mirza Mehdi Chans Darstellung der tschagataischen Sprache*" (Analecta Orientalia memoriae Al. Csoma de Körös dicata, Budapest, 1942–7) and by Prof. K. H. Menges in his study "*Das Čagataische in der persischen Darstellung von Mīrzā Mahdī Xān*" (Abhandlungen der Geistes- und Sozialwissenschaftlichen Klasse 1956, No. 9, Akademie der Wissenschaften und der Literatur, Mainz) (the latter hereinafter quoted as "*Menges op. cit.*"). Between them they cover the grammatical side of the subject sufficiently to absolve me from any further reference to it.

14. I would, however, remark that the use of so narrow a basis for his studies has led Prof. Menges into some droll errors. For example (op. cit. p. 648), he gives a list of eight important Çağatay writers with whose works our author was apparently unacquainted. In fact, as will be seen from Index X, six of them are in fact quoted, two of them actually in Part I. Again (same page) he completely fails to grasp the distinction drawn by our author between his Çağatay and Rūmī authorities. Furthermore (op. cit. p. 653) he misunderstands the difference between vowels *ba-* and *bilā iṣbā*^{c} (see para. 61 (5)), which he takes to be a matter of quantity. Finally (p. 659) he says that the Sanglax, Bābur Nāma and Persian lexicographers all use the "Osmanli" orthography to spell **köŋültaş** and that this has led to the "false pronunciation" **kūkaltaş** in Persian, whereas if he had had access to 308r. 8 and 9 he would have realized that "foster brother" really was **kökelteş,** derived from the Mongolian loan-word **kökel,** "wet nurse".

15. It should be added, to complete the list of previous publications, that in 1950 B. Atalay published in the Türk Dil Kurumu series (C. II 31) a work entitled "*Mirza Mehdi Mehmet Han: Seng-lâh—Lûgat-i Nevai*", 171 pp. of facsimile and 10 pp. of remarks. As Menges (op. cit. p. 647) points out, what it contains is merely a good reproduction of an indifferent MS. of Part I, of less value than Ross's edition.

16. Part II (26r. 29–26v. 23), described as a *xātima* (epilogue) to Part I, is very short. It is a list of 12 verses, phrases or individual words occurring in the works of Nawā'ī of which our author did not know the meaning. Not all the words concerned are Turkish, and it may well be that the text in these passages is corrupt. But the existence of this part does provoke the thought that in other cases of difficult verses our author may have been over-zealous in finding meanings for obscure words which were actually only scribal errors, with the result that he may have included in Part III some purely imaginary words with imaginary meanings. I have noticed in Part III a number of words which are otherwise

unknown and do not look Turkish; they are annotated "d." (for "dubious") in Index I.*

17. Part III (27r. 1–353r. 21), the main part of the book, is a Turkish-Persian dictionary, of which more below. There are relics of an original division into five "parts" (*cuz'*); the first, presumably beginning at 27r. 1, is not mentioned, but *cuz'* II, III, IV and V begin at 119r. 20; 203v. 7; 263v. 8 and 317r. 18 respectively. The fullest title is at 263v. 8, "part IV of the different kinds and varieties of grammatical forms (*ṣiyağ*)". *Cuz'* I contains the words beginning with *alif*, *cuz'* II those beginning with *bā* and *tā*, *cuz'* III those beginning with *cīm* to *fā*, *cuz'* IV those beginning with *qāf* and *kāf* and *cuz'* V the remainder. As the list of conjugational forms (see para. 57) in fully conjugated verbs is slightly different in each *cuz'*, it seems likely that each *cuz'* represents different stages in the author's work. Apart from that they do not seem to have any functional significance.

18. Part IV (353r.–end), described as a *taḏyīl*, "appendix", is a list of Arabic and Persian words and phrases found in the poetical works of Nawā'ī and his *Mahbūbu'l-qulūb* which have not, in the author's opinion, been adequately explained by previous lexicographers. The first entry "*āb-i ātaş-rang*, an idiom for wine" is a fair specimen. The subject is one remote from the interest of most Turkish scholars, and I shall not refer to it further.

DATE OF COMPOSITION

19. Two chronograms in verse written below the colophons of all the three MSS., and printed in *Ross's Introduction*, p. v, purport to give the date of the completion of the Sanglax. Unfortunately one adds up to A.H. 1172 and the other to A.H. 1173; but, splitting the difference, we can take the most probable date as A.D. 1759. So far as Çağatay proper is concerned, therefore, the book was compiled two and a half centuries after its golden age and at a time when the Turkish spoken in the areas with which the author was familiar was probably an Özbek of a type not very different from that represented in nearly all the texts and part of the vocabulary of Vambéry's *Ćagataische Sprachstudien*, Leipzig, 1867. Indeed, as shown in Index IV, there are numerous references to what must be 18th Century colloquial dialects. The point must be borne in mind when considering to what extent the book can be taken as a safe guide to Classical Çağatay, particularly in regard to a matter so essentially subject to secular change as pronunciation.

THE MANUSCRIPTS

20. The Sanglax has always been a rare book. Fatḥ ᶜAlī Xan Kacar (see para. 33), writing in Persia in about 1860, said so, and Pavet de Courteille, writing in Paris almost simultaneously, said in the Preface (p. iv) to his "*Dictionnaire Turc-Oriental*", Paris, 1870, that he greatly regretted that he had never seen a copy (though in fact he need not have gone further than London or Oxford to do so), and so was compelled to base his own work on an epitome of it, the *Xulāṣa-i ᶜAbbāsī*, in which, incidentally, he placed a wholly undeserved confidence. Even to-day no more than three copies are known:—the MS. belonging to the E. J. W. Gibb Memorial Trust, reproduced herein, and hereafter referred

* Examples are **uclıb, ucsarrak, ötleş, ökte, asabkur, bağlankaz, bağam, bağındaş, palal, balar, bandur**; there are a good many more.

to as "G."; MS. Or. 2892 in the British Museum, hereinafter referred to as "L." (for "London"); and MS. Elliott 341 in the Bodleian Library, hereinafter referred to as "O." (for "Oxford"). Menges (op. cit. p. 646, note 2) says that Prof. Henning has informed him that there is a second MS. in the British Museum. This is a misapprehension; the reference which he quotes is the cross-reference in the *Catalogue of Persian Manuscripts* to Or. 2892, the main entry of which is in the *Catalogue of Turkish Manuscripts*.

21. **G.** This is a very fine MS.; the scribe was not only a masterly calligrapher but also, subject to the limitation mentioned below, an accurate copyist. The MS. is in the same hand throughout with only very minor variations in script. The scribe did, however, suffer from one limitation; he was obviously a Persian, with little or no knowledge of Turkish. He was very careful in copying the main "red ink" entries of Turkish words (except some of the conjugational forms) and the Persian part of the text, but he could copy the Turkish quotations only mechanically and often faultily. For example, in copying the Rūmī verse in 43v. 13 *ᶜāqil iseŋ wérme köŋül bağına, zağ ṣifat düşme anıŋ ağıŋa*, by writing **dérme** and **yağına** in the first half he made the whole at first sight unintelligible.

22. The MS. contains 367 folios measuring 13¼ × 8¾ inches (33.5 × 22 cm.) of fine, thin, strong Oriental paper, pale buff and not watermarked. The written surface is enclosed within a frame measuring 10¾ × 6 5/16 inches (27.2 × 16.1 cm.) internally. Folios 1r., 27r. and 367v. are blank. There are 17 lines on fol. 1v.; 23 lines on fol. 26v.; 28 lines each on fols. 21r. and v. and 29v.; 30 lines on fol. 29r.; 20 lines, a colophon of two lines and two sets of chronographic verses on fol. 367r.; and 29 lines on all the other pages. The spacing is so regular that a "reference-finder" can easily be constructed by laying a slip of paper on almost any page and writing the numbers of the lines on each edge of it. The first five folios and the last are a little frail and have been enclosed in silk gauze; the rest of the MS. is almost perfect. It is encased in a contemporary leather binding, without flap, of a dark coffee colour, with decorations painted in gold on the inside and outside of both boards. The text is written in a beautiful clear *Nasxī* in red and black ink. The use of the two inks varies slightly between the various Parts. In Part III the Chapter and Section headings (see para. 55) and the main entries (Turkish words to be translated) are in red, also the word *şiᶜr* preceding verse quotations, the three *nuqṭas* which mark the ends of *bayts* in such quotations, less systematically the overlinings of such words as *al-şāhid*, *çunānkı* (*gūyad*) before quotations and the three dates on fol. 367r. All the rest is in black. Exceptionally the colophon and two chronograms are in a small, almost illegible *Nastaᶜlīq*. The colophon (text printed in *Ross's Introduction* p. v), which is followed by the impression in black of a seal, presumably the scribe's, bearing the words *niᶜma'l-mawlā niᶜma'l-naṣīr* (Qurān, Sūra 8, 41, no doubt a delicate compliment to his patron) is in two lines, the script of which differs sufficiently to suggest that the second was added later. The first line states that the MS. was finished in the month of Ṣaᶜbān, A.H. 1188 (Oct.–Nov. A.D. 1774), having been written by the command of Mīrzā Muḥammad Nāṣir, whose name is preceded by a string of high-sounding titles; the second line states that, after it had been submitted to the patron, it was, by his command, collated throughout with the author's original MS. It is perhaps more than a coincidence that this is also the name of the author's father (see *Ross's Introduction* p. vi). The identity of the two names and the fact that the author's MS. was

available for collation suggest that this beautiful MS. was commissioned by the author's father, perhaps for presentation to some distinguished patron or friend.*

23. **O.** Elliott 341 is described briefly in the *Catalogue of the Persian, Turkish, Hindustani and Pushtu Manuscripts in the Bodleian Library*, by Sachau and Ethé, Oxford, 1889, No. 1760, as "a manuscript of 322 folios measuring 13¼ by 8¾ inches with 29 lines to the page written in Naskhi; binding with flowers". It is written on a fine, thin European watermarked paper of dead white colour. The colophon states that it was transcribed for Hācī Luṭf ᶜAlī (the author of the Ataşkada) in A.H. 1186 (A.D. 1772–3). It was indisputably written by the same copyist as G.; almost the only technical differences are that the Chapter and Section headings in Part III (written in red in G.) are illuminated in gold and that the writing is slightly more compressed, so that the MS. covers 45 fewer folios; but its general appearance is slightly less attractive owing to the dead white colour of the paper.

24. **L.** Or. 2892 is described briefly in the *Catalogue of the Turkish Manuscripts in the British Museum*, by Charles Rieu, London, 1888, as "a manuscript of 369 folios measuring 15¼ by 14 inches, with 27 lines, 6¾ inches long, to the page, written on Italian paper by various hands in a more or less cursive Nestalik or Shikasteh-āmīz, apparently in the 19th Century". There is no colophon; the two chronograms are written in the vacant space on the lower part of the last page. The basic accuracy of the text, which seems rather high, is masked by its extreme unsightliness. The first hand is reasonably neat and attractive, at any rate for the first few pages; the others are nearly all hideous and one or two practically illegible.

25. A comparison of the three MSS. poses a pretty problem in textual criticism. As stated above, G., except in the texts of Turkish quotations and some of the conjugational lists, gives the impression of unusual accuracy, as indeed it should if it was collated with the author's original MS. But in spite of this there are at least three short omissions:—(1) in 4r. 15, where *nawᶜ-i şaşum* follows immediately on *nawᶜ-i çahārum*; (2) in 71r. 18, where the translation of **örkebçi** immediately follows the spelling of **urğacı**; and (3) in 112v. 2, where the translation of **éliklen-** is followed by the statement that it is conjugated

* The MS. is, generally speaking, so clear as to render it eminently suitable for reproduction, and experiment showed that it remained perfectly legible even when reduced by about one-third, which greatly reduced the cost of production. It has, however, four minor defects. First the paper of some leaves is so thin that ghosts of the writing on the back of the page appear in some of the photographs. Fortunately this defect is noticeable almost exclusively in the last few pages, containing the Arabic and Persian vocabulary, which is happily of secondary importance. Furthermore, the glazed surface of the paper is so easily damaged by erasure that corrections written over an erasion are sometimes hard to read. Again the ink is not waterproof and water stains and other marks obscure the text to some extent in the original and very much more in the reproduction. Finally the differing photogenic qualities of red and black ink produce a somewhat uneven appearance, and every photograph must be a compromise aimed at showing the red ink passages clearly without over-exposing, and so blurring, the black ink ones. An attempt has been made to reduce these disadvantages to a minimum by preparing a press copy from two separate sets of photographs, the clearer of the two alternatives being chosen for each opening. This has involved some retouching of unduly faint passages, usually those in red ink. Where damaged passages could not be rendered legible either by retouching or patching, the text has been copied in a footnote. This has not been done consistently in the lists of conjugational forms since, in these cases, a reader sufficiently persevering to plough through such lists can easily restore the missing words himself. The small variations in scale inevitable in such a voluminous work, but causing difficulty in the use of "reference-finders", are much regretted. Words in red ink have been overlined in the facsimile, since they would otherwise be indistinguishable, and a cross has been inserted in the margin opposite each main entry so that they can easily be picked out.

like other verbs ending in **-t-.** There are also cases, more particularly in the conjugational lists and occasionally elsewhere, of apparent small errors of one sort or another, misspellings, omissions of single words and the like. A selective comparison of the passages concerned with O. showed that all three omissions and nearly all the errors in G. reappeared in O. One or two of these errors, however, were corrected in a second hand. I was not looking for errors in O. which did not occur in G.; but no doubt some exist and I did happen to notice one by chance, the spelling of **çığıldu** (218v. 27); they are not likely to be numerous or important. Comparison of the same selected passages with L. was more fruitful; the second and third omissions could be made good and a number of errors corrected. Against the passage corresponding to 4r. 15 (where the first omission occurs) there is a marginal note *nawᶜ-i pancum mulāḥaẓa na-şud.* But even so, some errors common to all three MSS. still remain which could not have existed in the author's original MS., though they might go back to his fair copy. For example, apart from the omission in 4r. 15, in 173r. 22 all MSS. have **tozı** for **torı**; in 208v. 6 all place **carlat- çarlat-** among the verbs beginning with **çal**; in 319r. 16 all omit the translation of **mandağan**; and in 339r. 8 all write **yanğu** but spell out the word as **yanku.** Incidentally the omission in 4r. 15 also occurs in Atalay's text. The stemma of the MS. tradition must therefore be reconstructed as follows, A representing the author's original MS.; X the common archetype of the three existing MSS. (possibly the author's fair copy); Y the MS. in which the second and third omissions occurred; and Z a possible intermediary between L (19th Century) and X (pre-A.D. 1772); there may, of course, have been more links in the chain, but it is unlikely.

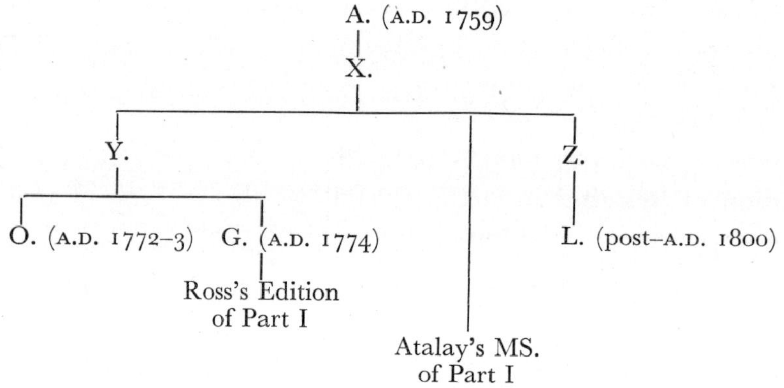

It is, of course, possible that somewhere in Asia other MSS. of the Sanglax still exist. There is no reason to suppose that Z has been destroyed, and the copy which Fath ᶜAlī Xān Kacar (see para. 33) saw in Persia in the middle of the 19th Century cannot have been L. or O., though it might have been G. But it is unlikely that any new MS. would provide any substantial improvement to the text of G., modified by the corrections from L. incorporated in the footnotes to the passages concerned in the facsimile and in Index I. There must be few Oriental works of comparable importance, of which we can say with equal confidence that we have the text practically in the form in which the author wrote it.

THE AUTHOR

26. Astonishingly little is known about the author, Muḥammad Māhdī Xān, as he calls himself (1v. 6); some biographical facts are set out in *Ross's Introduction*, pp. vi and vii,

and Menges (op. cit. p. 647). Briefly he had been, in modern terminology, a Civil Servant, the Private Secretary and Court Historiographer of Nādir Ṣāh, of whom he wrote two histories, the *Ta'rīx-i Nādirī* and the *Durra-i Nādirī*; but Nādir Ṣāh had been assassinated in A.H. 1160 (A.D. 1747), and the *Ta'rīx-i Nādirī* finished in A.H. 1161 (A.D. 1748), 11 years before the Sanglax was finished in A.H. 1172–3 (A.D. 1759); what he had been doing in the interim, and what post, if any, he held when he was writing the Sanglax we do not know. It is very likely that he was then, as I am now, just an old Civil Servant devoting his declining years to the study of Turkish philology. What is more important for estimating his capacity as a philologist is what can be learnt directly and by inference from the Sanglax itself.

27. Speaking perhaps with the undue indulgence of one old Civil Servant for another, I confess that I find him a rather agreeable old character. His own statement (IV. 6) that he had been from early years an eager reader of the works of Nawā'ī is fully borne out by the Sanglax itself. It is, of course, true that he was no etymologist (his etymology of **bosağa,** a Mongolian loan-word, in 134v. 10, and his derivations of **börk** from **börke-** (131v. 18) and **tab-** from **tabuk** (150v. 8) are merely typical examples of contemporary etymological technique), but he was a profound and original scholar much superior to his predecessors in the field of Çağatay lexicography. When he gives a quotation to illustrate the meaning of a word it is sometimes the same as one in the *Abuşka* (see para. 30), but more often than not he chooses quite a different one, when it would have been easier to copy the *Abuşka.* Indeed his knowledge was so great that when, as sometimes happens, a word is misspelt in the *Abuşka* with a supporting quotation, he can identify the passage and correct the error. For example under **üzgün** (74r. 1) he remarks that "the two Rūmī authors (one of whom was the author of the *Abuşka*) read the word **ürgün** with an **r** and supported it in their books with this quotation". The erroneous spelling and quotation will be found in the *Abuşka*, p. 101. Other engaging characteristics are the frankness, so rare among scholars, particularly of his period, with which he admits in Part II that there are passages and words that he does not understand, and the sense of humour which comes out in some of his criticisms of his predecessors. For example, in 79v. 16–18, he ends one such criticism with the words "although **ökte** does in fact mean *bī-hūda* ("nonsense") their explanations too are *bī-hūda*". Again, in 203r. 25, he ends an onslaught on Naṣīrī with the words "although he made one mistake about the (form of the) word and two about its meaning, in regard to the meaning (of the verse as a whole) he made three mistakes over a single word". Index X shows that he had read very widely, and IndexVA shows how careful he had been in noting Mongolian (sometimes only supposedly Mongolian) words in these authorities. Index VIII shows that he had at any rate a smattering of knowledge of a surprisingly wide range of foreign languages. Most surprisingly of all he had somehow heard of the Haitian word "cacique" and knew what it meant. The mention of the *yaŋı dunya* indicates that he got it from some Turkish authority.

28. At the same time there are some less attractive sides to his character. His proclivity for grinding out endless stereotyped and quite useless conjugations of verbs page after page points to a lack of appreciation of his readers' needs, and the fact that he devoted a whole *rasm* of Part I (24v. 3–25v. 20) to words misspelt in the works of Nawā'ī is evidence more of

pernicketiness than of broad scholarly judgement. Worst of all, perhaps, is his passion for fine language. He did not find the scope for this in the Sanglax that he had in the *Durra-i Nādirī*, that "linguistic *tour de force*" as Ross called it, but there are one or two passages in Part I which are pure gobbledygook; for example 2r. 17–19, where he obscures by a series of incongruous metaphors the simple statement that, when quoting familiar verses of Nawā'ī, he often does not trouble to give the author's name, but that extracts from other Çağatay authors are preceded by their names. Nevertheless, when all is said and done, his virtues greatly outweigh his defects, and his work is much the best of its kind.

THE EARLIER LEXICOGRAPHERS

29. In 1v. 8ff. the author gives a list of the earlier lexicographers whose works he had studied and, on the whole, found to be full of errors. These are "two Rūmī individuals whose names are not stated in their works" (usually referred to in Part III as *mu'allif-i Rūmī* or *mu'allifayn-i Rūmīya*), Tāli^c-i Harawī, Firāğī, Nadar ^cAlī (once, in 289v. 17, Nādar ^cAli) and Mīrzā ^cAbdu'l-calīl Naṣīrī (usually referred to in Part III as "Naṣīrī"). There are also five references (see Index XA. v.) to "the author of the *Mu'ayyadu'l-Fuḍalā*", who is probably not one of these.

30. It does not appear certain that the work of any of these authors has survived except that of one of the Rūmī individuals, whose work is quoted in 193r. 16 and 251v. 13 as *cāmi^c-i abuşğa*. This is the work published, with a useful introduction in French, by V. de Véliaminof-Zernof as "*Dictionnaire Djagatay-turc*", St. Petersburg, 1869. The identity of the two is proved by the fact that the two quotations mentioned above will be found on pp. 169 and 285 of the *Abuşka*, as this dictionary is called herein.

31. It is possible that the work of the second Rūmī individual is *al-luğat ^calā lisān Nawā'ī*, of which copies in Russia and Vienna are mentioned on p. 25 of the Introduction to the *Abuşka*, or perhaps the supposed epitome of the *Abuşka* referred to in Pavet de Courteille, op. cit., Preface p. ix (these two works may, of course, be identical). It is also, of course, possible that copies of the works of some of the other authors exist in the Soviet Union or elsewhere and will ultimately be discovered; the *Badāyi^cu'l-luğat* by an unknown author mentioned in p. 26 of the Introduction to the *Abuşka* may be one of them; but it is clear that the *Nāṣirī* (*sic*) of Mīrzā Qūlī Hidāyat referred to by that name in Pavet de Courteille, op. cit., Preface p. v, and by a different name in p. 27 of the Introduction to the *Abuşka* has nothing to do with the Naṣīrī of the Sanglax, and is a much later work. In any event we can bear the loss of these earlier works, if it is irreparable, with fortitude. Our author had clearly studied them very thoroughly, and the zeal with which he corrects their errors makes it very improbable that he would have omitted from his own work words which he found in them correctly translated. It seems that the primary authorities were the two "Rūmī" works, one of which, the *Abuşka*, we have, and the other of which may have been largely an epitome of it, but contained some original matter, since some quotations from "the Rūmī author", e.g. that in 111r. 22, cannot be traced in the *Abuşka*. On the other hand, the original matter in the rest cannot have been very voluminous, since our author points out (345v. 22) that the fact that the same error occurs in several of them clearly indicates that each of them slavishly followed his predecessors.

32. The special virtues of the *Abuşka*, which are not numerous, and those of the Sanglax are largely complementary. The earliest MS. of the *Abuşka* is dated A.H. 959 (A.D. 1552),* so the book must have been written hardly more than 50 years after the death of Nawā'ī in A.D. 1500 and 20 years after the death of Bābur in A.D. 1530. The author was, therefore, writing about what was still a living language and his notes on pronunciation, unfortunately scanty, must be treated with respect. Moreover both the author and his copyists were Turks and so understood what they were writing, in contrast with the copyists of the Sanglax, who probably did not (see para. 21). Unfortunately the book as a whole does not inspire the confidence which should *prima facie* be accorded to the work of an author who had such excellent potential sources of information to draw upon. Some of the errors exposed by the Sanglax, for example the gross mishandling of such a good Turkish word as *érdem* (99v. 3), are merely grotesque, and many of the entries aim at nothing more than turning unfamiliar Çağatay conjugational forms into familiar Osmanli ones. The author must have had access to some kind of literary tradition, for example he got the meaning of **ürgün** (**üzgün**) right (see para. 27), even though he got the spelling wrong and so destroyed the etymological basis of that meaning. Looking at the matter as a whole, it will, I think, be generally accepted that the *Abuşka* is certainly right only where the Sanglax agrees with it, that it is certainly wrong if the Sanglax disagrees with it, and that if it contains a word or meaning not contained in the Sanglax (there are very few) the entry should *prima facie* be regarded with suspicion.

A LATER ÇAĞATAY LEXICOGRAPHER

33. This is the convenient point at which to refer to the work of Fatḥ ᶜAlī Xān Kacar entitled alternatively the *luğat-i atrākīya* or the *bahcatu'l-luğāt*. The late A. A. Romaskevich described this work in his article (in Russian) "*A new Çağatay-Persian Dictionary*" in the miscellany "*Mir Ali Shir*", published by the Soviet Academy of Sciences, Leningrad, 1928, to commemorate the 500th anniversary of the poet's birth. The author, according to his autobiography, finally completed his work in A.D. 1862, towards the end of a long life largely devoted to the study of the works of Nawā'ī. His statement is that it was entirely his own work, derived from knowledge gathered in the course of a lifetime of private study, with the help of a few teachers and the opportunity to peruse a copy of the Sanglax for three days only. His account of the Sanglax, which he criticizes violently for specified deficiencies (op. cit. p. 90), is so completely divorced from the truth that it is hard to resist the conclusion that his object was to discourage his readers from searching for this rare book and so finding him out in a barefaced lie. In fact, so far as can be judged from the extracts given by Romaskevich, his work is largely a faulty transcription of the Sanglax. For example (op. cit. p. 95, note 6) he reproduces the very odd entry about the Haitian word "cacique" (see para. 27); again all the eight geographical notes (op. cit. p. 97) are direct quotations from the Sanglax, except that **akray** is an error for **ak saray, ıpa kuyruğı** for **ıpar kuyruğı** and **babğız** for **bayğız**; similarly of the tribal names (same page) **otuz iki, xalac** and **iştek** are correct and **öremiz** (for **ödemiş**) and **şıbak** (for

* See *Tarama Dergisi*, Vol. I, İstanbul, 1934, p. 48. I am indebted to Dr. Geoffrey Lewis for this reference.

şıban) incorrect quotations. The explanation of **öleŋ** as "a wedding song" (op. cit. p. 98) is another quotation, and the bit of folklore described under **töre** is taken from a passage in 44v. 23ff. (under **ak-/akıl-**). Nevertheless some of the passages quoted (op. cit. pp. 97 and 98), notably the account of the Kacar and the references to funeral and mourning customs, are original. It is very much to be hoped that our Soviet colleagues will re-examine this work in comparison with the Sanglax and extract any original passages of interest. It would also be interesting to know whether the explanations of the unintelligible words and phrases listed in Part II of the Sanglax are of any value. *Prima facie*, they are unlikely to be more than further exercises of the imagination (see para. 16 above).

THE AUTHORITIES QUOTED

34. A full classified list of the authorities quoted is contained in Index X. As Mīrzā Mahdī Khan himself says, Nawā'ī was his favourite author, and in 2r. 20ff. he gives a list of the 12 verse and nine prose works of Nawā'ī with which he was acquainted. Comparing this list with that in the *Abuşka* (Introduction p. 10) and the most recent comprehensive list of Nawā'ī's works, A. S. Levend's "*Nevā'īnin Eserleri*" in Türk Dili Araştırmaları Yıllığı, 1957,* it will be seen that, assuming no doubt correctly that *Arbaᶜīn Manẓūm* (Sanglax) and *Cihil Hadīṯ* (Levend) are identical, our author was familiar with all the known Turkish works of Nawā'ī with one important and two or three minor exceptions. The important exception is the *Muḥākamatu'l-luğatayn.* He was aware of the existence of this work and mentions it twice (117r. 2; 130v. 17), but he had never seen it. This is very much to be regretted; it would have appealed so much to his sensitive linguistic palate. Next after Nawā'ī his favourite Çağatay author was Bābur, whose *ta'rīx* (now commonly called the *Bābur-nāma*) he quotes extensively. His quotations from Bābur's poems, except two taken from the *ta'rīx*, seem to have been derived from the *Abuşka*. He also takes a few quotations from over a dozen other Çağatay authors. His range of Rūmī reading seems to have been more restricted, but included four or five dictionaries. His favourite Rūmī author, quoted over a hundred times, was Fuḍūlī, who is usually regarded as an Azeri author, but it is possible that the MS. which he used was extensively "Ottomanized". The 13 "proverbs" quoted were probably contemporary Özbek; 19th Century parallels can be found for at least two of them.

35. The most surprising of the Turkish quotations is that in 180r. 1 (partially repeated in 336v. 16) from the "*Oğuz-nāma*". This was from a text very close to, if not identical with, that of the well-known Paris MS. (Bibl. Nat. Supplément Turc 1001) in late Uyğur script (or perhaps the Mongol Official Alphabet), of which the best edition is that in "*Die Legende von Oghuz Qaghan*" by Bang and Rachmati (S.P.A.W. 1932, XXV). This text has always been a great mystery, but careful analysis shows that it was written, or re-written, in its present form after the Mongol invasion (it contains several Mongolian words), apparently in a North Western dialect, perhaps a very late form of Oğuz spoken in the neighbourhood

* The *Abuşka* list includes the *Sāqī-nāma*; Levend and the Sanglax list do not; but the five quotations from this work (see Index X B.) are all introduced by such words as "as he says", and in this context "he", not further defined, always means Nawā'ī; the omission from the list in the Sanglax was therefore either inadvertent, or due to its inclusion in some larger compilation.

of the Aral Sea in the 13th Century. Comparison between the two texts is hampered by the fact that the Paris MS. is damaged at this point (lines 358ff.). The two texts, with Bang and Rachmati's restorations in (brackets), are as follows:—

Sanglax **Oğuz Xan oŋ yakada** (v.L. **yakıda**)
Paris **Oğuz Xan beduk ordu . . . .** (**oŋ yakıda**
(S) **altı ak örge tiktürdi başına altun tofuk**
(P) **kırk kulac ıgaçnı tiktürdi anıŋ**) **başı**(**da**)**bir**
(S) **berkitken kırk kulaç yığacni tiktürdi.**
(P) **altun** (**dağuk koydı**)

The important difference is **tofuk** (**topuk**) "ball" in place of the improbable **dağuk** "fowl" restored by Bang and Rachmati from the next sentence.

36. Our author's system of quotation varies, but in some cases is fairly elaborate. A great many quotations are preceded merely by such words as *çunānki gūyad* "as he (i.e. Nawā'ī) says" or *al-şāhid* ᶜ*alayhi* "the evidence for this is", but many quotations from Nāwā'ī are preceded by the name of the work, and often the part of it, quoted. Occasionally a verse is quoted of which Mīrzā Mahdī Xān did not know the author; in those cases the words *lā adrī* "I do not know" or *şā*ᶜ*ir* "a poet" are used. All other quotations are preceded by the name of an author, or a book, or both, sometimes with a reference to the part of the book.

37. It will be seen that, in addition to the Turkish authorities, there are a good many extracts from Persian books, quoted to illustrate isolated Turkish or Mongolian (or supposedly Turkish or Mongolian) words. Most of these are from the *ta'rīx-i Waṣṣāf*, for which our author had an unbounded (many people would think, a misplaced) admiration; indeed his *Durra-i Nādirī* was written in imitation of it. The reason for these was our author's interest in the extraordinary jargon of Persian, heavily interlarded with Turkish and Mongolian words, which was evolved at the Ilkhanid court in the 13th Century and continued to exist in an attenuated form for at least another two or three centuries. It is no doubt this "language" which is indicated by the term *iṣṭilāḥāt-i Muğūl* (or *Muğūlīya*). Apart from one usage of **bay** (127v. 21), this term is applied only to the peculiar *mulamma*ᶜ poems of Waṣṣāf (see Index X E.); but it might almost equally well have been applied to some of the prose quotations. This odd idiom has recently formed the subject of a very interesting study by Prof. Minorsky in his paper "*Pūr-i Bahā's 'Mongol' Ode*" in B.S.O.A.S. 1956, XVIII/2. The non-Persian elements in it are often no more good Turkish than English loan-words in French like "smoking" and "five-o'clock" are good English in the sense in which they are used. Some of the words, it is true, in the "Mongol ode" are quite good Turkish both in form and meaning, but, on the whole, these form the minority. If a word in the Sanglax is illustrated by a Persian quotation, it is nearly always because the word does not exist in Turkish in the form or meaning quoted. The most characteristic words of this idiom are nouns formed from Turkish or Mongolian verbs (sometimes in a corrupt form) with the suffix **-mışı/-mişi,** that is the Turkish suffix **-mış/miş** with Persian **-ī** tacked on. This form is mentioned in 3v. 14–16 as a *ṭarīqa-i Muğūlīya*; Ross's edition is here unfortunately disfigured by a misprint, the key-words **asramışı** and **yaşamışı** being printed without the final **-ı.** The words listed in the Sanglax which can be identified as

having been taken from this idiom are collected in Index VII. It will be seen that of the 62 words (including duplicates) exactly half, 31, are in this form. Of the 83 non-Persian words collected in the Index to Minorsky's article six are in this form; two of them, **asramışı** and **tekemişi,** are common to both lists. The words in Index VII can also be examined from another angle, that of their etymological origin. It turns out, not surprisingly, that about one third of them are of Mongolian origin. But that is a mere fraction of the Mongolian words in the Sanglax, a subject more fully discussed in paras. 42ff. below.

THE LANGUAGES DEALT WITH

38. Deliberately or inadvertently, probably the latter, the epitomizers through whose very indifferent epitomes the contents of the Sanglax partially reached Western scholars like Zenker, Vambéry, Pavet de Courteille and Radloff, 19th Century Turkish scholars like Şeyh Süleyman, and the scholars of the Turkish Republic who compiled such works as the *Tarama Dergisi* and the *Türkçe Sözlük,* gave their readers the impression that the Sanglax was exclusively a Dictionary of Çağatay. This impression has occasioned some distress to such scholars as Prof. Menges, who has more than once* remarked that in that event Çağatay must have been a very heterogeneous language. But the most superficial study of the Sanglax shows that it is far from being a mere dictionary of Çağatay. Our author mentions in 2r. 16 the inclusion in his work of Mongolian and Rūmī words, but does not, so far as I can see, anywhere explain why, and it must be a matter of conjecture why he included as large a proportion of non-Çağatay elements as he did.

39. It is hard to say how many Turkish languages and dialects he recognized, but he seems to have thought that fundamentally there was one "Turkī" language with two slightly different literary varieties, "Cağatay" (*sic,* in his spelling) and "Rūmī", and a limited number of colloquial dialects. There are many references to grammatical and phonetic differences between the two literary varieties in Part I and to semantic and morphological differences in Part III. The nearest approach to a systematic discussion of the relationship between the two is in the passage (19r. 25–19v. 8) which begins "Since the reigning Sultans of Rūm and most of the tribes of that country are descended from the Tatar people (*él*), Turkī-yi Rūmī conforms with the Cağatay language, but because of contiguity and frequent communications and conversations with the Arabs they have

* For example, in his "*Glossar zu den volkskundlichen Texten aus Ost-Türkistan II*", A.G.S.K., 1954, No. 14, Akademie der Wissenschaften und der Literatur in Mainz, p. 710 s.v. **çüşkür-.** In this particular case, it is true, the lack of homogeneity is to be ascribed not to the inclusion of an additional, Rūmī, word in the Sanglax, but to errors by Radloff, but that is not typical. The only word for "to sneeze" in the Sanglax is **çüşkür-** (213r. 7); this is, as usual, reproduced in Vambéry's Ćagataische Studien p. 280 (**çöşkür-),** Pavet de Courteille p. 294, Şeyh Süleyman p. 156 (Kunos p. 51 **çüşkür-**) and Radloff W.B. III 2047 (**çöşkür-** "Dsch.") and 2201 (**çüşkür-** "Dsch."). **Tüçkür-** is quoted in W.B. III 1576 as "Dsch." on the authority of Vambéry, but the word does not occur in Vambéry; Radloff wrote "Dsch." by mistake for "O.T."; he took the word from Shaw's "*Sketch of the Turki Language*" Pt. II, Calcutta, 1880, p. 72; but the form is a dubious one even in "O.T." Burhan Şehidi's "*Uygursko-Kitaysko-Russkiy Slovar'* ", Peking, about 1952, has **tüşkür-** (p. 210), which is the form quoted in W.B. III 1591 as "Kir." (i.e. Kazax), with "Dsch." thrown in for luck. This is, however, an exceptional case of cumulative error. The normal errors which have given the impression that Çağatay is a heterogeneous language are best exemplified by the inclusion in the later Çağatay dictionaries of such forms as **ötüş-** (of a bird) "to sing" (as well as **eteş-**) and **etmek** "bread" (as well as **ötmek**), both of which are specifically described as "Rūmī" in the Sanglax.

Arabicized, corrupted and contracted some of their words. . . .". He did not know enough ancient Turkish history to understand when and why the two languages had diverged, and his explanation is, of course, erroneous, but he did appreciate the close connection between them.

40. As regards contemporary dialects, it will be seen from Index IV that there was great confusion in his terminology and probably also in his thoughts. The old Persian antithesis between Iran and Turan was very much in his mind, and the main dialectological antithesis is between the *Atrāk* (or *Özbekīya*, twice even *ahl*) of Turan (or Turan and Xʷārazm) on the one hand and the *Atrāk* of Iran (or Iran and Rūm) on the other, but there is occasionally an antithesis between the *Atrāk* of Iran and those of Rūm. There are a few references to the *Türkmenīya* or *Tarākima*, twice without further qualification, once to those of ᶜIraq (but whether ᶜ*Arabī* or ᶜ*Acamī* is not stated) and once to those of Xʷārazm. There are four references to the language of *Kāşğar*, two to that of the *Tatarīya* and a few scattered uses of other terms. The nearest approach to a systematic discussion of the difference between dialects is the passage (2r. 12ff.) in which he says that the *Özbekīyā* and the people of *Mā warā'u'l-nahr* (i.e. presumably Turan) pronounce the *kāf* of verbs like **kör-, kit-** and **kél-** as **k-,** while the Türkmenīya and the people of Xʷārazm (*sic*, and not, as might be expected, Rūm or Iran) pronounce these words in Persian fashion with a **g-** and that he regards both these forms as correct and does not distinguish between them, but that, in other cases, where the difference between **g** and **k** or vowels *ba-* and *bilā işbāᶜ* is significant semanticly he mentions the fact.* Again in 47r. 15 he says that the *Özbekīya* and *Türkmenīya* of Xʷārazm pronounce **alak-/alakış-** *ba-ḍamm-i alif*, which presumably means with a semi-rounded **a-** (the sound in English "awl"). To sum up, we can probably conclude that the dialect with which our author was most familiar was Özbek, that he had some knowledge of Anatolian and of the minor differences between that and Azeri and that he was aware of the separate existence of the Türki of Chinese Turkestan, the Türkmen dialects and the Tatar of the Volga valley, but his references to Xʷārazm are obscure.

41. The great majority of the Turkish words in the Sanglax are not described as belonging to any particular language, but there is sufficient evidence when a word is listed in two different forms in two different languages with cross-references to make it clear that our author regarded these undescribed words as Cağatay (so spelt), his name for the language of Nawā'ī. The only other large group of Turkish words belongs to what our author calls *Turkī-yi Rūmī*. They fall into two main classes, those which are solely Rūmī and those which are Rūmī in the sense of having a different meaning in Rūmī from that which they have in Çağatay. There is a small intermediate class of words which are synonymous in both languages but differ slightly in form. All these Rūmī words are collected in Index III. There are about 1,000 in all, of which just on three-quarters are only Rūmī. Where a word is described as "Rūmī", the derived forms, for example the causative forms of verbs, are often listed without this description, but as they too are obviously Rūmī they have been included in Index III in (brackets). These words do not form a homogeneous group. Those illustrated by quotations from Osmanli authors are, of course, Osmanli; those

* There are many examples of this, for example 106v. 29ff. (**ék-** and **ég-**); 66v. 21ff. (**or-, ur-, ör-** and **ür-**).

illustrated by quotations from Fuḍūlī may be Azeri rather than Osmanli proper. Others cannot be found in the standard Osmanli dictionaries, but occur in quotations in the *Tanıklariyle Tarama Sözlügü*, İstanbul, 1943ff. These seem to be old Anatolian words which never got a foothold in "high" Osmanli. Two or three, e.g. **ciwek, tum-, tumul-,** do not occur even in this authority but can be found in the *Söz Derleme Dergisi*, İstanbul, 1939ff. These seem to be purely colloquial Anatolian words. Some 60 words cannot be found even in that authority. Unless they can be traced somewhere we must conclude either that they are errors or that they are colloquial words now obsolete. The Turkish words belonging to other languages or dialects assembled in Index IV are numerically unimportant, about 40 in all, of which only half are peculiar to these dialects.

42. In addition to these pure Turkish words, a great many foreign loan-words are listed in the Sanglax. A good many of these were identified as such by our author and are so described, but a great many more were not. The largest group comprises the words called *Muğūl*, i.e. Mongolian. Those so described, and collected in Index V A., nearly 130 in number, of which nearly 100 are listed only as Mongolian words, fall into two main classes. The first, and larger, comprises perfectly recognizable Mongolian words, the second supposedly Mongolian meanings of personal names and the like painstakingly collected from the Persian historians, which seem to be purely imaginary deductions from false etymologies. There is a small intermediate class of Mongolian meanings of personal names which are either correct (e.g. **batu**) or not wholly imaginary (e.g. **cocı**). One word, **ṭayṣı,** so spelt, is described as Mongolian (it does, in fact, occur in the Mongolian dictionaries) with a cross-reference to **tayşı,** so spelt, which is described, more correctly, as Chinese (see Index VI C.). There is also a very small group of five words described as *Qalmaqī*, i.e. Kalmuk, collected in Index V B., of which three and perhaps a fourth can be identified as Mongolian.

43. In addition to these recognized Mongolian words, there is in the Sanglax a much larger group of words which our author regarded as good Turkish but which are, in fact, also Mongolian loan-words. These words, a little over 300, of which about 50 are duplicates of one sort or another, are collected in Index V C. It is fairly easy to recognize these loan-words and in picking them out I have been guided by three simple rules:—

(1) If a word can be shown to have existed in Turkish before the Mongol invasion, it can safely be assumed that it is genuine Turkish. (It will be noticed that on this principle some of the supposedly Mongolian words in Index V A. can be identified as Turkish loan-words in Mongolian.)

(2) If a word cannot be traced in Turkish before that date or explained etymologically as Turkish, but can be found in the Mongolian dictionaries, it can be tentatively identified as Mongolian.

(3) The identification becomes a practical certainty if the shape of the word is more Mongolian than Turkish (e.g. **otağa, égeci**), and even more so if it has a characteristic Mongolian suffix (e.g. **ögülge, ilbesün, erewül, borcın**).

44. One or two of the words in Index V C. have been entered with a query since, although I do not personally doubt that they are loan-words, the point is perhaps open to

debate. Conversely, it is very probable that there are some other loan-words in the Sanglax which have wrongly escaped inclusion in that Index.

45. What comes out more clearly than anything else from a careful study of the Sanglax is that one of the by-products of Mongol rule in the Turkish-speaking areas of the Near and Middle East was to introduce into all the Turkish languages of that area a much larger element of Mongolian than has ever been suspected. Some of these words, those in Index V A., were still recognized as Mongolian in the 18th Century; others had become so fully naturalized, at any rate in Çağatay, that their foreign origin had been forgotten. A good many of both classes soon became obsolete; for the existence of these in Turkish the only authority is the Sanglax and works indirectly copied from it. But others obtained such a hold that they still remain as ordinary constituents of the language. This is true not only, to some extent, of the modern descendants of Çağatay (Özbek and the like) and much more of the languages lying to the North and East of them in the Soviet Union (Kazax, Kirğiz, Mountain Altay, Tuvan and the like) but even, to a limited extent, of Republican Turkish. No-one, for example, has hitherto realized that **serin** "cool" is a loan-word, but it is a fact that it did not exist in any Turkish language before the Mongol invasion and is obviously derived from Mongolian *seri'ün*. It must surely have been by the irony of fate that the Sanglax, the only Turkish dictionary which gives even a hint, and that not a very clear one, of the extent of the Mongolian element in Çağatay, was such a rare book that the 19th Century lexicographers of the language never saw it and were compelled to rely on the epitomes which swept away ruthlessly this hint and much else of value in the original work. It was to these lexicographers that the language reformers of the early days of the Turkish Republic looked for "pure Turkish" words to replace foreign elements in Osmanli. The consequence was that a number of Mongolian or *iṣṭilāḥāt-i Muğūl* words, some quite clearly described as such in the Sanglax (e.g. **kurı/ultay**), were revived and introduced into Republican Turkish, often to replace Arabic words which had been incorporated in Turkish as early as the Karaxanid period, two centuries before the Mongol invasion.

46. The lists of Mongolian loan-words in Index V are accompanied by one, or if possible two, references to the original word as it appears in standard Mongolian dictionaries. Those used are:—

(1) Prof. E. Haenisch's "*Wörterbuch zu Manghol un Niuca Tobca'an*" (i.e. the "Secret History of the Mongols"), Leipzig, 1939, quoted as W.

(This contains a list of words in the Mongolian dialect spoken in China in the mid-13th Century.)

(2) Prof. N. N. Poppe's "*Mongol'skiy Slovar' Mukaddimat al-Adab*", Moscow-Leningrad, 1938, quoted as P.

(This contains a list of words in the dialect spoken in Persia in the early 14th Century, as represented in the Mongolian translation of Zamaxşari's *Muqaddimatu'l-Adab*.)

(3) Prof. J. E. Kowalewski's *Dictionnaire Mongol-Russe-Français*, Kazan, 1841ff., quoted as K.

(The standard, but now somewhat antiquated, dictionary of Classical Mongolian.)

(4) The *Mongol-English Practical Dictionary*, compiled by M. Haltod and others, the Evangelical Alliance Mission, 1949–53, quoted as H.

(The best available dictionary of modern written Mongolian.)

As explained in para. 4, I have substituted a single system of transliteration for the varying systems used in these four dictionaries.

47. The other two substantial groups of loan-words in the Sanglax are those borrowed from Arabic and Persian. These are collected in Indices VI A. and B. Our author identified a little over a dozen words or phrases as Arabic by origin, usually in a corrupt or turcicized form or with an altered meaning. There are about 50 more that he did not recognize. In the case of the Persian words which he recognized as such (a little over 50, including phrases) his formula usually is that a word is common to both languages, or that it is described as Persian in a Persian dictionary, or that it is a Persian word with an altered form or meaning. There are about another 130 Persian loan-words that he did not recognize.

48. There are also among the Çağatay words about 20 which are loan-words (mostly very early loan-words) from other languages, about half of them from Chinese. These are collected in Index VI C.

49. The loan-words in Rūmī are a special case. As the Sanglax is primarily a study of Çağatay, I have not devoted the same attention to the Rūmī material or tried to collect the loan-words contained in it, but where I have noticed such loan-words I have called attention to them in Indices I and III. Apart from the Arabic and Persian loan-words, which for the sake of completeness have been included in Indices VI A. and B., but marked "R." and italicized as duplicates (see para. 52), the majority (about 40) are Greek. There are also loan-words from the Romance languages or *lingua franca*, but it is often hard to say which, and six or seven from Latin, perhaps received via a Romance language or Byzantine Greek (**iskemle, büber, kalandas, gümrük, mard**) or Arabic (**çakır,** via *ṣaqr* from Latin *sacer*, and **çakırcı**). There are a few loan-words from other languages:—German (**kuruş**), Magyar (**palaska, şaranpaw**), Slavonic (**pilic, çete** (with **çeteci**), **kopusğa**), and Syriac (**çeleb,** with **çelebi**).

50. In addition, there are both in the Çağatay and in the Rūmī material some words which do not look Turkish and are probably foreign, but might be mere errors. These are marked "f." in Indices I and III, but I have not collected them in a separate Index since their status is so obscure.

51. It may be useful to close this section of the Introduction with some statistics. In Part III of the Sanglax there are, on my reckoning, about 6,536 entries, not counting separately the numerous conjugational forms included in the paragraphs devoted to most verbs, but including a few words mentioned in Part I or incidentally in Part III, but not included as main entries, and also a few errors of previous authorities (see sub-para. (5) below). This figure is, in a sense, a subjective one and other scholars might reach a slightly

different one. In reaching it, I have counted as only one an entry like **él** (112v. 3ff.), which deals with two quite different words meaning (1) "hand"; (2) "people", etc.; but I have counted as two, pairs of words like **él** and **ıl** which have the same spelling in Arabic script and so constitute a single "red ink" entry, but must be transliterated differently, whether the difference in pronunciation is mentioned, as in the case of **ék-** and **ég-** (106v. 29ff.), or not, as in the case of **él** and **ıl.** But the actual number of individual words, in the ordinary grammatical sense of the term, translated from Turkish (or other languages) into Persian is substantially less. To reach this net figure the following kinds of entries must be deducted:—

(1) Phrases containing two or more words of which the constituent parts are listed separately, e.g. those beginning with **iki** (109r. 16ff.) and **kara** (270v. 26ff.).

(2) The conjugational forms of the verb **ér-/é-** "to be" which are listed separately and not grouped under the infinitive like those of other verbs.

(3) Oblique cases, especially those of **ol** "he, that".

(4) Alternative spellings of a word already listed, e.g. **olca,** 86r. 12, as well as 86r. 3.

(5) The words misspelt in previous authorities, which I have included in the appropriate place (according to the Arabic alphabetical order) in Index I, marked E., to call attention to the fact that these words, many of which occur in the later dictionaries, do not really exist.

(6) The geographical, personal and tribal, etc., names collected in Index IX.

52. The entries enumerated in (1)–(5) above are italicized in Index I. In Index IX a good many names are contained in two or more sections (e.g. *Tağmac/Tamğac*) or are common nouns also used as names (e.g. **Ay, Tağ**), or are phrases made up of two common nouns (e.g. **Ilan otı**). All these have been italicized except, in the first case, names in the section to which they properly belong. Italics are used widely to avoid double-counting in some other Indices; in Index III for phrases, special Rūmī spellings of Çağatay words and words which have a different meaning in Rūmī; in Index IV for all words which are not peculiar to the dialect under which they are shown; in Index V for alternative spellings, Mongolian meanings of Turkish words and Mongolian meanings of names not italicized in Index X; in Index VI for foreign loan-words which have the same form as Çağatay words and for Rūmī words already indexed in Index III; and in Index VII for Turkish words and phrases which are included only because they have special meanings in the *iṣṭilāḥāt-i Muğūl.* All these italicized words and phrases are referred to herein as "duplicates".

53. After deducting from the gross number of entries, 6,536, the duplicates in Index I, 1,180 in number, and the names, less duplicates, in Index IX, 131 in number, there remains a net number of 5,225 words translated in the Sanglax. This too is a subjective figure; it includes such words as **abusun,** although it is not a main entry, because it occurs in the phrase **iki abusun** (109r. 16), but does not include **paykar** from the phrase **iki paykar,** because that is only one of hundreds of Persian loan-words used in Çağatay but not included in the Sanglax except perhaps in Part IV.

This figure of 5,225 can be broken down in various ways, of which the two most interesting are:—

Net number of entries				5,225
Deduct	Rūmi words, less duplicates	(Index III)	743	
	other Turkish words, less duplicates	(Index IV)	20	
	identified Mongolian words, less duplicates	(Index V A.)	94	
	identified Kalmuk words, less duplicates	(Index V B.)	2	
	identified Arabic words, less duplicates	(Index VI A.i.)	15	
	identified Persian words, less duplicates	(Index VI B.i.)	47	
	Iṣṭilāḥāt-i-Muğūl words, less duplicates	(Index VII)	49	
				970
Remainder	Çağatay words			4,255

Net number of entries				5,225
Deduct	Mongolian and Kalmuk loan-words, less duplicates	(Index V)	351	
	other loan-words, less duplicates	(Index VI)	220	
	Iṣṭilāḥāt-i-Muğūl words, less duplicates	(Index VII)	49	
	estimate of loan-words in Rūmī	(Index III)	125	
				745
Remainder	Turkish words			4,480
	Çağatay and dialects in Index IV		3,862	
	Rūmi, say		618	
				4,480

54. Three points must be emphasized. The first is that the appearance of precision given by these tables is completely spurious. Apart from the possibilities of mathematical error, all the figures are, in the ultimate analysis, estimates; they are compiled from a series of subjective judgements, and all of them probably contain errors and omissions; they have been calculated to the last unit only in the hope that these errors and omissions will, at any rate to some extent, cancel one another out. The second is that they relate solely to the contents of the Sanglax; they cannot properly be used as a basis for an estimate of the etymological constitution even of Çağatay and, of course, much less that of Rūmī. The third is that there is no doubt that both the residual figures, 4,255 and 4,480, are too high. Both include the dubious words marked "d" in Index I, some of which are likely to be purely imaginary, and the second includes also the words marked "f" in Index I, which are almost certainly foreign or imaginary.

THE ARRANGEMENT OF PART III

55. Part III is a sub-divided list of words and phrases in the alphabetical order of the Arabic-Persian alphabet. Apart from the (five) *cuz'* mentioned in para. 17, which are not morphologically significant, the largest unit of sub-division is the "Book" (*kitāb*), each of which contains all the words beginning with a particular letter, *alif*, *bā*, etc.; it should be noted that for this purpose *ᶜacami* letters are not distinguished from the *ᶜarabi* counterparts, so that, for example, Book II includes all the words beginning with **b-** and **p-** in a single list. Each Book is divided into three "Chapters" (*bāb*) for *al-maftūḥāt*, *al-maksūrāt* and *al-maḍmūmāt* respectively, that is, in Book I, words beginning with **a-** or **e-**, **é-**, **ı-** or **i-** and

o-, u-, ö- or **ü-.** Each Chapter is divided into a number of Sections, which do not seem to have a specific name,* containing words beginning with the "Book" letter vocalized with the "Chapter" vowel and followed by a particular letter; these Sections are prefaced with the words *ma*ᶜ*a'l-alif* (which occurs only rarely), *ma*ᶜ*a'l-bā* and so on. If, as is usually the case, the Section contains both verbs and other words, it is divided into two Sub-sections, the first containing the verbs and headed *mina'l-muştaqqāt*, the second containing other words and headed *mina'l- cawāmīd.* Within the individual Sub-sections the words are, in principle, arranged in alphabetical order; in practice, in those containing verbs the principle applies only to the basic Çağatay verbs, the derived (Passive, etc.) forms of each basic verb following it and preceding the next basic verb; the Rūmī verbs, if any, follow in a separate alphabetical order at the end. In the other Sub-sections the alphabetical order is so strict that alternative spellings of the same word (e.g. **olca** *ba- alif kaşīda*, 86r. 3, *ba- hā zada*, 86r. 12) may be separated quite widely.

56. Individual entries are made up of a series of components, but very few contain all of them. The broad arrangement is:—

(1) The word (in red ink).

(2) Its spelling (see para. 60ff.).

(3) Its language, if not Çağatay.

(4) The number of its meanings.

(5) (for each meaning, if more than one)

- (a) The meaning in Persian.
- (b) An alternative or more precise translation in Persian or some other language or languages.
- (c) The Çağatay form of a Rūmī word, or *vice versa.*
- (d) An illustrative quotation or quotations.

If a written word has two pronunciations, for example with ᶜ*arabī* and ᶜ*acamī* consonants, or vowels *ba-* and *bilā işbā*,ᶜ or different internal vocalization, two or three sets of components from (2) onwards may follow a single main "red ink" entry. The detailed application of this general arrangement varies between verbs and other words.

57. In the case of verbs, the form entered under (1) is the infinitive. Sometimes this is followed by an extended infinitive form in **-makhk/-meklik,** also in red ink. The principle governing these additions is obscure, but on its first occurrence the extended form was quoted in order to introduce a quotation containing such a form. The components following this entry may be a complete set, but examples of 5(b) are very rare so far as other languages are concerned. In the case of (2) only the root form, without **-mak/-mek** is spelt out. Under (5), but before (5)(d), a correction of an error by a previous authority is sometimes inserted if it relates to the meaning of the verb itself. Corrections to the form or meaning of a word (verbal form or non-verb) in a particular quotation follow the

* The word *dayl*, used in cross-references from a verbal form in a list of non-verbal words to its parent verb, seems to mean an individual paragraph in a section, not the section or sub-section as a whole.

quotation concerned. From this point entries relating to verbs follow one of three models:—

(i) There is a complete list of conjugational forms,* each written in red ink and followed by components (4) (if applicable), 5(a) and, sometimes, (d).

(ii) Only one or two conjugational forms follow, each written in red ink and followed by components 5(a) and nearly always (d), the entry ending with further instructions regarding conjugation beginning *wa bāqī ṣiyağ-i ān* or the like.

(iii) The infinitive is followed immediately by instructions regarding conjugation (*wa ṣiyağ-i ān . . . .*).

In the case of Rūmī verbs no instructions regarding conjugation are given since they do not follow the Çağatay model. Very occasionally it is stated that the verb is not conjugated or that only the forms already enumerated are used. In the case of verbs with more than one pronunciation, i.e. two or more (2)'s, and two or more verbs with the same meaning, the conjugations proceed side by side in a single entry, e.g. **or-, ur-, ör-** and **ür-** in 66v. 21 to 67v. 15 (53 lines), **ét-** and **it-** in 93r. 15 to 94r. 16 (60 lines), and **azğaş-** and **azık-** in 38r. 17 to 38v. 15.

58. In the case of words other than verbs, the entries follow the broad arrangement with two differences of emphasis. In the first place, components of type 5(b) are relatively common. The reasons for the additional translation vary. Often the Persian word first

---

* The term "complete list" is, of course, not strictly accurate. Our author seems, when he started Part III, to have compiled a standard list of conjugational forms which he considered adequate to exemplify the conjugation, and to have revised this list, perhaps in the light of experience, at the end of each *cuz'* (see para. 15). These changes seem to be progressive. The first list in the book, that under **at-** (27v. 18ff.) is as follows:— **atmak—attuk—atar, atadur—atmaydur—atğan, atarğan, atadurğan—at, atğıl—atma, atmağıl—atıŋ, atıŋız, atıŋlar—atmaŋ, atmaŋız, atmaŋlar—atman, atmasmén—atamén, atarmén, atadurmén, ataram—atarım, atmağım—atmağum—atıb, atıban, atmış—atmışaŋ—atmas—atması—atmadın—atıb bolmas, atsa bolmas, atmak olmas—ata almas—ata ata—atay, atayın—atsak, atğabız, atğaybız, atalı, atalıŋ—atğalı—atğac—atğucı—atğuca, atğunca, atğanca—atğum—atguŋ—atğusı—atğuluk—atğay, ata, atsa, atsun, atdék—atğudék, atardek.** This gives a total of 63 forms, of which 30, or nearly half, are duplicates. From time to time one or two extra forms are added in particular entries to introduce illustrative quotations. These usually disappear again immediately from the standard list. The standard list in *cuz'* II, see for example **bat-** (119r. 28ff.), is substantially the same as that in *cuz'* I, but with changes which on balance bring the total up to 64, including 30 duplicates. The conjugation of **yé-** (352v. 23ff.), the last verb in *cuz'* V, is substantially different and contains only 56 forms, including 31 duplicates. The oddest change in the standard list is one that occurs at the beginning of *cuz'* V in **layla-** (317v. 15ff.). Until that point the eighth and ninth entries had been the second person plural forms of the imperative, positive and negative; in **layla-** both these disappear and are replaced by **laylasaŋ, laylağabız, laylağaybız.** The only possible explanation is that our author, coming back after an interval and looking at his last entry, misread **kéwürmeŋ** as **kéwürseŋ** and completed the string **laylasaŋ** . . . . accordingly, overlooking the fact that these are merely the second person singular forms of the same tenses as those of which the first person plural forms, **laylasak,** etc., are listed a little later. This is merely one example of the quasi-hypnotic effect of writing out page after page of conjugational forms. Others are the numerous minor irregularities in the lists; one or two words are dropped out, or misspelt, e.g. **yama, yamağıl** for **yamama, yamamağıl** (337r. 9), and, in particular, *qāf* and *ğayn* appear sporadically in conjugations of verbs with front vowels and *kāf* (*gāf*) in conjugations of verbs with back vowels. Whether these errors are to be attributed to the author himself or the copyists (and both may be to blame) there is no good reason for seeing deep phonetic significance in them. All alike were Persians and lacked the instinctive feel of a Turk for the phonetics of his own language. The same is, of course, true of the copyists of the works of Nawā'ī and perhaps even of the master himself. The long and careful analysis of Çağatay phonetics in Menges, op. cit. p. 649ff., seems to me to be vitiated by his failure to take into account the possibility that the spelling irregularities on which his analysis is largely based are simple mistakes committed by persons who were not themselves Turks, for the most part at a time when Çağatay proper was already a dead language.

used has several meanings and the meaning intended has to be specified further, just as in English translations words like "swallow" have to be explained as "a bird" or "a gulp".* Often, too, the first translation is a general one, like "the name of a plant", and a more specific translation follows. This is sometimes in Persian, or in Persian and Arabic or some other language. The "other language" is most often not a language proper but *lisānu'l-ṭibb* "medical terminology"; examples are in 209r. 21; 254r. 7; 271v. 19 and, in an unusual formula, in 329v. 19, but there are a good many more. The remaining languages quoted are listed in Index VIII A.; the Turkish words concerned are mainly names of plants and animals and these equivalents and those from the *lisānu'l-ṭibb* were probably lifted from herbals and bestiaries used by our author; but it is hard to see why he should have quoted (incidentally accurately) the Russian and Kalmuk (see Index V B.) equivalents of **kamçi** "whip", unless it was to call attention, perhaps in a rather ill-chosen context, to his wide knowledge of languages. In the second place, the alternative meanings listed under (5) often go far beyond the proper limits of the Sub-section. First, if a conjugational form is homophonous with the word under treatment, it is mentioned separately at the end of the entry. For example under **açar** (32r. 26ff.) **açar** from **aç-** is mentioned. This may not be logical, but it is eminently sensible to remind someone who is looking up **açar** that it may be a verb. Secondly, after the Turkish meanings and verbal forms, homophonous foreign words are often listed; for example three Persian and one "Hindī" meanings of **açar** are listed. This, too, is sensible to the extent that such foreign words are likely to occur in Turkish works, particularly having regard to the proclivity of Çağatay (like Persian) poets for making the most ruthless puns, a practice to which frequent reference is made in notes on quotations in the Sanglax. But this hardly applies to some of the languages in Index VIII B., where all the languages concerned are collected; **kasık,** in Haitian "cacique", already mentioned in para. 27, is an extreme case, which can hardly be explained except as an example of innocent vanity.

THE ORTHOGRAPHY AND SPELLING SYSTEM OF THE SANGLAX

59. The English word "to spell" is ambiguous since it means both "to use certain letters to represent a word" and "to describe what letters are used to represent a word". To avoid ambiguity "orthography" is here used in the first sense and "spelling system" in the second. There are at least two orthographies in the Sanglax, that used for the Çağatay words, which is explained in 19r. 8ff., and that used for Rūmī words, which is called *imlā'-i Rūmī* and is no doubt merely the orthography of the Rūmī works which were consulted. The difference lies almost entirely in the fact that the first makes considerable use of vocalic *alif*, *yā* and *wāw* and the second very much less. The vowel-signs hardly appear at all in the Sanglax; they are occasionally applied to Persian and Arabic words to avoid ambiguity, and very occasionally to Rūmī words (e.g. **depele**–223r. 15).

60. Menges (op. cit. p. 649) suggests that the liberal use of vowel letters in Çağatay is best explained by supposing that it represents a letter for letter transcription of Uyğur orthography into Arabic script, but there are several good reasons why this cannot be so.

---

* These supplementary translations were usually omitted in the epitomes, with the result that erroneous translations of the initial translation occur in later works, e.g. those of Pavet de Courteille and Şeyh Süleyman.

The best is that if the Çağatay in the Sanglax is transcribed into the Uyğur script what comes out is often not legible according to the ordinary rules of Uyğur orthography. For example, forms like **ebm kmeci** (27v. 15), **ebuşğa** (27v. 17), **bt** (119v. 18) and **ptke** (119v. 19) are not possible in Uyğur script. The true explanation is to be sought elsewhere. Systems of Arabic orthography for recording unwritten Turkish languages must have been devised independently in several different places at several different times. The problems which then invariably arose are clearly explained in a passage (3r. 9ff.) in the Introduction to the 15th Century Arabic-Kıpçak vocabulary published with a translation by B. Atalay under the title "*Ettuhfet-üz-zekiyye fil-lûgat-it-Türkiyye*", İstanbul, 1945. "The Turkish language has no shape (*şakl*; that is, does not like Arabic have verbal roots from which various conjugational forms, nouns, etc., are formed by the addition of standard prefixed and suffixed letters and standard vocalic patterns), and for the lack of it confusion (*al-iltibās*) arises; so they have made (an arrangement) for all the nouns and verbs and indeclinable words in order that they may be read without 'shape' and confusion; it is that *fatḥa* is represented by *alif*, *kasra* by *ya* and *ḍamma* by *wāw*; for example the nouns 'wind' *yā alif lām* (i.e. **yel**), 'year' *yā yā lām* (i.e. **yıl**), 'road' *yā wāw lām* (i.e. **yol**) . . . . " and so on. This is, in fact, the orthography consistently used in that work, and if we had not the author's own explanation, and if the date (15th Century) was not quite incompatible with the theory, this too might have been regarded as another, and indeed a clearer, case of transliteration of Uyğur. Çağatay orthography is actually one link in a chain which goes back, probably without interruption, to the Karaxanid period; it is not notably different from the orthography of the Arabic script MSS. of the Kutaḏğu Bilig. When the Karaxanid Turks in the 10th (?) Century adopted Islam and with it the Arabic alphabet (in its early Persian variety with the triply dotted *fā* for **v**), the old Turkish long vowels were probably still sufficiently perceptible (as they were to Kāşğarī) to require at any rate some use of the vowel letters, and, as the vowel signs were probably not in current use for ordinary purposes, those letters were probably found to be so convenient for making written Turkish intelligible that they were used, without implication of vowel length, on a fairly extensive scale and continued to be so used down to the Çağatay period.

60. The spelling system in the Sanglax is elaborate and extremely helpful. It is hard to see why our author spelt some words out in full and others not at all, but when he spells a word out in part it is usually to call attention to an *ᶜacamī* letter or to supply a vowel not indicated by a vowel letter. Sometimes it is used simply to call attention to the difference in the pronunciation of two consecutive words. The indication of *ᶜacamī* letters is so consistent as to create a presumption that ambiguous letters not described as *ᶜacamī* are *ᶜarabī*.

61. The following are the principal rules governing the spelling out of words, with illustrative examples:—

(1) The initial letter, which can be inferred from the *kitāb* (see para. 55), and its vocalization, which can be inferred from the *bāb*, are not mentioned, unless it is necessary to call attention to the quality of the consonant (see (7) below), or the vowel (see (5) below).

126v. 27 **baltu** *ba-sukūn-i lām wa ḍamm-i tā-yi qarşat.*

(2) The spelling begins with the vocalization of the second letter, any other letter with the same vowel being mentioned simultaneously, and continues until all the letters

have been mentioned in a complete spelling out, or only some of them in an incomplete one.

127r. 12 **palaska** *bā bā-yi* ^{c}*acamī wa ba-fatḥ-i lām wa qāf wa sukūn-i sīn-i muhmala* (complete).

100r. 10 **irkiştek** *ba-sukūn-i rā wa şīn-i qarşat wa kasr-i kāf-i awwal wa fatḥ-i tā-yi qarşat* (incomplete).

(3) The vowel sounds are described, but there is no reference to the presence or absence of vowel letters except occasionally to the representation of final a/e by *alif* or silent *hā*.

51v. 16 **anda** *ba-sukūn-i nūn wa fatḥ-i dāl ba-alif-i kaşīda.*

86r. 12 **olca** *ba-sukūn-i lām wa fatḥ-i cīm ba-hā zada.*

(4) Front and back vowels can be distinguished only in the case of verbs.

66v. 21 **ormak** *ma*^{c}*a'l-qāf . . . . wa ba-işbā*^{c}*-i ḍamma* (**urmak**) . . . . **örmek** *ma*^{c}*a'l-kāf . . . . wa ba-işbā*^{c}*-i ḍamma* (**ürmek**).

(5) The vowels **i, u** and **ü** are described as *ba-* or *bā işbā*^{c},* similar vowels in preceding words in the same entry being by implication **é, o** and **ö**; vowels are only occasionally described as *bilā* (or *bidūn*) *işbā*^{c}; the point is very often left open, and in that case the indication is rather that the vowel is **é, ö** or **ö,** but this is often not so.

93r. 16 **étmek** (not spelt) "has six meanings . . . . and the last four are *ba-işbā*^{c}*-i kasra*" (**itmek**).

113r. 3 **élk** *ba-sukūn-i lām wa kāf . . . . wa bā kāf-i* ^{c}*acamī* (**élg**) . . . . *wa ba-fatḥ-i lām* (**élek**) . . . . *wa ba-işbā*^{c}*-i kasra wa fatḥ-i lām* (**ilek**).

66v. 21 (see (4) above).

(6) **B, c, t, n** and **y** are described as *bā-* and *cīm-i abcad, tā-yi qarşat, nūn* and *yā-yi xaṭṭay,* **r** and **s** as *rā* and *sīn-i muhmala* (**r** sometimes as *rā-i qarşat*), **z** as *ẓā-yi mu*^{c}*cama* or *ẓā-yi hawwaz* and **ş** as *şīn-i qarşat,* in order to distinguish them in case a *nuqṭa* is misplaced. The other letters can be sufficiently distinguished by their names.

See the examples under the other rules.

(7) The ^{c}*acami* letters **p, ç, g** and **j** (a very rare letter) are so described.

p 127r. 12 (under (2) above); **g** 113r. 3 (under (5) above); **ç** 208v. 5 **carlatmak** *ba-sukūn-i rā wa tā-yi qarşat wa fatḥ-i lām . . . . wa bā cīm-i* ^{c}*acamī* (**çarlatmak**).

j 262v. 17 **ğij** *ba-ẓā-yi* ^{c}*acamī.*

(8) The guttural nasal **ŋ** is sometimes, but not very consistently, indicated by the mention of *kāf ma*^{c}*a'l-imāla.*

118r. 2 **éŋek** *ba-sukūn-i nūn wa fatḥ-i kāf-i awwal ma*^{c}*a'l-imāla.*

(9) Instead of, or as well as, being spelt a word is sometimes said to be in the *wazn* of

---

* It should be noted that the phrase *bi'l-işbā*, in Kāşğarī's "Dīwānu'l-luğāti'l-Turk" has a different meaning from that which it has in the Sanglax; in the Dīwān it means "with back vowels"; for example in 496l. 10ff. of the facsimile (III 123 of Atalay's translation) **tōz** *bi'l-işbā*^{c} "dust" and **tuz** *bi'l-işbā*^{c} "salt" are so distinguished from **tōz** and **tūz** in their various meanings.

Considering that the particular purpose of this phrase in relation to unrounded vowels in the Sanglax is to distinguish between two front vowels, **é** and **i,** it is surprising that it is occasionally applied to *kasra* representing a back vowel, e.g. in 251r. 14. Its purpose there is to distinguish between **sırıl-** "to be quilted, basted" and **sıyrıl-** *ba-işbā*^{c}*-i kasra* "to be slipped", which is repeated in its full form in 259r. 18.

some Persian word, that is to have the same vocalization and sometimes some of the same consonants.

36v. 1 **ara** *bar wazn-i sarā wa* **ara** *bar wazn-i pāra.*

62. It should be added that in the case of some verbs, particularly Rūmī verbs, which our author had met only in written texts, he indicates back vowels where the verb really has front vowels, and vice versa, e.g. in 223r. 15 the infinitive suffix of (Rūmī) **depele-** is given as **-mak.** Attention is called to these errors in Index I.

THE PHONOLOGY OF THE SANGLAX

63. From what has just been said it will be seen that, apart from the question of front and back vowels, our author had equipped himself to denote scientifically the exact pronunciation of the words he was translating; but this is not to say that he always did so. To some extent this omission is probably deliberate. At the time he wrote, Classical Çağatay was probably already a dead language (see para. 19), and he was greatly confused by the existence in his time of alternative pronunciations of certain letters, for example initial *kāf* (see para. 40), both of which seemed to him to be equally correct. His perplexity was increased by the fact that Nawā'ī often made words rhyme with one another which were pronounced slightly differently; see, for example, 25v. 17ff. where he says that voiced and unvoiced consonants are made to rhyme as in **aç** "open" and **ac** "hungry" and that vowels *bā* and *bilā iṣbā*ᶜ are made to rhyme, **kéz** and **éz** with (Persian) **tīz** and **tuz** with **söz.** This probably made him more diffident than he need have been in indicating Çağatay pronunciations. If he had had the wider experience that we have he would have realized that bad rhymes are not peculiar to any time or language. Anyone who tried to fix English pronunciation by a study of the English and American poets would probably end in a worse state of confusion still.

64. The sounds which gave him most trouble were the gutturals. In the case of the front gutturals his dilemma is concealed by the fact that both **g** and **k** were represented by *kāf* (the dilemma remains for the transliterator); but in the case of the back gutturals, when he was genuinely uncertain whether a particular sound was voiced or unvoiced, he could not slide over the dilemma so easily. In the case of the final sound of the infinitive suffix he invented a special ligature like a "Scythian beast", a *qāf* with a *ğayn* growing out of its tail, see for example 27v. 18 **atmağ/k.** In the case of words other than verbs this ligature is not used and both forms are written out, whether the doubt relates to a medial guttural, as in 57r. 5 **ayakçı** *wa* **ayağcı**, or a final one as in 39r. 14 **azuğ** *ba-ḍamm-i zā wa sukūn-i ğayn-i mu*ᶜ*cama wa* **azuk** *ma*ᶜ*a'l-qāf.* Here the transliterator has an advantage, and in this and all other cases where a word is quoted in two forms the two sounds are written in succession separated by an oblique stroke, as **atmağ/k** above and many examples elsewhere, e.g. **e/énet-** in Index III. It is very probable that the process of devoicing final, and to a less extent medial, voiced consonants, which is a familiar phenomenon in other Turkish languages, for example Osmanli, was in full swing at the time when he wrote. Its most unfortunate effect was to blur the difference between the "possessive" suffix **-lığ/lig** and the "abstract" suffix **-lık/-lik.** Our author was well aware of the semantic difference between the two suffixes (see 23v. 24ff. and 317v. 28), and of the phonetic difference between their

Rūmī counterparts **-lı/-li** and **-lık/-lik,** but he could not isolate any phonetic difference in Çağatay.

65. He was also perplexed by the contrary phenomenon of voicing unvoiced initial consonants which could be observed in some contemporary dialects. He was aware that words which had unvoiced initials in Özbek had voiced initials in such dialects as Türkmen and that some words in Rūmī existed in both forms, e.g. **d/tapkur** and **d/tepele-,** but he seems to have been uncertain on which side of the fence Çağatay stood. Actually there is little doubt that it was not in the "voicing" class, and we are therefore bound to view with suspicion Çağatay spellings like 308r. 16 **gögümtül** *bā har dū kāf-i ᶜacamī.* This is certainly true of the numerous spellings with initial **c-**; there is, for example, no doubt at all that **Çağatay** is the right spelling, not **Cağatay,** the spelling plainly implied in 206v. 13, where it lies between **çağ** *bā cīm-i ᶜacamī* and **çağarak** *bā cīm-i ᶜacamī.* This is all the more vexing since both **c-** and **ç-** exist in Mongolian and loan-words in both classes, correctly spelt, occur in the Sanglax (see Index V). If we could be sure that Çağatay Turkish words retained initial **ç-** in all cases in the Sanglax as well as in reality, initial **c-** could be added to the other criteria for identifying possible Mongolian loan-words. In Rūmī the point does not arise since both initials occur in Osmanli, as well as in the Rūmī words in the Sanglax.

66. Nevertheless, the value of the spelling directions given in the Sanglax, in spite of their deficiencies, ambiguities and probable inaccuracies, must not be underestimated; they cast new light into many dark corners. The most important of these dark corners is that containing the closed **é.** A great deal of work on the identification of words containing this sound has been done since Vilhelm Thomsen first brought the matter out into the open some 50 years ago by his article in J.S.F.O. XXX on the letter used to represent it in the Yenisei inscriptions, the only letter with this value only in any native Turkish alphabet (except the Brahmi alphabet—see Türkische Turfantexte VIII—which hardly answers to this description). The distinction between *kasra ba* and *bilā işbāᶜ* in the Sanglax confirms the belief long held by some of us that the same distinction existed in the orthography of other Turkish languages but was never precisely stated by those who used them. Transliterators of Old Osmanli need no longer use the improbable form **didi** for "he said", which was clearly **dédi.** Indeed we can even confidently use the same letter in transliterating such words as **tégin** in Kāşğarī. At the same time, even in the Sanglax some discrimination is necessary. In 113r. 3ff. (see para. 61 (5)) the last three words are quite correctly transliterated **élg** "hand", **élek** "sieve" and **ilek** "ruler", and if we follow the system rigorously the first word meaning "beginning, first" must be transliterated **élk**; but there is overwhelming evidence that it was never anything but **ilk.** Similarly the spellings **ér-** "to be" and **ér** "man" for **er-** and **er** are improbable, even though confirmed by the Abuşka. It is, of course, possible that some open **e**'s were pronounced as **é** in Çağatay, but **élk** can hardly be anything except an error for **ilk.** There are, in fact, many examples in the Sanglax of alternative pronunciations like **e/épkin** and **e/érkec,** but there is no example of a statement that a word is pronounced with *kasra bā* and *bilā işbāᶜ* in the same meaning.

THE SIGLA IN INDEX I

67. Attention has now been drawn to most of the matters of interest which arise from the study of the Sanglax, but it would be ingenuous to suppose that a scholar interested in

some particular subject will willingly plough through the 730 pages of reduced facsimile which this volume contains in search of matter relating to it, without some help in reducing the volume of his labours. The various Indices will, it is hoped, provide acceptably classified lists of certain material. In addition, a set of sigla has been devised and is used in Index I to call attention also to other particular kinds of information not collected in separate indices. These sigla fall into six groups, and where members of more than one group are attached to a single entry they are separated by semi-colons. The groups are the following:—

(1) * This sign is attached to words the transliteration of which is uncertain (see para. 3).

†This sign is attached to words for which the Sanglax (and sometimes the *Abuşka* also) is the *earliest* authority, so far as my own researches have extended. In the case of words beginning with vowels and **c-/ç-** these researches have been so extensive that I think that the sign can be relied on. In the case of other words I cannot speak with the same assurance, but I have looked in all the obvious places.

‡ This sign is a refinement on †; it is attached to words for which the Sanglax (and sometimes the *Abuşka* also) is the *only* primary authority. For this purpose I regard later Çağatay dictionaries like Pavet de Courteille as secondary, as their information almost certainly goes back ultimately to one of these two primary authorities. The reservations made regarding † apply equally here. In a very few cases the sign has been attached to words which survive in 19th and 20th Century Özbek dictionaries and vocabularies.

(2) This group contains signs designed to summarize part of the contents of an entry.

S means that a word is spelt out in full, **s** that it is partially spelt. If these signs are lacking, the Sanglax guarantees only the first two letters and the vowel between them.

E means that the entry contains a correction of an error in a previous authority; if it follows **Q** or **q** (see below) the correction relates not to the meaning of the word in general, but to its meaning or form in a particular quotation.

C means that a verb is completely conjugated; **c** that two or more conjugational forms are listed, but not the complete series.

Q means that the entry contains two or more quotations, **q** that it contains one. **Q/q**(P) means that the quotation(s) is/are in Persian; all others are in Turkish.

X means that the entry contains a cross-reference to another entry; **x** means that the word concerned is mentioned in the line referred to but not as a main entry.

Y means that the entry contains a translation or translations subsidiary to the main translation.

(3) If a word is given more than one meaning, the number is shown in Arabic figures; if one or more of these is a verbal form, or a foreign word, these are indicated as V in the first instance and by a letter indicating the foreign language concerned in the second. For example 49r. 11 **al** 1, 1V, 2P, 3A, 1H means that **al**, apart from its meaning as a Turkish word, is a verbal form (imperative of **al-**) and has two meanings in Persian, three in Arabic and one in "Hindī".

(4) This group is used to record statements that a word is not Çağatay but belongs to some other language, e.g. Mongolian (**M**) or Rūmī (**R**), or the *iṣṭilāḥāt-i Muğūl* (I). Words described as common (*muştarak*) to Turkish and Arabic or Persian are marked **Aş** and **Pş.**

(5) This group is designed to call attention to words of certain specified classes, likely to interest particular scholars.

Z means that it is a zoological term, the name of an animal, the colour of its coat and the like (applied to about 400 words).

B means that it is a botanical term, the name of a plant, fruit or the like (applied to about 250 words).

F means that it contains matter of "folk-lore" interest (applied to about 250 words). The concept is a very nebulous one, and I do not feel confident that I have made the right selection; it includes entries containing descriptions of Turkish or Mongolian customs, names of weapons, garments, pieces of equipment (saddle, etc.) and the like.

N means that a word is recorded, exclusively or additionally, as a name; it is always followed by a further classifier, **g** for geographical, **p** for personal or **t** for tribal, names. (All these entries are collected in Index IX.)

h, attached almost exclusively to **Ng, p** or **t,** means that the entry contains some historical, or purportedly historical, matter, usually the latter.

(6) This group is devoted to personal observations, not to the actual contents of the entries.

a, m, p or the name of some language means that the word is, in my view, a loan-word from Arabic, Mongolian, Persian or the language named. Such words, other than Rūmī ones, are listed in Indices V C., VI A. ii, B. ii and C. It should be added, as a confession of illogicality, that some of the words marked "I" should be so marked under this group and not under group (4), since the designation is not based on an actual statement in the Sanglax.

d means that a word looks dubious and is likely to be an error of some kind (see para. 16).

e means that the form or meaning to be found in later lexicographers is erroneous in some respect. Such markings are mostly the result of chance observation; the later authorities contain many more errors, some cumulative, than are indicated here.

f means that a word is of a form unlikely to be Turkish and is therefore likely to be a foreign loan-word (see para. 50) or an error.

It should be added that in some cases where a word has several meanings or occurs in more than one Turkish language the numbers (group (3)) have been attached direct to sigla in groups (4), (5) and (6).

68. The following is a complete list of the sigla used:—

A an Arabic loan-word so described; **Aṣ** (see para. 67 (4)); **a** an Arabic loan-word not so described (see para. 67 (6)).

B a botanical term (see para. 67 (5)); **bi, bilāi.** see **S.**

C conjugated in full; **c** partly conjugated (see para. 67 (2)).

d a dubious word (see para. 16).

E an error by a previous authority (see para. 67 (2)); **e** an error by a subsequent authority (see para. 67 (6)).

F a folk-lore term (see para. 67 (5)); **f** a probably foreign word (see para. 50).

G the Gibb Memorial Trust MS. (see para. 21); **g** see **N.**

H a word in "Hindī"; **h** an entry containing historical matter (see para. 67 (6)).
I a word used in the *iṣṭilāḥāt-i Muġūl* (see para. 37).
L the London (British Museum) MS. (see para. 24).
M and **m** for Mongolian, as **A** and **a** *mutatis mutandis;* **mi** see **S**.
N a name; **g** geographical, **p** personal, **t** tribal, etc.
O the Oxford (Bodleian) MS. (see para. 23).
P, Pṣ and **p** (except in **Np**) for Persian as **A, Aṣ** and **a** *mutatis mutandis.*
Q two or more quotations; **q** one quotation; (**P**) in Persian.
R Rūmī (see para. 41); **R*** described as Rūmī, but not traceable in any Osmanli or Republican Turkish authority.
S spelt in full; **s** partially spelt; (**bi**) *ba-iṣbā*ᶜ (**bilāi**) *bilā iṣbā*ᶜ; (**mi**) *ma*ᶜ*a'l-imāla* (see para. 61).
T Turkish; **t** (except in **Nt**) ditto in combinations like **a-t, m-t, p-t.**
V a verbal form (see para. 67 (3)).
W explained by a *wazn* (see para. 61 (9)).
X contains a cross-reference; **x** is contained in a cross-reference (see para. 67 (2)).
Y contains a supplementary translation (see para. 67 (2)).
Z a zoological term (see para. 67 (5)).
*, †, ‡ see para. 67 (1).

THE PRESENT STATE OF ÇAĞATAY LEXICOGRAPHY

69. I can perhaps usefully close this Introduction by a brief summary of the conclusions which I have reached as the result of some years' study of the Sanglax and other Çağatay dictionaries. Apart from the work of Fatḥ ᶜAlī Xān Kacar (see para. 33) and the possibility of discovering new dictionaries, which are however unlikely to add much to our knowledge, anyone who wants to know more of the Çağatay language than is contained in the Sanglax and the Abuşka (the latter to be used with caution) must go to the original literary texts. The *Muḥākamatu'l-luġatayn* was not used by the author of the Sanglax, and a new edition of it, with a good index, is much to be desired; very little extra material is likely to be obtainable from the other works of Nawā'ī or the other authorities quoted in the Sanglax, considering the meticulous care with which our author combed them for material, but some extra material might be obtained from authors whom he did not consult, like Saqqāqī.

70. The "Eastern Turkish" material in Zenker's "*Türkisch-arabisch-persisches Handwörterbuch*", published in instalments from 1862 onwards, was probably derived from an epitome of the Sanglax; it is not an independent authority.

71. The vocabulary to Vambéry's *Ćagataische Sprachstudien*, published in 1867, was built up from two heterogeneous sources (1) an epitome of the Sanglax, and perhaps the *Abuşka* (though that work had not yet been published), representing genuine, but second-hand, Çağatay material with a good many errors, and (2) the author's own collection of contemporary words, mainly Özbek, with a few from Xiwa and Chinese Turkestan, some of which are valuable and interesting; but it is hard to distinguish between the errors in (1) and the genuine material in (2).

72. Pavet de Courteille's "*Dictionnaire Turc-oriental*", published in 1870, is a painstaking

and careful compilation of material from the *Abuşka*, an epitome of the Sanglax, Vambéry and the author's own studies of Ilminsky's edition of the *Bābur-nāma* and Abu'l-Ğāzī's *Sacaratu'l-atrāk*. Only the last two bring in additional material and the latter work is in 17th Century Özbek, not Classical Çağatay, which introduces an additional element of heterogeneity into the mixture.*

73. Şeyh Süleyman Efendi's "*Luğat-i Çağatay wa Turkī-yi ᶜUṯmānī*", İstanbul, A.H. 1298 (A.D. 1881), is based primarily on the *Abuşka*, one or more of the epitomes of the Sanglax, certainly Pavet de Courteille, possibly but probably not Vambéry, and the author's own collected material. It is known that he offered small rewards for "new" Çağatay words, and it may be suspected that some were invented just to qualify for the reward. It contains a number of quotations, some of which go back to the *Abuşka*, while others seem to be contemporary Özbek. The book is full of misprints, but it is a mistake to suppose that all the unintelligible translations, of which there are many, are mere misprints; some are unintelligent reproductions of matter from previous authorities. For example **çap** (p. 144) is translated (1)† *yağma, ğārat, talbīs, tadlīs* (which is merely an expansion of *talbīs wa tadlīs* in the Sanglax 204r. 26); (2) *qāf-wāw-şīn dāl-wāw yügür*; (3) *amr-i qatᶜ kardan.* Only comparison with the Sanglax will show that (2) is not *kuş* "a bird", *dū* (Persian "two"), but **koş** "run" (Turkish), **daw** "run" (Persian), and **yügür** "run" (Turkish). Those who seek an issue out of such troubles in the epitome and German translation, I. Kunos's "*Sejx Sulejman Efendi's Čağataj- Osmanisches Wörterbuch*", Budapest, 1902, are likely to be disappointed; for example the entry of **çap** (p. 39) extends only as far as *tadlīs*.

74. Radloff's great "*Versuch eines Wörterbuches der Türk-dialecte*", St. Petersburg, 1888–1911, takes material from all the dictionaries mentioned in the preceding four paragraphs and adds nothing extra except a few mistakes; but careful comparison shows that he did not incorporate all the material contained in any of them.

75. The fact is that these dictionaries are open to the same strictures as those contained in our author's criticism of his predecessors quoted in para. 31 above. Errors tend to be cumulative. For example **çiban** (215v. 14) was mistranscribed **çibay** in one of the epitomes. The word does not occur in the *Abuşka*, so Pavet de Courteille's only entry is **cibay** (*sic!*) "*clou, ulcére* (boil, ulcer)" (p. 301). Şeyh Süleyman, taking *clou* in its commoner meaning of "nail", reproduced this (p. 142) as **cibay** *çivi, mixce, pāra, carāhat, qibla* (or *qubla* ?), *mismār, mix* "nail, small nail, piece, wound, south or kiss ??, iron nail or wart, nail". Kunos (p. 53) reduced this to "wedge, nail; wound". Radloff enters the word three times:—III 2098 **çiban,** Osmanli and Karaim, "pimple, boil", with a number of quotations; III 2154 **çibay** (*sic*), Çağatay, "pimple, boil"; IV 155 **cibey** Çağatay, with a reproduction of Şeyh Süleyman's entry, untranslated. A good example of cumulative error going right back to one of the epitomes is **albutu,** translated in the Sanglax (49v. 25) *raᶜīyat, bāc guzār* "peasant, tax-payer" and described (correctly) as a Mongolian word. By an astonishing muddle the epitome turned this into *zaynat tāc kamar*, which Pavet de Courteille (p. 30) rendered "ornament, crown, belt". Şeyh Süleyman, who must have consulted the epitome

* On this subject see Abdülkadir İnan's article "*Ebugazi Bahadir Han ve Türkçesi*" in Türk Dili Araştırmalari Yıllığı, 1957.

† The paragraphing is mine; it is not in the original.

itself, amplified its text to *zaynat*; *tāc*; *zīb-i kamar* "ornament; crown; belt ornament" (p. 18), which Kunos (p. 62) reduces to **elbutu** (*sic*) "ornament, crown". Radloff, I 436, has **albutu,** Çağatay, with references both to Pavet de Courteille and Şeyh Süleyman, the latter quoted. Another instructive example is 62r. 19 **ötege** *xirs* "bear" (animal), described (correctly) as Mongolian. Pavet de Courteille (p. 44) reproduces this entry, adding the Mongolian form. There is nothing to show whether he took the hint from his source or made the discovery independently; the latter is the more probable. Şeyh Süleyman's entry (p. 25) is **ötege** *xirs, dubb, ayu, ayık,* all meaning "bear"; the last word is, of course, Çağatay and goes back ultimately to Sanglax 57v. 7; but it completely deceived Kunos, whose entry (p. 155) is **ötke** (*sic*) "bear, sober". Radloff's entry (I 1268) is **ötke,** Çağatay, from M. **ötege** "bear" (Ş.S. *xirs, dubb, ayu*). It will be seen that he avoided Kunos's mistake by the simple device of omitting *ayık*.

76. What has just been said is, I hope, a sufficient warning against the perils which lie in wait for those who rely on secondary authorities and do not go back to the fountain-head, the Sanglax. But I should not like to appear merely as one who condemns their errors without recognizing their merits. Pavet de Courteille, in particular, has done great service to Çağatay studies by his translations of quotations taken from the *Abuşka* and other sources. He, and all the other authors concerned, were earnest, and even dedicated, men whose sole purpose was to increase our knowledge. They worked under great handicaps and we should be grateful for their help, while forgetting their faults. If they had ever seen it, they would no doubt have echoed the plea in the concluding words of our author's preface (2v. 6), "wherever errors or defects exist, I beg those who notice them to correct them with the pen of kindness".

77. I trust that the same indulgence may be extended to myself. I have had occasion in the course of this Introduction to correct errors of many of my predecessors, I hope not too unkindly. I feel sure that my own work too suffers from errors and omissions, and I too beg that those who notice them will correct them with the pen of kindness.

78. I cannot close this Introduction without expressing my sincere gratitude to two of my friends. Mr. Victor Ménage, of the School of Oriental and African Studies of the University of London, has examined the Introduction and Indices with extreme care and made several valuable suggestions, particularly for removing asterisks in Index III. Dr. Charles Bawden, of the same School, has devoted the same attention to Index V with similar valuable results.

INDEX I. GENERAL INDEX

(Words listed as main entries in Part III of the Sanglax, in the order in which they occur, with the addition of words occurring elsewhere in Parts I and III).*

* In 30v. 12 *atağlığ* G, L, O is an error for *atalığ*.

* The additional words, which are indented, are mentioned incidentally in Part I or in the text of entries relating to other words in Part III. Where a word occurs several times in Part I, references which would add nothing extra are not given. The first word in each Section of the text (see para. 55 of the Introduction) is marked with a capital letter. "Duplicates" (see para. 52 of the Introduction) are printed in *italics*.

adaş W, Q, E.
27. adak Q, E, X; 2 1Ng, 1F.
33v. 5. adağlığ Y.
6. adra† W; m.
adun† W; M; Z.
aduncı† m-t.
7. adırğan† s, M.
edik W.
8. adım W.
Ar- C, X; x 158r. 11.
24. arı- S, C, Q, E, X; x 34r. 17.
34r. 15. arıt- s, c, q.
17. arıl- s, X; x 33v. 24.
18. ara-† C, q.
34v. 1. arat-†.
2. arala- C, Q; 2.
23. arba- C.
35r. 5. art- C, Q; 2.
arta-/artan- E 35v. 7.
24. artur-.
artıl- s, C, Q, E; 2.
35v. 17. ardlaş-† s, C (misspelt with *-mek*).
36r. 2. ardlaştur-‡ (misspelt with *-mek*).
3. arzı- S, C, Q; P.-T.
15. arğada-† C, Q; m.
aryak- E, 35v. 7.
36v. 2. Ara W, Q, X.
6. *ara ayı* s.
araba W, q, Y; (A); F.
7. *arasıda* x 36v. 2.
8. *arasıda mén* X; x 36v. 12.
9. aral q; 1m, 1Ng.
11. aralığ q.
12. *ara mén* Q, X; x 36v. 8.
15. aran q, X; 3.
17. arran† Q; qNg; 1Np.
21. erewül† W, X; m; x Özbekiya 323v. 10.
22. arayıcı yulduzlar s, Y; R.
23. arbağ W, Q; 2.
25. arpa s, W; 1B; 1Np.
26. arpağan B.
art S; 2.
27. artuk.
artuksı† q; 18r. 18.
28. artuksılığ‡ q.
29. artukmac‡.
37r. 1. ertiş S; Ng.
2. ard W; 1, 2P.
3. ardıca† q; 17r. 9.
4. arduc Y; B.
5. arazwarı‡ s, q; f; e.
6. arsalan s, X, Y; 1Z, 1F; x 40v. 11.
7. ersün† s; F.
8. arğac s, X; F.
9. arğamçı† S, q; m; x 71r. 23.
10. arğdal‡ s, q; m.
13. arğımak s, q; m?; Z.
14. arğuştak† S, Q, E; 2f; F.
18. arğun† 1Np; 2P.
20. arğış.
arğ/k s, q, X.
22. arka Y.
arkaluc S; R; F.
23. arg† W, q; 1p, 1Ng, 1H; x 99v. 23.
25. erkec W, X; Z; x 99v. 24; 306v. 17.
26. ergen W; R.
erkene kun‡ S; M; Ngh; e.
29. arlat† q; Nt.
37v. 2. arman† W, q; 1p; 1P.
4. armanlığ‡ q; p-t.
5. *aranduk*‡ Y; e; x 71v. 23.
ernek W, Y; 1, 1Ng.
6. arucan‡ F; x 70v. 29.
7. arusun‡ s; M.
8. *aruk* s, q, X; x 37v. 18.
9. erük S; 1, 1B.
10. arun‡ W; M.
11. arı S, q; 1, 1Z, 1V, 1P.
13. arış F; e; x 37r. 9; (see 100r. 24).
14. arığ s, Q, X; 3, 1Np; x 37r. 21; v.9, 21.
19. arığsızlık.
arığlığ q; 3.
21. *arik* X; x 37v. 19.
arılmay maradi‡ (q); t-a.
22. Az- C, Q, E; 2.
38r. 17. azgaş- / azık- } † S, C, Q, E.
azıt- E 38r. 23.
38v. 15. azğur- s, C, Q; 4r. 28.
39r. 5. azal-†.
Az 1, 1V, 1P.
6. az azğına q.
7. azağlak† s, q.
8. azak Ng.
9. azbuy‡ s, Y; B; e, f.
azğun q.
10. azğunluğ.
11. azlığ q.
13. azu W, Y.
azwa† W; B; e, f.
14. azuğ/k S, q, E; 1, 1P.
17. As- C, Q, E.
39v. 4. asıl- S, c, Q; 1, 1R.
10. astur- S.
11. asra- C, Q, E; m.
40r. 12. asrat- s, c, Q, E; m-t.
17. asral- s, c, q; m-t.
esri- x 74v. 8.
19. esenle- / esenleş- } S, X; R; x 223r. 1.
20A. *asa koy-* 1, 1R.
20. As Q; 1Z, 1ZR; 1Ng, 1V, 4P, 4A, 2H.
27. asabkur‡ S, q; d.
29. ast W, q.
40v. 2. astıdağı.
astığ/k.
astın S, q, X, Y; 2, 1P; x 40v. 5.
5. asır S, W, X; x 40v. 4.
6. asrar q; 1a, 1V, 1A; e.
8. asramışı I.
esergiş S; R.
9. asru W, Q.
11. *aslan* s, X, Y; x 37r. 7; 42r. 8.
12. aslanlığ q.
asman E 39r. 19.
13. asma S; 1, 1RB.
14. esen W, X; x 104v. 22.
asi R; x 40v. 16.
asığ S, q, X; 2.
16. asığlığ Q; 2.
19. Aş- S, C, Q, E; 1, 1R.
41r. 12. aşur-† s; 4v. 8.
14. aşa- S, C.
28. aşat- s.
aşkıl- E, 40v. 28.
29. aşuk- S, E, C, Q.
41v. 16. aşuktur- S.
18. aşla- R.
aşlan- s; r.
19. aşın- S, c, q; R.
21. aşındur- r.
22. Aş, 1, 1V.
aşar‡ 1, 2V.
23. aşam W, Q; 2, 3P.
28. aşama s, q.
42r. 1. eşkek S, q.

* *Örkemci* in the cross-reference is an error for *örkebci*.

** Main entry *aldara-* in error.

9. alak bulak.
ala kulang‡* Z; t-p?
12. alaman† q; 1, 1Ng; f.
14. alamancı‡ f-t.
alamancılığ‡ f-t.
alankawa† s; Nph.
16. alanc s, R*.
17. alaŋ s, q.
19. alaw† s, q; P; x 336v. 11.
20. alay 1R, 1V.
21. *alay bozan* X; R.
22. *ala yontlu* s; Np.
23. alp S.
alp arslan Np.
24. alpak† s; F; m.
25. albutu† s; M; F; e.
altaw S, q.
26. altawla† t-m.
27. altayı† s, q, E, X, Z; m; x 50r. 15; 220v. 13.
29. *al tamğa* Q, X; x 49r. 19; 161v. 14.
50r. 3. altmış 2.
altmışar 18r. 5.
4. *al tut.*
altun q, E, Y; x 247v. 8.
6. *altun bilge*‡ I.
7. *altun tamğa*‡ q(P); I; x 161v. 14.
9. *altun muğ*‡.
10. altı.
altışar 18r. 4.
altı yéti birqi^{c} q; t-a.
11. alçak.
alçaklığ.
12. alçu‡ s } m.
alçın‡ S } m.
alcı s, Y; R; (cf. 336v. 12).
13. *alcu taşı* Y; R.
aldağ X; 5v. 1.
14. aldağuc R.
eldewen s; R; F.
15. *alṭayı*† q, X; m; x 49v. 29; 220v. 14.
17. alğu bérgü q; 5v. 7.
18. alğu Nph.
19. alğut‡ S; F.
20. alğur‡ s; m.
alğun‡ s, M.*
alkar‡ 1Z, 1V.
21. alkış s.
alma 9r. 22.

22. *alma baş*‡ Z.
almalığ Ng.
24. alanca S; Np.
25. elencik s; Np; M.
27. aluc S, Y; R; B.
aluk E, 86v. 3.
28. alıs S; R.
alış bériş 5v. 7.
alış satış 5v. 8.
alığ satığ 5v. 8.
elik‡ M.
29. *al yaŋağ* S(mi) (read *surx rū*).
alıncak‡ 17v. 18.
Em W.
50v. 1. amac 1Pş, 3P; F; e; 25v. 21.
3. *em otı* B.
emizek S, Y; R.
4. emizekli R.
emizikli R (cf. 115r. 7).
5. *emek* X; R; x 115r. 3.
emekdeş r.
6. emlük S; F; ?x 271v. 19.
7. amıdun S; M (read *sukūn-i nūn*).
8. Aŋ- S, C, Q.
26. aŋdur-.
27. aŋla- s, C, Q.
51r. 18. aŋlat- s.
19. aŋdı- S, C, Q (misspelt with *-mek*).
51v. 5. *enet-* S, Y; R; (see 117v. 3).
eŋir- E, 107r. 29.
6. En W, Y; R.
7. enege† S, X, Y, E; 20r. 20.
10. ant S, q.
12. antutay‡ S, M.
anca S, q; 15v. 14.
14. ancak S, q; R.
15. ancılayın S; x 220v. 10; R 317v. 24.
16. anda† S, W, Q(P), X; F; m; x 284r. 6.
20. andağı.
andağın q.
21. andak W, q.
22. anduz S, Y; B.
24. andık X; R; Z.
25. *andın.*
ansız } q; 18v. 10.
ansızın } q; 18v. 10.

26. enişte S; R.
anğal‡ S; F; e, f.
28. anaktar S, Y; R; greek.
ankara W; R; F; greek.
29. ankut/d X, Y; Z; e; x 261r. 18.
52r. 2. aŋ† S.
aŋa 1, 1V.
3. *aŋaca.*
aŋsız } s, q; 2; e.
aŋsızin } s, q; 2; e.
5. aŋlak.
engenar S; R; B; greek.
6. *enler* R; 51v. 7.
enük W; R; Z; (see 118r. 10).
7. aŋız S(mi).
8. *anlar* q, X; 15v. 14; x 51v. 7.
10. *anı* Q, E.
anın E, 52r. 15.
18. *aniŋ* q.
21. Awla- S, C, Q, Y; 2.
52v. 14. awlat-s; 2.
15. awlan-s.
16. awlaş- s.
17. awun- S, C, Q.
53r. 4. awut- S, c, Q.
11. awucla- s, C, q.
24. awuclat- s.
25. awuclan- s.
26. awuclaş- s.
27. Aw q; 2; 17r. 19.
28. ewtünc S, q, X, Y; x 88v. 26, (error for *ötünc*).
53v. 1. awcı.
ewrüŋ S (error for *ürüŋ*).
2. awlak 17r. 23.
awuc s, q.
3. *awuc oyunı* R; F.
5. awurt S, q, Y.
7. awul S; A (*sic*, but an error).
8. awultaş†.
awuncak‡ s, q.
10. Aha‡ Q; F; f.
13. Aya- S, C, Q.
ayak- E 91r. 25.
ayan- E 110r. 12.
54r. 3. ayt- } S, C, Q; 12r. 25.
ayıt- } S, C, Q; 12r. 25.
54v. 3. aytış- s, c, q.

6. aytıl- s, c, Q.
11. ayr- / *ayır-* } S, C, Q.
28. ayrıl- S, c, Q.
55r. 2. ayrılış- s, c, Q.
6. ayırtla- S, C; 2; e.
19. ayırtlaş- s.
20. ayıl- S, C, Q, X; x 56v. 24.
55v. 6. ayıldur- S, c, q.
9. aylan-† S, (E), C, Q.
56r. 4. aylaş-‡ s.
5. aylandur-† s, q.
7. eyle- s, C, Q.
56v. 7. eylet-.
aynı- S, C, q, X, (misspelt with *-mek*).
23. aynıt- S, (misspelt with *-mek*).
24. ayın- S, q, X; R; x E 110r. 11.
26. Ay q; 3, 1Np.
28. aya q; 1, 1V.
57r. 1. iye S.
2. ayaz W; 1, 1Np.
aya/usalğu E 165r. 29.
ayağ/k q; 2; 19v. 14.
5. ayağ/kcı q.
6. eyegü S, W, X; x 92v. 2.
7. ayalğu† s, Q; m.
9. *ay baltu* Y.
ay toğdı Ng.
10. aycılığ q.
12. ayıd ağacı s, X, Y; R; B; f; x 57r. 27.
13. aydacı.
14. aydın S, q; 24v. 5.
16. ayrağ/k S; Z.
17. ayran W.
18. *ayru* s, q; x 57r. 24.
19. ayruk S, X, Y; 2, 1R, B.
21. ayruksı S; e.
eyrüm s, E; x 99v. 7.*
23. ayrı s, X; 1, 1Z, 1F.
24. ayrıc† S; Z.
25. ayrılış S, q.
27. ayrım s, X, (E).
ayıṭ ağacı X.
28. ayğır S, Y; Z.
aykak† S, q.
57v. 1. aylığ.

* In l. 22 and 23 *érdem* is misspelt *érwem*.

aylak W, Y; R.
2. eyle q; 1 (*or* ayla?), 1V; x 113r. 16.
4. ayırtğu‡ s.
aynuksı† s, q; e.
6. aywa Y; B.
ayu kulağı Y; R; B.
7. ayığ/k s, Q, Y; 1, 1Z.
10. ayığlığ.
10. ayıl S; 1F, 1V.
11. *ayım.*
Öp- S, C, Q.
27. öpüş- s.
28. öpül- s.
29. öpdür-.
öpre- } S, C, q, X; x 77r. 8 (spelt *opra-/opran-*); 93r. 4.
58r. 1. öpren- } S, C, q, X; x 77r. 8 (spelt *opra-/opran-*); 93r. 4.
22. Oba 1, 1Ng.
23. opa* s, q; f.
24. öbçin S, q; m.
26. öbçinlig/öbçünlüg q; m-t.
27. öpke S, Y.
öpkelig.
28. *öbücte* / öbüçin } † S, M.
29. öbüsün‡ S, Y; M; B.
58v. 1. öbüge‡ Q; m, e.
2. übük* X; 2Z; x 93r. 11; 188r. 16.
4. *übük* kuşı* Y; Z.
übül‡ M.
5. *oba* X.
opa X.
Öt- 1, 2R / ut- s(bi); 2 } C, Q, E.*
59r. 28. ötüş- s, C, q, X; 1, 1R; x 28v. 20.
59v. 14. *ötür-* / *otur-* } S, c, Q, E.
21. ötger- S, C, Q, E; x 59v. 15.
60r. 14. ötgeril- s, c, Q.
18. ötgeriş- s, c, q.
20. ötgen- S, E, C, Q, X; x 92r. 14.
60v. 11. utğuz-† S, C, q.
25. utğan-† S, C, q.
61r. 10. öte- S, C.

* The author correctly distinguishes between *öt-* "to penetrate" and (Rūmī) "to sing", *etc.* and *ut-* "to win", but "to singe" is *üt-*, not *ut-*.

24. ötel- s, c, Q.
27. otla- C, q; 2; 21v. 19.
61v. 16. otlat- s; 2.
16A. otlan- s; 2.
ötüz- E 59v. 18.
17. ötün- S, C.
62r. 1. Ot q, Y; 1, 3B, 1RB; 21v. 17.
3. *öt* 2V.
4. *ut* s(bi); 2V, 1H.
5. öte S; 2R; 2V.
8. otacı*‡ d.
*otaci Xaṭay**‡ Nt.
otağ/k X; x 66v. 16.
9. otağa q; F; m.
11. öteg.
otçı S, R.
12. oturak R.
utru S, q.
14. ötrüg.
ötrüggine q; 22v. 26.
15. ötgür† 2; 7v. 27.
16. ötgün S, Q; 1, 1F.
18. ötgünci q.
19. ötege‡ S, Y; M; Z.
20. ötleş ötleş*‡ Q, E; d.
25. otlağ/k.
otluğ/k q; 2.
27. ötlügen† S, Y; Z.
28. *ötelgü*† S, Y; Z; m; x 179v. 2, (see 95v. 11).
29. ötmek q, X; 1, 1V; x 30v. 26.
62v. 3. ötmekci Q.
5. ötme R.
utma (*for* ütme) s(bi).
7. otucı*‡ S; M.
ötür† S 1, 1V.
8. *otur* R V.
oturtma s; R.
9. ötürgü s, Y; F.
10. otuz q.
11. *otuz altı xaṭṭ* q; t-a.
12. *otuz iki* Nt.
13. ötüg q, Q(P); 1, 1I; 5v. 25.
ötünc x 53v. 1.
16. ötünci‡.
17. otuncı.
ot yém s, q; B.
19. Uç- s; 3; / 23. öc- Y } C, Q.
63v. 5. uçur- 3; / 7. öcür- } s, C, Q.
64r. 21. ucuş- S, E.

23. öceş- S, C, Q (misspelt with *-mak*).
64v. 11. öceştür- (misspelt with *-mak*).
uçra-† S, C, Q; m.
28. uçraş-† s, c, q; m-t.
65r. 2. uçrat-† / uçraştur-‡ } s, c, Q; m-t.
6. Uc q.
7. öc.
üç s.
8. *uç/öc* 2V, E.
9. uca S, Q; 1, 1F, 1R.
16. ucar*† W, X, Y; 1B, 1; f; x 245v. 25.
18. uçar*‡ 1 (read çidār), 3V.
üçer 1, 1V (öcer); 18r. 2.
19. üçergü S; F.
ocağ/k q; 2F.
22. ocağlak‡ B.
uçelesi† q; t-m. (v. 65r. 27).
24. uçan S, X.
25. ucan*† Ng.
öcew s, q.
26. üçewle/ücewlen q; t-m; 17v. 17.
ucru E 65v. 14.
27. ucsarrak*‡ s, q; d.
29. uçğur† s; 1, 1R (*band-i izār*); 7v. 26.
65v. 1. uçğun S, q.
2. uçğunluk.
3. *üç kat*† B.
üç kırlık‡ s; F.
4. ücgü S, q, Y; Z.
6. öcek*‡.
uclıb*‡ s; F; d.
7. uc/çmağ/k q: 1, 1V; sogdian.
9. uçma† q, X; x 65v. 11.
11. uçurum X; x ditto.
uc/çur† S, q, E; m.
14. ucuz s.
15. uçuş† S, Q, E.
18. uçuğ S, q, Y; 2, 2R; x 65v. 21.
21. uçuk X.
üç ok† q(P); Nth.
24. öcüg† s, Q, E; 2.
29. ocun* q; sogdian.
66r. 1. *üçün* q, X; 16r. 19; x 96v. 28.
3. üçünc S.
4. *üçünci* s.
uçça*‡ S, Q; Ng.
6. *üç yulduz*.
7. Oxşa- C, q; 2.
26. oxşaş- s, c, q.
29. oxşat- s, c, Q; 2.
66v. 9. Oxşaş Q; 1, 1V.
12. oxşuk*‡ s; Z.
13. *Öde-* / ödeş- } S, R; (cf. 61r. 10).
14. Öd S, Y.
ud X; x 92r. 20.
15. *oda* q, X; R; x 62r. 9; 66v. 20.
17. *ödek* s; R; 2; x 62r. 10.
18. ödemiş*‡ Nt.
ödlek† S.
19. üdür‡ S, Y; M.
20. ödünc S.
oda X.
21. Or- s, Y / ur- s(bi), X; 2 / 22. ör- s / 23. ür- s(bi), Y } C, Q.
67v. 15. orul-S / 16. urul- s(bi) / örül-s } c, Q.
21. ordur- s.
22. urdur- s(bi).
ördür- s.
ürdür- s(bi).
23. urun- S, C, Q.
68r. 11. uruş- C, q.
25. uruştur- q.
28. örte- S, C, Q.
68v. 22. örten- s, c, Q.
27. ürk- S, C, q, X; x 324v. 9.
69r. 11. ürküş- s.
12. ürküt- s, X; x 324v. 10.
13. örgen- S, C, Q; 2.
69v. 8. örget- s, c, Q; 2.
12. ürgüde- / *ürgüle-* } † s, E, C, Q, Y; 3v. 25.
ürgüre- E 69v. 13.
70r. 7. örle- S, C, q.
21. örlen- s, c, q.
23. orna- S, C, Q.
70v. 7. ornaş- s, c, q.
9. ornat- s, c, Q; 2.
13. ornuk-† S; e.
14. uranlaş-† s; m-t.
15. oranla- R.
16. öründle- S; R (misspelt with *-mak*).
17. öründlen- s; r (misspelt with *-mak*).
ürper- S, R; 2.
18. Ör† W, Q; 2; x 106v. 27.
21. ur Y, R.
22. *or/ur/ör/ür* V.
23. *ūr* 2P.
24. orağ/k W, Y.
25. orakçı q.
26. *orak kuşı* Y; R; Z.
uragan 7r. 24.
27. uran X; M; F.
71r. 1. oran R.
2. uranlaşmışı‡ I, m-t.
orba S, W; R; italian.
3. ört S, q.
4. orta S, Q.
7. *örte* V.
orta çağlığ q.
9. ortağ/k q.
10. urtağ/k s(bi) Ng.
11. ortancı q.
12. örtüg.
13. orçın‡ S, X, F; 1m, 1P; x 141v. 17.
14. ordu s, Q.
17. *orda* s.
orda bégi.
18. örs S; 1R; (1P *awirs*).
urgaçı† s.
örke S.
örkebçi†* S, Y; M; F; x 45v. 12.
19. ürker† Y.
20. örkesün s, Y; M; B.
ürkek†.
21. örkemci† S, q, X; Z.
23. örgen s, X.
ürkü s, q; 1, 1R.
25. örküc S; 2.
ürgün E 74r. 3.
26. ürkünc S, X.
27. ürkünclüg.
örmek q; 1F; 1V.
29. orman / ormanlik } R; B.
71v. 1. örme† S; 2.
2. *örmücek* s; R; Z; x 71r. 22; v. 19.
3. *orn* S, Q, X; 2; x 71v. 21.
6. örnek† s, X; x 305v. 18.

20. ögçe S, Y; 265v. 20.
öggçesiz R; 79v. 21.
21. ükre S, W.
22. *üksek* S, X; x 345r. 3.
23. öksürük Y.
öksük q.
24. öksiz S; R.
25. ögüt S; 1, 1V.
26. ügü S, q, Y; Z.
28. ögür S; 1, 1R.
29. ögürdi s; R (error for *öŋürdi*).
80r. 1. ögürğa S; x 89r. 13 (error for *oŋurğa*).
2. ögüz s; e.
öküz közi Y; R; Z.
3. ügüş S, Q, X; x 345r. 5.
5. ögülge S, q(P); I, m, e.
6. ökün s, Q, E.
10. ögün 1M, 1V.
11. ökünc S.
12. ögündüruk (*sic*) S; R; F; greek; 17v. 15.
13. ögündüre s, Y; r, greek.
15. Ol- S, E, X }
17. öl- s } C, Q.
81r. 11. ula- }
ulandur- } S, C, Q.
81v. 9. ulan- s, c, Q.
16. ulaş- }
üleş- } s, C, Q.
olak- Özbeg, Türkmen of Xwarazm 47r. 15.
82r. 16. ulu- S(bi), }
uluş- s, } C, Q, E, (misspelt with *-mek*).
82v. 12. oltur- 2; }
15. öltür- } s, C, Q, q(P); 4v. 11; x 59v. 16.
83r. 29. olturt- }
öltürt- } s, c, Q; 4v. 12.
83v. 8. olturğuz- C, q; 4v. 15.
23. olturuş- s, C, Q.
84r. 12. ölüt- S, C, Q.
26. ölceş- }
ölce- } ‡ s, C, q; F; m.
84v. 13. olcala-† s, C, q; m-t.
27. ölçe- s, C.
85r. 9. ulğay- S, C, Q, E, X; 2; x 85v. 13.
85v. 8. ulğayt- S, c, Q.
12. ulal- S, c, q, X; x 85r. 10.
14. Ol q; 15v. 15.
15. öl Q; 2.
18. *ol/öl* 2V.
19. ula‡ S(bi); M.
20. ölet.
ulaşık.
21. ulağ/k q; 1Z, 2F.
24. ultaŋ S, Q, X; F; e.
28. *ol turur* q.
86r. 1. olturuşluk.
2. olta S; R; italian.
3. olca Q; 1, 1m; x 86r. 12.
olcar E, 206v. 8.
7. ölceş‡ X; m; x 84r. 28.
8. ölçek S; q.
9. ölcemişi‡ I, m; x 86r. 7.
ölcey‡ M, 86r. 10, 12.
10. ölceytü‡ s; M; Nph.
12. *olca* S, X.
13. *olçih* Q; t-p.
uldaŋ x 85v. 27.
15. ölke† m.
16. ülgü s(bi); 2; x 124r. 17.
ölgüş‡ s; d.
17. ol luğ s, q.
18. öl lük s.
19. öleŋ S, Q; 1B, 1F‡, 1Ng.
25. *ulu taw* 1F; x 71r. 1.
26. ulus s, q; t-m.
27. ülüş s, q.
29. uluğ/k Q, E; 2.
86v. 5. oluk R.
uluğ/kluğ/k (G, O in error *uğ/kluğ/k*).
ölüg q.
7. ölügse s, q.
9. ölüke‡ s, M.
ululuğ X.
ölüm Y; 1, 1*‡.
10. ölümtük S, q.*
11A. ölümlük q.*
13. Omal-*‡ ("not conjugable").
14. um- S, q; R (misspelt with *-mek*).
16. umul- s, q; R (misspelt with *-mek*).
17. Oma† X (L . . . . *mafsal-rā gūyand*).
18. umac q.
19. omaça† S, X; x 86v. 18.
20. *omak*† X, q(P), E; h.
24. umanc s.
ömgen/*ömgün* s.
25. ömüdün‡ s, Y; M.
omuz s, Y.
25. Ön- S, C, Q, X; x 88v. 17.
87r. 14. öndür- S, c, q; 2.
17. una- S, E, C, Q.
87v. 6. unat- S, c, q.
8. unut- S, C, Q; 12v. 17.
26. unuttur- c, q.
28. unutul- S, c, Q.
88r. 3. ünde- S, C, X; x 116r. 27.
15. oŋar- S(mi), C, Y.
29. oŋarıl- s.
88v. 1. oŋal- S(mi), C, Q, X.
17. öŋ- X; R; x 86v. 26.
18. oŋul- c, q, X; R; x 88v. 2, (misspelt with *-mek*).
20. On.
ön V.
ün S(bi), q.
22. un Q.
24. ünen‡ M.
25. öntüc† S, q, X; x 53v. 1.
26. ondalık† s, Y.
27. ündür† S, Q, E; m.
89r. 1. *öndür* V.
ündürrek m-t.
2. onğay S, q, E.
oŋay E 89r. 4.
5. unkan‡ S; M; Z.
6. oŋ S, Q; 2.
9. üngü S; R.
10. öngür S, q.
12. oŋurğa S, X, Y.
14. üngülük s; r.
unut q; 1d, 1V; 5r. 29.
15. Uwan- S; R.
16. Uwa X.
uwad*‡ e, f.
uwadır*‡ s, X; x 308v. 28.
18. Oy- Y, }
uy- 2, } C, Q, E; x 294r. 29(?).
89v. 22. oyul- }
uyul- 2 } S, c, Q, E.

* *Ölümtük* is probably a scribal error for *ölümlük* in the passage quoted, in which, incidentally, it is misspelt, *-lü-* being omitted.

18. idi kut q(P); Np.*
19. *édiŋ* S, q; 16r. 25; x 99v. 12.
21. *édiŋiz* q; 16r. 26; x 99v. 14.
23. Ér- c, Q; 2; 5r. 4-7.
ır- R, 96v. 23.
97v. 1. éri- / éril- } S, C, Q.
24. érit- s, c, Q, Y.
27. ırcayıt-† s, C, q; m-t.
98r. 14. ırcay-† s, c, q; m.
17. ırğat- S, C, q.
98v. 2. ırğan- s.
3. ériş- S, C, Q, E.
27. ériştür-.
28. érik- S, C, Q, E.
99r. 15. irk- S; R.
irkil- S; r.
16. ırla- R; (see 349r. 9).
Ér / *éren* } S, Q; 2.
19. ér X; R.
ır R; (see 349r. 22).
ér V.
20. érenlik q.
22. érte S, Q; 3; x 99r. 20.
ertek E, 99v. 2.
28. érteki Q, E.
99v. 3. *ér taŋ*.
érdem S, Q, E; x 57r. 22, 23.
9. *érdük* q, X; 2V; 16r. 27.
10. *érdi* q, X; 2V; 16r. 24.
12. *érdiŋ* q, X; 2V; 16r. 26.
14. *érdiŋiz/érdıŋler* Q; 2V; 16r. 26.
17. *érse* X; 2V; 16v. 4.
18. *érseŋ* q; 2V; 16v. 4.
20. *érseŋiz* 2V; 16v. 4.
ırğat 1R; 1V; greek.
21. ırğay S; B; m.**
érk S, q.
23. *érg*† X; p.
24. *érkec* Q, X; 1Z, 1V; 16r. 28.
27. érkek s, Y.
28. érken s, Q, X; 1V, 1R; 16r. 27; x 100r. 11.
100r. 5. *érkenke* q.

* The etymology is a false one; the word is a corruption of *ıduk kut* "sacred majesty".

** The spelling phrase is corrupt in G, L and O; ? read *rā wa*[*yā wa fatḥ-i*] *ğayn* . . . .

6. *érkenlikin* q, X; x 100r. 10.
8. *érkenike* q.
érkenin q, X; x 100r. 7.
10. érkiştek‡ S, X; B; f; x 258r. 12.
11. *érkin* X; 16r. 27; x 99v. 29; 109v. 1.
12. érkene/*érkinek**† s, X; F; m, e.
13. érke† S, q, Y; 1Z, 1; f.
14. érlik.
15. ırmacuk R.
érmes q; 2V; 16r. 29.
16. *érmes érkin* q.
18. ırmak, 5r. 7.
érmen q; 2V; 16v. 2.
19. *érmeŋ* q; 2V; 16v. 3.
21. *érmiş* 2V; 16v. 3.
érn S, q.
22. *érür* 2V; 16r. 29.
23. *érürde* q; 2V.
24. *ériş* 1F, 1V; (see 37v. 13).
25. *érürsin* q; 2V.
26. irik S, q.
27. irikrek q, E.
100v. 3. iriklik q.
4. iriŋ S, Y, R.
5. Éz- S, C, Q; s(bilai), 25v. 26.
19. ézil- S.
20. izle- S, C.
101r. 4. izleş- s.
5. izlet- s.
İz q.
7. *éz* V.
És- C, Q; 7r. 5; 25r. 12.
21. éstür- c, q.
23. iste- s, C, Q; 11v. 11.
101v. 11. isteş- s.
istet- s.
12. istel- s.
13. ısıt- S, C, Q; 2.
28. ısın- s, c, q.
ısra- E 39v. 12.
ıska- Turks of Xwarazm, x 102r. 4.
102r. 2. ısla- S, X / 4. ésle- } C, Q, E.
102v. 6. ıslaş- s.
ıslan- s, C, Q; (2).
28. ıslat- s.
29. ısır- S, C.
103r. 16. ésirge- S, C, Q; 1, 1R.

103v. 5. éskir- / éskil- / 6. éski- } S, C, Q.
104r. 4. ésker- S, C, Q.
20. ésne- s, C, Q, Y.
104v. 6. ésnet- s, c, q.
9. ısmarla- R; p-t (G, O, in error, *ıslarla-*).
És (S(bi) is an error) q, X.
12. ıs q.
13. *ése*, 16v. 4; x 99v. 17.
14. *ésem* q; 16v. 5.
15. *éseŋ*, 16v. 4.
éseŋiz, 16v. 4.
16. ispir S, Y; R; Z; p.
17. *ıstı ot*‡ X; B; x 132v. 15.
iskele s; R; greek.
18. iskemle R; latin.
19. éski q.
20. ıslığ S, Y; R, (read *ba-Turkī*[*-yi Rūmī*]).
21. ısmarlama 2R.
ésen S, X; x 40v. 14.
22. ısıtma.
ısırğan otı Y; B.
ısırğa s, q, Y; f.
24. ısığ/k q.
25. *ısığ köl* Ng.
26. Éş- C, Q, E, Y; 2.
105r. 19. éşıl- s, c, q; 2.
21. éştür- 2.
22. işen- S, C, Q.
105v. 9. işendür-.
10. işne-‡ S, C, Q.
28. işnet- s.
29. işle- S, C.
106r. 11. işlet- s.
12. işlen- s.
13. éşit- C, Q.
28. éşittür- S.
29. éşitil- S, c, q.
106v. 2. İş W, Q; 2.
5. éş S(bilai) 1, 2V.
6. ıştan q, Y; 24v. 8.
8. işterek S, q; Pş.
10. iştek Nt.
12. işte s, Y; R.
işçi s, Q.
15. ışkırık S, X; 1F, 1; e; x 106v. 17.
17. iş kor.‡ e.
işkilik X; x 106v. 16.
iş küc; x 303v. 10.

* The spelling with back vowels is deliberate, see 4v. 28 and foll., but etymologically incorrect, probably dialectic.

20. élik S, q, X; 24r. 15; x 112v. 4.
21. ilik s(bi), Y.
22. Ém- C, Q.
113v. 5. émiz- S, C.
17. émizdür-.
18. émen- S, C, Q, E.
114r. 9. émgen- S, C, Q.
24. émget- s, c, q.
26. émgekle- C, q.
114v. 13 *Émes/émestür* Q; 16r. 26.
15. *émes bolsa* q.
16. *émen* Q; 16v. 2.
19. *émeŋ* q, E; 16v. 3.
23. émcek† q.
25. émdi q, 1, 1V.
26. *émdikece/émdike dégince.*
27. ımrağ S, q, q(P).
29. ımğa S; Z.
émgek s, Q, E, X; 2; x 50v. 5.
115r. 4. émegen† M.
émel‡ S, Y; M.
5. imir S, Y.
6. émizlik† 2.
émizik† s.
7. émizikli† 2 (cf. 50v. 4).
émiş } Q (G, L.O., in
8. *emiştür* } error -tük).
10. *émişsın/émiştürsin* q (ditto).
11. ımığ‡ S.
12. Én- S, C, Q.
27. éndür- c, Q.
115v. 2A. éneşle-† (*mayl-i nişīb kardan*).
2. inel-† S, C, Q.
17. ınan- C, q.
29. inci-† C, q.
116r. 12. incit-† s.
incin-† s.
13. incigir- S, C, q (G., O. in error *incir-*).
26. *inde-* S, C, Q, X; x 88r. 3.
116v. 14. indet- s, q.
16. ınık- S, C, q, E.
117r. 2. ıŋra- } s, (E), C. Q.
ıŋran- }
29. ıŋış-‡ S, c, q.
117v. 2. iŋle- } R.
iŋilde- }
3. énet- S; R; (see 51v. 5).
énen- s; r.
4. İn W, Q.
7. én s(bilai); 1, 1V.
8. ınağ/k q, E; 1, 1F.
11. ınamlı s.
ınan E 52r. 16.
12. *inen* X; Z; x 118r. 6.
ınanc S; 1, 1Np.
14. inewli† s.
15. incü S, Q, Q(P); X; 2, 1F; x 224v. 10.
20. incülük q.
21. inci s, q; 1, 1V.
23. incik† S; 2.
24. incike s, q; 2; x 95v. 24.
26. incikerek q.
27. ındaw† S, Y; B; f.
indekçi 7r, 17.
indür E 88v. 29.
28. éŋ S, Q.
118r. 1. inek S, E; 1, 1Z, 1P (*īnak*); E 118r. 13.
éneke x 51v. 8; E 118r. 13.
2. éŋek S(mi), q, E.
4. ingen S, q; Z; x 117v. 12.
6. *éngen* V.
7. éŋlik s, Q; 2.
9. iŋildü R.
10. énük S, X; Z.
12. ini S, q, E.
14. Éwür- S, C, Q.
29. éwrül- S, c, Q; 7v. 19.
118v. 11. éwrüş- s, C, Q; 2.
26. éw- S, R.
27. éwdür- r.
Éw q; X; x 92r. 16.
28. éwrül*‡ S; 1Ng, 1V.
29. *İyele*-† } S, C, q; (cf.
iyelen-† } 108r. 12).
119r. 20. Papatıya S, W, Y; R; greek.
21. babr ton‡ S, q; A-T.
24. bebek† W, X, Y, E; p; x 323r. 9.
28. Bat- C, q.
119v. 11. batur- S.
12. batlaş-† s.
13. Bat W, Q.
15. batrak q.
batak R, 119v. 17; 270v. 28.
16. batkak† X.
17. batman Y; 1, 1V.
18. batu S; M; 1, 1Np.
bet W.
19. petek S; R; greek (?), e.
peteke‡ S, Y; m.
20. petke‡ s, q; 2; f.
22. petik‡ s; F; f.
23. Baca† Pş.
24. bacanak R; F.
paçawra s; R; f.
26. Baxşı S, Q; chinese; E 120r. 12; 326v. 28.
29. Badalğa‡ S; p, e.
120r. 1. badak‡ W; Z; e, f.
2. bedenüs† s; Z; r, greek.
Bar- C, Q, E; 2.
120v. 22. barış- s, c, q.
26. barla-† X.
27. Bar q; 2, 1V, several P.
121r. 4. *bar ések* q.
5. *bar ésem.*
6. *bar éseŋ.*
bar ékec.
bar éken/bar érken.
barak Np. 95v. 13.
perewlik‡ s; f.
7. *bar biz* q.
perperem s, Y; R; B; f.
8. perpi S; B; r. f.
9. bartas q, X; 1Nph, 1Ng, 1Z; x 121r. 20.
15. bertik‡ S, q.
16. barça q, X; 2.
17. bardak s, R; x 310r. 9.
18. bars W, q, Y; 1Z, 1; p.
20. *barṭas* X.
barğa‡ S.
21. bark S.
perek E 193r. 13.
barlas S, q; Nt.
23. barlığ Q; 2.
25. barmağ/k 1, 1V.
26. barmaklığ 1R, 1V.
27. barandak*‡ Y; d.
28. barandakçı*‡ d.
barı Q, E; 1, 2A, 1P, 1Ng; x 121r. 17.
121v. 2. *barıca* q.
3A. *barıda* q; x 121v. 10.
4. parısa S, Y; R; B; greek (cf. 263r. 18).
5. barış Q.
7. barın Q.
9. *bar wa yok* q.
10. barınca X, q.
11. *barında* Q, 2.
14. *barangar* q, X; M; x

x 58v. 3.
16. Büt- C, Q; 5; 6r. 25; x 143r. 8.
129r. 12. bütker- C, Q; 5; x 143r. 11.
129v. 21. bütkeril- s; 5; 6r. 18, 22.
22. botra- } † S, E, C,
23. botraş- } Q*; m.
130r. 19. botrat- } † c, Q;
botraştur- } m-t.
23. But q.
24. *büt* V.
25. büte‡ (false etymology for next word).
26. buta† Q, E; 2; p.
29. bota Q; Z.
130v. 3. *buta*† X; p.
büte V.
4. botalığ.
bütew† s, q.
6. bütege*‡ B; f.
bütün Q; 24v. 25.
9. *büte/buta/bota* X.
buta 1Ng; 1P.
10. Bucağ/k W, q; 1, 1Np.
12. pucağ/k*† q; B.
14. *böcek* s; R; Z; (cf. 319r. 29).
15. bucurğad S; R; f.
16. buçuğ/k s; 1, 1R.
18. Buxsa-* S, C, q, Y.
131r. 6. Buxara q(P); Ng.
7. buxağu s, R; x 137r. 5.
puxak (*sic*) s; e.
8. *buxaw* s; x 137r. 5; (cf. 131r. 7).
9. Büdrü-† S, C, q, X, Y.
24. büdrüt-† s.
25. büdür- S; R; x 131r. 10.
26. buda- Y; R.
budan- s; r.
27. Budağ/k.
bodal*‡ f.
28. bodallık bodalıda*‡ q; f.
29. budandu s; R.
131v. 1. boday boday*‡ q.
3. bodur W; R.
büdene† S, Y; Z; m.

* The author insists that Tāli^c-i Harawī's front vowels are an error, but the word is derived from Mongolian *böte'ere-*.

Bur- C.
14. burul- s.
15. burun- s.
buruş- s; 2 or 3.
16. buruştur-.
17. börke- S, C, q.
132r. 3. börket- s.
börken- s, c, q.
6. borda-*‡ S, C, Q, E; m.
22. bordat-*‡ s; m-t.
23. burnaş-† S, C; 22v. 17.
132v. 7. Boran W, } † X.
borağan s, }
8. būrān P, Np.
purran*‡ s, W; Z; f.
burbay*† s, (E); f.
9. burtağ/k*‡ Q; m; x 205r. 8.
13. borc W, q.
14. burc/ç X.
15. burçak Y; 1B, 1, 1RB.
17. burçalık*‡ s; B.
pörcük* S; e.
18. pörçükli X; R.
19. borcın S, E; Z; m; x 247v. 8.
borçın S; Z; m.
20. bordağ/k m.
21. bursu*‡ S, X; B.
22. porsuk S, Y; Z.
25. burğu 1, 1R.
27. börk W.
28. börge s, Y; Z.
börgüt† s, q; Z; m; x 271r. 4, v. 3.
29. burma W; 3; x 132v. 21; 144r. 16.
133r. 2. *burn* S, q, X; x 133r. 15.
4. *burna* W, q, E; x 133r. 14.
6. *burna érkeni* q.
7. *burna çağ* q; t-m.
8. burnarak q.
9. *burnağı* q, X; 22v. 15; x 133r. 21.
10. buruşuk s.
11. burulğun S, X.
12. burun s, Q, X; 2; 24r. 19; x 133r. 4.
16. bürüncek S, Q; 2.
20. burunduruk Y; 1F, 1.
21. burunğı X.
22. böri Q, Y; Z.
24. borı Y; 1R, 1, 1

zabān-i Gurcī, 1H.
25. Boz- C, Q.
133v. 13. bozul- s, c, Q.
18. bozdur-.
19. bozla- C, q, Y.
134r. 4. Böz q, X; greek; x 147r. 27.
6. boz q; 1, 1Z, 1?P.
8A. buz X, Y.
8. *boz* V.
buzağu } s, q; Z; x
buzag (mis-spelling) } 118r. 11.
9. *buzaw*.
10. *buzaw başı*† Z.
11. *buzaw burnı* X.
bözçi greek -t.
bozçın E 132v. 17.
12. *boz doğan* S, Y; R; F.
13. bozlağ‡ q; Z.
14. bözlüg q; greek -t.
15. bozuğ/k q; 1, 1RF, 1Nt; x 65v. 23.
18. bozuğ/kluğ/k.
büzük R.
19. buzacı Nt.
Bus- C, Q, E.
134v. 5. püsgür- S; 2R.
6. Pus s; 2R.
7. bos s; MV.
8. *bus* 1V, 1P.
bosağa S, q; F; m; x 100r. 12.
bostağan E, 176r. 23.
10. püsgül S, R.
busu q.
12. bösün Y; M.
13. Buş- C, Q, E; e.
135r. 2. boşa- } C, Q.
boşan- }
135v. 1. boşat-.
2. buşurğan-‡ s, C, q.
17. Boş q; 2.
19. boşank‡ s; d.
puştu* s; X; R*.
püşük* 178v. 5.
20. Boğ- C, Q.
136r. 5. boğdur-.
boğuş-.
7. boğuzla- s, C, Q.
22. boğuzlat- s.
boğuzlan- s.
23. Buğ W, X; x 225v. 21.
24. buğa 1Z; 1Np; x 137r. 4.

* The correct Turkish form is *buğra*, which is borrowed by Mongolian as *buğura*; this form seems to be a muddle between the two.

** The second form is very dubious, and probably based on a scribal error.

* All these verbs should have front vowels; all MSS. change over to back vowels in the middle of the conjugation of *püle-*.

21. bitimlik‡.
22. Bıç- S, C; 2.
144r. 5. bıçıl- s.
6. Pic W (Y); 2R; p.
7. bıçak s, q, Y.
8. bıçğı S, Y.
9. biçek S, q, Y.
10. bıçın† S.
biçin q; 2; iranian.
12. Bıx- S, X; R.
13. Pıxtı s, X; R; p.
14. Bédew*‡ q; Z; d.
15. bide X; B; p.
16. Bér- C, Q, E; 2.
144v. 14. béril- S, c, q.
16. bırak- S, C, q.
29. bérki- } S, C, Q.
bérkiş- }
145r. 23. bérkit- } c, q.
bérkiştür- }
26. birik- S, C; x 145v. 9.
145v. 9. birikil- s, X.
birikış- s.
10. biriktür-.
11. Bir } q, E; 18r. 2.
birer }
13. *birerte* S, q.
15. birew s, q.
pirpirek E 263r. 29.
16. *bir dék* Q; x 145v. 22.
18. bérk S, q.
19. *bérkike* q.
20. birke q; 2.
22. *bir kibi* q, E, X.
bérgü 5v. 7; E 145v. 24.
25. bir künlik } Q.
bir künçilik }
27. birgine s, q.
29. birle/birlen Q; 16r. 21.
birlik 23v. 16.
146r. 2. *birin birin* q.
3. béri q.
bériki E 193v. 5.
birinci 17r. 20.
4. *bir yolı* q.
5. Béze- S, C, Q.
20. bézel- s, c, Q.
23. bézeş-.
24. bézet- s.
Biz W, q, Y; 3; 15v. 2; x 148r. 8.
27. *béz* X; x 134r. 6.
bézek.
bézekçi.

28. bézelik q.
29. *biz biz* X; 15v. 2.
pızlawuk‡ S; F.
146v. 2. *biz üz* q; R; x 147r. 29.
3. *biziŋ* s, q (read ba-nūn, etc., with L.).
6. *Bésrek*† q; Z; m; (cf. 122v. 10;) x 209r. 2.
8. Bişür- C, Q.
23. bişürt- s.
24. biş- c, q.
26. bışkar-‡ S, C, Q.
147r. 14. Béş }
béşer }
béşele† t-m.
béşelesi† t-m.
15. *béşelemiz*† t-m.
béşeleŋiz† t-m.
béşew s, q.
16. *béş barmak* (X); 1R, B; 1Ng.
18. *béş balığ* Ng.
19. bişme } 1, 1R.
bişi }
20. bışığ/k Q; 5r. 1; 24v. 4; x 147v. 9.
22. béşik q, Y.
23. bişim q.
24. Bığ‡ Q, E; 3.*
147v. 4. bığlamışı‡ q(P); I.
5. pığu‡ S; 1Z, 1Np (error for *payğu*).
6. Bıkın S.
pıktı R, x 144r. 14.
7. Bégen- S, C, q.
22. Bég S, Q; 2.
25. pīk q, E; P, (error for *payk*).
27. bégec X, E; x 148r. 5.
28. *bég börki* X; R; B.
29. béktaş Nph.
148r. 3. *pékter*‡ S, X; F; x 126v. 2.
5. bége† Q, E, X; x. 147v. 28.
8. bigiz S, X.
bégim q(E); x 43v. 15.
10. bigin Q.
13. Bil- s(bi), C, Q; 2; 18v. 17.

* *Bığ* as a crasis of *bıdık* "moustache" is possible, though *bıyığ* is a likelier reading; the other two meanings perhaps result from false readings, but may represent *bayık*, described by Kaşğārī as a "Ğuzz" word for "true, reliable".

148v. 6. bilin- s, c, Q.
10. bildür- C, Q.
25. bélgür- s, E, C, Q, E.
149r. 22. bélgürt- s, c, Q.
27. bile- q; R; E 351v. 2.
29. Bél q.
149v. 1. *bil* s(bi) 1V; 2P, 1H.
2. bilezik† Y; e, (misspelt *bilerzik*).
3. bilek q.
4. bélek q(P); 1, 1R*, 1P.*
8. bilekce.
bilen q; 16r. 2, (cf. 145v. 29).
9. bilew S, q; e; x 281v. 3.
11. *bél bağ* q.
12. *péltek*† S, q; 127r. 16.
13. bıltur q.
15. bılturğı q.
16. bildürge‡ S; 2; f.
bildirçin Z, x 300r. 28.
18. bélgü S, Q; 3.
21. bélgüt‡ q; Nt.
23. bélgürme q.
24. bélgülük q; 2.
25. *bile* Q; 3, 1V; 16r. 20 (cf. 145v. 29).
150r. 1. *bilesi* q, E.
3. *bile siz* q.
4. *béli bağlı* Z.
5. piliç W; R; Z; slavonic.
bilik Q; 3; 5v. 1.
8. biliklik X; x 150r. 9.
bileki/bileli E 150r. 2.
9. bilimlik q, X; x 150r. 8.
10. Béŋze- S, C; x 321r. 25.
24. béŋzeş- s.
béŋzet- s; x 127r. 20.
25. Bincik yam s; M*; Z.
26. biŋ S; X; R.
27. *biŋ kat* Y; R; e.
béŋz/béŋiz S(mi); x 127r. 29; 321v. 8.
28. béŋzeş s.
29. Biy (i.e. bī?) (X); Z; 262v. 14.
bibi† q; p; (see 143r. 6).

* *Bélek* "gift" is not Persian, but good Turkish; it is recorded by Kaşğārī.

* The translation given here is otherwise unknown and seems to be an error; the Rumī author's translation is, however, correct.

** So L; G, O spell infinitive *-mek* but all MSS. conjugate with back vowels.

27. talpın- s, C, Q, X.
159v. 15. talğa- C, Q, E.
160r. 9. talğan- s.
talık- S, C, Q; x 158r. 11.
22. talabı- S; R; x 159r. 28.
23. Tal Q, Y; 1B, 1R, 1V, 4P.
28. tala† W, Q; 1m, 1V, (L, O *sabz wa* . . . .)
160v. 2. talac‡ q, E; 1f, 1P.
5. talaz s; R; greek.
talaş 1, 1V; x 159r. 9.
6. talağ/k Y; 1, 1P (cf. 224v. 8).
7. talan q.
8. *talay* 1, 1M, 2V, (cf. 224v. 8).
9. telpek† S; f.
10. talax q, P.
11. talğa Q; 2; x 224v. 16.
14. talğalık.
talğ/kan Q, E.
19. talğum.
talğıc X.
20. talfāsa‡ q; P.
21. telegen‡ S; F; m.
22. tala*‡ Q; F.
24. talıcı R; x 160v. 20.
25. telim R.
talın E 336v. 26.
Tamız- S, C, Q; 4r. 28.
161r. 11. tam- c, Q, X.
19. tamla- R; x 161r. 11.
20. tamşı- S, C, Y.
161v. 4. Tam W, Q, X; 2, 1V; x 161v. 10.
7. temecemişi‡ qP; M (I).
10. tamcı q, X; x 161v. 7.
11. *temi/ür kazak* S (all MSS. have *kāf* for *qāf*).
12. temren W; R; F; f.
13. tamğa X; 2.
15. tamğacı q.
16. temel W; R; greek.
17. tamla S; R.
tamur S, q.
19. tamuğ/k q; sogdian.
21. Tan- S, C, Q; E 150v. 22.
162r. 10. tanı- S, C, Q.
26. tanış- s, c, Q.
162v. 2. tanıt- s, c, q.
4. tanıl- s.*
5. taŋ- S, C, Q, E.
27. taŋla- s, C, Q, E.
163r. 15. taŋlat- s.
16. taŋlan- s.
tanla- S, C, Q.
163v. 8. taŋırğa- S(mi), C, Q, E; x 164r. 12.
26. tanbala-‡ s, C, q; p-t.
164r. 12. taŋsukla- X.
Tenbük‡ S; F; H *or* p?
13. tanba‡ p.
14. tentek† S, W; m.
tansuğ/k s, q, X, E; x 164v. 4.
18. tanğ/kal‡ s, W, q q(P), E; d.
22. tankıldu R*.
taŋ W, Q, E, X; 2, 1p, 1V.
27. *taŋ yulduzı* q, Y.
29. *taŋ* q; 2Pş, 7P; x 164r. 27.
164v. 4. taŋsuğ/k X; x 164r. 16.
5. taŋla s.
5A. taŋlağı q.
6. taŋlalığ q.
7. taŋlay† s; m.
8. taŋut Ng, Nt.
tanga† Q; p; 20r. 19.
10. tanuğ/k q, E.
12. tanuğ/kluğ/k q.
14. tanış 2, 1V.
15. Tawsa-‡ S, C; d. (see *tawsan*).
26. tawsat-‡ s; d.
27. tawus- S, C.
165r. 11. tawşal-† S, C, Q, E.
165v. 1. tawşaldur-‡ c.
3. *Taw* W; 1 Özbek (X), 1R(p).
4. tawaçi*‡ s, Q.
7. tawar W; 1Z, 1M.
8. tawaşı W; R; a.
tawsan‡ S, W, Q, (X); 3.**
15. tawsamışı S; I; d; x 165v. 18.
16. tawusmışı s, q(P); I.
18. tawuş W, q.
20. *tawşan kurtı* Y; Z.

* The spelling *ma*^{c}*a'l-nün* is an error, as the conjugation is "*bā lām*".

** This is a misreading of the old Turkish word *tosun* "restive"; *tawsa-* was probably invented to explain it.

tawşancıl S, Y; R; Z.
21. tawuşkan s; 1Z, 1.
22. *tawuşkan uykusı* q.
23. tawuğ/k s, q, X, Y; Z; x 157r. 24.
25. *tawğ*‡ s, Q. (error for *tuğ*).
28. tawluğa/tawulğa s, Q, X, E; m; x 157v. 20; 224v. 28.
166r. 5. Tay- S, C, Q, E.
23. tayıt- S.
24. tayıl- S, X, c, Q; x 249v. 22.
166v. 2. taya- S, X, C, Q; x 166v. 20.
20. tayat- s, X; x 166v. 3.
21. tayan- s, c, q.
23. tayağla- C, q.
167r. 9. tayağlat- s, c, q.
11. tayağlaş- s.
12. tayağlan- s.
tayın- x 166r. 25.
13. Tayağ/k q(E); 2; x 271r. 6.
16. tayancak s.
17. teyze W, Y, R. (cf. 224v. 28).
tayşı S 1 Chinese, 1Np, (see 261r. 25).
18. tayğac S (spelt *tayğak*) q; 2.
20. tayğur s.
taylak† Z; x 173r. 10; 306v. 19.
21. *taymağur* d.
tayıncak S.
22. Topul-† S.
23. toparla- s; R.
toprağ sal- q; F; x 179v. 27.
26. Tüb Q.
29. tob/tub/töb/tüb, 16v. 11; x 189v. 6.
167v. 1. top s, Y; 3, 1P.
3. toparlak S; R.
4. topal† S, (see 261r. 26).
tupal‡ Pş, (P also *tubal*).
6. topalak s, Y; B.
8. topalaŋ† S.
töben q, E; (cf. 124r. 8; 343r. 14).
11. *tüb tüz*, x 225r. 3.
tob tolı R.

* This verb has back vowels; the front vowels in the earlier part of the conjugation are an error.

14. tuşlan- } C, Q.
tüşlen-
178r. 13. Töş Q.
16. tüş q.
17. tuş Q; 3.
24. tüş Q; 1, 1V.
28. *tuş* 3P.
29. tüşçilik q.
178v. 1. töşek W; (lexicographic note).
7. tüşkün.
tüşken*‡.
töşlük q (misspelt with *-luk*).
9. tüşlük q, X, (ditto).
toşuk E 288v. 9.
11. *töşük* Q, X.
14. Toğ- C, Q; 2.
179r. 9. toğur- s, c, Q; 4r. 27.
13. toğra- S, C, Q.
27. toğrat- s.
28. toğraş-.
29. toğral- s, c, q.
179v. 1. Toğalak†.
2. toğan X; Z, (see 261r. 29).
toğanak† s, X; Z; t-p.
3. toğay† s, X; f; x 180v. 28; 261v. 3.
4. toğdak† Z; m.
toğdarı*‡ Z, F; m?
6. toğrı q; 2.
8. toğğan q; 1, 1V.
10. toğğanliğ/k q.
11. toğma q.
12. toğur† 1m, 1V (cf. 172r. 15).
13. toğurka*‡ S; m, e.
14. toğuş.
15. Tüfkür-† C; p-t.
27. *tofrağ sal-* X.
28. *Tofrağ/k* X.
tüfürük } † S, X; p-t.
29. tüfürcek
180r. 1. tofuk q, X; 4.
3. Toku- S, C, q.
15. tokut- s.
16. tokul- s, c, q.
19. tokun- } s, C, Q.
tokuş-
180v. 12. tokundur- }
tokuşdur-
13. *tokta-* } c, Q, X; m;
toktaş-† } x 169v. 21.

19. *toktat-*† } c, Q, X;
toktaştur-† } m-t.
25. Tok.
tokac†.
26. tokal† f.
27. *tokay*† q, X; x 179v. 4.
29. toktaş‡ 1m-t, 1V.
toktamış† 1Nph, 1Nt.
181r. 2. toktawul‡ m.
tokrat*‡ Np.
3. toksabay*‡ S, X; F; f.
4. tokluk q; 2.
6. tokmar*‡ S; F; f.
7. tokmak Q; 1, 1Nt. 1R.
9. tokuz Q; F; 19r. 19; 20v. 15 (*k/kk*).
19. *tokuz atabeg.*
20. *tokuz ton* (X); B.
21. tokuzuncı q.
22. tokuş 2.
tokulğa‡ S; M; F.
23. tokum‡ F; m; x 347r. 14.
toka q, X.
25. tokka s.
26. Tök- 2, } C, Q, E.
tüg- S(bi)
181v. 27. tökül- } s, c, Q.
28. tügül-
182r. 9. töküş- } s, c, q.
tügüş-
12. töktür-.
tügdür- s.
13. tüket- s, C, Q, E.
182v. 2. tüken- s, c, Q; E 182r. 19.
6. tükre-*‡ S, C.
20. *tükür-* S, C, q; p-t (cf. 179v. 15).
183r. 4. tükelle-† s (see *tükel*).
Tük W, X; 1, 1P; x 188r. 15.
tökeb/teş E 181v. 3, 4.
5. *töker taşı.*
6. tükel.*
7. tügeli S, X; R; x 255r. 24.
tügen S, q.
9. tükeniş q.
10. tüküz‡ S, q; d.
11. tügün s, q; x 225r. 27.
12. tügme S, q, E.

* This is an old word, but the meaning given here is otherwise unknown and probably an error.

15. tügi S; B.
15. Tol- C, Q.
183v. 4. toldur- c, q.
7. tula-*‡ } S, C, q (cf.
töle- } 184v. 2).
184r. 8. tolğa- C, q, X; x 184r. 21.
20. tolğandur- c, q, X; x 184r. 9.
23. tolğan- } s, c, Q.
tolğaş-
28. tolun- S; R; x 91r. 25.
29. Tul s(bi), W, q, Y; 1, 1F.
184v. 2. tül Z.
-tul/-tül X.
3. *tul* 1P.
4. tola q; 1, 1V (*tula/töle*).
5. tolaşık†.
tolak†.
6. tulamışı } ‡ I.
tölemişi
tülen‡ s; M.
7. tolay s; 2, 1MZ, 3V.
8. tolğaş s, q; 1, 1V.
10. tolğama s, q.
12. tulf*‡ S, q; (A); e.
14. tölek q.
15. tülkü Z.
tolu Y.
16. tölük*‡ q, X.
17. *tölüküm hay tölüküm**‡ q; e.
18. tulum Y; m.
19. tulumba s; R; italian.
22. tolun q.
24. tolı S, Y; 1M, 1Nph.
25. Tomuş-*‡ S, C, Q; d.*
185r. 10. tomuştur-*‡.
11. tum- R.
tumul- r.
12. Tomağa† q, E; F; f.
14. tümen q; F; kuchaean.
16. tuman X.
17. *tümen* Q, E; F; x 71r. 14; 141v. 6.
22. tümengini*‡ s; 1 Özbek; 1R*; e.
23. tomruk s; R.
tumşuğ/k Q; 3.
28. tumucı R.
tomuzğan‡ S; Z.

* There is no other trace of this verb; it may be an error for *yumuş-*.

29. Tun-‡ S, C, q.*
185v. 7. tona- S, C; m.
20. tonal- s; m-t.
21. toŋ- / toŋul- } S, C, Q; 2.
186r. 21. töŋter- S, C, Q.
186v. 7. töŋteril- c, q.
9. tünle- S, C, q, (misspelt with -*mak*).
23. Tün Q, E; 2.
25. ton q; saka.
26. tun 1V, 1PNp, 1P, 2A.
28. tüner*‡ S, W; 1m, 2V.
187r. 1. tünegün s, q.
2. tonanma X; R; x 261v. 9.**
3. tonbak‡ q; F; p.
4. tonpuz*‡ S; B; f.
5. tonğuc‡ S, q; d, (? error for *tüŋür*).
7. tün kutar‡ S, W, q, E.
9. töŋ*‡ S, Q.
12. toŋ q; 1, 1V, 1P.
13. toŋuz S(mi); Z, 1.
14. *toŋuz balığı* Y; Z.
15. toŋuzlan kurtı } Y; / *toŋuzlan böcegi* } RZ.
tüŋlük s, Q, E.
18. tönlük*‡ R*.
19. Tuwağ s, W, Q, X; 2; x 188r. 23.
22. tuwurluğ/k*‡ s, q; F; (see 314r. 22).
24. Toy- S } C, Q; x / 25. tuy- s(bi) } 276v. 17.
187v. 19. toyğar- S, C, Q; 4r. 26.
188r. 6. tuydur- S(bi).
7. tuyla-† S, c, q; m.
10. Toy q, X, Y; 1, 1Z, (see 261v. 12).
12. tuy‡ X; d.¶
13. tuy*‡ d.
15. *tüy* X; R; x 183r. 5, (see 261v. 15).
toy/tuy 2V.
16. toyğar† X, Y; 1Z, 1V; x 49v. 1; 222v. 29.
17. toyğur.
18. toyğun*‡ S, W, q; Z.

* This is, no doubt, an error for *tüne-* which has the meaning given here.
** Misspelt *tonatma*.
¶ There is no other trace of such a word either in Turkish or Mongolian; it was probably inferred from the Mongolian loan-word *tuyla-*.

20. *toy kuşı* Z; x 188r. 12.
toymağur q; d.
21. tuynağ/k s, q, X; x 187r. 21; 188r. 12.
23. tüynek† B; m?
tuyuk S, Q.
29. toyumluk S; R.
188v. 1. Tép- S, C, Q.
14. tépiş- S.
15. tépil- S.
16. tépdür-.
tépre- / 17. tépren- } S, C, Q.
189r. 14. tépreş- s.
15. tépret- s, c, q.
17. tıpırçıla-*‡ S, C, Q; e.
189v. 5. *Tibbet* s, X; Ng; x 167v. 12.
tib tik q, X.
7. tibit†.
8. tépreşlik s.
tépük s.
9. *tébéngü* S, X; p?
10. *tépe* S, q, X; 2; x 167v. 26.
12. tipizlik*‡ e.
Titre- S, C, Q.
26. titreş- s.
27. titret- s, c, Q.
190r. 1. tit- S.
2. titil- S.
3. Tit u bit† q.
4. titretme q.
5. titregüc.
7. *tétik* q, X; x 152r. 17.
9. Tér- S, C, Q; 2.
190v. 13. térdür-.
14. téril- S; 2 } C, Q; 4v. / 15. tiril- S(bi) } 20.
191r. 9. tirilt-s, X; 4v. 19.
tiriltür- 4v. 20.
10. tirgüz- S, C, Q; x 191r. 9.
28. tire- S, C, q, X; x 191v. 21.
191v. 15. tirel- S, c, Q.
19. térge- S, C, Q; 2.
192r. 13. térkeş-*‡ S.
14. térle- S, C, Q.
28. térlet- s.
tırma- S, C, Q; 2.
192v. 17. tırman- / tırmaş- } s, C, q.
tırmala- R 192r. 29.
193r. 9. Tér q.

11. térek Q, E; B.
17. tirek 1, 1P.
18. tirsek S, q, Y.
20. térgek q.
21. térlik s, q; 2, 1R; x 57r. 27.
24. térem s, q(P); I.*
25. tırnağ/k.
26. tıralık*‡ q; d, e.
27. téri S, Q.
193v. 1. tırık‡ s; B.
tirik s, Q, E.
6. tiriklik.
tirikley‡ Q.
9. tiril s; R*; 1d, 1V.
10. térim s.
térimci‡ (*sic* in L, O).
11. tériŋ s, Q.
13. Tiz- S, C, q, X; x 173r. 24.
27. tizil- S, c, Q.
194r. 1. tézgin-† S, C, q, X; x 194r. 26.
15. tézgindür- c, q; x 194r. 26.
17. tizin-‡ S; d.
18. tizle-† R; p-t.
19. Tiz S (and s(bi)) Q; 1, 1p, 1V, 1P.**
22. tézek s, q.
23. tizek‡ s(bi), q; d.
24. tizgin S, X, Y; 1, 1V; x 92v. 3.
26. *Téskin-* X.
téskindür- X.
Téskeri† S, q, E, X; m; x 155r. 26.
29. Téş- C, Q; 6v. 27; E 349v. 19.
194v. 15. téşil- S, E, c, Q.
22. tişle- S, C, Q; 3v. 17; x 317r. 27.
195r. 11. tişleş- s, c, q.
13. Tiş q; 2.
15. *tiş sürgü* R.
téşkeri E 194r. 28.
téşük q, X; 25v. 16; x 178v. 11.
17. tişi.

* This is apparently a corruption of old Turkish *teŋrim*.
** There is an inconsistency here; *tiz* "knee" (*ba-iṣbā*^{c}) is implicitly distinguished from "swift", but in 25v. 27 that word too is rightly spelt *ba-iṣbā*^{c}; it is Persian.

Téftik‡ p. (cf. 157r. 25).
18. Tık- C, Q.
195v. 2. tıkıl- } s.
tıkılış- }
3. Tıkılış q.
5. Tik- S(bi) 3 } C, Q,
6. tég- s(bilai) 3 } (E); E 352v. 9.
196v. 2. tikiş- s } C, q.
3. tégiş- s(bilai); 2 }
27. tikil- S(bi), c, Q; 4.
197r. 10. tégür- S, c, Q; 4v. 16.
tégürt- 4v. 16.
18. tiktür- S, c.
21. ték tur- C, Q, E.
197v. 14. ték turğuz- c, q.
16. tékren-‡ s, C, q, (misspelt with *-mak*).
28. tékrendür-‡ (ditto).
tékşe- E 201v. 12.
29. tékirle-‡ S, C; x 198r. 12.
198r. 12. tékirlet-‡ X.
13. tékirlen-‡ s.
tékirleş-‡ s.
14. tikleş-† S, X; 2; x 226v. 1.
15. Ték Q; 3, 1‡d, 1Rp; x 226v. 5.
19. *tég* 3V.
20. tik s(bi), q; 1, 2V; x 226v. 5.
22. *tékek* s; X; R; B.
23. tiken q, Y; B.
24. tégdi*‡ S; 1, 3V.
25. tékre S, Q.
27. tégrü s, q.
28. tékirlek† S; 1, 1R; x 302r. 23.
29. tégirme s, q, X; x 224r. 12.
198v. 2. tégirmen s, q.
3. tikış S.
tégiş s, q.
5. *tégişce* s, q.
7. tikiklik q.
9. Tél- C, Q; 2.
199r. 4. télin- s; 2.
5. tile- } C, Q.
tileş- }
199v. 8. tilet- c, q.
9. tilen- s.
10. télbere-† S, C, Q; 3v. 26.
26. télberet-† s, c, Q.

200r. 1. télmür- s, C, Q.
18. Tél‡ 1, 1V.
19. til s(bi), W, q.
20. tilek S, q.
21. tilençi s, q; 7r. 26; x 222r. 12.
22. télew S.
23. télbe S, q.
24. télbelik q.
25. tılmac† s, X.
26. télük S, q; 5v. 1; 8r. 11; 25v. 16; x 198v. 9.
28. télik S; x 200v. 2.
29. télim s, Q; x 198v. 9; 200v. 2.
200v. 2. télin s, q.
4. Tim tim*‡ Q, E; 1, 2P.
6. tımar† X; 1Rp, 1P; x 235v. 22.
8. témsi tép‡ S.
10. témür S; 1, 1Nph.
12. *témür tiken* Y; 1F, 1B.
15. *témür kapu* s; Ng.
témür kazuk s; 2; x 273v. 3.
16. *témür kanat* s, q, (E), Y; Z.
19. *témür yalığ* s; Np.
20. Tın- S, C, Q, E; 1, 1R; 7v. 27; E 166r. 21.
201r. 15. tındur- c, Q, E; 1, 1R.
21. tiŋla- S, C, Q; x 226v. 28.
201v. 6. téŋşe- S, } C, Q, E,
7. téŋiştür- s, } X; x 202r. 2.
202r. 1. téŋteş- } † S, X; x
téŋteştür- } 201v. 7.
3. téŋeş- S, c, q.
6. téŋel-‡ (probably error for *téŋle-*).
teŋleş- S, C.
20. teŋleştür-.
-Tin/-tin x 227r. 2.
21. tınc S, q.
23. tınğu S; 2; x 227r. 3.
téŋ S, q; 1, 1P (*tang*).
25. téŋteş s; x 202r. 28.
téŋteşlik.
26. téŋri s, q.
27. téŋrilik.
téŋ kor s, X.
28. téŋlik.
tınmağur s, q, E; d; 5v. 11.

202v. 3. téŋiz s, q; 1, Np.
5. Téwre-*‡ S, C, Q.
20. téwret-*‡ s, c, q.
22. téwrel- } *‡ s, c, Q.
téwrül- }
27. Téwrük‡ S, Q, Y; 1, 1F.
203r. 2. téwe tikeni S; B.
3. *téwe kuşı* s, q, Y; Z.
4. Tıy- S(bi), C, Q, E; 6v. 17; E 201v. 2.
29. tıyıl- S, c.
203v. 3. Tıyık S(bi).
5. téyin S, Q.
-Ca/-ce
8. *-ca/-ce* 2; 17r. 5.
9. *-ça/-çe* 1, 1P.
11. Çap- S, C, Q; 4.
204r. 15. çapış- s, c, q; 3.
17. çapıl- s; 3.
18. çaptur- c, Q; 2.
24. çapğuda-‡ s.
25. çapğulaş-† s.
26. çabala- s; R; e.
Çap S; 1p; 4V.*
27. caba W; R.
28. çapağan, 7r. 24.
çabak S; Z.
çapan† S, Q.
204v. 2. çapawkı‡ S, q(P), X; I; d; x 205r. 12.
çapawul† s; I; t-m.
4. çapçı‡ S; 1, 1R, (p-t).
5. çapar† S, W, Q, X; p.
8. çapğulaş‡ 2.
9. çapğun† S, Q; 2, 2R; 8r. 5; x 132v. 7.
12. çapğuncı‡.
çapak S; R.
13. çabuk† s.
çapuk† s.
14. cebe s, X; 1R*, 1RF a.
15. Çat- S, C, Q.
205r. 1. çatla- s.
2. Cat q.
3. *çet* s, X.
4. çatağ† 1F, 1, (E).
5. çatal s; 2R.
6. çetele s, Y; R; F; greek.
7. çatğal‡ X; f.

All MSS. read *ba-turkī*; this probably means that in Turkish the Persian word *çap* "left" (opposite to "right") means, metaphorically, "deceit".

* Probably an error for synonymous Persian word *çangal*.

14. cawcı‡ S; M; e.
çawdur*‡ 1Np, 1M, 1Nt.
15. *çewrük* S, X; R; x 222r. 3.
16. *çewrünti* S, X; Y; R; B; x 222r. 5; 224v. 19.
18. cawşa*‡ s; f.
cewek‡ W, Q, 2; e.
20. çawluk‡ s.
çawlı*‡ F, x, 71r. 1.
21. çewüt‡ d. }
çewürme† S, X. }
22. çawuş S, Q, Y; 2.
27. cawun*‡ S, q, E, X; f; x 215v. 8.
29. -*Ca/ce/-ça/-çe* 4, (cf. 203v. 8, 9).
210r. 3. Cayka- }
caykat- s } † C, Q.
22. caykan- }
caykal- } † s, c, Q.
210v. 1. çeyne- S, C, Q, Y.
12. cay-† S.
13. Çay s, W; R.
14. çayan S, Q, X, Y; 2, 1R; x 222r. 15.
17. *ceyren*† W, q, X; Z; m; (see 205v. 28).
18. çayır† s, W, X, B; x 32v. 1.
19. çaykun‡ S.
çaylak s, Y; R; Z.
20. çaylan‡.
çayılğan‡ F; x 71r. 1.
21. Çubul-*‡ S, C, q, E; d.
211r. 4. çubult-*‡ s; d.
5. çubru- }
çubrul- } s, C, Q; m.
çubruş- }
28. çubrut- s, c, q, E; m-t.
211v. 3. Çöp S, Q; 1†m, 1.
7. çupan s; p.
çupan aldatan } Y;
atrak-i Tūrān } Z;
çupan aldayıcı R } p-t.
9. *çupan kuşı* Z; p-t.
10. çubçuk S, Q; Z.
12. çöpür S; 2.
13. çubuğ/k s.
cübe E 215v. 11.
Çot† s; F.
14. Cucut- S, C, Q.
27. cucurgen- S, C, q; e.
212r. 10. Çöçek S, q.
12. cocğa S; Z; x 118r. 11.
cücük S, q.
çuçun E 345v. 19.
14. cocı S; 1M, 1Nph.
17. Çox q.
çoxluk 23v. 28.
Çoḏın x 215v. 11.
18. Cörge-*‡ S, C, Q.
212v. 4. cörgen-*‡ s, c, Q.
10. çürü- S }
çuruş- s }
11. Curra‡ W 1, 1Zp?, 3P, 1PNg.
13. çur*‡ W, q; 2, 1P, d.
15. çurpa‡ S; Z; m, e; x 118r. 12.
çurtan s, Y; R.
16. çörçek† s, q, E; x 230v. 28.
19. çördük s, X, Y; R; B; x 325v. 28.
21. çorğa† s; m.
çörgeşük }
22. çörgük } *‡ s, q.
23. çörek otı s, Y; B.
24. çürük S, q.
25. çura‡ S; p, e.
cura s, W; P.
26. çurı*‡ S; p?
27. Çöz- S, C.
213r. 6. çözül- S.
7. Çüşkür- S, C, Q.
20. Cüşkür.
Cuğ† q; p.
22. çoğ q, X; 1, 1†F; x 214r. 3.
24. çoğan† S, W; 1, 1B.
25. coğurcuk† S; Z.
26. çuğul q; p.
27. Cufut S, q; a.
28. Çoku- S, }
çokuş- s, } C, Q, E.
213v. 19. çokul- S.
20. çokal-† S, C.
214r. 1. Çok q; X; 1, 1F; x 213r. 24.
çokar E, 207v. 19.
4. çokal S; R; f.
çokluk 1‡F, 1†, 1‡; x 92v. 2.
5. çokmar s; F.
6. çukur S, q.
7. Çöker- S, C, q; 4r. 29.
19. çökeril- s.
20. çök- c, q.
22. Çök s, Y.
23. cögeri*† S, X, B; f; x 214r. 25.
24. çökek s; 2.
25. çökelik s.
cögen*‡ X; B; f; x 214r. 24.
26. çöküç/ş S, X, Y; F; p; x 208r. 12.
27. çögür† S, Y; F.
28. Çulğa-† S, C, q.
214v. 9. çulğaş- }
çulğan- } s, c, q.
12. Cul Q, E; 2A.
15. çöl s, q.
16. çolak s.
17. çolpa S, q; 1, 1R; p.
18. çolpan S, W, Q, E, X, Y.
21. çolpu† S, f.
22. coldu*‡ S, W, q; f.
23. cülge‡ s, q; m.
25. çölmek S, Y; R.
26. Com- S, C, Q.
215r. 10. comur- S, c, Q; 4r. 27.
15. çömel- S; x 215r. 24.
16. Çum*‡ Q.
18. çomak s, Y.
19. cömele*‡ f.
çoman† f. (cf. P çamand).
cumca*‡ S, q(P); I(m).
21. çömçe s, X.
22. comurğan 1, 1V.
23. çömüş*.
çömüşlü* Xatay Nt.
24. Çonkay-*† S, X; f.
25. Contayı*‡ q; f.
27. çonkayıtma*‡ s.
28. cuŋ*‡ q; Z; p?
215v. 1. coŋ† q; chinese.
2. coŋ*‡ q.
3. *cüŋ* X; özbek.
4. *cung* q; P.
5. çüne*‡ S; M; Z.
6. Cöwe'ün kol S, X; M; x 127r. 4; 215v. 6.
cöwenğar s, q, X; M; x 215r. 6.
8. *cowun**‡ S, X; f; x 209v. 28.
9. Cuy-† S(bi); (see 347v. 13).
çuy-‡ x 215v. 10.
10. çuyun-‡ S, X.

11. *Çoyın* S, X (çoḏın).
Cébe E; A.
13. cıbar‡ s (t. with m. meaning).
çıpar s; Z.
14. çıban s; e.
cibir‡ S, X, Y; 1Z; 1M; x 222r. 9.
15. cibilger‡ S, q, E; f.
17. çibin s, q; Z.
18. Çıt-‡ S, C, Q.
216r. 3. çıtıkla-‡ s.
5. Çit 1 Kāşğar, 1R; x 205r. 3.
6. *çıt* V.
çıtuk† s, q.
7. çitgir S, W; M.
8. Çéçen† S, q, E; m.
10. çıçawut* S; Nt.
11. çéçek S, Q, E, Y; 1B, 1.
15. çiçe† Samarqandī; Xwarazmī.
16. cıcığ† s, q; x 217v. 14; 274v. 16.
17. Cıda- C, Q; m.
216v. 3. Cıda 1m, 1Vm.
4. Çırp-† S, C.
13. çırt-† S, C, q, Y; 3.
29. cırğa-† S, C, Q, E; m.
217r. 12. çırma- S, C, Q.
27. çırmaş- }
çırmal- } s, c, Q.
28. çırman- }
217v. 16. çırmat- }
çırmaştur- } c, Q.
20. çérikle- S, C, Q.
218r. 2. Cir/çir† W, q.
4. cır*‡ q; Z; d.
6. *cir** q; 1Ng, 1P.
7. çıray S, q; m; x 205v. 12.
9. çıraylığ Q; m-t.
12. çırpı S; R.
cırpıcı S, Y; R.
13. *cércer* S; R; a. (cf. 205v. 14).
14. circirek† S, q, E, X, Y; x 218r. 29.
17. cırğalaŋ S; Ng.
18. cırğamışı‡ S, qP; I (m-t).
19. cérge† S, Q; 2; m.

* Probably a corruption of the synonymous Persian word *xargāh*.

24. çérge† s, Q, X; 1F, 1RF; f.*
27. cérgelik† q; m-t.
28. çérgelik†; f-t.
çırlık S, X; R.
29. çıram* s, W; R*.
218v. 1. çırmaş Q; 1, 1V.
3. çırmaşlığ q; 2; 8r. 25.
4. cérib† W, q; a.
6. çérik S }
çérikçi s } Q; 18r. 18.
8. cırım*‡ S; Özbek.
9. Çiz- S(bi); R.
çizgin- S, c, Q; R; x 194r. 2.
12. Ciz u biz*‡ q.
14. cızlığ‡ X.
15. Cisgin† s.
16. Çığnan- S; R.
çığnat- s; r.
17. Cığ† W, q; x 219v. 22.
18. çığ s, q.
20. çığan S, q.
21. cığan.
cığa† S; 2; p.
22. cığı† S, X.
çığıt S, X; R.
23. çığır‡ S, q; 2; f.
25. çığırğu S; R.
26. cığıldan‡ S, X; f; x 220v. 14.
27. cığıldu‡ S; e.
çığın S; R.
29. Çık- C, Q.
219r. 15. çıkar- S, c, Q; 2.
22. çıkış- S, C, q.
219v. 5. Çık s, q; 1, 1V.
7. çıkrık S; X; F; x 219v. 11.
8. çıkrıkçı.
çıkğur S, q; d; 5v. 9.
9. çıkuk† s, q; e.
11. çıkır† S, X; x 219v. 8.
çıkış S, q.
13. Çék- s, C, Q; x 239r. 13.
28. çéktur- s.
29. çékiş- s.
220r. 1. çékil- }
çékin- } s.
2. çikre- S, C, q.
10. Çigit S, q; B; x 218v. 22.
11. çigdig‡ S; R*; B; e.

12. *çékdiri* s; R; (see 208r. 5).
13. çigelek† S; B; e; (cf. 220v. 1).
çékme 10r. 17 (cf. 208r. 9).
15. *çékmen*† X.
çégürtke* S, X; Z.
16. cégirdek‡ S; B; d.
17. çégirdek s; B; x 235v. 29.
çigildem‡ S; B.
18. *çigildem çéçegi*‡ Y; B.
19. *çékin** S, Q, X; 1B, 1; x 208r. 15.
22. çigin** s, q, E, Y; 2B, 1.
27. Cıla- M.
çıldıra- R.
28. *-Cıl/-cil* X.
29. çil Y 1‡; 2R, 1RZ.
220v. 1. çilek† S; B, (cf. 220r. 13).
cılamışı‡ q(P); M(I).
4. cılaw† S, Q; 1F, 1; p.
6. cılawlığ† p-t.
7. *-cılay/-ciley*† }
8. *-cılayın/* } S, Q; x
-cileyin† } 220r. 28.
10. çılbur† S, q(P); F; m.
11. çılpık† S.
12. cıldam† X.
13. cılğawa† S, X; Z; a.
14. cılğu‡ X; F; x 218v. 26.
çılğın S; R.
15. çélimlü s; R.
cile*‡.
16. cili*‡ S, Q, X.
19. cılı.
20. ciliye*‡; x 220v. 16.
Çimdi- S, C, q.
221r. 2. Cimcime*† S; a, e.
3. *cemceme**† s; A.
4. çımdığan† S (*nūn* misplaced in spelling out).
5. çimdik S.
cımıllığ‡ s; F.
6. Çine- S(bi), C, Q; m, e.
20. Çın s, q.

* The final *-y* of the main entry, not included in the spelling out, is no doubt a scribal error.
** *Kāf-i* ᶜ*acamī* is mentioned in both spellings, in the first it is an error for ᶜ*arabī*.

21. çin 1P, 1Np, 1Ng.
çıncanak‡ S, Y.*
çınğına 22v. 24.
22. çınkırak ⎫
23. çınkıraw ⎭ † S.
cıŋ*‡ S, Q; d.
25. çıŋrağu S; R.
26. ciŋseŋ*‡ S; F; chinese.
27. çénge† S, Q; f.
221v. 4. çingiz S, Q(P); 1N, 1Np.
8. Ciwli-‡ S, C.
19. çéwür- S, C, q.
29. çéwrul- S, c, Q.
222r. 3. Çéwrük S; 1, 1R; x 209v. 15.
4. çéwrünti ⎫ s, X; (see
çéwürme ⎭ 209v. 16).
5. *çéwürtke* S, Q; Z; x 220r. 15.
7. ciwek S; R (cf. Söz Derleme Dergisi, p. 279).
8. çiwit S; R.
9. ciwir‡ S, X, Y.
Çih S; R.
10. *cih* P.
Cı*‡ q; d.
11. *-cı/-ci/-çı/-çi.*
13. céyen*‡ W; F; e.**
çıyan s, Q; 1Z; 1; x 210v. 16.
15. çiye S, X; B.
16. cıyın*‡ S; f.
Hariş‡ S, q; a.
18. *ḥaqq kuşı*‡ Y; Z; a-t.
ḥöçek E, 212v. 16.
ḥawlan‡ W, q; A; e.
20. Xatun Q; 2; sogdian.
22. xaşa W; R; a (*ġāşīya*).
23. xakan X, q; h.
26. xak pelek‡ s, Q; F; p.
222v. 1. xan X; h; 1, 3P; x 222r. 25.
7. xata q; Ng; x 222v. 12.
8. xatay Nt.
9. xac/çır‡ W, q; Z.¶
10. *xi/ucir* P.
xaral‡ R*; f.

* In Kāşğarī *çıçalak*, of which this may be either a phonetic or a scribal corruption.

** Probably a Mongolized form of Turkish *yégen* with an altered meaning.

¶ Presumably a Mongolized form of Turkish *katır*.

11. xaşal S; 1R(a), 1P.
12. *xaṭa* q, X; Ng.
13. xaftan† X; p; x 274r. 7.
14. xalta‡ S; Qalmaq.
xalac s, q, q(P); Nth.
18. xallac s; 1Ng, 1P.
19. xalama‡ S; Z; f.
xanc‡ W; 1p, 4P.
20. xanca‡ W, q; 1f, 1P.
xanum x 45v. 15.*‡
Xu † 279r. 16.
22. xubul- c; M.
Xubla ‡ 279r. 16.
23. *Xuduk* s, q, X; 1Z, 6(?)P; 5v. 25; x 118r. 11; 284r. 7.
26. Xorulda- s, Y; R.
27. Xorata S; R; greek.
28. xoran R; greek.
xoros übügi X; R; Z; p-t.
223r. 1. xoşlaş- X; P-t, (misspelt with *-mek*); x 40r. 20.
2. Xırılda- s, c, q.
9. xırıldaş- s.
10. xırıldat- s.
11. Xırsız R; a-t.
xırzıma S; R; greek.
12. Xızan† S; p?
13. Xışıl S; R*.
Xına a.
xınalığ q; 1, 1Ng; a-t.
15. *Depele-* s; R, (misspelt with *-mak*); cf. 151r. 27.
16. Daban† W, Q; m.
17. dabğulı‡ S.
18. *dabku* S, X, E(?); x 151v. 1.
20. *dabkur*† S, q, X; 1, 1R; x 151v. 1; 261r. 9.
depengü R; p; x 151v. 17.
22. dabusun† S; M.
Daxı X; x 57r. 20; 224r. 5.
daxsar‡ W; Z; f, e.
23. Dada† W, q.
24. dādak‡ S ⎫ Q, q(P); p; (both
*dedek**‡ ⎭ words have final *kāf*).
223v. 1. dede 2R, 1P(E?).

3. Darı-‡ S, C, Q; d; x 223v. 19.
18. darış-‡ s, X; d.
20. darıl- S, X; R; x 153r. 13.
deril- R, (cf. 190v. 14).
21. Dara W; 1m, 2P.
22. dernek S; R.
daruğa q; m.
23. *derim éwi* X; R; x 226r. 26.
24. Des degirmi X; R; x 343r. 21.
25. *Daşırgan-* X.
26. *Daş* q, X; 4, 1Pş, 1P; x 157r. 6.
28. Dağ† q; 1Pş, 2P.
224r. 1. dağar‡ W; luğat-i Tātārīya.
2. dağan† W; X; f.
dağul s, q; P.
4. *dağı* q, X; x 57r. 20; 157v. 23; 223r. 22.
5. Defni W, Y; R; B; greek.
7. Dekşür- S, c, q; R.
8. Dek q; R.
9. *dék* q, (cf. 198r. 15).
12. *degirmi* S, X; R; x 198v. 1.
degle‡ S, q, X; m.
14. deŋlü S; R (*sağır nun* misunderstood).
15. degme S, q; R.
16. degül s, q; used only by the Turks of Rūm and Irān, not Çağatay.
18. Daldala-† S, C, q; m; x 224v. 2.
224v. 2. daldalaş- ⎫
daldalan- ⎭ s, X; m-t.
3. *dal-* X; R.
4. Dal q; 1†, 1B (cf. 160r. 23), 1P(q).
7. *dall* 2A.
8. *dalak* Y, (cf. 160v. 6).
dalaw*‡.
dalay† X; 3M; x 117v. 20.
10. *dalay lama*‡ S; M, Np; x 209v. 8.
11. dalbay† S, W, q; F; m; x 271r. 9.
13. dalda† W, q; m.
14. daldağay‡; d, m.

* *Dégil/n* in the idioms in which it is translated *pindārī* is clearly the imperative of dé-.

19. Zag† q; Pş.
21. zağar s, W; R; Z; f.
zağanos S, X; R; Z; greek.
22. zelek W; R*; f.
zengin W; R; p.
23. zengü‡ S; f.
Zügürd S; R; f.
24. zulan‡ W; M.
zunbuluk*‡ S, W, Y; p.
26. Zıbık S; 1‡, 1R; f.
27. zıbıkçi Y; R; f-t.
28. zırığ S; R*; p.
zirik† S, Y; B; p.
29. zık W; 1R*a, 1A.*
zılğıt‡ S; f, e.
228v. 1. zil W, Y; R; f.
2. Saba- S, C, q; m.
14. sapla- S.
saplan- s; 1, 1R.
15. Sap s; 2, 1R; 16v. 9.
17. sapa S; R.
18. sapağ S, Q.
20. saban W, Y; F.
21. sapan s, Y; 1F, 1Ng.
22. *saban okı* F.
23. sebed W, Y; R; F; p.
24. sebircek‡ S, X, Y.
25. *sap sarı* x 228v. 16.
sap sağ q; 2; x 228v. 16.
26. sapğun† S; F.
27. Sat- C, q.
229r. 7. satış- s.
satıl- s.
8. sattur-.
9. satğun al- C, q; 18v. 17.
20. sataş- S, c, q; R.
21. Satan*‡ S.
22. satığ s, q.
23. satığcı s, q.
25. satğucı.
Saç- S, C, Q.
229v. 9. saçıl- S, c, Q.
15. saçra- c, q.
17. Sac W, Q; 2, 1A, 1P.
21. *saç* 1, 1V; 25v. 21.
22. saçak s, q, Y; 3.
25. sac ayağ q, Y; R; x 224r. 2.
26. sacbağ q.
28. saçığ/k s, Q(E); 2.

* The translation *cān* must be corrupt or an error.

230r. 3. Saxla- C, q.
14. Saxtıyan† s, W, q; p.
16. *Sadu sadla-* X; R*; x 232r. 24.
17. *Sadak*† s, q, X; mʿ x 232v. 1; 261r. 5.
19. *sadu* S, X; R*; x 232v. 4.
Sarğar- S, C, Q, X; e.
230v. 6. sarğart- s, c, q.
8. sarsa-† S, C, X; e; x 230v. 18.
18. *sarsı-* s, X; R.
19. *sarar-* S; R; x 230r. 21.
sarkı- S,
20. sarkıt- s, } R.
20. sar- q; R.
22. sarmaş- S.
sarın- c, q; r.
Sarağ E 242r. 11.
24. sarağuc Pş.
25. sarp s, W; R.
sarpun S, R; f.
26. sart S, q; Nt; sanskrit; x 259v. 24.
28. sarç‡ S, (? corruption of Persian *sarkaş*).
serçek‡ X; Atrāk-i Īrān wa Rūm.
sarda*‡ W.
29. sarkut.
sarğ/kuk R.
231r. 1. serke† S; Z; m; (see 251v. 15).
sergi† S.
sarma R x 225v. 18.
2. sarmaşık† X, Y; B; x 231r. 11.
sarı q, X; 2, 2P.
5. sarıca X; 1Z, 1; x 271r. 15; 291r. 22.
6. sarığ q; 19v. 29; x 231r. 3.
7. *sarığ ağrık* q.
8. *sarığ kuş* q, Y; Z.
10. *sarı pustın* Nt; t-p.
sarı kawak s, Y; R; B.
11. sarigen (*sic?*) X; R*; B; x 231r. 2.
12. sarımtul‡.
Sazan balığ Y; R; Z; f.
13. Sası- S (misspelt with *şīn*).
14. sasıt- s.
15. Sasığ, 19r. 29.

Sağ- C.
25. sağıl- S.
26. sağal-† S, C, Q; 2.
231v. 14. sağalt-† s; 2.
16. sağın- S, C, Q, E; 3, (cf. 232v. 14).
232r. 18. sağındur- c, Q; 2.
23. sağu sağ- X; R; x 230r. 17.
24. Sağ Q, X; 4, 1V.
28. sağanak s; 2R.
29. *sağcı* e (cf. 232v. 20).
sağadak*‡ X; m.
232v. 1. sağrı S, Y; 2.
2. sağrak W, X; x 253v. 29.
sağlığ q; 3.
4. sağu S, X; R; x 230r. 19.
5. sağır s, W, Y.
sağırlık.
sağırtka‡ S, Y; Z; x 234r. 5.
6. sağış s, W, q.
8. sağın 2; 3V.
9. sağınc S, Q, E; 5v. 4.
14. *Sakın-* q; R, (cf. 231v. 16).
16. *Sak* q; x 138r. 4; 232r. 28.
17. sakağ W, q; e.
18. sakal q, Y; 20v. 16 (*sak/kkal*).
19. sakalduruk F.*
20. sakçi q, (cf. 232r. 29).
21. sakkar S; Z; f.
22. saksağan† Y; Z.
sakıt.**
sakkız S, Y; B.
23. *sakkız ağacı* Y; B.
24. Sek- R.
Sal- C, Q; 2; 11r. 15.
233v. 5. salın-
6. salıl- } s, c, Q.
10. sallan-† s, C, q; 2.
26. sallandur-.
Sal q; 1, 2V.
28. salaca R.
29. salt S, R.
salcuk Nph.

* All the MSS. misspell this word *sakaldurluk*.
** Apparently an error for *sevit* with triply-dotted *fā*, "Venus"; see *Kutadğu Bilig*, ed. Arat, v. 135 and Radloff's *Opyt* IV col. 501.

* In l. 14 L reads correctly *wa mu'allif-i. Rūmī īn lafẓ* . . . .

* In the first meaning this is an error for *sayı* (earlier *sayu*); this is probably also true of the third.

** The translation is inaccurate; the word here, and in line 17 above, is the old Turkish word *sayu* "every", common in early Uyğur.

* In line 4, in a false etymology of *sübüktegin* (for *sevügtégin*), *sübük* is described as Mongolian, but it is not in the ordinary dictionaries.

27. sürç- S, C.
242r. 6. sürçüş- s.
7. sürçül- s.
8. Surağ† Q, E; m.
12. süren† Q; x 242r. 19.
14. sürçe.
sorğu 5v. 6.
sorğuc R.
sürgewül S; t-m, I (?).
15. sürgü s, W; R.
16. *sürgü taşı* R.
sürgün.
17. sürme kilid R; T-P.
18. sürmişi† X; 2M, 1; (I).*
20. sürüci S; 2R.
21. soruş q; 1, 1V.
22. *sürüş* s(bi); V.
soruğ/k S, Q; 1, 1F†; x 251v. 20.
27. *soruğ küni* q.
28. sürüg S, Q.
242v. 1. Süz- C, q, Y; 3.
14. süzül- S, c, Q.
19. sözle- S, C, Q.
243r. 7. sözleş- s, c, Q.
12. sözlet- s. } c, q.
sözleştür- }
15. Söz; s(bilai) 25v. 29.
16. *süz* s(bi); 3V.
söz térgüci q.
17. *söz téger.*
18. sözçi S, q.
19. süzgüc s, q, Y.
21. süzme s.
süzük S, q.
22. Susa- S, C, Q; E 249r. 18.
243v. 5. susat- s.
6. sustay-‡ S, C, Q; p-t.
21. sustayıt-‡ S; p-t.
23. süs- S, Y; 2R.
süstür- r.
24. Susak S.
susam* S; R*; e.
25. susun*‡.
26. suğar- S, C, q, X; x 247v. 28.
244r. 7. suğarıl- S.
8. suğal- S, C, Q.
23. suğalt- s.

* *Luğat-i Muğulī* seems here to be an error for *iṣṭilāḥāt-i Muğūl*; the word is by origin Turkish, but typical of that "dialect".

24. soğla-*‡ S, C, q; e.
244v. 6. suğur-† S, C, Q; m.
19. suğruş-† S, c, q; m-t.
21. suğrul-† s, c, q; m-t.
24. Soğan, Y; B.
soğanlık Ng.
soğlı* S; R*.
25. *soğun** Y; Z, (see 249v. 1).
soğulcan† S, Y; Z.
26. Sok- C, Q, Y; 2.
245r. 12. sokul- S, c, q; 2.
15. sokuş- s; 2.
16. sokran- S; R.
Sokağ* W; 1Z, 1.
18. soksur† S; Z; m.
sokku S.
19. sokmağ/k† S, Q; 1, 1V.
22. sokur S; 3*; x 247r. 19.
23. sokkur‡ s.
24. sokuş.
sokum.
25. Sök- } C, Q; 2; 25r.
26. sög- s } 24.
245v. 14. sökül- s, c, q; 2.
17. söktur- s.
18. söküş- s.
19. sögle- s; R.
Sög† S; B.
20. sögdenis*‡ S; m.
21. sögdemişi*‡ q(P); I; m.
22. süksük S, q, X, Y; 1Z, 2R*, x 65r. 17.
25. sökel s; 2, 1P.
27. sökellik.
sögleme S; R.
sükü S; R; F; (misreading of *süŋü*); x 247r. 28.
sökücek*‡ F.
28. sögüd S; B.
sögüş 1, 1R.
29. sögünc† S, q; 5v. 4.
246r. 1. Sol- S, C, Q.
15. soldur-; 24v. 21.
sula-.
16. solu- }
soluk al- } R.
soluklan- }
17. Sol Q; 1, 1V; x 138r. 4.
19. solak 1R, 1Ng.
sülegey E 259v. 16.

* *Sokur* "blind" seems to be Mongolian; the other meanings are doubtful.

20. sülpük S; R }
solcuk* s; R* }
21. sulduz S; Nt.
sulṭān börki A-R; B; x 147v. 29.
22. solğun† S.
22. *sülgün* X; Z.
23. solutğan S; R.
suluk† S; q; 1F, 1; x 44r. 18.
25. soluk R.
26. sülük s, Y; Z.
sülügen s; R.
27. Sümür- S, C, Q, Y.
246v. 11. sümkür- S, Y.
12. Sümsük S; R.
13. sümkürük } S, Y.
sümük }
14. sümür sümür* R*.
15. Sun- S, 2 } C, Q.
16. sön- }
247r. 13. söndür- c, Q.
17. Sonkur q, X, E; 1Z, 1 Tātāriya wa Lakzīya; x 259v. 20.
20. söŋek S(mi), q.
21. soŋ S, Q; 2; 25r. 4.
24. soŋra S, q.
25. soŋrağı q; x 247r. 27.
26. süŋer† S, Y; greek.*
27. soŋğı X.
soŋğı uyku q.
28. süŋü X.
29. *soŋuŋca*** S, Q.
247v. 3. *soŋı* Q.
5. *soŋıca* S(mi) } Q; 17r.
soŋınca s } 9.
8. süne† S, X; 2; f; x 245r. 18.
9. Suwa- S, C, Q.
23. suwat- s.
24. suwal- s, c, Q.
28. *suwar-* S, X, C, Q; 21v. 19; x 243v. 26.
248r. 12. *suwur-*† S, C, Q, E; m; (cf. 244v. 6).
27. *suwurul-* S; m-t (cf. 244v. 21).
28. Suw (or *su?*) q; 4, 2P; 19v. 29.
248v. 2. suwdağın s, q.

* No doubt a Rumī word, though not so marked.
** So spelt in L; G and O incorrectly omit the second *kāf*.

* The main entry, beginning *sin alif* in all three MSS. is obviously corrupt.
** The correct Turkish form, in Kāşğarī, Kutadğu Bilig etc. is *sığun*; in Mongolian *soğun* (Kow. 1387) is used only for the female; this form is a muddle between both.

* "Pure" has front vowels in all other dialects; the back vowels here are an error or recent corruption; the second meaning is very dubious.

10. sılığ ağça R (error for *silik*).
11. *Sémir-* s, X; x 234r. 19.
12. *Sémiz* s; x 234v. 4.
Sın- S, C, Q.
28. sındur- c, Q.
256v. 4. sınık-† S, C, q; 2.
17. sınıktur-† c, q.
19. sına- S, C, q, (misspelt with *-mek*).
257r. 1. sınal- S, c, q, (ditto).
3. siŋ- S, C, Q.
28. siŋür- S(mi), c, Q.
257v. 8. siŋdür- s, c, q.
11. séŋre- S, C, q.*
22. siŋirle- S(mi), C; e.
258r. 4. siŋirlet- s.
5. siŋirlen- s.
Sén.
6. sın s(bi); 1, 1V.
7. *sīn* A.
séncileyin.
sındı W, Y; 1, 1V.
8. *séndürsin/sénsin* q.
10. sénsiz/sénsizin q; 15v. 10; 18v. 10.
11. sıngrak‡ S, X; x 100r. 10.
12. siŋek S(mi), q, X, Y; x 95v. 17.
14. siŋir S(mi), Q; 1, 1‡; x 155r. 16.
17. siŋirli yaprak X, Y; e; x 125r. 22.
18. siŋil S(mi), Q; 24r. 16; x 45v. 16; 92r. 22.
21. siŋillik.
siŋli, (see 258r. 20).
22. sénlik q.
sınuk 8r. 10; 25v. 12.
23. Séw- S, C, Q.
258v. 12. séwdür- c, q.
14. séviş- S.
15. séwin- S, C, Q; 24v. 10 (séwün-).
27. séwindür-.
sıwur- E 248r. 14.
28. Siwri S, R.
29. *sıwrı sıŋek* Y; R; Z; x 258r. 14.
séwgüm (*sic!*) s.
séwüklük } S, Q; 2.
259r. 1. séwiklik } S, Q; 2.

* Not recorded elsewhere, but cf. *seŋregü* in Kāşğarī.

3. *siwel* S, X, Y.
4. séwinc S.
5. séwici q.
6. Sıyır- S, C, q, Y.
18. sıyrıl- s(bi), X.
19. Şapat } † S, X.
şapalak } † S, X.
20. şebek s, W; R; Z.
Şatu S, q.
22. Şerilde- c, q.
24. Şaranpaw s, W; R; magyar.
25. Şaş- R; x 56v. 8; 206r. 1.
şaşur- r, (see 206r. 12).
26. Şaşğun R.
şaşı W, R; x 260r. 29.
şaşılık r.
27. Şağırdak‡ S.
şağıldak‡ s, Y.
29. Şefşel s, W; 2R*; f.
259v. 1. Şakka s; R; f.
şakırdi*.
2. Şalğurt‡ S; Z; x 209r. 2.
şalk? 317v. 8.
3. Şamar R; f; x 259r. 20.
Şawlum*‡ S; f; x 45v. 6.
4. Şay‡ W; f.
Şüdrün*† S, q, Y; m.
6. şu deŋlü R.
7. *şudurğu* X, Y; 1F‡; m?; 1Np; x 259v. 25.
8. Şor‡ Y; 1P, B, 1Nt.
9. şorak W, Y; R, p.
şurı E 310v. 22.
10. Şük 1; 1R*.
*şuk**‡ Y; Zend, Pazend.
11. şükkine q.
12. şükür*‡ S; m.
13. şükürci*‡ m-t.
Şol†.
şülegey*† S, Q, E, Y; m; x 179v. 29.
17. şulay‡ Özbegīya - i Tūrān wa Xwarazm.
Şomur*‡ M*.
18. Şundak/y q, X.
19. *şunkar* q, X; 1Z, 1F.
Şöyle* 128r. 12.
21. Şıba*‡ Y; f.
22. şıbak‡ S, q, X; 1B; 1; m.
24. şıban Nt.

şibike S; m, e.
25. Şıdurğu S, X; (1F‡, m?; 1Np) x 259v. 7.
26. Şıralğa‡ S, Q; 2; m.
29. şıram*‡ q; d.
260r. 1. şırdağ† q, X; 2; p; x 251v. 5.
4. şırlağan R; p.
5. şırlağancı r; p-t.
Şiş- C.
13. şişle- C, Q.
25. Şiş Q; 3, 1V.
27. şişik S.
28. şişman S; R.
Şığawul‡ S; I, m.
29. Şıl W, X, R.
şılan† S(bi), q; 1p, 1P.
260v. 3. şıltak† S, q; m.
4. şilim*‡ S(bi); m.
5. Şim-† S, C, q; m.
15. şımal-‡ C, Q.
27. Şimdi q; 1, 1V.
29. *şimdiye dek* s; R.
şimşek S; R.
261r. 1. Şén 3R.
şiŋ‡ S; 1, 1F; chinese?
3. şénlik 3r.
5. Şıwaran*‡ Y; B; p?
Şadak† X, Q; m.
şarş- R; x 230v. 9.
şaşı R; x 19r. 29.
8. *şayın* X; m.
şu R; x 19r. 29.
Ṭapanca R x 135v. 20.
9. *ṭabur* X; R; x 151v. 2.
10. Ṭaraz 2Ng, 4P, 1A.
12. *Ṭaş* R, (see 157r. 3).
13. ṭaşra R.
ṭaşrağı r.
Ṭağ X; 2R(1B); 19r. 28.
14. ṭağacar q(P); Np.
16. ṭağan Y; R; greek.
ṭağay/yı.
17. ṭağmac/ṭamğac Q(P); Nt, Ng, Np.
21. Ṭakıya a.
22. Ṭana W, X; Z; 1.
Ṭawar W; R; Z, (see 165v. 7).
23. *ṭawaşı* W, Y; R; a (see 165v. 8).
ṭawun s; R*.
Ṭay Z.

* A very dubious word; the Haydarabad MS. (see Gibb Trust facsimile 169r. 11) reads *ğunçaçı*, an unrecorded but possible p-t word for "concubine".

* "Leek" in Rumī is properly *pırasa* from Greek *praso*; *parısa* (121v. 4) is the better form; the Çağatay words no doubt derive from the same Greek root.
** L, O both read (*Rumīya*) *kebermek* in line 12.

22. katış-
katıl- } s, c, Q.
27. katıştur- c, q; x 265v. 26.
29. katıklaş- S, C, q.
266v. 13. katlan- s, C, Q, (X!); 2.
267r. 1. katra-
katna- } ‡ S, C; d; m?*
18. Kat Q; 1, 1R, 2V.
kat kat q 267r. 22.
23. katağan 1, Nt, 1.
katkak† q.
25. *katla* Q.
27. katlaw† s, X; F; x 126v. 2; 292v. 6.
katmar W; R; B; f.
28. katnaşık‡ d (? error for *kaynaşık*).
katış q.
29. katığ/k Q; 2; 19v. 24.
267v. 2. *katığ közlük* q; 19r. 5.
3. katılış† S, q.
4. katınc‡ S, X; F; e.
5. Kaç- S, C, Q.
16. kaçur- S; 4v. 8.
17. Kaç 1R, 1V, 1P.
18. kacar† q; 1m, 1Nt.
20. kaçağ.
kaçağcı.
kaçan S, q.
21. *kaçanğa tégrü* q.
21A. *kaçanğa ca* q.
22. *kacarcı*‡ m, (see 261v. 27).
kaçğun.
23. kaçğuncı.
kaçu† S ahl-i Tūrān wa Xwarazm.
kacır‡ S, q; Z; m.
27. kaçın‡ S, W; F.
28. Kada-† S, C; 2; m.
268r. 10. kadal-† s, c, q; m-t.
12. Kadağ/k‡ 2m.
13. kadağlık‡ Q, E; m-t.
17. kadırğa s; R; greek.
18. kadana q(R); r; italian.
19. kadağan‡ q; m; x 268r. 1.
20. Kara- S
21. karaş- s
karala- s } C, Q; m, m-t; 7r. 22.

* *Katra-* is probably borrowed from M. *katari-* "to trot"; *katna-* looks like an error for *kayna-*, cf. katnaşik.

268v. 18. karar- S, C, Q.
269r. 4. karart- s, c, Q.
7. karğa- C, Q.
19. karma- S, C, Q.
269v. 1. karmat- s, c, q, E.
5. karmaş- s, C, q.
17. karmaştur-.
18. karı- C, Q, E.
270r. 6. karıt- s.
7. karışla- S, C; e.
18. karışlat- s.
karıla- S, C, q.
29. karılat- s.
270v. 1. karık- S, C.
8. kar- S, q; R.
10. karış- S; r.
11. kars- S; R.
Kar 1, 1RV, 1A.
12. *karr*† A.
kara Q, E; 5, 1R; x 272v. 4.
26. *kara ağac* Y; R; B.
kara ağrığ q, Y; x 95v. 24.
28. *kara batak* s, X, Y; R; Z.
29. *kara baş* 1R, Z; 2 Atrāk-i Īrān; x 271r. 3.
kara bağ q; Ng; t-p.
271r. 2. karabına X; R; french; x 49v. 22.
kara boğaz X; 2R, Z; 1Ng.
4. *kara tal* X, Y; R; Z; x 271v. 3, 21.
kara tawuk s, Y; Z.
6. *kara tayak* Q; 19r. 4.
8. karatğu‡ s, X; F; m-t.
9. *kara tamğa* F.
10. *kara ton** Ng.
11. karaçu q, q(P).
14. *kara çörek otı* Y; B.
15. karaca X; x 231r. 6; 219r. 22.
kara çérik.
16. *karaxan* q(P); 2Np, 1Ng.
20. *kara düzen* R; F.
karar X; (A); x 262r. 17.
21. *kara su* q; Ng.
22. *kara şonkur* Np.
23. *kara şanba* q; t-p.
24. karağ Q, E.
27. karağcı q.

28. karağlığ q; E 268r. 15.
29. karağul† m; x 271v. 15.
kara kat B.
271v. 1. *kara kaş* Ng.
kara kalpak Nt.
kara kurut Y.
3. *kara kuş* X; Z.
kara kulağ 1Z, 1, 1R.
7. *kara kum* Ng.
kara kır Ng.
kara kırım Ng.
8. *kara kaytağ* Ng; x 281r. 29.
9. *kara göl* s; Ng.
10. *kara günlük* s; R; B.
karaltğu‡ s, Y; F.
karam E 270v. 24.
12. karamtul† s; 17r. 22.
karamuk Y; 2Z, 1F; x 209v. 17; 224v. 19.
14. karanğu q.
karanğuluk 23v. 13.
15. *karawul*† q, X; 1m, 1Nt.
18. karawunas s; Nt.
kara yonca Y; R; B.
19. *kara yémiş* X; B.
kara yiligi s.
20. karbıl çıbanı*‡ R*.*
kart S, (X); 2.
21. kartal X, Y; Z; x 271v. 3.
kartmak s, X.
22. kartuk S.
23. karçan s, W
karça S } Y; R*; Z.
24. karaca S, X, Y; R.
25. karçığay q, X; Z; m; 19r. 18.
26. *kardaş* q, X.
27. *kardaş kani* Y; R; B.
29. kars (qārs)‡ W; 1f, 1A.
kars (qars)/karṣ‡ W; 1f, 2A.
272r. 2. karsak s, W, Y; Z.
3. karşı s, q, Q(P); 1M, 1Ngh.
7. karşu s.
8. *karṣ*‡ X; x 271v. 29.
karğa 1Z; 1V.
9. *karğa büken* s, Y; R; B.
10. *karğa dölgi* s; R; B.

* Probably a misreading of *kızıl çıbanı*.

* The translation seems to be incomplete; there is no trace of the word in "Rūmī".

* Apparently a misspelling of *kığılcım*.

* Read *muxaffaf-i kalkdur-* with L.

kanda q; 2, x 281v. 1.
22. *kandın* Q; 2.
25. *kandaya dek* R*.
kandağay‡ s, q(P); M; Z; x 318v. 15.
27. kandur W; R*.
28. kanğalduruk‡ s, q, q(P), E; F.
278r. 2. kanka‡ S; F; f.
3. kankaraw‡ S; e; m.
4. kankı S.
kanklı S }
kaŋlı s } q; 1F, 1Nth.
9. kaŋşar† S; m.
10. kanlığ Q, Y; 3.
14. kanı q; 1, 1A.
15. *kanı tolğan* q.
16. kanık S; 1, 1Ng, 1V.
17. Kaw- }
kawla-‡ } C, Q, Y; (in Kāşğarī *kov-*).
278v. 11. kawdur- c, q.
12. kawul- S.
13. kawur- S, C, q.
23. kawrul- S, c, q.
25. kawuş- S, C, q.
279r. 8. kawuştur- S, c, q.
11. kawşa- }
kawşan- } R, (error for *kuşa-/kuşan-*).
12. Kaw W, q, E, Y.
18. kawak† 2P.
19. kawak ağacı Y; R; B.
kawçın E 345v. 20.
kawşak‡ S; e, (probably error for *kevşek*.)
kawğun‡ S, Q; 2; 8r. 1.
22. kawğuncı‡ q.
23. kawluc† S.
kawluk‡ s.
24. kawut S, Y; R.
25. kawucı S; R*.
kawur‡ S.
26. kawurcağ/k‡ q, Y; 3.
28. kawurcağcı‡ q.
29. kawurdağ/k‡ q.
279v. 2. kawursun S; Q; f.
5. kawursı‡ s.
kawurma 9r. 24.
kawurmac† s, q; 1, 1Ng.
7. kawuz‡ }
kawuzğa‡ } S.
8. kawuk S; 2 (also R).
10. Kaypan- S, C, X, Y; m; x 281r. 5.

22. kayt- S, C, Q, E.
280r. 6. kaytar- S, C, Q; 2; 8v. 14.
21. kaytış- S.
kayrıl- S, C, Q.
280v. 6. kayrıla-† s, C.
17. kayğur- S, C, Q.
281r. 5. *kayfan-* s, X; m; x 279v. 11.
6. kayna- S, C, Q.
17. kaynaş-.
18. kayır- S; R.
Kay q, X; 2, 1Np, 1M*.
21. kaya q.
22. kayaş Q, X; x 71v. 14.
25. kayalığ 1, 1Ng.
kayan 1†, 1M*(I).
26. *kayandın*†.
kayanı† q.
27. *kay bir* q.
28. kaytağ/k X; Ng.
29. *kayda* q; X; x 281r. 20.
281v. 1. *kaydın* q.
2. kaydu 2Nph.
3. kayrak† X; m.
kayru/ı.
4. kayrıtay s; m.
5. kayrıcı R.
kaysı q.
6. kayğ/ku q.
kayğuluk 23v. 13.
7. *kayğuluk kuş* Y; Z.
8. kayğanak† S (muddled), Y; f.
kaymak† Y.
9. kaynaşlık.
kaynak s; 1, 1R, 1Nt.
11. kaynawuk s; 2.
kayn S, X; x 281v. 17.
12. *kayu* S, Q; x 281r. 20.
14. kayuk S, q, X.
15. *kayı* S; 1, 1Nth.
16. kayış.
kayık R; x 281v. 15.
17. kayın s, X; 1, 1Ng; x 281v. 12; 345r. 2.
18. Kop- S, C, Q; 11r. 15.
282r. 3. kopar- s, c.
5. kobsa- S, C, q; e.*
16. Koba*‡ X; 1, 1Ng, 1 Qalmaqī; x 265r. 10.
17. kobağ/k* Ngh.

* In l. 5 read *ba-ğurīda nawāxtan* "to sing in a loud voice".

18. *koba kuşluk** (see 265r. 18).
kubtul E 291v. 24.
kobğa S, Q; 2; m.
21. kubala S, q(A); Nph.
22. kubur S; R.
23. kuburcuk Y; R.
24. kobuz S, Q; F.
26. kopusğa S; R; B; slavonic.
27. Kutur- S(bi), C, q, x 284r. 3.
282v. 10. kuturt- S.
11. *kutul-* S, C, Q, X; 4r. 18; 13r. 4; x 284v. 5.
28. kutkar- C, Q; 4r. 26.
kutkul- E 284v. 7.
283r. 16. kotanla-‡ S, C; m-t.
20. Kut 1M, 1A.
21. kutan‡ S, q; Z, m; x 288v. 21.
22. kotan‡ 2m.
23. kutluğ/k q; 1, 1Nph; 19r. 28.
25. kotur S, Q, Y; 2, 1Ng.
29. kotur botur*‡ S, q.
283v. 1. kutuz S, q, X.
3. Kuc- s(bi), C, Q.
20. kucuş- s, c, Q.
27. kucuştur-.
28. Kucağ.
kocğar S, Q; Z.
284r. 1. koca† p?
koca yemişi R; B.
2. koçı R; f.
Koxu.
3. *Kudur-* s(bi), c, q, X; 4v. 10.
kudurt- 4v. 12.
5. Kuda† S, X; m; x 51v. 17.
kuduz x 283v. 3.
6. kuduk q, X; 1, 1Z; x 222v. 25.
7. kuduman‡ s.
8. Kur- s(bi), C, Q; 2.
284v. 2. kurdur-.
kurul- S, q.
4. kurtul- S, c, q, E, X; x 282v. 11.
8. kurşa- S, C; 2.
21. kurşat- s; 2.
22. kurşal- }
kurşan- } s; 2.
23. korğada‡- S, C, q; m.

27. koŋğar- S(mi) }
koŋar- s(mi) } ‡C, Q; m; 7r. 5.
291r. 13. koŋğarıl-‡ m-t.
14. Kunacın† S; Z; m.
konaş }
15. konaşık } ‡ F; x 291v. 13.
17. konağ/k q; 1B, 1, 1R.
19. konağluk.
konalğa† q; t-m.
21. kunan S; Z; m.
konam*‡ S, X.
22. kunbul‡ q, E, X; A; x 290v. 9.
25. kondak† s; 2.
26. kunduz S, q; 1Z, 1Ng; x 76v. 27; 234v. 6.
291v. 1. *kunduz kırı.*
2. *kunda†* Z; p, (see 262v. 13).
konğur S, q(P); 1Z, 1Np.
4. *konğur öleŋ* Ngh.
6. konğrat }
koŋrat } s, q, E; Nt.
8. koŋğuz S(mi), Y; Z.
9. *ko ŋak* S(mi), X; x 291v. 28.
10. koŋşı S, X.
11. konuş S, q, X; 1, 1F.
13. Kuwan- S, C, Q; x 310r. 2, 28.
25. *ko-* c, q, X; R; x 292r. 1.
26. Ku Y; Z.
27. kowak*‡ S.
28. kowan Y; R.
kuwan V.
29. kowank*‡ S, X; d; x 291v. 10.
Koy- C, Q, X; 2; 11v. 10; x 291v. 25.
292r. 21. koyul-.
kuyla-‡ C; m.
292v. 2. kuylat-‡ s; m-t.
3. kuylan-‡ s; m-t.
Koy q; 1Z, 1V; 23r. 6.
koyar m 248v. 4.
5. kuyaş q.
6. kuyak S, X; F.
7. koyan S; Z; E 167v. 10.
8. *koyaŋ* S }
koyanğu s } *‡ q, Y; p?
10. koyçı S, q, E; 2.
14. kuyruğ/k Y; 2.
kuyruk salan Y; R; Z.
15. *koy kuşı* Z.
16. *koyn* S, Q, X; 2; x 292v. 21.
18. koyuk 2.
19. kuyum Y; R.
kuyumcı r.
koyun S, Q, X; 3, 1Z; 24r. 22; x 292v. 18.
24. *koyun gözi* Y; R; B.
koyı S, q, Y.
25. kuyı.
26. koyığı S, q.
27. Kıp- S, C, Y.
293r. 9. Kıp kırmızı.
Kıcış-† S, C, Q.
17. kıcığla-† C, q.
28. kıçkır- S, C, Q.
293v. 11. kıçkırış- S, c, q.
14. kıcırda- X; R; x 294v. 19.
15. Kiçkırış/k.
kıcı Y; B.
16. kıcış† s.
kıcığ† s, q, Y.
17. Kır- S, C, Q; 3; x 294r. 18.
294r. 13. kırıl- S, c, q; 3.
16. kırdur- 3.
17. kırp- S, C, q, X; x 293v. 19.
28. kırpıl- S.
29. kırk- S, C, q, X; x 346v. 28.
294v. 11. kırkıl-.
kırktur- q.
13. kırla-† S, c.
18. kırçıldat-† S, C, q, X; x 293v. 15.
295r. 3. kırçıldaş-.
4. kırığla-‡.
kır q; 1, 1 Kāşgar, 1R, 1, 3V, 2P.*
9. kırağ/k Q; 26r. 28; x 295v. 10.
11. kırağu S; R; (see 295r. 16).
kıran† Q; 1Fa, 1a, 1A; e.
16. *kıraw* S, Q, Y; (see 295r. 11).
18. kırpık† S, X.
19. kırpındı S; R.

* Under the second meaning read *marᶜā* for *maradī*.

20. kırtlış S, Q; 3.
22. *kır tékin* s; Ng.
23. kırğawul† q; Z; m.
24. kırğu Z.
kırğıc† S.
25. kırğız S, q(P); Nth.
27. kırk 1, 1Nt, 1V.
28. *kırk ayağ* Y; Z.
29. kırkılığ ‡.
kır kır S, q; 1, 1R.
295v. 1. *kırkız* s, qP; Ng, Nt; M(!).
3. *kır kıl* Y.
kırlağan çıbanı R.
4. kırmaça‡ s.
5. kırmız S, q, Y; f.*
6. kırnağ/k s, X; x 262v. 17.
7. kırığ/k† Q, q(P)**; 1, 1A, 1Nt, 1M; 26r. 28.
13. kırım q; Ng.*
15. Kızar- C, Q.
27. kızart- s, c, q.
29. kızı- S }
kızış- s } C, Q.
296r. 1. kızık- s }
27. kızıt- s, c, Q.
296v. 2. kızın- S; R.
kıjılda-‡ s; e.
3. Kız 1, 1R.
kızalağ‡ S; B.
4. kızamuk†.
kız oğlan.
kızğın R.
kız kardaş q.
5. *kız kuşı* Y; 1Z, 1RZ.
7. kızlığ 1, 1R.
8. kızığ s, q.
9. kıjığ‡ s.
kızıl Q; 2, 2Z.
13. *kızıl ala* Z.
14. *kızıl altun.*
kızıl alma Ng.
15. *kızıl ayağ* q; 1Z, 1; 19r. 4.
17. *kızıl palçığ* Y; R.
18. *kızıl bilge* q(P); I.
19. *kızıl tal* q; B.
20. *kızıl tüglü* q; Z.
21. kızılca s, Y; 2R.

* The Persian dictionaries describe this word as "Arabic" and the Arabic dictionaries as "Persian"; in any event it is not Turkish.
** In line 13 read *dar ta'rīx-i Wassāf* with L.

* Probably an error for *bilewle-*, which is recorded elsewhere with this meaning.

** Thetra nslations here, and those in the Abuşka which are quite different, though one quotation is the same, seem to be mere guesses; in the first meaning the word may be an error for *bilew*; the others are inexplicable.

* The spelling is muddled in G, but correct in L.

** These two words seem to be diminutives of Persian *kat/kad* "house" and *kac* "crooked".

* Probably an error for Persian *karkar* "fir tree" (Steingass).

24. *kān* P.
gence W; 1, 1P, 1Ng.
genc R.
25. gendü S, q; R.
26. kendir S, Y; R; B.
28. kens‡ S; d.
29. kenges Nt.
kend otı* R*; B.
301v. 1. Gewşe- S; 1, 1R.
2. kawla-‡ C, q; p-t.
12. Kewürke‡ S, q; m; 20r. 20; x 225v. 22.
13. kewrek S, W; R.
14. keweze S, Y; R.
15. kewzen W; Z; f.
kewş‡ S; d.
16. gewşek S; R.
16A. keweni S, W; R*.
16. Key- s(bi), C, Q; 12r. 28.
28. keydür- c, q.
302r. 1. keyil- s.
keymür- E 316r. 3.
2. Keybür‡ S, q, X; F; P; x 302r. 5.
5. keyli† W; a?
keymür‡ q, X; F; P; x 302r. 4.
6. keyn/keyin S, q.
7. *keyince* q.
9. Köpur- s, C, q.
20. köpürt- s.
köpul-‡ d.
21. Köp } S, q; E 311r. 28.
küp }
23. küpçek*† S, X.
köbcin S }
24. *köbcün* s } F.
köbcük }
küpçük s; R.
25. *köprek* q.
26. köprük S, q, Y.
27. göbek s.
köpek s; Z.
28. *köpek sarıg** Z.
köpelek S, q; Z.
302v. 1. göbelek*‡ s, Y; 2B.
4. köbenek s, Y; M; B.
köpük s, Y.
5. *köpük ṭaşı* Y; R.

6. köbün M.
köbe S, Y; M*; e.
8. küpe s; 1R, 1P.
köbeci* 1Ng, 1.
10. göpi*‡ S, X.
*köp yaġı** Q.
13. Küt- C, Q, X; x 303v. 22.
27. köter- S, C, Q; x 311v. 15 (R. *göter-*).
303r. 10. Kotawul‡ H-T; x 300r. 12.
11. *kotwal*‡ H-P.
12. kötel*‡ 1Z, 1P.
13. kötürüm† s.
14. kütük s; 1*‡, 1Ra.
köti S; R.
15. Köç- S, C, q.
25. köçür- S, c, q.
27. kücgen-‡ S, C.
303v. 8. küclen-.
9. küçükle- S.
10. Küc q, X; 2.
11. köç s 1, 4P.
14. *köç eri*‡ X; Nt; x 303v. 16.
küclük.
15. küclükgine q.
16. köçmen‡ X; Nt; x 303v. 14.
göcen S; R; Z.
17. küçük S; Z.
18. *kücün* S, Q.
21. *Güd-* X; R; x 302v. 14.
22. Güdüci S; R.
Kör- C, Q; 18v. 26.
304r. 16. körset- } S, C, Q; 4v.
körküz- } 15.
304v. 11. körün- S, c, Q.
16. körüş- S, c, Q.
20. güreş- S, C.
305r. 1. güreştür-.
körket- E 305r. 8.
2. körkey- S, C, q, E.
15. körüklen- s.
16. gürülde- } s.
gürüldeş- }
18. küre- S; R.
Güreş s.
güreşçi q.
20. gürbüz s, W; 1Rp, 2P.
22. gürbüzlük P-T.
23. körpe S; 2.
24. körtün S; R; F.
körçek*‡? x 318r. 12.

gürci‡ S; 1Z, 1Nt.
25. gürz 1R*, d; 1P.
kürek S; 3.
26. kürk s, X; 1, 1R*, 1; x 305v. 23.
28. görk s, Q.
305v. 2. kürke*† S, Q; f.
4. küreke*‡ S, W, Q, E; f; 20r. 20.
6. *görke bay* Q.
9. kürgen‡ s, X, E; 1, 1Nph; m.
11. görklük s, q.
12. görküz‡ S, q(P); 1I(?), 1V.
15. küren‡ S, q(P); 1, 1Ng; m.
17. görnek S, X; R; x 71v. 7.
18. kürenk† S, W; Zm, 3P.
20. körüşlük.
21. körük s, q, X, Y; 2.
23. gürüldü s; R.
Közet- } S, C, Q; x
24. közle- } 317r. 27.
306r. 18. közleş- s.
köz tut- c, Q; 19r. 7.
28. göze- S; R.
Köz q.
29. göz s, Q; 3 (including 306v. 4).
306v. 2. güz Q.
5. gözgü s.
közel*‡ s.
6. güzel s, q; 1, 1Z*‡.
7. gözlük s, q, Y; 1R, 1B.
10. gözeme S; R.
gözüŋ*‡ S, q; F; d.
12. Küs- q (mistranslated?)
13. göster- s; R.
14. *Küsew* q } x 309v. 4.
15. kusegü R }
köstebek s; R; Z.
16. köstek s; R.
kösem s, X, Y; R; Z; x 37r. 26.
18. Köşek } s, X; Z; x
köşelek } 173r. 10.
19. Gögert- S, C, Q; 2.
307r. 5. göger- q; 2.
kükte- E 307v. 17.
7. kökre- } C, Q.
kökreş- }
26. kükle-† C, Q; 2; p-t.
307v. 12. küklet-† s; 2; p-t.

---

* *Köbe* "slip-knot", or the like, is Mongolian (Kow. 2575; Haltod 227); *sacāf* and *farāwīz* both mean "fringe, edging" which is a reasonable development of meaning.

13. küklen-† s; 2; p-t.
14. Kük Q, E; 2p.
18. kök.
kūk 3P.
19. gög S, Q; 4; 22v. 20.
24. *gūg* 3P.
25. kükenek‡ s, X; P; Z; m.
26. gögeyin* S; Z; (cf. 310r. 20).
27. *gög boz* S, q.
28. kökrek† Q(E), X; 23r. 6; x 308r. 4, 15.*
308r. 1. kügerçin Z.
2. kügerçinlik 1, 1Ng.
köks q, E, X.
köksük E 308r. 4.
5. kökşün S; M.
gög karga s; Z.
göggine q; 22v. 22.
7. gög gömek‡ q(E); x 307v. 21; 309v. 9, 10.
8. kökel‡ m.
9. kökelteş q; m-t; 17v. 6.
10. gügem S; R; B.
11. köken‡ S; M.
kūkan 2P; 1HNg.
12. kükür*‡ S; luğat-i Kāşğar.
13. küküz‡ S; 1p, 1P.
küküzgine p-t; 22v. 23.
13. kökiis S, q, X; 24r. 13; x 308r. 1, 4.
15. gügüm R.
16. gögümtul† s, q; x 184r. 3.
17. Kül- C, Q, E.
308v. 5. külüş- S.
6. külümsü/e- s, C, Q.
19. Kül s(bi).
köl s(bilai), q }
21. *göl* s }
kül 1V, 2P.
22. gulac s, q, Y; p.
24. kūlāk q, 1Pş, 1P.
25. kölege S, Q, Y.
27. *külegec yüzlük.*
külegen.
külelir*‡ S, X; f; x 89r. 17.
29. külüfçe S; R*; p.

* L correctly has *köks* in l. 1 and 15 for *kös* in O.

külek s, Y; R; greek or p?
309r. 1. gülgü s, Q, X.
3. külük Z.
4. Göm- s, C, Q; 2.
15. gömül- S, c, q.
17. gömdür-.
18. gömür-*‡ S, C, Q.
28. gömürde- } s; R.
gümürden- }
29. Kümec q, q(P); 2Pş; x 27v. 15.
309v. 3. kümçuk (*sic!*)*‡ S, X; d.
4. gümrük s; R; latin.
5. kümes S; R; greek.
kümek† s, Q, E.
8. gümek*‡ s, Q, X; 2.
10. göm gög X.
11. kümele S } R; p.
küme }
12. kömür S, q, X; x 316r. 25.
14. *gömük*‡ s, q, X; 301r. 10.
15. gömüklük‡ q; 8r. 26.
16. gömüldürük S, Y; R.
18. Küŋren- S, C, Q.
310r. 1. künen-‡ S, X; d.
2. künendür-‡ d.
köŋül dön- R.
3. gönilen- S; R.
4. Gün S, X; 2, 1Nph; 22v. 14.
7. gön s(bilai), Y.
güne gün s, q.
8. *gūnā gūn* P.
9. güney† s, X.
gün batar.
gön bardak R.
10. *gün toğar.*
gün çiçegi R.
11. gündelik s; R.
köndelen‡ S, q, (E); m.
14. gündüz.
kündük P; e.
15. *künes* S, Q } *
20. küneş }
gön kulağı Y; R*; Z.
*göŋewün** S; Z; (cf. 307v. 26).

* The form *künes* is given, because the word is rhymed with words ending in *-s*; it is, of course, etymologically incorrect.

21. köŋlek s.
köŋlekçe q; t-p; 17r. 14.
köŋül 24r. 13.
22. *köŋül kalış* q.
24. günlük s, Y; 2R.
25. *güne karğar* S; Z.
göni s, W, Y; 2R.
27. gönilü 2R.
Güwen- S, X.
29. Güwenc S, q.
310v. 1. Köy- S, C, Q.
17. köydür- c, Q, E.
26. küymen-* S, C, Q.*
Köy 22v. 13.
311r. 8. küyew S, q; x 305v. 9.
9. *küyew otı* R; B.
10. küykenek† s, q, X; Z; m; x 307v. 25.
12. köynek s, Y.
13. köyük Q; 2.
15. Kipleş-‡ s, C; p-t.
27. Kip† q, E; p.
29. kipri‡ S, Y; Z (metathesis of *kirpi*).
311v. 1. *kipri tékin*‡ Y; Z.
kibi S, q.
2. Kit- C, Q.
15. kiter- s, C, Q, X; 4r. 29.
29. kitert- S.
312r. 1. kiteril- s.
2. kétür- s, C, q.
11. kétürt- S.
12. kétürül- S.
13. Kétmen s.
Kéç- S, C, Q.
24. kéçür- S, c, Q; 4r. 29.
27. kéçil- S.
28. Kiç q; p.
29. kéç Q; 1, 1V.
312v. 3. *kiç* 2P.
4. *kéç kurun* Q; t-a.
6. kicge*‡ S, q; 2; x 319r. 19.
7. kéçe.
8. géce.
8A. keçit q.
9. kicitken† s, Y; B.
10. kiciş.
11. kiçik s, q; 21v. 25.
12. gicik.
kécim*‡ Q, Y; p.

* This may be the correct form of the oddly spelt word *küyfen-* in Kāşğārī.

15. kéçi boynuzı Y; R; B.
17. *Giderek* s; R.
Kir- C, Q.
29. kirküz- S, C, q.
313r. 12. kiriş- C, Q; 18v. 22.
29. kirlen- S.
313v. 1. girneş-‡ S.
Kir W, q.
3. kérek.
kéreklik q.
4. kérpic s, q.
5. kirpik S, q.
6. kirtek*‡ S, q.
8. kirec S; R; f.
kirşen s.
9. kiriş S, q; 2.
10. giriş s, q.
12. Kéz- S, C, Q; s(bilai) 25v. 26.
23. kézdür- c, Q.
26. kéziş- S.
27. kizle- }
kizlet- s } C, q.
314r. 15. kizleş- s.
16. kizlen- s.
17. Kiz q, Pş.
18. gézek s, Q; 4.
21. gézékçi s.
22. *kiz tuwurluk**‡ S; (see 187r. 22).
23. Kés- C, Q; 9v. 15.
314v. 5. késiş- S, c, q.
7. késil- S, c, q.
9. késtür-.
11. késkület- S, C, q.
Kise E 197v. 5.
23. kések q.
késegen 7r. 24.
24. *késemen* q.
25. késkin S, Y.
26. késme S, q, X; 2.
29. késük s, Q.
315r. 1. késim S, Q.
5. Kişne- S, C, q.
11. Kiş q, X; 1Z, 7P.
13. kişen S.
14. kişi S, Q; 2.
kişir? Z; x 132v. 19.
18. *kişi kara* q, E.
20. Kifte‡ q; P.
22. Gégir- S, C, q, Y.
315v. 5. *Gégirdek*† S; (cf. 300v. 25).
gégirme S.
6. *kékiz*† S, q, X.

8. Kél- C, Q.
29. kéltür- C, Q, E.
316r. 15. kéltürt-.
16. kéltürül-.
16A. *-Kil/-gil* q.
17. *kél* V.
18. kéliş q.
19. kélin q.
20. Kim q; 2; 16r. 22.
22. *kimerse* S, q, X; 16v. 24.
23. kimsen S, q; chinese.
25. *kimesne* S; R; x 316r. 23.
kémür q, X; x 309v. 13.
26. kéme S, Q; x 65r. 24.
28. Géŋeş- S(mi), C, Q.
316v. 13. kéŋel-† }
14. kéŋiş-‡ } S.
15. kéŋelt-† }
16. kéŋiştür-† } S.
Ként/d S, q; sogdian.
18. kindik S, q.
19. géŋeş S, q; 1, 1V.
21. kéŋ }
kéŋiş } s.
-gine S, q, X.
23. Giwür- S, C, Q, (for earlier *kigür-*).
317r. 9. Giwe s, W; 1R, Z, f; 1P.
10. *Kiyir* S, Q, X.*
13. géyisi S; R.
kéyik q; Z.
14. kéyim q; 2.
15. kiyin q; 17r. 9; 24r. 17.
16. kéyünüklemişi‡ s, q(P); 2I; e.
19. La‡ Q, E; 2d, 1p.**
26. *-la-*.
27. laçın Y; 1Z, 1Nt, 1R; f.
28. *laçın kaya* 1R, 1Ng; f-t.
29. laş† q; 1p, 3P; e.
317v. 2. lağ lağ‡ q, X; 1p?, 1P; x 317v. 5.
3. *-lağ/k* X.
4. *law law*‡ q, X; 1p?, 2P; x 317v. 3.
6. Laba† W; M; tibetan *lama*.

* This word is morphologically impossible and must be a scribal error for *kiyin*.

** In the first two supposed meanings the word occurs only at the end of a verse, and is probably a scribal error for some exclamation like *ā*.

7. labaşak‡ M; e.
Lafadan S; R*; a; (cf. 317v. 7).
8. Lak S; X; 2Rp, 2P.
9. Lengec‡ S, Y; Z; (error for *yengec*).
10. langar S, q, Y; 1Pş, 2p, 2P.
15. Layla- C, q; p-t.
22. laylat- s; p-t.
23. laylan- s; p-t.
24. *-Layın/-leyin* S, X; R.
25. Löppek*‡ s, Y; B; f, e.
26. Luc‡ 1p, 1PNg.
luça‡ S, X; B; p.
27. Lodos R; greek.
Lurı kuşı Y; R; Z; a.
28. *-Lug/k/-lüg/k* (X); 3; 23r. 17.
318r. 2. Lök q; 1, 1R, 1Z, 1P, 3 Seistan.*
6. Luy M; 1Z, 2; chinese.
7. *-Lığ/k/-lig/k* (X); 5; 23r. 17.
10. lıman W; R; greek.
Mac‡ q, X; p.
12. Matal*‡ W, X; a.
mata‡ S, Y; Pş; Z.
12. Meṭellik‡ s, Q; a-t.
16. Max‡ q; d (error for *maç?*).
17. maxanık‡ (*sic*) S; F; a.
18. Madadhal‡ W; Özbekiya-i Tūrān; a?, e.
19. Marı-‡ S, C.
24. Mard† W; r; latin.
mersin S, Y; R; B; greek.
25. mergen† S; m; 19r. 10.
maral† S, W, Q; Z; m; x 249v. 1.
27. marul S, Y; R; B; greek.
28. marulcuk S; R; B; greek -t.
29. marıw*‡ M*; F.
318v. 1. Mez W; (in Kāşğarī *béz*).
2. Maşka‡ p.
Maşab*‡ q; f.
4. Makta- S, C, q; m.

* The word is not originally Turkish in any of these meanings, but to what extent they represent actual or corrupt Persian words is obscure.

12. Makta m, d.
makara S; R; f.
13. Meken‡ S, q(P), X; Daştī; Z; f.
15. mekkeki‡ S; Özbekiya-i Tūrān; f.
16. Meleş* Q; 1Nt, 1.
18. Mamuğ/k q; B.
19. *Man-* S, C, q; x 127r. 21.
26. mandur-.
27. maŋ- S, C, q.
319r. 6. maŋdur- c, q.
8. maŋra- S, C, q, X; x 320r. 9.
15. Mantar S, Y; R; B; greek.
16. mandağan‡ S, q; F; f.*
17. manṭal W; R*; a.
18. manklay† s, X; 2; m.
19. maŋ W; 1Z, 1V, (Kāşğarī *mān*).
20. maŋğıt Nt.
21. maŋlay† S, q; m; x 319r. 18.
22. mengel S; R; f.
mengüş Y; R; p.
23. maŋış† s(mi), q.
24. mana*‡ W, X; 1, 1P.
25. Maw‡ W; Z; f.**
26. mawı q; a.
27. May‡ W; Özbekīya; f.
mayruk S, q; (Kāşğarī *mayğuk*).
28. meyn/meyin; x 321v. 11.
mayuk E 318r. 11.
29. Möcek† s, Z; (cf. 130v. 14).
319v. 1. mucak*‡ Q; p.
3. möçelge‡ S; m.
4. möcene*‡ S; f.
moça*‡ S.¶
5. Mor W; 1R.
mör M.
murdar ağacı Y; B; p-t.
6. murğawul* S, q(P); Np.
8. morı*‡ 1 Kaşğar, 1Ng, 2P.

* All three MSS. leave a gap where the translation of this word should be.
** Probably Mongolian *ma'u* (S.107) "bad".
¶ L substitutes *manṣab* for *ᶜamal*.

10. Muz q, Y; x 319v. 11.
11. Müsün‡ X; M.
Muş*‡ 1, 1P; (cf. 321r. 4).
12. müşek‡ s, q, X; p.
14. muşmula S, Y; R; B; italian.
15. möşük† s, q, Y; Z; f.
16. Muşluk s, Y; R; 1B, 1; f.
18. Moğul Np; e.
19. moğulçın‡ q; m.
21. Mul*‡ W, q, E, Y; 1f, 3P, 1A, 1H; E 289v. 17.
25. möldür*‡ S, q, Y; m; x 225v. 20.
26. moloz S; R; f.
27. Muŋay- S, C, Q.
320 r. 7. muŋra-S, } C, Q, X; 3v. 25; x 319r. 9.
8. muŋraş- s,
muŋray-‡ s,
muŋurğa-‡ S,
320v. 1. muŋlaş- S, C, Q.
9. *Muna* S, q, (15v. 18).
10. munca S, q; 15v. 20.
12. *munda.*
mundağı q.
13. *mundağın.*
mundak Q; 2; 15v. 20; 17v. 4; x 259v. 18.
16. mondu*‡ S, Q, E; F.
21. monğal s; Nt.
22. muŋ S, Q; 1, 1H.
25. *muŋa* S(mi).
26. möngen Y; M.
muŋluğ Q; 2.
29. möngü S; 1M, 2Np.
321r. 2. *müŋüz* S(mi), q, X; x 141v. 23; 142v. 27.
4. muŋuş* q; (cf. 319v. 11).
5. monuğan m.
munuŋ q.
6. *-Mu/-mü* q; 1, 1P.
8. Muymul S, Y; R; Z; x 307v. 25; 311r. 12.
9. Mittin† s, q; P.
11. Mişe‡ S; p.
Mışır tawukı R; Z; a-t.
Mığ Y; 1, 2P.
12. Mégicin‡ S; Z; m.

Mıla qalmāğī 276v. 8.
13. mıltık† S, Y; f.
14. Mén- S(bilai) (*sic!*), C, Q.
23. méndür-.
minciş-*‡ S.
24. *méŋze-* S, X; x 150r. 10.
25. *méŋzet-* s, c, q; x 150r. 24.
27. *méŋzeş-* s; x 150r. 24.
28. Mén 15r. 26.
29. *mén mén/mén dürmén* Q.
321v. 2. ménce S, q.
3. mıncağ S, q, (Kāşğarī *munçuk*).
4. mındaw*‡ S; d.
méŋ S, q.
6. *miŋ* q, Y; 1, 1Nt; x 150r. 26.
7. *miŋ ayağ* Z.
méŋa (misspelling of *maŋa*).
méŋlığ (*sic*, **in error**). }
méŋli 1, 1Np. }
8. *méŋiz* X.
9. ménlik.
minisek*‡ (*sic* in L.).
10. Méye‡ S, X.*
11. Nerke‡ S (probably scribal error for *cérge*).
narı S, W, q.
12. *narırak.*
13. narın S; f, I?
14. Nesne S; R; (cf. 323r. 3).
Naṭas W; R; a; x 323v. 12.
Neğü Q, X; (*sic*, in error).
Nenek‡ x 119r. 25; 323r. 9.
16. Naw‡ q, Y; Pş.
19. newker† s, X; M; (error for *nöker*).
21. nawlık‡ q; Pş-t.
22. *Ne deŋlü* (*sic?*) R.
Nay‡ W, Q; F; 1p, 1P; x 218v. 27.
25. nayman† S; 1Nt, 1M.
Nutukçı‡ S, Q, E, X; m?

* This word is morphologically impossible and probably reproduces a scribal error.

322r. 1. Noğay Nt.
Noyat‡ S; qalmāġīya.
noya/ın† s; 1, 1‡; m.
3. né 16v. 7.
4. *-nı/-ni.*
néni q.
6. *né i/üçün.*
né érdi érkin.
né érkeni q.
7. Nébtes*‡ S, q; m, e.
9. *Nétmek* C, Q.
26. *Néte/ük* Q, X.
29. *nétkey* Q.
322v. 1. *nétti* Q; 3.
5. *nétib/nétiben* Q; 2.
8. Néçükleş- C, q.
13. Néçük s, q; x 322r. 29.
15. *néce* S, q; 17r. 13.
16. *néçe* s, q; 17r. 13.
17. *Nédin* q.
18. *Nési* q.
19. Nigende S; R; p.
20. *nége* S, q; x 321v. 16.
21. *Néyle-* C, Q.
323r. 1. *Néler* q.
2. *néyler* V.
3. Néme } S, Q, Y; (cf.
némerse } 321v. 14).
6. *némem* q.
7. Nének‡ S, q, X; x 119r. 25; 143r. 5.
9. *-nıŋ/-niŋ* q.
11. *néni* q.
12. *né néme* q.
13. *Néwcün* q.
14. Wax† W, q; p; x 323r. 17.
16. Warsakı R; f.
17. *Wah*† q, X; p.
19. -*Wul/-wül*† m; 7r. 21.
20. Wuh W, Q.
22. Wéresi S.
23. Wişne S; R; B; p; x 222r. 16.
24. Hepi S; R.
Har-† S, C, Q; x 158r. 11; (cf. 33v. 8).
323v. 9. *Herewül*† s, q, X; m; x 36v. 22.
10. haray*‡ q; d.*
11. harbatan‡ S; m.

* Probably a misunderstanding of Persian *har-* "all" and *ay* "month", the latter perhaps a scribal error for some other word.

12. harṭuman R; a.
herek W, X; R; f.
13. har yanı q; p-t.
Ham ol p-t.
14. Henek‡ s; f.
Hawalan- 1S, C, q, a-t.
22. Haw S, Q; (Kāşğarī I43 *o**).
26. Hayda-†.
27. Hay† W (hāy) q; p.
29. hay Q; p.
324r. 3. *hay tülügüm/hay tülüm* q; F.
5. *hay hay öleŋ/hay öleŋ* F.
6. Hopla- s, q(R); r; f.
8. Hoppuş*‡ s; Z; f.
9. hüpüşek*‡ Z; (cf. 58v. 2).
Hur- } † E, C, Q; x
hür- } 66v. 23.
29. hüret-*‡ C, q; m.
324v. 9. *hürk-*† X; x 68v. 28.
hürküt- S, c, q, X; x 69r. 13.
12. *Hürkünc* S, q; x 71r. 27.
13. Honıla-*‡ S, C, Q; m.*
23. Hona† S, Q; Z; m.
24. honı Y; r, greek.
25. Hıklawuk‡ s, Y.
Ya, q, X; 1, 1P§; x 340v. 27.
28. Yap- S, C, Q; 3, 1R; 19v. 4, 5.
325r. 16. yapıl- S, c, Q; 1R.
22. yapın- S, C, Q.
325v. 2. yapuş- s, C, Q, X; x 325v. 14.
14. *yapış-* s, X; x 325v. 2.
yapuşul-/yapışıl- s.
15. yapıştur-.
16. yapışturul- s, c, q.
18. Yab‡ 1, 1P.
19. yap S; 1, 1V; 1R, 1RV; 16v. 10, 11; x 223v. 25; 343r. 21.
21. yaba W, Y; F.
22. yapağ/k s; 1Z‡, 1R.
23. yapalak s; Z.
24. yaban W, Q; p.
26. yabancı S; R; p-t.
27. *yaban turak otı* X, Y; R; B; p-t; x 212v. 20.

* Probably misspelt with *-mek*; the Mongolian verb is (*h*)*onıla-* (Kow. 343).

28. *yabana* S; R; p.
29. yapar S; 1Np, 2V, 1RV, 1M*.
326r. 2. *yaprag/k* } s, q, E,
3. yapurğağ/k } X; x 333v. 11.
6. *yapu* R; (cf. 326r. 14).
yapucı r.
yapurğan E 326r. 5.
yapuşğan 1, 1V.
7. yapuğ/k Q; 2.
14. yapı‡.
yapıcı R; (cf. 326r. 6).
15. yapıncı† S, q; 1F, 1.
18. Yat- C, Q; 4v. 5; 24r. 8.
27. yatğur- S, C, Q.
326v. 5. yatış- S.
6. yatla- c, q.
yatur- 4v. 5.
10. Yat q, X; 1, 1V, x 327r. 15.
12. yatağ/k Q; 2.
15. yatağan S; 1R, 1.
16. yatsı S; x 332r. 8.
17. yatlığ s, Q; 2 (*sic* in all MSS.).
19. yatuğan† Q; m.
21. yatuğancı‡ q; m-t.
22. yatuk‡ s, q, E, Y.
24. yatış S, q.
Yaçan- E 152r. 18.
26. Yaxşı 15r. 18.
yaxşılar q, E; 1, 1V.
29. Yada-† C, Q; m.
327r. 12. yadat-† s, c; m-t.
13. *Yad* q, X; 1, 1P; x 326v. 10.
15. *yada taşı*† Q, Y; m-t; (see 205r. 21).
17. yadağ q; m-t.
18. Yar- C, Q, X; 26r. 28; x 348v. 24.
327v. 1. yardur-.
2. yara- C, Q, X; x 327v. 16.
16. yaran- S, c, q; x 327v. 2.
18. yaraş- s, C, Q; 2; 9r. 12.
29. yaru- } S, C, Q; 4r.
328r. 1. yaruş- } 21; 18r. 25.
19. yarut- } s, c, q; 16v.
yaruştur- } 21.
22. yaratıl- S, C, q.

* This word seems to be a misreading of *yarı*.

* In l. 23 L seems to have *biyik*, which is no doubt correct, for *bilik*.

* L omits the superfluous *wa ṣīn*, which is repeated in G from the previous entry.

26. *yalaŋlat-*‡ }
yalaŋaclat-‡ } c, q.
yalaŋlattur-‡ }
yalaŋaclattur-‡ }
335v. 1. yalbar- C, Q.
11. yalaŋlan-† } s.
yalaŋaclan-‡ }
12. yalçı- S, C, q.
18. yaldıra- C.
25. yaldırat- s.
26. yalduzla-† 2; r.
yalka-‡ S, C.
336r. 3. yalkı- C, Q.
11. yalkıt- s, c, q.
13. yalın- S, C, Q; 2.
25. yalab- S; R.
yaltaklan- s; R.
26. yalınlan- S; R.
27. yalınlandur- r.
Yalağ/k† q, Y.
336v. 1. yalaŋ/ngac s, Q, X.
4. yalaŋ s, Q; 2; x 336v. 4; 337r. 1.
7. yalaw‡ s, Q, E, X; 1, 1p.
yalawuz E 166r. 4; 336v. 9.
11. yalpak† S, X.
12. yaltaklığ Y; R.
yalçu S; R; (cf. 50r. 12).
13. *yalduz* R; (cf. 345v. 25).
yalduz kurtı } Z; (cf.
14. yaldırawuk } 345v.
möcek s, } 26).
yaldırak s.
yaldırayış s; R.
15. yalğan q.
16. yalğancı.
yalğancılık/
yalğanlık q.
17. yalğuz.
18. *yalğuzun* q.
19. yalkın† x 341r. 8.
20. yalman† W, Q; 2.
22. yelen*‡ S; F.
yalı W; R; 1, 1 greek.
24. yalın S, Q, E; 1, 1V.
28. yalınlığ q.
337r. 1. *yalınrak.*
yalıŋ s, q, X.
3. yalıŋlığ q.
4. yalıŋcak s; R.
yalıŋ kat S; R; e.
5. Yama- S, C, Q; 9v. 2, 29.

14. yamat- c, q.
16. yamal- s.
17. yamanla- S, C, Q; 2.
28. Yamac R.
yamağ/k Q; 1, 3R; 9v. 28.
337v. 3. yamağ/klığ q.
4. yaman q, Y; 1, 1M, Z; 15r. 18.
6. yamanlığ.
yemdü S }
yemdik s, R* }
yamgur q; x 333v. 3.
7. yamcı- P-T.
8. Yan- C, Q; 2; 10v. 24.
338r. 3. yandur- c, Q; 2.
10. yanc- S, C, q.
16. yancdur-.
17. yancıl-.
yandaş-‡ S, C, Q, E.
28. yandaştur-‡ c, q.
338v. 1. yaŋ- S, C, q.
8. yaŋıt- S(mi), c, q.
11. yaŋıl- s, c, Q.
16. yaŋşa- S, C, q.
23. yaŋkulan- R.
24. yaŋsıla- s, R.
Yan Q; 2, 1V, 3P.
29. yana Q, X, Y; 3, 1V; x 339r. 25.
339r. 3. yantak s, W; B.
4. yancak‡ s, q; F.
6. yancğay‡ s; 1, 1V.
7. yancuk.
8. yanku S; 1, 1R.*
10. yanğı S, q.
11. *yaŋ* W, q, X; 1, 1V; x 339r. 22.
13. yaŋa S; R.
yaŋacığ‡ d.
yaŋarak r.
14. yaŋağ/k s(mi), Q; 1, 1B.**
17. yenegen‡ S; Z.¶
18. yaŋla‡ S, Q; x 352v. 18.
20. yaŋlığ s, q; 23r. 29.
21. yaŋı S, q, X; 1, 1Ng; x 339r. 12; (see 352v. 18).

* All MSS. write *yanğu*, but the spelling gives *yanku*.
** "Nut" is properly *yağak* (in Kāşğarī, etc.); this is either a phonetic change of, or error for, that word.
¶ Error for *yaŋan* "elephant"?

23. yaŋış S; R.
yaŋıltmac† S; 2.
24. *yaŋı kurt* Y; R; Z.
25. *yana* Q, X; 3, 2V; 2P; x 339r. 2.
339v. 1. Yawaş-‡ s, C.
8. yawu- } C, Q.
yawuş- s }
25. yawut- } c, Q.
yawuştur- }
340r. 1. yewütke-‡ S, C, Q, X; x 352r. 22 (spelt *yewüt-*).
12. yawla- S, C.
18. *Yaw* (cf. 333v. 4).
yawaş q.
19. yawaşa W; R; p (for *lawāşa*).
20. yawçı‡ S.
yawçın E 345v. 20.
21. yawrı S; Z; x 118r. 12.
yawşan S, q, Y; B; x 259v. 22.
24. yawğan S, q.
26. yawlak s; x 317v. 4.
yawu S, W; R; p.
27. yawuz S, Q.
29. yawuğ/k s.
yawa‡ S; 1p, 1P.
340v. 1. Yay- S, C, q; 2.
11. yayıl- S, c, Q; 2.
17. yaykal- S, C, q.
23. yaykan- s; R.
24. yayakla- c, q.
25. yayla-.
26. Yay q, X; 2, 1‡, 2V; x 324v. 27.
29. yayak q.
341r. 1. yayan s; R.
2. yaypaŋ‡ S, q, E; x 331r. 9; 336v. 12.
5. yaycı S; 1, 1‡, 1Ng.
5. yaydak† S, W, q; Z.
7. yaykara s; R.
yaykın‡ S, X, Y; x 336v. 19.
yaylak 17r. 23.
8. yaylamışı I.
9. yaylım S, Y; R; 2.
10. yayma S; F.
yeyni S; R.
11. yayık S, Y; 1F, 1Ng.
12. Yupğa S, q; x 344r. 1.
14. yupğalık q.
15. Yut- C, Q.
27. yuttur- S, c, q.

* The word is Turkish in both meanings; *cut* (*sic*) "pestilence", etc., in Mongolian is a loan-word from Turkish.

* In the meaning "face" this must be a simple error for *yüz*.

9. yont 1Z, 1; x 297v. 7.
yont kuşı Y; R; Z.
10. *yonca* X; B; x 342v. 19.
yond R x 297v. 7.
yonka R.
11. yüŋ S, q.
12. *yüŋ* V.
13. *yöŋul* s(mi), X.
14. yuna*‡ S, X; F; p?
Yu- S(bi), C, Q.
347v. 6. yudur-.
7. yuwul- S.
8. yuwala- }
yuwalat- } X.
9. *Yuwa* W, q, Y; 1, 1Nt; x 89r. 16.
11. *yuwalak* s; R; (cf. 346v. 19).
12. yuwusğa‡ S.
yuwuş*‡ S, Y.
13. yuwundu S; R.*
Yuy- S, C; (see 215v. 9).
18. yuyul- c, Q.
22. Yiber- C, Q.
29. Yip S.
yıbar (see 93r. 8).
348r. 1. yiplik s.
Yét- S, C, Q, X; 2; 12r. 6.
17. yétiş- S, c, Q.
22. yétil- S, c, Q, E.
28. yétür- }
yétkür- }
yétkürt- } c, Q.
yétiştür- }
348v. 13. *Yéter* Q; 1, 2V.
16. yétek s, X.
yétmiş 18r. 6.
yétmişer 18r. 6.
17. yét/tti 20v. 10.
yétti ata q.
18. yéttiew (i.e. yéttew-?) q.
19. yétik s.
yétigen S, X.
20. *Yéd-* S, c, Q, R; x 348r. 2.
23. *Yédek* x 348v. 16.
yédi kardaş } R; x 348v.
yédiler } 20.
24. *Yır-* c, Q, X; 26r. 28; x 327r. 19.
349r. 1. yırt- S, C, q.

* L omits the superfluous final *-r* in G.

7. yırtış- s, c, q.
9. yırtıl- s.
yırla- S(bi), }
10. yérle- s(bilai), } C, q.
20. yırlaş- s.
yérleş- 21v. 21.
21. yırağra-‡.
Yér q; 21v. 19.
22. yır q.
23. *yır/yér* V.
24. *yér azuk* q; (see 353r. 20).
25. yırak.
yırakrakk/ğına q.
26. yıraw S, q.
27. yırtlas† s; 2.
29. yırtmac S; R.
yırtuk S.
yırtıcı s.
349v. 1. *yér kam* Q; (see 353r. 20).
5. *yér koyı* q.
6. *yér köki* Y; B.
yérlik yérin Q, E.
yırlıg E 349v. 8.
9. *yér néme* s, q; (see 353r. 21).
10. yırık.
Yézne S.
11. Yéş-*‡ C, Q, E.
22. yéşil-*‡ S, c, Q.
25. yéşin-*‡ S; 2.
27. Yığ- C, q; 19r. 14.
350r. 4. yığdur- c, q.
6. yığıl- }
yığılış- } c, q.
8. yığla- C, Q; 5r. 22.
22. yığlat- s.
23. yığlaş- s.
24. yığlamsın- s, C, q.
Yığ E 147v. 2.
350v. 3. yığac Q; 2.
5. yığlağu Q; 2; x 309r. 2.
7. yığınak† q.
8. yığı Q.
10. yığın S; 5v. 6.
11. *yıgınt* S, Y; Z; d.*
12. Yık- C, Q; 2; 19r. 15.
21. yıktur- 2.
yıkıl- c, Q; 11r. 15, 16.
25. Yıkuk S; 8r. 11; 25v. 12.
26. *yıkılğur* Q; d.
27. *yıkılmağur* d.

* Firağı's form *yağan* is correct.

28. Yikir-† S, C, q, X; x 351r. 6.
351r. 5. yikren- S, X; x 350v. 28.
6. *Yék* q; (see 334v. 23).
8. *yégen* S; (see 334v. 23).
yégülük q.
9. yigit s, q.
10. yigitlik.
yégirme s; 18r. 4 (*yégirmi*).
yégirmişer 18r. 5.
11. yégin S; R*.
yéginlik r*.
Yél- S, }
13. yıl- R, } C, Q.
24. yéldür- c, q.
26. yıldur- R.
yéle-*‡ S, C, Q, E.*
351v. 6. yélpi- S, C, q.
13. yéllen- S, C, q.
20. yélle- 21v. 21.
21. Yél 1, 1V; 21v. 19.
yıl 1, 1V; 20v. 20.
22. yélek† (*sic*) s, Q; 2, 1R.
24. yéleklik q.
25. yılan (*sic*) 1Z, 1; x 112v. 10.
26. *yılan otı* B (see 112v. 10).
27. *yılan balıgı* R; Z.
28. yılanğac Y; R*.
yéleŋ*‡ s, q.
29. *yılana ağu wéren* Y; Z.
352r. 2. *yılan yastuğı* X, Y; R; B; x 286r. 4.
3. yélpaze s; R }
yélpigüc s, q }
5. yélciley (*sic* in L.) q; 2.
6. yılcılık q; X; x 352r. 8, 13.
8. yılkı q, X; 17v. 11; x 352r. 7, 13.
10. yélke†.
yélken Q, Y.
12. yilgü*‡ Y; d.
13. yélgin‡ s; e.
yıllık/yillik q, X; 1, 1R; x 352r. 7, 8.
15. *yél yaparak* s; R.

* A dubious word, apparently connected with the synonymous verb *yal-* in Kāşğarī; the added second *-l-*'s do not occur in L.

INDEX II

Skeleton Cross-index to Index I.*

* See paragraphs 7 and following of the Introduction.

çöz	212v. 27.
Dé-	227r. 7.
Da/eb/p	223r. 15.
def	224r. 5.
daw	224v. 27.
ta/eb/p	150v. 8.
ṭab/p	261r. 8.
tef	157r. 25.
taw	164v. 15.
ṭaw	261r. 22.
dé/ı/ib/p	226r. 5.
déw	227r. 4.
dıw	228r. 7.
té/ı/ib/p	188v. 1.
téf	195r. 17.
téw	202v. 5.
du/üb	225r. 1.
duw	226r. 2.
to/u/ö/üb/p	167r. 22.
ṭop	261r. 26.
to/üf	179v. 15.
tuw	187r. 19.
Tac	152r. 18.
tuc	169v. 18.
Da/ed	223r. 23.
ta/et	151v. 18.
té/it	189v. 12.
do/ud/t	225r. 4.
tu/üt	168r. 1.
Dağ	223v. 28.
dax	223r. 22.
tağ	157r. 16.
ṭağ	261r. 14.
tak	157r. 25.
ṭak	261r. 21.
tax	152v. 3.
tık	195r. 18.
doğ	225r. 13.
toğ	178v. 14.
ṭoğ	261r. 29.
tok	180r. 3.
tox	169v. 20.
Deg/k	224r. 7.
tek	157v. 24.
dé/ig/k	226r. 9.
té/ig/k	195r. 18.
dö/üg/k	225r. 13.
tö/üg/k	181r. 26.
Da/el	224r. 18.
ta/el	158r. 11.
dı/il	226v. 26.
té/ı/il	198v. 9.
do/u/ö/ül	225r. 27.
to/u/ö/ül	183r. 15.
Da/em	224v. 20.
ta/em	160v. 25.
té/ı/im	200v. 4.
do/u/üm	225v. 20.
to/u/üm	184v. 25.
Dan	224v. 25.
deŋ	224r. 14.
ta/en/ŋ	161v. 21.
ṭan	261r. 22.
dé/ı/in/ŋ	226v. 28.
té/ı/in/ŋ	200v. 20.
do/u/ö/ün/ŋ	225v. 22.
to/u/ö/ün/ŋ	185r. 29.
ṭon	261v. 7.
Da/er	223v. 3.
ta/er	152v. 4.
ṭar	261r. 10.
dé/ir	226r. 23.
té/ı/ir	190r. 9.
du/ür	225r. 5.
to/u/ö/ür	170r. 13.
ṭor	261r. 26.
Des	223v. 24.
ta/es	155r. 21.
tés	194r. 26.
to/us	176r. 4.
Daş	223v. 25.
taş	155r. 29.
ṭaş	261r. 12.
té/iş	194r. 29.
düş	225r. 13.
tu/ö/üş	176r. 25.
Da/ey	224v. 28.
ta/ey	166r. 5.
ṭay	261r. 23.
déy	227v. 25.
té/ıy	203r. 4.
doy	225r. 2.
to/u/üy	187r. 24.
ṭoy	261v. 10.
taz	155r. 17.
diz	226r. 27.
té/iz	193v. 13.
du/üz	225r. 10.
to/u/ö/üz	173r. 22.
Ko/u	291v. 25.
Ka'a	263v. 8.
Kab/p	263v. 9.
kaf	274r. 7.
xaf	222v. 13.
kaw	278r. 17.
ḥaw	222r. 18.
haw	323v. 14.
kıp	292v. 27.
kıf	297v. 26.
kıw	299v. 4.
ğub	262v. 5.
ko/ub/p	281v. 18.
xub	222v. 22.
hop	324r. 6.
kow	291v. 13.
Ğac	261v. 27.
kac/ç	267v. 5.
xac/ç	222v. 9.
ğıj	262v. 17.
kıc/ç	293r. 9.
kıj	296v. 2 and 9.
ko/uc/ç	283v. 3.
Kad	267v. 28.
kat	265v. 25.
xat	222r. 20.
	222v. 7.
xaṭ	222v. 12.
kud	284r. 3.
ko/ut	282r. 27.
kuṭ	288v. 19.
xud	222v. 23.
Kağ	274r. 5.
kak	274r. 8.
xak	222r. 23.
ḥaq	222r. 18.
kığ	297v. 26.
kık	297v. 27.
hık	324v. 25.
koğ	288v. 21.
kox	284r. 2.
Ğal	262v. 2.
kal	274v. 21.
xal	222v. 14.
ğıl	262v. 18.
kıl	297v. 27.
ko/ul	288v. 23.
Kam	276r. 16.
ham	323v. 13.
kım	298v. 22.
ğum	262v. 13.
ko/um	290r. 17.
Ğan	262v. 3.
kan/ŋ	276v. 15.
xan	222v. 1 and 19.
ğın/ŋ	268v. 28A.
kın	298v. 27.
xın	223r. 13.
ğun/ŋ	262v. 13.
ko/un/ŋ	290v. 11.
hon	324v. 13.
Ğar	262r. 3.
kar	268r. 20.
xar	222v. 10.
ḥar	222r. 16.
har	323r. 24.
ğır	262v. 15.
kır	293v. 17.
xır	232r. 2.
ğur	262v. 7.
ko/ur	284r. 8.
xor	222v. 26.
hur	324r. 9.
Kas	273v. 5.
kıs	296v. 24.
ğus	262v. 12.
kus	287v. 3.
Ğaş	262v. 2.
kaş	273v. 10.
xaş	222v. 11.
kış	297v. 9.
xış	223r. 13.
ko/uṣ	287v. 5.
xoş	223r. 1.
Ğay	262v. 4.
kay	279v. 10.
hay	323v. 26.
kıy	299v. 6.
ko/uy	291v. 29.
Ğaz	262r. 25.
kaz	272v. 16.
kız	295v. 15.
xız	223r. 12.
ğuz	262v. 11.
ko/uz	287v. 17.
Keb/p	300r. 8.
g/kew	301v. 1.
hep	323r. 24.
kib/p	311r. 15.
kif	315r. 20.
giw	316v. 23.
g/kö/üb/p	302r. 9.
güw	310r. 27.
hüp	324r. 9.
Kec/ç	300r. 15.
g/ké/ic/ç	312r. 13.
g/kö/üc/ç	303r. 15.
ḥöç	222r. 18.
G/ked	300r. 19.
ket	300r. 12.
gid	312v. 17.
ké/it	311v. 2.
güd	303v. 21.
kö/üt	302v. 13.
Keg/k	300v. 22.
g/kég/k	315r. 22.
g/kö/üg/k	306v. 19.
G/kel	300v. 25.
ké/il	315v. 8.
g/kö/ül	308r. 17.
G/kem	301r. 6.

INDEX III. RŪMĪ WORDS*

Éw-, *ebe*, *awuc oyunı*, (ufacuk), (éwdür-), ufak, *ibik*, iplicek, uwan, efendi (gk.), üfür-, *epri-*; *iç ağa*, *uca*, *uçuğ*, ıçkır-, *uçğur*, ıçkırık;

aț, *it balığı*, *it boncuğı*, *it dirsegi*, *it xıyarı*, *ot*, öde-, ada, *oda*, öte, otçı, atğu, *ödek*, itgü, ötme, atmaca, *etmek*, *otur-*, oturtma, oturak, *ederek*, ödeş-, *ötüş-*;

ağ/k baba, *ağac delegen*, *ağac kawunı*, *ağac kakan*, *oğul otı*, ağla-, *ağ/klığ/k*, ıklığ, akın, oğun, (akıncı), oğra-, oğurlayın, oğraş-, ağırşak, *ağız yarı*, *ağzı açuk*, *oğuz*;

ege, *iki kardaş kanı*, ökçele-, ökçelet-, (ökçelen-), ögcesiz, öget, eglen-, ögündüre (gk.), ögündurük (gk.), *ögür*, égrice, ögürdi, égrik, *égrim*, egremci, ekseri (gk.), öksiz, ekez, öküz közi;

alı ko-, (*alı kon-*), aluc, alcı, *alcu taşı*, *alaca*, *alaca serce*, ılıcak, olta (ital.), eldewen, aldağuc, *ıldıra-*, ılığ/k, *ıllık*, oluk, alanc*, alıs, *alış-*, ılış ıl*, alay, *alay bozan*;

um-, *emek*, (emekdeş), umul-, emizek, emizekli, *emizikli*,

en-, öŋ-, ancak, (ancılayın), e/énet-, andık, anaktar (gk.), ankara (gk.), *enük*, üngü, üngülük, engenar (gk.), öŋül-, iŋle-, iŋilde-, iŋildü, *enler*, (énen-), enişte;

(ér-), *ır-*, ér, *ır*, ur, *orba*/oroba (ital.), ürper-, *orak kuşı*, ırğat (gk.), arkaluc, irk-, *ürkü*, irkil-, ergen, *érken*, ırmacuk, örümcek/*örmücek*, orman, ormanlık, iriŋ, oran, öründü, öründle-, (öründlen-), oranla-, örs, arayıcı yıldızlar;

as, us, *asa koy-*, *as/şı*, ispir (p.), üstele-, üstelet-, üstünle-, üstünlet-, üsküf (gk.), iskele (gk.), iskemle (lat.), *asıl-*, ıslığ, *aşlan*, uslan-, *asma*, ısmarla- (p.-t.), ısmarlama (p.-t.), osan, esenle-, esenleş-, ésirge-, esergiş;

aş-, uş-, aşı, işte, ışığ/k, éşkin, aşla-, işlek, (aşlan-), aşın-, uşundı, (aşındur-), uşur-;

ayu kulağı, ayıd/t ağacı, *öykün*, *öyle*, aylak, ayın-, oyundı, öyürtle-, (öyürtlen-), *ayruk*, uysal, uyuş-, öyüş*, uyaz;

üz, özle-, üzlü palçık, uzun éşek.

Papatıya (gk.), büber (lat.); pic (p.), paçawra (f.), *buçuğ/k*, böcek, bacanak, bucurğad (f.); buda-, *batak*, petek (gk.?), (budan-), budandu, (bedenüs gk.), bodur, büdür-; bıx-, boğaca, pık/xtı (p.), buxağu, bağlama, boğmak, boğna/uk, bağır-, pakır; *be/ég börki*, *pek*, bügi, bekle-, bükülüm, bekmez, fiker* (f.), beküri*, bögrülce; *bal kabağı*, bile-, *bula-*, balaban (f.), piliç (slav.), *baldırı kara*, buldurma, balığçıl, *bélek*, palaska (magyar); *ban-*, *ben-*, bön-*, biŋ, *biŋ kat*, boncuk, buncılayın, *pancar* (f.), *bandur-*, fınkır-*, buŋal-, puŋar, *beŋiz*, (*benze-*), *benzet-*; *borı*, (perpi), perperem, *burçak*, pörçükli, bardak, *burgu*, barmaklığ, f/parısa (gk.), warsakı (f.); pas, pus, bastuk*, bestil, basturma, fıskıya (a.), püsgül, püsgür-, besle-, fısıldu, fesligen (gk.), beslen-, basmak; paşa (p.); *béş barmak*, bişi/bişme, puştu*, fişek (p.), *başlığ*, başmak, wişne (p.); boyca boyca, *boyun buran*, poyraz (gk.); *biz üz*, *boz dogan*, *bozug/k*, büzük, bazlamac, bazar ertesi (p.-t.),)*bazar güni* p.-t.).

Caba, cebe (a.), çapçı (p.-t.), çiwit, çapak, *çapğun*, ciwek, çabala-, *çupan aldayıcı* (p.-t.), *çe/éwrük*, çewrünti; çit, çete (slav.), çeteci (slav.-t.), çedik, çetik, *çetik otı*, çatal, çetele (gk.), çatıldu; *çığıt*, çakıl, çokal, çakıldu, çağlama, çığın, (çığnat-), çığnan-, çakır (lat.), çakırcı (lat.-t.), çığırğu; çih, çeki, çigdig*, çé/ekdiri, çekmece; *çal-*, *çil*, çeleb (syriac), çolpa, çelebi (syr.-p.), *çalıcı*, çıldıra-, çalğu, çılğın, çalkuyın, çelik, çelim, çölmek, çélimlü, çelenk (f.); çam ağacı (A.-t.), *çam sakızı* (a.-t.), çemçe balığ, çamaşır (p.); çıŋrağu; çar (p.), *çeri*, çırpı, çırpıcı, çarcı, ce/ércer (a.), çördük, çurtan, çérge/*çerke*(f.), çırlık, çerilik, çıram*; çay, çaylak, *çayan*; çiz-, çizgin-.

Taw (p.), *tob tolı*, *tabu sağrakı*, *déwe tabanı*, dipi, déwecik*, *d/tapkur*, *dibek*, *țopal*, d/tepele-, diblik, dibelik, țawun*, *țapanca*, defni (gk.), *depengü* (p.), *țawar*, *t/țabur*, toparla-, toparlak, tebsi, t/țawaşı (a.), tawşancıl; tuc; dede, dutu, tutğal; *țağ*, toğdak (m.), toğdarı (m.?), takım, *tokmak*, țağan (gk.), *țoğan*, tuğur, toğurka (m.); dek, ték (p.), dögec, te/ékek, degül, d/tügeli, diklen-, (diklendür-), degme, tekne, *tékirlek*, *degirmi*, dekşür-; dal-, *tal*, tala-, dola*, talabı-, talıcı, delüce, *delüce toğan*, dilcek, daldırma, *dalğıcı*, dölük, telim, dilim, tulumba (ital.), dolamac, tolun-, dülengec, talaz (gk.); tum-, dümbelek (p.), tumucı, demed (gk.), temel (gk.), (tumul-), tamla-, tamla, *tümengini**, tımar (p.), tomruk, temren; *tın-*, diŋ-, dön-, *țana*, *dana burnı*, déne-, țonbay, țonat-, *tındur-*,

* See paragraph 40 of the Introduction.

(döndür-), tankıldu*, deŋlü, tönlük, dönüm, d/ṭonan-, *d/ṭonanma*, danaşık, toŋuzlan böcegi/*kurtı*; tar tağın*, tor top, torı, dürpi, dürpici, dürpil-, tercek*, *durak*, turğuz*, terki, (*terki bağı*), darıl-, *deril-*, tiril*, *dürlü*, torlak, térlik, derim éwi, durma, tırmala-, torun, dernek, dirsek; des degirmi, tasla-, taslak, tasalan- (p.-t.); *ṭaş*, *tiş sürgü*, düşün-, ṭaşra, (ṭaşrağı); doy-, *ṭoy-*, t/ṭüy, toyumluk, teyze/*deyeze*; *diz kapağı*, dizi, *dizgin*, tizle- (p.-t.), dizlik, düzme, *dizin dizin*, düzen, tazana (p.), düzenlik.

Ko-; *kaba kulağ*, *kaba kuşluk*, *kab/pa kab/pa yé-*, kapa-, kawucı*, kapat-, kawut, kapağ/k,kawak ağacı, (hopla-), kablu baka, kowan, kubur, kuburcuk, kabran (f.), kopusğa (slav.), kawşa-, kawşan-; kaç, *koca yemiṣi*, koçı, kıcırda-; *kuṭlu*, katmar (f.), kadana (ital.), kadırğa (gk.), koğ; kakı-, kakığanlığ, kakılcam, kakır-*, kakırdak, kakırma*, kakşak; kulb (a.), *kaldur-*, kaldurarak, kallukan (f.), kolan/ŋ, kalandas (lat.)*, *kolay*; *kum balığı*, kumral, komsı (a.); kın ağacı, (honı gk.), kanbıl otı (p.-t.), *kancık*, kandur*, kındur-, kındıra (a.), kındırğa (f.), *kandaya dek**, *konağ/k*; kar-, *kır*, *kır kır*, *kara*, *kara ağac*, *kara batak*, *kara boğaz*, *kara baş*, *kara tal*, *kara düzen*, *kara kulağ*, *kara günlük*, *kara yonca*, karbıl çıbanı*, karabına (french), kırpındı, karça(n)* (f.), kara/uca, *kurt bağrı*, *kurt kulağı*, xorata (gk.), harṭuman (a.), *kardaş kanı*, kurdasaŋ/*nı/nc* (f.), kurak, koruğ/k, *karğa büken*, *karğa dölgi*, *korku*, kırağu, xaral* (f.), xorulda-, kırlağan çıbanı, *karlankuç*, xoran (gk.), kars-, xoros übügi (p.-t.), (karış-), kuruş (german), xırsız (a.-t.), xırzıma (gk.); kısac, kıskan-, kuskun, kıskanc, kusundı, kasnak, (kasnakçı), kasırğa; *kuş etmegi*, xaşa (a.), *kaşka*, xaşal (a.), xışıl*, kaşmar (f.), kuşmar (f.); kıyı, kayık, kuyum, (kuyumcı), *koyun gözi*, kaynak, kayır-, kayrıcı, *kuyruk salan*; *kız*, *kız kuşı*, kuz, kazu, kazağuc, kızğın, *kızıl palçığ*, *kızıl qaṭīfa* (t.-a.), (*kızıl yumurta*), kızılca, *kızlığ*, kozalan*, kazma, kızın-, kazındu.

Gebe, hepi, giwe (f.), küpe, küpçük, *köpuk ṭaşı*, keweni*, *keber-*, *kebert-*, kewrek, *gewşe-*, gewşek, keweze; kéçi boynuzı, göcen; *güd-*, kedi, köti, güdüci, *kütük* (a.), *giderek*; gügem, gügüm, kekiz; külüfçe* (p.), külek (gk. or p.?), gelincek, *gelincek çicegi*, keler (p.); gem (p.), küme (p.), gemük, kümele (p.-t.?), gömüldürük, kemere, gümürde-, gemirdek, gümürden-, gümrük (lat.), kümes (gk.), kimesne; *gön bardak*, *gün çiçegi*, *gön kulağı*, gene, göni, kend otı*, gendü, gündelik, kendir, *köŋül dön-*, gönilü, günlük, gönilen-; (ger-), küre-, kerewid (gk.), *kārwān kıran* (p.-t.), gürbüz (p.), kirec, körtün, *kurk** (p.), kerki, kereke (a.), gürüldü, keremid (gk.), gerne-, görnek, gerneş-, kereste (p.), gürz*; köstebek, köstek, kest/dane (gk.), göster-, küsegü, kösem, *kesme*, kesmik, keser; géyisi; kez, göze-, *gözlük*, gözeme.

*Lafadan** (a.), *laçın* (f.), *laçın kaya* (f.-t.), lodos (gk.), lak/*lök* (p.), lıman (gk.), lurı kuşı (a.-t.), *-layın*/*-leyin*.

Makara (f.); moloz (f.); manṭal* (a.), mantar (gk.), mengel (f.), mengüş (p.); mor, (mard lat.), marul (gk.), marulcuk (gk.-t.), mersin (gk.); muşluk, mışır tawukı (a.-t.); muşmula (ital.), muymul.

Ne deŋlü; naṭas (a.); nigende (p.); nesne.

Rafadan (a.); ruzgar (p.).

Ṣu, *su başı*, *sap*, saw-, *suw kabarcuğı*, *suw yosunı*, sapa, sübe, *sübi*, sebed (p.), sıpkın, (sawul-), *saplan-*, siwri, *siwri siŋek*, (sawuş-); sac ayağ, süci, socuk*, sucuk, *sıçan otı*, sıçancıl, *sadu**, *sadu sadla-**, sütlegen, sataş-; sık, sağu, sağu sağla-, soğlı*, sıklık, sıkılcım, *sakın-*, sığın, sığınca, sıkındu, sağanak, *sığır dili*, *sığır kuşı*, sığırcı/uk, sokran-; sek, sükü (for süŋü), sigil, sögle-, sögleme, süksük*, sögüş; sıla, solu-, sülpük, salaca, solcuk*, salt, solutğan, *sulṭān börki* (a.-t.), sılığ ağca, solak, soluk, *soluk al-*, soluklan-, *salkum küpe*, sülügen, *salıncak*; *saman oğrısı*, sümür sümür*, sümsük, *semizlik otı*; sanu, *sancak*, sankı/u, sankulan-, (sünger gk.), sananık*, saŋsar; sar-, sür-, *sarı kawak*, (sıra gk.), sarp, sarpun, sérce barmak, *sırça*, sürüçi, sercek, *sırtak** (p.), sırık, sarkı-, sorğuc, sarkıt-, sarğ/kuk, sürgü, *sürgü taşı*, sarigen*, sırım, sarma, sırma, sürme kilid (t.-gk.), (sarın-), *sarar-*, *ṣarş-*, *sarsı-*; süs-, ṣaşı-, (süstür-), susam*; süye, seyyid ğazı nebiri* (a.-p.), sayığ, sayğu, soyğa, *sayığla-*, (sayğuluk), süylün; sızla-, sazan balığ (f.-t.).

Şu deŋlü; şebek, şefşel* (f.); şakka (f.); şük*, şıl; *şimdiye dek*, şamar, şimşek; şén, (şénlik); şorak (p.), şırlağan (p.), şırlağancı (p.), şaranpaw (magyar); *ṣaş-*, şaşı, şaşğun, (şaşılık), şışman, (şaşur-).

Yap-, *yap*, yapu, yawu (p.), (yapucı), *yapağ*, *yapıl-*, *yuwalak*, *yaban turak otı* (p.-t.), yabana (p.), yabancı (p.-t.), yuwundu, yawaşa (p.), *yéd-*, *yédi kardaş*, *yatağan*, *yédiler*, *yağ örüki*, *yağ çamur*, yağmur, yağrık, *yoxsul urğanı*, yağız; yegen, yégin, yéginlik, yüksük, *yügüş*; yıl-, *yél yaparak*, yalı (gk.), yalab-, yélpaze, *yalçu*, yaltaklığ, yaltaklan-, yıldur-, yaldırayış, *yalduz*, *yulduz kurtı*, yalduzla-, *yıllık*, *yulğun kozağı*, *yélek*, *yalıŋ kat*, *yılan balığı*, *yılan yastuğı*, yalıŋcak, yılanğac, yalınlan-, (yalınlandur-), yular; yamac, yemdik*, yaŋa, *yaŋı kurt*, yéŋi çeri, *yond*, *yont kuşı*, *yanku*, yonka, yaŋkulan-, (*yaŋarak*), yaŋsıla-, yaŋış, yarpı*, yurdu, yardım, yırtmac, yarmaca; yas/ṣ-, yus yumrı, yosun; yoş (a.); yaykan-, yaykara, yaylım, yayan, yeyni.

Zıbık (f.), zıbıkçı (f.-t.); zık* (a.), zağanos (gk.), zağar (f.); zügürd (f.); zil (f.), zelek* (f.); zengin (p.), zırığ* (p.).

INDEX IV. OTHER TURKISH LANGUAGES AND DIALECTS*

A. TŪRĀN

i. *ahl-i Tūrān wa Xʷārazm* kaçu.
ii. *baʿdī ahālī-yi Tūrān* 25r. 18 "say and write *kéle turğan* not *kéle türgen*".
iii. *atrāk-i Tūrān* 13r. 15 "use *-lıŋ/-liŋ* for 1st person plural of imperative"; *ağ bāzargān*; 205v. 11 *çār tāra* (p.), *çār pūd* (p.); *çupan aldatan.*
iv. *Özbekīya-i Tūrān.* eke, *taw* (for *tağ* "mountain"), madadḥal (a.), mekkeki (f.).
v. *Özbekīya-i Tūrān wa Xʷ ārazm* şulay.
vi. *Özbekīya* 8v. 12 "use *-ğın/-gin* for *-ğıl/-gil* in 2nd person singular of imperative"; *olak-* (for *alak-* 47r. 15); egü; tümengini; *cüŋ* (for yüŋ "wool"); cırım; may.
vii. "*a Samargandī* " çiçe.
viii. *Sartīya yüŋ* "wool" (215v. 3).

B. XʷĀRAZM

i. "*a Xʷārazmī*" *çiçe.*
ii. See also Ai and v and Cii.

C. TÜRKMEN

i. *iṣṭilāḥ-i Türkmenīya* tasa-; *yüŋ* "wool" (215v. 3).
ii. *Türkmenīya-i Xʷārazm olak-* (for *alak-* 47r. 15).
iii. *Tarākima-i ʿIraq dögüş-* (for *tégiş-* 196v. 4).

D. ĪRĀN

i. *ahl-i Īrān* çekme, çalma.
ii. *atrāk-i Īrān wa Rūm* numerous grammatical and phonetic characteristics in Part I (3v. 1, 5v. 3 and 21, etc.); *degül*; *karlankuc*; *salıncak*; *serçek.*
iii. *atrāk-i Īrān* kıkac (for Çağ. *burulğun* 133r. 12); keniz (for Rūmī *karabaş* 270v. 29).

E. MISCELLANEOUS

i. *atrāk-i ʿIrāq-i ʿArab* pancar.
ii. *atrāk-i Muğūl yont* (for Çağ. *kısrak* 297v. 7; in 347r. 9 *yont* is listed as an ordinary (Çağ.) word).
iii. *Daştı* meken (dubious, quoted from Ẓafar-nāma).
iv. *luğat-i Kāşğar çit*; *kır*; kükür*; morı*.
v. *luğat-i Tatarıya* dağar; *sonkur* ("blind", corruption of Mongolian *sokor*).

---

* See paragraph 40 of the Introduction.

INDEX V. MONGOLIAN LOAN-WORDS*

A. MONGOLIAN WORDS SO DESCRIBED

Öbücte/öbüçin *öbecin/öbetçin* W.120; *ebeçin* P.149.
übül *übül* W.157; *öbül* P.272.
öbüsün *ebesün* W.40; P.150.
éce *ecen* W.42; K.224.
acırğa W.4; P.97 (an old Turkish loan-word, metathesis of *adğır*).
ıtawun *ita(ğ)un* K.286; H.64.
otucı *şikasta band*; cf. *oktuçi-* "to cut in pieces" K.435; H.78.
ötege P.279; K.517.
adun *adu'un* W.3; *adu(g)un* K.70.
üdür W.158; P.273.
adırğan "hills and hillocks"; this word occurs in Kalmuk. See G. J. Ramstedt's Kalmükisches Wörterbuch p. 2a.
axsawurğa *aksarğa* K.134; H.9.
ögün *öge(g)ün* K.561; H.105.
ula *a'ula* W.10; *üla* P.372.
albutu *albatu* K.84; H.19.
élcigen *elcigen* P.152; K.211.
ölcey W.123; K.534.
ölceytü *ölceytü* K.535; *ölceyitey* H.111.
alğun "small mountain"; not traceable in M.; cf. *adırğan*.
elik "variegated"; cf. *alağ* W.4; K.74 (probably a Turkish loan-word).
éleke *helige(n)* W.75; *eligen* P.152.
ölüke *ölögey* K.531; H.110.
elencik "nourishing his people"; imaginary etymology of a personal name.
amıdun *amidu* W.7; P.100.
ömüdün P.276; H.111.
émegen *emege(n)* W.44; K.214.
émel *eme'el* W.44; *emél* P.154.
antutay *amtatay* W.7; *amtatu* P.101.
unkan *unağan* P.364; K.340.
ünen W.164; P.381.
örkebçi *erkebçı* K.264; H.57.
erkene kun "the lofty centre of a mountain"; imaginary etymology of a geographical name.
örkesün *örgesün* P.278; K.590.
arun *ari'un* P.105; *ari(ğ)un* K.144.
uran P.365; K.438.
orunci "beggar, petitioner"; *nomen agentis* from *orun* "representative" W.128 or *oron* "place", etc., K.447 (a Turkish loan-word).
ürünli* "grand-child"; probably connected with *üre* "seed, children, descendants" K.577; H.126.
arusun *arisun* K.146; H.30.
usun W.167; P.368.
işigey *isgay* W.83; *isegey/işigey* K.283.
üyle *üiyile* W.161; *üyle* P.375.

---

* See paragraph 42 and following of the Introduction

Batu "strong" W.13; P.113; correct etymology of personal name.
buxar "a learned assembly"; imaginary etymology of *Buxara*.
bahrawun kol (M.-T.) "right wing"; *bara'un* W.13; P.112; see baranğar.
bakuy "great"; imaginary etymology; see *déb*.
bulğan *buluğan* W.22; *bulğan* P.125.
bincik yam *asb-i çār-pāy*; not traceable in M.; *bincik* seems to be connected with Turkish *bin-* "to ride"; for *yam* see Pelliot's article in T'oung Pao, Vol. XXVII (1930), p. 192ff.
baranğar cf. *bahrawun kol*; *bara'un* and *ğar* W.60; P.175.
bos- W.19; P.122.
bösün *bö'esün* W.16; P.123.
bayandar "prosperous"; imaginary etymology of a personal name; perhaps supposedly *bayan* P.114; K.1083 with P. suffix *-dār*.
Cawcı *cōcay* K.2372; H.577.
cawdur "famous"; imaginary etymology of personal name; perhaps supposedly Turkish *çav* "fame" with a suffix, perhaps P. *-dar*.
cöwe'ün kol (M.-T.) "left wing"; *cao'ün* W.86; *cö'én* P.209; see cöwenğar.
cöwenğar cf. *cöwe'ün kol* and *baranğar*; *cao'un/cö'én* and *ğar*.
cibir *ci'ür* W.91; K.2354.
cocı "sudden, unexpected"; faulty etymology of personal name; from *coçi(n)* "guest, visitor" P.208; K.2392.
çitgir *çitkür* K.2159; *çidgür* H.534.
çağan *çaga'an* W.25; *çagan* P. 131.
cele* "a hat-guard, chin-strap" or the like; *cele* "a long rope for tying up an animal" K.2313; H.566.
cıla- "to desire, seek, pursue"; apparently inferred from I. *cılamışı*; the nearest parallel seems to be *cilbit-(ku)*, same meaning, K.2347; H.573.
cılamışı I., see *cila-*.
çüne* "jackal"; presumably *çino* "wolf" W.28; *çinā* P.134; "jackal" is properly *çökebüri*.
çingiz "king of kings"; imaginary etymology of a personal name, which is actually a Mongolized form of T. *téŋiz*, "sea".
Déb "good fortune, renown"; part of the imaginary etymology of the personal name *déb bakuy*; possibly suggested by M. *tab* "right, true" W.143; "well-being" K.1591.
tobçın *tobça'an* W.150; *tobçı* K.1821.
tabın "a company of 40 men"; this seems to be a simple misunderstanding of *tabin* "fifty" W.143; P.338; but there is possibly a T. word *tabı/un* meaning "company, herd" (cf. Russian *tabun* "herd") which got confused with the M. numeral.
tawar "brocade"; *tab/var* "treasures, precious things" W.143; K.1597, 1682; loan-word from T. tavar.
dabusun P.137; K.1602.
tuturğu/tuturğan *tuturğan* P. 356; K.1845.
taxuk/taxakuy "chicken"; loan-word from T. *takığu*; the oldest M. form is *takiya*, W.144, but other later forms exist in both languages.
tokulğa "horse-cloth"; deverbal noun from *toko-* "to saddle (a horse)" K.1798; H.419.
doğulan *dokulan* P.143; *dogolaŋ* K.1807.
tekemişi *takāpū-yi taᶜcīl wa surᶜat*; I., not traceable in M.; *tege-* means "to load" (K.1742) or "haul, carry on (a cart)" (H.407); "hurry, hurried" is *türgen* K.1953; H.442.
dalu P.138; K.1635.
tolı "mirror"; correct etymology of personal name; *toluy* P.350; *toli* K.1849.
tülen *tüle(g)en* K.1916.
d/talay *dalay* W.31; P.138; loan-word from T. *taluy*, which is probably itself borrowed from Chinese.
tolay *taolay/ta'ulay* W.145-6; ṭa'ūlay P.343; a very old loan-word from T. *tavşığan*.
düley P.147; K.1916.
temecemişi I.; from *temece-* W.149; P.345.
tarğun *tarğut* (plur.) W.146; *tarğun* P.341.
*dérsün** "numerous, abundant"; I., not traceable in M.; in the context quoted from Waṣṣāf probably the T. imperative "let them assemble" from *dér-*.
tosun W.152; P.351.
dayın *dayin* W.34; *dayn* P.138; very old loan-word from T. *yagı*.

ṭayşı "scribe, expert, master of an art"; *tayşi* K.1551; H.389; described as M., but *tayşı* is rightly described as Chinese (*ba-luğat-i Xitā'īyān*).
Ka'an W.54; K.732; loan-word from T. *kağan.*
xubul- "to rise from the dead"; *kubil-* "to be reincarnated" K.892; H.215.
kut "blessedness, good-fortune"; a T. word erroneously described as M.; the borrowed form in M. is *kutuğ* W.73; K.918.
kandağay W.59; K.724.
kınık "gracious"; imaginary etymology of a personal name.
kırığ/k "blocked, closed"; I., perhaps derived from *ka'a-* "to block, close" W.54; *ka(ğ)a-* K.734.
kırkız "forty men"; imaginary T. etymology, described as M., for a T. tribal name.
kurı/ultay "assembly"; not recorded in M., apparently an I. derivative (M. possessive noun/adjective) from *kuril* W.72; *kural* K.954, same meaning.
karşı "cemetery"; the T. loan-word *karşı* "castle" occurs in M., W.62; K.847; but the meaning "cemetery" is not recorded.
ğusun *ğudusun* W.71; K.1029.
ğaşun *ğaşi'un* W.62; *ğaşūn* P.178.
kay "firm, strong"; imaginary etymology of personal name.
kayan "torrent"; I., not traceable in M., where *kaya* K.819, H.174 means "the side" (e.g. of a mountain).
Köbe K.2575; H.227.
köbün *kö'ün* W.105; *köbe(g)ün* H.234.
köbenek *köbe/üŋ* K.2575, 2578; H.228.
köken "daughter"; *kö'üken* "child" W.104; *köbe(g)üken* K.2577.
kökşün "old, aged" K.2634; H.227; loan-word from T. *kökşin* "grey".
Laba "teacher" *lama* K.1961; H.485; from Tibetan *bla. ma*; note the more correct form in *dalay lama.*
labaşak *labaşik* K.1958; *labşik* H.484; from Tibetan *lba. ba* with suffix of indefinite article *śig.*
luy *lū* K.1965; H.486; from Chinese *lung.*
Möngü *möŋke* K.112; H.508.
möngen *müŋgü(n)* W.112; *möngü(n)* P.239.
mör P.239; H.510.
marıw* "an exclamation by a winner in a fight or competition"; perhaps I.; no obvious etymology, unless derived from *marğu-* "to refuse" K.2001; "to excuse oneself" H.494.
müsün K.2056; H.511.
Newker *nökör* W.119; *nöker* P.261.
nayman W.113; P.244.
Sübük* "heel", in an imaginary etymology of the T. personal name *Sübüktégin*; no trace in M.
subusun *subut* (plur.) W.136; P.327; *subusun* K.1391.
salur "sword blow", in an imaginary etymology of a tribal name; no trace in M.
Şomur* "lamp"; no trace in M.
*Yapar** "he suppresses all opposition"; imaginary etymology of a personal name.
yut "epizootic disease"; a T. loan-word with somewhat altered meaning; the normal M. form is *cut* K.2385; H.583 borrowed from a Turkish language in which initial *y-* had become *c-*.
yaman "goat", cf. *ımga* in Section C; *ima'an* W.82; *ima(g)an* K.309*.
yasun W.169; P.388.
*yazar** "great tribe"; imaginary etymology of a personal name.
Zulan "soft, smooth, gentle"; *sula(n)* "loose, free" P.327; K.1398.

B. LUĞAT-İ QALMAQĪ

Çekin "ear"; *çikin* W.27; K.2176.
*Koba** "armour"; probably an error for *kuya*; cf. *kuyağ* "armour" H.74; K.945.
xalta "gift"; not identified.
Mila "whip"; *mina'a* W.109; *minā* P.236; *mila(g)a* K.2025.
Noyat "the Qalmaqīya's name for their ruler"; plural of *noyan* W.119; P.260; cf. Section C.

* Regarding these words see M. Louis Bazin's paper "Noms de la 'Chèvre' en Turc et en Mongol" in Studia Altaica, Festschrift für Nikolaus Poppe; Harrassowitz, Wiesbaden, 1957. *Yaman* is a Kalmuk form, while *imğa* goes back to a more Classical form. There is no doubt that in Çağatay these are Mongolian loan-words, but M. Bazin makes out a convincing case for regarding *imağan* as an old Turkish loan-word in Mongolian.

C. MONGOLIAN WORDS NOT SO DESCRIBED

Öbçin "armour"; from *öbçin* "complete" K.507 (*öbçin kuyaktu* "armed from head to foot"); H.108.
öbçi/ünli/üg M.-T.
abağ/ka W.1; K.41.
e/öbüge *ebüge(n)* W.40; K.182.
abusun *abisin* K.43; H.11.
uc/çur *ucur* K.420; H.99.
uçra- *uçira-* W.157; *uça/ira-* K.418.
uçrat- }
uçraş- } M.-T.
uçraştur- }
otağa *otuğa(n)* K.386; H.79.
i/ötelgü *itelgü* K.287.
adunci M.-T. from *adun* (see Section A).
adra "waste land"; from *atar* K.61; H.14, same meaning.
égeci *egeçi* W.42; K.234.
ögülge "gift", I.; *öggülge* H.107.
alpak *olboğ* K.407; H.80.
ılbara- "to be scalded and blistered"; probably denominal verb from *ulabi/ur* "reddish" K.397; H.96.
ılbarat- M.-T.
ilbesün "a kind of duck"; obviously M., but *ilbe(g)esün* K.305; H.68 is translated "a fish lure, or bait".
alçu/alçın "escarpment"; not T., perhaps identical with alçu "instep" K.93.
olca W.123; P 265.
ölce-/ölceş- "to do homage"; probably deduced from I. *ölcemişi*; not T. and perhaps not properly M., but connected with *ölcey* (see Section A).
olcala- W.123; P.266.
ölcemişi I.; see *ölce-*.
ölceş M.-T. (?); see *ölce-*.
aldara- P.98; K.89.
aldarat- M.-T.
alt/ṭayı M. geographical name (W.172; K.84) used as a zoological term.
ılğa- *ilğa-* W.81; K.302 (the meanings are slightly different, but there is no other obvious explanation).
ilğawçı M.-T.
ılğamışı I.; see *ılğa-*.
alğur P.98; K.82.
ılğar M.-T.
ölke "province, city"; no trace in the pre-M. period, almost certainly M. *ölke* "an area on the sunny side of a mountain" W.123; K.535.
ımğa *ima'an* W.82; *imagan* K.309; cf. *yaman* in Section A.
anda W.7; P.102.
ündür *ündür* W.164; *öndür* P.276.
ündürrek M.-T.
erewül/*herewül* "reconnoitring patrol"; deverbal noun from *eri-* "to seek" W.45; P.163 (the *h-* is an erroneous prosthesis due to false analogy).
orçın *horçin* W.77; *orçin* K.468.
ırcay- *arcay-/ircay-* K.163, 325; H.33, 72.
ırcayıt- M.-T.
arğada- W.9; P.105.
arğdal the suggested etymology is false; the word is a deverbal noun from *arğada-*.
arğamçı *arğamci* W.9; K.154.
arğımak K.154 (the earliest T. occurrence is in the 14th cent. Chinese-Uyğur dictionary, which contains other M. words; it is more likely to be an M. loan-word in T. than vice-versa).
ırğay "a medicinal plant"; ? *arğuy* "wild sorrel, pasque flower" K.155; *irağuy* ditto H.71.

érkene/*érkinek* "the upper strut of a tent-door"; *bosağa* "the lower strut", q.v., is certainly M. and these words probably are too; they might be connected with *erkin* "high" K.268; H.58 or *erginek* (same references) "shelf, cupboard".

aral "island" W.8; P.104.

uranlaş- M.-T.; see *uran* in Section A.

uranlaşmışı I.

asra- *asara-* W.9; P.107.

asrat-
asral- } M.-T.

asramışı I.; see *asra-*.

ayalğu K.128; H.28.

oylan-
oylaş- } M.-T.; derivative forms of *oyila-* K.332; H.72.

Bawurçı *bas'urçin* W.12; *ba(g)urçin* K.1065.

peteke *böteke* P.123; *beteke* K.1068.

büdene *büdüne* K.1230; H.312.

botra- *böde(g)ire-* K.1229; *böte(g)ere-* H.309.

botrat-
botraş-
botraştur- } M.-T.

buğu W.21; P.124.

böke *bökö* W.17; *böke* P.123.

[bekewül "cook"; morphologically this word looks M., but the Farhang-i Cihāngirī is probably right in describing it as Hindi.]

balçağ/k "hand-guard, hilt (of a sword)" *baldağ* K.1079; H.275.

bölte/ü böri "hyena"; M.-T.; probably an error for *tölte/ü böri*; see *döltü*.

borçın "doe" } etymologically identical; *borçin sono* "a sort of duck" W.19; "grey gad-fly" K.1223;
borçın "female duck" } etymologically feminine form of *boro* "grey", a very old loan-word from T. *boz*.

borda- "to be fat, well-nourished"; from *borda/o-* "to fatten" K.1222; H.297.

bordat- M.-T.

bordağ/k "fat, well-nourished"; *bordoğu* ditto K.1222; "feed" H.297.

burtağ/k P.125; K.1222.

börgüt *börgüd* K.1262; H.311.

bosağa *bosoğa* W.20; *bos/şoğa* K.1173.

be/ésrek *beserek* K.1112; H.282.

Çöp "suitable, fitting"; *cöb* W.91; H.587.

çubru- *çuburi-* K.2202; H.544.

çubrut-
çubrul-
çubruş- } M.-T.

çéçen *seçen* W.133; *ç/seçen* K.1358.

cada/*yada* taşı M.-T. *cada* W.84; K.2275.

cıda- *çida-* W.27; P.132.

cıda *cida* W.89; P.205.

çağ/k "time" *çah* W.25; *çak* P.130.

çağdawul *çahdu'ulsun* W.25; *çağda(ğ)ul* K.2110.

çağarak *çağarik* K.2088; H.516.

çılbur *çilbur* W.27; *çilbu(ğ)ur* K.2166.

çalağay/*çalay* "sparrow-hawk"; apparently a corruption of *ca(ğ)almay şiŋkur*, same meaning, K.2248; H.554.

cülge K.2415; H.590.

cumca "shirt", I.; *çamça* W.25; *çamçay* P.130.

çine- P.134; K.2135.

çandawul corruption of *çağdawul*, q.v.

cankı *caŋgi* W.85; K.2242; probably a Chinese loan-word.

çurpa *çurba* K.2221; H.546.

cırğa- *cirğa-* W.90; K.2366.
çorğa "a narrow-necked jug"; from *çorğo* "tube, pump" K.2221; "spout, tap, gutter" H.543.
cérge *cerge* W.89; P.207.
cérgelik M.-T.
ceren/*ceyren* *céren* P.205; *ce(g)eren* K.2320.
ça/ıray *çiray* W.28; P.135.
çıraylığ M.-T.
Tobı "a cotton cap worn under a headdress"; apparently from *tobi* "a felt cap worn under a helmet" K.1818; H.422; but there may be some connection with T. *top*.
tobçımışı I.; probably from *tobçi-* K.1821; H.423, though the meaning is rather different.
d/tawulğa/*d/tawluğa* *du(ğ)ulğa* K.1810; H.475.
daban *daba'an* W.30; *daba(ğ)an* K.1595.
dotur "the lining of a garment"; *dotora* "inside" W.38; *dotar* P.143.
taka K.1569; H.392.
tok/xta- *tohta-* W.150; *tokta-* P.351.
toktawul deverbal noun from *tokta-*.
tok/xtat-
tok/xtamış
tok/xtaş- } M.-T.
toktaş
tok/xtaştur-
toğdak "bustard"; *toğodağ* K.1807; H.420.
toğdarı* "a kind of bustard"; connected with, or error for, *toğdak*.
tokum *tokom* K.1799; H.419.
toğur/*tur* "a hunting bird's perch"; *doğor* K.1812; H.469.
toğurka K.1815; H.421.
de/égle "overcoat"; *de'el/degel* "garment" W.34, 35; *dél* P.141.
tekeşmişi I., "bringing gifts and doing homage"; not related to *tekemişi* (Section A); "to do homage" is *meküyi-* K.2018; H.496/*meküski-* H.496; this may be a corruption of that word.
tala K.1629; H.399.
dalbay "a bird's wing used as a lure by falconers"; apparently from *dalba/dalba(ğ)a* "sail, banner" K.1636; H.452.
dalda "the back of the head; the back of anything behind which one hides"; *dalda* "screen, protection" W.31; P.138.
döltü "hyena"; *deltü* P.141; *deltey çinoa* H.463.
daldağay "a bird with a broken wing"; presumably derived from *dalda* in the sense that it tries to hide".
daldala- K.1640; H.452.
daldalan- } M.-T.
daldalaş-
telegen *telegen/tergen* W.147, 149; *tergen* P.349.
tulum K.1855; H.431.
tona- *tono-* W.151; K.1790.
tentek "stupid"; not Turkish; cf. *tendür dendür* "swaying" K.1690; "simple, simpleton" H.407.
taŋlay *tanklay* P.341; *taŋnay* K.1563.
dünen "four-year-old (animal)" *dönen* P.143; *dünen* K.1902; H.481.
tüner "stack of firewood"; cf. *tünerte-* "to be burnt" K.1902; H.438.
tur- See *toğur*.
dara "always, constant"; *dara* "one after the other" K.1663; H.454.
tarğa- W.145; K.1677.
tarğacı
targat- } M.-T.
tarğal-
tarğamışı I.; see *tarğa-*.
tarğas- M.-T.
daruğa W.33; K.1572.

torum H.426.
ṭorumtay *toromtay* K.1888; H.426.
tos- K.1831; H.423.
toskawul deverbal noun from *toska-* K.1831; H.423.
teseki "a slap"; no obvious T. etymology; perhaps connected with *tü(g)üşı* "the side of the jaw" K.1929; H.439; and *tü(g)üşide-* "to slap" H.439.
te/éske/iri *teskeri* P.350; *tesergü* H.410.
tuyla- P.354; K.1783.
tüynek "unripe melon"; no obvious T. etymology; perhaps from *tüynük* "smooth" K.1897; H.437.
Kabu K.756; H.161.
kabçur "tax"; misspelling of *kubçir* W.59; *kubçi(ğ)ur* K.901.
kabt/ṭurğay *kabturğa* P.285; *kabtağa* H.162.
kobğa *kobuğa* K.896; H.203.
kaban K.750; H.160.
kacar "lower vertebrae and bones of back and side"; probably from *kaca(ğ)ar* "bent, curved" K.815.
kacır K.819 (*kacir şibağun*); H.174.
ğ/kacarcı *ğacarçi* K.1003; H.247.
kada- K.773; H.166.
kadağ/k, kadağlık, kadağan, kadal- } M.-T.
kuda W.70; K.908.
kotan "fenced enclosure; lunar halo"; probably from *k/hotan* "willow-tree" W.73, 79; *udan* K.380, rather than *kota(n)* "fortress city" K.908; H.205, which is a Sanskrit loan-word, but the two concepts seem to be confused in *kota mandal* "circle, circumference" K.909; H.205.
kutan "pelican" W.73; K.909.
kotanla- M.-T.
katra- "to trot"; *katari-* K.781; H.165; see note in Index I.
ğılcay- "to lose one's senses"; morphologically M., but the only parallel *gilcey-* "to be crooked" H.255 is not very good.
kolansa *kolanska* P.301; *koloŋso* K.928.
komalak *koma'ul* W.65; *komo(ğ)ol* K.936.
kumar- *kumira-* K.935; H.219.
kumarğa(l) deverbal noun from *kumar-*.
kumarıl- M.-T.
hona *oona* K.336; H.73.
kancuğa *ğancuğa* K.981; H.241.
kunacın "two-year-old female (animal)"; mistranslation of *ğunacin* "three-year-old female (animal)" W.72; K.1021.
koŋğar-/*koŋar-* "to extract, pluck out"; c.f. *koŋkoyi-* "to hollow out, excavate" K.871; H.200.
koŋğarıl- M.-T.
kankaraw "a large camel-bell"; cf. *ka/oŋkinur* "small bell" K.730, 874; H.156, 201.
honıla- *onila-* K.343; H.74; from *honi* P.186.
kunan *kunan* W.72; K.865; *ğunan* K.1021; cf. *kunacın.*
ğıŋsı- "to run at the nose through smelling an acid vapour"; Abuşka p. 310 translates (of a dog) "to yelp and run away"; the latter is probably right, since the word seems to come from *ğaŋşi-* (of a dog) "to howl, yelp" K.982; H.241.
kaŋşar- "opposite, facing"; from *kaŋşiyar* "nose, face" K.729; H.156.
kara- W.60; P.292.
karatğu, karala-, karaş- } M.-T. from *kara-*.
harbatan "a troop of 100 men, or 10 picked men from the army"; mistranslated, plural possessive noun/adjective from *harban* "ten" W.75; P.181.

karaw/ğul *kara'ul* W.60; P.293.
karçığay W.61; P.293.
hüret- "to remove, send away"; probably M.-T. from *(h)üre-* "to perish, disappear" K.580; "to destroy, make disappear" H.126.
kırğawul *kirğool* K.2552; H.196.
korğada- *korğuda-* K.968; H.211.
karkıra *karkir* K.850; H.179.
korıya *koriya'an* W.67; *koriya* K.958.
koşun *koşi'un* W.68; *koşi(ğ)un* K.905.
kayp/fan- "to withdraw to one side"; from *kayibğana-* "to sway, wobble" H.153.
kuyla- "to bury"; *kuyila-* "to sheathe (a sword)" K.857; H.212.
kuylat- } M.-T.
kuylan- }
koyar in the phrase *su koyar* "a place where two rivers meet" is M. *koyar* "two" W.68; P.303.
kayrıtay "a title of high officials"; *kayiratu* "gracious, benevolent" K.713, possessive noun/adjective from *kayira(n)* "grace, favour" W.64; K.711, which is perhaps Arabic *xayr*, same meaning.
kayrak "whetstone"; *kayiraka(n)* H.154.
Kewürke *ke/ö'ürge* W.100, 105; *kö(g)e/örke* K.2629.
kökel "wet-nurse"; deverbal noun from *kökö-* "to suck, suckle" W.103; K.2633.
kükenek See *küykenek*.
köndelen W.104; H.224.
kürgen *küreken* P.229; *kürgen* K.2651.
küren *kür/küre* K.2636; H.237.
kürenk *küren/ŋ* K.2636; H.237.
küykenek/*kükenek* *küykünek* K.2563.
Möçelge K.2061; H.510.
makta- P.233; K.1998.
makta dubious deverbal noun from *makta-*.
moğulçın "like a Mongol", hence "whitish"; a fanciful translation of *moŋğolcı* "Mongolian" K.2031.
mégicin *megeci(n)* K.2017; H.496.
möldür "hail"; *möndür* K.2052; H.508.
manklay/maŋlay *maŋlay* W.107; *manklay* P.233.
monuğan M.-T. from *mono-* K.2028; H.501.
mergen "rifleman"; secondary meaning of *mergen* "wise, skilled" (e.g. skilled archer) W.109; K.2019.
maral W.108; K.1999.
Nébtes "comfort, freedom from care"; from *nebte* P.247; K.632 primarily "through", hence "thoroughly, cordially" and the like.
nutukçı a kind of bird (described); probably noun of action from *nuntuk/nutuk* "home camp, pasture ground" W.120; P.261 meaning "a domesticated hunting bird", cf. *şıdurğu* and *öbçin* for similar changes of meaning.
narın (probably I.) "special, superior" in phrases like *narın qalʿa, sarkar-i narın*; from *narin* "fine, accurate, good quality" W.114; P.246.
noyan W.119; P.260.
Saba- *saba-* K.1303; *sab-* H.322.
sübükle- supposedly M.-T.; see *sübük* in Section A.
suwur- etc. See *suğur-* etc.
sağadak/*s*/*şadak* *sa(ğ)adak* K.1294; H.319.
suğur-/*suwur-* *so'ora-/su'ora-* W.135; *su(ğ)ura-* K.1289.
suğrul-/*suwurul-* } M.-T.
suğruş- }
sokur "blind"; *sokor* W.135; *sokar* P.324.
sa/ohramışı I.; "negligence, defect", and the like; from *sağara-* "to become weak, dissolve, become less" K.1296 (misprinted *sağada-*); "to change (for the worse)" H.320.
soksur K.1408.
sögdemişi I.; "rest, relaxation"; from *seggere-* "to rest, relax" K.1367; H.332; probably error for *sögremişi*.
sögdeniş M.-T.; see *sögdemişi*.

salca "sheep tick"; *şalca* K.1449; H.361.
sandırak "delirium" etc.; M.-T. from *saŋda(ğ)ura-* "to be uneasy, perplexed" K.1291; H.318.
sandırakla- M.-T.
surağ K.1411; H.350.
se/érke *serkes* (plur.) W.134; *serge* K.1374.
sérin *seri'ün* P.320; *seri(g)ün* K.1371.
saydam "pure, even, smooth"; no obvious T. etymology; perhaps M.-T. from *sayida-* "to become good" H.316.
sayın W.133; P.315.
seyrün probably a misunderstood form of *sérin*, q.v.
Şıbak *şibān* (? error for *şibāk*) P.332; *şibağ* K.1475.
sibike *şibüge* W.139; P.332.
şı/udurğu "a lute"; from *şidurğu* "straight, simple, plain" P.332; K.1491; cf. *öbçin*, *mutukçı.*
şüdrün *şi'üder* W.142; *şi(g)üder* K.1513.
şığawul "official host"; deverbal noun from *ciğu-* "to support" K.2333; H.569; cf. *ciğuçi* "guide" K.2334; "guest" H.569.
şükür *şikür* K.1515; H.367.
şıltak W.140; P.333.
şülegey "saliva"; cf. *şilüget* (plur.) "a dribbling child" W.140; *şilügey* H.376.
şilim "gum, glue"; cf. *şilemde-* "to moisten" K.1493; H.375.
şim- *şimi-* W.141; *şime-* P.333.
şıralğa deverbal noun from *şira-* "to roast" W.141; P.335.
Yada- W.168; P.386.
yadat- } M.-T.
yadağ }
yada taşı See *cada taşı.*
yatuğan *yaduga(n)* K.2278; H.595.
yatuğançı M.-T.
yara W.169; P.387.
yosun "manner, style" W.171; K.2381.
yosunluk M.-T.

INDEX VI. OTHER LOAN-WORDS*

A. ARABIC†

i. ARABIC WORDS SO DESCRIBED

Ā, *mş.*; awul, *mḥ.* of *ḥawīlī* (a false etymology; the word is a secondary form of *ağıl*); ıxtıyar (*ixtiyār* with altered meaning); araba, *mḥ.* of *ᶜarrāda*. *Babr ton*, *mr.* (*babr* is actually a Persian loan-word in Arabic); bayır (*bāyir* with altered meaning). Cébe, *mḥ.* of *cubba*; *çek mḥ.* of *ṣakk*; cul (*cull*); *çam* (ağacı) R., *mḥ.* of *ṣamᶜ*. Ṭoppuz, *mḥ.* of *dabbūs*; tulf *mḥ.* and *mt.* of *tufl*; durluk *mr.* (*durr* with T. suffix -*luk*). Ḥawlan, *mḥ.* and *mt.* of *ḥawalān*; ka/ulmaş, *mḥ.* of *qul mā ṣi'ta*; kum/nbul, *mt.* of *qanbal*; ğ/karar, *mt.* of *ğarār*. *Sultān börki*, R., *mr.*; sırdaş, *mr.* (*sirr* with T. suffix -*daş*).

ii. ARABIC WORDS NOT SO DESCRIBED

Asrar "Indian hemp" (*asrār* with altered meaning). Fara "chick" (*farx*); faracı (Persian derivative from Arabic root); *fıskıya* R. (*fisqīya*). Cufut (corruption of *yahūd*, cf. Persian *cuhūd*); cılğawa (corruption of *cild qafā*); cimcime (*cumcuma*?); cérib (carīb); *ce/ércer* R. (*carcar*). *T/ṭawāṣī* R. (*ṭawaṣī*); takıya (taqīya). Kabaça (A.-P., *qabā* with P. suffix -*ça*); hawalan- (A.-T., denominal verb from *hawā*); ḥakk kuşı (A.-T. from *ḥaqq*); *kulb* R. (qulb); ğalaka (*ğalaqa*); *komsı* R. (corruption of *ğammāz*); xına (corruption of *ḥinā*); *kındıra* R. (corruption of *qinṭira*); xınalığ (A.-T.); *harṭuman* R. "dew" (probably a mistranslation; Redhouse lists A. *hurṭumān* "tares" as occurring in Osmanli); kıran (*qirān*); kurun (*qurūn*); xırsız R., "thief" (A.-T., corruption of *xayr* with T. suffix -*sız*); ḥarış "lost, non-existent" (corruption of *hirṣ* or *hariṣ*; the root *ḥaraṣa* gives quite inappropriate meanings); kurayşı "a Tatar cap" (*qurayṣī* means "belonging to the tribe of Qurayş"; the connection is obscure, but the word is fully spelt out, perhaps a false etymology for some other word); *xaşa* R. (corruption of *ğāṣīya*); *xaşal* R. "starch" (*xaṣal*, but not with this meaning in A.). *Kütük* R. "government register" (corruption of *kutub*); *kereke* R. (*karaka*, not good Arabic, ? corruption of "calico"); keyli (*kayla*). *Lafadan** R.; see *rafadan*; lurı (kuşı) R. (said to be a corruption of *nūrī*). Mawı (*māwī*); madadḥal "a woman's head-dress" (the form is attested by W. *namadmāl*, but seems impossible; perhaps an error for *madḥal* from *daḥala* "to conceal"); matal (*maṭal*); meṭellik (A.-T.); maxanık (with *kāf*) "fireplace" (corruption of *maxāniq* (plur.) "stoves in which silk-worms are stifled"); *manṭal* R. "door-bar" (perhaps a mistranslation; as Redhouse says, A. *manṭal* means "a vat for pressing grapes"); *mışır tawukı* R. (A.-T. "Egyptian bird, from *Miṣr* "Egypt"). Naṭas R. (*naṭās*). *Rafadan* R. "soft-boiled egg" (*rufadān*). *Sıla* R. "home, native country" (*ṣila*, but not in this meaning in A.). *Şewk** R. "honey" (the word might also be read *şö/ük* but no such word meaning "honey" is recorded in Osmanli; perhaps a misunderstanding of A. *ṣawk* "thorn", which is recorded in Osmanli). *Yoş* R. "unruly, quarrelsome" (otherwise attested only in S.D.D.; corruption of A. *waḥş*). *Ẓık* R* *cān* "soul" (this meaning is not otherwise attested and seems to be an error; *ziqq*, "water-skin", the A. meaning mentioned in the Sanglax occurs in Osmanli).

B. PERSIAN‡

i. PERSIAN WORDS SO DESCRIBED

İgdic/ş *mş.* (the word was probably borrowed from P., but is etymologically foreign to both P. and T.); alaw *br.*; amac *mş.*; arzı- *mr.*; işterek *mş.* Baca *mş.*; farfar *mş.*; *paşa* R., 222v. 4, *mḥ.* of *pādişāh*; paya *mş.* Çe/öküc/ş *mş.*; c/çalığ/k *mḥ.* of *cālāk*; çemen/çemender *mḥ.* of *çamand*; *çār pūd*, *çār tāra* (P. phrases, but not used in P.). Tupal

---

* See paragraph 47 of the Introduction.

† These fall into two classes, (i) those so described in the Sanglax, and (ii) those not so described. The first are usually described, if single words, as *muştarak* "common to both languages" (here "mş."), *mutarrak* "turcicized" (here "mt.") or *muḥarraf* "corrupt" (here "mḥ."). One or two phrases or compound words are described as *murakkab* "combined Arabic and Turkish" (here "mr."). The second are often used in meanings not known in Arabic proper and in forms somewhat differing from the Correct Arabic form.

‡ See the notes to Section A, which apply here *mutatis mutandis*. Some words are stated, not always correctly, to be Persian on the authority of the Burhān-i Qāti or the Farhang-i Cahāngirī. The letters "br." and "fr." are added after such words.

mş.; *tat mḥ.* of *dād*; dağ *mş.*; dağul *mt.* of *dāğūl*; tekew *mş.*, *mḥ.* of *takāb/takāw*; talfasa *mḥ.* of *talwāsa*; talax *mḥ.* of *talx*; dulana *br.*; *taŋ mş.*; tasma *mş.*; *daş mş.* Kawak (with *qāf's*) *mh.* of kāwāk (with *kāf's*); ğacğaw *mḥ.* of *ğajğāw*; ğurra *mş.*; ğaraw *fr. ğarw*; xoşlaş- *mr.* Kifte *mḥ.* of *kūfta*; *kükenek br.* (this word is M., see Index VC); kūlāk *mş.*; kempir *br.*; kümec *mş.* (*kūmāc*; this word is etymologically T. and a loan-word in P.); kündük (*kūndūk*); gandara- *mr.*; (gandarat- *mr.*); gürbüzlük *mr.* (*gurbuz* with T. suffix *-lük*); keyb/mür *br.*, *fr.* (*gaybur*); kīz *mş.* (a crasis of the old T. word *kiḏiz*); gezek *br.*; gezlik (*gazlak*). Langar *mş.* Mata *mş.*; mittin (*mītīn*). Naw *mş.*; nawlık P.-T. (*nāw* with T. suffix *-lık*). Rasık *mḥ.* of *rāsux.* Sibeki "yellowish" (*sībakī* in a meaning not known in P.); sarağuc *mş.*; *sürme kilid* R. *mr.* T.-P. Şor *mş.* *Ya* "or" *mş.*; yamçı *mr.* (*yām* with T. suffix *-çı*). Zag *mş.*

ii. PERSIAN WORDS NOT SO DESCRIBED

Abdan/abadan (*ābādān* with altered meaning); ax; axta; axtacı (P.-T.); ᶜallanbar "porter" (also listed in 316v. 23; apparently an A.-P. compound, but there is no apposite meaning for *ᶜallān* and it is probably corrupt); a/érg (*arg*); arman (*ārmān*); armanlığ (P.-T.); *ispir* R. "hawk" (probably a corruption of *işkira*, same meaning); *ısmarla-* R.; P.-T. (this goes back to a 12th cent. T. word *osparla-*, see J.R.A.S., 1942, p. 191ff., which is derived from Middle P. *ospār-* > modern P. *sipur-*); *ısmarlama* R., P.-T.; uşğun "sorrel" (corruption of *a/işxuwān*).

Bibi (*bībī*); *be/ébek* (*babak*); püpük (*pūpak*); pupuş (*pūpaş*); bıbay "feeble, powerless" (probably an error for *bī-bas*, same meaning); *pic* R.; bide "fodder" (not T., cf. *bada* "boiled rice"); buta "young branches; target" (*būta*); badalğa (corruption of *badraqa*); wax/h (*wāh*); *pık/xtı* R. (*pixtī*); bahlı (*bahla*); *bağılt/ţak* I. (*bağltāq*); bağışla- P.-T. (from *baxş*); bağışlat- P.T.; bağışlan- P.-T.; pūl; pūlak, *balış* I. (*bāliş*); bars (*pārs*); *fişek* R. (corruption of *mūşak*); wişne; piyāzi.

Çap (see Index I); çapçı P.-T.; çupan (*çūpān/şabān*); çapar; cadu "a kind of sparrow" (mistranslation, or metaphorical use of *cādū* "magic"); çadır (*çādar*); çax "fish-trap" (probably a corruption of P. *şax*); cuğ (*cūğ*); cığa (*cīğa*); çakal (*şağāl*); çuğul "an informer" (*çuğul*, same meaning, perhaps originally from M. *çoğil* "quarrelling" K.2192; H.539); cılaw (*calaw*); çolpa (said to be a corruption of *çulāh-pā*); cılawlığ P.-T.; çalapar (corruption of *çālāk-par*); *çamaşır* R. (corruption of *cāma-şūyī*); canağ/k (*canāğ*); *çar* R. (abbreviation of *çār-pūd*, see Sub-section i); çura; curra; çurı* "maid-servant" (probably a misreading of A. *ḥūrī*; alternatively a corruption of A. *cārīya*); çarkab (*çār-qab*); çarm; çaşta (corruption of *şaş-tā*); çaşn.

Taw R. (corruption of *tāb*); te/éftik (*taftīk*); dıwan (*dīwān*); d/tepengü (*tabangū* with altered meaning); tüfürcek/tüfürük "spittle", tüfkür-/tükür- "to spit" are all P.-T. words ultimately derived from *tuf/tufū* "spittle"; dādak/*dedek* (*dāduk*); *ték* R. (corruption of *tā ki*?); *dümbelek* R. (diminutive of *danbal*); tımar (*tīmār*); tanba; tönbek (*tanbak*); dunbul (*dunbal*, with altered meaning); tanbala- P.-T.; tanga; dangal; turma; *tasalan-* R. P.-T. (from *tāsa*); *tiz* "swift" (*tīz*); tazı (*tāzī*); tizle- P.-T.; *tazana* R. (*tāziyāna*).

Kıf (*qīf*); xaftan/*kab/ftan* (*xaftān*); xak pelek "leap-frog" (two P. words, but not recorded as a P. phrase with this meaning); ğalça; kaltaban (*qaltabān*); kalağay (with *qaf*; corruption of *kalāğī* with *kāf*); ham ol P.-T.; xanc; ğ/kunda (*ğunda*); har yanı P.-T.; ğur; *kur* "globular metal target" (*qūr*); *xoros übügi* R., P.-T.; hay (*hāy*); *koyaŋ*/koyanğu "sciatica" (Steingass lists *qūyan* and *kahankū* (the latter the P. translation of these words in the Sanglax) as dubious P. words); koz "nut" (*gawz*); xızan "people, relatives" (corruption of *xʷīşān*).

Kip (*kīb*); kawla- P.-T. (from *kāwīdan*); kipleş- P.-T.; kepenek (*kapanak*); kiç (*kīç*); kecek (*kacak*); kécim (*keçīm*); ketek (*kadak*, diminutive of *kad*); kükle- P.-T. (from *kūk*); küklet- P.-T.; küklen- P.-T.; küküz (*kūkūz*); küküzgine P.-T.; kal (*kāl*); gala; *külüfçe* R. (P. diminutive of A. *kufl* metathesized); gulac (*gulāc*); kelte (corruption of *kulūta*); *keler* R. (*kalār*); *gem* R. (*gām*); *küme* R. "hut" (*kūma*); *kümele* R. "hut" (perhaps error for plural *kümeler*); *kerwan kıran* R. P. (*kārwān*)-T.; *gürbüz* R. (*gurbuz*); kereç (*karāç*); kerek (*karak*); *kurk* R.* "chicken" (*kūrak*); *kereste* R. (*kirāsta*); kersen (*karsān*); keşir (corruption of *gazar*); gez (*gaz*).

La "mud" (*lāy*); luc (*lūc*); luça (abbreviation of *ālūça*); *lak* R.; laş (*lāş*); layla- P.-T. (from *lāy*); laylat- P.-T.; laylan- P.-T.

Mac (*māç*); max "kiss" (error for *māç*); mucak (*mūçak*); *mengüş* R. (*mangūş*); murdar ağacı P. (*murdār*)-T.; maska; mişe (for *bīşa*); müşek (*mūşak*).

Nay "a hawk's collar" (*nay* with altered meaning?); *nigende* R. (*niganda*).

Raxrax (corruption of *rāh rāh*); rawşan "a kind of triangular arrow-head" (this must be P. *rawşan* in a metaphorical (?) meaning); *ruzgar* R. (*rūzgār*).

Sebed R. (*sapad*); saxtıyan (*saxtiyān*); salla (1) "head-dress"; (2) "wedding gift" (morphologically not T.; P. *salla* means "basket", but A. *şila* is recorded in P. as meaning "gift"); saman "straw" (*saman* "clover"; *sāmān* has only inappropriate meanings); *sırtak* R.* (corruption of *şırdağ*, q.v.); sustay- P. (*sust*)-T.; sustayıt- P.-T.; *seyyid ğazi nebīri* R.*; A.-P. phrase with T. construction; sayra.

Şıwaran "the name of a *xākşīr*" (not, as Pavet de Courteille translates, "peach", but some smaller berry; morphologically P. but not in the dictionaries); şılan (*şīlān*); şırdağ (*şīr-dāğ*); *şorak* R. (şūra); *şırlağan* R. (corruption of *şīr- rūğan*); *şırlağancı* R.

Yawa "bread fried in oil" (*yāwa* "absurd, foolish" in metaphorical sense?); *yawu* R. (corruption of *yāwa*?); yaban (yabān); *yaban turak otı* R., P.-T.; *yabana* R. (extended form of *yabān*); *yabancı* R., P.-T.; *yawaşa* R. (corruption of *lawāşa*); yuna "felt saddle-cloth" (*yūn*, possibly a loan-word from T. *yüŋ* "wool").

Zunbuluk (metathesis of *zunbuğul*); *zengin* R. "rich" (corruption of *sangīn* "weighty"); *zırığ* R.* (*zirih*); zirik (corruption of *zirişk*).

C. OTHER LANGUAGES*

CHINESE

baxşı "scribe, secretary, surgeon", *po- shih* (G.9372, 9992).
bég "chief of a clan", *po* (G.9348 "leader of a hundred men").
çaw "paper-money", *ch'ao* (G.514).
coŋ "great, mighty", *chung* (G.2880).
çiŋseŋ "hereditary title of a court official"; perhaps *hsien-shêng* (G.4440, 9865 "elder, senior, term of address"), but cf. *şiŋ*.
tayşı "scribe, expert, master of an art", *ta* (or *t'ay*) *-shih* (G.10470 or 10573, and probably 9909).
kimsen "gilded leather" (in Kāşğari "gold leaf"), *chin- hsien* (G.2032, 4532 "gold thread").
luy "dragon" *lung* (G.7479).
şiŋ (1) "decision, settlement of a question"; (2) "part of a hereditary title"; no doubt Chinese, but not identifiable, perhaps two different Chinese words.

IRANIAN LANGUAGES

Parsik (of Turfan). kamuk "all", *hm'g*.
Saka. ton "garment", *ṯauna*.
Sogdian. uc/çmağ/k "paradise", *'wštmγ*.
ocun "(this) world", *''z'wn*.
ıxşıḏ "ruler", from *'γš'y-* "to rule".
tamuğ/k "hell", *tmw*.
xatun "lady", *χwt'ynh*.
ként "town, village", *knδ*.
Uncertain biçin "ape"; cf. Persian *būzīna*.

KUCHAEAN. tümen "10,000" *tumane/tmane*.

TIBETAN. *laba* "teacher" *bla-ma*.
labaşak "kind of garment" *bla-ba-śig*.

* Most of these loan-words are very old, but the two Tibetan words received through Mongolian, and probably one or two Chinese words similarly received, date only from the Mongol period. The references for Chinese words are the numbered characters in H. A. Giles' Chinese-English Dictionary, 2nd edn., London 1912. Languages from which loan-words occur only in "Rumi" are not included in this list.

INDEX VII. IṢṬILĀḤĀT-I MUĞŪLĪYA*

Ötüg; ağırlamışı; ögülge (m.); *al* (meaning "a red seal"), ölcemişi (m.), *altun bilge, altun tamğa*, ılğamışı; uranlaşmışı (m.); asramışı (m.).

Bağtak, bağılt/ṭak (p. or m.?), bığlamışı; (*bulğağ/k*, attested by Waṣṣaf as i.-iM., but good Turkish), balış (p.); baslamışı; başlamışı; *bay* (in the phrase *umarā-i bāy*).

Caw, çapawkı (probably scribal error for *çapawul*), çapawul (t.-m.); *çag* (m.); cılamışı (m.); cumca (m.); cırğamışı (m.).

Tobçımışı (m.?), tabın (m.), tawusmışı, tawsamışı (probably scribal error for *tawusmışı*); (*ṭağacar* personal name attested by i.-iM. quotation); tekemişi (m.); tekeşmişi (m.-t.); tulamışı, tölemişi; temecemişi (m.); (*tansux* 164r. 17, i.-iM. corruption of *tansuğ/k*); tarğamışı (m.), turğamışı (probably corrupt derivative of *turğur-*), térem (corruption of *teŋrim*), dérsün ("m.").

Kamlamışı; kırığ (m.), kurıltay (m.), kurmışı; kışlamışı; *kayan*; *kızıl bilge*.

Görküz (?); kéyünüklemişi.

Narın (? m.).

Sa/ohramışı (? m.); sögdemişi (? m.); sürgewül (? t.-m.), sürmişi.

Şığawul (m.).

Yağlamışı; yortawul (t.-m.), (*yarğu* as *bulğag/k*), yaraşmışı; yasakı (t.-m.), yasamışı; yaylamışı.

---

* See paragraph 37 of the Introduction.

INDEX VIII. FOREIGN LANGUAGES MENTIONED IN THE SANGLAX*

A. LANGUAGES IN WHICH THE EQUIVALENTS OF T. WORDS ARE QUOTED

ARABIC, *frequent.*
dialects:—*a^c^rāb-i Bağdād* 292v. 15.
ba- ^c^irāqī 220r. 19.
mağrabiyān 224v. 23. X.

"HINDĪ", *frequent.*

PERSIAN, *frequent.*
dialects:—*ba- isfahānī* 132v. 22; 271r. 5; 288r. 29.
ba-mazandarānī 271r. 5.
ba-ṣīrāzī 212v. 20; 261r. 5; 325v. 28.
ahl-i Tabaristān wa dāru'l-marz 319v. 15.

BERBER (*ba-luğat-i Barbarī*) 262v. 1 ("chenopodium" *aṭrīlāl* (?)).

COPTIC (*ba-Qibtī*) 259v. 8 ("soda-plant" *qāqlī*).

GREEK (*ba-Yūnānī*) 352r. 1 ("salamander" *sālāmandrā*).

RUSSIAN (*ba-zabān-i Rūs*) 278v. 8 ("whip" *pilāt*, i.e. *plet'*).

SPANISH (*ba-luğat-i Andalus*) 220r. 19 ("autumn crocus" *sūrancān* (?)) X.†

SYRIAC** (ba-Suryānī) 310r. 20 ("chameleon" *ḥirḏawn*) X.

B. LANGUAGES OF WHICH HOMOPHONOUS WORDS ARE TRANSLATED

ARABIC, *frequent.*

PERSIAN, *frequent.*
dialects:—*ahl-i Buxārā* 300v. 1 (*karak* "roof"; in Steingass).‡
ahl-i Siyistan 315r. 5 (*lūk* "ivy"; in Steingass).
Zand wa Pāzand 259v. 10 (*ṣūk* "bazaar"; in Steingass).

GEORGIAN (*ba-gurcī*) 133r. 24 (*böri** "bread").

HAITIAN (*ahālī-yi mamlakat-i yaŋı dunyā*) 273v. 10 (*kasık* "ruler, chief", i.e. "cacique").

LEZGIAN (*lakzīya*) 247r. 18 (*sonkur* "blind", a corruption of M. *sokor*, see Index V,C).

MAGRABĪ (*mağrabīyān*) 44r. 24 (*efendi* "God") X.

SPANISH (*ba-luğat-i Andalus*) 290r. 6 (*kulb* "a seed crushed and drunk to dissolve stones in the bladder") X.

SYRIAC (*ba-luğat-i Suryānī*) 112v. 7 (*él* "God") X.

---

* See paragraph 58 of the Introduction. Languages mentioned in both sections are marked X.

** *Hirḏawn* "chameleon" is in the Arabic dictionaries, so this should perhaps be classified as "Syrian Arabic", but in Section B "Syriac" seems more correct.

† *Sūrancām* (*sic*) is recorded in this sense in Dozy's Supplément aux Dictionnaires Arabes and at least one modern Arabic dictionary, but is probably a loan-word in that language.

‡ The Burhān-i Qāti^c^ is no doubt the authority from which both the Sanglax and Steingass quoted this and the two following dialectic meanings.

INDEX IX. NAMES

A. GEOGRAPHICAL

B. PERSONAL

C. TRIBES, CLANS, ETC.

INDEX X. AUTHORITIES QUOTED

A. LEXICONS

i. Arabic. al-Qāmūs; e.g. 214v. 12.
ii. Persian. Burhān-i Qāṭi^c } see Index VI, B (i).
Farhang-i Cahāngirī }
iii. Çağatay (see paras. 29-32 of the Introduction).
Mu'allifayn-i Rūmīya (one the Abuşka).
Tali^c-i Harawī.
Firāğī.
Nadar ^cAli.
Mīrzā ^cAbdu'l-Calīl Naṣīrī.
iv. "Rūmī".
Ḥalīmī-yi Rūmī* 160v. 12; 231r. 11; 275v. 29.
Ni^cmatu'llāh-i Rūmī* 275v. 29; 348v. 21.
Niṣāb-i Şāhidī-yi Rūmī* 210v. 15; 330v. 29.
Tuḥfatu'l-Mu'minīn 209r. 4.
Luğat-i Rūmī 279v. 9.
v. Probably Çağatay (see para. 29 of the Introduction).
Mu'ayyidu'l-fuḍalā 115r. 3; 118r. 4; 141v. 4; 178v. 4; 216r. 4.

B. ÇAĞATAY AUTHORITIES

Nawā'ī passim.
Nawā'ī (?), *^carīḍa ki ba-Badī^cu'l-zamān niwiṣta ast* 228r. 4; 315r. 18.
Nawā'ī (?), *Sāqī-nāma* 173r. 14; 217r. 26; 286v. 4; 326v. 20; 349r. 27.
Abā Bakr Mīrzā 336r. 23.
Bābur Pādişāh-*ta'rīx* about 250 quotations.
poems 13r. 15 (see Abuşka p. 36); 30v. 11 (see Bābur-nāma 196v. 8 of the facsimile, Gibb Memorial I); 75v. 29 (see Abuşka p. 108); 93v. 28 (same as 13r. 15); 160r. 28 (see Abuşka p. 171); 179v. 8 (see Abuşka p. 213); 203r. 14 (see Abuşka p. 196); 254r. 2 (see Abuşka p. 287); 295r. 5 (see Bābur-nāma 196v. 5).
Inşā'-i Buxārī 70v. 1; 110r. 14; 134r. 22; 208r. 1; 220r. 25; 235v. 5; 268v. 2 and 3.
Mīrzā Hācī Samarqandī 167r. 13.
maṯnawī-yi Sayyid Ḥasan 143v. 2.
Mīr Haydar (quoted as "Mīr Haydar" or "Haydar Télbe", with or without a reference to the *Maxzan*) 49r. 14; 66r. 1; 75v. 24; 95r. 20; 103r. 3; 138r. 6; 141r. 12; 146v. 6; 159r. 21; 164r. 15; 190r. 8; 197r. 13; 200v. 2; 201v. 10; 224r. 17; 229r. 24; 258v. 8; 307r. 29A; 322r. 28; 326v. 20; 342v. 14; 343v. 2; 345v. 18; 351r. 25.
Humāyūn Pādişāh *dar ^carīḍa ki ba-xidmat-i Bābur Pādişāh pidar-i x^wud niwista būd, wa naql-i ān dar kitābxāna-i Hind dīda şud* 113v. 29; 223r. 23 (same quotation, description varies slightly).
Sulṭān Ḥusayn Mīrzā 12v. 4; 38r. 23; 73v. 28; 91v. 10; 97v. 5; 105r. 25; 122r. 12; 123v. 7; 129r. 22; 132r. 4; 138v. 8; 139v. 3; 141r. 24; 146r. 22; 149r. 1; 153v. 5; 161r. 18; 171v. 13; 178r. 23; 182v. 7; 186r. 27, v.1; 192r. 17; 202v. 1; 227v. 4; 240r. 10; 243v. 8; 268v. 24; 275r. 29; 286v. 16; 290v. 23; 304r. 20; 306v. 12; 320r. 20; 326r. 16; 327r. 23; 337r. 22; 342v. 23; 352r. 22.
Ḥusaynī 39v. 19; 53v. 20.
X^wāca Kalān (*dar cawāb-i Bābur Pādişah*) 155r. 24 (see Abuşka p. 168).
Iskandar Mīrzā 100r. 14.

---

* Manuscripts of these three authorities are in the British Museum (see Catalogue of the Turkish Manuscripts in the British Museum, by Charles Rieu, London, 1888, pages 137b, 139b and 142b) and no doubt in other libraries. The second is extensively quoted in Tanıklariyle Tarama Sözlügü IV, Ankara, 1957. The third is probably identical with the Tuhfei Şahidî mentioned in Tarama Dergisi, İstanbul, 1934, Ip. 62.

Luṭfī 6v. 29; 41v. 5; 61r. 3; 73r. 7; 76v. 21; 87r. 12; 96v. 19 and 25; 98v. 29; 117v. 8; 152v. 7; 153r. 9; 169v. 17; 185v. 1; 188r. 20; 198v. 17; 207r. 4; 252v. 5 and 16; 282r. 3; 293v. 24; 305v. 11; 306v. 8; 321r. 26; 336r. 20.

Nāṣir 42r. 9; 62v. 18; 86v. 29; 97r. 14; 116v. 23; 118r. 5; 278r. 8.

Mullā Sāqī* 70r. 13; 84v. 5; 96v. 8; 99r. 11; 106v. 24*; 113r. 25; 135v. 9; 167v. 17; 171r. 14; 178v. 18; 217r. 3 and 6; 232v. 7; 261v. 28; 269r. 20*; 285v. 22*; 332v. 28*.

ᶜUbayd Xān Özbek 268r. 22.

Anonymous:—

(a) *Lā adrī* 4v. 20; 42r. 1 and 10; 49v. 12; 73v. 14; 74v. 27; 116r. 19; 206r. 6; 227r. 23; 232v. 20; 257v. 12; 266v. 15; 316v. 18; 323v. 10; 327r. 18; 339v. 11; 351r. 15; 352r. 10.

(b) *Šāᶜir* 113r. 4; 204v. 21; 330r. 8.

Proverbs (maṯal)** 43v. 11, 109v. 16; 115v. 20; 121r. 15; 160v. 17; 172v. 16; 178r. 17 and 20; 207v. 15; 255r. 29; 284r. 6; 285v. 20; 306r. 29.

C. RŪMĪ AUTHORITIES†

Fuḍūli (-yi Bağdādī) 5r. 5, 23, 24, 26 and v.29; 6r. 2; 7v. 14 and 16; 8r. 19 and 21; 9v. 13 and 19; 10v. 4, 20, 22 and 24; 11r. 2, 4 and 6; 12r. 12, 14 and v.25; 13r. 18; 15v. 4, 6 and 7; 17v. 5, 22, 23, 26 and 28; 18v. 29; 39v. 7; 43r. 6 and v.26; 45v. 10; 50v. 14; 56v. 25; 57r. 3; 66v. 16; 78v. 5; 86v. 15 and 16; 88v. 19; 89v. 5; 93v. 22; 96r. 10; 97r. 24 and 27; 122r. 27 and 28; 126r. 23; 127r. 19; 130v. 11; 138r. 12, 16 and v.26; 139v. 8 and 17; 141r. 18; 146v. 2; 154v. 29; 158r. 14; 204v. 22 and 23; 209r. 28; 218v. 10 and 11; 224r. 7 and 16; 225v. 23 and 25; 226r. 3, 4 and v.2; 229r. 21 and v.22; 230v. 20 and 23; 231v. 24 and 27; 232v. 14; 234v. 8, 10, 12, 14, 15 and 16; 236v. 13 and 15; 238r. 24; 239v. 14 and 19; 240r. 6 and v.5; 249r. 3; 252v. 11; 260v. 28; 270v. 17; 282r. 25; 284v. 3; 289v. 20; 290v. 26; 291v. 25; 300v. 11; 301r. 26; 305v. 29; 306v. 6; 325r. 8 and 10; 326v. 13; 332r. 6; 345r. 4; 347v. 10; 348v. 14; 351r. 13; 352v. 17.

Munaccim-i Rūmī (perhaps merely "a Rūmī astronomer") 275v. 26.

Nābī-yi Rūmī 127r. 22.

Nasīmī (-yi Rūmī) 208v. 17; 324r. 7.

Saᶜdu'l-Dīn Ṣafā-yi Rūmī (ki munšī-yi dānišmandī būda) dar ta'rīx-i āl-i 'Uṯmān‡ 5r. 6; 73v. 2; 97r. 24; 268r. 18; 270v. 18; 331v. 14.

Tācu'l-Tawārīx-i āl-i Uṯman‡ 10r. 22; 41v. 20; 300r. 22.

(Kitāb-i) Şamma (-i Rūmī) 229v. 26; 276r. 9.

Anonymous:—

(a) *Lā adrī* 76v. 13; 226v. 27.

(b) (*Saᶜir*) *bi-imlā'i'l-Rūmīya* 34r. 22; 242v. 17; 273r. 29.

(c) Şāᶜir-i Rūmī 43v. 13; 75v. 20; 142v. 17; 204v. 29; 242v. 18; 261v. 7; 270v. 9; 351r. 22.

D. OTHER TURKISH AUTHORITIES

Kalīla wa Dimna. The author clearly had two versions, one Çağatay and one Rūmī. The first is described in 110r. 25 as *Kalīla Dimna-i Turkī, ki ba-luğat-i Cağatay ta'līf namūda and*, the second in 10v. 8 as *Kalıla Dimna kb. a-lisān-i atrāk-i Rūm ta'līf karda and.* The latter may have been partly "normalized" with Çağatay spellings like ablative in *-dın/din*. In (a) and (b) below quotations with Çağatay or Rūmī spellings are marked Ç or R.

(a) *Kalīla Dimna* 71v. 12 (Ç.); 108v. 1 (Ç.); 109r. 9 (Ç.) and 10 (verse Ç.); 114r. 1 (Ç.); 186v. 8 (verse Ç.); 195r. 8 (verse Ç.).

(b) *Kalıla Dimna-i Turkī* 72r. 2 (Ç.); 75v. 21 (R.); 85v. 13; 229v. 16 (verse Ç.).

(c) *Kalīla Dimna-i Rūmī* (or the like) 10v. 8 (Ç.!); 10v. 26 (verse); 11r. 8; 80v. 14 (same as 10v. 26); 148r. 12 (verse); 149r. 28; 348v. 22.

Oğuz-nāma (see para. 35 of the Introduction) 180r. 1; 334v. 16.

---

* Except for those marked *, all these quotations are stated to be from the Gul-u Nawrūz-i Mullā Sāqī; some of the same quotations, including that at 285v. 22, appear in the Abuşka, being described as from the Gul-u Nawruz-i Luṭfī. The Sanglax nowhere corrects this ascription but it is presumably an error.

** These are probably contemporary Özbek proverbs; parallels to two of them will be found in the collection of proverbs in Vambéry's Cagataische Sprachstudien, Leipzig, 1867. With 121r. 15 compare No. 10 (p. 7) *ölümdin xorluk yaman*, and with 172v. 16 No. 7 (p. 7) *toyğa barsaŋ toyup bar*.

† The quotations listed below are usually, but not invariably, preceded by the words *ba-imlā-i Rūmīya*.

‡ These are alternative descriptions of the same work, which was published in İstanbul in A.H. 1279 (A.D. 1862–3). The quotation at 5r. 6 will be found in Vol. I, p.310.

E. PERSIAN AUTHORITIES

---

* These are all alternative descriptions of the *Cāmı^cu'l-Tawārīx* of Raşıdu'l-dın; the references in brackets are to the relevant pages in the Russian translation, "Rashid-ad-din, Sbornik Letopisey", Moscow, 1946 ff.

** 319v. 7 contains verse 7 of the poem published in Minorsky's "Pūr-i Bahā's ^cMongol' Ode", B.S.O.A.S., 1956, XVIII/2 (see para. 37 of the Introduction), with the variant readings contained in Wassāf (see Minorsky, p. 267), from whom the quotation may have been taken; but 235v. 16 is from a different poem.

† The passage is a reproduction of a quotation in Wassāf and does not agree exactly with the relevant passage (p. 28) in Mirza Muhammad's edition (Gibb Memorial, Vol. XVI).

‡ All these quotations, except 82v. 27 and 263r. 17, the latter illustrating a P. word, are described as *ba-iṣṭılāhāt-i Muğül* (or *Muğulīya*) and nearly all as *dar ğazal-i mulamma^c* (*ğ.-m. above*).

Turkish Text Reproduced and Printed by Lowe & Brydone (Printers) Ltd., London, N.W.10

بسم الله الرحمن الرحیم

الحمد لله الذی لا یستقصی حمده بلغات مختلفه والسنه شتی و خلق السموات والارض فی ستة ایام لا تری فیها
عوجا ولا امتا ولا یوصف ذاته باین و کیف و حیث و متی لا تاخذه السنة ولا تغلطه الالسنة تبارک و تعالی
والصلوة علی کلمة الله العلیا الذی نزل علیه الکتاب بلسان عربی مبین و نطق بالحق بشیرا و نذیرا للعالمین
والسلام علی آله واصحابه الذین لا یحتاج صدقهم الی الشاهد والبرهان و یتصف عندهم کل الحسن
بکل اللسان اما بعد چون بنده حقیر محمد مهدی ... از مبادی حال بخواندن اشعار امیر نظام الدین
... امیر علیشیر نوائی شوق تمام و بدانستن آن کلام میل مالاکلام داشت بعد از ...
تتبع ما صاحب مثنوی حالم گشت که لغات مشکله آنها را جمع سازد و بر معانی آن لغات کتابی پردازد اگرچه
بعضی از فضلا در تالیفات مذکور نیست و طالع نام هروی و فراغی و نعم علی و میرزا عبد الجلیل ...
بعضی از فضلا این فن کتابها بر لغت نوائی مدون ساخته اند اما چون در کمال اختصار بود و اکثر لغتها
که معنی معلوم ایشان نبوده تجاهل کرده بذکر آن نپرداخته اند و آنچه را هم بیان تحریر کشیده اند بعضی از ... خالی
... نسخه ... خوانده اند ... معنی ... قرار داده ... غلط ... شاهد ...
درست ... نه ... فاعل و مفعول ... کرده اند لهذا این کمینه ... دولت ...
خاقان ... سلیمان جاه شاهنشاه سکندر دستگاه ... افتاد با وصف ...
خدمت سلطانی و اشتغال بمشاغل دیوانی ... جنود ... و ضبط ...
و عرض مطالب جمهور ... قوانین و انجام مهام ... و تالیف این نسخه پرداخته
آنرا بترتیب حروف تهجی مرتب و هر حرفی را بحرکات ثلث منشعب ساخته هر باب را ... چند حرف نمود مثل

نوشت کتاب الالف باب المفتوحات حرف الالف مع الالف الی آخرها و بنای اشتقاق بر مصدری که علامتش ...
بود گذاشته انسیخ را در ذیل مشتقات مذکور ساخت و هر لغت که سماعی بودند در تحت جوامع ...
در ... ذکر نمود تا طالب در وادی ... فرهای ... نگشته بطریق سهل ... کر ... مطلب
مطلب کند و بنا بر صلابت الفاظ و صعوبت لغات از بستن کلام ... و بعضی از اشتباهات ...
... نکته ... شیوه ... بلکه از برای تصویب رای ...
اغماض در مقام خود ایراد کرد تا جواب ... شبهه ... کشته حمل ...
اختلاف معانی نکرده و لغات ... و الفاظ ... ایشانرا لفظ و معنی جدا ...
اگرچه ... لغت ... که ... حروف پ و چ و گ ... عجمی و عربی ...
و بلا اشباع شده اما چون حضرت نوائی ... و استاد این فن بود ...
جیم عجمی را با جیم عربی و حرکات مشبع را با غیر مشبع قافیه کرده چنانکه در ذیل ... از ...
قواعد منفرد با شواهد نگارش خواهد یافت لهذا ... بعضی جا از ذکر ...
و عربیه و مشبع و غیر مشبع نساخته ... اوز ... ترکیه ...
کم ... و ... انها با کاف عربی تلفظ ... و اهل ...
الفاظ ... با کاف عجمی ... لهذا قول هر دو فرقه را صحیح دانسته ...
عجمی و عربی ... مکرر بعضی جا که با حرف عجمی یا با اشباع معمول به فریقین ... لازم بود و بنا ...
در این تالیف مقصود بالذات حل لغات کتب منظومه و منثوره حضرت نوائی بود و بعضی از لغات ...
و رومیه ... از شواهد ...
اسم او دانسته قید نکرد ...
بمعرض بیان در آورد و آنچه از کتب نظم و نثر آنحضرت بنظر این کمینه رسیده که لغات آنها در این تالیف ...
دوازده جلد منظوم و نه جلد منثور است اما المنظوم غرایب الصغر و نوادر الشباب و بدایع الوسط
و فواید الکبر و حیرة الابرار و فرهاد و شیرین و لیلی و مجنون و سبعه سیاره و سد سکندری و لسان الطیر
و اربعین منظوم و نظم الجواهر اما المنثور محبوب القلوب و میزان الاوزان و خمسة المتحیرین و ...
و تاریخ ملوک عجم و مجالس النفایس و مناجات و وقفیه ...
شامل لغات مشکله فارسی و عربی ...
تمیزی ... هر لغت ... کتاب ... لغات فارسی و عربی ...
جلد منظوم ... شواهد ... لغات ...
... شاهد ... لغات فارسی و عربی ... محبوب
القلوب که ... مرغوب بود اکتفا نمود اگرچه ... تالیف ... نوشته ...
... کتاب ... ما ... اول ...

تتبع وتحقیق نیست و هیچ وجه شایسته اذعان و تصدیق نه والحق ضوابط و قواعدی که در لغت ترکی معین بوده
نه در لغت فرس هست ونه در لسان عرب وتمام صیغ آن موافق است با ضابطه علم ادب از انجا که دانستن انها
مرطالبان لازم بود آن ضوابط و قواعد را در ضمن این ترصیف وشش مبنا مرقوم و بشواهد و حجج مبرهن
و معلوم ساخته از ابمبانی اللغة موسوم نمود وچون الی الان کتابی در نحو و صرف ترکی احدی بر صرف و نحو
تالیف نکشته و تا این زمان نسخه بر این سیاق بر قواعد صیغ و داب اشتقاق آن تصنیف نیافته اولین رسالهٔ
که کاتب مؤلف بمدد بخت توفیق از روی استقرا و تحقیق پرداخته هرگاه قصوری و فتوری واقع شده باشد
از ناظران این نسخه بخانه لطف اصلاح نمایند

ترصیف اگرچه در لغت عرب مصدر اصل کلام وماخذ
صیغ است اما در لغت ترکی فعل امر مایه و اسطوانهٔ صیغ می باشد و علاماتی که از برای هر معنی موضوع و مقرر است
هر یک بر فعل امر ملحق گشته بالحاق آن علامات معنی مختلف و بمعنی دیگر منصرف میگردد و در وضع
هر صیغه تغییر لازم می باید سوای فعل امر که در هر حال بر حال خود باقی و جمیع علامات بدان راجع است مثل
آل و اور و کیت و کیل که فعل امر است هرگاه خواهند که مصدر بنا کنند ماق و ماک که علامت مصدر است
بر انها الحاق نمود، الماق و اورماق و کیتماک و کیلماک میگویند و اگر فعل ماضی اراده نمایند دی
بر انها منضم ساخته الدی و اوردی و کیتدی و کیلدی میخوانند و علی هذا القیاس و در بیان کلام جمیع
صیغ مشتقه انست که چون علامت ملحقه را از و حذف کنند فعل امر از ان صیغه باقی ماند و انچه ماورای آن
جوامد خواهد بود و گاه هست که علامتی بر علامتی دیگر انضمام یافته معنی علامت سابق را از ان لفظ منسلخ
و بمعنی دیگر منصرف میگرداند و دور که علامت فعل مضارع است بقاعدهٔ مقرره بر فعل امر الحاق یافته
فعل امر مفید معنی استقبال می سازد و غان و کان بر فعل مضارع علاوه گشته معنی استقبال را از او
نمود، بمعنی مصدر و فاعل و غیره منقلب میسازد و باید دانست که بنای استعمال صیغ از دو قسم بیرون نیست
یا با قاف و غین است یا با کاف و ایرهرد و قسم باید از روی سماع و اختیار باشد نه از روی قیاس و اختیار
هرچند که واغی در تالیف خود نوشته که ذکر قاف و کاف تخییر یست و طالع هروی نیز بتقریب ذکر معنی
نوشته که غین معجمه یا کاف بطریق تخییر بر اسم فاعل داخل میشود مثل قیلغوچی و بیلکوچی تا قول هردو
خالی از ربط و ناشی از سهو و خبط است زیرا که لفظ قیل که صیغه امر است یعنی بکن تانیث و تمام
آن با قاف و غین اشتقاق می یابد مثل قیلماق و قیلغای و قیلغوچی و اخوات انها و بیل یعنی بدان از کاف
و صیغ انها با کاف مذکور می گردد مثل بیلماک و بیلکای و بیلکوچی و اشباه انها و تغییر و تخییر در انها
بهیچ وجه راه نیست چنانکه ان شاء الله بتفصیل ذکر خواهد یافت مبنای اول در بیان وجوه صیغ و آن مشتمل
بر ده باب باب اول در بیان مصادر اگرچه نظر بضابطهٔ کلیه فعل امر جزو اتم الصیغ است بایست مقدم ذکر شود
لیکن بنا بر انکه در عربیت مصادر تقدم داشت تاسیاً له در این لغت نیز ذکر مصادر را مقدم ساخت و از ا
مبتنی بر دو فصل نمود فصل اول در مصادر عربیه و آن مشتمل است بر دو قسم قسم اول انست که بمعنی مصدر
و آن ماق و ماک است که در ذیل ترصیف بیان شد همچنانکه در لغت فرس مصدر انست که در اخر آن دال

مبنای اول
باب اول

یا تا و نون واقع شود مثل الماق یعنی گرفتن و کیلماک یعنی آمدن قسم دویم انست که بمعانی دیگر موضوع شده
اما بمناسبت مقام بمعنی مصدر هم استعمال می شوند و ان بر دو نوع است نوع اول صیغ است از انجمله
قسم اول فعل مضارع است مثل بارور یعنی میرود و چیکار یعنی میکشد و اغریر یعنی درد میکند و اینها بمعنی مصدر
و فاعل هم می اید چنانکه بارور را بمعنی رفتن گوید شعر سبکه تان ماربیلم لا دیوز لانیب هرزه
منصفا غرابلی اقبالا شور دیک بور دیک جا ضیمه و همچنین چیکار را بمعنی کشیدن در سبحه سیاره فرماید شعر
قلوا یمکوبجه دست رس منکا یوق غیر آه چیکار هیچ منکا یوق و نیز اغریر را بمعنی درد کردن استعمال کرده
الشاهد علیه شعر تندین او تونکی چیکا لار اغریر دین ایرماس شیونیم اندین قیلورمین نوحه کیم
آیرو توشار نجاندین تنیم قاعده باید دانست که صیغه مضارع هرگاه با ضمایر متصله انضمام یابد افاده معنی
مصدر میکند مثل باروری رفتن و چیکاری یعنی کشیدنش و اغریری یعنی درد کردنش و همچنین است بارورینک
و چیکارینک و اغریرینک و اگر با ضمایر منفصله استعمال شود بمعنی مصدر نمی اید و همان بمعنی مضارع می اید مثل
اینکه گویند بارور مین یعنی میروم و چیکار مین یعنی میکشم چون با میم ضمیر متکلم جمع شود اگر حرف را
که علامت مضارع است مضمومه یا مکسوره با میم ترکیب یابد بدستور افاده معنی مصدری میکند مثل
بغم را یعنی رفتنم و چیکاریم بکسر را یعنی کشیدنم و اگر مفتوحه بمیم ضمیر الحاق شود همان افاده معنی مضارع می نماید مثل
بار ورام یعنی میروم و چیکارام یعنی میکشم و علی هذا القیاس دیگر صیغی است که بمعنی حال استعمال می شوند مثل
آنارا و توکولا که انهارا بمعنی ریختن در سخن گویند شعر اقارا باشلادی یاش و توکولا باشلادی تیش
سفر برا قیتی قیلغیل که توشتی اشینکا ایش و از صیغی که بمعنی حال موضوع است قسم اول ان افاده معنی مضارع
و امر غایب نیز می کند چنانکه در ذیل باب دهم در بیان انها خواهد آمد دیگر صیغه مفرد غایب است از فعل مضارع
منفی مثل چیقماس یعنی بیرون نمی آید و ایشتماس یعنی نمی شود و آچماس یعنی نمیکشاید و کورماس یعنی نمی بیند و هرگاه با
حرف انضمام یابد بمعنی مصدر منفی می آید الشاهد علی الاول شعر چوق نوانی تاریدی لمحه منکا دین
سو دیار تور لار کیشی چوق ناسلیغ ایتیب بولسا تماشا الشاهد علی الثانی شعر تاو نا ای شیخ نوا ایشیماسینی
ایشیماس دیب پند کیم سینینک پندینک ایشتماسلیک انکا پندا ولمیش الشاهد علی الثالث شعر
یار اغزا چا سفنه دردیم سوزغالی تا پتیم سبب کیم جیجو کلوکلدین یا یوش میلادیکو اولیک لب الشاهد
علی الرابع شعر اول شوخ که میدان نظاری کورکا لمین نا اوریتغ کورماسکا نا اوریتا نوای نادی عمدا یعنی
فاعل منفی هم می اید چنانکه در ذیل فاعل بیان خواهد شد نوع دویم علامات است از انجمله لفظ تان و کان
که بطریق قیاس افاده معنی مصدر و فاعل میکند اما در بعضی الفاظ بمعنی ماضی و در بعضی بمعنی مفعول می آید و
استعمال آن بر دو گونه است اول انست که در اخر فعل امر در می آید مثل ساچغان که بمعنی افشانده و افشاننده
و بمعنی افشاندن گوید شعر خود شاچغاریدین چمن ملکیدا سلطان بولدی گل غنچه تا تلیغ کونکلیکا سالغان
کره امساک ایمیش و همچنین است کیلکان که بمعنی اینده و امده است و بمعنی آمدن هم آمده چنانکه گوید شعر
کوزوما کیلماس و چون کیلکان دا اول پوزالیما تیغ یخشی انکلاماس کیم کوز قوپسه او تر و دوز نایده

بدانکه اتراك روم وایران هرگاه خواهند که باین صیغه تکلم کنند اگر فعل امر آن مسکون الآخر است مثل آلغان و
وکیلکان غین وکاف را محذوف وسکون حرف آخر فعل امر را بحرکت مبدل ساخته آلن وکیلن میگویند چنانچه گفته
میشود والاندا یعنی چه گرفتن وکیلاندا یعنی چه درآمدن واگر حرف آخر فعل امر متحرك باشد مثل اشلاغان واوقوغان
ودیکان بدستور غین وکاف را ساقط ساخته بدل آن یای حطی مفتوحه در آورده باشلاین واوقوین ودین میگویند
باشلایاندا یعنی چه شروع کردن واوقویاندا یعنی چه خواندن ودیاندا یعنی چه گفتن وعلی هذا القیاس نوع دوم
انست که در آخر فعل مضارع در آید مثل اوزاتور واوزاتادور که غان بر انها ملحق شده بمعنی راهی کننده وراهی کنند
می آید تا بمعنی راهی کردن هم مستعمل است چنانکه شاهد بر اولرا در سبعه سیاره در داستان مسافر اقلیم
رابع بمعنی مصدر گوید شعر اوزاتورغان زمانی تلاندی چون اوزاتی دشامقغه یاندی واین نوع قلیل الاستعمال است
زیراکه در جمیع مولفات جناب نوایی زیاده بر این شعر شاهدی بنظر نرسید ومبنا علی استعمال بر صیغه ثانی آن
که اوتادورغان باشد وهمچنین است کیلودور وکیلادور که بالحاق لفظ کان افاده معانی مذکوره می نماید
چنانکه شاهد بر ثانی را در نسایم المحبة در ذکر خواجه عبد الرحمن کهوان که بمعنی آمدن فرماید که کینت اهلی
مولانا غه دیدیلار که خواجه سرینک کیلادورکانینکه خبر توری فلان خواجه اسدا برچو قورغه کریب تور دوقیغ
کافی هم بنا علی استعمال بر صیغه ثانیست که عبارت از کیلادورکان باشد وکیلودورکان قلیل الاستعمال است
دیگر میثل است که علامت مفرد مغایب است از فعل ماضی ودر بعضی از صیغ علامت مفعول وماضی مجهول است
که یای مصدری بران ملحق ساخته بمعنی مشکله واسم مصدر استعمال می نمایند مثل اسرامیشی یعنی نگهداری وپایشی
یعنی ساختگی واین طریقه منقولیه است تکمله بدانکه اتراك اسماء ذوات وصفات را خواسته اند که بصیغ فعلی تکلم
کنند سه حرف اختیار واشتقاقات را بر انها قرار داده اند حرف اول لاست مثل اشلاماق یعنی زیر کردن وتیشلاماق
یعنی بدندان گرفتن ودر بعضی جا لفظ فارسی را هم با این حرف مرکب ومشترك ساخته استعمال نموده اند مثل کارلاماق
بمعنی کاشتن چنانکه در نسایم المحبه در ذکر منصور حلاج بمعنی امر گوید که استادی بوعمرو بن عثمان مکی انکار نغایی
کیم الهی بیرادین انکا کارلاکیم اینینک اباغین کسیکای ودارغه تارتغای وازاین قسم است کارلاماق بمعنی ادا
کردن چنانکه در ذکر ابو العباس ارزیزی بمعنی ماضی گوید که بیر کون نمازینی [illegible] کارلادی وباشینی
مقنعه تارتیب چون نظر قیلدی [illegible] اوتوب یردی ونیز در ذکر عبد الرحمن بمعنی اداکند گوید که شیخ
قاشیغه کیلیب توراندا میتکان محلدا ایتلاکا یدورکه حج کارلاغای وازاین نوع است هوسلاماق
چنانکه بصیغه ماضی گوید شعر سلامت هوسلاندی شیخ وشاغندی که زهد بنیا ینکلیغ آسان ایردی نوع
حرف دوم میم است مثل یولدامان یعنی براه انداختن واوردکودامان یعنی سنگی زدن حرف سیم دا است مثل مونگلاماق
یعنی محزون شدن وتیلبه راماك یعنی دیوانه شدن وگاه هست که با لفظ فارسی هم ترکیب می نمایند مثل
کندراماق یعنی متعفن شدن وهمچنین است مشتقات انها قاعده از مصادر لغتم از انکه امر احادی باشد
مثل دیماك بمعنی گفتن ویماك بمعنی خوردن یا ثنائی باشد مثل قیلماق بمعنی کردن یا ثلاثی باشد مثل ایشتماك
بمعنی شنیدن از ابواب عشق منشعبه که در لغت عربی مستعمل است در لغت ترك زیاده بر معها ابواب ثلثه

که در ذیل مرقوم می گردد بنا نشده وهر یک باب سما چیست اول معنی انفعال است واستعمال آن بر شش نوع است نوع
اول انست که با لام مستعمل است مثل توتولماق یعنی گرفته شدن ویبار یلماك یعنی فرستاده شدن نوع دوم
انست که با نون مذکور میگردد مثل باغلانماق یعنی بسته شدن وکورونماك یعنی مرئی شدن نوع سیم انست که
جایز الوجهانست با لام ونون هر دو استعمال می شود مثل یاسالماق ویاسانماق یعنی ساخته شدن نوع چهارم
در معنی انست که ساختن اگر از جانب غیر باشد با لام واگر فی نفسه باشد با نون مذکور می گردد چنانکه شاهد
لامی را در خسرو شیرین در اتمام قصه چین گوید شعر یاساردا بولنا هر صنعت غه مشغول : یاسالغلیغ بولغوسی
عشرت غه مشغول : وشاهد نونی را بمعنی خود سازی در قسم سیم از محبوب القلوب گوید که ایرانلار یاسانماغی
که نمایش او چون دود خانه [illegible] وازاین قبیل است اورولماق بمعنی زده شدن واورونماق بمعنی
باین وآن زدن ومانند اینست قیلیلماق وقیلینماق یعنی کرده شدن چنانکه شاهد لامی را در قسم دوم
از محبوب القلوب در ذکر عشق فرماید که اگر کتاب لار تصنیف قیلیلسا ومجلدلار ترتیب بیتیلسا وشاهد
در نظم الجواهر در باب شباب گوید شعر تاری لیغ ایرور کونکلیکا سینما قحسرت : جاینغه تاری لیغنی
قیلینما قحسرت : نوع پنجم انست که با لام وبدون لام هر دو بطریق مستعمل است مثل ایریلماك و
ایریماك که هر دو بمعنی گداخته شدن باشد چنانکه شاهد بر اولرا در سد سکندری بصیغه ماضی
گوید شعر چو بیردینک ایکی لعلینکا نوشخند : اوبیات تین ایریلدی ایردا قند : وشاهد بر ثانی از صیغه
مضارع فرماید شعر عشقینک اوتین کرنوانی دیسا کیم املالی قرش سوزیدین کوبا تملم قوروروقرا ایریر
نوع ششم انست که هم با نون وهم بدون نون استعمال میشود مثل قالیناس وقالماس یعنی نمی ماند
الشاهد علی الاول شعر تا کیم اول کل سبز بولوت نیکلیغ هوانی بولمیشام : بزم عیشی یاد یدین اشکیم
قالیناس باده دین : وگاه هست که لام ونون جزو کلمه واقع میشود مثل قوتولماق بمعنی خلاص شدن وتاپیناماق
بمعنی اضطراب کردن دو قسم معنی مفاعله است وعلامت آن حرف شین است که بکلمه داخل میشود مثل اوروشماق
یعنی بیکدیگر زدن وتوتوشماق یعنی همدیگر را گرفتن وکوروشماك همدیگر را دیدن وگاه هست که شین را پیش از
کلام از برای تزیین سخن داخل میشود مثل قوروشماق بمعنی خشك شدن که مرادف قوروماق است وتاروشماق
بمعنی روشن شدنست که مرادف تایروماق است چنانکه در ذیل مبنا چهارم در ضمن زواید با شواهد مذکور
خواهد شد وگاه هست که شین جزو کلمه اتفاق می افتد مثل توشماك بمعنی افتادن که هرگاه خواهند که صیغه
مفاعله از آن بنا کنند توشوشماك می گویند یعنی بهم در افتادن سیم معنی تفعیل است که عبارت از استعداد
باشد واین در تحت ضابطه نیست که استقصا تواند شد زیرا که متعدی هر مصدری بیك نحو بنا می شود
چنانکه قوتولماق بمعنی خلاص شدنرا قوتقارماق وتویماق بمعنی سیر شدنرا تویغارماق وچوماق بمعنی
زدنرا چومورتاق وتوغماق بمعنی زائیدنرا توغورماق ویانماق بمعنی خطا کردنرا یازغورماق وآزماق بمعنی
کم کردنرا ازغورماق وتاماق بمعنی چکیدنرا تامیزماق واقماق بمعنی روان شدنرا آقیزماق وچوکماك
بمعنی فرو نشستن را چوکارماك وکیتماك بمعنی رفتن را کیتارماك وکچماك بمعنی گذشتن را کچورماك وکوچماك بمعنی

کوچیدنرا کوچورماک نیز میکویند و تعدی اکثری از مصادر بلفظ دور و توروتای قرشت بنا شده چنانکه
اورماق بمعنی زدنرا اوردورماق و سورماق بمعنی کیدن و پرسیدن را سوردورماق و توتماق بمعنی گرفتن را
توتترماق و اتماق بمعنی انداختن را اتتورماق و اوچراماق بمعنی دچار شدنرا اوچراتماق و سودراماق
بمعنی بیرون کشیدنرا سودراتماك میخوانند و در بعضی الفاظ که التقاء تا ثانی واقع میشود یك تارا حذف
مینمایند مثل اینکه تاتماق بمعنی چشیدنرا تاتورماق و یاتماق بمعنی خوابیدنرا یاتورماق میکویند اتاندرن بعضی
الفاظ اسقاط جایز نیست مثل متعدی اتماق و توتماق که ازرا البته اتتورماق و توتتورماق باید کفت چنانکه
در فوق مذکور شد و بعضیها نیز دال و تارا از دور و تور محذوف و حرف اخر فعل امررا مضموم و برای مهمله
منضم میسازند مثل اشماق بمعنی گذشتن و قاچماق بمعنی گریختن که متعدی انهارا اشورماق و قاچورماق
میخوانند و بعضیها حذف جایز نیست مثل الماق و چالماق که بمعنی گرفتن و نواختن که متعدی انهارا البته
الدورماق و چالدورماق باید مذکور ساخت و کاه هست که لفظ دور و تور جزء کلمه واقع میشود مثل تولورماق
بمعنی دیوانه شدن و اولتورماق بمعنی نشستن و اولتورماك بمعنی کشتن هرکاه خواهند که متعدی از آنها کنند تاکی
قرشت برآن ملحق ساخته تودورماق و اولتورتماق و اولتورتماك میکویند چنانکه شاهد بر ثالث به صیغه
جمع مخاطب از فصل امر در مقاله مجدهم در حیرت الابرار کوید شعر کیم بار دیسین بیرله همواره ایتینك
دای را اولتورتونك دیوارانیننك ∴ و متعدی بعضی از الفاظ بدو نوع استعمال میشود مثل اولتورماق
بمعنی نشستن که تعدی نیز را اولتورتماق و اولتورغوزماق و تعدی کورماك بمعنی دیدنرا کورساتماك و کود
کوزرماك میخوانند و دو علامت متعدی هم کاهی در یك صیغه اتفاق می افتد مثل تیکورماك بمعنی
رسانیدن که تای قرشت بران الحاق نموده تیکورتماك میکویند چنانکه در سد سکندری بمعنی تکلم
وحده فرماید شعر مغانی سیناهینی جان ملکیدین ∴ نی جان ملکیدین لامکان ملکیدین باتماق
بیرله تیکورتایین فوج فوج ∴ که تو دتون چریك نی حضیض فرواوج ∴ و همچنین است بیرلیماك بمعنی زده کردن
متعدی بیرلماك است اما بیرلیورماك هم میخوانند لا ادری شعر تیریکنی اولتورور کامم تینك
بیرلیتورماك اولوکنی مشکل ایرور و همکی این قواعد سماعیست بدانکه مصادر چون بمیم ضمیر متکلم
وحده اضافه شوند نظر بقاعده کلیه که در ذیل سیم چهارم از مبنا ششم نکارش خواهد یافت باید حرف اخر
علامت مصدر که میم است اضافه شود در آنصورت افاده معنی مصدر میکند مثل آلماغیم یعنی گرفتنم و کیلماکیم
یعنی آمدنم اما اکر بضم غین و کاف مذکور شوند افاده معنی مضارع منفی خواهد کرد مثل آلماغوم یعنی نخواهم
گرفت و کیلماکوم یعنی نخواهم آمد و غوم و کوم از جمله علامات جداکانه اند که در ذیل ابواب هم مذکور خواهد
شد خاتمه بدانکه قافی و کافی بودن مصادر و اسماء مصادر سماعیست اما اشتقاق صیغ انها قیاسیست یعنی انچه
از مصادر قافیست البته صیغش با قاف و غین و انچه کافیست با کاف اشتقاق مییابد مقام بحث اکر کویند که
چکونه است که ایلماك بمعنی بند و دام است کافیست و ایلماق بمعنی گرفتن و ایلیتماق بمعنی گرفتار شدن با صیغ مشتقه
قافیست جواب کوئیم که ایلیشماك بمعنی بند شدن مصدر ایلماك است که کافی است و ایلماق و ایلیتماق که

قافی اند مصادر جداکانه اند اما در معنا بیکدیکر نزدیکند اکر کویند که چکونه است که بیشیغ بمعنی پخته بلفظ کاف
شده و بیشماك که مصدر انست با صیغ مشتقه کافیست جواب کوئیم که این کلمه اکرچه خلاف قیاس واقع شده اما قول
استعمالست چنانکه در لسان عرب نیز ازین نوع کلمات شاذه هست فایده انچه اتراك روم و ایران قافی و کافی
مصادررا بسیار ملحوظ نمیدارند و بعضی از مصادررا کیف ما اتفق مذکور مینمایند چنانکه ایرماك بمعنی رسیدنرا
فضولی بغدادی علیه الرحمه با کاف مذکور ساخته و هوهذا باملائه الرومیه شعر خوش شدم ایرماك و لعدن
وصلنه پیراهن کبی شکه الوعماك استیرتك که اباغ دامن کبی ∴ و سعدالدین صفای رومی که منشی دانشمندی بوده
در تاریخ آل عثمان این مصدررا با قاف نا یمعنی بیان کرده و تا ایرماق که بمعنی نهر آب هم آمده مجنس ساخته و کفته
لب جویه وادب روم ایلی نامدارلرینی تعمیم ایتدکلری شقاق مقامندن ایرماقی کبی ایرماق کنارنده دعوت
ایلدی یعنی فلان پاشا بلك هنر رفته نامداران روم ایلی را بسبب رسیدن از مقام شقاقی که تعمیم کرده بودند
بکنار نهر دعوت کرد و عدم تعمید انجماعت بقاف و کاف مصادر بسبب انست که از بسیار صیغ ایشان قاف و کاف
محذوفست مثل انکه آلغان را آلن و کیلکان را کیلن و آلغوچی را الیچی و کیلکوچی را کیلیچی میکویند و ذکر ملخذ کاف
همان از مصادر اتفاق می افتد و هرکاه تخلفی در آن واقع شود مستلزم منقصتی نخواهد بود بر خلاف لغت جغتایه
که اکر مصدر قافی با کاف یا کافی با قاف مذکور شود سرایت بجمیع صیغ نموده معانی متناقضه از آن تولید خواهد
یافت باین جهة ایرادی در لغت جغتای مضبوط و مرعی است و نیز اتراك روم مصادررا هرکاه اضافه بیا متکلم
بعضی از حروفرا نماینده حرف اخر علامت مصدررا اعم از انکه قاف باشد یا کاف از برای تخفیف کلام ساقط می
سازند چنانکه المماق بمعنی گرفتن را میکویند که المامی یعنی گرفتنش و آلمادین یعنی از گرفتن و کیلماك بمعنی آمدن
میکویند که کیلماسی یعنی آمدنش و کیلمادین یعنی از آمدن و این الفاظ بمعنی نفی نیز استعمال میشود چنانکه
در ذیل باب هفتم در بیان نفی مفصلا با شواهد مذکور خواهد شد اما هرکاه با حروف قید استعمال شوند
افاده معنی اثبات میکنند چنانکه کویند آلماغه یعنی بکرفتن که مخفف آلماقغه است و کیلماکا یعنی بآمدن که
مخفف کیلماککا است و همچنین میکویند آلمالی دور یعنی کرفتنی است و کیلمالی دور یعنی آمدنیست و نیز صیغه متکلم
مع الغیر فعل ماضی که مصطلح و معمول به طایفه جغتای و عموم اتراك روم و ایرانست مثل ایلادوق یعنی
کردیم و یغلادوق یعنی کریه کردیم چون با بعضی از ضمایر و علامات انضمام یابد افاده معنی مصدر میکند مثل ایلادوغم
یعنی کردنم و اغلادوغم یعنی کریه کردنم الشاهد علیه من فضولی باملائه الرومیه شعر آه ایلادوکوم ...
ایچوندر شقان اغلادوغم غنچه خندانلق ایچوندر ∴ و همچنین است توکدوك یعنی ریختم توکدوکچه یعنی ... چنانکه فضولی
کوید شعر توکدوکچه تمامی غمنك اول آستانه ایچره ∴ پر پیرده ام اسیر که تو پراغی قان ایچره ∴ و ازین نوع است
و ازین نوع است اولدوق یعنی شدیم و اولدوغم یعنی شدنم و بودنم الشاهد علیه من فضولی شعر
فغان کیم باغریمنك اول لاله رخ تمازا ولدوغی بیلمز جکر برکا لمسنده داغ نیهان اولدوغی بیلمز. فصل دویم
در اسماء مصادر و آن سماعیست و بر دو نوع است نوع اول مختصاتند که همان معنی اسم مصدررا مفید اند از انجمله بیمك
انست که با تای قرشت می باشد مثل اونوت بمعنی فراموش و اویات بمعنی خجالت و بعضی با قاف و غین مستعمل است

مثل بوبروق یعنی فرمان و آلداغ یعنی فریب و بعضی با کاف نیز وارد شده است مثل بیلیلیت بمعنی اثر و تیلوك
بمعنی سوراخ و بعضی با شین متداول گشته مثل اوروش بمعنی جنگ و یوروش بمعنی رفتار و توروش بمعنی ثبات و
قیام و اوچوش بمعنی پرواز و برخی با میم مصطلح است مثل اولوم بمعنی مرگ و یولوم بمعنی معبر آب و بعضی با نون
و جیم مذکور است مثل سوکونج بمعنی شنام و ساغینج بمعنی اندیشه و خیال و قورقونج بمعنی خوف و برخی با لام
مشهور است مثل سیورغال بمعنی بخشش و احسان و یاساک بمعنی صف منتظم و مرتب و بعضی با نون استعمال می‌شود
مثل بیغین بمعنی جمعیت و یاغین بمعنی باران و بعضی با لفظ غو و کو واقع شده مثل یارغو بمعنی تفریق و سورغو بمعنی
و آلغو بمعنی اخذ و بیرکو بمعنی دهش و بعضی بدو سه وجه مستعمل است مثل الغوبیرکو و آلمش بیرش بمعنی داد و ستد
و آلیغ ساتیغ و الیش ساتیش یعنی خرید و فروش و قیلیغ و قیلیش بمعنی فعل و کردار و نظایر اینها بسیار است
نوع دویم از الفاظ مشترکه اند و آن لفظ غور و کور است مثل چیقغور یعنی در آمدن چنانکه گویند شعر
کور کالیج اول یوزنی باشیمغه اوردی یوزینی بلا کور که چیقغور کوز باشیمغه بلالار کیلتوریدو همت
تیناغور یعنی بی‌آسایش و بیقرار الشاهد علیه شعر محبتیم از ره‌مخانا نیدا بولغای کاشکی دردی اینك
تیناغور یجانیدا بولغای کاشکی و اید و علامت در بعضی الفاظ افاده معنی فاعل میکند چنانکه در باب ...

باب دوم

در بیان اسم فاعل مذکور خواهد شد باب دویم در بیان فعل ماضی و آن بر سه قسم است قسم اول علامات
که بمعنی ماضی موضوع‌اند و آن بر دو نوع است نوع اول دی و تی است و آن مشتمل است بر شش علامت که بر
بیست و چهار وجه استعمال میشود علامت اول دی و تی است که علامت مفرد مغایب است مثل آلدی یعنی گرفت
و کیتتی یعنی رفت دیگر دیلار و تیلار است که علامت تثنیه و جمع مغایب است مثل آلدیلار یعنی گرفتند و کیتتیلار
یعنی رفتند دیگر دینك و دونك و تینك و تونك است که علامت مفرد مخاطب است مثل آلدینك یعنی گرفتی
و اوردونك یعنی زدی و کیتتینك یعنی رفتی و توتتونك یعنی گرفتی دیگر دینکیز و دینکلار و دونکوز
و دونکلار و تینکیز و تینکلار و تونکوز و تونکلار است که علامات تثنیه و جمع مخاطب است مثل آلدینکیز
و آلدینکلار یعنی گرفتید و اوردونکوز و اوردونکلار یعنی زدید و کیتتینکیز و کیتتینکلار یعنی رفتید و توتتونکوز
و توتتونکلار یعنی گرفتید دیگر دیم و دوم و تیم و توم که علامات متکلم وحده است مثل آلدیم یعنی گرفتم
و اوردوم یعنی زدم و کیتتیم یعنی رفتم و توتتوم یعنی گرفتم دیگر دوق و دوق و توق و دوك و توك است که علامات متکلم
مع الغیر است مثل آلدوق یعنی گرفتیم و ساتتوق یعنی فروختیم و کیلدوك یعنی آمدیم و کیتتوك یعنی رفتیم
جهت اختلاف حروف و حرکات نهاده مبنا ششم در باب ابلا مسطور خواهد شد و گاه علامات متکلم مع الغیر
هست که جزء کلمه واقع میشود مثل توتوق بمعنی حایل و پرده و خونوك بمعنی خرگاه و اوتوك بمعنی کفش و موزه
قاعده موافق محاورات اتراك روم و ایران هرگاه علامات متکلم مع الغیر فعل ماضی با بعضی از ضمایر انضمام یابد
معنی موضوع له از او موضوع گشته افاده معنی مصدر خواهد کرد چنانکه در ذیل باب اول در بیان مصادر
تحریر یافت و بمعنی غیر متکلم مع الغیر نیز می‌آید چنانکه گویند یلادوك خانلر یعنی جفا نمودن
الشاهد علیه من فضولی علیه الرحمه ما بلاده الرومیه شعر ایله عشا مر جفا ...

صانمه کیم ضایع اولوبا یلادوکنك احسانلر و از این نوع است کوردوکنك کونکلم یعنی دلم که دیده بودی
چنانکه فضولی گوید شعر توتوشدی غم اودینه شاد کوردوکنك کونکلوم مقید اولدی اول ازادکوردنك
کونکلوم نوع دویم لفظ مان است مثل آلیبان یعنی گرفته و کیتیبان یعنی رفته و یلبان یعنی کرده الشاهد
علی الاخیر شعر چهره یا پیشك خسته جانیمنی آنکا زار ایلابان زلف سیغدینك تیلیه کونکلومنی
گرفتار ایلا نان و این لفظ بضمایر و روابط هیچ وجه اضافه نمیشود و اغلب انست که لفظ بان را مخفف ساخته
بمان بسا که اکتفا میکنند و آلیب و کیتیب و ایلاب می‌گویند الشاهد علی الاخیر شعر کاتب صنع چو
کهیکا پرایشنی رقم ایلاب سبز خطلار بحی غه بیر بی قضا منهم ایلاب و هرگاه خواهند که ضمایر منفصله و بعضی از
روابط استعمال نمایند در آن صورت الف و نون را از آخر مان ساقط سازند چنانکه گویند آلیبمن یعنی گرفته‌ام
و آلیب تور یعنی گرفته است و آلیب ایدی یعنی گرفته بود قسم دویم الفاظ مشترکه اند و آن بر دو نوع است
اول آنست که در بعضی جا افاده معنی مفعول و بعضی جا افاده معنی ماضی مجهول میکند و آن مشتمل است بر دو علامت
علامت اول میش است که ما بمعنی الماضی مثل آلمیش یعنی گرفته و اورمیش یعنی زده و قیلمیش یعنی کرده
المفعول و الماضی مثل آلینمیش یعنی گرفته شده و اورولمیش یعنی زده شده و این لفظ با ضمایر متصله و منفصله و
از روابط استعمال میشود مثل المیش من و المیشام یعنی گرفته‌ام و المیش سین و المیشانك یعنی گرفته و المیشدور
یعنی گرفته است و المیش ایدی یعنی گرفته بود و هکذا الحواتها و در اخر قسم دویم مضارع نیز در آمده افاده معنی ماضی
مثل الادورمیش یعنی میگرفته و اورادورمیش یعنی میزده و قیلادورمیش یعنی میکرده علامت دویم لفظ غان و کان است
که در باب اول در بیان مصادر مذکور شد اما بمعنی الماضی شعر تعالی الله زهی قدر و زهی ایمان جنتنی الیدوز لیلغان
کل یاشونغان برك کل بوتنكان شکر آندا یعنی تعالی الله چه قدر است در بستان الجنت است که در انجا گل واشده و
گل پنهان شده و شکر رویید اما بمعنی المفعول و الماضی المجهول مثل یاشورولغان یعنی پنهان شده و بوتکاریلکان یعنی
رویانیده شده و این صیغه در محاورات اتراك روم و ایران بتخفیف غین و کاف مستعمل است چنانکه در ذیل مصادر
مذکور شد و علامات انها که غان و کان باشد در اخر هر دو قسم مضارع نیز واقع میشود اما بمعنی الماضی
مثل اولورغان و الادورغان یعنی گرفته و کیلورکان و کیلادورکان یعنی آمده اما بمعنی المفعول و الماضی المجهول
مثل یاشونورغان و یاشونادورغان یعنی پنهان شده و بوتکاریلورکان و بوتکاریلادورکان یعنی رویانیده
و هر لفظ که الحاق یابد بالاشتراك افاده معنی فاعل و مصدر هم میکند چنانکه در ذیل مصادر در باب اول
نگارش یافت و در تحت اسم فاعل هم بیان خواهد شد و در معنی مصدری همان ضمایر متصله استعمال میشود مثل
یاشونغانی و یاشونورغانی و یاشونادورغانی یعنی پنهان شدنش و بوتکانی و بوتارکانی و بوتادورکانی یعنی
رویدنش و ضمایر منفصله مستعمل نیست نوع دویم صیغه مضارع منفی است مثل آلماس یعنی نمیگیرد و نمی‌گیرد
یعنی واقع میشود اما بمعنی ماضی منفی هم می‌آید یعنی نگرفته چنانکه گوید شعر شکنج طره سیدین کیم کونکلوم
بنفشه تورورا ما هنوز اچیلماس ایدی غنچه ناییده بدانکه فعل مضارع چون با روابط ماضی استعمال شود حکایت
حال ماضیه میکند مثل کیلور ایردی و کیلادور ایردی الشاهد علی الثانی شعر کیلادور ایردی

جیسم یعنی کوزکاج تایدی ای نوایی کچیتیم یعنی نادان او تروه باب سیم در بیان فعل مضارع و آن بر دو قسم است قسم اول
آنست که در آخر فعل امر رای مهمله در می آرند و آن بر دو نوع است نوع اول سماعیست و آن فعل امر مسکونة الاخر است
مثل ال یعنی بگیر و آت یعنی بینداز و بیر یعنی بده و چیک یعنی بکش که اینها را متحرک الاخر نموده بر رای مهمله منضم ساخته
اما حرکت حروف اخر اینها در تحت ضابطه نیست زیرا که سکون حروف اخر بعضی بضمه و برخی بفتحه تبدیل می یابد مثل اینکه ال
آلور بضم لام و آت را آتار بفتح تا و بیر را بیرور بضم را و چیک را چیکار بفتح کاف استعمال مینمایند و چنان نیست که
مضموم را مفتوح یا مفتوح را مضموم توان گفت و در این نوع تابع طریق استعمال می باید بود نوع دویم قیاسیست
و آن فعل امر متحرکة الاخر است مثل ایستا یعنی بخواه و یو یعنی بشو و دی یعنی بگو که اینها را بدون تغیر حرف حرکت
بر رای مهمله افزوده میگویند که ایستار یعنی میخواهد و یور یعنی میشوید و دیر یعنی میگوید و این هر دو نوع بمعنی مصدر
و فاعل هم می آیند چنانکه معنی مصدری با شواهد در ذیل باب اول در بیان مصادر مذکور شد و معنی
فاعل در تحت باب چهارم در بیان اسم فاعل نگارش خواهد یافت قسم دویم مشتمل است بر سه نوع تفصیلی نوع اول
مبتنی است بر سه قاعده قاعده اولی آنست که فعل امر مسکونة الاخر باشد حرف اخر را مفتوح و لفظ دور بر آن ملحق
مینمایند مثل آل و کیل که ازا آلادور و کیلادور میگویند یعنی میگیرد و می آید قاعده دویم آنست که اگر فعل امر
مفتوحة الاخر باشد مثل ایستا و اسرا و یا مضمومة الاخر باشد مثل یو و او و تو یای حطی بر آن ملحق و از بر لفظ
دور اضافه کرده میگویند که ایستایدور یعنی میخواهد و اسرایدور یعنی نگاه میدارد و یویدور یعنی میشوید و
اویدور یعنی میخواند قاعده سیم آنست که فعل امر مکسورة الاخر مثل دی و بی چون یا یست بدستور نوع دویم حرف
یا بر آن انضمام یابد و در بعضوعت التقا یاءین واقع میشد لهذا لفظ دور بر همان فعل ملحق ساخته اسرا
باشباع کسره تکلم کرده میگویند که دیدور یعنی میگوید و سیدور یعنی میخورد بحث اگر گویند که مسلم تماق
بمعنی منع کردن در وزن با دیماک بمعنی گفتن و یماک بمعنی خوردن بحسب ظاهر مساویست بچه جهت مضارع
دیماک و یماک دیر و دیدور و یر و سیدور و مضارع تماق تیبار و تیبادور می آید چنانکه گوید الشاهد
علی الاول شعر خالیسینی نیلاب نهان تو دتون نوائی خسته کیم ؛ تیبا اشکینی آه امر ایسغلادا کرا هین تیبار
الشاهد علی الثانی شعر بادورها کو یونکا یوق اختیاریم :: مینی هر نیچه کیم کونکلوم تیبادور :: جواب
گوییم که تماق چون باشباع کسره تلفظ میشود از جمله ثنائی و یای آن جزء کلمه است باین جهت مضارع آن تیبار و
تیبادور می آید و دیماک و یماک چون بلا اشباع تکلم میشود داخل احادی و حرف ثانی اینها که یای حطی باشد
بیان کسره است لهذا مضارع اینها دیر و دیدور و یر و سیدور می آید نوع دویم الفاظ مشترکه اند از انجمله غای
وکای و سوی و دیلت است که در آخر فعل امر در آید مثل آلغای و آلسون و آلدیلت یعنی بگیرد و کیلگای و کیلسون
کیدیلت یعنی بیاید و در بعضی مقام افاده معنی مفرد مغایب از فعل امر میکند چنانکه در ذیل امر مذکور خواهد شد
دیگر آنست که صیغه امر مسکونة الاخر را مفتوحة الاخر ساخته اند مثل تیشا یعنی سوراخ کند چنانکه در سنگلاخ کندی
در وصف سنان گوید شعر اوچی قطره سودین تاپیب چاشنی ؛ تیشانک کرینشا قطره سوتاشنی و همچنین است
تاربا یعنی بهم اعت شود چنانکه لطفی بطرزی جناس گفته شعر تا ایشیم توشتی بر آغزی تارایله ؛ کونکلوم ایلد

ساچی بزتارایله ؛ کوز توتار مین کیم کوزوم نینک سوی دین ؛ کونکلیدا تخم محبت تاریله ؛ و این صیغه بمعنی مصدر
و امر غایب و فعل لازم نیز می آید چنانکه معنی مصدری در ذیل باب اول با شاهد مرقوم شد و معنی امر غایب در تحت باب
ششم و معنی حال در باب هشتم مذکور خواهد شد فائده بدانکه علامت قسم دویم از فعل مضارع را که عبارت
از لفظ دور باشد چون با لفظ میش که از علامات ماضی است مرکب و ازابر منتسبات فعلی اضافه نمایند معنا
معنی استقبال می کند مثل ایسادورمیش بولغای یعنی میپوشیده باشد و قونغادورمیش بولغای یعنی از جا
میکنده باشد و قیلادورمیش بولغای یعنی میکرده باشد چنانکه در نسایم المحبه در ذکر شیخ ابوالحسن
خرقانی گوید که آنی آسماندین پرتار اتیانک سپله آسمیش بولغایلار و یسلی ایسادورمیش بولغای کیم بالادینی
و جیلادری قونغادورمیش بولغای و دریا لاردینی باشنه تیلادورمیش بولغای لار یردین تیرا تا اسماعها
باب چهارم در بیان اسم فاعل و آن بر دو قسم است قسم اول آنست که بر معنی فاعل موضوع اند و آن مشتمل است بر دو نوع (باب چهارم)
نوع اول قیاسیست و آن مبنی بر دو علامت است علامت اول غوچی و کوچی است که در آخر فعل امر در می آید مثل
آلغوچی یعنی گیرنده و کیلگوچی یعنی آینده تخطئه طالع هروی گوید در بیان معنی الغوچی که هرگاه بمعنی فاعل
بمعنی مصدر می آید و صیغه مبالغه نیز واقع می شود غلط کرده است غوچی و کوچی همان بر معنی فاعل وضع شده
و افاده معنی دیگر نمیکنند فایده اتراک روم و ایران چون خواهند که اسم فاعل بنا کنند غو و کو را از اسم فاعل ساقط
و حرف اخر ا بتحرکات بر حرف جیم مضاف مینمایند چنانکه آلغوچی و کیلگوچی و توتغوچی را آلیچی و کیلیچی و توتوچی گو
و علی هذا القیاس علامت دویم لفظ چی با جیم عجمی است که در اخر اسماء ذوات و غیرها در می آید مثل اوچی یعنی تیر گر
الشاهد علیه شعر بوزوق قبر یمنی کوزکان اوچی دکا ینغه اوخشاتغای ؛ فراقینک اوقی دین اندا کوزکو
سپکان و پرمرلان ؛ و همچنین است ایلچی یعنی کسی که مردم را بمهمانی طلب کند و بتیکچی یعنی نویسنده و چون در آخر
مصادر واقع شود آنرا بمعنی مفعول مصدری کردانند چنانکه در تاریخ بابری مذکور است که بابر چهار نیانی دولت
خواهلیق قیلسیز کا قشو لماقچی بولدی یعنی همراه شدنی و رفاقت کردنی شد و نیز گوید که یا عی لار زینت ایسنکا
استلا غماقچی ایدی ولت یعنی سوار شدنی بودیم وگاه هست که زاید بر کلام نیز استعمال میشود چنانکه در صفات
چهارم در ذیل زواید مذکور خواهد شد نوع دویم سماعیست و آن بر چند گونه است اول قول است که در آخر بعض
از الفاظ در می آید مثل قراول و یساول یعنی دیدبان و یساول یعنی ناظم و سازنده و بکاول یعنی سفرهچی و توقعاول
یعنی مستحفظ و اشباه اینها دیگر آنست که آخر امر مسکونة الاخر را مفتوح ساخته بر لفظ غان و کان می افزایند و آن
افاده معنی استدامت و شدت می کند مثل توتاغان یعنی دایم گیرنده و چاپاغان یعنی دایم تازنده و اوراغان
یعنی دایم زننده و کولاکان یعنی دایم خنده کننده و کیساکان یعنی بسیار برنده و ما یکون من هذا القبیل دیگر
جاق است مثل یاسانجاق که بمعنی خود ساز و خود آرا باشد چنانکه در تنبیهات محبوب القلوب گوید که یاسانجاق
مردانه بولمه سرکوپلات پروانه بولماس دیگر آنست که تیلاکا را که از الفاظ مشترکة المعنی است محذوف الکاف
و جیم بر آن ملحق ساخته تیلاچی گفته همان بمعنی سائل استعمال نموده اند چنانکه در لیلی مجنون گوید شعر
نون در کیشنکا تیلاچی نکی ؛ ایکیندا اتر سید و دیلنکی ؛ طابشاذاست قسم دویم الفاظ مشترکه اند و آن

بر دو نوع است نوع اول قیاسی است وان بر سه کونه است اول قسم اول فعل مضارع است مثل اچار یعنی میکشاید اچنا
بمعنی کشاینده نیز می آید چنانکه کوید شعر نالاریمن اچار بولسا یوز اولوغ بیزاد • بلبلنه نی ئانک کل اچلود
ضلله فریاد • و همچنین است کورار یعنی می بیند و ایشیتور یعنی میشنود و آیتور یعنی میکوید و آنکلار یعنی
می فهمد تا هر چه این لفظها را در مقاله مجد هم از تحفة الابرار بمعنی فاعل فرماید شعر لطف بیله ایلادی
انسان سیوقین بولیدا قیلدی سلیمان نبی یردی کورار کوزنی ایشیتور قولاغ آیتور تیل عطر نی انکلار دماغ
و بمعنی مصدر هم می آید چنانکه در باب اول در بیان مصادر ترقیم یافت دویم لفظ غان و کان است مثل یکان
و یرکان و ساچغان و ترکان که بمعنی کوینده و دهنده و افشاننده و چیننده در لسان الطیر در وادی حیرت
کوید شعر اول دیدی دیکان او زی یرکان او زی • بذل را ساچغان او زی ترکان او زی • و همچنین است یولغان
بمعنی شوینده چنانکه فرماید شعر بو تشنه مظلوم قانیغه قالیب یردی بهر آنی یوغان بحر اشکیم موجی
کولالتامش • و نظیر اینست جومورغان بمعنی غرق کننده و اوچورغان بمعنی پراننده چنانکه در باب هم
از محبوب القلوب در ذکر عشق کوید که عجب دود و سیع ایکرمی یوز عقل و هوش کیمه سین جومورغان
و تاعجب دود رفیع هر تیغی مینک زهد و تقوی باشین اوچورغان و بمعنی مصدر هم می اید چنانکه در ذیل باب
اول در بیان مصادر مذکور شد فایده بدانکه اتراک روم و ایران بقاعده که در ذیل مصادر بیان شد این صیغه
بتخفیف غین و کاف استعمال مینمایند مثل اینکه قیلغان بمعنی کننده را قیلن میکویند الشاهد علیه فضولی
بالملاء الرومیه شعر رعنالیغ ایله قامت شمشادی قیلن یاد • و لمی مجبل رخ امانیکی کوردکج و
نظیر اینست یلاکان بمعنی کننده که اترا ایلین بفتح یای حطی مذکور مینمایند ایضا منه ره شعر فضولی
ملامت ایلین سیدر سیلمزی • که بازار خون رسوا الرند ننک و نام اولمز • و این لفظ در معانی مصدری و
غیره با لغت جغتای انطباق دارد تتمه ذکر در لغت جغتای این علامت در اخر هردو قسم مضارع در می آید
مثل تازارغان و تازادورغان و ایورولادورکان که شاهد ثانی را بمعنی حضر کننده در عنوان داستان مراد
و رسیدن او با دمن کوید که ارمنیه تاغی کمربدا خارا تازادورغان ایل عجزین کوروب خارا تازارغه کمر
حسب اینکافی و شاهد بر رابع را بمعنی کردنده فرماید شعر چورولب سونکا کلادیم اولیش قوبون
اراغاشات • باشینغه ایورولادورکان تنیم غباری بیله • و بمعنی مصدر هم می اید چنانکه در ذیل
مصادر مذکور شد و در بعضی جا بمعنی ماضی و در بعضی جا بمعنی مفعول می آید سیم صیغه مفرد مغایب
از فعل مضارع منفی مثل اچماس که بمعنی نمیکشاید باشد اما چون با منتسبات نفی استعمال می شود بمعنی فاعل
منفی می آید چنانکه کویند اچماس بولسا یعنی نکشاینده باشد و بمعنی مصدر منفی هم مستعمل است چنانکه
در ذیل مصادر با شواهد مرقوم شد نوع دویم سماعیست و آن بر دو کونه است اول غور و کور مثل اوچغور
بمعنی تیز پر و تینغور بمعنی ستایش کننده و او تکور بمعنی کذرنده و همچنین است او یغا نماغور یعنی بیدار نشونده الشاهد
علیه شعر دیر میل یلای سه پیر صاحب نظر نینک کر دینی • ا کیم ایغانماغور نچیم کوز اچماس ایقودین ویدی
بعضی الفاظ افاده معنی اسم مصدر میکند چنانکه در ذیل باب اول در بیان اسماء مصادر مذکور شد تیزغون و

کونه است مثل غا و غون یعنی تعاقب کننده و لونکون یعنی کننده الشاهد علی الاول من سبعه سیاره شعر سود
دیلار کیمدین شتاب بیله • تیزغا و غونلا اضطراب بیله • و چون او تکون یعنی سبکاز هم هست شاهد ثانی بطریق ایما
مرد معنی دانو بوده شعر تیر باران غمینک جان و کونکول دین او تتی • افغا قدمی بلا بولماغین اریمیش او تکون • و نیز
فرماید شعر تیر باران فراق احبا جانی دین او تار • هیچ یامغور موندین ابا او تکون اولغا یموایکین • و مثل ایغت
چابغون بمعنی اسب تیز دو و باد و تند شدید و بمعنی مفعول هم می اید چنانکه در ذیل مفعول مذکور خواهد شد
و کاه هست که لفظ چی را که از علامات قیاسیه فاعلست بر آن الحاق مینمایند چنانکه شاهد بر اول در ذکر شیخ
الملوک در ذکر بهرام چوبینه کوید که بهرام پرویزغه تاو غونچی سپار یب او زی پادشا هلیقغه اولتوردی و شاهد
بر ثانی در لیلی مجنون در وصف حال مجنون کوید شعر بو نکته لار ایلابان شماره • او تکونچی لار ایلابان نظاره

باب پنجم

باب پنجم در بیان اسم مفعول وان مشتمل است بر دو قسم قسم اول الفاظیست که فی نفسه بمعنی مفعول موضوع اند مثل
سینوق بمعنی شکسته و مکوور و بیتیک بمعنی مکتوب و این نوع صیغ صفت مشبهه و اسم مصدر نیز واقع می شوند
مثل یقوق بمعنی خراب و منهدم و تیلوک بمعنی سوراخ و بویروق بمعنی فرمان قسم دویم الفاظ مشترکه اند و آن دو
نوع است نوع اول میش است که در بعضی جا افاده مفعول و در بعضی جا افاده ماضی میکند چنانکه در ذیل ماضی
بیان شد نوع دویم غان و کان است که در بعضی جا افاده معنی ماضی و در بعضی جا افاده معنی مفعول میکند
بمعنی الماضی کما ذکر نا بمعنی المفعول مثل قیلغان یعنی شده و تاپغان یعنی یافته چنانکه در باب هم از محبوب القلوب
در ذکر عشق کوید که بو تعریف قیلغان عشق معشوق وجودی بیله قایم دور و تواد تاپغان حالاتغه منسوب و
دایم و نظیر اینست بیتیکار یعنی مکتوب و نوشته چنانکه در وصف خود نیز دلان کوید که بمعنی چنانین
جاوالله بیتیکان کشاف کمان قیلغای و بمعنی مصدر و فاعل هم می آید چنانکه نکارش یافت قاعده بدانکه
اتراک روم و ایران این صیغه را بقاعده که در ذیل مصادر بیان شد بتخفیف مذکور مینمایند همچنانکه اولکان یعنی مرده
و اولغان بمعنی شده را اولن میکویند و شاهد بر معنی اخیر فضولی بغدادی کوید بالملاء الرومیه شعر خراب
اولن کونکل ای بت سننک مقامنکدر • تغافل ایلمه بیر قلچ داشیله ابادایت • و همچنین یانغان بمعنی سوخته را یانن
میکویند ایضا منه شعر دوزخه کیرمز ستمنکدن یانن • تا بلاجت دکل اهل عذاب تتمیم ذکر این علامت در لغت جغتای
در اخر هر دو قسم مضارع نیز در آمده افاده همان معانی میکند مثل تو تولورغان و تو تولادورغان یعنی کرفته شده
و تبیلورکان و بیتیلادورکان یعنی نوشته شده و بالاشتراک بمعنی مصدر و فاعل هم می آیند چنانکه در ذیل باب
اول و باب چهارم مذکور شد نوع سیم لیغ و لوغ و لیک و لوک است که بمعنی یای نسبت و یای مصدری و غیره اند
اما با بعضی الفاظ افاده معنی مفعول میکند مثل چیرماشلیغ یعنی پیچیده الشاهد علیه شعر رقعه دور
چیرماشلیغ مضمون صورتین • هیچ کیم ایتمادی عنوانی نینک مضمونیدین • و نظیر اینست کوموکلوک یعنی
مدفون چنانکه در خسرو شیرین در اژدها کشتن فرهاد کوید شعر کوموکلوک یرکا تا شید ور شبه کون • که
با روزن ایچره مینک باتمان دین اغزون • و ازین قبیل است بیتیک لیک یعنی مکتوب و نوشته شده چنانکه در خسرو
شیرین فرماید شعر قلیبدا داغی ایردی بتیک لیک • که اول بواسم دین تاپمیش اتیک لیک • و لفظ کوموکلوک

وبتیلیک لیک دد اینمقام مرادف کومولکان وکومولکان وکومولیش وبتیلکان وبتیلمیش استا تا اتبیلیک
بمعنی مفعول نیست بمعنی مدت وتیزی است نوع چهارم غون وکونا است مثل توتغون یعنی محبوس ومنقبض و بیرغون
بمعنی خسته وصبر کردن بمعنی ماندن ومطرود وا ینعلامت در بعضی الفاظ افاده معنی فاعل میکند چنانکه در ذیل
فاعل مرحوم شد باب ششم در بیان فعل الامر نحوی که در ذیل باب فاعل نگارش یافت صیغه مفرد مخاطب از فعل امر تا یه صیغ
جمیع علامات قایم و موتس را فقط کا هست که از برای مزید شان وتزیین بیان عیل وکیل بران ملحق مینماید
الشاهد علی الاول شعر قراکوزوم کیل مردم لوق اعیدی فن قیلغیل کوزوم قراسیدا مردم کبی وطن قیلغیل
الشاهد علی الثانی [illegible] سیاره شعر یا بوتنتیش ترکینی ایتکیل یا کم سیلکاج باشینک آلیب کیتکیل
والحاق این [illegible] ییر ببت اما مخصوص صیغه مفرد مخاطب از فعل امر و نهی است مثل قیلغیل وقیلماغیل واتیکیل
وایتماکیل وکا هست که حرف لام را در عیل وکیل بنون تبدیل مینمایند مثل تیلاکین که بمنزله تیلاکیل واقع
شده یعنی طلب کن چنانکه کوید شعر دیمانک که تماشلاری محراپیدا تیلاکین منکا که تماشلاری
محرابی وقت نور ود تیلاکیم و همچنین است دیکین که بعوض دیکیل ذکر شده و هو هذا شعر مین و منع دیری کم مرا
شایل آندا شه ساری ایقماس دیکین ای شیخ همتین مویا شوکت تین ایرکین مو واوزبکیه اغلب این نوع تکلم نمایند
فایده بدانکه صیغه مفرد مخاطب از فعل امر که اخر آن رای مهمله ما قبل مفتوح باشد از قبیل بار یعنی برو واختار
یعنی تفحص کن و قایتار یعنی برکردان کاه هست که حرف راء مضموم ساخته واو در اخر آن در می آرند چنانکه ذکر
غزل مذکور است شعر ای صبا اواره کونکلوم ایستا یوهر ان باروو وادی و تاغ و بیابانلاردین پریرلخشادو
تا پاکه آبی جونالسانک هر قایان غانم ایسا تا شینه ایورول قویون دیلت داغی آلداب تمایتار و نخلنه نصیری
این لغت را در دیباچه کتاب خود بمعنی مستقبل ذکر کرده وشعر اول را شاهد آورده و طالع هروی کفته که ند
او اخر جمع موضوع از برای امر غایب واو مضموم جهت طلب تاکید بکتابت در می آرند هرده و قول از خطا ناشی و
طبع از قول آن متحاشی است فایده بدانکه صیغه مفرد مخاطب امر کاه خواهند که تثنیه وجمع بنا کنند اکر فعل امر
مسکون الاخر باشد حرف اخر را متحرک ساخته نون وکاف ساکنین بر آن الحاق می کنند مثل کورونک وتوتونک
و آلینک وکیلینک وعلت اختلاف حرکات او رونک والینک در ذیل مبنا شش در باب ملا نکارش خواهد
یافت واکر متحرک الاخر باشد بدون تغییر حرف وحرکت اخر بر نون وکاف اضافه مینمایند مثل باشلانک
یعنی شروع کنید واوقونک یعنی بخوانید ودینک یعنی بکوئید وکاه هست که از برای مزید شان مخاطب وجمع
کلام نون وکاف خطاب را ترتیب داده بد و نوع دیکر استعمال مینمایند نوع اول انست که کاف بعد از نون را
بمناسبت مقام بقاعده که در باب ملا بیان خواهد شد مضموم یا مکسور نموده و زای هوز بران ملحق ساخته
کورونکوز وتوتونکوز والینکز وکیلینکز میکویند و هکذا اخواتها نوع دویم انست که لفظ لار که علامت
جمع حاضر وغایب است بر آن منضم ساخته کورونکلار وتوتونکلار والینکلار وکیلینکلار میخوانند الشاهد
علی الاول شعر کورونکلار عشق دشتین کیم نیم ولا دیخ یم کهی خانجش الفتین ددور کهی محلات شرار آنداقا امتا
چهار علامت است که چون بر صیغه مفرد غایب از فعل امر ملحق سازند افاده معنی استقبال هم میکند چنانکه در ذیل

باب هفتم در بیان مضارع مذکور شد علامت اول دیک است مثل اسرادیک یعنی نکهدارد الشاهد علیه
شعر کیم که کونکلین ایستا نامین عیکین تیلینی اسرادیک کیم تیلی تیغان کیشی نینک کونکلیدا آزار ایماس
و همچنین است سوردیک یعنی بپرسد واولدیک یعنی باشد ودیک بمعنی مثل ومانند هم می آید چنانکه در ذیل
مذکور خواهد شد علامت دویم سون است مثل اسراسون وسورسون وآلسون قاعده چون خواهند که
صیغه جمع مغایب بنا کنند لفظ لار که علامت جمع است بر علامت اول یا ثانی ملحق ساخته سوردیکلار و
سورسونلار میکویند الشاهد علی الاول شعر شام هجرانیم وصال اهلیغه بیلدیکه دهر ثانی سوردیکلار
نوای دیده کریانیدین و همچنین است ولدیکلار واولسونلار یعنی باشند چنانکه شاهد بر اول در بعد [illegible]
کوید شعر وطن غه یانیب خلوق اسوده دل ماری یزدین اولدیکلار راما بجل وا ینکونه علامت ضمیر از لفظ لار
که جمع است با هیچ ضمیر مرابطه انضمام نمی یابد علامت سیم غای وکای است مثل اسراغای یعنی نکهدارد و
یعنی بپرسد وکیلکای یعنی بیاید وکیتکای یعنی برود [illegible] مرادف است با اسرادیک واسراسون وسوردیک
سورسون وکیلدیک وکیلسون وکیتدیک وکیتسون علامت چهارم انست که فعل امر مسکون الاخر را مفتوح
الاخر ساخته الف را با لفظ کیراک یعنی باید مذکور سازند مثل باراشا کیراک بولغای یعنی لابد باید رفت
شا کیراک بولغای یعنی شبیه نباید باشد همچنانکه در تنبیهات محبوب القلوب در وصف عشق حقیقی کوید که قول
واضطرابلا انکا بارا شا کیراک بولغای وغلبات جذبات هم انکا اوخشا شا کیراک بولغای واز این قبیل است
کیرا کاله یعنی باید بکیرد وکیراک اورا یعنی باید بزند وعلی هذا القیاس باب هشتم در بیان نهی علامت نهی میم مفتوح که
که در اخر فعل امر در آید مثل بارما یعنی مرو وکیلما یعنی میا وکاه هست لام از نون تبدیل مینمایند مثل بارماغین
در این بحث مذکور است شعر بچه دیدیم اول صنم غه بارماغین یعنی مرو قیلما دعا ول ترک اخر بارماغین
یعنی رخت شراب موبچه کیم خوجه ای لیغ کور کوزدی ولی عقل حیرت قیلادی تیشلاب بارماغین یعنی انکشترا
وهمچنین است المانین که در این شعر بمنزله آلماغیل واقع شده شعر ای نوائی تیلاسانک دولت باقی باما
المانین دیر فنا بولیدین اسلاها وضع وميم مفتوحه کاه هست که در اخر بعضی کلمات وارد می شود اما بمعنی نهی
نمی آید وآن بر دو قسم است قسم اول انست که بدستور میم نهی در اخر فعل امر در می آید وآن سه موضع است
اول اسم جنس است مثل المأ یعنی سیب دویم بعضی از اسماء مصادر ومفعولات مثل ایکما یعنی خم و خمیده
چنانکه کوید شعر ایکما قدیمغه با قیب حسم قیل ایره و ناز دهر دیبا الحذی قامته عنانی کوژ
ونظیر اینست آسما یعنی اویزه و باسما یعنی نقش غالب زده وقاورما یعنی برشته [illegible] میم علامت مصدرات
که مصادر چون با بعضی از ضمایر استعمال نمایند قاف وکاف علامت مصدر را از برای تخفیف کلام محذوف
ساخته میم را الحاق میکنند مثل قیلماسی وکیلماسی یعنی کردنش و امدنش واین الفاظ افاده معنی
نیز میکند چنانکه کیفیت آن در بیان نفی مذکور خواهد شد قسم دویم انست که در اخر سایر الفاظ و
می شود وآن میم ضمیر متکلم وحده است که چون با لفظ غا وکا که حرف تعدی است جمع شود بعضی او قات حرف
تعدیه را محذوف و میم ضمیر را عوضا عن المحذوف مفتوح می سازند مثل خالیمغه وکونکلومکا که [illegible]

وکونکلونما میکویند چنانکه با شاهد در ذیل بیم دویم از مبنا شم مذکور خواهد شد قاعده گاه هست که
میم مفتوحه در فصل امر نیز جزو کلمه واقع میشود مثل یلما یعنی بپنه کن وسیرما یعنی برابد از نصوبت هرگاه خواهند که آن
صیغه را بمعنی نهی ادا کنند میم مفتوحه دیگر بر آن ملحق ساخته میکویند یاماما یعنی بپنه مکن وسیرماما یعنی
مریا باب هشتم در بیان نفی علامت نفی میم مفتوحه است که ما بین فصل امر و علامات صیغ واقع شود مثل آلماق یعنی نگرفتن
وکیلماماق بمعنی نیامدن وآلمادی یعنی نگرفت وکیلمادی یعنی نیامد وعلی هذا القیاس قاعده چون فصل بیتا
متولمای نامیه میکند هرگاه خواهند که صیغه مفرد مغایب منفی از ان بنا کنند بدو نوع مذکور میسازند نوع
اول انست که لفظ ماید در بر فصل امر الحاق میکنند مثل چاپماید و یعنی برق نیز نتانست ذیم بخاری
بولویتدادرد کاجودین کوزومکا هیچ نفس یوق که اوت چاپماید ور وان صیغه بمعنی ماضی منفی هم مستعمل آ
چنانکه شاهد آن در ذیل باب قیم در بیان ماضی گذشت نوع دویم آنست که لفظ ماس بر فصل امر ملحق میسازند
مثل آلماس یعنی نکرد و دیماس یعنی نمیکوید وان صیغه با لحاق بعضی از روابط بمعنی مصدر و فاعل منفی هم می آید
چنانکه در ذیل مصدر و فاعل نگارش یافت فایده رومیه ماس را در لغت خود مز با زاء معجمه مذکور میسازند
ودر معنی و مورد استعمال با لغت جغتای انطباق دارد مثل یازمز یعنی نمی نویسد و نوشتن و نوشتنی چنانکه
فضولی بغدادی بمعنی اخیر گوید شعر سینی ملک کورمدی یازمز اول ای عشقی گناه * ولی ازیلدی بویوزدین دیو ثوابه
تمیم ذکر صیغه متکلم وحده را بسه نوع استعمال مینمایند نوع اول انست که لفظ مان بر فصل امر الحاق میکنند
مثل کیسمان یعنی نمیبرم وایتمان یعنی نمیکنم قاعده گاه هست که حرف آخر فصل امر مسکونة الاخر را مفتوح ساخته
بر لفظ مان می افزایند مثل کیسامان که مرادف کیسمان باشد الشاهد علیه شعر بلا باشیمغه بسی کیلدی
قویمادیم عشقینک * کیسرایدی آخی یوق ایردی بولا بیله کیسامان * یعنی بلای بسیار بسرم آمد عشقت را ازو نگذاشتم
حالا صبح کن آنرا والا بالینها تقطع میکنم وهمچنین لیتامیدمن که بترکی رومی مرادف ایتامان وایتمان است مرادف
ایتمان باشد چنانکه فضولی بغدادی گوید باملاء الرومیه شعر ایده من ترک فضولی سر کوبین یار ینک *
نه قدر ظلم ایده سه بنکا خوشدر وطنم * یعنی ای فضولی هرگز ترک نمیکنم سر کوی یار را هر قدر ظلم کند بمن خوش است ظلم
ودر جمیع مولفات نوائی ودیوان فضولی زیاده بر این دو بیت شاهدی بنظر نرسیده من البدایع بدانکه در این
صیغه هرگاه میم را مفتوح ذکر کنند بنحویکه در ذیل قاعده فوق بیان شد افاده معنی نفی میکند اما چون میم را مکسور میکنند
سازند افاده اثبات میکند مثل اینکه گویند کیسامین یعنی میبرم وایتامین یعنی میکنم والامین یعنی میگیرم وعلی هذا
القیاس نوع دویم انست که نون را در لفظ مان مفتوح ساخته بر میم ضمیر متکلم وحده علاوه نموده میکویند کم تاپماینام
یعنی پیدا نمیکنم الشاهد علیه شعر چو خوبی نازلعا بر و تاپمانام علاج اینینک * قاشیغه مارغالی حیرانیمه
چاره ایلامینه * واین نوع در لغت جغتای قلیل الاستعمال است ودر جمیع مولفات جناب نوائی سوای این بیت شاهد
بنظر نرسیده اما بنای مکالمات اتراک روم وایران همگی بر این نوع است نوع سیم انست که لفظ ماس مین بر فصل
امر منضم شود مثل کیسماسمین وایتماسمین وتاپماسمین قاعده هرگاه میم مفتوحه جزو کلمه واقع شود مثل یاناق یعنی
بپنه چون خواهند که صیغ فعلی از آن بنا کنند مصدر را یاماماق میکویند یعنی بپنه کردن وچون بصیغه نفی تکلم کنند

میم مفتوحه دیگر علامت نفی در میانه فصل امر و علامت مصدر داخل کرده وازرا با سه میم مفتوحه ذکر کرده یاماماماق
میسازند یعنی بپنه نکردن وهمچنین است سیرماماق بمعنی بر بودن که منفی آن سیرماماماق می آید یعنی بر نبودن
وسایر صیغ را چو بنیم علامت مصدر از انها ساقط است با دو میم مفتوحه استعمال مینمایند مثل یامامادی یعنی
بپنه نکرد وسیرماماذی یعنی بر نبود وهکذا اخواتها من البدایع بدانکه دو لفظ اند که در بعضی مقام در صورت
مساوی ودر تقدیر مختلف می شوند وافاده معنی نفی واثبات هر دو می کنند وآن بر سه قسم است قسم اول
انست که صیغه مفرد مغایب منفی بدون تخفیف ومصدر مع التخفیف بضمیر مفرد مغایب اضافه شود مثل اولما
وقیلماس که مفرد مغایب منفی است واولما وقیلما که مصدر مخفف است در حالت اضافه هم بمعنی مصدر مثبت
وهم بمعنی مصدر منفی می آیند بیان سبب بدانکه در ترکی هرگاه حرف آخر کلمه ساکن باشد ضمیر آنرا یای حطی می آرند
مثل تاماش وکوز وتیش که تاماشی وکوزی وتیشی میسازند ونظیر انیست در فارسی کلمه مسکونة الاخر که ضمیر آنرا
همان شین تنها می آرند چشم ودندان ودست که چشمش ودندانش ودستش میکویند ودر ترکی هرگاه حرف آخر کلمه
مفتوح یا مضموم یا مکسور باشد ضمیر آنرا سی می آورند مثل اینکه میکویند تاماسی یعنی پدرش وکوزکوسی
یعنی آینه اش والچیسی یعنی رسولش واین لفظ بمنزله شین است که در فارسی در آخر کلمات متحرکة الاخر واقع می شود مثل
سفایش وروئیش وبینیاش وهرگاه خواهند که اولماس وقیلماس را که صیغه مفرد مغایب منفی است با ضمیر مفرد مغایب
مذکور سازند چون مسکونة الاخر اند ضمیر آنها را موافق قاعده مذکور یای حطی آورده اولماسی وقیلماسی میکویند یعنی
نشدنش ونکردنش واگر مخففات مصادر را که عبارت از اولما وقیلما باشد با ضمیر مفرد مغایب جمع کنند چون
مفتوحة الاخر اند لا محاله ضمیر آنها را سی باید آورد ودر آنصورت نیز اولماسی وقیلماسی میکویند یعنی شدنش وکردنش
پس متضمن معنی نفی واثبات هر دو خواهد بود واگر اسم باشد مثل آسما یعنی آویزه وچیکما بمعنی موزه که در سواری
میکشند بعلاوه معنی نفی واثبات مفید معنی آن اسم نیز خواهد بود چنانکه گویند آسماسی یعنی آویختنش و
نیاویختنش وآویزه اش وچیکماسی یعنی کشیدنش ونکشیدنش وموزه اش وهکذا اخواتها بمعنی النفی من نوائی علیه الرحمه
شعر عشق دین مخلصیما ایلاماس احبا بدعا * مستجاب اولماسی اینک مینی محروم نغمه تیلاک * یعنی احباب از برای
خلاصی من از عشق دعا کرده ومستجاب نشدن آن محزون را مدعا ومقصود است زیرا که نوائی اولماسیغه غا زمرا
وجان بکر راحت ملالت هجرایرور باعث بمعنی الاثبات در تاج التواریخ آل عثمان که باملاء رومیه تالیف یافته در ذکر
بنای مسجد ایا صوفیه مذکور است که مرآت ضمیر نقش پذیر اولن خاطره نک عرصه شهوده وجود خارجی کسو
سیله جلوه کر اولماسی منتهای بیتی ایدوکی تقریر ایتدی یعنی مرادی که در آینه ضمیر نقش پذیر شده جلوه گر
شدن آن در عرصه شهود با کسوه وجود خارجی منتهای نیت بودنش را تقریر کرد بمعنی النفی در کلیله دمنه ترکی که
بلغت جغتای تالیف نموده اند در داستان کشف وعقرب مذکور است تکیم کا کیم عادت بولور فعل ذمیم * مادر اولور
اندین اول بی اختیار تام وتاش دیمای چایان میتکاج تیکاره کونکلیدا کچماس قیلور قیلماسی کاره * یعنی عقرب
وسنگ نگفته بمحض رسید نیش زدن کار کردن ونکردن آن در دلش نمیگذرد بمعنی الاثبات من نوائی سقی
اوچوغ زخمی لبیده بیلکور وبیلکورماسین کوردیک * نشانه کیم که ایتار جان ارا داغ نمایمدین بیلکورما

در این شعر حاصل مصدر است یعنی هلاکت و معنی شعر اینست که زخم تیغ الل از لبش معلوم می شود علامتش را ببیند
کو که در میان جان از داغ نهان من نشانه میخواهد بمعنی النفی من نوائی شعر زخمیم اغزی بوتماسیدین
اویقوم اچمیش ای مرفیق کوبیابو اهرکا اویقو کیلتوروز خمیانه دوره یعنی از هم نیامدن دهان زخم خواب
ای رفیق کو یا این خمیازه ایست که امر زخم خواب بیکراست یعنی خواب برکت بمعنی الاثبات من فضولی با ملاة الرومیه
شعر دل که سرزنی لی اولر زلف پریشان اولمیش نوله جرمی که اسلیماسنه فرمان اولمیش یعنی نعش دل که
سرزن است از زلف پریشان شده است جرم او چیست که بر صلبش فرمان شده است قسم دویم انست که صیغه مفرد
منفی بدون تخفیف با لفظ دین که بمعنی از است انضمام یابد مثل ایلاماسدین واتماسدین یعنی از نکردن چنانکه
در کلیله دمنه که بلسان اتراک روم تالیف کرده اند مذکور است که وعده غدر و فا ایتماسدین آنی تادیب ایتدی
یعنی از وفا نکردن بوعده او را تادیب کردند تا هرکاه با لفظ مثل مذکور شود چون عدم ازلی و اثبات قبل
از برای ازل محال می باشد نفی در این مقام متضمن معنی اثبات خواهد بود چنانکه نوائی فرماید شعر باش اقادب
یونقرالیغ دوریناتولاد ادب دوستغرت ابلاماسدین بوزلمقل عصیانی دیرش یعنی سر سفید شده ترک ادب
روسیاهی است پیش از عزت کردن دوست عصیان از بس کن و نیز بهمین معنی کوید شعر عشق نخلی نینک بری
هجران ایمیش ای دوست لارش بو نصیحت نی منکر بر فاشق اولماسدین بورون یعنی اید وست بر نخل عشق هجر است
از این نصیحت برخورید پیش از عاشق شدن و نیز در سکندری در رزم اهرمن با فرهاد کوید شعر تو توب
بر کرز آندین سهمکین راق کیلیب ولغوم ین برقهر و کین راق آنی هم اورغالی یلنیب هواغه توشور
ماسلیقین بو یوون فرمان رواغه قسم سیم انست که صیغه مفرد مغایب منفی بتخفیف سین و کلمات مصدری تخفیف
قاف و کاف با حرف دین انضمام یابد که در آن صورت هم بمعنی مصدر مثبت و هم بمعنی ماضی منفی می آید و این قسم مصطلح اتراک
روم است و اینکه بمعنی مصدر مثبت می آید معلوم العله است زیراکه ها مصدر است که قاف و کاف کرحرف اخیر
علامات مصدر است برای تخفیف کلام از آن ساقط می شود چنانکه از شواهد معلوم می کردد بمعنی المصدر المثبت
من فضولی با ملاة الرومیه شعر معنبر سنبلونک دین المادین بوالمادوم سواد بو بر هوا الیق نکاسندین دکل
باد صبا دن دنث المادین مخفف الماقدین باشد یعنی از بو کرفتن از سنبل معنبرت رسوا شدم این رسوائی من از بو گرفتن
از باد صباست و که شعر هزبر سوالیغم فاش ایتمادین عالمه زار جسمیم اشک کرداب ده پنهان اولسه یک
ایتمادین مخفف ایتماکدین باشد یعنی از فاش کردن رسوائی من سر ابتلای لرجسم زار من اگر در کرداب اشک پنهان شود
هم . و نظیر اینست یا یماو اولما که مخفف یا یماق بمعنی سوختن و اولماق بمعنی شدن باشد چنانکه فضولی کوید شعر
ای فضولی شمع وش مطلو اچیلمز یا یمادین تا بلمکیم سنبلندن رشته جا نیم سنکلهد یعنی ای فضولی مثل شمع
مطلب از سوختن وا نمیشود تا بجا که از سنبلش در رشته جان رسد و نیز کلیله دمنه رومی مذکور است شعر
بن لوم چکم غم سودای زلفنک دین سنک چون که سن ال چکمدنک اغیار ایله یار اولمادین یعنی من بدست
کشیدم از غم سودای زلف تو چونکه تو دست نکشیدی از یار شدن با اغیار اما بمعنی ماضی منفی مجهول العله است
زیراکه شواهد اکر بمعنی مصدر منفی لا التباس کردد چون دیناس و تیلما سوح اشتباه انها میتوانست کفت کر مخفف انکلما

باشد لیکن چون هر جا بمعنی ماضی منفی مستعملست مخالفت با قیاس دارد و علتش معلوم نیست چنانکه کوید بمعنی الماضی المنفی
من فضولی با ملاة الرومیه شعر بو نه سر دور دستر عشقینک دیمادین هر کیسه یه شهره دوشمیش بن سنی سودوکوم بو
اوازه لر دیمادین بمعنی دیمامیش باشد یعنی اینچه سر است که سر عشقت را بهیچکس نکفته او ازها شهرت یافته که من ترا دوست
داشتم منه رحمه الله شعر سجده کاه ایتمشدی عشق اهلی قاشینک محرابینی میلمادین خیل ملائیک سجده آدم هنوز
میلمادین بمعنی میلمامیش باشد یعنی اهل عشق محراب بروی ترا سجده کاه کرده بودند هنوز خیل ملائیک سجده آدم نکرده
و که شعر می ایچمادین ایچیلر امیش باب مغفرت سو کندلر بو باید مپر مغان ایچرا ایچمادین بمعنی ایچمامیش باشد و در این
افاده معنی مصدر منفی هم میکند یعنی می نخورده باز از می نخوردن باب مغفرت وا نمیشد پیر مغان در این باب قسمها میخورد
و مثل اینست یتیشما و کوید و رماکه در کلیله دمنه رومی مسطور است که هنوز دوده یتشمادین تفا ندوه و کری ملامت خیم
ملامت دین باندیم یتیشمادین بمعنی یتیشمامیش باشد یعنی هنوز دودش نرسیده باز تفا ندوه و کری ملامت خیم
و نیز مذکور است که خصم آتلرک خانمانلرین ناردمار ایله کوید و رمادین آتلر آنک آب بوار ایله حیاتی لو جانین سوندوی
لر کوید و رمادین بمعنی کوید و رمامیش باشد یعنی خصم خانمان ایشان را با آتش هلاک نسوخته ایشان وجان و حیات
او را با آب هلاک خاموش کنند باب نهم در ذکر حال و بیان تکرار و آن مبنی بر دو کونه است مفرد و مکرر اما المفرد
مثل جاء زید لاعبا که در عربی مستعمل است یعنی آمد زید بازی کنان وذهب شاتما یعنی رفت شادی کنان اما المکرر
وجاء ربک والملک صفا صفا که در قران مجید وارد است و این هر دو کونه در ترکی بچهار قسم استعمال می شود قسم
اول آنکه اکر حرف آخر فعل امر ساکن است مثل مقیل یعنی بیفت و قوپ یعنی برخیز و یا ال یعنی بیفکن و کول یعنی بخند حرف آخر را
مفتوح ساخته برای بیان حالیه الف یا های هوز در آخر آن درآرند مثل یقیلا و قوپا یعنی افتان و خیزان و کونا و کوله
نظر افکنان و کولا یعنی خنده کنان چنانکه شاهد بر اول و ثانی در سبعه سیاره در داستان سعد کوید شعر
اورلرا یردی حصار دوری کام یقیلا قوپا تو تماین ایرانا الشاهد علی الثالث شعر قاشیدا خال هندوسی کافرلیک
که اهل دین قتل اوچون چقیب توروروکونا لادیر طامقنه الشاهد علی الرابع شعر عشق چوالیکا اوت یاقیب ایکو
کونعم سوزلاتیب هرساری کیم کولا باقیب در حالیه بیزنی سیغلاتیب و بتکرار هم مذکور میسازند مثل توتا توتا یعنی
کرفته کرفته و چاله چاله یعنی نوازان نوازان و باره باره یعنی رفته رفته الشاهد علی الاول والثانی شعر
کلکشت چمن خوشتور اکر ساقی و مطرب بو کیلسا توتا توتا واولسا چاله چاله الشاهد علی الثالث شعر فانی
نوائی برق تیغ دوره مکر اشاران اولغای باره باره قسم دویم اکر حرف آخر فعل امر مفتوح است مثل اوینا یعنی بازی کن
واسرا یعنی نگهدار وایستا یعنی طلب کن بدون استعمال میشود نوع اول انست که یای ساکنه در آخر آن در آورده میکویند
که اوینای یعنی بازی کنان و آسرای یعنی ضبط کنان وایستای یعنی طلب کنان و بتکرار هم مذکور میکردد الشاهد علی
الاول شعر اوینای اوینای ولتور و دیپرا و لوسنی کوزلار زینت شوخ قاتل الاجزی جانلار قصد قیغا اوینا تماغیل
الشاهد علی الثانی شعر کونکلا سر عشقینک آسرای آسرای ولد وم ای ساقی قدح توتقیکم خرابات اهلیغه تمام
اولنا فاش اولوش نوع دویم انست که یای مضمومه در آخر آن در آورده اوینایو واسرایو وایستایو میکویند چنانکه
شاهد بر اول او بمعنی بازی کنان در لیلی مجنون در وصف لیلی کوید شعر مزلا رسیله اوینایو تلاشا قوی اغماغن

اتیکالغاشا و شاهد بر ثالث اعنی طلب کنان فرماید شعر صبوحی بیتا یو ستکاج سحر ایچلدی باشلد
بو نوع دیر دا او تماس ایدی کا تیم ارا و این نوع تکرار غیر مستعمل است و سوای معنی حال افاده معنی دیگر نمیکند دیگر
و روابط هم انضمام می یابد قسم سیم اگر فصل امر مضمومة الاخر باشد مثل او قو یعنی بخوان و او یو یعنی بخواب ب
امر مفتوحة الاخر همان یای ساکنه را ملحق ساخته میگویند که او قوی یعنی قراءت کنان و او یوی یعنی خواب کنان
و تکرار هم مستعمل است قسم چهارم اگر حرف آخر فصل امر مکسور باشد مثل دی یعنی بگو و یی یعنی بخور چون التقا
یا با حرف یای بیان کسره موجب ثقل میگردد لهذا بهمان یای بیان کسره اکتفا کرده‌اند با اشباع کسره بلفظ می‌نمایند
و تکرار هم مذکور میگردد مثل دی دی کو یان و یی یی یعنی اکل کنان و این قسم رابع خاصه بدون تکرار افاده
معنی امر هم میکند چنانکه گویند دی یعنی بگوی و یی یعنی بخور و یی یعنی بنویس و علی هذا القیاس فائده
بدانکه این اقسام اربعه سوای نوع دویم از قسم دویم که عبارت از اوینا یو و ایتا یو و اشباه آن باشد بمعنی
دیگر نیز استعمال میشود از آنجمله هر گاه بر لفظ امر اضافه شوند افاده معنی امر میکنند مثل اینکه گویند یتا
یعنی دست بزن بعقب بیفکن و قویا بر یعنی رها بده و آلاکیل یعنی بگیر بیا و ایتای کور یعنی بخوان و قوی کور
یعنی بخوان و دی کور یعنی بگو دیگر هر گاه با مصدر استعمال شوند بمعنی مصدر می آیند مثل اینکه گویند آلا
کیلکا ندا یعنی در گرفتن آمدن چنانکه گوید شعر جان آلا کیلکا ندا سعی و اضطرابینغکه اولادی
آلماسانک هم تاپیغان چاغدا شتابینغکه اولادی و همچنین است آلا باشلادی یعنی گرفتن شروع کرد
و ایتای باشلادی خواستن شروع کرد و او قوی باشلادی خواندن شروع کرد و دی باشلادی گفتن شروع کرد
دیگر با ضمایر و منتسبات موافق اقتضاء آن ضمیر و نسبت معنی می‌بخشند چنانکه گویند آلامین یعنی میگیرم و ایتا
یعنی میخواهم و او قویمن یعنی میخوانم و دیمین یعنی میگویم و همچنین است آلاکیلمیش یعنی گرفته آمده الشاهد
غم نکدین اولتورماک ایشین تعلیم آلاکیلمیش اجل بو نوع استاد اولسا اول آزچا فدا نام هر بولغوسی واتن
قبیل است آلاکیلکای یعنی گرفته بیاید و ایتای الغای یعنی تواند خواست و او قوی الغای تواند خواند و دی
تواند گفت اما نوع دویم از قسم دویم بهما بمعنی حال اختصاص دارد و از این قاعده خارج است و با ضمیر و رابطه
و نسبتی استعمال نمیشود قاعده بدانکه قسم سیم و چهارم و نوع اول از قسم دویم هر گاه بتنهائی استعمال
افاده معنی متکلم وحده و مفرد مغایب و مفرد مخاطب نیز میکنند مثل ایتای یعنی بخواهم و بخواهد و بخواهی
و او قوی یعنی بخوانم و بخواند و بخوانی و دی یعنی بگوید و بگویم و بگوئی و در این معانی مرادف ایتا بین و
او قوبین و دیبین باشد چنانکه در کتاب در ذیل لغات مذکور است و قسم اول که عبارت از بیقیلا و قویا
و آلا و توتا و نظایر آن باشد از این قاعده خارج است و هر گاه خواهند که آن قسم را هم بایفما بی استعمال
باید که یای حطی را ملحق ساخته بیقیلای و قویای و آلای و توتای گویند تا مرادف بیقیلا بین و قویا بین
و آلا بین و توتا بین باشد فائده بدانکه رومیه هر گاه خواهند که لفظی را بمعنی حال ادا کنند اگر از اوامر مسکونة
الاخر باشد در آخر صیغ قاف و دق و در صیغ کاف و رک در می آرند مثل اینکه میگویند چاپار دق یعنی دوان دوان
و اوره دق یعنی نان و کیده رک یعنی رفته رفته و کیله رک یعنی آمده آمده و اگر از اوامر متحرکة الاخر باشد

یای مفتوحه در آخر آن در آورده تکرار مذکور میسازند مثل اینکه میگویند آغلایه آغلایه یعنی گریه کنان گریه کنان
و او قویه او قویه یعنی قراءت کنان و دیه دیه یعنی گویان گویان باب دهم در بیان تتمه علامات چون علامات نه صیغه
محتاج بشرح و بسط بود در ذیل نه باب یاد شد مذکر تتمه آن علامات میپردازد و آنها را بدو قسم منقسم میسازد قسم اول
در علاماتی که اوامر اعم از آنکه مسکونة الاخر باشد یا متحرکة الاخر بهمان حالت سکون و حرکت بر آن علامات منضم
و آن بر سه نوع است نوع اول علامات مفرده اند از آنجمله غاج و کاج است که بمعنی محض و مجرد و چون استعمال میشود
مثل آلغاج یعنی بمحض گرفتن و چون گرفت و تیکاج یعنی بمحض رسیدن و چون رسید و اسراغاج بمحض نگهداشتن
چون نگهداشت و دیکاج بمحض گفتن و چون گفت و این بدو طریق مستعمل است اول آنست که با لفظ چون استعمال
میشود چنانکه در لسان الطیر در مناجات گوید شعر هو ستم کم تندخوی دین ستیب اولچو سیکاج آه اوت
اوندین کیتیب دویم آنست که بدون لفظ چون مذکور میشود اما متضمن آن معنی هست چنانکه گوید شعر کوزونک
تا یمغه سیران ایتی ا مزنی نقد جان آلغاج ثینچوک کیم مست سرکار می غم نقل ایکان الغلج و کاج در لفظ کولاکاج
از این معنی خارج و از برای همان لفظ کولاکاج بمعنی خنده رو موضوع است فائده بدانکه رومیه این صیغه را بطریق
استعمال نمایند اول بهمین طریق و نوع که در لسان جغتای جاریست الشاهد علیه من فضولی علیه الرحمه الاکتاج
شعر جان چیقرتندین کونکل ذکر لبلی را ایلا کاج تن بولمز جان سنکی دین اول لفظی تکرار ایلاکاج دویم بالفظ
وجق مذکور میسازند چنانکه فضولی گوید شعر ای دین صبو قیل آه ایلمه یاری کورمجک بکا دشوار دور اول
کرسنکا آسان کورونور و همچنین است قیلمجق و ایدجک یعنی بمحض کردن و چون کرد دیگر غالی و کالی
که بدو معنی می آید اول بمنزله لام تعلیل است در عربی دویم بمعنی حتی است در عربی مثل قیلغالی یعنی برای کردن
و تا کرد و کیلکالی یعنی برای آمدن و تا آمد الشاهد علی الاول بالمعنی الاول شعر ایپاکلادیم ایشیب حیلا
زخمی او چون کو یا مقید قیلغالی خانلار قوشین هم اولدهر ابنا بینک المعنی الثانی شعر دود آهیم سر وید
چقتی و کلکون بولدی اشک قیلغالی ترک و فاسر و کل اندامیم منینک دیگر غو و کو است که افاده معنی حاصل
میکند مثل الغو بر کو یعنی داد و ستد و صو رغو یعنی پرسش و یلکو یعنی علامت دیگر ما ز است که علامت متکلم
وحده است از فعل نفی مثل المازیعنی نمیگیرم دیگر ماس است که علامت مفرد مغایب است از فعل نفی مثل الماس یعنی
نمیگیرد نوع دویم علامات مرکبه اند از آنجمله غوجه و غوبچه و غابچه و کوجه و کوبچه و کابچه است که بدو معنی
می آیند اول بمنزله الی باشد که در عربی مستعمل است افاده معنی غایت میکند دویم بمعنی وزن و مقدار و اندازه
باشد مثل اوشا تغوجه و اوشا تغوبچه و اوشا تغابچه یعنی تا شکستن و بقدر شکستن الشاهد علی الثانی بالمعنی الاول
شعر کونکول جراحتی غه یا ق وصال مرهمی نی فراق خار و سی پرله باشیم لوشاتغوبچه و همچنین است اتیغوجه و اتیغوبچه
و اتیغابچه یعنی تا گفتن و بقدر گفتن الشاهد علی الثالث بالمعنی الثانی من سیغه سیاده شعر اتیماقنه اگرچه بالمعنی
یوق اول سیغابچه اتیا الغویر یوق دیگر غولوق و کولوک است که افاده معنی تلبیس میکند مثل الغولوق یعنی گرفتنی
و کیکولوک یعنی پوشیدنی الشاهد علی الاول شعر صبر و قرار هوشنی آلماقلیغینک سیدهر ای جانلار نقصنکا
جانیمد در الغولوق الشاهد علی الثانی شعر نفیس کیلولوغ اولسا زنا لالانک تنیم غه هوش حسین نقشی حصیری باب

او رینغه برد یکنی غودیك وكودیك است كه بدو معنی می آید اول افادهٔ معنیٔ قابلیت می كند دوم معنی مماثلت
ومشابهت می آید چنانكه كویند اورغودیك یعنی زدنی وهمچنانكه بزند وساوورغودیك یعنی افشاندنی
وهمچنانكه بیفشاند الشاهد علی الاول والثانی یعنی الاول شعر بو كیچه آهیم ایروردوراننی برم اورغودیك
چرخ كلزاریدین انجم كل لادین ساوورغودیك و همچنان است بولغودیك بروجه شدنی وهمچنانكه بشود چنانكه سلطان
حسین میرزا یعنی اول فرماید شعر چون بودولت بولغودیك بولدی میسر وای كیم صحبتیم اول لحظه طالع دین
تابی كرنده ودر لسان الطیر یعنی ثانی كوید شعر باراییدی اول شه غه بیرینا اوغولی بولغودیك یوسف
آینینك الیغه قولی ونظر اینست ایتكودیك یعنی كردن وهمچنانكه بكند وشاهد آن در لسان الطیر یعنی ثانی كوید
شعر دردجامین توت یعنی نالم ایتكودیك عشق بهری كونكلومنا كاراینكودیك واز این قبیل است اشتیلیكو
یعنی شنیدن وهمچنانكه شنیده شود چنانكه در تاریخ بابری مذكور است كه اشتیلیكودیك نیمه ایشیتلنا
تقریر قیلغومدور یعنی چیزی كه قابل شنیدن باشد شنیده شود تقریر خواهم كرد دیكری میشانك است كه علامت مفرد
مخاطب است از فعل نامی مثل آسمیشانك یعنی اویخته چنانكه كوید شعر بو بیونوكا مشكین اپاكدین ای كونكلوم
آسمیشانك مایداخالیم سلیكاسین كیم بوبیونوما تا قیلیك كنكشد دیكری مایدور است كه علامت نامی مضارع
از صیغه نفی مثل آلمایدور یعنی نكرفته است ونمیكرد دیكر شش علامت است كه افادهٔ معنی استقبال می كند
اول غوم وكوم است كه علامت متكلم وحده است مثل آلغوم والغومدور یعنی خواهم كرفت وكیلكوم وكیلكومدور
یعنی خواهم آمد دوم غومیز وكومیز است كه علامت متكلم مع الغیر است مثل آلغومیز وآلغومیزدور یعنی خواهیم
كرفت وكیلكومیز وكیلكومیزدور یعنی خواهیم آمد سیوم غونك وكونك است كه علامت مفرد مخاطب است مثل الغونك
والغونكدور یعنی خواهی كرفت وكیلكونك وكیلكونكدور یعنی خواهی آمد ونظیر اینست اونوتغونك یعنی فراموش
كرد الشاهد علی الثانی شعر چون اونوتغونكدور مین ایلنی ایل سینی لاری چیكیك عیش جامین بواونوتغیلا
بیر ساعت اونوث چهارم غونكوز وكونكوز است كه علامت جمع مخاطب است مثل آلغونكوز والغونكوزدور یعنی
خواهید كرفت وكیلكونكوز وكیلكونكوزدور یعنی خواهید آمد پنجم غوسی وكوسی است كه علامت مفرد مغایب است مثل
آلغوسی وآلغوسیدور یعنی خواهد كرفت وكیلكوسی وكیلكوسیدور یعنی خواهد آمد فایده بدانكه ترکیه چون
خواهند كه لفظی را بمعنی ادا كنند غین وكاف را محذوف ساخته اكر لفظ امر آن مسكونة الاخر است حرف آخر را
متحرك می سازند همچنانكه آلغوسی وكیلكوسی را آلیسی وكیلیسی می كویند واكر متحركة الاخر باشد یای مفتوح در آخر آن
در آورده از لفظی علاوه می نمایند آغلا كه فعل امر مفتوحة الاخر است آنرا می كویند آغلایاسی دور یعنی كریه خواهد كرد
چنانكه فضولی بغدادی در مخمسات كوید با ملای الرومیه شعر ای كونكول عشق اهلنه هر شب كولاردنك شمع
بن دیمز میدیم كه آخر اغلایاسی دور كولن ششم غوسیلار وكوسیلار است كه علامت جمع مغایب است مثل آلغوسیلار
یعنی خواهند كرفت وكیلكوسیلاردور یعنی خواهند كرفت ومانند اینست اویغانغوسیلاردور یعنی بیدار خواهند كرد
الشاهد علیه شعر سوسیپیب ویغانغوسیلاردور بیزنی اویغانماسانك غنچه وصبح وصراحی غلغلی كولكوسیدور
فاعده همركاه خواهند كه صیغه سته را بمعنی نفی ادا كنند بدو طریق مذكور می سازند اول آنست كه مای نافیه را

فعل امر وعلامت مذكور آرند مثل الماغونك یعنی نخواهی كرفت وكیلماكونك یعنی نخواهی رسید وهمكذا الی آخرها دوم
آنست كه همان صیغ را بدون مای نافیه بر لفظ یوق الحاق می نمایند چنانكه میر در نحو كوید شعر ای نوایی
اوینا غونك یوق عشق یا یوز كورماكونك علم ایتیبیرین شغل وپ ومونز تركینی یكباره قیل یعنی ای نوایی عشق بازی
نكرده خواهی بود یار ونداد مخواهی بود علم خواسته زمین را ببوس وسخن را یكباره ترك كن ومثل اینست قولمغوی
وتوتولغونك یوق یعنی خلاصیت نخواهد بود الشاهد علی الثانی شعر زلفی دین ای نخم لیغ كونكلوم قوتولغو
بو متورور كیم سینینك هر حلقه زخمینكا اپرقلادی باث نوع سیوم حرف شرط است وآن بدو افادهٔ معنی شرط نیز
مستعمل است چنانكه مفصلاً در ذیل مبنا چهارم مذكور خواهد شد ومفرد آن سا است كه علامت مفرد مغایب
مثل اولتورسا یعنی بنشیند وبكشد وبا ضمایر خمسه نیز استعمال می شود اول سالار است كه علامت جمع مغایب
مثل اولتورسالار یعنی بنشینند وبكشند دوم سام است كه علامت متكلم وحده است مثل اولتورسام یعنی
بنشینم وبكشم سیوم ساق وسانك است كه علامت متكلم مع الغیر است مثل اولتورساق یعنی بنشینیم واولتورسانك
بكنیم واختلاف لفظ بسبب اینست كه مصدر نشستن قافی ومصدر كشتن كافی است چهارم سانك است كه علامت
مفرد مخاطب است مثل اولتورسانك یعنی بنشینی وبكشی پنجم سانكیز است كه علامت جمع مخاطب است مثل اولتورسانكیز
یعنی بنشینید وبكشید قسم دوم در علامات كه اخر امر مسكونة الاخر متحرك كه بر آنها انضمام می یابند وآنها نیز
دو نوع آمد نوع اول علامات مفرده اند از آنجمله لی است كه علامت متكلم مع الغیر است مثل آلالی یعنی بكیریم وآتالی
یعنی بكنیم وبعضی اتراك توران الالینك واتالینك میكویند چنانكه بابر پادشاه فرموده الشاهد علی الثانی
شعر خوش اول كه بهار فصلی بولغای بوستان ولغای طرب بیلا بابر عیش مانه كرم سا اسباب تیالینك ذکر انده
میر دین كزك وطعام وسین دین باده فایده بدانكه لفظ لی در لغت اتراك عدم افادهٔ معنی متی می كند مثل اولالی
یعنی ناشده چنانكه فضولی بغدادی كوید شعر كرمتارم عشق ولالی زاده دهر غم عشقه نی بوندین بتر
یا رب كرفتاری بت یعنی كرفتار غم عشق نا شده ام از ازاده دهر از این بدتر یا رب كرفتار كن دیكر یای است كه
ویین است كه بمعنی متكلم وحده ومفرد مغایب ومفرد مخاطب استعمال می شود مثل آلای والایین یعنی بكیرم وبكیرد
وبكیری واتای واتایین یعنی بكنم وبكند وبكنی دیكر نون وكاف ساكنتین است كه در فعل امر علامت جمع
مخاطب است مثل آلینك یعنی بكیرید واتینك یعنی بكنید واورونكوز یعنی بزنید نوع دوم علامات تركیبیه
وآن برد وكوند است اول قیاسی است از آنجمله دورغان ودوركان است مثل الادورغان یعنی كیرنده وكرفته
وكرمتن وكیلادوركان یعنی آینده وآمده وآمدن دیكر دورمیش است مثل آلادورمیش یعنی میكرفته وكیلا
دورمیش یعنی می آمده دوم سماعیست وآن لفظ تورغاج است مثل توبل تورغاج كه در این شعر مذكور است شعر
با خیمه كوزونك ظلمی ایماس ظلم بودور ظلم كیم مین تورا تورغاج تیلاكای مین یا نا مظلوم یعنی ظلم چشمت بجانم ظلم
ظلم اینست كه من ایستاده باشم تو مظلوم دیكر طلب كنی وهمچنین است اولتورا تورغاج چنانكه در شمائم الجنه مذكور
كوید كه معنی یار اردی كیچیك یاشلیغ وشوخ ایردی جمله اولتورا تورغاج سیكریلاولغ زینهار بومنغه
منبت یاغین دیبا را بردی یعنی مغنی بود خرد سال وشوخ بود در جمله بعض نشستن جسته بر كرد آن نغز سوار شده

مبنا دوم

پاهای خودرا بر پشکاوی یار میزد و در جمیع مؤلفات مرحوم نوائی بغیر از این دو شاهد بنظر نرسیده مبنا، دویم

در بیان کیفیت اشتقاق سیغ و آن مشتملست بر یک قاعده و دو شق اما القاعده بدانکه حرکات علامات

صیغ که بر فعل امر الحاق می یابد تابع حرکات فعل امراست یعنی اگر فعل امر مضموم الحرکه است مثل توت واور علامت هم

مضموم مذکور میشود مثل اینکه گفته میشود توتوم یعنی گرفتم و اوردوم یعنی زدم و اگر فعل امر مفتوح الحرکه یا مکسور

الحرکه باشد مثل آل و کیت در هر دو صورت علامت مکسور مشهور مثل آلدیم یعنی گرفتم و کیتیم یعنی رفتم و اگر خواهند

که از آنها فعل ماضی یا جمع مخاطب بنا کنند اگر مضموم الحرکه است سکون حرف آخر فعل امر را بضمه مبدل ساخته بنا نمایند مثل

توتوب یعنی گرفته و اوروب یعنی زده و توتونک یعنی بگیرید و اورونک یعنی بزنید و اگر مفتوح الحرکه یا مکسور

الحرکه است سکون حرف آخر را بکسره تبدیل میدهند مثل اینکه میگویند آلیب یعنی گرفته و کیتیب یعنی رفته و آلینک

بگیرید و کیتینک یعنی بروید اما این قاعده در لسان اتراک روم مرعی و ملحوظ نیست و اغلب آنست که در مفتوح الحرکه و مکسور

الحرکه نیز بضمه مذکور میسازند مثل اینکه میگویند که آلدوم و بیلدوم و آلوب و بیلوب و اشباه آن چنانکه

اشعار دیوان فضولی همگی دال بر اینست و بعضی از علامات نیز هست که حکم مبنیات دارند و این حکم از ایشان منفک

و کیفیت آنها مفصلا در ذیل مبنا ششم در اداب املا در تحت قواعد متفرقه مذکور خواهد شد شق اول

آنست که حرف آخر فعل امر الف باشد مثل آل یعنی بگیر و کیل یعنی بیا و صیغ این شق سوای قسم اول فعل مضارع آن کم

مخلف الاشتقاق و سماعیست و کیفیت آن در ذیل مبنا اول در بیان مضارع نگارش یافت بدو قسم اشتقاقی می باشد

قسم اول علاماتیست که فعل امر بهمان نحو مسکونة الاخر در آن علامات انضمام می یابد اول ماق و ماک است مثل آلماق یعنی

گرفتن و کیتماک یعنی رفتن بعد سیکردی و دی است مثل آلدی یعنی گرفت و کیتدی یعنی رفت دیگر دینک و تینک است

مثل آلدینک یعنی گرفتی و کیتینک یعنی رفتی دیگر علامات فعل ماضی است و چون حرف اول آن علامات دال و تا است شدید

در بعضی مقام بمتابعت و مناسبت کلمه ما قبل بحرف تا باید مذکور شود و وجه آن با علت اختلاف اعراب و تبدیل

کرده بعد در ذیل مبنا ششم مذکور میگردد دیگر دینکیز و دینکلار و تینکیز و تینکلار است مثل آلدینکیز و آلدینکلار

یعنی گرفتید و کیتینکیز و کیتینکلار است یعنی رفتید دیگر دیم و تیم و دوم و توم است مثل آلدیم یعنی گرفتم و کیتیم

رفتم و اوردوم یعنی زدم و توتوم یعنی گرفتم دیگر دوق و توق است مثل آلدوق یعنی گرفتیم و کیتتوک یعنی رفتیم

دیگر غان و کان است مثل آلغان یعنی گیرنده و گرفته و گرفتن و کیتکان یعنی رونده و رفته و رفتن دیگر غیل و کیل

مثل آلغیل یعنی بگیر و کیتکیل یعنی برو دیگر ماس است مثل آلماس یعنی نمیگیرد و کیتماس یعنی نمیرود دیگر مان است

مثل آلمان یعنی نمیگیرم و کیتمان یعنی نمیروم دیگر ماید است مثل آلماید یعنی نگیرد و نگرفته و کیتماید

یعنی نرود و نرفته دیگر میش است مثل آلمیش یعنی گرفته و کیتمیش یعنی رفته دیگر میشانک است مثل آلمیشانک یعنی

گرفته و کیتمیشانک یعنی رفته دیگر غوچی و کوچی است مثل آلغوچی یعنی گیرنده و کیتکوچی یعنی رونده دیگر غوچه

و غونجه و غانچه و کوچه و کونجه و کانچه است مثل آلغوچه و آلغانچه یعنی تا گرفتن و بقدر گرفتن و کیت کوچه و کیتکانچه

یعنی تا رفتن و بقدر رفتن دیگر غاج و کاج است مثل آلغاج یعنی بمحض گرفتن و چون گرفت و بگیرد و کیتکاج

بمحض رفتن و چون رفت و برود دیگر غالی و کالی است مثل آلغالی یعنی برای گرفتن و تا گرفته و کیتکالی یعنی برای

رفتن و تا رفته دیگر غای و کای و سون و دیک است و یک است مثل آلغای و آلسون و آلدیک یعنی بگیرد و کیتکای و

کیتسون و کیتدیک یعنی برود دیگر غولوق و کولوک است مثل آلغولوق یعنی گرفتنی و کیتکولوک یعنی رفتنی

دیگر غودیک و کودیک است مثل آلغودیک یعنی گرفتنی همچنانکه بگیرد دیگر غوم و کوم است مثل آلغوم یعنی خواهم

و کیتکوم خواهم دیگر غومیز و کومیز است مثل آلغومیز دور یعنی خواهیم گرفت و کیتکومیز دور یعنی خواهیم رفت دیگر غونک

و کونک است مثل آلغونک یعنی خواهی گرفت و کیتکونک یعنی خواهی رفت دیگر غونکوز و کونکوز است مثل آلغونکوز

یعنی خواهید گرفت و کیتکونکوز دور یعنی خواهید رفت دیگر غوسی و کوسی است مثل آلغوسی یعنی خواهد گرفت و کیتکوسی

یعنی خواهد رفت دیگر غوسیلار و کوسیلار است مثل آلغوسیلار دور یعنی خواهند گرفت و کیتکوسیلار دور یعنی

خواهند رفت دیگر سات یعنی اگر بگیرد دیگر سام است مثل آلسام یعنی اگر بگیرم و کیتسام یعنی اگر بروم

دیگر ساق و سالک است مثل آلساق یعنی اگر بگیریم و کیتسالک یعنی اگر برویم دیگر سانک است مثل آلسانک

یعنی اگر بگیری و کیتسانک یعنی اگر بروی دیگر سانکیز است مثل آلسانکیز یعنی اگر بگیرید و کیتسانکیز یعنی اگر بروید

قسم دویم علاماتیست که فعل امر مسکونة الاخر را متحرکة الاخر ساخته بر آن علامات اضافه مینمایند از آنجمله

لی است مثل آلالی یعنی بگیریم و کیتالی یعنی برویم دیگر ینا که و ین است مثل آلای و آلاین یعنی بگیرم و

بگیرد و بگیری و کیتای و کیتاین یعنی بروم و برود و بروی دیگر دور است مثل آلادور یعنی میگیرد و کیتادور

یعنی میرود دیگر دورمیش است مثل آلادورمیش یعنی میگرفته و کیتادورمیش یعنی میرفته دیگر دورغان و دورکان

مثل آلادورغان یعنی گیرنده و گرفته و گرفتن و کیلادورکان یعنی آینده و آمده و آمدن دیگر نکیز و نکلار

مسکونة الابتدا است مثل آلینک و آلینکیز و آلینکلار یعنی بگیرید و کیتینک و کیتینکیز و کیتینکلار یعنی بروید

دیگر ب و بان است مثل آلیب و آلیبان یعنی گرفته و کیتیب و کیتیبان یعنی رفته مثل اگر فعل امر مسکونة

الاخر را بعضی خواهند استعمال کنند سکون حرف آخر را مبدل بفتحه ساخته الفاظ های بیان فتحه در آخر آن در می آرند

و بطریق مفرد یا مزدوج مذکور میسازند مثل آلا و آلا آلا یعنی بگیر گیران اخذ کنان و اورا و اورا اورا یعنی بزن زنان

چنانکه کیفیت آن در ذیل ما بعضی از مبنا اول بیان شد شق ثانی آنست که حرف آخر فعل امر متحرک باشد و آن

از سه قسم بیرون نیست یا مضموم است مثل اوقو یعنی بخوان یا مفتوح است مثل ایلا یعنی بکن یا مکسور است مثل دی

یعنی بگو و هر یک از این اقسام ثلثه بر یک نهج بر علامات اضافه میشود و چون صیغ اقسام و انواع آنها به یک سیاق انتها

می یابد همه قسم را در تلو یک شق مندرج میسازیم و اختلافی که داشته باشد در ضمن توضیح بیان مینماید اول

ماق و ماک است مثل اوقوماق یعنی خواندن و ایلاماک کردن و دیماک گفتن دیگر دی است مثل اوقودی

یعنی خواند و ایلادی کرد و دیدی گفت دیگر دونک و دینک است مثل اوقودونک یعنی خواندی و

ایلادینک کردی و دیدینک گفتی دیگر دونکوز و دونکلار و دینکیز و دینکلار است مثل اوقودونکوز و اوقودونکلار

یعنی خواندید و ایلادینکیز و ایلادینکلار کردید و دیدینکیز و دیدینکلار گفتید دیگر دوم و دیم است مثل

اوقودوم یعنی خواندم و ایلادیم کردم و دیدیم گفتم دیگر دوق و دوک است مثل اوقودوق یعنی خواندیم و ایلادوق

کردیم و دیدوک گفتیم دیگر غان و کان است مثل اوقوغان یعنی خواننده و خوانده و خواندن و ایلاکان کننده و کرده

ودیکان کوینده وکفته وکفتن دیکر عیل وکیل است مثل او قوعیل یعنی بخوان وایما کیل بکن ودیکین
دیکر ماس است مثل اوقوماس یعنی نمیخواند وایلاماس نمیکند ودیماس نمیکوید دیکر مان است مثل اوقومان
یعنی نمیخوانم وایلامان نمیکنم ودیمان نمیکویم دیکر ماید طرست مثل اوقومایدور یعنی نمیخواند ونخواند وایلامایدور
نمیکند ونکرده ودیمایدور نمیکوید ونکفته دیکر میش است مثل اوقومیش یعنی خوانده وایلامیش کرده ودیمیش
کفته دیکر میشانلک است مثل اوقومیشانلک یعنی خوانده وایلامیشانلک کرده ودیمیشانلک کفته دیکر
ی وین است مثل اوقوی واوقوین یعنی بخوانم وبخواند وبخوانی وایلای وایلاین بکنم وبکند وبکنی ودیی ودیین
بکویم وبکوید وبکوی واوقوی وایلای بمعنی حال ودی بمعنی نیز استعمال می شود دیکر ب وبان است مثل اوقوب
واوقوبان یعنی خوانده وایلاب وایلابان کرده ودیب ودیبان کفته دیکر غوجی وکوجی است مثل اوقوغوجی یعنی خواننده
وایلاکوجی کننده ودیکوجی کوینده دیکر غوجه وغونجه وغانجه وکوجه وکونجه وکانجه است مثل اوقوغوجه واوقو
غونجه واوقوغانجه یعنی تا خواندن وبقدر خواندن وایلاکوجه وایلاکونجه وایلاکانجه تا کردن وبقدر کردن
ودیکوجه ودیکونجه ودیکانجه تا کفتن وبقدر کفتن دیکر قاج وکاج است مثل اوقوغاج یعنی بمحض خواندن
وچون خواند وایلاکاج بمحض کردن وچون کرد ودیکاج بمحض کفتن وچون کفت دیکر لی است مثل اوقولی یعنی بخوانیم
وایلالی بکنیم ودیلی بکوئیم دیکر غالی وکالی است مثل اوقوغالی یعنی برای خواندن وتا خوانده وایلاکالی برای
کردن وتا کرده ودیکالی برای کفتن وتا کفته دیکر غای وکای وسون ودیلک است مثل اوقوغای واوقو
سون واوقودیلک یعنی بخواند وایلاکای وایلاسون وایلادیلک بکند ودیکای ودیسون ودیدیلک بکوید دیکر
غولوق وکولوک است مثل اوقوغولوق یعنی خواندنی وایلاکولوک کردنی ودیکولوک کفتنی دیکر غودیلک وکودیلک است
مثل اوقوغودیلک یعنی خواندنی وهمچنانکه بخواند وایلاکودیلک کردنی وهمچنانکه کند ودیکودیلک
وهمچنانکه بکوید دیکر غوم وکوم است مثل اوقوغوم یعنی خواهم خواند وایلاکوم خواهم کرد ودیکوم خواهم
دیکر غومیز وکومیز است مثل اوقوغومیز دور یعنی خواهیم خواند وایلاکومیز دور خواهیم کرد ودیکومیز دور خواهیم
کفت دیکر غونکوز وکونکوز است مثل اوقوغونکوز دور یعنی خواهید خواند وایلاکونکوز دور خواهید کرد
ودیکونکوز دور خواهید کفت دیکر غوسی وکوسی است مثل اوقوغوسی یعنی خواهد خواند وایلاکوسی خواهد
کرد ودیکوسی خواهد کفت دیکر غوسیلار وکوسیلار است مثل اوقوغوسیلار دور یعنی خواهند خواند وایلا
کوسیلار دور خواهند کرد ودیکوسیلار دور خواهند کفت دیکر سا است مثل اوقوسا یعنی اکر بخواند وایلاسا اکر
بکند ودیسا اکر بکوید دیکر سام است مثل اوقوسام یعنی بخوانم وایلاسام اکر بکنم ودیسام اکر بکویم دیکر
سانک است مثل اوقوسانک اکر بخوانی وایلاسانک اکر بکنی ودیسانک اکر بکوئی دیکر سانکیز است مثل اوقوسا
نکیز یعنی اکر بخوانید وایلاسانکیز اکر بکنید ودیسانکیز بکوشید تذییل بدانکه علامتها که در طی این لفظ ذکر
شده باشند ای حرفی که میانه فعل امر واینها هست در می آرند مثل اینکه کفته میشود که اوقوید ور یعنی میخواند وایلا
سیکند واوقوید ورغان یعنی خوانده وخوانده وخواندن وایلایدورکان کننده وکرده وکردن واوقویدورمیش
یعنی میخوانده وایلایدورمیش میکرده اما ده حکومته الاخر چون التقاء یا بین واقع میشد موجب ثقل بود لهذا یای

مبنای
مسیم
باب اول

بیان کسره را باشباع تلفظ مینمایند چنانکه کفته می شود دیدوم یعنی میکوید ودیدورکان یعنی کوینده وکفته وکفتن
ودیدورمیش یعنی میکفته وهرکاه خواهند که معنی حال بیان کنند در آنجا هم بدستور ای حرفی آخر فعل امر مضمومة الاخر
الاخر در آورده بر سر مفرد بیامز دحج مذکوره میسازند مثل اوقوی یا اینکه کفته شود اوقوی او قوی یعنی خوانده وایلای
یا ایلای ایلامی یعنی کرده کرده وبطور اول بکونی الاخر بدستور باشباع بیا نمیشود مثل دی یا اینکه کفته شود دیکی
یعنی کویان کویان واین الفاظ بمعنی دیکر هم مستعملست چنانکه در محلش مذکور شد مبنای سیم در بیان ضمایر و اسما اشاره
وآن مشتملست بر دو باب باب اول در ضمایر وآن بر سه قسم است قسم اول ضمایر متصله اند که در آخر کلام واقع
میشوند از آنجمله م است که ضمیر متکلم وحده است مثل اینکه کفته می شود باشیم یعنی سرم وقاشیم یعنی ابرویم وکاه
که جزء کلمه نیز واقع می شود مثل اولوم یعنی مرک وبولوم یعنی مغز آب دیکر میز است که ضمیر متکلم مع الغیر است مثل
باشمیز یعنی سر ما وقاشمیز یعنی ابروی ما دیکر نون وکاف ساکنتین که ضمیر مفرد مخاطب است مثل باشینک یعنی
سرت وقاشینک یعنی ابرویت ودر صیغه امر نونی هم مخاطب است مثل آلینک یعنی بکیرید وآلمانک یعنی نکیرید
ونیز با ضمایر منفصله واسماء اشاره مصطلح است مثل سینک وسینینک واینینک وبوبونک واخوات اینها فقدر
اشاره ترکی تطبیکافت که در عربی در کلمه اولئک وذالک میباشد افاده اشاره معنی قریب وبعید میکند
بعضی جا بمعنی رابطه مفعول مستعملست چنانکه در ذیل روابط بیان خواهد شد ودر بعضی مقام خارج از معنی
زاید بر کلام است اما کلام نیز بدون آن ناتمام است دیکر نکیز ونکوز است که ضمیر جمع مخاطب است مثل باشینکیز
یعنی سر شما وکوزونکوز یعنی چشم شما وآلینکیز یعنی بکیرید واورونکوز یعنی بزنید دیکر ضمیر مفرد غایب است
بر دو کونه است اول ی است که در آخر کلمات مسکونة الاخر واقع می شود مثل باشی یعنی سرش وقاشی یعنی ابرویش دویم
سی است که در آخر کلمات متحرکة الاخر واقع می شود مثل اتاسی یعنی پدرش واویقوسی یعنی خوابش دیکر لار است که علامت
جمع می باشد مثل یخشیلار یعنی نیکان ویمانلار یعنی بدان وهرکاه با ضمیر غایب مذکور شود بمعنی جمع غایب می آید
چنانکه در هفت سیاره در مصالحه کلبنا هرام اکوید شعر چاره تاپماقه مجانم ایردیلار کیچه کوندوز
دیر ایلادیم یعنی چاره جستن جانم بودند وشب وروز ملازم بودند وهرکاه با نون وکاف خطاب جمع شود بمعنی جمع
می آید چنانکه در نوحه کردن بهرام در فراق کنیزک چینی خطاب بقوم وخیل خود کوید شعر قوم وخیلی که بندم
ایردینکلار دینام سرفکنده ایردینکلار یعنی ای قوم وخیلی که بنده ام بودید بکویم که سرفکنده ام بودید
جزء کلمه نیز اتفاق می افتد مثل ایلار یعنی میکند وزاید بر کلام هم واقع میشود چنانکه در مبنا چهارم در
زواید خواهد آمد قسم دویم الفاظی اند که مابین ضمایر متصله ومنفصله اشتراک دارند چون در ابتدای کلام
شوند بمعنی ضمایر منفصله اند ودر آخر کلام بمعنی ضمایر متصله اند واکر بتکرار مذکور شوند یکی افاده ضمیر ودیکری افاده
انتساب بضمیر میکند وآن چهار لفظ است اول مین است که بفارسی من وبعربی انا کویند ومین مین یعنی منم دوم
مین یعنی منم دوم فائده دوم وهیت این ضمیر اینها با یای ابجد وانتساب بضمیر اسامی متصله مذکوره میسازند چنانکه کویند
منم یعنی منم وبنم سلطانم یعنی سلطان من وبا ضمیر منفصل استعمال نمیکنند بخلاف جغتای که هر دو نوع را
مینمایند مثل الوم مین والورم ونوتادم مین ونوتادم یعنی میکیرم دویم سین است که بفارسی تو وبعربی انت

کویند و سین سین یعنی تو و چنانکه کوید شعر ای زهد بولوم اوریناکه بو مرحله ایچره مقصد غه جه سین سین
پیری یوز یمنک خط بهدین و اولغای سین یعنی بشوی ستیم بیز است که بفارسی ما و بعربی نحن کویند و بیز یعنی
مائیم و اولغای بیز یعنی بشویم فایده اتراک روم انتساب بضمیر اول بیز مذکور میسازند بلکه حرف آخر لفظ را مفتوح
زای معجمه بر آن ملحق میسازند مثل اینکه میکویند بیز بیز یعنی مائیم چنانکه فضولی کوید بامداد الرّویته شعر
اسیر درد عشق و مست جام حسن جو قاماییز وز مشهور اول لیلی سنکا مجنون بنکا دیرلر و همچنین میکویند که او جاقوز
یعنی او جاقیم الشاهد علیه شعر زاهدا کور سینه چاکی شعله سین بیزدین عاشق پیراو غباقوز بیز کیم سوزاند د
درود یواریمیز و مثل اینست قولیوز بکسر لام و ختم نای حطی یعنی غلام اوئیم و در شعر اهل بدد نک قولیوز او لدر
بیز جاندین عزیز یوسفا و لیله خودفروش اینکله یوخ بازاریمیز و همچنین جغتاییه میکویند که ایتاریز و
میکوریز یعنی میکنیم و رومیه میکویند که ایدیوز و میلوروز چهارم سیز است که بفارسی شما و بعربی انتم کویند
و سیز سیز یعنی شمائید و اولغای سیز یعنی بشوید و نیز افاده معنی سلب و نفی میکند مثل اینکه کویند سیز سیز یعنی بی شما
و هر سه معنی بصیغه ستاره در دیغای ولاد پادشاه کوید شعر بخت غه تاج تارک اولغای سیز شه قدم کو
مبارک اولغای سیز چون ازلدین شه جهان سیز سیز بولماسون یر نقش جهان سیز سیز ششم ستیم لفظی اند که ما بین
ضمیر و اشاره مشترکند از آنجمله لار باشد و آن الف ممدوده است که با لفظ لار که علامت جمع است جمع شده
بمعنی ایشان و آنها استعمال میشود دیگر آنت چنانکه کویند آنلار یعنی ایشان و آنها و انکا یعنی باو
یعنی بآن دیگر و آن با فارسی اشتراک دارد دیگر اول و شول و اوشالت که بمعنی آن و او استعمال میشود باب دوم
در اسماء اشاره و آن بر دو قسم است قسم اول آنست که مخصوص اشاره است و آن دو لفظ است اول بوست که بفارسی
این و بعربی هذا و هذه کویند الشاهد علیه شعر خطینک ایرماس کل اوزره سبزه باغ ارم دوربو سبزه
کون یوزینک اوزن سوادی دین رقم دوربو و همچنین میکویند که بولار یعنی اینها و بو دور یعنی اینست دویم مونست که
با بعضی روابط ترکیب یافته مثل مونکا یعنی باین الشاهد علیه شعر ازلهم سین ابدهم سین مجاولمه آخر کیم
آنکا یوق ابتدا بیله مونکا یوق انتها پیدا و همچنین است مونیم یعنی اینقدر و موندا یعنی در این و موندین یعنی از این و موندی
یعنی اینچنین و هرگاه تنها استعمال شود در آنصورت نون ساکن را مبدل بنون ساخته مونا میکویند چنانکه کوید
ایت لار دینک الیدا یوز پاره کونکولنی الدیم مونا کور هر بری نینک ایغزیدا بر پاره کونکول فایده باید دانست
که مورد استعمال هر یک از این دو قسم اشاره بعید کانه است و چنان نیست که اولین را بجای دویمین و دویمین را بجای
اولین مذکور توان ساخت تابع طبع بوده استعمال باید نمود قسم دویم الفاظیست که ما بین ضمیر و اشاره مشترکند چنانکه در
خاتمه مذکور شد مبنای چهارم در بیان الفاظی که بدون ترکیب افاده معنی نکنند و آنرا اهل ادب حروف کویند و آن مشتمل است
بر سه باب باب اول در روابط و آن مبنی بر دو قسم است قسم اول آنست که در آخر کلام واقع میشوند و آن روابط تقدیریست
و تقدیر محصور است بر سه نوع نوع اول آنست که بمعنی که رابطه مفعول است استعمال میشود از آنجمله دور حرفیست که در
مقابل یای ضمیر مفرد مخاطب واقع میشود حرف اول نون ساکنه است حرف دویم یای است چنانکه هر دو نوع کوید
دیما اغزین غنچه قدین سرو کیم ایل کور ماییش سرو نینک رفتاری نی یا غنچه نینک کفتاری نی کی کود هنش را غنچه قد

باب دوم

مبنای چهارم

باب اول

سرو که خلق ندیده رفتار سرو را و کفتار غنچه را و نون زاید نیز می باشد مثل اینکه کویند الغزیدا که مراد فالغزیدا
یعنی در دهنش و قدیدا که مراد قدیدا بود یعنی در قامتش و لفظ نی هرگاه در ابتدای کلام واقع شود افاده معنی استفهام
چنانکه در ذیل باب اول این مبنا مذکور شد دیگر نینک است چنانکه کوید شعر نیچه جودین تارتایین اول پریوشدین
نینک یوق مودو نیا یانی آیا ظلم ایله بیدادینک یعنی تا چند بکشم جور آن پریوش را نیست بانهایتی آیا ظلم باید
و در بعضی جا زاید بر کلام استعمال میشود چنانکه در مبنای چهارم در بیان زواید مرقوم خواهد شد نوع دویم نست که در
جا افاده معنی رابطه میکند و آن نون و کاف ساکنین ما قبل متحرکست که در آخر ضمایر منفصله واقع شده مثل
منینک و سینینک الشاهد علی الاول شعر هر کونکول الامی چون بولیش دلارامیم منینک اول سبب دین یوقتور
بر لحظه آرامیم منینک و همچنین است در اسماء اشاره از قبیل مونونک و اونینک الشاهد علی الاول و الثانی شعر
ایستانلار لیلی و مجنون حسن و عشقی دیر شان سین نظیری مین مونونک یاریم عودار ایشنک یعنی اکر از حسن و عشق
و مجنون مثال خواهی من نظیر مین سان و آن بمنزله این الفاظ با بعضی کلمات افاده معنی دیگر میکند مثل آنکه
میکویند منینک بیله یعنی با من و منینک دیم یعنی از منست و منینک مطلوبوم دور یعنی مطلوب منست و
هکذا اخواتها فایده کاه هست که از برای مبالغه دو علامت رابطه مفعول متوالی یکدیگر واقع می شود چنانکه
در خسرو شیرین در تحمید کوید شعر قلیبچون بر تخلیش مظهر کل جهان عقل خاشاکی بولوب کول فاطلوقانی
ایلتیب دریا نینک جهاندا قویماین اثاری اینینک یعنی طوفان فنا بر همه اشیا اصرار در جهان نگذاشته اثارش را و را
نوع ستیم انست که بمعنی بای تعدیه است و آن غا و غه و کاست الشاهد علی الاول شعر نامه شوقم کیشی عرض
ایلاهی الماس یار غه بر غلط بولغای جواب ایتماک طمع مین زار غه الشاهد علی الثانی شعر کوز کا تاکیردی خیال لینک سالوق
آهیم و همدیم با غلامیش مین فوزنا هر ساری شکاندین آنکا و کیفیت استعمال آن با موارد ذکر در ذیل مبنا ششم در
املا نکارش خواهد یافت قسم دویم روابط غیر تعدیه است و آن مشتملست بر دو نوع نوع اول حروفیست که در آخر کلام
واقع می شود و آنها مفرداتند از آنجمله با و چون است که بمنزله لام تعلیل است در عربی چنانکه کوید شعر هجر تیغی
کوبا و چون جسمیدا هر یون چیکدی بالش ای نوانی مین مذلت ایلا ری بودور بریم دیکر ایله و ایلادین و بیله و بیلان
و بیرله و بیرلانست که بمعنی مع است در عربی و لفظ ایله تحقیقا دیکر طرح که در کتاب الغه در ذیل الغات مذکور خواهد
دیکر دور ود و دورست که بمعنی هست می آید دیکر کیم است که بمعنی که مذکور میکردد الشاهد علیه شعر
در کیم یار دیو قمنکا آنکلا یار اینا داغی یوق و فا آندا نوع دویم حروفیست که با تمام ضمیمه کلمه تامه اند و در اول
اخر کلام مذکور میکرده و آن ای و ایر است که با علامات صیغه ماضی و غیره ترکیب یافته از آنجمله ایدی و ایردی است
یعنی بود چنانکه در لیلی مجنون کوید شعر لیلی که ایدی عرب بلاشی هم یار ایدی قیس مبتلاشی دیکر ایدینک و
ایردینک است یعنی بودی دیکر ایدینکر و ایردینکر و ایدینکلار و ایردینکلارست یعنی بودید دیکر ایدیم و ایردیم است
یعنی بودم دیکر ایدوک و ایردوکست یعنی بودیم دیکر ایکان و ایرکان بفتح کاف و ایکین و ایرکین بکسر کاف که بمعنی
باشد و زاید بر کلام هم می آید چنانکه در مبنای چهارم در ذیل زواید مذکور خواهد شد دیکر ایکاج و ایرکاج است یعنی
بودن و چون هست دیکر ایرور است یعنی هست دیکر ایماس و ایرماس است یعنی نیست و نباشد الشاهد علیه

شعر ایمان عمر شامی انجم قطره لار آهیم تغیدین پل نی نالنک کونکوز کوسین کرتیره قیلسا اوشبونم بیر کوش دیگر
ایمان و ایرمان است یعنی نیستم چنانکه در خاتمه حیرت الابرار گوید شعر گرچه ایمان قابل لطف و کرم لیکن
ایمان بیر یولی نومیدهم دیگر ایمانک و ایرمانک است یعنی نیستی دیگر ایمیش و ایرمیش است یعنی بوده دیگر ایسا
و ایرسا است یعنی باشد و اگر باشد دیگر ایسانک و ایرسانک است یعنی باشی و اگر باشی دیگر ایسانکیز و ایرسانکیز
یعنی باشید و اگر باشید دیگر ایسام و ایرسام است یعنی باشم و اگر باشم دیگر ایسالک و ایرسالک است یعنی باشیم و اگر باشیم
باب دوم در غیر روابط و آن بر دو قسم است قسم اول آنست که در ابتدای کلام واقع می شود و آن مبنی بر دو نوع است
نوع اول قیاسی است و آن نوایست که حرف استفهام است چنانکه گوید شعر ایله فانی بول که دانکیز نینک امکان
بولماغای کیم ایتالر موجود اکر یوقور دین توتماغای یلیلک و همچنین گویند نیده یعنی چیست نوع دوم سماعی
و آن آپ و ساپ و اشباه آنست که از برای مبالغه بر سر الوان در می آید مثل اینکه گفته شود آپ آق یعنی سفید محض
و سا ساریغ یعنی زرد محض و همچنین است قاپ قرا و قیپ قیزیل و کوم کوک و یاپ یاشیل و از اینگونه است بعضی
الفاظ اختصاص دارد مثل یاپ یاسی یعنی پهن محض و توپ تو یعنی مسطح محض و توپ توغری یعنی راست محض و تیپ تیک
یعنی راست شاخص و سا پ ساغ یعنی صحیح محض قسم دوم آنست که در انتها واقع می شود و آن مشتمل بر دو بیان
بیان اول آنست که افاده معنی حرفی میکند و آن بر دو نوع است نوع اول قیاسیست از آنجمله سا است که حرف شرط است و
با اوامر ترکیب می یابد و استعمال آن بر دو گونه است اول با حرف شرط فارسی که عبارت از اگر باشد دوم بدون
حرف شرط چنانکه میر علیشیر گوید شعر ای نوائی جانینک الغوم ده بیسا تا یغوریغیل جانغه
مونونک بیرله کرایتسا اکتفا قاعده بدانکه این حرف بغیر از اوامر با هیچ لفظی انضمام نمی یابد مگر لفظ یوق
که از او یوقسا گفته اند و این از شواذ است و در حقیقت یوقسا مخفف یوق ایسا و یوق ایرسا است
زیرا که هر سه لفظ بالاشتراک بیک معنی استعمال میشوند چنانکه در کتاب ما در ذیل لغات مذکور خواهد شد
وگاه هست که بالحاق و ایراد بعضی از منتسبات مفید سلب معنی شرط از حرف سا میشود مثل اینکه گویند
دیسا بولغای یعنی توان گفت چنانکه در فصل سیوم از محبوب القلوب در وصف اهل خرابات گوید کم
یخشی علی بیله ایشی یوق دیسا بولغای که عالم دا موندا کیشی یوق و همچنین است یاروتسا بولماس یعنی
روشن نتوان کرد و توتسا بولماس یعنی نتوان گرفت چنانکه در قسم سیوم از محبوب القلوب در ذکر حیا گوید که عمر
کیم و ناسیزه دور اندین امید کوزین یاروتسا بولماس محبوب که یوفا دور آندین وفا الغاو یدطمع توتسا
وگاه هست که حرف کلمه واقع میشود مثل کیم سه یعنی شخص و نیم سه یعنی چیز و باطسه یعنی شیرک دیگر مو است که
حرف استفهام است بمعنی آیا بود و این بد و طریق مستعمل است اول با لفظ آیا استعمال میشود چنانکه گوید شعر
میر بیله بوزونک تیم تیم اجر موایکین آیا یا شعله ما را بیر اخگر موایکین آیا دوم بدون لفظ آیا استعمال میشود
علیه شعر ساچینک رنگین عنبر مو دور مشک ختن مو لبین طعمی شکر مو دور و یا انکبین مو دیگر دین بمعنی از باشد
که آنرا بعربی من و عن گویند چنانکه گوید شعر اول پری محبوب بولغای دیب مینی یوانه دین چند دیک
چیقمان تو وکون کوشه ویرانه دین خطنه نوائی علیه الرحمه فرموده شعر فلک نیلوفری دین چشمه مهر

کسیده یوز ونکدا ایل دین اول چشمه قیلمیش نیلوفر سیدا و نصیری این شعر را از نسخه سقیمی چنین خوانده که یوز ونکدین ایل دین اوچشمه
قیلمیش نیلوفر پیدا و در قواعدی که در ابتدای کتاب خود نوشته ذکر کرده که در لغت ترک برای مزید تاکید دو لفظ دین از عقب
یکدیگر در می آرند و شعر مذکور را شاهد آورده سهو کرده دیگر دا و ده است که بمعنی ظرف زمان و مکان می آید که آنرا
فی گویند الشاهد علیه شعر بیر تو تغالی ولکا فوجکام کونکلدا ه یوق سیندا کونکول ایله که انم کونکولدا نوع
دوم آنست که بمعان مختلفه می آید و آن چاوچه است که در بعضی از مواضع قیاسیست و در بعضی سماعی اما قیاسی بدو معنی
می آید اول بمعنی انتهاست که آنرا بعربی الی گویند الشاهد علیه شعر بر تیره ایردی صبحدمیم شام غم غرچه تاشام
غم ایلا کامین صبحدم غرچه بولمیش انینک سفالی نوا ایغه جام و باده کوپ فرقا و شوق طرف سیله جام جم غرچه دوم
بمعنی قدر و مقدار باشد چنانکه گوید شعر لعلی دین بیر حرف سینوق کونکلومنی ایلار تا غنچه نقد جان بر شام یوقا تینک
الیدا تو قراغچه اما سماعی بر سه وجه است اول گویند که آر دیچه و سونکیچه و سونکینچه و کینچه و هر چه بار لفظ
یعنی از عقب الشاهد علی الاول شعر نوا بیا ابر عمرا ول شوخ ترکان جرتنده نوا تیلار ایتاک آندین یوکوره آر دیچه
الشاهد علی الثانی شعر چونکه سیتینک کوروب ولچه مزینحال الغولوب اوزکا کیلکاج نیه لولرخش سونکینچه یوکورا
دوم گفته میشود که اوز کا چه یعنی طور دیگر و نحو دیگر چنانکه گوید شعر التفات ایتی بو کوز مین قولغه اول شاه اوزکاچه
اوزکاچه آنکلاب مین ایمدی خالیمنی یاهه اوز کاچه سیم گویند کنچه یعنی چه طور و بالجیم عجمی هم بدو معنی بود اول گویند که
کونکلاکچه یعنی بکام دل الشاهد علیه شعر نی قول اسلام ارا توشکا کیم اول کافر نه مستا ول لیک کونکلاکچه
سیکو تیب سید ان نیاری دوم گویند کرنچه یعنی هرچند و چند تا چنانکه بمعنی هرچند گوید شعر طریق عشق ارا اودنی
چو فرد قیلسا بیراو خویدا نماس آنکا بیر کوکاچه ایرور لالارکاو و بمعنی چندتا فرماید شعر ایتادی جسم ایوی بیرهن
وای کیم تالمادی رهزن بیری کیم نچه روزن بولمادی و بفارسی بمعنی تصغیر باشد مثل باغچه و طاقچه یعنی باغ محقر و طاق
بیان دوم آنست که افاده معنی اسمی میکند و آن بر دو نوع است نوع اول قیاسیست و آن بر دو طریقه است طریقه اول
آنست که در همه جا بیک ملا استعمال میشوند از آنجمله آو است که از یک تا نه در آخر اعداد در می آید مثل بیراو یعنی یکی و ایکاو
دوتا و هکذا اخوات ها دیگر نچی است که در آخر تمامی اعداد در می آید مثل بیرینچی یعنی یکمین و ایکینچی یعنی دومین و علی هذا القیاس
دیگر تول است که در آخر الوان افاده معنی نیم رنگی میکند مثل آغیمتول یعنی مایل بسفیدی و قزیمتول یعنی مایل بسرخی و همچنین است
قرامتول و یاشیمتول و اشباه آنها دیگر لاغ و لاق است که مرادف زار و ستان است که بفارسی دکلزار و کوهستان استعمال میشود
و آن بمعنی مکانیست که متضمن کثرت و انبوهی باشد مثل توزلاق یعنی نمکزار و آولاق یعنی مکان پر صید و یایلاق و قیشلاق یعنی
که در تابستان و زمستان در آنجا اقامت نمایند دیگر دیلک است که به معنی استعمال میشود اول از ذات تشبیه است بمعنی تو
بود الشاهد علیه شعر طرفه خسارینک که حسن ایچرا ایرور کلدیک طرفه اق بو دور که کلزار ایرماس اول خسار دیک
دیگر در آخر صیغه مفرد مخاطب امر فعل امر در آمده آنرا بمعنی مفرد مخاطب مضارع میسازد چنانکه گویند باردیک یعنی میروی
و اسرادیک یعنی نگهدار الشاهد علی الاول شعر تیلبه کونکلومنی نوائی ضبط ایلاماک المادینک ایمدین حیک آندی
الیک هر نیاری بار ساباردیک الشاهد علی الثانی شعر ای نوائی تیلاکان زهد و صلاح کوز یوم کونکلیم
هم اسرادیک سیم گویند که سالغودیک یعنی انداختنی و چنانکه بیندارد و قرغالغودیک یعنی بر همزدنی و همچنان

بر همزه رد چنانکه شاهد بر هر دو معنی اول گوید شعر یار بولمیش اوزتاغه هجران طریقین سالغودیک عقل وجان و
کونکلوم خیلی هم قونغالغودیک و در آخر مثل مضارع نیز در آمده و بهمین معنی استعمال می‌شود مثل سالوردیک و قونغالوردیک
که مرادف سالغودیک و قونغالغودیک باشد و دیک بمعنی سالک هم می‌آید چنانکه در کتاب دال در ذیل لغات مذکور خواهد
شد و تبدیل دال بتا نیز جایز است فایده در محاورات تراکه روم دک بر وزن رک بحذف یای بیان کسره بمعنی تنها استعمال
میشود چنانکه فضولی گوید با ملاء الرومیه شعر شاملر انجم سایرم صبحه دک ای شب هجر نیکا یوم الحساب بکر
ماش و تاش است که افاده معنی مشارکت و معیت میکند مثل یولداش یعنی همراه و قارین تاش یعنی هم شکم و کوکلتاش
یعنی هم شیر و در این معنی با فارسی شرکت و شریکی معانی دیگر دارد که در کتاب تا و دال بطریق تحقیق نگارش خواهد یافت
طریقه دیگر انت که باختلاف مورد در املا اختلاف می‌یابند و چون در این مقام تعداد حروف مراد است و موارد استعمال
و وجه اختلاف در مبنا شتم مراد با ملامتر و ما نگاشته خواهد شد بذکر اجمالی اکتفا میرود از انجمله داغ و راک
که علامت فعل تفضیل است دیگر قی و غی و کی است که افاده معنی نسبت میکند مثل آنداغی یعنی انجائی و موندا غی یعنی
اینجائی و یلقی یعنی سالیانه و کیچه کی یعنی شبانه دیگر چه و کینه است که علامت تصغیر است مثل یومروقچه
یعنی مشتک و اسروک کینه یعنی مستک دیگر لیغ و لیق و لیق و لوق و لیک و لوک است که بمنزله یای نسبت و یای مصدر
و بمعنی صاحب است و معانی دیگر هم دارد چنانکه در کتاب لام در ذیل لغات مذکور خواهد شد نوع دیگر جماعت
از انجمله داق است که با اسماء اشاره ترکیب یافته مثل آنداق یعنی همچنان و موندا ق یعنی همچنین دیگر دو رو ق است که
بمعنی آلت است مثل بویوندوروق و آن آلتی است که در وقت تخم برکردن گاو کار بندند و او کوندوروق میلی است که
حلاجان پنبه را بدان از دانه جدا کنند دیگر لا و لای است که افاده معیت میکند مثل ایکالا و ایکالان یعنی تا
با هم و اوچالا و اوچالان یعنی سه تا با هم و حرف لا از مقوله تتمیم صوت نیز استعمال میشود چنانکه در بنای
چهارم در ذیل لغات خواهد آمد دیگر چاق و چاک است که در بعضی الفاظ بمعنی آلت مصطلح گشته مثل آلینچاق
و آن آلتی است که از برای زینت بر پیشانی اسب بندند و یا دغو چاق آلتی بود که بدان کند ه خورد کنند و یسلچاک
حایل و تعویذی که از گردن آویزند و چاق از علامات سماعیه اسم فاعل نیز هست مثل یاسانچاق یعنی خود آرا که در
ذیل باب چهارم در بیان اسم فاعل گذشت فایده در محاورات تراکه روم لفظ چاق و چاک هر گاه در آخر لفظی در آید
بمعنی محض و چون می‌آید چنانکه فضولی گوید با ملاء الرومیه شعر غرض فضولیه انجق النکه اولمکدر و لی عالدیل
هم سن اویبجی قاتل یعنی غرض فضولی همان در دست تو مردن است اما مخالفت آنهم چون تو قاتل باشی و نیز گوید شعر ال الد آلود
کزیملت اول کلرعنا انکین و هم ایدم کیم دوتر غاشو شید ا انکین یعنی آن گلرعنا چون نیر کند دامن ا پیت میگیرد
و هم میکند که مبادا لیت غاشو شید ا دامن اپکیرد و هر گاه با روابط و سنغنا بعضی استعمال شود افاده معنی دیگر کند
چنانکه گوید چیقه چقدم یعنی بیرون خواهد آمد و کیله جکم یعنی خواهد آمد الشاهد علی الاول من فضولی با ملاء
الرومیه شعر نیه اولغا نیم الدی قرارم بو کیچه چقا جقدر ظنکه نالهٔ زارم بو کیچه و از این قبیل است دیر جک اوله
یعنی اودین باشد و ایضا منه فی الترجیعات شعر باده مدین غیری که غم دفعنه بر جام تیر تعدی هرینه هر کیم قیو جک
اوله ایتر یعنی سوای باده که یک جام بدفع غم کفایت میکند نقد خود را هر که هر چیز دادنی باشد کم میشود بمنا خمار رد

در بیان فواید و آن حروفیست که از برای مزید شان و تزیین بیان استعمال می‌شود از انجمله ار است که در اعداد احاد در آید اوچ
مثل بیرار یعنی یک واوچار یعنی سه و تورتار یعنی چهار رو یوزار یعنی صد چنانکه در تاریخ الانبیاء در صفت قیصان بن
گوید کیم خلق دین یوزار یوزار کیشی ایرب بوپودی کیم کیفت لاد ناشاد بلای قاعده که اینچه از اعداد احاد فرآخرش یای
حطی باشد مثل ایکی و آلتی و یتی و سکز بی چو حرکت بر یا ثقیل است شین معجمه در میان در آورده ایکیشار و آلتیشار و
یتیشار و سکیزیشار میگویند و عددیش که بمعنی نه است بسبب سکون شین آخر کلمه است بیشار نخواستند و التمیز
و یتمیش را نیز آلتمیشار و یتمیشار باید گفت دیگر ایکان و ایرکان است الشاهد علی الاول شعر سین ایکان سین حو
تیلبه بوقسا ایرکان کیشیلار نبید سنگا ولی شیر تاشی محراپیدین نیه قبله قویدی سین ای خاج موجبدیر ایکان سین
که عاجز مین جواب دیش دیگر دور و تورر است چنانکه گوید الشاهد علی الاول شعر مغاذ افسیرای عشق وجهت
بلا دور سیرز که کونکلوم دین ایب صبر و شکیب اوتلار تا الادور سیرز تنعم اهل و نیم و صال الیح رد هجر اهلیغه نوا دیر سیز
آبر بیمالت کمزار و بنوا دور سیز بلا دور سیز یعنی بلائید و زار و بنوا دور سیز یعنی زار و بنوائید الشاهد علی الثانی
شعر نسرین کوز کوسیدا ایرساری سین یاری تاری ره چمن مسکین کوزکوز و تورر کل یوزی ایماس کوز کوزو تورر
مرادف کوزکوز دور باشد یعنی عود دیا دیم و نیز گوید شعر ناصل اعمای کونکول چو عشق اعیش اورکان آلتی اوکا
عمرونکلانی کیم حاصل تیلب تورر دین اونه و نیز از جمله روابط است چنانکه مذکور شد دیگر تو لو است که بمعنی شوق
واقع میشود الشاهد علیه شعر حیات بخش مینک مرحم ایمیشوک ای ساقی مکرکه واوینی ملال ایسیتمیکت
دیگر چی است که از مقوله تتمیم صوت برآورده می‌شود چنانکه در لیلی مجنون بطریق حسن خطاب بجوانان لیلی گوید
ای وادی یمین الحرام چی ایت مین سنکا امر تاشیکلاو چی و از برای تزیین کلام نیز مذکور میکردد چنانکه در لسان
الطیر فرماید شعر لیک سین مینک بیلیلیق آندین یراق تا بیمینک سیل لیق کمامکان دین یراق سیل بیلیلیق
و مینک بیل لیق مترادف مانند یعنی فارسیانه و همچنین است جریکچی که مرادف جریک باشد چنانکه در هفت سکندری
گوید شعر یوز دیغ قوی ایسین جریکچی کوبه اولیدین بنجه شاخ اونون ایریث و نیز علامت فاعل است چنانکه
در فصل چهارم از باب اول در بیان اسم فاعل گذشت دیگر سی است که در بعضی الفاظ واقع شده مثل آرتوقسی که مرادف
ارتوق بمعنی فزون باشد و نیز از روابط است چنانکه مذکور شد دیگر ش است که داخل بعضی از صیغ میشود مثل قورشاق
بمعنی خشک شدن که مرادف قوروماق باشد چنانکه در خسرو شیرین گوید شعر کمیر کو ماله سیله حسرو نیکوی
حوش اولوت تین کونکلوم آنداق بولدی محرورش که اندین شعله چون خاخیغه توشتی قورو شماق تیندا کی تاغیغه
توشتی و نیز در بهار لیلی بصیغه ماضی گوید شعر شهد لبی تابدین قوروشتی یوق یوقر پریکا با بو شتی
و همچنین است یار و شماق بمعنی روشن شدن که مرادف یار وماق است چنانکه در لیلی مجنون بصیغه ماضی گوید شعر
کیم او تلار بدین جهان یاروشتی لار بیغه بوشعله توشتی و در بعضی از صیغ علامت مفاعله است چنانکه در ذیل باب
اول در بیان مصادر نگارش یافت دیگر نینک و نونک است چنانکه گوید الشاهد علی الثانی شعر کوزونک نونک
الیدا نرکس کیلیب تا تیغ کوزلوک تا یوزونک تا شیدا کلا تیشین ساوغنغ یوز لولغ هر گاه لفظ نونک از مصرع خارج
شود باز افادهٔ همان معنی خواهد کرد چنانکه گویند کوزونک الیدا یا کوزونک نونک الیدا یعنی در پیش چشمت

مفعول نیز هست چنانکه مذکور شد دیگر عیل و کیل آست که در آخر صیغه مفرد مخاطبه از فعل امر و نهی در می آید مثل آ
و آلما غیل و کیل کیل و کیلما کیل دیگر لیغ و لیک آست که در آخر مضارع واقع میشود الشاهد علی الثانی شعر
جور و ظلمونک کرچه اولما کلیک نشان دور منکا چونکه سیزدین دور حیات جاودانی دیر منکا یعنی جور و ظلمت اگر
لغوردن نشانیست بمن چونکه از تست حیات جاودانی است بمن و معانی چند دارد که در کتاب لام در ذیل لغات و موارد
استعمال آنها در ذیل مبنا ششم در ادا بالملا مذکور خواهد شد دیگر لآست که از برای تتمیم صورت مذکور میباید چنانکه
کوید شعر قطون خولوق عارضینک و صفین نوائی قیلغالی لطف طبع ابیات تظمین در مکنون قیلدی کلا و بمعنی حیف و
افسوس نیز مستعمل است دیگرن ساکنه است مثل انتظار دیند او قرار دیند که مراد فاشطار ایدا و قرار ایدا باشد یعنی کرد
انتظارش و قرارش و این حرف بذکر و حذف هر دو مستعمل است چنانکه مع الذکر کوید شعر برای اوتی یعنی مر بنفه
برای انتظار ایندا که فی کونکلوم ابرو رهوشندانی صبیم قرار ایندا مع الحذف کوید خاطریم و یرا ملیغین
بیلکای پراو هجر ایندا اول که هر ساعت پراونی بو قلاغای و یرایندا نیکو بر تا قبل بکشورت مثل سین سیزین و آت
که مرادف سین سیز و آنسیز باشد یعنی چنو و بی او و همچنین آست پرین پرین که مرادف پر باشد یعنی لت الشاه
علیه شعر زلفونک کیم ایرور توکون توکون کونکلی ایل بولدی پرین پرین کرفتار نیک و این حرف ضمیر هم
مبنا پنجم
مرکب با رابطه مفعول نیز هست چنانکه نکارش یافت مبنا پنجم در بیان کلماتی که بر معنی خاص موضوع اند و افاده معنی
غیر موضوع له میکنند و آن بر دو قسم است قسم اول کلمات مفرد مانند کلچو بترکیب شوند مفید معنی غیر موضوع له
میباشند از آنجمله آلماق بمعنی گرفتن باشد که با بعضی کلمات بمعنی قدرت و توانائی می آید چنانکه کویند آلا آلماق
یعنی توانگرفتن و بارآلماق یعنی توان رفتن و با بعضی کلمات بمعنا خاص مصطلح است مثل کونکول آلماق یعنی دلجوئی
کردن و ساتغون آلماق یعنی خریدن دیگر بیلماک بمعنی دانستن است اما بدستور آلماق در صورت ترکیب افاده معنی
صورت و توانائی میکند چنانکه در خسرو شیرین در تدبیر دفع فرهاد کوید المصرع الاول الشاهد علی الاول و الثانی
علی الثانی شعر ولی کیلتو رماکیکا چاره بیلمان بو عجز ایدین اول الغیشکا باره بیلمان دیگر توشماک بمعنی افتادن
و فرود آمدن باشد که در صورت انضمام افاده معنی پرداختن میکند مثل اتا توشماک یعنی قبل ندازی پرداختن
چنانکه بصیغه ماضی در صیغه ستاره در داستان مسافر بحثم کوید شعر اضطراب الابلا بان اتا توشتی بیر ایکی
اوق ولی خطا توشتی دیگر کیرماک بمعنی در آمدن و داخل شدن باشد اما در صورت ترکیب بمعنی آغاز کردن می آید
چنانکه در تاریخ بابری صیغه ماضی انفعل بدین نهج مذکور است که عشرت پیمانه لارین تولدورو بمجلس اهلنه
تو تا کیر یشتی لار و صوق جاغیر لارین هم عمل اهلی بو تاکیر یشتی لار دیگر یازماق بمعنی نوشتن و خطا کردن با
اما بمعنی آغاز کردن هم مستعمل است چنانکه در تاریخ بابری مذکور است که خسرو شاه یا نا شیب کیلدیشیب
و اوروشا باز یب آبر یلیب امیرزا بدخشان سناری تارتتی و مانند اینست لفظ کور کرا مستاز دیدین آنا ارکا
مبالغه و تاکید با لفظ دیگر ترکیب یافته معنی لفظ ما قبل را متضمن معنی سعی بعضی امر مضرف می کردانند چنانکه
کویند میلا کور یعنی سعی در کردن کن الشاهد علیه شعر جفا قیلو ناری کلیم لا امونا میلا کوردی و قام
ایلکا قیلو سین ولی نکا میلا کور و این لفظ در محاوره اتراک مرتبه نیز استعمال می شود چنانکه فضولی کوید یا ملکا الرو

شعر دو تا کور کور بولیر ای اشک کیم منکیزم اکوکه بو صورت ظاهر نی کورد و کچه نقش پریزم آدر و از این کلمات یک
فارسی نیز بسیار است چنانکه میکویند بر امامی احد بر قرار آمد قسم دویم کلمات مرکبه اند و آن بسیار است از کنایات نانا
تاش و آلماق باشد و آن کنایه است از ظلم و ظلمت شام دیگر قولاغ توتماق است یعنی زمان کوش و تعهد کردن دیگر
تا باق با علاتماق است یعنی چیز غیر واقع بکسی اسناد دادن دیگر قیزیل یاق و آتا یاقاست و استعمال این دو لفظ
بالاز دو لج کنایه است از هجوم عام که پا را ورد الیه بلچوبپتی هجوم نمایند دیگر قاتیغ کوزلو است یعنی بخت چشم
آن عبارت از بی شرمی دیگر ساووق یوزلو است یعنی سرد رو و آن عبارت از بی مهر و خنک اطوار دیگر کلیک
آزماق باشد و آن کنایه است از فساد معده و تباهی هاضمه دیگر کوز توتماق است یعنی چشم داشتن و آن کنایه است از توقع
مبنا ششم تمهید
امری بودن و نظایر آن بسیار است مبنا ششم در ادا با ملا و آن مشتملست بر یک تمهید و چهار رسم تمهید بدانکه زبان
رسم الخط آن خاص کرترتیبش مطابق تحریر نیست و مضبوط و مقرر نیست در کتابت داخل لفظ میکردد مثل الف بیان فتحه و واو
بیان ضمه و یا بیان کسره که بکتابت در می آید اما بتلفظ در نمی آید و در بعضی از اسما و اعلام این قاعده مطرد نیست مثل ترکن
بمعنی تفنکچی و سنجق و سنجی وغیره و مولفین سلف تبدیل دال و تا را بیکدیگر مطرد کفته اند کو هر تحقیق را غلط سفته اند
بعضی را البته با دال و برخی را با تای قرشت باید مذکور ساخت مثل دیماک بمعنی کفتن و تیملو بمعنی منع کردن و
همچنین تبدیل غین و قاف و خا را بیکدیگر مطرد بیان کرده اند و این هم بیان واقعیت بلکه جهت که در اکثر جو
هر کاه تبدیل واقع شود غلط و معنی بر خلاف سیاق و غلط خواهد بود مثل یغماق بمعنی جمع کردن و یغماق بمعنی کشیدن
و یاغماق بمعنی باریدن و یاغین بمعنی باران که البته با غین باید نوشته شود بر خلاف یقما و یقماق بمعنی خراب کردن و
بمعنی افشردن و یا یقماق بمعنی از هضم و پیدا افتادن و مرهم بستن و یاقین بمعنی نزدیک که البته با قاف تحریر باید
و در صیغ و مشتقات آنها نیز همین ضابطه باید ملحوظ باشد تا معنی از اشتباه و اختلاف محفوظ باشد و از این قبیل
قرچقای بمعنی باز و قزقول بمعنی ناسور و قوز غونک یعنی کلاغ سیاه و قوزغالان بمعنی آشوب که حرف وسطی با غین آید
و بعضی دیکر با قاف مصطلح است مثل قورقو بمعنی خوف و ایقو بمعنی خواب و توقوز بمعنی نه و چاقین بمعنی برق و غلطه
طالع هروی در تالیف خود بتقریب معنی آلغوچی و آلقان نوشته که در بعضی مواد کاف عربی بموافقت استعمال و مخالفت
قیاس نایب مناب دال در می آید مثل ایتکان بمعنی ایدن و ایتکای بمعنی ایدای و کیتکای بمعنی کیدای سهو کرده
زیرا که لفظ ایدن و کیدن مخرف و مخفف ایتکان و کیتکان است که اتراک روم و ایران مصطلح ساخته بدان تلفظ
مینمایند لیکن در لغت جغتای مستعمل نیست چنانکه در ذیل مبنا اول در بیان ابواب صیغ مذکور شد اما ایدای و کیدی
در لسان فرق اتراک روم و ایران هم مستعمل نیست تا بطایفه جغتای چه رسد و لفظ اخراجی مخالف قیاس و استعمال
تمیز دیگر چون سلاطین سلیمان مکین روم و اکثر قبایل آذربایجان و بوم منشعب از ایل تاتار اند ترکی رومی با لسان جغتای موافقت
دارد لیکن رومیه بسبب مجاورت و کثرت محاورت و معاشرت با اعراب بعضی لغات را معرب و محرف و مرخم
ساخته اند چنانکه در اکثر جاها سین را بصاد مهمله و تای قرشت را بطای حطی بدل و تبدیل مینمایند مثل توراو
بمعنی تم و نوع که آنرا رومیه دلو مینویسند و توتلوغ بمعنی جسته و بنابر آن توطلو و تاغ بمعنی کوه را طاغ
بمعنی نام را آت و بمعنی اسب را آط مینامند و صوی بمعنی آبرا صو و آسیغ بمعنی نفع را آصی و صاسیغ بمعنی کندیدن را صاسیغ

مینویسند و در اکثر مواضع بیانات مشتمل که عبارت از الف و واو و یای خطی باشد از تحریرات ساقط میسازند و آنچه
حرف سین در آخر صیغه مفرد مخاطب از فعل نهی واقع شود مثل آلماس و نوتماس یعنی مگیر و آنرا الگن و توتمن باز ای
هوز مینویسند و نیز جغتائیه میگویند که اتیکاپز یعنی میکنیم و رومیه میگویند که ایدرز و در بعضی لغات نیز
مختلف الاستعمال اند چنانکه رومیه یا پناق را بمعنی ساختن بیان میکنند و در لغت جغتای یا شاق بمعنی ساختن و
یا پناق بمعنی پوشیدن استعمال میشود در رسم الخط ایشان نیز همان رسم الخط جغتائی است لهذا تحریر و تقریر آنرا
رعایت ازانکه تحریفات بنیاد در ایشان راه یافته جهت فساد لغت اگرچه در ترکستان نیز بجو نیکه در ابتدای دیباچه مذکور
شد اختلافات در السنه و لغات بعضی از طوایف خصوصا ترکمانیه و ازبکیه میباشد اما چون همگی اهل ترکستان
میباشند و زبان ایشان آمیخته خلط و تحریف نیست اساس سخن را بر قاعده و طریقه املای ایشان میگذارد و آنرا

رسم اول

رسم قسم میسازد رسم اول در بیان تغییراتی که بعنوان تخییر در حروف و حرکات واقع می شود و آن مشتمل است بر
سه فصل فصل اول در ابدال و آن بر دو قسم است قسم اول در ابدال حروف باید دانست که آنچه قاف و غین در آخر کلمه اتفاق
افتد ذوالوجهین و کاتب در نوشتن آن مختار بین الاشتراکست مثل یافراغ که نوائی علیه الرحمه در حرف غین با
و در حرف قاف با قاف قافیه کرده چنانکه گوید فی حرف الغین شعر ضعیف جسمیم اراپیری نینکا وسیدا
قودوغ میعاج اوزه دو یافراغ اویستکا یافراغ فی حرف القاف شعر باغ ایچره سنکا ساچتی گل آق دقیزیل یافراق
شه باشیغه آندا قیلیم ایل آق و قیزیل یا رماقی و از این قبیل است یاغ بمعنی پاو کاسه که در هر دو حرف بیان کرده
حرف الغین بالمعنی الاول شعر بولیندا نولق ایلاکیل باشدیر زخم کیم بو بول قطعیدا باش قیما قودور و
ایلغ فی حرف القاف بالمعنی الاول شعر وصلینکا کیم الدیتیشام لطف ایتیب عذر و سفه باق کیم قدم اوزین
سو بورناک کوزیله قویمان ایلغ بالمعنی الثانی شعر تشنه لبلار خالی بو وادیدا نی بولغای که سو کوز یا شیدور
اوتلوق لاله لار نجامی ایاق و نظیر اینت لیغ و لوغ که شاهد بر اقوال او هر دو بنا مذکور ساخته فی حرف الغین شعر
دوستلار کوپ زارلیغ قیلسام عجب ایرماسکه بار زار کونکلوم دوست جبیدین دبی آزارلیغ فی حرف القاف شعر
تحدیم آر تیقیلماق اولا آی بز صفه محرم لیق میسر بولسا خوشتوار یت لاری خلیفه همدم لیق و از این نوع است
بولاغ بمعنی چشمه که با هر دو لفظ منظوم ساخته فی حرف الغین شعر یارانا ضین سوغر چو زینا لدی کوز وم توکی سیلاب
ای نوائی سیله بالیغ غه کیراک موندا ق بولاغ فی حرف القاف شعر ای نوائی توبیا تا ز قطعین آسان ایلادینک
اشکیمن موندا ق که هرمنزلدا چیکتنیک یوز بولاق شوازاینگونه الفاظ بسیار است که هر دو طریق نوشته می شود
مثل قوروغ و قوروق بمعنی خشک و جراءت و منع و ساریغ و ساریق بمعنی زرد و تاتیغ و تاتیق بمعنی سخت و آغ و آق
بمعنی سفید نماینده بدانکه ابدال در فعل امریکه حرف آخر آن قاف یا غین باشد جایز نیست زیرا که آنچه استعمال آن
با قاف است البته با قاف نوشته میشود مثل یاق یعنی بسوز و سوق یعنی خراب کن و آنچه با غین است با غین تحریر می یابد
مثل یاغ یعنی بیار و ییغ یعنی جمع کن اما هرگاه علامات صیغ باشد اغلب آنست که آنچه در انتها واقع می شود با قاف
مذکور میگردد مثل الماق و توتماق یعنی گرفتن و الدوق و توتوق یعنی گرفتیم و آلناق و توتقاق یعنی
بگیریم و آنچه در وسط واقع می شود بحرف و با حرف غین نوشته می شود مثل الغای و توتغای و آلغوچی و توتغوچی

واشباه آنها و ذکر مصادر نیز با قاف مرجح است زیرا که نوائی علیه الرحمه مصادر را در نظم و در اوزان بهمه حروف
قاف بیان فرموده اند و هرگاه مصادر بحرف و ضمیری اضافه شد قاف مصدر در وسط اتفاق افتاده باشد بعضی اوقات قاف
آنرا بعضی با غین و بعضی با قاف مذکور ساخته اند چنانکه در این شعر ساماقیرا که مصدر است سالماغین با غین
ذکر کرده و با یاغین بمعنی باران قافیه نموده و هو هذا شعر فی جهان اولغای که نالم رعدایرور اشکیم یاغین برق دیر
کوزکا نجهان ایچره دم اوت سالماغین و با قاف نیز منظوم ساخته الشاهد علیه شعر نوائی کونکلی قایتین نو
اسرایب سین ای قاتل امیدیم بو ایدی کونکلوم نی موجه اسراماقینکغه مقام بحث اگر گویند که چون علامات تمامی
مشتقه با غین مرقوم است چرا باید مصادر را با قاف مذکور شود بلکه اولی آن بود که آنهم با غین استعمال شود یا علامات
صیغ هم تماشیا له با قاف مذکور کردد جواب گوئیم که چون اتراک در صیغ حروف وسط علامات را با غین و حرف آخر را
با قاف تکلم می کنند لهذا در اینجا تحریر تابع تقریرات است و در بعضی هم که مصادر را بصفت پیوسته بود املای آنها از همین
بنظر رسید دیگر هر الفی که در آخر کلمات واقع شود تبدیل آن بهای هوز مجوز است مثل آکیدا و آکیده و یا نیغا و یا نیغه
و آنجا و آنجه چنانکه هم در حروف الف و هم در حروف ها بنا نشده فی حرف الالف شعر برای اوتی مینی محرم و نغمه سرا
آنتظار اییدا که نی کونکلوم ایرور هوشیدا نی هوشم قرار بیدا فی حرف الها شعر سیه زلفونک بوزو خلوتی ساکن
کونکلوم خانمانیده سیلاب آندان کیمسا لغای تخرخان بلان قوش اشیا نیده فی حرف الالف شعر باغیر خونابیدین
ضعف اولدی غالب خسته جانیغا آغیر ایردی غذا عوداییم رحمت نا توانیغا فی حرف الها شعر نیه نی اوت ایدی
کیم نوشتی خانمانیمغه نیه نی شعله ایدی کیم توتاشتی جانیغه فی حرف الالف شعر بویندا ایندا کل نظاره قیلدیم خور
یمانی آنجا مدی تاشیندا باقیم رو خط مرغوب تماسلنجا فی حرف الها شعر کیشی و صال توقیلدی چپرله یا تعویذجه خیالی
شمع خه قیلسون نظر تا ملک آن تعویذجه و همچنین است اینتسا و ایتسه و اجرا و اجره و اوزرا و اوزره و یا نیما و یا نیمه و اشباه اینها
قاعده باید دانست که ابدال الف بها در دو مقام جایز نیست اول در کاف مفتوحه است که بمعنی یای تعدیه در آخر کلمات
استعمال می شود مثل منکا و سنکا و اوزکا و مینکا اما هرگاه کاف جز کلمه واقع شود از این قاعده خارج است مثل شکه بمعنی زد
و انکه و انکه بمعنی الاد و دایه که با های هوز مکتوب می شود و کوکه را بمعنی کوس نوازد و کوره را بمعنی کرسی که مراجعه شود
برو آن میگذارند با الف و با هر دو قسم استعمال میشود دوم در الف بیان فتحه است که در اواسط کلمات اتفاق می افتد
مثل آلماس و کیلماس و آتا و توتار و اشباه آنها و ابدال ها با الف در هیچ جا جایز نیست و آن نون مفتوحات که بدل حرف تعدیه
در آخر الفاظ در می آید چنانکه گوید شعر سنی مخلیندن سوالدی لعل میرآب اوستینه خضر کونا سینا المیز
آب حیوان اوستینه اما در نون مفتوحه که در آخر نیه [illegible] واقع شده مجوز است قسم دوم در ابدال حرکات و آن اینکه
و اینکان و ایکین و اینکین باشد که بفتح کاف و کسر کاف هر دو مستعمل است چنانکه از اینجا بمشکن و تیکن قافیه کرده
بفتح کاف مذکور ساخته الشاهد علیه شعر نیتیب توزاتای قدیکم جسمیم اشکن لار دور نیلاهب توزا و رای دم کیم
باغریم ایتکن لار دور یوزیم دیله موسولار کونکلوم منی آکیب ایمدیرین مثل الماد پیلا و بدعهد ایکا نلاد دور
و جای دیگر با چین و سین قافیه ساخته و بکسر کاف بیان فرموده چنانکه گوید شعر تا وار داغ عشقدا لیغ زلفین
مسلسل المجدی چین لاوه کرم میم ایکی تماشیکی لام آتینک تا النغ سین لاله دبنام حسن اهلینی کودنا ملک کر ظالملار دود

و قاتل ، کونکول آتور کوزای شاید که موندلغ ایرناس ابرکین لای فصل دویم در حذف از جمله غای و کای است که هرگاه تا بکی
ازضمایر منفصله اربعه استعمال شود ذکر و حذف یای آن تخییر است لشاهد طولی الاول فی الترجیحات مع الذکر
قیلمایارب آنی کیم بولغای مین ، اول پیکان و یوملکین دین مهجور مع الحذف شعر یاقیلی یردی کرنیا موصفة
تالنالار کلیمغه حسن بخلیغ سوبود کامیل لبی ، مع الحذف شعر شهر و کوردین ایلیک یوظا نماندین کیچکای
خانمادین کیم دیون ایکی جهاندین کیچکامین ، و نیز در لسان الطیر در داستان سیمرغ و هدهد هدهد در فطر تو کوید
شعر آنجه اوغای سیز بو یولدا مال و پر ، ایلاکای سیز قطع آنجه بحر و بر ، کیم و منالجاکا میغه یا تیکانیز ،
یا تمناسیدا جان ترک ایتکانیز ، و هرگاه تنها فی یا با ضمیر جمع یا با روابط و منتسبات فعلی ذکر شود یای آن مطلقا
قبول حذف نمیکند دیگر حرف تعدیه است در بعضی مواضع چنانکه کیفیت آن در ذیل رسم دویم نگارش خواهد
یافت فصل سیوم در تخفیف و آن بر دو قسم است قسم اول بعضی از حروف مشدده است از آنجمله چهار حرف مشدد
از اعداد که هم تشدید و هم تخفیف استعمال میشود اول اتکی است که بمعنی دو باشد دویم یتی است که بمعنی
هفت باشد چنانکه در خسرو شیرین در وصف پادشاه هر دو قسم کوید شعر شکوهونک جبهه سیدین جوکن یا
یتی قطره عرق دیک تیتیج ریا ، و هرگاه بمعنی سیدا باشد که صیغه مفرد مغایب از فعل ماضی است باید مشدد خوانده
شود و تخفیف در آن جایز نیست چنانکه در ذیل رسم چهارم از رساله نیز خواهد شد سیوم سکزات
که بمعنی هشت باشد چنانکه در صفت ستاره هر دو قسم کوید شعر پایه اهرنیدا سکیزانکا ستون آستیدا
برکیتیب سکیز کردون چمبر توقوزاست که بمعنی نه باشد چنانکه هر دو قسم فرماید شعر زهی جولانکهنک
افلاک اهن میدان لوا حنک برا فیقنکه توقوز کنبد بو توقوز کنبد خضرا دیک سفال استکه بمعنی [illegible]
قسم دویم بعضی از کلمات است که حرف اول آن یای حطی واقع شده که یارا تلب با لف و الف را در دیج حذف کرده
ده بجای [illegible] از آنجمله یوز بمعنی صد باشد چنانکه در سکندری در صنعت [illegible] یازیق بریری کوید شعر [illegible]
آتی لعب و کره اوتوب کیم سنان اوجی کوزمای [illegible] آیدنی [illegible] تیزلک ، یوروردی [illegible] فلک
فلک ، و بمعنی رو هم بهمین نحو مستعملست دیکر ییل بمعنی سال باشد چنانکه در فتح سکندری کوید شعر
کل عطری یوز ییللیق بولکیت یوز ایل ایلک اولوک جان تاپسون ایتیب یوز ییللیق و یوز ایل ایلک [illegible]
یکدیکراند یعنی صد ساله رسم دویم در کلمات و علامات که باختلاف موارد استعمال الحروف و حرکاتها اختلاف می یابد
و آن بر دو قسم است قسم اول الفاظ [illegible] و آن بر چهار نوع است نوع اول الفاظ که تابع حرف ماقبل اند و آن روابط
علامات است که حرف اول آن دال باشد هرگاه حرف ماقبل آنها تای قرشت باشد دال آنها با تای قرشت تبدیل می یابد
و اگر بای عجمی و جیم عجمی و سین مهمله و شین معجمه و قاف و کاف باشد استعمال آنها با دال و تا هر دو جایزست و دو جایز [illegible]
البته با دال استعمالست و ابدال جایز نیست از آنجمله دی است که علامت صیغه مفرد مغایب است از فعل ماضی
و همچنین است علامات چکانه آن که باز دانید ترکیب در مبنا اول در ذیل باب دویم تفصیل یافته دیکر دا و ده است
که بمعنی ظرف زمان و مکان بود که آنرا بعربی فی کویند دیکر دین است که بمعنی از باشد که آنرا بعربی من و عن کویند
دیکر دور و دور و دورو است که بمعنی است باشد دیکر هرگاه لفظ دور که حرف رابطه است در آخر فعل ماضی واقع [illegible]

رسم دویم

البته با تای قرشت استعمال میشود چنانکه کوید شعر کوزونکدین بلا قرا بولوبتور جانغه فراقینگ بلا بولوبتور
[illegible] شعر جیقیب عشق اوتی کوکسوم چاکیدین باشیدین آشیب توره ، بوادیکیم کان ییغلاغیغه اوزانچندین ادت
تو تاشیب هموده و همچنین است بولیشتور یعنی شده است و آشیب تور یعنی کذشته است و تو تاشیب تور یعنی درگرفته
نوع دویم آنست که تابع حرکت ماقبل [illegible] و آن ی و ی است که ضمیر مفرد مغایب است هرگاه حرف آخر کلمه ماقبل ساکن باشد مثل کوزی
و مانای حطی بر آنها ملحق سازند چه کوزی و تاشی کویند یعنی چشمش و ابرویش و اگر حرف آخر کلمه متحرک باشد یکی از حرکات ثلاث یا
یعنی مفتوح یا مضموم یا مکسور باشد مثل آتا و کوزکو و ایلچی ضمیر ازاسی می آرند مثل آتاسی و کوزکوسی و ایلچیسی [illegible]
آن نحو ذیل مبنا اول در باب هشتم شرح داده شد نوع سیوم آنست که تابع قافی و کافی بودن افعال اند که علامات [illegible]
و آن علامات تستلغ صیغ که اگر فعل از صیغ قافی باشد آنها با قاف و غین و اگر از صیغ کافی باشد با کاف مذکور میکردند
و تخلف از آن جایز نیست و این قاعده قیاسیست و مجموع است در بیان [illegible] اولش علامت است که تغییر در حرف آخر آن
واقع میشود اول ماق و ماک است که علامت مصدر است مثل اینماق یعنی پیدا کردن و ایتماک یعنی کردن دویم
ساق و ساک است که علامت متکلم مع الغیر است از فعل مضارع مثل تاپساق یعنی پیدا کنیم و ایتساک یعنی بکنیم چنانکه
شاهد بهر دو در خسرو شیرین در مدح [illegible] کوید شعر [illegible] تاپساق
[illegible] اندین [illegible] تاپساق ، بیجه کیم [illegible] الارا [illegible] عذر [illegible] دیکر
دوق و توق و دوک و توک است که علامات متکلم مع الغیر است از فعل ماضی مثل الکدوق یعنی کرفتیم و تاپتوق
یعنی پیدا کردیم و دیدوک یعنی کفتیم و ایتتوک یعنی کذشتیم چنانکه در سکندری در [illegible] دادن دارا
باسکندر کوید شعر دیدوک کیم جونونکنه آغاز ایمیش جفا لیقینکا [illegible] ایمیش ایشینکا [illegible]
تدبیرین ، جوکوردوک [illegible] و تولدوق [illegible] تقصیرین ، و وجه اختلاط [illegible] اول این رسم مذکور شده اند دیکر
شانزده علامتست که تغییر آنها در حرف اول واقع میشود و چون نمایز هر یک در ابواب مبنا اول [illegible] بیان صیغ
آن علامات مذکور شده اجمالا به تکرار آنها نمی پردازد و اما [illegible] مفردات و مرکبات اما المفردات اول که خان و کان
دویم غای و کای است سیوم قیل و کیل است چهارم غالی و کالی است پنجم غاچ و کاچ است ششم غو و کو است
اما المرکبات اول غوچی و کوچی است دویم غوچه و غونچه و غاچنه و کونچه [illegible] است سیوم غوم و کوم است چهارم
غومیز و کومیز است پنجم غونک و کونک است ششم غونکوز و کونکوز است هفتم غوسی و کوسی است هشتم
غوسیلار و کوسیلار است نهم غو دیک و کو دیک است دهم غولوق و کولوک است نوع چهارم آنست که تابع
کلمه ماقبل اند اعم از اینکه ماقبل از صیغ باشد یا از کلمات سایره و آن منحصر و منیافت بیان اول در الفاظی که از
حیثیت حرف مختلف شوند و آن چهار لفظ است اول غا و غه و کا است که بمعنی بای تعدیه است [illegible]
که افاده معنی انتساب میکند سیوم غینه و کینه است که بمعنی تصغیر آید چهارم راق و راک [illegible] است که افاده
معنی افضل میکند و استعمال آنها مبنی بر دو قاعده است قاعده اول قیاسیت و آن بر سه طریق است که در [illegible]
از این طریق ثلثه آن الفاظ تابع ماقبل کشته اگر ماقبل [illegible] آنها با قاف و غین و اگر کافیست با کاف مذکور [illegible]

میکردید اول آنست که باصیغ قافی یا کافی مذکور شوند دویم آنست که با اسامی که از انها صیغه قافی یا کافی
بناشده باشد انضمام یابند باید که از مصادر و صیغ مشتقه استدلال بر قافی و کافی بودن آن اسم نمود نسبت را
هم موافق آن بیان نمایند سیوم آنست که با کلمه که حرف اخر آن قاف یا کاف باشد استعمال شوند که بنابر قرب
مخرج نسبت قافی با غین و قاف و نسبت کافی با کاف مذکور میکرده قاعده دویم سماعیت و آن هم بر سه طریق است
اول آنست که قاف یا کاف در اول یا وسط کلمه ماقبل اتفاق افتاده باشد اغلب آنست که بسبب قرب مخرج
آن نسبت را تابع کلمه کرده و در کلمه قافی با غین و در کلمه کافی با کاف مذکور میسازند و گاه هست که برخلاف
این هم اتفاق می افتد دویم آنست که ماقبل از الفاظ سایره باشد اغلب آنست که با غین استعمال میشود و در بعضی
الفاظ با کاف مستعملست سیوم کلماتی اند که جایز الوجهان اند و هر دو قسم مستعمل اند توضیح در بیان کیفیت
استعمال الفاظ اربع لفظ اول خاوغه و کاست که به نوع قیاسی و به نوع سماعی استعمال میشود اما القیاسی
اول آنست که با مصادر و صیغ مشتقه مذکور شود چنانکه در این شعر تعدیه چیماقرا که مصدر قافیست با غین
و از کیرماک را که مصدر کافیست با کاف ادا نموده شعر آنچه بولدی تن او قونکدین ایچکاری تاشقاری بول
کیم اجل کیرماککا جان چیقماقغه دو رهجیلاری بولوش و همچنین لفظ قیلور را که از مشتقات مصدر قیلماقست بمعنی کردن
قیلورغه و توکار را که از مشتقات مصدر توکماکست بمعنی ریختن است توکارکا مذکور ساخته و هو هذا شعر
اولغوسی قان توکارکا اول کوز و قاشی قیلورغه بیداد و ظلم باعث ناز و عتاب انمه و گاه هست که یک صیغه
بدو معنی مستعملست و در اول معنی با صیغ قافی و در معنی دیگر با صیغ کافی اشتراک دارد مثل اولتور و بمعنی میکشید
و میکشد اگر بمعنی نشستن باشد چون اولتورماق که مصدر آنست قافی است او را اولتورغه باید گفت و اگر بمعنی کشتن
باشد چون اولتورماک که مصدر آنست کافی است اولتورورکا باید مذکور ساخت دویم اسامی است مثل سو و اوت
که بمعنی آب و آتش بود نسبت آنها را با غین مذکور ساخته سوغه و اوتغه میگویند زیرا که مصادر و صیغی که از آنها
بنا شده وضع استعمال ایشان با قاف است مثل سوارماق بمعنی آب دادن و اوتلاماق بمعنی آتش زدن و بیرویل
که بمعنی زمین و باد باشد نسبت آنها را بیرکا و ییلکا میخوانند باین جهت که وضع استعمال مصادر و صیغ آنها با کافست
مثل بیرلاشماک بمعنی جا کردن و ییللاماک بمعنی باد کردن و دانستن این موقوف به تتبع کامل است سیوم الفاظ است
که حرف اخر آن قاف و غین ملحقه باشد مثل تاغ و تاق بمعنی کوه که تاغغه میگویند چنانکه گوید شعر
تا هوای میل اولدی هجرینکا آندا قیلکیم یولوت تاغغه هر دم بیز لا نور هر ناش توکوب فریادیا یتیب و همچنین ایلاک
و کوک نه ملایک کا و کوککا میخوانند الشاهد علیه شعر انجم دیما کویاکه ملایک کا تو تاشتی اهیم اوقی
اوچقونلاری کیم کوککا بیتوردونک و از این قبیل است اولوق بمعنی بزرگ و کیچیک بمعنی کوچک که در صحت کننده
در خاتمه کا جا دارد گوید شعر اولوقغه اولوغغه عطا ایلاکون کیچیککا کیچیک جاشنا ایلاگون و هر گاه
حرفی ملحق کلمه و علامت در آید مانع تاقه منکشه باز علامت تابع قاف و کاف کلمه خواهد بود چنانکه در
خیر و شیرین حرف تعدیه کیچیک لار را با کاف و اولوغ لار را با قاف مذکور شده و هو هذا شعر کیچیک لارکا

کیچیک دور عمر اناسیغ اولوغلارغه اولوغ را قدر قیانی اما التماعیات اول کلماتیست که غین کاف و قاف
جزء آن کلمه باشد مثل قوش و کوز که تعدیه قوش با غین و تعدیه کوز کو با کاف مذکور شده الشاهد علی الاول
شعر قوشغه اوت تین دم بولور یوز وای کیم کونکلوم قوشی اهر نوا سرای آلماس اول لعل خنا را آتشنا الشاهد علی الثانی
علی الثانی شعر سپاه جسونکا پر مجه سیه رخشان تکلم بولغای قوباش کوز کوسیکا آهیم ستونی کر توتاش اولسونی
در تخلاف این هم واقع می شود چنانکه تعدیه کلا با غین ادا شده الشاهد علیه شعر کونکول کا جان بیله پیر دافینک
از دور قویینیه پیرهشم نیچه اتی کلاغه پیر دیم اهر زه تلالر لولسونی دویم الفاظ سایره است که فارسی از حرف غین و قاف
و کاف باشد اغلب آنست که تعدیه آن با غین مذکور میکردد چنانکه گوید شعر آستان زیب تا تنک یوق میتود
شام اشک واه که بولوت سقا سیغه کاهی صبا فراشیغه و تعدیه بعضی با کاف هم مذکور میشود مثل پیر او بمعنی یکی چنانکه
گوید شعر کر جیدای آلمای کونکول پیر شام پیر او کا تا کهاش با مرای یل ایجره جیدای آلغانیم مشهور ایتماین و نظیر آن
ایل بمعنی خلق الشاهد علیه شعر توتوب سنکا چوی لطف شاهی رحمت شفاعتینک اوروبا یکی جهان ایلیکا
ملاذ سیوم الفاظ جایز الوجهان اند مثل آنغه و آنکا که اسم اشاره است یعنی با وچنانکه شاهد برا قلعلم خسرو
شیرین در وصیت سهیلی حکیم گوید شعر تا پار چون دیوقدل اتیکیش سلیمان نی تنیل خانمین بولادنی
میلنا دولت آنغه تسلیم باریتی ایلاسون خاقانغه تسلیم الشاهد علی الثانی شعر لعلینک اول الوتکیم کونکول
مجر آنکا دیا کونکول ایمج ولبینک کوهر آنکا اما تا بای استعمال اغلب بحرف ثانیست و همچنین است لفظ کلبه که تعدیه
آنرا هم با غین و هم با کاف مذکور ساخته الشاهد علی الاول شعر کلانی بولغای کیم یوز نقطه برا کوکا یمین آیتی
سا انالار کلبه غه خس بکلیغ سوپورکا یمن آیتی الشاهد علی الثانی شعر تیره کلبه کا کریب جانا اولومدین ترک
ظلمت ایجرا خضر غرا ول نوع کیم آب حیاة و بعضی الفاظ هست که بدو معنی استعمال شده کاه هست که وضع استعمال نسبتهای
آنها در این معنی با غین و قاف و در این معنی با کاف می باشد نایندکا هرگاه کلمه که حرف اخر آن قاف باشد با غین تعدیه
جمع شود جایز است که حرف تعدیه را که جزو است تابع کلمه ساخته از آنهم با قاف نویسند چنانکه در خسرو شیرین گوید
شعر دیبان دیوانه سالسانبدلا یاقنه قوتولماق ولفرتا چیککای ایراقته اما در هر جا با غین نوشتن مخالف تکلم و لفظ
اتراکست هرگاه حرف کیری در میانه در آید در آنصورت بعینها غین را غین و قاف را قاف باید نوشت چنانکه گوید شعر تا کورون
یوزین قوپایش لغالی اشتیاقیغه کاه باشیغه ایورولور کاه توشار دو تاقیغه نایندکا بدانکه از الف نعم و ایران حرف
تعدیه را در هیچ جا مذکور نمیسازند اگر لفظ مسکونة الاخر باشد هما نحرف اخر را مفتوح ساخته بدل حرف تعدیه استعمال
می نمایند مثل اش و ایاغ که اشا باشه و ایاغه میگویند یعنی بسر و بپا و اگر متحرکة الاخر باشد یای مفتوحه در اخر آن در
می آرند مثل هوایه یعنی بهوا و سویه یعنی بآب و ایلحیه یعنی با ایلچی اگرچه در لغت جغتای نیز اسقاط حرف تعدیه برین نهج
جایز است اما بدور حضرت ساقط نمیکنند و در جمیع مؤلفات منظوم و منثور حضرت نوائی بغیر از سه مقام لفظی محذوف
التقایه بنظر نرسیده اول اوستیکا بود که کاف را حذف کرده نون مفتوحه در اخر آن در آورده اوستینه میگویند الشاهد
علیه شعر سبزه خطینک سوادی اهل خندان اوستینه خضر کویا سایه سالمیش آب حیوان اوستینه دویم ضمیر
متکلم وحده است که میم را مفتوح میسازند مثل جانیم و کونکلومه الشاهد علیها شعر کونکلوما پیکان نکلاهینک بر

قطره قطره سوایماش حالیما کوذه‌یك بعینه اول داغی کریان ایروش سیم نقد یرابت که با نون و کاف خطاب جمع
جمع شود که همان کاف خطاب را بدل حرف نقد یر مفتوح میسازند چنانکه کوید شعر کیلور ونکا یاسادیم کونکلوم
اوین یاسالور کلبه جو مهمان کیم کالج لفظ تیوی و کی است که افاده معنی انتساب میکند وان مشتملست بر دو نوع
قیاسی و یك نوع سماعی اما القیاسی فی الکلمات فیست که آخر آن غین و قاف یا کاف باشد مثل اولوغ و کیچیك و بلغ و کوك
که اولوغداغی و کیچیکداکی و تاغداغی و کوکداکی میکویند یعنی آنچه در بزرکست وانچه در کوچکست وآنچه در کوه است
وآنچه در آسمانست دویم اسامی است که وضع استعمال انها بر قافست مثل یول که مصدرش یولدا ماق بمعنی براه آمدن
و قافیست لهذا نسبتش را هم با غین مذکور ساخته یولداغی میکویند الشاهد علیه شعر طلب یولیداغی اواره لاذغه
مژده دینکیز که یولغه هادی یرورد وستم ملک حیش و پیر که بمعنی دوست چون استعمال آن بمعنی بیر کافست مثل کوبیز
که بمعنی دو بروشدنست نسبت آنرا یونیداکی میسازند چنانکه کوید شعر دیده‌دا ولسا چنك کمزیدا یستاد نه
جهان یوزیداکی دین احلیفه آینیك عریش اما السماعی اسامی و کلمات سایر اند که از آنها صیغه بنا شده که بر قاف
وکاف بودن انها استدلال توان کرد در آن تصوریا کر کافی بن کلمه باشد اغلب آنست که نسبتش با کاف مذکور میشود مثل
کونکول کا از اکونکولیداکی کویند الشاهد علیه شعر ن کونکلینی یوزادو دیده درد و غم نوائی نینك چو اول پری دور
برلا شویتیلبه کونکلیداکی و همچنین است کوی که آنرا کویداکی نامند چنانکه کوید شعر سیلادیم کیم اول الیلا پری
بغیدین خلاص تو قیلغان شیخ مغ کویداکی میخانه‌نی و از این قبیل است کون بمعنی روز که آنرا کونکی خوانند چنانکه
در مقاله سیم از حیرت الابرار کوید شعر بسکه سماع غزل و قول صوت بولوبان لول کونکی نماز ایلکا فوت
عین و قاف داشته باشد نسبت با غین بیان میشود و بعضی الفاظ مخالف این بیانند مثل سونکراغی بمعنی آخرین اما بوزنا
بمعنی اولین انقیاسیاتست زیرا که صیغ از آن بنا شده و بوراشماق بمعنی تقدم جستن مصدر آنست چنانکه شاهد
اولین را بمعنی آخرین و شاهد بر آخرین را بمعنی اولین کوید شعر وعده قیلدینك هم و ناهم قیل بروا ایتمادینك قیل
و فا و عده نکنه ایلخود بوزناغی یا سونکراغی لفظ تغنه و کینه آست که بمعنی تصغیر استعمال میشود وآن مشتملست بر یك
نوع قیاسی و یك نوع سماعی اما القیاسی مثل بومروق بمعنی مشت و کوز بمعنی کبود که بنا بر رعایت قرب مخرج نسبت بوکوز
با غین و نسبت کوزرا با کاف میکویند الشاهد علیه شعر یوزا و باد کا قویمادی ایلکین دیدیم یاریم و بای
تا شلا بان بومروقغینه قیلدی کوزومنی کوککینه اما السماعی الفاظ سایر است کاه هست که کلمات مرکبه
از قاف و غین را نسبتش با غین و کلمات مرکبه از کاف را نسبتش با کاف استعمال میشود مثل قوشغینه یعنی مرغك و کوکوس
کینه یعنی سینه‌اك و در الفاظی که عاری از این حروف باشد اغلب آنست که نسبت با غین مذکور میکردد مثل چیچغینه یعنی
واستك الشاهد علیه شعر جور ایله قیلدی بیدل لا یحفه یاری چیچغینه مهر ایله هر وعده کیم قیلدی یار
او تروق کینه اما نسبت جز بعض ململك معروف با کاف مستعملست و لفظ اتر و قکینه یعنی دروغك از جمله
چنانکه در ذیل قیاسی بر کلمه بیان شد لفظ جما دغ و راق هم الفاتست که بمعنی فعل تفضیل است وان مشتملست بر
قیاسی سه نوع سماعی اما القیاسیات اولا انست که با صیغ مشتقه استعمال میشود مثل اینکه اسم فاعل امر کا مخواهند
بنا کنند اگر قافیست نسبتش را هم با قاف مذکور سازند مثل آلغوچی راق یعنی کیرنده تر و اگر کافیست نسبتش با کاف بنا

نمایند مثل کیکوچیراك یعنی برنده تر دویم آنست که با الفاظی که از انها صیغه بنا شده مذکور شود مثل آچ بمعنی کرسنه
و توز بمعنی راست و چون آچماق بمعنی کرسنه شدن قافی و توزماك بمعنی راست شدن کافیست نسبت آچ را با قاف
و نسبت توز را با کاف مذکور ساخته میکویند که آچ راق یعنی کرسنه تر و توزراك یعنی راست تر سیم الفاظیست
که آخر آنها غین و قاف یا کاف باشد مثل سارغ راق یعنی سرد تر و یاووقراق یعنی نزدیك تر و چاکراك و تمناك
الشاهد علی الکافی شعر کوکراکیمید و صبح نینك پراهنی دین خاکراك کیر سیکیم شبنم توکولکان شین مدین
اما السماعیات آنست که با الفاظی که قاف و کاف داشته باشد مذکور شوند مثل قویراق یعنی سرازیر تر و کوکراك
یعنی بیشتر و کاهی تخلف هم واقع میشود دویم آنست که با الفاظ سایره استعمال شوند اغلب آنست که نسبت با غین و قاف
مذکور میشود مثل خوب راق و مرغوب راق الشاهد علیه شعر ای جمال و ناز و عشوه‌نك پری دین خوب راق
تا منینك مرغوب واندین کیم نیك مرغوب راق و با کاف هم مستعملست چنانکه در مقاله نوزدهم از حیرت الابرار
در وصف عشق کوید شعر هر نیچه کیم حسن دلاویز اغوش عشق او تی ایل کونکلی آرا تیزراك وشاهد بر دویم نیز
محبوب القلوب کوید که هر این کها بیند اکیم سار غا مید المنبع فه تر خد بولغای اول جانبی توت کا ایمکاکی آن طرق
کم راه خاطر فریب کیلکا کی و از این قبیل است بخشی راق و بهر الع چنانکه شاهد بر اولی در سکندری فرماید شعر
خردین ایرو غیب علمی براق ایرو بیخرددین خرد بخشی راق وشاهد بر ثانی از لیلی مجنون کوید شعر ضعف ایچره
غیب بولسا مشغوف بهر راك که تو میمانزل طبیعت ذوق سیم جایز الوجهانند
قاید کا اینکلمه در محاوره اتراك روم بمعنی حال و بنیان تکرار استعمال میشود مثل اینکه میکویند تا چاراق یعنی کریزان
کریزان و کیدراك یعنی رفته رفته و کیفیت آن در ذیل باب پنجم در مبنا للوك مذکور شد و در سیم الخط رومیه آنست
که بسقوط الف بنیان محمه تحریر باید یافت دویم آنست که از حیثیت حرف و حرکت مختلف میشوند از انجمله لیغ و لیغو و لیق
ولوق ولیك ولوك است که مترادف و بیك معنی استعمال میشوند و استعمال آن بر دو منوال است منوال اول
در اختلاف حرفست وآن مشتملست بر سه نوع قیاسی و سه نوع سماعی اما القیاسیات اول آنست که با صیغ مذکور شوند
با قافی مثل چیقماسلیغ یعنی بیرون نیامدن و با کافی مثل ایتماسلیك یعنی نکردن الشاهد علی الاول شعر
جیق نوائی قادینك حومنالمه میکل دین سود را یقودلا رکیشی چیقماسلیغ ایتیب بولسا تا شامك الشاهد علی الثانی
شعر تا و ماای شیخ نوا ایتی ایشیتما س دیب بیند کیم سینینك ایشیتماسلیکی انکا پند اولمیش دویم انست که با
الفاظی که از انها صیغه بنا شده مذکور شوند مثل آچلیغ بمعنی کرسنکی و توزلوك بمعنی راستی سیم انست که با کلماتی
که حرف آخر آنها قاف و غین یا کاف باشد استعمال شوند مثل داغلیغ یعنی داغدار و سباکلیك یعنی سپاهی چنانکه کوید
شعر ناکاه ای احباب دوران قیلما فای سپاه لیك بوقسا بیزدیك یوز تومان خانمان اوچون اولسا خرابك اما
السماعیات اول انست که با کلماتی که قاف و غین یا کاف داشته باشند مذکور شوند چنانکه در لیلی مجنون نسبت آغار ایماق
و نسبت سینکیل را با کاف بیان فرموده شعر سازاینی آغالیغ و سینکیل لیك کوپ بینادی سینکلی دین ایل لیك
و مثل اینست تاری لیغ یعنی بری و بیکیت لیك یعنی جوانی و کاه هست که مخالف این ضابطه استعمال میشود مانند
بیکلیغ که بمعنی ماننده باشد و از این قبیل است کم و کاستیلیغ که در مقاله دهم از حیرت الابرار فرماید شعر

کیم که بود وزاندا قیلیبدر است لیغ بوق تودا یتی غیر کم و کاست لیغ دوئیم الفاظ سایره اند کر غار علامت ایچ حرفی
باشند مثل دیوانه لیغ و فرزانه لیغ و اشباه آنها الشاهد علیه شعر عشقینکا اپر دیوانه لیق شو تونکا اپیر
فرزانه لیق اغیار دین بیگانه لیق ایلاب او زونکا آشنا و بنت بعضی الفاظ با کاف هم مستعملست مثل تیره لیک چنانکه
کوید شعر ساوغ آه یمدین بار و غلوغ آزولی کیپ تیره لیک تیشدا اول نیک لیغ کر تون بولغای او زون
کون قیسقاریث و نظیر انیست جیرلیک الشاهد علیه شعر منکا ایمدی سروایله کل مدلها یوقیلادی شرح
بویلوق کل جبین لیک لار هوا سیغ لادی سیم جایز الوجهاند مثل بیل لیغ و بیل لیک بمعنی سالیا نچنانکه در لسان
الطیر با قاف فرماید شعر لیک سیز منیک یلچی لیغ آیدین براق تا بیمی منیک سیل لوق کها مکاندین براق وکذا سیغه
سیاره با کاف کوید شعر کوکدین کتاردی چون تار لیغ تیم بیل لیک معاف تو تیتی خراج و در سد سکندری بدید
تسلط اسکندر بممالک دارا کوید مع القاف شعر سوزی نافذ ایردی ولی بول براق کیرا لغایردی برایکی بیل
براق مع الکاف شعر ایکی ملک ایرا یکی بیل لیک خراج چریک کا بیریب بخه کیم احتیاج و بتتبع متعدد رجوع شد
همین نحو مرقوم بود و از این قبیل است بیکانه لیغ و بیکانه لیک و کم لیغ و کم لیک سوال دوئیم در اختلاف حرکات
وانتم مستعملست بیک قاعده مناسب القاعده ما انکه اکر حرف ما قبل لام مضموم باشد لام نیز هم مضموم می آید مثل
تابغولوق بمعنی غمناک و قرانغولوق بمعنی تاریکی چنانکه کوید شعر کونکلوم بولور غمینک توفی هر لحظه تابغولوق
چو نشام بولدی هر نفس آرتار قرانغولوق و همچنین است نازکلوک یعنی نازکی الشاهد علیه شعر لطف کیم کیم سوده کل
عکسی مثل لیک کورونور حله نازکلوکدین هر بیاری غلط زلف بدنیک واکر حرف ما قبل مفتوح یا مکسور باشد لام نیز
مکسور مضموم میکردد مثل غمنا لیق یعنی غمناکی و بیرلیک یعنی اتحاد و سکون حرف آخر معتبر نیست مثل ویران
و مسلمان که در اینصورت هم مراعات حرکة ما قبل لام نسبت با کسره ادای شود چنانکه کوید شعر کوزونک کر
ایله یوزدین غمناللدی ویرانلیغ خدای او چون تی آنی یوقمو دور مسلمانلیغ مقام بحث اکر کویند که ظریف این
چه حضرت نوائی ناخوشلیغ را با سرکشلیغ قافیه فرموده اند و هو هذا شعر جانی خوشلوغ بیرله اول کافر تیرک
بیکا کیم اول خود الکو تالسا ایت آلماقته ناخوشلیغ بیله و همچنین در مقاله یازدهم از حیرة الابرار گفته اند شعر
سل کیمینا و رفاق و ناخوشلیقاوت کیمی کوید و رفاک و سرکشلیغی جواب کوییم که هرچند که بحسب ظاهر ناخوشلوغ را
ناخوشلیغ بکسر لام بیان کردن ناخوشی دارد اما مخالف قیاس نیست زیرا که شعرا تبعا تکلم لفظ خوش را بجهة امالة
غنه هم خانا اند و موش قافیه کرده اند باین جهة حضرت نوائی نیز جهة فتحه را دراین کلمه مراعات کرده نسبت آن را به
مذکور ساخته اند فایده در لسان اتراک روم و ایران مصطلحاتست که این لفظ را هرگاه بمعنی یای نسبت یا بمعنی صفات
استعمال شود بحذف قاف وکاف مذکور ساخته مراعات حرکت ما قبل نیز میکنند مثل شاملو یعنی شامی و دولتلو یعنی دولت
اما در لغت جغتای حذف جایز است و ترک مراعات حرکت ما قبل غیر جایز است مثل قراتاشلی و قراقویونلو که نام طایفه
و اکر بمعنی یای مصدری باشد حذف آن نه در لغت جغتای جایز است و نه در لسان اتراک روم و ایران و باید البته با قاف
وکاف مذکور شود مثل چوخلوق یعنی بسیاری و یالغوزلوق یعنی تنهائی و آشنالیق یعنی آشنائی و ایل لیک یعنی
یالیت و بیرلیک یعنی یکانکی دیکر سه علامت است از صیغ تانی علامت اول دیم و دوم قیم و قوم است که ضمیر متکلم

وحد است علامت دوئیم دیک و دوک و دینک و دونک است که ضمیر مفرد مخاطبست علامت سیم دینکیز و دونکوز
و دینکیز و دونکوز است که ضمیر جمع مخاطبست واستعمال اینها بر دو منوالست منوال اول در اختلاف حروفست
اکر حرف ما قبل اینها تای قرشت باشد اینها هم با تای قرشت مذکور میکردند مثل توتتی یعنی کرفت و کیتتی یعنی رفت
و اکر سین مهمله و شین معجمه و بای عجمی و جیم عجمی و قاف و کاف عربی باشد با دال و تا هر دو مستعملست مثل آسدی و
آشتی و اوپدی و اوپتی و اوچدی و اوچتی و یولوقدی و یولوقتی و توکدی و توکتی و هکذا اخواتها و با سایر حروف
البته باید با دال مذکور شود مثل اوردی و آلدی و بیردی و دیدی و غیرها و کیفیت آن در ذیل نوع اول از رکن سیم
از قسم ثانی بیان یافت منوال دوئیم در اختلاف حرکاتست اکر حرف ما قبل مضموم است حرف اول ضمایر هم مضموم ذکر میشود مثل
اوردوم و توتتوم یعنی زدم و کرفتم و اکر مفتوح یا مکسور است مکسور مذکور میکردند مثل سالدیم انداختم و یاتیم
خوابیدم و قیلدیم و اینیم کردم و هکذا اخواتها و بعضی از کلمات هست که بمنزله مبنیات اند و حرکات آنها از تغیر
مصونست چنانکه در ذیل قواعد سیم نحو بیان خواهد شد قسم دوئیم انست که بسبب ما بعد مختلف می شوند از آنجمله
بعضی از اسامی اند که حرف وسطای اینها مضموم یا مکسور باشد چون آنرا بحرف مضاف سازند باید حرف وسطی را
ساکن ساخته بر آن حرف اضافه نمایند مثل اوین بمعنی بازی و بویون بمعنی کردن و اورون بمعنی جا و اغیز
بمعنی دهن و باغیر بمعنی جکر و کونکول بمعنی دل و کوکوس بمعنی سینه و تاریم بمعنی شکر چنانکه شاهد برای این در نظم
الجواهر در صفت اکل کوید شعر تاریمنک بیله دوست بولماسانک اجر دور نیوچون کرایرا و خلیفه تاریمدین شد دور
و همچنین است یلیک بمعنی دست الشاهد علیه شعر چون ایلیک بیرماسر که اوپسام اولسه کا رایلیکنی
بر کیشی ایلکین او پای کیم اول الونا رایا رایلیکنی و مثل اینست سینکیل بمعنی همشیره کوچک چنانکه در لیلی مجنون کوید
شعر سا زا یتی انا لیغ و سینکیل لیک کوپ ایستادی سینکلیدین بحل لیک و بر این قیاس است کین بمعنی عقب
الشاهد علیه شعر بو زونک و صفین دیب ونکان تون در اشکیم توکا ایردیم تو توبانع کینین آی کیردی
قرانو فراقته پروین هم و از این قبیل است بورون بمعنی پیش و قبل و چون بمعنی معلم بر اعضای صورت آنرا هم بالحاق
بورون کویند و هرگاه بمعنی پیش استعمال شود حرکت را بسکون تبدیل نماید چنانکه کوید شعر بیشتی تورنغه
آنت که تونی بورون ایک یار و غلوغی بیله چونقع بولدی کنده دماغ و اکر بمعنی پیش استعمال شود بورنا بسکون را و
نون مذکور میشود و نظیر اینست قویون که بمعنی بغل و آغوش و کردباد و کوسفند باشد هرگاه بمعنی بغل و آغوش بحرف
اضافه شود ضمه یا را بسکون مبدل میسازند الشاهد علیه شعر کلامینک کوهری دیک تاپماس
کرچه صبا ایلکی یقا سین غنچه نینک یرتیب نچه کیم قوینین آختارمیش و هرگاه بمعنی کرداد و کوسفند استعمال
شود تغیر در اساس و حرکات آن را نمی یابد چنانکه بمعنی کرداد کوید شعر سینی سرکشته ایمان وادی هجرا
باث غصه تو فراقی واندوه سیلی دین قویوث دیکر الفاظ مسکونة الاخر اند که چون بحرف علامت افزوده شوند
حرف آخر را مضموم و بر آن علامت منضم میسازند مثل کوزونک یعنی چشمت و بورنونک یعنی بینیت و کوزوم یعنی چشمم
و بورنوم یعنی بینیم و اکر آن لفظ مفتوحة الآخر یا مکسورة الآخر باشد حرف آخر را مکسور نموده علامت انضمام میدهند
مثل باشینک یعنی سرت و تیشینک یعنی دندانت و باشیم یعنی سرم و تیشیم یعنی دندانم مقام بحث هرگاه کویند که

24v.

رسم سیم

چگونه صلابین شعر خورد دومه بخلاف قیاس خوردیمه نکجه حال واقع شده و هو هذا شعر هجرا احالیم کمی
بیهوشلوق کم غم بیمالک عشقینک اقبالیده تیل نظاره خواب و خوردیمه جواب همان گوئیم که در ذیل مبادو نیم
این سهو تبقریب ذکر ناخوشلیغ بیان شد رسم سیم در ذکر بعضی کلمات که مخالف قیاس واقع شده اند و آن بردو قسم
قسم اول آنست که مخالف استعمال است از انجمله ایلیک بمعنی دلک و بند و بیشیغ بمعنی پخته که در ذیل باب لک
از مبلغ اول دربیان مصادر مشروح تحریر یافت دیگر آیدین بمعنی مهتاب باشد و اصل آن آی تون است یعنی
ماه شب که از کثرت استعمال آیدین شهرت یافته چنانکه در لسان الطیر در داستان شیخ بایزید گوید شعر
بجه آیدین تا بدین روشن ایدی چرخ انجم وروی دین گلشن ایدی لفظ آیدین بمعنی لزنما نیز میتواند شد دیگر
ایشتان بمعنی پیجامه است و اصل آن ایچتون است دیگر ایکیلا است یعنی هر دو تا دیش را و بمعنی نیز اعتم باشد
چنانکه هر دو معنی بطریق ایهام گوید شعر ای کونکل گوید و در طمع تحیین تمنا مزهین بوایکیلا نینکدین کیم
الجماسدانا پند و بمعنی هر دو تا دیش را بابیتا بیکیلا مذکور شود ایکی مصطلح شده دیگر سیو و نماک بمعنی واوات
بمعنی دوست داشتن چنانکه گوید شعر ملکلیکن کونکل هر لحظه یوز قاینغو کیلور او ترو اگر هر زمان یوز
پر سیو و نماک لبارا یمار نرتاینغو و مثل اینست سیووب بمعنی دوست داشته چنانکه در ولادت مجنون گوید شعر
جاندین سیووب آنی بنوالالا هر کیم کر کوروب قیلیب عالالا و موافق قیاس بایت بکسر واو مذکور شود نیز اگر
بضم واو باشد اما سیووب بضم واو باید باشد مع هذا بضم واو استعمال نکرده و حضرت نوایی خود نیز سیوین مذکور
ساخته الشاهد علیه شعر ای نوایی بیکیتینک تطمینکا مثل ایتماسیوین کیم بصیب ولدی سکا
ادراک بیکیت و سیووب هم بایت بمتابعت کسر سین سیویب بکسر واو بیاید مع هذا در همگی نسخ سیووب
قسم دوم آنست که در مولفات حضرت نوایی بنظر رسیده و نسخ متعدده رجوع شد همه جا بر این نهج مرقوم بود
و آن بر سه نوع است نوع اول آنست که غلط محض است هم بر سهو القلم ناظم و هم بر تحریف نساخ اول محمول
شد از انجمله تینماسلیک کاست یعنی آرام نگرفتن چنانکه گوید شعر میل دینی کیم سالور که سه نی تینماسلیک
تینسان کونکلی انینک کیم کر کونکلدین چقاریب چون تینماق مصدر قافیت و منتسبات صیغ نیز تاماق استعما
می شود بایت تینماسلیغ مذکور شود عجب که سولدورما غای است یعنی افسرده نکند و این معنی مخالف مدعا
چنانکه گوید شعر کونکلون باغی اردو دخل قدی لیک قورتارمین کیم اول ایسیغ هوا سولدورماغای نوکس
هنا لیمینی بایت سولدورغای باشد یعنی نخل قدش در میان دل منست لیک میترسم که مبادا آن هوای گرم نهال نو رس
مرا افسرده کند دیگر تاپمادوک است یعنی نیافتم شعر تاپمادوک کلزار نخل بیخار ای باغبان و کرچه گلشن ارا
کل بوتماس ایرمیش خار سیز تاپماق بمعنی جستن از صیغ قافیت بایت تاپمادوق مذکور شود دیگر بو تونکیجا بیکرگا
یعنی تا باشب چنانکه در لیلی مجنون در خواستگاری و عروسی دختر نوفل گوید شعر سیل لا اکر بو عشق اراده ایردی
کونکلدین نه زیاده ایردی برمایدور ایدی ایکا وکا پوست بو تونکیجا وصل دولتی دست بایت بو تونکاجا شیخ
کافه مذکور شود تا معنی مطابق لفظ باشد زیرا که کاف در انجمله حرف تعدیه است و حرف تعدیه مبنی بر فتح می باشد
و بکسرا ما لکه نمیکند دیگر کوماست در این شعر شعر ای نوایی یار اگر دیر کیم اوزو نکی اوتغه سالا تر یالانک

25r.

ایلاه کا کو بیا جان او چون کو بیا نما کیل کو بیا مناسب مقام نیست بایت کو بیاز باشد یعنی ای نوایی یار اگر میگوید که
باتش بیداز بسبب تن برهنه کردن تعلل کن برای چه از تعلل بکن چون برهنه شدن سبب تاخیر در اجابت مطلوبست
امر یا لباس خود را بر آتش بیند له و اگر کو بیا باشد معنی این خواهد بود که بتن برهنه کردن مسوز در این صورت نه لطف سخن
و نه معنی سخن دیگر سونکیجه است یعنی از عقب تو چنانکه در وفات اسکندر از زبان مادرش خطاب با اسکندر گوید
که ماتم تو توپ شین ایتا المادیم بیریب جان سونکیجه میتا المادیم بایت سونکیجه با کاف خطاب مذکور شود
آن معنی عقیم است و حذف کاف خطاب در هیچ مقام جایز نیست و ضرورت شعری هم باعث بر حذف نبوده نوع دوم
آنست که مدخولست اما بر صحت محمول میتواند شد از انجمله ایلب بمعنی بو کرده چنانکه در مقاله دهم از حیرت الابرار
در وصف میخوارگان گوید شعر سیل سو بیرتا بینا ایچیب ال کیچ ساتی تا شیرتا بینا ایتیب کل کبی ایدمع الدال یعنی
بو مرایحه باشد بایتا یدیب با دال مذکور شود چون در بعضی الفاظ تبدیل دال به تا جایز است شاید در اینمقام نیز
واقع شده باشد دیگر قاازست که هر چند صیغه از صیغ کافی استعمال شده اول سود لا ارد و ورقا نست یعنی بر زمین کشد
چنانکه گوید شعر کراوملا شام ایتینک اول لزلف تا چین نیذ ورود شیراو زره سود الادمرقان بو یوندا غی سیم
و نیز ایناد و غانست یعنی وزنده چنانکه در دیباچه نظم بیت نثر گوید که ملات حوادثی بینینک اول تا تیغ ایناد و غان
مرمری نیکین تا بیچ و تحسین کیلا تور غانست که در عنوان سد سکندری بمعنی آمدن گفته که خاقان چین انینک قوبا
یلت کرم خولیوق بیله تیغ جهانگیر تارتیب کیلاتور غانی ایشیتیب سوفقا الماک بمعنی بر زمین کشیدن و ایناک بمعنی
و کیلماک بمعنی آمدن از مصادر کافی و اشتقاق تمامی صیغ آنها مبنی بر کافست بایت سود الادور کان و ایناد و رکان
و کیلادورکان مذکور شود بر خلاف قیاس با غین استعمال شده اگر چه حضرت نوایی در نسایم المحبه و محبوب القلوب همه جا
کیلادورکان با کاف نیز بیان فرموده و در تاریخ بابری هم کیلادورکان مذکور است اما در عنوان سد سکندری این لفظ
در هفت منظر با غین نماچ یافته و از بعضی خالی تر از این نیز مکتوبا و ملفوظا کیلاتورغان دیده و شنیده شد شاید جایز
باشد نوع سیم آنست که نه محمول بر صحت میتواند شد و نه بر سهو کاتب و آن بیت نقط است که در این شعر در قافیه خط واقع شده

رسم چهارم

شعر یوزدا خالینک دی ... تحریر ایتار خالدا لخط تامدی ... کون صفحه سیغه ... رسم چهارم در
بیان قواعد متفرقه و فواید مختلفه قاعده بدانکه علامات که از برای جمع از صیغ مفرد است یعنی لار و لار
و اسقاط میشود هرگاه حرف آخر کلمه با حرف اول علامت متحد باشد مثل سیغنوچی بمعنی گنجیده و یاغنوچی بمعنی آرنده
و تو ککوچی بمعنی ریزنده و سو ککوچی بمعنی دشنام دهنده ادغام جایز نیست اما در مقاربه صیغه ماضی که در ذیل باب دویم از مبلغ
اول گذشت هرگاه حرف آخر کلمه تای قرشت ماقبل مکسور باشد مثل بیت یعنی برس و ایت یعنی بگو چون لی که ضمیر مفرد
مغایب است و تینک که ضمیر مفرد مخاطب است در ملحق شود ادغام باید کرد مثل اتی یعنی کرد و بیتی یعنی رسید و
کردی و بیتینک یعنی رسیدی و این ادغام بمراعات حسن خط و صورت رسمی لفظ است که اگر ادغام نشود تعدد
هیئت مضحک در کتابت بهم خواهد رسید و اگر تای قرشت ماقبل مفتوح یا مضموم باشد مثل آت و توت
ادغام جایز نیست و هر دو تا را باید نوشت مثل آتتی یعنی انداخت و توتتی یعنی گرفت و آتتینک یعنی انداختی و توتتینک
گرفتی و علی هذا القیاس قاعده باید دانست که حرکات بعضی از علامات صیغ تابع حرکات کلمه ماقبلند یعنی اگر ماقبل

مضموم الحرکه است علامت هم مضموم مذکور میشود و اگر ما قبل مفتوح یا مکسور باشد علامت مکسور بیان می شود
چنانکه کیفیت آن در ذیل مبادی ثلثه مشروحاً نگارش یافته اما بعضی از کلمات و علامات هست که در لغت جغتای کلمات
آنها از تغییر محفوظ است و این قاعده در بارهٔ آنها غیر ملحوظ و آن بر دو نوع است نوع اول حروفیست که در هر حال مکسور اند
و مکسور شدن از آنها مرتفع از آن جمله میم است که ضمیر متکلم مع الغیر است و میم آن مبنی بر کسره می باشد مثل کوز و میز و کلمه
یعنی چشم ما و دل ما و باشیمیز و تیشیمیز یعنی سر ما و دندان ما دیگر حرف آخر کلمات است که بضمیر مفرد مخاطب اضافه شود
مثل اوزی یعنی خودش و کوزی یعنی چشمش چنانکه با رابطهٔ مفعول گوید شعر بو که زلفونک امیغه کونکلوم قوشی اوری
اوزین کورمایکینک ایی بیمرادی تیکماکیل باری کوزیش دیگر حرف آخر اسم فاعلات که عبارت از چی و چی باشد کر مکسور
اضافه میشود مثل توتقوچیم و قاپقوچیم یعنی گیرندهٔ من و ربایندهٔ من الشاهد علیهما شعر جنته کویونکا تامیشام
توتقوچیم تاپقوچیم اینیمکه و روش نوع دیگر آنست که مبنی بر رفع است از آن جمله دوق توق و دوق و دوکلوکات کر باشد با الف
که حرف اول آن علامات مضموم ذکر میشود مثل آلدوق و توتوق یعنی گرفتیم و دیدوک یعنی کفتیم و کیتوک یعنی رفتیم
نوع سیم بعضی از اسمات که ما قبل حرف آخر مضموم میشود مثل آچوق بمعنی کشاده و بولغانوق بمعنی درهم خورده
و سینوق بمعنی شکسته و یقوق بمعنی خراب و اشباه آن قاعده همچنانکه در عربیت اضمار قبل از ذکر لفظاً و رتبتاً
نیت واحد هم جایز است در ترکیم از آنقرار مستعملت چنانکه گوید شعر او قلاهرینک چالدی لار هر یان نوایی
کونکلینی بول لار ایتکاندیک تاغین دیوانه نینک و یرانه نینک یعنی ویرانه نینک دیواری فایده اگرچه موافق عربیت
در اسماء خروج از ضمه بکسره و از کسره بضمه جایز نیست و در افعال جایز است اما در ترکی در هر دو اتفاق می افتد در اسماء
سینوق بمعنی شکسته و تیشولع و تیلولع بمعنی سوراخ و یقوق بمعنی خراب و در افعال مثل دید و لع یعنی گفتیم و دید ولع یعنی
خوردیم قاعده اگرچه در لغات فرس همه جا میان جیم و پ و ژ و لعجمی فرق گذاشته و اشباع و عدم اشباع را هر حرکات
ملحوظ داشته اند اما در لغت ترکی چندان رعایت اینمعنی نمیکنند چنانکه جناب نوایی آچ را که امر از گشودن است
با آچ بمعنی گرسنه قافیه کرده و هو هذا شعر اول ترک خطانینک ایرور آندا قوزی تماچ کیم نازدین اولماغ
دیماک آلیند اگر کوز آچ آجلیغ دین اولای نینک مکرا ولدی کوزی بیمار تا آن ایچکالی تا ایل نیکا بولیش گرایملس آچ
و همچنین در غزل دیگر ماچ را بمعنی گیسو با آماج قافیه نموده و در ترتیب دیوان نیز جیم را بعد و قسم منقسم ساخته یکی آنکه
کلمه عربی بوده مثل تاج و محتاج آنها را بجیم ذکر کرده و آنچه کلمه فارسی و ترکی بوده مثل باج و کاج و ساج و آچ
آنها را جیم عجمی نامیده در تحت جیم عجمی مذکور ساخته و همچنین حرف جه را که جیم عربیت و بمعنی قدر و اندازه و نهایت است
با پلچه که جیم عجمی است قافیه فرموده و هو هذا شعر سرو و گل حسن ایچره بوقا ولسه و گلرخسار ده ایل هکیم قمری و بلبل
دامیین زارجه چون نوای کونکلینی سیندور دوغلک بیمدی بو تماک همکوا بر باس اینی چون هریان توشوب پرپارچه
و نیز اشباع را در قوافی منظور نداشته کثیر از کرات از کردیدن و این را که امر است از رسانیدن و بدون اشباع
کسره مصطلح است با خیز و تیز کر با اشباع تلفظ میشود قافیه نموده الشاهد علیه شعر قوش کیتوردی نامنک
و کونکلومنی قیلدی شعله خیز ایلاقی کوبا فناقی نینک سیلی بولاوتی تیزای نوایی چون صرصر توبو مسکرین رشید
خواه توتقیل کیشه خواهی جهان ملکینی کیز و همچنین توز بمعنی نمک را که با اشباع مستعمل است با سوز بمعنی سخن کر بلا اشباع

مذکور می گردد منقوش کرده چنانکه گوید شعر ای ملاحت شیوه لیک شیرین دوداغینک سوزی کا ای حکمت اهلی کونکلی
سالدی شکر شکل کا قوز ثمر و لیچسانک یا تنکلام قیلسانک او لکان جان تاپار اثر اشها تا بر دو راولدی تکلی جانبخش اول
نی سوزی قاعده چنانکه در لغت فارسی یا عربی بتداخل استعمال می شود لغت ترکی با فارسی و عربی بستداخلا هم گرد
میکردد اما استعمال مصادر و بعضی از روابط فارسی با لفظ ترکی معمول نیست چنانکه گویند که نخچی است و نیازلیست ما
بر عکس جایز است چنانکه گویند خوب دور و زبون دور و از ضمایر همان ضمیر متکلم وحده که عبارت از میم باشد مشترک
مستعمل بین اللغتین است چنانکه در ترکی میگویند آلورم و بفارسی میگویند گرمیگیرم و بعضی الفاظ فارسی نیز هست
که با روابط و نسبت فارسی ترکیب یافته و بیک معنی متداول گشته آن الفاظ مرکبه بر سبیل نظم است یا بر سم نقش کی
در سوق کلام ترکی استعمال میشود مثل رو برو چنانکه گوید شعر نی تاپیغ کونکلی بار آیا کیم وشول مهوش نینک
رو برو سیغه کیلور هر نفس انسان کوز کوفورد لفظ رو برو صیغه حرف تعدیه ترکی با فارسی جمع شده و همچنین است سر
الشاهد علیه شعر وصل دین محروم ایمن قیلساق فراق ایله بشر شاید او زنی بیر کاپر کون مهرمان اینکای فراق و نیز دربدر
المحبه در ذکر شیخ محیب الدین بر غش بطری پونیز گوید که قوم نینک طلبی کونکلی کا غالب اولدی و یا لغو را اویدا بر
ایلتور ایردی و از این قسم است سراسر چنانکه گوید شعر عالم ایشی سراسر غم سرکا کوی قیلماش ایکی توتوبان غمای هوبیامیق
فا یغوده و نظیر نیست تا بشام و بر دوام چنانکه در مقالهٔ دویم از حیرت الابرار گوید شعر او شبو صفت یوق کرتیمی
تا بشام قوی سحرو شامنی کیم بر دوام و از این نوع است در میان چنانکه در سد سکندری در بیان عدل اسکندر گوید
شعر کرک خیلی عصر جفای در میان الا دیجه نیکلیغ بوبیرنا کیان و شبیه نیست دو تاه بمعنی خمیده الشاهد
علیه شعر قد هر آیی باشی معنی ای ملکینیک دین تا چیب با شینی او غیر لار که بولدی ایله دوتاه و از اینگونه است
تنک چنانکه گوید شعر نوایی کر خرد ملکی داسودادین تنینک اولسا نکث تقدم او وحیل ایما دشتید امجنون وادی مین
وملتفت است تعداد الشاهد علیه شعر نیکلیغ بو از این قبل است باخراج چنانکه در پیمام ز تابدرکسکند در نماید شعر تمشیا میلیب چیشکر باخراج یا تاه مرکا کیم
احتیاج و عدیل نیست مروت و در محل الشاهد علیه شعر یا دهر اینداسرو قسیم عدیتینک ای عدل چان تعدیل
اینتام هنوز آزده و ترکه کیلدینک در محل و از این قبل است هم پاو پا برجا چنانکه گوید شعر یار اگر هم پاو پا
برجا ایسا بود و ر دو ای باشیغه هر لحظه اپور قیلماک بولود برکار ردیک و بعضی الفاظ نیز هست که بالکنایه یا بالتصریح
یک معنی خاصی مصطلح گشته در سوق کلام ترکی هم بهمان نهج استعمال میشود و اینمعنی بلفظ ترکی ادا نمیکردد مثل تردی
و تیر باران الشاهد علی الاول شعر و صلیغه محرم ایرما ستو نیعب هر بولیش ایکی تردامن کر تا تو غلوق برور لار تا
الشاهد علی الثانی شعر بو کر آهیم تیر باران بادوه کردون ساری غم سپاهی اینکالی کونکلوم کا دور قلاشاه راه حجر
کراز این گونه روابط و اصطلاحات در لغت جغتای مستعملست اما در تحریر آثار الدعه بیشتر استعمال میشود فایده
همچنانکه در سیاق فارسی بعضی از فتحهای ما قبل الف را مبدل بکسره و الف را بیای مجهوله مجانست کسره منقلب نمی سازند
مثل حساب و التفات و اعتماد که آنها را حسیب و التفیت و اعتمید میگویند در لغات ترکیه هم ابدال و قلب در اد
بعضی از کلمات مستعمل میدارند مثل اینکه قیراق بمعنی کنار را قیریق و آلماق بمعنی گرفتن را ایلماق و یارماق بمعنی شکافتن
برماق می نامند چنانکه شواهد آنها در کتاب الفصول ذیل لغات مذکور خواهد شد خاتمه در ذکر بعضی از اشغال حضرت

خاتمه

که معنی لغت و مضمون شعر مفهوم نگشته اولک ارانلک است چنانکه گوید شعر ای نوائی یار هجری غه بلا مهلک
ایمیش توکیم ارانلک منعفا اینکالی عشاقنی ابلار هلاک دیگر مضمون این شعر است شعر ساغینما بارچا بیشیغ سوزنی
طبع اتیار آشام بولور معنی و طعام چوایکیسی پختی و طبوخ دیگر ساقرغان است که در لیلی مجنون در وصف لمراوته گوید
شعر یالقوطی اولور سیم خضراء بولور آنگا چو جه فرش غبراء اعضاسیدا کیم بو توب یانکی پر توقماق ساری یرنی سنر ترش
توند کونی قیلور نونقشه سیزغان کا ایله مشکدین ساقرغان اگر چه تولغین روی علی قیاس و مناسب مقام
بمعنی ساقرغان که کلاغ ابلق نوشته اند و قزلغچ و بعضی هم متابعت کرده اند اما حقیقت آن نامعلوم نیست شاید معنی
سرشته و ممزوج باشد و معنی شعر لغیر این خواهد بود که نگارنده این نقش شبراعثات و کافور امیخته میکند
دیگر تومندیک است که در داستان پنجم از سبعه سیاره گوید شعر اچپی هر ایام جام نیلوفری تومندیکیم یاینا الغا
اول سیرتی دیگر چابون است که در لیلی مجنون در وصف شب گوید شعر ناکه لو کو چیکا کاوح یبان اوثی توشوغی
اتیب کوزینی چابوثی دیگر حاله است شعر حالا که مینر بولو اول میپله خوشخالی تیو چون کرتم قیلادی لاد
عمرغه خاله ولی شعر دیب ایردینک جان برای ولسانک ییتیشتی اول محل و کیم کلا سلطانه بیتکای جز کلالنیغ اوادم
خاله دیگر پچرپلپا است در سکندری شعر معنی اولوغ بیر نواسینی توزیپچر کوکاپلپا صداسینی توزدیکو
دیگر زیره کوپ ناغی است شعر نیتای کردون شبستانیدا انجم نی شمع ایجراه شفق کون نی سوزنای ایچکوم
اولنا زیره کوپ ناغی دیگر عروسک است که در لیلی مجنون در ابتدای کتاب گوید شعر قیش مهرنی چون اتیبان
ایتینک تارینک صدفین عروسک ایتینک دیگر موچی است شعر کرا یاغینک چیقتی اشکینک نینک سوودین
تا بیلیثای نوائی شکر اول کوی ایچره دهراینک موچی و در بعضی نسخ سوچی نظر رسیده تناس است کر در خسرو شیرین در
هرام چینی گوید شعر قرامغو کیچه اوح چیقنا یادینی اوتوب تناس فلک دین یوق یهادینی در یک نسخه طاس
و در یک نسخه تیماس فلک مرقوم بود و هر یک از این دو لفظ شعر موزون و معنی صحیح است لیکن بنسخ منعکس رجوع شد
تناس بود و تناس بکسر نون در فارسی بمعنی خوش و بی تشویش باشد و با این معنی هم که حمل شود بحسب معنی درست است اما بحسب
وزن درست نیست شاید که تناس در ترکی محرف تناس باشد او باللکه معنی شعر این خواهد بود که شب تاریک چون ترش
انکمان درآید خوش و بی تشویش از فلک نکر ازسها بجکمرد دیگر یا و مرغان است که در سد سکندری در وصف لشکر
روس گوید شعر ولی بادبالا اغرسا لغان کچیم سفرلات و با خیابا و مرغان کچیم چون این مقدمات از معلوم
و نامعلوم معلوم شد بمقصود رجوع و بذکر کتاب شروع می شود

27v

کتاب الالف باب المفتوحات حرف الالف مع الالف آآ بد و معنی می آید اول حرف ندا است چنانکه

گوید شعر بولونك لوزره هم کلامین هم قاری هم خسته حال بیرما قیبلوت خالیمه حسنونك زکاتی آ ابکیت

و دراجمعی با عربی مشترکست دویم مخفف آن بود که اسم اشارت است و آن با لفظ لار که علامت جمع است ترکیب یافته

بمعنی ایشان و آنها استعمال میشود الشاهد علیه شعر لای نوبت خیلیغه جانم بیج آ دم ارا بکوا الارخا تم سبن اول

آت کیم بولور خاتم آرا و با رابطه مفعولی نیز انضمام می یابد چنانکه گوید آنی یعنی آنرا مع البنا ابا جلد گویند و نیز نام محلیت

در نواحی کابل و ترکی و می زن قابله باشد و با بای عجمی خواهر بهتر که آنرا ایکاجی هم نامند ابا دان بمعنی خوب و خوش باشد

و آنرا آبدان نیز گویند و بفارسی بمعنی معمور ضد خراب بود آپ آغ و آپ آق با بای عجمی سفید محض و از برای مبالغه

موضوع است که از برای مبالغه مذکور میسازند چنانکه در دیباچه کتاب در ذیل ابجنیم نگارش یافت ابا غا و اباقا

عم را گویند ضرغام پسر بزرگ هولاکو خان بن تولی خان بن چنگیز خانست که بعد از پدر بر سریر سلطنت بر ازشت و چون اسم عم

هولاکو خان موسوم بوده باین جهت او را اباغا میگفتند آبدا ن مخفف اباد ان بمعنی خوب و خوش باشد چنانکه گوید شعر

بازاد فرشته قیاش صفحه سیغه و سفینکی شمکر کیم اول غلکی کاپه آبدان کاغذ و بفارسی اینادنکا . آب وشانرا دیو

حیوانات گویند اپریك با بای عجمی کهنه و مندرس و مجاز آدم بیرمسن را هم گویند ابسم بروزن هدم بمعنی ناکس باشد و آنرا

افسم هم خوانند اپکین با بای عجمی بروزن عمکین نخ سیاه الشاهد علیه شعر سنبلین کورکاج کو دونم و لدی قرانغوا نی

ساچی مونداق تیره یا خود ساچناغی اپکین مودود وی لتشعن ایله دودیکم ایلکینی خینا اوزه قیلمیش نگارش اول که کلکون کو

اوزره تونین اپکین ایلامیش و بکسر الف هم مستعملست ابم کاجی بفتح با و ضم کاف درستی است که از ابغار بهتر کی و نا

کلاغ و بعربی خباز ی گویند برکش مستدیر و بیمزه و کلش کوچك و سرخ مایل به تیرگی باشد ابو بضم با جلد ا گویند و آنرا

ابا و ابوکا هم نامند ابوشغه یعنی شوهر چنانکه در لیلی مجنون گوید شعر بیراندین ابوشغه در دوم نجی بیرماندین

اوغولعنم و شکنجی ابوکان تاغی نام کوهیست در دشت قپچاق که بیلمان اشتهار دارد مع التاء المثناة اتماق دو معنی دارد

اول انداختن دویم طالع شدن و این لفظ در طلوع صبح مستعملست و بدون لفظ صبح تنها نیز افاده این معنی میکند آتتی

انداخت و طالع شد آتتوق انداختیم و طالع شدیم آتار و آتادور می اندازد و طالع میشود الشاهد علی التاء

بالمعنی الاول شعر عشق آتی کیلتوراد و درخسته نوائی طرفی ناوك غمزه نی او لشوخ تا یان آتادوش و آتار بمعنی می اندازد

نامزد میکند هم می آید و در اینید و معنی ماخوذ از مصدر آتماقاست چنانکه مذکور خواهد شد و بمعنی فاعل و مصدر هم

استعمال میشود آتماید و دمی اندازد و نمی اندازد و نمی اند اخته است و طالع نمیشود و نشده است آتغان و آتارغان و آتادورغان انداز نده

و انداخته و طالع شونده و طالع شده و بمعنی مصدر هم می آید و آتار غان با مصدر آتماق هم اشتراك دارد آت و آتغیل

مفرد مخاطبه فعل امر و آت بمعنی نام و اسب و اسم الهی از الات شطرنج هم بود چنانکه در ذیل جوامد مذکور خواهد شد

آتما و آتماغیل مفرد مخاطبه فعل نهی آتینك و آتینکیز و آتینکلار جمع مخاطبه فعل امر آتمانك و آتمانکیز و آتمانکلار جمع مخاطب

از فعل نهی آتمان و آتمارمین نمی اندازم و طالع نمیشوم آتامین و آتارمین و آتادورمین و آتادورام می اندازم و طالع میشوم و آتام

و آتانم بمعنی نامم و نامزد میکنم هم باشد چنانکه مذکور خواهد شد آتایم و آتماغیم انداختم و طالع شدم و آتادیم بمعنی

نامیدم و نامزد کردم هم باشد چنانکه مذکور خواهد شد آتماغوم نخواهم انداخت و طالع نخواهم شد آتیب و آتیبان و

28r

آتمیش انداخته و طالع شده آتمیشانك انداخته و طالع شده آتماس نمی اندازد و طالع نمی شود بمعنی فاعل و مصدر نفی هم می آید

آتماسی انداختنش و نینداختنش و طالع شدنش و نشدنش آتما دین از انداختن و نینداختن و از طالع شدن و طالع نشدن

آتیب بولماس آتا بولماس و آتماقا و لماس نمیتوان انداخت و طالع نمیتوان شد آتا آلماس نمیتواند انداخت و طالع نمیتواند شد

آتا آتا امکان امکان و طلوع کنان و بدون تکرار هم باین معنی مستعملست آتای و آتایین بیندازم و بیندازیم و بیندازی

و طالع شوم و شوی و شویم الشاهد علی الاول بالمعنی الاول شعر دید نیایکیم خط اسیر آتای کونکلونکا اوقی دیبان

آتماغانی خطا ایلادوهینك لامو نیز بمعنی نام و نامزد کنم و کند و کنی چنانکه مذکور خواهد شد آتسا ی آتغای

و آتغای پیر و آتالی و اتالینك بیندازیم و طالع شویم و آتالی آتالینك یعنی نامیم و نامزد کنیم هم باشد آتغالی برای انداختن

و انداخته و برای انداخته و برای طالع شدن و تا طالع شده آتقانج چون انداخت و بینداز د بمعنی انداختن و چون طالع

شد و شود و بمعنی شدن آتقوچی انداز نده و طالع شونده آتقوجه و آتقونچه و آتقانچه تا انداختن و بمعنی انداختن و تا طالع

شدن و بمعنی طالع شدن الشاهد علی الاول بالمعنی الثالث شعر مصر آهیم ایسا دیم شامی هجران تاغیغه بخشید در

تانك آتقوچه یوباغ ها مون بولماس طالع هوی نوشته که آتقون یعنی کم زند و آتقونچه افاده تا گذشته است میاید

و شعر مذکور را شاهد آورد سهو کرده است الشاهد علی الثانی بالمعنی الثالث شعر ای نوائی بیل که تانك آتقونچه

بغلادم کیچه چرخ دیلك هر کیم که اول بد مهر سر کرداند وز آتقوم خواهم انداخت و طالع خواهم شد آتقونك

خواهی انداخت و طالع خواهی شد آتقوسی خواهد انداخت و طالع خواهد شد آتقولوق انداختنی و طالع شدنی آتغای

آتاو آتساو آتنون و آتدیك بینداز د آتقودیك و آتاردیك انداختنی طالع شدنی و همچنانکه بیندازد و طالع شود و نیز

آتاردیك بمعنی نامیدن و نامزد کردن و همچنانکه نامیده شود و نامزد کند چنانکه مذکور خواهد شد آتیشماق بمعنی

مفاعله است یعنی سنك و تیر و مثل آن بیکدیگر انداختن و صیغ آن بدستور شق اول الشین اشتقاق می یابد آتیلماق انداخته

شدن و صیغ آن با الام اشتقاق می یابد آتورماق بمعنی متعدی است یعنی انداز اندن و صیغ آن با لفظ تور اشتقاق

آتاماق بفتح تا دو معنی دارد اول نامیدن که بعربی عبارت از تسمیه باشد دویم نامزد کردن که آنرا بعربی خطبه گویند

آتادی نامید و نامزد کرد چنانکه بمعنی اول در سکندر نامه در صفت بنای سمرقند گوید شعر سکندر آتادی سمرقند

سمرقند فردوس مانند آتی و بمعنی ثانی در تاریخ الانبیا در ذکر حضرت موسی علیه السلام گوید که صفورا آلیغ من آتا

آتادوق نامیدیم و نامزد کردیم آتار و آتاید و می نامد و نامزد میکند چنانکه در خسرو شیرین گوید الشاهد علی الاول بمعنی

الاول شعر ملایم لار چون وجودیم تو پراقین مادیش هما نا کیم آتار لار رخته فرهاد و نیز گوید شعر نیا غه گرچه هر کیم

بولسا بانی آتار لار بانی اسمی بیرله آنی و آتار بمعنی می اندازد و طالع میشود هم باشد چنانکه مذکور شد و بمعنی فاعل و مصدر

هم می آید آتاناید و نمینامد و ننامیده است و نامزد نمیکند و نکرده است آتاغان و آتارغان و آتاید ورغان نامنده

و نامیده و نامزد کننده و کرده و بمعنی مصدر هم می آید و آتارغان بمعنی انداز نده و انداخته و طالع شونده و طالع شده

هم باشد آتا و آتاغیل مفرد مخاطب فعل امر چنانکه در حیرت الابرار در مقابله ایمان گوید الشاهد علی الثانی بالمعنی الاول

شعر دیر آتی افشان آتاغیل بیرا کیم ایشید و صبر ایله خوف و رجا و آتا پدر را گویند و بالمجاز مشایخ صوفیه مراد

هم نامند چنانکه در ذیل جوامد نگارش خواهد یافت آتاما و آتاماغیل مفرد مخاطب فعل نهی آتانك و آتانکیز و آتانکلار

جمع مخاطب فصل امر آتامانك و آتامانكيز و آتامانكلار جمع مخاطب فصل نهی آتامانان و آتاماس مین نمی نامم و نامزد نمیکنم آتای مین و
آتارمین و آتاید ورمین و آتادام می نامم و نامزد میکنم و آتادمین و آتادام بمعنی می اندازم و طالع می شوم هم باشد چنانکه مذکور شد
آتادیم و آتاماغیم نامیدیم و نامزد کردیم و آتادیم بمعنی انداختیم و طالع شدیم هم باشد چنانکه گذشت آتاماغوم نخواهم نامید
و نامزد نخواهم کرد آتاب و آتابان و آتامیش نامیده و نامزد کرده. الشاهد علی الاول المعنی الاول شعر بزمی وصالینکا
طالب تو تویلاهزین مطلوب محبتی دین آتینکی حبیب آتاب محبوب آتامیشانك نامیده و نامزد کرده آتاماس نمی نامد و نامزد
نمیکند و بمعنی فاعل و مصدر منفی هم می آید آتاماسی نامیدنش و نانامیدنش و نامزد کردنش و نکردنش آتامادین از نامیدن و نانامیدن
و از نامزد کردن و نامزد نکرده آتاب بولماس و آتاسا بولماس و آتاماقی ولماس نمیتوان نامید و نامزد نمیتوان کرد آتای آلماس
نمیتواند نامید و نامزد نمیتواند کرد آتابو و آتای آتای نامیده نامیده و نامزد کنان و بدون تکرار هم باین معنی مستعملست آتای
و آتامین بنامم و بنامد و بنامی و نامزد کنم و کند و کنی الشاهد علی الاول المعنی الاول شعر غمزه قاتل ایله کافر خونریز کوزی
دشمن جان مونالی آفت ایمان مودیین ونیز بمعنی بیندازم و بیندازد و بیندازی و طالع شوم و شود و شوی چنانکه گذشت
شد آتاساق و آتاغانیز و آتاغایز و آتالی و آتالیك بنامیم و نامزد کنیم و آتالی و آتالیك بمعنی بیندازیم و طالع
هم باشد چنانکه گذشت آتاغالی برای نامیدن و نامیده و برای نامزد کردن و تا کرده آتاغاچ چون نامید و نامند
و بعض نامیدن و چون نامزد کرد و کند و بعض کردن آتاغوچی نامنده و نامزد کننده آتاغوچه و آتاغانچه و آتاغونچه تا نام
و بقدر نامیدن و تا نامزد کردن آتاغوم نخواهم نامید و نامزد نخواهم کرد آتاغونك نخواهی نامید و نامزد نخواهی کرد آتاغوسی
نخواهد نامید و نامزد نخواهد کرد آتاغولوق نامیدنی و نامزد کردنی آتاغای و آتاسا و آتاسون و آتادیك بنامد و نامزد کند
و آتادیك بمعنی مانند پدر هم بود آتاغودیك و آتاردیك نامیدنی و نامزد کردنی و همچنانکه بنامد و نامزد کند و نیز آتاردیك
بمعنی انداختنی و طالع شدنی و همچنانکه بیندازد و طالع شود چنانکه مذکور شد آتالماق نامیده شدن و نامزد شدن
آتالدی نامیده شد و نامزد شد چنانکه بمعنی خبر در سکندرنامه در حاکم فرستادن سکندر با طراف عالم کوید شعر
آتالدی بیری مصر و بغداد غه یازیلدی بیری ملک نوشادغه و آتاق صیغ بر این سیاق و موافق شق اول بالالام اشتقاق می یابد
آتاشماق مصدر مفاعله است یعنی با هم ترنم کردن و خواندن و کوک نمودن و در رومیه او تو شماق بضم الف بانغمه استعمال یافته
آتاشتی ترنم کرد آتاشدیم ترنم کردیم آتاشودور آتاشادور ترنم میکند و آتاشور بمعنی فاعل و مصدر هم می آید آتاشاید و ر ترنم میکند
و نکرده است آتاشکان و آتاشوکان و آتاشادورغان ترنم کننده و ترنم کرده و بمعنی مصدر هم می آیند آتاش و آتاشکیل مفرد
مخاطب فصل امر آتاشما و آتاشماغیل مفرد مخاطب فصل نهی آتاشینك و آتاشینکیز و آتاشینکلار جمع مخاطب فصل امر آتاشمانك
و آتاشمانکیز و آتاشمانکلار جمع مخاطب فصل نهی آتاشمان و آتاشمامین ترنم نمیکنم آتاشامین و آتاشورمین و آتاشادورمین و
آتاشودورمین ترنم میکنم آتاشودیم و آتاشتیم ترنم کردیم آتاشماغوم ترنم نخواهم کرد آتاشیب و آتاشیبان و آتاشمیش ترنم کرده
الشاهد علی الاول غم سین قوناش بیله مناسب بین او بوندا خوبلار ایلا بیکیچکه کبرکالیدور آتاشیبان زار آتاشمیشانك ترنم کرده آتاشماس
ترنم نمیکند و بمعنی فاعل و مصدر منفی هم می آید آتاشماسی ترنم کردنش و نکردنش آتاشمادین از ترنم کردن و ترنم نکرده آتاشیب
بولماس و آتاشسا بولماس و آتاشماقی ولماس ترنم نمیتواند کرد آتاشا آلماس ترنم نمیتواند کرد آتاشا آتاشا ترنم کنان و بدون تکرار
هم مستعملست آتاشای و آتاشامین ترنم کنم و کند و کنی آتاشالی و آتاشکاینیز و آتاشکای و آتاشالی و آتاشالیك ترنم کنیم

آتاشغالی برای ترنم کردن و تا ترنم کرده آتاشغاچ چون ترنم کرد و کند و بعض کردن آتاشقوچی ترنم کننده آتاشقوچه و آتاشقونچه
آتاشقانچه تا ترنم کردن و بقدر ترنم آتاشقوم ترنم خواهم کرد آتاشقونك ترنم خواهی کرد آتاشقوسی ترنم خواهد کرد آتاشقولوق
ترنم کردنی آتاشقای و آتاشا و آتاشسا و آتاشسون و آتاشدیك ترنم کند آتاشقودیك و آتاشوردیك ترنم کردنی و همچنانکه ترنم
کند آتاغلاماق نامزد کردن آتاغلادی نامزد کرد آتاغلادوق نامزد کردیم آتاغلادور و آتاغلایدور نامزد میکند و آتاغلار
بمعنی فاعل و مصدر هم می آید آتاغلامایدور نامزد نمیکند و نکرده است آتاغلاغان و آتاغلاغان و آتاغلایدورغان نامزد
کننده و کرده و بمعنی مصدر هم می آید آتاغلا و آتاغلاغیل مفرد مخاطب فصل امر آتاغلاما و آتاغلاماغیل مفرد مخاطب فصل
نهی آتاغلانك و آتاغلانکیز و آتاغلانکلار جمع مخاطب فصل امر آتاغلامانك و آتاغلامانکیز و آتاغلامانکلار جمع مخاطب فصل
نهی آتاغلامان و آتاغلاماس مین نامزد نمیکنم آتاغلای مین و آتاغلار مین و آتاغلایدور مین و آتاغلادام نامزد میکنم آتاغلا
و آتاغلاماغیم نامزد کردیم آتاغلاماغوم نامزد نخواهم کرد آتاغلاب و آتاغلابان و آتاغلامیش نامزد کرده آتاغلا
میشانك نامزد کرده آتاغلاماس نامزد نمیکند و بمعنی فاعل و مصدر منفی هم می آید آتاغلاماسی نامزد کردنش و نکردنش آتاغلا
مادین از نامزد کردن و نامزد نکرده آتاغلاب بولماس و آتاغلاسا بولماس و آتاغلاماقی ولماس نامزد نمیتوان کرد آتاغلای
آلماس نامزد نمیتواند کرد آتاغلابو و آتاغلای آتاغلای نامزد کنان و بدون تکرار هم مستعملست آتاغلای و آتاغلایین نامزد کنم و
کند و کنی آتاغلاساق و آتاغلاغایز و آتاغلاغایز و آتاغلالی و آتاغلالیك نامزد کنیم آتاغلاغالی برای نامزد کردن و تا
کرده آتاغلاغاچ چون نامزد کرد و کند و بعض کردن آتاغلاغوچی نامزد کننده آتاغلاغوچه و آتاغلاغونچه و آتاغلاغانچه تا
کردن و بقدر آن آتاغلاغوم نامزد خواهم کرد آتاغلاغونك نامزد خواهی کرد آتاغلاغوسی نامزد خواهد کرد آتاغلاغولوق نامزد کردنی
آتاغلاغای و آتاغلاسا و آتاغلاسون و آتاغلادیك نامزد کند آتاغلاغودیك و آتاغلاردیك نامزد کردنی و همچنانکه کند
آتاغلاتماق مصدر متعدیست یعنی نامزد فرمودن و صیغ آن بدستور شق اول با تای قرشت اشتقاق می یابد آتاغلانماق بمعنی نامزد
شدن و صیغ آن با نون اشتقاق می یابد آتاغلاشماق مصدر مفاعله است یعنی نامزد یکدیگر شدن و صیغ آن با شین اشتقاق می یابد
آتغولاماق تیراندازی کردن آتغولادی تیراندازی کرد آتغولادوق تیراندازی کردیم آتغولادور و آتغولایدور تیراندازی میکند و آتغولار
بمعنی فاعل و مصدر هم می آید آتغولامایدور تیراندازی نمیکند و نکرده است آتغولاغان و آتغولارغان و آتغولایدورغان تیرانداز
کننده و کرده و بمعنی مصدر هم می آید آتغولا و آتغولاغیل مفرد مخاطب فصل امر آتغولاما و آتغولاماغیل مفرد مخاطب فصل نهی آتغولا
و آتغولانکیز و آتغولانکلار جمع مخاطب فصل امر آتغولامانك و آتغولامانکیز و آتغولامانکلار جمع مخاطب فصل نهی آتغولامان و
آتغولاماس مین تیراندازی نمیکنم آتغولای مین و آتغولارمین و آتغولایدورمین و آتغولادام تیراندازی میکنم آتغولادیم و آتغولا
ماغیم تیراندازی کردیم آتغولاماغوم تیراندازی نخواهم کرد آتغولاب و آتغولابان و آتغولامیش تیراندازی کرده آتغولامیشانك تیراندازی کرده
آتغولاماس تیراندازی نمیکند و بمعنی فاعل و مصدر منفی هم می آید آتغولاماسی تیراندازی کردنش و نکردنش آتغولامادین از تیراندازی کردن و تیر
اندازی نکرده آتغولاب بولماس و آتغولاسا بولماس و آتغولاماقی ولماس تیراندازی نمیتوان کرد آتغولای آلماس تیراندازی نمیتواند کرد آتغولابو
آتغولای آتغولای تیراندازی کنان و بدون تکرار هم مستعملست آتغولای و آتغولایین تیراندازی کنم و کند و کنی آتغولاساق و آتغولاغایز
آتغولالی و آتغولالیك تیراندازی کنیم آتغولاغالی برای تیراندازی کردن و تا کرده آتغولاغاچ چون تیراندازی کرد و کند و بعض کردن
آتغولاغوچی تیرانداز کننده آتغولاغوچه و آتغولاغونچه آتغولاغانچه تا تیراندازی کردن و بقدر آن آتغولاغوم تیراندازی خواهم کرد
آتغولاغونك تیراندازی خواهی کرد آتغولاغوسی تیراندازی خواهد کرد آتغولاغای و آتغولاسا و آتغولاسون و آتغولادیك تیراندازی کند

آتولادیلک و آتولادیک تیراندازی کردیم و همچنانکه کند آتولاتماق مصدر متعدیست یعنی تیراندازی کنانیدن و صیغ
آن با تمامی قرشت اشتقاق می‌یابد آتولاشماق بمعنی مفاعله است یعنی با یکدیگر تیراندازی کردن آتولاشای و آتولاشایین
تیراندازی بکنم و بکند و بکنی چنانکه در تاریخ بابری شاهد بر اول بمعنی اول مذکور است که منا داغیدا ایکی بیچه اوقاد
ایدی توشای یوسنک توده دماوقوم باریچه آتولاشای و باقی صیغ آن بدستور سابق اشتقاق می‌یابد آتلاماق تکاپو
وجست وخیز کردن چنانکه در لیلی مجنون خطاب دیک لیلی گوید شعر یار بیر آتلاماغینک ملاحتی دین باغلاب کوزی
خالتی دین آتدی تکاپو کرد آتلادوق تکاپو کردیم آتلادور و آتلایدور تکاپو میکند چنانکه شاهد بر اول [illegible]
در ذکر ابوالعباس نسائی گوید که عباس دیب تورکه دایم آیینک اتیسیکیدا آتلادور و ترهقیلور و آتلار بعضا [illegible] مستمر
می‌آید آتلانایدور تکاپو میکند و نکرده است آتلاغان و آتلارغان و آتلایدورغان تکاپو کننده و تکاپو کرده و بمعنی مصدر هم
می‌آید آتلا و آتلاغیل مفرد مخاطب از فصل امر آتلاما و آتلاماغیل مفرد مخاطب از فصل نهی آتلانک و آتلانگیز و آتلانگلار جمع مخاطب
از فصل امر آتلامانک و آتلامانگیز و آتلامانگلار جمع مخاطب از فصل نهی آتلاماسان و آتلاماس بین تکاپو نمیکنم آتلای بین و آتلای
و آتلایدورمین و آتلادرام تکاپو میکنم آتلادیم و آتلاماغیم تکاپو کردنم آتلاماغوم تکاپو نخواهم کرد آتلاب و آتلابان و آتلا-
تکاپو کرده آتلامیشانک تکاپو کرده آتلاماس تکاپو نمیکند و بمعنی فاعل و مصدر منفی هم می‌آید آتلاماسی تکاپو کردنش و نکردنش
آتلامادین از تکاپو کردن و تکاپو نکرده آتلاب بولماس و آتلاسا بولماس و آتلاماق اولماس تکاپو نمیتواند کرد آتلای آلماس تکا
پو نمیتواند کرد آتلایو و آتلای آتلای تکاپو کنان و بدون تکرار هم مستعمل است آتلای و آتلایین تکاپو کنم و کند و کنی آتلاساق
و آتلاغایمیز و آتلاغای بیز و آتلایلی و آتلالینک تکاپو کنیم آتلاغالی برای تکاپو کردن و تا کرده آتلاغاچ چون تکاپو کرد و کند و
بمحض کردن آتلاغوچی تکاپو کننده آتلاغوچه و آتلاغونچه و آتلاغانچه تا تکاپو کردن و جمع آن آتلاغوم تکاپو خواهم کرد
آتلاغونک تکاپو خواهی کرد آتلاغوسی تکاپو خواهد کرد آتلاغولوق تکاپو کردنی آتلاغای و آتلاسا و آتلاسون و آتلادیلک
تکاپو کنند آتلاغودیک و آتلاغودیک تکاپو کردنی و همچنانکه کند آتلاشماق با یکدیگر تکاپو کردن و جست و خیز نمودن و صیغ
آن با شین اشتقاق می‌یابد آتلاتماق مصدر متعدیست تکاپو فرمودن و جهانیدن و صیغ آن با تا و قرشت اشتقاق می‌یابد
آتلانماق مع النون سوار شدن آتلاندی سوار شد آتلاندوق سوار شدیم آتلانور و آتلانادور سوار میشود و آتلانغود
بمعنی فاعل و مصدر نیز می‌آید چنانکه بمعنی مصدر میگوید در خسرو و شیرین شعر کیل ای ساقی که اوتی عیش چاغی سنگا نو
ایمدی آتلانور آیاغی آتلانماید سوار نمیشود و نشده است آتلانغان و آتلانورغان و آتلانادورغان سوار شونده و سوار شده
و بمعنی مصدر هم می‌آیند آتلان و آتلانغیل مفرد مخاطب از فصل امر آتلانما و آتلانماغیل مفرد مخاطب از فصل نهی آتلانینک و
آتلانینگیز و آتلانینگلار جمع مخاطب از فصل امر آتلانمانک و آتلانمانگیز و آتلانمانگلار جمع مخاطب از فصل نهی آتلانمادو آتلا-
بین سوار نمیشوم آتلانامین و آتلانورمین و آتلانادورمین و آتلانورام سوار میشوم آتلانورغم و آتلانماغیم سوار شدنم آتلان-
غوم سوار نخواهم شد آتلانیب و آتلانیبان و آتلانمیش سوار شده آتلانمیشانک سوار شده آتلانماس سوار نمیشود و بمعنی فاعل و مصدر منفی
هم می‌آید آتلانماسی سوار شدنش و نشدنش آتلانمادین از سوار شدن و سوار نشده آتلانیب بولماس و آتلانسا بولماس و آتلانا-
و لماس سوار نمیتواند شد آتلانا آلماس سوار نمیتواند شد آتلانا آتلانا سواری کنان سواری کنان و بدون تکرار هم مستعمل است

آتلانای و آتلانایین سوار شوم و شود و شوی آتلانساق و آتلانغایمیز و آتلانغای بیز و آتلانالی و آتلانالینک سوار شویم آتلانغالی
برای سوار شدن و تا سوار شده آتلانغاچ چون سوار شد و شود و بمحض شدن آتلانغوچی سوار شونده آتلانغوچه و آتلانغونچه
آتلانغانچه تا سوار شدن و تا هنگام سوار شدن چنانکه در مقاله ششم از حیرت الابرار در وصف زنان گوید الشاهد علی الاول
بالمعنی الاول شعر ایلچیا کیل حاله سینی [illegible] کیمنا داغی چهره داتوتون در [illegible] آنکا همانک آتلانغونچا الا [illegible]
کار ایتیانک [illegible] آیینک [illegible] و نیز در مقاله شانزدهم از حیرت الابرار در وصف شراب خواران گوید بالمعنی الثانی شعر
[illegible] آتلانغوم سوار خواهم شد آتلانغونک سوار خواهی شد
آتلانغوسی سوار خواهد شد آتلانغولوق سوار شدنی آتلانغای و آتلانسا و آتلانسون و آتلاندیلک سوار شوند
آتلانغودیک و آتلانغودیک سوار شدنی و همچنانکه شود آتلاندورماق مصدر متعدیست یعنی سوار کردن آتلاندوردی
و آتلاندوردیلار و آتلاندوروب [illegible] سوار کرده چنانکه شاهد بر اول [illegible] در مقاله ششم از حیرت الابرار در وصف زنان گوید
شعر [illegible] و باقی صیغ بر این سیاق لفظ در اشتقاق
می‌یابد آیتقماق نام بر آوردن و مشهور شدن چنانکه گوید شعر بولنا [illegible] آتلانیب
مستلیغ بیرله آیتقماق [illegible] آیتقتی نام بر آورد آیتقتوق نام بر آوردیم آیتقور و آیتقادور نام بر می‌آورد و آیتقور بمعنی فاعل
و مصدر هم می‌آید آیتقماید نام بر نمی‌آورد و بر نیاورده است آیتقغان و آیتقورغان و آیتقادورغان نام برآرنده و نام بر آورده
و بمعنی مصدر هم می‌آیند آیتق و آیتقغیل مفرد مخاطب از فصل امر آیتقما و آیتقماغیل مفرد مخاطب از فصل نهی آیتقینک و آیتقینگیز
و آیتقینگلار جمع مخاطب از فصل امر آیتقمانک و آیتقمانگیز و آیتقمانگلار جمع مخاطب از فصل نهی آیتقمان و آیتقماس بین نام بر نمی‌آرم
آیتقامین و آیتقورمین و آیتقادورمین و آیتقورام نام بر می‌آرم آیتقورهم و آیتقماغیم نام برآوردنم آیتقماغوم نام بر نخواهم آورد
آیتقیب و آیتقیبان و آیتقمیش نام بر آورده الشاهد علی الاول شعر تیغ ایله باشیما کیلدینک که بو کون قتل ایتیشدا
خوبلار ایچرا بیر آیتقدین اولوبین آیتقیب و نیز در تاریخ بابری مذکور است [illegible] آیتقیب بدل لیک کا [illegible]
آیتقمیشانک نام بر آورده آیتقماس نام بر نمی‌آرد و بمعنی فاعل و مصدر منفی هم می‌آید آیتقماسی نام بر آوردنش و بر نیاوردنش آیتقما-
دین از نام بر آوردن و نام بر نیاورده آیتقیب بولماس و آیتقا بولماس و آیتقماق اولماس نام بر نمیتواند آورد آیتقا آلماس نام بر نمیتواند
آورد آیتقا آیتقا شهرت کنان و بدون تکرار هم مستعمل است آیتقای و آیتقایین نام بر آرم و بر آرد و بر آری آیتقساق
آیتقغایمیز و آیتقغای بیز و آیتقالی و آیتقالینک نام بر آریم آیتقغالی برای نام بر آوردن و تا نام بر آورده آیتقغاچ چون نام بر آورد
و بر آرد و بمحض بر آوردن آیتقغوچی نام بر آرنده آیتقغوچه و آیتقغونچه و آیتقغانچه تا نام بر آوردن و جمع آن آیتقغوم نام بر
آورد آیتقغوسی نام بر خواهد آورد آیتقغولوق نام بر آوردنی آیتقغای و آیتقسا و آیتقسون و آیتقدیلک نام بر آرند
آیتقغودیک و آیتقغودیک نام بر آوردنی و همچنانکه نام بر آرد والجوامد آت [illegible] بمعنی دارد اول اسب را گویند دوم نام
ج سیم آت از آلات شطرنج چنانکه در هشت بهشت گوید شعر [illegible] و آت [illegible]
[illegible] شعر نوایی ذکری [illegible]
[illegible] آت [illegible] شعر
[illegible]

307.x

ایلطالیق شدن جمع چنانکه در ذیل مصدر آتماق نگارش یافت آتا سه معنی دارد اول پدر را گویند دوم بمجاز مشایخ صوفیه و
زهاد را مانند پیر امراست لهذا نامیدن چنانکه در ذیل مصدر آتاماق مذکور شد اتابیک [illegible] با اتابیک بکسر با معنی [illegible]
و اتابک اتالیق را لالا و مربی اولاد سلاطین را گویند چنانکه در خسرو و شیرین در وصف [illegible] گوید شعر هم اول فرهاد که
ایردی اتابیک کوز و ب فرهاد خود آتی ادیک و لیک آتا آتا نکیم [illegible] کوپ یامیش سیز بیلیک [illegible] اول تو قیز ابیک
ف بو تصرف [illegible] و وجه تسمیه سلاطین اتابکیه باتابک آنست که چون سلاجقه اولاد خود را بامرا بکار میسپردند
واتراک امیر را بیک گویند آنها را اتابکان با ایشانرا باتابک تعبیر می کردند و آنکه بعد مرتبه اتابکیست و موافق تواریخ
از اتابکان سه فرقه بمرتبه سلطنت رسیدند فرقه اول جماعتی اند که در موصل و دیار بکر و شام پادشاهی کردند فرقه
دوم جماعتی اند که در آذربایجان بمرتبه سلطنت رسیدند فرقه سیم کروه سلغریان اند که در فارس سلطنت نمودند آتا دتونکا
عبارتست از دو بدل الحسن و ضرب و فنون سپاهیگری و آداب حرب بلد شد و آنرا آتیش تو توش هم گویند آتاغ نامزد آتا غلیغ دگر
دارد اول نامزد شده چنانکه در سبعه سیاره در وصف سهیل گوید شعر مهر لطیفه کونکلی با غلیغ ایدی کوییا
بو آنکا آتا غلیغ ایدی دوم نامیده شده چنانکه بابر پادشاه در تاخت طایفه هزاره فرماید شعر ایرانا غلیغ [illegible]
ایتولدی اهل و اولادی اسیر ایتولدی و مؤلف رومی بمعنی آتا غلیغ هم ذکر کرده سهو کرده آتالیغ بدو معنی بود اول بمعنی ابوت
باشد الشاهد علیه شعر ایوردو [illegible] اول آتالیغ آرزو بو پیر آتالیغ آرزو دوم نام
منصبی است معهود در ترکستان و خوارزم آت بوغزی کنایه است از خوراک اسب آترک بروزن بدمرک نام رودخانه ایست
حوالی جرجان آتسز بمعنی بی نام الجشد و نام پادشاه خوارزم است که معاصر سلطان سنجر بوده و مؤلف برهان قاطع نام
پادشاه مزبور را بکسر الف نوشته و گفته که بمعنی بی گوشت باشد و آن کنایه است از لاغر آتغو تبرک رومی ما کوی جولاه
بود اتکه بروزن فلکه لالا و مربی را گویند که بمنزله خدمتکار باشد چنانکه در تاریخ الملوک در ضمن جنگ شکسته
ورا را گویند که آتدا قحادث بوزلانمایکیم بولدا اولغیز بارتکه و پیر خواجه سرابرله تا لدی آتل بروزن قاتل نام رودخانه ایست
معروف که از حاجی ترخان گذشته بدریای خزر میریزد آتلانورا تاع و آتلانورا تاعی کنایه است از کاسه شراب که دروقت سودی
کیرند الشاهد علی الاول شعر ساقیا نم ایشیدین بولدی فراغ توغیل ایلدی منکا آتلانور المغ و شاهد بر ثانی در ذیل سیفه
آتلانور نوشته شد آتلیغ بروزن بارلیغ سه معنی دارد اول سوار را گویند چنانکه در سبعه سیاره در وصف شکار بهرام
گوید شعر آتدا آتلیغ فه حدیوق ایردی پدید صید غه هم عدد یوق ایردی پدید دوم گویند که ملان آتلیغ یعنی موسوم
بفلان الشاهد علیه شعر مجنونک علی بن [illegible] اوتا یماس دیکیم کونکول آتلیغ ضعیف بقرا ایلیکه منینک
سیم مجازا بمعنی نامدار و مشهور باشد چنانکه در خاتمه سبعه سیاره گوید شعر مین کمیذل و بختی آتلیغ میش بولسا
یوز سوکنچه همم او یا آتلیغ میش آتمه بسکون تا و فتح میم و جیم ترکی نعم نام پرنده ایست شکاری که آنرا باشه نامند آتمک بسکون
تا و فتح میم اتراک روم نانرا گویند و بلغت جغتای و تمک بضم الف مستعمل آتیش تو توش که مذکور شد آتار تو نارا باشد
وشاهد آنرا در تاریخ الملوک در ذکر اردشیر بابک گوید که اردوان باشورون لباس ضبر قیلب الار ینک آتدا اضبط در بیط
بیله آتیش تو توش لاریبن سیلاحی بیلا بیردی آتیشلیغ معنی ترکیبی آن عربی صاحب اکرم باشد چنانکه در تاریخ بابری
که فلان بابی تا تیغ او تی او زون بیر آتیشلیغ و یخشی ایتشلیغ ایکاندور یعنی فلان مرد نجیب اندازست آتیغ بروزن

x312.
اج

لانی چوب چهار پهلو است که مبدل ازظروف ساخته بر بهر بهره روغن کیرند آتیم گویند که او قآتی یعنی مسافت تیر پرتاب که آنرا عربی
غلوه السهم نامند مع الجیم من المشتقات آچماغ بتا جیم عجمی بمعنی کشودن آچی کشود آچوق کشودیم آچار یعنی آچادور بکشاید و آچار
ناعل و مصدر بمعنی آید چنانکه بمعنی کشاینده گوید شعر تا الان مین آچار بولسا بوز او لعودین [illegible] بیلیلغه بینا ملک کل آچکوردی
فرا و با آچار کلید را گویند چنانکه در ذیل مذکور خواهد شد آچا یدور بمعنی کشاید و نکشوده است آچقان و آچارغان و
آچادورغان کشاینده و کشوده و بمعنی مصدر هم می آید آچ و آچیل مفرد مخاطب فعل امر آچما و آچماغیل مفرد مخاطب فعل نهی
آچینک و آچینکیز و آچینکلار جمع مخاطب فعل امر آچمانک و آچمانکیز و آچمانکلار جمع مخاطب فعل نهی آچمان و آچماس مین بکشایم
آچامین و آچادورمین و آچادورمین میکشایم آچادیم و آچاغیم کشودم آچاغوم نخواهم کشود آچیب و آچیبان یعنی آچیش کشوده آچما
بمیکشاید و بمعنی فاعل و مصدر منفی هم می آید چنانکه بمعنی نکشودن گوید شعر باراغیر آچماسغه دردیم سیر [illegible]
کوب جیجو کلوکدین بایو شیبشلادیم کا اول ایکی لب آچماسی کشودنش و نکشودنش آچمادین از کشودن و نکشوده آچیب بولماس و آچیا بو
و آچماق او لماس نمیتوانکشود آچا آلماس نمیتواند کشود آچا آچا کشوده کشوده و بدون تکرار هم مستعمل آچای و آچاین بکشایم بکشاید
و بکشاق آچنا قو آچنایز و آچنای بز و آچابلی و آچالینک بکشایم آچیلابی برای کشودن و تا کشود آچقلاج چون کشود و
بکشاید و بمعنی کشودن آچوجی کشاینده آچوجه و آچوغنه و آچیغانچه تا کشودن و بمعنی کشودن آچوم خواهم کشود آچون ک
خواهی کشود آچوسی خواهد کشود آچولوق کشودنی آچنای و آچا و آچا و آچون و آچدیک بکشاید آچوبیلد آچارد
کشودنی و همچنانکه بکشاید آچیلماق کشوده شدن آچیلور و آچیلادور کشوده می شود و آچیلور بمعنی فاعل و مصدر هم می آید
چنانکه شاهد بر ثانی بمعنی مصدر در ذیل لغت آچار مذکور شد آچیلمایدور کشوده نمیشود و کشوده نشده است چنانکه
ثانی گوید شعر شکنج طره سیدین کیم که باز یلمایدور بنفشه تورود اما هنوز آچیلمایدور و باقی صیغ آن بدستور شتق اول
بالاسم اشتقاق می باید آچیلیشماق مصدر مفاعله است بکسر جیم و لام مع الشین بضم لام شدن و شکفتکی و انبساط کردن و صیغ
بدستور با مشتقات اشتقاق می باید آچتورماق مصدر متعدیست و صیغ آن با لفظ تور اشتقاق می باید آچیماق بکسر جیم تلخ شدن
آچیدی تلخ شد آچیدوق تلخ شدیم آچیر و آچیادور تلخ می شود و آچیر بمعنی فاعل و مصدر هم می آید آچیمایدور تلخ نمیشود
نشده است آچیغان و آچیرغان و آچیدورغان تلخ شونده و تلخ شده و بمعنی مصدر هم می آید آچی و آچیغیل مفرد مخاطب
امر آچیما و آچیماغیل مفرد مخاطب فعل نهی آچینک و آچینکیز و آچینکلار جمع مخاطب فعل امر آچیمانک و آچیمانکیز و آچیمانکلار جمع
فعل نهی آچیمان و آچیماس مین تلخ نمیشوم آچی مین و آچیرمین و آچیادورمین و آچیرام تلخ میشوم آچیدیم و آچیغام تلخ شدم
آچیغوم تلخ نخواهم شد آچیب و آچیبان و آچیمیش تلخ شده آچیمیشانک تلخ شده آچیماغ تلخ نمیشود و بمعنی فاعل و مصدر منفی
هم می آید آچیماسی تلخ شدنش و نشدنش آچیمادین از تلخ شدن و تلخ نشده آچیب بولماس و آچیا بولماس و آچیماق او لماس تلخ نمیشود
آچی آلماس تلخ نمیتواند شد آچی آچی تلخ تلخ شده و بدون تکرار هم مستعمل آچی و آچیین تلخ شوم و شود و شوی آچینا و آچینای
و آچینای بز و آچیلی و آچیلینک تلخ شویم آچیغالی برای تلخ شدن و تا تلخ شده آچیغلاج چون تلخ شد و تلخ شود و بمعنی تلخ شدن
تلخ شونده آچیغوجی و آچیغوجه و آچیغانچه تا تلخ شدن و بمعنی تلخ شدن آچیغوم تلخ خواهم شد آچیغونک تلخ خواهی شد
آچیغوسی تلخ خواهد شد آچیغولوق تلخ شدنی آچیغای و آچیغا و آچیغون و آچیدیک تلخ شود آچیغودیک و آچیردیک
تلخ شدنی و همچنانکه شود آچیتماق مصدر متعدیست یعنی تلخ کردن و مجازا بمعنی رنجه کردن با خاطر هم استعمال می شود

آجیتی تلخ کرد و سوزناک کرد چنانکه بمعنی اول گوید شعر زهر سی بیچه کوپ آجیتی نوائی آغزینی لعلی خاصیتی بله پرداغی کاسین چوچیتی
آجیتقان و آجیتورغان و آجیتادورغان تلخ کننده و سوزناک کننده و تلخ کرده چنانکه بمعنی سوزناک کننده گوید الشاهد
علی الاول شعر زخمیم آجیتقان دشنام اول لعل شکرخند ایرور ده وه توزلا ریمیش اول کمین قیلدیم کان یکم قند ایرور آجیت
و آجیتقیل مفرد مخاطب فعل امر بدو معنی چنانکه شاهد بر اول معنی اول گوید شعر شهد عیشینک زهرایتا دوردون
سینی او شبو جامدین خواه کاسینکی آجیت خواهی مذامینکی چوچیت و باقی صیغ برهمین سیاق موافق شود والا تای هر اشتقاق
می یابد آجیتماق سوزناک شدن زخم و جراحت که با خلش ملح شد الشاهد علیه شعر ناوکی تیغی الکرمیدین آجیتماق
فزون مضمر ایچیدا ... سیکلاید اتوزه آجیشتوق سوزناک شد آجیشور و آجیشادور سوزناک میشود و آجیشور
بمعنی فاعل و مصدر هم می آید آجیشماید و رسوزناک نمیشود ونشده است آجیشقان و آجیشورغان و آجیشادورغان سوزناک
شونده و شده و بمعنی مصدر هم می آیند آجیش و آجیشقیل مفرد مخاطب فعل امر آجیشما و آجیشماغیل مفرد مخاطب فعل نهی
آجیشینک و آجیشینکیز و آجیشینکلار جمع مخاطب فعل امر آجیشمانک و آجیشمانکیز و آجیشمانکلار جمع مخاطب فعل نهی
آجیشمان و آجیشماس مین سوزناک نمیشوم آجیشامین و آجیشورمین و آجیشادورمین و آجیشورام سوزناک میشوم آجیشوردم
و آجیشماغیم سوزناک شدنم آجیشماغوم سوزناک نخواهم شد آجیشیب و آجیشیبان و آجیشمیش سوزناک شده
آجیشمیشانک سوزناک شده آجیشماس سوزناک نمیشود و بمعنی فاعل و مصدر منفی هم می آید آجیشماسی سوزناک شدنش و
نشدنش آجیشمادین از سوزناک شدن و سوزناک نشده آجیشیب بولماس و آجیشا بولماس و آجیشماقی ولماس سوزناک
نمیتواند شد آجیشا آلماس سوزناک نمیتواند شد آجیشا آجیشا سوزناک شونده شونده و بدون تکرار هم مستعملست آجیشای
و آجیشایین سوزناک شوم و شود و شوی آجیشاق و آجیشغاینز و آجیشغایپز و آجیشالی و آجیشالینک سوزناک شویم
آجیشغالی برای سوزناک شدن و تا سوزناک شده آجیشغاچ چون سوزناک شد و شود و بمجرد شدن آجیشغوچی سوزناک شونده
آجیشغوچه و آجیشغونچه و آجیشغانچه تا سوزناک شدن و بعد از آن آجیشغوم سوزناک خواهم شد آجیشغونک سوزناک خواهی شد
آجیشغوسی سوزناک خواهد شد آجیشغولوق سوزناک شدنی آجیشغای و آجیشا و آجیشسا و آجیشسون و آجیشدیک
سوزناک شود آجیشغودیک و آجیشوردیک سوزناک شدنی و همچنانکه شود آجیشتورماق متعدی آجیشماق باشد یعنی
سوزناک کردن زخم و جراحت و صیغ آن بدستور لفظ تور اشتقاق می یابد آچیغلانماق مع النون والعین خشمناک شدن
الشاهد علیه شعر آچیغلانماقدور آیدین نی چوچوک سوزای کونکول خواه آچیغ سیغلامین خواهی شکرخند ایلایین
آچیغلاندی خشمناک شد آچیغلاندوق خشمناک شدیم آچیغلانور و آچیغلانادور خشمناک میشود و آچیغلانور بمعنی
فاعل و مصدر هم می آید آچیغلانماید و رخشمناک نمیشود و نشده است آچیغلانغان و آچیغلانورغان و آچیغلانادورغان
خشمناک شونده و شده و بمعنی مصدر هم می آیند آچیغلان و آچیغلانغیل مفرد مخاطب فعل امر الشاهد علی الاول
شعر آچیغلان کیم تو لالا ربیکنه که با ذرعیت غمشه دیز غایت ملیح آچیغلانما و آچیغلانماغیل مفرد مخاطب فعل نهی
الشاهد علی الثانی شعر جان بولوپتور لعلینک چوچوک ... ایام آچیغلانماغیل نکته سیم بولسا ای جان بعد از سوزلاریم
آچیغلانینک و آچیغلانینکیز و آچیغلانینکلار جمع مخاطب فعل امر آچیغلانمانک و آچیغلانمانکیز و آچیغلانمانکلار
جمع مخاطب فعل نهی آچیغلانمان و آچیغلانماس مین خشمناک نمیشوم آچیغلانامین و آچیغلانورمین و آچیغلانادورمین

و آچیغلانورام خشمناک میشوم آچیغلانوردم و آچیغلانماغیم خشمناک شدنم آچیغلانماغوم خشمناک نخواهم شد آچیغلانیب
آچیغلانیبان و آچیغلانمیش خشمناک شده آچیغلانماس خشمناک نمیشود و بمعنی فاعل و مصدر منفی هم می آید آچیغلانماسی
خشمناک شدنش و نشدنش آچیغلانمادین از خشمناک شدن و خشمناک نشده آچیغلانیب بولماس و آچیغلانا بولماس
و آچیغلانماقی ولماس خشمناک نمیتواند شد آچیغلانا آلماس خشمناک نمیتواند شد آچیغلانا آچیغلانا خشمکنان خشمکنان و
بدون تکرار هم مستعملست آچیغلانای و آچیغلانایین خشمناک شوم و شود و شوی آچیغلاناق و آچیغلانغاینز و آچیغلانغایپز و آچیغلانالی
و آچیغلانالینک خشمناک شویم آچیغلانغالی برای خشمناک شدن و تا شده آچیغلانغاچ چون خشمناک شد
و شود و بمجرد شدن آچیغلانغوچی خشمناک شونده آچیغلانغوچه و آچیغلانغونچه و آچیغلانغانچه تا خشمناک شدن و بعد آن
آچیغلانغوم خشمناک خواهم شد آچیغلانغونک خشمناک خواهی شد آچیغلانغوسی خشمناک خواهد شد آچیغلانغولوق
خشمناک شدنی آچیغلانغای و آچیغلانا و آچیغلانسا و آچیغلانسون و آچیغلانمدیک خشمناک شود آچیغلانغودیک
و آچیغلانوردیک خشمناک شدنی و همچنانکه شود آچیغلانماق مصدر متعدیست یعنی تلخ کردن و خشمناک کردن
آچیغلانور و آچیغلانادور تلخ میکند و خشمناک میکند الشاهد علی الاول شعر حدیثی اول تورور وبان تیریکونکه سوز
سوزنام ذاکر آچیغلانور اما چوچوک پیر مراسیخ و باقی صیغ آن بدستور شق اول باید اشتقاق می یابد آچیقماق مع القاف
گرسنه شدن آچیقتی گرسنه شد آچیقتوق گرسنه شدیم آچیقور و آچیقادور گرسنه میشود و آچیقور بمعنی فاعل و مصدر هم
می آید آچیقماید گرسنه نمیشود و نشده است آچیققان و آچیقورغان و آچیقادورغان گرسنه شونده و گرسنه شده و بمعنی
مصدر هم می آیند آچیق و آچیققیل مفرد مخاطب فعل امر آچیقما و آچیقماغیل مفرد مخاطب فعل نهی آچیقینک و آچیقینکیز و آچیقینکلار
جمع مخاطب فعل امر آچیقمانک و آچیقمانکیز و آچیقمانکلار جمع مخاطب فعل نهی آچیقمان و آچیقماس مین گرسنه نمیشوم آچیقامین و
آچیقورمین و آچیقادورمین و آچیقورام گرسنه میشوم آچیقوردم و آچیقماغیم گرسنه شدنم آچیقماغوم گرسنه نخواهم شد آچیقیب و
آچیقیبان و آچیقمیش گرسنه شده آچیقمیشانک گرسنه شده آچیقماس گرسنه نمیشود و بمعنی فاعل و مصدر منفی هم می آید آچیقماسی
گرسنه شدنش و نشدنش آچیقمادین از گرسنه شدن و گرسنه نشده آچیقیب بولماس و آچیقا بولماس و آچیقماقی ولماس گرسنه
نمیتواند شد آچیقا آلماس گرسنه نمیتواند شد آچیقا آچیقا گرسنه شونده گرسنه شونده و بدون تکرار هم مستعملست آچیقای و
آچیقایین گرسنه شوم و شود و شوی آچیقاق و آچیقغاینز و آچیقغایپز و آچیقالی و آچیقالینک گرسنه شویم آچیقغالی
برای گرسنه شدن و تا گرسنه شده آچیقغاچ چون گرسنه شد و شود و بمجرد شدن آچیقغوچه و آچیقغونچه و آچیقغانچه
تا گرسنه شدن و بعد از آن آچیقغوم گرسنه خواهم شد آچیقغونک گرسنه خواهی شد آچیقغوسی گرسنه خواهد شد آچیقغولوق
گرسنه شدنی آچیقغای و آچیقا و آچیقسا و آچیقسون و آچیقدیک گرسنه شود آچیقغودیک و آچیقوردیک گرسنه شدنی و همچنانکه
شود آچیقتورماق مصدر متعدیست یعنی گرسنه کردن و صیغ آن بدستور لفظ تور اشتقاق می یابد من الجوامد آچ گرسنه بکم
آچار با جیم عجمی و معنی دار دلوک کلیدرا گویند دویم فعل مضارع است یعنی میگشاید و بمعنی فاعل و مصدر نیز می آید
در ذیل آچماق مذکور شد و تغار بوده معنی بود اول نوعی از ترشی آلات باشد و آن زنجبیل و دارچینی و اشباه آن باشد که در
بر مربه کنند دویم مرهم آمیخته و ممزوج سیم زمین پست و بلند بود دوم زبان اهل هند عمل بودن احکام شریعت باشد آچا
با جیم عجمی و فتح میم و سکون یای حطی نام اهر دو اینست از یهود و درود ... بسکون جیم و کسر رای مهمله شتر دیبه کیا ...

کما آنرا چاپار هم نامند چنانکه در صفت سیاره در وصف شبدیز گاه بهرام گوید شعر قویتین سو و بوتاریجدین تم بوتابر
دین سوو تینی دین هم ارادا بولغان اولسا تورماغ آیرینه اسرآغان بولسا آچیغ آتی صرصر آچوق بفتح جیم عجمی بمعنی گشاده
باشد چنانکه در مقاله هفتم از حیرة الابرار در باب قانع گوید شعر کلبه سی آچیغ دین اولسا یاروق ایشیک ایل الیکه
دین اولسا آچوق آچه بفتح جیم عجمی زن پرستنده را گویند و بتشدید جیم کج بود که عمارات را بدان سفید کنند و آنرا عربی
جص خوانند آجیرغه بکسر جیم و سکون راء قرشت و فتح غین معجمه بلغت مغول بمعنی نر بود که آنرا فحل گویند آجیغ بکسر جیم
دو معنی دارد اول بمعنی خشم و غیظ بود دویم بمعنی تلخ باشد چنانکه هر دو معنی گوید شعر شیخ کو ترشی بین تلخ ی
مدحین دیدیم آجیغی کیلسا تانک یوچون کر آجیلیغ کیلادی حق لیکن مصادر و مشتقات هر یک مخالف است چنانکه ذیل
مشتقات بیان شد آجیلیغ خشمناک مع الخاء من المشتقات آختارماق تفحص کردن چنانکه گوید شعر قان بولوب
اینکان کونکول نی ایستایو اول مروت مداء فیه لا رخیلیغ کیلین لاردا آختارماقدا مرادیم آختاردی تفحص کرد آختاردق
تفحص کردیم آختارورو آختارادور تفحص میکند و آختارور بمعنی فاعل و مصدر هم می آید آختارمایدور تفحص نمیکند و نکرده
آختارمان و آختاروغان و آختارادورغان تفحص کننده و تفحص کرده و بمعنی مصدر هم می آیند آختار بسکون راء و آختارو
بضم راء و آختارغیل مفرد مخاطب از فعل امر الشاهد علی الثانی شعرای مبنا الحق کونکلوم ایستایو هربان مارو وادیغ تلغ ویتا
لار ایچ بیر آختارو تصیر بای لفظ را بمعنی تفحص ذکر کرده و شعر بجهت شاهد آورده سهو کرده آختارما و آختارماغیل مفرد
مخاطب از فعل نهی آختارینک و آختارینکیز و آختارینکلار جمع مخاطب از فعل امر آختارمانک و آختارمانکیز و آختارمانکلار جمع مخاطب
از فعل نهی آختارمان و آختارماس مین تفحص نمیکنم آختارامین و آختارورمین و آختارادورمین و آختارورم تفحص میکنم آختاردیم
و آختارماغیم تفحص کردنم آختارغوم تفحص خواهم کرد آختاریب و آختاریبان و آختاریش تفحص کرده آختارمیشانک تفحص کرده
آختارماس تفحص نمیکند و بمعنی فاعل و مصدر منفی هم می آید آختارمابی تفحص کردنش و نکردنش آختارمادین از تفحص کردن و تفحص
نکرده آختاریب بولماس و آختاریب بولماس و آختارماق اولماس تفحص نمیتوان کرد آختارا آلماس تفحص نمیتواند کرد آختارا آختارا
تفحص کنان و بدون تکرار هم باین معنی مستعمل چنانکه گوید شعر ناوکینک سپکا سینی آنداق یاشوردی بو کونکول تاما
آلمای جان نی تیغ [illegible] آختاره آختارای و آختارایین تفحص کنم و کند و کنی آختارساق و آختارغایمیز و آختارغای و آختارا
و آختارالینک تفحص کنیم آختارغالی برای تفحص کردن و تا تفحص کرده آختارغاچ چون تفحص کرد و کند و بمحض کردن آختارغوچی
تفحص کننده آختارغوسیدا آختارغونچه و آختارغانیچه تا تفحص کردن و مقابل آن آختارغوم تفحص خواهم کرد آختارغوبات تفحص خواهی کرد
آختارغوسی تفحص خواهد کرد آختارغولوق تفحص کردنی آختارغای و آختارسا و آختارسون و آختاردیلار تفحص کند
آختارغودیک و آختارور دیک تفحص کردنی و همچنانکه کند آختارماق بسکون الراء مع التاء مصدر متعدیست بمعنی متفحص شدن
و صیغ آن بدستور شق اول با تای قرشت اشتقاق می یابد آختاریشماق بکسر الراء مع الشین مصدر مفاعله است بمعنی با یکدیگر
تفحص کردن و صیغ آن بدستور با شین اشتقاق می یابد آختارلماق مع اللام بمعنی تفحص شدن و صیغ آن با لام اشتقاق می یابد
آختوملاماق بضم سین مهمله بدستی کردن و آقتوملاماق با قاف نیز استعمال می شود آختوملادی بدستی کرد آختوملادق
بدستی کردیم آختوملار و آختوملایدور بدستی میکند و آختوملار بمعنی فاعل و مصدر هم می آید آختوملامایدور بدستی نکرده
و میکند آختوملاغان و آختوملایدورغان بدستی کننده و بدستی کرده و بمعنی مصدر هم می آیند آختوملا و آختوملا

مفرد مخاطب از فعل امر آختوملاما و آختوملاماغیل مفرد مخاطب از فعل نهی آختوملانک و آختوملانکیز و آختوملانکلار جمع مخاطب
از فعل امر آختوملامانک و آختوملامانکیز و آختوملامانکلار جمع مخاطب از فعل نهی آختوملامان و آختوملاماس مین بدستی نمیکنم آختو
ملامین و آختوملایدورمین و آختوملارمین بدستی میکنم آختوملادیم و آختوملادیم بدستی کردم آختوملاغوم بدستی
خواهم کرد آختوملایب و آختوملایبان و آختوملایش بدستی کرده الشاهد علی الاول میر خسرو شیرین شعر شفق کون عجایب
چون قول الحزاب تب چو آختوملایب قویاش خاسینی و شایتیب آختوملامیشانک بدستی کرده آختوملاماس بدستی نمیکند و بمعنی فاعل
و مصدر منفی هم می آید آختوملامابی بدستی کردنش آختوملامادین از بدستی کردن و بدستی نکرده آختوملایب بولماس و آختوملا
و آختوملاماق اولماس بدستی نمیتوان کرد آختوملا آلماس بدستی نمیتواند کرد آختوملایو آختوملایو بدستی کنان و بدون
تکرار هم مستعمل آختوملای و آختوملایین بدستی کنم و کند و کنی آختوملاساق و آختوملاغایمیز و آختوملاغای و آختوملای
بدستی کنیم آختوملاغالی برای بدستی کردن و تا بدستی کرده آختوملاغاچ چون بدستی کرد و کند و بمحض کردن آختوملاغوچی
بدستی کننده آختوملاغوسیدا آختوملاغونچه و آختوملاغانیچه تا بدستی کردن و مقابل آن آختوملاغوم بدستی خواهم کرد آختوملاغو
بدستی خواهی کرد آختوملاغوسی بدستی خواهد کرد آختوملاغولوق بدستی کردنی آختوملاغای و آختوملاسا و آختوملاسون و آختو
بدستی کند آختوملاغودیک و آختوملاردیک بدستی کردنی و همچنانکه کند آختوملاتماق مع التاء بدستی کردن و صیغ آن موافق آن
با تای قرشت اشتقاق می یابد آختوملاشماق مع الشین بمعنی با یکدیگر بدستی کردن و صیغ آن با شین اشتقاق می یابد آختوملانماق
مع النون بدستی شدن و صیغ آن با نون اشتقاق می یابد من الجوامد آخ بعد از شاخ لفظ لیت که عبارة وای در مقام التحسر
و درد نالی گفته می شود و در فارسی بمعنی آفرین باشد آختا و آخته اسبی بود که تخم آنرا کشیده باشند و بفارسی آنچه کشیده شده با
مثل شمشیر کشیده شده از غلاف بر آورده شده آختاچی جلودار و جنیبت کش را گویند چنانکه در صفت سیاره
مسافر اللیل گوید شعر باغ آرا چونکه کیردی اول مجنون آختاچی الیکیدا ایدی گلگون آختیق بسکون خا و قاف
قرشت نواده باشد که آنرا رومیه تو روون گویند آخسا و [illegible] بفتح سین مهمله و غین معجمه و ضم واو و سکون راء بلغت
بند ترکش بود که آنرا بعربی منطقه الکنانه گویند آخسوم بضم [illegible] باشد چنانکه [illegible]
القلوب [illegible] گوید که آخسوم [illegible] دین خارج [illegible] نشانه و آقسوم
استعمال میشود مع الدال من المشتقات آداشماغ با یکدیگر خواندن و ترنم کردن و آنرا آداشماق هم گویند چنانکه [illegible]
مع التاء مذکور شد و صیغ آن نیز موافق صیغ آداشماق اشتقاق می یابد آداغلاماق همان آداغلاماق بمعنی نامزد کردن [illegible]
شد من الجوامد آدا بفتح دال ته و تل [illegible] گویند و [illegible] جزیره و خشکی بود که در میان آب باشد آداش
بر وزن باداش بمعنی همنام باشد الشاهد علیه شعرای خسته کونکول [illegible] عشقدا مجنون کمر کلیج سینی [illegible]
آداشینک ساغینور مین [illegible] گوید شعر اول پری [illegible] آندین [illegible]
منکا ایردی آداش و مؤلف [illegible] شعر [illegible] شاهد آورده
لفظ و معنی هر دو اختراعیست آداق چهار معنی دارد اول شهر [illegible] گویند و آن نام ولایتیست از ترکستان چنانکه در
در وصف سلطان [illegible] گوید شعر آنداکم غازی شه فرخنده بخت تاج الاین [illegible]
کیشی [illegible] که [illegible] آداق [illegible]

33v.

برخاستن وراه رفتن عادت نمایند ستیم نامزد بود چنانکه جزیره وخشکی را گویند که در میان آب باشد و در رومیه آنرا مخمسا خوانند اد
میگویند و در مجالس و بیم از مجالس النفائس یعنی امیر سعید کابلی مذکور است که مصراع محب لارمیتا نیکرکو یاغرسیز
کل یا عیدا خماری یارغه سیز کومین ولسلم ترتیم تینک تماشه کشه بیر شوخ ایروردیب یازغه سیز و مؤلف رومی کل یا عیدالا
کل لا امیدا خوانده و اداق را بمعنی وقت و موسم نوشته و شعر نوایی را شاهد آورده سهو کرده و بمعنی نامزد هم ذکر کرده و مؤلف
فرهنگ جهانگیری آداک با کاف فارسی بمعنی جزیره و خشکی میان آب نوشته آداغلیغ نامزد شده که آنرا عرب مخطوبه گویند
آدا بر وزن صدا زمین نامزروع و اراضی بایره را خوانند آدون بر وزن صابون بلغت مغولی رمه اسب بود آدوچی
گله بان یعنی راعی الخیل را گویند آدرغان بکسر دال و سکون رای مهمله بلغت مغولی یعنی تلوچه باشد آدیک بر وزن شیک
چکمه را گویند آدیم بر وزن قدم قدم و گام را نامند مع الراء المهمله من المشتقات آرماق خسته شدن و آنرا ارماق
نیز گویند آردی خسته شد آردوق خسته شدیم آرور و آرادور خسته می شود و آرور بمعنی فاعل و مصدر هم می آید
آرماید ور خسته نمیشود و نشده است آرغان و آرورغان و آرادورغان خسته شونده و خسته شده و بمعنی مصدر هم
می آیند آر بسکون را و آرو بضم او آرغیل مفرد مخاطبه فعل امر آرما و آرماغیل مفرد مخاطبه فعل نهی آرینک و آرینکیز و آرینکلار
جمع مخاطبه فعل امر آرمانک و آرمانکیز و آرمانکلار جمع مخاطبه فعل نهی آرماس و آرماس مین خسته نمیشوم آرامین و آرودورمن
آرادورمن و آروارم خسته میشوم و آرامین مخفف آراسیدورمین هم باشد یعنی درمیان آنم چنانکه در ذیل جوامد مذکور خواهد
شد آرورم و آرماغیم خسته شدنم آرماغوم خسته نخواهم شد آریب و آریبان و آرمیش خسته شده و آریب و آریبان بمعنی
پاک شده هم باشد و در این معنی با مصدر آریماق یعنی پاک شدن اشتراک دارند چنانکه مذکور خواهد شد آریشانک خسته
شده آرماس خسته نمیشود و بمعنی فاعل و مصدر منفی هم می آید آرماسی خسته شدنش و نشدنش آرمادین از خسته شدن و
نشده آریب بولماس و آرابولماس و آرماق اولماس خسته نمیتوان شد و آریب بولماس بمعنی پاک نمیتوان شد هم باشد آرالماس
خسته نمیتواند شد آرا آرا خسته شونده و خسته شده و بدون تکرار هم مستعمل است و آرا بمعنی میان نیز باشد آرای و آراین
خسته شوم و شود و شوی و بمعنی تفحص کنم و کند و کنی هم آمده و در این معنی با مصدر آراماق بمعنی تفحص کردن اشتراک دارند
چنانکه مذکور خواهد شد آرغاق و آرغایز و آرغای بز و آرلی و آرالینک خسته شویم و آرلی و آرالینک بمعنی تفحص کنیم
هم باشد و با این معنی ماخوذ از مصدر آراماق است آرغالی برای خسته شدن و تا خسته شده آرغلج چون خسته شد و
بمحض شدن آرغوجی خسته شونده آرغوچه و آرغانچه و آرغونچه تا خسته شدن و بقدر آن آرغوم خسته خواهم شد آرغونک
خسته خواهی شد آرغوسی خسته خواهد شد آرغولوق خسته شدنی آرغای و آرا و آرسا و آرسون و آردیک خسته شود
آرغودیک و آرودیک خسته شدنی و همچنانکه شود آریماغ بکسر را پاک و مصفا شدن و آنرا آریلماق با لام هم گویند آریدی
پاک شد آریدوق پاک شدیم آریور و آریدور پاک می شود الشاهد علی الاول من لسان الطیر شعر فسق تین نفس ایله الحکیم مادر
سوار ایرغوطه کیم اوردی ایش دله شعر بحر غرا [illegible] توشکان [illegible] موج شعر آریدینچه توتغان بولسا اوج و آریر بمعنی فاعل
و مصدر هم می آید آریمایدور پاک نمیشود و نشده است آریغان و آریرغان و آریدورغان پاک شونده و پاک شده و بمعنی مصدر
هم می آیند آریغیل مفرد مخاطبه فعل امر الشاهد علی الاول شعر دیرسین که یار عکسی سنکا توشکا [illegible] کونکول اول غبار
عنبرین آیینه سان آریغ و آریغ بمعنی پاک شوم و شود و شوی چنانکه در ذیل بیاید و بمعنی پاک و مصفا و زیبا هم باشد چنانکه در

34r.

ذیل جوامد مذکور خواهد شد آریما و آریماغیل مفرد مخاطبه فعل نهی آرینک و آرینکیز و آرینکلار جمع مخاطبه فعل امر آریمانک و
آریمانکیز و آریمانکلار جمع مخاطبه فعل نهی آریمان و آریماس مین پاک نمیشوم آریمین و آریرمین و آریدورمین و آریرام پاک میشوم
آریرم و آریماغیم پاک شدنم آریماغوم پاک نخواهم شد آریب و آریبان و آریمیش پاک شده الشاهد علی الاول شعر یار عکسی نینک
الوب جلوه کهی کیتی کیم خاطری مرآتی آریب وینه مجنون در وصف سلسله لیلی گوید شعر ایتی ترزی [illegible] آریب
اعضاسی خراشیدین تمیز آریب یعنی کوشش از خشت پوست پاک شده و اعضایش از خراش سرخ شده و مؤلفین رومی آریب را
بمعنی آریب نحیف و بمعنی جدا ذکر کرده اند یعنی بمعنی جدا ذکر کرده شعر نوایی را شاهد آورده اند وهمه اشتباه
بمعنی خسته شده نیز باشد و در این معنی با مصدر آرماق اشتراک دارند چنانکه گذشت آریمیشانک پاک شده آریماس
پاک نمیشود و بمعنی فاعل و مصدر منفی هم می آید آریماسی پاک شدنش و نشدنش آریمادین از پاک شدن و پاک نشده آریب بولماس
و آریسا بولماس و آریماق اولماس پاک نمیتوان شد و آریب بولماس بمعنی خسته نمیتوان شد هم باشد آریالماس پاک نمیتواند شد آری
آری پاک شونده و بدون تکرار هم مستعمل است آری و آریین پاک شوم و شود و شوی آریباق و آریغایز و آریغای بز
و آریلی و آریلینک پاک شویم آریغالی برای پاک شدن و تا پاک شده آریغاج چون پاک شد و بمحض شدن آریغوچی
پاک شونده آریغوچه و آریغونچه و آریغانچه تا پاک شدن و بقدر آن آریغوم پاک خواهم شد آریغونک پاک خواهی شد آریغوسی
پاک خواهد شد آریغولوق پاک شدنی آریغای و آریسا و آریسون و آریدیک پاک شود چنانکه شاهد بر اقلطه در باب ثلثی
محبوب القلوب در وصف زهد گوید کم هر سالک که بو مقامه [illegible] نفسانیت [illegible] آریغای
آریغودیک و آریدیک پاک شدنی و همچنانکه پاک شود آریتماق مع التا پاک کردن آریتماج چون پاک کرد و کند و بمحض
کردن چنانکه در تاریخ بابری [illegible] مذکور است [illegible] آریتماج [illegible] اوشوک
تمام بولادور و باقی صیغ آن بر این قیاس و با انضمام تای قرشت اشتقاق می یابد آریلماق مع اللام مرادف آریماق باشد یعنی پاک
و صیغ آن بالام اشتقاق می یابد آراماق بمعنی [illegible] تفحص کردن آرادی تفحص کرد آرادوق تفحص کردیم آرار و آرایدور تفحص
میکند و آرار بمعنی فاعل و مصدر هم می آید آرامایدور تفحص نمیکند و نکرده است آرا و آراغیل مفرد مخاطبه فعل امر و آرما
وسط هم باشد آرما و آرماغیل مفرد مخاطبه فعل نهی آرانک و آرانکیز و آرانکلار جمع مخاطبه فعل امر آرامانک و آرامانکیز
و آرامانکلار جمع مخاطبه فعل نهی آرامان و آراماس مین تفحص نمیکنم آرامین و آرارمین و آرایدورمین و آرارام تفحص میکنم
آرارم و آراماغیم تفحص کردنم آراماغوم تفحص نخواهم کرد آراسانک و آراغاسین و آراغای سین تفحص کنی الشاهد علی الاول [illegible]
الروبیه شعر [illegible] آراب و آرابان و آرامیش تفحص کرده
آرامیشانک تفحص کرده آراماس تفحص نمیکند و بمعنی فاعل و مصدر منفی هم می آید آراماسی تفحص کردنش و نکردنش آرامادین از
تفحص کردن و تفحص نکرده آراب بولماس و آراسا بولماس و آراماق اولماس تفحص نمیتوان کرد آرالماس تفحص نمیتواند کرد آرا و
آرای آرای تفحص کنان و بدون تکرار هم مستعمل آرای و آراین تفحص کنم و کند و کنی و خسته شوم و شود و شوی آراساق و
و آراغایز و آراغای بز و آرالی و آرالینک تفحص کنیم و آرالی و آرالینک بمعنی خسته شویم هم باشد آراغالی برای تفحص کردن
و تا تفحص کرده آراغاج چون تفحص کرد و کند و بمحض کردن آراغوچی تفحص کننده آراغوچه و آراغونچه و آراغانچه تا تفحص کردن
و بقدر آن آراغوم تفحص خواهم کرد آراغونک تفحص خواهی کرد آراغوسی تفحص خواهد کرد آراغولوق تفحص کردنی آراغای و

آراسا ما آراسون و آرادیك تحقیق کند آراغودیك و آرادیك تحقیق کردنی و همچنانکه کند آراماق متعدی است بمعنی تفحص
ساختن و صیغ آن با ثانی قرشات اشتقاق می یابد آرالاماق دو معنی دارد اول تفحص کردن دوم درمیان درآمدن
و میانجیگری کردن آرالادی تفحص کرد و درمیانه درآمد آرالادوق تفحص کردیم و درمیانه درآمدیم آرالار ها آرالایدور
تفحص بکند و درمیانه درمی آید الشاهد علی الاول والمعنی الاول شعر خضر ایله عیسی او لوب خط بیله لعلینکنه ایشی
بو کوروب بوایکا وی عارض و سیمانی آرالادی و آرالار بمعنی فاعل و مصدر هم می آید آرالامایدور تفحص نکند و نکرده است
و درمیانه درنمی آید و میانجی نشده است آرالا و آرالاغیل مفرد مخاطب فصل امر آرالاما و آرالاماغیل مفرد مخاطب فصل نهی آرالانك
و آرالانکیز ها آرالانکلار جمع مخاطب فصل امر آرالامانك و آرالامانکیز آرالامانکلار جمع مخاطب فصل نهی آرالامان و
آرالاماس مین درمیانه درنمی آیم و تفحص نمیکنم آرالای مین و آرالادیمین ها آرالایدورمین و آرالارام تفحص میکنم و درمیانه در
می آیم آرالادیم و آرالاماغیم تفحص کردم و درمیانه درآمدم آرالاغوم تفحص نخواهم کرد و درمیانه درنخواهم آمد آرالاب و
آرالاپان و آرالامیش تحقیق کرده و درمیانه درآمده آرالامیشانك درمیانه درآمده آرالاماس تفحص نمیکند و درمیانه درنمی آید
و بمعنی فاعل و مصدر منفی هم می آید آرالاماسی تفحص کردنش و نکردنش و درمیانه درآمدنش و درنیامدنش آرالامادین از تفحص
کردن و تفحص نکرده و از میانه درآمدن و درمیانه نیامده آرالاب بولماس و آرالاشا بولماس و آرالاماقی بولماس تفحص نمیتوان کرد
و درمیانه درنمیتوان آمد آرالای آلماس تفحص نمیتواند کرد و درمیانه درنمیتواند آمد آرالایو و آرالای ها آرالای تفحص کنان و درمیانه آمده
درآمده و بدون تکرار هم مستعملست آرالای ها آرالاین تفحص کنم و کند و کنی و درمیانه درآیم و درآید و درآیی چنانکه شاهد
بر اول بمعنی درمیانه درآیم در تاریخ بابری مذکور است که ملازمان تنبل غه قوشولماسون دیب آرالای آلدی و آرالاشاق آرالا
و آرالاغای ها آرالای ها آرالاینك تفحص کنیم و درمیانه درآییم آرالاغلی برای تفحص کردن و تا تفحص کرده و برای درمیانه درآمدن
و تا درمیانه درآمده آرالاغاچ چون تفحص کرد و کند و بمحض کردن چون درمیانه درآمد و درآید و بمحض درآمدن آرالاغوچی
تفحص کننده و درمیانه درآینده آرالاغوچه ها آرالاغونچه و آرالاغانچه تا تفحص کردن و بقدر تفحص کردن و تا درمیان درآمدن و بقدر
آن چنانکه شاهد بر ثانی بمعنی تا درمیان درآمدن در تاریخ بابری مذکور است که بو کون [illegible] بیك سکلاری باشلاب جمعیتی
آرالاغونچه تنبل کیلیب مغول لارغه قوشولغان ایکاندور آرالاغوم تفحص خواهم کرد و درمیان درخواهم آمد آرالاغونك تفحص
خواهی کرد و درمیان درخواهی آمد آرالاغوسی تفحص خواهد کرد و درمیان درخواهد آمد آرالاغولوق تفحص کردنی و درمیان
درآمدنی آرالاغای ها آرالاسا و آرالاسون و آرالادیك تفحص کند و درمیان درآید آرالاغودیك و آرالادیك تفحص کردنی
و همچنانکه کند و درمیان درآمدنی و همچنانکه درآید آرباماق افسون کردن آربادی افسون کرد آربار آربایدور افسون میکند
و آربار بمعنی فاعل و مصدر هم می آید آربامایدور افسون نمیکند و نکرده است آرباغان و آربارغان و آربایدورغان افسون
کننده و افسون کرده و بمعنی مصدر هم می آیند آربا و آرباغیل مفرد مخاطب فصل امر آرباما و آرباماغیل مفرد مخاطب فصل نهی
آربانك ها آربانکیز و آربانکلار جمع مخاطب فصل امر آربامانك و آربامانکیز و آربامانکلار جمع مخاطب فصل نهی آربامان و آرباماس مین
افسون نمیکنم آربای مین ها آربایدورمین و آربارمن افسون میکنم آربادیم و آرباماغیم افسون کردم آرباغوم افسون نخواهم کرد
آرباب و آرباپان و آربامیش افسون کرده آربامیشانك افسون کرده آرباماس افسون نمیکند و بمعنی فاعل و مصدر منفی هم می آید
آرباماسی افسون کردنش و نکردنش آربامادین از افسون کردن و افسون نکرده آرباب بولماس و آربابا بولماس و آرباماقی بولماس افسون

نمیتوان کرد آربای آلماس افسون نمیتواند کرد آربایو و آربای آربای افسون کنان و بدون تکرار هم مستعملست آربای ها آرباین افسون
کنم و کند و کنی آرباشاق و آرباغاینز ها آرباغاییز و آرباغلی و آربالینك افسون کنیم آرباغلی برای افسون کردن و تا افسون کرده
آرباغاچ چون افسون کرد و کند و بمحض کردن آرباغوچی افسون کننده آرباغوچه و آرباغونچه و آرباغانچه تا افسون کردن و بقدر
افسون کردن آرباغوم افسون خواهم کرد آرباغونك افسون خواهی کرد آرباغوسی افسون خواهد کرد آرباغولوق افسون کردنی
آرباغای ها آرباسا و آرباسون و آربادیك افسون کند آرباغودیك و آربادیك افسون کردنی و همچنانکه کند آرتماق
دو معنی دارد اول زیاد شدن دوم طی شدن آرتتی زیاد شد و طی شد آرتتوق زیاد شدیم و طی شدیم آرتار آرتادور
زیاد میشود و طی میشود و آرتار بمعنی فاعل و مصدر هم می آید آرتمایدور زیاد نمیشود و نشده است و طی نمیشود و نشده است آرتغان و
آرتارغان و آرتادورغان زیاد شونده و زیاد شده و طی شونده و طی شده چنانکه شاهد بر اول است بمعنی زیاد شده گوید شعر
خمی [illegible] آرتماینی [illegible] یکی [illegible] آنادی خضر و مسیح و بمعنی مصدر هم می آیند آرت و آرتغیل
مفرد مخاطب فصل امر آرتما و آرتماغیل مفرد مخاطب فصل نهی آرتینك و آرتینکیز و آرتینکلار جمع مخاطب فصل امر آرتمانك و
آرتمانکیز ها آرتمانکلار جمع مخاطب فصل نهی آرتمان و آرتماس مین زیاد نمیشوم و طی نمیشوم آرتامین و آرتادورمین و آرتارمن
آرتارام زیاد میشوم و طی میشوم آرتادیم و آرتماغیم زیاد شدم و طی شدم آرتماغوم زیاد نخواهم شد و طی نخواهم شد آرتیب و
آرتیبان و آرتمیش زیاد شده و طی شده چنانکه شاهد بر اول است بمعنی اول در خسرو شیرین گوید شعر [illegible]
آرتیب [illegible] ترتیب شاهد بر ثانی [illegible] سکندری گوید شعر تا اول
تنکری [illegible] بولوب [illegible] آرتیشان [illegible]
آرتیشانك زیاد شده و طی شده آرتماس زیاد نمیشود و طی نمیشود و بمعنی فاعل و مصدر منفی می آید آرتماسی زیاد شدنش و نشدنش
و طی شدنش و طی نشدنش آرتمادین از زیاد شدن و زیاد نشده و از طی شدن و طی نشده آرتیب بولماس و آرتا بولماس و آرتماقی
زیاد نتوان شد و طی نتوان شد آرتا آلماس زیاد نمیتواند شد و طی نمیتواند شد آرتا آرتا زیاد شونده شونده و طی شده و بدون تکرار
هم مستعملست آرتای و آرتاین زیاد شوم و شود و شوی و طی شوم و شود و شوی آرتاشاق ها آرتغای ها آرتغای ها آرتغلی و آرتالینك
زیاد شویم و طی شویم آرتغلی برای زیاد شدن و تا زیاد شده و برای طی شدن و تا طی شده آرتغاچ چون زیاد شد و شود و بمحض
شدن آرتغوچی زیاد شونده و طی شونده آرتغوچه و آرتغونچه و آرتغانچه تا زیاد شدن و تا طی شدن و بقدر آنها آرتغوم زیاد خواهم
شد و طی خواهم شد آرتغونك زیاد خواهی شد و طی خواهی شد آرتغوسی زیاد خواهد شد و طی خواهد شد آرتغولوق زیاد شدنی
طی شدنی آرتغای ها آرتسا و آرتسون و آرتدیك زیاد شود و طی شود آرتغودیك و آرتدیك زیاد شدنی و طی شدنی و
شود آرتورماق بمعنی زیاد کردن و صیغ آن بقرشات اول اشتقاق می یابد آرتیلماق بکسر التاء والحاء دو معنی دارد اول زیاد
دوم تکاپو کردن و قطره زدن آرتیلدی زیاد شد و تکاپو کرد آرتیلدوق زیاد شدیم و تکاپو کردیم آرتیلور ها آرتیلادور
میشود و تکاپو میکند و آرتیلور بمعنی فاعل و مصدر هم می آید آرتیلمایدور زیاد نمیشود و نشده است و تکاپو نمیکند و نکرده است
آرتیلغان ها آرتیلورغان و آرتیلادورغان زیاد شونده و زیاد شده و تکاپو کننده و تکاپو کرده و بمعنی مصدر نیز می آیند چنانکه شاهد
بر اول است بمعنی [illegible] گوید شعر آشکیم آرتیلغان [illegible] کیم [illegible] کونکلی
[illegible] آرتیل و آرتیلغیل مفرد مخاطب فصل امر آرتیلما و آرتیلماغیل مفرد مخاطب فصل نهی آرتیلینك ها آرتیلینکیز و آرتیلینکلار

35v

جمع مخاطب ماضی فعل ار آرتیلماتلنگ ع آرتیلمانکیز ع آرتیلمانکلار جمع مخاطب از فعل نفی آرتیلمان و آرتیلماس مین زیاد نمیشوم و تکاپو نمیکنم
آرتیلاهمین ط آرتیلورمین و آرتیلادورمین و آرتیلورام زیاد میشوم و تکاپو میکنم آرتیلورم ع آرتیلماغیم زیاد شدنم و تکاپو کردنم
آرتیلماغوم زیاد خواهم شد و تکاپو خواهم کرد آرتیلیب ع آرتیلیبان ع آرتیلیشن زیاد شده و تکاپو کرده الشاهد علی الاول ما
الثانی شعر بو کوروب هر کیم کا آرتیلیب مظلوم باش شوخ یاشلاری یتکه اوینارلار چوبو قمرک تیلیث و نیز مر سنکدی
در هنگام برکشیدن اسکنده از مصر میگوید شعر تینکیز ایلا ابان قطع و تاغ آرتیلیب یورودایردی بولار عزم مخلیث سیاه شعر
چنین است که تینکیز و تاغ قطع ایلا ابان آرتیلیب بول یورودایردی یعنی دریا و کوه را قطع و تکاپو کرده میرفت و ...
در این شعر آرتایب و آرتاییب و طالع هر دو را باب خوانده و بمعنی گذشتن و عبور کردن ذکر کرده اند الفاظ اختراعی آرت
آرتیلیشانلن زیاد شده و تکاپو کرده آرتیلماس زیاد نمیشود و تکاپو نمیکند و بمعنی فاعل و مصدر منفی هم می آید آرتیلماسی زیاد شدن
و نشدنش و تکاپو کردنش و نکردنش آرتیلمادین از زیاد شدن و زیاد نشده و از تکاپو کردن و تکاپو نشده آرتیلیب بولماس ع
آرتیلسا بولماس ع آرتیلما قالولماس زیاد نمیتوان شد و تکاپو نمیتوان کرد آرتیلماالماس زیاد نمیتواند شد و تکاپو نمیتواند کرد آرتیلا
آرتیلار زیاد شوند شوند و تکاپو کنان و بدون تکرار هم مستعمل آرتیلای ع آرتیلاین زیاد شوم و شوید شوی و تکاپو کنم و کنید
و کنی آرتیلساق و آرتیلغای ع آرتیلغای بیز ع آرتیلایلیع آرتیلالینک زیاد شویم و تکاپو کنیم آرتیلغالی برای زیاد شدن و
تا زیاد شده و برای تکاپو کردن و تا تکاپو کرده آرتیلغاچ چون زیاد شد و شود و بمحض شدن و چون تکاپو کرد و کند بمحض کردن
آرتیلغوچی زیاد شونده و تکاپو کننده آرتیلغوچه ع آرتیلغونچه و آرتیلغانچه تا زیاد شدن و بعد از آن و تکاپو کردن و بعد از آن آرتیلغوم
زیاد خواهم شد و تکاپو خواهم کرد آرتیلغونک زیاد خواهی شد و تکاپو خواهی کرد آرتیلغوسی زیاد خواهد شد و تکاپو خواهد کرد
آرتیلغولوق زیاد شدنی و تکاپو کردنی آرتیلغای و آرتیلار و آرتیلسا و آرتیلون ع آرتیلدیلر زیاد شود و تکاپو کند آرتیلغو
آرتیلودیلر زیاد شدنی و همچنانکه شود و تکاپو کردنی و همچنانکه کند آردلاشماق بسکون را و دال مهمله با یکدیگر ردیف
حلول شدن آردلاشتی ردیف شد آردلاشتولر ردیف شدیم آردلاشور و آردلاشادور ردیف میشود و آردلاشور بمعنی فاعل
و مصدر هم می آید آردلاشماید هم ردیف نمیشود و نشده است آردلاشکان و آردلاشورکان و آردلاشادورکان ردیف
شده و بمعنی مصدر هم می آیند آردلاش و آردلاشکیل مفرد مخاطب از فعل امر آردلاشنگ و آردلاشنکیل مفرد مخاطب از فعل نفی
آردلاشینک ع آردلاشینکیز و آردلاشینکلار جمع مخاطب از فعل امر آردلاشمانک ع آردلاشمانکیز و آردلاشمانکلار جمع مخاطب
نفی آردلاشمان ع آردلاشماس مین ردیف نمیشوم آردلاشایین و آردلاشورمین و آردلاشادورمین و آردلاشورام ردیف میشوم
آردلاشورم ع آردلاشماغیم ردیف شدنم آردلاشماغوم ردیف خواهم شد آردلاشیب ع آردلاشیبان ع آردلاشیشن ردیف شده
آردلاشیشانلن ردیف شده آردلاشماس ردیف نمیشود و بمعنی فاعل و مصدر منفی هم می آید آردلاشماسی ردیف شدنش و نشدنش آردلاشمادین
از ردیف شدن و ردیف نشده آردلاشیب بولماس ع آردلاشا بولماس ع آردلاشماقالولماس ردیف نمیتوان شد آردلاشاالماس ردیف
نمیتواند شد آردلاشا آردلاشار ردیف شونده شونده و بدون تکرار هم مستعمل آردلاشای ع آردلاشاین ردیف شوم و شوید و شوی
آردلاشساق ع آردلاشغای بیز ع آردلاشایلیع آردلاشالینک ردیف شویم آردلاشغالی برای ردیف شدن و تا شدن
آردلاشغاچ چون ردیف شد و شود و بمحض شدن آردلاشغوچی ردیف شونده آردلاشغونچه ع آردلاشغانچه و آردلاشغانچه
تا ردیف شدن و بعد از آن آردلاشغوم ردیف خواهم شد آردلاشغونک ردیف خواهی شد آردلاشغوسی ردیف خواهد شد آردلا

36r

ردیف شدنی آردلاشغای ع آردلاشلار ع آردلاشا و آردلاشسون ع آردلاشدیلر ردیف شود آردلاشغودیلر ع آردلاشغود
ردیف شدنی و همچنانکه شود آردلاشور بمعنی مصدر متعدی است یعنی ردیف ساختن کردن و صیغ آن با لفظ تور اشتقاق می یابد
ارزیماق بسکون راء و کسر زای معجمه نازیدن و ترکی صیغ نازیدن ارزیدی نازید ارزیدوک نازیدیم ارزیدو ارزیدیو نازیدند
علی الاول شعر خطوخان نقشیغه ارزیب آنکا دوقتی نبتت سبزه کیم سرچه گیاه خاستو آینه هم نفعی و ارزیدی بمعنی فاعل و مصدر
هم می آید ارزیمایدور نمی نازد و نمیانازیده است ارزیغان ع ارزیرغان ع ارزیدورغان نازیده و ارزیدو بمعنی مصدر هم می آید ارزی
و ارزیغیل مفرد مخاطب از فعل امر ارزیمای مفرد مخاطب از فعل نفی ارزینک ع ارزینکیز ع ارزینکلار جمع مخاطب از فعل امر
ارزیمانک و ارزیمانکیز ع ارزیمانکلار جمع مخاطب از فعل نفی ارزیمان ع ارزیماس مین نمیازم ارزیمین و ارزیرمین ع ارزیدورمین
ارزیرام می نازم ارزیرم ارزیماغیم ع ارزیماغوم نخواهم نازید ارزیب ع ارزیبان ع ارزیشن نازیده ارزیشانلن نازیده
ارزیماس نمی نازد الشاهد علیه شعر بصر ان کلی وکلشی طرفیغه ارزیماس کلکون میی لا جیجار تیغه ارزیماس بمعنی فاعل و
منفی هم می آید ارزیماسی نازیدنش و نازیدنش ارزیمادین نازیده ارزیب بولماس ع ارزیا بولماس ع ارزیماقالولماس
نمیتوان ارزید ارزیاالماس نمیتواند نازید ارزی ارزیار ع ارزیدیلر و بدون تکرار هم بمعنی مستعمل ارزیای ع ارزیاین بنازم و
بنازی ارزیساق ع ارزیغای بیز و ارزیغای بیز ع ارزیلیع ارزیالینک بنازیم ارزیغالی برای نازیدن و تا نازیده ارزیغاچ
چون نازید و نازد و بمحض نازیدن ارزیغوچی نازنده ارزیغونچه ع ارزیغانچه تا نازیدن و بعد از آن ارزیغوم
خواهم نازید ارزیغونک خواهی نازید ارزیغوسی خواهد نازید ارزیغولوق نازیدنی ارزیغای ع ارزیسا ارزیدیلر ع ارزیسون
بنازد ارزیغودیلر نازیدنی و همچنانکه بنازد آرغاداماق فریب دادن آرغادوق فریب دادیم آرغادا
و آرغادایدور فریب میدهد و آرغادا بمعنی فاعل و مصدر هم می آید آرغاداغان ع آرغادارغان ع آرغادایدورغان
فریب دهنده و فریب داده و بمعنی مصدر هم می آید آرغاداو آرغاداغیل مفرد مخاطب از فعل امر آرغاداما و آرغادامایغیل مفرد
مخاطب از فعل نفی آرغادانک ع آرغادانکیز ع آرغادانکلار جمع مخاطب از فعل امر آرغادامانک ع آرغادامانکیز ع آرغادامانکلار
جمع مخاطب از فعل نفی آرغادامان ع آرغاداماس مین فریب نمیدهم آرغادایمین ع آرغادارمین ع آرغادایدورمین ع آرغادارام
فریب میدهم الشاهد علی الثالث شعر مینی سیدل سنکا جان و ضیا ناقیرله یا دایمه مین بلی یمین طعنلی بو محنت بیرله
آرغادایدورمین آرغادارم ع آرغاداماغیم فریب دادنم آرغاداماغوم فریب نخواهم داد آرغادایب ع آرغادایبان ع آرغادایشن
فریب داده چنانکه شاهد بر او قلم ... التغایر فکر اشعار سلطان حسین میرزا گوید که معز و ن کو نکلینی آلداب
دلربای نینک کیلوری خبر نیچه سیب تورور و آرغاداب عشرت قولیغه و صل خبرین آیتیب تورور آرغادایشانلن فریب داده
فریب نمیدهد و بمعنی فاعل و مصدر منفی هم می آید آرغاداماسی فریب دادنش و ندادنش آرغادامادین از فریب دادن و فریب
نداده آرغاداب بولماس ع آرغادایسا بولماس ع آرغاداماقالولماس فریب نمیتوان داد آرغاداالماس فریب نمیتواند داد آرغادای
آرغادای فریب داده فریب داده و بدون تکرار هم مستعمل آرغادای ع آرغاداین فریب دهم و دهید و دهی آرغاداساق
و آرغاداغای بیز ع آرغاداغای بیز ع آرغادایلیع آرغاداالینک فریب دهیم آرغاداغالی برای فریب دادن و تا فریب داده آرغاداغاچ
چون فریب داد و بدهد و بمحض دادن آرغاداغوچی فریب دهنده آرغاداغونچه ع آرغاداغانچه تا فریب دادن و بعد از آن
فریب دادن آرغاداغوم فریب خواهم داد آرغاداغونک فریب خواهی داد آرغاداغوسی فریب خواهد داد آرغاداغولوق

ونیمه دادن آرغادماغای وآرغاطاسا وآرغاداسون وآرغادادیك فرینه هد آرغاداغودیك وآرغادارد یك فرهادی

وچنانکه بدخشان ایکامد ارابروفضل آره بروزن زاده بمعنی میان و وسط باشد وآنرا آرالیغ هم کویند ونیز بمعنی آرا اسید

در میان استعمال یعنی چنانکه باخیص بهر دو طریق کوید الشاهد علی الاول شعر کمخالینك که کونکلکر کوزار

ایرود کونکلیم آرا اسید لحدین قازایرود ونیز فرماید شعر کاه مجنون وشلیغی برله بولوب مضطرب کا بجاك

اولملیدین منتقل بجال مینک الشاهد علی الثانی شعر کونکلکیم اوطره بولغاندا لاله دود اول ای عشق دین

کوبیانات تلغ وادی ره ایلن آرالا بیکر پای حق شوالغ کویند اراه بروزن خوابه مخوف را است که آنرا بعربی

نامند من خسرو شیرین شعر ارابه دیماکیم کرد وزخرش بولوب خارایه که آسیدا شایش آرا اسیدا وآرا اسید بمعنی در میان

چنانکه شاهد آن مذکور شد اراسید مبین میان آنم وآرامین وآن بین هم کویند چنانکه نکارش خواهد

یافت آرالمین خشکی را کویند که در میان آب واقع شده باشد چنانکه در تاریخ بابری مذکور است کما شوکیتسی

سیلا پرآرال بار ایدی کیمن قالغان ایل لار آرال الحا کوروندی اکرچه آت ویراق بیله اوزلاریغ سالیب اوتتیلار

ونیز اسم شده از برای محلی که از ولایت خوارزم که مابین رود جیحون و رودخانه سیر واقع است آرالیغ وسط ومیان چنانکه

کوید شعر منا قیلا هجر خمارا یحیه لبیب مین خانیمه برقلعج بیله مینی تیل بوار الیغلیغ خلاص دامین وآرامین وارد آرا

سیلامین باشد یعنی در میان آنم الشاهد علی الاول شعر زلفی هجر بیدا بیم دودی هماتی توتتی مینی جدا اولوشوك

آرا مینک الشاهد علی الثانی شعر چون کیشی لیلی دین چتار مستور بینه عشق وجنون ای نوای بر عجب دور کیم

خلایق آره مین اران سه معنی دارد اول حجماتی که برای صید دم هکذا وحوش نصب کند چنانکه کوید شعر

سینک خجوف کیم بیکلادین وهمیدا لرانینک جرنلار قو تار و تیزایرکیم آلیدا اران کورکلیج دویم محوطه ایکرادر

خوابکاه دواب سازند سیم محال را کویند که هوای آن معتدل ومایل بکرمی باشد واین معنی مخصّص ازان باشد واران

نشد بلد در معنی بر دو اول محال قراباغ را کویند که مملکتی است معروف در آذربایجان چنانکه در سد سکندری کوید شعر

جو قیلادی اینی کونکلیدا ایدیجیم قراباغ ارانی ناتی قیلدی عزم ونیز کوید شعر که چو قیلدی قیشلاغ عزیمه شاه

قراباغ ارانی آرامکاه دویم اسم پیر طرس بن پهلوست که آذربایجان وارمن و فرغان برادران اویند و قراباغ اران

منسوب باوست اراول بروزن قراول جمعی را کویند که در وقت حرکت لشکر از عقب لشکر خصم در میانه میرفته باشند وآنرا

هراول نیز خوانند اداتجی بر نفر بکسر یای حطی وجیم ترکی رومی نام ستاره دو برادران بود که آنرا بعربی فرقدان کویند

ارباغ بروزن خلاق افسون را خوانند الشاهد علیه شعر زلفی سوچیا سید ابلها شلار نوائی نکته سین کیم جنون

کفار بیدور با خود بیلان ارباغ دیدمر وافسانه را نیز کویند چنانکه در محبوب القلوب کوید که نادانغه سوز عبالار ارباغ

آرباباغاجی بعربی عجا پاچورا کویند ونیز نام پادشاهی است از نسل چنکیز که بعد از سلطان ابوسعید بر تخت سلطنت

ایران نشست وآنرا آرپاخان نامند ارپاغانه کیاهی است بنوکرد و صحرا ها رسته مثل خوشه میبندد آرت بسکون راو

تای فوقیت عقبه وراه تنگ را کویند آرتوق وآرتوقی بمعنی زیاد وافزون بود چنانکه شاهد ثانی از سد سکندری کوید

شعر کیم اول ایاستان نباری چون باقشامین کوپ آرتوقی زبیل نکا ناقشامین ارتوقی لیغ زیادتی ونیز چنانکه در سد

سکندری در نعم کتاب کوید شعر جو حق دین ایدی کیلدی ایك وسلیغ قایو بیره کاکیم بولدی آرتوقی لیغ تقاح جیر لا

کویند که در قیمت و بقا وتمام و مقدار بر نوع خود مزیت داشته باشد آرتیش بسکون راو شین و کسر تای قرشت نام رود خانه

عظیم که فاصل است میان مملکت روس و بهرین تملاق آرد بروزن کارد بمعنی عقب باشد و بفارسی دنبه و بمعنی طرد او کابم رف

دویم بمعنی تقصیر و کوتاهی بود آردیجه یعنی از عقبش چنانکه کوید شعر نوایا ایرور اولدم خرکان برشده نوایلا حراینان

آندین بوکوردمه آرچه چیخ ارد وج نام درختی جبلی است که بفارسی مرس و بعربی عرعر کویند وآن نوعی است از سرو کوهیست

ارد واجی بفتح راو سکون زای معجمه سرودی است که در میان ترکان عراق معمول است چنانکه در میزان الاوزان کوید کر یا امراق

الجی ترکانه سیلسرودی شایع در مرکز آواز زوار عه دبرلار و آینینك بینی کوپراك هیج متمن الملدا بافلا نورد ارسلان بسکون را

وفتح سین مهمله شیر بود که آنرا بعربی اسد نامند ونیز نام برجی است از بروج فلکی واسلان تخفیف هم کفته می شود ارسوك

بسکون را وضم سین مهمله آلتی است نرچین که خبازان بدان خمیر از تنه ظرف خمیر کیر باشد ارغاج بسکون را وفتح غین معجمه

بود کارکاه نساجی را نامند و تارآنرا ارش نامند ارغاجی بسکون را وسیم وفتح غین معجمه وکسر جیم عجمی ریسمانیست که حمل

بار بر ستور بندد چنانکه در مناجات کوید که اکرچه پوش سین اولماسانك مدد اعمان وابشالك ارغاجی هی همان ارغدال بسکون را

وغین معجمه لفظیست مرکب از ارغ بمعنی هنر ودال بمعنی درخت که محل اخفا وکمین میباشد ومجاز شکستهای راه وکمینکاه را

کویند الشاهد علیه شعر زلفی بینك هرچو بیلیر نه دورین اهلیمه ارفدال ابجرا نادانمی اولمکان نکلنمکنش

ارغاق بسکون را وکسر غین معجمه اسب دونده پرزور بود چنانکه مثل است که تملاق آتغان تاریماس ارغاق منکان باریماس

ارغوشلی بسکون را وشین معجمه وضم غین وفتح تای قرشت یکنوع بازی است وآن بدین طریق باشد که یکی خم کشته دستها را بر روی

زانو میکذارد ودیکری آمده پا بر زمین زده از بالای او میجهد چنانکه کوید شعر خوش اولکر بمدا آی لار بسار دار ارغوشلی

شه آندا لمنوبر چالیب نولسه دیا توشوق ونیز نام یکنوع اصولیست در علم موسیقی چنانکه در میزان الاوزان در تصحیح لغت

توشوق کوید که بیه توشوقدر مکرر ارغوشلی اصولیدا شایعدر و بعضی اعداد ماولی اصولدکر بولور بتور و منوقمن آنکه

سهو انتم الفتح کرکتمانند ارغون نام یکی از اولاد قلیج ارسلان پادشاه روم است که نظام الدین ارغونشاه اشتهار دارد

ونیز نام پسر اباقاخان بن هولاکو خانست که سلطان احمد عم خود را کشته پادشاه شد و بفارسی به بمعنی آمده اول ارغونزاکم

وآن سازیست که موضوع افلاطونست دویم اسب تند وچالاك را نامند ارغیتش مفاصله غله را کویند ارغ بارق

بسکون را مخفف آریغ وآریق بمعنی مزبل الشاهد علیه شعر باده غم دفیغ ضین قیلود کیفیتین دیسانك بیلادیش آل ایلنکا

جامی ارضیانك کنایه دین اولوقتی آرما پشت بود که آنرا بعربی ظهر کویند ارقالوج بسکون را وجیم وفتح قاف وضم لام ترکی

رومی چیزیست که حمالان آنرا بر پشت و شانه بسته بار را بر بالای آن میکذارند ارک بروزن برك حصنی بود که در میان قلعه

سازند عموما چنانکه در حیرت الابرار در وصف قلعه هرات کوید شعر ارکی بیلك بارك تو قوز افلاکیك ایله کم کرد وکرة

خاکدین ونام قلعه ایست از قلاع سیستان خصوصا وبزبان اهل هند اسمیست از اسامی آفتاب ارکج بروزن سرکج بزیرساله

بز جشر و کله را کویند وآنرا از ترك روم کوسم نامند ارکن بروزن احسن ترکی رومی بمعنی بزن وفرزن بیشوهر باشد ارکنه توك

بسکون را وفتح کاف ونون اول وضم قاف موافق تواریخ ملعنت مغول معنی ارکنه شده معنی قون کرکوه باشد ومعنی ترکیبی آن

کمر کوه شد بود وآن نام کوهیست که بعد آزانکه ایلخان از تور بن فریدون شکست یافته مستاصل شد تیمان پسر ایلخان

انکوز پسر خال او بقلعه آنکوه کریخته در آنجا توطن کرد وقوم قیات ودرلکین در آنجا بهم رسیده فراوان شدند ارلات

اسم طایفه ایست از اتراک الشاهد علیه شعر ای نوائی مینی زار ایلادی بولوش کیم ارلات سنکا بولدی اونوت
هم بیلکوش ارمانه بروزن نوغان بمعنی حسرت و آرزو باشد چنانکه گوید شعر دیدیم او لبکالی لعل اینکان بیرلا نانی
ایمیش خضمات ارمانیدا اول خود لعل یکانی ایمیش و بفارسی نوعی از دارو باشد که بوی آن بسوی قرنفل ماند و بیخ دنجان
کند آرمانلیغ آرزومندی و حسرتناکی الشاهد علیه شعر ای نوائی سن خود ایتیب سین کیمه سین دیلبا تماسونک شاهی دین
حرمانلیغ و ناامیدین ارمانلیغ داغی ارندق زین پوش اسب بود که آن را بعربی غاشیه گویند ارناک بروزن ترانک
دارد اول النکشتر را گویند که بعربی عبارتها زبان باشد دویم نام کوهیست در ولایت خوارزم اوبچه طایفه قنات
در وقت نزول اردو کروه خود را بآن اسم آواز کرده پیدا نمایند و این نوع فریاد را اوران گویند اروسون بضم را و سین مهمله
بلغت مغولی پوست بود آروق بضم را بمعنی لاغر باشد الشاهد علیه شعر ضعفی کوبلوکدین نوائی نینک کم او
ناله بیش نی مناقی دور فضا بیلسا بولماغلیغ آروق و آریق بکسر را نیز مستعملست آروک بضم را و سکون کاف دو معنی دارد
اول مکث و درنگ دویم ... را گویند که در ... واقع شود دویم نام ... الو بود ارون بروزن ... بلغت مغولی
بمعنی خوب و خوش و پاکیزه باشد آری بکسر را دو معنی دارد اول زنبور را گویند چنانکه گوید شعر لب ... داغ ... نینک
جوجوک تیل بیرله کویا انکلاج ... شهد لیغ ... دویم بمعنی پاک و مصفا بود و از صیغ مشتقه نیز هست
چنانکه ... در ذیل مصدر ... مذکور شد و بفارسی بمعنی بله ... استعمال میشود آریش ... کارگاه نساجی کو
آریغ بکسر را بچهار معنی آمده اول بمعنی پاک و مصفا باشد چنانکه گوید شعر ای نوائی صبح ... ولدی شام ...
... شاید او ... جرم ... آریغ ... را گویند الشاهد علیه شعر غیر کودی باروراول اکت ...
تانی کوز بو ... آریغینک و هر دو معنی بطریق ایهام فرماید شعر بوزداهم ... کرتیراغ اون خط لاری ...
هر بیر کا ... آریغ سیم ... را نامند چنانکه در حیرة الابرار گوید شعر زر کرآ بیلمای ... آریغ
کوزلاری ... و باین معنی آروق بضم را هم مستعملست چنانکه در فوق مذکور شد چهارم نام ...
جنکیزت و آریق با قاف نیز باین معانی مستعملست آریغیزلیق ناپاکی آریغلیغ سه معنی دارد اول پاکی و طهارت دویم لاغری
سیم ... آریغلیغ ... چنانکه گوید شعر ... آریغلیغ سودین ...
آریق همان آریغ بود که بچهار معنی مذکور شد آریلمای ... و بالتخفیف ... را گویند چنانکه شاهد آن
در ذیل لغت آریغ نگارش یافت ... المشتقات آزماق دو معنی دارد اول راه کم کردن دویم بیخود شدن و با این معنی ابس
ازماق را هم گویند آزدی راه کم کرد و بیخود شد الشاهد علی الاول المعنی الثانی شعر بوزونک کوز کاج نوائی کونکلی
آندین ... دین بنداتش کیم او لمجنون ... آشفته حال اولمیش و له شعر نوائی آزدی یولدین چو کیمسی
جمیعه کوب ... طلب یولی نینک الان ... کونی موایرکین آزدوق راه کم کردیم و بیخود شدیم آزادور راه کم
میکند و بیخود میشود الشاهد علی الاول المعنی الثانی شعر کوزلاراو چادور مکر کم یاریم کیلا جدور ... ایرهم آزاد
مکر نکاریم کیلا جدور الشاهد علی الثانی بالمعنی الثانی شعر زخمیدین قان کوب قیا خود جنوندین ... کیم اول ...
گویند ... تیلبه کونکلوم آزه ... و مطالع هروی لفظ آزه را در این شعر نوشته که خبر از واحد غایب ماضی بمعنی
راه کم کرده است و شعر مزبور را شاهد آورده سهو کرده ... راه کم نکند و نکرده است و از خود بیرون رفته است

آزغان و آزاغان و آزادورغان راه کم کننده و کرده و بیخود شونده و بیخود شده و بمعنی مصدر نیز می آید چنانکه شاهد برای اول
بمعنی بیخود شدن در نسایم المحبه در ذکر قاضی حمید گوید که کوزی ... بیبی آزغان ... سماع نوکاندی ... و آزغیل
مفرد مخاطب امر آزیما و آزماغیل مفرد مخاطب ... آزینک و آزینکیز و آزینکلار جمع مخاطب ... امر آزمانک و آزمانکیز و
آزمانکلار جمع مخاطب ... آزمان و آزماس بین راه کم میکنم و بیخود میشوم آزامین و آزادورمین و آزارام
راه کم میکنم و بیخود میشوم آزابیم و آزماغیم راه کم کردم و بیخود شدم آزماغوم راه کم نخواهم کرد و بیخود نخواهم شد آزیب ... زنان
آزمیش راه کم کرده و بیخود شده الشاهد علی الاول بالمعنی الثانی شعر تاملدین افشانه جه عم تاپیغ آزیب قرهاد و ش ...
تانک آشوب بجد دشت اوفرار ... بمجنون مثال دیتوهم خرو شیرین کوید شعر ... آبخد شودروشین ... کمینه ...
آزیب سیلاد ... آزمیشان راه کم کرده و بیخود شده آزماس راه کم نمیکند و بیخود نمیشود و بمعنی اصل مصدر منفی هم می آید آزماغ
راه کم کردن و نکردن و بیخود شدن و نشدن آزمادین راه کم کردن و نکرده آزیب ... و آزیبا ... و آزمانیق ...
راه کم نمیتواند کرد و بیخود نمیتواند شد آزا آلماس راه کم نمیتواند کرد و بیخود نمیتواند شد آن آزمراه کم کنان و بیخود شده ...
بمعنی اول کوید شعر ای نوائی شکر کیم یول تاپتی ... کیم ... آزماغن آن ... و بدون تکرار هم مستعمل
آزای و آزاین راه کم کنم و کند و کنی و بیخود شوم و شود و شوی آزساق و آزغاییه و آزغای بیز و آزلی ... آزالیلک راه کم کنیم و بیخود شویم
آزغالی برای راه کم کردن و نا کرده و برای بیخود شدن و نا شده آزغاج چون راه کم کرد و کند و بمحض کردن و چون بیخود شد و شود
بمحض شدن آزغوجی راه کم کننده و بیخود شونده آزغوچه و آزغونچه و آزغانچه تا راه کم کردن و تا بیخود شدن و ... آزغوم
راه کم خواهم کرد و بیخود خواهم شد آزغونک راه کم کند و بیخود شود آزغوسی راه کم خواهد کرد و بیخود خواهد شد آزغولوق راه کم کردنی
و بیخود شدنی آزغای ... آزسا و آزسون و آزدیلک راه کم کند و بیخود شود آزغو ... آزاردیلک راه کم کردن و همچنانکه کنند
شدنی و همچنانکه شود آزغاشماق بسکون زا و شین و فتح غین معجمه و آزیقماق بکسر زا و سکون قاف ... کم کر ...
الشاهد ... شعر ... آزیقمان ... آزغاش ...
و آزیقتی راه کم کرد آزغاشوق و آزیقتوق ... آزغاشادور و آزیقادور ...
و آزیقور بمعنی فاعل و مصدر هم می آید آزغاشماید و آزیقماید ... آزغاشقان و آزغاشو ...
و آزیقغان و آزیقورغان و آزیقادورغان ... الشاهد علی الرابع بالمعنی الثانی من نسخه سیاره
اور کوداب یولدین آتی چیقغان ایمیش ... آزیقغان ایمیش و مطالع هروی آزیقغان ...
و مولف رومی آزیقغان با تای قرشت خوانده و نصیری هم متابعت کرده شعر مذکور را شاهد آورده ... سهو کرده ...
... شعر زلفیدا ... آزیقغان کاردانیم ...
نیز می آیند آزغاش و آزغاشقیل و آزیق و آزیقغیل مفرد مخاطب امر آزغاشماغیل و آزیقماغیل ...
... آزغاشینک و آزغاشینکیز و آزیقینک و آزیقینکیز و آزغاشینکلار ... جمع مخاطب ... آزغاشمانک
و آزغاشمانکیز و آزغاشمانکلار و آزیقمانک و آزیقمانکیز و آزیقمانکلار جمع مخاطب ... آزغاشمان و آزغاشماس بین و آزیقمان و
آزیقماس بین ... آزغاشامین و آزغاشورمین و آزغاشادورمین و آزغاشورام و آزیقامین و آزیقورمین و آزیقا
دورمین و آزیقورام ... آزغاشورام و آزغاشیم و آزیقورم و آزیقیم ... آزغاشماغوم آزیقماغوم

ازراه بدر خواهم رفت آزغاشیب‌ها آزغاشیبان‌ها آنغاشیمش و آزیغیجا آنیغیبان‌ها آزیغیمش از راه بدر رفته الشاهد علی
الاول شعر قویماسون بکچ بو لغه زنهار آزغاشیب هرگز قدم اهل هوشی کیم یو دیشاق قولیدین چیقیب الشاهد علی
الرابع شعر کوچیبسیم یو قیدین آی ایردیشیب لیکن هوش و کونکلوم یوق اوچی تهر نفس آندین آزیغیشتو نیز بحیرت
لا برله کویدیشنس آه دلبر کون آزیقیب کیچان بولدی چرا وجامای سیفه بیهمان آزغاشیمشانک‌ها آزیغیشانک از راه
رفته آزغاشماس و آزیغماس از راه بدر نرود و بمعنی فاعل و مصدر نفی هم می آید آزغاشماسی و آزیغماسی از راه بدر نرفتن و نرفتنش
آزغاشادین‌ها آزیغادین از راه بدر رفتن و از راه بدر رفته آزغاشیب بولماس و آزغاشا بولماس و آزغاشماق اولماس و آزغیب
بولماس‌ها آزیغا بولماس و آزیغماق اولماس از راه بدر نتوان رفت آزغاشا آلماس و آزیغا آلماس از راه بدر نتواند رفت آزغاشا
آنغاشلو آزیغا آزیغلا کم کنان و بدون تکرار هم مستعملست آزغاشای و آزغاشایین و آزیغای و آزیغایین از راه بدر روم
و بعضو بروی آزغاشاق و آنغاشغلیز و آزغاشغای بیز و آزغاشالی و آزغاشالیلی و آزیغاق و آزیغای بیز آزیغا
و آنیغالیلی از راه بدر رویم آزغاشغالی و آزیغغالی از راه بدر رفتن و تا بدر رفته آزغاشغاج و آزیغغاج چون از راه
بدر رفت و بمعنی رفتن آزغاشغوچی و آزیغغوچی از راه بدر رونده و آزغاشغوچه و آزغاشغونجه و آزغاشغای بیز و آزیغغوچه و آزیغغو
و آزیغغونجه از راه بدر رفتن و مقابل آن آزغاشغوم و آزیغغوم از راه بدر خواهم رفت آزغاشغونک و آزیغغونک از راه بدر خواهی
رفت آزغاشغوسی و آزیغغوسی از راه بدر خواهد رفت آزغاشغولوق و آزیغغولوق از راه بدر رفتنی آزغاشغای آزغاشا
و آزغاشلو آزغاشون و آزغاشدیک و آزیغای آزیغا و آزیغای و آزیغسون و آزیغدیک از راه بدر رود آزغاشغودیک
آزغاشودیک و آزیغودیک از راه بدر رفتنی چنانکه بدر رود آزغورماق بسکون زا و ضم غین معجمه متعدی
متعدیست بمعنی از راه بدر بردن و اضلال کردن آزغوردی از راه بدر برد آزغوردوق از راه بدر بردیم آزغوروروا آزغورا
از راه بدر بیبرد الشاهد الاول شعر زاهدا آهسکین نوائی هرنچه کیم سازلیلار پیر نوا برله مغنی‌لار بولدین آزغورید
و آزغورمق بمعنی فاعل و مصدر هم می آید آزغوردماید از راه بدر برد و نبرد و است آزغورغان و آزغورورغان و آن
غورادورغان از راه بدر برنده و بدر برد و بمعنی مصدر هم می آید آزغوروا آزغوریل مفرد مخاطب از فعل امر آزغورما و آزغور
ماغیل مفرد مخاطب از فعل نهی آزغورونک و آزغورونکیز و آزغورونکلار جمع مخاطب از فعل امر آزغورمانک و آزغورمانکیز و آزغورمانکلار
جمع مخاطب از فعل نهی آزغورسام از راه بدر برم آزغورامین و آزغورورمین و آزغوراین و میین و آزغوروی المی
بدر میبرم آزغورعدیم و آزغورماغیم از راه بدر بردیم آزغورماغوم از راه بدر نخواهم برد آزغورسانک و آزغورغایس و آزغورغای
از راه بدر ببری الشاهد علی الاول شعر کسنه کوسیکا یوز قویدیم بویولدین ماینا غوم ای نوائی هرنچه کیم یولدین آز
غورسانک یعنی آزغوروب و آزغورویان و آزغورمیش از راه بدر برده چنانکه در خسرو شیرین در تدبیر دفع فرهاد گوید الشاهد
علی الاول شعر بهر غیاثی آنینک دیلبا بلا میش صیید که دیوانیکای کیشینی آزغوروب قیلد سیاق شعر چنین است که دیو
نیشنی آزغوروب قیلد انیکای یعنی دیو تحفل از راه بدر برد و قید کند آزغورمیشانک از راه بدر برده آزغورماس از راه بدر برد
و بمعنی فاعل و مصدر منفی هم می آید آزغورماسی از راه بدر بردنش و نبردنش آزغورمادین از راه بدر بردن و از راه بدر نبرده
آزغوروب بولماس و آزغورا بولماس و آزغورماق اولماس از راه بدر نتوان برد آزغورا آلماس از راه بدر نتواند برد آزغورا آزغور
اضلال کنان و بدون تکرار هم مستعملست آزغورای و آزغوراین از راه بدر برم و بری آزغورماق و آزغورغای بیز و آزغور

و آزغورلی و آزغورالینک از راه بدر برویم آزغورغالی برای از راه بدر بردن و تا بردن آزغورغاج چون از راه بدر برد و بمعنی برد
بعض بردن آزغورغوچی از راه بدر برنده آزغورغوچه و آزغورغونجه و آزغورغانجه تا از راه بردن و مقابل آن آزغورغوم از راه
بدر خواهم برد آزغورغونک از راه بدر خواهی برد آزغورغوسی از راه بدر خواهد برد آزغورغولوق از راه بدر بردنی آزغورغای
آزغورا و آزغورسا و آزغورسون و آزغوردیک از راه بدر برد آزغوردیک و آزغورودیک از راه بدر بردنی چنانکه
ج آزالماق کم شدن و صیغ آن مولوش شواول اشتقاق می‌یابد من المحاسد آز بمعنی اندک باشد و نیز امر است از کمراه شدن اند
خوص چنانکه در ذیل اشتقاق گذشت و نیز هیچ واصل را گویند آز آزغینه یعنی کم کمک و اندک اندک الشاهد
علیه شعرای نوائی بهم آز آزغینه می‌مدرسه ذا دیر اداکیر که ابجاد شیخ تولا شاب تولا آزاغلاق بضم زا و سکون غین معجمه
اندک باشد چنانکه در تاریخ بابری مذکور است که چاپیون قوییدوق آزاغلاق هر ایرچاپیلدی آزاق نام شهریست اند
شمالی آزبوی بسکون زا و ضم یای تحتانی کشنیز باشد که آنرا بعربی جلجلان خوانند آزغون یعنی گمراه و آشفته چنانکه گوید
وصل کونیدین نوائی کونکلی ازیکی یو قی قیوه کوبر دولت هر کز اول اهل عشقینینک آزغونی دیک آزغونلوغ گمراهی و آشفتگی
آزلیغ بمعنی کمی و ضم بحا الشاهد علیه شعر چون تعضا لسیر بیمارکاهی از لیغ دیکله محض امواج لیغ دیم المحا الحوله ایل
سیاق شعر چنین است که ایل کاهی آزلیغ دین هولر مکله ایلا ما الد بحض امواج لیغ دود یعنی خلق از کمی کام هوار کله کردن بعض
ناهموار چیت آز و بر وفق ما زود ندان بیش بود که آنرا بعربی ناب گویند آندوا جوز خلوا صبر باشد و آن عصاره نباتیست که بر کرشه
برک کلم و بسیار ضخیم بود و آنرا انولع است آزرغ بضم زا و سکون غین معجمه و آزوق مع الالفاف بمعنی توشه و خوراکست الشاهد علی
الثانی شعرای نوائی کیم فناد شتیکاو تین مارجادین کیم بابا فلیغ آنداوک توشه سین لیغلدور آزوق و طالع هروی این
حاصل معنی آزناق تصور کرده و بمعنی کراه نوشته و ضیری هم متابعت کرده سهو کرده اند و آزوغ مع الغین بفارسی بعضی
پراستن باشد یعنی برید زیا خمای زیادتی از درخت مع البیت من المشتقات آسماق او بختن چنانکه در لیلی مجنون در کسی
پدر مجنون گوید شعر آسماق دین آبینک تارزلی قوشما ی قون کون اوتی اوچکالی با د و شما ی و منولف روی آسماق را همه این
سهوا آسمان خوانده و معنی نوشته آسمتی آوبخت آستوق آوبختم آسنار و آسنا دو دو می آویزد و اسله بمعنی فاعل و مصدر هم می آید
آسماید و دیمی آویزد و نیا و بختیه است آسغان و آسنار غان و آسنادرغان آویزنده و آوبخته الشاهد علی الاول المتوالثانی
شعر منعف دین کلبید اتو یماق ایتاسام ایلا میرد عنکبوت رشته آسغان بولسا هر یولا ید و بمعنی مصدر نیز می آید آس امر
امر است از آوبختن الشاهد علی الثانی شعر دیر اد ابدیت لیغ جو نامه سی ای منجه بونیوما آسقیل سو ماغلاجب آنی زیاد ایله
و آس سه معنی جامد نیز و لرد چنانکه در جوهر مناهده مذکور شود آسما و آسماغیل مفرد مخاطب از فعل نهی آسینک و آسینکیز و آسینکلار
جمع مخاطب از فعل امر آسمانک و آسمانکیز و آسمانکلار جمع مخاطب از فعل نهی آسامین و آسارمین می آویزم آسامین و آسارمین آسامان
و آسادام می آویزم آسادیم و آسماغیم آوبختم آسماغوم نخواهم آوبخت آسیب و آسیبان و آسمیش آوبخته چنانکه شاهد اول
در فهنبی گوید شعر جوسین چیکیبا تا افنیم تر اندسین تاج و زیب الا که دعوی ایله سوز آسیبی بیا منتهی ضیغ مدها از کلام
قصاید سبعه معلقه مشهورات آسمیشانک آوبخته چنانکه گوید شعر بو نیونکا مشکین اسیاکین لوکم طوبا دا آسمیشانک
تا بیدا حاصیم سیلکاسین کیم بو نیوما تا قیتنیک کنند آسماس نه آویزد و بمعنی فاعل و مصدر منفی هم می آید آسماسی نه آویختنش و نیاویختنش
آسمادین از آوبختن و نیاویخته آسیب بولماس و آسا بولماس و آسماق اولماس نمیتوان آوبخت آسا آلماس نمیتواند آوبخت آسا آسا

39v..

آویخته کان آویخته کان آسای و آسایین بیاویزم و بیاویزد و بیاویزی آساق و آسغانز و آسغای نزد و آسالی و
آسالینک بیاویزیم آسغلی برای آویختن و تا آویخته آسغلج چون آویخت و بیاویزد آسغوجی آویزنده آسغوسی و آسغوبیه و
آسغانجه تا آویختن و بمعنی آویختن آسغوم خواهم آویخت آسغونک خواهی آویخت آسغوسی خواهد آویخت آسغولوق آویختنی
آسمای و آسنا و آسسا و آسسون و آسدیک بیاویزد آسغودیک و آساردیک آویختنی و همچنانکه بیاویزد آسیلماق بکسر
الثین مع اللام مصدر انفعال است یعنی آویخته شدن و بترکی رومی مجاز بمعنی مصلوب شدن باشد آسیلغان آویخته شده
و آویخته شده چنانکه بمعنی اول گوید شعر اول الف دهر کیم عیان دهر هر طرفدین غم پیچ : مندی هجران دین آسیلغان سنگیو
پرچم سیله و بمعنی مصدر نیز می آید آسیلماسی آویخته شدنش و آویخته نشدنش و مصلوب شدنش و مصلوب نشدنش چنانکه
بغدادی بمعنی اثبات گوید شعر دل که سرزنیلی لولین زلف پریشان ایلیش نوله جرمی کم آسیلماسنه فرمان ایلیش
آسیلغوسی آویخته خواهد شد چنانکه در سد سکندری در قیمر کیمیر گوید شعر برادکیم طلع شهنه سی فیلغوسی
آیننک برله بوغزی دین آسیلغوسی و باقی صیغ بر همین سیاق موافق شق اول اشتقاق می باید آستورماق بکون سین و رای
مهمله و ضم تا مصدر متعدی یعنی آویزاندن و صیغ آن بدستور شق اول اشتقاق می باید آسراماق نگهداشتن الشاهد علیه شعر
فاش قیلمالیم اسرارچون کیم اسرای آلماس بیلن ایکنزه : امرکا لایدرین اسراماق یاری تمنا قیلما ایکنزه و طالع هر و هجر الف نوشته
سهو کرده اسرادی نگهداشت اسرادینک نگهداشتی چنانکه گوید شعر اسرادینک کوییدوکا لاعشاق مضطر کونکلینی
باغبان دیک کیم لوتون قیلغای صنوبر کونکلینی اسرادوق نگهداشتیم اسرار و اسرایدور نگاه میدارد الشاهد علی الاول گر
انجم آغزینه اکر تابع دور آغزینک نی عجب حرمت اسرارینی اوچون کیم اول اولوغدور بو کچیک و نیز اسرار بمعنی فاعل و مصدر می آید
چنانکه در صفت سیاره در طستان مشاق واقلیم نعیم بمعنی فاعل گوید شعر تخت اسرار کیشی بی یار ایلاجه : نقد المغنیه کوب
بنثار ایلاجه و در گرفتاری فرهاد در خسرو شیرین بمعنی مصدر فرماید شعر حصار ایکی اندا محکم جرخ تانتده : قیلب اسراه
اوچون حرم اهلینی بند : و بمعنی بنات نیز استعمال میشود چنانکه در ذیل جوامد گوهر خواهد شد اسراهایدور نگاه میدارد
نداشته است اسراغان و اسرغان و اسرایدورغان نگهدارنده و نگهداشته الشاهد علی الاول المعنی الثانی من جنسی شعر
بولماغیم سهوا تانک ایرماس کیم بو تانکلا خلق ارا : فاش بولدی اسراغان سرهانیم امرکا نوغ و بمعنی مصدر نیز می آید اسراهاسز
مفرد مخاطب نفی امر الشاهد علی الاول شعر دیبری برله می ایچسانک نوانی اسراحم بولسانغم ایریق اوتوغدین کرعه
لا افتلن الشاهد علی الثانی شعر اولمانی نینک کلش حسین خزان دین اسراغیل یارب : گل و شمشادین آسیبه زمان دین اسراغیل یا
آسراها و اسراغیل مفرد مخاطب نفی امر آسرانک و آسرانکیز و آسرانکلار جمع مخاطب نفی امر الشاهد علی الاول شعر خط و لعلی
قاشیدا آسراناک ادبی کیملانک ای خضر و مسیحا کستاخ : اسرامانک و اسرانیانکیز و اسرامانکلار جمع مخاطب نفی امر اسرامان و اسرا
نگاه میدارم اسرامیز و اسرامیمیز و اسرایدورمیز و اسرارام نگاه میدارم اسرایم و اسراغیم نگاه داشتم اسراغوم نگاه خواهم
داشت اسرابجا اسرایان و اسرامیش نگاه داشته اسراییشانک نگاه داشته اسرانماس نگاه میدارد و بمعنی فاعل و مصدر نیز هم
می آید اسراهایی نگاه داشتنی و نگاه نداشتنش اسرامادین از نگاهداشتن و نگاه نداشته اسراب بولماس و اسراها بولماس و
اسراماق اولماس نگاه نمی توان داشت اسرای المآس نگاه نمیتواند داشت اسراهو و اسرای اسرای ضبط کنان الشاهد علی ال…
شعر کونکلدا سر عشقینک آسرای سبرای اولدوم ای ساقی قدح بیر کیم خراباتا هلیغه نان بولسا فاش اولسون و بلا کوتاکیم

40r.

اسرای و اسراین نگاه نظر دم و نگاه طرب و نگاه داشته الشاهد علی الثانی المعنی الاول شعر نوایی فه عیدینک هجرانیدا پرتوق
یادکاراقنوم نیزاییک تا اسام الف دیک آنجانیم آمراآسراییش اسرهاق و اسرقاین و اسرقای نزد و اسرلیغ اسرالینک نگاه دیکم
الشاهد علی الرابع شعر جان و کونکول نیچه دیدی سرلیی اوزنی کیلکاج اول : و یانا قوینغا ایشونلار کونکلاج آنی ایچره آرا
اسرغالی برای نگهداشتن و تا نگاهداشته اسرقاج چون نگهداشت و نگاه داشته اسرغوچی نگاه طرزها الشاهد علیه شعر
آلما آنا نکنه هنتا لی دو غولکیم کوزنا میش بیز دیک : خاحول توقوزا تالیت بوتوزنا اسرغوجا یه اسرغوجم و اسرغوسی و اسرغو
تا نگهداشتن و بعده نگهداشتن اسرغوم نگاه خواهم داشت اسرغونک نگاه خواهی داشت اسرغوسی نگاه خواهد داشت
اسرغولوق نگهداشتنی چنانکه در تنبیهات محبوب القلوب گوید کمسل دین اسرغولوق در … اوین و توقوافدین اسرغولوق
دور کوزلاوین اسراغای و اسرها او اسرها اسراهون و اسرادیک نگاه میدارد الشاهد علی الاول شعر یادیوق طالع کیم پرلیهریک
آسراغای پرچم بزری در دورکیم ایا بکاکه … الشاهد علی الرابع شعر کیم کرکونکلین ایستاما شرع کین … اسرادیک
کیم تیلی تیغدان کیشی نینک کونکلیدا آزار ایماس : ولله شعرای نوانی تیلاکان زهد و صلاح : کوزنی و کونکلینی هم اسرادیک
اسراغودیک و اسرایدیک نگاه داشته و همچنانکه نگاه میدارد الشاهد علی الثانی المعنی الاول علی طریق الایهام شعر
آینیم باشیمنی … اکینکا جیک ای شهسوار : دیدی باش اسرایدیک ایرماس تیزلیک دین مرکیم : اسرایماق بکون سین و لام و فتح
مصدر متعدی یعنی نگهداری فرمودن اسرانیل اسرانماز نگهداری فرمودن چنانکه در دیباچه خسرو شیرین گوید شعر
الادغه آشکارا و نهانی کوز ایچرا اشات دیک اسرانیل آدی آسرانای و اسرانابین نگهداری فرمایم و فرمایید و فرمائی الشاهد علی
الاول المعنی الاول شعر کونکلو منا خالینک تجلیکا یدم بو قیلیچ کوزا و سیدا آنی مردم لادایجینداآسرانای و …
اسرانای براه این شعر بمعنی پنهان کردن ضمیمه در ثبت نمیده و باقی صیغ بر همین سیاق به دستور شق اول تا حرف اشتقاق می باید
اسرلماق مع اللام مصدر انفعال است یعنی نگهداشته شدن اسرالور نگهداشته می شود چنانکه در کیتی ختنین منطق
گوید شعر دم تو تولغاندین اولادا ایدیک تیلیبین اولکابی : سوز ناسون دیبیکیم سین جیر کیم نفس لادا اسرالغه بمعنی فاعل
نیز مستعملست و باقی صیغ بدستور حرف لام اشتقاق می باید اسنلماق بفتح سین و لام و سکون نون و اسنلشماق مع الثین
اتراک روم عبارت از داویختن بود من … اس … اول نام ولایتیست شمالی چنانکه در سد سکندری درو…
جهانگیری اسکندر گوید شعر چو مانم بولو جانب آس و روس : بولوب بوزلا ذی و جهد ینت … بتیم تا قم … گویند و آن
جانوریست معروف که از پوستش پوستین نازک دوزنکش سفید و سر دم آن سیاه باشد در خسرو شیرین شعر جهان شوخی در وی
قلیفیل احوالش که کمیش تون سیله کوندین کیش آنی سیم تبرکی روی جانوریست که آزار ابو ناسد چهارم امرا سد آویختن
چنانکه در ذیل مصدر آسماق گذشت و بفارسی نیز چهار معنی دارد اول سنگی باشد مدور که بدان غله آرد کنند دوم غله آرد
کویند سیم شتری بود که موی یا ذنب ریخته باشد چهارم نام قریه ایست از قرای فارس و بعربی هم پنج معنی آمده اول نام مرد
باشد دوم بقیه عسل را نامند که در شان انگبین مانده باشد سیم بقیه خاکستریست که در جایی مانده باشد چهارم ثلثها
عمارت را خوانند و بزبان هندی بمعنی امید است اول امید را گویند دوم کمان تیر اندازی باشد آسابقور بفتح سین و سکون نای
و رای قرشت و ضم قاف گوسفندی بود که آزاد در ستبخته باشد من سکندری فی ذم الاسرار شعر پرآو الیغه خوان جو
کیلتورگلین کیشی پرولی لون قو یله لو تور کلبین : پیالی آسابقوردین بولسا یالیغی داشت … بولوبطعن اولتا توان آست بوتفته…

عبارت از وداع کردن بود و اتراک توران خوشلاشمق گویند اسما قویماق
اویخته گذاشتن و باصطلاح اتراک روم

تخت منتخفق بود چنانکه کوید شعر تلمغ عاشقلیغ یوکیدین جم بولورغه یوق خلاص کورکه نی نوع اولدی خم حوّالدی
عشق آستیدا ثالف آستیداغی یا مُثین آستیغ وآستیق زیری که زنان در پشت آویزند آستین بسکون تین و نون و تکسر
تای قرشت دو معنی آرد اول بمعنی زیرین باشد که آن را عربی تحتانی کویند الشاهد علیه شعر نقطه خالینک سیدینی
لبینک آستیدا دور قطعه چولستین بولور هر برادا کیم یا نیلسا الب دویم حرکات کمر را خوانند و آن را آسر هم نامند و
آستین لباس معروفست که آن را عربی کم کویند آسر بکسر سین و سکون رای قرشت بروزن ظاهر حرکات کمره را کویند و آن را آستین
هم نامند آسرینك بود که کنج معرب آنست چنانکه در لسان الطیر آمده شعر پر ططنه ایدی مبهوت و دنك صبح طوام
آنینك غذاسی بردی بناك ترك اهلی دیك نمودلری آنینك جهد اندا لیك اسراری آنینك رومیه هم آنك را اسرار کویند
ونیز بمعنی نگاهبان چنانکه در ذیل اسراماق کذشت و جمع سر بمعنی راز بود اسرامیشی ضبط و نکهداری اسرکیش
بکسر میم و کاف عجمی و سکون راوشین قرشت بترکی مردی بمعنی حم و مرحمت آمده اسرو بروزن ابرو بمعنی بیناز باشد الشاهد
علیه شعر فرامتینك ایجرا ایشیم اضطراب بحر ابرو ترحم ایله کم خالیم خراب بحر ابرو ولی نوانی نوانی نج کورمه لغزنی
کیم اولیر جهوری حصر ابرو فانات اسلان بسکون سین شیر بمعنی اسد باشد و آن را ارسلان نیز نامند چنانکه کذشت
اسلانلیغ معنی لغوی آن شیریت واسدیت بود لیکن بمعنی دلیری و شجاعت استعمال شود چنانکه در مهیفه سیاره کوید
شعر دردایله جو ملقاج اسلانلیغ موش اولوب من ولعا یدیم جانلیغ آسمه بسکون سین و فتح میم آویزه را کویند و
ازالت روم دوجت تاکه ر نامند آسن بروزن رسن بمعنی صحیح وسالم و بکر الفیز مستعملست آسیغ بکسر سین و سکون
غین معجمه دو معنی دارد اول بمعنی نفع و فایده باشد چنانکه کوید شعر یار بی فای نی آسیغ اونکالا دی تیری چین جان
قاجان پرکای سبع الفاظی ایل یغیر تیری چین و آن را رومیه بتخفیف آسی کویند دویم بمعنی آویخته است آسیغلیغ بدو معنی آمده
اول بمعنی سودمند و با منفعت دویم آویخته را کویند الشاهد علیه شعر هر یان تیغ سالور کونکلوم آسیغلیغ دور انکا
بیل مقتل اهلیغه کیم کور دیع لادر فیلیغ ونیز صاحب علم کودن فرهاد کوید شعر ظلم آچما فمقالا اش تمای کیم الحق
اولعدی دهر کرامی ایمه پر لیع سیم اوزره یاز غیلیغ تا پلمین دیو بوبینیدا آسیغلیغ مع الثین من المثقات آشماغ
بسکون سین از حد کذشتن و تجاوز کردن باشد بترکی رومی بمعنی جستن نر وحوش و طیور بر ماده و جفت شدن آنها آشماد
می شود آشتی تجاوز کردیا الشاهد علیه شعر ظلم دین نا العزتا نلب یوق آشور ناوی ظلم ظلمی چو بز کا حد دین آشتی
آشتوق تجاوز کردیم آشار و آشادور تجاوز میکند و آشار دو معنی بکار دارد اول یعنی میخورد دویم بمعنی ماخوذ از
آشاماق است چنانکه مذکور شود تیم کله شترکه میکنید چنانکه در ذیل جوامد کفته خواهد شد و بمعنی فاعل و مصدر
نیز می آید آشمایه بمعنی تجاوز میکند نکرده است آشغان و آشار غان آشادور عام تجاوز کننده و تجاوز کرده و بمعنی مصدر نیز می آید
آنو آشغیل امراست از تجاوز کردن چنانکه در نوبه کری فرهاد در جیع فات خطاب باشلی چشم کوید الشاهد فی الحکایا
شعر نیاجی قتلیم ا سیمین آشغیل ایی یاشن و یوز مکا هر نی سیرین کیل اشا باش و طالع هروی آشغیل را لفظ والحد نیز
کرده نوشته که بمعنی ابهروا شو و نیز بهر را شاهد آورده و بعض ناس لفظ آشیلما را مصدر برای آن اختراع کرده و تو
که آشغیلما بمعنی از برداشتن و تیشه هم مناسبت کرده لفظ و معنی هر دو اختراعیست و آش دو معنی دارد اول
مقام را کویند بمعنی ترکی روی طعام است از پخته شدن طبور و وحوش آشماو آشماغیل مفرد مخاطبه از فعل ماضی آشیناك و

آشیتکو وآشینکلار جمع مخاطب از فعل امر آشمانك وآشمانکیز وآشمانکلار جمع مخاطب از فعل نهی آشماس و آشماس بین تجاوز منیکنم آشابور
وآشارمین وآشاد میمین وآشارام تجاوز میکنم وآشادمین وآشارلم بمعنی بیاشام نیز می آید و در معنی با مصدر اشاماق اشتراك دارد
آشادیم وآشماغیم تجاوز کرده ام وآشاد بمعنی آشامیده هم باشد آشماغوم تجاوز نخواهم کرد آشیب وآشیبان وآشیمش تجاوز کرده
الشاهد علی الاول شعر آشوروب حد دین نوانی هم نیاز و عجز بی یار ینك استغنا و ناز بی هر نچه حد دین آشیب آشمیشانك
تجاوز کرده آشماس تجاوز نمیکند آشماسی تجاوز کردنش و نکردنش آشمادین از تجاوز کردن و تجاوز نکرده آشیب بولماس و آشنا
و آشماق او لماس تجاوز نمیتوانکرد آشا آلماس تجاوز نمیتواند کرد آشا آشا تجاوز کنان و بدو نکرار هم مستعملست چنانکه صنایع
مذکورست که کاهی ایکی کون آشاکا هی ایج کون آشا ایستوراییم صبر آشا امراستان آشامیدن چنانکه در ذیل آشماق مذکور
خواهد شد آشای و آشایین تجاوز کنم و کنند و کهی بیاشام و بیاشامد و بیاشامی آشاق و آشغای بیز و آشغای بیز و آشالی
آشالینك تجاوز کنیم و آشالعاشلینك بمعنی بیاشامیم هم باشد آشغالی برای تجاوز کردن و تا تجاوز کرده آشغاج چون تجاوز کرد
و کند آشغوجی تجاوز کننده آشغوجی و آشغونجی و آشغانیچه تا تجاوز کردن و بعد تجاوز کردن آشغوم تجاوز نخواهم کرد آشغونك
تجاوز نخواهی کرد آشغوسی تجاوز خواهد کرد آشغولوق تجاوز کردنی آشغای و آشون و آشدیك تجاوز کند آشغودیك و آشادر
تجاوز کردن و همچنانکه تجاوز کند و اشاردیك بمعنی آشامیده و همچنانکه آشامیده شود هم آمده آشورماغ بفتح شین
و سکون را مصدر متعدیت یعنی کذرانیدن و تجاوز ساختن و صیغ آن بدستور شق اول با رای قرشت اشتقاق می یابد
آشاماغ بفتح شین خوردن و آشامیدن آشادی آشامید آشادو فاشامید نیم آشار و آشاید و رمی آشامد و آشار بکذرا معنی
دیکر باشد که در ذیل مضارع اشماق مذکور شد و بمعنی فاعل و مصدر نیز می آید آشا نماید و رمی آشامد و بیاشامیده است
آشاغان و آشارغان و آشاید و رغان آشامنده و آشامیده و بمعنی مصدر نیز می آیند آشا و آشاغیل مفرد مخاطب امر از فعل
و آشا بمعنی تجاوز کنان هم می آید چنانکه در ذیل اشماق کذشت آشا و آشانا مفرد مخاطب از فعل نهی آشانك و آشانکیز
آشانکلار جمع مخاطب از فعل امر آشامانك و آشامانکیز و آشامانکلار جمع مخاطب از فعل نهی آشامان و آشامارمین نمی آشامم
و آشادمین و آشایدورمین و آشارلم نمی آشامم و آشارمین و آشارام بمعنی میکذرم هم می آید چنانکه کذشت آشادیم و آشاغیم
آشامیدم و آشادیم بمعنی تجاوز کردم هم می آید آشاغوم نخواهم آشامید آشاب و آشامان و آشامیش آشامیده آشاماس نمی آشامد
و بمعنی فاعل و مصدر منفی نیز می آید آشاماسی از آشامیدن و نیاشامیدن آشامادین از آشامیدن و نیاشامیده آشاب
بولماس و آشامانا بولماس و آشاماق او لماس نمیتوان آشامید آشای آلماس نمیتواند آشامید آشا بو و آشالی آشای اکل و شرب کنان و بدون
نکرار هم مستعملت آشای و آشایین بیاشام و بیاشامد و بیاشامی و تجاوز کنم و کنند و کنی آشاساق و آشاغا بیز و آشاغای
و آشالی و آشالینك بیاشامیم و آشلی و آشالینك بمعنی تجاوز هم باشد آشاغالی برای آشامیدن و تا آشامیده
آشاغاج چون آشامید و بیاشامد آشاغوجی آشامنده آشاغوجی و آشاغونجی و آشاغانیچه تا آشامیدن و بعد آشامیدن
آشاغوم خواهم آشامید آشاغونك خواهی آشامید آشاغوسی خواهد آشامید آشاغولوق آشامیدنی آشاغای و آشاسا و آشا
و آشادیك بیاشامد آشاغودیك و آشاردیك آشامیدنی و همچنانکه بیاشامد و آشاردیك بمعنی تجاوز کردنی و همچنانکه
تجاوز کند هم می آید آشاتماق با تای قرشت مصدر متعدیت یعنی آشامانیدن و صیغ آن بدستور شق اول با تای قرشت اشتقاق
می یابد آشوقماق بضم شین و سکون قاف تعجیل کردن و طالع هروی آشوقماق بضم الف با بمعنی نوشته و نصیری هم نوشته کرده

سهو کرده اند آشوغمی تعجیل کرد آشوغوق تعجیل کردیم آشوقور و آشوقادور تعجیل میکند و آشوغور بمعنی فاعل و مصدر نیز می آید
آشوقمایدور تعجیل نمیکند و نکرده است آشوغمان و آشوقوغان و آشوقادورغان تعجیل کننده و تعجیل کرده چنانکه شاهد
اوله بمعنی اول در قسم سیم از محبوب القلوب در تنبیهات گوید که صبر ایله کوپ ایغلیغ ایش آچیلور ایشدا آشوغمان کونکلی سلوق
و بمعنی مصدر نیز می آید آشوق و آشوقیل مفرد مخاطب از فعل امر و آشوقغور ایشان را نیز گویند چنانکه در ذیل جوامد مذکور خواهد
شد آشوقما و آشوقمانغیل مفرد مخاطب فعل نهی الشاهد علی الثانی شعر حلولم ایچره ذوقی فراقیدا ای رقیب آشوقماغیل که
کرالک کیشی آشیغه آشوغونک و آشوغونکیز و آشوغونکلار جمع مخاطب از فعل امر آشوقمانک و آشوقمانکیز و آشوقمانکلار جمع مخاطب
الشاهد علی الاول شعر کیلسا آبنیر دا آشوقمالکیم فتح دین و لمایش نکته دان لیغ بیرله اول حضرتی ناشید اونکا ربنک
آشوغمان و آشوقمایمین تعجیل نمیکنم آشوقامین و آشوغورمین و آشوقادورمین و آشوقورام تعجیل میکنم آشوغوردم و آشوقماغیم
تعجیل کردم آشوقمادیم تعجیل نخواهم کرد آشوقوب و آشوقوبان و آشوقیش تعجیل کرده الشاهد علی الاول شعر آشوقوب بر لاب
علاجیمغه تیشیقنک ای مسیح نی عجب کرشوب لعلینک کلاهی انیز ایروه آشوقیشانک تعجیل کرده آشوقماس تعجیل نمیکند
فاعل و مصدر منفی نیز می آید آشوقماسی تعجیل کردنش و نکردنش آشوقمادین از تعجیل کردن و تعجیل نکرده آشوقوب بولماس آشوقا
و آشوقمای و آشوغماس تعجیل نتواند کرد آشوقا المالمار تعجیل نمیتواند کرد آشوقا آشوقا تعجیل کنان و بدون تکرار هم مستعملست آشوقا
و آشوقمایین تعجیل کنم و کند و کنی آشوقساق و آشوقغای بیز و آشوقمالیق آشوقالینک تعجیل کنیم آشوقماغلی برای تعجیل کردن
کرده آشوقماج چون تعجیل کرد و کند آشوقوچی تعجیل کننده آشوقوچی و آشوقوبجه و آشوقغانجه تا تعجیل کردن و تعجیل
آشیقغوم تعجیل خواهم کرد آشوقغونک تعجیل خواهی کرد آشوقوسی تعجیل خواهد کرد آشوقولوق تعجیل کردنی آشوقغای آشو
آشوقسا و آشوقسون و آشوقدیات تعجیل کند آشوقودیک و آشوقوردیک تعجیل کردن و همچنانکه تعجیل کند آشوقتورماق
بضم شین و نای قرشت و سکون قاف در اصل مصدر متعدیست یعنی تعجیل فرمودن و صیغ آن بر همین سیاق است بقیاس آشوقماق با
تمام اشتقاق می یابد آشلاماق بر کسر سین بمعنی پیوند کردن درخت باشد آشلاتماق بسکون شین و نون بمعنی پیوند کردن
آشیماق بکسر شین و سکون نون بر کسر دویم بمعنی سائیده شدن و فرسوده شدن آشیندی سوده و فرسوده شد
در تاج التواریخ آل عثمان در وصف مسجد ایا صوفیه با ملا در رومیه گوید که رخام و مرمرهاش مرمر جزین سیندین کیلکان
طاشیندی و ینه فرهاد تیشه سنکتراشلر تیشه لری شیندی آشیند در ماق مصدر متعدیست یعنی سائیده کردن
و فرسوده ساختن من الجوامد آش طعام را گویند و نیز اشاره است از تمام کردن چنانکه در ذیل مصدر آشماق گذشت آشار
کلمه شرط خوانند یعنی بمعنی تمام میکند و می آشامد چنانکه در ذیل آشماق و آشاماق نگارش یافت آشام بضم دال
دو معنی دارد اول بمعنی رتبه و طبقه بود چنانکه در وصف کوشک غنی هرات در دیباچه و قضانامه گوید که طرح لیکی
آشام ایوی نوبتی اشامی تیره لیک دین فراق شایش میوه داری آشامی بونوغولوقدین فراق اهلی کونکلی امدین نشان
دویم اکل و شرب بود چنانکه بمعنی شراب گوید شعر لعلی شوقین باشورور مین نان بوتوباتاغ مین آسراری الماک
اوزنی کلکون باده آشام الاکلاج و در اینمعنی با طعام مشترکت و بغیر سبب معنی دارد قلقتولات بقلم خلج دویم
نام ولایتیست ما بین شرق و شمال بنگاله که در ان ولایت عود خوب میشود سیم آب برنج پخته آشامه بفتح میم بغاذ
بمعنی طبقه و رتبه بود چنانکه گوید شعر کونکول خرابه سیدا اشالدی عاج مرتبه عشق که اول جهو البنا ید

بولدی چون دو آشامه اشکل بسکون شین و کاف ثانی و فتح کاف اول بر روی کشتی را خوانند لا ادری شعر بحر اشک ایچرا کی
کوز بولدی لعل زورق مثال ایکی صف کیرپیکلاری اشکل لار بولوبتور هر طرف اشلاو بسکون شین و واو طرفی بزرگیست کرا رشید
و چوب تراشیده در کنار چاهها گذاشته حیوانات را در میان آن آب دهند آشلیغ بکسر لام غله را گویند چنانکه در مجالس
النفایس در ذکر سید جعفر نوربخش گوید که پادشاه اعزاز و اکرام قلیغان دین سونکرا اسلیدا پیش ینک آلتون نارطاق
و ایکی یورح وار آشلیغ وجه معاش ایچون مقرر قیلدی آشلیغ ذخیره چی آشوغ و آشوق غوز آن باد که آنرا بعربی کعب گویند
چنانکه در تاریخ الانبیا در ذکر حضرت موسی علیه السلام و قارون گوید که موسی علیه السلام یرکا ایتی یا ارض خذیه
بر قارون نی آشوغیغه چه امریکا یا زنی آشوقولوسلیکلی استخوان سرزانو را گویند آشی بکسر شین چوبزن کاشتی ترکی روی شاخچه
نازک بود که بر بیخ درخت پیوند کنند مع الضاد اصلاهن با ملا در رومیه شیر بمعنی اسید بود و بلغت جغتای با بین توشته
می شود مع الغین المعجمة من المشتقات آغماق بالا رض و عروج کردن آغدی بالا رفت چنانکه ناصر گوید شعر اتی عاین کوتارد
کوک اوزرا آغدی مسیح امتی بینک تا نوسیدین بر ده فالغای مصطفی لاادری شعر طور موسی چیقتیم سازایلاهی کوککا
آغدی پرواز ایلادی آغدوق بالا رفتیم آغاردو آغادور بالا میرود و آغار بمعنی فاعل و مصدر هم می آید آغماید بالا
نرفته است آغمان و آغار غان و آغادورغان بالا رونده و بالا رفته و بمعنی مصدر نیز می آیند آغ و آغغیل مفرد مخاطب
از فعل امر و آغ بمعنی دام و برات سفید باشد چنانکه در ذیل جوامد تحریر یابد آغما و آغماغیل مفرد مخاطب فعل نهی آغینک
آغینکیز و آغینکلار جمع مخاطب فعل امر آغمانک و آغمانکیز و آغمانکلار جمع مخاطب فعل نهی آغمان و آغماس مین بالا نمیروم آغامین
و آغارمین و آغادورمین و آغارام بالا میروم آغادیم و آغماغیم بالا رفتیم آغاموم بالا نخواهم رفت آغسانک و آغیب
و آغیبان و آغیش بالا رفته آغیشانک بالا رفته آغماس بالا نمیرود و بمعنی فاعل و مصدر منفی هم می آید آغماسی بالا رفتنش
آغمادین از بالا رفتن و بالا رفته آغیب بولماس و آغماق و لماس بالا رفت آغا المالمار بالا نمیتواند رفت آغا آغا
عروج کنان و عروج کنان و بدون تکرار هم مستعملست آغای و آغایین بالا بروم و برود و بروی و همچنین آغساق و آغغای بیز و آغغلیه
و آغالی و آغالینک بالا برویم و آغسانک بمعنی تنک هم نباشد آغماغلی برای بالا رفتن و تا بالا رفته آغماج چون بالا رفت
و برود و بعضی رفتن آغوچی بالا رونده آغغوم بالا خواهم رفت آغغونک بالا خواهی رفت آغغوسی بالا خواهد رفت آغغولوق و
بالا رفتنی آغغای و آغسا و آغسون و آغدیات بالا رود آغودیک و آغاردیک بالا رفتنی و همچنانکه بالا رود آغدورماق
مصدر متعدیست یعنی عروج فرمودن و بالا فرستادن و صیغ آن بدستور با لفظ دور اشتقاق می یابد آغارماق بفتح غین و سکون
رای قرشت سفید شدن و با قاف نیز مستعملست آغاردی سفید شد آغاردوق سفید شدیم آغارور و آغارادور سفید میشود
الشاهد علی الثانی شعر غم شامی ایمانم صبح کرکو لعل شمعین ایچکان اشکیم سوبی بدر او لکه بر اقین آغارادور و آغارماید
ناصل و مصدر نیز می آید آغارماید و سفید نمیشود و نشده است آغارغان و آغارورغان و آغارادورغان سفید شونده و سفید
شده الشاهد علی الاول با المعنی الثانی شعر مخفی غمینک بازار دا بیغیلغان تیک جهان دود تینک نهان توتاردین آغارغان
سونکا کلادیم و بمعنی مصدر نیز می آیند آغار بسکون را و آغارو بضم را و آغارغیل مفرد مخاطب از فعل امر آغارماو آغارماغیل
مفرد مخاطب فعل نهی آغارمان و آغارماس مین سفید نمیشوم آغارامین و آغارادورمین و آغارادورمین و آغارورم سفید
میشوم آغاروروم و آغارماغیم سفید شدم آغارماغوم سفید نخواهم شد آغارمبه آغارماسان و آغارمین سفید شده

آغارمیشانك سفید شده آغارماس سفید نمیشود و بمعنی فاعل و مصدر منفی هم می آید آغارماسی سفید شدن و شدنش آغارماس
از سفید شدن و سفید نشده آغاریب بولماس و آغارسا بولماس و آغارماق اولماس سفید نمیتوانست آغارا آلماس سفید
نمیتواند شد آغارا آغارا سفید شونده سفید شونده و بدون تکرار هم مستعملست آغارای و آغاراین سفید شوم و شود و شوی
آغارماقه و آغارغاینر و آغارغای نیز و آغارالی و آغارالینك سفید شویم آغارغالی برای سفید شدن و تا سفید شده آغارغاچ
چون سفید شد و شود آغارغوچی سفید شونده آغارغوچه و آغارغونچه و آغارغانچه تا سفید شدن و مقدار سفید شدن آغارغوم
سفید خواهم شد آغارغونك سفید خواهی شد آغارغوسی سفید خواهد شد آغارغولوق سفید شدنی آغارغای و آغارلو آغا
و آغارغودك و آغارغودیك سفید شود آغارغودیك و آغارغودیك سفید شدنی و همچنانکه سفید شود الشاهد علی الاول
بالمعنی الاول شعر ایریاس اشکیم سیله کوزینك تیرازغان ... بیر موی بیر آغارغوم ... الیاس جان ... آغارماق
بسکون را و نای قرشت مصدر متعدیست یعنی سفید کردن و صیغ آن بدستور شق اول الحروف الاشتقاق می آید آغرماق
بسکون غین و کسر رای قرشت دو معنی دارد اول بدرد آمدن دوم رنجیدن آغریدی بدرد آمد و رنجید آغریدیلار بدرد آمدند
و رنجیدیم آغریر و آغرید و بدرد می آید و میرنجد الشاهد علی الاول المعنی الاول شعر خالی ... نوای کونکلی
اغیرابله کیم آغریغای ... قرا داغ ... توشوب وشاهد بر ثانی ... المحبه در ذکر ... الزمان کیبی
کوید که اول ... چون ... پادشاه ایشیکی ... آغریدی و آغریر بمعنی فاعل و مصدر نیز می آید
چنانکه بمعنی مصدری کوید شعر ... آغریر دین ایرماس ... آیرونو شا
جان دین ... آغریماید بدرد نمی آید و نمی رنجد آغریغان و آغریرغان و آغریدیرغان بدرد آینده و رنجنده و بدرد آمده و رنجیده
و بمعنی مصدر نیز می آیند آغری و آغرغیل مفرد مخاطب فعل امر آغریما و آغریماغیل مفرد مخاطب فعل نهی آغرینك و آغرینکز
آغرینکلار جمع مخاطب فعل امر آغریمانك و آغریمانکز و آغریمانکلار جمع مخاطب فعل نهی آغرایلی ... آغریالی جمع متکلم
اغریمان و آغریماس من بدرد نمی آیم و نمی رنجم آغریمین و آغریرمین و آغریدورمین و آغریرام بدرد آیم و میرنجم آغریم و آغریغام
بدرد آمدم و رنجیدم آغریغوم بدرد خواهم آمد و خواهم رنجید آغریب و آغریبان و آغریش بدرد آمده و رنجیده الشاهد
علی الاول المعنی الاول شعر ... کوپ ... ظلم ... آغریب ...
و درد ... آغریماس ... یوق ...
آغریماس بدرد نمی آید و نمی رنجد و بمعنی فاعل و مصدر منفی نیز می آید آغریماسی بدرد نیامدنش و رنجیدنش
آغریماغان بدرد نیامدن و نرنجیدن و نرنجیده آغریب بولماس و آغریسا بولماس و آغریماق اولماس بدرد نمیتوان
و نمیتوان رنجید آغری آلماس بدرد نمیتوان آمد و نمیتوان رنجید آغری آغری بدرد کنان و رنجان رنجان و بدون تکرار هم مستعملست
آغرای و آغرین بدرد آیم و آیند و ... آغریناق و آغریغای نیز و آغریلی و آغریلینك بدرد آییم و رنجیم
آغریغالی برای بدرد آمدن و تا بدرد آمده و رنجیدن و تا رنجیده آغریغاچ چون بدرد آید و آمد و چون رنجید و رنجد آغریغوچی
بدرد آینده و رنجنده آغریغوچه و آغریغونچه و آغریغانچه تا بدرد آمدن و مقدار بدرد آمدن و تا رنجیدن و مقدار رنجیدن
آغریغوم بدرد خواهم آمد و خواهم رنجید آغریغونك بدرد خواهی آمد و خواهی رنجید آغریغوسی بدرد خواهد آمد و خواهد رنجید
آغریغولوق بدرد آمدنی و رنجیدنی آغریغای و آغریغا و آغریسون و آغریدیك بدرد آید و رنجد الشاهد علی الاول

بالمعنی الاول شعر بابانان ... بلغای آغریغای ... کیم کوینادا باغیرم کاله ... عزاله ... یمتی
آغریغودیك و آغریغودیك بدرد آمدنی و همچنانکه بدرد آید و رنجیدنی و همچنانکه رنجد الشاهد علی الاول شعر
خسته کونکلوم ... پرلوسا ... ایرسا باغری آغریغودیك بالبارورش آغرتماق مع التاء مصدر
متعدیست یعنی بدرد آوردن و رنجانیدن و صیغ آن بدستور شق اول الحروف الاشتقاق می آید آغیرلاماق بکسر غین
و سکون رای قرشت سنکین داشتن و بالمجاز بمعنی تعظیم کردن استعمال می شود آغیرلادی تعظیم کرد آغیرلادو و تعظیم کردم
آغیرلامادینك تعظیم نکردی چنانکه فضولی کوید با ملاء روحیه شعر ... ساکن کو ... اوله ... سیکا ... پیر
ایچیم سوبله آغیرلامادینك ... آغیرلار و آغیرلایدور تعظیم میکند و اغیرلار بمعنی فاعل و مصدر نیز می آید آغیرلامیدور
تعظیم نمیکند و نکرده است آغیرلاغان و آغیرلایدورغان تعظیم کننده و تعظیم کرده و بمعنی مصدر نیز می آیند آغیرلا
و آغیرلاغیل مفرد مخاطب فعل امر آغیرلاما و آغیرلاماغیل مفرد مخاطب فعل نهی آغیرلانك و آغیرلانکز و آغیرلانکلار جمع مخاطب
فعل امر آغیرلامانك و آغیرلامانکز و آغیرلامانکلار جمع مخاطب فعل نهی آغیرلامان و آغیرلاماس من تعظیم نمیکنم آغیرلای
و آغیرلارمین و آغیرلایدورمین و آغیرلارام تعظیم میکنم آغیرلادیم و آغیرلامادیم تعظیم کردم آغیرلاغوم تعظیم خواهم کرد
آغیرلاب و آغیرلابان و آغیرلامیش تعظیم کرده آغیرلامیشانك تعظیم کرده آغیرلاماس تعظیم نمیکند و بمعنی فاعل و مصدر منفی هم
می آید آغیرلاماسی تعظیم کردنش و نکردنش آغیرلامادین تعظیم کردن و تعظیم نکرده آغیرلاب بولماس و آغیرلاسا بولماس و
اغیرلاماق اولماس تعظیم نمیتوان کرد آغیرلای آلماس تعظیم نمیتواند کرد آغیرلای آغیرلای تعظیم کنان و بدون تکرار هم
مستعملست آغیرلای و آغیرلاین تعظیم کنم و کند و کنی الشاهد علی الاول المعنی الاول شعر ... آغیرلای
ایت ... شکیم ... مردم اوق باغیردین ... یعنی نفس من ... نمی آید معنی
دیکر اینست که از ... ... نمی آید چکونه تعظیم کنم سکان ... از برای خواستن ... می باشد
آغیرلاشاق و آغیرلاغاینر و آغیرلاغای نیز آغیرلالی و آغیرلالینك تعظیم کنیم آغیرلاغالی برای تعظیم کردن و تا تعظیم کرده
آغیرلاغاچ چون تعظیم کرد و کند آغیرلاغوچی تعظیم کننده آغیرلاغوچه و آغیرلاغونچه و آغیرلاغانچه تا تعظیم کردن و تعظیم
کردن آغیرلاغوم تعظیم خواهم کرد آغیرلاغونك تعظیم خواهی کرد آغیرلاغوسی تعظیم خواهد کرد آغیرلاغولوق تعظیم کردنی
آغیرلای و آغیرلاسا و آغیرلاسون و آغیرلادیك تعظیم کند آغیرلاغودیك و آغیرلاغودیك تعظیم کردنی و همچنانکه تعظیم کند
آغیرلاتماق مع التاء مصدر متعدیست یعنی تعظیم فرمودن و صیغ آن بدستور با تای قرشت اشتقاق می یابد آغناماق بسکون
غین و فتح نون بر خاك غلطیدن که آن را اسب بی ... کویند آغنادی غلطید آغنادوق غلطیدیم آغنار و آغنایدور
می غلطد و آغنار بمعنی فاعل و مصدر هم می آید آغناماید و نمیغلطد و نغلطیده است آغناغان و آغنایدورغان
غلطنده و غلطیده و بمعنی مصدر هم می آیند آغنا و آغناغیل مفرد مخاطب فعل امر آغناما و آغناماغیل مفرد مخاطب فعل
آغنانك و آغنانکز و آغنانکلار جمع مخاطب فعل امر آغنامانك و آغنامانکز و آغنامانکلار جمع مخاطب فعل نهی
آغنامان و آغناماس من نمیغلطم آغنای من و آغنارمین و آغنایدورمین و آغنارام میغلطم آغنادیم و آغناغام غلطیدم
آغناغوم خواهم غلطید آغناب و آغنابان و آغنامیش غلطیده الشاهد علی الاول شعر لاله کون ... اول ...
... مینکر ... لاله زار ... آغنابتور ... الشاهد علی الثالث شعر ... پلاس ... اولای

43v.

کوزدن قرا الیلامیش بو قساقش جیران‌نی مثل‌ها بچه الآغنا میش آغنامیشالمق غلطیدن آغنامان بمعنی غلطکد ومعنی
فاعل ومصدر بمعنی هم آید آغنا ماق غلطیدن وغلطیدن غلطاندن از غلطیدن وتغلطید آغناب بولماق
وآغنالبولمار و آغناتا قاولمار بمعنی توان غلطید آغنای آلمان نمی‌توانند غلطید آغنایو و آغنای آغنای غلطان غلطان
وبدون تکرار هم مستعمل آغنای و آغناین بغلطم وغلطید وبغلطی آغناساق و آغنا غایز و آغنا غایز و آغنایلی
وآغنالند بغلطیم آغنا غالی برای غلطیدن وتا غلطیدن آغنا فاج چو تغلطید وبغلطد آغنا غوچی غلطنده آغنا
و آغنا غونجه و آغنا غانجه تا غلطیدن وبعد غلطیدن آغنا غوم خواهم غلطید آغنا غونک خواهی غلطید آغنا غو
خواهد غلطید آغنا غولو غلطیدنی آغنا غای و آغنا سا و آغنا سون و آغنا دیک بغلطد آغنا غودیک ها آغنار دیک
غلطیدنی وهمچنانکه بغلطد آغنا تماق مع الثنا مصدر مفاعله است با یکدیگر بر خاک غلطیدن وصیغ آن بتلخ
باشد اشتقاق مجا آغنا تماق مع التا مصدر متعدیست یعنی بر خاک غلطانیدن که از عربی تمریغ گویند وصیغ آن باتا
قرشت اشتقاق می‌یابد آغو تماق بضم ضین بمعنی مسموم شدن آغوتماق مع النون با زهر مغشوش کردن آغیللاماق بکسر ضین وسکون
لام اول ونون وفتح لام ثانی ناله کردن تا اهرا گویند چنانکه مثل است که آی آغیلاغونسا آیدلا یا غار کون ولا اولا
کوندا یا غار چون در اشتقاق آن منفعتی نبود بذکر مصدر اکتفا شد من الجوامد آغ سه معنی دارد اول آنچه موشا کرا گویند
چنانکه شاعر [illegible] وصف دنیا گفته با ملاحظه الرقیبه شعر عاقل ایسنگ دیرمه کونکل اغنه زاغ صفت دوشمانک
دوم بمعنی سفید بود وبا معنا تا قافیه مستعملست سیم ارابستن زعروج کردن وبالا رفتن چنانکه در بالا نوشته شد آغا برادر
بزرگتر را مانند آقاچه زنان کنیز منزبه را گویند چنانکه بیکم وخانم زنان محترمه را مانند آغاج دلکن بفتح دال ولام و
کاف وسکون نون وآغاج قاقن بفتح قاف وسکون نون بترکی رومی پرنده‌ایست سبز رنگ که بمنقار درخت را سوراخ کند و
بعربی قراع ونقار الخشب وبفارسی دارکوب سنبه گویند ومعنی گفته اند که نام مار در آن دارکوب باشد وبعربی صرد
مانند آغاج قاونی بضم واو وکسر نون بترکی رومی بادرنجبویه که آنرا بفارسی ترنج خوانند آغالیغ برادری چنانکه میر
مجنون گوید شعر سارا ایتی آغالیغ وسنیکل لیک کویا بیادی سینکلی دین بهل لیک آغ اوری بسکون رای قرشت
ضم کاف عجمی سراپرده را گویند وآن عبارتست از سراپرده که بطریق آلاچوق از چوب بنا زند آغ اوی آلاچوق را خوانند
وآن عبارتست از خانه مشبک که از چوب بنا زند الشاهد علیه شعر تاجول آغ اوید اولسا تاکر اهل عشق ایله
بلبل وهدهد ضیر بولغای قصر وله شعر نا سای دمرد بغلاسه دین آغ اوی جان کلتو ایمرا که کونکلونده
تار بقسا آندا کیر کلی ماه خرکاهیم آغ بابا بترکی رومی نام گوگرد باشد آغ بارزکان باصطلاح اتراک توران عبارتست از کار
از زیرک حیله وتلبیس باشد آلغ بابا سایغ زن پیر را گویند آغ یوغا و آغیوغا زن سفید از جنس کاو وکاومیش گویند و
نام یکی نوسیان بزرک سلاطین جنگیزیانست آغ بی بکسر بای ابجد پادشاه اروس را مانند آغچه درم ودینار چنانکه
منسوب در ظرفیات گوید با ملاحظه الرومیه شعر ظلم ایله آغچه ار آلو ظالم ایلرانعام خلقه منت ایله بلمز آنی کیم ایشدوکی
ظلمه کور [illegible] آغیل بروزن تارجل یعنی [illegible] اغزوق بضم الحال واثقال بود آغزیغ
بکسر بای قرشت بمعنی دم صبح ومعنی بخش هم باشد آغرق مخفف آغزیغ بود ونزل است از توجع وبدرد آمدن دمعا
شنفه دیکرم طرح چنانکه در ذیل معنی آغریاق گذشت آغرقیه غده ناک آغرین بسکون ضین ونون وکسر رای

44r.

قرشت بمعنی آهسته آمد ملتم از آنکه در رفتار باشد یا گفتار وکردار چنانکه گویند آغرین بور و یعنی آهسته برو و آغرین اور
یعنی آهسته بزن آغنز بسکون ضین وزای هوز دهن باشد وآنرا آغیز بکسر ضین هم گویند آغزی آچوق بترکی رومی نوعی از
عطرات وآن دائما بسته دهان کشاده وسخت بتراش نخودی که آنرا بعربی ناغره وبفارسی کبابه دهن کشاده گویند
آغسیرق بسکون ضین وقاف وکسر سین مهمله ورای قرشت یعنی عطسه آغ سونکاک بکوفع بازیست که در میان اتراک معروفست
وآن بر این نهج است که اطفال در شب مهتاب استخوانی را بعد پرانیده هر یک که آنرا پیدا کردند بطفلی سوار شده تا
که معهود اطفال است می برند چنانکه در محبوب القلوب در وصف پادشاه عادل گوید کم آیدین کیچه لار اتراک ضعفا
ایشی ایرغوشتک والطفال [illegible] شیلغ سونکاک آغلیغ بمعنی سفیدی بود واتراک روم بالهام سفید ابل گویند که از نان
بررو مانند آغوق بر وزن آهوز همزه مانند الشاهد علیه شعر شربت لعلینک قویوب نوش ایلابان حیوان سوی
بولغای آندا آق کیم قویوب حیوان سوین ایچکای آغوز بضم واو وسکون زای هوز شیر غلیظی است که سه چهار روز بعد
زائیدن دوشیده شود وآنرا بفارسی فله وفرشه وبعربی لبا مانند آغولوق زهرناک آغیر بکسر ضین وسکون رای قرشت
بمعنی سنگین وثقیل باشد الشاهد علیه شعر با غیر جوانلیغ ین ضعف اولدی غالب خسته جانیمنه آغیرا یردی عذا
عودا یری رحمت نا توانیمنه آغیر باقوجی یعنی گران فروش الشاهد علیه [illegible] شعر یا ناز خلاع غیر قلب
اشتغال آغیر باقوجی [illegible] آغیرشاق بسکون را وقاف وفتح شین قرشت بترکی رومی چوب مدوریست که در میان
دوک می باشد که رشته را بعد از تابیدن با آنجای پیچند وآنرا بعربی فلکة المغزل گویند ونیز تخته مدور را گویند که
بر سر ستون خیمه نصب کرده سر ستون را از خیمه بگذرانند واستخوان سر زانو وآنچه مثل آن باشد آغیرلامیشی اعزاز وتعظیم
آغیز بکسر ضین وسکون زای هوز دهن را گویند ومولف موید الفضلا که بنای تالیف کتاب خود بر تصحیح لغات عرب و
فرس وترک گذاشته آغیز را [illegible] السنه وافواه با زای معجمه مذکور است از رای مهمل با رای مهمله ذکر کرده در حرف الالف
مع الرا نوشته آغیز دیروق بکسر دال ابجد ورای قرشت وسکون قاف دهنه اسب بود که آنرا سولوق نیز خوانند وبعربی
حکمه وشکیمه گویند آغیز یاری بترکی رومی لعاب دهن باشد که آنرا بعربی ریق مانند آغیل بروزن عاقل دو معنی دارد
اول هاله ماه بود دوم محوطه ایست که برای خوابیدن گوسفندان سازند ودر این معنی با فارسی مشترکست آغیتول بکسر ضین
وسکون میم ولام وضم تای قرشت یعنی سفید مانند مع الفا افسم بسکون فا ومیم وفتح سین مهمله بمعنی ساعت معظم [illegible] اف
چنانکه در باب هفتم از محبوب القلوب در بیان ذکر گوید رباعی میخانه دجمی که ایرورا ده پرست ظاهر مین ایچکان
دین اولور کرم بهست منیک دین پر اهلس بوئی صفتمیحین اچکان آنی افسم اولسا تانک بوق سوست افندی
بفتح اول وثانی بمعنی زبان خداوند را گویند واتراک روم بمعنی خداوند وصاحب استعمال نمایند وعلما ودانشمند از امام [illegible]
مع القاف من المشتقات آقماق بسکون قاف وآقیلماق بکسر قاف وسکون لام روان شدن با آقیز و آقیلدی روان شد اق
آقار و آقاد و آقیلو و آقیلادی روان می‌شود چنانکه شاهد بر اول گوید شعر آقار قدحغه تا ما ریکا [illegible]
خمار اهلیغه نیماس [illegible] آقار تا ماری و آقار وآقیلور بمعنی فاعل ومصدر هم می آید شعر اول آی فراقیدا اشکیم
آقار رغه شام وسحر طلوع زهره [illegible] مشتری بر دوام اغیث وله شعر قیلدم کلار کوز رغه اکوزکان آنکلار [illegible] سیلین کیم
آقار رغه کیلکان اول بول لار سیله هر بهاری نا ندوپو دطالع هروی لفظ آقار رغه را از آقارماق بمعنی سفید [illegible]

نوشته که یعنی بغیدی مهیدن وشعر اخیر را شاهد آورده وبضعی هم متابعت کرده اشتباه کرده‌اند زیرا که مراد ناظم اگر بغیکی
می بوجا آقار ور غنایت ذکر کند وآقار ماسی آقاق بمعنی روان شدن باشد ودر مشتقات مصدر آقارلماق فصل الراء بیاید
فصل ثانی مع ما لسفید شدن وبغیدی مهیدن دراین شعر آقانه معنی نکند وآقار دو معنی جامد نیز دارد که در ذیل
جوامد مذکور خواهد شد آقماید ور وآقیلماید ور روان نمیشود وشده است آقمان وآقارغان وآقادورغان وآقیلغان
وآقیلورغان وآقیلادورغان روان شونده ورروان شده الشاهد علی الاول بالمعنی الثانی شعر دیماکو یوم دین ایل کمتوز
که بندایتمیش چین کلیخ اولوسی یوزدا لعلینک نوشی بن آقمان شکر لبلار و بمعنی مصدر نیز می آید چنانکه گوید
الشاهد علی الاول شعر حجری تیغدا کور کلیج غلوسین آقیزدیغان سیل الفنا دیک قویاشینک منزلی بولغاندا حوت
آق وآقماغ وآقیلماغ وآقیلغیل مفرد مخاطب از فصل الراء آقما وآقماغیل وآقیلما وآقیلماغیل مفرد مخاطب از فصل نهی آقینک وآقینکز
آقینکلار وآقمانک وآقمانکز وآقیلمانکلار جمع مخاطب از فصل الراء آقمانک وآقمانکز وآقمانکلار وآقیلمانک وآقیلمانکز و
آقیلمانکلار جمع مخاطب از فصل نهی آقمان وآقیلمان وآقماسمین وآقیلماسمین روان نمیشوم آقامین وآقادورمین و
آقارام وآقیلامین وآقیلورمین وآقیلادورمین وآقیلورام روان میشوم آقادیم وآقیلادیم وآقماغیم وآقیلماغیم روان شدم
آقماغیم وآقیلماغیم روان نخواهم شد آقیب وآقیبان وآقمیش وآقیلیب وآقیلیبان وآقیلمیش روان شده آقمیشانک وآقیلمیشانک
روان شده آقماس وآقیلماس روان نمیشود وبمعنی فاعل ومصدر منفی هم می آید آقماسی وآقیلماسی روان نشدن وروان نشدن
آقادیم وآقیلادین از روان شدن وروان شده آقیب بولماس وآقسا بولماس وآقماق بولماس وآقیلیب بولماس و
آقیلسا بولماس وآقیلماق بولماس روان نمیتواند شد آقا الماس وآقیلا الماس روان نمیتواند شد آقا وآقیلا روان روان
وبدون تکرار هم مستعملست آقای وآقامین روان شوم وشوی آقسام وآقسانگیز وآقسای وآقسابیز وآقالیک وآقیلالیک
وآقیلغاییز وآقیلغای وآقیلالی وآقیلالیک روان شویم آقغایلر وآقیلغایلر براو روان شدن وتا روان شده آقغاج
آقیلغاج چون روان شد وشود آقغوچی وآقیلغوچی روان شونده آقغوچه وآقغونچه وآقغانچه وآقیلغوچه وآقیلغونچه
وآقیلغانچه تا روان شدن وبعد ... روان شدن الشاهد علی الاول بالمعنی الاول شعر تانک ایمان جسیم آقیزغونچه
کوزوم کرتوکی اشک ... عجب برتنا ... آقغونچه ... الشاهد علی الثانی شعر بعزوم ناری کوزونک کوبا ...
کوزبود ... اولمهر ... آقغونچه ... آقیلغولوق وآقیلغولوق روان شدنی آقغای وآقا وآقسا
وآقتون وآقدیلک وآقیلغای وآقیلای وآقیلسا وآقیلسون وآقیلدیک روان شود الشاهد علی الثالث شعر
غم خدا ... آسیندا ... ترکانه ایاغ تور اینی بیله تا سالو قوز آقسا اوتوز چون در این خوانین مقولیست که در مجلس
شراب اگر یحیک نه پیاله واگر بیر دسی پیاله ... مینوشیده‌اند جناب نولیدی از لفظ توقوز واوتوز اینمعنی اراده نموده
اند آقغودیک وآقاردیک وآقیلغودیک وآقیلوردیک روان شدنی وهمچنانکه روان شود آقزماق وآقتورماق بکوی
تاف ... متعدیست یعنی روان کردن آقیزدی وآقتوردی روان کرد چنانکه شاهد بر اول ...
مصدر آقماق چه بیان آقمان نوشته شد آقیزدینک وآقتوردونک روان کردی چنانکه در صفت ستاره از زبان ...
درجمن نکشدن ... خطاب با آسمان کوید الشاهد علی الثانی شعر سین زا چون مهر یوقا یدی موجود مهر
فی البلاد ... اشکیم انجم مثل ... آقتوردونک دولتیم مهر یوقا ... آقیزدو وآقتوردو

آقتوردو روان میکند چنانکه در لیلی مجنون در صفت بهار کوید الشاهد علی الاول شعر دال ولاله ... صفحه بو
کیم شبنم برلا ... آقیزور وآقتورور بمعنی فاعل ومصدر هم می آید آقیزماید ور وآقتورماید ور روان نمیکند ...
آقیزغان وآقیزورغان وآقیزادورغان وآقتورغان وآقتورورغان وآقتورادورغان روان کننده وروان کرده وبمعنی مصدر
نیز می آید آقیزغیل وآقتور وآقتورغیل مفرد مخاطب از فصل الراء الشاهد علی الثانی شعر آقیزغیل ادم سیلاب ...
که جهان ... کونکول ... آقیزما وآقیزماغیل وآقتورما وآقتورماغیل مفرد مخاطب از فصل نهی
آقیزینک وآقیزینکز وآقیزینکلار وآقتورونک وآقتورونکز وآقتورونکلار جمع مخاطب از فصل الراء آقیزمانک
وآقیزمانکلار وآقتورمانک وآقتورمانکز وآقتورمانکلار جمع مخاطب از فصل نهی آقیزمان وآقیزماسمین وآقتورمان وآقتورماسمین
روان نمیکنم آقیزامین وآقیزادورمین وآقیزورمین وآقتورامین وآقتوروبمین وآقتورورمین وآقتورادورمین
وآقتورورام روان میکنم آقیزدیم وآقتوردیم وآقیزماغیم وآقتورماغیم روان کردم آقیزماغیم وآقتورماغیم روان نخواهم
کرد آقیزیب وآقیزیبان وآقیزمیش وآقتوروب وآقتوروبان وآقتورمیش روان کرده آقیزمیشانک وآقتورمیشانک روان کرده آقیزماس
وآقتورماس روان نمیکند وبمعنی فاعل ومصدر منفی هم می آید آقیزماسی وآقتورماسی روان کردن ... آقیزمادین وآقتورمادین
از روان کردن وروان نکرده آقیزیب بولماس وآقیزسا بولماس وآقیزماق بولماس وآقتوروب بولماس وآقتورسا بولماس وآقتورماق بولماس
روان نمیتواند شد آقیزا الماس وآقتورا الماس روان نمیتوان کرد آقیزا آقیزا وآقتورا آقتورا روان کنان وبدون
تکرار هم مستعملست آقیزای وآقیزامین وآقتورای وآقتورامین روان کنم وکنی آقیزالی وآقیزالیک وآقتورالی وآقتورالیک
روان کنیم آقیزغای وآقتورغای براو روان کردن آقیزغاج وآقتورغاج چون روان کرد وکند آقیزغوچی وآقتورغوچی روان
آقیزغوچه وآقیزغونچه وآقیزغانچه وآقتورغوچه وآقتورغونچه وآقتورغانچه تا روان کردن وبعد روان کردن آقیزغوم وآقتورغوم
روان خواهم کرد آقیزغونک وآقتورغونک روان خواهی کرد آقیزغوسی وآقتورغوسی روان خواهد کرد آقیزغولوق وآقتورغولوق
روان کردنی آقیزغای وآقیزا وآقیزسا وآقیزسون وآقیزدیک وآقتورغای وآقتورا وآقتورسا وآقتورسون وآقتوردیک
روان کند الشاهد علی الاول شعر توکیب ... باغیر قانینی ... ایله کیم ... آقیزغای تا ... آقیزدیک
وآقیزغودیک وآقتورغودیک وآقتوروردیک روان کردنی وهمچنانکه روان نکند آقارماق ... فلوماق بمعنی سفید شدن
که در حرف الفاء الفوقیة گذشت ومشتقات نیز به ستور مشتقات آنست من الجوامد آق ... آق بمعنی سفید بود چنانکه ...
زال دنیا در ردیف قاف بالملاحق ... قافیه کرده ... شعر سنبلینک سوکونکا یامیش آق ساچینی ایما تود
یوزی مهر ... آق ... ونیز ... شد چنانکه مذکور شد آق اورکا وآق اوی وآق بابا وآق بدرکانه وآق باشلیغ
وآقموغا وآقچه وآقچیل وآق سونکاک وآقتریق وآقلیغ وآقمتول ... بهمان صفت که در حرف ضاد مذکور شد آقان
برهان ... طایفه ایست از اتراک الشاهد علیه شعرای نوایی منکا برا اول صنم ...
کاقچاق وآقار شه ... سلکوت ... چنانکه در تاریخ بابری مذکور است که سلطان احمد میرزا ...
اوروشی اول ... نوایی سید آقار توزی ... غالب بولدی ... روان می شود چنانکه در ذیل آقماق
آقساغ آقساق بمعنی لنگ بود الشاهد علیه شعر ... مشکل ... عزیز ... کوز ...
آت آقساق ویول توزناق ... آتسراغ نام ... تاتاز ... ونیز نام ... در ... کابل

آقسنقر نام یکی از امراء کبار سلطان محمود سلجوقیست که اتابکان که در بلاد شام سلطنت کردند از اولاد او بودند
و زنکی بن آقسنقر نخستین آنطایفه بود و معنی ترکیبی آن آشنقار سفید باشد آقتوم بضم سین مهمله بمعنی برهنه است تا شلی
چنانکه گوید شعر ای ایچانک لو لماغیل آقتوم که پرده ردیدی که بو ایش اغلدی بنزنیک دیدار اکیوبا زوق و
آخسوم با خای منقوطه نیز بهمین معنی مستعملست چنانکه در الفمع الکاکسدت و بتولمنین و بمی و طالع هروی آقتوم را بمعنی
نادم و پشیمان ذکر کرده اند و در بعضی دلوین نیز کیره با زوق و در کمینه با زوق نوشته اند آقسین بسکون تا و نون
و کسر سین مهمله ایشبه شوخ سفلمه را گویند و از اشا و لوم نیز نامند آقشام شام را خوانند شعر همرا او اول شوخ
کونکلوم صیدا تیار در خسار لچین لطف آقشام قوش توتار غدوش اتیکاندیک چراغ آقیش بکسر قاف و سکون شین جریان
آب باشد آقمن بترکی رومی غارت و تاخت آقینجی غارتکر و تاخت کننده آقیندی مرادف آقیش بمعنی جریان آب بود
مع الکاف مع الشعاف اکیشمالک بسکون کاف و کسر شین قرشت ترش شدن و در بعضی مصطلحات اکلماک بسکون کاف
عجمی و نون و فتح لام بترکی رومی نشستن اکلنمز نمی نشیند چنانکه فضولی در مغشیات گوید باملاء الرومیه شعر
خواستجاب امسون قرشین فضولی خواجلات هجران اطلاق یوخو کوز کوز اکلنمز کونکل من الخوبدا کر بجمی بسکون کاف عجمی و میم
و فتح رای قرشت و کسر جیم عجمی بترکی رومی همین بود و آنرا اتراک توران ایرکامی گویند اکز بفتح کاف و سکون زای
هوز بترکی رومی ساق گندم و جو باشد که خوشه پیوسته است و بعضی از دو روی کیاه میمانند و آنرا اسپارس
ساری گویند اکری بسکون کاف و کسر سین قرشت بمعنی ترش بود که آنرا عربی خامض گویند اکه بفتح کاف
ها منون محروف آغاست یعنی برادر بزرک و این لفظ در میان اوزبک توران مصطلحاست و همه برادر را گویند چنانکه با بر شاه
در تاریخ خود گوید که بانیده سلطان پکوکی اکا دیر ایدیم و جیبه سلطان پکوکی سنکا دیر ایدیم و بانیده سلطان پکم مه
بولماسلوبود اکو بترکی اوزبکیه بمعنی تحسین باشد مع الکاف من المشتقات الماغ و الماقلیغ کرفتن الشاهد علی الاول شعر همرا و
فراد و هوشنی الماقلیغیلیک سیله شاید غالب آیتی سنکا جانیمدا ها الغولوق و ظالع هروی الماقلیغ را گرفتن و الغولوق را بمعنی
گفته شده ذکر کرده و شعر همرا شاهد آورده سهو کرده و نیز لفظیست که با بعضی کلمات افاده معنی غیر موضوع له میکند مثل
اوا الماق یعنی توان گرفتن و بارا الماق یعنی توان رفتن کونکول الماق بمعنی مجوی کردن و ساتغون الماق بمعنی خریدن الیمی
کرفت الالیمی توانست کرفت الدوق کرفتیم الا الدوق توانستیم کرفت الور و الانمیکرد و الور بمعنی فاعل و مصدر
هم می آید چنانکه بمعنی گیرنده در وصف شاه گوید شعر که پر کوجی اکر او لسون کنا و الغوجی شاه پر همه ایلیک بوقاره
و الور ایلیک قولی دهر الا الور می تواند کرفت المایدور نمیکیرد و نکرفته است الا المایدور نمیتواند کرفت و نتوانسته
کرفت الغان و الورغان و الادورغان کیرنده و کرفته الشاهد علی الاول بالمعنی الاول شعر آیر یا پر پریچین جان
کونکلونی حلم یلاپ پروین جانی هم الغیل چوبین دوبین کونکول الغان و بمعنی مصدر نیز می آید الی و الغیل
مفرد مخاطب فصل امر و الی شرح مخاطب در چنانکه در ذیل غیر مصادر مذکور شود الماد الماغیل مفرد مخاطب فصل
نهی الینک و الینکز جمع مخاطب فصل امر المانک المانکز و المانکلار جمع مخاطب فصل نهی المان و المامن نمیکیرم
الا المامن الا المامن نمیتوانم کرفت الامین الورمین و الادورمین و الورام میکیرم الا الورمین الا الورام متوانم کرفت
الورمیقام الامیم کرفتم الماغوم نخواهم کرفت الیب و الیبان و المیش کرفته المیشانک کرفته الا المیشانک

بسکون کاف و فتح سین مهمله بترکی رومی میخها کوچک بود که در
نجاری بکار رود و انچه بر میخ کوبیده شود آنرا قازوق گویند اکشی

توانسته کرفت المامین بکرده بمعنی فاعل و مصدر هم می آید الا المامین نتواند کرفت الماسی کرفتنش و نکرفتنش المادین
از کرفتن و نکرفتن چنانکه فضولی بمعنی کرفتن گوید باملاء الرومیه شعر عنبر سبلونک دین المادین بوطله دم صبا
بوی هوا یلی نیکاسندن دکل دماغ دن ادن هر الیب بولماس و الساب لماس و الماق اولماس نتوان کرفت الا الا کفته کرفته
و بدون تکرار هم مستعملست الای و الا بین بکیرم و بکیریم کرفته الا الا بین توانم کرفت و تواند کرفت و توانی کرفت و توا
کرفت الا الای و الا المایین توانم کرفت و نتواند کرفت و نتوانی کرفت و نتوانسته کرفت چنانکه شاهد برای اول معنی اخیر
خطاب محبوب گوید شعر تیغ تا رتیب دم الا الماس تیشینک باشیمه کویا خورشید نیکلیغ بولدا کوزده ولک
شتاب فراغی در تالیف خود الا الماس را بمعنی کرفته و ناکفته ذکر کرده و شعر همرا شاهد آورده سهو کرده الساف
و الغایز و الغای بزو الایلی بکیریم الا الساق و الا الغایز و الا الغای بز و الا الایلی و الا الا لینک توانیم کرفت
الغایلی برای کرفتن و تا کرفته بالمعنی الاول شعر الغالی دنیا عروسین ای که سانیسنک نقد دین عمر تا تیسغ ملیک
انکلا بوسناتیغ الیغ الا الغایلی برای اینکه تواند کرفت و تا توانسته کرفت الغاج چون کرفت و بکیرد و بکیری چنانکه
شعر کوزونک تانیغه سیراب ای لعزی نقد جان الغاج نحوکیم ستیکای می مفر نقدی را بکال الغاج الا الغاج چون
توانست کفت الغوجی کیرنده الغوجه و الغوبخه و الغانجه تا کرفتن و بقدر کرفتن الا الغوجه الا الغوبخه و الا الغانجه
تا تواند کرفت و بقدری که تواند کرفت الغوم خواهم کرفت چنانکه گوید شعر دیبا ایدینک الغوم نولی کونکلین
الغاج لونار رهنیک بخشی لا دا الماق یا نامالدر کونکلینی اندا قمودور الا الغوم کرفتن ممکن خواهد بود الا الماغوم
و الا الغوم بوق کرفتن ممکن نخواهد بود الشاهد علی الاول شعر اولوب ایجرا غیار صنینک دین نظر ایجرا سرادیم کیم الا الما
کنزا و الکونجه کرا بلا هسلم نطاره و الغونک خواهی کرفت الا الغونک کرفتن ممکن خواهد بود الماغونک و الا الغونک یوق
کرفتن ممکن نخواهد بود الغوسی خواهد کرفت الا الغوسی کرفتن ممکن خواهد بود الا الماغوسی و الا الغوسی یوق کرفتن ممکن
نخواهد بود الغولوق کرفتنت ممکن خواهد بود کرفتنی شاهد آن در ذیل الماق مذکور شد الغای و الا الغای الساف الغون و
الدیلت بکیرد الشاهد علی الخامس شعر نولدی کونکلین الکیستیغ سوری کان خانتی هم الدیلت کمجانی تید فیه هم کونکلی
الغای ابر مطرتش الا الغای و الا الساو الا الغون و الا الدیلت تواند کرفت الغودیلت و الوردیلت کرفتنی و بمجاز
بکیرد الشاهد علی الاول شعر باشی حالا کیم ایرهمرفوت نا الاین الیغه شد لیلت دین کچماین الیک یدین الغودیلت
الدورماغ مصدر متعدیست بمعنی کیرانیدن و کرفتار کردن الشاهد علیه شعر دیبا اول لر ابغضی اوچون کونکلی
الدورغولت اوزا بیکبر امنی هکن کیشی کونکلینی الدورماق و مجازا بمعنی دل ربیت آوردن و دیگو نیز استعمال میشود چنانکه
مطربی ایهام فرماید شعر اولیری لطف ابلا جان دیوانه لار کونکلینی الوش ببحث عشاق بیدلنینک کونکول الدورماغی
و مشتقات نیز متضمن این معنی میباشد الدوردی کرفتار کرد الدوردونک کرفتار کردی چنانکه شاهد آن در ذیل الدورماق
نوشته شد الدوردوق کرفتار کردیم الدورمه الدورمادور کرفتار میکند الشاهد علی الاول شعر اهل حال لار
احتیبا راجمانک دیده کیم هر کیشی اول یوزکا کوزنا الدوردی کونکلین الدوردوق و الدورمه بمعنی فاعل و مصدر نیز می آید
الدورماید و رکرفتار نمیکند و نکرده است الدورغان و الدیرمغان و الدیرادورغان کرفتار کننده و کرفتار کرده
مصدر هم می آید الدور و الدورغیل مفرد مخاطب فصل امر الدورمایا و الدورماغیل مفرد مخاطب فصل نهی الدورونک

وا الدورونکوز وا الدورونکلار جمع مخاطب از فصل امر الدورغانلی وا الدورغانکیز وا الدورغانکلار جمع مخاطب از فصل نفی
الدورغان نو الدورغانلار مین کرفتار میکنیم الدوراین وا الدورورمین وا الدورودام کرفتار میکنم الدوروروم و
الدورغانیم کرفتار کردیم الدورغانغو کرفتار نخواهیم کرد الدوروب وا الدوروبان وا الدورمیش کرفتار کرده الشاهد
علی الثانی شعر نوائی الدوروبان کونکلنی اکتابماش پراو تو رود که تولید ورجهاندا طلبلار الدورمیشانک
کرفتار کرده الدورماس کرفتار میکند و بمعنی فاعل و مصدر منفی هم می آید الدورماسی کرفتار کردنش و نکردنش الدور
از کرفتار کردن و کرفتار نکرده الدوروب بولماس وا الدورغا بولماس و الدورماق اولماس کرفتار نتوان کرد الدورالما
کرفتار نتواند کرد الدورا الدورا کرفتار کنان کرفتار کنان و بدون تکرار هم مستعمل است الدورای وا الدوراین کرفتار
کنم و کند و کی الدورناق وا الدورغانچ الدورغای ز الدوراغلی الدورالینک کرفتار کنیم الدورغالی برای کرفتار
کردن و تا کرفتار کرده الدورغاچ چون کرفتار کرد و کسی و کی الدورغوچی کرفتار کننده الدورغوچیا الدورغونچه
والدورغانچه تا کرفتار کردن و بقدر کرفتار کردن الدورغوم کرفتار خواهم کرد الدورغونک کرفتار خواهی کرد الدورغوی
کرفتار خواهد کرد الدورغولوق کرفتار کردنی الدورغای وا الدورول وا الدورنا وا الدورسون وا الدوردیلک کرفتار
الدورغوردیلک وا الدوروردیلک کرفتار کردند وهمچنانکه کرفتار کند الشاهد علی الاول شعر سین کونکل لیربانک
نوایغه کیمی سینک جدایلیغ ایرماس ولا هر دل لباغه کونکلنی الدورغودیک الیشماق بکسر لام و سکون شین قرشت مشدد
مفاعله است به معنی استعمال می شود اول بمعنی مفاوضه کردن باشد چنانکه در نم حسد کوید رباعی
جاهل که حسد بولغای نیت جمیلغه ضمن تعرابل کونکل دین آنکلا انا اوز کونزیدا کم کوزلانی الیشماقه چیک
تیغ سنم ایل کونزنی هم ادیغای وا اوز کونزنی هم تقدیم بالمجاز بمعنی مطاعنه و دستبازی کردن باشد سیم از هم ربودن
و از یکدیگر کرفتن بود و بترکی ربوغ بمعنی عادت کردن باشد و چون زکیفیت اشتقاق اتراک دوم مادرای اشتقاق لغات جغتای
در بعضی از نسخ ما هر بولسان تطابق داشت بمعنی عادت نوشته می شود الیشتیلار مفاوضه و مطاعنه کردند و از هم
ربودند و عادت کردند چنانکه بمعنی قیم دتا یخ نا بری مذکور است که بعضی ایچکی کلام خیابان باشند با بیسفر مرزا
منک کیشی بیله ایلیک الیشتیلار و نیز کوید که بیرایکی قاتلا او لطرفدین بو طرفدین قیلیچ الیشتیلار الیشوق
مفاوضه و مطاعنه کردیم و از هم ربودیم و عادت کردیم الیشور وا الیشادور مفاوضه و مطاعنه میکند و از هم می رباید
و عادت میکند و الیشور بمعنی فاعل و مصدر نیز می آید الیشمایدور مفاوضه و مطاعنه نمیکند و نکرده است و از
هم نمی رباید و نربوده است و عادت نمیکند و نکرده است الیشغان وا الیشمغان وا الیشادورغان صیغه فاعل و مفعول
و مصدر است از برای مفاوضه و مطاوضه کردن و از هم ربودن الیش وا الیشغیل امر مخاطب از فصل امر الیشما والیشا
مفرد مخاطب از فصل نفی الیشینک وا الیشینکیز وا الیشینکلار جمع مخاطب از فصل امر الیشمانلیز وا الیشمانکیز و الیشمانکلار جمع
از فصل نفی الیشمان وا الیشاین مین مفاوضه و مطاعنه میکنم و از هم میربایم الیشاین وا الیشورمین وا الیشادورمین و
الیشورام مفاوضه و مطاعنه میکنم و از هم می ربایم الیشوردوم وا الیشماغیم مفاوضه و مطاعنه کردیم و ربودیم الیشاغوم
مفاوضه و مطاعنه کردم خواهم ربود الیشیب وا الیشبان وا الیشمیش مفاوضه و مطاعنه کرده و از هم ربوده و عادت
کرده الیشمیشانک مفاوضه و مطاعنه کرده و از هم ربوده الیشماس صیغه نفی هر چهار معنی و بمعنی فاعل و مصدر منفی

می آید الیشماسی هر چهار معنی نفی و اثبات می آید الیشمادین از مفاوضه کردن و مفاوضه نکرده و از ربودن و نربوده
و از عادت کردن و عادت نکرده الیشیب بولماس وا الیشا بولماس و الیشماق بولماس مفاوضه و مطاعنه نتوان کرد و از هم
نتوان ربود الیشا الماس مفاوضه و مطاعنه نتواند کرد و از هم نتواند ربود الیشا الیشا مفاوضه کنان و مطاعنه
و ربوده کنان و عادت کنان و بدون تکرار هم مستعمل است الیشای وا الیشاین مفاوضه و مطاعنه کنم و کند و کی و ربایم و
رباید و رباتی الیشاق وا الیشغای ز وا الیشغای ز وا الیشالی وا الیشالینک وا الیشالی و ربایم و رباید و ربانی مفاوضه
کنیم و از هم ربایم والیشاق برکی رومی بسو عادت کنیم الیشغالی برای مفاوضه و مطاعنه کردن و برای از هم ربودن
مفاوضه و مطاعنه خواهیم کرد و از هم خواهیم ربود الیشغونکوز و مفاوضه و مطاعنه خواهید کرد و از هم خواهید
ربود الیشغوسلار مفاوضه و مطاعنه خواهند کرد و از هم خواهند ربود الیشغولوق مفاوضه و مطاعنه کردنی
و از هم ربودنی الیشغای لار وا الیشا لار وا الیشا لار وا الیشسونلار وا الیشسونلار مفاوضه و مطاعنه کنند و از هم
بربایند الشاهد علی الاول والمعنی الاخیر شعر ای نوائی یار بیله بولسا کونکلونک بخشی دوش کیم الیشغای لار
سیز کیبی دیبخواه لار و طالع هر دولی الیشغای را بمعنی قسمت کردن نوشته و الیشماق را مصدر برای آن قرار داده
لفظ و معنی هر دو اختراعیست الیشوردیلک وا الیشوردیلک مفاوضه کردند و از هم ربودند و همچنانکه مفاوضه و مطاعنه کند
و همچنانکه از هم برباید الیشماق مع النون مصدر افتعال است یعنی کرفتار شدن و صیغ آن بدستور مصدر الیشماق نون
می باید و بجای شین حرف نون داخل میشود الاتماق بکسر قاف و الامیشماق بکسر قاف و سکون شین قرشت هم بر آمدن و متولد
رویی از لفظ را بمعنی بیماو تاراج و زیر و زبر کردن نوشته و نصیحت هم متابعت کرده اند و از ترکیه و ترکانه خوانده
استعمال مینمایند الامی وا الامیشی هم بر آید الافوق وا الامیشوق هم بر آمدیم الاقورها الاتادور وا الامیشور وا الامیشا
بهم بر می آید والافور و الامیشور بمعنی فاعل و مصدر نیز می آید الاتمایدور بهم بر نمی آید و بیامده است الافغان و
الافورغان والامیشغان وا الامیشورغان وا الامیشادورغان بهم بر آینده و بهم بر آمده و بمعنی مصدر نیز می آید الاق و
الاقیل وا الامیش وا الامیشغیل مفرد مخاطب از فصل امر الاتما والاتماغیل وا الامیشما وا الامیشماغیل مفرد مخاطب از فصل نفی الا
قینک وا الافینکیز وا الافینکلار و الامیشینکیز وا الامیشینکلار جمع مخاطب از فصل امر الاتمانکیز وا الاتمانکلار و
الامیشمانکیز وا الامیشمانکیز وا الامیشمانکلار جمع مخاطب از فصل نفی الاتمان والاتمان مین والامیشمان وا الامیشمان مین
بهم بر می آیم الاتامین وا الافورمین وا الاتادورمین والافورام وا الامیشامین وا الامیشورمین وا الامیشادورمین وا الامیشورام
بهم بر می آیم الافوروم وا الامیشوروم وا الاتماغیم وا الامیشماغیم بهم بر آمدیم الاتاغوم وا الامیشاغوم بخواهم بهم بر آمد الاقیب
الاقیبان و الامیش وا الامیشیب والامیشبان وا الامیشمیش هم بر آمده الشاهد علی الاول شعر نوائیا چو سیه چکی
کونکلوم کا ملامت و زهد ایله تقوی بوزولدیلار الاقیب و شاهد بر ایج دم تاریخ بابری مذکور است که میرخسروانچه قرلباش
ایکاندور در ریطرف بیر سوز قاشی بر ایلساحاج عیب لار الامیشیب در طرف آچار لار الامیشمانک و الامیشمیشانک
بهم بر آمده الاتماس وا الامیشماس بهم بر نمی آید و بمعنی فاعل و مصدر منفی هم می آید الاتماسی و الامیشماسی بهم بر آمدنش
بهم بر نیامدنش الاتمادین والامیشمادین از بهم بر آمدن و بهم بر نیامده الاتا الماس وا الامیشا الماس بهم بر نتواند آمد
الاقیب بولماس وا الاتا بولماس و الاتماق بولماس و الامیشیب بولماس و الامیشا بولماس و الامیشماق اولماس بهم بر

تمام آمد الاتا آلاتما الامتشا الامتشا هم برآمد هم برآمدن و بدون تکرار هم مستعملست الاتای و الاتلیس یا الامتشای و
الامتشاین هم برآیم و برآید و برآیی الاتساق یا الاتالینک یا الامتشاق و الامتشالی یا الامتشالینک هم برآییم الامتشالی
و الامتشالی برای هم برآمدن و تا بهم برآمدن الامتاج یا الامتشاج چون هم برآمد و برآید و برآیی الامتوجی و الامتشوجی
هم برآینده الامتوجه و الامتونجه و الامتاجمط الامتشغوجه و الامتشانجه تا بهم برآمدن و بعد هم برآمدن الامتوم و
الامتشغوم هم خواهم برآمد الامتونک یا الامتشغونک هم خواهی برآمد الامتوسی یا الامتشغوسی هم خواهد برآمد الامتولوق
و الامتشغولوق هم برآمدنی الامتای یا الاتا و الاتسا و الامتون و الامتدیلی یا الامتشاع الامتشا و الامتشاد
الامتشون یا الامتشدیلی هم برآید الامقودیک یا الامتشغودیک یا الامتشغودیک هم برآمدنی و همچنانکه
هم برآمد الارتماق بسکون را و تای بعد از شین چشم را از غیظ خیره کردن اما بتنهایی افاده معنی نمیکند باید لفظ چشم را مذکور
ساخت الارتتی خیره کرد الارتتوق خیره کردیم الارتتوم و الارتنادی خیره میکند و الارتتور بمعنی فاعل و مصدر نیز می آید الار
تماید خیره نمیکند و [illegible] و نکرده است الارتغان و الارتتورغان
و الارتنادی فان خیره کننده و خیره کرده. و بمعنی مصدر نیز می آید الارت و الارتغیل مفرد مخاطب از فعل امر الارتماغیل
مفرد مخاطب از فعل نهی الارتینک یا الارتینکر یا الارتینکلار جمع مخاطب از فعل امر الارتمانک یا الارتمانکز یا الارتمانکلار جمع
از فعل نهی الارتمان و الارتماس بین خیره نمیکنم الارتامین یا الارتورمن یا الارتادورمین و الارتقام خیره میکنم الارتوروم و
الارتماغیم خیره کردنم الارتماغوم خیره نخواهم کرد الارتیب یا الارتیبان و الارتمیش خیره کرده. الارتمیشانک خیره کرده
الارتماس خیره نمیکند و بمعنی فاعل و مصدر نفی هم می آید الارتماسی خیره کردنش و نکردنش الارتمادین از خیره کردن و خیره نکرد
الارتیب بولماس و الارتسا بولماس یا الارتماق اولماس خیره نمیتوان کرد الارتا الماس خیره نمیتواند کرد الارتا الارتا خیره کنان
و بدون تکرار هم مستعملست الارتای یا الارتابین خیره کنم و کند و کنی الارتساق و الارتلی و الارتالینک خیره کنیم الارتا
برای خیره کردن و تا خیره کرده. الارتماج چون خیره کرد و کند الارتغوجی خیره کننده الارتغوجه و الارتغونجه و الارتماجه
تا خیره کردن و بعد خیره کردن الارتغوم خیره خواهم کرد الارتغونک خیره خواهی کرد الارتغوسی خیره خواهد کرد الارتغولوق
خیره کردنی الارتغای یا الارتا و الارتسا و الارتدون و الارتدیلی خیره کند الارتودیک و الارتغودیک خیره میکند و همچنانکه
خیره کند الداراماق بفتح دال و رای قرشت اضطراب کردن و بیقرار شدن و ظاهر هروی بمعنی فریب خوردن از خمره شعف
نوشته سهو کرده. الدارادی مضطرب شد الداراداوق مضطرب شدیم الدارادور یا الدارایدور مضطرب میشود الشاهد علی الاول
شعر یوکورماکلیک [illegible] کل [illegible] و الدارا بمعنی فاعل و مصدر نیز
الدارامایدور مضطرب نمیشود و نشده است الداراغان یا الداراغان و الدارایدورغان مضطرب شونده و مضطرب شده و
مصدر نیز می آید چنانکه شاهد اول بمعنی مضطرب شدن در تاریخ نابری مذکور است که بر سلطان الغ [illegible]
قاریلیغ دین موتا الدارا غلی دین [illegible] و نیز در یوسف میرزا خان کوبدا الدارا غالی دین یوکو یوب
کیلکو [illegible] الدارا یا الداراغیل مفرد مخاطب از فعل امر الدارامنا و الداراماغیل مفرد مخاطب از فعل نهی الدارانک
الدارانکر یا الدارانکلار جمع مخاطب از فعل امر الدارامانک یا الدارامانکر و الدارامانکلار جمع مخاطب از فعل نهی الدارامان
و الدارامیین مضطرب نمیشوم الدارایمن یا الدارامن یا الدارایدورمین یا الدارارام مضطرب میشوم الشاهد علی الاول

شعر آنکا آیغور سوزوم [illegible] چوبلدی [illegible] الدارا الدیم و
الداراماغیم فریب دادم الداراماغوم فریب نخواهم داد الدارایب یا الدارابان و الدارامیش مضطرب شده الشاهد علی
الاول شعر [illegible] خیلی الدارایب [illegible] خوش الدارامیشانک
مضطرب شده الداراماس مضطرب نمیشود الداراماسی مضطرب شدنش و نشدنش الدارامادین از مضطرب شدن و مضطرب نشدن
الدارایب بولماس و الدارا سا بولماس یا الداراماق اولماس مضطرب نمیتوان شد الدارا الماس مضطرب نمیتواند شد الدارا
و الدارا و الدارای اضطراب کنان و بدون تکرار هم بمعنی مستعملست الدارای و الداراین مضطرب شوم و شود و شوی
الشاهد علی الاول المعنی الاول شعر [illegible] الدا
الدارا ساق یا الدارا سایز یا الداراغای بیز و الدارالی یا الدارالینک مضطرب شویم الداراغالی برای مضطرب شدن و تا
مضطرب شده الداراماج چون مضطرب شد و شود الداراغوجی مضطرب شونده الداراغوجه و الداراغونجه و الدارامانجه
تا مضطرب شدن و بعد مضطرب شدن الداراغوم مضطرب خواهم شد الداراغونک مضطرب خواهی شد الداراغوسی
مضطرب خواهد شد الداراغولوق مضطرب شدنی الداراغای یا الدارا سا و الدارا سون و الدارادیلی مضطرب شود
الشاهد علی الاول شعر [illegible]
الداراردیک یا الداراغودیک مضطرب شده و همچنانکه مضطرب شود الدارا تماق بفتح التا مصدر متعدیست بمعنی
مضطرب کردن چنانکه در [illegible] بمعنی مضطرب کرده گوید شعر [illegible]
[illegible] و باقی صیغ بر همین سیاق موافق شق اول اشتقاق می یابد الدارا ماق بسکون لام و فتح دال فریب دادن چنانکه در
یکی از متعلقات [illegible] الدارادوق [illegible]
دادیم الدارار یا الدارایدور فریب میدهد و الدارار بمعنی فاعل و مصدر نیز می آید چنانکه بمعنی فریب دادن گوید [illegible]
بخاری شعر [illegible] الدارامایدور فریب
نمیدهد و نداده است الدارغان و الداغان یا الدارایدورغان فریب دهنده فریب داده و بمعنی مصدر نیز می آید الدارا و
الداراغیل مفرد مخاطب از فعل امر الشاهد علی الثانی شعر [illegible] تیغ کین یوز [illegible]
سوز [illegible] الداراغیل الدارانا و الداراماغیل مفرد مخاطب از فعل نهی الدارانک یا الدارانکر یا الدارانکلار جمع مخاطب از فعل
الدارامانک یا الدارامانکر یا الدارامانکلار جمع مخاطب از فعل نهی الشاهد علی الثانی شعر [illegible]
[illegible] الدارامان یا الدارامامین فریب نمیدهم الدارایمن یا الدارارمین یا الدارایدورمین
و الدارارم فریب میدهم الدارادیم یا الداراماغیم فریب دادم الداراماغوم فریب نخواهم داد الدارایب یا الدارابان یا الدارامیش
داده الشاهد علی الثانی شعر [illegible]
الدارابان الدارامیشانک فریب داده. الداراماس فریب نمیدهد و بمعنی فاعل و مصدر منفی هم می آید الداراماسی فریب دادنش
و ندادنش الدارایب بولماس و الدارا سا بولماس و الداراماق اولماس فریب نمیتوان داد الدارای الماس فریب نمیتواند داد الدارا یا الدارا
الدارای فریب داده فریب داده. و بدون تکرار هم مستعملست الدارای یا الداراین فریب دهم و دهد و دهی الدارا ساق یا الدارا غایز
و الداراغای بیز و الدارالی یا الدارالینک فریب دهیم الداراغالی برای فریب دادن و تا فریب داده. الداراماج چون فریب داد و دهد

آلداغوچی فریب دهنده آلداغوچیغا و آلداغونچه تا فریب دادن و نقیض فریب دادن آلداغوم فریب خواهم داد آلداغونک
فریب خواهی داد آلداغوسی فریب خواهد داد آلداغولوق فریب دادنی آلداغای و آلداسا و آلداسون و آلدایک فریب دهد
آلداردیک و آلداغودیک فریب دادید و همچنانکه فریب دهد آلداتماق مع التاء مصدر متعدی است [illegible] آلداتماق
بمعنی فریب دادنست و صیغ آن بدستور با حروف تاء قرشت اشتقاق می باید آلداشماق مع الشین مصدر مفاعله است بمعنی
فریب دادن آلداشیب و آلداشیبان و آلداشمیش فریب داده الشاهد علی الاول شعر عین وصل ایچرا ایشی ایل ا شکایت
ایکی باندین تغ ایستیب چالاریغ آلداشیب و باقی صیغ بدستور با حروف شین اشتقاق می باید آلدانماق بفتح الدال و سکون نون
مصدر انفعال است بمعنی فریب خوردن و صیغ آن با حروف نون اشتقاق می باید آلقاماق بسکون لام و فتح قاف دعای خیر کردن
چنانکه گوید شعر سین دانا ز اولدی [illegible] نیاز [illegible] عجب برسین [illegible] تارغاغان شای سینی اول آلقاماق و طالع
هر [illegible] آلقاماق [illegible] معنی کردن ذکر کرده مو شعر مرحوم بابر پادشاه هم آمده سهو کرده آلقادی دعا کرد آلقادوق
دعا کردیم آلقای دعا که آلقایه دعای کند و آلقار بمعنی فاعل و مصدر نیز می آید و فتح [illegible] گوید چنانکه ذکر
جواب مذکور خواهد شد آلقامایدور دعا میکند و نکرده است آلقاغان و آلقارغان و آلقایدورغان دعا کننده
و دعا کرده و بمعنی مصدر هم می آید آلقا و آلقاغیل مفرد مخاطب فعل امر آلقاما و آلقاماغیل مفرد مخاطب فعل نهی
آلقانک و آلقانکیز و آلقانکلار جمع مخاطب فعل امر آلقامانک و آلقامانکیز و آلقامانکلار جمع مخاطب فعل نهی آلقامان
و آلقاماسین دعا مکن آلقایمین و آلقارمین و آلقایدورمین و آلقارام دعا میکنم آلقادیم و آلقاغیم دعا کردم
آلقاماغوم دعا نخواهم کرد آلقاب و آلقابان و آلقامیش دعا کرده آلقامیشانک دعا کرده آلقاماس دعا نمیکند و معنی
فاعل و مصدر منفی هم می آید آلقاماس دعا کردن و نکردن آلقاب بولماس و آلقاسا بولماس و آلقاماق اولماس دعا نمیتوان کرد
آلقای آلماس دعا نمیتواند کرد آلقایو و آلقای آلقای دعا کنان و بدون تکرار هم مستعملست آلقای و آلقاسین دعا کنم و کند
آلقاساق و آلقاغایز و آلقاغای بیز و آلقایلی و آلقایلیک دعا کنیم آلقاغالی برای دعا کردن و تا دعا کرده آلقاغاچ
دعا کرد و کند آلقاغوچی دعا کننده آلقاغوچیغا و آلقاغونچه تا دعا کردن و نقیض دعا کردن آلقاغوم دعا خواهم
کرد آلقاغونک دعا خواهی کرد آلقاغوسی دعا خواهد کرد آلقاغولوق دعا کردنی آلقاغای و آلقاسا و آلقاسون و آلقاد
دعا کند آلقاغودیک و آلقاردیک دعا کردید و همچنانکه دعا کند آلماشتورماق بسکون لام و شین و رای قرشت ضم تا
با او حرکت دادن و تنها بی افاده معنی نمیکند لفظ با او باید مذکور ساخت و در صیغ آن نیز همین ضابطه ملحوظ است
آلماشتوردی با او حرکت داد آلماشتوردوق با او حرکت دادیم آلماشتورور و آلماشتورادور با او حرکت میدهد چنانکه در
لغز باسم مقراض گوید الشاهد علی الاول شعر [illegible] ؛ ایاغ اوجیدا [illegible] لار المنا
تا چان [illegible] آلماشتورور [illegible] ؛ [illegible] آلماشتورور بمعنی فاعل و مصدر
نیز می آید آلماشتورمایدور با او حرکت نمیدهد و نداده است آلماشتورغان و آلماشتورورغان و آلماشتورادورغان
با او حرکت دهنده و حرکت داده و بمعنی مصدر نیز می آید آلماشتور و آلماشتورغیل مفرد مخاطب فعل امر آلماشتورما و
آلماشتورماغیل مفرد مخاطب فعل نهی آلماشتورونک و آلماشتورونکیز و آلماشتورونکلار جمع مخاطب فعل امر آلماشتورما
و آلماشتورمانکیز و آلماشتورمانکلار جمع مخاطب فعل نهی آلماشتورمان و آلماشتورماسین حرکت نمیدهم آلماشتورامین و

آلماشتورورمین و آلماشتورادورمین و آلماشتورورام با او حرکت میدهم آلماشتوروم و آلماشتوردیم حرکت دادیم آلماشتورمایم
با او حرکت نخواهم داد آلماشتوروب و آلماشتوروبان و آلماشتورمیش با او حرکت داده آلماشتورمیشانک با او حرکت داده
آلماشتورماس با او حرکت نمیدهد بمعنی فاعل و مصدر منفی هم می آید آلماشتوروب بولماس و آلماشتورسا بولماس و آلماشتورا
آلماس با او حرکت نمیتواند داد آلماشتورا آلماشتورا با او حرکت کنان و بدون تکرار با این معنی مستعمل
آلماشتوراین و آلماشتورسین با او حرکت دهم و دهد و همچنین آلماشتورساق و آلماشتورغایز و آلماشتورغای بیز و آلماشتورالی و
آلماشتورالیک با او حرکت دهیم آلماشتورغالی برای با او حرکت دادن و تا حرکت داده آلماشتورغاچ چون با او حرکت داد و دهد آلما
شتورغوچی با او حرکت دهنده آلماشتورغوچیغا و آلماشتورغونچه تا حرکت دادن و نقیض حرکت دادن آلماشتورغوم با او حرکت
خواهم داد آلماشتورغونک با او حرکت خواهی داد آلماشتورغوسی با او حرکت خواهد داد آلماشتورغای و آلماشتورسا
و آلماشتورسون و آلماشتوردیک و آلماشتورغودیک و آلماشتوردیک با او حرکت دهد و همچنانکه حرکت دهد
آلاکیلماک کف ما آمدن و صیغ کیلماک در کاف خواهد آمد آلیقوماق بکسر لام و ضم قاف ترکی رومی بمعنی باز داشتن
آلیقوماق مع النون مکث کردن و باز داشتن من المجاهد آل [illegible] معنا آمده اول [illegible] کنید چنانکه گوید شعر
ای کونکول [illegible] یار آلیب ؛ خاطریم [illegible] یار آلیب ؛ دویم [illegible] خوانند چنانکه بمعنی جنون
و پشانی گوید شعر نوای آینکا یازغانی [illegible] ؛ [illegible] ؛ سیم بمعنی خدعه و مکر
باشد چنانکه در [illegible] آمده شعر حیله سی کوب آلی و آلداغی کوب ؛ مکرو دغا تونی سیله [illegible] ؛ چهارم
سرخ نیم رنک بود الشاهد علیه شعر [illegible] آل آیلادینک ؛ جان [illegible]
پا [illegible] شرکت [illegible] پادشاهان [illegible] خوانند که [illegible] لیغات [illegible]
می شود چنانکه [illegible] غزل ملمع با اصطلاحات مغول گفته شعر بر یارلیغ خوبی رخ خوب توشدی
تا خان شد بر همه خوبان ممالک ؛ وهم [illegible] سلطنت باید و [illegible] ذکر کرده کمال زین و [illegible]
[illegible] شکر [illegible] آن مواهب [illegible] گویند چنانکه در ذیل شاهد مذکور شود ششم [illegible]
در ذیل مصدر آلماق گذشت و [illegible] اول نوعی از ماهی [illegible] خوانند [illegible]
[illegible] نو زاینده را تا هفت [illegible] فارس میشود [illegible] سیم [illegible]
صبح و شام نباشد و هندی نام درختی است که از [illegible] حاصل میشود مانند [illegible]
نیز بکله برند آلابو وزن بالا دو معنی دارد اول بمعنی سرخ نیم رنک بود چنانکه [illegible] باشد [illegible]
نامند و [illegible] اشتراک دارد دویم هر چیز ابلق را گویند عموما و [illegible] خوانند خصوصا آلابولا لفظیست [illegible]
اللون والبلق چنانکه گوید شعر نون کوی حریری بولدی [illegible] ؛ چون جوادی آلابولا [illegible]
و مجاز بمعنی شوریده استعمال شود آلابکه بفتح بای ابجد و فتح کاف [illegible] نام یک نوع ارده است آلاتاغ نام کوهیست [illegible]
خراسان که مسکن اکراد است و نیز نام کوهیست در آذربایجان در حوالی ایروان آلاتوغان بفتح غین و سکون نون و آلاتوغانک
بفتح نون و سکون کاف نام پرنده ایست شبیه به باشه اما از باشه کوچکتر است آنچه بمعنی [illegible] بود که آنرا [illegible]
[illegible] بمعنی شبکه باشد و نیز نام یک نوع قماشیست [illegible] بلند [illegible] کوچک [illegible]

توی فاونیز کویند آلاچا بنون تا دهای شدید مختلف بود که برف و باران آمیخته باشد آلاچوق بضم جیم عجمی همان اتاک
که مذکور شد و آن خیمه ایست که صحرانشینان از چوب سازند چنانکه در خسرو شیرین در وصف بیشه طلسم دیو کوید شعر
ایچی کوییکان بغاج کاوا کی آچوق ٭ ولوب غول وشیا لمینفه آلاچوق ٭ الاخان والانان الفاظ مترادفه اند بمعنی مادر
الشاهد علیه شعر خانمان ین آیریب قیلغانک توغراغ ایچرا صیغ ٭ قیلما الطفونک مین الاخان والانانی ین جدا ٭
وله شعر کونکول ایتی که طفونک بارایدی ولی الاخان والانا یمیغه ناقد ٭ والانا را بمعنی جد کانه هست چنانکه
در ذیل مذکور شود آلار بسکون رای قرشت بروزن نکار اسم اشارة است یعنی ایشان و آنها آلاتاخته مرغیست از فاخته بزرگتر
وطوق کردن او سیاه و ناتمام و کوشت آن سمین بدن و مشهی و مجموع آن مستعمل بجز صالح میشود آلاتاراق احوال اراکو
الاقارضه کلاغ کبود است که از ابر بی صنعه نامند آلاترغان نام اردک هراتست که بعلقه اختیار الذین اشتهار دارد
آلاق بولاق مطرح نظر اوجه استعمال میشود بمعنی شوریده و بهم برآمده باشد و طالع هروی بمعنی التتبا والبق نوشته الا
جانوریست نقد زنبور و بد بو باکیاه تازه و سر کندم نار مولع باشد و آنرا بعربی ذرایح و بدیلجی ارپاس کویند و بلغت اصفهان
قتیمه زنبور است و موافق تحفة المؤمنین از سموم است له و خوردن سوختنه او با مرق کوشت کاو و به تنوره روغن زیتون جهة
کزند سک دیوانه نافعست آلامان دو معنی دارد اول نام مملکتیست از ممالک به فرنک لا ادری شعر بتغی بلماسیله
ویرانه هر الامان ایل لا ادری ٭ سرمحی صیحی بن خراب ایران وتوران ایل لا ادری ٭ دویم بمعنی یغما بود و مجاز طایفه غارتکر یغماگر
الامانچی کویند آلامانچی غارتکر آلامانچی لیغ غارتکری آلانقوا بفتح لام و قاف و سکون نون نام زنیست از قوم قیات چل ایلغار
که بی شوهر حامله شد و هنگام وضع حمل سه پسر آورد که بوزنجر پسر مهین اوست و مجموع خانان مغول از نسل بوزنجر اند بموافق
تاریخ روضة الصفا ظلم بمعنی بوزنجری در ایام خروج ابومسلم مروزی بوده آلانج بسکون نون و جیم بترکی رومی نی باشد
که مرد دو ضبه اول بکیرد آلانک بسکون نون و کاف عجمی بلند یهار اکویند که در اطراف نهرها بی شکسته باشد الشاهد علیه
شعر قطع قیلغونجه بادشتی اراپوزینک آلانک ٭ تاشلاب او ذلوکمی قدم دیرمنا جانی تابک ٭ و آلانک در این شعر کنایه از زن
و بلند بیت آلاو بسکون واو شعله و نایره آتش بود چنانکه کوید شعر عشقینک اوتی شعله سین مفرحتی الابجنون کونکو
ایله کیم دیوانه لاکم آلیم تیلار نی قیلماق آلاد و مؤلف برهان قاطع این لفظ را فارسی شمرده و معنی آتش شعله ناک نوشته آلای
بترکی رومی بمعنی جمعیت و کوکبه باشد و نیز از صنع مشتقه است چنانکه با معنی در ذیل آلماق نکارش یافت آلای بوزن با..
رومیه نام یکنوع نام یکنوع تفنگ است که آنرا قرابینه هم کویند آلاینتلی بسکون نون و تای قرشت نام پسر سیم تاغ خان بن ایلجی خان
و معنی آن صاحب البلو باشد آلپ بسکون لام و بای عجمی بمعنی پهلوان و بهادر بود و آلپ لار جمع انت آلپ ارسلان نام
معروف و معنی ترکیبی آن شیر دلیر باشد آلپاق بفتح بای عجمی پارچه باشد که بطرح و اسلوب ... از جانب ... بلعو از ...
و زینت و کرینان جامه بدوزند آلپوتو بضم با و تای قرشت بلغت مغول بمعنی رعیت و باج کذار باشد آلتا و بسکون لام و واو
فتح تا یعنی شش تا چنانکه کوید شعر فنای محض نیستلر بته ضروریه نیدین که یوتغه منهر تلیماس بو نوع آلتا و آلتا ولا
یعنی شش تا با یکدیگر آلتالی بفتح تا و کسر یای حطی جانوریست بزرک کربه که موی آن سنجاب است و پوست آنرا پوستین کنند و بدو..
دوزند چنانکه در خسرو شیرین در وصف چهار فصل کوید شعر قیزیل لعل تاجی یوق آنچه که سنجاب یوق آلتالی جبه باتقان
تاب و آنرا الطای نیز کویند و موجبیه آنرا حلمقا و نامند و فراغی سموا بمعنی پوستینه و بالاپوش و پوستین نوشته الثمنا

موافق شعر نوائی مهر و نیکین پادشاهان ترکت که در طرلیغات و فرامین میزده می شود چنانکه کوید شعر چونیاز
صفحه فه یار لیغ نا بسا رضا التمغا نیش ٭ شفوده ین حل قیلیب شکر قیلامینک مهر دیغانیم و له شعر بوزی کلچه رسانی قیلیک طرب
حکمی غه طغرا دوش ٭ بوزیدا امی کلی اول یارلیغ اوزره آلقغادوش ٭ و آنرا آلتیز کویند آلتمیش هیج لشکر که بعنوان طرح باشد
مدد شصت درم کویند آلتوت کنایه از هرج و مرج باشد آلتون طلا بود که آنرا بعربی ذهب و بفارسی زر کویند الشاهد
علیه شعر بوزنا باغی توپراغیدین آلما او شبو مثابه کیم بنجه توپراغ ایچیندا تپرسا آلتون سود اید در و طالع هروی تو
که بجبت انحل و وضع لغت موضوع از برای دانکست که با آن زر کشیده میشود سهو کرده آلتون یلکا احکام و یارلیغات
ترکی را کویند که مخصوص مالیات و محاسبات دیوانی باشد آلتون تمغا مهر و نیکین پادشاهان ترکت که در فرامین آب طلا
میشود و آن مخصوص عطایا و احسانات و آن حکم را یارلیغ الون تمغا کویند و صاف در جلد رابع تاریخ خود ذکر کرده
که جامه زرنکار را از خانه ... داشت و فرمان ... نشان که از ایشان آلتون تمغا خوانده اند واند آلتو بموغ زربفت
دیبای طلا باف را مانند آلتی عدد شش را کویند آلتی بیتی بیغ کنایه است از شش جهت و هفت آسمان چنانکه کوید شعر جمعا تو
پرده کیندین که عالم کو بیاسون ٭ آلتی بیتی بیغ سا لغیل ایکی اوچ نقاشا آلتماق بیت و دون و منازل آلتماقلیغ
بیتی آنچو بضم جیم و آلتمچی بسکون لام و نون و کسر جیم عجمی شدی پهلوی کوه را کویند آلتمچی بکسر جیم بترکی رومی آهک بود که آنرا
بعربی نوره خوانند آلتم طاشی بترکی رومی سنکیست سفید و همین و درخشان که آنرا بعربی کوکب الارض نامند آلدلغ بمعنی
فریب باشد و آنرا آلیز کویند چنانکه شاهد آن در ذیل آلمه مذکور شد آلداغچ بترکی رومی چاپلوس و فریبنده است آلدو
بفتح دال و واو رومیه حیله را کویند که قوشچیان بر دست کنند آلطالی همان آلتالی باشد که در فوق مذکور شد
الشاهد علیه شعر روشن آلماجرخ اله اوستیدین کوروبکان دوردی ٭ معوشیم یکیدا الطالی یله باشیدا کیش ٭
آلغوپر کو بمعنی کرنش و دادن و عبارت از دست باشد چنانکه کوید شعر ای نوائی جان الیب دیدی ... کامینک
دم امرا المان آنکا خالی بو آلغوپر کودین ٭ و نیز آلغو نام شهر خضاست که بتربیت آریغ بوکا نشو و نما یافته اخر موسر سلطنت
برخاسته بر آریغ غالب شد آلغوت بسکون لام و تای قرشت و ضم غین بمعنی نخیره و غله ایست که لشکریان بر سم خرج از والا
کیرند آلغور بسکون لام و رای قرشت بمعنی آهسته باشد آلغون بسکون لام و نون بلغت مغولی کوه کوچک بود آلقا
قوچ کوهی را نامند و نیز بمعنی دعای کنند چنانکه در ذیل اشتقاقات آلقاماق کذشت آلقیش بکسر قاف و سکون شین دعا
خیر را کویند آلما باش اسم یکنوع مرغابیست از جنس اردک که سر و کردن آن صندلی مایل بزردی باشد آلما لیغ نام شهری
از ترکستان که از آنجا تا بیش بالیغ دو هفته راه و از بیش بالیغ تا اجا بالیغ از جانب جنوب در راه بیابان که مغول آنرا یوغری
بول کویند چهل روز راهست و معنی ترکیبی آن سیبستان باشد آلنجه بفتح لام و جیم مفتوحه و سکون نون اسم پسر ترک
یافث بن نوح علیه السلام است و نیز نام پادشاهیست که تاتارخان و مغولخان پسران او بوده اند آلنجیک بسکون
و کاف و کسر جیم نام قبل خان نجد سیم چنکیزخانست و بلغت مغول بمعنی رعیت پرور باشد و در بعضی تواریخ مسطور است که
جد سیم را آلنجیک کویند آلوج بضم لام و سکون جیم بترکی رومی نام درخت جلی باشد که بفارسی آنرا کوجه کویند
و بعربی عویج نامند آلیس بکسر لام و سکون سین مهمله بترکی رومی بمعنی دور ضد نزدیک بود آلیک بلغت مغولی الموغ
آل یانکاغ بسکون لام و نون و غین معجمه و فتح یای حطی و کاف عجمی مع الامالة بمعنی سرخ روده بود موالمیم ام روزن

50v

کویند آناج آقول یعنی آهن که بهنکرآن برکوبن کاو و تبه زمین را بدان شیار کند و طا خین با جوب منبر کیت
و بغلر جوخا کی باشد که نشانه تیر را بدان نصب کنند و تخت پادشاهان را نیز کویند و بیك حصه از نهپ و جهان را نیز حصه
که هر قسمی بیست جهار آناج بود و آن افق کیاه دوای بود ازرك بکسر میم و فتح زای هوز و سکون کاف و تر که بر کی
مطلق کوله باشد که آنرا بعربی مخدبه صغار ربقار ثره خوانند از کلی بترکی روی چیزی را اطراد کویند و بکسر زای هوز
نامند که طفل خود را از شیر باز نکرفته باشد امك بترکی روی یعنی پیچ و نرحت باشد و آن مخفف ایکاك است
یعنی شرایت پیچ و نرحت املوك بسکون میم و کاف و ضم لام پوست کوسا له مرده است که از کاه پر کرده نزدیك مادر
تا تصور کوسا له خود کرده شیر دهد امیدوك بکسر میم و نون و ضم دال بلغت مغولی بمعنی پیچ و نرحت بود مع النون الاشتقاق
آنکا ق غ بسکون نون و کاف عجمی یاد کردن و فهمیدن و متذکر شدن آنکری یاد کرد و فهمید آنکمی و قیاد کردیم
و فهمیدیم آنکار و آنکا دور یاد میکند و میفهمد و آنکار بمعنی فاعل و مصدر نیز می آید آنکماید و یا هیکند و نکر است
و میفهمد و میفهمید است آنکمان و آنکار غان و آنکا دور غان یاد میکند و میفهمید آنکای که یاد کند یا فهمید
می آید آنکل آنکیل مفرد مخاطب از فعل امر آنکا و آنکا غیل مفرد مخاطب از فعل نهی آنکینك و آنکینکیر و آنکینکلار جمع مخاطب
از فعل امر آنکا نك و آنکا نکیز و آنکا نکلار جمع مخاطب از فعل نهی آنکمان و آنکا سن یاد میکنم و میفهمم آنکا میدور یاد
میکنم و نکرده ام و نفهمیده ام آنکامین و آنکا رمین و آنکا دور مین و آنکا رام یاد میکنم و میفهمم آنکیب و
آنکیبان و آنکیش یاد کرده و فهمیده چنانکه فضولی بغدادی با ملای آلروشیه کوید الشاهد علی الاول المعنی
الاول شعر لحظه لحظه لیبنك آنکیب بو جعك افغانلار قطره قطره ساچیلور دیده لرمدین تا ملار آنکیشانك یاد کرده و فهمیده
آنکا سن یاد میکند و میفهمد من اشار الطیر بالمعنی الثانی شعر آنکلاکیم سوز اوزکا معنی اوزکا دور معنی آنکا سن اوک
شاغل سوز کادور و بمعنی فاعل و مصدر نیز هم می آید آنکا یی یاد کردنش و نکردنش و فهمیدنش و نفهمیدنش آنکمادین
از یاد کردن و یاد نکرده و از فهمیدن و نفهمیده آنکیب بولماس و آنکا بولماس و آنکماقی بولماس یاد نمیتوان کرد و نمیتوان
فهمید آنکا آلماس یاد نمیتواند کرد و نمیتواند فهمید آنکا آنکا یاد کنان و فهم کنان و بدون تکرار هم مستعملست
و آنکا اسم اشاره نیز باشد یعنی او و آنکای و آنکایین یاد کنم و کند و کنی و بفهمم و بفهمد و بفهمی آنکاق و آنکغای
و آنکغای و آنکالی و آنکالینك یاد کنیم و بفهمیم آنکغلی برای یاد کردن و تا یاد کرده و برای فهمیدن و تا فهمید
آنکغاج چون یاد کرد و کند و فهمید و بفهمد آنکغوچی یاد کننده و فهم کننده آنکغوچه و آنکغو تجه و آنکغالیجه تا یاد
کردن و بقدر یاد کردن و تا فهمیدن و بقدر فهمیدن آنکغوم یاد خواهم کرد و خواهم فهمید آنکغو نك یاد خواهی
کرد و خواهی فهمید آنکغوچی یاد خواهد کرد و خواهد فهمید آنکغولوق یاد کردنی و فهمیدنی آنکغای و آنکای آنکا
و آنکغون و آنکدیلك یاد کند و بفهمد آنکغودیلك و آنکا دیلك یاد کردنی و همچنانکه یاد کند و فهمید و همچنانکه
بفهمد آنکدور تاتق غ مصدر متعدیست بمعنی متذکر ساختن و فهمانیدن و صیغ آن بدستور شوق و لیلی لفظ دو را شتقاق
می یابد آنکلا تاتق غ بسکون نون و کاف عجمی فهمیدن آنکلادی فهمید آنکلا دوق فهمیدیم آنکلادیم و آنکلادینك فهمید
و آنکلار بمعنی فاعل و مصدر نیز می آید آنکلاغان و آنکلاغان و آنکلایدورغان فهم کننده و فهمیده و بمعنی مصدر نیز می
آنکلا و آنکلاغیل مفرد مخاطب از فعل امر الشاهد علی الثانی شعر آنکلا غیل الخطاب ته دین کیم بولار بولماس نفع کرسنکا

51r

آنکلا اول بو جهاندین تخت و جاه دهر آنکلاتما و آنکلاتما غیل مفرد مخاطب از فعل نهی آنکلاتك و آنکلاتکیز و آنکلاتکلار جمع مخاطب
از فعل امر الشاهد علی الاول شعر خانقه شیخی دین بال انمز ناآنکلاتما دوق دیر پیر آنی خوب آنکلاتو را میکا آنکلاتما نك آنکلاتما
و آنکلاتمانکیز و آنکلاتمانکلار جمع مخاطب از فعل نهی آنکلاتمان و آنکلاتماس مین نمی فهمیم الشاهد علی الاول شعر
ای نوای تیلبه کونکلوم دردینی آنکلاتدی دیسام آنچه آیتور دیاو که کیم بیر لفظ آندین آنکلاتمان آنکلاتمایدور مین نمی فهمم
و نفهمیده ام چنانکه بمعنی اول کوید شعر نوای تیلبه مراب تا اول پری کوسیکا یوز لا نمیش ایشیتور مین فغان لیکن
حد یشین آنکلامایدور مین آنکلادیم بن و آنکلادیم بن و آنکلادیدور مین و آنکلادیلم می فهمم آنکلادیم و آنکلاتما نیم فهمید
آنکلاتماغوم نخواهم فهمید آنکلاتب و آنکلاتیان و آنکلاتمیش فهمیده آنکلاتماس نفهمیده بمعنی فاعل و مصدر نیز هم
می آید آنکلاتما دین از فهمیدن و نفهمیده آنکلاتما یی فهمیدنش و نفهمیدنش آنکلاب بولماس و آنکلا بولماس آنکلا
مالیا و لماس نمیتوان فهمید آنکلای آلماس نمیتواند فهمید آنکلابو و آنکلا آنکلا فهم کنان و بدون تکرار هم با جهمی
مستعملست آنکلای و آنکلایین بفهمم و بفهمند و بفهمی الشاهد علی الاول المعنی الاول شعر میا بیچ دهر ایچرا اکیم ایش بیرین
آنکلای بیانك مرزی ایرور هر ذره بینك تا هیو خورشید بین مصحم آنکلاسا ق و آنکلاغای و آنکلا غای بیز و آنکلا
و آنکلالینك بفهمیم آنکلاغلی برای فهمیدن و تا فهمیده آنکلاغاج چون فهمید و بفهمد الشاهد علیه بالمعنی الاول
شعر بود کوز تو تتوم تا ارغان کوز کا اول یوز بهر حدین آنکلاغاج مهر جالین یا دهی پنهان فسود آنکلاغوچی فهم کننده
آنکلاغوچه و آنکلاغوجه و آنکلاغالیجه تا فهمیدن و بقدر فهمیدن آنکلاغوم خواهم فهمید آنکلاغو نك خواهی فهمید آنکلاغو
خواهد فهمید چنانکه در صفه سباره در آغاز کتاب کوید شعر آمیاق هونلا خاجتا طاغو شکیم که اول ایچرا ایتیسا
آنکلاغوشی آنکلاغو لوق فهمیدنی آنکلاغای و آنکلاسا و آنکلادون و آنکلادیلك بفهمد الشاهد علی الرابع شعر
آنکلادیلك او تلو نغ بیزی کونکلوم فنیکلینغ مثلدی موم راکیم کورنا میشتور شعله نینك تا ثیرینی آنکلا ترد یك
و آنکلاغودیلك فهمیدنی و همچنانکه بفهمد آنکلاتما تو غ مع الیا مصدر متعدیست بمعنی فهمانیدن و صیغ آن بدستور
با حروف تا اشتقاق می یابد آنکدیماك بسکون نون و کاف عجمی و کسر دال کین کردن و مترصد شدن آنکدیدی کین کرد آنکدیدوق
کین کردیم آنکدیدیم و آنکدیدیدور کین میکند و آنکدیر بمعنی فاعل و مصدر نیز هم می آید آنکدیمایدور کین میکند و نکرده است
آنکدیکان و آنکدیرکان و آنکدیدورکان کین کننده و کین کرده و بمعنی مصدر نیز هم می آید آنکدیکیل مفرد مخاطب
از فعل امر آنکدیما و آنکدیماکیل مفرد مخاطب از فعل نهی آنکدینك و آنکدینکیر و آنکدینکلار جمع مخاطب از فعل امر آنکدیما
و آنکدیمانکیز و آنکدیمانکلار جمع مخاطب از فعل نهی آنکدیمان و آنکدیماس مین کین نمیکنم آنکدیمین و آنکدیر مین و
آنکدیدورمین و آنکدیرام کین میکنم آنکدیریم و آنکدیماکیم کین کردنم آنکدیماکوم کین نخواهم کرد آنکدیب و آنکدیکان
و آنکدیمیش کین کرده چنانکه در لیلی مجنون در وصف مجنون کوید الشاهد علی الاول شعر خلوتدا آنکا بو نوع لار
آنکدیب آنا سی کیندا این میش و نیز در فنا یم المحبه در ذکر خواجه ابو الوفای خوارزمی کوید که او غزی آنکدیب لار زینك
دستارین سر آب دهر الشاهد علی الثانی شعر اسرو یا الغان و علاحی دین کو میش اریدهان غنیم آنکدیبان پرجیه
توشتی ایلکیما او سولك کینه آندیشا نك کین کرده آندیماس کین نمیکند و بمعنی فاعل و مصدر منفی هم می آید آندیماس
کین کردنش و نکردنش آنکدیمادین از کین کردن و کین نکرده آنکدیب بولماس و آنکدیا بولماس و آنکدیماك اولماس کین

بسوان کرد آنکری والماس کمین بسوا کرد آنکری آنکمی کمین کمان کمین کمان و بدون تکرار هم مستعملست یعنی آنکری
و آنکمیین کمین کمم و کمد و کمجی آنکد یاك و آنکدیلی و آنکدیلیك کمین کمیم آنکمیکالی برای کمین کردن و تا کمین کردن آنکمیکا
چون کمین کرد و کمد آنکمیکوچی کمین کننده آنکمیکوچمی آنکمیکوچه آنکمیکاچه تا کمین کردن و بقصد کمین کردن آنکمیکوم کمین کنم
کرد آنکمیکونك کمین خواهی کرد آنکمیکوسی کمین خواهد کرد آندیکولوك کمین کردن آندیکای و آندیکا و آندیکون و آنکدی
کمین کند آنکدیکودیك و آنکدیدیك کمین کردنی و همچنانکه کمین کند آناتمك بفتح نون بالف کشیده و سکون تای قرشت
بترکی رومی بمعنی قطع کردن است جولیت بود که آنرا بعربی خفی گویند من الجوامد آن بروزن من بترکی رومی مفصل و بند استخوان
بود که آنرا بعربی زند گویند و ابن بفتح الف جمع آنت و آنلار نیز جمع آنت و آن در معنی با فارسی اشتراك دارد آناکا
بفتح نون و کاف عجمی زن مرتبه را گویند که از طفولیت خدمت کسی کرده بمنزله مادر باشد و آنرا آنکه دایناکا هم نامند
و عبارت از زن قابله نیز باشد که بفارسی دایه خوانند و مؤلف رومی ایناکا را بکسر الف مرادف اینی تصور کرده و بمعنی برادر
کوچك نوشته نصیری هم متابعت کرده انکه و انکه لفظ معول مصطلح است آنت بسکون نون و ضم تای قرشت بمعنی
سوگند باشد چنانکه در صبغه سیاره گوید شعر جزم قیلسانك بوایشه پنهانی آنت ایچیب این ایلانسانك آنی
آنتوتاك بسکون نون و ضم تای اول و فتح ثانی بالف کشیده بلغت مغول بمعنی شیرین بود آنجا و آنجه بسکون نون که
جیم یعنی آنقدر چنانکه گوید شعر خط و خال حسرتیدین آنجه اشکیم آقتی کیم ٭ هر کوزوم تونتی غبار و هر کوزوم کا توشتی
خال انجق بسکون نون و قاف و فتح جیم بترکی رومی بمعنی همان باشد چنانکه فضولی گوید ملامة الرومیه شعر
سنده مجنون دین فزون عاشقلیغ استعدادی وار ٭ عاشق صادق منم مجنونك انجق آدی وار انجیلاین بسکون نون و کسر
جیم و یای حطی و فتح لام بالف کشیده بمعنی آنچنان باشد آندا بسکون نون و فتح دال بالف کشیده و آنده بروزن خنده قبیله
گویند که دختر میگیرند چنانکه قودا قبیله را نامند که دختر میدهند و همچنانکه در میان اتراك روم و عجم مصطلح است که
در مقام بحث همدیگر را برادر و خال و عم میگویند در میان مغولیه و اتراك عادت آنست که یکدیگر را انده گویند چنانکه
در تاریخ وصاف مذکور است که شاهزادگان خون ز رخوردند و همدیگر را انده گفتند و در تاریخ رشیدی نیز ذکر شده که
ملازمان شخص را اندا گفتندی اندا آنداغی یعنی آنجاوی آنداغین یعنی آنجایی را چنانکه گوید شعر دیابو عالملدا اول آی
خوب جنت داغ کورنامیش مین آنداغی ایاریك یوزدا سونداغی خوب آنداق بروزن چارطاق بمعنی آنچنان باشد الشاهد
علیه شعر پر ایمیش جان الکدی اندا قیم ٭ ایدیکیم سلیدی آلا دینیلا یاردور شکر آب اندوز بسکون
نون و فتح های هوز و ضم دال نام درخت پلکوش است که آنرا بلبان از الطبرابن و قطشامی و نخل شامی گویند نام جمیع آلبها
و مرده هاست و گویند که جانوران نوا سود دارد آندر بقبر کی رومی جانوریست که از کرك و کفتار میزاید و آنرا سرلان نیز گویند
آندین یعنی از و آنیز و انیزین یعنی بی او چنانکه گوید الشاهد علی الثانی شعر دوست لار بوکیجه واقف بولونکوز کیم جفا
انیزین شفقته جانیم تن اول دین تاریخ بیت انشته بکسر نون و سکون شین قرشت و فتح تای قرشت بترکی رومی شوهر خواهر بود انغا
بسکون نون و لام و فتح غین معجمه یکنوع تیریست بزرگتر از تیر متعارف که سکان آن پهن و بزرك و مخصوص شکار وحوش باشد
انقتار بفتح نون و تای قرشت و سکون قاف و رای مهمله بترکی رومی کلید بود که آنرا بعربی مفتاح و مقلاد گویند انقره
بروزن نیزه بترکی رومی بمعنی سکار و شکار و نکالیف دیوانیست انقوت و انقودیکنوع مرغابیست از غاز کوچکتر و از اردك

بزرکتر

بزرکتر و ابلق از سفیدی و سیاهی و سرخی مایل بزردی و گوشت آن گرم و تر است و آنرا عقوقت نیز گویند و بعربی نحام خوانند
انك بسکون نون و کاف عجمی بمعنی عقل و فهم باشد آنکا اسم اشاره است یعنی باو و بمعنی با یکدیگران هم آمده چنانکه در فصل
آنکلاق یاد کرده شد آنکاجه یعنی تا باو آنکیسز بکسر نون و سکون زای هوز آنکیزین بکسر حین و سکون نون بمعنی بی
او و بمعنی بی عقل و نافهم الشاهد علی الاول شعر لبینك جواسیدا کیم وعده قیلدی انکسیزین ٭ یوق ایسه عمرایده ثمر سیدا
الدار اماندا ٭ دویم بمعنی نادان و غافل بود انکلاق فهم و ادراك را گویند انکار بسکون نون اول و رای مهمله و فتح کاف
عجمی و نون ثانی بالف کشیده بترکی رومی بمعنی کیاهیست انکلر بترکی رومی مفاصل عظام و بندهای استخوان بود انوك بروزن
سبك بترکی رومی بچه سباع و کلاب و وحوش باشد آنکیمز بسکون نون و زای هوز و بکسر کاف عجمی مع الامالة مجاز
...اعتبار را گویند که حاصل آن نابود شده و نشانه آن بر زمین مانده باشد آنلار یعنی ایشان و آنها و آنرا آلار نیز
نون هم گویند چنانکه در این شعر صنعه سیاره گوید و هر دو قسم شعر شاه الا بزه کوپ ییلا باجا انلار آنجه بوتون
کیم کان ایستب انلار آنی یعنی ایشان را چنانکه در سدّ سکندری در صفت خواجه خضر شاه از سکندر بهر آب حیات اولوشا
...ش گوید شعر دماغ غنچه خفت تاپیب یردی بولك قولاغ شا الماس ایردی بنفشه غه اول آنی بوجهت
خطا ایلادی که شه بو یروغیندین ابا ایلادی ٭ و لفظ آن در ابتدا شعر شاه و بعضی مسبوق است که پیشتر
شده و نیز گفته شعر نی تابیغ خال که هر بیت کیجه سی تیغ الی قویماش بزلیلن شتاب ایله آندین کولك الحق
نفره مایرب ٭ یعنی چه سخت خالیست که در شب هجر تو برای شایش کردن عمگساران اهل زمین از اشك و اندوه و اهل
نفره مایرب و مؤلف رومی لفظ آنرا در شعر سد سکندری و لفظ ایلین در شعر ثانی از نسخه سقیمی این بروزن طنین خوانده و
نوشته که بمعنی از برای آن و اشعار مزبوره را شاهد آورده و نصیری این را از تالیفه وی این بکسر الف و فتح نون اول
و سکون نون ثانی خوانده و نوشته که با سلوب عبارت بمعنی اندیشه است که رومیان میگویند و هم تشمر نیز استعمال
نموده لفظ و معنی هر دو اختراعیست آینك بتنهائی بمعنی او نیست اما در صورت ترکیب و اضافه بمعنی او می آید چنانکه در
اینك دیك یعنی مثل او و اینك بیله یعنی با او و اینك کیم یعنی از اوست و در بعضی جا بمعنی رابطه مفعول نیز استعمال میشود
چنانکه گوید شعر بو حسن و ناز ایرور دیکیم استهانی یوق نینك ٭ بر نفس یوق کیم کوکولدا یوز بلاسی یوق اینك
مع الواو من المشتقات آولاماق بسکون واو و فتح لام در معنی دارد اول شکار کردن دویم مالیدن بود که آنرا بعربی
دلك گویند و مالیدن بمعنی تطلیه را سهی تکالك میگویند آولادی شکار کرد و مالید آولاده و قیشکار کرده و مالید
آولادو آولایدور شکار میکند و میمالد و آولا بمعنی فاعل و مصدر نیز می آید چنانکه در مقامات شاه تر دم از جیر ... ایل
در صفحه مرد و نامرد بمعنی شکار کردن گوید شعر سو نقوراکر تیز نانی آولاد کوبی ٭ تیوزنی الکه پرداغی چیتماس ونی ...
جمع شکار هم آمده اولانایدورشکار میکند و نکرده است و میمالد و میمالیده است آولاغان و آولارغان و آولابدور غاشکار کند
و شکار کرده و مالنده و مالیده و بمعنی مصدر هم می آید آولاو آولاغیل مفرد مخاطب از فعل امر آولاماو آولانا مفرد
مخاطب از فعل نفی الشاهد علی الاول بالمعنی الثانی شعر کونكلا رنیك کیم مستخواب او دایر صر کوپ و لاماء هر باری
اوتیقوغه یار غان فتنه نی او یغاتما کوپ آولانك حا آولانکیز و آولانکلار جمع مخاطب از فعل امر آولاماتك و آولاماتکیز و آولاماتکلار
جمع مخاطب از فعل نفی آولانان و آولاماس مین شکار میکنم و میمالم آولای مین و آولارمین و آولامیدرمین و آولارام شکار میکنم

ومیمالم آولاریمو آولاناغیم شکار کردیم و مالیدیم آولاماغوم شکار نخواهم کرد و نخواهم مالید آولاسانکیز شکار
کنید و بمالید آولاب و آولابان و آولامیش شکار کرده و مالیده و شاهد بر اول از بمعنی ثانی در نسایم المحبه بتقریب ذکر
مشایخ صوفیه گوید که شیخ ابراهیم آجری خشت آولابتور و مؤلف رومی آولابتور را در این نسخ اولاتیب توز بفتح وا
وکسر تای قرشت خوانده و بمعنی خر کرده لفظ اختراعیست آولامیشانک شکار کرده و مالیده آولاماس شکار نکند
و نمیمالد و بمعنی فاعل مصدر منفی هم می آید آولامابی شکار کردنش و نکردنش و مالیدنش و نمالیدنش آولامادین از شکار
کردن و شکار نکرده و از نمالیدن و نمالیده آولاب بولماس و آولاسا بولماس و آولاماق اولماس شکار نتوان کرد
و نمیتوان مالید آولای آلماس شکار نمیتواند کرد و نمیتواند مالید آولایو و آولای و لای شکار کنان و مالیده مالیده
و بمعنی بدون تکرار هم مستعملست آولای و آولاین شکار کنم و کند و کنی و بمالم و بمالد و بمالی آولاساق و آولاغای
آولاغایمیز و آولابی شکار کنیم و بمالیم آولاغلی برای شکار کردن و تا شکار کرده و برای مالیدن و تا مالیده آولاغاچ
چون شکار کرد و کند و چون مالید و بمالد آولاغونچی شکار کننده و مالنده آولاغونچه و آولاغانچه و آولاغونچه
تا شکار کردن و بقدر شکار کردن و تا مالیدن و بقدر مالیدن آولاغوم شکار خواهم کرد و خواهم مالید آولاغو
شکار خواهی کرد و خواهی مالید آولاغوسی شکار خواهد کرد و خواهد مالید آولاغولوق شکار کردنی و مالیدنی
آولاغای و آولاسانلار و آولاسونلار و آولادیلر شکار کنند و بمالند آولاغودیلر و آولاردیلر شکار کردند و همچنانکه شکار کنند و مالند
و همچنانکه بمالد آولاتماق مع التاء مصدر متعدیست هم بمعنی یعنی شکار فرمودن و مالانیدن و صیغ آن بتجوید
شوق اول الحروف تا اشتقاق می یابد آولانماق مع النون مصدر انفعالست همان بمعنی شکار شدن می آید و صیغ آن با
نون اشتقاق می یابد آولاشماق مع الشین مصدر مفاعله است همان بمعنی باهم شکار کردن می آید و صیغ آن با شین
اشتقاق می یابد آوونماق بضم واو و سکون نون تسلی یافتن چنانکه در باب همدیم از حیرة الابرار در وصف بهار در حق
گوید شعر غنچه طفل ایشی آوونماق بولوبتور اونیا ماغی بارچا باشونماق بولوبتور آوونداپی تسلی یافت آووندوقتسلی یا
آوونور و آوونادور تسلی می یابد و آوونور بمعنی فاعل و مصدر نیز می آید آوونغان و آوونورغان و آوونادورغان
تسلی یابنده و تسلی یافته و بمعنی مصدر نیز می آیند آوون و آوونغیل مفرد مخاطب فعل امر آوونما و آوونماغیل مفرد مخاطب
نهی آوونونک و آوونونکیز و آوونونکلار جمع مخاطب فعل امر آوونمانک و آوونمانکیز و آوونمانکلار جمع مخاطب فعل نهی
آوونمان و آوونماس مین تسلی نمی یابم آوونماسمان و آوونالماسمین و آوونالمایدورمین تسلی نمیتوانم یافت الشاهد
علی الاول شعر زلفنو قدینک فرقتیدین نیچه قیلسام کشت باغ آوونالمان چمن نینک سنبل و شمشادیدین آوونامین
آوونامین و آوونادورمین و آوونورمن تسلی می یابم آوونوم و آووندیم تسلی یافتیم آوونماغوم تسلی نخواهم یافت آوونمامین
آوونماغوسی تسلی نیابم الشاهد علی الثانی شعر هجر بیتسا ... دیدیم آوونماغای مین بولیلک یا بنیاد ایرمیش ایچماک
باده گلفام تلخ آوونوب و آوونوبان و آوونوبمیش تسلی یافته آوونمیشانک تسلی یافته آوونماس تسلی نمی یابد و بمعنی فاعل
و مصدر منفی هم می آید آوونماسی تسلی یافتنش و نیافتنش آوونمادین از تسلی نیافتن و تسلی نیافته آوونوب بولماس و آوونا
و آوونماق اولماس تسلی نمیتوان یافت آوونا آلماس تسلی نمیتواند یافت آوونا آوونا تسلی یابان یابان و بدون
تکرار هم بمعنی مستعملست آوونای و آوونایین تسلی یابم و بیابد و بیابی آوونساق و آوونغای و آوونغای بیز

و آوونالی و آوونالیلار تسلی بیابیم آوونغالی برای تسلی یافتن و تا تسلی یافته آوونغاچ چون تسلی یافت و بیابد آوونغونچی تسلی یابنده
آوونغونچه و آوونغونچا و آوونغانچا تا تسلی یافتن و بقدر تسلی یافتن آوونغوم تسلی خواهم یافت آوونغولوق تسلی خواهی یافت آوونغوسی
تسلی خواهد یافت آوونغولوق تسلی یافتنی آوونغای و آوونسالار و آوونسونلار و آووندیلار تسلی یابند آوونوپ دیلر و
آوونوردیلر تسلی یافتند و همچنانکه تسلی بیابند آووتماق بضم واو و سکون تای قرشت مصدر متعدیست یعنی تسلی دادن
آووت و آووتغیل مفرد مخاطب فعل امر چنانکه گوید الشاهد علی الاول شعر هجران دین اسرو ملامت ... منکا مهی شعله
برخطه کونکلومنی آووت آووتونک و آووتونکیز و آووتونکلار جمع مخاطب فعل امر الشاهد علی الاول شعر ای نکار
اهلی اولدای کونکلینی خوشحال توتونک کر هلاکیم خبری ... آووتورکیم آووتونک و شاهد بر ثانی در تهانی محبوب القلوب
در وصف کوشناب گوید شعر احباب بسیکت تیکی غنیمت توتونکوز اوزنی تاریلیغ محنتی دین قوتقو تونکوز آبی هوا و ت
حسدین او تونکوز هر نوع ایله اوزنی نیچه کون آووتونکوز آووتمانک و آووتمانکیز و آووتمانکلار جمع مخاطب فعل نهی الشاهد
علی الثانی شعر ایل ملامتی نینک جانی ... قصدیجان کونکلومنی ... آووتمانکیز و باقی صیغ
بهمین منوال با حروف تا اشتقاق می یابد آووجلاماق بضم واو و سکون جیم بکف دست گرفتن آووجلادی بکف گرفت
آووجلادوق بکف گرفتیم آووجلادی و آووجلادیلار بکف میگیرد آووجلادور بمعنی فاعل و مصدر نیز می آید آووجلاغان بکف گیرنده
و گرفته است آووجلاغان و آووجلادورغان و آووجلایدورغان بکف گیرنده و بکف گرفته و بمعنی مصدر نیز می آید آووجلا و آووجلاغیل
مفرد مخاطب فعل امر آووجلاما و آووجلاماغیل مفرد مخاطب فعل نهی آووجلانک و آووجلانکیز و آووجلانکلار جمع مخاطب فعل امر آووجلاما
و آووجلامانکیز و آووجلامانکلار جمع مخاطب فعل نهی آووجلامان و آووجلامامن بکف نمیگیرم آووجلای مین و آووجلاپ مین و
آووجلاپ دورمین و آووجلارمن بکف میگیرم آووجلادیم بکف گرفتم آووجلاماغوم بکف نخواهم گرفت آووجلاب و
آووجلابان و آووجلامیش بکف گرفته الشاهد علی الاول شعر ... قلم ... آووجلاپ که ...
کیشیکا بو نوع دست آووچ آووجلامیشانک بکف گرفته آووجلاماس بکف نمیگیرد و بمعنی فاعل و مصدر منفی هم می آید آووجلاماسی
بکف گرفتنش و نگرفتنش آووجلامادین از بکف گرفتن و بکف نگرفته آووجلاب بولماس و آووجلاسا بولماس و آووجلاماق اولماس
بکف نمیتوان گرفت آووجلای آلماس بکف نمیتواند گرفت آووجلای و آووجلای ... بکف بگیرم آووجلاغای
برای بکف گرفتن و تا بکف گرفته آووجلاغاچ چون بکف گرفت و بگیرد آووجلاغونچی بکف گیرنده آووجلاغونچه و آووجلا...
و آووجلاغانچه تا بکف گرفتن و بقدر بکف گرفتن آووجلاغوم بکف خواهم گرفت آووجلاغولوق بکف خواهی گرفت
آووجلاغوسی بکف خواهد گرفت آووجلاغولوق بکف گرفتنی آووجلاغای و آووجلاسالار و آووجلاسونلار و آووجلادیلار بکف بگیرند
آووجلادیلار و آووجلاردیلار بکف گرفتند و همچنانکه بکف بگیرد آووجلاتماق مع التاء مصدر متعدیست یعنی بکف گیرانیدن
و صیغ آن با حروف تا اشتقاق می یابد آووجلانماق مع النون مصدر انفعالست یعنی بکف گرفته شدن و صیغ آن با نون
اشتقاق می یابد آووجلاشماق مع الشین مصدر مفاعله است یعنی با یکدیگر بکف گرفتن و صیغ آن با شین اشتقاق می یابد
من المجرد آو دو معنی دارد اول بمعنی صید و شکار باشد دویم شخص را گویند الشاهد علیه شعر ... عشق
الیکه استلا بولغای ... آوتوغ بسکون واو و نون و جیم ضم تا ...
کمان ... الشاهد علیه شعر ... آوتوغ ...

آل دیمان میلغا بحیلق و آنرا اوتوبچ بضم واو وشوچ نیز خوانند تُوچی مینا مرا نامند آورفات بسکون واو و نون
و کاف عجمی وفتح رای مهمله بمعنی پوش و نورانی بود و هوای صاف را نیز گویند آولاق شکارگاه آووچ بضم واو و کاف
چنانکه گوید شعر آووچ تا قادرین اوزا حوالیما نجحیرین رسیدی کونکلوم ایرور بو اصول ایله رتامن آووچ اوبونی
باصطلاح رومیه یکنوع قمار است و آن بدین نمط است که چیزی را مشت گرفته بپرسند که جفت است یا طاق هرکه مطابق
واقع بگوید بلخته باشد آوورت بضم واو وسکون رای مهمله وتای قرشت پری دهر باشد که آنرا بعربی شدق خوانند
چنانکه در سد سکندری در وصف لشام گوید شعر چیچن تاپسا یز ناالحکا سیغار نی تا لسا آوورتیغه یلرین یغار
آوول بضم واو وسکون لام مرضعی را گویند که ایلات در آنجا جمعیت کرده نشیمن نمایند و آن محرف حولی است که در عربی
بمعنی محوطه کوچک وگرداگرد سرا باشد آوولتاش همسایه را نامند آوونجاق بسکون نون وفتح جیم چیزی که بدان دل
فریفته تسلی دهند لاادری شعر بو فرمان دین سینوق کونکلوم سوینیدی بو معنی لیق آوونجاقدین آوونیدی
مع الها آهه آینه فولادی که در جنگ بر پیشانی اسب بندند چنانکه در سد سکندری در مدح بابر
گوید شعر مکر برق کاه شهنشه هوش آنکا آهه کوزکو بیر تخشی ... فرماید شعر یارنی
آهه یوزینک مدعا وتزیش ... کوزکو شعر چاقیب بر آوی آهه لار ارا ایشاری حکیم ...
باره لار دکیشاری ثم الیاء المثناة التحتانیة ایا ماق بفتح یای با الف کشیده بمعنی دریغ داشتن بود آیادی دریغ داشت آیادی
دریغ داشتی الشاهد علیه شعر موسوی که مشاشینی عقل ایله توزدونک فنا بولیدا یادنیک بر ... عقل مشا
آیادوق دریغ داشتیم آیاردا آیادور دریغ میدارد و ایار بمعنی ماضی مضارع نیز می آید آیامادور دریغ نمیدارد
و نداشته است آیا قان و آیا رغان و آیادیغان دریغ دارنده و دریغ داشته و بمعنی مستقبل نیز می آید آیا و آیاغیل
مفرد مخاطب از فعل امر یا کفن ... چنانکه دریغ مکن گفته شود آیامانا و آیاماغیل مفرد مخاطب از فعل نفی آیامانک
و آیامانکیز و آیامانکلار جمع مخاطب از فعل امر آیاماسانک و آیامانکیز و آیامانکلار جمع مخاطب از فعل نفی آیامادی و آیامادیم دریغ نمیدارم الشاهد
علی الاول شعر آیاغینکا بو که ملمان شار ... خاک بی دین او یا لورمین ای حکیم ملمانی آیاچین و آیارمین و
آیادورمین و آیارام دریغ میدارم الشاهد علی الثانی من حسینی شعر اوز فولامندین ... او نونکوچو آیارمین نی تانک
... ابلچرله دیبانک سوز لعل شکربار ایله آیادیم آیاماغیم دریغ داشتم آیاماغوم دریغ نخواهم داشت آیاب و
آیامان و آیامیش دریغ داشته الشاهد علی الاول شعر ... چیقتوابنانک سلکا ... دریغ ... تکار ...
آیاب ایرکینا ... اولعاده و در فصل بیست وششم از محبوب القلوب در وصف تجار گوید که نفیس اجناسی آیاچا یان کیما
آیامیشانک دریغ داشته آیاماس دریغ نمیدارد و بمعنی ماضی و مستقبل منفی هم می آید آیاماسی دریغ داشتنش و دریغ
نداشتنش آیامادینا نه دریغ داشتن و دریغ نداشته آیاب بولماس و آیا سا بولماس و آیاماق ... دریغ نمیتوان داشت آیای آلماس
دریغ نمیتواند داشت آیای آبای دریغ داشته دریغ داشته و بدون تکرار هم بهمین معنی مستعملست آیای آیامین دریغ
دارم و دارد و دارید و داشته آیامان و آیامایین دریغ ندارم وندارد وندارید ونداشته چنانکه در شعبه ستاره ...
اخیر گوید شعر آیامای آندین ... هیچ ایشته کما الخاصه کرمانک آیاناق و آیاغانه و آیاغای و آیلی و آیالیلک
دریغ دارید آیافلی برای دریغ داشتن وتا داشته آیاغاچ چون دریغ داشت ودارد آیاغوچی دریغ دارنده الخ

و آیاغونجه و آیاغانجه تا دریغ داشتن وبعد از دریغ داشتن آیاغوم دریغ خواهم داشت آیاغونک دریغ خواهی
داشت آیاغونجی دریغ خواهد داشت آیاغولوق دریغ داشتنی آیاغای و آیاسا و آیاسون و آیادیک دریغ دارد آیا
غوبیک آیلدی دریغ داشتی و همچنانکه دریغ طرح آیتماق بکسر یای حطی و تای قرشت آیتماق بجزای حطی
کفتن ... الشاهد علی الاول شعر ایتیلیدین کوردوم آنجه غصه کیم منیکا دین ... ایتماق بولماس نیهد امر
بولسا ایتیل آیتی کفت آیتوق بسکون یا و آیتوق بکسر یا کفتیم الشاهد علی الاول ... مجنون شعر ... آیتوق ...
سین ... بو ... الشاهد علی الثانی من سد سکندری شعر ... سوز
آیتیب ... آنکا ... آیتوق ... آیتور و آیتادور میگوید الشاهد علی الاول شعر دیبام ...
اهلینی کورکانلیک که ظالم ... کونکول آیتور کوزای ... وآیتور بمعنی فاعل ...
نیز می آید چنانکه بمعنی کوینده کوید شعر ... آنکا ... سوزدم آیتور ...
و بمعنی کفتن کوید شعر ... آیتور ... آغزینک ... یخشی ... سوز ... و
در منشات آمده که چون سیز ... آیتور ... آیتماید و ... میکوید و
آیتغان و آیتقان و آیتادورغان کوینده و کفته الشاهد علی الاول شعر تا دیدیم ... ایلاکه
کم آیتیغان ... بولمیش ... وشاهد ... بمعنی کفته ... المحبة ... ابو عبدالله کوید که
... که سیزنینک بو آیتادورغان سوز لا دینکیزدین او ... و بمعنی مستقبل نیز می آید چنانکه شاهد
اول را کوید شعر ... که ... آیتغاندیک ... ایمرا ... آیت
آیت و آیتغیل مفرد مخاطب از فعل امر الشاهد علی الاول شعر ای صبا حالیم ... سوزنی ... آیت بیغلادیم
... آیت الشاهد علی الثانی شعر ای ... آیتغیل
... آیتماق ... آیتمانک و آیتمانکیز و آیتمانکلار جمع مخاطب
از فعل امر آیتمانک و آیتمانکیز و آیتمانکلار جمع مخاطب از فعل نفی آیتماس میکوید آیتالماس نمیتواند کفت آیتالماسین
نمیتوانم کفت الشاهد علی الثانی شعر ... آیتا آلماس مین ... آیتا آلماسمن
آیتا سیم آیتورمین و آیتادورمین و آیتورام میکویم آیتماغوم و آیتماغیم کفتم آیتماغوم نخواهم کفت
آیتامین و آیتورمین و آیتادورمین میکوئی چنانکه شاهد ... المحبة در ذکر خواجه عبدالخالق غجدوانی
کوید که ... سین آیتاسین آیتیبو آیتیبادی
آیتمیش کفته آیتمیشانک کفته آیتماس نمیکوید و بمعنی ماضی و مستقبل منفی هم می آید آیتماسی کفتنش و نکفتنش
آیتمادین ... آیتیب ... آیتا آلماس نمیتواند کفت آیتا
آیتا کونانکوبان و بدون تکرار هم بمعنی مستعملست آیتای و آیتامین بکویم و بکوید و بکوئی آیتاق و آیتغلیز و آیتغای
و آیتالی و آیتالینک بکوییم آیتغلی برای کفتن و تا کفته آیتماج چون کفت و کوید آیتغوچی کوینده آیتغوچه و آیتغونجه و
آیتغانجه تا کفتن و بعد کفتن آیتغوم خواهم کفت الشاهد علیه شعر عرض ایتا لار ... آیکیجهان باد
آیتغوم ... آیتا المغوم ... چنانکه در ... داشته کوید

شعر آنما قنه اگرچه تا لغوم بوق اول آیتیفا نمحه آیتا آلغوم بوق آیتغونك نخواهی گفت آیتا آلماغونك آیتا آلغونك بوق
گفتنت ممکن نخواهد بود آیتغوسی خواهد گفت آیتا آلماغوسی آیتا آلغوسی بوق گفتنش ممکن نخواهد بود آیتغولوق
گفتنی آیتماغ آیتلو آیتیلو آیتون و آیتید بیك بگوید آیتغودیك و آیتوردیك گفتنی و همچنانکه بگوید آیتیشماق
بکسر تا و سکون شین مصدر مفاعله است با هم گفتن و مکالمه کردن آیتیشساق با هم مکالمه کنیم الشاهد علیه
شعر تا یمادیم اهل جهان یچرا آیدان همدمی کیم زمان آیسوچ ینیچرکا آیتیشساق دیبی و باقی صیغ بدستور شود
با شین اشتقاق می یابد آیتیلماق مع الکلام مصدر انفعالات یعنی گفته شد چنانکه گوید شعر وصلی دین دوی
سوز آیتای کیم ایماس ممکن و لیك خالی از عشق هم این طرز زمان آیتیلماغی آیتیلادی گفته میشود الشاهد علیه
شعر غریب قصه این عشق کیم تو کا نمادی هیچ اگرچه بو لغالی عالم بناسی آیتیلادی آیتیلیب گفته شده الشاهد
علی الاول شعر نامه و قاصد چه نامایاس نوانی دردی شرح کیم توکا نماس مجنبتی فی از لیب فی آیتیلیب آیتیلماغان
گفته نشده آیتیلغولوق گفته شدنی چنانکه گوید در سکندر نامه شعر دیدی کیم بو یراتیشور قیم تیلغولوق
بو آیتیلماغان نکته آیتیلغولوق و باقی صیغ بهمین سیاق با لام اشتقاق می یابد آیرماق بکسر یا و سکون را و قرشت
مصدر متعدیست یعنی جدا کردن و بسکون یا نیز استعمال میشود آیردی جدا کرد آیردوق جدا کردیم آیرادور
آیرادور جدا میکند و آیرغوچی بمعنی فاعل و مصدر نیز می آید آیرغان و آیرغان و آیرادورغان جدا کننده و جدا کرده
و بمعنی مصدر نیز می آید آیر و آیرغیل مفرد مخاطب از فعل امر آیرما و آیرماغیل مفرد مخاطب از فعل نهی آیرینك و
آیرینکیز و آیرینکلار جمع مخاطب از فعل امر آیرمانك و آیرمانکیز و آیرمانکلار جمع مخاطب از فعل نهی آیرمان و آیرماس من
جدا میکنم آیرامین و آیرور مین و آیرادور مین و آیرورام جدا میکنم آیرور من و آیرماغیم جدا کردنم آیرماغوم
جدا نخواهم کرد آیریب و آیریبان و آیریش و آیرمیش جدا کرده آیرمیشانك جدا کرده آیرماس جدا نمیکند
و بمعنی فاعل و مصدر منفی هم می آید آیرماسی جدا نکردنش و کردنش آیرمادین از جدا کردن و جدا نکرده آیریب
بولماس و آیرماب بولماس و آیرماق و بولماس جدا نمیتوان کرد آیرا آلماس جدا نمیتواند کرد آیرا آیرا جدا کنان جدا کنان
و بدون تکرار هم بهمین معنی مستعملست آیرای و آیرایین جدا کنم و کند و کنی آیرماق و آیرغای و آیرغای سیز و ایرغایلی
و آیرالینك جدا کنیم آیرغالی برای جدا کردن و تا جدا کرده آیرغاچ چون جدا کرد و کند آیرغوچی جدا کنند
آیرغوسیغوسی و آیرغابچه تا جدا کردن و بقدر جدا کردن چنانکه شاهد بن ثلث را بمعنی ثلث در دیباچه گوید
گوید که نصابنه مالعرکا بین ایرغوبچه الیکیم ایدا تا المادی آیرغوم جدا خواهم کرد آیرغونك جدا خواهی کرد
آیرغوسی جدا خواهد کرد آیرغولوق جدا کردنی آیرغای و آیرا او آیرماو آیرسون و آیر دیك جدا کند الشاهد علی
الاول شعر جان نقدین اجل ایرله ههنك ایکی بولیشلا آنداق که تا یب سودی آیرغایلیکی او ایرماق الشاهد علی
الخامس شعر آیرمان ساچینك سندین کونکل دیك اگر بند بند بمعنی مران آیر دیك آیرو دیك و آیرغودیك
جدا کردن و همچنانکه جدا کند الشاهد علی الاول شعر ضعف را اول کوچین سود ایرقولوم نا تیپ رقیب شید دین
آیرغودیك توب قیلما تا هجا دکوج آیریلماق بسکون یا و لام و کسر را مصدر انفعال است یعنی جدا شدن آیریلامیز و آیریلور
و آیریلامیز جدا میشود الشاهد علی الاول شعر فراق کونی دیمای کونز لا را میدی تان نعلا نك شیلور سیز

که بو کون کیتیچین آیریلادین آیریلغوسیدین جدا شدنی و همچنانکه جدا شود الشاهد علیه شعر تو نغالی شیرین لبنادی
شاخ شکر دیکیاد ماغیم دیبکه سوزیاد فدین ای آیریلغودیك تو تیز ماغیم و باقی صیغ بدستور با لام اشتقاق می یابد الشیما
بکسر را و لام و سکون شین قرشت مصدر مفاعلاتست یعنی از هم جدا شدن آیریلیشولار از هم جدا شدند چنانکه در لیلی
مجنون در جواب سلام گوید شعر هم اول کیچه آیریلیشتیلار آیریلیشتی اوز بولماین او ایدا نیه مات آیریلیشما ناز هم
جدا شونه و جدا شده و بمعنی مصدر نیز می آید چنانکه در لیلی مجنون در جواب داستان نوفل گوید که فلان منصوب الادنی
بی پرچین تایم آیریلیشاماداری و باقی صیغ بهمین سیاق با لام و شین اشتقاق می یابد آیرلاماق بکسر را و سکون را قاف قرشت
و فتح لام بمعنی از هم جدا کردن باشد و مجاز اتفرقی و تمیز نیك و بد کنند آیرلادی تفریق کرد آیرلادوق تفریق
کردیم آیرلادو و آیرلادیدور تفریق میکند و آیرلاغوچی بمعنی فاعل و مصدر نیز می آید آیرلاغان و آیرلاغان و آیرلادیغان تفریق کننده
و تفریق کرده و بمعنی مصدر نیز می آید آیرلا و آیرلاغیل مفرد مخاطب از فعل امر آیرلاما و آیرلاماغیل مفرد مخاطب
فعل نهی آیرلانك و آیرلانکیز و آیرلانکلار جمع مخاطب از فعل امر آیرلامانك و آیرلامانکیز و آیرلامانکلار جمع مخاطب
از فعل نهی آیرلامان و آیرلاماس من تفریق نمیکنم آیرلامین و آیرلادور مین و آیرلادیدورمین و آیرلارام تفریق میکنم آیرلادیم
و آیرلاماغیم تفریق کردنم آیرلاماغوم تفریق نخواهم کرد آیرلاب و آیرلابان و آیرلامیش تفریق کرده آیرلامیشانك تفریق کرده
آیرلاماس تفریق نمیکند آیرلاماسی تفریق نکردنش و کردنش آیرلاب بولماس و آیرلاماب بولماس و آیرلاماق و بولماس تفریق نتوان
کرد آیرلای آلماس تفریق نمیتواند کرد آیرلای و آیرلای آیرلای تفریق کنان و بدون تکرار هم بهمین معنی مستعملست آیرلای
و آیرلایین تفریق کنم و کند و کنی آیرلاغای و آیرلاغای سیز و آیرلاغایلی و آیرلالینك تفریق کنیم آیرلاغالی برای تفریق کردن
و تا تفریق کرده آیرلاغاچ چون تفریق کرد و کند آیرلاغوچی تفریق کننده آیرلاغوسیغوسی و آیرلاغابچه تا تفریق
کردن و بقدر تفریق کردن آیرلاغوم تفریق خواهم کرد آیرلاغونك تفریق خواهی کرد آیرلاغوسی تفریق خواهد کرد
آیرلاغولوق تفریق کردنی آیرلاغای و آیرلاسا و آیرلاسون و آیرلادیك تفریق کند آیرلاردیك و آیرلاغودیك
تفریق کردن و همچنانکه تفریق کند آیرلاشماق مع الشین مصدر مفاعلاتست یعنی با هم تفریق کردن و صیغ آن با شین
اشتقاق می یابد آیسلماق بکسر یا و سکون لام هشیار شدن و آن از روبته آیمماق با نون هم گویند آیسلدی هشیار
آیسلدوق هشیار شدیم آیسلور و آیسلادور هشیار میشوند و آیسلوچی بمعنی فاعل و مصدر نیز می آید آیسلغان و آیسلورغان و آیسلادورغان
هشیار شونده و هشیار شده و بمعنی مصدر نیز می آید آیسل و آیسلغیل مفرد مخاطب از فعل امر الشاهد علی الاول شعر
مجرا نما یخود ابسار امرنی نوانی ای شیخ آیچیل آلدی او سواك که مرانك دیماکه آیسل آیسلما و آیسلماغیل مفرد مخاطب
آیسلینك و آیسلینکیز و آیسلینکلار جمع مخاطب از فعل امر آیسلمانك و آیسلمانکیز و آیسلمانکلار جمع مخاطب از فعل نهی آیسلمان و آیسلماس مین و
آیسلامین هشیار میشوم آیسلورمین و آیسلادورمین و آیسلورام هشیار میشوم آیسلدیم و آیسلماغیم هشیار شدم
آیسلماغوم هشیار نخواهم شد آیسلیب و آیسلیبان و آیسلمیش هشیار شده آیسلمیشانك هشیار شده
آیسلماس هشیار نمیشود و بمعنی فاعل و مصدر منفی هم می آید آیسلماسی هشیار نشدنش و شدنش آیسلمادین از هشیار
شدن و هشیار نشده آیسلیب بولماس و آیسلماب بولماس و آیسلماق و بولماس هشیار نمیتوان شد آیسلا آلماس هشیار نمیتواند شد
آیسلا آیسلا هشیار شوان هشیار شوان و بدون تکرار هم بهمین معنی مستعملست آیسلای و آیسلایین هشیار شوم

وشوی آیلیناق و آیلیغاینو آیلیغای‌بز و آیلاسو آیلالینک هشیار شویم آیلیغالی برای هشیار شدن تا
هشیار شده آیلیغاج چون هشیار شد وشود آیلیغوچی هشیار شونده آیلیغوجو آیلیغونر و آیلیغانچه تا
هشیار شدن و بقدر هشیار شدن آیلیغوم هشیار خواهم شد آیلیغونک هشیار خواهی شد آیلیغوسی هشیار
خواهد شد آیلیغولوق هشیار شدنی آیلیغای و آیلاغا آیلیسا و آیلیون و آیلیدیک هشیار شود آیلیور دیلک آیلیغوبک
هشیار شدنی و همچنانکه هشیار شود الشاهد علی الثانی المعنی الاول شعر جام عشقی دین کونکول اول
ابره مست خرابی کیم قیامت بز سیغه تیکر و آیلیغوبیک ایماش آیلدرماق بکسر یا و سکون لام و رای قرشت و ضم
مصدر متعدی یعنی هشیار کردن آیلیدرغای هشیار کند الشاهد علیه شعر مست عشق و لیکن
یرنا کیل پیندای حکیم کیم کونکل آیلدرغای بو می نینک بخودین و باقی صیغ بر همین نهج بدستور شوق و اشتقاق ما
آیلیماق بسکون یا و نون و فتح لام بالف کشیده بمعنی کردیدن باشد و مؤلفین رومی آیلماق را بعضی کردیدن و بعضی
رجوع کردن و مشابه شدن نوشته اند و در باب بهم چیدن این شعر از صیغه سیاره شاهد آورده اند که شعر
پرده لار پیر یکا آیلانغان در انجمن اینچو تور لانغان و بمعنی مشابه شدن این شعر سنگ جسته اند که شعر کوز غیم از ون
تیغین هردم که اشکیم خیلی نینک قطره سی بحر و لدی تیدی آیلانیب تور قانغه هم و بمعنی جمع این شعر منشور و لغت المتحرین
موید مدعا ساخته اند که تا اول جمع غنه قیر نینک سوزی نینک صد تی تمام ظاهر بولوب اول عقیده لار یر آیلانیب
قیر نینک عقیده سیغه کیلدیلار و هم شواهد مذکوره همان بمعنی کردید نست چنانکه کردیدن در لغت فارسی بمعنی
رجوع و نکول و در زدن و سیر کردن است آیلانماق هم افاده آن معانی میکند و موارد استعمال این لفظ با فارسی مطابق است
سوای کردیدن بمعنی شدن که در ترکی با بعضی استعمال نمیشود آیلانغایلار کردیدند چنانکه در سد سکندری در مجادله
سکندر با موران کوید شعر تیشکا کلج سپر یکا آیلاندیلار ایکی قله دیک ایشکا قالدیلار آیلاندوق کردیدیم آیلانود
آیلانمیکرد دالشاهد علی الثانی شعر ای نوائی موجب سرگشته لیک ایرمیش جنون ایچکالی بوی نی هر نیا
باشیم آیلاندی و شوا آیلانماق بمعنی علم و مصدر متعدی آیدا آیلانغاید فرو میکردد و نکردید است آیلانغان و آیلانورغان
آیلانادورغان کردنده و کردیده الشاهد علی الاول والمعنی الاول شعر نیچوک کرقوس و فتح دوری به هر عکسی ایر صار
تا سیغم ایکیدین آیلانغان ایکی‌یاغه با منتش و شاهد معنی ثانی از صیغه سیاره در ذیل آیلانماق مسطور شد آیلان
و آیلانغیل مفرد مخاطب از فصل امر آیلانغل و آیلانغیل مفرد مخاطب از فصل نهی آیلانینک و آیلانینکیز و آیلانینکلار جمع مخاطب از فصل
آیلانمانات و آیلانمانکیز و آیلانمانکلار جمع مخاطب از فصل نهی آیلانغان و آیلانماس مین میکردم آیلانماس و آیلانمیزمین و آیلاندورمن
و آیلانور ایم میکردم آیلانغوسی و اتماغیم کردیدنم آیلانماغیم نخواهم کردید آیلانیب و آیلانیبان و آیلانمیش کردیده
آیلانمیشانک کردیده آیلانماس میکردد و بمعنی علم و مصدر منفی هم می آید آیلانماسی کردیدنش و نکردیدنش آیلانمادین
از کردیدن و نکردیدن آیلانیب بطاس و آیلانسا بطاس و آیلانماقای او لماس نمیتوان کردید آیلانا آلماس نمیتوان کردید آیلانا
آیلانما کردان کردان و صبوحی کرا هم با معنی مستعملست آیلاناقای و آیلانامین بکردم و بکردد و بکردی آیلاناق آیلانغا
و آیلانغاچی و آیلانابی و آیلانا لیسک بکردیم آیلانغالی برای کردیدن و تا کردیدن آیلانغاج چون کردید و تاکرد
آیلانغوچی کرده آیلانغوجو آیلانغونجو و آیلانغانجه تا کردیدن و بقدر کردیدن آیلانغوم خواهم کردید آیلانغونک

خواهی کردید آیلانغوسی خواهد کردید آیلانغولوق کردیدنی آیلانغای و آیلاناو آیلانسا و آیلانسون و آیلانیدیک بکردد چنانکه
در خسرو شیرین در وصف قصر شیرین کوید الشاهد علی الاول شعر رهایت میلدی آندای قصر عاوین که آیلانغای قلمچ
منهدور الشاهد علی الخامس شعر کونکول که نوشتی جنون وحشتی ده بایرکاهی قویوندای آهیم آنینک تیکراسیدا آیلانغای
آیلانغودیک آیلانورلیک کردیدنی و همچنانکه بکردد آیلاشماق مع آلتین مصدر مفاعلیست با هم کردیدن و صیغ آن با
اشتقاق مجاید آیلاندرماق بسکون یا و نون مصدر متعدیست یعنی کردانیدن چنانکه کوید شعر کوک تیکرماتک
آیلاندرماقی یا ستار باشینکا دیماآی دکون ویکیم باشینک ایرور سیاره در شرح و باقی صیغ بدستور لفظ و اشتقاق مجاید
آیلاماق بسکون یا بمعنی کردن باشد آیلادی کرد آیلادینک کردی آیلاما خفیف مکن ای آیلامانکیز نتوانستی کرد
چنانکه کوید شعر تیلیه کونکلونکی نوای ضبط آیلامی آلمادینک امیدی جیهان آندین یلیک هزار عاجزی بار دیک
آیلار و آیلاکردیم آیلار و آیلاسون میکند و آیلار بمعنی حاصل و مصدر هم می آید چنانکه بمعنی مصدر کوید شعر ایما ستود
قصه بلیکیم نام پر حیرت که تقصیر آیلاماس آیلارکا سپیلدا آیلامی آلور مستوان کرد چنانکه در خاتمه لیلی مجنون در وصف شیخ
شعر وجد بشا یغ ابر بصیر بالیغ سیمغ آیلادی آلم جو کهر باپیغ آیلامایدور نکند و نکرده است آیلاکان و آیلارکان
آیلاید کان نکنند و کرده چنانکه شاهد بر اول در معنی ثانی در لیلی مجنون کوید شعر ای حشت ن آیلاکان و طمنکا
یول آن میشام اولمه مانی آکاه و بمعنی مصدر هم می آیند آیلا و آیلاکیل مفرد مخاطب از فصل امر الشاهد علی الاول شعر
کونکلوم کا آیله لعل شکر خند آیله علاج فیلیغان کیچ نیمیغه کلمشد آیله فلاج و آیله بمعنی همچنان هم باشد چنانکه
ذیل جامد مذکور خواهد شد آیلاسا و آیلاماکیل مفرد مخاطب از فصل نهی آیلانک و آیلانکیز و آیلانکلار جمع مخاطب از فصل امر
آیلامانات و آیلامانکیز و آیلامانکلار جمع مخاطب از فصل نهی الشاهد علی الاول شعر ایا یکیلیاد و ستلار آهنت قیلار
انقعالیدین نفس ایمر ازغو شوار آیلامامات آیلامان و آیلاماس مین میکنم آیلامیمین و آیلارمین و آیلارمیزمین و آیلاکسیکیم آیلار ایم
و آیلاماکیم کردم آیلاماکوم نخواهم کرد آیلامیمین و آیلارمین و آیلایدورمن میکنی الشاهد علی الاول شعر جان پیرشیرین
مهلت جام او چون آیلکینکدا ایستغ نزع وقتی تزبت مزار ایتساب آیلارمین نزاع آیلاب و آیلابان و آیلامیش کرده آیلامیشانک
کرده آیلاماس میکند و بمعنی حاصل منفی هم می آید آیلاماسی کردنش و نکردنش آیلامادین از کرده و نکرده آیلاب بطاس
و آیلاسا بولماس و آیلاماقای او لماس نمیتوان کرد آیلای آلماس نمیتوان کرد آیلای و آیلای کیمان کمان الشاهد علی
الاول شعر باشیمنی آلماغان مین شجده شکر آیلار بورین اکر مروخرام جیغه بولسام شایه دیک هر شب سر کتکه
در صنم سکندر کوید شعر طریق آیلار کیردی میدان آل رافهر آیلاب یان قیلدی جولان اوا و لغت ثانی بدون تکرار هم
با معنی مستعملست آیلای و آیلادین بکنم و بکند و بکنی الشاهد علی الاول والمعنی الاول شعر نوا یتو دیدینک کو بیدین اتا
سلامت بول دیا نات آیلای تا مست آیلانات و آیلاکای نیز و آیلاکای و آیلاکیلیب بکنیم چنانکه شاهد بر اول در فرهاد و شیرین
کوید شعر عهدین او لد وک و اول عهد عهد آیلادی عادت آیلاکای ریخته قدم نیز آیلاکاج چون کرد و کند و
بجس کردن چنانکه بمعنی اول کوید شعر تاو نا عیل کو نکلو میزم لغونات محرم ارکم آیلاکاج قوشتی کیم آزاد تیب توسر
دام آیلاکاج آیلاکوچی کننده الشاهد علیه شعر جالیم کیم ایکان آیلاکوچی لیلی غم معروض مین سپید لایشن میلغوچی
دل لار غم معروض آیلاکوجو آیلاکو نجو و آیلاکانجه تا کردن و بقدر کردن آیلاکوم خواهم کرد من سکیک کجی شعر

دیمان کیم آنینک ناری عزم ایلاکوم ثم ابو بیرطکیم دیدبه رزم ایلاکوم ایلاکونک خواهی کرد چنانکه در بیان عنوان آدن کیلکند
بطلب خاقان چین کوید شعر یقین کیم بو سوزنی قبول ایلاکونک شیناز اهل ایساریه تر و ایلاکونک ایلاکو بیسخواهد کرد
ایلاکولوک کوی ایلاکای و ایلاکسا و ایلاکوتی ایلاکونک ایلادیکیند الشاهد علی الاول شعر دیمیش کیلسام نوائی سین ایلاکای
کیلیب کونکلی ایسار ایلاکای کاش الشاهد علی الرابع شعر نابیرلات سین تیلاعشق ایماس بیاز رشوط الیه یم شو اقیلماز ایلاکای
بابری نولی و طرشرط ایلادی لگا و ایلادی آنسا و ایلادی کسون و ایلادی الذیلیک توان کرد الشاهد علی الاول شعر ای نوائی
داغی بولانه سین کونکلونک داغی تکرسینی ضبط ایتسا الارکیم ایلادی انکا آنی ضبط ایلادی بیک و ایلاکو دیک کرد فی چنانکه
بکند ایلایماک مصدر متعدی نیست و معنی کنانیدن و صیغ آن بمنسوبه ای ابلاعت شتقاق بی یابد آینیماک بسکون
یا و کسر نون متغیر الحال شدن و آنرا چاشمال و شاشماک هم کوینید آینیدی متغیر الحال شد آینید ولک متغیر الحال شدهیم
آینیر و آینید و متغیر الحال میشود و آینیر بمعنی فاعل و مصدر هم می آید آینیماید و متغیر الحال نمیشود و نشده است
آینیکان و آینیرکان و آینیدورکان متغیر الحال شونده و شده و بمعنی مصدر هم می آید چنانکه شاهد بر اقول لسان الطیر
در داستان عشق گدا و شاهزاده گوید شعر ایلاهر اربیعی جوش بیز هر نیلاری بیل تو تماغینه یوییه کوهر نیلاری ییل توتی آینیکا
دین اول کلی فهه یول بیجو دا منزبی لوتفنه تلماش کوید یحلول آینی و آینیکیل مفرد غائب امر فعل الرآینیما و آینیما کیل مفرد
غائب امر فعل نهی آینیسک و آینینکیز و آینینکلار جمع غائب امر فعل الر آینیماسک و آینیمانکیز و آینیمانکلار جمع غائب امر فعل نهی آینیمان
و آینیماس مین متغیر الحال نمیشوم آینی مین و آینیر مین و آینیدورمین و آینیرم متغیر الحال میشوم آینیرم و آینیمام
متغیر الحال نشدهم آینیماکوم متغیر الحال نخواهم شد آینیب و آینیبان و آینیمیش متغیر الحال شده آینیمیشانک متغیر الحال
شده آینیماس متغیر الحال نمیشود و بمعنی فاعل و مصدر نفی هم می آید آینیماس متغیر الحال شدنش و شدنش آینیمادین
از متغیر الحال شدن و نشده آینیب بولماس و آینیسا بولماس و آینیماک اولماس متغیر الحال نمیتوان شد آینی الماس متغیر
نمیتواند آینی آینی تغیر حال کنان و بدون تکرار هم باین معنی مستعملست آینی و آینیمین متغیر الحال شوم و شوی
آینیسا لر و آینیکای بیز و آینیکای بیز و آینیلی و آینیلیک متغیر الحال شویم آینیکالی برای متغیر الحال شدن و ناشده آینیکاچ
چون متغیر الحال شود و بعد شدن آینیکوچی متغیر الحال شونده آینیکومه و آینیکو نچه و آینیکا نچه تا متغیر الحال شدن
آینیکوم متغیر الحال خواهم شد آینیکونک متغیر الحال خواهی شد آینیکوسی متغیر الحال خواهد شد آینیکولوک
متغیر الحال شدنی آینیکای و آینیسا و آینیسون و آینیدیک متغیر الحال شود آینیکوتی و آینیدیک متغیر الحال شدنی
و همچنانکه شود آینیماک بسکون یا و کسر نون مع التا مصدر متعدی نیست بمعنی محظوظ و متغیر الحال ساختن و صیغ آن بتوسط
شو او ل او تای فرشتا شتقاق بی یابد آینیماق بکسر یا و سکون نون بترکی رومی آینیماق بمعنی هشیار شدن باشد چنانکه
فضولی بمعنی از کوید با ملاحه الرومیه شعر شفا الطفل ایستین پیاره لعل نوش نفخان دن آیی هم اولماسی چیدر غافل
در مصنف نکنه دان غول بندای سه معنی دارد اول ماه بمعنی قمر باشد دوم ماه بمعنی شهر بود چنانکه بطریق ایهام کوید شعر
ن ماشخ بیز بقص هر مینکا ای منع لا یزال بر آی باشید اکمد سادی هیچ کیم ایکی هلال شینم حرف نونست وبیز نام پیراوقود
خان بن قراخانست که بعد از فوت کون خان برادرش بر تخت سلطنت نشست و اوضاع سخنا تا زطبقه مغولیه ملت ایا
به معنی آمده اول کیف مستعمل کوینید چنانکه در سل سکندری در وصف کوه یاجوج کوید شعر ایکی یوزانکا مناف

دیلمان فیا ثیمه بو تماعلندین نیچو ککیم آبادو بیم امراستاز دیمه نغ داشتیچنانکه در ذیل مصدر ایاناق کفت و بکسر الف عجمی
بود آیان بروزن نغان ریشه مفاضت بر از نامند و نیز نام غلام سلطان محمود سبکتکین است که معشوق او بوده ایاغ و ایاق ترکی
دارد اول پا را کوینید دوم کاسه و قدح را نامند و شواهد هر دو در باب ششم از دیباچه کتاب در ادب سلاح کارش یافته و فضولی رحمة
علیه الرحمه شاهد بر اول قول است و مبنی کفته شعر هر ماه بر ماس نخل الابد بصید دلی نوش ایمتین ای فضولی چیک الیغ لون
دین یلچیک ایاغ ایاقچی و ایاقچی عبارت از ساقی باشد چنانکه محمد سکندری کوید شعر ایاقچی کیتور جام می لب بلب که هو
اولدی هنکام عیش و طرب و اهل ایران کاسه شور و خود متکلم طلبع را کوینید که جمع کردن ظروف و سفلی یا مت ایا کونیم یا و الف کشیده
وضم کاف عجمی بروزن تکا یو استخوان پهلو را کوینید و ضم الف نیز مستعملست ایاالغوب بکون لام و ضم ضاد معجمه سکته را کوینید که از هند الحتر
نغمات بکشد چنانکه کوید شعر حال عیفه هجر یمد آزار تمام سرود یا رنو مصدد یغلیبه کونکول تولنا یا الغوبی من اسلای
شعر یاسید ایچلی هندی چالغوبی هندو بهر تام ایالنوا الغوبی آی یا الغوبی بتر نباشد که آن انغار چنانچ کمید آی تو غدی
نام عطلیعه لین ابوکات کابل و معنی ترکی آن یعنی ماه زاینید آیچی لیغ کوینید ایچی لیغ یعنی بگاه ماه ایکی آیچی کینغ بعنی چو ماه ماه
علی هذا القیاس الشاهد علیه شعر تا رغالش آیدا بر مین ایحادیم نا هیم سلا کاشکی برآ ایچلیغ ابو الحاجیم شاهیم سلا
آیدا آغاجی بکسر یا و سکون دال الز بکسر و منقوط در خت پیچ کش لست که آنرا بعربی نبخته لغابع و نبد خمته اور اوقاتسند و نجم آن لب
الشد کوینید و نیز که قاطع الشهوات و در وقت استسقاء نیز بکار برند و آبط با اطاع حطمی نیز استعمال میشود آیدا چی بهلوند
و ناهینا نزلشکر اخواستند آیدین بسکون یا و نون و کسر دال بمعنی بمنا باشد چنانکه در فرهاد و شیرین در وصف خزان کوید
شعر حلل قصر ایجرا هوات تا یتی تر حیل کو اکبی یلت کمپ لاه مکلل کوهر و نوب کو تیر کا آید بر یلت بوی قو یاش بمر دیشته می دین
تار و پودی و اصل وصیغ آن آیتو ب بمعنی ماه شب است که بتحریر یافته بر آیدین مشهور شده آیراق و آیراغ بسکون یا و فتح را
راب مهمله بر کوهی نزار کوینید و بعضی کوینید که جانوریست بشکل مرال که شاخهای چهید دارد و ایران بمعنی و بران دو معنی
آیر و بفتح را بمعنی جدا و منفصل باشد الشاهد علیه شعر کو یدین توشکان یراقی کونکلوم یرودآواره کیم ایرودور
آیرو خانمان دین توشوب آیروق بسکون یا و قاف و فتح راء مهمله بمعنی دیگر و آن بمعنی سپکانه نباشد دویم بمعنی دیگر بود که
داغی و طاغی نیز کوینید بنیم ترکی رومی نام کیاهیست در نهایت نازکی و طراوت که دوابان خوردن آن فربه شوند و آنرا بعربی
فرنیعه فردین نامند آیروقشی بسکون یا و قاف و ضم راء کسر معجمه بمعنی جدا که اندانست آیروم بضم راء و سکون میم بمعنی جمع کنکره
که در میان آب و رود خانها باشد و سوآمدن و محل بر ورام رالکه بمعنی اسلوب و فنون سیاهیکری آیروم خوانده و آیروم بمعنی فنون
سپاهیکری نوشته چنانکه در باب الف مکسوره در ذیل ایرام نکارش خواهد یافت آیری بکسر راء مهمله بمعنی دارد اول بمعنی
جدا و منفصل باشد که آنرا آیروهم کوینید دویم دو شاخه بود که بر کردن مجرمان نهند سیم شتر دو کوهان را نامند آیرس ج
بسکون یا و جیم و کسر راء مهمله شتر یو غور را کوینید آیریلش بسکون یا و شین و فتح و کسر راء و لام موضع انشعاب راه
جدا شدن هم آنرا اکوینید چنانکه در تاریخ بابری مذکوراست که قراتونینک بویی آیریلیشی دین بشر التی کینی سله تاریک
آیریم بکسر راء مهمله زین بود که آنرا تر لیک هم نامند و بضم بمعنی کرداب نوشته آبیق آغاچی همان ایدا غاجاست که
مذکور شد آیغیر بسکون یا و راء مهمله وکسر غین معجمه اسب نر بود که آنرا بعربی فحل کوینید ایقاق بسکون یا و قاف ثانی
و فتح قاف اول و الف کشیده بمادی و قول بیهوده را کوینید چنانکه در تنبیهات محبوب القلوب کوید کر نادانه سوز دعیان ایقاق

57v.

وکوپ دیماك بوزتامدو ویعنی تمام ونحن چنر هم استعمال کنند آیایغ بمعنی ماهیانه باشد ایلق برون المتوجد که
رومی بمعنی مفت بود که آنرا بفارسی رایکان ویترکی مجان خوانند ایله دو معنی دارد اول بمعنی مهمان باشد چنانکه
کوید شعر ایله کیم خضر ومسیح الیدا سبزه بیرله سو خطینک ولعلینک تا شیدا ایله بیل خضر ومسیح دو بیم ایراستاز کردن
چنانکه در ذیل مصادر کذشت آیرتعنو بکسر یا وسکون را وتای قرشت یعنی تیز وتفرق نیك وبد آینوقتی بضم نون
وکسر سین مهمله بمعنی عجیب وقریب باشد الشاهد علیه شعر نی اوچون کونکلوم بوکون آینوقتی شورانکیز ایرور عشقینك
اون کوبیا جانیم یا نار غیتنزایرور ایوا مه بود که آنرا بعربی سفرجل وبفارسی آبی نامند آیو قولاغی بترکی روی پنج بنایت
که چون بشکند دو خط صلیبی بهم جوفا از مشاهده شود لهذا بعربی عود الصلیب کویند آیغ و آیق بکسر یا دو معنی دارد
اول غربال باشد که آنرا بعربی دبا مند چنانکه در سد سکندری در وصف لشام کوید شعر آیغ لعیدین حنفیکیم نان ایرکن
آنی اتی کاسالماق خامکان یا یرقه مرکشار الطیر شعر کوهی تاغ ایچرا ایراسیغ توقوب اورکا بیتایردی آنی کوپ تاپن بوتوب
دو بیم بمعنی هشیار باشد آیغلیغ هشیلری آیل بکسر یا وسکون لام شکار شبیر اکویند فیزاسر تاز هشیلرشک چنانکه
کذشت آیسیم خواتون وبانوی حرم را کویند باب المضمونات حرف الالف مع الباء من المشتقات اوپماك با بای عجمی بوسیدن
اوپتی بوسید اوبتوك بوسیلیم اوبار واوپادو بمیبوسید واوپار بمعنی فاعل ومصدر نیزمی آید اوپمایدی میبوسید
ونبوسیده است اوپکان واوپارکان واوپادورکان بوسنده وبوسیده وبمعنی مصدر نیزمی آیند اوپ واوپکیل مفرد مخاطب
از فعل امر الشاهد علی الثانی شعر ای نوایی نفر بولسیدا ایراوپکیل هر قدم یعنی ولی بولدا قدم سیر ایچرا باش ایتا کیل
اوپلواوپما کیل مفرد مخاطب از فعل نهی اوپونك واوپونکیز واوپونکلار جمع مخاطب از فعل امر اوپمانك واوپمانکیز واوپمانکلار
جمع مخاطب از فعل نهی اوپمان واوپمارمین واوپمایدور مین نمیبوسم اوپماین واوپارمین واوپادورمین واوپارام میبوسم اوپادیم
واوپماکیم بوسیدم اوپاکوم نخواهم بوسید اوپوب اوپوبان واوپمیش بوسیده اوپمیشانك بوسیده اوپماس
نبوسد بمعنی فاعل ومصدر منفی نیزمی آید اوپماسی بوسیدنش ونبوسیدنش اوپمادین از بوسیدن ونبوسیده اوپوبولا
واوپابولماس واوپاالماس نمیتوان بوسید اوپا آلماس نمیتواند بوسید اوپا اوپا بوسه کنان بوسه کنان
وبدون تکرار هم بایمعنی مستعملست اوپای واوپاین بوسم وبوسد وبوسی اوپالی واوپکای واوپکایمیز واوپالی
واوپالینك بوسیم اوپکالی برای بوسیدن وتا بوسیده چنانکه بمعنی اول کوید شعر نامه بی قویونك ایکیم لشکر ا
ایلار کونکول اوپکالی چیقما قفه کوپا کیم شتاب ایلار کونکول اوپکاچ چون بوسید وبوسید اوپکوچی بوسنده اوپکوچه
اوپکوچه واوپکا بحه تا بوسیدن وبقصد بوسیدن الشاهد علی الثانی بالمعنی الثانی شعر کونا لعلی بیه کرتا لماس
اوپکونچه هوش حشوار بوس کونکلوم کمانیوبرسین لبخند انین اونی اوپکوم خواهم بوسید اوپکونك خواهی بوسید اوپکو
خواهد بوسید اوپکولوك بوسیدنی اوپکای واوپا واوپا واوپون واوپدیك بوسید چنانکه در لشکر کشی دارا
بجنك اسکندر کوید الشاهد علی الخامس شعر کیلیب رجا بیرا اوپدیا یلا جبلانم مونونك بیرله کیلادی بیلا خرام ایکو ایلك
واوپادیك بوسیدی وهمچنانکه بوسید اوپوشماك مع الشین مصدر مفاعله است یعنی یکدیکر را بوسیدن وصیغ آن بتود
شود اول ابنا مرشین اشتقاق می یابد اوپولماك مع اللام مصدر انفعالست یعنی بوسیده شدن وصیغ آن بالام اشتقاق می یابد
اوپدورماك مصدر متعدیست یعنی بوسانیدن وصیغ آن بالفظ مصدر اشتقاق می یابد اوپراماك بسکون بای عجمی وفتح را قرشت

58r.

واوپرانماك مع النون کهنه ومندرس شدن وآنرا رومیه ایپرمالد بفتح الف وکسر را کویند اوپرادی واوپرادی کهنه شد
اوپرادوك واوپراندوك کهنه شدیم اوپراروز واوپرایدور واوپرانورز واوپرانادور کهنه میشود واوپرار واوپرانور بمعنی فاعل ومصدر
نیز می آید اوپراکان واوپرارکان واوپرادورکان واوپرانکان واوپرانورکان واوپرانادورکان کهنه شونده وکهنه شده
وبمعنی مصدر نیزمی آید اوپرا واوپراکیل واوپران واوپرانکیل مفرد مخاطب از فعل امر اوپرما واوپرماکیل واوپرانما واوپرانماکیل
مفرد مخاطب از فعل نهی اوپرانك واوپرانکیز واوپرانکلار واوپرانینك واوپرانینکیز واوپرانینکلار جمع مخاطب از فعل امر اوپرمانك
واوپرمانکیز واوپرمانکلار واوپرانمانك واوپرانمانکیز واوپرانمانکلار جمع مخاطب از فعل نهی اوپرمان واوپرمارمین و
اوپرانمان واوپرانمارمین کهنه نمیشوم اوپرایمین واوپرارمین واوپرایدورمین واوپرارام واوپرانامین واوپرانورمین و
اوپرانادورمین واوپرانورام کهنه میشوم اوپرادیم واوپرانادیم واوپرانورم واوپراناکیم واوپرانماکیم کهنه شدم اوپراناکوم واوپرا
ناکوم کهنه نخواهم شد اوپراب واوپراباو اوپرانان واوپرامیش واوپرانیب واوپرانبان واوپرانمش کهنه شده اوپرمیشانك
اوپرانمیشانك کهنه شده اوپرماس واوپرانماس کهنه نشود وبمعنی فاعل ومصدر منفی نیزمی آید چنانکه بمعنی کهنه نشونده
شاهد براول اوپرماس محبوب القلوب کوید کر نیچه کیم توتنی رغایت بیرله کیسانك ایسکیرومس چونکه کیدم دیونك یا لانکه اوپرماس
توتن اول ایرور اوپرماسی واوپرانماسی کهنه شدنش ونشدنش اوپرمادین واوپرانمادین از کهنه شدن وکهنه نشدن
اوپراب بولماس واوپرانا بولماس واوپرامالماس واوپرانیب بولماس واوپرانا بولماس واوپرانماك اولماس کهنه نمیتوان شد
اوپرای آلماس واوپرانا آلماس کهنه نمیتواند شد اوپرای واوپرایای واوپرای واوپرانا اوپرانا کهنه شونده کهنه شونده وبدون تکرار
هم بایمعنی مستعملست اوپرای واوپراین واوپرانای واوپراناین کهنه شوم وشود وشوی اوپرالی واوپرالینك واوپراکای واوپراکایمیز
واوپرالی واوپرالینك واوپرانالی واوپرانکای واوپرانکایمیز واوپرانالینك کهنه شویم اوپرالی
واوپرانکالی برای کهنه شدن وتا کهنه شده اوپراکاج واوپرانکاج چون کهنه شد وشود اوپراکوچی واوپرانکوچی
کهنه شونده اوپراکوچه واوپراکونچه واوپراکانچه واوپرانکوچه واوپرانکونچه واوپرانکانچه تا کهنه شدن وبقصد کهنه شدن
اوپراکوم واوپرانکوم کهنه خواهم شد اوپراکونك واوپرانکونك کهنه خواهی شد اوپراکوسی واوپرانکوسی کهنه شو
اوپراکولوك واوپرانکولوك کهنه شدنی اوپراکای واوپراسا واوپراسون واوپرادیك واوپرانکای واوپرانلو واوپرانسا
واوپرانسون واوپراندیك کهنه شود اوپرادیك واوپراکودیك واوپرانودیك واوپرانکودیك کهنه شدی وهمچنانکه کهنه شود
من ابجوامد او با بدو معنی آمده اول خیمهای کوچك است که صحرانشینان در جایی زده اقامت نمایند ومجاز اهل اقامت را
نیز کویند دویم نام قصبه ایست از توابع هرات وبابای عجمی سفید ابرا خوانند که زنان بر رو مالند الشاهد علیه شعر اولکیم
اوپه وکلکونه دین نظاره قبل کیم یوقدر البته کیم رنکا ایرور اق ومرل اوپچین بسکون با ونون وکسر جیم عجمی لحنه را کویند
چنانکه در فرهاد وشیرین در ذکر طلسم سکندر کوید شعر ولیکن اوشبو یکپای تا فرق بولوبا وت تیلینمور او
ارلغو اوپچین لیك واوپچون لوك یعنی مسلح چنانکه شاهد بر ثانی در سد سکندری کوید شعر هرایچون لوك تنه قلب
کردوفرش که اندین توشوب هرا شو روشن اوپکا بسکون بای عجمی وفتح کاف شش بود که آنرا بعربی ریه خوانند اوپکالیك
کنایه از دلاور باشد اوپچته بضم با وسکون جیم عجمی وفتح تای قرشت اوپچین بضم با وکسر جیم عجمی وسکون نون بلغت مغولی بمعنی
خسته وکوفته ومریض وبیمار باشد اوبوسون بضم با وسین مهمله وسکون نون بلغت مغولی علف بود که آنرا بعربی حشیش کویند

ابوکا جد را کویند چنانکه در قضانامه اخلاقیه کوید که آتا ابوکام اول حضرت نینک آبا واجدادی خدمت لرنده اوغ
مراتب فه سزاوار ایردیلار و نیز در تاریخ الملوک در ذکر بهرام بن بهرام کوید که اتا ابوکا آتین آنکا قویدیلار ادبولک تا جیکه
جسر مرغان بود از قبیل خروس و هدهد و امثال آن و مجاز اهدهد را هم نامند و آنرا ابوپوپک و پوپوش نیز خوانند و در رومیه
ابلت بکسر الف و با استعمال نمایند ادبولک قوشی نام هدهد بود که آنرا افغان پوپو شانه سر کویند ادبول بلغت مغولی رستان باشد
ادبه بفتح بای هجا زده و او به با بای عجمی هان او با واو با باشد که در فوق مذکور شد مع الثامن المشتقات اوتمک بمعنی کذشتن
و نیز اسم جنس است از برای نان چنانکه در غیر مضاد مذکور خواهد شد و ترکی رومی بمعنی خوانند کی صرایید زمان شدکه مجاز
بیهوده کوئی و ژاژخائی را نیز کویند و چون با شتقاق ترکی رومی با اشتقاق لغت جغتای اختلافی دارد و صیغ مشتقه هر جا
که لغتها مطابق شود معنی رومی نیز مضاف معانی دیکر خواهد شد اوتماق باشباع ضمه بدو معنی آمده اول بردن مقارد و کرد رومیم
کله و پوست حیوانات و خوشه کندم را بشعله آتش نکاهداشتن که از مو و امثال آن پاک شود اوتتی کذشت و ترکی
رومی سرایید و باشباع کرو برده و بشعله پاک کرد اوتتوک کذشتیم و ترکی رومی سراییدیم اوتتوق باشباع کرو دیم
و بشعله پاک کردیم اوتار و اوتادور میکذرد و میسراید و باشباع کرو میبرد و بشعله پاک میکند ولوتار بمعنی
و مصدر نیز می آید چنانکه بمعنی کذرنده کوید شعر قیل شجستان تون لارین می دیر یاروق انداغ که چرخ مهر دین مجوی
مهر او قبر له اوتار ایامنی و نیز در سکند سکندری بیمار معنی آمده شعر چو آلدی جهان زهر من بلالش عدالت اوتاد
دهر الحیلیدی ماش و نیز بعنی اد اسکند و این معنی ماخوذ از مصدر اوتاماق بمعنی ادا کردنست چنانکه مذکور شود
اوتماید و ربمیکذرد و نکذشته است اوتکان و اوتارکان و اوتادورکان کذرنده و کذشته الشاهد علی الاول والمعنی
الثانی شعر سین ایتمای قضا بولمای مجرا سیمیکن جهان کار کاهیدا اوتکان قضا یا و بمعنی مصدر نیز می آید چنانکه بمعنی
کذشتن کوید الشاهد علی الاول شعر خوبلار هر دم اوتارسین سیز تا ماشیم ین ووکه باث هر نفس هجرینک منکا بو آی لاد
اوتکان برله سیل وله شعر نوای دفتر هجرینک نا زیب کوز توکی تخواین چو احسانک صحیفه کوکاسین تمان اوتکان
تهنه اوتغان و اوتارغان و اوتادورغان باشباع کرو برنده و کرو برده و بشعله پاک کننده و پاک کرده و بمعنی مصدر
نیز می آید اوت مفرد مخاطب فعل امر بعنی چهار معنی و معانی جامد هم دارد که در ذیل جوامد مذکور خواهد شد ان شاء الله تعالی
اوتکیل امر استانه بکذشتن اوتقا مفرد مخاطب فعل نهی امر چهار معنی اوتغیل امر استانه کرو بردن و بشعله پاک کردن تو بمعنی
در بیان معنی اوتغیل نوشته که دراز بکن و الینک اوتغیل بعنی دست دراز بکن و این معنی لخز اعتبت سهو کرده اوتونک
جمع مخاطبه فعل امر چهار معنی اوتونکوز و اوتونکلار جمع مخاطب استانه فعل امر بمعنی کذشتن و بردن و بشعله پاک کردن
اوتمانک جمع مخاطبه فعل نهی هر چهار معنی و تمانکیز و اوتمانکلار جمع مخاطب استانه فعل نهی بمعنی کذشتن و کرو بردن و بشعله
پاک کردن اوتمان و اوتمارمین و اوتمایدورمین نمیکذرم و باشباع ضمه کرو نمیبرم و بشعله پاک نمیکنم اوتامین
و اوتارمین و اوتادورمین و اوتارام میکذرم و کرو میبرم و بشعله پاک میکنم و اوتامین و اوتای مین و اوقارمین
و اوتارام بمعنی دامیکنم هم باشد و ترکی رومی بمعنی میسرایم اوتایم کذشتم و کرو بردم و بشعله پاک کردم صرایدم
و ادا کردم و در ابعض نامعصد اوتاماک اشتراک دارد اوتماکیم کذشتم و سراییدم اوتماغیم کرو بردم و بشعله پاک
کردم اوتماکوم نخواهم کذشت اوتماغوم کرو نخواهم برد و بشعله پاک نخواهم کرد اوتسانک نکهه ری و ترکی رومی

نبرات و باشباع کرو بری و بشعله پاک کنی اوتکاسین و اوتکای سین بکذری اوتغاسین و اوتغای سین باشباع کرو بری و بشعله
پاک کنی اوتوبغا و توبان بوا و تمیش کذشته و ترکی رومی سراییده و باشباع کرو برده و بشعله پاک کرده چنانکه شاه
براولرا بمعنی کرو برده کوید شعر اوی آل که جانز دینی اوتوشتور یارب نی بله مهر و فغا اوتوتوشتور ادمیشا لکن
و باشباع کرو برده و بشعله پاک کرده اوتماس نمیکذرد و ترکی رومی نمیسراید و باشباع کرو نمیبرد و بشعله پاک نمیکند
و بمعنی تامل و مصدر نفی نیز می آید اوتماس کذشتن و نکذشتن و سراییدن و نسراییدن و کرو بردن و بشعله
پاک کردن و نکردن اوتمادین از کذشتن و نکذشته و از سراییدن و نسراییدن و از کرو بردن و کرو نبردن و از پاک کردن
بشعله و پاک نکرده اوتوب بولماس و اوتسا بولماس نمیتوان کذشت و باشباع کرو نمیتوان برد و بشعله نمیتوان پاک کرد اوتا
الماس نمیتواند کذشت و نمیتواند کرو برد و نمیتواند بشعله پاک کرد اوتا اوتا کلمان کذران چنانکه کوید شعر نی نوع
اینکا یا بین هجرانکه تا غریبد و کونکلوش فراق انکیه لار بیچین اوتا اوتا نتیشیب توز تکرار هم مستعمل چنانکه
در نظم الجواهر در فهم کثرت کلام کوید شعر حلا دین اوتا هر کیم که کلام اولدی آنکا اول نوع کلام دین ملال اولدی آنکا
و ترکی رومی بمعنی خوانند کی بخان و باشباع برده برده و بشعله پاک کنان پاک کنان اوتای و اوتامین بکذرم و بکذرد
و بکذری و کرو برم و ببرد و ببری و بشعله پاک کنم و کند و کنی اوتسان بکذریم و ترکی رومی بسراییم اوتساق باشباع کرو
ببریم و بشعله پاک کنیم اوتالی و اوتالینک بکذریم و باشباع کرو ببریم و بشعله پاک کنیم اوتکالی برای کذشتن و اوتقالی
باشباع برای کرو بردن و تا کرو برده و برای پاک کردن با تش و تا پاک کرده اوتکاچ چون کذشت و بکذرد اوتغاچ چون
کرو برد و ببرد و چون بشعله پاک کرد و کند اوتکوچی کذرنده الشاهد علیه شعر قویا بو منزل ده سکن کاکونکولنی
زنهار شه انکا اوتکوچی یلدوزنی و مهمان نیکلیغ اوتغوچی کرو برنده و بشعله پاک کننده اوتکوسی و اوتکونچی و اوتکانچ
تا کذشتن و متعلق کذشتن الشاهد علی الثانی بالمعنی الاول شعر نی قطاع الطریق نزلی دور رباط
میل اوتکونچه اندین الخیال اتقوچبوا اتقونچه و اتغانچه باشباع تا کرو بردن و تا بشعله پاک کردن و متعلقات پاک کردن
اوتکوم خواهم کذشت اوتماکوم نخواهم کذشت چنانکه کوید شعر نولنی آتما کوجان کیز اکو آندین اوث
ندین که اوقسام یوز جاندین اوتماکوم آندین اوتغوم کرو خواهم برد و بشعله پاک خواهم کرد اوتکولک خواهی
کذشت اوتغولک کرو خواهی برد و بشعله پاک خواهی کرد اوتکوسی خواهد کذشت اوتغوسی کرو خواهد برد
و بشعله پاک خواهد کرد اوتکولوک کذشتنی اوتغولوق کرو بردنی و بشعله پاک کردنی اوتکای ایرکی میکذشت
چنانکه در نعت کوید شعر کولا کانک تا پتا ایردی جرم تراب آنکا کردون نینا وتکای ایردی جناب اوتغای ایردی
باشباع کرو می برد و بشعله پاک کند اوتاوار تسون اوتدیلک بکذرد و باشباع کرو برد و بشعله پاک کند اوتکودیک
کذشتنی و چنانکه بکذرد الشاهد علیه بالمعنی الاول شعر هم با دور دا هم یا نار دا اوتکودیک توز چرخ
جفا اول آی هجریدا آهیم اوتی کردون سارنی اتغودیک کرو بردنی و چنانکه کرو برد و بشعله پاک کردنی و چنانکه
پاک کند اوتاردیک بمعانی اوتکودیک و اوتغودیک باشد و نیز بمعنی ادا کردنی و چنانکه ادا کند و بمعنی مصدر
اوتاماک اشتراک دارد اوتوشماک مع الثین مصدر معامله است در دو معنی دارد اول انهم کذشتن در بهم
سراییدن و خواندن کردن بود و آنرا بلغت جغتای اتاشماک کویند چنانکه مذکور شد اوتوشتیلار انهم کذشتند و

اوتوشوك ازهم شراییدیم اوتوشولار واوتوشادورلار ازهم سیكه‌یندو باهم میسرایید واوتوشور

فاعل ومصدر نیز می‌آید اوتوشكان واوتوشوركان واوتوشادوركان ازهم كذرنده وازهم كذشته وبمعنی مستكم هم

می‌آیند اوتوشونك واوتوشونكوز واوتوشونكلار جمع مخاطب از فعل امر اوتوشماتك واوتوشمانكیز واوتوشمانكلار

جمع مخاطب از فعل نهی اوتوشمان واوتوشمامین واوتوشامین واوتوشورمین واوتوشادورمین واوتوشورام

ومی‌رایم اوتوشوب قیرلار ازهم كذشته‌اند چنانكه در ذكر الحبه در ذكر شیخ محیی الدین كوید كه هر بری الاردین

یانا پیریكا نظاره قیلیب اوتوشوبتورلار اوتوشماتك كذشته اوتوشماس نیكه‌زدو نغمه‌رایید و بمعنی فاعل و مستكم

هم می‌آید اوتوشماس كذشتن ونكذشتن وسراییدن ونسراییدن اوتوشمادین ازكذشتن ونكذشته وازسراییدن

اوتوشوب بولماس واوتوشنا بولماس اوتوشماك اولماس عنوان ازهم كذشت اوتوشا آلماس لار عنوان ازهم كذشت

اوتوشا اوتوشا ازهم كذشته كذشته وسراییده سراییده اوتوشای واوتوشامین بگذرم وبگذرم وبگذری اوتوشا

واوتوشكاپیز واوتوشكای‌پیز واوتوشلی واوتوشالیك ازهم بگذریم واوتوشالك تركی رومی یعنی سراییم

اوتوشكالی برای ازهم كذشتن وتا ازهم كذشته اوتوشكاج چون ازهم كذشت وبگذرد اوتوشكوچی كذرنده

اوتوشكوچه واوتوشكونچه واوتوشكانچه تا كذشتن وبقدر كذشتن اوتوشكو میدر ودر ازهم خواهیم كذشت اوتوشكونكوز

ازهم خواهید كذشت اوتوشكوسیلاردور ودر ازهم خواهند كذشت اوتوشكولوك ازهم كذشتنی اوتوشكایلاردور اوتوشو

واوتوشدیكلار ازهم بگذرند اوتوشكودیك واوتوشوردیك ازهم كذشتی وچنانكه ازهم بگذرند اوتورماك بضم تا

وسكون را مع الكاف مصدر متعدیست یعنی كذرانیدن وآن مخفف اوتكارماك باشد اوتورماق مع القاف یعنی نشستن

وان مخفف اولتورماق باشد اوتورمای نكذرانم ونكذرانید ونكذرانیدی چنانكه در خاتمه كتاب در خسرو شیرین در وصف

بعضی نكذرانند كوید شعر نا چیب بوینوع كل دین دانه انداش چوپان چوكم قویمای ایناندا اوتورمای وقتی دین پر لحظه سوین

طمع الملاحب بوسوصعدین آبروین ومؤلفین روحی قدرمای را در این شعر اوتورمای برای هنرخوانده وبعضی باختن وفرصت

ازدست دادن نوشته اند ونصیری هم متابعت كرده سهو كرده اند ونیز نشیند ونشیم ونشینی چنانكه شاعر عجمی

نشیند كفته شعر چاشتی هر كیشی پیشی تورمای بایم ساعت نوروبیر دم اوتورمای وسیغ اوتورماك واولتورماك

باغین بسكون شو اول الشقاق می‌آید اوتكارماك بسكون تا وراء قرشت وفتح كاف عجمی مصدر متعدیست یعنی كذرانیدن

كوید شعر مسكینیك آخر چو نوفراغ ویزنی اوتكارماك تورود مدفینك ایوانی غه كوك كنبدی دین ارتفاع اوتكار

كذرانید اوتكاردوك كذرانیدیم اوتكاردوعا اوتكاردوعی كذرانیداند الشاهد علی الاول شعر بیحولك قول العولما غایبتن بر

پریغه كرنجه كه كم لیكینی كورا را اوتكاردور كم پله واوتكاردور بمعنی فاعل ومصدر نیز می‌آید اوتكاریدو نمیكذرانند

ونكذرانیده است اوتكاركان واوتكاردوركان كذرانیده وكذرانیده الشاهد علی الاول والمعنی الاخیر شعر

چاكلاد بولغان شیم قانعلی وكوزده دیدی بلبل وعومعه دوركوهلار داوتكاركان نفس وبمعنی مصدر نیز می‌آیند

اوتكار بسكون را اوتكار بضم را اوتكاركیل مفرد مخاطب از فعل امر الشاهد علی الاول شعر نوك معترف دو

جرمی ضایب بین اوتكاركیم كرم اهلیغه لازم عفو دور جرم اعترافیدا الشاهد علی الثانی شعر سعی ایتیب كیلتور

میننك شاءنی دعوی جهاننا آلیدا بید الحكیم نینك داستانین اوتكاروا اوتكار ملوا اوتكاركیل مفرد مخاطب از فعل

اوتكاینك واوتكاینكیز واوتكارینكلار جمع مخاطب از فعل امر اوتكارماتك واوتكارمانكیز واوتكارمانكلار جمع مخاطب

فعل نهی اوتكارمان واوتكارماس مین نمیكذرانم اوتكارامین واوتكاردورمین واوتكارادورمین واوتكاردورام میكذرانم

اوتكاردورم واوتكارایم كذرانیدیم اوتكارایكوم نخواهم كذرانید اوتكارماتك واوتكاركامین واوتكاركای‌مین

بگذرانی نصیری سهو كرده نوشته كه اوتكاركای‌مین بمعنی فراغت دادن ونوعی كه او فراغت كند اوتكاریب اوتكاریشان

و اوتكاریش كذرانیده اوتكاریشانك كذرانیدی اوتكارماس نمیكذرانند وبعضی فاعل ومصدر متضمن نیز آیند اوتكارماس

كذرانیدن ونكذرانیدن اوتكارادین از كذرانیدن ونكذرانیده اوتكاریب بولماس واوتكارا بولماس اوتكارماك آلماس

عنوان كذرانید اوتكارا آلماس عنوانند كذرانید الشاهد علیه بتر حینه شعر مرهم اوتكارسا حدین سمدعی بیدادوم

اوتكارا آلماس صنالینك مدهاسی بیرین اوتكارا اوتكارا كذران كذران اوتكارای واوتكارایین بگذرانم بگذرانم

وبگذرانی اوتكاریالی واوتكاركاپیز واوتكاركای‌پیز واوتكارلی واوتكارالینك بگذرانیم اوتكاركالی برای كذرانیدن

وتا كذرانیده بالمعنی الاول من حیثیه شعر لعل ابرینك ایكی لبینك سوزونه شه مین اوتكاركالی شفتا بیر صد آفرینك

كه تمام بولدی لعل ناب آرا اوتكاركاچ چون كذرانید وبگذراند اوتكاردوچی كذرانیده اوتكاركوچه واوتكاركونچه

اوتكاركانچه تا كذرانیدن وبقدر كذرانیدن اوتكاركوم خواهم كذرانید اوتكاركونك خواهی كذرانید اوتكاركوسی

خواهد كذرانید اوتكاركولوك كذرانیدنی اوتكاركای‌دور واوتكاركای‌دور واوتكارسا واوتكارسون واوتكاردیك بگذراند

اوتكاردیك واوتكاركودیك كذرانیدی وچنانكه بگذراند اوتكاریماك بكسر را مع الكاف مصدر انفعالست یعنی كذرانیده

شدن اوتكارلور كذرانیده می‌شود چنانكه كوید شعر لبینك تا جسم ضعیف جوزی ایر صد اول نوع كه شه اوتكار

لعل آبدار ایچرا وبعضی فاعل ومصدر نیز می‌آید اوتكاریلیب كذرانیده شده الشاهد علیه شعر لبینك سوزی درانكا

قتر یل قولطه با غلاحینك با یوشه كه اوتكاریلیب توسیحقدین وثانی صیغ بعمین شیلاق با نضمام لام اشتقاق می‌آید

اوتكاریشماك بكسر راء مع الشین مصدر مفاعلتست یعنی باهم كذرانیدن اوتكاریشینك باهم بگذرانید الشاهد

شعر ای جهان وكونكول پر جیكر كا تار دیشنك اول كوی ساچی رحم تیمانلار دیشنك خال العسید ایر كانیم سوزین اوتكا

خایمون تیولرغه كیل السنایا البلر دیشنك وبلك همسیغ بعمین قیح باوجود این اشتقاق نیابد اوتكاماك بسكون تا ونون

كاف عجمی تقلید كردن بودو فراغی بعضی سبقت كردن وطالع هروی بمعنی نازیدن نوشته هر دو سهو كرده اند

اوپوتماك كوید اوتكاندی تقلید كرد اوتكاندوك تقلید كردیم اوتكانورم اوتكانادور تقلید میكند الشاهد علی

الاول شعر شوخلوق ره بین آنكا تقلید ایسار لار اشوخلار شیكرما كما الیكیم اوچنون چاشتیغه اوتكانورش واوتكانور

فاعل ومصدر نیز می‌آید اوتكانغایده تقلید نمیكند ونكرده است اوتكانكان واوتكانوركان واوتكانادوركان تقلید

كننده وتقلید كرده وبمعنی مصدر نیز می‌آید اوتكانكیل مفرد مخاطب از فعل امر اوتكانما واوتكانماكیل مفرد

مخاطب از فعل نهی الشاهد علی الثانی شعر كل چاجی كلبانك چیكاك ایشتورا بلبل سنكا آی وبیل فریاد قیلما اوتكا

اوتكاماكیل اوتكانینك واوتكانینكیز واوتكانینكلار جمع مخاطب از فعل امر اوتكانمانك واوتكانمانكیز واوتكانمانكلار

جمع مخاطب از فعل نهی اوتكانمان واوتكانماس مین تقلید نمیكنم اوتكانامین واوتكانورمین واوتكانادورمین واوتكانورام

تقلید میكنم اوتكانورم واوتكانایم تقلید كردم اوتكانغایكوم تقلید نخواهم كرد اوتكانیب واوتكانیبان واوتكان

تقلید کرده. الشاهد علی الاول شعر بو نادور چون جهان کلزارلاری کونکلوم قوشی بولماپ کل والی بلبل تقلید
اوتکانیب اوتکانمیشانلق تقلید کرده. اوتکانماس تقلید نمیکند و بمعنی فاعل و مصدر منفی هم می آید اوتکانماسی
تقلید کردن و نکردن اوتکانمادین از تقلید کردن و تقلید نکرده. اوتکانیب بولماس و اوتکانا بولماس و اوتکانماق
تقلید نمیتوان کرد اوتکانا آلماس تقلید نمیتواند کرد. اوتکانا اوتکانا تقلید کنان تقلید کنان و بدون تکرار هم
مستعملست اوتکانای و اوتکانایین تقلید کنم و کند و کنی اوتکانسا و اوتکانکاینز و اوتکانکای بز و اوتکانملی
و اوتکانالینک تقلید کنیم اوتکانکلی برای تقلید کردن و تا تقلید کرده. اوتکانکاچ چون تقلید کرد و کند
اوتکانکوچی تقلید کننده اوتکانکوچه و اوتکانکونجه و اوتکانکانجه تا تقلید کردن و بتقدیم تقلید کردن اوتکانکوم
تقلید خواهم کرد اوتکانکونک تقلید خواهی کرد اوتکانکوسی تقلید خواهد کرد اوتکانکولوک تقلید کردنی و اوتکا
و اوتکانا و اوتکانسا و اوتکانسون و اوتکاندیک تقلید کند چنانکه شاه میر او اول اراده محبوب القلوب بطریق
ترکی کوید که سیدزاده که لوبلی لارغه اوتکانکای میمون بنازنیغ و دوکم اشلیغ دین او ترکانیه امرکانکای اوتکاندیک
و اوتکانوردیک تقلید کردنی و همچنانکه تقلید کند اوتغوزماق بسکون تا و ضم زای هوز و ضم غین معجمه کرو و قمار را
باختن اوتغوزدی باخت اوتغوزدوق باختیم اوتغوزدور و اوتغوزادور می بازد و اوتغوزور بمعنی فاعل و مصدر منفی
اوتغوزماید و نمیبازد و نباخته است اوتغوزغان و اوتغوزورغان و اوتغوزادورغان بازنده و باخته و بمعنی مصدر
هم می آیند اوتغوزها و اوتغوزغیل مفرد مخاطب فعل امر اوتغوزماغیل مفرد مخاطب فعل نهی اوتغوزونک و
اوتغوزونکوز و اوتغوزونکلار جمع مخاطب فعل امر اوتغوزمانک و اوتغوزمانکیز و اوتغوزمانکلار جمع مخاطب فعل نهی
اوتغوزمای و اوتغوزماس مین نمیبازم اوتغوزامین و اوتغوزورمین و اوتغوزادورمین و اوتغوزورام میبازم اوتغوزوم
و اوتغوزماغیم باختنم اوتغوزماغوم نخواهم باخت اوتغوزوب و اوتغوزوبان و اوتغوزمیش باخته چنانکه در حیرت الابرار کوید
الشاهد علی الاول شعر [illegible] لاله شیش طاسی ارزاله بولوب کجستین کل اولوب [illegible] کوزکورو
جبین [illegible] اوتغوزوب اوتغوزمیشانلق باخته اوتغوزماس نمیبازد بمعنی فاعل و مصدر منفی هم می آید اوتغوزماسی
باختن و نباختن اوتغوزمادین از باختن و نباخته اوتغوزوب بولماس و اوتغوزا بولماس و اوتغوزماق ولماس نمیتوان باخت
اوتغوزا اوتغوزا المایه [illegible] تکرار هم باین معنی مستعملست اوتغوزای و اوتغوزایین ببازم و ببازد و ببازی اوتغوزسا
و اوتغوزسانکیز و اوتغوزغای بز و اوتغوزلی و اوتغوزالینک ببازیم اوتغوزغلی برای باختن و تا باخته اوتغوزغاچ چون
ببازد اوتغوزغوچی بازنده اوتغوزغوچه و اوتغوزغونجه و اوتغوزغانجه تا باختن و بتقدیم باختن اوتغوزغوم باخت
اوتغوزغونک خواهی باخت اوتغوزغوسی خواهد باخت اوتغوزغولوق باختنی اوتغوزغای و اوتغوزا و اوتغوزسا و اوتغوزسون
و اوتغوزدیک ببازد اوتغوزغودیک و اوتغوزوردیک باختنی و همچنانکه ببازد اوتغانماق بسکون تا و نون و فتح غین معجمه
مصدر انفعالست یعنی شرم کردن اوتغاندی شرم کرد اوتغاندوق شرم کردیم اوتغانور و اوتغانادور شرم میکند
و اوتغانور بمعنی فاعل و مصدر هم می آید اوتغانماید و شرم نمیکند و نکرده است اوتغانغان و اوتغانورغان و اوتغانادورغان
شرم کننده و شرم دیده و بمعنی مصدر هم می آید اوتغانا و اوتغانغیل مفرد مخاطب فعل امر اوتغانما و اوتغانماغیل مفرد مخاطب
فعل نهی اوتغانینک و اوتغانینکیز و اوتغانینکلار جمع مخاطب فعل امر اوتغانمانک و اوتغانمانکیز و اوتغانمانکلار جمع مخاطب

فعل نهی اوتغانمای و اوتغانماس مین شرم نمیکنم اوتغانامین و اوتغانورمین و اوتغانادورمین و اوتغانورام شرم میکنم
اوتغانورم و اوتغانماغیم شرم کردنم اوتغانماغوم شرم نخواهم کرد اوتغانیب و اوتغانیبان و اوتغانمیش شرم کرده الشاهد
علی الاول من لطفی شعر یار [illegible] بیله قیلمانکیز ای [illegible] چون آب حیات [illegible] اوتغانیب آندین [illegible]
شرم کرده اوتغانماس شرم نمیکند و بمعنی فاعل و مصدر منفی هم می آید اوتغانماسی شرم کردن و نکردن اوتغانمادین از شرم
نکرده اوتغانیب بولماس و اوتغانا بولماس و اوتغانماق ولماس شرم نمیتوان کرد اوتغانا آلماس شرم نمیتواند کرد اوتغانا
اوتغانا شرم کنان شرم کنان و بدون تکرار هم مستعملست اوتغانای و اوتغانایین شرم کنم و کند و کنی اوتغانسا [illegible] اوتغا
و اوتغانالینک شرم کنیم اوتغانغلی برای شرم کردن و تا شرم کرده. اوتغانغاچ چون شرم کرد و کند اوتغانغوچی شرم کننده
اوتغانغوچه و اوتغانغونجه و اوتغانغانجه تا شرم کردن و بتقدیم شرم کردن اوتغانغوم شرم خواهم کرد اوتغانغوسی شرم
خواهد کرد اوتغانغولوق شرم کردنی اوتغانغای و اوتغانا و اوتغانسا و اوتغانسون و اوتغاندیک شرم کند اوتغانغودیک
و اوتغانوردیک شرم کردنی و همچنانکه شرم کند اوتاماق بفتح تای الف کشیده یعنی ادا کردن باشد اوتادی ادا کرد
اوتادوق ادا کردیم اوتادور و اوتایدور ادا میکند و اوتار بمعنی میکند و بترکی رومی بمعنی میسر ایدهم آمده و در اینجا نکرده
ماخوذ از مصدر اوتماق است چنانکه گذشت و بمعنی فاعل و مصدر نیز می آید اوتامایدور ادا نمیکند و نکرده است
اوتا و اوتاغیل مفرد مخاطب فعل امر اوتاما و اوتاماغیل مفرد مخاطب فعل نهی اوتانک و اوتانکیز و اوتانکلار جمع مخاطب
فعل امر اوتامانک و اوتامانکیز و اوتامانکلار جمع مخاطب فعل نهی اوتامان و اوتاماس مین ادا نمیکنم اوتایمین و اوتارمین
و اوتایدورمین و اوتادورام ادا میکنم و بترکی رومی بمعنی میسر ایم هم باشد اوتاریم
و اوتاماغیم ادا کردنم و اوتاماغوم بمعنی گذشته هم باشد اوتاماغوم ادا نخواهم کرد اوتاب و اوتابان و اوتامیش ادا کرده
اوتامیشانلق ادا کرده اوتاماس ادا نمیکند و بمعنی فاعل و مصدر منفی هم می آید اوتاماسی ادا کردن و نکردن اوتامادین
از ادا کردن و ادا نکرده اوتاب بولماس و اوتا بولماس و اوتاماق ولماس ادا نمیتوان کرد اوتا آلماس ادا نمیتواند کرد اوتا
و اوتای و اوتای ادا کنان ادا کنان و بدون تکرار هم مستعملست اوتای و اوتایین ادا کنم و کند و کنی اوتاسا و اوتاغای بیز
و اوتاغای بیز و اوتالی و اوتالینک ادا کنیم اوتاغلی برای ادا کردن و تا ادا کرده. اوتاغاچ چون ادا کرد و کند اوتاغوچی
ادا کننده اوتاغوچه و اوتاغونجه و اوتاغانجه تا ادا کردن و بتقدیم ادا کردن اوتاغوم ادا خواهم کرد اوتاغونک ادا خواهی کرد
اوتاغوسی ادا خواهد کرد اوتاغولوق ادا کردنی اوتاغای و اوتاسا و اوتاسون و اوتادیک ادا کند و اوتاغودیک و اوتاردیک
ادا کردنی و همچنانکه ادا کند و اوتاردیک بمعنی گذشتی و همچنانکه بکند هم آمده و در اینجا بمعنی با مصدر اوتماق اشتراک دارد
اوتالماق مع اللام مصدر انفعالست یعنی ادا شدن اوتالدی ادا شد چنانکه در تاریخ بابری مذکورست که عید [illegible]
کومل [illegible] بقاسیدا اوتالدی اوتالغان ادا شونده و ادا شده چنانکه در [illegible] المحبه مذکور [illegible]
بمعنی ادا شده کوید که همیشه کونکلیدا اول [illegible] اوتالغان تابی [illegible]
بمعنی مصدر نیز می آید و [illegible] صیغ [illegible] و الاضافه [illegible] اشتقاق [illegible] اوتلاماق بغ و ضم [illegible] دار داول
آتش زدن و سوزاندن [illegible] اوتلادی آتش زد [illegible] اوتلادوق آتش زدیم [illegible] اوتلادور و اوتلایدور آتش میزند
و میزد چنانکه در لسان الطیر در داستان مجنون که الاغ خود را [illegible] در خرابه خوابیده بود کوید الشاهد علی

الثالث به المثنى الثالث شعر مرکبین کوتوی کما اوتلادیلر تیموب خارو خس غنه هر طرف اغزینه اوروب واوتلامق بمعنی ماحل و مصدر
بزمی آید اوتلاغنا بیله اتش میزند خواست و میچرد و میچرید است اوتلاغان واوتلادغان واوتلایدوغان اتش میزند
و چرنده و چرنده و بمعنی مصدر منفی آید و اوتلاسا اوتلاغیل مفرد غائب امر و اوتلاسا و اوتلاغیل مفرد غائب فعل نهی
و اوتلامانکیز اوتلاغیلار جمع غائب فعل امر و اوتلاماغانک و اوتلامانکیز و اوتلاماگیلار جمع غائب فعل نهی اوتلامان و اوتلاماغان
اتش میزنیم و میچرم اوتلای مین و اوتلارمین و اوتلایدورمین و اوتلارام اتش میزنم و میچرم اوتلایم و اوتلاماغیم اتش بزنم
اوتلاماغوم اتش نخواهم زد و نخواهم چرید اوتلاب و اوتلابان و اوتلامیش اتش زده و چرید اوتلامیشانک اتش زده و چریده
اوتلامادین از اتش زدن و اتش نزده و از چریدن و نچریده اوتلاماس اتش نمیزند و نمیچرد و بمعنی ماحل و مصدر منفی هم می آید
اوتلامالیی اتش نزدنی و نزدنش و چریدنش و نچریدنش اوتلاب بولماس و اوتلاشا بولماس و اوتلاماناق و لماس اتش نمیتوان زد و نمیتوان
چرید اوتلامای الماس اتش نمیتواند زد و نمیتواند چرید اوتلایو و اوتلاچی اوتلاچی اتش زنان اتش زنان و چریدن چریدن و به معنی تکرار
هم با یمعانی مستعملست اوتلامای و اوتلامایین اتش نزنیم و نزند و نزنی و نچرم و نچرد و نچری اوتلاماق و اوتلاماغلیق و اوتلاماغای
و اوتلامالی و اوتلامالیق اتش مزنیم و میچرنیم اوتلاماغلی برای اتش زدن و تا اتش زده و برای چریدن و تا چریده اوتلاماغاچ
چون اتش زد و بزند و چون چرید و بچرد اوتلاماغوچی اتش زننده و چرنده اوتلاماغوچیلار و اوتلاماغوچیسی و اوتلاماغانچه تا اتش زدن
و بعد از اتش زدن و تا چریدن و بعد از چریدن اوتلاماغوم اتش خواهم زد و نخواهم چرید اوتلاماغونک اتش خواهی زد
و نخواهی چرید اوتلاماغوچی اتش خواهد زد و نخواهد چرید اوتلاماغولوقی اتش زدنی و چریدنی اوتلاماغای و اوتلاماسا و اوتلاسا
و اوتلاماغدیدان اتش بزند و بچرد اوتلاماغودین و اوتلادیلار اتش زدنی و همچنانکه اتش بزند و چریدنی و همچنانکه بچرد
اوتلاماق مع التاسعه متعدیست بمعنی اوقاق بودن و چراندن و بمعنی آن به معنی هستو شتر و لامانه تا به تاشتغان

اوتلامق مع النون مصدر تعدیست بمعنی اتش به کرفتن و چرانیدن و بمعنی آن به هستو یامانه نوتانی اشتقاق می یابد
می یابد اوتونماک بضم تا و سکون نون بمعنی التماس کردن باشد اوتوندی التماس کرد اوتوندوک التماس کردیم اوتوندوم
و اوتونادور التماس میکند و اوتونور بمعنی ماحل و مصدر منفی هم می آید اوتونماید مرا التماس نمیکند و نکرده است اوتونکان
و اوتونورکان و اوتونادورکان التماس کننده و التماس کرده و بمعنی مصدر هم می آید اوتون و اوتونکیل مفرد مخاطب فعل امر
و اوتون هیمه را نیز کویند چنانکه مذکور شود اوتونما و اوتونماغیل مفرد مخاطب فعل نهی اوتونونک و اوتونونکیز
اوتونونکیلار جمع مخاطب فعل امر اوتونمانک و اوتونمانکیز و اوتونمانکیلار جمع مخاطب فعل نهی اوتونمان و اوتونمایمین
التماس نمیکنم اوتونایین و اوتونورمین و اوتونادورمین و اوتونورام التماس میکنم اوتونورغم و اوتونماغیم التماس کردیم اوتونماغوم
التماس نخواهم کرد اوتونوب و اوتونوبان و اوتونمیش التماس کرده اوتونمیشانکا التماس کرده اوتونماس التماس نمیکند و بمعنی
ماحل و مصدر منفی هم می آید اوتونمالیی التماس کردنش و نکردنش اوتونمادین از التماس کردن و التماس نکرده اوتونوب بولماس
و اوتونسا بولماس و اوتونماق اولماس التماس نمیتوان کرد اوتونا آلماس التماس نمیتواند کرد اوتونا اوتونا التماس کنان التماس کنان
و بدون تکرار هم با یمعنی مستعملست اوتونمای و اوتونمایین التماس نکنم و نکند و نکنی اوتونسا و اوتونکای
خواهد اوتونسه و اوتونالی و اوتونالیلک التماس کنیم اوتونماغلی برای التماس کردن و تا التماس کرده اوتونکاچ چون التماس کرد و کند
اوتونکوچی التماس کننده اوتونکوچیلار و اوتونکوچیسی و اوتونکانچه تا التماس کردن و بعد از التماس کردن اوتونکوم التماس خواهم کرد
اوتونکونک التماس خواهی کرد اوتونکوسی التماس خواهد کرد اوتونکولوک التماس کردنی اوتونکای و اوتونسون و اوتونکاندا

التماس کند اوتونکودیک و اوتونوب التماس کردنی و همچنانکه التماس کند اوتونکاندا بمعنی اوت بمعنی آمد اول البحر آتش کوکب
آتش چنانکه کوید شعر خوبلر خسار ریفه شالدی کلشا اوت ایله کیم کل خوبنی غبار اتشین خسار اوت دو قیم کیاه
کویند شیم ترکی رومی نیز بود جهارم دوا و مهلا اترا کویند که آنرا بعربی سم خوانند شم ارا
کدشتن هم ارات ارا یدن خوانند یکی کردن با شباع ضمه دو معنی دارد اول ارات از بردن آب و کرو دوقیم
انخوشه خاصل و کلمه تحسین ناترا باتش کرمش چنانکه مذکور شد و بزبان هندی کویند اوتا بفتح تا الف کشیده
ترکی و عربی و موضع استعمال شود اول کویند اوتابقا و اوتایان یعنی آنطرف و آن سو دوقیم کویند که اوتا کون یعنی
روز کذشته و اوتا دین یعنی از آن طرف و اوتا یعنی کذران و خوانندکان چنانکه
مصدر اوتمالی کذشت اوتاچی بیلاقیرا کویند و اوتاچی خطائی نام ادویه ایست اوبکه اوتلغ و اوتا نشین
که آنرا رومیه مخفف ساخته اوتا کویند اوتاغه بر طیور خوانند عموما و بر عمرکه بعلامت شجاعت و پهلوانی
جنگ بر سر زنند خصوصا چنانکه متضمن هر دو مضمون کوید شعر میلدیلوتار ارتا قیلدی اول ماتل شجاع
خورشید فاضیفه مثال خط شعلهوا اوتاک بمعنی ازا بود اوتچی بسکون تا و کسر جیم عجمی ترکی رومی طبیب و جراح باشد
که آنرا بعربی نتیجه نامند او تراق ترکی رومی نشیمن و جوش بود و اتراو بسکون تا و ضم را قرشت بمعنی مقابل و برابر
الشاهد علیه شعر نی ملالت خوب کیم ایلامیش او ترا یوز دشنام کلدی کیم اینک عار غنو کوز و تدین علیه
او تروک بمعنی دروغ باشد او تروک کینه بمعنی دروغ چنانکه کوید شعر جوز ایله هر فیلا بیلدی رقیبا بی
جین عینه مهر ایله هر وجه کیم قیلدی بی بار او تروک کینه او تنکو دو معنی دارد اول تند و یم دوقیم و کهمه
او تکون بسکون تا و نون و ضم کاف عجمی دو معنی دارد اول بمعنی کذرنده دوقیم نام یک نوع سکانیست چنانکه بطرق تکلم کوید
شعر تیرباران غمنک جان و کونکولدین او تی ای الله الله نیلابو باغین ایرمیش او تکونکو ولر شعر تیرباران
فراق احبا طاعتیدین او تار هیچ یامنع بونداز آیا او تکون و لغا غیولیکیش او تکونجه ا هکیذه دا کوبند چنانکه در
لیلی مجنون در ملاقات مجنون با یسات لیلی کوید شعر بونکته لار ایلا ایان شمار او تکونچی لار ایلا من نظاره کله
بفتح تا و کاف عجمی بمعنی ارده ملعقت مغولی خریبود که آنرا بعربی دیته خوانند او تلاش او تلاش بمعنی تو برو چنانکه کوید
مجر بویز او تلاش بلا هر دیدا بیغه شالمیش بمعنی سیل مجبور دین قو تولماق احتمال بن مر اعیل و نیز همین معنی فرماید شعر
غم و درد زندانی ایچرا کونکول کان تو شوب او تلاش او تلاش کرفتار لیغلاغی و لطالع هروی او تلاش او تلاش را بمعنی آتشین
آتشین نوشته و شعر بمعنی را شاهد آورد و بضی هم متابعت کرده هر دو سهو کرده اند و همچنین در تاریخ الانبیا
در ذکر احضار تخت بلقیس کوید که یا نبی من دیدیکیم کوز یوموب آچغونجه کیلتورای و اول تخت نی بلقیس منی او تکی
اوی ایچیندا قو یوب با جاسین مقفل قیلیب ایردی او تلاغ و او تلاق بمعنی علفخوار باشد او تلوغ او تلوق دو معنی دارد
اول مکانی را کویند که کیاه و علف بسیار داشته باشد دوقیم بمعنی آتشین و آتشناک بود الشاهد علیه شعر
ای نوانی هجر او تلوغ دشتی ایچرا انکلادیم آنی کیم بیلار هر دین قطعه ایرمیش سقش اتلو کان بسکون تا و ضم نون ولا
و فتح کاف عجمی پرندایست سیاه منقوش آواز که جالهای سفید دارد و آنرا بعربی سار و شارک خوانند او تلکو بفتح تا
و سکون لام و ضم کاف عجمی نام پرنده ایست شکاری که آنرا بعربی چرخ و صقر کویند او تماک نان

62 v.

روغن را خوانند چنانکه در حیرة الابرار در وصف قناعت گوید شعر کیم قورو وقاق و نان سوخته تو غراب میوث
که قرص خور و چشمهٔ حیوان دیبون ۰ و آنرا رومیه اتمك نمع الف کویند و معانی مشتقه از بجویت که در ذیل مسلاد
در این حرف کذشت او تماچی خبازرا مانند چنانکه در فصل سی و یکم از محبوب القلوب در وصف دهقان کوید که او تماجی
تنوری آندین قیزیق و خلاف بازاری آندین ایسیق و در نسایم المحبه در ذکر احوالات مشایخ صوفیه کوید که شیخ ابو بکر
خباز قدس سره او تماچی لیک کا مشهور بوده او بته بترکی روحی صدا و آواز و خواندن کبوتر بود و باشباع ضمه خوشه گندم
تازه را کوید که آنرا بشعله آتش نکه‌داشته پخته باشند و گله حیوانات را که با آتش نکه‌داشته از مو پاک کرده باشند
او توجی بضم تا و کسر جیم بلغت مغولی بمعنی شکسته بند باشد او تورر بضم تا و سکون را ی قرشت عمرا و ضمه را کویند
بزمار است از کلمهٔ ایندن چنانکه کذشت و بترکی روحی مار است از نشستن او توریته بسکون رای قرشت و تای ثانی و فتح میم ترکی
رومی جمع و دانه شمار کویند او تورکو بسکون رای قرشت و ضم کاف عجمی نام یک نوع الت بخاری است که بدان تخته را سوراخ
کرده میخ بر جای آن کوبند و آنرا غار بچاسکنه و بعربی مثقب کویند او تورر عدد سی باشد چنانکه کوید شعر
خلات نسل غرایب قوتمنکا بو شرط سیله ۰ که نامه تو قوتر و آقته ایچه منکا او توتر او توز الّتی خط چنانکه
کوید شعر میل نوا میمی هول خط سیله یارب غازیم ۰ کیم سرابرا سیدین آریلدی او توز الّتی خطوط او توز ایکی نام
از اتراك او توك در وصف دارد اول کفش و موزه را کوید الشاهد علیه شعر تاکیب سنجاق توزکالکون اوتو
قیلدی نیلنی خرام ۰ بوقینیك دیلك کیك برعاحسن بهار سیند ایسل ۰ دویم طومار ابواب وقایع و سرکذشت را خوانند چنانکه
در جلد سیم تاریخ وصاف در ذکر احوال جلال الدین سیوستانی مذکورات که چند او توك نوشت سراسر سرسری نیز اول
سرسری و نیز کوید که تفتیش آن او توکها و ایضاً الآن اول کها هم بعینه مترسل بعضی امرا بود او توکمی بر وزن آمده اول
انباچی را کویند دویم بمعنی همیه فروش باشد او تیم بسکون تای قرشت و کسر ای حطی نباتات دوا و غذای از رامسك
نامرد و وصف حضرت مریم علیها السلام کوید شعر سما روغ برله بیملو کی میلیبان قوت نفیسه اینك اعجازیدین
بوبرد یلونکان او ت بمعنی مع الجیم من المشتقات اوچما ق غ بسکون جیم عجمی چهار معنی دارد اول بمعنی طیران و پریدن دویم اوچ
ثانی اختلاج ثالث محو و معدوم شدن چهارم هشتم را کویند چنانکه بمعنی طیران و هشت بطریق ایهام کوید شعر
او قونکلین بیحیقاردیم کو بونکا میلسام هوا نامات بوق ۰ که اوچماق میلینی ملنا قفه بال و پرا برو مار عش ۰ و بمعنی افتادن
چشم فرماید شعر کوزلار اوچماقدین سلو سین کیم سنیم یادیم کیلو شرای کونکولکا بیخورنا قیل بردم که محو ادیم کیلوسی بلفظ
پریدن هر معنی که در فارسی مستعملست و بجماق نیز بهمان معانی در کلام ترك استعمال یابد اوچماق خاموش شدن شمع
بود که آنرا بعربی انطفا کویند الشاهد علیه شعر دمی که عشق او متیدا تا المغای اثرین دین ۰ عونه بولغو سی اوچماقته
هر منزین اوچتی چهار معنی دارد اول پرید ثانی اختلاج کرد ثالث معدوم شد رابع منطفی شد چنانکه در سکندری
در مخاطبات اسکندر کوید بالمعنی الثالث شعر او زوجکمت و مرا تشید بادی ۰ کب اوچتی دامیلکا تا الدی سواد و در خسرو شیرین
در ذکر فرهاد کوید بالمعنی الرابع شعر چانین کیم با رودی انواری آتینك ۰ چو اوچتی تا المادی اثاری آتینك اوچار بلفظ
مستقبل هر چهار معنی است الشاهد علی الاول بالمعنی الثانی شعر کونعم اوچار که هما یون بوزونکی کورکا عاجات بعنه
آنکا کبر بکاه او پلیل یکوثات بالمعنی الرابع شعر تیزلیبا یتیعنك نوله عشقینی کرچه او تا او چار اکی سونا چلو دادی

63 r.

بمعنی فاعل و مصدر منفی نیز آید اوچماید و ر بمعنی نپرد و نپریده است و اختلاج نکند و نکرده است و معدوم نشود و نشده
و منطفی نمیشود و نشده است اوچقان و اوچار کان و اوچاد و فان پرنده و پریده و اختلاج کرده و معدوم شونده و معدوم شده
و منطفی شونده و منطفی شده و بمعنی مصدر هم می‌آیند اوچکان و اوچار کان و اوچاد و رکان منطفی شونده و منطفی شده و بمعنی مصدر هم می‌آیند
اوچ امرست از پریدن و اختلاج کردن و زایل و منطفی شدن و عدد سه را نیز کویند اوچیل امرست از پریدن و اختلاج
کردن و زایل شدن اوچیل امرست از منطفی شدن اوچما مفرد مخاطب است از فعل نهی بمعنی چهار معنی اچاغیل نمی است از
پریدن و اختلاج کردن اچاکیل نفی است از منطفی شدن اچونك ها و چونکیز او چونکلار جمع مخاطب است از فعل امر چهار معنی
اوچماندع اوچمانکیز اوچمانکلار جمع مخاطب است از فعل نهی بمعنی چهار معنی اوچمان و اوچماس مین متکلم وحده است از مضارع منفی بمعنی
اوچمایمین اوچمایسین اوچماید بیز و اوچماید یلار منفی متکلم وحده است از مضارع مثبت بمعنی چهار معنی اوچادیم پریدم و اختلاج
و محو شدم و خاموش شدم اوچاغیم پریدیم و اختلاج و معدوم شدم اوچاکیم خاموش شدم اوچقوم نخواهم
پرید و اختلاج نخواهم کرد و معدوم نخواهم شد اوچاکوم منطفی نخواهم شد اوچوب و اوچوبان و اوچمیش پریده
و اختلاج کرده و معدوم شده و منطفی شده چنانکه در مقاله یازدهم از حیرة الابرار در وصف طلب علم کوید شعر
خلق کوپ و بو قیری یاری آتینك ۰ کوزدین اوچوب شمع دیاری آتینك ۰ و نیز در خسرو شیرین بهمان معنی کوید شعر
بوز یحین روشن ایلیب کوزنی کونین ۰ آنکا کوزدین اوچوب قرة العین ۰ و در لهار نظم سکندری آمده الشاهد علی الثالث
بالمعنی الثالث شعر بولار چون علم سازی کوچمیش ایدی ۰ دیکیل مشوی کنه اوچمیش ایدی ۰ اوچمیشانلیر بیرا اختلاج کرده
و معدوم شده و منطفی شده اوچماس مضارع منفی است بهر چهار معنی و بمعنی فاعل و مصدر منفی نیز می‌آید اوچماس
بمعنی نفی و اثبات بهر چهار معنی و مصدر می‌آید اوچمادین از پریدن و نپریده و از اختلاج کردن و اختلاج نکرده و از معدوم شدن
و معدوم نشده و از منطفی شدن و منطفی نشده اوچوب بولماس و اوچا بولماس نمیتوان پرید نمیتوان اختلاج کرد معدوم
نمیتوان شد منطفی نمیتوان شد اوچا آلماس نمیتواند پرید و اختلاج نمیتواند کرد و معدوم نمیتواند شد و منطفی نمیتواند شد
اوچا اوچا پران پران و اختلاج کنان و معدوم شوان و منطفی شوان و بدون تکرار هم بلفظ مستعملست اوچای و
اوچایین بپرم و بپرد و بپریم و اختلاج کنم و کند و کنی و معدوم و منطفی شوم و شود و شوی اوچاق و اوچایز و اوچماید
بپریم و اختلاج کنیم و معدوم شویم اوچالی و اوچکای بیز و اوچکای بیز منطفی شویم اوچالی و اوچالیبا پریم و اختلاج کنیم و معدوم
و معدوم شویم و منطفی شویم اوچقالی برای پریدن و تا پریده و برای اختلاج کردن و تا اختلاج کرده و برای معدوم شدن و تا معدوم
شده اوچکالی برای منطفی شدن و تا منطفی شده اوچقاج چون پرید و بپرد و چون اختلاج کرد و کند و چون معدوم شد و شود
اوچکاج چون منطفی شد و شود شعر عشق صفح و الفلح کونکولکا بو قتور و دخریره لیك ۰ اول صفتکیم شعله شمع و چکاج
بو لور دلخکر قرار اوچقوچی پرنده و اختلاج کننده و معدوم شونده اوچکوچی منطفی شونده اوچقونچا و اوچغونچا و اوچغانچا تا پریدن
قدم پریدن و تا اختلاج کردن و بعد از اختلاج کردن و تا معدوم شدن و بعد از معدوم شدن تا اوچکونچا و اوچکوچا
و اوچکانچه تا منطفی شدن و بعد از منطفی شدن اوچقوم خواهم پرید و اختلاج خواهم کرد و معدوم خواهم شد اوچکوم
منطفی خواهم شد اوچغونك خواهی پرید و اختلاج خواهی کرد و معدوم خواهی شد اوچکونك منطفی خواهی شد اوچقوسی
خواهد پرید و اختلاج خواهد کرد و معدوم خواهد شد چنانکه بمعنی اول کوید شعر اول پری اوچقوسی هر الیخ دین

آدمی بو نبه بولور معنا اوچکوسی منطفی خواهد شد اوچقولوق پریدنی واختلاج کردن ومعدوم شدن اوچکولو
منطفی شدن اوچقای پرد واختلاج کند ومعدوم شود اوچکای منطفی شود اوچا یا اوچسا و اوچون و اوچلی
پرد واختلاج کند ومعدوم شدنی وهمچنانکه معدوم شود چنانکه شاهد بر ثانی نیز یعنی اول گوید شعر
بوی وجیمین دی آلمان قوچقونینکلیغ نیری دیلک چیت لوغدین اوچقونینکلیغ اوچکودیلک واوچکونکلیغ منطفی شدنی
وهمچنانکه منطفی شود اوچار دیلک بمعنای اوچقودیلک واوچکودیلک باشد اوچورماق بضم جیم عجمی مع القاف
مصدر متعدی وچماق باشد که عبارت از پراندن ومختلج ساختن ومعدوم کردن بود من حیرت الابرار بالمعنی الاول
شعر تیلماک اوچون جیمینی وچورماقیغه باش آندا قیلیب تعبیه چوقاوق قناش اوچورماک مع الکاف متعدی
مصدر اوچماک باشد که عبارت است از منطفی ساختن بود چنانکه گوید شعر وه که کل شمعین اوچورماکلیک ایچون دور
قطره اوزی عقه بولوب تین دم غلطان تا مادم اوچوردی پرانید ومختلج کرد ومعدوم کرد ومنطفی کرد چنانکه بمعنی ثانی
ورابع بطریق جناس گوید شعر آهیم سیلی تو فراغین اوچوردی اشکیم سوی وتینی اوچوردی اوچورور واوچورادور
مضارع است بهرچهار معنی واوچورور بمعنی فاعل ومصدر نیز می آید چنانکه بمعنی پراندن در دیباچه محبوب القلوب گوید
که قونادلیغ صرصری اوچورور غبار وستیار نسترن نینک ساچلغان نافراغلاجی اوچورماید بمعنی پراند ونپراند است
ومختلج نمیسازد ونساخته است ومعدوم نمیکند ونکرده است ومنطفی نمیکند ونکرده است اوچورغان واوچورغانی اوچار
پراننده وپرانیده ومختلج کننده ومختلج کرده ومعدوم کننده ومعدوم کرده وبمعنی مصدر نیز می آید اوچورکان
دمکان و اوچورکان منطفی کننده ومنطفی کرده وبمعنی مصدر نیز می آید اوچورماق عبارت از پراندن ومختلج کردن ومعدوم کردن
ومنطفی کردن بالمعنی الاول شعر اوچورکه ای قویون کرال آی باشیغه ایو دایاین بودم که بولیدا تو فراغ پرله یکسان
یعنی ایزدم که درین او باخاک یکسان ای کرد با دمهیران که بر سر آنها بگردم بالمعنی الثالث شعر ای صبا گوزدین اوچور
ما نعلرن نینک دردینی کیم تیلیب بن سرمه مرو شاهجان نینک کردینی بالمعنی الرابع کوبی ساری هر کیچه کم عزم ایتیسا کونگل
ای چرخ اوچور شمع که اول یوتی یا نیکیماش وبیز عبارت از زیارت آمدن فال وظهور اثر خواب باشد چنانکه در ذیل جواهر
مذکور شود اوچورغیل امر است از پراندن ومختلج کردن ومعدوم کردن اوچورکیل امر است از منطفی کردن الشاهد علیه
شعر پر قویاش مشعلی دین خانیمه اوز عشق اوتی یوقا سیا شمع حیاتیمنی اوچورکیل یارب اوچورما مفرد مخاطب از فعل نهی
بهر چهار معنی اوچورماغیل مفرد مخاطب است از فعل نهی بمعنی مصدر اوچورماق اوچورماکیل مفرد مخاطب است از فعل نهی بمعنی
مصدر اوچورماک اوچورینک واوچورونگیز واوچورونگلار جمع مخاطب است از فعل امر بهر چهار معنی اوچورمانک واوچور
مانگیز واوچورمانگلار جمع مخاطب است از فعل نهی بهر چهار معنی اوچورغان واوچورماس مین میپرانم ومختلج میکنم ومعدوم میکنم و
منطفی میکنم اوچورامین واوچورورمین واوچوراورمین واوچورورام مختلج میکنم ومیپرانم ومعدوم میکنم ومنطفی میکنم
اوچوروب واوچوربان واوچورمیش پرانیده ومختلج کرده ومعدوم کرده ومنطفی کرده الشاهد علی الاول بالمعنی الاخیر شعر
چو یا روتوب یوزونک وتی فلک شبستانین اوپلتی دین اوچوروب همه طرف بجوم چراغ اوچورمثلا پرانیده ومختلج کرده
ومعدوم کرده ومنطفی کرده اوچورماس مضارع منفی بهر چهار معنی وبمعنی فاعل ومصدر منفی هم می آید اوچورغانی بمعنی نفی
واثبات بهر چهار معنی می آید اوچورغاندین بدستور اخوات بمعنی مصدر مثبت ونامنی منفی می آید اوچوروب بولماس و اوچورنا

نمیتوان پرانید ومختلج نمیتوان کرد ومعدوم نمیتوان کرد ومنطفی نمیتوان کرد اوچورا اوچورا پراندن پراندن ومختلج کردن
ومعدوم کنان ومنطفی کنان وبدون تکرار هم مستعملت اوچوراو اوچورایین پرانم وبپرانید پرانیدنی ومختلج ومعدوم ومنطفی
کنم وکنید وکنی اوچوراق واوچورایزها واوچورغای بپرانیم ومختلج کنیم ومعدوم کنیم اوچورالی واوچورکالی اوچورکالی منطفی
اوچورابی واوچورالینک بپرانیم ومختلج کنیم ومعدوم کنیم ومنطفی کنیم اوچورغالی برای پراندن وتا پراند وبرای مختلج کردن
وتا مختلج کرده وبرای معدوم کردن وتا معدوم کرده اوچورکالی برای منطفی کردن وتا منطفی کرده اوچورغاچ چون پرانید
وچون مختلج کرد وکند وچون معدوم کرد وکند اوچورکاچ چون منطفی کرد وکند اوچورغوچی پراننده ومختلج کننده ومعدوم
کننده اوچورکوچی منطفی کننده اوچورغوچه واوچورغونچه واوچورغانچه تا پراندن وبقدر پراندن وتا مختلج کردن وتا معدوم کردن و
معدوم کردن اوچورکوچه اوچورکونچه واوچورکانچه تا منطفی کردن وبقدر منطفی کردن چنانکه شاهد بر ثانی نیز یعنی اول در دیباچه
هشتم از محبوب القلوب در ذکر تجرید وقصه کلهنی گوید که ایل تیب اوتین اوچورکونچه آندین نخبر مالدی اثر اوچورغوم
خواهم پرانید ومختلج ومعدوم خواهم کرد اوچورکوم منطفی خواهم کرد اوچورغونک خواهی پرانید ومختلج ومعدوم
خواهی کرد چنانکه شاهد بر معنی اول اید در مناجات گوید که آخر اول قوشنی بوچامکه دین اوچورغونک اوچورکونک
منطفی خواهی کرد اوچورغوسی خواهد پرانید ومختلج ومعدوم خواهد کرد اوچورکوسی منطفی خواهد کرد اوچورغولوک
پراندنی ومختلج کردنی ومعدوم کردنی اوچورکولوک منطفی کردنی اوچورغای بپراند ومختلج ومعدوم کند اوچورکای
منطفی کند چنانکه شاهد هر دو را بمعنی پراند ومنطفی کند در نشات گوید که امید اولکیم عنایت چیندین وصل نسیمی ای
فراق تو فراغی نینک خس وخاشاکین اوچورغای وهدایت بولوتی دین قربت یاغینی لغیب هجران اوتی نینک اخکر وشعله سین
اوچورکای اوچوراو اوچورلا اوچورسون اوچوردیک بپراند ومختلج کند ومعدوم کند ومنطفی کند اوچورغودیک پراندنی که
پراند ومختلج ومعدوم کردنی وهمچنانکه مختلج ومعدوم کند الشاهد علیه شعر غم تونی صنعفا تیم آندا قیکم
اول کوزدین صبح انفاسی اوچورغودیک شمع بولمیش سیکیل یعنی تم سبک شده است همچنانکه انفاس صبح آنرا از کوی اوچورکو
پراند اوچورکودیک منطفی کردنی وهمچنانکه منطفی کند اوچورودیک بمعنای ذیل اوچورغودیک واوچورکودیک استعمال کرده شود
چنانکه در مقاله نایزدهم از حیرت الابرار بمعنی اوچورکودیک گوید شعر با مره شمعین اوچورودیک کریه عقل حیات
کتار وردیک سفیه اوچوشماق بضم جیم عجمی مع الثین مصدر مفاعله است یعنی با هم پرواز کردن وطالع هروی بمعنی
کج بحتی نوشته ونصیری هم متابعت کرده هرد وسهو کرده اند وصیغ آن بدستور شوالی الیشین قرشتاق شقاق می یابد
اوجاشماق بفتح جیم بالفکیده وسکون شین قرشت کاوش ومعارضه کردن اوجاشتی کاوش ومعارضه کرد شعر اجلیغه جان
آلوردا بیینکدی همجرینک نیچه کیم اول هو نونک پرله اوجاشتی پرده دین چیقغاچ یوزونک آلغالی قوغایی یاریغ یوزین قو برد
اوبات اوجاشتوق کاوش کردیم اوجاشورلار واوجاشادورلار کاوش میکند الشاهد علی الاول شعر آغزینک پیله پسته اوجا
یوچیلوغی دین سلمان که اوشول آغزی آچوق قامید بو توب توبرش واوجاشور بمعنی فاعل ومصدر هم می آید اوجاشماید کاوش نمیکند
ونکرده است اوجاشغان واوجاشورغان واوجاشاندورغان کاوش کننده وکاوش کرده وبمعنی مصدر هم می آید اوجاش واوجاشغیل
مفرد مخاطب از فعل امر اوجاشما واوجاشماغیل مفرد مخاطب از فعل نهی اوجاشینک واوجاشینکیز اوجاشینکلار جمع مخاطب از فعل امر
اوجاشمانک واوجاشمانکیز اوجاشمانکلار جمع مخاطب از فعل نهی اوجاشامن واوجاشورمین کاوش میکنم اوجاشامین واوجاشورمین و اوجا

واوجاشورام کاوش میکنم اوجاشورعم واوجاشاغیم کاوش کردنم اوجاشماغوم کاوش نخواهم کرد اوجاشیت واوجاشیان
واوجاشمیش کاوش کردما الشاهد علی الاول شعر اهل مسیح چه فهم ایلابان لونیات غه قالیپ اجل فراقینیک ایلکه
اولتوروبولاچون اوجاشیت اوجاشمیشانک کاوش کرده اوجاشماس کاوش نمیکند و بمعنی فاعل و مصدر منفی هم می آید
اوجاشماسی کاوش کردن و نکردن اوجاشمادین ناکاوش کردن وکاوش نکرده اوجاشیب بولماس و اوجاشسا بولماس و
اوجاشمای اولماس کاوش نمیتوان کرد اوجاشالماس کاوش نمیتواند کرد اوجاشا اوجاشا کاوش کنان کاوش کنان و بدون
تکرار هم بایعضی مستعملست اوجاشای عا اوجاشاین کاوش کنم و کند و کنی اوجاشاق واوجاشغایز و اوجاشغای پیز
واوجاشالیعا اوجاشالیک کاوش کنیم اوجاشغالی برای کاوش کردن و تاکاوش کرده اوجاشغاج چون کاوش کرد
وکند اوجاشغوچی کاوش کننده اوجاشغوسیدا اوجاشغوبجه و اوجاشغانجه تا کاوش کردن و بمقدار کاوش کردن اوجاشغو
کاوش خواهم کرد اوجاشغولک کاوش خواهی کرد اوجاشغوسی کاوش خواهد کرد اوجاشغولوق کاوش کردنی اوجاشغا
و اوجاشا و اوجاشسا و اوجاشسون و اوجاشدیک کاوش کنند اوجاشغودیک و اوجاشغودیک کاوش کردن و همچنانکه
کند اوجاشتورماق مصدر متعدیست یعنی بکاوش انداختن و صیغ آن بدستور با لفظ توم اشتقاق می یابد اوچراماق
بکون جیم عجمی و فتح رای مهمله دچار شدن اوچرادی دچار شد الشاهد علیه شعر سودا ورشته زحمت غه اوچرادی کونکلو
زلف و پلینک خیالدا فکر دقیقدین اوچرادوق دچار شدیم اوچرار و اوچرایدور دچار میشود الشاهد علی الاول
بلاد عشق تا که اوچرار او شبو تیلبه دیر اغزدا او تونی بو بلابه تا کهان دین اسراغیل البرت و اوچرار بمعنی فاعل و مصدر هم
می آید اوچرامایدور دچار نمیشود و نشده است اوچراغان او اوچراغان ها و اوچرایدورغان دو دچار شونده و دچار شده و منفی
نیز می آیند اوچرا و اوچراعیل مفرد غایب استمرار اوچراما و اوچراماغیل مفرد غایب استمرار منفی اوچرانک و اوچرانکیز و
اوچرانکلار جمع غایب استمرار اوچرامانک و اوچرامانکیز و اوچرامانکلار جمع غایب استمرار منفی اوچرامان و اوچرامایمن
دچار نمیشوم اوچرایمین ها و اوچرارمین و اوچرایدورمین و اوچرارم دچار میشوم اوچرایم و اوچرامایم دچار نشدم اوچرامای
دچار نخواهم شد اوچراب و اوچرابان و اوچرامیش دچار شده الشاهد علی الثانی شعر عقل او چوب نخود لوق ایلا دین
بولوقسا ناکهان کیم تیلبه لیق قیلغای پری اوچرابان اوچرامیشانک ده دچار شده اوچراماس دچار نمیشود
و بمعنی فاعل و مصدر منفی هم می آید اوچراماس دچار شدن و نشدن اوچراماسی دچار شدن و نشدن اوچرامادین
شدن و دچار نشده اوچراب بولماس و اوچراسا بولماس و اوچراناق و لماس دچار نمیتوان شد اوچرای الماس دچار نمیتواند شد
اوچرا بو و اوچرای اوچرای دچار شوان و بدون تکرار هم مستعملست اوچرای و اوچراین دچار شوم و شود و شوی اوچرانا
و اوچراغایز و اوچراغای پیز و اوچرالی و اوچرالینک دچار شویم اوچراغالی برای دچار شدن و تا دچار شده اوچراغاج چون
دچار شد و شود اوچراغوچی دچار شونده اوچراغوسیدا و اوچراغوبجه و اوچراغانجه تا دچار شدن و بمقدار دچار شدن اوچراغو
دچار خواهم شد اوچراغولک دچار خواهی شد اوچراغوسی دچار خواهد شد اوچراغولوق دچار شدنی اوچراغای و اوچراسا
و اوچراسون و اوچرادیک دچار شود چنانکه در داستان منافرالملیم اقول کوید الشاهد علی الاول شعر کونکلیکا اوچراغای
دلارای حاصل او لغای وصال یدیکامی اوچرادیک و اوچراغودیک دچار شدنی و همچنانکه دچار شود اوچراشماق مع التاء
مصدر مفاعله است بیکدیگر دچار شدن اوچراشیب بیکدیگر دچار شده چنانکه کوید شعر خوش تورور چیچی شام

ایکی یار اوچراشیب تا پیشیب پرلاییجه کرقوجوشوب یلا اشیب و باقی صیغ بدین قیاس بدستور شوق اول مع التاء
اشتقاق می یابد اوچراشماق مع التاء اوچراشتورماق مع الشین مصدر متعدیست یعنی دچار کردن اوچراتورماق
دچار میکند الشاهد علی الاول شعر ای نوای لولی اول نامهوان نغمه اوچراتورمین کیم مین نوادیک نا توان المیرکوی
اوچرات ولاچراتقیل دچار کن چنانکه شاهد برا اول در تحفة الابرار در مناجات میم کوید شعر ایبا سانا اولقوم خلایق
کوزنیکا اوچرات میینی خاصی بیهم و صیغ اوچراتسورماق با شین و لفظ تورمیز همین سیاق بدستور شوق اول اشتقاق می یابد
اوچ دو معنی دارد اول نوک و دم صرح چیزرا کویند چنانکه در وصف خنجر کرمنی مطلع کوید شعر سو سیله
شمع اوچینی هر ینهه الکد ینات نار و دیبی شعله نی سو برا کرجه روشن ایتما کد و محال دویم کمعنی انتقام باشد و بجیم عجمی
عدد سه را نامند و نیز امر است از پریدن و معدوم شدن و التماع کردن و منطفی شدن چنانکه در ذیل مضاد لرین
حرف کذشت و فوالغی حج را حاصل بعضا و اوجاشماق تصور کرده و بمعنی حریص بودن در خصوصیت نوشته سهو کرده اوجا
بفتح جیم با الف کشیده سه معنی دارد اول بمعنی پشت باشد الشاهد علیه شعر اوجاملدالی توقو لغان بیح اغریدیک کما
ارکو یا اولوغ ایرمیش شله اسر چون کوکسونکا قوی یدیم دلغ و نیز در تاریخ الانبیا در مقام تمام کردن حضرت ابراهیم
علیه السلام بنای کعبه را کوید که اول اوی تمامغه سیکاندین سونکرا شکر قیلیب اوجاسین کعبه دیوارینه قویوب
تفاخر ایتی و در میان اتراک رسم است که اسب و کوسفند را درست بخته پشت انرا ازبرای احترام مهمان زعیش مهمان می گذارند
و اکر در مجلسی این نوع طعام نباشد حمل بخست میزبان و بیوقعی مهمان کنند چنانکه در تتمه سکندری در ضیافت خاقان
شعر بی ده دیوه لو لخوان قیاسی ایمیس که توقون میک آت منینک اوجاسی ایمیس دویم مجاز ابعضی مجلس با استعمال
می شود سیم تبرکی روی بعضی سرین بود اوجا ر بمعنی دچار و معنی دیگرها اطعمه تلخ بود که آتش آن دیر ماند و آنرا
سوکسوک هم نامند و بعربی غضا کویند و دویم بلغ اراضاشد که آنرا میر جسوق کویند در اتراک خوانند تنها در استعمال نمیکند
بازار اوجار میکویند و با جیم عجمی بمعنی آمده اول جعد المار لیطه باشد دویم مدحسب بودن رحمانی معنی مشتق از فعل مضارع
چنانکه در ذیل مشتقات این حرف کذشت اوچار کو بفتح جیم عجمی و سکون دال بیقرشت و ضم کاف عجمی تکلم تیز باشد و جاغ
واجاق دو معنی دارد اول آتشدان مطبخ را کویند که در آنجا دیک بار نهند و بالمجاز دود مان و خاندان نیز اتراک نامند چنانکه
در فرهاد و شیرین در وصف خاقان کوید شعر بو الموغ دیر ایرضه لعز که اداغیش قوروقتاسون دیلان دولتی ناکام
دو بهم لو قراهنیات که بر کردن مجوسین و فهران نهند اوچا فلاق کیاه سه برکه ماند اوچا الاچی بمعنی مرتبه
اوچانکه در مجالس النفایس در مجلس هفتم در ذکر امیر تیمور کوید که تاوچی میخاد سیله چاپست و اوچا الاچی نا شین کیلتورسین
اوچان بفتح جیم عجمی با الف کشیده و سکون نون کشتی بزرگ را نامند چنانکه کشتی متوسط را کیمه و کوچک را قایق کویند و هم
ابجد نام محلیست از مضافات تبریز اوچاو بکون واو بمعنی تماچنانکه کوید شعر کونکلوم ایالیه والید میزعی کیم
بولمو غه فرد مرا نع تو پیغمبر لا اوشبو اوچاو اوچاو لا او اوچاولان یعنی جریه با هم چنانکه شاهد لعل ادن فرهاد
در طلسم کشودن فرهاد کوید شعر چیقیب شهزاده پرله شاه ایکا و لاه و نیز کیاهان سیله اوچاو لا اوجسا در اق بسکون
جیم و فتح سین مهمله با الف کشیده یعنی سمت بالا ارچنانکه در تاریخ بابری مذکور است که هر کیم نینک که لعلباری کو پرا کوب
ثانی اراق تولار لا او جمور بفتح الجیم عجمی سکون لام بی قرشت دو معنی دارد اول نیزه ای بود بر نیزه را خوانند دویم تیر کردی

66r.

اوخ

65v

66v.

کردن ناوخشانور باوخشانا نکتشبیه می کند و توصیف می کند الشاهد علی الثانی شعر اوخشانا ایدوب فیل الحمیا
اکچه دهقان سرو کلرو یعملسو وکلینی اوخشانا دوش و اوخشاتور یعنی ناول و مصدر منفی هم آید اوخشانغان و
اوخشاتور غان ناوخشانا نک تشبیه کننده و تشبیه کرده و توصیف کننده و توصیف کرده و یعنی ناول و مصدر منفی هم آید چنانکه
یعنی مصدر کوید الشاهد علی الاول شعر کلانی اوخشانماز اوچون نیار یعنیه کونیا ملغ لر اضطراب کونکلوم و
بلبل شیدا ایماس اوخشاتماغ اوخشاتماین تشبیه نکم وکند وکنی و توصیف نکم وکند وکنی الشاهد علی الاول المعنی الاول شعر
باغ کلکشتی اولیغان لیغده صحرا دنیا نش سرو قد ینکه [illegible] اوخشاتمابی اوخشاتقو صبا اوخشاتقو
اوخشانغانغه تا تشبیه کردن و بعدم تشبیه کردن و تا توصیف کردن و بعدم توصیف کردن چنانکه کوید الشاهد علی الاول
شعر دیه کیم ایرکین اول آی دینک قوباشغه نسبتی [illegible] اوخشاتقوچه نسبت [illegible] یعنی [illegible]
آیا قعلم تشبیه کردن نسبت [illegible] مینغ برین [illegible] یا ایدم الجامد اوخشاتر
یعنی تشبیه و مانند باشد شعر [illegible] اوخشان اول [illegible]
ودر شعر ای صنم [illegible] لیلی و مجنون [illegible] دلبر یعنی [illegible] اوخشار یعنی امثال آنها [illegible]
و مانند کردن ماخوذ از مصدر اوخشاماق است اوخشوق بضم شین و سکون [illegible] شتر [illegible] کوینده مع
الدال المشفقان اوداماق بفتح دال و او داشتن مع الشین [illegible] یعنی ادا کردن [illegible] مجاز یعنی [illegible]
[illegible] اودو مع الذال المهمله [illegible] که آنرا بعربی [illegible] کوینده و اینکه [illegible] اهل ایران [illegible]
غلطوات و امع واوی [illegible] باید نوشته بشود زیرا که [illegible] کاوات و کاهر ترکان لوی کوینده اودا [illegible]
و هرچه [illegible] باشد یعنی خانه [illegible] و آنرا [illegible] اوده [illegible] شعر [illegible]
اودام هر کوشه اولمیش [illegible] عند لیث اوداک مع الکاف [illegible]
و بالجملہ یعنی مجازات نیز مستعملت اودامیش نام [illegible] ایلنز ترکان اودلت بسکون دال [illegible] لام [illegible]
ترسنده و جنان بود اودود بضم دال و سکون [illegible] که آنرا بعربی [illegible]
اودونج بضم دال و سکون نون و جیم یعنی [illegible] اوده بفتح دال [illegible] مع الراء المشدد [illegible]
اوریاق مع القاف دور کردن که آنرا بعربی [illegible] کوینده و باشباع [illegible]
[illegible] کوینده اوریاک مع الکاف [illegible] تاسیدن و بافتن [illegible]
که از چشم [illegible] چنانکه [illegible] مذکور شود و باشباع [illegible] فریاد کردن باشد [illegible] سلطان [illegible]
بعربی چنان [illegible] را کلب نباح کوینده چنانکه [illegible] شعر [illegible]
[illegible] اوریا [illegible] ا بن کلوبنی لو [illegible] طرد [illegible] و باشباع
[illegible] فریاد کردن [illegible] الشاهد علی [illegible] المعنی الثانی شعر
[illegible] و باشباع [illegible]
[illegible] کردیم [illegible] او [illegible] اوریا [illegible]
[illegible] اول کوید شعر چو دهقان کیم [illegible] و باشباع

67r.

[illegible] فریاد می کند و [illegible] ناول و مصدر منفی هم آید چنانکه [illegible] او [illegible] افغان
کیم اول [illegible] اوریا [illegible] و [illegible] است و [illegible] و باشباع [illegible]
[illegible] اوریا [illegible] اوریاد [illegible] و اوریاد و ریغان [illegible] ونغان [illegible] چنا
شاهد بر [illegible] کوید [illegible] کونکول [illegible]
و یعنی ناول و مصدر منفی هم آید چنانکه شاهد بر اول [illegible] کوید [illegible] الاحتوشنا [illegible]
[illegible] و شاهد بر ثانی [illegible] دیوان کوید که اول [illegible]
[illegible] و [illegible] ایرکان [illegible] و سائر [illegible]
کرده و یعنی ناول و مصدر هم می آیند اورتمق [illegible] الدی [illegible] کوینده چنانکه
[illegible] اوریا [illegible] مصدر [illegible] اورتمق [illegible] مصدر [illegible]
امیرزاده کوید شعر [illegible] که مال الدنیا [illegible] دولت
اورکیل مفرد [illegible] اورکوتمق [illegible] مصدر [illegible]
و اوریا [illegible] اورتماق [illegible] و باشباع [illegible]
و فریاد [illegible] اورامین [illegible] و باشباع [illegible] و فریاد [illegible]
[illegible] چنانکه شاهد بر [illegible] اول کوید شعر [illegible]
لطف ایله احسان [illegible] و باشباع [illegible] چنانکه [illegible]
[illegible] بو سلیمان [illegible] کوید که [illegible] آنکا دیدی که [illegible]
[illegible] الشاهد علی الثالث المعنی الاول شعر [illegible]
[illegible] چنانکه شاهد بر اول [illegible] کوید شعر
ایکالنا [illegible] المعنی الثانی شعر [illegible]
دور [illegible] انقطاع اول [illegible] الوداع [illegible] و فریاد [illegible]
و اوروبان [illegible] دور کرده و بافته و باشباع زده و فریاد کرده اوریاتمک خطاب [illegible]
اوریاس [illegible] مصدر [illegible] ناول [illegible] منفی [illegible] آید [illegible] مصدر [illegible]
مصدر منفی می آید [illegible] مصدر مثبت و ماضی منفی می آید [illegible]
کرد و میتوان بافت و باشباع [illegible] و میتوان [illegible] کرد [illegible] اوریاماس [illegible] و باشباع [illegible]
زد و میتواند فریاد کرد اوریا اوریا دور کنان و بافته کنان و باشباع زده و فریاد کنان چنانکه در تاریخ [illegible]
[illegible] مذکور است که سلطان [illegible] و لا [illegible]
مستعملت اوریای و اوریا بین دور کنم و کند و کنی و [illegible] و باشباع زنم و [illegible] و فریاد
و کند و کنی اوریاق [illegible] دور کنیم و بیافیم و باشباع زنیم و فریاد کنیم اوریاغلی برای دور کرد
و نادر و کرده و برای زدن و تازده اوریاغالی برای بافتن و تابافته و برای فریاد کردن و تا فریاد کرده اوریاغاج چوند [illegible]

دکند و باشباع چون نزد و بزند چنانکه گوید شعر کونکلوم تیغ اورغاج آهیم دین هویدا بولدی دود شعله ننک
اوستیکا چون قویدونک سوسیدا بولدی دود اورکاج چون نیافت و بیافد و باشباع چون فریاد کند و کرد اورغنجی
دروکنند و باشباع نزند الشاهد علیه شعر مین آنکا حیران وایل منیک زخم اورسابو خرش بی خبر زخم اورغنجلا
داغی حیرانیم منینک اورکوچی بیافد و باشباع سلت فریاد کند اورغوجیدا اورغونجا اورغانجه نامه کردن و بقد
درو کردن و باشباع تازدن و بقد نزدن اورکوجیدا اورکونجه اورکانجه تابافتن و بقد بافتن و باشباع تا فریاد کردن
و بقد فریاد کردن اورغوم درو خواهیم کرد و باشباع خواهیم زد اورکوم خواهیم بافت و باشباع فریاد خواهم
اورغونک درو خواهی کرد و باشباع خواهی زد چنانکه در کشودن طلسم سفر او کوید شعر چیقیتا اورغونک آجای
ایستکه وق و یا منکه چون اورغونک البته اورکونک خواهی یافت و باشباع فریاد خواهی کرد اورغوسی درو خواهد
کرد و باشباع خواهد زد چنانکه در مقاله دویم از حیرة الابرار کوید سبلت سفاج ادا در غوسیده کامینی بافلاد
اول قدم احرامینی اورکوسی خواهد یافت و باشباع فریاد خواهد کرد اورغولوق درو کردنی و باشباع زدنی اورکولو
بافتنی و باشباع فریاد کردنی اورغای درو کند و باشباع بزند اورکای ببافد و باشباع فریاد کند اورغودا و اورسا
داورغون و اورغودیک ببافد و درو کند و باشباع بزند و فریاد کند اورغودیک درو کردنی و همچنانکه درو کند و باشباع
زدن و همچنانکه بزند چنانکه بمعنی زدن کوید بو کیجه آهیم ایرور در لنتی برهم اورغودیک حوح کان اریدین انجم
کل لادین ننا و اورغودیک اورکودیک بافتنی و همچنانکه بیافد و باشباع فریاد کردنی و همچنانکه فریاد کند اورادیک
بمعانی مذکور اورغودیک و اورکودیک استعمال شود اوروملماق بضم او و سکون لام مع القاف مصدر انفعالیت یعنی
درو شدن و باشباع ضمه یعنی زده شدن اوروملماک مع الکاف بهمان معنی بافته شدن می آید اوروملغان
و اوروملکان و اوروملدی درو شوند و درو شده و باشباع زده شوند و زده شد و بمعنی مصدر نیز می آیند اوروملکان و
اوروملکانلار و اوروملادیکان بافته شوند و بافته شده چنانکه شاهد بر اولماق بمعنی تانی کوید فی النعت شعر بارا
ایکا اوروملکان کیسوی عنبر شمیم بالیا تنسا المیش محمد را مازلفان ایکی میم و بمعنی مصدر نیز می آیند الشاهد علی الاول
من سکندرنامه فی النعت شعر اوروملکاندا تاسیچ تاب و شکنج ایکی عنبرین افعی اول حسم کنج و باقی صیغ برابن سیاق
از مصادر ثلاثی باغین و از مصادر کاف باکاف بدستور شود وله مضافه لام اشتقاق می یابد اوروماق مع القاف مصدر
متعدی اورماقست یعنی درو فرمودن و باشباع مضروب ساختن اوروماک مع الکاف متعدی اوروماک تا باشد یعنی
بافانیدن و باشباع بفریاد آوردن اوروناق بضم او و سکون نون خود را بر این و آن زدن اورونی خود را زد اوروندی
خود را زدیم اورونوردی اوروناردی خود را بزند و اورونور بمعنی فاعل و مصدر نیز می آید اورونماید خود را نمی زند
اورونغان و اورونغاننوا و اورونان خود را زننده و خود را زد الشاهد علی الاول المعنی الاول شعر یوزیدین اورتا
تاپسیوز آلیبد اکونکول شمع المعید اورونغان کبی پروانه کوییوب و بمعنی مصدر نیز می آیند اورون و اورونغیل مفرد مخاطب
از فعل امر الشاهد علی الاول شعر ای نوک بی طفل الاوقاونغان نرمان مجنون دینیان بو بهانه سیرله اورلیلی و ثمینک
شاری اورون و اورونیغه بمعنی جاو مکان هم بود چنانکه نا شاهد ذیل خواهد مذکور شود اورونا و اورونغیل مفرد
مخاطب از فعل نهی اورونونا سیو اورونکیز و اورونو نکلار جمع مخاطب از فعل امر اورونماغیل و اورونمانکیز و اورونمانکلار جمع مخاطب

از فعل نهی اورونان و اورونغان مین خود را نمی زنم اورونماین و اورونورمن و اورونادورمن و اورونورمن خود را میزنم
اورونورمو و اورونماغیم خود را نزدم اورونماغیم خود را نخواهم زد اورونوب اورونوبامن و اورونغیز خود را زده چنانکه
در سوکواری شیرین در ماتم فرهاد کوید شعر اورونوب آنجه شور و شین قیلدی که ضعفا ایلا بی یا نزیب صفلدی
اورونغاننک خود را زده اورونماس خود را نمی زند و بمعنی فاعل و مصدر منفی هم می آید اورونماس خود را نزدن
و نزدنش اورونمادین از خود را زدن و خود را نزده اورونوچی کانا اورونسا بو کالیو اورونماکانا خود را نمیتوان زد اورونا
المماس خود را نمیتوان زد اورونا اورونا خود را زده خود را زده و بدون تکرار هم مستعملست اورونای و اورونایین
خود را بزنم و بزند و بزنی اورونای و اورونایین و اورونغالی و اورونغای خود را بزنیم اورونغالی برای خود را زدن و تا خود را زدن
اورونغاج چون خود را زد و بزند اورونوچی خود را زننده اورونغوجیدا اورونغونجه اورونغونجا تا خود را زدن و بقدر خود را زدن
اورونغوم خود را خواهم زد اورونغونک خود را خواهی زد اورونغوسی خود را خواهد زد اورونغولوق خود را
زدنی اورونغای و اورونغالی و اورونسون و اورونسونلار و اورونغودیک اورونغودیک و اورونوردیک خود را زدنی و همچنانکه
خود را بزند اوروشماق مصدر مفاعلست یعنی سیکه کردن و کنایه از جنک و جدل کردن هم باشد چنانکه
کوید شعر بارو قیکر اولمادی شمع مرادینک آیتما کوبیوزیه کیشی قضا سیله بولماس اوروشماق ایلا اما یاغی و اوروشتی
مجادله کرد اوروشوق مجادله کردیم اوروشور و اوروشادور مجادله میکند و اوروشور بمعنی فاعل و مصدر نیز می آید
اوروشماید مجادله نمیکند و نکرده است اوروشغان و اوروشغان اوروشغانلار مجادله کننده و مجادله کرده و بمعنی مصدر نیز
می آیند اوروش و اوروشغیل مفرد مخاطب از فعل امر اوروشما و اوروشماغیل مفرد مخاطب از فعل نهی اوروشونک و اوروشونکیز
و اوروشونکلار جمع مخاطب از فعل امر اوروشمانک و اوروشمانکیز و اوروشمانکلار جمع مخاطب از فعل نهی اوروشمان و
اوروشماس مین مجادله نمیکنم اوروشامین و اوروشورمن و اوروشادورمن مجادله میکنم اوروشورمن اوروشماغیم جنک کرد
اوروشماغوم جنک نخواهم کرد اوروشوب اوروشوبان و اوروشیش مجادله کرده اوروشماس مجادله کرده اوروشماس مجادله
نمیکند و بمعنی فاعل و مصدر منفی هم می آید اوروشماسی مجادله کردنش و نکردنش اوروشمادین از مجادله کردن و مجادله
کرده اوروشوب بولا و اوروشا بولا و اوروشالای مجادله نمیتوان کرد اوروشا المماس مجادله نمیتواند کرد اوروشا اوروشا
مجادله کنان مجادله کنان و بدون تکرار هم مستعملست اوروشای اوروشا مجادله کنم و کند و کنی اوروشالی و اوروشغای
و اوروشغای بزما اوروشلی و اوروشالینک مجادله کنیم اوروشغالی برای مجادله کردن و تا مجادله کرده اوروشغاج چون
مجادله کرد و کند اوروشغوچی مجادله کننده اوروشغوجیدا اوروشغونجه و اوروشغانچا تا مجادله کردن و بقدر مجادله کردن اوروشغوم
مجادله خواهم کرد اوروشغونک مجادله خواهی کرد اوروشغوسی مجادله خواهد کرد اوروشغولوق مجادله کردنی اوروشغای
و اوروشا و اوروشسا اوروشغای مجادله کند اوروشغودیک و اوروشغودیک مجادله کردنی و همچنانکه مجادله کند اوروشتوروماق
مصدر متعدیست یعنی یکی بدیکری زنانیدن و با هم بجنک انداختن چنانکه بطریق لغز با سم نجم مرغ کوید شعر اول
فاج کیم قیلور کلاد تکلفاش کیم جونی سیر سکدین تولادی تمام کیم آتی اوروشتورماغیدین ایستار کام ناکام اوشا تغوید
آنی ناکام و صیغ آن بر این نهج با لفظ تور اشتقاق می یابد اورتاماق بکون را و فتح تا مصدر قربت سوز از دن چنانکه
کوید شعر یوزونک آچیب نی عجب یوزخانمانی اورتاماق کیم بولور پیر شمع و تی بیرله جهانی اورتاماق اورتادی

سوزانید شعر اشکنی ادا اورتادی تیغ غمنینک گرچه کویماس سو ایچرا توشکا خوش اورتادوا سوزانیم اورتادی
اورتایدور میسوزاند الشاهد علی الاول شعر بزم ارا اورتار نوای دنغمان سونکلوغ سرود ای مغنی چون قیلدیم
سیلوریسین ساز توزه و بمعنی فاعل و صفت نیز مستعمل چنانکه بمعنی مصدری گوید شعر جانیم اورتارکا اول اولوغ چهره
کلزار خلیل آنی روشن الیدکان کوکرد اورتی تابید اسیل اورتامایدکه نمیسوزاند و نسوزاند است اورتارکا ندا اورتارکان و
اورتایدورکان سوزاننده و سوزانده و بمعنی مصدر هم می آید اورتا واورتاکیل مفرد مخاطب امر فعل الشاهد علی الاول
شعر اولوغ اوت بیلا اورایینانک بوروب مغنی اورتاغی دین که اوتنی توتاشتور غالب کیراک خاشاک واورتا بمعنی
وسط و میان هم می باشد چنانکه در ذیل جامد مذکور شود اورتما واورتاماکیل مفرد مخاطب امر فعل نهی اورتانک و
اورتانکیز واورتانکلار جمع مخاطب امر فعل اورتامانک واورتامانکیز واورتامانکلار جمع مخاطب نهی فعل اورتامان واورتاماس مین
نمیسوزانم اورتای مین واورتارمین واورتایدورمین واورتارام میسوزانم اورتادیم واورتادیم کیم سوزاندم اورتاماکوم نخواهم
سوزانید اورتاب اورتابان واورتامیش سوزانیده الشاهد علی الاول شعر محبت اهلینی ولحسرتا که کوپ اورتاب
الارنینک آهی اوددین هراس کم قیلادور اورتامیشانک سوزانیده اورتاماس نمیسوزاند و بمعنی فاعل و مصدر نفی هم
می آید اورتاملیب سوزاندنش و نسوزاندنش اورتامادین ناسوزاندن و نسوزانیده اورتابیلا واورتانابولماس اورتالماناک و
نمیتوان سوزانید چنانکه در سد سکندری در آغاز داستان اسکندر گوید شعر اگرچه ایرمه موشک آتماق ایشی
بولوت نامونین اورتای آلماس کیشی اورتای بو واورتای اورتای احوال کنان و بدون تکرار هم مستعمل اورتای بو واورتای مین
بوزانیم و بوزاند و بوزانی چنانکه شاهد براول او بمعنی بوزاند گوید شعر کونکول اوتیرا پرکل هردین کوکسکا
داغ اورتای قیلا چرباب آیدورچه ناسیب آنداباغ اورتامی اورتانالو واورتاکاینز واورتاکای مز واورتابی واورتالنیات
بوزانیم اورتاکلای برای سوزاندن و تاسوزاندن اورتاکاج چون سوزانید و بوزاند اورتاکوجی سوزاننده اورتاکوجه
واورتاکونجه واورتاکانجه تا سوزاندن و بقصد سوزاندن اورتاکوم خواهم سوزانید دیماکدن سود نوای غه
اورتاکوم داغی جو کویدی جانی آتینک داغ اشتطار ایچرا اورتاکویلت خواهی سوزانید اورتاکوسی خواهد سوزانید اورتاکوکی
سوزانیدنی اورتاکاج اورتانلو اورتانسون واورتادیت بسوزاند الشاهد علی الرابع شعر دم اوتین تیلما قهوسی اولکو
اورتادیت کیم اول لعت هر زمان کونکلیکا یا قیلغو دیلتا نماس اورتاکودیک واورتاردیت سوزاندی و چنانکه بسوزاند
اورتانمات مع النون مصدر انفعالست یعنی سوخته شدن اورتانور واورتانادور سوخته می شود الشاهد علی الاول
شعر شمعدانیا اوت تورکه کردم اورتام افلاک اورتانورش آسرانسام کونکلوم کا جسم و جان غمناک اورتانورش واورتانور بمعنی فاعل
و صفت نیز می آید اورتانکان واورتانوکان واورتانادورکان سوخته شونده و سوخته شونده الشاهد علی الاول بالمعنی الثانی
شعر اولی قویاشتین آیرو اورتانکان بحمید قاینغوده کونکول ایچرا سوکیتان کونزا ارتمان دیلت سود و بمعنی مصدر
نیز می آید اورتانکوچی سوخته شونده چنانکه در آغاز عشقبازی لیلی و مجنون گوید شعر یوق یوقکه بوددی آه ایردی
اورتانکوچ جیبکا می ایردی و تاء صیغ بر نیاق باضافه حرف نون بدستور شواول اشتقاق می یابد اورکماک بکون راء
رمیدن و هورکماک و با های هوز نیز بمعنی مستعمل اورکی رمید اورکتوک رمیدیم اورکار و اورکادور میرمد
واورکار بمعنی فاعل و صفت نیز می آید اورکیکان رمیده اورکادورکان رمنده و رمیده

مصدر نیز می آید اورولک واورمک کیل مفرد مخاطب امر فعل اورکما واورکماکیل مفرد مخاطب نهی فعل اورکنک و
اورکونکوز واورکونکلار جمع مخاطب امر فعل اورکمانک واورکمانکیز واورکمانکلار جمع مخاطب نهی فعل اورکمان واورکماس مین
نمی رمم اورکامین واورکارمین واورکادورمین میرمم اورکادیم واورکادیم کیم رمیدم اورکاکوم نخواهم رمید
اورکوب واورکوبان واورکیش رمیده الشاهد علی الاول شعر اولوس دین اورکوب اونغوم دین داغی بولوب مین ولیک
یعنی رمیده نابود آشنا اول شوخ اورکیشانک رمیده اورکماس نمیرمد و بمعنی فاعل و مصدر منفی هم می آید اورکمای
رمیدنش و نرمیدنش اورکمادین نارمیدن و نرمیده اورکیبیلاس واورکابیلماس اورکابولماس نمیتوان رمید اورکاالماس
نمیتواند رمید اورکای اورکای رم کنان رم کنان و بدون تکرار هم مستعمل اورکای اورکای بین رم کنم کنید اورکاسات
اورکاینز واورکای بیز واورکای بیز واورکالی واورکالینک رم کنیم اورکالی برای رمیدن تارمیدن اورکاکاج
چون رمید و رمد اورکاکوجی رمنده اورکاکوجه واورکاکونجه واورکاکانجه تا رمیدن و بقصد رمیدن اورکاکوم
خواهم رمید اورکاکونک خواهی رمید اورکاکوسی خواهد رمید اورکاکوسی رمیدنی اورکاکای واورکاکای اورکساورکیون
اورکسین اورکاکوبلت اورکاکولت رمیده و چنانکه رمند اورکیشات منبع کاف مع الشین اردوف اورکماک بمعنی رم کردن باشد
وصیغ آن بدستور شواول باضافه شین قرشت اشتقاق می یابد اورکیشات منبع کاف مع التاء مصدر متعدیست یعنی رم دادن
و هورکیشات با های هوز نیز مستعمل وصیغ آن بدستور باضافه تای قرشت اشتقاق می یابد اورکانمات بکون راء و نون و میم
کافجی و مفتوح ارجاقل یعنی تعلیم کرفتن چنانکه گوید شعر سیزدین اورکانکان یکیبی لیلی وشین خالم و کیمی سیزدین اورکانکا
کیراک مجنون سیلاوه فرهاد عشق دیبم یعنی عادت کردن بود اورکاندی تعلیم کرفت و عادت کرد اورکاندوک تعلیم کرفتیم و
عادت کردیم اورکانور واورکانادور تعلیم می کیرد و عادت می کند واورکانور بمعنی فاعل و مصدر هم می آید اورکانامیدو تعلیم
نمیکیرد و نکرفته است و عادت نمیکند و نکرده است اورکانکان واورکانوکان واورکانادورکان تعلیم کیرنده و تعلیم کرفته و عادت
کرده و کننده و بمعنی مصدر هم می آیند اورکان و اورکانکیل مفرد مخاطب امر فعل الشاهد علی الاول بالمعنی الاول
شعر جانکوم ذخشنیمید انفه نیاسوریدی جامن دیلث شهسوار زلفات اورکان کیبلین جانیدث بالمعنی الثانی شعر
بیزنان دوستغه اورکان که بوده واصل اوش کیم زنان اهلیغه کونکلونکی دیبی اورکاشتیلا اورکانما واورکانماکیل مفرد مخاطب
نهی اورکانینکلار واورکانینکیز واورکانینکلار جمع مخاطب امر اورکانمانکیز واورکانمانکلار جمع مخاطب نهی
اورکانمان واورکانماس مین تعلیم نمیکیرم و عادت نمیکنم اورکانامین واورکانادورمین واورکانورام تعلیم میکیرم و عادت میکنم
اورکاندوم واورکاندیم کیم تعلیم کرفتم و عادت کردم اورکانغاکوم تعلیم نخواهم کرفت و عادت نخواهم کرد اورکانیب
واورکانیبان واورکانمیش تعلیم کرفته و عادت کرده الشاهد علی الاول بالمعنی الثانی شعر یار ایله مخوطیلکان کونکلو
ایبرداول نوع قوش کیم کیشیدین آیریلا آلماس کیچکیدین اورکانیب اورکانمیشانک تعلیم کرفته و عادت کرده اورکانماس
تعلیم نمیکیرد و عادت نمیکند و بمعنی فاعل و مصدر منفی هم می آید اورکانمایی تعلیم کرفتنش و نکرفتنش و عادت کردنش و نکردنش
اورکانمادین از تعلیم کرفتن و از عادت کردن و تعلیم نکرفته و عادت نکرده اورکانیب بولا واورکانابولماس اورکانالماس تعلیم نمیتوان
کرفت و عادت نمیتوان کرد اورکانا آلماس تعلیم نمیتواند کرفت و عادت نمیتواند کرد اورکانا اورکانا تعلیم کنان و عاد
کنان و بدون تکرار هم مستعمل اورکانای و اورکانایین تعلیم بکیرم و بکیرد و بکیری و عادت کنم و کنید و کنی اورکانسات

69v.

امر کانکا نیز و امر کانکای نیز و امر کانلی و امر کانلک تعلیم بکیریم و غادت تکیم امر کانکالی برای تعلیم کرفتن و تا تعلیم کرفته و برای
غادت کردن و تا غادت کرده چنانچه بمعنی قول کوید شعر کونکلنی آنتا را استاد ولی خال و خطینیک دوپر لوکی
الیدا اوکانکالی تیغا الیمیدا امر کانکاج چون تعلیم کرفت و بکیرد و چون غادت کرد و کند امر کانکوچی تعلیم کیرنده و غادت کننده
امر کانکوچیدا امر کانکوبجا امر کانکا بجه تا تعلیم کرفتن و بمقدار تعلیم کرفتن و تا غادت کردن و بمقدار غادت کردن امر کانکوم
تعلیم خواهم کرفت و غادت خواهم کرد امر کانکوسن تعلیم خواهی کرفت و غادت خواهی کرد امر کانکوسی تعلیم خواهند
کفت و غادت خواهد کرد امر کانکولوک تعلیم کرفتنی و غادت کردنی امر کانکای دا امر کانا و امر کانغا و امر کانون و امر کانولت
تعلیم بکیرد و غادت کند امر کانکو دیلت امر کانور دیلت تعلیم کرفتنی و همچنانکه تعلیم بکیرد و غادت کردنی و همچنانکه غادت
امر کاتماک مع الکاف مصدر متعدیست یعنی تعلیم دادن و غادت دادن امر کاتا الماس تعلیم نمیتواند داد و غادت نمیتواند
چنانچه مخفاولک کوید شعر یاد کوپ بملسا چا کو قیل نوائی نا الهکیم کل کا بلبل امر کاتا الماس و تا افغان قیلیب امر کانکوچه
و امر کانکوچه و امر کالتکا بجه تا تعلیم دادن و بمقدار تعلیم دادن چنانچه شاهد بر اولرا بمعنی ثلثی کوید شعر دیر پری
بو خرامات نیک ایوا بیندا نعقل کل کا سبق امر کانکوچه فرزانه کرات و همچنین یعنی تا غادت دادن و بمقدار غادت دادن یا
صیغ بر همین سیاق نا تای قرشا شتقاق می یابد امر کود ماک بضم کاف عجمی و فتح دال الف کشیده امر کولا ماک بضم لام بمعنی
بینکیزدن بود که آنرا بعربی نعاس کویند و مؤلف بدایع اللغة فی فرت ذکر کرده سهو کرده امر کودای و امر کولادی
بینکیزد امر کودا دو لتعا امر کولادولت بینکیزدیم امر کودایم امر کودایدوق و امر کولادوق بینکیزدیم چنانچه در مرقات بو نهان
کوید الشاهد علی الاول شعر بولوت ایلکه ... کیم تر کین امر کودار نا لیب ... و امر کودار و امر کولار
بمعنی فاعل و مصدر نیز می آید چنانچه بمعنی بینکیزنده کوید الشاهد علی الاول شعر امر کودار ایل ... کیم حقیقی کیچه
بولدین مرکیب ... چونکیم قیلمادی آکاه لیغ امر کودانا یدیم و امر کولانا یدیم بینکیزنمیزد نبوده است آوی
کودا کان امر کودار کان و ... امر کولادو کان و امر کولار کان امر کولاد کان بینکیزنده و بینکیزدنی و بمعنی مصدر نیز می آید
امر کودا و امر کودا کیل و امر کولا و امر کولا کیل مفرد غائب امر امر کودا نا و امر کودا نا کیل و امر کولا نا و امر کولا نا کیل
مفرد غائب مبالغه امر کودانلت و امر کوداکونکوز و امر کودانکلار و امر کولانلت و امر کولانکلار جمع غائب مبالغه
امر کودانا نلت و امر کودا نا نکلار و امر کولا نا نلت و امر کولا نا نکلار جمع غائب مبالغه امر کودانان و امر کولانان
و امر کولانان و امر کولا ناس مین بینکیزیم امر کودای مین و امر کودایدو مین و امر کودایم و امر کولای مین
امر کولادو مین و امر کولادیم و امر کولادیم بینکیزیم امر کودایم و امر کودایم و امر کودا ماکیم و امر کولا ماکیم بینکیزدیم امر کولا ماکوم و امر کودا ماکوم
بینکیز خواهم زد امر کودای و امر کودا باره امر کودا میش و امر کولا باره امر کولامیش بینکیزده چنانچه در سبعه
سیاره در داستان ... کوید الشاهد علی الاول شعر امر کوداب بولدین ... چقیشان امیش ... قول له
انیقیشان امیش امر کودامیشالت و امر کولامیشالت بینکیز زده امر کوداناس و امر کولاناس بینکیزنده و بمعنی فاعل و مصدر منفی هم
می آید امر کوداشلو امر کولاشلو بینکیز زدن و بینکیز زده امر کودانا دیق و امر کولا نا دیق بینکیز زدن و بینکیز زده امر کوداب بولالت و
امر کوداب بولماس و امر کودا ماق ... امر کولاب بولماس و امر کولا نا الت ... بینکی نمیتوان زد امر کودای الماس و اود
کولای الماس بینکی نمیتوان زد امر کودا ی ... امر کودای و امر کودای و امر کولای و امر کولای و امر کولای بینکیزان
و بد و ن تکرار هم بهمین معنی امر کودا و امر کودای و امر کولا و امر کولای بینکیزم و بینکیزنده

70r.

امر کادا نالت و امر کادا کا نیز و امر کادا کای نیز و امر کودا لی و امر کودا لینلت و امر کولا نالت و امر کولا کا نیز و امر کولا کای نیز و
امر کولا لی و امر کولا لینلت بینکیزیم امر کودا کالی و امر کولا کالی برای بینکیز زدن و تا بینکیز زده امر کودا کاج و امر کولا کاج
چون بینکیز زد و زند امر کودا کوچی و امر کولا کوچی بینکیزنده امر کودا کوچیدا و امر کودا کوبجا و امر کودا کا بجه و امر کولا کوچیدا و امر کولا
کوبجا و امر کولا کا بجه تا بینکیز زدن و بمقدار بینکیز زدن امر کودا کوم و امر کولا کوم بینکی خواهم زد امر کودا کوسن و امر کولا کو
بینکی خواهی زد امر کودا کوسی و امر کولا کوسی بینکی خواهند زد امر کودا کولوک و امر کولا کولوک بینکیززدنی امر کودا کای و امر کولا کا
و امر کودا سون و امر کوداد دیلت و امر کولا کای و امر کولا نا و امر کولا سون و امر کولا دیلت بینکیز زند امر کودا کو دیلت و امر
کودار دیلت و امر کولا کو دیلت و امر کولار دیلت بینکیزدنی و همچنانکه بینکیز زند امر تمالت بکسر نون و فتح لام با الف
امر تمادی بالف معروف امر تمادولت با الف ممدود امر تمار و امر تماید امر تمایدی بالف ممدود و امر تمار بمعنی فاعل و مصدر هم می آید امر تمایدی
بالف ممدود و مرفوعه است امر تما کان و امر تمار کان و امر تمایدو کان با الف ممدوده و با الف مرفوعه و بمعنی مستقبل هم می آید امر تما و امر تما کیل
مفرد غائب امر امر تمانا و امر تمانا کیل مفرد غائب مبالغه امر تمانلت و امر تمانکلار جمع غائب امر امر تما نالت
امر تمانانکلار و امر تمانانکلار جمع غائب مبالغه امر تمانان و امر تماناس مین بالف ممدوده امر تمای مین و امر تمای مین و امر تمایدو مین
و امر تمادیم بالف ممدوده امر تمادیم و امر تماکیم بالف مرفوعه امر تماکوم بالف خواهم رفت امر تماب و امر تمابان و امر تمامیش بالف مرفوعه
چنانچه در کل نور و زیارتسان آمده الشاهد علی الاول شعر که امر تما جیمیغ طا ... منارلار ... ایشیلا ... کا که
ابار لار ... امر تمامیشالت بالف مرفوعه امر تماناس بالف ممدوده و بمعنی فاعل و مصدر منفی هم می آید امر تمالت بالف مرفوعه زمنقر
امر تمادین بالف ممدوده و بالف مرفوعه امر تماب بولماس و امر تما ناب بولماس و امر تمانالت او الماس بالف نمیتوان رفت امر تمای الماس
بالف نمیتواند رفت امر تما یو و امر تمای ... بالف ممدوده ... و بد و ن تکرار هم بهمین معنی مستعملست امر تمای و امر تماین بالف مرفوعه
و بعد و بعد و بعدی امر تمانالت و امر تما کا نیز و امر تما کای نیز و امر تمالی و امر تمالینلت بالف ممدوده امر تما کالی برای بالف رفتن و تا بالف رفته
امر تما کاج چون بالف رفت و برود امر تما کوچی بالف رونده امر تما کوچیدا امر تما کو بجا امر تما کا بجه تا بالف رفتن و بمقدار بالف رفتن امر تما کوم بالا
خواهم رفت امر تما کونلت بالف خواهی رفت امر تما کوسی بالف خواهد رفت امر تما کولوک بالف رفتنی امر تما کای و امر تمانا و امر تما سون و
امر تمادیلت بالف برود امر تما کو دیلت و امر تمار دیلت بالف رفتنی ...
و امر ... بالف رفتنی و همچنانکه بالف برود امر تمالت مع النون بالف برآمدن امر تمانلت بالف برآمد چنانکه در تاریخ آلا
در ذکر عزیز علیه السلام کوید که مرکبی نینک چوروک سونکا کالریکا ماقی کوردی کیم بر بریکا متصل او لوب ... امر تماندی
و آیینک ... تاریلدی و ... صیغ بر همین سیاق تا نون اشتقاق می یابد امر تماق بسکون راء و فتح نون با الف کشیده
جا کردن امر تمادی جا کرد امر تمادوق جا کردیم امر تمار و امر تماید جا میکند و امر تمار بمعنی فاعل و مصدر نیز می آید امر تماید
جا میکند و نکرده است امر تماغان و امر تماغان و امر تمایدو غان جا کننده و جا کرده و بمعنی مستقبل نیز می آید امر تما و امر تماغیل
مفرد غائب امر امر تمانا و امر تماناغیل مفرد غائب مبالغه امر تمانلت و امر تمانکلار جمع غائب امر امر تما
و امر تمانانکلار و امر تمانانکلار جمع غائب مبالغه امر تمانان و امر تماناس مین جا میکنم امر تمای مین و امر تمار مین و امر تمایدو مین
و امر تمادیم جا میکنم امر تماریم و امر تماغیم جا کردیم امر تماغوم جا خواهم کرد امر تماب و امر تمابان و امر تمامیش جا کرده الشاهد
علی الاول شعر صنوبر کونکلیکا کونکلومنی او غشاتمانلت که امر تماب تورث ... آسیغه ... کونکلوم امر تمامیشالت

جاکرده. اورتاماس جاکه مینکند من از انشاء بخاری شعر فردی دوغم خندی ایری و غلشوقه نیرنا تا بکنج اورتاماس هر بیر الایماط
وبمعنی جای مصدر منفی نیز می آید او رساب بولماس و اورتاسابولماس و اورتاماقی ولماس جا نمیتوان کرد اورتای آلماس
جا نمیتواند کرد او رسابو و اورتای اورتای جاکان و بمعنی تکرار هم با جمیع مشتقات او رتای و اورتایین جاکنم وکنند
اورتاشاق و اورتاغاینه و اورتاغای نیز و اورتالیعا و اورتالینك جاکنیم اورتاغلی برای جاکردن و تاجاکرده اورتاغاچ
کرده وکنند اورتاغوچی جاکننده اورتاغوچه و اورتاغونجه و اورتاغانجه تا جاکردن و بمقام جا کردن اورتاغوم جا خواهم کرد
اورتاغونك جا خواهی کرد اورتاغوسی جا خواهد کرد اورتاغولوق جا کردن اورتاغای و اورتاشا و اورتاسون و اورتادیك جاکند
اورتاغودیك و اورتاردیك جا کردن و همچنانکه جاکند اورتاشماق مع الشین بایکدیگر جا کردن اورتاشیت جا کرده الشاهد
شعر مکن لیتا من تا ریتاق سکاتلادیکم جم را ممهر مسکن تو تو تبور لار سونکا لار اورتاشیب و با تاء صیغ نیز
با شین قرشت اشتقاق می یابد اورتاتماق باتای قرشت مصدر متعدی بمعنی جادادن و بالمجاز بمعنی محکم کردن باشد
اورتاتدو جا میسند چنانکه کوید شعر تارتاق ممکن ایماس او قونکی کونکلومدین یکم تاتا او قه نفس آنك
اورتاتادور اورتاتیب جاداده. چنانکه در مقاله هشتم از حیرت الابرار کوید شعر مسجد را اباد محیان تاتیب کوشه
محراب را کوب اورتاتیب اورتات مفرد مخاطب از فعل امر الشاهد علیه شعر دیمان اول آی اوقیسای دوست موغود
بوقسا اولشات کیم تاپیب شاهد ایله زلف قیغمه اورتات و با تاء صیغ بر همین نهج با تای قرشت اشتقاق می یابد اورنوقتاق
بسکون را و قاف و ضم نون دفعته خون از حلق و لشدن و هلاك کشتن اورتاتماق بسکون نون و شین اولاریکی
لشکر باشد دسته و نیز خوراید و وقت نزول چنانکه در بحث جو آمد در ذیل الفتا و ارزمذکور شود اورتالاماق
ترکی رومی تخمین کردن ولا شیئ جو معرفن اورونکلاماق بضم را و سکون نون و دال مهمله و فتح لام ترکی رومی بمعنی انتخاب
کردن باشد اورونداماق بسکون هر دو نون یعنی اثبات شدن اوریماك بسکون هر دو رای مهمله و فتح با عجمی ترکی
رویدن سبزه باشد و نیز بالمجاز راست شدن موی بر اندام و دمیدن خط نو خط را ز کوینده من الجوامد اورو زن نیز
معنی دارد اول بمعنی بلندی باشد چنانکه در خسرو شیرین در وصف اسب کوید شعر حرامی ایر کا چیقا قدار تو تون دیك
ایکلاماك دیمیشت اوزره قویوز دیك و در وصف کیم کوید شعر یولی او بو تاریب دکاماشی ملسا قویغ اولتوریکیمی
کامین ایلسا دویم مجاز از طرف بالای آب و سمت مرد نیز نسیم را کویند سیم ترکی رومی جانها و کوهها بود مثانند کرد کان که
در اعضا و کلوی و بر می آید و آنرا بعربی سلعه و بفارسی مغول ناسند و نیز از آراستن زدن و در و کردن و بافتن و فریاد کردن
ست چنانکه در ذیل مصدر اورماق و اورماك کذشت و بفارسی بمعنی مشت باشد عموما و مشتی را که بر دهن
و ناد و چشم و امثال آنها را نیز کویند که مغز شان ضایع و تیز شده باشد اوراقی اوراغ بر وزن سراغ داس بود
که آنرا بعربی محصد و منجل نامند اوراچی درو کر چنانکه در فصل سی و یکم از محبوب القلوب در وصف ظالمین کوید که
اوراچی نه آندین دهنه ب و باشاقچی تینك نا روبه آندین کوزی اوراق قوشی ترکی رومی جانوری باشد مبن زنك شبیه
بملخ که در صحراها و علفزارها بانك طولانی میکند و آنرا بعربی صرار کویند اوراغ بلغت مغولی بمعنی پیشه و صنعت با
وجوی بجمع طایفه از کت که هر وقت که خواهند دسته و فرقه بجمعی در دو سپید کنند آن تیر را با سم پیشه و صنعت فرا
وآن نوع فریاد را اوران و فریاد کردن را اورانلاشمیشی کویند چنانکه طایفه قیاتر ا اورحیان و منکیتیان را الای و کنکر را

جاوبی و خطای را اولوتا و قونغرات را جایلیغان و بعضی دوانه و برخی لولو آوا زنمایند و ترکی رومی بمعنی تخمین و قیاس باشد
اورتالاشمیشی اولاد کردن لشکریان باشد در وقت نزول اردو چنانکه در ذیل الهاد نکاشته شد اورمه بسکون را و فتح با
بروزن کرمه ترکی رومی بمعنی لباس درخت بود اورت بسکون را و تای قرشت سیم لت از برای آتش چنانکه در فوائد
کوید شعر کونزیم لسو ولیکن جا نید اورت بولوب هر زمان ایم با قماقدین کونزیم اورت اورتا بسکون را و فتح تای قرشت
بمعنی وسط و میان باشد الشاهد علیه شعر لابی که وصل الطیفه نامیشتو اتصال اول لام دور که اورتا
المیش آیی بلا ونیز کنایه از اواسط الناس است چنانکه کوید شعر نی اولونغ نی اورتانی کیم خلس و قاش بفیع آشنا
ایلامه خراش و امراض سوزاندن باشد چنانکه در ذیل مصدر اورتاماق کذشت اورتاچاغلیغ بمعنی میانه و وسط بود چنانکه
در فصل سی و هفتم از محبوب القلوب در ذکر کدخدائی کوید که اکر حسن اورتاچاغلیغ ده خوف و حاصل
دور اورتاغ و اورتاق شریك و سهیم را کویند الشاهد علیه جان تقدین اجل بیرله همرنیك ایکی بولیشان انداق که
تاپیب سوری آی غزای ایکی اورتاق و باشباع ختمه نام کوهیت در حدود قراقیم که محل بیلاق و قشلاق قرلغان بن
خان بوده و معنی ترکیبی آن کوه بلند باشد اورتانجی یعنی وسطی و میانین چنانکه در مقاله نوزدهم از حیرت الابرار
کوید شعر جوز نسالیب اورتانجی ایل او زن بوشوروش اتیب تکیه خیرالامور اورتوك لحاف و پوشش که بالای خود
اورچین بسکون را و نون و کسر جیم عجمی ملوکانه دیجان و کاشغر و آن نواحی را کویند چنانکه در بحر قلعه بخارا و کابل
اندرابچان تومان و در هندوستان پرکنه و در روم سنجق نامند و بفارسی بمعنی پایه و نزدبان بود اردو بمعنی
خیمه کاه سلاطین را خوانند الشاهد علیه شعر تا لار عجب ار اهد اشکیم اکو و بیهر باز خاب روستایی دیك کیم
حیرت ایلا کاتاموحد و کوروب و کدمز سیل سکه عجبی شعر یا نا الردو نی کیم سپهر برین بولوب آندا بچار کنن
اورده بفتح دال حرم را کویند یعنی خانه که منزل سلاطین و اکابر در آنجا باشند اورده سکی کیس سفید خرم باشد
اورس بسکون را و سین مهمله ترکی رومی سندان بود و بفارسی سرحد و کوهی باشد اورغاچی بسکون را و فتح غین معجمه
و کسر جیم عجمی بلغت مغولی انکشتوانه خیاطی بود که آنرا بعربی خسیعه خوانند اورکاد نام ستاره پروین بود که آنرا بعربی
ثریا نامند اورکاسون بفتح کاف و ضم سین مهمله و سکون نون بلغت مغولی خار بود که آنرا بعربی شوك خوانند اورکاك
رمنده و وحشی اورکانچی بسکون را و میم و فتح کاف و کسر جیم عنکبوت را نامند چنانکه در احوال او رفتار و در ذکر شد بازان
کوید شعر کور کلیر تیب شغله لیغ اوتدین سپندان آسیب اورکانچی تاری بیرله سندان و رومیه آنرا اور موچات و اورکوچ
کویند اورکان بفتح و سکون نون در بیابانها که در بادیه بار کنند و آنرا ارغامچی نیز خوانند اورکو بضم کاف
دارد اول بمعنی شنکی بود که آنرا بعربی نعاس کویند چنانکه در تاریخ بابری آمده که بعضی اورکوده و بعضی خواب آلود که سنك
اوچ ممری بولغان ایدی که سکبار سوراخ حقیقی دویم ترکی رومی بمعنی دم و وحشت باشد اورکوچ بسکون را و جیم و ضم کاف
سر شانه اسب و کوهان شتر را کویند و مجازا بلندی سر کوه را کویند اورکونج بسکون را و نون و جیم و ضم کاف بمعنی دم و
اورکونج لوك رمیده و صید کیر را کویند و هو رکونج تا هادی هم نیز مستعملست اورمالك بیکنوع شالیست نازك که از پشم شتر
می بافند الشاهد علیه شعر کیش و اورمالك قیدیدین او تعیش نی فوتایتمه کیم کیش قرلراق تولکو اورمالك یو تعادا
تاشالیر بعد و نیز بمعنی بافتن و بضم تابیدن باشد چنانکه در ذیل مصادر این حرف کذشت اورمان و اورماتلیق بیشه

ماده هر چیز را کویند اعم از آنکه انسان باشد یا غیر آن اورکا بسکون را و فتح کاف سرا
پرده را کویند اورکاچی بسکون را و با ابجد و فتح کاف و کسر جیم عجمی

جنكل و بیشه و نیستان بود اورمه بسكون را و فتح میم بهاء زده دو معنی دارد اول دانه ها كه بعد از آنكه در كرمابه
از آب كرم با آب سرد داخل شود در اعضا بهم رسد دوم بكونه رهنمایست كه مطرتی نوازد هن نیاف دا اورمچك بكون را
و ضم میم ترکی رومی عنكبوت بود اورت بسكون را و نون بمعنی جا و مكان شال الشاهد علیه شعر تورمیده یم
كوبا قریغان عشق اوتی آیدی بایشتوغان كباب اصنیدا هر یان داغ نهان ولنه شعر وصلینكا كوهرات تبسم لطف
انیسا خدنگ صفه ماق كیم قدم لوزین سو بویدای كندسپله قوبان ایاق و بمعنی عرض نیز استعمال می شود چنانكه در فارسی
گفته می شود كه فلان بجای فلان نهاده شد و آنرا اورون هم كویند اورنات بسكون را و فتح نون بمعنی مثال بود و رومیه
كورنات هم نامند اوروبضم را اجناء غله باشد اوروش بضم او و فتح بای ابجد تركی رومی لباس و پوشش باشد اوروش
بضم را و سكون شین قریشته حاصل مصدر اهر و شماوات بمعنی سپكی یكرزدن و بالمجاز بمعنی جنك و جدال استعمال می شود
الشاهد علیه شعر اول امین بیركا باشمنی غمیدین جان تلاشور دا فراقینك خیلی بیرله اول اورشوم بوتلاشیم دی
اوروغ و اوروق دو معنی دارد اول خویش و تبار و منسوبان و متعلقان را كویند چنانكه در تاریخ بابری مذكورست كه اوروغی
كیم خواجه میر انغه باشلاغ ایكیلادورلار ایدی مقامغه توشكانلار اوروغ كیلیب توشولار دوم تخم زراعت را كویند چنانكه
در كلیله دمنه مذكورست كه و فاسد تخم مزرعه سیدا آیككان اوروغ تنینك حاصلینی اوراراسیز و اوروغلوغ واوروقلوق
بمعنی خویشی و قرابت و انتساب بود چنانكه در تاریخ بابری در احوال محمد حسین میرزا كوید كه چون ارادۀ پیر نوع اوروغلوق
بولوب ایدی آنی آزاد ایتیم و نیز بمعنی دم ریختن باشد اوروقیاش از اتباعست نسل و تبار و خویش را نامند چنانكه در محبوب
القلوب كوید كه مروت و كرم نینك اوروقیاشی ایكه توانان تیر داشی و اوروق تاماش ایكیكیر دیج كفته می شود اما
تا یاش تنها مستعمل نیست بر خلاف اوروغ كه تنها نیز استعمال می شود اورولك بضم او و سكون كاف به معنی آمده
اول میانی بود كه در وقت چریدن بپای اسب بند نند دوم بمكث و در نات لشكر را كویند سیم تند دا آورا نامند كه بعربی
شمش خوانند اوروم بضم را و سكون میم طایفۀ ایست از اهل عجم كه در میان ملل مسیحیه با او در یوكج هم مشهور اند
و آنرا روم ایلی هم كویند اورومچك بضم را و سكون میم تركی رومی عنكبوت باشد كه آنرا اورمچك نیز كویند اورون
بضم را و سكون نون بمعنی جا و مكان بود چنانكه كوید شعر جان نكرچقفای و با خوب سیل اشیكم كوزدین چقمو
مین بابری اول كوكیلیمنی نهای تین اورون تحمد خالت استغفرا اورون بسكون را استعمال می شود چنانكه مذكور شد
اورونجی بسكون نون و كسر جیم بلغت مغولی بمعنی كما پیش بود اورونداو بضم را و دال و سكون نون تركی
بمعنی انجامك باشد اوروندوق بمعنی زین پوش باشد كه آنرا بعربی غاشیه كویند و بفتح الف در این مستعملست اوروملی
بضم را و سكون نون و كسر لام بلغت مغولی نیزه را خوانند كه آنرا بعربی اصفاد كویند اوره بفتح را بهاء زده
ستون را نامند مع الزاء المثلثات اوزبالك مع الكاف اوزباكلیك باشباع ضمه دو معنی دارد اول بمعنی كسیخته
كردن بود چنانكه در خسرو شیرین در وصف مرسب كوید الشاهد علی الاول شعر سقال آغی اوکا مبتر و دوش
تبه كلیك سبزه بی اصنیدا قرا بود دوش آنی اوزبالیك بیكیت بولماقی عهدا شاتمالی بولماق توره اوزماعیدا الشاهد علی الثانی
شعر وصلینكا خوی بیب ماونا ایشك دین سینی كیم كونكول اوزباكلیك ایشی صعب ایرور كا لیسیان دوم شاكردن باشكن
سكند بی شعر دیدی ججربیم بوق ایدی ای رفیق سوادی ماكی لوكا غای اولدیم غریق اوزبالوغ مع القاف اوزبالیغ

اوز

بسكون را بمعنی لاف امیز كفتن و اوزان خواندن و آن عبارتست از تصنیفات تركی كه خارج از وزن نظمست چنانكه در رساله
عروض كوید كه اوزان بلا رمینك اوزمانی هیچ وزن بیله راستی ایماس و نیز در كلیله دمنه تركی در مكالمۀ طوطی با داده با جغد
كوید كه اوزمی مینی نجات و قیلما قی كیشیكا الایق ایرماس اوزماق و اوزمو بمعنی اوزماق خرد غه موافق اوزدی كسیخته كردو شاكرد و اوزدی
خواند اینجو ولت كسیخته كردیم و شاكردیم اوزدوق اوزان خواندیم اوزلار و اوزادور میكسلد و شتاسیكند و اوزان نیز
و اوزار بمعنی اوزار هم میشود و دراز میشود هم باشد و در آخر بمعنی اوزخار مصدر اوزمانی بمعنی دراز شدنست چنانكه مذكور
شود و بمعنی فاعل مصدر هم می آید اوزمایدور میكسلد و میكسلد عبارتست و شتا میكند مكرزنات و میخواند و نیز آنكه
و اوزار كان و اوزادوركان كسیخته كننده و كسیخته كرده و شاكننده و شاكرده و بمعنی مصدر نیز می آید اوزغان و
اوزغان و اوزادورغان اوزان خواننده و اوزان خوانده و بمعنی مصدر نیز می آید اوز سه معنی دارد اول امر است از كسیختن
چنانكه كوید شعر ای كونكول امیدلارینك كلشن دوران دین اوزه هم كل و شمشاد دین هم لاله ریحان دین اوز دوم
امرست از شاكردن سیم امرست از اوزان خواندن و هشتم معنی دیگر دارد كه در ذیل جوامید مذكور خواهد شد اوز كسیل
امرست از كسیختن و شاكردن بالمعنی الاول شعر دوست كونكول لاخشم ایدین اوز كیلكو كونكولكیم توشا ایشترماس والكا
ایمیش اهدا كونكول الحباب كوشر اوزمیل امرست از اوزان خواندن اوزما مفرد غائب است فعل نفی هر دو مصدر اوزما
مفرد غائب فعل نفی مصدر اوزمانك اوزماعیل مفرد غائب فعل نفی مصدر اوزمانق اوزولت و اوزونكوز و اوزنكلا
جمع غائب فعل نفی هر دو مصدر اوزمان و اوزماس مین نمیكسلم و شتا نمیكنم و اوزان نمیخوانم اوزاین و اوزاتی و اوزادوبمن و اوزار
میكسلم و شتا میكنم و اوزان میخوانم و اوزایدین و اوزادام بمعنی دراز میشوم هم آمده اوزادیم كسیختم و شاكردم و اوزادیم
و دراز شدم اوزماكیم كسیختم و شاكردم اوزماغیم اوزان خواندم اوزماكوم نخواهم كسیخت و شتا نخواهم كرد اوزماغوم
اوزان نخواهم خواند اوزمیش اوزمیش كسیخته كرده و شاكرده و اوزان خوانده الشاهد علی الاول المعنی الاول شعر
بولدی پر كل هجر دین جسیم آجیلمان كلبنی عضو عضوین بسكه بنشاطب الكیش مین اوزوب اوزمیشانك كسیخته و شتا
كرده و اوزان خوانده اوزماس نمیكسلد و شتا نمیكند و اوزان نمیخواند و بمعنی فاعل و مصدر منفی نیز می آید اوزماسی
كسیختن و نكسیختن و شاكردن و نكردن و اوزان خواندن و نخواندن اوزمادین از كسیختن و نكسیخته و از شاكردن و
شانكرده و از اوزان خواندن و اوزان نخوانده اوزوب تولماد اوزما بولماد نمیتوان كسیخت نمیتوان شاكرد و اوزان نمیتواند خواند و اوزاالما
نمیتواند كسیخت شتا نمیتواند كرد اوزان نمیتواند خواند اوزا اوزا قطع كنان و شاكنان و اوزان خوان اوزان خوان و تكرار
تكرار هم مستعملست اوزای و اوزاین بكسلم و بكسلد و بكسلی و شاكنم و كند و كنی و اوزان بخوانم و بخواند و بخوانی و بمعنی دراز
شوم و شود و شوی هم آمده اوزالسا اوزكاینز و اوزكاینز بكسلیم و شاكنیم اوزماق و اوزغاینز و اوزمایز اوزان بخوانیم اوزامی
و اوزالینك كسسته كنیم و شاكنیم و بخوانیم و دراز شویم اوزمكالی برای كسیخته كردن و تا كسیخته كرده و برای شاكردن و تا شا
كرده بالمعنی الاول شعر ابا الطفال فیما اوزكلای آنجه حوینی اهاش كیم باركونكول لار الغابی اول بلا باغه حوش اوزغلی برای اوزان
خواندن و تا خوانده اوزكاج چون كسیخته كرد و كند و چون شاكرد و كند اوزغاج چون اوزان خواند و بخواند اوزكوچی
كسیخته كننده و شاكننده چنانكه در فصل ششم از محبوب القلوب در صفت صدر بمعنی اول كوید كه ظلم رشته سین اوزكوچی
و اوقاف بوزوفین توزكوچی اوزغوچی اوزان خواننده اوزكوچو و اوزكوچو و اوزكامجه تا كسیخته كردن و تمام كسیخته كردن

و ناشناکردن و بعلم شناکردن اوزغوچه واوزغوبخه واوزغانجه تا افزان خواندن و بغلم خواندن اوزکوم کیفته
خواهم کرد وشنا خواهم کرد اوزغوم اوزانخواهم خواند اوزکونك کیفته خواهی کرد وشنا خواهی کرد اوزغونك
اوزانخواهی خواند اوزکوسی کیفته خواهد کرد وشنا خواهد کرد بالمعنی الاول شعر توتوب ناط وطرحنکی زلفین
ایتماسرود که پریا اوزکوسی غم چیکی اوتالین آنینك اوزغوسی اوزانخواهد خواند اوزکولوك کیفته کردن وشناکردنی
اوزغولوق اوزانخواندنی اوزکلی بکلاند وشناکند اوزغای اوزانبخواند وزا واوزناوا اوزسون واوزدیك
بکلاند وشناکند واوزانبخواند الشاهد علی الرابع بالمعنی الاول شعر مرشدی کیم مخلصیم کفرطریقتیدین تیلادی
اوزلوکوم نونك مرشته سین اوزدیك کمزنادیم بوحصیر اوزکودیك کیفته کردن و همچنانکه کیفته کند وشناکردنی
و همچنانکه شناکند اوزغودیك اوزانخواندنی و همچنانکه بخواند اوزدیك مراد فاعل اوزکودیك واوزغودیك باشد
ونیز با مصدر اوزاتاق اشتراك دارد یعنی بهم زشدنی و همچنانکه درهم شود اوزوشمات بضم زای هوز مع التین مصدر اوزماق
یعنی باهم قطع کردن و باهم شناکردن اوزوشتی لار باهم قطع کردند وشناکردند چنانکه عمیدی قول گوید شعر
کوییدا ایت لارا اوزوشتی لار دنوانی خسته نی کیلم بما بان ظاهر که جیحق تاپدی تا شتی تاپدی دور اوزوشوب واوزوشولان واوزوشمیشتر
باهم قطع کرده و باهم شناکرده چنانکه در سکندرنامه در وصف یاجوج گوید الشاهد علی الاول بالمعنی الاول شعر
بحر عراق کم نوخم ونی اوزدیشان بیقلیغانینی الحال اوزوشوب سان و ثانی بهیج بمعنی ساق واوشول لعل الجوف
شیز الشقاق بجاید اوزولمات مع الکلام مصدر انفعال استعمال یعنی کیفته شدن بجای بمعنی کان اوزولوکان واوزولادی
کیفته شونده وکیفته شده الشاهد علی الاول شعر کونکول چو سیزدین اوزدوم شادلیغ ایمدی محال اولغانی
آچیلما تلیغ اوزولکان غنچه عدنی احتمال اولغا و ثانی مع سیغ رهین بفتح تا الام اشتقاق میاید اوزمانغ بفتح زای هوز و
واوزماناغ مع الکلام درانزشدن اوزادی واوزالدی دراز شد چنانکه در تشبیهات محبوب القلوب گوید الشاهد علی
الاول شعر چون کیتی سیکیت لیك واوزاینکاری لیغ دم شا وودی یعنی المادیغان هم ایسیغ اوزادوق واوزالدوق
درازشدیم اوزار واوزایدور واوزاپور و اوزالادور درازمیشود چنانکه شاهدبر اولرا در خمسة المتحیرین در وصف مولانا جامی
گوید که بونوع آثار وعلامات اندین کوپ منقولدور بشاتیار کامشغول بولسا سوز اوزارش واوزار واوزالور یعنی
و معلوم مینماید و اوزا رتبه معنی بکر آمده اول کیفته سیکندیم شناکند درازمیکند و معنی با مصدر اوزمات
اشتراك دارد سیم اوزانمیخواند ودر آن یعنی با مصدر اوزماق مشترکت میکنم شد اوزانیلیك واوزانمایدی دراز میشود شدن
اوزغان واوزغایدی واوزایدورغان واوزالغولوق الاول درازشونده ودرازشده و بمعنی معلوم میآید چنانکه شاهدبر اول
یعنی درازشدن در تاریخ ناری در ذکر درخت کیله نوشته که اوشبو یوراك دیك شاخ اوزاغان سانایی والولوغ غنچه
تاغل نینك بر کلاهی آچیلیب قطار کیبله کل لاری ظاهر بولور اوزاواوزاغیل اوزالعاواوزالقیل مفرد مخاطب از فصل امر اوزامای واوزانك
واوزالماوا واوزالماغیل مفرد مخاطب از فصل نهی واوزانك واوزانکیز واوزانکلا واوزانیك واوزانیکیز واوزانیکلا جمع مخاطب
امر اوزانیانك واوزانیکز واوزانانکلا واوزالمانك واوزالمانکیز واوزالمانکلار جمع مخاطب از فصل نهی اوزانان واوزانامن
و اوزالمان واوزالمامین درازمیشوم اوزانیمین واوزارمین واوزایدورمین واوزنام واوزلامین واوزالورمین واوزا
دورمین واوزالورام درازمیشوم واوزاین واوزلامین واوزالورام یعنی میکشم وشنا میکنم واوزانمیخوانم امد

چنانکه گذشت اوزاریم یکیمرا و اوزالورم بضم را و اوزانایم واوزالمایم درازشدیم ولوزلیم یعنی کیفتیم شناکردیم
واوزانخواندیم هم باشد اوزانغوم واوزالماغوم درازخواهم شد اوزاب واوزابان واوزامیش واوزالیب اوزالیسان
واوزالمیش درازشده چنانکه شاهدبر اول در تاریخ ناری در وصف کل خاسون مذکوراست که اوشبو برکیدین ایمیکا بولوب
برایلیك اوزاب نیه اوشبوخاسون برکلاهی آچیلادور اوزالمیشلك درازشده اوزانماس واوزالماس درازهمی نشود ودراز
و بمعنی فاعل و مصدر منفی هم میآید اوزاب بولماس واوزانا بولماس واوزاناق اولماس واوزالیب بولماس واوزالا بولماس
واوزالماق ولماس درازنتوان شد لعقل اولماس واوزالا آلماس درازنتواند شد اوزابو واوزای واوزای واوزالا اوزالا
درازشونده شونده وبدون تکرار هم باین معانی مستعمل چنانکه لطفی گوید الشاهد علی الثالث شعر کونکولنکه لالا
سنیزین اوزالوزاله یا توزختن چیچان لاری اوزغوم مکرغزاله یا تو اوزاغی ونلین واوزالا واوزالابین درازشوم وشودنی
واوزای واوزاین یعنی بکیلم و بکلاند و بکلی وشناکم وکند وکنی و اوزانبخوانم وبخواند و بخوانی هم باشد چنانکه گذشت
اوزناق واوزاغاینز واوزغایز و اوزلیق واوزلیك واوزلساق واوزاغاینز و اوزالغای بز و اوزالای واوزالالیك
درازشویم واوزالی واوزالسنك بمعنی بکیلیم و بکلاییم وشناکنیم و بخوانیم هم باشد اوزالغالی واوزاغالی برای دراز
شدن وتا درازشده اوزالماج واوزالغاج چون درازشد شود اوزاغوچی واوزالغوچی درازشونده اوزغوچه واوزغوبخه
واوزغانچه واوزالغوچه واوزالغانچه تا درازشدن وبقلم درازشدن اوزغوم واوزالغوم درازخواهم
اوزغونك واوزالغونك درازخواهی شد اوزغوسی واوزالغوسی درازخواهد شد اوزغولوق واوزالغولوق درازشدنی
اوزغای واوزغاوا واوزسون واوزدیك واوزالغای واوزالا واوزالسون واوزالدیك درازشود الشاهد علی
الخامس شعر یاشیم تادین اوزانتینك یکیم سینینك هم اوزالغای عیش اولیه یانچکه یاشینك اوزغودیك واوزالغودیك
واوزالودیك درازشدنی و همچنانکه درازشود اوزادیك مراد فاعل اوزغودیك باشد ونیز یعنی کیفته کردن و همچنانکه
کیفته شود وشناکردنی و همچنانکه شناکند ودرازبر دو معنی با مصدر اوزماق اشتراك دارد ونیز یعنی اوزانخواندنی
و همچنانکه بخواند ودرآن یعنی با مصدر اوزماق مشترکت اوزاتماق یا تاماق مصدر متعدی یعنی راهی کردن ودرازکردن
اوزاتتی راهی کرد ودرازکرد چنانکه بمعنی اول در حیرت الابرار در غزای عبدالله مبارك گوید شعر قهر الیه کافر تشکان
زبان جمله طهان ایردی میتماق تمان چونکه اوزاتتی آیدوخ سالی ایلدکه منیدین یوطنغ سالی ونیز تاریخ بیکی
در ذکر حضرت شعیب و موسی علیهما السلام گوید که آدم یعنی هشتدین جقاغوان عصا آنکا بیریب ای معنی اوزاتتی وقتی
بعنوان معنی ثانی گوید شعر هجران که خسته ولرتابیغ بیربستر بیلا الیغ اوزاتتی اوزاتوق راهی کردیم ودرازکردیم
سکهی بالمعنی الاول شعر سولوبنك کمکیلدی سوزآتیب بیلك آنکا منه ایتتوق اوزاتوقیرات اوزاتقان و
اوزانغان و اوزاتادورغان راهی کننده راهی کرده ودرازکننده ودرازکرده وبمعنی مصدر نیز میآید چنانکه در تحفه شاه
در داستان سافر اقلیم چهارم بمعنی راهی کردن گوید الشاهد علی الثانی شعر اوزاتوغان نوای آتلاندی چون اوزاتی
وثانی مع نایدی اوزات واوزاتقیل مفرد مخاطب از فصل امر بمعنی الشاهد علی الثانی بالمعنی الثانی من لیلی مجنون شعر
نی ظلم قیلور خدا ایلینی تا تغیل نی ظلم قولین اوزاتماغیل اوزاتای واوزاتایین راهی کنم وکند وکنی ودرازکنم وکنی
چنانکه شاهدبر اول را یعنی راهی کنم گوید شعر میرا ولمانا بوتوب ایا غلاحیب که لارتیمنی ایت تیلاتیب ایت

73v

لازم سازی اوزلاری و باقی صیغ بو نیاق تاناتای قوشتا اشتقاق می یابد اوز لاماق بزرگ کوچی خواستن و طلب کردن چنانکه
سعد الدین صفا در تاریخ آل عثمان نوشته که دید امیدلرنه اکمال ایچون سلطانات بلند در کاهینگ توتیای غبارین اوزلادیلر
ونیز کوید شعر اولیکیم یار ادم جانبین اهل یاد آنگ قوللوغی یولین کوزلار اول جانبه واسعیون مرزا جواهید اوزد معنی داد
اول بمعنی بلیغ وسفید صورتا هر باشد الشاهد علیه شعر ای ملاحت شیوه لیک شیرین دود اعنیک سوزنکا اوز شکر آبکا
کوییا سالدی شکرنکی کا اوتوز ونیز در نظم الجواهر کوید شعر تیل ایلدامی ین بولور بولت حاصل نهیز نوع نداسته
ملامت حاصل اوزجوزلا کاییدین انتقامت حاصل شاکت لیک دین ملی سلامت حاصل دویم بمعنی رو غارین بود
سیم مجاز ا بمعنی فوق وما بالا آمده شعرا ی سنکا تعمارت لیک طاماراکه کیم کوز و ب توز سوا اوزه سنبلی بو مقدار کرکش
چهارم عدد صد را کویند چنانکه در سبعه کبیر در رزم نامه قوبربری کوید شعر اوج اوز آلتمیش الی لعبه کوه
او توب کیم سال اجی کوزنای عزت ونیز در صباحت درای محیط کوید شعر آیری علمی اوز کتی بوزلات بوند مراد ابچوکیکم ملا
فلک بجم بمعنی خود و خویشتن است چنانکه در لسان الطیر در صفت سیمرغ کوید شعر تا نکا راجب چون کیلیش ایل الهز کشفه
با قیاس ایل بوزیلت ایله اشکال لیغة وموکافر ومان نسخه سقیمه مصرع اول را چنین خوانده که تانکار اجب ایل کیلیش اوز کوچالیغه
واوز کورا بعضی قرآن بمعنی خود و خویشتن نوشته لفظ اخراعیت سهو کرده شتم خویش و آشنا را کویند چنانکه در حیرت الابرار
در مصرع اخیر بمعنی خویش و خویشتن کوید شعر کیم که اوزی ایلادی یالغان سوزین کنبد برا ایلچین دیا مالغان سوزین کیمیه
کا یالغانچی دیبان قالسا آت بو آت ایله خار لانسا اوز و ینات لا ادری شعر آشنا لا انزنی تادار لیکن سیوار سکانکا نذ ینات
اوز ایلا محبت ایله ولیکن اوزنی یات هفتم ترکی وی کل چیند بود هشتم امر است از کیجمش نهم امر است نشا کردن دهم
امر است از اوزان خواندن چنانکه در ذیل اشتقاقات مذکور شد اوزاغوکون بضم ضین معجمه یعنی پر پرواز چنانکه در مقالة چهارم
از حیرت الابرار در نصیحت بدیع الزمان میرزا کوید شعر تا نکلا جیوق آندین بولور اوشو دور تین پر پار و قوشنور اوزاغوکون
اوزاق بمعنی دور و بعید باشد اوزالت بفتح زا و سکون کاف ماده دویه قوع و دنبال را کویند اوزالتش بکسر لام و کاف
و سکون شین قرشت یعنی رفتار چنانکه در لیلی مجنون کوید شعر تا الدیم اوز الیش و اوتوبت قولومنی کوز کورکم ایلانیان بوتوکی
اوزان علم رستا زیکنوع سرودی که خارج از اسلوب وزن و نظم است چنانکه در ذیل مصدر اوزماق کذشت اوزانکو
مرکابراکوبند اوزبک نام طایفه ایست معروف و آن سی و دو لو روغ می باشد که هر او روغی منشعب بچندین فرقه و طایفه است
اوز جبه بمعنی تقدم خودش چنانکه در سبعه سیکندر در وصف غلامان را بیعمد کوید شعر قولا ملا مربایحلقه شیدا لنغ
تا چیباوز جبا آلتونغه او مزملیغ اوزدیک کا یعنی مثل خود اوزره یعنی برو دوبالا چنانکه کوید شعر غارغ را اوزره
عین شکلیغ ده مظلوم لیات اوزره کونیزکرلر اوزره نقطه شکلیغ ده ک کوز فونک آستید الخال اوزلیک بفتح زا و سکون راء
قرشت دانهایست سیاه که آنرا می سوزانند و آنرا بفارسی سپند و بعربی حرمل کویند اوزکا بسکون زا و فتح کاف عجمی
دلرداول بمعنی غیر باشد چنانکه کوید شعر سوز لا شوی مین سایبه لاری ات یا وزا و ذوم پر اله مدام چون او تومدین افکا
بوق عالمدا اهمدن دیم منیت ونیز در خاتمه محبوب القلوب کوید که اوزولتدین اوزکادین یوزین تابار و اوزسونکی
ولوز کا سوزنی کونکلی تیجیقا ند دویم بمعنی خود دیکرا اوزکاکا یعنی بدیکری چنانکه سلطان حسین میرزا کوید شعر ای که در
کیم حسنی اوزکا کا پرمیش کونکول اوزکا کا برماک اچون ای بیکمان کونکلوم نی تا اوزکا جه بمعنی طور دیکر و بخودیکر باشد الشاهد

74r

علیه شعر جهرا ایدا ین خسته نینک هر لحظه خالی اوزکا چه لیک نا ولاید بیم نینک هر دم خیالی اوزکاچه اوزکونمک لطمانار
آبرا کویند که از آن ستوان کذشت و محتاج بشنا باشد چنانکه کوید شعر دردکوزکیم اییتا اساکیما بی غیم سو باغیه
راحتا یرمان کیم سودکیم سیلی نینک بار اوزکونی و موکیفین سو می اوزکون بار ای بهله خوانده با بمعنی نوشته و شعر من بوبیر شاه
آمده و بضبط هم مناسبت کرده اوزکینه سین کینه لفظ تصغیر است یعنی خود کرا الشاهد علیه شعر که وفا که نا
که افسوز سیله اوزکینه سین کوز کوروب هر لحظه دلبر لیغیدلبر تورلوک کینه اوزلوبا بحوق ترکی وی کل چیند بود
اوزلوک بمعنی خودی و هستی و انانیت باشد الشاهد علیه شعر خورق حنین رخ من بوای شیخ المناس پر دیش
باده پرماستیل که اوزلوک جنسیم رهون بولماسا و نیز بمعنی با خود بود چنانکه کوید شعر پیر او که دینغا ایمپا جیکا نبلد
اوزی دین اولکه بوونی صحوا و لوای بیه لوز لوک اوزولت به معنی آمده اول انکشتر الماسند چنانکه کوید شعر
تو تای جهاندا سلیمان سینی دایا جمشید نی مونکا جام وتا الدی نی آنکا اوزوک دویم بمعنی موی لا اچوق را کویند سیم بمعنی
پاره و کیسته باشد چنانکه در عنوان لیلی مجنون در وصف نظامی و خسرو کوید که هنیاما چون کیم کشفیجاد و کلام کیم بوی
آتینک آلیدا ایلینا المسلسله آئینک کوهر یسلکی کا تار تماق واوز نظمی نینک چهر و لت رشته مین و اوزوک تار
هم الاشره او لاماق اوزون دماند اوزون یالت ترکی وی کوی بازیت و آنچنان باشد که خود را در حکند
شخصی صبیان خطا بیند و دیکران را بیند و او نای خود را بجانب ایشان انداز دهر کدام که نیاید او بخورد او را بجانی
بدرون خط آید و این را بعربی بفارسی خرسک نامند اوزونک بسکون نون و کاف عجمی یعنی خود تو چنانکه کوید شعر
نوای ایستار اوینانک یا ر لعلی کا نصیحت ابازیش اوزونک دی ملیکا یرایا کلیابو لماکونیه بو لوموم اوزونکا بخود تو زرد
نخفف اوزوات یعنی برو دور بالا چنانکه کوید شعر وسیه اوزه زرور تطیغ ایکی قاشینینک یوزا اوزه جلوه کر بولغانی ایکی
طاوس ایره کلزار ایرا اوزیکا بخود ش اوز یدیک کا بمثل خود الشاهد علیه شعر آی خواسرا صبی پراوز یدیک کلستلا لقغدن
نرجم ایلا اساکامی اوزیکا مبتلا لا نه مع السین بر المثقات اوساغماق بفتح شین و سکون نون برابر شدن و فخر کردن
اوساندی بیزار شد اوساندوق بیزار شدیم اوسانور او سانادو بیزار میشود و اوسانیم بمعنی ماضی و مستقبل هم می آید
و سانماید و بیزار نمیشود و نشده است چنانکه در سبعه سیکندر در صباحت حمد را کوید المعنی الثانی شعر سنکا بو تمنا
توکا نماید و بیزار میشود و دین خمیه سا او ساغماغ مهراو سانمان تعاوسانونمان نعا و سانادو مرغان بیزار شوند و بیزار شده معنی
مصدر هم می آیند اوسانو تعا و سانغیل مفرد مخاطب امر چنانکه در نوحه کری بو دخطاب بهرام کوید الشاهد علی الشانی
شعر ای بیچم تیزی بر ساعت تا یا تغیل ثنی حرب و کینه مسهوا الذین او سانغیل اوسانما و اوسانماغیل مفرد مخاطب نهی
نهی اوسانینک و اوسانغیز و او سانینکلار جمع مخاطب امر اوسانمانک و اوسانکیز و اوسانماکیز جمع مخاطب نهی
اوسانمان و او سانماس مین بیزار نمیشوم اوسانامین و اوسانمابمین و اوسانادورمین اوسانوبمین بیزار میشوم اوسانوروم و اوسانما
بیزار شده ام اوساغاغوم بیزار نخواهم شد اوسانیب و اوسانیبان و اوساغیش بیزار شده اوساغیتانک بیزار شده اوسانماس
بیزار نمیشود بمعنی حال و مستقبل هر دو هم می آید اوسانماسی بیزار نشدن و بیزار نشدنش و اوسانمادین از بیزار شدن عنیز بیزار نشد
اوسانیب توکاکاو او سانا بوکاکا او سانماق وکاکا بیزار نمیتوان شد اوسانا المس بیزار نمیتواند شد اوسانا او سانیلر بیزار شوند و شوند
و بدون تکرار هم بهمین معنی مستعملست او سانای و اوسانمای و اوسانمای و اوسانمابین بیزار شوم و شود و شوی و شده اوسانماین بیزار نشوم

ونشود ونشوی ونشده چنانکه شاهد بر اولها بمعنی بیزار شده کوید شعر یار یوز یار مقیل بیر دی خزین کونکلیم هیچ
اوسانماغای نام محمله یار صرامیر کونکول اوسانا نا قیلو اوسانقای بیزو اوسانمالیغاو بانا لیت بیزار شویم اوسانماغ
برای بیزار شدن و نابیزار شده اوسانقلاج چون بیزار شده شود اوسانقوچی بیزار شونده اوسانقوسه و اوسانقوسو اوسانقا
نابیزار شدن و بقدم بیزار شدن اوسانقوم بیزار خواهم شد اوسانقونك بیزار خواهی شد اوسانقوسی بیزار خواهد شد
اوسانقولوق بیزار شدنی اوسانقاغ اوسانا او اوسانادا اوسانور اوسانادیك بیزار شوط الشاهد علی الاول شعر
منکا آنچه اوت شالدی مهر یوق کیم طبع کرآب حیا تلها آندین اوسانقای اوسانقودیك او اوسانقودیك بیزار شده و همچنانکه
بیزار شود اوسانه صراق مصدر متعدیست بمعنی بیزار کردن و صیغ آن با لفظ اشتقاق می باید اسرو ماك بکون سین
وضم رای مهمله مست شدن و مستی کردن و اسیراك بفتح الف و کسر را نیز مستعملست چون اسروك که بمعنی مست باشد ضم
الف مطرد شده و نظر بقاعده کلیه مصدر و اشتقاقات نیز بضم الف می باید اهدا مضمومات الف ذکر کرده شد
اسرودی مست شد اسرودولت مست شدیم اسرودی اسرودیلر مست شدند و اسرور بمعنی فاعل و مستانه
اسرومایدور مست میشود و شده است اسروکان و اسروکان و اسرودیرکان مست شونده و مست شده چنانکه شاهد بر اولرا
در تفهیمات محبوب القلوب کوید که سیرا لاکان آییلور و اسروکان تاییلور و بمعنی مصدر نیز می آید اسرو و اسروکیل مفرد
از فصل امر اسرو مطلوب است اکیل مفرد فی طلبه از فصل نهی اسرونك و اسرونکوز و اسرونکلار جمع مخاطبه از فصل امر اسروماك
اسرومانکیز یا صحرانکلار جمع مخاطبه از فصل نهی اسرومان و اسرومادین مست نمیشوم اسرومین و اسرومین و
اسرومایدورمین و اسرورام مست میشوم اسرودوم و اسرودیم مست شدم اسروماکوم مست نخواهم شد اسروب
اسرومان و اسرومیش مست شده اسرومیشانك مست شده اسروماس مست نمیشود و بمعنی فاعل و مستانه بمعنی هم
می آید اسروماسه مست شد خرم و نشئه خرم اسرومادین از مست شدن و مست نشده اسروب بولماس و اسروا بولماس
و اسروماقولیق مست نمیتوان شد و اسروی آلماس مست نمیتوانند شد اسروکی اسروکی مستی کنان و بلغت ترکیه هم
با معنی مستعملست اسروی غا و اسروبین مست شوم و شود و شوی و شده اسروساق و اسروکاییز و اسروکاییم و اسرو کی
و اسرو لیلیك غا اسروب مست شویم اسروکالی برای مست شدن و تمام شده اسروکاچ چون مست شد و شود
اسروکوچی مست شونده اسروکوچه و اسروکونچه و اسروکالیچه تا مست شدن و بقدم مست شدن اسروکوم
مست خواهم شد اسروکونك مست خواهی شد اسروکوسی مست خواهد شد اسروکولوك مست شدنی اسروکاغی و
اسروغلو اسرومنی با صرید مست شود اسروکدیك با صرید مست شدنی و همچنانکه مست شود اوسماغ بکون سین
کوشت از استخوان پاك کردن و تنها بی افاده این معنی نمیکند باید لفظ استخوان مذکور شود اوسماك مالوف شدن و کم
کردن اوسدی کوشت از استخوان پاك کرد و عادت کرد اوسارو اوسادور استخوان پاك میکند عادت میکند و سخنان و
اوسا غان اوسادیغان کوشت از استخوان پاك کننده و پاك کرده و بمعنی مصدر هم می آید اوسکان و اوسارکان و اوسادورکان عادت کننده
و عادت کرده چنانکه از این مصرع ظاهر میشود لا الهی ع نوغان بولوسکان بیریم دیبلو لمامحنت آستیدا اوسمور مفرد
از فصل امر بمعنی اوسغیل استخوان پاك کن ولوسکیل عادت کن اوسونك و اوسونکوز و اوسونکلار جمع مخاطبه از فصل
هر دو معنی اوسما مفرد مخاطبه از فصل نهی هر دو معنی اوسماغیل استخوان پاك مکن اوسماکیل عادت مکن اوسمانك و اوسما نکیز

و اوسمانکلار جمع مخاطبه از فصل نهی هر دو معنی اوسماس و اوسماس مین استخوان پاك نمیکنم و عادت نمیکنم اوسامین و اوسادورمین
و اوسادورمین و اوسارام استخوان پاك میکنم و عادت میکنم اوسادیم استخوان پاك کردیم و عادت کردیم اوسماغیم استخوان
پاك کردیم اوسماکیم عادت کردیم اوسماغوم استخوان پاك نخواهم کرد اوسماکوم عادت نخواهم کرد اوسوب و اوسوبان
اوسمیش استخوان پاك کرده و عادت کرده اوسمیشانك استخوان پاك کرده و عادت کرده اوسا او اوسا استخوان پاك کنان و عادت
کنان و بدون تکرار هم مستعملست اوسولماق بضم سین و سکون لام کوشت از استخوان پاك شدن اوسمافلاغ
بمعنا المرطلب کسی تحقیق و استمزاج کردن بنحویکه آن شخص نفهمد اوسلاغماق بسکون سین و نون و فتح لام ترکیب سر و هوش شدن
اوستالاماك بفتح تای قرشت و اوستولاماك بسکون سین و نون وضم تای قرشت ترکیب سر و تاق شدن اوستالاماك بفتح تا
اول و سکون تای ثانی و اوستولاماك بضم تای طول و سکون نون و تای ثانی مصدر متعدیست بمعنی ساختن مزاج و امید
او س بر وزن طوس ترکیب سر و بمعنی هوش باشد او سال بفتح سین با الف کشیده و سکون لام بمعنی قصور و تقصیر و اهمال
چنانکه در سد سکندری کوید شعر یودوش بیهید ابها اس ایر دی او سال کو چار روا تو شاردا با بار دی چیال
و نیز در تاریخ بابری مذکور است که بی تجربه لیغدین موندا قا او سال بولدی و بمعنی ضایع و معطل نیز استعمال میشود چنانکه
در سد سکندری کوید شعر چو با بدی کیشی پلکالی ریم خال که او ز خدمتین بو چون ایمیش او سال و بمعنی و تاریخ
آمده که بیزلار نی موندا قا مخاصره و قیلیب قوبلار ا اکر بادی بیر غه بیتما سانکیز اوی او سال بولغو سید و را و سان بضم النون بر
روی معنی کاهل باشد او ست بر وزن پوست بالا و فوق را کویند الشاهد علیه شعر سبز مخطینك سوادی لعل خندان
او ستنه خضر کویا سایه سالمیش آب حیوان او ستنه او ستون بسکون سین و نون وضم تای قرشت بدو معنی آمده اول بمعنی
فوق و فایق باشد چنانکه کوید شعر کیشی کیم ایلکی او ستون تیلاسه بنما قیلسون تو لیدا ز هو لا اهل و کرخن سوی
و نیز در سد سکندری کوید شعر چو بولدی بیری نقطه کاه محیط قوبی سو و او ستون سپهر بسیط و در تاریخ بابری
مذکور است که بو باغلار نینك او ستونی تمام آت چاپتورلیك هموار و صحرا دویم حرکات صحیحه را خوانند او ستید الحیاة الا بین
او سروك بمعنی مست و مخمور بود الشاهد علیه شعر بن نوع تاپدی جاپیکان مستانه و یکا او لبحا لت که تون تا انفوایدی
رخشینده ازی او سروك و لیمن لیلی مجنون شعر نو فل چریکی داغی چکیب صفه او سروك تیو لار کیبی ایاچ کفه دی و ب یا
دا ز بزمی آیدا و سروك را لت بمعنی تو ببمعنی نشاط ترمم استعمال می شود چنانکه کوید شعر یو قوت عجب لعلینك دین
اسخود لو حمود آتین ایرمش چونکه او سروك را لت بولور اول مو کا لب شیرین ایرمش او سروك کینه بمعنی مستك مخمورك
الشاهد علیه شعر اسرو یا لمان و عده سیدین کو عیش ایر دی جان غنیم انکه پیان بر کیمه تو شتی ایلکیم او سروك کینه
او سکوف بسکون سین و فا و ضم کاف نیکنوع کلاهیست که فرقه از عسکر روم بدان اختصاص دارند نیز تا غه را کویند که بر
سر چخ و شاهین کنند او سون بضم سین و سکون نون ملفت مفتوحه آب بود مع الثروات اشتقاقات اوشاتماغ با تا عرفات
بمعنی شکستن چنانکه در ترجیع کوید شعر اوشاتماقای بیتا سا تانك بو سنبل لار فی ثم قیدا و لماآثرا اوشبود و در سد
اوشاتتی شکست اوشاتوق شکستیم اوشاتور و اوشاتادور میشکند و لوشاتور بمعنی فاعل و مصدر نیز می آید
اوشاتماینور نمیشکند و شکسته است اوشاتغان و اوشاتوغان و اوشاتادورغان شکننده و شکسته و بمعنی مصدر هم می آید
اوشاتغ اوشاتغیل مفرد مخاطبه از فصل امر اوشاتما و اوشاتماغیل مفرد مخاطبه از فصل نهی اوشاتینك و اوشاتینکیز

اوش

واوشاتینکلار جمع مخاطبه نفعل امر اوشاتمانك واوشاتمانکز واوشاتمانکلار جمع مخاطبه نفعل نهی اوشاتمان واوشاتماس مین

نمیشکنم اوشانامین واوشانورمین واوشاتادورمین واوشاتورام میشکنم اوشاتوروم واوشاتماغیم شکستنم اوشاتماغوم

نخواهم شکست اوشاییب واوشاییبان واوشاتمیش شکسته اوشاغیشالك شکسته اوشاتماس نمیشکند وبمعنی فاعل ومصدر

منفی هم می آید اوشاتماسی شکستنش ونشکستنش اوشاتمادین ازشکستن ونشکسته اوشاییب بولماس واوشاتماقالی

واوشاتیبا بولماس نمیتوان شکستن واوشاتا الماس نمیتواند شکستن واوشاتا اوشاتا شکسته شکسته وبدون تکرار هم مستعملست

اوشاتای واوشاتاین بشکنم وبشکند وبشکن وشکسته چنانکه شاهد براول وبرا بمعنی اول کوید شعر تیمغه عشق دا

پردیم شکست یعنی اول اوت ٭ یار دهرغه اوشبو قورو قیمه نی دیدیم اوشاتای اوشاتینا قدواوشاتمایمز واوشاتمای بیز و

اوشاتملی واوشاتالیك بشکنیم اوشاتغلی برای شکستن وتاشکسته اوشاتغاج چون شکست وشکند اوشاتقوجی

شکننده اوشاتقوجه واوشاتقونجه واوشاتغانجه تاشکستن وبعدم شکستن الشاهد علی الثانی بالمعنی الاول شعر

کونکول جراحتی غه تاق وصال مرهمی نی ٭ فراق غاره سی پرله تاشیم اوشاتغونجه اوشاتغوم خواهم شکست اوشاتغونك خواهی

شکست اوشاتغوسی خواهد شکست اوشاتغولوق شکستنی اوشاتغای واوشاتا واوشاتسا واوشاتون واوشاتدیك شکند

الشاهد علی الاول شعر اول شوخ کونکلوم آلدی یایب جسمیمه شکست ٭ بیر لحظه دیك که شاخن اوشاتغای ثمر یله اوشانغوالت

واوشاتوردیك شکستی وهمچنانکه بشکند اوشاتماق بسکون لام واوشاتیلماق بجر تای قرشت وسکون لام مصدر انفعالست

یعنی شکسته شدن اوشاتلغان واوشاتلورغان واوشاتلادورغان واوشاتیلغان واوشاتیلورغان واوشاتیلادورغان

شکسته شونده وشکسته شده چنانکه شاهد براول بمعنی اخیر کوید شعر خطیبنك عمی دین اوشاتلغان قلم کبی بدنیم

ایجیدا نا کبو هر طرف ضعیف سونکاك وبمعنی مصدر نیز می آیند اوشالغای واوشاتیلغای شکسته شود الشاهد علی الاول

شعر کونکول کانا وکینك تاکیر دی بچه خطین ایلا زمین ٭ که بوشیشه ایچیدا اول داغی تاکه اوشاتغا حیث اوشا تسنا

واوشاتیلسا هرکاه شکسته شود الشاهد علی الثانی شعر هجری جسمیدا سونکاکلار نی اوشاییب کوید ورو

یعنی اوت با تراق یا نار کوپراك اوشاتیلسا اوتون ٭ وباقی صیغ رهین شاق وموافق قاعده مقررم شق اول اشتقاق می یابد

اوشماقغ نبکوزیشین ترکی وبلی ازاطراف هجوم کردن وبکجا جمع شدن اوشوشماقغ متهاجم ساختن چنانکه شاعر رومی کوید باملاحه ارو

شعر کیلینك آغیز ایلانك الاوشوبونك ٭ بومرغ وحشی بی دامه دوشوروك اوشاغاق بحجر شدن چنانکه در

ترکی در باب سیم در داستان نار کوید که جمیع جانورانیم شو شهدن او شانوز خصوصا نوع بشرمن زهرمدن فاتاشان

من انجماد آوش روزن دوش ودو معنی دارد اول نام ولایتیست از ترکستان که تخت سلیمان هم کویند ودر دومنزلی آنست

واوست دویم اسم اشارتست چنانکه حیدر تیلبه در مخزن کوید شعر توت غم ومحنت سیله کونکلوم نکی خوش غافل

اینا نك هرم ودم غا سینك اوش ٭ وبرای مبالغه بسیار هم اشاره قریب وبعید داخل میشود مثل اوشبو یعنی این واوشاك

آن اوشاغ واوشاق یعنی ریزه وحقیر بود الشاهد علیه شعر بو نوم سینك عکسی کا جی قیلدی کوبونك سینك اوشاغ

تاشین ٭ کمال عشق کورکیم کهرباایچادا تار کاهیم ٭ ونیز در مقاله بیستم از حیرت الابرار کوید شعر کلکا سحر وتنی بر ورده حلوه

باغ ٭ کیج تیشانك تیراراو غلان اوشاغ اوشاق بفتح شین مخفف ومحرف اوش اول باشد یعنی آن چنانکه کوید شعر

دیما کیل هذا ای مغنی کیم اونوم تاپمیش خراش ٭ قیل اوشال جهان سیله کونکلوم دین انده صوتین ونیز بارشاه فرموده

شعر فغانیم آشتی بلبل مین نمی بوق دمم قول دین ٭ بنی ایراوشال کلدین کونکولدا خاریم ناب ونیز اطلاعات شکسته شدن

چنانکه کذشت اوشانجه بمعنی آنقدر باشد الشاهد علیه شعر حیات نقدینی نیلای کیم سیفروش آلماس ٭ اوشانجه مونغه

که یا نیغای خمار زلالم شیم اوشانداق یعنی همچنان چنانکه در نشات همه کتب بابر در هم کوید که مطلوب اوشانداق کیم حیا

تنیکه المراد امیض شیخ دین نشاط کلی الحیلمای اوشبو یعنی همچنانکه کوید شعر کونکلونك دور لعل تاشینکدین

ایچیدا یك مولادیکا یشیم خلق اوشبو بیدین دیلار آنی دورهدن اوشغون بسکون شین ونون وضم غین معجمه دینار کو

اوشمو نجه وانچو نجه چاپلیق یعنی اینقدر چنانکه در یکی سکنه همه کلمه خانان دین یا اسکله کوید الشاهد علی الثانی

شعر ولیلی انی کاسونلار کرقیلادینك بیان ٭ الا دین قیل اوشمونجه چاپلیق یمان اوشوش بمعنی آن باشد چنانکه کوید

شعر بیر کون آهیم دین اوشول بدمهر کونکلی یشافای ٭ نیچه کیم تولادیر تاپتیغ تا مارلوتین کلار اوشونکی باشلغ

اوغ

وسکون نون وکسر دال ابجد ترکی ودو معنی هجوم بود که از چند جا واقع شود وسغ لغتین المشتقات اوغورلادی دزدیدن کان

معروفست اوغورلادی دزدید ومسلك نکنه ری شعر سغاج ادوره کر بولسا ویز بینك یانکاغ ٭ کونا میر کا هر نی اوغور

زاغ اوغورلادوق دزدیدیم اوغورلادیا اوغورلادیك تحسین دزدید واوغورلادی بمعنی فاعل ومصدر نیز می آید چنانکه در خسرو

شیرین در دو صفت شیرین بمعنی مصدر کوید شعر سوادخالی لوغزی لیقغه مانند ٭ کیلیب کوندوز کونکلنی اوغورلار

قند ٭ اوغورلادی تورهوسکرنهانی ٭ شکر تومیش ویا تورتومیش آنی لوغورلامایند صغیند د ودزدیده است

اوغورلاغان واوغورلارغان واوغورلایدورغان دزدنده ودزدیده وبمعنی مصدر نیز می آیند اوغورلا واوغورلاغیل

مفرد مخاطب نفعل امر اوغورلانك واوغورلاناغیل مفرد مخاطبه نفعل نهی اوغورلانك واوغورلانکز واوغورلانکلار جمع مخاطب

از فعل امر اوغورلامانك واوغورلامانکز واوغورلامانکلار جمع مخاطب نفعل نهی اوغورلامان واوغورلاماس مین نمی دزدم

اوغورلامین واوغورلارمین واوغورلایدورمین واوغورلارام میدزدم اوغورلایم واوغورلاماغیم دزدیدنم اوغورلاماغوم

نخواهم دزدید اوغورلاب واوغورلابان واوغورلامیش دزدیده اوغورلامیشالك دزدیده اوغورلاماس نمیدزد وبمعنی فاعل

ومصدر منفی هم می آید اوغورلاب بولماس واوغورلاسا بولماس اوغورلاماقالماس نمیتوان دزدید اوغورلای آلماس نمیتواند دزدید

اوغورلای واوغورلای اوغورلاین زدی کمان وبدون تکرار هم مستعملست اوغورلای واوغورلاین بدزدم بدزدد بدزدی

دزدیده اوغورلاساق واوغورلاغایمز واوغورلاغایمز واوغورلالی واوغورلالیك بدزدیم اوغورلاغلی برای دزدیدن

وتادزدیدن اوغورلاغاچ چون دزدید وبعد دزدید اوغورلاغوچی دزدنده اوغورلاغونجه واوغورلاغونجه واوغورلاغانجه تادزدیدن

وبعدم دزدیدن اوغورلاغوم خواهم دزدید اوغورلاغونك خواهی دزدید اوغورلاغوسی خواهد دزدید اوغورلاغولوق دزدیدنی

اوغورلاغای واوغورلاسا واوغورلاسون واوغورلادیك بدزدد اوغورلاغودیك واوغورلادیك دزدیدنی وهمچنانکه بدزد

اوغورلاتماق مع التا مصدر متعدیست یعنی بدزد دادن وصیغ آن موافق شق اول باضافه تای قرشت اشتقاق می یابد اوغورلانماق

مع النون مصدر انفعالست یعنی دزدیده شدن وصیغ آن بانون اشتقاق می یابد اوغورلاشماق مع الشین با یکدیگر دزدیدن

وصیغ آن باشین اشتقاق می یابد اوغولجاماق بسکون لام وفتح جیم بالف کشیده تعظیم کردن اوغولجادی تعظیم کرد اوغولجا

تعظیم کردیم اوغولجارو اوغولجابدور تعظیم میکند واوغولجار بمعنی فاعل ومصدر نیز می آید اوغولجامایدور تعظیم

نکرده است اوغولجاغان واوغولجارغان واوغولجایدورغان تعظیم کننده وتعظیم کرده وبمعنی مصدر نیز می آیند

اوغوبجاق المحق الجابی مفرد مخاطب از فصل امر اوغوبجامان واوغوبجامانغیل مفرد مخاطب از فصل نهی اوغوبجامانك وا اوغوبجانكز و
واوغوبجانكلار جمع مخاطب از فصل امر اوغوبجامانك وا اوغوبجامانكز وا اوغوبجامانكلار جمع مخاطب از فصل نهی اوغوبجامان عا اوغوبجامانی
تعظیم نمیكنم اوغوبجای مین وا اوغوبجارمین وا اوغوبجادیم صدمین وا اوغوبجادام تعظیم میكنم اوغوبجادیم وا اوغوبجادلیم تعظیم
كردیم اوغوبجالماغوم تعظیم نخواهم كرد اوغوبجاب عا اوغوبجامان وا اوغوبجامیش تعظیم كرده اوغوبجامیشالت تعظیم كرده
اوغوبجاماس تعظیم نمیكند وبمعنی فاعل ومصدر منفی هم می آید اوغوبجامابی تعظیم كردن ونكردن اوغوبجالماغان تعظیم
كردن تعظیم نكرده اوغوبجاب بولماس عا اوغوبجانا بولماس وا اوغوبجاماقی ولماس نمیتوان كرد اوغوبجالماس تعظیم نتواند
كرد اوغوبجایو وا اوغوبجالی واوغوبجای تعظیم كنان وبدون تكرار هم مستعملست اوغوبجای وا اوغوبجامین تعظیم كنم وكنكند
وكرده اوغوبجاساق وا اوغوبجاغاییز وا اوغوبجاغاییز اوغوبجالی وا اوغوبجالینك تعظیم كنیم اوغوبجامابای تعظیم كرد
وتا تعظیم كرده اوغوبجاغاچ چون تعظیم كرد وكند اوغوبجاغوجی تعظیم كننده اوغوبجاغوجه وا اوغوبجاغونجه وا اوغوبجاغا
تا تعظیم كردن وبعلامه تعظیم كردن اوغوبجاغوم تعظیم خواهد كرد اوغوبجاغونك تعظیم خواهی كرد اوغوبجاغوسی
تعظیم خواهد كرد اوغوبجاغولوق تعظیم كردن اوغوبجاغای عا اوغوبجاسا وا اوغوبجاسون وا اوغوبجادیك تعظیم كند
اوغوبجاغودیك وا اوغوبجاردیك تعظیم كردن وهمچنانكه تعظیم كند اوغراشماق وا اوغراشماق بتركی رومی بمعنی جنگیدن
بود كه آنرا بعربی مضادمت كمیند اوغراشتوم دچار شدم لاادری شعر غریب پرده نشین دلربا یه اوغراشتوم كورونك
كورونك نه كورنمز بلایه اوغراشتوم ونیز در محاورات اتراك روم بمعنی چسبیدن استعمال میشود چنانكه كویند كه فلان كوی
ننك اوزرینه اوغرادیم یعنی از حوالی فلان قریه گذشتم من الجامد اوغ دو معنی دارد اول چوبهای فوقانی الاچوق را
كویند الشاهد علیه شعر ایلی آق اوی اوغلاغی قاتلیغ مشم بولمیش تیتین آندا مرهم لوقمیله كرای مه خركر نشین
ونیز در مفردات كوید شعر سیل بولید اماد شتی اش كانیم ایماس كوزا الاچوغیلاری ننك دودیكان اوغلاری دوز
دوم موزه ایست كه از پوست چرم … اوغان بفتح غین بالف كشیده وسكون نون نام جناب احدیت عز اسمه شاهد
چنانكه در سبعه سیاره در مكالمه خاقان با فرهاد كوید شعر بوكون بو نه شكر كیم قیلدی اوغانیم سینی منك آیغه كیم
بولغای كاتیم مؤلف رومی اوغان را بجای باب الف مضمومه اسم جناب باری جل ذكره ذكر كرده وبكجا لفظ او اوغان آ
اشاره بعنید صوغان انتهای در فن فهرسه … نوشته وشعر … نزد شاهد آورده ونیز لطفی در نعت گفته
شعر اول آدم غه ودیعت قویدی تینكری اوغان اوشبو سوز بیلما … لین ومطالع هروی اوغان را
بحضرت پناه سر گفته كه بمعنی ادعیه است كه در حال استعاذه خوانده شود واین شعر از لطفی شاهد آورده وهر دو سهو كرده اند
اوغری دزد را كویند اوغلاغ وا اوغلاق بزغاله چهار ماهه را نامند ونیز نام برج جدی است اوغلان بسكون غین
ونون پسر وفرزند را خوانند ومجازا پسر امرد را هم كویند ونیز اولاد خوانین مغول را اوغلان وغلان كویند چنانكه شاهزادكان
عجم را میرزا وشاهزادكان روم را سلطان كویند اوغلان آتی جند بید … بود وآن خشبه سان آبی ستكر تركی آنرا
قنقز كویند اوغور بسكون راء غین فرشت دو معنی دارد اول سمت ومقصدی باشد كه بآنطرف توجه وروكند دویم بمعنی
بركت وسعادت بود وفراغی اوغوز بن قراخان بن مغول خان را كه بازای هوز است ودر بیان اتراك وكتب تواریخ اسم او
از بیانست اوغوز را غیر معجمه خوانده وباین معنی ذكر كرده اوغورلوق بد ومعنی آمده افلاك دوزدی باشد الشاهد علیه شعر

غارضینك كوردوم نهان اشلات یلادی تینكری قاش یاشوردون تا الماس اوغورلوق اوی ولكیم بولنا یاش دیوب صاحب
اوغورلاین بتركی رومی بمعنی دزدوار وبطریق دزدی … یكرطرف كه در ذیل مشتقات ذكر یافت اوغوز بسكون
هوز اسم پسر قراخان بن مغول خانست كه طایفه مغولیه بدو منسوبند واوزاق وكوزاق پسران او بوده وموافق تاریخ
اوغوزخان قیاس انجانان ترك جمال داشت كه جمشید اعظم نسبت با ملوك عجم بود واولصاف تركان را اعتماد او كه ذكر
سلطنت خود خراسان وعراق عجم بكرفت ملك مصر وشام وروم ومرزهان ایرا تصرف نكرد وبتركی رومی بمعنی كم هوش ونادان
اوغوش بسكون شین قرشت … فرتوت وحاضر كمیند اوغول مع اللام فرزند را نامند اوغول اوتی بتركی رومی …
باشد اوغون مع النون بتركی رومی بمعنی كار … نعود كه آنرا بعربی قات خولند مع القاف من المشتقات اوقراماق و
اوقراماق همان اوپرلماق واوپراماق بمعنی كهنه ومندرس شدن باشد كه در حرف ها كذشت اوقراك بضم
رای قرشت بتركی رومی بمعنی تیف كردن من الجامد اوقاق بتركی رومی بمعنی ریزه وحقیر بود اوقاجوق مصغر او بود باشد
بمعنی حقیر است اوقراغ بسكون قاف وغین وفتح رای قرشت بالف كشیده رخت وپلاس را كویند چنانكه در تاریخ بابری مذكورست
كه مستیغ خالیتید العبد الله تون لو فراغی … اوفكا بمعنی قهر وخشم وآنرا اوپكا با یای فارسی نیز كویند
مع القاف من المشتقات اوقوماق خواندن اوقودی خواند اوقودوق خواندیم اوقور واوقویدور میخواند الشاهد
علی الاول شعر انكا … اوقیب نامنك اوقور اول صنم واوقور
بمعنی فاعل ومصدر نیز می آید چنانكه بمعنی فاعل كوید شعر كر اوقورهم … هم قبولی
توشا … وبمعنی مصدر فرماید شعر اوقوردا آقی باشیم … كه هر دو
نامه غه مدادا … اوقوماینك نمیخواند ونخوانده است اوقوغان وا اوقورغان وا اوقوید ورغان خواننده وخوانده
وبمعنی فاعل ومصدر نیز می آید چنانكه بمعنی مصدر كوید الشاهد علی الاول شعر ای نوایی قیلما غا … اكر
دیوانه مین اول پری صفیش اوقوغان سالدی دیوانیم دیرایل اوقو وا اوقوغیل مفرد مخاطب از فصل امر اوقوما وا اوقومانك مفرد
مخاطب از فصل نهی اوقونك وا اوقونكوز وا اوقونكلار جمع مخاطب از فصل امر اوقومانك وا اوقومانكیز وا اوقومانكلار جمع مخاطب از فصل نهی
اوقومان وا اوقوماسمین نمیخوانم اوقوریمن وا اوقورمین وا اوقویدورمین وا اوقورلام میخوانم اوقوروم وا اوقوماغیم خواندنم
اوقوماغوم نخواهم خواند اوقوب وا اوقوبان وا اوقومیش خوانده اوقومیشالك خوانده اوقوماس نمیخواند وبمعنی فاعل
ومصدر منفی نیز می آید اوقوماسلیك خواندن ونخواندن اوقوماغان … از خواندن ونخواندن اوقوب بولماس … اوقوبولماغی ونتواند
نمیتوان خواند اوقوی آلماس نمیتواند خواند اوقوی خواندن اوقوی خوانده وبدون تكرار هم مستعملست اوقوی و
اوقوین میخوانم ومیخواند ومیخوانی وخوانده الشاهد علی الاول المعنی الاول شعر …
بلبله تا اوقوی بیل مقالا … اوقوساق وا اوقوغایمیز وا اوقوغایمیز وا اوقوی نخوانیم چنانكه شاهد بر …
در مجلس دویم از مجالس النفائس … مولانا شرف الدین علی یزدی كوید كه بو جماعت لطفا الدین …
بولدونك سیفناك … اوقوغالی برای خواندن وتا خوانده اوقوغاچ چون خوانده … شعر
ای نوایی … خواستن چنانكه در خمسه
المتحیرین كوید كه مولانا … اوقوغوجه وا اوقوغونجه وا اوقوغالی

تا خواندن وبقصد خواندن چنانکه در رسیدن نامه فرهاد بشیرین کوید الشاهد علی الثانی با لمعنی الاول شعر

اوقوغونجه بو مکتوب شادی دین حبیب یوز قاتلاغ آشوبا و اوقوغوم خواهم خواند او قوغونلنی خواهی خواند اوقوغوسی خواند

خواندلد اوقوغولوق خواندنی او اوقوغای او اوقوسا او اوقوسون او اوقودیلنه بخوانند او اوقوغودیلی او اوقودیلی خواندنی دیچه لکه بخوانند

اوقوشماق مع الشین مصدر مفاعله است یعنی با یکدیکر خواندن وصیغ آن مانند اوقوشتی او لدیا فرهنگ اشتقاق مییابد

اوقولماق مع اللام مصدر انفعال است یعنی خوانده شدن او اوقولوبدر او اوقولور او اوقولمیش خوانده شد الشاهد علی الاول

مرتضی الابرار شعر ای بو قولوب سکه عدل آینکا خطبه دولت او اوقولوب بینکا وصیغ آن بسیار لازم اشتقاق مییابد

اوقوتماق مع التا مصدر متعدیست یعنی خواناندن وصیغ آن با تای قرشت اشتقاق مییابد اوقلاماق در معنی طرد

دوبم از جای بلندی بتحصیل تیر تا بکردن اوقلادی تیر زد وپرتاب کرد او اوقلادیکیز تیر زدید وپرتاب میکند وا اوقلادیم بمعنی

هم می آید اوقلاماید او اوقلادو تیر نمیزند و نزده است وپرتاب نمیکند و نکرده است اوقلاغان او اوقلاغان او اوقلادی او بتیرزنینه

و نزده و پرتاب بکنند و کرده و بمعنی مصدر هم می آید او اوقلا او اوقلاغیل مفرد مخاطب فعل امر او اوقلادما او اوقلاماغیل

مفرد مخاطب فعل نهی او اوقلاتی او اوقلادیکیز او اوقلادیکلار جمع مخاطب فعل امر او اوقلاما نکیز او اوقلاما نکلار جمع مخاطب

نهی او اوقلادیم او اوقلادیم تیر نمیزنم وپرتاب نمیکنم او اوقلادیمین او اوقلادیمین او اوقلادیم او اوقلادیم تیر میزنم وپرتاب میکنم

اوقلاغوسیدور او اوقلاغوسیم تیر زدنیم وپرتاب کردنیم او اوقلاغوم تیر نخواهم زد وپرتاب نخواهم کرد او اوقراماق بفتح راء قرشت

آهسته صدا کردن اسب بود در طلب علف که آنرا بعربی تحمحم کویند چون اشتقاق صیغ آن منتج نماید بنوشتن کرمصدر اکتفا شد

الحمد او اوقچ بمعنی طرد او اول تیر را کویند الشاهد علیه شعر تاشینک دین تو شوب بین یراق یادین او اوقچ ملک منکا منه

دین بولدی کو یا بدن او اوق دیدیم بالمجاز چو بنهایت هر اهل دانند که مانا ای همانا هر آینه بون بوشند چنانکه کوید شعر او ویکرا اوق

تیرا نده ساکنه خاطر جمع ایماس نه عجب کراس یوقوقر کنیدکردان را اوقچو بنهایت الاعلا لاچوقچ را اوق کویند بسیم بمعنی انداختم

و فی الفورانشد الشاهد علیه تو شوم اد بیکیم کوونکا اوق او درنام ایلکیم اوپ کوونک طالع کرا ولی او اوق میتکام اوق

سیکاندیم اویقودین چهار رم بمعنی خامت شعر نوا یا ثلمه او لفیض خانقاه ایچره غم نهایت کاپرور خوشیر اوق آنداوق

ایکانیم و نیز بمعنی مقصد از لسان الطیر کوید شعر سلامت شاخی بیرله طوبی بولسا بوق او کوینی نوت بیشه دین بریار او اوق

بجهم بمعنی هم استعمال میشود چنانکه کوید شعر نوای و کلشن که پیر کل دین باروق منکا بس بورور کنج بیت الحزن او اوق وهم با این

کوید شعر مسکینفث ایشار نوای نیسه جنت اهل زهد موبجا او اوق بولور تفاوت عالم و جاهل ابل معنی شرانیت کرنوای

مسکن ترا میخواهد و اکر زهد جنت نسیه را هم اینقدر در میان عالم و جاهل تفاوت می باشد و مولفین رهنیه او اوق را بمعنی کرد

نقد مند نسیه فهیده معنی نوشته اند و شعر نیز بعد الشاهد آورده اند تغییر هم مناسبت کرده و فرا بعی کفته که در مطلع

ترکی کویند که فلان فلان بت و خشاد وا این او اوق بعنوت باشد در صورت معنی هم اختراعی ولا یعنی است او اوقاد بر نهایت

که آنرا بفارسی کلنک کویند و زلف آنرا بر حقیقه و کلاه خود نصب کنند الشاهد علیه شعر قیلدی علم او اوقتا او تاغسین اول

قاتل شجاع خورشید فارضیفه ها با خط شغلاغ او اوقلاغو او اوقلاق اتلاوی تیری کرخیمه آشیابه دون بفتن کنند و نیز چوبی باشد

بادرات کرخیمه را نزابدان بند کنند و آنرا بعربی مرزاق و منوال و بقلمری و رتبه کویند او اوقوش بمعنی قراءت و خواندن بود

او اوق بیلاشنی بترینا دیود چنانکه در فرهاد و شیرین در صفت فرهاد با اژدها کوید شعر چو اژدر هم نجم او کلکه روانه

او قفه هر جم او لدی بر نشانه اکرچه اژدها بلر ابر بوی خزانه ولیکن اوول الوق بیلاچنی او اوق پران مع الکاف من المشتقات

اوکماک بسکون کاف عجمی در منقوط در اول مدح و ستایش کردن باشد چنانکه در فرهاد و شیرین در وصف فرهاد کوید شعر

اینلک اول کوهر والا اسوا بد صد که بو او وکما کهدین استغناسی او در بیم بمعنی جمع کردن بود او کدی مدح کرد و جمع کرد او کدا

مدح کردیم جمع کردیم او کاردا وکا دور مدح میکند وجمع میکند چنانکه شاهد بر اول المعنی منضرد مخاطب فعل امر کوید

شعر زهد ایلهای کر نوائی فنا وکا دین کورد لات ایشول عمر وکلوات ایمیش هلم میخانه ایمیش ودر حیرة الابرار بمعنی کوید

عهد اشطیح قهر کیم تو کان صیقلج پاره سید ضمیریم اوکاو وکار بمعنی نامل و مضمون نیز می آید چنانکه در هم بیتا

در خاتمه کتاب بمعنی مدح کردن کوید شعر ایل اوکادین کونکل لیشاد ایتمان کهنوش آمد غرا اعتبار ایتمان او کاید و مدح نکند

ونکرده است وجمع نمیکند و نکرده است او کانکان او کارکان واو کاد ور کان مدح کننده و مدح کرده وجمع کننده وجمع

بمعنی مصدر نیز می آید او کاو وکیکیل مفرد مخاطب فعل امر در معنی الشاهد علی الاول المعنی الثانی شعر دردی محنت تا

ای مخزون کونکول جانخفه اولث هرنی افزون کیلسا آندین جسم وبرانمنه اوک اوکا واوکاکیل مفرد مخاطب فعل نهی

او کونلک او کونکونز او کونکلار جمع مخاطب فعل امر او کانکیز واو کانکلار جمع مخاطب فعل نهی او کانلو او کامایین

مدح نمیکنم وجمع نمیکنم او کایین واو کارمین واو کایدورمین او کارام مدح میکنم وجمع میکنم او کایم او کاکیم مدح

کردیم وجمع کردیم او کاکوم مدح نخواهم کرد وجمع نخواهم کرد او کوبع او کوبان واو کمیش مدح کرده وجمع کرده چنانکه

در مقاله نوزدهم از حیرة الابرار در وصف عشق کوید الشاهد علی الاول المعنی الثانی شعر آرتا سید عشق کر بیمنم او کاچ

هر کیمی بیر غم ایا غین تو کوب او کیشانک مدح کرده وجمع کرده او کیاس مدح نمیکند وجمع نمیکند و بمعنی حال و مستقبل

هم می آید او کابی مدح کردنش و نکردنش وجمع کردنش و نکردنش او کادین از مدح کردن و مدح نکرده و از جمع کردن

او کوب تولغا او کا تولغانه مدح میتوان کرد وجمع میتوان کرد او کا آلغای مدح میتواند کرد وجمع میتواند کرد

در مقاله سیم از حیرة الابرار در وصف بدیع الزمان میرزا کوید بالمعنی الاول شعر هم کر ایل صنعی دین او تمیش ایشه یوزدین

اینک او کا آلغای کیشی او کا او کا مدح کنان وجمع کنان و بدون تکرار هم مستعملست او کای او کایین مدح کنم و

و جمع کرده واو کای بمعنی تا چیزی بونا اما دیجی و نا برابر نیز استعمال میشود او کاک او کاکاپنو او کاکای او کالی او کالینک

مدح کنیم وجمع کنیم او کاکالی برای مدح کردن و تا مدح کرده و برای جمع کردن و تا جمع کرده او کاکاچ چون مدح کرد و کنکله

جمع کرد و کند او کاکوچی مدح کننده وجمع کننده او کاکوچی او کاکونچه او کاکانچه تا مدح کردن و بقصد مدح کردن و تا

جمع کردن و بقصد جمع کردن او کاکوم مدح خواهم کرد وجمع خواهم کرد او کاکونک مدح خواهی کرد وجمع خواهی کرد او کاکوسی

مدح خواهد کرد وجمع خواهد کرد او کاکولوک مدح کردنی وجمع کردنی او کاکای او کالا او کاسا او کاسون او کادیلی مدح کند

جمع کند چنانکه در صفت سیاوش کوید الشاهد علی الثالث بالمعنی الاول شعر کیم جواهر نی آلیغه او کسا تل فضلت کینی آینه

او کسا او کاکودیلی او کارلتی مدح کردن و جمع کردن و جمع کند او کولمک مع اللام دو معنی داد

اول ستوده شدن دویم جمع شدن او کولدی ستوده شد و جمع شد الشاهد علیه بالمعنی الثانی شعر کونکول آنچه

او تونکلین او کولدی بیکانی کیم باشاق سیله بوبلا من جمع ان خوش دو اوکولکان او کولکان واو کولادور کان ستوده شده

و ستوده شده وجمع شونده وجمع شده چنانکه در فرهاد و شیرین شاهد بر اول معنی جمع شده کوید شعر آچیلیش هر طرف پرکلشن کل

اوکولکان هرنیلری پرخون کلی وبمعنی مصدر نیز می آید اوکولوب وا وکولونان وا وکولمیش ستوده شدن جمع شد چنانکه
در حیرة الابرار کوید الشاهد علی الاول والمعنی الثانی شعر معرکه دا ازالیپ رستمی ایشلاری اوزیدو کولوب ایلی و تا
سبع برابن سیاق بالالام اشتقاق می یابد اوکونماک بضم کاف عجمی وسکون نون بمعنی مفاخرت ومباهات وخود را ستودن باشد
چنانکه در خمسه المتحیرین کوید که امیر ظاهرو باطنیم منه موجب مباهات وقوانماق ودینی وآخرتیم منه باعث افتخار و اوکونماک اندی
اوکوندی خود را ستود اوکوندیلر خود را ستودیم اوکونورها اوکونادور خود را می ستاید چنانکه فضولی کوید الشاهد
علی الاول ابتلای آکرونتیه شعر اوکونور دیدیم که حیرانیم ازلدن یوزینکا اولدی معلوم بولا اماندا کرچه تمامیاشی واوکو
بمعنی فاعل ومصدر هم می آید اوکونماندین خود را می ستاید وستوده است اوکونکان وا اوکونورکان وا اوکونادورکان خود را ستاینده
خود را ستوده وبمعنی مصدر هم می آید اوکون وا اوکونکیل مفرد مخاطب فعل امر اوکونمان وا اوکونمانکیز اوکونانکلار جمع مخاطب
فعل نهی اوکونمان وا اوکونماس مین خود را نمی ستایم اوکونامین وا اوکونورمین وا اوکونادورمین وا اوکونورام خود را می ستایم اوکونور
وا اوکوناکیم خود را ستودیم اوکوناکوم خود را نخواهم ستود اوکونوسا وا اوکونوبان وا اوکونمیش خود را ستوده اوکونمیشاملک
خود را ستودن اوکونماس خود را نمی ستاید وبمعنی فاعل ومصدر منفی هم می آید اوکونماسی خود را ستودن ونستودن اوکونمادین
از خود را ستودن وخود را نستوده اوکونوب بولغای وا اوکونا بولغای خود را نمیتوان ستود اوکونا آلغای خود را نمیتواند ستود اوکونا اوکو
خود را ستایشکنان وبدون تکرار هم مستعملست اوکونای وا اوکونایین خود را بستایم وبستاید وبستایی اوکونالک وا اوکونکا
وا اوکونکای ... اوکونالی وا اوکونالینک خود را بستاییم اوکونکالی برای خود را ستودن وتا خود را ستوده اوکونکوچی خود را
اوکونکوچی وا اوکونکونچه وا اوکونکانچه تا خود را ستودن وبمقدار ستودن اوکونکوم خود را هم ستود اوکونکولیک خود را
خواهی ستود اوکونکوسی خود را خواهد ستود اوکونکولوک خود را ستودنی اوکونکای وا اوکونلوا اوکونسلوا اوکونسون وا اوکونکای
خود را بستاید اوکونکودیلوا اوکونوریلک خود را ستودنی وهمچنانکه خود را بستاید اوکورماک بضم کاف وسکون رای
قرشت بهایهای کریستن بالصوت شدید الشاهد علیه شعر ایشیم تاغ اوزره هر یاز اشک سیلابینی بهر ناکه دو
فراق آشوبیدین هردم بولوت ینکلیغ اوکورناکه قرا اوکوردی هایهای کریست چنانکه در لیلی مجنون کوید بخشی نامزد
لاد کبی اوکوردی نوفل باریسی اشک دیلت یو کوردی علد کوردوک های هایکه کردیم اوکورورو اوکورادورها های های کریه می کند
واوکورو بمعنی فاعل ومصدر نیز می آید چنانکه بمعنی مصدری کوید شعر شامناممی تولاکیم عرب اینادر اوکونکلوم
ای مغنی چالا باشلا اوکورور کوکته قویوزی یعنی ای مغنی بنواز قوپوز شروع کن در ساز هایهای کریه کردن اوکورنابیلکی
هایهای کریه میکند ونکویماست اوکورکان وا اوکورورکان وا اوکورادورکان هایهای کریه کننده وکریه کرده وبمعنی مصدر نیز آ
اوکور وا اوکورکیل مفرد مخاطب فعل امر اوکورمانکوا اوکورماکیل مفرد مخاطب فعل نهی اوکورونک وا اوکورونکوز وا اوکورونکیز
جمع مخاطب فعل امر اوکورمانک وا اوکورمانکیز وا اوکورمانکلار جمع مخاطب فعل نهی اوکورمان وا اوکورماس مین هایهای نمیکنیم اوکورامین و
اوکوروریمین وا اوکورادورمین وا اوکوروریلار هایهای میکریم اوکوردوم وا اوکورکانیم هایهای کریه کردیم اوکورناکوم هایهای کریه نخواهم کرد
اوکوروب وا اوکورونابان وا اوکورمیش هایهای کریه کرده الشاهد علی الاول شعر کر نولسا مفرط افغان اینتا جانا
قیلمه عیب سیز منداغ الغایتکان کونکول سوکیدا سیغلاغا اوکوروشا اوکورمیشاملک هایهای کریه کرده اوکورماس هایهای
کریه نمیکند وبمعنی فاعل ومصدر منفی هم می آید اوکورماسی هایهای کریه کردن ونکردن اوکورمادین ...

کریه کردن وهایهای کریه نکرده اوکوروب بولماس وا اوکورا بولماس اوکورا آلغای هایهای کریه نمیتوان کرد اوکورا آلماس هایهای کریه
نمیتواند که اوکورا اوکورلا ... هایهای کریه کنان وبدون تکرار هم مستعملست اوکورای وا اوکورایین هایهای کریه کنم وکند وکنی
اوکورالیک وا اوکورکای بیز وا اوکورالی وا اوکورالیک هایهای کریه کنیم اوکورکالی برای هایهای کریه کردن وتا کریه
کرده اوکورکاچ چون هایهای کریه کند اوکورکوچی هایهای کریه کننده اوکورکوچه وا اوکورکونچه وا اوکورکانچه تا هایهای
کردن وبمقدار کریه کردن اوکورکوم هایهای کریه خواهم کرد اوکورکونک هایهای کریه خواهی کرد اوکورکوسی
هایهای کریه خواهد کرد اوکورکولوک هایهای کریه کردنی اوکورکای وا اوکورلا وا اوکورسا وا اوکورسون وا اوکوردیلک هایهای
کریه کند اوکورکودیلک وا اوکورودیلک کریه کردنی وهمچنانکه کریه کند اوکوسماک وا اوکوسلاماک بضم سین مع الکاف کم شدن
اوکوسدی وا اوکوسکودیک کم شد چنانکه در لسان الطیر در توحید کوید الشاهد علی الاول شعر بیر یوزین بالمفرع بی
بیله بیوتی کرد چرخ کل اطلس یوناغدین اوکوسدی ونیز در استغنا کوید الشاهد علی الثانی والاول شعر تاغ بیله ییغدی
سینک یوق بولماغین بیر بیوزی بیرین بیر قمم اوکوسلدی ساغین سدین تاغ بی پرله لموب بولسا یوق اوکوسدی تونچه
برابا فراغ اوق اوکوسوداک وا اوکوسلد ولک کم شدیم اوکوسورا اوکوسودور اوکوسادور کم می شود اوکوسورا اوکوسوریمی
فاعل ومصدر هم می آید اوکوسماید ... اوکوسماید ور کم نمیشود ونشده است اوکوسکان وا اوکوسورکان وا اوکوسادورکان
اوکوسکلان اوکوسوکاران وا اوکوسوکان کم شونده وکم شده وبمعنی مصدر هم می آید اوکوسوا اوکوسکیل وا اوکوسول وا اوکوسکیل
مفرد مخاطب فعل امر اوکوسونکوا اوکوسونکیل وا اوکوسلوا اوکوسماکیل مفرد مخاطب فعل نهی اوکوسونک وا اوکوسونکیز وا اوکوسونکلار ...
اوکوسونکوز وا اوکوسکلا جمع مخاطب فعل امر اوکوسمانک وا اوکوسمانکیز وا اوکوسمانکلار جمع کوسمانات وا اوکوسمانکیز وا اوکوسمانکلار
جمع مخاطب فعل نهی اوکوسمان وا اوکوسماس مین وا اوکوسماس من کم نمیشوم اوکوسامین وا اوکوسورمین وا اوکوسادورمین
اوکوسوریمیز اوکوسلامین وا اوکوسوریمین وا اوکوسلادیم ... کم میشوم اوکوسدوم وا اوکوسورومیز اوکوسکانیم ... اوکوسولماکیم کم شدیم
اوکوسناکوم ... کم نخواهم شد اوکوسوب وا اوکوسوبان وا اوکوسمیش کم شده اوکوسمیشاملک
اوکوسمیشاملک کم شده اوکوسماس وا اوکوسماس کم نمیشود وبمعنی فاعل ومصدر منفی هم می آید اوکوسماسی ...
کم شدن ونشدن اوکوسمادین از کم شدن وکم نشده اوکوسوب بولماس وا اوکوسا بولماس اوکوسا آلماس ... اوکوسا آلغای
اوکوسوب بولمادوا اوکوسا بولمادوا اوکوسا آلماس کم نمیتوان شد اوکوسا آلماس کم نمیتواند شد اوکوسای اوکوسای
اوکوسلا اوکوسلا کم شده کم شده اوکوسای وا اوکوسایین وا اوکوسالی وا اوکوسالیک کم شوم وشود وشوی وشده اوکوسالک وا اوکوسا...
اوکوسالیک وا اوکوسالیک کم شویم اوکوسکالی وا اوکوسکالی برای کم شدن وتا کم شده اوکوسکاچ اوکوسکاچ
چون کم شده شود اوکوسکوچی وا اوکوسکوچی کم شونده اوکوسکوچه وا اوکوسکونچه وا اوکوسکانچه اوکوسکونچه
اوکوسکانچه تا کم شدن وبمقدار کم شدن اوکوسکوم وا اوکوسکوم کم خواهم شد اوکوسکونک وا اوکوسکونک کم خواهی شد
اوکوسکوسی وا اوکوسکوسی کم خواهد شد اوکوسکولوک وا اوکوسکولوک کم شدنی اوکوسکای وا اوکوسا وا اوکوسون وا اوکوسدیلک
اوکوسکای وا اوکوسلا وا اوکوسا وا اوکوسلون وا اوکوسلدیلک کم شود الشاهد علی الاول شعر بیغلامانی اوکم میلاد ...
ابکی آریغ آریلیب اوکوسکای ... الشاهد علی الثانی شعر ترینیشه سیداعمر ... اوکوسناغم یوق ای ساقی کلیم تولا
ایله پیاله اوکوسکودیلک وا اوکوسودیلک ... کم شدنی وهمچنانکه کم شود اوکوتماک بضم سین مع التا ...

يعني كم كردن اوكسوتورواوكوتالمكم سكند الشاهد على الاول شعر نا يمطلسيفه نال معنى ايرند غلر فكيم غمم ...
ديرفنا ميخانه آندين كوث واوكسوتو يعني فاعل مصدر منزيه آيد چنانكه در لسان الطير يعني كم كنند كويد مصر اوكسوتلمك
تغير ايله امكانى يوقى اوكسوتوملكا قيلمج دوره داغى اوق اوكسوتها وكتكيل مفردنها المبلغ فضل الهامل الشاهد على الاول شعر
جان وكونكومنى ...ليمكا كايلامه يبن يامان آنوق قايله عدين يوقسا ياسين اوكسوت وناقى صنع برهمن ساقيه دستور شود
تاتاى قرشت اشفاق مى يابد اوكوتمالك بضم كاف عجمى وسكون تاى قرشت يعنى آرد كردن باشد اوكريالك بسكون كاف
وكسر راى قرشت يعنى جنبانيدن كمثلو ولشال آتى آمد اوكچه لاانا العطو كچه لاثمالك بسكون كاف وتاى قرشت وفتح جيم عجمى ولام
تركى رومى معنى دارد اوكله ميمنزين باشلد كويند كه آنى اوكچه لاتى يعنى اسب را پاشنه زه و ميمنز ... صرصح كرد
اسب بود عقب پاى اسب بكر اوكچه لاثمالك مع الكون مصدر انقصا است مجروح شدن پاى اسب بود از پاشنه پاى اجنبى بكر
من الجامد اوكات بفتح كاف عجمى بالف كشيده وسكون تاى قرشت تركى رومى معنى نرم وهموار بود اوكاى بفتح كاف عجمى وسكون
ياى حطى نا پدرى ونا مادرى ونابرادرى را كويند چنانكه در تاريخ الملوك در ذكر كيكاوس وقصه سياوش كويد كه سودا
اوكاى آنلسى آنكا عاشق بولوب ايردى ومعناى شهه نيز دارد كه در ذيل مصدر اوكمالك كذشت اوكما بسكون كاف وفتح
تاى قرشت معنى بيهوده وچوچ باشد واوكته با هاى هوز نيز با معنى مستعملست الشاهد عليه شعر نا يحاچون عمر لو تار
فوجكيم بولاتع عشرت سيله عيش تركن كيم بو بيهوده فلتا وكتادر بو نوع اوكوت واوكته حقى نى واقع اولماپوتقيد دن اغار
خانچ بين اوكته ده قيلمرى دين كيشيكا بيزرا اوكوت ونيزدر قسم يم ار محبوب القلوب در تسبيهات در وصف لا محلس
كها اوكته براوين قيلمنا نابوده اولدزمان پشيمان بولماقتى نسود ومؤلف مرمية وندر على معنى ... وخمبيلات
شدن نوشته اند وطالع هروى بتقريب معنى اوكوت نوشته كه اوكتا دو معنى بخانيد نست كه از لوازم نصيحت آ
وندر على ونصيري هم مساعت كرده اند وفراغ اوكتا اوكوتدر ايدفهم شموده معنى بنزلت وپند ونصيحت ... هكى
شعر اورا شاهد آورده اند اكرچه معنى اوكتا بيهوده است مناى بيانهم بهوده است اوكتا ليك كلدى بيهوده وچوچ كردن
وتوالتسهيلى اوكتاى نام پسر سيم چنكيزخانست كه بعد از پدر پادشاه شد ... ممالك خطا وشيوه وشيمه
وطا بوده اوكچه بسكون كاف عجمى وفتح جيم عجمى پاشنه بود كه آنرا بعربى عقب نامند واتراك روم كوينلد فلان كمسنه
اوكچه اينيچ يعنى پرو نعلى كرده كه جراحه ايزار اوكچه سيمز خوانند يعنى ثبات قدم ندارد اوكرا بسكون كاف وفتح راى قرشت بيرون
شعر آتش رشته را كويند اوكسالك بسكون كاف واول وثانى وفتح سين مهمله يعنى بلند ... تنع باشد وآنرا بوكسالك هم كويند
اوكسولك بمعنى صرفه بود كه آنرا بعربى سقا الخوانند اوكسولك يعنى كم واندك چنانكه كويد شعر مينى كرسفيه دراچر الاد
اوسرولت قانلك كنوه مكا قيليرتيو لسانده دين اوكسولك اوكسيز بسكون كاف فتح هاى هوز وكسر سين مهمله تركى رومى عنان ...
يتيم وبى پدر ومادر باشد اوكوت بضم كاف عجمى وسكون تاى قرشت پند ونصيحت را كويند چنانكه شاهد بر آن دو خزينه الغنا
اوكتا كذشت ونيز امر است از آرد كردن ونرم كردن دانه اوكور بضم كاف عجمى ... رايت شبيه بسخن كه چشمها آتش ... خند
چنانكه در ليلى مجنون در وصف شب كويد شعر نا كه اوكونچكا كاكى يسان اوتى نوسونغى ليتيبه كوز يغچا ... آهان
بوف وكوف وبوم وجغد نامند ومؤلف برهان قاطع اوكوز ناريش شمرده وبا معنى نوشته اوكوز بضم كاف عجمى وسكون راى قرشت
اسپ عمليايانه بود كه وقت نماذ يان جتن آنجا باشد وباصطلاح روميه بمعنى مالوف وبا نوراست اوكوز بضم كاف

پركى رومى بمعنى اول ومقدم بود اوكوغه بضم كاف عجمى وسكون راى قرشت وفتح ضمه ... مهرهاى پشت باشد كه آنرا بعربى فقرات الظهر
نامند اوكوز بسكون راى هوز هوامل كاو را نامند اوكوز كوزى بتركى رومى نام كياهيست كه آنرا بفارسى بكاو چشم وبعربى
عين البقر كويند اوكوش بضم كاف عجمى وسكون شين قرشت بمعنى بسيار و فراوان بود چنانكه كويد شعر فغان كه هجرين آنكلاى
اوكوش العرنيكا ترحم ايتمادى دل مهرى يوق صنم نيكا وكلمه شعر خوان وصليدا اوكوش نعمت داده راغيار روزى ايتمادى كام
اول نوع تنم مايرب ودرهجران تو ... يوكوش نيز مستعمل اوكولكا بضم كاف عجمى اول وفتح ثانى وسكون لام بمعنى صله وجائزه
آمده چنانكه در تاريخ مطلع السعدين مذكوراست كه اوكولكه وانعام فراوان بلشكريان داد اوكون بضم كاف سه معنى دارد
اول بمعنى غير بود چنانكه در حيرة الابرار كويد شعر كوز كه ايبوركى آنينك خلقيتى چيزى اكى كوز مالك ايكن صحبتى
بردين اوكون چون نيمه موجود ايماس كه كان آنيا يكى ايرورشرلك وبش ونيز درمجلس كه در تعداد الاى المى كويد
شعر بولاردين اوكون بردى عقل وحواش سينى قيلدى هم تابيشه هوش اش وطالع هروى بمعنى خوان ... نوشته
وشعر نهم بزار نستى مكتوب شاهد آورده دويم بلغت مغولى بمعنى سيه بود كه آنرا بعربى شحم نامند سيم امر است از
خود راستودن چنانكه در ذيل مصدر اوكونمالك كذشت اوكونج بضم كاف وسكون نون وجيم ندامت وپشيمانى را كويند
ومؤلف برهان قاطع اوكنج برودن شطرنج بفارسى نيز ذكر كرده وبا معنى نوشته اوكولهورق بضم كاف عجمى ودال مهمله ...
قرشت وسكون نون وقاف تركى رومى ميلى است كه حلاجان پنبه دانه را بدان از پنبه جدا كنند اوكونده بفتح راى ... مهمله
چوبى باشد كه بر سر آن سيخى از آهن نصب كرده بجهت كاو وخر خلانند تا در راه روند وآنرا بفارسى غاوشنك خوانند مع الاوكز
من المشتقات ... مع القاف شدن وبودن الشاهد على الاول والمعنى الاول شعر غميم كو پ آتيا الماس ميزيانكا كو...
هلاك اولماق ايچيدا يوز قيليج زخمى عجيب بكو كسوم خاك خاك اولماق وآنرا بولماق ... كويند وطالع هروى اولماق را مع القاف
مردن نوشته سهو كرده اولمك دا ولماكليك مع الكاف بمعنى مردن باشد الشاهد على الاول شعر كوردين كيتمك و...
اولمك منكا نينك بولسا قانانك كه جلاد ... كه لعل ناتى لعتى ع الشاهد على الثانى شعر جمع ظلم ... كرچه اولمان
ثنا بعده منكا ... كسيدين ده حيات جاودان ده منكا اولدى شد بودو اولدى شيم اولماقلق ...
اولور بضم لام ميشود بمعنى فاعل مصدر منزيه آيد اولا بفتح لام دو معنى دارد اول بميرد چنانكه كويد شعر بولكه
تيغى تيليشماسين بو درين بوزاولادن حسن اهيشكيم بولسا كوپ قصاب قوى مردارا ولاش دويم بمعنى پيوند ميكند وبامعنى
مشتق از مصدر اولاماق بمعنى پيوند كردن باشد چنانكه نكارش يابد و بمعنى فاعل مصدر مزبور آيد چنانكه بمعنى اول
كويد شعر ديما كه كيم دى اودتى قتل وتى تامنام راه كيم اول الفكيمى بردى اولار دا اجابنم ... ونيز بمعنى ... كويد شعر
اى نواى المكيل اندين بوزنا كيم ... اجل بكيم اجل ... اولار كاه ... كاى شايد بجا ال اولادور ميشود و ميميرد ...
نميشود و ... است و ... اولمايد بمعنى نميشود و ... چنانكه بمعنى اخير كويد شعر بو كه
اولاعمردين اميدم ... اولمايد ... براى انعام كه بوباده ... اولوم ... اوليات اولغان ... اولاعان
شونده وشد الشاهد على الاول والمعنى الثالث شعر عشق بحرى ... بيرو ... كيم كر بو قاندين تراولغان
ترا ولغان وبمعنى مصدر مزبور آيند اولكان ... اولاكان ميرنده ومرده الشاهد على الاول والمعنى الثانى
شعر لب ... شوكيدا اولكان ... كو يونكدا ازلفيد ... ايلاك ... بوليش لعلى ... آنينك وبمعنى مصدر مزبور آمده

چنانچه کوید الشاهد علی الاول شعر منانم او زونکا توت که اولادسین کتاه ایله بو جرم طفیلنک اولکانیکانی قورود
جزغ اول امراستانرشدن وبودن ومردن چنانکه مرثیه مجنون بمعنی اول کوید شعر ای دشت نیل الکان بوطن کاه
بول آزمیشام اول زمانی آنکاه وسه معنی نمامدم دارد که باشو اهد دخیل جامد مذکور خواهد شد اولغیل امراستانرشدن
اولکیل امراستانمردن اولما مفرد مخاطب ازفعل مضموم بمعنی وللغیل نهی استانرشدن اولماکیل نهی استانمردن
اولونک واولونکوز واولونکلار جمع مخاطب ازصیغه امرمضموم بمعنی اولمانک واولمانکیز واولمانکلار جمع مخاطب نهی
اولمان واولماسین نمیشوم ونمیمیرم اولامین واولادورمین میشوم ومیمیرم الشاهد علی الثانی بالمعنی الثانی شعر
ای سیجیم اولادورمین مردم قدم ایت رنجه بو بیمار دیناری اولورمین واولورام میشوم اولادرمین واولادرام میمیرم وپیوند
میکنم دارد بمعنی مصدر اولاناق مشترک اولورم واولماغیم شدنم وبودنم اولادیم واولماکیم مردنم واولادیم بمعنی پیوند کردم
هم باشد اولماغوم نخواهم شد ونخواهم بود اولماکوم نخواهم مرد دنوبدا واولوبدا واولمیش شده ومرده الشاهد علی المعنی
الاول والثانی شعر ایکی کوزونک ولبینک عمی دیش مینرخسته اولوبدا اولوبتر بلدیم اولمیشانک شده ومرده آیکا
نمیشود ونمیمیرد وبمعنی فاعل ومصدر بمعنی هم می آید چنانکه بمعنی شدن کوید شعر نوایی اولمبیغه غانم عراق ایچکا
مکوز اهتمال هر بیر مرجع امکاناکه شدن وشدنش چنانکه بمعنی نفی واثبات هردو بطریق ابهام کوید شعر عشوه دین
البلامان احباب دغا مستجاب اولماسی نینک معنی نغمه تیلاک ونیز بمعنی مردن ومردنش اولمادین ازشدن وناشده وازمردن
ومرده چنانکه بمعنی شدن در کلیله ودمنه بملاء الرمیته آمده شعر بن الوم چیکدوم غم سودای زلفونکدین سنسک
چون حسن الجیکذ نک اغنا ایله نیا واولمادش اولوب کیهانا ولولسا بولماس نمیتوان شد ونمیتوان مرد اولماق اولماس
نمیتوان شد اولماک اولماس نمیتوان مرد اولاالماس نمیتواند شد ونمیتواند مرد اولا اولا شده شده ومرده مرده وبلکه
تکرار هم مستعمل اولای واولایین بشوم وبشود وبشوی وشده چنانکه شاهد بر تکلم بمعنی اول کوید شعر ای نو
مبلا بلاده بینک بیره اهل قولوم کردیناناک مقبول اولای دار اولما بو مرده ودایله ونیز بمعنی بمیرم وبمیرد وبمیرد ومرده الشاهد
علی الاول بالمعنی الاول شعر دیماهر دم بسکنه البلای بیره واقوی کیم اولای کیم اولوال ولغونک دو دور بعد مرده تا
ایله ونیز بمعنی پیوند کنم وکنی وکند وکرده اولساق بشویم وباشیم اولسانک بمیریم اولغایمز واولغای بشویم وباشیم چنانکه
باول بمعنی ثانی در خاتمه سبعه سیاره در بظوفی دنیا کوید شعر سین دمین چو دکیم اولغایمز آخر بکیم قوپی دین قوتولغا
آخر اولکانیز واولکانی بمیریم واولای واولای لنک بشویم وباشیم بمیریم وپیوند کنیم اولغلی برای شدن وناشده اولکانی
برای مردن وتامرده اولغاج چون شده وشود الشاهد علیه شعر جمالین وصف ایتارمین همه ایم اول کلعذار اولغاج
قورووق شاخ ایله کیم ظاهر تیلور کل لادبها را اولغاچ اولکاج چون مرد وبمیرد اولغوچی شونده اولکوچی میرنده
اولغوجی اولغوچی اولغانچه تا شدن وبقلم شدن چنانکه در سبعه سیاره در داستان منا ز اقلیم کوید الشاهد علی
الاول بالمعنی الاول شعر بولماسا رحمت لغوجه آکاه کیتکو دیک مین باشیم آیتا کما اولکوچی واولکوچه اولکانچه تا مردن و
مردن الشاهد علی الاول بالمعنی الاول شعر جرغه سین بر نالوانی غمه ایدی اولکوچه بش نیم عیش بجر اطرا الجرین اولغا
حیکیث الشاهد علی الثالث شعر کبینک نوشی زکاتر ملاحت اهلیغه بر بیر بولسانک اولوب مین حسرتیدین جان نه یوق
اولکانجه ملاجمشد اولغوم خواهم شد وخواهم بود اولکوم خواهم مرد الشاهد علیه شعر کردیانک تبلیم سوزینی

یوق دیکوم یوقای مسیح اولکوم اوطان پراه پیدم هم مینی همراز میلسا اولغونک خواهی شد وخواهی بود شعر هامونکی
ایلادبان امرزنی نفسی خوش نکیم می دیکل بیچ نمین اولغونک اوحانی بولکونک خواهی مرد الشاهد علیه شعر
چونکه آنینر اولکونک ملحقیشیم دیم کیم آیرلماغه دوش با مدلول ازضیغه اولکونچه تطویل ای کونکول ولغوچی خواهد شد
وخواهد بود اولکوچی خواهد مرد اولغولوق شدنی وبودنی اولکولوک مردنی اولغای شود وباشد وباشلغ بمعنی بود
شود اولکای بمیرد چنانکه کوید شعر باهری کونکلوم هوشی چشمینک وقد دیر احکر کامیت بر کلا سنکلیم کما ولکای
ممتی کوهر ابیث اولالاد وامقا الادر واولسولادر واولسونلادر بشوند وباشند بمیرند چنانکه مصدر کندری بمعنی باشد کوند
الشاهد علی الاول شعر وطیبه بانبیخ لوقاسوده دلنه مامر عنونه اولوبسکلاد لها محال ولغوسلیکر اولوبدیک شدلی نو
بشوم الشاهد علی الاول بالمعنی الاول شعر اکر بولسا بو زمان عذا میلغامین شیب ولغودیک بولساجاتان منکا الکو
دیک بن اولادبین سردخام وهمچنانکه عیرم الشاهد علی الاول بالمعنی الاول شعر توشکا لی لجانیمه بمام کوزونک حالی
اولکودیک مین که بی صعب ایروخسته لیغیتر واولادریک بمعنی پیوند کردن وهمچنانکه پیوند کند هم آمده ودر بمعنی لحوند
مصدر اولاناقاست اولاناق بفتح لام واو اولاندورماق بسکون نون وراو وضم دال مصدر متعدی بمعنی بند کردن
وپیوستن رشته مرتیمان نیکان اولادی اولاندوردی بند وپیوند کرد اولادوق واولاندوردوق بند وپیوند کردیم
اولادو اولادیم اولاندوریرو اولاندوراللا بند وپیوند میکند واولار بمعنی بمیرد هم باشد چنانکه دخیل اولمانک کذشت
واولار واولاندورور بمعنی فاعل مصدر هم میاید اولانایدور واولاندوراییم بند وپیوند نمیکند ونکرد مات الا قا
اولادان واولایدوغان اولاندورغان واولاندوردوغان اولاندورادورغان بند وپیوند کننده بند وپیوند کرده وبمعنی مصدر هم می اید
اولاواولادیل واولاندور واولاندورغیل مفرد مخاطب ازفعل امر چنانکه شاهد بر ثالث برای مناجات کوید که آلمی اول سپل الغنی اکا هلیغ
بیتکوروبو هشیار الغنی بی اشتنا هلیغ غه اولاندوراولانا واولاماغیل واولاندورماغیل مفرد مخاطب
نهی اولانک واولانکیز واولانکلار واولاندورونک واولاندورونکیز واولاندورونکلار جمع مخاطب ازفعل امر اولامانک واولامانکیز واولاما
اولاندورمانک واولاندورمانکیز جمع مخاطب ازفعل نهی اولادین واولادیم واولاندورایین واولاندورادیم واولاندورمایین واولاندورمادیم
بند وپیوند میکنم واولادمین واولادام بمعنی میمیرم هم آمده چنانکه کذشت اولانام واولاغامیم اولماغایمین واولاندورمادیم
اولاندوراین واولاندوردایمین بند وپیوند نکنم چنانکه شاهد بر اول بمعنی ثانی در تاریخ الانبیا هرذکر ایوب علیه السلام
وفریب دادن شیطان زوجه حضرت را کوید که شیطان آیتی کما کرکیم اولاوسنکی کیسیب منکا بیرسانک کیم سا چمغه اولاسام موبجه
بیاسین بیرورمین اولانار اولانارمین اولاندورارمین بند وپیوند میکنیم او لادیم بکسر اولاندوردوم بضم راو
اولاماغیم اولاندورماغیم بند وپیوند کردیم اولادیم بمعنی مردیم هم آمده اولاناغوم واولاندورماغوم بند وپیوند نخواهم کرد
اولاب اولابان واولامیش واولاندوروب واولاندورموشان واولاندورمیش بند وپیوند کرده اولامیشالیک واولاندورمیشالیک بند کرده وپیوسته
اولاناس واولاندورماس بند وپیوند نمیکند وبمعنی فاعل ومصدر بمعنی هم آمده اولاناسی واولاندورماسی بند وپیوند کردن
نکردن اولانادیو واولاندورمادین از بند وپیوند کردن وپیوند کرده اولاب بوتیا واولاسا بوتیا واولاناق ممکن واولاندوراب
اولاندوربوتیا بولماس وا ولاندورماق اولماس بند وپیوند نمیتوان کرد اولای الماس واولاندوراالماس پیوند
نمیتواند کرد ونمیتواند تابیدا ولایوا ولای اولای واولاندوراولاندوراب بند وپیوند کنان وبدون تکرار هم مستعمل اولای واولا

داولانقلی داولاندورالینک بند وپیوند کنم وکنده کنی وکرده ونیز اولای وا ولاین یعنی بشوم وبشود وبشوی وببرم وببرد
وببری اولاناق وا ولالی وا ولالینک وا ولاندورناق وا ولاندورالینک وا ولاندورالینک بند وپیوند کنیم ونیز اولالی وا ولالینک
یعنی بشویم وببریم اولاماج وا ولاندورماج چون بند وپیوند کرده کند اولاغوچی وا ولاندورغوچی پیوند کننده وتابنده
اولاغوچیه وا ولاغوچیغه وا ولاغانچه وا ولاندورغوچیه وا ولاندورغوچیغه وا ولاندورغانچه تا بند وپیوند کرده وبعد پیوند کردن
اولاغوم وا ولاندورغوم بند وپیوند خواهم کرد اولاغونک وا ولاندورغونک بند وپیوند خواهی کرد اولاغوسی وا ولاندورغوسی
بند وپیوند خواهد کرد اولاغولوق وا ولاندورغولوق بند وپیوند [illegible] پیوند کردنی اولاماق
اولاسا وا ولاسون وا ولادیلار وا ولامیش [illegible] بند وپیوند کنند اولاغور [illegible] ولاندورغور
اولاندورماق بند وپیوند کردنی وهمچنانکه بند وپیوند کند واولاغور بمعنی [illegible] وهمچنانکه [illegible] آمده وکذا
ماخوذ از مصدر اولاماق است چنانکه مذکور شد اولاناق مع النون مصدر انفعالست یعنی پیوستن وبند وپیوند شدن
اولانمه پیوسته الشاهد علیه شعر یا ناعشق ایلکیدین حالیم اولاندی ایلیغ لارغه فراق آشوبیدین تا الدعه ایشیم
دشوار ایلیغ لارغه ونیز در فرهاد وشیرین در وصف فرهاد گوید شعر بود کیم بولدی بو دانای ماهی مرضلارغه اولاندی
جسمی داغی اولانغان وا ولانورغان وا ولانادورغان پیوسته شوند وپیوسته شده وتابیده شوند وتابیده شده الشاهد
علی الاول بالمعنی الاخیر شعر تالیبان زلفونک را تا بی نوا جسمی تاب سیلاکا کی بولمای [illegible] اولانغان تار کبی
وبمعنی مصدر نیز می آیند اولانیش اولانماق اولانمیش پیوسته شدن وتابیده شدن الشاهد علی الاخیر بالمعنی الاول
بانکی آی [illegible] سیل ایلاکا ندیک اولانمیش [illegible] هلالی [illegible] موافق [illegible]
می باید اولاشماق مع الشین والقاف مصدر مفاعله است یعنی بیکدیکر پیوستن وبند شدن اولاشمات مع الشین الکاف
یعنی تقسیم کردن چنانکه گوید شعر کیم [illegible] اولاشماک ایستانانک ای کوهر [illegible] سیل [illegible] کیم [illegible] دیلک
سیلماس [illegible] اولاشتی پیوست وتقسیم کرد بالمعنی الاول شعر [illegible] آشفته [illegible] تسلسل [illegible] اولاشتی
اولاشتوق پیوستیم اولاشتوک تقسیم کردیم وتقسیم اولاشور اولاشادور می پیوندد وتقسیم می کند واولاشور بمعنی فاعل و مصدر
نیز می آید چنانکه بمعنی تقسیم [illegible] هری گوید شعر هر اولاشور [illegible] قرص مهر الغان آی [illegible]
اولاشماید ونشده است ونمیشود وتقسیم نمیکند ونکرده است اولاشغان وا ولاشورغان وا ولاشادورغان پیوسته شونده و
پیوسته شده وبمعنی فاعل ومصدر نیز می آیند اولاشکان وا ولاشوکان وا ولاشادورکان تقسیم کننده وتقسیم کرده وبمعنی فاعل ومصدر
نیز می آیند چنانکه شاهد بر اول را بمعنی مصدری در عنوان یکی از مقطعات گوید که [illegible] تحفه [illegible] ولوشکا [illegible]
اولاش مفرد مخاطب است از فعل نهی هر دو مصدر اولاشغیل مفرد مخاطب است از هر دو مصدر اولاشماقا ولاشکیل مفرد مخاطب
از فعل امر هر دو مصدر اولاشمات الاشما مفرد مخاطب است از فعل نهی هر دو مصدر اولاشماغیل مفرد مخاطب است از فعل نهی مصدر اولاشما
اولاشاکیل مفرد مخاطب است از فعل مصدر اولاشماک اولاشنک وا ولاشنکیز وا ولاشنکلار جمع مخاطبه از فعل امر هر دو مصدر اولاشما
اولاشمانک وا ولاشمانکلار جمع مخاطبه از فعل نهی هر دو مصدر اولاشمان وا ولاشمارمن نمی پیوندم وتقسیم نمیکنم اولاشامین اولاشورمن
اولاشادورمن اولاشورام می پیوندم وتقسیم میکنم اولاشوردم پیوستم وتقسیم کردم اولاشماغیم پیوستیم اولاشماکیم تقسیم کنم
اولاشمابوم نخواهم پیوست اولاشماکوم تقسیم نخواهم کرد اولاشیب اولاشیبان وا ولاشیپ پیوسته شده وتقسیم کرده الشاهد

علی الاول بالمعنی الاول شعر فلک نینک بلکا معی غه کاج اولمیش قیاش حریق آنکا آهیم ستونی بیلا عدوی پیوند اقیکیم
اولاشیپ تو شدی یعنی پیوسته شده گوید شعر چون احلیغه اولاغانلار ابولا آنی [illegible] پیوسته [illegible] اولاشتی ترد
وبمعنی تقسیم کرده هم [illegible] گوید کمینه عراق ولایتلارین اولاشیب [illegible] اولاشمالی پیوسته شده تقسیم کرد
اولاشماس پیوسته نمیشود وتقسیم نمیکند وبمعنی فاعل ومصدر نفی هم می آید اولاشماس پیوسته شدنی و [illegible] تقسیم کردنی
ونکردنی اولاشمادین از پیوسته شدن وپیوسته نشده واز تقسیم کردن وتقسیم نکرده اولاشیب [illegible] اولاشمالی
پیوسته نمیتوانند وتقسیم نمیتوانند کرد اولاشا الماس پیوسته نمیتواند شد وتقسیم نمیتواند کرد اولاشا اولاشا پیوسته
شونده وتقسیم کنان وبدون تکرار هم مستعمل است اولاشای وا ولاشاین پیوسته شوم وشوی [illegible] وتقسیم کنم وکند کنی
اولاشالی وا ولاشالینک پیوسته شویم وتقسیم کنیم اولاشماق [illegible] پیوسته شدن وتا [illegible] اولاشکالی برای تقسیم
کردن وتا تقسیم کرده اولاشاج چون پیوسته شد وشود اولاشکاچ چون تقسیم کرده کند اولاشغوچی پیوسته شونده
اولاشکوچی تقسیم کننده اولاشغوچیه وا ولاشغوچیغه وا ولاشغانچه پیوسته شدن وبعد از آن اولاشکوچیه وا ولاشکوچیغه وا ولاشکانچه
تا تقسیم کردن وبعد تقسیم کردن اولاشغوم پیوسته خواهم شد اولاشکوم تقسیم خواهم کرد اولاشغونک پیوسته خواهی
اولاشکونک تقسیم خواهی کرد اولاشغوسی پیوسته خواهد شد اولاشکوسی تقسیم خواهد کرد اولاشغولوق پیوسته شدنی
اولاشکولوق تقسیم کردنی اولاشغای پیوسته شود چنانکه گوید شعر بار الیدیم که حقیقت غه اولاشغای لغرحال النما
بوروش عشق مجازیم بادره اولاشکای تقسیم کند اولاشا وا ولاشسا وا ولاشسون وا ولاشدیلار پیوسته شود وتقسیم کند اولاشقوک
پیوسته شدنی وهمچنانکه پیوسته شود اولاشکودیک تقسیم کردنی وهمچنانکه تقسیم کند اولاشودیک بمعنی اولاشغودیک و
اولاشکودیک باشد اولوماق باشباع ضمه ضم لام واولوشماق مع الشین ناله کشیدن ساختن ونشان الدامثال آن
اولودی وا ولوشتی ناله کشید الشاهد علی الثانی شعر مینینک خاطیمه افغان چکتی احباب کیم کویونکا کیم
اسلاهم اولوشتی اولوروا ولویده وا ولوشور واولوشادور ناله می کشد چنانکه از جانب فرهاد خطاب شیرین گوید الشاهد علی الاول
تیکد مرکویونکا را ایت لار کا حالت فراغت چه ره در لار دا ملالت بیلیب کیم منکا بی شمیمی شادیش اولور لار هوا یکین
هر تون غرادیش واولور وا ولوشور بمعنی فاعل ومصدر نیز می آیند اولومایده وا ولوشمایدور ناله نمیکشد ونکشیده است اولوکان و
اولوغان واولوبدکان واولوشکان واولوشورکان وا ولوشادورکان ناله کشنده وناله کشیده وبمعنی مصدر نیز می آیند اولو وا ولوکیل
اولوش وا ولوشکیل مفرد مخاطب است از فعل امر اولوماو اولوماکیل وا ولوشماو اولوشماکیل مفرد مخاطبه از فعل نهی اولونک اولونکیز وا ولونکلار
اولوشونک وا ولوشونکیز وا ولوشونکلار جمع مخاطبه از فعل امر اولومانک وا ولومانکیز وا ولومانکلار وا ولوشمانکیز وا ولوشمانکلار جمع مخاطبه
نهی اولومان وا ولومارمن اولومایدورمن اولوشمان وا ولوشمارمن وا ولوشمایدورمن ناله نمیکشم اولورمن وا ولورمن
اولویدورمن وا ولورام وا ولوشامین وا ولوشورمن وا ولوشادورمن وا ولوشورام ناله می کشم اولودوم اولوشدوم اولوغایم اولوشغایم
ناله کشیدم اولوماغوم وا ولوشماغوم ناله نخواهم کشید اولوب اولوبان وا ولوبین وا ولوشوب وا ولوشوبان وا ولوشمیش
ناله کشیده الشاهد علی الاول شعر ای نوائی ولما کیم انکا عبدلوك آنینک کویدا این ایت لاری پردم اولوب پرخته هوردی
وطالع هروی اولوبراد [illegible] نبشته که فعل ماضی بمعنی مرده است واز قبیل مجاز مشارفه است بمعنی نیست الشاهد علی
الرابع من لیلی ومجنون شعر اول لحمه نینک اوستیدا اولوشوب [illegible] الارایدی دزه شوب ونومیدلیک [illegible] ولوشما

ناله کشیده اولنماش و اولنماش ناله نکشیده و بمعنی فاعل و مصدر نفی هم می آید [illegible] ناله کشیدنش و
نکشیدنش اولنمادیغی از ناله کشیدن و ناله نکشیدن [illegible]
[illegible] ناله نتوان کشید [illegible]
کشیده [illegible] ناله بکشم و بکشد [illegible]
[illegible] ناله بکشیم [illegible] برای ناله کشیدن [illegible]
[illegible] چون ناله کشید و بکشد [illegible] ناله کشد [illegible]
[illegible] تا ناله کشیدن و بقدر ناله کشیدن [illegible] ناله کشیدنی [illegible]
[illegible] ناله بکشد الشاهد علی الثانی شعر [illegible]
[illegible] ناله می کشیدند
چنانکه [illegible] کوید الشاهد علی [illegible] شعر [illegible]
[illegible]
[illegible] ناله بکشید [illegible] چنانکه کوید شعر [illegible]
[illegible]
ترکیب آن ایستادن بود لیکن [illegible] باید نوشته شود چنانکه [illegible]
ناف نقاش [illegible] کوید شعر [illegible]
مع الکاف یعنی کشش الشاهد علیه شعر [illegible]
[illegible] نشست و کشت [illegible] نشستیم [illegible] کشتیم [illegible] می نشیند و می کشد الشاهد
الثانی بالمعنی الثالث [illegible]
[illegible] چنانکه در نفحات الانس [illegible] شیخ صدر الدین قونوی [illegible] مولانا جلال الدین [illegible]
[illegible] کوید که شیخ دیدی که سجاده [illegible]
و هرکاه [illegible] چنانکه [illegible]
و منکند و نکشته است [illegible] نشسته و نشسته الشاهد علی الاول بالمعنی الثانی
[illegible]
[illegible] چنانکه [illegible] الشاهد [illegible]
بالمعنی الاول شعر [illegible]
شاهد [illegible] کوید شعر [illegible]
[illegible] چنانکه [illegible] کوید شعر [illegible]
[illegible]
[illegible]

[illegible] نشستم و کشتم [illegible] نشستم [illegible]
کشتم [illegible] نشسته و کشته [illegible] نشسته و کشته
[illegible] نشستن و نکشتن و کشتن و نکشتن
[illegible] از نشستن و نشسته [illegible] می توان نشست و می توان کشت [illegible]
نمیتوان نشست [illegible] نمیتوان کشت [illegible] نمیتواند نشست و نمیتواند کشت [illegible] نشسته [illegible]
[illegible] بنشیند و بنشینم و بنشینی [illegible]
و بکشد و بکشی و کشته چنانکه شاهد [illegible] بکشم کوید شعر [illegible]
[illegible] بنشینم [illegible] بکشیم [illegible] بنشینم و بکشیم الشاهد علی الاول
بالمعنی الاول شعر [illegible]
برای نشستن و نانشسته [illegible] برای کشتن و ناکشته بالمعنی الاول شعر [illegible]
[illegible] چون نشیند و بعضی [illegible]
چنانکه در [illegible] کوید که [illegible]
[illegible] چون کشته و بکشد و بعضی کشتن چنانکه کوید شعر [illegible]
[illegible] نشسته چنانکه [illegible]
کوید شعر [illegible] کشد چنانکه [illegible]
[illegible]
[illegible] خواهم نشست [illegible] خواهم کشت
چنانکه کوید شعر [illegible]
خواهی نشست [illegible] خواهی کشت [illegible] خواهد نشست [illegible] خواهد کشت الشاهد علیه شعر [illegible]
[illegible] شعر [illegible]
[illegible] نشستی [illegible] کشتی [illegible] شعر [illegible]
[illegible] کوید که [illegible]
[illegible] بنشیند [illegible] بکشد شعر [illegible]
[illegible] بنشیند و بکشد الشاهد علی الرابع بالمعنی الاول شعر [illegible]
[illegible] چنانکه نشیند [illegible]
شعر [illegible]
بکشد بالمعنی الثانی شعر [illegible]
[illegible] چنانکه [illegible] کوید شعر [illegible]
[illegible]

83v.

مصدر ثانی بمعنی نشاندن وکافی بمعنی تل فرموده بنشاندا ولتورتونك دا ولتورتونكوز واولتورتونكلار بنشانید وتمثیل نفرمایند
چنانکه در مقاله هر دو هم انجمن الابرار جعفی اول کوید شعر کم دیع جوخلیل نها سیرنقت حکم سیاستیه میلدی
کیم ار دیبین ربله هوا تیغنینك داعرا اولتوردوتوب ودیوارا تینیك اولتورتوب دا ولتورتوبار دا ولتورتمش نشانده
فرموده چنانکه در خسرو شیرین فرموده الشاهد علی الاول بالمعنی الاول شعر توشا لکاج توبا طکامر اجزا لیلهد کی
لیك اولتورتوب آنی وهو ومعنی بطریق ایهام فرماید الشاهد علی الثانی شعر قتل حکی بیلا جنا اولتورتهان عاشق عشق
چون کیم سین اکمل مین تقدیم ایلا ایرام اولتورتاوی داولتورتابین نبشانام ونبشانانید ونبشانانی وتمثیل نفرمایم ونفرماید
تعریف الشاهد علی الثانی بالمعنی الاول شعر ای نوا دیر سین اولغامت نی کونکلوم دین جهار شی نهال اولتورتابین
اولتورتدم تجاوزیند و نابعی صیغه بعینه سنا قیولتق تی اول الجنا منلوتورتشالشفاق می باید اولتورغوزماق مصدر متعدی
یعنی نشاندن اولتورغوزدوق نشاندیم اولتورغوزدورا ولتورغوزادور می نشاند چنانکه شاهد براول ایراد یافته شم
از محبوب القلوب دزد کرادب کوند که معجب خسیم خاطرنیه انشا ینت ذومتن اولتورغوزدور ولولتورغوزور بمعنی فاعل معنی
هم می آید اولتورغوزماید ونی نشاند ونشانده است اولتورغوزغان دا اولتورغوزغان دا اولتورغوزادور غان نشانده ونشا
وبمعنی مصدر هم می آید اولتورغوزو دا ولتورغوزغیل مفرد مخاطب از فعل امر اولتورغوزماو ا ولتورغوزماغیل مفرد مخاطب از فعل نهی
اولتورغوزونك دا ولتورغوزونکوز دا ولتورغوزونکلار جمع مخاطب از فعل امر اولتورغوزمانك دا ولتورغوزمانکز دا ولتورغوزمانکلار
جمع مخاطب از فعل نهی اولتورغوزمان دا ولتورغوزملس من نمی نشانم اولتورغوزاین دا ولتورغوزوبین دا ولتورغوزاینم دا ولتورغوزمی نشانم اولتور
غوزدو دعا ولتورغوزماغیم نشاندیم اولتورغوزماغوم نخواهم نشانید اولتورغوزوبدا ولتورغوزوبان دا ولتورغوزمش
نشانده اولتورغوزمیشلك نشانده اولتورغوزماس نمی نشاند اولتورغوزماسی نشاندش ونشاندش اولتورغوزمادین
از نشاندن ونشانده اولتورغوزوب بولغانا ولتورغوزماغو بولغانا ولتورغوزماقو کلا ایموان نشانید اولتورغوز آلماس نمیتوان
نشانید اولتورغوز اولتورغوزا نشانده نشانده وبدون تکرار هم مستعملت اولتورغوزای دا ولتورغوزاین نبشانم ونشانی
ونبشانی ونشانده اولتورغوزماق دا ولتورغوزمایز دا ولتورغوزغای دا ولتورغوزالی دا ولتورغوزالینك نبشانیم اولتورغوزماقلیغ
برای نشاندن وتا نشانده اولتورغوزغاج چون نشانید ونبشاند ومحض نشاندن اولتورغوزغوچی نشاننده اولتورغوزغوم
اولتورغوزماغیم دا ولتورغوزغونچه تا نشاندن وبقدر نشاندن اولتورغوزغوم خواهم نشانید اولتورغوزغونك
خواهی نشانید اولتورغوزغوسی خواهد نشانید اولتورغوزلوق نشاندنی اولتورغوزیلکا دا ولتورغوزیلتا دا ولتورغوزیمنا دا ولتورغوز
دا اولتورغوزدیلك نبشاند اولتورغوزدیلتو دا ولتورغوزمیلك نشانده وهمچنانکه نبشاند اولتوروشماق بضم تا وراء
وسکون شین شاکن شدن وفرونشتن اولتوروشتی فرونشتا الشاهد علیه شعر نوائی هجراو تیغلیغا اندالطغنا
جوادردیم باده دین سوا ولتوروشتی اولتوروشتوق فرونشتیم اولتوروشور دا ولتوروشادور فرومی نشیند اولتوروشور
بمعنی فاعل ومصدر هم می آید اولتوروشما بدر فرونمی نشیند ونشسته است اولتوروشقان دا اولتوروشوکان دا اولتوروشاندور
فرونشانده وفرونشسته وبمعنی مصدر هم می آید اولتوروش دا اولتوروشغیل مفرد مخاطب از فعل امر اولتوروشما
دا اولتوروشماغیل مفرد مخاطب از فعل نهی اولتوروشونك دا اولتوروشونکوز دا اولتوروشونکلار جمع مخاطب از فعل امر اولتوروشمانك
دا اولتوروشمانکیز اولتوروشمانکلار جمع مخاطب از فعل نهی اولتوروشمان دا اولتوروشمارمین فرونمی نشینم اولتوروشامین

84r.

اولتوروشوبمین دا اولتوروشاد ورمین دا اولتوروشورمین فرومی نشینم اولتوروشور ورم اولتوروشمایم فرونشستم اولتوروشماغوم
فرونخواهم نشست اولتوروشوبدا ولتوروشوبتا ولولتوروشمیش فرونشسته الشاهد علی الثالث شعر ا وقونلارکونکلوکا
بتکماس دین غبار دین ایردی کونکلوم دا غبار اولتوروشمیش نا سو سپتیك آندا پیکاندین اولتوروشمیشانك فرونشسته
اولتوروشماس فرونمی نشیند وبمعنی فاعل ومصدر منفی هم می آید اولتوروشماسی فرونشستنش ونشستنش اولتوروشمادین
از فرونشستن وفرونشسته اولتوروشوب بولغانا ولتوروشا بولغانا ولتوروشا آلغای فرونمیتوان نشست اولتوروشا آلماس فرونمیتواند
نشست اولتوروشا اولتوروشا فرونشسته نشسته وبدون تکرار هم بمعنی مستعملت اولتوروشای دا اولتوروشاین فرو
نشینم ونشیند ونشیند نشسته اولتوروشا قدا ولتوروشغایز دا اولتوروشغای ز دا اولتوروشالی دا اولتوروشالینك
فرونشینیم اولتوروشماقلیغ برای فرونشستن وتا فرونشسته اولتوروشغاج چون فرونشست ونشیند اولتوروشغوچی
فرونشیننده اولتوروشغوسیدا ولتوروشغونچه دا ولتوروشغانچه تا فرونشستن وبقدر فرونشستن اولتوروشغوم فرونخواهم نشست
اولتوروشغونك فرونخواهی نشست اولتوروشغوسی فرونخواهد نشست اولتوروشغولوق فرونشستنی اولتوروشغا دا ولتوروش
ا ولتوروشا دا ولتوروشغو دا ولتوروشیلك فرونشیند دا ولتوروشغودیلك دا ولتوروشودیلك فرونشسته وهمچنانکه فرونشیند
اولتومات بضم لام وسکون تای قرشت ترکردن اولتومتی ترکرد اولتوتوك ترکردیم اولتوتور اولتوتادور ترمیکند و
اولتوتور بمعنی فاعل ومصدر نیز می آید واولتوتوراید یلار یعنی ترمیکردند چنانکه در نسایم المحبه مذکور ابوعبدالله اندلسی
کوید که آن ارق سو بار ایردی اصحاب بین بیر بیتلار ایردی کیم آنی ایچکای شیخ ابومحمد بیمی کیم بوغز ونکی اول ایل اوشبو دستور بیله
بوغز اولتوتورایردیلار اولتوتمایدور ترمیکند وترکرده است اولتوتکان دا اولتوتوکان دا اولتوتادورکان ترکننده وترکرده و
بمعنی مصدر هم می آید اولتوت دا اولتوتکیل مفرد مخاطب از فعل امر اولتوتما دا اولتوتماکیل مفرد مخاطب از فعل نهی اولتوتونك دا اولتوتونکوز
اولتوتونکلار جمع مخاطب از فعل امر اولتوتمانك دا اولتوتمانکز دا اولتوتمانکلار جمع مخاطب از فعل نهی اولتوتمان دا اولتوتمسمین ترنمیکنم
اولتوتامین دا اولتوتوبمین دا اولتوتادورمین دا اولتوتورام ترمیکنم اولتوتدوم دا اولتوتماکیم ترکردیم اولتوتماکوم ترنخواهم کرد اولتوتوبتا
اولتوتکایمین دا اولتوتکایمین ترکنم چنانکه شاهد برثالث در نسایم المحبه مذکور ابوبکر جوشنی کوید که کونکلوم تا زغینه مقدار
که بوغز ومنی اولتوتکای مین اولتوتوب اولتوتوبان دا اولتوتمیش ترکرده اولتوتمیشانك ترکرده اولتوتماس ترنمیکند وبمعنی فاعل و
منفی نیز می آید اولتوتماسی ترکردنش ونکردنش اولتوتمادین از ترکردن وترنکرده اولتوتوب بولغانا اولتوتا بولغانا ولتوتا آلغای اوتما
ترمیتوان کرد اولتوتا آلماس ترنمیتواند کرد اولتوتا اولتوتا ترکنان ترکنان وبدون تکرار هم مستعملت اولتوتای دا اولتوتاین
ترکنم وکنند وکنی وکرده اولتوتالی دا اولتوتالینك ترکنیم اولتوتماقلیغ برای ترکردن وتا ترکرده اولتوتغاج چون ترکرد
وکند اولتوتغوچی ترکننده اولتوتغوسیدا اولتوتغونچه دا اولتوتغانچه تا ترکردن وبقدر ترکردن اولتوتغوم ترخواهم کرد اولتوتغونك
ترخواهی کرد اولتوتغوسی ترخواهد کرد اولتوتغولوق ترکردنی اولتوتکای دا اولتوتما دا اولتوتسا دا اولتوتون دا اولتوتدیلك ترکند اولتوتدی
اولتوتدیلك ترکردنی وهمچنانکه ترکند اوبجاشماق بفتح جیم وسکون شین قرشت اوبجاماق بحذف شین تعظیم کردن
باین طریق که یك زانو بر زمین گذاشته زانوی دیگر را برداشته بعد از آن دست را بالای سر گذاشته زانوی آن بزمین زند وبعضی
باین قسم تعظیم را بدین مغول او بجاش کویند وبعضی چنین کفته اند که هم نباشد اوبجاشتی تعظیم کرد اوبجاشتوق تعظیم کردیم
اوبجاشور دا اوبجاشودور تعظیم میکند واوبجاشور بمعنی فاعل ومصدر نیز می آید اوبجاشا یدی تعظیم نمیکند ونکرده است اوبجاشقان

84v.

واولغلاماق کا لغلو اولغلاشاده کلوف تعظیم کننده وتعظیم کرده، و بمعنی مصدر منفی هم آید اولغلاش و اولغلاشکیلی مفرد مخاطب امر

امر اولغلاشماق واولغلاشماکیل مفرد مخاطب فعل نهی اولغلاشنگ و اولغلاشنگیز و اولغلاشنگلار جمع مخاطب فعل امر اولغلاشمانگ

اولغلاشمانگیز و اولغلاشمانگلار جمع مخاطب فعل نهی اولغلاشمان و اولغلاشماس مین تعظیم نمیکنم اولغلاشامین و اولغلاشورمین و

اولغلاشادورمین و اولغلاشوردم تعظیم میکنم اولغلاشقوم و اولغلاشقایم تعظیم کردیم اولغلاشاکوم تعظیم نخواهم کرد اولغلاشا

اولغلاشیبان و اولغلاشیش تعظیم کرده، اشاهد علی الاو تلان کرلوی نور [illegible] شعیم کیب سکلاریله اوزوپوروغی

نوسوبی بیله اولغلاشیب کوروشوب اولغلاشیشالک تعظیم کرده، اولغلاشماس تعظیم نمیکند و بمعنی فاعل و مصدر منفی هم آید

اولغلاشماسی تعظیم کردنش و نکردنش اولغلاشمادین از تعظیم کردن و تعظیم نکرده اولغلاشیب کیلا و اولغلاشا بیلا و اولغلا

شا اولغلاشالماس تعظیم نمیتوان کرد اولغلاشا الماس تعظیم نمیتواند کرد اولغلاشا اولغلاشا تعظیم کنان و بدون تکرار هم

مستعملست اولغلاشای و اولغلاشایین تعظیم کنم و کند و کنی و کرده، اولغلاشسا اگر و اولغلاشالی و اولغلاشالیک تعظیم کنیم اولغلاشقالی

برای تعظیم کردن و تا تعظیم کرده، اولغلاشقاچ چون تعظیم کرد و کند اولغلاشقوچی تعظیم کننده اولغلاشقوچه و اولغلاشقونچه

اولغلاشقانچه تا تعظیم کردن و بعد از تعظیم کردن اولغلاشقوم تعظیم خواهم کرد اولغلاشقونک تعظیم خواهی کرد اولغلاشقوسی

تعظیم خواهد کرد اولغلاشقوتاق تعظیم کردنی اولغلاشقای و اولغلاشا و اولغلاشنا و اولغلاشسون و اولغلاشدیک تعظیم کند

اولغلاشقودیک و اولغلاشوردیک تعظیم کردنی و همچنانکه تعظیم کند اولچالاماق بفتح جیم ولام کیب کردن و غنیمت کردن

اولچالادی کیب کرد چنانکه گوید سعشو کورزونک جورعم وحشی نعام اولچالادی تماشینک خیلی دا اولکیم حشر

ایلین تا الاغای اولچالادوق کیب کردیم اولچالاروی و اولچالایدیکه کیب میکند و اولچالار یعنی فاعل و مصدر منفی هم آید اولچالاماس

کیب نمیکند و نکرده است اولچالاغان و اولچالاخان و اولچالایدیم کیب کننده و کیب کرده، و بمعنی مصدر منفی هم آید اولچالا

و اولچالاغیل مفرد مخاطب فعل امر اولچالاما و اولچالاماغیل مفرد مخاطب فعل نهی اولچالانگ و اولچالانگیز و اولچالانگلار

جمع مخاطب فعل امر اولچالامانگ و اولچالامانگیز و اولچالامانگلار جمع مخاطب فعل نهی اولچالامان و اولچالاماس مین کیب نمیکنم

اولچالامین و اولچالارمین و اولچالایدورمین و اولچالاوردم کیب میکنم اولچالادیم و اولچالاماغیم کیب کردیم اولچالاماغوم کیب نخواهم

کرد اولچالابان و اولچالابان و اولچالامیش کیب کرده، اولچامیشالک کیب کرده، اولچالاماس کیب نمیکند و بمعنی فاعل

مصدر منفی هم می آید اولچالاماسی کیب کردنش و نکردنش اولچالامادین از کیب کردن و کیب نکرده، اولچالاب و اولچالا

اولچالا اولچالاماس و اولچالاماق اولماس کیب نمیتوان کرد اولچالای الماس کیب نمیتواند کرد اولچالاییو و اولچالای اولچالای کیب کنان

و بدون تکرار هم مستعملست اولچالای و اولچالاین کیب کنم و کند و کنی و کرده، اولچالاسا و اولچالاکای و اولچالایلیک کیب کنیم اولچالاغالی

برای کیب کردن و تا کیب کرده، اولچالاغاچ چون کیب کرد و کند اولچالاغوچی کیب کننده اولچالاغوچه و اولچالاغونچه

اولچالاغانچه تا کیب کردن و بعد از کیب کردن اولچالاغوم کیب خواهم کرد اولچالاغونک کیب خواهی کرد اولچالاغوسی

کیب خواهد کرد اولچالاغولوق کیب کردنی اولچالاغای و اولچالاسا و اولچالاسون و اولچالادیک کیب کند اولچالاغودیک و او

اولچالادیک کیب کردنی و همچنانکه کیب کند اولچاماق بفتح جیم یعنی اندازه کردن اولچادی اندازه کرد اولچادوق اندازه کرد

اولچار و اولچایدور اندازه میکند و اولچار یعنی فاعل و مصدر منفی هم آید اولچا و اولچاغیل مفرد مخاطب فعل امر اولچاما

و اولچاماغیل مفرد مخاطب فعل نهی اولچانگ و اولچانگیز و اولچانگلار جمع مخاطب فعل امر اولچامانگ و اولچامانگیز و اولچامانگلار

85r.

جمع مخاطب فعل نهی اولچامان و اولچاماس مین اندازه نمیکنم اولچامین و اولچارمین و اولچایدورمین و اولچاوردم اندازه میکنم اولچادیم

اولچاماغیم اندازه کردیم اولچاماغوم اندازه نخواهم کرد اولچابان و اولچابان و اولچامیش اندازه کرده، اولچامیشالک اندازه کرده

اولچاماس اندازه نمیکند و بمعنی فاعل و مصدر منفی هم می آید اولچاماسی اندازه کردنش و نکردنش اولچامادین از اندازه کردن

و اندازه نکرده، اولچاب و اولچا و اولچا اولچا اولچاماس و اولچاماق اولماس اندازه نمیتوان کرد اولچای الماس اندازه نمیتواند کرد اولچایو و اولچای اولچای

اندازه کنان و بدون تکرار هم مستعملست اولچای و اولچاین اندازه کنم و کند و کنی و کرده، اولچاسا اگر و اولچالی و اولچالیک

اندازه کنیم اولچاغالی برای اندازه کردن و تا اندازه کرده، اولچاغاچ چون اندازه کرد و کند اولچاغوچی اندازه کننده اولچاغوچه

اولچاغونچه و اولچاغانچه تا اندازه کردن و بعد از اندازه کردن اولچاغوم اندازه خواهم کرد اولچاغونک اندازه خواهی کرد

اولچاغوسی اندازه خواهد کرد اولچاغولوق اندازه کردنی اولچاغای و اولچاسا و اولچاسون و اولچادیک اندازه کند

اولچاغودیک و اولچاوردیک اندازه کردنی و همچنانکه اندازه کند اولغایماق بسکون لام و یای حطی و فتح غین معجمه دو معنی دارد

اول بمعنی عظیم و بزرگ شدن باشد و قسم مجاز ا بمعنی پیر و معمر شدن استعمال میشود و اولغالماق نیز بایمعنی استعمال میشود اولغاید

بزرگ شد و پیر شد چنانکه در تاریخ الانبیا در ذکر کشتی ساختن حضرت نوح علیه السلام بمعنی اول گوید که اول حضرت [illegible]

یغاچ بنچه سیل دین سونکرا اولغایدی اولغایدوق بزرگ شدیم و پیر شدیم اولغایور و اولغایدور بزرگ [illegible] میشود و اولغا

بمعنی فاعل و مصدر منفی هم آید اولغایما دو بزرگ و پیر نمیشود و نشده است اولغایغان و اولغایوغان و اولغایادورغان بزرگ

شونده و بزرگ شده و پیر شونده و پیر شده و بمعنی مصدر منفی هم آید چنانکه گوید لشاهد علی الاول لمعنی الثانی شعر

[illegible] عشق ایچرا عمرم زاهد ا قوی زهد ایرشادین کیشی موندا قا ولوغ صنعت خا ولغاندا [illegible] ومطالع هروی اولغایغان

ماخوذ از اولمالت بمعنی مردن دانسته و بعضی هم [illegible] ذکر کرده، و شعر میرزا شاهد آورده، سهو کرده است اولغای و اولغایغیل

مفرد مخاطب فعل امر اولغایما و اولغایماغیل مفرد مخاطب فعل نهی اولغاینگ و اولغاینگیز و اولغاینگلار جمع مخاطب فعل امر اولغایمانگ

و اولغایمانگیز و اولغایمانگلار جمع مخاطب فعل نهی اولغایمان و اولغایماس مین بزرگ نمیشوم و پیر نمیشوم اولغایامین و اولغایورمین و اولغا

یادورمین و اولغایوردم بزرگ میشوم و پیر میشوم اولغایدیم و اولغایماغیم بزرگ شدیم و پیر شدیم اولغایماغوم بزرگ و پیر

نخواهم شد اولغایبان و اولغایبان و اولغایمیش بزرگ شده و پیر شده چنانکه شاهد بر اول است بمعنی ثانی در تاریخ الملوک

در ذکر تفویض [illegible] سلطنت [illegible] میگوید که [illegible] دشا [illegible] چون [illegible]

ایردی کوشه توتوت عبادتغه مشغول بولدی اولغایمیشالک بزرگ شده و پیر شده اولغایماس بزرگ نمیشود و پیر

نمیشود و بمعنی فاعل و مصدر منفی هم می آید اولغایماسی بزرگ شدنش و نشدنش و پیر شدنش و نشدنش اولغایمادین از بزرگ

شدن و بزرگ نشده اولغایب کیلا و اولغاینا بیلا و اولغایماق اولماس بزرگ نمیتوان شد و پیر نمیتوان شد اولغایالماس بزرگ

نمیتواند شد و پیر نمیتواند شد اولغایا اولغایا بزرگ شده بزرگ شده و پیر شده پیر شده و بدون تکرار هم بایمعنی مستعملست

چنانکه در مجالس نهم از مجالس النفایس در صفت ظاهری بمعنی اول گوید که کچمات لیکن اکفشد [illegible] منسوب بود و معمول

ایامدا آندین نظم لار [illegible] اولغایا کوپراک بولدی و مؤلف روحی اولغایارا در این مصرع اولغایاز خوانده و بتای

نوشته اولغایاز موافق اشتقاق غلطات افاده معنی نمیکند اولغایساق و اولغایسا نیز و اولغایسای نیز و اولغایالی و اولغایالیک

بزرگ شویم و پیر شویم اولغایغالی برای بزرگ شدن و تا بزرگ شده و برای پیر شدن و تا پیر شده اولغایغاچ چون بزرگ شد و شود

وبرهند وشود چنانکه بمعنی اولهم تاریخ یا بری مذکور است که کفر لا سوا ولغا یغلم تضیرتی یا را ولغا یغوچی بنرلت شوند

برشونده اولغا یغوسه ولغا یغوچی الغا یغاکا نابنرلت شدن وبتلمیر شدن چنانکه شاهد بر ثانی از بمعنی اولهم تاریخ الملوک

در ذکر اردشیر بن شیرویه کوید که چون اردشیر کیچیک ایردی بهم چنین نی وزیر قیلدیکیم اولغا یغوبمه ملک تدبیرنی قیلدی

اولغا یغوم بنرلت خواهم شد وبر خواهم شد اولغا یغونک بنرلت خواهی شد وبر خواهی شد ولغا یغوسی بنرلت

خواهد شد وبر خواهد شد ولغا یغولوق بنرلت شدنی وبرشدنی اولغا یغای دا ولغا یا وا ولغا یسا وا ولغا یوب

اولغا لیوب بنرلت شوده برشوده چنانکه شاهد بر ثالث از بعد نظم الجواهر در صفت کوید شعر باش اولغا یسا الماس

دوده دروده بلکیم ملوسبهو الطلسد دوده در ده اولغا یغوچیل دا ولغا یوچیک بنرلت شدنی وهمچنانکه بنرلت شود وبرشدنی

وهمچنانکه بر شود اولغا یماق بسکون لام و یای حطی و تای قرشت وفتح غین معجمه مصدر متعدیست یعنی بنرلت کردن

اولغا یتیبعا ولغا یتیبا ما ولغا یتمیش بنرلت کرده چنانکه در لسان الطیر در صفت شاکرد ارسطو کوید لشاهد علیه

شعر ایلا بار آنی حکیم اوجیند جلقه شاکردلار ایچرا چیند آنکا محو ملا حظهی آیتیبان طفل ایکان دین آیینه

اولغا یتیبان وبیز در لیلی مجنون در صفت ولادت مجنون کوید شعر بولماینا ظاهری غم ودرد اولغا یتیبان آنی

در دیده قشونلیقی صنع بر چین نمی مبولقی تنی اول لاصنا فه نای قرشت اشتقاق مییابد اولالماق بفتح لام اول وسکون تانی

مرادف اولغا یماق باشد یعنی بنرلت شدن تا ولاکیب بنرلت شد چنانکه در کلیله دمنه ترکی مذکور است که بازبچه اولالیب قالغان

چیکری من الجوا ملید اول بفتح معنی دارد اول اسم اشارت است یعنی آن چنانکه شاهد بر آن کوید شعر اول الف دیت

قد لطافتا ایچرا بولدی چیکا اون صفرد یلتا بولدی آنینک ضمیمه در قرم آغیز دویم بمعنی رطب وتر باشد الشاهد علیه شعر

اونک حرینک کونکلوم کا توشکا چ کویدیکیم کوزندین کیم کوبا ر اول وقو ردو قچون نیستانقه توشتی اوت وهمه در معنی کوید شعر

ای نوانی مینکا انهان ایتما اول آی رقعه سین چوزنکا اول دبر همیشه اشلاریتما قیرله بینک سیم مجاز بمعنی آب ودریا

استعمال میشود من کمکدی شعر سورب کیمه نی ولکا آندا قکر طیش هول موغه قیلدیلار آهنک سیر همچنانکه ابرامرت از

شدن وبودن چنانکه مذیل اولماق کذشت بچم امراست از بودن چنانکه مذیل ولماک مذکور شد اولا باشباع ضمه

وفتح لام با الف کشیده بلغت مغولی کوه بلند بود اولات بمعنی رکی باشد اولاشیق رشته ضریان نیم جهید وسبک شده

اولاغ واولاق سه معنی دارد اول مرکب سواری را کویند چنانکه در مجلس چهارم از مجالس النفائس در صفت خواجه قطب الدین

کوید که توشتا او چا غدا اولاغلاری یوقا ریمیش بغایت بیلکیشی قول لاز بغیه اوزلارین کوزنا ریتیقو شتا اوزلار مثلا

ندیم بمعنی بلت وقاصد بود که از جانبی بجانبی صغیر ساده باشد سیم کاری بی اجرت باشد ومولف برهان قاطع هم بغاربی این معنی

ذکر کرده. اولتانک بسکون لام ونون وکاف عجمی وفتح تای قرشت پوستی بود که برته کفش وموزه دوزند لشاهد علیه شعر

کل مقصود عندا ولیبتی بو بو اسیر بندا کیم تا بانغه تیکان بولدی نیه بر اولتانک وبیز در حیرت الابرار در منقبت کوید شعر

اوتوک اولتانیچه نعلین آنکا بولوب بر قلم اوزنی کویز آنکا ومهمن لفظات که عوام آنرا بمعرض اجنه بجای دشنام استعمال

نموده الدنک میکویند وازان قبیل است لفظ دینک که بمعنی دشنام میکویند واصل آن تنکاست وآن عبارتست از ملقی باشد که

چوب ودرخت نامه دو بیا از آن میوه کذاشته برای فروختن میکرده اند اول تو دو ر یعنی آنت وآن شعر شاهد آنست شعر

مغاج برله باشا قیم تندا تا المیشر اول تو دوده برهم جنوندیکیم فراقینک دوقینی چمیهما اسیند ود دوم ومکان منتصل

نشسته شود بمعنی نشیند وملکه مدی آید چنانکه در ذیل شقاق کذشت اولتورو شلوق بمعنی مسکن ووطن باشد چنانکه

کویند لواده فم اولتورو شلوق تو بر دینکا کی غوارزم است اولتشه بسکون لام وفتح تای قرشت بجار زمینی که روی باجا وبنایی کنند

اولجا دو معنی دارد اول کیب وغنیمت را کویند که در جنك از دشمن بدست آید چنانکه در حیرت الابرار کوید شعر ایکا او جول اول

که جلادت قبلوبر دو قدرت آنی ایلا عوت قیلور دویم بمعنی اندازه باشد چنانکه کوید شعر سنا ایقان آنجا تو بدو لت حلم تو ام

نکار ایچره که اولجا داغ ایله تمام جمال اخلاق وبولا المداد ایچره ووبیز در فصل نجم از محبوب القلوب در ذکر عاشق کوید که اول آن

کیفیتین سود پا لادا اولجه جابیدین بو حالت معلوم بولدیکیم سیاست هنکامیدا منظوری حاضر بولمیش آنرا اولجه نیز کویند

اولجامیش یکنوع تعظیمیست که در میان اتراک معمولست وکیفیت آن در ذیل مصدر اولجاشماق مذکور شد وآنرا الجمیشو هم نامند

اولجاک بسکون لام وکاف وضم جیم عجمی مقیاس وآلت کیل وذرع ومرشته که بآن اندازه کیرند چنانکه کوید شعر ازین

بردین کنار بتیب آسرا دیم بر کلاده کیمکی کوزدا آلیبان رشته بیر له ایا غی اوز بیدین اولجاک اولجامیشی بمعنی تعظیم واحترام وپیش کش

کذرانیدن بود اولجایتو بسکون لام ویای حطی وفتح جیم با الف کشیده بلغت مغولی تو بمعنی صاحب ولجای بمعنی بخت وبرکت شده

ومعنی ترکیبی آن مبارک ومیمون وصاحب میمنت بود ونیز نام پادشاهیست که بانی سلطانیه است وپسر ارغون بن اباقای بن هلاکو

خانست ونیز اولجای نام دختر غازانخانست که در حباله شاهزاده بسطام بوده واصل اولجای قوتلوغ میکشد اولجه بسکون

لام وفتح جیم بنهار زده. همان اولجا بمعنی کیب وآنقدر باشد که در جوق نکارش یافت ونیز بجیم عجمی بمعنی اینجه بود الشاهد علیه

شعر خامه جان تینسکا چو استکیلوم انکلا خماسین اولچه خامه غه منینک بحر هجران ایتمش ونیز در فرهاد وشیرین

در صفت خزاین خاقان کوید شعر خزاین دغاکیم بو نیز بحر ایله کان تا شیب نقد بیتی آندا اولچه امکان اولکا ولایت وشهر را

کویند وآن معروفست اولکو باشباع ضمه وضم کاف عجمی دو معنی دارد اول بمعنی اندازه بود دویم بمعنی بیم ترازو مانند اولکوش

بضم کاف عجمی وسکون شین قرشت بمعنی افسرده وپژمرده باشد اول لوغ مع العین بمعنی مرده بود چنانکه در لسان الطیر

کوید شعر هر نی بوریر اولدی یکان دیلت تو ریتیش بولوغ واول کومغ بولوب دفع اوزنادین اولتوک مع الکاف بمعنی

تری وطراوت باشد اولنک بفتح لام وسکون نون وکاف عجمی بمعنی دارد اول سبزه وسبزه زار را کویند چنانکه کوید شعر

الماری غبان زلالیبر بیر بر آیینه کون انجم وکول عکسیدو رآیدا ز یا جین واولنک وله حیرت الابرار شعر کوک اولتک

الماری داهر کونه در دانجم ایله دایره لاجورد دویم یکنوع سرودیست که در میان اتراک شایعست وآن این نحواست که چون عروس

بعد از آنکه عروس بحجله می آمد دختران نزد او جمع شده سرود ونوادر وصف داماد تصنیفات میخوانند وهمچنین در خانه داماد

نیز جوانان جمع شده برقص وخوانندگی عروس را میستایند واین شعر شهرت باین معنی منسوب سکندریه شعر مغنی نوز

چینکه ونزند احیلک نواچیک که بی های اولنک های اولنک سیم نام محلی است مابین همدان وکابل که مسکن طایفه

هزاره است اولوناه بضم لام مخفف ومحرف اولوغ ناغ باشد یعنی کوه بنرلت ونیز طایفه خطای که نام فرقه است از فرقه

در وقت نزول لشکر برای سپاه کردن بیکدیکر فرقه خود را بآن اسم اعلان میکنند اولوس بسکون سین مهمله بمعنی خلق وجماعت بود

الشاهد علیه شعر تو تولمیش ایردی غضب بن اولوسنی قیلدی اسیر قوباش تو تولسا بلی قسه دهر آنکا تابش اولوش بسکون شین قرشت

بمعنی حصه وبهره وسهم باشد قطعه چو عشق دردو بلاغه جهانغه اوردی صلا تخستین اولوش منی جهانغه اوردی صلا دین الله

اون اولوشیدین توقوزین آلدیم اولوشیم یا بیم که قالدی آن انر وجهانغه اوردی صلا اولونو واولوق یعنی بنرلت عظیم چنانکه شاه

برثان را کویند شعر آندین قلیچکا یلماس ایکان کفر کا بردین کیم بوا بیمر حقیدا جلب دا آنغا نا دلوق نوکه شعر بنفشه

منینک نیچه بولیش ملاغی مونجه اولوق که اول سنینک خطینکا هندودور قدمه تابوق و مقلهم و می اولوق قرایر اهیب شعر

الوق بالف ممدوده خوانده و بمجرو قیاس یعنی اشفته حال و دلکیر نوشته و ظاهر هروی و نصیری هم بتا بعت کرده انهم

ایشان شبهه نیست زیراکه معنی شعر اینست که چو بنفشه مجنون نمرات دمش غش شده واو خط ترا غلام هندوی کج پای کج

سریراست دقیم المجانه و همرا کویند سیم ترکی و جی معنی ناو دار باشد اوقلوغ و اوقلوق یعنی بزرکه و بیجا اولوک

مرده را کویند الشاهد علیه شعر آرزو ایله بیلکا آیدا غان سرناکی خنش خم سوی بین اولوک عمرا یلا کانور

آرنو اولوکا بفتح سین مهمله جیفه و مردار را نامند چنانکه در فرهاد و شیرین در نامه فرهاد کوید که شعر بولا

ایچرا با بردی بیر ضعیف ایت منینک دیلغا ایرو مجرو بخفایت جبیر لار حسمینی مجروح ایتا دلغ اولوکا ایمدی آندا

کیم سورولت زاغ اولوکه بفتح کاف بلغت مغول یعنی کهواره باشد اولولوغ مخففا ولوغلوق یعنی بزرکی و پردیت اولوم

تو یعنی طرد او کی یعنی اید بود ندیم کف شیشتو را کویند که آنرا بعربی زبد خوانند اولومتولت بضم لام و تا فرشت و سکون

و کاف یعنی نیم مرده و نیم جان باشد الشاهد علیه شعر ایکی بو نوع غالب جسم اومتولت مور قلیغغه شوق تشریفینا رایلتور غاز ایم

اولو ملولوک ایاردین رو هرکار الیلتور یعنی چنانکه کشتی بر غالبی که در حالت کشتن میکند تسلل و اطاله کرده دم راست

میدانند هر هزکار میکنند و هم انرا او و قتی که برای قتل من می آید و صل برمید ارنم مع المیم من المشتقات اوملماق بفتح میم اول

سر ابیز یر و عقب را پنالا کردن و چون قابل اشتقاق نبود کرمصدر انکف لشد اومملت بسکون میم اول ترکی عروی توقع کردن

و امید داشتن چنانکه ضبولی بغیر ادی یعنی مفرد خاطب از فعل نهی کوید با ملکا الزومیته شعر هر دم دیردن لو بمه ضبولی

دوای درد صبرایله اول که دردو دیم هم دوا و یر هرادی مولملت بضم میم اول ما مول باشد چنانکه ضبولی یعنی مصلاح

کوید با ملکاه الرومیه شعر کولرا چلوق او سوا و دهنکدین مکر او لدی جزوکیم لایتجزی یرا نکا اهل دانا نجیدا اوما

استخوان مفصل را کویند و او خانا هم نامند او ماج بکون آشیت که از آرد بجوشانند چنانکه در سد سکندری در وصف

کوید شعر مناهات فیلماس سها کدین کلاچ عمین بولماس ایراپنا یا دغان او ملاج لوما چا بفتح میم و جیم عربی با لف کشیده هما

اونا باشد که مذکور شد لوما ق مخفف و تماق یعنی قبیله باشد و در او غوزنامه مسطور است که بعد از او غوز خان کو

خان پسر بزرکتر او که بر تخت نشست مجلس عشرت آراسته بیست و چهار تن از اعیان و پسر های بزرک که از کنیز بوجود آمده بودند

در پیرون خرکاه نهاد که دوازده تن در بیرون خرکاه نشسته و دوازده تن اسب شاهزاده ها را نکاه داشته انچه از نسل این

تن بهم رسیدند آنها را او ماق نامیدند واو ماق بمعنی اورو غ باشد یعنی خویش و تبار و قراغی در تاریخ خود بیغوما و بزرکی تو

معنی او چهنیلت لوما نغ بسکون نون و جیم بمعنی توقع و امید باشد او مکان بفتح کاف عجمی بیشهای حلقوم و استخوانهای

حلق و سینه باشد او مورت بضم میم و دال ابجد بلغت مغولی شلوار بود که آنرا بعربی سرابیل کویند او موز بسکون زای هوز یعنی

دوش راست که آنرا بعربی غاتق و منکب نامند مع النون مع الیات او مالت بسکون نون رویدن و از التدوم اونکالت

اثقیف روید اونیوت روییلیم او ناروا و نا دود میروید و او نا ر یعنی راضی میشود هم آمده و بایمعنی مشتق از مصدر

او نا ماقات چنانکه مذکور شود و نا عل مصدر هر دو معنی هم می آید او نماید و ر نمیروید و نرویده است او نکاب و

او نا رکان عاد او نا درکان رویند و رویده الشاهد علی الاول من الامر شعر سمار و غ سراه یملوکنی میلیسان فوت نفشغه

* چو غماز مر بولسالار رهیهات مسکین مور نیناک جانی اولو ملوک کشتی و واجب القتل چنانکه کوید شعر یوز آلماد یولیدین قتلیمغه

آینناک غمازی دین بلکیل بو بردین اونکان اوت یمنی و بمعنی بیشه بیز ایچه آیند اوت واونکیل مفرد مخاطب از فصل امر او اون

معانی جامه هم دارد چنانکه در ذیل جو لمه مذکور خواهد شد اونما و اونما کیل مفرد مخاطب از فصل نهی او نو تلو نو کو

او نو نکلار جمع مخاطب از فصل امر او نما نک وا و نمانکیز او نمانکیز جمع مخاطب از فصل نهی او نما ر و او نماس مین نمیروییم او نامین وا و نا د

و او نادور مین وا و نا رام میرویم او نا ر مین وا و نا رام بمعنی راضی میشوم هم آمده وقد ر یمعنی مصدر او ناماق اشتر العداد سبید

او نا بیم او نا کیم رو بیده ام وا و نا بیم بمعنی راضی شده ام هم باشد او نما کوم نخواهم روئید او نوب وا و نو با ن و

او نمیش روئیده بیشانک روئیده او نما س نمیروید و بمعنی فاعل و مصدر منفی هم می آید او نما بیه تو نیز

و نروئیده نیز او نما دین ازرو ییدن و نرویده او نوب بو لغا او نما بو لغا وا و نما لغای لغا نمیتواند روئید او نا

آلماس نمیتواند روئید لو نما لو نما روئیده روئیده و بدون تکرار هم مستعمل است او نای وا و نا بین بدویم و بروید

و بروند و روئیده و نیز یعنی راضی میشوم و شود و شوی و شده او نسا لت بروییم او نا لها و نا لیک برویم و راضی شویم

او نکالی برای روئیدن و تا روئیده او نکاچ چون روئید و بروید او نکو چی روئنده او نکو چه وا و نکو غه وا و نکا نچه

تا روئیدن و بقدم روئیدن او نکوم خواهم روئید او نکو نلت خواهی روئید او نکو سی خواهد روئید او نکو لوک

روئیدنی و بترکی رومی یعنی حیله و معالج هم بود او نکای غا و نا و اوقنا طو نکو غا و نما بیرو ید چنانکه لطفی کوید الشاهد

علی الاول شعر او نکای ایری جرومنه ایچرا زکش چون لطفی ابرو هکغزو نلت قتلی او نکو دین طوتما دیلیدر و سیدی و چنانکه

بروید وا و نا ر دیلت یعنی راضی شده و چنانکه راضی شود هم می آید الف او نما بسکون نون و رای مهمله و ضم دال المصدر

متعدیست یعنی رو یا نیدن و نیز یعنی لغت حق و سبز کردن هر فی استعمال میشود او ند ر کان وا و ند و ر کان واو ند ر ما دور کان

رو یا نیده و رو یا نیده چنانکه شاهد بر اقل را بمعنی اول در مقام مجید کوید که کوکدین یا مغور ایندرکان و یردین نبات

او ند ر کان و با شی صنع بر همین سیاق و مولغو ثوق و ل الصنا مذ الفظ در اشتقاق میاید او نا ماق بفتح نون با لف کشیده

یعنی راضی شدن و ند رعلی سهوا یعنی راضی کردن نوشته او نادی راضی شد او نا مادی راضی نشد چنانکه در تاریخ

الانبیا کوید که قابیل او زسینکلیسی نینک حسنی جهتیدین آنکا مایل ایردی او نا مادی کیم هابیل کا بیرکا یلار او نادوق راضی شدیم

او نا ردو لو نا ید هر راضی میشود و او نا ر یعنی سبز میشود هم آمده چنانکه در ذیل او نما لت مذکور شد و بمعنی فاعل و مصدر منفی نیز آید

او نا ما ید و نمر راضی نمیشود و نشده است و نا غان وا و نا غان وا و نا ید هر غان راضی شونده راضی شده و بمعنی مصدر هم می آیند

او نا و او نا غیل مفرد مخاطب از فصل امر او نا ما وا و نا ما غیل مفرد مخاطب از فصل نهی او نا نک وا و نا نکیز وا و نا نکلار جمع مخاطب

از فصل امر او نا ما نک وا و نا ما نکیز وا و نا ما نکلار جمع مخاطب از فصل نهی او نا مان وا و نا ما س مین راضی نمیشوم الشاهد علی الاول شعر

ناموغ او یتغه او نا بمجر بیلک و یتغه او نا مان باشیم با روز غجیدا رمین فرا قنکا جید ا مان او نای مین وا و نا ر مین وا و نا یدور

او نا رام راضی میشوم وا و نا ر مین وا و نا رام یعنی میرویم هم آمده او نا دیم وا و نا ما غیم راضی شدم وا و نا بیم بمعنی میرویم هم

باشد او نا ما غو مر راضی نخواهم شد او نا ب وا و نا با ن وا و نا میش راضی شده او نا میشا نلت راضی شده او نا ما س

راضی نمیشود و بمعنی فاعل و مصدر منفی هم می آید او نا ما بسی راضی شدنش و نشدنش او نا ما دین ازراضی شدن و راضی نشده

او نا ب بو لغا وا و نا سا بو لغا وا و نا ما قالی الماراضی نمیتواند شد او نای آلماس راضی نمیتواند شد او نا بو لغا و نای او نا راضی شده راضی شده

و بدون تکرار هم مستعمل است او نای وا و نا بین راضی شوم و شود و شوی و شده و نیز یعنی برویم و بروید و بروند و رو ئیده

اوناشاق و اوناغانزوا اوناغای‌نزوا اونابلی‌و اونالینک راضی شویم و اونالی بمعنی بوویم هم باشد اوناغالی برای راضی شدن و تا
راضی شده اوناغاج چون راضی شد وشود اوناغوچی راضی شونده اوناغوچه و اوناغونچه و اوناغانچه تا راضی شدن و بمعنی راضی
شدن اوناغوم راضی خواهم شد اوناغونک راضی خواهد شد اوناغوسی راضی خواهد شد اوناغولوق راضی شدنی
اوناغان و اوناسالو و اوناغولوادیک راضی شود الشاهد علی الاول شعر ای نوای هیچ سیلمازکیم اوناغایموکونکول آنکا موبخه
اجنبی بولار که ارشاد ایلادیم اوناغوبدور و اونارلیک راضی شدن و همچنانکه راضی شود و اونادیک بمعنی رسیدن و همچنانکه رسید
هم می‌آید اوناتماق بفتح نون و سکون تای قرشت متعدیست یعنی راضی کردن و اوناتوچه و اوناتونچه و اوناتقانچه تا راضی کردن و بمعنی
راضی کردن الشاهد علی الثانی بالمعنی الثانی شعر میرا اولمادی خان‌زادلک ولیک بولای دیدین که تا ملادی
جانیم آنی اوناتونجه و باقی صیغ برین نهج مو افق شق اول با تای قرشت اشتقاق می‌یابد اونوتماق بضم نون و سکون تای قرشت
فراموش کردن اونوتتی فراموش کرد اونوتتوق فراموش کردیم اونوتوردی و اونوتادور فراموش میکند و اونوتور بمعنی
فاعل و مصدر هم می‌آید اونوتغان و اونوتوغان و اونوتادورغان فراموش کننده و فراموش کرده الشاهد علی الاول بالمعنی الثانی
من سکندری شعر دیمانکیم مینی یاد ایتیب شاد قیل اونوتمایلار سینکی برابر یاد قیل و بمعنی مصدر هم می‌آید اونوتمایدور
فراموش نمیکند و نکرده است اونوت و اونوتقیل مفرد مخاطب از فعل امر الشاهد علی الاول شعر وجودم اوریادینک
ای عشق ایمدی ترکیم تو تت خدای اوچون که مینی قایدا کوردونک آندا اونوت و اونوت بمعنی فراموش هم باشد اونوتماغیل و اونوتما
اونوتماغیل مفرد مخاطب از نهی الشاهد علی الثانی من فرهاد و شیرین شعر اونوتماغیل که تا هجرانی سیلادی مینی
بر نامه برله قیلمادینک یاد اونوتونکلار و اونوتونکیز و اونوتونکلار جمع مخاطب از فعل امر اونوتماننکیز و اونوتمانکلار جمع مخاطب
از نهی اونوتمان و اونوتماسمین فراموش نمیکنم اونوتماسمین و اونوتورمین و اونوتادورمین و اونوتور فراموش میکنم اونوتورکم و اونوتغوم
فراموش کردیم اونوتماغوم فراموش نخواهم کرد اونوتوبجا و اونوتوبان و اونوتمیش فراموش کرده اونوتمیشانک فراموش کرده
اونوتقاس فراموش نمیکند و بمعنی فاعل و مصدر منفی هم می‌آید اونوتماس فراموش کردنش و نکردنش اونوتمادین از فراموش
کردن و فراموش نکرده اونوتوب بولمای و اونوتا بولماماق و اونوتماق اولماس فراموش نمیتوان کرد اونوتا آلماس فراموش نمیتواند کرد اونوتا
اونوتا فراموش کنان اونوتای و اونوتاین فراموش کنم و کند و کنی و کرده اونوتاق و اونوتغای‌مز و اونوتغای‌سز و اونوتالی و اونوتالینک
فراموش کنیم اونوتقالی برای فراموش کردن و تا فراموش کرده اونوتغاج چون فراموش کرد و کند اونوتغوچی فراموش کننده
اونوتغوم فراموش خواهم کرد اونوتغونک فراموش خواهی کرد الشاهد علیه شعر چون اونوتغونکدور سین المنی ال
سینی ناری چیکیب عیش جاسین بو اونوتماغلار بیر ساعت اونوت اونوتغوسی فراموش خواهد کرد اونوتغولوق فراموش کرده
اونوتقالی و اونوتالا و اونوتسا و اونوتسون و اونوتدیک فراموش کند چنانکه در پیغام اسکندر بخاقان چین گوید الشاهد علی
الرابع شعر مسلم تو تار بولسا بوراز بنی اونوتدیک مقالات ناسازینی اونوتغودیک و اونوتوردیک فراموش کردنی
و همچنانکه فراموش کند اونوتولماق مصدر متعدیست یعنی فراموش فرمودن و اونوتولماغایمن و اونوتولماغایمن فراموش
نفرمایم الشاهد علی الاول شعر غرضیم بوکه او نوتولماغایمن اوزنی آنکا گوسیداکیم افغان که و بیکار چیکیب
و باقی صیغ برین نوال موافق شق اول با لفظ تو اشتقاق می‌یابد اونوتولماق بضم نون و تای قرشت و سکون لام مصدر لازمست
یعنی فراموش شدن اونوتولوب و اونوتولادور فراموش میشود و اونوتولور بمعنی فاعل و مصدر هم می‌آید چنانکه در باب فراموشکاری

اهل حسن در سخن قطعه بطرق بمعنی مصدر گوید که حسن اهلی نینک کونکلی نیسان وفا اندا اونوتولوری نینک سیاقی
اونوتولغایمو آیا فراموش شود الشاهد علیه شعر سیلمان اونوتولغایمو ایکاندور منکا هجر باکوبر الغایر بو تالاد شواز
و باقی صیغ برین نهج بالام اشتقاق می‌یابد اوندامات بسکون نون و فتح دال مهمله از زدن و دعوت کردن و اشنیدمات کسبه
الف هم گویند اوندادی دعوت کرد اوندادوک دعوت کردیم اوندار و اوندایدور دعوت میکند و اوندار بمعنی فاعل و
هم می‌آید اونداغایدور دعوت نمیکند و نکرده است اوندالگان و اونداگوچی و اوندایدورگان دعوت کننده و دعوت کرده
بمعنی مصدر هم می‌آیند اوندا اوندانک و اونداینکیز و اوندانکلار جمع مخاطب از فعل امر اوندامانک و اوندامانکیز و اوندامانکلار جمع مخاطب
نهی اوندامان و اوندامسمین دعوت نمیکنم اوندارمین و اوندایدورمین و اوندادام دعوت میکنم اوندارم اوندادیکیم
دعوت کردیم اونداماغوم دعوت نخواهم کرد اوندابجا و اوندابان و اوندامیش دعوت کرده اوندامیشانک دعوت کرده
اونداماس دعوت نمیکند و بمعنی فاعل و مصدر منفی هم می‌آید اونداماسی دعوت کردنش و نکردنش اونداماداین از دعوت کردن
و دعوت نکرده اونداب بولمای و اونداماق بولماماق اولماس دعوت نمیتوان کرد اونداما آلماس دعوت نمیتواند کرد
اوندایو و اوندای اوندایلی دعوت کنان و بدون تکرار هم مستعملست اوندای و اوندایین دعوت کنم و کند و کنی و کرده
اوندا شالی و اونداغای مز و اونداغای سز و اونداغالی و اوندالینک دعوت کنیم اونداغالی برای دعوت کردن و تا دعوت کرده اونداغاج
چون دعوت کرد و کند اونداغوچی دعوت کننده اونداغوچه و اونداغونچه و اونداغانچه تا دعوت کردن و بمعنی دعوت کردن اونداغوم
دعوت خواهم کرد اونداغونک دعوت خواهی کرد اونداغوسی دعوت خواهد کرد اونداغولوق دعوت کردنی اونداغای و
اوندالسا و اونداسون و اوندادیک دعوت کند اونداغودیک و اوندادیک دعوت کردنی و همچنانکه دعوت کند اونکارماق بسکون
نون و رای قرشت و فتح کاف عجمی مع الامالة بمعنی راست کردن نکار بود که آنرا بعربی اصابت گویند اونکاردی راست کرد
اونکاردوک راست کردیم اونکارور و اونکارادور راست میکند و اونکارور بمعنی فاعل و مصدر نیز می‌آید اونکارمایدور راست نمیکند
و نکرده است اونکارغان و اونکارغوچی و اونکارادورگان راست کننده و راست کرده و بمعنی مصدر هم می‌آیند اونکار بسکون را
اونکار و بضم را و اونکارغیل مفرد مخاطب از فعل امر اونکارمای و اونکارماغیل مفرد مخاطب از نهی اونکارینک و اونکارینکیز و اونکارینکلار
جمع مخاطب از فعل امر اونکارمانک و اونکارمانکیز و اونکارمانکلار جمع مخاطب از نهی اونکارمان و اونکارماسمین راست نمیکنم اونکارارمین
اونکارادورمین و اونکارادورمین راست میکنم اونکاردوم و اونکاریم راست کردیم اونکارماغوم راست نخواهم کرد اونکاریب
اونکاربان و اونکارمیش راست کرده اونکارمیشانک راست کرده اونکارماس راست نمیکند و بمعنی فاعل و مصدر منفی هم می‌آید
اونکارماسی راست کردنش و نکردنش اونکارمادین از راست کردن و راست نکرده اونکاریب بولمای و اونکارا بولماماق و اونکارماق اولماس
راست نمیتوان کرد اونکارا آلماس راست نمیتواند کرد اونکارا اونکارا راست کنان و بدون تکرار هم مستعملست اونکاری
اونکارایین راست کنم و کند و کنی و کرده اونکاراق و اونکارغای مز و اونکارغای سز و اونکارالی و اونکارالینک راست کنیم اونکارغالی
برای راست کردن و تا راست کرده اونکارغاج چون راست کرد و کند اونکارغوچی راست کننده اونکارغوچه و اونکارغونچه
اونکارغانچه تا راست کردن و بمعنی راست کردن اونکارغوم راست خواهم کرد اونکارغونک راست خواهی کرد اونکارغوسی
راست خواهد کرد اونکارغولوق راست کردنی اونکارغای و اونکارسا و اونکارسون و اونکاردیک راست کند چنانکه شاهد برین
مثل گوید که ایش اولدی مرکرا قه اونکارا اونکارغودیک و اونکاردیک راست کردنی و همچنانکه راست کند اونکارلماق

مجمریل وایلماق لام بمعنی راست شدن کار باشد و تا بع صیغ برین فتح با الام اشتقاق می یابد اونکالماق بسکون نون
ولام وفتح کاف عجمی مع آالاملاله به شدن وصحت یافتن والتیام یافتن واتراک ردوم اونکولمک بضم کاف کویند اونکلد
به شد اونکالدوق به شدیم اونکالور یا اونکالادو به میشود واونکالور بمعنی فاعل مصدر منفی هم می آید اونکالمایدکه به
نمیشود ونشده است اونکالغان او نکالغوای اونکالادرغان به شونده و به شده وبمعنی مصدر هم می آید اونکال اونکالور
مفرد غایب امر وفعل امر اونکالدی اونکالمغیل مفرد غایب فعل نهی اونکالینک اونکالینکز واونکالینکلار جمع غایب فعل امر
اونکالماتک اونکالمانکز اونکالمانکلار جمع غایب فعل نهی اونکالماس اونکالمس بمعنی نشوم اونکالامین اونکالورمین و
اونکالامیز اونکالورمیز به میشوم اونکالایبی اونکالیبان اونکالمیش به شده اونکالمیشانلیک به شونده اونکالماس نمیشود
وبمعنی فاعل مصدر منفی هم می آید اونکالمایی به شدنش ونشدنش اونکالمادین از به شدن و به نشده اونکالیسکو
اونکالسا اونکالادی او اونکالماقالیک به نمیتوان شد اونکالماس به نمیتواند شد اونکالا اونکالا به شونده به شونده
تکرار هم مستعملست اونکالایی اونکالایین به شوم وشود وشوی وشده اونکالناقو اونکالغلی اونکالغای اونکالا
اونکالالیک به شویم اونکالغلی برای به شدن وتا به شده الشاهد علیه بالمعنی الاول شعر کیل کلیح کونکلیکا دا
اوشتی اونکالغالی تیر محفله نار نار غیل که دلفکار مین هنوز اونکالغاچ چون به شد وشود اونکالغوچی به شونده
اونکالغوجه اونکالغونچه اونکالقانچه تا به شدن و بعد به شدن اونکالغوم به خواهم شد اونکالغونک به خواهی شد اونکالغوسی
به خواهد شد اونکالغولوق به شدنی اونکالغای او اونکالا اونکالسا اونکالدیلار به شوند الشاهد علی الاول شعر
کونکلوم لکا بوزتومان نیش اصر ساچرا از ایلامانیاله وصالینک نوشیدین او لا زخم لاله کون اونکالغای دیب و کله شب
کونکول ضعفی کمر اولماس فرقتینکدا اوه لونکالغا ایمو مرضی کیم قیلور هر دم بلیت زهری اشامی اونکالغودیک اونکالور
به شدنی وچنانکه به شود اونکملک بسکون نون وکاف عجمی بترکی رومی بر وییدن بمعنی لغت جغتای اونمک کویند
چنانکه مذکور شد اونکولمک بترکی رومی به شدن ودر لغت جغتای اونکالماق کویند اونکولمیش به شده چنانکه
فضولی کوید ملکه الرومیه شعر جگر یدا دایله هر دم که اول زخم اوز زخم هیچ بر دم که دیدم اونکمش اونکولمش
کونکلوم ترلیکوامدادون عرصه نه را کویند ونیز اراسته ورسیدن چنانکه در ذیل صنم اونمک کذشت وباشباع ضمه
ندده حتی اراد اوکا صدا وآواز را کویند الشاهد علیه شعر اوچکارمین عشق ارا اولغ کرجاده کوه بیت ملفاخان
ایت تیلک که فریاد ایلاکای آهو کورب دوم هر چیز منقوش ماننده عموما چنانکه در سکندری کوید شعر اوشاق
تمداوون توز چهره مانند ابریهر ولیکن بری توز بری تمدا برور وآن را خوانند خصوصا الشاهد علیه شعر مین بتلاکا
وصل وآینک کونکلم لغایارایله سنکا ایکی ماش ارایسند اکرالتا البته اولوش وزان بلفسنجنکی بمعنی راست وصد وصد و درصع
لونتوچ بسکون نون وجیم وضمهای فوقیت بمعنی ترین ودین باشد چنانکه کوید شعر ایغه باش توید ودم اماتنغ ایله
آبرنادی باش یاس بوکیلم بیوع بوتومد آنینکا دستوچ وآنرا اوتوچ نیز کویند اوندالیق بسکون نون وفتح دال وکسر لام عبارت
از بهملت باشد که آنرا امری عشق خوانند اوندرو بسکون نون وراء فوقیت وضم دال بمعنی ضعیف وملبد بود چنانکه در
سیاره کوید شعر ایلهاک پنجهم غیرلزبی اوندو ایتها دسیم خصل زبی ونیز در سه سکندری فرماید شعر میلو یازجاما
عمارتین بیت بر عمارای اوند وصعفا جفه شکست وطالع هوی اوند ودر ابن شعرا خیرا نیز بکسر الف خوانند بمعنی غلت

مدو وخصامت جثه نوشته سهو کرده ونیز اراسته ورسیدن چنانکه در ذیل صنم اونمک وطالع کذشت اندو بلند
بلند تر اونغاسی بسکون نون ویای جبلی وفتح غین معجمه با الف کشیده بمعنی ابزار و وسایل اندلو بود چنانکه در فصل بیت مفهم
از محبوب القلوب در وصف اهل سوق کوید که ایلکلاری آتینک سودی اونغای آکیب آغیر یاتماق آتینک مضرویی و کاموکلیفن
دومیه اونکای بفتح کاف عجمی کرده وبمعنی ومیه نوشته حضرت مذکور از محبوب القلوب شاهد آورده اند وتصیر باستاک
عونه وبعلاجمان بمعنی جبینه ودوته شده نیز مذکور ساخته اونقاب بسکون هردو نون وفتح قاف با الف کشیده ملقب
کره اسب وکره خر باشد اونک بسکون نون وکاف عجمی وبمعنی آمده اولمرات بمعنی ثواب باشد الشاهد علیه شعر عیش کیلمو
ایشیم یرفلغز صیدا اونک خانقه کفی هوس ایلاها مین آندین سوتک ونیز در فصل چهارم از محبوب القلوب در ذکر پادشاه
ظالم کوید که خطا رلی لونک کیلما سا دخل یی لاکر شرکت بلکه نقیض تونغا لاکر خصمت دویم ارست صنعچه باشد چنانکه
کوید شعر کرمین ابستا نوازی که کیتی طلعتا یتتب ثانمه معلوم ایماس سولوق لی دیره هر ا اونک اونکو بسکون نون
وضم کاف عجمی بترکی رومی بمعنی لجاج ووصل وستیزه کار باشد اونکور بسکون نون وراء مهمله وضم کاف عجمی کوشه دامن
باشد چنانکه در خصایم الحرمه در ذکر شیخ ابو علی فارمدی کوید که چون سماع دین فارغ بولدیلار شیخ توتیمنا لدی وقتکا
تبرتیشیب ولاسنوایر دیلار شیخ بر ینک سیله سپر اونکورنی آلیب باشغه قوی بوجار لادی که ای ابو علی طوسیجا بیلسین اونکوره
بسکون نون وراء مهمله بضم کاف عجمی وفتح ضین معجمه فترات ظهر بود که آنرا اوکره خرم کویند وبفارسی پشته مانند
اونکولوک حیله وعلاج بود اونوت بمعنی فراموش باشد الشاهد علیه شعر ایله درد وغمینکا اوکاندیم کیم اونوت
بولدی منکا عیدی روطوتی ونیز آنرا اسناد فراموش کردن چنانکه کذشت مع الواو من المشتقات اوانوق بفتح واو وسکون نون بترکی
رومی بمعنی بی حس شدن من ابجوامدادات اشنا نهمرغان باشد وآنرا بواهم مانند اواد مرز کنار که در عراق کویند اوادی بکسر
دال وسکون راء مهمله بمعنی افتادن ستور باشد وآنچه از قسطلان ینکه چارپا بیلع پهلو افتاده نتواند برخاست وآنرا اوکلا کیر
کویند مع الیاء من المشتقات اویماق بسکون یا به پنج معنی آمده اول بمعنی کاویدن باشد که آنرا بعربی تنویر کویند دویم بمعنی
زخم دیتن وماستدن بود سیم بمعنی موافقت ومتابعت کردن باشد چهارم قبیله را مانند پنجم انکشتوانه خیاطی را
چنانکه در ذیل جامه کاری خواهد آمد اویدی کاوید وبت وموافقت کرد چنانکه بمعنی اول در آغاز عشق مجنون و
احوال لیلی کوید شعر تیرنا غلامین چو ینکا فویدی تیرنا غ تیرنا غجه یکی اوییدی ومعنی شعر اینست که ناخنها را چون برید
کذاشت بعد هر ناخنی بهر کاوید وطالع هروی مصرع اخیر را از نسخه سقیمی باین نحو خواند که تیرنا غ تیرنا غ چاپیر اولدی و حاپیر
بمعنی سینی نوشته که آب از آن تراوش کند در تصحیح معنی شعر از خواهد بود که چون ناخن ابرید وکذاشت ناخنها را سیوشد
که آب از آن تراوش کند معهذا چاپیر کیاه ریزه ایست که در بیشه آن در هم پیچد ودر زیر درختان وجاهای نمناک میروید و
اوولنچ ولفظ صرف ومعنی اخر بی ست وبمعنی زخم بت در تاریخ بابری مذکور است که شهسوار نمینک باشید نی کف دسته
سونکا کی قیلیجی الیب کیکالمر شیوا عیدیلار مخشی یلدی ایدوق کاوید یم وتسیم وموافقت کردیم اویارو ا و یادو رمی کاوید
وموافقت می کند اویار بمعنی فاعل ومصدر نیز می آید چنانکه در تاریخ بابری بمعنی زخم بندنده مذکور است که صمد نینک باشید
ادنیارکیشی یوق ایدی ایشولار زخم سیله نا بردی او یماید ور بمیکاود ونکاویده است وبمیندده و بسته است وموافقت کند
ونکرده است او یغان واو یلمغان واو یادور غان کاونده کاوید وبندنده وبسته وموافقت کنند وموافقت کرده چنانکه

شاهد بر اول لمه بمعنی کاویده در لیلی و مجنون دمو نات لیلی خراشیدن نادم مجنون سوی خود آکوید شعر اویغنا نالر آچیدا
کیم سینیب قان کونرچیه لاری دیل آغزیقان و بمعنی مصدر نیز می آید اوی کا ویغیل مفرد مخاطب از فعل امر بمعنی
الشاهد علی الاول بالمعنی الاول شعر کوزوم اوی ای بلیت قمرانی که اول کوزداس بو کوزدین سونکرا آقتی واوی بمعنی
جامه هم آمده که در ذیل جامه بکنند نوشخواهد شد اویماق و یماغیل مفرد مخاطب از فعل امر بمعنی الشاهد علی الاول
بالمعنی الثالث من فضولی شعر ای فضولی جمع اهلی ومسجد توتیش سن ر میسکده توت اویمه بوکرایه او یونک و
اویونکوز و اویونکلار جمع مخاطب از فعل امر و نیز از راسته خواب کردن چنانکه بیایید اویماق و اویمانکیز و اویمانکلار جمع مخاطب
از فعل نهی اویماس و اویماس مین یعنی کاوم نمیبندم موافقت نمیکنم لو یامین و اونارمین واو یادوم و اویارام میکاوم و میبندم
و موافقت میکنم اویادیم و اویاغیم کاویدم و بستم و موافقت کردم اویاغوم بخوام کاوید و نخوام بست و موافقت نخوام کرد
اویغای ایردیم میکاویدم و میبستم و موافقت میکردم چنانکه بمعنی اول کوید شعر اویغای ایردیم کونزدین زاغ پرسه
بیلسام ایردی کیم بیر نظر دین ناشیه بو خیه بلالار کیلدی بصر اویوب و اویوبان و یمیش کاویده و بسته و موافقت کرده
اویوب و اویوبان بمعنی خواب کرده هم آمده در این معنی با مصدر اویوماق اشتراک دارد اویمیشانک کاویده و بسته
موافقت کرده اویماس نمیکاود و نمیبندد و موافقت نمیکند و بمعنی عل و مصدر منفی هم می آید اویماسی کاویدنش و
نکاویدنش و بستنش و نبستنش و موافقت کردنش و نکردنش را و بمادین از کاویدن و نکاویده و از بستن و نبسته و از موافقت کردن
و موافقت نکرده اویوب کوبیلماو دیه و یکا قاماق آلماس نمیتوان کاوید و نمیتوان بست و موافقت نمیتوان کرد و اویوب بولماس
بمعنی خواب نمیتوان کرد هم باشد اویا آلماس نمیتواند کاوید نمیتواند بست نمیتواند موافقت کرد اویا او یا کاوش کنان و
بسته بسته و موافقت کنان و بدون تکرار هم با همین معنی مستعملست اویای و اویا یین بکاوم بکاود بکاوی ببندم ببندد
ببندی و موافقت کنم و کند و کنی اویسا قیغا و یغانیز و اویغای نیز و اویلی و اویالینک بکاویم و ببندیم و موافقت کنیم اویغای
با کاویدن و با کاویده و برای بستن و با بسته و برای موافقت کردن و تا موافقت کرده اویغاج چون کاوید و بکاود و چون بست
و ببندد چون موافقت کرد و کند اویغوچی کاونده و بندنده و موافقت کننده اویغوم خواهم کاوید خواهم بست و موافقت
خواهم کرد اویغونک خواهی کاوید خواهی بست موافقت خواهی کرد اویغوسی خواهد کاوید خواهد بست موافقت خواهد کرد اویغو
کاویدن و بستن و موافقت کردن اویکیلو اویلا و یسا اولا و یکیلو بکاود و ببندد و موافقت کند اویغودیک و اویادیک
کاویدنی و چنانکه بکاود و ببندد و چنانکه ببندد و موافقت کردن و چنانکه موافقت کند اویلماق بضم یا و سکون لام
مصدر انفعالست بمعنی کاویده شدن و بسته شدن و موافقت کرده شدن اویول و اویلغیل مفرد مخاطب
از فعل امر بمعنی الشاهد علی الاول بالمعنی الاول شعر ای کوز آیینه اوزکا یونکمو اکی یلتیش سین هوس هم تیغ دین
اویول یاخود نوازدین اویال و الطالع هر دو با نسخه سقیم بود و لفظ اویول و اویالرا در مصرع اخیر اویالخوانده و اویال
اول را بمعنی کندن و ثانی را بمعنی جدا شدن نوشته سهو کرده است اویولیب و اویولوبان و اویولمیش کاویده شده و
بسته شده و موافقت کرده شده الشاهد علی الاول بالمعنی الاول شعر تا بیلیم درد و بلا غملار لا ریدین اویولوب یود اکیم
غنا خانه لاری دین تیشلیش و تایی صیغ بر این سیاق موافق اویولماق اشتقاق می یابد اوید و رماق مصدر متعدی
یعنی کاواندن و زخم بسته کردن و موافق و متابع ساختن و باقی صیغ بر این نسق لفظ دو می شود کرد اویوشماق مع التثنیه

مصدر مفاعله است هم بمعنی هجوم کردن و متابعت یکدیگر نمودن باشد و صیغ آن موافق مشتقات اویماق اشتقاق می یابد
اما بدل لام شین مذکور میشود اویوماق بضم با بمعنی خواب کردن بود و آنرا اویوقلاماق هم گویند اویودوق خواب کردیم
اویو و اویوید و مخواب میکند الشاهد علی الاول شعر لوی کا بیتکو نیمیسا بیوز اللابانیم آغزیناه چون یلو یو صبح والم
ددح و روانیم دین کیتار و اویو بمعنی فاعل و مصدر نیز می آید چنانکه شاهد بر اول لمه بمعنی فاعل گوید شعر کونکلو تیجا
حیف یلانسا اویو هوش ایسا اویو بولسا الیغ ایلکیاشین قویماسه بیر اویو نایدود خواب نمیکند و نکرده است اویوغان
اویوغان و اویوید و اویوغان خواب کننده و خواب کرده و بمعنی مصدر نیز می آید اویو و اویوغیل مفرد مخاطب از فعل امر الشاهد علی الاول
شعر شام غم اولنوردی یونماشادی مین شاد اویو به تا بیغوا بی تقصد بیلمان سیرتا بیغودین آزاد لو تو اویوملا اویونا غیل مفرد
مخاطب از فعل نهی اویونک و اویونکیز و اویونکلار جمع مخاطب از فعل امر و نیز از راسته کاویدن و بستن و موافقت کردن چنانکه گذشت
اویوماغیل و اویوماغیز و اویومانکلار جمع مخاطب از فعل نهی اویوماس و اویوماس مین خواب نمیکنم اویو مین و اویو میدا و اویو میمین و اویودا
خواب میکنم اویودوم و اویوغیم خواب کردم اویوغوم خواب نخواهم کرد و میکنه اویوناداو اویومیش خواب کرده چنانکه شاه
بر افلاطون تاریخ الانبیا گوید که حضرت نوح علیه السلام اویوب ایردی و عورت عضوی آچیلیب ایردی حام کوروب کولدی و
اویوب و اویوبان بمعنی کاویده و بسته و موافقت کرده نیز آمده چنانکه گذشت و اویومیشان خواب کرده آویوماس خواب نمیکند
الشاهد علیه شعر دیبا نا لنکدین لو یوماس کیچه لار لا ایدیم کیم تا لنک ایماش کیلملسا یمار لار ارغا او یقوایت اضافه دین و بمعنی فاعل
و مصدر منفی هم می آید اویوماسی خواب کردنش و نکردنش لو یوماد ین از خواب کردن و خواب نکرده اویوب بولماس و اویوماق
اویونلتی و کا خواب نمیتوان کرد و اویوب بولماس بمعنی نمیتوان کاوید و نمیتوان بست و موافقت نمیتوان کرد هم آمده اویوی آلماس
خواب نمیتواند کرد و یو یوغای آلنام خواب توانم کرد چنانکه گوید شعر اویوی آلنام ایشیکینک توفرلغی یا ستانیسان سلطنت
تخته چیقماق تیلاغان و یغانیسان اویوی اویوی خواب کنان و بدون تکرار هم مستعملست اویوی اویوین خواب کنم
و کند و کنی و کرده اویوماق و اویوماییز و اویوغای نیز و اویونک و اویونلیک خواب کنیم اویوغالی برای خواب کردن و تا خواب کرده اویوغاچ
چون خواب کرد و کند اویوغوچی خواب کننده اویوغوم خواب خواهم کرد اویوغونک خواب خواهی کرد اویوغوسی خواب خواهد
کرد اویوغولوق خواب کردن اویوغیلو اویوغیلا و اویوسا و اویوغیچا و اویوغودیک خواب کند اویوغودیک و اویوردیک خواب کردن و چنانکه خواب کند
اویوتماق بضم یا و سکون تای قرشت مصدر متعدیست یعنی خوابانیدن الشاهد علیه شعر غفلت دین کوز طالع
اویغاتسا لار ایلیک اول ایلا لار اویوتماق ایچون افسانه غه مشغول ایدیم و اویوتیب و اویوتقان و اویوتمیش خوابانیده الشاهد علی الاول شعر
خلق دین غافل ایمیش قتل میلوش کونز آچار فتنه ضایلی اویوتوب و باقی صیغ بر همین منوال موافق مشتق اول یا نای قرشت اشتقاق می یابد
اویالماق بفتح یای الف کشیده و سکون لام خجل شدن اویالدی خجل شد اویالدوق خجل شدیم اویالورداو یالدو خجل میشود
الشاهد علی الثانی شعر نهان نوآشکار نوازی بن اول ماقیغ کا یوجا قیلیب یه کا جوای اله دهش و اویالیب یعنی خجل شده
هم می آید اویالغان اویالور غلو و اویالادورغان خجل شونده و خجل شده و بمعنی مصدر نیز می آید چنانکه گوید الشاهد علی الاول اندین آرو
اویالماین کورکاندا جان قیلدیم فدا قیلما انکر یحیین که قیلیش مین اویالغان دین بوادیش اویالغاو اویالغیل مفرد مخاطب از فعل امر چنانکه
شاهد بر اول در ذیل مصدر اویولماق مذکور شده اویالما اویالماغیل مفرد مخاطب از فعل نهی اویالینک و اویالینکیز و اویالینکلار
خجل میشوم اویالماسو اویالماسانک و اویالمانکلار خجل میشوم اویالماروم اویالماغیم خجل شدیم اویالماغوم خجل نخواهم شد

اویالغامین طو یاتغای بن خجل شوم الشاهد علی الثانی شعر جون تاشی باشینکنه یاغدی سیعیب اتیا اغامی ثقصور ملکم
بوسوز تشلادین اویالغای بن اویالیب وا ویالیبان وا ویالمیش خجل شده اویلماز خجل نمیشود وبمعنی فاعل ومصدر منفی هم
می آید اویالماسی خجل شدنش ونشدنش اویالیب بولماس او یالنا بولماس او یلماقا ولماس خجل نمیتوان شد اویالا آلماس خجل
نمیتواند شد اویالاویالا خجل شوان اویالاوا ویالامین خجل شوم وشود وشوی وشده لو یالنا قدا ویالغا ینجا ویالغای
وا ویالالی طوا ویالالینک خجل شویم اویالغالی برای خجل شدن وتا خجل شده اویالغاج چون خجل شد شود اویالغوچی خجل شونده
اویالغوم خجل خواهیم شد اویالغونک خجل خواهی شد اویالغوسی خجل خواهد شد اویالغولوق خجل شدنی اویالغای او یالغای
وا ویالسون طوا ویالدیک خجل شود اویالغودیک وا ویالورد یک خجل شدنی وهمچنانکه خجل شود اوینماق بکون نوک
شدن الشاهد علیه شعر ایجیب کرد ونجه ساغر کاش آندا اقیجود اولسام کیم ایکیمیز سودین هم بولماغای وینماغیم امکا
اوینماندی بیدار شد اوینماندوق بیدار شدیم اوینمانور او ینمانماس بیدار میشود واوینمانور بمعنی فاعل ومصدر منفی
اوینمانماید ور بیدار نمیشود ونشده است اوینمانمان واوینمانورغان ببعا واوینمانادورغان بیدار شونده وبیدار شده وبمعنی مصدر
می آید اوینمان واوینمانیل مفرد مخاطب از فعل امر اوینمانماواوینمانماقیل مفرد مخاطب از فعل نهی اوینمانسنواوینمانسنکر اوینما
جمع مخاطب از فعل امر اوینمانمانلر واوینمانمانکز واوینمانمانکلار جمع مخاطب از فعل نهی اوینمانمان واوینمانمانغاس بیدار نشوم اوینماقا
واوینمانورمین واوینمانادورمین وا وینمانور لم بیدار میشوم اوینمانوردم واوینمانادم بیدار شدم اوینماغوم بیدار خواهم شد
اوینمانسنواوینمانسنان واوینمانمش بیدار شده الشاهد علی الاول شعر واوینمانسیع اویقودین مهر شعبین تا رتیل
کوز آچیب هر کوشه دین پرنشه نی بیدار قیل واوینمانماشاندک بیدار شده اوینمانماس بیدار نمیشود چنانکه کوید شعر وله بوکی
دوریکیم کونمانیم چرخ دین اوتسوت که اولناز اویقوسیدین حتما غونجه مهرا وینماغاش وسیاق نظم چنین است که مهر حتما
اولناز اویقودین اوینماغاس یعنی تا آفتاب دمیابد وا از خواب بیدار نمیشود لیکن نصیری لفظا وینماغاس را خبر مهر دانسته
ونوشته که مهر اوینماغاس یعنی آفتاب طالع نمیشود وبغیر تغیر اینست لا الجته واوینماغاقم بمعنی طالع شدن نیز
اشتباه او الطهر من الثمرات وبمعنی فاعل ومصدر منفی هم می آید واوینماسی بیدار شدنش ونشدنش واوینماسیب بولماس اوینماسا
بولماس واوینماقا ولماس بیدار نمیتوان شد اوینمانا آلماس بیدار نمیتواند شد واوینمانا اوینمانا بیدار شوان بیدار شوان اوینمانای
واوینمانامین بیدار شوم وشود وشوی وشده اوینمانناق واوینمانغاپیز واوینمانغای پیزها اوینمانالی واوینمانالینک
بیدار شویم اوینمانغالی برای بیدار شدن وتا بیدار شده اوینمانغاج چون بیدار شد وشود من فرهاد وشیرین شعر بو توش
کوکز کا نلار اوینمانغاج هولدم بولوب واقف بو ایشدین اهل غالر اوینمانغوچی بیدار شونده اوینمانغوجه واوینمانغوجه واوینما
تا بیدار شدن وبمعنی بیدار شدن اوینمانغوم بیدار خواهم شد اوینمانغونک بیدار خواهی شد اوینمانغوسی بیدار خواهد شد
اوینمانغولوق بیدار شدنی اوینمانغای واوینمانا واوینمانسا واوینمانسون واوینمانادیک بیدار شود اوینمانغودیک و
اوینمانودیک بیدار شدنی وهمچنانکه بیدار شود اوینمانماق مع التا مصدر متعدیست یعنی بیدار کردن اوینمانورواوینما
بیدار میکند الشاهد علی الثانی شعر بختیم اوینمانماس کرچه فرعیم دمراهلین اولوم اویقوسیغه بارغانلار اینا اوینمانادو
واوینماتور بمعنی فاعل ومصدر هم می آید چنانکه بمعنی مصدری کوید شعر ای نوائی منیم تون کوز ایلغیغه قویوب
اوینماتوغه حشم جیحون الهلابان میغاداوبواوینمانک واوینمانیل امرا ستا نبیدار کردن الشاهد علی الاول شعر شعلیکی

غزالینکینی ناز اویقوسیدین اوینمانماس تا اویقولاری کیتسون کلزلر ایجینیا اوینمات اوینمانغوسیلادی دهیبیدار نخواهند کرد چنانکه کو
شعر منوسیبیب اوینمانغوسیلادی دیمه جیغالهینما نماننات فیه وجه وصراحی غلغل کولکیله وبات صیغ بر این سیاق
موافق شوال اول نا نائی قرشنا اشقاق می یابد اوینمولا ناق خواب کردن اوینماناق بازی کردن الشاهد علیه شعر چمن اونو
برله آلمه دین نقدینا ب دین واقف اول بوشمشه برله بولماس اهل عرفان اوینماناق اوینادی بازی کرد اوینادوق بازی کردیم
اوینار واوینایدور بازی میکند واوینار بمعنی فاعل ومصدر منفی هم آید اوینامادور بازی نمیکند ونکرده است اوینامان
اوینارغان واوینایدورغان بازی کننده وبازی کرده الشاهد علی الاول لمعنی الاول شعر لوح هشیم دین آیکر مرید لا اله دنی
اول اوینارغان کبی یغلاج اونیم یاله دهش وبمعنی مصدر هم می آید اوینا واوینا غیل مفرد مخاطب از فعل امر الشاهد علی
الثانی شعر شوخلوغ دین بوکه بلغ ایجرا ایتلادیم اوینماناق کوزلادیم نیک لمغیر امید ابرهیم اوینا غیل اوینا منا
واوینامانا غیل مفرد مخاطب از فعل نهی اوینانک واوینانکز واوینانکلار جمع مخاطب از فعل امر اوینامانک واوینامانکز اوینامانکلار جمع مخاطب
از فعل نهی اوینامان واوینامانس بازی نکنم اوینایمن واوینایدورمین واوینایورم بازی میکنم اوینادیم واوینامانغیم
بازی کردیم اوینامانغوم بازی خواهم کرد اوینابتور اوینابان واوینامش بازی کرده الشاهد علی الاول شعر
اوینایب اولتوردی نوایی کوزونک حینی بار بکیم اکر بود عاصیش اوینامیشاننک بازی کرده اوینامالس بازی نکند
وبمعنی فاعل ومصدر منفی هم می آید اوینامانسی بازی کردنش ونکردنش اوینامانادین از بازی کردن ونکرده اوینایب بولماس
اوینایالماس واوینامانا قا ولماس بازی نمیتوان کرد اوینایالماس بازی نمیتواند کرد اوینابوواوینای اوینای بازی کنان الشاهد
علی الاول من لیلی مجنون شعر قیزلار بیله اوینایو تولاشه قوی یانغما فین ابتکالی تماشا الشاهد علی الثانی شعر
اویناای اویناای اولتور دوریبر اولوسی کوز لار اینک شعر تابل الاحراب جانالدی قصد نیغه اویناتماغیل وبدون تکرار هم مستعمل
اویناای اوینامین بازی کنم وکند وکنی وکرده چنانکه شاهد براولها بمعنی ثانی کوید شعر بوشهسوار کیم کوی
اویناما قغه ایجیش می عنه سوی ابوکان باشیم آلیقه اوینای اوینانا ق واوینا غایبز ولوینا غایبز واوینا غای اوینا لیک
بازی کنیم اوینا غالی برای بازی کردن وتا بازی کرده اوینا غاج چون بازی کرد وکند اوینا غوچی بازی کننده باشد
علیه من لسان الطیر شعر ایکی شطرنج اوینا غوچی ادشاده عرصه شطرنج فه الملاد کشاد لوینا غوم بازی خواهم کرد اوینا
بازی خواهی کرد اوینا غوسی بازی خواهد کرد اوینا غولوق بازی کردنی وهمچنانکه بازی کند اوینا تماق مع التا
مصدر متعدیست یعنی بازی فرمودن اوینا توروواوینا تادور بازی میفرماید الشاهد علی الثانی شعر لب کمخندان اقیدین
تاش وکوزین اوینالادور اوینای اوینای مستی بجله نخان مغیلاتنادوش وباقی صیغ بر این منوال موافق شوال وبا ثنای قرشنا اشقاق
می یابد اوینا شماغ مع الشین مصدر مقابله است یعنی با هم بازی کردن وصیغ آن بدستور یا شین قرشنا اشقاق می یابد
اوبا تماغ بفتح تای فوقانیه وسکون قاف یعنی فرو کردن کواکب باشد وآنرا رومیه تولوتماق کویند ومثلطن مرتبه
ابا تماق بفتح الف نوشته اند وطالع هروی بمعنی کردید نذکر کرده او باتتی غروب کرد چنانکه کوید شعر اوبه
جون قوتاش اول آل کعبه تا لدی دهریار وتماق چوبا ردی مهر بهان نا آمت دوران اکبر وارش اوبا قوسی واوبا تادو غروب میکند
الشاهد علی الاول شعر حسن دوری غه ونا یوق بو قوتاش بات اوبا قور خوبلادین خوش ابرو یخش لینغ ذکتی متبلغ
واوباقور بمعنی فاعل ومصدر منفی آید اوبا قمایدور عرضه منکند ونکرده است اوباقغان واوباقوغان واوباقادورغان

غروب کننده و غروب کرده و بمعنی مصدر هم می آید چنانکه شاهد بر اول مصرع مصدری گوید شعر برده یابنلج یونکا توتقان
باشیم آتماقی همراه و باتماقدا اقوش تاپی یا بیلمان دیك شفق او باقی ملولی اتمیل مفرد مخاطب از فصل امر او باتما و او باتما غیل
مفرد مخاطب از فصل نهی او باقینك و او باقینکیز و او باتینکلار جمع مخاطب از فصل امر او باتمانلار و او باتمانکیز و او باتمانکلار جمع مخاطب از فصل نهی
او باتقان و او باققان مین غروب میکنم او باتاسین و او باتورمین و او باتادورمین و او باتورام غروب میکنم او باتوردوم و او باتماغیم
غروب کردیم او باتماغوم غروب نخواهم کرد او باتقی و او باتقان و او باتمیش غروب کرده چنانکه در لیلی مجنون در صفت
نوفل با قبیله لیلی گوید الشاهد علی الاول شعر هر تون غه که اول اوتنی یاقیب عمر لختی تون دا بین او باقیب یا بمیشانک
غروب کرده او باتماس غروب نمیکند و بمعنی فاعل و مصدر منفی هم می آید او باتماسی غروب کردنش و نکردنش او باقیب بولکان
او باقماسلیق او باتماقا و باقماقلیک غروب نمیتوان کرد او باتاالماس غروب نمیتواند کرد او باتا او باتا غروب کنان غروب کنان
تکرار هم مستعمل است او باتمای و او باتمایین غروب کند فکم و کنی و کرده او باتقا قچا و باتقانیز و او باقمای بیز و او باتکو و او باتقا
غروب کنیم او باتقالی برای غروب کردن و تا غروب کرده او باتقالاچ چون غروب کرد و کند من سلطان حسین میرزا شعر
آتجا او باتقالاچ یا ناکونکلوم نی بوزو بلی لغزلوغوم تیرشامیم اندهدین سغل ادام کوپ دم دایله او باتقوچی غروب کننده
او باتقوسیدا و باتقوسیدا و باتمقا تا غروب کردن و بقصد غروب کردن او باتقوم غروب خواهم کرد او باتقونك غروب خواهی کرد
او باتقوسی غروب خواهد کرد او باتقولوق غروب کردن او باتقای بیدا و باتمادا و باقسالدا و باتقاندا غروب کنند او باتقود
او باتقودیك غروب کردن و همچنانکه غروب میکند اویلانماق بسکون یا و نون مع القاف بمعنی تفکر کردن بود و آنرا رومیه
دوشونماك گویند اویلانماك بسکون یا و نون مع الکاف یعنی صاحب خانه شدن و آن بالمجاز بمعنی زن گرفتن و زن گرفتن
کردن چنانکه در لیلی مجنون در جواب کله که از پی لیلی از جانب مجنون گوید شعر اویلانماك ایشی که نسبت ایستینك
بزکا اوزا ایشینکیکی همت ایستینك اویلاندی تفکر کرد و زن گرفت اویلاندوق تفکر کردیم اویلاندوك زن گرفتیم اویلانور
اویلاناتور تفکر میکند و زن میگیرد و اویلانور بمعنی فاعل و مصدر هم می آید چنانکه بمعنی زن گرفتن گوید شعر طلاق
برآتی کیم ده هر ایرا ساو سین غریب الملکا ایماس اویلانور بیری غریب اویلانماید که تفکر نمیکند و نکرده است و زن نمیگیرد و نگرفته
اویلانغان و اویلانورغان و اویلاناتورغان تفکر کننده و تفکر کرده و بمعنی مصدر نیز می آیند اویلانکان و اویلانورکان و اویلانادورکان
زن گیرنده و زن گرفته و بمعنی مصدر نیز می آیند اویلان مفرد مخاطب از فصل امر مصدر اول اویلانماق و اویلانماك اویلانغیل
مفرد مخاطب امر مصدر اول اویلاناق اویلانکیل مفرد مخاطب امر مصدر دوم اویلانماك اویلانما مفرد مخاطب از فصل نهی هر دو مصدر
اویلانماغیل مفرد مخاطب از فصل نهی مصدر اول اویلانماقا و اویلانماکیل مفرد مخاطب از فصل نهی مصدر دوم اویلانماك اویلانینك و اویلانینکیز
اویلانینکلار جمع مخاطب از فصل امر هر دو مصدر اویلانمانك و اویلانمانکیز و اویلانمانکلار جمع مخاطب از فصل نهی هر دو مصدر اویلانمان
و اویلانمادورمین تفکر نمیکنم و زن نمیگیرم اویلانامین و اویلانورمین و اویلانادورمین تفکر میکنم و زن میگیرم اویلاندوم تفکر
کردم و زن گرفتم اویلاندیم تفکر کردیم اویلاندیم زن گرفتیم اویلانماغوم تفکر نخواهم کرد اویلانماگوم زن نخواهم گرفت
اویلانیب اویلانیبان و اویلانمیش تفکر کرده و زن گرفته اویلانمیشانك تفکر کرده و زن گرفته اویلانماس تفکر نمیکند و زن
نمیگیرد و بمعنی فاعل و مصدر منفی هم می آید اویلانماسی تفکر کردنش و نکردنش و زن گرفتنش و نگرفتنش اویلانمادین اینکه تفکر
کردن و تفکر نکرده و زن گرفتن و زن نگرفته اویلانیب بولماس و اویلانا بولماس تفکر نمیتوان کرد و زن نمیتوان گرفت

اویلاناماق اویلانالماس تفکر نمیتوان کرد اویلانماك اویلانالماس زن نمیتوان گرفت اویلانا آلماس تفکر نمیتواند کرد و زن نمیتواند گرفت اویلانا
اویلانا تفکر کنان و زن گیرنده اویلانای و اویلانایین تفکر کنم و کند و کنی و کرده و زن بگیرم و بگیرد و بگیری و گرفته اویلانقا
اویلانقالی و اویلانقای بیز تفکر کنیم اویلانغا و اویلانکا و اویلانکای بیز زن بگیریم اویلانقالی و اویلانالی تفکر کنیم
و زن بگیریم اویلانقالی برای تفکر کردن و تا تفکر کرده اویلانکالی برای زن گرفتن و تا زن گرفته اویلانقالاچ چون تفکر کرد و کند
اویلانکالاچ چون زن گرفت و بگیرد اویلانقوچی تفکر کننده اویلانکوچی زن گیرنده اویلانقوچه و اویلانقوسیغا
تا تفکر کردن و بقصد تفکر کردن اویلانکوچه و اویلانکوسیغا تا زن گرفتن و بقصد زن گرفتن اویلانقوم تفکر خواهم
کرد اویلانکوم زن خواهم گرفت اویلانقونك تفکر خواهی کرد اویلانکونك زن خواهی گرفت اویلانقوسی تفکر خواهد کرد
اویلانکوسی زن خواهد گرفت اویلانقولوق تفکر کردن اویلانکولوك زن گرفتن اویلانقای تفکر کند اویلانکای زن
بگیرد اویلانا و اویلانسا و اویلانسون و اویلاندیك تفکر کند و زن بگیرد اویلانقودیك تفکر کردن و همچنانکه تفکر کند
اویلانکودیك زن گرفتن و همچنانکه بگیرد اویلانوردیك همان بمعنی اویلانقودیك و اویلانکودیك باشد اویلاتماق
بسکون یا مع التاء بمعنی تفکر کردن بود و صیغ آن بدستور مشتقات اویلانماق است اما بدل نون تا داخل می شود
اویوشماك بضم یا مع الشین ترکی رومی بمعنی افسرده شدن خون در عضو باشد چنانکه گویند اناق اویوشدی یعنی پا خفتن
که آنرا بعربی خدر گویند اویورتلماك بسکون تای قرشت و فتح لام ترکی رومی بمعنی انتخاب آمده اویورتلنماك مع النون یعنی
انتخاب شدن اویکونماك بسکون یا و نون و ضم کاف ترکی رومی بمعنی تقلید کردن باشد و در لغت جغتای اوتکانماك
گویند من اثبو امد اوی هفت معنی دارد اول خانه را گویند چنانکه در این بیت گوید شعر حیکا الارتن دین اومن
چون او قیچقار ریحان هم چقار اویدین بایل چیقیقان کبی تعظیم ابچون مهمان سیله تدیم کام انسند العمر از انکه زباشد یا ماده
چنانکه در حیرة الابرار در وصف اسب گوید شعر جنبش کردون کورونان توسینی اوی کیم بودوب یا بجار آتینك خرمنی
خرمن او لی بولمانا نیمو چون مدلش دایر ایتار سیر و توز اتیا سر خرام و دیگر در مقاله بیستم در وصف خانه فریدون گوید شعر
تهری دین ارشی ریان کوردی بیم اوردی باشین اوی سوتی ایچکان بیتم سیم تام برج ثور است چهارم شاکاو بود و اینکه شا
کاهرا اهل ایران اود نیل با بالعکس نویسند از اغلاط و لغو است زیرا که اوی بمعنی گاو باشد و او بمعنی نهره است که آنرا بعربی مراغ
گویند پنجم آرامست از گاو بدن ششم آرامست از زخم و تن هفتم ارامست از مسامحت کردن چنانکه در ذیل مصدر اویناق گذشت
او یا بفتح یا بالف کشیده شیء کمچه را گویند و آنرا سیکیل هم نامند اویات دو معنی دارد اول بمعنی شرم و خجالت بود الشاهد
علیه شعر بو کیم تا لیب نور او لکی هر یا احیات منکا حیات تا المامیش از بحکه ا اویات منکا و له شعر چو قویلیم عشق آتی
هر بیلدو ده بوانه دین داغی ثیای قرها در مجنون بلبل و پروانه دین داغی جیچین کانه بولدم عشق اله آشنا الغدی بو انشکا
آشنا الار دین اویات سیکانه دین داغی دوم بمعنی عیب و فضاحت باشد چنانکه گوید شعر کوپ اسروانسین اید یرکل اویات تو
قولوم دین توشوب سیبسا پیمانه ماکه و همچنین در عنوان یکی از مقطعات نوشته که خطش تراش قیلوردین یار اماسلیغ اتبا
قیلور و یارا ردیماکین اویات بیلوش و بمعنی اول نیز استعمال میشود چنانکه در خاتمه حیرة الابرار فرماید شعر کیما یویادی
زمان حیات قیلغانیم ایش کیلماکان آندین اویات اویا تیلیغ بمعنی شرمنده و عیبناك باشد الشاهد علیه بالمعنی الاول شعر
هر اید آتین تریکلیك دین او یاتلیغ مین ولیك مبند اوی قیصر احل بولیشه اهمال ایلامیش او یا ز بسکون زای هوز نیز کوی

خوبکر باشد که آنرا اعراب بغداد زنبران کویند ونیز پشه را نامند اوبالت بسکون کاف پوست شکوده بکار میباشد
باشد که جمع کرده پوستین دوزند و پوست سرآنرا چوقلوق کویند اوباکو استخوان پهلو بود وبفتح الفین مستعملست چنانکه
در الف مفتوحه کذشت اوبان بسکون نون جلوله باشد وآنرا تزکین هم نامند اوبداجی بسکون یا وفتح دال وکسر
جیم عجمی خادم رئیس شرع را کویند که برای تعلیم آداب صوم وصلوة بدهات رود اوبداق جائی بکمر وصنا که بود که در آن
آن علف وکیاه دوشیده باشد اوبیال بسکون یا و لام وفتح سین مهمله بالف کشیده اتراک روم شخصی را کویند که هر چه
شود فهمیده بلا تصور تصدیق کند اوبغاغ واویغاق بمعنی بیدار بود چنانکه در مقاله بیستم از حیرة الابرار کوید شعر
توشه بن حوری که پیچان ایروث اوبغلغ ایتار مضمر که شیطان ایرمز اوبغاغلیق سیدلری چنانکه در صحیفه سیاره کوید
شعر دیرمین ایلاجی مرحمه بیر طلب نظر نینک کوزینی آه کیم اوبغاغو بختیم کوز آچماس اوبقودین اوبغور بسکون یا
قرشت وضم غین معجمه است کفته اند که در زمانی که میان اوغوز خان وپدرو اعمام جهت دین وملکت نزاع افتاد بعضی از اقربا
جانب اوغوز را کرفتند وخدمت ایشان را اوبغور لقب نهاد یعنی تابع وپیوست ومؤلف ظفرنامه کفته که معنی اوبغور پیوستن وبا
همدیکر است ومؤلف تاریخ حبیب السیر تقریری کرده احوال ایدی قوت حاکم آن طایفه که در عهد چنکیزخان بوده اوبغور
الف ضبط کرده الحاصل نام طایفه ایست از اتراک اوزبکیه که منسوب بآن فرقه اند واعجب مایل العزیمات میباشد اوبقو بسکون
بسکون یا ونون وضم ضین معجمه بمعنی بیدار شدن وبرپا بودن وموافق باشد اوبقو خواب را کویند اوبقوجی یعنی خواب ناکسر النوم
چنانکه کوید شعر کیمایان خالیفه کوزنا الماس عجب یوقیکیم ایرمش اول قرکوز آلا انجیم شال لیلیت اوبقوجی اوری قیزی
خادمه وکنیز حرم را کویند اوری قیزلیغ یعنی خدمتکاری حرم چنانکه در صحیفه سیاره کوید شعر بار جاخادملاری پیکلیغ
باشوروب کوندر ارجری تیکلیغ پری اوری قیزلیغی اخدمت کوش زلان جون کیم پریلیک برو روپوش اوبکا بسکون یا وفتح
کاف بمعنی قهر وخشم بود اوبکالیک یعنی خشمناک وقهرآلود اوبلوق باشباع ضمه وسکون یا وقاف وضم لام را نیز کویند
آنرا بعربی مخدّ نامند اوبلوک بسکون یا وکاف وضم لام بمعنی خوار باشد چنانکه در توحید کوید شعر ذاتی ولکو
توللت اوب سینکین منکی کین برکید عالم بوعالم ایجرا اوبلوک قولونک حاجبله آدم اوبله بفتح لام هما زده بمعنی ادلاو
دت ظهور را کویند وهم بترکی درو بمعنی مهمان بود و باشباع ضمه بلغت مغولی بمعنی شغل وکار باشد اوبیاق بدو معنی آمده اول
انکشوانه خیالی را کویند که از استخوان وغیر آن درست نمایند استاد علیه شعر کوز اسرو تیکیم آیینک اوبیامغه
بیلمان کیم کونعم آجی ایکین آندا پاسونکاک مواپکین دوم قبله را نامند وسه معنی مصلحی نیز دارد چنانکه در ذیل اشتقاق
نوشته شد اوبیه بسکون یا وفتح میم حانوه خیک وملک بود که آنرا تولوم هم کویند وبعربی زق کویند اوبین بسکون
یا ونون بمعنی بازی وهزالت وآنرا اویون هم خوانند اوبناش معشوقه را کویند واوبناشلیغ یعنی معشوقه داری و
معشوقبازی چنانکه در قطعات کوید شعر چه نوکر کابر دینکا خانزت نیه کیلیب تیلسه خدمت نیغ قولداشلیغ
بیل انداق که جنونک غمه بر تانک ملاقی نیه ایساکای تیماق اوبناشلیغ اوبناقدرسی بود که آهو آنرا باستاد ویبه
خوابکاه خود ساخته باشد اوبوز بضم یا وسکون زای هوز مطلق بره را خوانند اوبوش بسکون شین قرشت بترکی روم بمعنی
بموج وغیره آمده اوبوق بسکون نشان باشد که در صحرا ها برای علامت بکذارند اوبوت بضم یا وسکون همان اوبن
بمعنی بازی وهزل بود چنانکه کوید شعر اوینابدولتوردی نواسنی کونونک چونی ایرکین اکربو دوراوبون اوبونجی

شعر حلوه قیلدی نظر فضا سید ا:: نوم واوبغاغلیق الراسیدا اوبغاغو یعنی بیدار نشونده الغاهد علیه

بمعنی بازیکر چنانکه در لسان الطیر در تشبیه روزکاه بعرصه شطرنج کوید شعر موبغه بینا دهما فکین دردیم چون
اوبونجی بیلما قیغه میل ایتم اوپوندی بسکون نون وکسر دال بترکی رومی بمعنی مفعل باشد که نا خوانده بمهمان بیانی رود ونیز
بمعنی کاوینه شد وبقا اوپوندی جاک کیبا زا کویند با بلکوار حروف دالف مع الباء من المشفا ایرامالت بسکون باء عجمی وضم
رای مهمله وایراتمالت مع النون همان اوپرالمالت ولوپرالمالت بمعنی کهنه وصند بر باشد که در مضموم الف مذکور شد
ایراتمالت مع التاء مصدر متعدیست بمعنی کهنه کردن اپیتمالت بکسر با وسکون نون بمعنی خیسیدن بود اپیتمالت
مع التاء مصدر متعدیست یعنی خیسانیدن اپیتیبا اپیتیبا وا پیتمیش خیسانیده چنانکه شاهد بر اول در تاریخ
بابری مذکور است که در ذکر ایام محاصره مذکور است کسیمار جالدیری رو تقلیب تراشه سینی دوفه اپیتیب آتنه پوهم الا اپکه
چون اشتقاق آن منتج مایه نبود بزواید امالات نشد باقی صیغ هم نیز بتقویم مواقف قاعده شواول شتوم کرد در تزاحوامد اپیار
بفتح بای عجمی وسکون رای قرشت مثل وعنبر وجوهر خوشبو را کویند اپیار قوزو 2 نام قصبه ایست از مواضع سمرقند
که آنرا شیراز وسیلاجرنا و قوهم نامند ایپک بر وزن زیر لعاب ریشم باشد بعنا چه بترا کویند که بعربی خطیره ابریشم
ایت بکسر با بترکی رومی تاج مرغان بود که آنرا حضانیه اوبوات کویند ایپکین نخ سیاه وبفتح الفین مستعملست چنانکه نمانکه
در مفتوحات الف نوشته شد ایپلیت بسکون یای عجمی وکاف وکسر لام رشته پنبه را نامند ونیز علقوات که آنرا بعلیه رشته
کیشکا
وسو وبعربی عرق مدینی کویند چنانکه در تاریخ المحبه در ذکر خواجه عماد خلج کوید که بوسو رجحت غره تیپ توم کیم هر
رشته رحق بولسا کیم تکلا عرآ تی اپلیک دیرلار چون رشته خواجه نینک تقریر غه باعلا حسا تخلف بر اول اغر بغم بولو
اپلیجات بسکون بای عجمی وکسر لام وفتح جیم بترکی رومی همان رشته بود که مذکور شد مع التاء من المشتقات اپتمالت
بشش معنی آمده اول کردن دوم چیزی را با دست زدن وافکندن سیم کم ومفقود کشتن چهارم پنهان دیدن شدن پنجم بو کردن
وچهار معنی اخیر با اشباع کسره مذکور میکرد دشتم نام کوهیست که ما بین سمرقند وشهرسبز واقعست چنانکه در ذیل حوادث مذکور
خواهد شد اپتی کرده و با الاشباع افکنده مفقود شد پنهان شد بو کرد چنانکه در خاتمه تاریخ الملوک کوید المعنی الاول
شعر دیبا نکیم ما بوالکدی ول هجران جمانز آنیدی ونیکلیغ اپتی نهان المعنی الثانی شعر چو منقدین اپتی آیینک زمتو
کیم الکدی جهاندار لیغ تخته بنی ومعنی ثالث در تبنیهات محبوب القلوب کوید که حق یولیدین جقمغان اپتی وتوزبار زمان مقصود
بتی ومعنی رابع در لیلی مجنون در احوال مجنون فرماید شعر بر لحظه شور ایجیندا اپتی اولموغ دمیدین آنی تیغ اسوک
کردیم چنانکه کوید شعر اپج نوانی بی که منم اپتوک طبیب عشق دین غصه مخمور نیه زنک ایمش باقوت ناب وبا اشباع
افکندیم ومفقود شدیم وپنهان شدیم و بو کردیم اپتار وا اپتا دور میکند و با اشباع می افکند ومفقود میشود وپنهان میشود وبو میکند
وا اپتار بمعنی ماضی ومصدر هم می آید چنانکه در مقاله بیستم از حیرة الابرار در حکایت خواجه حماد بر اپتار بمعنی کم شدن کوید
شعر یوقا اپیدی بو یولدا منکار رهمای تینکری سینی قیلدی آنکا رهنمای یول اپتاری سینی هراسان قیلیب بولیغ هراسیم
آنان قیلیب اپتمایدور ومیکند ونکرده است وباشباع نمی افکند ونیفکنده است ومفقود نمیشود ونشده است وپنهان نشده است
نمیشود وبو نکرده است ونمیکند اپتکان واپتاکان واپتا دورکان کننده وکرده وبا اشباع افکننده وافکنده ومفقود شونده
وپنهان شونده وشده وبو کننده وبو کرده چنانکه بمعنی مفقود شده کوید شعر اول توکان کیم تیلبه را اپتکان کوزوکلکا
اورتادیم تا پیداری نا پیدا اول آزنینک قوالوغیه سیلکورو وبمعنی مصدر نیز می آید چنانکه بمعنی کردن کوید شعر

وصل ایتمك اره عنان تیلنمك اشك دم لادرین * شايل نیم لا دیغیب ایتكان کبی نوأل ایت مایتكیل بكن و باشباع بیفكن و نقود
شو ونهان شو و بوكن الشاهد على الاول المعنى الاول شعر ای كه فضل ایتمك دین اوزنی سر و خلق آزاد ماییت * هر پریشان نقش
منصف نی كاك دیلك شاده ایث ما المعنى الثانی شعر ای خیم صل ایبیب نان شابلایت جسمی كم فرایی منفی بن آمداو
كه برلك كما بر حضر نیز بطر یق تجانس كوید شعر ای رقیب منزنی آنكا كر تو قسانك ایث بز كام رحم ایت آیناك كوبردین ایث
یعنی بار رحم كن واز كوی او كم شو كه چه بار دوز نجه عشقنك شعله سی پرزنی اوز ایلنك سیله اولنا ایلایت یعنی بار ابد كشح
بانطوف بیند لز الشاهد على الثانی المعنى الاول شعر كه كماى شوخ مینی باشینك ایچون بیاد ایتكیل یا باشینكدین ایو
ودوعب بیر بیلی آزاد ایتكیل * وایت بلا اشباع یعنی كوشت و بالاشباع یعنی سك هم باشد چنانكه در جواهر منكور خواهد شد
ایتا وایتماكیل مفرد مخاطب از فعل نهی ایتینك و ایتیكیز و ایتیكلار جمع مخاطب از فعل امر و باشباع یعنی سند شوید
ودر این معنی با امر حضد ایتیماك اشتراك دارد چنانكه بیاید ایتمك ایتمانكیز و ایتمانكلار جمع مخاطب از فعل نهی ایتامین و
ایتادین ما بناء بر معنا ایتادام میكنم نفی متكلم ومنفقود میشوم ونهان میشوم و بو میكنم ایتادیم ایتمادیم كردیم و باشباع
انكندیم ومنفقود شدیم ونهان شدیم و بو كردیم ایتاكوم نخواهم كرد و باشباع نخواهم افكند و منفقود نخواهم شد و نهان نخواهم
شد و بو نخواهم كرد ایتاتان وایتماس میب میكنم و باشباع نمی افكنم ومنفقود نمیشوم ونهان نمیشوم و بو نمیكنم ایتاسین ایتاز
وایتاسه میكند و باشباع می افكند ومنفقود میشود ونهان میشود و بو میكند الشاهد على الاول المعنى الاول
شعر كل نار یتماده بلبل چون كم كوردی كلكشت ایتاسین كلشن را ایتیب وایتیبان ایتمش كرده و باشباع افكنده
ومنفقود شده ونهان شده و بو كرده چنانكه شاهد برای اول این معنى نهان شده كوید شعر بر یكیت كلكلتیما حسن
سی چو كم كلاج ایتیب ببحهد خلق دین اولایث وشاهد برای ثالث این معنى منفقود شده كوید شعر بلبه كونكلوم كاب
زلفونك ایچون ایتمش ایدی كیجه میخانه ارامت و پریشان تا بینم و معنى بو كرده در حین الابرار در وصف شراب فرماید
الشاهد على الاول شعر سیل سویین تا پیا ایچب مل كوش ساقی تاشین تا پا ایتیب كلكی و بیز دماغ انسه سكندری بوستان
كوید شعر كل عطری بو ز یلی لیق بو لكیتیب بو ز ایل لیك اولوك جان تا بسی چون ایتیب ایتیب و ایتیبان یعنی بنیل
هم می آید چنانكه بیاید ایتمیشانك كرده و باشباع افكنده ومنفقود شده ونهان شده و بو كرده ایتماس نمیكند و
باشباع نمی افكند ومنفقود نمیشود و بو نمیكند و بمعنى فاعل و مصدر منفی هم می آید ایتماسی بمعنى مصدر مثبت و مصدر منفی
ایتمادین بمعنى مصدر مثبت و مصدر منفی می آید چنانكه بمعنى كردن كوید در فصولی بالملاة الرومیه شعر سنی در شوق الیم
تا شی ایتمادین عالم زار جسمم اشك كرد اندی نهان او لسه بلد ایتیب ایتما و ایتماك آیتما نمیتوان كرد و باشباع
نمیتوان افكند ومنفقود نمیتوان شد ونهان نمیتوان شد و بو نمیتوان كرد ایتا ایتیا كرده كرده و باشباع افكنده افكنده
ومنفقود شده ونهان شده و بو كان و بدون تكرار هم مستعمل ایتای ایتایین بكنم و بكند و بكنید كردیم
شاهد برای اول لحم مناجات كوید كه نوعاید موجود ایتای دینانك كن فیكون عبارتی انكا كافی و باشباع بیفكنم و بیفكند
و بیفكنید ومنفقود شوم وشوید و شوید و بو كنم و كند و كنید ایتا ایتاكا و ایتكای بز و ایتالر ایتالیك بكنیم الشاهد على الثانی
من یا بر بادشاه شعر خوش اولكم نهان فضلی بیعد شاده * بو لغان جان لبنك سلبی نازی آماده * كز بویلنانا اسباب ایتا لیك
ویكانه * میندین كرك وطعام وسیندین باده * و باشباع بیفكنیم ومنفقود شویم ونهان شویم و بو كنیم ایتماسا لكوا ایتماكاین

~~ایتكای بز و ایتالر ایتالیك بكنیم الشاهد على الثانی من یا بر بادشاه شعر خوش اولكم نهان فضلی بیعد شاده * بو لغان جان لبنك اسلامه~~
~~نازی آماده * كز بویلنانا اسباب ایتا لیك ویكانه * میندین كرك وطعام وسیندین باده * و باشباع بیفكنیم ومنفقود شویم ونهان~~
و بو كنیم ایتماسلك و ایتماكاین و ایتماكای ایتماسلانك نمی كنیم چنانكه شاهد برای این معنى نكیم كوید شعر كون بیلك
منفق نجه هوی و نالامی چیتماییلك كوب بیلك چقنایی بیكونیكم بولغاینی بیر یله بت ایتكایلی برای كردن و تاكرده بولسانك
برای افكندن و تا افكنده و برای منفقود شدن و برای نهان شدن و تا شده و برای بو كردن و تا كرده ایتكاچ بمعنى كردن و بمعنى افكندن
و بمعنى منفقود شدن و بمعنى نهان شدن و بمعنى بو كردن ایتكوچی فاعل مضارع منكور چنانكه در حیرة الابرار در توحید
كند كوید شعر جسم سپهرنی سیر ایتكوچی روح تو باشنی سیر ایتكوچی ایتكوم خواهم كرد چنانكه در صفه بیان
علم مدلا ادام كوید كه توقف قیلوریی فهم ایتكوم * و كه كیدلكونك ولیك سیر كیتكوم و باشباع خواهم افكند و منفقود خواهم شد
ونهان خواهم شد و بو خواهم كرد ایتكونك خواهی كرد و باشباع خواهی افكند و منفقود خواهی شد و نهان خواهی شد و بو خواهی
ایتكوسی خواهد كرد چنانكه كوید شعر چون لحد كوب قضا پیت ایتكوسی توسن لعینك * توسن كردون ركابینكه تكا
بولدی توت و باشباع خواهد افكند و منفقود خواهد شد و نهان خواهد شد و بو خواهد كرد ایتكای و ایتای و ایتسا و ایتسون و لیتدن
بكند و باشباع بیفكند و منفقود شود ونهان شود و بو كند چنانكه شاهد برای اول این معنى منفقود كوشود كوید شعر
رشكدین دیرمین كه مهر ایتسون سپهر ایاینیدین * ما رشك ایتكای ایمابوان اچرا آینیك یا بیدین * ایتكویلیك ایتاید ایتكای
و همچنانكه كند چنانكه شاهد برای اول این معنى لسان الطیر كوید شعر دم دجامین توت مینی زار ایتكودیك * عشق صهبای
كونكلومنا كلدار ایتكودیك * یعنی دم دجام را بمن بكر همچنانكه مرا زار كند و همچنانكه دم عشق دل من كلزار كند و باشباع افكنده نی
و همچنانكه بیفكند و منفقود شدنی و همچنانكه منفقود شود ونهان شدنی و همچنانكه نهان شود و بو كردنی و همچنانكه بو كند
ایتیلماك مع اللام مصدر انفعالست یعنی كرده شدن و باشباع افكنده شدن و منفقود شدن و از صیغه مشتقات بمعنى
معنى استعمال میشود ایتیلدی كرده شد چنانكه ذكر ملوك عجم كوید كه آرای احوال ایدین اجمال طریقی بیله اختصار ایتیلدی
افكنده شد و منفقود شد ایتیلسا كرده شود چنانكه در باب حاز محبوب القلوب در ذكر عشق كوید كه هر بر یدا اگر كتا بلار
تیلسا و مجلد لار ترتیب ایتیلسا و باشباع افكنده شود و منفقود شود و باقی صیغ برین نهج موافق شق اول الام اشتقاق یا بم
ایتیشماك مع الشین مصدر مفاعلاتست یعنی با یكدیگر كلكری كردن و همدیكر را بادست افكندن و از مصدر مشتقات بمعنى
می آید ایتورماك بكون تای اول وضم تای ثانی مصدر متعدیست یعنی متعدی كرد افكند انیدن و از صیغه بمعنى
مستعملست و متعدی كم شدن ونهان شدن ایتورماك بالای واحد و ایتكورماك استعمال میشود چنانكه بیاید ایتاكر تیماك
بكاری منادرت كردن ایتا باشلاماق بكار شروع كردن چنانكه در باب حیم از محبوب القلوب در ذكر نوهد كوید كه
فوایدی هر منداینا باشلادهای ایتا نساق باشباع دست زدن و بر انكیختن چنانكه بمعنى مفرد مخاطب از فعل امر در صیغه
در استا نهنا فراقلیم سیم و مكالمه حكیم ابا سعد و نقل حلم كوید شعر زال غینك كوكسكا اور و بایتاسانك كره بولوم
حیم وضال ایتورماك بضم تا و سكون را قرشت ایتكورماك بكون تا و را وضم كاف منفقود كم كردن ایتوردی و ایتكوردی
كم كردی الشاهد على الاول شعر ای تیلبه كونكول حیقاد نیك و لزلف حمدین * كو یا كه قرانقو كیجه دا یولنی ایتوردونك ایتوك
و ایتكو مایدیكم بمیكند و نكرده است ایتوردوك و ایتكوردوك كم كردیم ایتوردو و لار ایتورایدرلار ایتكوردولار و ایتكورایدر كم كرد كند

وایتوردود وایتکوردود بمعنی فاعل و مصدر منفی نیز می آید ایتورکان وایتوردوکان وایتوردوکان وایتکورکان وایتکوردوکان و
ایتکوردوکان کرکند و کم کرده الشاهد علی الاول المعنی الثانی شعر عشق صحراسیدا ر افاقیل ایتورکان ارسنیی بولدیلار
و بید پروانه ایتر اتسبت و بمعنی مصدر هم می آید ایتور وایتور کیل وایتکور وایتکور کیل مفرد مخاطب از فعل امر ایتورنا وایتوریا کر
وایتکورنا وایتکورنا کیل مفرد مخاطب از فعل نهی ایتورونک وایتورونکو وایتورونکلار وایتکورونک وایتکورونکو وایتکورونکلار
جمع مخاطب از فعل امر ایتوریزلار وایتوریزلار وایتوریزلار وایتکورنکلار وایتکوریزلار جمع مخاطب از فعل نهی ایتورمان
ایتورماس مین وایتکورمان وایتکورماس مین کم نمیکنم ایتورامین وایتورورمین وایتوراورمین ایتورورمن وایتکورامین وایتکوروورمین
ایتکوراورمین وایتکورورمین کم میکنم ایتوروردوم وایتکوروردوم ایتورکیم وایتکورکیم کم کردم ایتورماکوم
ایتکورماکوم کم نخواهم کرد ایتورمیش وایتورمیشور وایتکورمیش وایتکورمیشور کم کرده ایتورمیشانک وایتکورمیشانک
کم کرده ایتورماس وایتکورماس کم نمیکند و بمعنی فاعل و مصدر منفی هم می آید ایتورماسی وایتکورماسی کم کردنش و نکردنش ایتورمادین
وایتکورمادین از کم کردن و کم نکرده ایتوروب بولماس وایتوریا بولماس وایتورماک آلماس وایتکوروب بولماس وایتکوریا بولماس و
ایتکورماک آلماس کم نمیتوان کرد ایتورا آلماس وایتکورا آلماس کم نمیتواند کرد ایتورا وایتکورا ایتکوراکم کان کم کنان و
نکرار هم مستعملست ایتورای وایتورایین وایتکورای وایتکورایین کم کنم و کند و کنی و کرده ایتورسانک وایتورکاینز وایتورکای
ایتورالینک وایتکورسانک وایتکورکاینز وایتکورکای وایتکورالینک کم کنیم ایتورکالی وایتکورکالی برای کم کردن و تا کم کرده
ایتورکاچ وایتکورکاچ چون کم کرد و کند ایتورکوچی وایتکورکوچی کم کننده ایتورکوچنی ایتورکانچه وایتکورکوچنی وایتکورکانچه
وایتکورکانچه تا کم کردن و بمقدار کم کردن ایتورکوم وایتکورکوم کم خواهم کرد چنانکه در لیلی مجنون در پیغام دادن لیلی
بپدر مجنون گوید الشاهد علی الاول شعر خیلینکنی بوداشت دین ایتورکوم سونکرا داغی تنغ قهر سورکوم ایتورکونک
ایتکورکونک کم خواهی کرد ایتورکوسی وایتکورکوسی کم خواهد کرد ایتورکولونک وایتکورکولونک کم کردنی ایتورکای وایتورکاسیسا
وایتورکاسیسا وایتورسون وایتورلیت وایتکورکای وایتکورسا وایتکورسون وایتکورلیت کم کند ایتورکودیک وایتوروردیک
وایتکورکودیک وایتکوروردیک کم کردیم و هچنانکه کم کند ایتیماک باشباع و بکسر تای قرشت شد شدن ایتیدی شد
ایتیدولع شد شدیم ایتیر و ایتیدور شد میشود و ایتیر بمعنی فاعل و مصدر هم می آید ایتیماید و شدنی و ناشدنی
ایتکان و ایتیرکان و ایتیدورکان شد شونده و شده و بمعنی مصدر هم می آید ایتی وایتیکیل مفرد مخاطب از فعل امر ایتما وایتماکیل
مفرد مخاطب از فعل نهی ایتینک وایتینکیز وایتینکلار جمع مخاطب از فعل امر و بصیغه ایتیماک لم اشتراک دارد چنانکه
ایتیمانک وایتیمانکیز وایتیمانکلار جمع مخاطب از فعل نهی ایتیمان وایتیماس مین شد نمیشوم ایتیمن وایتیرمین وایتیدورمین وایتیرام
شد میشوم ایتیرمن وایتیماکیم شد نخواهم شد ایتیماکوم شد نخواهم شد ایتیمیش وایتیمیش شده وایتیب وایتیبان
بمعنی شدن و کرده شده هم می آید ایتیمیشانک شده ایتیماس شد نمیشود چنانکه گوید شعر ایشکینی
کوروبتیز بولور کونکلی همانده آری ایتیماس چونکه سوی بالاسا فولاد و بمعنی فاعل و مصدر منفی هم می آید ایتیماسی شد
و نشدنش ایتیمادین از شد شدن و شدن ایتیب بولماس وایتیا بولماس وایتیماک آلماس شد نمیتوان شد وایتیب بولماس
بعضی بجای اینکه کرد و بنهایت نمیتوان شد هم آمده ایتا آلماس شد نمیتواند شد ایتا ایتا شد شده شده و بمعنی تکرار هم
مستعملست ایتا ایتیین شد شوم و شود و شوی و شده ایتیسانک وایتیکاینز وایتیکای و ایتیلی وایتیلینک شدیم

ایتکالی برای شد شدن و تا شده ایتکاچ چون شد شد شود ایتکوچی شد شونده ایتکوچنی وایتکانچه
تا شد شدن و بمقدار شد شدن ایتکوم شد خواهم شد ایتکونک شد خواهی شد ایتکوسی شد خواهد شد
ایتکولونک شد شدنی ایتکای وایتیسا وایتسون وایتیلیت شد شود ایتکودیک وایتیوردیک شد شدیم و هچنانکه شد
ایتیمالک بکسر تای اول و سکون تای ثانی مصدر متعدی بمعنی شد کردن چنانکه گوید شعر ترا ز امر محمد لاین ایتیماک
ایشینک حیا تخلیق کیسکان قیا قیا تقشینک و طالع هوی این لفظ را مصدر لازم دانسته ایتیماق نوشته سهو کرده
ایتتی شد کرد چنانکه در سلیمه و تحفه گوید که بزرد نینک سپل آشنا دن اعندین جبار لیغ نا سده نا ده معنی عنه
نه نیشین ایتیتی ایتیتور وایتیتاد کنند میکند وایتیتور بمعنی فاعل و مصدر هم می آید چنانکه بمعنی مصدری در فصل بیت و شینم
از محبوب القلوب در ذکر صوفیان ریایی گوید که سوالی طمع نیشین ایتیتورکالی مو هان ایتیتماس شد نمیکند بمعنی فاعل و مصدر
منفی هم می آید چنانکه بمعنی فاعل گوید شعر ایرلیت ینو چون دو ره شاخ اوزره کلبن برکی سوهان دیلیت ایتیماس بولسا ملبنک
ایچونغنچه سیکانین ثمی اگر غنچه سکان خود را برای جان بلبل تند نکند باشد چرا برک کلبن در شاخ مثل سوهان در شتاس
ایتکالی برای تند کردن و تا تند کرده چنانکه بمعنی اول گوید شعر بلادا را چو مین اولدم بلا مبتلی لا اینیغ نی تانک ایتکالی
لوح نزلیم اولنا بیلادی و تای صنع برانستاق موافق قاعده شود اول ماضی فحرف تا اشتقاق بی یاید ایتاکلاماک ده معنی
دارد اول آنکه دامن زدن دوم جنیزا در دامن کردن ایتاکلادی دامن زد و در دامن کرد ایتاکلادوک دامن زدیم و در دامن
کردیم ایتاکلار وایتاکلایدور دامن میزند و در دامن میکند وایتاکلار بمعنی فاعل و مصدر هم می آید ایتاکلاماید دامن نزند
و نزده است و در دامن نمیکند و نکرده است ایتاکلاکان وایتاکلارکان وایتاکلایدورکان دامن زننده و دامن زده و در دامن کننده
و در دامن کرده و بمعنی مصدر هم می آید ایتاکلا وایتاکلاکیل مفرد مخاطب از فعل امر ایتاکلاما وایتاکلاماکیل مفرد مخاطب
از فعل نهی ایتاکلانک وایتاکلانکیز وایتاکلانکلار جمع مخاطب از فعل امر ایتاکلامانک وایتاکلامانکیز وایتاکلامانکلار جمع مخاطب از فعل نهی
ایتاکلامان وایتاکلاماس مین دامن نمیزنم و در دامن نمیکنم ایتاکلامین وایتاکلارمین وایتاکلایدورمین وایتاکلارام دامن میزنم و در دامن میکنم
ایتاکلاکیم وایتاکلاماکیم دامن نزدنم و در دامن کردنم ایتاکلاماکوم دامن نخواهم زد و در دامن نخواهم کرد ایتاکلاب وایتاکلاب
وایتاکلامیش دامن زده و در دامن کرده چنانکه شاهد بر اول از معنی ثانی در مخزن گوید شعر کیلدی
ایتاکلاب کمرشا هوار قیلسا قبول اولوغ قولیده نی نهضول ایتاکلامیشانک دامن زده و در دامن کرده ایتاکلاماس دامن
نمیزند و در دامن نمیکند و بمعنی فاعل و مصدر منفی هم می آید ایتاکلاماسی دامن زدنش و نزدنش و در دامن کردنش و نکردنش
ایتاکلامادین از دامن زدن و دامن نزده و از دامن کردن و در دامن نکرده ایتاکلاب بولماس وایتاکلایا بولماس وایتاکلاماک آلماس دامن
نمیتوان زد و در دامن نمیتوان کرد ایتاکلاماک آلماس دامن نمیتواند زد و در دامن نمیتواند کرد ایتاکلایو وایتاکلای ایتاکلایو دامن زنان
و در دامن کنان و بدون تکرار هم مستعملست ایتاکلای وایتاکلایین دامن بزنم و بزند و بزنی و زده و در دامن کنم و کند و کنی و کرده
ایتاکلاسانک وایتاکلاکاینز وایتاکلاکای و ایتاکلالی وایتاکلالینک دامن بزنیم و در دامن کنیم ایتاکلاکالی برای دامن
زده و تا دامن زده و برای در دامن کرده و تا در دامن کرده ایتاکلاکاچ چون دامن زد و زند و چون در دامن کرد و کند ایتاکلاکوچی
دامن زننده و در دامن کننده ایتاکلاکوچنی وایتاکلاکانچه تا دامن زدن و بمقدار دامن زدن و تا در دامن کردن و بمقدار در دامن
کردن ایتاکلاکوم دامن خواهم زد و در دامن خواهم کرد ایتاکلاکونک دامن خواهی زد و در دامن خواهی کرد ایتاکلاکوسی

دامن خواهند زد و در دامن خواهد کرد اتاکلاکو لوک دامن زدن و در دامن کردنی اتاکلاکای اتاکلاسار اتاکلاهون ه

اتاکلادیک دامن زده بود و در دامن کند اتاکلاتمالک مع التا مصدر متعدیست یعنی دیگری را به دامن زدن آتش و در دامن کردن

امر کردن و صیغ آن با تای قرشت اشتقاق می یابد اتاکلاشمالک مع الشین مصدر مفاعله است یعنی با هم آتش را دامن زدن

و چیزی را با یکدیگر در دامن کردن و صیغ آن با شین اشتقاق می یابد اتاکلانمالک مع النون مصدر انفعالست یعنی دامن زده

شدن و در دامن کرده شدن و صیغ آن با نون اشتقاق می یابد من الجوامد اتک دو معنی دارد اول ... را گویند

ماند چنانکه مطربوتچاس گوید شعر ... آیت تا ...

و چهار معنی دیگر دارد که در ذیل الف مصدر اتیمالک نگارش یافت اتیالک بمعنی ... بود که آنرا بعربی ذیل گویند و بالجاندامنه

و کناره ... هم نامند چنانکه در خسرو و شیرین در ... فرهاد گوید شعر اتیالک ...

ابردی ... نوشیدلار ... خرم و شاد بولوبلار ... اتا ... عب الکشک بود

چنانکه گوید شعر کرایت ... قیلاالتقابو آتی تاک ... آزادوزوی

هم خوانند اتالکو پرنده ایست شکاری که آنرا بفارسی چرخ و بعربی صقر گویند اتاد ون بفتح تا و ضم واو و سکون نون

مغولی بمعنی کبک باشد که تیهو معرب آنست بالیعی ... جانوریست در آب که ... شود و بفارسی ...

و بعربی ... گویند ایت برات نام پادشاهیست معروف که او غوز خان با او جنگ کرده شکست یافت بالاخره

شده ایت بورنی نام نواییست که آنرا در اصفهان ... نامند و آن ... مثل ... و ... گلش

ایت ... ترکی ... بود ایت خیابی ... ایست ... آنرا بعربی ...

ایت دیرنا سکی ... و آن کوشتی بود که در ... چشم ...

و آنرا بفارسی ناخنه و بعربی ظفره نامند ایت سیکا سک ... بود ایت نماناصت شپرک باشد که آنرا بعربی خفاش

خوانند ... باصطلاح ... بمعنی ... باشد اتیمالک نام کوهیست که مابین سمرقند و شهر سبز

واقعست و معانی ... هم دارد که در ذیل ... حروف نگارش یافت ... باشباع کسره و کسر تای قرشت

دارد اول بمعنی مقصود ... شده است دویم بمعنی ... باشد الشاهد علیه شعر ...

... شعر ...

... چنانکه ... فرستادن ...

... شعر ... ایسیکی ...

تای قرشت و کاف ... و آنرا ... هم میگویند مع الجیم من المشتقات ایچماک بمعنی

بمعنی شرب و نوشیدن باشد چنانکه گوید شعر ایچماکیم زاهدا ... الفا

مودین ... هم گویند ایچتی نوشید ایچتوک نوشیدیم ایچادوا ... نوشید

می آید ایچاید ... نوشند و نوشید چنانکه شاهد ...

گوید شعر ... شاهد ...

در تاریخ بابری مذکور است که فلان ... ایچادورکان ... بمعنی ...

می آید چنانکه ... شاهد ... نوشید

که شیخ ... ایچادورکان ... آلیب ... ایلیکند

... مفرد مخاطب ... مذکور خواهد شد ایچما

ایچماکیل مفرد مخاطب ... جمع مخاطب ...

الشاهد علی الاول شعر ... لفظ ایچما ...

ایچماسمین نمینوشم ایچمابیم ... ایچماکوم ... نوشید ایچما

... چنانکه شاهد ... گوید شعر ...

... نوشیده ایچماسا ... نوشید و بمعنی

و مصدر ... هم می آید ایچماک ... از نوشیدن و نوشیده چنانکه بمعنی نوشیدنکو

من ... شعر ... ایچادین ...

ایچمان ... نمیتوان نوشید ایچا آلماس نمیتواند نوشید ایچا ... نوشان ... ایچای

ایچامین بنوشم و بنوشد و بنوشی و بنوشید ... برای نوشیدن ... نوشید

ایچکاج چون نوشید و بنوشد ایچکوچی نوشنده الشاهد علیه شعر ای نوائی ...

... نوشیدن ... چنانکه شاهد ...

بمعنی ... شعر ...

و شاهد ثالث ... گوید شعر ...

دین ایچکوم ... نوشید ... خواهی نوشید ... خواهد نوشید ایچکولوک نوشیدنی و بمعنی

... باشد چنانکه در فرهاد و شیرین ... گوید شعر ...

... ایچکاندین ...

ایچدیک بنوشد الشاهد علی الخامس شعر ... ایچدیک ...

... ایچورمالک ... ایچور ...

... نوشاندن ... ایچوردی نوشانید ...

هم می آید ... نوشاند ... نوشانند و نوشانید ...

هم می آید ایچور و ایچورکیل مفرد مخاطب ... مفرد مخاطب ... ایچوروب ...

جمع مخاطب ... جمع مخاطب ... ایچورامین ...

ایچوروب ... نوشانید ... نوشانید ...

ایچورمیش نوشانیده ... نوشانیده ... ایچورماسی ... نوشانیدن و

نوشانیدن ... از نوشانیدن و نوشانید ... نمیتوان نوشانید ایچورا آلماس

ایچورا آلماس ... نمیتواند نوشانید ایچورا ... نوشانیده ...

مستعملت ایچوراری وایچوراییمن نصحاک نوشاند ونوشانیدن ونوشانید وایچوراشیرا ایچوکاپیز وایچورکاینر وایچورلمار ایچوراینک
نوشانیم ایچوکلی برای نوشانیدن وتا نوشانیدن ایچورکاج چون نوشانید ونوشاند چنانکه در فرهاد وشیرین کوید
فرهاد کوید شعر لب خطن سوتن ایچورکاج دایم عشق بولوب هر کم هری سرمایه عشق ایچورکوچی نوشانیدن ایچورکوچه
وایچورکونمچوا ایچورکابچه نوشانیدن وبعقدم نوشانیدن ایچورکوم خواهم نوشانید ایچورکونک خواهی نوشانید
ایچورکوسی خواهد نوشانید ایچورکولوک نوشانید ایچوکلی وایچورار وایچورناطا ایچورسون وایچورماک بنوشاند ایچورکودوک
ایچورمدوک نوشانیدن ویچنانکه بنوشاند ایچیشما لت مع التنزیع مصدر مفاعله است یعنی باهم نوشیدن وصیغ آن موافق
قاعده شق وللتنزاشتقاق می‌یابد ایچیلماک مع الکلم مصدر انفعال است یعنی نوشیده شدن وصیغ آن بالالام اشتقاق
یابد ایچغیسنا تنغ بکون جیم عجمی ونون وکسر غین معجمه بمعنی شدن من کل ونوعر ملکاشه شعر ایلیک دین ایچغینب
شالدی نانکیغاب باربر اغین تیشلادی الدی وباتی صیغ برین فیح موافق شق ول اشتقاق می‌یابد ایچمیر تاق بترکی روی بعضی
یعنی برجستن کلو وآن عبارت از فواق زدن باشد من الجولمد ایچ برون هیچ یعنی اندرون وباطن بود الشاهد علیه
شعر می ایچ دهر ایچرا کیم ایچ سری دین آنکلادی دبنان مزی ایرورهرزونینک ماهیتی خورشید بن بهم در معنی
ایشی تیرین هم دین شد یعنی ایراث از نوشیدن چنانکه کذشت ایچیا همشیره بزرک را کویند وبلغت مغولی یعنی
وخداوند بود ایچ آغا باصطلاح رومیه خدمتکار امرد باشد که آنرا ایچ اوغلان هم کویند واتراک توران بمعنی
چوره نامند ایچ آغز یعنی مرض اسهال بود چنانکه در سنایا لمعجبه مذکور ابراهیم خواص کوید که ایچ اغزینی سیله اونی ایچد
هر جلسه که نفاسا بولورای یعنی غسل قیلورایردی ایجان بفتح جیم مشدده وسکون نون کندم وکنجد را بود که بریان کرده کویند
بیشیرنی امیخته مجموع ایچ اوغلان همان ایچ آغا باشد که در فوق مذکور شد ایچره یعنی درمیان الشاهد علیه شعر
مشکین خطینک اول یوزه کیچکلکون هرقایچره توعنبری کویاکه ساچلدی شفق ایچره ایچرکو بکسر جیم عجمی وسکون رای قرشت
وضم کاف تکلفی بزرای نامند ایچقیرتق بترکی رومی برجستن کلو باشد که آنرا بفارسی غنک وبعربی فواق کویند ایچکا
یعنی نازکتر من لطفی شعر قیلدیم دینام ایچکارک سیلینی بوقمتوری کیشی نینک که قیل وقالی ایچکارک بسکون رای ولی فتح
رای ثانی بمعنی اندرون تر باشد چنانکه در لیلی مجنون در احوال مجنون کوید شعر کونکلوم اوبن ای تا یغوبرلان جسم
اولینه تر اغوبرلان ایچکارک اوی ایچره غصه تاپی بل فرقت اوتی سنک التهابی ایچکارک بیکسر رای یعنی اندرون بیکسر
یعنی شرب ونجمع بود چنانکه در لیلی مجنون در عرض مجنون قل کوید شعر کونکلوم اوبن ای تا یغوبرلان جسم ~~...~~
برلان ~~ایچکارک اول ایچره غصه تاپی~~ شعر آیین طریقه قوید لار بیزنی ایچکوایری بچه کونه کوندوز ایچکولوک یعنی شراب
نوشی ونوشیدنی باشد ومست وشرابخواره هم کویند چنانکه شاهد آن در ذیل مصدر ایچماک کذشت ایچکی یعنی اندرونی
چنانکه لطفی کوید شعر اول ایدزینک دولتی دین توغدی کونکلدا نینک کونی حسن طالع کور کراولد ایچکا ایچکی بجری
ایچماک بوستین را کویند وبمعنی نوشیدن هم باشد چنانکه در ذیل اشتقاق مذکور شد ایچون بضم جیم عجمی بمعنی لام تعلیل
وبای سببیت است الشاهد علیه شعر کوزلارینک ادرم ایچون قیلسا عتاب ایرمار عجب باربعین کیم بولوب الارزنارنک
مزاج واوچون بضم الف نیز بهمین معنی مستعملت ایچن ارا بکسر جیم عجمی ایچن آره یعنی در وسط ودرمیانه الشاهد علی الاوکیر
جان وکونکول نچه دیدی اسرلی اونزینی کیلکلاج اولیک وه یانا قوزغا لیشتی لارکه کلاج آنی ایچن ارا الشاهد علی الثانی

فی الترجیعات شعر نچه مغفلین ایشاب دیدیم می ایچون تیلاسی ایچن آره منکانه ونیز در تاریخ الملوک مذکور اسکندر
کوید که ملوک طولیغ ترا بران ربچه اول بعضی قیلدی کیم ایچ بونا آلتمیش مسلیفه جه الارا ایچن را و از تلع قیلیب
تا بینیلی ضربی متمادی مع ایچا اختیار مرد معتبر کم نیک را کویند چنانکه در تاریخ بابری مذکور است
که اولوغ اختیار کیشی ایدی وبیان اتراک والعراب دهم نیز مصطلحات است ومجاز امشلیغ وروشنی قوم را هم کویند وبمعنی مروت
اخشید بکون خا وذال معجمه وکسر شین قرشت پادشاهان فرغانه را کویند ومؤلف تاریخ روضة الصفا کفته که بمعنی
لسان الترک ملک الملوک مع الدال من المشتقات ایدلاماک بوکرد ایدلاماک بو کردان ایدلادی بو کرد ایدلا ایدلا بو میکند ایدلار
تا مل میکند هم می آید ایدلاماینور بوعنکند ودیکر صیغ مشتقات ایدکانوار ایدکوار نیالکار بوکردن وبو کرده وبمعنی ...
هم می آید ایدلا وایدلا کیل مفرد مخاطب از فعل امر ایدلانک وایدلانکیز وایدلاکلار جمع غائب ...
آید بو ورایحه را کویند چنانکه در لسان الطیر کوید شعر ...
ایدی ممالک وسکر و اوتنی ولیدی ونیز در تاریخ بابری در وصف ... مذکور است که ...
تنزیل کل ایدی کیلور لا لکلو ... ایدیلک یعنی بوی خوش چنانکه کوید شعر ...
افغان قیلمانی وه که بو ... ایدی دک نسخه آل ...
چنانکه کویند عتاب ایدیرک یعنی عتاب کنان هر قصه ایدرک یعنی قصه کنان آیدی به معنی آمد ...
بود چنانکه ناصر کوید شعر شکر ایتینک هر دم ایدی ... تا ایدی مظلوم ...
تدویم بمعنی بود باشد چنانکه در لیلی مجنون کوید شعر لیلی که ایدی عرب ... هم ... سیم یعنی
بوی ایدیش بکون شین قرشت ظروف واوانی را نامند الشاهد علیه شعر ... تکلف ...
بی تکلف ... ونیز در ... کوید شعر
با نا ... عتاب ... یعنی ...
که در عهد چنکیز خان بود ومؤلف تاریخ حبیب السیر ... کفته که معنی آن خداوند دولت است ایدک
بکسر دال وسکون نون وکاف عجمی یعنی بودی چنانکه در لسان الطیر کوید شعر بود ... ایدینک
عاشق وواله ... ایدینکیز یعنی بودید لاف ... یعنی لاف زن بودید چنانکه ...
ساده از زبان ... خطاب بقوم وخیل کوید شعر ... لاف زن ...
الرابع من المشتقات ایرنماک بمعنی لازم ومتعدی کرده وآمده یعنی رسیدن ورسانیدن ... لازم ...
مرد ومستعملت چنانکه فضولی بغدادی بمعنی لازم آنرا ما کاف مذکور ساخته وسعد الدین ... در تاریخ آل عثمان ...
با قاف بیان نموده وشاهد هر یک نظما ونثرا در ذیل باب اول از مبنا اول در دیباچه کتاب ... ایرودمیرتکیر
الشاهد علیه بالمعنی الثانی شعر ... ملک تیغ ... کراچ اولسه ...
ونیز یعنی ... رسیدی ورسانیدی چنانکه فضولی کوید بالمعنی الاول بالملاحظه الرفیعه شعر ...
قدینی ای سر بلند ... سلطنت تختینه ایرورنینک ... ونیز یعنی بودی ...
ایرما ... رسید ورسانید چنانکه شاهد ... ونیز ... مجبوب القلوب در حکایت ملوک

Margin: ایغ — اید — ج — ایر

97v.

کوید. که تمرقر صیغه ایلکینک ایرماسا توغلاجما الوتماک هم مقتضم بعض ایریماک مختلط و ایریمالتی مع اللام کداخته شد
ایریدی ایریلدی کداخته شد چنانکه در یوسف و زلیخا موسی جوانی کوید الشاهد علی الثانی شعر
ایکی لعلینکا توتیجهد اونات تین ایریلدی ایرایدی قندا ایریلتی و ایریلدی کداخته شدیم ایریدیم و ایریلدیم و ایرلتی
کداخته می شود الشاهد علی الاول شعر عشقینک وتین کرنوانی دیلکیم ایلاجم قتم سوزیدین کونکلم قلم تورود
ایریدوات من سلطان حسین میرزا شعر بو و اثر کونکلیکا و بولادا آهیمدین ایریره اوزکا جسدو دبوتا تیغ لیغ بحرایلا
اوزکا جنه و ایرید و ایریلور یعنی فاعل و مصدر تیز هم آمد ایریماسید قنر غمینکا ازد و نکداخته استا ایرکان و ایرکان
ایریلدیرکان و ایرلیکا و ایریلورکا ایریلدوکا کداخته شونی و کداخته شده و بمعنی مصدر هم می آید ایری و ایریکیل و ایریکل
ایریلکیل مفرد مخاطب امر ایریتملو ایریماکیل و ایریملو ایریماکیل مفرد مخاطب نهی ایرینک و ایریتکیز و ایرینکلار
ایریلسنک ایریلسنکز و ایریلسنکلار جمع مخاطب امر ایریماسنک و ایریماسنکلار و ایریلماسنکلار جمع مخاطب نهی
ایریکان و ایریکای تیرین و ایریکان و ایریماس
کداخته شوم ایریکیمین ایریمین و ایریلکیمین ایریلادورمین و ایریلورام کداخته می شوم
ایریکیم ایریلورم و ایریلکیم کداخته شدیم ایریکوم و ایریلکوم کداخته نخواهیم شد ایریکای ایرسارین و ایریماس
ایریلیب ایریلیباتا ایریلیش کداخته شده چنانکه در فرهاد و شیرین در توحید کوید الشاهد علی الاول شعر دیکیم قم
اوت تونمای ارام ایریت کوک ایله کیم بر تصرفاشون خام ایریکیشا و ایریلیشا نک کداخته شدن ایریماس و ایریلماس
کداخته نمیشود و بمعنی فاعل و مصدر منفی هم می آید ایریماسی و ایریلماسی کداخته شدن و نشدن ایریلمادین ایریلمادین
از کداخته شدن و کداخته نشده ایریب توکماک و ایریلیب توکماک ایریماک آلماک و ایریلیب توکماک ایریماک آلماک
کداخته نمیتوان شد ایریکلا و ایریلکالماس کداخته نمیتواند شد ایری ایری ایریلا ایریلا کداختن کداختن
تکرار هم مستعمل ایری ایریمین ایریلیب ایریلادین کداخته شوم و شود و شوی و شد ایریتا النعار ایریکانز و ایریکای
ایریتماک ایرتماک ایریلماک تعار ایریلیب ایریلیکار ایریلادی و ایریلادی لنیک کداخته شوم ایریکای ایریلکای
برای کداخته شدن تو تا کداخته شد ایریکاج و ایریلکاج چون کداخته شد و شود ایری کوچی ایریلکوچی کداخته
شونده ایریکوچی و ایریکوچی و ایریکا نجی ایریلکوچی و ایریلکانجی کداخته شدن و بعد از کداخته شدن ایریکوم
ایریلکوم کداخته خواهم شد ایریکیلک ایریلکولک کداخته خواهد شد ایریکوسی و ایریلکوسی کداخته خواهد شد
ایریکولوک و ایریلکولوک کداخته شدنی ایریکای و ایریلکای ایریلاب و ایریلاب ایریلا و ایرپیسا ایرلیکای
ایریلون و ایریلدیلیک کداخته شود ایریکودیک ایریلیک و ایریلکودیک و ایریلوردیک کداخته شدنی و همچنانکه کداخته
ایریتماک مع التاء مصدر متعدیست یعنی کداختن که آنرا بعربی اذابه کویند ایریتی کداخته کرد الشاهد
ناش ایریتی و ه که خسرو کونکلیکا کلا ایتمادی شعله لاد کیم تیشه سیدین سیکویدی فرهادینک ایریت و ایریتکیل مفرد مخاطب
امر الشاهد علی الاول شعر ای نوایی جون سنی کو یدورسی جرخ ایمدی نی سود آه او تیدین سین آنی خوامی قربت
خوامی ایریت و تلک صیغ بعض جو او تو تو او لا بای قرشا شقاقی می باید ایریتماق بسکون طو تمای قرشت فتح جیم
الف کیدی مصدر متعدیت غودلر کردن دندان باشد در حالت خنده و این لفظ تنهایی مستعمل نیست باید لفظ دندان
مذکور شود ایرجاییتی دندان غودلر کرد ایرجاتیتی ایرجاتیکوس دندان غودلر میکند و ایرجاتیو ر بمعنی فاعل و مصدر هم

٦٠

98v.

می آید ایرجاتماد و ر دندان غودلر میکند و نکرده است ایرجاتمادی و ایرجاتیو غان و ایرجاتیلیادورمان دندان غودلر کننده
و غودلر کرده و بمعنی مصدر هم می آید ایرجاتیب و ایرجاتیغیل مفرد مخاطب امر ایرجاتما و ایرجاتماغیل مفرد
امر فعل نهی ایرجاتینک و ایرجاتینکز و ایرجاتینکلار جمع مخاطب امر ایرجاتمانک و ایرجاتمانکز و ایرجاتمانکلار جمع
امر فعل نهی ایرجاتیمان و ایرجاتیماس مین غودلر میکنم ایرجاتیامین و ایرجاتیورمین و ایرجاتادورمین و ایرجاتیودا غودلر
ایرجاتیور و مو ایرجاتیماکیم غودلر کردیم ایرجاتیماکوم غودلر نخواهیم کرد ایرجاتیب و ایرجاتیبان و ایرجاتیمیش غودلر کرده الشاهد
علی الاول شعر بو کلشن غنچه سیدا ژاله ماریار کیم تیش ایرجاتیب کولا و لاشنه بلبل نوحه سیغه بو غالیبعد این ایرجاتیشا
غودلر کرده ایرجاتماس غودلر نمیکند و بمعنی فاعل و مصدر منفی هم می آید ایرجاتماسی غودلر کردن و نکردن ایرجاتمادین از غودلر
کردن و غودلر نکرده ایرجاتیب بولماس و ایرجاتیب بولماس و ایرجاتیماکا و لماس غودلر نمیتوان کرد ایرجاتیما آلماس غودلر نمیتواند کرد
ایرجاتیا ایرجاتیا غودلر کنان و بدون تکرار هم مستعمل ایرجاتیای ایرجاتیاین غودلر کنم و کند و کنی و کرده ایرجاتیساق و
ایرجاتیسا ایر و ایرجاتیسالر و ایرجاتیتا النیک غودلر کنم ایرجاتیغالی برای غودلر کردن و تا غودلر کرده ایرجاتیماج چون غودلر کرد
و کند ایرجاتیغوچی غودلر کننده ایرجاتیغوچی و ایرجاتیغانجی تا غودلر کردن و بعد غودلر کردن ایرجاتیغوم
غودلر خواهم کرد ایرجاتیغونک غودلر خواهی کرد ایرجاتیغوسی غودلر خواهد کرد ایرجاتیغولوق غودلر کردنی ایرجاتیغای و
ایرجاتیتا و ایرجاتیتا و ایرجاتیغون و ایرجاتیدیلیک غودلر کند ایرجاتیغودیک و ایرجاتیغودیک غودلر کردنی و همچنانکه غودلر
ایرجاتیماق بسکون راو و یای حطی غودلر شدن دندان در حالت خنده ایرجاتیدی ایرجاتیادور غودلر میشود چنانکه الشاهد
در لسان الطیر در جواب هدهد کوید شعر نفس یکیمرله کیم قیلسا نا نک هر ادیش ایرجاتیدور او لکام دیر شیطان غنچه تیش ایرجا
غودلر شد چنانکه کوید شعر سین کیم و کملاک سوزی جون غنچه ایچره ژاله عیان ایل الرا ایرجاتیادی هر کز چو لدا ایرغنچه تیش
و باب صیغ مواقف شوال الشتقاق می باید ایرغاتماق بسکون راو و یای قرشت و فتح ضم جیم با الف کشیده جنباندن ایرغاتیه
جنبانید ایرغاتوق جنباندیم ایرغاتور و ایرغاتادور جنباند و ایرغاتور بمعنی فاعل و مصدر هم می آید ایرغاتماید جنباند
و نجنبانیده است ایرغاتغان و ایرغاتوغان و ایرغاتمادوغان جنباننده و جنبانیده و بمعنی مصدر هم می آیند ایرغات و ایرغا
مفرد مخاطب امر ایرغاتات ترکی رومی بمعنی عمله و فعله باشد ایرغاتما و ایرغاتماغیل مفرد مخاطب نهی ایرغاتینک و ایرغا
و ایرغاتینکلار جمع مخاطب امر ایرغاتمانک و ایرغاتمانکز و ایرغاتمانکلار جمع مخاطب نهی ایرغاتمان و ایرغاتماس مین
نمیجنبانم ایرغاتامین و ایرغاتورمین و ایرغاتادورمین و ایرغاتورام میجنبانم ایرغاتورم و ایرغاتمادیم جنباندیم ایرغاتما
نخواهم جنبانید ایرغاتیب و ایرغاتیبان و ایرغاتمیش جنبانیده چنانکه در صفت سیاره در صفت عدل پادشاه کوید الشاهد علی
الاول شعر آندا نوشیروان کبرا باقضای باشیدا ایرغاتیب آکهی قاقضای ایرغاتمیشامک جنبانده ایرغاتماس نمیجنباند
و بمعنی فاعل و مصدر منفی هم می آید ایرغاتماسی جنباندن و نجنباندن ایرغاتمادین از جنباندن و نجنبانده ایرغاتیب بولما
و ایرغاتا بولماس و ایرغاتماق او لماس نمیتوان جنبانید ایرغاتا آلماس نمیتواند جنبانید ایرغاتا ایرغاتا جنبانده جنبانده و
بدون تکرار هم مستعمل ایرغاتای و ایرغاتایین بجنبانم و بجنباند و بجنبانی و جنبانده ایرغاتساق و ایرغاتسالر و ایرغاتسنک
ایرغاتالی و ایرغاتالینک بجنبانیم ایرغاتغالی برای جنبانیدن و تا جنبانیده ایرغاتغاچ چون جنبانید و جنباند ایرغاتغوچی
جنباننده ایرغاتغوچی و ایرغاتقانجی تا جنبانیدن و بعد جنبانیدن ایرغاتغوم جنبانیدن خواهم جنبانید ایرغاتغونک

۹۸۷

خواهی جنبانید ایرغاتغوسی خواهد جنبانید ایرغاتغولوق جنبانیدنی ایرغاتغای وایرغاتاو ایرغاتسالار ایرغاتنور
ایرغاندیلت بجنباند ایرغاتغودیلت وایرغاتودیلت جنبانیدنی وهمچنانکه بجنباند ایرغاتماق مع النون مصدر ایرغاتماق
یعنی جنبیدن وصیغ آن مثل مشتقات مصدر ایرغاتماق اشتقاق می یابد اما بدل تا حرف نون داخل میشود ایریشماک بکسر الف
وسکون شین قرشت پیروی کردن واز قفا رفتن ومتابعت کردن باشد چنانکه گوید شعر نوا بیا توتار اهل فنا بجا تیلوبین
ایریشماک ایستار ایناناک ایشته هم آلا زقفا ایریش وطالع هروی بمعنی کاوش کردن ذکر کرده ایریشتی از قفا رفت
ایریشتوک از قفا رفتیم ایریشور وایریشادور از قفا میرود وایریشور بمعنی فاعل ومصدر هم می آید ایریشایدی از قفا میرود دو نرفته
ایریشکان وایریشوکا وایریشادورکان از قفا رونده واز قفا رفته وبمعنی مصدر هم می آید چنانکه شاهد بر اول او بمعنی مصدر گوید
شعر تا چاپانکیم اول شاه ایریغ توتلوغ ابهرمین زار ایریشکانی شاغیفا یلادوتاچان کر بر کینی پر کهر یلجیکته ایریش و
ایریشکیل مفرد مخاطب امر الشاهد علی الاول شعر ای نولک چابکونک تونک ایناسانک یابوسینق بوینونکا
ابپ تاقا قامیدی چله ایت بیتک ایریش وطالع هروی بمعنی کاوش کردن نوشته وشعر بر نوبر شاهد آورده سهو کرده
منزل لیلی مجنون الشاهد علی الثانی شعر کیم یار فتله سینی ایریشکیل تمای نیلبری که تاردیلار تیشکیل ایریشما ایریشمانک
مفرد مخاطب نهی ایریشینک ایریشینکیز ایریشینکلار جمع مخاطب امر ایریشمانک ایریشمانکیز وایریشمانکلار جمع مخاطب
نهی ایریشمان وایریشماس مین از قفا نمیروم ایریشامین وایریشورمین وایریشادورمین ایریشورکا از قفا میروم ایریشوردیم ایریشام
از قفا رفتیم ایریشماکوم از قفا نخواهم رفت ایریشیب وایریشیبان وایریشیبتن از قفا رفته الشاهد علی الاول شعر
نوا اخرهم عودین ناغیم تو تغاندا گوید هردم فلک سابری ایریشیب طرغان اوچقونلارهم فغانیم فاسیناق شعر خیز است که در
ناغیم تو تغاندا فلک سابری فغانیم غا ایریشیب طرغان اوچقونلار عودین گوید وهردم و نیز در لیلی مجنون گوید شعر
هر قوم غرکه مقدمی تیشیب پیوشت کیبک آنی ایریشیب ایریشیبانک از قفا رفته ایریشماس از قفا نمیرود
وبمعنی فاعل ومصدر منفی هم می آید ایریشماسی از قفا نرفتن ونرفتن ایریشمادیت از نفقی کردن واز قفا رفته ایریشیب
بولماس وایریشیب بولمامیو ایریشماک اوکما از قفا نمیتوان رفت ایریشا آلماس از قفا نمیتواند رفت ایریشا ایریشا پیروی
وبدون تکرار هم مستعمل چنانکه در غنایم المحبه در ذکر شیخ ابو علی فارمدی گوید که شیخ کوردم که تا لین آیل
باردو ایریشی مین داغی الا رحمة ایریشا باردو ایریدیم ایریشای وایریشاین از قفا بروم و برود و بروی و بروید ایریشا
ایریشکاینه وایریشکای وایریشاو ایریشالینک از قفا برویم ایریشکالی برای از قفا رفتن و تا برفته ایریشکاج چون رفته
رفت و برود ایریشکوچی از قفا رونده ایریشکوچا وایریشکونچا ایریشکیما از قفا رفتن وبقلم از قفا رفتن ایریشکوم از قفا
خواهم رفت ایریشکونک از قفا خواهی رفت ایریشکوسی از قفا خواهد رفت ایریشکولوک از قفا رفتنی ایریشکای
ایریشلی ایریشا وایریشکورنوا ایریشیلمت از قفا برونده الشاهد علی الثالث شعر کونکول وزیدم نوالیکولی
طوفیدین نیتانک امیدی ایریشا ایتلاجی اول کوی ارا کونکلومنی یا نغای تیتی ایریشکودیلت وایریشودیلت از قفا
رفتنی وهمچنانکه برود ایریشتورماک مصدر متعدیست یعنی از قفا فرستادن و رسانیدن وصیغ آن ما بنا معلوم لفظ
اشتقاق می یابد ایریکماک بکسر الف وسکون کاف دلگیر شدن ایریکتی دلگیر شد ایریکتیم دلگیر شدم چنانکه
لطفی گوید شعر ایریکتیم بوصفا سیز سیکاک مجرو تیلاب مین سیر قیلماق کلشن ایچره ایریکتونک دلگیر شدم ایریکور ایریکا

۹۹۲

دلگیری شود وایریکور بمعنی فاعل ومصدر هم می آید ایریکماید دلگیر نمیشود ونشده است ایریککان وایریکوکان و
ایریکادورکان دلگیر شونده ودلگیر شده وبمعنی مصدر هم می آید ایریک وایریککیل مفرد مخاطب امر ایریکلا ایریکنکار
مفرد مخاطب نهی ایریکینک ایریکینکیز ایریکینکلار جمع مخاطب امر ایریکمانک ایریکمانکیز وایریکمانکلار جمع مخاطب نهی
ایریکمان وایریکماسمین دلگیر نمیشوم ایریکامین وایریکورمین وایریکادورمین وایریکورام دلگیر میشوم ایریکوردیم وایریکادیم
دلگیر شدیم ایریکماکوم دلگیر نخواهم شد ایریکیب ایریکیبان وایریکیبتن دلگیر شده چنانکه در لیلی مجنون گوید الشاهد
علی الاول شعر پرکون ایریکیب مهمود بش نوشتی باشغه هوای مکتب مولف وطالع هروی بمعنی بیزاری شود برخاستن تو
وطالع هروی بمعنی برخاستن ذکر کرده وهر دو تیغمبر ببیت هاسهو کرده اند ایریکیبتی دلگیر شده ایریکماس
دلگیر نمیشود وبمعنی فاعل ومصدر نفی هم می آید ایریکماسی دلگیر شدن ونشدن ایریکیب بولکا وایریکیب بولماس وایریکا الماد
دلگیر نمیتواند شد ایریکا الماس دلگیر نمیتواند شد ایریکا ایریکا دلگیر شده دلگیر شده وبدون تکرار هم مستعمل ایریکای
ایریکامین دلگیر شوم وشود وشوی وشید ایریکای وایریکایمن دلگیر شوم وشود وشوی وشید چنانکه شاهد بر اول
بمعنی دلگیر شدن در کل نوروز شعر حکایت خرکوش ایریکای اولدا داغی آنو ایریکا
ایریکاینه وایریکایمه وایریکالی وایریکالینک دلگیر شویم ایریککالی برای دلگیر شدن وتا دلگیر شده ایریککاج چون دلگیر شد
وشود ایریکوچی دلگیر شونده ایریکوچا وایریکونچا وایریکاچنا تا دلگیر شدن وبقلم دلگیر شدن ایریککوم دلگیر خواهم شد
ایریککونک دلگیر خواهی شد ایریککوسی دلگیر خواهد شد ایریککولوک دلگیر شدنی ایریککای وایریکا وایریکا و
ایریککای وایریککیلت دلگیر شدنی وهمچنانکه دلگیر شود ایرکمک بسکون را وکاف ترکی رومی بمعنی جمع کردن تا ایرکیلماک
بکسر کاف وسکون لام بمعنی جمع شدن ایرلاماق بترکی رومی بمعنی سرائیدن وخواندن بود من الجوامد ایر بسکون را اول
فتح را وسکون نون مرد را گویند چنانکه در تاریخ الملوک ذکر سلطنت همای بنت بهمن گوید الشاهد علی الثانی شعر
باتا پرنچه کون همای آکری ملکت ایرلار ایریلی تیمکا مالدی ملکت وبالجا زاز اده مرتبا زنا نامند چنانکه گوید شعر
تیلار مین فضرسین فطع قیلغای مین ایرلار دیلت باغیر وقیل بولات بیرکاله سیدین اوزکا زادا ایمه وایرکون
به معنی دلیر داول مخفف ایرتاست یعنی اول وقت ندیم بمعنی برود باشد سیم ایرتاسته رسیدن وملحق شدن ایرانلیک آزاد
مردی وجوانمردی باشد الشاهد علیه شعر راست لیغدا سرو ازادی بیکت لیک باغیدین پاکلیک العمل خشا بی
ایرانلیک کاشیدین ایرتا بسکون را وفتح تا عربی ... به معنی استعمال میشود ولی بمعنی ساتو باشد چنانکه در جلال النفا
گوید که بو روزنا اونکان شعرا وایرتا کیجکان ... ستاره در داستان مثنوی اقلیم رابع گوید شعر چون دیدکان
بولدی نکته سنگ دیدیکیم ایرتا چاغدا دهلی ارا تدیم اول وقت را گویند چنانکه در تاریخ نابری مذکور است که آندا قرا
تا بیکیم قیش مینزل الار مناسب ... ایرتا یان جمعیت قیلیب غنیم دفع غیرمتوجه بولغانیلار بیم بالمجاز ابتدای صبح را تا
چنانکه اقسام اول شب را گویند شعر ایرتا و آقشام غمیم آندا ق ترتیب پیرله دهر کیم کونومکا یوق طلوع صبح فرق شام کی
ونیز در فرهاد و شیرین گوید شعر قدم بار و اوزده هر بار یتا الدیم کیم اوزنی تلعه دین تا شقاره سا الدیم که
حیل ایمو کینیب ایرتا و کیچه تا منیا یمو مین آندین خبر هیچ ایرتا کی بمعنی قدیمی باشد الشاهد علیه شعر چرخ دین
ای کونونیل کر بولیش تیکودیلت سیل اشکیدین خلل بو ایرتا کی تجانه غه ولله شعر هر تانک ایرتا چکا کردون

تنغی قیلیمه تانك تماس کیم باردور اول دشمنلاریمیزا ایرتاکیم قوله شعر ای نوائی هجر یدین بیکلار کوبوبدور ولیبوغا
دیمادی کیم بیلار اول عشاق ایچیندا ایرتاکیم وطالع هر بیلی ترتاك را بمعنی سوختن نوشته و بشعر مزبور استشهاد جسته
شاهد او شاهد بر صحت ایرتانك یعنی اول صبح ایردام بسکون را ومیم وفتح دال فنون فروسیت وآداب سپاهی کویند
کویند چنانکه در تاریخ الملوك در ذکر الب شیر اتابك آمده که چون بلوغ حد بیغه میتی تا برجا سپاهیلیك پیله ایرداملیکانه بولوب
شهرت توتی ونیز در فصل پنجم از مجالس النفایس در ذکر میر حیدر کوید که سپاهیلیغیدا هم ایرداملار که بولور اوق اتماق
جلد وقیلیچ چاپماق اداخابك وسایر جلادتلار آنجه بارکیم عصری نینك اهلی بیند قیلورلار ومؤلف رومی یکجا ایردام را
در این نسخه آیروم بمد الف وضم را خوانده ودر الف مضمومه با یمعنی ذکر کرده ویکجا ایردام خوانده ودر الف مکسوره بیان
نموده ودر هردو جا همین مصرع را از مجالس النفایس شاهد آورده وبعضی هم متابعت کرده آیروم وایردام را
دانسته با یمعنی نوشته اند سهو کرده اند ایردوك مرادف ایدوك باشد یعنی بودیم چنانکه کوید شعر عشق ارا
غایت سیز بلیتای کونکول هجر بیر دشوار ایکن کورمامیش ایردوك بلا ونیز بمعنی رسیدیم ورسانیدیم وملحق ساختیم ایردی
مرادف ایدی باشد یعنی بود الشاهد علیه شعر بیوك کعدین ایرو هر طرف ناقه میل تمنداوزره ایکیلو ایردی
اول قد نازك ونیز بمعنی رسید ورسانید ایردینك مرادف ایدینك باشد یعنی بودی چنانکه در سبعه سیاره در ذکر آن
مناظر اقلیم اول کوید شعر سین کر عجبی منکا ایمس ایردینك یار وهمراه بو جلیس ایردینك ونیز بمعنی رسیدی ورسانیدی
ایردینکیز ایردینکلار یعنی بودید الشاهد علی الاول شعر ای شکیب وصبر کون بود منکا یارلیغ هم بولماسا
تیکرامدا خود یار ایردینکیز وشاهد بر ثانی در سبعه سیاره در نوحه کردن بهرام در فراق کنیزك چینی کوید شعر
که بیلدیم ایردینکلار نی دنیا ... ایردینکلار ... ایرلاف ... لاف وضم ومضاف ودال
ونیز بمعنی رسیدید ورسانیدید ایرسا از ادات شرط ومرادف دیناست یعنی اکر باشد چنانکه شواهد وکیفیت آن در دیباچه
مثال چهارم از دیباچه مفصلا نکارش یافته ونیز بمعنی اکر برسد وبرساند ایرساناك اکر باشی چنانکه کوید دیریری
ایلکیدین زنادسیلکا باغلامیش تبت قاشیدا ایلماس ایرسانك سجده بی اکراه قایت ونیز بمعنی اکر برسی واکر برسانی
ایرسانکیز اکر باشید واکر برسید واکر برسانید ایرغات بترکی رومی عمله وفعله باشد ونیز از ترسانیدن خبساندن چنانکه
ایرمی بسکون را وفتح میم چوب شیر خشت را کویند ایرك بسکون را وکاف دو معنی دارد اول بمعنی اختیار وقدرت باشد
چنانکه در سد سکندری در نعم سکندر با دیو سازان کوید شعر سپه بولدی خندقی را ایلسیر ایلك تاپا آلمادی
آنکا جمع ایراك دویم حصن تعمیر را کویند که در وسط قلعه سازند وبا یمعنی بفتح الف نیز مستعملست چنانکه در باب الف
مفتوحه کذشت ایرکاج بز نر سه ساله ونیز نر بیشرو کله را کویند وبفتح الف مستعملست ومذکور است
چنانکه کوید تا بماس ایرکاج یعنی هنوز نرسیدکا الشاهد علیه شعر ایشادینك دنیلی وسین توشاکی محبوب دیك
تا بماس ایرکاج کام لعلی دین پشیمان بولدی توت وکیماس ایرکاج یعنی هنوز نیامده چنانکه کوید وکر شعر کیلماس ایرکاج
ریدلار بیسفه کنمان ابتاما کرکتاد بولساناك ایجب داغی تو توبیر جام کیت ایرکاك بفتح کاف اول وسکون ثانی
یعنی نر باشد که آنرا در انسان مذکر ودر اسب فحل کویند ایرکان بفتح کاف وسکون نون یعنی هست الشاهد علیه
شعر نوائی اولدی بریر وبلاهوا سیدا کیم دیدوك خرد لیغ واول اسرو تیلبه ایرکاندور وبکسر کاف نیز مستعملست

چنانکه بطریق جناس وایهام فرماید شعر دیمانی ایرکین نوائی نینك حیلاجودار اوماغی ومخاطبکیم هر نیکیم کامیاب الیک
میرزا بینکا مصرع اول اطلاعیت مضایست که مکو نوائی را چه اختیار است در چیلا ودار شدن معنی دیکر اینست که مکو نوائی را
که میل حود دار شدن نوائی چراست ومرا چه اختیار هر چه کوهان میرزا بر کشد ونیز لفظ ایرکین که در روابط استعمال شود
الشاهد علیه شعر ای زاهد منکا ری مقصودی کوناکیمسین ایرکین سین جو غدرت خامه سید بن ظاهر ایتما ولیس معنی
وایرکان بفتح کاف بترکی رومی عزیز غیر منا قبل باشد ایرکانکا بودن چنانکه در دیباچه فرهاد وشیرین کوید شعر اوزنك
سود ونك رقم تا صلاح نولمه شیء لعلو سعید ایرکانکا خامه ایرکانلیکین یعنی بودنش را چنانکه در سد سکندری که
دانا با سکندر کوید شعر آمینك دفعی لیبا بن ایلینه توزرای آنکا اول کیم ایرکانلیکین کور کوزرای وایرکانیم ...
ایرکانینکا بودنش چنانکه در دیباچه فرهاد وشیرین آمده که دلکش ایرکانینکا باعث فرهنی طوق آسیدین طغرا در ایرکانین
مرادف ایرکانلیکین باشد یعنی بودنش را چنانکه در سبعه سیاره در توحید کوید شعر ... ایرکانین کیشی بیلماس
بیلماس کیشی ... کیچو ایشه بیلماس ایرکیشتاك بسکون را وشین قرشت وکسر کاف اول وفتح تای قرشت دانه سنجد ...
آن که دراز ومدور باشد وآنچه دانه چنین بود آنرا اسیغراق نامند ایرکیب مرادف همان ایرکان بود در فوق شرح یافت
ایرکنه وایرکنك بسکون را وفتح کاف اول ونون چوب بالای خانه را کویند چنانکه چو بیز ... تو بسیار ...
ایرکه بسکون را وفتح کاف بهار زده دو معنی دارد اول کره لب باشد که آنرا بعربی بط کویند دویم بمعنی غنج ودلال بود
اسکندر میرزا کوید شعر ایرکه چاقی ایرك نادر ... ناصح مینی تو نغیل ... ایرلیك بمعنی ... وآزاده
بود ایرماق بترکی رومی معبر ایرماق باشد یعنی ... ایرماس نیست ونباشد الشاهد علیه شعر ...
نوز کورددم واشکیم باغدی یا مغرور ایرماس عجب بولغان ... ونیز بمعنی نمیرسد ونمیرساند ایرماس ایرکین
نمیباشد ونبوده باشد چنانکه کوید شعر ای نوائی بوکه دهر ازدین بوز افت ... ایرماس ایرکین تا بماین اوله
افت دهر این وقوف ایرماق نهر را کویند ایرمان نیستم ونباشم چنانکه کوید شعر باده نوش کرم نعیم بولسا ...
محبوبی کرطیبیه ایرماس آنکا ایرمان حریف ونیز بمعنی نمیرسم ونمیرسانم ایرمانك نیستی ونباشی لاادری شعر کربار ...
عشق بو نوع اوینابیدین هیچ کیشی چین تاپیغان ایرمانك الحق یعنی اکر با همه عشق باخته ... اشناسنده وشناسنده
باشی الحق ونیز بمعنی نمیرسی ونمیرسانی ایرمیش بوده ونیز بمعنی رسیده ورسانیده ایرن بسکون را ونون لب را کویند
الشاهد علیه شعر صفحه جسونکا اجابحر ... ای یمین ... اوخشاشو کیم ... قونباش ... ایرو
هست ومیرسد ومیرساند ایرود در بودن ودر رسیدن ورسانیدن چنانکه در خاتمه خسرو وشیرین در وصف ...
کوید بالمعنی الاول شعر ایرور دا کوکب ... ایروهین ... عالم آرا ایریش تار نشاجی را کویند و
ارایستانیه روی کردن ورسیدن چنانکه کذشت ایرورسین هستی چنانکه در سد سکندری در فضیلت عفو کوید شعر ایرود
سین واول کره ابرودین بابی آفرینش ... ونیز بمعنی میرسی ومیرسانی ایریك بکسر را وسکون کاف یعنی درشت
باشد چنانکه کوید شعر هجر تاشی ... شالیسی ... ای کونکول عشق ... ایریك ایرکاك
درشت تر چنانکه در مکالمه حکیمانه ارسطو با اسکندر در باب منع نزاع کوید شعر ... ایریك اوزره
معده معدن ... ایماس وکرمنع قیلدی ... نی ایش ترکی ... سپلیندی که کوب طبعی ...

1557

ایریکالی آتینت بمعنی واجب نورووره مینونت برله هم نا بیاشا اشناغ بولور واجب والمحله بهلاق تراغ وموافق
ایریکالت را ما خوبا را بنا مشتهر نموده بمعنی صبح نمود برخاستن و زودتر نوشته اند و شعر بیوبرلیشا هدا آمرزه اند
معنی هنر متابعت کرده سهو کرده اند ایریکلیت بمعنی رشتی و خشونت بلشدا الشاهد علیه شعر اوز لوکونلجه
کیسما کاکا نولی بیل کیم بومتورومرد هر ایریکلیت لاریدین بخشی ایکالی اینیلت بکسر را و سکون نون وکاف عجمی
جرک ودیم بود که آنرا بعربی ملل و فیح نامند مع آنرا من المشتقات ایمز ما لت بسکون زا لیا سیدین لیز
اینجوك شاسیدیم ایزارعا یزارد وسینا بد وایزار بمعنی فاعل و مصدر هم می آید اینما بدور نمیا ید وتا سیده ایکا
ایزارکان ایزادوکا شاسنده شا سیده و بمعنی مصدر هم می آیند این و این کیل مفرد مخاطب فعل امر الشاهد علی الاول
چون نوایی وصل تاپقایمدی پرده وا ی ی بمعشر تیبین بکم هر باخود آب حیوان بیرلماینا الشاهد علی الثانی بمعنی شاقا
جا میمدا ایز کیل هم کیم هر نیجه اول بولسا آچیغ بولمغوسیده وی مجمل اندین جوجوات ایز نشان قدم واثر پا رام کویند
چنانکه در ذیل جوامد مذکور شود ایزنما و ایزنماکیل مفرد مخاطب فعل نهی ایزینك عا ایز ینکرها ایزینکلار جمع مخاطب فعل امر
ایزنمانك ها ایزنماکرها ایزنماکلار جمع مخاطب فعل نهی ایزمان وایزماس مین نمیابیم ایزامین ها ایزادمین وایزادورمین و ایزادام
میابیم ایزاریم ها ایزماکیم شاسیدم ایزماکوم بخواهم شاسید ایزیمو ایزینان وایزمیش شانیده ایزمیشانلت
شانیده ایزماس نمینماید و بمعنی فاعل و مصدر منفی هم می آید ایزماسی شاسید نشو و شاسید نشی ایزمادین ایزمانلت
و شاسیده اینب بولماو ایزنا بولماس و ایزمالت ایکمال نمیتوان شاسید ایزا الماس نمیتواند شاسید ایزال ایزاغل شاسیده
و بدون تکرار هم مستعمل آنرا ایزاین بشاید بشاسید بشانی شاسیده الشاهد علی الاول بالمعنی الاول شعر شیرین جیدین
ایزی خان شیر سیدین قیل هدن طلمتنی کمین تیره لیوای خضر و چشمنکی ین زلالت ایزسالت وا ایزکا پنو ایزکای پنو ایزکال ایزالسلت
بشاییم ایزکلی برای شاسیدن و شاسیده ایزکاج چون شاسید و بشاید ایزکوچی شاسیده ایزکوچه و ایزکالجه
تا شاسیدن و بقدر شاسیدن ایزکوم خواهم شاسید ایزکونك خواهی شاسید ایزکوسی خواهد شاسید ایزکولوك شاسید
ایزکلو ایزنا و ایزنیلدا ایزدیلك بشاید ایزکودیلک ها ایزاردیلك شاسیدنی و همچنانکه بشاید ایزیلماك بکسر زا و سکون لام
یعنی شاسیده شدن و صیغ آن موافق تشوا ولك الام اشتقاق می یابد ایزلاماك بسکون زا و فتح لام پی جستن و اثر قدم را
کردن ایزلادی پی جوئی کرد ایزلادولت پی جوئی کردیم ایزلا دوایزلایدور پی جو میکند و ایزلار بمعنی فاعل و مصدر هم
می آید ایزلامایدور پی جوئی نمیکند و نکرده است ایزلاکان و ایزلارکان ها ایزلایدورکان پی جوئی کننده و پی جوئی کرده و
مصدر هم می آیند ایزلا و ایزلاکیل مفرد مخاطب فعل امر ایزلاما و ایزلاماکیل مفرد مخاطب فعل نهی ایزلانك وایزلاکنر
ایزلانکلار جمع مخاطب فعل امر ایزلامانك و ایزلامانکر و ایزلامانکلار جمع مخاطب فعل نهی ایزلامان و ایزلاماس مین پی جوئی نمیکنم
ایزلای مین و ایزلارمین ها ایزلایدورمین ها ایزلادام پی جوئی میکنم ایزلادیم و ایزلاماکیم پی جوئی کردیم ایزلاماکوم پی جوئی نمیکنم
ایزلاماو ایزلاباو ایزلامیش پی جوئی کرده ایزلاماس پی جوئی کرده ایزلامیشانك پی جوئی کرده ایزلاماس پی جوئی نمیکند و بمعنی فاعل و مصدر منفی هم می آید
ایزلاماسی پی جوئی کردنش و نکردنش ایزلامادین از پی جوئی کردن و پی جوئی نکرده ایزلاب بولماو ایزلاسا بولماو ایزلامالت ایزلامالت او لماس
پی جوئی نمیتوان کرد ایزلای الماس پی جوئی نمیتواند کرد ایزلا یو ایزلای ایزلای پی جویان و بدون تکرار مستعمل ایزلای ایزلاین
پی جوئی کنم و کند و کنی و کرده ایزلاسالت ها ایزلاکای ها ایزلاکای بو ایزلاسلت ها ایزلالسلت پی جوئی کنیم ایزلاکالی برای پی جوئی کردن

1514

و تاپ جوی کرده ایزلاکاج چون پی جوئی کرد و کند ایزلاکوچی پی جوئی کننده ایزلاکوجه ها ایزلاکالنجه تا پی جوئی کردن و
بقدر پی جوئی کردن ایزلاکوم پی جوئی خواهم کرد ایزلاکونك پی جوئی خواهی کرد ایزلاکوسی پی جوئی خواهد کرد ایزلا
کولوك پی جوئی کردیم ایزلاکالی ایزلاسا و ایزلاسنی ها ایزلادیلت پی جوئی کند ایزلاکودیلك ها ایزلاردیلك پی جوئی کردنی و همچنانکه
پی جوئی کند ایزلاشماك مع الشین مصدر مفاعله است یعنی یکدیگر پی جوئی کردن و صیغ آن مانند اشتقاق می آید
ایزلامالت مع التاء مصدر متعدیت پی جوئی فرمودن و صیغ آن مانند قرشتاشقاق می یابد ایزلاتمادین ایز نشان
و اثر پا را کویند چنانکه کوید شعر اولیری برله ایکاو تا چاق خلدیو نا ینما غای کیما و خا راو لغمدین سراد
ایماستورمیندا ایز و نیز آمده است نمایید چنانکه گذشته مع الیاء من المشتقات ایماك بعنی وزیدن نسیم باشد ایسدی
وزید ایسه دولت وزیدیم ایسارها ایسادور میوزد و ایسار بمعنی فاعل و مصدر هم می آید ایسا بدر نمی وزد و نوزیده آ
ایساکان ها ایسادورکان وزنده و وزیده چنانکه شاهد من الشعر بمعنی اول ای مرد بیلاچند بولان کوی که ظلمت خوانی
بنفشه اول تا تنغ ایسادی غالیه صر صری حنکمن تا بتی ایس و ایسکیل مفرد مخاطب فعل امر الشاهد علی الاول
شعر قو پای باد صبا جانان سارنی چاره مسیح انفاسین کلینغ جان ساری ارن واین باشیلاع کسره بمعنی هوش و عقل
نیز آمده چنانکه در ذیل جوامد بیاید ایسما و ایسماکیل مفرد مخاطب فعل نهی ایسینك ها ایسینکرها ایسینکلار جمع مخاطب
از فعل امر ایسمانك و ایسمانکر و ایسمانکلار جمع مخاطب فعل نهی ایسمان ها ایسماس مین نمیوزم ایسامین ها ایسادورمین ها ایسلاده
ایسادام میوزم ایساریم ها ایسماکیم وزیدیم ایسماکوم بخواهم وزید ایسیب ها ایسبان ها ایسمیش وزیده ایسمیشانك
وزیده ایسماس نمیوزد و بمعنی فاعل و مصدر منفی هم می آید ایسماسی وزیدنش و نوزیدنش ایسمادین از نوزیدن و نوزیده
ایسیب بولماو ایسا بولماو ایسماك ایکمالت نمیتوان وزید ایسا الماس نمیتواند وزید ایسا ایسا وزان وزان و بدون
تکرار هم با همین معنی مستعمل و ایسا الزادات شرط نیز باشد یعنی اگر باشد ایسای ها ایساین بوزم و بوزد و بوزی و وزیده
ایسالی ها ایسکانو ایسکای بو ایسکای ایسالسلت بوزیم ایسکالی برای وزیدن و تا وزیدن ایسکاج چون وزید و بوزد
ایسکوچی وزنده ایسکوجه ها ایسکوجه و ایسکالنجه تا وزیدن و بقدر وزیدن ایسکوم خواهم وزید ایسکونك خواهی وزید
ایسکوسی خواهد وزید ایسکولوك وزیدنی ایسکای ها ایسا و ایسونی بوزد ایسکودیلك ها ایساردیلك وزیدنی
و همچنانکه بوزد ایستورماك مصدر متعدیت یعنی وزانیدن ایستورکوسی خواهد وزانید الشاهد علیه شعر
صبح چون اینی صبا ایجکل قدح کیم بولمغونك سین و کوپ ایستورکوسی بو باغ اراده از صبا و نالی صبح بر ساقی مرا
شو اول ما لفظ و اشتقاق می یابد ایستاماك بفتح تا خواستن و طلب کردن ایستادی خواست ایستادولت خواستیم
ایستار و ایستایدور میخواهد الشاهد علی الثانی من فرهاد و شیرین شعر بو نوع ایستایدور ای عالمی
که قیلغای فکر تینك دیوان خیالی و ایستار بمعنی فاعل و مصدر هم می آید چنانکه بمعنی فاعل کوید شعر خوب ایستدی
کونکلو منی احتیار بولسا اندین اهرکا خوب خوبراق بود هرکه یوق و لدلستاندین خوبراق ایستامایدور نمیخواهد و نخواسته
ایستاکان ها ایستایدورکان خواهنده و خواسته و بمعنی مصدر هم می آیند ایستا و ایستاکیل مفرد مخاطب فعل امر
ایستاما و ایستاماکیل مفرد مخاطب فعل نهی ایستانك ها ایستانکر و ایستانکلار جمع مخاطب فعل امر ایستامانك ها ایستامانکر و ایستامانکلار
جمع مخاطب فعل نهی ایستامان و ایستاماس مین نمیخواهم ایستای مین و ایستارمین ها ایستایدورمین و ایستادام میخواهم ایستادیم و ایستاماکیم

121

خواستم چنانکه شاهد براقل الملک کوید شعر کونکولی خالدو باغیرنی شکاف ایتلیمنا ابنیلق قلبی سله خیری بر ورنما
ایستاماکوم نخواهم خواست ایستا و ایستاماس نخواستی ایستامیش نخواسته ایستامیشکا خواسته ایستاماکی نخواهد و بمعنی ما
و مصدر منفی هم می آید ایستامای خواستن و نخواستن ایستاب کوپلا و ایستاماس بوپلا و ایستاماک الکستوان خواست ایستا
الماس نمتواند خواست ایستایو و ایستای ایستای خواهان خواهان الشاهد علی الاول شعر صبوحی ایستایو سنکاج
سحر لعلیدی ایشیک بو غنچه بردالو تماس ایدی کانیم ارا و بدون تکرار هم مستعمل ایستای ایستاین نخواهم و نخواهد
و نخواهی و خواسته ایستاماس و ایستاکا بخواه ایستاکای بخواه ایستلیا ایستاماس نخواهیم ایستاکالی برای خواستن و تا خواسته ایستاکا
چون خواست نخواهد ایستاکوچی خواهند ایستاکوچی ایستاکوغه ایستاکانچه تا خواستن و بقدر خواستن الشاهد علی الثانی
بالمعنی الاول شعر ایستاکوغه ای کونکول هر دم دوا ایستاکیل کیم دوا تا پملاق تماستور مکن ایکی ادم دیمند ایستا
خواهم خواست ایستاکونک خواهی خواست ایستاکولوک خواستنی ایستاکودیک و ایستادوک خواستنی و چنانکه نخواهد چنانکه
در خاتمه کتاب حیرت الابرار کوید الشاهد علی الاول بالمعنی الثانی شعر دیناملک ایستیکیم میلاکا دیک بلند بولنما
ایستاکودیک دلپسند ایستاشماک مع الشین باهم خواستن و از یکدیگر خواستن و صیغه آن باشین اشتقاق می یابد ایستلغا
مع التا مصدر متعدیست یعنی طلب فرمودن و صیغه آن با تای قرشت اشتقاق می یابد ایستالماک مع اللام مصدر مجهول
یعنی خواسته شدن و صیغه آن باللام اشتقاق می یابد ایسیتماق بکسرتین و سکون تای قرشت کرم کردن و بالمجاز بمعنی
تب کردن باشد چنانکه کوید شعر کونکلی ما ایلدین دهر بغیه یوق و کیم مینی الایلادی راضی ایسیتما قیغه ولیکن
قورقوتوب واستعمال المجاز از لفظ بحقیقت غالبست ایسیتتی تب کرد ایسیتوق تب کردیم ایسیتور
تب میکند و ایسیتور بمعنی فاعل و مصدر هم می آید ایسیتادی تب میکند و نکرده است ایسیتغان و ایسیتورغان
ایسیتادورغان تب کننده و تب کرده الشاهد علی الاول بالمعنی الثانی شعر ایسیتغان تا زین جسمینکه بردن
توب توشتی تاب الهجر ابر و بیر آتشین کل برکی کیم تابتغای کلاه الهجر و به همین معنی کوید شعر بیجهم اوتاری جانیم هم
آچیغ سوزدین بری معنی جوجو کلوکدین ایسیغانغه آچیغ شربت ایردور شرابنا تمغ و بمعنی مصدر هم می آید ایسیت و
ایسیتغیل مفرد مخاطب از فعل امر ایسیتما و ایسیتماغیل مفرد مخاطب از فعل نهی ایسیتسینک ایسیتسینکلار ایسیتکیم ایسیتاین
ایسیتورمین ایسیتادور ایسیتوک تب میکنیم ایسیتورمیز ایسیتماکیم تب کردنم ایسیتماکوم تب نخواهم کرد ایسیتیب ایسیتسا
ایسیتمیش تب کرده ایسیتمیشانک تب کرده ایسیتماس تب نمیکند و بمعنی فاعل و مصدر منفی هم می آید ایسیتمای
تب کردن و نکردن ایسیتمادین از تب کردن و تب نکرده ایسیتیب کوپلا و ایسیتسا بوپلا و ایسیتماک الماس تب نمتواند کرد ایسیتا
الماس تب نمتواند کرد ایسیتا ایسیتا تب کنان و بدون تکرار هم مستعمل ایسیتای ایسیتاین تب کنم و کند و کنی و
کرده ایسیتسانک و ایسیتغانی و ایسیتغای و ایسیتالی و ایسیتالیکیم ایسیتغالی برای تب کردن و تا تب کرده ایسیتغا
چون تب کرد و کند ایسیتکوچی تب کننده ایسیتکوچی و ایسیتکوغه و ایسیتغانچه تا تب کردن و بقدر تب کردن ایسیتکوم
تب خواهم کرد ایسیتکونک تب خواهی کرد ایسیتکوسی تب خواهد کرد ایسیتکولوک تب کردنی ایسیتکاق و ایسیتکا و
ایسیتکوک و ایسیتدیک ایسیتسیلکنی کند ایسیتکودیک ایسیتکودیکنی تب کردنی و چنانکه تب کند ایسیتماق مع الکاف
شدن ایسیتیب کرم شد ایسیتیکیم کرم شدم الشاهد علیه شعر بوزی نظاره سی دفع ایلادی سادوغ

نسیم بنی یالانیک کهای کوی آفتاب روط ایسیتدیم و باب و صیغه بعنوان مشتقات مصدر ایستماق اشتقاق می یابد لیکن بدل تانون تا
میشود ایلاناماق بکسرتین و فتح لام بمعنی بو کردن و استشمام باشد چنانکه کوید شعر پرکل عجب دیدیم تو نای الغریبه
داغ پرکا بیمو بیتان عطری بسنا عفیفه فراغ برکین چوجلوشا بلادی بوم بیله زلغ ایدی بمکنیک ایلاماقنه بوجیف تسلغ
و اتراک خوارزم ایسغاماق هم کویند ایلاماک کوش بمعنی دادن و بمعنی شنیدن ایلادی بو کرد و شنید ایلاماذی
بو نکرد و نشنید چنانکه در تاریخ الانبیا در دعوت کردن هود علیه السلام قوم عاد را باسلام کوید که هود ایلیک بیل
آلاوین ایمانغه دعوت قیلیب الا رغنلت و جبار لیغدین آنینک سوزین ایلاماذیلار ایلامادینک بو نکردی و نشنید
الشاهد علیه بالمعنی الثانی شعر بو نلاف وفا اوردونک مینک تیغ جفا سور دو لک هرنیچه که یالاردیم هیچ ایلادی
بلمقی ایلادوق بو کردیم ایلادوک شنیدیم ایلادی و ایلارم ایلادور بو میکند و میشنود و ایلادی بمعنی فاعل و مصدر منفی هم می
ایلاماید بو نمیکند و نکرده است و نمیشنود و نشنیده است ایلاغای و ایلاغان و ایلایدورغان بو کننده و بو کرده و بمعنی مصدر
نیز می آید ایلاکان و ایلاکای با ایلاید و کان بمعنی شنونده و شنیده و بمعنی مصدر هم می آیند ایلا مفرد مخاطب از فعل امر
مصدر ایلاماق و ایلاماک ایلاماغیل مفرد مخاطب از فعل امر مصدر ایلاماق ایلاکیل مفرد مخاطب از فعل امر
ایلاماک ایلاما مفرد مخاطب از فعل نهی هر دو مصدر ایلاماغیل مفرد مخاطب از فعل نهی مصدر ایلاماق ایلاما
مفرد مخاطب از فعل نهی مصدر ایلاماک ایلاکیل و ایلاکیلار جمع مخاطب از فعل امر هر دو مصدر ایلاسانک و ایلاسانکلار
ایلاماسانکلار جمع مخاطب از فعل نهی هر دو مصدر ایلاسام و ایلاسامین بو میکنم و میشنوم ایلاسامین و ایلایین و ایلایدورمین
ایلارم بو میکنم و میشنوم الشاهد علی الخامس بالمعنی الثانی شعر ایلارم کونکلی نینک نغمه سینی ایشکا کیم
آنچه آن نایش بمنا عفیفه بیتوری اس منات بید ایلادیم بو کردیم و شنیدم ایلاماغیم بو کردنم ایلاماکیم شنیدنم
ایلاماغوم بو نخواهم کرد ایلاماکوم نخواهم شنید ایلاب و ایلاسا و ایلامیش بو کرده و شنیده الشاهد علی
الاول بالمعنی الاول شعر تیلادیم ایلاب ایلادیب عنفستکی که اولتام لطار عنفستکی که لیبنکی معنی شعر اینکه
کا هی که بوسیم روبت را و کاهی لب را بو کرده بو کرده عنفستر الطلب میکنم و مطالع هوی لفظ عنفستر از شعر از نسخه سقیمی عشق
خوانده و در بیان معنی ایناماک با نضلت نوشته که کاه بمعنی پنهان نمودن هم می آید از آنجمله است از تمثال کاخضای عشق را
ذریعه ادراک منظور مال نموده شعر تیلادیم ایلاب ایلادیب عنفستکی که اولتام که یوز و نکیکر لبینکی
و چهار استشمام کرده اول آنکه بلفظ عشق شعر موزون نمیشود ثانیا اینکه این شعر مطلع غزلست و عشق ای قافیه نمیشود سیم
ایلاماک بمعنی پنهان نمودن نیامده غلط آشکارا است چهارم اینکه مسلمانا که با این معنی باشد آن معنی از نرنط فارج است و در بو طفر
ایلامیشانک بو کرده و شنیده ایلاماس بو نمیکند و نمیشنود و بمعنی فاعل و مصدر منفی هم آمده ایلامای بو کردن و نکردن
و شنیدن و نشنیدن ایلامادین از بو کردن و بو نکرده و از شنیدن و نشنیده ایلاب بوپلا و ایلاسا بوپلا بو نمیتوان کرد
و نمیتوان شنید ایلاماق و کلا بو نمیتوان زد ایلاماک اوکلا نمیتوان شنید ایلای الماس بو نمیتواند کرد و نمیتواند شنید ایلای
ایلای ایلای بو کنان و استماع کنان و بدون تکرار هم با جمعلی مستعمل ایلایکا و ایلایین بو کنم و کند و کنی و کرده و
و شنود و شنوی و شنیده چنانکه شاهد براقل الملک بمعنی بو کیم کوید شعر دیدیم ایلایعی عنبرین زلفونکنی آل اشیم بوض
دیدی کیم سین تیلیه تا شنید اعجب سودا ایمیش ایلاماق ایلاغای زد ایلاغای بو کنیم ایلاماک و ایلاکای بر

ایلاگای بشنویم ایلاغبلی وایلالینک بوکنیم وبشنویم ایلاغالی برای بوکردن وتا بوکرده ایلاکالی برای شنیدن
وتا شنیده ایلاغاچ چون بوکرد وکند ایلاکاچ چون شنید وبشنود ایلاغوچی بوکننده ایلاکوچی شنونده ایلاغوم بو خواهم
کرد ایلاکوم خواهم شنید ایلاغونک بوخواهی کرد ایلاکونک خواهی شنید ایلاغوسی بو خواهد کرد ایلاکوسی خواهد شنید
ایلاغولوق بوکردنی ایلاکولوک شنیدنی ایلاغای بوکند ایلاکای بشنود ایلاغسا وایلاغسون وایلاغدیک
بوکند وبشنود ایلاغودیک بوکردن وهمچنانکه بوکند ایلاکودیک شنیدن وهمچنانکه بشنود ایلاغودیک یعنی
ایلاغودیک وایلاکودیک نباشد ایلاغماق مع الشین همه کوه ابوکردن وصیغ آن بدستور الشین اشتقاق میابد ایلاماق
مع النون در معنی اول یعنی بوبرداشتن ومنعقد شدن باشد ددقیم بمعنی خمیدن بود ایلاندی بوبرداشت وخمید
ایلاندوق بوبرداشتیم وخمیدیم ایلانور وایلانادور بوبر میدارد ومیخمید وایلانور یعنی فاعل ومصدر هم
می آید ایلانمایدور بوبر نمیدارد وبرنداشته است ونخمید ونخمیده است ایلانغان وایلانوغان وایلانادورغان
بوبردارنده وبوبرداشته وخمنده وخمیده الشاهد علی الاول بالمعنی الاول شعر عشق وصحبت خلیفه توشکای بی
تابلیغ الشام زخمی ایلانغان بوراننیتکه رهینه وبمعنی فاعل ومصدر منفی نیز می آید چنانکه شاهد بر اول یعنی بوبرداشتن
شعر بوکه کونکلوم ایتینک تیشلادی آغزین تاچوهرت یا اوتی یا خود اینک ایلانغانی بولیش سبب ایلان و
ایلانغیل مفرد مخاطب فعل امر ایلانغنا وایلانغاغیل مفرد مخاطب فعل نهی ایلانمالغا ایلانسنکیزا ایلانکلار جمع مخاطب
فعل امر ایلانکیز وایلانکنکیز جمع مخاطب فعل نهی ایلانمان وایلانغامین بوبر نمیدارم ونمیخمیم ایلانامین ایلانور
وایلانادورمین وایلانورام بوبرمیدارم ومیخمیم ایلانوروم وایلانغانیم بوبرداشتم وخمیدم ایلانغاغوم بو
نخواهم برداشت ونخواهم خمید ایلانیب وایلانبنان وایلانمیش بوبرداشته وخمیده ایلانغانانک بوبرداشته
وخمیده ایلانماس بوبرنمیدارد ونمیخمید وبمعنی فاعل ومصدر منفی هم می آید ایلانمایسیی بوبرداشتن وبرنداشتن
وخمیدن ونخمیدن ایلانمادین از بوبرداشتن وبوبرنداشته واز خمیدن ونخمیده ایلانیب بولماس و
ایلانغا بولماس وایلانماقالولماس بونمیتوان برداشت ونمیتوان خمید ایلانا آلماس بونمیتواند برداشت ونمیتواند
خمید ایلانا ایلاناکدان کذان وخمیده خمیده وبدون تکرار هم مستعملست ایلاناای وایلانابین بوبردارم
وبردارد وبرداری وبرداشته ونخمیم ونخمید ونخمیی ونخمیده ایلانا وا ایلانغایرا ایلانغای ایلاناق
ایلانالینک بوبرداریم ونخمیم ایلانغالی برای بوبرداشتن وتابوبرداشته چنانکه بمعنی لعز کوید شعر تالم آلا
بولدی باغریم مایره سیبی یلانغالی کیم یا خمیدین او تماس ایل توتمای قولاغ بوله بوبولدی وبرنجی خمیدن ونخمیده
ایلانغاچ چون بوبرداشت وبردارد وچون خمید ونخمید ایلانغوچی بوبردارنده وخمنده ایلانغوچه وایلانغو
ایلانغانچه تابوبرداشتن وبقدر بوبرداشتن وخمیدن وبقدر خمیدن ایلانغوم بوخواهم برداشت ونخواهم خمید
ایلانغونک بوخواهی برداشت ونخواهی خمید ایلانغوسی بوخواهد برداشت ونخواهد خمید ایلانغولوق
بوبرداشتنی وخمیدنی ایلانغای وایلانسا وایلانسون وایلانغودیک بوبردارد ونخمید ایلانغودیک وایلانغودیک
بوبرداشتنی وهمچنانکه بوبردارد وخمیدنی وهمچنانکه بخمید ایلاتماق مع التا مصدر متعدیست همان بمعنی
بود وصیغ آن با تای قرشت اشتقاق می یابد ایبرماق بکسر بین وسکون یای بدان کزیدن ومجاز بمعنی خوردن مستعملست

اما معنی مجاز آن بحقیقت غالبست ایبردی کزید وخورد ایبردوق کزیدیم وخوردیم ایبرور وایبرادور میکزد
ومیخورد وایبور یعنی فاعل ومصدر هم می آید ایبرمایدور نمیکزد ونکزیده است ونمیخورد ونخورده است ایبرغان وایبرکان
وایبرادورغان کزنده وکزیده وخورنده وخورده چنانکه میکویند دوغا له چمارم نحز یعنی خورنده کوید الشاهد علی الاول
شعر هرکز نچوک سیغدی آینینک دیک قوماره آرتوق ایبرغان قوشارایت لاد توبان وبمعنی مصدر هم می آید ایبر
وایبرغیل مفرد مخاطب فعل امر ایبرنکا وایبرماغیل مفرد مخاطب فعل نهی ایبرینک وایبرنکیز وایبرنکلار جمع مخاطب
فعل امر ایبرمانکیز وایبرمانکلار جمع مخاطب فعل نهی ایبرمان وایبرماس مین نمیکزم ونمیخورم ایبرامین وایبرور
وایبرادورمین وایبرورام میکزم ومیخورم ایبرورم وایبرغانیم کزیدیم وخوردیم ایبرماغوم نخواهم کزید ونخواهم خورد
ایبریب وایبربنان وایبرمیش کزیده وخورده ایبرمیشانک کزیده وخورده ایبرماس نمیکزد ونمیخورد وبمعنی فاعل و
منفی هم می آید ایبرمایسی کزیدن ونکزیدن وخوردن ونخوردن ایبریب بولماس وایبرا بولماس وایبرماق آولماس
نمیتوان کزید ونمیتوان خورد ایبرا آلماس نمیتواند کزید نمیتواند خورد ایبرا ایبرا کران کران واکل کنان اکل کنان
وبدون تکرار هم مستعملست ایبرای وایبرابین بکزم وبکزد وبکزی وبکزید وبخورم وبخورد وبخوری وبخورده ایبرناق وایبرغایرا
وایبرغای وایبرالینک بکزیم وبخوریم ایبرغالی برای کزیدن وتا کزیده وبرای خوردن وتا خورده ایبرغاچ
چون کزید وبکزد وچون خورد وبخورد ایبرغوچی کزنده وخورنده ایبرغوچه وایبرغانچه تا کزیدن وبقدر کزیدن
وتا خوردن وبقدر خوردن ایبرغوم خواهم کزید وخواهم خورد ایبرغونک خواهی کزید وخواهی خورد ایبرغوسی خواهد
کزید خواهد خورد ایبرغولوق کزیدنی وخوردنی ایبرغای وایبرسا وایبرسون وایبردیک بکزد وبخورد ایبرودیک
وایبرودیک کزیدنی وهمچنانکه بکزد وخوردنی وهمچنانکه بخورد ایبرکاماق بکسر با وسکون را وفتح کاف عجمی یعنی دریغ
داشتن بود واتراک بعیم بمعنی رحم کردن استعمال کنند ایبرکادی دریغ داشت وترکی رومی رحم کرد ایبرکادوک دریغ داشتیم
ورحم کردیم ایبرکارو وایبرکایدور دریغ میدارد ورحم میکند وایبرکار یعنی فاعل ومصدر هم می آید ایبرکامایدور دریغ
نمیدارد ونداشته است ورحم نمیکند ورحم نکرده است ایبرکاکان وایبرکایدورکان دریغ دارنده ودریغ داشته و بمعنی
هم می آید ایبرکا وایبرکاکیل مفرد مخاطب فعل امر ایبرکاماکیل مفرد مخاطب فعل نهی ایبرکانک وایبرکانکیز وایبرکانکلار
جمع مخاطب فعل امر ایبرکامانک وایبرکامانکلار جمع مخاطب فعل نهی ایبرکامان وایبرکاماس مین دریغ
ایبرکایمین وایبرکارمین وایبرکایدورمین وایبرکارام دریغ میدارم ایبرکادیم وایبرکاماکیم دریغ داشتم
ایبرکاماکوم دریغ نخواهم داشت ایبرکاب وایبرکابنان وایبرکامیش دریغ داشته الشاهد علی الاول شعر عجب شفقه
دهر غارونینک کیم ایبرکاب آنی خطیب له منبل ادیب کاتب وینزیه وفضل سبب وشم از محبوب القلوب دوز کرنجار کوید
که نفس لجنانسی بی ایاب چابان نکماسا ولذیذ اغذیه ایبرکاب قورغوغان بیاسا وبترکی رومی بمعنی رحم کرده ایبرکا
دریغ داشته ایبرکاماسا دریغ ... نبرد وترکی رومی بمعنی رحم نمیکند وبمعنی فاعل ومصدر منفی هم می آید ایبرکاماغا دریغ دا
نداشتن وترکی رومی بمعنی رحم کردن ونکردن ایبرکامادین از دریغ داشتن ودریغ نداشته واز رحم کردن ورحم نکرده
ایبرکاب بولماس وایبرکانا بولماس وایبرکاماق آولماس دریغ نمیتوان داشت ایبرکای آلماس دریغ نمیتواند داشت ایبرکابر
ایبرکای ایبرکای دریغ دارنده دریغ دارنده وبدون تکرار هم مستعملست ایبرکای وایبرکابین دریغ بدارم وبدارد وبداری

وداشته ایبرکاسانك وا ایبرکاکابزوا ایبرکاکای بزوا ایبرکالی وا ایبرکالینك دریغ بداریم ایبرکاکالی برای دریغ داشتن
وتا دریغ داشته ایبرکاکاچ چون دریغ داشت وبدارد ایبرکاکوچی دریغ دارنده ایبرکاکومه وا ایبرکاکونچه وا ایبرکاکاغچه تا
دریغ داشتن وبقصد دریغ داشتن ایبرکاکوم دریغ خواهم داشت ایبرکاکونك دریغ خواهی داشت ایبرکاکوسی دریغ خواهد
ایبرکاکولوك دریغ داشتنی ایبرکاکای وا ایبرکاسا وا ایبرکاسون وا ایبرکادیك دریغ دارد ایبرکاکودیك وا ایبرکادیك
دریغ داشتنی وهمچنانکه دریغ دارد ایسکیرماك بکون سین هر او کسر کاف اول وا ایسکیلماك مع اللام بمعنی کهنه شدن
وایسکیماك بضم طا ولام هم کویند ایسکیردی وا ایسکیلدی کهنه شد الشاهد الاول شعر عشوه کلاردا غیدین
جان پرده سین کوراکیم بو عیرا ایسکیردی عالم شاهلاری تعداسیدین الشاهد علی الثانی شعرای نوایی کوتفرابنا
بو قناچرخ نینك اطلس کیدینك کان ایتغا قیتا ایسکیلدی تونی ایسکیردوك وا ایسکیلدوك کهنه شدیم ایسکیردور
وا ایسکیرور وا ایسکیلور وا ایسکیلادور کهنه میشود وا ایسکیره وا ایسکیلور بمعنی فاعل ومصدر هم می آید ایسکیرمایدور
ایسکیلمایدور کهنه نمیشود ونشده است ایسکیرکان وا ایسکیروکان وا ایسکیرادورکان وا ایسکیلکان وا ایسکیلورکان
ایسکیلادورکان کهنه شونده وکهنه شده الشاهد علی الاول بالمعنی الثانی شعر حقیقت عشق اونی کوکسوم ضاکیدین
باشیمدین آشیب توشتی بو ایسکیرکان بغلچه اطلی بچندین اوت تونا شیب توش وبمعنی [illegible] هم می آیند ایسکیرو
ایسکیرکیل وا ایسکیلکیل مفرد مخاطب فعل امر ایسکیرماغیل وا ایسکیرماکیل وا ایسکیلما وا ایسکیلماکیل مفرد مخاطب فعل نهی
ایسکیرنك وا ایسکیرنکیز وا ایسکیرنکلار وا ایسکیلنك وا ایسکیلنکیز وا ایسکیلنکلار جمع مخاطب فعل امر ایسکیرمانك و
ایسکیرمانکیز وا ایسکیرمانکلار وا ایسکیلمانك وا ایسکیلمانکیز وا ایسکیلمانکلار جمع مخاطب فعل نهی ایسکیرمان وا ایسکیرماس مین
ایسکیلمان وا ایسکیلماس مین کهنه نمیشوم ایسکیرامین وا ایسکیرورمین وا ایسکیرادورمین وا ایسکیرورام وا ایسکیلامین و
ایسکیلورمین وا ایسکیلادورمین وا ایسکیلورام کهنه میشوم ایسکیرورم وا ایسکیلورم وا ایسکیرماکیم وا ایسکیلماکیم
کهنه شدنم ایسکیرماکوم وا ایسکیلماکوم کهنه نخواهم شد ایسکیریب وا ایسکیرپان وا ایسکیرمیش وا ایسکیلیب وا ایسکیلپان
ایسکیلمیش کهنه شده چنانکه در لیلی مجنون کوید الشاهد علی الثانی شعر کیم ایسکیرپان نچا رختی میل ایتیناسقلغان
درختی ایسکیرمیشانك وا ایسکیلمیشانك کهنه شده ایسکیرماس وا ایسکیلماس کهنه نمیشود وبمعنی فاعل ومصدر منفی هم می آید
ایسکیرماسلیك وا ایسکیلماسلیك کهنه شدنش ونشدنش ایسکیرمادین وا ایسکیلمادین از کهنه شدن وکهنه نشدن ایسکیریب
بولماس وا ایسکیرپنا بولماس وا ایسکیرانا اولماس وا ایسکیلیب بولماس وا ایسکیلنا بولماس وا ایسکیلانا اولماس کهنه نمیتوان شد
ایسکیرا آلماس وا ایسکیلا آلماس کهنه نمیتواند شد ایسکیرا ایسکیرا وا ایسکیلا ایسکیلا کهنه شده کهنه شده وبتکرار
هم مستعملست ایسکیرای وا ایسکیراین وا ایسکیلاین وا ایسکیلای کهنه شوم وشود وشوی وبشده ایسکیرکای وا ایسکیرکای
وا ایسکیرکای بزوا ایسکیرکالی وا ایسکیرکالینك وا ایسکیلکای بز وا ایسکیلکالی وا ایسکیلکالینك
کهنه شویم ایسکیرکالی وا ایسکیلکالی برای کهنه شدن وتا کهنه شدن ایسکیرکاچ وا ایسکیلکاچ چون کهنه شد بشود
ایسکیرکوچی وا ایسکیلکوچی کهنه شونده ایسکیرکومه وا ایسکیرکونچه وا ایسکیرکاغچه وا ایسکیلکومه وا ایسکیلکونچه وا ایسکیلکاغچه تا
برای کهنه شدن وتا کهنه شدن ایسکیرکوم وا ایسکیلکوم کهنه خواهم شد ایسکیرکونك وا ایسکیلکونك کهنه
خواهی شد ایسکیرکوسی وا ایسکیلکوسی کهنه خواهد شد ایسکیرکولوك وا ایسکیلکولوك کهنه شدنی ایسکیرکای وا ایسکیرسا

وا ایسکیرسون وا ایسکیردیك وا ایسکیلکای وا ایسکیلسا وا ایسکیلسون وا ایسکیلدیك کهنه شود ایسکیرکای وا ایسکیرسا
ایسکیرسون وا ایسکیرکودیك وا ایسکیلکای وا ایسکیلسا وا ایسکیلسون وا ایسکیلدیك کهنه نشود چنانچه مشاهده است
در قسم سیم از تنبیهات محبوب القلوب کوید کهدینانك لطافتی صنایع والقای سیده وتیلاحشامك کریلاسینك ایسکیرتیم
کیدورا ایسکیرکودیك وا ایسکیروردیك وا ایسکیلکودیك وا ایسکیلوردیك کهنه شدنی وهمچنانکه کهنه شود ایسکارماك
بکون سین هرای قرشت وفتح کاف قبول کردن وبجناب درآوردن ایسکاردینك قبول کردی ایسکاردوك قبول کردیم ایسکارور
وا ایسکارادور قبول میکند وایسکارور بمعنی فاعل ومصدر هم می آید ایسکارمایدور قبول نمیکند ونکرده است ایسکارکان و
ایسکارورکان وا ایسکارادورکان قبول کننده وقبول کرده وبمعنی مصدر هم می آیند ایسکارو وا ایسکارکیل مفرد مخاطب فعل امر
ایسکارما وا ایسکارماکیل مفرد مخاطب فعل نهی الشاهد علی الاول شعر کیچه کلبه مکینانك مدعی مضمونی ایسکار
تولون آی سیرابتا ردا ات هولردین تا مایلی واتی ایسکارنیك وا ایسکارنکیز وا ایسکارنکلار جمع مخاطب فعل امر ایسکارمانك
وا ایسکارمانکیز وا ایسکارمانکلار جمع مخاطب فعل نهی ایسکارمان وا ایسکارماس مین قبول نمیکنم ایسکارامین وا ایسکارورمین وا ایسکا
دورمین وا ایسکارورام قبول میکنم ایسکارورم وا ایسکارماکیم قبول کردنم ایسکارماکوم قبول نخواهم کرد ایسکاریب
وا ایسکارپان وا ایسکارمیش قبول کرده ایسکارمیشانك قبول کرده ایسکارماس قبول نمیکند وبمعنی فاعل ومصدر منفی هم می
ایسکارماسلیك قبول کردنش ونکردنش ایسکارمادین از قبول کردن وقبول نکرده ایسکاریب بولماس وا ایسکارانا اولماس قبول
نمیتوان کرد ایسکارا آلماس قبول نمیتوان کرد ایسکارا ایسکارا قبول کنان وبدون تکرار هم مستعملست ایسکارای وا ایسکاراین
قبول کنم وکند وکنی وکرده ایسکارمای وا ایسکارماین قبول نکنم ونکند ونکنی ونکرده الشاهد علی الثانی بالمعنی الاول
شعر مو ایچنام بجناب ایسکارماین کورسو مین بو قوعیت ماکبیدا بوالیمد اچون بمعنوب بما سن آنکا د ایسکارکای ایسکا
کابزوا ایسکارکای بزوا ایسکارکالی وا ایسکارکالینك قبول کنیم ایسکارکالی برای قبول کردن وتا قبول کرده ایسکارکاچ چون قبول
کرد وکند ایسکارکوچی قبول کننده ایسکارکومه وا ایسکارکونچه وا ایسکارکاغچه تا قبول کردن وبقصد قبول کردن ایسکارکوم
قبول خواهم کرد ایسکارکونك قبول خواهی کرد ایسکارکولوك قبول کردنی ایسکارکای وا ایسکارسا وا ایسکارسون وا ایسکار
قبول کند ایسکارکودیك وا ایسکاروردیك قبول کردنی وهمچنانکه قبول کند ایسناماك بکون سین وفتح نون وسین
دره کردن که آنرا بعربی تثاوب کویند الشاهد علیه شعر بنچه اویقیسام آه اولوم کیمدین بالغیر خومانی خالش ایسناماك
بو ابسناکوزداتی عجب اول نوع نایش ونیز در لیلی مجنون در وصف بهار کوید شعر باش غنچه ایسناماك بولور ...
ژاله نو شوبا غنچه بولور تیش ایسنادی دهن دره کردن ایسنادوك دهن دره کردیم ایسنار وا ایسنایدور دهن دره میکند
وایسنار بمعنی فاعل ومصدر هم می آید ایسناکان وا ایسنارکان وا ایسنایدورکان دهن دره کننده وکرده وبمعنی مصدر هم می آیند
ایسنا وا ایسناکیل مفرد مخاطب فعل امر ایسناما وا ایسناماکیل مفرد مخاطب فعل نهی ایسنانك وا ایسنانکیز وا ایسنانکلار
جمع مخاطب فعل امر ایسنامانك وا ایسنامانکیز وا ایسنامانکلار جمع مخاطب فعل نهی ایسنامان وا ایسناماس مین دهن دره نمیکنم
ایسنامین وا ایسنارمین وا ایسنایدورمین وا ایسنارام دهن دره میکنم ایسنایم وا ایسناماکیم دهن دره کردنم ایسناماکوم
دهن دره نخواهم کرد ایسنایب وا ایسناپان وا ایسنامیش دهن دره کرده ایسنامیشانك دهن دره کرده ایسناماس دهن
دره نمیکند وبمعنی فاعل ومصدر منفی هم می آید ایسناماسلیك دهن دره کردنش ونکردنش ایسنامادین از دهن دره کردن

و دهن بهم ننکرده. اینتاب بولماس و اینتاشا بولماس و اینتامانک اولماس هرزه بمعنوان کرد اینتای آلماس دهن بهم نمیتواند

اینتابوما اینتای اینتای هرزه کان و بدون تکرار هم مستعملست اینتای ها اینتاین دهن بهم کم و کی کرده اینتان

ها اینتاکانیزها اینتاکای بیزها اینتالی ها اینتالینک دهن درو کنیم اینتاکالی برای بهم کردن و ناکرده اینتاکاج چون

کرد کند اینتاکوچی هرزه کند اینتاکوجه ها اینتاکونجه ها اینتاکانجه تا دهن بهم کردن و بقدم آن اینتاکوم دهن

خواهم کرد اینتاکوبی دهن بهم خواهد کرد اینتاکولوک دهن بهم کردنی اینتاکای ها اینتاشا ها اینتاسون ها اینتاذیلک

دهن بهم کند اینتاکوچیک ها اینتاچیلک دهن بهم کردنی و همچنانکه کند اینتاماک مع التا مصدر متعدیست یعنی

دهن در کشانیدن اینتاتور ها اینتاتادور دهن بهم میکشاند الشاهد علی الاول شعر ظاهر ایلا اوزینی ایلماهیم

هر بنده آغوسوه کوی موندا قاینتاتور آغو نفس جینک اوینتوسه و تا قی صیغ بر این منوال موافق شق اول الحاق تا قرشا اشتقاق

می یابد آسلاد الاتاق بتر که روی سپردن و توصیه و تودیع کردن و تا اصلا دهم مستعملست من الجوامد ایس باشلغ

دارد اول هوش را کوینید چنانکه در فرهاد و شیرین در کرفتاری فرهاد کوید شعر هم آخر کوز کوز و بیکر نهانی

قیلیب یوز ریوا ایله بیهوش آیی ادبی یو قلوقدا ایلاب بکرو ترو یی اماغ باشیغه شاسیب بند و زنجیر و اتراک دوم اوس

بضم الف استعمال نمایند دویم بمعنی رایحه و بو باشد الشاهد علیه شعر شمیم زلف وصلیدین اییشتیم نکته بیر کون

ابر ودر بیل لاله که مثک ناب ایی کیماس مشامیدین ایسا از ادات شرط است یعنی باشد و اکر باشد و کیفیت استعمال

در صنائع اچهارم در دیباچه خمسه که رشته اینام باشم و اکر باشم الشاهد علیه بالمعنی الاول شعر مین که هر دم دو

سپدا اینار دین زار اینام دوست لا رعیب ایتماسون دشمن لار نعیه یار اینام اینانک باشی و اکر باشی اینانکیز باشیلکز

باشید التعبیر بسکون سین مهملة و فتح شین و تای محمیه ترکی روی بند عابت شکاری که آنرا بفارسی باز و بعربی بازی کویند

ایستی اوت فلفل بود که آنرا بوبر نیز نامند و اتراک روم بوبر کویند سکله بفتح کاف و لام ترکی رومی خانی

که در آنجا بکشتی نشیند و از کشتی در آیند اسکمله ترکی رومی کرسی و صندلی باشد که بر روی آن طعام خورند و نشیند

ایکی کهنه را کوینید الشاهد علیه شعر ضعیف تن اغمیسکدین بونا ایسکی بولغان دلغه هر ایسکی داغ بوشاح

اوزیره یر قورووق یا پولغ اسلغ بسکون سین و ضم و کسر لام ترکی اوازی بود که از منقار طیور برآید و آنرا بعربی صفیر کویند

اسمارلمه ترکی رومی دو معنی دارد اول بمعنی پیغام بود دویم بمعنی تفویض باشد ایسن بفتح سین و سکون نون یعنی صحیح و سالم

و بفتح الف نیز مستعملست اییتمه تب ایسرغان اوتی کیاهیت دوایی که آنرا بفارسی کونه و بعربی انجم کویند ایسرغه

بسکون را و فتح غین معجمه کوشواره باشد که از ابریشم قرط نامند چنانکه در باب هفتم از حیرة الابرار کوید شعر

التون ایسرغه کر قولاغ آغر یتوزشرجال او تو کدو هم که اماغ آغریتور ایسیغ و ایسیق بمعنی کرم و حار باشد الشاهد علیه

شعر سنا و وقاهیم کیم چیکار مین کرم اولوم آتقا منه اتاش چشمه لار دا سو بولور ایسیغ هوا بولغای سنا دوق ایسیغ

نام ولایتی است که مسکن ترک بر نانت بوده مع الثین من المشتقات ایشماک بدو معنی آمده اول رشته را بیکدیکر تابیدن

دویم زمین را کاویدن که آنرا بعربی نقر کویند ایشتی تابید و کاوید ایشتوک تابیدیم و کاویدیم ایشار ها ایشادی

میتابد و میکاود و ایشار بمعنی فاعل و مصدر هم می آید و نوایی علیه الرحمه در فرهاد و شیرین در وصف قصر شیرین

وارتفاع آن اشار آن قصر کفته که شعر تاپیب عقل ارتفاعی نهنک شماره ایکی مینک قاری هر بیر ایشاره یعنی عمل شما

ارتفاعش را جسته هر آشارش دو هزار زرع است و مولف رومی ایشار را سهو اوزین مصرع ایشار خوانده و ایشار را بهمزه

الف مکسور بمعنی کندن و کاویدن ذکر کرده و شعر مذکور را شاهد آورده و از برای موزونی این مصرع را چنین تصحیح کرده

که ایکی مینک تاری حد هر بیر ایشاری معنیش بی معنی معتمم شاهد مزبور شاهد مستغنیست ایشماک و ایشماید ها بدو

تابیدهاست و میکاود و نکاویدهاست ایشکان ها ایشلرکان ها ایشادورکان تابید و تابیده کاوند و کاوید و بمعنی مصدر

هم می آیند ایش و ایشکیل مفرد مخاطب از فصل امر الشاهد علی الاول بالمعنی الاول شعر بیلی تاری هجریدین جسیم تو

ناریت ای قلک رحم ایت بو ایکی رشته نی بیر کا ایش و ایش بمعانی دیکر هم آمده که در ذیل غیر مصادر مذکور خواهد

ایشماو ایشماکیل مفرد مخاطب از فصل نهی الشاهد علی الثانی بالمعنی الاول شعر کنند ز لعل تو نات ایشا الماج و تاب

کونکول شکم سینه ایشماکیل اطناب لیسروه ایشینک ها ایشینکیز ها ایشینکلار جمع مخاطب از فصل امر ایشمانک ها ایشماکیز

ایشمانکلار جمع مخاطب از فصل نهی ایشمان ها ایشماس مین نمیتابم و نمیکاوم ایشلس ها ایشار مین ها ایشاتورمین ها ایشار می تابم و میکاوم

ایشاریم ها ایشماکیم تابیدیم و کاویدیم ایشماکوم نخواهم تابید و نخواهم کاوید ایشماس نمیتابد و نمیکاود و بمعنی

فاعل مصدر منفی هم می آید ایشماسی تابیدنش و نتابیدنش و کاویدنش و نکاویدنش ایشمادین از تابیدن و تابیدن

و از کاویدن و نکاویدن ایشیب تو لماها ایشاتو لما ها ایشمال آلماها نمیتوان تابید و نمیتوان کاوید ایشا آلماس نمیتواند تابید

نمیتواند کاوید ایشا ایشا تابیده کنان و کاویده کنان و بدون تکرار هم مستعملست ایشای و ایشاین تابیم و تابیک

و نتابی و تابیده و بکاوم و بکاود و بکاوی و کاویده ایشانک ها ایشکانیز ها ایشکایز ها ایشالی ها ایشالینک بتابیم و بکاویم

ایشکالی برای تابیدن و تا تابیده و برای کاویدن و تا کاویده ایشکاج چون تابید و بتابد و چون کاوید و بکاود ایشکو

تابیده و کاونده ایشکوچی ها ایشکونجه ها ایشکانجه تا تابیدن و بقدم تابیدن و تا کاویدن و بقدم کاویدن ایشکوم خواهم

تابید و خواهم کاوید ایشکونک خواهی تابید و خواهی کاوید ایشکوسی خواهد تابید و خواهد کاوید ایشکولیک تابیدنی و کاویدنی ایشکا

ایشلماک ایشتوریلماک تابیده شدن الشاهد علی الاول بالمعنی الاول شعر ایتی ایچون تیلار ایشکای طناب وجانیک که

ایلکا رشته جان تابرجا پیچ و تابدار ایشلمانک مع اللام تابیده شدن دو رشته بیکدیکر و کاویده شدن ایشلکا

ایشلوکان ها ایشلادورکان تابیده شده و کاویده شده چنانکه در ولادت فرهاد کوید الشاهد علی الاول بالمعنی الاول شعر

ایشلکان رشته سی تاب و نادین ثبیتلکان باغری جکاک قضادین و باقی صیغ بر این نهج با لام اشتقاق می یابد

مصدر متعدیست یعنی تابانیدن و کاوانیدن و صیغ آن با لفظ تور اشتقاق می یابد ایشانماک بفتح شین و سکون نون

بمعنی مطمئن بودن و اعتماد کردن باشد ایشاندی مطمئن شد ایشاندیک مطمئن شدیم ایشانور ها ایشانادور مطمئن میشود و

بمعنی فاعل و مصدر هم می آید ایشانمایدور مطمئن نمیشود و نشده است ایشانکان ها ایشانورکان ها ایشانادورکان مطمئن شونده

و مطمئن شده چنانکه سلطان حسین میرزا فرماید الشاهد علی الاول بالمعنی الاول شعر کر حسینی کونکلی صیدین اولاناس اول

باغری تاش بوسنکدل دلبر کیم کیسک سیلاس ایشانکان تاماغ اوزره و بمعنی مصدر هم می آید ایشان ها ایشانکیل مفرد مخاطب

ایشانما و ایشانماکیل مفرد مخاطب از فصل نهی چنانکه شاهد بر اول در تنبیهات محبوب القلوب کوید که تو غفلت

ایشانمانک ها ایشانینک ها ایشانینکیز ها ایشانینکلار جمع مخاطب از فصل امر ایشانمانک ها ایشانمانکیز ها ایشانمانکلار جمع مخاطب

ایشانمان ها ایشانماس مین مطمئن نمیشوم ایشانامین ها ایشانورمین ها ایشانادورمین ها ایشانورمن مطمئن میشوم ایشاناغاکیم مطمئن

ایشانماکوم مطمئن نخواهم شد ایشانیب وایشانیبان وایشانمیش مطمئن شده چنانکه شاهد بر اول در تاریخ بابری مذکوراست که
بیننك بکلیکی ایشانیب حوصله سیدین آرتوق بیمه لاولاسه وا قیلدی ایشانمیشانك مطمئن شده ایشانماس مطمئن نمیشود
وبمعنی فاعل ومصدر منفی هم می آید ایشانماسی مطمئن شدنش ونشدنش ایشانمادین از مطمئن شدن ومطمئن نشده وایشانیب
وایشانغانی بولماس وایشانمالی اولماس مطمئن نمیتوان شد ایشانا آلماس مطمئن نمیتواند شد ایشانا ایشانا اعتماد کنان وبدون
تکرار هم مستعملست ایشانای وایشانایین مطمئن شوم وشود وشوی وشد ایشاناك وایشانکایمز وایشانکای بز و
ایشانملی وایشاناالینك مطمئن شویم ایشانکالی برای مطمئن شدن وتا مطمئن شده ایشانکاچ چون مطمئن شد وشود
ایشانکوچی مطمئن شونده ایشانکوچه وایشانکونچه وایشانکانچه تا مطمئن شدن وبقدر مطمئن شدن ایشانکوم مطمئن خواهم شد
ایشانکونك مطمئن خواهی شد ایشانکوسی مطمئن خواهد شد ایشانکولوك مطمئن شدنی ایشانکای وایشانماغای
وایشانسون وایشانسونلار مطمئن شود ایشانکودیك وایشانوردیك مطمئن شدنی وهمچنانکه مطمئن شود ایشاندرماك
مصدر متعدیست یعنی مطمئن کردن وصیغ آن بر بن نهج بالفظ در اشتقاق می یابد ایشناماك بسکون شین وفتح نون درخشیدن
ایشنادی درخشید ایشنادوك درخشیدیم ایشنار وایشنایدور می درخشد الشاهد علی الاول شعر سین که تو
سین ماهرولار جلوه ایلکنده رولیك کیجه ایشنار قیرت نوری مهر چیقفاچ سلکولور وایشنار بمعنی فاعل ومصدر هم
می آید چنانکه در لسان الطیر بمعنی درخشنده کوید شعر اوچغون اولدی عازم چرخ برین قالدی تا دوران ارا ایشنا
چیبین ایشنا ماید ودر معنی درخشد ونمی درخشد است ایشناکان وایشنایدورکان درخشنده ودرخشید
وبمعنی مصدر هم می آید چنانکه شاهد بر اول از معنی مصدری درغرایب المحبه در ذکر امرایه مجهوله کوید کر بر
که ایشناکانی کوککا تیتی ایشنا وایشناکیل مفرد مخاطبه فعل امر ایشنا نا وایشناکیل مفرد مخاطبه فعل نهی ایشنانك
ایشنانکز وایشنانکلار جمع مخاطبه فعل امر ایشنانانك وایشنانانکز وایشنانانکلار جمع مخاطبه فعل نهی ایشناما
وایشناماس مین نمی درخشم ایشنای مین وایشنارمین وایشنایدورمین وایشنارام می درخشم ایشنایم وایشنانای
درخشیدیم ایشناماکوم نخواهم درخشید ایشناب وایشنابان وایشنامیش درخشیده ایشنامیشانك درخشیده
ایشناماس نمی درخشد وبمعنی فاعل ومصدر منفی هم می آید ایشناماسی درخشیدنش ونادرخشیدنش ایشنامادین از درخشیدن
ونادرخشیده ایشناب بولماس وایشنا بولماس وایشنانالماس نمیتوان درخشید ایشنای ولماس نمیتواند درخشید ایشنا
وایشنا ایشنای درخشان درخشان وبدون تکرار هم مستعملست ایشنای وایشنایین بدرخشم بدرخشد بدرخشی
درخشید ایشناناك وایشناکایمز وایشناکای بز وایشنالی وایشنالینك بدرخشیم ایشناکالی برای درخشیدن
وتا درخشیده ایشناکاچ چون درخشید وبدرخشد الشاهد علیه شعر برق هردم چاقیلیب ایشناکاچ اوقتره بولود
یعنی اوشموندین آلیك عمر چراغیغه حباب ایشناکوچی درخشنده ایشناکوچه وایشناکونچه وایشناکانچه تا درخشیدن
وبقدر درخشیدن ایشناکوم خواهم درخشید ایشناکونك خواهی درخشید ایشناکوسی خواهد درخشید ایشناکولوك
درخشیدنی ایشناکای وایشناسا وایشناسون وایشنادیك بدرخشید ایشناکودیك وایشناردیك درخشیدنی وهمچنانکه
بدرخشد ایشناتماك مع التا مصدر متعدیست یعنی درخشان کردن وصیغ آن بر بن نهج قیاس بانای قرشت اشتقاق می یابد
ایشلاماك بسکون شین وفتح لام کار کردن ایشلادی کار کرد ایشلادوك کار کردیم ایشلار وایشلایدور کار میکند

وایشلار بمعنی فاعل ومصدر هم می آید ایشلامایدور کار نمیکند ونکرده است ایشلاکان وایشلارکان وایشلایدورکان کار کننده کار
کرده وبمعنی مصدر هم آید ایشلا وایشلاکیل مفرد مخاطبه فعل امر ایشلاما وایشلاماکیل مفرد مخاطبه فعل نهی ایشلانك وایشلانکز
ایشلانکلار جمع مخاطبه فعل امر ایشلامانك وایشلامانکز وایشلامانکلار جمع مخاطبه فعل نهی ایشلامان وایشلاماس مین کار نمیکنم
ایشلای مین وایشلارمین وایشلایدورمین کار میکنم ایشلادیم وایشلادیم کار کردم ایشلاماکوم کار نخواهم کرد ایشلاب
وایشلابان وایشلامیش کار کرده ایشلامیشانك کار کرده ایشلاماس کار نمیکند وبمعنی فاعل ومصدر منفی هم می آید ایشلاماسی
کار کردنش ونکردنش ایشلامادین از کار کردن وکار نکرده ایشلاب بولماس وایشلا بولماس وایشلا آلماس کار نمیتوان کرد ایشلای
آلماس کار نمیتواند کرد ایشلای وایشلای ایشلای کارکنان کارکنان وبدون تکرار هم بایمعنی مستعملست ایشلای وایشلاین کار
کنم وکند وکنی وکرده ایشلاناك وایشلاکایمز وایشلاکای بز وایشلالی وایشلالینك کار کنیم ایشلاکالی برای کار کردن وتا کار
کرده ایشلاکاچ چون کار کرد وکند ایشلاکوچی کار کننده ایشلاکوچه وایشلاکونچه وایشلاکانچه تا کار کردن وبقدر کار کردن ایشلاکوم
کار خواهم کرد ایشلاکونك کار خواهی کرد ایشلاکوسی کار خواهد کرد ایشلاکولوك کار کردنی ایشلاکای وایشلاسا وایشلاسون
وایشلادیك کار کند ایشلاکودیك وایشلاردیك کار کردنی وهمچنانکه کار کند ایشلاتماك مع التا مصدر متعدیست
یعنی کار فرمودن وصیغ آن موافق مثل اول بانای قرشت اشتقاق می یابد ایشلانماك مع النون مصدر انفعالست یعنی کار کرده شد
وصیغ آن بانون اشتقاق می یابد ایشتماك شنیدن ایشیتی شنید ایشیتوك شنیدیم ایشیتور وایشیتادور می شنود
وایشیتور بمعنی فاعل ومصدر هم می آید ایشیتمایدور نمیشنود ونشنیده است ایشیتکان وایشیتورکان وایشیتادورکان
شنونده وشنیده وبمعنی مصدر هم می آید ایشیت وایشیتکیل مفرد مخاطبه فعل امر ایشیتما وایشیتماکیل مفرد مخاطبه فعل نهی
ایشیتنك وایشیتنکز وایشیتنکلار جمع مخاطبه فعل امر ایشیتمانك وایشیتمانکز وایشیتمانکلار جمع مخاطبه فعل نهی
ایشیتمان وایشیتماس مین نمیشنوم ایشیتامین وایشیتورمین وایشیتادورمین وایشیتورام میشنوم ایشیتوردوم وایشیتدیم
شنیدم ایشیتماکوم نخواهم شنید ایشیتیب وایشیتیبان وایشیتمیش شنیده ایشیتمیشانك شنیده ایشیتماس نمیشنود
وبمعنی فاعل ومصدر منفی هم می آید چنانکه بمعنی نشنیدن کوید شعر تا ومنا ای شیخ نواسیغ ایشیتماس سیب بیندکیم
سیننك بندینك ایشیتماسلیك آنکا بند اولمیش ایشیتماسی شنیدنش ونشنیدنش ایشیتمادین از شنیدن ونشنیده
ایشیتیب بولماس وایشیتا بولماس وایشیتا آلماس نمیتوان شنید ایشیتا آلماس نمیتواند شنید ایشیتا ایشیتا استماع
کنان وبدون تکرار هم مستعملست ایشیتای وایشیتایین بشنوم وبشنود وبشنوی وشنید ایشیتاناك ایشیتکایمز
وایشیتکای بز وایشیتالی وایشیتالینك بشنویم ایشیتمانك وایشیتماکایمز وایشیتماکای بز وایشیتمالی وایشیتمالینك
نشنویم چنانکه شاهد بر رابع را در تاریخ الانبیا در دعوت حضرت نوح علیه السلام کفار را کوید که اول دعوت سوزین
آیتسا ایشیتمالی دیب قولاغلارین توتار ایردیلار ایشیتکالی برای شنیدن وتا شنیده ایشیتکاچ چون شنید وشنود
ایشیتکوچی شنونده ایشیتکوچه وایشیتکونچه وایشیتکانچه تا شنیدن وبقدر شنیدن ایشیتکوم خواهم شنید ایشیتکونك خواهی
شنید ایشیتکوسی خواهد شنید ایشیتکولوك شنیدنی ایشیتکای وایشیتسا وایشیتسون وایشیتسونلار بشنود ایشیتکودیك
وایشیتوردیك شنیدنی وهمچنانکه بشنود ایشیتتورماك بکسر شین وسکون تای اول وضم تای ثانی مصدر متعدیست
یعنی شنوانیدن وصیغ آن بالفظ تور اشتقاق می یابد ایشیتیلماك بکسر شین وتا وسکون لام مصدر انفعالست یعنی شنیده

شد تا ایشیتلکوریك وایشیتلور دیك معلوم شدنی وهمچنانکه مسموع شود وشاهد بر اول معنی اولدر تاریخ باری بعد کوکا
کما ایشیتلکوریك نیمه ایشیتیلسا تقریر قلغوسیدور من الجوامد ایش بر معنی خویش بدو معنی طرح اول معنی کا بنا شد الشاهد علیه
شعر سیغلا غنام کونکلومکا ایشیم آه دردا الوطلیم دیر اوتعنه کیم یا معموریاغار آتینك نشانه بدو معنی ابرو دویم بالمجاز بمعنی دو
کاذ لرا استعمال میشود چنانکه کوید شعر غم تا پار جهرینکا الشکیم ایچره کونکلوم پلوسین ایش کهنی تا بغان کیبی ایل غایب دیدی
ارا و بلا اشنلغ به معنی آمد اول معنی سلح وازینا ط بود چنانکه کویند ایکیمیز بیر ببرکا ایش ایلا یعنی بطبین وایش بولدی
یعنی مربوط شدند دویم امرست از بایدن تیم امرست از کاویدن چنانکه در ذیل مصدر ایشماك کذشت ایشان صرفا بچ نون آ
بمعنی بیرجانه که آنرا مربی ازار کویند الشاهد علیه شعر اوی ایچره هم کتابه هم ازاده ضرورت قودیوکا ایکان جا
قیلماق یوقا یرسا اول اوی وخشا بیر کیشیکا که آنرا بولماغای تیشان وسیلباق اشترك بسکون شین وکاف عنق
قرشت بمعنی موج بود خواه از دریا باشد وخواه از تالاب وروودخانه چنانکه در مقاله دهم از حیرة الابرار در باب درویشی
کوید شعر توزکور و نوبه مهر چو توبرغان سوده ایکری بولوبر اشترك اورغان سوده ودر بعضی از ملهب مشترك باشند
بسکون شین وفتح تای قرشت نام ظلیفه ایست از اوزبکیه که در سمت شرقی ملغار بخشند وموضع سکنای ایشان تمام
ایشته بفتح تای قرشت ترکی رومی اسم اشارتست بمعنی اینك وعربی یعنی هذا ایشیم بکسر جیم عجمی احکا رود مباشر کار دره کو
چنانکه در مثنوی سکندری کوید شعر کرا ایش ایلشیغه توشتی یه اولوق نیمه ایش اولوق ایشیچی تایغولوق ونیز در مثنوی سیاره
در داستان مسافر اقلیم سیم کوید شعر ایلا معنی از ره آزاده سفرلیغ این اتمالك آماده ایشیم لا داون کوزلی کیچیلکا
تا که بولدی مرتب اول اسباب ایشقریق بسکون شین وکسر قاف اول در ای قرشت بدو معنی بود اول کوزه ایت اولدر که سوراخ
در دشت آن قرار مید هند چون اطفال باد در آن مید هند صدا میکنند وآنرا ایشکلانیز نامند دویم ترنجی را کویند که باد
نیم داشته باشد ایش کوچ بمعنی کارد کار باشد ایشکلان بمعنی اول ایشقریق بود چنانکه مذکور شد ایش کوچ از اتباع آ
بمعنی کار روا بود چنانکه لفظ کار بتنهائی استعمال میشود ولفظ بار بتنهائی مستعمل نیست بر هم از انقرالمغز دم
کفته میشود لیکن کوچ تنها افاده معنی نمیکند ایشکن بکسر کاف وسکون نون ترکی رومی تنها راست بود المجاز آ
خوشنو را هم کویند ایشلك بفتح لام وسکون کاف باصطلاح رومیه بمعنی کار کرده وکار آزموده باشد ایشیم ایشوق کوبی
طرح اول بمعنی روشن ومنور باشد دویم ترکی رومی کلاه خود بود وبضم ب ترکی رومی بمعنی پهلوان نوشته ایشیك بکسر شین
خانه وسرا باشد الشاهد علیه شعر قوتیکم نوشنا آهیم کوزتاری بین چقا الماس بیراونکلیغ که قالغانی ایشکنا ع
سنار ایچره فله مثنوی چاکلیك کوکسوم ایشیکه حیم اوی بیت الحزن اولا ایشیك نینك حلقه سیدور
ایشکاکی بلغت مغولی بند بود ایشین برقم اکویند بن ملک شعر بولوتکوکا ایشین ایشناب
تار یا عیب یا معمور آید مع الطاء ایطلغی بسکون طاء حطی کسر غین معجمه حرف طا را کویند مع الظاء المعجمه ایظلغی بسکون ظا — ایط × ایظ
حرف ظا را کویند مع الغین ایغیر باشباع کسره وکسر غین معجمه وسکون را روز بروز ضعف آن قوه میافزاید — ایغ
مع القاف ایق بروزن تیغ طرف نشیب مرود ورود خانه را کویند ونیز بمعنی باشد ضد آن اکر — ایق
سمت علیا وطرف بالای مجنب باشد وزمانند ایقلیغ ترکی رومی نام سازی بود که آنرا بغاجه کانچه وغیره کوینده
مع الکاف من المشتقات ایکماك بسکون کاف بمعنی کاشتن بود وباکاف عجمی بمعنی خم کردن باشد ایکتی کاشت ایکدی باکاف عجمی خم — ایك

ایکوتك کاشتیم ایکمونك باکاف عجمی خم کردیم ایکار وایکادور میکارد وباکاف عجمی خم میکند وایکار بمعنی فاعل ومصدرهم می آید
ایکماید ونمیکارد ونکاشته است وباکاف عجمی خم نمیکند ونکرده است ایکگان وایکلرکان وایکادورکان کارنده وکاشته
چنانکه شاهد بر اول معنی اول در بحر نامطبوع کوید شعر بوکاشدا ای دهقان نیمه آزمون ایتیم وباغلیغی ایکگانکا بحر
بر بوقودن وباکاف عجمی بمعنی خم کننده وخم کرده وبمعنی مصدرهم می آید ایکت وایکیکیل مفرد مخاطبه فصل امر ایکیلوایکیکیل
مفرد مخاطبه فصل نهی ایکینك وایکینکیز وایکینکلار جمع مخاطبه فصل امر ایکمانك وایکمانکیز وایکمانکلار جمع مخاطبه فصل نهی
ایکان وایکماسمین نمیکارم وباکاف عجمی خم میکنم ایکامین وایکارمین وایکادورمین وایکارام میکارم وباکاف عجمی خم میکنم
بکارید ایکماکیم کاشتیم وباکاف عجمی خم کردیم ایکاکوم نخواهم کاشت وباکاف عجمی خم نخواهم کرد ایکیب وایکیبان وایکیمیش کاشته
وباکاف عجمی خم کرده ایکیمشانات کاشته وباکاف عجمی خم کرده ایکماس نمیکارد وباکاف عجمی خم نمیکند وبمعنی فاعل ومصدر منفی هم
ایکیاسی کاشتنش ونکاشتنش وباکاف عجمی خم کردنش ونکردنش ایکمادین از کاشتن ونکاشته وباکاف عجمی از خم کردن وخم نکرده
ایکیب بولماس وایکیا بولماس وایکماك بوماس نمیتوان کاشت وباکاف عجمی خم نمیتوان کرد ایکا آلماس نمیتواند کاشت وباکاف عجمی خم
کرد ایکا ایکا کاشته کاشته وباکاف عجمی خم کنان خم کنان وبدون تکرار هم مستعملست ایکای وایکاین بکارم وبکارم ونکارم
وکاشته وباکاف عجمی خم کنم وکند وکنی وکرده ایکالك وایکگانیز وایکگای نیز وایکالو ایکالینك بکاریم وباکاف عجمی خم کنیم
ایکگالی برای کاشتن وتا کاشته وباکاف عجمی برای خم کردن وتا خم کرده ایککاچ چون کاشت وبکارد وباکاف عجمی چون خم کرد وکند
ایککوچی کارنده وباکاف عجمی خم کننده ایکگوچیدا ایکگوچیدو ایککاچه تا کاشتن وبقدر کاشتن وباکاف عجمی تا خم کردن وبقدر خم کردن
ایکگوم خواهم کاشت وباکاف عجمی خم خواهم کرد ایکگونك خواهی کاشت وباکاف عجمی خم خواهی کرد ایکگوسی خواهی کاشت وباکاف
وباکاف عجمی خم خواهی کرد ایکگولیك کاشتنی وباکاف عجمی خم کردنی ایکگای وایکا وایکسا وایکسون وایکیلیك بکارید وباکاف
عجمی خم کنید ایکگودیك وایکاردیك کاشتی وهمچنانکه کاشته شود وباکاف عجمی خم کردنی وهمچنانکه خم کرده شود
ایکیلماك مع اللام کاشته شدن وباکاف عجمی خم شدن ایکیلدی کاشته شد وباکاف عجمی خم شد چنانکه کوید شعر
ضعفلیغ جسمیم ایکیلدی کثرت بیکانیدین وشاخ غلح نینك شاخی خم ایکگان بادین کورونك وباقی صیغه موافق اول
بالام اشتقاق می یابد ایکتورماك مع التا مصدر متعدیست بمعنی کاراندن وصیغ آن بالفظ تور اشتقاق می یابد ایکدورماك
مع الدال باکاف عجمی مصدر متعدیست بمعنی خم فرمودن وصیغ آن بالفظ دور اشتقاق می یابد ایکدیرماك مع الدال باکاف عجمی
مصدر متعدیست بمعنی خم فرمودن وصیغ آن بالفظ دیر اشتقاق می یابد ایکیرماك بکسر کاف عجمی وسکون رای قرشت دو معنی دارد
کردانیدن دویم بطلراب معنی رشته تابیدن استعمال میشود ایکیردی کردانید وتابید چنانکه بمعنی ثانی کوید شعر ایکیردی
نعتینك نوابی کوزاو جیبرله اکر باقنامك مطبع اولغای آنکا نساج المسلج ایکیردیك کردانیدیم وتابیدیم ایکیردور
ایکیرادور میکرداند ومیتابد وایکیرور بمعنی فاعل ومصدرهم می آید ایکیرمایدور نمیکرداند ونکردانیده است ونتابیده است
ایکیرکان وایکیرورکان وایکیرادورکان کردانندهو کردانیده وتابنده وتابیده الشاهد علی المعنی الرابع شیخ انکه بیرم ایکیر
ایسیله کونا چیکیلیب ایکینیکا انحش لیغ تیکیلیب وبمعنی مصدرهم می آید چنانکه شاهد بر اولین معنی کردانیدن
در عنوان داستان بهرام کوید که خسرو وبهرام خانی تا باب توشوبی ودیدانیه بیر قوغان ایکیرکانی واونیه قورغانی
ارك دولت خسرو ایکیرکان قلعه بنیاد ده بفیه کیرکانی وحق امروی ایکیرکان ایدر فصل انکیرکان باالف مفتوحه

ساکن خوانده و بمعنی کردانیدن درمفتوحات الف نوشته اند و صورت مذکور را شاهد آورده سهو کرده ایکرو ایکرکیل مفرد ناظر
انفصل امر و ایکرنام کیاهیست تلخ چنانکه مذکور شود ایکرنا و ایکرنا کیل مفرد غائب نفصل نهی ایکرنیک و ایکرنیکز و ایکرنیکلار
جمع غائب نفصل امر ایکرنا نک و ایکرنا نکز و ایکرنا نکلار جمع غائب نفصل نهی ایکرنارمن و ایکرنا رمن میکردانم و میتابم ایکرکی
و ایکرور بین و ایکرادور بین و ایکرور ام میکردانم و میتابم ایکرور رم و ایکرنا کیم کردانیدم و تابیدم ایکرنا کوم نخواهم
و نخواهم تابید ایکریب و ایکرپان و ایکرپش کردانیده و تابیده ایکرپشانک کردانیده و تابیده ایکرنا س میکردانند
ایکرنا س میکردانند و بمعنی فاعل و مصدر منفی هم می آید ایکرنا ی کردانید نش و تابیدنش ایکرنا دین
از کردانیدن و نکردانیدن و از تابیدن و نتابیدن ایکریب بولماس و ایکرنا بولماس و ایکرنا لماس نمیتوان کردانید
تابید ایکرا لماس نمیتوان کردانید و نمیتوان تابید ایکرا ایکرا کردانید کردانید و تابید تابید و بدون تکرار هم مستعملست
ایکرای و ایکرایین بکردانم و بکرداند و بکرداننی و کردانیده و بتابم و بتابد و بتابی و تابیده ایکرنا ک و ایکرکا نیز و ایکرکای
و ایکرلی و ایکرالینک بکردانیم و بتابیم ایکرکالی برای کردانیدن و تا کردانیدن و برای تابیدن و تا تابیدن ایکرکاچ
چون کردانید و بکرداند و چون تابید و بتابد ایکرکوچی کردانند و تابنده ایکرکو و ایکرکانچه و ایکرکونچه تا کردانیدن
و مقدم کردانیدن و تا تابیدن و مقدم تابیدن ایکرکوم خواهم کردانید و خواهم تابید ایکرکونک خواهی کردانید و خواهی
تابید ایکرکوسی خواهد کردانید و خواهد تابید ایکرکولوک کردانیدنی و تابیدنی ایکرکای و ایکرلا و ایکرنا و ایکرسون
ایکردیک بکرداند و بتابد ایکرکودیک ایکرور دیک کردانیدنی و همچنانکه بکرداند و تابیدنی و همچنانکه بتابد ایکارتما
بفتح کاف بمعنی لازم و متعدی هر دو آمده یعنی کردیدن و کردانیدن چنانکه در خسرو شیرین در وصف اسب بمعنی کردیدن
کوید شعر خرامی اسرکا چقماغدا قوتون دیک ایکارمانک و قتی شتافتن قوبون دیک ایکاردی کردید و کردانید
ایکاردیک کردیدیم و کردانیدیم ایکاردور و ایکارادور میکردد و میکرداند شاهد علی الاول بالمعنی الثانی شعر
کهی کرست ایکاردور باد پا خود حیلی با ربودا راضه قویون میتکاچ املکیم خاشاکنی و ایکارور بمعنی فاعل و مصدر هم می آید
ایکارمایدور میکردد و نکردیده است و میکرداند و نکردانیده است ایکارکان و ایکارورکان و ایکارادورکان کردنده و کرداننده
و کردانندی و کردانیده و بمعنی مصدر هم می آید ایکارو ایکارکیل مفرد غائب نفصل امر و ایکار بمعنی زین هم باشد چنانکه
شود ایکارنا و ایکارنا کیل مفرد غائب نفصل نهی ایکارنیک و ایکارنیکز و ایکارنیکلار جمع غائب نفصل امر ایکلمانک و ایکارنانک
و ایکارنانکلار جمع غائب نفصل نهی ایکارنان و ایکارناس مین میکردم و میکردانم ایکارامین و ایکارادورمین و ایکارادور
و ایکارادورام میکردم و میکردانم ایکارنادوروم و ایکارنا کیم کردیدم و کردانیدم ایکارنا کوم نخواهم کردید و کردانید ایکاریب
و ایکاریان و ایکارپش کردیده و کردانیده شاهد علی الاول بالمعنی الثانی شعر کوک ابلقینی ایکاریب ای قوناش
سنان تار تیغ مکر بو نوبه قیلدینک عیان نبرد سنکی ایکارپشانک کردیده و کردانیده ایکارناس میکردد و میکرداند
بالمعنی الاول شعر ایکارناس کوک حصاری دورینه ترک فلک کوکاج ایو وظالف اشهبین پرخشان ضرور چابکسوارین ایکارنا
کردیدنش و نکردیدنش و کردانیدنش و نکردانیدنش ایکارنادین از کردیدن و نکردیدن و از کردانیدن و نکردانیدن ایکاریب بولماس
ایکارنا بولماس و ایکارنا لماس نمیتوان کردید و کردانید ایکارالماس نمیتواند کردید و کردانید ایکارا ایکارا کردان کردان
و کردانده کرداننده و بدون تکرار هم مستعملست ایکارای و ایکارایین بکردم و بکردد و بکردی و کردیده و بکردانم و بکرداند

ایکارنانک و ایکارکانیز و ایکارکای نیز و ایکارلی و ایکارالینک بکردیم و بکردانیم ایکارکالی برای کردیدن و تا کردیدن و برای
کردانیدن و تا کردانیدن ایکارکاچ چون کردید و بکردد و چون کردانید و بکرداند ایکارکوچی کردنده و کرداننده چنانکه بمعنی اول در لیلی
مجنون در صفت نوفل با قبیله لیلی کوید شعر دشت اهنی ایکارکوچی قوبولادین آشوبدا ابله کیم قویولادین ایکارکو و ایکارکونچه
و ایکارکانچه تا کردیدن و مقدم کردیدن و تا کردانیدن و مقدم کردانیدن ایکارکوم خواهم کردید و کردانید ایکارکونک خواهی
کردید و کردانید ایکارکوسی خواهد کردید و کردانید ایکارکولوک کردیدنی و کردانیدنی ایکارکای ایکارلا و ایکارنا و ایکارسون
ایکاردیک بکردد و بکرداند شاهد علی الاول بالمعنی الثانی شعر قوبون نیکلیغ ایکارنا ارشین اولشوخ دم اوبان
دیک بیندین کیم اشبو سمند ابلسه و کوپچماش ایکارکودیک و ایکارور دیک کردیدنی و همچنانکه بکردد و کردانیدنی و همچنانکه
ایکارتماک بفتح کاف و کسر را و سکون شین قرشت مصدر مفاعله است یعنی با هم کردیدن ایکارتیکان و ایکارتیشوکان و ایکارتیکان
و ایکارکان با هم کردنده و با هم کردیده و بمعنی فاعل و مصدر نیز می آید چنانکه شاهد بر اول معنی با هم کردیدن در تاریخ بابری
که قراول کیشی سی ایلیک آلیشیب اراکهست ایکارتیشکان علا اکین دین هایون نینک قراولی سیدی بولغاچ او تغییم تا چار
سیلمادی نتوانست کوید چنانکه در تاریخ بابری مذکورست که علا قلی و عواقب حقیقی دین منینک سیلمایکارتیشا تیمادی و تا قیصر
نسح موافق قول ما بجاق شین اشتقاق می یابد ایکالاماک بفتح کاف و لام مالک و صاحب شدن ایکالادی مالک شد چنانکه
در مجلس دوم از مجالس النفایس در وصف شاه بدخشان کوید که سلطان ابو سعید میرزا آلاردین صاتقاندی و ملک لارین
ایکالادوک مالک شدیم ایکالا و ایکالایدور مالک می شود و ایکالار بمعنی فاعل و مصدر هم می آید ایکالاماید ور مالک نمیشود
و نشده است ایکالاکان و ایکالاکان و ایکالایدورکان مالک شونده و مالک شده و بمعنی مصدر هم می آید ایکالا و ایکالا
مفرد غائب نفصل امر ایکالاما و ایکالاما کیل مفرد غائب نفصل نهی ایکالانک و ایکالانکز و ایکالانکلار جمع غائب نفصل امر ایکالاما
و ایکالامانکز و ایکالامانکلار جمع غائب نفصل نهی ایکالامان و ایکالامان مین مالک نمیشوم ایکالای مین و ایکالادورمین و ایکالادور
و ایکالادورام مالک میشوم ایکالادیم و ایکالاماکیم مالک شدم ایکالاماکوم مالک نخواهم شد ایکالاب و ایکالاپان و ایکالاپ
مالک شده ایکالامیشانک مالک شده ایکالاماس مالک نمیشود و بمعنی فاعل و مصدر منفی هم می آید ایکالاس مالک شد
و شدنش ایکالامادین از مالک شدن و مالک نشدن ایکالاب بولماس و ایکالانا بولماس و ایکالانا لماس مالک نمیتوان
ایکالا الماس مالک نمیتواند شد ایکالا ایکالا و ایکالای ایکالای مالک شونده شونده و بدون تکرار هم مستعملست ایکالای و ایکالایین
مالک شوم و شود و شوی مثل چنانکه شاهد بر اول کلام معنی اول در صفت میان در داستان ملا فرا آقلیم بقیم از زبان زید
خطاب با جمل تیخانه کوید که شعر بار بینان اول نقود دین ایکالاب یا لات و منات سانی کیلای ایکالماک و ایکالار
و ایکالای نیز و ایکالالی و ایکالالینک مالک شویم ایکالاکالی برای مالک شدن و تا مالک شدن ایکالاکاچ چون مالک شد و شود
ایکالاکوچی مالک شونده ایکالاکو و ایکالاکوچه و ایکالاکانچه تا مالک شدن و مقدم مالک شدن ایکالاکوم مالک خواهم شد
ایکالاکونک مالک خواهی شد ایکالاکوسی مالک خواهد شد ایکالاکولوک مالک شدنی ایکالاکای و ایکالالا و ایکالاسون
ایکالادیک مالک شود ایکالاکودیک و ایکالادیک مالک شدنی و همچنانکه مالک شود ایکلاماک بسکون کاف عجمی و نون و فتح
لام مکث کردن ایکراماک بسکون کاف عجمی و نون و فتح را و قرشت هجوم کردن و چون اشتقاق صیغ آنها منتج نا یافته بود بذکر مصدر
اکتفا شد من ابجد ایلیک بسکون کاف عجمی آتی است که بدان رشته تابند و آنرا بفارسی دوک و بعربی مغزل کویند مرض المغزل را

هم گویند چنانکه در کلیله و دمنه مذکور است که پرا کو طبیب قاتیغه کیلیب قورساغ آغریغی دیو قرارسیز بولوب ایحد
ایت ینلنا ایکه منینک ساغینچی دین ترازله بغلاب ایکا بفتح کاف عجمی بمعنی نالان و نالنده بود الشاهد علیه شعر
کتاروری غلتیغ عشقینک شعله کیلیب یری دین و طوفیچون ایکاسی کیلدی اول لعل جمیلدین ایکاچ بفتح کاف و سکون جیم
که در آخر کلمات افاده معنی هنوز میکند الشاهد علیه شعر ایلکا شام اولمیش نوا یغیه بوزونکین صبح ایرور کیم
ساغینسون روز و شامین بار ایکاچ صبح و صال و له شعر نی اوت تور روز بوکه تیماس ایکاچ ایریب آتیغ اول ایرم کوکسو
یردین ون تاش کیم الکیم و نیز در حیرة الابرار در وصف شعرای سلف گوید شعر میچیکیان مار جاسی عزم ایتی کالان ترمغه
تیماس ایکاچ تیتی لا دیر طالع هر وی بمعنی نهایت و غایت نوشته و گفته که صبا جمعا ایکاچ یعنی تا صبح و اقشام جه ایکاچ
یعنی تا شام و شعر بوبر را از حیرة الابرار شاهد آورده این ترکیب اختراعی و معنی نهایت بی‌نهایت معنی است هر گاه
خواهند استعمال نمایند صباحغه دیکن و اقشامغه دیکین تا صباحغه جه و اقشامغه جه باید گفت ایکاچی بفتح کاف
عجمی و کسر جیم همشیره بزرگ را گویند چنانکه در تاریخ الانبیا در ذکر حضرت زکریا و یحیی علیهما السلام گوید کم ایکالاچی ننک
حرم لاری ایکاچی و سینکیل ایردیلار و نیز در ذکر حضرت یعقوب علیه السلام گوید که اول شرع دا ایکی ایکاچی سینکیلا
نی بر کیشیکا نکاح قیلما قروا ایردی ایکار بفتح کاف عجمی و سکون رای قرشت زین بود که آنرا بعربی سرج نامند مرسل
سکنه ببه شعر یعنی تیز رو خوش خارا شکن باری کرک زور و بلری پیلتن مرصع ایکا بیرله زرین تا بیب یا نا غاشیه
کوهرآگین تابیب و نیز اطلاق زین کردن و کردانیدن چنانکه گذشت ایکار جهار لج را گویند ایکاک سوهان را نامند الشاهد
علیه شعر اوزلو کونلت میدی ینکیسنا اکا اوتلب بیل کیم یو تور روده هر ایر یکلیک لار ایدین بخشی ایکاک و آنرا سوهان
ساختمه اکه گویند و بعربی مبرد نامند ایکالا بمعنی هر دو چنانکه در تاریخ بابری مذکور است که معتر آنداق بولدی کیم بلخ
میرزا ظفر میرزا بیله بر ره بولغاندا ایکالا میرزا نینک نیکلیغ بیرله ایجلکای ایکالاسی هر دو نا پیش ایکالا میز هر دو ما
چنانکه در پند دادن پدر مجنون مجنون گوید شعر مین بیله و لول ضعیف سیله کیل ایکالامیز کا چلو ایله ایکالا نیکز هر دوی ما
شما ایکان بفتح کاف یعنی هست و نیز لفظ زاید نیست که در روابط استعمال میشود چنانکه گوید شعر یوزیجهد ایلیم
کونکلومنی الیبایدی قتل ایلاجه بیلامیر یوینکی جهد ایکان لاجر دوش و بکسر کاف نیز مستعمل است ایکا نجه تا بودن و مقدار بودن
یعنی اجر گوید شعر عشق و هجران اوتیدین غارمین ایکانجه یوز میننک بولدی اغبار ضا شکیم المی بر عارضین یکانکا بیور ترا
علیه شعر جانیم بیلینک شهیدی ایکانکا تانوق تورور هر آنکا نقیه بولغان کفن ارا ایکانلیکی بو ایکانین یعنی بود ترا
چنانکه شاهد بر ثانی را گوید شعر طرح عشق را اسرنی جو فرد قیلسا بیر وحدت تیماس انکا بیر کونکلنجه ایر عملاری ایکاو ایکاو
یعنی هر دو چنانکه در فرهاد و شیرین گوید شعر خزان بی ایکاو کا قیل دی تسلیم قیلیب خاتم حرمیشین داغی تفهیم ایکاو لایکاو
هر دو با هم الشاهد علی الثانی شعر نی خوش بولغای ایکاو لان مست بولساق وصل باغنده قولوم بولسا آینینکنی بو سفندا
و آغزیم دو داغیندا ایکاو کا هر دو ایکاوار بفتح کاف و واو با الف کشیده و رای بی‌نقطه بمعنی دو کس باشد ایکاو لیک یعنی دو
چنانکه گوید شعر اگر سیز هم بیم بولسانک ایکاو لیک بخشید هم بولغا ابد عمری اکرنا پنام او زومنی دیسا رام یا الغوز
ایکره بسکون کاف عجمی سبحه بود که آنرا بعربی بعیر اخوانند ایکلیچ و ایکلیش بر سر زن کنفش اشتی باشد که بیایر جنبی بود
و ما ده زنجیر اکدیش بر وزن طبیب ده معنی دارد اول اتصال و امتزاج دو چیز را گویند بایکیک کردیم محبوب طلوع را خوانند و اب

دو چیز را هم گویند شاید در این معنی مشترک باشد ایکری بسکون کاف فارسی و کسر رای قرشت دو معنی دارد اول بمعنی کج و ناراست
بود چنانکه گوید شعر قاشینکا ایرلو یا آلمان کهسر دیر و دیدی که سحبه راست ایماس ایکری بولادی چوینه محراب دوییم باشد
باشد که آنرا بفارسی چنگ و بعربی بربط خوانند الشاهد علیه شعر نوا اکر تیلار جتاملت تو تمراق که ایکری دین کوی
لبلا بیچه یرو بی بلیک حیکار آوازی و بعربی بمعنی در حیرة الابرار گوید شعر توز دور دور ایکری علی ناسازی بروق ایکری
بولور ایدی که ناساز ایرو قله شعر خلق طعن ایتسا نولی ایکیلیک المقلوق ایکری نیکلیغ کمقیلور بل اثری بر مضاد
و مؤلف رومی ایکری را بمعنی در نوشته و شعر بوبر را شاهد آورده بابجاز بمعنی در استعمال میشود اما در این شعر بمعنی کج بمعنی
ایکریجه بترکی رومی نوعیست از سکر ایکریک بترکی رومی سطح آب بود که دابر انیز گویند ایکری لیت کچی نلر استی ایکری ده
بمعنی گرداب نباشد چنانکه گوید شعر چرخ بحر قعری قیلغان تمنا ذره لار مهر غواصین بو ایکریم بحر مسر گرداب کورنک
و بترکی رومی نمدیست که بر زیر زین افکنند ایکلیک در ونا که چنانکه در کلیله و دمنه مذکور است که ایکلیکلین زیر
دارو دین اگرچه سیلوبر کا اینینک سنا غالوری اول دار ودین دو دیو بینی ایو رو رسه شعر تا پیتیم شرف یوز ونک سیله ای یار
خوش لقا دایکلیک کونکولکا بولدی سینینک صحبتینک دوا ایکما بمعنی چنین بود الشاهد علیه شعر یوز ونکا
هر تار ویدین ایکما قاش ایر ور اخود بتی آیدا ایکی هندو غه واقع اولدی بیچوه ایکن بسکون کاف عجمی و نون دو معنی دارد اول
سر دوش و کتف را خوانند چنانکه در لیلی مجنون در حکایت بیخود شدن و بدوش کشیدن دایه او را گوید شعر ایکینکا
قویوب بیر یغی طلبی آنداق که قوبا شی جرخ زلبی دوییم مجاز بمعنی باز و آمده چنانکه گوید شعر قدینک خرامی ایکینک
جفلبی او کونا دی غریب نخل که دایم ایرور آنکا بشلنغ و آنرا ایکین بکسر کاف نیز گویند ایکنه بسکون کاف عجمی و فتح نون
باشد که آنرا بعربی ابره نامند ایکی آبو سون بمد الف و ضم بای ابجد و سین مهمله دو همشیره را گویند ایکی اوج تقاب کنایه
از هیولی و صورت و موالید ثلثه چنانکه شاهد آن در الف مفتوحه در ذیل الکی مذکور شد ایکی سکر عبارت از جهار بود که
آنرا دو پیکر نامند چنانکه در خسرو شیرین در مطلع گوید شعر طرب ایلاب جنا دیم ایکی پیکر قوبا بر ضیا آیلد الماتین یکورب
ایکی توه لیک یولوم یعنی راه دو لشتره و آن کنایه است از افق که مطلع صبح صادق و کاذب است چنانکه در لیلی مجنون گوید شعر
چون مهر سیهر بولدی یا روتیق ایکی توه لیک یولومنی تو تتی ایکید ادو باره چنانکه در داستان هفتم از سبعه سیار گوید
شعر کیشی اولکا نکا تیغ کین سورماس بیر اولوکنی ایکید اولتورماس ایکیر بکسر کاف و سکون رای قرشت نام گیاهیست
که بعمه به در بهشکم نافع است و آنرا بفارسی صبح گویند و بهترین آن در سپاهان بود و نیز آنرا ستاره رشته نامیدن و کرده اند
چنانکه در ذیل صندل بیکرنا که گذشت ایکیرا د بفتح رای اول و سکون ثانی یعنی دوتا چنانکه در صحبت المتحیرین
در وصف عبدالصمد کاتب گوید که غلط سیز مصرع بیتیماکای بعضی بیر دا بیر دا بیکیرا دا بیکه آر تو قا پیات هم تراقیلب تور
بفتح میم علی در سیتر را گویند ایکیز بکسر کاف و سکون رای هوز بمعنی توام باشد الشاهد علیه شعر بو زونکنا توناش
با تو نایش یو زونک بو ایکان که نادی بی ایکا ن فرقی ایماس نیچوک که ایکیز ایکیسی هر دو یش ایکیشا د یعنی هر دو نا ایکی تا د
ترکی رومی کاهیست که آنرا بفارسی خون سیاوشان و بعربی دم الاخوین گویند ایکی لیک بمعنی دوی بود در لیلی مجنون
وصل ایلادی ایکی لیکنی ماتیح دو جهدن تو تتی ساتیح ایکین بکسر کاف و سکون نون به پنج معنی استعمال شود اول کشت و
زرع را گویند چنانکه گوید شعر خطینک باشی جیکا لی خالینک کهرو نماس کو کلری چون ایکین کم بولدی دانه تو

مشغا بر کبر نماید از جمله روابط است و بمعنی اثبات استعمال میشود الشاهد فیکه شعر زلفو ینکا خال عجم را سیه
نقطه و بیت بوزو ینکا لنلف و دوا یکبندا و الایکن سیم لفظ زاید یست که از برای تزیین کلام در روابط واقع می شود چنانچه
کوید شعر دیو اهل ایمرمنک تاریخ ایلاهیندا اسیو کفر اهل ایمرسین کبی بار موایکین بکث ولو سعترسین ایکین
سو نوانی تیلبه بو قسا پرکان کیشیلاهیند بسنکا و با معنی با نیم کاف نیز مستعملت چنانکه در فوق مذکور شد چاپ
مرادف ایکیسین باشد بمعنی و تابش و در معنی مخالف تیلمس و موافق استعمالات چنانکه بطریق ایهام کوید شعر ای کونکو
کوید مطلع نمین تمام عین بوایکین تبوچون کرهرکز ایلاهاش ایا تا پند بیم بیهان مضی دو باشد چنانکه در تاریخ بابری مذکور
که باغنو تیر اتکان ندین سو نمات بین ایکین جا پشیب کیلا باشلادیلر و با کاف عجمی و دوش و کتفه را کوید و مجاز ابا تو دار
نامند چنانکه کوید شعر یاشیل تون وایکینینک پرله تامینک ولعروه کمایکی بایندین آریلیش لیکی اخضر ...
بکسر کاف و سکون نون و جیم بمعنی توتیم باشد چنانکه در بستی سکندر بی در پیغام پادشاه کشمیر اسکندر کوید شعر ایکنج
اول که بار آنجه افتو کریم مولجب سیکان بار جاسینی جا کریم ایکینجی بکسر جیم بمعنی دوبین چنانکه کوید شعر ایجب کرکه
شاغر کاش آیدا قیتجو داولسام کیم ایکینجی سور دیر هم بو للغاتی معانی غنیم امکان ایکینجی بکسر کاف و دال و سکون نون و
عصر را کوید ایکینکر یعنی تمام هر دو چنانکه در جناب لنز مکارم دینا کوید شعر اکر ایکینکرا اسید لواقع اما
یقین که مقصد الحقیقه تا پماغو نک قربت ایکی یوز لوک بعضی دورو نماید الشاهد فیکه شعر ایکی یوز لوک بولمانک
ایل بو باغ نینک جناکلی کر قزارو دیر یوزی لیکن تا نا پرنار غار دور مع اللاتم من المشتقات ایلماق کرمتن و سنطر کرمتن
چنانکه کوید شعر کیر بیکینک یا یمیش کونکول لار ایلغا بی قلاب لار تپیلیدور او لشوخ نینک کونکو لونی کونزکا ایلماقیم
ایلدی کرفت المدوق کرفتیم ایلار و ایلاد دور میکرد چنانکه مثل است که دولتا کرسینی کونزیکا ایلادین تیلاتما سا
آن اوزی تیلادی والادیعنی میبرد و بمعنی فاعل و مصدر نیز می آیدا یلما ید دور میکرد و نکرفت و بمعنی مصدر نیز هم می آید
ایلغان و ایلادیغان و ایلادیغان کیرنده و کرفته و بمعنی مصدر نیز می آیدا یلما غان و ایلماید دیغان نکیرنده و نکرفته و بمعنی مصدر نیز
هم می آیند چنانکه بمعنی نکرفتن در فرهاد و شیرین در بی التفاتی موکلین فرهاد با رخسرو کوید شعر ایتمک حکمینه
پروا ایلماغانی ایشاسین کونزکا مطلق ایلماغانی ایلماتیلیقیل مفرد مخاطب از فعل امر الشاهد علی الاول شعر عمر او تمایش
اندیشه قیل و هر نفسه بو فتوح میر بیل ای شه کمانی کونزکا ایلکیم نی کدا قا لورنی شه والمعنی بی فایده هم طرح کردند
جوامد مذکور شود ایلماو ایلماغیل مفرد مخاطب از فعل نهی ایلینک عا ایلینکیز و ایلینکلار جمع مخاطب از فعل امر ایلما نک و ایلما نکیز
ایلما نکلار جمع مخاطب از فعل نهی ایلمانک ایلماس مین عمیکیرم الشاهد علی الاول من عبید خان اوزبک شعر کل باشلیغی تیلمان
نظرونینکا جمالینک باریلیه کونزکا ایلمان سرونینی نمازینکا لینک باریلیه ایلادمین و ایلادیمین و المتنفیه ایلادیم میکردم و ایلادیمین
والادرام بمعنی میخیمم هم باشد ایلادیم کا ایلما غیم کرفتیم ایلماغوم نخواهم کرفت ایلسانک و ایلغای و ایلغای بکیری الشاهد علی
الثانی شعر هر نیچه کیر بیک سنا نیغه تولانی کونکلینی هر زمان ایلغای مین ای بد مهر آی پر کونزکا ایل و ایلغای مین بمعنی
ایلغادسیکی هم آمده ایلیب و ایلیبان و ایلیش کرفته ایلیشانک کرفته ایلماس عیکیرد و بمعنی فاعل و مصدر منفی هم می آید
ایلماسی کرفتن و نکرفتن ایلماس نکرفتن ایلماسی از کرفتن و نکرفته ایلیب بولماو ایلماس تکلیف نمیتوان کرفت ایلا الماس نمیتواند کرفت
ایلا ایلا کرفته کرفته و بد و تکرار هم مستعملت ایلادی و ایلادمین بکیرم و بکیرد و بکیری و کرفته و بجنه کم و کند

و کرده و در این معنی با صیغه مصدر المحلال الا شتراک لطرد ایلیناق و ایلیناییز و ایلینای نیز و ایلادیلو ایلادیلینک بکیم و بکیرد
و ایلا لینک بمعنی بخته کیم هنم آمده ایلینا لی برای کرمتن و تاکرفته و شاهد آن در ذیل ایلیناق مذکور شد ایلینلیچ جون کرفت
و بکیرد ایلینوجی کیرنده ایلینوجی و ایلینو بخه و ایلینا بخه تاکرمتن و بمعنی کرمتن ایلینوم خواهم کرفت ایلینون خواهی کرفت ایلینو
خواهد کرفت ایلینولوق کرفتنی ایلینای و ایلاد و ایلاسا و ایلسون و ایلدیک بکیرد الشاهد علی الثانی شعر تدبیک
جمند اکورو بیلغان اکر سوین کونزکا ایلسا انما نا کر اکو را کا یعنی لچ وطالع هر بچی بیا و ایمعنی ایلیز کویدن نوشته
سهو کرده ایلینونک و ایلادولک کرفتنی و جمانکه بکیرد الشاهد علی الاول ایلینو نیکول شعرای نوایی اولیه پیو شدن وفا
کوز تو تماغیل کیم جنون اهلینی اسلاکونزکا ایلینو بلیتماس ایسلدور ماغ مصدر متعدیست یعنی بند کردن و کران شدن
صبح آن برای سیاق با قلطه در اشتقاق می آید ایلیناق بکسر لام و سکون نون در معنی ایمعنی را و ابند و کرفتار شدن ریعم
کرم شدن و در اکثر در و معنی ایلیز شدن نوشته سهو کرده ایلینادی بند و کرفتار شدیم کرم شد ایلینادیم بند و کرفتار
شدیم و بیم کرم شدیم چنانکه بمعنی اول کوید شعر باچی کونکول تقوی بشیات هر نیکا باغلادی تاپری و ایلیدی بسین کد
که بین بو نوع ایلینادیم و بمعنی ایلینادیم آمد بر شعر آمیدیم بمالف و کسر خوانند و بمعنی منوع شدن از جم کت
نوشته و شعر ایمعنی شاهد آورده و طالع هر دو جسم با این نحو معنی کفته و بسلاحیت آن ایلیناق ر است ایلیحاقان تراریا
لفظ و معنی در و لغز اعلا است و ایلینادیم را بکره ایلیناق نوشته که بمعنی بر شدیم و ایلیز شدیم نمی هم مناسبت که ایلینادی
بند و کرفتار شدیم و بیم کرم شدیم ایلینور و ایلینادور بند و کرفتار میشود و بیم کرم میشود الشاهد علی الاول المحو ایلیناتا
بخاری شعر فارس و خالینکا وابسته ایرور بغزده رحمه توش دوز اغمه ایلینورکا سوو دانه ایچون و ایلینور بمعنی فاعل و مصدر
هم می آید ایلینایدیبر کرفتار میشود و نشده است و بیم کرم میشود و نشده است ایلینفان و ایلینورغان و ایلینادیرغان بند و کرفتار
شونده و کرفتار شده و بیم کرم شونده و بیم کرم شده و بمعنی مصدر هم می آیند چنانکه شاهد بر اول بمعنی کرفتار شدن در تاریخ بابری
در طریق شدآهو مذکور است که کیک ایلینفا دین سونک بیراق کتار کا تانیم بولغای ایلین ها ایلینفیل مفرد مخاطب از فعل
ایلینما و ایلینماغیل مفرد مخاطب از فعل نهی ایلینینک و ایلینینکیز و ایلینینکلار جمع مخاطب از فعل امر ایلینمانک و ایلینمانکیز
و ایلینمانکلار جمع مخاطب از فعل نهی ایلینمان و ایلینماس مین بند و کرفتار میشوم و بیم کرم میشوم ایلینور و ایلینمام بند
کرفتار شدم و بیم کرم شدم ایلینماغوم بند و کرفتار نخواهم شد و بیم کرم نخواهم شد ایلینیب و ایلینیبان و ایلینیش بند
و کرفتار شده و بیم کرم شده چنانکه شاهد بر اول بمعنی اول در تاریخ بابری مذکور است کهایکی قولاغوزین کیبین ایلکا لیبکا توت
جاینیم کیراکلی اوقا ایلینیش لدی ایلینیش ایلینماس بند و کرفتار شد و بیم کرم شد ایلینماس بند و کرفتار نمیشود و بیم کرم نمیشود و بمعنی
فاعل و مصدر منفی هم می آید ایلینماسی بند نشدن و نشده نشد و بیم کرم شد و نشده نشد ایلیناماد بی بانبد شده و بند نشده و از
بیم کرم شدن و بیم کرم نشده ایلینیب و لمس و ایلینسا بولماس و ایلیناماقی و لماس بند و کرفتار نمیتوان شد و بیم کرم نمیتوان شد
ایلینا آلماس بند و کرفتار نمیتواند شد و بیم کرم نمیتواند شد ایلینا ایلینا بند و کرفتار شده شده و بمعنی تکرار هم مستعملت
ایلینای و ایلینایمین بند و کرفتار شوم و شود و شوی و شده و بیم کرم شوم و شود و شوی و شده ایلیناق و ایلینفای نیز
و ایلینالی و ایلینا لینک بند و کرفتار شوید و بیم کرم شوید ایلینغالی برای بند و کرفتار شدن و تا بند و کرفتار شده و برای بیم
کرم شدن و تا بیم کرم شده ایلیناچ چون بند و کرفتار شد و شود و چون بیم کرم شد و شود ایلینوچی بند و کرفتار شونده و بیم کرم شونده

١١٥٧

ایلینغوجیغا ایلینغوچه و ایلینغانچه تا بند و گرفتار شدن و بقدر کم قلیل شدن و تا نیم کم شدن و بقدر نیم کم شدن ایلینغوم
گرفتار خواهم شد و نیم کم خواهم شد ایلینغونک بند و گرفتار خواهی شد و نیم کم خواهی شد ایلینغوسی بند و گرفتار خواهد
شد و نیم کم خواهد شد ایلینغولوق بند و گرفتار شدنی و نیم کم شدنی ایلینغای و ایلینا و ایلینسا و ایلینسون و ایلینار
بند و گرفتار شود و نیم کم شود ایلینغودیک و ایلینوردیک بند و گرفتار شدنی و همچنانکه شود و نیم کم شدنی و همچنانکه
ایلیتماق مع التاء مصدر متعدیست همان بمعنی نیم کم کردن باشد چنانکه در لیلی مجنون در بیان پیری لیلی گوید شعر
یوزلاندی آتا سیغه ایلیتماق تیر سوز ... بن ایلیتماق و صیغ آن موافق ... او لتا تای قرشت اشتقاق ... ایلیشماک
مع الثاء بمعنی بند شدن چیزی بجائی و کائی بودن از مصدر و صیغ مشتقه بسبب ماخوذ بودن از لفظ ایلمک است
که بمعنی دام باشد ایلیشتی بند شد ایلیشتوک بند شدیم ایلیشور و ایلیشادور بند میشود و ایلیشور بمعنی فاعل و مصدر
هم می آید ایلیشماینور بند نمیشود و نشده است ایلیشکان و ایلیشورکان و ایلیشادورکان بند شونده و بند شده و بمعنی مصدر
هم می آید ایلیشور و ایلیشکیل امر مفرد غایب از فعل امر ایلیشما و ایلیشماکیل امر مفرد غایب از فعل نهی ایلیشینک و ایلیشینکیز
جمع غایب از فعل امر ایلیشمانک و ایلیشمانکیز و ایلیشمانکلار جمع غایب از فعل نهی ایلیشمان ایلیشامین بند شوم
ایلیشامیز و ایلیشورمیز و ایلیشادورمیز و ایلیشورم بند میشوم ایلیشورم و ایلیشماکیم بند نشدیم ایلیشماکوم بند نشد
شد ایلیشیب و ایلیشسان و ایلیشکیش بند شده ایلیشمانک بند نشدن ایلیشماس بند نمیشود و بمعنی فاعل و مصدر منفی
هم می آید ایلیشمابی بند نشدن و نشده ایلیشیب بولماس و ایلیشا بولماس و ایلیشماق اولماس بند نمیتوان شد
ایلیشا آلماس بند نمیتواند شد ایلیشا ایلیشا بند شده بند شده و بدون تکرار هم مستعملست ایلیشای و ایلیشاین بند شوم
و شوی و شده ایلیشانک ایلیشکاینه و ایلیشالی و ایلیشالینک بند شویم ایلیشکالی برای بند شدن و تا بند شده
ایلیشکاج چون بند شد و شود ایلیشکوچی بند شونده ایلیشکوچه و ایلیشکونچه و ایلیشکانچه تا بند شدن و بقدر بند شدن
ایلیشکوم بند خواهم شد ایلیشکونک بند خواهی شد ایلیشکوسی بند خواهد شد ایلیشکولوک بند شدنی ایلیشکای و
ایلیشسا و ایلیشسون و ایلیشسد و ایلیشاسد بند شود ایلیشکودیک و ایلیشوردیک بند شدنی و همچنانکه بند شود
ایلیشتوماق مصدر متعدیست بمعنی بند کردن و صیغ آن ما الفظ توان اشتقاق نمی یابد ایلغاک آمد و امثال آن را با پروزن
بجنبش و امال کردن ایلادی بجنبت ایلار و ایلایدور بجنبد الشاهد علی الاول شعر کیم بلاجین قاجا آلغای کوزقلب
دور و ایلار خلق ایلشاونده پرویزن املاک ایلادی و ایلار بمعنی ... و بمعنی فاعل و مصدر هم می آید ایلاکو ایلاکیل مفرد
غایب از فعل امر ایلاما و ایلاماکیل مفرد غایب از فعل نهی ایلانک و ایلانکیز و ایلانکلار جمع غایب از فعل امر ایلامانک و ایلامانکیز
و ایلامانکلار جمع غایب از فعل نهی ایلامان ... ایلاماغا ... الشاهد علی الثانی
شعر مجنون دیک ایلاهوین تا یکیم یله چیقو ... کو تا که ... اول ایلادیکیم دین · و ایلاهوین و ایلاهرام بمعنی
بجنبم و نیم باشد ایلادی بجنبانیدم ایلاماکیم نجنبیدم ایلاماکوم نخواهم جنبانید ایلابان و ایلامیش بجنبیده
ایلامیتا المنجنه ایلاماس نجنبد و بمعنی فاعل و مصدر هم می آید ایلاماسی نجنبیدن و نجنبیده ایلاماغا دین از جنبیدن و
نجنبیده ایلاب بولماس و ... نمیتوان جنبید ایلای آلماس نمیتواند جنبید ایلایو ایلای ایلای بجنبه کنان
و بدون تکرار هم مستعملست ایلای و ایلایین بجنبم و بجنبی و بجنبه الشاهد علی الاول المعنی الاول شعر

١١٦٢

کردنام کیم کو یکه تو فراغین ایلادی کوزجاقه سین هنیات توشو کا لولی پریشان پرله غزال الشکاین ... کوکی
و در همین معنی با مصدر ایلماق اشتراک لفظی دارد ایلاکاننغا ایلاکایز و ایلاکای یز و ایلاکای و ایلاکلانک ... و ایلاکجی و ایلاکلانک
بجنبیم هم آمده ایلاکالی برای بجنبیدن و تا بجنبه ایلاکاج چون بجنبت و بجنبد ایلاکوجی جنبیننده ایلاکوچه و ایلاکونچه و ایلاکانچه
تا بجنبد و بقدر بجنبیدن ایلاکوم خواهم بجنبت ایلاکونک خواهی بجنبت ایلاکوسی خواهد بجنبت ایلاکولوک بجنبیدنی ایلاکای و ایلاسا
و ایلاسون و ایلادیک بجنبد ایلاکودیک و ایلاردیک بجنبیدنی و همچنانکه بجنبد ایلباراماق بسکون لام و فتح با ابجد و قاف
بخته شدن و آبله کردن بعضو از گرمی آب ایلبارادی آبله کرد ایلبارار و ایلبارایدور آبله میکند الشاهد علی
من حیرت الابرار شعر کیم که ... ایلکوسیلو ایلبارارش و ایلبارار بمعنی فاعل و مصدر
ایلباراماید و هم آبله نمیکند و نکرده است ایلبارغان و ایلبارغان و ایلباراردورغان آبله کننده و آبله کرده و بمعنی مصدر
ایلبارا و ایلبارا غیل مفرد غایب از فعل امر ایلبارما و ایلبارماغیل مفرد غایب از فعل نهی ایلبارانک و ... آبله مکن
ایلبارانیب و ایلبارارمین و ایلبارایدورمین و ایلبارارام آبله میکنم ایلباردیم و ایلبارادیم آبله کردم ایلبارامادیم ...
نخواهم کرد ایلبارار ... ایلبارامیش آبله کرده ایلبارامیشمک آبله کرده ایلباراماس آبله نمیکند و بمعنی فاعل و
منفی هم می آید ایلباراماسی آبله نکردن و نکرده ایلبارمادین از آبله کردن و آبله نکرده ایلبارا ... بولماس و
ایلبارماق اولماس آبله نمیتوان کرد ایلبارا آلماس آبله نمیتواند کرد ایلبارایو و ایلبارای ایلبارای آبله کنان و بدون تکرار هم مستعملست
ایلبارای و ایلبارایین آبله کنم و کنی و کند ایلباراساق و ایلباراغایمیز و ایلبارالی و ایلبارالینک آبله
کنیم ایلباراغالی برای آبله کردن و تا آبله کرده ایلباراغاج چون آبله کرد و کند ایلباراغوچی آبله کننده ایلبارغوچه و ایلباراغانچه
ایلبارغانچه تا آبله کردن و بقدر آبله کردن ایلبارغوم آبله خواهم کرد ایلباراغونک آبله خواهی کرد ایلباراغوسی آبله خواهد کرد
ایلبارغولوق آبله کردنی ایلبارغای و ایلباراسا و ایلباراسون و ایلبارادیک آبله کند ایلبارغودیک و ایلباراردیک آبله کردنی
و همچنانکه آبله کند ایلباراتماق مع التاء مصدر متعدیست بمعنی پختن و آبله دار کردن کرمی آب عضو را ایلباراتیب ایلباراتما
ایلباراتمش آبله دار کرده چنانکه در حیرت الابرار در وصف کرمی آب گوید الشاهد علی الاول شعر ... آنکاچون المغ ...
سوجوشی ... ایلبارالیتب و باقی صیغ ... اشتقاق میابد ایلتماک بسکون لام و ضم تای قرشت بردن ...
رد چنانکه در اغاز لیلی مجنون در وصف پادشاه گوید شعر چون بار ایلیتی بخت خاوندانه تا ... بالجمله
برنجه منزل هر نوع مراد آمد ... ایلیتی از شعر ... خوانده نوشته که معنی کرم کردن بر
مرصع اشاهد آمده سهو کرده ایلیتوک بردیم ایلتور و ایلتادور میبرد الشاهد علی الاول شعر قضا ازادی ...
آی کون ... دوشش ... ایلتور و ایلتور بمعنی فاعل و مصدر هم می آید چنانکه
برنده گوید شعر نام المتور ... شرح ... مینک ... اولونغان ...
ایلتا الور و ایلتا آلادور یعنی میتواند برد چنانکه شاهد ... الاولی گوید شعر آنجا نیم ایلتا
الور ... ایلتکان و ایلتورکان و ایلتادورکان بری
برنده و برده چنانکه در لسان الطیر شاهد اولی ... در لسان الطیر گوید شعر ... ایلتکان
نفع تقوی و عبادت ایلتکان و بمعنی ... ایلتکان ...

ومعنی مصدر هم می آید ایلیت وایلیتکیل مفرد غائب امر فصل امر الشاهد علی الثانی شعر ای نوائی شاه لاغ چون گل لار
منکری یوق ایلیتکیل هم تنکری کاهیفه شئ اقه لاذ ایلیتما وایلیتماکیل مفرد غائب امر فصل فی ایلیتیپ وایلیتیکیل ایلیتکلا
جمع غائب امر فصل امر ایلیتمانات وایلیتمانکیز وایلیتمانکلار جمع غائب امر فصل فی ایلیتمان وایلیتما رمین بیرم ایلیتایین وایلیتارمین ایلیتار
ایلیتارام میبرم ایلیتایم وایلیتماکیم بردیم ایلیتماکوم بخواهم برد ایلیتیب ایلیتماس والمیمش برده الشاهد علی الثانی شعر
تعلیم ایتیتیبت ایلاحسولامر ایلیتیپان کو بونکه دمی کیم بار ورجنت غه ظلمات تیغی دین بولغان شهید ایلیتماستان برده ایلیتما
نمیبرد وبمعنی فاعل ومصدر منفی هم می آید ایلیتماس برد نش ونبرد نش ایلیتمادین از برده ونبرده ایلیتیب بولکا وایلیتساتون
ایلیتمات اولکا نمیتوان برد ایلیتا آلماس نمیتواند برد ایلیتا ایلیتا برده برده وبدون تکرار هم مستعملست ایلیتای وایلیتایین ببرم
وببری وبرده ایلیتا آلکا وایلیتا آلمایین نتوانم بردن نتواند بردن نتوانی بردن توانسته برد چنانکه شاهد بر ثانی را معنی لیلی
در لیلی مجنون در وصف پیر لیلی کوید شعر اوت قهرینه اولمایین هم آوردین خیلی دین ایلیتا آلماین کرد ایلیتسالت و
ایلیتکاینز وایلیتکای بز وایلیتای وایلیتالیک ببریم چنانکه شاهد بر رابع را در فرهاد وشیرین در کفتار فرهاد کوید شعر
ببرید بیب سودیلی خسرو غه تنکری بریدیب ایلیتایلی باشینی آبرو والمیتکالی برای بردن وتا برده ایلیتکاج چون برد
ایلیتکوجی برنده ایلیتکوچی وایلیتکوچی وایلیتکانچا بردن وبقدر بردن ایلیتکوم خواهم برد الشاهد علیه شعر تیغ ایکن
کونکول وتیغه تیکمن برمادینک ایلیتکومدور آه کیم توبراقیغه اول سوحسرتین ایلیتکونک خواهی برد ایلیتکوسی خواهد
ایلیتکولوک بردنی ایلیتکای وایلیتکای وایلیتساو ایلیتسون وایلیتک برد الشاهد علی الاول شعر دوردین غمکین مین ای ساقی قدح
سیلینی هی توغوصاتا ایلیتکای کونکلوم دین غمی سو ایلیتکودیل ایلیتوردیلت بردی وهمچنانکه برد ایلیتیرامق بکونه
وکنزای قرنت وفتح زای مهمله درخشیدن ودرمیمنه ایلیترامق کویند ایلیترادی درخشید ایلیترادوی درخشیدم
ایلیترام ایلیترایدور میدرخشد الشاهد علی الاول شعر اختری دورخ عشاقده لختر خالیغه اولکم توبایلیترایم
تولی نشک شوید وبی وایلیترا بمعنی فاعل ومعنی هم می آید ایلیترا ساید وتمیدرخشد فددرخشید است ایلیتراغان
ایلیتراغان وایلیترایدور رغبا درخشنده ودرخشیده وبمعنی مصدر هم می آید ایلیترا وایلیترا غیل مفرد غائب امر فصل امر ایلیترا ما
ایلیتراغیل مفرد غائب امر فصل فی ایلیترانک وایلیترانکیز وایلیترانکلار جمع غائب امر فصل امر ایلیترانات وایلیترانکیز وایلیترانکلار جمع غائب
امر فصل فی ایلیترانات وایلیترانا رومین میدرخشم ایلیترایمین وایلیترارمین وایلیترایدور وایلیترام میدرخشم ایلیترایم وایلیترانام
درخشیدم ایلیترانماکوم بخواهم درخشید ایلیتراب وایلیترابان وایلیترامیش درخشیده ایلیترامیشانک درخشیده ایلیتراماس
نمیدرخشد وبمعنی فاعل ومصدر منفی هم می آید ایلیتراماس نمیدرخشید نشو ندرخشید نش ایلیترامادین از ندرخشیدن
ایلیتراب بولماس وایلیترابولماسلا وایلیترا اولماق نمیتوان درخشید ایلیتراولماس نمیتواند درخشید ایلیترابو وایلیترای ایلیترای درخشان درخشان
وبدون تکرار هم مستعملست ایلیترای وایلیترایین بدرخشم وبدرخشد وبدرخشی وبدرخشید ایلیترانماق وایلیترانماین ایلیتراغای
ایلیترالی وایلیترالیک بدرخشیم ایلیتراغلی برای درخشیدن وتا درخشیده ایلیتراغاج چون درخشید وبدرخشید ایلیتراغوچی
درخشنده چنانکه در محبوب القلوب کوید کم زربفت کسوت لیلت دنیا کزین نجات وسبد ایلیتراغوچی حسین ایلیتراغوچ
ایلیتراغوچه وایلیتراغانما درخشیدن وبقدر درخشیدن ایلیتراغوم خواهم درخشید ایلیتراغونک خواهی درخشید ایلیتراغوسی
خواهد درخشید ایلیتراغولوق درخشیدنی ایلیتراغای وایلیتراغا وایلیتراسون وایلیتراشون ایلیترالیت بدرخشد ایلیتراغودیک وایلیترادی

درخشیدنی وهمچنانکه بدرخشد ایلغاماق بمعنی ایلغار کردن باشد یعنی شدن مرکب راندن وبمعنی تجسس وتفتیش نیز می آید ایلغادی
ایلغار کرد ایلغادی وقد ایلغادی ایلغار کردیم ایلغار وایلغایدور ایلغار میکند وایلغار بمعنی فاعل ومصدر منفی هم می آید وفاعل مصدر نیز
ایلغانایدور ایلغار میکند ونکرده است ایلغاغان وایلغاغان وایلغایدوغان ایلغار کننده وایلغار کرده وبمعنی مصدر هم می آید
ایلغا وایلغاغیل مفرد غائب امر فصل امر ایلغاما وایلغاماغیل مفرد غائب امر فصل فی ایلغانات وایلغانکیز وایلغانکلار جمع غائب
امر فصل امر ایلغانانات وایلغانانکیز وایلغانانکلار جمع غائب امر فصل فی ایلغامان وایلغامارمین ایلغار نمیکنم ایلغای مین و
ایلغارمین وایلغایدورمین وایلغارام ایلغار میکنم ایلغارم وایلغامایم ایلغار کردیم ایلغاماغوم ایلغار نخواهم کرد ایلغاب
وایلغابان وایلغامیش ایلغار کرده چنانکه در خاتمه سبعه سیاره کوید الشاهد علی الثانی شعر آز کیشی بر له هر طرف
کیتمیش خصمی ناشیفه ایلغابان بیمیش ایلغامیشانک ایلغار کرده ایلغاماس ایلغار نمیکند وبمعنی فاعل ومصدر منفی هم
ایلغاماسی ایلغار کردنش ونکردنش ایلغامادین از ایلغار کردن وایلغار نکرده ایلغاب بولماس وایلغابولماس وایلغاماق
ایلغار نمیتوان کرد ایلغای آلماس ایلغار نمیتواند کرد ایلغایو وایلغای ایلغای ایلغار کنان وبدون تکرار هم مستعملست ایلغای وایلغایین
ایلغار کنم وکند وکنی وکرده وایلغانماق طایفه هم هست ایلغانای وایلغاغای بز وایلغالی وایلغالیک ایلغار کنیم ایلغاغلی برای
ایلغار کردن وتا ایلغار کرده ایلغاغاج چون ایلغار کرد وکند ایلغاغوچی ایلغار کننده ایلغاغوچه وایلغاغوچه وایلغاغانچه تا ایلغار
کردن وبقدر ایلغار کردن ایلغاغوسیز دور ایلغار خواهیم کرد چنانکه در تاریخ بابری مذکورست که غوربند شکی دین حبیب آلار ایلغاغای
اوستیکا ایلغاغوسیز دور ایلغاغونکوز دور ایلغار خواهید کرد ایلغاغوسیدور ایلغار خواهند کرد ایلغاغولوق ایلغار کردنی ایلغای
وایلغاسا وایلغاسون وایلغادیک ایلغار کند ایلغاخودیک وایلغاردیک ایلغار کردنی وهمچنانکه ایلغار کند ایلیکلاماق بدست آوردن
ودستگیر کردن ایلیکلادی بدست آورد ایلیکلادوک بدست آوردیم ایلیکلاد وایلیکلایدور بدست می آورد وایلیکلار بمعنی فاعل ومصدر هم
می آید ایلیکلانمایدور بدست نمی آورد وبیاورده است ایلیکلاکان وایلیکلارکان وایلیکلایدورکان بدست آورنده وبدست آورده وبمعنی
مصدر هم می آید ایلیکلا وایلیکلاکیل مفرد غائب امر فصل امر ایلیکلانات وایلیکلانکیز وایلیکلانکلار جمع غائب امر فصل
ایلیکلامان وایلیکلامارمین بدست نمی آرم ایلیکلایمین وایلیکلارمین وایلیکلایدورمین وایلیکلارام بدست می آرم ایلیکلادیم
وایلیکلادیم بدست آوردیم ایلیکلاماکوم بدست نخواهم آورد ایلیکلاب وایلیکلابان وایلیکلامیش بدست آورده چنانکه شاهد
در تاریخ الملوک کوید که ضیاء الدین چون ایل بود ولوبا بردی توراالمای تاجی اما آنی قاووب ایلیکلاب فریدون خراسیغه سنکا
ایلیکلامیشانک بدست آورده ایلیکلاماس بدست نمی آرد وبمعنی فاعل ومصدر منفی هم می آید ایلیکلاماسی بدست آوردنش ونیاوردنش
ایلیکلامادین از بدست آوردن وبدست نیاورده ایلیکلاب بولغای وایلیکلابولغای وایلیکلاما اولغای بدست توان آورد
ایلیکلای آلغای بدست تواند آورد چنانکه در مکتوب ششم از منشات کوید که ظلمت درتاسید بن مقصود کوهر نیز وایلیکلای آلغای
ایلیکلایو وایلیکلای ایلیکلای دستگیر کنان وبدون تکرار هم مستعملست ایلیکلای وایلیکلایین بدست بیارم وبیارد وبیاری
وآورده ایلیکلانات وایلیکلاسیز وایلیکلای بز وایلیکلالی وایلیکلالیک بدست بیاریم ایلیکلاغلی برای بدست آوردن
وتا بدست آورده ایلیکلاکاج چون بدست آورد وبیارد ایلیکلاکوچی بدست آرنده ایلیکلاکوچه وایلیکلاکوچه وایلیکلاغانچه تا بدست
آوردن وبقدر بدست آوردن ایلیکلاکوم بدست خواهم آورد ایلیکلاکونک بدست خواهی آورد ایلیکلاکوسی بدست خواهد آورد
ایلیکلاکولوک بدست آوردنی ایلیکلاکای وایلیکلاسا وایلیکلاسون وایلیکلادیک بدست بیارد ایلیکلاکودیک وایلیکلاردیک

بدست آوردن و همچنانکه بدست بیارد ایلیکلاشماك مع الشین مصدر مفاعله است با یکدیگر دست بازی کردن و بدست آوردن و صیغ
موافق شو اول الحروف شین اشتقاق می یابد ایلیکلانماك مع النون مصدر انفعالست یعنی دستگیر شدن و بدست آمدن و صیغ آن با کاف
و شین اشتقاق می یابد من الجامد ایلیکچار بمعنی آمده اول دست را گویند الشاهد علیه شعر ای نوائی خسته کونکلونکنه مدد دوتماغ
راست آتنداق کیم ضعیف ایلیکا یوروق قوت عصا یا آنرا ایلیك هم خوانند و ایل و ایلیك عبارت از پنجه تا بند دست و قول قیلرز از
پنجه تا سر دوش باشد دویم بمعنی اهل و خلق و گروه بود چنانکه بمعنی اول دویم گوید شعر بو تار یا نا تلیغ آنکا کیم کیرایا مان ایل ال
کوموار ایلیك اورغان میلو ایلیکی قرا تیم سال را نامند سیم مال الماسند چهارم امرات از گرفتن چنانکه در ذیل مصدر ایلیماق
گذشت و بالمجاز بمعنی رام و مطیع نیز استعمال میشود و مقابر یوچیل را گویند که تا قلمه صغیر باشد و بر زبان ترکانی نام یکی از ماهها
العجمیست حمل اسمه ایلاك پرویزن بود که آنرا بعربی منخل خوانند الشاهد علیه شعر مجرشا بحر دونی باشیم ناغد ...
بولدی انجم پراکه چرخ چنبری کونیا ایلاك ایلان دو معنی دارد اول بمعنی مر بود که در روابط استعمال میشود دویم مار را گویند
و آنرا ییلان هم نامند ایلاکه بفتح کاف بلغت مغولی حکم باشد ایلان اوتی نباتیست که در دمین مار و کلمر آنجا روید
و بر روی زمین پهن میشود و نیز نام محلیست از توابع سمرقند ایلای بفتح لام با الف کشیده و یای مخلوط زده بمعنی برابر و حضور بود
چنانکه در لیلی مجنون در وصف بدیع الزمان میرزا گوید شعر جو دیکایلا سیدا تو قوز املاك افلاك تا شید اتو ...
بسکون لام و نون و فتح بای ابجد و ضم سین مهمله نام نوعی از زرد است ایلتی بسکون لام و کسر تای قرشت دو برادر که هر کدام زن
داشته باشند زنها را ایلتی یکدیگر گویند و آنرا بفارسی یاری نامند ایلچی با جیم عجمی رسول و پیغام رسان را خوانند الشاهد علیه شعر
نوائی که تا پاسوخا الدین خبری خیال ایلچی سینی کرچه یوز باری حیا روث و نیز هرود پیاچه دعصته در الفاظ رمناع خود گوید که
سرحد بیکلاری ایلچی سی نینک نحوی و آلانی دیکو اهلاجی سیله تا یتار بناق نینک یعنی ایلچیکان بکسر جیم و فتح کاف بمعنی لغت
مغولی خر بود که آنرا بعربی حمار گویند ایلچی لیق دو معنی دارد اول بمعنی رسالت و سفارت بود دویم گویند که مینک ایلچی لیقیمی
هزینماله چنانکه در لسان الطیر در وصف سیمرغ گوید شعر لیك سیز مینک ایلچی لیق آندین یراق تا دیبی نینک ییل لیقی کا امکان قلندی
یراق ایلخان نام پادشاهیست از اولاد اوغوز خان که آخرین خوانین مغول بوده و تور بن فریدون براو غالب آمد و نیز فرقه مغول ...
خود را ایلخان گویند یعنی سلطان الطایفه ایلدام بمعنی سریع و چابك باشد الشاهد علیه شعر ای اجل گوید ایلدام باشیم
قبل آغزیم کیم ایلامیش هجر اشکیم سیلین ایلدام ضعف جسمیم نی نیکیل ایلد ایلیق سرعت و چابکی باشد چنانکه در سکندری گوید
شعر تا پارکوی چو کاندین ایلد ایلیق ولیکن بولوب آخر آرام لیق ایلدکو نه بسکون لام و دال ابجد و زای هوز اسم اولین طبقه اتابکان
افراسیاب خانست که ملك ارسلان بن طغرل پیشرو بوده ایلدیریم برق را گویند حیرت الابرار تذییل آلیدا آوه خالندیك ایلدیریم
او تروسیدا خاشاك دیك ایلدیس بسکون لام و زای هوز و کسر دال ابجد ریشه و بیخ درخت و نبات را نامند ایلغاد استعجال
در راندن اسب و بمعنی مضارع و فاعل و مصدر هم می آید چنانکه در ذیل ایلغاماق گذشت ایلغامیش دو معنی دارد اول ایلغاد کردن
دویم بمعنی تفحص و تفتیش بود ایلغاوچی بسکون واو و کسر جیم عجمی ایلغار کننده را گویند و آن مخفف ایلغاغوچی باشد ایلغای نام
طایفه ایست از ترکمانیه بمعنی ... ایلغار کنم و کند و کرده ایلمق دو معنی دارد اول ایلچی است را نامند دویم گویند که یوز ایلمق
یعنی ... چنانکه هر دو بمعنی ... در حیرت الابرار در ذم اسراف گوید شعر آت آنکا تا رتارکه یوز ایلمقی باث سیم آنکا
بر ده که بوز ایلمقی یان یعنی اسب با و میکشد که صد ایلمقی دارد و سیم باو بسد هد که صد ایلمقی دارد و نطالع هر ...

.٧ ٤.٢ و صیغ آن بانون اشتقاق می یابد ایلیکلانماك مع تا مصدریست متعدی یعنی دستگیر فرمودن

مأخوذ از ایل و عنین و بمعنی اتباع و اشبلو نوشته سهو کرده ایلکار راك بمعنی پیشتر و اقدام بود چنانکه در سکندری در فتن
اسکندر بتسخیر خطا گوید شعر عنایت قیلیب شاه عالی مقام توقف سیز ایلکار را لیع المجه خرام ایلکاری بکسر پیش مند پیرو بود الشاهد
علیه شعر اختر نور روز که راجع اولور کا مستقیم جو یشو خلو ... کیبن کیلسا ایلکاری ایلك بسکون لام و کاف اول
و ابتدا را گویند چنانکه شاعر گفته شعر ایلك ا فقها آیتی یادا ... سوبلانا کی سوز کر ابنیاد ... و با کاف عجمی بمعنی پیشانی
الشاهد علیه شعر نیچه خورشید ... کویا قرا یمیش کوکیف تا قیلیب ... و بفتح لام پرویزن بود
کسر و فتح لام هر دو معنی دارد اول نام محلی باشد از ولایت حصار ترکستان دویم پادشاهان شهر بخارا را گویند مثل ابو الفرج ...
تا ایلك و خان قبله یغما و تتار ... حرز ... ایلیك بکسر لام ...
دنیا چند دیوان گوید شعر ایلیك ... ایل لیك ...
اول گویند که یوز ایل لیك یعنی صد ساله چنانکه ... گوید شعر کل عطری ...
بول کیتیب یوز ایل لیك اولوك خان تاپیب جون ... دویم بمعنی ... متصل نوشته شود ...
میکند چنانکه هر دو معنی گوید شعر ... ایل لیك دین ...
یعنی سالیانه چنانکه در صفه ... گوید شعر نیه خوار ... ایل لیقان و آنرا
روم بالمجاز بمعنی واجب و مرسوم استعمال نمایند ایلماك و ایلمك بسکون لام و کاف و فتح میم بمعنی دام و بند باشد الشاهد علیه
عیش صراحت ... صید ایلا ... کرچه ... سیدین ایلماکیم و نیز قلاب و زنجیری را گویند
که بدان چقه و عینك را بهر بند کنند که نیفتد ایمن بفتح لام بمعنی مع بود ایسا ... مراد ... بمعنی مع باشد که در ... الفاظ
واقع میشود و نیز از رسانیدن و غربال کردن چنانکه در ذیل مصدر ایلانماك گذشت و بفتح العین بمعنی آمده چنانکه در حرف
الف مفتوحه مع اللام مذکور شد ایلیجاق بترکی رومی مصغر ایلیغ بود یعنی نیم گرم ایلیش ایسل بکسر لام و سکون شین ...
بترکی رومی بمعنی حال باشد ایلیغ و ایلیق دو معنی دارد اول نیم گرم را گویند الشاهد علیه شعر تان توکار کونکلی ...
نینك واشك ایکی کوزی اولکو ... کیماسا ایسغ ایلیغ دویم ترکی ... نام ... که آنرا اقلیم هم گویند
مذکور شد ایلیك بکسر لام و سکون کاف دستعار نامند چنانکه گوید شعر تنفه تاش ... تیش زخمی کرسا الدی ...
تا ... ایلیکا کونکلاك سیز بدن بینك سیز ایلیك و آنرا ایل و ایلك هم خوانند چنانکه در فوق مذکور شد و با شباع کسره مغز
استخوان باشد که آنرا بعربی مخ گویند مع المیم من المشتقات ایماك مکیدن ایمدی مکید و بمعنی ما هم باشد ایمدو
مکیدیم ایما و ایما دور میمکد چنانکه شاهد بر ثانی را در تاریخ الانبیا در ذکر حضرت موسی علیه السلام گوید که صند و قی
کیلتورد یلار ایسه آچتی ... طفل کوردی کیم ... ایماد ... و ایمار بمعنی فاعل و مصدر هم می آید ایمایدور میمکد و ...
ایکان و ایمارکان و ایمادورکان مکنده و مکیده بمعنی مصدر هم می آیند چنانکه شاهد بر اول بمعنی مصدری در کل نور روز میلاد
ثانی آمده شعر سوت امیکاندا سعادت دایه بولدی تیلی چو صفاح هنر ... ایم و ایمکیل مفرد مخاطب از فعل امر
ایما و ایما کیل مفرد مخاطب از فعل نهی ایمنیك و ایمینکیز و ایمینکلار جمع مخاطب از فعل امر ایما نك و ایما نکیز و ایما نکلار
جمع مخاطب از فعل نهی ایمان و ایماس مین میمکم ایمامین و ایمارمین نفی ... ایمادیم و ایماکیم مکیدیم ایماکوم
نخوام مکید ایمیغ ایمیان و ایمیش مکید ایمیشانك مکیدی ایماس میمکد و بمعنی فاعل و مصدر منفی هم می آید

ایم

ایماسه مکیدنش و مکیدنش ایمادین از مکیدن و مکیده ایمیب بولماس و ایمنا بولماس و ایماک اولماس نمیتوان مکید ایما آلماک
نمیتواند مکید ایما ایا مکید مکیده و بدون تکرار هم مستعملست ایمای و ایماین بمکیم و بمکد و بمکی و مکیده ایمنا لط ایمکا بیرد
ایمکای بیز و ایما و ایما لینک بمکیم ایمکالی برای مکیدن و تا مکیده ایمکاج چون مکید و بمکد ایمکوچی مکنده ایمکوجه ایمکوبجه
ایمکابجه تا مکیدن و بعد مکیدن ایمکوم خواهم مکید ایمکونک خواهی مکید ایمکوسی خواهد مکید ایمکولوک
مکیدنی ایمکای و ایما و ایمسا و ایمسون و ایمدیلک بمکد ایمکویدیلک و ایماویدیلک مکیدنی و همچنانکه بمکد ایمیزماک بکسر همزه و سکون
زای هوز و فتح میم و سکون کاف است یعنی مکانیدن و شیر دادن ایمیزدی شیر داد ایمیزدوک شیر دادیم ایمیزدور
ایمیزگوسی شیر میدهد و ایمیزور بمعنی فاعل و مصدر هم می آید ایمیزماید ور شیر نمیدهد نداده است ایمیزکان و ایمیزمکان
ایمیزمکا شیر دهنده و شیر داده و بمعنی مصدر هم می آید ایمیز و ایمیزگیل مفرد مخاطب فعل امر ایمیزما ایمیزماکیل مفرد مخاطب
از فعل نهی ایمیزینک و ایمیزینکیز و ایمیزینکلار جمع مخاطب فعل امر ایمیزمانک و ایمیزمانکیز و ایمیزمانکلار جمع مخاطب فعل نهی ایمیزمان
ایمیزماسمین شیر نمیدهم ایمیزامن و ایمیزورمین و ایمیزایدورمین و ایمیزدورمین شیر میدهم ایمیزودوم ایمیزاکیم شیر دادم ایمیزاکوم
شیر خواهم داد ایمیزسه و ایمیزسیان و ایمیزمیش شیر داده ایمیزمیشانک شیر داده ایمیزماس شیر نمیدهد و بمعنی فاعل و مصدر
منفی هم می آید ایمیزماسی شیر دادنش و ندادنش ایمیزمادین از شیر دادن و شیر داده ایمیزیب بولماس و ایمیزنا بولماس و ایمیزماک
شیر نمیتوان داد ایمیزا آلماس شیر نمیتواند داد ایمیزا ایمیزا شیر داده شیر داده و بدون تکرار هم مستعملست ایمیزای ایمیزاین
شیر بدهم و بدهد و بدهی و داده ایمیزنا لط ایمیزکای بیز و ایمیزکای بیز و ایمیزالی و ایمیزالینک شیر بدهیم ایمیزکالی برای شیر دادن
تا شیر داده ایمیزکاج چون شیر داد و بدهد ایمیزکوچی شیر دهنده ایمیزکوچه و ایمیزکوبجه ایمیزکالیجه تا شیر دادن و بعد
شیر دادن ایمیزکوم شیر خواهم داد ایمیزکونک شیر خواهی داد ایمیزکوسی شیر خواهد داد ایمیزکولوک شیر دادنی
ایمیزکای و ایمیزا و ایمیزسا و ایمیزسون و ایمیزدیلک شیر بدهد ایمیزکودیلک و ایمیزوردیلک شیر دادنی و همچنانکه شیر بدهد ایمیزدور ... ایمیزمسکنیم
ایمیزماک است یعنی شیر خورانیدن و مشتق آن بالفظ دو اشتقاق می آید ایمانماک بفتح میم و سکون نون احتراز کردن و
کردن ایمانمدی احتراز کرد ایماندوک احتراز کردیم ایمانورمن و ایمانادور احتراز میکند و ایمانور بمعنی فاعل و مصدر هم می آید
ایمانمایدور احتراز نمیکند و نکرده است ایمانکان و ایمانوکان لط ایماناد ورکان احتراز کننده و احتراز کرده و بمعنی مصدر هم می آید
ایمان و ایمانکیل مفرد مخاطب فعل امر ایمان بمعنی قسم هم آمده ایمانا و ایماناکیل مفرد مخاطب فعل نهی ایمانینک و
ایمانینکیز و ایمانینکلار جمع مخاطب فعل امر ایمانمانک لط ایمانمانکیز و ایمانمانکلار جمع مخاطب فعل نهی ایمانمان لط ایمانماسمین احتراز
نمیکنم ایمانامین و ایمانورمین لط ایمانادورمین و ایمانورمین احتراز میکنم ایمانودوم لط ایمانماکیم احتراز کردیم ایماناکوم احتراز نخواهم کرد
ایماینب ایمانیبان لط ایمانمیش احتراز کرده. الشاهد علی الاول شعر مین کیم وکستاخ ایلکینک دیبان ایمانماکان
ایلانینک نینک چون کف پایین و پار مین ایماینب. و لطالع هروی یاینب اول نظر شعرا ایماینب خوانده و ایمانماک را بمعنی
آن قرار داده و نوشته که ایمانماک عبارت از ... و ایشان امورات و غیره هم متابعت کرده لفظه معنی هروی احتراز
ایمانمیشانک احتراز کرده ایمانماس احتراز نمیکند و بمعنی فاعل و مصدر منفی هم می آید ایمانماسی احتراز کردنش و نکردنش ایمانمادین
از احتراز کردن و احتراز کرده ایماینب بولماس و ایمانا بولماس و ایمانماک اولماس احتراز نمیتوان کرد ایمانا آلماس احتراز نمیتواند کرد ایمانا
ایمانا احتراز کنان و بدون تکرار هم بمعنی استعمال میشود چنانکه در عینیه که طامون پادشا. مخدمت پادشاه نوشته

و بعینه دیده شد چنین برید کمعادلام تا بوغید ا قهرقا ایمنه عرضه داشتا ولیکم ... کلسله دینه مسئله کوارست کر
احتراز کرم و کرده ... ایمانا ...
ایمنه هر طرف نه نظر ... ایمانای و ایمانای احتراز کنم و نکنم ... کرده حیات
شاهد براقطر بمعنی احتراز نکند در تاریخ بابری مذکور است ... که سلطان حسین میرزا که اتا سید ایمانمای و تینکری
قورقای هنوز ... ایمانماک ایدی ایمانسانک و ایمانکای بیز و ایمانای و ایمانالینک احتراز کنیم ایمانکالی برای
کردن و تا احتراز کرده ایمانکاج چون احتراز کرد و کند ایمانکوچی احتراز کننده ایمانکوچه و ایمانکوبجه ایمانکابجه تا احتراز کرد
و بعد احتراز کردن ایمانکوم احتراز خواهم کرد ایمانکونک احتراز خواهی کرد ایمانکوسی احتراز خواهد کرد ایمانکولوک احتراز
ایمانکای و ایمانا و ایمانسا و ایمانسون و ایماندیک احتراز کند ایمانکودیک و ایمانوردیک احتراز کردنی و همچنانکه احتراز کند
الشاهد علی الاول المعنی الثانی شعر توتلشغان ... ایمانکوسیدیک وچنون ...
ایمکانماک بسکون میم و فتح کاف ... رنج و زحمت کشیدن ایمکاندی رنج کشید ایمکاندوک رنج کشیدیم ایمکانور و ایمکانادور
رنج میکشد ایمکانور بمعنی فاعل و مصدر هم می آید ایمکانمایدور رنج نمیکشد و نکشیده است ایمکانکان و ایمکانورکان لط ایمکا
رنج کشنده و رنج کشیده و بمعنی مصدر هم می آید ایمکان و ایمکانکیل مفرد مخاطب فعل امر ایمکانما و ایمکانماکیل مفرد مخاطب
فعل نهی الشاهد علی الثانی شعر ...
ایمکانینک و ایمکانینکیز و ایمکانینکلار جمع مخاطب فعل امر ایمکانمانک و ایمکانمانکیز و ایمکانمانکلار جمع مخاطب فعل نهی
ایمکانمان و ایمکانماسمین رنج نمیکشم ایمکانامین و ایمکانورمین لط ایمکانادورمین و ایمکانورمین رنج میکشم ایمکانودوم
و ایمکانماکیم رنج کشیدیم ایمکانماکوم رنج نخواهم کشید ایمکانماسانک لط ایمکانماکاسین و ایمکانماکای مین رنج نکشی
علی الثانی شعر نوائی ... ایمکانماکاسین ... ایمکانیب و ایمکانیبان
و ایمکانمیش رنج کشیده الشاهد علی الثانی شعر ...
ایمکانیبان و ایمکانمیشانک رنج کشیده ایمکانماس رنج نمیکشد و بمعنی فاعل و مصدر منفی هم می آید ایمکانماسی رنج کشیدنش و نکشیدنش
ایمکانمادین از رنج کشیدن و رنج نکشیده ایمکانیب اولماس رنج نمیتوان کشید ایمکانا آلماس رنج نمیتواند کشید ایمکانا ایمکانا رنج
رنج کشان و بدون تکرار هم مستعملست ایمکانای و ایمکانایمن رنج بکشم و بکشد و بکشی و کشیده ایمکانا لط ایمکانکای بیز و
ایمکانکای بیز و ایمکانالی و ایمکانالینک رنج بکشیم ایمکانکالی برای رنج کشیدن و تا رنج کشیده ایمکانکاج چون رنج کشید و بکشد
ایمکانکوچی رنج کشنده ایمکانکوم رنج خواهم کشید ایمکانکونک رنج خواهی کشید ایمکانکوسی رنج خواهد کشید ایمکانکولوک
رنج کشیدنی ایمکانکای و ایمکانا و ایمکانسا و ایمکانسون و ایمکاندیک رنج بکشد ایمکانکودیک و ایمکانوردیک رنج کشیدنی
و همچنانکه رنج بکشد ایمکاتماک مع التاء ... رنج دادن ایمکاتیب و ایمکاتیبان لط ایمکاتمیش رنج داده الشاهد علی
الثالث شعر نوائی نخسته ... ایمکاتمیش ...
باتای قرشتا شقاق ... ایمکالاماک ... رفتن اطفال شیرخوار را گویند ایمکالادی ...
ایمکالادوک ... ایمکالادور ... و ایمکالادور بمعنی فاعل و مصدر هم می آید
ایمکالامایدور ... و نرفته است ایمکالاکان و ایمکالاورکان ... و راه
و راه رفته الشاهد علی الاول المعنی الاول شعر ...

اولنورکوبی بو ایمکاکیم و بمعنی مصدر هم می آیند ایمکاکلاو ایمکاکلاکیل مفرد مخاطب از فصل امر ایمکاکلاما و ایمکاکلاما کم
مفرد مخاطب از فصل نهی ایمکاکلافت و ایمکاکلانکیز و ایمکاکلانکلار جمع مخاطب از فصل امر ایمکاکلامانک و ایمکاکلامانکیز و ایمکا
مانکلار جمع مخاطب از فصل نهی ایمکاکلانان و ایمکاکلاماس مین بدست و پاره میرود ایمکاکلادی مین و ایمکاکلادیم
دیدیمین و ایمکاکلادام بدست و پاره میروم ایمکاکلادیم و ایمکاکلاماکیم بدست و پاره رفتم ایمکاکلاماکوم بدست و پاره
نخواهم رفت ایمکاکلاب و ایمکاکلادبان و ایمکاکلامیش بدست و پاره رفته ایمکاکلامیشانک بدست و پاره رفته ایمکا
بدست و پاره میرود و بمعنی فاعل و مصدر نفی هم می آید ایمکاکلاماسی بدست و پاره رفتن و نرفتنش ایمکاکلامایین از
رفتن بدست و پاره رفته ایمکاکلاب بولماس و ایمکاکلانا بولماس و ایمکاکلامانک اولماس بدست و پاره نمیتوان رفت
ایمکاکلادی الماس بدست و پاره نمیتواند رفت ایمکاکلایو و ایمکاکلادی ایمکاکلادی خیزان خیزان و بدو بدو تکرار هم مستعملست
ایمکاکلادی و ایمکاکلادین بدست و پاره بدوم و برود و بروی هرجه ایمکاکلاسانک و ایمکاکلاب و ایمکاکلالینک بدو
پاره رویم ایمکاکلاکالی برای بدست و پا رامیش و تا راه رفته ایمکاکلاکاج چون بدست و پاره رفت و برفته ایمکاکلاکوبی
بدست و پاره رونده ایمکاکلاکوم بدست و پاره خواهم رفت ایمکاکلاکونک بدست و پاره خواهی رفت ایمکاکلاکوسی
بدست و پاره خواهد رفت ایمکاکلاکولوک بدست و پاره رفتنی ایمکاکلاکای و ایمکاکلاسنا و ایمکاکلاسون و ایمکاکلا
بدست و پاره رود ایمکاکلاکودیک و ایمکاکلاردیک بدست و پاره رفتنی و همچنانکه برود من ایجو امدا یماس و یماستور
یعنی نیست الشاهد علی الاول شعر حیات بخش ایدا اولجه عکس زیاده محل حیرت ایماس جور عکسیدین دور دراح الشاهد
علی الثانی من لیلی مجنون شعر خرمن یاری توشسا پرشرارم مکویا کیدین ایماستور آنکا چاره ایماس بولسا یعنی نباشد
در حیرة الابرار که وصف سخن کوید شعر تیرا نوالی و نوا دیما کیل هرنی ایماس بولسا روان ایکیل ایمان یعنی نیستم
الشاهد علیه شعر جهان اهلی نفاقیدین قاتان تاریشام ایمان ایمن تیلادین اول جهانی تا یقا مین شلیدا ستا الندا دم
در خاتمه حیرة الابرار کوید شعر کرچه ایمان قابل لطف وکرم لیک ایمان هم بیلی نومید هم و نیز امراست از احتراز کردن
چنانکه در ذیل مصدر ایماماک کذشت ایمانک یعنی نیستی الشاهد علیه شعر ای نوالی دم بودم دود تو غنیمت باده
ایچ از کاهیدم کامیتار یتماسکا چون واقف ایمانک یعنی ای نوائی دم بردم است غنیمت دان و باده بخور چون برسیدن
نرسیدن دم دیگر واقف نیستی و مؤلف رومی در بیان معنی ایمانک کفته که چون قافیه در شک و جنک واقع شده کاف
از روی ضرورت و ندرت داخل شده لیکن در وقت خطاب تکلم عنی شود این ادعای غلطی است بلکه کاف علامت خطابست که در مقام
خطاب البته باید تلفظ شود والا افاده معنی متکلم وحده خواهد کرد یعنی نیستم چنانکه در ذیل ایمان مذکور شد ایمانک
نیستی است چنانکه در تاریخ الملوک در ذکر همایون پادشاه کوید که دل ارابی انکا کورکوز دیلار کیمزنی توشکا ایماک
کیکا سونکیلدی ایمدی یعنی حالا باشد الشاهد علیه شعر میدا ایسا عکسینی کوز آیکیلیم اوپکالی باشکوتونان
ایمدی یعنی کیم تا بیم عرلغنان و نیز بمعنی میکید چنانکه در تحت مصدر ایماماک کذشت ایمدی یکا جوابی بیکادیکیم یعنی تا حال
ایماغ بسکون میم و غین معجمه و فتح رای قرشت بمعنی مطلوب و مرغوب و محبوب بود چنانکه کوید شعر بو بلاخیزدن وادم که نوائی
اول آی نیچه سیک که رنا موزعشق آنکا ایماغ ایتادورمن دهمچنین و صاف در غزل ملمع با اصطلاحات مغول کفته شعر ای ترک
نازنین که دلفروز و مهوشی اینان دلربای و ایماغ او نیشی ایمیا بسکون میم و فتح غین معجمه بزکوهی را کویند ایمکاک بسکون میم و

نم کاف عجمی دو معنی دارد اول بمعنی جمع و شفقت بود الشاهد علیه شعر نفسینک ایتیا شخلوغ چرخ ایمکا کیدین تیلادث
لطفلی تیزاق که نبر لیلا عرفات پراله ادیث دوم بمعنی بدست و پاره رفتن اطفال را خوانند چنانکه در ذکر طفولیت فرهاد کوید شعر
قدم اوردی و ترک مهد قیلدی قوبوب ایمکاک ایمکاک عیدو که جهد قیلدی و روسیه آنرا بعربی سلاخنه امات کویند و صاحب مولد
الفضلا ایمکا را بلام با معنی نوشته سهو کرده ایمکان ملبغت مغولی زن بود ایمیل بفتح میم و سکون لام بلغت مغولی زین
باشد که آنرا بعربی سرج نامند ایمیس بکسر میم و سکون زای معجمه بخاری بود که از زمین متصاعد شده و روی هوا را فرو کیرد
آنرا بعربی ضباب و بفارسی نژم خوانند ایمیزلیک جای لوله و زنبیر دهنده ایمیزلیک بکسر میم و زای معجمه لوله کوزه
و ابریق و امثال آن بود و لوله هر چیز را کویند ایمیزیکلی دو معنی دارد اول لوله دار دوم بنزبیر دهنده باشد ایمیش و
ایمیشتوک یعنی بوده است الشاهد علی الثانی شعر حیات بخش بیمیانده مع ایمیشتوک ای ساقی مکر که واوینی علا
اتیب قیلیب سین اح و نیز در خسرو شیرین در خبر آمدن شاپور از جانب فرهاد کوید شعر مونکا تیکر و کرما لا سالغ
ایمیشتوک شیری که دشت و کامی تلغ ایمیشتوک ایمیش مین و ایمیش توک سین یعنی بوده الشاهد علی الثانی شعر
کونکول آوردا ایجب لر با ایمیشتوک سین و نطر باکه بلا جنجرا ایمیشتوک سین ایمیغ بکسر میم و سکون غین معجمه بمعنی لرزیدن
بر بود مع النون من اشتقاقات ایمناک بسکون نون فرود آمدن و نازل شدن ایندی فرود آمد ایندوک فرود
آمدیم اینادور فرود می آید الشاهد علی الاول شعر کر قونا شدی بیلا دیوز ونجی کرم بو ملچیکا تیغ ایلکا جریمی بوانا
جون آسما ندین بولغت و اینار بمعنی فاعل و مصدر هم می آید اینمایدور فرود نمی آید و ینامدا است اینکان و ینارکان نازل شده
فرود آینده و فرود آمده و بمعنی مصدر هم می آیند چنانکه کوید الشاهد علی الاول شعر قو یاش کلبه کا اینکاندین منکا یو
تا تلا خویشتر افتد مراشامه موی روشن ایلکان شمع شبستانیم و اینکان بمعنی نام هم آمده چنانکه در دیباچه مذکور خواهد شد
این و اینکیل مفرد مخاطب از فصل امر اینما و اینما کیل مفرد مخاطب از فصل نهی اینینک و اینینکیز و اینینکلار جمع مخاطب از فصل امر
اینمانک و اینمانکیز و اینمانکلار جمع مخاطب از فصل نهی اینمان و اینماس مین فرود نمی آیم ایناسین و ینارسین و اینادور نیز و اینادام
فرود می آیم اینادیم و اینما کیم فرود آمدیم اینماکوم فرود نخواهم آمد اینیب و نیبان و اینمیش فرود آمده اینمیشانک فرود
اینماس فرود نمی آید و بمعنی مصدر نفی هم می آید اینماسی فرود آمدنش و فرود نیامدنش اینادین از فرود آمدن و فرود
و فرود نیامدن اینیب بولماس و اینا بولماس و اینمانک اولماس فرود نمیتوان آمد اینا آلماس فرود نمیتواند آمد اینا اینا فرود
فرود آمده و بدو و تکرار هم مستعملست ایناوی و اینایین فرود بیایم و بیاید و بیایی و آمدن اینسانک و اینکای و اینایلی
فرود بیایم اینکالی برای فرود آمدن و تا فرود آمده چنانکه بمعنی اول کوید شعر اینکالی کوکدین بلالار تو دور
نلا هجر او بی دین تا دتنام تاب و شکن لیک د و دانه اینکاج چون فرود آمید و بیاید چنانکه در تاریخ بابری در ذکر منعاقات
کوید که بو کوتل دین اینکاج کشتی در کا عالمی ملاحظه قیلود اینکوچی فرود آینده اینکوسی و اینکو بیچه و اینکا بچه تا فرود آمد
و نقل فرود آمدن اینکوم فرود خواهم آمد اینکونک فرود خواهی آمد اینکوسی فرود خواهد آمد اینکولوک فرود آمدنی
اینکای و اینا و اینسا و اینسون و ایندیلک فرود بیاید اینکودیک و اینادیک فرود آمدنی و چنانکه فرود بیاید و ربنا ک مصدر
بمعنی فرود آوردن آید و روی اینید و در تا باید فرود آورده الشاهد علی الاول شعر بولماسا اولت تماشی حالیم ایپرا جلوه ساز
مثاله عدکا فرمین ارباش اینید و روب قیلسام نماز اینید و رکالی فرود آوردن و تا فرود آورده چنانکه بمعنی اول کوید شعر کر

توتنا قاغ اوچین جنون دیو ای سیمرغ سنگ باران خاخت بر ما ستو ری آتی ایند هر کلبه وناقی صبغ برین فهم سوافق شد و الفاظ بود
اینا ملاماق بیلیت کرده و صیغ آن بیستم باشین تر شتا اشتقاق میابد
اشتقاق می یابد اینا الماک بفتح نون با الف کشیده و سکون لام زاری و ابرام و الحاح کردن چنانکه در فصل بیت و یکم از مجموع
القلوب در ذکر حفاظ گوید که لئیم سیرت و کلادو دلارا ایتمو جو چا لقوجی هر ار لیغ و اینا الماک سیله آلقوجی اینا لدی الحاح
کرد اینا لدیم الحاح کردم چنانکه گوید شعر وصلیز اجتناب کوپ اینا لدیم تاودی کو یکدین میتی بولنا مبرم شیوه ملته
کنا مروودا بروود اینا لدوک الحاح کردیم اینا لور و اینا لادور الحاح میکند و اینا لور بمعنی فاعل و مصدر هم می آید اینا لما
الحاح نمیکند و نکرده است اینا لکان و اینا لورکان و اینا لادورکان الحاح کننده و الحاح کرده و بمعنی مصدر هم می آیند اینا ل و اینا لکیل
مفرد مخاطب فصل امر اینا لما و اینا لماکیل مفرد مخاطب فصل نهی اینا لینک و اینا لینکز و اینا لینکلار جمع مخاطب فصل امر اینا لمانک
اینا لمانکز و اینا لمانکلار جمع مخاطب فصل نهی اینا لمان و اینا لماس مین الحاح نمیکنم اینا لامین و اینا لورمین و اینا لادورمین و اینا لورام الحاح میکنم
اینا لورم و اینا لما کیم الحاح کردیم اینا لماکوم الحاح نخواهم کرد اینا لیب و اینا لیبان و اینا لیبس الحاح کرده الشاهد علی
الاول شعر قاریب نجالغه تا لدیم کر یار قیلماس رحم بیچوک که طفل کبی اراسهلا جنسام اینا لیب بنللیشانک الحاح کرده
اینا لماس الحاح نمیکند و بمعنی فاعل و مصدر منفی هم می آید اینا لماسه الحاح کرده نشد و نکرده نشد اینا لمادین از الحاح کردن و الحاح نکرده
اینا لیب بولماق و اینا لسا بولماق و اینا لماق اولماق الحاح نتوان کرد اینا لا الماس الحاح نمیتواند کرد اینا لا اینا لا الحاح کنان
و بدون تکرار هم مستعملت اینا لای و اینا لا این الحاح کنم و کنند و کنی و کرده اینا لساک و اینا لکاییز و اینا لکای بیز و اینا لیلی
و اینا لینک الحاح کنیم اینا لکالی برای الحاح کردن و تا الحاح کرده اینا لکاج چون الحاح کرد و کند اینا لکوچی الحاح کنند
اینا لکوجه و اینا لکونجه و اینا لکاغه تا الحاح کردن و بقدر الحاح کردن اینا لکوم الحاح خواهم کرد اینا لکولک الحاح خواهی
کرد اینا لکوسی الحاح خواهد کرد اینا لکولوک الحاح کردنی اینا لکای و اینا لسا و اینا لسون و اینا لدیک الحاح کنند
اینا لکودیک و اینا لوردیک الحاح کردنی و همچنانکه الحاح کند اینا نماق باور کردن اینا ندی باور کرد اینا ندوق باور
کردیم اینا نور و اینا نادور باور میکند و اینا نور بمعنی فاعل و مصدر هم می آید اینا نماید ور باور نمیکند و نکرده است اینا نغان
و اینا نورغان و اینا نادورغان باور کننده و باور کرده و بمعنی مصدر هم می آیند اینان و اینا نغیل مفرد مخاطب فصل امر اینا نما
اینا نماغیل مفرد مخاطب فصل نهی چنانکه مثل است کر اینا نماغیل دوستونکغه ساماتان تقار بوستونکغه اینا نینک و اینا نینکز
اینا نینکلار جمع مخاطب فصل امر اینا نمانک و اینا نمانکز و اینا نمانکلار جمع مخاطب فصل نهی اینا نمان و اینا نماس مین باور نمیکنم اینا نامن و
اینا نورمین و اینا نادورمین و اینا نورام باور میکنم اینا ندیم باور کردیم اینا نماکوم باور نخواهم کرد اینا نیب و
اینا نیبان و اینا نغس باور کرده اینا نغشانک باور کرده اینا نماس باور نمیکند و بمعنی فاعل و مصدر منفی هم می آید اینا نماسه
باور کرده نشد و نکرده نشد اینا نمادین از باور کردن و نا باور نکرده اینا نیب بولماق و اینا نسا بولماق و اینا نماق اولماق باور نتوان کرد اینا نا
الماس باور نمیتواند کرد اینا نا اینا نا باور کنان و بدون تکرار هم مستعملت اینا نای و اینا نا این باور کنم و کنند و کنی و کرده
اینا ناق و اینا نغاییز و اینا نغای بیز و اینا نیلی و اینا نینک باور کنیم اینا نغالی برای باور کردن و تا باور کرده اینا نغاج چون باور کرد و کند
اینا نغوچی باور کننده اینا نغوجه و اینا نغونجه و اینا نغاغه تا باور کردن و بقدر باور کردن اینا نغوم باور خواهم کرد اینا نغولک
باور خواهی کرد اینا نغوسی باور خواهد کرد اینا نغولوق باور کردنی اینا نغای و اینا ناقا و اینا نسا و اینا نسون و اینا ندیک باور کنند
اینا نغودیک و اینا نوردیک باور کردنی و همچنانکه باور کند اینجیماک رنجیدن اینجیدی رنجید اینجیدوق رنجیدیم اینجیر

اینجیدور رنجد و اینجیر بمعنی فاعل و مصدر هم می آید اینجیماید ور نرنجد و نرنجیده است اینجیکان و اینجیرکان و اینجیدورکان
رنجنده و رنجیده و بمعنی مصدر هم می آیند اینجی و اینجیکل مفرد مخاطب فصل امر و اینجی را هم گویند اینجیما و اینجیماکیل مفرد مخاطب
فصل نهی اینجینک و اینجینکز و اینجینکلار جمع مخاطب فصل امر اینجیمانک و اینجیمانکز و اینجیمانکلار جمع مخاطب فصل نهی اینجیمان و
اینجیماس مین نمی رنجم اینجی مین و اینجیر مین و اینجیدور مین و اینجیر ام می رنجم اینجیدیم رنجیدم اینجیماکوم نخواهم رنجید اینجیب و
اینجیبان و اینجیبس رنجیده اینجیبشانک رنجیده اینجیماس نمی رنجد و بمعنی فاعل و مصدر منفی هم می آید اینجیماسه رنجیده نشد و نرنجید
اینجیمادین از رنجیدن و نرنجیده اینجیب بولماس و اینجیسا بولماس و اینجیماک اولماس نمیتوان رنجید اینجی الماس نمیتواند رنجید اینجی اینجی
رنجان رنجان و بدون تکرار هم مستعملت اینجی و اینجی این رنجم و رنجد و رنجی و رنجیده اینجیسای ما رنجمامین رنجم و نرنجد رنجی و
رنجیده چنانکه شاهد بر اول او معنی رنجی گوید شعر ای نوائی کرد بنانک کوب اینجیسای دورا هلادین هر زه دیر لا ایا علتو
لار قبلما اغیل پروا بیز اینجیساک و اینجیکاییز و اینجیکای بیز و اینجیلی و اینجیلینک برنجیم اینجیکالی برای رنجیدن و تا رنجیده
اینجیکاج چون رنجید و رنجد اینجیکوچی رنجنده اینجیکوم خواهم رنجید اینجیکولک خواهی رنجید اینجیکوسی خواهد رنجید
اینجیکولوک رنجیدنی اینجیکای و اینجیسا و اینجیسون و اینجیدیک برنجند اینجیکودیک و اینجیردیک رنجیدنی و همچنانکه رنجد
اینجیتماک مع التا مصدر متعدیست بمعنی رنجانیدن و صیغ آن با تای قرشت اشتقاق می یابد اینجینماک مع النون مصدر لازمست
بمعنی رنجیده شدن و صیغ آن با نون اشتقاق می یابد اینجیرماک بسکون نون و را و کسر جیم و کاف عجمی ناله زاری کردن اینجیکردی
ناله زار کرد اینجیکردوک ناله زار کردیم اینجیکرور و اینجیکرادور ناله زار میکند و اینجیکرور بمعنی فاعل و مصدر هم می آید
اینجیکرماید ور ناله زار نمیکند و نکرده است اینجیکرکان و اینجیکرورکان و اینجیکرادورکان ناله زار کننده و ناله زار کرده
و بمعنی مصدر هم می آیند اینجیکر و اینجیکرکیل مفرد مخاطب فصل امر اینجیکرما و اینجیکرماکیل مفرد مخاطب فصل نهی اینجیکرمان
و اینجیکرماس مین ناله زار نمیکنم اینجیکرامین و اینجیکرورمین و اینجیکرادورمین و اینجیکرورام ناله زار میکنم اینجیکردوم
اینجیکرماکم ناله زار کردیم اینجیکرماکوم ناله زار نخواهم کرد اینجیکریب و اینجیکریبان و اینجیکریبتر ناله زار کرده الشاهد علی
الاول لا ادری شعر چرخ ظلمیدا که بو غزو معنی قریب سیلادیمین ایکاری چرخ کبی اینجیکریب سیلادیمین اینجیکریبشانک
ناله زار کرده اینجیکرماس ناله زار نمیکند و بمعنی فاعل و مصدر منفی هم می آید اینجیکرماسه ناله زار کرده نشد و نکرده نشد اینجیکرمادین
اینجیکرمابولماس و اینجیکرساک اولماس ناله زار نمیتوان کرد اینجیکرا الماس ناله زار نمیتواند کرد اینجیکرا اینجیکرا ناله زار کنان و
بدون تکرار هم مستعملت اینجیکرای و اینجیکراین ناله زار کنم و کند و کنی و کرده اینجیکرساک و اینجیکرکاییز و اینجیکرکای بیز
اینجیکرلی و اینجیکرلینک ناله زار کنیم اینجیکرکالی برای ناله زار کردن و تا ناله زار کرده اینجیکرکاج چون ناله زار کرد و کند اینجیکرکوچی
ناله زار کننده اینجیکرکوجه و اینجیکرکونجه و اینجیکرکاغه تا ناله زار کردن و بقدر ناله زار کردن اینجیکرکوم ناله زار خواهم کرد
اینجیکرکولک ناله زار خواهی کرد اینجیکرکوسی ناله زار خواهد کرد اینجیکرکولوک ناله زار کردنی اینجیکرکای و اینجیکرسا
و اینجیکرسون و اینجیکردیک ناله زار کند اینجیکرکودیک و اینجیکروردیک ناله زار کردنی و همچنانکه ناله زار کند ایندا ماک
بسکون نون و فتح دال دعوت کردن و بخانه طلبیدن و آنرا اوندا ماک هم گویند ایندادی دعوت کرد ایندادوک دعوت کردیم ایندار
و اینداید ور دعوت میکند و ایندار بمعنی فاعل و مصدر هم می آید ایندامایدور دعوت نمیکند و نکرده است ایندا کان و
ایندارکان و ایندایدورکان دعوت کننده و دعوت کرده و بمعنی مصدر هم می آیند ایندا و ایندا کیل مفرد مخاطب فصل امر چنانکه

حیرت الابرار کوید الشاهد علی الاول شعر اینداتکلف بیله احتیاج جلالمالمانا بله اطلاغی اینداتنا وایندا ناکیل مغرک طلب
انفصل فی ایندانك واینداتکیز واینداتکلار جمع خاطب ازفصل امر ایندانانك واینداتکیز واینداتکلار جمع خاطب ازفصل نفی
ایندانان واینداناس مین دعوت میکنم ایندامین واینداربین واینداید صربین واینداراه دعوت میکنم ایندایها ایندالکا
دعوت کردیم ایندالکوم دعوت نخواهم کرد ایندااب واینداپان واینداميش دعوت کرده چنانکه در حیرت الابرار در حکایت تمام
ویر خلیرکش کوید الشاهد علی الاول شعر دیدی که بیرکون تیلیبان جشوغام ایندالیبیم نادیه اهلین تمام ودر تاریخ
نوشتن فرهاد وشیرین کوید الشاهد علی الثانی شعر کوروبمین آندا مردم لوق نشانی کوزومدا ایندابان مردم
ایندامیشانك دعوت کرده ایندا ناس دعوت نمیکند وبمعنی فاعل ومصدر منفی هم می آید ایندا ملبی دعوت کردن ونکردن ایندا
از دعوت کردن ودعوت نکرده ایندااب بولماس و ایندا ابولماس و ایندا مانك املماس دعوت نمیتواند کرد ایندا ای آلماس دعوت نمیتواند
کرد ایندا ابو ایندا ای ایندای دعوت کنان وبدون تکرار هم مستعملست ایندای وایندا یین دعوت کنم وکنند وکنی وکرده ایندالنا
وایندالکا یز وایندا کای یز وایندالی وایندالینك دعوت کنیم ایندالکالی برای دعوت کردن وتا دعوت کردن ایندا کاج چون دعوت کرد
وکند ایندا کوجه دعوت کنند ایندالکوجه وایندالکابجه تا دعوت کردن وبقدر دعوت کردن ایندالکوم دعوت خواهم کرد
ایندالکونك دعوت خواهی کرد ایندالکو سی دعوت خواهد کرد ایندالکولوك دعوت کردنی ایندالکای وایندالسا وایندالسون و
ایندالدیك دعوت کند ایندالکودیك وایندالردیك دعوت کردن ایندالکای وایندالسا وایندالسون وایندالدیك دعوت کند
ایندالکودیك وایندالردیك دعوت کردن وهمچنانکه دعوت کند ایندالتمالی مع الکاف مصدر متعدیست دعوت فرمودن وچنانکه
طلبانیدن چنانکه در لیلی ومجنون در عروسی مجنون کوید شعر خوش وقت اولوبان قوپوب طرب نالی ایندالتی قبیله اهلینی
وصیغ آن بر نسق قاتالای تر شتالی اشتقاق می یابد اینیقماق بکسر نون وسکون قاف والف کرفتن اینیقتی الف کرفت
اینیقتوق الف کرفتیم اینیقور واینیقادور الف میکرد واینیقور بمعنی فاعل ومصدر هم می آید اینیقماید ورا الف نمیکرد
ونکرفته است اینیقمان واینیقمور غان واینیقادورغان الف کیرنده والف کرفته وبمعنی مصدر هم می آید اینیق اینیقغیل
مفرد مخاطب ازفصل امر اینیقما واینیقماغیل مفرد مخاطب ازفصل نهی اینیقینك واینیقینکیز واینیقینکلار جمع مخاطب ازفصل امر اینیقمانك
واینیقمانکیز واینیقمانکلار جمع مخاطب ازفصل نهی اینیقمان واینیقماس مین الف نمیکیرم اینیقامین واینیقورمین واینیقادورمین
اینیقورام الف میکیرم اینیقورم واینیقماغیم الف نکرفتم اینیقماغیم الف نخواهم کرفت اینیقیب واینیقیبان واینیقمیش
الف کرفته اینیقمیشانك الف کرفته اینیقماس الف نمیکیرد وبمعنی فاعل ومصدر منفی هم می آید اینیقماسی الف کرفتن ونکرفتن
اینیقمادین از الف کرفتن وهنوز الف نکرفته چنانکه نامه بمعنی لمانی کوید شعر کچیك ایکان ایت نفسینك اینیقمادینا ولتور
کماولتور ور سیق چونکیم اولالدی اولدی والیچوق بعنی سگ نفس کوچك بوده وهنوز الف نکرفته اورا بکش که چون آن بدخو بزرک شد
ترا می کشد وسولف رومی اینیقمار را بمعنی بزرك شدن نوشته وشعر مذکور را شاهد آورده اینیقیب بولماس و اینیقیا بولماس و
اینیقماق ولماس الف نمیتوان کرفت اینیقا آلماس الف نمیتواند کرفت اینیقا اینیقا الف کرفته کرفته وبدون تکرار هم مستعملست
اینیقای واینیقایین الف بکیرم وبکیرد وبکیری وکرفته اینیقساق واینیقغای یز واینیقغای یز واینیقغالی اینیقغالیك
الف بکیریم اینیقغالی برای الف کرفتن وتا الف کرفتن اینیقغاج چون الف کرفت وبکیرد اینیقغوچی الف کیرنده اینیقغوجه
اینیقغوجه واینیقغانجه تا الف کرفتن وبقدر الف کرفتن اینیقغوم الف خواهم کرفت اینیقغونك الف خواهی کرفت اینیقغوسی

الف خواهد کرفت اینیقغولوق الف کرفتنی اینیقغای واینیقسا واینیقسون واینیقدیك الف بکیرد اینیقغودیك و
اینیقوردیك الف کرفتنی وهمچنانکه الف بکیرد اینکراماق وانکرامق بسکون نون وکاف عجمی نالیدن باشد ومولف رومی
اینکرامالی را بالکاف ذکر کرده وگفته که نوائی علیه الرحمه در محاکمة اللغتین فرموده اند که اینکرامالی العه سینکرامالی العه مایله
ماشورون آهسته بیغلاماق دور واین شعر از نوائی شاهد آورده شعر اینیا ناسا معد اهلیدین عشقینکونینهان الاماسا
کیمه لا رکه اینکرامالی العه وا تیم که سینکرامالی چون محاکمة اللغتین بنظر فقیر رسیده واین شعر هم در دیوان ندوای
نوائی ملاحظه شده وامکار انجا بنیر نشنا هو نیاشت وصیغه مشتقه که در دیوان ملاحظه شد باغین بود لهذا قول مولف
رومی را مناط اعتبار ندانسته آن را با قاف مذکور کرد اینکرادی واینکرادی نالید اینکرادور واینکرادور ق نالیدیم اینکرادو
اینکرایدور واینکرا نور وانیکرا نادور می نالد واینکرار واینکرا نور بمعنی فاعل ومصدر هم می آید اینکرامایدور واینکرامایدور
نمینالد ونالیده است اینکراغان واینکرا قان واینکرا یدورغان واینکرا قنغان واینکرا نورغان واینکرا دورغان نالنده وناله
وبمعنی مصدر هم می آید چنانکه شاهد بر رابع را کوید شعر ضعف دین اینکرا نا نیم ایرانینك غذا نلار دیك هودیم عشق اهلی
نینك بیلکا آتشناپیده اینکرا واینکرا غیل واینکرا ناق واینکرا نقیل مفرد مخاطب ازفصل امر اینکرانا واینکرا ناقیل واینکرا ناد
اینکرا ناغیل مفرد مخاطب ازفصل نفی چنانکه شاهد بر ثالث را تصنیفات محبوب القلوب کوید که دوست جور یدین اینکرا ناد شمن
سیلدیدین کونکرا ما اینکرا نك اینکرا نکیز اینکرا نکلار واینکرا نینك واینکرا نینکیز واینکرا نینکلار جمع مخاطب ازفصل امر
اینکرا نمانك واینکرا نمانکیز واینکرا نمانکلار واینکرامانك واینکرامانکیز واینکرامانکلار جمع مخاطب ازفصل نفی اینکرامان واینکرا ما
واینکرا نمان واینکرا نماس مین نمی نالم اینکرای مین واینکرار مین واینکرا یدورمین واینکرا امین واینکرا نور مین واینکرا یدور
واینکرا نور لم می نالم اینکرا دیم بکسر نون ثانی واینکرا نوروم بضم رای مثلثی واینکرا ماغیم واینکرا ماغیم نالیدم اینکرا ماغوم اینکرا ما
نخواهم نالید اینکرا سام واینکرا سام واینکرا ماس مین واینکرا نماس مین واینکرا نغای مین نالم الشاهد علی الرابع شعر
ایچمای بوز باشا قای کل چیب اینکرا نام الم تا پارتا باسیغه بیراوکه خار وبار ورث اینکراب واینکرا بان واینکرا میش واینکرا
اینکرا نیبان واینکرا میش نالیده الشاهد علی الثالث شعر قبینك هم ایینك هم کونکلوما کو یونکلاد شمن دور کر توندا
تا بمیش افغان واینکرا میش اینکرا میشانك تا بید اینکرا ماس واینکرا ماس نمی نالد وبمعنی فاعل ومصدر منفی هم می آید
اینکراملبی واینکرا ملبی نالیدن ونالیدن اینکرا مادین واینکرا مادین از نالیدن ونا ناله نکرده اینکراب بولماس واینکرا
اینکرا ماقا ولماس واینکرا نیب بولماس واینکرا نابولماس واینکرا ماق املماس نمیتواند نالید اینکرای آلماس واینکرا نا آلماس نمیتواند نالید
اینکرا یو اینکرای اینکرای واینکرا نا اینکرانا نالان نالان وبدون تکرار هم مستعملست اینکرای واینکرا یین واینکرا نا واینکرا نا یین
وبنالد وبنالی ونالیده اینکرا ساق واینکرا نغای یز واینکرا نغای یز واینکرا نالی واینکرا نالیك بنالیم اینکرا غالی واینکرا نالی
برای نالیدن وتا نالیده اینکرا غاج واینکرا نغاج چون نالید وبنالد اینکرا غوجی واینکرا نغوجی نالنده اینکرا غوجه اینکرا نغوجه
واینکرا غانجه واینکرا نغوجه واینکرا نغوجه واینکرا نغانجه تا نالیدن وبقدر نالیدن اینکرا غوم واینکرا نغوم خواهم نالید اینکرا
واینکرا نغونك خواهد نالید اینکرا نغوسی واینکرا غوسی خواهد نالید اینکرا غولوق واینکرا نغولوق نالیدنی اینکرا غای اینکرا سا
و اینکرا سون واینکرا دیك واینکرا نغای واینکرا نا واینکرا سون واینکرا نسا واینکرا اندیك بنالد اینکرا غودیك واینکرا ردیك و
واینکرا نغودیك واینکرا نوردیك نالیدنی وهمچنانکه بنالد اینکشماق بسکون نون وشین قرشت وکسر کاف عجمی نالیدن

باشد اینکشیب واینکشبان واینکشمیش را له زار کرده چنانکه شاهد بر اول در تاریخ بابری مذکور است که نماز خفتن
نماز آنجه چاپغو دا باغدیکیم مین اینکشیب ولتوروب بدیم اینکلاماک واینکیلدا ماک بترکی بمعنی نالیدن ونالان
بود اینا تماک بفتح نون وسکون تای قرشت بترکی بمعنی خصی کردن انسان واخته کردن استر را گویند اینا تماک مع النون بمعنی
خصی شدن واخته شدن من المجامد این برون نکین سوراخ وخانه جانوران را گویند چنانکه در حیرة الابرار گوید بمصر
منونکرا تیبان با الغان وحین دین خپکار اضیق اغون برله این دین وبیز در فرد کرد وخانه ایوب خلف در حیرة الابرار گوید
شعر تارایق سیمهانغه بولوبلی بدی غم قوبی یعنغه باغلادی بغر باهم حرف بادم اینی عمیر وسعایب است وخرکیلنه نیست
یعنی بموش سوراخ شکن غم شده بود بدمشر غربال هم بت وبلا اشتلع بمعنی عزو بهنا بود ونیز امر است از فرود آمدن چنانکه
در ذیل مصدر انیماک کذشت ایناغ واپناق بمعنی ندیم ورفیق ومصاحب باشد چنانکه لطفی گوید شعر تا یدا مجنون بالود
ابدی مضطرب غم دیشیدا کرمنینک دیک تاپنا ابر محاول بویولد ابر ایناغ ومؤلف رومی تفاوت در معنی ایناغ وایناق
قرار داده یکی را مصاحب بی تکلف ویکی را بمعنی نایب ومقرب نوشته وتمر علی قیصیری هم متابعت کرده اند ونیز در دولت
خوانین ترک نام منصبی است معهود که مقربان مصاحب را بآن اختصاص دهند ایناق بفتح نون با الف کشیده وسکون
بمعنی صاحب اعتبار باشد ایناق شرح کمیند وآن مخفف اینکار باشد چنانکه در ذیل مذکور خواهد شد ایناغ بفتح نون
اول وسکون ثانی وجیم بمعنی امر بود ونیز اسم خاکمری بوده که در عهد سلطان ارسلان دختر امیر محمد بن ایلدکز بحباله نکاح
درآورده قوتلوغ ایناغ از وی متولد شده اینادلی بسکون واو وکسر لام سوراخ وکودالی را گویند که بچه صید کنده باشد
اینجو بسکون نون وضم جیم چیه بمعنی آمده اول مروارید کویند الشاهد علیه شعر دیلینک واینجو تیشلاریدنک
حسرتیدین نوادی نینک جسمی واشکی پارد ودوره رشته در تمنی آثار وله شعر کوز مجری یاش شیشه کیبیه دم اینجو غوش
یاسیلدی او شبوعجه ایله یوز ناری اینجو سی دویم بمعنی ملوک باشد سیم املاک در قنات خاصه دیوانی را خوانند چنانکه در تاریخ
وصاف مذکور است که ضبط نواحی مملکت دیوان تمامت املاک امرا جمیع ممالک با اینجو در آوردند ودر تاریخ مرآت الادوار مسطور
که امیر محمود شاه اینجو اسنا بر این اینجو مسکشت که ضابط املاک خاصه سلاطین مغول بود وآنرا ایشان اینجو کویند واینجو
لشکر باشد والای مانند اینجولوک بمعنی مملوکیت باشد چنانکه در تحفه اخلاقیه کوید که آزاده لارنینک اینجولوک
کا کرماک طمودین تشنق وبنده لارنینک آزاد. لیقغه چقارامیدیدین توقی اینجی بکسر جیم زن را کویند چنانکه در
تاریخ الملوک در ذکر سلطنت همای بنت بهمن کوید که شعر یا نا پر نجه کون همای آلدی ملک ایرانلار بار بیا اینجی کا قالدی ملک
ومعانی شتفه هم دیده که در ذیل مصدر اینجیماک مذکور شد اینجلک بسکون نون وکاف وکسر جیم بند سنا قا بود که آنرا ایلقاب
شتالنک کویند و مجاز اینند قلم دست اسبرا مانند اینجکا بکسر جیم وفتح کاف دو معنی دارد اول بمعنی نازک بود چنانکه در شیعه
سیاره در تعریف کردن دلارام هرام را بصید گور کوید شعر دیمادی نازنین حدیثی نی یوق جکتیدا قولصدقدین اینجکا اوق
دو تیم آزار بمتا عرض کسند اینجکا رالک بمعنی نازکتر الشاهد علیه شعر کونکلوم آجیلماس دبی بوبد نبر از دن ایله
که عکم تو کون اینجکار الک تارد ین اینداو بسکون نون و واو وفتح دال نام آیت شبیه بکنجد که روغن آنرا در تطلیه شتران
بکار میبرند وآنرا در ایران معیدا وکویند اینک بسکون نون وکاف عجمی بمعنی کونه و عارض بود چنانکه کوید شعر سالغوچ
مالمنه اوتعارضنی آچ کیم جهانی کوید ورود اول اوتلوغ اینک وله یوزی یا نیغ باشی آق تر ظاری کر اوتکا حیف اینکی تر بل

کوزی تاشی قرا اینکت لاترکا وبفتح نون وسکون کاف دو معنی دارد اول تماده کاو باشد دوم آلت رجولیت را مانند وتولک رومی
اینا لد را بمعنی برادر کوچک نوشته وتقیری هم متابعت کرده وبعبارتی بسم اشاره ومصغر این بود اینکالک بسکون نون وفتح کاف
اول عجمی مع اللام اله یعنی آنرا گویند ابن سلطان حکندی شعر اول الدج کوندا بل بولدی آنداقیز یون که بولدی اینکا کلاهر کا قولوغ
ومولف موید الفضلا اینکالک با الام بمعنی نوشته غلط خوانده است اینکان بسکون نون واول نولان وفتح کاف عجمی نام روشتر شتر
نام روباب ناقه حضرت صالح علیه السلام گوید شعر میلدی سلیمان دعوتینی قولدیلار چو معجزه قولدی حوتین حیقتی انکان تمک
ناغیننک مضروبین وآنرا مخفف ساخته اینا زهم کویند ونیز بمعنی فرود آیند وفرود آمده وفرود آمدن باشد چنانکه در ذیل اینماک کذ
اینکلیک بسکون نون وکاف عجمی وکسر لام دو معنی دارد اول کویند که قوباش اینکلیک یعنی خورشید چهره چنانکه در مناجات کوید
قوباش اینکلیک لار هواسیدا باشیمنی بولدها یلانا دو یم بمعنی غازه وکلکونه بود که زنان بر چهره مالند الشاهد علیه شعر
ن زلال واتیش کلدوره که بستان شاهدی الیحر آرایش بو اینکلیک داغی اول کونر کوپله اینکیلک بترکی رومی بمعنی ناله بود
اینوک بضم نون وسکون کاف بچه سباع وکلاهبار کویند چنانکه بچه کوسفند وآهو وامثال آنرا قوزی ولرکا وکاومیش وکرکدن
واشباه آنرا بوزاو واغو وکودغو ونظایر آنرا خودوک واز خوک را جوجه واز فیل وحوش وحشرات رابالاو ازند روز و
وکبک را جوجه واز بلبه طیور را بالا مری نامند اینی بکسر نون برادر کوچک را کویند چنانکه در شیعه سیاره کوید شعر
ای سنکلیغ ونا او غولنیکلیغ شه غمخدمت قیلوردی قولنیکلیغ ومؤلف رومی اینماک واینا کا هم بمعنی برادر کوچک نوشته
وتقیری متابعت کرده مع الواو من المشتقات ایووریالک بضم واو وسکون رای قرشت کردانیدن چنانکه کوید شعر
سن دین یوز ایوورالک منکا ممکن یوق اکرچه هرنار یعنی آکینکه که کیلدیم یوز ایوور دونک ایو وریک کردانید ایوورد
کردانیدیم ایوورد بسکون واو وایوورادور میکرداند وایوورور بمعنی فاعل ومصدر هم می آید ایوورغاید ونمیکرداند
ونکرداننده است ایوورکان وایوورکا وایوورادورکان کرداننده وکرداننده وبمعنی مصدر هم می آید ایوورغا ایوورکیل مفرد مخاطب
از فعل امر الشاهد علی الاول شعر قدح سین یا قیامیران بین اسرو ایو وره ناغر که سرکردان میں اسرو ایوورناو ایوورناکیل مفرد
مخاطب از فعل نهی ایوورغوت وایوورونکوز وایوورونکلار جمع مخاطب از فعل امر ایوورمانکوز وایوورمانکلار جمع مخاطب از فعل نهی ایوورمان
وایوورمادین نمیکردانم ایوورامین وایوورورمین وایووراد ورمین وایوورادورام میکردانم ایوورسام وایوورغایم کردانیدم ایوورغایم میکردانم
کردانید ایوورو وایوورووبان بسکون واو وایوورمیش کردانیده ایوورمیشانک کردانیده ایوورغاس نمیکرداند ونمیکرداند بمعنی
فاعل ومصدر منفی هم می آید ایوورملس کردانیدنش ونکردانیدنش ایوورغادین از کردانیدن ونکردانیده ایووب یوبان و
ایوورسا ایوورسالا وایوورسانک اکرتا نمیتوان کردانید ایوورالماس نمیتواند کردانید ایوورا ایوورا کردانیده کردانیده وبعضی تکرار هم
مستعملست چنانکه در فصل بیت دیجهانیم از مجبوب القلوب در ذکر کداها کوید که پوستین ایوورکیما کلاری جوانلیغ وسعیت دن
نشانه ایوورای وایوورالین بکردانم وبکرداند وبکردانی وکردانیده ایوورتالک وایوورکارم وایوورکای یوزم ایوراکای یر الفلیکردیم ایوورکای
برای کردانیدن وتاکردانیده ایوورکاچ چون کردانیده بکرداند چنانکه در فرهاد وشیرین در احوال فرهاد کوید شعر ایوورکاچ نیز سین
دور فلک دوارث بولوبا لقانا اضیکا چرخ دوار ایوورکوجی کرداننده ایوورکوچه وایوورکونید وایوورکابحه تا کردانیدن وتقدیر کردانیدن ایوورکو
خواهم کردانید ایوورکولک خواهی کردانید ایوورکولک کردانید ایوورکولک خواهد کردانید ایوورکوی کردانید ایوورکای وایووراوا ایوورمانا یوعی یوردوک
بکرداند ایوورکولیت وایووروبلک کردانیدنی دیجهانکه بکرداند ایوورولمالک مع الکاف بسکون واو وضم رای قرشت بمعنی کرمید بود چنانکه

کوید شعر ای نوای اوز قوپاشیم باشیغه ایوروبلکم بحوالق کیم باشیغه کردون قوپاشی ایورولوب ابو رولوب ایوروبلدی
میکرید ا ش هد علی الاول شعر بر اولوغ طاعت نوداول بت سهرتین قیلمالق نظر چون آشنا یوزین کوروب خاطر مشتاق ایورولدی
وایورولکم بمعنی فاعل و مصدر هم آید ایورولکا وایورولکای و ایورولکم کردنده و کردیدن چنانکه شاهد بیت ثالث اینجنی اولکوید شعر
چو دوک سونکلاریم اولیش قویون اراخاشاک باشیغه ایورولادور کان تنیم غبار چپله و بمعنی مصدر منفی هم آید ایورولما
کان وایورولمادوکا نکردنده و نکردیدن شاهد علی الاول بالمعنی الثانی شعر تیلی جرقمه ایورولکان باهندو که بولدی
نکته سی کوب غیب حضنیغه ناخ و بمعنی مصدر منفی هم می آید چنانکه بمعنی نکردیدن کوید شعر دیما لفظین کیم تیلی ایورولماکا
دین دودسینوق کیم تا پارتار آغزی دین چیقمونجه کوپ زار لفظ ایورولکا ایورولکیل مفرد مخاطب از فعل امر چنانکه در مکافات
مجنون نا آهو کوید لشاهد علی الاول شعر اوشبوقیلسنک بیله خرامانیغ مجنون جشمی نا ریو مقامانیغ در ایله بوروون بو کوز قراقلار
ایورو باشیغه ولحیا تقدین وایورولماغلاتی هم هست چنانکه در ذیل ایجامد مذکور خواهد شد ایورولکلی برای کردیدن و تا
کردیدن بالمعنی الاول شعر خس اماس کرداب اکیم باشینکا ایورولکلی سوا و نه سرکشته عاشق جسمی نینک خاشاکی دور
و باقی صیغه بر این سیاق موافق شواول الام اشتقاق می یابد ایوروشمالت مع الشین براوون چیزی کردیدن و المجاز بمعنی کاوش کردن استعمال
میشود چنانکه در تاریخ بابری مذکور است که سمرقند ایوروشمالا داعیه بیچپله انکا کیشی لاییسا یب سمرقند لاشیب ایوروشوکاوش
کرد ایوروشولت کاوش کردیم ایوروشور وایوروشادور کاوش میکند ا ش هد علی الاول شعر کونکول اشیغلا غیرنا زین بین
آن نا ایر نفس آهیم یا تا را و نغمه چو اطفال ایوروشولادو ایوروا غزون وایوروشو بمعنی فاعل و مصدر هم می آید ایوروشماید
کاوش میکند و نکرده است ایوروشکان وایوروشکان نو ایوروشادورکان کاوش کننده و کاوش کرده و بمعنی مصدر هم می آید ایوروش وایوروشکیل
مفرد مخاطب از فعل امر ایوروشما وایوروشماکیل مفرد مخاطب از فعل نهی ایوروشونکت وایوروشونکوز وایوروشونکلار جمع مخاطب از فعل نهی چنانکه
شاهد بر ولعل در تیام المحبه نیز در کرشیخ با یزید بسطامی کوید که جواب قیلدی کیم چین آتی ولکا ایوروشمانکت ایوروشمان و
ایوروشماس مین کاوش نمیکنم ایوروشامین وایوروشادور مین ایوروشونکا کاوش میکنم ایوروشورویم وایوروشماکیم کاوش کردنم ایوروشاکوم کاوش
نخواهم کرد ایوروشوب وایوروشوبان وایوروشوش کاوش کرده ایوروشماقال کاوش کرده ایوروشماس کاوش نمیکند و بمعنی فاعل و مصدر منفی
هم می آید ایوروشماسلیکا کاوش کردنش و نکردنش ایوروشمادین از کاوش کردن و کاوش نکرده ایوروشوب الماس و ایوروشالمای و ایوروشمالت
کاوش نتوان کرد ایوروشا آلمان کاوش نمیتواند کرد ایوروشا ایوروشا کاوش کنان و بدون تکرار هم مستعملست ایوروشای وایوروشای
کاوش کنم و کند و کنی و کرده ایوروشالی وایوروشکای نیز وایوروشکاوشالی ایوروشالیکا کاوش کنیم چنانکه شاهد بر ثالث در تاریخ
مذکور است که سمرقند ایلینی بن کیلکو نجه ایوروشکای بیز ایوروشکالی برای کاوش کردن و تا کاوش کرده ایوروشکاچ چون کاوش کرد و
ایوروشکوچی کاوش کننده ایوروشکوچی وایوروشکونجه ایوروشکاغا تا کاوش کردن و بقدر کاوش کردن ایوروشکوم کاوش خواهم کرد ایوروشکو
کاوش خواهی کرد ایوروشکوسی کاوش خواهد کرد ایوروشکولوک کاوش کردنی ایوروشکای وایوروشالا ایوروشالا ایوروشی وایوروشسه
کاوش کند ایوروشکودیک وایوروشمادیلیکا کاوش کردن و همچنانکه کاوش کند ایو ملت بسکون واو و ضم کاف بمعنی تعجیل کردن باشد
ایودومیت مصدر متعدیست یعنی تعجیل فرمودن من المجوامد ایو بسکون واو خانه را کویند شعر زنبور نینک ایوی کبی
ماغیم تیشوب تیشوب لعلینک خیالی هر تیشوک ایچیندا الیکیش وآنرا اوی نیز خوانند ایورولت بسکون واو و لام و ضم رای
مهمله نام ولایتی است نزدیک شهر بصره و نیز امرست از کردیدن چنانکه کذشت مع الباء من المشتقات الاهمال والایخبار مع النون

بفتح با و لام با لفکنیدن یعنی ما لک و صاحب شدن ایالادی و ایالاندی ما لک شد ایالادوک و ایالاندولدوک ما لک شدیم
ایالادو ایالایدور وایالانور و ایالادور ما لک می شود ایالاندو وایالانور بمعنی فاعل و مصدر هم می آید ایالانایدور وایالانمایدی
ما لک نمیشود و نشده است ایالاکان وایالارکان وایالایدورکان وایالانکان وایالانورکان وایالادورکان ما لک شونده و ما لک
و بمعنی مصدر هم می آید ایالاما ایالاکیل وایالان وایالانکیل مفرد مخاطب از فعل امر ایالاما وایالاماکیل وایالانما وایالانماکیل
مفرد مخاطب از فعل نهی ایالانینک وایالانینکیز ایالانینکلار جمع مخاطب از فعل امر ایالانمانک وایالانمانکیز ایالانمانکلار جمع مخاطب
نهی ایالایان وایالاماسمین وایالانمان وایالانماسمین ما لک نمیشوم ایالایمین وایالادورمین وایالایدورمین وایالارمن ایالا
ایالانورمین وایالانادورمین وایالانورمن ما لک می شوم ایالایم وایالانورمن وایالاماکیم وایالانماکیم ما لک شدم ایالاماکو
ایالانماکوم ما لک نخواهم شد ایالاب وایالابان وایالامیش وایالانیب وایالانیبان وایالانمیش ما لک شده چنانکه در
سیاره در کاملة بهرام با نوای در غالم خوابکوید لشاهد علی الاول شعر ایالاب تاج و دولت وسکون تا میش لونکانیغ همچی
ایالامیشانک وایالانمیشانک ما لک شده ایالاماس وایالانماس ما لک نمیشود و بمعنی فاعل و مصدر منفی هم می آید ایالانما وایالانما
ما لک شدن و نشدن ایالامادین وایالانمادین از ما لک شدن و ما لک نشده ایالاب بولماس وایالاب بولما وایالاماک ایمکان
ایالانیب بولماس وایالانا بولماس وایالانماک اولماس ما لک نتوان شد ایالای آلماس وایالانا آلماس ما لک نمیتواند شد ایالا
ایالای ایالای وایالانا ایالانا ما لک کنان و بدون تکرار هم مستعملست ایالای وایالایین وایالانای وایالانایین ما لک شوم
و شوی و شده ایالاسالی وایالاکای بیز وایالاکای بیز وایالانسالی وایالانکای بیز وایالانکای بیز وایالانالی
ایالانالینک ما لک شویم ایالاکالی وایالانکالی برای ما لک شدن و تا ما لک شده ایالاکاچ وایالانکاچ چون ما لک شد و شود
ایالاکوچی وایالانکوچی ما لک شونده ایالاکونجه وایالاکاغا وایالانکونجه وایالانکاغا تا ما لک شدن
و بقدر ما لک شدن ایالاکوم وایالانکوم ما لک خواهم شد ایالاکونک وایالانکونک ما لک خواهی شد ایالاکوسی وایالانکوسی
ایالاکولوک وایالانکولوک ما لک شدنی ایالاکای وایالاسا وایالاسون وایالانکای وایالادیک وایالانسا وایالانسون و
ایالادیک ما لک شود ایالاکودیک وایالانکودیک وایالانوردیک ما لک شدنی و همچنانکه ما لک شود جزو ثانی
ثانی تبغنش بعضی از صیغ کتاب الباء باب المفتوحات حرف الباء مع الباء پیاتیه بفتح هر دو بای عجمی و یای حطی و کسر تای قرشت
بر وزن بطاویه برهمکی روحمام نبا بیت که آنرا افراهیب بابونه کویند بر توت بسکون با و رای مهمله و ضم تای قرشت
از عربی و ترکی و آن جامه ایست که در جنک پوشند زیرا که بر بالای دیبا پوشیده میشود و نیز جبه جامه بود که رستم زال در
روز جنک میپوشیده و بعضی کویند که آن از پوست کوان دیو بوده و از برای توضیح آنرا بر لفظ توت که بمعنی قبا باشد
چنانکه در سه مکندری در تنم بارق بر بری کوید شعر پلنکینه بر کستوان آتشه کیبیب ترتن خلق آفا شفقه بیک
بر وزن نمک مردم چشم بود که آنرا بعربی انسان العین کویند و آنرا تنک هم خوانند و ببک وبنبال نیز کویند مؤلف کوید
که کاف این لفظ کاف تصغیر ظاهرست که بعضی از عین رافت آنرا بیک خوانده اند یعنی پدرک و بعضی آنرا در خلوت حدقه دل
پس هفت پرده جا نشین دیده اند بآن مناسبت ننک نامیده اند یعنی نادرک و اینکه بکسر با و نون استعمال میشود تحریف
اما تحریف مشهور و مصطلح و معمول به است مع التاء من المشتقات باتماق فرو رفتن باتوق در دفتیم باتار و باتادور
فرو میرود و باتار بمعنی فاعل و مصدر نیز می آید باتاید فرو میرود و فرو نرفته است باتقان و باتار غان و باتادورغان فرو رفته

دفرورفته بمعنی مسلم هم می‌آید بات و باتقیل مفرد مخاطب از فعل امر و بات بمعنی زود هم باشد باتما و باتماغیل مفرد مخاطب
فعل نهی باتینک و باتینکیز و باتینکلار جمع مخاطب از فعل امر باتمانک و باتمانکیز و باتمانکلار جمع مخاطب از فعل نهی باتمان و باتماس مین
فرونمیروم باتامین و باتارمین و باتادورمین و باتارام فرو میروم باتماس فرو نمیرود و بمعنی فاعل مصدر منفی هم می‌آید باتماسینکه
بفرو رفتن تو باتارینکه بفرو رفتن تو باتیب و باتیبان و باتیش فرو رفته باتیشانک فرو رفته باتسا بولغای و باتیب بولغای
فرو توان رفت باتا آلغای فرو تواند رفت باتا باتا فرو رفته فرو رفته باتای و باتایین فرو بروم و برود و بروی و رفته باتسا
و باتغاینن و باتغای بزد و باتالی و باتالینک فرو روم باتغالی برای فرو رفتن و تا فرو رفته باتقاج چون فرو برود و رفته
باتغوچی فرو رونده باتغوچه و باتغاینچه تا فرو رفتن و بقدر فرو رفتن الشاهد علی الثانی بمعنی الاول شعر سینی بوق
تینکات ایوصر هجرینک بابرلنی تیدین که یاغدی تینیم تاش ایچکا باتغونچه تاتا آلغانینکچه بقدری که فرو تواند رفت
باتغومیز دور فرو خواهیم رفت باتغونکوزدور فرو خواهید رفت باتغوسیلاردور فرو خواهند رفت باتماغوم و باتغوم یوق
فرو نمیخواهم بود باتا آلماغوم و باتا آلغوم یوق فرو رفتن ممکنم نخواهم بود باتغولوق فرو رفتنی باتغای و باتا و باتسا
و باتسون و باتدیک فرو رفت باتقودیات و باتاردیلک فرو رفتنی و همچنانکه فرو رود باتورماق بضم تای قرشت و سکون رای
مهمله مصدر متعدیست یعنی فرو بردن و صیغ آن بر نسق اشتقاق می‌آید بتلاشماق بسکون تا و شین قرشت مواجهه و روبرو
شدن من المواجهه بات بروزن مات بمعنی زود و سریع باشد الشاهد علیه شعر یاریان هر نیچه بات کیلسا کور دونور منکا
یکج کیلسان کینسا کورونور منکا بات و بات بات یعنی زود زود چنانکه گوید شعر تیغی بات بات زخم اوراردین زار جسیم
میلدی ضعف زمزم اولسون کیم کوپ ایچسا تینکوریدور آزار سو باتراق بمعنی زودتر بود الشاهد علیه شعر دیب سین کرنوا
کیلکوم داغی اولتورکوم اول اولدی بوحسرتدین کیل تینکری ایچون باتراق باتقاق بمعنی آنست که گل و لای آن چسبنده باشد
و پای اسب و آدم بدان فرو رود و بعضی آنرا باتاق گویند باتمان وزنیست معین که آنرا بفارسی من گویند و نیز بمعنی فرو نرود چنا
ذکر رفت باتو بضم تا بلغت مغولی بمعنی سخت و صلب باشد و نیز نام یکی از خوانین ترکانست که بنا بر این نام اشتهار دارد بت بروزن کت
دو و فارض را گویند بتک بتای عجمی بفتح تا و سکون کاف بترکی رومی کنده و محمل بود بتکه بتای عجمی و فتح تا و کاف بهاء رده و صله
وسنکان طعم باشد که آنرا بعربی تامضه خوانند و بسکون تا دستار را گویند که بر سر پیچند و نیز بالمجاز بمعنی دستار بعضوا اند الحن از
برای نشاط استعمال میشود چنانکه در تاریخ بابری مذکورست که بر باره سی سونیتا و لوغلوغی فر اعتمید قیلیب تبلیج لار ری
ایلیک لاریکا آلیب شمشیر بازلیغ قیلیب تیکه میلا باشلاغیلار پتیک بتای عجمی و کسر تا چوبهای کوچک و باریک را مانند کرده
بوشیدن سقف خانه بر چوبهای تیر دوخته ند و بر روی آن نی و خاشاک ریخته اندود کنند مع الجیم باجه دو زن و دیجه نزنان را باج
گویند و در این معنی با فارسی مشترکست باجناق بترکی رومی دو شخص را خوانند که زنهای ایشان خواهر یکدیگر باشند باجاوره
بتای عجمی و رای مهمله و فتح زاء و سکون واو و رومیه کرباس کهنه را گویند عموما و آستری را مانند که مطبخیان ظروف را بدان پاک
کنند خصوصا مع الخا بخشی بسکون خا و کسر شین نویسنده و دبیر و خواننده و جراح را گویند چنانکه بمعنی نویسنده و دبیر گوید باخ
شعر عشق ابواب بازار غم بخشی جسمیم خامه سی خامه کیم تیغ فراقینک بالادی باشیمنی شوق و نیز در مکتوب شمانه شات گویند
مبا حدین توشن منقعه جدوپین دیر آقشامنغه جاولتوروب انجه ایشی تیلورلار کیم نجد دیوان نجد نویسنده بخشی و بخشه یز
جمیلا آلما غالبلار و در تاریخ بابری مذکورست که مغول جراح هم بخشی دیر مع الذال المهمله بدالغه بفتح دال باد

بار

وسکون لام بمعنی بوسه باشد بدق بروزن ورق جانوریست بدبو که شیر از بوی او نفرت کند و اگر در جامه افتد آنجامه تا پاره
بوی زشت دهد و آنرا باسوسمار دشمنی تمامست بدنوس بفتح دال و ضم نون خروس را گویند مع الرا من المشتقات بارماق سه معنی
دارد اول بمعنی رفتن باشد دوم بمعنی سلوک کردن سوم بمعنی انگشت را مانند چنانکه در هر سه معنی بطریق ایهام گوید شعر بارمای تینکلا
بارماقین کوکاج نوای غالینی هم حیات و هم اولوم کوردوم آنینک بارماقیدا بارماق تلیغ همانا بمعنی رفتن و سلوک کردن بود نیکو
مجریرا گویند که در اطراف نشیمن ساخته شود چنانکه در ذیل جامه مذکور خواهد شد باردی رفت و سلوک کرد شعر
بیزه شامیم نعم قیلدی مظالم الهلالی یخشی باردی هر بالمینغ لار دا شینی اهه صبح بار دو تند فتیم و سلوک کردیم باردینک رفتی
کردی چنانکه خطاب بعشوق بجانب فرهاد بمعنی ثانی گوید شعر منکا ای عشق همه دانه تلبدی نیاث قصوری قیلمادینک مردانه باردینک
بارور و بارادور میرود و سلوک میکند چنانکه در مقاله دوم از حیرة الابرار بر مثل کت نویسنده ظالم بالارباب ده گوید الشاهد علی
الاول المعنی الاول شعر کیفیت تیننا دلیبی برابکی عوان طلما بوخواجه آلای پهلوان بر خط ایتیب پرکاب شرو اوندین کیم حق
آنینک ایلکیغی قیلغان رقم شاه نیغه کرچه بو بارور بخشیلار ترلتا بیله هم بخشی بارور بخشی الاهو معنی نیت که نویسنده یکی بیغ و ده
خطی نویسند که خود ستاره قلم کند اکرچه این بیت ترک رفته و خوب واقع آید اما بار ترک هم رفته خوب بخش میکند و مولف
رومی بخشیلار را در این شعر بخشیلار خوانده و بوبارور را صفت بخشی فهمیده و بتعریف کر لغت بخشی نوشته که بوبارور بخشی
یعنی کاتب خوب عجم و شعر زیر را شاهد آورده سهو کرده است الشاهد علی الاول و الثانی شعر کوکلوم نا لیسان بعض
کبی بارور ایلیکدین نبضینک شاتی کونهام که طبیب ایلکی باردوش و بارور بمعنی فاعل و مصدر هم می‌آید چنانکه بمعنی سالک گوید
شعر دیکه نان باردی الم لار دیوز لاینب هر داغینه ضعف افزا می باقیلا استوردی اردهجاغینه بارغاق و بارور
و سلوک کننده و سلوک کرده الشاهد علی الاول بالمعنی الاول شعر خوش اول ارزندی که بارغان کلبه دیر کلش فنا بارغان دیلت
قاسلکیکا چون دار فنادین باشقال الولغای و نیز شاهد بر ثالث را بمعنی بهر نسایم المحبه دوز کرمنای گوید کراوله پیچ غم سیمی
سوریلا کر بارادور غان کیشیغ بان باردی اول دروشی دیدی کر بو بوزو قه کیر دی و بمعنی رفته گوید شعر تیغ سیدا دینک
بیله بارغان شهید عشق نینک درستخیز دهر ابرا هرقطره تا فدین توشوب و بمعنی مصدر هم می‌آید چنانکه شاهد بر اولر بمعنی
رفتن گوید شعر طالعم و وداع ایتیم آج اول یوزینی دمیکیم زاد ادی بلینای چو بو بارغان بیله باردیم بار ر بسکون را و بار ر
بضم را و بارغیل مفرد مخاطب از فعل امر الشاهد علی الثانی شعر ای صبا آواره کونکلوم ایستا بوهر یان بارو وادی و ناغ و
بیابانلار نی پیرپر آختار و الشاهد علی الثالث شعر آتیمان کیل کیل داعی قیلغیل توقف لحظه کیلکاج او قابارغیل و سلی
جا بمعنی آلغیل بارکیل بارسا و بارساغیل مفرد مخاطب از فعل نهی بارینک و بارینکیز و بارینکلار جمع مخاطب از فعل امر بارمانک و بارمانکیز
بارمانکلار جمع مخاطب از فعل نهی بارمان و بارماس مین نمیروم بارورمین و باردورمین و بارادورمین و باروزام میروم و سلوک میکنم
علی الاول بالمعنی الاول شعر دیب بمیش هر کیم آنینک باشین کیتور ینا لطفا تیاش باشیم الیب اینک اول قاتلنی ایستای بارمین
بارغامین و بارغای مین بروم و سلوک کنم بارماغامین و بارماغای مین نروم و سلوک نکنم الشاهد علی الاول شعر عشق بزی غه
یتیب بارماغامین چونکه سینی تار تادور اول لناری بوبزتار بیله نغمه جنک بلا ... میرود و بمعنی فاعل و مصدر منفی هم می‌آید
بارماسینکه برفتن تو و سلوک نکردن تو بارورونکه برفتن تو و سلوک کردن تو بارمیب و بارمیان و بارمیش رفته و سلوک
کرده الشاهد علی الاول بالمعنی الاول شعر خس کبی جسمیم غم هجران شعله سین اودونک باریب برق فتنه غا شاکهنی گوید و بدونک بارت

ونیز در خسرو شیرین در حرکت خاقان و فرهاد بجانب یونان گوید شعر تا یالی اولوغ عزم دین آوازه تاریث ایشیتکاچ خلق توپ
آن تاریث تارتیشانات رفتنه وسلوک کرده بلمنا یولغای وتارب تولغا توانرفت وسلوک توان کرد تارا آلغای توانرفت وسلوک
تاره تاره رفته رفته وسلوک کنان الشاهد علیه بالمعنی الاول شعر نوایی اوندین تاریغ دور شکر آشنا زاق اولغای تاره تاره
وبدون تکرار هم مستعملت تارتعه تارابین بروم وبرود وبروی ورفته وسلوک کنم وکند وکنی وکرده چنانکه شاهد بر ثانی معنی
اول گوید شعر ساقیا اصرلوک ایله مشکل ایرمس قطعی آتینکث دیرسین اوندین تارابین جلسقه قوی دور یعنی تارساق تعا بغا بیزو
تارغای بیز ز تارایلی تارالینک بروم وسلوک کنیم الشاهد علی الرابع بالمعنی الحسنین یقول علیه بیت تاریسغ کوییدا یولی یماروق
ساقیا می توت که بوقا تلا بلمراپ اونکاچه تارغیلی برای رفتن وتلرفته چنانکه معنی ثانی گوید شعر غم خزاین ظاهر ایتیش چهره
زر دیم مینینگ تارغالیسل دیلت بهارناز پرومدیم مینینگ ونیز بمعنی برای سلوک کردن وناسلوک کرده تارغاچ چون رفته و
برود ومحض رفتن وچون سلوک کرد وکند ومحض کردن تارغوچی رونده وسلوک کننده تارغوچیه وتارغوچه فتارغاچه تارغوتن بوشکه
رفتن چنانکه در شوق سفر کعبه معظمه گوید الشاهد علی الثانی بالمعنی الاول شعر اوماردین تقدم تا که تارغوچه کام که بولغای
میسر منکا اوشبو کام ونیز بمعنی ناسلوک کردن وبقدم آن تارا آلغایسنکچه بقدمی که توانرفت وبقدم یک سلوک توانی کرد
الشاهد علیه بالمعنی الاول شعر ای نوایی ایستاسانات دور اهل طلبدین جلا حش افرناد شیشه کام وتارا آلغایسنکچه تار
تارغوم خواهم رفت تارغونک خواهی رفت تارغوسی خواهد رفت چنانکه گوید شعر تیرع بولدی علمه سیکاسینک اوتکانکا تین
کونکولم چون قوناش تارغوسی ظالمدین قرانغو کیلکوسی تارمایغوم تارغوم یوق رفتنم نخواهد بود تارا آلماغوم فتارا آلغوم یوق
رفتن وسلوک کردن هم کم نخواهد بود تارماغونک تارغونک یوق رفتنت وسلوک کردنت نخواهد بود تارا آلماغونک تارا آلغونک یوق
توانایی رفتنت وسلوک کردنت نخواهد بود تارماغوسی وتارماغوسی یوق رفتنش وسلوک کردنش نخواهد بود تارا آلماغوسی و
تارا آلغوسی یوق توانایی رفتنش وسلوک کردنش نخواهد بود الشاهد علیه بالمعنی الاول شعر سین خود اولکوم شکر کیم اولوم
تارا آلغوسی یوقتور تیغ هجری زخمیدین بو نوع کیم قاییم تاروث تارغولوق رفتنی وسلوک کردنی الشاهد علیه بالمعنی الاول شعر
منع دیری غم هجرین مینی منع ایتما ای رفیق بو یول ایرور چو اهل ملامتغه تارغولوق تارغاغ تارلغا تارلغا تارغوتار یلث بر ود دیوانی
کند الشاهد علی الخامس بالمعنی الاول شعر تیلبه کونکلوم کیمی نوایی ضبط ایلای آلمادینک ایمدی چیک آندین الیلت مرتبای
تارتماتلبوتارغوتین تارغوتتورتین وتاروز دیلتین رفتنم وهمچنانکه بروم وسلوک کردنم وهمچنانکه سلوک کنم الشاهد علی الاول الثانی
الاول شعر موتونک دیک کیم نادیر یلا نوتی معنیه ساغزه کونکول خالیغه واقف بول که اوزدین تارغودیک توزتین تارتیشماغ
مع آلتین ارباب مفاعله است یعنی با یکدیگر صلح کردن وسلوک نیک کردن باشد چنانکه در سکندر نامه در رسوله فرستادن خاقان
چین نزد سکندر گوید شعر تاالیب صلح دین سوز بیار کای رسول تارتیشماق طریقینی تیلغای قبول تارتیشق صلح کرد تارتیشتوق
صلح کردیم تارتیشیر وتارتیشادور صلح کند تارتیشغان فتارتیشودغان فتارتیشادورغان صلح کننده وصلح کرده ومعنی ضد هم می آیند
تارلامانوغ تفحص وجستجو کردن چنانکه یوقلاماق بمعنی تفحص عدم شی باشد وصیغ آن مستور شق والاشتقاق می آید من الجوسد
تار سه معنی دارد اول بمعنی موجود باشد دویم بمعنی هست چنانکه بمعنی اولی نوایی گوید شعر تند لوق منعین من نوع ایلای آنکا کیم
اوزکا اینینک برانیشی یار اول اسا تارآبینک تاری الحواری تند شیم آراسته رفتن چنانکه در ذیل مصادر تارتماق گذشت وبغارتی مواشی برهان
تا ملع بمعنی رسته وغرلطقاش لابچه بریث توان برداشت وبر که مرهت مرحمت واجازت وکرت ونوبت وبیخ وبن هر چیز وجای انبوه چیزها شد

دریا باد وچوپار وضایع ساختن ومکان وبلیلی کنند وفرچه صلابرده وتارکا تو تاروحدست دهل غزان در حیوانات دهیم
اندوه دیبا روانبار سر کن که بچه کم نوعی بمعنی مرادست دیزند ومثال زیفا یطرلان وآرد بیخ وارزن که بچه بهنور مهیا کرده تا
ونام دهی از ولایات طوس وآنچه تا نه ضعف مصر که انرا بشند وانچه نوعیند کان نوعیند وماکولات ومشارب انبار کنند ونیز مرادیک
باشد چنانکه گوینده کار وبار بلمزدیدالله یعنی باشیم الشاهد علیه شعر خوشتو بولساق ایلکا ولاهمیرمیزین دیش سنکا
دنیا ده بیشسا مرغم بین دیش بولساق تارتیبا لحوصفه محرمیزین دیش منع در عطا بولسا در بین دیش بار ایسام بانم
تارایسانات باشی تار ایکاچ یعنی هنوز بجه چون نباشد تارایکان وتارایرکان تماهت تاولیک تارماو جمع فرد وسکون
یستانی تار بیز هستیم شعر جادو شمع دیبای دیبپری کم قتلی کر با بیزا سوق ولاحش پر پرم نفتح مرد وقای تیغ تنکری
رومی نام نباتیست که آنرا تغلربی خرفه وبعربی بقلة الحمقا گوینده پرپهم با هردو تا بعی مهمی وسکون رای مهمله جیدو ام تارنشند
بر تاس نام پسر کماری بن یافث بن نوح علیه السلام است وکماری انرا ولاد نامزد که نه ولدیافث است وکیفیت احوال او بر سبیل اجمال آن
که چون نوح علیه السلام یافث را نامزد بلاد مشرق کرد او در تحول وسیم جبلنکا وبروایتی هم ساوک رحل اقامت انداخت هر یک
از پسران را بملکی مخصوص کردانید وکماری در حدود ببلغار نشین تر یافته دار آنجا توطن نمود وامر او بپر شد یکی بغار ودیگری
بر هر یک گوشه کرفته بنام خود عمارت کردند ودو نا موضع بجانب بیت الحرد مازو پوست آنها ملبوسات ترتیب داده فروختند که
منسوب باشان بنام ایشان مشهور شدند چنانکه در مدح سکندر گوید شعر جوانغار یدا ایردی بر تاس روس کو کیلی خیلی
دیک تاباندیده وشورش وهمچنین نام روباهیست سیاه فام منسوب بدان مملکت که از پوست آن پوستین سازند وبر طاس لطای حطینه آنه
ونیز نام یکی از دستارهای ست بر تیک بکون را وکاف وکسرتای قرشت ترکیبی استخوان بود چنانکه در زبان اتراک مثل است کراولو کول
خوار لیغ وسینوقدین بر تیک تلیمان تارجا دو معنی دارد اول بمعنی مهه چنانکه گوید شعر ای کراسینک نینلنکه ای تاریجا اهل دنیا
تاج کیم کلاسینک دور آنکا یوق تلیم ایله تخت احتیاج وبمعنی دویم هم گوینده دویم معنی تهت تارداق بکسون را وفتح دال آن
رویی کونو وابریق بود تارس بروزن طرس جانوریست حمنده از پلنک کوچکتر که آنرا ارام کرده مانند سکان شکاری سید صوش تارنقها
وآنرا بفارسی یوز وبعربی فهد گویند وشاهد آن را در تنگری محبون در وصف اسب گوید شعر تارس آهو مغلب ملاحظه یتدیش تاغلیعی کوپی
تخالتیدیش ونیز بجانب ترکیبا الملیله را گوینده بر طاس همان بر تاس باشد که مذکور شد تارغا بکون را وفتح میم جیم تارغا بود
تارق بکون را وقاف با ادی بطریق تغاراجه مذکور شود چنانکه گوینده لوحو تارق یعنی خانمان وخانه وانائث البیت بولاس بکو
را وسین مهمله وفتح لام نام طایفه ایست از اتراک که سلاطین کم کانیه هند وستان از آن فرقه اند شعر ای نوایی بینلامی ال تغان
بیله بر لاسنی کیم پر ده کونکلوم کا خالامانثل ولیشغع مکش تارلیغ دو معنی دارد اول بکا لفا رو فرنچ گوینده الشاهد علیه
ای نوایی جهتینک دیز قیلسا فارا ولکمر کالمثی یوق عجب یوچون که سیزنین پر کا اول تارلیغ دویم بمعنی هستی باشد چنانکه
لیلی مجنون در مصراع گوید شعر تارلیغ تونین ایکی دین نالیب چیت یوقلوق کرنیا فلا بان ورثه تارماغ وتارمان انکشترانه
ونیز بمعنی رفتن بود چنانکه در ذیل مشقات مذکور شد تارماقلیغ بترکی روی از رعایت کاز سنک با چوب از برای تکیه کردن
در کنار مهتابی وباغچه ترتیب دهند وآنرا در عرف عادت محجر گویند ونیز بمعنی رفتن چنانکه در مشقات مذکور شد بر ندق زین پوش
که آنرا بعربی غاشیه گویند بوندیخی فاشیه کش تارسی یعنی هم چنانکه گوید شعر قراردو خال مخطط کنوقنسیک
مکر تارسی گوید وردی قوناشینگ ونیز در فرهاد شیرین گوید شعر شهی کیم تنکری دین سیعی کوشش تاپلی شه لادرین آر توق

تاپتی بخشش و طالع هروی باریعنی بمعنی دیگر نوشته بمعنی بخشش نوشته و بشر نیز خجسته سهو کرده و بعربی دو معنی دارد اول
بمعنی خاتون و دوم بمعنی تراشنده و بفارسی بمعنی حاصل و بهر حال استعمال میشود و بنظم قصیده ایست در هند و ستان باریجه
بمعنی راه هست و مقدم بودن چنانکه در سد سکندری در پیغام رای هند با سکندر گوید شعر قولی بولغانین شدا اوتوبتاشتا
ماریدا کم کوروب انکی آی مشکین هلال لینک باریدا پر تسبیه بفتح تای عجمی و سین مهمله و کسر رای مهمله بترکی رومی سبزی بود که از آن
کندنا و بعربی کراث گویند و از حروف قرینه بمعنی سبزی است چنانکه مذکور خواهد شد باریش بمعنی خرام و رفتار بود شاهد
علیه شعر کورماکان خضر سوی نینک باریشین کیل و کور آب حیات نیمه خرامش و نیز باریش کیلیش بمعنی رفت و آمد باشد
بیکت لیکیم باریبان کیلدی باشیم قالدی یانیغ فنا یولیدا بونیکلیغ ایمیش باریش و کیلیش باریت بمعنی همراه شر چنانکه گوید شعر
وعده لار وصل ضرکیم ایلاب ایدینک بی جهت باریبان و تونولدی باریق و نیز گویند که یوق و بارین یعنی نیست و هست را چنانکه
گوید شعر نوائی او لکیشی تاپتی فراغ عالمدین که همتی کوزی تینلا کوردی یوق و بارین اینینک باریو یوق یعنی هست و نیست الک
علیه شعر کونکل غم نکین کتار کا بارو یوقا شوب مرنغ مبو غنیمی صدقه یعنی کیم یوق و باریم فدا باریجه مرادف باریم شاهد
بمعنی راه هست و مقدم بودن چنانکه در لیلی مجنون گوید شعر امکانی باریجه ایلادین جهد تا کیم قیلادی آنی سنکا هم مهد باریند
بد معنی استعمال شود افل یعنی بودن الشاهد علیه شعر بوحضالار دین کم کونکلو ماغ قیلا میل نیهار اول مزده
جانیم طرینا لیسکو فرات یوقیم یعنی بهر مقام چنانکه گوید شعر ایرمس پاد بارینداتیم دستین جیف انکاکیم شکر باریند
ایشی دایم شکایت توریر انغاد معرف بمراوفق قول باشد و آن بلغت مغول یعنی طرف است بود چنانکه در سد سکندری گوید شعر
باز با انغار آنکا خیل شرق زمین سمرقند دین تا که سرحد چین مع التزا سبز بوزن و رز گوشت تازه را گویند که در زیر زخم
روید و گوشت زاید است که در زیر پوست بر آید و آنرا بعربی غده گویند با زار ایرتا سبی بترکی رومی روز دوشنبه بود با زار کونی
روز یکشنبه را نامند با زلانا ناج بترکی رومی یکنوع حلوائیست که آنرا بفارسی تو بر تو گویند بزلک نام پرنده ایست بزنگ توغاول
باس ماده که پت بالهای آن سفید است و یکنوع دیگر هست که سر و منقارش سفید است مع السین من الشقات باسماق از الفاظ مشترکه
است و با هر نفعی معنی خاص استعمال میشود مثل انکه گویند کونکول باسماق یعنی دل آرام گرفتن و دشمن باسماق بر خصم غالب شدن و
ماتاق یوقو باسماق مغلوب کردن باده و خواب تیل وایاغ باسماق پا بر روی چیزی گذاشتن و مهر باسماق یعنی مهر زدن و توز باسماق فغان
باسماق یعنی گرد فرو گرفتن و غم فرو گرفتن و بترکی رومی معنی خاموش دارد چنانکه در ذیل جوامد مذکور خواهد شد باستی
ماضی معانی مذکوره است یول ا باستی یعنی دل آرام یافت چنانکه گوید شعر یار هجرانیغ دین نوائینی باقو قوتانکیز کیم هجب
ایش کا بوران باستی کونکول تونا دی هم می باستی یعنی شراب مغلوب کرد چنانکه در سبعه سیاره در داستان مسافر اقلیم دکر نیز
سعد نکوبا شعر رنکی بخش قویدی قلعه فتح سعد نی غار ابچیدا باستی باسار و باسادور و سوی ضایع معانی مذکوره است چنانکه
شاهد بل علیه در سد سکندری در وصف شنا بمعنی فرو میکرد گوید شعر باسیب هیم بولغاج کراتبا رآتی هم ولشکر دیلی کیم
باسار قالماتی باسماید و در فرو میکرد و فرو نگرفته است چنانکه در تاریخ بابری گوید کر هنوز اولوسنی یمشی باساید و کو بولغانیبدور
و بمعنی آرام میگرفت گوید کر تاغ بوی بر ایچی لیق یول یدی ولایت هم هنوز کونکول تا باسماید و ا بردی باسغان و نا باسا و باسغان نتاباساندور
بمعنی فاعل و مفعول و معتد می آیند چنانکه در سد سکندری بتقریب کراجی را بمعنی آرام گرفتن گوید شعر سوز آتیت آنینک
شاری سالمانی کوز ین ه آنکا تیکرو کیم تابتی قاصدا او زینی کونکول باسغانین چونکه فهم ایتی شاه سئوال ایتیب اها نه ایلادی کماه

مغلوب کرده گوید شعر بخشیم اوینا تماس بو نوع صوفی دین لفرا یا میلة میز که مرادا ایتو نی تا سغالا دین بیرین اوینا الی و بمعنی گذاشته
گوید شعر کرا یاغی خوشی بینک تاوتماک میسر بولمناس کونزنا لیب هر برکیم کو سبانک ایلاغ باسغانین ایوت بارس و باسغیل مفرد مخاطب از
فعل امر باسما و باسماغیل مفرد غائب نفی باسینک و باسینکیز و باسینکلار جمع غائب از فعل امر باسماینک و باسماینکیز و باسماینکلار
جمع غائب از فعل نهی باسیب و باسیبان و باساباسیمش آرام گرفته و غالب شده و مغلوب کرده و پا بر روی چیزی گذاشته و فرو گرفته و مهر زده
چنانکه شاهد بر اول را بمعنی مغلوب کرده در مقالة نهم از حیرة الابرار در وصف مستان گوید شعر که بیقلیب کلکو بوپ و لحظه
مستانه لیب هر بایی قولا هوس بیله کلکو بوپ سیقلیب پی به پی بر طیفیلغا ندا باسیب آی می و بمعنی پا بر روی چیزی گذاشته گوید
شعر تا غیننا ماک نابه غم شاه ملول یرغا تنغا نیمدین باسیب اولتوروا شام بو نوع تا لاجا چاپی یرنی کجا نیمدین و نیز بمعنی مغضوب سایر ان المنبر
در داستان شیخ صنعان گوید شعر باسیب و تکان ایل قلیب بیدا آنکا یوق ولی یوز آنجه دین پروا آنکا و هم چنین شاهد بر ثانی
در حیرة الابرار بهمین معنی گوید شعر اولکه اوشا توب باسیبان تیشه نی قیلما دی ایاغ زخمی دین اندیشه نی شاهد بر ثالث بمعنی فرو گرفته
گوید شعر کونکول که تا تیغ سپاهی بیله زلعابتی قیلسا اولاکی که کونکول نی باسیب تورور غلغلنی شاهد بر رابع بهمین معنی گوید
شعر مین کیبی مجنون نی هم باسیب شو ذلت کردیکیم مهر و لیلا سرنخم لیله دلبعی تیر عرا باسیدین باسغای آرام یابد و غالب شود و مغلوب کند
و پایگذارد و فرو گیرد و مهر زند چنانکه بمعنی پایگذارد گوید میر سلطان حسین میرزا شعر یوز غم ایرور ایچرا الدی هجرانیدا خسته حالیم
بر قدم باسغای موپ بو کلبه احزان ارا و بمعنی مهر زند گوید شعر کونکلوم بحرالیم لار چون بوتتی قویدی حلاج عشق خازن اول
بیکلیغ که باسغای مهر ابواب او سینه باسغاج چون آرام یافت و یابد و چون غالب شد و شود و چون مغلوب کرد و کند و چون پا
گذاشت و گذارد و چون فرو گرفت و گیرد و چون مهر زد و بزند چنانکه بمعنی مهر زند گوید شعر خاتم لعلینک اکر آغزیمغه تنکا
تنسا لاگوم مهر ابیار دا موم تا پوشغان کبی باسغاج اوزوک جون بنیا و تمامی صیغ این مصدر مثل بجار و نقد معنی سب تا مالات بوضع
میشد بذکر بعضی از آنها اکتفا شد باسیلماق آرام گرفتن و مغلوب شدن و در زیر پا ماندن و فرو گرفته شدن و مهر زده
باسیلدی آرام گرفت و مغلوب شد و در زیر پا ماند و فرو گرفته شد و مهر زده شد چنانکه در تاریخ بابری بمعنی آرام گرفته شد
که فلان نینک پر آیداغ ان بو کوری پراو نینک پر کوزم یاغی نی تاریغ تا الغان تا و چون تا یاغلاتیم تا یاغ آستیدا خانه مصنفی ایل بوسا
تین تمام باسیلدی لار و جای دیگر گفته که غوغا باسیلدی باسیلغاج چون آرام گرفت و گیرد چون مغلوب شد و شود و چون در زیر
پا ماند و بماند و چون فرو گرفته شد و شود و چون مهر زده شد و شود چنانکه در سد سکندری در اغاز نظم کتاب بمعنی در زیر پا ماندن
گوید شعر کونکلومدا قوت نجیبینکلا دورش بیوک کیم اباغ استیدا قالسا مور باسیلغاج که تا بخید لسا مور ضعیف ناخوش خلقی
و لغای آیا حریف باستوریا توغ مصدر متعدی است یعنی آرام دادن و غالب ساختن و مغلوب ساختن و پا گذاشتن و فرو گرفتن و
مهر زدن چنانکه صیغه ماضی آنرا بمعنی پا گذاشته در تاریخ الملوک در ذکر بهرام گوید کر بهرام در یا بجانه دین کرجستان سپاهی دشت تحافیق
دین چیقب خوارزم نا باستوروب جرجان نواحی سیدا جا تا تغه شیخون ایوب و نیز صیغ بر همین سیاق اشتقاق می یابد باسیرقاماق
بسبب خواب پریشان نا غلبه کابوس در خواب مضطرب کردن چون اشتقاق و صیغ آن منسجم با مذکور نمود بذکر مصدر اکتفا رفت باسلماق
بسکون سین و فتح لام بترکی رومی بمعنی پرورده شدن بود باسلادوک پرورده یم باسلادوکم پرورده یم فضولی گوید با ملاء الرومیه شعر
جان دیر کونکل او لغمزه یکیم موجه زمانلر جان ایچره سنی باسلادوکم آننک ایچون دور باسلمنک پرورده شدن چنانکه فضولی
بمعنی ماضی گوید با ملاء الرومیه شعر کوز منه باسلنوب قیمت بولن سکانکی کورود وغ صدفده کوهر ولان قطره بارانه تنکر تدم

122v.
(ج)

من الجوامد پاس. باتای عجمی رو زطاس ترکی رومی بمعنی زنک بود که آنرا بعربی صدا گویند باستورمه ترکی رومی گوشت قدید باشد
باستوق بضم با و سکون تا و قاف ترکی رومی نوعی حلوا است که از شیره انگور پخته تهیه کرده هم می پزند و در وقت مزه برشته سازند
بکار میبرند و آنرا بستیل هم نامند و اعراب جلد الفرس در نشانات و دیار حجاز قمر الدین گویند و آنچه اهل ایران شیره انگوری که نقوع
آورده مین کرده مغز بادام بر آن پخته آنرا باستوق نامند باسروق بکون ... رای عماله پوششی بود که برای ... نادو تا از بزرگ
خیمه و آلاچوق و اسب میکشند باسغون باسغو مغلوبیت باسقاق شحنه و داروغه و لایت را خوانند باسقیچ نرد بان را گویند
باسلامیشی یعنی غلو ساختن و فرو کردن باسماق ترکی رومی زینه و پله ایست که پا بر آن نهاده بالا روند و نیز دو تخته کوچک
بشکل نعلین که بر یا فندکان حقوت باشد که پا بر بالای آن گذاشته حرکت دهند و معانی مصدری در ذیل اشتقاقات مذکور شد
باسمه نقشی بود که بر قالب برقانها و کاغذها زنند الشاهد علیه شعر طرفه آبی دو صفا رینک کوک آنکا ما و باش انجم
اتینک شکه باسمه قیلغان ذرجلی و نیز در بند ترجیع در وصف نیا گوید شعر ایاغ الیکیداکی ... اوت توفی زر
باسمه سی آندین شرارهٔ بستیل ترکی رومی همان باستوق بود که در فوق مذکور شد سرک برون بعضی ... را گویند
و بکسر یا نیز مستعملست مع الشین من المشتقات باشلاماق بچهار معنی آمده اول شروع کردن دویم متوجه ساختن گویند شعر
عقل او ییلیدی عنانین باشلاماق نامع نبود تیلبه کیم دشت و مرکب دوم یوزلدی بوله آنکا سیم بلدی کردن چهارم راهی
کردن باشلادینک شروع کردی و متوجه ساختی و بلدی کردی و راهی کردی چنانکه در خاتمه سد سکندری بمعنی اول گوید
شعر بوله مشونغه کیم ایلادب شنابه توکا باشلادینک خامه دین در تایب باشلادوق شروع کردیم و متوجه ساختیم و بلدی کردیم
و راهی کردیم باشلادی باشلادی و شروع میکند و متوجه میسازد و بلدی میکند و راهی میکند و باشلادی بمعنی فاعل مصدر هم می آید
چنانکه بمعنی بلدی کننده تاریخ باری مذکور است که باری غلامان آیدان بولا باشلادی کیشی کیلتور تا دیلام باشلادی و شروع میکند
و نکوئه استا باشلاغان و باشلاغان و باشلاغای شروع کننده و شروع کرده و متوجه سازنده و متوجه ساخته و بلدی کننده و بلدی کرده
و راهی کننده و راهی کرده و بمعنی مصدر هم می آید باشلاتو باشلاماق مفرد مخاطب از فعل امر بچهار معنی چنانکه در خسرو شیرین
شاهد اول را بمعنی رابع گوید بیت همین هند و عربیت آتشکه غریبا شلا عذاب برخلاف یلد اوتا بحر باشلا با شلاغیل با شلاغیل با شلا
مفرد مخاطب از فعل نهی باشلاغیل و باشلاغیل و باشلاغیل جمع مخاطب از فعل امر باشلانکیز و باشلانکیز و باشلانکیز جمع مخاطب از فعل نهی
باشلادی باشلامادیم شروع میکنم و متوجه میسازم و بلدی میکنم و راهی میکنم باشلای ین و باشلای ین و باشلای ین باشلا
شروع میکنم و متوجه میسازم و بلدی میکنم و راهی میکنم باشلاغای شروع میکند و متوجه میسازد و بلدی میکند و راهی میکند
و بمعنی فاعل و مصدر معنی هم می آید باشلاماسنکه شروع نکردنت و متوجه نساختنت و بلدی نکردنت و راهی نکردنت باشلا
شروع کردنت و متوجه ساختنت و بلدی کردنت و راهی کردنت باشلادی و باشلادی باشلامیش شروع کرده و متوجه ساخته
و بلدی کرده و راهی کرده چنانکه شاهد اول را بمعنی بلدی کرده در تاریخ الانبیا در ذکر حضرت خضر علیه السلام گوید که
ذو القرنین حیوان سوی خیالی بیله ظلمات غه کیرکاندا خضر علیه السلام آنی باشلادی کیرتی و نیز در سبعه سیاره گوید شعر
حکم قیلدیکه او لطرف سور و نکوز تا نکلادبا شلاب یولینی کیلتوروب نکوز و شاهد ثانی را بمعنی روانه کرده در سد سکندری
گوید شعر بو نیکلیغ سیه باشلاباب ایکی شاه که بر کونجی لیک تا الدعا و لمرسل باشلاماق خطاب شخص واحد باشلا
بر لکای باشلادی بر نکلش و شروع میتوان کرد و متوجه توان کرد و راهی توان کرد باشلادی الفاعش شروع تواند کرد و

123r

تواند ساخت و بلدی تواند کرد و راهی تواند کرد باشلادی و باشلاجی باشلاجی شروع کنان و متوجه سازان و بلدی کنان و راهی کنان باشد
بکرار هم مستعملست باشلاجی و باشلایین شروع کنم و متوجه سازم و بلدی کنم و راهی کنم و باشلامه مفرد غائب و مفرد مخاطب بمعنی ماضی منفی
نیز می آید باشلاغای و باشلاغای و باشلاغای باشلاغای باشلاغیل شروع کنیم و متوجه سازیم و بلدی کنیم و متوجه سازیم و بلدی کنیم و راهی کنیم
چنانکه در خسرو شیرین در داستان سهیل حکیم گوید الشاهد علی الرابع المعنی الثالث شعر بو مشکل نکته حلی اول جلوه ز
آتینک شاری بو یوپنانک باشلابی یولی باشلاغای برای شروع کردن و تمام کرده و برای متوجه ساختن و تا متوجه ساخته
و تا بلدی کرده و برای راهی کردن و تا راهی کرده چنانکه در فصل هفتم محبوب القلوب در ذکر کاتب غلط نویس یعنی برای راهی کردن گوید
که اول سفالی عرفه تا باشلاغالی یخشی وا یاسین مالک در ضرخ فه تا باشلاغالی یخشی و در تاریخ باری بمعنی برای بلدی کردن مذکور است
که هلی مرده دین تاپیب یول باشلاغالی کیلتورکای بلاغ باشلاغاچ چون شروع کرد چون متوجه ساخت چون بلدی کرد چون راهی کرد
چنانکه بمعنی اول گوید شعر تاینماس سین بیمانک المنی کیم نعتدی باشلاغاچ آشنا لاردین بورون بیکانه تیلادی سینی محشر
باشلاغوچی فاعل مطلقی مذکور باشلاغوچی باشلاغوچی باشلاغاچه تا شروع کردن و مقدار شروع کردن تا متوجه ساختن و
و تا بلدی کردن و مقدار بلدی کردن و تا راهی کردن و مقدار راهی کردن باشلاغای آلغاغینچه مقدار یکه شروع توانی کرد و متوجه توانی
ساخت و بلدی توانی کرد و راهی توانی کرد باشلاغومیز دور شروع خواهیم کرد و متوجه خواهیم ساخت بلدی خواهیم کرد و راهی
خواهیم کرد باشلاغونکوز دور شروع خواهید کرد و متوجه خواهید ساخت بلدی خواهید کرد و راهی خواهید کرد چنانکه در مقاله
چهارم از حیرة الابرار بمعنی ثانی در وصیت سکندر گوید شعر قرقه چون باشلاغونکوز دور یوقتم نعش تابدین جهان
بر فولوتم باشلاغوسیلار دور شروع خواهند کرد متوجه خواهند ساخت بلدی خواهند کرد راهی خواهند کرد باشلاماغوم
باشلاغوم یوق شروع نخواهم کرد متوجه نخواهم ساخت و بلدی نخواهم کرد و راهی نخواهم کرد باشلاغای و باشلاغوم یوق شروع
کردن ممکن نخواهد بود متوجه ساختن ممکن نخواهد بود بلدی کردن ممکن نخواهد بود راهی کردن ممکن نخواهد بود باشلاغونکوز لوق
شروع کردن متوجه ساختن بلدی کردن راهی کردن باشلاغای باشلاغان باشلاغون باشلادیک شروع کند و متوجه سازد
و بلدی کند و راهی کند چنانکه در باب دویم از محبوب القلوب شاهد اول را بمعنی اول در ذکر زهد گوید که عبادت سایجی بینا باشلا
در ریاضت فوایدی هر وقت لایتا با باشلاغای باشلاغودلیک و باشلاغودلیک شروع کردن و همچنانکه شروع کند و متوجه
ساختن و همچنانکه متوجه سازد و بلدی کردن و همچنانکه بلدی کند و راهی کردن و همچنانکه راهی کند باشلاماق مع النون
مصدر انفعالست یعنی شروع شدن و توجه کرده شدن و بلدی کرده شدن و فرستاده شدن باشلانغان و باشلانغان و باشلانغان
فاعل و مفعول و مصدر هر چهار معنی می آید چنانکه شاهد اول را بمعنی فرستاده شدن در لسان الطیر در مدح حضرت
حضرت رسالت گوید شعر ایلتکان اول لار ایدی باشلانغان هم اول ایساکان هم اول باعث باشلانغان هم اول و باقی صیغ
بر فوق قاعده شق اول از انواع اشتقاق می یابد باشلاشماق مع التا مصدر مشترکست یعنی شروع فرمودن و متوجه گردانیدن و
فرمودن و راهی ساختن و باقی صیغ بر قاعده شق ثانی از انواع اشتقاق می یابد باشقارماق بچهار معنی آمده اول انجام دادن دویم متوجه
ساختن چنانکه در فرهاد و شیرین گوید شعر کیشی یوبان ساری یارماق کیرا کتورشغان اول ناقه باشقار ماق کیر کتورگیم
بلدی و راهنمائی کردن چنانکه در مقابل بیت و چهارم از محبوب القلوب در ذکر واعظ گوید که یورو مالکان یولغه ایلتی
باسما با ... بی یولدین چیقار ماق و در چهارم راهی کردن الشاهد علیه شعر ای نوای تاریاین دین کونکلی

باشقان یوقسا بوزغمی انکا هم نید ور باشقارماغیم وکه ایضاً تیلبه راب هدیم بولیر غایب نولون تیمکیم تیز کا آنی عقل کوبی
ساری باشقاماقدور دایش باشقاردوق انجام دادیم متوجه ساختیم بلدی کردیم راهی کردیم باشقاردوم باشقاردوک انجام میدهد
ومتوجه میسازد وبلدی میکند وراهی میکند وباشقار در بمعنی فاعل ومصدر هم می آید باشقارماید که انجام نمید هد ونکند
ومتوجه نمیسازد ونساخته است وبلدی نمیکند ونکرده است وراهی نمیکند ونکرده است باشقارغان وباشقاروچی وباشقارادورغان
انجام دهنده وانجام داده ومتوجه سازنده ومتوجه ساخته وبلدی کننده وبلدی کرده وراهی کننده وراهی کرده وبمعنی مصدر هم
می آیند باشقاد بکوبز را باشقار وبفتح او باشقارغیل مفرد مخاطب از فعل امر الشاهد علی الاول بالمعنی الرابع شعر
الآکیل ور بولسا مجنون شیوه وبی نختیار قویماغیل او زاختیار یغه بو ساری باشقار ق من سلطان حسین میرزا شعر آخار ورد
تا چنانک اول کونکلوم که مجنون شیوه دور هر نیچوک بولسا عالم صحراسی ساری باشقار ق باشقارماو باشقارغیل مفرد مخاطب
از فعل نهی باشقارینک وباشقاریکیز وباشقارینکلار جمع مخاطب از فعل امر باشقارماینک وباشقارمانکیز وباشقارمانکلار جمع مخاطب از فعل نهی
باشقاریمان وباشقارماس مین انجام نمیدهم ومتوجه نمیسازم وبلدی نمیکنم وراهی نمیکنم باشقاراسین وباشقارورمن وباشقارادورمن
باشقارودام انجام میدهم ومتوجه میسازم وبلدی میکنم وراهی میکنم الشاهد علی الثالث بالمعنی الاول شعر پلیب کوبنا
بالغیز بار ورمین بو ایشی او نرا شیم دین باشقار ورمین بالمعنی الرابع بضمیر الخطاب شعر عدم یولیغه کرچه باشقارورسن
پراولماک پرله آندین قولغارورسین باشقارماس انجام نمید هد ومتوجه نمیسازد وبلدی نمیکند وبمعنی فاعل ومصدر منفی هم
می آید باشقارماسینکغه با انجام ندادنت ومتوجه نساختنت وبلدی نکردنت وراهی نکردنت باشقاروروبکه با انجام دادنت
ومتوجه ساختنت وبلدی کردنت وراهی کردنت باشقاریب وباشقاریبان وباشقارومیش انجام داده ومتوجه ساخته وبلدی کرده وراهی
کرده چنانکه در حیرة الابرار گوید الشاهد علی الاول بالمعنی الثالث شعر وحکوتیلاب حیلی غه برلن ونوانکر کله مینک
یولسا بولوبیشی تانغ ایله توبرتینی توروکون باشقاریب حیلی نی بول عقبه سیدین قولغاریث باشقارمیشانک الخطاب بمعنی ماضی
باشقارساپولغای وباشقاریب بولغای انجام تواند داد ومتوجه تواند ساخت وبلدی تواند کرد وراهی تواند کرد باشقارا وباشقارا انجام
داده متوجه سازان بلدی کنان راهی کنان وبمعنی تکرار هم مستعملت باشقاراي وباشقارایین انجام دهم ودهد ودهی ودهیم
سازم وسازد وسازی وبلدی کنم وکند وکنی وکرده وراهی کنم وکند وکنی وکرده چنانکه در لسان الطیر شاهد بر اول معنی
گوید شعر دیدی کیم سن خیل غه بولوب باشقاراي بیلکانیم جه خیلنینگ آیب باراي باشقارغانی وباشقارغایمیز وباشقاری
باشقارالیک انجام دهیم ومتوجه سازیم وبلدی کنیم وراهی کنیم باشقارغالی برای انجام دادن وتا انجام داده وبرای متوجه ساختن
وتا متوجه ساخته وبرای بلدی کردن وتا بلدی کرده وبرای راهی کردن وتا راهی کرده باشقارغاج چون انجام داد ودهد
وچون متوجه ساخت وسازد چون بلدی کرد وکند وچون راهی کرد وکند باشقارغوچی فاعل صیغه باشقارغوچه
باشقارغودک وباشقارغانچه تا انجام دادن وبقدر انجام دادن وتا متوجه ساختن وبقدر متوجه ساختن وتا بلدی کردن وبقدر بلدی
کردن وتا راهی کردن وبقدر راهی کردن باشقارالغاینچه بقدری که انجام تواند داد ومتوجه تواند ساخت وبلدی تواند
کرد وراهی تواند کرد باشقارغوسیدور ونا انجام خواهیم داد ومتوجه خواهیم ساخت وبلدی خواهیم کرد وراهی خواهیم کرد
باشقارغو نیکوز دور بدستور خطاب بجمع حاضر باشقارغوسیدور بخطاب بجمع غایب باشقارسیلغوم وباشقارغوم یوق انجام
نخواهیم داد متوجه نخواهیم ساخت بلدی نخواهیم کرد راهی نخواهیم کرد باشقارالماغوم وباشقارا آلغوم یوق انجام دادن ممکنم

نخواهد بود بلدی کردن ممکنم نخواهد بود راهی کردن ممکنم نخواهد بود باشقارغولوق انجام دادنی ومتوجه ساختنی وبلدی
کردنی وراهی کردنی باشقارغای باشقارلو باشقارسا باشقاریوغ باشقارولیا انجام دهد ومتوجه سازد وبلدی کند وراهی کند
باشقارغودیک باشقارور دیک انجام دادنی وهمچنانکه انجام دهد ومتوجه ساختنی وهمچنانکه متوجه سازد وبلدی کردنی وهمچنانکه بلدی
کند وراهی کردنی وهمچنانکه راهی کند من الجوامد باشاق بمعنی تمام اول یکانرا گویند الشاهد علیه شعر ناوکینک
اوزره باشاق گویا ابر رجب نبات کیم کونکول کا یولیار اول شکل یکان دین جوجوت نعیم بمعنی خوشه باشد چنانکه مطربتار گفتا
شعر کونکول نینک مزرعی کیم ناوکینک دین او لدی یوزون باشاقی ترنالک وچون کیلکا یکر ودابله مجنون باشاچی دوهم
اول یکان کرانا سنداوم بمعنی خوشه چین بود چنانکه در فصل سیوم یکلماز مجنوب القلوب ذکر کرده است گوید کیم اراقچی اندین ترکی
باشاچی نینک یاروب آندین کورنی باش توبان نصم ای فوقیت وفتح بای ابجد وسکون نون بمعنی زیر رسر نکون باشد چنانکه
در حیرة الابرار در نعت اسناد گوید شعر چرخ که مهر آلتونی بیلاهر زمان یوزینی آیتینک قرایلاه جهان باشوروبلغم دوبین
هر شهر کا کوما رباش توبان آفی سیپم ثمیم تومن روبی بهمو اباش توبان باسیم هم بمعنی نوشته باشچی الله علیل هم زمانرا گویند باشقه
بمعنی جداگانه الشاهد علیه شعر قیلور فرمان بهینک اشلیتینک تو توب باشقه باشقه الارآیتی و نیز بمعنی دیگر چنانکه گوید
شعر اوجی خم ایکنه یرله کوزیدغ ناسیاع شعه آسفار چینی بامان کوزینی کاسون بولدی کونکول جمکا کافلابیلیت باشلاغ
همان بمعنی باشلاماق باشد که در ذیل مصادر گذشت باشلیغ دو معنی دارد اول جواد ومرتبی خواندا الشاهد علیه شعر
باشلاغی یمی لار عشق اهلی هجران دشتیدا وامق وفرهاد ایله مجنون نوایی باشلیغ وهمچنین در تاریخ الملوک ذکر اسکندر گوید
که تورت یونمکیم خداستیدا اردی افلاطون آلتی باشلیغ دوم ترکیب رومی کلاه کی بکام باشد که بر سر اسپ بندند ونیز گفته میشود
که باشلیغ باشیغه بولور یعنی هر صاحب سر در خود میشود باشماق به بمعنی بوداوک کوتاه بکساله را نامند دویم کفش
نوینده سیم ترکی رومی مستعمل بود که زنان بر سر بندند باشی اولکو نام برج میزان باشد چون حیدر دو ذاولی آن سنا غامتشاز
برابر میشود لهذا باین اسم تسمیه یافته باشی دماتلیق بضم الکنایه از مغرور وسرکش بود مع العین من المشتقات باغلاماق
بستن چنانکه گوید شعر دیمیری خدا همی غنای که سیلوی باغلادینک سیل کیم او شبو باغلانماقغه بارایدی عزاز شهر باغلادی
بستیم باغلار وباغلامید ور می بندد وباغلار بمعنی فاعل ومصدر هم می آید باغلاماید ور نمی بندد ونبسته است باغلاغان
باغلارغان وباغلایدورغان بند نده وبسته الشاهد علی الاول بالمعنی الثانی شعر نی کوروندکا میسکنچه نیشکر شیرین وتورش
نی تینک سندی یلینکا باغلاغان سیل باغة وبمعنی متعدد هم می آید باغلا وباغلاغیل مفرد مخاطب از فعل امر باغلاما وباغلاماغیل
مفرد مخاطب از فعل نهی باغلانک وباغلانکیز وباغلانکلار جمع مخاطب از فعل امر باغلامانک وباغلامانکیز وباغلامانکلار جمع مخاطب از فعل نهی
باغلامان وباغلاماس مین نمی بندم باغلایمین وباغلارمین وباغلایدورمین وباغلادرام می بندم باغلاماس نمی بندد وبمعنی فاعل
ومصدر منفی هم می آید باغلاماسینکغه به نبستن تو باغلاغینکغه به بستن تو باغلاب وباغلابان وباغلامیش بسته باغلامیشا
بسته باغلاسا بولغای وباغلاب بولغای تواند بست باغلای وباغلای باغلای بسته کنان چنانکه در سکندر نامه
در آغاز داستان اسکندر گوید شعر پری طول کمدا راسیل مقبللیغ عزم پری بوکه سد باغلایبوا تیغ عزم وبمعنی تکرار هم مستعملت
باغلای وباغلایین ببندم وببندد وببندی وبسته باغلاسا قد باغلاغیز وباغلامیز وباغلالی باغلاغیلیک ببندیم باغلاغالی برای بستن
وتا بسته باغلاغاج چون بست وببندد باغلاغوچی ببندنده باغلاغوچه وباغلاغونچه وباغلاغانچه تا بستن وبقدر بستن باغلای

124v.

آلقاینینکه معنیسی که قولوق بت باغلاغوسیز دور خواهیم بت باغلاغوسنکوز دور خواهید بت باغلاغوسیلار دور خواهند بت
باغلاغاغوم و باغلاغوم یوق بخواهم بت باغلاغولوق آلماغوم و باغلاغی آلغوم یوق بستن محکم نخواهم بود باغلاغولوق بستن باغلاغای
باغلاغا و باغلاغوتیغا باغلادیك ببندید باغلادیك شاهد علی الاول شعر بو نفعك شوقیدا لشکیم کمندلار ایچوزا اله باغلاغیش باغین
اول نوع کیم دور باغلاغالیب بیلیر ایچره باغلاغودیك و باغلاغوچی بستن و همچنانکه ببندد باغلاتماق مع التاء مصدر متعدی بت
مبنی بنا اندن صیغه آن بدستور باتای قرشت اشتقاق می یابد باغلاتماق مع النون مصدر انفعال است یعنی بسته شدن باغلانغان
و باغلانغان و باغلانمه غان بسته شوند و بسته شد شاهد علی الاول المطلع الاخیر شعر لعل لبا بغیشلیك دیکان سوزنی
ایشتکان قیلماغای آبحیوان بیله باغلانغان دهر کونکولی ثوب معنی مصدر هم می آید باغلاتغای و باغلانسا و باغلانسون و باغلانیدك
بسته شود شاهد علی الاول شعر ماشین کوکلاج حسن ایلا باغلانمه ایل کم نیك باغلانغای . هیچ کیم کوز توتا لار ایلانکی آبها شکار
او لغاج . و باق صیغه بر این نهج بانون اشتقاق می یابد باغلاشتورماق بهم بستن بهمدیگر پیوستن باغلاشتوردوق بهم بستیم
باغلاشتوردو و باغلاشتوردی بهم می بندد و باغلاشتورغو فاعل معنی هم می آید باغلاشتورامیدور و بهم می پیوندد و پیوسته
باغلاشتورغان و باغلاشتورغان و باغلاشتورادورغان بهم پیوندند و بهم بسته و بمعنی مصدر هم می آید باغلاشتور و باغلاشتورند
مفرد غائب فعل امر باغلاشتورسا و باغلاشتورسون مفرد غائب فعل نهی باغلاشتورونکیز و باغلاشتورونکیز باغلاشتورونکلار
جمع غائب فعل امر باغلاشتورسانک و باغلاشتورسانکیز باغلاشتورسانکلار جمع غائب فعل نهی باغلاشتورمان و باغلاشتورمادین
بهم می بندم باغلاشتورامین و باغلاشتورورمین و باغلاشتورادورمین و باغلاشتورودورام بهم می بندم باغلاشتورسام بهم می بندد
و بمعنی فاعل و مصدر هم می آید باغلاشتورماسینکه نبستن تو بهمدیگر باغلاشتوروروونکه نبستن تو بهمدیگر باغلاشتورسا
و باغلاشتورمانید باغلاشتورمیش بهم بسته باغلاشتورمیشان بهم بسته باغلاشتورماب او لغای باغلاشتورووب بولغایم توان
باغلاشتورا آلغای بهم تواند بست چنانکه شاهد بر لغی امیر بیلیمیوان کوید کر خواسیم فیما بیل او لغو تکرار یکی پیچ خم دیکا
مربوط باغلاشتورا آلغای باغلاشتورا باغلاشتوراییم بسته کمان و بند و تکرار هم مستعملست باغلاشتوراییم باغلاشتورایین
بهم بندم و ببندد و ببندی و بسته باغلاشتوربا قد باغلاشتورغایز و باغلاشتورغایز و باغلاشتورالی باغلاشتورالینك
بهم ببندیم باغلاشتورغالی برای بهم بستن و تا بهم بسته باغلاشتورغاچ چون بهم بست و ببندد باغلاشتورغوچی بهم بندند
باغلاشتورغوچه و باغلاشتورغوچه و باغلاشتورغانچه تا بهم بستن و بقدر بهم بستن باغلاشتورا آلقاینینکه معنیسی که قولی
بهم پیوست باغلاشتورغوسیز دور بهم خواهیم بت باغلاشتورغوسنکوز دور بهم خواهید بت باغلاشتورغوسیلار دور
بهم خواهند بت باغلاشتورغاغوم و باغلاشتورغوم یوق بهم نخواهم بت باغلاشتورا آلماغوم و باغلاشتورا آلغوم یوق
بهم بستن محکم نخواهم بود باغلاشتورغولوق بهم بستن باغلاشتورغالی باغلاشتورالاردو باغلاشتورسالار و باغلاشتور
سونلار و باغلاشتوردیکلار بهم ببندند چنانکه شاهد بر اول لطف مقاله شانزدهم از محبوب القلوب در وصف شراکه یک
بنی شفقت بیله بیتیکرا باغلاشتوریغا ملایم بیوعل و انوسین بتیمانك دین آشوریغا ملایما باغلاشتورودیك و باغلاشتوروردیك
هم بستن و همچنانکه بهم ببندد باغیشلاماق بخشیدن یعنی عفو کردن و عطا کردن باغیشلادوق بخشیدیم باغیشلادی باغیشلا
می بخشد و باغیشلاغو بمعنی فاعل و مصدر هم می آید باغیشلانا بدو می بخشد و بخشیده است باغیشلاغان و باغیشلاغان باغیشلاغ
بخشند و بخشیده و بمعنی مصدر هم می آید باغیشلا و باغیشلا مفرد غائب فعل امر باغیشلاسا و باغیشلامای مفرد غائب فعل

125r.

باغیشلاسانک و باغیشلاسانکیز و باغیشلاسانکلار جمع غائب فعل امر باغیشلامانك و باغیشلامانکیز و باغیشلامانکلار جمع غائب فعل نهی
باغیشلامان و باغیشلامادین می بخشم باغیشلادیم و باغیشلادیمین و باغیشلایدورمین و باغیشلادیم می بخشم باغیشلامیش
می بخشد و بمعنی فاعل و مصدر هم می آید باغیشلاماسینکه نبخشیدن تو باغیشلاماسینکه نبخشیدن تو باغیشلا
و باغیشلاییان و باغیشلامیش بخشیده باغیشلامیشان بخشیده باغیشلاماب او لغای و باغیشلاب بولغای تواند بخشید باغیشلا
آلغای تواند بخشید باغیشلایو و باغیشلای باغیشلای مخوکان و عطا کان و بند و تکرار هم مستعملست باغیشلایای باغیشلایین
بخشم و ببخشد و ببخشی و بخشیده باغیشلاغا قد باغیشلاغایز و باغیشلاغایز و باغیشلالی و باغیشلالینك ببخشیم باغیشلاغالی
برای بخشیدن و تا بخشیده باغیشلاغاچ چون بخشید و ببخشد باغیشلاغوچی بخشنده چنانکه مشارکه به شرح خاوند تحلیل کپ تو دعا
باغیشلاغوچی مهم چهار نفر بیشتر ایسا ایش آلا ایرور باغیشلاغوچه و باغیشلاغوچه و باغیشلاغانچه تا بخشیدن و بقدر بخشیدن
باغیشلا آلقاینینکه معنیسی که قولوب بخشید باغیشلاغوسیز دور بخواهیم بخشید باغیشلاغوسنکوز دور بخواهید بخشید باغیشلاغوسیلار
خواهند بخشید باغیشلاغاغوم و باغیشلاغوم یوق نخواهم بخشید باغیشلای آلماغوم و باغیشلای آلغوم یوق بخشیدن محکم نخواهم بود
باغیشلاغولوق بخشیدنی باغیشلاغای و باغیشلاغا و باغیشلاغوتیغا و باغیشلادیك ببخشید باغیشلادیك و باغیشلادیك
بخشیدنی و همچنانکه ببخشد باغیشلاتماق مع التاء مصدر متعدی بیت یعنی بخشانیدن و صیغه آن بانای قرشت اشتقاق می یابد
باغیشلانماق مع النون مصدر انفعال است یعنی بخشیده شدن باغیشلانغان و باغیشلانغان و باغیشلانمه غان بخشیده شوند
و بخشیده شد چنانکه شاهد بر اول لطف مقاله سیزدهم در وصف معراج کوید شعر ایتی هم چیم ایچرا مشکل تو دورور یا
باغیشلانغان ایل الیمیز داخل تو دورور و بمعنی مصدر هم می آید و باقی صیغه بر این نهج بانون اشتقاق می یابد باغیماق تنگ کردن
زیاد کردن باشد من الجوامع باغ بند رشته را کویند شاهد مکیه شعر رشته زلفیدا ایلیدین هر لحظه نی کونکول
پر قوشیدور کیم تاچیب تور کیا اتلیغی بیله و بمعنی کارزار و پهلو دشمن را مانند باقام بر وزن آرام باپیچ طشله بر دیوار
حمیده و حمایل شکسته برای محافظت تکیه دهند باغری قرا پرنده ایست بزرکتر از کبوتر مخطط بالوان مختلفه منهدی آن صاحب
وسینه آن سیاه و در صحرا بی آب سنکلاخ میباشد آکاهدیکه شعر بو ملزم توکان ایکیم کونکول کونکلوم المدور کونکلوم تو
غم دشت ارا باغریقرا دوروش و آنرا باغیرتلاق هم نامند و بمعنی سنکخوار و بعضی قطاه کویند باغلامه ترکه رویی نام یکیمن
که پیکت کهسته تلوراحد باغلیغ بمعنی بسته باشد چنانکه کوید شعر کونکول توشیدور دین غفلت باداری بیله چیبین
باغلیغ ایرور چنکوت تاری بیله باغ یا پراغی بنافه یا پراغی در متبوای دوای کمان را بفارسی سپر خیاط و بعربی لسان الحمل کویند
رومیه سینکیربلی یا پراغی هم نامند باغیر دو معنی دارد اول جکر را کویند شاهد مکیه شعر جکر کوند در شکیم ...
باغیر بواشلی خلطان بیله ممزوج دویم بیرکی و مسی ملاریست از فرزاد کردن باغیرلاق بجکر رفتن و سکوتان ملاوت ...
لام باغریتر اباشد چنانکه کذشت باغیرداق پارچه و بند عبود که مرکب و بوی شکر کوبك بندند باغیرساق روده ...
کویند باغیش دو معنی دارد اول اند و طلنا بخیمه بو دویم منسل از نوخارا نامند باعینشدا مرجع فستق باشد
چمادراتو کویند چنانکه مشفقه سیاه و داستان از اقلیم هفتم کوید شعر خاطر پر مسافر ورداق نکته دین کونکول
حقه دردان تیلدی باغیشدا او لتور و بیناد شه دخلین کر چرخ کهنه نهاد قیته تاریخ بابر عند کوراشکر پسلا
نینك تعظیمی نه قوبوب کوروشتوم سلطان العرخطاو نك قولدا باغیشدا او لتورغوفو دوم باعیندا ش سرزانو ضا باشدچنانکه

125r.

کوید شعر ایماس آیکون ایکی ابغیداشین کوک زلبی برکیمیش تولاقیه دیکه هیچ ینکا آنی القیتی افغانیم بغتاق بروزن
چماق ابریشمی است که مغولیه مانند کیسو تابیده بموی سر خود پیوند میکنند و زنان آنرا مکلل کرده بکلاه دوخته بسر میگذارند
چنانچه وصاف در جلد ثالث تاریخ در ذکر کیخاتو خان کوید که چون بغتاق زرین خود از فرق الغ خاتون کردون بیغتا دیز
در غزل ملمع با صطلاحات مغولیه کوید بغتاق تو خورشید فلک راست سراغوچ قد جوش تو سرو خرامان نما اللث وله اماده کشت
بورک قمرتا نهاده بغتاق آل برزیرچ چرم آتشی و مؤلف برهان قاطع این لفظ را فارسی شمرده بمعنی کلاه و فرجی نوشته و کفته
با طای حطی هم آمده بغلتاق و بغلطاق ارغالق باشد چنانچه شاعر کفته شعر کرم زنید بغلطاق او کشاید کان جا کر بسته باند
جیب پر هنش و مؤلفین رومی نوشته اند که لباس نیمه داریست که در زیر جبه پوشند و مؤلفین فرهنک
جهانکیری هر دو لفظ را فارسی ذکر کرده و کفته که نوعی از فرجی باشد و صاحب برهان قاطع بمعنی جامه و کلاه و فرجی بر کستوان
نوشته بغلنقاز بسکون غین و نون و زای هوز و فتح لام و قاف قاز سرخ را کویند چنانچه در تاریخ بابری در صفت اینتا
مذکور است که اسر و کوپ بغلنقاز قالین بغلنقاز اوچیب قات امرغاندا تیز یل پر لار ایکا کوپ و نوبکه کوپ ایکا ندور
برهان قاطع ذکر کرده که پرنده ایست ابلق که پا و کردن دراز و منقاری سرخ دارد و نوشته که بجای حرف آخر رای قرشت هم بنظر آمده
بغنجاق بفتح غین و جیم عجمی و سکون نون قلم زرین دست و پای اسب را کویند و بجای غین قاف هم می آید مع القاف من المشتقات
باقماق نکاه کردن باقیق نکاه کردیم باقار و باقاد و بنکاه میکند باقار بمعنی فاعل و مصدر هم می آید چنانچه
در لیلی مجنون در معراج بمعنی مصدری کوید شعر جونکه کوزی توزت اولوب باقار دین تا پیچ نظار هم اول ... دین
باقامید و ر نکاه میکند و نکرده است باقمان و باقارغان و باقاد و رغان نکاه کند و نکاه کرده و بمعنی مصدر هم می آید
چنانچه کوید الشاهد علی الاول شعر سبزه خطینک کوز و مینی یار و بور باقمان زنانی کوپ نظر قیلنا اکر میتی الیجرکود
باق و باقیل مفرد مخاطب از فعل امر باقماو باقماغیل مفرد مخاطب از فعل نفی باقینک و باقینکز و باقینکلار جمع مخاطب از فعل امر باقماینک
باقماینکز و باقماینکلار جمع مخاطب از فعل نفی باقمان و باقماس مین نکاه نمیکنم باقایین و باقارمین و باقادورمین و باقار ایم نکاه میکنم
باقماس نکاه نمیکند و بمعنی فاعل و مصدر منفی هم می آید باقماسینکغه نکاه نکردنت باقار سینکغه نکاه کردنت باقیب
باقیبان و باقیش نکاه کرده باقیشانک نکاه کرده باقسا بولغای و باقیب بولغای نکاه توان کرد باقا الغای نکاه تواند کرد
باقا با قتا نکاه کنان نکاه کنان و آنکاه باقا بمعنی نظر باد چنانچه در تاریخ بابری مذکور است کلمه کابلغه باقا غزنی همیشه ارزانی
تورور بدون تکرار هم مستعمل باقای و باقایین نکاه کنم و کند و کنی و کرکه باقساق و باقغایز و باقغای بز و باقای و باقالینک
نکاه کنیم باقغالی برای نکاه کردن و تا نکاه کرد باقغاج چون نکاه کرد و کند باقوچی نکاه کننده باقوچه و باقوغچه
باقماغچه تا نکاه کردن و بقدر نکاه کردن باقا الغاینیکچه بقدر یکه نکاه توانی کرد باقغومیز دور نکاه خواهیم کرد
باقغو نکوزدور نکاه خواهیم کرد باقغو سیلار دور نکاه خواهند کرد باقماغوم باقغوم یوق نکاه نخواهم کرد باقا الماغوم
باقا النغوم یوق نکاه کردن ممکن نخواهد بود باقغولوق نکاه کردنی باقغاق و باقاو باقسا و باقسون و باقدیلک نکاه مکند باقماغای
باقماسا باقماسون باقمادیک نکاه نکند چنانچه شاهد بر ثانی را در حیرة الابرار کوید شعر باقماسا دهقان چمنین تون و کون
نخل ترین آنکا قوروغان اوتون یکی از مؤلفین رومی باقماسا را باقانسا با یای حطی خوانده و در باب یای مفتوحه بمعنی حفظ
نکند نوشته و شعر مذکور را شاهد آورده سهو کرده باقغودیک و باقاردیک نکاه کردن و چنانچه نکاه کند باقیشماق مع الثنی

مصدر مفاعله است بمعنی هم نکاه کردن و باقی صیغ موافق شقاو لباشین قرشت اشتقاق بجا بدان باقیلماق مع الالم بمعنی نکاه کرده شدن
و صیغ آن با لام اشتقاق بجا بد باقتوزماق روی چیزی را بجانب چیزی کردن و متوجه ساختن باقتوزدی متوجه و مایل ساخت چنانچه
در سد سکندری تبقریب تعریف عشق کوید شعر اول اینه کیم سکندر ایتی چولاددین آنی سیکرا یتی کیم رو ایچیک ...
باقتوزدی آیینه غزلک سلیم باقتوردوق متوجه و مایل ساختیم باقتوردونک متوجه ساختی باقتوردولار متوجه ساختند باقتورور بمعنی فاعل و مضارع می آید
باقتورغای بدور متوجه نساخته است باقتورغان و باقتورماغان و باقتوردورغان متوجه ساخته و متوجه ساختن بمعنی فاعل و
می آید باقتور و باقتورغیل مفرد مخاطب از فعل امر باقتورما و باقتورماغیل مفرد مخاطب از فعل نفی باقتورینک و باقتوروینکز و باقتورینکلار جمع
مخاطب از فعل نفی باقتوردان و باقتورماس مین متوجه نمیسازم باقتورامین متوجه میسازم و باقتوردورمین و باقتورور ایم متوجه میسازم باقتورماس
متوجه نمیسازد و بمعنی فاعل و مصدر منفی می آید باقتورماسینکغه متوجه ناساختنت باقتورورسینکغه متوجه ساختنت باقتوریب
باقتوریبان و باقتوریش متوجه ساخته باقتوریشانک متوجه ساخته باقتورا بولغای و باقتوریب بولغای متوجه توان ساخت باقتور
الغای و باقتورا الغای متوجه تواند ساخت چنانچه در تاریخ بابری مذکور است که بیانه نواحی سینی بجا بیت الافغانلار کور قاندین اول
وعده واستمالت بیله بیز کا باقتورغالی لار باقتورا باقتورا متوجه کنان و بدون تکرار هم مستعمل باقتوراي و باقتورايين متوجه
سازم و سازد و سازی و سازند باقتورساق و باقتورغایز و باقتورغای بز و باقتورالینک متوجه سازیم باقتورغالی برای متوجه ساختن
و تا متوجه ساخت چنانچه بمعنی اول در تاریخ بابری مذکور است که حسن یعقوبی وعده لار بیله میرزاغه باقتورغالی کیلکان ایکاند
باقتورغاج متوجه ساخت و سازد باقتوروچی متوجه سازنده باقتوروچه و باقتوروغچه و باقتورماغچه متوجه ساختن و بقدر متوجه ساختن
باقتورا الغاینیکچه بقدر یکه متوجه توانی ساخت باقتورغومیز دور متوجه خواهیم ساخت باقتورغو نکوزدور متوجه خواهید ساخت
باقتورغو سیلار دور متوجه خواهند ساخت باقتورماغوم باقتورغوم یوق متوجه نخواهم ساخت باقتورا الماغوم باقتورا النغوم یوق
متوجه ساختن ممکن نخواهد بود باقتورغولوق متوجه ساختنی باقتورغاق و باقتوراو باقتورسا و باقتورسون و باقتوردیک متوجه سازد
مز انجو امد باقوی بلغت مغولی بمعنی بلند بود باقه و باقرچاق لاک پشت باشد و آنرا تاشباقه و تاشباقه نیز نامند و بعربی
کشف خوانند و اتراک روم قابلو باقه و توسباقه کویند باقیر با ثانی عجمی ترکی روی مس بود که آنرا بعربی صفر نامند و بمعنی خلیم با
که بروی مس نشیند باقیش بمعنی نکاه چنانچه کوید شعر یوزین کوروکاج باشیغه توشتی شکرن لفظ داتی نیلایکیم بیر
باتیشدا یوز بلا باشیغه کیلتوردوم باقیشلیغ نظرکاه و جای تفرج را نامند نیز کویند چنانچه باقیشلیغ یعنی آهو نکاه
بقنچاق همان بقنچاق باشد که در کتاب لباس مع الغین مذکور شد مع الکاف من المشتقات بکلک بسکون کاف و فتح لام ترکی عربی
بمعنی باز داشتن باشد بکلور یعنی باز میداریم چنانچه فضولی بغدادی کوید بیت ملاه الروضه ترجمه ایکلا درمه کوبلی
بکلر ویز لشکر سلطان عرفانو ولایت بکلر ویز من انجو امد بک با بای عجمی و وزن بلک بمعنی جمیع و همه بود چنانچه در نظم
در ذکر پهلوان محمد چپه یار و تحقیق ایم او کوید کلخیوق لیغ کیشی ... تحقیق ... یلدی چپه بایغر قرار تا بی یعنی بار جاغر یاد و بر ...
رومی بمعنی محکم و متین و استوار باشد و بفارسی بیهنر و خود پسند و خود رای را خوانند و نیز مرادف الات چنانچه کوید
وبك یعنی آلات خانه بکاول خوانسالار را کویند چنانچه در سد سکندری کوید شعر تو کا تکلاج ایشن شاه بیاردان
بکاول کیلیب تا بیدی دستارخوان و مؤلف فرهنک جهانکیری در بیان معنی خوانسالار کفته کر چاشنی کیر باشد که آنرا ترکی
توشمال و هندی بکاول کویند بلک بوریه بکاول بجی ترکی رومی کل بستان افروز بود که آنرا سلطان بوریکی نامند

تاج خروس گویند بکتر بروزن ناتر نوعی از سلاح جنگ باشد و آن پارچهای آهنست که بهم وصل کرده بطرز قبا دوزند چنانکه
در افغان نظم سنگلاخ مذکور است گوید شعر سالیب ترنه سوز جوشن و بکترینی توپ و باش ... نظم پاک افسرین بکتر بکتر
جو هم مذکور شیلر ندو مثلا و هم گویند بکتر بترکی رومی جنا باشد و ... نوشته کرده
شراب و شراب خوردن بود و پیاله شراب را نیز گویند یعنی ... هم آمده است باکمی بترکی رومی بمعنی ... بود که
آنست مع اللام من المشتقات بالالا مانع بمعنی گذاشتن و توالد کردن عموم حیوانات و جانوران بالالادی توالد کرد
چنانکه در تاریخ الملوک در ذکر سلطنت خسرو پرویز در وصف ... گوید که ... را ایردی و آنینگ
فیل هندوستان ... بالالادی بالالادی بالالاید و در توالد میکند بالالار بمعنی ... هم می آید
بالالا نا یدو توالد نمیکند و نکرده است بالالامان ... توالد کند و توالد کننده بمعنی ... هم می آید
بالالاو بالالاعیل مفرد ... بالالانا و بالالاعیل مفرد ...
از فعل امر بالالانا ... بالالامان ... توالد میکنم بالالای من ...
بالالادام توالد میکنم بالالامایس توالد نمیکند و بمعنی فاعل ... بالالامانسیکنه ... توالد کرد
بتوالد کردنت بالالابه ... بالالامیش توالد کرده چنانکه در مقاله دوم ... گوید
اول شعر چون بولور ایردی ... توالد کرده بالالانا
بالالاب ... توالد توان کرد بالالای ... توالد توانی کرد بالالایو ... توالد کنان و بدون ... هم مستعمل است
بالالای بالالاین ... توالد کنم و کند و ... بالالاساق ... بالالاغای ... توالد کنیم بالالاغلی
توالد کردن و تا توالد کرده بالالاغاچ چون توالد کرد و کند بالالاغوجی توالد کننده بالالاغوجه و بالالاغا تا توالد
کردن و ... توالد کردن بالالا ... توالد تواند کرد بالالاغو ... توالد خواهیم کرد بالالاغو ... توالد
خواهید کرد بالالاغو ... توالد خواهند کرد بالالاغوم ... توالد نخواهم کرد بالالاماغوم بالالاغوم ... توالد
محکم نخواهد بود بالالاغولوق توالد کردن بالالاغای ... توالد کند بالالاغویدن ... توالد کند
و همچنانکه کند من الجوامد بالا عسل را گویند الشاهد علیه شعر لعلی دین کا ... شیرین ...
... ایچم ... کاج بالایوعه ... نوعی از مسکرات است که از ... العسل ترتیب ... چنانکه در تاریخ مطلع السعد
مذکور است که انواع مشروبات و مسکرات از باده و ... و بال و مثلث و عرق مرتب داشته اند و بعربی ... نوعی از
باشد و بفارسی ... آمده اول ... از حیوانات دست بود از کتف تا سر ناخن و ... از جانوران پرنده جناح باشد ... نوعی
ناهیست که بنیاد ... بود ... و فساد بسیار کند و در ... مشترکست ... کردن و امراء
... بالای بمعنی قامت و فوق باشد بالا بچه جانوران را نامند چنانکه گوید شعر ...
... آشیان ... بالاد بروزن تالار ... بود که آن ...
... بالاغنه یعنی ... و لطیفه ... بالتو بسکون لام و ضم تا قرشت ... گویند چنانکه
در تاریخ الانبیا مذکور است که حضرت ابراهیم علیه السلام ... بالتو ...
و آنرا بعربی فاس گویند بالچاغ و بالچاق بفتح جیم عجمی بالف کشیده آهنی که ما بین تیغه و قبضه شمشیر ... میکند ...

شعر ... قانیم ... اولیکا ... بالچاقی بالچیغ باتای عجمی که
جیم عجمی گل بود که آنرا بعربی وحل گویند بالدیر ... بود که در ... باشد و نصیری ... نوشته بالدرغان
ساق ... باشد که آنرا بفارسی ... و بزبان ... گویند و آن ... و بلند ... شبیه
... و بالدیرقرا بترکی رومی ... باشد که آنرا بعربی ...
النبرخوانند بالش بکسر لام ... آن نوشته که بالش ...
که بها آن ده دینار باشد ... بالش ...
بالش ... هندوستان نوشته کرده
موافق تواریخ ... معروف
بال قاباغی بترکی ... شیرین بالیغ ... شهر و ولایت بود چنانکه ...
مشهور است ... گویند الشاهد علیه شعر ای ...
... بالیغ ... بکسر لام اول و جیم عجمی و سکون ... بالیغچین مع النون بترکی رومی ... است که آنرا ...
بو تیمار و ... و بعربی ابوالحزین ... گویند بالیقچه باتای عجمی و بفتح لام و قاف و سکون سین مهمله بترکی رومی ...
باشد بلقته باتای عجمی و فتح لام و تای قرشت و سکون قاف و بلقیدرق مع الدال المهمله ... باشد ...
باتای عجمی بروزن ... چنانکه در تاریخ بابری در وصف ... مذکور است ...
و ... بلنباتن ... بفتح لام و تای ابجد بالف کشیده و سکون نون بترکی رومی ... که آنرا
... و بعربی صقر گویند و بفارسی ... بلبلات باتای عجمی بروزن ...
گویند که در زبان او لکنت باشد ... چنانکه مذکور خواهد شد ... نام کوهیست معروف ...
... مع النون من المشتقات ... بسکون نون و کاف عجمی ...
بمعنی شبیه و مانند کردن بود الشاهد علیه ... شعر ...
... و بلغت ختای ... چنانکه ...
... شبیه و مانند شدن ... بسکون نون بترکی رومی یعنی ... و آنرا بلغت ختای ...
... فرو بردن چنانکه ... گوید ... شعر ...
... بانای عجمی بروزن ...
عراق عرب ... گویند و آن گیاهیست که بفارسی ... خوانند ...
... بند و در ... بود که بدان ...
... چنانکه گوید شعر ...
بروزن ... گویند که از ...
دویم نوعی ... بسکون نون و کاف عجمی ...
باشد ... بترکی رومی ... بود و بلغت ختای ... مع الواو باو بروزن ...

بضم واو وسکون رای قرشت و کسر جیم بمعنی طلخ باشد چنانکه در مهمات محبوب القلوب در خاتمه کتاب در نقل تنخ بملوک کوید
که هارون دیدی کیم کیاکین نحراندین بیشکورای دیاکین باوه حی خانه دین بو بیراری مع المد الفا جیلی بجلی باشد چنانکه
در خاتمه محبوب القلوب کوید کر اکر شونقار اینا موه بیت سپلیسکه اهل ارذکا دیوق هم شکر دو دکرا ایلیکیک بصل اینچی بجلی
تاکادیوق مراو قتولی بلغت مغول طرف راست بود چنانکه جوانغار طرف چپ باشد و برانغار و جوانغار بعرف
آنهاست مع الیاء المثناة المشقات بایمیا ق غ بجیا غنی شدن بایدوق غنی شدیم بایر و بایدور غنی میشود و
بایر بمعنی فاعل و مصدر هم می آید بایماید ور غنی میشود و نشده است بایغانور بایرغان و بایدورغان غنی شونده و غنی شده و
مصدر هم می آید بایی و بایغیل مفرد مخاطب فعل امر بایما و بایماغیل مفرد مخاطب فعل نهی بایینک و بایینکیز و بایینکلار
جمع مخاطب فعل امر بایمانک و بایمانکیز و بایمانکلار جمع مخاطب فعل نهی بایمان و بایمامین غنی نمیشوم بایمین و
بایرمین و بایدورمین و بایرام غنی میشوم بایماس غنی نمیشود و بمعنی فاعل و مصدر منفی هم می آید بایماسینکه غنی نشد
بایر سینکه غنی شدنت بایمیغ بایمیان و بایمیش غنی شده چنانکه در سد سکندری در وصف پری دانشمندان کوید بیت
الاولق نیچه بولسا الا دیم ایچره اسن تا پارلا کمال ایچره و بعجز باشقان شای دانش ایچره بایمیش کتاردین نیچه ایسکیزیکه کتا
بایمیشانک غنی شده بایمیا بولغای و بایمیب بولغای غنی تواند شد بایمیا آلغای و بایی آلغای غنی تواند شد بایی بیایی غنی شده
غنی شده و بدون تکرار هم بایمعنی مستعملست بایی و بایبین غنی شوم و شود و شوی و شده بایمیا قه و بایغانیز و بایغای
بایلی و بایلینک غنی شویم بایغیلی برای غنی شدن و تا غنی شده بایمیاج چون غنی شد و شود بایغوچی غنی شونده
بایغوچه و بایغوچه بایغانچه تا غنی شدن و بعد غنی شدن بایی آلغانینکچه بعد ازینکه غنی تواند شد بایغومیز دور غنی
خواهم شد بایغونکوز دور غنی خواهید شد بایغوسیلار دور غنی خواهند شد بایماغوم و بایغوم یوق غنی نخواهم شد بایی آلماغوم
بایی آلغوم یوق غنی شدن ممکن نخواهد بود بایغولوق غنی شدنی بایغای بایمیاغای بایغوسون بایی دیک غنی شود بایغودیک و
بایر دیک غنی شدنی و همچنانکه غنی شود من المجرد بای سه معنی دارد اول غنی که کویند الشاهد علیه شعر چون یوی
کونکلا سوادین اشک نیار وت یوق آچیب کیم دردم سیز ایلیکا بای ایل فرزند و بیزلا التزکات دویم کهینه کر بای بیری یعنی بنیاد داد
بنت کرد چنانکه در محبوب القلوب در فصل بیت و دویم در ذکر مطرب و مغنی کوید که با اهل الله کیم ارغنون اونی دین دیر فه
کردی و دین و اسلام نقدین مغبچه لار عز بای پیری سیم تا اصطلاح مغولیه امرای بای عمومی باشد که رو برنامجات قطع و فصل
حکام را نوشته بنا بنا در جمع برنامجات کرده اکر حکمی بر خلاف قانون از امرای دیوان صادر شده باشد ازخواست نمایند بای غانو
چندایت که آنرا بایقوش هم کویند و بفارسی جغد نامند باید و بسکون یاء و ضم دال نام یکی از خوانین چنگیزیست که قبل از ایلخان تو
بر تخت سلطنت ایران نشست بایسر بکسر یا اکر چه در عربی بمعنی خراب ضد آباد باشد اما در ترکی بمعنی خاتم معبوده و در اصطلاح
در فنایم المحبه در ذکر خواجه محمد خسی کوید کر ارسلان نوه نی الار ایلا ایکا قو بویلا و نزی بیسک بایغ چقیپ اولتوردی بایری
بسکون یا و کسر رای قرشت بمعنی قدیمی باشد چنانکه در مجالس النفایس در وصف سید حسین کوید کر آنا بابادین بو در کاه نینک بایری
بلکه نوعما سید دور بایغیز بسکون یا زای هوز و کسر غین معجمه در بلاد غیرات و آن نام ولایتیست از توابع هرات که رپته آغا
در کمال و فصاحت چنانکه کوید شعر اغزینک سپاه تینک لیک تا الاشمر پسته اویا الماس اول آغزی آجوق بایغیزی نیسلف
بو چلو مین کوزش بایقوش جغد باشد که آنرا بای خاتون نیز نامند باید نام پسر کوله خان بن اوغوز خانست و بلغت مغول بمعنی ...

باشد بایه چوبی بابا و بمعنی بدن شایه عمومیت و زیبانه بود چنانکه در سد سکندری در وصف هوت کوکوید شعر کو دوه نوب
نکه سیدین جدی بابه اسد قیماق نینک آستیدا لیا سایه و در اصطلاح انا مطلق مشترکست و بفارسی بمعنی تقدمه و بنا و
مرتبه و نرد بان باشد بیات بعضی بیات به معنی آمده اول بمعنی خداوند بود دویم نام پسر دوین کونخان بن اوغوز
سیم نام فرقه ایست که نحوها عبد الله ابا الغازی بحب طوایف ترکمان میشمارند و منسوب به بیات خان بن کونخان صید استدیان
نام دوایست معروف که آنرا سوسن کویند بجهت دیتمین بدن و تقویت بصر نافعست چون تلخ آن غیر مستعمل از بلای ترنج
شیرین آنرا شیرین بیات خوانند بیرق بسکون یاء و قاف و فتح رای قرشت علم کوچک را کویند و نیز قصب التسوانا مانند که بر میان
استلزی نصب کنند و اسبی که کوه را بیرق کویند که بر قرار کرفت سیه بر وزن بضم رو معنی ولی داول صید را خوانند الشاهد
شعر موافق کیل دیلا بولین کونور روزایله بیرش چمن بوبا شیل خلعت بینک سوهوانیم هم تعیم نوعی از پای خفیف ایست
منقلی عراقی اما از آن تلخ تر باشد چنانکه در مقاله شاتر دهم از حیرة الابرار در وصف خود نمایان کوید شعر کونکل الف
ایتیب آز و هوس بین یکان قایمیجه وسین پر مکر دین کیا پر مکر هم دیما شنم دیکیل تر لیک آینک آستیدا پر دیکیل بیتال
مع الکلیم ماد بیاز کویند و آنرا بیه نیز خوانند و ستطار مع الراء المهمله بعربی مفاتح آرا ردوا بد تا مانند بسله یعنی مهمن بتکه
در لیلی مجنون کوید شعر مجنون او فوغوشبیله نامه ضمغا ایتی تیشا انامه و آنرا بویله و شویله هم کویند با بصمو با
حرف التاء مع التاء بوبر بتکرر و عمفا اشد بوبوش بضم هرد و بای عجمی هدهد شانه بسر را کویند و مؤلف برهان قاطع نوبر
بر وزن روکش بمعنی نوشته پوپوک با هر دو بای عجمی مضموم تاج مرغانرا مانند تاج خروس و هدهد و امثال آن و مجاز هدهد
هم خوانند و آنرا او بوک نیز کویند و مؤلف برهان قاطع بوبک و پوپک بر وزن خوبک و بو بو و بو بو و بوبویه بمعنی شانه سر هدهد
نوشته حرف التاء مع التاء المشقات بوتماک به پنج معنی آمده اول رو بیدن کیاه و سبزه دویم التیام یافتن زخم و جراحت سیم ساخته
شدن و انجام یافتن چنانکه در صحیفه سیاره در داستان نمرد کوید شعر حکم تیلادی کم آلتون و کینون تخت بولا کلکا
چهار ایسون چهارم بعمل آمدن و حاصل شدن پنجم وثوق و اعتماد کردن بوتتولک رو بیدیم التیام یافتیم و ساخته شدیم و
بعمل آمدیم و اعتماد کردیم بوتتونک رو بیدی و التیام یافتی و ساخته شدی و بعمل آمدی و اعتماد کردی چنانکه بمعنی اخیر کوید
شعر دوستلار حق غم تمت قیلیا ش هر نی دشمن دیدی بوتتونک باری بوتار و بوتا دور میروید و التیام می یابد و ساخته
میشود و بعمل می آید و اعتماد میکند الشاهد علی الاول المعنی الاول شعر کیچه تن نوع بوتای کیر بکینک خیالید کوز منکا
ایکنه بوتار تا نحنه سیکر و ستر ارا و بوتار بمعنی فاعل و مصدر هم می آید چنانکه بمعنی ساخته شدن در سد سکندری کوید شعر
که بوایش بوتلکا تاپیلدی جهت نی نوع امیدی کا ناکوراه مصلحت بوتماید و برمیروید و نروییده است و التیام نمی یابد و ناساخته
و ساخته نمیشود و نشده است و بعمل نمی آید و نیامده است و اعتماد نمیکند و نکرده است بوتکان و بوتارکان بوتادوکان رستیده
و روییده و التیام یابنده و یافته و ساخته شونده و شده و بعمل آینده و بعمل آمده و اعتماد کننده و اعتماد کرده چنانکه شاهد بر او
بمعنی روییده در لیلی مجنون کوید شعر اوستیکا یاغیب غبار محنت بوتکان ایلغینه خار محنت و بهمان معنی فرماید شعر بوتکان
او قشار دیکاسین هر یان قیزیل تال اهره ورک هر بار دین سیکا ملایی بو جسم خون آلودرا و بمعنی بعمل آمده در وصف نیم لوتاک
مسلمانه تا یکی بابر و مند کوراست که در مضار زدیک مقترت و عزیز آن ضمیر کیچه لیک فرصت قالیب ایشی خا غیر مهالک ایدی مقرر
در کیم موند اق بوتکان کیشی اندا ق شکست تاپغای و بمعنی مصدر هم می آید بوتماکان و بوتمادوکان نرویید و التیام نیافته

وساخته نشده وبعمل نیامده واعتماد نکرده چنانکه شاهد براول بطریق جناس کوید شعر تیغ عشقینک یلمزسید هر بوتماکان
یعنی الیام نیافته در دیوهر کیمکا آتیب بوتماکان یعنی اعتماد نکرده هر بر اسید هر آهیم اوقی دین آندا کل یاخودکیا هی
بوتماکان یعنی نرسیده و بمعنی فاعل و مصدر منفی هم می آید بوت وبوتکیل مفرد مخاطب از فصل امر بمعنی چنانکه از
از معنی ثانی وجناس را بطریق ایهام کوید الشاهد علی الاول شعر وصل ایلادیب واعی تماکیلکوسی تیغ هجر یتکان
اولغان کونکول بوسوزکا بوت وبوت بمعنی ران هم بود چنانکه در غیر منصب نکار شراید بوتا و بوتا کیل مفرد مخاطب
از فصل امر بمعنی چنانکه بمعنی خامس کوید الشاهد علی الاول شعر دیبام که ترک عشقینک ایتای بوتما ای پری
کیم تیلبه لا تجدید شیکا کوپ اعتنا ربوق بوتونک عبوتونکو بوتونکلار جمع مخاطب از فصل امر بوتماتک بوتماتکیز بوتمانکلار
جمع مخاطب از فصل نفی چنانکه بمعنی خامس کوید الشاهد علی الاول شعر نوائی ترک عشق ایستیم دیبا بوتمانک کر بوتماسلار
کیتیهر سوز ایشیتسا اصر واتود یوانه دین داغیغ ونیز بهمین معنی کوید الشاهد علی الثانی شعر ظلم ایله یقرحالیک تلیغان
یعنی هم باقیب بوتکا دوریعنی دنیا الادا اول خلاصه بی بوتما نکیزنا بوتمان وبوتماس بمعنی نمی رویم والیام نمی یابم و انجام نمی یابم
و بعمل نمی آییم واعتماد نمی کنیم بوتامین و بوتامین بو تادورمین وبوتادام میرویم والیام می یابیم و انجام می یابیم و بعمل می آییم واعتماد
می کنیم بوتماس نمی رود والیام نمی یابد و انجام نمی یابد و بعمل نمی آید واعتماد نمی کند چنانکه بمعنی ثانی در مثنوی سیاره کفته
فرخ شاه کوید شعر دیدی بو عجز بیرله بوتماس ایشیم بار دور و دور تینکریم ایوق ایباکیشیم و بمعنی فاعل و مصدر منفی هم می آید
بوتماسینکا بنرسیدنت و بالیام نیافتنت و با انجام نیافتنت و بعمل آمدنت و با اعتماد نکردنت بوتوب و بوتوبان و بوتوبتیش
دوییده والیام یافته و ساخته شده و بعمل آمده و اعتماد کرده چنانکه شاهد بر اول را بمعنی رسیده کوید شعر بوزو
آغزینک غمی دین کوزیاشیم چون آتیکل آچیلیب غنچه بوتوب و بهمان معنی در مدح پادشاه کوید شعر سوین کیم حق ایلیجی بحفظ الحیات
بوتوب ما برجا اندین نهال حیات و بمعنی ساخته شده در خسرو شیرین در وصف قصر فرهاد کوید شعر بوتوب القصه هر
صوای ایاسا لدی باغ عرجنت مثالی ونیز بهمان معنی در سبعه سیاره در داستان ماه فرخ کوید شعر تاشیبان آندا انشد
خوشبوکه بوتوب اولعمارت دلجو بوتمیشانک خطاب شخص واحد حاضر بوتسا بوتکیلا بوتوب بوتکیلا نمیتوان رسید والیام نمیتوان یافت
وساخته نمیتوان شد و بعمل نمیتوان آمد و اعتماد نمیتوان کرد چنانکه شاهد بر ثانی بمعنی اول وخامس بطریق ایهام کوید شعر
دیب ایمیش پرکون کیلیب کونکلی یارا سین بونکارای کیلسا بونکیل ای کونکول بوسوزکا خود بولماس بوتوب بوتا الماس نمیتواند رسید
والیام نمیتواند یافت ساخته نمیتواند شد و بعمل نمیتواند آمد و اعتماد نمیتواند کرد بوتا بوتا رسیده رسیده والیام یا
یافته و ساخته شده شده و بعمل آمده آمده و اعتماد کنان و تدوین تکرار هم با یک معنی بمعنک بوتای بوتایین بروییم والیام
یابیم و انجام یابیم و بعمل آییم و اعتماد کنیم و بمفرد مخاطب و مفرد مغایب و ماضی نیز بهمین نحو استعمال میشود بوتسا بوتکای بوتکاین
بوتای بوتالینک برویم والیام یابیم و ساخته شویم و بعمل آییم واعتماد کنیم بوتکالی برای رسیدن وتا رسیده و برای الیام
وتا الیام یافته و برای ساخته شدن وتا ساخته شده و برای بعمل آمدن وتا بعمل آمده و برای اعتماد کردن وتا اعتماد کرده چنانکه
برای انجام یافتن و ساخته شدن در سبعه سیاره در داستان نهر کر کوید شعر ایکی مینک ما بمان آلتون ایتی طلب بوتکالی
اولمقاه عیش طرح بوتکاج چون روشید و روید چون الیام یافت و یابد چون ساخته شد و شود چون بعمل آمد و آید چون
اعتماد کرد و کند بوتکوچی رونده والیام یابنده و ساخته شونده و بعمل آینده و اعتماد کننده بوتکوچه و بوتکونچه و بوتکانچه

تا رویدن و بقدر رسیدن وتا الیام یافتن و بقدر الیام یافتن وتا ساخته شدن و بقدر ساخته شدن وتا بعمل آمدن
و بقدر بعمل آمدن وتا اعتماد کردن و بقدر اعتماد کردن بوتا آلغانیکچه بقدر یکه توانی رسید والیام توانی یافت و ساخته توانی
شد و بعمل توانی آمد واعتماد توانی کرد بوتکوسیز بود خواهیم رسید والیام خواهیم یافت ساخته خواهیم شد و بعمل خواهیم آمد
اعتماد خواهیم کرد بوتکوسیز دور خطاب بجمع حاضر بهمین معنی بی بوتکوسیلار دور خطاب بجمع غایب بهمین معنی بوتماکوم
بوتکوم یوق نخواهم رسید والیام نخواهم یافت و ساخته نخواهم شد و بعمل نخواهم آمد و اعتماد نخواهم کرد بوتا آلغوم
بوتا آلغوم یوق رسیدن ممکن نخواهد بود والیام یافتن ممکن نخواهد بود و ساخته شدن ممکن نخواهد بود و بعمل آمدن
ممکن نخواهد بود و اعتماد کردن ممکن نخواهد بود بوتکولوک روییدنی والیام یافتنی و ساخته شدنی و بعمل آمدنی و اعتماد
کردنی بوتکای بوتیا بوتسا و بوتسون و بوتدیک بروید والیام یابد و ساخته شود و بعمل آید و اعتماد کند چنانکه در مقاله
نهم از حیرة الابرار شاهد بر دویم را بمعنی دویم کوید شعر مثلنا بلا زخم لا تری چاره سی بوتسا غنا او تلار عشینک بلموی
بوتکیدیک و بوتاردیک روییدنی و همچنانکه بروید والیام یافتنی و همچنانکه الیام یابد و ساخته شدنی و همچنانکه
ساخته شود و بعمل آمدنی و همچنانکه بعمل آید و اعتماد کردنی و همچنانکه اعتماد کند و شاهد بر اول را بمعنی رسید نخ کوید
شعر بوتکودیک ایردی وصل ایله کونکلوم جراحتی هجران تیلیجی بیرله یانا پاره قیلدیلار بوتکار غالت نخ معنی طرد اوک
روپانیدن دویم الیام دادن سیم ساختن و انجام دادن چهارم بعمل آوردن پنجم پوشانیدن بوتکاردی رویانید والیام د
وساخت و بعمل آورد و پوشانید چنانکه در سبک ملکه ری در شکن طلسم باد کشمیر بمعنی سیم کوید شعر ایکی خنده سایه
روان ماردیلار ش کج وخشت ایله رب بوتکاردیلار و بمعنی پنجم در تاریخ الانبیا در ذکر حضرت سحق علیه السلام کوید که عمری
بونیکتا نکایستکاندین سونکرا مینکری تعالی حکیمن بوتکادی بوتکاردور بوتکارادور میرویاند والیام میدهد و میسازد
و بعمل می آرد و میپوشاند بوتکار و بمعنی فاعل و مصدر هم می آید بوتکار نماید و دیگر ویاند و نرویانیده است والیام نمیدهد
نداده است و نمیسازد و نساخته است و بعمل نمی آرد و نیاورده است و نمیپوشاند و نپوشانیده است بوتکارکان و بوتکاردورکان
بوتکاردوکان رویانید و رویانیده والیام دهنده و داده و سازنده و ساخته و بعمل آرنده و آورده و پوشاننده و پوشانیده
مصدر هم می آید بوتکار بکونل بوتکار و نصم را و بوتکارکیل مفرد مخاطب از فصل امر پنج معنی چنانکه شاهد بر اول
بمعنی پنجم در شبهات محبوب القلوب کوید که اوزونکنی زیبا لباس خیالیدین اوتکاز لباس زیبا الیقین بیلا حسانک بیرلا بونکی بو
و شاهد بر ثانی بمعنی دویم سلطان حسین میرزا فرموده شعر ایستا مان کیلسا یا ناکونکلوم شکافین تا بما قاش وه کر پرهیم
فی یوب اول چالک کوکسوم بوتکارماو بوتکارماکیل مفرد مخاطب از فصل نفی بوتکارتیک بوتکارتکیز بوتکار بوتکارمانکلار جمع مخاطب
بوتکارمالت و بوتکارمانکیز بوتکارمانکلار جمع مخاطب از فصل نفی بوتکارامان بوتکارماس مینرو یانم والیام نمیدهم و نمیسازم و بعمل نمی آرم و
نمیپوشانم بوتکارامین و بوتکارورمین بوتکاردورمین میرویانم والیام میدهم و میسازم و بعمل می آرم و میپوشانم بوتکارماس
نمیرویاند والیام نمیدهد و نمیسازد و بعمل نمی آرد و [illegible] و بمعنی فاعل و مصدر منفی هم می آید بوتکارماسینکا بنرویانیدنت
و با الیام ندادنت و بنساختنت و بعمل نیاوردنت و بنپوشانیدنت بوتکاریب و بوتکاریبان و بوتکاریش رویانیده والیام داده و ساخته
و بعمل آورده و پوشانیده چنانکه شاهد بر اول را بمعنی ساخته در تاریخ در وصف زلزله و خرابی بوالقصه مذکورست کر پچینو
لیغو اینکاریب و قصر خاقانی بوتکاریب و بمعنی پوشانیده در تاریخ الانبیا در ذکر تفاخر حضرت ابراهیم علیه السلام بعد از تمام کنبه

گوید که خطاب کیلدی کیم ... سین ... بوتکاریبین ... بوتکلر ...

والتیام داده و ساخته و بعمل آمده و پوشانیده بوتکایا بولغای و بوتکایب بولغای توان رویانید التیام توان داد و توان ساخت

و بعمل توان آمد و توان پوشانید بوتکارا بوتکارلار رویندکان و ترمیم کنان و سازنده ساخته و حاصل کنان و پوشاننده کان

تکرار هم بمعنی مستعمل بوتکادایم ... رویانم والتیام دهم و بسازم و بعمل آرم و بپوشانم ... مفرد غائب و مخاطب

نیز بهمین نحو می آید ... بوتکارالیم برویانیم والتیام دهیم و بسازیم و بعمل آریم و بپوشانیم

بوتکلرکالی برای رویانیدن و نارویانیده و برای التیام دادن و نا التیام داده و برای ساختن و ناساخته و برای بعمل آوردن

و نابعمل آمده و برای پوشانیدن و ناپوشانیده چنانکه ... گوید شعر

... مصرع ...

... چون رویانید و برویانید

و چون التیام داد و بدهد و چون ساخت و بسازد و چون بعمل آمد و بیاید و چون پوشانید و بپوشاند بوتکارکوچی رویاننده

والتیام دهنده و سازنده و بعمل آرنده و پوشاننده ... تا رویانیدن و ...

تا التیام دادن ... تا ساختن ... تا بعمل آمدن ... توانی رویانید والتیام

داد و بعمل توانی آمد و توانی پوشانید بوتکارکومیز دور خواهیم رویانید التیام خواهیم داد خواهیم ساخت بعمل خواهیم

آمد خواهیم پوشانید بوتکارکونکوز دور خطاب بجمع حاضر بوتکارکوسیلار دور خطاب بجمع غایب بوتکلماکوم و بوتکارکوم یوق

نخواهم رویانید و التیام نخواهم داد و نخواهم ساخت و بعمل نخواهم آمد و نخواهم پوشانید بوتکارا آلماغوم و بوتکارا آلغوم یوق

رویانیدن ممکن نخواهد بود و التیام دادن ممکن نخواهد بود و بعمل آوردن ممکن نخواهد بود و پوشاندن ممکن نخواهد بود

بوتکارکولوک رویانیدنی و التیام دادنی و ساختنی و بعمل آمدنی و پوشانیدنی بوتکلکای و بوتکارا ...

بوتکاردیک برویاند و التیام دهد و بسازد و بعمل آید و بپوشاند چنانکه شاه بابر ... در تاریخ بابر ... گوید

که ... بوتکار ...

رویانیدنی و همچنانکه برویاند و التیام دادنی و همچنانکه التیام دهد و ساختنی و همچنانکه بسازد و بعمل آمدنی و همچنانکه

بعمل بیاید و پوشانیدنی و همچنانکه بپوشاند بوتکاریلماک مع الکاف مصدر انفعالست بمعنی رویانیده شدن و نیز

ملتئم شدن و نیز ساخته شدن و همچنانکه بعمل آمدن و نیز پوشانیده شدن و صیغ آن بر سیاق ما تقدم اشتقاق می یابد بوترماق

بکون تا و فتح راء مهمله و بوتراشماق مع الشین پریشان و منتشر و متفرق شدن ... بوترماک با کاف مذکور

ساخته و بمعنی ... نوشته سهو کرده بوترادی و بوتراشتی متفرق شد الشاهد علی الاول شعر ...

... بوترادی ... بوترادوق و بوتراشتوق متفرق

شدیم بوترار و بوترایدور و بوتراشور و بوتراشادور متفرق می شود الشاهد علی الاول شعر ...

... کیم هوای مشک و عنبر ... بوترایدور ... و بوتراشور بمعنی فاعل و مصدر هم می آید ...

بوترامایدور متفرق نمیشود و نشده است بوتراغان ... بوتراشغان ...

متفرق شونده و متفرق شده و بمعنی مصدر هم می آید چنانکه شاهد ... از خسرو شیرین گوید که ...

تاغ و دشتغه بوتراشغانلاری ... بوتراش و بوتراشغیل مفرد غائب لفظ الحال ... و بوتراشما و

بوتراشماغیل ... بوتراشنکلار جمع غائب لفظ الحال

چنانکه گوید الشاهد علی الاول شعر ...

... جمع غائب لفظ الحال ...

بوتراشماس مین متفرق نمیشوم ...

متفرق میشوم ... بوتراشماس متفرق نمیشود و بمعنی فاعل و مصدر منفی هم می آید ... متفرق

نشدن تو ... متفرق شدنت ... بمعنی

... متفرق شده الشاهد علی الثالث شعر ...

... متفرق شده ... بوتراشا بولغای ... متفرق تواند

... متفرق تواند شد ... متفرق شوان ...

... متفرق شوم ...

... متفرق شویم ... برای متفرق شدن و نامتفرق شده ...

... چون متفرق شد ... متفرق شونده ...

... نامتفرق شدن ...

... متفرق خواهیم شد ... متفرق خواهید شد ...

متفرق خواهند شد ... متفرق نخواهم شد ...

... متفرق نتوانم شد ... متفرق شدنی ...

... متفرق شوید ...

... متفرق شدنی ... بوتراماغ و بوتراشماغ مصدر متعدی بمعنی متفرق

ساختن ... متفرق کردن چنانکه شاه ... گوید شعر ...

... متفرق کنم ... الشاهد

علی الاول ...

... اشتقاق ... چنانکه ... خسرو شیرین ...

شعر ...

و اعتماد کردن چنانکه ...

... درخت ... چنانکه ... گوید شعر

...

...

...

شتر را گویند خصوصاً چنانکه در لیلی مجنون در وصف پدر لیلی گوید شعر بوتام دینار او لعفت اعرابی کیم قالماس ردمیدین
اثر هیچ ونیز در تاریخ الانبیا آمده که قوم صالح علیه السلام دین برمعجز غریب تیلادیلار کیم خارا تاش دین غا تیلیب چقا
نیو چقا عیل جهارم نقوش و کلها باشد که نساجان بروی دیبا و غیره بافند و بوته نیز نویسند و معانی مشتقه هم دارد
در ذیل عمده بوتماک گذشت بوتالیغ یعنی بجاطر و بوته طره بوتا و بسکون واو بمعنی بوت و حکومتیان زصلب بود که نند و
نداشته باشد چنانکه گوید شعر تاریتیان تیغ جفا باغریمی یوز چاک ایلادی بار بی ادا کیم دیر ایدیلار ایل بالغری توبا
بوتکه بفتح تا و کاف عجمی هار زده نام یکنوع گیاهیست که در صحراها بوته بوته میروید بوتون بمعنی درست باشد الشاهد کلیه
ای نوای توت بوتون بوعهد دا ایمانه نی چون بوتون لوک یوقتور مرا ایل عهد ایله پیمانیده ونیز بطریق تمثیل فرماید شعر
چرخ تاریتیب جمران بوتون قویمادی اغریمینی پرضم بوتون تونکا بلریب بزنی بچال ایلادینک نی باشیغ ایریشی یاریب بوتون
بوته همان بوتا باشد که در فوق مذکور شد ونیز نام ولایتیست در حدود شاهجهان و مغار بوطرنه بود که از کل حکمت شانند
و زر و سیم در آن گذارند و بوته معرب آنست مع الجیم بوجاغ و بوجاق بر وزن اوجاق دو معنی دارد اول کنج و ضلع خانه را
چنانکه فضولی گوید مادامه الکرومیه الشاهد علی الاول شعر دمادن جاودشدی بوجاغ باکمی فضولی دار الامانی دن عبارت
بوجاغی دویم نام ملکیست از قریم و با باء عجمی و جیم قلیچ خربزه دهند و انبود که مغز آنرا خوردن پوست آنرا نباشد چنانکه در
تمایم المحبه بتقریب ذکر تم شیخ گوید که شیخ خدمتی بار بدیلار اول او لملا قالدا تاون سید و باربدی پوچاغی خواجه سار
تاشلادی لا انر غایت طلب جرار تیدین اول بوجاغی تیر دیبی اله سیدیلار بوجات بفتح جیم تا آنکه دوم حشرات الارض را گویند که
جانوریست مثل لعاب که در میان استخوان سفید میلت هم بچه دارد نقل دانه لوبیا که برکیاها و درختان میچسپد بوجر ماده
بضم جیم و سکون رای مهمله و دال و فتح غین معجمه بترکی رومی چرخیست که بدان لنگر کشتیها از دریا میکشند بوجوغ و بوجوق بضم جیم
و بود و معنی دارد اول کور را گویند که بینی او بهم کشته معیوب شده باشد دویم بترکی رومی بمعنی نصف بود مع الخا من
المشتقات بوخسانماق بضم کوه و خا فتح سین مهمله کریدر کلو کرکشتن از شدت اندوه که آنرا بعربی غصه گویند و مؤلفین بدیع بمعنی کریه کردن
عاشق بهجر از معشوق نوشته گفته اند که حضرت نوائی این لغت را در محاکمة اللغتین باین معنی تصحیح نموده و این شعر را نوشته که مجنون
اند وهیدا بوخسامین سیلاب آلمان سیناتی و هلاک جیمله قو یوب بغنا یه عزم ایتای بدبو انهای معتمد جمع شدایی شعر
نظر رسید منع این دعوی موقوف بمحاکمه است بوخسادوق غصه ناک شدیم بوخسا دیو بوخسا ندیو غصه ناک میشود و بوخسار بمعنی فاعل
و مستعمل هم می آید بوخسلماید غصه ناک نمیشود و نشده است بوخسا قان بوخسار قان بوخسایتقا غصه ناک شونده و غصه ناک شده
و بمعنی مستعمل هم می آید بوخساو بوخسایل مفرد مخاطب فعل امر بوخساناو بوخسانماک مفرد مخاطب فعل نهی بوخسا لمقه بوخسانکیز
و بوخسانکلا جمع مخاطب فعل امر بوخساناملا بوخسانکیز و بوخسانکلا جمع مخاطب فعل نهی بوخسمان و بوخساناس بمعنی غصه ناک نشود
بوخساس بوخسارین بوخسا بوخسادیم بوخسارام غصه ناک میشوم بوخسا ماس غصه ناک نمیشوی و بمعنی فاعل و مستعمل هم
می آید بوخسا ناسی غصه غصه ناک نشدن تو بوخسار ایکه غصه ناک شدن تو بوخساب بوخسابان بوخسامیش غصه ناک شده
و بوخسا بین بمعنی غصه ناک شده ام چنانکه شاهد بوخساق لیلا آن در ذیل مصدر مذکور شد بوخسا میشا غصه ناک شده بوخسا نماتو
بوخساب بولغای غصه ناک تواند شد بوخسای القای غصه ناک تواند شد بوخسایو بوخسابای بوخسا غصه ناک شوان بود و تکرار هم
مستعملست بوخساو بوخساین غصه ناک شوم و شود شوی و شده بوخساناق بوخسا غا بزرو بوخساغای بزرو بوخسالی بوخسا

غصه ناک شویم بوخساغلی برای غصه ناک شدن و غصه ناک شدن بوخساغاچ چون غصه ناک شد و بوخساغو بوخساغو
شوند بوخساغوجه بوخساغونی بوخساغانیمه تا غصه ناک شدن و بقدر غصه ناک شدن بوخسا آلغایغه بقدر غصه ناک
بوخساغو میز دور غصه ناک نخواهیم شد بوخساغو نکوز دور غصه ناک خواهید شد بوخساغوسیدور غصه ناک خواهند شد بوخسا
ناغوم بوخساغوم یوق غصه ناک نخواهم شد بوخسالی آلغوم بوخسالی آلغوم یوق غصه ناک شدن ممکن نخواهد بود بوخساغو
غصه ناک شدنی بوخساغایو بوخسانسا بوخسانسو بوخسادیک غصه ناک شو بوخساغویدی و بوخساغودای غصه ناک شدنی
و همچنانکه غصه ناک شود من الجوامد بخارا اسم شهریست مشهور از ماوراء النهر و مؤلف حبیب السیر گفته که اشتقاق لفظ بخارا
از بخار است و معنی بخار بلغت مغول جمع علم باشد بوخاغو بضم ضین بترکی رومی زنجیر بود که بر پای ستور و بهم زانوی بندند ...
با پای جوی و چستر و رسنه را گویند که بر خیم و اجات بندند بوخاو بسکون واو بمعنی حلوا باشد که بکردن ... کشند و با الخا ... گویند
که بر پای ستور و بهم زانو بندند مع الدال من المشتقات بودروماق بسکون دال و فتح رای مهمله سکندری خوردن و بسر در آمدن که آنرا بعربی
عثار و عثره گویند و رومیه بودروماق بضم دال و سکون رای مهمله گویند بودرودی سکندری خورد بودروماس سکندری
نخورد چنانکه در لغتهای نظم الجواهر گوید که جاده بی سیر دا طبع توسن تیز کامی کا اهل یودروماس سوادی تقلید ایلام حرف نخوا
بودرومای بودرودوک سکندری خوردیم بودروغو بودرویدور سکندری خورد و بودروغوچی بمعنی فاعل مستعمل هم می آید بودرو
نماید سکندری نمیخورد و نخورده است بودروغو بودروکیل مفرد مخاطب فعل امر بودرونا و بودروناکیل مفرد مخاطب فعل نهی بودرونک
بودرونکوز بودرونکلا جمع مخاطب فعل امر بودرونامانک بودروناکیزو بودروناکلا جمع مخاطب فعل نهی بودروسون بودروماس سکندری نخورم
بودرومین بودرومیز بودرویدین سکندری نخورم بودروماس سکندری نخورد و بمعنی فاعل و مستعمل هم می آید بودروماس
سکندری خوردن تو نخوردن تو بودروماسینکا سکندری نخوردنت بودروونکا سکندری خوردنت بودروبوب بودروماغ بودرومیش
سکندری خورده بود بودرومیشالک سکندری خوردنی بودروناق بودروغای سکندری توان خورد بودرویالغای سکندری
تواند خورد بودروی بودروی سکندری خورده خورده بودروی و بودروین سکندری نخورم و نخورد و نخوری و نخورده
بودروناک بودروغای بودروکای بزرو بودرغای بزرو سکندری نخوریم بودرو کلای برای سکندری خوردن و تا سکندری خوردن بودروچ
چون سکندری خورد و نخورد بودروغوچه بودروغوجه بودروغایغه تا سکندری خوردن و بقدر سکندری
خوردن بودروی آلغاینکه بقدر سکندری توان خورد بودروغومیز دور سکندری خواهیم خورد بودروغونکوز دور سکندری
خواهید خورد بودروغوسیدور سکندری خواهند خورد بودروناغوم بودروغوم یوق سکندری نخواهم خورد بودروی آلماغوم
بودروی آلغوم یوق سکندری خوردن ممکن نخواهد بود بودروغای بودروناو بودروسون و بودرودیک سکندری بخورد
بودروغودیلو بودروغودیک سکندری خوردن و همچنانکه سکندری نخورد بودروتماک مع التا مصدر متعدیست بمعنی سکندری
دادن و بسر در آمدن و صیغ آن بدستور بتای فوقیت اشتقاق می یابد بودرماک بضم دال و سکون رای مهمله بترکی رومی بمعنی
سکندری خوردن باشد بودا ماق بترکی رومی پراستن باغ و درخت باشد از شاخ زاید که آنرا بعربی تشذیب گویند بودانماق
مع النون پیراسته شدن باغ و درخت از شاخ زاید من الجوامد بوداغ و بوداق شاخ درخت را مانند بودال بمعنی بوداو
باشد بودالیق و بودالیه بمعنی صاحب جام جای خود چنانکه در تاریخ بابری مذکور است که جوانغار برانغار و قول
و دا اول هر طایفه بودالیق بود الیدا نوشوب هر قول الوز توشیدین یر اغلاعیب بوداندو بسکون نون و ضم لام

بزرگ رومی چوبهای پیرنوات که در وقت قطع کردن از درخت فرو می‌ریزد بوداى بوداى بیکنوع سرود حیثیت مخصوص ایجیکه
چنانکه در آخر رساله عروض فرموده که چون اوزان لاهرنینک اوزان ناعی و اوزن بکلاه نینک بوداى بوداى هم وزن ناپلیمه
ایماس ایردی آنکا قترض قیلیلادی بودور بوهزن شتر بزرگ رومی یعنی کوتاه قد و قصیر القامه بود بودنه بفتح دال مهمله
و نون بها زده بیلد برچین باشد که آنرا بعربی سلوی نامند مع الرأ من المشتقات بورناق پیچیدن و تابیدن بوردوق
پیچیدم بوداد و بورادور می‌پیچد و بوداد بمعنی فاعل و مصدر هم می‌آید بورماید ورنمی‌پیچد و نپیچیده است بورغان و
بورمقان و بورادورغان پیچنده و پیچیده بمعنی مصدر هم می‌آید بور و بورغیل مفرد مخاطب از فعل امر بورماد و بورماغیل مفرد مخاطب
از فعل نهی بورونک و بوروبکوز و بورونکلار جمع مخاطب از فعل امر بورمانک و بورمانکیز و بورمانکلار جمع مخاطب از فعل نهی بورماس و بورماس من
نمی‌پیچم بورامین و بورامیز و بورادورمین بورادورام می‌پیچم بورماس نمی‌پیچد و بمعنی فاعل و مصدر منفی هم می‌آید بورماسینکه نپیچیده
پیچیدنت بوروب پیچیده بورمیش و بورمیشان پیچیده بورمیشانک پیچیده بورساپولغای و بوروب بولغا توان پیچید بولالغای
تواند پیچید بورا بورا پیچنده پیچنده بوراى بورابین پیچم و پیچید و پیچی و پیچیده بورساق و بورغلیز و بورغای
بورابلغیه الینک بپیچم بورغالی برای پیچیدن و تا پیچیدن بورغاج چون پیچید و پیچید بورغوچی پیچنده بورغوجه
بورغونجه و بورغانجه تا پیچیدن و بمقدار پیچیدن بورا آلغانینکجه بمقدار یکه توانی پیچید بورغونکوز دور نخواهید پیچید بورغوسلار
خواهند پیچید بورماغوم و بورغوم نخواهم پیچید بورالماغوم و بورا آلغوم یوق پیچیدن نمی‌توانم بود بورغولوق پیچیدنی
بورغای و بورغایلوبیهون ... پیچید بورغودیک و بورادیک پیچیدنی و همچنانکه بپیچد بورولماق مع اللام پیچیده شدن
بورومناق مع النون خود را بچیزی پیچیدن بوروشماق مع الشین پیچیده شدن و بمعنی درهم کشیده شدن و بمعنی درهم
کشیده شدن پوست و مانند آن از حرارت آتش و شکنج یافتن از آن نیز هم استعمال میشود بوروشتورماق مصدر متعدی
آنست و صیغ آن موافق اول با لفظ توان اشتقاق مییابد بورکاماق بسکون را و فتح کاف سر پوشیدن و این لفظ متضمن
الفاظ مناسب بمعنی چیزی بلباس پیچیدن و بورک بمعنی کلاه ما خوذ از این معنی است که لفظ سر است بورکادی سر پوشید چنانکه
گوید شعر باغ ارا خطا بیجوراغ بینکرین مینه ایرب شاه نقابیب غنچه زنکاری لباسیدا ساسین بورکادی بورکادوک سر را
پوشیدیم بورکار بورکادور سر را می‌پوشد و بورکار بمعنی فاعل و مصدر هم می‌آید بورکامایدور سر را نمی‌پوشد و نپوشیده است
بورکاکان و بورکاکان بمعنی کاسه سر را پوشنده و پوشیده و بمعنی مصدر هم می‌آید بورکا و بورکاکیل مفرد مخاطب از فعل امر بورکاما
و بورکاماکیل مفرد مخاطب از فعل نهی بورکانک و بورکانکیز و بورکانکلار جمع مخاطب از فعل امر بورکامانک و بورکامانکیز و بورکامانکلار جمع
مخاطب از فعل نهی بورکامان و بورکاماس من بورکامایمن نمی‌پوشم بورکای مین و بورکارمین و بورکایدورمین و بورکادورام می‌پوشم بورکاماس
نمی‌پوشد و بمعنی فاعل و مصدر منفی هم می‌آید بورکاماسینکا نپوشیدنت بورکاسینکا بپوشیدنت بورکاب و بورکابان
و بورکامیش سر پوشیده بورکامیشانات سر پوشیده بورکاسا بولغای و بورکاب بولغای سر توان پوشید بورکای آلغای
سر را تواند پوشید بورکا بورکا سر پوشان پوشان بورکای و بورکاین سر بپوشم و بپوشد و بپوشی بورکاسات و بورکابیز
بورکای بیز و بورکاکالی و بورکالینک سر بپوشیم بورکاکالی برای پوشیدن و تا پوشیدن بورکاکاج چون سر پوشید و بپوشد
بورکاکوچی سر پوشنده بورکاکوجه و بورکاکونجه و بورکاکانجه تا سر پوشیدن و بمقدار پوشیدن بورکای آلغانینکجه بمقدار یکه سر را
توانی پوشید بورکاکومیزدور سر را نخواهیم پوشید بورکاکونکوزدور سر را نخواهید پوشید بورکاکوسیلاردور سر را نخواهد

پوشید بورکاماکوم و بورکاکوم یوق سر را نخواهم پوشید بورکای آلماغوم و بورکای آلغوم یوق سر پوشیدن نمی‌توانم بود بورکاکولوق
سر پوشیدنی بورکاکای و بورکاسا و بورکاسون و بورکادیک پوشید بورکاکودیک و بورکادیک سر پوشیدنی و همچنانکه بپوشد
بورکانماق مع النا مصدر متعدی است یعنی سر را پوشاندن و صیغ آن موافق اول با تای قرشت اشتقاق می‌یابد بورکانماق
مع النون مصدر انفعالیست یعنی پوشانده شدن بطریق تلطف بورکانیب پوشانده شده چنانکه سلطان حسین میرزا فرماید
شعر اوزنا بینب قالغلیج او تیمغه مجنون ایستا دغیردین اولتوروبعین طرفرایش کوبکیم کولونی بورکانیب و باقی صیغ
سیاق با نون اشتقاق مییابد بوردا ماق بسکون را و فتح دال با الف کشیده فربه و پروار شدن بوردادوق پروار شده ایم
بوردا ر بوردایدور پروار میشود و بوردار بمعنی فاعل و مصدر هم می‌آید بوردامایدور پروار نمیشود و نشده است بوردا غان و
بورداغان و بوردایدوغان پروار شونده و پروار شده چنانکه در سد سکندری در وصف زمستان گوید الشاهد علی الاول و کل
الثانی شعر مونونات یوبزیدا می‌میطی لعل تاب آنینک ایچیدا بوردا قان بط کباب و نیز در بعیسنات سفر وذم حضر
گوید شعر کتکدا قالیب بوردا غان زاکیان و مضلومی و چاقمه سود و زیان و موافقی دیگر بعضی مرغی نوشته که بر سر
بخواند و شعر اخیر را از سد سکندری شاهد آورده اند و بعضی هم متابعت کرده اشتباه کرده اند بوردا و بورداغیل مفرد
مخاطب از فعل امر بوردا ما و بوردا ماغیل مفرد مخاطب از فعل نهی بوردانک و بوردانکیز و بوردانکلار جمع مخاطب از فعل امر بوردامانک
بوردامانکیز و بوردامانکلار جمع مخاطب از فعل نهی بوردامان و بوردا ماس من پروار نمیشوم بوردای مین و بوردا رمین و بوردایدورمین و بوردادورام
پروار میشوم بوردا ماس پروار نمیشود و بمعنی فاعل و مصدر منفی هم می‌آید بوردا ماسینکه پروار نشدنت بوردا رینکه پروار
شدنت بوردا ب و بوردا بان و بوردامیش پروار شده بوردامیشانات پروار شده بوردا سا بولغای و بوردا ب بولغای پروار توان شد
بوردای آلغای پروار تواند شد بوردا بوردا پروار شوان بوردای و بوردایین پروار شوم و شود و شوی و شده
بوردا ساق و بوردا غایز و بوردا غای بیز و بوردا غالی و بوردا لینک پروار شویم بوردا غالی برای پروار شدن و تا پروار شده بوردا
چون پروار شد و شود بوردا غوچی پروار شونده بوردا غوجه و بوردا غونجه و بوردا غانجه تا پروار شدن و بمقدار پروار شدن
بوردای آلغانینکجه بمقدار یکه پروار توانی شد بوردا غونکوز پروار خواهیم شد بوردا غونکوزدور پروار خواهید شد بوردا غوسلار
پروار خواهند شد بوردا ماغوم و بوردا غوم یوق پروار نخواهم شد بوردای آلماغوم و بوردای آلغوم یوق پروار شدن نمی‌توانم
بوردا غولوق پروار شدنی بوردا غای و بوردا ساو بوردا سون و بوردا دیک پروار شود بوردا غودیک و بوردا دیک پروار شدنی
و همچنانکه پروار شود بوردا تماق مع التا مصدر متعدیست یعنی فربه و پروار کردن و صیغ آن با تای قرشت اشتقاق می‌یابد
بورناشماق بسکون را و شین و فتح نون بیکدیگر تقلاع و سبقت جستن و پیشی گرفتن بورناشتوق پیشی گرفتیم بورناشور و
بورناشادور پیشی میگیرد و بورناشور بمعنی فاعل و مصدر هم می‌آید بورناشماید ور پیشی نمیگیرد و نگرفته است بورناشغان
بورناشوغان و بورناشادورغان پیشی گیرنده و پیشی گرفته و بمعنی مصدر هم می‌آید بورناش و بورناشغیل مفرد مخاطب از فعل امر بورناشما
و بورناشماغیل مفرد مخاطب از فعل نهی بورناشینک و بورناشینکیز و بورناشینکلار جمع مخاطب از فعل امر بورناشمانک و بورناشمانکیز و بورناشمانکلار
جمع مخاطب از فعل نهی بورناشمان و بورناشماس من پیشی نمیگیرم بورناشامین و بورناشورمین و بورناشادورمین و بورناشادورام پیشی میگیرم بورناشماس
پیشی نمیگیرد و بمعنی فاعل و مصدر منفی هم می‌آید بورناشماسینکه به پیشی نگرفتنت و بورناشورینکه به پیشی گرفتنت بورناشیب
بورناشیبان و بورناشمیش پیشی گرفته بورناشمیشانات پیشی گرفته بورناشسا بولغای و بورناشیب بولغای پیشی توان گرفت بورناشا آلغای

پیشی تواند کرفت بوزناشا و بوزناشا تعلم جویان و بدو ونکرا هم مستعمل است بوزناشای و بوزناشایین پیشی بکریم و بیکرد دیگری
و کفته بوزناشساق و بوزناشغاینی و بوزناشغای بزه بوزناشلیه بوزناشالنام پیشی بکریم بوزناشغلی برای پیشی کرفتن و تاشتی
بوزناشفلاج چون پیشی کرفت و بیکرد بوزناشغوجی پیشی کیرنده بوزناشغوجیه بوزناشغا تا پیشی کرفتن و نقل پیشی کرفتن
بوزناشا الغانیه بمعنی بیکرد پیشی تواند کرفت بوزناشغو نیز و پیشی خواهیم کرفت بوزناشغو نخود و پیشی خواهید کرفت بوزناشغو بولادا
پیشی خواهند کرفت بوزناشا غوم و بوزناشغوم بوق پیشی نخواهیم کرفت بوزناشا الماغوم و بوزناشا القوم پیشی کرفتن و حکم نخواهد بود
بوزناشغولوق پیشی کرفتنی بوزناشغای و بوزناشا و بوزناشس و بوزناشدیک پیشی کرفتنی و همانکه بیکرد من الجوار
بوران بروزن توران و بوراغان بفتح را و ضمن معجمه برف و باد شدید باشد بهم آمیخته بود که آنرا چاپقون نیز کویند و بوران
بفارسی نام دختر پرویز است که بعضی موضوع است بُران با باء عجمی بمعنی بر آن شتر را نامند که نر ماده باشد بوزای
بسکون را و فتح ثای ابجد با الف کشیده در طرف راز را خوانند و فرانغی نوشته که بود ... با بود بوزناق نام کوزنا
... الشاهد علی الاول شعر نوای خاصیل ایت همت ... بکیم ... هوا ایلغانلار مقصد ... نشت بوزناقی
الشاهد علی الثانی شعر ایتما کلیلد ... شکل مقصد ... بن بکیم بارش ... آقساق ... بوزاق
و در فصل هفتم از محبوب القلوب حضرت ... که بوزدین ... که ... بوزناق چاپش
پیله اوزین ضایع ایتیب بورج بمعنی درج ... آقل ... را کویند چنانکه در ... محبوب القلوب
کوید که مفلس ... آسا که ... سقال آراسته ... کمال ... بود و با جیم عجمی ... بمعنی
مشبهات و آنرا ایستی اوت نیز نامند و اتراک ... بورکویند بورچاق نوعی از حبوبات شبیه نخود که نهال آن ...
مینا شد و آنرا بعربی خلر کویند بتشدید لام و ... کوچک را خوانند که ... دانه نخود باشد ...
که آنرا بفارسی ... و بعربی جلبان کویند بورچالیق بسکون را و فتح جیم عجمی ... لاله صحرائی را کویند بورچوک با بای عجمی و
جیم عجمی مضمومه و رای مهمله و کاف ساکنه ... کوچک که بشکل ... از ابریشم سازند بورچوقلی ... بود
که آنرا بلغت ختای ... کویند بورچین بسکون را و نون و کسر جیم عجمی ... آهوی ماده را کویند و با جیم عجمی ...
... بوزچین خوانند ... بوداغ و بورداق بمعنی ... باشد
بورسو بسکون را و ضم سین مهمله کیاهی بود که در ... خشک کنند و ... هند و آنرا ...
بورسوق با بای عجمی بسکون را و قاف و ضم سین مهمله حیوانیست که آنرا ... و باصفهانی ... و بعربی وشق ...
کویند و آن ... باشد کوچک که ... و بعضی از پوست و خطهای سفید و سیاه دارد و از پوست و پوستین سازند
و هر چند ... که ... باشد کوشت و ... الغذا و ... کوشت ... آن ...
دافع ... پوستین پوست ... و ... نامات بورغو شاخی ... که آنرا نامند نفیر نوازند
و ... دو می ... بود که ... کردن ... که ... نصب کرده ... و ... ازمیان ...
و ... دو ... نامند ... کویند که آنرا بعربی ... خوانند بورک بر وزن ترک ... باشد
بورکا بفتح ها ... بود که آنرا بعربی ... نامند بورکوت بضم کاف عجمی و سکون تای قرشت بمعنی عقاب باشد
... شعر کیردی بورکوت ... یعنی عقاب ... دیدی ... بورمه بر دن

... باشد که از ... چون آنرا ... بهم آید و جمع شود ... نامند که ...
... کنند ... و آبها ... دهند ... بود که ... و آبها ... که چون آنرا ... آید بود
بسکون را و نون ... چنانکه کوید شعر ... که ... بوزنیغلای یار ... چون ... کنه
... و آنرا ... کویند بورنا بر وزن ... بمعنی اول و ابتدا و مقدم باشد چنانکه در حیرة الابرار کوید شعر ایش
کون ... بوزنا ... با یای ... بمعنی
ذکر کرده بوزنا ایرکانی مقدم ... چنانکه ... کوید شعر ... کیم ...
بوزنا ایرکانی ... بوزناچاغ بمعنی زمان ... چنانکه در حیرة الابرار کوید شعر ... بوزناچاغ ...
و دو ... بوزناراق ... الشاهد علیه شعر ... جان
کونکول ... بوزناراق ... بوزناقی بمعنی ... و اولین و نخستین باشد چنانکه کوید شعر
... و آنرا ... کویند
بضم ... شدن ... آتش ... بورولغون بضم ...
و سکون لام و نون ... بورون بضم ... بمعنی ... اول
باشد الشاهد علیه شعر ای کونکول ... بورون ...
بوزنا هم کویند چنانکه ... نامند چنانکه ... کوید شعر بوردون ... بیله ...
... بورون ... و آنرا ... بور
کویند چنانکه مذکور شد بورونچاق بضم را و سکون نون و کاف و فتح جیم ... بمعنی ... اول ... زنان را کویند چنانکه
کوید شعر ... بورونچاق ... اول ... ایکی ... بر ...
از محبوب القلوب ... نعت کوید که ... بورونچاق ... کوروس ...
... الشاهد علیه شعر ... ایرکان ...
بورونچاق ... و آنرا بعربی خشام نامند و این ماخوذ از
بورون بمعنی ... باشد ... و ... کویند و این ماخوذ از بوردون بمعنی تقدم باشد بوردنتی یعنی اولین و
نخستین و آن ... بوزناقی باشد بوری کرک بود که آنرا بعربی ذئب نامند الشاهد علیه شعر ... که یوسف ...
اولدی ... هر ... کوید شعر ... فرهاد و شیرین کوید شعر ... شاز ... آی ...
آج بوریا ... طعمه ... نفیر باشد که آنرا نوازند و بزبان ... و هندی ... کویند ...
من المشتقات بوزناغ خراب کردن الشاهد علیه شعر زهد و تقوی بوزدی ... ایلاحکا ... شکوکیم عشق ... جنون
بوزناق بیله آبادانیا ... بوزدوق خراب کردیم بوزایدو بوزادور خراب میکند الشاهد علی الثانی شعر نوا ...
... شکیب ... بوزادور ... و بوزار ... می آید بوزنایدور خراب میکند
و ... است بوزغان ... و بوزادورغان خراب کننده و خراب کرده و بمعنی ... هم می آیند بوزوبوزغیل ...
... الشاهد علی الاول شعر ... بوزغای ... کونکول ... بوزناک ...

علی آلکانی شعر جانبانسی بوزغیل نیدین که محرف این وشه خلاف شرع و فاقیلمینک اول ابنا احداث و بوزلسیله و موفهم کرکا
ویغ را هم گویند چنانکه در ذیل جوا مد مذکور خواهد شد بوزغاو بوزغانغیل مفرد مخاطب از فعل نهی بوزونک و بوزونکوز و
بوزونکلار جمع مخاطب از فعل امر بوزغانک و بوزغانکیز و بوزغانکلار جمع مخاطب از فعل نهی بوزغان و بوزغاسین خراب مکنم بوزامین و
بوزارمین و بوزاد و بوزمین بوزارام خراب میکنم بوزغاس خراب نمیکند و بمعنی فاعل و مصدر منفی هم می آید بوزغاسینکه خراب نکرده
تو بوزارسنکه بخراب کردن تو بوزوب و بوزوبان و بوزوبش خراب کرده بوزوبشانک خراب کرده بوزغابولغای و بوزوب بولغای خراب
توان کرد بوزالغای خراب تواند کرد بوزا بوزا خراب کنان بوزای و بوزاین خراب کنم و کند و کنی و کرده بوزسلو بوزغلیز و
بوزغای یز و بوزمای و بوزالینک خراب کنیم چنانکه در سکندری در نظام الملک کشمیر گویند استشهد علی الرابع شعر قید حکمت اسوده
الجاه بوزلی الادیمیرف حاشا بوزغالی برای خراب کردن و تا خراب کرده بوزغاج چون خراب کرد و کند چنانکه در مقالة المدوازده
از حیرة الابرار در صفت ظلمه گوید شعر می پیله بوزغلج قاری نینک خالینی شاهد او چون هم بسیار ورزالینی بوزغوجی
خراب کننده بوزغوچی و بوزغوچه و بوزغانچه تا خراب کردن و بقدر خراب کردن بوزا آلغاسینچه بقدر یکه خراب توانی کرد بوزغوز دور
خراب نخواهیم کرد بوزغونکوز دور خراب نخواهید کرد بوزغوسیلار دور خراب نخواهند کرد بوزغاغوم بوزغوم بوق خراب نخواهم کرد
بوزالماغوم بوزا آلغوم بوق خراب کرده نخواهم بود بوزغولوق خراب کردن بوزغاغو بوزاو بوزغاو بوزغون و بوزرد بلت
خراب کند بوزغودیلک و بوزدیلک خراب کردن و همچنانکه خراب کند بوزولماق مع اللازم خراب شدن بوزولغان خراب شده
و خراب شد چنانکه بمعنی ثانی گوید شعر همراه و ...ین سیندی کونکلوم ایستا مانا زنصرتینک پناه شاید کونکلی
بوزونغانغه بوزوغ دیوار ... معنی مصدر هم می آید بوزولغودیک بوزو لوزدیلک خراب شدنی و همچنانکه خراب شود الکه
علی الاول المعنی الثانی شعر تیلبه زابا تیکان کونکول ایدیمه کیرسا کا لاز سیغلاب ایل کونکلی بوزولغودیک جکار
الا در شاهد بر ثانی معنی اول در تحفة اخلاقیه گوید که بوم دیده و خانها اوا سیندا ...ایب تولاز تالجان بوده
دیلک بولسا سیل دین سیل ... قصیح برابر نسا قبالالام مواقع فاعل مقرر اشتقاق می یابد بوزدور ... مصدر متعدی است
یعنی خراب فرمودن و سنیع آن بالفظ ... اشتقاق می یابد بوزلاماق فریاد نامه شتر باشد ... چنانکه آن را بعربی حنین گویند
و مجاز انعره و فریاد نام زده ... خوانند که بناله حزین باشد بوزلاددوق فریاد کردیم بوزلادی و بوزلایدور فریاد میکند و بوزلار بمعنی
فاعل و مصدر هم می آید بوزلامایدور فریاد نمیکند و نکرده است بوزلاغان و بوزلاغان و بوزلایدیغان فریاد کننده و فریاد کرده بمعنی
مصدر هم می آید بوزلا و بوزلاغیل مفرد مخاطب از فعل امر بوزلاما و بوزلاماغیل مفرد مخاطب از فعل نهی بوزلانک و بوزلانکیز و
بوزلانکلار جمع مخاطب از فعل امر بوزلامانک و بوزلامانکیز و بوزلامانکلار جمع مخاطب از فعل نهی بوزلامان و بوزلاماسین فریاد مکنم بوزلادین
بوزلارمین و بوزلایدورمین بوزلارام فریاد میکنم بوزلاماس فریاد نمیکند و بمعنی فاعل و مصدر منفی هم می آید بوزلاماسینکه فریاد کردن
و نکردنش بوزلاماسینکه بفریاد نکردن تو بوزلارسنکه بفریاد کردن تو بوزلاب و بوزلابان و بوزلامیش فریاد کرده چنانکه در
نوحه کری فرهاد و یاد کردن خاقان را ... گوید استشهد علی الاول شعر بو تام دیکا بوزلاب اوکوزسا جفا تاشین بیوفا کیم
او دیسام بوزلامیشانک فریاد کرده بوزلاسا بولغای و بوزلاب بولغای فریاد توان کرد بوزلاب آلغای فریاد تواند کرد بوزلای بوزلای بوزلادی
فریاد کنان بوزلای و بوزلاین فریاد کنم و کند و کنی و کرده بوزلاساق و بوزلاغای یز و بوزلاسالی و بوزلالینک
فریاد کنیم بوزلاغالی برای فریاد کردن و تا فریاد کرده بوزلاغاج چون فریاد کرد و کند بوزلاغوجی فریاد کننده بوزلاغوچه

بوزلاغوچه و بوزلاغانچه تا فریاد کردن و بقدر فریاد کردن بوزلای آلغاسینچه بقدر یکه فریاد توانی کرد بوزلاغومیز دور فریاد نخواهیم
بوزلاغونکوز دور فریاد نخواهید کرد بوزلاغوسیلار دور فریاد نخواهند کرد بوزلامالغوم و بوزلاغوم بوق فریاد نخواهم کرد بوزلای الماغوم
بوزلای آلغوم بوق فریاد کرده محکم نخواهد بود بوزلاغولوق فریاد کردن بوزلاغای و بوزلاسا و بوزلاسون و بوزلادیلک فریاد کند
بوزلاغودیلک و بوزلاردیلک فریاد کردن و همچنانکه فریاد کند من الجواهد بوز شش معنی دارد اول کرباس گویند چنانکه
در فصل بیت و هفتم از محبوب القلوب در وصف اهل سوق گوید که آلوردا کتانی بوز دیبا تاردا بوز و سفید اکتاندین
آر نوقسونه ب و آن از ترکانیه و رومیه بین و بعربی بز خوانند دوم رنگ کبودی مایل بسفیدی را گویند سیم اطلاق سلیله
نامند چنانکه میرد و معنی گوید شعر کونک حلاسیدین اولور خوانکه منکنک بوز تو فراغ بولسا استنکلا ...
چهارم مرد فهیم خوشخوی را نامند ... سیم اسب را گویند ...
در پی جمد گویند ششم اسب را خراب کردن چنانکه در ذیل مصدر بوزماق نوشته شد بوزا اغو بفتح میم و بوزک
بسکون کاف و بوز او بسکون واو بچه گاو و گاو میش و کرکدن و امثال آن را نامند چنانکه شاهد بر ثالث در تاریخ نام و گوید
که بر بوزاو لیغ کرکدن کا جیقیب قالجا پری ایا اضیغی حنکل همنا الدی بوزاو نلشبی جانوریست که کرنده است از عقرب بزرگه جا
دارد و سران شکل ... است بوزاو بوزنبی زهریست که از بن ناخن بر آید و آن را رومیه دانه بوز گویند بوز
یعنی کرباس باف بوزدومان بسکون زا و نون و ضم دال و فتح عین بالف کشیده بترکی رومی چماق بود و آن چوبی است که سر آن
کنده باشد و بعربی دبوس گویند بوزلاغ بنا ده دراج و قرغاول را گویند چنانکه در تاریخ بابری در صفت ... گوید کمر
که نیه پرده راج دو ... ی قرغاولینک بوزلاغی زنک لیلت بولور بوزلوک یعنی کرباسی چنانکه گوید شعر کمر
لباس ملاحت اموش ایل ... کرایکی حلیه لیغ اولسون وکرتنی بوزلوک بونوغ و بوزوق سه معنی دارد اول ویرانه ما
چنانکه گوید شعر ایلکا ممرینک بار بوز وغ کونکلوم ... تا ... تابیدین محروم ...
دوم بترکی رومی بمعنی طنبور ... که شش تار و هفت تار دارد سیم نام طایفه ایست از اتراک از نسل اوغوز خان که وجه تسمیه
آن در باب الف مضمومه در ذیل الفت اوغوز ذکر یافته بوزوغلوق و بوزوقلوق یعنی ویرانی بوزوک بترکی رومی دبوس گویند
اعم از آنکه از انسان باشد یا سایر حیوانات و طیور بوزچی بضم و فرو ش نام طایفه ایست از ترکان ... التین ... المشتقات بوسماق
کمین کردن و هر گوشه پنهان شدن بوستی کمین کرد چنانکه در لسان الطیر در وصف ابراهیم ادهم گوید شعر پر کون
ایکندا او تون جمیله ... بوستی لار ... اطراف ... تیلفلبل آینک سلوک امتحان
من انشاء بخاری شعر سواد کاکلونک ... بوستی ... کم یاشونغای ... علی
بمعنی تند و غضبناک شدن و رنجیدن نوشته سهو کرده بوستوق کمین کردیم بوسا بوسا دو بکمین میکند بوسار بمعنی
فاعل و مصدر هم می آید بوسمایدور کمین نمیکند و نکرده است بوسغان و بوسغان و بوسایدیغان کمین کننده و کمین کرده بمعنی مصدر هم
می آید بوسغیل مفرد مخاطب از فعل امر بوسما و بوسماغیل مفرد مخاطب از فعل نهی بوسونک و بوسونکوز و بوسونکلار جمع مخاطب
از فعل امر بوسمانک و بوسمانکیز و بوسمانکلار جمع مخاطب از فعل نهی بوسمان و بوسماسین کمین مکنم بوسامین و بوسارمین و بوسایدورمین
کمین میکنم بوسماس کمین نمیکند و بمعنی فاعل و مصدر منفی هم می آید بوسماسینکه کمین کردن و نکردنش بوسماسینکه
بکمین نکردن تو بوسارسینکه بکمین کردن تو بوسوب و بوسوبان و بوسمیش کمین کرده بوسمیشانک کمین کرده بوسا بولغای و
بوسوب بولغای کمین توان کرد بوسا آلغای کمین تواند کرد بوسا بوسا کمین کنان بوسای و بوساین کمین کنم و کند و کنی و کرده

چهارم مرد فهیم خوشخوی را نامند و مؤلف فرهنگ جهانگیری این لفظ فارسی شمرده و گفته
که اسب شد و تیز را بوز نامند و مرد صاحب فهم را بواسطه تیزی فهم بوز گویند
پنجم بمعنی یخ بود که انرا موز هم خوانند و

بوس

134v.

بوساق و بوسغاپرو بوسغای‌نره بوسنالیعنی بوسنالیلک کیکن کیم بوسغای برای کمین کردن و تا کمین کرده بوسغاچ چون کمین کرده کند
بوسغوچی کمین کننده بوسغوچه بوسغونچه و بوسغانچه تا کمین کردن و بعد از کمین کردن بوسنا آلغانیکه بعد از آنکه کمین تواند کرد بوسغو
مینه بود کمین خواهم کرد بوسغوکوز کمین خواهید کرد بوسغوسیلار کمین خواهند کرد بوساغوم یوق کمین نخواهم کرد
بوسنا آلماغوم بوسنا آلغوم یوق کمین کردن محکم نخواهد بود بوسغولوق کمین کردن بوسغای بوسنالیو بوسا و بوسون و بوسیلار
کمین کند بوسغودیلیک بوسنادیلک کمین کردن و همچنانکه کمین کند بوسکورمالک بکون سین و رای قرشت و ضم کاف عجمی ترکی
روی دو معنی دارد اول خصم را بحمله و هیبت پراکنده کردن دویم آب باد هوا افشاندن مولف گوید بوس با بای عجمی ترکی رومی بکار
بوده بمعنی کم شدن هوا استعمال میشود و نیز هوای غبار آلود گویند و غبار را بادم منقبض هم الملاحق میشود و با بای عربی بلغت مغول
از برخاستن و بلغت جغتای از استار کمین کردن و غبار بر مجفف بسنه باشد بوساغه بفتح سین بالف کشیده و ضم [illegible] آستا
ده مه گویند الشاهد علیه شعر او باین دیر بوساغانیغ دیه کربان بلیر ب بایستاناغ دیر آستانینگ لشکستجان
این لفظ معروف و مترادف بوسه گاه خواهد بود بوسکول با بای عجمی و سکون سین و لام و ضم کاف عجمی ترکی رومی منکله باشد
بمعنی کمین باشد چنانکه در سد سکندری در وقت سکایاجوج گوید شعر کینیکه مینامیز ادا ز نامی عالم [illegible]
رای بوسوعه آلارنی چو [illegible] ایتیت کیلیب خندق اهلینی محبوط ایتیت بوسون بلغت مغول پیش بود که آنرا بترکی
قبل خوانند مع الشین المثلثات بوشماق زبان رسیدن بوشتی زبان رسید چنانکه گوید شعر ایلیگی [illegible]
بوشماس ای شیخ کف پاینگ کیم اوپتوم تیبوشتی بوشمادی زبان نرسید چنانکه در تاریخ بابری مذکور است که سلطان احمد
قنبل [illegible] بوغرسینه [illegible] لاب سیقتی لاردی بوشمادی بوشار و بوشادو زبان نرسید چنانکه شاهد برا اول در فصل
از محبوب القلوب بدین وصف مکتبه گوید که اول قوم [illegible] دراند و مفهی آز توشار آنرا ق کیشیکا [illegible]
و بوشار بد و معنی هم آمده اول سست میشود دویم خالی میشود و در اینده بمعنی [illegible] بوشاناقات و بمعنی [illegible]
هم می آید بوشما بد و معنی زبان عیز رسید و نرسیده است بوشغان و بوشاغان بوشادو زبان رسنده و زبان رسید و بمعنی [illegible]
هم می آید و بوشاغان با مصدر بوشاناق اشتراک دارد بوشاب زبان عیز رسید و بمعنی [illegible] هم می آید بوشماسینکه
زبان نرسیدن تو بوشارینکه زبان نرسیدن تو بوشوبه بوشوبان و بوشمیش زبان رسیده الشاهد علی الثالث شعر
ن بالد پادکونکول شاری شا السلیخ که هرتی زلال کمزکوسینی نایه تیر [illegible] بوشمیش و مولف رومی بوشمیش را در این
شعر بمعنی شدن بفلفلت و دن و نجیدن و نجنوشیدن نوشته و بقضی هم تسامح کرده و مطابق هروی بمعنی خالی
شدن ذکر کرده و شعر مذکور را شاهد آورده اند در شبهه ایشان شبهه نیست بوشا آلغای زبان تواند رسانید بوشغالی برای
زبان رسیدن که زبان رسید بوشغاچ چون زبان رسید و رسند بوشغوچه و بوشغونچه و بوشغانچه تا زبان رسیدن و بعد
زبان رسیدن چنانکه در [illegible] استحکام [illegible] رای هند گوید الشاهد علی الثانی بمعنی الثانی شعر
تیلین مفتاری قیلیب نکته سنج کر بوشغونچه خود تیمادی بولد انج و مولف رومی بوشغونچه را بحضر [illegible]
و پریشان دل شدن نوشته و شعر مذکور را شاهد جسته بوشغوچی زبان خواهد رسید بوشغولوق زبان رسیدن
بوشغای و بوشا و بوشسا و بوشسون و بوشدیلک زبان رسید الشاهد علی الاول شعر ایا فقه کربانی بوشغای [illegible]
کراولنا بادبه دین کمنه سفا ملحوظ بوشغودیلک و بوشادیلک زبان رسیده و همچنانکه رسید و بوشاردیلک بمعنی سست

135r.

و همچنانکه سست شود و خالی شده و همچنانکه خالی شود هم می آید و در میند و بمعنی صیغه مصدر بوشاناق اشتراک طرفین
و چون بمعنی از صیغه دو معنی موافق نمی آید که حذف کرد آنها بر طرف بوشاناغ و بوشاتاق بد و معنی آمده اول سست شدن دویم
شدن بوشادی و بوشاتدی سست شد و خالی شد بوشادوق بوشاتدوق سست شدیم و خالی شدیم بوشار و بوشا بد در بوشانود
بوشانادور سست میشود و خالی میشود چنانکه از لغزی که بر لعل لطیفه اند موضع مسطور است الشاهد علی الاول المعنی الاول شعر
اکر بو نوع ایاس چون بی امیون بلمیاق کوبیراک بوشار جی آلار ثانی آنکا جوهی اولوبته هم ونیز بوشار بمعنی [illegible]
و باین معنی با مصدر بوشماق اشتراک طرفین چنانکه گذشت و بمعنی اول با مصدر هم می آید بوشاناید بوشانادیت
و خالی میشود و نشده است بوشا فاری بوشلرغان بوشاید غان بوشانغان بوشانغان و بوشانالمیست شونده و سست شده و خالی شونده
و خالی شده و بمعنی مصدر هم می آید و بوشلوقان با مصدر بوشماق اشتراک دارد بوشلو بوشاغیل و بوشان و بوشاتقیل امر [illegible]
بوشانا و بوشانافیل و بوشاناو بوشانا امر مخاطب بفعل مفرد چنانکه شاهد مثالش بمعنی اول در تنبیهات محبوب القلوب گوید
بو شانما هیچ خانیا شانما و بوشاناما بوشانکیز و بوشاتکیز و بوشانگلار و بوشانغالار و بوشاننکیز و بوشانکلار جمع مخاطب بفعل نهی بوشانما
بوشانکلار و بوشانماننک بوشانما نکیز و بوشانمانکلار جمع مخاطب بفعل نهی بوشانمان و بوشانماس بمعنی بوشانماس بسته شود
خالی شوم بوشامین بوشادین بوشایدمین بوشارام بوشاناین بوشانورمین بوشانادورمین و بوشانور دام سست میشوم
خالی میشوم بوشاناسروم بوشاناس سست میشود و خالی میشود و بمعنی اول با مصدر نفی هم می آید بوشاناسینکه بوشانماسینکه
بست نشدن تو و خالی نشدن تو بوشاریکه بوشاوینکه بست شدن تو و خالی شدن تو بوشاب و بوشاماب و بوشامیش
بوشانیب و بوشاینکو بوشامیش سست شده و خالی شده چنانکه شاهد برای اول معنی سست شده در تاریخ بابری مذکور است که ناتمل خلال
میلب تا بریلدیم تنک بوشاب ایکاند عراکارا یو ولدی و بمعنی خالی شده در آخر فنا یم المحبة دعوکر آراغ نارین گوید که اولغر ملک
ایمر و با شارین تا ببلیرووک بوشاسیتالمع بوشاینشالمنسست شده و خالی شده بوشانلبولغای و بوشاب و شایب بوشانا
و بوشاینب و بوشاغاسست تواند شد و خالی تواند شد بوشا آلغای و بوشانا آلغای سست تواند شد و خالی تواند شد بوشایو بوشاکا بوشاب
و بوشانا بوشامنا سست شوان و خالی شوان و بد بن تکرار هم با مشتق می آید بوشاناو بوشانیس و بوشاناتکو بوشاتلین سست شوم
و شود و شوی و شد و خالی شوم و شود و شوی و شد بوشاناق و بوشاقانیز و بوشاقایز و بوشاکادو بوشالیلحد بوشاناق و بوشاناکه
بوشانغای بزر و بوشانالی و بوشاناق سست شویم و خالی شویم بوشاغلی و بوشاناغالی برای سست شدن و تا سست شدن و برای خالی شدن
خالی شده بوشاغاچ و بوشاتفاچ چون سست شد میشود و خالی شد میشود بوشاغوچی و بوشانوچی سست شونده و خالی شونده
بوشاغوجه و بوشاغونجه و بوشاغانجه و بوشانوجه و بوشانونجه و بوشانغانجه تا سست شدن و بعد سست شدن و تا خالی شدن و بعد
خالی شدن بوشا آلغانینکه و بوشانا آلغانینکه بعد از آنکه سست تواند شد و خالی تواند شد بوشاغوسیدور و بوشانغوسیدور
سست خواهم شد و خالی خواهم شد بوشاغونکیزدور و بوشانغونکیزدور سست خواهید شد و خالی خواهید شد بوشاغوسیلار
و بوشانغوسیلار سست خواهند شد و خالی خواهند شد بوشاغوم یوق و بوشاماغوم بوشانماغوم و بوشانغوم یوق سست نخواهم شد خالی
نخواهم شد بوشا آلماغوم و بوشا آلغوم یوق و بوشانا آلماغوم بوشانا آلغوم یوق سست شدن محکم نخواهد بود و خالی شدن
محکم نخواهد بود بوشاغولوق بوشانغولوق سست شدنی و خالی شدنی و بوشاغای و بوشاسا و بوشاسون و بوشادیلک و بوشانغای
بوشانا و بوشانسا بوشانسون و بوشاندیلک سست شود و خالی شود و بوشادیلک و بوشاندیلک و بوشانمیش و بوشانغوسیدور بیست شده و همچنانکه

ست شود و خالی شدن و همچنانکه خالی شود بوشاماق مصدر متعدیست یعنی سست کردن و خالی کردن و صیغ آن بر این نهج
با تای قرشت اشتقاق می یابد بوشورغاماق بسکون را و نون و فتح غین بمعنی متاسف شدن بوشورغاندوق متاسف
شدیم بوشورغانور و بوشورغاناد ور متاسف میشود و بوشورغانور بمعنی فاعل و مصدر هم می آید بوشورغانایدور متاسف نمیشود
و نشده است بوشورغانغاو بوشورغانورغان بوشورغانادور متاسف شونده و شده و بمعنی مصدر هم می آیند بوشورغادی بوشورغانغیل مفرد
المخاطب فعل امر بوشورغانیلار بوشورغانغیل مفرد غائب فعل نهی بوشورغانینک و بوشورغانینکیز بوشورغانینکلار جمع المخاطب فعل امر بوشورغاماینک
بوشورغاماینکیز بوشورغامانکلار جمع المخاطب فعل نهی بوشورغاناین بوشورغانام بوشورغانورمن و بوشورغانورام متاسف میشوم بوشورغامایمن و بوشورغانورمن
بوشورغانادورمن متاسف میشوم بوشورغاناس متاسف نمیشود بمعنی فاعل و مصدر نفی هم می آید بوشورغاماسینکغه بمتاسف
نشدن تو بوشورغانورینکغه بمتاسف شدن تو بوشورغانینک بوشورغانیبان بوشورغانیش متاسف شده الشاهد علی الاول
من کل نور دور ملامت لی شعر بوشورغانیب چیقلدوی غنچه تیز ٭ تیلادی تیلنا پرجان خونریز بوشورغانیشانک متاسف
شدن بوشورغانابولغای بوشورغانیب بولغای متاسف تواند شد بوشورغانا آلغای متاسف تواند شد بوشورغاناماس
نگان بوشورغاناین بوشورغاناین متاسف شوم و شود و شوی بوشده بوشورغاناق بوشورغاناینکیز و بوشورغانغایمیز بوشورغانغیل سود
متاسف شویم بوشورغانغالی برای متاسف شدن و تا متاسف شده بوشورغاناج چون متاسف شده شود بوشورغانوچی متاسف
شونده بوشورغانوچه و بوشورغانوجه بوشورغانغاچه تا متاسف شدن و بقدر متاسف شدن بوشورغانا آلغانیچه بقدر یکه متاسف
توانی شد بوشورغانورمن نبود متاسف خواهیم شد بوشورغانغوسیدورمن متاسف خواهید شد بوشورغانغوسیلاردور متاسف
خواهند شد بوشورغاماغوم بوشورغانغوم یوق متاسف نخواهیم شد بوشورغاناالماغوم بوشورغانا آلغوم یوق متاسف شدن هم
بود بوشورغانغولوق متاسف شدنی بوشورغانغاییه بوشورغانلو بوشورغانسلو بوشورغانون و بوشورغانیک متاسف شود
بوشورغانودیک بوشورغانیک متاسف شدنی و همچنانکه متاسف شود من الجواهد بوش دو معنی دارد اول بمعنی خالی باشد
چنانکه در فرهاد و شیرین در گفتار فرهاد گوید شعر چو قوینای بندرا بر عضونی بوش دنیا غنچه کیتورکالیلارکی
هوش دویم بمعنی سست بود بوشلوق بسکون نون و قاف بمعنی سست بود بوشتو با تای عجمی بترکی روم بمعنی تفنگ کونکی
که آنرا طبانچه گویند مع الغین من المشتقات بوغماق بمعنی خفه کردن و گلو را تنگ فشردن باشد و بترکی روم بمعنی کردن زدن
بود بوغدوق خفه کردیم بوغادور بوغادور خفه میکند الشاهد علی الاول شعر کیمکا کیم دولاب چرخ یلک بنالوره کشته
بیلک بوغوزنابیره بوغار قیلغان کبی فرهاد و چنغ ٭ و بوغار بمعنی فاعل و مصدر هم می آید بوغماید و بوغمایدور خفه نمیکند و نکرده است
و بوغغان و بوغادورغان خفه کننده و خفه کرده و بمعنی مصدر هم می آیند بوغ و بوغغیل مفرد المخاطب فعل امر بوغما
بوغماغیل مفرد غائب فعل نهی بوغونک و بوغونکیز بوغونکلار جمع المخاطب فعل امر بوغماینک بوغماینکیز بوغمانکلار جمع المخاطب فعل نهی
بوغمان و بوغمایمن خفه نمیکنم بوغامن و بوغارمن و بوغادورمن بوغارام خفه میکنم بوغماس خفه نمیکند و بمعنی فاعل
و مصدر نفی هم می آید بوغماسینکغه بخفه نکردن تو بوغارینکغه بخفه کردن تو بوغوب و بوغوبان و بوغیش خفه کرده بوغیشانک
خفه کرده بوغابولغای بوغیب بولغای خفه تواند کرد بوغا آلغای خفه تواند کرد بوغا بو غا خفه کنان و بتکرار
هم بامعنی مستعملست بوغای و بوغاین خفه کنم و کند و کنی و کرده بوغاق و بوغایاینکیز و بوغغایمیز و بوغالی و بوغالینک خفه کنیم بوغغالی
برای خفه کردن و تا خفه کرده بوغغاج چون خفه کرد و کند بوغوچی خفه کننده بوغوچه و بوغوجه بوغغاچه تا خفه کرد

و بقدر خفه کردن بوغا آلغانیچه بقدر یکه خفه توانی کرد بوغغوسیدورمن خفه خواهیم کرد بوغغوسیدور خفه خواهید کرد
بوغغوسیلاردور خفه خواهند کرد بوغماغوم بوغغوم یوق خفه نخواهیم کرد بوغا الماغوم بوغا آلغوم یوق خفه کردن محکم هم
بود بوغغولوق خفه کردنی بوغغای و بوغلو بوغسلو بوغغوسی بوغادیک خفه کننده الشاهد علی الاول شعر از غم او ولدوم کیم
اجل بوغوزو بوغای کیم نه ابرو مرقاب مجنون آنکا هر لحظه التفاتیم با رهت بوغوزیک قدرم بیلک خفه کردن و همچنانکه خفه
کند بوغوزلاماق مصدر متعدیست بمعنی ذبح کردن و صیغ آن بر این نهج بالتلاطم اشتقاق می یابد بوغوشماق مصدر
یعنی یکدیگر را فشردن و همدیگر را خفه کردن و کنایه است از نهیب و گریبان شدن و صیغ آن بر این سیاق با شین قرشت اشتقاق
بوغوزلاماق بسکون زای هوز و فتح لام ذبح کردن بوغوزلادوق ذبح کردیم بوغوزلار و بوغوزلایدور ذبح میکند بوغوزلار
بمعنی فاعل و مصدر هم می آید بوغوزلاغان و بوغوزلادورغان و بوغوزلاینیمیز ذبح کننده و ذبح کرده و بمعنی مصدر هم می آیند بوغوزلا مفرد
ذبح میکند و نکرده است بوغوزلا و بوغوزلاغیل مفرد المخاطب فعل امر چنانکه شاهد بر اطلاق بر صیغه مستاره دو بیت ای جمع آدم
با کینرک چینی گوید شعر سونکرا آتیمادا بخشی کوزلاسانک هم برایقدین توروب بوغوزلا ای غیرلا ناز بوغوزلاماغیل
مفرد غائب فعل نهی بوغوزلانک و بوغوزلانکیز بوغوزلانکلار جمع المخاطب فعل امر بوغوزلامانک و بوغوزلامانکیز بوغوزلامانکلار جمع المخاطب
فعل نهی بوغوزلامان بوغوزلامایمن ذبح نمیکنم بوغوزلارمن و بوغوزلایمن و بوغوزلایدورمن ذبح میکنم بوغوزلاماس ذبح
نمیکند و بمعنی فاعل و مصدر نفی هم می آید بوغوزلاماسینکغه بذبح نکردن تو بوغوزلارینکغه بذبح کردن تو بوغوزلاب و بوغوزلابان
و بوغوزلایش ذبح کرده الشاهد علی الاول شعر کونکلوکا هجر تیغی کیم اورور ایردین بیرلیق سالدی بوغوزلابانی توش
دیلک توکوب تا ن لمشطری البلاهه و بوغوزلاشانیک ذبح کرده بوغوزلابولغای و بوغوزلاب بولغای ذبح تواند کرد بوغوزلا آلغای
ذبح تواند کرد بوغوزلای و بوغوزلاین ذبح کنم و کند و کنی و کرده بوغوزلاق و بوغوزلاینکیز و بوغوزلایلی ذبح کنیم بوغوزلاغالی
برای ذبح کردن و تا ذبح کرده بوغوزلاغاج چون ذبح کرد و کند بوغوزلاغوچی
ذبح کننده بوغوزلاغوچه و بوغوزلاغوجه بوغوزلاغاچه تا ذبح کردن و بقدر ذبح کردن بوغوزلای آلغانیچه بقدر یکه ذبح توانی کرد
بوغوزلاغوسیدورمن ذبح خواهیم کرد بوغوزلاغوسیدور ذبح خواهید کرد بوغوزلاغوسیلاردور ذبح خواهند کرد بوغوزلاماغوم
بوغوزلاغوم یوق ذبح نخواهیم کرد بوغوزلای آلماغوم بوغوزلای آلغوم یوق ذبح کردن محکم نخواهد بود بوغوزلاغولوق ذبح کردنی
بوغوزلاغای و بوغوزلاغلو بوغوزلاسلو بوغوزلاسون و بوغوزلادیک ذبح کند بوغوزلاغودیک بوغوزلادیک ذبح کردنی و همچنانکه ذبح
کند بوغوزلاتماق مع التاء مصدر متعدیست یعنی ذبح فرمودن و صیغ آن با تای قرشت اشتقاق می یابد بوغوزلانماق مع النون
مصدر انفعالیست یعنی ذبح شدن و صیغ آن با نون اشتقاق می یابد من الجوامد بوغ بدو معنی دارد اول بخاری که از آب
جوشیده و دیگ طعام و اشباه آن بر آید و آنچه از زمین و کوه متصاعد شود آنرا دمه ملن خوانند بوغا گاو و گاو میش را گویند
و نام پسر شیخ بورنوک که جد هشتم چنگیز خان باشد بوغاجه بترکی روم بمعنی گلو و حلقوم باشد و آنرا المغت خفتا
بوغوز مانند بوغاق بروزن سراغ هوای مختنق را خوانند و آنرا بوغساق نیز خوانند بوغامه چادرشب و ساروقی که آن رخت
چنانکه در تاریخ ناری مذکور است که محمد حسین میرزا قورقچی دین توشک خانه قرچب گریب توشک بیلک بوغجامه سفیه
اونینک بافلانیب توز بوغجه بر نه بفتح جیم عجمی و سکون رای مهمله و فتح میم و بوغجی بکسر جیم عجمی دستمانی را گویند که برای بسته
بودن خانهای کمان بگوشهای کمان می اندازند بوغداق بروزن تخماق گرهی را مانند که در تنه درختان باشد بیغدای گندم بود

136

وبرج سنبله را هم خوانند بوغدایق بکسر یای حطی نام پرنده ایست که آنرا همای گویند بغرا بروزن طغرا بکوع آشیست تعریف
که وا منعی آن بغراخانست که در آغاز دولت سلاجقه پادشاه چین و ختا بوده و آن آش را بنام او موسوم ساخته بغراخانی گفتند و بعضی
تصحیف نموده بغراخانی خوانند و آن برین نحوست که خمیر را مثل رشته باریک نمایند و آش پزند بوغرات بروزن خطرات نام
والی قلماقست که در عهد اسکندر از اتباع دارا بوده بوغز بسکون فین و زای معجمه گلو و حلقوم را گویند الشاهد علیه
مینکا لج اول قاتل ایرور بوغز و مدا ایکی بار باغیش تیغی اوزمین کورکوز و ب سورکیلدی یانار نالنار ناغیش وجاز را بمعنی علیق و خور النده
نیز استعمال میشود چنانکه در تاریخ بابری بهر دو معنی و صفت فیل مذکور است که بوغزی خیلی اولوغ دور برقطار بتوه نینک بوغزیغی
برقیل بوار از بوغوز بضم فین هم گویند بوغماق بترکی معنی کردن زدن باشد که آنرا بعربی تعصبا نامند و نیز بمعنی خفه کردن بود چنانکه
مذکور شد بوغناق بسکون غین و قاف و فتح نون با الف کشیده و بوغنوق بضم نون هوای مخبث تیره را گویند که بترکی
بود که در کلمات به معنی گرد باد هم آمده بوغو آهوی نر را گویند شعر بیلدا حیوان وشلدی ایلکی دین ارکا اینا کونکول
الیدا یم کیم آرزو قیلغای بوغو شاخید اکل و نیز مرسفه ستاره گوید شعر کوکنی صید الاردین اول حنکل وا تم ایردی تولا
غو و مرك بوغور بضم فین و سکون رای مهمله شتر دو کوهان بود که نر و ماده از آن هم میرسد بوغورداق دو معنی دارد
استخوان دو طرف حلقوم را گویند دویم خوشه بود که تازه سر زده باشد و آنرا بوغورداق نیز خوانند بوغوز بضم فین و سکون
زای هوز بمعنی گلو و حلقوم داب بود که مذکور شد بوغون بضم فین و سکون نون بند و مفصل را گویند که در اعضای آدمی
و تنه درخت باشد چنانکه گوید شعر بیز بوغون ایرماس سونکاکدین رشته جانیم اراسی عقده لفونک دین توکونکلادر
دمی که بوتار بمدا باش و نیز در سکندری در وصف چوپ گوید شعر بولوچشم ... آیرو آیرو بوغونی پراپی لیك کر بولغای
سراپ توکونی بوغنه بکسر غین و فتح نون طنازیه ... شارم و معتبر لفظ اینلیت یعنی اینك چنانکه مجالس النفایس در ذکر مولانا
سغدی گوید که بوغنه مثل بیچی هیچه با ملاقان او چون امید اولکیم تینکری انکلر رحمت ایلمیش بلفای یعنی برای خوبك گفتن
ازملك امید آنکه خدا با و رحمت کرده باشد و مولف ... بمعنی مثل این و همچنین نوشته سهو کرده مع القاف من المشتقات
بوقتورماق جمیع ادوات ... درکین گذاشتن بوقتوردوق درکین گذاشتیم بوقتورور و بوقتورادور درکین میگذارد و بوقتورور بمعنی
فاعل و مصدر هم می آید بوقتورماید درکین نمیگذارد و نگذارده است بوقتورغانی بوقتورغایی بوقتورادور درکین گذارنده و درکین گذاشته
و بمعنی مصدر هم می آید بوقتور و بوقتورغیل مفرد مخاطب از فعل امر بوقتورما و بوقتورماغیل مفرد مخاطب از فعل نهی بوقتورونك
بوقتورونکیز بوقتورونکلار جمع مخاطب از فعل امر بوقتورمانك بوقتورمانکیز بوقتورمانکلار جمع مخاطب از فعل نهی بوقتوریان و بوقتوریامین
درکین میگذارم بوقتورارمین و بوقتورورمین و بوقتورادورمین ... بوقتورورام درکین میگذارم بوقتورماس درکین نمیگذارد
و بمعنی فاعل و مصدر منفی هم می آید بوقتورماسینکا بدرکین نگذاشتن تو بوقتورورینکا بدرکین گذاشتن تو بوقتوروب و بوقتوروبان
بوقتورمیش درکین گذاشته بوقتورمیشانك درکین گذاشته بوقتوروب ... درکین گذاشته ایم بوقتورا بولغای
و بوقتوروب بولغای درکین توان گذاشت بوقتورا آلغای درکین تواند گذاشت بوقتورا بوقتورا درکین گذاشته گذاشته
بوقتورای بوقتوراین درکین بگذارم و بگذارد و بگذاری و گذاشته بوقتوراق و بوقتورغایمیز و بوقتورایلی
و بوقتوراینك درکین بگذاریم بوقتورغالی برای درکین گذاشتن و تا درکین گذاشته بوقتورغاچ چون درکین گذاشت و بگذارد
بوقتورغوچی درکین گذارنده بوقتورغوچه بوقتورغونچه تا درکین گذاشتن و بقدر درکین گذاشتن بوقتورا آلغانیچه

137

بقدریکه درکین توانی گذاشت بوقتورغومیز بود درکین خواهیم گذاشت بوقتورغونکیز بود درکین خواهید گذاشت بوقتورغوسیلار بود
درکین خواهند گذاشت بوقتورمالغوم و بوقتورغوم یوق درکین نخواهم گذاشت بوقتورا آلماغوم و بوقتورا آلغوم یوق درکین
گذاشتن محکم نخواهد بود بوقتورغولوق درکین گذاشتی بوقتورغای و بوقتورای و بوقتورسا و بوقتورسون و بوقتوردیلك درکین
بگذارد بوقتورغودیك و بوقتوردیك درکین گذاشتی و همچنانکه بگذارد من المجامد بوقتا همان بوقات که بحرف با
مع الغین مذکور شد بوقاغو و بوقاق همان بوغاغو و بوغاق و بمعنی طوق و زنجیر باشد که بحرف با مع الکاف گذشت بوقورمه
جمعی را گویند که کمین کرده از عقب خصم درآیند بوقورداق همان بوغورداق باشد که بحرف با مع الغین گذشت مع الکاف
من المشتقات بوکماك خم کردن و ته کردن بوکدوك خم کردیم و ته کردیم بوکار و بوکادور خم میکند و ته میکند و بوکار بمعنی
فاعل و مصدر هم می آید بوکگان و بوکارکان و بوکادورکان خم کننده و ته کننده و خم کرده و ته کرده چنانکه شاهد بر اول
بمعنی اخیر در مقاله شانزدهم از حیرة الابرار در وصف خود نمایان گوید شعر بوکرکی اوچون ایچکاری بوککان عیان اث
حرص و هوا قوشلاریغه آشیانث و بمعنی مصدر هم می آیند بوك و بوككیل مفرد مخاطب از فعل امر بوکا و بوکاکیل
مفرد مخاطب از فعل نهی بوکونك و بوکونکیز و بوکونکلار جمع مخاطب از فعل امر بوکمانك و بوکمانکیز و بوکمانکلار جمع مخاطب از فعل نهی
بوکان و بوکاسمین خم میکنم و ته میکنم بوکامین و بوکارمین و بوکادورمین ... بوکارام خم میکنم و ته میکنم بوکماس خم میکند و
ته میکند و بمعنی فاعل و مصدر منفی هم می آید بوکماسینکا بخم نکردنت و بته نکردنت بوکارینکا بخم کردنت و بته کردنت
بوکوب و بوکوبان و بوکمیش خم کرده و ته کرده بوکمیشانك خم کرده و ته کرده بوکا بولغای و بوکوب بولغای خم توان کرد
و ته توان کرد بوکا آلغای خم تواند کرد و ته تواند کرد بوکا بوکا خم کنان و ته کنان بوکای و بوکاین خم کنم و ته کنم و
کنی و کند بوکای و بوکاینکیز و بوکالینك خم کنیم و ته کنیم بوکالی برای خم کردن و تا خم کرده و برای ته کردن
و تا ته کرده بوککاج چون خم کرد و کند و چون ته کرد و کند بوککوچی خم کننده و ته کننده بوککوجه و بوککونجه و بوککانچه
تا خم کردن و بقدر خم کردن و تا ته کردن و بقدر ته کردن بوکا آلغانیچه بقدریکه خم توانی کرد و ته توانی کرد بوککومیز دور
خم خواهیم کرد و ته خواهیم کرد بوککونکیز دور خم خواهید کرد و ته خواهید کرد بوککوسیلار دور خم خواهند کرد و ته خواهند کرد
بوکماکومیز بوککوم یوق خم نخواهم کرد و ته نخواهم کرد بوکا آلماغوم و بوکا آلغوم یوق خم کردن محکم نخواهد بود و ته محکم نخواهد بود
بوککولوك خم کردنی و ته کردنی بوککای و بوکا و بوکسا و بوکسون و بوکیلك خم کند و ته کند بوککودیك و بوکادیك خم کردی
و همچنانکه خم کند و ته کردی و همچنانکه ته کند بوکلمك بضم کاف و سکون لام بوکرایماك بسکون کاف و یای حطی مع رای
مهمله خمیدن و ته شدن بوکلادوك و بوکرایدوك خمیدیم و ته شدیم بوکولور و بوکولادور و بوکرایور و بوکرایادور خمیده
میشود و ته میشود و بوکولور و بوکرایور بمعنی فاعل و مصدر هم می آید بوکلمایدور بوکرایماید و رخمیده و ته نمیشود و نشده است
بوکولکان ... بوکولکان و بوکولاکان و بوکرایکان و بوکرایورغان خم شونده خمیده و ته شونده و ته شده چنانکه بمعنی خمیده در
در فرهاد و شیرین در وصف ... فرهاد کش گوید شعر قدی ایکی بوکولکان پرخلیل فلك زالی کبی حیلت سکالی و بمعنی مصدر
هم می آیند بوکول و بوکولکیل و بوکرای و بوکرایکیل مفرد مخاطب از فعل امر بوکولما و بوکولماکیل و بوکرایما و بوکرایماکیل مفرد مخاطب
از فعل نهی بوکولونك و بوکولونکیز بوکولونکلار و بوکراینك و بوکراینکیز و بوکراینکلار جمع مخاطب از فعل امر
بوکولمانك و بوکولمانکیز و بوکولمانکلار و بوکرایمانك و بوکرایمانکیز و بوکرایمانکلار جمع مخاطب از فعل نهی بوکولمان و بوکولمان

137v.

بوکرایمان و بوکرایاماس خم میشوم و نه میشوم بوکولامین و بوکولوبمین و بوکولادورمین و بوکولورام و بوکرایامین و بوکرایمدین و بوکرایلمکمیکلانکز
خم میشوم و نه میشوم بوکلماس و بوکرایاماس خم میشود و نه میشود و بمعنی حاصل مصدر منفی هم می آید بوکلماسینکا و بوکرایماسینکا
بخم شدن تو به نشدن تو بوکولوبمنکلو بوکرایوبدنکا بخم شدن تو و به نشدن تو بوکولوبانغ بوکولمیش
بوکرایب و بوکرایبیان و بوکرایمیش خمیده و نه شده التاسع عشر الرابع شعر چرخ شکوفه کوتانقد بو نکو رغو ضیغ
بنکرلنکا هرتون کمانیکی بوکرایب آیلانه دوش بوکولبشانک و بوکرایمیشانک خمیده و نه شده بوکولنا بولغای
و بوکرایب بولغای
بوکولوب توکلو بوکرایناربولغای خم توان شد و نه توان شد بوکولا آلغای و بوکرایا آلغای خم تواند شد و نه تواند شد بوکولا بوکولاد
بوکرایو بوکرا یا بوکرایا خمیده خمیده و نه شده شده بوکولای و بوکولامین و بوکرایای و بوکرایاس خم شوم و نه شوم و شود و شوی
شده بوکولسا و بوکولکای مزو بوکولکای مزو بوکولالسا و بوکولاسیو بوکرایسا و بوکرایکای مزو بوکرایکلسین و بوکرایلسا و بوکرایانک
خم شویم و نه شویم بوکولکاج و بوکرایکاج چون خم شد و نه شد بوکولکوچه بوکرایکوچی خم شونده و نه شونده بوکولکوچیه
بوکولکونه و بوکولکاینه بوکرایکونه و بوکرایکاینه خم شدن و نه خم شدن و تا خم شدن و نه خم شدن بوکولا آلغانچه
بوکرای آلغانچه مقدور که خمیده و نه توانی شد بوکولکونیز و بوکرایکونیز نم خواهیم شد و نه خواهیم شد بوکولکوسیز بوکولکوسدور
بوکرایکوسیز دور خم خواهید شد و نه خواهید شد بوکولکوسیدور و بوکرایکوسیدور خم خواهند شد و نه خواهند شد
بوکولماکوم بولکوم یوق و بوکرایماکوم و بوکرایکوم یوق خم نخواهم شد و نه نخواهم شد بوکولا آلماغوم و بوکولا آلغوم یوق و بوکرایا آلماغوم
بوکرایا آلغوم یوق خم شدن ممکن نخواهد بود بوکولکای و بوکولای و بوکولسون و بوکولدیلر و بوکرایکای و بوکرایلو بوکراینا
و بوکرایسون و بوکرایدیلر خم شود و نه شود بوکولکودیلر و بوکولوبدیلر و بوکرایکودیلر و بوکرایوبدیلر خم شدنی و همچنانکه خم شود و
شدنی و همچنانکه نه شود بوکرماک بفتح کاف عجمی و سکون را فریاد کردن کاصل کنند و مجاز فریاد کردن از کلو بود بسوت
شدید بوکربدوک فریاد کردیم بوکردی و بوکرادور فریاد میکند و بمعنی حاصل مصدر هم می آید بوکرمایدور فریاد نمیکند
و نکرده است بوکرکان و بوکرمکان و بوکرادرکان فریاد کننده و فریاد کرده و بمعنی مصدر هم می آید بوکره و بوکرکیل مفرد
غایب فعل امر بوکرنا و بوکرنکیل مفرد مخاطب فعل نهی بوکرونک و بوکرنکو و بوکرونکلر جمع مخاطب فعل امر بوکرمانک
بوکرمانکیز و بوکرمانکلار جمع مخاطب فعل نهی بوکرمان و بوکرماس مین فریاد نمیکنم بوکرامین و بوکرادورمین و بوکرمادورمین و بوکرکای
فریاد میکنم بوکرماس فریاد نمیکند و بمعنی حاصل مصدر منفی هم می آید بوکرماسینکا بفریاد نکردن تو بوکرکونکا بفریاد کردن
تو بوکرعب و بوکروبان و بوکرمیش فریاد کرده بوکرمیشانک فریاد کرده بوکرسابلکا و بوکروب بولغاله فریاد توان کرد بوکرا آلغا
فریاد تواند کرد بوکرا بوکرسا فریاد کنان بوکرای و بوکرامین فریاد کنم و کند و کنی و کرده بوکرسانک و بوکرکای
و بوکرکای مز و بوکرسالی و بوکرالیسلک فریاد کنیم بوکرکالی برای فریاد کردن تا فریاد کرده بوکرکاج چون فریاد کرده و کند
بوکرکوچی فریاد کننده بوکرکوچه و بوکرکوچه و بوکرکاینچه تا فریاد کردن و بقدر فریاد کردن بوکرا آلغانچه مقدور که
فریاد توانی کرد بوکرکومیزدور فریاد خواهیم کرد بوکرکوندور فریاد خواهید کرد بوکرکوسیدور فریاد خواهند کرد
بوکرمادومبوکرکوم یوق فریاد نخواهم کرد بوکرا آلماغوم و بوکرا آلغوم یوق فریاد کردن ممکن نخواهد بود
بوکرکولوک فریاد کردن بوکرکای و بوکراو و بوکرسون و بوکردیلر فریاد کند بوکرکودیلر و بوکروبدیلر
کردن و همچنانکه فریاد کند بوکرلمان بفتح کاف عجمی و سکون تای قرشت پیش آب خار بر آمدن و صیغ آن موافق اول الشقاق

138r.

بوکما لمانوغ بفتح کاف عجمی ترکی و بمعنی غلتیدن کردن و تفتیح باشد من الجواهر المسند بوکما پهلوان و کشتی گیر را گویند که بر اشکال
تامی و غالب باشد بوکسک بفتح کاف عجمی و سکون تای قرشت سد و بندی که پیش آب بندند بوکر بسکون کاف عجمی ترکی
قرشت هینکاه و کرده کاه را گویند و آنرا بوکر هم خوانند و بعربی خاصره نامند بوکرالک تلوه و کرده را گویند بوکر الکی جمع
باشند که ایشان را در جنکگاه بعنوان طرح دمیدن و چنانکه از طرف بمین یساق بوکرالک و از چپ سول بوکرالک هم گفته
بوکرو بجه بسکون کاف عجمی و لام و ضم را و فتح جیم بوکرو بجوات بضم جیم کاف فرزند ترکی رومی خار نایب شبیه بنا ملا می کوچک
که آنرا لوبیا گویند بوکسا بسکون کاف و فتح سین مهمله با لاتراز کمر را گویند چنانکه میرحیدر در وصف عزیمت تیمور گوید
بیتها نیکری کوید شعر کوردی که پر حمر ایاغی ایلی یوق بوکسا بیچه همچو بایریم بهلی یوق وینز بمعنی تنه کند خم کند بوکر
حمار بوکر بمعنی هینکاه باشد که در فوق مذکور شد بوکر تکن بسکون لام و تای قرشت و نون و فتح کاف عجمی ثانی نبات خار که
در برک و شکل شبیه بدرخت کل سرخ و ثمر ش در شکل و حجم مثل توت سیاه که آنرا بعربی علیق نامند مرکب القوی است و
اجزای او جامع و حابس نفث الدم و مجفف و منفرد و مقوی احشاست بوکولوم بترکی رومی ولی بود و شکنج جامه و جمیع
قامت و اشیا آنرا گویند بوک بحکم کاف عجمی ترکی رومی بمعنی بر افروز باشد منه اللحم من المشتقات بوینا تغ
اول شدن و تیم بودن سیم یافتن و دراز کردن باشد چنانکه فضولی گوید با ملاحا الرومیه شعر عم او غوبر لعشق ما زارن
نقد عمر یح بولق اولمز سود سودا دیمان او لمغ املق بولا آلما قلیغ توان شد و توان بودن چنانکه گوید شعر جمکم
بولوب خفاجه روزی بولساجم ایرماس بولا آلما قلیغی سوز غنیم که نوبف خابل بیلالک بمعنی قسمت و حصه کردن و
جدا کردن الشاهد علیه شعر کونکلوبنی کمز لاوی آلدی نیشانلت ایکی بولالک شیراهلی دین خرایلی کسکا قولتیا السین و دوتایغ با
بولاناک بمعنی تقسیم کردن دیده شد بولدی به معنی آمده اول شد حتیم یافت چنانکه فضولی در وصف حمام مطلوب گوید
با ملاح الرومیه شعر اولدی پاپوش شریف مشرف لب حوض بولدی دیدار لطیف مضاد دید تمام سیم سد کرده الشاهد
علیه شعر سیل اشکیم و دی ایکی بولدی عالم ملکوی کوینا غالم ایردی بغدا دو اشکیم و دی شط بولدوق شدیم و یافتیم
بولدوک خصه کردیم بولور که در بضم لام اول میشوند و میباشند و می یابند چنانکه بمعنی میباشد گوید شعر در دو دم
اولوم خالی بولور لا حی مفوحه کبرینا الارخا الیم سوراینر کلبه احزانیمه و بولور بمعنی فاعل و مصدر هم می آید چنانکه بمعنی
شدن در صیغه نسیلسر دو غضب کرد زهر اهر د لاد ام را گوید شعر دیری او زجانیمه نوقیلدی پروای بولور بن بیلا ایشنی
بیلدیم وای و نیز در گلستان الطیور در مصراع فرماید شعر ایریلادی آتیف ایلیفه توشب خوشه نجیر بولور غمیاد و شوب
بولادلاد بفتح هر دو لام حصه میکنند و بولا بمعنی فاعل و مصدر هم می آید بولادور میشود و میباشد و می یابد و حصه
میکند چنانکه بمعنی میباشد گوید شعر بیکت لار ایشی پرده در لیغد و ایدی بولادو رکونکول پرده لیغلا حصه را غرض
بولا آلور و بولا آلادور میتواند شد و میتواند بود و میتواند یافت و حصه میتواند کرد الشاهد علی الاول المکی الاول شعر منکا کر
ماکی اولشوخ نینک وصال الولغای بولا آلور که بوکرسانک داغ خیال الولغای و نیز در نسایم المحبه در ذکر ابو عبدالله دینوری
کوید که خاطر بوکونکول کونکلوجاوالدی بولا آلورکر آلت سیز هم کونکلوکای بولماید و میشود و شده است و نمی یابد و نیافته است و
حصه نمیکند و نکرده است بولغان و بولورغان و بولادورغان شونده و شده باشنده و بوده و یابنده و یافته چنانکه شاهد برای
بمعنی شده گوید شعر بیر تو تار کونکلوم کا کرد و زدین جدا بولغان بلا جانلاد و درج پوانه کونکلوم دین خط بولغان بلا

و در سد سکندری بمعنی بوده گوید شعر چو بولدی مطیع آندا بولغان اولوس قیریم برله فتح ایلادی اندلس و شاهد بر ثالث را
بمعنی شونده در دیباچه المحبه در ذکر مشایخ گوید که دریا الارداغ قیر بولادو ارفان کیمسه فی توتو بالم قیرا قیه چقارماق و بمعنی مصدر
هم می آید چنانکه بمعنی بودن گوید شعر اولتورودلار همه نیك بولنام اولادین بولماسام بولماغان خانا سینك
بر له بلا بولغان بلا یعنی میتکشدم را اگر همدم تو باشم و میمیرم اگر نباشم جانا همراه تو نبودن بلاخست و بودن بلاخست چنانکه شاهد
بر اولرا بمعنی شدن گوید شعر مالك عاشق اوزانیب پروانه دیك دم اوزار فاق بولغاسیدین بختی بارق بلبل کبی بسیار گوی و بولغان
اهل خطای و قلماق سمور را گویند بولکان و بولکان و بولادورکان حصه کننده و حصه کرده و بمعنی مصدر هم می آید بولماغان
بولمایدورغان یعنی نشونده و نشده و نباشنده و نبوده و نیابنده و نیافته چنانکه بمعنی نشده گوید شعر بولماغان بولسا
عیان نعت زنعیه محفی یار فانیم فی ایدی کوسیلی ایت لار کیمه فوفا ایلامان و همچنین سلطان حسین میرزا فرماید شعر اوچ اگر
تو تنی نیکا کیردی یانا توفراغ ارا بولماغان بولسا سرشکیم بحر یدین طوفان مجل یعنی اوج اگر گرفت چرا باز میان خاك رفت اگر
از بحر سرشکم طوفان محل نشده باشد و مؤلف رومی از نسخه سقیمی بولماغین بولسا بکسر ضین خوانده و شعر مزبور را شاهد آورده
بولماغین بولسا یعنی شده نشده باشد و این کلمه خالی از معنی است و بمعنی مصدر منفی هم می آید بولماکان و بولمایدورکان نحصه نکننده
و حصه نکرده و بمعنی مصدر منفی هم می آید بول امر است از شدن و بودن و یافتن چنانکه بمعنی باش گوید شعر
جهان لذاتینی شیرین کورار سین لیك بیل فکیر وش کرمتار اولمه واقف بول که قند و قیدا بر و روماند و نیز امر است از حصه
کردن و بمعنی فراوان هم آمده بولماسا مفرد مخاطب از فعل نفی مصدر بولماك و بماق بولغیل امر است از شدن و بودن و
یافتن الشاهد علیه بالمعنی الاول شعر ای نوائی یتا احبا نك غم تینکیز یکا اساجل کشتی باده بوررون تا پغیل و بولغیل ملاح
بولکیل امر است از حصه کردن بولونك و بولونکوز و بولونکلار جمع مخاطب از فعل امر هر دو مصدر بولماسون بولمایکیز
جمع مخاطب از فعل نهی هر دو مصدر بیتا ن و بولماس بین نمیشوم و نمیباشم و نمی یابم و حصه نمیکنم بولویسین و بولوزام میشوم و
میباشم و می یابم بولارمین و بولادورام حصه میکنم بولامین و بولادورمین حصه میکنم و میشوم و میباشم و می یابم بولماس نمیشود
و نمیباشد و نمی یابد و حصه نمیکند و بمعنی فاعل و مصدر منفی هم می آید بولماسینکغه نشدنت و نبودنت و نیافتنت
بولماسینکا بحصه نکردنت بولونکغه شدنت و بودنت و یافتنت بولارینکا بحصه کردنت بولوب و بولوبان و بولمیش
شده و بوده و یافته و حصه کرده چنانکه شاهد بر اول را بمعنی شده گوید شعر سها بولسا شبستانینکدا طالع بولوب دو کوکب
قوناشدیك ظالم ارا و بمعنی بوده در سد سکندری در تکمیل خمسه خطاب بطالع و بخت فرماید شعر بورونقدین چو کوکب
باریلیغ دبی تیبی سیزدین مدد کار لیغ کیجملیار کاییمدین بولوب تاشیما اولوغ مددها سنا الدینکیز یاشیما و مؤلف رومی بولوب برا ازان
از نسخه سقیمی بولوب نا یای حطی خوانده و در بابای مغموسه بمعنی راه آمده و شد نوشته و شعر مزبور را استشهاد جسته بمعنی راه
بجای نیارد و بمعنی حصه کرده در فرهاد و شیرین در شوق العشق گوید شعر بولوب قرص مه تا تانی ایکی کیشی آنرا قکه بولکای
تانی ایکی و شاهد بر ثالث را بمعنی یافته فضولی بغدادی گوید با ملاحت گر رتبه شعر ملك هم او لیکه بولمیش صفاکر موقیت
قرار و بمعنی ولمیش بو بزمده رقاص بولمیشانك شده و بوده و یافته و حصه کرده و لتا بولغا و بولوب بولغا بوده باشد [illegible]
علی الاول شعر بولسا بولغای سرو قدلار ابر پیرکار دم ملیح سرو کلر و یوم منیمك لیکن اررود اسیر و ملیح و لی بولسا بولغای الیکا ب
دولت مسیرای کونکول ئی بر کالیکی دسته نا کی جنا الغام توت و نیز بمعنی توان یافت و حصه توان کرد بولا آلغای تواند شد

و تواند بود و تواند یافت و حصه تواند کرد بولسا بولماس و بولوب بولماس نمیتوان شد و نمیتوان بود و نمیتوان یافت چنانکه شاهد
بر اول را بمعنی اول در باب هفتم از محبوب القلوب در ذکر توحید گوید که اوز وفیات دین سکانه بولماس غیبه و بجنونه آشنا بولماس
و نیز بحصه نمیتوان کرد بولا آلماس نمیتواند شد و نمیتواند بود و نمیتواند یافت و حصه نمیتواند کرد بولماق و بولماقلیق
[illegible]
[illegible]
[illegible]
چنانکه در خسرو شیرین بمعنی اول گوید شعر [illegible]
بولغالی برای شدن و تا شده و برای بودن و تا بوده و برای یافتن و تا یافته الشاهد علیه بالمعنی الاول شعر [illegible]
[illegible] بولکالی برای حصه کردن و تا حصه کرده بولغاج
و بولا تورغاج چون شد و شود و بجبر شدن و چون یافت و یابد بجبر یافتن چنانکه بمعنی اول در تحفه [illegible]
[illegible]
بولکاج چون حصه کرد و کند و بجبر کردن چنانکه در خسرو شیرین در شوق العشق گوید شعر [illegible]
[illegible] بولغوچی و بولغونچه و بولغانچه تا شدن و بقدر شدن و تا بودن و بقدر
بودن و تا یافتن و بقدر یافتن چنانکه شاهد بر ثالث را بمعنی بقدر بودن گوید شعر [illegible]
[illegible] بولکوچی و بولکونچه و بولکانچه تا حصه کردن و بقدر حصه کردن
بولا آلغانیچه بقدری که تواند شد تواند بود تواند یافت و حصه تواند کرد بولغوم خواهم شد و خواهم بود و خواهم یافت
چنانکه در سبعه سیاره در داستان مسافر اقلیم دوم گوید بالمعنی الثانی شعر [illegible]
بولغوم بولکوم حصه خواهم کرد بولغونك خواهی شد و خواهی بود و خواهی یافت الشاهد علیه بالمعنی الاول شعر [illegible]
[illegible] بالمعنی الثانی شعر [illegible]
[illegible] بولکوسی حصه خواهد کرد [illegible]
یوق نخواهم شد و نخواهم بود و نخواهم یافت بولماکوم و بولکوم یوق حصه نخواهم کرد بولا آلماغوم و بولا آلغوم یوق شدن
و بودن ممکنم نخواهد بود و یافتن ممکنم نخواهد بود و حصه کردن ممکنم نخواهد بود بولغولوق شدنی و بودنی و یافتنی بولکولوك
حصه کردنی بولغای باشد و شود و بیابد بولکای حصه کند چنانکه شاهد آن در ذیل بولوب مذکور شد بولا آلغای
تواند شد و تواند بود و تواند یافت و حصه تواند کرد الشاهد علیه بالمعنی الاول شعر [illegible]
[illegible] الشاهد علی الاول بالمعنی الاول
شعر [illegible] الشاهد علی الثالث بالمعنی الاول
شعر [illegible] تواند شد
تواند بود چنانکه شاهد بر اول را در تنبیهات محبوب القلوب گوید شعر [illegible]
[illegible] الشاهد علی الاول بالمعنی الاول شعر [illegible]

طامرچیتیز اینینک سیری بردصراغو بولادیز یعنی تواند یافت وحصه تواند کرد بلغودیک وبولودیک شدنی وبودنی همچنانکه
نبود وناشد ونافتنی همچنانکه بیاید وشاهد بر اول اعدر لسان الطیر یعنی همچنانکه باشد کوید شعر بار ایدی علوقیشه
فه برنیبا اوغول بولغودیک یوسف آیینک کیدا قول وتین سلطان حسین میرزا بهمین معنی فرمایند چون بود دولت بولغودیک
بولدی میسروای کیم معتنیم ول لحظه طالع ضعفودین تاپتی کرنده بولغودیک مین یعنی شدنی ام الشاهد علیه شعر کر بود کام
کوزوز نار لغای قصیه بولغودیک مین دیر ارامت وپریشان غامت وشاهد بر ثانی را بمعنی اول در خسرو شیرین در کرفتاری فرهاد
کوید شعر بولودیک تیر چدم شاریچ اسیم انکا تیشه کوهزنانک آخر یم سالغیتم بولکودیک وبولاردیک حصه کردنی و
همچنانکه حصه کند بولوماق مع النون بودن وموجود شدن ونایافت شدن بولوماس یعنی پیدا شد ونایافتنی شود
وجدا ومنقسم نمیشود ودر رومیه بولونمز کویند چنانکه فضولی بغدادی کوید با ملاحة الرومیه شعر عکس نالمز سیکم
کوز کوبه باقسم ضعفدین عالم صورتم برشیدا بولونمز کبی بولوماک مع النون جدا ومنقسم شدن بولوماسی یعنی نباشد
ونایافت شود وجدا نشود چنانکه بمعنی جدا نشود در ابتداء فرهاد وشیرین در مناجات کوید شعر اوتومدا یوقتر یکلیک
مهری تابین سویوم یقلو قیا بابی سلیچ بولونغای تو فراغیم کونفادین نیمی یوق وجود ومدا هوادین بولوشماق مع الشین
از باب مفاعلات یعنی با هم شدن وبودن وهمدیکر را یافتن بولوشماک بایکدیکر تقسیم کردن بولوشوب با هم شده
بوده چنانکه بمعنی اول در مقاله دوازدهم از حیرت الابرار در صفت عابد کوید شعر کینت نینک ارادی بریکی جوان
ظلمات بو خواجه الارجیلوان پریی پرله بولوشوبایله دوست کیم کیشی کیم کوریسه دیکای مغز وپوست وبیز یعنی همدیکر را یافته
وبا هم تقسیم کرده بولاناق سه معنی دارد اول بزرکی روی یعنی یافتن بود دویم مخفف بولغاناق باشد یعنی آلودن سیم بکنج
آش رفیقلیت چنانکه در ذیل خواهد مذکور خواهد شد بولاناک بمعنی حصه کردن باشد بولانادیم یعنی یافتم وآلوده
نکردم وحصه نکردم چنانکه فضولی بمعنی یافتم کوید با ملاحة الرومیه شعر جکیم داغنه مرهم بولانادیم سندن
نیجه آه الایلیم آه یابند جکریم بولغاناماق مع النون بولغاشماق مع الشین آلوده شدن وشوریده شدن وبهم آمیختن بولغاندی
وبولغاشتی آلوده شد وشوریده شد وآمیخته شد الشاهد علی الاول المعنی الثانی شعر کوزوم بولغاندی مع اشکدین وای
کورونک کولا کیدین عماند آشوب ودر هند سکندری در بزم دلراوسکندر کوید الشاهد علی الثالث بالمعنی الثانی شعر
دیبا مین که قوزغالدی غالم ایلی که بولغاشتی بهستر ظارم ایلی بولغاناد وقاد بولغاشوق آلوده شدیم وشوریده شدیم
وآمیخته شدیم بولغانور وبولغانادور وبولغاشور بولغاشادور آلوده میشود وشوریده میشود وآمیخته میشود الشاهد علی الاول
بالمعنی الاول والثانی شعر آشوب که اول کوزلاریدا آیلاناد ودیا غلاجبین وجان بود رودین اور تاناد ودیع یا غایت
اوسرو کلوک دین بولغاناد ودور اول است کبی کر بولغانور یا غلاناد ودور وبولغانور وبولغاشور یعنی فاعل ومصدر هم می آید
بولغانایمدور بولغاشمایدور آلوده نمیشود ونشدهات وشوریده نمیشود ونشدهات وآمیخته نمیشود ونشدهات بولغانغان
بولغانیغان وبولغانادوغان وبولغاشقان وبولغاشوغان وبولغاشادوغان الاینده وآلوده شده وشوریده وشوریده شد وآمیزنده و
آمیخته شده شاهد بر اول بمعنی آلوده شده شعر یا نازنا لیفه یاغزی آغزیغای هر کهه کیم کونکای باغیرپرکاله شیک
تا نفه بولغانغان مثله یعنی وشوکفه ومی بولغانغان ازادراین شعر بوبیا لغان خوانده وبمعنی زیک شده نوشته وشعر مذبور را
شاهد آورده سهو کرده لفظ اخترا عیست بولغان وبولغانیل وبولغاش وبولغاش عیال مفرد غائب امر فعل امر بولغامنا

وبولغانماغیل بولغاشما بولغاشماغیل مفرد غائب امر فعل نهی بولغانینک وبولغانینکیز بولغانینکلار بولغاشینک وبولغاشینکیز و
بولغاشینکلار جمع غائب امر فعل امر بولغانمانک وبولغانمانکیز بولغانمانکلار وبولغاشمانک بولغاشمانکیز وبولغاشمانکلار
جمع غائب امر فعل نهی بولغانامن وبولغانامین وبولغاشامن وبولغاشامن مین آلوده میشوم وشوریده میشوم وآمیخته میشوم
بولغانامین وبولغانورمین وبولغانادورمین وبولغانوراموبولغاشامین وبولغاشورمین وبولغاشادورمین وبولغاشور رام
آلوده میشوم وشوریده میشوم وآمیخته میشوم بولغاناس وبولغاشماس آلوده نمیشود وشوریده نمیشود وآمیخته نمیشود یعنی
فاعل ومصدر منفی هم می آید بولغاناسینکنه وبولغاشماسینکنه با آلوده نشدن تو وبشوریده نشدن تو وبا آمیخته نشدن تو
بولغانورونکنه وبولغاشورونکنه با آلوده شدن تو وبشوریده شدن تو وبا آمیخته شدن تو بولغانیب وبولغانیبان و
بولغانمش وبولغاشیب وبولغاشیبان وبولغاشمش آلوده شده وشوریده شده وآمیخته شده الشاهد علی الاول المعنی الثالث شعر
کورعنیم افزون لوغین هردم که اشکیم جیل نینک قطره سی بحر اولدی امیدی بولغانیب تورقانغنه هم الشاهد علی الرابع شعر
یوز کاشانسا کونکلوم احوالین نکایو قوق کناه کوز یاشیم کیم بولغاشیب جیقسا باغیرقانی بیله بولغانیشانک وبولغاشیشانک آلوده شده
وشوریده شده وآمیخته شده بولغانا بولغای وبولغایب بولغای آلوده تواز شد وشوریده تواز شد وآمیخته تواز شد
بولغاناالغای وبولغاشاالغای آلوده تواند شد وشوریده تواند شد وآمیخته تواند شد بولغانا وبولغاشا وبولغاشا آلوده
وشوریده شوریده وآمیخته آمیخته بولغاناغ وبولغانایبرع بولغاشنکو بولغاشاین آلوده شوم وشوریده شوم وآمیخته شوم وشوکه
وشده بولغانساقه بولغانغایزع بولغانغایزع بولغانالیع بولغانالینکه بولغاشساقه بولغاشغایزع بولغاشغایزع بولغا
وبولغاشالینک آلوده شویم وشوریده شویم وآمیخته شویم بولغانغای وبولغاشغای برای آلوده شدن وتا آلوده شده وبرای شده
شدن وتا شوریده شده وبرای آمیخته شده وتا آمیخته شده بولغاناج وبولغاشاج چون آلوده شد وشود چون آمیخته شد
وشود بولغانغوچی وبولغاشغوچی آلوده شونده وشوریده شونده وآمیخته شونده بولغانغوچه وبولغانغوچه بولغانغانجه
بولغاشغوچه بولغاشغونجه بولغاشغانا آلوده شدن وبقدر آلوده شدن وتا شوریده شدن وبقدر شوریده شدن وتا آمیخته
شدن وبقدر آمیخته شدن بولغانا آلغانینجه وبولغاشا آلغانینجه بقدر یکه آلوده تواند شد وشوریده توانی شد وآمیخته
توانی شد بولغانغوسیدور وبولغاشغوسیدور آلوده خواهیم شد وشوریده خواهیم شد وآمیخته خواهیم شد بولغانغوز دور
وبولغاشغوز دور آلوده خواهید شد وشوریده خواهید شد وآمیخته خواهید شد بولغانغوسیدور وبولغاشغوسیدور آلوده
خواهید شد وشوریده خواهید شد وآمیخته خواهید شد بولغانماغوم بولغانغوم یوقه بولغاشماغوم وبولغاشغوم یوق
آلوده نخواهم شد وشوریده نخواهم شد وآمیخته نخواهم شد بولغانا الماغوم بولغانا آلغوم یوقه بولغاشا الماغوم وبولغاشا
آلوده شدن ممکن نخواهد بود وآمیخته شدن ممکن نخواهد بود بولغانغولوق وبولغاشغولوق آلوده شدنی وشوریده
شدنی وآمیخته شدنی بولغانغای بولغانا وبولغانسا وبولغانون وبولغانادیع بولغاشغای بولغاشا وبولغاشون
بولغاشدیک آلوده شود وشوریده شود وآمیخته شود بولغانودیک بولغانوردیک بولغاشودیک بولغاشوردیک آلوده شده
وهمچنانکه آلوده شود وشوریده شدنی وهمچنانکه شوریده شود وآمیخته شدنی وهمچنانکه آمیخته شود بولغاتماق
مصدر متعدیست یعنی آلوده کردن وشورانیدن وآمیختن بولغاتور وبولغاتادور وبولغاتور وبولغاتادور آلوده میکند ومی شوراند ومی میزد
الشاهد علی الاول بالمعنی الاول شعر کیم سیکت لیک داملود تو بیر سیکت لیک ولدوز قاری بولغاتور سقاین تیسا

تدح چالیق و شاهد بر ثالث از معنی اول در تنبیهات محبوب القلوب گوید که خشم هر چه حقیر بولسا کونکول قوزغاتور خشم
اوشاق بولسا کوز بولغاتور بولغار و بولغاتور بمعنی حاصل مصدر هم می آید بولغاب و بولغابان و بولغامیش و بولغا بیت
بولغاتیبان و بولغامیش آلوده کرده و شوریده چنانکه شاهد بر اول از معنی اول در تاریخ الانبیا در ذکر برادران یوسف علیه السلام
گوید که کونکلاکین توی تاپیغه بولغاب یوسفی بیچه سیدی دیب تاملیغ کونکلاکین یعقوب علیه السلام تاشیغه کیتور
و شاهد بر ثانی از معنی اول در لیلی مجنون گوید شعر توندیرغیه بولغابان قولیغ برله ایلاجرا ایدی بحر بولیغ و صیغ
بولغاماق موافق شوقیم و صیغ بولغا تماق موافق شوق اول کاشتقاق می یابد بولدورماق دنداکردن و سکت کردن و بازا
بولدوردوق باز ایستادیم بولدوردوم و بولدورای بونی باز ایستد و بولدوردور بمعنی حاصل مصدر هم می آید بولدوردایدو باز
و نا ایستاده است بولدورغان و بولدورورغان بولدوردورغان باز ایستنده و باز ایستاده و بعض مصدر هم می آید علیحده و بولدرغ
مفرد غائب از فعل امر بولدورنا و بولدورغاغیل مفرد غائب از فعل نهی بولدورمغل و بولدورونکوز بولدوروز جمع غائب از فعل امر
بولدورغانک و بولدورغانکیز و بولدورغانکلا جمع غائب از فعل نهی بولدورغان و بولدورغایمن باز نمی ایستم بولدوراین و بولدورغای
و بولدورادورمن و بولدورورام باز نمی ایستم بولدورماس باز نمی ایستد و بمعنی حاصل مصدر نفی هم می آید بولدورماسلیکتین باز
نه ایستادن تو بولدوروبونکه به باز ایستادن تو بولدوروب و بولدوروبان و بولدورمیش باز ایستاده چنانکه در تاریخ
بابری مذکور است که آتیم بولدوروب تیور ایرالکاسونیز گوید که آتیم بولدوروب ایدی و تاغ هم بر کوچه کا باووق بارایدی
بولدوریشانک باز ایستاده بولدورتابولغاو بولدوروپ بولغایی تواند باز ایستاد بولدورا آلغای تواند باز ایستاد بولدورا
آلمادی نتوانست باز ایستاد چنانکه در تاریخ الملوک در ذکر یزدجرد بن شهریار گوید که هر ایندین دشمن لار ایسیلاقاتابیغ
و مدتی ایلیک ایاغ اورمدی بولدورا آلمادی و نیز در تاریخ بابری در وصف غنیم مذکور است که بر ایکی اوق آتتی لار بولدورا
آلمادیلار قاچا پرده ایلاجر بولدورا بولدورا دنداکنان و بولدورغاوبولدوراین باز ایستیم و ایستد و بق
و ایستاده بولدورناق و بولدورغا بز و بولدورغای بز و بولدورابلی و بولدورالیسنک باز ایستیم بولدورغالی برای
باز ایستادن و تا باز ایستاده بولدوغاج چون باز ایستاد و ایستد بولدورغوچی باز ایستنده بولدورغوچی و بولدورغونجه
و بولدورغانچه تا باز ایستادن و بقدر باز ایستادن بولدورا الغانیچه بقدریکه باز تواند ایستاد بولدورغوسیدور نخواهیم
باز ایستاد بولدورغوکودور خواهید باز ایستاد بولدورغوسیلاردور خواهند باز ایستاد بولدورماغوم و بولدورغوم یوق
نخواهم باز ایستاد بولدورا آلماغوم و بولدورا آلغوم یوق باز ایستادن هم نخواهد بود بولدورغولوق باز ایستادنی
بولدورغای و بولدورغاو بولدورغاناو بولدورسنک و بولدوردیک باز ایستد بولدورغودیک و بولدوروردیک باز ایستادنی و همچنانکه
باز ایستد بولاماق بابا عجمی بمعنی پف کردن باشد چنانکه در مجالس النفایس در وصف مولانا عبد القهار گوید کرا وتی
کوب بولاماکدین ماده قولاغی شار بابریب کربولدی و نیز در عنوان نثر لیلی و مجنون از مکتب گلستان گوید که بهار نزاکت
نفس نفس ایسکان نسیم لار بولاماکی بیله لاله حمراقین نار وتغانل بولادوک پف کردیم بولادو و بولادور پف میکند
بولای بمعنی حاصل مصدر هم می آید بولاماید و پف نمیکند و نکرده است بولاکان و بولادیکان و بولادوکان پف کننده
پف کرده و بمعنی مصدر هم می آید بولاو بولاکیل مفرد غائب از فعل امر بولانا و بولاماکیل مفرد غائب از فعل نهی
بولانک و بولانکیز و بولانکلار جمع غائب از فعل امر بولامانک و بولامانکیز و بولامانکلار جمع غائب از فعل نهی بولامان و بولماس

پف نمیکنم بولای مین و بولامین و بولایدورمن و بولادورمن پف میکنم بولاماس پف نمیکند و بمعنی حاصل مصدر منفی
هم می آید بولاماسلیکته پف نکردن تو بولاریکنه بپف کردن تو بولاب و بولابان و بولامیش پف کرده چنانکه
سبحه سیاره گوید شاهد علی الاول شعر کمیه بوغریغه تیغ سوکاغو عرضیمین بولاب و بولاغو بولایشانک پف کنا
بولانا بولغای و بولاب بولغای پف توان کرد بولای آلغای پف تواند کرد بولای و بولای و بولای پف کنان پف کنان
بولای و بولایین پف کنم و کند و کنی و کرده بولاناق و بولاغای بز و بولاغای بز و بولابلی و بولالینک پفکنیم بولاغالی برای
پف کردن و تا پف کرده بولاغاج چون پف کرد و کند بولاغوچی پف کننده بولاغوچی و بولاغونچه بولاغانچه پف کردن و
پف کردن بولای آلغانیچه بقدریکه پف تواند کرد بولاغوسیدور نخواهیم کرد بولاغوکودور خواهید پف
بولاغوسیلاردور خواهند پف کرد بولاماغوم و بولاغوم یوق پف نخواهم کرد بولای آلماغوم و بولای آلغوم یوق پف کردن هم
نخواهد بود بولاغولوق پف کردن بولاغای و بولاناو بولاسونکو بولادیک پف کند بولاغودیک و بولادیک پف کند
و همچنانکه پف کند بولاشماق مع الشین باهمدیگر پف کردن و صیغ آن بدستور ابشین قرشت اشتقاق می یابد بولاتماق
مع التاء مصدر متعدیست بمعنی پف فرمودن و صیغ آن با تاء قرشت اشتقاق می یابد بولاماق مع النون بمعنی پف کرده شد
و صیغ آن با نون اشتقاق می یابد بولاماق بول بمعنی فراوان و بسیار بود چنانکه حیدر تلبه در هجو کوید شعر خلق
ایدی و حاصل بولغ کیلکان ایزی برله تیلاکی یاندی یوق و نیز ترکیب شدن و بودن و حصه کردن چنانکه در تحفه
و بولماک کشت و بابای عجمی لطیوس گوید الشاهد علیه شعر چو بیدی قبا آغزی کونکلومنی آنکا داغ ایلادیم اغلاغانیدیک ایت
جر له تیلاکان او سیکا بولاغ بولاشق آلوده و شوریده هم آمده بولاغ و بولاق دو معنی دارد اول چشمه آب نا سند کرا ز زمین
جوشیده بر آید چنانکه شاهد بر دو معنی شش مبانی اللغه در اداب ملاحظه گفته تاخت دو بسا بسیار خواسته که معنی آن چا
باشد بولاغ او تی گیاهیست که در کنار آبها روید و برگش شبیه برگ تره تیز لعات و آنرا بعربی حرف الماء گویند بولاک
بمعنی فرقه و گروه بود چنانکه فضولی بغدادی گوید با ملاحه الرومیه شعر جیفه دنیا دکل کرکس کبی مطلوب بز بر بولاغمقا
لوز قاف قناعت بکلدوزلار و آنرا بولوک هم گویند بولاماج و بولاماق یکنوع آش صفتی است که از آرد میزند و بولاماغی
گوید کهن هم باشد و ترکی مرو بمعنی یاش و در انیش بود چنانکه در مولای اشتقاق این حرف گذشت بولباد خراب شدنی چنانکه
در لیلی مجنون در وصف مجنون گوید شعر جز بیر کیشی کیم سپهر بولباد بیلماس یا نا پر آنینیک کولباد بولتو بولته بوی شکسته
که آنرا بعربی ضبع گویند بولجار محل و موعدی باشد که از برای اجتماع لشکر لاجرات مقرر و معین کرده چنانکه در خمسه نرین گوید
شعر چریکا ایلایابان میعاد بولجار من شیکندری شعر تیننک آنیننک جاروبو
شه روم الیچرله سکار یغه من سکطا یختیین میرزا شعر چرخ دیکانده و آیرای کلر خونکدین کل تاغنچ ای حسینی فراق والمن
نیننک بولجاری دوش و نیز در تاریخ بابری در وصف جنگ سمرقند مذکور است که دروازه لار و کرداکرد قلعه نیننک صنیعکی بولجا
لارا و لاشیلدی و کازرستان دروازه سی شیریم لقمای نیننک بولجاری ایدی و دروش اولطرفدین بولغار و چون بولجاریحه غافل
بولدور یره باصطلاح رومیه دیت و قصاص و نفای که بایلدر از ای گناه نسبت بجرم بعمل آید بلغار نام مملکتیست که منسوبست
بلغار بن کاری بن یافث بن نوح علیه السلام است و کاری که از اولاد یازدهم کانز یافث است در حدود بلغار زمینی خوش
یافته در آنجا توطن نمود و اورا دو پسر شد یکی بلغار و دیگری برطاس و هرات گوشه گرفته بنام خود عمارت کردند و این مملکت

که بلغار عمارت کرد بنام او مشهور شد و بولغار یعنی آلوده میکند چنانکه در ذیل بولغاناق گذشت بولغاغ و بولغاق انقلاب واشفتگی چنانکه گوید شعر دیما کونکلونک ملکی نای خاقدین بو نوع اولمیش خراب تا بو کشور اهلیغه توشتی فراقینک بولغاغی وبمعنی منقلب واشفته هم استعمال میشود چنانکه وصاف در غزل ملمع باسلطان الحمات مغولیه گوید شعر تا نا یا غی عشق بو زهر کشته برون تاختیه بولغاق شد این کار پریشان بما للث وان لفظ را مولف موید الفضلا فارسی شمرده وبمعنی ازدحام وغوغا نوشته ومولفان برهان قاطع وفرهنگ جهانگیری بلغاک غوغا واشوب ذکر کرده اند وصاحب فرهنگ جهانگیری گفته که بل بمعنی بسیار وغاک بمعنی غوغا واشوب باشد مولف گوید که اصل لغت صحیح همان بولغاق است که مذکور شد ولفظ ترکی ومعانی مولفان دیگر ازتحقیق دوراست ودور نیست که بلغاک محرف بولغاق باشد واگر لفظ فارسی باشد دره منوچهر فتح هم بود بولغان مغولیه سمور را گویند ونیز بمعنی شونده وشده وشدن باشد چنانکه در ذیل مصدر بولماق گذشت بولغانچوق بمعنی انقلاب واشفتگی بود چنانکه در تاریخ الانبیا بتقریب ذکر حضرت الیاس علیه السلام گوید که خرقیل دین سونکرا بنی اسرائیل ارا سیدا سیاست حیثیتی دین کوپ بولغانچیغلیغ واقع اولدی بولغانوق ابکل آلو را گویند بولغور بسکون لام وراء مهمله وضم غین معجمه گندم نیم کوب بود بولک بفتح لام وسکون کاف بمعنی فرقه وگروه باشد که در فوق نوشته شد وبا تاء عجمی بولکی بود که در گوشهای کمان در زیر چله گذارند وآنرا بفارسی زاغ کمان خوانند اشاهد علیه شعر تارا غلاغه دین بولکی خان زه سیا بن جله ولا ایمیش تاشینک یا بن نوایی صد نیفه کرا بیتا سانک فیرطاق بولوت ابر را گویند بولوك بضم لام معنی پادشاه باشد او که قوم وگروه را گویند چنانکه در سد سکندری در ذکر اشکانیان گوید شعر مورخ که بلمزدی ملوک عجم بو تیکلیغ تیلدیر داستانی رقم که اول توقوز ایردی اوچونجی بولوك که بارا بری بیله عالم ایچرا ملوك تعبیرها طوایف را گویند که مستعمل بجند نیزه وقریه بود چنانکه در هند پرگنه ودر کابل وبخوان تومان ودر مملکت فرغانه اورچین خوانند لیکن در تاریخ بابری همه جا بولاك بفتح لام بمعنی فرقه وگروه وبولوك بضم لام بمعنی دهات وولایت مذکوراست وبلوك بفارسی طرف شراحیه باشد وبعضی گفته اند که طرفیت که آنرا بشکل حیوانات ساخته باشند وبشکل شتر را هم نامند بولوم بمعنی ثبات وپایداری باشد چنانکه در تاریخ بابری در وصف تخمینی مذکوراست که بیا بست وبجرات وبولوم بیزه وصح النون بن التشقا بومنك بسکون نون بترکی رومی بمعنی خرف وفرتوت باشد من الجوامد بونجوق خرمهره بود که آنرا بعربی خرزه گویند بونچلاین بترکی رومی یعنی اینچنین بند ور برونت برزور بیهانه بود که بدان توبره وجوال واشال آنها دوزند وکنایه از کرناریاختن وریسمان برپای بستن وبفتح باشد بزبان آید چنانکه باشاهد در ذیل بای مفتوحه مذکور شد بونکوز بسکون نون وزاء معجمه وضم کاف عجمی مع الامالة شاخ حیوانات را گویند وآنرا بونوز ومونکوز هم خوانند بونکار بابای عجمی بسکون نون وراء مهمله وفتح کاف عجمی مع الامالة بترکی رومی چاه آب وچشمه آب بود ومجاز گوشه چشم را هم خوانند مع الواو بو اسم اشارت است یعنی این چنانکه گوید شعر کونکول لدا قطره تا بلار باغلاغان ابر نسان غمانا کیم نظر با غیدا شو قینکدین آچیلغان ارغواندور شو بولوغ بولوق بمعنی هیئت بود که عبارت از تشخص باشد چنانکه اول لوغ بمعنی هویت باشد وآن عبارت از تشخص خارجی بود من لسان الطیر شعر مرنه بود یا اولدی یکاندیك تور یقین بولوغ واول الوغ بولوب مع امرادی ثم الیاس التشقا بویاماق بمعنی رنگ کردن باشد بو یادوق رنگ کردیم بویار وبویاید رنگ میکند وبویا بمعنی فاعل مستقبل هم می آید بویاماید رنگ نمیکند ونکرده است بویاغان وبویارغان وبویادورغان رنگ کننده ورنگ کرده وبمعنی مصدر هم می آیند بویا وبویاغیل

مفرد مخاطب از فعل امر بو یاسنا وبو یامنا عیل مفرد مخاطب از فعل نهی بویانك وبویانکیز وبویانکلار جمع مخاطب از فعل امر بویامانك وبویامانکیز وبویامانکلار جمع مخاطب از فعل نهی بویامان وبویاماس مین رنگ نمیکنم بویای مین وبویارمین وبویاید مین وبویاکای رنگ میکنم بویاماس رنگ نمیکند وبمعنی فاعل ومصدر منفی هم می آید بویامسنکه بی رنگ نکردن تو بویارینکه به رنگ کردن تو بویاب وبویابان وبویامیش رنگ کرده بویلیشانك رنگ کرده بویاسا ولغای وبویاب بولغای رنگ توان کرد بویای آلغای رنگ تواند کرد بویایو وبویای بو یای رنگ کنان رنگ کنان بویای وبو یای ین رنگ کنم وکند وکنی وکرده بویاساق وبویاغانیز وبویاغای بیز وبویالی وبویالیك رنگ کنیم بو یا غلی برای رنگ کردن وتا رنگ کرده بو یا غاج چون رنگ کرد وکند وبویاغوچی رنگ کننده بویاغوچی وبویاغوچه وبو یا غانچه تا رنگ کردن وبقدر رنگ کردن بویای آلغانچه بعد مرتبه رنگ توانی کرد بویاغو میز دور رنگ خواهیم کرد بویاغو چیدور رنگ خواهید کرد بویاغو سیدور رنگ خواهد کرد بویاملغو بویاغو یوق رنگ نخواهیم کرد بویای آلماغوم وبویای آلغوم یوق رنگ کردن ممکنم نخواهم بود بو یاغولوق رنگ کردنی بویاغای وبویاسا وبو یاسون وبو یادیك رنگ کند بویاغو دیك وبویارم دیك رنگ کردن وهمچنانکه رنگ کند بویالماق مع اللام رنگ شدن بویالسا رنگ شود چنانکه گوید شعر هجر تیغیدا لبی شوقیدین قسا تا مان باشیم لعل اولور کو یا بویالسا هر طرف قانیمغه تاش وباقی صیغ آن بدستور شوق اول الامثال می باید بویلاماق بسکون یای حطی قد کرمش بویلادوق قد کرفتیم بویلار وبویلایدور قد میکرد وبویلار بمعنی فاعل ومصدر هم می آید بویلاماید وبقدر نمیکند ونکرفته است بویلاغان وبویلارغان وبویلادورغان قد کیرنده وقد کرفته وبمعنی مصدر هم می آیند بویلا وبویلاغیل مفرد مخاطب از فعل امر بویلاما وبویلاماغیل مفرد مخاطب از فعل نهی بویلانك وبویلانکیز وبویلانکلار جمع مخاطب از فعل امر بویلامانك وبویلامانکیز وبویلامانکلار جمع مخاطب از فعل نهی بویلاماس وبویلاماس مین قد نمیکنم بویلای مین وبویلار مین وبویلایدور مین وبویلادام قد میکنم بویلاماس قد نمیکرد وبمعنی فاعل ومصدر منفی هم می آید بویلامابی قد کرفتنش ونکرفتنش بویلاماسنکه بقد نکرفتنت بویلارینکه بقد کرفتنت بویلاب وبویلابان وبویلامیش قد کرفته بویلیشانك قد کرفته بویلاسا بولغای وبویلاب بولغا قد توان کرفت بویلای آلغای قد تواند کرفت بویلایو وبویلای بویلای قد کرفته کرفته وبدون تکرار هم مستعملست بویلای وبویلای ین قد بکیرم وبکیری وکرفته بویلاساق وبویلاغانیز وبویلاغای بیز وبویلالی وبویلالیك قد بکیریم بویلاغالی برای قد نکرفتن وتا قد کرفته بویلاغاج چون قد کرفت وبکیرد بویلاغوچی قد کیرنده بویلاغوچه وبویلاغانچه تا قد کرفتن وبقدر قد کرفتن بویلای آلغانچه بقدریکه قد توانی کرفت بویلاغو میزدور قد خواهیم کرفت بویلاغو چیدور قد خواهد کرفت بویلاغو سیدور قد خواهد کرفت بویلاماغوم وبویلای آلماغوم یوق قد نخواهم کرفت بویلای آلماغوم یوق قد کرفتن ممکنم نخواهد بود بویلاغولوق قد کرفتنی بویلاغای وبویلاسا وبویلاسون وبویلادیك قد بکیرد بویلاغو دیك وبویلارم دیك قد کرفتنی وهمچنانکه قد بکیرد بویلاشماق مع الشین با یکدیکر قد کرفتن بویلاتماق مع التاء مصدر متعدیست یعنی قد کیرانیدن وصیغ آنها موافق شوق اول اشتقاق می باید بویورماق امر فرمودن بویوردوق فرمودیم بویورور وبویورادور میفرماید وبویورور بمعنی فاعل ومصدر هم می آید بویورماید نمیفرماید ونفرموده است بویورغان وبویورغان وبویورادورغان فرماینده وفرموده وبمعنی مصدر هم می آیند بویور وبویورغیل مفرد مخاطب از فعل امر بویورما وبویورماغیل مفرد مخاطب از فعل نهی الشاهد علی الثانی نوبو بوماغیل نیه صبری طبیب تینکری اوچون که او شوبو شربت یا سن ایچمدی سنان کلورمنکا بویورونك وبویورونکیز وبویورونکلار جمع مخاطب از فعل امر بویورمانك وبویورمانکیز

142v.

بویماتکلار جمع غائب از فعل نفی بویورمانه و بویورغاس مین نمیفرمایم بویراسین و بویورمین نمیفرمایم بویورماس نمیفرماید

و بمعنی فاعل و مصدر منفی هم می آید بویورماسینکه نفرمودن تو بویوروب بفرمودن تو بویوروب و بویوروبان و بویورمیش

فرموده بویورمیشلیک فرموده بویورماغ بولغای و بویوروب بولغای توان فرمود بویورا الغای تواند فرمود بویورا بویورا فرما

بویورای و بویورای یین نفرمایم و بفرماید و بفرمایی و فرموده بویورماق و بویورغایسیز بویورالی و بویورالسنک

بفرمائیم بویورغالی برای فرمودن و تا فرموده بویورغاچ چون فرمود و بفرماید بویورغوچی فرماینده چنانکه در خاتمه

سد سکندری گوید شعر هنر بود ایشنی بویورغوچی دور هنر هم ولی لاف اورغوچی دور بویورغوچی بویورغوچی

تا فرمودن و بقدر فرمود بویورا الغاینکجه بمعنی بقدر توانی فرمود بویورغوسیز دور خواهیم فرمود بویورغوسیدور نخواهید

بویورغوسیدور خواهند فرمود بویورمانغوم بویورغوم یوق نخواهم فرمود بویورا الماغوم بویورا الغوم یوق فرمودن نتوانم نخواهد

بویورغولوق فرمودنی بویورغاغ بویورا بویورنابویورغون و بویور دیلک نفرماید بویورغودیک بویوردیک فرمودی

و چنانکه بفرماید بویوره یماتاق بضم یا و سکون را مصدر متعدیست یعنی بیکدیگر آمرا ساختن و صیغ آن تا آنای قریشت اشتقاق

اشتقاق میابد بویورملماق بکون یا و لام و ضم را مصدر انفعالست یعنی فرموده شدن و صیغ آن با لام اشتقاق

یابد من انجا مد بوی دو معنی دارد اول قامت را گویند چنانکه در خسرو شیرین در تحویل حمل گوید شعر قیلور توتون پر

کون سیله اینات اتار لیکن بوی برله ساچین تینات دوم نام رستنیست که آنرا بفارسی شنبلیله و بعربی حلبه نامند

بوی اوتی همان شنبلیله باشد بویاغ و بویاق رنک صباغی را خوانند بویاغلیغ یعنی رنکین چنانکه گوید شعر قیننک

دین لاله دیک تورچاک خاک اولغان کونکول نیکا کیم همتا زار ایلیش بویاغلیغ هم گویلک بوی باش بمعنی سراپا باشد مجازا

لباس و پیکر گویند الشاهد علیه من سبعه سیاره شعر هوادین بولدی هر زاری نامش بوی باشی اوسیدا ایدی خانه بیچه بو

باصطلاح اتراک روم یعنی شخص و اندام باندام چنانکه شاعر رومی گوید با ملاحه الرومیه شعر بویجه بویجه عرض است فقیر

یازد جمع ایتیب سرو دلر لشکر دو نثر بویداش بمعنی هم قد و هم اندام باشد چنانکه گوید شعر باغبان کیم سروا وذر

ایلابیش پیوند کل سرو بویلوق کلرخوم بوی قسا بیداشی مود وقد بویراز با بای عجمی و سکون یا و زای هوز و فتح رای مهمله

رومی بادی بود که از میانه مشرق و شمال وزد بوی روغ و بویرذق امر و فرمان را گویند الشاهد علیه شعر اکر یامان و اگر بخشی

کیمه یوق آزادی نیدین که بو برو عجی بخشی یا نیانغه دو صنف ونیز نام برادر تابانک خان زغا کوزنامیار باشد که چینکیز خان

نمان با او خبات کرده بعمل بدر لشکر او مرا مقلوب ساخت بوی دوعجی فرماینده بویرولتو و بویورولدی بمعنی مرد و فرمان بود

و مجازا احکام و ارقام را خوانند که از جانب سلاطین و ارباب حکم صادر شود بولیوغ و بویلوق قطیلغ و لیوبامین و تمک

و کاف افاده معنی نسبت و معیت و ذو و ذا کند و از این بوکلام نیز استعمال شود چنانکه گویند سرو بولیوغ یعنی سروقامت

ملیه شعر منکا ایمدی سرو ایله کل منفا ... سرو بولیوغ کل جبین لیلی لاله ... یعنی همچنین چنانکه

شعر تا جان دعران منکا بیر بویله عشقی و اکوی کای که اوراکامنش یعنی ... بوینوز بسکون یا و زای هوز

و ضم نون شاخ حیوانات را گویند و از او بونکوز و سونکوز هم نامند بوین بسکون یا و نون و بویون بضم یا بمعنی گردن بود

چنانکه مرحوم گوید شعر ای کونکول آخر قیلیب خطیفه قیلدیم بویون و کمسیغه بوینو موغه تقوید یلادینک

و بو بون نا شیما قبمعنی گردن خاریدن باشد و آن کنایه است از خجل شدن چنانکه گوید شعر ای نوای بو نادیم اهلیغه

143r

کیم الار تا شیدلا باش انیدور کان ایل بوبین تاشیب بو یون بو ران بت که رومی مرغیست سبزوات نایل بسرخی که تاجی بر سر دارد نامند

هد هد و آنرا بفارسی کاسکینه و بعربی شقراق نامند و نیز گویند که مرغیست سیاه زنگ و بطوق الثیر که آنرا بعربی اخیل گویند و بتازی

شهوا بست چنانکه بمثل الشام من الاخیل گویند بو یوندوروق آلتیست از چوب که بر گردن گاو گاو بندند وآنرا

یوغ و بعربی نیر نامند باب المکسورات حرف الباء بیناک مردمک چشم را گویند الشاهد علیه شعر ایماس بوجهالکه گوزغا

تیککاندا تاب توروریا پیشیب یین شوق یین بینا کیم و آنرا نیناک هم گویند بکسر نون و قاف و فتح گاف بیناب بمعنی پیاب

بیدست و پا باشد بیسبر بفتح بای ثانی و سکون رای مهمله ماتراک روم فلفل را گویند و آنرا بوتیرم نامند بیبی بکسر هر دو

بای ابجد خاتون را گویند مع التاء المثناه بیتماک بسکون تا بمعنای بمعنی آمده اول رسیده زخم و سبزه دوم التیام

زخم و جراحت یعنی ساخته شدن و انجام یافتن چهارم بعمل آمدن و حاصل شدن و در این بمعنی مرادف بوتماک باشد چنانکه

با صیغ در ذیل با مضمومه گذشت و صیغ این نیز از این ... الاشتقاق می یابد بیتکورماک مصدر متعدیست بمعنی بود

اول رویانیدن دوم التیام دادن سیم ساختن و انجام دادن چهارم بعمل آوردن و حاصل کردن و در این بمعنی مرادف

بوتکارماک باشد چنانکه در با مضمومه گذشت بیتکور و بیتکورادور میرویاند و التیام میدهد و میسازد و حاصل میکند بیتکورو

بمعنی مصدر هم می آید چنانکه در فصل سیم از محبوب القلوب بمعنی حاصل کردن گوید که یا لغان حکم بیتکوره کلیم ... تشریح

واو تروک پروانه بیتکور ... صیغ برین سیاق اشتقاق می یابد بیتیماک بکسر تا بمعنی نوشتن بود چنانکه

در مقاله دوازدهم از حیرت الابرار در منقصت ... گوید شعر اول کر طریقی بیتیمات ... کتاب تعلم ایله ... کرد خوش

بیتیدی نوشت چنانکه در نامه نوشتن شیرین بفرهاد گوید شعر بیتیدی ... سطر مکتوب دیبای ... سطر کیم ... نقطه

بیتید ورک نوشتیم بیتیره بیتید ورمینویسد چنانکه در افغان نظم سد سکندری در وصف مولانا جامی گوید الشاهد علی

الثانی شعر قویب توراتواریخ و افسانه سین بیتید عهد ... بیتیرمعنی فاعل و مصدر هم می آید چنانکه

بمعنی نویسنده در مجالس النفایس در وصف خواجه ابوالوفا خوارزمی گوید که خواجه و صاحب دین کشی بیتیرمو لنسا ملی بیتیماک

کرا ... و نیز در عنوان یکی از مقطعات گوید که غلط بیتی کاتب ماسیدا قلم سورماک و بمعنی نوشتن گوید شعر ایماس غیمی باز اد

چلغد لیزوفشان کاغذ که شعله چیکتی بمعنی بیتیرمان کاغذ و هم در سد سکندری در نظم کتاب فرماید نوعایت کر لعیم

هر باشان ایدی بوز آنچه بیتیر وقت آشنا ایدی و در مقاله شانزدهم از حیرت الابرار گوید شعر یوزیدا ... نشان

همه بیتیر کاورق ... و نیز در خمسه المتحیرین در ذکر مولانا جامی گوید که اول حضرت بیتیر لی فصوص و نصوص و منکوک و اکثر

تومینیک حمد مکتبی ... نظر الابرار بیتماید دور می نویسد و نوشته است بیتیکان و بیتیرکان و بیتید ورکان نوشته

و نوشته چنانکه شاهد بر اول با بمعنی نوشته در خاتمه خمسه المتحیرین نوشته که اول آلا بیتیکان ... رسید ...

آنسکلیات مختصر ... مفید رساله هیچ کیم بیتماید و ربهی و بیتیکیل مفرد غائب از فعل امر چنانکه شاهد بر اول

در رسایم المحبه در ذکر شیخ احمد راعی گوید که هم آلتی کاغذنی امتحان او چون کیلتهوری که ای شیخ منینک و چون تعویذ بیتی

بیتیاو بیتیماکیل مفرد غائب از فعل نهی بیتیماکه بیتیکر و بیتیسنکلار جمع غائب از فعل امر بیتیمانک و بیتیمانکر و بیتیمانکلار

جمع غائب از فعل نهی بیتیمان و بیتیمان مین نمینویسم بیتی مین و بیتیر مین و بیتید ورمن و بیتیرام مینویسم بیتیماس نمینویسد

و بمعنی فاعل و مصدر منفی هم می آید بیتی الماس نمیتواند نوشت چنانکه در مقاله دوازدهم از حیرت الابرار در وصف یاقوت

مستعصی کوید شعر کیم باری مصحف بیتیما کیم ایشی ایله که آندا ق بتی آلماس کیشی بیتیما سیکا بنوشتش بوستی
چنانکه در مثنوی سید حسن کوید شعر نی نظمی برابر نام مینی مو نالش که حرفی بولغای آنینک تمراک بیتیسار بیتیکوی دین آنجم
قوت منکا که بولماس تیریکا فرصت منکا بیتیب بیتیبان و بیتیمیش نوشته و بیتیب و بیتیبان یعنی نویسیده و نوشته
و سلخته و خامل کرده نیز باشد بیتیمیشانک نوشته بیتیسا بولغای و بیتیب بولغای توان نوشت بیتی آلغای تواند نوشت
بیتی آلماغای نتواند نوشت چنانکه در قصیده کوید شعر لمعیمهر دیمی بولوریی و اردی بودیل بیتی آلماغای عطارد بیتی بیتی
نوتیان نویسان بیتی بیتیمین نویسیم و نویسد و نویسی و نوشته بیتیاق و بیتیکانه و بیتیکای نیز و بیتیلی
بیتیلینک بنویسم چنانکه شاهد بر همه است در مقاله سیم لز نزهة المتحیرین در ذکر مولانا جامی علیه الرحمه تالیف نسخه معما
کوید که الا دید یلدا کیم بو تشویشین تار تماپر بیتیلی بیتیکالی برای نوشتن و نوشته بیتی [illegible] چون نوشت و بنویسد
بیتیکوچی نویسنده چنانکه در محبوب القلوب کوید که بیتیکوچی کا هم پرده فاصله هم بیتیکوچی [illegible] بیتیکو و بیتیکونچه
بیتیکانچه تا نوشتن و بقدر نوشتن بیتی آلماسنکچه بقدر یکه توانی نوشت بیتیکو میز بود نخواهیم نوشت بیتیکو نکوز بود
نخواهید نوشت بیتیکوسیلار بود نخواهند نوشت بیتیماغوم و بیتیکوم یوق نخواهم نوشت بیتی آلماغوم و بیتی آلغوم یوق نوشتن
ممکن نخواهد بود بیتیکولوک نوشتنی بیتیکالی و بیتیسون و بیتیلار و بیتیکالار بنویسند الشاهد علی الرابع شعر
جنونوم دین پریومغه هم سودا اثر قیلسا بیتید یکالار کوزی کونکلوم قوشیدین توکنا تان تعوید و سیاق شعر
که کوزی کونکلوم قوشیدین تان توکسا تعوید بیتید یکالار بیتیکو بیلن و بیتیر دیلک نوشتنی و همچنانکه بنویسد الشاهد
علی الثانی بالمعنی الاول شعر دیبا جلوق شرح دین نامه یازکیم کویا صفحه و خامه ایرماس بیتیر دیک بیتیماک بکسر با و ...
و سکون تای ثانی مصدر متعدیت یعنی نویسانیدن بیتیتی نویسانید چنانکه در سکندر نامه در فتح کشمیر کوید
شعر سکندر او قوغلچ بیتیتی مثال که بر کیل کالی بولماک آشفته حال و باقی صیغ بر این سیاق ما تای قرشت موافق
قول اشتقاق می آید بیتیلماک مع اللام یعنی نوشته شدن بیتیلدی نوشته شد الشاهد علیه شعر عشقیم ...
وامق و مجنون غه او بردی خطی که عشق دفتریدا بو روز تراق بیتیلدی یلار و باقی صیغ بر نهج بالام اشتقاق می آید من الجوامد بیتیسیک
بکسر با و سکون کاف مکتوب و نوشته را خوانند شعر بیتیکینک دین که سوادینی کورو جان تاپتیم ظلمات ایچره مثلا چشمه حیوان
تاپتیم و مولف فرهنگ جهانگیری و صاحب برهان قاطع این لفظ را در تالیف خود فارسی شمرده بمعنی نوشته آورده اند بیتیم لیک
یعنی صاحب ترکیب و صاحب اندام مع الجیم من المشتقات بیچماق بکسر با و جیم عجمی یعنی قطع کردن و مجاز بمعنی جدا ساختن و درو کردن
بود بیچتی درو کرد بیچتوق درو کردیم بیچار و بیچادور درو میکند و بیچار بمعنی فاعل و مصدر هم می آید بیچا بدون قطع
میکند و نکرده است بیچان و بیچارغان و بیچادورغان درو کننده و درو کرده و بمعنی مصدر هم می آید بیچ و بیچیل مفرد مخاطب
از فعل امر بیچاو بیچا غیل مفرد مخاطب از فعل نهی بیچ ماسون بیچ ماسیم و بیچ ماس کالار جمع مخاطب از فعل امر بیچانک و بیچانکیز و بیچانک لار
جمع مخاطب از فعل نهی بیچمان و بیچمامین درو میکنم بیچامین و بیچار مین و بیچادور مین و بیچار ام درو میکنم بیچامس درو نمیکند
و بمعنی فاعل و مصدر منفی هم می آید بیچماسینکنه بدرو کردن تو بیچار ینکنه بدرو کردن عیب بیچیلدی بیچیمیش درو کرد
بیچیشانان درو کرده بیچاب بولغای و بیچیب بولغای درو تواند کرد بیچا آلغای درو تواند کرد بیچا بیچا درو کنان [illegible]
بیچای و بیچا نین درو نمی کند و نمی کرد بیچاق و بیچانه و بیچانیز و بیچالی و بیچالینک درو کنیم بیچغالی برای درو

کردن و نادر و کرده بیچتاج چون درو کرد و کند بیچتوچی درو کننده بیچتوچه بیچتونه و بیچا غنان درو کنند [illegible]
بیچا آلغاینکچه بقدریکه درو توانی کرد بیچتو میز دور درو نخواهیم کرد بیچتو نکوز دور درو نخواهید کرد بیچتوسیلار دور درو
نخواهند کرد بیچاماغوم و بیچتوم یوق درو نخواهم کرد بیچا آلماغوم و بیچا آلغوم یوق درو کردن ممکن نخواهد بود بیچتولوق
درو کردنی بیچمای و بیچالو بیچسا و بیچسون و بیچدملک درو کند بیچتودیک و بیچاردیک درو کردن و همچنانکه درو کند بیچتوریک
مصدر متعدیست یعنی درو فرمودن بیچیلماق مع اللام یعنی درو شدن و صیغ آنها موافق قول اشتقاق می آید
من الجوامد بیچ بکسر با و جیم عجمی ترکی روح نطفه بود که از حرام منعقد شده باشد که آنرا بعربی نغل کویند و مجاز اشلتر ...
نامند که از نسل و بنیاد برآید بیچاق با جیم عجمی کارد باشد که آنرا بعربی سکین خوانند الشاهد علیه شعر نوا نظم را
تیغ زبانین ایله سوردی کیم بیچاق نامراو بیاتیدین اوزنی او لتورا کا کاسکا کی بیچمی بسکون جیم عجمی و کسر میم بیچمه آرنا
که آنرا بعربی منشار کویند بیچک بفتح جیم عجمی و سکون کاف بمعنی موزن بود که آنرا بعربی ابن نامند چنانکه کوید
شعر یار امنی تیککالی الجشینلار بیچک بولیکن بیچکاری شنه خانیم بولیا اپیک بولیکن بیچن بکسر جیم عجمی و سکون نون
دو معنی دارد اول بمعنی حصاد و درو باشد دوم بوزینه را کویند چنانکه در سد سکندری در وصف لشام کوید شعر بیچن ...
تا ابیکا سیغار... تالسا او وو صفعه لکی یغار و نیز بحساب ترکی نام سال بوزینه است مع الخاء من المشتقات بیخاق
بسکون خا ترکی روی معنی بیزار شدن باشد که آنرا اوسانماق هم خوانند من الجوامد بیخی با یای عجمی و سکون خا ترکی روی
کوشت ابرات که افسرده سیکند و بقتی با قاف نیز بایمعنی مستعملست مع الدال بید او اسب دهد را کویند چنانکه در
سکندری در وصف اشکر عرب کوید شعر علم لا انقرا او سنا لارحم قرا بیدا و او مزیم بر کستوانلار حم قرا بیده علف و یونجه را
نامند که بر همه تا بیده خشک کنند و آنرا بوجه هم خوانند مع الرا من المشتقات بیرمالک بمعنی دادن باشد
و نیز از کلماتیست که از برای مبالغه یا تزیین [illegible] آید بر کلام ذکر میشود چنانکه کویند تو تا بیر الک یعنی کرفتن و تو تا بیر
یعنی عطا کردن بیر دوک داد بیرورم و بیرادور میدهد و بیرو بمعنی فاعل و مصدر هم می آید چنانکه میر سکی
در مقاله بنجم از حیرت الابرار کوید شعر بیل که عطا مبلغا لیکیم ... سیم برهکا لیکیم برصرمستحق بیرنا یدو صمید ...
بیرو بیرکیل مفرد مخاطب از فعل امر الشاهد علی الاول شعر غم اولتورصینی قوتیب بند و پر قدح بر کیم مقلوم ... بیرتالک
یوق افیون و نیز در حیرت الابرار کوید شعر ساقی آلیب کیل قدح خوشکوار پر که آلیب تاپای آنی خواجه وار و مولف
برکه الیب را درین شعر برلای آلیب خوانده و بیرلای آلیب را نوشته که یعنی خواند که کم و بیکم اکرچه بتصحیف خوانده اما
نخوانده و نیز در آخر بعضی کلمات از برای مبالغه داخل میشود چنانکه در فرهاد و شیرین کوید شعر بوده لار کیم کوز و معنی
آندین آچیتیک منینک الیکیم بیله فالمغه سا چیتینک که الارغه داغی آندین عطا بیر غنی الار غه داغی آلی تو تابیر محمد ...
کفته میشود که تو تابیر یعنی بکیر بیرماو بیرما کیل مفرد مخاطب از فعل نهی الشاهد علی الثانی شعر مرادی کر ایماس حالار کیم
الهی بیرما کیل عاشق مرادین بیرینک و بیرینکیز و بیرینکلار جمع مخاطب از فعل امر بیرمانک و بیرمانکیز و بیرمانکلار جمع مخاطب از فعل نهی
بیرمان و بیرمامین عیندم بیرامین و بیرو رمین و بیرادورمین میدهم الشاهد علی الاول شعر ای کیم تنیمغه جان بیرامین دهر ...
دین اولسام بی آیرو توشکو جا سیندیک ریفوقدین بیرالاین و بیرا آورین و بیرا آلادو رمین میتوان داد چنانکه در نظم ...
مرام و ملاقات ملذ کوید الشاهد علی الثانی شعر کیشیکا اول بیرمی صلای کرات نظرینک آلیدا جالی کرات

معنی چون تاپیب قوبدوب تیپ برا آلوربن اوتونکا فکیلون برنا یب تمنید هد و بمعنی فاعل و مصدر منفی هم می آید چنانچه پخاسینکا

بندادنت بیروونکا بلادنت بیربوپ بیان قبیر بیش داوه بربیشانک داده برها بولغای قیریب بولغای تواندادبرا آلغای

تواند داد برا ابیرا داده داده وبدون تکرار هم مستعمل است برا اچ برا ابین بدهم وبدهد و بدهی داده برها الغیرکا برز

برکای برزپیرالی ویرا لینلک بدهیم برکالی بلی دادن و نادادن چنانچه در مقالة النجم از حیرة الابرار کوید المعنی الاول شعر

مشعلی بلیغ ایسانان سکلالی لقمه تا تیغ لار ساچان ممتلی برکاچ جوز دادو بدهد چنانچه کوید شعر تا نیاید ام اهلینی کیم

اول که جان قیلسا نامت فدا حالینکا نسیم برکاچ دهر کردون تا نیماش برکوچی دهند چنانچه میرت سکندری در جواب

سکندر بسوال دارا کوید شعر تیلاب بیچنه کوپ بولما یمختغه توشن هوا تونی اول سینه برکوچی قوش برکوچه و برکونچه

برکانچه تادادن و نقد دادن الشاهد علی الاول المعنی الاول شعر نراهد ابرکوچه ینداییله اوزونیک ترلر زیا سید برکیل

اوزونکا آتیغوجه ناینه فه پندبرا آلغا ینکچه بقدر یکه تولابی داد بیر کوم خواهم داد الشاهد علیه شعر چرخ دونکا

که آمیدین یورو اولچومینی برری بربادبین آنی داغی بیر کوم برباد برکونک خواهی داد برکوسی خواهد داد برها کوم

برکوم یوق نخواهم داد برا الماغوم بیرا آلغوم یوق دادن مکمم نخواهد بود برکولوک دادنی برکای برا اوپیر سلو برسون

و برد بلت بدهد چنانچه در لسان الطیر در مکالمه دختر ترسا با شیخ صنعان کوید الشاهد علی الرابع شعر ذوق ایله

شیخ اوزنی بیهوش ایلادی نکته دین آغزینی خاموش ایلادی ایمدی اوز حالیدا دیبپ دیلت جواب اولچیمزاق آلنکا تیلاله

خطاب برکودیلک تغییر دیلک دادنی و همچنانچه بدهد بیر سیلما لت بکسر را و سکون لام معنی داده شدن بیر یلکاچ بیر ایله

بیر ایلکویلیوب تغییر لیدیلت داده شود الشاهد علی الثالث شعر وصلی کیر بولماس سیر بیز تویبان جان دهان کیربلیا

اوترو جا بولماق ایماس امکان عوض و بلت صیغ بیرتسانی بالام اشتقاق میاید برا قمساق بفتح را و سکون تا فم رها کردن

بیرا قتوق رها کردیم برا قور و برا قادور رها میکند بیرا قمع بمعنی فاعل و مصدر هم می آید برا قمایدور رها میکند و نکرده ا

برا قمارع برا قمیایع برا قادیم رها کنند رها کرده و بمعنی مصدر هم می آید برا ق و بیرا قنیل مفرد مخاطب امر برا قنا

برا قنا قیل مفرد مخاطب صله برا قینک و برا قینکز و برا قینکلار جمع مخاطب فعل امر برا قمانک و برا قمانکیز و برا قمانکلار

جمع مخاطب صله برا قمایع برا قماس بین رها منیکنم برا قماسیم و برا قورمین و برا قادورمین و برا قورام رها سیکنم برا قماس رها منیکند

و بمعنی فاعل و مصدر منفی هم می آید برا قماسینکمنی رها نکردنت برا قوروینکنی رها کردنت برا قمیبو برا قیبان دو ایقیش رها کرده

الشاهد علی الاول شعر جهانی بیرکیمنانک آنکلا خواص کیم بلا بوکیدین قوتولوب هر کیشی بی برا قیپ برا قیشا لمس رها کرده

برا قتنا وتلتاو ایب بولمای رها توان کرد برا قما آلغای رها تواند کرد برا قما برا قما رها کان رها کنان و بدون تکرار

مستعمل برا قمایع برنا ابین رها کنیم و کند و کنی و کرده برا قشا قع برا قما برا قغای برم برا قفاری برم برا قتا و او انالیک رها کنیم برا قتغالی

بلی رها کردن و ناردها کردن برا قماج چون رها کرد و کند برا قغوجی رها کنده برا قغوجه بیرا قغوچغه و برا قما غه تا رها کردن

و بقدر رها کردن برا قما آلغا ینکچه بقدر یکه رها تواند کرد برا قتیمین دور رها خواهیم کرد برا قغو تنکیز دور رها خواهید کرد برا قغو

سیلادور رها خواهند کرد برا قغاغوم برا قغوم یوق رها نخواهم کرد برا قما آلماغوم بیرا قما آلغوم یوق رها کردن ممکن نخواهد بود برا قغولوک

رها کردنی برا قماع برا قلماسلو برا قتوق وبرا قدیک رها کند برا قغو دیک بیرا قغو دیک رها کردنی و همچنانچه رها کند

بیرکیمک میکون ملوکه کاف و بیرکیمناک مع آتشین محکم شدن برکید و لفعیر کیشتولک محکم شدیم برکو برکید دو

برکیشو و برکیسادور محکم میشود و برکیرو برکیشور بمعنی فاعل و مصدر هم می آید برکیمایدور محکم نمیشود و نشد است برکیکان د

برکیرکان و برکید صرکان برکیشکان و برکیشمرکان و برکیساد صرکان محکم شوند و محکم شده الشاهد علی الاول المعنی الثانی

شعر عشق ارا بینر لمزغیما لوزدام ایمچارمین قان داغی بل ایمکارمین هجرا و قیدین برکیکان سکان داغی و بمعنی مصدر هم می آید چنانچه شا

را اول در معنی محکم شدن کوید شعر ای نوائی اریدیا آینیک املر دوریا یوقمی تان برکیکانداغی بلغزماس شوخ ستمکاری به تیشن برکی و

برکیکیل و برکیشو و برکیشکیل مفرد مخاطب امر برکیما و برکیما کیل و برکیشما و برکیشما کیل مفرد مخاطب صله برکینک و برکینکیز

برکینکلار و برکیشینک برکیشینکیز و برکیشینکلار جمع مخاطب فعل امر برکیمانک و برکیمانکیز و برکیمانکلار برکیشمانک برکیشمانکیز

برکیشمانکلار جمع مخاطب صله برکیمالا و برکیماسین و برکیشمان و برکیشماس مین محکم نمیشوم برکیمین و برکیمین و برکید و مین

برکرام و برکیشامین و برکیشور مین و برکیشادور مین برکیشورام محکم میشوم برکیماس و برکیشماس محکم نمیشود و بمعنی فاعل و مصدر منفی

هم می آید برکیماسینکا و برکیشماسینکا محکم نشدنت برکیرینکا و برکیشورونکا محکم شدنت برکیب و برکیبان و برکیشیب و برکیشیب و

برکیشبان و برکیشیش محکم شده الشاهد علی الرابع شعر قوش بالیب صید ایتماکیل کیم غلمی یوق برکیشیب خانه قوشی تشکه

تا برکیلغان کجلت ملا بیدین برکیمیشانک و برکیمیشانک محکم شده برکیما بولغای و برکیب بولغای و برکیشا بولغای

برکیشیب بولغای محکم توان شد برکی آلغای و برکیشا آلغای محکم تواند شد برکی و برکیشا برکیشا محکم شده محکم شد

برکیمین و برکیشای و برکیشا بین محکم شوم و شود و شوی و شده برکیمای و برکیمایع برکیشمای و برکیشمای محکم نشوم و نشود

و نشوی و نشده الشاهد علی الاول بالمعنی الاخیر شعر قرلغ ایرماس کیم قیلمیش مین کوزوم سیلی بولین محکم سرشک این ملکیم

اول یول برکیمای تیلمیش تر شیع نم برکیسا الغو برکیکانیز و برکیکای یزو برکیلی برکیلنیک و برکیشانک و برکیشکای بیز

برکیشکای بیز و برکیشکیلی و برکیشانیک محکم شویم برکیکالی و برکیشکالی برای محکم شدن و نامحکم شده برکیکاچ و برکیشکاچ

چون محکم شده شود برکیکوچی و برکیشکوچی محکم شونده برکیکوچه و برکیکونچه و برکیکانچه و برکیشکونچه و برکیشکونچه و برکیشکانچه

تا محکم شدن و بقدر محکم شدن برکی آلغا ینکچه و برکیشا آلغا ینکچه بقدر یکه محکم تواند شد برکیکومیزدور و برکیشکومیزدور محکم خواهیم

برکیکونکیزدور و برکیشکونکیزدور محکم خواهید شد برکیکوسیدور و برکیشکوسیدور محکم خواهند شد برکیکوم یوق و برکیشکوم یوق

برکیشکوم یوق محکم نخواهم شد برکی آلماغوم و برکی آلغوم یوق و برکیشا آلغوم یوق محکم شدن ممکن نخواهد بود برکیکولوک

برکیشکولوک محکم شدنی برکیکای و برکیسا و برکیسون و برکیدیک و برکیشکای و برکیشا و برکیشا و برکیشسون و

برکیشدیک محکم شود برکیکودیک برکیردیک و برکیشکودیک و برکیشور دیک محکم شدنی و همچنانچه محکم شود

برکیتماک و برکیشتورماک مصدر متعدیست بمعنی محکم کردن برکیتکان و برکیتورکان و برکیتادورکان و برکیشتورکان و برکیشتوروکان

و برکیشتورادورکان محکم کننده و محکم کرده الشاهد علی الاول المعنی الثانی شعر ناوکینک چیکمان کرچه مالیش

آنکا جان ریشه سی کوچ سلادین چیقغان تن امکان نریشه برکیتکان ها ان و بمعنی مصدر هم می آید و بات صیغ بیرتسانی ساق

میاید بر کیماک بکسر راو سکون کاف متحد شدن برکیولت متحد شدیم برکورو برکادور متحد میشود برکور معنی

فاعل و مصدر هم می آید برکیمایدور متحد نمیشود و نشد است برکاکان و برکورکان و برکادورکان متحد شونده و متحد شده و بمعنی مصدر

هم می آید بیرک و بیرکیکیل مفرد مخاطب امر برکیما و برکیما کیل مفرد مخاطب صله بیرکینک و بیرکینکیز

برکینکلار جمع مخاطب فعل امر برکیمانک و برکیمانکیز برکیمانکلار جمع مخاطب صله بیرکیمان و برکیماس مین متحد نمیشوم

1457

بریکامبرع بریکوبین بیریکادوبین بیریکیبسیر بیکورام متحد میشوم بریکاس متحد نمیشود و بمعنی فاعل و مصدر منفی هم می آید
بریکماسینکا متحد نشدنت بریکوونکا متحد شدنت بریکیوبریکیان و بیریکمش متحد شده بریکیشانات متحد شده
بیریکنا بولغای بیریکیب بولغای متحد توان شد بیریکا آلغای متحد تواند شد بیریکا بیریکا متحد شوان بیریکای و بیریکاین
متحد شوم و شود و شوی و شده بیریکیناک و بیریکاناز و بیریکگای بز و بیریکالی و بیریکالینک متحد شوم بیریکگالی برای متحد شدن و تا
متحد شده بیریکگاچ چون متحد شد و شود بیریکوچی متحد شونده بیریکوبیریکگیچه و بیریکگانچه تا متحد شدن و بقدر متحد
شدن بیریکا آلغانیچه بقدریکه متحد توانی شد بیریکومیزدور متحد خواهیم شد بیریکونکوزدور متحد خواهید شد
بیریکوسیلاردور متحد خواهند شد بیریکاکوم و بیریکوم یوق متحد نخواهم شد بیریکا آلماغوم و بیریکا آلغوم یوق متحد شدن ممکن نخواهد
بود بیریکگولوک متحد شدنی بیریکگای و بیریکگاو بیریکاو بیریکسون و بیریکگیلیک متحد شو بیریکگودیک و بیریکودیک متحد شدنی
و همچنانکه متحد شود بیریکیلمالک مع الکاف مرادف بیریکاک بمعنی متحد شدن باشد بیریکیشمالک مع التاء مصدر مفاعله
یا یکدیگر متحد شدن بیریکتورمالک مصدر متعدیست یعنی متحد کردن و صیغ هر یک از مصادر ثلثه موافق شق اول اشتقاق می آید
من الجوامد بیرو بیرار هر دو بیک معنی باشد یعنی محتاج باشد الشاهد علی الثانی شعر اکر عشاقینکا نرم ایچره بولسه بیرار نیلیک
نوای دیلک بیرار جان غرساله هم یاد قیلیغ بیر نوا الاخری نوایی بیرار لفظ مرکب فهمیده ازرا بمعنی نوبت و کرت نوشته و شعر نوایی را شاهد آورده
سهو کرده بیرارسته بفتح راء اول و تاء قرشت هنازده و سکون راء ثانی بمعنی کاهی و بعضی وقت چنانکه کوید شعر بو کیم فراق
اوتیدین خبر بیرار ایتی میتی امزی بیرارسته خبرسیز بولمایکین آیا وله شعر کهی کرکه کوزلاسین زهر چشیم تانک ایحاس بولور چو یاد ام نینک کیم
سی بیرارسته تلخ بیرو بسکون واو بمعنی یکی چنانکه در هشت بکندری کوید شعر سکندر صفی دین بیرو سوردی خرش آیینک دیک
که توشکای جانین دین درخش بیریلک یعنی مانند هم الشاهد علیه شعر یوزونک بیرله جانا قویاش بیردیلک اولغای قوباش
بیرله نموا کر بولسا بیردیلک و همچنین در حیرت الابرار در صفت صوفیه کوید شعر حالا اصحاب داغی بیردیلک بیم لیغدا باری بیزدیک
بیرلک بسکون راء و کاف بمعنی محکم و استوار بود چنانکه در هشت بکندری در بزم ردعا باوجش کوید شعر کجک محکم اولغاج چیکیب
قیلدی بت آیینک دیک که بیرلا اولسانا می هر شستی بیرکیکا بمعنی چنانکه در لیلی مجنون کوید شعر چون بار ایدی
ایلکایم افات بیریکیکانا مایل اولدی ایاغ وحالتی بیرکا دو معنی دارد اول بمعنی همراه باشد دویم کوینده کا اون قیلمیش یعنی یکرا مرا
کرده چنانکه کوید شعر اول الفکیم شیل ایله چیکتینک طغرینک یاینده حسن ایچیند ایرکا اون قیلمیش باینده اخالکی
بیرکیبی مرادف بیردیلک بود یعنی مثل هم و مانند هم چنانکه در مقاله پنجم از حیرت الابرار کوید شعر بولنا کمراتک فکر ایله
شاه زمان بخشیغه بخشی و یامانغه یامان ایکیسیدین بیرکیبی آلسا حساب مملکتی ایچرا توشار انقلاب و شعر لفظ را وی بجهوا
از لفظ ادمیز شعر بیرکیبی و بیرکوسی بیاسین مکتوب خوانده و بمعنی ادنی ذکر کرده و شعر نوایی را شاهد آورده شاهدش بر خلاف
مدعا شهادت میدهد بیرقونلوات و بیرکونی لیک یعنی یکروزه بود الشاهد علی الاول شعر نوایی نظم الامین قویکیم کوز ببر
کونلوکا ایرماس اکر یوزییل حیقاسیانک طمع بحری بیر دور کونی الشاهد علی الثانی من سکندری شعر صدو یتوبیر کونی لیک
بولغه تنده بوهم بولمادی فکرو رای ایجره کند بیرکیشه بکسر کاف عجمی و فتح نون مصغر لک باشد چنانکه در مقاله پنجم از حیرت
الابرار در نصیحت بدیع الزمان میرزا کوید شعر کوبر کهن بیرتجله دا بولدی قیل حیرانا باسیل دین اطاعت قیلدی هدم منزلی
کاشانه سی هر بیرین بیرکینه قوشرانه سی بیرلان و بیرلنه بمعنی مع در روابط استعمال میشود چنانکه در سبعه سیاره در دا

1462

ساتر اقلیم اول کویا الشاهد علی الاول شعر تولا ایلاب سرشک بیرلان کوزیدا آیتا باشلادی غنا بو دین سوز الشاهد علی الثانی
شعر کونکول سام قاشینک بولورمین توزوانیم بیرله نشان وایکی بیرو بیرچو بولمس نوایی بیرله نون بیرین بیرین بمعنی یک یک
چنانکه کوید شعر زلفونک کیم ایوور توکون توکون کوکله ایل بولدی بیرین بیرین کرفتلونک بیری بمعنی ستوطوف باشد
الشاهد علیه شعر بیر نخله تیر کوزوب صینی بیر نخله اولتوروب کلدیم بو کونزا اویون وقتی که تاملاری بیر نیما بمعنو
یکجا رو بود چنانکه کوید شعر بیریولی بیرزنی اوتونوتک ناموس التفات ایتما بیر او تونوتک نامیس مع الزاء من مشتقات بیرلمالک
بفتح زاء آراستن بیزادولک آراستیم بیزادیم بیزا ایدو دی آراید و بیزار بمعنی فاعل و مصدر هم می آید چنانکه بمعنی آراستن کوید
شعر بیزار داغ فار ضینک مشاطه حیوان چشمه سی ایچره متوشوب کلکونه کلکون قیلیش بیر ماه حاجیر اسینک بیزانماید معنی آ
و بنا راسته است بیزاکان معلوم کان و بیزایدورکان آراینده و آراسته و بمعنی مصدر هم می آیند بیزا و بیزاکیل مفرد
مخاطب فعل امر بیزانما و بیزانماکیل مفرد مخاطب فعل نهی بیزانک و بیزانکیزو بیزانکلار جمع مخاطب فعل امر بیزانما
بیزانانکیزو بیزانمانکلار جمع مخاطب فعل نهی بیزانمان و بیزانماسون نمی آرایم بیزای مین و بیزارمین و بیزایلدیم و بیزارام می آرایم بیزانما
نمی آراید و بمعنی فاعل و مصدر منفی هم می آید بیزانمسینکا بنیاد راستن تو بیزاینکا بآراستن تو بیزایبو بیزامان و بیزامیش
آراسته الشاهد علی الاول شعر کوکسوم آچتیم هر طرف قیلدی کمان اول طفل کیم لااله الا دیر لیم بیزایبین داغ خونالود ایما
بیزامیشانک اراسته بیزانسا بو لغانو بیزایب بولغانی توان آراست بیزای الغای تواند اراست بیزایبو و بیزای بیزای اراسته کمان
بیزامو آیا بنیاد ایم و بنیاد اید و بنیاد ایدی و آراسته الشاهد علیه بالمعنی الاخیر شعر یوزینی کل لاله دین بیزامو یوزیمنی قربان
البلادین ایتم یاموزونکا ستکلدی تا نالادیم یوزینی قربان بیلکاج بیزای و بیزاین بنیاد ایم و بنیاد اید و بنیاد ایدی و آراسته بیزانک
بیزاکا و بیزاکای بیز و بیزالی و بیزالینک بنیاد ایم بیزاکالی برای آراستن و تا آراسته بیزاکاچ چون آراست و بنیاد اید بیزاکوچی
آراینده بیزاکوچه بیزاکوچو بیزاکانچه تا آراستن و بقدر آراستن بیزای آلغانیچه بقدریکه توانی آراست بیزاکومیزدور
خواهیم آراست بیزاکونکوزدور خواهید آراست بیزاکوسیلاردور خواهند آراست بیزانماکوم و بیزاکوم یوق نخواهم آراست
بیزای آلماغوم و بیزای الغوم یوق آراستن ممکن نخواهد بود بیزاکولوک آراستنی بیزاکای و بیزاکاو بیزاسون و بیزاکیلیک
بنیاد اید بیزاکودیک و بیزاردیلک آراستنی و همچنانکه بنیاد اید بیزالمالک مع اللام آراسته شدن بیزالکان و بیزالکان
و بیزالادوکان آراینده و آراسته الشاهد علی الاول المعنی الثانی شعر ای که کورمای بین قوروق شاخی بیزالکان کل کله
محو باشید نه ایرجسم انکا عرفیه باق من سلطاحمین بیزار شعر سبزه وکل دیک خطی بیرله یوزین مرشح ایتای سبزه و کل
دین بیزالکان باغ رخسارین مودی و بمعنی مصدر هم می آیند بیزاشمالک بایکدیکر آراسته شدن و صیغ آن بالشین اشتقاق
می یابد بیزاتمالک مع التاء مصدر متعدیست یعنی آراسته کردن و صیغ آن با تمامی قرشت اشتقاق می یابد من الجوامد بیز بروزن
بحهنا بمعنی آمده اول بمعنی ما بود که آنرا بعربی نحن کویند و این در ابتدا واقع میشود دویم در آخر کلمه در آمده افاده انتساب بغیر میکند
چنانکه مرد و معنی کوید شعر زهد مین و کوثر بیز دو مغ دیری نیدین کیم بیز هر بلاکش بیز مین نوش یا چش سیم در قرآ
که آنرا بعربی مخنف کویند حمایم کرباس بود که آنرا بوبز هم خوانند و بعربی ترنامند بیزاک آرایش بیزاکچی آرایشکر
بیزاکلیک آراسته و باز بود چنانکه کوید شعر قیزلاشید بیزاکلیک سر بسر کل بیرکیدی تلنو تلنو انواع الیه کوه بلا
بولغان تنیم بین بیزبیز مانیمو از اوریمیه بیزودکو نیند بیزلادوق با بای عجمی و سکون زاء و ضمه و قاف و فتح لام و ضم واو

146v.

که بود که اطفال آنرا مدور ببرند و اطوار آنرا از اندام طرح کرده دیمان از آن که تمامینه تاب دانه در کشاکش بما آرند صدا می از آن
بر می آید ییز و ز بترک موی یعنی نمایم چنانکه فضولی گوید با ملات الزمنیه شعر اسیر درد عشق و مشتاق حسن چوق اما پرکوه مشهود
اولان لیلی منکا مجنون سنکادیر لیز نیک نون و کاف شاکینش اکر چه بنزله کاف خطابیست در حرف ما کاهی زاید بر کلام
استعمال میشود چنانکه در این شعر واقع شده شعر محنات بحین ما یعنی د و در زمان کاشانه یمیز اولدی کو یا اژدها کالی
یز نیک و ایرانه میزه در اینجا همان معنی ما باشد و نا به آن ربط کلام نیز هست چنانکه در دیباچه کتاب در صفت چهار رمنکا تر یانی صبح
التین بیسلیک شتر و تفره را گویند چنانکه میر حیدر در معزن گوید بیت اولیکیم القصه نی کیم خامه و قاش سیدالار اول ایسرلک
ایی بو قلم و شولعه فرهنگ جها نگیری و صاحب برهان قاطع بیسراک بضم سین ضبط کرده و ظاهرا بیسر ترکیه بمعنی شتر جوان پر قوت
و شتر جوان که مادرش تازی عربی و پدرش دوکوهان باشد نوشته است مع الیون الشقات بیشهوا التغصین بمعنی پختن باشد اکر چه
بیشیغ که معنی حاصل مصدر است یعنی پخته نافین واقع شده از المنقرا بات مصدر و مشتقات آن تماما نباشد لیکن مخالف
قیاسی است که موافق استعمال است الشاهد فیه شعر سو سو سوانیلدین چون نابو د میلدیبیر بولی سین بیشور مالت
هر زمان پراعز کاجه سودانی بوز بیشوروک یختیم بیشوروب بیشور دور میزدو بیشور و یعنی حاصل مصدر هم بیشوراماید دور
یمیزد و پخته است بیشورکان بیشورکان بیشوار دورکان پزنده و پخته و بمعنی مصدر هم می آیند چنانکه گوید الشاهد علی
الاول شعر خیالینکنه سو ابیشورکان الهاب ی مناعیمی آشفته اول شاک سازاده بیشرو بیشوردیک مفرد مخاطبه امر
بیشور بیشوراکیل مفرد مخاطبه فضل الامر بیشورونک بیشوروبکوز بیشورونکلار جمع مخاطبه فضل الامر بیشورا نکیز بیشورا نکیز
بیشورانکلار جمع مخاطبه فضل امر بیشوراغ بیشوراس مین یمنیم بیشورامین بیشورو بیشورکیم بیشورادور بیشورادام میزم
بیشوراس یمیزد بمعنی حاصل مصدر بمعنی هم می آید بیشورماسنکا نپختن تو بیشورورونکا پختن تو بیشوروب بیشورو
بیشورمیش پخته بیشورمیشانک پخته بیشورنا بولغا عوبیشوروب بولغا توان پخت بیشورا آلغای تواند پخت بیشوراباشورا پزان
پزان بیشوراغ بیشوراسین بپزم و بپزد و بپزی و پخته بیشورسا العیشو کالیز و بیشوکای پزد بیشورلیو بیشورانیک
بپزیم بیشورکالی برای پختن و تا پخته بیشورکاج چون پخت و بپزد بیشورکوچی پزنده بیشورکو چه و بیشورکو پخته و بیشورکو پخته
تا پختن و بقدر پختن بیشورا آلغا ینچه بقدر که تواند پخت بیشورکو میزدو خواهیم پخت بیشورکو نکوزدور خواهید
بیشورکو سیلاردور خواهند پخت بیشورماکوم بیشورکیم بوق نخواهم پخت بیشورالماغوم و بیشورالقوم یوق پختن مکم نخواهد بود
بیشورکو لوک پختنی بیشوکای بیشار و بیشوربلو بیشورسون و بیشورد دیلک بپزد بیشور کوید بیشورنک
پختنی و بپخته چنانکه بپزد بیشوریماک بیکون را و نای قرشت مصادر متعدیست یعنی پز اندن و صیغ آن بدستور موافق بیشور
با حرف تا اشتقاق می یابد بیشیماک مصدر انفعالیست یعنی پخته شدن و تذکر یافتن بیشیق پخته شدن و تذکر یافت
چنانکه در آمدن مجنون بقبیله گوید المعنی الاول شعر هر یاری تیشتی بو حکایت کیم هوش لنکا ایلامیش سرایت ایکی نکلدا
بو خیال بیشتی نوفل نمدا می خبر تیشتی و صیغ آن موافق بو اول اشتقاق می یابد بیشقار دنا و بیکون شین ورای مهمله و فتح تا
یعنی تذکر کردن و مخاطب بیاندن بیشقار دو ق تذکر کردیم بیشقار دور بیشقار ادور تذکر میکند و بیشقارور یعنی حاصل و مصدر
هم می آید بیشقار ما بد و تذکر میکند و نکردنات بیشقارغان و بیشقار دورغان و بیشقار ادورغان تذکر کننده و تذکر کرده و بمعنی
هم می آیند بیشقار و بیشقار عیل مفرد مخاطبه فضل الامر بیشقار سا و بیشقار زا غیل مفرد مخاطبه فضل فی بیشقار ینک

بیشقار ینکیز و بیشقار ینکلار جمع مخاطبه فضل الامر بیشقار لیکلار جمع مخاطبه فضل بیشقار دیان
و بیشقار ما بن تذکر نمیکنم بیشقارامین و بیشقار و رمین و بیشقار ادورمین و بیشقار و را تذکر میکنم بیشقار ماس تذکر نمیکند
و یعنی حاصل و مصدر نفی هم می آید بیشقار ماسینکه تذکر کردن تو بیشقار ور ونکه تذکر کردن تو بیشقار لیق بیشقار ناب
بیشقار میش تذکر کرده بیشقار میشانک تذکر کرده بیشقار نابولغای و بیشقار اب بولغای تذکر توان کرد بیشقارا آلغای تذکر
تواند کرد بیشقارا بیشقار سا دا تذکر کنان تذکر کنان بیشقار ای و بیشقار ابین تذکر کنم و کند و کنی و کرده بیشقار ایلی
بیشقار ابین تذکر نکنم و نکند و نکنی و نکرده چنانکه شاهد بر این معنی نکرده گوید شعر کونکول کامر نصیب و اقراد
نیدی پر و دمین پر غرای که بیشقار ما این پر غر او نوعتش بیشقار سا و بیشقار لیز و بیشقار غای و بیشقار لی و بیشقار لیز تذکر کنم
بیشقار غالی برای تذکر کردن و تا تذکر کرده بیشقار غاج چون تذکر کند و مجرد کردن بیشقار غوچی تذکر کننده بیشقار غو
بیشقار غو چه و بیشقار غانچه تا تذکر کردن و بقدر تذکر کردن بیشقار ا آلغا ینچه بقدر که تذکر تواند کرد بیشقار نا غو و بیشقار
بیشقار ماغانچه تذکر نکردن و بقدر نکردن چنانکه شاهد بر این معنی اول در تنبیهات محبوب القلوب گوید که سوز نی کونکولدا
بیشقار ماغو نجه تیلکا کیتورما بیشقار غو میز دور تذکر خواهیم کرد بیشقار غو نکوز دور تذکر خواهید کرد بیشقار غو سیلار دور
تذکر خواهند کرد بیشقار غوم و بیشقار غوم یوق تذکر نخواهم کرد بیشقار الماغوم و بیشقار القوم یوق تذکر کردن من نخواهد بود
بیشقار غولوق تذکر کردنی بیشقار غای و بیشقار ا و بیشقار سا و بیشقار سون و بیشقار دیلک تذکر کند بیشقار غودیلک
بیشقار ور دیلک تذکر کردنی و همچنانکه تذکر کند من انجا مد بیش بیشاد عدد پنج را گویند بیشالا مرغ تا بیشالا
مرغ تا یش بیشالامین مرغ تای شما بیشالا انکز مرغ تای شما بیشا و بکون و او یعنی پنج تا چنانکه گوید شعر خوا
حسن ایله مقصود بیلادی و صلاتی کونکولی نی تا پیکاج عضو بیش ایماس بو بیشا او بیش ارمغاق بترکی نوع علم کیاهیست دولت
که از ملحقات از اسفید چکی هم گویند و نیز نام کوهستانیست از ممالک ری و گمبر و بسیار است و آن را هار حبال الغ انکت
نامند و آب سفید مو و دان آنجا خیزد بیش بالیغ نام شهریست از ممالک ترکستان که از آنجا تا خانبالیغ از جانب جنوب بیش راه بیانانا
که معمول آنرا بو غری اول گویند چهل روزه راهست بیشمه و بیشی نانهای کوچک باشد که در روغن پزند و مرقوه
نان که خمیر شرا با تخم مرغ برهم زده در روغن میپزند بیشی گویند بیشیغ و بیشیق بمعنی پخته بود چنانکه در تاریخ بابری
در وصف میوه هند گوید که بیشیغی یا یمان ایماس خام لیقیدا غریب پیمز و دور و بمعنی پخته شدن هم استعمال میشود چنانکه مرقوم
طوطی گوید که بان لاد و قب بیشیغ المغا تا تعه کیلور بیشیک کهو لو باشد که آن را عربی مهد نامند چنانکه در فرهاد
و شیرین در ولادت فرهاد گوید شعر بیشیک ده هیلاجینی و خطلت بولو بو بیز نوش لب دستان کرتی بیشیمه تکلمدیکی
چنانکه در تاریخ بابری مذکور است که بر پسوت بیشیم خرما و عوق در زات میلیله بیستیغ العفن بیشنغ به معنی آمده اول
بدوت را گویند دویم بمعنی میا و ساخته و آراسته بود چنانکه در فرهاد و شیرین گوید شعر کیتوریب شراب در پرده
که بولدی کونکولو مینیر بوید و بو درد باشیغه در چیکاسدین بو لعه تیغ بودم نزم نشاطی الدکی لیغ من بهار سکند ری سفر
کراولرایله میلدی هر ایشی بیغ مونکا خوشنیب ایلامیدی بار وتیغ شیم بمعنی قصد و عزم و آهنک باشد الشاهد علیه
شعر نیچه کیم مینا او بر نشه لار ناشی اضدر چیکار چتر دیک کیمنی پر از ایلاما کلیله محلنا بیغ و نیز در سد سکندری
در مثل دار اکوید شعر اول ایکی کیشی هم راق یلا دیان آینک مثل عزه اتفاق بیلا جان که جوز مثل غوسی بر کا اولیغ مثل

آنکا پر بورو زاق چیکب تیغ قتل هنیز دم لیلی مجنون کبی شعر اوزر قیلیبنی الیا امیش ایدی بیغ پنهان قیلیب ایدی بهر لیغ بیغ
و شلفین رومی یکی بیغ را در این شعر لخیر بیغ و مصراع این شعر بابای خجلی خوانده و بمعنی جانب و طرف کرده نوشته و دیکری بیغ مع الف
خوانده و بمعنی جیم و محقوق کر کرده و هر دو شوند که مطلع از لیلی مجنون معنی شاهد آورده اند سهو ایشان جیم و محقوق است
بیغلامیشی بمعنی اختکی و اراستکی بود چنانکه در جلد رابع و ما فسند کور است که در سلخ درج سطوبینا بیغلامیشی و قضا
بیغلامیشی کردند بیغو بابای عجمی بضم فتح معجمه نام خان و نصرت سنکاری شبیه بنا زامان از بان کو چکتر که کهنشک دامثال
بدان صید میکند و نیز نام پادشاهیت معروف که سلجوقان نجانب و حکومت خوارزم منسوب بود مع القاف بیقین
بکتواف و سکون نون هیلو و هیکاه را کویند مع الکاف من الشقات بیکانماک بفتح کاف عجمی و سکون نون پسندیدن
بیکاندوک پسندیدیم بیکانور و بیکانادور می پسندد و بیکانور بمعنی فاعل و مصدر هم می آید بیکانماید و د نمی پسندد و
نپسندیده است بیکانکان و بیکانورکان و بیکانادورکان پسند کننده و پسندیده و بمعنی مصدر هم می آید بیکان بمعنی بیکانکیل
مفرد مخاطب فعل امر بیکانماو بیکانماکیل مفرد مخاطب فعل نهی بیکانینک و بیکانینکیز و بیکانینکلار جمع مخاطب فعل امر
بیکانمانک و بیکانمانکیز و بیکانمانکلار جمع مخاطب فعل نهی بیکانمان و بیکانماس مین نمی پسندم بیکانامین و بیکانورمین
بیکانادورمین بیکانورم می پسندم بیکانماس نمی پسندد و بمعنی فاعل و مصدر منفی هم می آید بیکانماسینکا به نپسندیدن تو
بیکانوردونکا به پسندیدن تو بیکانینک و بیکاینان و بیکانمیش پسندیده بیکانیشانک پسندیده بیکانسا
بولغای و بیکانیب بولغای پسند توان کرد بیکانا آلغای پسند تواند کرد بیکانا بیکانا پسند کنان پسندکنان بیکانمای
بیکانامین پسند کنم و کند و کنی و کرده بیکانمای و بیکانمایین نپسندم و نپسندد و نپسندی و نپسندیده الشاهد
علی الاول بالمعنی الاخیر شعر چیککاندا نقاش قضا اول لعل و کل رخ صورتین کو یا بیکانمای تاشلامیش لوح ایله آنی کون
هیاتین بیکانسانک بیکانسانکیز و بیکانسانکای بیکانسالی و بیکانالینک پسندیم بیکانکالی برای پسندیدن
و تا پسندیدن بیکانکاج چون پسندید پسندند بیکانکوچی پسند کننده بیکانکوچه بیکانکونچه تا پسندید
و بعد از پسندیدن بیکانا آلماسینکه بعد مشکه توانی پسندید بیکانکومیز دور خواهم پسندید بیکانکونکدور خواهد
پسندید بیکانکوسیدور خواهند پسندید بیکانماکوم و بیکانکوم یوق نخواهیم پسندید بیکانا آلماغوم و بیکانا آلغوم نی
پسندیدن ممکن نخواهد بود بیکانکولوک پسندیدنی بیکانکای و بیکانامیکا فنا و بیکانانون و بیکانندیلیک
بپسند و بیکانکودیلک و بیکانوردیلک پسندیدنی و همچنانکه بپسندد من ایجوا مید بیک با کاف عجمی بخفف بیک
بمعنی رفیع و بلند و بزرک باشد و مجاز از مولا و سلطان و حاکم و امیر را کویند چنانکه در حیرة الابرار کوید شعر تولغه
که بیک میلنا تواضع فزون رشته دخ ایلکها وزنکا اوزون و نیز در وصف پادشاه کوید شعر شه لا ادب دین
تیکیبان یرکا کوز سوزدا تنا بیکلاه کا نی امکان سوز و بابای عجمی بفلزی بمعنی امضا باشد چنانکه در حیرة الابرار آورده شعر
لطمه فرهد هدنی که محتاج ابوعت بیک بیل لرجه باشد تاج ابوعت و طالع هروی بیک بمعنی تا مدار بیت این شعر بیک تا به
ابجد خوانده و بیک را بمعنی قیاس بمعنی خرو سن ذکر کرده و بشعر نوای استشهاد جسته لفظ و معنی هر دو خراب است بیکاج زنان
محترمه را کویند و از آن بیکه هم خوانند و مؤلف رومی بمعنی خترنوشته و ضیری هم متابعت کرده بیک بورد که بر کی
ده کل بستان افروز بود و آن را سلطان بورکه هم نامند بیکایش نام یکی از پادشاهان خوارزم است و نیز نام شحنیت از

انسا لکان طریقت که طایفه بیکچی در روم لوما و مولا و مرشد خود دانسته او بنا و قی خودها با و نسبت میدهند در معنی ترکمان آن بلد
بکی بمعنی سنان بزرک باشد و بیک بمعنی هم مولا و هم خداوند بود و مؤلف برهان از الملح این لغت را فارسی تصور نموده و نوشته که بمعنی بهرام
و جلوه کن و کفته که کویند ترکیست وجه مناسبت اصلا معلوم نشد بیکتر بابای عجمی و سکون کاف و فتح تا و قرشت زره اراد
سلاح جنک باشد وان با زنجای آهن است که بطریق قلبیکی یکدیکر وصله دوخته در جنک پوشند و آن را بکتر هم کویند چنانکه
شاهد آن در حرف بای مفتوحه مع الکاف نوشته بیکه زنان محترمه را کویند و آن مخفف بیکاج باشد بیکه رک
الشاهد علیه شعر عشق اکر بولسا هوای نفس دین پاک ای کونکول یوق تفاوت دلبرینک کر بیکه بولسون کر میرک
دکه شعر لیلی و شیرین کا هم ایله کیمی القات بیکه کا چون یوق کز براوی قیزا ایله ایدین و بمعنی محبوب نازنین
دلحشه نوشته بیکیز بکسر کاف عجمی هفت زای هوز نیرقشر اکویند و آن را بیز هم نامند بیکیم خاتون بزرک را کویند چنانکه در
تاریخ بابری در وصف زنان سلطان حسین میرزا کوید که فلان غنچه چی لیق مرتبه سیدین بیکیم لیک مرتبه سیغه ترقی قیلدی
و مؤلف رومی بمعنی زن بیشوهر و زنی که فرزند نیاورده باشد نوشته اند و ضیری هم متابعت کرده بیکین بمعنی مانند
بود الشاهد علیه من غیرشانه شعر هیچ کیم ملک بقا سلطانی بولغای بولیکین تا نی محض اولمای سلطان ابوالغازی بیکین
و در کلیله دمنه در وصف کوه مذکور است با املاء الرومیه شعر سولوی در بیکین منبع نور سواد دیده سیکی عیب دن دور
مع الکاف من الشقات بیلماک باشباع کسره دانستن و در صورت ترکیب افاده معنی توانستن و توانائی هم میکند چنانکه شاهد آن در
ذیل بیلمان مذکور خواهد شد بیلدی ولک دانستیم بیلور و بیلادور میداند و بیلور بمعنی فاعل و مصدر هم می آید بیلماس میداند
نمیداند و ندانسته است بیلکان و بیلورکان و بیلادورکان داننده و دانسته و بمعنی مصدر هم می آید بیلکانکاچه و بیلادورکانکاچه
تا بدانند چنانکه شاهد بر اول لطف بیاچه و تتمه مدیحه کوید که بو قیزلیق شراب ایلا هر یلا قوی کوتوب بیلدا حیدی ذلت
بیش و حکومت آلغانی ضیعت بیلکانکاچه بیل و بیلکیل مفرد مخاطب فعل امر بیلما و بیلماکیل مفرد مخاطب
فعل نهی بیلینک بیلینکیز و بیلینکلار جمع مخاطب فعل امر بیلمانک بیلمانکیز و بیلمانکلار جمع مخاطب فعل نهی
بیلمان و بیلماس مین نمیدانم چنانکه شاهد بر اول لطف در مصرع اول این شعر از خسرو شیرین در تعریف فرهاد کوید شعر
ولی کیلتور مکا چاره بیلمان بو عجزیم دا اول ایشکا مایه بیلمان تا ره بیلمان یعنی عنوانم نیست بیلا آلمان یعنی بیلا آلماس مین
نمی توانم دانست الشاهد علی الاول شعر یار نا کیم یوم اوزومنی پله آلمان سین سیز کیلکه پر خطه تحمل قیلا آلمان سین سیز
بیلاممو بیلورمین و بیلادورمین و بیلورام میدانم بیلماس نمیدانند و بمعنی فاعل و مصدر منفی هم می آید بیلماسینکا ندانستن تو
بیلورونکا بدانستن تو بیلیب و بیلیبان و بیلمیش دانسته بیلمیشانک دانسته بیلسا بولور و بیلیب بولور میتوان دانست
چنانکه شاهد بر اول لطف در غرائب الصغر در وصف نوروز عید بیک خوارزمی کوید که طبیعتینک ن تعدیه قوت و لطافت سار
انکا بینی شعری دین بیلسا بولور بیلا آلور میتواند دانست بیلا بیلا دانسته دانسته و ندانسته بیلکای هم چنانک
چنانکه کوید شعر عمری بیلا بایش سیری کیتمانک کیرانک آخر کیم شیتمه آندین مینی حیران بیلا باریم بیلای و بیلای بین بدانم
و بداند و بدانی و دانسته بیلسانک و بیلکاینز و بیلکای و بیلالی و بیلالینک بدانیم بیلکالی برای دانستن و تا
بیلکاج چون دانست و بداند الشاهد علیه شعر یار فه بیلکاج اچنا جیمینی بولمادیم کیمسه کا یا نا محتاج بیلکوچی
داننده بیلکوچه و بیلکاچه و بیلکونچه تا دانستن و بعد از دانستن الشاهد علی الثانی بالمعنی الاول شعر یار ینک دیدیلای

غیر بیله نادره ایجب تورر• تحقیقی بیلکو بخرنی تا نالجرکه بو تو بیش بیلا آلغا سینکچه بقدر یکه توانم دانست بیلکومیزده
خواهیم دانست بیلکونکوزدور خواهید دانست بیلکوسیلاردور خواهند دانست بیلماکوم بیلکوم یوق نخواهم
دانست بیلا آلماغوم بیلا آلغوم یوق دانستن ممکن نخواهد بود بیلکولوک دانستنی ممنوع تمنا اروشانداهم باشد
چنانچه شاهد آن در ذیل جوامد مذکور خواهد شد بیلکای بیلا و بیلکای بیلمیلوب بیلیلیک بداند الشاهد علی الخامس شعر
جاه نینک زیبی ضرکیم حسن بیلا بیلیلیک کیم زینتی کیلمادی جاه اهلیغه احسان ینکلیغ بیلکوبیلیک بیلوردیک دانستی د
چنانچه بداند بیلیغانک مع النون دانسته شدن بیلینکاچ چون دانسته شد و شود چنانچه در سد سکندری در
وصیت اسکندر یادرش کوید شعر بیلینکاچ که بو نوع ایمیش هرکات اولا بوینی اوزونکا بول آموزکار بیلینکای
بیلینلو بیلینکی و بیلینیلیک دانسته شود چنانچه در سد سکندری در وصف حال اسکندر کوید الشاهد علی الاول شعر
بیلینکای دیبلکاندا ایرپارلیثی که خلق اینمادی تینکریکا نداق کیشی و باقی صنع برین شایق با نون موافق اول الشفاق
بیلدورماک مصدر متعدیست یعنی فهمانیدن معلوم کردن بیلدوردوک فهمانیدیم بیلدوردی و بیلدوراد ود
بفهماند و بیلدوردی بمعنی فاعل و مکمل هم می آید بیلدوردا بیدی بفهماند و نفهمانیدن است بیلدورکان بیلدوردکای
بیلدوراد ورکان فهمانیده و فهمانیده و بمعنی مفعول هم می آیند بیلدوردی و بیلدور کیل مفرد مخاطب فعل امر بیلدورمااه
بیلدورماکیل مفرد مخاطب فعل نهی بیلدوروک و بیلدوروکیز بیلدورونکیز جمع مخاطب فعل امر بیلدورمانک و بیلدور مانکیز
بیلدورمانکلار جمع مخاطب فعل نهی بیلدورمانو بیلدورماس یعنی فهمانم بیلدورماین بیلدوردین بیلدوراد ورسین بیلدوردی
سفهمانم بیلدورماس بفهماند بمعنی فاعل مصدر هم می آید بیلدوروماسینکا نفهمانیدن بیلدوروونکا
نفهمانیدن بیلدوروب بیلدوروبان بیلدوروبمیش فهمانده بیلدورمیشانک فهمانده بیلدورماباولغای بیلدوروب تونه
توان فهمانید بیلدورا آلغای تواند فهمانید بیلدورا بیلدورا تفهیم کنان بیلدوراری و بیلدوراین بفهمانم و نفهماند
نفهمانی و فهمانده بیلدورمانک بیلدورکاسین و بیلدوردکای بین بفهمانی الشاهد علی الثانی شعر تیلبه لیک ایلا بولوا
ای صبا خالیمنی مکرو اولپری فرخ تقریری پله بیلدورکاسین بیلدورمانک بیلدورکاینزو بیلدوردکای بیتو بیلدورابلی
بیلدوراینک بفهمانم بیلدورمکالی برای فهمانیدن و تا فهمانیده چنانچه بمعنی اول کوید شعر بیکنه تا یمنی تونکی
عشق ایمدبی ناتسیغ کیلسا لا ارفرهادایله مجنون آنکا بیلدورکالی بیلدوردکاج چون فهمانید و بفهماند بیلدوردکوچی
فهمانیده بیلدوردکوچه بیلدوروبوتی بیلدوردکا بخشه تا فهمانیدن و بعد فهمانیدن بیلدورا آلغانینکچه بقدر یکه توانم فهمانید
بیلدورکومیزدور نخواهیم فهمانید بیلدورکونکوزدور خواهند فهمانید بیلدورکوسیلاردور نخواهید فهمانید بیلدورماکوم
بیلدورکوم یوق نخواهم فهمانید بیلدورا آلماغوم و بیلدورا آلغوم یوق فهمانیدن ممکن نخواهد بود بیلدورکولوک فهمانیدنی بیلدوردکای
بیلدورا بیلدورماگید ورسون بیلدوروردیک نفهماند بیلدوردی کیمدیک بیلدوروردیک فهمانیدنی و چنانچه بفهماند بیلکورماک
بضم کاف عجمی مصدر لازم است بمعنی معلوم شدن باشد و مولفین روی وفا الم هروی مرادف بیلدورماک فهمید بمعنی فهمانیدن
نوشته اند و نصیری هم متابعت کرده سهو کرده اند و بیلکورماک متعدی آنست چنانچه معلوم خواهد شد بیلکوردی
معلوم شد الشاهد علیه شعر ایچرا سبکه توللغان اوکینک هریان الغایرناس که رکلاهدیک او تونک سیلکوردی جسم
نا توانیم دیث و له شعر هجرنامی کوزیاشیم باشیدین آشتی ایله کیم سو بولی هرتار ملالیم جسم لاربیلکوردی کوزر

من سلطانین سوزلر شعر ایلاریدیم عشق نینک رسوا الاریغه سوزیش بولغای سواسوزوم لاد ایرکانی بیلکوردی
بیلکورمادی معلوم نشد چنانچه کوید شعر شام هجریم تیره دورانداق که کوندوزهم بولوب هر نیچه کیم احتیاط ایتیم
قیاش بیلکورمادی بیلکوردوک معلوم شدیم بیلکوروز و بیلکورادور معلوم میشوم الشاهد علی الاول شعر سین
که یوق سین نامرو لادجلوه ایلاملار لاروليك کیمه اینشار قوت نوی هم حقفاج بیلکوردی که سیرلجانکالاشیرین
نیدیم بیلکوروز صحیتم بن اولوک سین دیتیرای نیاغ بن بیمارین الشاهد علی الثانی شعر ایله تا منیع کونکولو
ایچره تو کان اهرتاب سین کیم لاله نینک غنچه سید بیلکوراه دور تاشیده و بیلکوروز بمعنی فاعل مصدر هم می آید بیلکورکان
روبی بیلکوروز ایمعنی سفهماند نوشته و این شعر را شاهد آورده شعر زلفی و صلین ایستا شام خسار مهر افروز بیلکور
یو قجب چون سیل کیلیشی بیلکوروز نوروزی دین و همین شاهد خلاف معنی او را سفهماند بمعنی معلوم میشود معلوم
میشود و معنی شعر اینست که آمدن سال از نوروز معلوم است بیلکورماید و معلوم نمیشود و نشده است بیلکورکان بیلکوردکان
بیلکورادورکان معلوم شونده و معلوم شده الشاهد علی الاول المعنی الثانی شعر ضعف لیغ جیمیده بیلکورکان بو غولامه
هیاتین آنکا یاندا شغان توکلالار نینک شبیهی تارلار و بمعنی مصدر هم می آیند بیلکوروز و بیلکورکیل مفرد مخاطب فعل امر
بیلکورماو بیلکورماکیل مفرد مخاطب فعل نهی بیلکوروک بیلکوروکیز بیلکوروزنکیز جمع مخاطب فعل امر بیلکورمانک و بیلکورماسکیز
بیلکورمانکلار جمع مخاطب فعل نهی بیلکورماین بیلکورماین معلوم نمیشوم بیلکورماسینکا نامعلوم نشدن بیلکوروونکا نامعلوم شده
بیلکوروب بیلکوروبان و بیلکورمیش معلوم شده بیلکورمیشانک معلوم شده بیلکورابولغای بیلکوروب تواند معلوم
شد بیلکورا آلغای معلوم تواند شد بیلکورا بیلکورا معلوم شده معلوم شده بیلکورای و بیلکوراین معلوم شوم
و شوی معلوم بیلکورمانک بیلکورکاینزو بیلکورکای بیتو بیلکورابلی و بیلکورالینک معلوم شوم بیلکورمکالی برای معلوم شدن
و تا معلوم شده الشاهد علیه بالمعنی الاول شعر قتل عام اینکاج که تا چون عشقی دین هر بولهوس جسمیما جان کیردی
عشقیم آیدا بیلکورکالی بیلکوردکاج چون معلوم شد و شود بیلکوردکوچی معلوم شونده بیلکوردکوچه و بیلکوروبوتی بیلکوردکا بخشه
تا معلوم شدن و بعد معلوم شدن بیلکورا آلغانینکچه بقدر یکه معلوم توانم شد بیلکورکومیزدور معلوم خواهیم شد
بیلکورکونکوزدور معلوم خواهید شد بیلکورکوسیلاردور معلوم خواهند شد بیلکورماکوم و بیلکورکوم یوق معلوم نخواهم
شد بیلکورا آلماغوم و بیلکورا آلغوم یوق معلوم شدن ممکن نخواهد بود بیلکورکولوک معلوم شدنی بیلکورکای و بیلکورا
بیلکوربلو بیلکوربوب بیلکوردیک معلوم شود بیلکوردیک بیلکوروردیک معلوم شدنی و چنانچه معلوم شود بیلکورتماک
بسکون لام و راء مهمله و تای قرشت مصدر متعدیست یعنی معلوم کردن بیلکورتوب بیلکورتوبان بیلکورتمیش معلوم کرده چنانچه
در فرهاد و شیرین خطاب بصبح کوید الشاهد علی الاول شعر شادم آهیمنی بیلکورتوب دینک دین کوزوم یاشینی
آنکلاتب شبنمینک دین بیلکورتمای و بیلکورتماین معلوم نکنم و نکند و نکنی و نکرده چنانچه شاهد بر اول را بمعنی معلوم
نکرده در خطاب فرهاد با وحوش کوید شعر منکا بیلکورتمای سیکرلیسیکم بن دیا یغیه قرینلیریماس لیکیم بن و با ای
صیغ برین سابق با تای قرشت اشتقاق می یابد بیلاماق بتر که رومی چیزیرا نیک فسان کشیدن و تیز کردن چنانچه در
کلیله دمنه ترکی رومی در وصف کوه با بلاجورتیه مذکور است که ان بخار دور کار قطع بود و تاننه دیش بیلاردی من الجوند
بیل کمر کیمیدالشاهد علیه شعر بیلینک و آغزینک حدیث در زینیریلمان تیغ ایکل ایاسیلو نیهان موبحرتو شمشیر

میل و تال و باشباع کسره امر است از دانستن و بفارسی آلتی است آهنین که باغبانان و امثال ایشان زمین را بدان بکنند و پارو
کشتی را هم نامند و نیز نام صوبه ایست در هندوستان شبیه به غرجل که از آن مرا شارزند بیلاتر زلیک دستینه بود که زنان
بدست کنند و آنرا بفارسی دست برنجن و بعربی سوار گویند بیلالک بمعنی بود اول بنادم را گویند چنانکه گوید شعر
تا یمقا قولیشیمال تیغی چیکماکه قیلوش قیل بولادی قیلیچ دین بهوین اول اسیم بیلالک دویم بمعنی هدیه و نوباوه باشد میوه
فرهنگ جهانگیری بامعنی طرب شمرده و این شعر را از سلطان سلوچی شاهد آورده شعر خاک و خاشاک سرایت میفرستد
هر صباح گلشن فردوس را فراش بر رسم بلاک سیم تیر که روی زمین را بدو پشته خاک بود کرنا را از آنرا سوراخ سوراخ کرده تا
و بفارسی نوعی از پیکان باشد که آنرا مانند بیل کوچک سازند و آنرا پیکان شکاری نیز نامند و در این معنی بلک بحذف الف
بیان فتحه نوشته میشود بیلاگجه دو شاخه چوبی که بردست مجرمان و محبوسین زنند بیلان لفظیست که در آخر کلمات بمعنی مع
واقع میشود چنانکه در توحید گوید شعر تا پناق عجیب فکر و تخیل بیلان سینی بیتبانک ظالعقل و فراست بیلان سنکا بیلوو
بفتح لام و سکون واو و سنک فساز باشد چنانکه گوید شعر بلا ارا چومین او لدعم بلا قیلیجا لعینی نیتا نک نیتکا
لوح نزاریم اولنابیلاو بیلبا غ کمربند را نامند الشاهد علیه شعر فی کمرندی تا مینیکه نیشکرشیرین دوتو
فی آنینک بندی بیلینکا با غلاغان بیلباغچه بیلیتات با بای عجمی و سکون لام و کاف و فتح تای قرشت بمعنی الکن بود چنانکه
گوید شعر نوائی اول یوز و لب شوقیدین ناگه نواچیکیه دم اوراماس بلبل و طوطی که بو یوره کیچه اوله بیلانک بیلتور
بمعنی پارینه الشاهد علیه شعر اولنا دیب یردیب نوای تیر کوزلری وصلیم سیله بیلتورا ولکا ملاحتیله آتی برابر بولدی
و در فتنه بیلدیر گویند بیلتور بمعنی پارینه اله چنانکه گوید شعر اولمانیکه معزورحسن ای شوخ لعینکیم باغ اورای سیر
بیلتور کل لاردین بیری سیل ایماس بیلدورکا بسکون لام و رای مهمله و ضم دال و فتح کاف عجمی دو معنی طره اول قسمی از
باشد که بقبضه شمشیر یا تازیانه تعبیه کرده دسته از آن بگذرانند دویم چوبی که حلقه کرده بوضع خام دام سیا
بدان صید طیور نمایند بیلکو بسکون لام و ضم کاف عجمی بمعنی تمغا و نشان و علامت باشد الشاهد علیه شعر جان ارا دا فی
کورروب عاشق بغمینی آنکلادی اول کیشی دیت کیم تاینغای اوز تولین بیلکو کوروب ولا نوائی ایچ قدح و فانی اول کم تاپتی بقا
برا و که تا پماد یلا ابل ایاغ وسیلکو سین و بالمجاز بدو معنی هم می آید اول نشانه تیر دویم تخلص چنانکه در خاتمه منطق الطیر
در تبدیل تخلص خود از نوائی بفانی گوید شعر فیض تیکاچ اول مغانی دین منکا تاپتی بیلکو نظم فانی دین منکا بیلکوت
نام طایفه ایست از اتراک چنانکه گوید شعر ای نوائی مین ار ایلچه بیر لوحش کیم مر ارلات اونوت بولدی منکا
هم بیلکوت بیلکورتا بمعنی اثر و علامت باشد الشاهد علیه شعر اوچ قر نحی لیدا بیلکور و بیلکو طلبین کورلیت
نشانه کیم کرا بیتار جان ارا داغ نهانیم دین بیلکولوک بمعنی معاد او دو نشاندار باشد چنانکه در دو معنی بطریق ایهام گوید
شعر عشق و تیدین قوللوغونک داغینی قویدوم کوکسوما اوزنی بو نوع ایلادیم عشق اهلی ایچره بیلکولوک بیله بمعنی
می آید اول بمعنی همچنین بود که در ابتداء کلمه در می آید و آنرا بعربی کذلک گویند دویم بمعنی مع در آخر کلمه استعمال میشود
چنانکه بمعنی اول گوید شعر طرفه کوم کیل که غنان تارتمای اول شوخ دمی سونک بیله قاتیغ لیغ بیله خالیمنی بیلیب سیم
یعنی با یکدیگر الشاهد علیه شعر دایم قاشینکدا بولنا نوائی محبلیماس گل چهره بلبل اولنا نیتانک متصل بیله جهار دم
بمعنی دانسته و فهم کنار باشد چنانکه گوید بیله باردیم یعنی دانسته نفهم و شاهد آن در ذیل مشتقات مصدر بیلماک مرقوم شد

بیلورسی یعنی یا او و هم او شر چنانکه در تحفه بیلورسی دوستان زبان از اقلیم هفتم گوید شعر کیم کیلور تا مر خطای نوازش تی
بیرکیز خوب نهادش و توغلیقین بیلورسی یعنی این ترا بیلاف و بیلاکی خوانده هر دو لفظ را مرادف یکدیگر بامعنی نوشته
شعر را و در شاهد آورده اند سهو کرده اند بیلهسیز بمعنی مراهیه چنانکه گوید شعر نوائی همرهم تا الدعیتیلانک
شکرة جاهی که سیار تار تیبکز بیله بیله سیز بیلی تاغلی یکنوع برنده ایست شبیه بباز که دم او دراز و دو رنگ
دم او سفید و همه انگشت سفید است بیلیچ بعضی قلیج ترکی را بدین جهت طیوری را نامند بیلیلیک بمعنی علم و دانش
بود چنانکه در سد سکندری در وصف حکما گوید شعر بیلیک اوچی فکر تلاری منزلی باری آیدا حل مشکلی
معلوم و دانسته هم استعمال میشود چنانکه از این شعر معلوم و دانسته میشود شعر چو الدلان و انجم تیمار الحید
که نا هیچ ایلکا بو لغای بیلیک و مجاز بمعنی پند و تعلیم و ارشاد هم می آید بیلیک لیک یعنی عالم و دانشمند و بمعنی آگاه
هم باشد و از ابیلیملیک نیز گویند بیلیم لیک مرادف بیلیک لیک بود چنانکه بمعنی عالم و دانشمند در تاریخ بابری
که محمد ندقا سر و بیلیم لیک کیشی ایدی مع النون من المشتقات بینکزامالک بسکون نون و کاف عجمی و فتح زای هوز شبیه
و مانند شدن بینکزادولک شبیه شدیم بینکزارو بینکزایدور شبیه میشود و بینکزار بمعنی فاعل و مستقبل هم می
بینکزامایدور شبیه نمیشود و نشده است بینکزاکان و بینکزارکان و بینکزایدورکان شبیه شونده و شبیه شده و بمعنی مصدر هم
می آید بینکزاو بینکزاکیل مفرد مخاطب از فعل امر بینکزاماو بینکزاماکیل مفرد مخاطب از فعل نهی بینکزالک
بینکزانکیز و بینکزانکلار جمع مخاطب از فعل امر بینکزامالک بینکزامانکیز و بینکزامانکلار جمع مخاطب از فعل نهی بینکزامان و بینکزاماس
شبیه نشوم بینکزای و بینکزارمین و بینکزایدورمین و بینکزادم شبیه میشوم بینکزاماس شبیه نمیشود و بمعنی فاعل و مستقبل منفی
هم می آید بینکزاماسینکا شبیه نشدن تو بینکزارینکا شبیه شدن تو بینکزاب بینکزاماان و بینکزامیش
(بینکزاو بینکزای بینکزای)
شبیه شده بینکزامیشاملک شبیه شدن بینکزاسا بولغای و بینکزاب بولغای شبیه توان شد بینکزالغای شبیه تواند شد
شبیه شونده شونده بینکزای و بینکزامیس شبیه شوم و شود و شوی و شده بینکزسالک بینکزاکاینز و بینکزاکای بیز
بینکزالی و بینکزالینک شبیه شویم بینکزاکالی برای شبیه شدن و تا شبیه شده بینکزاکاچ چون شبیه شد و شود کر
بینکزاکوچی شبیه شونده بینکزاکوچیدور بینکزاکونیز و بینکزاکانچه تا شبیه شدن و بعد شبیه شدن بینکزیلغانیکچه تعلقیه
شبیه توان شد بینکزاکومیزدور شبیه خواهیم شد بینکزاکونکوزدور شبیه خواهید شد بینکزاکوسیلاردور شبیه خواهند شد
بینکزاماکوم و بینکزاکوم بوق شبیه نخواهم شد بینکزاعلی الملفوم و بینکزای العوم نوع شبیه شدن محکم نخواهد بود بینکزا
شبیه شدنی بینکزاکای و بینکزای و بینکزاسالو بینکزاسون و بینکزادیلیت شبیه شود بینکزاکودیلیت و بینکزاردلیت شبیه شدنی
و همانکه شبیه شود بینکزاشمالک مع الشین مصدر مفاعله است بیکدیگر شبیه و مانند شدن بینکزاماتالک
مع التا مصدر متعدیست یعنی تشبیه کردن و صیغ آنها موافق شق اول اشتقاق می یابد من الجوامد بینجک یام بکوز
نون و کسر جیم بلغت مغولی اسبا چاپای بود بینک بسکون نون و کاف عجمی بترکی و مهلدو هزار بود و در لغت جغتای با میم استعمال
بنک تامات بترکی روی چیزیست که نا شکسته کوسفند میباشد و آنرا بفارسی هزار خانه و هزار لا باشد بینکز
بسکون نون و کاف عجمی و زای هوز و بینکیز بکسر کاف عجمی مع اللاحقه بمعنی گونه و بشره بود بینکیزش بکسر زای هوز بمعنی
مشابهت مع الیا بی رتیلا را نامند و لوزبکیه تو لان امیر بیلت را گویند بی بی خواتین بیلت را خوانند چنانکه

در قسم ثنیم از مجموب القلوب کوید که خواجه کیم بی وباریدا دعلک کا آیلانغای بی بی نینک هم عشق ایتاکی قولغه بولغانغای
بیازی با بای عجمی یکنوع سکانیست و بالمجاز تیر را کویند که آن نوع سکان باشته باشد چنانکه در تاریخ ابو سعید کورکان
کهلادن قیرغاول و بودنه ون بیازی بیله آتیب کم ازایاردی بیه بفتح بای و بهاء زده مار دنبان بود بییک بکسر یا و سکون کاف
بلند و بزرک را کویند چنانکه بمعنی بلند و عالی کوید شعر فلک قویغاج سرو اکر توشسا ایاغین او بکلکی یوق عجب
کیم بیتاولورغایه قوپاش بیغاج بییک شوکله تیغ کیم باشیمغه یتکوردونک توقف قیلماغیل سونغان ایتماس بییک یرن
قولی بولغای ولنه دهر باغی نینک کلی اوتدور بییک شجاری دود بیلیکا پر اول کلنی و اوت سالغیل اشجار یغه هم
مؤلف حبیبی بیت را در این شعر بتیک بتای قرشت خوانده و بمعنی ویده نوشته سهو کرده است کتاب التا باب المفتوحات
حرف التا مع الباء الموحدة المشتقات تاپماق قغ پرستیدن و اینها خود از تاپوقات چنانکه در ذیل لعوامد مذکور خواهد شد و بالباء
عجمی یعنی یافتن تاپتوق پرستیدیم و یافتیم چنانکه بمعنی ثانی کوید شعر مدبری تاپتوق نولینی سلامت دین یراق کوید کیم
اولدی نوح و فیکلیغ جهانده شهرتی تاپار و تاپادور پرستد و می یابد و تاپار بمعنی فاعل و مصدر هم می آید تاپمادور
نمی پرستد و نپرستیده است و نمی یابد و نیافته است تاپقان و تاپلغان و تاپادورغان پرستنده و پرستیده و یابنده و یافته
و بمعنی مصدر هم می آید چنانکه بمعنی یافتن کوید الشاهد علی الاول شعر سبل نوایی که طلب بیله تاپلماس مقصودی لیک تاپقای
داعی بار ایلیکا البته طلب تاپ و تاپغیل مفرد مخاطب فعل امر تاپما و تاپماغیل مفرد مخاطب فعل نهی تاپنک و تاپینکیز
تاپنکلار جمع مخاطب فعل امر تاپمانک تاپمانکیز و تاپمانکلار جمع مخاطب فعل نهی تاپمان و تاپماس مین نمی پرستم و نمی یابم تاپایمن
تاپادورمین و تاپادورمن تاپا بام پیدا اسیکم تاپماس نمی پرستد و نمی یابد بمعنی فاعل و مصدر منفی هم می آید و یافتن و یافتنش
تاپماسلیغینه نپرستیدنت و نیافتنت تاپلمسلیغینه نپرستیدنت و نیافتنت تاپیب و تاپیبان و تاپمیش پرستیده و یافته تاپیدی
پرستید و یافت الشاهد علیه المعنی الثانی شعر نظر اهلیغه کردی خیلی کیلدی سر رهه سیل مدین اوق روشن سرمه ای
کوز تاپمیشانک نظامی قیل ایدی تاپا الغوسی تاپ بولغای توان پرستید و توان یافت تاپا الغای تواند پرستید و تواند
یافت تاپا تاپا پرستش کنان و پیدا کنان تاپای و تاپایین بپرستم و بپرستد و بپرستی و پرستیده و بیابم و بیابد و بیابی
و یافته تاپمای و تاپمایین صیغه نفی چنانکه شاهد بر اولرا بمعنی نیافته و نیابد در صیغه سیاره در داستان مسافر اقلیم هفتم کوید
شعر خواجه سلیمان کمستا یرهم ایسانغ تاپمای لو عقو حادور موبا او یقانغ معنی شهرتیت که خواجه عبید اند کرست تاهشنا
و نیابد که در خوابت یا سیدله و مؤلف حبیبی تاپمای را تاپمای بانون خوانده و بمعنی عید لاند نوشته و شعر نیز براش شاهد آورده
سهو کرده است تاپساق و تاپساپزو تاپساغای یزو تاپلی و تاپالینک بپرستیم و بیابیم چنانکه شاهد بر اول بمعنی ثانی در خسرو شیرین
در رسیدن فرهاد بکوه ارمن کوید شعر بونیکلیغ بیله عمر نوح تاپساق بدن کوپ راک اندین موح تاپساق تاپیلی برای
و تا پرستیده و برای یافتن و تا یافته تاپغاج چون پرستید و چون پرستد چون یافت و بیابد تاپقوچی پرستنده و یابنده تاپقوچه
تاپقوچه و تاپغانچه تا پرستش کردن و بقدر پرستیدن تا یافتن و بقدر یافتن چنانکه شاهد بر ثانی را بمعنی یافتن کوید
شعر استادام ای خضر کیلکا یمن قیلیب جان بیله طوف کعبه کوی ین خبر تاپغونچه بارغا نیملیز ایل تاپا آلغاینکچه بقدر که
تواند پرستید و تواند یافت تاپغوسیزدور خواهیم پرستید خواهیم یافت تاپغونکیزدور خواهید پرستید و خواهید یافت
تاپغوسیلاردور خواهند پرستید خواهند یافت تاپماغونکیزدور نخواهید پرستید نخواهید یافت چنانکه در صیغه

سیاره در داستان مسافر اقلیم اول کوید الشاهد علی الثانی بالمعنی الثانی شعر کیم تیلاب موندا تاپغونکوزیوقتوردی تاپشورمین
و طریق اوقتورمن تاپا آلماغونکیزدور و تاپا آلغونکیزیوق پرستیدن ممکن نخواهد بود تاپقولوق پرستیدنی و یافتنی چنانکه
در تاریخ الانبیا در ذکر قوم حضرت موسی علیه السلام صنعت کاو کوید که پراوی کیم اولرتاپیشلیغ هرزکی تاریخ بولغای تاپقولوق
بولدیلار تاپیناغ تاپاو و تاپناو و تاپسون و تاپید ملت بپرستد و بیابد الشاهد علی الناس بالمعنی الثانی شعر منجه
جانیمغه ای یناق تامیز پر قطره می کیم اوزین تاپید کونکول خط الدنیا خانماسین تاپغولیک و تاپاردیک پرستیدنی و
چنانکه پرستد و یافتنی چنانکه بیابد و شاهد بر اولرا بمعنی یافتنی در تاریخ الانبیا کوید که چون بنی اسرائیل بونوبتیه ستلک
الآر تاپقودیک بار نماید و تابینماق قغ مع النون خم شدن برای نیاز و پرستش کردن و ساجد شدن تابینور و تابینادور
ساجد میشود چنانکه در مقاله هفدهم از حیرت الابرار کوید الشاهد علی الاول شعر جان نچوک بولغای آنینک تاشیغه کیم
تابینور حق بیله بت قاشیغه و تابینور بمعنی مصدر هم می آید و باقی صیغ بر این سیاق قیاس شود و از این اشتقاق می یابد تاپیلماق
مع الکاف با بای عجمی یعنی یافته شدن تاپیلغوسیدیک و تاپیلوردیک یافته شدنی و چنانکه یافته شود الشاهد علی الاول بالمعنی
الاول شعر ایلیمغه دشتی مجنون کونکول آواره دور کیم پری لار ایستاکان بیرله تاپیلغوسیدیک ایماس و باقی صیغ بر این سیاق تالام
اشتقاق می یابد تاپشماق قغ بکسر بای عجمی و سکون شین مصدر مفاعلات یعنی همدیکررا یافتن تاپیشور و تاپیشادور همدیکر را می یابند
و تاپیشور بمعنی مصدر هم می آید چنانکه شاهد آن در ذیل لغت تاپغونکوزیوقتور نکاشته یافت و صیغ آن بر این سیاق تاپشتین
اشتقاق می یابد تاپشورماق قغ بسکون بای عجمی و راء مهمله و ضم شین سپردن چنانکه کوید شعر لبینک هجرا غاکی تن ار کونکلو
حبس ایتیم بیرک کیم جان نیز الیغ ریسم دور توبر لغنه تاپشوردوق تاپشوردوق سپردیم تاپشورور و تاپشورادور می سپارد
و تاپشورور بمعنی فاعل و مصدر هم می آید تاپشورماس و نسپارد و نسپرده است تاپشورغان و تاپشورمایدور و تاپشورغانلار سپرنده
و سپرده و بمعنی مصدر هم می آید تاپشور و تاپشورغیل مفرد مخاطب فعل امر تاپشورما و تاپشورماغیل مفرد مخاطب فعل نهی
تاپشورونک و تاپشورونکیز و تاپشورونکلار جمع مخاطب فعل امر تاپشورمانک و تاپشورمانکیز و تاپشورمانکلار جمع مخاطب فعل نهی
تاپشورمان و تاپشورماس مین نمی سپارم تاپشورامین و تاپشورادورمین و تاپشورادورمن می سپارم تاپشورماس نمی سپارد
و بمعنی فاعل و مصدر منفی هم می آید تاپشورماسلیغینه نسپردنت و تاپشورمسلیغینه نسپردنت تاپشوریب و تاپشوریبان و تاپشورمیش
سپرده تاپشوردی سپرد تاپشورا الغوسی بولغای تواند سپرد تاپشورا آلغای تواند سپرد تاپشورا تاپشورا
سپرده سپرده تاپشورای و تاپشورایین بسپارم بسپارد و بسپاری و سپرده تاپشورساق و تاپشورسابزو تاپشورغایبزو تاپشورای
تاپشورالینک بسپاریم تاپشورغالی برای سپردن و تا سپرده تاپشورغاج چون سپرد و بسپارد تاپشورغوچی سپارنده
تاپشورغوچه و تاپشورغونچه تا سپردن و بقدر سپردن تاپشورا آلغاینکچه بقدر که تواند سپرد تاپشورغوسیزدور خواهیم سپرد
تاپشورغونکیزدور خواهید سپرد تاپشورغوسیلاردور خواهند سپرد تاپشوراغوم تاپشوراغوم یوق نخواهم سپرد تاپشورالماغونکیزدور
تاپشورا آلغوم یوق سپردن ممکن نخواهد بود تاپشورغولوق سپردنی و چنانکه بسپارد تاپتورماق قغ مصدر انفعال یعنی
سپرده شدن و صیغ آن بالالام اشتقاق می یابد تپه لاماق قغ بفتح تای عجمی و لام تیره کردن بپای برو فرو زدن و بمجاز بمعنی کشتن و هلاک
کردن باشد من الجواهر تابان بر وزن داماان باشته یا بود که آنرا بعربی حصب کویند و بفارسی بمعنی درخشان و نورانی باشد
چنانکه بمعنی کهید شعر اول سبیین تیره دور کونکلوم اوبی هجرانی دین کیم ایماس تابان کوزوم شمعی آنینک تابانی دین

151v.

تاپقو بمعنی طعن و سرزنش بود و آنرا دابقو نیز باشد تابقور سه معنی دارد اول بمعنی فوج و گروه باشد و آنرا دابقور هم
گویند و در عثمانیه بتخفیف تابور خوانند دویم تحمیل و تکلیف زاید بر خراج را خوانند و آنرا تاپقور باضم هم نویسند سیم چرخ روپ
کتل کش بود و آن چرمیست که از میان زین کشیده می شود تابو سغراتی باصطلاح عثمانیه کنایه از پیاله باشد که در بزم شراب
بجهت یکدیگر نوشند و تابو مخفف تابوغ باشد تابوغ و تابوق بمعنی سجده و پرستش باشد و بالمجاز بمعنی استعمال شود که
بجهت تعظیم را خوانند که در ترکستان و دولت خوانین مغول معهود و مستمر است و آن چنان باشد که شخصی در برابر پادشاهان
سر برهنه کرده خم شود و دست بر سر و پیشانی گذارد چنانکه الشاهد علیه شعر قول الولدی نانگلاچیدا داغ کوپکو ... چنان
وفات برسیدا بسکیم نوایی ایتی تابوق ولة زخمیغه یرکهنا توهین حیقسا اول بوسکیم مانگلاحی ... باز ... ایلیب
ایلاریمین تابوق دیم بمعنی خدمت و بندگی بود چنانکه در نامه نوشتن شیرین بفرهاد گوید شعر وحوش ایرمیش شینک
آلینکا خادم سناء ایرمیش تابوغونکا ملازم و نیز در مکتوب بهم از منشات گوید که التماس قیلیلور کیم اول پریشان ابتاغه
کیم تابوغه تاپشورولدی تامل حقارتیغه باقماغای ملاحظه قیلیلماغای تابوغساق بفتح سین مهمله بالف کشیده تابوجی
تابوجی بکسر جیم عجمی بمعنی پرستش کننده و خدمتکار بود تابین بر وزن کابین باصطلاح مغول چون جماعتی بجهل رسند
آنرا ملک تابین گویند و باصطلاح اتراک توران جمعی را نامند که در تاخت و کیسه شریک باشند و نیز از رستاخیز پرستش و نیاز و تسلیم
کردن و با بمعنی اخوذ از تابیناق است چنانکه مذکور شد تبسی بسکون با و کسر سین مهمله تبرکه روی سینی کوچک بود
که آنرا مجمعه گویند تپل با بای عجمی بوزن اجل و تپل اسیغ اسب سارپ پیشانی را خوانند تپنکو بفتح بای عجمی
و سکون نون و ضم کاف عجمی دامنه زین را گویند الشاهد علیه شعر تالدی همینک دین آی بوزیدا ای جالت نشان کوبا
جولان کونه آی تپنکوا پلا عنیت وله شهسوار یرنینک ایا فین و بکا ... آی ایله کون هر بیری بیر تپنکو لوریند
در رتبه آنرا دینکو نامند و با بای ابجد بفارسی تخته صندوق مصر و زنبیل و سبد و کیسه حجام و عطار را خوانند مع التاء المثناة
تاماق و چیدن تانتوق چشیدیم تاتار و تاتادود بچشد و تاتار بمعنی فاعل و مصدر هم می آید و نام طایفه هم
که منسوب بتاتار خانند چنانکه در ذیل جوامد بیان شود تاتایدور بچشد و بچشیده است تاتقان و تاتاغان و تاتقان
چشنده و چشیده و بمعنی مصدر هم می آید تات فتاتغیل مفرد مخاطب از فعل امر تات سه معنی دارد هم چنانکه در ذیل
مذکور خواهد شد تاتاتما و تاتاتعیل مفرد مخاطب از فعل نهی تاتینک و تاتینکیز و تاتینکلار جمع مخاطب از فعل امر تاتمانک
تاتماینکیز و تاتماینکلار جمع مخاطب از فعل نهی تاتار تاتارمین بچشم تاتامین و تاتاسین و تاتادور تاتارم بچشم تاتاماس
نچشد و بمعنی فاعل و مصدر منفی هم می آید تاتماسینکه نچشیدن تو تاتاریکه بچشیدنت تاتیب و تاتیبان و تاتمیش
چشیده تاتمیشانک چشیده تاتنا توقتا و تاتیب بولغای تواند چشید تاتا الغای تواند چشید تاتا تاتا چشان
چشان تاتای و تاتاین بچشم و بچشد بچشی چشید الشاهد علی الاول المعنی الاول شعرای نوایی شربت لعلی
ایرور جان بخش لیک شعفدین اولسام نه حیم دیکامین آنی تاتای تاتای و تاتاین بچشم و بچشد و بچشی بچشید الشاهد علی
الاول بالمعنی الاخیر شعر خواجه حسنی ایچرو سبزی خطسیز و تون لبی سینی آکه اول نعیم و نعمه دین تاتای تونیز تاتساق
تاتغانی تاتماغانا تالینک بچشیم تاتقالی برای چشیدن و تاچشیدن تاتغاج چون چشید و بچشید تاتغوجی چشنده تاتغوچه
تاتغوچه تاتقانچه تا چشیدن و بقدر چشیدن تاتا الماینچه بقدریکه نتواند چشید تاتغوسی دور خواهیم چشید تاتغو کور دور

قاق

152r.

خواهید چشید تاتغوسیلار دور خواهند چشید تاتماغوم و تاتغوم یوق نخواهم چشید تاتا الماغوم و تاتا آلغوم یوق
چشیدن ممکن نخواهد بود تاتغولوق چشیدنی تاتغالی تاتسا و تاتسا تونده تاتمادیک بچشد تاتغودیک و تاتاردیک چشید
و همچنانکه بچشد تاتوزماق بضم تا و سکون زای مهمله مصدر متعدیست یعنی چشانیدن تاتوزماس بمچشاند چنانکه
در حیرت الابرار در ذم اسراف گوید شعر مشتهی ایل بوزا ... لقمه تاتوزماس ... و باقی ... براز سیاق
اشتقاق می یابد من الجوامد تات به معنی آمده اول بمعنی مزه و لذت و طعم بود دویم زنگ تاجیک را گویند چنانکه در حیرت
الابرار در وصف ظلم ظالم گوید شعر چه داغی ... آنیا سینی ... سیم محرف داد
بمعنی عدل باشد و داد کفتن کنایه است از فریادی که مظلوم در مقام دادخواهی و تظلم کند چنانکه در مقاله ... در حیرت الابرار
در حکایت شیر و دراج گوید شعر ... بیان دام آرا اول مبتلا ... تات ... تاریخ ... بهتر
ذکر دراج همین شعر بهمین کیفیت مذکور است و آنرا داد هم گویند چنانکه در ذیل ... نیز بهمین معنی مستعملست و نیز ارستان خسرو
چنانکه در ذیل تاتماق گذشت تاتار نام پسر الینجه خان بن کیوک خانست و کیفیت احوال آنست که الینجه خان را دو پسر آمد
شکر یکی را تاتار نام کردند و دیگری را مغول و چون الینجه خان بمرتبه شیخوخیت رسید و پسران بزرگ شدند نصف مملکت
بتاتار خان و نصف دیگر را بمغول خان داد و از طبقه تاتاریه هشت نفر سلطنت کردند و آخرین ایشان سونج خانست که پادشاه
آن طبقه بود منتهی شد و فرقه کرجال تاتار نامیده میشوند منسوب بتاتار خانند و از طبقه مغول در ذیل لغت مغول مذکور
خواهد شد و بمعنی بچشد چنانکه نگارش یافت تاتلیغ یعنی با مزه و در عثمانیه آنرا محرف ساخته تاتلو گویند و بمعنی شیرین
و سفلات استعمال نمایند تیتلک بکسر تای ثانی و سکون کاف مرضی را گویند که در حالت بیماری از شدت مرض هزل و شوخی کرده
سخنان بیکنه باشد چنانکه گوید شعر ... کوز ونکا شوخلوق آیین ایرور ... ایله کیم بیمار الار ... بولور بمعنی سبک و نکبه
تابین نیز منسوبات مولف وی بمعنی حب و خیالات وکار ... نوشته و طالع هروی بمعنی صحیح ... کرده و شعر بر ... است آورده سهو کرده مع الجیم تاجاماک بفتح جیم و سکون نون اباء و خودداری کردن و فراغی این لفظ را سهوا تاجاماق با بای حطی
و در باب یای مفتوحه ذکر کرده تاجاندیم اباکردم تاجاماندیم ابانکردم الشاهد علیه شعر مغ ... تبلاکی عجانی
مزه که دیدیلار ... تاجاماندیم تاجاندوق اباکردیم تاجانور و تاجاناددور ابامیکند و تاجانور بمعنی فاعل و مصدر هم می آید تاجان
تاجاماینادور ابامیکند و نکرده است تاجاغان تاجاغان و تاجانادور ... اباکننده و اباکرده و بمعنی مصدر هم می آید تاجان
تاجانغیل مفرد مخاطب از فعل امر تاجاما و تاجاماغیل مفرد مخاطب از فعل نهی الشاهد علی الاول شعر ... تونکیاسین ...
تاجاماکیم سینکا ایش ... نوناق ولیکن ... تاجانینک و تاجانینکیز و تاجانینکلار جمع مخاطب از فعل امر
تاجامانک و تاجاماینکیز و تاجاماینکلار جمع مخاطب از فعل نهی تاجامان و تاجاماس مین ابا میکنم تاجامین و تاجاسین و تاجادور تاجاناس
ابا میکنم تاجاماس ابا میکند و بمعنی فاعل و مصدر منفی هم می آید تاجاماسینکه ابا نکردنت تاجانوریکه باناکردنت تاجاب و
تاجیبان و تاجامیش اباکرده تاجامیشانک اباکرده تاجانا بولغای و تاجاب بولغای با تواند کرد تاجانا الغای ابا تواند کرد تاجانا
تاجاتا اباکنان اباکنان تاجاناى و تاجاناین اباکنم و کند و کنی و کرده تاجاسا و تاجاغانیز و تاجاغانای و تاجاتای و تاجاتا
اباسیم تاجاغالی برای اباکردن و تا اباکرده تاجاغاج چون اباکرد و کند تاجاغوجی اباکننده تاجاغوچه و تاجاغو
تاجاغانچه تا اباکردن و بقدر اباکردن تاجانا الغاینچه بقدریکه ابا نتوانی کرد تاجاغوسی دور ابا خواهیم کرد تاجاغوکور دور

قاج

152v. تاخ × تار ×

الماخواهید کرد تاجانغوسیلاردورا بالماخواهند کرد تاجاماغوم تاجانغوم یوق المانخواهم کرد تاجاماماآلماغوم تاجاماآلغوم تا
کردن ممکن نخواهد بود تاجانغولوق اباکردن تاجانناي تلجاماقتا جانسلاقتا جانسون تلجاندیك اباکند تاجانغودیك
تاجانغودیك اباکردن وهمچنانکه اباکند مع الخا تاخوق وتخاقوی ملفت مقولت مرغ باشد که آنرا بعربی دجاجه گویند
ونیز نام شالبیت از شالهای ترکی تاخوق غلاف سدقد ترکتراکوینید مع الرامن المشتقات تاراماق تخمرزمانی افکند
شانه کردن تارادوق شانه کردیم تارارو تارایدور شانه میکند وتارامعنی فاعل ومصدرهم می آید چنانکه بمعنی مصدر آمده
شعر تارادر احتدی لیغ نرلفین مسلسل ایلادی حین لاد کرمیم ایکنر لفی ایکی لام اینك تارلغ سین لارینا تارالماماایدور شانه میکند
وتکرده است تارامان وتاراماغان تارایدورغان شانه کنند وشانه کرده وبمعنی مصدرهم می آید چنانکه لطفی گوید شاهد
علی الاول شعر سنبلونکنی تاراغاندا گل اوزه تانکلا عرق کیم بولوتلوغ کیچه سینك البته بولماس شبنمی تارا وتاراغیل
مفرد مخاطب الفعل الامر شاهد علی الاول شعر کرکونکول لا نری جلادی وطن ایستابر بولسانك بیش توکونکلا نرفی زلفونکنی
تارای قرا کونرنی تاراناقتا ولفاغیل مفرد مخاطب الفعل الامر تارانك وتارانکیز وتارانکلار جمع مخاطب الفعل الامر تارانالغ وتارالمانکیز تا
جمع مخاطب الفعل الامر ~~تارانکیز تارانالکلار جمع مخاطب الفعل الامر~~ تارامان وتارالماس مین شانه نمیکنم تارای مین وتاراد
تارایدورمین وتارارام شانه نمیکند وبمعنی فاعل ومصدرهم می آید تاراماسینکه بشانه نکردنت تارانکیه بشانه کرد
تالمب وتارابان وتارامیش شانه کرده تارامیشانك شانه کرده تاراشاتولغای تاراب بولغانه شانه تواند کرد تارالغای شانه
تواند کرد تاراپوعتا رای تارای شانه کنان تارای وتارایین شانه کنم وکنید وکهی وکرده تاراسا قدتاراغایز وتارا
غایز وتاراگای شانه کنیم تاراغلی برای شانه کردن وتماشانه کرده تاراغاج چون شانه کرد وکند تاراغوچی شانه
کننده تاراغوچه تاراغونجه تاراغانچه تا شانه کردن وتعقیب شانه کردن تارای آلغانینجه بتقدیریکه شانه توانی کرد تاراغوسیر
شانه خواهیم کرد تاراغوچرده شانه خواهید کرد تاراغوسیلاردور شانه خواهند کرد تاراغوم تاراغیم یوق شانه نخواهم کرد
تارالماغوم وتارا آلغوم یوق شانه کردن ممکن نخواهد بود تاراغولوق شانه کردن تارلغای تاراسلوقتا راسون تارادیك
شانه کند چنانکه شاهد بر شانه در لسان الطیر در حکایت شیخ ابوالعباس قصاب گوید شعر کیم هرخوش یاسی مرخنده ماك
کیم ماجان پر بزکش اوغلی هم سقال کیم آنی سیل لار چیکیب یوب تاراغای بونرنان پرمو بجا دیشکا یانرلغای تاراغوسیدیك تارات
شانه کردن وهمچنانکه شانه کند تاراتماق مع التاء مصدر متعدیست یعنی شانه کنانیدن وصیغ آن بدستور مانای قرشت اشتقاق
می یابد تارالماق مع اللام یعنی شانه شدن وصیغ آن بالام اشتقاق می یابد تاریماق بکسر الجیم افشاندن تاریدون
تخم افشاندیم تاریسو تاریدور می افشاند چنانکه در لسان الطیر در کالمه هدهد بامرغان گوید الشاهد علی الاول شعر
فسق تخمین نفس ایله اولکیم تاریش سوال ایرغوسیدیك کیم اودوی آرین وتاریر بمعنی فاعل ومصدرهم می آید تاریماید ور نمی افشاند
تلریغان قتاریغان وتاریدورغان افشانده وبیفشاند وبمعنی مصدرهم می آید تاری وتاریغیل مفرد مخاطب الفعل الامر تاریغا
تاریغیل مفرد مخاطب الفعل الامر تاریك وتاریکیز وتاریکلار جمع مخاطب الفعل الامر تاریمانك وتاریمانکیز تاریمانکلار جمع مخاطب
الفعل الامر تاریمان وتاریماس مین نمی افشانم تاریمیم تاریر مین وتاریدورمین وتاریسام نمی افشانم تاریماس نمی افشاند وبمعنی
فاعل ومصدر منفی هم می آید تاریماسینکه بیفشاندنت تاریمیکه بافشاندنت تاریب وتاریبان وتاریمیش افشانده
علی الاول شعر کوینی قیلدی نوائی جوشیاده تخم مهر نکلی بوموزرعه تاریب وتاریمیش بمعنی پی وعقب هم بود چنانکه در...

153r

جوابد مذکور خواهد شد تاریمیشانك افشانده تاریقیابولغاو تاریب بولغای تواند افشاند تاریغای آلغای تواند افشاند
تاری تاری افشان افشان تاریغا تاریغین بیفشانم وبیفشاند وبیفشانی وافشاند چنانکه شاهد بر اقل مذکور شاید
گوید شعر اول شوخ یوز واشیکنکا با قماس نوایا غم غنچه زعفران یوز ونکا اغوان تاریغای تاریغلی وتاریغالی
وتاریغاچ تاریغینک بیفشانیم تاریغلی برای افشاندن وتا افشانده تاریغاج چون افشاند وبیفشاند تاریغوچی افشاننده
تاریغوچه تاریغونجه تاریغانچه تا افشاندن وتعقیب افشاندن تاری آلغانینجه بتقدیریکه تواند افشاند تاریغوسیدور خواهم
افشاند تاریغونکزدور خواهید افشاند تاریغوسیلاردور خواهند افشاند تاریغاغوم وتاریغوم یوق نخواهم افشاند
تاریالماغوم وتاری آلغوم یوق افشاندن ممکن نخواهد بود تاریغولوق افشاندنی تاریغای وتاریغلتا تاریسون وتاریدیك
تاریغودیك وتاریدیك لیفشانند وهمچنانکه بیفشاند
بیفشاند تاریماتاقغ مع التاء مصدر متعدیست یعنی افشاناندن وصیغ آن بر منهج تا نامی قرشت اشتقاق می یابد تاریلماق
مع اللام یعنی افشانده شدن تخم وبذر تاریلغاغ وتاریلغان تاریلسا وتاریلسون وتاریلدیك افشانده شود چنانکه شاهد بر...
به سمجناس گوید شعر تاابشیم توشتی بر آغزی تاراماله کونکلومی ساری شاچی بر تارا یلة کوزتو تاصین کیم کونونوم
دین کونکلیدا تخم محبت تاریلیة وصیغ آن بر این سیاق بالام اشتقاق می یابد تاریقماق بکسر اول وسکون ظاف دلتنك شدن
الشاهد علیه شعر اولتور وبیل تخم دینا اول شوخ حیقاق غلایدی شرخوش اطلا واهل مجلس دین تاریقماق خلابیدی و
رعیته دار یلیاق گویند تاریقتوق دلتنك شدیم تاریقور وتاریقادور دلتنك میشود وتاریقور بمعنی فاعل ومصدرهم
می آید تاریقمایدور دلتنك نمیشود وشده است تاریقغان وتاریقوغان وتاریقادورغان دلتنك شونده ودلتنك شده
مصدرهم می آید تاریقماغان قتاریقمایدورغان دلتنك نشونده ودلتنك نشده چنانکه شاهد بر اقل اطلغ بمعنی دلتنگی در لسان الطیر
گوید شعر مین قوشیده مین چمن دین چیقماغان دشت ووادی سیریدا تاریقماغان وبمعنی مصدر منفی هم می آید تاریق
تاریقغیل مفرد مخاطب الفعل الامر تاریقما وتاریقماغیل مفرد مخاطب الفعل الامر الشاهد علی الاول شعر کوب تاریقما ای کونکول
اول شوخ هجرانی اراشایدلو شبوادیشه اوقا ییدی لیکن جبوده تم تاریقینك قتاریقینکیز وتاریقینکلار جمع مخاطب الفعل الامر تاریقمانك
تاریقمانکیز وتاریقمانکلار جمع مخاطب الفعل الامر الشاهد علی الاول شعر نوائی تاریقسا تاریقمان خوبلار تاریقما الحکیم من غالفویی ونری وبی
فغان زلزلی آینینك تاریقمان وتاریقماسمین دلتنك نمیشوم تاریقامین وتاریقورمین وتاریقادورمین وتاریقورام دلتنك میشوم
تاریقماس دلتنك نمیشود وبمعنی فاعل ومصدر منفی هم می آید تاریقماسینکه بدلتنك نشدنت تاریقوتکنه بدلتنك شدنت
تاریقیب تاریقیبان وتاریقمیش دلتنك شده الشاهد علی الاول شعر دوستلار بوکیچه واقف بولونکوزکیم چیقلادی
آتینزین شیفته جانیم تن ایدی دین تاریقیب تاریقیشانك دلتنك شده تاریقیب بولغاو تاریقیب بولغانه دلتنك تواند شد
تاریقا آلغای دلتنك تواند شد تاریقا تاریقا دلتنك شوان تاریقای تاریقایین دلتنك شوم وشود وشوی وشده
تاریقیناق وتاریقغایز وتاریقغلی وتاریقغالینك دلتنك شویم تاریقغلی برای دلتنك شدن وتا دلتنك شده
تاریقغاج چون دلتنك شد وشود تاریقغوچی دلتنك شونده تاریقغوچه قتاریقغونجه وتاریقغانچه تا دلتنك شدن وبعد
دلتنك شدن تاریقا آلغانینجه بتقدیریکه دلتنك توانی شد ~~تاریقا آلغانینجه بتقدیریکه دلتنك توانی شد~~ تاریقغوسیدور
دلتنك خواهم شد تاریقغونکزدور دلتنك خواهید شد تاریقغوسیلاردور دلتنك خواهند شد تاریقماغوم قتاریقغوم یوق
دلتنك نخواهم شد تاریقا آلماغوم وتاریقا آلغوم یوق دلتنك شدن ممکن نخواهد بود تاریقغولوق دلتنك شدنی تاریقغا
153r

و تاریقلو تاریقسا و تاریقسغو تلیرقلیق دلتنک شونده تاریقمویلیک و تاریقمودیک دلتنک شدنی و همچنانکه دلتنک شولی
مصدر متعدی است بمعنی تنگ کردن و صیغ آن برین سیاق با لفظ نور اشتقاق می یابد تارتماق بسکون را و تای قرشت یعنی
کشیدن و مطلق به لفظ کشیدن و قسم بر هم تنگ کشیدن و ترازو کشیدن و صورت کشیدن و باز کشیدن و نفس کشیدن و امثال
آن و در ترکی علاوه آنها بمعنی اختلاج چشم هم استعمال میشود و مؤلف رومی تارتماق را بمعنی نوشیدن و نوشتن هم نوشته
و از برای نوشیدن مصرع اول این شعر سلطان حسین میرزا استشهاد جسته و هو هذا شعر ... تارتارمین اول
بد خوی بیننک کوییا تینکری یعنی ... و برای نوشتن از تاریخ الملوک ... الا کفاف
این فقره را شاهد آورده ... جمیع اقالیم و بلاد ... یاساب و در هر دو
سهو کرده زیرا که از آن مصرع میکشیدن مقصود شاعر است نه می نوشیدن و از فقره تاریخ نقش کشیدن منظور است
نه نقش نوشتن معهذا این فقره در وصف مانی نقاش که در زمان شاپور بوده یعنی مانی ... مثال عالم را کشیده
اقالیم بلاد را مشروح ساخت تارتوق کشیدیم تارتار و تارتادور میکشد و اختلاج میکند الشاهد علی الاول و ...
الاول شعر چون ... یکا کیر کونکلک عاقبت خالانی سود کرسپهر ... تارتار لانه بو قوت
رسیدن فرهاد بارمن گوید بالمعنی الثانی شعر ... سالور ... ایلکای تارتاد
بمعنی فاعل و مصدر هم می آید تارتماغدور میکشد و نکشیده است و اختلاج میکند و نکرده است تارتقان و تارتغان و تارتادور
کشنده و کشیده و بمعنی مصدر هم می آید تارتو با تقبیل مفرد مخاطب از فعل امر الشاهد علی الاول شعر ای نوائی کرتیلاسن
یار وصلین تاپماسین ... عالم دین ... و باری دین ... و شاهد بر ثانی ...
خواهد شد تارتما و تارتماغیل مفرد مخاطب از فعل نهی تارتینک و تارتینکیز و تارتینکلار جمع مخاطب از فعل امر الشاهد علی الثانی
... چون ... تارتینکیز ... تارتمانکلار جمع مخاطب
از فعل نهی تارتمان و تارتماس من میکشم تارتماسمن ... قاقاط دام میکشم تارتاسین و تارتارسین و تارتارسیز
میکشی چنانکه شاهد بر اول ... گوید شعر ... دین اول ... تارتاسین افغان
فریاد و شاهد بر ثانی ... فرهاد ... اوناخسرو فرماید شعر ... تارتادورسین ... اشقام
تارتادورسین تارتماس ... و بمعنی فاعل و مصدر نفی هم می آید تارتماسینکفه ... بکشیدنت تارتیب
تاپماق ... کشیده تارتمیشانک کشیده ... تارتیب ... آیا توان کشید تارتا آلغایمو آیا تواند
کشید الشاهد علیه ... تارتا آلغایمو ... تارتا تارتا کشان
کشان تارتای و تارتایین بکشم و بکشد و بکشی و کشیده الشاهد علی الاول بالمعنی الاول شعر یارب ...
تیغ تارتای ... الشاهد علی الثانی بالمعنی الاول شعر عاشق ... زماندین تارتای
اولکه آشوب ... تارتاینک ... بکشیم چنانکه ... فرهاد
الشاهد علی الرابع شعر ... تارتغالی برای کشیدن و تا کشیدن
تارتماج چون کشید و بکشد تارتغوچ کشنده تارتغوچی ... تارتغانچه تا کشیدن و معتمد کشیدن چنانکه ...
... الشاهد علی الثالث بالمعنی الثانی شعر ... تارتیب

آلیغه بات تارتا آلغاینکچه بمقدمه ... توانی کشید تارتغوسیدور ... خواهیم کشید تارتغونکزدور خواهید کشید تارتغوسیلاردور
خواهند کشید تارتماغوم تارتغوم یوق نخواهم کشید تارتا آلماغوم تارتا آلغوم یوق کشیدن نتوانم نخواهد بود تارتغولوق
کشیدنی تارتغای و تارتقای و تارتسا و تارتسون و تارتدیلار ... بکشد الشاهد علی الاول شعر ... تویغه
توشسام ... سوبلیه ... تارتغوسی ... کشیدنی و همچنانکه بکشد تارتاد
تیشماق مع الشین ... فاصله است یعنی ناهموار کشیدن و کشاکش کردن و صیغ آن ... تیشماق آول
باشین اشتقاق می یابد تارغاماق و تارغاشماق مع الشین ... تارغالماق مع اللام ... پراکنده شدن تارغادوق
تارغاشوق و تارغالدوق پراکنده شدیم تارقار و تارقایدور و تارغاشور و تارغاشادور و تارغالور و تارغالادور پراکنده میشود
الشاهد علی الخامس شعر ای نوائی ... سین ... منکا ... تارغالور تارغا
تارغاشور و تارغالور بمعنی فاعل و مصدر هم می آید ... تارغالماید ... پراکنده نمیشود ... تارغاماز
تارغاغان و تارغایدیغان و تارغاشقان ... تارغالغان و ... تارغالادورغان
پراکنده شونده و پراکنده شده و بمعنی مصدر هم می آید تارغا و تارغاغیل و تارغاش و تارغاشغیل و تارغال و تارغالغیل
مفرد مخاطب از فعل امر تارغاما و تارغاماغیل و تارغاشما و تارغاشماغیل و تارغالما و تارغالماغیل مفرد مخاطب از فعل نهی
تارغانک و تارغانکیز و تارغانکلار و تارغاشینک و تارغاشینکیز و تارغاشینکلار و تارغالینک و تارغالینکیز و تارغالینکلار
جمع مخاطب از فعل امر الشاهد علی الاول شعر ... تارغانک ... سیز ... همری
دین ... الشاهد علی الرابع شعر ... تارغاشینک ... تیشبسا ...
آهیم ... دین علم ... تارغامانک و تارغامانکیز و تارغامانکلار و تارغاشمانک و تارغاشمانکیز و تارغالمانک
تارغالمانکیز و تارغالمانکلار جمع مخاطب از فعل نهی تارغامان و تارغاماسمین و تارغاشمان و تارغاشماسمین و تارغالمان و تارغالماسمین
پراکنده نمیشوم تارغایمین و تارغارمین و تارغایدورمین ... تارغاشامین و تارغاشورمین و تارغاشادورمین و تارغالورمین
تارغالامین و تارغالورمین و تارغالادورمین و تارغالورام پراکنده میشوم تارغاماس و تارغاشماس و تارغالماس
پراکنده نمیشود و بمعنی فاعل و مصدر نفی هم می آید تارغاماسینکفه و تارغاشماسینکفه و تارغالماسینکفه پراکنده نشدنت تارغانکفه
تارغاشونکفه و تارغالونکفه پراکنده شدنت تارغاب و تارغابان و تارغاشیب و تارغاشیبان و تارغالیب
تارغالیبان و تارغالمیش پراکنده شده الشاهد علی الرابع شعر ... پریشان ... جمع اولوب
... تارغامیشانک و تارغاشمیشانک و تارغالمیشانک پراکنده شده تارغاب
تارغاب بولغای و تارغاشیب بولغای و تارغالیب بولغای ... پراکنده تواند شد تارغای آلغای و تارغا
تارغا آلغای پراکنده تواند شد تارغای و تارغای و تارغاشای و تارغالای ... پراکنده شو
تارغای و تارغایین و تارغاشای و تارغاشایین و تارغالای و تارغالایین پراکنده شوم و شود و شوی و شده تارغانا
تارغانا و تارغاغای و تارغالای و تارغالینک و تارغاشنا ... تارغاشغای و تارغاشالینک ... تاد
تارغانا ... تارغالغای ... تارغالا لینک پراکنده شوم ... تارغاشغالی ...
پراکنده شدن و تا پراکنده شدن تارغالج و تارغاشغاج و تارغالغاج چون پراکنده شد و شود چنانکه ...

154v

منازل اقلیم بصیم و بتخانه شکستن نزید کوید الشاهد علی الاول شعر وبیح یله شام اولی ایشیلک آچلیب ایل بر تتر ایشیکا
میل قیلیب . تارغالج باریغا ایل بر هر جیت اول ایشیکنی مقفل ایلاجبه بهت تارغاغوچی و تارغاشقوچی تارغالغوچی پراکنده
شونده تارغالغوچی و تارغاغوچی و تارغاشغوچی و تارغاشتغوچی و تارغالنغوچی و تارغالغاتغوچی پراکنده
شدن و بقلب پراکنده شدن تارغای الغای ایشنکیه و تارغاشا الغای ایشنکیه و تارغالا الغای ایشنکیه پراکنده توانی ساختن تارغاغوسی بودور و تارغاشقوسی
بیدور و تارغالغوسی بودور پراکنده خواهیم شد تارغاغوسی کزبدور و تارغاشقوسی کزبدور و تارغالغوسی کزبدور پراکنده خواهید شد تارغاغوسیلار بودور
تارغاشقوسیلار بودور و تارغالغوسیلار بودور پراکنده خواهند شد تارغاماغوم و تارغاغوم یوق و تارغاشماغوم و تارغاشقوم یوق و تارغالماغوم
تارغالغوم یوق پراکنده نخواهم شد تارغای الماغوم و تارغای الغوم یوق و تارغاشا الماغوم و تارغاشا الغوم یوق و تارغالا الماغوم
تارغالا الغوم یوق پراکنده شدن ممکن نخواهد بود تارغاغولوق و تارغاشقولوق و تارغالغولوق پراکنده شدنی تارغاغای
تارغاسا و تارغاسون و تارغادیلت و تارغاشغای و تارغاشا و تارغاشسا و تارغاشسون و تارغاشدیلت و تارغالغای و تارغا
غالا و تارغالسا و تارغالسون و تارغالدیلت پراکنده شود چنانچه شاهد بر اول است در منتخبات خان چون نزد سکندر
مرتباس نشانت کوید شعر اگر تارغاسا هر طرف لشکر رسول اولسا و خسرو و صف شکن و شاهد بر ثانی درخیابان المحبة ذکر
ابو المحسن طرزی کوید که هر کیشی طغا مدین اوز مرسینی الغای و هر یخطه سر پر لار به سیله بولغای لار و تارغاشقایلار تارغا
مودیلت و تارغادیلت و تارغاشقودیلت و تارغالغودیلت پراکنده شدنی و همچنانکه پراکنده شود تارغامتاق
مع التاء المصدریة متعدیت یعنی پراکنده کردن چنانکه مسک سکندری در کیسه کشودن اهل نجل کوید شعر آچلر ریحان یما
کا مچ تارغاتماقچی هر طرف آنکا اوزکا پر طمعا قچی تارغاتماسا و تارغاتماغیل منوچا المرسل الشاهد علی الثانی شعر صبا زلفین
آچیب تارغاتماغیل عجون کونکول لار نی شکسکن ایلاصیلار سیر ورک نجیاغان آندا تارغاتغالج چون پراکنده کردو کند
الشاهد علیه شعر نیم صبح خیلی سنبلی لعونکنی تارغاتغلج سوادی تونجر مشک سوره دین هرا ان غبار ایلتوز و تا قونیغ
برای نباق با تاتای قرشاق شبقاق می یابد من الجوامد تار عمنی تنگ و ضیق باشد چنانکه کوید شعر تنکری چیش لولپرییکر
انداق تار آغیز کیم کیشی بیلماس که آندا یوق و صیل المر آغیز و بفارسی هم و معنی دارد اول عمنی تیره و تاریک بود دقیم تار تناجی آچی
تاراغ تاراق بمعنی شانه بود که آنرا بعربی مشط خوانند الشاهد علیه شعر ماجرا ولغای زلفینک سود الاری تارغ
کونرونه جسیم تاراغ نیکلینی سار خچکاتیل تاراغلیغ و تاراقلیغ شانه دار خوانند تارانغو و تانکغو بسکون نون و کاف
عجمی و ضم غین معجمه بکوچ دختی است شبیه بسپیدار که در کنار رودخانها و انهار وید الشاهد علیه شعر تاستیننک تارانک
بلعو تارانک سرو رعنا و تارانغو را و آنرا بولغون هم کویند و بعربی طرفا و بفارسی کز نامند تاراولیت بسکون واو فتحها
و فتحلی تاتامین مطویقه از وجه استعمال شود بترکی رومی بمعنی تاروما ر ترت و برت ازاتیا عنه بمعنی تارومار بود چنانکه
در تاریخ نابری مذکور است که کیشی قراسینی ترت و برت قیلدی و بفارسی ترت و برت کویند تاتیش و تاتیشق بسکون راء کشتا
وشیدن قرشت یعنی کشاکش چنانکه شاهد بر اول در تاریخ نابری مذکور است که بوقیش بعنوع تلاشو تلاتیش بیله او تی تاتیغ
یعنی حشر که چنانکه ~~شاهد بر اول در تاریخ نابری مذکور است~~ در بسط سکندری کوید شعر تیبب هر طرفدین اولوس نه
لاریغ اوکوش تاتیغ و تحفه هر لاریغا ترچوق سیر شدن و دلیا شدن از علف بهاری ترجلت بترکی رومی برهنه و بیحار
چنانکه فضولی در محبات کوید با ملکه الرومیه شعر بیله سن محبوب و بوخ نظاره نکا غافلدن تابا واکر ترجلت سجوب

155r

ساد یوب بجلت سا النانک نقاب ترخان بروزن دهقان دو معنی دارد اول کسی را کویند که از جمیع تکالیف دیوانی معاف و مسلم
باشد طایفه مرصفا را زغنایم به بیت او امت به بری مقرر دارند و بدون رخصت بنار کاه پادشاه در آید و تا نه کنا ماقی ما فیه نشود
پرسش نمایند دویم نام طایفه است از اعاظم اولوس جغتای و وجه تسمیه آنست که وقتی که اولوک خان تموچین بسکون بیر خود
بکوتن چنکیز خان متمم کشته اراده کرد که سحرکاه بر سر او هجوم به اوران میان بر او دیکی از امور ت واقعه را ترخان نوش خود تنفس سرک
در انزمان دو کودک که از کله شبرآمده بودند این سخن را شنیده متوجه اردو چنکیز خان کشته او را از این خوا
مطلع ساختند و چنکیز خان آن دو کودک را که خبر قصد اولک خان آورده بودند تا نه بطن ترخان ساخت و طایفه ترخان که
در ولایت ماوراء النهر هستند از نسل ایشانند و بفارسی نیز دو معنی دارد اول سبزی است که آنرا بعربی طرخون کویند
دویم اسم ابو نصر فارابی بوده ترخیق ترس بروزن سر برد و معنی دارد اول بمعنی معکوس باشد دویم سرکین را کویند به تفاریق معنی
خوف و بیم بود تارقاجی بسکون راء و فتح غین معجمه و کسر جیم جامه متفرقه را کویند که از ولایتی کوچ داده بولایتی دیکر ساکن سازند
تارقامیشی متفرق و پراکنده شدن ترغون بلغت مغولی بمعنی فربه باشد ترکی بسکون راء و کسر کاف بترکی رومی بمعنی ترک
ترکی باجی قرات را کویند تارلا بسکون راء و فتح لام مزرعه را نامند ترلان جوارح پرنده معروف که آنرا اچاولغ نیز تارلیغ
شکی ترنا بسکون راء و کاف و فتح نون حنا و حنین باشد تاریغ ارزن را کویند الشاهد علیه شعر تاریغ کبی سوکو لور
بلنکام لبیغ پرله . تاریغ تاریغ که سیغیشتوردی الکونین تاریغ و در این شعر مصرع اول از لفظ تاریغ ارزن مقصود است
در مصرع ثانی دانه ارزن چنانکه از لفظ جاسم جنس مفهوم میشود و اکر کویند جو معنی دانه مراد میباشد فیز در خیابان
المحبة در ذکر خواجه مظفر احمد کوید که بر کون ایتو نایردی که پیمانه تاریغ دین بردانه شیخ ابو سعید ابو الخیر عهید و باقی تاجرانی
مین مین تاریمش بکسر طا و میم و سکون شین بمعنی عیب بود که آنرا اسینکر هم کویند و بفارسی نیز مانند صیر بیغوز ریمش کوید
چنانکه در ذیل تاریاق مذکور شد مع الرباستان بروزن ناز شمشیر کویند که سر شربعلت کجلی مونداشته باشد چنانکه
شعر مناسب ایما تاز باشیغه تاج تونا غه نو توغیغه نی احتیاج و نیز بمعنی کسان الطیر بطراخیام مرغان کوید شعر چون مسنز
اوزن حیقتی بهمن تازدین قالدی قوبی سار ق تاجور و بفارسی بمعنی اخش باشد و محبوب و بسیار هر بدلهم کویند و بمعنی مصله
بر آمده تازقرا نام مرغیست بمقدار که سر آن موی ندارد ترنه بفتح زا و نون بهارده بترکی رومی مضراب طنبور بود تازی
نوعیست از سک شکاری که بتازند که معروفست و بفارسی بمعنی عرب بمع التنین من الشفات تاشا تاق باصطلاح ترکانست
سوختن نفس باشد از خستکی دویدن تاسلاماق بسکون سین بترکی رومی چیزی بر و جود طبع بجز اسناد دادن تاسه لانماق
بفتح سین و لام و سکون نون بترکی رومی یعنی مضطرب شدن من الجوامد تاسکی بفتح سین بمعنی سیلی بود که آنرا بفارسی تپانچه
و بعربی لطمه کویند تسکیره بسکون سین و کسر کاف و راء مهمله بمعنی معکوس باشد چنانکه خواجه کلان در جواب بر باد
نوشته شعر الطاف ظرافت و لطافت قیلادین نتیجه فرد ایمز تومان نزاکت قیلادین کرهند وایشی تسکیره ایکان نو جوش
ایسیغ بردین منافع طرافت قیلادین و تیسکاری بفتح تا و فتح کاف نیز مستعملست تاسلاق بترکی رومی بضم تا مطبوع را کویند
تسمه چرم خام و دوال چرمی را کویند الشاهد علیه شعر تولوبدا انبدا جنون تسمه سیز منکر لینکای پریوشی که میینب و قولغه
آنسا جیلا جوه و آنرا تامیش هم کویند و موق لغات فرهنک جهانکیری و برهان قاطع از لفظ ایران یزد کر کرده اند مع التین المنشفا
تاشماق بسکون شین طغیان کردن آب و امثال آن و سرشار و افزون شدن تاشتی طغیان کرد چنانکه کوید شعر تفوقو

تاز
تاس
ج
تاش

کولك یوزیکا کلکون ایناس کیم فراقینکا بن نوایقا تاشتی ناشتوق طغیان کردیم تاشا وتاشا دور طغیان میکند وتاشار
معنی فاعل ومصدر هم می آید تاشما یدور طغیان نمیکند ونکرده است تاشغان وتاشار غان وتاشادور غان طغیان کننده وطغیان کرده
وبمعنی مصدر هم می آیند تاشی وتاشغیل مفرد مخاطب از فعل امر وتاشر امثال غایب هست که در ذیل جواهر مذکور خواهد شد
تاشماو تاشماغیل مفرد مخاطب از فعل نهی تاشینك وتاشینکز وتاشینکلار جمع مخاطب از فعل امر نقل کردن هم باشد چنانچه
در ذیل تاشیماق مذکور شود تاشمانك وتاشمانکز وتاشمانکلار جمع مخاطب از فعل نهی تاشمان وتاشماس مین طغیان نمیکنم تاشامین
تاشار مین تاشادورمین تاشارام طغیان میکنم تاشماس طغیان نمیکند وبمعنی فاعل ومصدر منفی هم می آید تاشماسینکه بطغیان
نکردنت تاشارینکه بطغیان کردنت تاشیب تاشیبان وتاشمیش طغیان کرده الشاهد علی الاول فلك نینك پرده سی دین
بو کیم تیلدی شفق کلکونات مکر کیم یوزی دین کوزیاشیم خونابی تاشیب تورور وینز مقاله اول از حیرت الابرار کوید شعر ذاتنغه دریا
قدم چون تاشیب بیریان از لب آن ابدین آشیب ذکر فی التمجید من لیلی مجنون شعر هم اوشبو او توم تاشیب جهاندین هم
آشیب آسماندین وتاشیب وتاشیبان بمعنی حمل ونقل کرده نیز آمده ودر این معنی ما خوذ از مصدر تاشماق است چنانچه مذکور شود تاشیما
طغیان کرده تاشا بولغای وتاشیب بولغای طغیان توانکرد وتاشیب بولغای بمعنی حمل ونقل توان کرد هم باشد تاشا الغای
طغیان تواند کرد تاشا تاشا طغیان کنان تاشای وتاشایین طغیان کنم وکند وکنی وکرده تاشناق وتاشغاق
تاشغای بز وتاشاوتاشالینك طغیان کنیم تاشغالی برای طغیان کردن وتا طغیان کرده تاشغاج چون طغیان کرد وکند تاشغوچی
طغیان کننده تاشغوچی وتاشغوچه وتاشغانچه تا طغیان کردن وبقدر طغیان کردن الشاهد علی الثانی بالمعنی الاول شعر قدحه
باده ترکیبی نه فرق تاشغونچه ای ساقی که غم زهریغه جامیم تولوب تورور بلکه تاشیب تورور وطالع هروی برای لفظ تاشغونچه تاشغو
مصدر قرار داده وشعر زبور را شاهد آورده تاشغوماق لفظ اختراعی وبمعنی لب هر کاه تاشغوماق بمعنی سیداشت ومصدریست
از صیغه بایست تاشغونچه مذکور شود تاشا آلغاینکچه بقدریکه طغیان تواند کرد تاشغومیز دور طغیان خواهیم کرد
تاشغونکوز دور طغیان خواهید کرد تاشغوسیلار دور طغیان خواهند کرد تاشاغوم وتاشغوم بوق طغیان نخواهم کرد تاشا آلماغوم
تاشا آلغوم یوق طغیان نکردن ممکن نخواهد بود تاشغولوق طغیان کردن تاشمای وتاشا وتاشاسلیك تاشغون وتاشلیق طغیان کند
تاشغود بلیك وتاشلدیلیك طغیان کردن وهمچنانکه طغیان زکند تاشیماق بکسر شین نقل کردن از جائی بجائی تاشید
نقل کرد تاشیدوق نقل کردیم تاشیر وتاشید ونقل میکند وتاشیر بمعنی فاعل ومصدر هم می آید چنانچه بمعنی نقل کردن
در قره هاد وشیرین در وصف قصر فرهاد چنین کوید شعر تاشیر غه تاش وخشت وبیل ارابه توتوب چین ایجرا آباد وخرابه
ونیز در لیلی مجنون در ذکر حالات مجنون کوید شعر که شغلی کیناك تاشیرغه تبعیل یا سنا رایدی اول کینالدیله سیل ودر لسان
الطیر در حکایت خر سلطان کوید شعر بو کلا بان ایکی کاپ بدلانه بولك بولك تاشیردین تللالاین ایکیند اتولك تاشیرلار ایدی
نقل میکردند چنانچه در فرهاد وشیرین در خارا تراشی فرهاد کوید شعر بو رونوایکی ویز خاراکز بهت تاشیرلار ایدی سنکان خلق
تاشمایدور نقل نمیکند ونکرده است تاشیغان وتاشیرغان وتاشیدورغان نقل کننده ونقل کرده وبمعنی مصدر هم می آیند تاشی
تاشیغیل مفرد مخاطب از فعل امر تاشیما وتاشیماغیل مفرد مخاطب از فعل نهی تاشینك وتاشینکز وتاشینکلار جمع مخاطب از فعل
الشاهد علی الاول شعر نولق فاغ اولدی غمدین دردین اشتند ختن فا کوییکا تاشینك وهم بو سرعه سکندری کوید شعر
دیدی شه هم سیز کا فانیو را نکیز ولیکن بو کشور ابراقر یا نکیز تاشینك هم یکیم بولسنا ایلاب شتاب که بولك

تاما سون رشته تاب والماس ر طغیان کردن هم باشد ودر این معنی ماخوذ از تاشماق است چنانکه کذشت تاشیماسنکاه
تاشیمانکز وتاشیمانکلار جمع مخاطب از فعل نهی تاشیمان وتاشیماس مین نقل نمیکنم تاشیر مین وتاشیر مین وتاشیدور مین وتاشیرام
نقل میکنم تاشیماس نقل نمیکند وبمعنی فاعل ومصدر منفی هم می آید تاشیماسینکه بنقل نکردنت تاشیرینکه بنقل کردنت
تاشیب وتاشیبان وتاشیمیش نقل کرده الشاهد علی الاول شعر کونکول اچا کیکا کام تیمه خطینك مکری تولا میلیش دیکیز
کور که خیل مور سکن ایچره تاشیب تورور وتاشیب وتاشیبان بمعنی طغیان کرده هم آمده چنانچه کذشت تاشیغان تا نقل کرده
تاشیا بولغای وتاشیب بولغای نقل توان کرد وتاشیب بولغای بمعنی طغیان توان کرد هم باشد تاشی الغای نقل تواند کرد تاشی
تاشی نقل کنان تاشی وتاشیین نقل کنم وکند وکنی وکرده تاشیناق وتاشیغای بز وتاشیغالی وتاشالینك نقل کنیم تاشیغالی
برای نقل کردن وتا نقل کرده تاشیغاج چون نقل کرد وکند تاشیغوچی نقل کننده تاشیغوچه وتاشیغونچه وتاشیغانچه تا نقل
کردن وبقدر نقل کردن تاشی آلغاینکچه بقدریکه نقل تواند کرد تاشیغومیز دور نقل خواهیم کرد تاشیغونکوز دور نقل خواهید
کرد تاشیغوسیلار دور نقل خواهند کرد تاشیماغوم وتاشیغوم یوق نقل نخواهم کرد تاشی آلماغوم وتاشی آلغوم یوق نقل کردن ممکن نخواهد
بود تاشیغولوق نقل کردن تاشیغای وتاشیسلو تاشیغون وتاشید سیلك نقل کند الشاهد علی الاول شعر
هلا کیم ایلاکنا اول یا لعل ابنا کلیلا این لباس تامات که تو فراغیم تاشیغای کلاه اینکا الماه وتاشیدیلك بدو معنی هم آمده اول بمعنی
مثل نك آن نقیم مثل بیرودن آن چنانکه در ره سعی بطریق تجانس کوید شعر یا غدی جوهر نیك ادتی جوهر نیك تاشیدیلك
یعنی باریدی تیر جوهرت مثل نیك جوهرت میلدی خان کونکلوم ایچره هم تاشیدیلك وخون کرد روان ولم را هم مثل بوتش تاجیلی ناهیم
ایا غیغه سپهر کوزیاشیم نینك لعل وصدرین تاشیدیلك لعل ودر اشك چشم را نقل کند تاشیغودیلك وتاشیرودیلك نقل کرد
نقل کند تاشیماق مع النون بمعنی انفعالست یعنی نقل شدن از جائی بجائی تاشین وتاشینغیل مفرد مخاطب از فعل امر
الشاهد علی الاول شعر نوای خانقه داغ فنك وجانینك اولمیش قید بولاردین خلص ایتلر مین نادیری سا ریغ تاشین
تاشینغای وتاشیناو تاشیناق تاشینغون وتاشیندیلك نقل کند چنانچه در فرهاد وشیرین در طوفانی شدن نیل کوید الشاهد علی
الخامس شعر روان بیتکوی بیلا هر طرف زر صرف یا نکی آی زهره خدین تیمن وهرا که بولماسین بورون بوسیل زیاده تاشیند
موند اشاه وشاهزاده وباقی صیغ برین سیاق با نون اشتقاق می یابد تاشیماق مع التا مسند متعدیست یعنی نقل فرمودن تاشیتما
تاشیتا وتاشیتا وتاشیتقون وتاشیتدیلك نقل فرماید چنانچه در مکالمه فرهاد با خسرو آمده بهرام بطرب بمداین کوید الشاهد
علی الاول شعر مداین شهر آدم دین آریتغای خطا ملکیکا تو فراغین تاشیتغای وباقی صیغ برین نهج با تای قرشت ا
می یابد تاشیماق بکسر شین وسکون قاف کوفته وپخته وناخوش شدن در هیچ شدت تاشیقتوق پخته شدیم تاشیقتور
تاشیقادور پخته میشود وتاشیقور بمعنی فاعل ومصدر هم می آید تاشیقمایدور پخته نمیشود ونشده است تاشیقغان وتاشیقور غان
تاشیقادورغان پخته شونده وپخته شده وبمعنی مصدر هم می آیند تاشیق وتاشیقغیل مفرد مخاطب از فعل امر تاشیقما وتاشیقماغیل
مفرد مخاطب از فعل نهی تاشیقینك وتاشیقینکز وتاشیقینکلار جمع مخاطب از فعل امر تاشیقمانك وتاشیقمانکز وتاشیقمانکلار جمع مخاطب
نهی تاشیقمان وتاشیقماس مین پخته نمیشوم تاشیقامین وتاشیقور مین وتاشیقادور مین وتاشیقورام پخته میشوم تاشیقماس پخته نشود
وبمعنی فاعل ومصدر منفی هم می آید تاشیقماسینکه بپخته نشدنت تاشیقورینکه بپخته شدنت تاشیقیب وتاشیقیبان و
تاشیقمیش پخته شده تاشیقیشالك پخته شده تاشیقا بولغای وتاشیقیب بولغای پخته توان شد تاشیقا الغای پخته تواند

شد تاشیقا تاشیقا خسته شوان تاشیقماق فتاشیقابین خسته شوم شود وشوی وشاید تاشیقنا وقتا تاشیقتابیزو تاشیقتا
تاشیقلی قتاشیقالینک خسته شویم تاشیقماقلی برای خسته شدن و تا خسته شدن تاشیقماچ چون خسته شد تاشیق
خسته شوند تاشیقموغیبو تاشیقمو بخود تاشیقما بخه تا خسته شدن و بعد خسته شدن تاشیقا آلغاسینکیم بعد هرکه خسته
توانی شد تاشیقمومیزدور نخسته نخواهیم شد تاشیقموکیزدور خسته خواهید شد تاشیقموسیلاردور نخسته خواهند شد تاشیقما
تاشیقموم یوق خسته نخواهم شد تاشیقا الماغوم قتاشیقا آلغوم یوق خسته شدن ممکن نخواهد بود تاشیقمولوق خسته شد
تاشیقفای وتاشیقلقا تاشیقنا قتاشیقسون خسته شود تاشیقمودیلیک قتاشیقمودیلیک نخسته شده
خسته شود تاشلاماق دو معنی دارد اول بمعنی بیرون انداختن باشد چنانکه گوید شعر ای نوائی ایله خوش بولکر فرهادا
دین سیل که فوتی تاشلاماقته دوییم یعنی سنگ زدن تاشلادوق انداختیم وسنگ زدیم تاشلا تاشلا
می انداز وسنگ میزن الشاهد علی المعنی الاول شعر کونکول تاشلادی قرا سین دا غلاریم قویدی غم هردان حنون
دین دیوانه ساچغان دیک هردان و تاشلادی یعنی هم می آید تاشلامایدی بیرون نمی انداز دو نمیند اخته است و
نمیزند ونزده است تاشلاغان قتاشلاغوان قتاشلایدورغان انداز نده وانداخته وسنگ زننده وزده وبمعنی مصدر هم می آیند
تاشلاو قتاشلاغیل مفرد مخاطب تاشلاسا وتاشلاغیل مفرد مخاطب تاشلاکیز وتاشلانکلار
جمع مخاطب تاشلانکیز وتاشلانکلار جمع مخاطب تاشلامان قتاشلامانمن نمی اندازم وسنگ نمیزنم
تاشلاسین قتاشلاسون تاشلاماسین نمی انداز دو سنگ نمیزند و بمعنی
منفی هم می آید تاشلاماسینکه بانداختنت وسنگ زدنت تاشلاب قتاشلاباق
تاشلامیش انداخته وسنگ زده تاشلامیشانک انداخته وسنگ زده تاشلابولغای وتاشلاب بولغای توان انداخت
وسنگ توان زد تاشلایالغای توان انداخت وسنگ توان زد تاشلاغای تاشلادی وتاشلای انداخته انداخته وسنگ
زنان سنگ زنان تاشلای بیندازم وبیندازی وانداخته وسنگ بزنم وبزند وبزنی تاشلا
تاشلاغانیم تاشلاغای بیندازیم وسنگ بزنیم تاشلاغالی برای انداختن و انداخته و برای سنگ زدن و
تاسنگ زده تاشلاماچ چون انداخت و بیندازد وچون سنگ زد و بزند چنانکه بمعنی اول گوید شعر
ایتینک تاشلاماچ هر تاشلاغوچی اندازنده وسنگ زننده
تاشلاغو تاانداختن و بعد از انداختن و تا سنگ زدن و بعد سنگ زدن تاشلاغوسی
بعد هرکه بیرون توانی انداخت و بعد هرکه سنگ توانی زد تاشلاغومیزدور نخواهیم انداخت وسنگ نخواهیم زد تاشلاغو
خواهید انداخت وسنگ خواهید زد تاشلاغوسیلاردور خواهند انداخت وسنگ خواهند زد تاشلاماغوم قتاشلاغوم یوق
نخواهم انداخت وسنگ نخواهم زد تاشلای آلماغوم قتاشلای آلغوم یوق انداختم ممکن نخواهد بود وسنگ زدنم ممکن نخواهد
تاشلاغولوق انداختنی وسنگ زدنی تاشلاغای قتاشلاغا وتاشلاغوچی تاشلامیسین بیندازد وسنگ بزند تاشلاغو تاشلا
انداختنی بیندازد وسنگ زدنی سنگ بزند تاشلاتماق مع التا معلوم متعدیست یعنی اندازاندن
درجم فرمودن تاشلاتقومایدی یعنی می اندازانید و درجم فرمود چنانکه در تاریخ الملوک بمعنی اول
گوید که ایکین لادین تاشلاتقو وباب آن بستور تاشی قرشت اشتقاق

تاشلانماق مع النون یعنی انداخته شدن وسنگ زده شدن و صیغ آن با نون اشتقاق تاشقیر فانماق بکسر
مهمله ونون وفتح غین معجمه سوده شدن تمام وسنگ وصیغ آن موافق اول اشتقاق
من المواحد تاش بروزن آش بچهار معنی بود اول سنگ را گویند الشاهد علیه شعر
قیلدی تاشیدین دوییم بمعنی ظاهر و برون باشد چنانکه گوید شعر
که تاشینک واترا تاشقار
باشد و بادا مستعملست چهارم در لغتیر لفظی که واقع میشود افاده معنی
وبا فارسی نیز مشارکت چنانکه شاعر گفته شعر
استعمال میشود مثل
هم واقع میشود یعنی چنانکه شاعر گفته شعر
تاشبافقه سنگ پشت باشد که آنرا باقه و باقه چاناق هم گویند و بعربی کشف خوانند تاشقوت
بمعنی ظاهر و بیرون وآن تاشقی بمعنی خارجی و بیرونی بود چنانکه گوید شعر
تاشقی
تاشقی ادوب تاشقی لیغ بمعنی خارج
چنانکه در مقاله ششم سلطان گوید شعر تاشقی
آیینک تاشکینت بکسر کاف وسکون نون وتای قرشت نام شهریست از ماوراء النهر
منسوب بنجاست تاشلیغ بمعنی سنگلاخ باشد مع الغین تاغ به معنی بود اول کوه را گویند الشاهد علیه شعر تاغ
لیغ دوییم نام درختی است که آتش
آن دیر ماند و آنرا بعربی غضا خوانند سیم نام چهارم
دوییم مرغ را خوانند تغا بچهار معنی
اول تغاری که دوییم چنانکه در تاریخ وصاف
خان که مکاییل چنانکه تغاری
ظرفیست چنانکه در تاریخ وصاف
تاروق
از تاعوق مرغ بود که آنرا تاووغ وتاووق وبعربی دجاجه
خوانند مع الفا تغنتاک تاماق بمعنی
جای بستن آن چنانکه گوید شعر
عشق
شعر اول کینه

157v.

نوشته که بیغو نام گذاشت و شعر میرزا بر سبیل شاهد آورده سهو کرده. تاموق بضم تا و قاف و واو دود. می بندد و تاقالر یعنی حاصل کند

هم می آید چنانکه بمعنی صنوبری گوید شعر ای غنچه که ترکیب جمع هوفه بو غنچه‌نه تا قلر غنچه‌ی ناریلق تاقماید بمعنی نبندد و

تاقغان و تاقارغان حفاظ و حراغان بندند و بسته چنانکه شاهد تاقلماغ بمعنی تاختن گوید شعر تاق قوغاق بوینیغه دیبا ملناب

کورلدی بوینیغه کیم تاقغان تو سهو شکن سرش و بمعنی مصدر منفی هم می آید تاقت و تاقتیل مفرد مخاطب از فعل امر تاقتا و تاقتاغیل

مفرد مخاطب از فعل نهی تاقینک و تاقینکیز و تاقینکلار جمع مخاطب از فعل امر تاقمانک و تاقمانکیز و تاقمانکلار جمع مخاطب از فعل نهی تاقمان و تاقما

می بندم تاقامین و تاقارمین و تاقادورمین و تاقارام می بندم تاقماس نمی بندد و بمعنی حاصل مصدر منفی هم می آید تاقماسینکغه

نبستنت تاقارینکغه ببستنت تاقیب و تاقیبان و تاقیش بسته الشاهد علی الثالث شعر تاقیم جهان لنازی بعد

جمعی کمر تاله سیدین زیریغ تاقیش لو کمر اکدین بیبین تاقیشانات بسته تاقنا و لغا و تاقیب و تاقه توار بت تاقا آلغای تواند

تاقا تاقا بسته کنان تاقای و تاقایین ببندم و ببندد و ببندی و بسته الشاهد علی الثانی بالمعنی الاول شعر

دکلدین ایب تاقایین کوکسوم داغلاردین دردو بلا حیکلار کا عشق بلا تاراز ق تاقساق و تاقسانیز و تاقسای نیز و تاقلی

تاقایلیک بجندیم تاقلغالی برای بستن و تابسته چنانکه در حیرة الابرار گوید شعر زلفیکا مشغول الیرور شاهد زیبه تاقای

مین یراقتین جان بیر بسیز لیقتیم یوق باقلغالی تاقلاج جوز بت و به بندد تاقوجی بندنده تاقوجی و تاقوجیغه تاقاغه

تابستن و بقدر بستن تاقا آلغای نیکه بقدر یکه توانی بست تاقغوسیدور خواهیم بست تاقغوسی اکیز دور نخواهید بست تاقغوسیلاد

خواهند بست تاقماغوم و تاقغوم یوق نخواهم بست تاقا آلماغوم و تاقا آلغوم یوق بستن نمکم نخواهد بود تاقغولوق بستنی

تاقغای و تاقا و تاقسا و تاقسون تاقماسین ببندد تاقغوسیلک و تاقاردیک بستیم چنانکه بندد تاقمالیا و تاقیلغ مع اللام بسته

شدن و منع آن بالام اشتقاق می یابد من المجوامد تاق نام درختیت که اثر هیزم آن دیر بماند و آن را تاغ هم گویند چنانکه

در حیرة الابرار گوید شعر توف یوزی آلتون بیله حدولکا بلکه اوتولیت تا قایی زحل آنکا تیز مرمسد سکندری درو

اسب گوید شعر هم آلتون ایکار داغی آلتون لجام هم آلتون تاقادغی آلتون ستام و مولف برین تاق را بمعنی توقه کرده و یا زحلقه

زرانه دارد باشد در تالیف خود فکر کرده و شعر میرزا بر سد سکندری شاهد آورده و تصویب هم متابعت کرده و فراغی در شرح دیگر

تاق و لغان تاقادا لغا خوانده و تاق را بمعنی نیز و دلغاد را بمعنی درش نوشته چنانکه عبداشتباهات ایشان در ذیل تاق و لغا مذکور خواهد

شد تاقوق بسکون ظاف و ضم تا و قوشت خلاخی بود که بروی ترکش صندوق کشند و با خاین مستعمله تاقوق بضم تاف و لهما

تاخوق بمعنی مرغ بود که منکه شد تلت و تجی بکسرتان بمعنی یکرا شد چنانکه در حیرة شیل گوید شعر باخاغه

تقیم حمیلر دوش ووصفت بهجتیم تقی لر دوش وآن را داغی هم گویند تاقیم مع الیم باصطلاح جوهریه اسباب تجمل را گویند مع الکاف

تلت دو معنی دارد اول بمعنی تحت ضد فوق بود دوم بمعنی فردتنها باشد صفاریسی موافق برهان تاملع اندر شده و قلیل را گویند

و هر نوع زدن را خوانند عموما و زدن دست بر کفل را هم که گشتین در دست نشیند خصوصا و نام گیاهی هم هست که دیوان کنند

نار سر بوید و ده مصدر آن کافه میسلار ندو بمعنی تند رفتن و تیز دویدن نیز آمده تکالت بترکی رومی تالک انکور باشد و نهال آن تا

اشجار را مانند تکامیشی بلغت مغولی تکاپوی تعجیل و سرعت بود تکادر بسکون واو آهو را گویند که از میان دم و تر کوه و بعضی ها

ایستاده و بعضی‌ها خاروان و بعضی‌ها خاخشک و بعضی‌ها خاسیز باشد و آن لفظ عرف و مشترکست تکسند لغطیست که از ترکی

و خاجی و آن کمربندیست که از ابریشم و پشم می بافند و بلیک سر آن تکمه یا مهره و بسر دیگر آن انگله نصب کنند و آن مهره یا تکمه را

158r

در آن انگله اندازند تا بر میان بسته شود و انواع آن فوطه و مثال آن چند و یکنوع کمربستن را هم گویند و آن چنانست که از روی

ظرافت و جنائی کمر راست بسته گوشه کمربند را از یکطرف دراز آویزند چنانکه در حیرة الابرار گوید شعر بیلیکا اندرشه

قیرین بنلبیب لبکه ظرافت بیله تک نیدا بیتیب تکش بر وزن حبش نام یکی از پادشاهان خوارزم است که معاصر البحرلان

بوده تکشمشی پیشکش کردن اندن و زمین بوسی که در خدمت سلاطین بعمل آید تکنه بفتح کاف و نون پارچه سفیدیست که

زنان آن را چکن دوزی کرده بسر بندند و بسکون کاف بترکی رومی ظرفی باشد مدور و بزرگ که از چوب تراشیده در میان آن ته

شویند و خمیر کنند و مجازا زنا و کوچک مدور را گویند که بر آن نشسته از آب عبور نمایند تکشفتم کاف مشدد بدو معنی آمده اول

بز نر باشد که آن را بعربی جدی و تیس گویند چنانکه در سد سکندری در وصف کوه گوید شعر کورونوب تکه سیدین جلو

اسد تپلاجغی بنینک آسیدا شاید دوم نام طایفه ایست از ترکمانیه و بغارسی نیز بدو معنی دارد اول کعبلد و فصل را مانند و دوم

سرگین گاو را و امثال آن که بدست هزار ساخته خشک کنند تکیش در اوغوزنامه بتقریب گوید بعد از جنس ذکر است که بعد از آن

سه پسر داشته که نام آنها ایل تکین و قوزی تکین و سبکتکین بوده و معنی تکین بزبان ترکی نیکو صورت باشد مع اللام من الثلاثی

تالمناق دو معنی دارد اول بمعنی خسته شدن باشد و آن را آرماق و هالماق و تالیقماق و تاوشالماق نیز گویند دوم بمعنی

رفتن بود اعم از آنکه بآب باشد یا بغیر و امثال آن تالدی خسته شد و فرو رفت الشاهد علیه بالمعنی الاول شعر قولدی

ای خضر همیم خسته نوایی قولینی کیم بو یول بیله سیدین ماعوزی آنینک تالدی نیه نیز بهایم صفحه در بهمه سیلی در گوی

هرام در کم شدن دلارام گوید شعر کیم تنی سوساییب قونیب تالدی هر جیمی فرست لوق تالدی و بمعنی نانی فضولی

در بنک و باده گوید شعر بحر فکرت تینکیز نیه تالدی جوخ اوزی بیر لمشوق تیقیلدی تالدوق خسته شدیم و فرو رفتیم

تالوردی تالادور خسته میشود و فرو میرود و تالورد بمعنی حاصل مصدر هم می آید تالمایدور خسته نمیشود و نشد است و فرو نمیرود

و نرفته است تالغان و تالورغان و تالادورغان خسته شوند و خسته شده و فرو رونده و فرو رفته الشاهد علی الاول

بالمعنی الاول شعر قیل اوز لوت دستی نعلی ایسنا تالمت مقصد مفر آسایش نی تالمت تینسا حیم بحر بیابان قطعید اتالغا

و بمعنی مصدر هم می آید و تالغان هر چیز مسموق را گویند خصوصا و گندم بریشته مسموق را خصوصا چنانکه در ذیل جوامد مذکور خواهد

شد تال و تالغیل مفرد مخاطب از فعل امر و تال بمعنی درخت بید و شاخه درخت نیز باشد چنانکه مذکور خواهد شد

تالما و تالماغیل مفرد مخاطب از فعل نهی تالینک و تالینکیز و تالینکلار جمع مخاطب از فعل امر تالمانک و تالمانکیز و تالمانکلار جمع

از فعل نهی تالمان و تالماس مین خسته نمیشوم و فرو نمیروم تالامین و تالورمین و تالادورمین خسته می شوم و فرو میروم تالغای

تالغایمین خسته شوم و فرو روم الشاهد علی الثانی بالمعنی الاول شعر اولا رمین یتارمین مقصد عیفه یا غناق امکان

بدر معنی پله یول اشدیب دین کرچه تالغایمین تالماس خسته نمیشود و فرو نمیرود و بمعنی حاصل مصدر منفی هم می آید تالماسینکغه

بخسته نشدنت و بفرو نرفتنت تالورینکغه بخسته شدنت و بفرو رفتنت تالیب و تالیبان و تالمیش خسته شده و فرو رفته

الشاهد علی الاول بالمعنی الاول شعر الکل یامینی سیل دی الماس ای نوایی بولغیه سیدین آنینک تاغری مکو تالیب توش

الشاهد علی الثالث من سد سکندری شعر طبیعت که خود کسالت تورور تردد آنکا صعب حالت تورور خصوصا که تا

تالمیش اولغای بیش قاتیغ یوییدین تالمیش اولغای بیش تالمیشانلک خسته شده و فرو رفته تالسا بولغای و تالیب بولغا خسته توا

و فرو توان رفت تالا آلغای خسته تواند شد و فرو تواند رفت تالا تالا خسته شوان و فرو کنان و تالاسین و ...

را هم کویند تالای وتالاین خسته شوم وشود وشوی وشد وفرو روم ورود وروی ورفته نیز بمعنی غارت کنم وکند وکنی
وکرده وبداخ بمعنی اخذ از مصدر تالاماقست چنانکه نکارش یابد وتالای بمعنی بیمار هم آمده وبلغت مغولی پیشانی را کویند
چنانکه در ذیل جلد مذکور خواهد شد تالساق وتالغای وتالغایمیز تالالیق تالالینك خسته شویم وفرو رویم وتالای بمعنی
غارت کنیم هم می آید تالغانلی برای خسته شدن وتا خسته شده وبرای فرو رفتن وتا فرو رفته تالغاج چون خسته شده
وچون فرو رفته بود تالغوچی خسته شونده وفرو رونده وخواص تالغوچه وتالغونچه وتالغانچه تا خسته شدن وبعد
خسته شدن وتا فرو رفتن وبعد فرو رفتن تالآلغانینچه بقدری که خسته توان شد بقدری که فرو توان رفت تالغوسیدر
خسته نخواهید شد وفرو نخواهید رفت تالغوسیلاردور خسته نخواهند شد وفرو نخواهند رفت تالماغوم تالغوم یوق خسته نخواهم
شد وفرو نخواهم رفت تالالماغوم وتالالغوم یوق خسته شدن محکم نخواهد بود وفرو رفتن محکم نخواهد بود تالغولوق
خسته شدنی وفرو رفتنی تالغای وتالسا وتالسون وتالدیك خسته شود وفرو رود تالغودیك وتالوردیك خسته
وهمچنانکه خسته شود وفرو رفتنی وهمچنانکه فرو رود الشاهد علی الاول المعنی الاول شعر هجر ارا ایخغر فرخ یتقلغم تورت
کیم ایعمت بوبه اوطانغدین بو وادی ایچره باغریم تالغودیك تالدورماق مصدر متعدیست بمعنی خسته کردن وفرو
وغوص فرمودن وصیغ آن موافق شق اول الفاظ عمر اشتقاق می یابد تالاماق بفتح لام غارت کردن وبرکسی ومی بمعنی کزیدن
سك باشد تالادی غارت کرد وسك کزید تالار وتالایدور غارت میکند وسك میکزد وتالا بمعنی امر حاضر هم می
آید چنانکه در لیلی مجنون در مکالمه مجنون با زید بمعنی غارت کننده کوید شعر سین ایکی الاردین اولسانك سجادغی
تالاردین اولسانك تالامایدور غارت نمیکند ونکزیده است وسك نمیکزد ونکزیده است تالاغان وتالارغان وتالایدورغان غارت
کننده وغارت کرده وبمعنی مصدر هم می آید تالا وتالاغیل مفرد مخاطب بفعل امر تالاما وتالاماغیل مفرد مخاطب بفعل نهی
تالانك وتالانکیز وتالانکلار جمع مخاطب بفعل امر تالامانك وتالامانکیز وتالامانکلار جمع مخاطب بفعل نهی تالامان وتالاماس
غارت نمیکنم تالایمین وتالارمین وتالایدورمین وتالارام غارت میکنم تالاماس غارت نمیکند وبمعنی فاعل ومصدر منفی
هم می آید تالاماسینکغه بغارت نکردنت تالارینکغه بغارت کردنت تالاب وتالابان وتالامیش غارت کرده وسك کزیده
تالامیشانك غارت کرده تالاشابولغای تالاب بولغای غارت توان کرد تالای آلغای غارت تواند کرد تالای آلغانی
تالای آلماغای نتوانی غارت تواند کرد چنانکه شاهد علی المعنی فصل هم از محبوب القلوب در ذکر لشکریان کوید
تالای آلغانی تالاماق وچون در تکادیك سنه ونیا فراخی تالاماق تالایو وتالای تالای غارت کنان وبدون تکرار هم
مستعملست تالای وتالاین غارت کنم وکند وکنی وکرده ونیز بمعنی خسته شوم وشود وشوی وشد وفرو روم ورود وروی
ورفته تالاسا قع تالاغایمیز وتالاغایلا تالاینك غارت کنیم وتالای بمعنی خسته شویم وفرو رویم هم می آید تالاقاچ
چون غارت کرد وکند تالاغوچی غارت کننده تالاغوچه وتالاغونچه وتالاغانچه تا غارت کردن وبعد غارت کردن تالای آلغانچه
بقدری که غارت توان کرد تالاغومیز وغارت خواهیم کرد تالاغونکوزدور غارت خواهید کرد تالاغوسیلاردور غارت نخواهند
کرد تالاماغوم وتالاغوم یوق غارت نخواهم کرد تالای آلماغوم وتالای آلغوم یوق غارت کردن محکم نخواهد بود تالاغولوق غارت
کردنی تالاغای تالاسا وتالاسون وتالادیك غارت کند الشاهد علی الاول شعر کونکلونك جور وغم وزحمتین تمام اولجا الادی
تاشینك خیالیدا اولکیم حبش ایلین تالادی تالاغودیك وتالاردیك غارت کرده وهمچنانکه غارت کند تالاتماق مع التا

مصدر متعدیست بمعنی غارت کنانیدن وصیغ آن با تای قرشت اشتقاق می یابد تالانماق مع النون بمعنی غارت شدن وصیغ آن
با نون اشتقاق می یابد تالاشماق مع الشین بمعنی کوشش کردن وجنگ کردن بود چنانکه کوید شعر تاوکینك کونکلوم کیم کاج خان
تالاشماق بوایکیش کیم میلی سینکا نی کونکلوم حیله خانیم الحاصل ونالاش جان کنایه است از حالت نزع وسکرات وبالمجاز بمعنی جنگ
کردن هم می آید تالاشتی کوشش کرد وجنگ کرد الشاهد علیه بالمعنی الاول شعر لبینکدین جان تالاشیب کوچکالی
هجر اوکونکلوم اولار حالتدا اول بیمار ریك کیم جان تالاشیب تورور تالاشتوق کوشش کردیم وجنگ کردیم تالاشور وتالاشا
کوشش میکند وجنگ میکند وتالاشور بمعنی فاعل ومصدر هم می آید تالاشمایدور کوشش وجنگ نمیکند ونکرده است تالاشغان
تالاشورغان وتالاشادورغان کوشش کننده وکوشش کرده وجنگ کننده وجنگ کرده الشاهد علی الاول المعنی الاول شعر باشاق
اوستیدا تالاشغان کبی منم لکالاری دشت عشقینك اراعشاق ایله سیکان تالاشورمین وبمعنی مصدر هم می آید تالاش وتالاشغیل
مفرد مخاطب بفعل امر وتالاش بمعنی کوشش وجنگ هم بود تالاشما وتالاشماغیل مفرد مخاطب بفعل نهی تالاشینك وتالاشینکیز وتالاشینکلار
جمع مخاطب بفعل امر تالاشمانك وتالاشمانکیز وتالاشمانکلار جمع مخاطب بفعل نهی تالاشمان وتالاشماسمین کوشش نمیکنم وجنگ نمیکنم
تالاشامین وتالاشورمین وتالاشادورمین وتالاشورام کوشش میکنم وجنگ میکنم الشاهد علی الثالث بالمعنی الثانی شعر
آچیغیم کیلکالی کوزین آچیغ باده غه ترجیح خوداهلی جوقلیلار بیهوده دان تالاشورمین وشاهد بمعنی اول در ذیل تالاشغان
مذکور شد تالاشماس کوشش نمیکند وجنگ نمیکند وبمعنی فاعل ومصدر منفی هم می آید تالاشماسینکغه بکوشش نکردنت
بجنگ نکردنت تالاشورینکغه بکوشش کردنت بجنگ کردنت تالاشیب وتالاشیبان وتالاشمیش کوشش کرده وجنگ کرده تالاشمیشانك
کوشش کرده وجنگ کرده تالاشابولغای وتالاشیب بولغای کوشش وجنگ توان کرد تالاشا آلغای کوشش وجنگ تواند کرد
تالاشا کوشش کنان وجنگ کنان چنانکه در لیلی مجنون بمعنی اول کوید شعر المراد دین ایکیلیسی تالاشا اولار دمن تیلی جان
تالاشای وتالاشاین کوشش وجنگ کنم وکند وکنی وکرده تالاشاق وتالاشغایمیز وتالاشغایلیك وتالاشالینك کوشش وجنگ کنیم تالاشغالی
برای کوشش وجنگ کردن وتا کوشش وجنگ کرده چنانکه بمعنی اول کوید شعر کویا که نال وجان چین ایره خی کیم تاری چو
یوق جان تالاشغالی اولنال ایتالار تالاشقاچ چون کوشش وجنگ کرد وکند تالاشغوچی کوشش کننده وجنگ کننده
چنانکه بمعنی اول در عنوان یکی از مقطعات کوید که یو تطری اولتورماق تالاشغوچیلار کیم هند وحبشه دان آلاردین یوقطری ایرور
ونیز حبیه سیل تیلبه بهمان مضمون در مخزن کوید شعر کیمکا کم همت نظری توش بولور کوکا تالاشغوچی اوچلار توش بولوتر تالاشغوچه
تالاشغونچه وتالاشغانچه تا کوشش وجنگ کردن وبعد از کوشش وجنگ کردن تالاشا آلغانینچه بقدری که کوشش وجنگ توانی کرد
تالاشغومیزدور کوشش وجنگ خواهیم کرد تالاشغونکوزدور کوشش وجنگ خواهید کرد تالاشغوسیلاردور کوشش وجنگ نخواهند کرد
تالاشماغوم وتالاشغوم یوق کوشش وجنگ نخواهم کرد تالاشا آلماغوم وتالاشا آلغوم یوق کوشش کردن وجنگ کردن محکم نخواهد
بود تالاشغولوق کوشش کردنی وجنگ کردنی تالاشغای وتالاشسا وتالاشسون وتالاشدیك کوشش وجنگ کند تالاشغودیك
تالاشوردیك کوشش وجنگ کردنی وهمچنانکه کند تالاشتورماق مصدر متعدیست بمعنی کوشش فرمودن وبجنگ انداختن
وصیغ آن برین نهج بالفظ فوق اشتقاق می یابد تالپینماق بکسر بای عجمی وسکون نون طپیدن از ملشد چنانکه در محاکمه شیرین با
بانو کوید شعر بالیغ خلی بو بولغای سودین آیرو که تالپینماقدا اولغای ییتابان سوز ورفتیه تالپیماق کونکلوم تالپینه
طپیدم تالپینور وتالپینادور میطپید بمعنی فاعل ومصدر هم می آید چنانکه بمعنی مصدری کوید شعر جسمیم اکر کوباد

کنکول تالپینوی یعنی لیناس کیم که ایکی کاتوشا اوت یوتجب اضطراب آنکا تا لپینمایدود نمیطپید و نطپید طپسنا تالپینبا
تالپینوغان و تالپینادوغان طپیده وطپیده و بمعنی مصدر هم می‌آید تالپین و تالپینیل مفرد غائب المتفعل الرا تالپینما فا تالپینما غیبل مفرد
غائب المنفصل تالپینک و تالپینکزو تالپینکلار جمع غائب المتفصل الرا تالپینمانک و تالپینمانکزو تالپینمانکلار جمع غائب المنفصل تالپینما
تالپینماس مین نمیطپیم تالپینامین و تالپینومین تالپینادور مین تالپینورام میطپیم الشاهد علی الثالث شعر تالپینومین
اشك اوا هرهم که تیشلا هر لیلیوغ کیم تینکیز کا توشتی‌غان و هیچ بر یلاهر اضطراب تا لپینانك و تالپینمالیمن تالپینغالی میطپو
چنانچه شاهد بر این واحد نظم ابو الجواهر کوید که نفس امیلا هر غنچه که تالپینغالی می‌کوپ کرچه بو توتون لولك تیلا هنانك سینغای
سین کوپ تالپیناس منطپید و بمعنی اصل مصدر منفی هم می‌آید تالپینما سینکه بنطپید نت تالپینورونکه بطپید نت
تالپینغیب و تالپینبان و تالپینمیش طپیده تالپینمیشانك طپیده تالپینا بولغای و تالپینیب طپیده توان طپید تالپینا
الغای تواند طپید تالپینا طپیان چنانچه میرسی کنده در مقدمه کتاب کوید شعر طلب بولیدا تالپینا تیرلما
فی دشلو مترلغه تیمالك ثنا تالپینای و تالپیناییین بطپم و بطپید و بطپیع طپیده تالپیناق و تالپینغانیز و تالپینغلی
تالپینلی و تالپینالینك بطپیم تالپینغالی برای طپیدن و تا طپیدن تالپینغاج چون طپید و بطپید تالپینغوجی طپید
تالپینغوجی و تالپینغوجه تالپینغانجه تا طپیدن و بقدم طپیدن تالپینا الغانینکچه بقدریکه تواند طپید تالپینغوسیزدور نخواهم طپید
تالپینغوسی کوردور نخواهید طپید تالپینغوسیلادور نخواهند طپید تالپینما غومدور تالپینغوم یوق نخواهم طپید تالپینا الماغوم
تالپینا الغوم یوق طپیدن محکم نخواهد بود تالپینغولوق طپیدنی تالپینغای و تالپینا و تالپینسا و تالپینسون و تالپینادیك
بطپید تالپینغو دیك و تالپینودیك طپیدنی و همچنانچه بطپید تالغاماق دو معنی دارد یکی فرق کذاشتن و امتیاز دادن
تالغادوق فرق کذاشتیم و امتیاز دادیم تالغا رقتالغا یدور فرق میکذارد و امتیاز میدهد و تالغار بمعنی فاعل و مصدر هم می‌آید
تالغانا یدور فرق نمیکذارد و نکذاشته است و امتیاز نمیدهد و نداده است تالغاغار و تالغار غان و تالغایدور غان فرق کننده
و فرق کذاشته و امتیاز دهنده و داده و بمعنی مصدر هم تالغا و تالغاغیل مفرد غائب المتصل الیه تالغا بمعنی موج دریا و
هوا نیز بود تالغانا و تالغاناغیل مفرد غائب المنفصل الیه تالغانك و تالغانکز و تالغانکلار جمع غائب المنفصل الیه و معنی الغه
سهوا تالغانك را شتوی از تالغاق بغیه کندم بر شته قیاس کرده نوشته که یعنی آتش کرمه بپوزانید تالغانما تالغاناکز
تالغانانکلار جمع غائب المنفصل الیه تالغامان و تالغاماس مین فرق نمیکذارم و امتیاز نمیدهم الشاهد علی الاول بالمعنی الاول
شعر سانا مجرا اندین اول لدرم ایلا حیل بجد مینی تری تولا کیم ناده یا لخو یوز هر ایکانی تالغاما ولنه شعر امیر نوائی دود اکر
بو دم معنی سا تیکلی سین تولا قوی کیم مین آتینك شاف و دو دین تالغامان تالغایمین و تالغادین و تالغایدیمین و تالغالم
فرق میکذارم تالغاماس فرق نمیکذارد و بمعنی فاعل و مصدر منفی هم می‌آید تالغاماسینکچه بی فرق نکذاشتن و با امتیاز ندادن
تالغابنکچه بی فرق کذاشتن و بامتیاز دادن تالغاب تالغابن و تالغامیش فرق کذاشته و امتیاز داده الشاهد علی الثالث
بالمعنی الثانی شعر دیلا سنا قی ایلکیدین مناب موخوشتوم یوقنا دردم هر زمان آندین کیلنا اولغو شتوم کیم آنی تالغامیس تالغامیشانك
فرق کذاشته و امتیاز داده تالغاما بچکاو تالغاب توبنه فرق توان کذاشت و امتیاز توان داد تالغای الغای فرق تواند کذاشت
و امتیاز تواند داد تالغایو تالغای و تالغای تفریق کنان و امتیاز دهان تالغاعه تالغاین فرق کذارم و کذارد و کذارید
و کذاشته و امتیاز دهم و دهد و دهید و داده تالغاشاق تالغاغانز و تالغاغای‌نز و تالغا تالغالینك فرق بکذارید و امتیاز بدهیم

تالغاغلی برای فرق کذاشتن و تا فرق کذاشتیم و امتیاز دادن و تا امتیاز داده تالغاغاج چون فرق کذاشت و بکذارد
تالغاغوجی فرق کذارنده تالغاغوجه و تالغاغوجه تالغاغانجه تا فرق کذاشتن و بقدم فرق کذاشتن و امتیاز دادن و بقدم
تالغای الغانینکچه بقدریکه فرق توان کذاشت و امتیاز توان داد تالغاغوسیزدور فرق خواهیم کذاشت و امتیاز خواهیم داد
تالغاغوسی کوزدور فرق خواهید کذاشت و امتیاز خواهید داد تالغاغوسیلادور فرق خواهند کذاشت و امتیاز خواهند
تالغاماغوم و تالغاغوم یوق فرق نخواهم کذاشت و امتیاز نخواهم داد تالغای الماغوم تالغای الغوم یوق فرق کذاشتن و امتیاز
دادن محکم نخواهد بود تالغاغای و تالغاسا و تالغاسون تالغادیك فرق بکذارد و امتیاز دهد تالغاناغای و تالغانانسا
تالغاناسون و تالغانادیك فرق نکذارد و امتیاز ندهد الشاهد علی الرابع بالمعنی الاول شعر برا وکه بخشی ایمان بخشیدین
نراغ ایسان ابجلداتالغانادیك بخشی کرایانان ناده تالغاغو دیك و تالغادیك فرق کذاشتنی و همچنانچه فرق بکذارد و امتیاز دهد
و همچنانچه بدهد تالغاماق مع النون فرق کذاشته شدن و صیغ آن با فعل اشتقاق می‌یابد تالیقماق بکسر لام
و سکون قاف خسته شدن تالیقتوق خسته شدیم تالیقور و تالیقادور خسته میشود چنانچه در تاریخ بابری مذکور
که بوش آت سیز اوت قدیمه بو روب تالیقور و تالیقور بمعنی فاعل و مصدر هم می‌آید تالیقمایدور خسته نمیشود و نشده است
تالیقمان و تالیقوغان و تالیقادورغان خسته شونده و خسته شده و بمعنی مصدر هم می‌آید تالیق و تالیقغیل مفرد غائب المتصل
تالیقما و تالیقماغیل مفرد غائب المنفصل تالیقمان و تالیقماس مین خسته نمیشوم تالیقامین و تالیقورمین و تالیقادورمین و تالیقورم
خسته میشوم تالیقماس خسته نمیشود و بمعنی فاعل و مصدر منفی هم می‌آید تالیقماسینکچه بی خسته نشدن تالیقمیشنکچه بی خسته
شدن تالیقیب تالیقیبان و تالیقمیش خسته شده الشاهد علی الاول شعر چابکوم تیز سوار تند شد عنداده حقیقت
مین سونکغه بیتا الماان بوکوبهر دا تالیقیب تالیقمیشانك خسته شده تالیقا بولغا و تالیقیب بولغه خسته توان شد
تالیقا الغای خسته تواند شد تالیقا تالیقا خسته تا خسته تالیقای و تالیقاین خسته شوم و شود و شوی
و شدی تالیقشاق و تالیقغانیز و تالیقغای‌نز تالیقالی و تالیقالینك خسته شویم تالیقغالی برای خسته شدن و تا
شدن تالیقغاج چون خسته شد و شود تالیقغوجی خسته شونده تالیقغوجه و تالیقغانجه تا خسته شدن و بقدم
خسته شدن تالیقا الغانینکچه بقدریکه خسته توان شد تالیقغوسیزدور خسته خواهیم شد تالیقغوسی کوزدور خسته
خواهید شد تالیقغوسیلادور خسته خواهند شد تالیقماغوم و تالیقغوم یوق خسته نخواهم شد تالیقا الماغوم تالیقا الغوم
تالیقغای و تالیقسا و تالیقسون و تالیقغودیك و تالیقودیك خسته شدنی
خسته شدن محکم نخواهد بود تالیقغولوق خسته شدنی و همچنانچه خسته شود تالابماق بفتح لام و کسر باء ابجد
ترکی رومی بمعنی طپیدن زمان شد من الجوامد تال نام درخت بید بود که آنرا بعربی خلاف کویند الشاهد علیه شعر کونکلو
هیشه تالکبی تیترا سا نبتالمث کیم وصل نکخر بیر یسله دایم خلاف دوم قلمه بو تکالنکا اوخشار بکاسین هر یان تیرتیلا
تالاوندروبرات هر یلدین سیکاندلار نیك بو جسم خونا لود ادا و نیز از کرستان خسته شدن و غوص کردن و فرو رفتن و ترکی
رومی شاخچه درخت بود و بفارسی چنار معنی دارد و اول درخت شبیه بهزنا است که در دیار هند میشود و از درخت بوهم چنین
کویند که دیم طبق مس و برنج و نقره و طلا و امثال آن تیم دو پیاله کوچك کم عمق که از آلات خنیاکران هند است چنانکه بر هم زنند
باشد که آنرا تال هم کویند و بعربی برکه نامند تالالا بروزن بالاسبزه و سبزه را خوانند من باب پادشاه شعر
خاطرنی بهار دضیلدا اکشتا الادور کوز نو مرنیز نیك لاله دشتا الادور خوش اول لحظه تالالار بلیب کشتا ایتسا مزکلا

160v.

کیم لطیف و دلکش تالادور و نیز در تاریخ بابری در وصف ولایات کابل مذکور است که چیکین تالا ادرتی بسیار بخشی بولور
و بمعنی نفس زنان از خستگی و غوص کنان هم باشد چنانکه در ذیل مصدر تالماق گذشت تلاج چشم نیلچ شهلا را گویند
چنانکه گوید شعر نرگس اول کوز دیلیماس ای باغبان کوز ایماس آنچ اوچون کیم بوپری قماج ایرور اول پر تلاج و مؤلف برهان
بمعنی چشم کج نوشته و مضیرج هم متابعت کرده و طالع هروی بمعنی غارت زده ذکر کرده هر دو شعر بی بصیرا شاهد آورده اند
سهو کرده اند و بفارسی بمعنی تالان و فغان بود تالان بازای معجمه ترکی رومی کرد باد را گویند تلاش یعنی کوشش و جنگ
چنانکه شاهد آن در ذیل مصدر تالاشماق مذکور شد تالاغ و تالاق سپرز بود که آنرا بعربی طحال خوانند و بعضی ز
عراق بفارسی پلرچه تنبان و شلوار باشد تالان یعنی غارت و تاراج چنانکه در مقالهٔ شانزدهم از حیرت الابرار گوید
شعر اولکه جهان دایلادسنا تالان اوچون مایم ایروم نعمت الوان اوچون تالای دو معنی دارد اول بمعنی فراوان و بسیار
دویم بلغت مغولی پیشانی بود و نیز مفاعلی مشتقه هم دارد که در ذیل مصدر تالماق و تالاماق مذکور شد تلپک
بسکون لام و کاف و فتح بای عجمی کلاه را گویند تلخ بفتح لام مخرف تلخ باشد چنانکه باغ و تاغ قافیه کرده شعر
عیب کیمادین شیرین لیکنکه آچیغ سوزنی یماس غریب جوجوک میوه بولسا اخته تلخ تالغاو تالغه بمعنی موج باشد چنانکه
حلیمی رومی در کتابی که بلغت نوشته در وصف کمرنا گوید که ... تالغه ...
اولور ... بمعنی انقلاب دریا و هوا استعمال میشود چنانکه در تاریخ بابری در وصف چشمهٔ غزنین مذکور است که اکر نجاست
بو چشمه فه تاسالار تالغا و طوفان و یامغور و چاپقون بولور تالغا تیوق بمعنی متموج و آشوب آلود بود تالقان
تالقان گندم برشته را گویند که کوبیده غذا سازند خصوصا و هر چیز نرم کوبیده را خوانند عموما چنانکه در فرهاد
و شیرین گوید شعر ... تالقان ... و در دیوان است
مثل است که در مقام ... گویند که تاغنی تالقان ایتیم یعنی کوه را ...
کردم و مقصود ... طالع هروی تالقان ...
... سهو کرده اند تالغوم بمعنی ... و انقلاب هوا را گویند تالغیج ...
... تالمی خوانند تلغاسه ... بود الشاهد علیه ...
قات قات ... تالغلسه ... تلکن بفتح لام و کاف عجمی و سکون نون ...
ساخته میشود تاله بروزن لاله ... چنانکه گوید
تاله تاله ... و له شعر ...
... تالبجی ...
نیلم ... بمعنی فراوان و بسیار بود مع المیم من المشتقات تامیزماق بکسر میم و سکون زای هوز مصدر متعدیست
یعنی چکانیدن تامیزدوق چکانیدیم تامیزدی تامیزدور چکاند و تامیزور بمعنی فاعل و مصدر هم می آید تامیزاید
میچکاند و بچکانیدن است تامیزغان و تامیزغوچی ... چکانید ... و بمعنی مصدر هم می آیند تامیز
تامیز غیل مفرد مخاطب از فعل امر الشاهد علی الاول شعر ... تامیز دیدی ...
آنکاباده ... تامیزما و تامیزماغیل مفرد مخاطب از فعل ... تامیزنکیز ... جمع مخاطب از فعل ...

161r.

تامیزمانک و تامیزمانکیز و تامیزمانکلار جمع مخاطب از فعل نهی تامیزمان و تامیزماس مین بمعنی چکانم تامیزاس مین و تامیزماس من و تامیزدوق
تامیزورام میچکانم تامیزماس نمیچکاند و بمعنی فاعل و مصدر منفی هم می آید تامیزماسیکنه نچکانیدنت تامیزورمو نکنه نچکاند
تامیزمانولغاو تامیزیب بولغاسی توان چکانید تامیزا آلغای توانم چکانید تامیزا تامیزا چکیده کنان تامیزای و تامیزایین
بچکانم و بچکاند و بچکانی و بچکانید تامیزغای و تامیزغایمیز و تامیزغایسن و تامیزسانک بچکانیم تامیزغالی برای چکانیدن
تاچکانید تامیزغاچ چون چکانید و بچکاند تامیزغوچی چکاننده تامیزغوچیو تامیزغوچیه و تامیزغاچه تاچکانیدن و تاچکانیدن
چکانیدن تامیزا آلماس نکه سعدم چکه توان چکانید تامیزغوسیدور خواهیم چکانید تامیزغونکیزدور خواهید چکانید تامیز
غوسیلار دور خواهند چکانید تامیزماغوم و تامیزغوم بوق نخواهیم چکانید تامیزا الماغوم و تامیزا الغوم بوق چکانید ...
بود تامیزغولوق چکانیدنی تامیزغالی لار و تامیزالار و تامیزمالار و تامیزماسلار و تامیزدیلار بچکانند الشاهد علی الاول
شعر ... تامیزوب ...
چکانیدنی و چنانکه بچکاند چنانکه شاهد بر اول ... شعر دوستلار ...
... تامغاق بمعنی چکیدن باشد ... تامغادو ...
الشاهد علی الاول شعر ... الشاهد علی الثانی شعر ...
... که بدن کلبه ... و تامنا ... بمعنی فاعل و مصدر هم می آید تامنغان
تامنارغان ... چکیده و چکید الشاهد علی الاول و المعنی الثانی شعر ...
ملاحتی ... و بمعنی مصدر هم می آیند تامغاج چون چکید ... الشاهد علیه شعر ...
تامغاج خزان ... تامغوچی چکنده چنانکه گوید شعر ...
تان تامغوچی ... تامغودیلت ... چکیدنی و همچنانکه بچکد
الشاهد علی الاول و المعنی الاول من سلطان ... شعر ... تامغودیلت
... تاملانماق ترکی رومی بمعنی ... چکیدن
باشد تامشماق بسکون میم و کسر شین قرشت کم کم نوشیدن و لذت از باقی بردن که آنرا بعربی مص گویند تامشیدی
کم کم نوشید تامشیدوق کم کم نوشیدیم تامشیر و تامشیدور کم کم مینوشد و تامشیر بمعنی فاعل و مصدر هم می آید تامشیمایدی
کم کم مینوشد و نوشید است تامشیغان و تامشیرغان و تامشیدورغان کم کم نوشنده و کم کم نوشید و بمعنی مصدر هم می آیند
تامشی و تامشیغیل مفرد مخاطب از فعل امر تامشیما و تامشیماغیل مفرد مخاطب از فعل نهی تامشینک و تامشینکیز و تامشینکلار جمع مخاطب
از امر تامشیمانک و تامشیمانکیز و تامشیمانکلار جمع مخاطب از فعل نهی تامشیمان و تامشیماس مین کم کم نمینوشم تامشی مین و تامشیرمین و تامشیدوم
تامشیرام کم کم مینوشم تامشیماس کم کم نمینوشد و بمعنی فاعل و مصدر منفی هم می آید تامشیماسیکنه بکم بکم نوشیدنت تامشیر
بکم بکم نوشیدنت تامشیماتولغا و تامشیب بولغا کم کم توان نوشید تامشی آلغای کم کم تواند نوشید تامشی تامشی کم کم
نوشان چنانکه گوید شعر ساقی ... تامشی تامشی ... تامشیو و تامشیین کم کم
نوشم و نوشد و نوشی و نوشید تامشیسا ... تامشیغای ... تامشیغالی برای کم کم
نوشیدن و تا کم کم نوشیدن تامشیغاج چون کم کم نوشید و بنوشد تامشیغوچی کم کم نوشنده تامشیغوچه ... تامشیغا

1617.

تا کر کوشیدن و بمقدار کم کم نوشیدن تامشی آلقاینکه بمقدار کم کم توانی نوشید تامشیغونبزیکه کم کم خواهیم نوشید تامشیغونکیز

کم کم خواهید نوشید تامشیغوسیلاردور کم کم خواهند نوشید تامشیماغوم وتامشیغوم یوق کم کم نخواهم نوشید تامشی آلماغوم

تامشی آلغوم یوق کم کم نوشیدن ممکن نخواهد بود تامشیغای تامشیپاو تامشیون و تامشیدلیک کم کم نوشید تامشیغودک

تامشیردلیک کم کم نوشیدنی و همچنانکه نوشیدن اجواسد تام بروزن بام سه معنی دارد اول دیوار سرای باشد الشاهد

شعر کیا بیم جز باغیز یوق کرچه آهیم بار آیینکه دیک کیم توشادور ایئم اچره چوکاینب قوش اوچسا تامیمدین دویم بمعنی قطره

بود چنانکه بدو معنی سید سکندری در وصف رفعت قصر خاقان کوید شعر یامین دین آشیناک تامی تام کوریاکان ...

شعله نامیغه سیکوریاکان و آنرا تامچی هم نامند چیم اراست ز چکیدن تماجامیشی لغت مغولیست بمعنی مضایقه ...

چنانچه در تاریخ وصاف در بیان جلوس ارغون خان مذکور است که چون المچی غدمت هولاجو رسید در جواب گفت با ارغون تماجامیشی

میمنی مضایقت نکا میرود و نیز در تاریخ فازانی در ولیعهد کردن چنگیز خان اوکتای را ذکر کرده یافته که جغتای ...

مناداکه چون من در کمترین سخن براه دیکر کرده در دولت تماجامیشی کند تامچی قطره باشد الشاهد علیه شعر فلک ...

ظلمی که تیتیمیش خسته کونکلوم تین هیچ کیکیم تامچی برار عوض کوپ تامیب مغاک ایتمیش و آنرا تام هم کویند تمرقزلک

بکسر میم و سکون راء قرشت و فتح قاف و زای هوز قرآن مجید را خوانند و بضم میم هم کفته اند تمرتن بروزن رامین ترکی

رومی پیکان تیر بود تمغا علامت و نشان و آلتی که بدان چیزها را مهر و نشان کنند و دواب را داغ نمایند و تمغه که از ...

عشور و خرج دیوان دهند و نیز مهر و نشان فرامین پادشاهان را کویند آنچه بآب زر باشد آلتون تمغا و آنچه بسرخی باشد

آل تمغا و آنچه بسیاهی باشد قراتمغا کویند تمغاچی فاعل و مباشر فعل تمغا را کویند چنانکه در خاتمه لیلی مجنون بتقریب

نصیحت شاهزاده در وصف تجار و عمله ظلم کوید شعر تمغاچی ایتیب تاشیغه جولان مرهم تیلاکای زکات حولان ...

بروزن فلک ترکی رومی بمعنی اساس و بنیاد بود تامله بسکون میم و فتح لام رومیه قطره را کویند تا مو بضم میم و سکون کاف

قرشت مراد دریشه درخت چنانکه در سد سکندری در وصف سپاه کوید شعر چنار الیکی یلیت تیتراب ایل اچره بی ولی ...

اول بر لب یل برغه سی اکرچه ایلیک تیتراب اول برلب وش تامورلار دور ره ایله کیم آبکش تاموغ و تاموق دوزخ را کویند

الشاهد علیه شعر فراق ایچرا نمار ایدی کیم رقیب بعینه هم تاموغ دین اینماس ایدی کیم امشاف بولدی ... النون

من المشتقات تاماق بسکون نون انکار کردن چنانکه کوید الشاهد علی الاول شعر عشق اکر بولسا که ...

ای کونکول تاناغیم ایچره دور ربوا یشه چو حق دیر کوه تاندی انکار کرد چنانکه در یکی از مقطعات ...

کوید شعر ... و تاندی آخر که آندین ... او قلار قلیغ ... لفظ تاندی

مشتق از تاناق بمعنی شناختن دانسته و ندانسته بمعنی دانستن نوشته و شعر ... شاهد آورده سهو کرده تاندوق انکار

کردیم تانار و تانادور انکار میکند و تانار بمعنی فاعل ... هم می آید چنانکه بمعنی انکار کننده کوید شعر ...

شهید ... انکار میکند و نکرده

تانغان و تانارغان و تانادورغان انکار کننده و انکار کرده و بمعنی مستقبل هم می آید تابن و تاغیل مفرد مخاطب از فعل امر

تاناو تاناغیل مفرد مخاطب فعل نهی الشاهد علی الاول شعر ... نوائی ... عاشق او لغامیوری ...

موالکه مجنون ... تانینک و تانینکیز و تانینکلار جمع مخاطب فعل امر تانمانک و تانمانکیز و تانمانکلار جمع مخاطب فعل

1624

انکار نمیکنم تانامین و تانارمین و تانادورمین و تانارام انکار میکنم تانماس انکار نمیکند و بمعنی فاعل و مصدر منفی هم می آید

تانماسینکه انکار نکردنت تانارینکه انکار کردنت تانیب و تانیبان و تانمیش انکار کرده الشاهد علی الثانی

شعر نوائی ... چون ... آنکا کیماس اولوم ... کر آیتمیش تانمیش و تانیب و تانیبان بمعنی شناختن

هم باشد و در آنجا بمعنی ماخوذ از مصدر تانیماق باشد تانمیشانک انکار کرده تانسابولغای تانیب بولغای انکار توان کرد

تانا آلغای انکار تواند کرد تانسا تانسا انکار کند تانای و تانایین انکار کنم و کند و کنی و کرده تانمای و تانمایین انکار نکنم و نکند

و نکنی و نکرده تانساق و تانغای بز و تانغای بز تانالیقا تانالینک انکار کنیم تانغالی برای انکار کردن و تا انکار کرد تانغاج

چون انکار کرد و کند تانغوچی انکار کننده تانغوچی و تانغانچه تا انکار کردن و بمقدار انکار کردن تانا آلغاینکه

بقدر یکه انکار توانی کرد تانغومیزدور انکار خواهیم کرد تانغونکوزدور انکار خواهید کرد تانغوسیلاردور انکار خواهند

کرد تانماغوم و تانغوم یوق انکار نخواهم کرد تانا آلماغوم و تانا آلغوم یوق انکار کردن ممکن نخواهد بود تانغای و تاناو تانسا

تانغون و تاندیلک انکار کند تانغودیلک و تانار دیلک انکار کرد بس و همچنانکه انکار کند تانیماق و تانیماقلیغ بکسر نون

شناختن چنانکه در سد سکندری کوید الشاهد علی الثانی شعر انکا کیم ... نکته دان ... اولوغ ایش ...

تانیماقلیغ حرفی تانیدی شناخته تانیدوق شناختیم تانیر و تانیدور میشناسد و تانیر بمعنی فاعل و مصدر

هم می آید چنانکه بمعنی مصدری در حیرت الابرار در وصف شاعر ... کوید شعر ... تانیر بمعنی ...

حقدین اولیامای ... تانیمایدور نمیشناسد و شناخته است تانی و تانیغیل مفرد مخاطب امر

امر تانیما و تانیماغیل مفرد مخاطب فعل نهی تانینک و تانینکیز و تانینکلار جمع مخاطب فعل امر تانیمانک و تانیمانکیز و تانیمانکلار

جمع مخاطب فعل نهی تانیمان و تانیمارمین نمیشناسم تانیمین و تانیدورمین و تانیرام میشناسم تانیماس نمیشناسد

و بمعنی فاعل و مصدر منفی هم می آید تانیماسینکه نشناختنت تانیرینکه بشناختنت چنانکه در لیلی مجنون ...

مجنون ... کوید شعر قاچاسلیغیم ایردی تانیماسدین ... تانیرینکه ... تانیب و تانیبان

تانیمیش شناخته و تانیب و تانیبان بمعنی انکار کرده هم باشد چنانکه مذکور شد تانیمیشانک شناخته تانیسا بولغای

تانیب بولغای توان شناخت تانی آلغای تواند شناخت تانی تانی شناخته شناخته تانی و تانیین بشناسم و بشناسد

و بشناسی و شناخته تانیساق و تانیغای بز و تانیغای بز تانیلی ... بشناسیم تانیغالی برای شناختن و تا شناخته تانیغاج

چون شناخت و بشناسد تانیغوچی شناسنده تانیغوچی و تانیغانچه تا شناختن و بمقدار شناختن تانی آلغاینکه

بمقداریکه توانی شناخت تانیغومیزدور خواهیم شناخت تانیغونکیزدور خواهید شناخت تانیغوسیلاردور خواهند شناخت

تانیماغوم و تانیغوم یوق نخواهم شناخت تانی آلماغوم و تانی آلغوم یوق شناختن ممکن نخواهد بود تانیغولوق شناختنی

تانیغای و تانیسا و تانیغون نواند یلک بشناسد تانیغودیلک و تانیردیلک بشناختنی و همچنانکه بشناسد و شاهد بر اول ...

... که ... تانیشما ... مصدر مفاعله است بمعنی

همدیکر را شناختن تانیشتی لار همدیکر را شناختند چنانکه در ملاقات لیلی با مجنون کوید شعر ... تانیشتی لار ...

... تانیشیب و تانیشیبان و تانیشمیش همدیکر را شناخته الشاهد علی الاول شعر ...

... تانیشیب ... تانیشای و تانیشایین همدیکر را شناسیم و شناسد و شناسید

تشلخته چنانچه شاهد بنائی بمعنی شناسد کوید شعر عاشق و معشوق بولماق بیرین تانیشماین پیرایجکلوکین

باشقه کوزیا اهل دهلی تانیماس و باقی صیغ برین هم باشین اشتقاق می‌یابد تانیتماق غ مع التاء مصدر متعدی بمعنی شناسا

تانیت و تانیتقیل امر است یعنی شناساندن چنانچه در مقالات ششم نصیحت الابرار در غزل حضرت الله علیه گوید شعر

پرده چابینی یعنی بنکلابن آریت صفا داسوی ایلکا اوزونکنی تانیت و باقی صیغ باتای قرشت اشتقاق یابد تانیلماق مع النون

بمعنی شناخته شدن و صیغ آن با لام اشتقاق می‌یابد تانکماق غ بسکون نون و کاف عجمی بمعنی تعجب و حیرت باشد تانکلا

لاد بعشند چنانچه در فرهاد و شیرین در دولت فرهاد گوید شعر هر بیر وحله ایچره باقلابان حیرت مرصع مهد ایچره تانکلا

جست و مطالع هر و تانکلاماق اصل که بمعنی سرزنش کردنست مصدر باب تانکلتی قرار داده و بمعنی تعجب دن ذکر کرده و شعر

شاهد آورده سهو کرده تانکلدوق بتیم تانکار تعلقدار همی نمی‌بندد و تانکلار بمعنی فاعل و مصدر هم می‌آید چنانچه در دولت

باسک لیلی کوید شعر قاینن تنی دین چوایلادی کم ماقلاجعا بالانی عجبکم اوزونکلا کیکی آنکا جل ایتی تاب یاشیدین آتی

کلکل ایتی چون بولدی آنی تانکاردین آزاده یمز چوایله ندیم قیلدی بیناده تانکماق یعنی بند و نبسته است تانکغان

تانکلغان و تانکلادرغان بسته و بسته الشاهد علی الاول المفعول الثانی شعر یار غم تانکغان ما مو ظاهری بیر بوب

باشیعه تاج لعل و یاقوت ایلامیش اول تاجه زیر قراق و بمعنی مصدر هم می‌آید تانکتا تانکیل مفرد مخاطب امر الشاهد

علی الاول شعر کم اولسام دیبری تانک سیلیم زنار ایله مجکم منکا تابوت یوش ایلامه غا دیری پاجیبیدین و تانکیل مخاطبه

جامه هم طرد که در ذیل مذکور خواهد شد تانکا و تانکا غیل مفرد مخاطب امر تانکیله و تانکینکیز تانکینکلا

جمع مخاطب امر الشاهد علی الاول شعر چوستا و لدعم بنا بیله یوینکوزی تانکینک امشا لغان تعشیم لیکا اسینه

تانکیم تانکمانک و تانکمانکیز و تانکمانکلار جمع مخاطب نفی تانکمان و تانکمادین می‌بندم تانکامین تانکلارمین و تانکادورمین

می‌بندم تانکماس نمی‌بندد و بمعنی فاعل و مصدر منفی هم آمده تانکماسینک که نبستنت تانکارینکه که بستنت تانکیب تانکبان

تانکیش بسته چنانچه در فرهاد و شیرین در فراق فرهاد گوید الشاهد علی الاول شعر تانکیب داغ و بنفشه چرخ قید ببوند

کند او که کند و بند او بند و نیز در لیلی و مجنون در حال مجنون گوید شعر تانکیبرا و ستیکا آیی بهیت عزم ایلادیلار

ببله فرحیت در حیرت الابرار در مصارع گوید الشاهد علی الثانی شعر م تانکیبان آلیدا جزاکم هم ظان تیز بولوب

جلوه کرالشاهد علی الثالث شعر دیبری خالصیفه چیکابن موسیلی چست کیم غنچه زنلودین تانکیش لیکابیر بیرت

تانکیشانلا بسته تانکاتوغتا و تانکیب بولغانه نوازیست تانکا تانکا بند بند بند تانکای و تانکا بیندم

بند و بندی و بسته تانکاق و تانکاپیر و تانکای پیر و تانکادیلار بیندیم تانکلای برای بستن و تاکسته تانکلی چوبت

و بیند تانکوی بندد تانکوسعا تانکونکوز و تانکماسما بستن و بعد بستن تانکا آلغا نینکیجه معتبر نیکه توانی بستا تانکونکیز

خواهیم بست تانکونکوز خواهید بست تانکوسیلار و نخواهند بست تانکماغوم تانکوی نیکیم نخواهیم بست تانکا آلماغوم

تانکا الغوم یوق بستن مکمن نخواهد بود تانکولوق بستنی تانکای و تانکا و تانکا و تانکون و تانکلا بندد تانکونیلی تانکلا

بستنی و همچنانکه ببندد تانکلاماق مع الغ بسکون نون و کاف عجمی بمعنی سرزنش کردن و طعن و توبیخ باشد چنانچه در قسم دویم از محبت

القلوب در باب توبه گوید که ناشایسته احوالین انکلا ماقه و ناباینته فعالین و تانکلاماق و مطالع هر و تانکلاماق قرار

تعجب دن ذکر کرده و شعر در فرهاد و شیرین در بیان معنی تانکیلادور در ذیل تانکماق مذکور شد شاهد آورده سهو کرده

تانکلادوق سرزنش کردیم تانکلادی و تانکلادیسن سرزنش کنید چنانچه شاهد بر او لطائف لسان الطیر در صفت حیرت گوید شعر بوقنی

بیلماس ایلر بیمی هم آنکلاماس فی بولادرنی تانکلادور تانکلاماس و تانکلار بمعنی فاعل و مصدر هم می‌آید تانکلاماید سرزنش

نمیکند و نکرده است تانکلاغان و تانکلاغوچی و تانکلادیغان سرزنش کننده و سرزنش کرده و بمعنی مصدر هم می‌آید تانکلا و تانکلاغیل

مفرد مخاطب امر تانکلانکا و تانکلانکیز مفرد مخاطب امر فعل الشاهد علی الاول شعر نوا او اصوات ایساسوچ و شاهد

از ادراکات قضا چیکتی بودم قیم بیر تانکلانک و تانکلانکیز و تانکلانکلار جمع مخاطب امر تانکلامانک و تانکلامانکیز و تانکلاما

جمع مخاطب فعل نفی تانکلادیمان و تانکلاماسمین سرزنش نمیکنم تانکلادیمین و تانکلادیمین و تانکلایدور تانکلاماس سرزنش نکنم تانکلاغا

سرزنش نمیکند و بمعنی فاعل و مصدر منفی هم می‌آید تانکلاماسینکه به سرزنش نکردنت تانکلارینکه به سرزنش کردنت تانکلاب

تانکلابان و تانکلامیش سرزنش کرده تانکلامیشانک سرزنش کرده تانکلاما بولغای و تانکلاب بولغای سرزنش توان کرد تانکلاماس آلغای

سرزنش تواند کرد تانکلای و تانکلای تانکلایی تانکلایی سرزنش کنان تانکلای و تانکلایین سرزنش کنم و کند و کرده تانکلاسا

تانکلاغای و تانکلاغای و تانکلاغای که تانکلاغای سرزنش کنیم تانکلاغلی برای سرزنش کردن و تا سرزنش کرده تانکلاغاچ چون سرزنش

کرد و کند تانکلاغوچی سرزنش کننده تانکلاغوسی و تانکلاغونکیز و تانکلاغایه تا سرزنش کردن و بعد سرزنش کردن تانکلا

آلغانینکچه بعد بیکه سرزنش توانی کرد تانکلاغونکیز و سرزنش خواهیم کرد تانکلاغونکوز و سرزنش خواهید کرد

تانکلاغوسیلار و سرزنش خواهند کرد تانکلاماغوم و تانکلاماغوم یوق سرزنش نخواهم کرد تانکلای آلماغوم تانکلای آلغوم

سرزنش کردن ممکن نخواهد بود تانکلاغولوق سرزنش کردنی تانکلاغای و تانکلاسا و تانکلاغون و تانکلادی سرزنش کند

تانکلاغولی و تانکلادیلار سرزنش کردنی و همچنانکه سرزنش کند تانکلاماق غ مع الثاء بمعنی مطعون شدن و صیغ

آن با تای قرشت اشتقاق می‌یابد تانکلاماق غ مع التون یعنی مطعون شدن و صیغ آن با نون اشتقاق می‌یابد تانلاماق

بسکون نون و فتح لام بمعنی برگزیدن و انتخاب کردن باشد چنانچه کوید شعر ایتا سانانک خازلکو نکول ایتلسا تردد یوق

کیم تولیدا الآخرنی تانلاماق تردیدی دوش تانلادی انتخاب کرد الشاهد علیه شعر عالم اهلیدین کیم اول آنینی نواسی

تانلادی سیلمادیکیم عشقیدین اولوز عالم بولور تانلادوق انتخاب کردیم تانلادی و تانلادید انتخاب میکند و تانلار بمعنی فاعل و مصدر

هم می‌آید تانلاماید یا انتخاب نمیکند و نکرده است چنانچه کوید شعر قولی بن عشق نینک کیم تانلامایدور جفت سیز سیند

سه فی قولدین تانلاغان و تانلاغوچی و تانلادیغان انتخاب کننده و انتخاب کرده و بمعنی مصدر هم می‌آید چنانچه شاهد بر او

کوید شعر صدقه سی ایلامک معنی و ودی اوپ و سلاهای کیم ضعیف ایتمیش اولوردین تانلاغانی مرض تانلا و تانلاغیل مفرد

مخاطب امر تانلا ماو تانلاغیل مفرد مخاطب امر فعل تانلانک و تانلانکیز و تانلانکلار جمع مخاطب امر تانلامانک و تانلاما

تانلامانکلار جمع مخاطب فعل نفی تانلامان و تانلاماسمین انتخاب نمیکنم تانلادیمین و تانلادیمین و تانلادورمین انتخاب میکنم تانلاماس

انتخاب نمیکند الشاهد علیه شعر عشق یکی بزم نینک سینغان سفالی ایچره کیم بجام جمشید جامین تانلاماس همت آنکا

تانلاماسینکه با انتخاب نکردنت تانلارینکه با انتخاب کردنت تانلاب و تانلابان و تانلامیش انتخاب کرده چنانچه در فرهاد و شیرین

گوید الشاهد علی الاول شعر خطا و چین دا تانلاب نازنین لار ملاحت بیرله آفرین لار و نیز در وقفیه گوید که کیفیات

تزیین خود پیوند الآخرنی سلطنت امورینه متعلق ایشلار کفایتی ایچون سایر تانلاب و خاصه غلامیدین سیچیب

الشاهد علی الثانی شعرای نوایی چون نیخازا هلیغه اصلا یوق ونا تانلاماغونک هرکز و فا اهلی الآخرنی تانلاب الشاهد

163

علی الثالث شعر کر نوائی نا رودیلت بوق ظالم ایمروز عجب کیم کین بیط الملوی موشاهد دین آنی تانلاغیش تانلامیشانلک انتخاب کرده
تانلاشابولغای وتانلاب بولغای انتخاب توان کرد تانلای آلغای انتخاب تواند کرد تانلای تانلای وتانلای بو انتخاب کنان تانلای
تانلامین انتخاب کنم وکند وکنی وکرده تانلاماق وتانلاغای تانلاغایمز وتانلاکو وتانلاغیلیا انتخاب کنیم تانلاغالی برای انتخاب کردن
وتا انتخاب کرده تانلاغاج چون انتخاب کرد وکند تانلاغوچی انتخاب کننده تانلاغوسیز وتانلاغوسیز قتانلاغاغه تا انتخاب کردن بتقدیم
انتخاب کردن تانلاغای آلغایسنکه بعد بیکه انتخاب توانی کرد تانلاغومیز بودو انتخاب خواهیم کرد تانلاغونکوز دو انتخاب خواهید کرد
تانلاغوسیلار دور انتخاب خواهند کرد تانلاغای غوم وتانلاغوم یوق انتخاب نخواهم کرد تانلای آلماغوم قتانلای آلغوم انتخاب کردن
محکم نخواهد بود تانلاغولوقا انتخاب کردنی تانلاغای وتانلاساو تانلاغون وتانلاغیلیا انتخاب کند تانلاغودیلت تانلاغولیا انتخاب
کردن وهمچنانکه انتخاب کند تانکرقا مانا ق بسکون نون وراء مهمله وکسر کاف عجمی مع الاماله وفتح غین معجمه تعجب کردن
تانکرقادوق تعجب کردیم تانکرقار وتانکرقاید ور تعجب میکند وتانکرقار بمعنی حال مستقبل هم می آید تانکرقامایدور
تعجب نمیکند ونکرده است تانکرقاغان وتانکرقاغان قتانکرقاید وران تعجب کننده وتعجب کرده وبمعنی مستقبل هم می آید تانکرقا
تانکرقاغیل مفرد مخاطب فعل امر تانکرقانا وتانکرقانکیز مفرد مخاطب فعل نهی الشاهد علی الاول شعر روایه عجز کیشی دنیام
تانکرقامانا ای شیخ اول ایشه چون ایرایتب تصرف خدا ماجرا الشاهد علی الثانی شعر یوز نکی پرده دادینام پری
تانکرقاماغیل مینی موقیل ادی بمعنون اوزی فنان موایماش تانکرقانک وتانکرقانکیز تانکرقانکلار جمع مخاطب فعل امر
تانکرقامانک وتانکرقامانکیز وتانکرقامانکلار جمع مخاطب فعل نهی تانکرقامان وتانکرقامایمین تعجب نمیکنم تانکرقای مین
تانکرقای مین وتانکرقاید ورمین تانکرقادام تعجب میکنم تانکرقاماس تعجب نمیکند وبمعنی حال ومستقبل منفی هم می آید تانکرقاماسیکه
تعجب نکردنت تانکرقانکه بتعجب کردنت تانکرقاب وتانکرقابان وتانکرقامیش تعجب کرده چنانکه شاعر در کل ونوکر
کوید الشاهد علی الاول شعر المیکدین ایچیمیب المیغمی سالدی تانکرقاب المرزا فین تیشالشی عطالدی ومؤلفین درکی
این لفظ را تانکرقاب بازای هوز خوانده شعر زبهر شاهد آورده اند وبفیرء هم متابعت نموده سهو کرده اند
تانکرقامیشانک تعجب کرده تانکرقاشابولغای وتانکرقاب بولغای تعجب توان کرد تانکرقای آلغای تعجب تواند کرد
تانکرقای وتانکرقای قتانکرقای بو تعجب کنان تانکرقای وتانکرقامین تعجب کنم وکند وکنی وکرده تانکرقاساق قتانکرقاسا
تانکرقاغایمز وتانکرقاغالی وتانکرقالیت تعجب کنیم تانکرقاغالی برای تعجب کردن وتا تعجب کرده تانکرقاج چون تعجب
کرد وکند تانکرقاغوچی تعجب کننده تانکرقاغوسیز وتانکرقاغوسیز تانکرقاغاغه تا تعجب کردن وبتقدیم کردن تانکرقا
آلغایسنکه بعد بیکه تعجب توانی کرد تانکرقاغومیز دور تعجب خواهیم کرد تانکرقاغونکوز دور تعجب خواهید کرد تانکرقا
غوسیلار دور تعجب خواهند کرد تانکرقاماغوم وتانکرقاغوم یوق تعجب نخواهم کرد تانکرقای آلماغوم وتانکرقای آلغوم یوق
تعجب کردن محکم نخواهد بود تانکرقاغولوق تعجب کردنی تانکرقاغای وتانکرقاساو تانکرقاسون قتانکرقادلیت تعجب کند
تانکرقاغودیلت قتانکرقاردیلت تعجب کردنی وهمچنانکه تعجب کند تنبه لامانا ق بسکون نون وفتح بای ابجد پیشتر دم را محکم
کردن تنبه لادوق دم را محکم کردیم تنبه لار وتنبه لاید ور دم را محکم میکند وتنبه لار بمعنی حال ومستقبل هم می آید تنبه لامایدور
محکم نمیکند ونکرده است تنبه لاغان وتنبه لاغان وتنبه لاید ورغان دم را محکم کننده ومحکم کرده وبمعنی مستقبل هم می آید
تنبه لا وتنبه لاغیل مفرد مخاطب فعل امر تنبه لاما وتنبه لاماغیل مفرد مخاطب فعل نهی تنبه لانک وتنبه لانکیز وتنبه لانکلار جمع

164

مخاطب فعل امر تنبه لامانک وتنبه لامانکیز وتنبه لامانکلار جمع مخاطب فعل نهی تنبه لامان وتنبه لامایمین دم را محکم نمیکنم تنبه لای مین
تنبه لای مین وتنبه لاید ورمین وتنبه لادام دم را محکم میکنم تنبه لاماس دم را محکم نمیکند وبمعنی حال ومستقبل منفی هم
می آید تنبه لاماسیکه بدم محکم نکردنت تنبه لانکه بدم محکم کردنت تنبه لامیشانک دم را محکم کرده
تنبه لاشابولغای وتنبه لاب بولغای دم را محکم توان کرد تنبه لای آلغای دم را محکم تواند کرد تنبه لای تنبه لای وتنبه لابو
دم را محکم کنان تنبه لای مین وتنبه لای دم را محکم کنم وکند وکنی وکرده تنبه لاساق وتنبه لاغایمز وتنبه لاغالی وتنبه لالیت
دم را محکم کنیم تنبه لاغالی برای دم محکم کردن وتا محکم کرده تنبه لاغاج چون دم را محکم کرد وکند تنبه لاغوچی دم را محکم
کننده تنبه لاغوسیز وتنبه لاغوسیز تنبه لاغاغه تا محکم کردن وبتقدیم محکم کردن تنبه لای آلغایسنکه بعد بیکه دم را محکم توانی کرد تنبه
لاغومیز دور دم را محکم خواهیم کرد تنبه لاغونکوز دور دم را محکم خواهید کرد تنبه لاغوسیلار دور دم را محکم خواهند کرد تنبه لاما
غوم تنبه لاغوم یوق دم را محکم نخواهم کرد تنبه لای آلماغوم وتنبه لای آلغوم یوق دم را محکم کردن محکم نخواهد بود تنبه لاغولوق
محکم کردنی تنبه لاغای وتنبه لاساو تنبه لاسون وتنبه لادیلت دم را محکم کند الشاهد علی الاول شعر فی دولتا ولغوسی
اول کون نوایی غمکیم یا ده ایویکا اینلاب اچیشیب یشکی نتنبه لاغای تنبه لاغودیلت تنبه لاردیلت محکم کردنی وهمچنانکه
محکم کند تانکوتلانماق مرادف تانکرقاماق است یعنی تعجب کردن من الجوامد تنبولت بسکون نون وکاف وضم
بای ابجد خیمه کوچک را کویند که در زبان چادر نیز زده شود وبعضی کویند این لفظ هندیست تنبه چوبیست که
پشت در بندند تنسک بسکون نون وکاف وفتح تای قرشت بمعنی چنکال مجهول وسفینه را المند تانسوغ
تانسوق بسکون نون وضم سین مهمله چیزی را کویند که کتاب وغریب ونادر باشد چنانکه میر حیدر مجذوب کوید شعر
اناکه بودا بن امدی خیال اوتراغ کیلتوروی بو تانسوغ مثال وازا تانسوق هم کویند ومؤلف برهان قاطع تنسخ بر
وزن فرسخ را بمعنی نوشته وکفته که تنسوق معرب آنست سهو کرده زیراکه تنسوق لفظ ترکیست وتنسخ معرب آنست چنانکه وصاف
در تاریخ طرح اصطلاحات مغولیه تنسخ را با رخ و پاسخ قافیه کرده تنغال بسکون نون وفتح غین تنغال بمعنی القا
بر وزن بیجال صبح را کویند که ظلام وکل باشد چنانکه در سکندر کوید شعر بوینکلینج چیرلت بخشیراق قال ایله
ایکی سیلدا جمع اولدی تنغال ایله ومطالع هروی بمعنی کل عنیف نوشته وشعر بهر شاهد آورده سهو کرده ونیز در تاریخ
مطلع السعدین در عزیمت امیر تیمور بهمت خطا مذکور است که کلانتران اولوس نسخه تنغال از تواچیان بزرک ستد جمع
آمدن سپاه باشد وجوانب رفته تانغلدو بترکی رومی بمعنی وازو ترک باشد تانک بر وزن بانک سه معنی دارد اول صبح
کویند الشاهد علیه شعر صبح دولت یوزونکلای توسن کردون سنکا اشهب باشینکا وسید ایکی دم ایله که تانک باشید
کوکث دویم بمعنی تعجب بود چنانکه کوید شعر اشکیلت آمی قراسولار کونه مدین مجراها تانک یوق ادبایم چو بولیشتور منکا اشرم
تله شعر نونو قمچی باشیغه سوقور تومافر حوتانک یماس که بولغوسی سبب رنج واضطراب آیینک ومؤلف وی تانک یما را بند
شعر از نسخه سقیمی تانکلسانک بفتح کاف خوانده وتانکلسانک را بمعنی محو ونهند نوشته لفظ ومعنی هر دو اخراعیست سیم نواری
کویند که بر کمرد واب بندند وآن را شاک هم نامند وپر ار است از رستن وتجیدن چنانکه در ذیل مصدر تانکماق مذکور شد تانکلد
ولدوزی ستاره صبح بود که در بعضی هنگام صبح طالع شود وازا نغار سه ناهید کویند چنانکه در مثنوی در وصف بسیکیز کوید
شعر جمال اپرانوش وقتی خورشید دیک تنک بر وزن جنک مد ومعنی آمد اوکل نواری کویند که بر کمرد واب بندند دویم بمعنی

بتمه باشد و مجاز انک بار را نامند چنانکه در صد سکندری گوید مصرع نیا بود و پدر پدر امغر و ارمرخت. تاینجب شک لار
چرخ کولمرخت. و در فارسی هم باین معنی استعمال میشود و بفارسی هفته معنی طرد او لفظ صحیح است تقیم منضمه باشد را
خوانند که معمران فنقاشان اظهار منصب خو برا زکنند عموما و نکاخانه شا نبی را کوینید خصوصا و از الرنهایم تا
سیم در کوه چهارم نزدیک پنجم نایاب ششم نام و لایتی بدخشان هفتم تیر عضلیری بود تانکوغ و تانکو ق همان تانسوغ
تانسوق بود که در فوق نکارش یافت. تانکلا بسکون نون و کاف عجمی یعنی فردا باشد الشاهد علیه شعر نزاهد الا تانکلا
کوش مسی دین کیب دیماسهز کیل که میخانه اوا خوش تو تملیا و مزنی بو کوش تانکلا تیغ یعنی نسیب بفردا اجل فرداچنانکه
در صفه سیلرم دمو سفیر بے کوید شعر کیم بو کون تانکلا لیغ بولو بتورمین عمر بخان عذمی قو لو بتورمین تانکلا عصکو
نون و کاف عجمی و یای حطی کام دهن را کوینید تنکوت نام و لایتی است از ممالک خطا و نام طایفه ایست از قلماق تنکه
زر رایج را خوانند الشاهد علیه شعر کیرلک قو یاش دبری شکه بولسا بیغانه چو یو سنو موغلیکی بحرغه بما تیلسا لموله شر
طرفه آو دصدفارینک کوزلک آنکا ما و ی لباش انجم آتینک شکه با سیم ملغان زرحلی تانوغ و تانوق شاهد و کواه تا
چنانکه در حیرت الابرار در توحید کوید شعر وحدت ذاتیغه قویاش ثینک تانوق. نره دین افزون و قویاشتین یار و ق
و مؤلف ور ی تانوق را بمعنی پاسبان نوشته سهو کرده است تانوغلوغ و تانوقلوق شهادت و کواهی الشاهد علیه شعر
آسرا دیم سینی کوزا بحر او تا ش. تاینما ایوکا تانوغلوق آسیغینک. یعنی ای اشک ترا بمردن دیده نکه کردم کواهی داد نبو
بخون من نفع تو بود. تانیش بمعنی معروف و شناسا بود و مجاز ابمعنی آشنا هم استعمال شود و نیز از استاز شناختن مع لواو کرد
المشتقات تاوسا ماق بسکون واو و فتح سین مهمله از فرو کود البتا بجستن و بجا الا کی کنش تاوسادوق جسته تاوسا
تاوساید و بجهد و تاوسار بمعنی فاعل و مسند هم می آید تاوسانا ید بمحمد و بجسته است تاوساغان تاوساغان تاصلغلد
جسته و جسته و بمعنی مسند هم می آید تاوسا و تاوساعیل مفرد مخاطب از فعل امر تاوساما و تاوسلمافیل و بهمه مخاطب
تاوسانک و تاوسا بکر و فلو سا. نکلا جمع مخاطب از فعل امر تاوسا ماتک و تاوسلمانکر و فلو سانکلا جمع مخاطب از فعل نهی تاوسامان و تاوسلمانین
مجهم تاوسای مین و تاوسامین همتا ماید مرتاوسا ایجهم تاوسلماس بجهد و بمعنی فاعل و مسند منفی هم می آید تاوسلماسنکه
بجستن تو تاوسا رنکنه بجستن تو تاوساب و تاوسامان و تاوسامیش جسته تاوسامیشانک جسته تاوساسا بولغا
تاوساب بولغه توان جست تاوسای لغای توان جست تاوسای و تاوسای فما وسا یو جسته کان تاوسای و تاوساین بجهم و
بجهی و جسته تاوسا ساق و تاوسا غای مرتاوسا غای بزه تاوسلی و تاوسالیک بجهیر تاوسا غلی برای جستن و تا جسته تاوسا غاج
چون جست و بجهد تاوسا غو جی جهنده تاوساغو جه و تاوساغو بحر و تاوسا غاتا جستن و بقصد جستن تاوسای آلغای نکه بقصد بجهد
توان جست تاوساغو میز بدور خواهیم جست تاوساغو کوز دور خواهید جست تاوساغو سیلار دور خواهند جست تاوساما
تاوساغوم یوق نخواهم جست تاوسای آلماغو و تاوسا آلغوم یوق جستن محکم نخواهد بود تاوساغو لوق جستنی تاوساماق و تاوساسا
تاوساسون تاوساداین بجهد تاوساغویدی تاوسار ایک جستنی و همچنانکه بجهد تاوسا بماتاق مع التاسه در تعدیت یعنی
جهاندن و صیغ آن با تای قرشت اشتقاق می یابد تاووسماق بضم واو و سکون سین مهمله بمعنی تکمیل و تفویض و تمام نمودن باشد
تاووسوق تکمیل کردیم تاووسور تاووسادور تکمیل میکند و بمعنی فاعل و مسند هم می آید تاووسماید در تکمیل میکند و
نکرده است تاووسغان و تاووسغان تاووسادوغان تکمیل کننده و تکمیل کرده و بمعنی مسند هم می آید تاووس و تاووسغیل

مفرد مخاطب از فعل امر تاووسماو تاووسماعیل مفرد مخاطب از فعل نهی تاووسونک و تاووسونکیز و تاووسونکلار جمع مخاطب از فعل امر تاووسمانک
تاووسمانکیز تاووسمانکلار جمع مخاطب از فعل نهی تاووسمان و تاووسماس مین تکمیل نمیکنم تاووسامین و تاووسور مین و تاووسادور مین
تاووسورلار تکمیل میکنند تاووسماس تکمیل نمیکند و بمعنی فاعل و مسند منفی هم می آید تاووسماسینکه بتکمیل کردنت تاووسو
بتکمیل کردنت تاووسوب و تاووسوبان و تاووسمیش تکمیل کرده تاووسمیشانک تکمیل کرده تاووسا بولغا تاووسوب تکمیل توان کرد
تاووسا الغای تکمیل توان کرد تاووسا تاووسا تکمیل کنان تاووسای و تاووسلین تکمیل کنم و کنند و کنی و کرده تاووسا و تاووسغای
تاووسغای بزه تاووسلیکا و تاووسلیک تکمیل کنیم تاووسغلی برای تکمیل کردن و تا تکمیل کرده تاووسغاج چون تکمیل کرد و کند
تاووسغوچی تکمیل کننده تاووسغوچه تاووسغو بحر تاووسغاغا تکمیل کردن و بقصد تکمیل کردن تاووسا آلغای نکه بقصد بکه
تکمیل توان کرد تاووسغو میز بدور تکمیل خواهیم کرد تاووسغو کوز دور تکمیل خواهید کرد تاووسغو سیلار دور تکمیل خواهند کرد
تاووساغوم یوق تکمیل نخواهم کرد تاووسا آلماغو و تاووسا آلغوم یوق تکمیل کردن محکم نخواهد بود تاووسغو لوق
تکمیل کردنی تاووسغای تاووسادی تاووسا تاووسون تاووسدی تکمیل کند تاووسغو دیک و تاووس دیک تکمیل کردنی و همچنانکه
کند. تاوشاماق بسکون واو و لام و فتح شین قرشت خسته و مانده شدن تاوشالدوق خسته شدیم تاوشالور
تاوشالادور خسته میشود الشاهد علی الاول شعر ضعف اودی بسیدا چون اورودونک قدم امزلوکی تاوشالور یولنوزون
دور بو آغیر یو کنی کوتارکان تاوشالور و تاوشالور بمعنی فاعل و مسند هم می آید تاوشالماید و رخسته نمیشود و نشده آ
تاوشالغان و تاوشالوغان و تاوشالادوغان خسته شونده و خسته شده الشاهد علی الاول المعنی الثانی شعر فرقتینک بجهدن
بولغلی خلاص اولسام عجب ای بخاص آغیر او یقو یه بلمی غاندیک تاینغ امیکا کرا تاوشالغان و بمعنی مسند هم می آید تاوشا
تاوشالغیل مفرد مخاطب از فعل امر تاوشالما و تاوشالماغیل مفرد مخاطب از فعل نهی تاوشالینک و تاوشالینکیز و تاوشالینکلار جمع مخاطب
از فعل امر تاوشالمانک و تاوشالمانکیز و تاوشالمانکلار جمع مخاطب از فعل نهی تاوشالمان و تاوشالماس مین خسته نمیشوم تاوشالامین
تاوشالور مین و تاوشالادور مین خسته میشوم تاوشالماس خسته نمیشود و بمعنی فاعل و مسند منفی هم می آید تاوشالماسینکه
بخسته نشدنت تاوشالورینکه بخسته شدنت تاوشالیب و تاوشالیبان و تاوشالمیش خسته شده تاوشالمیشانک خسته
شده تاوشالا بولغای تاوشالیب بولغای خسته توان شد تاوشالا الغای بخسته توان شد تاوشالا تاوشالا خسته شوان
تاوشالای و تاوشالاین خسته شوم و شود و شوی و شده تاوشالساق و تاوشالغای و تاوشالغای بزه تاوشالالی و تاوشالالیک
خسته شویم تاوشالغلی برای خسته شدن و تا خسته شده تاوشالغاج چون خسته شده شود تاوشالغوچی خسته
تاوشالغوچه تاوشالغو بحر و تاوشالغاغا تا خسته شدن و بقصد خسته شدن الشاهد علی الثالث المعنی الثانی شعر غم یوکی
آستیدا تاوشالدوم دی بجر اینک میوه التفات اتیسالک داغی مین بزر تاوشالغانجه قیل تاوشالا آلغای نکه بقصد بکه
خسته توان شد تاوشالغو میز بدور خسته خواهیم شد تاوشالغو کوز دور خسته خواهید شد تاوشالغو سیلار دور خسته
خواهند شد تاوشالماغوم و تاوشالغوم یوق خسته نخواهم شد تاوشالا آلماغو و تاوشالا آلغوم یوق خسته شدن محکم نخواهد بود
تاوشالغو دیک جسته شدنی و همچنانکه خسته شود الشاهد علی الاول المعنی الاول شعر حله کل بکی یر استینک یوره
جانیم ایزابیت بولسا آیینک آستیدا نا که تینینک تاوشالغو دیک یعنی حله از برک کل کردی اکر نا کاه بدنت در زیر آن بر
کل خسته شدنی باشد از بیره جان من کن دوا غی بز لغت را از بغته سیقعی بوینا لغو خوانده و بایانا لغو را بضم تا یعنی از ابر کاهید

نوشته وشعر مزبور را شاهد آورده لفظ و معنی اختراعیست تاوشالدورماق مصدر متعدیست یعنی خسته کردن
خسته کردن تاوشالدوردی خسته کرد و شاهد آن در ذیل تاوشالغوچه نگارش یافت و باقی صیغ موافق شق اول تا آخر
در اشتقاق می‌باید من الجوامد تاو بر وزن گاو و محرف تاخ بمعنی کوه بود که از بچه توران بآن لفظ تلفظ نمایند و مطالع
اتراک دعم بمعنی فرصت نباشد تواچی بکسر جیم عجمی چاوچی باشد و آن عبارت از شخصی بود که از جانب پادشاهان فرمان
بایشان الاحکام صادر نمایند فرامین ناصر شود چنانکه در صحیح سکندری گوید شعر چرچیکا الیچیان سیغاد بوبجارد تواچی
هر طرف تیکجو دیعاو لغات و نیز در مجلس هفتم از مجالس النفایس در ذکر احوال امیر تیمور و سیاست کردن سه نفر مقصر گوید تواچی
میعاد پیله چاپب بلیرب و خلالاسی نینک بلشین کیلتوروب تو آد بر وزن هار اسم جنس است جمع ستور و چارپایان را گویند
و بلغت مغولی بمعنی قماش بود تواچی بر وزن مواشی ترکی رومی خواجه سرا باشد توسن بسکون واو و نون و فتح سین
مهمله بر وزن رهزن سه معنی دارد اول سرکش و چموش باشد چنانکه گوید شعر ای بحتل قیلما غیل کوب توسن لیغ دوران
کیم عشوق بر کاسنا لدی فاجر لیغ وفزیان لوق وله شعر هزنی دوران دین کیلور تیلیم خوشتراری رفیق نقع چون یوق اوزنی
کریوز قانلا توسن ایلا کیل بوتیز دم خسرو و شیرین هر کس فرستادن خسرو بجو لستکار شیرین کوید شعر بیبا ر دیکار و انلار
شابرغ پریب بیرا و کاسوز نینک اختیاری کوپ ایضو لا هر بایده یولوب بالاهوم ایکی توسن بی قیلما یلاد ملایم وان نیز سان
باشد دویم بالمانه که بیکار گویند چنانکه هم درو معنی فرمایند شعر چون لحظه کوپ قضا پستانیکو بی توسن لیغنیک توسن
کردون کا بینکه نگاه بولدی توث سیم نفس اجرت رحم دوختر تخته ‌را مانند الشاهد علیه شعر کوبیکا کیر کا نیما
توسن ایدیم لیک بولدعم تو را تورا محتاج تاوسامیشی بسکون واو و فتح شین مهمله و کسر میم و شین قرشت یعنی سرکشی و جنگ
تاوسمیشی بضم واو و سکون سین مهمله بمعنی نفو نفیر باشد چنانکه در ابتدای جلد سیم تاریخ و صاف مذکور است که تومان
توکا ترابنلر بر لحه تاوسمیشی کرد و نیز گوید که حکومت ایجو را بطغاجار نوبین تاوسمیش نمود و اینکه در اکثر تواریخ این لفظ
در اینمقام تاوسامیشی نوشته اند ناشی از سهو کاتب یا مورخ خواهد بود تاووش بر وزن چاووش صدا را گویند عموماً و آواز
یار را گویند خصوصاً الشاهد علیه شعر تاووش کیم اونغا شیدین کیلنادیرمین بلمزی تاشیمد قراایشیلیدین شایه کر کاج نشا
مین کیم قویاشیمد ه تاوشان قوینی اسم جنسیست که آنرا بفارسی کوکره ‌ات و بعربی خنضا خوانند تاوشانجیل بسکون واو
نون و لام و فتح شین قرشت و کسر جیم ترکی رومی عقاب بود که آنرا بفارسی اله ‌نامند تاوشقان بضم واو و سکون شین قرشت
خرگوش را باشد و نیز نام سالیست از سنا لهای ترکی و تاوشان مصحف آنست تاووشقان او یقو یی کنایه از غفلت بود چنانکه خسرو
شیرین گوید شعر تاووشقان اویقوسی آندین آلیب هوش شا هنیب لیری دین خواب خرگوش تاووغ تاووق بضم واو
مرغ خانگی باشد چنانکه در صحیح سکندری در مکالمه سکندر با سوالی را گوید شعر بو بیوری که سوز بیلا آبجه تاووق
که کجد را بیفه بولغای تاووق و آنرا بلغت مغولی تاعوق تاحوق و تاقوی و بعربی دجاجه خوانند و سکون واو و فتح
ان بزی و امراب چنانکه گوید شعر اوزنی سوا لیغ ایلما علم کرنا وغونکا کوک نوا سین شقه ناسی صحو شاحین خلوه
است و نیز در فرهاد و شیرین در سنک انداختن فرهاد گوید شعر نیزه ناش آتیب یدی روان سونکا صحجه تاوغونیک
تاولوغا بسکون واو و ضم لام تاولغا ضم واو و سکون لام کلاه خود را نامند الشاهد علی الاول شعر مدی جوشن ارکی
اشنکت دیک کیم اوق چرکیتا و لوغا اولا اوق اوزی رجکا زنکلیغ و شاهد ثانی را صحیح سکندری در وصف لشکر چین فدکر

روی کلاه خود گوید شعر تاوولغا داچینی بالاو دلپذیر کیب جوشن او سیدا چینی حریر تا ز داو لوغه و داو ولغه نیز خوانند
و مؤلف رومی در فرائد هر دو را بی شعر از نسخه سقیم بآن نحو خوانده اند که ع تا غا دا لغا داچین یا لو ر پذیر و فرائد الغار معنی
دوش تصویر کرده و تاقار را بآن مناسبت بمعنی نیز نوشته و مؤلف رومی تا قار را بمعنی تو قر که عبارت از حلقه زبانه دار باشد نوشته
و دالغار را بمعنی کلاه خود بیان نموده و بلا و زر اهم سکار نگذاشته و صنع معنی برای آن کرده بجز بیان بمعنی درخشان مذکر
در صبری هم مناسبت کرده الفاظ و معانی هم اختراعیست مع الیا من المشتقات تا لمیما قع بسکون یا بمعنی لغزیدن بود
چنانکه در صحیح سکندری در آغاز نظم کتاب گوید شعر بو یول قطعیدین تایما لغنیک خدایدی سو بخمه سو ستا یماغنیک
دایدی تایدوق لغزیدیم تایار و تایادور میلغزد و نیز تایار بمعنی تکیه می‌دهد و با معنی تاخود از مصدر تایا ملاق است
و معنی فاعل و مصدر هم می‌آید تایما یادور میلغزد و لغزنده است تایغان و تایادورغان لغزنده و لغزیده و بمعنی تکنده
هم می‌آیند تای و تایغیل مفرد مخاطب از فعل امر تایما و تایما غیل مفرد مخاطب از فعل نفی تاینیک و تایینکیز و تاینکلار
جمع مخاطب از فعل امر تایغانلار و تایمانیکز و تایما نکلار جمع مخاطب از فعل نفی تایمان و تایماس مین میلغزم تایامین و تایارمین
تایادورمین و تایادورام یعنی میلغزم و تایلرمین و تایارام با مصدر تایاماق نیز اشتراک دارد بمعنی تکیه میدهم تایماس میلغزد
و بمعنی فاعل و مصدر منفی هم می‌آید تایماسینکینه نبلغزیدنت تایارینکینه بلغزیدنت و تایلرینکینه با مصدر تایاماق اشتراک دارد
یعنی بتکیه کردنت تایب و تابیبان و تاییش لغزیده تایمیشانلت لغزیدی تایساوینکا فایب تواند لغزید تایالا
تواند لغزید تایا تما یا لغزان لغزان تایای و تایین بلغزم و بلغزد و بلغزی و لغزیده و نیز یعنی تکیه دهم و دهد و دهی
و داده تایساق و تایغای بزو تایغای بزو تالکا و تایالیک بلغزیم و تایلی یعنی تکیه دهیم تایغیلی برای لغزیدن و تا لغزیدن تایغالی
چون لغزید و بلغزد تایغوچی لغزنده تایغوچیه و تایغوچه و تایماغیه تا لغزیدن و بقدر لغزیدن تا یا آلغای تنکجه مقدر که تواند
لغزید تایغو میزدی و خواهیم لغزید تایغونکوز دو خواهید لغزید تایغو سیدلار و در خواهند لغزید تا لغوم و تا لغوم بود
لغزیدن محکم نخواهد بود تایغولوق لغزیدنی تایغای و تایا و تایا فایدیوی تایدیلت بلغزد تایما فای تایماغای یا سلغای نباید
لغزد چنانکه شاهد بر اول از در فرهاد و شیرین در ارشاد خضر علیه السلام فرهاد را بجشودن طلسم سقراط گوید شعر
دیما نیکیم تایما فای اول یولدا کامینکث سانا غلیغ کام ایله بولسون خرامینکث یعنی اینست کر اگر بگوش که در آن راه قدمت بلغزد
باید که رفتنت بشمار قدم نباشد و مؤلف رومی تایما فای را در این شعر تینما فای بکسر تا و سکون نون خوانده و تینما فای را بمعنی سست ورزن
نوشته و شعر مزبور را شاهد آورده سهو او ظاهر است زیرا که تینما فای بمعنی انبار نجید نباشد و این معنی بمقام موقع لستانیغو
تایار دیلت لغزیدی و همچنانکه بلغزد و تایلردیلت نیز با مصدر تایاماق اشتراک دارد چنانکه مذکور شود تایمیماق بکسر با
و سکون تای قرشت مصدر متعدیست یعنی لغزاندن و صیغ آن بدستور تای قرشت اشتقاق می‌یابد تایلیماق بکسر یا و سکون
لغزیده شدن و آنرا اتراک روم تایماق گویند مع الکون تایلیدیلار لغزیده شدند الشاهد علیه شعر توز قوی نوا
ایا غینک عشق کوپیدا کیم آندا اشک سوودین ایل کوپ تایلیدیلار تایلیغان و تایلوغان تعالیلدعه مع الغزیده شونده و لغزیده
شده چنانکه شاهد بر اول را بمعنی اول در هفتم سیم از تنبیهات محبوب القلوب گوید که ایشدا آشوفنان کوپ تایلیود کوپ
تایلیغان کوپ بیقیلیو و بمعنی مصدر هم می‌آید تایلیب و تایلیبان فاعلیش لغزیده شده چنانکه شاهد بر اول در آخر
حیرة الابرار در عنوان سخن گوید که اول فول حکایتی دکیم ایا غی تایلیب یا غلیغ آشنی شاه نینک با شی کاسه سیفه آوکر

تایلغاج چون لغزیده شد و شود چنانکه در سد سکندری در فضیلت عقل گوید شعر کنه لا یبدا کیمسا بولسا السیز تاییلغاق
الیاغ بولغای اول دستگیر و تایاق صیغ بزین یاق با لام اشتقاق می یابد تایاماق نعتج تای با الف کشیده یعنی تکیه دادن و
تایاماقیز بهمین معنی باشد تایادوق تکیه دادیم تایادوق و تایادور تکیه میدهد و تایار با مصدر تایاماق نیز اشتراک
دارد یعنی میلغزد چنانکه گذشت و بمعنی فاعل و مصدر منفی هم می آید تایانمایدور تکیه نمیدهد و نداده است تایاغان
تایادورغان تکیه دهنده و تکیه داده و بمعنی مصدر هم می آید تایا و تایاغیل مفرد مخاطب الامر تایاما و تایاماغیل
مفرد مخاطب النهی تایانک و تایانکیز و تایانکلار جمع مخاطب الامر تایامانک و تایامانکیز و تایامانکلار جمع مخاطب النهی
تایامان و تایاماسمین تکیه نمیدهم تایای من و تایارمین و تایادورمین و تایادام تکیه میدهم و تایادام نیز با مصدر
تایاماق اشتراک دارد یعنی میلغزم چنانکه مذکور شد تایاماس تکیه نمیدهد و بمعنی فاعل و مصدر منفی هم می آید تایاماسلیک
بتکیه ندادنت تایاماینکه بتکیه دادنت و تایاینکه با مصدر تایاماق اشتراک دارد تایاب و تایاپان و تایامیش تکیه
داده الشاهد علی الاول شعر هم یسایان بولین قطع المهالک دشوار ایروش ضعف دین کیم بوروین قولا تایاب
دیوار هذا الشاهد علی الثالث شعر قوبدی اول سرو دیونی بو خاکی تن بیمار غه شمع نیکلیغ کیم تایامیشلار آنی دیوار
تایامیشانک تکیه داده تایاسا بولغای و تایاب بولغای تکیه تواند داد تایای آلغای تکیه تواند داد تایای تکیه
دهان تایای و تایایین تکیه بدهم و بدهد و بدهی و داده و نیز با مصدر تایاماق اشتراک دارد یعنی بلغزم و بلغزد و بلغزی
و لغزیده تایاسا و تایاغایمن تایاغای و تایالی و تایالینک تکیه بدهیم و تایالی بمعنی بلغزیم هم باشد تایاغالی جهة
تکیه دادن و تا تکیه داده تایاغاج چون تکیه داد و بدهد تایاغوچی تکیه دهنده تایاغوسی و تایاغوچی و تایالغا
تا تکیه دادن و بقصد تکیه دادن تایاغالی تایالغانینکه بقصد تکیه تکیه توانی داد تایاغومیزدور تکیه خواهیم داد
تایاغوسیدور تکیه خواهند داد تایاغوسیلار تایاغوسیدور تکیه خواهند داد تایاماغوم و تایاغوم یوق تکیه نخواهم داد
تایاماغومدور و تایامغوم یوق تکیه دادن بحکم نخواهد بود تایاغولوق تکیه دادنی تایاغای و تایاسلا و تایادیق تایادیک تکیه
دهد تایاغوسی و تایارلیک تکیه دادنی و چنانکه تکیه دهد و تایاریک هم با مصدر تایاماق شرکت چنانکه گذشت
شد تایاماق مع التاء مصدر متعدیت یعنی تکیه دادن و در معنی با تایلماق مرادف و مطابق و معنی صیغ با یکدیگر موافق
صیغ او با تای قرشت اشتقاق می یابد تایانماق مع النون تکیه کردن عموما و به پشت تکیه کردن خصوصا تایانغادیک یعنی مثل
تکیه کننده و پشت بدبولادی الشاهد علیه شعر ضعفیم اچره قیلدی ناسیفه تایانغاندیک تموز هر یانان کونجانک
یا بوسنغان کونی بینک دبولادی و تای صیغ بدستور بانون اشتقاق می یابد تایاقلاماق چوب زدن و آن ماخوذ از تایاق یعنی
چوب دستی بود چنانکه در عالم التفاسیر در صفت پیری گوید که بیرکیسینکا کیم تلق لا تمین اول ایشیش بیکیتی آشنای رای
بیله بارینا سا سیغیا نه الفاظیلیه بخشی آنینیکا ایشیو تایاقلاغانیه ذاتی صیدیقلو ایشی تایاغلادوق چوب زدیم تایاغلا
تایاغلادی چوب میزند و تایاغلار بمعنی فاعل و مصدر هم می آید تایاغلاماس چوب نمیزند و نزده است تایاغلاغان
تایاغلادورغان چوب زننده و چوب زده و بمعنی مصدر هم می آید تایاغلا و تایاغلاغیل مفرد مخاطب الامر تایاغلاما و تایاغلاماغیل
مفرد مخاطب النهی تایاغلانک و تایاغلانکیز و تایاغلانکلار جمع مخاطب الامر تایاغلامانک و تایاغلامانکیز و تایاغلامانکلار جمع مخاطب
النهی تایاغلامان و تایاغلاماسمین چوب نمیزنم تایاغلای من و تایاغلارمین و تایاغلادورمین و تایاغلادام چوب میزنم تایاغلاماس

چوب نمیزند و بمعنی فاعل و مصدر منفی هم می آید تایاغلاماسلیک بچوب زدنت تایاغلاماینکه بچوب زدنت تایاغلاب تایاغلاپان
تایاغلامیش چوب زده تایاغلامیشانک چوب زده تایاغلاسا بولغای و تایاغلاب بولغای چوب تواند زد تایاغلای آلغای چوب تواند
زد تایاغلای و تایاغلایین تایاغلای چوب زنان تایاغلای و تایاغلایین چوب بزنم و بزند و بزنی و بزنیم تایاغلاغاق تایاغلای
تایاغلای بزند تایاغلایلی و تایاغلالینک چوب بزنیم تایاغلاغالی برای چوب زدن و تا چوب زده تایاغلاغاج چون چوب بزند و بزنه
تایاغلاغوچی چوب زننده تایاغلاغوسی و تایاغلاغوچی و تایاغلاغالی تا چوب زدن و بقصد چوب زدن تایاغلای آلغاینکه بقصد
چوب توانی زد تایاغلاغومیزدور چوب خواهیم زد تایاغلاغوسیدور چوب خواهند زد تایاغلاغوسیلار چوب خواهند زد تایاغلا
ماغوم و تایاغلاغوم یوق چوب نخواهم زد تایاغلاماغوم و تایاغلاغوم یوق چوب زدن بحکم نخواهد بود تایاغلاغولوق چوب
زدنی تایاغلاغای و تایاغلاسا و تایاغلادیک چوب بزند تایاغلاغودیک و تایاغلادیک تایاغلاریک چوب زدنی و چنانکه
زند تایاغلاتماق مع التاء مصدر متعدیت یعنی چوبکاری فرمودن تایاغلاتتی چوبکاری فرمود چنانکه در سد سکندری
در داستان بارق بربری گوید شعر اجازت سوز ین عرض قیلغاچ قورب تایاغلاتتی قرا یلدیان استوروب و تایا
صیغ بدستور تای قرشت اشتقاق می یابد تایاغلاشماق مع الشین مصدر مفاعله است یعنی همدیگر را چوبکاری فرمودن
و صیغ آن با شین اشتقاق می یابد تایاغلانماق مع النون یعنی مضروب شدن و صیغ آن با نون اشتقاق می یابد من الجوامد
تالغ و تایاق بمعنی تکیه باشد و آن حاصل مصدر تایاماق بمعنی تکیه دادنست و بالمجاز چوب بستر را گویند چنانکه میر نظامی
راست شعر اوخشاتی قامتینک عرعر و صنوبر نیلغبان بجلوه سیماسار ایریمیش الفدین تایاغی و مولف فرهنگ جهانگیری
این لفظ را تاباق با بای ابجد خوانده و فارسی تصور کرده و بمعنی چوبدستی نوشته و صاحب برهان قاطع نیز متابعت کرده صیغ و شواهد
که در ذیل مصدر تایاماق و تایاغلاماق مذکور گشته بر سهو ایشان بر برهان قاطع است تایاغاق بفتح یا و سکون نون گیه
کاه تیزه بروزن سبیضه بترکی درمی همشیره مادر بود که آنرا بعربی خاله خوانند تایمش بسکون یا و کسر شین قرشت لغت
ختائیان بمعنی بسیر رقا قرق و نام استاد بود و ختائی هم نامند تایغاج بسکون یا و قاف و فتح غین معجمه با الف کشیده
جای لغزیدن را نامند و بسیار گوید و کثر الکلام را هم گویند لا ادری شعر ای بیکت بولما حدیث و گفتگو یونگ سیکیل
آدمی خلقه اهانت بستکوهر تایغان تیل تاینوس بضم نون معجمه و سکون را مهمله بسیار لغزش تایلاق شیریه ساله را
تایلاغود هرکز لغزش نکنند تایغاجاق بکسر یا و سکون نون و قاف و فتح جیم با الف کشیده مکان لغزیدن را گویند بالعموما
حرف التاء مع الباء من المشتقات توپولماق بضم تای مهمله و سکون لام خودبه فوج لشکر خصم زدن و صیغ آن
بدستور تو قول اشتقاق می یابد توپارهاماق بفتح تای مهمله و سکون رای قرشت برکی روی یکجا جمع کردن و گرد نمودن توپ ناساما
کنایه از خاک انداز آن باشد و آن چنانست که از برای سپید کردن چیز در پرده در خانه تاریک خاک ریخته جمعی که ملتنه
در دی بایشان باشد با گرانه تاریک در آمده دست با خاک میرسانند که شاید آن تیره بختی مسروق را بجا بیند از تند
چنانکه گوید شعر نوای فراقینکدین اول نوع ایتی که کردی تاپیلماس غمینک ساتسا تو پراغ بر الجاما توب بدو معنی آمده
اول بمعنی ضیر و بیخ و بن باشد چنانکه در خسرو شیرین در تمجید گوید شعر کمی کیم علم دریاسی تا پسه توج بتی للاشیر توبی تالیب توبی
دوم و در لیلی مجنون گوید شعر بو لور قرا برتوبی کابانا ق بولماس عرب با بحر با شی چیقارماق و نیز گوید شعر عشق یا غیند
ز و ایلکی اسیدیم نخلین یوق که شاخین او شاتیب بلکه توبین هم قوندار یب دوم لفظیست که از برای مبالغه واقع می شود

مثل توبتوز و توب توغری یعنی بیسار است و مسطح و با بای عجمی سه معنی دارد اول فوج و جمعیتی را گویند که یکجا فراهم آمده باشند
دوم گوی مدور بود که آنرا بعربی کره نامند سیم المجاز توپی را گویند که بجانب خصم اندازند و آنرا بعربی مدفع خوانند
و بفارسی طاقه اقمشه و امتعه بود توپارلاق بفتح بای عجمی و لام و سکون رای مهمله و قاف ترکی روی چیزی بود که طارا
گویند توپال بفتح بای عجمی و سکون لام دو معنی دارد اول لنگی باشد که پای او بزمین نرسد و باسر پنجه راه رود دوم برانه
نقره و مس و امثال آنرا گویند که در وقت پتک زدن از آن جدا شود و در این معنی با فارسی مشترکست و بفارسی با بای محکم
استعمال میشود توپالاق بفتح بای عجمی بیخی است بقدر زیتون و بزرگتر از آن و سیاه و اندرونش سفید و خوشبو که بلبان
سعد و بفارسی مشک زمین گویند مدر بول و مفتت حصاة و مفتح عروق و مجفف جراحات و جمیع سم عقرب شرابا و ضمادا
نافعست توپالانک بفتح بای عجمی و لام و سکون نون و کاف عجمی باد شدید گردامیز بود که باران نداشته باشد توبان بمعنی کون
و واژگون و سرازیر بود الشاهد علیه شعر یوزی توبان توشوبان مرکبینک ایزیکا قالت ییرا و زره قرمنی تیلمان کبی
کدای تلاش و مؤلف رومی توبانرا دربن شعر توبان با تاف و یای حطی خوانده و توبانرا بمعنی زیر و پایین نوشته و شعر مذکور
استشهاد جسته و نصیری هم متابعت کرده هردو سهو کرده اند توبتوز یعنی راست است و مسطح محض توبتوی ترکی
پر و مملو محض تبت بتشدید باء مفتوحه نام شهریست از ملک چین که مشک خوب از آنجا حاصل شود و بکسر تا نیز گفته اند
توبچاق بسکون بای عجمی و قاف و فتح جیم عربی اسبی را گویند که اندامش جمع و گرد و فربه باشد چنانکه در فصل هشتم از محبوب القلوب
در وصف فناق گوید که کونکول لاری توبچاق سکریتیور دین آرام تاپماق اوزلاری عاجز الانک توز کا چاپماق و از او توبچاق
هم گویند توبچین نام پادشاهیست که چنگیزخان بوضع سیاسات امور ملکی نوشته توبچیپیشی بمعنی اجتناب از توبه
و در هشت اندیشه کردن باشد توبراغ و توپراق خاک را گویند الشاهد علیه شعر بو که تیشه ایتیلای کوزخاک
پاییره یه غه بیل ککو همزبی قوا توپراقغه همسنک ایلادینک توبیز یعنی بیمار عمیق که نه نداشته باشد مثل کل و نوره
سلاحهای شعر مکمل جیبه لیک آتلار کچیم پوش جهان توبیز تینکزدیک با شلادی جوش توپتازغان با بای عجمی توپی
باشد که بجانب خصم اندازند توبیته آغاج نام محلیست از مواضع آذربایجان که مابین شیروان و گرجستان واقعست توپوز بفتح
بای عجمی مشدد و سکون زای هوز آن آلتی است آهنین که سر آن بطریق چماق مدور باشد و آنرا بعربی دبوس گویند و توپوز و
آهنین توپوق بضم بای عجمی مفصل پا بود که آنرا بفارسی بژول و بعربی کعب نامند توبولغو نام درختیست صلب و سخت
که از چوب آن دسته قمچی سازند توبه چاق همان اسب توبچاق بود که مذکور شد توپه بفتح بای عجمی دو معنی دارد اول تل بلند را
گویند چنانکه در فرهاد و شیرین گوید شعر فلک سوری توپه سین لار دمیتینک فخ توباشدین آخرین لا ربهتینک فخ که کوهی
بس مع ابوالفه سا الدینک بیلک راک توپه نینک توفراغین آلدینک و در تاریخ نا برینامه گفته است که پشه دین ایلکاری
توپه او ستیکا چیقیلم تدبیم فرق سر را مانند الشاهد علیه شعر تو پامی بیر زیش الیکی تینک ایتیر بیر پله که هر کیشی که
بیتیب گویدا باشیمغه قامت و بکسر تا نیز باشد و معنی مستعملست توبی بکسر بای بی رونق چوبی عرقچین شبیه دار بود که آنرا
زیر دزیر کلاه خود بر سر کذارند چنانکه در وصف لشکر برطاس و روس گوید شعر تا و ولغا لاری توپی بکلیغ الیغه او تا
باش او زره شادیغ قوش بری چون کلاه خود طایفه برطاس و روس بشکل عرقچین هم میباشد لهذا توبی مانند وصف کرده
و در جای دیگر کلاه خود لشکر او زبک را چون مغفر و طاس چرکسی ذکر کرده یعنی سکانی چنانکه در باب جیم مع الرا مذکور شد

شد توبیه بکسر بای ابجد و فتح یای حطی المذبان را گویند که در صحرا چرید فربه شده باشد مع التاء المثناة توتماق بمعنی گرفتن
و داشتن باشد چنانکه گوید شعر گوز الیر توتقاندا کیم کوز توتماق او ناس جز المه آلن توتفیل کیم الم خیلینیا یالار بابال یعنی صبر آمده
چشم که خیال چشم میتوان داشت آنرا بچیز که حیل الم را پامال میکند یعنی شراب را و لفظ گرفتن و داشتن هر معنی که در فارسی استعمال
میشود توتماقی در ترکی بهمان معنی می آید مثل اینکه گویند که چنین شد یعنی متصور کرد و همچنین کاسه داشتن و پایدار داشتن و چشم داشتن
و اشباه آنها توتنوق گرفتیم و داشتیم توتار و توتادور میگیرد و میدارد و توتار بمعنی فاعل و مصدر هم می آید توتماید و
میگیرد و نگرفته است و نمیدارد و نداشته است توتغان و توتارغان و توتادورغان گیرنده و گرفته و دارنده و داشته چنانکه
شاهد بر اول بمعنی گرفته گوید شعر ای نوائی شاه چتری سایه سیندین غار یعلات توتغان الیر لولی آشفته پرچم راه انش بمعنی
مصدر هم می آید چنانکه شاهد بر اول بمعنی داشتن در ذیل توتماق مذکور شد توت و توتغیل مفرد مخاطب امر فصل الرکنا
علی الاول المعنی الثانی شعر ساقیا در جامیمکدین منکا توت توشیدین و لیلغی یوزنیر غوت توتوبرلابار
اوروب توت خانقه سرغوتین یر مغنی بساناقه وله شعر قصر جاه ینکینه سپهر اجید ایوان بوازیتوت هم سهی
دین بیریله یکسان بولدی توته توت یعنی مچو کر و شاهد بر ثانی بمعنی او در ذیل توتماق گذشت توتما و توتماغیل مفرد
مخاطب نهی توتونک و توتونکیز و توتونکلار جمع مخاطب امر توتمانک و توتمانکیز و توتمانکلار جمع مخاطب نهی توتار
توتارمین بگیرم و بمیدارم توتامین توتارمین و توتادورمین و توتادورام میگیرم و میدارم توتماس بمیگیرد و نمیدارد و بمعنی فاعل
و مصدر منفی هم می آید توتماسینکنه نگرفته و نداشته توتارینکنه بگرفته و بداشته توتوب و توتوبان و توتمیش
گرفته و داشته توتمیشانک گرفته و داشته توتسا بولور بمعنی توتیب بولور میتواند داشت الشاهد علی الاول شعر چون از قسمین
ایل کامی پله عقل الدیلادی عشق دین توتسا بولور بخلاق معدوم توتسا بولغای توتوب توتالغای توان گرفت و توان داشت توتالغای
تواند گرفت و تواند داشت توتا توتسا گرفته گرفته و داشته چنانکه معنی ثانی گوید شعر کلک چین جو
اکماق و مطربی بو کیلسا توتا توتا و اولیر چاله سرچاله توتای توتاین یعنی بگیرم و بگیرد میگیری و گرفته و بدارم و
بدارد و بدارید و داشته چنانکه شاهد بر اول را بمعنی قول گوید شعر بوکلش کل لاری نینک چون و ماسی یوقتورای بیلا
توآچیلغای توتای کیم سین قنانینک کوکلرین آشور دونک و توتای خاشاک دود ناکرا هم گویند که با آتش نگهدارند
که تا در بگیرد توتساق و توتسانه و توتسای و توتکاو توتالیک بگیرم و بدارم توتغالی برای گرفتن و تا گرفته و برای داشتن و تا
داشته توتغاج چون گرفت و بگیرد چون داشت و بدارد توتغوچی گیرنده و دارنده چنانکه در مکتوب لیلی بمجنون گوید شعر
مریاری او رایهید یا نانک تکیلت دین توتغوچی کاز دم اتیاکلیک دین توتغومی و توتغونچه و توتغانچه تا گرفتن و بقدر گرفتن و تا
داشتن و بقدر داشتن چنانکه شاهد بر ثانی را بمعنی بقدر گرفتن گوید شعر هر کیشی کیم یر صیندا پر سینماء دیلک سا هو ابر
تانک ایلمایین کوکی کر توتغونچه ماشاک و آهی تاین توتا آلغانینچه بقدر یکه توانی گرفت و توانی نگهداشت توتغوم و توتغوسیدیم خواهم گرفت
و خواهم داشت توتغونکی و بخواهی گرفت و خواهی داشت چنانکه بمعنی اول گوید شعر تیره لیکده در تیتو توتغونک صفا
خای گوش ایها الساقی لنادم ساکه خذ طلسما توتغوسیدیه خواهد گرفت و خواهد داشت بالمعنی الاول شعر ساقیا جام
دایم غنیمت دور حیات توتغوسیدیهم چون اجل کاسینی دوار غامت توتالغوم و توتغوم یوق نخواهم گرفت و نخواهم داشت توتا
الماغم و توتالغوم یوق گرفتن ممکن نخواهد بود و داشتن ممکن نخواهد بود توتغولوق گرفتنی و داشتنی توتغای و توتلو و توتسا

توتسون توتديك بيجيد و بدار دار الشاهد على الاول بالمعنى الاول شعر كونكلوم اكر كاج انيسيم بولدى توتغايمو ايكاش
بمنظاندا هيچ كيم بو نوع مهمات سرانجام ايتش و در تاريخ الملوك در فوت اسكندر بمعنى ثانى كويد كه وصيت قيلدى كيم تا الار ايلين
تابوت دين تاشقارى چيقارغايلار كيم عالم اهليغه موجب تنبيه بلكه عبرت بولغاى كيم عالم دين ايليك تارتا توتغايلار
معنى كشيده دار تورسا شاهد بمعنى ثانى كويد شعر شاه غازى ايشيكين تينكرى بيبى توتسون كيم تا توتالار ضربها الاك
خانلار ضربلار و شاهد بمعنى ثانى كويد شعر كيمنى مينديك خانقه دين سوردى لار اهل صلاح مضمم توتديك
نادرى ارا اوباشيق توتنوديك و توتلديك كرفتم و همچنانكه بكيرد و داشتى و همچنانكه بدارد توتولماق مضمم تاين توكول
كرفته شدن توتولدى كرفته شد چنانكه در خاتمه حيرت الابرار كويد شعر آيتوريغه چونكه قويولدى كونكول آيتماى
اوليت توتولدى كونكول و باقى صيغ بر اين سياق بالاتمام اشتقاق مى يابد توتوزماق مصدر متعدى يعنى كيرانيدن
وصيغ آن با لفظ توز اشتقاق مى يابد توتابير مالك بمعنى داشتن و بيرواك اكرچه بمعنى دادن باشد اما در بعضى از كلمات كه اير الدى شود
افاده معنى لغوى نميكند بلكه از براى مبالغه است توتابر و توتابر كيل بمعنى بدار چنانكه شاهد براول اين معنى ثانى در خاتمه
كتاب فرهاد و شيرين كويد شعر بو دم لار كيم كونكول مينى آيدين آچتينك مينينك بيلكيم بيله ظالمغه سان چتينك كه الارغه
داغى آيدين عطايش غمى لار ضر داغى آئى توتابر توتابر كاى و توتابرو توتابر اى توتابر غيرتوتابر ديك بدار الشاهد على الرابع بالمعنى الثانى
شعر شيخ و اهل خانقه تينكرى توتابرسون منكا حق يولين كم كه كيلى ديرها اوباشيق توتوشماق مع الشين و
توتاغلاشماق از باب مفاعله است يعنى همديكر را كرفتن توتوشتى لار و توتاغلاشتى لار همديكر را كرفتند چنانكه در صفت سياه
در وصف شكار بهرام كه زيركه شكار كاه كور بهرام شد كويد الشاهد على الاول شعر سى ايله پيرچين توتوشتى لار مضمم انكلاباتوق
جوشتى لار توتوشتوق و توتاغلاشتوق همديكر را كرفتيم توتوشور لار و توتوشادور لار و توتاغلاشورلار و توتاغلاشادور لار همديكر را ميكيرند
توتوشماى دور لار و توتاغلاشماى دور لار همديكر را نميكيرند و نكرفته اند توتوشغان و توتوشقان و توتاشادورغان و توتاغلاشغان و
توتاغلاشقان و توتاغلاشادورغان همديكر را كيرنده و كرفته و بمعنى مفعول هم مى آيند توتوش و توتوشغيل و توتاغلاش و توتاغلاشغيل
مفرد مخاطب از فعل امر توتوشماو توتوشماغيل و توتاغلاشماو توتاغلاشماغيل مفرد مخاطب از فعل نهى توتوشونك و توتوشونكوز و
توتوشونكلار و توتاغلاشينك و توتاغلاشينكيز و توتاغلاشينكلار جمع مخاطب از فعل امر توتوشمانك و توتوشمانكيز و توتاغلاشمانك و
توتاغلاشمانكيز و توتاغلاشمانكلار جمع مخاطب از فعل نهى توتوشامين و توتوشاسين و توتاغلاشامين و توتاغلاشاسين ميكيرم
توتوشامين و توتوشادورمين و توتاغلاشامين و توتاغلاشادورمين و توتاغلاشورمين ميكيرم
توتوشماس و توتاغلاشماس نميكيرد و بمعنى فاعل و مستقبل منفى هم مى آيد توتوشماسينكيز و توتاغلاشماسينكيز نكرفتيد توتوشونكيز
توتاشونكيز نكرفتيد توتوشوب و توتوشوبان و توتوشيبان و توتاغلاشيب و توتاغلاشيبان و توتاغلاشيبش همديكر را كرفته
الشاهد على الاول شعر يوق ايريكه كه ناديريدا قول لار توتوشوب بولنا يو القصه ادام ياى منكا دم هست و شاهد
رابع در تاريخ بابرى جنس هندوكوه است كه بر افغان بيله چابقولاشيب توتاغلاشيب و ليكى تاريخ دين بيله اوق اچى لار
توتوشيبان و توتاغلاشيبان همديكر را كرفته توتوشا بيلكا و توتوشا بيلكاو و توتاغلاشا بيلكا و توتاغلاشا بيلكاى همديكر
توان كرفت توتوشا آلغاى و توتاغلاشا آلغاى همديكر توان كرفت توتوشا و توتوشاو توتاغلاشا و توتاغلاشا همديكر را كرفته كرفته
توتوشاى و توتوشايين و توتاغلاشاى و توتاغلاشايين همديكر را بكيريم و بكيريد و بكيرند و كرفته توتوشاق و توتوشقاق

توتوشقالو و توتوشالبك و توتاغلاشاق و توتاغلاشالبك همديكر را بكيريم توتوشغالي
توتاغلاشغالى براى همديكر را كرفتن و تا كرفته توتوشقاچ و توتاغلاشقاچ همديكر را كرفت و بكيرد توتوشغوچى و توتاغلاشغوچى
همديكر را كيرنده توتوشغوچى و توتوشغانچه و توتاغلاشغوچى و توتاغلاشغانچه همديكر را كرفتن و تا كرفتن
توتوشا الغاى و توتاغلاشا الغاى و توتاغلاشا الغانيكيز همديكر كه همديكر را توانى كرفت توتوشغوسى و توتاغلاشغوسى در همديكر را خواهيم كرفت
توتوشغونكز بيدور و توتاغلاشغونكز بيدور همديكر را خواهيد كرفت توتوشغوسى لار دور و توتاغلاشغوسى لار دور همديكر را خواهند كرفت توتوشماغوم
توتوشماغوم يوق و توتاغلاشماغوم و توتاغلاشماغوم يوق همديكر را نخواهم كرفت توتوشالماغوم يوق و توتاغلاشالماغوم و توتاغلاشا الماغوم
همديكر را كرفتن ممكن نخواهد بود توتوشغولوق و توتاغلاشغولوق كرفتنى توتوشماقلار و توتوشوماقلار و توتوشولار
و توتوشديلار و توتاغلاشديلار و توتاغلاشسالار و توتاغلاشسونلار و توتاغلاشديكلار همديكر را بكيرند
توتوشغوچيلار و توتوشولدى و توتاغلاشغوچيلار همچنانكه بكيرد توتوشتورماق و توتاغلاشتورماق مصدر متعدى
يعنى دو نفر را بهمديكر بستن و كرفتن وصيغ آن با لفظ توز اشتقاق مى يابد توتاشماق بفتح تا و شين و سكون شين بمعنى
دركرفتن استعمال شود اما از آنكه دركرفتن آتش باشد با مصاحبت توتاشتى دركرفت چنانكه در ترجيعات كويد شعر تاناى
ديب خبر و شبو مقصود دين توتاشتى بى تيم ايله محبتيم توتاشتى و توتاشادور دركيرد توتاشور مصدر هم مى
توتاشماى دركرفته است الشاهد على الاول بالمعنى الثانى شعر
منكا ... مى آيند
چنانكه شاهد ... حيرت الابرار كويد
توتاشقالى توتاش و توتاشغيل مفرد مخاطب از فعل امر
توتاشماو و توتاشماغيل مفرد مخاطب از فعل نهى توتاشينك جمع مخاطب از فعل امر توتاشمانك و توتاشمانكيز
توتاشمانكلار جمع مخاطب از فعل نهى توتاشمان و توتاشمانك توتاشادورمين
توتاشماس بمعنى فاعل مى آيد توتاشماسينكيز بهمديكر توتاشورونكيز
توتاشيب و توتاشيبان در كرفته توتاشمايين در كرفت توتاشا آلغاى
تواند دركرفت توتاشا و توتاشا دركرفته دركرفته توتاشاى و توتاشايين دركيرم و دركيرد و دركيرى و دركيرد كفته توتاشاق
توتاشغايمز و توتاشغاى و توتاشا آلغاى براى دركرفتن و تا دركرفته توتاشقاچ چون دركرفت و دركيرد
توتاشغوچى دركيرنده توتاشغوجه و توتاشغونچه تا دركرفتن و بقدر دركرفتن توتاشا آلغانينكيز بقدر نيكه توانى دركرفت
توتاشغوسى دور خواهيم دركرفت توتاشغوسى خواهيد دركرفت توتاشغوسى لار دور خواهند دركرفت توتاشماغوم يوق
نخواهيم دركرفت توتاشا الماغوم و توتاشا الماغوم يوق دركرفتن ممكن نخواهد بود توتاشغولوق دركرفتنى توتاشماى و توتاشليو توتاشا
توتاشتورماق دركيرد توتاشقودلمق و توتاشتورديك دركرفتنو همچنانكه دركيرد توتاشتورماق مصدر متعدى يعنى در
كيرانيدن توتاشتوردى دركيرانيد الشاهد عليه شعر فتيله لار توتاشتوردى مكر غنيمكا قويلارداغ
انطار كونكول و باقى صيغ بر اين سياق موافق شق اول با لفظ توز اشتقاق مى يابد توتالماق بفتح تا و لام
ولام با الف كشيده و سكون نون از براهه راه بستن آمدن و صيغ آنها موافق شق ثانى اشتقاق مى يابد من الجوامد توتاش

منفصل و هم پیوسته چنانکه گوید شعر حسن دیوانی اخر مطلعده اول پیوسته تاش کاتب تقدیر آتینک مصرع لاتین
یازمیش توتلتوقلار سرکهنم بالشیکه بولماسا تانیغه تاش کیم نوعی پرقلانیغه تانوغلوقا کرچه یاش کیم نوعی [illegible]
کرتن چنانکه گذشت توتاشتوروق تندنک و دسته خاشالعبود که بدان آتش افروزند وآنرا توتروق و توتغوتیز گویند
و معرب ضم میخوانند توتاغان یعنی اهیم گیرنده واین لفظ مرکب است و مبلغ استعمال میشود توتای خلشا العدود [illegible]
که بدان آتش افروزند الشاهد علیه شعر غفلیلم بحود لغ ایچون توتینیان تغیله دود ایله دموا [illegible]
اوت یلمیلیب ونیز معانی مشقه دارد چنانکه در ذیل مصدر توتماق گذشت توتروق دسته خاشالعبود که بان آتش
افروزند چنانکه گوید شعر اوچین ایردی عشق اوتی خرد بیلیتیغی دیشوق گوید صوب هران بو توتروق یله دوش
قیلدیلار هر دوکه شعر ای نوایی عشقی هر کیم یار دعقانی اینتاسنا بیر یوز یندا نا یلغای توتروق اوچون خس بر کیمی و آنرا
توتاشتوروق و توتغوتیز نامند توتی به رمزن کیمی دعد و بحور را گویند توتغاق بکوی تای ثانی ولام و فتح عین مهمله
خوشخال بتکیکه روی سر ریشم باشد توتغو همان یعنی توتاشتوروق و توتروق است که در فوق مذکور شد توتغون یعنی گرفتار
و محبوس الشاهد علیه شعر هراوینغ ایجره تامللیشلار مهر بین کونکول وه تاچان بولغای بزینک توتغون بدنیدین خلاص
توتغونلوق گرفتاری و محبوسی توتماج یک نوع آشی است و آن چنان است که خمیر را پهن پهن بریده بپزند توتورغان و توتورغو
بلغت مغولی بزغ بود که آنرا سپرچه نیز گویند توتوت بجاد بره و خالی نامند که بر سر گیرند چنانکه در لسان الطیر
در داستان شیخ صنعان گوید شعر منظری آندین آسیلغان پرتوتی بر قیاشقه اولبولوب [illegible]
از برای پرده واونیا نغمه را محذوف ساخته تتق نویسند و مولف برهان تا بلع این لفظ را [illegible] شمرده بمعنی چادر و پرده
بزرگ نوشته توتوقلوغ و توتولوق یعنی گرفتگی و انقباض و بمجاز اعمی کسوف و خسوف نیز استعمال میشود چنانکه
لطفی راست شعر یانکیا یکا ندا کورثادی هیچ کیم آی توتولغونین جز ایچون توتیان [illegible] توتوم
دو معنی دارد اول بمعنی کف [illegible] دوم ترشی و حموضات را گویند و بفارسی [illegible] مع الجیم توتج بتاچ
رومی نوعی از ظروف است که آنرا روی گویند و بفارسی [illegible] نامند و نیز [illegible] و آن نام شهری است [illegible]
باهرقیب باهواز توجار ابرتلیرلیک و هوای [illegible] را خوانند مع الخا توختاتماق و توختاشماق فرونشستن و آرام یافتن
توتمانماق و توختاشماق با لام مستعملست توختادوق و توختاشوق آرام یافتیم توختایدور آرام مییابد و [illegible]
نامل و مسند هم میآید توختامایدور آرام نمییابد و نیافته است توختاغان و توختاغلغان و توختایدوغان و توختاشغان و
توختاشورغان و توختاشادورغان آرام یابنده و آرام یافته و بمعنی مصدر هم میآید توختا و توختاغیل و [illegible] امر مفرد مخاطب
از فعل امر توختانلو و توختاناغیل و توختاشا و توختاشماغیل امر مفرد مخاطب از فعل نهی [illegible]
جمع مخاطب از فعل امر [illegible] جمع مخاطب از فعل نهی توختامان
توختامایمن و توختاشمایمن آرام نمییابم [illegible] و توختاشایمن و توختاشورمن
توختاشادورمن و توختاشورمن آرام مییابم توختامان و توختاشمان آرام نمییابد و بمعنی نامل و مسند نفی هم میآید [illegible]
بآرام نیافتند [illegible] آرام یافتند [illegible] توختاشمیش
آرام یافته و نیز توختامیش نام پادشاه خوارزم است که معاصر امیر تیمور بوده و در میان ایشان معارضات اتفاق افتاده توختامیشالیق

توختاشیغای [illegible] آرام یافته [illegible] آرام توانیافت توختای آلغای
توختاشای آلغای آرام توانید یافت توختای توختیای و توختایو و توختاشا و توختاشا آرام یافتن توختای و [illegible]
آرام یابم و یابد و یابی و یافته توختاشا [illegible] و توختاشلی و [illegible] و توختاشا و توختاشقای
توختاشلی و توختاشلیلینک آرام یابیم توختاغالی و توختاشغالی برای آرام یافتن و تا آرام یافته توختاغلیچ و توختاشغلیچ چون آرام یافت
و یابد توختاغوچی و توختاشغوچی آرام یابنده توختاغوچه و توختاغونچه و [illegible] و توختاشقونچه و توختاشغانچه
تا آرام یافتن و بعد از آرام یافتن توختاالغاینک و توختاشاالغاینک بقدریکه آرام توانی یافت توختاغو دیر و توختاشغو دیر
یافت توختاغو دکوزه و توختاشغو دکوزه آرام خواهی یافت توختاغوسیدور و توختاشغوسیدور آرام خواهند یافت توختاغولوق
توختاشغولوق آرام یافتن توختاغای و توختاشای و توختاسون و توختاشسون و [illegible] و توختاشا و [illegible]
و توختاشدیلر آرام یافتند الشاهد علی الاول من لسان الطیر شعر [illegible] توختاغای دیب
[illegible] توختاغودیک و [illegible] آرام یافتم و چنانکه بیاید توختاتماق مع التا و
توختاشتورماق مصدر متعدی بمعنی آرام دادن و فرونشاندن توختاتالماس و توختاشتورالماس آرام نتواند داد الشاهد علی
الاول شعر ای حکیم [illegible] هیچ کیم کیم کاج آنی توختاتالماس [illegible]
مع الرا من المشتقات تورماق [illegible] بمعنی ایستادن بود چنانکه [illegible] پادشاه گوید
شعر [illegible] بمعنی ماندن و مکث کردن الشاهد علیه شعر
[illegible] تورودوق ایستادیم و
ماندیم توردونک ایستادی و ماندی چنانکه [illegible] گوید شعر نوایی [illegible]
کاروان‌دین [illegible] توردونک [illegible] الشاهد علی الاول المعنی الثانی شعر [illegible]
[illegible] بمعنی ماندن گوید شعر
یعنی [illegible] و نیز ایستاده است و ماندست تورغان و
[illegible] ایستنده و ایستاده و مکث کننده و مکث کرده چنانکه شاهد [illegible] گوید شعر
[illegible] تورغان [illegible] گوید شعر [illegible]
[illegible] ثابت [illegible] چنانکه گوید شعر [illegible]
[illegible] تورغان [illegible] و ایستاده است [illegible]
الشاهد علیه شعر ای نوایی [illegible] تورغیل امر مفرد
مخاطب از فعل امر الشاهد علی الاول المعنی الثانی شعر [illegible]
[illegible] تورغیل امر مفرد مخاطب
[illegible] جمع مخاطب از فعل امر [illegible] جمع مخاطب از فعل نهی [illegible]
[illegible] تورماس [illegible]
[illegible] الشاهد علی الثانی شعر ای نوایی [illegible]

رضه رضوان لها تورماس نمی ایستد و نمی ماند و بمعنی فاعل و مصدر منفی هم می آید تورماسینکه بنا ایستادنت و بنماندنت چنانکه
در صفحه سیاره مداستان مناظر اقلیم هفتم بمعنی ثانی می گوید شعر شهر دا تورماسینکه یمان قیل باشینک ایب کینارکا
ایمان قیل تورورینکه بایستادنت و بماندنت تورویمه تورویان و توروش ایستاده و مانده تورویشانک ایستاده و مانده تورو
بماس و تورا بولماس نمیتوان ایستاد و نمیتوان ماند چنانکه در خمسه خسرو شیرین در بیوفائی دنیا گوید الشاهد علی الثانی شعر
بونیکلیغ اوبدا یعنی تورنا بولماس که ظلم بر هم آندا امرنا بولماس تورا بولغاو توروب بولغه توان ایستاد و توان ماند تورالغای
تواند ایستاد و تواند ماند تورا تورا ایستاده ایستاده و مانده مانده چنانکه بمعنی ثانی گوید شعر کوسیکا کیرکالیمدا توسن ایشیم
لیک بولدم تولا تورا معطلش و بدو زنکاره هم مستعملت توراع و توراین بایستم و بایستد و بایستی و ایستاده بمانم و بماند و بمانی
و مانده چنانکه شاهد بر اول اطلاع بمعنی بمانم گوید شعر ایتکیم نچه حمد نیک سونکچه بویه اولاق تا که اوتنانک یافینا
سین نه اوتکونچه توراین تورناق و تورغلیز و تورغای یزو تورغلی بمعنی المنیک بایستیم و بمانیم تورغالی برای ایستادن و تا ایستا
و برای ماندن و تا ماندن تورغاج بمعنی ایستادن و هنوز ایستاده چنانکه گوید الشاهد علی الاول شعر بار دور و محراب
تورغلج بت قیلغاندیک سجود بجه قیلسام مثله قدتا ملالغ اثرنیک تار شود دوز تورا تورغاج یعنی من ایستاده ام
و برخاسته الشاهد علی الثانی شعر جانیغه کزونک جلی یان ظلم بوده ظلم کیمین تورا تورغلج تیلادکا یعنی تا ظلوم
تورغوچی ایستنده و مکث کننده تورغوسی و تورغونه و تورغاغنه تا ایستادن و بقصد ایستادن و تا ماندن و بقصد ماندن
الشاهد علی الثانی بالمعنی الاول شعر چو اول کافر چیپار کوزنا الماغای سیزای بسلمان الله که سین بعاوه کونکلو عوغا ایب
تورغوسی الکدم دیم تورا آلغای نیکچه بقصد که توانی ایستاد و توانی ماند تورغوسیز دور نخواهیم ایستاد و نخواهیم ماند
ایستاد و نخواهید ماند تورغوسیلار دور خواهند ایستاد و خواهند ماند تورغلغوم دور و تورغوم یوق نخواهم ایستاد و نخواهم ماند
الشاهد علی الاول بالمعنی الاول شعر گرچه اغیار دین الما قیلیغ ایما سوز سینی ممکن تورغلغوم دور یاقیبان آنجه کما امکان تا الآ
تورا آلماغوم دور و تورا آلغوم یوق ایستادن ممکن نخواهد بود و ماندن ممکن نخواهد بود تورغولوق ایستادنی و ماندنی تورغای
تورغای و تورسون و تورسونلار بایستد و بماند الشاهد علی الاول بالمعنی الاول شعر جفاغه توزولک و توزوق باغینکا زلفونک
نچوک که سایه منزلی که هر توبرغای تورغوز تورغودیک و تورادیک ایستادنی و همچنانکه بایستد و ماندنی و همچنانکه بماند
تورغوزماق مصدر متعدیست بمعنی طرح اول برخیزاندن دویم و اداشتن تورغوزدوق برخیزانیدیم و واداشتیم تورغوزدور
تورغوزادور برخیزاند و وا میدارد و تورغوزغوچی بمعنی فاعل و مصدر هم می آید تورغوزماید و برنخیزاند و بنخیزانده است تورغوزغان
تورغوزغان و تورغوزدوقان برخیزانده و برخیزانیده و واداشته و بمعنی مصدر هم می آید تورغوزو و تورغوزغیل مفرد امر
امر الشاهد علی الاول بالمعنی الثانی شعر کراهل تورغوزادی جسمیم و اول ای گویدای دو ستلار نشیم قبار ع آندا ایرم توروز
تورغوزمانک تورغوزمایکه تورغوزمانکلار جمع مخاطب از فعل نهی تورغوزمای و تورغوزماس برنخیزانم و وا نمیدارم تورغوزامین و تورغوزورمین
تورغوزادیمین و تورغوزارام برمیخیزانم و وامیدارم تورغوزماس برنخیزاند و وا نمیدارد و بمعنی فاعل و مصدر منفی هم می آید تورغوزماسینکه
برنخیزانیدنت و بوا نداشتنت تورغوزوبونکه برخیزانیدنت و بواداشتنت تورغوزوب و تورغوزوبان و تورغوزمیش برخیزانیده و وادا
تورغوزای و تورغوزاین برخیزانم و برخیزانیم برخیزانی و برخیزانید و وادارم و وادارد و وادارید و واداشته تورغوزمیشانک منو
خیزانیده و واداشته تورغوزا بیلغای و تورغوزولغای توان برخیزانید و توان واداشت تورغوزالغای تواند برخیزانید و تواند واداشت

تورغوزاو تورغوزا برخیزانیده برخیزانیده و واداشته واداشته تورغوزغای و تورغوزاین برنخیزانم و نخیزانید و نخیزانی و نخیزانید
و وا ندارم و ندارد و ندارید و نداشته چنانکه بمعنی وا نداشته در خسرو شیرین گوید شعر سومین تورغوزماین کوزیما لعلینک
تا ویغه آیب اشکی دین سو تورغوزماق و تورغوزغالیزو تورغوزغای یزو تورغوزالی تورغوزالیلی برخیزانیم و واداریم تورغوزغالی برای
برخیزاندن و تا برخیزانیدن و برای واداشتن و تا واداشتن و تا واداشته تورغوزغاج چون برخیزانید و برخیزاند و چون واداشت
و وادارد تورغوزغوچی برخیزاننده و وادارنده تورغوزغوسی و تورغوزغونه و تورغوزغاغنه تا برخیزانیدن و بقصد برخیزانیدن و تا
واداشتن و بقصد واداشتن تورغوزا آلغاینکیچه بقصد که توانی برخیزانید و توانی واداشت تورغوزغوسیز دور نخواهیم برخیزانید و
خواهیم واداشت تورغوزغونکیز دور خواهید برخیزانید و خواهید واداشت تورغوزغوسیلار دور نخواهند برخیزانید و خواهند واداشت
تورغوزالغوم دور تورغوزغوم یوق نخواهم برخیزانید و نخواهم واداشت تورغوزا آلماغوم دور تورغوزا آلغوم یوق برخیزاندن و واداشتن ممکن
نخواهد بود تورغوزغولوق برخیزاندنی و واداشتنی تورغوزغای و تورغوزا و تورغوزسون و تورغوزسونلار برخیزاند و واداشت
تورغوزغودیک و تورغوزدیک برخیزاندنی و واداشتنی و همچنانکه برخیزاند و وادارد تورالماق بضم تای مثناة ... تولید
یافتن و بهم رسیدن تورادولت تولید نیافتیم تورادوع تورالیدور تولید می یابد و تورادوعی بمعنی فاعل و مصدر هم می آید تورانماید و تولید
می یابد یافته است تورالماید و تورالماید بودی یعنی تولید نیافته بود چنانکه در تاریخ الملوک در وصف آن درخت گوید کا
دو هزار سال آندین صاحب جمال عراق تورانماید و تورانمایدی تورالکان و تورالدوقان تولید یابنده و تولید یافته چنانکه
برا و کیم حلاحت بیره گل و نیلوفر گوید شعر آتینک توغان تورالکان بیری کتمیش اول الیدا کیچکیلغان همرتوز و بیرتورا
مفرد مخاطب از فعل امر تورالنا و تورالنکیل مفرد مخاطب از فعل نهی تورالنانک و تورالنکیز و تورالنکلار جمع مخاطب از فعل امر تورالمانک
تورالمانکیز تورالمانکلار جمع مخاطب از فعل نهی تورالمان و تورالماسمین تولید نمی یابم تورالامین و تورالارمین و تورالادورمین و تورالارام
تولید می یابم تورالماس تولید نمی یابد و بمعنی فاعل و مصدر منفی هم می آید تورالماسینکا بتولید نیافتنت تورالیبینکا بتولید
یافتنت تورالیبو تورالیبان و تورالمیش تولید یافته چنانکه شاهد بر اول امر قسم الحجه در ذکر ابو عبدالله برتی گوید که
دیدار ایجادین بیدی کیم مالکه احداثه تورالیبور تورالمیشانک تولید یافته تورالا بولغای و تورالیب بولغای تولید توان یافت تورالغای
تولید تواند یافت تورالای و تورالای تورالایو تولید یابان تورالای و تورالاین تولید یابم و یابد و یابی و یافته تورالیشانک و تورالای بیز
تورالکای یزو تورالغالی و تورالغالینک تولید بیابیم تورالکالی برای تولید یافتن و تا تولید یافته تورالکاج چون تولید یافت و بیابد
تورالکوچی تولید یابنده تورالکوسی و تورالکونه و تورالکاغنه تولید یافتن و بقصد تولید یافتن تورالا آلغاینکچه بقصد که تو تولید
توانی یافت تورالکوسیز دور تولید خواهیم یافت تورالکونکیز دور تولید خواهید یافت تورالکوسیلار دور تولید خواهند یافت نیافته
تورالکوم یوق تولید نخواهم یافت تورالا آلماغوم دور تورالا آلغوم یوق تولید یافتن ممکن نخواهد بود تورالکولوق تولید یافتنی
تورالکای و تورالسون و تورالسونلار تولید بیابد تورالکودیک و تورالدیک تولید یافتنی و همچنانکه تولید یابد تورتماق
مع التاء مصدر متعدیست بمعنی تولد ساختن و صیغ آن برین نهج با تای قرشت اشتقاق می یابد توردوک باشباع ضمه و سکون
و تای قرشت فرو بردن تورتتوک فرو بردیم تورتادور فرو میبرد و تورتادوچی بمعنی فاعل و مصدر هم می آید تورتمایدور فرو برده
فرو برده است تورتکان و تورتکانلر و تورتادورکان فرو برنده و فرو برده و بمعنی مصدر هم می آید تورت و تورتکیل مفرد مخاطب از فعل امر
تورتغاو تورتماکیل مفرد مخاطب از فعل نهی تورتونکلار و تورتونکیز و تورتونکلار جمع مخاطب از فعل امر تورتمانک و تورتمانکیز تورتمانکلار

بجمع خاطر پریشان یعنی توزیتا نمق توزغان تین فرو نمیرم توزتامین یعنی توزتادی و توزتادم فرو میرم توزیتماس فرو
نمیرد و بمعنی فاعل و مصدر هم می آید توزتاسینکا بفرو بردنت توزلاریکا بفرو بردنشه توزتوبه توزتوبانه توزیتش
فروبرده توزیتیشانک فروبرده توزتیا بولغاه و توزتوب بولغه فروتوان برد توزتا آلغای فرو نتواند برد توزیتا توزیتا
بلع کنان و فرو برده توزتای توزتا بین فرو بریم و فرو بری و برده توزتقانیم توزتکاند و توزتکلیپ توزتلیپ توزتالینک
فرو بریم توزتکالی برای فرو بردن و نافرو برده توزتکاج چون فرو برد و برد چنانکه در صفت کیمیه در وصف ...
شعر امرو بحر اقلیم شالفورد چلش سیف توزتکاج سدره اسنا ماق شیاق توزیان است که شکاج توزتوب ...
آسا آسا و بمعنی چون رسید مثل مثلثه فرو برده توزتکوی فرو بریم توزتکوچ توزتکوچ توزتکاجه ۲ فرو بردن و ...
فرو بردن توزتا آلماینکه بعد نیکه فرو توانی برد توزتکیمز ... فرو خواهیم برد توزتکوز ... و خواهید برد توزتکیلار
فرو خواهند برد توزتکام و توزتکوم یوق فرو خواهم برد توزتا آلماغوم توزتا آلغوم یوق فرو بردن ممکن نخواهد بود توزتکوله
فرو بردنی توزتکای و توزتا توزتسا و توزتسون و توزتید بلک فرو برد توزتکودیک نمی فرو برد و همچنانکه فرو برد توزتسله
مع الکسر بیکیک فرو بردن و صیغ آن با اضافه شین قرشا شقاقی نیاید توزتقلغاک مع الکاف بمعنی فرو برده شدن توزیغ
الی بالالف اشتقاق می یابد توزلانماق بسکون را و فتح لام دو معنی دارد اول نقش دوختن دویم بدام شبکه انداختن توزلادی نقش
دوخت و بدام انداخت چنانکه سلطان حسین میرزا بمعنی ثانی گوید شعر ... سیلغاج چرخ ...
اول چیبین ... توزلادی هران یتیمنی آیلاجیب توزلادوق نقش دوخت و بدام انداخت توزلار و توزلایدور نقش میدوزد
بدام می اندازد و توزلار بمعنی فاعل و مصدر هم می آید توزلانمایدور نقش نمیدوزد و نقش دوخته است و بدام نینداخته
توزلاغان و توزلاغان و توزلایدورغان نقش دوزنده و نقش دوخته و بدام اندازنده و بدام انداخته و بمعنی مصدر هم می آیند توزلا
توزلاجیل مفرد مخاطب از فعل امر توزلانا و توزلاتیل مفرد مخاطب از فعل نهی توزلانک و توزلانکیز و توزلانکلار جمع مخاطب از فعل امر
توزلامانک و توزلامانکیز و توزلامانکلار جمع مخاطب از فعل نهی توزلاسان و توزلاسامین نقش میدوزی و بدام می اندازم توزلای مین و
توزلایمین ... توزلادام نقش میدوزم و بدام می اندازم توزلاماس نقش نمیدوزد و بدام نمی اندازد و بمعنی فاعل و مصدر هم
می آید توزلاماسنکه نقش نه دوختنت و بدام نینداختنت توزلاسنکه نقش دوختنت و بدام انداختنت توزلاب و توزلاباب و
توزلامیش نقش دوخته و بدام انداخته توزلامیشانک نقش دوخته و بدام انداخته توزلاسا بولغه و توزلاب بولغه نقش توان
دوخت و بدام توان انداخت توزلای آلغای نقش نتواند دوخت و بدام نتواند انداخت توزلایو و توزلای و توزلای نقش دوزان و
بدام افکنان توزلای و توزلای مین نقش بدوزم و بدوزد و بدوزی و دوخته و بدام بیندازم و بیندازد و بیندازی و انداخته
توزلاساق توزلاغانی و توزلاغای چرو توزلاب و توزلای لک نقش بدوزیم و بدام بیندازیم توزلاغالی برای نقش دوختن و تا نقش دوخته
و برای بدام انداختن و تا بدام انداخته توزلاغاج چون نقش دوخت و بدوزد و چون بدام انداخت و بیندازد توزلاغوچی نقش دوزنده
و بدام اندازنده توزلاغوچی و توزلاغوچی و توزلاغاچه تا نقش دوختن و بعد از نقش دوختن و تا بدام انداختن و بعد از بدام انداختن توزلای
آلماینکه بعد نیکه نقش توانی دوخت و بدام توانی انداخت توزلاغومیز دور نقش خواهیم دوخت و بدام خواهیم انداخت توزلاغوکدور
نقش خواهید دوخت و بدام خواهید انداخت توزلاغوسیلار نقش خواهند دوخت و بدام خواهند انداخت توزلاغوم و توزلاغوم یوق
نقش نخواهم دوخت و بدام نخواهم انداخت توزلای آلماغوم و توزلای آلغوم یوق نقش دوختن و بدام انداختن ممکن نخواهد بود توزلاغو

نقش دوختنی و بدام انداختنی توزلاغای و توزلاسا و توزلاسون و توزلادیلک نقش بدوزد و بدام بیندازد توزلاغودیک و توزلایدی
نقش دوختنی و همچنانکه بدوزد و بدام انداختنی و همچنانکه بیندازد توزلانماق مع النون نقش دوخته شدن و بدام انداخته شدن
توزلانغان و توزلانغان و توزلانماغان نقش دوخته شونده و نقش دوخته شده و بدام اندازه شونده و بدام انداخته شده چنانکه شاهد
اقبال بمعنی نقش دوخته شده در صفت سیاه در وصف سلاح در رزم پادشاه گوید شعر ... آیلاغان ...
لانغان و بمعنی مصدر هم می آیند و مؤلف ... ها بمعنی ... و بسته ذکر کرده و ... نوشته که ... بماند د
کشد و طالع هروی توزلانغان با زای هوز خوانده و بمعنی انتظام داده نوشته و ... شاهد آورده سهو کرده
و بالف صیغ برین نهج با نون اشتقاق می یابد من المجاهد توزد هشت معنی دارد اول آنچه مشتبه یافته شود ... که
... و توری که زنان بر سر می اندازند چنانکه بمعنی دوم گوید شعر ... نوائی ...
که سین اول ... دویم صدر خانه را گویند چنانکه ... شعر ... که
که بولدی ... ایکی ... و نیز در لسان الطیر ... شیخ صنعان گوید
شعر ... فردوس آیین ... توزدا ... کردوز ...
آندا ... دیم ... بوستان ...
دین ... توزکمید ... سیم بمعنی محاذی و برابر باشد چنانکه در ... گوید که ...
... و نصیر ... که ... کلمه ... چهارم بمعنی ... بود ... ششم ... بمعنی ... پنجم ... و بمعنی ... است ... بمعنی ... مستعمل شود چنانکه گوید
کتیب ... رفته است و آمده است و بمعنی ... هفتم نام شهری است ... فریدون که ولایت توران
منسوب بوست هشتم ... ایستادن و ماندن چنانکه در ... گذشت ... که
که در آشنا کند و بمعنی ... و بمعنی ... هم باشد و معشوق و مطلوب ... گویند و بمعنی
منافت و ... و بمعنی ... بود و نام دختر ایرج است که زن منوچهر باشد توراق ... که ...
کرده ... توراق ... نام ... شبیه ... که ... شیر ... گویند
توزتو ... چنانکه شاه ... در تاریخ ... که ... توزلاد ...
یعنی هر چهار ... توزت او ... طایفه ارلات و برلاس و ترخان ... اعظم ... من حیرت ... شعر
آندا ... که ... توزت ... و شاید ... حضرت ... طایفه ... و کیان و
و ساسانیان باشند که بعد از حضرت آدم تا زمان بعثت حضرت خاتم ... سلطنت کردند و کنایه از چهار ... ستون
که عبارت از هند و روم و ایران و توران باشد و ربع مسکون هم ... شد توزت انا کنایه است از امهات سفلی که
عبارت از عناصر اربعه باشد چنانکه در صفت گوید شعر ... خورشید ... که ...
یعنی ... توزت آتا ... کنایه از کتب اربعه آسمانی است که عبارت از فرقان و انجیل و زبور و توریه باشد توزتا ... یعنی چهار
چنانکه گوید شعر ... ذات ... و لعناصر ... توزتاو ... با کو
واو و فتح لام با الف کشیده یعنی چهار تا با هم توزتوب ... مربع باشد توزتوج ... با و کو

نون وجیم بمعنی چهارم بود چنانکه در مقاله نوزدهم از حیرة الابرار کوید شعر سینی قلکنی که قیلیب ستدین هر بیری برشم ایله
بولدی منیر اوچ قویاش بو قلمی تیلدی شتاب مشعله تورتونج اوی اراسا الدی تاب تورتونجی یعنی چهارمین الشاهد علیه
شعر نیلامین تورتونجی کردون نینک تاری بهرنجیم کورمامیش طالع دانا هیم دیک توقوز کردون بیکیت تورسوق بکوف
را وقاف وضم سین مهمله دو معنی دارد اول مشکی است که بشکل مطهره دوزند تا از مشک کوچکتر و از مطهره بزرکتر باشد دوم کوشه
چابوق بود که اندر طرف لباس در پیش کمر بالای جیب بکذارند تورغاق بدو معنی آمده اول پاسبان و نکهبان و کشیکچی را کویند
دوم معنی پاسبانی و حراست هم باشد چنانکه شاه بیلبیسی کفته شعر بر مرکه میمون تو قدم نوبت تورغاق میران و مهان برعلیک
باری دویم نام طایفه ایست از اوزبک و مولف فرهنگ جهانکیری و صاحب برهان قاطع این لفظ را بفتح تا نیز بر وزن چماق خوانده
و فارسی تصور کرده با معنی نوشته اند تورغامیشی بمعنی اخراج و دور کردن باشد چنانکه در جلد خامس تاریخ وصاف مذکور است
اکر سیور سیورغامیشی کند و اندیشهای دور دراز خاطرش تورغامیش تورغانی برله یعنی سرا پا و چنانکه هاتف الشاهد علیه شعر
تورغانی برله بر آتشیلر مد دولت شوخ کیم یوق و بار بیلی باشتین ایاقی کوید مهر تورغانیم برله یعنی سرا پا و چنانکه هاتف الشاهد
علیه شعر کوزنام قاشیلی بولمدین تورغانیم برله فغان وای بر بهر بیر چوبطانا نوک برله توتی تورغای بکون را
و یای حطی وفتح غین معجمه بالف کشیده پرنده ایست از کنجشک بزرکتر که آنرا بفارسی چکاوک و بعربی هدهد کویند چنانکه در تاریخ
در وادی فتح وفنا کوید شعر یعنی تومان مینک لاله وکل ابرغا یالغ تورغای وبلبلی قیلغو دیک هلاک ودر تحفه
از محبوب القلوب کوید که کبوتر فقه آندین مستیلق و تورغای فقه آندین نشاط وهم مستیلق و آنرا بالطای حطی هم نویسند
و نیز نام پهلوانی بود که کانت و بفتح را هم مستعملست چنانکه در کتاب ظفرنامه مذکور خواهد شد تورغو بکون را وضم عین معجمه
حریر نفیس و بافته ابریشمی را کویند چنانکه مثلست که تو و فقه لیربانک تو پوتمادور غوتونک کیسلر و نخان اقماشی ازا
که سلاطین حکام و ارکان چسپانند چنانکه کوید شعر نامه سین جان پرده سیله چرخادیم کیم عشق اوراقی الجناب آلفای نشانیم باشد
تورغو کیریب وطالع هروی بمعنی مکتوب بمهر کرکرده و مصرع بوبطرز شاهد آورده سهو کرده و مولف برهان تورغو تملو
و فارسی تصور کرده و بمعنی بیرام نوشته تورغود نام طایفه ایست از ایله تورغوز برون هر چیز تکرر کرده چو بکنده بود که
بر پشت در اندازند و آنرا بفارسی مترس کویند و نیز اهرست زیر خز اندک و داشتن چنانکه در پیل عنده تقر بغوز ناق کذشت
تورغون ثابت وایستاده و نیز تورک ترک اسم یافث بن نوح علیه السلام است که ابو ترکان یافث اوغلان کویند و شیخ
ملیح در تفسیر خود ذکر کرده که یاجوج و ماجوج از اولاد یافث اند و یافث پدر ترکست توکان بفتح کاف و جمع توکان
ترکان مولف تاریخ حبیب السیر کفته که اولاد و احفاد او غوزخان بعد از توالد و تناسل یه بیست و چهار شعبه شدند و کروهی
از ایشان که در ولایت خراسان و ماوراء النهر متوطن شدند باقتضای آب و هوا اشکال اطفال ایشان از صورت ترکیبه در آمد
و مردم ایشان را ترکمان کفتند یعنی ترک مانند و نیز کفته که ترکمان قومی علیحده اند سوای ترکان و موافق ظفرنامه ترکان طایفه
را مانند که از نسل ترک بن یافث اند ترک بمعنی کاف بخاطر کویند که در قهستان آخر ترکان فرهنگ و نیز در ترکتام سود دستکرد
. وهل نمی مقصور و قیش چنانکه در مقاله عروض که نوانی علیه الرحمة تالیف نموده به ریان اصر ان مذکور است کریانا سروکی
دو میم ان زکیب نرلار بو لفظ آنکا علم بولوب تورلار واول محل شمر مقصور و زینداوا قع دور تورلاق بفتح لام بالف کشیده
مزن و مهجوان مرد نو خواسته را خوانند و نیز کوچک ایداللهلاد را کویند که امرد و نو رس باشد تورلوق لمیدن و میدن و

وحشت وتلواسه تورلوک بضم لام بمعنی نوع وقسم باشد الشاهد علیه شعر یعنی بو انمغه یوزشکونا راد وقوم وخیلیمدین
که مجنون نهن تورلوک ظلم کیم قیلیش عرب قیلیش ودوم سیه معرب کویند تورموجاق بضم میم وفتح جیم بالف کشیده کیاهیست معروف
که از انبیو زید دور اطعم آن برشی مایلست تورنا و تورنه شال نفیس باشد که از کمرک و پشم نرم بافته شود چنانکه در وصف خواجه
نقشبند کوید شعر اطلس کردون بیله مینک زیب وفر تورمه تونی آسیدا کوک آستر لیک اوشول تورمه بیچهر تارایله تورما و تورا
رشد ابیون بلبلهٔ تورنا بر وزن حنا پرنده ایست بکوه بزرک که کردن دراز دارد و پر دیدم او را بعربی زنند و از ابها زنبکالنک
کویند شعر سرو نازیم باشیدا تورنا پرین کورکیم ایرمش شمع نینک باشیدا کول بولغان پریشان تلریک تورود داز اداتی
رابطه است چنانکه کویند ایب تورور یعنی کرفته است بریب تورور یعنی داده است و با این معنی اداء لغز مستعملست توروش
بمعنی ایستادکی و ثبات و درنک بود چنانکه در تاریخ ملوک کوید که افراسیاب توروش برنادی غمی یوز قیاتاری و در تاریخ تاری
هم در وصف فاغنه مذکور است که باغی لیق یورش و توروش بیلا المادیلار تورودم شتر بچهٔ دو ساله را کویند و یکساله را
کشک و کوشلک و سه ساله را نایلاق نامند و همچنین اسب نری بود که آنرا برنادیان بجهانید از ان نتاج حاصل کنند تورون بترک
رومی نواده را کویند تورنه بفتح را بتشدید آمده اول بمعنی نسب و نژاد باشد چنانکه در تاریخ نابری مذکور است که در وش تیمورخان
تورن و موچه بیله موندین اولوغ ایدی دویم شاهزادکان و اولاد پادشاهان را کویند الشاهد علیه شعر خم غذایی اولماسیند
قاف ترکانه ایاغ تورهٔ آیینی بیله تا ماسا توقوز آقتا او توز و این شعر مشعر است بر قوانین خوانین ترک و آن چنانست که چون در
مجلس شراب یکی پیاله دهند اکر بیچکه بترجمان آن نه پیاله و اکر بر یزد سی پیاله میخورند سیم بمعنی رسم و قانون بود چنانکه در شیبانی
نامه خطاب بیابانی کوید شعر تورهٔ بیله بارش اصول توت خانقه سر قویتین بر یمینی چیانانقه و نیز در تاریخ کزیده نقل شاه
ابوالمظفر مذکور است که کار عشق بدیکرست و تورهٔ سلطنت دیکر چهارم بلطافت بمعنی ایدکوید که چنکیزخان بنا کذاشته چهارم
چوبهای بلند و تختهای اهر است که باز بجهت قلاع و حصار پر دهند بر یکدیکر پیوسته حصار لشکر مینارند و در عقب آن ایستاده مشغول
جنک میشوند چنانکه کوید شعر مغ ایشیکین تورهٔ دیک یاپ یوزونکا کیم کیدون قویاش سنان جبک طوبیلاسا و اش کوزدن نورد
و نیز در سد سکندری کوید شعر ارابه چایلد دو ریغیه باند اشیت ایکی دور دین هم حصاری آیشیب ارابه اوزه تورهٔ پوست ولو
تورهٔ کیدیم اخلوق همدست ولوبث تورهٔ باخالاجرا بله سندو دبث کیمن ایلدابان کیند اهل شت و طالع هروی بمعنی توپ نوشته و شعر
مزبور را از سد سکندری شاهد آورده سهو کرده و بفارسی شغال را کویند و مولف برهان قاطع بمعنی بوغاوهم نوشته که بر تکدی
پای ستور کذارند توزری بترکه روی یکنوع لوبیت مخصوص و آن نرنک سرخ مایل بتیره کی باشد مع الزام المشتقات توزماک
باشباع ضمه سه معنی دارد اول تحمل کردن و آنرا توزلاماق هم کویند دویم ساختن و آراستن و کوک کردن سیم مهره برشته کیدن
و انتظام دادن و با این معنی بخیر توزماق هم مستعملست توزدی تحمل کرد و ساخت و آراست و انتظام داد چنانکه بمعنی اول کوید شعر
هجران اقتزدی نولدی وصل ملکین پردوبات آندا قاییش تلفانفه موندین کم کیرا کاس جولدور توزدوک تحمل کردیم و ساختیم و آنا
و کوک کردیم و انتظام دادیم توزارو توزادور تحمل میکند و میسازد و انتظام میدهد چنانکه شاهد بر اولها بمعنی آیند در وصف کوه
زمن کوید شعر یهی لاحچله لیلی بعزم عشرت تونلام لارا آنداکا هی بزم عشرت و توزار یعنی تاملی و مسکن هم می آید توزماید در تحمل نکند
و نکردهاست و نمیسازد و نساخته است و نمی آراید و نیاراسته است و انتظام نمیدهد و نداده است توزکان و توزارکان و توزادور کان
تحمل کننده و سازنده و ساخته و آراینده و آراسته و کوک کننده و کوک کرده و انتظام دهنده و انتظام داده چنانکه شاهد بر اولها

× تورز ×

173v.

بمعنی نازنده کوید شعر فلات ظالم دولت ابتی تامیتیم ختم تاشینک هر بیری توزکان همدین معنی کولککن مفرماید شعر نا مطیع بر
اونیدین مفعول اوله ایشه کیم بو نوالی توزکان کوسرنا چایب تشو معنی مشید هم می اید چنانچه شاهد بر اقول معنی
اوستن دمعنون سکندری کوید که خاقان ینک اسکندر اعچون ضیا ماسبا بین توزکلب توزن و توزکیل مفرد مخاطب
از فعل امر بمعنی الشاهد علی الاول المعنی الرابع شعر ای مغفچون نهان دار نیم پیلو رمین ساز توزه تارینان توزکلوغ
نواسانینک بیله آواز توزا الشاهد علی الثانی بالمعنی الرابع شعر ای طبع روش معنی کرنوانی کونکلینی اینسا نسالنا هر حاله
بجال الیانماک توزکیل قوبض و توزمغلی بخامه هم طرح چنانچه در ذیل جامه مذکور خواهد شد توزنا و توزناکیل مفرد مخاطب
از فعل نهی توزونک و توزونکیز و توزونکلر جمع مخاطب از فعل امر توزمانک و توزمانکیز و توزمانکلر جمع مخاطب از فعل نهی توزامین
تحمل میکنم و میسازم و می آرایم و کوک میکنم و انتظام میدهم توزمامین و توزمابین تحمل نکنم و نسازم و نیارایم و کوک نکنم و انتظام ندهم
الشاهد علی الاول بالمعنی الاول شعر توزکامین هرچند بولسا تیرم هجران توزلماد [illegible] کر تعیین [illegible] که ایام وصال التیمادور
توزماس صیغه نفی است از فعل مضارع و بمعنی فاعل و مصدر منفی هم می اید توزماسینکا تحمل نکردنت نساختنت نیاراستنت
بکوک نکردنت با انتظام ندادنت توزا دینکا تحمل کردنت و بساختنت و باراستنت و بکوک کردنت و با انتظام دادنت توزو
توزوبان توزوتیش تحمل کرده و ساخته و آراسته و کوک کرده و انتظام داده چنانچه در فرهاد و شیرین در ولادت فرهاد کوید
الشاهد علی الاول بالمعنی الثالث شعر توزوب [illegible] آینک [illegible] بالمعنی الخامس شعر
کولار [illegible] توزمیشانک خطاب با [illegible]
توزا بولغای [illegible] تحمل توان کرد و توان ساخت و توان آراست و کوک توان کرد و انتظام توان داد توزا آلغای تحمل تواند کرد
و تواند ساخت و تواند آراست و کوک تواند کرد و انتظام تواند داد توزا توزا تحمل کنان و ساخته کنان و آراسته کنان
کوک کنان و منتظم کنان و بعد از تکرار هم مستعمل چنانچه در سد سکندری در معامله سکندر و دارا معنی ثالث کوید شعر [illegible]
[illegible] توزای و توزایین [illegible]
و فعل [illegible] شاهد بر اقول معنی [illegible] و بنا نم [illegible] سکندری در جواب رسول دارا کوید شعر اینک [illegible]
توزای آنکا اولکیم ایرکانلیکین [illegible] توزای [illegible] توزالینک تحمل کنیم و بسازیم و بیارایم و کوک کنیم
و انتظام دهیم توزکلی برای تحمل کردن و تا تحمل کرده و برای ساختن و تا ساخته و برای آراستن و تا آراسته و برای کوک کردن و تا کوک
کرده و برای انتظام دادن و تا انتظام داده توزکاچ چون تحمل کرد و کند چون ساخت و سازد و چون آراست و آراید چون کوک کرد و کند
چون انتظام داد و دهد توزکوچی فاعل هر پنج معنی چنانچه در فصل ششم از محبوب القلوب [illegible] کوید که
اوقات [illegible] توزکوچی [illegible] توزکا [illegible] تا تحمل کردن و بقدر تحمل کردن و تا [illegible]
و بقدر ساختن تا آراستن و بقدر آراستن و تا کوک کردن و بقدر کوک کردن و انتظام دادن و بقدر انتظام دادن توزا [illegible]
تحمل توانی کرد و توانی ساخت و توانی آراست و کوک توانی کرد و انتظام توانی داد توزکومیز [illegible] تحمل خواهیم کرد و خواهیم ساخت
و خواهیم آراست و کوک خواهیم کرد و انتظام خواهیم داد توزکوسیز [illegible] تحمل خواهید کرد و خواهید ساخت و خواهید آراست
و کوک خواهید کرد و انتظام خواهید داد توزکوسیلار [illegible] تحمل خواهند کرد و خواهند ساخت و خواهند آراست و کوک خواهند کرد و انتظام
خواهند داد توزکولوک تحمل کردن و ساختن و آراستن و کوک کردن و انتظام دادن توزکاو [illegible]

174r.

تحمل کند و بسازد و بیاراید و کوک کند و انتظام دهد چنانچه در سد سکندری در مقابله سکندر با دارا کوید شعر [illegible]
[illegible] توزکوسیک [illegible] تحمل کردن و چنانچه کند [illegible]
بسازد و آراستن و چنانچه بیاراید و کوک کردن و چنانچه کند و انتظام دادن و چنانچه دهد توزاتمالک [illegible]
[illegible] ساخت و آراست [illegible] الشاهد علیه بالمعنی الاول
شعر [illegible] کوید شعر
[illegible] توزای [illegible] توزانتوک ساختیم و آراستیم [illegible]
آراید [illegible] الشاهد علی الاول بالمعنی الاول شعر دینام [illegible]
[illegible] توزاتماید [illegible]
[illegible] توزاتکان [illegible] ساخته و آراسته [illegible] چنانچه
ساخته [illegible] شعر [illegible] توزاتکان [illegible]
[illegible] توزات [illegible] توزاتماکیل [illegible]
[illegible] جمع [illegible] توزاتمان [illegible]
میکنم توزاتمامین [illegible] توزاتماس [illegible]
فاعل [illegible] می آید توزاتماسی [illegible] توزاتماسینکا [illegible]
و بنیاراستنت [illegible] توزاتیب [illegible]
ساخته و آراسته [illegible] چنانچه در لیلی مجنون در وصف پادشاه کوید الشاهد علی الاول بالمعنی الاول شعر [illegible]
[illegible] توزاتمیشانک ساخته و آراسته [illegible] توزاتا بولغای [illegible] توان ساخت
و توان آراست [illegible] توان کرد توزاتا آلغای تواند ساخت و تواند آراست [illegible] تواند کرد توزاتا توزاتا ساخته کنان و آراسته
کنان [illegible] توزاتای [illegible] بسازم و بسازد و بسازی و ساخته و بیارایم و بیاراید و بیارایی و آراسته [illegible]
و کرده چنانچه شاهد بر اول معنی [illegible] کوید شعر [illegible] توزاتای [illegible] توزاتایم [illegible]
[illegible] توزاتکانی [illegible] بسازیم و بیارایم [illegible] چنانچه شاهد بر اول [illegible] خسرو شیرین
[illegible] کوید شعر [illegible] توزاتکلی برای ساختن و ساخته [illegible]
آراستن و تا آراسته و برای [illegible] کردن و [illegible] کرده توزاتکاچ چون ساخت و سازد و چون آراست و بیاراید و [illegible] کرد و
[illegible] ساختن و [illegible] کردن چنانچه شاهد بر [illegible] فرهاد [illegible]
[illegible] کوید شعر توزاتکوچی [illegible] توزاتا آلغای [illegible] توانی ساخت
و توانی آراست و [illegible] توانی کرد [illegible] نخواهیم ساخت و نخواهیم آراست [illegible] نخواهیم کرد [illegible] نخواهید ساخت
و نخواهید آراست و [illegible] خواهید کرد [illegible] نخواهند ساخت و نخواهند آراست [illegible] خواهند کرد [illegible]
نخواهم ساخت و نخواهم آراست [illegible] نخواهم کرد [illegible]
ساختن و آراستن [illegible] کردن [illegible] بسازد و بیاراید [illegible] کند چنانچه [illegible]

از حیرت الابرار در وصف راستی گوید الشاهد علی الاول المعنی الثالث شعر بولسا ایلیک ابکری ایلیک ایچره ایلیکی کیسما کلاه [illegible]
مکر توزانکو عیلت و توزاتور دیلک ساختنی و همچنانکه بنلزد و آراستنی و همچنانکه بنیاد ایمارت کردن همچنانکه راست کند [illegible]
بفتح زا به معنی طرد اول ساخته شدن دویم آراسته شدن سیم راست شدن ضد کج باشد توزالدی ساخته شد [illegible]
شد و راست شد چنانکه در فرهاد و شیرین در حشر قصر چهار فصل فرهاد گوید المعنی الثانی عشر توزالدی [illegible]
کلش بولدی نینک آستیدا اکر و نیز حمد بیلا چیچیلی جنون گوید شعر موندا قیچی توزالدی [illegible] الیق بونوع اولدی
آنا آنا الیق توزالکای و توزالاو و توزالسا و توزالسون و توزالدی ساخته شود و آراسته شود و راست شود چنانکه در [illegible]
بلبل و گل گوید الشاهد علی الاول المعنی الثالث شعر بیرای کوشلی که هر بیر کال توزالکای چو یاد ایتکانی و [illegible]
و در حکایت [illegible] گوید الشاهد علی الثالث بالمعنی الثانی شعر که تا انکلاه که ایل بولنا و ادی [illegible] توزالسا ایکی [illegible]
صفدر و باقی صیغ برین سیاق بفتح زا مع الکلام اشتقاق می یابد توزالیشماک مع کثرت معنی مفاعله است یعنی باهم [illegible] کردن
و بلهم آرایش کردن و باهم راست شدن و صیغ آن باشین اشتقاق می یابد بضم زا و سکون لام به معنی بو جلو [illegible] شدن دویم
شدن [illegible] باشد توزولدی منتظم شد و کوک شد چنانکه در فرهاد و شیرین در شکستن المراهرمن گوید المعنی الاول شعر
هو [illegible] به عشرت انجام توزولدی و صفتکیم [illegible] و نیز [illegible] گوید المعنی الثانی شعر [illegible]
مجودی توزولدی [illegible] و نیز [illegible] گوید شعر [illegible] آهنک
جفا بینا توزولدی توزولور توزولادور منتظم میشود کوک میشود الشاهد علی الاول المعنی الاول شعر [illegible]
که صفت [illegible] توزولسا [illegible] و توزولور معنی فاعل و مصدر هم می آید و باقی صیغ برین [illegible]
مع الکلام اشتقاق می یابد توزولوشماک عقب یکدیگر قطار شدن و باهم کوک شدن و صیغ آن باشین اشتقاق می یابد توزلاماک
بسکون زا و نون و فتح لام بالف کشیده به معنی متحمل شدن [illegible] چنانکه گوید شعر [illegible] آنا [illegible]
توزلاماک آنا [illegible] توزلاماق متحمل شدن توزلاندوق متحمل شدیم توزلاندوق منکوب شدیم
توزلانورم توزلانادور متحمل میشود و منکوب میشود و توزلانور به معنی مصدر هم می آید توزلانماید و متحمل نمیشود و نشده است و منکوب
نمیشود و نشده است توزلانکان و توزلانوکان و توزلاناندکان متحمل شونده و متحمل شده و به معنی مصدر هم می آیند توزلانغان و توزلانورغان و
توزلانادورغان منکوب شونده و منکوب شده و به معنی مصدر هم می آیند توزلان مفرد مخاطب از فعل امر و مصدر توزلانکیل مفرد مخاطب
از فعل امر و مصدر توزلانماک توزلانغیل مفرد مخاطب از فعل امر و مصدر توزلاناق توزلانما مفرد مخاطب از فعل نهی و مصدر توزلانماک
مفرد مخاطب از فعل نهی و مصدر توزلانماک توزلانماغیل مفرد مخاطب از فعل نهی و مصدر توزلاناق توزلانینک و توزلانینکیز و توزلانینکلار
جمع مخاطب از امر و مصدر توزلانماک و توزلانماینکیز و توزلانماینکلار جمع مخاطب از فعل نهی و مصدر توزلانمان و توزلانماس مین
متحمل نمیشوم و منکوب نمیشوم توزلانامین و توزلانورمین و توزلانادورمین و توزلانورام متحمل میشوم و منکوب میشوم توزلاناس
متحمل نمیشود و منکوب نمیشود و به معنی فاعل و مصدر نفی هم می آید توزلانماسینکا متحمل نشدنت توزلانماسینکه منکوب نشدنت
توزلانوجاق متحمل شدنت توزلانوچقه منکوب شدنت توزلانیبان و توزلانیب توزلانیبان و توزلانمیش متحمل شده و منکوب شده توزلانمیشانک
متحمل شده و منکوب شده توزلانسا بولغای و توزلانیب بولغای متحمل تواند شد و منکوب تواند شد توزلانا آلغای متحمل تواند شد و منکوب تواند
و توزلانا توزلانا متحمل کنان و منکوب شوان توزلانای و توزلانایین متحمل شوم و شود و شوی و منکوب شوم و شود و شوی [illegible]

توزلانا آلدو توزلانکای بیز توزلانکای بیز متحمل شویم توزلاناسا قو توزلانغای بیز توزلانغای بیز منکوب شویم توزلانکای و توزلانا الیک
متحمل شویم و منکوب شویم توزلانکالی برای متحمل شدن و نامتحمل شدن توزلانغالی برای منکوب شدن و نامنکوب شدن توزلانکاچ
چون متحمل شد میشود توزلانغاچ چون منکوب شد میشود توزلانکوچی متحمل شونده توزلانغوچی منکوب شونده توزلانکوچه توزلانغوچه
توزلانکانچه تا متحمل شدن و مقدار متحمل شدن توزلانغوچه و توزلانغانچه تا منکوب شدن و مقدار منکوب شدن توزلانا آلغانیکه
مقدار یکه متحمل تواند شد و منکوب تواند شد توزلانکوسیدور متحمل خواهیم شد توزلانغوسیدور منکوب خواهیم شد توزلانکوسی و
متحمل خواهید شد توزلانغوسی منکوب خواهید شد توزلانکوسیلار دور متحمل خواهند شد توزلانغوسیلار منکوب خواهند شد توزلانا
توزلانکوم بولوق متحمل خواهم شد توزلانا غوم و توزلانغوم بولوق منکوب خواهم شد توزلانا آلماغوم و توزلانا آلغوم متحمل شدن ممکن نخواهد
بود منکوب شدن ممکن نخواهد بود توزلانکولوک متحمل شدنی توزلانغولوق منکوب شدنی توزلانکای متحمل شود توزلانغای
منکوب شود توزلانا و توزلانسا و توزلانسون و توزلاندیک متحمل شود و منکوب شود توزلانکودیک متحمل شدن و همچنانکه شود توزلانغو
منکوب شدنی و همچنانکه منکوب شود توزلانور دیک یعنی توزلانکودیک و توزلانغودیک باشد توزلاماق بفتح زا و لام و سکون نون
به غلطیدن توزلاندوق به غلطیدیم توزلانور و توزلانادور به غلطد و توزلانور به معنی فاعل و مصدر هم می آید توزلاناید
به غلطد و نغلطیده است توزلانغا و توزلانورغان و توزلاناندوغان به غلطنده و به غلطیده و به معنی مصدر هم می آیند توزلان
توزلانغیل مفرد مخاطب از فعل امر توزلانمان و توزلانماغیل مفرد مخاطب از فعل نهی توزلانینک و توزلانینکیز و توزلانینکلار جمع مخاطب از فعل امر
توزلانماینکیز و توزلانماینکلار جمع مخاطب از فعل نهی توزلانمان و توزلانماس مین به غلطم توزلانامین و توزلانورمین و توزلانایین و توزلانو
به غلطم توزلاناس به غلطد و به معنی فاعل و مصدر نفی هم می آید توزلانماسینکه به غلطیدنت توزلانوچقه به غلطیدنت
توزلانیبان و توزلانیب توزلانمیش به غلطیده توزلانمیشانک به غلطیده توزلانسا بولغای و توزلانیب بولغای به تواند غلطید توزلانا آلغای
به تواند غلطید توزلانا توزلانا به غلطان غلطان توزلانای و توزلانایین به غلطم و غلطد و غلطی توزلاناسا و
توزلانغای بیز و توزلانغای بیز به غلطیم توزلانغالی برای به غلطیدن و نابه غلطیدن توزلانغاچ چون به غلطید
توزلانغوچی به غلطنده توزلانغوچه و توزلانغانچه تا به غلطیدن و مقدار به غلطیدن توزلانا آلغانیکه مقداریکه تواند
به غلطید توزلانغوسیدور به خواهیم غلطید توزلانغوسی و به خواهید غلطید توزلانغوسیلار دور به خواهند غلطید
توزلانا غوم توزلانغوم بولوق به خواهم غلطید توزلانا آلماغوم توزلانا آلغوم به غلطیدن ممکن نخواهد بود توزلانغولوق به غلطیدنی
توزلانغای توزلانا و توزلانسا و توزلانسون و توزلاندیک به غلطد توزلانغودیک و توزلانور دیک به غلطیدنی و همچنانکه به غلطد توزلانا
مع الکلام مصدر متعدی به غلطاندن و صیغ آن با تای قرشت اشتقاق می یابد توزوماک بضم زا و سکون نای قرشت کرد برانگیختن
توزوتولوک کرد برانگیختیم توزوتور و توزوتادور کرد برانگیخت و توزوتور به معنی فاعل و مصدر هم می آید توزوتماید و کرد بر
نمی انگیزد و نینگیخته است توزوتکان و توزوتورکان و توزوتادورکان کرد برانگیزنده و برانگیخته و به معنی مصدر هم می آیند توزوت و توزوتکیل
مفرد مخاطب از فعل امر توزوتما و توزوتماغیل مفرد مخاطب از فعل نهی توزوتونک و توزوتونکیز و توزوتونکلار جمع مخاطب از فعل امر توزوتمانک
توزوتمانکیز و توزوتمانکلار جمع مخاطب از فعل نهی توزوتمان و توزوتماس مین کرد بر نمی انگیزم توزوتامین و توزوتورمین و توزوتادورمین
کرد برمی انگیزم توزوتماس کرد بر نمی انگیزد و به معنی فاعل و مصدر نفی هم می آید توزوتماسینکا بکرد بر نینگیختنت توزوتوچقه بکرد
برانگیختنت توزوتوب و توزوتوبان و توزوتمیش کرد برانگیخته توزوتمیشانک کرد برانگیخته توزوتسا بولغای و توزوتوب بولغای بکرد

توان برانگیخت توزیتا آلماغای که تواند برانگیخت توزیتا توزیتا کرد انگیزی که توزیتای و توزیتاین کرد برانگیزم
و برانگیزی و برانگیخته توزوتقاق و توزوتغاپ توزوتغای چزه توزوتملی و توزوتالیک کرد برانگیزیم توزوتغلی برای کرد
انگیختن و تا کرد انگیخته توزوتغاج چون کرد برانگیخت و ملا انگیزد توزوتغوچی کرد برانگیزنده توزوتغوچیوتی و توزوتغوتا
تا کرد برانگیختن و چند مرتبه کرد انگیختن توزوتا آلغای تنکه بتقدیم که کرد توانی برانگیخت توزوتغوسیز به و نکرد خواهیم برانگیخت توزوتغوجی
کرد خواهید برانگیخت توزوتغوسیلار که و کرد خواهند برانگیخت توزوتا مغوم توزوتغوم یوق کرد نخواهم برانگیخت توزوتا آلماغوم توزوتا
الغوم یوق کرد انگیختنی محکم نخواهند بود توزوتغولوق کرد انگیختنی توزوتغای توزوتالیق توزوتغوسلانوق توزوتقوچی توزوتقدیک کرد برانگیختی
توزوتغوچیلیک و توزوتوغدیک کرد انگیختنی و همانکه برانگیزد من الجوامد توز دو معنی دارد اول گرد و غبار که بند دویم بن کوتاه
چنانکه در فصل سین و شین از مجنون العقلاء به وصف نوکران کلاغی نعت گوید کمسقالین تریقیلیکی قولاغی توزیکلار ایه الار آشفته
حال آشفته حال قوینغا ملاحت و باشلاغ ختم دولت به معنی دارد اول لغات باشد شعر خواهم خواجه سبزی خط سبز و توزیلیه
سین [illegible] تا تمامی توزین دویم بمعنی طرح و مسطح بود چنانکه در مقاله بیستم از حیرة الابرار در وصف ظلم گوید
و خرابی مملکت گوید شعر باغ وصل المجانی بی کا توزی ظلم و طمع یولدی و بی بکا پیش سیم بلاد اصول و شعار ملک چنانکه
الابرار در وصف بزرگان گوید شعر تلغ ایله توزنی توان و کون باشقلیب خیلی ببلی خصبه سیدین قوتقلیب چهارم بمعنی راست
صحیح باشد شعر تدبیک توزیغل کلان لرلم توزی که توزلشیاقه بولتی شایه هم توزی پنجم راست صندوق و کیسه
شعر دینام بود بکلجه اون وکر توزی میکن دین پس ایاس بوسوزنی پل توزی ششم راست بمعنی نادق و موافق بود چنانکه گوید
شعر سوقد لالا کزی وکرتوزی میلک دین یا خاص پری بزنیک بیله توزی هفتم پوست درخت با دام کوچک است که محمد استعمال
بر کمان چسپانند او را توس هم گویند و توسح معرب آنست هشتم راست از تحمل کردن نهم راست از تاختن دهم راست از آراسته کردن یازدهم
راست از سر برشته کشیدن دوازدهم راست گوار کهن سال چنانکه در ذیل مصدر توزولاک گذشت و بعضی بمعنی ساخت دانسته
بود و نام شهریست نزدیک با هواز و بمعنی جمع کنند و برآید و کشند و حاصل کنند هم استعمال شود توزآغاجی نوعی از درخت که
هم آن خدنگ بلخ باشد و از انبار هیزم کوبند و تون که بر کار چند پوست آنست توزاغ و توزاق دام را نامند چنانکه در
شیرین گوید شعر بلا ابحرو فراغی بوله کیلیش تقولونه او زانیبی به کیلیش و آنرا دوزلغ هم گویند توزانات بفتح زاء و سکون
نون و کاف عجمی زمینی بود که خاک آن نرم باشد چنانکه در یکی از قطعات گوید شعر بیلیم دلیل شاهزاده پویه ایلدم قوم و توزانات
یوشاغ تاغ و خلع نصرتاتیغ توزاق بسکون زاء و قاف و فتح منی مهمله سنگی است مدور بزرگ که دستنو که در صحرا طلیه کند و بوته
تانک بمروی آن کشیده شده و جمع آن از چیز نرم میده پست که چون دست بدان برسد بهد شکافته شود توزلوغ و توزلاغ بسکون زاء
وقاف و فتح لام با الف کشیده نام شهری بود چنانکه در تنبیهات محبوب القلوب گوید که ایتی ز الاصبحینی ایرا ملاغ کوکی با ملو یخس
توزلاغه توشسا تو صحکی تو تار توزلوغ و توزلوق بمعنی نمکین و ملیح باشد الشاهد علیه شعر حرکت قیلنا بلی توز توکلی
شهد آغاد توزلوق ایل کمیری یوقین کبی شیرین خرکات توزلوک یعنی راست چنانکه گوید شعر یوچین ایچره خلق سوییی کمی
عی یوق توزلوک ایله کیم هشغلرایقی شباثوله شعر کونکول کلان لیغی کجایکی ملیک قیلو اول شوخ ای بولدی قیلنا ایدی تماشی کبی
توزلوک توزنهک بمعنی ساخته و آراسته و منتظم باشد الشاهد علیه شعر کونکول خراسیدین آبادی دیر و که بولدی توزوک
حریم ملک ارا کتابشنک عدالتی بار و نیز در خسرو شیرین گوید شعر برا وکیم تاپه شه لیغدین برناست توزوک بولسا ایشی

نیک اصیلت و بمعنی انتظام و آراستگی هم استعمال شود چنانکه در صفت کندنیدن مده شعر فی کیم آنکا توزداق ابرغا متوزه
توزوکلوک لغیر لیکیلیکا نخرین بجوک و مجازا بمعنی آباد و معمور هم مستعمل توزوکلوک به معنی مابعد لیک بمعنی انتظام و شایستگی و
آراستگی بود و تقویم بمعنی نظم و ساخته و آراسته باشد و مجازا بمعنی آبادی و معموری هم می آید الشاهد علیه شعر بوزوقلیک
کونکلوم ایمدی مم سپاهی حجکا کوپلی بحرش توزوکلوک کورتا کیل هر کز بو سیکلینغ کیم سیو بهیز دولت ثم الثلثی من المشتقات توسماق
بسکون سین باییدن توستی بایید چنانکه در لسان الطیر در صفت ابراهیم ادهم گوید شعر توستی لا دیو لیغلی تطالعین مانت
تلغیلی آیتنیک سلوکین امتحان توستوق بایید توستا بعنی توستادو بیستا باید و بمعنی فاعل مصدر مفعول هم می آید توسمایدینیمی
و بایید است توسغان بعنی توستاغان بعنی توستاد و غان باید و بایید و بمعنی مصدر هم می آید توسی و توسغیل مفرد فعل امر
توسیلو توسیناغیل مفرد فعل امر توسوک بعنی توسونکیز و توسونکلار جمع فعل امر توسماک و توسمانکیز و توسمانکلار
جمع فعل امر توسمانگ بعنی توسماس مین کیم بیکم توسا بین و توسا دین بعنی توسا نیم توسارام میسا یم توسماس نمیبا باید بمعنی فاعل
منفی هم می آید توسماسین که بنیا شدنت توسا تین که بنیا باید نیست توسوب بعنی توسوبان بعنی توسمیش باید چنانکه شاهد
مقامات هم در ذکر شیخ محمود بخاری گوید که مسوال اهلی مجاهل الایلا بین توسوب مکنی جایکو دو بنیه تیلا لار ایری
و نیز در تاریخ ناریخ ملوک است که بولنی توسوب او روشو باشنی لار تو سمیش نایایید توسیا بو لغا او تو سعیکه تواند باید
توسیا آلغای تواند باید توسیا توسیا ملاحظه کنان توسای بعنی توسا بین باشیم و بباید و بیاید و بایید توسیاق بعنی توسغلیق بیسیمان
توقالی بعنی توسیالی حسبا یم توسغلی برای بایید و تا نبایید توسغاج چون بایید و بیاید توسغوچی باینده توسغوجیه
توسغوجی و توسغابجه تا بایدن و مقدار بایدن توسیا آلغای تنکه مقدار یکه تو انی بایید توسغوسیز و نخواهیم بایید توسغوسیدور
بایید توسغیلاخ و نخواهند بایید توسماغوم یوق نخواهم بایید توسا آلماغوم توسا آلغوم که بایید محکم نخواهد بود
توسغولوق بایندنی توسغای بعنی توسا لو توسا لو توسیک توسدیک بباید توسغوبولمه توسا رلیک باینده و همانکه بیا
من الجوامد توس بسکون سین بر وزن آمده اول بمعنی توز باشد که بر کمان و امثال آن بچسپند شعر تاوکیک نیک پوستا
رنگی تون لیبوش یا که کونکلومدین که پران او تی بیقیش آنکا دویم بمعنی پشت درخت و خلاف بدو طالع هروی نوشته که
محدث و مکمل تمام لست توستوغان بسکون سین و نون و ضم تای قرشت و فتح عین مهمله کنولوله دار و ابر توری گویند الشاهد علیه
شعر قامیغ اولتوردی یمنی تو تضیل آنا غمی توستوغان کیم بی منبع اولتوری که کا آجیغ آغوده و که عشر هلال ناسوده
در کرامت بکیم توقتسا نابو تقلیب یو کونوب توستوغان ایچید اغیز فرداغی یعنی کاسه آبخوری نوشته و مولفین برهی از لغت
اشتباها بوستاغان با بای ابجد خوانده و به حرف بایمعنی کرج کشتی مانند ذکر کرده اند و نصیری بهم متابعت کرده توسقا و لعنت
و لام و فتح قاف و ضم واو نگهبان و محافظ او باشد توسلوق یعنی نگهبانی و قافی بزاد توسون ملعف مضحک و فتن ترکی
ثم الثانی من المشتقات توشماک باشباع ضمه فرود آمدن و افتادن و هر کاه با لفظ کورکوب شود تا دنه معنی پر پلا ختن کند چنانکه شاهد
در فصل تا نیمه مذکور میشود و تنها نانی اماده ایمعنی کند توشتی فرود آمد و افتاد و آنا توشتی بمعنی تیر انداز و طرف چنانکه در عجه
مرداستان منازمیم گوید شعر اضطرا لیبلاد ان آنا توشتی پرایکی او ق بیلی خطا توشتی توشوک فرود آمدیم و افتادیم تو
توشادو توشادو می آید و می افتد الشاهد علی الاول المعنی الثانی شعر توشار کونکلومکا اول یوزیدین تری کو کسوم شکافی
پورونو دون بی بی بولغای قیلسانک ای تیغ قضا اوسع و توشار بمعنی فاعل مصدر هم می آید و بلا اشباع یعنی سیکراند توشما ید

توس

ج

توش

فرود نمی آید و نیامده و نمی افتد و نیفتاده توشکان و توشادورکان فرود آینده و آمده و افتنده و افتاده و پرنده و پرداخته
الشاهد على الاول بالمعنى الاول شعر عشق توشتی زاغی عینك منقاری دهر ازقوت نزلت کویا توشکاند ورود لکلنیك
هلاکی لاشیفه و بمعنی مصدر هم می آیند چنانکه شاهد براوقرا بمعنی افتادن کوید شعر قیلوکی جسیم که هر نیك
سوز علمیچه تولغانوش اوتمه توشکاندین نشان هیچ ایله تابی آینك توشو توشکیل مفرد غائب ماضی قبل امر توشو مطلبا
هم دلرد چنانکه در ذیل جواب باشواهد مذکور خواهد شد توشما و توشماکیل مفرد غائب ماضی نفی توشولنك و توشکون
توشونکلار جمع غائب ماضی قبل امر توشمانك و توشمایکز و توشمانکلار جمع غائب ماضی نفی توشمان و توشماسمین فرو نیاییم و نیافتیم و نپریدم
توشامین و توشارمین و توشادورمیز توشارام فرود آییم و می افتم و می پرم و توشارمین و توشارام بلا اشباع بمعنی میکترم هم
مستعملست توشماس فرود نمی آید و نمی افتد و بمعنی فاعل و مصدر نفی هم می آید توشماسینکا بفرود نیامدنت و نیفتادنت
و نپریدنت توشارینکا بفرود آمدنت و بافتادنت و بپریدنت توشوب توشوبان و توشمیش فرود آمده و افتاده و پریده
توشمیشانك فرود آمده و پرداخته توشا بولغانی توشوب بولغانه فرود توان آمد و توان افتاد و توان پرداخت توشا الغای فرود
تواند آمد و تواند افتاد و تواند پرداخت توشا توشا ترولکان … توشاغ توشایین فرود آییم و آید و آیی و آمده
و بیفتم و بیفتد و بیفتی و افتاده و نیز بامصدر توشامات اشتراك طرد یعنی بکترانم و بکتراند و بکترانی و کترده توشسات
توشکایز و توشکاو توشکاو توشانینك فرود آییم و بیفتیم و بپرداریم و توشلی بلا اشباع یعنی بکترانیم توشکالی برای فرود آمدن و ا
و افرود آمده و افتاده و پرداخته بالمعنی الاول شعر عجب یوق صالحیلی توشکالی ترتیب بیلن نزلث کراشك وآه او قابیل
نینك کوز و کونکلینی باك ایلاهر بالمعنی الثانی شعر توشکالی قدینك هوایی باشنا اولش لرا باش لر اکیتیم الف بیلن قان
الغدیك باش لرا توشکاج چون فرود آمد و بیاید و چون افتاد و بیفتد توشکوجی فرود آینده و پرداززنده توشکوجه توشکونچه
تا فرود آمدن و بعد فرود آمدن و تا افتادن و بعد افتادن چنانکه شاهد بر … بمعنی تا افتادن کوید شعر …
توشکان حوادث اوتیدین مانع ایماس کوزیاشیدین کرچه کوز توشکونچه بیرنم دهر منکا توشا آلغا منقصد یکه فرود تواند
آمد و تواند افتاد توشکومدور خواهم فرود آمد و خواهم افتاد توشکونکدور خواهی فرود آمد و خواهی افتاد چنانکه
سکندر … بالمعنی الثانی شعر نچه کیم عقل ابجر دهر ز بردست بیلور کیم تاپان
توشکوسید … توشماکوم و توشکوم یوق فرود نخواهم آمد و نخواهم افتاد توشا الماغوم توشا آلغوم یوق فرود آمدن
و افتادن ممکن نخواهد بود توشکولوك فرود آمدنی و افتادنی توشکای و توشسا و توشسون و توشدیك فرود بیاید
و بیفتد توشماکای و توشماسا و توشماسون و توشمادیك فرود نیاید و نیفتد الشاهد على الاخر بالمعنى الاخر شعر …
توشدیك توشمادیك … توشکودیك … توشادیك فرود آمدنی و همچنانکه فرود
و افتادنی و همچنانکه بیفتد چنانکه بمعنی افتادن کوید الشاهد على الاول شعر ایله زنجیری تو دوز لغونك قمر …
توشکودیك بولمیش … آیینك و توشلریك بلا اشباع یعنی کتریدن و همچنانکه بکتراند توشورماك فرود
آوردن و افکندن توشوردی فرود آورد و افکند چنانکه در تنبیهات کوید کهجا لوتغه که آیینك دیك سینك …
سیاست تیغی بیله باشین … توشوردی توشوردوك فرود آوردیم و افکندیم توشوردور فرود می آورد و می افکند
توشور و بمعنی فاعل و مصدر هم می آید توشوراید … فرود نمی آرد و نیاورده است … و نیفکنده است توشوکان و توشوغان

توشوردورکان فرود آورنده و فرود آورده و افکننده و افکنده و بمعنی مصدر هم می آیند توشورو توشورکیل مفرد غائب ماضی قبل
توشورما و توشورماکیل مفرد غائب ماضی نفی توشورولت و توشورونکز و توشورونکلار جمع غائب ماضی قبل امر توشورمانکیز و
توشورمانکلار جمع غائب ماضی نفی توشوردان و توشورارمین فرود نمی آرم و نمی افکنم توشورامین و توشورورمین و توشوراراستم توشورام
فرود می آرم و می افکنم توشورماس فرود نمی آرد و نمی افکند و بمعنی فاعل و مصدر نفی هم می آید توشورماسینکا فرود نیاوردنت
و نیفکندنت توشورورونکا بفرود آوردنت و افکندنت توشوروب و توشوروبان و توشورمیش فرود آورده و افکنده توشورمیشانك
فرود آورده و افکنده توشورا بولغانی توشوروب بولغانی فرود توان آورد و توان افکند توشورا الغانی فرود تواند آورد و تواند افکند
توشورا توشورا فرود آورنده کان و افکننده کان چنانکه در تاریخ نابری مذکور است که توشورا توشورا کیچه … توشو
توشوراین فرود بیاورم و بیاوری و بیاورد و بیفکنم و بیفکنی و بیفکند توشورالی … توشورکای بیز
توشورالی و توشورالینك فرود بیاوریم و بیفکنیم توشورکالی برای فرود آوردن و تا فرود آورد و برای افکندن و تا افکندن توشو
چون فرود آورد و بیاورد و چون افکند و بیفکند توشورکوچی فرود آورنده و افکننده چنانکه بمعنی اول …
در وصف صبر کوید که … توشورکوچی … توشورکونچه تا فرود آوردن
فرود آوردن و تا افکندن و بعد افکندن توشورا الغا … فرود تواند آورد و تواند افکند توشورکوم
فرود خواهم آورد و خواهم افکند توشورکونکدور فرود خواهید آورد و خواهید افکند توشورکو … فرود خواهند آورد
و خواهند افکند توشورماکوم و توشورکوم یوق فرود نخواهم آورد و نخواهم افکند توشورا الماغوم توشورا آلغوم فرود آوردن و افکندن
ممکن نخواهد بود توشورکولوك فرود آوردنی و افکندنی توشورکای و توشورسا و توشورسون و توشوردیك فرود
بیاورد و بیفکند توشورماکای و توشورماسا … فرود نیاورد و نیفکند و همچنانکه بیفکند توشورمالت بکو
و تای قرشت مصدر متعدیست فرود آوراندن و افکنانیدن توشورتوب و توشورتوبان … فرود آورانیده و افکنانیده چنانکه
… الشاهد على الاول شعر توشورتوب هول سبزه اوزره سپاه …
بارکاه … و باقی صیغ بر این سیاق و اضافه تای قرشت اشتقاق می یابد توشولماق … فرود آورده شدن و افکنده شدن
توشولکاج چون فرود آورده شدند و شوند و چون افکنده شدند و شوند … بالمعنی الاول شعر
توشولکاج … و باقی صیغ بر این نهج بالالحاق … توشماك
مع الشین مصدر مفاعله است یعنی … افتادن و صیغ آن … اشتقاق می یابد توشامالت …
بمعنی کتردن بود توشادولت کتردیم توشادور توشایدور میکترد الشاهد على الاول شعر چون …
خارا … فرود …
و می افتد چنانکه کذشت توشامایه … کترده … و بمعنی مصدر هم
و توشارکان با اشباع بمعنی فرود آمده و فرود آورده و افکنده و افکنده هم می آید چنانکه ذکر رفت توشا و توشایکز
مفرد غائب ماضی قبل امر توشا و توشاکیل مفرد غائب ماضی نفی توشانك و توشانیکز و توشانکلار جمع غائب ماضی قبل امر توشامان
توشامانیکز و توشامانکلار جمع غائب ماضی نفی توشامان و توشامارمین … توشایمین و توشارمین و توشایدر … توشارام میکترم
و توشارمین و توشارام با اشباع با مصدر توشماك اشتراك لفظ دارند یعنی فرود می آیم و می افتم توشاماس نمیکترد و بمعنی فاعل و مصدر

177a.

منقوص می آید توشاماسینکا نبکترونت توشارینکا بکترونت و باشباع یعنی فرود آمدنت و افتادنت توشاب و توشاناق
توشلمیش کترلمه الشاهد علی الاول شعر هنر قیم توشابو لارینی میخانه دا کوینا زهران یا پشغان صدلار
دهر توشلمیشانک کترده توشاناتو تفاقوشاب وجه توانکترد توشاالقای تواندکترد توشای وتوشای وتوشایو کترد
توشلغ توشابین بکترم و بکترد و بکتری و کتردو و باصله توشماله هم اشتراک دارند چنانکه مذکور شد
توشاناله توشاکاینز توشاکاینز توشلیهتوشانیک بکتریم و توشلی باشباع یعنی فرود بنایم بنشیم توشاکلی
کتردن و تاکتردن توشاکاج چونکترد و بکترد توشاکوچ کترنده توشاکوجه توشاکوجه توشاکانجه تاکتردن و
کتردن توشای آلقانینکی بمعنی تواناکترد توشاکومیز بودن خواهیم کترد توشاکونکوز بودن خواهید کترد توشاکوسل
خواهند کترد توشاناکوم توشاکوم یوق نخواهم کترد توشای آلماغو توشای آلغوم یوق کتردن ممکن نخواهد بود توشاکان
کتردن توشاکای توشانلیق توشاسون و توشادیلک بکترد توشاکودیک توشارادیک کتردن و همچنانکه بکترد ور
باشباع نامصدر توشماله عین اشتراک دارد توشانماک مع الکنا مصدر متعدیست یعنی کترانیدن و مبسوطش بودن
آن بانامی قرشی اشتقاق می یابد توشالماک مع الکلام کترده شدن توشالیب توشالیبان توشالمیش کترده شده چنانکه
شاهد برا ولر در مقاله دهم از حیرت الابرار کوید شعر حصن هواده توشالیب مغرب شه عزم دلسیل خیلی حبیب کینی
توشالکاج چون کترده شد و شود الشاهد علیه من خسرو شیرین شعر توشالکاج بو دیناملکا دانی اصلی دلنک
لیک اولتورتو ینکوث و باقی صبح برین سباق بالالام اشتقاق می یابد توشلانماق دچار و مقارن شدن توشلانمات چاشتکاه
کترانیدن توشلاتدوق دچار شدیم توشلاتدولک چاشتکاه کترانیدیم توشلاتور و توشلاتادور دچار شود و چاشتکاه
و توشلاتور بمعنی حاصل مصدر هم می آید توشلاتادور و دچار نیشود و نشد است و چاشتکاه نیکترانیدو نکترانیدست توشلاتنان
توشلاتغان و توشلاتادورغان دچار شونده و دچار شده و بمعنی مصدر هم می آیند توشلانغان و توشلاتورکان توشلاتادورکان چا
کترانینده و کترانیده و بمعنی مصدر هم می آیند توشلات مفرد مخاطب فعل امر و مصدر توشلاتغیل مفرد مخاطب فعل امر مصدر
توشلاتماق توشلاتکیل مفرد مخاطب فعل امر مصدر توشلاتماک توشلاتما مفرد مخاطب فعل نهی و مصدر توشلاتماغیل
مفرد مخاطب فعل نهی مصدر توشلاتماق توشلاتماکیل مفرد مخاطب فعل نهی مصدر توشلاتماک توشلاتینک و توشلاتینکیز توشلاتینکلار
جمع مخاطب فعل امر و مصدر توشلاتماک توشلاتماینکیز توشلاتماینکلار جمع مخاطب فعل نهی هر دو مصدر توشلاتغان و توشلاتماغان
دچار نیشوم و چاشتکاه نمیکترانم توشلاتامین و توشلاتورمین و توشلاتادورمین و توشلاتورام دچار میشوم و چاشتکاه میکترانم
توشلاتماس دچار نیشود و چاشتکاه نمیکترانید و بمعنی حاصل مصدر منفی هم می آید توشلاتماسینکنه بدچار شدنت
توشلاتماسینکا بچاشتکاه نکترانیدنت توشلاتورونکنه بدچار شدنت توشلاتورونکا بچاشتکاه کترانیدنت توشلاتیب
توشلاتیبان و توشلاتمیش دچار شده و چاشتکاه کترانیده چنانکه شاهد برا قوله بمعنی اول در تاریخ نابری مذکور است که جوی بنا
دین محرکوچیب تاغ وقادا توشلاتیب تمامچین باغ و قادین تیپارده وله توشلاتیشانک دچار شدن و چاشتکاه کترانیدن
توشلاتسا و توشلاتیب توشلاتسه دچار تواند شد و چاشتکاه توان کترانید توشلاتا آلغای دچار تواند شد و چاشتکاه
تواند کترانید توشلاتانا و توشلاتانا دچار شوان و چاشتکاه کتران توشلاتاید و توشلاتاین دچار شوم و شوی
و شده و چاشتکاه بکترانم و بکترانند و بکترانی دکترانید توشلاتاسا قرتوشلاتانیاز و توشلاتانایز دچار شویم توشلاتسا

178a.

توشلانکانز و توشلانکای بز چاشتکاه بکترانیم توشلاتنالی دچار شویم و چاشتکاه بکترانیم توشلاتنالی برای دچار شدن
تا دچار شدن توشلاتنالی برای چاشتکاه کترانیدن و تا چاشتکاه کترانیده توشلاتغاج چون دچار شد و شود توشلاتغاج
چون چاشتکاه کترانید و بکترانید توشلاتغوچی دچار شونده توشلاتکوچی چاشتکاه کترانیده توشلاتغوچی توشلاتغو
توشلاتغانجه تا دچار شدن و بقدر دچار شدن توشلاتکوچی توشلاتکوچه توشلاتکانجه تا چاشتکاه کترانیدن و بقدر
چاشتکاه کترانیدن توشلاتا آلغانینکیز بمعنی دچار توانی شد و چاشتکاه را توانی کترانید توشلاتغومیز دو دچار خواهیم
شد توشلاتکومیز بودن چاشتکاه خواهیم کترانید توشلاتغونکوز بودن دچار خواهید شد توشلاتکونکوز بودن چاشتکاه خواهید
توشلاتغوسیلار دچار خواهند شد توشلاتکوسیلار بودن چاشتکاه خواهند کترانید توشلاتماغوم و توشلاتغوم یوق دچار نخواهم شد
توشلاتماکوم و توشلاتکوم یوق چاشتکاه نخواهم کترانید توشلاتا آلماغو و توشلاتا آلغوم یوق دچار شدن ممکن نخواهد بود و چا
کترانیدن ممکن نخواهد بود توشلاتغولوق دچار شدنی توشلاتکولوک چاشتکاه کترانیدنی توشلاتغالی دچار
چنانکه در باب دهم از محبوب القلوب در ذکر عشق کوید که اول تماشا حوسانیدین و اول نظاره استدعا سانیدین
توشلاتغای و قیلمی یوزلانکای توشلانکای چاشتکاه بکترانید توشلاتا و توشلاتسا و توشلاتغون و توشلاتدای دچار
و چاشتکاه بکترانید توشلاتغودیک دچار شدنی و همچنانکه دچار شود توشلاتکودیک چاشتکاه کترانیدنی و همچنانکه
توشلاتوردیک بمعنی توشلاتغودیک و توشلاتکودیک باشد من الجواسد توش شیر بمعنی طرف و کینه را کویند
در شمایم الحبه در ذکر بابا سنکو کوید که تیمور بیک خراسان عزیمت بیرکا بابا فوتی نینک تیشنی آلیب تیمور بیک
آلیب تورتیمور بیک دیب توره که خراسان ایری بوزی نینک کوکیدیب تورلا بابانزکاحوالا قیلدی و نیز در تاریخ نابری
مذکور است که بعضی قوش نینک بوتایی بخشی بولور بعضی نینک آلتی بخشی بولور بعضی نینک آلتی یخشی بولور و دیم خوابیت کلام
چنانکه مثل است که دشمن نی دیماس توشکالی کیماس تیم بمعنی مقارن بود چنانکه کوید شعر زلف دهر اینو قیلکله
اوتیغه جراشی دود یا بنا کوشیغه توش بیر کیکا نا بحیب دهر کهات و نیز بمعنی مقارن و بمعنی خواب بطریق جناس کوید شعر
صبح اوبیقوسین اول که ایلادی ترلث زرق و دیعزین اوزیکا توش کورکای اول که فضلتدین ایتی نوم صبح توشین مکر
که توش کورکای و نیز مثل است که تینک بولماغونچه توش بطاس آرمت و طرفها کوید چنانکه در سید سکندر
کوید شعر خانقه مکر دشت سلی بایردی بزم آلالاینبان شمر توشی صلدی عنم و توش توشین یعنی سمت چنانکه کو
شعر کونکولنی چاک چاک اینکالج تیشتی او قهر ایرزین اوتون قویا فنه کو ایکیم بولاوت نینک توش توشین باریش
و توش توشین یعنی از هر طرف چنانکه سلطان حسین میرزا کوید شعر عشق تیغی دین تیمدای من توبان نصل والف پرکلا
نیکلیغ که توش توشین کیلیش کیوق بیم بمعنی نیم رهن و منتظر باشد چنانکه بطریق جناس کوید شعر توشدا کور
غارضین کونکلومنی بندیدی عشق ایلة اول عقربکم تیکیم توش دو تی خورشید ایتماکای و نیز بمعنی سیاره در داستان مسافر
اقلیم اول کوید شعر را مردی مهمانراغه خواجه قدم کیلدی چون خواجه کیلدی مهمان ژهیم توشکا تیکو و طعام
ایدی سیکولوکلار دا زیب و زینتلیدی و نیز در مثنوی در وصف سید حسن کوید شعر جمال ایرا نا نک باتی ناهید دیک
کال ایرا توش وتی خورشید دیک شتو امر از فرود آمد زنان شد و بفارسی بمعنی طرد اول قوت و توانی دو یم طاقت سیم
خوراک بقدر احتیاج باشد و از تحف توشه است و مؤلف فرهنگ جهانگیری بمعنی بدن هم نوشته توشیچی شیلک یعنی بقدر نیم روز

وچاشت روز چنانچه در تاریخ تابری در وصف جولکای نخچوان مذکور است که ناصله توشی لیک بولدمر توشلک بودی
توشلک خاشاک مستعد توشانالد بمعنی کسترده شدن ولیم هم شده از برای جیاط و غیر آن که در وقت خواب واستراحت کسترانند
و مؤلف فرهنگ جهانگیری لغت توشک را ظاهرا بپهی شمرده و بمعنی نه جانه نوشته و مؤلف برهان قاطع گفته که بمعنی برخوابه
که جنار تا نهالی باشد و بمعنی جوابه هم نوشته و صاحب مؤید الفضلا که بنای تالیف کتاب خود را بر لغت عربیه نهاده
و ترکی کذاشته موشولد و پیشولدا که در ترکی بمعنی کربه است وآنرا بعربی سنور خوانند توشک خوانده و توشکرا کلمه
ترکی بمعنی نهالیت بمعنی کربه نوشته و مؤلف برهان قاطع نیز از مؤید الفضلا این معنی را ذکر کرده و هم تصحیف خوانی کرده شتر کربه
معنی نوشته اند توشکون بمعنی غلوک و افتاده نباشد توشکان کلمه تمام بود توشلوق چنانکه معنی او اول بمعنی
القدم باشد دویم بالمجاز بمعنی تنومند و جسیم و زورمند استعمال شود چنانکه در تاریخ الملوک المعتبره مذکور است
تخته اولتوردی چون آندین اولوغراق و تن و توشلوق ایلیا دا بردی الاره آتینکت خدمتی قاتیغ کیلور
و نیم روز بود و وقتیکه آنرا توشلوق نامند چنانم کویند توشلوق توشتی بمعنی سمت سمت چنانکه در خسرو شیرین کوید
تا باب قویغانی دابتو حیل توشتار کاملیدا لا توشلوق توشتی بیل توشوک هرف و مراد ... بمعنی ... بود
علیه شعر ... توشولغ توشوک باغریم بوطرفداق ... وله شعر
کوککه کوز آچیبان ... توشوب تایان که آتیب جان ... اگرچه این کلمه که اصل مصدر
بمعنی نامیز مستعمل ... مشتقات ... استعمال میشود ... مع الغین من المشتقات توغماق
در معنی ... الشاهد علیه شعر سوردیک بولسا بوکلشدا آنا ... توغماقی ... کلماغ
او غول دیم مجازا بمعنی طالع شد ... توغدی زاید و طالع شد توغدوق زاییدیم و طالع شدیم توغار و توغادور
میزاید و طالع میشود و توغار بمعنی فاعل و مصدر هم می آید توغماس ... نمیزاید و نزاییده است و طالع نمیشود و نخواهد شد توغمغان
توغمانغان و توغاد ... نزاییده و طالع نشده چنانکه شاهد بر اول معنی ... در کل ... مذکور
شعر آینک توغغان ... قشری ... بعنی طالع شونده در لیلی مجنون کوید شعر
... توغغان زاییده ... بمعنی طالع شده فرماید شعر تاشینک ... توغغان
... طالع ... بمعنی ... هم می آید چنانکه بمعنی زاییدن کوید الشاهد علی
شعر ... توغغان ... و توغغا زهرا
نامند توغ و توغیل مفرد مخاطب از فعل امر توغما و توغما غیل مفرد مخاطب از فعل نهی توغونک و توغونکیز ... جمع مخاطب
از فعل امر توغمانک و توغمانکیز و توغمانکلار جمع مخاطب از فعل نهی توغمان و توغمار مین نمیزایم و طالع نمیشوم توغاسین هم توغار مین
توغادور مین و توغار ام میزایم و طالع میشوم توغماس نمیزاید و طالع نمیشود و بمعنی فاعل و مصدر منفی هم می آید توغماسینکا
نزاییدنت و طالع نشدنت توغانینکه بزاییدنت و بطالع شدنت توغوب و توغوبان و توغیش زاییده و طالع شده
علی الاول المعنی الثانی شعر تاش ... منجم چونکه کوردی بی نقاب دیدی کوریکم ... توغوب ... آفتاب
توغمانک زاییده و طالع شده توغا توغا و توغوب و توغیب توان زایید و طالع شد توغا الغای توان زایید و طالع توان شد
توغا توغا زاییده زاییده و طلوع کنان توغای توغایین بزایم و بزاید و بزاید و بزاییده و طالع شوم و شود و شوی و شده

توغمای و توغمایین سبنه نفی توغای و توغایین باشد چنانکه بمعنی نزاییده کوید شعر حیات ... چون ... اهل ...
بولسون ... اولاجاه لند ... توغای ... اول ... بیکانه ... توغشا ... توغشا ... توغشای ... توغشای ... طالع شود
توغشلی برای زاییدن و نزاییده و برای طالع شدن و نطالع شده توغشاج چون زاید و بزاید چون طالع شده و شود
توغوچی زاینده و طالع شونده توغوب و توغوبدور و توغونجه تا زاییدن و بقصد زاییدن و تا طالع شدن و بقصد طالع شدن
توغا آلغا ... توانند زاییده و طالع توانی شد توغومیز ... خواهیم زایید و طالع خواهیم شد توغونکیز
زایید و طالع خواهید شد توغوسیلار ... خواهند زایید و طالع خواهند شد توغاغوم ... توغوم یوق نخواهم زایید و طالع نخواهم
توغا الماغوم ... الغوم یوق زاییدن و طالع شدن ممکنم نخواهد بود توغولوت زاییدنی و طالع شدنی توغاغو توغا
توغسا و توغسون ... بزاید و طالع شود توغوبدیک ... زاییدنی و چنانکه بزاید و طالع شدنی و چنانکه طالع
شود توغورماق مع الراء المهمله مصدر متعدی بمعنی زایانیدن توغورور ... میزایاند و توغورور بمعنی فاعل و مصدر
هم می آید چنانکه بمعنی زایانیدن در تاریخ الانبیا در ذکر موسی علیه السلام کوید که ...
بولوب ... احتیاج بولدی توغوروب و توغوروبان و توغورمیش زایانیده چنانکه در ... الابرار کوید الشاهد علی
شعر ... شیطان ... ییک ... بولوبان ... و ...
دیک ... توغوروب ... توغراماق ... بیکوزین ...
ریزه کردن توغرادوق ریزه کردیم توغراب و توغرابدور ریزه کرده و توغرار بمعنی فاعل و مصدر هم می آید توغرامایدور ...
و ... است توغراغان و توغراغان و توغرادیم ... ریزه کننده و ریزه کرده و بمعنی مصدر هم می آید توغرا و توغراغیل مفرد
توغرامای ... توغراماغیل مفرد مخاطب از فعل نهی ... توغراناک توغرانکیز ... جمع مخاطب از فعل
امر توغرامانک ... جمع مخاطب از فعل نهی توغرارمن ... ریزه میکنم توغرارسین و توغراسیز ...
توغرارام ریزه میکنم توغراماس ریزه نمیکند و بمعنی فاعل و مصدر منفی هم می آید توغراماسینکه بریزه نکردنت توغرامینکه
بریزه کردنت توغراب و توغرابان و توغرامیش ریزه کرده چنانکه در مقالات ... الابرار در وصف ظلمت کوید الشاهد
علی الاول شعر ... توغرابسون ... الشاهد علی الثانی شعر ...
پاره ... توغرامیش ... ریزه کرده توغرابولغای و توغراب ...
ریزه توان کرد توغرا الغای ریزه توانند کرد توغرای و توغرای و توغرایو ریزه کنان توغرای و توغرایین ریزه کنم و کند و کنی و کند
توغرایساق و توغرایسا ... توغرالی ... ریزه کردن و تا ریزه کنند توغراغاج چون ریزه کرد و کند
توغراغوچی ریزه کننده توغراغوب و توغراغونچه تا ریزه کردن و بقصد ریزه کردن توغرای آلغای ... ریزه
کند توغراغومیز ... ریزه خواهیم کرد توغراغونکیز ... ریزه خواهید کرد توغراغوسیلار ... ریزه خواهند کرد توغراغوم
غوم یوق ریزه نخواهم کرد توغرا الماغوم و توغرای الغوم یوق ریزه کردن ممکنم نخواهد بود توغراغولوق ریزه کردنی توغراماق توغرا
توغراسون و توغرادیک ... ریزه کند توغراغودیک و توغرادیک ریزه کردنی و چنانکه ریزه کند توغراتماق مع التاء متعدی
یعنی ریزه کنانیدن و صیغ آن با تمامی توغراماق اشتقاق می یابد توغراشماق مصدر مجهول است بمعنی یکدیگر ریزه کردن و صیغ آن با تمامی
اشتقاق می یابد توغرالماق مع اللام یعنی ریزه شدن توغرالدیم ریزه شدم الشاهد علیه شعر ...

179

موجه زخم نیز هست. و از قبیل قلتبان بالیدا بیله توغرالدیم و باقی صیغ بر بن سیاق بالام استقاق باید برابر مجاهد توغالاق بمعنی توغ
باشد توغانات یک نوع از جوارح شکاری بود که آنرا اولکو گویند توغانلک بفتح نون و سکون کاف نام پرنده ایست شبیه بباشه
اما از باشه کوچکتر و آنرا الا توغان و الا توغانک نیز نامند توغای بسکون یای حطی هم دمی است که در صحرا و دشتها بماند
و آنرا توغای هم گویند توغلاق مرغیست آبی کبود رنگ و بزرگ شبیه بمرغابی توغدق مرغیست شبیه بمرغ از جنس هو بره که
آنرا با باز و شاهین شکار کنند و چون باز و شاهین خواهند که او را بگیرند فضله خود را بر سر و روی آنها انداز(د) و خود را خلاص کند
و از نجاست که در عرب مثل زنند که ان الحباری سلاحها سلاحها توغری دو معنی دارد اول راست شدن و دروغ را گویند دوم
بمعنی برابر و محاذی بود چنانچه در تاریخ بابری در وصف کابل مذکور است که نیه پرچشمه خواجه عبد الصمد توغری سیدادیدکه خواجه
روشنائی در بر لاد توغغان همراه و اولوالانجام را گویند من بابر پادشاه شعر عزرایله صبا بیتکل الخیدا غیغه فی کل کر
سه تا یا غیغه دیکیل ولغی اشیاقایله بایردیث نغار دیکیل سلام توغغا یغغه و نیز بمعنی زاینده و زاییدن بود چنانکه
ذیل توغاق گذشت توغغان لیغ و توغغان لیق بمعنی حمله دوم و اولوالارحامیت باشد چنانچه در تاریخ بابری در وصف قرنبا
مذکور است که اول طبقه دین هر کیم کمینینک سر و قیتیم فه توشتی ایلیکیمدین کیلکا بغه توغغان لیغینی بجا کیلتوردوم توغما غا
خوانند چنانکه در بهار(ستان) النقایه در وصف میر حیدر جبوجی گفته که آلادین بو دوم کا نینک بابری بلکه توغما سید ... توغوز بفتح
میم و سکون رای مهمله نیمی جوارح را نامند و نیز اطلاق است از نازا یاسیدن توغوزها بضم غین و سکون زای مهمله و فتح قاف قرشت
بمعنی خیمه و خرگاه باشد توغورش بمعنی زادگی بود چنانکه گویند توغوشلوق یعنی صاحب اصالت و نجابت مع الفاظ المشتقات
تونکوریات تف کردن تونکوردولغ تف کردیم تونکوردو و تونکوراددو تف میکند و تونکور و بمعنی فاعل و مصدر هم می آیند
تونکورادایدور تف میکند و نکرده است تونکوروکان و تونکوروکان و تونکوراددوکان تف کننده و تف کرده و بمعنی مصدر هم می آیند
تونکور و تونکورکیل مفرد مخاطب از فعل امر تونکورنیا و تونکورنکیل مفرد مخاطب از فعل نهی تونکوروبیک و تونکوروز و تونکوروزلار
جمع مخاطب از فعل امر تونکور نیانک و تونکور نیا بیکیز و تونکور نیانکلار جمع مخاطب از فعل نهی تونکور نیا نم تونکور نیا من تف نمیکنم تونکورامیز
تونکوروجی و تونکوراددوجی و تونکوروچی تف میکنم تونکوریماس تف نمیکند و بمعنی فاعل و مصدر منفی هم می آید تونکوریاسیکا
تف نکردنت تونکوروپ و تونکا تف کردنت تونکوروب و تونکوروبان و تونکوروبیش تف کرده تونکوربیتالک تف کرده
تونکوریابولغا و تونکوروب بولغه تف توان کرد تونکورآلغای تف تواند کرد تونکورا تونکورا تف کنان تونکورای و تونکوراین
تف کنم و کنند و کنی و کرده تونکورناک و تونکورکاینز و تونکورکایز و تونکورلی و تونکور الیسک تف کنیم تونکورکالی
برای تف کردن و تا تف کرده تونکورکاج چون تف کرده کند تونکورکوچی تف کننده تونکورکوچه و تونکورکوچه و تونکورکوچکا تف کردن تونکور
تف کردن تونکورآلغا ینکیم یعنی میتوانیکه تف توانی کرد تونکورکوسیز دودن تف خواهیم کرد تونکورکونکیز دو تف خواهید کرد تونکور
دوسیلارد و دن تف خواهند کرد تونکوریا کوم و تونکورکیم یوق تف نخواهم کرد تونکور الماغوم و تونکور الغوم یوق تف کردن نتوانم
بود تونکورکولیک تف کردن تونکورکای و تونکورلاو تونکورسا و تونکورسون و تونکور بیلک تف کند تونکورکوده
تونکوروبدیلک تف کردن و همچنانکه تف کند توفراغ بالما ق غ کنایه از خالی بودن باشد از برای پیدا کردن چیز بنود بود چنانکه
شاهد آن در ذیل توپراغ نگارش یافته بر ابجوامد توفراغ توفراق همان توپراغ و توپراق بمعنی خاک بلند که مذکور شد توقاس
بفتح فاوراء مهمله و توقوچالت بسکون را و کاف و فتح جیم آبی را گویند که از دهن انداخته شود و آبی که از دهن روان شود و زراشوله

180

باشد توقوق بمعنی کرد و ملجا باشد لیکن بجا از ابتدا بمعنی ستمات اول قتله خیمه را گویند چنانکه در اوغوزنامه مسطور است که
اوغوزخان اونک یاناما آلتی قاره کاتیکتوردی باشینه آلتوق توقوق بر کیتکان یغرق قولاج سغاجی تکتوردی دیبته قل
کوچک را خوانند سیم فورلق پا بود که آنرا توپچیقیز خوانند مع القاف من المشتقات توقونا قوغ بضم تا بالمعنی توقودوق یافتیم
توقودوق یدور بیبافد و توقور بمعنی فاعل و مصدر هم می آید توقونا یدور نمیبافد و نبافته است توقوغان و توقوغان و توقولغان
بافته و نبافته و بمعنی مصدر هم می آیند توقو و توقوغیل مفرد مخاطب از فعل امر توقوما و توقوماغیل مفرد مخاطب از فعل نهی
توقونک و توقونکوز و توقونکلار جمع مخاطب از فعل امر توقومانک و توقومانکیز و توقومانکلار جمع مخاطب از فعل نهی توقوماس نمیبافم
توقویین و توقویمن و توقویلاین و توقورام میبافم توقوماس نمیبافد و بمعنی فاعل و مصدر منفی هم می آید توقوماسیکنه نبافتنت
توقوونکنه بیافتنت توقوب و توقوبان و توقومیش بافته توقوغیشالک بافته توقوماق بولغا و توقوب بولغا توان بافت
توقوی آلغای تواند بافت توقوی توقوی بافان بافان توقوی و توقوین ببافم و ببافد و ببافی و بافته توقونای و توقوناین
صیغه نفی توقوی توقوین توقوی آلمای و توقوی آلماین نتوانم بافت و نتواند بافت و نتوانی بافت و نتوانسته که بباید چنانکه
شاهد بر ثانی را بمعنی نتواند بافت در نعت گوید شعر قوپاش نینک شعاعی خط طی مسیح توقوی آلماین بجز نکا بوریا توقونا
توقوغای و توقوغایمیز و توقولی و توقویلیک توقوبالیم بافیم توقوغالی برای بافتن و تا بافته توقوغاج چون بافت و ببافد توقوغوچی بافنده توقوغوچه
توقوغوچه و توقوغاغه تا بافتن و بعد بافتن توقوی آلغاینکیم یعنی میتوانی بافت توقوغوسیزدودور خواهیم بافت توقوغونکوزدو خواهید با(فت)
توقوغوسیلار دودور خواهند بافت توقوماغوم و توقوغوم یوق نخواهم بافت توقوی آلماغوم و توقوی آلغوم یوق بافتن ممکنم نخواهد بود
توقوغولوق بافتنی توقوغای و توقوسا و توقوسون و توقوبیلیک ببافد توقوغودیک و توقوردیک بافتن و همچنانکه ببافد توقوماق
مع التا مصدر متعدی است بمعنی با قاندن و صیغ آن بدستور بنای قرینه اشتقاق می یابد توقولماق مع اللام بمعنی بافته شدن
توقولغان و توقولوغان و توقولادوغان بافته شونده و بافته شده ما شاهد علی الاول از المعنی الثانی یعنی سید سکندر بمعنی شعر دیما یکم
یوز توپمان جان نورغه سوا مولجید انامر الحیب صبر توقولغان کوجنس بیا ارا اوکوش ایمیز نغشی دریا ارا و بمعنی مصدر هم می آیند
و باقی صیغ بر بن سیاق بالام اشتقاق می یابد توقونماق مع النون و توقوشماق مع الشین بهم خوردن در هم چیزی بشد اندر وی
شدت و متضاد شدن توقوندی و توقوشتی بهم خورد چنانکه در خسرو شیرین در طوفان دریا گوید الشاهد علی الثانی شعر
هانا کوککا بیکیم سو توقوشتی فلک کنبد لاجی نینک مستغفی توقشتی توقوندوق و توقوشتوق بهم خوردیم توقونور و توقونادور
توقوشور و توقوشادور بهم میخورد و توقونور و توقوشور بمعنی فاعل و مصدر هم می آیند توقونمایدور و توقوشمایدور بهم نمیخورد و نخورده است
توقونغان و توقونورغان و توقونادورغان و توقوشغان و توقوشاغان و توقوشادورغان بهم خورنده و بهم خورده
و بمعنی مصدر هم آیند توقون و توقونغیل و توقوش و توقوشغیل مفرد مخاطب از فعل امر توقونما و توقونماغیل و توقوشما و توقوشماغیل
مفرد مخاطب از فعل نهی توقونونک و توقونونکوز و توقونونکلار و توقوشونک و توقوشونکوز و توقوشونکلار جمع مخاطب از فعل امر توقونمانک
توقونمانکیز و توقونمانکلار و توقوشمانک و توقوشمانکیز و توقوشمانکلار جمع مخاطب از فعل نهی توقونمان و توقونمامین و توقوشمان و توقوشمامین
بهم نمیخورم توقونامین و توقونورمین و توقونادورمین و توقونورام و توقوشامین و توقوشورمین و توقوشادورمین و توقوشورام بهم میخورم
توقونماس و توقوشماس بهم نمیخورد و بمعنی فاعل و مصدر منفی هم می آید توقونماسیکنه و توقوشماسیکنه بهم نخوردنت توقو(نوب)
و توقوشوب و توقونکنه
توقونوب و توقونکنه بهم خوردنت توقونوب و توقونوبان و توقونمیش و توقوشوب و توقوشوبان و توقوشمیش بهم خورده توقونسا بولغه

توقوب بولغای توقوشا بولگای توقوشیب بولگیم توان خورد توقونا آلغای وتوقوشا آلغای بهم تواند خورد توقونا توقونا
توقوشا توقوشا بهم تصادم کنان توقونای توقوناین وتوقوشای وتوقوشاین بهم خوریم وخورد وخوری وخورده توقونای توقونای
توقوشای وتوقوشاین بهم نخوردم ونخورد ونخوری ونخورده چنانچه شاهد براول است بمعنی نخورده در سد سکندری در پیغام دادن دارا
باسکندر گوید شعر ولی بن اوچون کیم کیچکوی ناشینک توقونمای توردورناشغه هرگز باشینک توقونا وتوقونغا
توقونغای چیز وتوقولماى وتوقونالیک وتوقوشاق وتوقوشغلیق وتوقوشغای چیز وتوقوشالی وتوقوشالیلغیم خوریم توقونغالی وتوقوشغالی
برای بهم خوردن وتا بهم خورد توقونغلیچ وتوقوشغلیچ چون بهم خورد وخورد توقونوچی وتوقوشوچی بهم خورنده توقونوغچه
توقونوغلوق وتوقوناچ وتوقوشوچه وتوقوشوغلوق وتوقوشغا برای بهم خوردن وتا بهم خوردن توقونا آلغاسیکه وتوقوشا آلغاسیکه تا که بهم
توان خورد توقونغوسیدور توقوشغوسیدور بهم خواهیم خورد توقونغوسیدور توقوشغوسیدور بهم خواهید خورد توقونغوسیلاردور
توقوشغوسیلاردور بهم خواهند خورد توقوناغوم یوق توقونغوم یوق وتوقوشاغوم یوق وتوقوشغوم یوق بهم نخواهم خورد توقوناغوم توقونغوم
بهم خواهم خورد توقونا آلغوم یوقدور توقوشا آلماغوم توقوشا آلغوم یوق
توقوناماغیدور توقوشغوم یوق بهم خوردن ممکن نخواهد بود توقونغولوق توقوشغولوق بهم خوردنی توقونغای وتوقونادور توقونا
توقونسون وتوقوندیك وتوقوشغای وتوقوشادور وتوقوشسون توقوشتی بهم خورد توقونغودیك وتوقونوردیك وتوقوشقودیك وتوقوش
بهم خوردن وچنانکه بهم خورد توقوندورماق وتوقوشتورماق مصدر متعدی است یعنی تصادم ساختن وتوقو چیزرا
بیکدیگر از روی شدت زدن وصیغ توقوند موافق بالفظ درس وازتوقوشتورماق باتوقوشتماق می یابد توقتاماق وتوقتاتماق
یعنی آرام یافتن وباحرف خا نیز مستعملست چنانکه در ذیل توختاماق وتوختاشتاماق نگارش یافت توقتا وتوقتاغیل وتوقتار
توقتاس غیر مفرد خاطب امر فعل است شاهد علی الاول شعر دیبلیعیش سن یرغدنك آتغوم نوایی کونکلیکا توقتا آنچه کیم قرار توق
کونکلنی توقتاناى توقتاماس وتوقتاشماس آرام نمی یابد شاهد علی الاول شعر کونکلوم ایچره توقتاماس لعلینك خیالی بیر زمان
نی عجب ولسام بو زخیم دین چهره تان بارون وبمعنی فاعل ومصدر منفی هم می آید توقتا غالی وتوقتاشقالی برای آرام یافتن
وتا آرام یابنده چنانکه در لسان الغیب شاهد براول است بمعنی لغوی گوید شعر آشکار ایلادی نجا تحت توقتاغالی آندلنا
بنگهت توقتاتماق وتوقتاشتورماق مصدر متعدیست یعنی آرام دادن وبدل قاف خاء معجمه نیز استعمال میشود توقتاتو
توقتاتادور وتوقتاشتورور وتوقتاشتور آرام میدهد شاهد علی الثانی شعر کیم کاچ اول آنی یاتمن دور کیم تاتار قیلمای
لیك بحود لوغ ایله کونکلوم امزین توقتاتادور توقتات وتوقتاتغیل وتوقتاتتغیل وتوقتاشتور وتوقتاشتورغیل مفرد خاطب امر فعل است
شاهد علی الاول شعر کونکلوم گاه دینالك اول سنکاچ آت تیماسون سعی ایتیب توقتات کونکلونی اسرافیل نهاد
کونکل توقتاتای وتوقتاتغای وتوقتاشتورغای وتوقتاشتورای آرام بدهم وبدهد وبدهی وداده شاهد علی الاول بالمعنی الاول
شعر خرد کونکول سهی توقتاتای دیدیم کیم بوزولدی یکر یکبحیلین کوروب یالی سیلیه وبالف صنم توقتاماق بر زبان اکابر
قوت وزن توقتاشتورماق بالفظ توقتشقاق می یابد من انجاهد توقت بمعنی رسید گرسنه باشد توقماچ چوبی که درشت بد
بکار برند ناکوفته نکرده و آنرا غاز بیرون می نامند و تقریبا آن بود که کازران دروقت جامه شستن میزنند توقالرون
گویند که از جهه زنان کوچکتر و بمنزله خدمتکار باشند توقتای بچه و حیواناتی که در میرود خانها باشد چنانکه در تاریخ
بنکویدیست که خان ییرهندا بوقراسو آنداق توقتای یورو نوب کیلیب بعد کیم ایچندا ابراهیرو توسکوبیر بولغای وآنرا توقتا
نیز گویند توقتاش بضم ثانی ساکن بود ونیز اسمیست از آرام یافتن توقتامیش نام یکی از خواتین خوارزم است که در عهد امیر تیمور بود

با او مخالفت کرده ومکرر محاربات میان ایشان واقع شد آخر بقتل رسید ونیز نام طایفه ایست از ترکمان وبمعنی آرام کرفته هم باشد چنانکه
در ذیل صناید گذشت توقتاوول مستحفظان قلاع را گویند توقرات نام پادشاه طماق است که در عهد اسکندر از اتباع او بود
توقرا بای بسکون قاف وتای حطی وفتح سین مهمله وبای ابجد بالف کشیده کسی باشد که چوب بر دست گرفته در برابر سلاطین ایستاده خدمت کند
واهل ایران آنرا ایشیك آقاسی وبعضی دیگر صحبت گویند توقسلوق یعنی سیری بعد از گرسنگی بمعنی نرم بودن وپر خوردن و فراغت بود چنانکه
تاریخ الانبیاء در ذکر یوسف علیه السلام وتعبیر خواب فرعون گوید که یتی بیل توقلوق بولوب نیه یتی بیل قحط بولغوسیدور
توقمار بسکون قاف ورای مهمله وفتح میم بجکو تیر بیست بپیکان که بجای پیکان گره میماند تکمه از چوب یا استخوان در آن نصب کنند
توقماق در معنی چرا وترکیب آلیسته معروف که بدان میخ چادر بر زمین کوبند چنانکه در تاریخ الانبیاء در ذکر نمرود و فرعون شده
گوید که ایش پیرکا بیتی کیم توقماق یا ساتی کیم متصل آهنك باشیغه پرلاوراولار ایردی دویم نام طایفه ایست از ازبك چنانکه در
التصغامه مذکور است که شعر کوبو دیمی نیری بیرزاتی ده بحمد ایکم ترك تعماده مرحیمه مشتمل لاچی را هم گویند توقوز عدد نه
که آنرا بعربی تسعه خوانند وچون عدد الافلاک نه واشکال رقم هندیه نیز نه وعدد سلاطین طبقه مغول هم نه است که اول ایشان
مغول خان وآخر ایشان ایلخان باشد وبعضی از مورخین هم عدد اولاد یافث را که ابو الترك است نه شمرده اند که عبارت از ترك وترك
وسقلاب وخزر وچین وکیماک وخازان وخرو باشد لهذا ترکان تیمنا اعتقاد اکثر حساب را بر نه گذاشته اند چنانکه در حیرت الابرار
گوید شعر ساقی ادب شرطینی آنا ده توت ایکیما توقوزیکونوب باده توت ونیز در سد سکندری گوید شعر کیلیب قویلادی
باشیغه تاج نش لباس نیرایو سینکا زرین کمر باناالیج توقوز دولت کا نیغه توت وحیه برله آهنك با نیغه وله سلع
هری که اشیا کیلیب توقوز توقوز آیدین صیاکیلیبا وچون هدیه وپیشکش از هر جنس که باشد نه نه ترتیب میدهند لهذا هدیه
وپیشکش را نیز بالجمال توقوز نامند چنانکه گوید شعر چون بیتی قات بیرکا کیر کوکلك قامت خالای سود کرسیهلاچلسیدین آنیکه
تا تنادولا توقوز وموافق شرع نبوی نیز زینت عدد نه بر اعداد دیگر وضوح دارد نیز براکه عدد اسماء حسنای الهی نود ونه است کری
از نه عشرات ونه احادی وعدد کلیات عالم امکان مجملا هزار است که از تضعیف نه بلعتبار لزوم زوجیت در مخلوقات بظهور آمده
وچون کمال نبوت حضرت خاتم الانبیا علیه الصلوة والسلام ختم شد عدد از ولج اطهار آنحضرت هم نه مقرر شد توقوزتالك کنا
از آباء علوی که عبارت از نه فلك باشد توقوز توت نام درختیست که نه بوست طرد وچوب آن در کمال صلابتست وآنرا توقوز یوق
هم گویند توقوز بحی یعنی نهمین الشاهد علیه شعر بیك قصرنیه توقوز بحی فلك اول الطلس که باهل الملایل فرشتان
توقوش تا گوی جولاهه را نامند وبمعنی سه وبهم خوردن دوچیز از روی شدت باشد توقولغه بضم قاف وسکون لام
وفتح غین معجمه بلغت مغول جل اسب باشد توقوم بالان بود که بر پشت دواب نهند وجل اسب را هم گویند توقه یعنی اسباب تجمل
واثاثیه چنانکه در تاریخ نابری مذکور است که دیلدیکیم توقه توقه سیلابا الحی لیك قیلغزنی قوبیلی تکلفانه کیلکیل بهانمود
خوانند وبا تاء مشدده به تازی حلقه فرانه در بود که از آهن وبرنج واشال آن ساخته ننده تیر وشمشیر را از آن بحکم آیند مع
مز المشقات توکات یعنی تخمین وبمعنی لازم ومتعدی هر دو استعمال میشود وبا شباع ضمه وسکون کاف عجمی بمعنی کردن باشد چنانکه
صعب لیخ حبیبمدا ده مهران یونعلادین کره تاك لیغیه ابر کچه توکون توکالکال توکمی ریخت توکری باکاف عجمی کوزدا
علیه شعر زار حبیبما بو حولدیم تیم نینك سا ابو ده کیم نیه پرلا توکلدی توکون هر تارخه توکار وتوکادور بریزد
الشاهد علی الاول تارلغونك ایچرکیم اشکیم توکلر کافزنك مرو تسبیح تا ربا رشته ناره وتوکار بمعنی فاعل ومصدر هم می آید

توك ×

چنانچه در افغان نسخه سیاره در وصف شیخ نظامی بمعنی ریختن گوید الشاهد علی الاول شعر ویخچه نی ثبات ایله شکر توکا
کاه شیکن قبلب کمی شکر دی ذلله . هم راشین تا قدم ویبکیم قاودی لار الشام ابد فیق . قنیم اوستیندا توکار تاشیم جزاول
تاش اتیماکیل و مؤلف عربی توکانماشیم ایمدی شعر توکانماشیم دشتعدها را خوانده و توکاتاش را بعضی قتاس یعنی لعل ملمع بود
وشعر مزبور را شاهد آورده . و بعضی هم متابعت کرده اند و دم خاره نیز توکاباش را بای ابجد ضبط کرده . و بمعنی مصدر کو ریختن
سهو کرده اند و باکاف عجمی یعنی کو میزند . چنانچه در حیرت الابرار در وصف لئیم گوید شعر بشیر [illegible] توکه تلیر ما لئیم صدایم
تا یاره کونکلی بیم دینا کیم آچا تا نکلا باخود بو کونس توکار اول توکونکا یا نامیرتو کونش توکمایدو یعنی بزد و ریخته است و کو میزند
وزده است توککان و توکارکان و توکادورکان ریزنده و ریخته و باکاف عجمی یعنی کو زننده و کو زده . چنانچه شاهد بر اول گذشت
کو زده گوید شعر دم [illegible] توککان کبی پنهان خرد اهلی کو لیک کونکلوم ایمر [illegible] داغ اوز [illegible]
و بمعنی مصدر هم می آیند توله و توککیل مفرد مخاطب از فعل امر توکما و توکماکیل مفرد مخاطب از فعل نهی توکونک و توکونکوز
توکونکلار جمع مخاطب از فعل امر توکمانک و توکمانکیز و توکمانکلار جمع مخاطب از فعل نهی توکان و توکارمین میریزم و باکاف عجمی کو میزنم
توکامین و توکلومین و توکادورمین و توکادام میریزم و باکاف عجمی کو میزنم توکارسن میریزی و باکاف عجمی کو میزنی و بمعنی فاعل و مصدر
منفی هم می آید توکاسینکا بریختنت و باکاف عجمی بکو زدنت توکارینکا بریختنت و باکاف عجمی کو زدنت توکوب و توکوبان و
توکیش ریخته و باکاف عجمی کو زده . چنانچه گوید الشاهد علی الاول شعر هر بیری [illegible] آنکلا [illegible] جهاسیدین جناب
بو کو لالالکیم توکوب [illegible] شته [illegible] در صفت [illegible] الابرار در وصف [illegible] گوید الشاهد علی الثانی
شعر لنه که [illegible] توکوبان [illegible] ناشیل [illegible] توکیشلیک ریخته و باکاف عجمی کو زده . توکتا و توکتا
توکوب [illegible] توان ریخت و باکاف عجمی کو توان زد توکالماله نتوان ریخت و باکاف عجمی کو نتوان زد توکا توکا ریزان ریزان و
باکاف عجمی کو زنان توکا باشلادی یعنی ریختن آغاز کردی چنانچه در خاتمه سد سکندری گوید شعر بودم [illegible]
کیم ایلاب شتاب توکا باشلادی [illegible] خامه دین [illegible] و باکاف عجمی کو زدن آغاز کردی توکای و توکاین بریزم و بریزد و بریزی و
ریخته [illegible] شاهد علی الاول المعنی الاول شعر [illegible] توکای [illegible] که تا [illegible]
کانیم [illegible] و باکاف عجمی یعنی که بزنم و بزند و بزنی و [illegible] توککوچی ریزنده چنانچه گوید شعر [illegible] لاله زار
لاله تاپین توککوچی [illegible] و باکاف عجمی یعنی کو زننده توککوچه و توککوچی تا ریختن و بقدر ریختن و باکاف
عجمی تا کو زدن و بقدر کو زدن توکالغانیچه [illegible] و باکاف عجمی [illegible] توککوم خواهم ریخت
و باکاف عجمی کو خواهم زد توککونک خواهی ریخت الشاهد علیه شعر ای نوایی [illegible] توککونک سرشک
[illegible] دولت [illegible] آب و دانه [illegible] و باکاف عجمی کو خواهم زد توککوسی خواهد ریخت و باکاف عجمی کو خواهد زد توکماغوسی
توککوم یوق نخواهم ریخت و باکاف عجمی کو نخواهم زد توکالماغوم [illegible] ریختن ممکن نخواهد بود و باکاف عجمی کو زدن ممکن
نخواهد بود توککوک [illegible] و باکاف عجمی کو زدنی توککای و توککا [illegible] بریزد و باکاف عجمی کو بزند توکوکونکوز
توکارلیک [illegible] بریزد و باکاف عجمی کو بزند [illegible] توکولماک [illegible] شدن [illegible]
شعر توکلماک [illegible] عشاق آرزو [illegible] که تیغ عشق [illegible] و باکاف عجمی یعنی کو زدن
توکولدی ریخته شد و باکاف عجمی کو زده شد چنانچه در فرهاد و شیرین گوید شعر [illegible] چون سوز توکولدی

می اینتاب شه مدح مانند کو لدی توکولور و توکولادور ریخته میشود الشاهد علی الاول شعر هر بیرین تا که کونکول
سینه دی آتار توبی طوفان شیشه سیلیکیم توکولور بدی چون تاتی شکست . و باکاف عجمی کو میشود و توکولور یعنی فاعل و مصدر هم می آید
توکولکان و توکولورکان و توکولادورکان ریخته شونده و ریخته شده الشاهد علی الاول المعنی الاخیر شعر یعنی رکشه جیمی تاغ ایله
قان لاله زار ایتمیش قویون یا خود توکولکان لاله زار ایمره کنار ایتمیش سینا قوشرجیز است که یا خود قویون توکولکان
زار ایمره کنار ایتمیش و باکاف عجمی کو شونده و کو شده و بمعنی مصدر هم می آیند توکولما و توکولماکیل مفرد مخاطب از فعل امر یعنی ریخته شو
و باکاف عجمی یعنی کو مشو چنانچه گوید الشاهد علی الاول شعر چو [illegible] بو چمن غنچه و گلیدا و فا توکولما غنچه کبی لیک
کل مثل لیک آچیل توکولودیلت و توکولوردیلت ریختی و چنانچه ریخته شوی الشاهد علی الاول المعنی الاول شعر توکولکای
ایدی جسمیم [illegible] سونکاکلادی ایله مکرکه [illegible] عشق اول سونکاکی [illegible] باقی صیغ برین نسق موافق توکولما لازم
میکرد توکوشماک [illegible] بیکدیکر ریختن و باکاف عجمی یعنی کو زدن باشد توکوشکان و توکوشورکان و توکوشادورکان بیکدیکر ریزنده
و ریخته و باکاف عجمی کو زننده و کو زده . و بمعنی مصدر هم می آیند چنانچه شاهد بر اول امعنی کو زدن [illegible] داستان
کرتا [illegible] فرهاد گوید [illegible] آتینک کفتار [illegible] توکوشکانلار [illegible] و باقی صیغ برین قیاس
باشین قرشتا اشتقاق می یابد توکونماک مصدر متعدیست یعنی [illegible] و صیغ آن بالفظ تمام اشتقاقی نیاید [illegible]
باکاف عجمی یعنی کو زنانیدن و صیغ آن بالفظ در اشتقاق می یابد توکاتماک مع الثا مصدر متعدیست یعنی تمام کردن توکاتو
تمام کردیم و توکاتور توکاتادور تمام میکند و توکاتور یعنی فاعل و مصدر هم می آید چنانچه بمعنی مصدر در مقاله سیم از خمسة
المتحیرین در احوال ملا جامی و شرح او بتالیف کتاب نفحات بنویسد گوید که از فرصت اتوکاتوریکا موفق بولدیلار [illegible]
تمام میکند و نکرده است توکاتکان و توکاتورکان و توکاتادورکان تمام کننده و تمام کرده . و بمعنی مصدر هم می آیند چنانچه در مقاله
سیم از خمسه المتحیرین در بیان تالیفات ملا جامی گوید که الا ابجد [illegible] کور بولفانی [illegible]
تحفه الاحرار نی بنیاد قیلیب اول تقریب سیله توکاتکانلاری بود استاندند که [illegible]
در نسخه مذکوره توکاتکانلاری خوانده و توکاتکانلاری را نوشته اند که یعنی تقصیر شد و خواسته شد که تمام شد کذا
مزبور را شاهد آورده اند و بعضی هم متابعت کرده . سهو کرده اند لفظ و معنی هر دو لخیر است توکات و توکاتکیل مفرد
مخاطب از فعل امر الشاهد علی الثانی شعر [illegible] توکاتکیل که [illegible] هر لب تشنه [illegible] ترشح تا ملا ف
توکاتما و توکاتماکیل مفرد مخاطب از فعل نهی توکاتینکلار توکاتینکر و توکاتینکلار جمع مخاطب از فعل امر توکاتمانک و توکاتمانکیز و توکاتمانکلار
جمع مخاطب از فعل نهی توکاتامن و توکاتامن تمام میکنم توکاتامین و توکاتورمین و توکاتادورمین و توکاتادام تمام میکنم توکاتاسن
تمام میکنی و بمعنی فاعل و مصدر منفی هم می آید توکاتماسینکا تمام نکردنت توکاتورینکا تمام کردنت توکاتیب و توکاتیبان و
توکاتیش تمام کرده . توکاتشلیک تمام کرده توکاتا بولغا و توکاتا بولمای تمام نتوان کرد توکاتالغای تمام توان کرد توکاتای
تمام کنان توکاتای و توکاتاین تمام کنم و کنند و کنی و کرده . توکاتا لادور و توکاتکای و توکاتکای [illegible] توکاتماغای [illegible] تمام کنیم
توکاتکالی برای تمام کردن و تا تمام کرده توکاتکاچ چون تمام کرد و کند توکاتکوچی تمام کننده توکاتکوچه و توکاتکونچه
توکاتکانچه تا تمام کردن و بقدر تمام کردن توکاتا الغانچه بقدریکه تمام توانی کرد توکاتکوم دور تمام خواهیم کرد توکا
توکونکوز دور تمام خواهید کرد توکاتکوسی دور تمام خواهند کرد توکاتکوم و توکاتکوم یوق تمام نخواهم کرد توکاتا الماغوم

توکانا آقنوم بوقتام کردن محکم نخواهد بود توکانکولوک تمام کردن توکانکای حتو کانلو تو کانسا و توکانسون و توکاندیلک
تمام کند تو کانکودیلک و توکاتوردیلت تمام کردن و همچنانکه تمام کند توکاماک مع النون تمام شدن توکانکاچ توکانا
توکانسا و توکانسون و توکاندیلت تمام شود چنانکه در تعلیم کردن فرهاد سنکتراشی را از نادر گوید الشاهد علی الاول شعر
سینلردین تیشه در آسوده بولغای توکانکای جبه ایش دین سوده بولغای توکانکوجه و توکانکانجه تا تمام شدن و بمعنی
تمام شدن الشاهد علی الثانی بالمعنی الاول شعر اولاد ایلاکانوکانکونجه ایچ فاش هم اولدی نظر برهم اولدی نقاش و تبع
صیغ برنسق باوزن اشتقاق میباید توکاماک بسکون کاف وفتح دال مهمله مسدود کردن توکادی مسدود کرد الشاهد
من کلام الفنین بولغ شعر نوغینک جیقتی و اغیار جهری تا پتی بول تاوکیک سکابنی تاکو نکلوم شکابن توکادی توکادم
مسدود کردیم توکار و توکاید ور مسدود میکند و توکار بمعنی فاعل و مصدر هم می آید توکاماید مسدود نمیکند
و نکرده است توکاکار و توکارکان و توکاید و رکان مسدود کننده و مسدود کرده و بمعنی مصدر هم می آیند توکولو توکاکیل مفرد
غائب امر فضل امر توکانلو توکاماکیل مفرد غائب النهی توکانکه و توکانکز و توکانکلار جمع غائب فضل امر توکاماتک و توکاما
توکامانکلار جمع غائب فضل نهی توکانان و توکاناس مین مسدود میکنم توکای مین و توکار مین و توکایدور مین توکادم مسدود کردیم
توکاناس مسدود نمیکند و بمعنی فاعل و مصدر منفی هم می آید توکاماسینکا بمسدود نکردنت توکارینکا بمسدود کردنت
توکاب و توکابان و توکامیش مسدود کرده توکامیشانک مسدود کرده توکاسابولغای و توکاب بولغه مسدود توان کرد
توکای آلغای مسدود تواند کرد توکای توکای و توکای تو کای بو مسدود کنان توکای و توکاین مسدود کنم و کند و کنی و کرد
توکلسا و توکاکانچه توکاکای بز و توکالی و توکانیل مسدود کنیم توکاکالی برای مسدود کردن و تا مسدود کرده توکاکاچ
چون مسدود کرد و کند توکاکوجی مسدود کننده توکاکوچه و توکاکونچه و توکاکانچه تا مسدود کردن و بمعنی مسدود کردن
توکای آلغاینکه بمعنی مسدود توانی کرد توکاکومیز بو مسدود خواهیم کرد توکاکونکوز دور مسدود خواهید کرد
توکاکوسیلار دور مسدود خواهند کرد توکاماکوم و توکاکوم یوق مسدود نخواهم کرد توکای آلماقوم توکای آلقوم یوق مسدود کردن ممکن
نخواهد بود توکاکولوک مسدود کردن توکاکای و توکاسلو توکاسوه و توکادیلک مسدود کند توکاکودیلک و توکاکورتیلک مسدود کرده
و همچنانکه مسدود کند توکرماک بضم کاف و سکون رای مهمله تف کردن توکردی تف کرد چنانکه گوید شعر انجم
ایرماس چرخ ظلمین خالیه آنکلاب قضا تیره رخسار نینه مینک تاملاغ کوردی بو کیچه تف کردیم توکورور و توکورادور
تف میکند و توکورور بمعنی فاعل و مصدر هم می آید توکورمایدور تف نمیکند و نکرده است توکورورکان و توکولادورکان
تف کننده و تف کرده و بمعنی مصدر هم می آیند توکورو توکورکیل مفرد غائب امر فضل امر توکورما و توکورماکیل مفرد غائب النهی
فهی توکورونک و توکورونکیز و توکورونکلار جمع غائب فضل امر توکورمانک و توکورمانکیز و توکورمانکلار جمع غائب فضل نهی توکورمان و توکورماس
تف میکنم توکورامین و توکورورمین و توکورادورمین و توکورام تف کردیم توکورماس تف نمیکند و بمعنی فاعل و مصدر منفی هم
می آید توکورماسینکا بتف نکردنت توکورونکا بتف کردنت توکوروب و توکوروبان و توکورمیش تف کرده توکورمیشانک تف کرده توکوره
بولغه و توکوروب بولغه تف توان کرد توکورا آلغای تف تواند کرد توکورا توکورا تف کنان توکورای و توکوراین تف کنم و کند
و کنی و کرده توکورسا و توکورکانچه و توکورکای بز و توکورلی و توکورالینک تف کنیم توکورکالی برای تف کردن و تا تف کرده
توکورکاچ چون تف کرد و کند توکورکوجی تف کننده توکورکوچه و توکورکونچه و توکورکانچه تا تف کردن و بمعنی تف کردن

توکورا آلغاینکه بمعنی تف توانی کرد توکورکومیز دور تف خواهیم کرد توکورکونکوز دور تف خواهید کرد توکورکوسیلار دور تف
خواهند کرد توکورماکوم و توکورکوم یوق تف نخواهم کرد توکورا آلماقوم و توکورا آلقوم یوق تف کردن ممکن نخواهد بود توکورکولوک
تف کردن توکورکای و توکورسلو توکورسوه و توکورسون تف کند توکورکودیلک و توکورکورتیلک تف کرده و همچنانکه تف کند
توکاللاماق بفتح کاف و سکون لام اول تفحص و جستجو کردن و صیغ آن موافق توکماک است اشتقاق میباید من الجوامد توکل
بر وزن غولک مهره گویند مرصیه توپخانه صفار موافق برهان قاطع بمعنی چشم باشد توکاریاپی سنگهای ریزه که بر
سر راه و فرش کنند الشاهد ... تفحص و جستجو شد
توکللی بالکسر با الف کشیده و کسر لام ترکی رومی بمعنی جمیع و قابل الفهم مستعملست توکان بضم کاف عجمی و سکون نون
داغ را گویند الشاهد علیه شعر ... توکالمرکیم ... شاهی کو ...
توکانش ... چنانکه ... توکانیشی است ...
توکوز بضم کاف و سکون زای معجمه بمعنی تمام و کامل باشد چنانکه گوید شعر ... سرکرد
یوم ایره ... توکوز توکون بضم کاف عجمی گره ... الشاهد علیه شعر ...
اوالمای ... توکمه بسکون کاف عجمی و فتح میم ...
بر لباس ... چنانکه گوید شعر ... توکانکیم ...
دین ... آن را خود از توکاک بمعنی ... بوده ... لفظ ترکی ... استعمال مینماید ...
بفتح تا نوشته سهو کرده توکی بکسر کاف عجمی ... مع الکلمة من المشتقات تولماق بمعنی پر شدن باشد
چنانکه در فصل ... اهلیدیک ... تولماق یوق
تولدوق پر شدیم تولادور و تولادور پر میشود و تولار بمعنی ... آمده ...
بامصدر تولاماق و تولامانک اشتراک دارد چنانکه مذکور خواهد شد و بمعنی فاعل و مصدر ... آید تولمایدور پر نمیشود
نشده است تولغان و تولارغان و تولادورغان پر شونده و پر شده الشاهد علی الاول بالمعنی الثانی شعر کونکلوم آنداق
قان ... تولغان ... و بمعنی مصدر هم می آیند تول و تولغیل مفرد
امر فضل امر تولما و تولماغیل مفرد غائب فضل نهی تولونک و تولونکیز و تولونکلار جمع غائب فضل امر تولمانک و تولمانکیز و تولمانکلار
جمع غائب فضل نهی تولمان و تولماس مین پر میشوم تولامین و تولارمین و تولادورمین تولادم پر میشوم و تولارمین و تولارم بمعنی
می آیایم ... و پر عوض ... مستعملست ... تولاماق و تولامانک مشترکست تولماس پر نمیشود بمعنی فاعل
هم آید تولماسینکا بپر نشدنت تولارینکا بپر شدنت و بامصدر تولاماق و تولامانک مشترکست ...
و آراسته و عوض کنم و پر عوض کنم و کند و کنی و کرده و تولاسی ... که در ذیل جوامد مذکور خواهد شد تولکالی
تولغای بز و تولغای بزه و تولالی و تولالینک پر شویم و تولالی بمعنی ... عوض کنیم و پر عوض کنیم هم آمده تولغالی برای پر شدن
و تا پر شده چنانکه بمعنی ... گوید شعر ... تولغاچ ...
تولغاچ چون پر شد و شود تولغوچی پر شونده تولغوچه و تولغونچه و تولغانچه تا پر شدن و بمعنی پر شدن الشاهد
علی الاول بالمعنی الاول شعر ... تولغوچه ... تولا آلغاینکه ...

پر توانی شد تولتوم پر خواهم شد چنانکه در صفت سیاره در داستان سنا فراقلیم دقیم گوید شعر جهرا اگر چه غم سیله تولغوز
تا بدا بولسام آلار سیله بولغوم تولغونک پر خواهی شد تولغوسی پر خواهد شد تولماغوم و تولغوم یوق پر نخواهم شد تولماللا
و تولا آلغیم پر شدن حکم نخواهد بود تولغولوق پر شدنی تولغای و تولاو تولسا و تولسون و تولدملیت پر شود
تولغودلیق و تولاردلیق پر شدنی و همچنانکه پر شود و تولاردیک با مصدر تولاماق و تولاماک اشتراک دارد تولدملیت
مصدر متعدی است بمعنی پر کردن تولدرغوچی پر خواهد کرد چنانکه در سد اسکندری در فوت اسکندر گوید شعر کیتوریا ایا
باده و قویغل زاغ تولا توت منکا سلغر الوداع دی یغنم آنکلا سیغانی که تولدرغوچی چیغ نماشی و صیغ آن بدستور
لفظ در اشتقاق می باید تولاماق بفتح لام اسب آراستن از برای تعزیه تولاماک بمعنی عوض کردن باشد عموما و بر عوض کردن
گویند خصوصا و توالت خاص احمد آفتت تولادوق اسب آراستیم تولادوک عوض کردیم و توالت کردیم تولار و تولایدور
اسب می آراید و عوض میکند و توالت می کند و تولار بمعنی پر میشود هم می آید و در این معنی با مصدر تولماق اشتراک دارد
چنانکه مذکور شد و افاده معنی فاعل و مصدر هم میکند تولامایدور عوض نمیکند و نکرده است و اسب نمی آراید و نیز بالمعنی
و توالت نمیکند و نکرده است تولاغان و تولاغان تولایدورغان اسب آراینده و آراسته و بمعنی مصدر هم می آید تولاکان
تولایدورکان عوض کننده و عوض کرده و توالت کننده و توالت کرده و نیز بمعنی مصدر می آید تولا مفرد غائب امر
و بمعنی ملوحه نباشد تولاغیل مفرد غائب امر حاضر مصدر تولاماق تولاکیل مفرد غائب امر حاضر مصدر تولاماک تولاغا
مفرد غائب امر حاضر هر دو مصدر تولاماغیل مفرد غائب امر حاضر مصدر تولاماق تولاماکیل مفرد غائب امر حاضر مصدر تولاماک
تولانک تولانکیز و تولانکلار جمع غائب امر حاضر هر دو مصدر تولامانک و تولامانکیز و تولامانکلار جمع غائب امر حاضر هر دو مصدر تولامانک
تولامادیم اسب نمی آرایم و عوض نمیکنم و توالت نمیکنم تولایمن و تولارمن و تولایدورمن و تولارام اسب می آرایم و عوض میکنم و توالت
میکنم و تولارمن و تولارام با مصدر تولماق نیز اشتراک دارند چنانکه گذشت یعنی پر میشوم تولاماس اسب نمی آراید و عوض
نمیکند و توالت نمیکند و بمعنی فاعل و مصدر منفی هم می آید تولاماسینکه با اسب نیاراستنت تولاماسینکا بعوض نکردنت و بر توالت
نکردنت تولارینکه به اسب آراستنت و بر پر شدنت تولارینکا بعوض کردنت و بتوالت کردنت تولاب و تولابان و تولامیش اسب آراسته و
عوض کرده و توالت کرده چنانکه شاهد بر او لعل بمعنی اخیر در تاریخ بابری در وصف توش مذکور است که توزتانی و الت الت ای خولجه
خولجه آلیب یدی ایکی ایچ تولاب یدی تولامیشانک اسب آراسته و عوض کرده و توالت کرده تولاسا تولغاکو تولاب تولغا اسب توان
آراست و عوض توان کرد و توالت توان کرد تولای آلمه اسب تواند آراست و عوض تواند کرد و توالت تواند کرد تولای تولای
تولایو اسب آراسته کان و عوض کنان و توالت کنان تولای و تولاییین اسب بیارایم و بیاراید و بیارایند و آراسته
و عوض کنم و توالت کنم و کنند و کنی و کرده و با مصدر تولماق هم اشتراک دارد چنانکه گذشت یعنی پر شوم و شود و شوی و شد
و تولای معانی خامس هم دارد چنانکه مذکور خواهد شد تولاساق و تولاغانیز و تولاغای بیز اسب بیارایم تولاساک و تولاکابیز
تولاکای بیز عوض کنیم و توالت کنیم تولالی اسب بیارائیم و عوض کنیم و توالت کنیم و بمعنی پر شویم هم می آید تولاغلی برای اسب
آراستن و تا اسب آراسته تولاکالی برای عوض کردن و تا کرده و برای توالت کردن و تا توالت کرده تولاغاچ چون اسب آراسته
بیاراید تولاکاچ چون عوض کرد و توالت کرد و کند تولاغوچی اسب آراینده تولاکوچی عوض کننده و توالت کننده تولاغوچه
تولاغونچه و تولانچه تا اسب آراستن و بمقدار اسب آراستن تولاکوچه و تولاکونچه و تولاکانچه تا عوض کردن و تا توالت کردن و بمقدار

تولاپی آلغانینکه بمقداری که اسب توانی آراست و بمقداری که عوض توانی کرد و بمقداری که توالت توانی کرد تولاغوسیز دور اسب نخواهیم آراست
و تولاکیسیزدور عوض نخواهیم کرد و توالت نخواهیم کرد تولاغونکیزدور اسب نخواهید آراست تولاکونکیزدور عوض نخواهید کرد و توالت
نخواهید کرد تولاغوسیلاردور اسب نخواهند آراست تولاکوسیلاردور عوض نخواهند کرد و توالت نخواهند کرد تولاماغوم و تولا
غوم یوق اسب نخواهم آراست تولاماکوم تولاکوم یوق عوض نخواهم کرد و توالت نخواهم کرد تولاماللا تولای آلغوم یوق اسب آراستن
محکم نخواهد بود و عوض کردن و توالت کردن هم حکم نخواهد بود تولاغولوق اسب آراستنی تولاکولوک عوض کردنی و توالت
کردنی تولاغای اسب بیاراید تولاکای عوض کند و توالت کند تولاسلوق تولاسون تولادیک اسب بیاراید و عوض کند و
کند تولاغودیک اسب آراستنی همچنانکه بیاراید تولاکودیک عوض کردنی و توالت کردنی و همچنانکه کند تولاردیک همچنانکه
تولماق و تولاماق و تولاماک اشتراک دارد و بمعنی تولغودیک و تولاغودیک و تولاکودیک باشد تولغاماق مصدر
متعدی است بمعنی پیچیدن و تولغاندی هم گویند تولغادوق پیچیدیم تولغار و تولغایدور می پیچد و تولغار بمعنی فاعل و مصدر
هم می آید تولغامایدور نمی پیچد و نپیچیده است تولغاغان و تولغاغان و تولغایدورغان پیچنده و پیچیده و بمعنی مصدر هم می آید
تولغا و تولغاغیل مفرد غائب امر حاضر تولغاسلو تولغامادیم تولغاماغیل مفرد غائب امر حاضر تولغانک و تولغانکیز و تولغانکلار جمع غائب امر
حاضر تولغامانک و تولغامانکیز و تولغامانکلار جمع غائب امر حاضر تولغامادیم نپیچیدم تولغایمن و تولغارمن و تولغاییدورمن و تولغارام
تولغارام می پیچم تولغاماس نمی پیچد و بمعنی فاعل و مصدر منفی هم می آید تولغاماسینکه بنپیچیدنت تولغارینکه به پیچیدنت تولغا
تولغاماینکه تولغامیش پیچیده تولغامیشانک پیچیده تولغاسا و تولغای و تولغاب و تولغاوان پیچید تولغای آلغای توانی پیچید تولغا
تولغاکو تولغایو پیچان پیچان تولغای و تولغایین بپیچم و بپیچد و بپیچی و بپیچد تولغاساق و تولغاغانیز و تولغاغای بیز و تولغالی تولغا
به بپیچیم تولغاغالی برای پیچیدن و تا پیچیده تولغاغاچ چون پیچید و بپیچد تولغاغوچی پیچنده تولغاغوچه و تولغاغونچه و
تولغاغانچه تا پیچیدن و بمقدار پیچیدن تولغا آلغانینکه بمقداری که توانی پیچید تولغاغوسیزدور نخواهیم پیچید تولغاغونکیزدور نخواهید
پیچید تولغاغوسیلاردور نخواهند پیچید تولغاماغوم و تولغاغوم یوق نخواهم پیچید تولغای آلماغوم و تولغای آلغوم یوق پیچیدن حکم نخواهد بود
تولغاغولوق پیچیدنی تولغاغای و تولغاسلو و تولغاسون و تولغادیک بپیچد الشاهد علی الاول شعر اگر تیغ امرینا اول تاثل بو یون سونکیده
بیتای آخره ... کمنا بوینین تولغاغای حیفینک ... تولغاغودیک و تولغاکودیک پیچیدنی و همچنانکه بپیچد تولغاندی
بمعنی تولغاناق باشد یعنی پیچیدن لکن تولغاندی ... چنانکه مولانا لطفی در توحید گوید الشاهد
علی الاول شعر چون قویونی ... سود الیکر ... تولغاندی و باقی صیغ بر بن سیاق باشد و
اشتقاق می باید تولغاماق مع النون تولغاتماق مع التاء پیچیده شدن تولغانغان و تولغانورغان و تولغاناد و غایب و تولغانتا
تولغاشورغان و تولغاشادور ... پیچیده شوند و پیچیده شد و بمعنی ... هم می آید چنانکه گوید الشاهد علی الاول شعر قاریتیم
ایجره تینیم تولغانماین ... لا اله ... تولغانیب و تولغانیبان ... تولغانمش و تولغا
تولغاشان و تولغاشمیش پیچیده شده الشاهد علی الاول شعر ... جسیم ماننده اوتغه توشکان تیل ... بیک
اور تاموزمین تولغانیبت الشاهد علی الرابع شعر ... شعله کیم ... رنج و محنت ... تولغاشیب
تاشیمدین تولغاشیت و باقی صیغ تولغاماق با نون واز تولغاشماق با شین ... اشتقاق می باید تولوغماق بضم لام و سکون نون
ترکی و بمعنی غروب کردن آفتاب و باید کواکب باشد من الجوامد تول باشلغ بر وزن پولچی ... دارد اول زن بیشوهر

که آنرا بعربی ارمله کویند الشاهد علیه شعر بغایت حیله کیدهمزالکردوش اکر ایرین حتی قیلسیل بو تولدین
دوم اسبی که برای تعزیه آراسته باشند حیم نلج کوسفند کاه را کویند چنانکه ام اوات تشبیه است که در آخر الوان واقع شود
چنانکه کویند آلقیمتول یعنی مایل بسفیدی و همچنین است قیزیمتول و کوکومتول و یاشیمتول و اشباه آن و بفارسی بمعنی چنک و
پرخاش بود تولا بمعنی پرهملو باشد الشاهد علیه شعر ماپل ایا غیزنی قیلدی بی تاب تولاء خوسینینک ایسکی غالبینی
که جواب تولا ونیز آمده است از آراستن اسب تعزیه و عوض کردن و توالت کردن تولاشیق بکسر شین بمعنی پیچیده بود تولاق
پا تابه را کویند تولامیشی اسب آراستن برای تعزیه و عوض کردن و توالت کردن تولاف مع النون بلغت مغولی هیمه و هیزم باشد
تولای مع الیا بمعنی آمده اول بمعنی جمیع و همه بود دوم جمعیکه با حداث فتنه همداستان باشند بیکدیکر با این لفظ
اجاغ نمایند سیم بلغت مغولی لخوکوش را کویند و معانی شقه هم طرح چنانکه در ذیل مشتقات مذکور شد تولغاش مع الکسر
بمعنی پیچ و تاب بود الشاهد علیه شعر کوزلاری تیخ جبرا شاو تولغانا ینتالک تالدی چوز سیلی نینک حیرنا ش و تولغا
ونیز امر است از پیچیده شدن تولغامه بفتح غین و میم جمع را کویند که چون فوج با خصم مقابل شوند ایشان از کمین خصم در آمده بجنک
مشغول شوند چنانکه در تاریخ بابری مذکور است که مغول لارنی تولغامه یا شاد و قیلیم غنیم کیشی سی یا و وتی کیلکلنج بو ایکی
بولاک تولغامه اونک قولدین سول قولدین غنیم نینک آرقاسیغه ایسرولکایلار تولف بسکون لام و فا بعضی و ترک
شغل باشد الشاهد علیه شعری تولفی نینک مرتبه سی بیلکه مرحوم لیغ ـ دفع ایتکالی دیر اهلیغه کرچیکا ادوده
تو لک بفتح لام بمعنی جارح و طیور و در عوض آن پر تازه بر آمدن چنانکه در وصف خزان چار مصرع فرهاد کوید شعر چمن
نینک هریغاچی شاخ قوشی بولو بطاری تولک ایامیغه توش تولکو روباه را کویند تولو بحرک بود که آنرا بفارسی
ژاله و بعربی حالوب و برد کویند تولوك اجناس ماکول بود سوای غله که آنرا آشلیغ نامند و در تاریخ بابری مذکور است که
قیشلاق و قلانتیب ایدی با زیلا آشلیغ تولوک تالمایدی ایدی تولوکوم هی تولو کوم بکنوع سرود بیت که در جشن و سور سرایند
چنانکه در حیرة الابرار کوید شعر تله سرودی چله نا النام قولوش قیلسام اداهی تولو کوم هی تولوکوش تولم خیك بود
که آنرا بعربی زق خوانند تولومبه بسکون میم و فتح بای ابجد باصطلاح رومیه چاهیست که چوب بطری تودنك درازی بدان تعبیه
کرده اند و بحرکت آن چوب آب از چاه بیرون آید و نوع دیکر هست که در صندوق تعبیه کرده هر جا خواهند نقل مینمایند و
آب بمیان آن ریخته بجنبانید که بتیغهای آنرا حرکت دهند آب مقدم بچستن و نوع دیکر در نهایت شدت از آن میجهد و احراق که در
استنبول واقع میشود بدان خاموش مینمایند تولون یعنی پر و مملو و تولون آی بمعنی بدر کامل باشد چنانکه در وصف لخری کوید
مطلوب کوید شعر اون تولون آینینک قراغیندین چو آکدینلدا اون هلالی کیرکی قو پراقنه هلال آلیغی تولون آینه جان
تو بهلی بکسر لام بلغت مغولی آینه بود که آنرا بعربی مرآت و مغولی نامند و نیز نام پسر کوچك چنکیز خان است که پدر هولاکو باشد
و خواین چنکیزیه که در ایران سلطنت کردند از نسل او میند مع الیم المشتقات تو موشماق بضم میم و سکون شین نوشته ملول
و ساکت ده نجی نشستن تو موشوق ملول نشسته الشاهد علیه شعر از لدارندنجیخال اولدی مورین ولمغلوتلر ازاهد
تو موشتی تو موشتوق ملول نشستم تو موشور و تو موشادو ملول می نشیند تو موشم بمعنی فاعل و مصدر هم می آید تو موشماین نملول نمی نشیند
و نشسته است تو موشغان و تو موشغلیو تو موشادغلی ملول نشسته و ملول نشسته و بمعنی مصدر هم می آید تو موشر و تو موشغیل مفرد
معاطبه ملل الشاهد علی الاقل شعر عشرت بیتکیم جیغ آلیدا اتقا وت یو قو قصه جز خواه بنم ایچر و ساع ایستخواه کج ایچر تومون

تومْ

تو موشا و تو موشماغیل مفرد مخاطب از فصل امر تو موشونك و تو موشونکز و تو موشونکلا جمع مخاطب از فصل امر تو موشماك و تو موشماکز و تو موشما
جمع مخاطب از فصل نهی تو موشمان و تو موشمازمین ملول نخواهیم نشست تو موشامین و تو موشورمین و تو موشادورمین و تو موشور ملول می نشینم
تو موشماس ملول نمی نشیند و بمعنی فاعل و مصدر منفی هم می آید تو موشماسیکه بملول ننشست تو موشمونکه بملول نشسته تو
تو موشو و تو موتمش ملول نشسته تو موتیشانك ملول نشسته تو موشسا و تو موشوب و تو موشوبنه ملول تواند نشست تو موشا آلغا
ملول تواند نشست تو موشا تو موشا ملول نشسته تو موشای و تو موشایین ملول نشینم و بنشیند و بنشینی و نشسته تو موشغا
چون ملول نشست و بنشیند تو موشغوچی ملول نشیننده تو موشغونچه و تو موشغونچه و تو موشغا نحتا ملول نشستن و بعدم ملول نشستن
تو موشا آلغاینچه بقدر یکه ملول تواند نشست تو موشغومیز و بملول خواهیم نشست تو موشغونکز دور ملول خواهید نشست
تو موشغو سیلار دور ملول خواهند نشست تو موشماغوم و تو موشغوم بوقملول نخواهم نشست تو موشا آلماغوم تو موشا آلغوم یوق ملول نشستن
محکم نخواهد بود تو موشغولوق ملول نشستنی تو موشغای و تو موشا و تو موشسا و تو موشونو تو موشدیك ملول نشیند تو موشغودور
تو موشودیك ملول نشستی و چنانکه بنشیند تو موشتورماق مصدر متعدی است ملول و ساکت در کنجی نشاندن و صیغ آن
بدستور لفظ متعدی اشتقاق می یابد تو مماق بترکی رومی یعنی آب فرو رفتن تو مولماق باب فرو رفتن شدن من الجوامد
تو ماغه کلاه چرخ و شاهین که آنرا بعربی قلنسوة الطیر خوانند چنانکه در لسان الطیر در مناظره هدهد با سنقور کوید شعر
باشیما آلتون تو ماغه تاج نرج چو رعنی خوشیله میلیش تاجیش و مؤلف ره نی سهوا بمعنی او تاغه و تیل هم نوشته و شعر مزبور را
شاهد آورده تومان بسه معنی آمده اول عدد ده هزار را کویند الشاهد علیه شعر نرعونك فرامیدا تومان تبله حیف
کم مقامع کیمود دوم موضعه سال و ماه ف و باز نسبت مغولیه هر امیری را که صاحب ده هزار لشکر باشد امیر تومان نامند و
اهل ایران نیز ده هزار دینار را یك تومان کویند دویم بخار غلیظی است که از زمین متصاعد شده روی هوا را فرو کیرد و آنرا
مه خوانند سیم ولایات کوچك و قصبات را کویند که در تحت ولایت بزرک بود چنانکه در دیباچه و نغینه میرسید تهرکی
مناسب حالیه کوید شعر پریسی توشوز شاری حکیم وقتم پرسی تومان شاری احمدی علم و نیز در تاریخ بابری در وصف
کابل مذکور است که سمرقند و بخارا دا و بو نواحیدا ولایتچه لارنی بکم نیه پراولوق ولایت نینک تحتیدا بولغای تومان دیر
لار و صاحب نوشته که کنایه از بسیاری است و در بعضی ولایات هزار و در بعضی ده هزار را میکویند که
برهان قاطع این لفظ را فارسی شمرده نوشته که تومان قصبه ایست که صد ده در تحت آن جمع باشد هر دو سهو کرده اند
توماکینی بسکون نون اول و کسر کاف عجمی و نون ثانی امر بچه یا پای و انتها و طرف اسفل هر چیز را کویند و مومیه حلو کشو را
خوانند تومروق بسکون میم و ضم رای مهمله بترکی رومی کنده بود که بر پای محبوس نهند تو موشوغ و تو موشوق منقار طیور را نامند
چنانکه کوید شعر ایا کلبندا تو زبر غنچه یا خم لیغ سیکان هر یان که بلبل نینک تالیب تو قرآندا تو موشوغ سرله تر باغی و نیز بمعنی
هم استعمال شود اول بینی را کویند چنانکه در لیلی مجنون خطاب به لیلی کوید شعر یا تیب ایکاکینك الیکیکا قویبانك
تو موشوغینك او تسول ایشیك کا قویبانك دویم دماغه کوه را نامند چنانکه در خسرو و شیرین در وصف فرهاد کوید شعر
امر یخود تاغ و تو موشوغ دیك آنکا باش ولی تو موشوغ کیم اول بولغای فراناش و نیز در لسان الطیر در وادی معرفت کوید شعر
باشیغه اول کیم سو قعبا یردی قول پرتایا سینك تو موشوغین شرح ایتی اول تو موشتی بترکی رومی یعنی آب فرو رفتن تو موزغان
بضم میم و سکون زای هوز و نون و فتح غین معجمه حیل باشد که آنرا بعربی خنفسا کویند مع النون المشتقات تو ناتیق تسکو

تون

نون تیره و تاریک شدن قندی تیره شد توناد و توناد ور تیره میشود چنانکه لطفی گوید الشاهد علی الاول شعر
یننظرها کوز تونار بیلاس یوزونک ماهیتین موبجه روشن بولدی کیم اولدی دل و جان اوتراکان و توناب معنی حاصل مصدر
می‌آید و هیمه داین گویند که بر سر هم چیده شعله میسازند و تیره یعنی برهنه کرد و در این معنی با مصدر توناماق اشتراک دارد
تونغان و تونارغان و توناد ورغان تیره شونده و تیره شده و بمعنی مصدر هم می‌آیند توناس تیره نمیشود توناالماس تیره نمیتواند شد
تونوب و تونوبان و تونیش تیره شده تونساتوتغاتوتوب بولغنه تیره توان شد تونغاچ چون تیره شد و شود تونغوچی تیره شونده
تونغوسی و تونغونجه و تونغانجه تا تیره شدن و بقلم تیره شدن تونغای و توناو تونسا و تونسون و توندیک تیره شود و تونغو
تونارلیک تیره شدنی و همچنانکه تیره شود توناماق بفتح نون بالف کشیده یعنی برهنه کردن تونادی برهنه کرد
توناد و توناید ور برهنه میکند و تونار بمعنی فاعل و مصدر هم می‌آید و تیره یعنی تیره میشود و در این معنی با مصدر توناماق اشتراک
دارد و هیمه را هم گویند که بر سر هم چیده انشرد هند توناغان و توناید ورغان برهنه کننده و برهنه کرده و بمعنی مصدر
هم می‌آیند توناو و تونایل مفرد مخاطب فعل امر توناماو و تونامایل مفرد مخاطب فعل نهی تونانک و توناینکز و تونانکلار جمع مخاطب
فعل امر تونامانک و تونامانکز و تونامانکلار جمع مخاطب فعل نهی تونامان و تونامارمین برهنه نمیکنم توناین و توناینه
تونارام برهنه میکنم تونارمین و تونارام بمعنی خبر و تیره میشوم هم باشد توناماس برهنه نمیکند و بمعنی فاعل و مصدر
منفی هم می‌آید تونامانسینکنه برهنه نکرده تونارینکنه برهنه کردنت تونابتو تونابان و تونامیش برهنه کرده توناب
برهنه کرده تونابولغای و توناب توتغنه برهنه توان کرد تونابو و تونای تونای برهنه کنان و بدون تکرار هم مستعملست
تونای و تونایاین برهنه کنم و کند و کنی و کرده توناساق و تونافاین و تونافای برهنه کنم تونالیک برهنه کنم تونامالی
برای برهنه کردن و تا برهنه کرده توناغاچ چون برهنه کرد و کند و بحض کردن توناغوچی برهنه کننده توناغوچه
توناغونجه و تونافانجه تا برهنه کردن و بقلم برهنه کردن تونایالغانینکچه بقلم چه برهنه تولدی کرد توناغومیزدور
برهنه خواهیم کرد توناغونکزدور برهنه خواهید کرد توناغوسیلاردور برهنه خواهند کرد تونامانغوم و توناغوم
برهنه نخواهم کرد توناالماغوم و تونا آلغوم یوق برهنه کردن محکم نخواهد بود توناغولوق برهنه کردن توناغای و تونانسا
تونلسون تونادیک برهنه کند توناغودیک و تونارلیک برهنه کردنی و همچنانکه کند توناماق بفتح اللام برهنه شدن و سیخ
با لام استنقاق می‌آید تونکماق بسکون نون و کاف عجمی و تونکلماق بسکون نون و لام و ضم کاف عجمی یخ بستن و منجمد
شدن و دلسرد شدن می‌آید تونکدی و تونکلدی یخ بست و سرد شد تونکدم و تونکلدم یخ بستم و سرد شدیم تونکاد
تونکارمن و تونکولورمن یخ میبندم و افسرده میشوم و تونکار و تونکولور بمعنی فاعل و مصدر هم می‌آیند چنانکه بمعنی یخ بنده
و منجمد و دلسرد بیت گوید الشاهد علی الاول شعر سفر قیلغان آدمجام دمشق سنا وفدا تونکار کمیکا آرام بند
تونکماید ور تونکلماید یخ نمیبندد و نبسته است تونکغان و تونکارغان و تونکادورغان و تونکولغان و تونکولارغان و تونکولادورغان
یخ بنده و یخ بسته و سرد شونده و سرد شده و بمعنی مصدر هم می‌آیند تونک و تونکیل و تونکول و تونکولکیل مفرد مخاطب فعل
امر الشاهد علی الثالث بالمعنی الثانی شعر تیرتی باشیدا قرا تینین اکر کیب تیماینک اربیمیچ کال سیله اول خاصل ایلکان
تونکول و تیره دیره لا بر در وصف لکوید شعر بوخو دیا سرخم سین ایستار کونکول کربو کونکول بولنا سین آیندین تونکول
و تونک کونه سرنک را هم گویند چنانکه در ذیل بولسه مذکور خواهد شد تونکما و تونکمایل مفرد مخاطب فعل نهی تونکلمه

تونکونکز و تونکونکلار و تونکولونک و تونکولونکز و تونکولونکلار جمع مخاطب فعل امر و تونکمانک و تونکمانکز و تونکمانکلار و تونکولمانک و
تونکولمانکز و تونکولمانکلار جمع مخاطب فعل نهی تونکمان و تونکمارمین و تونکولمان و تونکولمارمین یخ نمی‌بندم و سرد نمیشوم تونکامین و
تونکارمین و تونکادورمین و تونکارام و تونکولامین و تونکولورمین و تونکولادورمین یخ میبندم و سرد میشوم تونکمار و تونکولماس
یخ نمی‌بندد و سرد نمیشود و بمعنی فاعل و مصدر منفی هم می‌آید تونکماسینکنه و تونکولماسینکنه یخ نبستنت و سرد نشدنت و تونکارینکنه و تونکولارینکنه
یخ بستنت و سرد شدنت تونکوب و تونکوبان و تونکیش و تونکولوب و تونکولوبان و تونکولمیش یخ بسته و سرد شده
در خسرو و شیرین گوید الشاهد علی الاول بالمعنی الاول شعر قرو چشمه سی هر یان تونکوب موزو اولغان قطره لار کوهیدا
یولدوز و شاهد برابع را بمعنی ثانی در محبوب القلوب در وصف پری گوید که عجب عجب مرض کا تیدین حیات دین تونکولوب
تونکیشانک و تونکولمیشانک یخ بسته و سرد شده تونکابولغای و تونکوب بولغای و تونکولسا بولغای و تونکولوب بولغای یخ توان بست
و سرد توان شد تونکا تونکاو تونکولا تونکولاو یخ تواند بست و افسرده تواند شد تونکای و تونکاین و تونکولای و تونکولاین یخ بندم
و بندد و بندی و بسته و سرد شوم و شود و شوی و شده تونکا قه و تونکغاینه و تونکغاینه و تونکالی و تونکالیک و تونکولساق
تونکولغاینه و تونکولغاینه و تونکولالی و تونکولالیک به بندیم و سرد شویم تونکالی و تونکولالی برای یخ بستن و تا یخ بستن و سرد
شدن و تا سرد شده تونکغاچ و تونکولغاچ چون یخ بست و ببندد و چون سرد شد و شود تونکغوچی و تونکولغوچی
یخ بنده و سرد شونده تونکغوچه و تونکغونجه و تونکغانجه و تونکولغوچه و تونکولغونجه و تونکولغانجه تا یخ بستن و بقلم یخ بستن و تا سرد شدن و
بقلم سرد شدن تونکالیکچه و تونکولالیکچه بقلم چه یخ توانی بست سرد توانی شد تونکغومیزدور و تونکولغومیزدور یخ خواهیم بست و سرد خواهیم
شد تونکغونکزدور و تونکولغونکزدور یخ خواهید بست و سرد خواهید شد تونکغوسیلاردور و تونکولغوسیلاردور یخ خواهند
بست و سرد خواهند شد تونکماغوم و تونکغوم یوق و تونکولماغوم و تونکولغوم یوق یخ نخواهم بست و افسرده نخواهم شد تونکا الماغوم
تونکا آلغوم یوق و تونکولا الماغوم و تونکولا آلغوم یوق یخ بستن و سرد شدن محکم نخواهد بود تونکغولوق و تونکولغولوق یخ بستنی و سرد شدنی
تونکغای و تونکای و تونکسا و تونکسون و تونکغودیک و تونکغای و تونکولغای و تونکولسا و تونکولسون و تونکولدیک یخ ببندد و سرد شود
چنانکه شاهد برای اول بمعنی اول در تاریخ بابری در وصف حمام مذکور است که ایسیغ هوا لاردا آنداق سیرین بولغای کیم باو و تونکغودیک
کیم کیشی ناو و صدین تونکغای تونکغودیک و تونکاردیک و تونکولغودیک و تونکولوردیک یخ بستنی و همچنانکه به بندد و سرد شدنی
و همچنانکه سرد شود تونکارماق بسکون نون و کاف عجمی و رای مهمله و فتح تای قرشت واژگون کردن تونکاردی واژگون
کردیم تونکارور و تونکارادور واژگون میکند و تونکار بمعنی فاعل و مصدر هم می‌آید تونکارماید ور واژگون نمیکند و
نکرده است تونکارغان و تونکارورغان و تونکارادورغان واژگون کننده و کرده و بمعنی مصدر هم می‌آیند تونکار و تونکارکیل مفرد
مخاطب فعل امر تونکارما و تونکارمایل مفرد مخاطب فعل نهی تونکارینک و تونکارینکز و تونکارینکلار جمع مخاطب فعل امر
تونکارمانک و تونکارمانکز و تونکارمانکلار جمع مخاطب فعل نهی تونکارمان و تونکارمارمین واژگون نمیکنم تونکارمین و تونکارادور
تونکارادورمین و تونکارارمین واژگون کنم تونکارماس واژگون نمیکند و بمعنی فاعل و مصدر منفی هم می‌آید تونکارماسینکنه واژگون
نکردنت تونکارینکنه واژگون کردنت تونکاریب و تونکاریبان و تونکارمیش واژگون کرده الشاهد علی الاول من سلطان
میرزا شعر تا چیتم یوسفا اولنوریب تو دیو زخم واندوه ایله یارتلوبن بتیرالاک روز کلرین تونکاریب تونکارمیشانک واژگون
کرده تونکارابولغای و تونکاریب بولغای واژگون توان کرد تونکارا تونکاراو واژگون تواند کرد تونکارای تونکاراین واژگون

کان تونکخارلو تونکخارلاین   واژکون کم وکند وکی وکرده الشاهد علی الاول من سلطان حسین میرزا شعر ای حسنی چنغ طی
بیله بولسامین دلبقی لشك طوفانی بیله کعودنا ناسین تونکخارای تونکخارمالدو تونکلرکاینز و تونکلرکای واژکون
تونکلرکالی برای واژکون کردن و ناکرده تونکلرکاج   چون واژکون کرد وکند تونکخارکوچ   واژکون کننده تونکلرکوچی
تونکلرکوچه و تونکخارکاغه تا واژکون کردن و بقصد واژکون کردن تونکخارا آلغایمن بجهیلش کون خواهیم کرد تونکخارکونکوز بود
واژکون خواهید کرد تونکلرکیسلا تورور واژکون خواهند کرد تونکلرکایم و تونکخارکوم یوق   واژکون نخواهم کرد تونکخارالا
تونکخارالکنیم یوق واژکون کردن محکم نخواهد بود تونکخار کولوك   واژکون کردنی تونکخارکای و تونکخارا و تونکلرلو تونکخارسیون
تونکلرلیك   واژکون کند تونکلرکوجیك و تونکلرکوچیك واژکون کردنی و همچنانکه کرده شود تونکلرتاك   واژکون شدن تونکخاریلدی
واژکون شد چنانچه در کلیله دمنه گفته اند شعر کوبوترکا چو شاهین حمله قیلدی جهان کوزیا باشیغه تونکخاریلدی
و ناقص بر سیاق بالالام اشتقاق می یابد تونلاماق   بسکون نون و فتح لام شبگیر کردن تونلادی شبگیر کرد تونلادو
شبگیر کردیم تونلاریتو تونلایدور شبگیر میکند و تونلار بمعنی فاعل و مصدر هم می آید تونلاغای دور شبگیر خواهد کرد
تونلاغان تونلارغان و تونلاریمیز شبگیر کننده و شبگیر کرده و بمعنی مصدر هم می آید تونلا و تونلاغیل   مفرد مخاطب امر
تونلانکیز تونلاغیل مفرد مخاطب فعل نهی تونلامانك و تونلامانکیز و تونلامانکلار   جمع مخاطب فعل نهی تونلاماسانکیز و تونلاماسا
جمع مخاطب فعل نهی تونلاماغان و تونلاماغایمین   شبگیر نکنم تونلاماسین و تونلامانکیز شبگیر نکنیم تونلاماس
شبگیر نمیکند و بمعنی فاعل و مصدر منفی هم می آید تونلاماسنکیز   شبگیر نکردنت تونلاماینکیز   شبگیر نکرده تونلامیش
تونلامیش شبگیر کرده چنانچه شاهد بر اول در تاریخ بابری مذکور است که هر لحظه تونچپا با آتلانیلدی میدان یولی بیله کیلیب تونلاغ
کوتلادین تونلاب و تونچغرض و قیدا چیتو تواجی سیدا هر لحظه لارجا سلدی تونلامیشا تاك   شبگیر کرده تونلاسا بو تونلاغای تونلاب تونلاغا
شبگیر توان کرد تونلاغا آلغای   شبگیر تواند کرد تونلای تونلای تونلای و تونلایو   شبگیر کنان تونلای و تونلایین شبگیر کنم و کند
و کرده تونلاسا قونلاغا یز و تونلاغای یز و تونلاغو و تونلاینك   شبگیر کنیم تونلاغالی   برای شبگیر کردن و تا شبگیر کرده تونلاغاج
چون شبگیر کرد و کند تونلاغوچی   شبگیر کننده تونلاغوچه و تونلاغوچی و تونلاغاغه تا شبگیر کردن و بقصد شبگیر کردن تونلای آلغای
قدم به شبگیر نتوانی کرد تونلاغومیز   شبگیر خواهیم کرد تونلاغوسیز دور   شبگیر خواهید کرد تونلاغوسلار دور   شبگیر خواهند کرد
تونلاغوم و تونلاغوم یوق   شبگیر نخواهم کرد تونلاغای آلماغوم و تونلاغای آلغوم یوق شبگیر کردن محکم نخواهد بود تونلاغولوق   شبگیر
کردنی تونلاغای و تونلاسا و تونلاغون و تونلادیك   شبگیر کند تونلاغودیك و تونلاردیك   شبگیر کردنی و همچنانکه شبگیر کند
نون   بمعنی آمده اول بمعنی تاریك و مظلم باشد میر سپهسالار شعر ای موز آقشام چو حقیقی ظالم ادا مدیدیکیم قیلدیلار
بیزنی قرا او نصیب تون آقشام دا سهوا بمعنی شب نوشته در دیم مجازا بمعنی شب استعمال شود چنانکه در فصل چهارم از محبوب القلوب
در وصف پادشاهان ظالم گوید که یا روق کوزی تیره تون دیا سها کور دونا دو دیما کان مدبر سیم قبا را کوینید چنانکه بمعنی تنا
و شب بطریق جناس گوید تا منزیل تون ایچره بولدی جلوه کرناهیم منینك   مهرا بتا رهر تون شفق خون لبی ایچره اضطرابی چهارم
ام ستاره تیره و خیره شدن چشم چنانکه در ذیل تونناق گذشت و بفارسی تام شهرهیت از مضافات خراسان و کلهم تمام رالم تا
و بعربی هم دو معنی طرفا و ملقا و کاه منطقه باشد دیم روده کوسفند را کوینید تونار   بفتح نون با الف کشیده و سکون رای مهمله تون
جار هیمه فراوان بود که بر سر هم چیده شعله میسازند و نیز فعل مضارع مصدر تونناقاست یعنی چشم تیره و خیره میشود و مصادر

مصدر تونناماقاست یعنی برهنه کردن تونناکون   بفتح نون اول و ضم کاف عجمی دونکشته را گویند چنانچه میرعلیشیر
گوید شعر تانکلا جیله چون توناکوند صبحدم شیل کمسنکا ناالدی بو کون بیل بودم تونامتا   بترکی رومی معنی او سیکر
باشد و اثاثه و کوکبه ملوك را نیز گوینید و بلوال و نظار چیچی‌نیز مستعملت توبنك   شلزیت بشکل غلمان کوچك که آن را سر
گران نولند شعر فقای بارا اولدی تونباك نوبنید دمش که خوشتر و فصل ایچرا خلیلیغ لا از تونبوز   بسکون نون و ضم
جیم و زای عجمه در سنولست بلند و صلبر و لبریك که دسته دسته همچاها غنا لسر رویید و ازان حصیرها و غلزالها بافند تونوج
بسکون نون و جیم و ضم جیم فرزند اولین اخولتند چنانکه در تاریخ بابری مذکور است که سلطان احمد میرزا نیز تونوجی پدر
بولدی منینك تونغوج فرزند ایم بو ایدی تونغطار   بسکون نون و رای مهمله و ضم قاف و فتح طای حطی بمعنی پرنظر کشیکچی
و پاسبان را گوینید که شب پاسداری کند چنانکه در وصف پادشاه گوید شعر تونغطار آندا بخت بیدل بیغای صبحدم تیرکو
دم خدایا بیناق و صاحب برهان قاطع طلوع شمرده و بمعنی شمع بلبریك نوشته که تا صبح سوزد و حقیقت آن معلوم نیست تونك   بکون
نون و کاف عجمی به معنی آمده اول کوزه من تونك را کوینید الشاهد علیه شعر ای تولب بخت و غمدین تاچار بولسا تانك
کرالدی بولسه می لیغ تونك سور من کولعزادینك سینك شرب حکم دیم شعر مار چو تونك و قدح بر لیم جام صفلا
خورشید نام دوم بمعنی سرو بود الشاهد علیه شعر آ. واشکیدین ابرو داوت و سواپچرو فا شوق زاهدان غم آنکا کوتریغ
اولغیل کر تونك سیم امرلست ایغ بستن و سرد شدن چنانکه گذشت و بفارسی بمعنی کمینه بود تونکوز   بسکون نون و ضم
مرای حطی و ضم کاف عجمی خوك را کوینید و نیز نام سالی است از سالهای ترکی تونکوز یالیغی نوعیست از ماهی که آن را بعربی جولفین
خوانند تونکوزلان قرتیمی و تونکوزلان بوجیکی بترکی رومی جنگل باشد که آن را بعربی خنفسا نامند تونکلوك   بسکون نون و کاف
اول عجمی روزنه خانه را کوینید الشاهد علیه شعر تا لنا پر توتام امر حقیقت انداز خباعی چوقه بر قوبالستور تونشا مراودی
تونکلوکدین باروق و نیز در لیلی مجنون گوید شعر آندا ق که تنیمد صدآتدا مجنون هم تونکلوکچه هم ایشیکچه روش وظالم کوی
بمعنی منتهای خانه نوشته و شعر بر بهوا را شاهد آورده سهو کرده تونلوك   بترکی رومی بمعنی از دحام و کثرت وانبوهی باشد شاخ الوان
توواغ   بفتح واو بر وزن سراغ دو معنی دارد اول بمعنی ستم ستور باشد چنانکه گوید شعر نوع یب او بیکاریدین ولغالیت ایاغیش
اوپا آلمان سمندری نینك توواغین و نیز در لیلی مجنون در مکالمه مجنون با نوفل گوید شعر یوز و صد لعل شمینك
تو واغی باشیمه عمر کیمینك ایاغی   و آن را توبناغ هم کوینید دویم سرپوش هر چیز را کوینید عموما و بر قمر اطلسند خصوصا و بمعنی
باد الیغز مستعمل است توو صرلوغ تو دورلوق   بضم واو و لام و سکون رای مهمله تهدی باشد که با طرافی خیمه والاچوق کشیده شود
مکتبه شعر ابجکلیری اول کل تق و صلوضی کونا تاشلا هر بیتاش ای مسلمن اشیم لطفا ماندا بان اول این دارغم الیا این المشعاك
تو بماق   بسکون یا یعنی سیر شدن چنانکه گوید شعر حسن دین تونباقا یا من کوکه بحل خوب ابرونت توبغای ابدیم بو تنا
ابدی یوسف کنعانچه خوب و باشلغ فتحه بمعنی فهمیدن بود توید و ق   سیر شدیم و باشباع فهمیدیم توباد و تو نیادور
سیر میشود چنانچه شاهد بر اول در لیلی مجنون گوید شعر خالیم غمی غیب تونیاصوابر کمن کوزم دینی اونیاد و ابر کمن و باشلغ
یعنی میفهمد چنانکه در تاریخ بابری مذکور است که شام توبار چا قطاع غا نام الولار توبار لار و تونبلمه بمعنی فاعل و مصدر هم می آید
دو نماید و سیر نمیشود و نشده است و نفهمید و نفهمیده است تونیغان و تونیارغان و تونیاربغان سیر شونده و سیر شده و باشلغ فهمنده
فهمیده و بمعنی مصدر هم می آید تونی و تونیغیل   مفرد مخاطب امر چنانکه شاهد بر ثانی را بمعنی اول گوید عشقنی تنه ایتی

خورشید منشاند صد مو اول * حسنی دین در بین که تو نیل ماه کفنا ند صد مو اولی و توی معانی نجا مده هم دارد چنانکه ذیل
جوامد مذکور خواهد شد . تومناو تویما عیل مفرد تحالمبانه فصل نهی تویونک و تویونکز و تویونکلار جمع تحالمبانه فصل امر
تویمانک و تویمانکز و تویمانکلار جمع تحالمبانه فصل نهی تویمان و تویماس مین سیر نمیشوم و باشتباع نمیفهمم تویامین و تویارمین
تویادورمین و تویا رام سیر میشوم و باشتباع میفهمم تویا حقتیمامین و تویتمای مین سیر شوم الشاهد علی الاول شعر خالک
یونعم قراکوتویمامین خسار وی مین * کوکوز وم نینک مردمین خسار هیه خالا ایتکامین و باشتباع یعنی نفهمم تویماس سیر نشود
و باشتباع نفهمد و بمعنی فاعل و مصدر منفی هم می آید تویماسینکه سیر نشدنت و باشتباع نفهمیدنت تویارینکه سیر شدنت
و باشتباع بفهمیدنت تویوب و تویابان و تویمیش سیر شده و باشتباع فهمیده تویمیشانک سیر شده و باشتباع فهمیده تویلوتغه
تویوب توتغه سیر توان شد و باشتباع توان فهمید تویا آلغای سیر تواند شد و باشتباع تواند فهمید تویا تویا سیر شونده
سیر شونده و باشتباع فهم کنان فهم کنان تویای و تویاین سیر شوم و شود و شوی و شده و باشتباع نفهمم و نفهمد و نفهمی و فهمیده
تویاقه و تویغای نرو تویغای پز و تویایلی و تویالینک سیر شوم و باشتباع بفهمم تویغلی برای سیر شدن و تا سیر شده و برای فهمیدن
تا فهمیده تویغاج چون سیر شد و شود و باشتباع چون فهمید و فهمد تویغوجی سیر شونده و باشتباع فهمنده تویغوجه و تویغونجه
تویغانجه تا سیر شدن و بقدر سیر شدن و تا فهمیدن و بقدر فهمیدن چنانکه شاهد بر اول بر این معنی تا فهمیدن گوید شعر
نوا اوت هاوند و سپاهان سرله بر بردین * حسینی تویغونجه کیم سنکا آهنگ حجاز اولمیش * و در این شعر بمناسبت مقام اسم ما نیکا ایهام
که حسینی مخالف طرف بطریق ایهام ادا نموده . تویا آلغاینکیم معتمد بکه سیر توانی شد و توانی فهمید تویغوم سیر خواهم شد
چنانکه در سبحه سیاره در داستان مسافر اقلیم اول گوید شعر مین ایلیت داجاندین ارتویغوم * تیرلیا اولتام ولطف یوز تویغوم
تویغونک سیر خواهی شد و باشتباع خواهی فهمید تویغوسی سیر خواهد شد و باشتباع خواهد فهمید تویماغوم و تویغوم یوق سیر
نخواهم شد و باشتباع نخواهم فهمید تویا لماغوم و تویا لغوم یوق سیر شدن محکم نخواهد بود و باشتباع فهمیدن محکم نخواهد بود
تویغولوق سیر شدنی و باشتباع فهمیدنی تویغای و تویای و تویسا و تویسون و تویدیک سیر شود و باشتباع بفهمد تویغودیک و تویادیک
سیر شدنی و همچنانکه سیر شود و باشتباع فهمیدنی و همچنانکه بفهمد تویغارماق بسکون یا و راء مهمله و فتح غین معجمه الف کشیده
مصدر متعدیست یعنی سیر کردن و مصدر متعدی فهمیدن تویدور اقی آید چنانکه بیاید تویغاردوق سیر کردیم تویغار
تویغارادو سیر میشود و تویغارور بمعنی فاعل و مصدر می آید تویغارمایدور سیر نمیکند و نکرده است تویغارمان و تویغارمان
تویغارادیان سیر کننده و سیر کرده و بمعنی فاعل و مصدر هم می آید تویغار و تویغار عیل مفرد تحالمبانه فصل امر و تویغار نام نو
هم هست چنانکه در ذیل جوامد مذکور خواهد شد تویغارماو تویغارماعیل مفرد تحالمبانه فصل نهی تویغارنکلار و تویغارنکز
جمع تحالمبانه فصل امر تویغارمانک و تویغارمانکز و تویغارمانکلار جمع تحالمبانه فصل نهی تویغارمان و تویغارماس مین سیر نمیکنم تویغارامین و تویغا
تویغارادیرمین و تویغاررورامین سیر میکنم تویغارماس سیر نمیکند و بمعنی فاعل و مصدر منفی هم می آید تویغارماسینکه سیر نکردنت تویغاردورنکه
سیر کردنت تویغاریب و تویغابان و تویغارمیش سیر کرده چنانکه در تحفه کوی فرهاد و خاقان ایاد کردن گوید الشاهد
علی الاول شعر قلمی تویغاریب خسرو خفا ندین * تیلا شناسکه قایمی آتدین * و در لیلی مجنون در مکالمهٔ پدر مجنون با مجنون گوید
الشاهد علی الثانی شعر آچ تویغابان یالانکی یاتتم اولدوم دیکانم اسینی ایتتم * و در لیلی مجنون سیر کرده تویغارشا تویلغای
تویغاپ تویغه سیر توان کرد تویغارالغای سیر تواند کرد تویغارا تویغارا سیر کنان سیر کنان تویغاری و تویغارای سیر کنم و کند و کنی

و کرده تویغارماقه تویغارغایزو تویغارغای پز و تویغارایلی و تویغارالینک سیر کنیم تویغارغالی برای سیر کردن و تا سیر کردن تا
در لسان الطیر در مدح خلیفه ثانی بمعنی اول گوید شعر خوان بذلدین جهان اهلی تویوب * اول و زین تویغارغالی کبی اورونب
تویغارغاج چون سیر کرد و کند تویغارغوچی سیر کننده تویغارغوجه و تویغارغونچه و تویغارغانجه تا سیر کردن و بقدر آن تویغارالغاینکیم
بقدریکه سیر توانی کرد تویغارغومیز و سیر خواهیم کرد تویغارغوسیدور سیر خواهید کرد تویغارغوسیلاردور سیر خواهند کرد تویغارغا
تویغارغوم یوق سیر نخواهم کرد تویغارالماغوم و تویغارالغوم یوق سیر کردن محکم نخواهد بود تویغارغولوق سیر کردنی تویغارغای و تویغارای و تویغارسا
تویغارغودیک و تویغارادیک سیر کند و همچنانکه سیر کند تویدورماق باشتباع ضمه و سکون یا و راء مهمله
و فتح دال مهمله مصدر متعدیست یعنی جهاندن و صیغ آن با لفظ در اشتقاق می آید تویلاماق بسکون یا و فتح لام الیز انداختن و لکد
پراندن تویلاب و تویلابا و تویلامیش الیز انداخته چنانکه شاهد بر اول در نسایم المحبه در ذکر شیخ سیف الدین باخرزی گوید که ماده
آت نینک جلاوین تو توب قولدا بشیغی آتر اندوردا آت سرکشلیغ قیلیب عنانیز الیب تویلاب یو کوردی چون ذکر باقی صیغ نیز
نبود بزواید الاطناب ننمود موافق شق ان با شتقاق می آید من جوامد تویی هفت معنی دارد اول جشن و مجمع سور را گویند عموما
چنانکه گوید شعر می بولوب ایشکیم فدا باغریم سرود افغانلاریم * کیلینک اهل عشق کیم غم خلیفه تویی ایتماسام * و سوم
خوانند خصوصا دویم توغدری باشد که آنرا توی قوشی هم نامند و بفارسی هوبره و بعربی حباری گویند سیم محفف توشاغ بمعنی
بود چنانکه تویلاشاق بمعنی الیز انداختن ماخوذ از این لفظ است چهارم صیغ را نامند چنانکه مصطلح است که دو ابکشیده را
بعد از آنکه بیا بند گویند که تویمین تویتوم اگر بحسب معنی اینست که بعینی و نقش هم آنرا گرم اما بالمجاز بمعنی عینی استعمال شود
پنجم ترکی رو بمعنی موی باشد و آنرا توک هم خواهند ششم امراست از سیر شدن هفتم باشتباع امراست از فهمیدن و بفارسی بمعنی انده
توبیغای بر بغایت از کجشک بزرگتر و بلند پرواز و بیز پرکه آنرا از آن رو تغ آملج و لکن و آملج قافن و خروس و بو کور و الجه سرحه
هم نامند و بفارسی خول و بعربی قرام و نقار الخشب خوانند و نیز امراست از سیر کردن چنانکه گذشت تویغور تغد سیر شونده و
سیر دایمی تویغون بسکون یا و نون و ضم غین معجمه بر وزن پرخون نوع سفید هر یک از جنس طیور را گویند عموما و باز سفید را نامند
خصوصا الشاهد علیه شعر خیل زحمت نه بنیجا توشکان صفا اهلی ایرور * ایله کیم تانک تویغونی توشکای سیرولت خان
ارا تویی تویشی توغدراست که مذکور شد تویماغود کرسنه دایمی و هرکز سیر نشونده چنانکه لطفی گوید شعر بو تویماغود
کوز و مکا تو ر صد کمیز ماکان کبتی آی دیک یوز یعنیه بنجه که بو مبتلا دیا تماد تویناغ و تویناق بسکون یا و فتح نون با لف کشیده
و ناخن ستور گویند چنانکه در لیلی مجنون فرماید شعر تویناغ ایماس انکلا شام کا هی * بو قیش قلم او جیفه سیاهی * و از تو و اق
و تو و اق هم نامند چنانکه مذکور شد تویناک مع الکاف خنزیر نیم سیر باشد تویوق بضم یای حطی و سکون قاف بمعنی جناس بود
که نوعی از صنایع بدیعیه است چنانکه در حیرة الابرار در منقبت شعر گوید شعر انکلا ماین سوزدا تویوق بحرینا تا دیی بود
بلکه فنون و بحری ثم جناس در ترکی بحر بیت مخصوص که آنرا بحر تویوق نامند و آن وزن رمل مسدس مقصور است چنانکه در رساله عروض
که نوایی علیه الرحمه تالیف کرده چنین نوشته که ترک اولوسی بتخصیص جغتای خلقی ارا شایع دور کیم اوزان لیکم آلاره بودین اول دور
لا تبلغ یاشا با مجلس لار دا آیتورلار سهر دیسی بو نوع دور کیم ایکی بیت فه مقرر دور و سجع و قیلور لار دیکم بتجنیس آتیلغای و اولعه زنتج
مسکرس مقصور دور آنداق کیم شعر یا ربا ولعتهد وشکر یالبمودون * یا مکر شهد و شکر یالبمودون * جانیمه پیوسته ناوک تما
غمزه او مین قاشیغه یالبمودون تویولوق بضم یا و لام و سکون نیم و تا فیز کهر وی قیمت بود که از نا الجسم پیدا آید ایب

المکسورات حرف التاسع الباء من المشتقات تیپماك بسکون باء عجمی لگد زدن و پازدن چنانکه در مقاله سیزدهم از حیرة الابرار گوید شعر
جوم ن بتیما کنکان قویش کو نا چت * تیپکان ایاغ دین کیلو ر حت * تیپدوك لگد زدیم تیپار و تیپادور لگد میزند و تیپا
بمعنی فاعل و مصدر هم می آید تیپاید ور لگد میزند و زده است تیپکان و تیپارکان و تیپادورکان لگد زننده چنانکه شاهد
اول معنی اول در ذیل مصدر مذکور شد و معنی مصدر هم می آیند تیپ و تیپکیل مفرد مخاطب از فعل امر الشاهد علی الثانی شعر
دید بلا ر چیدا بله تو سن لیغین ایلینک اوکوت * کیم دیدی تیپکیل و منیر بی اوشات ای واعظ تیپما و تیپماکیل مفرد مخاطب
از فعل نهی تیپینک و تیپینکیز و تیپینکلار جمع مخاطب از فعل امر تیپمانک و تیپمانکیز و تیپمانکلار جمع مخاطب از فعل نهی تیپان و
تیپار مین پامیزنم تیپامین و تیپار مین و تیپا سه مین و تیپا دا م پا میزنم تیپاس لگد میزند و بمعنی فاعل و مصدر منفی هم می آید
تیپماسینکا بلگد نزدنت تیپار ینکا بلگد زدنت تیپیب و تیپیان و تیپمیش لگد زده تیپمیشانک لگد زده تیپسا و تیپگا
تیپیب بولغای لگد تواند زد تیپا تیپا لگد توانند زد تیپا آلغای لگد توانند زد لگد زنان تیپای و تیپاین لگد بزنم
و بزند و بزنی و زده تیپا الد و تیپکا بیز و تیپکای بیز و تیپکا و تیپا لیلی پا بزنیم تیپکالی برای لگد زدن و تا لگد زده تیپکاج چون لگد
زد و بزند تیپکوچی لگد زننده تیپکوچه تیپکونچه تیپکانچه تا لگد زدن و بقدر لگد زدن تیپا آلغاینچه بقدر یکه لگد
زد تیپکو بیز دور لگد خواهیم زد تیپکو نکوز دور لگد خواهید زد تیپکو سیلار دور لگد خواهند زد تیپا کونك و تیپکونك تو
لگد نخواهی تیپا آلماغونك و تیپا آلغونك تو لگد زدن ممکن نخواهد بود تیپکو لوك لگد زدن تیپکای و تیپای و تیپسون و تیپسه بك
لگد بزند تیپکودك و تیپار دیك لگد زدن و همچنانکه لگد بزند تیپشماك بکسر باء عجمی و سکون شین قرشت مصدر مفاعله
یعنی بیکدیگر لگد زدن و صیغ آن با شین اشتقاق می یابد تیپیلماك بکسر باء عجمی و سکون لام لگد زده شدن و صیغ آن با لام
می یابد تیپدورماك مصدر متعدی یعنی لگد زنانیدن و صیغ آن با لفظ دور اشتقاق می یابد تیپراتماك بسکون باء عجمی
و فتح راء مهمله و تیپرانماك بالحاق نون حرکت کردن و جنبیدن و تیپرانماقلیك و تیپرانماقلیك هم بهمین معنی است چنانکه شاهد بر
الجمید گوید شعر قو پماغی ممکن ایماس تو ر ملکه تیپرانماقلیکی تاپملسا جانجز لیلینک ننکه سید بن لجان عنا تیپرادی و تیپرانیدی
حرکت کرد چنانکه در شیلی مجنون در ملاقات دیدن مجنون با دختر نوفل گوید الشاهد علی الاول شعر نوفل کوزی بان بو طرفه حالات قریه
کو یا وسیله مقالات * قوپتی داغی ایکا تیپرادی دیك * مو یحره کیشیکان کیبی نیك * و نیز در تاریخ الانبیاء در ذکر عزیر علیه السلام گوید
مرکبین سینیب اوز شمر یغه تیپرادی تیپرادوك و تیپرانیدوك حرکت کردیم و در تاریخ بابری شاهد بر اول چنین مذکور است که موفق الحاکم
تیزاوق تیپرادوك بر اوچ یول باردوق تیپرایو و تیپرایدور تیپرانور و تیپرانادور حرکت میکند و تیپرایو و تیپرانور بمعنی فاعل و مصدر هم
می آیند چنانکه شاهد بر اول بمعنی مصدری گوید شعر ای نوای میل قیلما جا ملکه ایستار جاهدا دوست * بیلکان که تیلاب
ایتا الد تیپرارکا بولغای بین مصدر شاهد بر ثانی را بمعنی مصدری در حیرة الابرار در وصف فقها گوید شعر آیتا تاغه دستان ادبیکا ن
تیپرا نور یچه اوروب کوچ * تیپرایدور و تیپرانایدور حرکت میکرده است تیپرارکان و تیپرارکاچ تیپراکی حرکت کننده و تیپراکی
کرده و بمعنی مصدر هم می آیند تیپرا و تیپرا کیل و تیپران و تیپرانکیل مفرد مخاطب از فعل امر چنانکه در حیرة الابرار در وصف سخن گوید
الشاهد علی الاول شعر تیپرا نوای و نوا ییا کیل * هر نی ایماس بولسا ر عاد تیپا کیل * تیپرما و تیپرماکیل و تیپرانما تیپرانماکیل مفرد مخاطب
من الشاهد علی الرابع شعر آیتا سانا ملنا ولمنچه باشینکا تیکار کای قلم * دیریبی بولیدین تو قرا فید یك تیپرانماکیل تیپرانک و تیپرانکیز
تیپرانکلار جمع تیپرانینك و تیپرانینکیز و تیپرانینکلار جمع مخاطب از فعل امر تیپرانمانک و تیپرانمانکیز و تیپرانمانکلار و تیپرانمانکلار جمع مخاطب

تیپرانان و تیپرانماس مین و تیپرانمان و تیپرانماس مین حرکت نمیکنم تیپرایو مین و تیپرار مین و تیپرایدور مین و تیپرانام و تیپرانامین و تیپرانور مین و
تیپرانادور مین و تیپرانورام حرکت میکنم تیپرانماس و تیپرانماسور حرکت نمیکند و بمعنی فاعل و مصدر منفی هم می آید تیپرانماسینکا
تیپرانماسینکا بحرکت نکردنت تیپرار ینکا و تیپرانور ینکا بحرکت کردنت تیپراب و تیپراپان و تیپرامیش و تیپرانیب و تیپرانیپان و تیپرانمیش
حرکت کرده تیپرامیشانك و تیپرانمیشانك حرکت کرده تیپرابولغای و تیپراب بولغای و تیپرانیب بولغای و تیپرانیب بولغای حرکت توان کرد
تیپرای آلغای و تیپرانا آلغای حرکت تواند کرد تیپرای و تیپرایو و تیپرانا و تیپرانا سنا حرکت کنان تیپرانالی و تیپرانالی و تیپراکای بیز
تیپرالی و تیپرانیلی و تیپرانسانك و تیپرانکای بیز و تیپرانکای بیز و تیپرانالی و تیپرانالی حرکت کنیم تیپراکالی و تیپرانکالی برای حرکت کردن و تا حرکت کرده
تیپراکاچ و تیپرانکاچ چون حرکت کرد و کند الشاهد علی الثانی شعر اول قوپاش و صلیدا امزنی ریشکدین کم الیدام * شایه
با نیمدا تیپرانکای نو هم یلاطرش تیپراکوچی و تیپرانکوچی حرکت کننده تیپراکوچه و تیپراکونچه و تیپراکانچه و تیپرانکوچه و تیپرانکونچه
تیپرانکانچه تا حرکت کردن و بقدر حرکت کردن الشاهد علی الخامس بالمعنی الاخیر شعر کو نوای ضعفی تیپرانکوچه با ر ایردی و لیك
مجراوی کو کسیکا کیم ستیکدی بیله تیپرانمادی * تیپرای آلغاینچه و تیپرانا آلغاینچه بقدر یکه حرکت تواند کرد تیپراکو بیز دور و تیپرانکو بیز دور
حرکت خواهیم کرد تیپراکونکوز دور و تیپرانکونکوز دور حرکت خواهید کرد تیپراکو سیلار دور و تیپرانکو سیلار دور حرکت خواهند کرد تیپراکاکوم
تیپراکوم یوق و تیپرانکاکوم و تیپرانکوم یوق حرکت نخواهم کرد تیپرای آلماغوم و تیپرای آلغوم یوق و تیپرانا آلماغوم و تیپرانا آلغوم یوق حرکت کردن ممکن
نخواهد بود تیپراکولوك و تیپرانکولوك حرکت کردنی تیپرا کای و تیپرانکای و تیپرانسا و تیپرانسون و تیپرادیك و تیپرانکای و تیپرانا و تیپرانسا و تیپرانسون
تیپرانغایك حرکت کند تیپراکودیك و تیپرادیك و تیپرانکودیك و تیپرانغیدیك حرکت کردن و همچنانکه حرکت کند تیپرشماك مع التعدی
با یکدیگر حرکت کردن و صیغ آن با شین اشتقاق می یابد تیپراتماك مع الناصدر متعدی است یعنی متحرك ساختن و جنبانیدن
تیپراتکوچی جنبانندن چنانکه در شمایل الحبه در ذکر ابو علی رضی گوید که تا نکلادیکای مین که الاریننك باش تیپراتکوچیلاریدین
مین و باقی صیغ آن بدستور با تای قرشت اشتقاق می یابد تیپرچلاتماق بکسر باء عجمی و میم عجمی و سکون راء مهمله و فتح لام بالف کشیده
بمعنی دست و پا زدن و طپیدن بود تیپرچلادوق دست و پا زدیم تیپرچلادیم و تیپرچلادیك و دست و پا میزند چنانکه ملا ...
در کل و نوروز گوید الشاهد علی الاول شعر تیپرچلادی چو مرغ نیم بسمل * اوزی اوزی بیرله سوز لاشو ر عنادل * و تیپرچلا دور بمعنی
فاعل و مصدر هم می آید تیپرچلایدور و دست و پا میزند و زده است تیپرچلاغان و تیپرچلادی و تیپرچلایدور دست و پا زننده و زده
و بمعنی مصدر هم می آیند تیپرچلا و تیپرچلا کیل مفرد مخاطب از فعل امر تیپرچلاما و تیپرچلاماغیل مفرد مخاطب از فعل نهی تیپرچلانکلار
تیپرچلانکیز و تیپرچلانکلار جمع مخاطب از فعل امر تیپرچلامانك و تیپرچلامانکیز و تیپرچلامانکلار جمع مخاطب از فعل نهی تیپرچلان تیپرچلامان
دست و پا میزنم تیپرچلای مین و تیپرچلار مین و تیپرچلایدور مین و تیپرچلایو مین دست و پا میزنم تیپرچلاماس دست و پا نمیزند تیپرچلاماس
دست و پا نزدنت و بمعنی فاعل و مصدر منفی هم می آید تیپرچلارینکا بدست و پا زدنت تیپرچلاب و تیپرچلاپان
تیپرچلامیش دست و پا زده چنانکه شاهد بر اول در تاریخ بابری مذکور است که بیر کرلع بوزاوی و تنکا کو یوب تیپرچلاب
یاتادور بو خوزلاب هر کیشی شیرالفه الدی تیپرچلامیشانك دست و پا زده تیپرچلاب بولغای و تیپرچلاب بولغای دست و پا توان زد
تیپرچلای آلغای دست و پا تواند زد تیپرچلای و تیپرچلایو و تیپرچلایو دست و پا زنان و طپان تیپرچلای و تیپرچلایین
دست و پا بزنم و بزند و بزنی و زده تیپرچلاغای و تیپرچلاغای بیز و تیپرچلاغای بیز و تیپرچلای و تیپرچلالیلی دست و پا بزنیم تیپرچلاغالی
برای دست و پا زدن و تا دست و پا زده تیپرچلاغاچ چون دست و پا زد و بزند تیپرچلاغوچی دست و پا زننده تیپرچلاغوچه

189v.

تیرچیلاغوغه و تیرچیلاقماغه تا دست و پا لرزدن و بمعنی دست و پا لرزیدن تیرچیلاغی آلمانینکه بمعنی اینکه دست و پا توانیتز تیرچیلا
غوسیز بود دست و پا خواهیم لرزید تیرچیلاغوغیز بود در دست و پا خواهیند لرزید تیرچیلاغوسیلار بود در دست و پا خواهیند لرزید تیرچیلا
ماغوم و تیرچیلاغوم یوق دست و پا نخواهم لرزید تیرچیلای آلماغوم و تیرچیلای آلموم قید دست و پا لرزیدن ممکن نخواهد بود تیرچیلاغوچی
دست و پا لرزیدن تیرچیلاغای و تیرچیلاغنا و تیرچیلاغسون و تیرچیلادیلر دست و پا لرزند تیرچیلاغودیلر و تیرچیلاردیلر دست و پا لرزید
و همچنانکه برزند من الجوامد تیت بفتح تای مشدده همان تیت است که در باب تای مضمومه ذکر شد تیب تیک یعنی راست
بینا و دلست چنانکه گوید تو تبوز یعنی همواره بسیار هموار و در تاریخ بابری مدکور است که بر تیب تیک اینش بین ایتیب و زدن اوزا
تنکی دین او توب یعنی از بالا نشیب بینایلر است تیب آمده از نشیب های کنار دولانبی گذشته تیبیت بکسر با و سکون تای ثانی
پشم نرمی بود که از زیر موی بز و قوربرآید تیرا شلیسک بسکون بای عجمی صاحب جنبش تیبولت بضم با عجمی یعنی لنگر باشد
تیبینکو بفتح با و سکون نون و ضم کاف عجمی دامنه زین بود و بفتح تا نیز مستعملست چنانکه شاهد آن در باب تای مفتوحه گذشت
تیبه بفتح با عجمی دو معنی دارد اول کفش مرا گویند دوم مثل اینکه ناشد چنانکه هرد و معنی را تواندار گوید شعر
خیال تیبلچاقی نوالی باشیند امنزلکه قودین که پیرتپه دین بلیرلی ری دیکی بولاغ و تو پیره بضم تا نیز نامند و معنی استعمال میشود
تیپین تیبلت زمین گل که از سم ستور کوفته شده از باشد مع التا من المشتقات تیترا ماک بسکون تای ثانی مضطرب شدن و
لرزیدن چنانکه در لیلی مجنون در وصف بیماری لیلی گوید شعر شمشادینه تیترانالعبید اش تاپلی سیلی دین ایله کیم سپیدار
تیترا دولت لرزیدیم تیترادی تیترایدو در سیلرزید و تیترا یعنی فاعل و صفت هم می آید تیترا ماید و رمیلرزد و لرزنده است
تیترا کان و تیترا رکان و تیترا ید مکان لرزنده و لرزیده چنانکه شاهد برنالش را بمعنی اول در فصل یای و همه از محبوب القلوب بجهت ذکر
زنان گوید که کبر که ایکی ننا تاجنه عانه سور بکای تیترا بیدیکان باشغه تیترا کیج سا بخنای تیترا و تیترا کیل مفرد مخاطب
از فصل امر تیترا نا و تیترا نا کیل مفرد غالبه از فصل امر تیترا ننک و تیترا نکیر و تیترا نکلار جمع غالبه از فصل امر تیترا نا ملک و تیترا
تیترا نا نکلار جمع غالبه از فصل نهی تیترا مان و تیترا ماس مین عیلرزیم تیترای مین و تیترا مین و تیترا مین و تیترا میسلرزیم تیترا ماس
عیلرزید و بمعنی فاعل و صفت مصنوع هم می آید تیترا ماسینکا نبلرزیدت تیترا رسینکا بلرزیدت تیترا بد تیترا نا بع تیترا میش
لرزیده تیترا میش انک لرزیده تیترا نا تو لغنه و تیترا ب تو لغنه توان لرزید تیترا ای لکنای تواند لرزید تیترا ی و تیترا یو
لرزان لرزان تیترای و تیترا این بلرزیم و بلرزید و بلرزند و لرزیده الشاهد علی الاول المعنی الاول شعر نچه دنیم او نا تیترای
د لربا لار کوسیداش ای سلطانلار بولوب بین کافرستاندین سلولت تیترا نا لک و تیترا کای نزه تیترا کای بزو تیترا لی و تیترا لیک بلرزید تیترا کا
برای لرزیدن و تا لرزیده تیترا کاج چون لرزید و بلرزید تیترا کوچی لرزنده تیترا کو جه تیترا کو غوبه تیترا کا غه تا لرزیدن و معقدار لرزیدن
تیترای تیغانینکه بعضی که توانیند لرزید تیترا کو میز بود در خواهیم لرزید تیترا کو نکو بود در خواهیند لرزید تیترا کو سیلار بود در خواهند
لرزید تیترا نا کوم و تیترا کوم یوق نخواهم لرزید تیترای آلماغوم و تیترای آلغوم قید لرزیدن ممکن نخواهد بود تیترا کو لوک لرزیدنی تیترا کای
تیترا سا و تیترا سون و تیترا دیک بلرزند تیترا کودیک و تیترا ردیک لرزیدند و همچنانکه بلرزند تیترا تماک مع الکسر تا ام لرزیدن
و صیغ آن با شین اشتقاق می یابد تیترا تماک مع التا مصدر متعدیست یعنی لرزانیدن و بمعنی لازم هم مستعملست یعنی لرزیدن چنانکه
در خسرو شیرین در وصف بیماری شیرین گوید شعر جزا تیبر له تیترا نماک نشانی تو پاش تیلسه نخیل لالم سوزانی تیترا تورنکا لمثل
و لرزیدن کردنش چنانکه بمعنی اول در لیلی مجنون در وصف بیماری لیلی گوید شعر او لغنه که لطف دین ایدی کان تیل تیترا توسه کان نمک

190r.

تابانی صیغ برزیساق با تای قرشنا اشتقاق می یابد تیتمات بسکون تای ثانی چیزی را با دست پاره پاره کردن و پنبه را از دانه
جدا کردن و اشباه آن و صیغ آن موافق تیتول اول الشتقاق می یابد تیتیلماک بکسر تای ثانی و سکون لام از هم پاره پاره شدن
و از هم پاشیدن و صیغ آن با لام اشتقاق می یابد من الجوامد تیت و تیت ازاتباعست یعنی از هم پاشیده و پاره پاره چنانکه
گوید شعر مین کیم و اسلام کیم تجاره بیرا لمخرقه الیلاعی او لیب تینیت الطفا الحنا لی تیت و تیت تیل نما بمعنی لرزیده باشد
الشاهد علیه شعر قویاش تیل چمو پیرله تیر کلیم ایلا کلاح سروش منکا تیترا تا توشی تیزو تیکلیغ لسطو ابلا او تیترا کج
تیلمای چیقه است که سر آن دانهای کوچک و بر نجهای الوان بجهة زینت می آویزند و همیشه لرزانست چنانکه گوید شعر
تیترا کیچ ایر خاص مصحح کیم قویاش قاش اهندوش خوشه پروین شاعلی خطا از قیلدی مکان تیتیک شنجشی را گویند که در دست
مرض هزال و تندی و شوخی نیابه برایام تیمت کند چنانکه حیله تیلبه در مخزن گوید شعر ایرکیشی ایمکا که استیل حالت بو
همچه پنجه سینسا ایتیک دال بولوش و بفتح تای اول نیز مستعملست چنانکه در تای مفتوحه گذشت مع الرا من المشتقات تیرمات
بسکون رای مهمله بمعنی بود اول بمعنی چیدن باشد و در طرب لفظ چیدن بر مهملا ملاق و تیرمر شود و در ترکی از اقرار استعمال
میوه چیدن و سخن چیدن و بنا چیدن و گل وگیاه چیدن و غیر آن دوم بمعنی بر چیدن جمع کردن باشد چنانکه گوید
شعر با ذل ایلکی بو قاری سایل قولین کرکیل فویتی تینک بولمو تیرمادک و تا چاق خومیل بنده و نیز تحیرة الابرار در فنم
گوید شعر هم سا چاری بهمل و هم تیرماک هم آتورمه خورده و هم پیرهای تیردی چیدو بر چید چنانکه در لیلی مجنون بمعنی اول گوید
شعر تا مه که سیز هزینی تیردی بو بحر فصیله جلو بیردی من سعی تیلیز بو بحکم کیم سیهر شنبد تاز غالم اهلیغه بولدی
شنبد نازش نیلکون مو صبه فضا بردی بو النجم مرا آتدا کوب تیردی تیر دولت چیدیم و بر چیدیم تیرادی تیرا دو در بچید
بر بچید چنانکه در مقاله سیزدهم از حیرة الابرار در بلبلها بخیر گوید الشاهد علی الاول با المعنی الثانی شعر مهر تیرادی
کساجنا کیتی بولدی تیرای کمر کا کمرتا العاقیتی و تیرادی با مضارع و مستعمل تیرا ماک نیز انشان استطر در بمعنی ایستد کسند صارت کردن هم
می آید و بمعنی فاعل و صفت هم استعمال بی شود تیراید و رمیچیند و میچیند و بر میچیند و بر بچیندست تیر کان و تیرا کان و تیرا یدکان
چینده و چیده و بر چینده و بر چیده چنانکه شاهد بر آغل را بمعنی چیده گوید شعر لعل امراق ابحر بر بیرله کان تیرکان کسی
نامه همی پیراو ایتم تیم شکیم تایدم و بمعنی بر چینده در لسان الطیر در هوای توحید گوید شعر اوله بید بچکان از ظرپکان اوده
بذل انسا لچنا نا مزی تیرکان نا مزی و بمعنی معهده هم می آیند چنانکه گوید الشاهد علی الاول شعر تیر لدان کیم عیش تیلدی عنحا
قرن لالش تیرنا الایاندا ناشا فیرکان کوی پیکان او لوش و تیر کان بمعنی برست کسند صارت کرده صارت کرده هم مستعملست تیر کا نکا غه
بمعنی نا بچینده و نا بر چینده چنانکه در بهایه و صنعه گوید که سیمر دلینا ایکی بو کولو بخوشه تیرنا کیدا آفشا نغمه رفع نهفتنا
بر دین دیک بر آ نعوج دانه تیر کانکا غه تیر و تیر کیل مفرد غالبه از فصل امر تیرنا و تیرنا کیل مفرد غالبه از فصل هی الشاهد علی
الاول شعر چون تو بو بتوبه توان جسیم ایست تا شیح بن تیرنا ای کرد و نغذا تیکلیغ نیه خاجغه تاش و تیرنا در صنعه تخاما
امر چینک و نا خن زدن باشد چنانکه در دیل امضاء مند کو خواهد شد تیر نیک و تیر نیکیز و تیر نیکلار جمع غالبه از فصل امر تیرنا
تیرنا نکو تیرنا نکلار جمع غالبه از فصل نهی تیر مان و تیر ماس مین بچینم و بر بچینم تیرامین و تیرامین و تیرادو مین و تیر امام بچینیم و بر بچینیم
و تیرامین و تیرامام بمعنی ایست میکنم هم مستعملست تیر ماس بچیند و بر بچیند و بمعنی فاعل و صفت منفی هم می آید تیرماسینکا
بچیند و بر بچیند تیر ایسنکا بچیندت و بر چیندت و نیز بمعنی ایست کردنست تیب و تیرنا نو تیرمیش چیده و بر چیده

تیریشانك چه وبرچه تیرنا بولغای وتیریب بولغای توان چید وبرچید تیرا آلغای تواند چید وبرچید تیرا تیرا چیده
وبرچیده بچیده تیرلی معنا بین . بچینم وبچیند وبچینی وچیده وبرچینم وبرچیند وبرچینی وبرچیده ونیز بمعنی لنکم وکندوکای [illegible]
تیرماك وتیرکاینزو تیرکای بز وتیرلسه لغیر لینك . بچینیم وبرچینیم وتیرلی بمعنی ایستکیم هم باشد تیرکالی برای چیدن وتلچیدن
برای برچیدن وتابرچیدن تیرکاج چون چید وبچیند وچون برچید وبرچینید تیرکوچی چیننده وبرچیننده [illegible]
در نظم الجواهر در صفت چمن کوید شعر سیز تیرکوچی کرده [illegible] ظاهر ایلتلش هر چیزنی نینك سنك من ظاهر ایتیلتیز تیرکوچه
تیرکوبغو تیرکانغه تاچیدن وبقصد چیدن تابرچیدن وبقصد برچیدن تیرا آلغانینکچه بقدری که تواند چید وبرچید
تیرکوم خواهم چید وبرچید تیرکونك خواهی چید وبرچید چنانکه بمعنی [illegible] خسرو وشیرین در صفت فرهاد کوید شعر
بونی کلترلی بچین چون صد دیر کونك فی آتاغیکیم افرونك انصاف بر کونك تیرکوسی خواهد چید وبرچید تیراکوم وتیرکوم یوق
نخواهم چید ونخواهم برچید تیرا المالغوم وتیرا الغوم یوق چیدن وبرچیدن ممکن نخواهد بود تیرکولوك چیدنی وبرچیدنی
تیرکای وتیرا تیرنلو تیرسون وتیر دیك . بچیند وبرچیند چنانکه در محبوب القلوب کوید الشاهد علی الاول المعنی الاول شعر
کیم سوزنی تیرب تنسوچ آنغه یغه یکای نا الغای دو صفح ایتینک دودی خمیرکای الشاهد علی الثالث والرابع شعر وصل [illegible]
دین دیانك کیم هدعی کل تیرغلسون تیرخا تیرسون امرنا بالمغربیه بوزونك خار وخش تیرکودیك وتیراردیك چیدنی وچیدنی
وهمچنانکه بچیند وبرچیند تیرادردیك بمعنی ارستکردی وهمچنانکه ارستکندم می آید ودرا بمعنی بجمعه تیرا لغا لاشتراک ذکر تیر [illegible]
مسمی متصل تیرغا لغات بمعنی برچیدن وبرچیدن کردن وصیغ آن با لفظ واشتقاق می یابد تیریلماك بکسر طا وسکون لام
طرو اول چه شدن دویم برچه شدن سیم باشباع کسر یعنی زنده شدن وزندگی کردن چنانکه کوید شعر کونکلی ایتینك هجر الی
جاندین ساولی که یوقیبن سینیز تیرلیمالك احتمالی تیریلدوك چه وبرچه شدیم وزنده شدیم وزندگی کردیم تیریلور وتیریلادور
چه وبرچه میشود وزنده میشود وتیریلور بمعنی فاعل ومصدر هم می آید تیریلماید چه نمیشود وقشلاق وبرچه نمیشود وزنده
نمیشود وقشلاق تیریلکان وتیریلمکان وتیریلادرکان چه شونده وچه شده وبرچه شونده وبرچه شده وزنده شونده وزنده
شده چنانکه شاهد بالقلعا بمعنی چه شده کوید شعر معنی خلوت دین ایحد الحلی مخ دیر یتیریکان تاشلاغانك که چه خوش
دم کوب تیریلکان کنبد ودهلیز لفظ کوب در این شعر جای تو ایهام اداشده یك معنی اینست که کنبد ودهلیزی کهنم چه باشند
خوش هواست وبمعنی مصدر هم می آیند تیرلیه تیریلکیل مفرد خاطب المنفصل الرجاء چنانکه شاهد برا ولرا بمعنی زندگی کن کوید
شعر نوالی اله تیریلکیم او یاتیبن او لما کاسین اکه رسول علیه السلام بولسا شفیع تیریلما وتیریلماکیل مفرد خاطب المنفصل
تیریلسانك تیریلسنکیز نهی [illegible] جمع خاطب المتصل الر تیریلماك وتیریلمانکیز وتیریلمانکلار جمع خاطب المنفصل
جمع خاطب المنفصل تیریلمان وتیریلماس مین چه نمیشود وبرچه نمیشوم وزنده نمیشوم تیریلمسین وتیریلور مین
تیریلادورمین تیریلورام چه وبرچه میشوم وزنده میشوم تیریلماس چه وبرچه نمیشود وزنده نمیشود بمعنی فاعل وصفت
منفی هم می آید تیریلماسینکا بچیدنت بر چیدنت وبزنده شدنت تیریلوروکا بچه شدنت وبرچه شدنت وبزنده شدنت
تیریلسه وتیریلسا وتیریلمیش چه وبرچه شده وزنده شده تیریلیشانك چه وبرچه شده وزنده شدهٔ تیریلسا توانغلو تیریلیب تو
چه وبرچه توان شد وزنده توان شد تیریلا آلغای چه وبرچه تواند شد وزنده تواند شد تیریلا تیریلا چه وبرچه
برچه وزنده شوان زنده شوان تیریلای وتیریلایین چه وبرچه شوم وشوی وشوند وبرچه شوید وزنده شوم وشوی وشوند

که اساس آنرا بسیار چه باشند خوش هوا است و معنی دیگر اینست که کنبد و هلیزی

تیرلسانك وتیرلیکاینزو تیریلکای بز وتیریلا الی تیریلا الینك چه وبرچه شویم وزنده شویم تیریلکالی برای چه وبرچه شدن وچه
وبرچه شدن وبرای زنده شدن وتلمزنده شدن تیریلکاج چون چه وبرچه شده شوی وچون زنده شده شوی تیریلکوچی چه
وبرچه شونده وزنده شونده تیریلکوچه تیرلکوبغو تیریلکانغه تا چه وبرچه شدن وبقصد آن وتا زنده شدن وبقصد زنده شدن
تیریلا آلغانینکچه بقدری که تواند چه وبرچه تواند زنده شد تیریلکوم وتیریلکوم یوق نخواهم چه وبرچه نخواهم شد ونه زنده نخواهم شد
تیریلکونك وتیریلکونك یوقتور چه وبرچه نخواهی شد ونه زنده نخواهی شد چنانکه بمعنی لطیف کوید شعر ای نوایی یار هجری درد یدا
اولماکه طالبیش چون تیریلکونك یوقتور اپسلر کایوقی هالدیش تیریلماکوسی تیریلکوسی یوقتور چه وبرچه نخواهد شد
وزنده نخواهد شد تیریلکولوك چه وبرچه شدنی وزنده شدنی تیریلکای تیریلکو تیریلسون تیریلا تیرسون وتیریلاینچه وبرچه
وزنده شود تیریلکودیك وتیریلوردیك چه وبرچه شدنی وهمچنانکه چه وبرچه شود وزنده شدنی وهمچنانکه زنده شود
تیرلیتمالك بسکون لام وتای قرشت مصدر متعدی تیریلماك است یعنی زنده کردن وازا تیرکوزماك هم کویند وصیغ آن با تای قرشت
اشتقاق می یابد تیرکوزماك بسکون رای مهمله وزای عجمه وضم کاف عجمی زنده کردن تیرکوزدوك زنده کردیم تیرکوزور وتیرکوزادور
زنده میکند وتیرکوزور بمعنی فاعل ومصدر هم می آید تیرکوزماید زنده نمیکند وتیرکوزماس تیرکوزا آلور زنده میتواند کرد الشاهد
شعر غمزانك او لتوریبان نوایی نی بار سوزبیله چون تیرکوزا الور لبینك تیرکوزکان وتیرکوزوکان تیرکوزادورکان زنده کننده وزنده کرده
ومعنی مصدر هم می آیند تیرکوز وتیرکوزکیل مفرد خاطب المنفصل الراء الشاهد علی الاول شعر نوایی اولدی هلاك غمینك
ایجره تیرکوز آنی ینچه نشان تو ناتین الاکدیم اولوب تصحیح سیاق شرحنرات که چه نشان تو تاین بقصریح الاکدیم اولوب [illegible]
علی الثانی شعر بر قدح می برله تیرکوزکیل نوایی مینچه دیر ایشکیدا غمهجور اولوب نی کلیمیا تای تیرکوزماد وتیرکوزماکیل
مفرد خاطب المنفصل تیرکوزونك وتیرکوزونکوز وتیرکوزونکلار جمع خاطب المنفصل الر تیرکوزماك وتیرکوزمانکیز وتیرکوزمانکلار جمع خاطب المنفصل
تیرکوزمان وتیرکوزماسمین زنده نمیکنم تیرکوزامین وتیرکوزورمین وتیرکوزادورمین زنده میکنم تیرکوزماس زنده نمیکند وبمعنی فاعل
ومصدر هم می آید تیرکوزماسی زنده کردنش ونکردنش تیرکوزماسینکا بزنده نکردنت تیرکوزورونکا وتیرکوزکانینکا بزنده
کردنت تیرکوزوب وتیرکوزوبان وتیرکوزکیش زنده کرده تیرکوزیشانك زنده کردهٔ تیرکوزا بولغای وتیرکوزیب بولغای زنده توان کرد
تیرکوزا آلغای زنده تواند کرد تیرکوزا وتیرکوزا زنده کنان زنده کنان تیرکوزای وتیرکوزایین زنده کنم وکنی وکنند وکنید وکنم
علی الاول ما المعنی الاول شعر دیب ایدینك جهدیدین اولسانك تیرکوزای پیغ الملة آرزو اولتوردی وه اوتکاریکل [illegible]
دین تیرکوزمالك وتیرکوزکاینزو تیرکوزکای بز وتیرکوزالی وتیرکوزالینك زنده کنیم تیرکوزکالی برای زنده کردن وتا زنده کرده چنانکه بمعنی اول
کوید شعر کیلدی تیرکوزکالی منعضم کوروب اولعیسی دم کیلکالی هم اوزاتیبن قیلدی صلی کینکا فهم تیرکوزکوجی زنده کننده
تیرکوزکوچه تیرکوزکوبغو تیرکوزکانغه تا زنده کردن وبقصد زنده کردن الشاهد علی الاول المعنی الاخیر شعر مینك بلاکش قلب
قتل کنه تا زیاندی مینی تیرکوزکوچه عمرلی ثواب ابلاه اش تیرکوزا آلغانینکچه بقدری که زنده توانی کرد تیرکوزکوم وتیرکوزکوم یوق زنده نخواهم کرد
تیرکوزکونك وتیرکوزکونك یوق زنده نخواهی کرد تیرکوزکوسی وتیرکوزکوسی یوق زنده نخواهد کرد تیرکوزالمالغوم
تیرکوزا الغوم یوق زنده کردن ممکن نخواهد بود تیرکوزکولوك زنده کردنی تیرکوزکای وتیرکوزکو تیرکوزسون وتیرکوزسون زنده کند
تیرکوزکودیك تیرکوزوردیك زنده کردنی وهمچنانکه زنده کند تیرماك نقیض را یعنی نصب کردن وراست کردن منضم کردن
باشد وازا تیرکاماك هم کویند تیرادی راست کرد چنانکه در قیام الحجه در ذکر ابو یعقوب زیزی کوید که این زیزی یلیک

191v.

اوجاق‌جایی بیرکا تیرادی و کوکین بوتاری یقیلب کوزین کوککاتیکی تیرادوک راست کردیم تیرادیم تیرایدور راست میکند

وتیرار یعنی چپید و برچپند و بمعنی فاعل و مصدر هم می‌آید تیرارغایدور راست میکند مضی نمات تیرارکان و تیرایرکان و تیرایدورکان

راست کننده راست کرده و بمعنی مصدر هم می‌آید و تیرارکان یعنی چپنده و چپیده و چپیدن و برچپنده و برچپیده و برچپیدن

مستعملست تیرا و تیرا کیل مفرد غائب امر فعل الرباعی تیرانک و تیرانکیز و تیرانکلار جمع غائب فعل الامر تیراماتک و تیراماتکیز

تیراماتکلار جمع غائب فعل النهی تیرامان و تیراماس مین راست میکنم تیرایمن و تیرایدورمن و تیرایدورمن و تیرارمن راست میکنم و تیرارمن

و تیرارم یعنی میچپینم و برمیچپینم هم مستعملست چنانچه گذشت تیراماس راست نمیکند و بمعنی فاعل و مصدر نفی هم می‌آید تیراماسینکا

براست نکردنت تیرارینکا براست کردنت و بچپیدنت و برچپیدنت تیرابیب تیرابان و تیرامیش راست کرده تیرامیشانک راستگانک

تیرالماق تراب بولغای راست توان کرد تیرای آلغای راست تواند کرد تیرای تیرای و تیرای بو راستکان راستکان تیرای و تیرایمن

راستکنم و کند و کنی و کرده و بالمصدر نیز اشتراک دارد یعنی چپنم و بچپید و بچپیدو برچپنم و برچپید و برچپنی تیراساک

تیراکاینرو تیرکاینرو تیرالی و تیرالینک راستکنیم و تیرالی و تیرالینک یعنی بچپنیم و برچپنیم هم آمده تیراکالی برای راست کردن و تا

راست کرده تیراکاچ چون راست کرد و کند تیراکوچی راست کننده تیراکوچه و تیراکونچه و تیراکانچه تا راست کردن و بقصد راست کردن

تیرای آلغانینکچه بقدر یکه راست توانی کرد تیراکوسیزدور راست خواهیم کرد تیراکونکیزدور راست خواهید کرد تیراکوسیلاردورلار

خواهند کرد تیراناکوم و تیراکوم یوق راست نخواهم کرد تیرای آلماغوم و تیرای آلغوم یوق راست کردن ممکن نخواهد بود تیراکولوک تیرا

کردن تیراکاع تیراسلو تیراسونی تیرادیلک راست کند تیراکودیلک تیرادیلک راست کردنی و چنانکه راست کند تیرادیلک

بمعنی چپنده و برچپنده و چنانکه چپید و برچپید هم باشد و بعضی معنی با مصدر نیز اشتراک دارد چنانچه گذشت تیرالماک

بفتح را و سکون لام ضب شدن و تیر شدن و راست شدن تیرالکان و تیرالورکان و تیرالادورکان راست شونده راست شده الشاهد علی

الاول المعنی الثانی شعر توفیلغا الم تیرتیرتیجیسیم هلاک و ضعف ینه کونکلومدین تیرالکان هوای سپکان کونکلونک

و بمعنی مصدر هم می‌آید تیرالیب تیرالیبان و تیرالمیش راست شده الشاهد علی الثالث شعر باغریدین که کوکوم کاسپکان تیرا

عشقنک او قیدین نوک سپکان ایرمیش و باقی صیغ بر نسق بالا اشتقاق می‌یابد تیرکاماک بسکون را و فتح کاف عجمی بمعنی یاد

اول ماخذه و پرسش کردن چنانکه در خسرو شیرین در ذکر ولادت فرهاد گوید شعر خلایق هر بری قیلماتیرکاماک یوق تیلغا

یامان قیلدینک دیبانک یوق دیدیم چوب و ستوران بجائی راست کردن و نتیجه دادن و با معنی تیرنانک هم کوییلدیکادوک پرسش کرد

راست کردیم تیرکادیم تیرکاید و راست میکند پرسش میکند و تیرکار یعنی فاعل و مصدر هم می‌آید تیرکامایدور پرسش نمیکند

راست نمیکند و نکرده است تیرکاکان و تیرکاکان و تیرکایدورکان پرسش کننده و پرسش کرده و راست کننده راست کرده و بمعنی مصدر

هم می‌آید تیرکاو تیرکاکیل مفرد غائب فعل الامر و بمعنی تیرکانا و تیرکانایل مفرد غائب فعل نهی هر دو معنی تیرکانک

تیرکانکیز و تیرکانکلار جمع غائب فعل الامر تیرکامانک و تیرکامانکیز و تیرکامانکلار جمع غائب فعل نهی تیرکامان و تیرکاماس مین پرسش نمیکنم

راست نمیکنم تیرکایمن و تیرکایدورمن و تیرکارمن پرسش میکنم راست میکنم تیرکاماس پرسش نمیکند راست نمیکند و بمعنی فاعل

و مصدر نفی هم می‌آید تیرکاماسینکا بپرسش نکردنت و براست نکردنت تیرکارینکا بپرسش کردنت و براست کردنت تیرکاب و تیرکابان

تیرکامیش پرسش کرده و راست کرده چنانکه در نصیحت‌نامه گوید الشاهد علی الاول المعنی الاول شعر نی بولکیم نادانی علیالابین

کیننکه لار دا تو یدی الیکین لارکه تیرکاب تاریغان و کیلکان کیشی تحصیل الامان هر کیم ایشیتی و دو فعاله تجز حیرتها الاله الآله کرد

ت پطیث

192r.

الشاهد علی الثانی بالمعنی الثانی شعر سیر دل کو ددم بر این حرف بیر قیپاق تاسیفه بوکلاب تیکن جسم او بیر الیجان اولیغ

بکوزی تیرکابان لولوی یکاسفا اوین ستون الشاهد علی الثالث بالمعنی الاول شعر لعمه رخنا دیله امز ادی عشاقنی بغیر تحسین کو

زادلار دین تیرکامیش تیرکامیشانک پرسیده و راست کرده تیرکاسا بولغای و تیرکاب بولغای پرسش توان کرد و راست توان کرد تیرکای آلغای

پرسش تواند کرد و راست تواند کرد تیرکای و تیرکایه تیرکایو پرسشکان و راستکان تیرکای و تیرکایین پرسش کنم و کند و کنی

و کرده و راستکنم و کند و کنی و کرده تیرکاسا اگر تیرکاینرو تیرکاینرو تیرکالی و تیرکالینک پرسش کنیم و راست کنیم تیرکاکالی

برای پرسش کردن و تا پرسش کرده و برای راست کردن و تا راست کرده تیرکاکاچ چون پرسش کرد و کند و چون راست کرد و کند تیرکاکوچی

پرسش کننده و راست کننده تیرکاکوچه و تیرکاکانچه تا پرسش کردن و بقصد پرسش کردن و تا راست کردن و بقصد

راست کردن تیرکای آلغانینکچه بقدر یکه پرسش توانی کرد و راست توانی کرد تیرکاکوسیزدور پرسش خواهیم کرد و راست خواهیم کرد

تیرکاکونکیزدور پرسش خواهید کرد و راست خواهید کرد تیرکاکوسیلاردور پرسش خواهند کرد و راست خواهند کرد تیرکاناکوم

تیرکاکوم یوق پرسش نخواهم کرد و راست نخواهم کرد تیرکای آلماغوم و تیرکای آلغوم یوق پرسش کردن ممکن نخواهد بود و راست کردن ممکن

نخواهد بود تیرکاکولوک پرسش کردنی و راست کردنی تیرکاکای و تیرکاسا و تیرکاسون و تیرکادیلک پرسش کند و راست کند چنانکه

شاهد بر ثانی و معنی اول در مکتوب چهارم و یکی از منشآت گوید که یاتیش تواچی بیر هر کون آلارنینک کیلکانی کیلکالاکانین تیخشی تیرکا

تیرکاکودیلک عتیرکادیلک پرسش کردنی و چنانکه پرسش کند و راست کردنی و چنانکه راست کند تیرکشماک بسکون را و شین

و فتح کاف عربی پیچیده شدن و قطعا از عصب هم رفتن و صیغ آن موافق شق اول اشتقاق می‌یابد تیرلاماک بسکون را و فتح لام

عرق کردن تیرلادوک عرق کردیم تیرلادیم تیرلار و تیرلایدور عرق میکند تیرلار یعنی فاعل و مصدر هم می‌آید تیرلامایدور عرق نمیکند و نکرده

تیرلاکان و تیرلارکان و تیرلایدورکان عرق کننده و عرق کرده چنانکه شاهد بر اول اعمی اول در تنبیهات محبوب القلوب گوید که تیرلاکان

آتیلوروا و سرکان تا تیلورو بمعنی ثانی و اسلطان حسین میرزا فرماید شعر تیرلاکان صوش یوزونک نونکا ایله لطوپارکیم کرد

تادوک اولوق بولوق هر کوکل سیرابدی و بمعنی مصدر هم می‌آیند تیرلا و تیرلاکیل مفرد غائب فعل امر تیرلاما و تیرلاماکیل

مفرد غائب فعل نهی تیرلانک و تیرلانکیز و تیرلانکلار جمع غائب فعل امر تیرلامانک و تیرلامانکیز و تیرلامانکلار جمع غائب فعل

نهی تیرلامان و تیرلاماس مین عرق نمیکنم تیرلایمن و تیرلایدورمن و تیرلارمن عرق میکنم تیرلاماس عرق نمیکند و بمعنی

فاعل و مصدر نفی هم می‌آید تیرلاماسینکا بعرق نکردنت تیرلارینکا بعرق کردنت تیرلاب و تیرلابان و تیرلامیش عرق کرده

تیرلامیشانک عرق کرده تیرلاسا بولغای و تیرلاب بولغای عرق توان کرد تیرلای آلغای عرق تواند کرد تیرلای و تیرلایو عرقکان

عرقکان تیرلای تیرلایین عرق کنم و کند و کنی و کرده تیرلاسا اگر تیرلاکاینرو تیرلاکاینرو تیرلالی و تیرلالینک عرق کنیم تیرلاکالی

برای عرق کردن و تا عرق کرده تیرلاکاچ چون عرق کرد و کند تیرلاکوچی عرق کننده تیرلاکوچه و تیرلاکانچه تا عرق

کردن و بقصد عرق کردن تیرلای آلغانینکچه بقدر یکه عرق توانی کرد تیرلاکوسیزدور عرق خواهیم کرد تیرلاکونکیزدور عرق خواهید

کرد تیرلاکوسیلاردور عرق خواهند کرد تیرلاناکوم و تیرلاکوم یوق عرق نخواهم کرد تیرلای آلماغوم و تیرلای آلغوم یوق عرق کردن ممکن

نخواهد بود تیرلاکولوک عرق کردنی تیرلاکای و تیرلاسا و تیرلاسون و تیرلادیلک عرق کند تیرلاکودیلک عتیرلادیلک عرق کردنی

و چنانکه عرق کند تیرلاتماک مع التاء مصدر متعدیست یعنی بعرق آوردن و صیغ آن با تای قرشت اشتقاق می‌یابد تیرنا

بسکون را و فتح میم بالف کشیده بمعنی چنگ و ناخن زدن بود و در تبه تیرنا لاتاق خوانند و بالمجاز بمعنی خراشیدن هم استعمال

تیرنادوق چنك وناخن زدیم تیرنالمو تیرنا یدور ناخن چنك منزلهٔ الشاهد علی الاول شعر مرهم اودینه کو نیکول غمین
تیرنادا ول شوخ ضعب توشوبتو ول انکلرفه ایش و تیرنار یعنی کاهل و مضارع هم می آید تیرنا یدور چنك وناخن بزنید
و تعالست تیرنا فان یعنی تیرنا زنان و تیرنا یدور زنان چنك وناخن زنند وزده و بمعنی مضارع هم می آید تیرنا و تیرنا غیل مفرد
غائب امر فاعل امر و تیرنا در مصدر تیرنالك صیغه نهی آید یعنی مزن چنانکه مذکور شد تیرنا و تیرنا غیل مفرد غائب امر فاعل
تیرنالك تیرنا یکز و تیرنانکلار جمع غائب امر فاعل امر تیرنانك و تیرنانکز یعنی تیرنانکلار جمع غائب امر فاعل امر تیرنا مای تیرنامای
چنك وناخن نزنیم تیرنامیع تیرنا زمین یعنی تیرنا یدور مین و تیرنادم چنك وناخن بزنیم تیرنا بم تیرنا بارم تیرنامیش چنك وناخن
زده چنانکه شاهد براول لطرامی کلی بجون کوید شعر امرکا جی شینا فه جلی تیرناب ترمشو چینی دشته پرله چیراب ثور
در تاریخ الانبیا در قصهٔ حضرت آدم علیه السلام و کشته شدن قابیل کوید که قابیل قارفه بیرنی تیرناب و منقاریلا تاز
الشاهد علی الثانی شعر کوسید ایتا لام منوکه تیرنابان که تیشلا ابان ضعف دین ولکاندا پر دین ...
تیرنامیشالمش چنك وناخن زده تیرنا شابو یعنی تیرنا بولغه چنك وناخن توان زد تیرنا ای آلغای چنك وناخن توان زد تیرنای ...
تیرنا بو چنك وناخن زنان تیرنای یعنی تیرنا بین چنك وناخن نزنم و نزند و نزنی زده تیرنا نا ق یعنی تیرنا نا بق تیرنا غای ...
تیرنالیك چنك وناخن بزنیم تیرنا غلی برای چنك وناخن زدن و تاز زده تیرنا غلج چون چنك وناخن زد و بزند تیرنا غوجی
چنك وناخن زننده تیرنا غوچه و تیرنا غوچه یعنی تیرنا غانچه تا چنك وناخن زدن و بعد از ناخن زدن تیرنا ای آلغا یشکچه بعد بیکچه
وناخن توان زد تیرنا غو میزدور چنك وناخن خواهیم زد تیرنا غو تکو زدور چنك وناخن خواهید زد تیرنا غوسی ...
وناخن خواهند زد تیرنا ما غوم و تیرنا ما غوم یوق چنك وناخن نخواهیم زد تیرنا ای آلماغوم و تیرنا ای آلغوم یوق چنك وناخن نزنم
محکم نخواهد بود تیرنا غولوق چنك وناخن زدنی تیرنا غای و تیرنا سا و تیرنا سون و تیرنا دیك چنك وناخن بزند تیرنا غودیك
تیرنا ردیك چنك وناخن زدن و همچنانکه بزند تیرنا بما ق مع النون و تیرنا شماق مع الشین با چنك وناخن خسیك
و بنا الازمن تیرناندوق و تیرناشوق تا چنك بنا الازمنیم تیرنا نوم تیرنا نادم تیرنالشو و تیرنا شادور با چنك بنا الامیردور
تیرنانوس و تیرنا شوس یعنی فاعل و مصدر هم می آید تیرنا نمایدور تیرنا شمایدور با چنك بنا الامیر و زنقه است تیرنا نمان و تیر
نانوغان یعنی تیرنانادوغان و تیرنا شمان یعنی تیرنا شوغان و تیرنا شادوغان تا چنك بنا الاروند و بنا الارفته و بمعنی مصدر هم می آید
تیرنادع تیرنا شیل و تیرنا لش و تیرنا شیل مفرد غائب امر فاعل امر تیرنا نماو تیرنا نماغیل و تیرنا شماو تیرنا شماغیل مفرد غائب امر فاعل امر تیرنا شنك
تیرنا شنکز و تیرنا شنکلار و تیرنا شیك و تیرنا شنکز و تیرنا شنکلار جمع غائب امر فاعل امر تیرنا شنك و تیرنا شنکز و تیرنا شنکلار تیرنا شماك و تیرنا شمانکز تیرنا شما
جمع غائب امر فاعل امر تیرنا نماع تیرنا نماس و تیرنا شماع تیرنا شماس یعنی با چنك بالامیر و هم تیرنا نامین و تیرنا شمین تیرنا نامین تیرنا نو
تیرنا شامین تیرنا شمین تیرنا شنقین تا چنك بالامیر هم تیرنا نماس و تیرنا شماس با چنك بالامیر و بمعنی فاعل و مصدر منفی هم می
تیرنا ماسنکه تیرنا شماسنکه با چنك بنا الارمنت تیرنا نمونکه و تیرنا شمونکه با چنك بالارمنت تیرنا نیب تیرنا نیسان و
تیرنا غنشو تیرنا شیغ تیرنا شیغا تیرنا شیش با چنك بالارفته تیرنا غیشا و تیرنا شیشا تا با چنك بالارفته تیرنا نا بوقعابی
تیرنا نیب تیرنا شیب تیرنا شاب ... با چنك بالاتوان مرفت تیرنا نا آلغه تیرنا شا آلغای تا چنك بالاتوان مرفت تیرنا نا و تیرنا نا
تیرنا شا و تیرنا شا چنك زنان و بالارفته کنان و بدون تکریر نیز استعمال می شود چنانکه در سکندر نامه ...
کوید الشاهد علی الاول شعر طلب یولدا تا لیبنا تیرنانا ... تیرنانا ... تیرنا شا و تیرنا شا

با چنك بنا الابروم و برود و بروی و رفته تیرنا نا ق و تیرنانقانبزو تیرنا نا ای بزو تیرنا نالیق تیرنا شا ق و تیرنا شلیزو تیرنا شلیق
تیرنا شالیق یعنی تیرنا شالی با چنك بنا الابرویم تیرنا نغلی و تیرنا شغلی برای الازمن و تا با چنك بالازمن تیرنا نغاج و تیرنا شغلج
چون با چنك بنا الارفت و برود و بعضی تیرنا نغوجی و تیرنا شغوجی با چنك بنا الاروند تیرنا نغوجه و تیرنا نغوچه
تیرنا نغا و تیرنا شغوجه تیرنا شغوجه تیرنا شنا مابنا الازمن و بعد از الازمن تیرنا نا آلغا یشکچه و تیرنا شا آلغا یشکچه بعد بیکچه با چنك بنا الاوا
رفت تیرنا غو میزدور و تیرنا شغو میزدور با چنك بنا الاخواهیم رفت تیرنا غو تکو زدور و تیرنا شغو تکوزدور با چنك بنا الاخواهید رفت
تیرنا غوسیدور و تیرنا شغوسیدور با چنك بنا الاخواهید رفت تیرنا ما غوم و تیرنا ما غوم یوق و تیرنا شماغوم و تیرنا شماغوم یوق با چنك بنا الا
نخواهم رفت تیرنا نا آلماغوم تیرنا نا آلغوم یوق و تیرنا شا آلماغوم و تیرنا شا آلغوم ... چنك بنا الازمن محکم نخواهد بود تیرنا غولوق و تیرنا شغولوق
با چنك بنا الازمنتوق تیرنا غای و تیرنا نا و تیرنا نا سون و تیرنا ندیك و تیرنا شغای و تیرنا شا و تیرنا شا سون و تیرنا شدیك با چنك
بنا الارود تیرنا نغودیك و تیرنا نوردیك و تیرنا شغودیك و تیرنا شوردیك با چنك بنا الازمنتوق و همچنانکه برود من الجوامد ستیس ...
کوینده الشاهد علیه شعر کل کبی یوز ... هوشومدین ... کرچه ... دم ...
تیرالك بد و بمعنی ... اول درخت سپیدار بود چنانکه کوید شعر آیینك ... تیرالك ...
رولوب باشیغه تا ریتیان ... و نیز در خسرو شیرین در وصف خزان کوید شعر تیرالك ...
تا دیغ آغزیغ ... برك با نای عجمی خوانده و کفته که برك بمعنی ورق ... از آن
سوزن سازند و زنان آنرا بر سر زنند و همیشه ... و مطالع هروی کفته که ترك
بند ایت ... که بر اغنام ... و شعر ثانی را از خسرو شیرین شاهد آورد
و جامع ابوشقه بمناسبت شعر ثانی بمعنی نهال از زعفران نوشته ... بمعنی ... زبان ...
سکه ... در وصف یاجوج و ماجوج کوید شعر ... تامیش ... دوییم ...
کویند و بفارسی آبلمان ... باشد که در روی آب دیك جوشان و روغن جوشان از جوش ... بکون ... کاف و فتح
سین مهمله بند و مفصل ... بود که آنرا بفارسی آرنج و بعربی مرفق کویند الشاهد علیه شعر ...
او چون هر توت ... تیرکالك بکون ... و فتح کاف ...
علیه شعر ... تیرلیك بکون ...
لام ... که جامه کوتاه باشد که بجهت حفظ ... بر زیر خالق پوشند چنانکه کوید شعر ...
و کلکون تیرلیك اوزه دین سوسن و کل ...
... پوشند ... شعر ...
... فرهنك جهانکیری این لغت را با شاهد در فرهنك خود مذکور ساخته تیرناغ و تیرناق
بمعنی ناخن باشد ... الت بود که شیره را بعد از انکه ... استعمال ... چنانکه کوید شعر
... خضر و چشمه ... تیری ...
... الشاهد علیه شعر ...
سونکاك لیکن سونکاك ... هند کویند شعر ... کیلب

193v

شلغمه دارچینی تیری تیزیق بکسر تا و فا اسم کیاهیست که از جنس سوزن و بوشیه بهمنه است تیزلیک بکسر
معنی تیزی بود چنانچه کوید شعر کیلکان ایتیش اولیم اولکانلارین تیر که مزکانی تیزلیک بوجهدین و یخشیلیق اولمالی
منکا و نیز در داستان بهرام از شیعه سیاوش کوید شعر نیه جاه تیپ الخیاری بات تا بمای ولیخیل ننک کوپ الحیات
تیزیکیدین سور و بیجی صورت حال ظاهر آنکه لب که مخمور در احوال تیزیکیدین سور یعنی از تیزی اش پرسید و مولف و نیز تیزکی
دین را در این شعر تیزیکی با بای ابجد خوانده و کفته که دیره حک نسنه یعنی چیز داده فیر بیوریکی صحیح اولیت شخص شعر
شاهد آورده و نصیری هم متابعت کرده سهو کرده اند لفظ و معنی هر دو اختراعی است تیزکلیک نزدیک تیزیکلای
الشاهد علیه شعر سنکا صید اولغالی عریان بولوبمین تا جان بولدی تیزیکلای توشن جادو وله شعر کمزوبیمین کیر
بیکیمی باشدین ایاغ تیشکان کونکول خالین قوشیدهر کیم تیزیکلای بولیش اولغایلار یوبالین و نیز به معنی سکندری کوید
شعر چون قاب اینی تیزقاز مامی بیشه تیزیکلای کوزلار ایردی هیشه تیزیل بسکون لام تیزکی روی یعنی جان و حیات بلکه
و نیز امر است از تیزیل شدن چنانچه کذشت تیزیم بسکون میم خوشه بود که بعد از درو در میان خرمنکاه بماند تیزلمچی کوچی
کویند که خوشهای برخیته را از میان خرمن جمع کند تیزنیک بسکون نون و کاف عجمی بمعنی عمیق بود چنانچه کوید شعر
غرقه بولدی ناتوان جسمیم سرشکیم بحریدا کیم سوخته تیزنیک بولسا جو بهرنا کا هیق و نیز به معنی سکندری کوید شعر
تالینکیشی اولغاندا جنبش ماتی تیزنیک بحر بولدی غرق بیش ماتی سخ الزا من المشتقات تیزنالک بسکون زای معجمه بمعنی برشته کشید
کنید و ازانه نیز ماله هم نامند تیزدی برشته کشید چنانچه در لیلی و مجنون خطاب مجنون کوید شعر هم تدعو هلنا ذا
الملک ام لطف و بهاد اکوهر پاک خامه سیله اول که سینی تیزدی کوهر نی قرا اینکاکا تیزدی تیزدوک برشته کشیدیم
تیزار و تیزادور برشته میکشد و نیز امر بمعنی فاعل و مصدر هم می آید تیزنماید در برشته نمیکشد و نکشیده است تیزکان
تیزکان و تیزادورکان برشته کشنده و برشته کشیده و بمعنی مصدر هم می آیند تیز و تیزکیل مفرد مخاطب از فعل امر تیزنک
تیزکیل مفرد مخاطب از فعل نهی تیزنک و تیزنکز و تیزنکلار جمع مخاطب از فعل امر تیزنامک و تیزنمانکیز و تیزنمانکلار جمع مخاطب نهی
تیزنار و تیزارمن برشته میکشم تیزامن و تیزارمین و تیزادورمین و تیزادورم برشته میکشم تیزماس برشته نمیکشد و بمعنی فاعل
و مصدر منفی هم می آید تیزماسینکا برشته نکشیدنت تیزارینکا برشته کشیدنت تیزیب و تیزیبان و تیزمیش برشته کشیده
تیزمیشالک برشته کشیده تیزنا بولغای و تیزیب بولغای برشته تواند کشید تیزا الغای برشته تواند کشید تیزکوسی [illegible] برشته
بکشم و بکشد و بکشی و کشیده تیزنالک و تیزکای تیزو تیزالی و تیزالینک برشته بکشیم تیزکالی برای برشته کشیدن و تا برشته
کشیده تیزکاج چون برشته کشید و بکشد و بعض کشیدن تیزکوچی برشته کشنده تیزکوجه و تیزکانجه تا برشته
کشیدن و بمقدار کشیدن تیزا آلغانینچه بمقداریکه برشته تواند کشید تیزکومیزدور برشته نخواهیم کشید تیزکونکوزدور برشته
خواهید کشید تیزکوسیلار دور برشته خواهند کشید تیزناکوم و تیزکوم یوق برشته نخواهم کشید تیزا آلماغوم و تیزا آلغوم یوق برشته
کشیدن محکم نخواهد بود تیزکولوک برشته کشیدنی تیزکای و تیزایکای تیزنهاد و تیزسون و تیزدیات برشته کشد تیزکودیک و تیزدیک برشته
برشته کشیدنی و همچنانکه برشته کشد تیزمالت بکسر زا و سکون لام یعنی برشته کشیده شدن تیزیلکان و تیزیلورکان و تیزیلادورکان
برشته کشیده شونده و برشته کشیده شده چنانچه کوید الشاهد علی الاول کالمعنی الاخیر شعر کولار [illegible] تیشینک کمزی
اشکیم تیزیلکان انجو سلیک توزوب قطرالار قله شعر تیشلاد [illegible]

194r

ایجود شد بمعنی مصدر هم می آید و باقی صیغ بر مثال اول الامر اشتقاق می یابد تیزکینماک بسکون زا و نون و کسر کاف عجمی بمعنی پیوند
باشد و آن را چرکینماک هم کویند و تیکیماک هم کویند تیزکیندولک دوزیدیم تیزکینورم تیزکینادورم دوزم تیزکینادور دوزد
مصدر هم می آید تیزکینماید دوزد دوزنده و دوزیده است تیزکینکان تیزکینورکان تیزکینادورکان دوزنده و دوزیده و بمعنی مصدر هم آیند
تیزکین و تیزکینکیل مفرد مخاطب از فعل امر و تیزکین بمعنی ملابس هم بود چنانکه در [illegible] خواهد شد تیزکینما
تیزکینماکیل مفرد مخاطب از فعل نهی تیزکینینک و تیزکینینکیز و تیزکینینکلار جمع مخاطب از فعل امر تیزکینمانک و تیزکینمانکیز و تیزکینمانکلار
جمع مخاطب از فعل نهی تیزکینمان و تیزکینماس مین دوزم تیزکینامین تیزکینورمین تیزکینادورمین تیزکینورکه دوزم تیزکینماس
دوزد و بمعنی فاعل و مصدر منفی هم می آید تیزکینماسینکا بدوزی تیزکینورسنکا بدوزی تیزکینیب و تیزکینیبان
تیزکینمیش دوزیده الشاهد علی الاول شعر تیزکینیب ایله کیم فوبون آیلادی ایله کیم تو تون زخمی نالب [illegible]
بلا [illegible] تیزکینیشا [illegible] تیزکینا بولغای و تیزکینیب بولغای دوزد تواند تیزکینا آلغای دوزد تواند تیزکینا تیزکینا
دوزم دوزد تیزکینای تیزکینایین دوزیم دوزد [illegible] تیزکینکای و تیزکینکای تیزکینکلی [illegible]
دوزیم و دوزد تیزکینکالی برای دوزیدن و تا دوزیده تیزکیناج چون دوزید و دوزد و بعض دوزیدن تیزکینکوچی دوزنده
تیزکینکوجه و تیزکینکانجه تا دوزیدن و بمقدار دوزیدن تیزکینا آلغانینچه بمقداریکه دوز تواند تیزکینکومیزدور دوزیم
خواهیم دوزد تیزکینکونکوزدور دوزیم خواهید دوزد تیزکینکوسیلاردور خواهند دوزد تیزکیناکوم و تیزکینکوم یوق دوز نخواهم دوزد
تیزکینا آلماغوم و تیزکینا آلغوم یوق دوزیدن محکم نخواهد بود تیزکینکولوک دوزیدنی تیزکینکای و تیزکینلوتیز کینا و
تیزکینسون و تیزکینیدیک دوزیدنی تیزکینکودیک و تیزکینیدیک دوزیدنی و همچنانکه دوزند تیزکیلماک بمعنی متعدی است یعنی
دوزدادن و دوختن تیزکیلدور دوخت تیزکیلدی هم رسید چنانکه کوید الشاهد علی الاول شعر منا [illegible]
هر لحظه باشیمنی خار دصایو ورسانلک جوهر سوفنیل بوسر کردان شلبری و باقی صیغ بر مثال اول لفظ در اشتقاق می آید [illegible]
بکسر زا و سکون نون بدون زا نوشتن و صیغ آن بدستور موافق اول الاشتقاق می یابد تیز لالماک تیزکی روی یعنی تعجیل کردن
من الجوامد تیز بمعنی تند و سریع باشد چنانکه در لیلی و مجنون کوید شعر تیبیدا ایل فوبون آشیمه دم پراله او [illegible]
و نیز امر است از برشته کشیدن چنانکه کذشت و باشباع کسره زا نیز نامند الشاهد علیه شعر مست بولسام آستانینک
بر منکا باش قویماغی و حلیم کیم متکیه میلغای من تیز تیکی ناستانیب و نیز در خسرو و شیرین در صفت زمستان کوید شعر [illegible]
سیله معلق دم ایلاکب ایکی تیزکو کو اچر عکس ایلاب و بغلار سی یعنی سنک باشد تیزلت بفتح زا و سکون دال ابعاد کویند قطعه شعر
شاو نغدا تاپچیان او ت شعله سیدین تیزلک د [illegible] ایلماتدم آهنت و باشباع کسره دال باشد که جزل و استعمال آن از دهن [illegible]
الشاهد علیه شعر تیزلک آلغان انغه کیم حیکاد یهر وق توغیر یوق تورهر صفالی یولوق تیزکین بسکون زا و نون و کسر کاف عجمی
اسب بود که آن را سمند بی عنان و زمام خوانند و اتراک روم دیزکین نامند و نیز امر است از دوزدن چنانچه کذشت مع الیتین من المشتقات
تیسکیمالک و تیسکیندورماک همان تیزکیماک و تیزکیندورماک باشد که در حرف الشام الزا کذشت من الجوامد تیسکاری بسکون سین و
فتح و کسر راء مهمله همان تیسکیری بمعنی معکوس بود چنانچه در مقالة النبی وشم از محبوب القلوب در ذکر ملاحظان حرامنک کوید کر [illegible]
او نیغه تیسکاری مینک صرغایلار و شهر نینک کوی و محلاتیغه کیزده کالملار و مولفین زهی تیسکاری باشین قربشت خوانده با معنی [illegible]
کرده اند و قصر نظر نموده را شاهد آورده امد مع الیتین من المشتقات تیشمالت یعنی مصالح کردن الشاهد علیه شعر شول [illegible]

1947.

نهدوم قوقلوسون ده پچه ایکنه پیرله نقب تیشماق لطفه بولادیغه تیشتوک سوراخ کردیم تیشار و تیشادور سوراخ کند
و تیشلار بمعنی فاعل و مصدر هم می آید بیتشماید و سوراخ نمیکند و نکرده است تیشکان و تیشارکا و تیشادورکان سوراخ کننده و بمعنی
کرده و بمعنی مصدر هم می آید تیش و تیشکیل مفرد مخاطب فعل امر الشاهد علی الاول شعر لمرء کوریکیم کونکلونی تیشنلک
یول بولوپ غمزه کیم عشقینی ترک ایتکیل دیبان کوکسومنی تیش تیشما و تیشماکیل مفرد مخاطب فعل نهی تیشینک و تیشینکیز و تیشینکلار
جمع مخاطب فعل امر تیشماننک و تیشمانکیز و تیشمانکلار جمع مخاطب فعل نهی تیشمان و تیشمارمین سوراخ نمیکنم تیشامین و تیشارمین
تیشادورمین تیشادورام سوراخ میکنم تیشماس سوراخ نمیکند و بمعنی فاعل و مصدر منفی هم می آید تیشماسینکا بسوراخ نکردنت
تیشارینکا بسوراخ کردنت تیشیب و تیشیبان و تیشیمیش سوراخ کرده تیشیپتور سوراخ کرده تیشتانوک [illegible] تیشیب
سوراخ توان کرد تیشا آلغای سوراخ تواند کرد تیشا تیشا سوراخ کنان تیشای و تیشایین سوراخ کنم و کند و کنی
و کرده تیشاک و تیشکای من و تیشکای سن و تیشالی تیشالیلی سوراخ کنیم تیشکالی برای سوراخ کردن و تا سوراخ کرده تیشکاچ
چون سوراخ کرد و کند و بمعنی سوراخ کردن تیشکوچی سوراخ کننده تیشکوچه تیشکونچه تیشکاغه تا سوراخ کردن و تقدم سوراخ کردن
تیشای آلغاینکچه بعد بیکه سوراخ توانی کرد تیشکومیزدور سوراخ خواهیم کرد تیشکونکیزدور سوراخ خواهید کرد تیش
کوسیلاردور سوراخ خواهند کرد تیشاکوم و تیشکوم یوق سوراخ نخواهم کرد تیشا آلماغوم تیشا آلغوم [illegible] سوراخ کردن نکنم نخواهد بود
تیشکولوک سوراخ کردن تیشکای و تیشالی [illegible] سوراخ کند چنانکه شاهد بر [illegible] در
سنان باد مشا کوید شعر [illegible] و شاهد بر الثانی [illegible] کوید
[illegible] تیشا الار [illegible] تیشکودیک تیشادور [illegible] سوراخ کردنی
سوراخ کند تیشلماک بکسر تین و سکون لام بمعنی سوراخ شدن باشد و طالع هروی تیشلماق با تاء نوشته و بمعنی خراشیدن ذکر
کرده لفظ [illegible] و سقیم است تیشلکان و تیشلوکان و تیشلان [illegible] سوراخ شونده و سوراخ شده چنانکه [illegible] در [illegible]
کوید الشاهد علی الاول بالمعنی الثانی شعر [illegible] تیشلکان رشته [illegible] تیشلکان [illegible]
هم می آید تیشلماغ و تیشلماسین سوراخ نشوم و نشود و نشوی و نشده چنانکه شاهد بر افلا بمعنی سوراخ نشود کوید شعر
[illegible] تیشلماس [illegible] تیشلکودیک تیشلودیک سوراخ شدن
و چنانکه سوراخ شود الشاهد علی الاول بالمعنی الاخر شعر [illegible]
[illegible] تیشلکودیک [illegible] الاستقاق می باید تیشلاماک بسکون شین و فتح لام بدندان کزیدن
[illegible] برای کزیدن [illegible] محافظت کردن تیشلادوک بدندان کزیدیم تیشلار و تیشلادور بدندان میکزد و تیشلار بمعنی فاعل
و مصدر هم می آید چنانکه بمعنی مصدر میکوید شعر بوکه کونکلوم [illegible] تیشلار [illegible]
[illegible] تیشلاماید و بدندان نمیکزد و نکزیده است تیشلاکان و تیشلادورکان بدندان کزنده و بدندان کزیده و بمعنی مصدر
هم می آید تیشلا و تیشلاکیل مفرد مخاطب فعل امر تیشلاما تیشلاماکیل مفرد مخاطب فعل نهی تیشلانک و تیشلانکیز و تیشلانکلار جمع مخاطب
فعل امر تیشلامانک تیشلامانکیز تیشلامانکلار جمع مخاطب فعل نهی تیشلامان و تیشلامارمین بدندان نمیکزم تیشلامین و تیشلارمین و تیشلادورمین
تیشلادورام بدندان میکزم تیشلاماس بدندان نمیکزد و بمعنی فاعل و مصدر منفی هم می آید تیشلاماسینکا بدندان نکزیدنت
بدندان کزیدنت تیشلاب و تیشلابان و تیشلامیش بدندان کزیده الشاهد علی الاول شعر آشفته ساچینی [illegible] و تیشلاب

1952.

کرچه میلوبر پریشان سنبلغه تیشلار اله و له شعر بولدی [illegible] جسمیم [illegible] تیشلادی تیشلاب
[illegible] الشاهد علی الثانی شعر [illegible]
[illegible] تیشلاجان [illegible]
[illegible] تیشلادیم [illegible] بدندان کزیده تیشلاتا [illegible] بدندان توان کزید تیشلای آلغای بدندان تواند کزید
تیشلادی تیشلادی و تیشلای بدندان کزیده کنان تیشلای و تیشلایین بدندان بکزم و بکزد و بکزی و کزیده تیشلاکاج چون
بدندان کزید و بکزد و بمعنی کزیدن تیشلاکوچی بدندان کزنده تیشلاکوچه و تیشلاکونچه تیشلاکاغه تا بدندان کزیدن و تقدم بدندان کزیدن
تیشلای آلغاینکچه بعد بیکه بدندان توانی کزید تیشلاکوم دور بدندان نخواهم کزید تیشلاکونک دور بدندان خواهد کزید تیشلاکو
بدندان خواهد کزید چنانکه در کلیله و دمنه [illegible] شعر هر کیم [illegible] تیشلاب
کوسیلار تیشلاکوم و تیشلاکوم یوق بدندان نخواهم کزید تیشلای آلماغوم و تیشلای آلغوم یوق بدندان کزیدن نکنم نخواهد بود
تیشلاکولوک بدندان کزیدنی تیشلاکای تیشلاسون و تیشلادوک [illegible] بدندان بکزد و تیشلادی [illegible] بدندان کزیدنی و چنانکه
بدندان بکزد تیشلاشمالک مع [illegible] بمعنی مفاعله است یعنی یکدیکر را بدندان کزیدن و با یکدیکر جنگ کردن بدندان کزیدن تیشلاشیب و
تیشلاشیبان و تیشلاشمیش بدندان کزیده چنانکه کوید الشاهد علی الاول شعر بوراکیم [illegible] تیشلاشیب
کیم یا تا یو [illegible] بعضی [illegible]
شعر [illegible] کوید کرنی [illegible]
چوب کوده زمین [illegible] تیش سیور کو بترکی رومی [illegible] تیشوک یعنی سوراخ الشاهد علیه شعر [illegible]
[illegible] تیشوک [illegible] ساخته توشوک [illegible] تمام کویند لیکن
مصدر و صیغ مشتقه تمامی بکثرت استعمال میشود و بضم تا درست نیست تیشی یعنی ماده و انثی مع الفا تیقیتک پشم [illegible]
از [illegible] مع القاف من المشتقات تیقماق یعنی انباشتن و طپانیدن چنانکه کوید شعر [illegible]
[illegible] تیقتوق طپانیدیم تیقار و تیقادور و میطپاند و تیقار بمعنی فاعل و مصدر
می آید تیقمایدور نمیطپاند و نطپانیده است تیقغان و تیقارغان و تیقادورغان طپاننده و طپانیده الشاهد علی الاول المعنی الثانی
شعر [illegible] تیقغان [illegible] و بمعنی مصدر هم می آید
تیق و تیقغیل مفرد مخاطب فعل امر تیقما و تیقماغیل مفرد مخاطب فعل نهی تیقینک و تیقینکیز و تیقینکلار جمع مخاطب
فعل امر تیقمانک و تیقمانکیز و تیقمانکلار جمع مخاطب فعل نهی تیقمان و تیقمارمین نمیطپانم تیقامین و تیقارمین و تیقادورمین
تیقادورام میطپانم تیقماس نمیطپاند و بمعنی فاعل و مصدر منفی هم می آید تیقماسینکغه بنطپانیدنت تیقارینکغه بطپانیدنت
تیقیب و تیقیبان و تیقمیش طپانیده تیقیشانک طپانیده تیقتا بولغه و تیقیب بولغه توان طپانید تیقا آلغای تواند
طپانید تیقا تیقا انباشته کنان تیقای و تیقایین بطپانم و بطپاند و بطپانی و طپانیده تیقغا و تیقغای بر
تیقغای بز و تیقغالی تیقغالیلی برای طپانیدن و تا طپانیده تیقغاچ چون طپانید و بطپاند و بمعنی طپانیدن تیقغوچی طپاننده
تیقغوچه تیقغونچه تیقغاغه تا طپانیدن و تقدم طپانیدن تیقا آلغاینکچه بعد بیکه توانی طپانید تیقغومیزدور خواهیم طپانید
تیقغونکیزدور خواهید طپانید تیقغوسیلاردور خواهند طپانید تیقغاغوم و تیقغوم یوق نخواهم طپانید تیقا آلماغوم

1957 تیغا آلغوی بو قطلیپاندن محکم نخواهد بود تیقتولوق لیپاندن یعنی تیقغای مقلو تیقسلو تیقسون تیقندیک بطلپاند تیقتود یک و
تیقار دیک لیپاندن و همچنانکه بطلپاند تیقیلماق بکسر لام و تیقیلیشماق بکون لام و سکون یا و شین قرشت با جمعیت و ازدحام
بجای و طپیدن و صیغ تیقیلماق بالام و از تیقیلیشماق بالام و شین اشتقاق یابد بن ابجوامد تیقیلیش بمعنی ازدحام و فلو
چنانکه در تاریخ نابری مذکور است که آنداق تیقیلیش بولدی کیم نی ایلکاری کیلا والدیلار نی تاچقانیغه یول تاپا آلدیلار مع
الکاف و التشدید تیکماک باشباع کسره و سکون کاف سه معنی دارد اول بمعنی دوختن بود چنانکه کوید شعر جان رشته سینی چرمادیم
اوتونکه وای کیم تیکنک ناغیزینی یلرهی و تیکماککا تاریوق دویم بالمجاز بمعنی نصب کردن باشد سیم غرس کردن درخت بود و
اشباع با کاف عجمی به معنی آمده اول خوردن چیزی بچیزی از قبیل تیر و سنگ و زخم و امثال آن الشاهد علیه شعر تیغ ظلمی تیکماکی
دین الامسا ایل کونکلی بیم تیکماسون غیر غیغه دیب کونکلوم توهم ایلاکای دویم رسیدن سیم آزردن تیکتی دوخت و نصب کرد
و غرس کرد چنانکه در داستان هفتم از سبعه سیاره کوید بالمعنی الاول شعر بیلکاج اول عوض خاطر ایاکی تیکتی ایکی قولنی آیب
خاکی و معنی با کاف عجمی سیم و حدی کوید شعر وصال الحمنی ایکینم فراقنا یتم و نا فالنی تیکتیم جفا تا یتم تیکتی
بلا اشباع با کاف عجمی یعنی خورد و رسید و آزرد الشاهد علیه بالمعنی الاول شعر تابینک سو قید اجسیم قرخونا بیر وه
هر جون تاشی آنکا کیم تیکتی لعل ناب ایروه و نیز در خسرو شیرین در طلسم کشودن فرهاد کوید شعر چو تیکتی اول لخت ترواتا
بقیلدی بو خند نیک امکن نکونساش و نیز تام یکنوع هوا یست چنانکه در ذیل جو امد مذکور شود تیکار دوزد و رسید و نصب
و غرس میکند و بلا اشباع با کاف عجمی میخورد و میرسد و می آزرد و تیکار بمعنی فاعل و مصدر هم می آید چنانکه در فصل بپ هشتم
از محبوب القلوب در وصف اهل سوق بمعنی آزرنده کوید که مینک کا تیکار نی یوزکا المامدین آلاغه یوق پرهیز اوبات و باکاف عجمی
مع اللاشباع بمعنی دوختن کوید شعر کوزنی همندری نظیغه توغیاندا کاشکی آندا تیکارکا ایلاشا کیم بیکلا تی یعنی شیش و باکاف عجمی بلا
اشباع بمعنی رسیدن فرماید شعر قیلیم حیفنی ایبانک بیلکا اموره تیغ چیکت تا تیکاردین ایاب یرکین اینا کین و اول الحدید تیکماید
عمید و زد و نه دوخته است و نصب و غرس نکند و نکرده است و بلا اشباع نمیخورد و نخورده است و نمیرسد و نرسیده است و نمی آزرد و نیازرده
تیککان و تیکار کان و تیکادورکان مع اللاشباع دوزنده و دوخته و نصب و غرس کننده و نصب و غرس کرده چنانکه شاهد بر اول
بعض دوخته کوید شعر قامتیم دال و نیاتیم کلرنک ایبره تا نازایلا دال و کل تیککان هالی اصره آرام ایلاه دینک و باکاف عجمی بلا اشباع
یعنی خورنده و خورده و رسنده و رسیده و آزرنده و آزرده چنانکه در فضایل الحبه در ذکر ابو طاهر کرد شاهد بر اول در باب ناغ زندکو
بمعنی غرس کرده و رسیده کوید که مینک انام ملکیدا امری تیککان و منکا میراث تیککان درخت دین ایره و بمعنی رسیده هم می آید
چنانکه باکاف عجمی بلا اشباع بمعنی خوردن در حیرت الابرار در وصف فرهاد کوید الشاهد علی الاول شعر آرقاغه دستاری و جی
تیککان تیر اوجری برله اموریب کردن ونیز در خسرو شیرین کوید شعر او چوب تیککا نداز دستی آهنکث که بلیبان اوق جاج
فرستی آهنکث و بمعنی رسیدن فرماید شعر التون ابزمیب اریب کونکاز شادی خالص بولورش فی عجب شاد ظرسه یوزه تیککان سالی
ایمکان منکا تیک و تیککید مع اللاشباع امر است از دوختن و نصب و غرس کردن چنانکه شاهد بر اول بعض اولکوید شعر
ای نوای اول سیخادم قو یاش چین امر دیغ زخم او صیو ایکیه سی و مرهم تاری بیله تیک وتیک چیزیست بیناده هم کویند چنانکه در
جو امد کور خواهد شد و با کاف عجمی بلا اشباع امراست از خوردن و رسیدن و آزردن و تیککیل نیز مرادف آنست تیکما و تیکما کید
مفرد مخاطب مضاف امر نیک تیکینکاه تیکینکر و تیکینکلار جمع مخاطب مضاف امر تیکماک و تیکما نکر و تیکما نکلار جمع مخاطب مضاف نفی

1962 تیکمان و تیکمان بین بمیدوزم و نصب و غرس نمیکنم و با کاف عجمی بلا اشباع نمیخورم و نمیرسم و نمی آزرم تیکماس نمیدوزد و نصب و غرس
نمیکند و با کاف عجمی بلا اشباع نمیخورد و نمیرسد و نمی آزرد چنانکه بمعنی نمیرسد کوید شعر آغزینکا تیکماس هلال زینک برله سوزنینک
خورشید بر لهٔ نمرزینک و مؤلف روحی نوشته که معنی لیاقت ندارد یعنی لیاقت ندارد و بمعنی فاعل و مصدر منفی هم می آید چنانکه
رسیدن کوید شعر فهم ایتایخشی یامان و صلینک منکا تیکماس کیم بخشی لار دین یخشی یین بین یامان لار دین یامان و در
فرماید شعر او قونک کونکلوم کا تیکماس دین غباری یردی کونکلوم دا غباری ولتور و شمیش تا سو سیپتینک آندا یکانیدین و
عزالدین در تاریخ الملوک در ذکر سلطنت تمراز اد کوید که ایلغینه ایتا قیب محلاقینه سوداراینلار کیم تیکماس کیچه سلطنت خبا
قیلسه سزا بی بود و هر تیکما سینکا تبد و ختنت و نصب و غرس نکونت و با کاف عجمی بلا اشباع نخورونت و نرسیدنت و نیازردنت
تیکار تیکا تبد و ختنت و نصب و غرس کردنت و با کاف عجمی بلا اشباع بخوردنت و برسیدنت و بیازردنت تیکیب و تیکیبان قه تیکیر
دوخته و نصب و غرس کرده الشاهد علی الاول کا المعنی الاول شعر مین نازلیغان کبی در لعل ارامیلنا من نظر کوز کرمت
نین تیکیب مین اول لب خندان لرا و در سکندر نامه کوید بالمعنی الثانی شعر یا خندقا آیدا موند و تیکیب تا لین نیشکرلی
که هندو تیکیب و با کاف عجمی بلا اشباع یعنی خورده و رسیده و آزرده چنانکه شاهد بر اول در معنی خورده در مجالس النفایس
وصف ریاضی کوید که شاکردلاری تاغ کیشی تکا بلیر بتلش بیما الاینیب بقیرغه تیکیب اولوب ایریشو بمعنی رسیده در سکندر
در وصف دارا کوید شعر بو لوب کوپ کیانی ایش لمداشا آنکا تیکیب بمعنی الت میراث آنکا تیکیشاتک دوخته و نصب و غرس
کرده و با کاف عجمی بلا اشباع خورده و رسیده و آزرده تیکنا بو لنای و تیکیب بولغنه توان دوخت و نصب و غرس توان کرد و با کاف
عجمی توان خورد و توان رسید و توان آزرد تیکا آلغای تواند دوخت و نصب و غرس تواند کرد و با کاف عجمی بلا اشباع تواند خورد و تواند
تیکا تیکا و دوزان و دوزان و نصب کنان و غرس کنان و با کاف عجمی بلا اشباع تا ند خورده تا ند رسید و آزرده ایریدی
رسید و تواند آزرد تیکای و تیکای بین بدوزم و بدوزد و بدوزی و دوخته و نصب کنم و کند و کنی و کرده و با کاف عجمی بلا اشباع
و تیکای
بخورم و بخورد و بخوری و خورده و برسم و برسد و برسی و رسیده و بیازرم و بیازرد و بیازری و آزرده تیکنا ای تیکای کل تیکا کای بیز
تیکالینک بدوزیم و نصب و غرس کنیم و با کاف عجمی بلا اشباع بخوریم و برسیم و بیازریم تیکای کلی برای دوختن و تا دوخته و برای نصب
و غرس کردن و تا کرده و با کاف عجمی بلا اشباع برای خوردن و تا خورده و برای رسیدن و تا رسیده و برای آزردن تا آزرده تیککاج
چون دوخت و بدوزد و بمحض دوختن و چون نصب و غرس کند و بمحض کردن چنانکه بمعنی بمحض غرس کردن کوید شعر او قونک
کونکلوم کا تیککاج قطره تا نالهٔ آمتی کیم کوره ایش نهال آنداق کیم آبی تیککاج اوق بولغای شیدا و با کاف عجمی بلا اشباع چون خورد
و بخورد و بمحض خوردن و چون رسید و برسد و بمحض رسیدن و چون آزرد و بیازرد و بمحض آزردن تیککو جی فاعل معانی
تیککو چه و تیککو غه و تیککا نغه تا دوختن و بمقدار دوختن و تا نصب و غرس کردن و بمقدار آن و با کاف عجمی بلا اشباع تا خوردن و بمقدار
و تا رسید و بمقدار رسیدن و تا آزردن و بمقدار آزردن تیکا آلمایدر بمقدار تواند دوخت و نصب و غرس تواند کرد و تواند
و تواند رسید و تواند آزرد تیککو میدور خواهیم دوخت و نصب و غرس خواهیم کرد و با کاف عجمی بلا اشباع خواهیم خورد و
خواهیم رسید و خواهیم آزرد تیککو نکو زد و در خطاب بجمع حاضر تیکمان تیکما تیککو سیلار در صیغه جمع غایب تیکمان تیکما کوم
تیککو بو ق نخواهم دوخت و نصب و غرس نخواهم کرد و با کاف عجمی بلا اشباع نخواهم خورد و نخواهم رسید و نخواهم آزرد تیکا آلماغوم تیکا آلغوم
دوختن و نصب و غرس کردن محکم نخواهد بود و با کاف عجمی بلا اشباع خوردن و رسیدن و آزردن محکم نخواهد بود تیککولوک دوختنی
و نصب و غرس کردنی و با کاف عجمی بلا اشباع خوردنی و رسیدنی و آزردنی تیککای تیکاو تیکلی تیککو نوتیک بلند بلند و نصب و غرس کند

و باکاف عجمی بجوید و بسد و بیرزد تیکیکودیلنتیکاردیک دو جنتی و همچنانکه بدوزد و نصب کردن و همچنانکه نصب کند و باکاف
عجمی خون ریزد و همچنانکه بجوید و بسیدنی و همچنانکه برسد و لمزیدنی و همچنانکه بخیزد تیکیشمالک مع الیاء ضمیر مفعول
یعنی با هم خیالی کردن و باکاف عجمی بلا اشباع دو معنی دارد اول تبدیل و معاوضه کردن دوم بیکلیکویدیک و ملاقی کردن و مجازاً
بمعنی جنک کردن هم مستعملست و همین لفظات که ترکمن و اوزبک حرف ساخته دو کوشفاک میکویند تیکیشوک با هم خیالی
کردیم و باکاف عجمی تبدیل کردیم و ملاقی و جنک کردیم تیکیشوبلار تیکیشادورلار با هم خیالی میکنند و باکاف عجمی تبدیل میکنند
و تیکیشیم بمعنی فاعل و مصدر هم می آید و تیکیشایدورلار با هم خیالی میکنند و نکرده اند و باکاف عجمی تبدیل میکنند و نکرده اند
و جنک میکنند و نکرده اند تیکیشکالو تیکیشوکان تیکیشادورکان با هم خیالی کننده و خیالی کرده و باکاف عجمی تبدیل کننده و تبدیل کرده
و ملاقی و جنک کننده و کرده و بمعنی مصدر هم می آیند تیکیش و تیکیشکیل مفرد مخاطب امر فعل امر تیکیشما و تیکیشما کیل مفرد
مخاطب نهی فعل نهی تیکیشسینلار و تیکیشسینکیز تیکیشینکلار جمع مخاطب امر فعل امر تیکیشمانکیز تیکیشمانکلار جمع مخاطب فعل نهی
تیکیشمان و تیکیشماسمن متکلم وحده از فعل نفی تیکیشامین و تیکیشورمین و تیکیشادورمین و تیکیشودورام خیالی میکنم و باکاف عجمی تبدیل میکنم
و ملاقی و جنک میکنم تیکیشماس مفرد غایب از صیغه مضارع منفی تیکیشماسینکا بخیالی نکردنت و باکاف عجمی تبدیل
نکردنت و ملاقی و جنک نکردنت تیکیشورینکا بخیالی کردنت و باکاف عجمی تبدیل کردنت و ملاقی و جنک کردنت تیکیشیب و
تیکیشبان و تیکیشمیش خیالی کرده و باکاف عجمی تبدیل کرده و ملاقی و جنک کرده تیکیشیشالغ خیالی کرده و باکاف عجمی تبدیل کرده
و ملاقی و جنک کرده تیکیشالغای و تیکیشیب توغای خیالی توان کرد و باکاف عجمی تبدیل توان کرد و ملاقی و جنک توان کرد تیکیشا
آلغای خیالی تواند کرد و باکاف عجمی تبدیل تواند کرد و ملاقی و جنک تواند کرد تیکیشا تیکیشا خیالی کنان و باکاف عجمی تبدیل کنان
و ملاقی کنان و جنک کنان تیکیشای و تیکیشایین خیالی بکنم و بکند و بکنی و کرده و باکاف عجمی تبدیل و ملاقی و جنک کنم و کند و کنی
و کرده و باکاف عجمی تبدیل و ملاقی و جنک کنم و کند و کنی و کرده تیکیشالی و تیکیشکالی و تیکیشکای و تیکیشالیک تیکیشالینک
خیالی بکنیم و باکاف عجمی تبدیل و ملاقی و جنک بکنیم تیکیشکالی برای خیالی کردن و تا خیالی کرده و باکاف عجمی برای تبدیل کردن
و تا تبدیل کرده و برای ملاقی و جنک کردن و تا کرده تیکیشکاچ چون خیالی کرد و کند و باکاف عجمی چون تبدیل کرد و کند و چون ملاقی
و جنک کرد و کند تیکیشکوچی فاعل صیغه مذکوره تیکیشکو تیکیشکیچه تیکیشکالیچه تا خیالی کردن و بعد خیالی و باکاف عجمی تا
تبدیل کردن و بعد تبدیل کردن و تا ملاقی و جنک کردن و بعد از آن تیکیشا آلمای بنکیم نمیتوانم خیالی توانی کرد و باکاف عجمی
تبدیل توانی کرد و جنک توانی کرد تیکیشکوسیدورمن خیالی خواهیم کرد و باکاف عجمی تبدیل خواهیم کرد و ملاقی و جنک خواهیم کرد
تیکیشکونکوزدور مخاطب جمع حاضر تیکیشکوسیلار مخاطب جمع غایب تیکیشکولوک خیالی کردنی و باکاف عجمی تبدیل کردنی و ملاقی
و جنک کردنی تیکیشکالیلار و تیکیشالار و تیکیشالار تیکیشسونلار و تیکیشکای خیالی کنند و باکاف عجمی تبدیل کنند و ملاقی
و جنک کنند چنانکه شاهد براول بمعنی اخیر در تاریخ نابری مذکوراست که فرمان بولدی که برانغار جوانغار هم بویرونغیم
سله تیکیشکایلار جوانغاردین فلان بویرونغ قتیکیشی تیکیشکودیلنه تیکیشوریالیک خیالی کردنی و همچنانکه خیالی کند و باکاف
عجمی تبدیل کردنی و همچنانکه تبدیل کند و ملاقی و جنک کردنی و همچنانکه کند تیکیلمالک مع الاشباع بکسر کاف و سکون لام بمعنی
دارد اول دوخته شدن دوم نصب شدن سیم فرو شدن درخت و مجازاً بمعنی مستظهر شدن هم استعمال میشود تیکیلو و تیکیلکا
دوخته میشود و نصب و فرو میشود چنانکه شاهد براول بمعنی اول در محبوب القلوب کوید که باشلاریغه کل ها نغانک آلاردین

یوزونکا تیکان سانجیلوری کراول سانجاغی در قلبسانک باغریغه چوکیر تیکیلوسی و بطنرا بمعنی مستظهر میشود و تیکیلور بمعنی فاعل
و مصدر هم می آید تیکیلکان و تیکیلوکان و تیکیلادورکان دوخته شونده و دوخته شده و نصب و فرو شونده و شده چنانکه شاهد
براول بمعنی دوخته شده کوید شعر ای نوای آچتی کوکسوم نینک تیکیلکان چاکینی نامه سی تونوم دا بیکم اضطرابیدین کونکول
مستظهر شونده و مستظهر شده هم مستعملست و بمعنی مصدر هم می آید تیکیل و تیکیلکیل مفرد مخاطب فعل امر به معنی نیز از این
مستظهر شدن چنانکه کوید الشاهد علی الاول شعر ای نوای سعی ایله چون وصل الماسین بهلادی یار لطفیغه تیکیل ایمدی غیرنی
نونکول تیکیلیب تیکیلیبان و تیکیلیش دوخته شده و نصب و فرو شده الشاهد علی الاول المعنی الثانی من حیرت الابرار
شعر تا تیکیلیب او شبو بیت نامرکا بولدی مهیا بوا ولوغ کارکا و نیز بمعنی مستظهر شده تیکیلکای و تیکیلکای و تیکیلکای
تیکیلدیلر دوخته شود و نصب شود و فرو شود چنانکه شاهد براول بمعنی ثانی کوید شعر لعلکون می باشند
بولساکیشی نینک ای حریف نفعی کوپ ای کیم تیکیلکای تا جیدا شهوار لعل و نیز بمعنی مستظهر شود و باقی صیغ بر سیاق بالا اشتقاق
می یابد تیکورمالک بضم کاف عجمی و سکون را مصدر متعدیست یعنی رسانیدن چنانکه در مقاله دهم از حیرت الابرار کوید شعر
کایماس ایلیکا نفع تیکورمالک هم اولورتیل ایلکا و بمعنی مصدر منفی کوید شعر جهان خاکی ایره کلوخ مانی نا پاک اینالک تیکورمانی
اولی ملوث اولسه کلوخ تیکورمی رسانید الشاهد علیه شعر بوزوغ کونکلومنی کوزیاشیم بوسیردی تیکوردی سیل
ویرانیغه آفت تیکورا باشلادی رسانیدن آغاز کرد چنانکه حیدر تلبه در معرض دزد کراولیبی و مردی قافله در صفت خانم طی
کوید شعر بولدی بیکیت سوز لاکی دین منفعل کوپ تیکورا باشلادی خاتمه تیل تیکور و تیکورادور میرساند چنانکه شاهد
براو لعل در مقاله ششم از حیرت الابرار در تعریف بیسلاطین کوید شعر مهمی خفی دا ایره دیلار نوشی ایچیدین تیکوریشلار تیکورما
تیکورانکو تیکورمالکا رسانید الشاهد علی الاول شعر کوز تیکورمانک ای پری لار کیم کونکلوم چشمه سین اولپری و حور رضوان تیرشکی مین
ایلاهیمیش تیکورکای بمعنی کو تیکورنا و تیکورورون و تیکوردیلر برسانند الشاهد علی الاول شعر کونکلوم اندیشه سی و صلینک
در هوا سیدبو کیم حورادیغه تیکورکای چاره دیر خیال اندیش و باقی صیغ بر همین سیاق اشتقاق می یابد تیکورمالک بسکون کاف
و رای مهمله و ضم تای ثانی فرشته مصدر متعدیست یعنی دوزانیدن و نصب فرمودن تیکورودولار دوزانیدیم و نصب فرمودیم تیکوندور
تیکورادور میدوزاند و نصب میفرماید و بمعنی فاعل و مصدر هم می آید و باقی صیغ آنهم بر همین نهج بسکون کاف با لفظ تور اشتقاق می یابد
تیک تورماق ساکت و خاموش ایستادن تیک توردوق ساکت ایستادیم تیک توراور تیک توردور ساکت می ایستد تیک توراو
بمعنی فاعل و مصدر هم می آید تیک تورمایدور ساکت نمی ایستد و نا ایستاده است تیک تورغان تیک تورغان تیک تورادورکان ساکت
ایستنده و ایستاده و بمعنی مصدر هم می آیند چنانکه شاهد براول بمعنی مصدری در تاریخ الملوک در ذکر بهرام چوبینه کوید
که پرویز جواب بر نمای الار آنینک تیلی تورغاندین اول ایشکا رضا منهم قیلماق تهمتی سیله هرموزنی هلاک قیلیب تیک توردی تور
مفرد مخاطب فعل امر الشاهد علی الاول شعر تا نکلادی کوثر اوچون دیریسین بوکونی ایچماکیل تیک توراغ زاهد نوای سین کیمی ساقی
مود می تیک تورما و تیک تورماغیل مفرد مخاطب فعل نهی چنانکه در آغاز نظم سبعه سحریه کوید الشاهد علی الثانی شعر
سخنی سر و حریفانه جیک پراون پرله تیک تورماغیل ایا نه جیک تیک تورونکلار تیک تورونکیز تیک تورونکلار جمع مخاطب فعل امر تیک توراالنک
تیک تورمانکیز و تیک تورمانکلار جمع مخاطب فعل نهی تیک تورمان و تیک تورماسمین ساکت نمی ایستم تیک تورورمین و تیک توراادورمین و تیک توراادورام
تیک توراالم ساکت می ایستم تیک توراادورمین و تیک توردوم ساکت ایستادم چنانکه شاهد براو در نظم خمسه نجبه در ذکر خانی

کوید که معنی مطلوب اونیله تیمه او قمچین بز سنکا قولاق سانغلج تیله توتمارسین تیک توتقاس تمام ایستد و بمعنی اول
منقوش هم می آید تیک توزماسینکه شاکت ناینادنت تیک توزرونکه و شاکت ایتادنت تیک توزوب تیله توتقان
شاکت ایتاده تیک توزوب تانک شاکت ایتاده تیک توزوب تیک تارناید توز ایتادنه شاکت تیزوان ایتاد چنانکه در داستان ششم
سیلو کوید کلا شاهد علی الاول شعر صند لا لیسیدا تیک توزوب بولماس مسلکی کیمنا یاشوروب بولماس ظالم هر دو کینا را
در این شعر از خمسه سیتیو کیا بیقوتیلیم خواند و کینا را بحقر تیاس معنی نامه نوشته و شعر به ملا شاهد آورده
توتماولنای تیک توربو شاکت تواز ایتاد تیک توزوا آغای شاکت تواندا ایتاد تیک توزوا شاکت ایتاده ایتاده
تیک توزای تیک توزن شاکت بایتیم و بایتید و بایتی وایتاده چنانکه در بنای الطبیر کوید کلا شاهد علی الاول شعر
ظالیم عنی توتای بارنا بتای سوزچین باتیک توزای بیلمان بیناقی تیک توزناق و تیک توزمانو تیک توزمای بز تیک توزلیب توزلاز
شاکت بایتیم تیک توزغلب برای شاکت ایتادن و ناشاکت ایتاده تیک توزلاج بمحض شاکت ایتادن تیک توزغوجی شاکت
مذکور تیک توزغوجه و تیک توزغوزه و تیک توزغاغه تا شاکت ایتادن و بمقدار شاکت ایتادن تیک توزا آقانینکه بمقدارچه کم
توانی ایتاد تیک توزغوزه و شاکت خواهیم ایتاد تیک توزغوزیرد و شاکت خواهید ایتاد تیک توزغوسیلادرد و شاکت خواهند
تیک توزغانموم و تیک توزغوم یوق شاکت نخواهیم ایتاد تیک توزالمغوم تیک توزالغوم یوق تا شاکت ایتاد بحکم نخواهد بود تیک
توزغولوق شاکت ایتادن تیک توزغاغو تیک توزایتیک توزماو تیک توزغوچون و تیک توزدور بانشاکت باید تیک توزغودیک تیک توزلار
شاکت ایتادن و همچنانکه باید تیک توزغوزناق مصدر متعدی است بمعنی شاکت ساختن تیک توزغوزیه شاکت ساخت
چنانکه در خمسه المحبه دو کوید کلا شاهد علی هیتی شیخ سیلا او توز سیدا اولتوروب بارد علی ایتکوالملق شیخ مجلس
اهلیغه تیک توزغوزدی و باق صیغ برناق اشتقاق بی باید تیکرانا ق تبکون کاف و فتح راء مهمله بمعنی درهم زدن و کوبیدن
چنانکه در خمسه آزاد خود کوید شعر هر شام حرفه تیکرو تیکرانا قوینة بولا و برنا و لایتیه اتیدا تیفا قایتی شی مصیبه تیکرانا
کوبید تیکرانا بدق درهم زدیم تیکرانور تیکرانا درهم درهم زدند و تیکرانور معنی فاعل و مصدر هم می آید تیکرانا باید درهم زد
تیکرانات تیکرانشان و تیکرانور فان و تیکرانا درهم زند و درهم زند درهم زده و بمعنی مصدر هم می آید تیکرانیل مفرد غایب
امر تیکرانا مل و تیکرانا غوچی تیکرانمان و تیکرانا اکچی مخاطب تیکراتمان تیکرانا اکاس و تیکرانا اسین تیکرانور مین و تیکرانا اکو باغم
درهم زنم تیکرانماس درهم نزند و معنی فاعل و مصدر هم می آید تیکرانا سینکه درهم نزنده تیکرانورکه درهم زنده تیکرانب
تیکرانمان و تیکرانیش درهم زده تیکرانا تیکرانافا نیکرانیب درهم زد و تیکرانا ناب درهم زده درهم زد تیکرانا غیه درهم زده
تیکرانا تیکرانا درهم زدن درهم زدن تیکرانا ناو تیکرانکاچی درهم زدن و درهم زده تیکرانا ق و تیکرانا پازه تیکرانا ناو ... درهم
تیکرانکوچی تا درهم زنم تیکرانغلب برای درهم زدن و نادرهم زده تیکرانلاج بمحض درهم زدن تیکرانغوچی درهم زنده تیکرانغو
تیکرانغوغه تیکرانا غه تا درهم زدن و بمقدار درهم زدن تیکرانا آقانینکه بمقدار چه درهم توانی زد تیکرانغوزیرد درهم خواهیم
تیکرانغوزه درهم خواهید زد تیکرانغوسیلادرد درهم خواهند زد تیکرانغوم و تیکرانغوم یوق درهم نخواهم زد تیکرانا الکان
تیکرانا الغوم یوق درهم زدن بحکم نخواهد بود تیکرانغولوق درهم زدن تیکرانا نای تیکرانا نای تیکرانا ناو تیکرانغوچون تیکرانغودیک درهم زند
تیکرانغودیک تیکرانغولیک درهم زدن و همچنانکه درهم زنند تیکرانور درهم زنو ق در اینجا سخن و صیغ آن بدستور لفظ مذکور اشتقاق تیکرانماق
تیکرالاماق بکسر کاف و سکون راء مهمله و فتح لام مصدر متعدی است بمعنی غلطاندن و تیکرالاتماق متعدی کوید تیکرالا دولو غلطاندن

تیکرلادی و تیکرلایدور میغلطاند و تیکرلار بمعنی فاعل و مصدر هم می آید تیکرلانایدور میغلطاند و نغلطانید باست تیکرلا
تیکرلار کان و تیکرلانیپ کان غلطانده و غلطانیده و بمعنی مصدر هم می آید تیکرلا و تیکرلاکیل مفرد غایب امر از فعل امر تیکرلا ما
تیکرلانالکیل مفرد غائب امر از فعل نیه تیکرلالمعتیکر لانکیز و تیکرلانکلار جمع غائب امر تیکرلا ما نلغ تیکرلانا نکیز و تیکرلا نا جمع غائب امر
تیکرلا مان و تیکرلا ناس مین میغلطانم تیکرلا سین و تیکرلاسیز و تیکرلایدور و تیکرلا نام میغلطانم تیکرلاناس میغلطاند و بمعنی
فاعل و مصدر هم می آید تیکرلامانسینکا نغلطاند تیکرلارینکا نغلطاند نغلطانید تیکرلا بو تیکرلا ما دور تیکرلانیش غلطانده تیکرلا
میشانک غلطانده تیکرلا سابولغانه و تیکرلاب بولغانوا زغلطانیده تیکرلا ای آغای تواندغلطانید تیکرلا ای تیکرلا ای و تیکرلا یو
غلطانده غلطاندن تیکرلا لاغو تیکرلا لاینین نغلطانم و نغلطاند و نغلطانبی و غلطاندن تیکرلانسالغو تیکرلا کالیمز و تیکرلا ناوی و تیکرلا
نغلطانیم تیکرلا کابی برای غلطاندن و ناغلطانیدن تیکرلا لاکاج بمحض غلطاندن تیکرلا کوچی غلطاننده تیکرلا کوجه
تیکرلا کوغه تیکرلا کاغه تا غلطاندن و بمقدار غلطاندن تیکرلا آقانینکه بمقدار چه توانی غلطانید تیکرلا کوسیزد و تیکرلاکوم
تیکرلا کونکه و ... نخواهید غلطانید تیکرلاکوسیلادرد و نخواهند غلطانید تیکرلا ناکوم و تیکرلا کوم یوق نخواهم غلطانید تیکرلا
الملغوم و تیکرلا لای آلغوم یوق غلطانیدن بحکم نخواهد بود تیکرلا کای و تیکرلا سلو تیکرلا سون و تیکرلا دیلت غلطاند تیکرلا کوید
تیکرلا ردیک غلطاندنی و همچنانکه نغلطاند تیکرلا تماک مصدر متعدی است از تیکرلا ماک باشد و صیغ آن با تای
قرشت اشتقاق می باید تیکرلا ماک مع النون تیکرلا تماک مع الشین بمعنی غلطیدن بود و صیغ تیکرلا تماک با نون و از
تیکرلا تماک با شین اشتقاق می باید تیکلاتماک و تیکلا تماک تیکلیک بسکون کاف و شین قرشت و فتح لام دو معنی دارد اول تیز
نگاه کردن و دقیم راست ایتادن و با دال ابجد مستعمل است ما مواهد تیلت بیج معنی لمده اول المرادات تشبیهات که در آخر الفاظ
مشهوره بمعنی مانند باشد و مولد استعمال آن در دیباچه کتاب در صنایع مام نکاشته آمد دویم بمعنی شاکت و خاموش بود چنانکه شاه
آن در ذیل صیغ تیک توزماق مذکور شد سیم بمعنی فریفتها چنانکه کوید شعر منظور حسن و جمال العولادی یوز تیلک آنداق کیم
شاد ایتیب عالم الهین تیلک مینی عرو بز صیلدی و له جمعلادیبی بادین یا رو معتمد تیلدینک آزاده تیلک مینی دود ایدیم
چهارم تحت سند خود الکو نید پنجم حرف ترجی است بترکی رومی بمعنی کاش و کاشکی باشد ششم راست از رسیدن هفتم راست خوردن
بمعنی تصادم هشتم راست از رسیدن چنانکه در ذیل مصادر کذشت و این سه معنی اخیر با فعل بیز مستعملست و با شلغ کسره سه
اول بمعنی راست منزیج و بمعنی جنید بود الشاهد علیه شعر اولتلیغ توتلوقای بصر نصر فاندا تعظیمیم ضرب تیک شیلکیم خاتانا
کوبید کاسه بولغای بیت دویم راست زدن و بمعنی سیم راست زغضب کردن چنانکه کذشت تیکالک بفتح کاف بمعنی تا کانکو بود
و ماننده را نجا بیا همه نامند و بفتح تا نیز استعمال می شود تیکان خار باشد که آن را بعربی شوک نامند شعر سیلاجه کبی کلاف تیکی زاده
کونکلوم بولمر بلبل بیری دایم تیکانلاستیکری تیکون کاف عجمی و کسر دال ابجد ایت که از بوت و نمد دوزند و نیز بمعنی رسید و بضرب
خورد و لرزید تیکرا بسکون کاف و فتح راء قرشت دوره و المراعرا کونید و آکچت شعر ثمینیکه لکن بولغلج املاک لوله
دیر پروانه لار او ریلاه تیکرلنالا کریچرخ و له شعر بوز فلک فلک تیکراسید اخط مود و بنا صنع ترکانه قوبلاس تیلک تیوره
بحریرا و چون ایتمیش مدبر خط تیکرو بفتح راء قرشت لفظیست موضوع از برای انتهاکه بمعنی حتی استعمال میشود الشاهد علیه
شعر خوبلاره قول بولدیلار ولیکن پر یلاره تا چی لاره خوبلاره نیکم سوز فلک ایردی بو یرکا تیکرو خوت تیکره بکسر کاف و اول
رای مهمله و کاف ثانی و فتح لام غلطان را کونید و اتراک دوم چرخ عراده را مانند تیکیه بفتح میم بمعنی بده چنانکه تاریخ

1987

بابوری منذ کهراست که شکل وشمایلی دیب بولوق تیکرمه سغال لیغ قوبا یوزلوك تنبل کیشی ایدی دروتبه آزاد کمر میکونید

× تیکرمان مع النون سیار اکویند الشاهد علیه شعر کوك تیکرمان ناشی آیلاند ورناق ایسار باشیمه دیما آی وکون بوکیم

× باشیم اوزه سیلدرد قهر تیکمش بکسر کاف وسکون شین بمعنی خیالت بود وبا کاف عجمی سه معنی دارد اول یعنی ببکلیکر رسیدن دوم

تلاشی وهیم خوردن وجنك کردن چنانکه درمقاله دلار ابا اسکندر کوید شعر ایکی شاه هرنا برابرش ونکرید آ یاشا ازکری

× برله تیکیش ونکرید آسیم بمعنی لرزش بود تیکیشجه بفتح جیم یعنی تا هنکام تلاشی ورسیدن بیکلیکر چنانکه درسد سکندری

درنعوت پادشاهی کشمیر ضیرورز بن ملو کوید شعر مقصر بو نوع ایکیلم ایکی آیی بولاق کشمرنیك اوزره دفتو فرایی بوسیادیله

× جمع الیلاب سپاه تیکیشجه باریغه بیرپنج داه تیکیك لیسك دوخته شدن چنانکه درزبانیم الحبه درذکر شیخ عبد

القادر کیلانی ودچارشدن بدزدان با وکوید که اوغری دیدی که نینك بار دیدیم قرق آلتون دیدی قانی دیدیم تونومدا

× تیل دمع اللام من المشتقات تیلماك دو معنی دارد اول سوراخ کردن وآن ماخوذ از تیلوك باشد دویم جزبر اخط خط وشرحه شرحه

بریدن وآن ماخوذ از تیلیم است یعنی قلچ برید تیلدی سوراخ کرد وشرحه شرحه برید چنانکه بمعنی اخیر کوید شعر جکرکبا

میل ایتماکان ایسا اولست نوایا نینکا باغر ینکی هرطرفنی تیلدی وله شعر بند ایشیتیب دوستلار هجر کیم سیله یار اولمانکی

کیم مینك باغریم تیغ هجر بیله تیلدی تا تیلدوك سوراخ کردیم وخطخط بریدیم تیلادر وتیلادور سوراخ میکند وشرحه شرحه

میبرد وتیلادر بمعنی فاعل ومضارع هم می آید وبا مصدر تیلماك هم اشتراك دارد یعنی طلب میکند تیلماید ودرسوراخ نمیکند

ونکرده است وشرحه شرحه نمیبرد ونبریده است تیلکان وتیلادرکان وتیلادورکان سوراخ کننده وسوراخ کرده وشرحه شرحه برنده وبمعنی

مصدر هم می آیند تیل وتیلکیل مفرد مخاطب از فعل امر تیلما وتیلماکیل مفرد مخاطب از فعل نهی تیلینك وتیلینکیز

تیلینکلار جمع مخاطب فعل امر تیلمانك وتیلمانکز وتیلمانکلار جمع مخاطب از فعل نهی تیلمان وتیلماس من سوراخ نمیکنم وشرحه شرحه

نمیبرم تیلادور من وتیلادورمن وتیلادور من وتیلادرام سوراخ میکنم وشرحه شرحه میبرم چنانکه لطفی شاهد براول ومعنی ثانی درذکر

اخراج مجنس کوید شعر دلبرا توشتوم ایلینکدین تیلادورمن یعنی بزبان افتادم سیندین اوزکانی جهاندا تیلادورمان یعنی طلب

نمیکنم تجنیس این مصرع ناقص است کوریبیم توشامینینك ایلیکیم آرتا سیندین دستم لار کوب تیلادورمن یعنی شرحه شرحه میبرم

تیلادورمن وتیلادرم با مصدر تیلماك نیز اشتراك دارد یعنی طلب میکنم تیلماس سوراخ نمیکند وشرحه شرحه نمیبرد وبمعنی فاعل و

منفی هم می آید تیلماسینکا نسوراخ نکردنت ونخطخط نبریدنت تیلادرینکا بسوراخ کردنت وبشرحه شرحه بریدنت وبطلب کردنت

تیلیب وتیلینان وتیلمیش سوراخ کرده وشرحه شرحه بریده چنانکه بمعنی ثانی کوید شعر تیلیب اغزیمنی عشقینك تیغی هجرینك

اویقسه بتوراب عمیم نزیمی دچون کونکلوم اوقی بحرهٔ کباب ایلادر تیلیشانك سوراخ کرده وشرحه شرحه بریده تیلنا بولغای تیلیسا

سوراخ توان کرد وشرحه شرحه برید تیلا آلغای سوراخ تواند کرد وشرحه شرحه تواند برید تیلای وتیلای بن سوراخ کنم وکند وکنی وکرده

وشرحه شرحه ببرم وببرد وببری وببرید با مصدر تیلماك نیز اشتراك دارند تیلنا لیغ تیلکای من وتیلکای یز وتیلای لینك سوراخ

کنیم وشرحه شرحه ببریم وتیلای لی وتیلای لینك بمعنی طلب کنیم هم باشد تیلکالی برای سوراخ کردن وتا سوراخ کرده وبرای خط خط بریدن

تیلکاج مصدر سوراخ کردن شرحه

وتا بریدن تیلکو محل سوراخ کنند وخط خط برنده تیلکو جه تیلکو نچه و تیلکانچه تا سوراخ کردن وبقدر سوراخ کردن تا شرحه شرحه

بریدن وبقدر شرحه شرحه بریدن تیلا آلغایسنجه بقدریکه سوراخ توانی کرد وبقدریکه شرحه شرحه توانی برید تیلکوسیدر ز سوراخ

خواهیم کرد وشرحه شرحه خواهیم برید تیلکو نکوز دور سوراخ خواهید کرد وشرحه شرحه خواهید برید تیلکوسیلادیر سوراخ

1992

خواهند کرد وشرحه شرحه خواهند برید تیلماکوم دور تیلماکوم یوق سوراخ نخواهیم کرد ونخط نخواهیم برید تیلا آلماغوم

× تیلا آلغوم یوق سوراخ کردن نمیکنم نخواهد بود وشرحه شرحه بریدن ممکن نخواهد بود تیلکولوك سوراخ کردن وشرحه شرحه

×× بریدنی تیلکای تیلادور تیلسا وتیلسون وتیلادیك سوراخ کند وشرحه شرحه ببرد تیلکودیك وتیلادیك سوراخ کردنی

سوراخ کند وشرحه شرحه ببرید بیرید بیغی وچنانچه ببرد وتیلادردیك نیز با مصدر تیلماك اشتراك دارد تیلیماك مع النون

سوراخ شدن وشرحه شرحه بریده شدن وصیغ آن بانون اشتقاق می یابد تیلاناك وتیلا تماك بمعنی خواستن وطلب کردن

باشد تیلادوك وتیلا تنوك طلب کردیم تیلادر وتیلادیدور وتیلاتور وتیلاتادور طلب میکند تیلادور بمعنی فاعل ومصدر

هم می آید وتیلادر با مصدر تیلماك نیز اشتراك دارد یعنی سوراخ میکند وشرحه شرحه میبرد تیلاتماید وتیلاتماید وطلب نمیکند ونکرده

تیلاکان وتیلادیدورکان وتیلاتکان وتیلاتورکان وتیلاتادورکان طلب کننده وطلب کرده وبمعنی مصدر هم می آید چنانکه

شاهد بر ایجاد این معنی از داستان نوفل ومجنون کوید که نوفل کین عرصه سیغه آت سوروب دا وتیلادیکانلاری تیلادر تیلادکیل

تیلادرم تیلادکیل مفرد مخاطب از فعل امر تیلاتما وتیلاتماکیل وتیلاتماکیل مفرد مخاطب از فعل نهی تیلانك تیلاتینکز وتیلاتینکلار وتیلادینکلار

تیلاتینکز وتیلاتینکلار جمع مخاطب از فعل امر الشاهد علی الاول شعر دوستلارکا کش اوراسیر ورایمنی تیلاتنك تا یمان کیلتوسا نکز

مردیغه جایمنی تیلاتنك تیلاتمانك وتیلاتمانکز وتیلاتمانکلار وتیلاتماغلار جمع مخاطب از فعل نهی تیلاتمان وتیلاتماس من

تیلاتماس من طلب نمیکنم الشاهد علی الاول شعر تا لبینك والمی بولدوم تیلادیم آب حیات سوفینی تیلادیم کیشی کیم واده غه بو

مغلوب تیلادیر من وتیلادیمن وتیلادیدور من وتیلادرام وتیلاتاشامن وتیلاتمن وتیلاتادر من وتیلاتورام طلب میکنم وتیلادرمن وتیلادرام

با مصدر تیلماك نیز اشتراك دارند تیلادرمن وتیلادرمن وتیلادرمن طلب میکنم چنانکه شاهد براول لطفی در تنا زالطبر درحکایات بلحیم کوید

شعر نیدی ولیکیم من تیلادیمن قالدی لوك لخ دین من بولطف تو تغایدلو الشاهد علی الثالث شعر دیدیم نظم اهلی نینك

کیم بولغای جیدی هاتف نوای بولغای اولکیم من تیلادیم صرین اکر بولغای وتیلادیر من یعنی سوراخ میکنم وشرحه شرحه میبرم هم آمد

تیلاما تیلاتماس طلب نمیکند وبمعنی فاعل ومصدر منفی هم می آید تیلاتماسینکا تیلاتماسینکا بطلب نکردنت تیلادکینکا تیلاتورکا

بطلب کردنت تیلاب وتیلاتیب وتیلامیش وتیلاتیب تیلاتیشیب تیلاتمیش طلب کرده الشاهد علی الاول شعر خام کونکلوم کیم تقاضا

تیلاب افغان قیلورش بارده صد اول طفل دیلکیم سیغلاغای حلوا اوچون تیلامیشانك وتیلاتمیشانك طلب کرده تیلاتا بولغای و

تیلاتا بولغای وتیلاتیب جهته طلب توان کرد تیلای آلغای وتیلاتا آلغای طلب تواند کرد تیلای وتیلای وتیلاتای وتیلاتا تیلاتا خواها

وطلب کنان چنانکه شاهد براول لطفی درلیلی مجنون درآمدن قاصد ابن سلام نزد مادر لیلی کوید شعر مقصود لاری جوابلاجهان نامر

باسنم تیلادیو نا لیب قوبلاش وینز درباب ششم از محبوب القلوب درحکایت کوهرافتادن از تاج پرویز کوید که خلعتینی نادی بیله

جقاریب بلار واول کوهر طالب تیلادیو لار تیلار وشاهد بر ثانی لعل بدعوی دکاردر حال مجنون کوید شعر بولادی غه شانی سایمان بانوسلار

تیلادیشا ابان تیلای وتیلاتیر وتیلاتا وتیلاتا یین بطلبم وبطلبد وبطلبید وتیلای وتیلاتا بن با مصدر تیلماك نیز اشتراك دارد

تیلاتا نعیلاکای ز وتیلاکای ز وتیلالی وتیلالینك وتیلا تشالی وتیلا تشکای ز وتیلاتا تشلی وتیلاتا لینك طلب کنیم

وتیلالی وتیلالینك با مصدر تیلماك نیز اشتراك دارد تیلاکالی وتیلاتا شکالی برای طلب کردن وتا طلب کرده تیلاکاج وتیلاتشکاج بطلب

کردن الشاهد علی الاول شعر نوایا غمی جانیم الوداسی ایتیب ساغیندی کیم تیلاکاج اوشبو نا نوازبر ناش تیلاکوچی تیلاتکوچی طلب کننده

چنانکه شاهد براول در زبانیم اغنیه درذکر ذوالنون مصری کوید که اول فرزند تیلاکوچی نینك یولداشی شد ودر تیلاکوجه وتیلانکوجه

بیلاکلاغیغ تیلاکنکومه تیلاکنکوبه و تیلاکنکاغه تا طلب کردن و تعلیم طالب کردن چنانچه میر در لیلی مجنون در مصرع کوید الشاهد علی الثانی
شعر چون نار تاشیدا بار تاپتی امیدنی تیلاکاغه ایا تاپتی تیلاکی آلماسنکه تیلاکنکا آلماسنکه تعلیم که طلب تولی کردنیلاکونیز
تیلاکونیز دو خواهیم طلب کرد تیلاکونکوزه و تیلاکنکونکوزه خواهید طلب کرد تیلاکوسیلار بود و تیلاکنکوسیلار خواهید طلب کرد
تیلاکنکاکوم تیلاکوم یوق و تیلاکنکاکوم تیلاکنکوم یوق نخواهم طلب کرد تیلاکی آلماغوم تیلاکنوم یوق و تیلاکنکا آلماغوم تیلاکنکا آلغوم طلب کرد
محکم نخواهد بود تیلاکای و تیلاکنکای تیلاکسون تیلاکنسون تیلاکنکای تیلاکشای تیلاکشسون و تیلاکشد یلک
طلب کند الشاهد علی الاول شعر درد و بلا و غصه نی کونکلوم اراکیتوردی عشق دوستلاین پراد کبی کیم تیلاکای تا
تیلاکوملک تیلاکنکوملک و تیلاکنکومک تیلاکتوزملک طلب کردن و همچنانکه طلب کند و شاهد بر اول معنی ثانی در تاریخ نابرعهد کلدرت
کلکونکول تیلاکوملک تحقیق خبر کیلتوردی تیلاکمتالک مصدر متعدیست یعنی طلبانیدن تیلاکتی لار طلبانیدند
مجنون شعر کیم قتیرفه ملم اوچون مرغث هر یان چو تیلاکتی لار یوق و سنغر آن تا تای قرشتا اشتقاق می یابد تیلاکنک
مع النون خواسته شدن و سنغر آن با نون اشتقاق می یابد تیلبه رامالک بسکون لام و فتح تای ابجد و رای مهمله با الف کشیده
دیوانه شدن تیلبه رادوق دیوانه شدیم تیلبه رادو تیلبه راید و دیوانه میشود الشاهد علی الاول شعر [illegible]
تیلبه بولوبدین که تیلبه راد براتی [illegible] زخم اتیار تیشیم و تیلبه رار معنی فاعل و مصدر هم می آید تیلبه رماق
دیوانه میشود و تیلبه رار تیلبه راکان تیلبه راکان دیوانه شوندم و دیوانه شده و معنی مصدر هم می آید
تیلبه رار تیلبه راکیل مفرد غائب از فعل امر تیلبه راسا تیلبه راکیل مفرد غائب از فعل نهی جمع غائب از فعل نهی تیلبه راسان تیلبه راسا تیلبه دیوانه
میشوم تیلبه رادیم تیلبه رادیک تیلبه رادی [illegible] دیوانه میشوم الشاهد علی الثانی شعر [illegible]
دیرار تیلبه رادین غصه دین کیم [illegible] تیلبه راماس دیوانه نمیشود و معنی فاعل و مصدر نفی هم می آید
تیلبه رامانلیغ بدیوانه نشدنست تیلبه رامنکا بدیوانه شدنست تیلبه رار [illegible] دیوانه شده الشاهد علی الاول
شعر تیلبه راب کونکلی نوای [illegible] نفعی و سلسله زلف ایله [illegible] تیلبه راماسانک دیوانه
تیلبه رانابو [illegible] دیوانه توانشد تیلبه رای آلغای دیوانه توانشد تیلبه رای تیلبه رای تیلبه رای دیوانه شوان
تیلبه رایین دیوانه شوم و شوی و شود و شوید الشاهد علی المعنی الاول شعر جانغه [illegible]
بله تینکری وچون سناقیا جامیدا [illegible] تیلبه رای تیلبه رای تیلبه راکان [illegible]
شویم تیلبه راکالی برای دیوانه شدن و تا دیوانه شدن تیلبه راکاج مجنون دیوانه شدن تیلبه راکوجی دیوانه شونده تیلبه
تیلبه رادو تیلبه راکانه تا دیوانه شدن و بعد دیوانه شدن تیلبه رای آلغایسنکه تعلیم دیوانه توانی شد تیلبه راکومیزدور
دیوانه خواهیم شد تیلبه راکوزدور دیوانه خواهید شد تیلبه راکوسیلار دیوانه خواهند شد تیلبه راکوم تیلبه راکوم یوق دیوا
نخواهم شد تیلبه رای آلماغوم [illegible] دیوانه شدن محکم نخواهد بود تیلبه راکولوک دیوانه شدنی تیلبه راکای تیلبه راسا
تیلبه راسون تیلبه رادیک دیوانه شود تیلبه راید [illegible] دیوانه شدنی و همچنانکه دیوانه شود تیلبه راتمالک
مصدر متعدیست یعنی دیوانه کردن تیلبه راتیب تیلبه راتیب تیلبه راتیب دیوانه کرده الشاهد علی الثالث شعر نوای
نینک جنونی عیب قیلمانک کیم آنی تیلبه راتیب پریوش تیلبه راتکاج چون دیوانه کرد و بعد دیوانه کردن من مجنونانه شعر
دیر آید نینک [illegible] تیلبه راتکاج ظلم [illegible] کیتیب و باقی صیغ بر سیاق تاتا

وزنشا اشتقاق می یابد تیلمورمالک بسکون رای مهمله و ضم میم با نماندن چشم در طلب طالبه نظر کردن تیلموردوک تا
ماندیم تیلموردیم تیلمورادور ناظر میماند الشاهد علی الاول شعر [illegible] هر توتار نیکونکلومغ کوزوم بیکه
تیکو مصدم بولیغه تا بیتیلمورور و تیلمورور معنی فاعل و مصدر هم می آید تیلمورمایدور ناظر نمیماند و نماندست تیلموری
تیلمورکان تیلمورادور منتظر ماندن و منتظر مانده و معنی مصدر هم آیند تیلمور و تیلمورکیل مفرد غائب از فعل امر تیلمورسا
تیلمورماکیل مفرد غائب از فعل نهی تیلمورون تیلمورونکیز جمع غائب از فعل امر تیلمورماسون تیلمورماکاید جمع
از فعل نهی تیلمورمان تیلمورادین ناظر نمانم تیلمورمایین تیلمورادین تیلمورادیز تیلموری منتظر بمانم تیلمورانک تیلمورکاریز
تیلمورکاییین تا ناظر بمانی الشاهد علی الثانی شعر یوق که کوز نابید کیم چون ناظر [illegible] بر اقیش [illegible]
ای کوز تیلمورکاسین تیلمورماس ناظر نمیماند و معنی فاعل و مصدر نفی هم می آید تیلمورماسینکا بنا ظر ماندن تیلمورو
بناظر ماندنست تیلمورو تیلمورماید تیلمورمیش ناظر مانده الشاهد علی الاول شعر تا تل کوز و نک که اول [illegible]
یا قیاس منکا کوزوم چه کیم تیلمورماسا تیلمورور تیلمورمیشانک ناظر مانده تیلمورسا تیلمورسا [illegible] ناظر توان ماند تیلمورا آلغای
ناظر توانی ماند تیلمورا تیلمورا نظاره کنان نظاره کنان تیلمورای تیلمورایین ناظر بمانم و بمانی و بماند الشاهد علی
المعنی الاول شعر نه کوییدین [illegible] جیقسا ایلیا تین [illegible] تیلمورای تیلمور
تیلمورکلی و تیلمورکالی برای تیلمورکالی تیلمورکانیم تیلمورکالی برای ناظر ماندن و تا ناظر ماندن چنانچه [illegible] کوید شعر ای نوای کوز
بوزیدین آلماق الماس [illegible] آرتوق [illegible] تیلمورکالی تیلمورکاج بعد از ناظر ماندن تیلمورکوجی نظاره کننده
تیلمورکوچی تیلمورکونچه تیلمورکاغه تا ناظر ماندن و بعد ناظر ماندن تیلمورا آلغایسنکه تعلیم ناظر توانی ماند تیلمورکومیزدور ناظر خواهیم
تیلمورکوزدور ناظر خواهید ماند تیلمورکوسیلار بود ناظر خواهند ماند تیلمورکوم تیلمورکوم یوق ناظر نخواهم ماند تیلمور آلماغوم
تیلمور آلغوم یوق ناظر ماندن محکم نخواهد بود تیلمورکولوک ناظر ماندنی تیلمورکای تیلمورسا تیلمورسون تیلمورکیل ناظر ماند
تیلمورسون تیلمورکای ناظر ماندنی و همچنانکه ناظر ماند من الجوامد تیل بکسر تا و سکون یا المستعمله است در اصطلاح کو دلنکه
شرح بریدن چنانچه کذشت و با شباع کسره بمعنی زبان باز اکویند چنانچه کوید شعر ظلم اهلی خلق [illegible] تیل
بار ایله کیم سباع اجار [illegible] تیلاک بفتح لام و سکون کاف بمعنی طلب و مسئلت باشد الشاهد علیه شعر تا [illegible]
وصلین ایستاب [illegible] دعا ای نوای تا [illegible] یوق آنداق [illegible] تیلاک تیلانجی بسکون نون و کسر جیم عجمی کداونا
وبند چنانچه در لیلی مجنون در توحید کوید شعر نون در [illegible] تیلانجی [illegible] تیلاو بفتح لام
و سکون واو بمعنی بهادر و دلیر باشد تیلبه بسکون لام و فتح تای ابجد یعنی دیوانه الشاهد علیه شعر [illegible] مجنون [illegible]
میم حقفاج آنقان باشلار [illegible] تیلبه کینی دین [illegible] تیلبه لیک یعنی جنون و دیوانگی چنانچه
سیار در وصف ملا جامی کوید شعر چونکه [illegible] تیلبه لیک بولدی [illegible] تیلماج بفتح میم بالف کشیده
و سکون جیم ترجمان را خوانند که واسطه در میان دو شخص بود لغتی را از زبانی بزبانی نقل نماید و از او تیلماج هم نامند تیلوک
بضم لام و سکون کاف مصرع را کویند چنانچه در مقاله [illegible] از حیرت الابرار در وصف ملا جامی کوید شعر [illegible]
باشید لکو لکولوک دام کبی [illegible] تیلیک بکسر لام و سکون کاف خطوط و شبهاتی بود که از آثار پای [illegible]
در جاده زمین هم رسد تیلیم بسکون میم یعنی قاچ بریده الشاهد علیه شعر [illegible]

تاشلاب تیلادرکا الارینیك تادی قطعا تیلما انکیز وله شرکیم که ملحینی دیدی تیجه تیلیم تیلادی تیلغای آنی نیجه تیلیم
تیلمین بسکون نون مرادف تیلیك وتیلیم باشد دو معنی طرد اول خطوط وشبهائی بود که درجادهٔ زمین بهم رسد چنانکه
در مقالهٔ اول النهرین کوید شعر عجوز ونای بعدم عامه یول کیلکان ازی بیرله تیلین ایردی یول دوییم تلچ بریده را کویند
مع المیم تیم قیم ازاتباعست یعنی کل گلچیانچه کوید میرله یوزونك تیم تیم لعمرو ایکان آیا یاشعله ارا بیر لیکمو ایکان آیا
وله لعل لعل قاوذره بیر بیرك کل تیرکان کبی نامه جیرادایتیم تیم سرینکیم تامید قروطالع هر وی تیم را بمعنی چکیدن قطره
بمعنی چکید چکیده نوشته سهو کرده وتیم در فارسی دو معنی طرد اول کاروانسرای بزرك راکویند دویم بمعنی دره باشد تیما
باصطلاح رومیه حکومت ولایت کوچك بود که درتحت ولایت بزرك باشد وآنرا سنجق هم نامند وبفارسی خدمت ومحافظت
ومزارعی باشد تیمی تیب بسکون میم وبای ابجد وکسر سین مهمله وتای قرشت لفظیست که در مقام تردید در میانه نفی واثبات
استعمال کنند مثل اینکه هرکاه خواهند که بکویند که صدای میشنود ونمیشنود وامری میفهمد ونمیفهمد وبوی استشمام میکند
ونمیکند میکویند که تیمی تیب تیمور بضم میم وسکون رای مهمله بمعنی آهن باشد ونیز نام پادشاهیست معروف که توران وهند
مسخر کرد وبا ایلدیرم بایزید خان پادشاه روم جنگ کرده براو غالب آمد وچون داماد امیر حسین والی بلخ بوده بان گورگان
ملقب ومشهور شد وسلاطین هند وستان از نسل اویند تیمور تیکان خاریست سه پهلو که از آهن وفولاد ساخته بر
دشمن بریزند وبفارسی خارخسك نامند ونیز نام گیاهیست که آنرا خارخسك کویند وآن بری وبستانی باشد وبری شبیه
بنبات هندوانه وشاخهای او خاردار ومنبسط بر روی زمین وثمرش صلب سه پهلو واز نخود کوچکتر است مرکب القوی ومدر بول
ومسکن درد مثانه است تیمور قاپو بفتح قاف بالف کشیده وضم بای عجمی قلعه‌ایست در دربند راکویند تیمور قازوق بضم زای معجمه و
سکون قاف آخر یعنی میخ آهن ونیز نام ستارهٔ جدی وبسبب اینکه قطب است وحرکتش محسوس نیست باین اسم تسمیه یافته تیمور قانات
بفتح نون بالف کشیده وسکون تای قرشت مرغی را نامند که تازه پر وبال برآورده باشد وآنرا بفارسی نیخ پر کویند الشاهد
شعر تاکونکولدین باش چیقارمیش هر طرف سیکالارینك قوش بالا سیدیك بولوبتور کیم بولور تیمور قانات ومؤلف رومی نوشته
که بجوجهٔ اردکت تیمور قانات کویند تیمور بالیغ بفتح تای حطی بالف کشیده وکسر لام وسکون غین لقب پدر سلجوق است که از الندشت ور اسیب
شیخ کانی باین لقب نامیدند مع النون من المشتقات تیناتی بسکون نون بمعنی آسایش وآرام کرفتن بود چنانکه کوید شعر
ضعف وقتی کوبی دین چیقما قتحمل ایلا حسام ایکی قدم ایلادم تیناتقا ییتا رمین هایبت وترکی رومی بمعنی سخن کفتن وحرف
زدن باشد تیندی آرام کرفت ومؤلف رومی این لفظ را بمعنی نبوز شدن از مشقت هم نوشته سهو کرده تیندوق آرام
تینار تینادور آرام میکیرد وتینار بمعنی فاعل ومصدر هم می‌آید تینمایدور آرام نمی‌یابد وبنا مه است تینغان تینار قان
تیناعرقان آرام کیرنده وآرام کرفته وبمعنی مصدر هم می‌آیند تیس وتینغیل مفرد مخاطب از فعل امر چنانکه در خسرو
شیرین در آغاز کتاب کوید الشاهد علی الاول شعر بوایشد الی تا یانر بر لحظه نوتیش بیتور سیتمی تینیك وسیتغه متن
الشاهد علی الثانی شعر ای سیحا برنفس تینغیل که بار میش دم سلامت جانلار اوینایب ول قوناشی باشیم کیلتور کانی تیما
تیناعیل مفرد مخاطب از فعل نهی الشاهد علی الثانی شعر سین آبی ایسانا کین تیناعیل بر لحظه کیم بالالث اکر مطلوب تابمش
اندین ایریمیش هم طلب تیلیش تینیك تینسنکیز و تینسنکلار جمع مخاطب از فعل امر تیناتك وتینما نکیز وتینما نکلار جمع
از فعل نهی تینان وتینارمین آرام میکیرم تینارسین وتینارسیز تینادورمیز تینارام آرام میکیرم تینسام وتینغامین وتینغاین

الشاهد علی الثانی شعر ایتا رام بوزمارلاونکا بیمن علم صدر سیدیش تا زمانی تینغامین دور اهلی تینیك غوغا سیدین تینماس
آرام نمیکیرد وبمعنی فاعل ومصدر منفی هم می‌آید تینما سلیغ آرام نکرفتن چنانکه کوید شعر بوکهن دیر ایچرا تینما سلیغ فن الفنا
تون وکون خاطر نجیه تا مان سودا بیدین تیندم ظافانش ونیز کوید شعر ای نوای دهر بوقوبای تینما سلیغ تورودش تینغاسین
کونکلا سانك پروا یوق ونا بزغیه هم ودر این شعر تینما سلیك با کاف مذکور است وهو هذا شعر میل دینی که سالور کهنه
تینما سلیك کا تینیبان کونکلی آسینك کیم که کونکلودین چیقاریش ودر این لفظ شعر مخالفت قیاس واستعمال واقع شده زیرا که منظور شاه
منعقد در صیغ تینماق تاپلمشت وآهنم با بیت تینما سلیغ نه مذکور شود وذکر آن با کاف سوای سهو کاتب احضرت ناظم وهمی نخواهد
تینما سینکفه با رام نکرفتنت تینما سینکفه با رام کرفتنت تینیب وتینیبان وتینمیش آرام کرفته تینمیشانك آرام کرفته
تینناسولغای وتینیب بولغای آرام توان کرفت تینا الغای آرام تواند کرفت تینا تینا اسایش کنان تینغای وتینابین
آرام بکیرم وبکیرد وبکیری وکرفته الشاهد علی الاول شعر نوای دیساتك کیم زمانی تینغای زمانا اهلیدین الحکیل اجتناب
تیناق وتینغانی روتینغای بر وتینالی وتینا لیك آرام بکیریم تینغلی برای آرام کرفتن وتا آرام کرفته تینغاج بمعنی آرام کرفتن
تینغوجی آرام کیرنده تینغوجه وتینغوجه وتینغاجه تا آرام کرفتن وبقدر آرام کرفتن تینا الغا تینکجه بقدریکه آرام توانی کرفت
تینغومیزدو آرام خواهیم کرفت تینغونکیزدو آرام خواهید کرفت تینغوسیلاردو آرام خواهند کرفت تیناغوم وتینغوم یوق آرام نخواهم
کرفت تینا الماغوم تینا الغوم یوق آرام کرفتن ممکن نخواهد بود تینغولوق آرام کرفتنی تینغای وتینا وتینسا وتینغون وتینک
آرام بکیرد تینغو دیك وتینار دیك آرام کرفتنی چنانکه آرام بکیرد وشاهد بر اول بمعنی تاریخ تابری مذکور است که کونکول
تینغو دیك جواب شافی تابمادیم تیند ومرزفانغ مصدر متعدی بیت بمعنی آرام دادن باشد وترکی رومی یعنی سخن در آوردن تیندو
تیند ورادو آرام میدهد الشاهد علی الاول شعر تیند ورمای وجیقاتینی خاکر روشن خیر ایله کیم آبادلیا دو ویرانه فهر
وتیند ورور بمعنی فاعل ومصدر هم می‌آید وترکی رومی یعنی سخن در می‌آورد تیند ورتیند وریتیند ور اظهارات از آرام دادن چنانکه شاهد
بر اول کوید شعر یوزونك کوزلاك تیلاب تا بماس نوای کونکلی نا الماقدین خدای اوچون الیب برقعنی آسنیك کونکلینی تیندورغ
وطالع هروی تیندور ماق را تیند ورغالیك باکاف مذکور ساخته وهمان معنی بحرف در آوردن نوشته وشعر بوبر را شاهد آورده
وتیند ور ترکی ایشان بتکلم ساختن باشد آرام دادیدا الشاهد علیه شعر تینما غو اعنیا رخاطر الادیان کوب اضطراب مجرا قتلیم
اوچون سین دین کونکول تیند وردونکوزه وباقی صیغ بر این سیاق بالفطه وما شقاق می‌آید تینکلا ناق بسکون نون وکاف
عجمی وفتح لام شنیدن وغور سخن کردن تینکلادوق شنیدیم تینکلادینك شنیدی تینکلا مادینك نشنیدی الشاهد علیه
شعر درونیکفه قولاغ سالغوم دیب مستجیب کیلدینك خالیم نیجه شرح ایتیم سوز تینکلا مادینك باری تینکلادور
تینکلادیدور میشنود وتینکلار بمعنی فاعل ومصدر هم می‌آید تینکلا مایدور نمیشنود ونشنیده است تینکلاغان وتینکلاغوان وتینکلادی
شنونده وشنیده وبمعنی مصدر هم می‌آیند تینکلا وتینکلاغیل مفرد مخاطب از فعل امر چنانکه در خاتمهٔ سد سکندری کوید الشاهد علی
الاول شعر معنی سوزوم تینکلا آخر کبی حزین نغمه ساز ملل خرکبی تینکلاما وتینکلاماغیل مفرد مخاطب از فعل نهی تینکلانك و
تینکلانکیز وتینکلانکیزلار جمع مخاطب از فعل امر تینکلامانك وتینکلامانکیز وتینکلامانکیزلار جمع مخاطب از فعل نهی تینکلانان وتینکلارمن میشنوم تینکلا
تینکلارسن وتینکلادورمین وتینکلارام میشنوم تینکلامان نمیشنود وبمعنی فاعل ومصدر منفی هم می‌آید تینکلاماس تینکلاماسینکفه تینکلاتت
تینکلامینکفه نشنیدنت تینکلاب وتینکلابان وتینکلامیش شنیده تینکلامیشانك شنیده تینکلاسا بولغا وتینکلاب بولغا توان شنید

201v

تینکلاغوآلغالی تواند شنید تینکلاش بتینکلاغو تینکلای با استماع کنان وغورکنان تینکلای وتینکلابین بشنوم وبشنود وبشنو
وشنید تینکلاغانی وتینکلاغانی وتینکلاغای نیز وتینکلاغالی تینکلاغای بشنویم تینکلاغالی برای شنیدن وتا شنیدن تینکلاغاج
محض شنیدن تینکلاغوچی شنونده تینکلاغوچی وتینکلاغوچی وتینکلاغوچی ناشنیدن وبقدر شنیدن تینکلای آلغای تینکلای بقدرکه
توان شنید تینکلاغومیزدو ونشنواهیم شنید تینکلاغونکوزدو نشنواهید شنید تینکلاغوسیلار دو نخواهند شنید تینکلاغوم
تینکلاغوم یوق نخواهم شنید تینکلای آلماغوم وتینکلای آلنوم یوق نشنیدن محکم نخواهد بود تینکلاغولوق شنیدنی تینکلاغانی
تینکلاسون وتینکلادیلر بشنود تینکلاغودیک وتینکلادیک شنیدن وهمچنانکه بشنود تینکشانالک بکون نون
وکاف عجمی وفتح شین قرشت وتینکیشتورمالک بکاف عجمی بمعنی سنجیدن وموازنه کردن باشد وتینکشاتماق وتینکلاشتورماق
هم بهمین معنی استماع شده تینکشادی وتینکیشتوردی سنجید چنانکه در لسان الطیر در ذکر خواجه نقشبند علیه الرحمه گوید الشاهد
علی الثانی شعر تاکمونیدی کونیکا چیقیه کلب سیکورین یا کلیلک آنی طلب چون آنینک برله تینکیشتوردی اونی
ناله قیلدی اشکلار الیب کوزیدین تینکشار وتینکشاید ووتینکیشتور وتینکیشتوراسنجید چنانکه میر حیدر مقاله ششم از مخزن
گوید الشاهد علی الاول شعر هرنیکه اوکیتیسالک آلهم اغدا تنغ عزکوب بلرنجالی تینکشالر بهجم ومولفین روچی تینکشار را
در این شعر تینکشار بمجهول نون خوانده وبمعنی جمع کردن وچیدن نوشته ونظیری هم متابعت کرده سهوکرده اند لفظی مرود
اخترای است وتینکشاو وتینکیشتور بمعنی امر حاضل ومفرد هم می آیند تینکشانا بید وتینکیشتوربا بسنجید وبسنجید ای
تینکشاکان وتینکشاید ورکان وتینکیشتورکان وتینکیشتورکای وتینکیشتورا بسنجند وبسنجید بمعنی سنجید نیز هم می آیند تینکشا وتینکشا
تینکشام وتینکیشتورم کلمه مفرد غائب از فعل امر تینکشاما وتینکشاماکی وتینکیشتوربا تینکیشتورنا ماتینکشامانای تینکشا
تینکشالر جمع غائب از فعل امر تینکشانای وتینکشانای وتینکشانا جمع غائب از فعل ماضی تینکشانالر تینکشاماس وتینکیشتور
تینکیشتورماس تینکشایین وتینکشایین وتینکشایدمین وتینکشارام وتینکیشتورامین وتینکیشتورمین وتینکیشتورمین وتینکیشتو
میسنجم تینکشامار وتینکیشتورماس میسنجد وبمعنی حاضر ومفرد منفی هم می آید تینکشاماسینکا وتینکیشتورماسینکا مسنجیدنت
تینکشارنکا وتینکیشتورور نمیسنجیدنت تینکشاب وتینکشابان وتینکشامیش وتینکیشتوروب وتینکیشتورمان وتینکیشتورمیش
سنجیده تینکشامیشانک وتینکیشتورمیشانک سنجیده تینکشانا بولغای وتینکشاب بولغای وتینکیشتوربا بولغای وتینکیشتوربولغان سنجید
تینکشا آلغای وتینکیشتورا آلغای تواند سنجید تینکشای وتینکشایو وتینکشایو وتینکیشتوراو وتینکیشتورا موازنه کنان تینکشکه
تینکشایین وتینکیشتورای وتینکیشتورای بسنجم وبسنجد وبسنج وبسنجید تینکشانالو وتینکشاکای نیز وتینکشالی وتینکشا
تینکیشتورنالی وتینکیشتورکای نیز وتینکیشتورای وتینکیشتوربنای بسنجیم تینکشالی وتینکیشتورکالی برای سنجیدن وتا سنجیدن
تینکشالاج وتینکیشتورکاج محض سنجیدن تینکشاکوچی وتینکیشتورکوچی سنجنده تینکشاکوچی وتینکشاکوچی تینکشاکوچی وتینکیشتور
تینکیشتوروب وتینکیشتورکانا سنجیدن وبقدر سنجیدن تینکشا آلغای وتینکیشتورا آلغای بقدرکه توانی سنجید تینکشاکومیزدو
تینکیشتورکومیزدو نسنجیم سنجید تینکشاکونکوزدو وتینکیشتورکونکوزدو نخواهید سنجید تینکشاکوسیلاردور وتینکیشتورکوسیلاردور نخواهند
سنجید تینکشاماقوم تینکشاقوم یوق وتینکیشتورماقوم وتینکیشتورکوم یوق نخواهم سنجید تینکشای آلماغوم وتینکشای آلغوم یوق وتینکیشتورا
تینکیشتورا آلغوم یوق سنجیدن محکم نخواهد بود تینکشاکولوک وتینکیشتورکولوک سنجیدنی تینکشاماکای وتینکشاسا وتینکشاسون
تینکشادیلر تینکیشتورکای وتینکیشتورا وتینکیشتورسا وتینکیشتورسون تینکشاکودیک وتینکشاردیک وتینکیشتورکودیک تینکیشتور

202r

سنجیدنی وهمچنانکه بسنجد تینکشاشماق بکون نون عجمی وشین معجمه وفتح تای قرشت تینکشاشتورماق بضم تای ثالثه
بکون رای مهمله مرادف تینکشاماق وتینکیشتورماق باشد یعنی سنجیدن وموازنه کردن خود بمعنی الاطاله بفکر مصادر آنکه
نمود صیغ آنها نیز مواقع شود اول اشتقاق می یابد تینکشاشماق بکون نون وشین قرشت وفتح کاف عجمی بمعنی مفاعله است یعنی
با یکدیگر سنجیدن وموازنه کردن تینکشاشوک با یکدیگر موازنه کردیم چنانکه در نظم المحبه در ذکر سیدی آتا گوید
خواجه احمد یسوی تینک قرابتی دور دربیت دورکه مین واحمد تینکشاشوک مین بیسیک ارادیم دونا قوسنغ بر بیعنی موافق شود آن
اشتقاق می یابد تینکلاشماق مساوی شدن وصیغ آن بجهان صیغ الام اشتقاق می یابد تینکلاشماق بکون نون وکاف عجمی
وشین معجمه وفتح لام مساوات جستن وبا هم مساوی شدن تینکلاشتورماق مساوی شدن تینکلاشی تینکلاشتورم تینکلاشادورم مساوی میشوم
وتینکلاشتورمین بمعنی فاعل ومصدر هم می آید تینکلاشماید ودر مساوی میشود ونشده است تینکلاشکان وتینکلاشتورکان تینکلاشادور
مساوی شوند ومساوی شده وبمعنی مصدر هم می آیند تینکلاش وتینکلاشجیل مفرد غائب از فعل امر تینکلاشتا وتینکلاشماکیلمدو
غائب از فعل ماضی تینکلاشیلد وتینکلاشیکر وتینکلاشیکر جمع غائب از فعل امر تینکلاشمای تینکلاشماکیر وتینکلاشماکی جمع غائب از فعل
تینکلاشمان وتینکلاشمارمین مساوی میشوم تینکلاشامین وتینکلاشتورمین وتینکلاشادورمین تینکلاشتورام مساوی میشوم تینکلاشماس
مساوی میشود وبمعنی فاعل ومصدر منفی هم می آید تینکلاشماسی مساوی شدن نیز نشدنش تینکلاشماسینکا مساوی نشده تینکلاشتوره
تینکلاشکانینکا تینکلاشادورکا مساوی شدنت تینکلاشیب وتینکلاشیبان وتینکلاشمیش مساوی جسته تینکلاشمیشانک مساوی جسته
تینکلاشا بولغای وتینکلاشیب بولغای مساوی توان شد تینکلاشا آلغای مساوی تواند شد تینکلاشا وتینکلاشا مساوات جویان تینکلاشای
تینکلاشایین مساوی شوم وشود وشوی وشوید تینکلاشالی وتینکلاشکای نیز وتینکلاشکای نیز تینکلاشالی وتینکلاشتا مساوی شویم تینکلاشکالی
برای مساوی شدن وتا مساوی شده تینکلاشکاج محض مساوی شدن تینکلاشکوچی مساوی شونده تینکلاشکوچه وتینکلاشکو
تینکلاشکانچه تا مساوی شدن وبقدر مساوی تینکلاشا آلغای بقدرکه مساوی توانی شد تینکلاشکومیزدور مساوی نخواهیم
تینکلاشکونکوزدور مساوی نخواهید شد تینکلاشکوسیلاردور مساوی نخواهند شد تینکلاشماکوم وتینکلاشکوم یوق مساوی نخواهم شد
تینکلاشا آلماغوم تینکلاشا آلغوم یوق مساوی شدن محکم نخواهد بود تینکلاشکولوک مساوی شدنی تینکلاشکای تینکلاشا
تینکلاشسا وتینکلاشسون تینکلاشکودیک مساوی شود تینکلاشکودیک وتینکلاشتوردیک مساوی شدنی وهمچنانکه شود تینکلاشتورماک مشدد
متعدی است یعنی با هم مساوی کردن وصیغ آن بدستور لفظ مذکور اشتقاق می یابد من الجوامع تینغ بکون نون ودیم بمعنی
آسوده وآرمیده بود الشاهد علیه شعر کرنالاکوبغه دیرایتنغ املادیم توتالادیکم غصه دین بو طعنه ایرکانی باهیم سلپا دیشیم
تینغو بکون نون وضم غین معجمه بمعنی مکث وآرام بود ومجازا تنها ماندن یا تنها رفتن را گویند تینک بکون نون وکاف عجمی
بمعنی برابر ومساوی چنانکه گوید شعر چو یار الیلارا امیش ایرسا جلوه حسن تینک اولدی کعبه سیله دیر وسومنات تینکا وتینکا
مقابل ونظیر خوانند تینکتاش بفتح تای قرشت وسکون شین معجمه بمعنی کفو وهمتا باشد تینکتارلیک بضم لام وسکون یا بمعنی برابری
وهمتائی تینکری بکسر رای مهمله اسم جناب باری تعالی است در لسان الطیر شعر خان چون ثنی مطلق وازلیکاکای تینکری مسیره
آغلز ایلکاکای تینکری لیک یعنی خدائی والوهیت وبمعنی خدائیت والهیت نا معده تینک قور بضم تای وسکون رای مهمله بمعنی نظیر
وکفو وهمتا بود وازاینکاش هم نامند تینک لیک تساوی وبرابری تیناعو ر بفتح میم وضم غین معجمه وسکون رای مهمله
یعنی بی قرار وبی آرام چنانکه گوید شعر تحتیم آنهوده جانا نیدا بولغای کاشکی دردین تینک تیناغور حابیدا بولغای کاشکی

202v.

من سلطانحسین میرزا شعر غنچه خندا ز لطف بیب کونکلوم دا تا لدی خار خار تیتما غوز خا ننغنه آیتین دنیا ده . باری فنا ث دغو آفت

تیتماغوز معنی نون معنی هم میکند و ضعیف و ناتوان میشود نوشته و شعر لغیرا شاهد آورده و بعضی هم متابعت کرده لفظ

معنی هر دو خطا صریح است تیتنکیز مکسر کاف عجمی و زای عجمه دریا را گویند الشاهد علیه شعر سو قدین اشکا یم و عزقا لوب بی کلا

مین نمیث بکم تیتنکیز داکم ادبیار اسراف ق کیراک دمین و نیز نام پسر چهارم اوغوز خان بن قراخان بن مغول خانست که هشتم خانان مغول

بوده مع الواو من المشتقات تیوراماق بکون واو و فتح رای مهمله دوختن که بطریق کوک باشد و بیخ کشیدن تیورای

دوخت تیوراد وک دوختیم تیوراردیتوراربود سید و نیز بمعنی فاعل و مصدر هم می آید تیورامایدور و نمید مد دوخته

تیوراکان تیورارکان تیورابیدورکان دوخته و دوخته و بمعنی مصدر هم می آید تیوراو تیوراکیل منوط المنفصل تیوراماسا

تیوراماکیل منوط المنفصله تیورامامه تیوراتیکم تیورانکلار جمع مخاطب المنفصل تیوراماتیم تیوراماتیکم تیوراملکلام مخاطب

المنفصله تیورلیان تیوراماس من غیبه هم تیورای من تیورارمین تیورابدورمین تیورارام میدوزم تیوراماس نمیدوزی

فاعل و مصدر منفی هم می آید تیوراماسینکا بدوختند تیورابیکا بدوختند تیورابه تیورابان تیورامیش دوخته الشاهد

علی الاول شعر تیتیب لمغزیمی عشقینک تیغی هجرینک اوقیغه تیوراب عمیم زری ایچون کونکلوم اوقی ایچره کبابلار و نیز

الابله کوکید شعر ظلم نو ده اوشبوکه پرناتوان علم تیلالب شمری بن ولغا یروان تیوراب یالغینی آیینک هر تیکان هر تیکان

اوستیله کوز تیکان الشاهد علی الثانی شعر شه ایکیدامو تکه لیک خلعت غم پرنیان میث میغلانده پرا له آلیب

تیوراپان کیکان قراتیش تیوراپیشانک دوخته تیوراتنا بولغای تیوراب بولغای تواند دوخت تیورای آلغای تواند دوخت

تیورای تیوراری و تیورایو دوزان دوزان تیورای تیوراریتن بدوزم و بدوزد و بدوزی و دوخته تیوراکاندیو تیوراکای

تیورابلی بدوزیم تیوراکیلی برای دوختن و تا دوخته تیوراکاج مجرد دوختن بیجون دوخت و بدوزی تیوراکوب دوزنها تیوراکی

تیوراکونه تیوراکاغه تا دوختن و بقصد دوختن تیوراکی لغا ینکه بقصدیکه تولیده دوخت تیوراکومیز دوز خواهیم دوخت

تیوراکونجزیدو بخواهید دوخت تیوراکونیلار بدو خواهند دوخت تیوراماکوم تیوراکوم بوق نخواهم دوخت تیورای الماغوم و

تیورای آلغوم قوق دوختن ممکن نخواهد بود تیورا کولوند وختی تیوراکای تیوراماغیتورابوم تیوراندیک بد دوزیدت تیوراندیک

دوختی و همچنانکه بدوزند تیوراتمان مع التا مصدر متعدیست یعنی دوزانیدن تیوراتای و تیوراتایین بدوزانم و بدوزاند

و بدوزانی و دوزانیدن الشاهد علی الاول المعنی الاول شعر کیل که غمزات ایچره سینکا تاقیبان نجان رشته سیز کونکلوم جانکا

کبی کوکسوم شکافین تیوراتای و صیغ آن باتای قریش اشتقاق می یابد تیورالماق مع الیای تیوریلماق بضم رای مهمله و سکون لام

یعنی دوخته شدن تیورالدی و تیوریلدی دوخته شد الشاهد علی الثانی شعر بیجه افغان میلانام تانک یوقیراکیم کونکلیکا

هم اوشبو تیوریلدی شکلده زمانغ ابرها قدی تیورالیسه تیورالیبان تیورالیش و تیوریلوبه تیوریلو تیوریلیش دوخته شده

الشاهد علی الاول شعر قبل چون میلدینک کونکولی بوکهن تیکاک ایکان اوملاینکیم تالدیلاره جان برده سیغه تیورالیب

الشاهد علی الرابع ناله ناله خلوتینک کوکسوم کاکو یاسیدی کیم تیورولیبتوراتوان کونکلوم پرپر ناله لار ونباقی صیغ آنها سیاق

از تیوریلماق نفهمید و انتیوریلماق بضم و او و فاعل شقاقی باید من الجواهد تیورولماق بکون واو و کاف و ضم رای مهمله

دلبد اول بمعنی کرد و متحد باشد چنانکه کوید شعر کل ایماس کلبنده تا ملنغ داغ ایره کیم نسترن تیورولماک ایلی تیوراماسوق فوتانه

رهم ای معشوق دله شعر داغی کوپ تن دن که خرقم نا پیشرای بیمین بدن آنکلاهر تیورولماک یمروز آستیده تیورولماک توکان دو ...

203r.

و میل آهنی بود که بر وسط سنگ زیرین دستاس نصب کرده سنگ بالا را از آن کلم اندیک میکرداننده کران ابعم محمود

گویند نیز تیکانه بفتح واو بمان ت و کاف و کسر تای قرشت شترخار باشد و آن کیاهیست که ترنجبین بر آن بنشیند و شکوفه زرد

بواسیر نافعست نیز تویش بضمتاه و کسر شین معجمه شترمرغ بود که آن را مرغ ابعامه نامند کویند چنانکه در تنبیهات محبوب القلوب

گوید که تیوه تویشی یکلاهب کوچابو الماروچادرناتن اجپا د حیا بولملس مع الیای المشتقات تیماق بالاشباع

منع کردن چنانکه در تاریخ تابری سند کورلستکه چاپنونی تاوغان چیریک نینک تیماقینینک خیلی اشکالی دارد و فراهی بعضی کمنا

نوشته سهو کرده تید نینک منع کرد الشاهد علیه شعر مکرسنا چنکوی تید نینک قشه دیکیم پریشانغا النیلخینکه

قویار باشیر تیار و تیادور منع میکند چنانکه شاهد اول و ثانی در مبنا اول از دیباچه کتاب در فضل تیم هر بیان فصل

مضارع متعرم شده و تیار بمعنی فاعل و مصدر هم می آید تیمایدور منع نمیکند و نکرده است تیغان و تیارغان و تیارکان

منع کننده و منع کرده چنانکه شاهد اول علا بعضی او لکوید شعر کیم که کونکلین ایسانماس عمکین تلخواسار دیلک کیم تیلین

تیغان کیشی تینک کونکلیدا آزالمیاش و بمعنی مصدر هم می آیند تیماغان و تیمایدورغان منع نکننده و منع نکرده چنانکه شاد

بر اولر بمعنی اقل صر باب هفتم از محبوب القلوب کوید که شاه دا زین اسرار ما قدا تیلین تیماغان باشی ایرب تق تیغیل مقرر بهما

از فصل امر الشاهد علی الاول شعر کیم نونک که کم ایله یوز دین فه سالدی دیر المنغ خدای اوچون تیقاکین یوقه محمد یلمانیلنغ

الشاهد علی الثانی شعرای نوای فصل بیسار چالنانک ایل تیل آغزیدین نظم دیم تیلنی تصیل نوریتیم سوم آغزیلیقامیل

منوط المنفصل الشاهد علی الثالث یعزیابر بیاد شاه شعر تیماعیل دیوانه کونکلوم نی که رسوا بولماد بیب عاشق اولغایمو ایدی اول

تیلبه رسوا بولماسا تینیک و تیمینکلار و تیمنکیز جمع مخاطب المنفصل تیماتک و تیماتکیز تیمانکلار جمع مخاطب المنفصله تیمانکیز

منع میکنم الشاهد علی الاول شعرای کونکول غلوتچا سین سینکوم رهدین اولکونک ایمدی تیمان نیغ افغان چیک و نوا دا بیله

تیمین و تیمارمین و تیمادورمین تیمادام منع میکنم تیماس منع نمیکند و بمعنی فاعل و مصدر هم می آید تماسیکه منع نکردنست تیکه

منع کردنست تیتیب و تیتیبان و تیمیش منع کرده الشاهد علی الاول شعر ناله دین عشق که کونکلومنی تیب تیتی فراق ایدی لیقیله

نفان چیکیکیل و فریاد تیکیل و نیز در خسرو و شیرین در آمدن خسرو به مشاطه از من در صفت فرهاد گوید شعر تیب اهل اسباغیبن منک

قاریغه دین دیمار برلیلیر دین کیم هم یاره هین تیتیشانک منع کرده تیساتولغای و تیب تولغای منع تواند کرد تیا الغای منع تواند کرد

تیا تیا منع کنان منع کنان تیسام تیسا بین منع کنم و کند و کنی و کرده تیا آلمای تیا آلمایین منع نتوانم کردن نتواند کرد

ونتوانی کرد و نتوانسته کرد چنانکه در خسرو و شیرین در حکایت جبال فرهاد کوید الشاهد علی الاول المعنی الثانی شعر ایشکا

عشق و عاشقلیغ سر دیر دین تیا آلمای کمزیدین ایی سردین و معنی شعر اینست که چون شود سر در عشق و عاشقی را منع نتواند کرد چون

خود در رد عشق را و نصیحت این لفظ را در این شعر تیا آلمای بالنون خوانده و نوشته که یعنی آرام نتوانم کرفت و شعر ز بر را شاهد آورده

اگرچه در لفظ بلند غلط و در معنیش غلط کرده اما در معنی به غلط در تلفظ کرده تیساق تیماقانیز تیماغای نه تیتکا تیبالینک منع کنیم

تیعلی برای منع کردن و تا منع کرده تیعاج مجرد منع کردن تیغوچ منع کننده تیغوچه و تیغوجه تیماغیه تا منع کردن بقصد منع کرده

تیا الغایینکچه بقصدیکه منع توانی کرد تیغومیز دو منع خواهیم کرد تیغونکوز دو منع خواهید کرد تیغوسیلار دو منع خواهند کرد

تیماغوم تیغوم یوق منع نخواهم کرد تیا آلماغوم تیا آلغوم یوق منع کردن ممکن نخواهد بود تیغولوق منع کردنی تیما تیلادیسا

جسونه تیدیلر منع کند تیغود بلنه تیاردیک منع کردید و همچنانکه منع کند تیسلما تق بکسر و سکون لام ممنوع شدن تیسلکی

203r.

× ×

تیجی ×

202v.

×

تیو ×

×

× ×

× (ح)

ا؎

ممنوع شد چنانکه در تاریخ بابری مذکوراست که تینکری براست کیلتوردی چیرلیک تیلادی تیلغاندیك یعنی کالممنوع چنانکه در تاریخ
بابری آمده که آتمنی اوقلادیم بوتنا الانیلاردی برنیمه تیلغاندیك بولدیلار و باقی صیغ برتیلاق الام اشتقاق می یابد من الخوابد
تیتق بکسر تای حطی مع الاشباع و سکون قاف بمعنی منع باشد چنانکه در تاریخ بابری مذکوراست که بوردون ولایت لار ایاغی
ایدی حطی تیتق میتق بولمایدی و نیز گوید که هر نیچه بوبو سونلوق سوزلار آیتیب منع قیلور لار یتتوقفه کیرماس یعنی منع پذیر نشود
تیتین بکسر تای حطی و سکون نون سحاب را گویند شاهد چغتایه شعر تیتین و تامن غراک شوخلار اوز ایکی ییرتا بیر له
یمرکا چیککاندین کونکول اچیتاب ایرور وله شعر کیب عمر ایله کیتر ایمر و میلیار غالیغ ایپاك لباس ایله توتماغ صالحمی تولا تیتین تیك
اوز توکی اوق بولدی جانیغه آفت فریبیه تیننك پریچین کیلدی وزناشیغه بلا جزء ثالث تیفش و تغیر بعضی از صیغ کتاب الجیم

باب المفتوحات حرف الجیم مع الالف چا دوجه بچند معنی آید اول بمعنی غایت و نهایت باشد دویم بمعنی وزن و مقدار آید و در معنی
نیز مستعمل چنانکه گویند کیوچه یعنی از عقب و از کاچه یعنی تا بر دیگر و نیچه یعنی چگونه و بالجیم عجمی هم بدو معنی بود اولکه گویند
یعنی یکجا پرهن و بیچه یعنی چند تا و هر چند و شواهد آنها در ذیل ابنا چهارم تکاشف یافت و بفارسی علامت تصغیر باشد مثل باغچه و ما
مع الباء من مشتقات چاپماق و چاپمان قیلیغ باجیم عجمی و سکون باء عجمی چاپمار یعنی آمده اول تاختن بمعنی دویدن باشد چنانکه در
شیرین در جستجوی فرهاد گوید شعر کیشیلار هر طرف چاپماق کیرا کوز تاپان بولسا انی تاپماق کیرا کوز دوییم بمعنی دوانیدن بود سیوم
تاختن بمعنی غارت کردن آمده چهارم بمعنی شمشیر زدن و زخم زدن و بریدن بضرب واحد باشد چنانکه در مقاله هشتم از حیرة الابرار گوید
شعر قتل ایشیکا چو تانی دین چیکتی تیغ باشین آینك چاپماق اوچون سیلدی تیغ و نیز در خسرو شیرین در وصف کوهکن فرهاد فرماید
شعر آینك دیك خاره چاپماق ایتی بنیاد که حقتی تاغدین گرد و نغمه فریاد و ایکی چاپماق یعنی از میان دو نیم کردن چنانکه شاهد آن
در ذیل چاپیب مذکور میگردد چاپتی دوید و دوانید و غارت کرد و شمشیر زد چنانکه بمعنی ثانی گوید شعر تیغ تارتیب تالچوز لاکز ناشیغه
چون چاپتی رخش تندین اوچتی بو که هر ان ناش و ناشین اوچتی تاج چاپتوق دویدیم و دوانیدیم و تاختیم و شمشیر زدیم چاپادور
چاپادور میدود و میدواند و غارت میکند و شمشیر میزند و چاپار بمعنی فاعل و مصدر هم می آید چنانکه بمعنی اول تاختن گوید شعر
سرکران مین عشق دین چاپارنك باشیمنی پامالحبر لیغ کیم چاپار مرداو خش اوزو لوتو طلا فای فراز دین و نیز در سد سکندر در وصف شمشیر زدن
بمعنی شمشیر زدن فرماید شعر تلیع بوق هلال درخشنده اول چاپار و قیدا بر قمر خشنده اول چاپتان و چاپاغان چاپادورغان
دویده و دوانده و دوانیده و غارت کننده و غارت کرده و شمشیر زننده و زده چنانکه شاهد بر اول بمعنی نوازنده در خسرو شیرین گوید
شعر قدم قویدی و کیردی قصر ایچره کمندادیو چاپقان تیغ خونریز و بمعنی مصدر هم می آیند چاپ و چاپتیل مفرد مخاطب بالتحال
چاپماق چاپیلنید مفرد مخاطب المبتنی للمجهول چاپینك و چاپینکیز و چاپینکلار جمع مخاطب المبتنی الرجا باتك و چاپانکیز و چاپانکلار جمع مخاطب
از فعل نهی چاپمان و چاپماس مین میدوم و میدوانم و غارت میکنم و شمشیر میزنم چاپامین و چاپارمین و چاپادورمین و چاپاداصیدوم و میدوانم
و غارت میکنم و شمشیر میزنم چاپاماس مفرد مخاطب از صیغه نفی مطلق مذکور چاپیب و چاپیبان و چاپیبیش دویده و دوانیده و غارت
کرده و شمشیر زده و شاهد بر اقل از معنی در ویده در مجلس هشتم از مجالس النفایس گوید که تیمورخان ارانتی که نواحی سغاد سیله چاپیب ایردی
اوچالامینک باشین کیلتوردون و بمعنی دوانیده در خسرو شیرین در معراج گوید شعر چاپیب براق همه رخشین چو یکره بولوب اول
اسفرسعد اکبر و بمعنی شمشیر زده فرماید شعر دیدی باشیمنی چاپیب طعمه ایلیت ایتلاریمنکا دیدی بو یوکدین اوز طلیش باقیله من اکبر
و نیز در سد سکندری در وصف رزم سکندر با دلدار بمعنی دو نیم زده گوید شعر فلك ترک کردو نی ایکی چاپیب آیننك هر برسیکا بیر مینا

چاپیشانك دویده و دوانیده و غارت کرده و شمشیر زده چاپسا و لغای و چاپیب و لغیه توان دوید و دوانید و غارت کرد و شمشیر
توان زد چاپا الغای تواند دوید و دوانید و غارت تواند کرد و شمشیر تواند زد چاپا چاپا دوان دوان و دوانیده کنان دوان
کنان و شمشیر زنان و بدون تکرار نیز باعضاف مستعملست چنانکه در تاریخ بابری بمعنی تاختن کنان مذکوراست که حیرتان یلی چاپیبون چاپ
آن لار نیغ خراب قیلدیلار چاپای و چاپایین بدوم و بدوم و بدوی و دوید و بدوانم و بدواند و بدوانی و دواند و تاخت کنم
و کند و کنی و کرده و شمشیر زنم و بزند و بزنی و زده چنانکه شاهد بر اول در مقاله هشتم از حیرة الابرار در باب و فا بمعنی شمشیر زنم گوید
تند بولوب قاتل پولاد چنك دیدی یکینکیزنی چاپای بیدرنك چاپناق و چاپغانیز و چاپغای برو چاپالی چاپالینك بدویم و
و تاخت کنیم و شمشیر زنیم چاپغالی برای دویدن و تا دوید و برای دوانیدن و تا دوانید و برای تاخت کردن و تا تاخت کردن و برای
شمشیر زدن و تا شمشیر زده چنانکه بمعنی برای شمشیر زدن در سد سکندری گوید شعر قایادلیت بیلیید اکم اوزره تیغ کردین جهتی
بیلدیغ چاپغاج بمحض دویدن و بمحض دوانیدن و بمحض تاخت کردن و بمحض شمشیر نواختن چاپقوچی دونده و دواننده و تاخت کننده
زننده چاپقوچه و چاپقوچه و چاپغانچه تا دویدن و تا دوانیدن و تا تاخت کردن و تا شمشیر زدن و بمقدار آنها چاپقومیز دوشت
دوید خواهیم دوانید و تاخت خواهیم کرد و شمشیر خواهیم زد چاپقوکز دو و جمع خاطب چاپقوسیلار دو و جمع مغایب چاپقولوق
دویدنی و دوانیدنی و تاخت کردنی و شمشیر نواختنی چاپغای و چاپا و چاپسا و چاپسون و چاپدیك بدود و بدواند و تاخت کند
و شمشیر بزند چاپقودیك و چاپاردیك دویدنی و همچنانکه بدود و بدواند و همچنانکه بدواند و تاخت کند و همچنانکه تاخت
کند و شمشیر زند و همچنانکه شمشیر بزند و شاهد بر اول بمعنی همچنانکه بدود در تاریخ بابری مذکوراست که بو تلغ لار بیننك او ستون
تمام آت چاپقودیك هموار دور چاپیشماق مع الشین المعجمه با یکدیگر دویدن و دوانیدن و بیکدیگر شمشیر زدن چاپیشیب چاپیشیا
چاپیشیش با هم دویده و دوانیده و بیکدیگر شمشیر زده چنانکه شاهد بر اقل از بمعنی دوانیده در سد سکندری گوید شعر یمنا
آتلاغین بحرا را چاپیشیب اوکوشیغ ایله بیر بیرین تاپیشیب و باقی صیغ برتیلاق تاپیشماق اشتقاق می یابد چاپیلماق مع اللام
آمده اول دوانیده شدن دویم تاخت شدن سیوم جدا شدن بضرب شمشیر را شنا آن و صیغ آن بالام اشتقاق می یابد چاپتوراق
مصدر متعدیست دو معنی طرد اول بمعنی دوانیدن بود دویم بمعنی تاخت فرمودن باشد چاپتوردی دوانید و تاخت فرمود چنانکه
خسرو شیرین گوید بالمعنی الاول شعر کیشوبان نوفه چاپتوردی چاپتوردی و تاباتی چلیتوردی بوسیر عزمه تاباتی که قیلدی بیسر دشتا ناتش چاپتورسیش دوانیده
و تاخت فرموده چنانکه شاهد بر اول بمعنی اول در سبعه سیاره گوید شعر اول مشافری آنغه میند و کیل چاپتورو بخند شعفه
منکو کیل چاپتورایغ چاپتوراین بدوانم و بدواند و بدوانی و دوانیده و بتازم و بتازد و بتازی و تاخته چنانکه شاهد بر اول
در افسانه سکندری گوید شعر بیلیك تختی اوزره چقیب اولتوراین خیال الجی بین هطرف چاپتوراین و باقی صیغ بر نهج بالفظ تو
اشتقاق می یابد چاپقوداناق بسکون بای عجمی و ضم قاف معجمه و فتح دال و دشدید با برف و باران بوزیدن و صیغ آن موافق و قیم اشتقاق
می یابد چاپقولاشماق بفتح لام و سکون شین معجمه بیکدیگر شمشیر زدن و ستیزه و نبرد کردن و صیغ آن موافق اول اشتقاق می یابد
چاپالاماق بفتح بای ابجد و لام بترکی روی بمعنی دست و پا زدن من ابجوامد چاپ باجیم و بای عجمی ترکی بمعنی تلبیس و تدلیس باشد
و نیز اراتست از دویدن و دوانیدن و تاخت کردن و قطع کردن و شمشیر نواختن بضرب واحد چاپسا برو زن با بابر کوروی بمعنی
و عطیه است چاپاغاغان دایم تازنده چاباق باجیم عجمی و فتح بای ابجد و سکون قاف ماهی بیزه را گویند چاپان باجیم عجمی و بای عجمی
و سکون نون لباس پشمی و نیلم و دانا مند انك شاهد چغتایه شعر ایرور چند یتیمنك نونك کلای آق کلیم کورونمه چاپانلیا قلیغ

204v.

چاپانی اوزده ماموق وکه شعر داغ امرلرکا چاپانیم ایچ وتاشی ناملادی باغلادیم هم چاپاندین ظللدی کرایسکی ماموق

چاپاوتی باجیم عجمی وبای عجمی مفتوحه وسکون واو وکسر تاف چپاول بضم واو وسکون لام بر سر خصم تاختن و غارت کردن چنانکه

در تاریخ وصاف چپان تاختن بخارا مذکور است که جمله هزار سوار بتق وابکار تا البه بتمویه براندند پس چپاوقیان با لشکر تعقب

رسیدند ونیمه ازان اسیران بر گرفتند فآنرا چپه می گویند چاپچی بسکون بای عجمی وکسر جیم عجمی [illegible] دو معنی دارد اول حلاج

گویند دویم تعمیه شخصی را گویند که قول وفعل او مبنی بر تلبیس باشد چپر باجیم عجمی وبای عجمی [illegible] محوطه ایست که از

خس وخاشاک وچوب ترتیب دهند چنانکه در نسایم المحبة مذکور است [illegible] گوید که شاه ابو الغازی [illegible] خان ابر

میشلاهر که چپر تودوه [illegible] در تاریخ بابری [illegible] ولایات هند مذکور است که خس [illegible]

[illegible] الطال کیفت یاشهر بولدی وانچه [illegible] کویند چاپقولاش بمعنی [illegible]

زدن بود چاپقون بسکون بای عجمی ونون وضم قاف معجمه دو معنی دارد اول بمعنی تاخت [illegible] شعر

[illegible] چاپقون [illegible] کویند که [illegible] الشاهد [illegible]

[illegible] وکوزناشیم چاپقوندیک [illegible] دو معنی دارد [illegible]

[illegible] دویم بمعنی دست بهم زدن بود که آنرا بعربی صفقه خوانند چاپقوچی فارسی کرچیق باجیم عجمی وفتح بای عجمی و

سکون قاف بترکی رومی چراغ چشم باشد که آنرا بعربی رمص نامند چاپوق بضم بای ابجد [illegible] باجیم عجمی کیی بود که کند

صورت [illegible] شمشیر داشته باشد جبه بفتح بای [illegible] بدو معنی آمده اول بمعنی [illegible] باشد دویم اسلحه را نامند

وبلغت جغتای جبا [illegible] سع التاسز المشتقات چاپماق وچاپماقلیغ باجیم عجمی وسکون بای [illegible]

ودو چیز [illegible] وسر بهم آوردن چاپتی هم پیوست چاپتوق هم پیوستیم چاپتار وچاپتادور هم می پیوندد وچاپتاد

تامل ومستقبل می آید چاپتایدور می پیوندد وپیوسته است چاپتغان [illegible] وچاپتا دورغان هم [illegible] وبهم پیوسته و[illegible]

می آیند چاپتی وچاپتیل مفرد [illegible] چاپتا وچاپتاغیل مفرد [illegible] وچاپتا دو معنی [illegible] که در ذیل [illegible]

مذکور خواهد شد چاپتینک وچاپتینکیز وچاپتینکلار جمع [illegible] چاپتانک وچاپتانکیز وچاپتانکلار جمع [illegible]

هم می پیوندم چاپتامین وچاپتامیز [illegible] هم پیوندم چاپتاماس هم می پیوندد وبمعنی [illegible] می آید چاپتیب و

چاپتیبان وچاپتیش هم پیوسته چنانکه [illegible] شعر [illegible]

چاپتیش [illegible] چنانکه فضولی بغدادی علیه الرحمه گوید [illegible] شعر

[illegible] آتشی [illegible] چاپتوبانرا با دو توبان قافیه کرد

وگفته شعر [illegible] وتوبان [illegible] چاپتیشانک هم بسته وبرافراخته چاپتاب

چاپتیب گفته هم توان بست وتوان برافراخت چاپتا الغای هم تواند بست وتواند برافراخت چاپتا چاپتا هم پیوسته کمان چاپتای

چاپتامین هم پیوندم وپیوندد وپیوندی وپیوسته چاپتاق وچاپتغانیز وچاپتغای وچاپتالی هم پیوندم چاپتغلی برای بهم پیوستن وبا هم پیوسته

چاپتاج چون هم پیوست وپیوندد چاپتوچی هم پیوندد چاپتوغه وچاپتغاچه تا بهم پیوستن [illegible] بهم پیوستن چاپتوغه

هم خواهیم پیوست چاپتوغی دور هم خواهید پیوست چاپتوسلادور هم خواهند پیوست چاپتولوق هم پیوستنی چاپتغای و

چاپتوچاپتولوچاپتوغو چاپتدیک هم پیوندد چنانکه شاعر رومی شاهد برآن آورده گفته شعر [illegible] چاپتوق کوز

205r.

[illegible] آنه باش [illegible] هم پیوستنی وچنانکه می پیوندد چاپتلاماق باجیم عجمی یعنی ترکیدن بود وصیغ آن موافق

[illegible] اشتقاق می یابد من الجوامد چپت [illegible] که ایشان [illegible] نامند وکلمه ایشان [illegible] داشتن الخیمه

در حیرت الابرار گوید شعر [illegible] چپت [illegible] باجیم عجمی [illegible] را گفته اند شعر

بکسر جیم عجمی یعنی کنار استعمال کنند چاتاغ [illegible] که [illegible] وبالجمله [illegible]

در شغل وعمل [illegible] میخوانند ومؤلف برهان قاطع از [illegible] چاتال مع اللام بترکی رومی چیزی دو شاخ را گویند

وبجانب [illegible] چاکار [illegible] نامند چاتاله بفتح لام [illegible] بترکی رومی چوبی بود که از برای ضبط [illegible]

وازانجا [illegible] خوانند چاتغال بسکون تا ولام وفتح غین معجمه [illegible] وسایر ترکیب [illegible]

بود [illegible] گویند چاتلاغوچ بسکون تا وفتح لام [illegible] که بفارسی بن وبعربی حبة الخضراء نامند چاتما

بفتح میم دو معنی دارد اول [illegible] چوب [illegible] دویم [illegible] چنانکه [illegible] دو معنی [illegible]

الابرار گوید شعر [illegible] وچاتما [illegible]

سیمان چاتمادیا [illegible] ظلم وغضب [illegible] بفتح تای [illegible] بترکی رومی بمعنی [illegible] بود

چنه چی یعنی تاخت کننده که آنرا بلغت جغتای چاپاوتی گویند چاتی بکسر تای [illegible] سه پایه بود که [illegible] از آن آویزند چنانکه

در نسایم المحبة مذکور است که [illegible] گوید [illegible] بتکلف [illegible] وبا [illegible] آسینک [illegible]

[illegible] چیتک بکسر تا وسکون کاف بترکی رومی کربه باشد که آنرا بعربی هر [illegible] گویند

چیتک [illegible] بترکی رومی [illegible] بود که [illegible] گویند وکل آن [illegible] کربه باشد وآن از جمله [illegible]

چاتیلدوق بسکون لام وضم دال [illegible] بود مع الحاخ [illegible] که [illegible] کند وآن [illegible]

که [illegible] مثل [illegible] آبشار [illegible] که بنا لای آن [illegible]

[illegible] جنکو [illegible] بود مع الجیم چاجاک باجیم اول عجمی وثانی عربی مفتوح [illegible]

که آنرا بفارسی [illegible] گویند مع الدال چادر [illegible] خیمه را گویند که از کرباس [illegible] ووانچه از چوب [illegible]

والاچوق نامند چادو نام یکنوع [illegible] است چنانکه [illegible] شعر [illegible]

جادو [illegible] سنک یده باشد که آنرا یده تاشی [illegible]

ویاده تاشی هم گویند وبعربی حجر المطر نامند چدیک باصطلاح اتراک روم یکنوع [illegible] است که ساق بلند دارد وزنان آنرا [illegible]

میپوشند مع الراء من المشتقات چارلاماق بمعنی صدا زدن وندا وآواز کردن باشد چارلادو [illegible] چارلار [illegible] چارلاید [illegible]

الشاهد علی الاول [illegible] عشق [illegible] چارلار [illegible]

بمعنی فاعل ومستقبل هم می آید چارلاغان وچارلاغان [illegible] چارلاید [illegible] صدا زننده وصدا زده وبمعنی مضارع هم می آید [illegible]

مفرد [illegible] چنانکه در حیرت الابرار گوید الشاهد علی الاول شعر [illegible] چارلار [illegible]

چارلاتلو [illegible] مفرد [illegible] جمع [illegible] چارلاتنکلار [illegible]

[illegible] چارلاغان وچارلاغان [illegible] چارلادو [illegible] وچارلادام [illegible] چارلاماس [illegible]

وبمعنی فاعل ومستقبل منفی هم می آید چارلاب وچارلابان [illegible] چارلامیش صدا زده [illegible]

جالاوی آکنای صدا تولکند جالای جاردلادو جارلاو صدا زنان جارلای جارلامین صدا زنم و زنید بی و زنده جالوانلق و جالانلاغا

جالاغلیر و جالولی و جالولینک صدا زنیم جارلاغلی برای صدا زدن و تا صدا زده جارلاماج چون صدا زده و زنند بعضی صدا زدن

چنانکه در تاریخ الانبیا در ذکر جرجیس راهب و متهم شدن او بزنا کوید که شامه اول غرابه خیتاجه ابلیک قاریغنه قو یوب جاناودی

سونکرا تا دینلا بحی طفلی جارلاماج طفل لبیک دیب جواب بردی جالاغوجیم صدا نزند جالاغوسیر و جالاغوا قا صدا نزد

و بقدر صدا زدن جالاغومیز بزنیم صدا خواهیم زد جالاغوکز بزنید صدا خواهید زد جالاغو سیلار زدند صدا خواهند زد جارلاغولوغ صدا

زدنی جالاغای جالاغو سلیم جالاغاسون جارلاغو دیلت صدا زند جارلاغو دیلت صدا زدنی و همچنانکه زند جلرلاماق مع

مصدر متعدی بنا بر صدا زدن کردن و صیغ آن بدستور باتای قرشت اشتقاق می یابد من الجوامد جار بمعنی ندا و آواز بود چنانکه خسرو

شیرین کوید شعر جریک کا الامان میغاد بو جارث تو اچو هر طرف سنکورد ی اول جار ... و در این شعر لفظ ...

تقسیم کرده و نوشته که بمعنی اخباری باشد که برای سفر از جانب پادشاه بلشکر شود و شعر بر بعد شاهد آورده و مضیره هم ثابت کرده

سهو کرده اند و نیز اسم طایفه ایست از اکراد که در کوهستانات حوالی کنجه سکونت دارند و باجیم عجمی بترکی رومی یکنوع بافته ایست

که آنرا اتراک توران چارتاره و چادر بود کویند و بفارسی چادرشب ... بعربی ... کویند و مخفف چلم هم باشد چرای

باجیم عجمی بمعنی چراغ و چمن و مرغزار را کویند و چرای بجیم نیز مستعملست چار تو بده چارتارع یکنوع بافته ایست ...

شاهد بر ثانی ... محبوب ... بیان ... کوید که ... ایکی ... تون ... کان ...

شقاوت اکرچه لفظ ... ما چون ... مصطلح است و در فارسی غیر مستعمل لهذا در ذیل لغات ترکی نکارش یافت ...

... ترکی رومی ... باطراف آن آهن ... خوب ... کویند چرچی باجیم عجمی ... ترکی رومی ...

و ... فروش بود که آنرا بعربی صید لانی نامند چارقب بسکون را و بای ابجد ... کیسه کربان والطراف دامن ...

بجای ... و ... آهن کویند الشاهد علیه شعر شفق چنین ... سید بن چارقب ... شفق ...

... بسبب ... هشتم از منشات کوید که ... سیدین ...

قول لا ... چارقب ... چرکس باجیم عجمی و سکون را و فتح کاف و کسر سین مهمله یکنوع سکانیست ...

... چنانکه در ظرب ... واروی مصطلح است الشاهد علیه شعر ... چوشن ... آینک ...

کیم اوق چرکسی ... و ... سکان ... حیرت الابرار در وصف پادشاه کوید شعر شعله ... چرکسی

... زمانه ... شعله ... در وصف سپاه امیرک کوید شعر کو ... یار و ... کو ...

باش ... و ... چرکسی چون کلاه خود طایفه اوزبک ... آنرا چرکسی مانند کفته یعنی سکانی در جای دیکر کلاه خود

... مانند ... مانند کفته یعنی ... مانند چنانکه در ... منظومه باشاهد ...

چارکه باجیم عجمی و سکون را و فتح کاف شادروان و خیمه و خرکاه را کویند چنانکه کوید شعر ... چارپا ... تو ...

جایکه بلبل ... ایچاره ... سپاه ... و بترکی رومی نام خیمه کوچکی است که آنرا ... کویند و بکسر جیم هم

مستعملست چرمر باجیم عجمی بمعنی زیر پوست بود الشاهد علیه شعر عجب ... ای ... اوز ... چر ...

آسیاب جرن بفتح را و سکون نون آسیا کویند شعر سینک ... و ... الزمان ... جرتلار ...

کیم ... کاج چاروقا باجیم عجمی و ضم را ... کویند که ... آن ... باشد چرک ... ترکی رومی بمعنی ... تاش

و آن مخفف چیرات است و جری ... بمعنی ... مع الثین من المشتقات جاشماق مضطرب شدن و ... آنراشم ...

جاشوق مضطرب شدیم جاشار و جاشادور مضطرب میشود و جاشار بمعنی فاعل و مصدر هم آید جاشغان و جاشاغان و جاشاردر

مضطرب شونده و مضطرب شده و بمعنی مصدر هم می آیند جاش و جاشغیل مفرد فی المبنی للفعل الامر جاشما و جاشماغیل مفرد

از فعل نهی جاشینک و جاشینکز و جاشینکلار جمع فی المبنی للفعل الامر جاشماتک و جاشماتکز و جاشما تکلار جمع فی المبنی للفعل نهی جاشمای

مضطرب نشوم جاشاسین و جاشار سین و جاشادر ... مضطرب میشوم جاشماس مضطرب نمیشود جاشیب و جاشیبان ...

مضطرب شده الشاهد علی الاول لا ... شعر ... مضطرب ...

جاشماسلک مضطرب شدن جاشنا بولغای جاشیب ... مضطرب تواند شد جاشا الغای مضطرب تواند شد جاشا ...

مضطرب شوان جاشای جاشاین مضطرب شوم و شود و شوی و شده جاشا ... جاشغای ... جاشلو جاشالنک مضطرب

شویم جاشغالی برای مضطرب شدن و تا مضطرب شده جاشقاج چون مضطرب شده شود و بعضی شدن جاشغوچی مضطرب

جاشغوجه جاشغونه و جاشغا تا مضطرب شدن و بقدر مضطرب شدن جاشغوسیدر ... مضطرب خواهیم شد جاشغوکزدور مضطرب

خواهید شد جاشغوسیلار ... مضطرب خواهند شد جاشغولوق مضطرب شدنی جاشغای جاشلو جاشنا و جاشون و جاشدیک

مضطرب شود جاشغو دیلت جاشار دیلت مضطرب شدنی و همچنانکه شود جاشیرماق بکسر شین و سکون را و مهمله مشکل

متعدی بمعنی مضطرب و پریشان و پاک کردن و صیغ آن بکسر شین باتای قرشت ... اشتقاق می یابد من الجوامد جاش

باجیم عجمی و بسکون واو و جاش و باش از اتباعست بمعنی پریشان و پراکنده جشته باجیم عجمی و سکون شین و فتح تای قرشت

لمبو ... و بجیم هم مستعملست و بفارسی بمعنی طعمه و طعام اندک باشد جشن هنکامه عیش و طرب و مجمع ضیافت

بود چنانکه در تاریخ الملوک در وصف جمشید و اتمام قلعه اصطخر کوید که چون بو عمارت تو کاندی عالم سلاطین و اشراف و اکابر

یغیب ... جشن ... مع الغین من المشتقات چاغلاماق باجیم عجمی دو معنی دارد اول تصور و کمان کردن دویم ملاحظه وقت

کردن چاغلادی تصور کرد و ملاحظه وقت کرد چنانکه در حیرت الابرار کوید الشاهد علی المعنی الاول شعر ایتکبی ...

اوزنی ... چاغلادیم و در سد سکندری فرماید بالمعنی الثانی شعر ... سکندر ...

و ... چاغلادیم چاغلادوق تصور کردیم و ملاحظه وقت کردیم چاغلارم و چاغلارور تصور میکند و ملاحظه وقت میکند و چاغلار

بمعنی فاعل و مصدر هم می آید چاغلاغان و چاغلاغوچی و چاغلاغان تصور کننده و تصور کرده و ملاحظه وقت کننده و کرده و بمعنی مصدر

هم می آیند چاغلا و چاغلاغیل مفرد فی المبنی للفعل امر چاغلاما و چاغلاماغیل مفرد فی المبنی للفعل نهی چاغلانک چاغلانکز و چاغلا

جمع فی المبنی للفعل امر چاغلاماتک ... جمع فی المبنی للفعل نهی چاغلاماسمین تصور نمیکنم و ملاحظه وقت نمیکنم

چاغلادیمین ... چاغلایدیر ... تصور میکنم و ملاحظه وقت میکنم چاغلاماس تصور نمیکند و ملاحظه وقت نمیکند

فاعل و مصدر منفی هم می آید چاغلاب و چاغلابان و چاغلامیش تصور کرده و ملاحظه وقت کرده چنانکه در ولادت فرهاد کوید

الشاهد علی الاول بالمعنی الاول شعر ... اول کشوردا چاغلاب ... کار ... و در مقاله سیزدهم

از حیرت الابرار در داستان ... کوید الشاهد علی الثانی بالمعنی الاول شعر ... چاغلابان ...

تا ... باغلابان و در سد سکندری کوید بالمعنی الثالث شعر ... چاغلابان ...

... چاغلابان چاغلامیشانک تصور کرده و ملاحظه وقت کرده چاغلاتا بولغای و چاغلاب ... تصور توان کرد ...

206v.

وقت توان کرد چاغلایالغای تصور تواند کرد و ملاحظه وقت تواند کرد چاغلادی چاغلاجی چاغلادیو تصور کنان و ملاحظه وقت
کنان چاغلادی چاغلایبن تصور کنم و کند و کنی و کرده و ملاحظه وقت کنم و کند و کنی و کرده چاغلاداق چاغلادیو چاغلادیک
چاغلادیلر چاغلادیلک تصور کنیم و ملاحظه وقت کنیم چاغلاغلی برای تصور کردن و تا تصور کردن و برای ملاحظه وقت کردن
و تا ملاحظه وقت کردن چاغلاغاچ چون تصور کرد و کند و بمجرد تصور کردن و چون ملاحظه وقت کرد و بمجرد کردن چاغلاغوچی
تصور کننده و ملاحظه وقت کننده چاغلاغوجه چاغلاغونجه چاغلاغانجه تا تصور کردن و بمقدار تصور کردن و تا ملاحظه وقت کردن
و بمقدار ملاحظه وقت کردن چاغلاغوسیدور تصور خواهیم کرد و ملاحظه وقت خواهیم کرد چاغلاغوسیدورمیز تصور خواهید کرد
و ملاحظه وقت خواهید کرد چاغلاغوسیلاردور تصور خواهند کرد و ملاحظه وقت خواهند کرد چاغلاغولوق تصور کردنی
ملاحظه وقت کردنی چاغلاغای چاغلادیلر چاغلاغوچی چاغلادیلر تصور کنند و ملاحظه وقت کنند چاغلاغوزلیق چاغلادیلر تصور کردنی
و همچنانکه تصور کنند و ملاحظه وقت کردن و همچنانکه ملاحظه وقت کنند من الجوامد چاغ باجیم عجمی دو معنی دارد اول وقت
و زمان را گویند چنانکه گوید شعر شامدین کم سون نزهتلان آستیدا منکم چاغیم کیم که کم نایدهر بلورین دسته کوزکو
آستیدا و بعضی در غزل ملح با اصطلاح مغولیه گوید شعر تجنیس سرزلف توکرد آنچه نکرد نش در چاغ جغاتای مغولان اختیار
دوم بمعنی صحیح و درست بود الشاهد علیه شعر کونکلی اول بیوزا ونی دین خلق ایچرا چاغ ایتادور یا نی خوب بیکی تاشی بیلک
چاغ ایتادور جغاتای بفتح غین و تای قرشت و سکون یای حطی اسم پسر دوم چنگیزخانست که ما وراء النهر و ختن و کاشغر و پیش
بالیغ تا قراقیم در تحت سلطنت او بوده و اولوس جغتای بدو منسوبست و از اجغتای نیز گویند چنانکه گوید شعر نوایی ایلا کلا
خافقه ایرور عاشق که ترک قول لاری آتینک جوجی بود و جغتای چاقاراق باجیم عجمی و فتح قاف و رای مهمله و سکون الف تخته
سوراخ دار و مدور که بر بالای آلاچوق گذارند و سرچوبهای آلاچوق را بدو گویند از آن بیرون کند چاغان باجیم عجمی و فتح غین
و سکون بلغت مغولی بمعنی آمده اول کهروز عید را گویند دوم بمعنی سفید باشد چاغاناق باجیم عجمی و فتح غین و نون و سکون تا
آتنج و بند دست را نامند چاغداول باجیم عجمی و سکون غین و لام و فتح دال غنیم ولوقوجی را گویند که لشکر را رانند و وقت
از اطراف لشکر خبردار باشند و طلایه طرح کنند چنانکه در تاریخ نادری مذکور است که کیچه چاغداول اوقدغه
اولوغ عجمی دین تانک آتقونجه آت اوسیدا اوقایدیلار و آن را چنداول هم گویند چاغلامه باجیم عجمی و سکون غین و فتح لام و
ترکی درمیم بمعنی صدا و آواز بود چاغلیغ دو معنی دارد اول بمعنی قدر و مقدار و اندازه باشد چنانکه گوید شعر …
جالینک خواندا ای همیش … چاغلیغ … شعر …
ایسه جسمین یا بار چاغلیغ لباسی … دوم بمعنی صحت و درستی بود چاغیش باجیم عجمی و کسر غین و سکون یای حطی …
الشاهد علیه شعر چاغیزنی غافل ایسانک … چاغیرغه باجیم عجمی
و کسر غین اول و سکون رای مهمله و فتح غین ثانی شاپشان بود که آنرا غلیواج و دوران و بعربی حظله خوانند الجیم العجمی مع القاف
من المشتقات چاقماق باجیم عجمی بمعنی دارد اول گزیدن مار و عقرب و امثال آن دوم بدگویی و سعایت کردن سیم فولاد آتش زنه
بود که آنرا بعربی قداحه گویند چنانکه در ذیل جوامد نوشته خواهد شد چهارم بمعنی قدح و قداحه باشد یعنی چاقماق زدن چنانکه …
الکبر در حکم کردن مجنون الحق گوید شعر … چاقماق … کوز یا رو نور شعله … بمعنی درخشیدن
و برق باشد که آنرا بعربی و مضمع تلالؤ و لمعان گویند چنانکه گوید شعر … چاقماق قهوش …

207r.

یاقماق اوچون میلنغانلیک اوت چاقماق قهوش چاقیق گزیدن و سعایت کرد چنانکه در تاریخ الملوک مذکور که کیکاوس
بمعنی ثانی گوید که سودابه او کای ناسی آنکا عاشق بولوب ایردی کام حاصل قیلالمادی اوز قوم خوجه دین کیکاوس قاشیدا آنی اوری
بیله بدنام قیلیب چاقتی و نیز بمعنی چقماق زد و درخشید و درخشانید چاقار و چاقادور میگزد و سعایت میکند و چقماق میزند
و میدرخشد و میدرخشاند چنانکه لطفی شاعر شاهد بر اول ایل بمعنی ثانی گوید شعر کونکلی اوستیدا توقوب نیچه یاشی آغیر لانکا
ایلکا تا چاقار بمعنی حول خوب یا غی دور و چاقار بمعنی فاعل و مصدر هم می آید و نیز بمعنی منزل و مکان باشد چنانکه در ذیل
نگارش خواهد یافت چاقغان و چاقادورغان گزنده و گزیده و سعایت کننده و کرده و چقماق زننده و زده و درخشنده و …
و درخشاننده و درخشانیده و بمعنی مصدر هم می آید چاق و چاقغیل مفرد مخاطب امر چاقاو چاقغیل مفرد مخاطب
چاقینگلار چاقینکیز چاقینکلار جمع مخاطب امر چاقای چاقایلی و چاقایلیک چاقانکلار جمع مخاطب امر چاقام چاقامن میگزم
و سعایت میکنم و چقماق میزنم و میدرخشم و میدرخشانم چاقامن و چاقادورمن و چاقادورم میگزم و سعایت میکنم و
چقماق میزنم و میدرخشم و میدرخشانم الشاهد علی الثالث بالمعنی الثالث شعر برق یا سرکیم اوت چاقارمین …
تاغ ایله بولمش … چاقماس … نمیگزد و سعایت نمیکند و چقماق نمیزند و نمیدرخشد و نمیدرخشاند
نامل و مصدر منفی هم می آید چاقیب چاقیبان چاقیش گزیده و سعایت کرده و چقماق زده و درخشیده و درخشانیده و شاهد …
… شعر برو هر دم چاقیبان …
در حکم کردن مجنون الحق … چنانکه شاهد آن در ذیل چاقماق نگارش یافت چاقیشانک گزیده و سعایت کرده
و چقماق زده و درخشیده و درخشانیده چاقسا بولغای چاقیب بولغه توان گزید و سعایت توان کرد و چقماق توان زد و توان درخشید
و درخشانید چاقا چاقا گزان گزان و سعایت کنان و چقماق زنان و درخشان درخشان و درخشانیده کنان چاقماغ و چاقماق
بگزم و بگزد و بگزی و گزیده و سعایت کنم و کند و کنی و کرده و چقماق بزنم و بزند و بزنی و زده و بدرخشم و بدرخشد و بدرخشی و درخشیده
و بمعنی متعدی نیز استعمال میشود چاقسام چاقسانگ چاقسا چاقسای چاقالینک بگزیم و سعایت کنیم و چقماق بزنیم و بدرخشیم
چاقغالی برای گزیدن و تا گزیدن و برای سعایت کردن و تا سعایت کردن و برای چقماق زدن و تا چقماق زدن و برای درخشیدن
و تا درخشیدن و درخشانیدن چاققاچ بمجرد گزیدن و بمجرد سعایت کردن و بمجرد چقماق زدن و بمجرد درخشیدن و درخشانیدن چاقغوچی
گزنده و سعایت کننده و چقماق زننده و درخشاننده و درخشنده چاقغونچه چاقغوجه چاقغانچه تا گزیدن و بمقدار گزیدن و تا سعایت کردن
و بمقدار سعایت کردن و تا چقماق زدن و بمقدار چقماق زدن و تا درخشیدن و درخشانیدن و بمقدار آن چاقغوسیدور خواهیم گزید
و سعایت خواهیم کرد و چقماق خواهیم زد و خواهیم درخشید و درخشانید چاقغوسیلاردور … خطاب جمع حاضر چاقغوسیلاردور
جمع غایب چاقغولوق گزیدنی و سعایت کردنی و چقماق زدنی و درخشیدنی و درخشانیدنی چاقلتاغ چاقماغ چاقماقنا و چاقتون
چاقدیلک بگزد و سعایت کند و چقماق بزند و بدرخشد و بدرخشاند چاقغودیلک چاقارلیک گزیدنی و همچنانکه بگزد و سعایت کند
و همچنانکه سعایت کند و چقماق زدنی و همچنانکه بزند و درخشیدنی و همچنانکه بدرخشد و بدرخشاند چاقیلماق بکسر قاف و
سکون لام به سه معنی بود اول گزیده شدن دوم سعایت کرده شدن سیم درخشیده شدن آتش و برق که آنرا بعربی التماع و ایماض گویند
چاقیلغان و چاقیلادورغان گزیده شونده و گزیده شده و سعایت کرده شونده و سعایت کرده شده و درخشان شونده و درخشانیده شده الشاهد
علی الاول بالمعنی الاخیر شعر مرکچی نینک غلو دین هر دم چاقیلغان اوتا یمش کیم کونکول آلیغ ضعیف و بقراری بهم مینک

ونیز در خسرو شیرین گوید شعر دو چوبه اوچی و فیروزه خرگاه • آیینه ایکی کاچی مه ایله ماه • قاندوق زرین و سیمین کیم قاملغان
کواکب بیک سپهر اوزره چاقیلغان • و بمعنی مصدر هم می آید چنانکه شاهد بر اول بمعنی درخشیدن گوید شعر ای که سوزونک
کبه تاچان کویدی بو زوق کونکلونک • وی • غار ضمینک اوتی چاقیلغاندا بو کاشانه کویوب چاقیلیب چاقیلیناد چاقیلیش کرده
و سعایت کرده شده و درخشیده شده الشاهد علی الاول بالمعنی الثالث شعر کمزه مکا اوت چاقیلیکاج غم دین اشیکیم آتار
تاچان که مناعقه توشکاج توکار ناغین نی بیچاث ونیز در حیرة الابرار در صفت شیخ نظامی علیه جناس گوید شعر خزی
ینک بعیدین اوت چاقیلیب رخشی دامی تیزلیک اوت چاقیلیب چاقیلغاج چون کرده بوکرده و بمعنی کرده شدن و چون غایب
کرده شد و شود و بمعنی سعایت کرده شدن و بمعنی درخشیده شد و شود و بمعنی درخشیده شدن بالمعنی الثالث شعر چاقیلغاج المنة
حسنونک منکا قالماس ثبات • ثبر اوکانی اثر قالغای کبر برق و شیغه اوزه ا بمنیش چاقیلغوسی کرده خواهد شد و سعایت کرده خواهد
درخشیده خواهد شد چنانکه در زمین بمعنی ثالث گوید شعر ده تاچان نقه سیکرو عشقینک کاجیدین کوزوم ناه لحظه اوت
بس تو بعد که جلوه عشقینک یا قیا اوت کیم جلوه هم واوت چاقیلغوسی
چاقیلغوسی و باقی صیغ بر سیاق مواقعه اول بالالم اشتقاق بیابد چاقیشماق بکسر قاف و سکون شین بهم خوردن و تضاد
نمودن و صیغ آن موافق شق اول با شین معجمه اشتقاق می یابد چاقماناق بسکون قاف و ضم نون و چاقناشماق مع التین
منقلب شدن و بهم بر آمدن صیغ چاقماناق موافق شق ثانی و صیغ چاقیشماق موافق شق اول اشتقاق بیابد چاقماتماق
چاقماشتورماق مصدر متعدیست یعنی منقلب ساختن و صیغ آنها موافق شق اول اشتقاق بیابد چاقیلداماق بکسر قاف مشدد
و سکون لام و فتح دال صدا کردن چیزی که در جوف چیزی باشد چاقیلداتماق مع التا متعدی آنست یعنی صدا در آوردن
چنانکه مثل است که سین تاشاونک چاقیلدات باغیرلارینی تخان مجهور من الجوامد چاق همان چاغ بمعنی وقت و زمان
و در هیت باشد که در حرف عین مذکور شد چاقار بفتح القاف مع الراء المهمله بمعنی آکویند که از زیر و رو شمه بد قلعه که جمعی در آنجا
محوطه و حصاری ساخته شکی نمایند چنانکه در مذمت یوسف خواجه گوید شعر بابور ایردیم چاقار غه کاه کاهی شمیم نینک
سوزی کونکلومکا باتاردین • چو یوسف خواجه چاقی امیدی ایرمان • ایتوردی بیزنی آخر اول چاقاردین و مولف رومی چاقار را بمعنی
شمر چوقار بضم جیم خوانده و بمعنی جمع شدن نوشته سهو کرده • در تاریخ بابری مذکور است که محمد سلطان میرزا پسر قند نینک تاثر ور
غاینده چاقلردی بر مدرسه سالیب توری چاقال شغال را گویند چاقچالاغای بمعنی انقلاب و بر هم خورد که باشد چنانکه گوید شعر
تاچان که مست بولوب حقه اول توبایش اوردین تمام شهر غه توشکای غغان و چاقچالاغای چاقماق فولاد آتش زنه بود که آنرا
قداحه و مقدحه گویند چنانکه در مقاله هشتم از حیرة الابرار در باب وفا گوید شعر تاشکه چاقماقدین اولغای برق تیز تومار
ابکالایین اولدفراق • چاقماشیق بسکون قاف اول و آخر و فتح نون و کسر شین یعنی انقلاب و برهم خوردگی چاقمیش بکسر قاف و سکون میم
سه معنی دارد اول خم و شکل را گویند دویم ازرق چشم را مانند سیم ترکی روی عمر فیج است و آن پرنده ایست شکاری سیم و فکر تیز
سقر گویند چاقیرتانات نام یکنوع ریاحین است چاقیرچی رومیه جلاد را گویند چاقیل بترکی رومی سنگهای ریزه بود چاقیلناق
بسکون لام و فتح تای قرشت و سکون کاف آخر چکیده دوغ بود که آنرا جوشانیده خشک کنند و آنرا عرب اقط و ترکی قروت هم
گویند یعنی کشک چاقیلداق بفتح دال ابجد سیا بود که آب دان میرید و صدا می کند و مجازا شخص پرگو را گویند که بسیار چانه
میزنند چاقیلداد بضم دال ابجد که ربو صدا و آوازی بود که از خوردن دو چیز بهمدیگر بهمرسد چاقین بسکون نون برق تبا
چنانکه گوید شعر حمزه یو لعطاله تهمیم دیدای کال خرمنی کیم چاقین خرمن غه توشکان نینک جهنا تاثیر بار • و نیز بمعنی لمعه برق و آتش

الجیم العجمیه مع الکاف چک سه معنی دارد اول بمعنی عهد بود که باشد من انشا بلطف شعر عشق اهلی قضا بدل اریغ کیم چکتین آجناعی بو
فنه لاز ایل عقلی غه چیزای اشر ایرماس لار دویم صکوک و سجلات و بروات را گویند و این لفظ مسک بود چنانکه گوید شعر جان بربه
و ملینکی بیع اینکانی یازدیم کونکلومه • در ره عشق ایکی کاهیم چکلیک کونکلوم چکیم سیم بمعنی قرعه آمده چنانکه در تاریخ الملوک
در ذکر ضحاک گوید که اول هر کون ایکی کیشی اولتورور ایردی که نیغ کیشی بو ملنلیک ناامستایر خلوت من قل اولو را بردی چکچه برنج
بچه چشم محو و والده را گویند چکری با صطلاح رومیه نام یکنوع کشتی است چکچه بفتح میم و ضم میم نهاد زده بترکی روی بد و معنی هید
اول صندوقچه کوچک را گویند دویم نام قصبه ایست از ممالک روم که در نزدیکی استنبول واقع است چکمن بسکون کاف و نون وفتح
میم دو معنی دارد اول بارانی را مانند الشاهد علیه شعرای نوایی کلفشان چکمن سیله اولکه عذار • نی عجب اشکینکنی نامنقور الخیاله
فی ذیز در ابتدای لیلی مجنون گوید شعر یا زیما مغوری سیکاج ایلادینک بات • بیر چکمونی یا اشیل قزلات • دویم نام موضعیست در حوالی
اندخود من عمال بلخ و مولف رومی بمعنی چکمه و چاقشور نیز ذکر کرده سهو کرده • چکمه با صطلاح اهل ایران موزه ساق بلند دیت که
تیماج و پوست دوخته در ساوری بر پا کنند چکوج چکوش از ابزار یست که زرگران و مسگران بدان کار کنند و آنرا عرب مطرقه
نامند الشاهد علی الثانی شعر کو کومه فرنا حید اعشقینک بلا اسمیاریغه • بر کیتوردا ابلاهی فرهاد سیغین چکوش • و با ضمیر
نار بی بیشتر کت و ضم جیم عجمی هم مستعملست چکه بفتح کاف عجمی هاء زده دو معنی دارد اول بمعنی ریک باشد که آنرا اقوم نیز گویند دویم چکیم
میوه ایست که در کوهستانات اندجان و فرغانه باشد و بتشدید کاف عربی شقیقه دو طرف پیشانی بود که آنرا عرب صدغ خوانند
چکی بر وزن نیکی با صطلاح رومیه وزنی باشد معین و آن مساوی صد و چهل حقه است و هر حقه چهار صد درهم و هر درهم چهار دانک
چکین بد و معنی آمده اول سبزه و گیاه باشد دویم نخاله بوتهانی بود که از ابریشم ده دهند و باین دو معنی بکسر جیم هم مستعملست و بلغات روم
کوشن را گویند و بکاف عجمی در انتهای سیله کوچک است که در میان پلوتک دارد هم میرسد و عم تیز دارد الجیم العجمیه مع اللام من المشتقات
چالماق و چالماقلیغ نواختن و بترکی رومی کنایه از بوجدن و دزدیدن هم باشد چالدوق نواختیم چالور و چالادور نیز نواز و نوازد
و چالور بمعنی فاعل و مصدر هم می آید چالغان بمعنی الهغان • چالادورغان نوازنده و نواخته و بمعنی مصدر هم می آید چالغ چالغیل مفرد
فعل امر و چال سه معنی جامد هم دارد که در غیر مصادر مذکور خواهد شد چالماو چالماغیل مفرد فعل امر بر غلیه چالینک و چالینکز
چالینکلار جمع غائب با فعل امر چالمالانک چالمالینکز و چالمانکلار جمع غائب با فعل نهی چالمادیم چالماس من نمینوازم چالماس
چالادور چالورام مینوازم چالماس نمینوازد و بمعنی فاعل و مصدر منفی هم می آید چالیب چالیبان چالمیش نواخته چالمیشانک
نواخته چالغانا بولغای چالیب بولغاچه توان نواخت چالالغای تواند نواخت چالالاو چاله چاله نوازان نوازان
چنانکه گوید شعر کلکت چون جوشتو را کرتاقی و مطرب بولکیله تو نانوتا و اول چاله چاله چالای چالاین نوازم و نبولند و سوازد
و نواخته چالنا و چالغایز و چالغای چالالی چالالینک نوازیم چالغالی برای نواختن و تا نواخته چالمناج چون نواخت
و بعضی نواختن چالغوچی نوازنده چالغوچی چالغوچی چالغاچه تا نواختن و بعد نواختن الشاهد علی الثالث بالمعنی الثانی
شعر ای نوایی نوحه آهنکیدا کوپ قیلدینک فغان • ابهدی مجلس مطربی بو نغمه نی چالغانچه معلوم • خواهیم نواخت چالغوسی
خواهید نواخت چالغوسلار نیز • خواهند نواخت چالغولوق نواختنی چنانکه در فرهاد و شیرین گوید شعر بو غاره در که بول
دین آلغولوق دمش • آیینک کوس رحیلی چالغولوق دمش • چالناغی چالاو تیغ سازو چالسورنی چالدیک نوازد چالغودیک و چالاردیک
و حتی و مهنا نکه نغخا زدا الشاهد علی الاول بالمعنی الاول شعر ساقیای تو بس معنی نوحه آهنکو چالکیم سنا • عزم اهلیش کرسه حک

چاقنودیك چالیغماقلیغ مع النون وچالیشماق چالیشماقلیغ مع اللام یعنی نواخته شده چالینغوچی چالینغو
نواخته خواهد شد چنانکه شاهد برا قلعادر سنکلاخ کوید شعر پنجه بولسه خیلینك راکوز چیل چالینغوچی
اوزره کوس رحیل شاهد ثانی را در فرهنگ ایام الحجه در ذکر معشوق طوبی کوید که بو نوبت موندا اصرار ورلارینجه کوندین سونکرا
سینمك در کاهینکا چالینغوسی دور وباقی الفاظ این نهج موافق شق اول اشتقاق می یابد چالیشماق وچالیشماقلیغ مع الشین هم نواختن
و مجازا بمعنی کوشیدن هم استعمال میشود وباقی صیغ بدستور یاشین اشتقاق می یابد چارلاماق بسکون را وتای قرشت وفتح لام انجار
و باجیم عجمی چشم را از چشم خیره کردن و تشهلك اماده معنی نکند باید لفظ چشم مذکور شود وصیغ آن موافق شق اول اشتقاق می یابد
من الجوامد مع الجیم چالا بر وزن بالا بلغت مغولی منکوله باشد که مغولیه بر سر کلاه دوزند چلایر نام طایفه ایست از اتراك
مع الجیم العجمیه چال چال به سه معنی بود اول ریش دو موی را کویند عموما و اسپی را نامند که موی آن سرخ و سفید باشد خصوصا چنانکه
کفته شعر چون شاه کند بر اسب چالش چالش دشمن کند از دل چو نالش نالش دویم شتر بچه را خوانند سیم آبدنغ را کویند و از نوکشه هم
باشد چنانکه در ذیل جامد کذشت و بترکی رومی ام ازین دیدن و دیدن بود و بفارسی شش معنی دارد اول کودال دویم کرو قمار سیم
چهارم رغبت که بر دو قسم است کوچکترا چال و بزرکترا خرچال کویند و بعربی حباری و بفارسی هوبره نامند پنجم نام دهیست از [illegible]
ششم نام دهیست از بدخشان و بزبان هندی نیز [illegible] به معنی آمده و [illegible] را ملك چال خوانند و دو کروه یک فرسخ باشد هفتم قمار سیم
نوعی باشد از ماهی و سروری در فرهنك خود بمعنی ماشقالداغ ذکر کرده چالاپ بفتح لام و بای عجمی و سکون رای مهمله مکیات که عنکبوت
آنرا بمیان پرده خود می تند و هرکاه از حرکت فارغ شود باو چسبیده می ایستد چالاسین چالك و چالاك و آنرا چالشم کویند
چالاماق مرغ موش کیر بود و آنرا چالای هم کویند چالای به سه معنی باشد اول مرغ موش کیر است دویم نام طایفه ایست از اتراك سیم بمعنی
نوازم و نوازد و نوازی و نواخته چنانکه در ذیل مصدر چالماق کذشت چلب بر وزن ثعلب بترکی رومی بمعنی جناب [illegible] باشد چنانکه
نسیمی میکوید شعر چلب سنی نچه شیرین دوداغلو یارا تمیش که سلسبیل او ناموره لبلرینك نزلالندن وبفارسی دو معنی دارد اول کج
کویند که در بقله خانه نوازند دویم بمعنی فتنه و آشوب بود چلپك بسکون لام و کاف وفتح بای عجمی نوعی نانیست نازك که در روغن پزند
چنانکه در قضانامه مدینه کوید که شعبان آینینك درتاسیدا کیم برات بولغای چلپك او قوزی تمام حلوا ایکیه باتمان چالپاو
بسکون لام وواو وفتح بای عجمی و چالپوق بسکون لام و قاف و ضم بای عجمی موضعی را کویند که آب ایستاده کل و خلاب شده باشد چلبی
بفتح لام و کسر بای ابجد و یای حطی نویسنده و شاعر و خوانا و دانا و ظریف الطبع را کویند چالغو بترکی رومی بمعنی ساز بود چالت بسکون لام و تای
قرشت چست و چالاك چالقوین بضم قاف و کسر یای حطی و سکون نون بترکی رومی پشت خوابیدن و بر قفا افتادن را کویند که آنرا بفارسی ستان
و بعربی سطیح خوانند و بعضی بمعنی ستان و بن ستان نوشته همانا در نسخه از لغات رومیه لفظ ستان را در تحت لغت چالقوین ستان
و با بمعنی ذکر کرده اشتباه او واضحست چالمه بسکون لام وفتح میم فوطه و دستاری بود که بر سر بندند و باصطلاح اهل ایران یکنوع مشربه است
که از تلاطین دوخته در جوار جهازها بر فاش بربندند و با آن آب خورند چلنك بر وزن پلنك بترکی رومی شهپر مرغ باشد و مجازا [illegible]
که جوانان نامی از طرآت ساخته بکلاه خود نصب کرده بعلامت دلیری و پهلوانی بر سر زنند و در اینجا تعبیه منظور است
چالیمچی نوازنده و آن مخفف چالغوچی است و بترکی رومی بمعنی مرده و زنده باشد چالیش بمعنی کوشش بود و نیز [illegible] کوشش کردن و شوکت
فرهنك جهانکیری لفظ چالش را نامی شمرده و بمعنی رفتار از روی ناز و تکبر ذکر کرده و از اشعار شاهد آورده مولانا خسرو شعر
بمدار نشد و چالش آغاز کرد [illegible] شیخ سعدی [illegible] سر خصم را کرد با الش کنیم [illegible] شاهد [illegible]

لغت چال مذکور شد اشغال مذکور هیچ یك دلالت بر رفتار نمیکند بلکه هما بمعنی کوشش از آنها مفهوم میشود چلیش هیز
دو تخمه را کویند یعنی یم و نر ماده میشان هر یك از جنس خود باشد و آنرا شالغونچه هم نامند و شتر دو تخمه را ابرلغ خوانند چالیغ وچالوق
باجیم عربی و عجمی ابتر را کویند که جلف و تند باشد و آن محرف چالالواست الشاهد علی الاول حشو کرو ایشیم بولسه را کب بوشیخ
ایکا انمالسوی توسن اتلانیب چون کیم ایر بهد چالیغ چلبیك بر وزن [illegible] بترکی رومی فولاد جوهردار باشد و مؤلف تحفه المؤمنین
جلیك را باجیم ابجد نوشته که اسم ترکی فطاله است چلیم بر وزن حلیم بترکی رومی بمعنی [illegible] و درستی ترکیب بود چالین
و سکون نون آتش زنه باشد که آنرا چقماق هم کویند چنانکه در خسرو شیرین کوید شعر [illegible]
چالین [illegible] المعجم العجمیه مع المیم من المشتقات چالماق و چالماقلیغ بسکون میم ونون وفتح لام بمعنی صوت و اکراه حرف زدن
[illegible] باکراه حرف زدیم [illegible] باکراه حرف میزند و [illegible] بمعنی فاعل و مصدر هم می آید [illegible]
[illegible] باکراه حرف زننده و حرف زده و بعضی مصدر هم می آیند [illegible] مفرد مخاطب فعل امر [illegible]
مفرد مخاطب فعل نهی [illegible] جمع مخاطب فعل [illegible]
[illegible] باکراه حرف میزنی [illegible] باکراه حرف [illegible]
[illegible] بمعنی فاعل و مصدر نفی هم می آید [illegible] باکراه حرف زده [illegible] باکراه حرف [illegible]
[illegible] باکراه حرف [illegible] باکراه حرف [illegible] باکراه حرف زدن [illegible]
[illegible] باکراه حرف نیم [illegible] باکراه حرف [illegible]
[illegible] چون باکراه حرف [illegible] باکراه حرف زننده [illegible] باکراه حرف [illegible]
[illegible] باکراه حرف خواهیم زد [illegible] باکراه حرف خواهند زد [illegible]
باکراه حرف [illegible] باکراه حرف بزند [illegible] باکراه حرف زدن
و چنانکه نزند من الجوامد چماشیر بر وزن طباشیر بترکی رومی لباسی درخت بود که آنرا او د به هم کویند چام آغاجی بترکی رومی نام درخت
صنوبر بود و آن محرف شمع آغاجی است زیراکه چوب آن بسبب دسومت مانند شمع میسوزد چمچه قاشق بزرکیست که از چوب و مس سازند
بدان آش بر هم زنند چمچه بالیغ بترکی رومی یکنوع ماهی است که آنرا بفارسی کفچلیز کویند چام سقیزی بترکی رومی صمغ درخت صنوبر
که از [illegible] خوانند چمن بر وزن دمن و چمند [illegible] کاهل و بدماغ بود که آنرا بفارسی چمند و بعربی
حرون کویند چنانکه شاهد ثانی را در فصل [illegible] کوید که [illegible]
[illegible] زیراکه در لغت [illegible]
نامند و بلغت جغتای [illegible] را کویند و بفارسی بمعنی باغ و بستان و سبزه زار خرم باشد [illegible] آمده مع النون چاناق
جاناق دو معنی [illegible] چنانکه کوید الشاهد علی الثانی شعر [illegible]
[illegible]
[illegible] ذکر کرده که [illegible]
که بر اسب بسته میشود جناق [illegible] شاهد آورده سهو کرده دویم نام طایفه ایست و با جیم عجمی کاسه را نامند چنانکه
[illegible] و باده کوید [illegible] الرقیه شعر [illegible] وجنام باجیم عربی

209v.

مفارسی کروی باشد که دو کره را هم به مبندند و آن معروفست و مؤلف برهان قاطع گفته که با اول مضموم طاق پیش مزراب باشد
و با اول مضموم دامنهٔ زین و تسمهٔ رکاب بود جندک بر وزن فندک مردهٔ ملبوس را نامند چانق باجیم عجمی و سکون نون و قاف بترکی
رهی هول را نامند چانقتا بسکون نون و فتح قاف چنگال چانقی بسکون نون و کسر قاف بمعنی منزلت و شوکت باشد چانک
بر وزن بانک منزلت و جرس و ناقوس بود چنگا و چانکا باجیم عجمی و سکون نون و فتح کاف عجمی مع الاماله ملت اسفل باشد که آنرا چا
گویند چنگلک باجیم عجمی قلاب بود و آن آلتی است که از آهن سازند و سر آن کج و تیز باشد مع الواو چاو بر وزن نکاو دیگ [illegible] جاو
اول معروف یا و بمعنی [illegible] باشد و صاحب تاریخ روضة الصفا در وصف حصار بامیان که از ولایت غزنین است نقل کرده که چنگیزخان
بعد از سوختن و ویران کردن آن موضع را چاو بالیغ نام نهاد یعنی شهر بد در اصطلاح یعنی شهر دشمن انسب است دویم نام شهریست که در سمت شرقی
جنوبی خانبالیغ واقع شده از خانبالیغ تا آنجا یکماهه راه مسافت است و الایلچه که کنیه مغولیه است در آنجا می باشد و باجیم
عجمی [illegible] و بمعنی آمده اول که بمعنی آواز باشد چنانکه گوید شعر زاهد اعشقینکی باشیدا [illegible] آندین سونکرا کیم خالیم تشیع ایله
سالدینک باری مالمغه چاو دویم کاغذ پاره ایست مربع طولانی که در عهد خواتین مغول بشکل خاص [illegible] پادشاه را بر آن نقش کرده
در عوض زر با آن معامله میکرده اند و وصاف در جلد دویم تاریخ خود در بیان احوال ایچاوی که در عهد کیخاتو خان رایج بود مذکور
ساخته که هیات و صورت چاو [illegible] پیرامن سطح کاغذ پاره مربع مستطیل چند کلمه بخط خطائی نوشته و بر بالای آن لا اله
الا الله محمد رسول الله سکه [illegible] نقد ساخته و فروتر از آن ایرنجین تورجی تحریر کرده در میان دایره کشیده خارج از [illegible]
و از نیم درهم تا ده دینار رقم زده مترو[illegible] شد چاوجی بسکون واو و کسر جیم نام بلغت مغول پاشنه پا بود چلودود باجیم عجمی نام پسر
کیوک خان بن اوغوز خان است و بلغت مغول بمعنی صاحب ناموس باشد و نیز نام طایفه ایست از ترکمان چاودرولت باجیم عجمی و سکون واو و کاف
و ضم رای مهمله بترکی رومی کوکناب بود و بکسر جیم نیز مستعملست چاودرونی باجیم عجمی و سکون واو و نون و ضم رای مهمله و کسر تای قرشت بترکی
رومی دانه ایست سیاه که در میان گندم روید و آنرا قرامو قده لوجه نیز گویند و بفارسی شیلم و شملک و زوان نامند و اکرکا کوکرد
[illegible] نام باشد جوشه بفتح شین معجمه [illegible] شنبوف را گویند جوکت بر وزن زغلک لون [illegible] بود چنانکه گوید
شعر کلکون تون اوزرا جوک نقش آچیلمادی لالا [illegible] و بمعنی رنگ هم استعمال شود چنانکه [illegible] در وصف
طبور هند فرماید شعر [illegible] چاودلوق باجیم عجمی و سکون واو و [illegible]
چاوتو چاودورمه باجیم عجمی و ضم واو و سکون رای مهمله و فتح میم محوطه و دیوار [illegible] و سراپرده و امثال آنرا گویند که بدور خانه
و خیمه بکشند و بکسر جیم هم استعمال میشود چاوش باجیم عجمی و ضم واو و سکون شین معجمه بدو معنی آمده اول چوبداران است که
عبارت از یساول و ایشیک آقاسی باشد چنانچه در افسانهٔ [illegible] سیاره گوید شعر چاوش بخت ایشیکدا حاضر بولکیم کیرار [illegible]
قبله [illegible] قولی و نیز در خاتمه انتخاب فرماید شعر کیشی بوزنن پادشاه اولسه تخت کره و جهان پناه اولسه تیتی کوک
گنبدیدا آرامی چاوشی بولسه چرخ [illegible] دویم کسی را گویند که پیش پیش قافله رفته و بلدی نموده بحرکت و نزول ایشان را اخبار کند
باشد [illegible] الشاهد علیه شعر عشق چاوشلاری بوز قافله [illegible] کوچوبین [illegible] روان ایلاکیز
و نیز در لیلی مجنون گوید شعر آنداق تاپیان بو خیل چاووش کیم بولغان ایکین اول [illegible] چاودن بضم واو و سکون نون
هنر را گویند شعر دهر [illegible] و صلکا [illegible] بوستون کیم [illegible] و بضم جیم هم باجیم عجمی مستعملست
و نوکر رومی بمعنی چاپغون نوشته که عبارت [illegible] باشد که شدید [illegible] سهو کرده جه بچند معنی استعمال شود اول لغات

جاو

جه

210r.

جای

وانتهاد دویم وزن و مقدار [illegible] گویند امر کلمه بمعنی [illegible] گویند [illegible] و آنرا چه بمعنی [illegible] و باجیم عجمی گویند کوتکاه
معنی یکجا [illegible] و پنجه یعنی [illegible] و طاقچه بمعنی [illegible] و طاق [illegible] و تفصیل آن در دیباچه کتاب مذکور است مع الیاء المثناة
چایقاماق و چایقاماقلیغ چایقاتماق و چایقاتماقلیغ مع الکاف مصدر متعدی است بمعنی جنبانیدن و چرخانیدن و بهم زدن و این مصدر [illegible]
و هوا و شعله ما را استعمال میشود چایقادوق چلقانوت جنباندیم چایقادور چلقادور چایقاتور و چلقاتادور جنباندند [illegible]
الشاهد علی الثالث شعر تاشی فراقیدا [illegible] چلقاتور [illegible] کولاک و چلقاتادور [illegible]
معنی فاعل و مصدر هم می آید چنانکه شاهد بر اول [illegible] مصدر گوید شعر کوزوم [illegible] آچیم [illegible]
[illegible] قطره قطره [illegible] چایقاقان چلقاقان [illegible] و چایقاتقان و چایقاتورغان جنباننده
و جنبانیدن و بمعنی مصدر هم می آید چایقاو چایقاغیل و چایقات و چایقاتغیل مفرد غائب فعل امر الشاهد علی الثالث شعر
بزم [illegible] ای ساقی هوش [illegible] آینک چایقات چایقاتما و چایقاتماغیل [illegible]
مفرد غائب [illegible] چایقاتمان و چایقاتمانکیز و چایقاتمانکلار و چایقاتیننک و چایقاتینکیز و چایقاتینکلار جمع غائب [illegible] چایقاتما
چایقاتمانکیز و چایقاتمانکلار و چایقاتمانک و چایقاتمانکیز و چایقاتمانکلار جمع غائب [illegible] چایقاتمانکلار [illegible] چایقاتما و چایقاتماس
جنبانم چایقادیم [illegible] چایقادیمیز [illegible] چایقاتادورمین و چایقاتادورمین و چلقاتادورمین [illegible]
چایقاتماس چایقاتماس [illegible] و بمعنی فاعل و مصدر هم می آید چایقاب و چایقاتیب [illegible] و چایقاتیب [illegible]
جنبانیده چایقاتیب [illegible] و چلقاتیب [illegible] و چایقاتیب [illegible] توان جنبانید چایقای آلغای و چایقاتا آلغای تواند
جنبانید چایقای [illegible] و چایقاتادیغان متحرک [illegible] چایقاتادین و چایقای [illegible] و چایقاتادین [illegible] جنبانم و جنباند و جنبانی
و جنبانید چایقاتماق [illegible] چایقاتماغلیق [illegible] و چایقاتماس [illegible] و چایقاتماغیر و چایقاتنای [illegible] و چایقاتا و چایقاتالنکیز
[illegible] جنبانیم و چایقالنک [illegible] چایقاالماق بمعنی [illegible] آید چایقاتالی و چایقاتالی برای جنبانیدن و جنبا[illegible]
چایقاغاج و چایقاتقاج چون جنبانید و جنباند و [illegible] جنباندند چایقاتقوچی و چایقاتقوچی جنباننده چایقاتقوچی [illegible]
چایقاتقاغیر و چایقاتقوچی [illegible] جنباندن [illegible] جنباندن چایقاتقوسی [illegible] جنبانید چایقاتقو [illegible]
چایقاتقو [illegible] جنبانید [illegible] جنبانید [illegible] چایقاتقوسی [illegible] چایقالغای و چایقاتاسا
چایقاسون و چایقادیلک [illegible] چایقاتاسا [illegible] چایقاتدیلک [illegible] جنباند چایقالغو دیلک [illegible] دیلک [illegible]
جنباندنی [illegible] جنباند چایقاتماق و چایقاتماقلیغ مع النون چایقالماق و چایقالماقلیغ مع الکاف بمعنی جنبیدن و حرکت کردن
آب و هوا و شعله الشاهد علی الثانی شعر [illegible] چایقالماق [illegible]
چایقاتادور و چایقالور و چایقالا [illegible] الشاهد علی الاول شعر مضطرب [illegible] موج [illegible]
[illegible] الشاهد علی الثالث شعر [illegible] آهیم [illegible]
و که شعر [illegible] که چایقالورسا [illegible] بولسا چراغ [illegible] که اکیل [illegible]
بولسا چراغ چایقالور چایقالغان [illegible] چایقالغان و چایقالادورغان [illegible] و جنبیده چنانکه شاهد [illegible]
بمعنی [illegible] گوید شعر [illegible] آهیم [illegible] چایقالغان و بمعنی مصدر هم می آید
چنانکه شاهد بر [illegible] بمعنی مصدر گوید شعر [illegible] چایقالغان [illegible]

در بیان ضبط و ناق بمعنی برین ساق اشتقاق می یابد چاپاناماك و چاپانامالیك بسکون یا و فتح نون بمعنی چاپیدن بود که آنرا عربی
مضغ گویند چاپنادور چاپیلیم چاپنار و چاپانایدور میچاپید چنانکه در مهرالمسلمین در باب سوم گوید الشاهد علی الاول
گاو تماك لطف ایچون چاپانارانا بیچ رواده کریانا یو [illegible] چاپاناکان و چاپانایدورکان چاپیده و چاپیده و بمعنی مضغه
می آیند چاپانا و چاپاناکیل مفرد مخاطب فعل امر چاپانا و چاپاناکیل مفرد مخاطب فعل نهی چاپاناماك و چاپاناملیك و چاپاناکلا
جمع مخاطب فعل امر چاپاناماك و چاپانامانکلار جمع مخاطب فعل نهی چاپانامان و چاپاناماس بمعنی چاپیم چاپانای مین و چاپانار مین
چاپانایدور [illegible] چاپانادام میچاپیم چاپاناماس نمیچاید و بمعنی فاعل و مصدر هم می آید چاپاناب چاپاناباریش چاپیده چنانکه در لیلی
مجنون در وصف لیلی گوید الشاهد علی الاول لحشر [illegible] چاپاناب و شاپیب [illegible] چاپاناشالك
چاپیده چاپاناشا [illegible] چاپاناب [illegible] چاپانای الغای تواند چاپید چاپانای چاپانای و چاپانایو چاپیده کان چاپانای [illegible]
بچاپیم و بچاپید و بچاپد و بچاپیده چاپاناناك و چاپاناکاین و چاپاناکای [illegible] چاپانالی و چاپانالیك بچاپیم چاپانالی برای چاپیدن [illegible]
چاپاناکاچ چون بچاپد بچاپیده و محض چاپیدن چاپاناکوچ چاپیده چاپاناکوچ [illegible] چاپاناکا [illegible] چاپیدن [illegible]
چاپاناکومیز دو نخواهیم چاپید چاپاناکوکوز [illegible] نخواهید چاپید چاپاناکوسیلار [illegible] نخواهند چاپید چاپاناکوك چاپیدنی چاپاناکا و چاپاناسا
چاپاناسونه چاپاناد [illegible] بچاپید چاپاناکودیل چاپاناردیك چاپیدنی و همچنانکه بچاید چاپیا [illegible] بسکون یا بمعنی هوائی شدن تیر باشد
و معنی آن موافق شوال و الاشتقاق می یابد من الجوامد چای با جیم عجمی بمعنی نای ترکی ورود بزرگ که از سیل و آب بود [illegible]
بلند نا خیشك چایان با جیم عجمی و فتح یا و سکون نون عقرب باشد و برج عقرب را مانند من [illegible] شعر چایان نوش
[illegible] ابتدای [illegible] و ترکی رومی [illegible] که آنرا [illegible] خوانند چنانکه در [illegible]
شاهد [illegible] شعر [illegible] عقرب چایان [illegible] دم دور [illegible] و چنان [illegible]
چیان [illegible] گویند الشاهد علیه شعر [illegible]
کویا لاله [illegible] و آنرا [illegible] مانند چایپر با جیم عجمی [illegible] که از [illegible] و [illegible]
نیز گویند چایقون با جیم عجمی بسکون یا و نون و فتح قاف جنبش آب و هوا را مانند چایلاق با جیم عجمی مع القاف ترکی دو [illegible] باشد که [illegible]
[illegible] خوانند چایلان با جیم عجمی مع النون بمعنی [illegible] بود چایلغان بکسر یا و سکون لام و نون و فتح غین [illegible]
تو [illegible] باب المضمومات حرف الجیم مع الباء الثقالة [illegible]
با جیم عجمی و ضم با و سکون لام پوسیده شدن چوبولدوق پوسیده شدیم چوبولور و چوبولادور پوسیده می شود و بمعنی فاعل و مصدر هم می آید
چوبولغان و چوبولوغان و چوبولادورغان پوسیده شونده و پوسیده شده الشاهد علی الاول بالمعنی الثانی شعر بولادی [illegible]
[illegible] و معنی [illegible] هم می آید و [illegible] چوبولغا [illegible]
شاهد آمده [illegible] چوبول و چوبولغیل مفرد مخاطب فعل امر چوبولما و چوبولماغیل مفرد مخاطب فعل نهی چوبولونك و چوبولونکوز
چوبولونکلار جمع مخاطب فعل امر چوبولمانك و چوبولمانکلار جمع مخاطب فعل نهی چوبولماس و چوبولماس پوسیده نمیشوم چوبولامین
چوبولورمین و چوبولادورمین و چوبولوبان پوسیده میشوم چوبولماس پوسیده نمیشود چوبولوب چوبولوبان و چوبولیش پوسیده شده چوبولیشالك
پوسیده شده چوبولسا [illegible] و چوبولوب [illegible] پوسیده تواند شد چوبولالغای پوسیده تواند شد چوبولا چو بولا پوسیده شوان
چوبولای چوبولاین پوسیده شوم و شود و شوی و شده چوبولساق [illegible] چوبولغای [illegible] چوبولغای [illegible] پوسیده شویم چوبولغالی

برای پوسیدن شدن و تا پوسیده شدن چوبولغاچ چون پوسیده شد و شود و محض شدن چوبولغوچی پوسیده شونده چوبولغوجه
چوبولغوسی چوبولغانچه تا پوسیده شدن و مقدم پوسیده شدن چوبولغومیز دور پوسیده نخواهیم شد چوبولغوکوز دور پوسیده نخواهید
شد چوبولغوسیلار دور پوسیده نخواهند شد چوبولغولوق پوسیده شدنی چوبولغاو و چوبولاو چوبولسا و چوبولسام چوبولساك پوسیده
چوبولغودیك چوبولوردیك پوسیده شدنی و همچنانکه شود چوبولتماق و چوبولتماقلیق مع التاء مصدر متعدی بمعنی پوسانیدن و معنی آن
با نای قرشت اشتقاق می یابد چوبورماق و چوبورماقلیق با جیم عجمی و ضم با و سکون [illegible] و چوبورلماق و چوبورلماقلیق مع اللام چوبوروش
چوبورشماقلیق مع الشین المعجمه از پی هم [illegible] چوبوردوق چوبورلدوق [illegible] چوبوروشتوق [illegible] چوبورادور چوبوریدور
چوبورلور و چوبورلادور و چوبوروشور و چوبوروشادور [illegible] چوبورادور چوبورلور چوبوروشور [illegible] و مصدر هم می آید
چوبورغان چوبورادورغان چوبوریدورغان چوبورلغان چوبورلوغان چوبورلادورغان چوبوروشغان چوبوروشوغان و چوبوروشادورغان
از پی هم [illegible] شونده [illegible] و معنی [illegible] هم می آید چوبور و چوبورغیل چوبورل و چوبورلغیل چوبوروش و چوبوروشغیل مفرد مخاطب فعل
چوبورما و چوبورماغیل و چوبورلما چوبورلماغیل چوبوروشما چوبوروشماغیل مفرد مخاطب فعل نهی چوبورونك و چوبورونکوز چوبورونکلار چوبورلونك
چوبورلونکوز و چوبورلونکلار و چوبوروشونکوز جمع مخاطب فعل امر چوبورمانك چوبورمانکوز چوبورمانکلار و چوبورلمانك [illegible]
چوبورلمانکلار چوبوروشمانك [illegible] جمع مخاطب فعل نهی چوبورماس [illegible] چوبورلماس [illegible] چوبوروشماس [illegible]
از پی هم [illegible] چوبورامین چوبورورمین چوبوریدورمین چوبورلامین چوبورلورمین چوبورلادورمین و چوبوروشامین و
چوبوروشورمین و چوبوروشادورمین از پی هم [illegible] چوبوراب چوبورلاب چوبوروشوب چوبوروب چوبورلوبان و چوبورلیش و چوبور
چوبوروشوبان چوبوروشیش از پی هم [illegible] چنانکه شاعر [illegible] تاریخ [illegible] گفته [illegible]
[illegible] شاهد علی التاسع [illegible]
[illegible] چوبوروشوب [illegible] چوبورلوب از پی هم [illegible] چوبوروب [illegible] چوبورغالی [illegible]
چوبوروشا [illegible] از پی هم [illegible] تواند شد چوبوراالغای و چوبورلاالغای و چوبوروشاالغای از پی هم [illegible] تواند شد چوبوری چوبوری
چوبورلای چوبورلا و چوبوروشا چوبوروشای از پی هم [illegible] شوان چوبوری [illegible] چوبورلای چوبورلاین و چوبوروشای چوبوروشاین از پی
هم [illegible] شوم و شود و شوی و شده چوبورساق چوبورغای [illegible] چوبورغای [illegible] چوبورلساق [illegible] چوبورلغای [illegible]
چوبورلای [illegible] چوبوروشاق [illegible] چوبوروشغای [illegible] از پی هم [illegible] شویم [illegible]
چوبوروشغالی از پی هم [illegible] شدن و تا [illegible] چوبورغاچ چوبورلغاچ چوبوروشغاچ [illegible] از پی هم [illegible] شود و شده و محض شدن چوبورغوچی
چوبورلغوچی چوبوروشغوچی از پی هم [illegible] شونده چوبورغوچه [illegible] چوبورغانچه [illegible] چوبورلغانچه و چوبورغانچه
چوبوروشغانچه چوبوروشغانچه از پی هم [illegible] شدن و مقدم شدن چوبورغومیز دور و چوبورغوکوز دور چوبوروشغوسیلار دور از پی هم [illegible] خواهیم [illegible]
چوبورغوکوز دور چوبوروشغوکوز دور از پی هم [illegible] خواهید شد چوبورغوسیلار دور و چوبورلغوسیلار دور و چوبوروشغوسیلار دور از پی هم [illegible]
چوبورغولوق چوبورلغولوق چوبوروشغولوق از پی هم [illegible] شدنی چوبورغاو چوبوروشاو چوبوروسون چوبوروردیك چوبورلسا و چوبورسا و چوبورلا
چوبورلسون چوبورلسیك چوبوروشغای چوبوروشا و چوبوروشا و چوبوروشون و چوبوروشدیك [illegible]
شود چوبورغودیك چوبوروردیك چوبورلغودیك چوبورلوردیك چوبوروشغودیك چوبوروشوردیك از پی هم [illegible] و همچنانکه شود چوبورتماق
چوبورتماقلیق مع التاء مصدر متعدی بمعنی از پی هم [illegible] کردن چوبورتماك و چوبورتمانکیز چوبورتمانکلار از پی هم [illegible] الشاهد علی [illegible]

شعر سین کو یار مین مجرا ام مردم او توم تیزاتیکا لی · ای نم اهلی وصل افسانه سین چو بو نمانیکز · و فراقی مجنون ناس دو معنی بر آن قرار داده
اول به معنی و آمدن اعضای آدمی از چوب طبرلیک دویم رسیدن زمانه فرو ماندن سوختن و سیاه شدن و شمر ز بر جدا جدا آورده هر دو معنی
اخرا و لا یعوا است و ناقص بر بنیاد تا ای قرشت اشتقاق می یابد من الجوامد مع الجیم العجمیه چوپ با بای عجمی دو معنی دارد اول به معنی شاتیه و نوا (ج)
بلسند چنانچه در خسرو شیرین گوید شعر چو واندیشه توشتی کو نکیلکا چوب · روان دیدی الماراعدیکم قوپ مرسعه سیاره شعر
شاهلیغ خلعتی قدینک بیله چوب · شاهلار هندی بم اباعینکا کوپ مز سج سنجکده ری شعر کاهی خود آزاردی کوپ بولسا هم
سیاست طریقه چوب بولسا هم دویم خاشاک را گویند چنانچه در لیلی مجنون در احوال مجنون گوید شعر تا تلیغ کونزلیتکان بیله چوب
کیرپکلاری دین حساب اکوپ چوپان با بای عجمی مفتوحه شبان را گویند چوپان آلداتان بلغت اتراک توران و چوپان آلداغی بلغت
اتراک دعم نام مرغیست کوچک شبیه بناشه و چنان به زمین نشیند که هر که آن را ببیند تصور کند که قوت برخاستن و پریدن ندارد
همینکه پیش او روند پرواز نموده دورتر نشیند و آن را به فارسی شبان فریبک گویند چوپان قوشی نام مرغیست کبود مایل به زردی
که از گنجشک کوچکتر است چو بچوق با هر دو جیم عجمی و سکون بای ابجد و قاف گنجشک بود چنانچه در سد سکندری گوید شعر بچه بولسا
چو بچوق غه لجاد و لغت کوسیدین میلوم صید کر کوپ طرب · و هم در تاریخ الملوک در صفت تاج خسرو پرویز گوید کر منیک کو هر بیله مکللیب
ایدیلار هر بیری چو بچوق یوموتقه سیچه · چوبود بضم بای عجمی و سکون دال مهمله بدو معنی آمده اول هوی بزرگ و سفید را گویند دویم
جنگل و بیشه بر درخت را مانند چو بوخ و چو بوق بضم بای ابجد شاخچه نازک چوب نازک باریک را خوانند مع التا چوت بالجیم عجمی جوت
تیشه را گویند و آن آلتی است از آهن که نجاران بدان چوب تراشند مع الجیم من المثناة چو جو تمال چو جو تماکلیک بضم هر دو جیم و سکون تای جوج
قرشت به معنی شیرین و لذیذ کردن باشد چو جو توک شیرین کردیم چو جو تورو چو جو تادور شیرین میکند و چو جو تور به معنی فاعل و مصدر هم می آید
چو جو تکان چو جو توکان و چو جو تادورکان شیرین کننده و شیرین کرده و به معنی مصدر هم می آید چو جوتدو چو جو تیکیل مفرد مخاطب از فعل امر الشاهد
علی الاول شعر شهد عشقینک نظر ابتلار کردی نیز او شوتجام دین · نوایکا مینکا آجیغ خواهی مذاقینکا چو جوت · و در خسرو شیرین در وصف
ملا نظامی گوید الشاهد علی الثانی شعر نوایی کیم مریدی بولدی صدق ارادت بیله انکا معنی ده صدر حمول کو هر بیله کونکلین ایدی تعسل
حمول شکر بیله کامین چو جو تکیل چو جو تماو چو جو تماکیل مفرد مخاطب از فعل نهی چو جو تونکیز و چو جو تونکلار جمع مخاطب از فعل امر
چو جو تمانک چو جو تمانکیز و چو جو تمانکلار جمع مخاطب فعل نهی چو جو تسان و چو جو تار مین شیرین میکنم چو جو تامین و چو جو تورمین چو جو تادور مین و چو جو
شیرین میکنم چو جو تماس شیرین نمیکند و به معنی فاعل و مصدر منفی هم می آید چو جو توبه چو جو تو بان چو جو تمیش شیرین کرده چو جو تمیشانک شیرین
کرده چو جو تسا بولغه و چو جو توب بولغه شیرین توان کرد چو جو تا الغای شیرین تواند کرد چو جو تا چو جو تا شیرین کنان چو جو تای
چو جو تا یین شیرین کنم و کند و کنی و کرده چو جو تسانک چو جو تکای بیز و چو جو تکالی و چو جو تالیک شیرین کنیم چو جو تکالی برای
شیرین کردن و تا شیرین کرده چو جو تکاچ چون شیرین کرد و کند و محض کردن چو جو تکوچی شیرین کننده چو جو تکوچه و چو جو تکونچه
تا شیرین کردن و بعد شیرین کردن چو جو تکو سیز دور شیرین خواهیم کرد چو جو تکو نکیز دور شیرین خواهید کرد چو جو تکو سیلار دور شیرین
خواهند کرد چو جو تکو لوک شیرین کردنی چو جو تکای چو جو تلو چو جو تسلو چو جو تستون و چو جو تدیلیک شیرین کند چو جو تکو دیلیک و چو جو تور دیلیک
شیرین کردنی و همچنانچه کند چو جو کاناک و چو جو کانماک بضم هر دو جیم و سکون دال مهمله و نون و فتح کاف عجمی دو معنی دارد شکفته شدن
چنبره شدن که باصطلاح لغاشانه خم گویند چو جو کاندوک شکفته شدیم چو جو کانور چو جو کاندور شکفته میشود و چو جو کانور
به معنی فاعل و مصدر هم می آید چو جو کاناخان و چو جو کانوکان و چو جو کاندورکان شکفته شونده و شکفته شده و به معنی مصدر هم می آید چو جو کان

چو جو کانکیل مفرد مخاطب از فعل امر چو جو کانما و چو جو کانماکیل مفرد مخاطب از فعل نهی الشاهد علی الاول شعر خوبلار لعلی حیاتیمه
چو جو کانماکه باز اوزی هر نچه چو جو لادی مجرا اهمی کوپ چو جو کانینک و چو جو کانینکلار جمع مخاطب از فعل امر چو جو کانما
چو جو کانمانک و چو جو کانمانکلار جمع مخاطب از فعل نهی چو جو کانما و چو جو کانمار مین شکفته میشوم و چو جو کانورمین و چو جو کاندور مین
چو جو کانورام شکفته میشوم چو جو کانماس شکفته نمیشود چو جو کانیب و چو جو کانسان و چو جو کانمیش شکفته شده چو جو کانمیشانک شکفته
شده چو جو کانسا بولغه و چو جو کانیب بولغه شکفته توان شد چو جو کانا الغای شکفته تواند شد چو جو کانا چو جو کانا شکفته شوان
چو جو کانای چو جو کانایین شکفته شوم و شود و شوی و شده چو جو کانسانک چو جو کانکای بیز و چو جو کانکالی و چو جو کانالیک
شکفته شویم چو جو کانکالی برای شکفته شدن و تا شکفته شده چو جو کانکاچ چون شکفته شد و شود و محض شدن چو جو کانکوچی
شکفته شونده چو جو کانکوچه و چو جو کانکونچه تا شکفته شدن و بعد از آن چو جو کانکو سیز دور شکفته خواهیم شد چو جو کانکو نکیز دور
شکفته خواهید شد چو جو کانکو سیلار دور شکفته خواهند شد چو جو کانکو لوک شکفته شدنی چو جو کانکای و چو جو کانلو و چو جو کانسا
(ج) چو جو کانتون و چو جو کاندیلیک شکفته شود چو جو کانکو دیلیک و چو جو کانور دیلیک شکفته شدنی و همچنانچه شود من الجوامد چو چالت با هر دو
جیم و سکون کاف ظرف سفالین را گویند چنانچه در تنبیهات محبوب القلوب گوید که سفال چو چالت هر داش دین عنیک چقار تهمت
پر هم دین آن توق یا ناس چو جغه به سکون جیم ثانی و فتح غین معجمه بچه خوک را مانند چو جوک بضم جیم ثانی و سکون کاف به معنی شرم
باشد الشاهد علیه شعر یار آغیز آچماغنه در دیم سوزلاری تا مینم سبب کوپ چو جو کلوک دین یا یوشمیشلار مکر اول ایکی لب
جوجی بکسر جیم ثانی و بلغت مغول به معنی ناکاه و نیز نام پسر مهین چنگیز خانست که ممالک سقسین و قپچاق و خوارزم و ترکستان و بلغار
و اوکالک تا خدود روس در تحت سلطنت او بود و اولوس جوجی به منسوبست و در تاریخ غازانی وجه تسمیه را چنین نوشته اند که جوجی
در راه در وجود آمد چون راه مخوف بود مجال ترتیب گهواره نیافتند مقداری آرد را خمیر کرده او را در آن پیچیدند تا اعضا بدر دنیا نیابد بدین سبب
جوخ نام او جوجی کردند که ناکاه در وجود آمده است مع الخا چوخ به معنی بسیار باشد چنانچه گوید شعر اول پریوش جو جرینیک مین تیلبه
جور دیک شیدا سی چوخ · نی عجب گر بولسا عالم ملکیدا غوغاسی چوخ · مع الراء من المثناة مع الجیم العجمیه چورکاماک چورکانماک بسکون رای مهمله و فتح
کاف عجمی سوختن و هم پیچیدن تغ آتش و هوا پوست و مو و امثال آن را چورکادی سوخت و هم پیچید چنانچه در خاتمه لیلی مجنون گوید
شعر چون امر بیغ خزان بیلی نا ووغ نیم باز اغیق و روتی چورکادی هم · چورکادوک سوختیم و هم پیچیدیم چورکادور چورکایدور سوزند
و هم پیچید و چورکار به معنی فاعل و مصدر هم می آید چورکاکان و چورکارکان و چورکایدورکان سوزنده و سوخته و هم پیچنده و پیچیده به معنی مصدر هم
می آید چورکاو چورکا کیل مفرد مخاطب از فعل امر چورکاما و چورکاماکیل مفرد مخاطب از فعل نهی چورکانک و چورکانکیز و چورکانکلار جمع مخاطب
از فعل امر چورکامانک و چورکامانکیز و چورکامانکلار جمع مخاطب از فعل نهی چورکامان و چورکامار مین نمیسوزم و هم نمی پیچم چورکای مین
چورکارمین و چورکایدور مین چورکارام میسوزم و هم می پیچم چورکاماس نمیسوزد و هم نمی پیچد چورکاب و چورکامان و چورکامیش
سوخته و هم پیچیده چنانچه در حیرت الابرار در مقاله دویم گوید الشاهد علی الثانی شعر اوت حیکیان شعله بیباکی چورکاب
انجم بیله افلاکنی چورکامیشانک سوخته و هم پیچیده چورکاسا بولغه و چورکاب بولغه توان سوخت و هم توان پیچید چورکای الغای
تواند سوخت و هم تواند پیچید چورکای چورکای و چورکا چورکا و سوزان سوزان پیچان پیچان چورکای و چورکایین بسوزم و بسوزد و بسوزی
و سوخته هم بپیچم و بپیچد و بپیچی و پیچیده چورکاسانک چورکاکای بیز و چورکاکالی و چورکالیک بسوزیم و هم بپیچیم الشاهد علی
الرابع بالمعنی الثانی شعر ای نوایی عشق پرده سی گر چه رسوا المعجزی · اول نی میدانیده کیم نامه آنی چورکالی · چورکاکالی برای سوختن

و تلوسته و برای چیدن و تا چیدن چرکاکاچ چون چید و چید و بخش چیدن چرکاکوجی هم چیدن چرکاکوجه و چرکاکوغانه

چرکاکاغه تا چیدن و بقدر چیدن چرکاکومیزدر و در هم خواهیم چید چرکاکونکه بود هم خواهید چید چرکاکوسیلاغرید

هم خواهند چید چرکاکولوك هم چیدنی چرکاکای چرکاسلر چرکاسون چرکاتالیم هم بچید چرکاکودیك و چرکاکو ایلیك هم چیدنی

و همچنانکه به چید چرکاتالنغ چرکاتمان کلیك مع النون چیده شدن و در هم کشیده شدن و سیاه سوخته شدن از شعله و تف ×

[illegible]

چور ×

[illegible]

× چور

[illegible]

[illegible]

× چوش

[illegible]

× جوغ ×

[illegible]

جوف ×

×× جوق

[illegible]

بمعنی فاعل و مصدر هم می آید چوقوغان و چوقوغان و چوقوبیدرغان و چوقوشغان و چوقوشمزلوق چوقوشا نیز کود کند مو کرده و بمعنی مصدر هم می آید
چوقوچو و قوغیل و چوقوش و چوقوشقیل مفرد مخاطبه فعل امر چوقوناو چوقوناغیل و چوقوشاو چوقوشاغیل مفرد مخاطبه فعل نهی چوقوملغه چوقونکوز
چوقونکلاده چوقوشونك و چوقوشنکوز و چوقوشنکلاده جمع مخاطبه فعل امر چنانکه در لیلی مجنون خطاب بکرمهای اعضا بدن لیلی گوید الشاهد علی الاول
نظم کمزه منی چوقونك تیمنی تیشلانك آیینك کوزین و تیشین یا اشیلاغلانك چوقوماناك و چوقوماینکز و چوقومانکلاده و چوقوشمانك و چوقوشمانکز
چوقوشمانکلاده جمع مخاطبه فعل نهی چوقوسان و چوقوغان بین و چوقوشاسن بین و چوقوشمان بین کود نمیکنم چوقوری بین و چوقوربین و چوقوبیدور بین و چوقورام
چوقوشامین و چوقوشمیزمین بمعنی نمی آید چوقوشنکوکسیکیم چوقوناس و چوقوشماس کود نمیکند و بمعنی فاعل و مصدر منفی هم می آید چوقوب چوقو
چوقوپیش چوقوشوب و چوقوشوبان و چوقوشمیش کود کرده الشاهد علی الاول نظم زاغ که چوقوب آتمز ایتکان کونکلومدین
تیراغ ایله اوزنی ناتوان کونکلومدین اعضاسیدا کم اثر قیم قودی منقار ایله جنکیدا نشان کونکلومدین الشاهد علی الرابع
نظم زاغلار کوسیدا کونکلومنی چوقوشوب اوزنیلا توشقونغ ایتماس هیچ آغزیدا بربر کندیدین چوقوشیلك و چوقوشیتا کود کرده
چوقوشایولغه چوقوب یولغه و چوقوشایولغه و چوقوشوب یولکود توان کرد چوقوی آلغه و چوقوشا آلغه کود تواند کرد چوقوی چوقوی چوقوشاموق
کودکان چوقوی و چوقوبین و چوقوشای و چوقوشایین کودکم وکند وکنی ورکنم چوقوتاقر چوقوغانز چوقوغای زو چوقوبلد چوقولنك و چوقو
چوقوشغانز و چوقوشغای زو چوقوشا و چوقوشالنکود کنیم چوقولکا و چوقوشغلی برای کود کردن و تا کود کرده چوقولج و چوقوشغلج چون کود کرد
وکند و مجص کردن چنانکه شاهد بر لغت در تاریخ الانبیا در کر موسی علیه السلام و قصه عوج گوید کر صانع کانینان قدرت اظهار
مثل در قیلدی کیم اول تاغ اوستیدا اولتوروب چوقولج آنداق تیشلدی که عوج نینك بوینینه توشوب تن هلاك قیلدی و
مؤلف رومی بمعنی جمع شدن نوشته و فقره مذکوره را شاهد آورده و بعضی هم متابعت کرده سهو کرده اند چوقوغوچی و چوقوشغوچی کوب کننده
چوقوغوسی و چوقوغوجه و چوقوغانجه و چوقوشغوجه و چوقوشغونجه و چوقوشقالا کود کردن و بعد کود کردن چوقوغوسیز دور و چوقوشغوسیز کود نخواهیم کرد
چوقوغوسیز سز و چوقوشغوسیز سیز کود نخواهید کرد چوقوغوسیلار دور و چوقوشغوسیلار دور کود نخواهند کرد چوقوغولوق و چوقوشغولوق کود کرده
چوقوغای و چوقوسا و چوقوسون و چوقودیك و چوقوشغای و چوقوشا و چوقوشا و چوقوشسون و چوقوشدیك کود کند چوقوغودیك
چوقودیلك و چوقوشغودیك و چوقوشماساکود کردن و همچنانکه کند چوقولماق و چوقولمالیغ بفتح قاف و سکون لام کاوبین شدن وکود شدن و معنی آن
موافق اول یا لام اشتقاق می یابد چوقالماق و چوقالماقلیغ بفتح قاف اول و سکون لام بمعنی زیاده و افزون شدن باشد چوقالدی
زیاد شدیم چوقالیبد چوقالادور زیاد میشود و چوقالور بمعنی فاعل و مصدر هم می آید چوقالغان و چوقالورغان و چوقالادورغان زیاد
شونده و زیاده شده و بمعنی مصدر هم می آیند چوقال و چوقالغیل مفرد مخاطبه فعل امر چوقالما و چوقالماغیل مفرد مخاطبه فعل نهی چوقالنك
چوقالینکز و چوقالینکلاده جمع مخاطبه فعل امر چوقالمانك و چوقالمانکز و چوقالمانکلاده جمع مخاطبه فعل نهی چوقالدی و چوقالاس مین زیاد نمیشوم
چوقالامین و چوقالورمین و چوقالادورمین و چوقالورمن زیاد میشوم چوقالماس زیاد نمیشود و بمعنی فاعل و مصدر منفی هم می آید چوقالیب و چوقالیبان
چوقالمیش زیاد شده چوقالمیشانك زیاد شده چوقالالغای و چوقالیبولغای و چوقالیب بولغه زیاد تواند شد چوقالا آلغای زیاد تواند شد چوقالا و چوقالا
زیاد شوار چوقالای و چوقالایین زیاد شوم و شوند و شوی و شد چوقالسا و چوقالغای و چوقالغای و چوقالای و چوقالای زیاد شوم
چوقالغلی برای زیاد شدن و تا زیاد شده چوقالغاچ چون زیاد شده شود و مجص شدن چوقالغوچی زیاد شونده چوقالغوسی چوقالغوجه
چوقالغانچه تا زیاد شدن و بعد زیاد شدن چوقالغوسیدور زیاد خواهیم شد چوقالغوسیز سیز زیاد خواهید شد چوقالغوسیلار دور زیاد
خواهند شد چوقالغولوق زیاد شده چوقالغای و چوقالا و چوقالسا و چوقالسون و چوقالدیك زیاد شود چوقالغودیك و چوقالورلیك زیاد شدنی

جوك

و همچنانکه شود من الجوامد چوق دو معنی دارد اول بمعنی بسیار باشد چنانکه در تنبیهات محبوب القلوب در وصف کذاب گوید که نهمد و
اضافی چوقتور اما یا لغایت یا منا ارزاق منقی بو قتور و چوق باخانیز بمعنی مستعملست دویم منکله را گویند که برسر کلاه دوزند و اینمعنی در طایفه قلماق
بمعنی جمع القاب و لا قلماق در زمانهات سلاطین باشی چوقلوق اولوس نینك اولوغ تمورچی نویند و چوق با ضم جیم نیز باین معنی استعمال می شود
چوقال بفتح قاف و سکون لام بترکی رومی برکستوان بود که بر اسب بندند چوقلوق به معنی آمده اول پوستین سر خاب باشد که هم کرك
از آن پوستین دوزند و آن چه مشکی است آنرا اوباك گویند دویم بمعنی فروختن و کرت سیم بمعنی منکله دار بود چوقمار بفتح میم بالف کشیده و
سکون رای مهمله کوزه و عود و اشنان آنرا نامند چوقور بضم قاف و سکون رای مهمله بمعنی کود باشد الشاهد علیه نظم چوقور فرق تو
چوکونز کو پیا قوی ضعیفتی نظر قیلور او یا فی دین چوقوردا ینهان دور الجیم مع الکاف من المشتقات چوکارماق و چوکارماقلیق با جیم عجمی و فتح کاف
و سکون رای مهمله فرونشاندن چوکاردیلار فرونشانیدند چنانکه در لیلی مجنون گوید بوغالت ایچیندا نا بیناج آچی برنامه چوکاردیلار و
نامه اوزنی قویدیلار آب چوحت ایلیکن ایلغینیلا انکلیلار ... چوکاردوك فرونشاندیم چوکارور و چوکارادور فرو می نشاند و چوکارور
بمعنی فاعل و مصدر هم می آید چوکارکان و چوکاررکان و چوکارادورکان فرونشاننده و فرونشانده و بمعنی مصدر هم می آیند چوکار و چوکارغیل
مفرد مخاطبه فعل امر چوکارما و چوکارماغیل مفرد مخاطبه فعل نهی چوکارینك و چوکارینکز و چوکارینکلاده جمع مخاطبه فعل امر چوکارمانك
چوکارمانکز و چوکارمانکلاده جمع مخاطبه فعل نهی چوکارمان و چوکارماس مین فرونمیشانم چوکارامین و چوکاررمین و چوکارادورمین و چوکارورمن
فرومینشانم چوکارماس فرونمینشاند چوکاریب و چوکاریبان و چوکارمیش فرونشانده چوکارمیشانك فرونشانیده چوکارا آلغای
چوکاریب بولغه فرو تواند نشانید چوکارا آلغای فرو تواند نشانید چوکارا چوکارا فرونشانده فرونشانده چوکارای و چوکارایین
فرونشانیم و بنشاند و بنشانی و بنشاند چوکارسا و چوکارغای زو چوکارغای زو چوکارغلی و چوکارالینك فرونشانیم چوکارغلی برای فرو
نشاندن و تا فرونشانده چوکارغاچ چون فرونشست و نشسته و مجص نشستن چوکارغوچی فرونشاننده چوکارغوجه و چوکارغونچه
چوکارغانچه تا فرونشاندن و بعد فرونشاندن چوکارغوسیز دور فرو خواهیم نشانید چوکارغوسیز سیز فرو خواهید نشانید
چوکارغوسیلار دور فرو خواهند نشانید چوکارغولوق فرونشانده چوکارغای و چوکارا و چوکارسا و چوکارسون و چوکاردیك فرونشاند چوکار
چوکارغودیك فرونشاندنی و همچنانکه نشاند چوکالماق و چوکالماقلیك بکسر رای مهمله و فتح لام فرونشانده شدن و معنی آن موافق
اول یا لام اشتقاق می یابد چوکالماق و چوکالماقلیك فرونشستن چوکوب و چوکوبان و چوکمیش فرونشسته الشاهد علی الاول
نظم ... دیدی کیم بر کروه ماجرا ایدوك بیز شاری ختن دین ... قیلبان کیمسنی ... کولاب چوکوب ...
پاك و نا ... موافق شق اول اشتقاق می یابد من الجوامد چول با جیم عجمی اسم مسند فرو نشستن باشد که آنرا بعربی ... گویند
چوکاری بفتح کاف عجمی و کسر رای مهمله ایست که ساق آن بلند و شبیه به نی و دانهای آن شبیه بدانهای ذرت و خوشه انگور است و آنرا آ
دهند و مثل گندم آرد کرده نان میپزند و آنرا جوکان هم گویند چوکالك با جیم عجمی و فتح کاف بمعنی فرو نشسته در لب بود و بمعنی ...
استعمال شود چوکالیك بکسر لام و سکون کاف آخر و دفع ترشیلست که آنرا چکیده کرده بجوشانند جوکان بفتح کاف عجمی و سکون نون ...
باشد که هنگام کوهر شد چوکوج و چوکوش با جیم عجمی و ضم کاف و سکون شین معجمه ... که نقره کاران و مسکران بدان کار کنند و آنرا بعربی مطرقه
گویند و بفتح جیم هم مستعملست چنانکه در جیم مفتوحه گذشت چوکور بضم کاف عجمی و سکون رای مهمله سازیست معروف که آنرا ... گویند

جول

الجیم مع اللام من المشتقات چولغاماق و چولغاماقلیغ مع الجیم العجمی و سکون لام و فتح غین پیچیدن چولغادوق پیچیدیم چولغاتیب
پیچید و چولغار بمعنی فاعل و مصدر هم می آید چولغاغان و چولغاغان و چولغایدورغان پیچنده و پیچیده و بمعنی مصدر هم می آیند چولغا و چولغاغیل

مفرد مخاطب افعل امر چولغانا ما و چولغاناکیل مفرد مخاطب افعل نفی یعنی مپیچ چنانچه شاهد برا ولیا [illegible] محبوب القلوب گوید که چون
ما یلغانغه چولغانا و چون آیتا الکرسی لی ایلغانغه بولغانا ما چولغانالدی چولغانیکیز و چولغانا نکالیکا جمع مخاطب افعل امر چولغانا ما نکه چولغانا
چولغانا نکلار جمع مخاطب افعل نفی چولغانا نارع و چولغانا مین نمی پیچم چولغانای مین چولغاسیز چولغانا یدو مین چولغا دا م مپیچم چولغانا
نمی پیچید و معنی فاعل و مصدر نیز هم می آید چولغاناب و چولغاناباو چولغانامیش پیچیده چولغامیشانات پیچیده چولغانا ساب و لغان و چولغاناب بولغانه
توان پیچید چولغانای آلغای تواند پیچید چولغانای چولغانای چولغانا بو پیچید پیچیده چولغانه و چولغانا مین پیچم و پیچید و پیچیدن
چولغاناق چولغانا غاینز و چولغانا غای نز و چولغانا و چولغانا پیچیم چولغانا غلی برای پیچیدن و تا پیچیدن چولغانا غاج چون پیچیده و پیچیدن
پیچیدن چولغانغوچی پیچنده چولغانغوچه و چولغانغوچیه و چولغانا غانچه تا پیچیدن و مقدار پیچیدن چولغانغو سیز و دو نخواهیم پیچید چولغانغوسی
خواهید پیچید چولغانغوسی لار دو در نخواهند پیچید چولغانغو لوق پیچیدنی چولغانا غای چولغانا سلوچ چولغانلوق چولغاناسی پیچید چولغانغودک
چولغانادیک پیچیدنی و چنانچه پیچید چولغاناشماق و چولغاناشقلیغ مع الشین و چولغانا تماق و چولغانا تماقلیغ مع النون پیچیده شدن
چولغانیشیغ چولغانیشیان و چولغانیشیشو چولغانیشیو چولغانیشیان و چولغانا غیش پیچیده شده الشاهد علی الاول شعر کم بو چیرماشقان
آچیلغاندام ایکی رشته و بیلک حمایت چیلسا تا بیتار اهم پر پره کا چولغانیشیب و صیغ چولغاناشقاتاشین واز چولغانا تماق تا بنون موافق شق اول
می باید من الجوامد چول چول عربیت چنانچه صاحب قاموس گفته الجل بالضم والفتح ما تلبسه الدابة لتصان به اما با و او بیان
و در ترکی بضم جیم مستعمل است و آن یعنی پوشش حیوانات باشد چنانچه گوید شعر مجنون باشینی جهد دین آلماس ایکی اصلاده کو لیلی ایتی چنک
جولیدین تا پسه مصلا و بالمجاز تنیده عنکبوت را هم مانند من گفته مجنون شعر اورکا چی شیبا اقدا جولیتی تریاب توشو غیشی رشته پراه
متولف در معنی جل بفتح جیم بمعنی تنیده عنکبوت ذکر کرده و شعر نیز بهمان شاهد آمده و با جیم عجمی نیز آن جی آب را گویند چنانچه در خمسه
گوید شعر بلشیم آلیب دنیا ای نا دا یله جول حول مقصد ایری توقوم دور دور بول چولاق با جیم عجمی کسی را گویند که از دست معیوب باشد
چولپا بسکون و فتح بای عجمی با الف کشیده یعنی لاغر زبون باشد چنانچه در تاریخ بابری مذکور است که فلان را که چه سوز بکا الوزاید تیلی چولپا
ایدی و از آن در معنی نیز چولپا گویند چولپان با جیم عجمی و سکون لام و نون و فتح بای عجمی بر وزن سلطان نام ستاره بود که آن را بترکی زهره
میرن و بعربی شعری و بفارسی کاروانکش گویند الشاهد علیه شعر قوباشنی بو طلسم ای کر دون اول آیینه ایلجهان تشبیه آغیز کیم چولپان
کوزلاینکو آی آنکا تاش او لسون و که نشان که مزونک بیاض و سوداینی کوز کلی چولپانغه شا الماد یم نظور چرخ نا هیفه فراغی یعنی سلطان
نوشته و شعر اول را شاهد آمده سهو کرده چولسو با جیم عجمی و سکون لام و ضم بای عجمی با لاپش بود که از شاخهای نازک بافته
بالا بند چولد و بسکون لام و ضم دال بر وزن خوشبو یعنی ساله و خیازه باشد چنانچه گوید شعر نوا ولعینا دی بغاز طلوعین بورکن
رحایتی چوقیلدی جلد لیغ ایمدی کیرا لدانکا جلدو چولکا بفتح کاف عجمی فضا زمین مسطحی را گویند که در میان دو کوه واقع شده باشد
اعم از آنکه با آب و سبزه باشد یا زمین خشک چنانچه در سد سکندری در وصف کوه یاجوج گوید شعر چو بیتی لار ایرماس لیم ولد
آچوق چولکا ای یرده خوب و سرخ و خوشبو یعنی صحرای سبز آباد نوشته چولمک با جیم عجمی و سکون لام و کاف و فتح میم بترکی و روی بلسمان
و دیک سفال بود که آن را بعربی قدر نامند و دیک مسین را هم گویند مع المیم من المشتقات چوماق و چوماقلیغ بسکون میم زیر آب
فرو رفتن و غوطه زدن الشاهد علی الاول شعر مانغوریغه چوماقدین غرض طالبغه وصل او لدی که غواص و لما کیکا غرق او لوب
گوهر بر به باعث چومدوق با بفرو رفتیم چوما و چوما دور با بفرو میرود و چوما ریعنی فاعل و مصدر هم می آید جوماغانده چوما غان
چوما غان با بفرو رفته و فرو رفته و معنی مصدر هم می آید جوم و جوماسیل مفرد مخاطب افعل امر جوما و جوما غیل مفرد مخاطب

افعل نفی جومانک و جومانکیز و جوما کلاجم جمع مخاطب افعل امر جومانک و جومانکیز و جوما نکلار جمع مخاطب افعل نفی جومان و جومانمن
با بفرو میروم جوماسین و جومارمین و جومارمیز جومادارم با بفرو رفتم جوماس با بفرو میرود و معنی فاعل و مصدر نیز هم می آید
جوموب و جوموبا و جومیش با بفرو رفته جومیشانک با بفرو رفته جومیشا تولغان و جوموب تولغان با بفرو توانم رفت جوما آلغای با بفرو
تواند رفت جومنا جومنا غوطه زدن جومای و جومایین با بفرو بروم و بر و دو بروی فرو رفته جومناقه جومغایز و جومغای بیز
جومغایلیعو جومغا لیلار با بفرو بروید جومغالی برای فرو رفتن و تا فرو رفته بالمعنی الاول شعر جومغلی قویاس قعره و قیتی دیک
سوینکا کلا دراشک اشلاد ادام کیم بجبیا یان الماس ایم بو جهش جوماج چون با بفرو رفت و بعد بعض فرو رفتن جومغوچی با
فرو رونده جومغوچیه و جومغوچیز و جومغانچه تا با بفرو رفتن و مقدار فرو رفتن جومغوسیز دو در با بفرو نخواهیم رفت جومغوسی
با بفرو نخواهید رفت جومغوسی لار دو در با بفرو نخواهند رفت جومغولوق با بفرو رفتنی جومغای و جوماد و جوسا و جومسون و جومدیک
با بفرو رفته الشاهد علی الاول شعر اشک بحریدا اکر جسمیم غریق او لماس نیتانک یوق آنکا اول مرتبه کیم جومغای تینکیز غه توشه
خرج جومغودیلته جومار دیک با بفرو رفتنی و چنانچه فرو رود جومرتاق و جومرتا قلیغ بضم میم و سکون رای مهمله مصدر
متعدی یعنی آب فرو بردن و غوطه دادن چنانچه در سد سکندری گوید الشاهد علی الاول شعر بلا سیلی غه تینکیز ایچرا
موج زن جومرتاق او لوسی یو مینکینک جومرتدی با بفرو برد چنانچه گوید شعر کونکلوم کرداب جسم غه جومرتدی ایما
تو بجه له و بعرق غه غضنفر جومرتغان و جومرتغان و جومرتا رمز ما با بفرو برد و فرو برده چنانچه شاهد به اقلیم یعنی اول مرتبه ایماز
در محبوب القلوب در ذکر عشق گوید که بحری در وسیع دریکیه بو نه عقل و هوش کیمسین جومرتغان و با قی صیغ بر قیاس بضم میم و لغات
ای مهمله موافق شق اول الشتقاق می باید جومالماک و جومالما کلیک با جیم عجمی و فتح میم و سکون لام بر سر دو پا نشستن و صیغ آن بر قیاس
موافق شق اول الشتقاق می باید من الجوامد چوم با جیم عجمی لفظیست که از برای مبالغه بمعنی هیچ و تمام استعمال میشود چنانچه گوید
شعر تیل لیلا یلاخلیق یوزدینی چوم قرا کیم عمراو توبی دوست کو نکلی غه تیلدی یوز تومان تقصیر بیله و نیز در لیلی مجنون گوید شعر دانغو
جهان یوزین چوم اولدی نوع که کوک یوزین ایتم چوماق با جیم عجمی چوب دستی بود که بشکل کفچه آن کند مانند و آن را بعربی دبوس خوانند
جوماله کلو بنده تازه انلمند جومان بر وزن دخان کاهل و تنبل را خوانند جومجا بسکون میم و فتح جیم ثانی یعنی پیراهن تلیسه چنانچه مصنف
در جلد رابع در کیفیت احوال هلاکوخان ذکر کرده که در بیلیک او کتای قاآن آمدن که قاعده پادشاه پیران مارا ابتبات دیده و اقدیمی
قبای بالایی که موجب را دیر باشد اما هلاکو واو لاد او تربیت جومجاطرند یعنی پیراهن و با هر دو جیم عجمی قاشوق نیز گویند که از چوب و مس سازند
بدان دیک بر هم زنند و با معنی نیز بفتح جیم هم مستعمل است چنانچه در جیم مفتوحه گذشت جومرغای بمعنی آب بازی باشد و نیز یعنی آب فرو
چنانچه در ذیل مشتقات مذکور شد جومورت یک نوع کفگیر بیت که از چوب تراشیده بدان از دیک طعام بکشند جومولوخای نام
ارو غی است از اوزبکیه مع النون من المشتقات جونغایماق و جونغایماقلیغ با جیم عجمی بسکون نون و بای حطی و فتح تای مرادف جونالماک باشد یعنی
بسر دو پا نشستن و صیغ آن موافق شق اول الشتقاق می باید من الجوامد جونتای بسکون نون و فتح تای قرشت و کسر یای حطی خم چین کوچک
که آن را دو خانه میسازند چنانچه در لسان الطیر در داستان شیخ صنعان و مکالمه دختر ترسا با او گوید شعر ایلاننک دعوی
ماسین داغی آل بو لدا خرج ایلامکا جونتایسیکه نالک جونغا یمه با جیم عجمی و سکون نون و تای قرشت و کسر یای حطی بر وزن دندانه کوشه
بسر دو پا نشستن جونک بسکون نون و کاف عجمی بجمله بعضی آمده او لترمار کش را گوینده الشاهد علیه شعر با خیل ایچ بونک
کیم او لا آی زهره دیک تیز ایماس جنک کیم لیلی عمارسین جنکار خامون ارا و متولف بهار ظلم ملایم شمرده و نوشته که شتری باشد

که منونه اهرا بن یا ر بکشیده باشند دویم بمعنی بزرک و عظیم باشد چنانکه کوید شعر بار کشلاه غه نامنی قاچان تیلغای ناه تیو نینک
کونکلی کیجیک ده مکا ایرور چکری جونک سیم کشتی و سفینه را نامند چنانکه در خسرو شیرین کوید شعر ایکی یو نجونک حد سیز هر بری کینک
ملک جو بکنی هر برتو تابین نینک قرقه تیری آینک جمع فرهنای ایکیتی ایچرا بهر کردان تا لیب آی جهادرم اوزبکیه موی و پشم را کویند و از این
وساریه یونک نامند و بفارسی مجموعه نظم و نثر را خوانند چنانکه در سد سکندری در مساحت دریا کوید شعر کمه کیم اول الحراقیر له
تولوب سفینه بولوب دیماکیم جنک اولوب و الملاقان اسم بالمجاز و لهذا که مشترکست جونه با جیم عجمی و فتح نون هها زده بلغت مغولی شغال
(جوو) مع الواو جواوین قول بفتح واو و ضم همزه و سکون نون بلغت مغولی جهت چپ بود که خالی از انتقال اشتهار دارد جوانغار بسکون نون
و رای مهمله و فتح غین معجمه عرف جوانغار قول باشد بلغت مغولی یعنی جهت چپ چنانکه در سد سکندری کوید شعر جوانغار دا ایلکر
ایلی یسارئ یا نا سناری بر طاسیغ بر برئ جوون بضم واو و سکون نون هم او کویند و بفتح جیم هم با همین معنی مستعملست چنانکه شاهد آن
(جوی) در ذیل جیم مفتوحه نکاشته شد مع الیاء من المشتقات جویماق و جویماقلیغ با شباع ضمه و سکون یا بمعنی بر داشتن و نابود کردن باشد و با جیم
بمعنی کم شدن بود جویوناق و جویوناقلیغ با جیم عجمی و ضم یا و سکون نون مرادف جیماق باشد بمعنی کم شدن و صیغ آن موافق شق اول
(جیب) اشتقاق می یابد من الجوامد جوبین با جیم عجمی بکسر با و سکون نون حرفی چوبی باشد و ان آهن لبخته است باب المکسورات من الجیم مع الباء جبه
و آن ترکی جبه باشد چنانکه در قاموس مذکورست که الجبه ثوب معروف و الدرع و بترکی بمعنی اسلحه و پوشیدنی باشد و فراغی جباء
جیم بمعنی یکلاهی بر نکن نوشته که عورتان بسر اندازند سهو کرده جیبار مع الراء المهمله هوای نمناک مترشح باشد و با تای عجمی اسپید کو
که کلها و نباتات دیکر در اعضا داشته باشد جیبان با جیم عجمی مع النون دمل و قرحه بود که در اعضا بر آید جیبی بکسر با و سکون
مهمله بزکوهی بود و نر ا جیرین کویند و بفارسی شوکا و بعربی ایل نامند و بلغت مغولی بمعنی بالا باشد که از آن بعربی جناح خوانند جیلکا
بکسر با و سکون لام و رای مهمله و فتح کاف عجمی تمام اسب بود چنانکه در حیرة الابرار کوید شعر خشیفه امرمان ایکاری مرنکار ملکه جیلکا
آنکا کوهر نکار و فراغی بمعنی یراق زین نوشته جیبین با جیم عجمی مکسور باشد الشاهد علیه شعر عجب خندانا منونو خالینک مونوی
(جیت) ابرو مجبین … ایاکم شهد اینا ای اول کلبرلر اوزع قویمنیش چیتی مع التاء من المشتقات چیتماق و چیتماقلیغ با جیم عجمی و مکسور تای قرشت
بمعنی رو ترش کردن و انقباض وجه و شبهات افاده اغمض میکند باید لفظ رو مذکور باشد چیتی رو ترش کرد چنانکه
قنائیم المحبه در ذکر ابو الادبان کوید که شیخ سوزینینک آهر یله جرا بین چتتی و او تیر چقتی چیتوق رو ترش کردیم چیتار
چیتادور رو ترش میکند و چیتار بمعنی فاعل و مصدر هم می آید چیتار مو چیتار دور چیتا سو دور آیا رو ترش میکند چنانکه شا
بزنالت در زم صوت مطرب در تاریخ بابری مذکورست که مو نونک اوقوشیدین بر جی قولاقین توتا سود و بینه بر جیماری
چیتا مود و د چیتقان چیتلرغان و چیتا دورغان رو ترش کننده و رو ترش کرده و بمعنی مصدر هم می آید چیت و چیتغیل مفرد
از فعل امر و چیت مغانی دیکر دارد که در ذیل جوامد مذکور خواهد شد چیتام و چیتماغیل مفرد مخاطبه فعل نهی چیتمنک و چیتمنکیز
چیتمکلته جمع مخاطبه فعل امر چیتمانک و چیتمانکیز و چیتمانکلار جمع مخاطبه فعل نهی چیتمان و چیتماس مین رو ترش نمیکنم چیتاین
چیتا سن و چیتا دور و چیتادام رو ترش میکنم چیتماس رو ترش نمیکند و بمعنی فاعل و مصدر منفی هم می آید چیتیب و چیتیبان
چیتمیش رو ترش کرده چیتمیشلک رو ترش کرده چیتسا بلغنه و چیتیب بولغای رو ترش تواند کرد چیتا آلغای
تواند که چیتا چیتا رو ترش کنان رو ترش کنان چیتای و چیتاین رو ترش کنم و کند و کنی و کرده چیتماغ و چیتماغا
چیتماغیز و چیتالی و چیتالینک رو ترش کنیم چیتماغلی برای رو ترش کردن و تا رو ترش کرده چیتماج چیت رو ترش کرده و کند

بعض

عبس کردن چیتوچی رو ترش کننده چیتوچه و چیتوبچه و چیتماقچه تا رو ترش کردن و بعد که رو ترش کرد کن چیتومرد
رو ترش خواهیم کرد چیتونکوز دور رو ترش خواهید کرد چیتوسلار دور رو ترش خواهند کرد چیتولوق رو ترش کردنی
چیتماغ چیتما چیتما چیتیمون و چیتدیلک رو ترش کند چیتودیک و چیتاردیک رو ترش کردنی و همچنانکه کو چیتیلاغ
چیتیلدماقلیغ با جیم عجمی بکسر تای قرشت و سکون لام با سر انکشت نیش کرفتن و صیغ آن بدستور خواتم موافق شق اول اشتقاق می یابد
من الجوامد مع الجیم العجمیه چیت بلغت کاشغری بمعنی کنار باشد و بترکی دیوار حصار و حایط بود که از چوب ساخته شود
و نیز استاد رو ترش کردن چنانکه کذشت چیتوق بضم تا شخص منقبض ترش رو را کویند قطعه ده را وا آنی دیکیل دو تمند
کیم برا و سانا عجل یمان دل بسته خسته بو طان حیرا بین کورسانا چیتوق جانی چیتماس آنی کمه کلیج خسته چیتکیر بسکون تای قرشت
(جیچ) و کسر کاف عجمی بمعنی نوکیر بلغت مغولی لشکر را نامند مع الجیم چیجان و چیچن با دو جیم عجمی و فتح تا و سکون نون [illegible]
کویند چنانکه در قسم دویم لزجوبة الفلوب در وصف خود پند ان کوید که اوز الکیلار دانا و چیچان و در ملفوظ
مستحسن و مولف رومی نوشته که کسی باشد که عاقل نباشد اما خود را عاقل و دانا داند چیچاووت با دو جیم عجمی و فتح تا وضم
واو و سکون تای قرشت نام طایفه ایست از اوزبکیه چیچک با دو جیم عجمی و فتح تا بی و سکون کاف دو معنی دارد اول شکوفه و
الشاهد علیه تیمور زمان چیقار وران هر طرف سکان الار نینک کوزا ایرور ایقور که تو پلاغدین چیچکلار آشکار ایتیش دویم بمعنی آبله را کو
که آن را بعربی جدری نامند چنانکه بطریقه ایهام فرماید شعر یوز و ینکا آبله زخمی دین لعل کا حال البلاه نیجو لنکه باغ تا پلمنم چیچو
آچیلدی چیچک و سرهری و مولف مویدالفضلا این لفظ را ملاحی تصور کرده و بمعنی کل نوشته و صاحب ادات الفضلا بمعنی خال رخسار کرد
و صاحب شرفنامه با بمعنی جای جیم دویم خاذ کرکرده همه سهو کرده اند چیچسه با دو جیم عجمی و فتح ثانی جنازه
بمعنی هیشه و بزرک مسموع شد چیچیغ بکسر جیم ثانی و فتح جیم که احته دنبه کوسفند باشد چنانکه در لزجوبة و تحفه مذمه کوید
(جید) که اکرابت تابلماسا چیچیغلیغ آش بو ب نفرتفه بر کالماه ر مع الدال من المشتقات جیداماق و جیداماقلیغ بمعنی تحمل کردن بود جیدادوق
تحمل کردیم جیدار و جیدا ایدور تحمل میکند و جیدار بمعنی فاعل و مصدر هم می آید جیداغای و جیداغانی و جیدا بنیان تحمل کند و تحمل کرد
و بمعنی مصدر هم می آیند جیدا جیداغیل مفرد مخاطبه فعل امر الشاهد علی الاول شعر ای که برآی عشق دین آشفته مین وصل ایستا
هر جفا قیلسا جیدا امر و فع و جیدا ایتسا تونز و جیدا معنی جبا نیز طرد یعنی نیز جیداما و جیداماغیل مفرد مخاطبه فعل نهی جیدامنک
جیدانکلار جمع مخاطبه فعل امر جیدامانک جیدامانکیز و جیدامانکلار جمع مخاطبه فعل نهی جیدانار و جیدانار مین تحمل نمیکنم جیدای من
جیدای الماس مین و جیدا لمانا باید تحمل نمیتوانم کرد الشاهد علیه شعر حسرتا ولتوردی میناری مع کسوتها تها ایکم جیدا المکان بو کون
دین سونکرا آینک هجرانیغه جیدای مین و جیدا سین و جیدا ایدور و جیدا دام تحمل میکنم جیداماس تحمل نمیکند و بمعنی فاعل و مصدر منفی
هم می آید جیدا و جیدابان و جیدامیش تحمل کرده چنانکه شاهد بر اول در مصرع اول از محبوب القلوب در ذکر سخا کوید کر عالم
اهلی نینک تا تیغ رنج واریت ملاحتی فه جیدا سون لا ز حیدامیشالک تحمل کرده جیداسا و تغه و جیداب بولغای تحمل تواند کرد جیدای الغا
تحمل تواند کرد جیدای جیدای و جیدا ابو تحمل کنان جیدای و جیداین تحمل کنم و کند و کنی و کرده جیداسا و جیداغای
جیداغایز و جیداینک جیدالینک تحمل کنیم جیداغالی برای تحمل کردن و تا تحمل کرده جیداغاج چیدا تحمل کردن و تحمل کردن
جیداغوجی تحمل کننده جیداغوچه و جیداغوبحه و جیداغانغه تا تحمل کردن و بعد تحمل کردن جیدای اغوجه و جیدای آغوبحه و جیدای الغا
تا تحمل تواند کرد و بعد که تحمل تواند کرد الشاهد علی الثالث شعر کر جیدای المای کونکول … بر او کا ناکهان بار عاملی ایچو حید

آلغلیغه مشهور است اینها یبن جیدا غوسیزدور و تحمل خواهیم کرد جیدا غونکوزدور و تحمل خواهید کرد جیدا غوسیلار دور تحمل خواهند کرد جیدا غولوق تحمل
کردن جیدا غای و جیدا ماسا و جیدا سون و جیدا دیک تحمل کند چنانچه شاهد بر اولها در حدیث کوید شعر کیم که مونی توزه المادی جیدا
که اوزی توق و قونکجی بولغای آچ جیدا غو دیک و جیدار دیک تحمل کردن و همچنانکه تحمل کند من الجامد جیدا یعنی نیزه و نیزه ایراسته تحمل کند
چنانکه در ذیل مشتقات گذشت مع الراء المهمله من المشتقات چیرپاتیغ و چیرپاتیلیغ با جیم عجمی و سکون رای مهمله و بای عجمی [illegible] زدن و نواختن
باشد اما مخصوص زدن سیلی یا چوب نازک باشد بر عضو برهنه و اشباه آن چنانچه کسی کسی را سیلی چرپاق و سفاج چپاق چرپتوق زدیم
چرپار چرپادور میزند و چرپار بمعنی حاصل و مصدر هم می آید چرپغان و چرپارغان و چرپادورغان زننده و زده و بمعنی مصدر هم می آید
چرپ و چرپغیل مفرد مخاطب [illegible] چرپینک و چرپینکیز [illegible] مفرد غایب [illegible] چرپسون و چرپینکلار جمع مخاطب [illegible]
چرپانک و چرپانکیز و چرپانکلار جمع [illegible] چرپایان و چرپایین [illegible] چرپایمیز [illegible]
[illegible] چرپسانک و چرپیش [illegible] چرپیشانک [illegible] توانزد [illegible] توانمزد و چرپاچرپا
زنان زنان [illegible] چرپاین [illegible] چرپانک [illegible] زده [illegible] چرپغای [illegible] برای زدن و نازدن
چرپماج چون زده و برند و بمحض زدن [illegible] چرپقوچی زننده [illegible] تازدن و بعد از زدن چرپتوسیزدور خواهیم زد
چرپتونکوزدور خواهید زد چرپتوسیلار دور خواهند زد چرپتولوق زدن چرپغای و چرپادو [illegible] چرپادیک [illegible]
چرپاردیک زدن و همچنانکه زند چرپتاق و چرپتاقلیغ با جیم عجمی و سکون تای فوقانی [illegible] بمعنی مستعمل و کمتر ابیزدن که آنرا
بفارسی [illegible] کویند [illegible] سیم لوبیات [illegible] دندان شکستن که آنرا بعربی [illegible]
و تنبهات بی افاده این معنی نیکند باید لفظ ساز و تیغ و غیره ذکر شود چرپتوق نواختیم و ناکی زدیم تلبب کردیم چرتار و چرتادور مینوازد
و ناکی میزند و تلبب میکند و چرتار بمعنی حاصل و مصدر هم می آید چرتغان و چرتارغان و چرتادورغان نوازنده و نواخته و ناکی زننده
و زده و تلبب کننده و کرده و بمعنی مصدر هم می آید چرت و چرتغیل مفرد مخاطب لفظ امر چنانکه شاهد بر اول امر [illegible]
[illegible] کوید شعر [illegible] ترکانه ساز مقام نوا [illegible] ترکی حجاز چرتسا و چرتغیل مفرد مخاطب [illegible] چرتسنک
چرتینکیز و چرتینکلار جمع مخاطب لفظ امر چرتسون و چرتسونلار جمع غایب [illegible] چرتایین [illegible] مینوازم و ناکی زنیم
و تلبب میکنم چرتایین و چرتامین [illegible] چرتادورمان مینوازم و ناکی میزنم و تلبب میکنم چرتماس صیغه مستقبل منفی است و بمعنی حال
و مصدر منفی هم می آید چرتیب [illegible] چرتیش نواخته و ناکی زده و تلبب کرده چرتیشانک نواخته و ناکی زده و تلبب کرده
چرتسا [illegible] چرتیب [illegible] توان نواخت و ناکی توان زد و تلبب توان کرد چرتا الغای تواند نواخت و ناکی تواند زد و تلبب تواند کرد
چرتا چرتا نوازان نوازان و ناکی زنان و تلبب کنان چرتای و چرتایین بنوازم و بنوازد و بنوازی و نواخته و ناکی بزنم و بزند
و بزنی و زده و تلبب کنم و کند و کنی و کرده چرتساق و چرتغای [illegible] چرتالی و چرتانینک بنوازید و ناکی بزنیم و تلبب کنیم چرتغالی
برای نواختن و نانواخته و برای ناکی زدن و نازده و برای تلبب کردن و ناکرده چرتماج چون نواخت و بنوازد و ناکی زد و بزند و چون تلبب
کرد و کند چرتقوچی نوازنده و ناکی زننده و تلبب کننده چرتقوجه [illegible] تا نواختن و تا ناکی زدن و تا تلبب کردن و بعد از آن
چرتقوسیزدور خواهیم نواخت و ناکی خواهیم زد و تلبب خواهیم کرد چرتقونکوزدور جمع مخاطب [illegible] چرتقوسیلار دور جمع غایب
چرتقولوق نواختن و ناکی زدن و تلبب کردن چرتغای و چرتا و چرتسا و چرتسون و چرتدیک بنوازد و ناکی بزند و تلبب کند چرتقو
چرتاردیک نواختن و ناکی زدن و تلبب کردن و همچنانکه بنوازد و ناکی بزند و تلبب کند چرغاناق و چرغاناقلیغ بسکون [illegible]

بالف کشیده بمعنی عیش و نشاط کردن بود و [illegible] که از برای مرغ شکاری تیر بر هوا انداختن باشد چرغادوق عیش کردیم
چرغار چرغایدور عیش میکند و چرغار بمعنی حاصل و مصدر هم می آید چرغاغان و چرغارغان و چرغایدورغان عیش کننده و عیش کرده و بمعنی
مصدر هم می آیند چنانچه شاهد بر اول [illegible] کوید شعر [illegible]
[illegible] چرغا و چرغاغیل مفرد مخاطب لفظ امر چرغانک و چرغانکیز [illegible] مفرد غایب [illegible] چرغانک و چرغانکیز و
چرغانکلار جمع مخاطب لفظ امر [illegible] جمع غایب [illegible] چرغایین [illegible] عیش میکنم چرغایین
چرغایین و چرغایمین [illegible] چرغادام عیش میکنم چرغاماس عیش نمیکند چرغاب و چرغابان [illegible] عیش کرده [illegible]
[illegible] کوید الشاهد علی الاول شعر [illegible] چرغابیشانک
عیش کرده چرغابتوانغای [illegible] عیش توان کرد چرغاالغای عیش تواند کرد چرغایو و چرغای و چرغای عیش کنان چرغای
چرغایین عیش کنم و کند و کنی و کرده چرغاساق و چرغاغای [illegible] چرغالی عیش کنیم چرغاغالی برای عیش کردن و نا
عیش کرده چرغاغاج چون عیش کرد و کند و بمحض کردن چرغاغوچی عیش کننده چرغاغوجه و چرغاغانجه تا عیش کردن و بعد از
عیش کردن چرغاغوسیزدور عیش خواهیم کرد چرغاغونکوزدور عیش خواهید کرد چرغاغوسیلار دور عیش خواهند کرد چرغاغولوق عیش
کردن چرغاغای و چرغاسا و چرغاسون و چرغادیک عیش کند چرغاغودیک و چرغاردیک عیش کردن و همچنانکه عیش کند چرپانان
چرپاناغلیغ با جیم عجمی و سکون [illegible] میم پیچیدن چرپادی پیچید چنانچه کوید شعر [illegible] ناهیم باشیغه چرپا
[illegible] آهیم چرپادوق پیچیدیم چرپار و چرپایدور می پیچد و چرپار بمعنی حاصل و مصدر هم می آید چرپار [illegible] پیچد چنانکه در
مجنون [illegible] مجنون از [illegible] بلیلی کوید شعر [illegible] چرپادی [illegible] چرپاغان
چرپارغان و چرپایدورغان پیچنده و پیچیده الشاهد علی الاول بالمعنی الثانی شعر [illegible] چرپاغان [illegible]
بلمان اول مکتوب [illegible] و بمعنی مصدر هم می آید چرپا و چرپاغیل مفرد مخاطب لفظ امر چرپانک و چرپانکیز
مفرد غایب [illegible] چرپانک و چرپانکیز و چرپانکلار جمع مخاطب لفظ امر چرپاسون و چرپاسونلار جمع غایب [illegible]
چرپایین و چرپایمین [illegible] چرپادورمان می پیچم چرپاماس نمی پیچد و بمعنی حاصل و مصدر منفی هم می آید
چرپاب و چرپابان [illegible] پیچیده چرپابیشانک پیچیده چرپابتوانغای پیچیدن تواند چرپاالغای تواند پیچید چرپایو چرپا
پیچان پیچان چرپای و چرپایین بپیچم و بپیچد و بپیچی و پیچیده چرپاساق و چرپاغای [illegible] چرپالی بپیچیم چرپاغالی برای پیچیدن
و ناپیچیده چرپاغاج چون پیچید و بپیچد و بمحض پیچیدن چنانچه [illegible] کوید شعر [illegible] چرپاغاج [illegible]
[illegible] آسان [illegible] چرپاب [illegible] و [illegible] آسان [illegible]
قطع کردن [illegible] پیچیدن [illegible] آسان [illegible] چرپاغوچی پیچنده چرپاغوجه و چرپاغانجه تا پیچیدن
و بعد از پیچیدن چرپاغوسیزدور خواهیم پیچید چرپاغونکوزدور خواهید پیچید چرپاغوسیلار دور خواهند پیچید چرپاغولوق پیچیدن چرپاغای
[illegible] چرپادیک بپیچد چنانکه شاهد بر ثالث [illegible] نامه کوید شعر [illegible]
اینه [illegible] چرپاغودیک و چرپاردیک پیچیدن و همچنانکه بپیچد چرپاشماق و چرپاشماقلیغ مع الشین چرپالماق و چرپالماقلیغ
و چرپانماق و چرپانماقلیغ مع النون [illegible] چرپاشادور و چرپالور و چرپالادور و چرپانادور [illegible]
علی الاول شعر باشیغه چرپاشور [illegible] الشاهد علی الثانی شعر [illegible]

217v.

بزه دور که چرناشاده‌ی کونکلدا ایوزوز لغونک خیالی تورسیله تاملی الشاهد علی الخامس شعر انجم ایرماس قطره لار کوک استغید اله
عیان دوحا آهیم کیم فلک طاقیغه هر تون چرناتور و چرناشور و چرنالور و چرناتور بمعنی تامل و مصدر هم می آیند چرناشقان و چرنا
شوغان و چرناشامغان و چرنالغان و چرناتورغان و چرنالادورغان و چرناشقان و چرناتورغان و چرنالادورغان بمعنی شوند و بمعنی مشتق الکا
علی الاول المعنی الثانی شعر تنیم اول رشته نلغونکغه چرناشقان خیال اولمیش الشاهد علی الرابع شعر تاشینلا بحر رشته جانغه
چرنالغان کونکول عنکوتیدیم کیم ایلجی بولمیش ایرا الشاهد علی السابع شعر بر قبیله انکلا ایل همیله المشوخ دین
جانغه مرتا موغ که چرنالغان کیلور کاز ایله و بمعنی مصدر هم می آیند چنانکه کوید الشاهد علی السابع شعر کوب بلوماردیک
چرناتقلیم هجر یلدیم اینماس که فاطمه ایچیدا هر طرف داغ نمایندی چرناشقای چرناشاو چرناشا و چرناشور و چرناشد بیک
چرنالغای و چرنالا و چرنالسا و چرناشون و چرنالدیک و چرناتغای و چرنالو چرنا فسلو چرنالور چرنالدیک بمعنی شود الشاهد علی
الاول شعر موج ایلیغ آستیدا اولکاندین تاجان تا منلی وقوف ارسلان بکیم کوککا چرناشقای بوشو کوک چرناشیب و چرناشیبان و
چرناشیش و چرناشیب و چرنالبان و چرنالمیش و چرنا و چرنالمکو چرنا یمش بمعنی شده الشاهد علی الاول شعر کوبدیم و اولغای تابی
رشته جانیدا دور شمع تاریدیک که کول بولغاندا توویش چرنالشیب الشاهد علی الرابع شعر بیلکا کوزو نلنا و لغایف
یوزدا چرنالیب کویا بولمیش سلطان او تغه زنار بیزنا لیب الشاهد علی السابع شعر تاب لبنغ کیسوسیغه چرنالمیش رکشته فی
کم ناده ولده ایکی قویون برزادبولغای چرنا یتب چرناشقوچه چرناشقوچه و چرناشقاچه و چرنالغوچه چرنالغاچه و چرنالغوچه
چرناشغوچه و چرنایغاچه بمعنی شدن و بمعنی شدن الشاهد علی الثالث شعر باده ایچ بوکلرکه ضعیفه کوب فکر ایتما کیل کیم انکا
هر نفس چرناشقا یغه حیرت کیلتورور و باقی صیغ بریساق انچرناشا و قاپشیو انچرنالماق با الام و انچرناتماق با نون اشتقاق می یابد
چرناتماق و چرناتماقلیغ بالفای قرشت و چرناشتورماق و چرناشتورماقلیغ مصدر متعدیست یعنی پیچاندن چرناتغای بیی
چرناشتورغای بیی بیچاند چنانکه شاهد بر او لطایف تنبیهات محبوب القلوب در خاتمه کتاب در حکایت بهلول وهارون کوید کم کشش
کیسنام شایدستادم چرناتغای بیی و بمعنی باشتین ایاغ بولادغه تا انغا الحجر تا ننغای بیی چرناتیب چرناتبان چرناتمیش و
چرناشتوریب و چرناشتوریان و چرناشتوریب الشاهد علی الرابع شعر ملکه قرار یغه جانیم رشته سیی چرناشتورمیش جانیم کیم جیات
جاودانه ایلا تا جرام و باقی صیغ بر بعیو نجع موافق تتوا ول اشتقاق می یابد چریکلاماق با جیم عجمی و کسر را و سکون کاف فتح
لام بالف کشیده لشکرکشی کردن چریکلاماق لشکر کشیدیم چریکلادیم و چریکلادی و لشکرکشی میکند و چریکلادی بمعنی فاعل و
هم می آید چریکلاکان بمعنی چریکلادیغان و چریکلاتیغان کشنده و لشکر کشیده و بمعنی مستمر هم می آیند چنانکه شاهد بر اول بمعنی
در تاریخ بابری مذکورست که اول چریکلاکانی دین متوهم بولوب چریکلا و چریکلاکیل مفرد مخاطب از چریکلاسا و چریکلادا کنند
مفرد مخاطب چریکلادی چریکلاکای و چریکلاکای جمع مخاطب چریکلالار چریکلاسا چریکلاکای چریکلاسینلار چریکلاسنکیز جمع مخاطب
چریکلار لو چریکلالار لشکر کشیم چریکلادیم چریکلادین چریکلادیلار چریکلادی و چریکلاکالی لشکر کشیدیم چریکلادیم لشکر کشید چریکلا
چریکلالیم چریکلاسین لشکر کشید چنانکه شاهد بر او تاریخ بابری مسطورست که ارغون چریکلاکیل کیلکیلاران یا تاسیدا اولتوردو تولا
چریکلاماسانک لشکر کشیده چریکلاسا و لغای و چریکلاب و لشکر کشید چریکلاتیلار لشکر نواند کشید چریکلاش و چریکلاش چریکلا چریکلا
لشکرکشی کان چریکلاکو چریکلادین لشکر بکشیم و بکشد و بکشید چریکلالار لشکر چریکلاکانیز و چریکلادیکان و چریکلادی کله فعل چریکلا
لشکر بکشیم چریکلاکالی برای لشکر کشیدن و تا لشکر کشیده چریکلاکاچ چون لشکر کشید و بکشد و بمحض لشکر کشیدن چریکلاکونچه

218r. (ج)

لشکر خواهیم کشید چریکلاکونوز بود لشکر خواهید کشید چریکلاکوسیلار و لشکر خواهند کشید چریکلاکولوک لشکر کشنده چریکلاکلاکی
چریکلاتلو چریکلاتسون چریکلاکیلیک لشکر بکشد چریکلاکودیک و چریکلاکردیک لشکر کشنده و همچنانکه لشکر بکشد بن الحوامد جیرب بکلنه
بترسه معنی دارد اول اماد وصل و قرحه را کویند چنانکه در عنوان کتاب لیلی مجنون کوید که مجنون نونک آتاسی آنی عشق بادیه سیدین کیلتورو
کعبه طوافیغه بارغان و اول مناجات بیله کونکلیدا کی جیرن بارغان و با نیمتی با جیم عجمی هم مستعملست دوییم نام پرنده ایست که فوج فوج سیر
چنانکه در تاریخ بابری در وصف نوعی از آن پرنده کوید که منات قوین فوغی نینک قیزیل رنکی باز بو جنس بود نه جیرب یک جیل جیل اوچار ستر
نام رود خانه ایست که از حوالی تاشکند جاریست چنانکه در تاریخ بابری مذکورست که سوندین بو رود ارا قجیر سوی نینک کنار یدا اوق
شکت تاپیب از دیلاهر و بغایر یی کودیر کویند و آن نوعیست از پوست کوزن که آزاد باشد و زینت میکنند جیزی با جیم عجمی فتح لای
و سکون یای حطی بمعنی چهره و شکل و رخسار بود چنانکه در حیرت الابرار کوید شعر اکر چرایی رشک قمر بولماسا لعل لبی تنک شکر بولماسا
چرای لیغ لفظیست مرکب از لیغ که بمعنی نسبت و صاحب است مثل اینکه کوبتر چرای لیغ یعنی کبوتر شکل چنانکه در سکندری در وصف
آیینه چینی کوید شعر بیرسا اول حق زادمه روا ایدی نیه ناموش رنه کونکو ایدی قولیدین بو کوزکو یراق کیتماس که کوزکو چرای لیغ
یادا ایتمادی و نیز در تاریخ الانبیا در ذکر داود علیه السلام کوید که کوچ ایکه بیر عجب زنکی لیغ فرشته کیم کبوتر چرای لیغ ایردی عرضه دن
کیب آیینک تماشیدا قوندی جیرپ با جیم عجمی و سکون را و کسر یای عجمی سنکی کرده یی همه بدین باشد جیرجی با جیم عجمی و سکون را
یای عجمی و جیم ترکی رومی کاذر بود که آنرا بعربی قصار کویند جیرجیر بکسر هر دو جیم و سکون هر دو را و بعربی بر ترکی رومی چند چوب
که هم پیوسته بطریق چرخ میکردانند و بدان پنبه از تخم جدا میکنند جرجرک بکسر هر دو جیم و سکون هر دو را و لام کاف و فتح را ی
جانوریست شبیه بملخ که در تابستان در شدت کرما در جنگلها بسیار صدا میکند چنانکه در حیرت الابرار ایزد کرستوغه کوید شعر
یاوه کوب آیتور دایری جرجرک چرخ کوبا در صدا ایری فرفرک و آنرا اتراک روم چرلیق و بعربی جرد کویند و نصیری بحضن قلیل نوشته
که مرغیست که فریاد میزند جیرغالانک بسکون را و نون و کاف عجمی و فتح جیم و لام بالف کشیده نام عشرتکاه و سیرکاهیست از منزهات
دار الملک هرات جیرغامیشی بسکون را و فتح جیم و کسر میم و شین معجمه بمعنی عیش و عشرت بود چنانکه وصاف در جلد رابع در وصف سلطان
خدا بنده محمد بجانب مصر کوید که در سلخ جبلو غیا و جیر غامیشی کردند جیرغاو جیرکه بسکون را و فتح کاف عجمی بمعنی سلاله و صف و قطار بود
چنانکه در مناجات کوید شعر الهی بو قوا ایردیم بار اییمتینک لطف ایردیم اولوغلار جیرکاسیکا تامینک و در تاریخ بابری در بیان حال دوشمن
که در مرتبه متساوی بوعند مذکورست که سوندا قرار تاپتی کیم جیرکا دایر دیبی بو قضاری تو دوغای تا الدانیه بر علو خه جیقتغای و مجاز آ
جنوع شکاریست که صفوف از اطراف حلقه زده و حشرا میان میکرند چنانکه کوید شعر انکا دیم تیلمیش کوزی آلغان کونکول صید نحه
قصد هر طرفدین چرکا تویزکان جیلا کاین کوروب و نیز در حیلی مجنون فرماید شعر جرکا آرا تالمیش ایردی مجنون دعوی یکیت عهدیدن او رون
و با جیم عجمی بمعنی شادروان و خیمه و خرکاه باشد چنانکه در مقاله شانزده هم از حیرت الابرار در لاف شرابخواران کوید شعر بیز کیشی رشک
ایکوجه چرکام تاپتی منیک کیشی آلالا متوجه اولکام تابتی و نیز در تاریخ بابری مذکورست که عمر شیخ میرزا نینک اوز کا بیکلاری و بیکلاری
فراخ حال لاری ولایت و یر وموجه و چرکا و وجه استقامت میسر بولدی و تیزکه رومی یکنوع خیمه ایست کوچک که آنرا نمطلدیری نامند
و بفتح جیم هم مستعملست چنانکه در مفتوح با جیم مذکور شد جیکالیک یعنی هم سلک و هم قطار و هم رتبه چنانکه در سکندری
کوید شعر ون تو تسا او لوغی باشیدا ایکملیک ی قیلنا ایکمکی او لنغ جیرکا لیک و با جیم عجمی بمعنی صاحب خیمه و خرکاه باشد جرلیوق
با جیم عجمی بسکون را و قاف و کسر لام ترکی بدی همان جرجرک بود که در فوق مذکور شد جیرم با جیم عجمی بمعنی پیرنم ترکی رومی شرار آتش

چیرماش بمعنی پیچ وخم آمده چنانکه گوید شعر ای نوائی یوزیدین دیکه آچو تا یوقلدی زلفینی بیعا که هم تیره تورور هم چیرماش
دیر در مقاله دهم از حیرة الابرار در بیان عشق گوید شعر بیز بولوب توز توکیدین مرتفع چیرماش اوچون بند البار تاب کند
ونیز امر است از چیرماشمق چنانکه گذشت چیرماشلیغ یعنی پیچیده شده الشاهد علیه شعر زلفنه دور چرخ چیرماشلیغ
که مضمون تصویریدین هیچ کیم ضمیم اتمادی معنولی نینک تصویری دین ونیز بمعنی پیچ وخم باشد جیبیب بروزن غریب مساحت شعث
دنبع دو شصت نمرا گویند چنانکه در لسان الطیر توحید گوید شعر برجیب بیر قالماغان آفاق را املکه بو کاپاس زیلی
طاق را چیرلیت باجیم عجمی وکسر را وسکون کاف چیریکچی بکسر جیم عجمی ثانی بمعنی لشکر باشد الشاهد علی الاول شعر چیریکی
غم سپاهی کمر که کونکلوم دشتیدا ... الشاهد علی الثانی من سکندری شعر
بوندغ قوریاسین چیریکچی کیبت اول دین بیچه شاخ اوتون آتیریب جیرپیم بکسر طا وسکون میم المرتبه خوانند که او خوانند مع الرا
بمعنی من المشتقات جیزنالت باشناع کسر ... بمعنی خط کشیدن بود جیزکینمالت باجیم عجمی وسکون زا ونون وکاف جیز
ترکی بمعنی کوبیدن ودر هم زدن باشد چنانکه قصوبی ضدادی گوید با املاء الترکیه شعر کا کلنات تاب باشینکا جیزکینالت
ایستغالدم ای ... شعر نوله ...
دنیاییه شا ... من الجوامد ... صدا را گویند که ...
مخون کتاب ... الشاهد علیه شعر ...
چنتی ... جیرلیغ ...
دجیم مع الجیم مذکور شد مع السین جیسکن باجیم عجمی وسکون سین ونون وکسر کاف عجمی ... باشد که از شدت ... جیس
متحد شود مع الغین المعجمه من المشتقات جیغناماغ باجیم عجمی وسکون غین ونون ... جیغ
مع التا معنده متعدیت بمعنی ... جیغ بروزن تیغ بمعنی فریاد وفغان بود الشاهد علیه شعر
کیمکا کیم ده لا ... بوغزین ایب ... فریاد جیغ و باجیم عجمی ...
ابزنی وچوبهای باریک ساخته از پیش در خانه وخرگاه آویزند چنانکه گوید شعر پرده کینکاج ... ایروش بول
لار دین جیغ نینک ... جیغان بفتح غین با الف کشیده وسکون نون مقدمرا گویند چنانکه گوید شعر
تیند ... وجیغانی ... وباجیم عجمی خاله زاد ... جیغنه بفتح غین ...
بمعنی پر باشد ... جیغی بکسر غین همان جیغ باشد بمعنی فریاد وفغان جیغیت باجیم عجمی وکسر غین
وسکون یای قرشت ترکی ... جیغنس باجیم عجمی وکسر
غین وسکون زای ... چنانکه در تاریخ بابری مذکور است ...
جیقیب ... که آنرا ... باجیم عجمی وکسر غین اول وضم غین ثانی وسکون
ترکی ... بمعنی صدا وفریاد بود جیغیلداب بکسر غین وسکون لام ونون وفتح دال ...
... جیغلدو وبکسر غین وسکون لام وضم دال ...
باجیم عجمی وکسر غین وسکون نون ... مع القاف من المشتقات چیق
جیقماق وجیقماقلیغ بمعنی برآمدن باشد جیقتی برآمد جیقتوق برآمدیم جیقاو جیقادور برمی آید وجیقار بمعنی فاعل

مصدر هم می آید چنانکه بمعنی مصدری گوید جیقارغه بو ویرانه دین ... جیقمان جیقارغان و
جیقادورغان برآینده وبرآمده الشاهد علی الاول والثانی بالمعنی الثانی شعر آغزیدین جیقمان ...
جیقارغان رشته ... وشاهد بر ثالث ...
دین جیقادورغان ... بمعنی مصدر هم می آیند وجیقارغان باسیغه ...
مذکور خواهد شد جیقو وجیقغیل مفرد مخاطبه ... الشاهد علی الثانی شعر ای ... جیقیل ...
یم شباب ایامیغه نسبت ... از شیب وجو قنغیت ...
جیقماغیل مفرد مخاطبه ... جیقینک جیقینکلار جمع مخاطبه ... جیقمانکلار جمع مخاطب
جیقمان وجیقماس ... جیقار ... جیقادور ... برنمی آید ...
جیقیب وجیقینکو جیقیش برآمده ... جیقا آلمای ... جیقا جیقا
برآمده برآمده جیقاین برآیم وبرآید وبرآیی وبرآمده جیقساق ... جیقالی جیقالینک برآییم جیقغالی
برای برآمدن ... شعر ... جیقغالی ...
کونکول جیقغاج چون برآمد وبرآید ... جیقغونچه جیقغوچی ...
جیقغوسی ...
جیقیشقدیک ... الشاهد علی الاول شعر ...
... جیقارماق ... بفتح قاف وسکون را مهمله مصدر متعدی ...
بدرآوردن وکنایه از ... جیقاریلیدی ...
که بایمین ... جیقارغان ...
... چنانکه
جیقارلیغ جیقارغای ... الشاهد علی الاول المعنی الاول شعر ...
... جیقارغاچ چون برآورد ...
گوید شعر ...
... جیقیشمالیغ ... جیقیشوق خوش برآمدن ...
جیقیشادور خوش برمی آید ... جیقیشقان ... خوش برآینده وخوش برآمده
مصدر هم می آید جیقیش وجیقیشغیل مفرد مخاطبه ... گویند چنانکه ...
جیقیشما وجیقیشماغیل مفرد مخاطبه ... جیقیشینک ... جمع مخاطبه ...
جمع مخاطبه ... جیقیشماس ... خوش برنمی آید چنانکه گوید شعر ...
... جیقیشتیم ... جیقیشمیش خوش برآمده ...
جیقیشا ... خوش توان برآمد ... خوش برآمده ...
جیقیشاین خوش برآیم وبرآید وبرآیی وبرآمدن جیقیشساق ... جیقیشقالی برای خوش برآمدن

ما خوش بر آمد چقیشماج چون خوش بر آمد و بر آید بمعنی بر آمدن چقیشقوچی خوش بر آینده چقیشقوسه چقیشقو چقیشما
تا خوش بر آمدن معقد خوش بر آمدن چقیشقومیز دو بخوش خواهیم بر آمد چقیشقونکیز دو بخوش خواهید بر آمد چقیشقوسیلار دو
خوش خواهند بر آمد چقیشقولوق خوش بر آمدنی چقیشماغ چقیشلار چقیشلو چقیشتی چقیشدیک خوش بر آید الشاهد علی
الاول شعر منکا دهر پیری مطلب بوزاهد یوهو طالب تا جان صحبت چقیشماغی چون کیم تین تیلبه اول الله چقیشقودیک
چقیشقودیک خوش بر آمدنی و بمعنی خوش بر آید من الجوامد چقوق باجیم عجمی لفظیست که ترک و تازیک در حین راندن ستور
کنند چنانکه در لیلی مجنون خطاب با علی لیلی بطریق ایهام فرماید شعر یلرا صلی تا وعبلی ول آستانه کیمسه سینی چقوق یاشاند
فیز امراستا بر آمدن چقتریق بسکون را و قاف مضموم کسراء مهمله چرخی که گوید که پنبه و ابریشم بدان بریسند و در دولا
و آنرا چقر هم گویند چیقر بمجی کیم ازاستند که چرخ را بساز د بانکرداند چیقتقور بسکون قاف و راء مهمله و ضم جیم عجمی
چنانکه گوید شعر کم کاج اول یونی باشیمغه لوردی ایندی تیغ بلاکم که چقتقور کم باشیمغه قولاد کیلتو روب چقوق شم
بر آمدن چنانکه در مقالات دهم از حیرت الابرار در وصف سیاه خانه بود شعر قاشتلاغ یکو نکل اوو دیک سینوق تر الاری
دین چقوق چقیر بکسر تا و سکون راء مهمله هما چقتریق بمعنی چرخ باشد که در شد چقیش بکسر تا و سکون شین معجمه خروج
از تنگنای بفضای وسیع باشد چنانکه در تاریخ بابری مذکور است که او شبو سو نوک کنک در دین چقیشیلر جهار باغ بوبور دوم
مع الکاف من المشتقات چیکما کلیما باجیم عجمی بمعنی کشیدن بود چیکتی کشید چنانکه در مقالات چهار دهم از حیرت الابرار در شکایت
از اهل لدکوید شعر یکا دنیا الیا اهالی چرخ دون کیمی که چیکتی بیه سیلدی بی نکون چیکوک کشیدیم چیکار چیکادو بکشد و چیکا
فاعل و مصدر هم می آید چیکماکان چیکماکان چیکما بدو کان کشنده و کشیده و بمعنی مصدر هم می آید چیک چیکیل مفرد مخاطب
از فعل امر چیکما و چیکما کیل مفرد مخاطب از فعل نهی چیکینکیز و چیکینکلار جمع مخاطب از فعل امر چیکمانک چیکمانکیز و چیکمانکلار
جمع مخاطب از فعل نهی چیکمان و چیکماس مین نمیکشم چیکایین و چیکلار مین چیکارم و چیکار ما سیکشم چیکماس نمیکشد و بمعنی فاعل
مصدر منفی هم می آید چیکب و چیکیبان و چیکمیش کشیده چیکمیشا ملکشیدند چیکتنا بولغای و چیکیب بولغای تواز کشید چیکا الغای
تواند کشید چیکا چیکا کشان کشان چیکای و چیکاین بکشم و بکشد و بکشی و کشیدم چیکاک و چیککایر و چیکگای و چیکابکیم الشاهد
علی الرابع شعر دهر ایله دیر آیل چیکابلی چیکا لعبچه سجده لرابعا چیککا بلی برای کشیدن و تا کشیدن المعنی الاول شعر
تنکری خلق ایتمیش بعینه کوبا چیکماکا بلی کیم دی یوق کیم با س ین خلق ایدا اندین ملول المعنی الثانی شعر قورودی چیکماکالی تا اندین
کوزوم نقاب قیزیل تپای ابنی سینز اولور چون بولور نقاب قیزیل چیکاکاج چوز کشید و بکشد و بمجرد کشیدن چیکاکوچی کشنده چنانکه
در مقالات دوازدهم از حیرت الابرار در وصف ظالم کوید شعر چستم یلینوچی بادا اولوب بارجاستم چیکاکوچی بادا اولوب چیکاکو
چیکاکو بچه کاچیکا کاجه ناکشیدن و بمقدار کشیدن چیکاکومیز دو بخواهیم کشید چیکاکونکیز دو بخواهید کشید چیکاکوسیلار دو بخواهند کشید
چیکاکولوک کشیدنی چنانکه در لسان الطیر در خاتمه کتاب گوید شعر بولماغای کیم نرگسی تیلبه لیک چیکاکولوک بولغای مهلاجی
دین ایلیک چیکاکانی چیکاکا چیکاکونی چیکاکالینکند چنانکه در خاتمه لیلی مجنون در وصف عشق گوید الشاهد علی الثالث شعر اول نی
وجود دین ایتسه زایل چون بولدی ایکینچی سیکاما مایل یوق یوق که ایکینچی آنی چیکا کونکلیکا وصال ایمیز اکیا چیکاکودیک چیکلار دیک
کشیدنی و همچنانکه بکشد چیکتوریاناک و چیکتوریا کلیک بضم اول تا و سکون راء مهمله مصدر متعدیست بمعنی کشانیدن و صیغ آن هو
شوار اول با لفظ تو را اشتقاق می یابد چیکشماک و چیکشما کلیک مع الشین مصدر مفاعله است بمعنی بایکدیگر کشاکش کردن و با هم کشیدن

و صیغ آن باشین اشتقاق می یابد چیکلماک و چیکلما کلیک مع اللام و چیکینماک و چیکینما کلیک مع النون بمعنی باب انفعال است
یعنی کشیده شدن و صیغ آن بزبن سیاق با لام اشتقاق می یابد چیکرا ماک و چیکرا ماکلیک بسکون را و کاف و فتح راء مهمله با الف کشیده
چشم باز نماندن از خشکی دماغ که آنرا بعربی سهر گویند چیکرادی چشم باز نماند چیکرار و چیکرایدور چشم باز نمی ماند چیکراب
فاعل و مصدر هم می آید چیکراکان و چیکراکان و چیکرایدورکان چشم باز نماننده و چشم باز نماند و بمعنی مصدر هم می آید چیکراب
چیکراباب و چیکرامیش چشم باز نمانده چنانکه در حیرت الابرار در وصف شب گوید الشاهد علی الثانی شعر رابعه دین الیلدی بو سوز
شب اجم شستگی بدمانعین حشت ایله که اولدی بو چو تا نیراتیب چیکرایسان کوزلاری لو یقو کیتیب چیکراسا بولغای و چیکراب بولغای
چشم باز نتوان نماند چیکراکای لغای چشم باز تواند نماند چیکرابو چیکرای چیکرای چشم باز نماند باز نماند چیکراکالی برای چشم
باز نماندن و تا چشم باز نماند چیکراکاج چون چشم باز نماند و بماند و بمجرد ناماندن چیکراکوچی چشم باز نماننده چیکراکوجه و چیکراکو بچه
چیکراکا بچه تا چشم باز نماندن و بمقدار چشم باز نماندن چیکراکای چیکراکاسلار چیکرا سون و چیکرا دیک چشم باز نماند چیکراکیدیک و چیکرادیک
چشم باز نماندنی و همچنانکه باز نماند من الجوامد چیکت باجیم عجمی و کسر کاف عجمی و سکون تا قرشت پنبه دانه را گویند الشاهد علیه شعر
اشلت جهرنید اکوز نعم آق بولدی آنتا قکیم ناموغ شاله اشلت اولما موغ دین یا قدی آنداق کیم چیکت چیکرلیک باجیم عجمی و سکون
راء و کاف عجمی و فتح دال ابتر که روی مسجد بحره البتی بود که مجاز آنرا برای تحلیل الطعام بکار برند چیکریری باجیم عجمی و کسر دال و راء مهمله ترکی
روی بام بچنبره کشته است چیکلاک باجیم عجمی و فتح کاف عجمی اول و لام و سکون کاف ثانی در تبیت شبیه بدل کنجشک و در آن بها نه بیز بود
شبیه بدان نها ق که در قوت پیا باشد و سیدفان آن سرخ تیره و ترش شیرین و کیاه او بمقدار شیری و بکثر شبیه به برک کل سرخ است و مقوی دل
و دماغ و مطفی صفرا و در طب بدقت چیکن همان چکن بمعنی نازنین بود که با شواهد در جیم مفتوحه مذکور شد چیکوریکای باجیم عجمی
و ضم کاف اول عجمی و سکون طا و تا قرشت و فتح کاف ثالث ملخ را گویند و آنرا جیرتکا نیز نامند چیکردک بکسر کاف اول عجمی و سکون راء
و کاف ثانی و فتح ذال سخت نرم حنکلی را خوانند و با جیم عجمی دانه را گویند که در میان میوه باشد چیکلدام باجیم عجمی و کسر کاف عجمی و سکون لام
میم و فتح دال پسته را که را نامند چیکلدام چیکی نام مولیت شبیه به بن چهار پنج و نایل پاستلام و سنامش بقدیم مشروب و نامه نا
تو ترش ایدی می نماند و آنرا بلغت اندلس میجان و بعزانی لعبت بربری گویند چیکمن باجیم عجمی و کسر کاف عجمی و سکون نون دو معنی دارد اول
بمعنی حین و گیاه باشد چنانکه گوید شعر چیکنم را بربری سبزه خطی کو نکلوم را بحر که دیبیم آن چیکن بو چیکن کو یا اولدی علیمکی
قیناغ کیم کونکولنی صاد قیساغ سیکین قیز در تاریخ بابری در وصف بحرای غور بند مذکور است که چیکن تا لا لا او تی بسیار یخشی بولور دوم معنی بجاد
بو تهانی بود که از ابریشم در زند و فتح جیم تیز باشد و معنی مستعملست چنانکه در جیم مفتوحه مذکور شد و با کاف عجمی سه معنی دارد اول
سیاه را گویند که در میان شلغم بکار برند و از قبیل شلتوک است تیز دارد دویم سرد و ترا نامند سیم نام نباتیست که آنرا المبا اسطوخودوس
خوانند و از مسهلات وتقویت دل و تزکیه مشهور که کند و مولف در وی چیکن را بمعنی حصه و کره نوشته سهو کرده است در شبهه لو از آن
انشاء بطریت که گفته شعر عشق اهلی قتبا یدالا دینکیم چیکن آچیای بوقصه لا از ایل عقلیغه چرناش ایرمولار و در این شعر ماتو
در لفظ چیکن جز و کلمه نیست بلکه چیک بمعنی عقده و کره باشد و یا و نون در آخر آن ضمیر مفرد بمخاطب و رابطه مفعول است چیکن یعنی کردش
مع اللام من المشتقات چیلاماق بلغت مغول بمعنی خواستن و طلب کردن و رانیدن بود چلا در بخا ق باجیم عجمی ترکی و یعنی دیوانگی کردن
من الجوامد چیل بعض زینل لفظیست که در آخر الفاظ افاده معنی نماند میکند چنانکه کوینک آچیل یعنی سفید مانند و آچیل جیل آچی
و با جیم عجمی مرغ کوچک را گویند و تبریزی روی پیه یعنی دلرم اولا ایرور را نامند دویم بر نده ایست که آنرا بفارسی تیهو خوانند و لیعه موچ سروآ

ستم فله بلند که در یکجا تل کند چیلاك باجیم عجمی و فتح لام و سکون کاف نباتیست بری که میوهٔ ان سرخ و شیرین است چیلامیشی بلغت
مغولی معنی راندن بود چنانکه در تاریخ وصاف مذکور است که پادشاه آفتاب در دار دوی آسمان بر سمند طلوع نشست و جیلو لالان اشعهٔ
ضیا انجمن انجم را چیلامیشی کرده متفرق کردانیدند و نیز در مقامات سلطان احمد و ارغون خان کفته که ارغون را با لشکر بکه بوجود
پیلشتی است چیلامیشی کنان بپایهٔ تخت کیوان رفته آمدند جیلاو بفتح لام و سکون واو عنان اسب باشد چنانکه کوید شعر ای عنان
اختیار حقیقی بکیر الهی که دین بویه دادهر شاری طول چابك که تا پیشاری جیلاو و نیز مجاز اعنی حاجه و بیش پای اسب جلو را کویند چنانکه
سلیمان کدهری کوید شعر اولوس الیدا ابندر آزاد لار جیلاو دامثیب بویه شهزاده لار جیلاو لیغ بمعنی همعنان بود چنانکه ندای
بابری در وصف جنك امیر بکته مذکور است که جیلاولیغ کیلادور مرا بنغلدا م برشان بایمای جیلاولیغ یا تا در لار جیلادی بفتح لام و
یای حطی و سکون جیلاپن بکسر یای حطی و سکون نون بمعنی مثل و مانند باشد الشاهد علی الاول شعر ای وبیل دیوانه و مستا و ملخیدکین
دینك بیل جیلاپنی اول آی اردو حرحطه آییل ای کونکول و نیز در تاریخ الملوك مذکور است کو یلدکر فیلقوس لیکندر نی اوغول جیلاکی
اسراب و تعهد قیلدی و همچنین کفته میشود که آنجیلاپین یعنی مثل آن و بو جیلاپین یعنی مانند این جیلیبور باجیم عجمی و سکون لام و دال
مهمله و ضم بای ابجد شیء اسبرا کویند چنانکه در تاریخ وصاف آمده که مرکب دش را جیلبور کفته از شیر از برون آورد چیلیق باجیم
و سکون لام و قاف و کسر بای عجمی چراغ چشم را کویند و چیلیق لیغ کوز یعنی چشم چراغ الود جیلدام مرادف ایلدام بمعنی زود و سریع باشد
جاماو بفتح میم معجمه با الف کشیده و واو بهلوی حیوانیست ببچه که کنبکه موی آن سرخ است و از پوست آن پوستین دوزند و از ان ابالی
و الطای هم نامند جیاعنو ملاحظات که از کردن توش آویزند و آزان و جیغبلد از نیز کویند جلغین باجیم عجمی و سکون لام و نون
و کسر غین معجمه ترکی روی دیوانه و از عقل بیکانه را کویند جلیملو باجیم عجمی ترکی روی یعنی دست و پا دار چیله بمعنی راندن و نکاپو باشد
جلی بکسر لام دو معنی دارد اول طوق قرانبراست و آن حلقهٔ آهن بود که بر کردن مجرمین نهند الشاهد علیه شعر طوقلا بوبلیش جلی
تا نظرغه ایمان اهلینی حلقه لار نحیر لغونك رشته سی زاریه و نیز در مقالات ضدهم از حیرة الابرار کوید شعر هر تاری چوه یغا جی جلی
سفیله هند عکه چکلار لا دحلی با خاس عربان و سر اهرقا رود سود بن بارعه بجر او نیز در خمسه بن در وصف ملامران و قیم
عمادی کوید فی النعت شعر مذار الطرفیدا هر تاری کالاث جلی لیك نچه کردن بسته قول لاث و آزا جلبه هم نامند دوم جای کم را
کویند جلیه طوق نجا و نیز بمعنی سلاسل مع المیم من المشتقات چیمدیالك و چیمدیا کلیك باجیم عجمی و سکون و کسر دال نیشکونج کرفتن یعنی
با دو سر انکشت کزیدن چیمدیدی نیشکونج کرفت چیمدیدوك نیشکونج کرفتیم چیمدیر و چیمدید و رد نیشکونج میکیرد و چیمدیر بمعنی مصدر
هم می آید چیمدیر ایدی نیشکونج میکرفت چنانکه در لیلی مجنون در حالات مجنون کوید شعر چیمدیر ایدی اینك لار نی هر دم
چاینار ایدی ینك لار نی هر دم چیمدیکان و چیمدیرکان و چیمدیورکان نیشکونج کیرنده و کرفته و بمعنی مصدر هم می آید چیمدیکای و چیمدیکد
مفرد مخاطب بفصل امر چیمدیا و چیمدیاکیل مفرد مخاطب بفعل نهی چیمدینك و چیمدینکیز و چیمدینکلار جمع مخاطب بفعل امر چیمدینکیز و چیمدیانکیز
چیمدیانکلار جمع مخاطب بفعل نهی چیمدیمان و چیمدیاس نیشکونج نمیکیرم چیمدی من و چیمدیمایمن و چیمدیمیز و چیمدیمای نیشکونج میکیرم
چیمدیماس نیشکونج نمیکرد چیمدیب و چیمدیمان و چیمدیمیش نیشکونج کرفته چیمدیمیشانك نیشکونج کرفته چیمدیالغای و چیمدیب بولغای
نیشکونج توان کرفت چیمدی الغای نیشکونج تواند کرفت چیمدیکای نیشکونج کرفته کرفته چیمدی چیمدی من نیشکونج بکیرم و بکیرد
و بکیری و کرفته چیمدینك و چیمدیکانی و چیمدیکالی نیشکونج بکیرید چیمدیکالی برای نیشکونج کرفتن و تا کرفته چیمدیکاچ
چون نیشکونج کرفت و بکیرد و بمحض کرفتن چیمدیکوچه و چیمدیکونچه تا نیشکونج کرفتن و بقدر کرفتن

(ج)

جیمدیکو بیزدور نیشکونج خواهیم کرفت جیمدیکونکوزدور نیشکونج خواهید کرفت جیمدیکوسیلاردور نیشکونج خواهند کرفت جیمدیکولوك نیشکونج
کرفتنی جیمدیکای و جیمدیسلر جیمدیسون و جیمدیلك نیشکونج بکیرد جیمدیکودیك و جیمدیر دیك نیشکونج کرفته و همچنانکه بکیرند من الحوامل جیمه
بکسر هر دو جیم و سکون میم اول و فتح میم ثانی جای را کویند که آب ایستاده کل شده باشد جیمه یکه چون شخصی در آنجا بیفتد غرق شود و فتح
جیم بمعنی کاسه سر بود جیمدیغان باجیم عجمی و سکون میم و کسر دال و نون و فتح غین معجمه با الف کشیده پر نرم مرغان را کویند خصوصا آنکه
فر را خواسته خصوصا جیمدیك باجیم عجمی و سکون میم و کاف و کسر دال نیشکونج جیمسیلیغ بکسر میم و سکون لام اول و کسر لام ثانی پرندهٔ
کویند که بر کمر آویزند و مقنعه را خوانند که زنان بر سر اندازند مع النون من المشتقات چینامالیك و چینامالیك بالاشباع باجیم عجمی و فتح
نون با الف کشیده سنجیدن و تصور کردن چینادیم تصور کردیم چینامادیم تصور نکردیم چنانکه در مکتوب پنجم از منشات کوید
که مشهد غه کیلکاندین عرض بوا بردی کیم اوز و صدای آنچه قوت چینامادیم چیناردی و چینایدور تصور میکند و چینار بمعنی فاعل
و مصدر هم می آید چینار ایدی تصور میکرد چنانکه در تاریخ بابری در وصف سلطان ابراهیم پادشاه هند مذکور است که او زیاد
بیکلار بیلاینك کا یاوو قیل چینار ایدی چیناکان و چینارکان و چینایدورکان تصور کننده و تصور کرده و بمعنی مصدر هم می آید چنانکه
شاهد برا و لما در قضیه مدرسه کو یکدکر بو حضیره هیچ نوع خدمتغه امز قابلیتیم نی چیناکان جهتدین لاجرم تمنا لار ایتیکین یوزیکا
قیلیب ایردیم چینا و چیناکیل مفرد مخاطب بفعل امر چینامانا و چیناماکیل مفرد مخاطب بفعل نهی چینانك و چینانکیز و چیناناکلار
جمع مخاطب بفعل امر چینامانك و چینامانکیز و چینامانکلار جمع مخاطب بفعل نهی چینامان و چیناماس من تصور نمیکنم چینای من و چینایمن و چینایمیز
چینادام تصور میکنم چیناماس تصور نمیکند و بمعنی فاعل و مصدر منفی هم می آید چیناب و چینابان و چینامیش تصور کرده چینا
تصور کرده چیناب بولغای و چیناب بولغای تصور توان کرد چینا الغای تصور تواند کرد چینای بو و چینای جیناب تصور کنان
چینای چینای من تصور بکنم و بکند و بکنی و کرده چینانك و چیناکای و چینای و چینالیك تصور کنیم چیناکالی برای تصور کردن
و تا تصور کرده چیناکاچ چون تصور کرد و بکند و بمحض کردن چیناکوچه تصور کنند چیناکوچه و چیناکونچه تا تصور کردن
و بقدر تصور کردن چیناکو بیزدور تصور خواهیم کرد چیناکو نکوزدور تصور خواهید کرد چیناکوسیلاردور تصور خواهند کرد چیناکو
تصور کردنی چیناکای و چیناسلر چیناسون و چیناسیلك تصور کند چیناکودیك و چینارديك تصور کرده و همچنانکه تصور کنند من الجوامد

(ج)

جبن باجیم عجمی ذات ستره بر وغ را کویند چنانکه کوید شعر ای کونکول آهنکی دیرسین کیم و املا تماشا جین ایرور کو نکلیکا
سرایت ایلاکانا و بمعنی بعضی شکنج بود و نام یکی از چهاران دوازده مکانه یافث هم بوده و نیز اسم ولایتیست معروف چنبی ناق باجیم اول
عجمی و سکون نون اول و قاف و فتح جیم و نون ثانی انکشت کوچك باشد که آنرا بعربی خنصر نامند چنقراق باجیم عجمی و سکون نون و قاف ثانی
و کسر قاف اول و فتح رای مهمله و جی نیقراو بسکون واو چوبی را کویند جینك بسکون نون و کاف عجمی بعنی شریك تاخت و تاز را کویند
الشاهد علیه شعر ترکتاز ایلایب کونکول الکدینك اجلادین بوز اخان حصه آیریا آنکا یوچون که ایرمار ایردی جینك و له شعر
غارت اسلام و دین یا الغوز قیلور سین کویا سیله بیما الاجایو قخاجت که بولغای کیسه جینك جینکو بسکون نون و کاف و فتح رای مهمله
و ضم غین معجمه ترکی روح و نام جریر باشد جینکانك بسکون هر دو نون و هردو کاف عجمی و فتح سین مهمله نام منصبیست مخصوص که لمرزه ترکی
خانان ترك بدان اختصاص یافته اند که نایب پادشاه بوده اند جینکه باجیم عجمی و سکون نون و فتح کاف عجمی نوعیست مخصوص که در عرق و سیما
زن مصدر دست یکدیکر را کرفته برای عزت عروسی میرقصند و میخوانند چنانکه در میزان الاوزان در بیان سرودها کوید که یا ناچینکه دوره
ترك اولوسی زلف و قیز کوچوده ر طوی لار یدا آیتور لار و اول سرودی در بغایت موثر و ایکی نوع دهر نوعی هیج وزن پیله ار

اینلس و بر نوع چریت آنیلور که منسج مطوی موقوف بجی دوده و یا بار لفظی بی ردیف در سفینه مذکور تیلولار آنداقیم شعر
تاموچین دین ایسیب کلدی سنا تاپ یناش کیم دیمین توشتی لوت لحانیم ارا یا بایاش و از آنجاست که در صنعت تجنیس یعنی [illegible]
کفته شعر منی تو نوب چینکه منیداچنک نواچیک که می هایل و لنک هایل و لنک نوای چیعتر لنیک چرکاد دو تور و دو ناندغ
سه تار چنک دو تار چینکیز باجیم عجمی بسکون نون و زای معجمه و کسر کاف عجمی موافق تاریخ روضة الصفا لغت مغولی بمعنی شاه شاهان
و او پادشاهیست معروف که با کثر اقالیم تسلط یافت و نام اصلی او تموچین بوده چنانکه شاعر گفته شعر هادیم نام توچینکیزخان ازان کی
تو خصال تموچین هوان ازین رو که معنی چینکیزخان شاه شاهان بود شاه شاهان بترکی زان و وصاف در جلد رابع تاریخ خود از تاریخ جهانکشای جوینی
کرده که بیت چینکیزی کفت که تراجنکیز نام کردیم و معنی چنکیز بحر باشد و بعد از لفظ چنکیز بجای چینکیز که صیغه جمع است بدل کرده چینکیز نام
خواند مع الواو من المشتقات جولیما و جیولیما کلیک بسکون واو و کسر لام آشفته کویی و هذیان باشد جیولیدوک هذیان کفتیم جولیدر و جیولیدر
هذیان میکوید و جیولیر بمعنی فاعل و مصدر هم می آید جیولیکان و جولیکان و جیولیدکان هذیان کوینده و هذیان کفته چنانکه شاهد آن اکما
بمعنی اول در فصل بیت چهارم از محبوب القلوب بعد ذکر و لطف کوید که او یقود اسوز دیکان جولیکان بولور اول دیکاندیک قبلغان نی
دیکان بولور جیولی و جیولیکید مفرد غایب المستقبل از جولیما و جیولیما کیل مفرد غایب المستقبل جیولینک و جیولینکز و جیولینکلار جمع
غایب المستقبل از جیولیماک و جیولیما نکز و جیولیما نکلار جمع غایب المستقبل جیولیمان و جیولیماس مین هذیان نمیکویم جیولماین و جیولمیمین
جیولیمدین و جیولیرام هذیان میکویم جولیماس هذیان نمیکوید و بمعنی فاعل و مصدر منفی هم آید جولیسه جولیسان و جیولیمیش هذیان
کفته جیولیمیشالیک هذیان کفته جیولینا بولغان و جیولیب بولغان هذیان تواند کفت جیولی آلغای هذیان تواند کفت جیولی جیولی
هذیان کویان جیولیو جیولیین هذیان بکویم و بکوید بکوی و کفته جیولینا لیک جیولیکای و جولیکای بن و جیولیلینک هذیان
بکویم جیولیکالی برای هذیان کفتن و تا هذیان کفته جیولیکاچ چون هذیان کفت و بکوید بمحض کفتن جیولیکوچی هذیان کوینده جیولیکو
جیولیکو و جیولیکانه تا هذیان کفتن و بعد هذیان کفتن جیولیکوسی دور هذیان خواهیم کفت جیولیکو دور هذیان خواهید کفت
جیولیکوسیلار دور هذیان خواهند کفت جیولیکولوک هذیان کفته جیولیکای بیز جیولیسا جیولیسون جیولیسنک هذیان بکوید جیولیکودیک
جیولیولیک هذیان کفتن چنانکه کوید جیوردالات جیوردنالیکلیک باجیم عجمی بضم واو و سکون رای مهمله مصدر متعدیست یعنی کردانیدن
جیوردوک کردانیدیم جیوردی و جیوردی و میکرداند و جیورر بمعنی فاعل و مصدر هم می آید جیوردکان و جیوردکان جیوردی کردانیده
و کردانیده و بمعنی مصدر هم می آید جیوره و جیوره کیل مفرد غایب المستقبل جیوره و جیوردا کیل مفرد غایب المستقبل جیوردونک
جیوره و نکز و جیوره و نکلار جمع غایب المستقبل از جیوره نک جیوره نکز جیوره نکلار جمع غایب المستقبل جیوره ماس من نمیکردانم
جیوره میین جیوره میدین جیوره ماس نمیکرداند و بمعنی فاعل و مصدر منفی هم می آید جیوره و جیوریان و جیوره میش
کردانید الشاهد علی الاول شعر اول قویوند [illegible] بار یعنی باشیدین جیوره [illegible] آنرا داییپ جیوره میشاند
کردانید جیوره [illegible] کردانید جیوره آلغای تواند کردانید جیوره [illegible] جیوره کای [illegible]
بکردانیم جیوره کالی برای کردانیدن و تا کردانیده جیوره کاچ چون کردانید و بکرداند و بمحض کردانیدن جیوره کوچی کردانیده جیوره کوچه
جیوره کوسی [illegible] تا کردانیدن و بعد کردانیدن جیوره کو [illegible] خواهیم کردانید جیوره کوسی دور خواهید کردانید جیوره کوسیلار دور خواهند
کردانید جیوره کولوک کردانیده جیوره کای [illegible] و جیوره دیک بکرداند جیوره [illegible] بکرداند [illegible] چنانکه
بکرداند جیوره [illegible] بسکون واو و لام و ضم رای مهمله بمعنی کهنه و ژنده باشد جیوره [illegible] کوینده [illegible]

علی الاول شعر وصلینک [illegible] پروانه وار جیوره لوب [illegible] جیوره [illegible]
جیوره [illegible] پروانه [illegible]
[illegible] باجیم عجمی بسکون
و کاف [illegible] باجیم عجمی و سکون واو و ضم رای مهمله و جیوره
بضم واو و سکون [illegible] جیوره [illegible] بضم واو و سکون رای مهمله
[illegible] چنانکه در تاریخ الانبیاء در قصه حضرت سلیمان علیه السلام کوید که [illegible] سلیمان علیه السلام [illegible]
[illegible] ایوب علیه السلام کوید که [illegible] آلتون [illegible]
[illegible] باجیم عجمی بکسر واو و سکون [illegible]
[illegible] باجیم عجمی بکسر واو و سکون رای مهمله [illegible] باجیم عجمی
[illegible] باجیم [illegible]
چنانکه در تاریخ بابری مسطور است که [illegible]
و باجیم عجمی [illegible] چنانکه در دیباچه کتاب [illegible]
جیان [illegible] باجیم عجمی [illegible] چنانکه
[illegible] محبوب القلوب [illegible] چنانکه
در صراح کوید شعر [illegible] باجیم عجمی
[illegible] جیین بکسر یا و سکون نون [illegible]
[illegible] چنانکه در مقاله [illegible] کوید شعر [illegible]
[illegible] کویند حولات [illegible]
حولانات [illegible] چنانکه در لیلی مجنون [illegible] کوید شعر [illegible]
[illegible] کتاب [illegible]
[illegible] چنانکه در تاریخ بابری مذکور است که [illegible]
[illegible] چنانکه [illegible] کوید شعر [illegible]
[illegible] خاقان مرادف قاآن باشد یعنی ملک الملوک چنانکه [illegible]
[illegible] کوید شعر [illegible]
[illegible] پادشاهان چین را خصوصا چنانکه [illegible]
[illegible] نوشته که خاقان [illegible]
[illegible] و آن [illegible]
چنانکه [illegible] الابرار کوید شعر [illegible]
[illegible] در تاریخ بابری در وصف [illegible] مذکور است که [illegible]

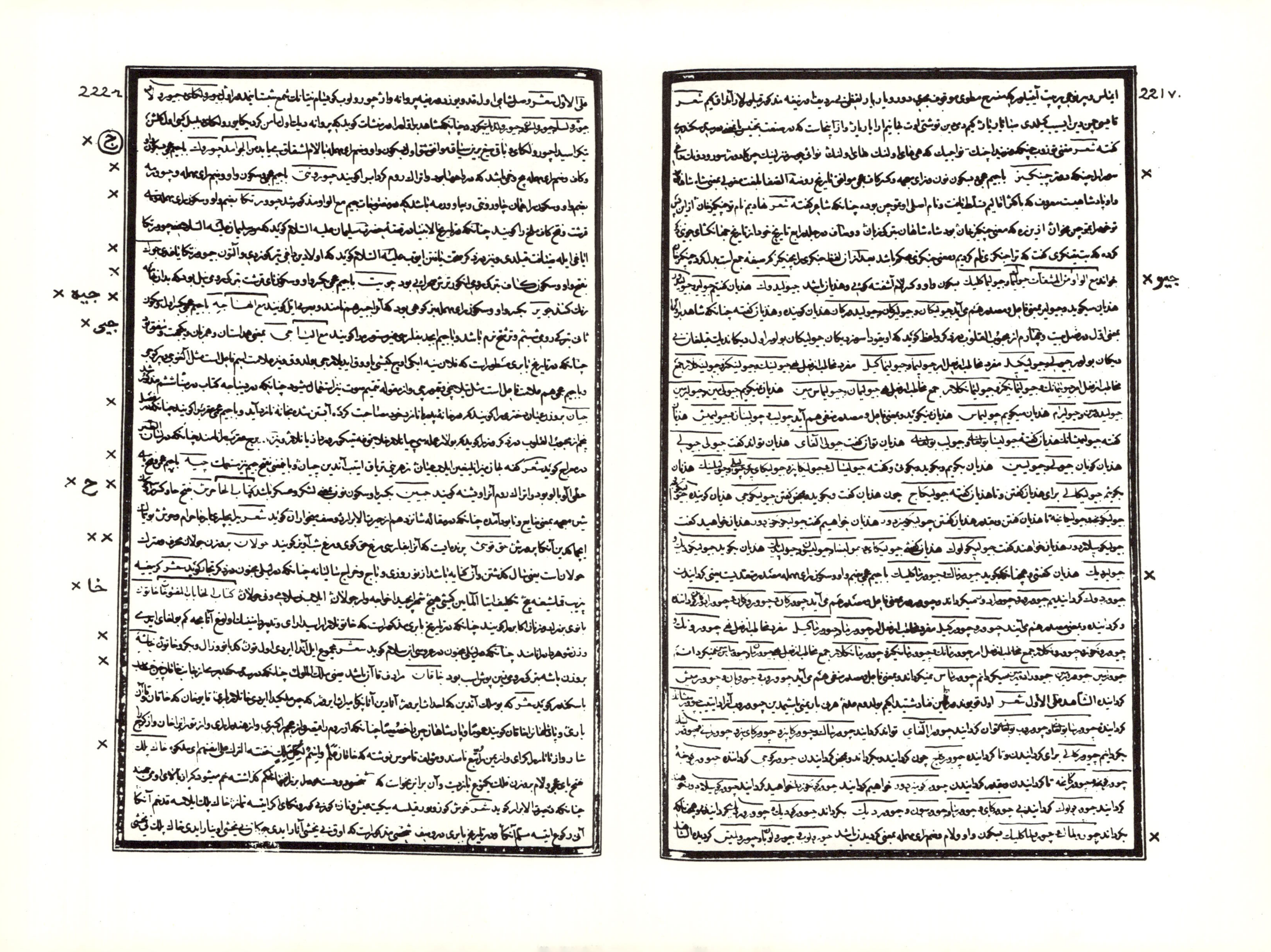

ناچار ایدی خان بمعنی پادشاه بود و باین جهت پادشاهان ترکستان را خان گویند و چون سلاطین روم منتسب ایلخانند خود را خان نامیدند
و بعد از انکه ترکستان و خان را متصرف شدند لفظ سلطانی را که بلغت عرب بمعنی پادشاهست بر خانی افزودند و اینکه در ایران حکام و
اعیان دولت را خان گویند همچنین از این نگاه داشت که چون سلاطین روم از عظم شان الملک قاسم پادشاهی بامرا و اعیان خود
ایشان را پاشا نامیدند که مخفف پادشاه باشد بعد از انکه پادشاهی ایران بخاندان صفویه منتقل شد ایشان هم علی رغم سلاطین
اعیان دولت خود را خان و فروتر از آنرا سلطان لقب دادند و بعد از انکه سلطنت هند بدودمان گورکانیه انتقال یافت خود را
پادشاه نامیده بطریقه ایران اعیان و اکابر دولت خود را بخطاب خانی اختصاص دادند و خان بفارسی دیه بمعنی اول خانه صرف شده
دوم ربالمد را گویند سیم علی و شان زنبور را گویند ختا اسم ملکی است معروف که چین دار الملک آنست چنانکه در
گوید شعر یا نابر قصه بی ایلچی بشناق تشابکا ضر کون جنس خانی ثبا ملای جغتای نیز مستعملست ختای اسم ... ازبکیه
مخیر بمعنی حریر استر را گویند چنانکه در تاریخ الملوک دور کوهستان آمده که آنقه ایشاکی نور ... اول ...
و با جیم عجمی نیز مستعملست و بضم و کسر اول بفارسی بمعنی خوب و زیبا و جمیل باشد خزال بترکی رومی جوالهای بزرگ بود که از پلاس دوزند
خشل بفتحتین قرشت و سکون لام بترکی رومی آهار بود که بر قماش و کاغذ مالند و بفارسی نوعی از حلواست که آنرا مقل گویند
ازرق مشهور و برای بواسیر نافعست خطا همان مملکت ختا باشد که مذکور شد چنانکه گوید شعر قیامت دشتی ...
بیز لاقنات خطا خانی ... بالشلاتی خطا الاولئی ختنان یکنوع لباسیست که از زر و طرف جاک دارد ...
آنرا تعریف نموده قتان هم نامند خلته بسکون لام و فتح تای قرشت بلغت جغتائی بمعنی هدیه و پیشکش باشد خلج بفتح لام ...
از اتراک الشاهد علیه شعر نوائی آن کلایخانلا مرد ... حرب و کرجنتای یعقه ترکمان و خلج و در جامع رشیدی مذکور است که
در عهد اوغوز خان فرزندی از زن سپاهی متولد شد آن ضعیفه بسبب قحط ... قوت ... لاجرم سپاهی ...
دید که ... گرفت ... شغال ... از وی ... و کباب ساخته بزن خود داد تا سیر خورده شیر پیدا آمد
چون اوغوز خان از این قضیه مطلع شد گفت قال آچ یعنی نان گرسنه و این لفظ از کثرت استعمال بخلج تبدیل یافت خلج بضم لام مشدد
نام شهریست از ترکستان که مشک خوب از آنجا آرند و بفارسی بمعنی خوشبو نیز آمده خلمه بفتح لام و میم ... را گویند خنج بر وزن
رنج زخم را مانند که ... باشد و بفارسی موافق برهان قاطع بمعنی نابع و باطل و نفع و سود و عیش و طرب و ناز و کرشمه بود خنجه بر وزن
پنجشاخچه نازک بود که از درخت روید چنانکه در تاریخ ناری مذکور است که تال النجه لاریدین ... بارماغچه ... دیک ...
و بفارسی آواز ... باشد که هنگام مباشرت از بینی بر می آید باب المضموم حرف الخاء مع الواو خوبولناتغ بلغت مغولی مرده ... آمدن باشد
خوبولغان مرده ... کما از کوه برآمدن باشد و بمعنی فاعل و مصدر هم می آید و سیغ آن موافق شق اول الاشتقاق می آید مع الدال خودوت
بضم دال که ... نامند ... ناکس و ناجنس اولادین کیشی بولسون دیبان ... چیکه ... لطیف ... خود ...
قیلسانک تربیت ایت بولمس ... ایشاک بولماس ... آدمی و آنرا قودوق نیز خوانند و بفارسی بمعنی پریشانی طبیعت باشد ...
رشک و حسد و قهر و خشم و غلت ... خوردن ... باشد مع الراء المهملة خوردولداناتغ بضم راء و سکون لام
فتح دال مهمله بترکی رومی نفیر کشیدن و صدا کردن ... خواب ... که آنرا ... گویند ... خوراته بفتح راء با الف
کشیده و تای قرشت ... بترکی رومی ... باشد خوران بترکی رومی دست ... خوروز ... خوبوک بترکی رومی ...
مرغیست ... که آنرا ... و تو بغار ... هم نامند و بعربی قراع و قمار الحبت گویند ...

خوشلاشماک لفظیست مرکب از فارسی و ترکی که بمعنی ولع کردن باشد و وجه اشتقاق آن ... باب المکسور من حرف الخاء مع الراء الشاهد
خیرلداماق و خیرلداناق ... بکسر و سکون لام نفیر کشیدن و صدا کردن سلاح و کلاب است از گلو در حالت خشم که خواهند بجانب کسی جستن
کنند و همچنین خرخر کردن شخص مخنوق را گویند خیرلدادی از گلو نفیر کشید خیرلدا یور و خیرلدایدور از گلو نفیر میکشد خیرلدار بمعنی ...
هم می آید خیرلداغان و خیرلدارغان ... خیرلداسه اگر از گلو نفیر کشد و نفیر کشنده و بمعنی مصدر هم می آید خیرلداب و خیرلدامو خیرلدایش
از گلو نفیر کشیدن چنانکه در لیلی مجنون در وصف ... الشاهد علی الاول شعر ... خیرلداب ...
خیرلداب خیرلدامناس از گلو نفیر نکشد ... و بمعنی فاعل و مصدر نفی هم می آید خیرلدایو و خیرلدای خیرلدای از گلو نفیر کشان خیرلدا
برای نفیر کشیدن و تا نفیر کشیده خیرلداغاج چون از گلو نفیر کشید و بجکد و بجز کشیدن خیرلداغوچی از گلو نفیر کشنده خیرلداغو
و خیرلداغو و خیرلداغانجه تا از گلو نفیر کشیدن و مقدمه نفیر کشیدن خیرلداغای و خیرلداسا خیرلداسون و خیرلدا دیک از گلو نفیر کشیده خیرلدا
و خیرلدابولیت از گلو نفیر کشیدنی و همچنانکه بجکد و باب ... موافق شق ثانی اشتقاق می آید خیرلدا شما ... مع الثاء ... از گلو نفیر
کشیدن و بجز افتادن و سیغ آن موافق شق اول الاشتقاق می آید خیرلدا تماغ مع الصاد ... بمعنی ...
از روی خشم و بجز اندازختن و سیغ آن نانای قرشت اشتقاق می آید من الجوه ... از ... را گویند ...
بسکون لام و کسر زای معجمه و فتح میم بترکی رومی آهک باشد مع الزاء المعجمه خزان بفتح زای معجمه با الف کشیده و سکون نون ...
مع الشین المعجمه خشل بکسر شین و سکون لام بترکی رومی ... مع الیاء خینا حنا بود که بر دست و پا بندند خینا لیغ حنا
بسته الشاهد علیه شعر خوشا اولکیم خزان ... تا ...
در داغستان که مسکن طایفه لکزیست ... باب ... مع الدال من المشتقات ... دامامق بفتح ... بترکی رومی
بمعنی کشتن و هلاک کردن بود من الجواهر ... دابان بر وزن ... را گویند چنانکه در تاریخ ... مذکور است که ...
توشکاندا ... دابا ... دیر ...
بسکون با و ضم ... و کسر لام ... را گویند دابقو بسکون با و ضم ... بمعنی ... و ... باشد و ... گویند ...
در تالیف خود ... نوشته است ... که ... از برای ...
دابقور بسکون با و راء مهمله و ضم ... بمعنی ... است چنانکه ... گوید شعر ...
دابقور دابقور ... که از میان ... کشیده شود و آنرا دابقوریز خوانند ...
دابوسون بضم با و سین مهمله و سکون نون بلغت مغولی ... دابجی بمعنی ... باشد و آنرا داغی ... گویند ... بر وزن
افزبکشک ... نامند مع الدال دادا بر وزن بابا ... گویند چنانکه ... بادشاه ... بادشاه ...
بود و نقل آن در ... داشت ... داداک باد الاول ... الف
فتح دال ثانی و سکون کاف دادک کنیز را گویند چنانکه در محبوب القلوب ... گوید ... داداک ...
دادک دین ... دوشرو ... ششم ... مقتم ... محبوب القلوب ... گوید که ...
دادک لاری ... فرهنگ جهانگیری بفارسی ... ذکر کرده و شعر ... را شاهد آورده و هو هذا شعر ...
... دادک ... و مولف برهان قاطع دادک بضم ثانی بر وزن ... بمعنی ...
... اول ... دادک لار ... آی ... خورشید ...

223v

قول دده‌لەدین خاصل اولغانلیك توقعده میرزا مغول دده بترکی رومی جدّ پدر پدر و مادر پدر را گویند و بالمجاز مشایخ زهّاد و صوفیان را هم

و مولف فرهنگ جهانگیری این لفظ را طرحی شمرده و نوشته که پیر و پیشوای طایفهٔ قلندران را خوانند و جانوران درنده را هم گویند و صاحب قاموس

ذکر کرده که کنیزک که نیکو را نیز گویند عموماً و کنیزک پیر صحالی که از طفلی خدمت کسی کرده باشد خصوصاً مع الراء من المشتقات داریماق مرادف داریقماق بجهت عجمی

شدن و دور کردن باشد چنانچه گوید الشاهد علی الاول شعر اسروقیبول آزیقیب داریماق هر باری سوسوش برای صید صیدنی بولغای

داریغیشلیق شرح چنین است که ای صید صید نی بولغای پریوبان داری یعنی ای صید صید چه شود یك بانیلوفر و کن داریغی رو کرد

داریدوق رو کردیم داریرود اریدی رو میکند و داریر بمعنی فاعل و مفعول هم می آید داریرایدی رو میکرد چنانچه در صفحه

دولتسان نیجم درقصه بنابر وصیل گوید شعر هر طرفدین داریرایدی صیدی شه فه ایرجی پناه ایشی قیدیغی داریغانی و داریغان

داریدیغان رو کننده و رو کرده و بمعنی مصدر هم می آیند داریعمود داریغیل مفرد مخاطب از فعل امر چنانچه شاهد بر اول در ذیل صید مذکور شد

داریغیل و داریغانا عیل مفرد مخاطب از فعل نهی داریبلغه و داریبکرو و داریبکلار جمع مخاطب از فعل امر داریغانك و داریغانیگز و داریغانکلار جمع

مخاطب از فعل نهی داریغان و داریغان مین رو میکنم داریغیمین و داریغمن مین و داریغیمغودار رام رو میکنم داریغاس رو نمیکند و بمعنی اعل

و مصدر هم می آید داریغبدار بان و داریعیش رو کرده چنانچه شاهد بر اول در تاریخ الملوك دو گوهر گوید که حضرت

معز سیدین سلکی کازوال العایب و شاهد بر ثانی در رساله دو گرد مهم از حیرت الابرار و در حق اهل ظلم گوید شعر حاصل و شولد و یکا

بلا داریبان تا یوبلا بلکه بوبا داریبان دائیمی شانك رو کرده داریغیاوپغای و داریب توالماغ و توانکرد داریغاغای رو تواند کرد

داری داریب رو کنان داریغی داریغین رو کم و کند و کنی و کرده داریغای و داریغانم و داریغلایم و داریغلار داریغیلی و کیم داریغیلی برایم که

و تا رو کرده داریغاج چون رو کرده و کند و بحض کردن داریغوچی رو کننده داریغومه و داریغوجه و داریغانچه تا رو کردن و بقدر رو کردن

داریغوسیز بیرون روی خواهیم کرد داریغوسیز رو در رو خواهید کرد داریغوسیلار بود رو خواهند کرد داریغولوق رو کردنی داریغای و داریغا

داریغی و داریغیش رو کند چنانچه شاهد بر اول در باب دویم از محبوب القلوب بیرزگر زهد گوید که هر نا الشکه بی مقامیه داریغای

و ملفقی باینت شرع سیله نفسانیت لوقی دین آریغای داریغودیک و داریریک رو کردنی و همچنانچه رو کند داریشماق مع الشین الفوقانیة المبلّغ

مع الشین مرادف داریماق باشد یعنی رو کردن و بچاه شدن و بمعنی باب مفاعله نیز می آید یعنی بهمدیگر رو کردن و صیغ آن باشین اشتقاق می آید

داریلماغ بکسر طا و سکون لام ترکی رومی بمعنی دلتنگ شدن بود و آنرا جغتائیه داریقماق گویند دیماك ترکی رومی بمعنی جمع شدن

من الجوامد دارا بروزن خارا بمعنی همیشه و مدام باشد و بفارسی دو معنی دارد اول پسر دارا بن بهمن است که معاصر اسکندر بوده دویم گروه

که در دبه خم نشسند دنبك بسکون را و کاف و فتح نون ترکی رومی مجمع و انجمن را گویند دارغه خاکروب و شهر را نامند چنانچه در مجالس

النفایس مذکور است گوید که داروغه دین تاچپ تانمان ایرکانین کیشی بیلماس دیسیم ایوی ترکی رومی الاجوق بود و بلغت جغتای گرمی

گفته شود مع السین المهمله درس دکری باصطلاح رومیه بمعنی مقصود و درس لفظ ایدیست که از برای مبالغه مخصوص بیکدیگر و تو

مثل بوس بوصری و ناپ پاسنی مع الشین المعجمة من المشتقات داشیرماق همان تاشیرماق بمعنی لنگیدن ستمر از سنگ بالمشلکه در ....

مفتوحه مع الشین مذکور شد من الجوامد داش مرادف تاش باشد که بمعنی سنگ بیرون و در صومعت آمده چنانچه در حرف تای مفتوحه مع الشین

با شواهد گذشت و بفارسی کوه و سفال بیز را گویند چنانچه گوید شعر خواهم لیلی خیالا الا تین بیشوریکا کراو ایشیم شعله لیغ کوتکلیوم بوستان

لاله کو یا داش ایرمش و داغ بمعنی یا فارسی مشترکست و بفارسی بمعنی گلستان هم نوشته اند مع الغین المعجمه داغ نشان و گل باشد که از پشت آب

و شراب و امثال آن در جامه هم رسد الشاهد علیه شعر بکه قوید و تك و کوسه کوتکلومنی آلغان نتاغ داغ جسیم اوليش قرم اول کلیم

224r

که توبین داغ داغ قویدم بمعنی یا فارسی مشترکست و بفارسی دو معنی دارد اول معروفست دویم مضمونی که شلوار چند بغل بسته دامنها را برنگ

تاتار بلغت تاتاریه بمعنی جنگ وجنگ باشد دامان بروزن تابان سه پایه بود که آنرا بعضی سلاح ابامی خوانند داغل بضم غین معجمه

و سرایت داغول بمعنی غبار و مکار و صحرا ازو نباشد چنانچه در مصطلحات و هشتم از محبوب القلوب بصورت کتابان گوید شعر که بولاغی

کیم که اونی بدبر و ماه صرا اکمیلنانك نظر پوافلی دور د امی بمعنی بیکر باشد چنانچه گوید شعر باشیمه قویش آشیانید و دامی

سیه دامغ شاهین عشق ایجرا مونداق بحتا ایله افتراقیت و آنرا تق و تاق و داغی نیز گویند مع الفاء دمی بروزن بخی ترکی رومی نام

درختیست که در طرف مرغزار سبز می باشد و بچوب بخور اننده بوی خوش دهد و آنرا ترکی ابرش خاروبار آنرا حب الغار نامند مع الکاف

من المشتقات دکشورماك بسکون کاف و را مهمله و شین معجمه ترکی رومی یعنی تبدیل کردن دکشوردوم تبدیل کردم و عنوان

الرومیه شعر خانق فصل تکلکون شراب تانه دکشوردوم سو بجنك و دودین تا لهوافانه دکشوردوم من الجوامد دك

ترکی رومی بمعنی نهایت و غایت بود چنانچه گفته شود که صباحدن رواحه دك یعنی از صبح تا شام که بعربی حتی گویند دیك بمعنی

مانند بود اگرچه با یای بیان کرده شده میشود و لیکن چون نوای علیه الرحمه با الف ناتیه کرده با زنیت در مفتوحه نیز مذکور

و هو هذا شعر بیلك قصید نه تو فیز و نجی نات اول الجلك که با بینا الملاء با فرش دك و تفصیل آن در حرف تای مکسوره مع الکاف نگارش ...

دکری بکسر کاف عجمی و سکون را مهمله ترکی رومی بمعنی مدور باشد و آنرا بلغت جغتای تیکرمه گویند دکله بسکون کاف

و فتح لام و تانیت آستین کوتاه که بر بالای لباس پوشند چنانچه گوید شعر یاشیل یکلیك کمسا بیغ دکله دین که هندی تامات خزان

درختی بدرهم برابر ناخضر شاخ و دیکلادی ودیکله بکسر دال الیزا بمعنی مستعمل چنانچه منکو خواهد شد دکلو بسکون کاف فتح

ترکی رومی بمعنی نوع و قسم بود گویند که نه دکلو یعنی چه نوع و چه قدر و او دکلو یعنی آن نوع و آن قدر دکمه بسکون کاف عجمی و فتح میم

ترکی بمعنی نفع و فواید بود چنانچه فضولی بغدادی گوید با ملاحظه الرومیه شعر دیمز ... دکمه قیدی جکم ...

بر آزاد ماتم دکل بضم کاف عجمی بمعنی دکل بین بعضیستی چنانچه حمید تلیه در مخزن گوید شعر ای گدا ... عشق ضعیف ...

بو مجلس فه دکل بین حریف و این لفظ در لغت جغتای مستعمل نیست در میان اتراك روم و ایران مستعمل است مع اللام من المشتقات دلالاماق

دالالماق بفتح هر دو دال کشیده و لام ثانی و سکون لام اول پشت جیزی خزیدن و پنهان شدن دالالادی بپشت خزید دالالادی

بپشت خزیدیم دالالادی دالالاید و ... بپشت می خزید دالالار بمعنی فاعل و مصدر هم می آید دالالامق دالالادی دالالایدو ... بپشت

خزنده و خزیدن و بمعنی مصدر هم می آید دالالاودی دالالاغیل مفرد مخاطب از فعل امر دالالامانی و دالالاماغیل مفرد مخاطب از فعل نهی

دالالالار و دالالانکیز و دالالانکلار جمع مخاطب از فعل امر دالالاماسون دالالامانکیز و دالالامانکلار جمع مخاطب از فعل نهی دالالامان و

دالالاماس بپشت نمیخزم دالالادیم دالالاریمن دالالاییکلار دالالار بپشت میخزم دالالاماس بپشت نمیخزد و بمعنی فاعل و مصدر نیز هم

می آید دالالاغ دالالادی دالالاغوی دالالامیش بپشت خزیده الشاهد علی الاول شعر نی محمد اله اوابولدی ایل تفرج ایتیب مین ملکا

تدین کلدی ایلدین دالالاسیانك بپشت خزیده دالالاسانکو دالالاب تو نقه بپشت توان خزید دالالای لغه بپشت توانم خزید

دالالابدغ دالالای دالالابی بپشت خزیده خزیده دالالای دالالای بین بپشت بخزیم و بخزی و خزیدن دالالاسا دالالاغانزو دالدا

لاغای برو دالالبلو دالالبسك بپشت بخزیم دالالاغلی برای پشت خزیدن و تا پشت خزیدن دالالاغاج چون پشت

خزید دالالاغوجی چون پشت خزید و بخزد و بمحض خزیدن دالالاغوچی بپشت خزیده دالالاغوجه و دالالاغوچه دالالاماغه تا پشت

خزیدن و بقدر پشت خزیدن دالالاغوسیز بپشت خواهیم خزید دالالاغونیز دو پشت خواهید خزید دالالاغوسیلار دو بپشت

دالالاغولوق بپشت خزیدن بی دالالاغای د الدالاساغو الدالاسوق و دالالادیك بپشت خزیده دالالاغویلجو الکلاه یك بپشت خزیدن بی
و همچنانکه بخزد دالالاشماقلیق و دالالاشماقلیغ مع الشین و دالالاماقلیغ و دالالاماقلیغ مع النون مرادف دالالاماق باشد
دالالاشماق و باشین و انما دالالاماق بالنون اشتقاق می یابد الماغ بترکی رومی همان تالماق بمعنی فرو رفتن بآب و غوطه کردن باشد چنانکه
در لغه مفتوحه مع اللام بالشاهد مذکور شد من الجواهر دال بمعنی باشد اول کتف و پشت را گویند دویم درخت
چنانکه گوید شعر تامیم دال و باشیم کلمك ابرصو تانار ایله دال وکل
و لنه و را که بطلوع شجر بریده میده وزند بهمین مناسبت دال بترکی گویند سیم
گویند چنانکه فردوسی در صفت گفته شعر هوا پر ز تیر شد دال
اول بمعنی راهنماست دویم عشوه گری نامند دالاق سپر بود که آنرا بعربی طحال خوانند دالاو مع الواو
بلغت مغولی دریا باشد و نیز قول بعضی کرا خوانند و از املاك
مخصوص کار سلاطین خاصه باشد ایشانرا نامند دالایلامآ بفتح هر دو لام و سیم و سکون یای حطی نام کسیه
واقع شدن و شمر خاو در سمت شرقی و جنوبی خطا میباشد که از حابا لیغ تا آنجا یکماهه راه مسافت است دالبای بسکون لام و یای
و فتح بای ابجد بمعنی چارپای بالی بود که توشمان آنرا بر هم بسته جوارح شکاری را بدان طلب کنند کذا لشاهد علیه
چیماق ایرمه دالبای و او نافه سیله که بال و پر بوایسه ممکن اولماز اوله پرواز دالدا بمعنی باد پا پشت سر و عقب هر چیزرا گویند
که در آنجا پنهان شوند چنانکه گوید شعر دمر ایلچیری دین ا ولدم تاکی بیخانه بونی کیم بر عصا چینلیکو بدالدا بی هرخلیفسا ...
مرغی را نامند که بال آن شکسته باشد دالدیرمه بسکون لام و رای مهمله و کسر دال و فتح میم بترکی رومی شاخ درختی بود که در خوانسار
بر بالای آن زنند تا ریشه محکم کرده سبز شود و از آنجا کنده در جای دیگر بکارند و آنرا بعربی ... و بفارسی ... نامند دالغا همان
دالغا بمعنی موج و انقلاب آب و هواست که در حرف تای مفتوحه مع اللام مذکور شد دالغیچ بترکی رومی غوطه خور باشد دالو
الو بلغت مغولی شانه و دوش بود که آنرا بعربی کتف نامند دالوجه بضم لام و فتح جیم بترکی رومی دانه ایست که در میان گندم روید
و سیاه باشد و آنرا قرابوق و چاورنی هم گویند چنانکه در جیم مفتوحه مع الواو گذشت دالوجه طوغان بترکی رومی مرغی است شبیه
شبیه شاهین که آنرا بعربی صقر الصقار گویند مع النیم دامارلوق بفتح میم با الف کشیده و سکون رای مهمله و قاف و ضم لام ...
مرچیم نامند دمد بمعنی ... بترکی رومی ... تنباکو بود که آنرا خشک کرده باشد ... خلری باشد سه پهلو ...
فندق که مغزی در میان دارد و چون بر لباس رسد جدا نشود و عصاره آنرا چون بدهانی که کیک بسیار باشد بیفشانند همه ...
و آنرا بعربی حسک و مغزیانرا حب الاسیر و بفارسی ... خوانند دمره کو بسکون میم و فتح رای مهمله و ضم کاف دمراتکی بکسر میم و کاف
و فتح راو سکون تای قرشت و دسیرا و بسکون واو ... باشد که در اعضا ... خارش کند و پوست ... و آنرا بعربی ... و بفارسی ...
و هندی داد گویند مع النون دنکل بمعنی جنکل بود و ... مکسور ... و الملحا خوانند ...
رومی بمعنی ... ایست که از بن ناخن بر می آید دانیشوق بکسر نون و شین و سکون قاف باصطلاح رومیه بمعنی مذاکره بود و مشاوره بود
مع الواو داوون بضم واو و سکون لام ... که هوا از تیره کند داوولغا بضم واو و سکون لام و فتح غین معجمه ...
بسکون واو و ضم لام و فتح ... تاوولغا و تاولوغه بمعنی ... که با شواهد در ذیل یای مفتوحه مع الواو مذکور شد مع الیاء داینا ...
بفتح یا با الف کشیده و زای معجمه ... بترکی رومی همشیره مادر بود که آنرا بعربی خاله گویند داین بکسر یا و سکون نون بمعنی بلند

بمعنی خصم و دشمن باشد المضمومات حرف الدال مع الباء دوبدورون بضم هر دو دال و رای مهمله و سکون بای ابجد و نون صدای کوفتن باید
چنانکه گوید شعر چو کوچه دین قولاغیم دوبدوروب ایشیتا کونکول دو کولدارایله کیم اولتار ... و نیز چوبیستکر ...
در وقت ... دو بدون یعنی راست ... و آنرا توتوبتوز هم گویند چنانکه ...
مع التاء دوتوق بضم تا بترکی رومی بمعنی ... و کر ... باشد دوتور ... مع الدال دوداغ بفتح دال ثانی و سکون غین معجمه لب
باشد و آن معروفست دودوك بضم هر دو دال نایی بود که آنرا بعربی مزمار خوانند مع الراء المهمله من المشقات دورمالك بسکون
بترکی رومی یعنی ... من الجوامد دوراق بترکی رومی محل اقامت و توقف دورچی بسکون راو کسر ... بترکی رومی ...
سوهانیست که آنرا مرسمن خوانند دورچی بکسر ... بمعنی ... لفظی است مرکب از عربی و ترکی ...
که زنان ... باشد چنانکه در فرهاد و شیرین در وصف ... گوید شعر ...
بود ... دورمن بسکون را و نون و فتح میم نام آروغست ... بسکون را و فتح میم باصطلاح رومیه ...
کمانرا ... شود مع الزاء المعجمه دوزاغ دوزاق دام صیاد را نامند الشاهد علی الاول شعر ...
... که ... و نیز نام ... از توابع ... که در ... است ...
بسکون نون و کاف و کسر لام بترکی رومی ... باشد دوزکون بسکون را و نون و ضم کاف عجمی ... آراسته بود ...
و فتح میم ... را گویند مع الشین دوشونك بضم شین و سکون نون بترکی رومی ... مع الغین المعجمه دوغولان
بلغت مغولی ... بود که آنرا بعربی ... خوانند مع الکاف من المشقات دوکولماك ... بضم کاف عجمی و سکون لام و فتح
دل باشد الشاهد علی الاول شعر ... دوکولمك ... و ...
دو کوکلنالعدیه شد ... دوکوك ...
که بمعنی ... است ... و دوکوك را گفته که ...
در معنی ... کرده ... که در ... تا ... بیدار میکند و دوکولادی ...
دوکولاروب ... چنانکه شاهد بر اول ... در ذیل ... و دوکولار ...
دوکولتکا ... دوکولدار ... و بمعنی ... دوکولماق ...
دوکولابا دوکولامیش ... دوکولایوعود ... دوکولاغو دوکولانی ... دوکولاکالی برای ... کردن ...
چون ... دوکولاکوجی ... دوکولاکوجه ... دوکولاکا ...
... دوکولادی ... و همچنانکه ... کندن من الجوامد دوکلی بفتح کاف عجمی بترکی
رومی بمعنی جمیع و همه باشد و آنرا توکلی هم گویند چنانکه گذشت دوکج بفتح کاف عجمی و سکون جیم بترکی رومی توکماق بود که آنرا بعربی مدقه
دوکاج بسکون کاف عجمی و جیم و فتح میم نان کم باشد که در روغن مالیده بخورند و آنرا ... نامند دوکوك بضم کاف اول و سکون ...
... گویند دوکولك بضم کاف اول عجمی و فتح لام و سکون کاف ... بود دوکون بضم کاف عجمی و سکون نون ...
بمعنی ... باشد و آنرا توکون هم نامند ... مع اللام من المشقات دولاماق ... دولاماقلیغ ...
و آنرا دولاشوماق ... دولاشتورماقلیغ هم گویند دولادی ... دولادوق ... دولادیم ... دولاید ... دولاتی ...
... می آید دولاغان ... دولایان ... دولاو ... دولاغیل ...

225v.

دولاناود ولاناعیل اسفرد غالب انفعل نهی دولانلغ دولاینکورود ولانکلار جمع غالب انفعل امر دولاناتلغ دولانانیکورود ولاناتکلار جمع غائب
انفعل نهی دولاناود ولاناس بین نمی چیم دولای بین دولار بین بعد ولابدمین ود ولا دام نمی چیم دولاناس نمی چپیده بمعنی ناصل و مستقبل
هنم می آید دولابود ولابعد ولامیش چپیده دولامیشانک چپیده دولانابولغای ود ولاب بولغه توان چپید دولاالغای توانم چپید
دولایوود ولایی دولایی چغازیچان دولای ود دولایین بچیم و بچپد و بچپیده دولاناود ولاغایرود ولاغای یرود دولاعود ولای بچیم دولانا
بای چپیدن و تا چپیده دولاغاچ چو بچپد و بچپد و بجز بچپیدن دولاغوجی چپیده دولاغوجه دولاغوچیزود ولاغا تا چپیدن و تعلیم
چپیدن دولاغومیز ود خواهیم چپید دولاغوتکیز ود خواهید چپید دولاغوسیلار ود خواهند چپید دولاغولوق چپیدنی دولاغای
دولاسونک دولادیک بچپید دولاغودیک ود دولاردیک چپیدنی د چنانکه بچپید ولاشورناق ود ولاشوراقلیغ مرادف دولاناق
و دولاناقلیغ باشد یعنی چیزی که لایق چپیدن باشد و صیغ آن باشند با لفظ تو موافق در اول اشتقاق بی یابد ولاشماق ود ولاشماقلیغ
مع الیثن چپیده شدن دولاشیب ود دولاشما ود ولاشمیز چپیده شده الشاهد علی الاول شعر نوایی ترکلار نینک ترکی تو تسه
عیب قیلما ملکیم آنکا پر ترکان موش نهی عکوری دولاشیب تورش دنا و صیغ برین سیاق باشد بخلاف لفظ تو در اشتقاق بی یابد من الجوامد دولاغ
بر وزن لالاغ پاتابه بود که آنرا پاپیچ گویند دولاشنق هم چپیده دولاناج بترکی رومی گرداب بود دولانه بفتح نون آلوچه جنگلی
ومؤلف برهان قاطع گفته که میوه ایست شبیه بسیب کوچکی آن در باغ و صحرا هر دو بهم میرسد در رنگش سرخ میشود و لذتش مانند آلو
میخوش باشد و یکدانه خسته و دانه طرود دولامه بلغت مغولی بمعنی کر باشد که آنرا بعربی اصم خوانند دولتو بسکون لام و ضم تاء
جانوریست از جنس کفتار چنانکه در ... گوید شعر ... دولتو ... دولت بمعنی
بترکی رومی بمعنی رام و نرم ... باشد دولمت بسکون لام و کاف و فتح میم جانوریست زهردار شبیه بعنکبوت که آنرا بعربی رتیلا گویند
ومؤلف فرهنگ جهانگیری و برهان قاطع ... دولمه بسکون لام و فتح میم ... آنست که به و سیب و امثال آنرا از تخم خالی کرده
میان آنرا از گوشت قیمه پر کنند و این مشتق از دولماق بمعنی پر شدن باشد دولامه بفتح لام و میم آنست که برگ تاک و اشباه آنرا از گوشت قیمه
پر کنند و این مشتق از دولاماق بمعنی پیچیدن بود و در رومیه آنرا سارمه گویند و دولامه در معنی مرادف ... و دلنکچ بفتح لام
و کاف عجمی و سکون نون و جیم بترکی رومی ... باشد که آنرا فلیولج گویند دوله بفتح لام بترکی رومی ... بود که آنرا ...
دوبله بجر لام متحرک باشد که آنرا ... دومان بجارست که از زمین متصاعد شود و آنچه از آتش ...
و دیک و امثال آن صعود کند آنرا بوغ نامند دومبلاک بسکون میم و کاف و ضم بای ابجد فتح لام بترکی رومی ... کوچک بود دومری
بسکون میم و کسر ... باشد و ... هم گویند ... مع النون من المشتقات دونمک بترکی رومی
بمعنی برگشتن باشد دونکول دونمک یعنی ... شدن ... دونه دونه یعنی گردان گردان و کشته من فضولی ... بالملاحه
الرقیه شعر ای فضولی ناوک آهلیه الدیم انشاء دونه دونه ... دونه ... دونه دونه
کرد ایلدیم من فضولی بالملاحه الرقیه شعر ای فضولی یاره دونه ... سدق ... الله
اللهیم دونانمک بفتح نون اول و سکون نون ثانی بترکی رومی بمعنی تزیین و آراسته شدن است و ازا طونانماک هم نامند من الجوامد
دونلنمه ... گویند دونانمه بفتح نون اول و میم ... و سکون نون ثانی بترکی رومی ... آمدن اول ... بود
که در میان آن توپ و چراغخانه باشد دونانم بمعنی تزیین و آرایش باشد دونانما بمعنی آراستگی و آیین بود و کوکبه و اثاثه پادشاهی را هم گویند
و آنرا طونانما هم خوانند دونبول بسکون نون و لام و ضم بای ابجد ... که دانه بسته باشد

دونکوز

226r

دونکوز بسکون نون ... بترکی ... دونم بضم نون و سکون میم بترکی رومی بمعنی جریب است که ...
مساحت اراضی ... دونوغ بر وزن ... جیبت ...
بترکی رومی بمعنی تحمل کردن بود ... گویند ... بالملاحه الرقیه شعر قیلالی
مجنون کبی ... فضولی شعر ... بالمعجمه ...
اعتبار ... فضولی آتش ... مع الباء من المشتقات دیبسانماق ... بسکون یای ابجد و فتح سین مهمله
پای کوفتن بود دیبسانادی پای کوفت دیبساندوق پای کوفتیم دیبسانادیم ... دیبسانور پای میکوبد و دیبسار بمعنی حال و مستقبل هم می آید
دیبسادار بردی پای میکوفت چنانکه ... علیها
اول ... دیبسانغان ... دیبسانغان پای کوبنده ...
و بمعنی مستقبل هم می آید دیبسا و دیبساغیل مفرد غائب انفعل امر دیبسا ... خواهد شد دیبسا
دیبساغیل مفرد غائب انفعل نهی دیبسانک دیبسانکود دیبسانکلار جمع غائب انفعل امر دیبسانامانک دیبسانامانکود دیبسانامانکلار جمع غائب
انفعل نهی دیبسانام دیبسانامانس بین پای نمیکوبم دیبسای بین ... دیبسابدین ... دیبسانامس ...
نافل ... هم می آید دیبسانب ... دیبسامیش پای کوفته چنانکه ... الشاهد علی الاول
شعر ... دیبساب ... آلدا
... دیبسامیشانک پای کوفته دیبسانابولغای ... دیبساب بولغه پای توان کوفت دیبسا ... بود
دیبسا ... دیبسای ... پای بکوبم و بکوبد و بکوبی و کوفته دیبساناق ... دیبساغای ...
پای بکوبم دیبساغلی برای پای کوفتن و تا پای کوفته دیبساغاچ چو پای کوفته ... دیبساغوجی پای کوبنده دیبساغو
دیبساغونه ... تا پای کوفتن ... دیبساغومیز ... پای خواهیم کوفت دیبساغوتکیز ... پای خواهید کوفت دیبساغوسیلار ...
خواهند کوفت دیبساغولوق پای کوفتنی دیبساغای ... دیبسادیک ... پای کوفتنی ...
بگوید من الجوامد دیب دو معنی دارد اول بلغت مغولی بمعنی ... چنانکه گفته خواهد شد دیب باقوی نام ...
خان بن ترک ... و بلغت مغولی معنی دیب بخت ... و معنی باقوی ... دیبسا بسکون با و فتح سین مهمله ... استعمال ...
... که آنرا ... دیک ... از اوجاق ... چنانکه مذکور شد
دیبلک بفتح با و سکون کاف ... الکفار ... دیبلیک
بسکون با و کسر لام بترکی رومی ... جمیع ... دیب ... که ... باشد و آنرا
... مع الراء المهمله دیرسون بسکون را و نون و ضم سین مهمله بلغت مغولی بمعنی فراوان و بسیار آمده
... در تاریخ ... گوید که چون نوبت خلیفه ... آن ... لشکر ... یعنی بسیار تا کار ... آمد
دیریم بکسر را و سکون یا و میم ... آنرا ... استعمال نمایند مع الزاء المعجمه
دیزقالپاغی بترکی رومی ... باشد دیزهن بترکی رومی بمعنی ... دیزلیک بترکی رومی ... که سپاهیان ایشان از ...
دوجه ... دیزی بکسر ... که آنرا بعربی سلک گویند و بمعنی ...
... استعمال شود دیزین دیزین بترکی رومی بمعنی رشته رشته و سطر سطر و صف صف مع الکاف من المشتقات دیکلاشماق ...

بسکون کاف و شین قرشت و ضم لام ... معنی ... اول تیز نگاه کردن دوم راست بستادن و با تای قرشت نیز مستعملست دکلمک بسکون کاف و
نون و فتح لام بترکی معنی آسوده شدن باشد چنانچه فضولی بغدادی کوید بامیلا الرتبه شعر یا ... دکلمک
دکلکچه دکلنون ... سن ... مصدر متعدی ... کردن من الجوامد دیلک بمعنی استمال
میشود اول از ادات تشبیه است بمعنی مثل و مانند بود چنانچه کوید شعر یوق ... دیلک دشمن ... دیلک
دوم بمعنی ... و خاموش باشد و باید و بمعنی با تای قرشت نیز مستعملست سیم ... مفرد ... واقع میشود افاده معنی مترد
مناسب میکند چنانچه کوید ... بیعنی ... الشاهد علیه شعر تیلبه کونکلوم ... دیک ...
آندین ... دیلک ... چنانچه کوید ... دیلک ... صبد
جمع از اسم فاعل حذف نموده بدل آن ... افاده معنی قابلیت ... میکند چنانچه ... را کوید ...
یعنی ... چنانچه ... خوانند ... دکلاچه دیکله بسکون کاف عجمی ...
آستین کوتاه که بر بالای لباس پوشند الشاهد علی الاول شعر ... دیکلاچه ...
ابنا ... شعر ... حاشیه ... دیکلاچی ... آزاد ...
چنانچه ... مع الکاف کذشت دیکیل بکسر کاف عجمی و سکون لام یعنی ... چنانچه کوید شعر کل ...
بوز غنچه دیکیل ... دیکیل
... شعر ...
دیکیلانغ ... دیکین بکسر کاف عجمی و سکون نون ...
اول الی و حتی بود که از برای انتها موضوعست چنانچه ... کوید شعر ... دیکین
خان ... کوید شعر ... تراش و
همچنین در حیرت الابرار در آغاز نظم کتاب کوید شعر ... سوفه ...
بنیاد ... دوم بمعنی ... چنانچه کوید شعر ... جمال الدین ... دیکین ...
آستیدین آفتاب و نیز کوید شعر دیکین ...
و نیز در مقاله شانزدهم از حیرت الابرار در وصف ... شعر ... دیکین ...
... سیم ... چنانچه کوید شعر ... دیکین ...
ابرکین ... بکسر کاف و سکون نون و فتح جیم بمعنی الی و حتی بود که از برای انتها موضوعست چنانچه کوید شعر ...
ایلیکدین ... و نیز ... کوید شعر عالم ... خسرو و خاقان ...
دیکیجه ... بمعنی ... کاف ...
... چنانچه ... مع اللام دکلت بسکون لام و کاف و فتح جیم عجمی ...
... دلیم ... بترکی ... که آنرا ... کویند ... شعر دلیم دلیم دلیم ... کیل ...
... دلیم ... مع النون ... دینکلاماق بسکون نون و کاف عجمی و فتح لام ... دینکلاماق بمعنی شنیدن ...
بود که در حرف تاء مکتوبه مع النون بیان شد و ... اشتقاق می یابد دینکلمک بسکون نون و کاف عجمی ...

شده باشد دیانات بفتح نون بترکی ... بمعنی ... کردن ... که آنرا ... کوید چنانچه کوید
شعر ...
چنانچه ... کتاب ...
ایات ... مع الواو دیوه تاتاغ بفتح تای قرشت و ... بترکی ... شتر ...
و آنرا ... دیوه ... که ... دیوه چیك بترکی ...
جانوریست شبیه بملخ اما ... مع الیا
من المشتقات ... یعنی ... و دیلاك که ...
و افعال آنست با صیغ مشتقه ... کفت دیدوك کفتیم
دیدوك ... الشاهد علی الاول شعر ...
الشاهد علی الثانی شعر ...
فاعل و مصدر هم می آید چنانچه ... کوید شعر ...
اول هم ... کوید شعر ...
در داستان اول کوید شعر ... فرماید شعر
... چنانچه ... کوید ...
علی الاول بالمعنی الاول ... کوید شعر ...
... شیخ الاسلام ... در مقاله ... از حیرت الابرار آمده شعر ...
دیکاندین ... مفرد ... الشاهد علی
الثانی شعر ...
دیدال ... مع الکاف کذشت ... مفرد ... جمع ... الشاهد علی
الاول شعر ... الشاهد علی الثانی شعر ...
دینکیز ... جمع ... الشاهد علی الثانی شعر
دیانیکز ...
الشاهد علی الاول لا ادری ...
دیدوم ... دیرام ... الشاهد علی الثانی ... شعر ...
... الشاهد علی الثالث شعر ...
... الشاهد علی الثالث شعر ...
ای ... چنانچه ... کوید الشاهد علی الاول
شعر ...
دیبان ... الشاهد علی الاول شعر ...

وله شعر دیب ایدیم بین کیم نوائی خالیغه یکتن خبر ایلا ایسا اصلی عمرنی تا یا نیلمه قیلیبدین تا کیملیث الشاهد علی الثانی
شعر کیجه کیلدیکم ده حیبا و حلوا و کلی و کیلمادی کیم الاریکا کیچه تانک آتنوبجه ایتوکلادی یتیشا تانک کیچه دیبا بولغنه
دیب بولغنه نوازکشند دیکا الغای نواند کفت چنانچه کوید شعر صبیم فغه کیم دی الغای کیم منکا بو بولدا هم بولی مکرشا هیم کیم
دره حشنو یوحمه آلما هیم دیبا بولور میتوان کفت چنانچه سلطان حسین کوید شعر خامه ده جسیم ولمخان رشته سبی کبی
مینو کیم منبع ایله تولیغا نما لغید یو حیبا بولمز الکند دیب بولماس دیبا بولمادی بیاد املا میتوان کفت الشاهد علی الثانی شعر
نقطه موهوم فغه قسم نیز اتشالمت برئ دیبا بطالرلار آیینک یوق آغزی نینک مقدارچه الشاهد علی الثالث شعر عالم
ایچرا آدم دیبا الدی اولملس کیم جاه ایله مولغای منکا تا نون الملار ایمز کاچه دیئ دیمین بکویم و بکوید بکوی و کفته الشاهد
علی الاول بالمعنی الاول شعر نکوم نکلوم ایمار لیله که چاشی موسیئی یوق ایشا شیفته جان ایچرا نهان دی موسیئی
دیسکیم کیلدیم کیلمه مو چاه تا السکیم کوید شعر یوق الینکا سوزدیکا نارانکا ولاچین دیکان سوزنی دار انکا
الشاهد علی الثانی بالمعنی الاول شعر تا شی ایلین مویدین کوزی قراسین مویدین کونکلوم اهری نینک دردو بلاچین مویدین
کوزی قرلین موسین کونکلوم اهری نینک دردو بلاچین مویدین دیسالدو دیکانیز دیکای نزم دیلی دیلینک بکویم الشاهد علی الرابع
برا اوکه منوچهر ایله مثلدی تهمیم نینی من نوع یو قیلی کیم قیلدی محترم بیزنی وینز دو خاتمه سکندری کوید شعر دغا الحق
فضل و دانش ایلیئ هم آمیزدیو نزهم آمیز دیکمی بیکلیب بار کمتن و تاکفته بالمعنی الاول شعر او نوائی بولمادا آینیک یادیدین غافل دی بیتی
اولدونک دیکا الحکیم اول امینوی دایلا الملوس دیخج چون کفت و بکوید و مکفتن الشاهد علیه شعر دیکاج ابحاب اشیفه ایلور دولی
لاد نی بیله قوباش یعنواب و جند دیکوی کوینه چنانچه ده ضل بوییم از مجوب القلوب کوید که شاهنشه مینا طاحین جهز دیکوی
وآینینک آخرتی نمی یکوجو یکوجه دیکو به و دیکا بجه تاکفتن و بقدم کفتن چنانچه در صفل بجه سیاره در وصف بهرام کوید الشاهد
علی الثانی بالمعنی الاول شعر فامتهی دیکو بجه چرخ دبی یتره کوز الیلادی آینینک ولچی و ینز در خمسه شیرین در وصف خسرو فرهاد کوید
الشاهد علی الثالث بالمعنی الثانی شعر دیکانجه بلکه یوز انجه تکلف تکلف با سپیدا تا الماس ناسف دی آلتوجه دی النونجه
دی الغانجه تا نوازکفت و بقدر چه نوازکفت چنانچه ده صل سکندری کوید الشاهد علی الثالث بالمعنی الثالث شعر بزی
جثه ایچرا ز بروست راق یا نا پر حقیر ایردی و پیت طرق آنکا بجه قوت مونکا آغجه منعف دی الغانجه قوت دی الغانجه ضعفه دیکو
خوام کفت چنانچه کوید شعر پر ضعیف بار توپ هر لیکن قولاغینکه دیکوم یوزیا متین توت بو طریقین ای یکتیر هیدا یشت
دیکونک خواهی کفت چنانچه در خاتمه خسرو شیرین کوید شعر نیامی بجه دیکونک سوزنی هذیان بو هذیان لالارنی قوی چیکنکر
دیکوسی خواهد کفت بکولوک کفتنی چاشی دیسا ود یسوی دیدیک بکوید الشاهد علی الاول شعر ایل پری دیوزنی دیکای کیمکان
خوب لیک ایرمه موپری زادیم مینینک یوز آغجه خوبا دیکودلیکئ دیردیک کفتو و چنانچه بکوید و شاهد با ولطا و وصف الله
حسین کا زرکامی کوید که غالبا سبب طابتیلی مولحد بو تونورا عزکا مینکودلیک حیثیتی یو قلیدی دیبشما الیکو دیبشما کیلک بجهراد
شین بمعنی مقاطله است یعنی بهم کفتن و مکالمه کردن الشاهد علی الاول شعر رشک دین عشقینک تو تلرمین خان و کونکلوم
فغان بعد مالاس ایل تبرین دیبشما لیکا مو سیله دیبشکان دیبشوکان و دیبشادور کان بهم کوینده و بهم کفته و بمعنی مصدر هم کوید
چنانچه شاهد با ولطا بآ معنی در صفه سیاره کوید شعر او زیکا کیلکاچ اول ایکی کلخواه دیبشکاندین و لمادیم آکاه
دیبشیمانه دیبشمیش بهم کفته الشاهد علی الاول شعر کیمسه یاریدن خوشتورغم دیبشیب و انکالشیب یا تیه کا هوج

اولنمونا کامیوبا یعلاشیب و تلقو بیغ بیزسا ق مواقو ثق اول اشماق دیب یا بد دیلیما العقدیلیما کیلیک بکسر جیم و سکون لام کفته کینک
دیلکان دیسلیم کالان دیلیا چه مکان کفته شوید و کفته شد چنانچه شاهد با ولطا بمعنی ثانی در صفه سیاره کوید شعر کوشه دا
ممکن دیلکان زچر خلق ین غا لیچ چند العزلت کیزدیلکویس کفته خواهد شد در صفه سیاره شعر چو دیلکو چا ملا
قولی شاه مدحین بوروند دیبالدا ملیدیلیکوسی ایردی کفته نخواهست شد چنانچه در صفه بدیع الزمان میرزا کوید که ولایت
شهرت سیز آکیب دو مرینیو سو دنیا حلیو حلکا بانی قیلا انیکرا ایردی یو قدیلما کوجلی ایردی و تلقی بیغ بیزیغ مالام اشقاء
می یا بدین الجوامد دیو مضم یا تریکه دوی بمعنی کویان و کفته باشد شعر کنت کنزا آشکارا ولسو نبی یوجمله عالم کند نی
دیوان بجهت مخولیتما الشوعلولی کلیزات پادشاهان و حکام و دفترخانه طلسیبارا کوپند چنانچه در صل سکندری در صفه
باسکندر کوید شعر بولمبچ سلیقی تیسمر تلمغا نغر لج که اندین ایدی دو ستلوقه دواج سکر شاه دیوالیفه کیما یش قیا
ایچرا سکر تیپا میر فی در صفه سیاره در داستان قیم کوید شعر بلو موفق مالیز ایتی دیبولنئ شاه الدیلا درجه فه بند ایتیب آنی دیوم
کینید که شعرا اشعار خود را در آن ثبت و جمع نمایند و نیز دیوان را نامند چنانچه بمعنی دیوم و ینم در خاتمه خمسه شیرین در صف
بمعنی بخود کوید شعر نی صلات ایچرا که پرفرمان سلار دیم آیینک صنطوفه پر دیوان سار دیم بود یوان تو تبا اولکشور ساند اق
که دیوان تو ترناکای ممتزیا آندا ق و بمعنی تنیم در تاریخ باری مذ کورات که بعضی بکلاه زنی بخشیلاه و دیوانه بیله آتی تینی سرکار
نیلا ب کنز یلکیمه لاز ینکا و ستیکا میتین قیلیلادی چنانم علس بجا مکه را و داد خواهی را کوبند چنانچه در تاریخ باری
که دیوان تامرنا فلدین سونک سیرفه آلاینب و بفارسی جمع شیاطین بود کتاب الراء المهمله باب المفتوحات حرف الالف راسوق
بوزن فاسق و آن معروف است و روبتیج معرب آنست که عبارتانی ترکی سوخته باشد اصطلاحی است از برای سنکی که زنان آنرا بر ابرو
میکشند مع الجار خرخ بفتح هردو حاء و سکون راء و بمعنی خطخط راه راه چنانچه کوید شعر خیال خیلی کمربرکا
کیلمرکا دیرکیا ثیونوم که بول بولا اولو بتو سر شکدین سخرخ مع الفاء رمدان بفتح راء بروزن همدان بترکی روی سینه تیم برشتر را کوبند
مع الواو روشن بروزن جوشن بکوبم سکاینت سه پهلو و بترکی بمعنی دریچه و منظر باشد و بفارسی معروف باب المضمومات زرکا
باصطلاح اتراک دروم نیم و باد بود و بفارسی بمعنی زمانه و ایام باشد کتاب الزاء المعجمه باب المفتوحات سنجوری باشد کانی شبه
و نانج معرب آنست شعرای نوائی شام عمدین آیرو یوقتور صبح وصل آقایرو ولیکرترار توبه هرنی نیز ایتساز الث و آن با فارسی شترا
دارد زغش بفتح غین بروزن بقریتر کی ردی کلب معلوم بود زغنوس بفتح غین و ضم نون و سکون سین مهمله ترکی روی نوعی از جوز
شکاریت کما آن المغزل نامند زلت بروزن ملات ترکی روی بمعنی ایمکو آشناره بود زنبکن بروزن زنجکن ترکی روی بمعنی
و نا الدار زنکو بسکون نون و ضم کاف عجمی بروزن بازاکوینه باب المضمومات زوکورد بضم کاف عجمی و سکون رای مهمله و دال ترکی روی بمعنی کماو
آمده زولات بروزن ملاس بلغت مغولی بمعنی نرم و لین باشد زنلوق بسکون نون و قاف و ضم یای ابجد و لام بروزن التسلم آنرا با
که کبی دهان خود برباد کند و دیکری چنان دستبرآن زند که آن باد از دهان او و باصدا بجهد و آن را بفارسی زانغر کوبند و مولف
قالع زبغل بفارسی بای معنی نوشته باب المکسورات زیق بکسر یای ابجد و معنی دارد اول شخص کوتاه کردن کوتاه قامت را کوبند دوم
دوی چو مینه بود که زنان چو مینه باز آنرا بکار برند زیقی بترکی روی مزی را خوانند که مناجقه کند و چو مینه باز باشد
بغلر بمعتری و سعتر لم کوبند زرنخ بکسر او و سکون نون مهمله رو ینه در دانامند زرنک بکسر رای مهمله و سکون کاف زرشک با
که آنرا بمعرب انبر باریس خوانند زق بروزن بدو ترکی روی جاز اکوبند و ضرب بمعنی خیک و مشک باشد زلغت بسکون لام قطه

قرشت و کرغین جمه بمعنی ململه است و آن چنانست که مردان و زنان در وقت شادی بر دها و نرد مقرر المکند دولیه برغین میل
بترکی رومی سنج باشد که در نقاره خانها نوازند و بعربی صنج نامند کتاب السین المهمله باب الفتوحات من المشتقات ساباتماق ساباتیغ ساب
بفتح با و با الف کشیده با چوب و نی پنبه زدن و حلاجی کردن چنانچه شاهد بر اول از اوله در فصل الواو عجوب الظلو بعرزه کو سلطان زمان کوید
که مجنون لار چرخ اونی سدی چیله آیننک دماسیغه نغمه ساز کیم لار ماسوغ ساباق کو سحاوین بیله آیننک آلقیشی نغمه پرداز
سابادی حلاجی کرد سابارو سابایدور حلاجی میکند و بمعنی فاعل و مصدر هم می آید ساباغار و ساباغان و سابایدورغان
حلاجی کننده و حلاجی کرده و بمعنی مصدر هم می آیند سابلونا باعیل مفرد غائب المبنی للمفعول سابالدی ساباعیل مفرد غائب المبنی
فی سابانک و سابانکز و سابانکلار جمع غائب المبنی للفاعل سابانالدی سابانکیز سابانکلار جمع غائب المبنی للفاعل سابالی سابانار
حلاجی میکنم سابای میز سابار میز سابایدور میز سابادام حلاجی میکنم ساباماس حلاجی نمیکند و بمعنی فاعل و مصدر منفی هم می آید
سابابک سابابان سابامیش حلاجی کرده سابالیشان حلاجی کرده سابابا سابابولغای ساباب برفته حلاجی توان کرد سابا الغه
حلاجی تواند کرد سابابیو سابای سابای حلاجی کنان سابای سابابین حلاجی کم و کند و کنی و کرده ساباناق ساباغای
ساباغای بولنا بالیک سابابالینک حلاجی کنیم ساباغلی برای حلاجی کردن و تا حلاجی کرده ساباغاچ چون حلاجی کرد و کند
ساباغوچ حلاجی کننده ساباغوجه ساباغونجه ساباغانچه تا حلاجی کردن و بقصد حلاجی کردن ساباغوسیز دور حلاجی خواهیم کرد ساباغو
حلاجی خواهید کرد ساباغوسیلار دور حلاجی خواهند کرد ساباغولوق حلاجی کردنی ساباغای ساباسلو ساباسون سابادیک حلاجی کند
ساباغودیک سابادیک حلاجی کردن و همچنانکه حلاجی کند سابلاماق بسکون بای عجمی و فتح لام بمعنی رشته بهم رسیدن سابلاندی
مع النون کشیده شد رشته بهم رسیده بود و بترکی رومی بمعنی اتصال و سونیا متن باشد من الجوامد ساپ بابای عجمی بمعنی حاصل و اول
رشته و جنس امله را کویند دویم لفظیست که از برای مزید تاکید استعمال شود چنانچه کویند ساپساری یعنی زرد محض ساپساغ یکی
صحیح و صحیح این لفظ مخصوص چین و جاست سیم بترکی رومی دسته شمشیر و کارد و تیر و امثال آنرا نامند ساپا بفتح بای عجمی و الف کشیده
بترکی رومی خارج راه و کنار شهر را کویند ساپاغ بفتح بای عجمی و الف کشیده و سکون غین معجمه ساق برک و دسته هر چیز را خوانند
چنانچه در لیلی مجنون در وصف خزان بمعنی ساقه کوید شعر هر برک که خسته و لرزانتی بر ریشته اپاغ اغرایتی کو یا توپیدا اوموزدن
بولدی اوزونا بلکا زاپاغی و بمعنی دسته کوید شعر هر کونه کیم اخز بخسته ظاهر قیلیبان ساپاغی دسته ساپان بعضی تاتارچوبی
باشد که بر سر آن آهن نصب کرده زمین را شیار کنند که بعربی فدان کویند و با بای عجمی دو معنی دارد اول کلاه خن بود که آنرا بعربی مقلاع نامند
دویم نام علفیستان از محال تهران که در کنار جوی جغتای واقع است ساپان اوتی چوب دراز زیت که بر سر چوب شیار نصب کرده دهقانان
آنرا بدست کرفته کاو میرانند سبد بعضی ترکی رومی طرفیست که از نی و شاخه تر درست کرده میوه و امثال آنرا در آن کذارند
و آنرا بعربی سله و بفارسی ساوین کویند سبدجک بکسر تا و سکون زای مهمله و کاف و فتح جیم استخوان نرم بود که آنرا غضروف
و بعربی غضروف نامند ساپاره نرده ئی تمام ندرد ساپاخ دو معنی دارد اول صحیح دویم حیشاله چنانچه در تاریخ بابری مذکور
که مینساباغ توربیب بر بولاک او نزیبی ساترا بیقلغا ایلادی ساپنوب بسکون بای عجمی و نون و ضم غین معجمه حبه و نیزه ایست شکل حجه
که صیادان بدان ماهی صید کنند مع التاتار المشتقات ساتماق ساتماقلیغ فروختن ساتوق فروختیم ساتار ساتادورمین فروشنده ساتار سات
فاعل و مصدر هم می آید ساتقا ساتارغان ساتادورغان فروشنده و فروخته و بمعنی مصدر هم می آیند ساتات و ساتقیل مفرد
غائب المبنی للمفعول امر ساتماو ساتماعیل مفرد غائب المبنی للفاعل ساتینکلار جمع غائب المبنی للفاعل ساتمانک ساتمانکلار جمع

غائب المبنی للفاعل ساتمان و ساتمادین میفروشم ساتامیز و ساتارمیز ساتادورمیز ساتادام میفروشم ساتماس نمیفروشد و بمعنی فاعل و مصدر
منفی هم می آید ساتیب ساتیبان ساتیش فروخته ساتیشاندک فروخته ساتابولغای ساتیب برفته توان فروخت ساتا الغای
تواند فروخت ساتاق ساتاتیر ساتا لغای ساتالیک ساتقای بفروشیم ساتقالی برای فروختن و تا فروخته ساتقاچ چون فروخت
و بفروشد چون فروختن فروختن ساتقوچ فروشنده ساتقوجه ساتقونجه تا فروختن و بقصد فروختن الشاهد علی الثانی شعر
ملالی این یتوی جیبه پیراهسا ساتقون آل خورش و چربه پیراهه جمانه ساتقونجه ساتقوسیز دور خواهیم فروخت ساتقوسی دور خواهید
ساتقوسیلار دور خواهند فروخت ساتقولوق فروختنی ساتقای ساتسلو ساتسون ساتادیک بفروشد ساتقودیک ساتادیک فروختنی
و همچنانکه بفروشد ساتیشماق و ساتیشماقلیغ مع التا بمعنی فاعلیه است بجهة که فروختن و صیغ آن باشتقاق میباید ساتیلماق
ساتیلماقلیغ مع اللام بمعنی فروخته شدن و صیغ آن بالالام اشتقاق میباید ساتقون الماق ساتقون الماقلیغ مصدر متعدی است بمعنی
و صیغ آن با لفظ قر اشتقاق میباید ساتقون الماق ساتقون الماقلیغ خریدن ساتقون آلدی خرید ساتقون آلورسا ساتقون آلادور
بمعنی فاعل و مصدر هم می آیند ساتقون آلقان ساتقون آلغار ساتقون آلادورغان خرنده و خریده و بمعنی مصدر هم می آیند ساتقون آل
ساتقون آلغیل مفرد غائب المبنی للفاعل چنانچه شاهد بر اول در فیل ساتقون آلدی مذکور شد ساتقون آلسون ساتقون آلغیل مفرد غائب المبنی
ساتقون آلینک ساتقون آلینکیز ساتقون آلینکلار جمع غائب المبنی للفاعل ساتقون آلادور ساتقون آلامین ساتقون آلانکلار جمع غائب المبنی للفاعل ساتقون آلا
ساتقون آلادور میخرم ساتقون آلامیز ساتقون آلارمیز ساتقون آلادورمیز ساتقون آلماس نمیخرد و بمعنی فاعل و مصدر منفی هم می آید
ساتقون آلیب ساتقون آلیبان ساتقون آلمیش خریده ساتقون آلیشان خریده ساتقون آلابولغای ساتقون آلا الغای
تواند خرید ساتقون آلا الغای خرید ساتقون آلا ساتقون آلاتیر ساتقون آلالغای بخرم و بخرد و بخری و خریده ساتقون آلاق ساتقون آلغای
ساتقون آلالیک ساتقون آلغالی بخریم ساتقون آلغالی برای خریدن و تا خریده ساتقون آلغاچ چون خرید و بخرد و بخرد خریدن ساتقون آلغوچی خرنده
ساتقون آلغوجه ساتقون آلغونجه ساتقون آلغانچه تا خریدن و بقصد خریدن ساتقون آلغوسیز دور خواهیم خرید ساتقون آلغوسی دور خواهید خرید
ساتقون آلغوسیلار دور خواهند خرید ساتقون آلغولوق خریدنی ساتقون آلغای ساتقون آلسلو ساتقون آلسون ساتقون آلادیک بخرد
علی الثالث شعر عشق اهلی ساتقون آل ایرینک تو تیاسیدین قیلغیل تر ازو ایکی کوزوم نینک قراسیدین ساتقون آلغودیک
آلادیک خریدنی و همچنانکه بخرد ساتاشماق بفتح تا و سکون شین بترکی رومی بمعنی بسته شدن و چاق شدن باشد ساتاشدی در بسته شد چنانچه
مثنوی کوید شعر دل در شده تمام سلسله منکوینیه اول لحظه یکم ساتاشدی کوز دوم زلف در حلقه من احوامد ساتان بفتح تا و الف کشیده ساج
و سکون نون تمام ران بود تا سر انکشتان ساتیغ بکسر تا بمعنی فروخت باشد ساتیغ الیغ یعنی خرید و فروخت و داد و ستد چنانچه کوید
شعر آلقالی دینلو دین ای کیم ساتیننک نقد جان عمر ساتیب مرلعالماق انکلاو بو ساتیغ الیغ ساتیغچی بکسر تا دلال و دست فروش را
کویند که چیزها را دست بدست کرداند و بفروشد چنانچه میر حقیقیه در مخزن کوید شعر بر عشق کور و بیلمل بونی بولغانی کیلدیکی ساتیغچی
تا شیغه نی دلال و ساتقوچی هم فروشنده را کویند چنانچه در ذیل مصدر ساتماق کذشت مع الجیم من المشتقات ساچماق و ساچماقلیغ بجیم
بمعنی پاشیدن و افشاندن بود الشاهد علی الاول شعر یا تاهریم اینیم ساچما مقرر که بلغیدین لاله که بولیشتی لاله دیک ساچیلغ
کونکول برکا له برکا له ساچوق افشاندیم ساچار ساچادور می افشاند و ساچار بمعنی فاعل و مصدر هم می آیند ساچقان ساچار
افشاننده و افشانده و بمعنی مصدر هم می آیند چنانچه کوید الاول شعر خرده ساچاندین جمله کیم سلطان بولدی کل
غنچه تا تیلیغ کونکلیکا تا لغان کو امساله اینمیش ساچ شلیخیند مفرد غائب المبنی للفاعل چنانچه در سیر الابرار در ترک دنیا کوید

الاوّل شعر چه خورشید دیك ایلیکینکی آچ آنلانیکیم سیم ایسالما للمغه ساچ و ساچ کیسه را هم کویند ساچماو ساچماغیل مفرد
مخاطب از فعل امر ساچینك ساچینکز و ساچینکلار جمع مخاطب از فعل امر ساچمانك ساچمانکز و ساچمانکلار جمع مخاطب از فعل نهی ساچمان و
ساچمارمین نمی‌افشانم ساچامین و ساچارمین می‌افشانم ساچادورمین و ساچادورام می‌افشانم ساچماس نمی‌افشاند و بمعنی فاعل و مصدر منفی هم می‌آید
ساچیب و ساچیلو ساچیمیش افشانده ساچیشانك افشانده ساچسا بوله و ساچیب بولغوراز افشاند ساچا آلغای تواند افشاند ساچالغای
افشانده افشانده ساچای و ساچایین بیفشانم و بیفشاند و بیفشانی و افشانده الشاهد علی الثانی بالمعنی الاول شعر تا افشاه
یتساکو نکلونیا اولادهٔ ذو قیدیق گنج خیالدین ساچایین هر طرف تحفه ساچاق و ساچار و ساچاچا و ساچلوساچا بیمسلیم پکما
برای افشاندن و تا افشانده ساچقاج چون افشاند و بیفشاند و بخیر افشاندن ساچقوچی افشاننده ساچقوچه ساچقوچی و ساچقا تا افشاند
و تقدیم افشاندن ساچقو سیردور خواهیم افشاند ساچقو سیزدور خواهید افشاند ساچقو سیلاردور خواهند افشاند ساچقولوق افشاندنی
ساچقای ساچیلو ساچیلا و ساچیلسون و ساچیلدی بیفشانند ساچقودیك ساچارلیك افشاندنی و همچنانکه بیفشانند ساچیلماق خوانند الخلیع
بجیم عجمی مع اللام افشانده شدن ساچیلغان و ساچیلورغان و ساچیلادورغان افشانده شونده و افشانده شده الشاهد علی الاول بالمعنی
شعر تاپوه ونك زنار زلفونکی ساچیلغان سویدیك کشور اسلام ارا یوزمینك بنا تاپمیش خلل و بمعنی مصدر هم می‌آید چنانکه در فرهاد و
شیرین کوید الشاهد علی الاول شعر بولولار کیم کوزوم آندین آچیتینك سینیك ایلیکیم یله قالمغه ساچیتینك تمنا سیز کونکلومدین
المه ساچیلغان برله توفراغ ایجره ساچیلماق ساچیلاتیغو ساچیلورتو ساچیلدی آنکا افشانده میشوید الشاهد علی الاول شعر کمزوم حسنی عجل
میلدیم ای جواهرنینك که بادی هم آنینك او قو مقدم بیغه ساچیلمیغن ساچیلغوسی افشانده خواهد شد چنانکه کوید شعر تا تم اشکی دری
توفراغینکا ساچیلغوسی کوهر ایم فلك دین باشینکا ساچیلدی تورت و باقی صیغ سیاق موافق اول الام اشتقاق بیابد ساچراماق
جستن ساچرادی جست چنانکه در کلیله دمنه ترکی مذکوراست شعر تقدیر ایلی دین جعقضا ایچیده ساچرادی بیلیکیل کم سود تیلماس
اینلیك دغیفه ستر من الجواهد ساج بمعنی دو معنی دارد اول آهنیست مدور شکل چپرکم بر روی آن نان پزند دوم مویسر را کویند
چنانکه با آملج قافیه کرده گفته شعر جونغه توشتی صنوبر قدینک دین ایله که سو بولوب یاغیغه نزیه ایزلادی باشیدا ساج
نیز در جنك توغل با قبیله یلی کیم کوید شعر ماکی کوتیزنیك قیلیب قاش قیرقب لیکن ساچ امرینغه نانش و بجای اکیمیز امانند شعر ایکادی
آشفته سودای ما ضیمر کلافنینك تا المیلیدین آندا ایکیم تو براشتی اول آشفته ساچ و بمعنی تخته را کویند و بفارسی ساج و درختیست هندی بقدی
درخت چنار برك و صلب و نایل بینا هیچ پرك و نوشبو و بزش مستطیل بمقدار فوفل باشد و اهل هند آنرا ساکونه خوانند و باجیم عجمی
هم بمعنی موی سر و کیسو بود و نیز امر است از افشاندن ساچاق با جیم عجمی سه معنی دارد اول ریشه را کویند که از نخ و ابریشم بافند چنانکه
کوید شعر آل ساچاق آلتین ... سیم ساقی ... و آنرا بعربی هدب کویند دوم سفره باشد
که در وقت طعام بکسترانند و آنرا بعربی سماط نامند سیم طرح بیش عمارت باشد و از چهار قست از تخته بندی که از پیش سقف سر بر آمده شود
ساج ایاغ ترکی دو سه پایه باشد که آنرا بعربی منصب و بفارسی سه پایه خوانند و ساج ایاغ بوم ... ساچیماغ منقر
که با هم مثلث ... چنانکه در کتاب شمر آمده شعر تنبه بطین اوچ اوشاق بولدوز ... ساج ایاغ کنوا ... بولغای
کیسوی صنوبولست که از ابریشم بافند الشاهد علیه شعر ساچباغینکدین چیقضان آیا سنبل پرچین ... یاتیرمین ...
ایکی ... بودرش ساچیق و ساچق بکسر جیم عجمی دو معنی آمده اول نثار و شاباش را کویند چنانکه کوید شعر هر کیشی ایلکیکاسیق
بیر ... ملکی ساچیقین ... تقسیم ایلکدینك دوم نقد و جنسی باشد که در هنکام دامادی از خانه داماد بخانه عروس ...

چنانکه در تاریخ بابری مذکوراست که خلیفه تینك اولوغ قزینیه ما هم بیك خینك کیماکا اوغلی ... ساچیغی کیلدی ... ساچیغ
نیز کوید که ایکنچی قزینی طوی و این ... آلغان ساچیقنی کلتوردی و سولغه ... چنانکه بیان لفظ ... شمرده و ...
با همین معنی نوشته سهو کرده مع الخاء المعجمه المشتقات ساخلاماق ... ساخلاماقلیغ یعنی نکهداشتن ساخلاد ... ساخلاد
نکاه میدارد ساخلادی بمعنی فاعل و مصدر منفی هم می‌آید ساخلادی ساخلادی ... نکاه داشته و بمعنی ...
می‌آید ساخلا و ساخلاغیل مفرد مخاطب از فعل امر ساخلانك و ساخلانکز و ساخلانکلار جمع ...
مخاطب از فعل امر ساخلامانك و ساخلامانکز و ساخلامانکلار جمع مخاطب از فعل نهی ساخلارمین نکاه میدارم ساخلادی ...
مین و ساخلادی ... ساخلاماس نکاه نمیدارد و بمعنی فاعل و مصدر منفی هم می‌آید ساخلاب ساخلاتکو ساخلاکیش
نکاه داشته ساخلامیشانك نکاه داشته ساخلاسا و ساخلاب بولغای ... ساخلایالغای نکاه تواند داشت ساخلاغای ... نکاه ...
ساخلای ساخلای نکاه داشته نکاه داشته ساخلای ساخلایین نکاه بدارم و بدارد و بداری و داشته ساخلاغاچ ساخلاماق ...
ساخلاکو و ساخلالیل ... نکاه بدار ... ساخلاغلی برای نکاه داشتن و تا نکاه داشته ساخلاغاچ چون نکاه داشت و بدارد و بجز نکاه داشتن
ساخلاغوچی نکاه دارنده چنانکه در محبوب القلوب کوید که خالف نفس لا ... و ... ساخلاغوچی ...
تند بادی ساوورماقدین ساخلاغوچی ساخلاغوچه ساخلاغوچه ساخلاغاچه تا نکه داشتن و تقدیم نکه داشتن ساخلاغو سیزدور نکاه
داشت ساخلاغو سیزدور نکاه خواهید داشت ساخلاغو سیلاردور نکاه خواهند داشت ساخلاغولوق نکاه داشتنی ساخلاغای و ساخلاغانا
ساخلاغون و ساخلادیك نکاه دارد ساخلاغودیك ساخلادیك نکاه داشتنی و همچنانکه نکاه دارد ... تعیشان سکون خا
و کسر تای قرشت و فتح تای حطی ... پوستی بود که دباغت شده باشد چنانکه در تاریخ الملوك در ذکر فریدون کوید که
اولوغ تربیت قیلیب علم قیلغان سختیانی ... قیلدی و آنرا بعربی ادیم کویند مع الدال المهملة المشتقات ساد و ساد و ساداماق ...
تو مه کردن بود و آنرا ساقو ساغماق هم کویند من الجواهد ساداق ... تعصدق و ساداق بفتح دال ترکش را نامند چنانکه در ...
الطیر ... و صفت و شاه ... کوید الشاهد علی الرابع شعر بورادین سر ... کوت آنکا ساداق و تا القان ... آنکا ...
مستعملست ساد و بضم دال ترکی رومی توحه ... نامیان بود و آنرا ساغونیز کویند مع الراء المهملة المشتقات ساریغاریماق و ساریغارماق
بسکون هر دو رای مهمله و فتح غین معجمه با الف کشیده بمعنی زرد شدن باشد الشاهد علی الاول فی التوحید شعر قویاشنه
که قیزاریتاق کاه ساریغارتماق ایرور ... که صنعونك باعید ابارار اول صفت ... کل ... آنرا ساریغاق کویند
ساریغار دوق نمی‌دوشیم ساریغارمین ساریغارادور زرد میشود و ساریغار و بمعنی فاعل و مصدر هم می‌آید ساریغار ساریغارد ساریغا ...
ساریغارادور ... زرد میشود و زرد شده و بمعنی مصدر هم می‌آید چنانکه کوید الشاهد علی الاول شعر جهره ساریغارغان ساتی آرزای کونکول
نینك ناله سی با جمیع ... خزان ... الا ... ساریغا و ساریغا خیل مفرد مخاطب از فعل امر ساریغار و ساریغالماغیل مفرد مخاطب
از فعل نهی ساریغا بینك و ساریغاینکز و ساریغاینکلار جمع مخاطب از فعل امر ساریغامانك ساریغامانکز و ساریغامانکلار جمع مخاطب از فعل نهی ساریغامان
ساریغامانیز ... زرد نمیشوم ساریغارامین و ساریغارمین ... ساریغادورام زرد میشوم ساریغارماس زرد نمیشود و بمعنی فاعل و مصدر منفی
هم می‌آید ساریغاب ساریغاتا و ساریغامیش زرد شده ساریغامیشانك ... زرد شده ساریغاسا بولغای و ساریغاب تولغای زرد تواند شد
ساریغارالغای زرد تواند شد ساریغار ... زرد شده ساریغای و ساریغایین ... زرد شوم و شود و شوی و شده
ساریغایانا ... ساریغاری بوز ساریغاغای ... زرد شوم ساریغارتغلی برای زرد شدن و تا زرد شده ساریغارغاج چون زرد

شد مشود و بمعنی نزد شدن سارغار غوجی نزد مشونده سارغار غوجیه [illegible] تا نزد شدن و بقیه نزد شدن
سارغار غو نزد دور نزد خواهیم شد سارغار غونکیز نزد خواهید شد سارغار غو سیلار نزد خواهند شد سارغار غولوق نزد شدن
سارغار غاج [illegible] نزد شود الشاهد علی الثالث مصرع یوز و جیهه [illegible]
شاخ اونده شاخ و برکیم [illegible] سارغار غایکم [illegible] نزد شدنیه و همچنانکه نزد شود
سارغار غو دیلت [illegible] د شد [illegible] چنانکه کوید مصرع بو بنکلیغ کیم [illegible] شعلکون تان [illegible]
سارغار غو دیلت [illegible] سارغار تماق [illegible] بسکون هو و سماری مهمله و تای قرشت مصدر متعدی است یعنی نزد کردن
سارغایب [illegible] نزد کرده چنانکه [illegible] کوید الشاهد علی الاول مصرع [illegible]
سارغار تبان بوزار لار دیلت سارینغ آغریغ بیله بمار لار دیلت و باقی صیغ [illegible] بالتاء قرشت اشتقاق می یابد سارسماق [illegible]
هر دو سین مهمله و سکون رای مهمله بمعنی [illegible] شدن و لرزیدن و جنبیدن [illegible] بود و در رومیه صرح فی استعمال [illegible]
[illegible] لرزید [illegible] و مصدر هم می آید [illegible]
ولرزیده و بمعنی مصدر هم می آیند [illegible] مفرد غائب [illegible]
[illegible] جمع غائب [illegible]
[illegible] و بمعنی فاعل و مصدر هم می آید [illegible] لرزیده
[illegible] لرزید [illegible] تواند لرزید [illegible] لرزان
[illegible] بلرزیم و بلرزید و بلرزی و لرزیده [illegible]
برای لرزیدن و تا لرزیدن [illegible] چون لرزید و بلرزید و بمحض لرزیدن [illegible]
و بعد لرزیدن [illegible] خواهیم لرزید [illegible] خواهید لرزید [illegible] خواهند لرزید [illegible] لرزیدنی
[illegible] بلرزد [illegible] لرزیدنی و همچنانکه بلرزد [illegible]
بترکی و بمعنی [illegible] بود که مذکور شد [illegible] بفتح رای اول و سکون رای ثانی بترکی و بمعنی [illegible] شدن [illegible]
بسکون را و کسر [illegible] مع الثانی بترکی و بمعنی فروهشتن و آویختن [illegible] بترکی و بمعنی [illegible]
بغدادی صیغه [illegible] کوید [illegible] مصرع [illegible]
اینجه دو شدی [illegible] بسکون را [illegible] و فتح میم با الف کشیده یعنی [illegible]
[illegible] مصرع [illegible] چشم [illegible]
مقام من الحوامد [illegible] که بوده [illegible]
[illegible] لفظ با فارسی مشترکست سرب با بای عجمی بر وزن ضرب بترکی و بمعنی [illegible]
بسکون [illegible] نون و ضم بای عجمی [illegible] سارت بسکون را و تای قرشت [illegible]
کوید چنانکه [illegible] کوید [illegible]
سارج بسکون را و جیم [illegible] ایران [illegible]
بعد از [illegible] را خوانند سرقوت بمعنی [illegible] تو ت بترکی و بمعنی فروهشته و آویخته بود

سرکه بسکون را و فتح کاف بر اخته را کویند [illegible] بسکون را و فتح کاف عجمی [illegible]
و اشال آنرا نامند [illegible] نام کیاهیست که بر درخت بپیچد و آنرا بعربی عشقه و لبلاب [illegible] خوانند [illegible]
[illegible] سالیغ بمعنی [illegible] باشد [illegible] چنانکه کوید مصرع [illegible]
[illegible] اول [illegible] سالیغ [illegible] نام شهریست معروف از ولایت [illegible]
[illegible] نام [illegible] کویند [illegible] نام [illegible]
[illegible] کویند و مؤلف [illegible] نوشته اند سالیغ یعنی [illegible]
چنانکه کوید مصرع [illegible] سالیغ [illegible]
نامند چنانکه کوید مصرع سالیغ [illegible] سالیغ قوش نوعی از [illegible]
که آنرا [illegible] خوانند چنانکه [illegible] در وصف لشکر [illegible] کوید مصرع [illegible]
[illegible] سالیغ قوش [illegible] نام [illegible] بفتح قاف و واو با الف کشیده بترکی و بمعنی [illegible]
بود که آنرا [illegible] کویند [illegible] نوشته [illegible] بترکی و بمعنی [illegible] عشقه است که آنرا [illegible] عاشق
نامند چنانکه مذکور شد [illegible] مع الزاء المعجمه [illegible] بترکی و بمعنی نوعی ماهیست [illegible]
[illegible] مع السین من المثقفات [illegible] بکسر سین [illegible]
متعفن شدن [illegible] مع الثانی مصدر متعدیست یعنی [illegible] و متعفن کردن [illegible]
[illegible] مع الغین المعجمه من المثقفات [illegible]
دوشیدن [illegible] دوشیدیم [illegible] دوشید [illegible] بمعنی فاعل و مصدر هم می آید [illegible]
دوشنده و دوشیده و بمعنی [illegible] هم می آید [illegible] مفرد غائب [illegible] کویند چنانکه
خواهد شد [illegible] مفرد غائب [illegible] جمع غائب [illegible]
جمع غائب [illegible] دوشیدند [illegible] بمعنی فاعل
و مصدر هم می آید [illegible] دوشیده [illegible] دوشیده [illegible] تواند دوشید [illegible]
تواند دوشید [illegible] دوشیده [illegible] بدوشیم [illegible] دوشیده [illegible]
[illegible] بدوشیم [illegible] برای دوشیدن و تا دوشیدن [illegible] چون دوشید [illegible]
[illegible] دوشنده [illegible] تا دوشیدن و بعد دوشیدن [illegible] خواهیم دوشید [illegible]
دوشید [illegible] خواهند دوشید [illegible] دوشیدنی [illegible] بدوشد
[illegible] دوشیدنی و همچنانکه بدوشد [illegible] بفتح غین و سکون لام دوشیده شدن [illegible]
لام موافق [illegible] بفتح غین و سکون لام دو معنی دارد اول [illegible]
[illegible] صحیح شدیم [illegible] صحیح میشود [illegible]
و مصدر هم می آید چنانکه [illegible] کوید مصرع [illegible]
[illegible] صحیح شونده [illegible] و بمعنی مصدر هم می آید [illegible]

مفرد مخاطب از فعل امر ساغالماق ساغالمادی فعل ماضی مفرد مخاطب از فعل نهی ساغالسانک ساغالسنکیز ساغالسنکلار جمع مخاطب از فعل امر ساغالمانک و
ساغالمانکیز ساغالمانکلار جمع مخاطب از فعل نهی ساغالمادی ساغالماس مین صحیح نمیشوم و هشیار نمیشوم ساغالامین ساغالادورمین و ساغالورمین
ساغالورمان صحیح میشوم و هشیار میشوم ساغالسام ساغالسامین ساغالغای مین صحیح شوم و هشیار شوم چنانکه میر نجبا طریقی
ایهام کوید الشاهد علی الاول بیت درد جامی برله یتوای ساقی دمار یتیم کیم ولا یمین عشق کویدا ساغالسام بیرزمان ساغالما
صحیح نمیشود و هشیار نمیشود و بمعنی فاعل و مصدر منفی هم می آید ساغالیب ساغالیبان و ساغالیبان صحیح شده و هشیار شده چنانکه میر سعیه
سیاره کوید الشاهد علی الاول بالمعنی الثانی بیت زنکی بخش قیدی تلغه فه بی سحدنی غار ایچیدا باشیدی ساغالیب صحیح جود نذری
اونینک خالیغه آیلاغدی ساغالیبان صحیح و هشیار شده ساغالساو لغه ساغالیبتو لغه صحیح و هشیار توان شد ساغالالغه
صحیح و هشیار تواند شد ساغالالای ساغالالای صحیح و هشیار شوان ساغالالای ساغالالاین صحیح و هشیار شوم و شود و شوی و شده
ساغالساق ساغالغای یز و ساغالغای یز ساغالسالی و ساغالسانک صحیح و هشیار شویم ساغالغالی برای صحیح و هشیار شدن تا صحیح و هشیار شده
ساغالغاج چون صحیح و هشیار شد و شود و بعض شدن ساغالغوچی صحیح شونده و هشیار شونده ساغالغوجه و ساغالغوجه ساغالغا
تا صحیح و هشیار شدن و بعد صحیح و هشیار شدن ساغالغوم زد صحیح و هشیار خواهیم شد ساغالغوم زد صحیح و هشیار خواهد
ساغالغوسیلار صحیح و هشیار خواهند شد ساغالغولوق صحیح و هشیار شدنی ساغالغای ساغالغای ساغالسانک ساغالسلو ساغالسلی ساغالدی
صحیح شود و هشیار شود الشاهد علی الاول بالمعنی الثانی بیت قوی بعضیه تزاهد و او تلوغ دیم دین دم قیل تیلیه اینا مکافی یوق تیم
ساغالغای پندا ایله ساغالغودیک ساغالور دیک صحیح و هشیار شدنی و چنانکه صحیح و هشیار شود ساغالتماق ساغالتماق قیلیغ
بسکون لام و تای قرشت مصدر متعدیست یعنی صحیح کردن و هشیار کردن و باقی صیغ آن بدستور شق اول المصانعه تای قرشت اشتقاق می یابد
ساغنماق و ساغینماق قیلیغ بجر ضین و سکون نون سه معنی دارد اول یاد کردن دویم تصور کردن سیم حفظ کردن الشاهد علی الاول بالمعنی
الاول بیت ده یجه بونی ساغینماغی او نو تو تونک پرهیز باساغینماغی اخوداونو تماغی او نوت ساغیندیم یاد کردم و تصور کردم
و حفظ کردم چنانکه بمعنی ثانی کوید بیت یکجه بار دی یار یعاندین تالمادی حیران کونکول آتیدا استعمال ساغیندیم بار ایشی جیران کونکول
ساغیندیلار یاد کردند و تصور کردند چنانکه بمعنی اول در تاریخ بابری مذکور است که جیرلیک اولیادی ساغیندیلار جیرلیک ایکیلار تاریخ حماقه
بوی قویدیلار ساغینور و ساغیناد و یاد میکند و تصور میکند و حفظ میکند و ساغینور بمعنی مصدر هم می آید چنانکه بمعنی یاد
کردن در محکوم بجیم از منشات کوید که یوسف علی دین تو للوقته بیساز دیم الا تقریبی یله کا هی یحصد نیکی ساغینور خاکم سیر
ساغینغای و ساغینغایم ساغیناد و یاد کننده و یاد کرده و تصور کننده و تصور کرده و حفظ کننده و حفظ کرده و بمعنی مصدر هم می آید
ساغینیب و ساغینیبان مفرد مخاطب از فعل امر بمعنی الشاهد علی الاول بالمعنی الثانی بیت سرانجام ایلمالدا ایریمیشلی نوائی خضر عمری
صبر بولدی ساغینی ولد شعر دیما کوپلی نفس کیم دنیا عوضین صدقیل اویدا بعضی دیک ساغینی بکاره باد دم سنکا بالمعنی الثالث من قصیدی
نه ما بلاحال رویته بیت چقمه یارم کیمه را اغیار جهیدن ساغینی سن مه اوچ ملاحت سن بونقصانده سنکا و له شعر ترحم قیل
بو کولبیش تدبیه و هم ایله آمیمدین ساغینی چمایه ناکه یاعی راوقای کمان ابرو و ساغینی نهانی غلمدین هم دارد که دوزخ جوابد نکته جاهل
ساغینماو ساغیناحیل مفرد مخاطب از فعل نهی بمعنی الشاهد علی الاول بالمعنی الثانی بن فضولی ما ملاء الروبته شعر سعاجوهر تهنکلک امه دم
ایل ساغنغه سوویدای نشه اول سراب سنکا ساغینلی و ساغینکیز و ساغینکلار جمع مخاطب از فعل امر ساغینماتک و ساغینماتکیز و ساغینما
جمع مخاطب از فعل نهی ساغینمان و ساغینمامین یاد میکنم و تصور میکنم و حفظ میکنم ساغینامین ساغینورمین ساغیناد و ساغینورمین ساغینامیکم

وتصور میکم

وتصور میکم و حفظ میکیم الشاهد علی الثانی بالمعنی الثانی شعر کیم رقیبیم بولسا بیرکیم یار المحبر النفات غالم اهل ساغینورمین کیم سنکا
بولمیش رقیب بالمعنی الثالث شعر ساغینورمین کیم ساغینی اجراسیدین دیب کرده مجال شیخ کافر ملحوادبی کوچا لسام ساغینماس یاد نمیکند
و تصور نمیکند و حفظ نمیکند و بمعنی فاعل و مصدر منفی هم می آید ساغینیب و ساغینیبان و ساغینمیش یاد کرده و تصور کرده و حفظ کرده الشاهد
علی الاول بالمعنی الاول شعر یوز و زلفونکنی ساغینیب کیلیشام ای مه جبین کیچه منی کیچه منی کیچه منیای کوندوزی دوزخ آلیش
آرزو و اشتیاق نوشته و شعر بیجرانشا هدا و ترکه سهو کرده و نیز تریکنی مجنون کوید بالمعنی الثانی شعر اولکان ساغینیب غنی
آبی پراویکا یکوردیلار بهانی ساغینمیشانک یاد کرده و تصور کرده و حفظ کرده ساغینالو لغه و ساغینیبلو لغه یاد توان کرد و تصور توان کرد
و حفظ توان کرد ساغینالغای یاد تواند کرد و تصور تواند کرد و حفظ تواند کرد ساغینا ساغینا یاد کنان و تصور کنان و
حفظ کنان ساغیناغای و ساغینالین یاد و تصور و حفظ کنم و کند و کنی و کرده ساغینسا و ساغینغای و ساغینغای یز و ساغینالغالی
یاد کنیم و تصور کنیم و حفظ کنیم ساغینغالی برای یاد کردن و تا یاد کرده و برای تصور کردن و تا تصور کرده و برای حفظ کردن و تا حفظ کرده
ساغینغاج چون یاد و تصور و حفظ کرد و کند و بعض یاد و تصور و حفظ کردن چنانکه بمعنی اول کوید شعر ناله نغمه کیم ایل
دین هان ایلار کونکول سینی ساغینغاج نیه بیخود مان ایلار کونکول ساغینغوچی یاد کننده و تصور کننده و حفظ کننده ساغینغوجه
ساغینغوجه و ساغینغاجه تا یاد کردن و بعد یاد کردن و تا تصور کردن و بعد تصور کردن و تا حفظ کردن و بعد حفظ کردن ساغینغوم
یاد خواهم کرد و تصور خواهم کرد و حفظ خواهم کرد چنانکه بمعنی اول کوید شعر خلدار ابولسام آنینک کوبین ساغینغوم ده تیانک
غربت بیجره ایلاچناک ایل منزل و ماوای بابا ساغینغونک یاد خواهی کرد و تصور خواهی کرد و حفظ خواهی کرد ساغینغوسی یاد خواهد کرد
و تصور خواهد کرد و حفظ خواهد کرد ساغینغولوق یاد کردنی و تصور کردنی و حفظ کردنی ساغینغای و ساغینسا ساغینغای ساغینغای
ساغیندیک یاد کند و تصور کند و حفظ کند الشاهد علی الاول بالمعنی الثانی شعر خلق شومیدین تو کولدی جسم اول ینکلیغ
کیم سونکا کلاهدار الم کورکان ساغینغای نال ایر قدر ساغینودیک و ساغینور دیک یاد کردنی و تصور کردنی و حفظ کردنی و چنانکه
کند و تصور کند و حفظ کند ساغیند و ساغینماق و ساغیند و ساغیلیغ مصدر متعدیست یعنی متذکر ساختن و تحذیر فرمودن الشاهد علی الاول
بالمعنی الاول شعر کاوونتی یار بو محزونی وه کیم کونکلونا بار آیه هردم ساغیند صفا قدیمام سین هم او نوت ساغیند ده متذکر ساختیم
و تحذیر فرمودیم بالمعنی الاول شعر ریکانه پرست اولمه ساغیند و هر دم اوز و منی او ز تور قانی دا ایلاچنا یکانه نی ریوا ساغیندنه عید
متذکر کن و تحذیر بفرما بالمعنی الاول شعر ای نوائی کام ناپمای کرمین اول دعم عشق ارا ایم که تاپسام کام آنکا کا هی ساغیند و غول میسه
ساغیندورماین متذکر کنی و تحذیر بفرمایی چنانکه در تاریخ الانبیا در قصص حضرت یوسف علیه السلام بمعنی اول کوید که سویج غرآبیق
کیم سالت ریا نغمه بایب اعتبار تا پسانک میسی ساغیند و صفای سین و باقی صیغ برین سیاق الفقط در اشتقاق می یابد ساغو ساغاق ساغاق
دوینه نحصه کردن ساغیناز باشد و از اسادو ساد لا ساق و هم کویند چنانکه کذشت من الجواهر ساغ بفتح معنی بود اول معنی هشیار ما
الشاهد علیه شعر لعلی دین مست اولوبان بار دیم خمار دیم مرضی لمزی می ده هر بوکه هم اصروک و هم ساغ ایتا دقی دویم صحیح و تندرست
کویند چنانکه هر دو معنی طریق ایهام کوید شعر اکر نوائی ایکی نرکینک خیالی بیله مریض و مست جهاندین او تار سین دولتیل ساغ
سیم بمعنی هشیاری و تندرستی هم باشد چنانکه بمعنی هشیاری کوید شعر لبینی حوطلی ضلیم جونغه بولدی بدل می ایچسا تراوی
ساغقا ایل بادوش کهر و نوره جها درم طرفه است از انا مسند و با یمنوی افاق نوشتمات بجم امسار دو شیدن ساغاناق بفتح غین و نون با
شیده ترکی و رومی طراز شدید بدی بود که زود بشکند و نیز غبار ابخاد شده که از ان املاقی شود ساغیخی مستحفظ ساغداق ترکن اکوی

وآنرا سدق وصداق وساطاق هم خوانند ساغرغ بکون غین وکسر زای معجمه که قفل را نامند ومجازا بوستکل اسب خر بود که دامن کرده

وآنرا بفارسی کچخت کویند سغراق بمعنی مجاق که نوعی از مطهره را کویند ویکر بر هم مشعلت ساغلنغ دوستوق طرف را کوئه معنی بو سیدن

مشیره هنده باشد چنانکه در مقطعات کوید شعر ملازنایکم قویوب منک دین او یتیش اینام منی دین آیتو قساغلیغ او یکو

ذکر بمعنی صحت وتندرستی بود سیم هشیار را کویند ساغو بمعنی ضمیر کرد نوعی از نامند وآنرا ساغو نیز خوانند چنانکه مذ

ساغری بکسر غین بمعنی شلوار بود که آنرا بعربی امم والمروش کویند ساغرلیق یعنی کری ساغیرتقه بکسر غین وسکون رای

وتای قرشت وفتح قاف جانوری است که در بهشتیم سنکون میشود و برا عضای ایشان میچسبد وآنرا بعربی قراد وبفارسی کنه نامند ساغیش

بسکون شین بمعنی تابش بمعنی شمار وحساب باشد چنانکه ملا لطف الله در کل ونوروز کوید شعر سنکا بولدا س میر آلتی بنن زاده تابع

لا یساغیشدین هم زاده ساقین چند معنی دارد اول کوسفند شیر دار را کویند دویم در مقابله عشق وستی ودیوانکی وبیماری الم

میشود یعنی آنرا ستادن کردن و تصور کردن وحذر کردن چنانکه در ذیل مصدر اقتیناق کذشت ساغینچ بکسر غین وسکون نون

وجیم بمعنی تصور واندیشه وخیال بود چنانکه در سکندرنامه در مصراع بمعنی تصور کوید شعر بو بودین وجودی لباسین سویوب

باشیدین تعین لو اسین قویوب وجودی عدم کرئیل لیکب ساغینچ وجود وعلم دین بولوب کونکلی تنج ودر مقاله اول از حیرت الابرار

در بیان قلم کوید شعر کافروموزن سالدی تیلسالک ساغینچ نی آنکا یاسروین بونات کونکلی تنج کوید وزبان خلق

تاخود این ویکم شفق ویکم سعید وطالع هروی ساغینچ را در این شعر از نسخه سقیمی تاپنج نامفانی وتای عجمی خواندند وتاپنج را بمعنی نیاز کرد

وسفر هزبور را اشاهد آورده لفظ ومعنی اعتراض است مع القاف من المشتقات ساقیماق بترکی رومی حفظ کردن چنانکه فضولی

بغدادی بمعنی امر کوید بامثله الرومیه شعر مطرب آقلامیمه سرو دنکله فضولاختینه بن ئیل استکندن ساقن قوبا ستناد کر

من الحواسد ساقت فطرت را کویند چنانکه بطریق تجنیس فرماید شعر اولماسا آیما کلرخ ساقی اجالیم خراب یوق ایسنا سامقدل

کلکون جام مولغیر کتاب سقاغ بمعنی اباغ عنبر را نامند چنانکه کوید شعر بقادیلک قربا کرنا یان سینیک سمین

سقاغینکه ایتالدیلک هم نایان ایرنا رقشا آکنام اپاغینکه سقال لحیه باشد که آنرا بفارسی ریش خوانند الطلب

حکیم شعر ولیکه کافر بولوب یشکی قیلور خالیق آقسقالیغه کولار خلق نی رسوالیق سقال دلوق عقدار ارب بولوکرنیا

بمروکذارند که مثل ریش از زیر چانه آویخته شود سامچی نکهبان ومستحفظ را کویند لاادری شعر ابراهیم اوغلی ایدی اشچو

سامچی سی ثینک یولاوج نوفدی آتدین بار جانینک اول یانچی سی ساقار تشدید قاف مفتوحه وسکون رای مهمله اسب پیشانی

سفید باشد ساقساغان کلاغ ابلق بود که آنرا بعربی عقعق نامند سقیت نام شلم بریغات سقیز بکسر قاف وتشدید

وسکون زای هوز بمعنی است که از درخت بن در آید وآنرا بعربی علک البطم خوانند سقیز آغاجی نام درختی است که آنرا بعربی

بطم کویند مع الکاف سکمک بترکی رومی خراسیدن اندروی زبود عموما وخرام کبک را کویند خصوصا مع اللام من المشتقات سالماق

سالماقلیغ بمعنی انداختن باشد وبمعنی اضطراب کردن ومضطر ساختن در اهم استعمال شود ودر این معنی لازم ومتعدی هر دو می آید لیکن بمعنی

لفظ لجتها آن افاده ایمعنی میکند چنانکه بمعنی لازم کوید الشاهد علی الاول شعر کوزپله کونکلوما بولمیش کوییا وصلینک نی

کیم کونعم اجمامی نیز اولدی وکونکلوم سالماقی ونیز کوید شعر اوبقومنا یه لاریدین کیتا عمر تنبنی که با شیم برکا اورب

که یوزیم سالماق امثی سالدی انداخت واضطراب کرد ومضطر ساخت سالا باشلادی انداختن شروع کرد واضطراب کردن شروع

ومضطر ساختن شروع کرد چنانکه در مرثیه دن فرهاد وشاپور راجنبه کوید المعنی الثالث شعر سالا باشلادی هردم بلرم کونکلی ایستب

لا ادری – ککلیکدلیک ایتم مسکم کلوب قهقهه ایتم کیرلنم س یجری کبی کلب سکره آدمه

منعت داره کونکلی سالمی سالادی ویعنی انداختن واضطراب بکند ومضطرب بسازد الشاهد علی الاول والمعنی الثانی شعر کیم ایکم اول

کوزی رادیب کیتسا آندین ایت اوبن ایت اوبن معنی پیلپه کونکلوم سالور هجران توبی ونیز قصه خسرو وشیرین کوید شعر کوزوم تار نلدی

ایار کیلکاج سالور کونکلوم مکر که لرکیلکاج لشاهد علی الثانی المعنی الاول شعر پرادغی یاکونکلوم کافرغ ملان سالادور برو

بیای که بو ایش منکا ملازسالادور وسالورعی نامل مستمر هم می آید چنانکه بمعنی انداختن کوید شعر کافر ع یکم بسی کبی خیا

آتشنا کجاری اوت سالوردی یکشور اسلام ارانی ایکی ا ونیز تمام طایفه ایت از ابرالت چنانکه در ذیل جامه مذکور خواهد شد سالغان

سالورغان سالادورغان انداختن واندازد وانداخته واضطراب کند واضطراب کرده ومضطرب سازد ومضطر ساخته وبمعنی مستمر هم آید

سال وسالقیل مفرد مخاطب امر یعنی سالچوب که از چوب وتخته یکدیکر بسته برآن نشسته از آب بکذرند چنانکه

در ذیل جوامع مذکور خواهد شد سالکوسالماغیل مفرد مخاطب نهی سالینک وسالنکیز وسالنکلار جمع مخاطب امر سالما

سالماینکیز سالماینکلار جمع مخاطب نهی سالمان بمعنی سالماس مین بمعنی اندازم واضطراب کنم ومضطرب سازم سالامین وسالورمن

سالادورمن سالغوم بمعنی انداختم واضطراب کردم ومضطرب ساختم سالغامین بمعنی ننداختم واضطراب نکنم ومضطرب نسازم چنانکه

شاهد بر این بمعنی اول وثالث بطریق ایهام کوید شعر کونکول اضربدم نوایی کوب لطوفیدین نیسالمک ایمدی ایر پیشا ایت لاری

ایلکونکلی را کونکلومنی سالغای مین سالماس یعنی نیندازد واضطراب نکند ومضطرب نسازد وبمعنی فاعل ومصدر نفی هم می آید سالیب

سالیب سالمیش انداخته واضطراب کرده ومضطرب ساخته چنانکه شاهد بر اول لطیفه اول قصه خسرو وشیرین کوید شعر بلا کوه

سیغه سالیب قدمنی ملامت او یجوغه تاریب علمی ومجنونیم که بی در طریق یار بی چنین مند کم راست که اکر بیکادر آیدان بیکت لاکه کنکول

سالیب ایدیلار هند وستانداتور ناقفه راشی اتمالر یبلایار شاهد بر ثانی بمعنی لازم کوید شعر کونکلوم سالیباز بنض کبی باروز الیک

نبضینک شاری کور شام که طبیب الیکی بار اد وتر سالمیشاتک انداخته واضطراب کرده ومضطر ساخته سالساتوتقا وسالیب توتقای تواند انداخت

واضطراب توان کرد ومضطرب توان ساخت سالا الغای تواند انداخت واضطراب تواند کرد ومضطرب تواند ساخت سالا سالا

انکان امکان واضطراب کنان ومضطرب کنان وبدون تکرار نیز بامعنی مستعملت چنانکه بمعنی اول کوید شعر تاشیدا خیال هندوی

کافر این بحر که اهل دین مثلی ایچون چیب تور بعر کیم سالادیر طاقعه ونیز فرماید کغ نشاط زمید اساتی ماهوش برخوش شراوش ایت

ایاغ تو قسا قولیما الا ملح ایچ سالای وسالایی بیندازم وبیندازیم وبیندازی واندازد واضطراب کنم وکند وکنی وکرده بینکش

سالنم وسالنزیم وسالنزی وساخته سالسا قتسالغایتر وسالغایتر وسالسائیلی وسالاالیک بیندازیم واضطراب کنیم ومضطرب سازیم سالمانا

سالماغاسین وسالماغای سیز مبنید ازید واضطراب کنید ومضطرب سازید چنانکه شاهد بر ثالث ایر معنی ثالث در منشات کوید کر

سیز دین کو براد شکست لار تو شکان اینکری تعالی پناه ده سیفیب کونکول سالماغای سیز سالغالی برای انداختن وانداختن

وبرای اضطراب کردن وتا اضطراب کرده وبرای مضطر ساختن وتا مضطر ساخته سالغاج چون انداخت وبینداز وبمحض انداختن وچون

کرد وکند وبمحض کردن وچون مضطر ساخت وسازد وبمحض ساختن سالغوچی انداز ومضطراب کند ومضطرب سازد چنانکه بمعنی اول

کوید شعر فتنه کوز لو کلادر دیا یوقی برمیش کمز وینکمک سالغوچی برچا باقاقسله فالمغه ریسالغز کوزنی سالغوچی سالغا

سالانداختن وبعدم انداختن وتا اضطراب کردن وبعدم اضطراب کردن وتا مضطر ساختن وبعدم مضطر ساختن چنانکه شاهد بر ثانی او بمعنی

انداختن کوید شعر شکر لار صلدیلیک سنکا با قتیبیرا وکیم لیحدین کونکل برقالر مطلو سالغوچه خافلیغ کام ثانی وشاهد بر ثالث

معنی کوید شعر جامه سنیک دیر دوسالدینک ایله مسکین بیرنی دنج آیمان آندا دوام دردن سالغان مثل سالغوم ودو

واضطراب خواهیم کرد و مضطرب خواهیم ساخت تالغوتقوزدی نخواهید انداخت واضطراب خواهید کرد و مضطرب خواهید ساخت تالغو
سیلار دور خواهند انداخت واضطراب خواهند کرد و مضطرب خواهند ساخت تالغولوق انداختن واضطراب کردن و مضطرب ساختن
تالغای و تالغینی تالغاسی تالغوچی تالدیلیک بیندازد واضطراب کند و مضطرب سازد تالغودیلیک تالغوردیلیک انداختنی و همچنانکه
بیندازد واضطراب کردن و همچنانکه اضطراب کند و مضطرب ساختنی و همچنانکه مضطرب سازد الشاهد علی الاول المعنی الاول شعر
یار دیولیشرل و تلمزنه هجران طریقین تالغودیلیک عقل و هوش و جان و کونکلوم خیل هم قیزنا تالغودیلیک تالیناق و تالیناتیلیغ مع الفوقانی
تالیماق و تالیماقلیغ مع اللام انداخته شدن تالیندی و تالیلدی انداخته شد الشاهد علی الثانی شعر یا قاشلیغ
قیلدی چیقاریب قتل اوچون بوغونغیه تالیلدی یکرویش تالینور و تالیناد و رو تالیلور و تالیلدوک انداخته میشود الشاهد
الثالث شعر عجایب قطع برمیزیلدا کلای مصرع امرین ایدین تش کیشی تیر اینابن هم قطع اولور هم تالیلور تاکام تالینغاج و تالیلماغاج چو
انداخته شده شود و بعض انداخته شدن چنانکه شاهد بر اول معنی اول در کتاب الطیر درذکر مصراع کویه مشرقی بیلاسع نوهم
اوزدین تالیناد بوتالینغاج فی تالیماقلیغ تالیناد وتالینغ برین تالیق اشتقاقی یا بینا اللاتماق و تالماقلیغ بسکون لام
اول و فتح ثانی در معنی طرح اول آویزان شدن از درخت و مانند آن باشد دویم معلق آویزان شدن تالماندوق خراسیدیم و آویزان شدیم
تالماغوم تالمادوم خراسید و آویزان میشود و تالماغومچی فاعل و مصدر هم می آید تالماچار تالماغوچی تالماندورماقلیغ خراسیدن
و خراسید و آویزان شوند و آویزان شده و بمعنی مصدر هم می آید تالمادی تالماغیل مفرد غائب امر فعل امر تالماتا و تالماغیل
مفرد غائب امر فعل تالماسون تالماسونلار جمع غائب امر فعل تالماغانلار تالماغانکز تالماغانکلار جمع غائب
مفرد تالماغان تالماغاس نفی خراسیم و آویزان نخواهیم تالماغوسیز تالماغاسیز تالماغوسیکز خراسیم و آویزان شوم تالماغار
خراسید و آویزان میشود و بمعنی فاعل و مصدر منفی هم می آید تالماغاچ تالماغانچه تالماغونچه بلغز خراسیده و معلق آویخته شده الشاهد
علی الاول المعنی الاول شعر تالماغیب چوزلفلوه الجه خلقنی واله مبتلو هم تدرعیبی هم اندام معراض ایبیه چوتالماغانیا نخراسم
و آویزان شده تالماغیلو تالماغوتالماغ تالماغب تالماغانغه توان خراسید و آویزان توان شد تالماتا التالغو تواند خراسید و آویزان تواند شد تالماتا
تالماتا خراسان نخراسان و آویزان آویزان و بدون تکرار هم بدین معنی مستعملست تالماتای و تالماتایین بخراسم و بخراسد و بخراسی و بخراسید
و آویزان شوم و شود و شوی و شید تالماتایق تالماتاییز تالماتاسین و تالماتاسینلار تالماتایلیک بخراسیم و آویزان شویم تالماتاسیلار
خراسیدن و ناخراسیده و برای آویزان شدن و تا آویزان شده تالماغاج چون خراسید و بخراسد و بمحض خراسیدن و چون آویزان شده شود
و بمحض شدن تالماغوچی خراسنده و آویزان شونده تالماغوچه تالماغوچیه تالماغانغه تا خراسیدن و بقدر خراسیدن و تا آویزان شدن
و بقدر آویزان شدن تالماغوسیز و نخواهیم خراسید و آویزان نخواهیم شد تالماغوسیکز نخواهید خراسید و آویزان نخواهید شد تالماغ
سیلار دور خواهند خراسید و آویزان خواهند شد تالماغولوق خراسیدنی و آویزان شدنی تالماغای تالماغاو تالماغاس تالماغ
تالماندیلیک بخراسد و آویزان شود تالماغودیلیغ تالماغوردیلیک خراسیدنی و همچنانکه بخراسد و آویزان شدنی و همچنانکه آویزان شود
تالماغومای مصدر متعدیست یعنی معلق آویزان ساختن و صیغ آن با لفظ در اشتقاق بی یا بدین الحواس تالماناک چیزیست که از چوب
در ترتیب داده بر بالای آن رشته از ابنهای عمق که بزند الشاهد علیه شعر جو مغلبی قیناس قصر ضوی بیک سونکاکالاراشلیکن
طرفه کوکیم تیه بیان ایار اسابیم بود و نیز آمر است از انداختن و اضطراب کردن و مضطرب ساختن دلچنانکه در ذیل تالماق گذشت تالا
بزرگ و بی تخته باشد که امواتزا برو و آن غسل دهند تالت بسکون لام و تای قرشت ترکی و بمعنی فرد و تنها بود تلجوق التمجیت

از اهل اعتبار تحقیق کنم که تحقیق خواهم میکرد سلاطین سلاجقه از اولاد او بیندیم و افاق تمام داشتند و نسب او بوجهیرا اربشالغزالیا
میرسد و مؤلف برهان قاطع سلجوق بر وزن طوق نوشته سهو کرده زیرا که ملاحظه در ذیل لغات سلجوق که سلجوقی بمعنی الغزو مسیم
صف سلجوق باشد مرکاه بر وزن طوقی بود مخفف آن هم بفتح جیم تا بیست استعمال شود سلجه بسکون لام و فتح جیم بهلو و بنهلو تا
کوچک که بر طی بچسبد چنانکه در لیلی مجنون در وصف سلیلی لیلی گوید شعر تان قهمای سلجه کیمی کاجلرل کابتیب یوتکا...
و آن اسلحه غیر نیز هم نامند و بمعنی قراول و بضاعت هم که گویند سالغوت بسکون لام و واو و تای قرشت و ضم میم ...
خوانند که از برای لشکریکانه در مملکت واقع شود و آنرا البغ هم گویند در قدیم گذاشتن آغروق ولبر بتکین باشد در خانقان السمان
بسکون لام و نون و قاف و کسر میم و فتح جیم در بیمانیست که المقال الزمخشری آویخته بر آن رشته خمیر حرکت دهند و آنرا از التنگه
و ایران سالیغاق و بمعنی ادوجمه و بتلبیه مادیچ گویند و از اهل خوارزم سالیقیغلی استعمال شد و از محالف ماسلات سالغین
مع الغین المکسوره سالقین مع القاف المکسوره نیم خشکت که در مقام حکم بوزد شعر حیوان سوژنی مشهور...
د مید ورسالقین بیلان ستار جانانیم کوپاکهجوالم لیتمینن سالغوم بسکون لام و سیم و ضم ثالث خوشه انگور و امثال آن بود که آنرا بعربی
عنقود نامند سالغوم کوپه بضم کاف و فتح های عجمی با اصطلاح روپیه بکجو کوشولر آیت خوشه طره ایوان نام بیزنارغ خان بن
اوغوزخان است و دراوغوزنامه بمعنی آنرا ملقب مغول تحقیق نوشته اند و نیز نام طایفه ایست از ترکان که منسوب باو بیند و معانی
مشقه هم دارد که در ذیل مصدر سالماق ذکر شد سالماق بمعنی انداختن دو معنی دارد اول استر و شالیت که بر سر چند خیمه هیرابت که
در ایام بهار و جشن بجانه داماد فرستد و بعبارت سید و مزیتیل گویند که چیزها در آن گذارند و ببرند سالیغ سالتق ...
بود اول توجیه ملکی را گویند که از برای لشکریکانه در مملکت واقع شود الشاهد علی الاول شعر فرمایدیکیم تیشلرنکا حرز ...
زاق عشق اهلی اجرا قتل اوچون سالسالماقالیغ و آنرا سالغوت هم نامند چنانکه مذکور شد دویم بمعنی سراغ و نشان باشد چنانکه
در تاریخ بابری مذکور است که تا چنان لاارتبینک خبر بیماروق سالیغ بر دیلا دویم بمعنی خبر بود چنانکه مؤلف ظفرنامه در بیان
امیر تیمور با توقتمش خان مذکور ساخته که هرچند سپاه مخالف بعد سیکی کیمیر سیند و بنیز و شمشیر و سالیغ جمله می آمد اینان
بزخم تیر با نمیکردانیدند مع المیم المثلثات سمیرماق مع الراء المهمله فربه شدن و بکسر هم مستعملست سمیردی فربه شد سمیردی
سمیرادی فربه میشود و سمیرور بمعنی فاعل و مصدر هم می آید سمیرکانی سمیرفرکان سمیرادی و ...گان فربه شونده و فربه شده و بمعنی مصدر
می آیند سمیرو سمیرکید مفرد غائب امر فعل امر سمیرماو سمیرماکید مفرد غائب امر فعل امر سمیرسنک سمیرنکز و سمیرنکلار جمع غائب امر
سمیرنانک و سمیرنانکز سمیرنانکلار جمع غائب امر فعل سمیرایین سمیرور فربه شوم سمیرامین و سمیرور و ... سمیرادورمین و سمیرورم
فربه میشوم سمیرغاس فربه نمیشود بمعنی فاعل و مصدر منفی هم می آید سمیرمه سمیرمیان و سمیرمیش فربه شده سمیرتانک فربه شده
سمیریاتو لغای سمیرب تو لغای فربه توان شد سمیرالغای فربه تواند شد سمیرا سمیرا فربه شونده شونده و بدون تکرار هم مستعملست سمیرای
سمیرایین فربه شوم و شود و شوی و شید سمیرالیق و سمیرکایق و سمیرالی و سمیرالینک فربه شویم سمیرکالی برای فربه شدن و تا شده
سمیرکاج بمحض فربه شدن سمیرکوچی فربه شونده سمیرکوچه سمیرکوچکه و سمیرکاغه تا فربه شدن و بقدر آن سمیرکومیزدور فربه خواهیم
شد سمیرکوسیز دور فربه خواهید شد سمیرکوسیلار دور فربه خواهند شد سمیرکای سمیرا و سمیرا سمیرسون سمیردیک فربه شود سمیرکودک و
سمیرودیک فربه شدنی و همچنانکه فربه شود من الجوامد سالناتان بمعنی باشد اقلکا بود که آنرا بعربی گویند دیمم نام بلدیست
که ذب سلاطین سالنابیه بلوچستان و بمعنی هفت معنی دارد اول نظام و اندازه کار دویم قرار و آرام سیم شهر و قصبه چهارم تخت و ...

234v.

بم قونو قدرت ششم نشانه نیز هفتم بمعنی بیترلت سانان اوغزچی بترکی رویی که کتان بود که آنرا مبری [illegible] خوانند جمع کند برفان
و معنی سمرقند است و آن شهریست مشهور در ماوراء النهر و معنی ترکی آن به سمرلیت و سمر نام پادشاهیست از ترک که بانی آن دیه که معمور
ایام شهر شده و در تاریخ بابری در وصف سمرقند مذکور است که مغولیه و اتراک آنرا سمیز کند گویند مع الزاء المعجمه سمیز بکسر میم
سکون زای معجمه بمعنی فربه و فربه شدن و بکسرتین هم مستعملست سمیزلیک فربهی چیزلیک اوتی بترکی و چاق خوش باشد که آنرا مبری
بقلة الحمقا گویند سامسون بسکون میم و فتح نون و ضم سین مهمله ثانی نام ولایتی است از ممالک قسطنطنیه روم و نیز نام یکقوم سگی است که
در دریا که از آن مملکت بهم میرسد و باسم آن ولایت شهرت یافته [illegible] نام ولایتست اما بوت آن جانوره که هم از آن
ولایت می آرند باسم آن ولایت مینامند و از این قبیل است پوستی که از بلغار می آرند و آنرا بلغار میگویند مع النون من المشتقات سانماق و سانماقلیغ
بسکون نون قیاس کردن صریحه با کاف استعمال نمایند ساندوق قیاس کردیم ساندورمانادو قیاس بکند چنانکه فضولی گوید بالاملا
الرومیه فی المشتقات شعر سانا مه که ناله زارم انکا اثر قیلمادی آنی مرهم ایله ملالده [illegible] و سانامق بمعنی فاعل و مصدر هم می آید
سانامغیل مفرد مخاطب فعل امر الشاهد علی الاول من فضولی بالاملاء الرومیه شعر بولونور مردده مایتمرس گلستانده که
حقه سنده غنچه نینک سان یکم [illegible] وسان بمعنی شمار و عدد نیز [illegible] هم باشد سانامغیل مفرد مخاطب
فعل نهی چنانکه فضولی [illegible] گوید الشاهد علی الاول بالاملاء الرومیه شعر [illegible] سانما که
احباب خالندن [illegible] حبیب سانیلق سانیلچر [illegible] جمع مخاطب فعل امر سانامانك سانمانکر سانمانکلار جمع مخاطب
الشاهد علی الاول من فضولی بالاملاء الرومیه شعر پرتو خورشید سانمانکیز [illegible] آفتابن [illegible] کیم کروب
[illegible] سانامس من قیاس میکنم الشاهد علی الاول من فضولی بالاملاء الرومیه شعر جاکلار کوکسمده سانمانکیم [illegible]
کونکلمنک شمرنبه [illegible] سانامادو [illegible] قیاس میکنم چنانکه شاهد [illegible] فضولی
در مقطعات گوید بالاملاء الرومیه شعر [illegible] سانامس قیاس بکند
و بمعنی فاعل و مصدر منفی هم می آید [illegible] قیاس کرده [illegible] قیاس کرده [illegible] توان کرد
سانامالغای قیاس تواند کرد سانانا قیاس کنان و بعضی تکرار هم بامعنی مستعملست سانانای [illegible] قیاس کنم و کنند [illegible]
سانامناق هم اشتراک طرح چنانکه بیاید [illegible] قیاس کنیم [illegible] اشتراک طرح [illegible]
برای قیاس کردن و تا قیاس کرده سانغاج چون قیاس کرد و کند [illegible] قیاس کردن سانغوچی قیاس کننده [illegible]
تا قیاس کردن و [illegible] قیاس کردن [illegible] قیاس خواهیم کرد [illegible] قیاس خواهید کرد [illegible] قیاس خواهند کرد [illegible]
قیاس کردن [illegible] قیاس کند [illegible] قیاس کردن و همچنانکه قیاس کند [illegible]
باسعد [illegible] اشتراک طرح [illegible] شمردن [illegible] شمردیم [illegible]
چنانکه در مقاله [illegible] الشاهد علی الاول [illegible]
فاعل و مصدر هم می آید [illegible] چنانکه شاهد [illegible] اول گوید [illegible]
کام [illegible] هم می آید [illegible] مفرد مخاطب فعل امر [illegible]
[illegible] جمع غائب [illegible]
[illegible] الشاهد علی الاول [illegible]

235r.

[illegible] سانالماس [illegible] سانا مام [illegible] و بمعنی فاعل و مصدر منفی هم می آید [illegible]
[illegible] شمرده چنانکه خسرو شیرین [illegible] علیه السلام گوید الشاهد علی الاول شعر
[illegible] سانامایدی [illegible]
شاهد آمده [illegible] هم مناسبت کرده [illegible] شمرده [illegible]
شمرده [illegible] شمرده و بدون تکرار هم بامعنی مستعملست [illegible]
و بامعنی [illegible] اشتراک طرح چنانکه گذشت [illegible]
و بامعنی [illegible] مشترکت [illegible] برای شمردن و تا شمرده [illegible] چون شمرد و شمرده [illegible] شمردن [illegible]
[illegible] شمردن و بعضی شمردن [illegible] تا توان شمرد و مقدور [illegible] توان شمرد چنانکه در مقاله [illegible]
ازحیرة الابرار در وصف کمال [illegible] گوید الشاهد علی الثالث بالاملاء الرومیه شعر [illegible]
[illegible] و بامعنی ذکر کرده لفظ اخراجیست [illegible]
شمرد [illegible] خواهید شمرد [illegible] خواهند شمرد [illegible] شمردن [illegible]
[illegible] و همچنانکه [illegible] بفتح نون و سکون لام یعنی شمرده شدن [illegible]
[illegible] شمرده شوم الشاهد علی الثالث شعر اگر احباب [illegible]
[illegible] اشتقاق [illegible] بسکون نون و قاف و کسر دال [illegible]
بالف کشیده بمعنی هذیان گفتن [illegible] هذیان گفتیم [illegible] هذیان [illegible] میگوید [illegible]
و مصدر هم می آید [illegible] هذیان گوینده و هذیان گفته و بمعنی مصدر هم می آیند [illegible]
[illegible] مفرد مخاطب فعل امر [illegible] مفرد مخاطب فعل نهی [illegible] جمع مخاطبه
[illegible] جمع مخاطب فعل نهی [illegible] هذیان میگویم [illegible]
[illegible] هذیان میگویم [illegible] هذیان میگوید و بمعنی فاعل و مصدر منفی هم می آید [illegible]
[illegible] هذیان گفته [illegible] هذیان گفته [illegible] هذیان توان گفت [illegible]
هذیان تواند گفت [illegible] هذیان گویان و بدون تکرار هم بامعنی مستعملست [illegible]
هذیان بگویم و بگوید و بگوی و گفته [illegible] هذیان بگویم [illegible]
برای هذیان گفتن و تا هذیان گفته [illegible] چون هذیان گفت و بگوید و بعض گفتن [illegible] هذیان گوینده [illegible]
[illegible] تا هذیان گفتن و بعضی هذیان گفتن [illegible] هذیان خواهیم گفت [illegible] هذیان
خواهید گفت [illegible] هذیان خواهند گفت [illegible] هذیان گفتنی [illegible]
[illegible] هذیان بگوید [illegible] هذیان گفتنی و همچنانکه بگوید [illegible]
بسکون میم نیش زدن عقرب و نیز زدن [illegible] آن بجای فرو بردن [illegible] بسکون نون و شین قرشت و کسر جیم بمعنی
مفاعله است مطاعنه کردن و [illegible] و نیز زدن و صیغ آنها بهمین [illegible]
فروشدن [illegible] الشاهد علی الاول شعر [illegible]

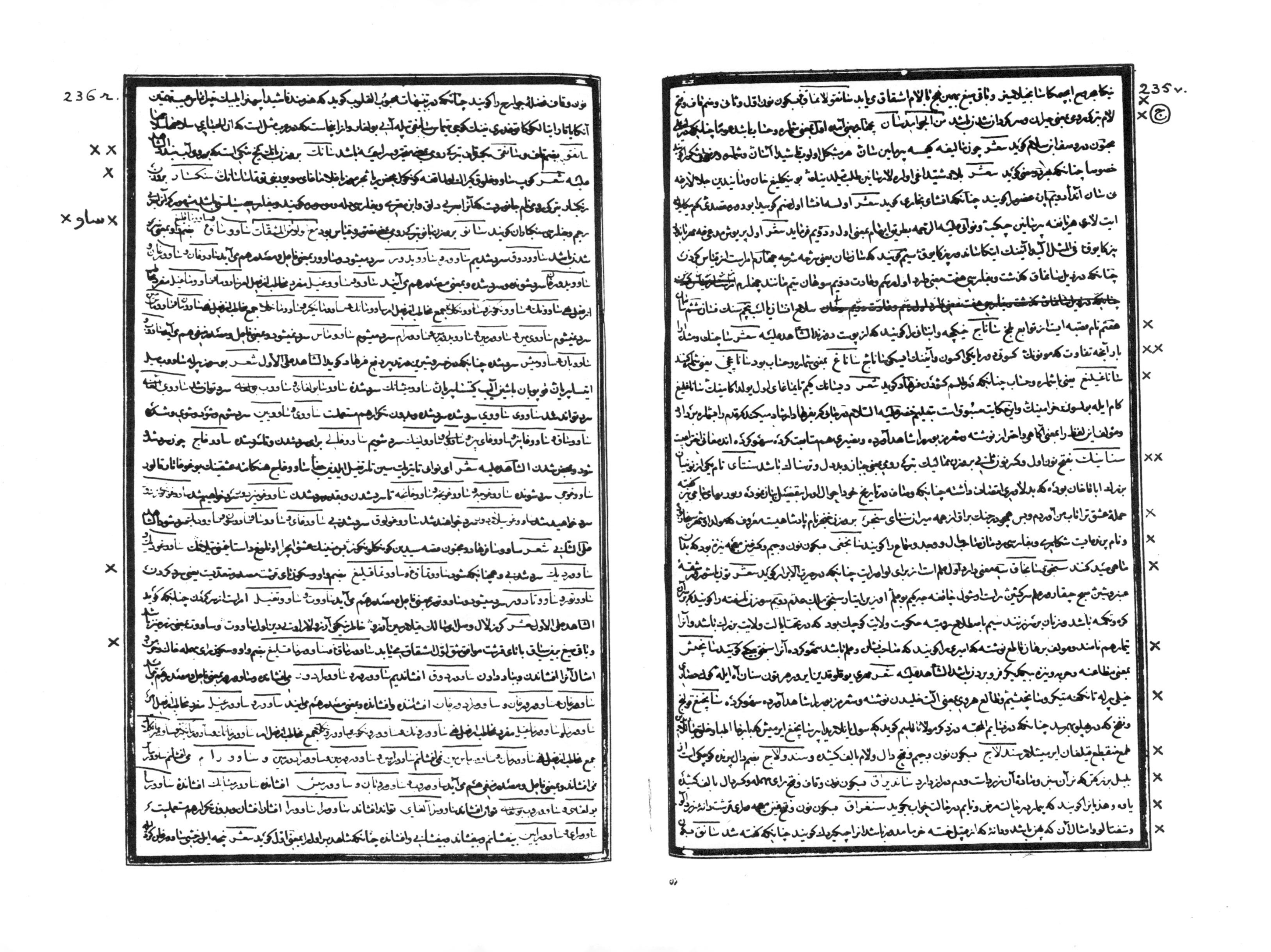

(ج)

[illegible]

[illegible]

کوزیاروتوب سوزبرامتن باشیماتو قزاغلغزنی شاودماق شاودمانزو شاودمانیزو شاودرسلوغنا ودرلسنک
بیفشانیم شاودرغالی برای افشاندن وتا افشاندن شاودرغوجی افشاننده چنانکه درباب چهارم از محبوب القلوب در وصف ظلمت
کوید که سیلی دودرخرمن شاودرغوجی شاودرغوجه شاودرغونجه شاودرغاجه تا افشانند وبعد افشاندن شاودرغوسیزدور
خواهیم افشاند شاودرغونکردور خواهید افشاند شاودرغوسیلاردور خواهند افشاند شاودرغولوق افشاندنی شاودرغای شاودراو
شاودرسلار شاودرغوسا وجودیک بیفشاند شاودرغودیک شاودرغانیفه وهمچنانکه بیفشاند الشاهد علی الاول شعر
بوکیچه آهیم یعنی بوغاننی برهم اورغودیک چرخ کلزار دین انجم کل لار دین شاودرغودیک وله شعر سیکریم کوبرشاودرغودیک
ایسار جهرازی لطف ایتیب ای کل سحاب وصل نینک سیکوریمش شاودرلماق شاودرلماقلیغ بسکون واو ولام وضم راء مهمله افشانده
وبنا داده شدن شاودرولغو شاودرلغیل مفرد مخاطب فعل امر الشاهد علی الاول شعر مین چکیب نعره اولای ایل غافل بولسون
شاودرولای چرخ نکون ای هجر دین برباد بولک شاودرولای شاودرولایب افشانده وبنا داده شوم وشود مثوی وشده چنانکه در
مجنون از نوای مجنون کوید الشاهد علی الثانی بالمعنی الاول شعر بوغدای کوپ تمام ورلانیش شاانما کجه شاودرلانیش شادرولغای
شاودرلانماس ودرلساو دورلسون شاودرلدیلار افشاندشوها الشاهد علی الاول شعر ایله شاودرولنای عناصر هرتوز کیم ایلغای
نشان بوواد دین ازانا وناق صیغ برینج بسکون واو وضم راء بالام اشتقاق بی یابد شاودماق بسکون واو وفتحه دوی رنج کوفت شاو
رنج کن چنانکه صنو برآیکوید با ملاد الروتیه شعر دوتوب توشلر باشیمه اشیان فریاد کیلیشلر چوای آهیم اوده سم باشیم
شاووغوطلی شاودملماق بضم واو وسکون لام وشاودشماق مع آلتین بمعنی جدا شدن ورنج شدن باشد شاوولوب
شاوولوبانچنا وولیش وشاوو شوبه شاووشوانما ووشمیش رنج شده چنانکه شاهد علی ما ضبوله کوید با ملاد الروتیه شعر جیم کیم
کیز کونکلوم جسم وجانمدین نیم بو باشیمدین ساوولوب اول کسته ماندین نیم من اخواهید شاوو بمعنی جدا ومنفصل باشد الشاهد علیه
شعر هشتو باشیمدین حقا ییب وز لوکومنی اوردی تیغ آنی بلشیدین شاوایتیب اشنی تنیمدین قیلدی شاو وبترکی رومی از استان رنج کردن
چنانکه در ذیل شاووناق مذکور شد وبفارسی چنان معنی طرح واوکاچ کنترات دیعیم فرقه نمرکوید سیم بو ته باشد خلص در
که بلند جان قیب بیلنکر باشد عدوضیان کم سیله بجلاز تباسیله دابدان تبند چهار بمعنی سایدن بود شاووت بضم واو وسکون
تای قرشت نیمی ناسند وبنرابرت از شود کردن چنانکه کذشت شاووت بوزان یکجوع سکانیت دراز وبلویلت کر ازانغار شی
کویند شاودوغ وشاودوق بمعنی بیرد وبلرد شاودولوق سردی چنانکه کوید شعر نوای سیله کونکلومکا اوت شالکیم زمان اهلی
کونکلومکا اوت شالکیم زمان اهلی شاوولوق آتیغ عقیل پیشانه کم کونکلومنی شاووقیتشلار سوغات هدیه وارمغان کویند
ستان شعر تیللیار صرچان مقالاتن هر نیوال تحفه سیله سوغاتن شاوغوت بسکون واو دوم نون وضم ضین معجمه اشتی نامند کران
جامه وجامی برآمده مخملک کوهنه باشد مع الماسیما معنی معنوانها الکدز باشد سمیته بعضی نسخه سفیه واحوتر اخواست مع الیا
مزلمیقان ساپماق وساپماقلیغ بسکون یا شمردن شایدوق شمرد یمین شاپای شاپا دودن سیشمار دیمتایلار معنی فاعل ومصدر هم می آید
شاپغار شاپارغان وشاپادرغان شمارند شمرده وبمعنی مصدر هم می آید شنای وشاپغیل مفرد مخاطب فعل امر بشای رود خا
خشک ووقت وشمار راهم کویند شاپملو شاپغاینغیل مفرد مخاطب فعل نهی شاپینک وشاپینکز وشاپینکلار جمع مخاطب از فعل امر
شاپمانک وشاپغاینکز وشاپمانکلار جمع مخاطب فعل نهی شاپمان وشاپغایمن بمعشمار م شاپایین وشاپاپاریین وشاپاپدورمیز شاپاپارام میشمارم
شاپماس بمشمارد وبمعنی فاعل ومصدر منفی هم می آید شاپیب شاپیناو شاپغیش شمرده شاپیشالک شمرده شاپیناوشد وشاپیب ونغا

توان شمرد وساپا الفنای تواند شمرد شاپاپ شاپا شمرده شمرده وبدون تکرار هم مستعملت شاپای شاپابین بشمارم وبشمارد وبشمارد
وشمرده شاپنماق وساپنغانیز وشاپغلونیز وشاپکالغانابا بشمارید شاپغیلی برای شمردن وتا شمرده شاپغاج چون شمرد وبشمار دیکوئیم
شمردن شاپغوجی شمارنده شاپغوجه وشاپغونجه وشاپغانجه تا شمردن وبعد شمردن شاپغوسیزدور خواهیم شمرد وشاپغونکردور خواهید
شمرد شاپغوسیلاردور خواهند شمرد شاپغولوق شمردنی شاپغای وشاپا وشاپا شاپسون وشاپسایک بشمارد وشاپغونیک وشاپلوینک شمرد
همچنانکه بشمارد شاپلماق وشاپلماقلیغ بجیم وسکون لام شمرده شدن وصیغ آن با لام اشتقاق ی یابد شاپلماق وشاپلماقلیغ
بسکون یا بمعنی انتخاب کردن باشد شاپلادوق انتخاب کردیم شاپلادی وشاپلادیلار انتخاب میکند وشاپلار بمعنی فاعل ومصدر هم می آید شاپلاغان
شاپلارغان وشاپلایدورغان انتخاب کننده وانتخاب کرده وبمعنی مصدر هم می آید شاپلا وشاپلاغیل مفرد مخاطب فعل امر شاپلاما
شاپلاماغیل مفرد مخاطب فعل نهی شاپلانک وشاپلانکز وشاپلانکلار جمع مخاطب فعل امر شاپلاماتک وشاپلامانکز وشاپلامانکلار جمع مخاطب
شاپلامان وشاپلاغایمن انتخاب میکنم شاپلایین وشاپلاپاریین وشاپلاپدورمیز وشاپلاپارام انتخاب میکنم شاپلاماس انتخاب نکند وبمعنی فاعل
ومصدر منفی هم می آید شاپلاپ وشاپلاپ انتخاب کرده الشاهد علی الاول شعر یارب اولکا کل موده مرآهیم تونیدین قرا
یا اوتاغالار ایچینده بین شاپلاب الغان فرقه شاپلامیشالیک انتخاب کرده شاپلاپناوشد وشاپلاپ وبوغه انتخاب توان کرد شاپلای آلغای
انتخاب تواند کرد شاپلاپوز وشاپلاپ سلیلارای انتخاب کنان وبدون تکرار هم بامعنی مستعملت شاپلامی شاپلادی بین انتخاب کنم وکند وکرد
وکرده شاپلاماق وشاپلاغانیز وشاپلاغونیز وشاپلاغالی وشاپلالینک انتخاب کنید شاپلاغلی برای انتخاب کردن وتا انتخاب کرده شاپلاغاچ
چون انتخاب کرد وکند ومحض انتخاب کردن شاپلاغوجی انتخاب کننده شاپلاغوجه وشاپلاغونجه وشاپلاغانجه تا انتخاب کردن وبعد انتخاب کرده
شاپلاغوسیزدور انتخاب خواهیم کرد شاپلاغونکردور انتخاب خواهید کرد شاپلاغوسیلاردور انتخاب خواهند کرد شاپلاغولوق انتخاب کردنی
شاپلاغای وشاپلاسا وشاپلاسون وشاپلاسایک انتخاب کند شاپلاغودیک وشاپلادیلک انتخاب کردی وهمچنانکه انتخاب کند شاپلاتماق وشاپلاتماقلیغ
مع التاء مصدر متعدیست انتخاب کنانیدن وصیغ آن با تای قرشت اشتقاق ی یابد شاپلانماق وشاپلانماقلیغ مع النون انتخاب شدن
شاپلانیب وشاپلانیبان وشاپلانمیش انتخاب شده الشاهد علی الاول شعر لیلی ومجنون وفرهاد ابد یلار ورونی حبیب بالغیم وا له
کیم سین تا لیب سین شاپلانیب ومنکه قرو بی شاپلانیب یعنی شمار وحساب نوشته وشعر نیز بوراشاهد آمرد مسهو کرده وقیغ ین
بانون اشتقاق ی یابد سیغاناق بسکون یای حطی وفتح فا وسیپاناق بمعنی وپراکنده کردن باشد چنانکه در تنبیهات محبوب القلوب
کوید کر اکرچه تیلنی اسرایناق کونکول کا محنت تهم ایماس وزنی سیپلاناق نا شنفه آفت تهرچیز در باب چهارم در وصف ظلمت کوید کر محبتی
دم که تعدی سیپاناق پیله اوکسماس ودر مشتقات نیز بای عجمی بدل فا استعمال مینمایند برای اختصار با شتقاق صیغ مع الفا اکتفا
سیغادی خرج کرد چنانکه در لسان الطیر در مکالمه کبک وهدهد کوید شعر وجه فرآنز کوندا با دین سیغاوی کوم آغاز جون
اول ایشنی آنکا خرج سیغادوق خرج کردیم سیغار وسیغاید ور خرج میکند وسیغار بمعنی فاعل ومصدر هم می آید چنانکه در خمزه
کوید شعر منکا سیغمادی ایتیکای محنت ورنج آنکا سیغلوفه تا لقای مخزن وکنج ونیز در فصل بیت وششم از محبوب القلوب در ذکر تعارکه کوید که
یا وارث سیپلرا وچون بیغیشغای با خادثه قهر غاروچون تاراغلغای سیغاغان وسیغارغان وسیغایدورغان خرج کننده وخرج کرده بمعنی
مصدر هم می آیند سیغا وسیغاغیل مفرد مخاطب فعل امر سیغاما وسیغاماغیل مفرد مخاطب فعل نهی سیغانک وسیغانکز
سیغانکلار جمع مخاطب فعل امر سیغامانک وسیغامانکز وسیغامانکلار جمع مخاطب فعل نهی سیغامان وسیغاغایمن خرج میکنم سیغایین
سیغاریین وسیغایدورمیز وسیغاپارام خرج میکنم سیغاماس خرج نمیکند وبمعنی فاعل ومصدر منفی هم می آید سیغاپ وسیغاپان وسیغامیش

خرج کرده . سیغامیشانک خرج کرده سیغاسابولغای سیغاب بولغای خرج توان کرد سیغا آلغای خرج تواند کرد سیغاب سیغای
خرج کنان وبدون تکرار هم مستعملست سیغای سیغاین خرج کنم وکند وکرد وکرده سیغاسای سیغامایین خرج نکنم ونکند ونکرد
ونکرده . چنانچه شاهد براو لرا بمعنی خرج نکند در تنبیهات محبوب القلوب کوید که مجنون لار دینکی سیغاماس تیرکان کچه سیماسلیق
سیغاساق سیغاغایز سیغاغای بیز سیغالی سیغالینک خرج کنیم سیغاغلی برای خرج کردن وتا خرج کرده سیغاغاج چون خرج کرد
کند وبمعنی خرج کردن سیغاغوچی خرج کننده چنانچه میرحیدر در مقالة اول المخزن کوید شعر هر نی که تاز غاندیم وسیغادیم تمام
تیلدیم آنی سیغاغوچی غه حرام سیغاغوچه سیغاغونچه سیغاغانچه تا خرج شد تا خرج شدن سیغاغوسیز دور خرج خواهیم کرد
سیغاغوسیز دور خرج خواهید کرد سیغاغوسیلار دور خرج خواهند کرد سیغاغولوق خرج کردنی وهمچنانچه خرج کند سیغالماق
سیغالماق قلیلنج مع الفا واللام وسیالماق مع الباء العجمیه خرج وپراکنده شدن ودر مشتقات نیز باء عجمی بدل نا داخل میشود سیغالدی
خرج وپراکنده شد چنانچه کوید شعر عقل ودین نقدی نی نادیر دا ایکر ناس ایکاش مبتلا منبجه لار بولیدا سیغالدی سیغالو
سیغالاندور خرج وپراکنده میشود الشاهد علی الثانی شعر باده تونت نقد حیا تمنی ایکی منجه جان تا با بیر لحظه چون بونقد
سیغالوش وسیغالور بمعنی فاعل ومصدر هم می آید سیغالغان سیغالورغان وسیغالادورغان خرج وپراکنده شونده وشده الشاهد
علی الاول المعنی الثانی شعر فنا دیر ایکردین نقدی برباد اولدی تاپنغوم یوق که جمع املا بدو هر کز خرابات بیر سیغالغان
وبمعنی مصدر هم می آید سیغالغوچیلیک وسیغالوردیک خرج وپراکنده شدنی چنانچه شود الشاهد علی الاول المعنی الاول
شعر ای کونکول نقد حیاتینک قیل فنا بولیدا مرف حیفا یعنی کر بولسه هم فوح ایچون سیغالغودیک ثنا قیبنع برین سیاق
بالام اشتقاق می یابد سیاباغلامق وسیاباغلاماق قلیلنج بفتح یا ولام وسکون غین معجمه بمعنی بیهوده وهذیان کفتن باشد واتراک روم
سایغلاماق بکسر یا استعمال نمایند سیاباغلادی هذیان کفت سیاباغلادور وسیاباغلایدور هذیان میکوید وسیاباغلاد بمعنی فاعل ومصدر هم
می آید سیاباغلاغان وسیاباغلادورغان هذیان کوینده وکفته وبمعنی مصدر هم می آیند سیاباغلاو سیاباغلاغیل مفرد مخاطب
امر سیاباغلانک وسیاباغلانکیز مفرد مخاطب از فعل امر سیاباغلانکیز وسیاباغلانکلار جمع مخاطب از فعل امر سیاباغلاسون وسیاباغلاسونلار
سیاباغلاسونلار جمع مخاطب از فعل نهی سیاباغلامان وسیاباغلاماس تین هذیان مکویم سیاباغلایمین وسیاباغلایدورمین سیاباغلادیم
هذیان میکویم سیاباغلاغاس هذیان میکوید وبمعنی فاعل ومصدر منفی هم می آید سیاباغلاغای سیاباغلاغاندین سیاباغلاغانیش هذیان کفته
سیاباغلاغانانک هذیان کفته سیاباغلاب بولغاغای وسیاباغلاب بولغای هذیان کفت سیاباغلای آلغای هذیان تواند کفت سیاباغلاب وسیاباغلای
سیاباغلای هذیان کویان سیاباغلای وسیاباغلاغاین هذیان بکویم وبکوید وبکفته وکفته سیاباغلاغاق وسیاباغلاغیز وسیاباغلاغای بیز
سیاباغلاغالی وسیاباغلاغلینک هذیان بکویم سیاباغلاغلی برای هذیان کفتن وتا کفته سیاباغلاغاج چون هذیان کفت وبکوید
وبمعنی کفتن سیاباغلاغوچی هذیان کوینده سیاباغلاغوچه وسیاباغلاغونچه وسیاباغلاغانچه تا هذیان کفتن وبعد کفتن سیاباغلاغوسیز دور هذیان خواهیم
کفت سیاباغلاغوسیز دور هذیان خواهید کفت سیاباغلاغوسیلار دور هذیان خواهند کفت سیاباغلاغولوق هذیان کفتنی سیاباغلاغای وسیاباغلا
سیاباغلاسون وسیاباغلاغودیک هذیان بکوید سیاباغلاغودیک وسیاباغلارلیک هذیان کفتنی وهمچنانچه بکوید سیراماق وسیراماق قلیلنج
بفتح سین مهمله بالف کشیده سراییدن وخواندن نماز کویند چنانچه شاهد براول در عنوان خسرو شیرین کوید که فرهاد نینک علم
وجود کلشنی غه کیلکان ثمن قلم بلبلی تیلیدین سیراماق سراییدن سرایید چنانچه در خسرو شیرین در خبر بردن شاپور شیرین کوید الشاهد علی
الاول شعر غم ککیم آنکلامیش ایدی حکایت بار این سیرادی آنداق کیم حکاوت سیرادوق سراییدیم سیرادی وسیرادور سراید سیر

وسیراشور بمعنی فاعل ومصدر هم می آید سیراغان وسیراغان وسیرادورغان سراینده وسراییده وبمعنی مصدر هم می آید سیراو سیراغیل
مفرد مخاطب از فعل امر چنانچه در لسان الطیر کوید الشاهد علی الثانی شعر سیراغیل ای طوطی شیرین کلام نطق شیرینکیله مقام
سیراغانی وسیراغاغیل مفرد مخاطب از فعل نهی سیرانک وسیرانکیز وسیرانکلار جمع مخاطب از فعل امر سیراسون وسیراسونلار وسیراما
جمع مخاطب از فعل نهی سیراماس وسیراماس مین مسرایم سیرایمین وسیرایدورمین وسیرادورمین مسرایم سیراغاس بسراید وبمعنی
فاعل ومصدر منفی هم می آید سیراماغان وسیرامیش سراییده سیرامیشانک سراییده سیراب بولغای وسیراب بولغای توان سرایید سیرای آلغای
تواند سرایید سیرابو وسیرای سیرای سراید سراینده وبدون تکرار هم بامعنی مستعملست سیرای وسیراین بسرایم وبسراید وبسراید
وسراییده سیراساق وسیراغایز وسیراغای بیز وسیرالی وسیرالینک بسراییم سیراغلی برای سراییدن وتا سراییده سیراغاج چون
سراید وبسراید وبمعنی سراییدن سیراغوچی سراینده سیراغوچه وسیراغونچه وسیراغانچه تا سراییدن وبعد سراییدن سیراغوسیز دور خواهیم
سراییدن سیراغوسیز دور خواهید سرایید سیراغوسیلار دور خواهند سرایید سیراغولوق سراییدنی سیراغای وسیراسا وسیراسون
سیرادیک وسیرادیک بسراید الشاهد علی الاول شعر نامه سین قوش کیتورور سیراسا اوصافینک یوقتجه چونکه بولماس ایماننک
سیراغودیک وسیرارلیک سراییدنی وهمچنانچه بسراید سیراشماق وسیراشماق قلیلنج مع الثاء المثلثه بیکدیکر سراییدن وصیغ آن باشین موافق
شود ولی اشتقاق می یابد سایغلاماق بکسر یا ترکی رومی بمعنی هذیان کفتن است من الجواهد سایغ بمعنای بسیار باشد اول وقت چنانچه
کنند چنانچه کوید شعر سین لبینک سوز فان سای ومیزغان یوتار مین ای حبیب سینی ایچیکلیکم منکا هوز حجرکه لیش
نوعی بود که در تابستان خشک ودر زمستان سیل وآب از آن جاری شود ودر کو آن را نیز کویند الشاهد علیه شعر بوردا
اول ساز ادین که تنکولکا نظرغه سایغ تاشی ملیک بنجه باقسه باش کهرو قوث وله شعر سیل الاکیم تمکار کوزوم نایتی سایغینک تا
تاشی وظالع هر دو بمعنی فلاخن نوشته وشعر مزبور را شاهد آورده بمعو کرده سیم بمعنی حساب وشمار باشد چنانچه کوید شعر لم
تا المادی کدود باشینغه اوزن اغانث هرتوکی سای حیفا تاشی بله سینه نه بوزا غان وله شعر تنم اکر بولسا باشیم مینک هرتوکی سایی
بنانانک موجه تلش کیم نامه ور لار دل ربا الاربلشیه وبا بمعنی سایو بعضم نایز مستعملست چنادم ارانک زیردن چنانچه سند کوید شد سایاغ
بفتح یا بالف کشیده یعنی شهلراه رونده ورهرو چنانچه در لسان الطیر کوید شعر کوهی تاغ ایچرا ایرآپیغ تو توب امر کابیب یدی آلتی
کوب قان بو توث رام اولغونچه بیب یردی اول ساباغ کوندا ایکی نالالاو الکوینه تاباغ سیدام بسکون میم بمعنی سیدان بمعنی صاف وهموار
وامعن باشد چنانچه در تاریخ بابری در وصف سنکاره که عبارت از نارنکی باشد کوید که وجمعی تبنغ دیلک تورمو نونک تریچیسیدا
دوزنا هموار ایلس سیدغازی نیری بترکی روی سنکنجات سفید عنم وسبک که در میان سنک رخام یافت میشود وجمیع سیاه در چشم
سیرک بسکون یا وکاف وفتح راء مهمله بمعنی متخلل وکم حجم ورقیق بود که آن را بفارسی شل خوانند سایرو بروزن ناهر وبمعنی ایا
الشاهد علیه شعر کرنوای سایروایردی مجنون غم لمعیدا تیرانا الماس چو جوهر ایکیکا توبیه غفی من فضول املاء الدوریه شعر غم بولنده
بن کیعدو بقال دیسه مجنون عجب سایرو یه دشوار دور هم لیلی ایتمک ساغ المن سایرون بسکون یا ونون ونفسم راء مهمله هوای مرد
باشد سیره بسکون یا وفتح راء مهمله بولمزوه پر نده ایست کوچک تر از جنس کنجشک کر مانند بلبل خوش آواز است سایغو بضم غین معجمه ترکی رومی
شمار وحساب باشد عنبر عنبر تر از تفکر واندیشه بود سایغولوق بمعنی اندیشه ناک واندیشه ناکی سایو بضم با بمعنی شماره وحساب چنانچه
کوید شعر غنچه کولکوسیکا ای بلبل کونکول کیپراکنما تاغ نیکاکه هر کل سایو بوز خار بولغامو ایدی ونیز در صفه سیاره در سقراط ابرام
از فراق معشوق کوید شعر باشیدینکه ایلاهی تاره هرتوکی سایو بولدی پاره سایغ بترکی رومی بمعنی هذیان بود سایین بسکون یا

238v. سوب

وسکون نون بمعنی خوب و برگزیده و منتخب باشد و نیز لقب باتو خان بن جوجی خان بن چنگیز خانست که در میان اتراک بسایین خان
اشتهار دارد و ثانیا ... نام قلعه ایست در آذربایجان از توابع تبریز باب المضمومات حرف السین مع الباء من المشتقات سوپورماک و
سوپورماکلیک بضم بای عجمی و سکون رای مهمله جاروب کردن سوپوردوک جاروب کردیم سوپورور و سوپورادور جاروب میکند سوپورود
بمعنی فاعل و مصدر هم می آید سوپورغان و سوپورغان و سوپورادورکان جاروب کننده و جاروب کرده و بمعنی مصدر هم می آید سوپورود
سوپورکیل مفرد مخاطب از فصل امر چنانچه در صحیفه سیاره در آغاز داستان گوید الشاهد علی الاول نثر کیل و جمع سوپورکیل ای ...
گردباشت ... سوپورغانسال سوپورنا و سوپورنا ... مفرد مخاطب از فصل ... سوپورونک و سوپورونکیز و سوپورونکلار جمع مخاطب امر ...
سوپورسانک و سوپورسانکیز سوپورسانکلار جمع مخاطب از فصل ... سوپورغان و سوپوراین و سوپورایم و سوپورامین جاروب کنم ...
سوپورادیم جاروب میکنم سوپورماس جاروب نمیکند و بمعنی فاعل و مصدر منفی هم می آید سوپوروب و سوپورغان و سوپورمیش
جاروب کرده سوپورمیشان جاروب کرده سوپورنابولغای و سوپوروب تولغه جاروب توان کرد سوپوراآلغه جاروب تواند کرد
سوپوراسوپورا جاروب کنان و بدون تکرار هم مستعملست سوپورای سوپوراین جاروب کنم و کند و کنی و کرده سوپورسانک
سوپورکای بیز و سوپورکای بیز و سوپوروکای و سوپوراینلر جاروب کنیم سوپورغالی برای جاروب کردن و تا جاروب کرده سوپورکاچ چون جاروب کرد
و بحث کردن چنانکه در خوشه چین ... گوید نثر سوپورگاچ ... چیکیلدی ترکیبکا ... زاغ سوپور
جاروب کننده سوپورگوچی و سوپورگوچی و سوپورغلیغ تا جاروب کردن و بقدم جاروب کردن سوپورکومیزدور جاروب خواهیم کرد سوپورکونکیز
جاروب خواهید کرد سوپورکوسیدور جاروب خواهند کرد سوپورکولوک جاروب کردنی سوپوردای و سوپورلار و سوپوربار و سوپورتو و
سوپورتدای جاروب کند سوپورتکوچی و سوپورتدیلک جاروب کردن و همچنانکه جاروب کند سوپورتغالیک بسکون تا
مصدر متعدیست بمعنی جاروب کنانیدن و صیغ آن بر نسق ... اشتقاق می یابد سوپورولماک و سوپورولماکلیک مع ...
جاروب شدن و صیغ آن بدستور بالا اشتقاق می یابد سوبولماک و سوبولماکلیک بضم با و سکون کاف و فتح لام بمعنی پی کردن
و قطع کردن ... باشد سوبولدوک پی کردیم سوبولار و سوبولادور پی میکند و سوبولادو بمعنی فاعل و مصدر هم می آید سوبولکه
سوبولغان و سوبولادوکان پی کننده و پی کرده و بمعنی مصدر هم می آید سوبولکو سوبولکیل مفرد مخاطب از فصل امر سوبولانی و سوبولانگ
مفرد مخاطب از فصل ... سوبولنک و سوبولنکیز و سوبولنکلار جمع مخاطب از فصل امر سوبولکای و سوبولکایلار جمع مخاطب ...
سوبولغایم و سوبولاین پی کنم سوبولامیز و سوبولامیز پی کنیم سوبولادیم و سوبولایم پی میکنم سوبولماس پی نکند و بمعنی فاعل
و مصدر منفی هم می آید سوبولوب و سوبولغان و سوبولمیش پی کرده سوبولمیشان پی کرده سوبولابولغه و سوبولوب تولغه پی توان کرد
سوبولای آلغای پی تواند کرد سوبولا و سوبولا و سوبولا پی کنان و بدون تکرار هم مستعملست سوبولای و سوبولا
پی کنم و کند و کنی و کرده سوبولسانک و سوبولکای بیز و سوبولکای بیز و سوبولکای پی کنیم سوبولغالی برای پی کردن و تا پی کرده
سوبولکاچ چون پی کرد و بحث کردن سوبولغوچی و سوبولغوچی پی کننده سوبولغلیغ تا پی کردن و بقدمی
کردن سوبولکومیزدور پی خواهیم کرد سوبولکونکیزدور پی خواهید کرد سوبولکوسیدور پی خواهند کرد سوبولکولوک پی کردنی
سوبولکای سوبولتو و سوبولتماق پی کند سوبولکودای و سوبولتدیلک پی کردن و همچنانکه پی کند ...
بضم با و زای ... بمعنی مستطیل و دراز کشیده باشد و این لفظ بخصوص طول جسم و اندام استعمال میشود چنانکه گوید سوبا بویلوق
... و سوبابویلو یعنی کشیده قامت و سوبی ... مستعملست سوبا ... بمعنی شمعیه و دار و ... سوبایی سوار ...

239r سوت سوج سود

... گویند سوپورکو بضم بای عجمی و کاف عجمی و سکون رای مهمله جاروب باشد چنانچه در ... الابرار در وصف ... گوید نثر
شام ... سوپورکوسی ... سوبوسون بضم با و سین مهمله و سکون نون ...
سوبوت ... سبکتکین نام پدر پادشاه ... سلطان محمود سبکتکین ...
... قدم است زیرا که ... سوبولماق ... بمعنی ...
... سوت ... بفتح تا و الف کشیده و کسر رای مهمله ... واستخوان ... سوتلاکان بسکون تا
و نون و فتح لام و کاف عجمی ... بنا ... که آن ... نباشد مانند ... و از ... است چون ...
... سوج ... بضم جیم ...
بضم جیم و سکون ... ترکی ... و آن ...
... سوجی بکسر جیم ... بمعنی شیرین و لذیذ سوجی ... بمعنی ...
الشاهد علیه نثر ... سوجی ... تاریخ الانبیا ...
یوسف علیه السلام و ... عزیز مصر ...
زندان ... سود ... بمعنی شراب باشد مع الدال ... سودراماک ... بسکون دال و فتح رای مهمله با الف کشیده
بر زمین کشیدن ... بمعنی کشیدن ... و لفظ سودراتا ... کشیدن
سودرادوک کشیدیم سودرار و سودرایدور میکشد و سودرا بمعنی فاعل و مصدر هم می آید چنانکه ... گوید نثر ...
اولسا ... سودرار ... سودرایدورکان کشنده و کشیده
مصدر هم می آید سودرا سودراکیل مفرد مخاطب از فصل امر الشاهد علی الاول نثر سودرا ...
شاید ... مفرد مخاطب ... سودرانک ... جمع مخاطب
الشاهد علی الاول نثر ... شاد ...
از فصل امر سودرانک و سودرانکیز و سودرانکلار جمع مخاطب از فصل ... سودرامان و سودراماس ... سودرایین و سودرایم ...
سودرارام میکشم سودراماس نمیکشد و بمعنی فاعل و مصدر منفی هم می آید سودراب ... سودرامیش کشیده سودرامیشان
کشیده سودرانابولغه سودراب تولغه توان کشید سودرای آلغه تواند کشید سودرا و سودرا کشان کشان چنانچه شاهد
... سکندری ... گوید نثر ... سودرای ...
سودری ... و شاهد ... الذین و ... گوید که ...
سودرای سودرای ... و بدون تکرار هم مستعملست سودرای و سودرایین بکشم و بکشد و بکشی و کشیده سودرانانک
سودرکای بیز و سودرکای بیز ... بکشیم چنانچه در ... گوید الشاهد علی الرابع نثر ... سودرغالی ...
... سودراطلی برای کشیدن و تا کشیده سودراکاچ چون کشید و بحث کشیدن سودرکوچی کشنده سودراغو
سودراغلیغ تا کشیدن و بقدم کشیدن سودرکومیزدور خواهیم کشید سودرکونکیزدور خواهید کشید سودرکوسیدور خواهند
کشید سودرکولوک کشیدنی سودرکای ... بکشد سودرکودای ... کشیدنی و همچنانکه بکشد
الشاهد علی الاول ...
مع ... الشاهد علی الاول نثر ...

239 v.

کیلیب سوررا تیغیلیک بمعنی کشانیدی چنانکه گوید مصرع کوروبالکو بونی ارازار لیغیم تنه بولوب سوکالی تا اشقا رایت [illegible]
سوریلتیننک وباقی صیغ برین سیاق تاناى [illegible] شقاق مجاید سوررلتما سوررلتما کلیک مع التاء المهمله کلب بمعنی کشیدن
وصیغ آن تاثین اشتقاقی بی یابد سوررالماک وسوررالما کلیک مع المیم بمعنی کشیده شدن وآن مرادف [illegible] باشد چنانکه
شود سوررالمو حکم لادود بمعنی کشیده میشود الشاهد علی الاول مصرع یکانا چنک سوررالور کلمه کا کیرتا ملک خم بولوب [illegible]
اولغان زمان آنداق که تا پنهانی طولوث وسوررالو بمعنی فاعل ومصدر هم می آید سوررالکانی سوررالکانی سوررلادکا بمعنی کشیده
وکشیده شده چنانکه در لیلی مجنون در ترباى لیلی ومجنون گوید الشاهد علی الاول بالمعنی الثانی مصرع سوررالکان خطیبله [illegible]
بولی کیم قوم [illegible] بولی تاشا ابیدی لوث الشاهد علی الثانی بالمعنی الاول مصرع کراملا نام لیلینک اولغاى تابیدین [illegible]
سوررالادکان بویاندا [illegible] واین شعر در دیوانهاى حضرت ناظم سوررالادوغان مرقوم است اما غالب [illegible] است شاید [illegible]
واشتباه باشد وبمعنی مصدر هم استعمال میشود وباقی صیغ برین سیاق بالالام اشتقاق بی یابد مع الراء المهمله [illegible] سوروساق
سورتالیغ دو معنی دارد اول پرسیدن دویم [illegible] چنانکه [illegible] ایهام گوید الشاهد علی الاول مصرع دیدی [illegible]
سوراتین موکه تا پنهاى بین حیات پرحیات تلزم خود [illegible] آتیننک سورتاغی سوریتاک وسوریتا کلیک باشباع [illegible] بمعنی
اول بمعنی راندن بود چنانکه در نوحه کری هرام چینی در رفنات هرام گوید الشاهد علی الاول شعر تا فاول اژدها سورتا الی آخر
تانی ول اهرمن اولتورنا الی آخر ونیز در داستان خسرو شیرین گوید که تلخ وسفید [illegible] تلخ سورتاک دویم مجاز بمعنی شیار کردن زمین
سیم ترکی رومی بمعنی نالیدن بود چنانکه فضولی گوید باملاء الرومیه مصرع ایاغینک توزینه یوز سوروب [illegible]
یوزین یوزکه شبنم بوبادین کلبرک [illegible] سوردی پرسید ومیکید وباشباع راند وشیار کرد ونالید چنانکه بمعنی اول [illegible]
شیان گوید مصرع چون کوروب اوصفت یاناز خالیم سوردی خالیم [illegible] وبمعنی ثالث فرماید مصرع کوبا [illegible] خطینک [illegible]
لبینکین سوردی [illegible] کیم لباس اولدی [illegible] کون آنکا [illegible] سوروب پرسیدیم ومیکیدیم چنانکه گوید مصرع هرقطره [illegible]
قانغان پرده اولوب [illegible] سوروق لعلینک نه قیل ایرمیش سوردیک راندیم وشیار کردیم [illegible] نالیدیم [illegible]
میپرسد ومیمکد وباشباع میراند وشیار میکند ومینالد الشاهد علی الاول بالمعنی [illegible] فضولی باملاء الرومیه مصرع [illegible]
هر صبح سوریلرکون یوزینی غالبا آندین آنکا حاصل اولوبدر بو شرف سورار بمعنی سراغ میکند هم می آید ودر بعضی ماخوذ از مصدر
است چنانکه خواهد آمد وبمعنی فاعل ومصدر هم مستعمل چنانکه بمعنی پرسنده گوید مصرع نه ضعف دور که سورار [illegible]
[illegible] کونکا ایما [illegible] توان [illegible] ودر فصل [illegible] از محبوب القلوب در ذکر [illegible] وجفت کاوان [illegible] راندن گوید که دهقان
[illegible] سورار [illegible] آنداق که آدم سورغان وسورغان وسورادورغان پرسنده وپرسیده ومیکنده ومیکیده وبمعنی مصدر هم می آیند سورکان
سورکان وسوریادوکان [illegible] ورانده وشیار کننده وشیار کرده الشاهد علی الاول بالمعنی الاخیر مصرع [illegible] که سورکان [illegible]
[illegible] حقیقی [illegible] وبمعنی مصدر هم می آید سورد مفرد غالب الفصل [illegible] بمعنی سوریتا [illegible]
[illegible] چنانکه [illegible] گوید مصرع یولدین آخر سوریتا سلطان مین دیبان درویشی یا [illegible] اولدیو [illegible] درویش
هم سلطان [illegible] سوریتا [illegible] سورکیل بران وشیار کن سوریتا کیل مران وشیار کن بالمعنی الاول
[illegible] سوریتا کیل کیم کونکول [illegible] سورونک سورونک [illegible] سوروق
جمع غالب الفصل امر [illegible] سوریاناک وسوریانکز وسوریانکلای جمع غالب الفصل امر [illegible] سوریان [illegible]

240 r.

نیمکو وباشباع منرانم وشیار میکنم [illegible] سورى او آم پرسم ومیکیم وباشباع میرانم وشیار میکنم و
سورار ام بترکی رومی بمعنی [illegible] لم المصدر [illegible] مبنی براغ میکنم سورناس نپرسید ونمیکید ونمیراند
وشیار نمیکند سورانیب بترکی رومی بمعنی نالیده سوروب وسوروبان سوروبش پرسیده ومیکیده چنانکه [illegible] گوید الشاهد
علی الاول مصرع [illegible] تا [illegible] هم آخری نینک [illegible] تابان سوروب ونیز [illegible] میکند
نظم [illegible] گوید بالمعنی الثانی مصرع [illegible] سوروب [illegible] وباشباع بمعنی رانده وشیار کرده
وبترکی رومی بمعنی نالیده چنانکه فضولی گوید الشاهد علی الثالث باملاء الرومیه مصرع درد [illegible] یوزینه سوروب [illegible]
یوزى کیم [illegible] پرسیده ومیکیده [illegible] وشیار کرده [illegible] توان پرسید وتوان میکید
وباشباع توان راند وشیار توان کرد سورا آلغاى تواند پرسید وتواند میکید وباشباع تواند راند وشیار تواند کرد سورا سورا
پرسان پرسان ومیکیده میکیده وباشباع رانده رانده وشیار کنان [illegible] هم مستعمل است وبمعنی مصدر هم می آید چنانکه بمعنی
پرسیدن گوید مصرع [illegible]
مصرع [illegible] کونکول [illegible]
وپرسیده ومیکیدن ومیکیده چنانکه [illegible] گوید مصرع [illegible]
[illegible] وشیار [illegible] وکرده [illegible]
وکرده [illegible] پرسیم ومیکیم [illegible] باشباع برانیم وشیار کنیم [illegible]
[illegible] پرسیم ومیکیم وسراغ کنیم [illegible] وباشباع بمعنی برانیم وشیار کنیم سورغالی
براى پرسیدن وتا پرسید وبراى میکیدن وتا میکید چنانکه بمعنی اول گوید مصرع [illegible]
سورغالی [illegible] وبراى میکیدن [illegible] گوید مصرع [illegible]
[illegible] سورکالی براى راندن وتا راند وبراى شیار کردن وتا شیار کند چنانکه بمعنی اول فرماید مصرع [illegible]
[illegible] سورغاج چون پرسید وپرسید [illegible]
وچون میکید [illegible] سورکاج چون راند وبراند [illegible] وچون شیار کرد وکند [illegible] چنانکه [illegible]
هرام چینی شیرویه را گوید بالمعنی الاول مصرع بولوب شیرویه اولمکدین آگاه توهم دین که [illegible] سورغوج [illegible]
ومیکنده بالمعنی الاول مصرع [illegible] سورکوج
راننده وشیار کننده سورغوجه [illegible] سورغانجه تا پرسیدن وبقدر پرسیدن وتا میکیدن وبقدر میکیدن [illegible]
سورکانجه تا راندن وبقدر راندن وتا شیار کردن وبقدر شیار کردن چنانکه در نوحه کری هرام چینی در رفنات فرهاد گوید بالمعنی الاول
مصرع [illegible] سورغوم خواهیم پرسید وخواهیم میکید
سورکوم خواهیم راند وخواهیم شیار کرد سورغونک خواهی پرسید وخواهی میکید سورکونک خواهی راند وخواهی شیار کرد سورغوسی
خواهد پرسید وخواهد میکید چنانکه [illegible] خلق تا اسکندر [illegible] تکلیف سلطنت گوید بالمعنی الاول مصرع
[illegible] خواهد راند وشیار خواهد کرد سورغولوق [illegible]
ومیکیدنی سورکولوک راندنی وشیار کردنی چنانکه در خسرو شیرین گوید بالمعنی الاول مصرع [illegible]

برایش کورولتم اولسه کور کولوك دعه سورغای پرسیدن بمعنی چنانچه کوکلتاش بالمعنی الاول لمشرای نوایی کیم سوراولیه لساسینی آولر نی
دشتا صو سورغای مکر غول بیابان دین خبر سورکای براند وشیلر کند سورلیسون ادسون [illegible] سوردیلك بپرسد بمعنی و باشباع براند
شیلر کند الشاهد علی الثانی بالمعنی الثالث شعر سورسا سبدان ایبرام بالت بوکورمالیك صابرشیم کیم جهان ملیك ندین کریبولکای
الشاهد علی الرابع بالمعنی الاول شعر شام هجرانیم وسال الحلیفه چه تفسیقه دعه آن سوردیکلار نوایی دیلی کرلیادین و سورا
وسورسا و سیرلیدون ترکی مرومی یعنی بنالد چنانچه شاهد براین رافضولی بغدادی کوید ملای الزوینه شعر آیینك بو لنده [illegible]
سورینه لر یوز بغلمام نکه ملات حیلی جوه آدم ایتماک نفس قرآنم سورغودیك پرسیدنی و همچنانچه بپرسد و مکیدنی و همچنانچه
بمکد سورکودیك رانیدنی و همچنانچه براند وشیلر کردنی و همچنانچه شیلر کند سورردیك [illegible] سورغودیك و سورکودیك باشد و
نیز بامصدر سوراملاق اشتراك دارد یعنی سراغ کردنی و همچنانچه سراغ کند سورماق و سورغوماقلیغ مصدر متعدیست یعنی
پرسیدن و مکیدن و امر کردن سوردرماق [illegible] کلیله مصدر متعدیست دیکر برا راندن وشیلر امر کردن و صیغ آنها بدستور
بالفظ مصدر اشتقاق می یابد سورولماق و سورولماقلیغ بضم را و سکون لام پرسیده شدن و مکیده شدن سورولماك و سورولماکلیك
باشباع ضمه رانده شدن و بالمجاز بمعنی شیلر شدن نیز میباشد و صیغ سورولماق بامیم مهمله و صیغ سورولماك بالکاف موافق [illegible]
می یابد سوروشماق و سوروشماقلیغ بضم را و سکون شین پرسیدن و مکیدن سوروشماك و سوروشماکلیك باشباع ضمه منجر شدن
سوروشوق پرسیدیم و مکیدیم سوروشتوك منجر شدیم سوروشتیلار پرسیدند و مکیدند و منجر شدند چنانچه در داستان [illegible]
سیار در قصه سهیل و غبار کوید المعنی الاول شعر قوپوبان [illegible] سوروشتیلار [illegible] سوروشور
سوروشادور میپرسد و میمکد و بمعنی میشود و سوروشور بمعنی فاعل و مصدر هم می آید سوروشغان و سوروشقان و سوروشادورغان پرسنده
پرسیده و مکنده و مکیده و بمعنی مکیده هم می آید سوروشکان و سوروشقان و سوروشادورغان منجر شونده و منجر شده و بمعنی مسلکم هم می آیند
سوروش مفرد مخاطب از فعل امر بمعنی سوروشما مفرد مخاطب از فعل نهی بمعنی سوروشغیل امر استبا پرسیدن و مکیدن و
سوروشماغیل نهی استبا از پرسیدن و مکیدن سوروشکیل امر استبا منجر شدن سوروشماکیل نهی استبا منجر شدن سوروشوك و سورو
سوروشونکلار جمع مخاطب از فعل امر بمعنی [illegible] سوروشمانك و سوروشماکیز و سوروشمانکلار جمع مخاطب از فعل نهی بمعنی سوروشمان و سوروشامن
میپرسم و میمکم و منجر میشوم سوروشامن و سوروشورمن و سوروشادورمن [illegible] میپرسم و میمکم و منجر میشوم سوروشامس منجر شد و
نمیمکد و منجر نمیشود و بمعنی فاعل و مصدر منفی هم می آید سوروشوب سوروشوبان و سوروشوبن پرسیده و مکیده و منجر شده چنانچه در ملامات
مراحی باشاهد کوید الشاهد علی الاول بالمعنی الاول شعر [illegible] سوروشوب [illegible]
سوروشمانان پرسیده و منجر شده سوروشا الغاه سوروشوبالغاه توان پرسید و توان مکید و منجر توان شد سوروشا الماه تواند پرسید
و تواند مکید و منجر تواند شد سوروشا سوروشا پرسان پرسان و مکیده مکیده و منجر شده شده و بدون تکرار هم مستعملست سوروشا
سوروشایین بپرسیم و بپرسید و بپرسیم و بمکم و بمکد و بمکی و مکیده و منجر شوم و شود و شوی و شده سوروشساق و سوروشغاییز
سوروشغاییز بپرسیم و بمکیم چنانچه شاهد براول [illegible] فرماید شعر [illegible]
ینکلیغ [illegible] سوروشساك و سوروشسانکیز منجر شویم سوروشسا و سوروشسانك
بپرسیم و بمکیم و منجر شویم سوروشغالی برای پرسیدن و تا پرسیدن و برای مکیدن و تا مکیدن سوروشکالی برای منجر شدن و تا منجر شدن
سوروشقاج چون پرسید و بپرسد و چون پرسیدن و بمحض پرسیدن و چون مکید و بمکد و بمحض مکیدن سوروشکاج چون منجر شد و شود و بمحض شدن

سوروشغوچی پرسنده و مکنده سوروشکوچی منجر شونده سوروشغوچه و سوروشغوغه و سوروشغانچه تا پرسیدن و بمقدار پرسیدن تا مکیدن
و بمقدار مکیدن سوروشکوچه و سوروشکوغه و سوروشکانچه تا منجر شدن و بمقدار منجر شدن سوروشغوسیدور خواهیم پرسید و خواهیم مکید
سوروشکوسیدور منجر خواهیم شد سوروشغوزدور خواهید پرسید و خواهید مکید سوروشکوزدور منجر خواهید شد سوروشغو
سیلاردور خواهند پرسید و خواهند مکید سوروشکوسیلاردور منجر خواهند شد سوروشغولوق پرسیدنی و مکیدنی سوروشکولوك
منجر شدنی سوروشغای بپرسد و بمکد سوروشکای منجر شود چنانچه در فضل بیت وشتم از مجمع الغلو [illegible] ملاکور کوید که
ایش آنکلا تیکای کر [illegible] سوروشغای و [illegible] سوروشون
سوروشدیك بپرسد و بمکد و منجر شود سوروشغودیك پرسیدنی و همچنانچه بپرسد و مکیدنی و همچنانچه بمکد سوروشکودیك
منجر شدنی و همچنانچه منجر شود سوروشوردیك مرادف سوروشغودیك باشد سوروشماق و سوروشماقلیغ
بضم شین معجمه و سکون لام پرسیده شدن و مکیده شدن و صیغ آن بالام اشتقاق می یابد سوراماق و سوراماقلیغ بضم را
سراغ و تفتیش کردن باشد سوراادوق سراغ کردیم سورارد و سورار [illegible] سراغ میکند و سورار [illegible] سوراماق [illegible]
دارد یعنی میپرسد و میمکد و باشباع ضمه یعنی میراند وشیلر میکند [illegible] چنانچه در ذیل [illegible]
و بمعنی فاعل و مصدر هم می آید سوراغان و سورارغان و سورارادورغان سراغ کننده و سراغ کرده و بمعنی مصدر هم می آید [illegible]
سورا مفرد مخاطب از فعل امر [illegible] سورامانک مفرد مخاطب از فعل نهی [illegible] سورانکلار جمع مخاطب از فعل امر بمعنی
سورانکیز جمع مخاطب از فعل نهی [illegible] سورامان و سورامین سراغ نمیکنم سورارمین و سورارمین و سورادورمین سراغ میکنم
سوراماس سراغ نمیکند و بمعنی فاعل و مصدر منفی هم می آید سوراب و سورابان و سوراپین سراغ کرده چنانچه شاهد براول [illegible]
[illegible] کوید که حضرت [illegible] علیه السلام [illegible]
[illegible] کوید که [illegible]
[illegible] فرماید که [illegible]
سراغ کرده سورابولغای و سوراب بولغای سراغ توان کرد سوراای الغای سراغ تواند کرد سوراای و سوراای سراغ
و بدون تکرار هم مستعملست سورای و سوراین سراغ کنم و کند و کنی و کرده و نیز بامصدر سوراماق و سوراماك اشتراك دارد
چنانچه در ذیل آن مصادر مذکور شد سوراساق و سوراغاییز و سوراغاییز و سوراساك [illegible] سراغ کنیم و سورای و سوراینك یعنی
بپرسیم و بمکیم و باشباع برانیم وشیلر کنیم سوراغالی برای سراغ کردن و تا سراغ کردن سوراقاج چون سراغ کرد و کند و بمحض کردن سوراغوچی
سراغ کننده سوراغوچه و سوراغوغه و سوراغانچه تا سراغ کردن و بمقدار سراغ کردن سوراغوسیدور سراغ خواهیم کرد سوراغوزدور سراغ
خواهید کرد سوراغوسیلاردور سراغ خواهند کرد سوراغولوق سراغ کردنی سوراغای و سورارنا [illegible] سراغ کند سوراغودیك و
سورادیك سراغ کردنی و همچنانچه سراغ کند و سوراغودیك با مصدر سوراماق و سوراماك اشتراك دارد چنانچه مذکور شد سوراتماق
سوراتماقلیغ بفتح را و سکون تا مصدر متعدیست یعنی سراغ و تفتیش کنانیدن سوراتتی و سوراتمان و سوراتغان [illegible] سراغ امر فرمود چنانچه
در تفحص کردن خرو شیرین مرکوید الشاهد علی الاول شعر [illegible] آیینك دیك [illegible]
صیغ برین ساق مانای قرشت اشتقاق می یابد سوراشماق و سوراشماقلیغ مع الشین بمعنی مضاطلمات با یکدیگر سراغ کردن و صیغ
باشین اشتقاق می یابد سورالماق و سورالماقلیغ سراغ و تفتیش شدن و صیغ آن بالام اشتقاق می یابد سورالماك و سورالماکلیك باشباع ضمه

وسکون واو تای فوقانی بمعنی نالیدن باشد و در [illegible] سیقتاک گویند سیقتوک نالیدیم سیقتادور نالد و سیقتامق بمعنی حاصل

مصدر هم آمده سیقتکان و سیقتاکان سیقتادورکان نالنده و نالیده و بمعنی مصدر هم می آید چنانچه گوید الشاهد علی الاول شعر

سیقتکان دیک کوزیم یوزیمه یتیشقیمه [illegible] کوزیادو [illegible] ایلکیدین [illegible] دابولسا اولیلاک سیقت و سیقتکیل مفرد حاضر

از فعل امر سیقتا و سیقتاکیل مفرد غائب از فعل نهی سیقتونک و سیقتونکز جمع غائب از فعل امر سیقتامانک و سیقتامنکز

سیقتامنکلار جمع غائب از فعل نهی سیقتادیم سیقتادین سیقتادی [illegible] سیقتادوق [illegible] سیقتاماس

نالد و بمعنی حاصل مصدر نیز هم می آید سیقتوب [illegible] نالیده سیقتیشانک نالیده سیقتابولغای [illegible]

توان نالید سیقتا آلغای تواند نالید سیقتا سیقتا نالیده نالیده سیقتای سیقتاین [illegible] نالیدن

الشاهد علی الاول بالمعنی الاول شعر [illegible] غالب وکلکون [illegible] تابیب آلیغه اول [illegible]

[illegible] سیقتکانک سیقتکاپز و سیقتکای پز و [illegible] سیقتکالی برای نالیدن و تا نالیدن سیقتکاج چون

نالید و نالد و بعض نالیدن سیقتکوچی نالنده سیقتکوچه سیقتکونچه تا نالیدن و بقصد نالیدن سیقتکوسیزدور

خواهیم نالید سیقتکوسیدور خواهید نالید سیقتکوسیدور خواهند نالید سیقتکولوک نالیدنی سیقتاچی و سیقتاچیلیک

سیقتدیک بنالد سیقتکودیک و سیقتاردیک نالیدنی و همچنانکه بنالد سیقتورنک و سیقتورماکلیک [illegible]

لفظ [illegible] مصدر متعدیست [illegible] نالیدن امر کردن و صیغ آن بدستور لفظ [illegible] اشتقاق می یابد سیقتوتماک و سیقتوتماکلیک

مع الثنین بمعنی مفاعله است یعنی بیکدیگر نالیدن و صیغ آن بانثین اشتقاق می یابد سیقتوشماک و سیقتوشماکلیک مع اللام یعنی [illegible]

و صیغ آن باللام اشتقاق می یابد سیرکاماک و سیرکاماکلیک بسکون رای و فتح کاف عجمی بزمین کشیدن سیرکادور کشیدیم سیرکادور

سیرکایدور [illegible] و [illegible] سیرکاکان بمعنی حاصل مصدر هم می آید سیرکاکان و سیرکاکان [illegible] کشیدن و کشیده و بمعنی مصدر

هم می آید سیرکا و سیرکاکیل مفرد حاضر از فعل امر سیرکاما و سیرکاماکیل مفرد غائب از فعل نهی سیرکانک و سیرکانکز

سیرکانکلار جمع غائب از فعل امر سیرکامانک سیرکامانکز جمع غائب از فعل نهی سیرکادیم سیرکادین سیرکادی [illegible]

سیرکایدور [illegible] سیرکاماس [illegible] میکشند و بمعنی حاصل مصدر منفی هم می آید سیرکاب سیرکابان و سیرکامیش کشیده سیرکا

میانانک کشیده سیرکابولغای و سیرکاب بولغای تواند کشید سیرکای آلغای تواند کشید سیرکای و سیرکای سیرکای کشان کشان

و بمعنی تکرار هم مستعملست سیرکای سیرکاین بکشم و بکشد و بکشی و کشیده سیرکانک و سیرکاپز و سیرکای پز و سیرکالی برای

بکشیم سیرکالی برای کشیدن و تا کشیدن سیرکاکاج چون بزمین کشید و بکشد و بعض کشیدن سیرکاکوچی کشنده سیرکاکوچه و سیرکاکو

سیرکاکانچه تا کشیدن و بقصد کشیدن سیرکاکوسیزدور خواهیم کشید سیرکاکوسیدور خواهید کشید سیرکاکوسیدور خواهند کشید

سیرکاکولوک کشیدنی سیرکاکای و سیرکاکای سیرکاسون سیرکادیک بکشد سیرکاکودیک و سیرکاردیک کشیدنی و همچنانکه بکشد

سیرکاتماک و سیرکاتماکلیک بسکون رای و نون و فتح کاف عجمی بزمین کشیده شدن سیرکانیب سیرکانیبان و سیرکانیش کشیده شده

الشاهد علی الرابع من لغات [illegible] نیغ و هجران منعی دین [illegible] امکان یا من [illegible] کوینکا [illegible]

و تا فوقانی صیغ بریناق با نون اشتقاق می یابد سیرچماک و سیرچماکلیک بسکون رای و جیم عجمی لغزیدن سیرچتوب لغزیدیم سیرچادور

میلغزد و سیرچاب بمعنی حاصل مصدر هم می آید سیرچکان و سیرچکاکان سیرچادورکان لغزنده و لغزیده و بمعنی مصدر هم می آید سیرچ و سیرچکیل

مفرد حاضر از فعل امر سیرچما و سیرچماکیل مفرد غائب از فعل نهی سیرچانک و سیرچانکز جمع [illegible] سیرچماسین و سیرچماین و سیرچادیم

میلغزم سیرچماس نمیلغزد و بمعنی حاصل مصدر منفی هم می آید سیرچوب سیرچوبان و سیرچیش لغزیده سیرچیشانک لغزیده سیرچاتوبولغای

سیرچوب بولغای تواند لغزید سیرچا آلغای تواند لغزید سیرچا سیرچا لغزان لغزان و بمعنی تکرار هم بمعنی مستعملست سیرچای و

سیرچاین بلغزم و بلغزد و بلغزی و لغزیده سیرچانک و سیرچاپز و سیرچای پز و سیرچالی و سیرچالیک بلغزیم سیرچکالی برای لغزیدن و

تا لغزیدن سیرچکاج چون لغزید و بلغزد و بعض لغزیدن سیرچکوچی لغزنده سیرچکوچه و سیرچکونچه و سیرچکانچه تا لغزیدن و بقصد لغزیدن

سیرچکوسیزدور خواهیم لغزید سیرچکوسیدور خواهید لغزید سیرچکوسیدور خواهند لغزید سیرچکولوک لغزیدنی سیرچکای و

سیرچای و سیرچاینا و سیرچون و سیرچیدیک بلغزد سیرچکودیک و سیرچاردیک لغزیدنی و همچنانکه بلغزد سیرچتماک و سیرچتماکلیک

مع الثنین یا یکدیگر لغزیدن و صیغ آن بانثین اشتقاق می یابد سیرچلماک و سیرچلماکلیک بضم جیم عجمی و سکون لام لغزیده شدن و

آن باللام اشتقاق می یابد من الجوامد سوراغ بمعنی تفحص و تفتیش باشد و بمعنی نشان و اثر و خبر هم استعمال میشود چنانچه گوید

شعر او خرابات اهلی سوراغین [illegible] ایتمیش بو طرف کیلیشام تابیب سوراغ اول [illegible] کیراک [illegible] گوید شعر

[illegible] و [illegible] اوکوز [illegible] تابیب [illegible] [illegible] از [illegible] و خوداران

درویش گوید که روا بولغای کیم [illegible] ویرانه [illegible] ناشور [illegible] سراغ [illegible] [illegible] ذکر

کرده سهو کرده سوران غریو و آواز بلند باشد که لشکریان بجمعیت و از دحام بکنند چنانچه در خمسه [illegible] گوید شعر

چو [illegible] در [illegible] و وحشی لا اربات سوران سالیب یا [illegible] توشتی لا اربات و له شعر سوران بو [illegible] تا بو [illegible]

[illegible] سورچا بسکون رای و فتح جیم عجمی بمعنی لغزش بود سورغوج [illegible] که روی [illegible] بود که [illegible] سورکاول بسکون [illegible]

و فتح کاف عجمی و ضم واو و جمعی [illegible] گویند که از عقب لشکر راندن لشکر مامور باشند سورکو بضم کاف عجمی چوبی [illegible] که [illegible]

بدان زمین تخم افشانده را هموار کند تا تخم پوشیده شود سورکوتا [illegible] که بر روی آن [illegible] اصلاح کند سوروین

[illegible] و [illegible] سورمه کلید لفظیست مرکب از ترکی و فارسی و با صطلاح [illegible] کلیدیست که از چوب ساخته بدان [illegible]

نصب میکنند و بت و کشاد آن با دست [illegible] مزلاق گویند سورنای بلغت مغولی دو معنی دارد اول بمعنی شادی [illegible]

بود دوم غریو و آواز بلند باشد که در جنگ بطریقه خود بکنند و آنرا بلغت جغتای سوران گویند و نیز بمعنی پرسش [illegible]

سوروجی بضم اول کیم [illegible] سوروجی [illegible] نیز جمله [illegible] گویند که همراه [illegible] الزمر [illegible]

سوروش بمعنی استفسار باشد چنانچه در خاتمه [illegible] گوید شعر چون [illegible] و لیکن [illegible] سوروی [illegible]

اول سوروشتین [illegible] خسته کونکلونکا [illegible] و نیز [illegible] پرسیدن و [illegible] شدن سوروغ سوروق

بضم او سکون آخر دو معنی دارد اول بمعنی پرسش و سؤال و احتساب بود چنانچه در خاتمه [illegible] گوید شعر [illegible]

[illegible] [illegible] [illegible] [illegible] بولسه [illegible] باشیقلی [illegible] ستون و خون [illegible]

اسند چنانچه در سد سکندری در وصف لشکر [illegible] گوید شعر [illegible] ستون [illegible]

و مجازا [illegible] گویند که [illegible] گوید شعر [illegible] یول [illegible]

بارغای اول که [illegible] سوروق سوروغ کوف [illegible] پرسش گویند یعنی [illegible] الشاهد علیه شعر نوای [illegible]

سوروغ کونکلی [illegible] سوروک بضم او سکون کاف بمعنی گله [illegible] الشاهد علیه شعر [illegible]

کونکلین [illegible] سوروک [illegible] شعر [illegible] سوروک [illegible] چوپانی [illegible]

مع الزاء المعجمة من المشتقات سوزماق با لکاف بمعنی صاف کردن باشد و در دو مقالت نیز از لفظ استعمال میشود اول در حالتی که طعام و حلوای پخته
بالخود جمع کرده از مواضع سیل نشیب کند و آنرا بعربی کوز لاستعدیم نازل کرد چشم و دوم در حالت شمار با غلبه حجاب ما تنبهای اثنا
دو معنی میکند باید لفظ طیرا چشم هندکی میشود مثل اینکه کوینه توش اهرین سوزادیمایلغان کوزین سوزادور سوزدوک صاف کردیم
خار و سوزادور صاف میکند و معنی فاعل و مصدر هم می آید سوزکان و سوزارکان و سوزادورکان صاف کننده صاف کرده
مصدر هم می آید سوزو سوزکیل مفرد خطاب فعل امر الشاهد علی الاول شعر نی ایچیم زهد علم طاسین آلکر وای پیرینک
بیلای چون خرابات اهلی ابجرا باده سوزش و بغار ... سوز و کمال باشد سوزما و سوزماکیل مفرد خطاب فعل نهی سوزونك
سوزونکیز و سوزونکلار جمع خطاب فعل امر سوزماسه سوزماییکیز و سوزماکلار جمع خطاب فعل نهی سوزاین سوزارمین صاف کنیم
سوزامیز سوزارمیز و سوزادورمین و سوزارام صاف میکنم سوزماس صاف نمیکند و معنی فاعل و مصدر منفی هم می آید سوزو
سوزوبان سوزوبش صاف کرده سوزمیشانك صاف کرده سوزابولمای و سوزابولغای صاف توان کرد سوزا آلمای صاف نتواند کرد
سوزا سوزا صاف کنان و بدون تکرار هم بهمین معنی مستعمل سوزای سوزاین صاف کنم و کنند و کنی و کنید سوزسانك سوزکای بیز و
سوزکای سیز و سوزالینك صاف کنیم سوزکالی برای صاف کردن و تا صاف کند سوزکاچ چون صاف کرد و کند و کنی
سوزکوچی صاف کننده سوزکوسی سوزکونچه و سوزکالیغه تا صاف کردن و بقصد صاف کردن سوزکومیزدور صاف خواهیم کرد
سوزکوچیدور صاف خواهید کرد سوزکوسیلاردور بهمان معنی خواهند کرد سوزکولوك صاف کردنی سوزکای و سوزاو سوزماو سوزیك
سوزدیك صاف کند سوزکودیك و سوزاردیك صاف کردی و همچنانکه کند سوزیلماق و سوزولماق بالکاف بضم زا و سکون لام صاف شدن
منیز بدو معنی استعمال میشود چنانکه کویند قوش سوزولادی یعنی پرید بالخصوص از برای فرود آمدن جمع میکند و کویند سوزولادی
یعنی پشت چشم نازک میشود از حالت خمار و غلبه خواب سوزولدی صاف شد و پرید بالطیور جمع شد و پشت چشم نازک شد چنانکه
شاعر بمعنی اخیر کوید با ملاحظه الرعیه شعر خمار باده چون کوزینه طولدی کوز ... ابر کروش سوزولدی سوزولوب و سوزولوبان
سوزولمیش صاف شده و پرید بالجمع شده طیور و پشت چشم نازک شده چنانکه شاعر بمعنی اخیر گفته با ملاحظه الرعیه شعر
سوزولمیش نرکسینك چشم سیاهی ایله ... مستانه نکاهی و باقی صیغ بین سیاق قبالالام اشتقاق به یابد سوزلانماك و سوزلاماق الکاف
مبکو نظر بفتح لام حرف زدن و گفتن سوزلادی حرف زدیم سوزلار و سوزلایدور حرف میزند سوزلار بمعنی فاعل و مصدر هم می آید
سوزلاکان و سوزلارکان و سوزلایدورکان حرف زننده و حرف زده و بمعنی مصدر هم می آید چنانکه در تعلیم الجواهر کوید الشاهد علی الاول شعر سیل
الیدا ... بولدی غرابت خاصیل بمعنی ملاحت و ظرافت خاصیل اونی سوزلاکاندین استفلدت خاصیل ... لیکیدین ملاحت
خاصیل سوزلامان و سوزلامایدور حرف نزننده و حرف نزده و بمعنی حرف نزدن و نکفتن هم می آید چنانکه در حیرة الابرار در وصف ملاحت
کوید الشاهد علی الاول شعر نکته سوزلاکلیغ ایتیم تاشی تاپسا حقیقت ادن جاشی ... حقیقت کوهر ... رشته
سوزین سوزلامان کان ... سوزلا و سوزلاکیل مفرد خطاب فعل امر الشاهد علی الاول شعر ... ای نوله سوزلا واضح استانیم
عشق ارا مجنون و فرهاد ... مجنون قصه سی افسانه دور الشاهد علی الثانی من لسان الطیر شعر ایا ... مقصود اسلی ... سوزلاکیل
مرغ کیم سوزلا سمن آندین سوزلاکیل سوزلامه ... سوزلا ... سوزلا و سوزلاییکیز جمع خطاب فعل امر سوزلامانك سوزلاماییکیز
جمع خطاب فعل نهی سوزلامان و سوزلامامین حرف نزنم سوزلامای و سوزلامیمیز و سوزلا ... سوزلا دام حرف نمیزنم سوزلاماس
حرف نمیزند و بمعنی فاعل و مصدر منفی هم می آید سوزلاب و سوزلابان و سوزلامیش حرف زده الشاهد علی الاول شعر ...

غالب و لیکن تیلیمه لال اردی بیلماینچه یوتقو ... کونی خیالینك بیلا سوزلاب غافل قالمیش سوزلاتمانك حرف زنید سوزلاتماق و سوزلاتغون بر
حرف توان زد سوزلای آلماس حرف نتواند زد سوزلای بو و سوزلای و سوزلای حرف زنان و بدون تکرار هم بهمین معنی مستعمل سوزلای و سوزلاین
حرف بزنم و بزنند و بزنی و بزنید سوزلاسانك سوزلاکای بیز و سوزلاکای سیز و سوزلالینك حرف بزنیم سوزلاکالی برای حرف زدن و
تا حرف زند سوزلاکاچ چون حرف زد و بزند و بزنی سوزلاکوچی حرف زننده چنانکه کوید شعر کوپ سوزلاکوچی ...
بولماش هر کیم ... پشیمان بولماس سوزلاکوسی سوزلاکونچه و سوزلاکالیغه تا حرف زدن و بقصد حرف زدن سوزلاکومیزدور حرف خواهیم
زد سوزلاکوچیدور حرف خواهید زد سوزلاکوسیلاردور بهمان حرف خواهند زد سوزلاکولوك حرف زدنی سوزلاکای سوزلاماو سوزلادیك
حرف زند سوزلاکودیك ... حرف زدی و همچنانکه حرف زند سوزلاشماق و سوزلاشماقلیق مع الشین المعجمة با کسی مکالمه
کردن سوزلاشور و سوزلاشادور مکالمه میکند الشاهد علی الاول شعر سوزلاشور مین ... لال اردیلا ...
چون او ... مکالمه کرده ... سوزلاشیب سوزلاشیبان و سوزلاشمیش مکالمه کرده الشاهد علی الاول شعر
فرقت ... باشیغه ... سوزلاشیب ... سوزلاشقوچه و سوزلاشقانچه
تا مکالمه کردن و بقصد مکالمه کردن الشاهد علی الثانی بالمعنی الاخیر شعر ...
اولای ... سوزلاشکونچه ... باقی صیغ بین سیاق قیاس اشتقاق به یابد سوزلاتماق و سوزلاتماق مع التاء و سوزلا ...
... برای حرف زدن ... چنانکه در وصف ...
در وصف ... الشاهد علی الاول بالمعنی الاول شعر ...
شاه ... سوزلاتکالی ... باقی صیغ بین سیاق الاشتقاق به یابد من الجوامد سوز
سخن را کویند و بالاشباع ... انصاف کردن و پشت چشم نازک کردن ... الجمع کردن ... چنانکه ... سوزتیکو
سخن چین ... الشاهد علیه شعر سوز ... سوز تیکان
بکنای ... سخن ... چنانکه مضمون ...
... الشاهد ... شعر ... سوز کوچ بسکون زاء ...
کاری ... الشاهد علیه شعر ...
سوزمه بفتح ... شراب ... سوزوك ... بکسر کاف ... چنانکه کوید شعر تا تیغ ...
ایاغ ... سوز ... مع التاء المهملة من المشتقات سوسامق و سوساماقلیق ... فتح سین ...
بمعنی تشنه شدن باشد سوسادوق تشنه شدیم سوسار و سوسایدور تشنه میشود سوسار بمعنی فاعل و مصدر هم می آید
سوساغان و سوسارغان و سوسایدورغان تشنه شونده و تشنه شده و بمعنی مصدر هم می آید سوسا و سوساغیل مفرد خطاب فعل امر
سوسامانك و سوسامانغیل مفرد خطاب فعل نهی سوسامان و سوسامامین تشنه نمیشوم سوسامای و سوسامیمن و سوسابوقمین و سوسادام تشنه نمیشوم
سوساماس تشنه نمیشود و بمعنی فاعل و مصدر منفی هم می آید سوساب و سوسابان و سوسامیش تشنه شده الشاهد علی الاول شعر ...
اولدی ... شعر ...
تا ... تشنه شده سوسابولمای و سوسابولغای تشنه توان شد سوسا آلمای
تشنه نتواند شد سوسای سوسای ... تشنه شده و بدون تکرار هم مستعمل سوسای و سوسایین تشنه شوم و شوند

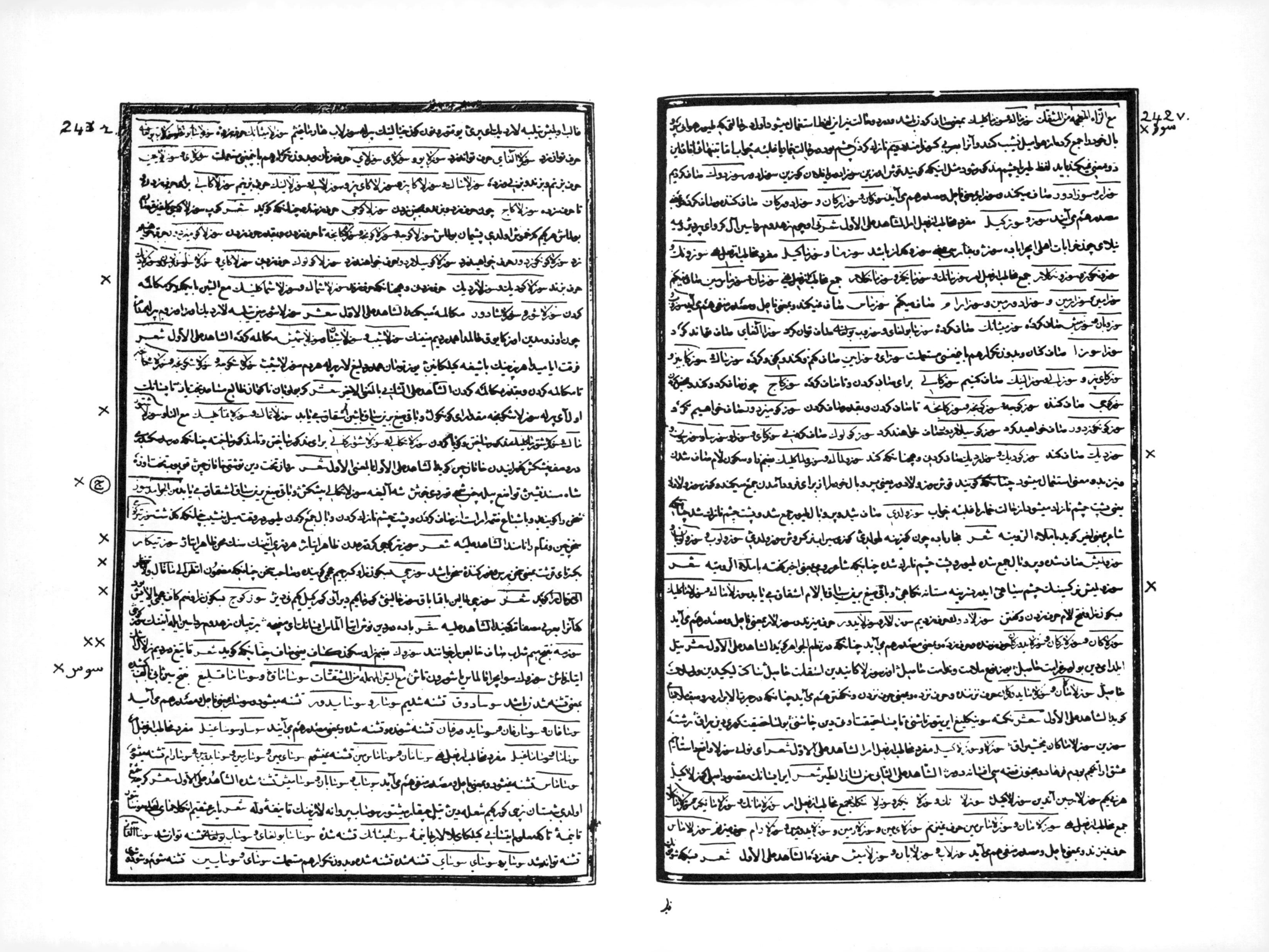

243v.

وشده سوناتلقو سونالماپزو سوناغاییزو سونالی و سولالینک تشنه شوم سوناغلی برای تشنه شدن و تاتشنه شدن

سوناغاج چون تشنه شده شود و بعضی تشنه شدن سونالغوجی تشنه شوند سوناغوچه و سوناغوغه و سوناغانچه تا تشنه شدن

وبقدر تشنه شدن سوناغومیزدور تشنه خواهیم شد سوناغونکیزدور تشنه خواهید شد سوناغوسیلاردور تشنه خواهند

شد سوناغولوق تشنه شدنی سوناغای و سوناسا و سوناسون و سونادیل تشنه شود سوناغودیک و سوناجودیک تشنه شدنی

و همچنانکه تشنه شود سوناتماق و سوناتما قیلیغ مع الکاف مصدر متعدیست یعنی تشنه کردن وصیغ آن برین فهج بانای قرشت اشتقاق

می یابد سوستاتماق و سوستاتما قیلیغ بسکون سین و نای حطی و فتح تای قرشت با الف کشیده بمعنی سست شدن باشد چنانکه

آغاز نظم سکندری گوید الشاهد علی الاول شعر بو بول قطعی دین تاپماغینک نی ایدی کم رو بغمه سوستاتماغینک نی ایدی

سوستایدوق سست شدیم سوستایورو سوستایادور سست میشود الشاهد علی الاول من سلطان حسین میرزا شعر ضعف تن دیدم

که اول آرام جانیم سوستایور جانیم آسیب خسته جسم ناتوانیم سوستایور و سوستایوروب بمعنی فاعل و مصدر هم می آید سوستایما

سوستایوغان و سوستایادورغان سست شونده و سست شده و بمعنی مصدر هم می آید سوستای سوستایغیل مفرد مخاطب فعل امر سوستایما

سوستایماغیل مفرد مخاطب نهی سوستاینک و سوستاینکیز و سوستاینکلار جمع مخاطب فعل امر سوستایمانک و سوستایمانکیز و سوستایمانکلار

جمع مخاطب فعل نهی سوستایما و سوستایماس سست نمیشوم سوستایامین و سوستایورمین و سوستایادورمین و سوستایورمین سست میشوم الشاهد علی الثانی

شعر هجر بیچاره بولدم منجه کیم سیغلادیم وصل امیدی داغی تاپیلم سوستایوروب ولکودین سوستایاس سست نمیشود بمعنی

فاعل و مصدر نفی هم می آید سوستایب سوستایبان و سوستایش سست شده چنانکه در سکندری بعد گوید شعر

گوید الشاهد علی الاول شعر اوکم نام ایدی آق تاچیمنی یابیب کیلیب اوز و مکا کیمی سوستاییب سوستایتماک سست شده

سوستایساتو و سوستاییب بولغان سست توان شد سوستایا آلغان سست تواند شد سوستایا سوستایا سست شده سست شده

و همچنین تکرار هم مستعملست سوستای سوستایین سست شوم و شود و شوی و شده سوستاتماق و سوستاتماقیز و سوستایماغایز و سوستایما

سوستایالینک سست شوم سوستایغلی برای سست شدن و تا سست شده سوستایماج چون سست شد و شود و بعضی شدن سوستایغو

سست شونده سوستایغوچه و سوستایغوچه و سوستایغانچه تا سست شدن و بقدر سست شدن سوستایغومیزدور سست خواهیم شد سوستایغو

سست خواهید شد سوستایغوسیلاردور سست خواهند شد سوستایغولوق سست شدنی سوستایغای و سوستایا و سوستایسا و سوستایسون

سوستایدیک سست شود سوستایغودیک و سوستایوردیک سست شدنی و همچنانکه سست شود سوستاتماق و سوستاتما قیلیغ

بسکون سین ثلثه و تای ثلثه و فتح تای اول و کسر یای حطی مصدر متعدیست یعنی سست کردن وصیغ آن برین سیاق بانای قرشت اشتقاق می یابد

سوسمک بسکون سین ترکی رومی بدو معنی دارد اول شاخ زدن باشد که آنرا بعربی مناطحت گویند دویم نا کتشدن گویند سوسادور

مصدر متعدیست یعنی ثلثه نیفوغنا کتشدن کردن برالجو اند سوساق بفتح سین و سکون نون و قاف جیجه و ملعقه بود که بدان دیک برهم زنند سوسم

بفتح سین و سکون میم ترکی رومی بمعنی حیران و متحیر باشد سوسون بضم سین و سکون نون آبدو نوع و آب طابوری گویند که در ته ظرف نشیمن شود

مع الشین المعجمه من المشتقات سوفامایاق و سوفامایا قیلیغ بفتح ضمن با الف کشیده و سکون زای مهمله تشنه را آب دادن و سیراب کردن و از اسوفار

هم گویند سوناسوق سیراب کردیم سوفاردیم و سوفاردور سیراب میکند و سوفاروب بمعنی فاعل و مصدر هم می آید سوفارغان و سوفارغلی

سوفارادورغان سیراب کننده و سیراب کرده و بمعنی مصدر هم می آیند سوفار و سوفارغیل مفرد مخاطب فعل امر سوفارما و سوفارماغیل مفرد مخاطب

از نهی سوفارینک و سوفارینکیز و سوفارینکلار جمع مخاطب فعل امر سوفارمانک و سوفارمانکیز و سوفارمانکلار جمع مخاطب فعل نهی سوفارمان

وفازیور

2442

سوفارمامین سیراب نمیکنم سوفارامین و سوفاریورمین و سوفارادورمین سوفاریور سیراب میکنم سوفاریب سوفارییان و سوفاریش سیراب کرده

چنانکه شاهد براوصاف تاریخ بابری چنین مذکورست که کوپ ولد باشیدا قوشولدا سوفاریب آتی تیندورونب آلدندوق سوفاریشانک

سیراب کرده سوفاریا بولغای و سوفارییب بولغان سیراب تواند کرد سوفارا آلغان سیراب تواند کرد سوفارا سوفارا سیراب کنان

هم مستعملست سوفاری و سوفاری سیراب کنم و کند و کنی و کرده سوفاریاق و سوفاریاقیز و سوفاریقیز و سوفارالینک سوفارالیسلت

سیراب کنیم سوفارغلی برای سیراب کردن و تا سیراب کرده سوفارغاج چون سیراب کرد و کند و بعضی کردن سوفارغوجی سیراب کننده سوفارغو

سوفارغوچه و سوفارغانچه تا سیراب کردن و بقدر سیراب کردن سوفارغومیزدور سیراب خواهیم کرد سوفارغونکیزدور سیراب خواهید کرد

سوفارغوسیلاردور سیراب خواهند کرد سوفارغودیک و سوفارودیک سیراب کردنی و همچنانکه سیراب کند سوغالماق و سوغالما قیلیغ

بفتح ضمن با الف کشیده و کسر رای مهمله و سکون لام سیراب شدن و صیغ آن برین سیاق بلا رای مکسوره و الحاق لام اشتقاق می یابد سوغالماق

و سوغالما قیلیغ بفتح ضمن با الف کشیده و سکون لام فرو رفتن آب بزمین و خشک شدن آب باشد که آنرا بعربی نضوب گویند سوغالدی

خشک شد الشاهد علیه شعر ای کونکل سوغالدی اشکیننک سعی ایلا کیل که تا که سیرهم والی جانیم کمرای سوغالماغای بین سوغالا

سوغالادورغان خشک میشود سوغالوب بمعنی فاعل و مصدر هم می آید سوغالغان و سوغالغان و سوغالادورغان خشک شونده و خشک شده

و بمعنی مصدر هم می آید سوغال و سوغالغیل مفرد مخاطب فعل امر سوغالما و سوغالماغیل مفرد مخاطب فعل نهی سوغالینک و سوغالینکیز

سوغالینکلار جمع مخاطب فعل امر سوغالمانک و سوغالمانکیز و سوغالمانکلار جمع مخاطب فعل نهی سوغالمان و سوغالماس خشک نمیشوم

سوغالامین و سوغالورمین و سوغالادورمین و سوغالورمن خشک میشوم سوغونساتان و سوغالماس و سوغالماغای خشک نشود سوغالماس

سوغالماغایمین و سوغالماغایمین خشک نشوی چنانکه شاهد بر ثالث در ذیل لغت سوغالدی مذکور شد سوغالماس خشک نشود و بمعنی

فاعل و مصدر نفی هم می آید سوغالیب و سوغالیبان و سوغالمیش خشک شده چنانکه شاهد بر اول در حسبه المتقین در صفات اسرار گوید

که دمیغ کیم اول تینکزلار سوغالیب سوغالیا بولغان و سوغالیبان خشک شده سوغالیا بولغای و سوغالیب بولغان خشک تواند شد سوغالا آلغای

خشک تواند شد سوغالا سوغالا خشک شده شده و بدون تکرار هم مستعملست سوغالای و سوغالایین خشک شوم و شود و شوی

وشده سوغالاناق و سوغالانایز و سوغالغایز و سوغالالی و سوغالالینک خشک شویم سوغالغلی برای خشک شدن و تا خشک شده سوغالغاچ

چون خشک شده شود و بعضی خشک شدن سوغالغوجی خشک شونده سوغالغوچه و سوغالغوچه و سوغالغانچه تا خشک شدن و بقدر

خشک شدن سوغالغومیزدور خشک خواهیم شد سوغالغونکیزدور خشک خواهید شد سوغالغوسیلاردور خشک خواهند شد

سوغالغولوق خشک شدنی سوغالغای و سوغالا و سوغالسا و سوغالسون سوغالدیک خشک شود سوغالغودیک و سوغالوردیک

خشک شدنی و همچنانکه خشک شود سوغالتماق و سوغالتما قیلیغ بسکون لام و تای قرشت مصدر متعدیست یعنی خشک کردن

آب وصیغ آن برین فهج با تای قرشت اشتقاق می یابد سوقلاماق و سوقلاما قیلیغ بسکون ضمن و فتح لام با الف کشیده و نون مجهول

فرو بردن سوقلادوق فرو بردیم سوقلادی و سوقلادور فرو می برد و سوقلاب بمعنی فاعل و مصدر هم می آید سوقلاغان و سوقلاغان

سوقلادورغان فرو برنده و فرو برده و بمعنی مصدر هم می آیند سوقلا و سوقلاغیل مفرد مخاطب فعل امر سوقلاما و سوقلاماغیل مفرد مخاطب

از نهی سوقلانک و سوقلانکیز و سوقلانکلار جمع مخاطب فعل امر سوقلامانک و سوقلامانکیز و سوقلامانکلار جمع مخاطب فعل نهی سوقلامان

سوقلاماس فرو نمیبرم سوقلامین و سوقلایمین و سوقلادورمین و سوقلایورمن فرو می برم سوقلاماس فرو نمیبرد و بمعنی فاعل و مصدر نفی

هم می آید سوقلاب و سوقلابان و سوقلامیش فرو برده چنانکه در سکندری در تعقل دلرا گوید الشاهد علی الثانی شعر بیر سوقلاب

کرده کاجی غنیمتی توکوب برکالامن آتینک بیلمی سوقلاتیشالمدی فروبرده سوقلاتیبولدی بوقلا فروتوان برد سوقلای آلقای فروتواند برد
سوقلایبو سوقلای بوقلای فروبرده فروبرده و بدون تکرار هم مستعملست سوقلایج سوقلاین فروبرم وببرید ببرده سوقلاتماین
سوقلاتمای بیز سوقلایبدو سوقلا لینک فروبریم سوقلاتملی برای فروبردن وتا فروبرده سوقلاماج چون فروبرد و بمجرد
فروبردن سوقلاتقوچی فروبرنده سوقلاتقوچیو سوقلاتقوچیغو سوقلاماغجه تا فروبردن و بمقدار فروبردن سوقلاتقوسیز بدون فروخواهیم برد
سوقلاتقو نکوزبد فروخواهید برد سوقلاتقوسیلار بدو فروخواهند برد سوقلاتقولوق فروبردنی سوقلاتمای فروبرد سوقلاتسلو سوقلاتسون و
سوقلادیلر فروبرد سوقلاتقودیلر سوقلار دیلر فروبردند وهمچنانکه فوبرد سوقورتاق سوقورتا قیلیغ بضم قاف وسکون راء مهمله چیزرا
از چیزی بیرون کشیدن و در آوردن مثل تیغ از غلاف وپیکان از زخم وموازینهاست وامثال آن سوقوردی در آورد من لغة بعنون شعر
یعنی که سوقوردی تیغ نیبالی کونکلی ایرسالدی خاک امنی خاک سوقوردو فرو آورد سوقورور و سوقورادور در آورد و سوقوروب
بمعنی مصدر هم می آید چنانچه در مجالس النفایس در وصف مولانا سیمی گوید که سکسفر مقیدان سیقاجی کولکا سیدا ایاغیدین تیکان
سوقور صرفه مشغول ایکاند سوقوران سوقوروغان و سوقورادوغان در آورنده و در آورد و بمعنی مصدر هم می آید سوقور سوقورغیل
مفرد غایب از فعل امر سوقورما و سوقورماغیل مفرد غایب از فعل نهی سوقورونک و سوقورونکوز و سوقورونکلار جمع غایب از فعل امر سوقورمانک و سوقور
مانکلار جمع غایب از فعل نهی سوقوران سوقورناس مین در نمی آیم سوقورامین و سوقوروین سوقورادورمین سوقوردیم در آوردم سوقورماس
در نیاورد و بمعنی فاعل و مصدر منفی هم می آید سوقوروب و سوقوروبان و سوقوریش در آورده سوقوریشانک در آورده سوقوریبولغای و
سوقوروب بولغه توان در آورد سوقورا آلغه تواند در آورد سوقورا سوقورا در آورده در آورده و بدون تکرار هم مستعملست سوقوراین
سوقورین در آرم و در آرید در آرید و در آورده سوقورتا و سوقورغاینو سوقورغاینز و سوقورغایدو سوقورغای لینک در آریم سوقورغالی برای در آوردن
و تا در آورده سوقورغاج چون در آورد و بمجرد در آوردن سوقورغوچی در آرنده سوقورغوچیو سوقورغوچیغو سوقورغلیقتا در آوردن و بمقدار
در آوردن سوقورغوسیز دور در خواهیم آورد سوقورغو نکوز دور در خواهید آورد سوقورغوسیلار دور در خواهند آورد سوقورغولوق در آوردنی
سوقورغایدو سوقورلاری سوقورسالار و سوقورسولار و سوقوردیلر برکشید الشاهد علی الثالث شعر تیغ قادا بیرلی لینکا ام زیباسین
آندین بو طمع ابن هجران سیله بیر سوقورسا الاینتیم سوقورغویدیک سوقوروردیلر در آوردن و همچنانکه در آوردنی سوغورتماق و سوغورتما قیلیغ
بسکون غین وشین معجمه وضم راء مهمله بیچکی تیغ کشیدن و در آوردن تیغ وامثال آن سوغورشتیلار در آوردند چنانچه در تاریخ بابری مذکور
که اوجینه چقماق دچون امر وشتی لار وبر بریکا قیلیچ سوغوروشتیلار و باب صیغ بر پیغ اشتقاق بی باید سیوزد لماغ و سوزولما قیلیغ مع الکاف
کشیده شدن و در آورده شدن سوغولغان و سوغولورغان کشیده شونده سوغولالالینک کشیده شونده و کشیده شده و بمعنی مصدر هم می آید چنانچه شاهد
اول در کلیله دمنه مذکورست که غالیکیم آتینک [illegible] بومحل [illegible] سوغولغانی بخشی [illegible] وصیغ آن با الام اشتقاق می باید
سوقان پناه بود که آنرا بعربی [illegible] گویند سوقاقلیغ نام محلیست در خلیج قلعه تفلیس گرجستان و معنی ترکی آن [illegible] تان ناشه سو علی
بسکون غین وکسر لام ترکیبی [illegible] کتاب بود سوغوت نوعی از [illegible] کوهی باشد که از [illegible] گویند سوغولکان بضم غین وسکون لام و
نون وفتح جیم کم [illegible] وباریک که در جاهای نمناک وکنار آبهای اندک بهم رسد واز آن [illegible] خوانند مع الفاء فی المثقال سوقماق
سوقما قیلیغ به [illegible] اول فروکردن [illegible] گویند [illegible] سوقماق
راهنمای [illegible] منشعب شود چنانچه [illegible] سوقتوق فروکرده [illegible] سوقا دود
سیکند [illegible] سوقمان و سوقارغان و سوقاد وغا فروکننده و فروکرده [illegible]

سوق و سوقغیل مفرد غایب از فعل امر سوقما و سوقماغیل مفرد غایب از فعل نهی سوقونک و سوقونکوز و سوقونکلار جمع غایب
از فعل امر سوقمانک و سوقمانکیز و سوقمانکلار جمع غایب از فعل نهی سوقار و سوقارمین فرو میکنم و میکوبم سوقامین و سوقامین
سوقادورمین و سوقادورام فرو میکنم و میکوبم سوقماس فرو نمیکند و نمیکوبد و بمعنی فاعل و مصدر منفی هم می آید سوقوب و سوقوبان و سوقیش
فرو کرده و کوبیده سوقیشانک فرو کرده و کوبیده سوقیبولغای و سوقیب بولغای فرو توان کرد و توان کوبید سوقا آلغای فرو تواند
کرد و تواند کوبید سوقا سوقا فرو کنان و کوبیده کوبیده و بدون تکرار هم مستعملست سوقای و سوقاین فرو کنم و کنید و بکوبم و
بکوبید و بکوبند سوقاق و سوقغای [illegible] سوقغایلینک فرو کنیم و بکوبیم سوقغالی برای فرو کردن و تا فرو کرده
کوبیدن و تا کوبیدن سوقغاچ چون فرو کرد و [illegible] سوقغوچی فرو کننده و کوبنده
سوقغوچیو سوقغاچه تا فرو کردن و بمقدار فرو کردن و تا کوبیدن و بمقدار کوبیدن سوقغوسیز دور فرو خواهیم کرد و خواهیم کوبید سوقغونکوز دور
فرو خواهید کرد و خواهید کوبید سوقغوسیلار دور فرو خواهند کرد و خواهند کوبید سوقغولوق فرو کردنی و کوبیدنی سوقغای و سوقتا و سوقتا
و سوقتو و سوقتو دیلر فرو کردند و کوبیدند الشاهد علی الاول بالمعنی الاول شعر شایداول لیغولو باش کلبنکا سوقغای بیرکچه
ای نوایی منتظر بولماده وسالمغز بیت سوقوبیدیک سوقارتیلار فروکردند و همچنانکه فرو کرد و کوبید الشاهد علی
شعر یار ایکا کلبه اغرانیمه کیرمامین تانکلا ایمایش کیم بانش سوقوبتیلار باش بوبوزوق کاشانه سوقولماق و سوقولما قیلیغ بضم قاف
وسکون لام دو معنی دارد اول فروشدن و کوبیده شدن سوقولوب و سوقولوبان و سوقولمیش فروشده و کوبیده شده چنانچه در
سکندرنامه گوید الشاهد علی الاول بالمعنی الاول شعر ای سوقولوب سکنه عدل آتینکا خطبه دولتنا و قولوب ایشنکا و باقی صیغ بر سیاق
بضم قاف والحاق لام اشتقاق می باید سوقوشماق و سوقوشما قیلیغ مع الشین بیکدیگر فرو بردن و بیکدیگر کوبیدن و صیغ آن با شین اشتقاق
می باید سوقرانماق بسکون قاف وضم راء مهمله بستر کردن رو بر آن جهت فرو بردن بجهت بخن کشتن ولند لند کردن من الجواهر سوقمه
برمزن براق دو معنی دارد اول نوعی از جنس آهو ست اما از آهو بزرگتر که شاخ آن را دسته کارد می سازند و بعضی ماده را گفته است دوم کوچه
تنک را مانند سوقتور بسکون قاف وراء مهمله وضم صاد مهمله نوعی از پرندگان باشد و آنرا سونرم خوانند سوقتو بسکون قاف واو دو ضم
ثاء وهاون چوبین بزرگ را مانند سوقماغ و سوقماق راه باریک بود که از راههای بزرگ منشعب شود و آبادی رسد چنانچه در خسرو
شیرین در وصف طلسم شعر گوید شعر یوله بیر سوقماق ایکی ایرمخلوق آتینک مرزاری آنداقیکیم کماده و نیز نهریست از ملطام اهرین گوید
شعر با سیب مخلص بولین نو فراغی آتینک جیب هر نیله بهینک سوقماغی آتینک و نیز بمعنی فرو کرده و کوبیده باشد چنانچه در [illegible]
گذشت سوقود بضم قاف وسکون زای مهمله جای بود که آب آن خشک شده باشد و مجازا بمعنی کم استعمال می شود و لکن
گویند که آب حدیقه او بطرفه رحشمش بعجان افتاده باشد دوم چاه خشک را مانند و نافع خشک شده اسب و دواب بعلوقه تا تواند گویند
سوقوش بمعنی مطالعه و حربه هم فرو بردن باشد سوکوندین راهم گویند سوقوم دواب که برای اکل آن را ذبح کنند مع الکاف من المشتقات
سوکمک و سوکما کلیک دو معنی دارد اول بمعنی شکافتن باشد دوم بمعنی دشنام دادن چنانچه گوید الشاهد علی الاول شعر ای سلطان
دیب سوزبیاق تمنا سیز قیلادی مین که سوکماک ایلتی بینان لب کویا سیدین و بمعنی لب یا کاف عجمی هم استعمال می شود سوکی شکاف
و دشنام داد چنانچه در سبعه سیاره در داستان جیم گوید بالمعنی الثانی شعر آغزیغه هر بی کیلکاین سوکی بیرکیشی بیر قیچلیغ بغاج
توکمی سوکار و سوکادور سیشکافد و دشنام میدهد الشاهد علی الاول بالمعنی الاول شعر بولوب آغزینی آی مهری کوبا سکاد
تیدین یوق اشکنی بو یمای توکلر و سوکماک بمعنی فاعل و مصدر هم می آید سوکان و سوکا دوکان شکافنده و دشنام دهنده

ودشنام داده و بمعنی مصدر هم می آید سوکله و سوکلکیل مفرد غائب امر نفی الحاضر سوکا و سوکا کیل مفرد غائب امر نفی غائب
سوکنلر و سوکنکز و سوکنکلار جمع غائب امر نفی الحاضر سوکانکز و سوکانکز سوکانکلار جمع غائب امر نفی غائب سوکان و سوکارمین نمیشکنم
ودشنام نمیدهم سوکامین و سوکارمین و سوکاده مین و سوکادام میشکنم و دشنام میدهم سوکامس نمیشکند و دشنام نمیدهد
و بمعنی حال و مصدر منفی هم می آید سوکوبه سوکوبان سوکیش شکافته و دشنام داده سوکیشانک شکافتنی و دشنام داده
سوکنابولغای سوکوب بولغای توان شکافت و دشنام توان داد سوکا آلغای تواند شکافت و دشنام تواند داد سوکا سوکا
شکافته شکافته و دشنام داده داده و بدون تکرار هم مستعملست سوکای سوکامین بشکافم و بشکافند و بشکافی شکافته
ودشنام بدهم و بدهد و بدهی و داده سوکنالک و سوککانزر سوککانیزر سوکالی سوکالینک [illegible] سوککالی
برای شکافتن و تا شکافته برای دشنام داد و تا دشنام داده سوککاج چون شکافت و شکافند [illegible] دشنام دهد
و بمجرد دادن سوککوجی شکافنده و دشنام دهنده سوککوچه و سوککوچه و سوککانچه تا شکافتن و بمجرد شکافتن و تا دشنام
و بمجرد دشنام دادن سوککوسیزدور نخواهیم شکافت و دشنام خواهیم داد سوککونکوزدور نخواهید شکافت و دشنام خواهید داد
سوککوسیلاردور نخواهند شکافت و دشنام خواهند داد سوککولوک شکافتنی و دشنام دادنی سوککای سوکاقو و سوکنا و سوکون
سوکدیلت بشکافد و دشنام بدهد سوکاکاج سوکاناقو کاسون سوکادیلت شکافد و دشنام دهد چنانکه مولانا [illegible]
ازجهت الابرار و ماکوید بالمعنی الاول شعر رازلیین تیککان ایسن سوکانا [illegible] کونکلیدا ایرمز توکانا سوکودیلت
سوکاردیلت شکافتنی و چنانکه بشکافد و دشنام دادن و چنانکه دشنام دهد سوکولمالک و سوکولماکلیک مع الالف شکافته
ودشنام داده شدن سوکولکان و سوکولمرکان سوکولکانی شکافته شونده و شکافته شده الشاهد علی الاول بالمعنی الثانی شعر
کولار زانی سوکولکان جسم زار [illegible] سیغاداغلیمو [illegible] سوکولکان [illegible] و نیز بمعنی دشنام داده شونده و دشنام داده شده
و بمعنی مصدر هم می آیند و باقی صیغ بر سیاق الام اشتقاق می یابد سوکتورمالک و سوکتورماکلیک بضم تا و سکون رای مهمله مصدر متعدیست
یعنی شکافانیدن وصیغ آن بالفظ تور اشتقاق می یابد سوکوشمالک و سوکوشماکلیک مع الشین بمعنی مقابله است یعنی یکدیگرا دشنام دادن
وصیغ آن باشین اشتقاق می یابد سوکلاماک بسکون کاف عجمی ترکی رومی بمعنی پخته کردن کوشت بود من الجوامد سولت بالکاف عجمی ارزن
که پوست آن را کرفته باشند سوکدانیس بسکون کاف عجمی و سین مهمله و فتح دال مهمله و کسر نون بمعنی نظاره بود یعنی هیچ تماشا کردن
سوکلامیشی نبدون اضطراب رومی آسودگی هم زدن در ظفرنامه در جنگ توقتمش خان گفته که هرچند لشکر دشمن حملهای پیاپی کردند اما
که فرود آمده سوکلامیشی کرده بودند از جای نجنبیدند سوکسولت بضم و سین و سکون واو و کاف عجمی بضم وجیست که در
براک روید و چون خشک شود در پیشهای آن مرغان از خاک برآمده در هوا پرند چنانکه در لیلی مجنون گوید شعر
عشاقتی که بولدی توفراق هجران کورونوب سوکناکلاری آق شوکوله کوکم چو بولدی بوده یا نفای پانزی اسه دوه نوده آوز
او خار هم مانند و بعربی عضا کویند و ترکی رومی زقلر دیرت نام خارد باشد و نیز اسبی را کویند که اندام اشه باشد سوکل بفتح کاف
بمعنی خسته و بیمار باشد و نیز کور را کویند که از عضوی معیوب بود و بفارسی نیز دیت که بسبب آنچه در کشته را افتند معانی اشتین بیک کر
نزدیکت سوکلیت بیماری سوکلمه بسکون کاف عجمی و فتح لام و میم ترکی رومی کوشت نیمه پخته بود سوکو بضم کاف ترکی رومی نیز بود سوکو
شاخهای کوچک است که تراشیده سیخچه کرده بالای آتش کباب کنند سوکود بضم کاف عجمی و سکون دال مهمله نام درخت بیدست سوکوش بمعنی
دشنام باشد و در بعضی نسخ بمعنی ناسزا هم مانند سوکونج بضم کاف عجمی و سکون نون و جیم دشنام را کویند الشاهد علیه شعر اکو سیچ

اولکی

اولوکوی بتر که نهر ایری من نطق ایر بیرکه سوکونج تیله لولولمتیر [illegible] مع الکاف من المشتقات سولماق و سولماقلیق بسکون لام عجمی
افسرده شدن باشد سولدوق افسرده شدیم سولمز سولادور افسرده شود سولور بمعنی حال و مستقبل هم می آید سولغان و سولانغان
سولادورغان افسرده شونده و افسرده شده و بمعنی مصدر هم می آید سول و سولغیل مفرد غائب امر الحاضر سولسون و سولسون جمع غائب امر سولکای سولسید
سولما و سولماغیل مفرد غائب امر نفی الحاضر سولونلار و سولونکز و سولونکلار جمع غائب امر نفی الحاضر سولمانکز و سولمانکلار جمع غائب
امر نفی غائب سولمان و سولمارمین افسرده نمیشوم سولامین و سولارمین و سولادرمین و سولادورمین افسرده میشوم سولماس افسرده نمیشود
و بمعنی حال و مصدر منفی هم می آید سولوبه سولوبان و سولمیش افسرده شده الشاهد علی الاول شعر کلابغا نه واکی کل کبی سولوب جشوقید
کلابکی تر نینک اوردنا سیدا اشتناه سولیشانک افسرده شدنی سولنا بولغای سولوب بولغای افسرده توان شد سولا آلغای افسرده
توان شد سولا سولا افسرده افسرده و بدون تکرار هم مستعملست سولای و سولامین افسرده شوم و شود و شوی و شده سولنای و سولمایین
افسرده شوم و شود و شوی و شده الشاهد علی الاول بالمعنی الاخیر شعر بیک ایوریلی اوزکل سولمای توکلار جیش خزان سیلغا
کونکلونکنی ای بلبل حجاز کلزار عنیه سولناق و سولغالیر و سولغای بزم سولالی و سولالینک افسرده شویم سولغالی برای افسرده شدن و تا
شده سولغاج چون افسرده شد و بمجرد شدن سولغوجی افسرده شونده سولغوچه و سولغوچه و سولغانچه تا افسرده شدن و بمجرد افسرده
سولغوسیزدور افسرده نخواهیم شد سولغونکوزدور افسرده نخواهید شد سولغوسیلاردور افسرده نخواهند شد سولغولوق افسرده شدنی
سولغاج سولاقو و سولناقو سولون و سولادیلت افسرده شود سولماغاج سولمالمقو سولمایالمقو سولمادیلت افسرده نشود الشاهد علی الثانی شعر
شیخ پلاسی بوز چابر نالا هندیم و نلت [illegible] سیله اوتلاردین کراک برلیغ امیدینک سولمانامسولغودیک سولودیلت افسرده شدنی
افسرده شود سولدرماق و سولدرماقلیق مصدر متعدیست یعنی افسرده کردن و صیغ آن با لفظ در اشتقاق می یابد سولاماق آشامیدن
و صیغ آن بدستور شولتیی اشتقاق می یابد سولماق و سولماقلیق و سولوماق بمنابح ترکی رومی بمعنی نفس کشیدن و از برای آسایش نفس
مکث کردن من الجوامد سول جانب چپ را کویند چنانکه در شاهنامه کوید شعر سنان اونک قولیدا ایچکیم سنون سول
ایکندا آقالقان کیلیب لعلکون ملت کرمین ایستانوا دیکه کمشان الحاسین تیب نامه معلوم یاس سول قولیدین دیوا اونک میز ارات از
افسرده شدن چنانکه کذشت سولاق ترکی رومی بمعنی بود که دست چپ کار کرده باشد و نیز نام طعمه ایست از ولایت روس که در حسن
قلعه در بند واقع شده میان الجدیدها الکائیران و هرات سولپوت بسکون لام و کاف و ضم باء عجمی سولجوق بسکون لام و واو و فتح جیم ترکی
رومی بمعنی افسرده باشد سولدوز بسکون لام و زای معجمه و ضم دال مهمله نام طایفه ایست از اتراک سلطان بهرک لفظیست مرکبه ترکی
ترکی ترکی رومی کل جیبان اغری باشد سولغون بسکون لام و نون و ضم غین معجمه بمعنی افسرده سولکون بسکون لام و نون و ضم کاف عجمی
تذرو را کویند و آنرا رومیه سولیلوز نامند سولوتقان بضم لام و سکون تای قرشت و نون و فتح غین معجمه ترکی رومی ملت بمعنی النفس بود سولو
بضم لام و سکون قاف سه معنی دارد اول دهنه اسب را کویند دویم چیز آبدار را کویند چنانکه در تاریخ الانبیا در ذکر حضرت سلیمان علیه
و باران طلبیدن قوم کوید که بوطبع سیله کیم قرابولوت سولوق بولور اول بولوتی تیلادیلار ییم ترکی رومی کویند که سولوق آلیم یعنی نفس بکشم
ودم زدنم سولوق بسکون کاف ترکیم سیاهیست که در آنجا بم میرسد که خون میمکد و آنرا بعضی زلو و دیوچه و بعربی علق کویند سونکان
بفتح کاف عجمی و سکون نون ترکی رومی مرغ باشد و آنرا زنک سرخیست که نقاشان بکار برند مع میم من المشتقات سومورماق و سومورماقلیق بضم
و سکون رای مهمله مکیدن نوشیدن و آنرا بعربی مص کویند الشاهد علیه شعر بو فصل ایچرا ملاحت تاشیدین سلطان ایلاغای که
جکاکای سومورماکلایوز بکا جام قالقانین سومورد [illegible] نوشیدیم سومورمو سومورادور میشوند سومورمین بمعنی حال و مصدر هم می آید

سوم

246v

سوسوکانی سومرکانی سومرادوکان نوشنده ونوشیده ومعنی مصدر هم وآیند سومرم سومرکید مفرد غائب المستقبل الی سومریم

سومرنکید مفرد غائب المستقبل الی سومرونک وسومرنکوز سومرنکلار جمع غائب المستقبل الی سومرسنانك وسومرنکیز وسومرنکلار جمع غائب

المستقبل سومرمان وسومرامین منوشم سومرابین وسومرسین وسومرامین وسومرام منوشم سومرنام وسومرکامین وسومرکامین

نوشم الشاهد على الثالث شعر ایله جهران تیلاهین تیلاهین نیچه ملالا قلمی قیق کیم نهت جلیس تولا تو قنالك سومرکامین آنی سومرناس

منوشید ومعنی فاعل ومصدر هم می آید سومرونبه سومرونان وسومرمیش نوشیده سومرسنانك نوشیده سومرسنا بولغای

سومرب بولغه توان نوشید سومرا آلغای تواند نوشید سومرا سومرا نوشان نوشان وبدون تکرار هم مستعملست سومرای

سومرامین بنوشم وبنوشد وبنوشی ونوشیده سومرسنانك سومرکانیزم سومرکانیزم وسومرکای وسومرالیلی بنوشیم سومرکالی برای نوشیدن وتا

نوشیدن سومرکاج چون نوشید ونوشد ومحض نوشیدن سومرکوچی نوشنده سومرکوجه سومرکوبه وسومرکاغه تا نوشیدن

وبمعنی نوشیدن سومرکوبیزدو نخواهیم نوشید سومرکونکوزدور خواهید نوشید سومرکوسیلادردو نخواهند نوشید سومرکوالك

نوشیدنی سومرکای سومرام سومرام سومرنا وسومرسون وسومرمیك نوشد سومرکودیك وسومرمیك نوشیدنی وچنانکه نوشد

سومرکوسنانك بسکون میم وراء مهمله وضم کاف آبی که بخاك کردن که آنرا بعربی امتغاط کویند چون اشتقاق آن منتج نباشد نیست بلکه مضاهی اکتفا

میشود وصیغ آن موافق شد ولا اشتقاق نمی یابد من الجوامد سوموك بسکون میم وکاف وضم میم وسین مهمله بترکی تنخواه کویند که هرجا

مظنه اکل بود آنجا خانه شود سومکورولك بسکون میم وکاف ثانی وضم کاف اول وراء مهمله و سوموك بضم میم وسکون کاف آبی بهم بوده

آنرا بعربی ظلا کویند سوموه سوموتیرکی هویج یعنی پهوپه چنانکه کویند سوموه سوموه سوموك بیلك پنهان آشفته وبهوده سخن نیز

مع النون من المشتقات سوناماق بضم نا قلنغ بسکون نون وقاف ولازم ومتعدی هردو آمده هم بمعنی دراز شدن وهم بمعنی دراز کردن استعمال میشود اکنا

على الاول بالمعنى الثانى شعر ایستاسا نانك تیلیم چهقلرقیل تیغ اصالا یکیم نو بنانك سوچین بو یون سوتامادا خود تقصیر ایاشسونما

سونالیك بمعنی خاموش شدن آمده باشد سوندی دراز شد ودراز کرد وخاموش شد چنانکه در سفینه سیاره در داستان اول کوید المعنی

الاول شعر سوندی تو فراغ امنوتن نزاری باشغه چیکتی پلاه اولنبارینی سوندوق دراز شدیم ودراز کردیم سوندولك خاموش شدیم

سونار سونار دور دراز میشود ودراز میکند وخاموش میشود وسونار بمعنی فاعل ومصدر هم می آید سونغان سونارغان وسونادورغان درازشونده

ودرازشده ودرازکننده ودرازکرده چنانکه در لسان الطیر بمعنی دراز کرده کوید شعر لیك عثمان کیم کلاجی اول ملتفت شمع اولتوربیب سونغان

ایاتین تیلدی جمع وبمعنی مصدر هم می آید سونکان وسوناکان وسونادوکان خاموش شونده وخاموش شده وبمعنی مصدر هم می آید سون

امرست از دراز شده ودراز کردن وخاموش شدن چنانکه بمعنی اولی کوید شعر ای نوائی قول سراچه بیك بو یونی وجغالی تیلمانا باری

سلاجی بوبیغه ایلکینکونی سونما نهی است از هر سه معنی سونغیل امرست از دراز شدن ودراز کردن سونکیل امرست از خاموش شدن

سونماغیل نهی است از دراز شدن وکردن سونماکیل نهی است از خاموش شدن سونونك وسونونکوز وسونونکلار جمع غائب المستقبل از هر دو معنی

سونمانك سونمانکیز وسونمانکلار جمع غائب المستقبل هر دو معنی سونامن سونامین درازشوم ودراز کنم وخاموش شوم سونامیز وسونامیز

سونادورمیز سونارام دراز شوم وکنم وخاموش شوم سوناس دراز نشود ونکند وخاموش نشود وبمعنی فاعل ومصدر نفی هم می آید

سونوب وسونوبان وسونمیش درازشده ودراز کرده وخاموش شده سونمیشانك دراز شده ودراز کرده وخاموش شده سونا بولغای سونا

دراز توان شد وتوان کرد وخاموش توان شد سونا آلغای دراز تواند شد وتواند کرد وخاموش تواند شد سونا سونا دراز شده شده

ودراز کنان وخاموش شده شده وبدون تکرار هم مستعملست سونای وسونایین دراز شوم وشود وشوی وشده ودراز کنم وکند وکنی وکرده

247r

وخاموش شوم وشود وشوی وشده سونساق وسونسانیز وسونسانکیز وسونکلاینیز سونتانك وسونکایبینیز دراز شویم وکنیم سونتا

سونالینك دراز شویم ودراز کنیم وخاموش شویم سونغالی برای دراز شدن وتا دراز شدن وبرای دراز کردن وتا دراز کردن سونکالی برای

خاموش شدن وتا خاموش شدن سونغاج برای دراز شدن وتا دراز شدن وبرای دراز کردن وتا دراز کردن وبمعنی دراز کردن چنانکه در مثل شمس

از حیرت الابرار در باب حیای نوشیروان کوید المعنى الاخير شعر سونغلیچ الیکینی ایزو ترنی تیلاب تیغ کمینه بیچه ترکین سالغای سونغاج

چون خاموش شد وشود ومحض خاموش شدن سونکوچی دراز شونده ودراز کننده سونکوچی خاموش شونده سونغوچه وسونغوچه

سونغانچه تا دراز شدن وبمعنی دراز شدن وتا دراز کردن وبمعنی دراز کردن سونکانچه وسونکانچه وسونکانچه تا خاموش شدن وبمعنی خاموش

شدن سونغوسیز دور دراز نخواهیم شد ونخواهیم کرد سونغوسیزدور خواهیم شد ونخواهیم خاموش شد سونغوسیز دور دراز نخواهید شد ونخواهید کرد سونغوسیز

خاموش نخواهید شد سونغوسیلاردور دراز نخواهند شد ونخواهند کرد سونکوسیلاردور خاموش نخواهند شد سونغولوق درازشدنی

ودراز کردنی سونکولوك خاموش شدنی سونغای دراز شود ودراز کند المعنی الثانی شعر تلغ اولکیم کنونوم کیکای جمال العالم آرای

کوز یمنی سونغایاق تیلنا م هوس سونغای که پایین سونکای خاموش شود چنانکه در خمسه بدیع کلاله فرهاد با خسرو هر خاك اکنا

کوید شعر غزم اینچاچ بیدین سونکای برین شیراقتم ستیزانی ارکانکای برین سوناقی سوناقی وسوناتینك وسونادیك دراز شود وکند سونقاغ

شود سونکودیك دراز شده ودراز کرده وچنانکه دراز شود وکند سونکودیك خاموش شده وچنانکه خاموش شود سونا بوعلت

مرادف سونکودیك وسونکودیك باشد سونده وسونادیك کلیك مصدر متعدیست بمعنی خاموش کردن آتش سونده وسوندیلاق

خاموش میکند الشاهد على الاول شعر غنچه صلیم آچلمیم فراقیم سوندوم هر نیجی کیم کلمه کالی ملایم سلوچین سوندورماك

سوندورکالیس وسوندورکاین خاموش کنی الشاهد على الثانى شعر اشك لیله کونکلم اوتی وچارن تیغ توت سانیایم بو سبباله مکوالونلیك

سوندورکالیش سوندورکوچی خاموش کننده چنانکه در لسان الطیر در مجموعه القلوب در ذکر کملع کوید که هر ملوی کوده غنچه سوندورکوچی

ونا فی صیغ برین سابقا اشتقاق می یابد من الجوامد سونقور دو معنی دارد اول پرنده ایست شکاری از جنس چرغ که آنرا شنقار نیز کویند چنانچه

خسرو شیرین کوید شعر نیکاخودچیقا سون سونقور جهلدین کوروب شوکت صدا چون اکیا ندین دویم تا ناریه ولکرتیر کوزه نابینا کرسند

که آنرا خصاییه سونقور نامند وظالع هرویچ آنرا سنقور بفتح سین ضبط کرده ونوشته که جانوریست شبیه بموش که پوست آنرا چون بر عضو مفلوج

بندند نفع دهد سهو کرده سونکاك بسکون نون وکاف ثانی وفتح کاف عجمی ولام مع الامالة بمعنی استخوان بود چنانکه کوید شعر ای تن خاك

خدنکنکا نشان بولغان کیمنا لاشم بو معنی قوروق باشیم کیمنا لدا وضرب سونکاك سونك بسکون نون وکاف عجمی بمعنی در صحبت وبعد ازان

چنانکه کوید شعر عشق کیلتمرنیا ایشیم دین منالغ میدا اونك خانقه بکوموسل اداماین آندین سونك وبالمجاز بمعنی اخر نیز استعمال شود چنانکه

در بهر نامطبوع کوید شعر اوتلا ملیکیدا بر سفینه لیکن بوخسته اشعار یدین حلی سونك ایلیکیدا شیشه ایچره یی لیکن اصرعی لعلی دیك

مرادف سونکرا بسکون نون وکاف وفتح طاء مهمله بعد وعقب الشاهد علیه شعر اولکاینمدین سونکرا کیلدی هم طلبیدی عیادقا ویغو

که کیم باشیغه سمیش قو یلش اویغا غادیم سونکونی یعنی آخرین چنانکه کوید شعر ومدمقبلدینك هم غنام قتل چپدو امیلما دینك

میل وغلو مدنکه یا خود بویراغی یلسونکراغی سونکو بسکون نون وراء مهمله وفتح کاف عجمی جرمیست متخلخل شبیه بنمد کم خورده کرحون

آب کلارند آبرا بخود کشد وآنرا بعربی اسفنج ابجو وبفارسی ابرکمن کویند سونکمی مرادف سونکراغی بود یعنی آخرین سونکمی اد نیتو کنایه از

خواب مرده باشد الشاهد علیه شعر نوا یسا او توبان عمر غفلتا بچرا دیریغ که سونکمی او یقوغه کونرسیل ایتار دا او یغاندیر سونکو بسکون

وضم کاف عجمی نیز بود ما را از اتراك رعم سو کو نامند سونکوبه بسکون هر دو نون وکاف ثانی وضم کاف اول یعنی لرزشت و نوائی علیه الرحمه

دهمه محکمه‌ای از زبان نادران کند خطاب با سخنهء دوتا و سونکونجه بحذف کاف خطاب مذکور ساخته هما نا ماناتی از بهوالنسم
بود و هو هذا شعر که نا تم توتوب تین ایتا الماتیم بیرب لجان سونکونجه سیا الماتیم یعنی تام کرفته شین نتوانستم کرد و جان داده
از جست نتوانستم رسید سونکونجه یعنی الخواموش شدن و بقدر خواموش شدن باشد سونکی یعنی آخر چنانچه در مرثیه سید حسن گوید
هرکز اتیکا یموا ایدیم دولت وصلینکی طمع سپلنام ایدی که سونکا اینده فرقت بولغای وبیر در مقال المستم از حیرت الابرار گوید شعر
تون سپله تا صبح موافق دمه صبح اولکاذب سونکی صادق دمه صبح سونکچه بکون نون مع الاماله و کبکاف عجمی و فتح جیم سونکجه
بکون هر دو نون و کسر کاف یعنی از عقب الشاهد علی الاول شعر اینکی بنجه سمند نیک سونکچه پویه ایلای تاکها اوتنا تک باقیان سونکی
اونکونجه توراری الشاهد علی الثانی شعر تا بو طرف که قویاش نینکیغ اولغای کار بار ویرا سونکیجه منا یه شل لیت بو خاکسار بارود
سونه بفتح نون دو معنی دارد اول المرده نول کویند و ثانیا مصابو چیز نامند دویم معنی طلا باشد که آنرا آلتون هم خوانند مع الواو
از المشتقات سوواماق سوواماق بفتح واو با الف کشیده بمعنی ذوق کردن باشد چنانچه در مقاله نوزدهم از حیرت الابرار نظم یافته
ملککت گوید شعر اوی سوواماق نینک کوچ هم تملادی لبکه بوا ثر نلفوجه هم تملادی سووادوق اندوه کیم حادث سوواید
اندوه میکند الشاهد علی الاول شعر بو کیم اندیشه و غم یا مضری یخانه دین لوتماس سوولکی یا که پردیر تامی اضده کوپلاین ...
بمعنی فاعل و مصدر هم می آید سوغان سوولغان و سووایدوغان اندوه کننده و اندوه کرده و بمعنی مصدر هم می آید سوواو سوو
مفرد غائب ماضی نقل انتها سوواما و سووامالیغ مفرد غائب ماضی نقل نفی سوواتکی سووایکر سووانکلار جمع غائب ماضی نقل انتها الشاهد علی
الاول شعر سووانکا ولای اوی نیک تا بینی با الجنیغ یا ساتبان سکریم منیک او یینی هجر که توبراغ ایتا دی سوواماتک سووانکار سوو
جمع غائب ماضی نقل نفی سووامام سوواماس مین اندوه میکنم سووای بن سوواس بن سووای ایدیم سووادام اندوه نمیکنم سوواماس
اندوه میکنم سوواماس اندوه نمیکند و بمعنی فاعل و مصدر نفی هم می آید سوواب سووابان سووایش اندوه کرده سووایماس اندوه
کرده سووابیری سوواب تورین اندوه کرده ام الشاهد علی الاول شعر ایماس کو کسوما ایکی افلاک باب یاب لالالامه کیم سوواب یتانا
چقماغای کونکلوم خولیپدین سووانسا یلغای اندوه توان کرد سووایو سووایو سووای اندوه کمان و بدون تکرار هم مستعملست
سووای اندوه کنم و کند و کنی و کرده سووا ناق سووغایز سووغای سوو تاوه سووا اندوه کنیم سوواغلی برای اندوه کردن
کرده سوواغاچ چون اندوه کرد و کند و بمجرد کردن سوولغوچی اندوه کننده سوولغوچه و سوولغونچه تا اندوه کردن
اندوه کردن سوواغونیزدو اندوه خواهیم کرد سوولغونیزدو اندوه خواهید کرد سوولغوسیلاردو اندوه خواهند کرد سوواغولوق اندوه
کردن سوواغالاری سووا شکالاری سووا سولاری سووادیکلار اندوه کنند الشاهد علی الرابع شعر خیالیمان کو جسیم فدهم سوو وادیکلا
که باشیتن نا ایاغ هجرا و فلاح سیرلع یارا بولدم سوواغودیلک سووارادیلک اندوه کردن و چنانچه اندوه کند سووایماناق
سووایتماق قیلماق مع التاء مصدر متعدیست یعنی اندوه فرمودن و صیغ آن نا لمع قریشت اشتقاقی یابد سووالماق سووالماق قیلماق مع
اللام اندوه شدن سووالغان سووالغان و سووالادوغان اندوه شونده و اندوه شده چنانچه در لیلی مجنون در صفت ابوالدین
مجنون گوید الشاهد علی الاول با لمعنی الثانی شعر توفراغلاری را ایانکی لیا لغان هم بالجنون یوزی سووالغان و بمعنی مصدر هم
می آید چنانچه در صفه سیان گوید الشاهد علی الاول شعر خجریه تا نیبان تو فراغ یا لجنغ الجراهیدی سووالغان جلغ دیتی
صیغ بریجی بالام اشتقاقی یابد سووالماق و سوواریاماق قیلماق بفتح واو و سکون رای مهمله بمعنی سیراب کردن و آنرا سوواریماق هم
چنانچه مذکور شد سووارادوق سیراب کردیم سووارادوق سوواراد و د سیراب میکند و سوواراد و بمعنی فاعل و مصدر هم می آید چنانچه

گوید شعر مینو کیم اینی چقماغای سایریغ کل لالاکه هفتاق تا بینا طلوع آندین سووارادور چاغدا بستانین سووارغان و سووارقان
سوواراد و قان سیراب کننده و سیراب کرده و بمعنی مصدر هم می آید سووارغ سووارغیل مفرد غائب ماضی نقل سووارادلو سووارماغیل
مفرد غائب ماضی نقل نفی سووارماغان سووارینک سووارینکلار جمع غائب ماضی نقل سووارانک سووارانکیز سووارمانکلار جمع غائب ماضی
سووارارمان و سووارماس مین سیراب میکنم سووارامین و سووارارمین سووارادور مین سوواریب تورمین سیراب میکنم سووارایب سوورمیش
سیراب کرده سووارمیشانک سیراب کرده سوواراماس سیراب نمیکند و بمعنی فاعل و مصدر نفی هم می آید سووارماغانی ماقتا سووار
سیراب توان کرد سووارا آلغای سیراب تواند کرد سووارما سیراب کنان و بدون تکرار هم مستعملست سووارادکا سووارا
سیراب کنم و کند و کنی و کرده سووارناق سووارغایز سووارغایمز سووارادی سووارانک سیراب کنیم سووارغلی برای سیراب کردن
و تا سیراب کرده چنانچه بمعنی اول در تاریخ الانبیاء در ذکر موسی علیه السلام گوید که ایل کالاا را سیوا او لنجاه تا شیغه سووارغالی کلیتوردی
سووارغاچ چون سیراب کرد و کند و بمجرد کردن سووارغوچی سیراب کننده سووارغونچه سووارغانچه تا سیراب کردن و بقدر
سیراب کردن سووارغونیزدو سیراب خواهیم کرد سووارغونکوزدو سیراب خواهید کرد سووارغوسیلاردو سیراب خواهند کرد سووارغو
سیراب کردن سووارغلوق سووارلوق سووارلاسوو سووارغو سووارغ یلنیراب کند سووارغودیک سووراب لب سیراب کردنی و چنانچه سیراب کند
سووراماق و سووراماق قیلماق بضم واو و سکون رای مهمله کشیدن و در آوردن لباس از بدن و رسته از لباس اشلاه آن چنانچه گوید الشاهد
علی الاول شعر بیرضا ب دورتیکار حالتدا کو کسوم چاکینی ایب سووراماق کونکلیکیم جیوه تطیلغان چاکدین و مولتین سوورماق
بکسر سین نوشته و سین مکسور ذکر کرده‌اند سهو کرده‌اند سووروردی کشید و در آورد چنانچه در آغاز مثنوی لیلی مجنون گوید
شعر خیالی ایلادی تاریبان بیقلیش حیکرتنی غافت لباسیش یوقیم بولباسنی سووروشی کیم جیمی بن آنی اوتنه امودی سووروردی
در آوردیم سووروردی سووروبان در آورده و بمعنی فاعل و مصدر هم می آید سوورغان سوورغان سووراید ان در آرنده
در آورده الشاهد علی الاول با لمعنی الثانی شعر مرثیه کیم مهلک یا دام آغوتیکی انکاهیم کیم کفن جسیغا غیدین سوورغان تلمز الحسن
و بمعنی مصدر هم می آید چنانچه شاهد برا ولعل آنمعنی در تنبیهات محبوب القلوب در ذکر مقامی حلیم گوید کرا کنش ایرسالا ایچو کورسا
سووروغاندین سونک یورینکا ازبیلکه حولاس سووروغ سووروغیل مفرد غائب ماضی نقل سووروماغیل مفرد غائب ماضی نقل نفی
سووروپدور سووروپکنو سوورونکار جمع غائب ماضی نقل سوورونکیزلار جمع غائب ماضی نقل سوورودان سوورونکیز
آرم سووروامین و سوورورمین سووراد و ریبین سوورولم در می آرم سوورماس در نمی آرد و بمعنی فاعل و مصدر نفی هم می آید سوورو
سووروب و سووروپیش در آورده سوورشانک در آورده سووروباتورینه و سوورییب توبعاو توان آورد سوورا آلغای در توانند
آورد سووروا سوورا در آورد در آورده و بدون تکرار هم مستعملست سووراد سوورارین در آرم و در آری و در آرد و در آورد
سووروناق سووروغایز سوورغایمز سووراتی سووراتکیز در آریم سووروغلی برای در آوردن و تا در آورد سووروغاچ چون در آورد
و در آرد و بمجرد در آوردن سووروغوچی در آرنده سووروغونچه سووروغانچه تا در آوردن و بقدر در آوردن سووروغونیزدو خواهیم
در آورد سووروغونکوزدو خواهید در آورد سووروغوسیلاردو خواهند در آورد سوورغولوق در آوردن سوورغای سووراشوند
سوورورون سوورور دیلک در آرد سووروغودیک سووروریدیک در آوردن و چنانچه در آرد سووروناق و سووردیماق قیلماق
بضم واو و رای مهمله و سکون لام کشیده شدن و در آورده شدن و صیغ آن بر سیاق با الام اشتقاق می یابد من الجوامد سو آبرا
گویند و آنمعروفست و بمعنی رواج و رونق و جاه و عزت و آبرو استعمال شود چنانچه گوید شعر بیلیک زولفونک خیالین شرح ایتار من

248v.

سوبوه تشنه ومعیبن لملینكا تالمره ورمره خانیما سوق وفلرجه جوجانب سوطرفی تاشد ومناحب رهان تالع [illegible] بوشنا ومنكر

كرده مولات كوید كه خان ضو ومعنی روشنا ئیست كه عوام از ابحر یف سوكویند سودا فین منهج الآنجر را كه مراد بوبعینو [illegible]

درسكی سكندر ی دوه صید ز اسكندر وتفرج كه محیط كوید سوسوطفین ایله كودی عیان تكر [illegible] كه مانیان سوسیز لیغ

بآبی حتا یا رجو می بتركه رومی حباب روی آب بود سوقو نا د موضعی را كویند كه دو آب بهم [illegible]

میزد خصوصا سوتو یجی جمعی را كویند كه آب [illegible] سووات بفتح واو وسكون تای قرشت موضعی را كویند كه [illegible]

سیراب كنند وآب بر طرف [illegible] سوق وفق بفتح واو [illegible] سوبو سونه بتركه [illegible]

سبز جیت كه در روی آب جمع شود و آنرا [illegible] مع الماء [illegible] بمعنی تسلی وتصبر باشد مع البیان المتعلق

سویمنا ق وسوبما قلیغ مبكون یا بمعنی كندن لباس پوست بود كه [illegible] وسلخ باشد سویدوق كندیم سوبار و سوبادر

میكند وسوبار بمعنی فاعل ومصدر هم می آید سویمان وسوبازمان وسوبادورمان كننده وكندن وبمعنی مصدر هم می آیند سویه سوبیل مفرد

غائب المنفصل [illegible] سوبما [illegible] مفرد غائب المنفصل [illegible] سوبونكلار جمع غائب المنفصل [illegible]

سوبانكلار جمع غائب المنفصل [illegible] سوبمیق سوبمیق [illegible] سوبادورم میكم سوبما س [illegible]

فاعل ومصدر [illegible] كنده سوبمیشانك كنده [illegible] تواند كند سوبا آلقای

تواند كند سوبا سوبیا كنده كنده وبدون تكرار هم مستعملست سوبای سوباین بكنم وبكند [illegible] كنده سوبیا ق وسوبیاین وسوبیغای

سوبلی [illegible] مكنیم سوبیغالی برای كندن وتا كنده سوبیغاج چون كند وبكند [illegible] كندن سوبیقوجی كننده سوبنو تیزرود

خواهیم كند سوبنو [illegible] خواهید كند سوبنو [illegible] خواهند كرد سوبیغولوق كننده سوبیغا [illegible]

بكند چنانكه در حیرت الابرار در وصف مستان كوید الشاهد علی الاول سعر [illegible] ایله كه سوبیغا [illegible]

كفن سوبیغو [illegible] كننده وچنانكه بكند سوبلما ق وسوبلما قلیغ مع الكاف كنده شدن لباس وپوست سوبیغا [illegible]

سوبلادورمان كنده شوند وكنده شدن چنانكه مكنده شدن پوست روی محبوب كوید الشاهد علی الاول المعنی الثانی سعر [illegible]

برك كل [illegible] حسبانیده [illegible] كالبانیدن وبمعنی مصدر هم می آیند وبلفه صیغ برین سایق بالالم اشقاق

می یابد [illegible] سوبدمرما قلیغ دیكر را كندن پوست ولباس او كردن وصیغ آن بدستور بالفظ در اشتقاق می یابد سویلانمات

سویلما كلمك باشباع ضمه لفزیدن ودوكانه شدن تیر را كویند یعنی بدو بیرون رود جسته [illegible] باشباع بمعنی كفتن باشد

سویلادی دوكانه شد وكفت سویلادی سویلایدور دوكانه میشود میكوید سویلادی بمعنی فاعل ومصدر هم می آید سویلكان سویلا [illegible]

سویلا [illegible] دوكانه نشونده وشده وكوینده وكفته وبمعنی مصدر هم می آیند سویلاماس دوكانه نمیشود ونمیكوید وبمعنی فاعل ومصدر منفی

هم می آید سویلامیق سویلاماپن وسویلامین دوكانه شده وكفته الشاهد علی الاول بالمعنی الاول شعر [illegible]

آتسانچ [illegible] وكر خود [illegible] آتسام سویلا [illegible] وله سعر [illegible]

آرام ایستاكای كونكل [illegible] سویلا آلقای دوكانه تواند شد وتواند كفت سویلا یو وسویلامی سویلامی دوكانه شد وكفته

وبدون تكرار هم مستعملست سویلانی وسویلایین دوكانه شود وشده وبكویم وبكوید وبكوبد كفته سویلاكالی برای دوكانه شدن

وتا دوكانه شده وبرای كفتن وتا كفته سویلاكاج چون دوكانه شد وشود وبمحض شدن وچون كفت وبكوید وبمحض كفتن سویلاكوجی

دوكانه شونده وكوینده سویلاكومه سویلاكوبجه وسویلاكانجه تا دوكانه نشدن وبمحض دوكانه شدن وتا كفتن وبمحض كفتن سویلاكوبی دوكانه

249r.

خواهد شد وخواهد كفت سویلانكولوك دوكانه نشدنی وكفتنی سویلاكاج سویلماتا سویلاسون وسویلادیلك دوكانه شود وبكوید

سویلاكودیلك سویلا [illegible] دوكانه شدنی وچنانكه شود وكفتنی وچنانكه كفته شود سویلاتما العصف مع التیمن مكالمه كردن چنانكه

[illegible] كوید امام الروحیه سعر لطف ایله [illegible] اول سوایله سویلاشمكه [illegible] وهم آو كوید امام [illegible]

سعر ایله آغزینك شكر یكم سویلشن [illegible] سنكا كرچه [illegible] برابر لفظ وصیغ آن ما بین اشتقاق می یابد سیورغا

سیورغاما قلیغ بضم یا وسكون رای مهمله وفتح غین معجمه احسان وبخشش كردن سیورغادوق احسان كردیم سیورغار وسیورغاییدور

احسان میكند چنانكه در دیباچه وقصیده كوید الشاهد علی الاول سعر چولمینت لار [illegible] تا [illegible]

داغی [illegible] بو پر كرسواب [illegible] اولی [illegible] اراده بولور [illegible] ایكن [illegible] كیم [illegible] بو پر [illegible] سیورغا [illegible]

وسیورغار بمعنی فاعل ومصدر هم می آید سیورغاغان وسیورغاغان وسیورغاغان احسان كننده واحسان كرده وبمعنی مصدر هم

آیند سیورغا وسیورغاغیل مفرد غائب المنفصل [illegible] سیورغانا وسیورغاناغیل مفرد غائب المنفصل [illegible] سیورغاملك وسیورغایكر وسیورغاپلار

جمع غائب المنفصل [illegible] سیورغانانك وسیورغانانكز وسیورغانانكلار جمع غائب المنفصل [illegible] سیورغانان وسیورغانامین احسان میكنیم سیورغایین

سیورغامین وسیورغاییدورمن سیورغادیم احسان میكنم سیورغاماس احسان نمیكند وبمعنی فاعل ومصدر منفی هم می آید سیورغاب وسیورغاپان

سیورغامیش احسان كرده سیورغامیشانك احسان كرده سیورغاپ تولغه احسان توان كرد سیورغای آلقه احسان

تواند كرد سیورغایو وسیورغای سیورغای احسان كنان وبدون تكرار هم مستعملست سیورغای سیورغاین احسان كنم وكند وكرد

سیورغاناق سیورغالی سیورغای [illegible] سیورغالی احسان كنیم سیورغاغالی برای احسان كردن وتا احسان كرده سیورغاغاج چون

كرد وكند وبمحض كردن سیورغاغوجی احسان كننده سیورغاغوجه وسیورغاغونچه وسیورغاغانچه تا احسان نكردن وبمحض احسان كردن

سیورغاغوسیزمن احسان نخواهیم كرد سیورغاغوسیزدور احسان نخواهید كرد سیورغاغوسیلاردور احسان نخواهند كرد سیورغاغولوق احسان كند

سیورغاغای وسیورغاسا سیورغاسون سیورغادیلك احسان كند سیورغاغودیلك وسیورغادیلك احسان كردنی وچنانكه احسان كند سویناماك

سویناماقلیغ بفتح یا وسكون نون شكفته كردن [illegible] سوسیماق وسكون [illegible] خوانده [illegible] كرده سویناندور

تنكه كیم سوینادور سویناپادور تنكه میكند سویناندور بمعنی فاعل ومصدر هم می آید سویناكان وسوینادوكان سوینادوكان تنكه كننده

وتنكه كرده وبمعنی مصدر هم می آیند سوینایه سوینانكیل مفرد غائب المنفصل سوینا [illegible] سوینا [illegible] مفرد غائب المنفصل [illegible]

سوینانك وسوینانكو سوینانكلار جمع غائب المنفصل [illegible] سوینانك سوینانكز سوینانكلار جمع غائب المنفصل [illegible] سوینامین

تنكه میكنیم سوینامین وسوینادورمن سوینادیم تنكه میكنم سویناماس تنكه نمیكند وبمعنی فاعل ومصدر منفی هم می آید

سوینامیش وسویناپ [illegible] تنكه كرده سوینامیشانك تنكه كرده سوینافنا ولغای سوینایب ولغه تنكه توان كرد سوینا آلقای تنكه

تواند كرد سوینا سوینا تنكه كنان وبدون تكرار هم مستعملست سوینای وسوینایین تنكه كنم وكند وكرده سوینالی وسویناكا

سویناكای [illegible] سوینالی وسوینالیك تنكه كنیم سویناغالی برای تنكه كردن وتا تنكه كرده سویناغاج چون تنكه كرد وكند وبمحض كردن

سویناغوجی تنكه كننده سویناغوجه وسویناغونچه وسویناغانچه تا تنكه كردن وبمحض تنكه كردن سویناغوسیزدور تنكه خواهیم كرد سویناغو

تنكه خواهید كرد سویناغوسیلاردور تنكه خواهند كرد سویناغولوك تنكه كردنی سویناغای سوینافسا سوینا [illegible] سوینادیلك تنكه كند

سویناغودیلك سوینادیلك تنكه كردنی وچنانكه تنكه كند سایتا الجمله [illegible] مكون یا ولام اول كسر جیم [illegible]

وجستن [illegible] سوی اصل ونسب را كویند [illegible] كندن پوست ولباس سویماق مكون یا وفتح [illegible] از العدم [illegible]

249v

سیب

پوشیده کویند سوبیوت کوزنی کویند الم از آنکه نر بلند باشد یا ماده، و نر آنرا بوغو و ماده را مارال نامند سوبلوت بسکون یا و نون و فتح لا
ترکی رومی بمعنی تند رو باشد سیویونله این احسان دایمی نماند چنانکه در مسلم مکه چنین داده ساختن اسطرلاب و آینه اسکندری
کوید شعر اول اینکا که حکمت ایلی چیکتی دیو غ سلطانا پیشه دین جیحون العجم کم کار ریحی اول کنج المال کرش که یونانی ایلکا سیموا لا
سویه بفتح یای بعلیه ده ترکی رومی عصا و ملقه را کویند باب الکلمات حرف الیاء مع الباء المثناة سپماق و سپماقلیق بسکون یای عجمی
افشاندن بود سپیدی افشاند سپاکیرشتی شروع بافشاندن کرد چنانکه در غنایم المحبه مذکور میر خشابوی که مکر تاغ
بیل اینا دایر عجب بیلک اوستیکا چقتی افشانی با غنی بیب سپلنار و سپاکیرشتی و چون ییماک بمعنی بول کردن است سپاکیرشتی هم
خوانده میتواند شد یعنی بول کردن شروع کرد سپاردی سپادور نمی افشاند الشاهد علی الاول سحر کرنوان غره تاغ آشفته بو
تا نالیغ یاش چون سپیلار هم بوعزونک اوتغه عنبر کلمه لوک و سپیلار بمعنی فاعل و مصدر هم می آید سپکار سپادار و سپادورکا افشان
و افشاندن بمعنی مصدر هم می آید سیب و سیپکیل مفرد مخاطب بفعل امر و نیز سپکیل افشای بناهست که در شرح نهم امیری چنانکه
در ذیل جواهر مذکور خواهد شد سپما و سپماکیل مفرد مخاطب بفعل نهی سپینک و سپینکیز و سپینکلار جمع مخاطب بفعل امر
سپمانک و سپمانکیز و سپمانکلار جمع مخاطب بفعل نهی سپیمان و سپمارمن نمی افشانم سپاصن و سپارمن و سپادیغیم و سپار
می افشانم سپماس نمی افشاند و بمعنی فاعل و مصدر نفی هم می آید سپیب و سپیمان و سپمیش افشانده سپیشانک
افشانده سپیبا و لغای و سپیب تولغای تواند افشاند سپا الغای تواند افشاند سپا سپیبا افشانده افشانده و بعضی
بتکرار هم مستعملست سپای و سپایین بیفشانم و بیفشاند و بیفشانی و افشانده سپیبانک و سپیکای و سپیکایی و سپابیلسای و ایسیند
بیفشانیم سپکالی برای افشاندن و تا افشانده سپکاج چون افشاند و بیفشاند و بعضی افشاندن سپکوسی افشانده سپکو
سپکو چه و سپکالیچه تا افشاندن و بقدر افشاندن سپکومیز دور خواهیم افشاند سپکونکوز دور خواهید افشاند سپکو سیلار
خواهند افشاند سپکولوک افشاننده سپکای سپاو سیبا و سپیسو و سپیدیک بیفشاند چنانکه در مقاله سیم در هم از جرت
اله برابر دریاب ربابی نغم کوید سحر شیشه که مرخسارا امنی سپکای کلاب طاقی اسرکار آنی آرزو لاب سپکوریک و سپیلر ...
افشاننده و بیفشاند سپیلماک و سپیلماکلیک بکسر یای عجمی و سکون لام منون افشانده شدن سپیلکان و سپیلوران و سپیلادقمه کا
افشانده شونده و افشانده شده چنانکه شاهد بر اول و ثانی بمعنی ثانی در همشات کوید کرد قمی ولکل و لاله لارا را سیبدلا ... سپیلکان
وسنبل بیرا با ... دن نمونه کود کوز و دایره ی و بمعنی مصدر هم می آید سپالماق و سپالماقلیغ بفتح یای عجمی و سکون لام و را
تا بیلماق بمعنی لغزیدن باشد سپالدوق لغزیدیم سپالدی و سپالادور میلغزد و سپالور بمعنی فاعل و مصدر هم می آید سپالغان
سپالورغان و سپالادرغان لغزنده و لغزیدن و بمعنی مصدر هم می آیند سپال و سپالغیل مفرد مخاطب بفعل امر سپالما و سپالماغیل
مخاطب بفعل نهی سپالینک و سپالینکیز و سپالینکلار جمع مخاطب بفعل امر سپالمانک و سپالمانکیز و سپالمانکلار جمع مخاطب بفعل نهی سپا
سپالماس نمیلغزم سپالامین و سپالورمین و سپالادورمین میلغزم سپالماس نمیلغزد و بمعنی فاعل و مصدر نفی هم می آید
سپالیب سپالیبان سپالغاندین لغزیده سپالیشانک لغزیده سپالیب تولغای و سپالیب تولغای لغزیده سپالا الغای تواند لغزید
سپالا سپالا لغزان لغزان و بعضی تکرار هم مستعملست سپالای و سپالایین بلغزم و بلغزد و بلغزی و لغزیده سپالیانک
سپالغای و سپالغایز و سپالالی و سپالالینک بلغزیم سپالغالی برای لغزیدن و تا لغزیده سپالغاج چون لغزید و بلغزد و بعضی لغزیدن
سپالغوچی لغزنده سپالغوچه و سپالغونچه تا لغزیدن و بقدر لغزیدن سپالغومیز دور خواهیم لغزید سپالغوکوز دور خواهید لغزید

250r

سپالغوسیلار دور خواهند لغزید سپالغولوق لغزنده سپالغای سپالای و سپالسا و سپالسون بلغزد سپالغلیک بلغزیم سپالماق
لغزیدنی و چنانکه بلغزد سپالاناق و سپالاناقلیغ بفتح لام و ... و همزاد اکردن و آنرا اسپالاق الم کویند سپقارماق و سپقارماقلیغ
بسکون یای عجمی و فتح قاف با الف کشیده ظرف آب و شراب را بسر کشیدن و تمام نوشیدن بجوییکه چیزی از آن باقی نماند سپقاردی
تمام نوشیدیم سپقاردی و سپقارادور تمام مینوشد و سپقارور بمعنی فاعل و مصدر هم می آید سپقارغان و سپقارورغان و سپقارادورغان
تمام نوشنده و تمام نوشیده و بمعنی مصدر هم می آیند سپقار و سپقارغیل مفرد مخاطب بفعل امر سپقارما و سپقارماغیل مفرد مخاطب
بفعل نهی سپقارینک و سپقارینکیز و سپقارینکلار جمع مخاطب بفعل امر سپقارمانک و سپقارمانکیز و سپقارمانکلار جمع مخاطب بفعل نهی سپقارا
سپقارماس تمام نمینوشم سپقارامین و سپقارورمین و سپقارادورمین تمام می نوشم سپقارماس تمام نمینوشد و بمعنی فاعل و مصدر نفی
هم می آید سپقاریب و سپقاریبان و سپقارمیش تمام نوشیده سپقاریشانک تمام نوشیده سپقاریب تولغای و سپقاریب تولغای تمام تواند نوشید
سپقارا الغای تمام تواند نوشید سپقارا سپقارا نوشان نوشان و بعضی تکرار هم مستعملست سپقارای و سپقارایین
تمام بنوشیم و بنوشد و بنوشی و نوشیده الشاهد علی الاول والمعنی الاول شعر ساقیا برا دیکیم ... شرطی بولکیم
تو قنالی لبالب سپقارای سپقارغای و سپقارغایز و سپقارالی و سپقارالینک تمام بنوشیم سپقارغالی برای تمام
و تا نوشیده سپقارغاج چون تمام نوشید و بنوشد و بعضی نوشیدن سپقارغوچی تمام نوشنده سپقارغوچه و سپقارغونچه
تا تمام نوشیدن و بقدر تمام نوشیدن سپقارغومیز دور تمام خواهیم نوشید سپقارغوکوز دور تمام خواهید نوشید
الشاهد علی الثانی بالمعنی الاول شعر ...
سپقارغوسیلار دور تمام خواهند نوشید سپقارغولوق تمام ...
~~...~~
~~...~~

ج

الشاهد علی الاول والمعنی الاول شعر ...
سپا بفتح با خاکیست که برای ضیافت لشکر هنگام جنگ در یک طرف ... سپاغاق بفتح یای عجمی
و میم با الف کشیده و سکون نون و قاف جای لغزیدنست ... و آنرا سپرغاق هم کویند ...
فارسی لخشان خوانند سپیاد بفتح یای عجمی و سکون واو بمعنی ماهیت و مدلل باشد سپیقین بسکون یای عجمی و نون و کسر قاف ترکی
آلتیست بشکل پنجه که از آهن سازند ... و آنرا اعراب ظاله نامند سپیکیل بسکون یای عجمی و نون و کسر کاف عجمی ...
... که در پیش آدم ... سپیکی بفتح یا و کسر کاف مع الیا ... چنانکه کوید سحر ...
... اما چون در لغت ترکی بمعنی ...

سیج

مصطلح شده و در فرس مستعمل نیست ... سپجان ...
و بفارسی شک کویند سپجانجیل بفتح جیم عجمی ...
کبجشک صید کند و آنرا بفارسی ... سپچکان ...

مبیخ

ایوب خلف بادنرم کوید سحر ...

سیر

سیخ بروزن میخ آنرا کویند ... سیر یا ک ...

باشد سیرنادی ربود چنانکه مصرعی در وصف دنم بادقیر بری کوید شعر چو تابیب علی سیدینی سیرنادی یامیب
امرسیاهی فه هم کیرنادیغ وطالع هوی سیرناقرا تالف ویک سیم مصدر مقرر داده وبمعنی آرام وتوقف نوشته وشعر ...
شاهد آمده . چهار غلط دریک لفظ اتفاق افتاده . اول آنکه مصدر سیرناغ کامیت وثانی بیت دویم آنکه مصدر سیرنادی
بیت سیرنانالک با دویم است واکی سیرناقی بود ماضی آن سیرندی می آمد سیم اینکه سیرناماق وسیرنانالک هیچیک بمعنی آرام وتوقف
سیرناماق لفظیست بمعنی ومعنی سیرنانالک ربودن چهارم اینکه آرام وتوقف در این شعر معنی ندارد سیرنادیم ربودم الشاهد وله
شعر صنعم دیر اچرامستا ولسانم مینی عقلین نی نالک شیخ دستارین کمه مسجه کیر کلیج سیرنادیم وینه در خاتمه خسروشیرین
کوید شعر آتینک بیلیت سیرنادیم وجعیر تاج که باشی طیلسانه بولدی محتاج سیرنا عسیرنا یه ود میربایند وسیرنا معنی فاعل و
هم می آید سیرناکان وسیرناکان سیرنایده کان ربایند و ربوده وبمعنی مصدر هم می آیند سیرنا وسیرناکیل مفرد مخاطب فعل
سیرنا ناو سیرنا ناکیل مفرد مخاطب فعل نهی سیرنانک وسیرنا نکیز وسیرنا نکلار جمع مخاطب فعل امر سیرنانانک وسیرنا نانکیز
جمع مخاطب فعل نهی سیرنان وسیرنامین سیرنایم سیرنای بیز سیرنا بیز سیرنابدیز سیرنادیم سیرنایم سیرناناس نیربایند وبمعنی فاعل
ومصدر منفی هم می آید سیرناب سیرنابان سیرنامیش ربوده الشاهد علی الثانی شعر خرابات اهلی عور و داغ دیر کیم کو بیده
ساقی دوایوق سیرنابان تا جاغدین امرکاشیخ دستارین سیاق شرحین ایت که خرابات اهلی عور وسا دیرکیم داغ کو بیده ونک
دستارین سیرناب تا چاغدین امرکا دوایوق سیرنامیشانک ربوده سیرنانابونه وسیرناب بولغایی توان ربود سیرنای آلغه
تواند بود سیرنایو وسیرنای سیرنای ربوده ربوده وبدون تکرار هم مستعملت سیرنای وسیرنامین برابیم وربایند وربایده
سیرناناتمه سیرناکابین وسیرناکای بین ربایی الشاهد علی الاول شعر ای نوای حسنت بیر ابچرا کیم سیرنانانک ربودی الافرس
لایق دولولد دستار وفرش سیرنانالد سیرنا کابیز سیرناکای بیز وسیرناتی وسیرنانیلیبرایم سیرنا کالی برای ربودن وتا ربوده
چون ربود ورباید ومحض ربودن سیرناکوچی ربایند سیرناکوچی سیرناکو بخه وسیرناکا بخه تا ربودن ربودن سیرناکو میزدد
خواهیم ربود سیرناکو تخردور خواهید ربود سیرناکو سیلاخ دور خواهند بود سیرناکو لولک ربودنی سیرناکای سیرنانا وسیرنا
سیرنادیک ربابید الشاهد علی الاول شعر شاه ایرناس پرتوی نوشکاج اودیم حتی هم کو یاک چو کمه بستان که ادسیرناکای شمع
ناریوق سیرناکو دیک وسیرنار دیک ربودن وهمچنانکه رباید سیرنامالک وسیرنا ماکلیک مع الکلام معنی ربوده شدن وسنح آن
مرینساق بالالام اشتقاق یابد سیریغماق وسریغمافیلیغ بجیم وسکون فاء معنی کیختن باشد الشاهد علی الاول شعر بلماسنا
ایردی جیلیلی پریوش صلیفه تیلمسه دیک ویرانه لار سایر سیریغماق تمایدی سیریغتوق کریختیم سیریغتود سیریغادو سیکرد
وسیریغقو معنی فاعل ومصدر هم می آید سیریغقان سیریغقو غانه سیریغقا ید دیغان کریزنده وکریخته وبمعنی مصدر هم می آیند سیریغ
سیریغقیل مفرد مخاطب فعل امر سیریغما وسیریغماغیل مفرد مخاطب فعل نهی سیریغینک وسیریغینکیز سیریغینکلار جمع مخاطب فعل
سیریغمانک وسیریغمانکیز وسیریغمانکلار جمع مخاطب فعل نهی سیریغمان وسیریغمامین عنکریزیم سیریغماس سیریغقومین سیریغادورمین
سیریغقورام مبکریزم سیریغماس ممکریزد وبمعنی فاعل ومصدر منفی هم می آید سیریغیب سیریغمان وسیریغمیش کریخته سیریغیشانک
کریخته سیریغنا بولغای وسیریغیب بولغای توان کریخت سیریغا آلغایی تواند کریخت سیریغا سیریغا کریزان کریزان وبدون تکرار
هم مستعملت سیریغای وسیریغایین بکریزیم وبکریزد وبکریزی وکریخته سیریغقاناق وسیریغغاییز وسیریغقانایمز وسیریغقای بیز سیریغای
بکریزیم سیریغقانی برای کریختن وتا کریخته سیریغقاج چون کریخت وبکریزد ومحض کریختن سیریغقوچی کریزنده سیریغقوچه وسیریغقوچه

سیریغقاغنه تا کریختن وبعد از کریختن سیریغقومیزدور خواهیم کریخت سیریغقونکیزدور خواهید کریخت سیریغقوسیلار دور خواهند کریخت سیریغقولوق کریخته
سیریغقای سیریغا سیریغینا وسیریغسون وسیریغقیدیک بکریزد سیریغقودیک وسیریغقوردیک کریختن وهمچنانکه بکریزد وسیریغقوما
سیریغتورماق وسیریغتورالیغ مصدر متعدیست بمعنی کریزانیدن وسنح آن بدستور الفاظ اشتقاق می یابد سیریغماق وسیریغمالیغ بکسر ومعنی بخیه
زدن باشد سیریغدوق بخیه زدیم سیریغدوم سیریغدی بخیه میزند وسیریغو معنی فاعل ومصدر هم می آیند سیریغغان وسیریغقان و
سیریغغان بخیه زننده وبخیه زده وبمعنی مصدر هم می آیند سیریغ وسیریغیل مفرد مخاطب فعل امر سیریغما وسیریغماغیل
مفرد مخاطب فعل نهی سیریغینک سیریغینکیز وسیریغینکلار جمع مخاطب فعل امر سیریغمانک وسیریغمانکیز وسیریغمانکلار جمع مخاطب فعل نهی
سیریغان سیریغامین بخیه میزنم سیریغامیز سیریغیدورمین سیریغادورمین وسیریغادورام بخیه میزنیم سیریغماس بخیه نمیزند وبمعنی فاعل
ومصدر منفی هم می آید سیریغیب سیریغان وسیریغمیش بخیه زده سیریغیشانک بخیه زده سیریغینا بولغای وسیریغیب بولغای بخیه
توان زد سیریغا آلغای بخیه تواند زد سیریغا سیریغا بخیه زنان وبدون تکرار هم مستعملت سیریغای وسیریغایین بخیه
بزنم وبزند وبزنی وزده سیریغیناق وسیریغغاییز وسیریغغای بیز وسیریغقای بیز سیریغالی بخیه بزنیم سیریغقالی برای بخیه زدن وتا
زده سیریغقاج چون بخیه زد وبعد از آن ومحض زدن سیریغقوچی بخیه زننده سیریغقوچه سیریغقو بخه وسیریغقا بخه تا بخیه زدن و
بعد از بخیه زدن سیریغقومیزدور بخیه خواهیم زد سیریغقونکیزدور بخیه خواهید زد سیریغقوسیلار دور بخیه خواهند زد
بخیه زدن سیریغقای سیریغا سیریغسون وسیریغقیدیک بخیه بزند سیریغقودیک وسیریغقوردیک بخیه زدن وهمچنانکه بخیه بزند
سیریلماق وسیریلمالیغ مع الکلام بخیه دوزی شدن وباشباع کسره بمعنی لغزیده شدن باشد سیریلدی بخیه دوزی شد
لغزیده شد سیریلور وسیریلادور بخیه دوزی میشود وباشباع لغزیده میشود الشاهد علی الاول بالمعنی الثانی شعر ...
خانقه فه ... اشیخ قوت معنی ... که کام ... ساقی ... سیریلوکامیم وسیریلور بمعنی فاعل ومصدر هم می آید
سیریلغان وسیریلوغان وسیریلادوغان بخیه دوزی شونده وبخیه دوزی شده الشاهد علی الاول بالمعنی الثانی شعر اول بولوت
لباس ... سیریلغان خط لادی ... بار آتینک ... توشکای بولوت ... وباشباع بمعنی لغزیده شونده ولغزیده شده وبمعنی
مصدر هم می آیند سیریل وسیریلغیل مفرد مخاطب فعل امر سیریلما وسیریلماغیل مفرد مخاطب فعل نهی سیریلینک وسیریلینکیز
سیریلینکلار جمع مخاطب فعل امر سیریلمانک وسیریلمانکیز وسیریلمانکلار جمع مخاطب فعل نهی سیریلمان سیریلمامین لغزیده نمیشوم سیریلادورمین
سیریلورمین وسیریلادورمین وسیریلورام لغزیده میشوم سیریلماس بخیه دوزی نمیشود ولغزیده نمیشود وبمعنی فاعل ومصدر منفی هم می
آید سیریلیب وسیریلینان وسیریلمیش بخیه دوزی شده ولغزیده شده سیریلیشانک بخیه دوزی شده ولغزیده شده سیریلینا بولغای
وسیریلیب بولغای توان لغزید سیریلا آلغای بخیه دوزی تواند شد ولغزیده تواند شد سیریلا سیریلا بخیه دوزی شده ولغزان
لغزان وبدون تکرار هم مستعملت سیریلای وسیریلایین لغزیده شوم وشود وشوی شده سیریلیناق وسیریلغاییز وسیریلغای بیز وسیریلای
سیریلکینک لغزیده شویم سیریلغالی برای بخیه دوزی شدن وتا شدن وبرای لغزیده شدن وتا شدن سیریلغاج چون بخیه دوزی
شد وشود ومحض شدن وچون لغزیده شد وشود ومحض شدن سیریلغوچی بخیه دوزی شونده ولغزیده شونده سیریلغوچه وسیریلغوچه
تا بخیه دوزی شدن وبعد از آن وتا لغزیده شدن وبعد از آن سیریلغومیزدور لغزیده خواهیم شد سیریلغونکیزدور لغزیده خواهید
سیریلغوسیلار دور لغزیده خواهند شد سیریلغوچی بخیه دوزی خواهد شد ولغزیده خواهد شد سیریلغولوق بخیه دوزی شده ولغزیده
شدن سیریلغای سیریلا سیریلنا سیریلسون وسیریلادیک بخیه دوزی شود ولغزیده شود سیریلغودیک وسیریلوردیک بخیه دوزی شدنی

وهمچنانکه شود والمزینیشنده وهمچنانکه شود سیرتماق وسیرجیا تلمغ بجیم وسکون لام وقرشت مصدر متعدیست یعنی
دمنعیه بودن نوصیغ آن بدستور ثانی قرشت اشتقاق می‌یابد من الجواهر سیر نام رودخانه ایست عظیم که از هندیا بیرون آمده تا
گذشته به دریا در آید خوارزم بعد چون انتقال الحیاء یابد سیرام بفتح را وسکون میم نام ولایتیست از ترکستان که بنا کرده
ومولانا ابو نصر بود ونیز گفته‌اند که شهریست که بنا کرده ولایت الغون وامرات سیرت بسکون را وتا قرشت شانه
گویند سیرتاق اتراک دم بالاپوش را نامند و اتراک قولن شیرداغ گویند چنانکه مذکور خواهد شد سیرلان
بسکون را وتا ونون وفتح لام جانوریست شبیه بگفتار که اندرون هم می‌رسد وکفش او هم گویند سرچه بسکون را وفتح جیم
بمعنی شیشه وآبگینه باشد چنانکه حیدر تلبه در هجو گوید شعر ایرکیشی ایکاکا اینیک غلک بولور سرچه
سینسا اینیک والد بولور صورتیه مجاز بمعنی تند وتیز هم استعمال نمایند سرچه بابنا ق بترکیب وحالت کوبلت بعد که
آنرا سربی خضر نامند سرداش لفظیست مرکب از لغتین بمعنی همراز باشد الشاهد علیه شعر ای کونکل این ترلد عشقی
ملفاش ایتماکیل ثمین سنکا ستریم دیدیم سین ایلنی سرداش ایتماکیل سیرقاق وسیرتاق زمینی را گویند که در هوای سرد از تنخ برنج
لرزیده شود سیرکالک بفتح کاف تاجیکی بمعنی بیخواب وبیخوابی باشد که آنرا سربی سحرخوانند بالمعنی الاول شعر سین اولدم الله کی
نازامیقوبی دین ایدکونگ آچماس ینوچ آندین که هرازشایی بولغای کمزلار بو سیرکالک بالمعنی الثانی شعر دیما امیقوبین کونکول
هجران تونی آچیلمادی فنیلا آلفای اجل امیقوبیرله سیرکالکم جامع اینشه بمعنی چولها الودشدن هم چسبیدن چشم نوشته و
نصیر هم بمعنی چسبیدن چشم ذکر کرده ونظام هروی سیرکالد بازای هوز نوشته وبمعنی لاینیدن مذکور ساخته وهر سه شعر مذکور آورده
آورده اند سیرکه بسکون را وفتح کاف بزرگ هم را نامند شپش بزرگ را هم نامند که در بدن وجامه بهم رسد وآنرا ایغار نیز شپش
گویند سیرمه ترکیب وی نقده بود وآن مفتول دراز است که چین کرده باریک برید ده در زیر دوزها بکار برند سیرکه بفتح را
مانندی چیز بسته وپهلوی هم چسبیده را گویند ومؤلف برهان قاطع بفتح اول ودوم بهمین معنی ذکر کرده وبجای لفظ صف یکی آورده
ودانه برشته کشیده نیز استعمال می‌شود سیریغ بخیه باشد که بر جامه زنند الشاهد علیه شعر پرده سلطنت چون ارتی
زاهد ایشی خرقه از بره فوی آسیغ موجه سیریغ سیریغ لیغ یعنی بخیه دار چنانکه گوید شعر ای نوالی او لتی یاش وسلیق که الیغ
ایتکالی تمام ایلادی بین سیریغ لیغ دلق دوکدون وار قد سیریق بکسر دو مثنیه چوب باشد که عمود ادا وآهنین سوروق باشد که بر جهت
بالمعنی تکلم می‌شود ونیز دانا سند خصوصا سیریزبترکی وه وه والد کا باشد سیرین بمعنی خنک ونارد بود سیرنجاق بالا شنا
بکسر را وسکون نون وتا قاف وفتح جیم جای بلند لغزنده باشد که اطفال در ایام نشسته لغزیده بپایین آیند وآنرا اسیا نجاق هم نامند چنانکه
مع الزاء المعجمه سیزماق وسیزما قلیغ بسکون زا بمعنی نقش کردن بود چنانکه در حیرة الابرار در وصف خواجه نقشبند گوید شعر جلانشه چکیب
هیچ معنا قشنی سیزماقا ایچون آنرا اقشا قشینی سیزماک وسیزماکلیک دو معنی دارد اول فهمیدن دوم ترشح کردن سیزدی بمعنی آن
نقش کرد وفهمید وترشح کرد بالمعنی الاول شعر نقطه مشک دهر بویا غلبی آینک جبین را آکهر سوادینی نقوش سیزدی بیاض دیزلارا سیزا
سیزادور نقش میکند وفهمید وترشح میکند چنانکه شاهد برای او رابمعنی ثالث بمعنی آن تمثیل گفته اند مشیلسین فی تونیاک که منک
ایچکا آندین ولیسیزاری بمعنی از کوزه همان بردن تراود که در اوست وسیزار بمعنی فاعل ومصدر هم می‌آید چنانکه بمعنی نقش کننده گوید شعر
عشق دشتیدا قویون ایرماس که مین دیوانه ده دشتدا راسیرکیته لیلی خطین سیزار بر کلادور وبمعنی نقش کردن گوید شعر نیما فاناللماس اولی
خالیدا ریکی سیزادوا سیر تیننکی کوریبان نقاش سیزمارع سیزارغان وسیزادورغان نقش کننده ونقش کرده الشاهد علی الاول المعنی الاول

جاکم

چنانکه در ترتیب المجنون گوید شعر نون کوی تیلیق نقش سیزغان کافورایله مشک تیزغان بالمعنی الثانی شعر بو یمقیلیم ذا آچی
اوچی کا اسید اپری نقش سالغیمانیب اوچون سیزغان آینک جاقیغه وبمعنی مصدر هم می‌آید سیزکان وسیزارکان وسیزادورکان فهمنده
وفهمیده وترشح کننده وترشح کرده وبمعنی مصدر هم می‌آید سیز امریست از نقش کردن وفهمیدن وترشح کردن ومعانی دیگر مذکور
جوامد یا شواهد مذکور خواهد شد سیزغیل امر از نقش کردن چنانکه گوید شعر ای مصور لطف ادیب سیزغیل سینی خاتمانغه توش ایله کیم
توشکای یوزی بو دینه حیرانغه توش سیزکیل امریست از فهمیدن وترشح کردن سیزما نهی است از هر سه معنی سیزما قیل نهی است
از نقش کردن سیزماکیل نهی است از فهمیدن وترشح کردن سیزینک وسیزینکیز وسیزینکلار جمع مخاطب للحاضر سیزمانک وسیزما
سیزمانکلار جمع مخاطب للحاضر سیزمارم سیزمارمن نقش نیکنم ونیفهمم وترشح نیکنم سیزلیمن وسیزارمن وسیزادورمن وسیزارکا نقش میکنم
ومیفهمم وترشح میکنم سیزماس نقش نیکند ونیفهمد وترشح نیکند وبمعنی فاعل ومصدر نفی هم می‌آید سیزیب وسیزیبان وسیزمیش
نقش کرده وفهمیده وترشح کرده الشاهد علی الاول المعنی الاول شعر مکر فرهاد خاو دین سیزیب تا خیر باتی بیلان متعدد دور کو
شیرین لب لعلی شکر ایتین ودحجر شیرین مرکبغلای فرهاد گوید بالمعنی الثانی شعر سیزیبان ریحی که اول غربت اسیری هماناغوت کی
دشمن ستیم دوده مقاله هنم از حیرة الابرار در اتحاد بحسن وعشق گوید بالمعنی الثالث شعر قطره لار اول غنجه ذکر ما را چشمه سوی
دین سیزیبان اولچاه از سیزمیشانک نقش کرده وفهمیده سیزیشا بولغانه وسیزیب بولغانه نقش توانکرد وتوان فهمید وترشح توان کرد
سیزا الغای نقش تواند کرد وتواند فهمید وترشح تواند کرد سیزا سیزیر نقش کنان وترشح کنان وفهمکنان بمعنی حال هم مستعملست سیزلی
سیزاین نقش کنم وکنند وکنی وکرده وبفهم وفهمند وبفهمی وفهمیده وترشح کنم وکنند وکنی وکرده سیزباق وسیزغایز وسیزغای نقش کنیم
سیزیناک وسیزکایز وسیزکای بفهمیم وترشح کنیم سیزلی وسیزالیک نقش کنیم وبفهمیم وترشح کنیم سیزغلی برای نقش کردن وتا نقش کند
بالمعنی الاول شعر چهره سیزغلی بو قیرد سنکا خالیعنی نامه الا رکالت تحریر چهره تحریر اینا این سیاق شعر چنین است که چه سنزا سعده
بیرد سنکا خالی یعنی سیزیدن رقتای که برای نقش کردن بتو خالم واحد ناشد چه لطف ناصحا اما ملک سیزکم سیزکالی برای فهمیدن وتا فهمید
وبرای ترشح کردن وتا ترشح کرده سیزغاچ چون نقش کرد وکند وبمحض نقش کردن چنانکه گوید شعر اول پریوش صورتین سیزغلیج مسلم ایکاندی
کیم خوبلیق ایلکان دیوانه بو تمثال المیش سیزکاچ چون فهمید وفهمکند وبمحض فهمیدن وچون ترشح کرد وکند وبمحض کردن چنانکه گوید
تاریخ بابری بمعنی اوله اند کرامت که نقیر حلوی وسلطان حسین میرزا بولوب تبدیل اوله مصدر بقابلیت تبدیل بولوب سیزکاچ تمرالملکی سیزغوچی
نقش کننده سیزکوچی فهم کننده وترشح کننده سیزغوجه وسیزغوجه وسیزغاجه تا نقش کردن وبمجرد نقش کردن سیزکوجه وسیزکوجه وسیزکاجه تا فهم
کردن وبمجرد فهم کردن وتا ترشح کردن وبمجرد ترشح کردن سیزغوسیزدر ونقش خواهیم کرد سیزکوسیزدور خواهیم فهمید وترشح خواهیم کرد
سیزغوسیزدیز نقش خواهید کرد سیزکوسیزدور خواهید فهمید وترشح خواهید کرد سیزغوسیلاردور ونقش خواهند کرد سیزکوسیلاردور خواهند
فهمید وترشح خواهند کرد سیزغولوق نقش کردنی سیزکولوک فهمیدنی وترشح کردنی سیزغای نقش کند سیزکای بفهمد وترشح کند سیزا
سیزنا وسیزسون وسیزدیک نقش کند وبفهمد وترشح کند سیزغودیک نقش کردنی وهمچنانکه نقش کند سیزکودیک فهمیدنی وهمچنانکه
فهمد وترشح کردنی وهمچنانکه ترشح کند سیزاردیک مرادف سیزغودیک وسیزکودیک باشد سیزیلماق وسیزیلما قلیغ بکسر زاء معجمه ولام
بمعنی نقش شدن باشد وصیغ آن با الام اشتقاق می‌یابد سیزیلماک وسیزیلماکلیک مع الکاف فهمیده شدن سیزیماک وسیزیماکلیک
مع النون مترشح شدن وصیغ سیزیلماک بالام وانیسیزینماک با نون اشتقاق می‌یابد سیزغورماق وسیزغورما قلیغ بسکون زای معجمه وضم راء
مهمله وضم غین معجمه بمعنی نقش کردن با نوک کلک وامثال آن سیزغورغان سیزغورغان وسیزغوردغان بمعنی مصدر هم می‌آید سیزغور وسیزغورغیل

مفرد غائب المستقبل امر سیزغورسا و سیزغورغای مفرد غائب المستقبل سیزغورغونک و سیزغورغونکیز و سیزغورغونکلار جمع غائب المستقبل امر سیزغورسانک
سیزغورسانکیز و سیزغورسانکلار جمع غائب المستقبل سیزغورغایلار سیزغورامین و سیزغوراسمین میگدازم سیزغورامین و سیزغورورمین و سیزغوراردیم و سیزغورادیم
میگدازم سیزغوراس میگدازد و بمعنی فاعل و مصدر هم می‌آید سیزغوروب و سیزغوروبان و سیزغورمیش گداخته چنانکه در سنگلاخ
گوید الشاهد علی الاول سعشر ایشیتیم کم جنون صحرا نورد کم باشیمنی تاغ ایدی سوز و صدق نچه مونکلیغ تین ایردی یراق تینین سیز
غوروب ایردی علی فراق من لطفی سعشر و نادالمعنی باتی فراق دیباری نچه کم سیزغوروب آلتون دیک امتحان قیلدی سیزغورسانک گدا
سیزغورسانک توانستی و سیزغوروب توانسته توان گداخت سیزغورا الغای تواند گداخت سیزغورا سیزغورا گدازان گدازان و بعد گذار
هم مستعملست سیزغورای و سیزغورامین بگدازم و بگدازی و بگدازی سیزغوراق و سیزغورغایمیز و سیزغورغایمیز و سیزغورالی و سیزغورلیک
بگدازیم سیزغورغالی برای گداختن و تا گداخته سیزغورغاج چون گداخت و بگدازد و بعض گداختن سیزغورغوچی گدازنده سیزغورغود
سیزغورغوچی و سیزغورغانچه تا گداختن و بقدر گداختن سیزغورغوسیدور خواهیم گداخت سیزغورغوسیدور خواهید گداخت سیزغورغوسیدور
خواهند گداخت سیزغورغای و سیزغورا و سیزغورنا و سیزغورغون سیزغوردیانه بگدازد و سیزغوردیک و سیزغوردیک گداختنی همچنانکه گدا
سیزلاماق بترکی رومی مصدر ثریا ناله زار کردن سیزلار ناله زار میکند من فضولی بالملاحه الرومیه سعشر میل ایتمس تیغ یمینی جهدیم ×
یارنانک دکلیم سیزلارالوم حیلاد و نمونه نمودنت سیزلیدا نالد بترکی رومی مصدر ثریا کردن من الجواهر سیز بمعنی تهی اول × ج ×
جمع غائب المط شد بمعنی شما دو بیم چون با ضمیر جمع غائب المجمع افاده معنی اینها تا کند چنانکه گوید سیز سیز بمعنی شما بسیم در آخر کلمات ملحق
معنی نفی میکند مثل اینکه گوید سیز سیز بمعنی شما چنانکه شاهد بمعنی بیصبه سیاره در ذیل ابجا سیم از دیباچه کتاب نکلارش نامت
و نیز الرسات نقش کردن و فهمیدن و ترشح کردن چنانکه در ذیل اشتقاقات گذشت و بفارسی بمعنی سند قنیز باشد سیزکالک بکون تلوحکا ×
ثلثی و فتح کاف عجمی در چشم اکنی نید چنانکه لطفی گفته سعشر ناماشیمیم اعلاه تی تیبر کا کیمدین باش آتار سو بولالافلادین حقارجی نلغ
او میجه یاقسه تاز سیزنید و سکون نون و ضم دال المهمله ترجمه بود که از جایی ترشح کند مع البتر المهمله سیزکانماک و سیزکانماکلیک × سیس ×
بسکون یا و نون و فتح کاف از خواب و از غلبه دهشت جستن چنانکه در خسرو شیرین در ماتم فرهاد گوید شعر بیتب کیدون نقش سیزکا
بوقی توشوب غائب المطلوب تیراغنا گیتیت بوق سیزکاندوک جستیم سیزکانور و سیزکانادور جستند الشاهد علی الاول سعشر ناقیا
بری کهم شاهی غارهردیق پرپیشان توشکوروب بوخته دایم سیزکانور و سیزکانور بمعنی فاعل و مصدر هم آید سیزکانکان و
سیزکانکان و سیزکانادوکان جستن و جسته و بمعنی مصدر هم می‌آیند سیزکان و سیزکانکیل مفرد غائب المستقبل امر سیزکانما و سیزکانما
مفرد غائب المستقبل چنانکه گوید الشاهد علی الثانی سعشر کوز یوموب اچتو یخه نال او نیانماس اویقوده سینی نا الیم دیر هر شای جرک
سیزکانماکیل سیزکانینک و سیزکانینکیز و سیزکانینکلار جمع غائب المستقبل امر سیزکانمانک و سیزکانمانکیز و سیزکانمانکلار جمع غائب المستقبل
سیزکانماسینلار و سیزکانامین سیزکانامین و سیزکانورمین و سیزکانادوعه سیزکانورامن میجهم سیزکانکاین بجهی من لسان الطیر سعشر
چون اجل تیغیدین سیزکانکاین غفلتینک اویقوسیدین اویغانماسین سیزکانماس بجهد و بمعنی فاعل و مصدر منفی هم می‌آید
سیزکانیب و سیزکانیب و سیزکانمیش جسته الشاهد علی الاول سعشر کوکی یخود لوغوم دین سیزکانیب تو قسام ادیمه جیبت
بیلیدا جرنا شیبالی شوق غنیک از الوحیا غنیدا سیزکانیشلیک جستن سیزکانا بولغای و سیزکانیب بولغای توان جست سیزکالغای
تواند جست سیزکانا سیزکانا جهان جهان و بدون تکرار هم مستعملست سیزکانای و سیزکانایین بجهم و بجهد و بجهی جسته سیزکانا
سیزکانکالیز و سیزکانغای و سیزکانا و سیزکانالیک بجهیم سیزکانغالی برای جستن و تا جسته سیزکانکاج چون جست و بجهد و بجهند

جستن سیزکانکوچی جهنده سیزکانکوچه و سیزکانکانچه تا جستن و بقدر جستن سیزکانکوسیدور و خواهیم جست سیزکانکوسیدور
خواهید جست سیزکانکوسیدور خواهند جست سیزکانکولوک جستنی سیزکانکای و سیزکانا و سیزکاناغا و سیزکانغو و سیزکاندیک
بجهد الشاهد علی الاول من لیلی و مجنون سعشر میتی یوتیک یوز یکانمالماه سیزکانکای اوز اویقوسیدین اول ماه سیزکانماکای
سیزکانماسا و سیزکانماسون و سیزکانماکدیک بجهد الشاهد علی الاول سعشر چالای کوکوم دیک تیکیت آغزیمغیم کم کهکلاو مرغ
سیزکانماکای بچه غضایه م دین سینمک سیزکانکودیک و سیزکانورالیتیم و همچنانکه بجهد مع الغین المعجمه من المشتقات سیغماق و سیغماقلیغ × سیغ
بسکون یا و فتح غین گنجیدن باشد و سیغیشماق و تمام ناتر شتوطالع هر ویرسیغماق با نامعا با خصیص ذکر کرده و سیغماق بمعنی آمیزش باشد
چنانکه مذکور خواهد شد سیغدوروق گنجید یرسیغار تعیینا دور میگنجد و سیغار بمعنی فاعل و مصدر هم می‌آید سیغار و
میتواند گنجید الشاهد علیه سعشر ضعف کوکیل کیم قدره نال لالان سیغماز کهی نجه سیغیت دیم سیغماالوراتیناله حال لیک
سیغمایان سیغمایان و سیغمادوغان گنجنده و گنجیده و بمعنی مصدر هم می‌آیند چنانکه شاهد در اول در ذیل سیغماالور نوشته شد
سیغ و سیغغیل مفرد غائب المستقبل امر سیغسا و سیغغای مفرد غائب المستقبل سیغینک و سیغینکیز و سیغینکلار جمع
غائب المستقبل امر سیغسانک و سیغسانکیز و سیغسانکلار جمع غائب المستقبل سیغغایلار سیغامین بگنجم سیغامیز و سیغارمین و
سیغادور می‌گنجیم سیغاس بگنجد و بمعنی فاعل و مصدر منفی هم می‌آید سیغیب و سیغیبان و سیغیمیش گنجیده سیغا
گنجیده سیغا بولغای و سیغیب بولغای توان گنجید سیغا الغای تواند گنجید سیغا سیغا گنجید و گنجید و بدون تکرار هم مستعمل
سیغای و سیغایین بگنجم و بگنجد و بگنجی و گنجید سیغاق و سیغغایمیز و سیغغایمیز و سیغالیک بگنجیم سیغغالی برای گنجید
و تا گنجید سیغغاج چون گنجید و بگنجد و بعض گنجیده سیغغوچی و سیغغوچه و سیغغانچه تا گنجیدن و بقدر گنجیدن الشاهد علی الاول
بالمعنی الثانی سعشر یتوری ایرا سوغیمی بولسا او سیغانماس لالا الم برابر بیسغغوچه یانه بکرا سیغغوسیدور و خواهیم گنجید سیغغو
خواهید گنجید سیغغوسیدور خواهند گنجید سیغغولوق گنجیدنی سیغغای و سیغا و سیغاغا و سیغغون و سیغدیک بگنجد سیغغودیک و سیغادیک گنجید
و همچنانکه بگنجد چنانکه در سنگلاخ گوید الشاهد علی الاول المعنی الثانی شعر ولیکن بود مرا کمانیشه ای ابا سیغغودیک
بارجا آرایشه سیغیشماق و سیغیشماقلیغ مع آلتی مرادف سیغماق است یعنی گنجیدن و صیغ آن باشتقاق می‌آید سیغورماق × ×
سیغورماقلیغ بفتح و سکون را مهمله مصدر متعدی سیغماق است یعنی گنجانیدن سیغوردوق گنجانیدیم سیغورور و سیغورادور
میگنجاند و سیغورور بمعنی فاعل و مصدر هم می‌آید سیغورغان و سیغوروغان و سیغورادوغان گنجاننده و گنجانیده و بمعنی مصدر هم
می‌آیند سیغور و سیغورغیل مفرد غائب المستقبل امر چنانکه در سنگلاخ در ذکر ملوک عجم گوید الشاهد علی الاول شعر معنی عجم
ایجرا نوعنیل نم سیغورا آیراذ کرملو عجم سیغورسا و سیغورغای مفرد غائب المستقبل سیغورغونک و سیغورغونکیز و سیغورغونکلار جمع غائب
المستقبل امر سیغورسانک و سیغورسانکیز و سیغورسانکلار جمع غائب المستقبل سیغورغایلار سیغورامین بگنجانم سیغورامین و سیغورورمین
سیغورادورمین و سیغوراس میگنجاند سیغوراس نمیگنجاند و بمعنی فاعل و مصدر منفی هم می‌آید سیغوروب و سیغوروبان و سیغورمیش گنجانیده
چنانکه در بیضه سیاره در موصفه گوید الشاهد علی الاول شعر جرعه طلب ایچنده اناش سیغوروب امزنی اول بجرم گنجیدا المشبوب
مقاله نوز در هم از حیرة الابرار در وصف سیاه چمره گوید شعر نظم ادبغه تیشکالالاری معلوم آنکا باش سیغوروب پرچه مظلوم آنکا ولی کا
سیغوروب با حار ترشحی از نیخه سیغی سیقیب بگنجان ملاحق اند و گفته که سیغماق فعل متعدی است و بمعنی گنجانیدن باشد و سیقیب
فعل ماضی آنست و نون برای مماثله تبدیل یافته سیغیر سیر گفته می‌شود و شعر بورا شاهد آمده سهو کرده الفاظ اخر اعمیت سیغور

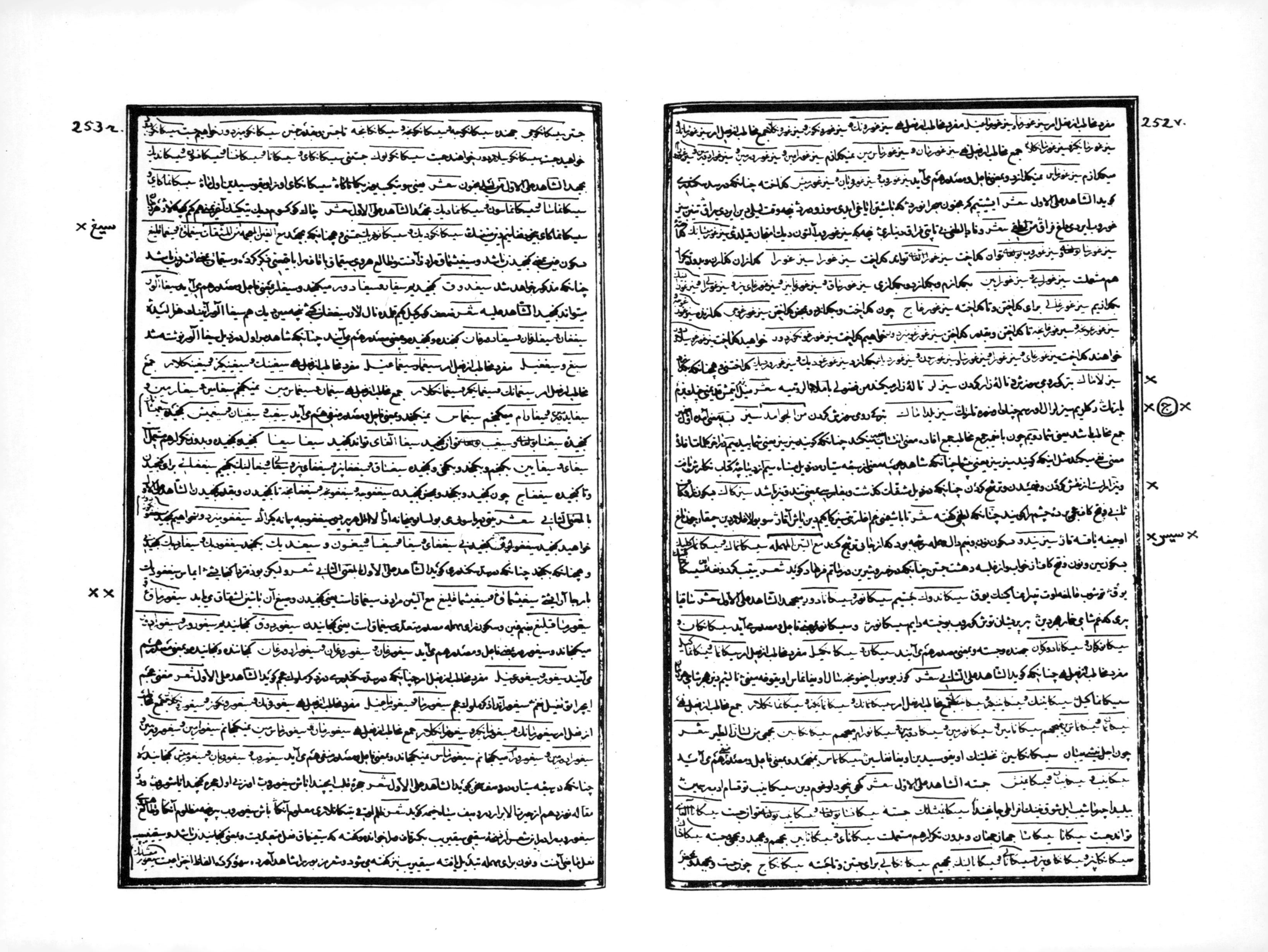

253v.

کجلینغ سیغورنابوتخا و سیغورسب تغاتوران کجانید سیغورا الغای تواند کجانید سیغورا سیغورا کجان کجان و بدون تکرار هم
مستعملست سیغورای و سیغوراین بکجانم و بکجاند و بکجانی و کجانیده سیغورماق و سیغورغلیز و سیغورغای بز و سیغورالی و سیغورالینک
بکجانیم سیغورغالی برای کجانیدن و تا کجانیدن سیغورغاج چون کجانید و بکجاند و بجهت کجانیدن سیغورغوجی کجانندن سیغور
سیغورغوچه و سیغورغاغه تا کجانیدن و مقدم کجانیدن سیغورغو میزدور خواهیم کجانید سیغورغو کوزدور خواهید کجانید سیغور
کجانیدنی سیغورغای سیغورا سیغورنا سیغورچن سیغوردیک بکجاند چنانچه در دیباچه نظم الجواهر کوید که کلدسته سندی
کم دلیجن اداجاشا کی سیغورغای سیغورغودیک سیغوروردیک کجانیدنی و همچنانکه بکجاند سیغمشورماق سیغمشورماقلیغ مصدر
متعدی سیغیشماق است بمعنی کجانیدن و صیغ آن با لفظ تور اشتقاق می یابد چنانچه در لیلی مجنون کوید لشاهد علی الاول المعنی لنا
شعر مرهمید که اول سیپه فی کوه دوش توش توشتین آتینک شلری یوکوه دوش بار یوفه ایژ آنکا یالیناماق تاممکن آتینک ساری سیغیناما
و طالع مرهی سیغیناماق تاتان ذکر کرده و بعضی کجانیدن نوشته سهو کرده سیغیندی کجیده شد و ملتجی شد چنانکه در مراتع
سکندری کوید بالمعنی الاول شعر یا منی راق سیغیندی و منالاریتا نانث و منالامجیفه اتصال ایلاجان نیکیم ایتابان الیا
ایردی هوش تاب یفه حق تیکوب دست برش سیغیندیم کجیده شدم و ملتجی شدم بالمعنی الثانی شعر چو تینغ حکمی منکا بولک
دمل بولتی رزه که ایل تاجیب آنکا اوق بین ضعیف خسته سیغیندیم سیغیندوق کجیده شدیم و ملتجی شدیم سیغینور و سیغینادور
کجیده می شود و ملتجی می شود و سیغینور بمعنی فاعل و مصدر هم می آید سیغینغان و سیغینورغان و سیغینادورغان کجیده شونده و کجیده
شده و ملتجی شونده و ملتجی شده و بمعنی مصدر هم می آید سیغین و سیغینغیل مفرد خطاب المنفصل امر و سیغین کاو کوهی را هم کویند
سیغینما و سیغینماغیل مفرد خطاب المنفصل نهی سیغینینک و سیغینینکیز و سیغینینکلار جمع خطاب المنفصل امر سیغینمانک و سیغینمانکیز و سیغینمانکلار
جمع خطاب المنفصل نهی سیغینمان و سیغینماس مین کجیده نمی شوم و ملتجی نمی شوم سیغینامین و سیغینورمین و سیغینادورمین و سیغینادام
کجیده می شوم و ملتجی می شوم سیغینماس کجیده نمی شود و ملتجی نمی شود بمعنی فاعل و مصدر منفی هم می آید سیغینیب و سیغینیبان و سیغینمیش
کجیده شده و ملتجی شده سیغینمیشانک کجیده شده و ملتجی شده سیغیناتورغا و سیغینیب تولغه کجیده توان شد و ملتجی توان شد
سیغینا آلغای کجیده تواند شد و ملتجی تواند شد سیغینا سیغینا کجیده شده شده و ملتجی شده شده سیغینای و سیغینایین کجیده شوم
و شود و شوی و شده و ملتجی شوم و شود و شوی و شده سیغینسان و سیغینسانکیز و سیغینغای بز و سیغینالی و سیغینالینک کجیده شویم و ملتجی
شویم سیغینغالی برای کجیده شدن و تا کجیده شدن و برای ملتجی شدن و تا ملتجی شدن سیغیناج چون کجیده شد و شود و بجهت
شدن و چون ملتجی شد و شود و بجهت شدن سیغینغوجی کجیده شونده و ملتجی شونده سیغینغوچه و سیغینغاغه
تا کجیده شدن و مقدم کجیده شدن و تا ملتجی شدن و مقدم ملتجی شدن چنانکه شاهد بر ثانی بر این معنی تقدم کجیده شدن کوید شعر
... بولمیش هست و غم خیلی کونکلوم کشورین کیم نشاط آتدا سیغینغونچه نشانی تا المامیش سیغینغو میزدور کجیده خواهیم شد و ملتجی خواهیم
شد سیغینغو کوزدور کجیده خواهید شد و ملتجی خواهید شد سیغینغو سیلاردور کجیده خواهند شد و ملتجی خواهند شد سیغینغو
کجیده شدنی و ملتجی شدنی سیغینغای سیغینا سیغینغان سیغینغودیک سیغینوردیک کجیده شود و ملتجی شود سیغینغودیک سیغینوردیک
کجیده شدنی و همچنانکه کجیده شود و ملتجی شود سیغیندورماق سیغیندورماقلیغ مصدر متعدی معنی آن
یعنی ملتجی ساختن و صیغ آن با لفظ دور اشتقاق می یابد من الحوامض سیغراق بسکون غین و قاف و فتح رای مهمله با الف کشیده کنیزک اولمدار بود
و بفتح سین هم مستعملست و مجازا پیاله و قدح شراب خوری را مانند سیغو بسکون غین اول و ضم ثانی بمعنی کجانیش بود چنانکه در تاریخ

254r.

بابری مذکورست که اکیچه نیلکا آلغوچه سیغو بیز قویه قوبدیک واقعه ایدی سیغناق بسکون غین و فتح نون با الف کشیده
دو معنی دارد اول پناهکاه و جای محفوظ کویند که با آنجا پناه برده شود دویم کوچ خیلی است چنانکه بابر پادشاه فرماید حشر
خیلی حرمی سیغنیناک بولماسا بابر نی ثانی بابری خطی ایلسو خط سیغناق مودور سیغیر بکسر غین و سکون رای مهمله کاو را
کویند سیغیرچماچ بسکون را و فتای قرشت و جیم و فتح میم با الف کشیده کله تا ن کاو را کویند سیغیرچین پرنده ایست سیاه رنک
که نقطهای سفید دارد و آنرا بفارسی سار نامند سیغیرچوقه سیغیرجوق ترکه ربوجاه سیغیرچین بمعنی سار باشد و از سیغیر
هم خوانند سیغیر دیلی بترکه دیلی کیاهیست که آنرا بعربی لسان الثور و بفارسی کاوزبان نامند سیغیر توحش بترکه دیکی نیکان
سیغیرچین بمعنی سار باشد سیغیر قویروق کیاهیست شیر دار که بر کشت زمین معروف و شاخ زیاده بر ... و آنرا المنان
الطب ماهیزهرج و بعربی سم السمک کویند چو آنرا کوبیده در آب اندازند ماهی بیحس شده بر روی آب آمده صید شود سیغین بکسر غین
و سکون نون روییه کاو کوهی را نامند و تیز امراست از کجیده شدن و ملتجی شدن چنانکه کذشت سیغینچه بکسر غین و سکون نون
و فتح جیم ترکه دوی چوبین و حصار کوچک و موضعی باشد که بدان پناه برند مع الفاء من المشتقات سیغماق و سیغماقلیغ بمعنی افشردن بود
سیغتوق افشردیم سیغار و سیغادور می افشرد و بمعنی فاعل و مصدر هم می آید سیغتغان و سیغارغان و سیغادورغان افشارنده
و افشرده و بمعنی مصدر هم می آید سیغ و سیغغیل مفرد خطاب المنفصل امر سیغما و سیغماغیل مفرد خطاب المنفصل نهی سیغینک و
سیغینکیز و سیغینکلار جمع خطاب المنفصل امر سیغمانک و سیغمانکیز و سیغمانکلار جمع خطاب المنفصل نهی سیغمان و سیغماس مین نمی افشرم
سیغامین و سیغارمین و سیغادورمین و سیغادام می افشرم سیغماس نمی افشرد و بمعنی فاعل و مصدر منفی هم می آید سیغیب و سیغیبان و
سیغمیش افشرده ما شاهد علی الاول شعر هر کوزومدین آقا دور ... خونلوغ ... سیقیب
سیغمیشانک افشرده سیغاتورغا و سیغیب تولغه توان افشرد سیغا آلغای تواند افشرد سیغا سیغا افشرده افشرده و بدون تکرار
هم مستعملست سیغای و سیغایین بیفشارم و بیفشارد و بیفشاری و افشرده سیغسان و سیغسانکیز و سیغغای بز و سیغالی و سیغالینک بیفشاریم
سیغغالی برای افشردن و تا افشردن سیغاج چون افشرد و بیفشرد و بجهت افشردن سیغغوجی افشارنده سیغغوچه و سیغغاغه
تا افشردن و مقدم افشردن سیغغو میزدور خواهیم افشرد سیغغو کوزدور خواهید افشرد سیغغو سیلاردور خواهند افشرد
سیغغولوق افشردنی سیغغای و سیغا و سیغغون و سیغدیک بیفشارد سیغغودیک سیغادیک افشردنی و همچنانکه بیفشارد
سیغلماق و سیغلماقلیغ بکسر قاف مع اللام افشرده شدن سیغیلغان و سیغیلورغان و سیغیلادورغان افشرده شونده و افشرده شده بمعنی
علی الاول المعنی الثانی شعر بولدی یوزینک یاد ... تمانا ... نالش ... و لیش مین سیغیلغان ... و
مصدر هم می آید و باقی صیغ به دستور الام اشتقاق می یابد سیغتالماق سیغتالماقلیغ بمبالغه و افراط کردن از روی تکلف سیغتالدی
کویند سیغتالدوق با افراط کریه کردیم سیغتالور و سیغتالادور با افراط کریه میکند و سیغتالور بمعنی فاعل و مصدر هم می آید
سیغتالغان و سیغتالورغان و سیغتالادورغان کریه کننده و کریه کرده و بمعنی مصدر هم می آید سیغتا و سیغتاغیل مفرد خطاب المنفصل امر
سیغتالما و سیغتالماغیل مفرد خطاب المنفصل نهی سیغتالینک و سیغتالینکیز و سیغتالینکلار جمع خطاب المنفصل امر سیغتالمانک و سیغتالمانکیز و سیغتالمانکلار
جمع خطاب المنفصل نهی سیغتالمان و سیغتالماس مین با افراط کریه نمی کنم سیغتالامین و سیغتالارمین و سیغتالادورمین و سیغتالادام با افراط کریه میکنم
سیغتالماس با افراط کریه نمیکند و بمعنی فاعل و مصدر منفی هم می آید سیغتالیب و سیغتالیبان و سیغتالمیش با افراط کریه کرده سیغتالمیشانک با افراط
کریه کرده سیغتالاتورغا و سیغتالیب تولغه با افراط کریه توان کرد سیغتالا آلغای با افراط کریه تواند کرد سیغتالای و سیغتالایین کریه کنم

و بدون نکول هر متعلت سیقتاتو سیقتاماین بافراط کریه کنم و کند و کنی و کرده سیقتاساق و سیقتاماپز و سیقتاغای و سیقتاغای...

بافراط کریه کنیم سیقتاقلیلی برای کریه کردن بافراط و نا کریه کننده سیقتاقاج چون بافراط کریه کرد و کند و مجمل کردن سیقتاغوچ

بافراط کریه کنند سیقتاغوچه و سیقتاغونه و سیقتاقاغه بافراط کریه کردن و نا کریه کرده سیقتاغونیزدود بافراط کریه خواهیم کرد و سیقتا

بافراط کریه خواهید کرد سیقتاغوسیلاردود بافراط کریه خواهند کرد سیقتاغولوق بافراط کریه کردن سیقتاغای و سیقتاسا و سیقتا

سیقتادیلت بافراط کریه کنند سیقتاغودیلت و سیقتاردیلت بافراط کریه کردن و همچنانکه کند سیقتالماق و سیقتالماقلیغ مع الکاف العجمی

سیقتاماق بمعنی کریه کردن بطرز لطافت است و مشتق آن با الاما شتقاقات است یا بمعنی ماهی الکوش جنکرا آنها پرداخت سیقتاتماق و سیقتاتماق

مع التا المصدریه بمعنی بافراط کریانیدن سیقتاتتی کریانید الشاهد علیه شعر اول آی کولا کولامیز ایاغ... بمعنی سیقتای

بمعنی یا یکه سیقتانتی بمعنی سیقتالمین و سیقتاتای مین و سیقتاتورمین و سیقتانادیرمین و سیقتاتورار بافراط میکنیم الشاهد علی الثالث

شعر هجران کیدا بوزمغ کونکلوم ادا یا بعد یار غالم اهلین سیقتاتورمین آه. وافتاد در دامی و تا باقی بمعنی بدستور تا ...

اشتقاق و ما بعد من الجامد سیق بترکه و بی بمعنی تنک دتنکنا و متراکم تا شد بمعنی لشکر هم آمده و نیز از رستاخیز چنانکه کذ

سیقلیق بترکه و بی بمعنی جا و اول تنکی و مضایقه شدد و بیم ضمیر و آملزی کلمه ضمیر طبور جر آید سیقیش بمعنی فشار بود

سیقیلمق برابطه الحرمه بمعنی تنکنا و متراکم تا شد سیقیسد بترکه و بی افشرده هر چیز بود که آن را بعربی عصاره کویند و ما ...

بمعنی عصر و شیره درخت هم استعمال میشود مع الکاف من المشتقات سیکاک و سیکیناکلیک سیکون کاف عجمی و کسر را بی مهمله و سیکنات

سیکینا کلیک بکمه کاف عجمی و سکون تاء مهمله بمعنی جستن بود و جستن از خواب و جستن از غلبه و دهشت را سیکانماک کویند چنانکه

مذکور شد سیکریدیه سیکریدی جست الشاهد علی الاول شعر تاش ایریق وه کهنه رو کونکلیکا کا را ینمادی شعله

کیم تیشه سیدین سیکریدی فرهادنینک سیکرو و سیکریدی و سیکریه سیکردادور بمعنی الشاهد علی الاول شعر کوبلیم

سوفادین قطره سیکریدی یلی چون تکلم و توی علیکدین چقار و بالفظ سیکرکان و سیکرکان و سیکریدورکان و سیکرکان

سیکرورکان و سیکرادورکان جهنده و جسته چنانکه در خسرو شیرین در وصف قصر چا و شل فرهاد کوید الشاهد علی الاول

بالمعنی الثانی شعر سدف کونجوس لیلا هر ایان آیتی سوبو سودین سیکریکان هر قطره اینجی بمعنی صدم کم می آیند سیکری و سیکری

سیکر و سیکریکیل مفرد غالب از فصل امر سیکریا و سیکریپا ادیل و سیکریا و سیکریپا کیل مفرد غائب از فصل امر سیکرینک و سیکرنکز

سیکرینکلار و سیکرنک و سیکرونکز و سیکرینکلار جمع غالب از فصل امر سیکریانک و سیکرلانکر و سیکریانکلار و سیکرمانک و سیکرمانکز

سیکریانکلار جمع غائب از فصل امر سیکریامن و سیکرامن و سیکرامن و سیکرماس من بمعنی سیکرومن و سیکرومن و سیکریدورمن

سیکریرام و سیکرابیر و سیکرای من و سیکرورمن و سیکرادورمن و سیکریرام بمعنی سیکرماس و سیکرمیاس منفی دو عنوان

مستقبل و هم می آیند سیکریر و سیکربان و سیکریمش و سیکریر و سیکریش و سیکریاش جسته سیکرینمانک و سیکرمانک جسته

سیکرپا بولغای و سیکریپتولغای و سیکریپا بولغای و سیکرپا بولغوا جست سیکری آلغای و سیکرا آلغای توانست سیکری سیکری

سیکرا سیکریپا جست و جسته سیکری و سیکری و سیکرای و سیکرامن بمعنی بجهند بمعنی جسته سیکریانک و سیکرانه

سیکرکای و سیکرلی و سیکیلینک و سیکریانک و سیکرکانز و سیکرکای بیز و سیکرلی و سیکرالینک بمعنی چنانکه شاهد

منابع داده در شایم الجنه ذکر مولانا جلال الدین محمد رومی کوید کر بیری با یا بر بکادیب تیر که کیلینک بو تام دین یا نا بیر کادیب تیر که

کیلینک بو تام دین یانا بیر تامه سیکرلی سیکرجالی و سیکرلیلی برای جستن و تاجسته سیکریکلیج و سیکرکاج چون جست و بمعنی

جستن سیکریکوجی و سیکرکوجی بمعنی سیکریکوچه و سیکریکوچه و سیکریکوچه سیکرکوچه و سیکرکوغه و سیکرکاغه نا جسته

بقاء جستن سیکریکونیز دور و سیکرکونیز دور و نیز خواهیم جست سیکریکونکوز دور و سیکرکونکوز دور خواهید جست سیکریکوسیلار دور و سیکرکو

خواهند جست سیکریکولوک و سیکرکولوک جستنی سیکریکای و سیکریکا و سیکرکونو و سیکریدیک و سیکرکای و سیکرا و سیکرا سیکر

سیکریتی و سیکردیلت بمعنی چنانکه شاهد بر هنر داور قسم دیم انجوب القلوب در وصف عیوانکان کوید کما کوید ...

دین لوکاییل سیکرینا سیکریکودیلت و سیکریدیلت و سیکیریکدیلت و سیکرکدیلت بمعنی جستنی و همچنانکه بمعنی سیکریتمالک و سیکریتماکلیک

سکون کاف عجمی و کسر را مع التا و سیکرتماک و سیکرتماکلیک بکاف و سکون را مع التا المصدریه بمعنی جهانیدن سیکریتماک

سیکرتادور و سیکرتیر و سیکرتاداددور بمعنی جهانید الشاهد علی الاول شعر ایله صیدار ایجره کیم یش تا اول لیا بکولار کیم بکاری بین

چرخ اندره سیکرتنکو سیلیدور کیش و نیز بمعنی آمارین بج با تای تورشه و اوشوق اول الشقاق ما بعد من الجامد سیکرتمه بکونی

کاف عجمی و تای قرشت و کسر و فتح میم موضع شد و نیز در اعضای عصب و بار لیجه و کره او ما کویند کم بخطر لهاوت و پی بیدار از آنجا تاشد

چنانکه در تاریخ نابری مذکور است که تا ... اوچه و سیکرتمه یول لادین تو شولدی سیکنمر بکسر کاف و سکون را مع هم مشدد

هشتم را مانند بتشدید کاف نیز مستعملست چنانکه در مطرح محمد سیستان کوید شعر بایه او رینیدا سیکنمر آنکلاتوت

آسیتا ابر کیمت سیکنمر کرد و ث و مفار و معنی جستن و الکلاه اختص ستوده بود سیکیل بکسر کاف عجمی و مترکی و می ترکیب

که دو دست و اعضا بر آید و آن را بعربی ثولول کویند مع الکاف من المشتقات سیلماق و سیلماقلیغ بمعنی پاک کردن سیلادوق پاک کن

سیلادی و سیلادور و پاک میکند و سیلار بمعنی دست مالید و با مخفی یا خود از مصدر سیلاماک است و بمعنی امل و مصدر هم می آید

سیلغان و سیلاغان و سیلادوغان پاک کننده و پاک کرده و بمعنی مصدر هم میاید سیل و سیلغیل مفرد غالب از فصل امر سیلسا

سیلماغیل مفرد غالب از فصل امر سیلینک و سیلینکز و سیلینکلار جمع غالب از فصل امر سیلسانک و سیلسانکز و سیلسانکلار جمع غالب

فصل سیلمان و سیلمامن بالعکس سیلامین و سیلارمین و سیلادیرمین و سیلادورمن و سیلاام پاک میکنم و سیلاماس ماسکنا ...

اشتراک دارد بمعنی دست مالم سیلماس پاک نمیکند و بمعنی ام و مصدر منفی هم می آید سیلسه و سیلمه و سیلیش پاک کرده ...

پاک کرده ما تولغای سیلیب تولغای پاک توان کرد سیلا آلغای پاک تواند کرد سیلای و سیلاین پاک کنم و کند و کنی و کرده سیلسا

سیلغانیز و سیلغای بیز و سیلارکای و سیلادیکای و سیلادیکای پاک کنیم و سیلادیکای و سیلادیکای پاک کنند و معنی دست مالم سیلغالی برای

پاک کردن و تا پاک کرده سیلغاج چون پاک کرد و کند و مجمل کردن سیلغوچی پاک کننده سیلغوچه و سیلغونه و سیلغاغه تا پاک کرده

و بمعنی پاک کردن سیلغونیز دور پاک خواهیم کرد سیلغونکز دور پاک خواهید کرد سیلغوسیلار دور پاک خواهند کرد سیلغولوق

پاک کردن سیلغای و سیلاو سیلنا و سیلون و سیلادیلت پاک کند سیلغودیلت و سیلادیلت پاک کردن و همچنانکه پاک کند سیلماق

سیلماقلیغ بکسر لام اول و سکون ثانی و سیلنماق و سیلنماقلیغ مع النون بمعنی پاک شدن و مشتق سیلینمک بالام ... سیلماق ...

اشتقاق ما بعد سیلاماک و سیلاماکلیک بفتح لام دست کشیدن و مجازا بمعنی بر خود خوب و مهربانی کردن استعمال میشود و بمعنی ...

هم نوشته سهو کرده سیلاماک بضم ... بکشیدن چنانکه کفته شد سیلادی دست کشید و مهربانی کرد چنانکه در لیلی مجنون

کوید بالمعنی الاول شعر باشین سیلادی فراق او بار کیم ... بوناش ... سیلار و سیلادیدور دست میکشد و مهربانی میکند

و سیلاب بمعنی امل و مصدر هم می آید و نیز بمعنی بالعکس ... سیلاماق اشتراک دارد سیلاکان و سیلادیکان و سیلادیکان دست

و دست کشیده و مهربانی کننده و مهربانی کرده چنانکه شاعر ... بمعنی مهربانی کننده ... کوید کما باین سیلاکان اینینه ...

255v

آباد و بمعنی مصدر هم می آید سیلاچو سیلاچو کیل مفرد غائب المستقبل سیلاچا و سیلاچا کیل مفرد غائب المستقبل سیلاتنك
و سیلاکلار جمع غائب المستقبل سیلاتماتك و سیلاتماکر سیلاتماکلار جمع غائب المستقبل سیلاتان و سیلاتاسین دست میکنم و مرزانی میکنم
سیلاویمن و سیلاریمن سیلاریقز سیلارام دست میکنم و مرزانی میکنم و سیلاریمن و سیلارام بمعنی پاك میکنم هم باشد سیلاماس
دست نمیکند و مرزانی نمیکند و بمعنی فاعل و مصدر منفی هم می آید سیلاتبو سیلاتان و سیلامیش دست کشیده چنانکه در لسان الطیر
خطاب بباز گوید الشاهد علی الاول شعر شاه الیکو سکینك بولغای صدام لعنتك ول تارتیب بید مکان بر مقام ایلکی سیلامیش
الیکو برتو بالینکا جنکو روب سنقل ابله چنکا لینکا ومیز دتاریغ الانبیا مذکر کاظاب الاخد و دکویکم الیکاری باریسیلا
اوجاسیفه الیکین سیلاب ازدها بولدین چیقیب غوغا وتی لار ونیزه یم الحبه مرزه کر ادیب احمد که نابینا بوده کوید کر
بلطاق بیله سیلاب یب تورکه ایناکو باشیغه اوخشار وهم مذکر بمجنون در لغت مجنون با وحوش کوید الشاهد علی الثانی
شعر کاهی ایچیبان یونولوک چیقیش کاه سیلاتبان آینك سیرنیش و بمعنی مرزانی کرده هم باشد سیلامیشاند دست کشیده
کرده سیلاتنا بولغای سیلاب ولغه دست تواز کشید و مرزانی تواز کرد سیلاب آلغه دست تواند کشید و مرزانی تواند کرد سیلاتو
دست کشان و مرزانی کنان و بدون تکرار هم مستعمل سیلای و سیلاین دست بکشم و بکشد و بکش و کشیده و مرزانی کنم و کند و کن
و کرده سیلاتناك و سیلاکاتر و سیلاکای تر سیلاکای سیلای دست بکشیم و مرزانی کنیم و سیلاتلی و سیلالینك بمعنی پاك کنیم هم باشد سیلاکالی
برای دست کشیدن و تا دست کشیده و برای مرزانی کردن و تا کرده سیلاکاچ چون دست کشید و بکشد و بعض کشیدن و چون مرزانی
کرد و کند و بعض کردن سیلاکوچی دست کشنده و مرزانی کننده سیلاکوچه و سیلاکوچیز و سیلاکاچنار تا دست کشیدن و بقدر دست کشیدن
و تا مرزانی کردن و بقدر مرزانی کردن سیلاکومیز دور دست خواهیم کشید و مرزانی خواهیم کرد سیلاکونکوزدور دست خواهید کشید و مرزانی
خواهید کرد سیلاکولار دور دست خواهند کشید و مرزانی خواهند کرد سیلاکولوك دست کشیدنی و مرزانی کردنی سیلاکای و سیلا
سیلاتون و سیلادیك دست بکشد و مرزانی بکند سیلاکودیك و سیلاگودیك دست کشیدنی و بمعنی انکه دست بکشد و مرزانی بکند و بمعنی انکه
بکند سیلاتمانك و سیلاتماکلیك مع التاء مصدر متعدی است بمعنی دست کشانیدن و مرزانی فرمودن و صیغ آن بدستور تا اول مشتق
می یابد سیلاتماك و سیلاتماکلیك مع التاء مصدر مفعول است بمعنی بکسی دست کشیدن و مرزانی کردن و صیغ آن با تاء اشتقاق می یابد
سیلاتماك و سیلاتماکلیك مع النون مصدر انفعال است بمعنی دست کشیده شدن و مرزانی نامتن و صیغ آن با نون اشتقاق می یابد
سیلکماك و سیلکماکلیك بسکون لام و کاف تکاندن سیلکدوك تکاندیم سیلکادی و سیلکاید ور میتکاند و سیلکاکاد بمعنی ماضی
و مصدر هم می آید سیلکاکان و سیلکاکان سیلکادور تکاننده و تکانیده و بمعنی مکنده هم می آید سیلك و سیلکاکیل مفرد غائب
المستقبل سیلکا و سیلکا کیل مفرد غائب المستقبل سیلکینك و سیلکینکر و سیلکینکلار جمع غائب المستقبل سیلکماتك
سیلکماتکر و سیلکماتکلار جمع غائب المستقبل سیلکامن میتکانم سیلکاکامین و سیلکامین و سیلکادور میتکانم سیلکماس
نمیتکاند و بمعنی فاعل و مصدر منفی هم می آید سیلکیب و سیلکبان و سیلکمیش تکانده سیلکیشانك تکانیده سیلکا و لغا و سیلکیک
توان تکانید سیلکا آلغه تواند تکانید سیلکا سیلکا تکان تکان و بدون تکرار هم مستعمل سیلکای و سیلکاین تبکانم و بکا
و تکانی و تکانیده سیلکاك و سیلکاکای تر و سیلکا و سیلکالینك تکانیم سیلکاکالی برای تکانیدن و تا تکانیده سیلکاکاچ
چون تکانید و تکاند و بعض تکاندن سیلکوچی تکاننده سیلکوچه و سیلکاچنا تکاندن و بقدر تکاندن سیلکومیز دور
خواهیم تکانید سیلکونکوزدور خواهید تکانید سیلکولاردور خواهند تکانید سیلکولوك تکاندنی سیلکاکای و سیلکا و سیلکا

256r

سیلکودیك و سیلکودیك تکاند چنانکه تکاند سیلکودیك و سیلکادیك تکاندنی و بمعنی انکه تکاند سیلکیتماك و سیلکیتماکلیك مع النون بکسر الکاف
تکانده شدن سیلکینیب و سیلکینبان و سیلکینمیش تکانده شده چنانکه در لسان الطیر در داستان مرغ گوید الشاهد علی الاول شعر
سیلکینیب چون ایچره توشمش برچی تا بمیش آیدین ز سبز و خرجی کشودی و باقی صیغ را بر سالق با نون اشتقاق باید سیلاق بفتح لام
رومی مخفی وطن و مسکن باشد سیلکینماك تعویذی بود که از کاغذ و امثال آن ساخته باشند ... شعر
امر شام تلك پری لار ... سیلکینماك ...
بین مذکور ... نوشته ... و در ...
سیلیغ ... باشد الشاهد علیه شعر ...
سیلیغ ... شعر ...
چو ... سیلیغ ... چنانکه گوید شعر ...
... سیلیغ ... نوشته سیلیغ آنچه ...
بود که ... باشد مع المیم المثقلة سیمیرماك مع الراء المهملة فربه شدن ... مستعمل چنانکه ...
در ذیل مفتوحات ... مع الراء المعجمة فربه مع النون من المثقلات سینماك مع النون شکسته شدن
سیندی شکسته شد سینار و سینا دور شکسته می شود ... سینا ...
هم می آید سینغان و سینغان و سینا دور شکسته شده ... الشاهد علی الاول ... شعر ...
اولسا ... مفرد غائب المستقبل ...
... سینماتك ... سینماتکلار ...
... سینماکلار جمع غائب المستقبل ... شکسته میشوم سینامین و سینامیز ...
سینادام شکسته میشوم سینماس شکسته نمیشود و بمعنی فاعل و مصدر هم می آید سینیب و سینیبان و سینمیش شکسته شده
شکسته شده سینا ... شکسته ... سینا ... سینا شکسته شکسته و بدون تکرار هم
مستعمل سینای و سینایین شکسته شوم و شود و شوی و شد ... سینا ...
سینغای ... شکسته شویم ... سینغالی برای شکسته شدن و تا شکسته
شده ... سینغاچ ...
شکسته شد و شود و بعض شکسته شدن سینغوچی شکسته شونده چنانکه در لسان الطیر ... گوید شعر ...
کیم ... سینغوچه و سینغاچنا تا شکسته شدن و بقدر شکسته شدن سینغو
خواهیم شکست سینغونکوز خواهید شکست سینغوسی خواهند شکست الشاهد علیه شعر ...
... سینغولوق شکسته شدنی سینغای و سینا و سینا ... سینادیك شکسته شود
سینادیك شکسته شدنی و بمعنی انکه شکسته شود الشاهد علی الاول بالمعنی الثانی من لسان الطیر شعر ...
سینغودیك ... و سینادیك ... بمعنی ... و بمعنی انکه ...
مصدر متعدی ... الشاهد علی الاول شعر ...

256v

سیندورتاق هان ابریش سیند و مرغودلنه سیند و مرغودلنکش و همچنانکه بشکند الشاهد علی الاول المعنی الثانی شعر سیناسا

کوکلوم غنچه بیکم سنك بادان فراق بولدی غم لتو جسم دین هر باره دین سیند و مرغودلك و در خسرو شیرین در وصف فرهاد کو

کوید المعنی الاول شعر حباب بکی غنچه لیغ آفته تونیغ آسیب سیند و مرغودلك بو سینه تیغ و تاقی مینغ برتیغ با القطعه استغنا

می یابد سینقماق و سینقماقلیغ بکسر نون و سکون قاف شکسته حال و شکسته دل شدن و مجازا بمعنی ناتوان شدن استعمال

می شود سینقتی شکسته حال شد چنانکه در فرهاد و شیرین در مجوبی فرهاد کوید شعر چو کونکلی هجر ایله تاشیدین سینیقتی

زنان فصد ایلادی اهل حقیق سینقور و سینیقادور شکسته حال میشود و سینقور بمعنی فاعل و مصدر هم می آید سینقغان

سینقوغان و سینقادوران شکسته حال شونده و شکسته حال شده و بمعنی مصدر هم می آید سینق و سینقغیل مفرد غائب

امر فصل امر سینقما و سینقماغیل مفرد غائب المنفصل فی سینقینك و سینقینکز و سینقینکلار جمع غائب المنفصل امر سینقما و سینقماخکز

سینقماخلار جمع غائب المنفصل فی سینقمان و سینقمارمین شکسته حال نمیشوم سینقامین و سینقورمین و سینقادورمین و سینقومن

شکسته حال میشوم سینقماس شکسته حال نمیشود و بمعنی فاعل و مصدر منفی هم می آید سینقیب سینقیبان سینقیمیش

شکسته حال شده سینقیمیشانك شکسته حال شدن سینقا اولغه و سینقیب تونه شکسته حال توان شد سینقا الغای شکسته

حال شوم و شود و شوی و شده سینقغای و سینقغای بز سینقغای بز سینقالی سینقالیك شکسته حال شوم سینقغالی برای شکسته

حال شدن و تا شکسته حال شده سینقغاج چون شکسته حال شود و شد و بعد شدن سینقغوچی شکسته حال شونده سینقغوجه

سینقغوجه و سینقغاخه تا شکسته حال شدن و بعد آن سینقغوسیزدور شکسته حال خواهیم شد سینقغوسیزدور شکسته

حال خواهید شد سینقغوسیلاردور شکسته حال خواهند شد سینقغولوق شکسته حال شدنی سینقغای و سینقا و سینقسا

سینقسون و سینقیدلك شکسته حال شود سینقغوسیدلك و سینقوردیك شکسته حال شدنی و همچنانکه شکسته حال شوده

سینقتورماق شکسته حال و شکسته دل شدن و مجازا بمعنی ناتوان کردن باشد سینقتورغای و سینقتورا و سینقتورسا و سینقتورسون

سینقتورلك شکسته حال کند الشاهد علی الثالث شعر کیم وفا اهلین سینقتورسا بیلور مین آنچه کیم کوپ پنهان [illegible]

کوپ سود هم و سینغ آن برین سیاق با لفظ توان اشتقاق می یابد سیناماق سینامالیك بفتح نون امتحان کردن سینادوك امتحان کردم

سینار و سینایدور امتحان میکند و سینار با مصدر سیناماق هم اشتراك دارد یعنی شکسته میشود و بمعنی فاعل و مصدر هم می آید سیناغان

سیناغان و سینایدوکان امتحان کننده و امتحان کرده و بمعنی مصدر هم می آید سینا و سیناکیل مفرد غائب المنفصل امر سینانا و سیناماکیل

مفرد غائب المنفصل فی سینانك و سیناکیز و سیناکلار جمع غائب المنفصل امر سینامانك و سیناماکیز و سیناماخلار جمع غائب المنفصل فی

سینامان و سینامارمین امتحان نمیکنم سینایمین و سینارمین و سینادورمین و سینارمن امتحان میکنم و سینامانك با مصدر سیناماق اشتراك

دارد یعنی شکسته میشوم سینامار امتحان نمیکند و بمعنی فاعل و مصدر منفی هم می آید سیناب و سینابان و سینامیش امتحان کرده

سینامیشانك امتحان کرده سینانا بولغای و سیناب بولغای امتحان توان کرد سینای آلغای امتحان تواند کرد سینای و سینای سینای

امتحان نکنم و بدون تکرار هم مستعملست سینای و سینایین امتحان بکند و نکنم و نکنی و نکرده چنانکه شاهد بر [illegible]

از مرتبة الابرار بمعنی اخیر کوید شعر کیم نی که ایلادی [illegible] کوپ سینامای [illegible] سینالك و سیناه

سیناکای بیز و سینالی و سینالیك امتحان کنیم سیناغالی برای امتحان کردن و تا امتحان کرده سیناغوچی دور و امتحان خواهیم کرد سیناغوسی

امتحان خواهید کرد سیناغوسیلار دور امتحان خواهند کرد سیناغولوك امتحان کردنی سیناغای و سینانا و سیناسا و سینادیك امتحا

۱۱.ل ۷ خال تواند شد سینقا سینقا شکسته خال شده شده وبدون تکرار مستعملست
سینقای و سینقایین شکسته

257r

کند سیناکودیك و سیناردیك امتحان کردن و همچنانکه امتحان کند سینالمالدو و سینالمالیك بفتح نون و سکون لام امتحان شدن

سینالیب سینالیبان و سینالمیش امتحان شده چنانکه شاهد بر اول اعلام مکتوب شصت و نهم کوید که [illegible]

سینکنه اعتماد قالیب تور و هر تا بیو معلوم بولوب و سینالیب [illegible] تاقی مینغ برین سیاق با لام اشتقاق می یابد سینکماك و سینکماکلیك

بسکون نون و کاف عجمی سه معنی دارد اول منجذب شدن یعنی بخود فرو کشیده شدن دوم خوش کردن سیم هضم کردن و فرو خوردن

تحمل کردن هم استعمال میشود در معنی که سر خود را بزیر پر و بال کشد آنحالت را هم سینکماك کوید سینکه منجذب شده بخود فرو کشیده شد

و خوش کرد و هضم کرد چنانکه بمعنی اول در تاریخ الانبیاء مذکور ولادت حضرت رسول صلی الله علیه و آله و سلم کوید که [illegible]

سینکدی سینکار و سینکادور منجذب و بخود فرو کشیده میشود و خوش میکند و هضم میکند چنانکه شاهد بر [illegible]

هشتم از مرتبة الابرار در باب [illegible] کوید شعر یا که سینکار [illegible] سینکار بمعنی فاعل و مصدر

هم می آید سینکگان و سینکاکوان و سینکادورکان منجذب شونده و منجذب شده و خوش کننده و خوش کرده و هضم کننده و هضم کرده و بمعنی مصدر

هم می آید سینک و سینککیل مفرد غائب المنفصل امر سینکما و سینکماکیل مفرد غائب المنفصل فی سینکنك و سینکیکز و سینککلار

جمع غائب المنفصل امر سینکمانك و سینکماکیز و سینکماکلار جمع غائب المنفصل فی سینکمان و سینکمارمین منجذب نمیشوم و خوش نمیکنم و هضم

نمیکنم سینکامین و سینکارمین و سینکادورمین سینکامن منجذب میشوم و خوش میکنم و هضم میکنم سینکماس منجذب نمیشود و خوش نمیکند و هضم

نمیکند و بمعنی فاعل و مصدر منفی هم می آید سینکیب و سینکیبان و سینکمیش منجذب شده و خوش کرده و هضم کرده چنانکه شاهد بر اول

[illegible] کوید المعنی الاول شعر سینکیب [illegible] کوید

الثانی شعر [illegible]

توتی بولوب سینکمیشانك منجذب شده و خوش کرده و هضم کرده سینکا بولغای و سینکیب [illegible] منجذب توان شد و خوش توان کرد و هضم توان کرد

سینکا آلغای منجذب تواند شد و خوش تواند کرد و هضم تواند کرد سینکا سینکا منجذب شد شده و خوش کنان و هضم کنان چنانکه

کوید المعنی الثانی شعر [illegible]

سینکای سینکایین منجذب شوم و شود و شوی شده و خوش و هضم کنم و کند و کنی و کرده سینکالی و سینکگالی و سینکاکای بیز و سینکگا

منجذب شویم و خوش کنیم و هضم کنیم سینکگالی برای منجذب شدن و تا منجذب شده و برای خوش کردن و هضم کردن و تا کرده سینکگاج چون

منجذب شد و شود و بعد شدن و چون خوش و هضم کرد و بعد کردن سینکگوچی منجذب شونده و خوش کننده و هضم کننده سینکگوچه

سینکگوچه و سینکگاچه تا منجذب شدن و تا خوش کردن و تا هضم کردن و بعد آنها سینکگوسیزدور منجذب خواهیم شد و خوش خواهیم

و هضم خواهیم کرد سینکگوسیزدور منجذب خواهید شد و خوش و هضم خواهید کرد سینکگوسیلاردور منجذب خواهند شد و خوش

کرد و هضم خواهند کرد سینکگولوك منجذب شدنی و خوش کردنی و هضم کردنی سینکگای و سینکگا و سینکسا و سینکسون و سینکدیك

منجذب شود و خوش کند و هضم کند چنانکه در لسان الطیر در صفت استغنا کوید الشاهد علی الثالث المعنی الثالث شعر [illegible]

یوز تومان بحر عمیق قطره [illegible] سینکماکای و سینکماسا و سینکماسون و سینکمادیك منجذب نشود و خوش نکند و هضم

نکند الشاهد علی الاول المعنی الاول شعر [illegible] سینکگودیك و سینکادیك منجذب [illegible]

و همچنانکه شود و خوش کردن و همچنانکه کند سینکورماك سینکورماکلیك بسکون نون مع الاول و ضم کاف عجمی مع الراء المهمله [illegible]

و خوش کردن و هضم کردن [illegible] و خوش میکند و هضم میکند [illegible]

بمعنی فاعل و مصدر هم می آید چنانکه بمعنی هضم کردن گوید شعر ای کونکول ایلکین جفا سین سینکوروردین اولکونک ایمدی بمان سینی افتاد
جلک دریا دایله سینکوردوم مجذوب ساختم و خوش کردم و هضم کردم چنانکه در حیرة الابرار گوید المعنی الثانی شعر جون منی شیدا
آشفته حال بیله تماغه سینکوردوم خیال سینکورنام و سینکورکامین و سینکورکای مین مجذوب سازم و خوش کنم و هضم کنم چنانکه
در فرهاد و شیرین در تعریف منع فرهاد از زبان خسرو گوید الشاهد علی الاول المعنی الثالث شعر سینکورنام غصه دین اولماد کرا
ایشیمکا بارجا ایل کولماله کیراکوت ونیز در سفینه سیاره گوید الشاهد علی الثالث بالمعنی الثالث شعر شه دین ولی ... لیغ کرکورکای
مین جوصله نایلیکیم سینکورکامین سینکورکوچی مجذوب سازنده و خوش کننده و هضم کننده چنانکه در تنبیهات محبوب القلوب ... صانع
بمعنی ثالث گوید که خام لازمی بیشیم کوچی و طعام لازمی سینکورکوچی دناق صنع برین سایل قه ضم کاف عجمی و رای مهمله موافق شوق والشفاق
سینکورماک و سینکورماکلیک بسکون نون و کاف عجمی مصدر متعدیست یعنی جذب کنانیدن و خوش فرمودن و فرو خورانیدن سینکورور
سینکورودرباغ مجذوب فرموده و خوش فرموده و فرو خورانیده چنانکه سبعه سیاره در داستان بهرام گوید الشاهد علی الاول المعنی
الثالث شعر چونکه کل صلدین ... تکاریب کرودون ... المجاز ... کیسترودی ... سینکورور
مثل و عیشوناق صنع برین ... اشتقاق می یابد سینکورانماک و سینکورانماکلیک بسکون نون و کاف عجمی و رای مهمله با لفکیند ازری
حزن آهسته گریه کردن چنانکه گوید لا ادری شعر ایستاسام دردا جلادین عشقنکی پنهان ایلماک کیمه لارکه اینکرانا کور ... تیم
که سینکرانماک سینکرادی گریه کرد سینکرار سینکراید و گریه میکند و سینکرار بمعنی فاعل و مصدر هم می آید سینکراکان و سینکراکای
سینکرایدرکا گریه کننده و گریه کرده و بمعنی مصدر هم می آید سینکراو سینکراکیل مفرد مخاطب فعل امر سینکرانما و سینکراناکیل مفرد
مخاطب نهی سینکرانک و سینکرانکز و سینکرانکلار جمع مخاطب فعل امر سینکرانمانک و سینکرانمانکز و سینکرانمانکلار جمع مخاطب نهی
سینکرانان و سینکرانامین گریه میکنم سینکرارمین و سینکراورمین و سینکرایدورمین سینکرارکه گریه میکنم سینکرامس گریه میکند و بمعنی فاعل و
منفی هم می آید سینکراب و سینکرامان و سینکرامیش گریه کرده سینکرامیشانک گریه کرده سینکرالسابولغای و سینکراب بولغای گریه تواند کرد سینکرای
گریه تواند کرد سینکرایو و سینکراو سینکرای گریه کنان سینکرای و سینکرایین گریه کنم و کند و کی و کرده سینکرلساک و سینکراکاینز و سینکرا
سینکرلی و سینکرالیلی گریه کنیم سینکراکالی برای گریه کردن و تا گریه کرده سینکراکاچ چون گریه کرد و کند و محض کردن سینکراکوچی گریه کننده
سینکراکوچه و سینکراکوچه و سینکراکاغه تا گریه کردن و بعد گریه کردن سینکراکومزدو گریه خواهیم کرد سینکراکونکزدو گریه خواهد کرد
سینکراکوسیلار گریه خواهند کرد سینکراکولوک گریه کردن سینکراکای و سینکراسا و سینکراسون و سینکرادیک گریه کند سینکراکودک
کردن و چنانکه گریه کند سینکرلاماک و سینکرلاماکلیک بسکون نون و رای مهمله و کاف عجمی مع الاماله پی کردن یعنی عصب پا قطع کردن
سینکرلادیک پی کردیم سینکرلادم سینکرلایدور پی میکند و سینکرلار بمعنی فاعل و مصدر هم می آید سینکرلاکان و سینکرلاکای
پی کننده و پی کرده و بمعنی مصدر هم می آید سینکرلاکان و سینکرلایدرکا پی کننده و پی کرده و بمعنی مصدر هم می آید سینکرلا
سینکرلاکیل مفرد مخاطب فعل امر سینکرلاما و سینکرلاماکیل مفرد مخاطب نهی سینکرلانک و سینکرلانکز و سینکرلانکلار
جمع مخاطب فعل امر سینکرلامانک و سینکرلامانکز و سینکرلامانکلار جمع مخاطب نهی سینکرلامان و سینکرلامای میکنم سینکرلامین
سینکرلارمین سینکرلایدورمین و سینکرلادم پی میکنم سینکرلامس پی میکند و بمعنی فاعل و مصدر منفی هم می آید سینکرلاب و سینکرلاب
سینکرلامیش پی کرده سینکرلامیشانک پی کرده سینکرلاسابولغای و سینکرلاب بولغای پی تواند کرد سینکرلاغای پی تواند کرد سینکرلایو
سینکرلای و سینکرلای پی کنان و بدون تکرار هم مستعملست سینکرلای و سینکرلایین پی کنم و کند و کی و کرده سینکرلاساک و سینکرلاکاینز

سینکرلاکاینز و سینکرلالی و سینکرلالیلک پی کنیم سینکرلاکالی برای پی کردن و تا پی کرده سینکرلاکوچی پی کننده سینکرلاکوچه و سینکرلاکوچه
سینکرلاکاغه تا پی کردن و بعد پی کردن سینکرلاکومزدو پی خواهیم کرد سینکرلاکونکزدو پی خواهید کرد سینکرلاکوسیلار پی خواهند
سینکرلاکولوک پی کردن سینکرلاکای و سینکرلاسا و سینکرلاسون و سینکرلادیک پی کند سینکرلاکودک پی کردن و چنانکه پی
سینکرلاتماک سینکرلاتماکلیک مع التاء مصدر متعدیست دیگری را بقطع عصب پا و پی کردن امر فرمودن و صیغ آن بدستور بالا
اشتقاق می یابد سینکرلانماک و سینکرلانماکلیک مع النون پی شدن و صیغ آن بانون اشتقاق می یابد من الجوامد سین
کلام ضمیر مفرد مخاطبست یعنی تو و در آخر کلمه افاده انتساب بضمیر مذکور کند چنانکه گویند سین سین یعنی تو تو و باشباع کسره
آمده اول بمعنی ... اکوید دوم امر است از شکسته شدن ونیز حرفیست از حروف تهجی سینجلاین مثل تو سیندی
هندی کان بود که آن را بعربی مقراض گویند ... یعنی شکسته شد چنانکه در ذیل سیماق ... سیندوردین و سین سین
یعنی تو تو الشاهد علیه شعر آیریلیب ... جان بیله کونکلوم ... رحم ایلاب ... جانی هم آغیل ... سیندوردین
کونکول آلغان سین سیز و سین سیزین یعنی تو الشاهد علی الثانی شعر یا ناسین سیزین ... غم بولوب ...
سینغراق بسکون نون و غین معجمه و قاف و فتح رای مهمله دانه زرد آلو و شفتالو و امثال آن که چون باشد و هر دانه که مثل دانه خرما در آن
باشد از آن ... گویند چنانکه مذکور شد سینکاک بسکون نون و کاف اخر و فتح کاف عجمی اول مع الاماله پشه و بعضی آن را
بق و بعوضه خوانند ... التوحید شعر الهی عجز ایلاب ... سینکاک بیله ...
واتا ... سینکاک و پشه ... سینکاک ... سینکیر بسکون نون و رای مهمله و کسر کاف عجمی مع الاماله رک
دار ... و پی ... چنانکه گوید ... سین ... سینکیرد ...
تویم ... چنانکه در خسرو و شیرین گوید ... سینکیر ...
پر ... کاهیست ... هم گویند ... لسان الحمل و ...
بارهنک سینکیل بسکون نون و لام و کسر کاف عجمی مع الاماله خوام ... را گویند چنانکه گوید شعر ای ... صاحب ...
آتانک ... سینکیل ... سبعه سیاره فرماید شعر سین هم ایمدی ...
بولغیل ... سینکیل بولغیل ... بسکون ... چنانکه از زبان مجنون در وقت وداع ...
گوید شعر ... سینکیل ... سینکیل ... سینکیل ... سینکیل
در ذیل سینکیل مذکور شد سین لیک یعنی تو ... کنایه ... چنانکه گوید شعر ... سین لیک وصل ...
طلب ... سیوناک و سیوناکلیک بسکون واو دوست داشتن
علی الاول شعر ... سیوناک ... الشاهد
شعر ای ... سیوناکلیک ... سیودوک دوست داشتیم
سیوادور دوست میدارد و سیوار بمعنی فاعل و مصدر هم می آید چنانکه بمعنی فاعل گوید شعر اول ... سیوار
تا ... سیوکان و سیوار کان و سیوادورکان دوست دارنده و دوست داشته چنانکه گوید الشاهد علی الاول
المعنی الثانی شعر ... دوست ... سیوکانیم ... و بمعنی مصدر هم می آید
سیو و سیوکیل مفرد مخاطب فعل امر الشاهد علی الثانی شعر ... سیوکیل ... ای ...

برآیینک دیك تا فی خوب سیونا سیوناکیل مفرد غائب مخاطب سیوینك سیوینکیز و سیوینکلار جمع غائب مخاطب الرع
سیونانك و سیونانکیز سیونانکلار جمع غائب مخاطب سیونان و سیونامن دوست میدارم سیوارمن و سیوامیز و سیوادور
سیوامام دوست میدارم سیوناس دوست میدارد و بمعنی حال و مستقبل نیز هم می‌آید سیوب و سیونان و سیومیش
دوست داشته سیومیشانك دوست داشته سیونا بولغا و سیوب بولغه دوست تواند داشت سیوا آلغای دوست تواند داشته
سیوا سیوا دوست داشته و بدون تکرار هم مستعملست سیوای و سیوا ایمن دوست بدارم و بدارد و بداری دوستدا
سیونالك سیوکای مز و سیوالی و سیوالینك دوست بدارید سیوکالی برای دوست داشتن و تا دوست داشته سیوکاچ چون
دوست داشت و بدارد و مجرد داشتن چنانکه گوید شعر جان نقوشی ایرتاندی سیوکاچ یار نینك او تلوغ یوزینی نیلاکای کوینا ...
بولغای شمع ایله پروانه دوست سیوکوچ دوست دارنده چنانکه حیدر تیلبه گوید شعر غالیه سیوکوچ ناخنینك تملنی
عنبر نالماس ینتار کلنوی سیوکوچه و سیوکونچه و سیوکانچه تا دوست داشتن و بقدر دوست داشتن سیوکومیز دور دوست خواهیم داشت
سیوکونکیز دور دوست خواهید داشت سیوکوسیلار دور دوست خواهند داشت سیوکولوك دوست داشتنی سیوکای و سیوای و سیوسا
سیوسون و سیوسونلار دوست بدارد سیوکودیك و سیولدیك دوست داشتیم و همچنانکه دوست دارد چنانکه در تاریخ بابری در وصف
مظفر میرزا مذکور است که سیوکودیك اخلاق و لفظ ... هم بود یاتیبدی سیود و رمالك و سیود و رالیك مصدر متعدیست یعنی خود را محبوب کردن
سیودورکالی برای آنکه خود را محبوب کند و تا محبوب کرده چنانکه معنوی اول گوید شعر دیمانیکزا و لیکم سیوارمین نیکا فانینکوی تو کا
لطف آرتوق کوردکونده آرتوقی راق سیودورکالی و صیغ آن بر این قیاس با لفظ دور اشتقاق می‌یابد سیونیماك و سیونیماکلیك بکسر واو و
شین بمعنی معامله است یعنی یکدیگر را دوست داشتن و صیغ آن باشین اشتقاق می‌یابد سیونماك و سیونماکلیك بکسر واو و سکون نون بمعنی
شادی کردن باشد سیونیدوك شادی کردیم سیونوپ و سیونیادور شادی میکند و سیونور بمعنی حال و مستقبل هم می‌آید سیونیکای
سیونوکاچ سیونادی شادی کنند و شادی کند و بمعنی مستقبل هم می‌آید سیونیه سیونکیل مفرد غائب مخاطب الشاهد علی الاول
شعر ای نوایی یکتینینك نظمینی کامیل اینسا سیونکیم نصیب ولدی سنکا مناصب دراك یکیت الشاهد علی الثانی شعر
سیونکیل ای کونکول آنکه جمینکا پر لطف کیلدی لودان ای خان حضورون کیم حیات جاودان کیلدی سیونینك سیونینکیز و سیونینکلار
جمع غائب مخاطب سیونیمانك و سیونیمانکیز سیونیمانکلار جمع غائب مخاطب سیونیمان و سیونیمامن شادی میکنم سیونامین سیونیوز
سیونادور سیونور شادی میکنم سیونیاس شادی میکند و بمعنی حال و مستقبل نفی هم می‌آید سیونیب سیونیبان سیونیمیش
شادی کرده سیونیمیشانك شادی کرده سیونیبا بولغه و سیونیب بولغه شادی توان کرد سیونیا آلغه شادی تواند کرد سیونیا سیونیا
شادی کنان و بدون تکرار هم مستعملست سیونیای و سیونیا ایمن شادی کنم و کند و کنی و کرده سیونیالی و سیونیکایز سیونکالی
سیونیلی و سیونیالینك شادی بکنیم سیونکالی برای شادی کردن و تا شادی کرده سیونکاچ چون شادی کند و کند و مجرد کردن
سیونکوچه شادی کننده سیونکوچه و سیونکونچه و سیونکانچه تا شادی کردن و بقدر شادی کردن سیونکومیز دور شادی خواهیم کرد سیونکونکیز
شادی خواهید کرد سیونکوسیلار دور شادی خواهند کرد سیونکولوك شادی کردنی سیونکای و سیونیا و سیونیسا سیونسون و
سیونیدیك شادی کند سیونکودیك سیونودیك شادی کردن و همچنانکه شادی کند سیونیدورماك و سیونیدورمالیك مصدر متعدیست
یعنی شادی کردن و صیغ آن بر این قیاس با لفظ دور اشتقاق می‌یابد من الجوامد سیونچی بسکون واو و کسر را ترکی رومی غنیمت
هر چیز را گویند سیونچی سینکالی ترکی رومی پیشه بود که آن را ابریشم تو آمند سیوکوم بسکون واو مهر و محبت سیوکولوك

بضم واو و لام و سیوکلیك بکسر واو و لام و سکون کاف بمعنی محبت باشد چنانکه در شمایل الحبیبه مذکور کفیل جهان کوینکر دیدیلار
یین حق نینك نوع سیله پرستش قیلورین عیدی آیینك مهر و سیوکلوکی مخصوص بادت و المقصود تو تار و بمعنی محبوب و دوست داشته نیز
آمده چنانکه در منشآت گوید که سیوکلیکیم بارچا مجموعه زاده لارینك مجموعی و منینك سیوکلیکیم ... السینی برینکیزکه بولسه
بفتح واو و سکون لام دانه ایست صلب که در دست و اعضا در می‌آید و آن را رومیه سیکیل و بعربی ثولول گویند سیونچ بکسر واو
و سکون نون و جیم بمعنی مژده و نوید بود سیونچی بمعنی مژده کاننده چنانکه گوید شعر ... کون بولغای که اول غایب سفردین کیلکای
دیب اسینابانمین دین سیونچی تیلار اندین خبر مع الیاء سیلاماق و سیلانماق قیلیق بکسر یا و سکون لام بمعنی لغزیدن باشد که آن را
بعربی ازلاق گویند مثل اینکه ناست یار روغن دار ازطرف و از هر جهت یا دست فشرده یا پاك کند سیلادوق لغزیدیم سیلاب و سیلا
سیلادور سیلغزاند و سیلار بمعنی حال و مستقبل هم می‌آید سیلانان و سیلادور سیلار دورغان لغزانده و لغزاننده بمعنی مستمر هم
می‌آینده سیلار و سیلارمیل مفرد غائب مخاطب سیلاینا و سیلاماغیل مفرد غائب مخاطب سیلاینك و سیلاینکیز و سیلاینکلار جمع
غائب مخاطب سیلاینالك و سیلاینالکیز سیلاینالکلار جمع غائب مخاطب سیلاغان و سیلاماسمین نمی‌لغزانم سیلامین و سیلار ور و سیلار
سیلادور میلغزانم سیلاناس نمی‌لغزاند و بمعنی حال و مستقبل نفی هم می‌آید سیلاب سیلابان و سیلامیش لغزانده سیلامیشانك
لغزانده سیلابولغای و سیلاب بولغه توان لغزانید سیلا آلغای تواند لغزانید سیلای و سیلا ایمن لغزانیده لغزانیده و بدون
تکرار هم مستعملست سیلای و سیلا ایمن بلغزانم و بلغزاند و بلغزانی و لغزانده سیلاناق و سیلاغای و سیلاغایمز و سیلالی و سیلاینك
بلغزانیم سیلاغالی برای لغزاندن و تا لغزانده سیلاغاچ چون لغزاند و مجرد لغزاندن سیلاغوچی لغزاننده سیلاغوچه و سیلاغونچه و سیلاغانچه
تا لغزاندن و بقدر لغزاندن سیلاغومیز دور لغزانیم خواهیم لغزانید سیلاغونکیز دور خواهید لغزانید سیلاغوسیلار دور خواهند
لغزانید سیلاغولوق لغزانیدنی سیلاغای و سیلا و سیلاسا و سیلاسون و سیلادیك بلغزاند الشاهد علی الجامس شعر یوز و سیل
یوزاك تاریخ دوره دینك که کیلمادی ثالث اجل الملکی اول غائبی آندین سیلادیك سیلاغودیك و سیلادیك لغزانیدنی و همچنانکه بلغزاند
سیلانماق سیلانماقلیق باشباع کسره و سکون لام لغزیدن چنانکه باشتقاق در حروف الیاء مع الراء مذکور شد کتاب الشین المعجمه
باب المفتوحات حرف الشین مع الباء شاپات بفتح بای عجمی و سکون تای قرشت و شاپلاق بفتح بای عجمی و لام و سکون قاف سیلی بود که بر صفحه
و آن را رومیه شمار گویند شبلت بفتح بای ... ترکی رومی نوعی از بهرینه بود مع التاء شاتاتو بضم تا ... گویند چنانکه در
الجنبه مذکور شیخ شمس الدین علی لالا گوید که یکی واقعه دو گوردی که بر شاتو قویوپتور لار آسمانغه چه و بر او بوشاتو باشید اتو و تو
مع الراء من المشتقات شارلداماق صدا کردن آبی که دفعه ریخته شود و صدای آبشار و امثال آن را هم گویند شارلداب شارلدابان
شارلدامیش دفعه ریخته شده چنانکه شاهد بر اول در تاریخ بابری در تعیین توپ مذکور است که هر آینه دین اریکان آلات سودیك
شارلدالیط لب فه کیروی و باقی صیغ بر این نهج موافق شق اول الشقاق می‌یابد من الجوامد شاراپنو بسکون نون و فتح بای عجمی بر وزن قرانقو
ترکی رومی نام آلتی است که آن را آبدزدك گویند مع الشین المعجمه من المشتقات شاشماق بترکی رومی بمعنی مضطرب شدن شاشماق ... مضطرب
متحد است یعنی مضطرب شدن من الجوامد شاشقوت بترکی رومی مضطرب شاشی بر وزن کاشی ترکی رومی بمعنی احول شاشیلیك
احولی مع الغین المعجمه شاغرداق بکسر غین و سکون را و مهمله و قاف و فتح دال مهمله آوازی بود که از خوردن دو چیز سخت که بهم رسد
بکسر غین و سکون لام چرکیست که در دنبه و موی زیر شکم و گرد ران گوسفند جمع می‌شود و بعربی ذو ... و بفارسی ... گویند
مع الفا شافشاك بسکون فا بر وزن یغماق ترکی رومی لباسی بود که ناچسبان و از هم دریده باشد و موافق اندام نباشد و مجاز کسی را گو

که عقل و فهم و کفتکوی او پریشان باشد مع القاف شتاق با قاف مشدد بر کتی بمعنی هزل و استهزا باشد شاتر دی ... که ابهام
دو چیز بیکدیکر مسموع شود مع الکاف شالغورت بسکون لام و را مهمله و تای قرشت و ضم غین معجمه حیوان درنده و درنده را مانند
مع المیم شامار بترکی رومی طناب خیمه و سیل بود که بر چشم فرو زنند مع الواو شاولوم بسکون واو و میم و ضم لام بمعنی جلف و شنیع و ناسزا
باشد مع الیا شای بروزن جای صاحب حکمت و فنا و کار سودمند و با منفعت را کویند باب المضموم حرف الثین مع الدال شودر
بسکون دال و نون و ضم را مهمله بمعنی ترشح و شبنم و قطرات ریزه باران بود که آنرا بعربی طش کویند الشاهد علیه شعر
بیتسا یو نعخطینکا کریان کنتم اشکیم اولسا اول کل و بو سبزه نینک شودر و فی دیك شود کلو بفتح دال بترکی رومی یعنی آنقدر و آن نوع
شودر عنو نام سازیست که آنرا عود کویند و نیز نام پادشاه تنکوت است که معاصر چنکیز خان بوده و از آن شیده عرفوم خوانند
مع الرا المهمله شوره کیاهیست شبیه باشنان و اسفند و علفیست شوره تلخ که شتر بخوردن آن راغب و بامزاج او موافق است و آنرا بقطعی
قاقلی و بعربی تلکم و بفارسی و ترکی شوره کویند و نیز نام طایفه ایست از ترکمانیه شوارق بمعنی سراغ بترکی رومی ...
که آنرا بعربی سبخه نامند مع الکاف شوك دو معنی دارد اول ... کنار را کویند دوم بترکی رومی بمعنی ... باشد و بلغت زند
و پازند بمعنی انار است که بعربی رمان نامند شوك کینه یعنی ... کنار را چنانکه کوید شعر ... یادلی کاشتن اباغ
با الفاز ... شوکه بضم کاف و سکون را مهمله چتر را کویند و آن سایبانیست که
بر سر سلاطین نکهدارند شوکه چی چتردار بود مع اللام شول اسم اشارتست یعنی آن شولاکای بفتح لام و کاف عجمی و سکون
حطی ... باشد که از دهن روان شود و آنرا بعربی ریق کویند چنانکه بطریق لف و نشر ... سعدی بونده ...
که کوزی آغزی ... ایل ... آثار شولاکای ... و نیز ... لابرار کوید شعر ...
چون ... آغزی ... شولاکای ... و مولف ... شولاکای را بسین مهمله خوانده و ... سین ... کرده و شعر ...
شاهد آورده سهو کرده شولای ... توران و خوارزم ... لفظ را استعمال نمایند مع المیم شوم بضم میم
را مهمله بلغت مغولی بمعنی چراغ باشد مع النون شونداق و شونداغی ... مراد ... بود ... و همچنین الشاهد علی الاول
شعر یا ... شونداق ... یا ... نام و نشان ... شقشاد ...
از جنس چوغ که ... و آنرا ... نامند و نیز ... پادشاهان و سلاطین را کویند چنانکه در تاریخ نابری ...
هر شیخ ... که هر شیخ ... و کوتر خانه ... شقشاد بولدی باب المکسور من حرف الشین مع الباشیبا
بمعنی ... باشد و بفارسی ... شیباق بفتح با و سکون ... ترکی باشد که آنرا ... خوانند ...
... در هنکام پوشش ... سعدی ...
... شیبان ... شبیکه ... بفتح کاف ...
کویند مع الدال شید ... بضم دال مهمله ... و سکون را مهمله ... شیر ... مع الذال ...
مع الرا المهمله شیر ... بفتح کاف و سکون لام ... کویند چنانکه ... محبوب القلوب
در وصف ... کوید که ...
وحشه که از کوشت شکار ... چنانکه در تاریخ نابری ... شکار ...
بوز ... شیر ... مقام و الملکه شیر ... چنانکه ...

دفنیه کوید که ... شیر ... بیلدا ... شیرداغ ...
دارد ... کلند ... بجای تکلتو در زیر زین کذارند و بجای فرش ... جامه ...
چشوار آستین کوتاه که بر بالای لباس پوشند چنانکه کوید شعر ... شادین ...
موکبیش ... شیرداغ ... مولف برهان قاطع لفت شیرداغ را ... و بمعنی ... فرهنك خود ذکر کرده شیرلا
بترکی رومی شیرینت بود ... شیرلا ... مع الثین المعجمه من المشتقات شیشماك و شیشماکلیك
بمعنی ورم کردن آمده شیشتی ورم کرد شیشار و شیشادور ورم میکند شیشار بمعنی فاعل و مصدر هم می آید شیشکان و شیشادی
شیشادورکان ورم کنند و ورم کرده و بمعنی مصدر هم می آید شیش و شیشکیل مفرد ... شیش بمعنی سیخ هم باشد چنانکه
بیاید شیشماو شیشماکیل مفرد ... شیشینك ... جمع ... شیشماکز
شیشمانکلار جمع ... شیشماس ورم میکند بمعنی فاعل و مصدر ... شیشیب و شیشبان و شیشمیش ورم
شیشیشانلر ... شیشیب ... ورم توان کرد شیشا آلقای ورم تواند کرد شیشا شیشا ورم کنان ...
هم ... شیشای شیشاین ورم کنم و بکند ... شیشکالی برای ورم کردن و تا ورم کرده شیشکاج چون ورم کرده
و ... کردن شیشکوچی ورم کننده شیشکوچه و شیشکینه و شیشکابخه تا ورم کردن ... ورم کردن شیشکای و شیشا
شیشسون و شیشدیلت ورم کند شیشکودیلك و شیشارلیك ورم کردن و همچنانکه ورم کند ... و شیشلامکلیك سیخ
زدن شیشلادی بسیخ زد چنانکه کوید شعر ...
شیشلامیش ... بسیخ میزند ... شیشلار ... فاعل و مصدر هم می آید شیشلاکان ... شیشلایدورکان بسیخ زننده و بسیخ زده و
مصدر هم می آید شیشلاغو شیشلاکیل مفرد ... شیشلادنك و شیشلانکز
شیشلانکلار جمع ... شیشلاخماین بسیخ میزند شیشلانکی
شیشلادین و شیشلایدیر ... شیشلاخام بسیخ میزند ... شیشلاماس بسیخ نمیزند بمعنی فاعل و مصدر منفی هم می آید شیشلاب و شیشلاکان و شیشلامیش
بسیخ زده الشاهد علی الاول شعر ... شیشلاب ... شیشلامیشدیر
بسیخ زده شیشلاکای ... شیشلاغو ... شیشلای ... بسیخ زنان و ...
مستعملست شیشلامی شیشلامین ... بسیخ ... شیشلاکای ... بسیخ
برای سیخ زدن و تا بسیخ زده شیشلاکاج چون بسیخ زده ... شیشلاکوچی ... شیشلاکوچه شیشلاکابخه
تا بسیخ زدن ... بسیخ زدن شیشلاکو ... بسیخ خواهیم زد ... بسیخ خواهند زد ...
بسیخ زدن شیشلاکای و شیشلاشا ... شیشلاسون و شیشلاخو بلت بسیخ زند شیشلاکودیلك و شیشلارلیك بسیخ زدن و همچنانکه بسیخ زند
من الجوامد شیش ... بمعنی بود ... سیخ را کویند الشاهد علیه شعر ...
باغر ... اوریا ... بالمجاز ... کوچك را مانند که بر ... چنانکه کوید شعر ...
آند ... شیشیك بکسر شین و سکون کاف ...
متوهم شیشمان بسکون شین و نون و فتح میم بالف کشیده بترکی رومی ... مع الغین المعجمه شیغاول بفتح ...
و ضم واو و سکون لام ... کویند مع اللام شیل ... بترکی رومی ... آنرا ... نامند شیلان ... باشد

کسره و فتح لام بالف کشیده و سکون نون سماط سلاطین و امرا و اطعام طعام را گویند چنانچه در خاتمهٔ حیرة الابرار گوید شعر خدمت را

باد ایدی پیر قول آنکا پایه خدمت ته بکاول آنکا برکون آیینک برسید اشیلان خلقی شاه هم اشتهار لغات خالقی و بعضی ضبط آن

شلتاق بسکون لام و قاف و فتح تا بترکی دعاوی دروغ و تخیل بیجا باشد چنانچه در تاریخ الملوک در ذکر سلطنت بوراز دخت گوید که

جمیع اکاسره را فی دین تا الغان شلتاق لار بجمیع لطایفه تا منیشلادی شیلیم باشباع کسره و فتح لام و کسر لام و سکون میم بمعنی باشد

که بدان کاغذ و امثال آنرا بچسبانند مع المیم شیمالت بسکون میم بمعنی میکیدن باشد شیمدوک میکیدیم شیمارم شیما دور میکد

و شیمار بمعنی فاعل و مصدر هم می آید شیمکان و شیملکان شیمادکان میکند و میکیده و بمعنی مصدر هم می آیند شیم و شیمکیل مفرد

انجیل ار شیمنا و شیما انجیل مفرد غالبانه حاضر شیمنک شیمنکز و شیمنکلار جمع غالبانه حاضر شیمانک و شیما انکز

شیما انکلار جمع غائبانه شیمان و شیمانمین میمکم شیمای بین و شیمادیم شیمادم شیمادم میمکم شیمانک میمکرد

فاعل و مصدر بمعنی هم می آید شیمیب و شیمیبان شیمیش میکیدن الشاهد علی الاول شعر شیمیب تو تنام کوی جوان

دولت ذوقین کو کلش قیز ارغان باده دین کل یا پراغی سنکلیغ دو داغیدا شیمیش الک میکیده شیمنا توانمه و شیمیب توان میکید

شیما الغای تواند میکید شیما شیمنا میکنده میکنده شیمای شیمایین میکم و میکد و میکی و میکید شیمانک و شیمکابز

شیمکلیز و شیمانکی شیمانیک میکیم شیمکابی برای میکیدن و تا میکیده شیمکاج چون میکید و میکد و بعضی میکیدن شیمکوجی

میکنده شیمکوجه و شیمکیجه شیمکابجه تا میکیدن و بعد میکیدن شیمکومیز بود خواهیم میکید شیمکونکوز بود بخواهید میکید شیمکوسی

خواهند میکید شیمکولوک میکید بی شیمکای و شیمایمنا شیممسون و شیمیدیک میکد شیمکودیک و شیمادیک میکیدی و همانچه

میکد شیما الماغ و شیما الماسلیغ بمعنی نانید زباشد چنانچه کنید قولیشما الماق بمعنی سبق الاکرذن و آستین برزدن شیما الدی

آستین برزدیم شیما الدیم شیما الادور آستین برمیزند و شیما لور بمعنی فاعل و مصدر هم می آید شیما لغان و شیما لوزقان و شیما الادرغان آستین برزده

و برزده و بمعنی مصدر هم می آیند شیمال و شیما لغیل مفرد غالبانه حاضر الشاهد علی الاول شعر نایما قولیشمال دیقیق کم

میلوش تل یولاتیفلیغ ین بورون اولیس یلاده شیمالنا و شیما الماغیل مفرد غالبانه حاضر شیما النک شیما النکز و شیما النکلار

جمع غالبانه حاضر شیما الماک و شیما الماکز و شیما النکلار جمع غالبانه حاضر شیما الماک شیما الماس بین آستین برنمیزنم شیما الامین و

شیما الومین و شیما الادور شیما لورلم آستین برمیزنم شیما الماس آستین برمیزند و بمعنی فاعل و مصدر منفی هم می آید شیما لیب و شیما لیبان

شیما لمیش آستین برزده الشاهد علی الاول شعر ای نوایی قیلما کیمایه مراول صروف شیکا ثری بیا الی اعجب صلیغ تلمز شیما لیب

نما لمیک شیما المیشانک آستین برزده شیما الیبا و شیما لیب بوقانه آستین توان برزد شیما الا الغای آستین تواند برزد شیما الای شیما الا

آستین برزنان و بمعنی تکرار هم مستعملست شیما الای شیما الایین آستین برزنم و برزند و برزنی و برزده شیما الماق و شیما الغایز و شیما الغای بیز

شیما الاخی شیما الالیک آستین برزنیم شیما الغابلی برای آستین برزدن و تا برزده شیما الغاج چون آستین برزدند و بعضی برزدن شیما الغوجی

آستین برزننده شیما الغوجه شیما الغوچه و شیما الغاجه تا آستین برزدن و بعد آستین برزدن شیما الغومیز بود آستین خواهیم برزد شیما الغوکوز

آستین بخواهید برزد شیما الغوسی بود آستین بخواهند برزد شیما الغولوق آستین برزدن شیما الغای شیما الا و شیما الا و شیما السون

شیما الدیک آستین برزند شیما الغودیک و شیما الودیک آستین برزدن و همانچه برزدن الحواسی شیمدی یعنی الحال و الفعل

چنانچه ضیلی گوید بابلاغه الرویته مصغ سوددی مجنون نوبتین شیمدی تنیم سودای عشق دو دو دیر لمهرنان بر اشقینک بدر ازنیدی

و نیز بمعنی میکید شیمدی بردک بفتح تا و دال ثانی بترکی رومی بمعنی نا خال شیمشک بسکون میم و کاف و فتح شین ثانی بترکی رومی بمعنی برق باشد

مع النون شین بترکی رومی سه معنی دارد اول لقب و طرنیا الدرا گویند دوم بمعنی معمور و آباد بود سیم کون و نام را نامند شنک بسکون

نون و کاف قطع و فصل امور باشد و نیز نام منصبی است معهود چنانچه خوانین مغولیه امرای معتبر را که مامور بقطع و فصل قضایا بالمشاهده

شنک گویند شینلیک بسه معنی بود اول شادی و طرنیا کی باشد و بمعنی جهت توبه و تغنک دا که بلغا الهام بر خالی کنند شینلیک

نامند و سیم آبادی و معموری را خوانند سیم گویند که آق شینلیک یعنی سفید چهره و صفید فام و در سایر الوان نیز بهمین نحو استعمال میشود

مع الواو شیوران بفتح واو و نام حاکمی بود و آنرا در شیراز شعر اد گویند کتاب الصاد صداق بمعنی نایاخ و صدق بمعنی و رق

ترکی باشد الشاهد علی الاول شعر صداق یاپاغی کلم ایلیکی کاستان تو تیمش یوز او قصیدا حسی بو قال الشد خاطر نالیک وله ستکا

یا ندا شماقا یساب تا تلیم یا آهیم او ق بولدی حسد دین بر طرفی تر اینیکا بر یان صدا فنکه الشاهد علی الثانی من سیمه سیار حشر

دیما ییر نا زنین صد پشنی یوق حیکوی اول صدقه دین یا یخیکا اوق و آنرا شادق و شادمان گویند و باسم طله نیز مستعمل مسابین بمعنی

ستاین باشد که در ذیل سین مفتوحه مذکور شد کتاب الطا باب المفتوحات مع البا طابور بترکی رومی بمعنی صف و بمعنی فوج و

باشد مع الرا طراز نام شهری است در حد و حدود چین که حسن خیز باشد و مشک خوب از آنجا آرند علم یکی از ولایات بدخشان هم هست و بنیادی

کلاه کاخامه با فعل گویند عموما و نیز بیشکو و کلاه خانه مشکو را نیز گویند و مقسم را هم نامند و بمعنی آراستن و ساختن چیزها و نقش و نگار

و زیب و زینت و آرایشی کرد و ظرز و نمط هم آمده و بمعنی میل خامه مخترعات را گویند و آن معرب است مع الشین طاش بترکی رومی بمعنی

سنگ و بیرون بود طاشره و طشره بترکی رومی بمعنی بیرون طاشره جی بمعنی بیرونی مع العین طاغ بترکی رومی بمعنی کوه بود و در لغت

جغتای با تا و قرشت مستعملت و نیز نام هیمه ایست که آتش آن دیر بماند طغاجار نام یکی از امیران بزرگ که در عهد هلاکو خان و اباقا خان

بوده چنانچه وصاف در غزل اسلام با صطلاحات مغولیه گوید شعر در غیرت کش چشم تو هم خوی طغاجار در رونقه کی برزلف تو طوماتا

طالت طغان بترکی و مغولی طرفی باشد پس که در اینجا کو کو دما و هو اشناء آن برنیاز کنند و آنرا بفارسی طبقه گویند طغای و طغایی برادر نامیاشد

که آنرا بعربی خال نامند طغاج و طمغاج نام قرائیست از کشغر چنانچه گوید شعر امیر ابت مغول و لغای آینیدا ای آیلا مسلمان پیکان

آن نا الماق بود صبوری قا بیسه طمغاج شوم و کم فرهنگ جهانگیری طمغاج بتقدیم میم نام ولایتی است از ترکستان نوشته و این شعر از نظامی

شاهد آورده شعر چیکل از لغت بر طمغاج بنده خرلخ شوشی بر چاچ بنده و نیز گفته که نام پادشاه سمرقند باشد و پادشاه تبت و نیز ادام گفته

این شعر از خاقانی شاهد آورده شعر تاج بربود از سر مهراج زنان یا به طمغاج خان کرد آفتاب و مولف تاریخ حبیب السیر ذکر کرده که نام

خاکی است که تکش خان پادشاه خوارزم را بحکومت ری نصب داده بود مع القاف طاقیه بکسر قاف کلاهی است که بر سر گذارند مع الو

طاقانه بمعنی خانه گوشاله در ماله باشد و بکحاله را باشماق گویند مع الواو طوار بمعنی صومعه بترکی رومی بمعنی حیلها را در ایدی و طواشی

باشد طواشی بمعنی خواجه بترکی رومی خاجه سرا بود که آنرا بعربی خصی گویند طاون ضم واو بترکی رومی سقف خانها باشد مع الیا طای

کره اسب کساله و دو ساله را نامند طاید و نام شهری در ترکستان مشتمل بر چهار فرسنگ در چهار فرسنگ که تماما آن بنا کرده مستقر

بود و خان ایلخ را که بجنکا خوانین مغول بود و مترو کستانیت طایشی بسکون یا و کسر شین قرشت بلغت مغول بمعنی نوسینده و خاذق و ماهر و استاد

باشد باب المضمومات مع الباء طوبال بترکی رومی لنگ را گویند که پای او بزمین نرسد مع الراء المهمله طرغای بسکون را و یای

و فتح غین معجمه بر زبان درست که آنرا بفارسی ساسر و بعربی هدهد گویند و نیز نام پدر حضرت امیر تیمور کورکان است طاب اه

بفتح را نیز مستعملست چنانچه در ظفرنامه در وصف حسب و نسب امیر گوید شعر قرلشان نژادی طراغای نام جهانش بکام و سپهرش بکام مرحف

بضم را و سکون غین معجمه بر زبان درست که آنرا بفارسی ساسر و بعربی هدهد گویند طوغان بکسر شین و مع الغین طوغان یکنوع از جوارح شکاری است که آنرا بلغاری شکار شکر زاولکوی

و بجاز اشجاع خصم افکن را هنم نامند و نیز نام پادشاهیست معروف و نام یکی از ندماء مقرب سلطان احمد و ارغون خان بوده که مولد او
قهستان بوده و نصیرای میرزا لیف خود مذکور ساخته که طوغان لغت رومی است و با طاء حطی غلط است غلط نوشته اگر رومی باشد
بطریق اولی با بیا طا نوشته شود طوغای ج وبجی را گویند که در میمون و دخان نها باشد و با تاء قرشت نیز مستعملت طغرا نشان XX
بود که از جانب پادشاهان در ابتدا فرامین و احکام با آب طلا نوشته یا بسرخی رقم شود چنانچه گوید شعر کونکول پرده سی
اوسینه داغ عشقینک بو طغرا اضر نقش خاتم بولوبتور وله شعر یا زلر غه مطلع صبح اوزره نو بر نو طغرا قیاش طلاء سی
دین ماده الیعینات زمحل طغرل بسکون غین و لام و ضم رای مهمله نام پرنده ایست شکاری و نیز نام پادشاهیست معروف از سلجوقیه
که الپ ارسلان پسر او بوده مع النون غین المثلثه طوناتما لتبرکیری بمعنی آرایش دادن و مکمل و مزین ساختن چنانچه شاعر رومی گوید ملمعا گر و طون
شعر طوناتیش غضب فرخندن ملی کومیش قندیل ایله صبحن جایی طوناتماک مزین و آراسته شدن من الجوامد طوناتما ترکی ج
بمعنی زین و آراستگی بوده کوکبه و اثاثه پادشاهی را گویند و با دال الابجد و تاء قرشت هم مستعملست طونبای بسکون نون و یای حطی و
بای با الف کشیده ترکی رومی گاو باشد که آنرا بعربی بقر گویند مع الیا طوی جشن و بجمع را گویند که عروسی و سور و عرس بدل خاصه مشهورست طوی
چنانچه در مکلح کردن اسکندر روشنک و همین را گوید شعر کل و سبزه امامید ابولد بطوی بولوبکلش آیین بیله شهرکوی و ترکی
رومی و بمعنی طار دارنده ایست که آنرا بفارسی هوبره و بعربی حباری گویند دوم بمعنی موی بود طونیون بسکون یای حطی و نون و ضم
من معجمه فمان تو تیغون باشد که در حرف تاء مضمومه مذکور شد کتاب العین المهمله باب المفتوحات مع الراء عراس با راء مشدد و سکون سین عا
زیاد خیر را گویند چنانچه در مقطعات گوید شعر عمریز ایله کچوروب غفلت ایله نکته اوزینه که ملار خواکش برابینک دمرکه
تغافل بیوزیدین قیلغای الغای پاپچراش مع اللام علکچر بفتح لام مشدد و با یای ابجد و سکون نون و رای مهمله بمعنی جلال و بار کثر باشد
چنانچه در صبحه سیاره در داستان بهرام گوید شعر بیله شهره ایره که برعجلج جرخ ملکی دین الکان اخراج الیلاتان قطع دشت و
تاغ ایله روذ انکا کلتوردی پیوسته مرود نیمه کون زمیدایمرا بولدی صرنک بولدی پاخر کوبا سو کوب لشنک مع النون عنقوت
مرغابیست معروف از غاز کوچکتر و لذا او را طوغان نیز گویند انقوت و انقود نیز گفته شود چنانچه در الف مضمومه گذشت باب المکسورات عیرلیدیما عی
بکسر عین و سکون لام از کلو صدا کشید و زشلوع بود دو حالتی که بسوی صید یا آدمی آغاز حمله کند عیرلیدادی صدا کشید و عیرلیدار عین
فاعل مصدر هم می آید عیرلیدا غان عیرلیدیغان عیرلیدی غان صدا کشنده و صدا کشید و بمعنی مصدر هم می آید عیرلیدیا عیرلیدیغان
مفرد غائب انفعل امر عیرلیدا ما عیرلیدیما ناعیل مفرد غائب انفعل نفی عیرلیدانک عیرلیدانکز عیرلیدانکلار جمع غائب انفعل امر
عیرلیدانانک و عیرلیدانانکز عیرلیدانانکلار جمع غائب انفعل نفی عیرلیدا ناس صدا نمی کند و بمعنی فاعل مصدر نفی هم می آید عیرلیداب عیرلیدایا
عیرلیدامیش صدا کشیده چنانچه در لیلی مجنون گوید لشاهد علی الاول شعر کاهی کهغضب بیله عیرلیداب کوهوز اسیدیکی
عیرلیداش عیرلیدا شاتوغه و عیرلیداب توبغه صدا تواند کشید عیرلیدای المکیه صدا تواند کشید عیرلیدا بو و عیرلیدای عیرلیدیه صدا کشان و ملکو
تکرار هم مستعملت عیرلیدا علی برای صدا کشیدن و تا صدا کشیدن عیرلیدا غاج چون صدا کشید و کشید و بمعنی کشیدن عیرلیدکو
صدا کشنده عیرلیدا غوجه عیرلیدا غوچه عیرلیدا غایجه تا صدا کشیدن و مقابله صدا کشیدن عیرلیدا غاچ عیرلیداسا عیرلیداسو عیرلیدا یک
صدا بکشد عیرلیدا غو یک عیرلیدار دیک صدا کشیده و همچنانچه بکشد کتاب العین المعجمه باب المفتوحات مع الالف مع الجیم غجرجی غاج
بفتح جیم اول و کسر ثانی و سکون رای مهمله دلیل و بلد را گویند چنانچه در کل و نوروز گوید جناب و آمدن شعر غجرچی باشلار ایرکان بمعنی اقیش
پروانان ارسلان بولیغه کیتمیش غجغا و بسکون جیم و دو او معروف عرقاوت که بفارسی مشهور بکاو قطار باشد و بجاز دسته خار ریتکه

ازدار

که از برای غربال بر کردن غربند که الیز ایلا اجته جست و خیز کند چنانچه گوید شعر سقالی شیخ ریا فرقه کیچه کیلدی حرام و ملکو لالا
ایشالک بو بینیه یکمال اعجمانه و طالع هروی غرما او امیر شیرازی نسخه سعی یا بتو خواند و با تقوا نوشته که رشته ایست که بکنکل غاز
انجمنه زینت ستو لیغانیه الدمستر ز لیتماشا هد آورده لفظا و معنی و جو جز احیست مع الراء المهمله من المشتقات غاربلاغ غاربالماغ بسکون غین و غار
مهمله بمعنی غربال کردن بود غاربار دی غربال کرد غاربار و غاربار را دور غربال میکند و غاربالیدو رینی فاعل و مصدر هم می آید غاربالار
غاربالار و غاربالیدو تکرار غربال کنند و غربال کرد و بمعنی مصدر هم می آید غارباربع غاربار جیل مفرد غائب انفعل امر غاربالماینا
مفرد غائب انفعل نفی غاربالینک غاربالینکز غاربالینکلار جمع غائب انفعل امر غاربالمانک و غاربالمانکز و غاربالمانکلار جمع غائب
انفعل نفی غاربالمانکو غاربالماس بین غربال نمیکنم غاربالادیم غاربالادیمیز غاربالادوق غاربالادیلار غاربالیدیکم غربال میکنم غاربالاس غربال نمیکند
و بمعنی فاعل و مصدر نفی هم می آید غاربالایب غاربالیبان غاربالیش غربال کرده غاربالیشانک غربال کرده غاربالیب تو اند
غاربالیب بو لغه غربال تواند کرد غاربالا را آلغای غربال تواند کرد غاربالا غانا غاربالاغانا غربال کنان و بعد تکرار هم مستعملست غاربالابی
غاربالا این غربال کنم و بکند بکن و کرده غارباریاق غاربالاو غاربالار غاربالارغای غاربالارزی غاربالالیک غربال کنیم غاربالاغالی برای غربال کردن و
غربال کرده غاربالاغاج چون غربال کرد و بکند و بمعنی کردن غاربالاغوجی غربال کننده غاربالا غوجه و غاربالاغوچه و غاربالاغایجه تا غربال
کردن و مقابله غربال کردن غاربالا غو سینر دو غربال خواهیم کرد غاربالاغوچیز دو غربال خواهید کرد غاربالاغو سیلار دو غربال خواهند کرد
غاربالا غو تو غربال کرد غاربالاغای غاربالاغا لو غاربالاغاو غاربالاغون و غاربالار دیک غربال کند چنانچه در خسرو شیرین در صفت
شیرویه شیرین گوید لشاهد علی الثالث شعر سپهر اول ایمتی آختا حادیرش فنا و نکان ایشی غاربالماغ ایر منکا از زیرا گر
مینک دمیالدی عشقینکا ارهوای جهان بین غاربالاغو دیک غاربالاردیک غربال کردن و همچنانچه غربال کند من الجوامد غرار بعضی گفته اند ج
جوال را گویند چنانچه در صحبه سیاره در داستان مانو فیروزه و بوست گوید شعر هر نیبتیکم بار ابر دی غار ایجرا ایچی
شالدی بر غرار ایجرا تا که ایلیک غرار ابرست تولادی هر غرار ایجرا ایچوب بولادی و در رسال الیفات حضرت نوایی با قاف رقم است و در تحفه
اتراک دوم غرار را ضرار یعنی مستعملت و غراره بعربی جوال شبکه دار بود که بطریق تعریب یا قند کاه و امثال آن کنند معنی آخر برهان قاطع آنرا
فارسی شمرده اما با این ذکر ساخته و با یعنی نوشته و در هر دو صورت لفظ و معنی یکی بنزدیک است چون احتمال غیرست که قرابها تلفظ
و غرابی مرادی باشد در بابانه نیز مذکور خواهد ساخت و طالع هروی بمعنی متاس قرار یا قاف بمعنی سند قد نوشته و شعر بعینه شاهد آورده
سهو کرده غرغیچی بسکون را و کسر یای حطی و جیم عجمی بند ترکش و بند شمشیر و بند سپر و امثال آن بوده چنانچه در تاریخ بابری مذکور است
که پراوق داوو لغاسیغه او دودم و ده پراوق تا لغانینی غرغیچی بیله کوکلاوی اصر دوم غز و بفتح رای مهمله و زده شنهای تاریک و مضاف
کویند که در کل آیینها رو یدالشاهد علیه شعر کرنوای کاکل شکوه بیرزآیماس جعد مطلا تاب رولیک و لداس نشکیل اغرو دمولفه فرهنک
جهانگیری غرو بر وزن سر و حل بفارسی عبوی ذکر کرده و این شعر از حکیم اسدی شاهد آورده شعر یکی کشته چون چون نکن تند و هیچ
در بیشه نبید و غرو و مولف برهان قاطع بمعنی رنا بی قلم نوشته مع الزاء المعجمه غازان غلزان شش محمد کرد او لاد یلتوبا بوقنا نوچ غاز
در مقطعات گوید شعر المه و کلاب تامیناتو قوه نه لمع یر ما س او لمغ غار انغه راغبتیکم رحم فنا بی ثبنیک غلزانی ثوندی زهم اوبه ایما
مناسب دو یم کا تهای جن زا ناسدیتیم تو قیه من فر لمغ داگوید بچا دم ظالیفه مسالوبی تو کا نفرهم خود دارید و تمر و اشکریتی ایم و زارتی
کنند چم نام مملکتیست از ممالک روس و شم نام پادشاهیست معروف از سلسله مغولیه که در بلاد ایران سلطنت کرده بشرف اسلام مشرف
شد و پادشاهی با حقه او در عهد او انقراض یافت و پدرش ارغون خان بن اباقا خان بن هلاکو خانست و شنب غازان در تبریزنا و مدفن اوست

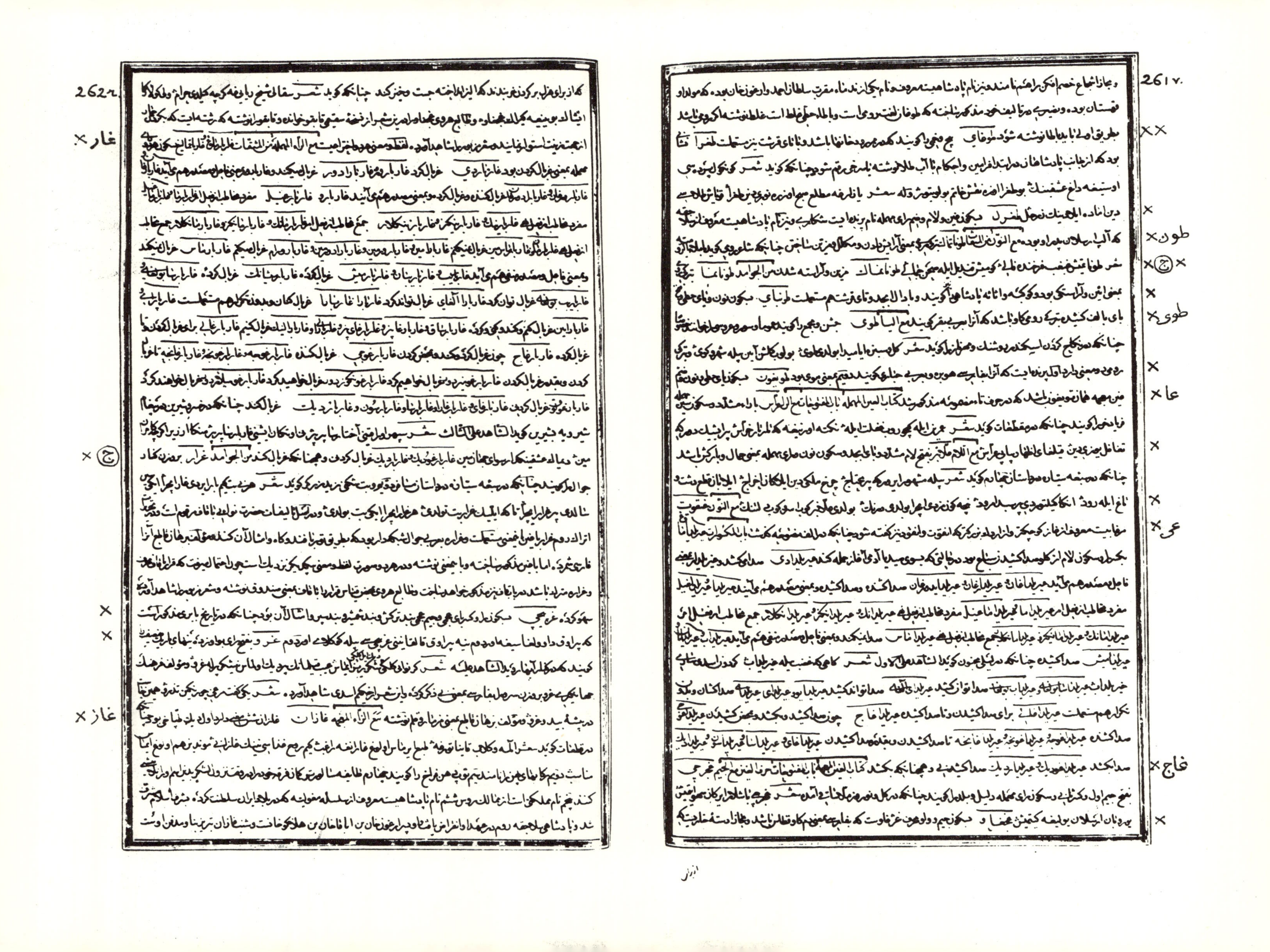

غازاناچی کناهیت که بلغت بربری المریلال کویند وشبیه است شلغ اوبجهکال غاز وآنرا تجهیت بنابر بزه وتیره ومغایبت لج وملا

رلج وجالی الآلات نفس ومنفتح سده وتنقی کرده وشانه است مع الثین المعجمه غاشون بلغت مغولی بمعنی تلخ بود مع الکاف غلجه

بسکون لام وفتح جیم عجمی بمعنی پست وکوتاه باشد وبفارسی روستا وده نشینان وناشرا کویند غلکه بفتح لام وکاف بمعنی کلید چوبی را

کویند که در پشت در بساخته شود مع الیاء غلیداق بسکون یای حطی نام ولایتی است نزدیک بدشت قبچاق که تیرهای آنجا بصحت ورایت [illegible]

باشد ونشکند وبعربی بمعنی کریم باشد چنانچه در قاموس آمده که الغیداق الرجل الکریم باب المضمومات قوبچاچی بسکون با وفتح جیم عجمی اول

وکسر ثانی خدمتکار حرم را کویند چنانچه در تاریخ بابری در صدد احوال سلطان حسین میرزا مذکور است که فلان قوبچه چی لغت مرتبه [illegible]

بیکم لیک مرتبه سیغه نزتی قیلدی شعر بسکون زای [illegible] بر وزن پرصدای [illegible] وسلغ بود چنانچه در [illegible] در وصف

کوید شعر [illegible]

وبفارسی [illegible] کویند [illegible]

[illegible] خوانند [illegible] لفظیست مشترک که بترکی [illegible] باشد چنانچه [illegible]

کوید شعر [illegible] کویند غوز

[illegible] ترکان که در زمان سلطان سنجر [illegible] خراسان را مسخر کردند کما فی القاموس غوسون بضم سین مهمله وسکون نون بلغت مغولی

[illegible] کنیز مدخوله را نامند [illegible] مستعملست غونده [illegible]

کننده وآنرا تیلا هم کویند وبترکی [illegible] هم خوانند غونک بسکون نون وکاف [illegible] مانند الشاهد [illegible] شعر [illegible]

[illegible] واز [illegible] هم کویند باب المکسورات مع الراء المهمله غرناق

از الفاظ مشترکه است [illegible] کنیز وجاریه را نامند ودر عربی بمعنی جمیل باشد چنانچه در قاموس مذکور است الغرناق [illegible] الشاب الابیض

الجمیل جمع غرانیق ودر ترکی [illegible] مستعملست مع الزاء المعجمه غزش [illegible] بود که از انداختن تیر وسنگ وامثال آن برآید مع الکاف

[illegible] بسکون لام ویای حطی وفتح جیم [illegible] باشد [illegible] یدی از [illegible]

[illegible]

[illegible]

[illegible]

[illegible]

[illegible] از خود [illegible]

[illegible]

[illegible] از خود [illegible]

[illegible] از خود [illegible]

[illegible] از خود [illegible]

[illegible] بسکون نون وکاف [illegible] باشد [illegible] که دماغ از استشمام رایحه تند [illegible]

[illegible]

فرستخ [illegible] وبمعنی مصدر هم می آید غینکشیغیل مفرد غایب امر [illegible]

مفرد غایب [illegible] جمع غایب [illegible]

[illegible] الشاهد علی الاول شعر [illegible]

[illegible]

[illegible]

[illegible] برای فرستادن و [illegible]

[illegible]

[illegible]

[illegible] بفتح نون [illegible] چنانچه در [illegible]

از دیباچه کتاب [illegible] الشاهد علیه شعر [illegible]

[illegible] بسکون نون وکسر [illegible] چنانچه کوید شعر [illegible]

[illegible]

[illegible]

[illegible] کتاب لغات باب المفتوحات حروف الفاء مع الراء المهمله فرب

بفتح را وکسر جیم [illegible] فرفر [illegible]

چنانچه در [illegible] کوید شعر [illegible]

[illegible] شعر [illegible]

[illegible] فرکه [illegible] کویند فربه [illegible]

کویند چنانچه [illegible] کوید شعر [illegible]

فربه [illegible] الشاهد علیه شعر [illegible]

[illegible]

[illegible] مع السین المهمله فسلکن بسکون سین [illegible]

[illegible]

[illegible] مع اللام فلفس بسکون لام وسین [illegible] مع الیاء فیقود [illegible]

[illegible] باب المکسورات [illegible] مع الراء المهمله [illegible]

[illegible] شعر [illegible]

[illegible]

[illegible] چنانچه [illegible] کوید شعر [illegible]

[illegible]

شاهد آمده و این حرف بدون تحقیق پرانده قرشت بفتح راء مشدده و سکون سین و تاء قرشت صداق کماز چماق اسب و راندن شلك اوشال
آن بر آید چنانکه در سد سکندری در وصف اسب گوید شعر قولاق سیری اشوب چیقیب ایله شالیب‌ال ایلغیغه قرشتایله ونیز در خسرو شیرین
در صفت اندازی فرهاد گوید شعر اوچیب تیلکا انداضربتی آنینك که باریب اودون بیغاچ قرشتی آنینك مع الیاء المهمله قسقیه قسقیه
ابوالباز الدر وهم قولوز دانگویند قسلدو بکسر سین و سکون قاف و ضم دال ترکی رومی آهسته سخن گوش کی سخن گفتن مع الیاء الموحده من المشتقات قسقیرماق
صدا بر آمدن از منخر بینی و هو لا یختلط بالنفخ و آوار و میته قسقیرماق خوانند من الجامد قسلك بفتح شین و سکون کاف ترکی رومی هوشك
بود که در وسیمای آتش بازیها آتش در هند که هوا بلند شود و قطار قسقیر را کم گویند که باروط در آن ریزند مع الکاف قسکر بودن
جگر ترکی رومی کلکونه و غازه باشد که زنان بر روی مالند مع النون قسقیرماقغ بسکون نون و راء مهمله و کسر قاف ترکی رومی صدا بر آمدن از منخر
بینی بود جزو چهارم بیغنن و تفسیر بعضی از صیغ مشتقه کتاب القاف باب المفتوحات حرف القاف مع الالف قاآن
بمعنی شاه . شاهان باشد باین جهه مغولیه اعظم پادشاهان خود را که پادشاهان دیگر تابع او باشند قاآن گویند مع الباء من المشتقات قاپماق
مکو بیای عجمی دست ربودن و باد هر کز نتوان و اشباه آن الشاهد علیه شعر ای نوائی بلبه کویی ایلچی نینك خاتینکا کیم منتوماق
قاپماغو دین یار لیغلاغو ایماش و سیناق جز اینکه کنار کویی ایلچی نینك کیمه توتماق قاپماغو دین خالیکا یار لیغلاغو ایماس قاپدی
ربودیم قاپارم قاپا دور میربایدو قاپار بمعنی فاعل مستعمل هم می آید قاپمانه قاپاغان و قاپدوغان ربایند ربوده و بمعنی مستعمل هم می
قاپه قاپغیل مفرد مخاطب فعل امر قاپلغقا قاپاغیل مفرد مخاطب فعل امر قاپینك و قاپینکیز و قاپینکلار جمع مخاطب فعل امر قاپماغان
قاپمایکیز و قاپمانکلار جمع مخاطب فعل امر قاپمیس و قاپارمیس و قاپادورمیس قاپا دام میربایم قاپمان قاپماسمین بمیربایم قاپیپ و قاپیبان
قاپمیش ربوده قاپمیشین ربوده اش را قاپمیشانك ربوده قاپیپتور و قاپیپتوربیز ربوده ایم قاپماس نمیرباید قاپماسلیغ
نربودن قاپماس بولسا نرباید تا باشد قاپادورمیش بولغه سیر بوده باشد قاپا قاپا ربوده ربوده و بدون تکرار هم مستعمل قاپایو
ایا ربایم و بر باید ونربای قاپما یو نربوده قاپساق و قاپغای قاپمای قاپساك قاپنك برایم قاپغانی برای ربودن و قار بوده قاپغاچ
چون ربوده بر باید و بمعنی ربودن قاپغوچ گیرنده و ربانیده الشاهد علیه شعر خسته کویوب کما یا میشام بیکش تونفوجیم ایتینك دوره دست
قاپغوچه قاپغو سیز قاپغانجه تا ربودن و بقصد ربودن قاپغوده ور خواهیم بود قاپغو سیکور خواهی بود قاپغوسیدو ربوده خواهد بود
قاپغولوق ربودن قاپغای و قاپغاپسه و قاپیپتی قاپیدیك بر باید قاپغو میلیك تمیز نوقاپدیلك مین ربود که نام قاپیشماق مکررا بی عجمی ربودن
ربوده از هم ربودن و صیغ آن تا این قرشت اشتقاق می یابد قاپسماقغ کر مته ربوده شدن و صیغ آن با لام اشتقاق بی یابد قاپتورماقغ
مصدر متعدی و صیغ آن با لفظ قاپ اشتقاق می یابد قاپاماقغ بفتح با ابجد احاطه کردن و محصور ساختن و با بای عجمی ترکی رومی بمعنی سد کردن
بود قاپادوق محصور کردیم و با بای عجمی ترکی رومی سد کردیم قاپادیم قاپادی محصور کردید و قاپادی بمعنی سد کرد و سد میکند بمعنی فاعل
هم می آید قاپاغان و قاپاغان و قاپادوغان محصور کنند و محصور کرده چنانکه شاهد بر اول بمعنی تاریخ تاریخ نذکور است کرغالی
قاپاغان یوسونلوق قیلیب اولتوروب ایدی و بمعنی مصدر هم می آیند قاپاقا قاپاغیل مفرد مخاطب فعل امر الشاهد علی الاول شعر
قاپاپتالا دوسلی خلوتیدا لمینی ای کمدون قیچه جوار بنیداد اول آی نینك قاپالغاچی و با بای عجمی ترکی رومی از سد کردن
قاپاناقا قاپاناغیل مفرد مخاطب فعل امر قاپانك قاپانکیز و قاپانکلار جمع مخاطب فعل امر قاپاناغان و قاپانکلار جمع مخاطب فعل امر
قاپای قاپارمیس قاپامادیم قاپادم محصور کنیم الشاهد علی الثالث شعر مکرالیتوریری لارای فونوکیتیلیه کونکلومنی کم تو
نماید در نیچه کیم جسم او سیندا قاپادم میش قاپامان و قاپامادین محصور نکنیم قاپاب و قاپابان و قاپامیش محصور کرده چنانکه در

بیت الشاهد علی الاول شعر کیلور ایردیم الجنم داوای نسبوق بولوب نو فرزانه داد البدایت کما آقاموب توش توشوم دین قاپاپ
منکا قاپی لار احتنا بلاهلی دست قاپامیین محصور کرده قاپاب یزو قاپاب توریبیز محصور کرده ایم قاپاماس محصور نکند
قاپاماسلیغ محصور نکردن قاپاماس بولسا محصور نکند باشد قاپادورمیش بولغه محصور کرده باشد قاپایو و قاپای قاپا یلی
محصور کنان و بدون تکرار هم مستعمل قاپایو ای محصور کنیم و کند و کی قاپانایو محصور کرده قاپاساق و قاپاسیز
قاپاغای یزو قاپلی و قاپالینك محصور کنیم قاپاغالی برای محصور کردن و تا محصور کند که قاپاغاچ چون محصور کرد و کند و بعض کرد
قاپاغوچی محصور کننده قاپاغوچیه و قاپاغوچیز و قاپاغانجه تا محصور کردن و بقصد آن قاپاغوسیدور محصور خواهم کرد قاپاغو سیکور
محصور خواهی کرد قاپاغوسیدور محصور خواهد کرد قاپاغولوق محصور کردن قاپاغای قاپاسه قاپاسوی قاپادیلیك محصور کند قاپاتو
توربی قاپادیلیمین محصور کرده ام قاپالماقغ مع اللام المهمله بمعنی محصور شدن قاپالغان قاپالوران و قاپالادوغان محصور شونده
و محصور شده و بمعنی مصدر هم می آیند چنانکه شاهد بر اول گوید شعر تیلبه کونکلوم قاپالغان سودا شیدای تیماینکر قیلدی عمر ثانی
ایچرا کوپ قاپالغاندین بوایرور قاپالماغلیق و قاپالماغلیغین محصور شوی الشاهد علی الثانی شعر دشت سودا قاپالغان جنون دیلکا
قاپقیم شیدان فرقتا لیچرا میندیك قاپالماغلیغ و قاپالماغلیغ بو مسباق بالام لشفاق می یابد قاپارماقغ بفتح با و سکون راء مهمله آبله کردن
و مجازا بمعنی ورم کردن هم استعمال میشود و رومیه از ترس ساختن که بیک گویند و بمعنی اخیر استعمال نمایند قاپادوق آبله کردیم و ورم کردیم
قاپاردی آبله میکند و ورم میکند الشاهد علی الاول بالمعنی الاول شعر فراقدین اینانیق ایاقیم دیدار انچقاروب کرکو طبیب الحکیم
باب نامی قاپاروش و قاپاردی بمعنی فاعل و مصدر هم می آید قاپارغان و قاپارغان و قاپاردوغان آبله کننده و آبله کرده و ورم کننده و ورم کرده
چنانکه شاهد بر اول بمعنی آبله کرده گوید شعر اولوچوغ ایرورقا قاپارغان لعل صح اتراسیفه شیشه طلا جیوان سوبین المیش اوس احیا
وله ایچیدا سوتیکا اسیدا ایاش قاپارغان شکل ایله سیز سیزین پرتلز قویغان داغ مجرا رغو کونه نو و بمعنی مصدر هم می آیند قاپار قاپارغیل
مفرد مخاطب فعل امر قاپاراغیل مفرد مخاطب فعل امر قاپارینك قاپارینکیز و قاپارینکلار جمع مخاطب فعل امر قاپارمیس قاپارمیس
قاپارنکیز و قاپارنکلار آبله میکنم قاپارمان آبله نمیکنم و ورم نمیکنم قاپاریپ قاپاریپان قاپاریش آبله کرده الشاهد علی الثالث
بالمعنی الاول شعر جیجوکلوکلا دین سوبا گوید مرکایچی دین ... قاپارمیشدیلیم قاپاتی لعل آقتین یاکیلیغ دودا قینك قاپارمیشین آبله کرده
و ورم کرده اش قاپارمیشانك آبله کرده و ورم کرده قاپاریپ یزو قاپاریپ توریبیز آبله کردیم و ورم کردیم قاپارماس آبله نمیکند و ورم
نمیکند قاپارماسلیغ آبله نکردن و ورم نکردن قاپارماس بولسا آبله نکند باشد قاپارادورمیش بولغه آبله و ورم نکرده باشد قاپا
قاپارا آبله کنان و ورم کنان و بدون تکرار هم مستعمل قاپارایو آیا آبله و ورم کرد و کند و کی قاپارمایو آبله و ورم نکرده قاپاراق
قاپارغای یزو قاپارغای قاپارلینك آبله و ورم کنیم قاپارغالی برای آبله و ورم کردن و تا کند که قاپارغاچ چون آبله و ورم کرد و کند
و بعض کردن قاپارغوچی آبله کننده و ورم کننده قاپارغوچیه و قاپارغوچیز تا آبله و ورم کردن و بقصد آن قاپارغوسیدور آبله و
خواهم کرد قاپارغوسیکور آبله و ورم خواهی کرد قاپارغوسیدور آبله و ورم خواهد کرد قاپارغولوق آبله کردن و ورم کردن قاپارغای
قاپارسه و قاپارسون و قاپاردیلیك آبله کند و ورم کند قاپارغالیك توریپ و قاپاریپ توربی آبله کرده ام قاپارتماقغ بسکون راء مهمله و تاء قرشت
مصدر متعدی یعنی آبله دار کردن و ورم دار ساختن و رومیه آنرا کبر تماك گویند بمعنی اخیر استعمال مینمایند قاپارتیب قاپارتیپان و قاپارتمیش
آبله دار کرده و ورم دار ساخته چنانکه در سد سکندری گوید الشاهد علی الاول بالمعنی الثانی شعر تماشا تیلیب عرض انصاف دین قاپارتیب
از این دعوی و لاف دین و باقی صیغ بر این قیاس قاپاتماقغ بفتح با و تاء قرشت اشتقاق می یابد قاپاسماقغ بسکون با و فتح سین مهمله با هم کشیدن تا پنهان شدن

264v.

گرمش و فرو کردن چنانچه در داستان بهرام از بیعه ستیان در صفت غبار و سهیل گوید شعر ایله تاریغ ایلاکینا سیغادیکیم تاچانیکیم بوایش بولدی
نچه کوندین سونک اولغلوسکا ف تاپساناق بوایکی چیرلک آن و تولکف روی طی تاپساناق را در آن شعر تاپساناق خوانده و تاپساناق را باخیون شنه
و شعر مزبور را شاهد آورده سهو کرده تاپسادوق درمیان گرفتیم تاپسادوق تاپساید ور درمیان میگیرد و تاپسار بمعنی حاصل مصدر هم می آید
تاپسار غه تاپساغان و تاپساید وغان درمیان گیرنده و درمیان گرفته و بمعنی مصدر هم می آید تاپسا و تاپسا عیل مفرد غائب امر فعل امر
تاپسامه و تاپسامه عیل مفرد غائب امر فعل نهی تاپسانک و تاپسانکیز و تاپسانکلار جمع غائب امر فعل امر تاپسامانک و تاپسامانکیز و تاپسامانکلار جمع غائب
امر فعل نهی تاپسای مین و تاپسای بیز و تاپساید ورمین تاپسارم درمیان میگیرم تاپسامان و تاپساماس مین درمیان نمیگیرم تاپسابو و تاپسابان و
تاپسامیش درمیان گرفته الشاهد علی الثانی شعر تان تور کونکلوم ... تاپساباش کام الدرحضرت ...
الشاهد علی الثالث شعر ... کونکول تابلمیش ... تاپسامیشین درمیان گرفته
تاپسامیشانک درمیان گرفته تاپساماس درمیان نمیگیرد تاپساماسلیغ درمیان نگرفتن تاپساماس بولسا درمیان نگرفته باشد تاپسالی
بیش بوقته درمیان نگرفته باشد تاپسایو و تاپسای تاپسه درمیان گرفته گرفته و بعض تکرار هم مستعمل تاپساغو آیا درمیان گیرد
و بگیرد و بگیری تاپسامایو درمیان نگرفته تاپساسا و تاپساغای بیز و تاپسالی و تاپسالینک درمیان بگیریم تاپساغالی
برای درمیان گرفتن و تا درمیان گرفته تاپساغاچ چون درمیان گرفت و بگیرد و بمحض گرفتن تاپساغوچی درمیان گیرنده تاپساغوچه و تاپساغونچه
تاپساغاغه تا درمیان گرفتن و بعد از آن تاپساغوم دور درمیان خواهم گرفت تاپساغونک دور درمیان خواهی گرفت تاپساغوسیدور درمیان
خواهد گرفت تاپساغولوق درمیان گرفتنی تاپساغای و تاپساسه و تاپسالسون و تاپسالیک درمیان بگیرد تاپساغویلیک ... درمیان گرفتنی
تابقارماق بسکون با ... درمیان ... تابقاردوق درقاب گذاشتیم تابقارور و تابقارادور
درقاب میگذارد و تابقار بمعنی حاصل مصدر هم می آید تابقارغان و تابقاریدوغان و تابقارادورغان درقاب گذارنده و درقاب گذاشته و بمعنی مصدر
می آید تابقار و تابقار عیل مفرد غائب امر فعل امر تابقارما و تابقارما عیل مفرد غائب امر فعل نهی تابقارینک و تابقارینکیز و تابقارینکلار
جمع غائب امر فعل امر تابقارمانک و تابقارمانکیز و تابقارمانکلار جمع غائب امر فعل نهی تابقارای مین و تابقارای بیز تابقارادورمین درقاب میگذارم تابقارمان و
تابقارماس مین درقاب نمیگذارم تابقاریبه تابقاریبان و تابقارمیش درقاب گذاشته تابقارمیشین درقاب گذاشته اشرا تابقارمیشانک درقاب گذاشته
تابقارماس درقاب نمیگذارد تابقارماسلیغ درقاب نگذاشتن تابقارماس بولسا درقاب نگذاشته باشد تابقارادورمیش بوقته درقاب نگذاشته
باشد تابقارا تابقارا درقاب گذاشته گذاشته و بعض تکرار هم مستعمل تابقارغو تابقارالی مین درقاب گذارم و بگذارد و
بگذاشته تابقارساناق ... درقاب بگذاریم تابقارغالی برای درقاب گذاشتن و تا درقاب گذاشته
تابقارغاچ چون درقاب گذاشت و بگذارد و بمحض گذاشتن تابقارغوچی درقاب گذارنده تابقارغوچه و تابقارغونچه تابقارغاغه تا درقاب گذاشتن
و بعد از آن تابقارغوم دور درقاب خواهم گذاشت تابقارغونک دور درقاب خواهی گذاشت تابقارغوسیدور درقاب خواهد گذاشت تابقارغولوق
درقاب گذاشتنی تابقارغای و تابقارسه و تابقارسون و تابقاردیلک درقاب بگذارد تابقارغویلیک ... درقاب گذاشتنی
تابلاماق لفافه کردن و ملفوف کردن تابلادوق ملفوف کردیم تابلادی و تابلایدور ملفوف میکند و تابلار بمعنی حاصل مصدر هم می آید تابلاغان
تابلاغان و تابلایدورغان ملفوف کننده و ملفوف کرده و بمعنی مصدر هم می آید تابلا و تابلا عیل مفرد غائب امر فعل امر تابلاما و تابلاماعیل
مفرد غائب نهی تابلانک و تابلانکیز و تابلانکلار جمع غائب امر فعل امر تابلامانک و تابلامانکیز و تابلامانکلار جمع غائب فعل نهی تابلای مین
تابلای بیز و تابلایدورمین ملفوف میکنم تابلامان و تابلاماس مین ملفوف نمیکنم تابلابان و تابلامیش ملفوف کرده و لفافه کرده

265r.

علی الاول شعر ... باشینکه تابلاب ... تابلامیشانک
کرده تابلامیشانک ملفوف کرده تابلاماس ملفوف نمیکند تابلاماسلیغ ملفوف نکردن تابلاماس بولسا ملفوف نکرده باشد تابلادورمیش بوقته
ملفوف نکرده باشد تابلایو و تابلای تابلای ملفوف کرده و بعض تکرار هم مستعمل تابلاغو آیا ملفوف کند و بکند تابلامایو ملفوف نکرده
تابلاسا و تابلاغای بیز و تابلالی و تابلالینک ملفوف کنیم تابلاغالی برای ملفوف کردن و تا ملفوف کرده تابلاغاچ چون ملفوف کرد و کند و بمحض کردن
تابلاغوچی ملفوف کننده تابلاغوچه و تابلاغونچه تابلاغاغه تا ملفوف کردن و بعد از آن تابلاغوم دور ملفوف خواهم کرد تابلاغونک دور ملفوف خواهی کرد
تابلاغوسیدور ملفوف خواهد کرد تابلاغولوق ملفوف کردنی تابلاغای و تابلاسه و تابلاسون و تابلادیلک ملفوف کند تابلاغویلیک ... تابلاغویلیک
ملفوف کردنی تاپاماق بابای عجمی ... کنایه ... چون ... ظرفی را گویند ...
باشد خصوصا چنانچه در تاریخ الانبیا در ذکر ابراهیم علیه السلام گوید ... خلیل مصری ...
تابی ... تابا ... چنانچه در تاریخ بابری مذکور است ...
شکل ... ولایت اندجان ...
... بعضی ... استعمال ...
تابارچوق ... چنانچه در خاتمه حیرة الابرار گوید شعر ...
مقدمه ... تاپاغان ... چنانچه در حیرة الابرار در وصف میخوارگان گوید
شعر ... تاباق و تاباغ ... اول ... دوم ...
نامه ... شعر ... تاباق ...
...
چشم را گویند چنانچه گوید شعر ... تاباغ ...
... تاباق ... کنایه است از ...
... تاباقولاغ ... گویند
تاپاتامیق ... تاپال بمعنی ... بود
و نیز ... چنانچه گذشت تامان ...
... چنانچه ... گوید شعر ...
تپتال بسکون با و لام و فتح تای قرشت با الف کشیده ... چنانچه در تاریخ بابری مذکور است که ...
بولغای ایدی و نیز ... تپتان ... چنانچه گوید
شعر ... تاتورغای ...
و ضم تای قرشت و فتح ... تچاق ...
آن ... و ... اصحاب تواریخ ... ذکر کرده اند که ...
که ... یافت ...
جنگ کشته شده بود ...

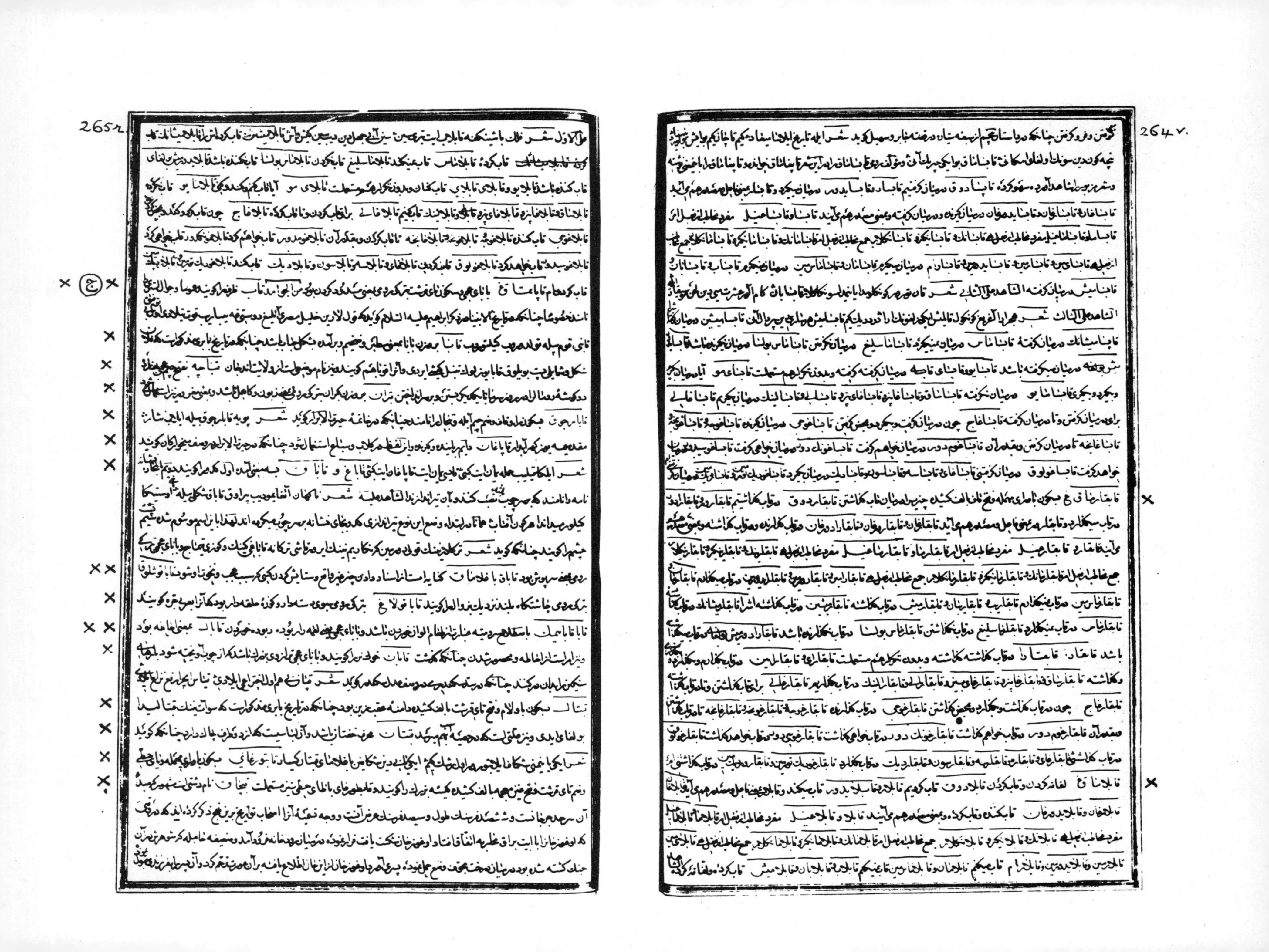

265v.

تابوبجاق نام نهاد در لسان عوام تبچاق اشتهار یافت وارو س و اکثر ایلات دشت را تابع او ساخته امرا بجلو آبا آن فرهنا دو سعلاّلی
در آنمت پادشاهی کرد و نیز نام طایفه ایست که از نسل او می باشند چنانکه ملوکفته شعر کون قوم قبچاق لسر حبش شمار ها الاصل آن
یك چش و نام پسر تنبکرخان بن اوغوز خان هشم هست چنانکه در اوغوزنامه بتقریب ذکر وجه تسمیه تالماق مسطور است که اوغوز خان
ایت براق را دفع کرد جمعی از لشکر او غوز خان که زنان و اموال ایت براق را غارت شده بودند
لیت تر از اولاد او که دید ند لو لاد او
دشت قبچاق گویند
شیراز انانیکه
شمیلیز آز

266r

[illegible]

تات و شین و جیم لام با یکدیگر یافت شدن تاپیلاشتوق ... یافت شدند چنانکه میرزا سکندر در حکایت سلطان ابو سعید کورکان گوید شعر
تاپیلماسی لار ایشنه حد دین فزون ٭ عداوت بیننده الیمه چکی ازون ٭ تاپیلادور یافت میشود و تاپیلادورلار یافت شوند
و مصدر هم می‌آید تاپیلماقان و تاپیلاشورغان و تاپیلاشادورلار یافت شوند و یافت شده و بمعنی مصدر هم می‌آید تاپیلاشتوق تاپیلاشیل
مفرد غائب از فعل امر تاپیلسون و تاپیلا شما ... مفرد غائب از فعل نهی تاپیلماسون و تاپیلماسونلار جمع غائب از فعل امر تاپیلسونلار
تاپیلماسونلار جمع غائب از فعل نهی تاپیلاسین و تاپیلاسیز و تاپیلادی یافت شد تاپیلدیم تاپیلدوک تاپیلدیلار تاپیلماس
یافت نشوم تاپیلماغای ... تاپیلغایمن یافت شوم تاپیلغایسین یافت شوی تاپیلغایسیز یافت شوید تاپیلغایلار یافت شوند
تاپیلیب ... یافت شده‌ام تاپیلماس ... یافت نشدن تاپیلماس بولسا یافت نشود اگر ...
بولسای یافت شده باشد تاپیلغان تاپیلغان یافت شده و بدون تکرار هم مستعملست تاپیلماسا ... ایا یافت شوم و شود
تاپیلماس و یافت نشده تاپیلاسا و تاپیلاسای و تاپیلاسایمن و تاپیلاسالار و تاپیلاسانک یافت شوم تاپیلغالی
برای یافت شدن و تا یافت شده تاپیلغاج چون یافت شد و شود و یافت شدن تاپیلغوچی یافت شونده تاپیلغوسی و تاپیلغوسی
تاپیلغالی تا یافت شدن و مقدم یافت شدن تاپیلغوسیدور و تاپیلغوسیدورلار یافت خواهد شد تاپیلغوسیدور تاپیلغوسی
تاپیلغوسی لوق یافت شدنی تاپیلغای ... یافت شود تاپیلغوسیدیک تهی ... تاپیلماق
دیلمین یافت شدنم تالدرماق بسکون تاو نون ... بمعنی ... تحمل و شکیبائی کردن و ثبات قدم ... تالدرماق
تالدرماق (تالدرمای) ... بالکاف استعمال نمایند و دویم چند لا شدن تحمل کردن و چند لا شدن چنانکه در سد سکندری در حال ... گوید المعنی الاول شعر
تیشکلیج ... ایکی ... دیک ... شعر ... بولسا ...
چونکه ... تالدوردی ... تالدوردوق تحمل کردیم و چند لا شدیم تالدورور تالدورادور تحمل میکند و چند لا میشود و
تالدورو ... و مصدر هم می‌آید تالدورغان ... تالدورغان تالدورا دو ... تحمل کننده و تحمل کرده و چند لا شونده و بمعنی مصدر هم
می‌آید تالدورغو ... مفرد غائب از فعل امر تالدورما ... تالدورسون ... جمع غائب از فعل امر ...
تالدورماسون ... تالدورساق ... تالدورماغای ... تالدوردیم تحمل کردم و چند لا شدم تالدورماس
تالدورماس ... تحمل نکنم و چند لا نشوم تالدورسام ... تالدورسانک ... تحمل کرده و چند لا شده ... تالدورسا ...
شود ... تحمل کرده و چند لا شده تالدوربیرماس ... تحمل کرده‌ام و چند لا شده‌ام تالدورماس ... تحمل نکند و چند لا
نشود الشاهد علیه بالمعنی الاول شعر ... ٭ ... تالدورماس
تالدورماسلیغ تحمل نکردن و چند لا نشدن تالدورماس بولسا تحمل نکند اگر باشد و چند لا نشود اگر باشد تالدوراسان ... تحمل کرده
و چند لا شده باشد تالدورغان تالدورغان تحمل کرده و چند لا شده و بدون تکرار هم مستعملست تالدورماسو ایا تحمل کنم و کنند
شوم و شود و شوی تالدورغای ... تحمل کرده و چند لا شده تالدورغای ... تالدورغایلار ... تالدورغالی ... تحمل کنیم
شویم تالدورغالی برای تحمل کردن و تا تحمل کرده و برای چند لا شدن و تا چند لا شده تالدورغاج چون تحمل کرد و کند و بمعنی کردن و چون
چند لا شد و شود و بمعنی شدن تالدورغوچی تحمل کننده و چند لا شونده تالدورغوچیدور تالدورغالی ... تا تحمل کردن و مقدم تحمل کردن
و تا چند لا شدن و مقدم آن تالدورغوسیدور تحمل خواهم کرد و چند لا خواهم شد تالدورغوسیدور تحمل خواهی کرد و چند لا خواهی شد تالدورغوسی
تحمل خواهد کرد و چند لا خواهد شد تالدورغولوق تحمل کردنی و چند لا شدنی تالدورغای و تالدورغای ... تالدورغون و تالدورغوسیدیک

تحمل کند و چند لا شود تالدورغوسیدیک ... تالدورسین تحمل کند و چند لا شوند ... تاراماق بسکون تاو ... تاراماق
بفتح نون با الف کشیده قطره زدن و جوشیدن و چکیدن تارادوق و تاپادوق قطره زدیم تارادور ... تاپادور
... و مصدر هم می‌آید چنانکه ... آلمبری ...
... تارغان ... تاپان ... تاپاغان ... قطره زننده و قطره زده و بمعنی مصدر هم
آید تارا تارا ... تاپا تاپا ... مفرد غائب از فعل امر ... تاراگیل و تاپاگیل ... مفرد غائب ...
... جمع غائب از فعل امر ... تاپاسون ...
تارایسین تاراسین ... تارادیم ... قطره زدیم ... تارامادیم ...
... قطره نزنم ... تاراب ... تاپاب ... تارامیش و تاپامیش ... قطره زده چنانکه شاه ...
... تاراب ... تارامیشمن و تاپامیشمن قطره زده‌ام تارامیشلار ... قطره زده تاراب
تاراب ... تاپاب ... تاراماس و تاپاماس قطره نزند تاراماسلیغ و تاپاماسلیغ قطره نزدن تاراماس بولسا
تاپاماس بولسا قطره نزند اگر باشد ... تاراسای و تاپاسای ... تارای و تاپای
قطره زنان و بدون تکرار هم مستعملست تارای و تاپای ... تاراساق ... تاراغای ...
تاراغای ... تاپاغای ... و تاپاغای ... قطره بزنیم تاراغالی برای
زدن و تا قطره زده تاراغاج و تاپاغاج چون قطره زد و زند و بمعنی زدن تاراغوچی و تاپاغوچی قطره زننده تاراغوچیدور
تاراغوسی و تاپاغوسی ... تا قطره زدن و مقدم قطره زدن تاراغوسیدور و تاپاغوسیدور قطره خواهم زد تاراغوسی دور
تاپاغوسیدور قطره خواهی زد تاراغوسیدور ... قطره خواهد زد تاراغولوق و تاپاغولوق قطره زدنی تاراغای و تارا
تاراسون ... تاپاسون ... تاراسالار ... تاپاسالار ... قطره زنیم ... تاپا ...
قطره زده‌ام ... تات. بمعنی ... چنانکه گوید شعر چون ... ٭ ...
کسب ... آینکه ... ٭ ... گوید شعر ... ٭ ...
و ... سکندری در وصف ... گوید شعر بولا المیلین ... ٭ ... ٭ ...
... بولا المیلین یعنی ... تالماق یافت شدن ...
... و ... تات تات یعنی ... طبقه طبقه چنانکه گوید شعر ... تات تات ... ٭ ...
... گوید ... تاتاغان اسم ... یافت شود ... یافت شده باشد تاتاق
یعنی ... و صلب چنانکه ... در تاریخ ... ٭ ...
... تاتلاو ... نوبت و کرت باشد الشاهد علیه شعر ... ٭ ...
... تاتلاو ... نوبت ... چنانکه میرزا سکندر گوید شعر ... ٭ ...
مثال ... تاتلاو و ... بسکون واو ... هم گویند ... بسکون ...
و ... تاتش ... آشوب و انقلاب تاتش بمعنی ... چنانکه گوید شعر ... ٭ ...
لعلکون ... ٭ ... تاتیغ و تاتیق ... بمعنی ... و صلب ... الشاهد علیه

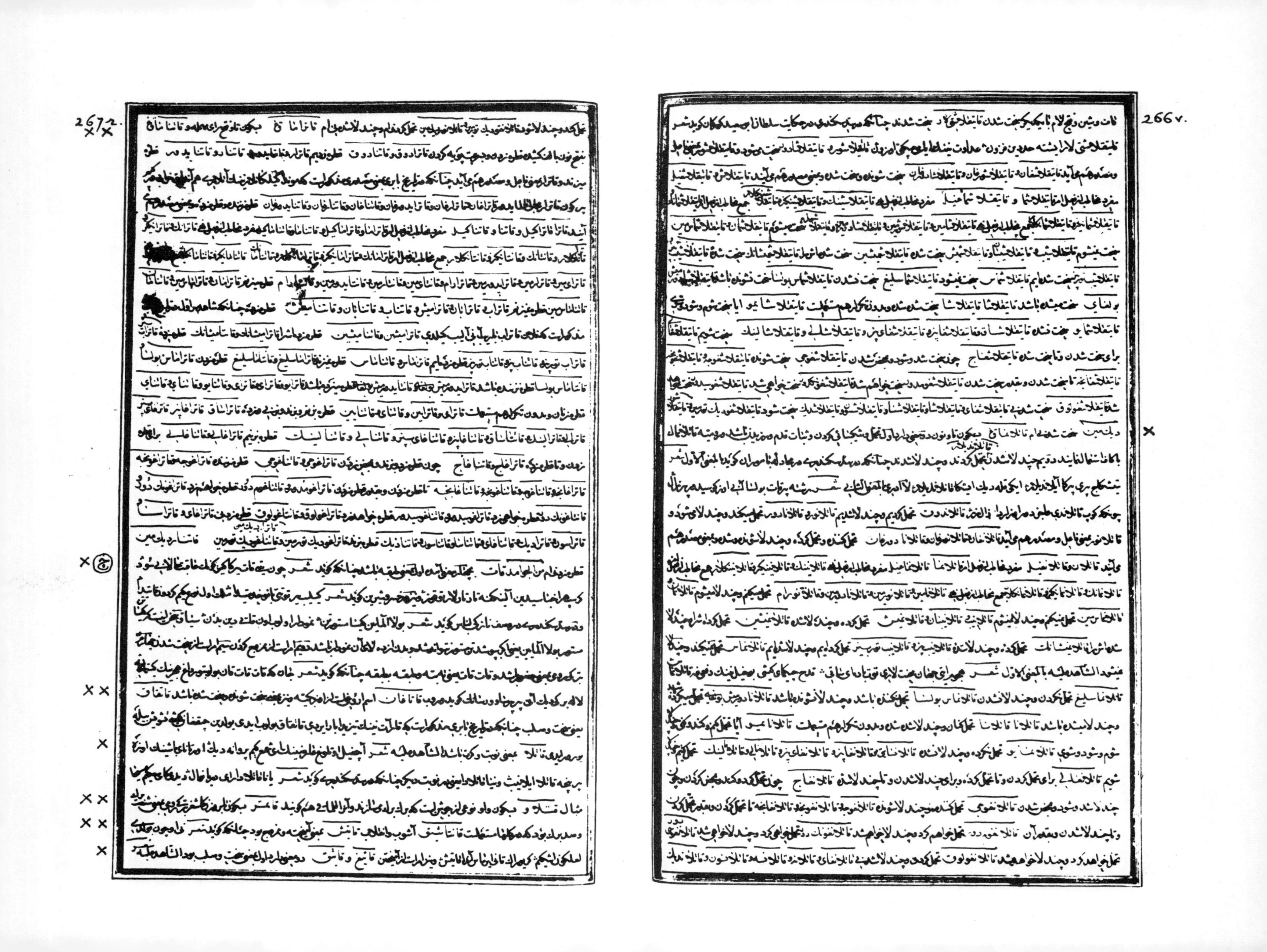

معرفاتیغ کونکلونک ایچرا تاپاید ابولسون بولسا هم فی المثل ایراول کیم ینکلیغ که بوکنا قاش لرا دیم ادام و تا تحریر شد که چنانکه درچغتای هم
انجم دتا الابرار درباب مناعت کوید شعر تیغ کونکول ایراله تاپتیق بیزا دماغ بر کوکبر اوسنق براه کلاج تاپتیغ کمزلوک کنایه از چیره چشم باشد
الشاهد علیه شعر کمزونک نونک آلیدا زکرکیل تاپتیغ کمزلوک یوزونک تاپشیدا کل آتیش ساووغ یوزلوک تاپیلیش بکسر تا و لام
و سکون شین سکا فرا کویند که صرانجا دوا بهم بیوند د چنانکه در تاریخ بابری آمده که اندرآب سو نینک تاپیلیشیدا و قت سولدی تاپینج
بکسر تا و سکون نون و جیم هدیه و تکلف باشد که بمجمع مخیج و روبی براى اما دو مناسبت ... از اقوسانست هم کویند مع الجیم من المشتقات تاپجاق
باجیم عجمی کینجش تاپچوق کرینجیم تاپچاق تاپچادو سیکرین و چاپلر مخفیا مع مصدر هم می‌آید تاپجان و تاپچارغان و تاپچادورغان کرینچک
و معنی مصدر هم می‌آید تاپچ و تاپچیل مفرد مخاطب فعل امر تاپچا و تاپچاغیل مفرد مخاطب فعل نهی تاپچینک و تاپچنکز تاپچنکلار
اشاه ... تاپچیکلار ... کر کاروسق ... بن دنیا کملود
جمع مخاطب فعل امر تاپچانک و تاپچانکیز و تاپچانکلار جمع مخاطب فعل نهی تاپچامین و تاپچارمین و تاپچاتکیز و تاپچاتکیزلر تاپچاین
تاپچارمین منیکرنم تاپچای تاپچیپان و تاپچیش کرینچه تاپچیشین کرینچه اشراقا تاپچیشانک کرینچه تاپچیپ و تاپچیپتر
کرینچه ایم تاپچاس منیکرنم تاپچا سلیغ نکرینجن تاپچاس بولسا نکرینجن باشد تاپچادورمیش بولغای سیکرینجه باشد تاپچا تاپچا کرنزا
کرزان و بدون تکرار هم مستعملست تاپچا یمو آیا بکرنم و بکینه و صکرینی تاپچمایو نکرینجه تاپچاوقه تاپچاپز و تاپچای بزو تاپچا
تاپچا لینک بکرنیم تاپچلی برای کرینجن و تاکرینجه تاپچاج چون کرینجه و بکرینه و بجن کرینجن تاپچوغی کرینه تاپچوغه و تاپچغچه
تاپچانچه تاکرینجن و بعد کرینجن تاپچونم خواهم کرینجت تاپچونک خواهی کرینجت تاپچوسی خواهد کرینجت چنانکه میر سکاکی
در تشکی دن امزی دا رابله در حق مقابله اسکندر کوید شعر بری دپ که کوکلاج قرا تاپچوسی بری عیب که منم ایشیکی آچسونکا تاپچونو
کرینجن تاپچای و تاپچوتا چسه تاپچون و تاپچدیک بکرینه الشاهد علی الکل المابس شعر تاپچدیک اول کمدی ... کیم اول لب خندان کیرانک
احتراز اتکای ابدین مرکشیکا خان کیرانک تاپچودیک نوزمین کرینجوله تاپچوماق بفتح جیم عجمی مع الرا المهمله مصدر متعدیست یعنی
کرزاندن و سیع آن بینیاق باجیم مضمومه مزی مهمله الشقاقی یابد من الجواسد قاچ بتر که روبه معنی حفه باشد ونیز اهل استر کرینجن بولونه
حیفه خونخ و امثال آنرا کویند تاپچار دو معنی دارد اول المتخواه بن نعرات پت و چلوار کویند چنانکه در تاریخ بابری مذکور حسن یعقوب کوید
که قرانغو کیجه دا امیرلیغ نینک ورت او و حسن یعقوب نینک تاپچلیغیغه بیکتا تاپچارینی بیرو نرا قامز حیلیغه کرشتلر بولدی دیم ام نلکفل
از تاراک تاپچاق بمعنی کرینجه تاپچا بمعنی کرنزاعه کویند تاپچان بفتح جیم عجمی و سکون نون کرینجه وقت چنانکه کوید شعر کی داد
تاوسین سحرباب کمرکیل قطره لار نقطه لار یکلیغ کرونیبا تاپچاپ تاپچاتیا تاپچنه تاپچلیغه سیکرو یعنی تاپجی و تاپجه و مثال الشاهد علیه شعر
تاپچا نفعه بولای اوز بولوک مستقی ایچرا تینک خوش او لکه چلوه کهیم وادی فلکونام مجرمی یعنی بلد و دلیل تاپچون بمعنی کرینجه
تاپچوسی کرینجه تاپچو بضم جیم عجمی با سطلح اهل توران منجارکم کرینی باشد که از پل جمله و اقع شد تجنیه بکسر جیم و سکون یا و ها
کرکس بود که آنرا بعربی نسر کویند چنانکه در تاریخ الانبیا در ذکر عوج بن عنق کوید که عوج جهان دین بر صند و قینیک تپرت پایه سیغه
تپرت تجنیه نی با فلاب ... صند و قینه کردی و کوینلکه کرکس بیلان ... برد و فرسنگ قطع می‌کند بدلیل انکه مهما از زعفران آید
واو کمان برکان کرده ... مسافت آن ... از ... و از خواص اوست که ... حرا
در وقت خواب بلغجم و اتی پوشد و تا هزار سال عمر میکند تاجین بکسر جیم عجمی ... لاچین ... سیل که خرد و بزرگ جمعت خود
مراعات نماید ... که سیل ... آمد ... و آنرا تاچین کویند مع الدال من المشتقات تا دامامغ بفتح دال الف کشیک محمود
کردن و الحاح بمعنی عجکم کردن نیز آید تا دادوق متحمل کردیم تا دارو تا دا یدغه متحمل میکند و تادار بمعنی فاعل و مصدر هم می‌آید

تادامانغ تادامانغ تادا یدرغان متحمل کننده و کرکیمی بمعنی مصدر هم می‌آید و لفظ تدقرکه خال دتو شیجات و مکالمات مصطلح شده است
معمولست که بالمجنسه تاکید استعمال می‌شود تادا و تاداغیل مفرد مخاطب فعل امر تادامانا و تادامانغیل مفرد مخاطب فعل نهی
تادانک و تادانکیز و تادانکلار جمع مخاطب فعل امر تادامانک و تادامانکیز و تادامانکلار جمع مخاطب فعل نهی تادای مین و تادارمین و تادایده
تادادام متحمل میکنم تادامان و تادامس مین متحمل نمیکنم تادابدو تادابان و تادامیش متحمل کرده تادامیشانک متحمل
کرده تادابرو تادابتور متحمل کرده ایم تاداماس متحمل نمیکند تادامان سلیغ متحمل نکرده تاداماس بولسا متحمل نکرده باشد
تادایدورمیش بولغای متحمل نکرده باشد تادا یو تادای تادای متحمل کنان و بدون تکرار هم مستعملست تادای مو آیا متحمل
کند و کی تادامایو متحمل نکرده تاداناق و تادافای بز و تادافای بزو تادای و تادالینک متحمل کنیم تاداغلی برای متحمل کردن
و تاکرده تاداقاج چون متحمل شد و شود و متحمل شدن تاداغوچی متحمل کنند تاداغوچه و تاداغونچه تادافانچه تا متحمل
شدن و بعد متحمل شدن تادالغومد و رمتحمل خواهم کرد تادالغونکدور متحمل خواهی کرد تادالغوسیدور متحمل خواهد کرد
تادامغولوق متحمل کردن تادامای و تاداسلو تادالیق و تادادیک متحمل کند تادالغوسیک نویرسی تادارتیک متحمل کردنیم تادالماق
مع الکلام متحمل و صبر کردن تادالیب و تادالیباو تادالمیش متحمل و صبر کرده الشاهد علی الاول خسرو کونکل ملالات ایریمجرمانم
بر لب بچول که سید بیقلغای ... تکلم ... تادالیپ و تناقص صیغ ... الالام اشتقاقی یابد من الجواسد تادا غوده دو
دو معنی دارد اول کیمیخ داکویند ... تدال ... کدام ... الوان قمشه دیکر مستعملست تادافلیه
بمعنی متحمل و صبر کرد باشد چنانکه میر کمال ... فرهاد بمعنی محکم کوید شعر غضب پرله بوبیوری شاه ... الشاهد ... المثله
بچارش کیم ... تادافلیع قول الامیر رست بلبر ... ... تادافلیغ ... شعر ... تادافلیغ ... اعجله
خواند و قرا ... باز و ذکر کرده و شعر ... شاهد آمده ... مناسبت کرده ... سهو کرده اند لفظ و معنی آن خراست و ... تاریخ
بابری بمعنی متحمل ... کوکلات ... تاداغلیغ ... تارونغه ... سفینه
تادانه کنن که بر بالای حوبین ... چنانکه در تاریخ آل عثمان با ملاء رومیه مذکورست که کیلوه او لان کهاری چقلوب تاپادوغه
محکم تادانماس ... خان تادا خان ... مذکور شد و ظاهرا بمعنی اکید و تدریج استعمال می‌شود چنانکه در تاریخ بابری
مذکورست که آتلیغ بایاق جیرجکار کاتیغین ... الرای المهمله من المشتقات تارامانغ ... تارامانغ ... کشیده و
تاراشماق مع الکین و تاراکشماق مع الکاف المفتوحه بمعنی نکاه کردن باشد تارادوق معنی تاراشوق و تارالادوق نکاه کردیم تارادوق
تاراشور تاراشادور تارالادور تارالایدیغ نکاه میکند و تاراد و تاراشور و تارالادور بمعنی فاعل و مصدر هم می‌آید چنانکه بعید خان ... شاهد
بمعنی مصدر کوید شعر قرابلا ... تارالاب و تکانه دین کونکل ... او لکالدی ... تاراغان ... خان
تاراشغان و تاراشورغان و تاراشادرغان و تارالاغان و تارالایدورغان نکاه کننده و نکاه کرده و بمعنی مصدر هم می‌آید
و تارالدرغان بالمصدر ... بمعنی باهم شدن هم اشتراک دارد تاراغیل و تاراش و تاراشغیل و تارالا و تارالاغیل مفرد
مخاطب فعل امر تارامانا و تاراماغیل و تاراشما و تاراشماغیل و تارالاما و تارالاماغیل مفرد مخاطب فعل نهی تارانک و تارانکیز و تارانکلار و تاراشینک
تاراشینکلار و تارالانک و تارالانکیز و تارالانکلار جمع مخاطب فعل امر تارامانک و تارامانکیز و تارامانکلار و تاراشمانک و تاراشمانکیز
تارامانکلار و تارالامانکیز و تارالامانکلار جمع مخاطب فعل نهی تارای مین و تارارمین و تارایدورمین و تارارم و تاراشامین و تاراشورمین
تاراشادورمین و تاراشورام تارالای مین و تارالادین و تارالایدیرمین و تارالارام نکاه میکنم تاراماس مین و تاراشماس مین و تاراشماس مین

268v.

قارالانان بمعنی قارالمان است نکاه میکنم قاراب وقارابان وقارامیش قاراشیب قاراشیبان قاراشیمش قارالاب و قارالابان و
قارالامیش نکاه کرده الشاهد علی الاول من انشاء بخاری شعر یارا اولتورکالی انشابی کوزوم قاشیدا ایکن کمانیکا ولان اوق و قاسینی
تورغوب تورغی قاراب و له شعر عشق یولیدا خطر پیدا ایرور واقف بولوب که کیمنینک دا بلالار باقیشیب تورغی قاراب [5]
علی الرابع شعر شاهد ولدی قیلیب مثل منا داشیدا جسمیم کردیغ کوروب هرکیشی کویلاه قاراشیب تورقوشا هد بر تابع من قبیل القتال
منه کم شد قارامیش قاراشیمیش و قارالامیشین نکاه کرده اشرالا قاراشیبان و قاراشیمیشان و قارالامیشانان نکاه کرده قاراب بیز و قاراب تورور
قاراشیب بیز و قاراشیب تورور و قارالاب بیز و قارالاب تورور نکاه کردیم قارالماس و قاراشماس و قارالاماس نکاه نمیکند قارالماسلیغ و قاراشماسلیغ
قارالاماسلیغ نکاه نکردن قارالماس بولسا قاراشماس بولسا و قارالاماس بولسا نکاه نکنند باشد قارالایدور بولغای و قاراشادور و قارالایدور بولغای نکاه کند
باشد قارالایو و قارالای و قاراشا قاراشا و قارالایو و قارالای قارالای نکاه کنان و بدون نکرار هم مستعمل است قارالیو و قارالاشا
و قارا لای بو ایا نکاه کنم و کند و کنی قارالمایو و قاراشمایو و قارالامایو نکاه نکرده قارالسانک و قاراغاسین و قاراغای بیز و قاراشسانک
قاراشغاسین و قاراشغای بیز و قارالاسانک قارالاغاسین و قارالاغای بیز الشاهد علی الاول شعر تا یقین بیلدی خارج بنجام کنزاده
دین قارالاسانک بولغوسیدور کم قارالساق و قارالغای بیز و قاراغای بیز و قارالیلی و قارالسنک و قاراشساق و قاراشغای بیز و قاراشغای بیز
قاراشلی و قارالاسانک و قارالاساق و قارالاغای بیز و قارالاغای بیز و قارالی و قارالالینک نکاه کنیم قارالغالی و قاراشغالی و قارالاغالی برای نکاه کردن
و تا نکاه کرده قارالغاچ و قاراشغاچ و قارالاغاچ چون نکاه کرد و کند و بعضی کردن قارالغوچی و قاراشغوچی و قارالاغوچی نکاه کننده قارالغوچه
قارالغانچه و قاراشغوچه و قاراشغانچه و قارالاغوچه و قارالاغانچه تا نکاه کردن و بعضی نکاه کردن قرالغوم دور
قاراشغوم دور و قارالاغوم دور نکاه خواهم کرد قارالغوسی دور و قاراشغوسی دور و قارالاغوسی دور نکاه خواهی کرد قارالغوسیدور و قاراشغوسیدور و قارالاغو
نکاه خواهد کرد قارالغولوق و قاراشغولوق و قارالاغولوق نکاه کردنی قارالغالی و قاراشاسون و قارالاسون و قارادیک و قاراشغای و قارالاشه و قارالاشه قارا
قارالشدیک و قارالاغای و قارالاشه قارالاسون و قارالادیک نکاه کند قارالغودیک تورورمن و قارادیک تورورمن و قاراشغودیک تورورمن و قارالاغودیک
نکاه کردنیم قارا رنا و تغ بفتح راء اول و سکون رای ثانی بمعنی سیاه و تیره شدن باشد و نیز کلیه است نهکده شدن که متضمن کود و تیره
و اغتباش و کدورات قارا ری سیاه شد چنانکه در مجلسکه کدی مرد ستان بلبل مزاغ کوید شعر چو بلبل ایا نا قیلدی بودکدا
قارادی چو ابینه ا افریه زاغ نیما کا جوابا ملادی بحنه کوش بیرالیب بلبل دیک اولدی خموش قارا ردی و سیاه و مکدر شدیم قارا
قارارادو سیاه می شود الشاهد علی الاول شعر سونک کرتیین کرکهزوم آلمرلاسی تا الملک تینک توبی دا چو بیرلا الحمد زمان قارا ر
و قارارو بمعنی فاعل و مصدر هم می آید قارارغان و قارارو غالی قارارادورغان سیاه شوند و سیاه شده چنانکه شاهد بر اول ایراد میشود سکنی کوید
شعر قونا ش چقاننحیات ولغای تیره تون ایچرا اول آی کیلسا نوالی نینک فراقی ایچرا قارارغان مونکلاریندا اوتیز بیرو شاتکوید کرمه بیرین قارارغا
کوزکا نورم بونی ولغان کونکلکا سرو رستغشتی مز سکلاه حمی بیرلا شعر زلفی جهرچین پریشان خاطر ایروا میکن جهر شامی بیت قارار غان
بر نکایم بوایکن و بمعنی مصدر هم می آیند قارا رغا قارارغیل مفرد مخاطب امر قارارنا و قارارغا غیل مفرد مخاطب الفعل الیه قارار بینک
قارار بیکر و قارارسانکلر جمع مخاطب امر قارارسا لیغ و قارار ساکر و قارار اکنکلر جمع مخاطب الفعل الیه قارار الیین و قارار بیر تورورسین قارارادوره و قارار در کسیاه
میشوم قارار غان و قارار غایسین سیاه میشوم قارار سیه قارار ساره قارار میش سیاه شده قارار بیشین سیاه شده اشرا قارار یشانک
سیاه شده قارار بیز و قارار بیب تورور سیاه شده ایم قارار ماس سیاه نمیشود قارار ماسلیغ سیاه نشدن قارار ماس بولسا سیاه نشونده باشد
قارارادور مش بولغای سیاه میشده باشد قارارا قارارا سیاه شده و بدون نکرار هم مستعمل قارارای مو آیا سیاه شوم و شود

269r.

و شوی قارار ما یو سیاه نشده قارار سانک قارار غاسین و قارار غای بیز و قارار غای بیز قارار غالی بلغا قارار الی سیاه شویم قارار غالی برای سیاه شدن و تا سیاه شده
قارار غاچ چون سیاه شد و شود و بعضی شدن قارار غوچی سیاه شونده قارار غوچه و قارار غونچه و قارار غانچه تا سیاه شدن و بعضی سیاه شدن
قارار غوم دور سیاه خواهم شد قارار غونکدور سیاه خواهی شد قارار غوسیدور سیاه خواهد شد قارار غولوق سیاه شدنی قارار غا
قارار و قارار سون و قارار دیک سیاه شود قارار غودیک تورورمن قارار دیک تورورمن سیاه شدنی ام قارار تماق بکسر رای مهمله و نون تعدیه
مصدر متعدیست یعنی سیاه کردن قارار تور و قارار تادور سیاه میکند الشاهد علی الاول شعر ای نوایی شلم خود بنا بیرو تینک یوزی
آق ایرور لیکن قارا ر تور ... ... ایشان ازان قارار تای و قارار تایین سیاه کنم و کند و کنی و کرده چنانکه ... کوید الشاهد علی الاول
بالمعنی الاول شعر کوزونکنا کاسولا حسرت ... ایل کوزی ... و ناقیغم بیغ ... اشتقاق می یابد قارغاماق یعنی
نفرین کردن قارغادوق نفرین کردیم قارغار و قارغار مین نفرین میکند و قارغار بمعنی فاعل و مصدر هم می آید قارغاغان و قارغالغان و قارغایدور
نفرین کننده و نفرین کرده و بمعنی مصدر هم می آیند چنانکه کوید الشاهد علی الاول شعر سیندا نازا ولدی ... انازا ... عجب
بیم سین آی قارغاغان ... ... الامیش قارغا و قارغاغیل مفرد مخاطب الفعل الیه قارغانا و قارغاناغیل مفرد مخاطب الفعل الیه قارغانک
قارغانکیز و قارغانکلار جمع مخاطب امر قارغاسانک و قارغاسانکیز و قارغاسانکلار جمع مخاطب الفعل الیه قارغای بین و قارغار مین و قارغایدور مین و قارغار دار م
نفرین میکنم قارغالغان و قارغاغان مین نفرین میکنم قارغاب و قارغابان و قارغامیش نفرین کرده قارغامیشانک نفرین کرده قارغاب بیز و قارغاب تورور
نفرین کرده ایم قارغاماس نفرین نمیکند قارغاماسلیغ نفرین نکردن قارغاماس بولسا نفرین نکننده باشد قارغایدور میش بولغای نفرین میکرده
باشد قارغایو و قارغای قارغای نفرین کنان و بدون نکرار هم مستعمل قارغای و قارغایین نفرین کنم و کند و کنی و کرده چنانکه ... کوید
ترجیع شاهد ثانی را بمعنی نفرین کند کوید بولوب تنده ... قیلدی عزم ... قارغامیو آیا نفرین کنم و کند
و کنی و قارغامایو نفرین نکرده قارغاسانک و قارغاغاسین و قارغاغای بیز و قارغاغای بیز و قارغالینک نفرین کنیم قارغاغالی برای نفرین کردن و تا نفرین کرده
قارغاغاچ چون نفرین کرد و کند و بعضی کردن قارغاغوچی نفرین کننده قارغاغوچه و قارغاغونچه و قارغاغانچه تا نفرین کردن و بعضی آن قارغاغو
نفرین خواهم کرد قارغاغونکدور نفرین خواهی کرد قارغاغوسیدور نفرین خواهد کرد قارغاغولوق نفرین کردنی قارغاغای و قارغاسه و قارغا
قارغادیک نفرین کند قارغاغودیک تورورمن و قارغادیک تورورمن نفرین کردنیم قارنا ماق بفتح نون و تقدیم الف کشیده یعنی پر بودن قارنادی پر بود
من مکر شاهد شعر ... ... قارنا دو قر بودیم قارنادی قارنایدور ...
بمعنی فاعل و مصدر هم می آید قارناغان قارنارغان قارنایدورغان ... و بمعنی مصدر هم می آیند قارنا و قارناغیل مفرد مخاطب
از فعل امر قارنانا و قارناناغیل مفرد مخاطب الفعل الیه قارنانک و قارنانکیز و قارنانکلار جمع مخاطب الفعل الیه قارنانکلار و قارنا
جمع مخاطب الفعل الیه قارنای مین و قارنار مین و قارنایدور مین و قارنار مین ... قارناغان ... قارناب و قارنابان و قارنامیش پر بوده ...
در بستان ... ... کوید [5] شاهد علی الثانی ... ... ایله ...
... قارنامیشین ... قارنامیشانک پر بوده قارناب بیز و قارناب تورور
پر بوده ایم قارناماس پر نمی باشد قارناماسلیغ پر نبودن قارناماس بولسا پر نبوده باشد قارنایدور میش بولغای پر میبوده باشد قارنایو قارنایو
پر بوده و بدون نکرار هم مستعمل قارنامایو آیا پر باشم و پر باشد و پر باشی قارنامایو پر نبوده قارناسانک و قارناغاسین و قارناغای بیز و قارنا
قارنالینک پر باشیم قارناغالی برای پر بودن و تا پر بوده قارناغاچ چون پر بود و پر باشد و بعضی پر بودن قارناغوچی پر باشنده قارناغوچه و قارناغونچه
قارناغانچه تا پر بودن و بعضی پر بودن قارناغوم دور پر خواهم بود قارناغونکدور پر خواهی بود قارناغوسیدور پر خواهد بود قارناغولوق

تلرغاناى قماغاناسه وتلرغاسون تورغاندیك برابد تلرغانوبیك تورغیچ تلرغاولیدین بو تغلم تارتماق ع مع الثاء المثلثه مصدر متعدی
یعنی ربایانیدن تارتات تارتقا تغیل اربستاند ربایانیدن چنانکه در خبر وشیرین کوید الشاهد علی الاول شعر بوتون لاد کیم
کونزدین آندین آچتینك سینك الیکیم بیله قالمقه ساچینینك آیرغاچ بد الیه بوبینوادین نواسیز الارغه تارتاتیل هوادین فتوی
رومی تارتاتیل ازاین شعر تارتاتیل با یای حطی خوانده وسیم آرا اثنا قافیه نهیده و نوشته که یعنی اهل و عزیز تمکن و شتر بر بصر لشاه آورده
منصوری هم مناسب کرده لفظه معنی هرده وهرغ ولا بمعنی است وباقی صیغ آن بدین سیاق بانای قرشتاشقا قی یابد تارتاشماق ع بسکون راء
التین المهمله بمعنی مقابله است یعنی از هم ربودن وبیکدیگر ربودن وبالجان بمعنی کشتی گرفتن استعمال می شود اما بجان غالب حقیقت است تارتاشتوق
کشتی گرفتیم تارتاشور وتارتاشادی کشتی میگیرد وتارتاشور بمعنی فاعل ومصدر هم می آید تارتاشقان وتارتاشقوان وتارتاشادی فاردکشتی گرفته وکشتی گیر
وبمعنی مصدر هم می آید تارتاشت تارتاشقیل مفرد غائب المتصل الامر تارتاشا وتارتاشما فیل مفرد غائب المتصل الحال تارتاشسینك وتارتاشیکر تارتاشا
جمع غائب المتصل الامر تارتاشاتك وتارتاشتیکر وتارتاشماتحلاصر جمع غائب المتصل الحال تارتاشالیین وتارتاشوریق تارتاشادین وتارتاشماکشتی میگیریم
تارتاشمان وتارتاشماس مین کشتی نمیگیرم تارتاشیبه تارتاشیبتاع تارتاشمیش کشتی گرفته الشاهد علی الاول شعر قالبا مدلنا اتلیتماسه
قالب ولعوم ایله کیم خوشیله کونکلوم تالاشوروشار اکاولان تارتاشیب تارتاشیبین کشتی گرفته اصل تارتاشمسانك کشتی گرفته تارتاشیب
تارتاشیب تورین کشتی گرفته ایم تارتاشماس کشتی نمیگیرد تارتاشماسلیغ کشتی نگرفتن تارتاشماس بولسا کشتی نگیرد باشد تارتاشادورمیش [illegible] کشتی
میگرفته باشد تارتاشا تارتاشا کشتی گرفته گرفته وبدون تکرار هم مستعمل تارتاشای تارتاشاین کشتی بگیرم وبگیرد وبگیرند گرفته
تارتاشساق وتارتاشغا پر وتارتاشغای پر وتارتاشای وتارتاشا کشتی بگیریم تارتاشغالی برای کشتی گرفتن وتاکشتی گرفته تارتاشغاچ چون کشتی
گرفت وبگیرد وبمحض گرفتن تارتاشقوچی کشتی گیرنده تارتاشقوچی وتارتاشقوچا وتارتاشغانچه تاکشتی گرفتن ووقت کشتی گرفتن تارتاشقوسیدور کشتی
خواهم گرفت تارتاشقوسی دور کشتی خواهی گرفت تارتاشقوسیدور کشتی خواهد گرفت تارتاشقولوق کشتی گرفتنی تارتاشقای وتارتاشقای تارتا
تارتاشقوسه تارتاشادیك کشتی بگیرد تاتارتاشقودیك تورین وتارتاشقوریك کشتی گرفتنی تارتاشتورماق ع مصدر متعدی یعنی کشتی گیرانیدن
وصیغ آن بدستور بلفظ تورماق اشتقاق می یابد تارتیماق ع بکسر ثالث بمعنی پرشدن باشد تارتیدوق پرشدیم تارتیر تارتیدور پرمیشود
تاریر بمعنی فاعل ومصدر هم می آید چنانکه بمعنی مصدر کوید الشاهد علی الاول شعر زلفونغه ای مشك ایستاردین تاریچه بنده لیغ
یوق صدینك [illegible] بو سودادین اوزونکنی ساتماکوب یعنی ای مشك تا پرشدن بزلف [illegible] ازاین سودا بکذر
بسیار خود فروشی مکن [illegible] این شعر [illegible] خوانده [illegible] نوشته ومنصوری [illegible] ذکر کرده تاریغان فاعل
تاریغان پرشونده وپرشده چنانکه شاه صاحب [illegible]
[illegible] وبمعنی مصدر هم می آید چنانکه کوید الشاهد علی الاول شعر [illegible]
[illegible] تاری وتاریغیل مفرد غائب المتصل الامر [illegible]
پرهم باشد [illegible] مفرد غائب المتصل الحال تارینك تارینکیز تارینکلار
جمع غائب المتصل الامر تاریغانك وتاریغانیکر وتاریغانکلار جمع غائب المتصل الحال تاریمین وتاریمین وتاریدیمین وتاریرام پر میشوم تاریمان
تاریمان [illegible] تاریب تاریبان تاریبیش پرشده الشاهد علی الاول شعر [illegible]
[illegible]
[illegible]

تارتیماسلیغ پرنشدن تارتیماس بولسا پرنشده باشد تارتیدورمیش بوده پرشده باشد تارتیب تارتیب پرشده پرشده وبدون تکرار
هم مستعمل است تارتیسو آیا پرشوم وشود وشوی تارتیبایو پرشده تارتیاق وتارتیغاپر وتارتیغای پر وتارتیغالی تارتیغالینده پرشوی برتارتیغلی
برای پرشدن وتاپرشده تارتیغاچ چون پرشد وشود وبمحض شدن چنانکه کوید شعر نوتیکت تیکون تیفیکم تارتیغاچ آنکلادیم
کیم بیك لارحسنی بازار میش بیك [illegible] چاقی خوب تارتیغوچی پرشونده تارتیغوچه وتارتیغونچه تاپرشدن ووقت
پرشدن تارتیغوم دور پرخواهم شد تارتیغونکدور پرخواهی شد تارتیغوسی دور پرخواهد شد تارتیغولوق پرشدنی تارتیغای وتارتیغه
تارتیغونوتارتیدیك پرشود تارتیغودیك تورین وتارتیدیك [illegible] پرشدنیام تارتیتماق ع مع الثاء مصدر متعدی یعنی پرکردن وصیغ آن بدستور
بانای قرشتاشقاق می یابد تارتیلماق ع بکسر لام وسکون شین وفتح لام بمعنی وجب کردن باشد تارتیلادوق وجب کردیم تارتیلادور
تارتیلاید ور وجب میکند وتارتیلادور بمعنی فاعل ومصدر هم می آید تارتیلاغان وتارتیلاغوان وتارتیلاید ورغان وجب کننده ووجب کرده و
مصدر هم می آید تارتیلا وتارتیلا وتارتیلاغیل مفرد غائب المتصل الامر تارتیلاغنا وتارتیلاغاغیل مفرد غائب المتصل الحال تارتیلاسینك تارتیلایکر
تارتیلانکلار جمع غائب المتصل الامر تارتیلانانك وتارتیلانیکر وتارتیلانکلار جمع غائب المتصل الحال تارتیلادیمین وتارتیلادیمین وتارتیلادیمین وتارتیلادیم
وجب میکنم تارتیلاماس تارتیلاماسمین وجب نمیکنم تارتیلادیب وتارتیلاغان وتارتیلامیش وجب کرده تارتیلامیشین وجب کرده است
وجب کرده تارتیلادیب تورین تارتیلادیب تورمن وجب کرده ایم تارتیلاماس وجب نمیکند تارتیلاماسلیغ وجب نکردن تارتیلاماس بولسا وجب نکرده
باشد تارتیلاید ورمیش [illegible] وجب میکرده باشد تارتیلادیو تارتیلادی تارتیلادی وجب کنان وبدون تکرار هم مستعمل است تارتیلادی [illegible]
آیا وجب کنم وکند وکنی تارتیلاغایو وجب کرده تارتیلاغاق وتارتیلاغاپر وتارتیلاغای پر وتارتیلاغالی وتارتیلاغالینك وجب کنیم
تارتیلاغالی برای وجب کردن وتاوجب کرده تارتیلاغاچ چون وجب کرد وکند وبمحض کردن تارتیلاغوچی وجب کننده تارتیلاغوچه
تارتیلاغونچه تارتیلاغانچه تاوجب کردن ووقت آن تارتیلاغوم دور وجب خواهم کرد تارتیلاغونکدور وجب خواهی کرد تارتیلاغوسیدور وجب خواهد
کرد تارتیلاغولوق وجب کردنی تارتیلاغای وتارتیلاغسه وتارتیلاغسون وتارتیلادیك تا وجب کند تارتیلاغودیك توریین وتارتیلادیك وجب کردنی
تارتیلاتماق ع مع الثاء مصدر متعدی یعنی وجب کنانیدن وصیغ آن بانای قرشتاشقاق می یابد تارتیلاماق ع بکسر لام والف با
کشیده بمعنی کر کردن وبیحودن باشد تارتیلادوق کر کردیم تارتیلادور تارتیلاید ور کر میکند وتارتیلادور بمعنی فاعل ومصدر هم می آید تارتیلاغان
تارتیلاغان وتارتیلاید ورغان کر کننده وکر کرده وبمعنی مصدر هم می آید تارتیلا وتارتیلاغیل مفرد غائب المتصل الامر تارتیلاغنا وتارتیلاغاغیل
مفرد غائب المتصل الحال تارتیلاسینك تارتیلایکر تارتیلانکلار جمع غائب المتصل الامر تارتیلانانك وتارتیلانیکر وتارتیلانکلار جمع غائب المتصل الحال می
تارتیلادیمین وتارتیلادیمین وتارتیلادیمین وتارتیلادیم کر میکنم تارتیلاماسمین کر نمیکنم تارتیلادیب تارتیلادیب تارتیلامیش کر کرده چنانکه
در تاریخ تابری در وصف خیل منکرات که بقا لوا ولوطغه یار اشادور تارتیلادیب سانلرلاری تارتیلامیشین کر کرده اش تارتیلامیشانك
کر کرده تارتیلادیب تورو تارتیلادیب تورمن کر کرده ایم تارتیلاماس کر نمیکند تارتیلاماسلیغ کر نکردن تارتیلاماس بولسا کر نکرده باشد تارتیلادور
میش بولغه کر میکرده باشد تارتیلادیو وتارتیلادی تارتیلادی کر کنان کر کنان وبدون تکرار هم مستعمل تارتیلاغایو آیا کر کنم وکند وکنی
کر کرده تارتیلاغاق وتارتیلاغاپر وتارتیلاغای پر وتارتیلاغالی تارتیلاغالینك کر کنیم تارتیلاغالی برای کر کردن وتاکر کرده تارتیلاغاچ چون کرد وکند وبمحض
کردن تارتیلاغوچی کر کننده تارتیلاغوچه تارتیلاغونچه تارتیلاغانچه تاکر کردن ووقت کر کردن تارتیلاغوم دور کر خواهم کرد تارتیلاغونکدور
کر خواهی کرد تارتیلاغوسیدور کر خواهد کرد تارتیلاغولوق کر کردنی تارتیلاغای وتارتیلاغسه وتارتیلاغسون وتارتیلادیك تا کر کند تارتیلاغودیك توریین وتارتیلا
دیك مین کر کردنیام تارتیلاتماق ع مع الثاء مصدر متعدی یعنی دیگری را کر کردن فرمودن وصیغ آن بدستور بانای قرشتاشقاق می یابد

تاریتما قرغ بمعنی جمع الفاظ برهم افتادن چشم را گویند و تنها ای افاده این معنی نمی کند باید لفظ چشم مذکور شود تاریقتی برهم افتاد
تاریقوی و تاریقاد و برهم می افتد و تاریقیو بمعنی حاصل مصدر هم می آید تاریقمار و تاریقمارت تاریقاد و فارسی برهم افتادم و برهم افتاد و مرتبتی
هم می آید تاریقیسه تاریقیسان و تاریقیش برهم افتاده اشیا تاریقماس برهم می افتند تاریقماسلیغ برهم
افتادن تاریقماس برهم افتاده باشد تاریقیاد و مرتبش بولغای برهم می افتاده باشد تاریقیا تاریقیا برهم افتاده افتاده و مرتبه تکرار
هم مستعمل است تاریقماسلی برای برهم افتادن و تا برهم افتاده تاریقیا الغای برای آنکه برهم تواند افتاد و تا تواند افتاد تاریقملیح چون
برهم افتاده و بیفتد و بعضی افتادن تاریقیوپ برهم افتاده تاریقیوجی تاریقیوبجه و تاریقیابجه تا برهم افتادن و مقابل آن تاریقیوبیده برهم
خواهد افتاد تاریقیولوق برهم افتادنی تاریقماسلیق و تاریقیمه و تاریقسه و تاریقسوی و تاریقدیلک برهم بیفتد تاریقیودیلک تاریقیوردیلک
برهم افتادنی و همچنانکه بیفتد و با قیاس چون بمعنی موافقت ندارند اشتقاق آن مجاز بود تارماق بکون را ترکی و بمعنی
و داخل کردن باشد چنانکه شلوار و جی صیغه ماضی آن را گفته بالملاحه الرومیه شعر توبراغی ایچره سو قاریدی بیله کرمه کوسترود
ایله و بلغت جغتای چوب بیت کمان و کریان جنگ بشر آن نصب کرده بدان صید طیور کنند چنانکه در ذیل جام مذکور خواهد شد تاریشماق
بکسر اول و سیم قرشت بمعنی منع و داخل شدن تارسماق بکون اول و سیم مهمله ترکی و بمعنی لباس فراخ را کوتاه کردن و تنگ کردن من الجوامد تاد
بیفزا گویند ترکی و بمعنی ارسال منع کردن و به عربی میر را نامند یعنی سردهم باشد و بلا ترکی ز و بمعنی چشم و کمر کرده بود قرا قا ن ا
تشریح ضرا آمده ام گفتمی سیاه باشد چنانکه گوید شعر خلقین الیب تمرهر اولدی و سیمین یرقرا تون سوادی پرایکی کاندیشه ما نورونا
نوییم ملت کابوس بود و آنجا القاست که در خواب بسبب امتلاء معده و صعود بخار بفارض آدمی میشود الشاهد علیه شعر شام هجر ایچنی
شرح ایلادی الملای و نعمت دینی اول قرا باسقان کیچه بیلکیم آتینک چقماس اونی ثیم مجاز امدا هم خوانند چنانکه گوید شعر غم اولتالا
کولار تا شینکه کیم تیلماش خلیط اولوب بوقرا منع خامه تقلیدش وله شعر یوزو نمک اخال الصفحه دانا میغان کبوی قرا خالینک ملاح تو
ایصریکیم قرا دا باش جفا دم ترکی رومی بمعنی ناجل هم باشد چنانکه فضولی بغدادی گوید بالملاحه الرومیه شعر دمادم مردم چشم ایچره قان
زلف و خالینکدن بلی اکثر مشاهیر اهل هنر ایش قرادن دمش و در تاریخ آل عثمان بالملاحه رومیه مذکور است کبری کبیه طوب تو قوندقی کوفوق
احماسندن عرو مرسل ایتسه کرک جم بطریقه ابتلام گویند کمه کالا قرا یعنی مرطب و رواجی چنانکه در تاریخ الانبیا در ذکر موسی علیه السلام و فرار بسبب
از فرعون گوید که پر لحظه دین سونکرا ایل کالاقرا سین اول چاه باشنفه سو دار لمی کیلتو رو وکالا ایتمانی گفته میشود اما قرا بتهای
بامعنی مستعمل نیست شتم گویند کمر کمیتی قرا اتباع و سایر الناس را نامند چنانکه در منشآت مرحوم بدیع الزمان میرزا گوید که ایش کوجی کمیتی
قرا سیدیکا قویماسا تیکن بمعنی زراق بولغای و لذا اعجات که ملوک طوایف را که بعد سپهر آمده قراخانی خوانند و در مجالس النفایس
الندایس در وصف فخرالدین گوید که کمیتی قرالم دین دمه یعنی از اتباع و منسوبان منت دیم مفیدی کلمه و حدی است و من لفظ رومی و بیم غیر از لفظ قرا
جز کلمه تصنیم کرده و نوشته که قرالم یعنی آمیخته و ممزوج و مصنف توضیح ذکر کرده که یعنی خویش و قوم و فقیر هم بر موجب شاهد ایراد و دو نسخه
کمیتی قرالم را بمعنی خویش نزدیک مفلح و واسع نوشته هر دو سهو کرده اند دار آزقره و قاره هم گویند چنانکه با شاهد در ذیل مذکور خواهد شد
قرا آغاج ترکی رومی نام درختی است که ثمر آن چون بخشک شود از جوف آن ریشه سنکوز کرده و آن را به عربی ثمرة البق و بفارسی درخت ناسیده است را آغرنچ
مرضیست که آن را به عربی جمره و سیوطی شقاقلوس گویند و در فرس زن دام نامند چنانکه گوید شعر کمره عجر یلیغی ناراتی قرا آغریغیه
کوفتاریق قرا بانا ق بفتح تا و طا و بعد و تلاوت شده و سکون قاف ترکی رومی نام مرغابیست سیاه رنگ که آن را ترکی جغتای قاشقالداغ و بفارسی می نامند
گویند قرا باش ترکی رومی نام بلبل بود و آن را الدار انکیتمر اکوینمد و مهمان نشناختم قرا باش نامند قرا باغ نام ولایتی است در آذربایجان

که منسوب بلزان بن فارس است چنانکه در سیر سکندری گوید چو قیشلاق اینو ایردی کونکلید اجزم قرا بلغ از آن شارعی ملای
عزم و شمر کنه ط از اللت آنست قرابنسه بکسر بای ابجد و فتح نون ترکی رومی یکنوع تفنیکست که آن را آلماهی چوزن هم خوانند قرا بوغان
ترکی رومی نام بلبل بود و آن را قرا باش هم گویند و نیز یکنوع گنجشکیست که زیر گلوی آن سیاه است و نام موضعی هم هست قرا دشت قچاق
قرا تال ترکی رومی پرنده ایست قوی جثه که آن را به عربی عقاب و بلغت جغتای بهرکوت گویند قرا تاو و ق بضم واو و سکون قاف مرغیست سیاه
منقار و پایها و منوچه مایل به سرخی و مقدم قبرده است و آن را با صفهانی غرقاز و بلار گیلانی توکا نامند و کوشت او چه کولی و ملایم الیبا
و ملیح نامحست قرا تاباق کنایه ایست از هجوم تمام و ضعفای او باش که با چوب و دست جنگ کنند چنانکه در تاریخ بابری مذکور است که
اشوی تینک بیرابرو لوند ولونا ایشقی بیرلیتیب قرا تایاق قیلیب لشو نینک تاش قوزغالیشدا بغی لازبیی ضربه است ایرکیکا تیقیب دیتیز
گوید کر او شفه یکر کلیح اوشدا هم بیرایل یاق قرا تایاق قیلیب غریب مراسماس امرا اوردا اوشردین تاولاب قرا تغو بسکون تا و میم ضم
الشات که توپچیان از نا العیور بهم دسته جا نوران شکاری را بدان لطمه کنند و آن را دالباعی نیز گویند قرا تمغا فرمان پادشاهان
ترک را گویند که مهر و نشان آن زیبا و ملاعبت آمیخته است قراتون نام حلیست که ما بین ولایت کابل و سیکنهار واقع
قراچو رجال شایسته را گویند چنانکه در تاریخ بابری مذکور است که پادشاه علیه الرحمه فرموده است کیلکاچه بر قراچو کیشی او منبله شر
تیلفای و در تاریخ بابری مذکور است که پادشاه علیه الرحمه فرموده است کیلکاچه و ستاق در ذکر یاساق چنگیز خان و بیان احوال جوجی بن
چنگیز گوید که یاساق که در هر کس او واضع احوال شایان خانیت ندانند و هنوز این قاعده مطرح است و بدین یک مزلت او برغ آمی
قراچی متنا و یخانند و مصیر مرجع یعنی یناق نوشته قراچورک ادیق سیاه دانه بود که بر روی نان پاشند نباتش شبیه برازیانه و گلش بزرد نما
بسفید است و آن را به عربی شونیز نامند قراجه یکنوع زهریست که در زبان ها بهم میرسد و آن بر دو نوع است نوع دیگر را بیشه نامند قراچه بیان
لشکرشان و قراجات نام استن او لاد مغول لغات و اوغوزخان بیرلو بوده و نیز نام پادشاه هندست که معاصر اسکندر بوده و نام محلی
از محال عینک قشلاق صلوات طوایف و هیات از عوالم آنکسار که بحو مصر سر به آید و مجموعا تابع خود میسازد قراخان نامند و مقام ایشان
ذکر کرده که نوبتی یکی از ملوک عجم بر خان ترکستان تاخته بعزو متحف و هدایای بسیار با آن دیلم فرستاده از آنجمله غلامی بود صبحی و آنغلام
در قطوخان حسیات خود نموده او را بمجلس خویش برآورده و در روز برعکس از انقلاب تربیه یافته تا کار مرجع کرده خان را بقتل رسانید و پادشاه شد از آن
او را قراخان خواندند قرا دوزن ترکی رومی نام یکنوع طنبوریست که جملار الحاد و قرا د بمعنی جوال باشد چنانکه شاهد آن در ذیل کتاب
مرقوم شد قراسو نام رودخانه ایست که از سمت بخارا آمده در صحرا رود خواهد و داخل جیحون میشود چنانکه سلطان حسین گفته گوید شعر کیم بلک
ایمان سی کیم نوالی و نتکا نی اول جانان بیاری تبیان کر نه قراسو غضبا خلاجی تیر غا بیلاجی چراپه ئل قرا سنقور نام سلطان حسین بن ملکشاه پادشاه هرات
قراشنبه کنایه است از هفته سیاه و نحوست ایام هفته چنانکه در صحیفه سیاه و مجلس آرایش بیرام گوید شعر دالیکا ایرد ای طرب هر قراشنبه
شه فضا برد ایی و لحظه قراشنبه قراغ و قاراغ مردمک چشم را گویند الشاهد علیه شعر قا اهلی ایاغی توپراغ شرحین بلیزلار بولسا الك
قراغی مو حل ایله لیغی فی اوز کامرا دایمه و له شعر باشتین ایاغ تا الالت تیم اوفدم کرکتان دماغ ایرمن حسنونک کاتیلغا ای تیلوهر بری
بر قراغ ایردی دمی کفوی قراغ را بمعنی باز و نوشته و بسبب اینکه ما لهرز نام قراغی گویند بمعنی نگاه و تا الان هم ذکر کرده و بمعنی سیاه نیز گفته و
و نیشری هم متابعت کرده هر سه معنی مجهول و غیر معقول است قراقچی بمعنی راهزن و قطاع الطریق بود الشاهد علیه شعر کونکول کلادیتلی
تالیح ایتارکا یاپا مناقشه برقع آتینک دین دوربگه یوزرا بخلاقه قراقچی کاروان کهرکاچ قراقلیغ بمعنی قحط و غلا بود چنانکه در ختم
گوید کر خلایق محظ و قراقلیغ او چون است غفاره ماداد و زکاوه رقراغوله دید ناباز نامند قراقات ثمره جنگلی است بقدر فلفل که در ترشی کلمرد

قراقاش نام ضلعیست قراقانیاق نام طایفه ایست از مغول که در حجت شمال خوارزم در کنار رود سیحون سکونت دارند قراقوروت آبکوت
که جوشانیده غلیظ آنرا کشک سازند ومایه آنرا با دیگر بجوشانند تا بحدی که منعقد شود وآن بسیار ترش و سرد وخشک وسکن حرارت
خوفست وآنرا بعربی مصل گویند قراقوش عقاب بود که آنرا بوربکوت هم گویند ودرمیته قرنال وقراتال نامند قراقولاغ جانوریست
درنده از گربه بزرگتر و گویند که دایما از عقب شیر راه رفته چون جانوری صید شیر بخورد و بعد از آنکه شیر صید را گذاشته از خوردن آن فارغ
شود باقی مانده را او بخورد و بدین سبب شیر گوش گفته اند ازینجا است که در بخارای دیگر در بخارا قراقولاغ گویند و در مملکت روم چون امثال آن در خانه
اعیان وامرا در خانه پادشاهان برای استخبار واختبار خانه باشند و چون از آنها دور و خبر مطلع شوند و خبر برسانند و آنرا ادارکان
گویند قراقوم نام ولایتیست قراقیر بسکون رای مهمله نام موضعیست در دشت قپچاق ما بین رود کرکان واترک قراقیزیم نام شهریست
از ممالک ترکستان که از آنجا تا خانبالیغ و هم از آنجا تا تبت که سرحد ختای است چهل روزه راهست قراقیتاغ اصل آن قراقیاتاغ است
یعنی کوه بلند سیاه وآن نام ضلعیست از ولایات داغستان که مسکن طایفه لکزیانست قراکول بضم کاف عجمی وسکون لام نام موضعیست
از ماوراءالنهر قراکونلوک بضم کاف عجمی اول ولام وسکون نون وکاف ثانی بترکی رودی بمعنی بود که آنرا ایسه سایله گویند قراکلق بسکون
لام وتای قرشت بضم غین معجمه ملاحیست که زراعت کار هنا صبت کند تا خانها را از سیاهی آورده کرده داخل شوند وآنرا بعربی لعین نامند
قراستول بسکون میم وضم تای قرشت زنیست مایل بسیاهی باشد قراوق بسه معنی طرحی اول آسیو است سرخ رنگ شبیه بالوبالو که آنرا بعربی
زعرور گویند دوم دانهایست سیاه که در میان گندم پیدا شود وآنرا بفارسی شیلم وضحان نامند چون با گندم برهم طلا کنند نان تلخ شود
سیم جانور آبله سیاه را گویند که المقابل الحمرة سال بر آمده آن خطرناکست قراتغو بفتح غین معجمه ظلم وتاریکی بود الشاهد علیه شعر هر دم ایستا
تیلبه کونکلوم عشقی کمان ایلا مانک ثم برق لامع فی قرانغو ابو داینهان ایلا مانک قراوول بضم واو مخفف قراقول و بمعنی محافظ باشد یعنی
دیده بان چنانکه گوید شعر تاش اصو خال سیلن سوابولی تو قراول ... عقل وهوش کیلبی اصوباتته قراقچی طلالخ ... ونیز نام طایفه ایست
از اعراب نزدیک دمها تا اصل ایشان از ترکانست که از عهد سلاطین مغول در میان آن طایفه ساکن اند و در آن زمان قراول بوده اند و اکنون
بآن اسم موسوم اند قراوناس بضم واو نام طایفه ایست از مغول که بمعنی مشهور اند قراونجه بترکی رومی نوعی از سیب باشد که آنرا بفارسی
دیواسیب وبلسان الطب حند قوقی گویند قرامیش میوه ایست که آنرا آلو هم نامند قراییکلی بکسر یای حطی ... ولام وکاف
کاف بلدرقین وزانو را گویند قریل چپانی بترکی رومی جغل آگله باشد قارت بسکون رای مهمله وتای قرشت ... شبه بود که آنرا بفارسی
پیوک نامند واتراک بعضی زشت و قوی هیکل را گویند قرتال مخفف قرانال باشد که آنرا بعربی عقاب و بفارسی دال گویند قارتماق
بسکون رای مهمله وتای قرشت پرده ایست که از زیر بر روی زخم و جراحت می بندد وآنرا قاسما قه هم نامند قارتوق بسکون را وقاف ثانی وضم تای
قرشت شاخ حجامت را خوانند قرچان باجیم عجمی بوزن مرجان و قرچه بسکون رای مهمله وفتح جیم عجمی بترکی رومی پرنده ایست از گنجشک
کوچکتر که رنگ آن زرد مایل بسیاهی است که آنرا بفارسی زرد و بعربی وطواط گویند قرچه بفتح رای مهمله وجیم بوزن ... بترکی رومی بمعنی
بلند بود که آنرا قارچه هم نامند و بعربی عضد گویند قرچغای بلند شکاری بود که آنرا بعربی بازی خوانند بزبان الطیر شعر
قرچغای قیلدی عنان کشتاچی کوکوب چنکال ایله منقار ایچی قارداش برادر را گویند وآن مخفف قارنداش بمعنی هم شکم بود الشاهد
علیه شعر ترجمه قاش ایله سیر ایدا ... قارداش قاینی بترکی رومی
خورشای و شاربات که آنرا بعربی دم الاخوین خوانند وآن صمغیست خالص ... گویند عصاره گیاه بخیست که از سقوطر و نواحی هند آید
قارت بوزن پارس شال وآنچه برکمر بندند و بعربی بمعنی سوای سخت باشد قرس بوزن درس بمعنی درشتی و هم زن باشد که آنرا قرص هم

خوانند و بعربی صفقه گویند و قرص بعربی بمعنی نیش و گزیدن آمده چنانکه در قاموس مذکور است القرص اخذک لحم انسان باصبعیک حتی تولمه
قارساق بفتح سین مهمله بوزن چارباغ نام حیوانیست از سنجاب بزرگتر که از بلاد روس و ترک آرند پوستش سرخ و سفید و ابلق بود
وکمتر از سنجاب و قاقم نباشد وآنرا بفارسی فنک گویند قرشی بکسر شین معجمه نام ولایتیست از ماوراءالنهر که در جهت جنوب سمرقند
واقع است وآنرا نسف ونخشب هم گویند و حکیم بن عطا ماه مقنع را از چاه سفر بیرون آنرا طالع کرد و بلغت مغولی کهر خانه است چنانکه
در تاریخ نادری مذکور است که قرشی منسوب به آن تیمور که در خانه مغول است ... قرشیدن ... تاریخ روضة الصفا ذکر کرده که
کبک خان در حدود فرسنگی نخشب قصری بنا کرد و بمغولیه قصر را قرشی گویند لهذا آن ولایت بقرشی اشتهار یافت و وصاف در تاریخ خود در
بیان احوال اقبال تنها از گفته که قرشی بزبان ایشان معتبر از کاخ خانیت و بارگاه سلطنت است قارشو بضم شین معجمه برابر و محاذی را
گویند قرص همان قرس بمعنی درشت زن باشد که در فوق مذکور شد قارغا کلاغ را گویند و نیز امریست از نفرین کردن چنانکه گویی
قارغبوکن بضم بای ابجد و فتح کاف وسکون نون بترکی رومی نام دوائیست که از جمله سمومات است وآنرا بعربی قاتل الکلب و خانق النمر
وبفارسی کچوله خوانند قارغه دولکی بضم دال وفتح لام وکسر کاف عجمی بترکی رومی حنظل باشد وآن نباتیست شبیه به تماته کرده
میروید وبغایت تلخ است قارغاشا بفتح غین و شین معجمتین بمعنی نزاع و دعوا بود قارغیش بکسر غین وسکون شین بمعنی نفرین باشد
شاهد آن در بیان معنی آلقیش مذکور شد و نیز در بیت سکندری در وصف عدل گوید شعر خدو دولغ ایکم بولمر ایلدین تون وکون آلقیش
خانی قیلسه قارغیش قوتی آقفردی و قارغیش بای در این شعر قارقاش بفتح غین خوانده و بمعنی غلبه و غوغا ذکر کرده است قرقره بمعنی جلوپ نام رقصیست
بچلنت که زیر گلوی آن سیاه است چنانکه در تاریخ نادری مذکور است که تورنا و قرقره و اولوق قوشلارتالین و بچه بولمرین ... تاج ... آن
در وصف تخموز مذکور است که فلان سمیع دستار بی یا پایمال جواب قرقره ... غلامزاده ... برهان مع است که
در هر جنگ هم ملامت جادری بهم میزنند ومجاز آن پرهای زیر قرقره گویند چنانکه گوید شعر یلبرانا وکاکل بوده آهیم تونی
دین قراریا اوتاقه لارایچیندین شایلیجه الکتان قرقره قارلاغوچ بسکون را ونون وجیم عجمی بترکی روم وایران پرستوک باشد که آنرا بعربی
خطاف نامند قارلواج بضم لام وفتح واو و قارلوغاج بضم لام وفتح غین معجمه وسکون جیم پرستوک باشد چنانکه در شیبانیات مذکور است الخلوب
دیب کوسم گوید که حق کوی قوش نینک ... ذکر آسوری تاشیدا قلار ... نینک ... قارلیغ نام
طایفه ایست از اتراک و در تواریخ وجه تسمیه آن برین نهج مذکور است که چون اوغوزخان از ولایت غور و غرجستان بسمت قدیم خود مراجعت
نمود در زمستانی ... بسیار ... اوغوزخان ... چکس از لشکریان تخلف نماید بجهة کثرت برف از کاروان بماندند ... که
آمدند اوغوزخان آن جماعت را قارلیغ لقب نهاد قارناق ... ماهی گیران چنکال بر سر آن نصب کرده بدان شکار ماهی کنند و بترکی
بمعنی ... بود چنانکه در ذیل مشتقات مذکور شد قارن بسکون را ونون شکم و شکنبه را نامند وآنرا قارین هم گویند
چنانکه ... در سد سکندری گوید شعر قارین دین ... نواه ... کورباس ... ایستار ...
توق یارلیغ ... آینک قارین اوق ... نام یکی از ملوک سلف بود و نیز نام جادرانی است که در این فن معلم داستا
فرهاد بود چنانکه در خسرو شیرین گوید شعر یا ناتوتی ... یا نا ... قارنی یاردق ...
بود که آنرا بفارسی اسبغول نامند و نیز نام موضعیست در جهت جنوب ... قارو بضم را بمعنی عوض باشد الشاهد علیه شعر
اوشبو ... ایستاکیل ... کونکلوک ... سنکا ... قارو و نیز در میان ... معمول است که با لعکس
دهد در حصه دیگر بدل آن ... پیاله ... گویند واکر دو پیاله باشد قوش پیاله مند چنانکه گوید شعر

272v

کام شاقی لبالب ایدین تاپتیم اما آلدی جان ای که دهان زین قوش ایچتینک فاضل اولماقا دوردین وله شعر هر قوشونکه منزه ایله تارتیغ
تارتیشام اجل پرچمین هم حیله تاپ قوش و قاره پله و ظالم هروی بمعنی شراب کهنه و شعر بویمای شاهد آورده [illegible]
نوشته است درست نوشته تاروجه بضم را و فتح جیم ترکی ردیمی بمعنی باز و بود که از ابریشم سفید بافند تره و تا رکه بمعنی رشته
قراوقاقا استعمال می شود که در مقوقه مذکور شد چنانکه شاهد بایشین را بمعنی سیاه گوید شعر زلفلار اصیدا ایلا خمال ایستاکه کونکولاتی
کوزونک شب شکار اول نوع یکیم قیلغای کیبان ناتاره صید شیا قیخر اینیت که اول نوع هم تاروکیبان شب شکار صید قیلغای کوزونکی
حالیوا انباع ومتابع نابریبند کولت که شعر قیربان ترکان ناظرهم جیسنی ایلادوک بند کیشی تاره سینی تارب بمعنی بو داولکه یوس
کیند و آنمه وقت دوییم بمعنی نوع باشد چنانکه در سنگ سکیپسی گوید شعر طناپ که مسلح قیلدی قولاج قیلیب اوتی بیلیت تاری
بریغلیغ در مردو بمعنی خسرو شیرین در مکاله جماعت خار اکن بافرهاد گوید شعر ایر صاچ سیل که خان تارتیب هیشه اوشالمالی
تیبین وتیشه مشقت دین سیکت [illegible] که تارتیش ایکی اوچ [illegible] سیم تلم آتی ایت که با چیزها [illegible] کند چنانکه در
سکبجی گوید شعر تاری هم تیموردین آنکا بولدی خاص که ایل بولدی کوکرکا [illegible] چنانم با نصر گویند و آن [illegible]
دوش ناسرانکشتان چنانکه در لغز بلبم [illegible] گوید شعر تانات کوپ [illegible] ایله بیر [illegible]
کرچه تاری در [illegible] استظهار و بچند بمعنی شتقه هم آمده چنانکه در ذیل مصدر تارتماق گذشت تاریلیغ بمعنی بری و کهولت [illegible]
الشاهد علیه شعر بیکت لیک اولدی [illegible] کهولتا ولدی خزان دیکای بو سوزنی تلریلیغی [illegible] تاری بکیر
و شکنبه را نامند و از انها رن بسکون را هم گویند چنانکه با شواهد در مقوقه مذکور شد تاریجه بسکون نون جیم [illegible]
قوم و چنعم خوانند تاریداش برادر را گویند چنانکه در سنگ سکیپسی در مخالفت گوید شعر تاریداش تاپسا [illegible]
کیمسکا بی باشیق مع الزاء المعجمه من الشقاقات تارتماق بمعنی کندن باشد تاز دوق کندیم تارار و تازار [illegible]
چنانکه بمعنی سکیپسی گوید شعر مردتامین تازار [illegible] ایله شیرین دهر لیک بولدی [illegible] تازغان و تازارغان
تازدیعیم کنده و کنده الشاهد علی الاول المعنی الثانی شعر کونکل [illegible] اوقونک [illegible] ایکما کلیلدا [illegible]
تازغان مکان در و اول و شاهد ثانی الشعر بمعنی اول در عنوان داستان خسرو شیرین گوید [illegible] تازا [illegible] کوروب [illegible]
کرچت ایتکانی و بمعنی [illegible] هم می آید چنانکه شاهد بر اول [illegible] بمعنی فرماید شعر [illegible] فرهادیکم [illegible] تازغایلیم
تیشه و تامین دین اولمای [illegible] لفظ تا در ابتدا شعر مجهول و معطوف [illegible] و تازغان چیزیست که از چوب [illegible]
چون ازا و جاق برکیرند بر بالای آن گذارند و نیز امر است از تحصیل کردن چنانکه در ذیل مصدر تازغاماق مذکور خواهد شد تازو تازغیل
مفرد مخاطب لفعل امر تازسا و تازیلغیل مفرد مخاطب لفعل نفیه تازینک و تازینکیز و تازینکلار جمع مخاطب لفعل امر تازانک و تازینکیز
جمع مخاطب لفعل نفیه تازاسین و تازارمین [illegible] تازار [illegible] تازغای مین بمعنی کنم [illegible] الشاهد علی الثانی
و منه مصل ایتسا اولیشیرین صنم [illegible] فرهاد [illegible] کنده تازمیشین کنده اش
تازمیشانک کنده تازپیره و تازپ توپه کنده ایم تازغاس عمیکند تازغاسلیغ نکندن تازغاس بولسا نکنده باشد تازادو [illegible] میکند
باشد تازا تازا کنده کنده و بدون تکرار هم مستعمل تازای مو آیا بکنم و بکند و بکنی تازمایو نکنده تازماقه تازغاسیز
تازغای و تازغای تازلنک بکنیم تازغانی برای کندن و تا کنده تازغاج چون کند و کند و بعد کندن تازغوچی کننده تازغوجه تازغوچ
تازملغه تا کندن و بقصد کندن تازغو [illegible] خواهم کند تازغوسی [illegible] خواهد کند تازغولوق کندنی

273r

تازغای و قان تلمه و تازغون و تازغیلیک بکند تازغوچیلیک تو [illegible] و تازارلیک [illegible] کنده ام تازد [illegible] دیگر را بکند اکر کردن [illegible]
آن بدستور با لفظ در اشتقاق می یابد تازیشاق بکنند مع آکتن با هم کندن و صیغ آن با لفظ اشتقاق می یابد تازیماق بکسر زاء
مع اللام کنده شدن و صیغ آن با لام لشتقاق می یابد تازغاماق بسکون زاء و نون و فتح غین معجمه بالفکین و بمعنی تحصیل کردن و از الفاظ
هم گویند تازغاندوق تحصیل کردیم تازغانور تازغانادور تحصیل میکند الشاهد علی الاول شعر دیماس [illegible] نوا [illegible]
عشق ایچرا [illegible] سیلما آتون [illegible] تازغانور و تازغانور بمعنی حاصل و مستعمل هم می آید تازغانغان تازغانغان تازغانادور
تحصیل کننده و تحصیل کرده چنانکه [illegible] فرهاد و شیرین گوید الشاهد علی الاول با المعنی الثانی شعر [illegible]
ریاضت [illegible] تازغانغان [illegible] بمعنی [illegible] می آید تازغان و تازغانغیل مفرد مخاطب لفعل امر [illegible] تازغان [illegible]
ذیل مصدر تازغاماق گذشته [illegible] خواهد آمد تازغانغیل و تازغانماغیل مفرد مخاطب لفعل نفیه تازغانینک و تازغانینکیز و تازغانینکلار جمع
از فعل امر تازغانمانک تازغانینکیز و تازغانمانکلار جمع مخاطب لفعل نفیه تازغانامین و تازغانورمین و تازغانادورمین [illegible] تحصیل میکنم تازغانمان
تازغانماس مین تحصیل نکنم تازغانیب [illegible] تازغانیش تحصیل کرده الشاهد علی الاول [illegible]
[illegible] حاصل [illegible] تازغانیپ [illegible] تازغانیشین تحصیل کرده تازغانیپ [illegible]
تحصیل کرده ایم تازغانغاس تحصیل میکند تازغانغاسلیغ تحصیل نکردن تازغانغاس بولسا تحصیل نکنده باشد تازغاناده [illegible] تحصیل
میکرده باشد تازغانا تازغانا تحصیل کنان و بدون تکرار هم مستعمل تازغانای مو آیا تحصیل کنم و کند تازغانمایو تحصیل نکرده
تازغاناقه تازغانغایسیز و تازغانغای [illegible] تحصیل کنیم تازغانغالی برای تحصیل کردن و تا کرده تازغاناج چون تحصیل کند
و بعد تحصیل کردن تازغانغوچی تحصیل کننده تازغانغوچه تازغانغوچ تازغانغوچه تا تحصیل کردن و بقصد تحصیل کردن تازغانغو [illegible] تحصیل
خواهم کرد تازغانغوسی [illegible] تحصیل خواهد کرد تازغانغولوق تحصیل کردنی تازغانغای تازغانغای [illegible]
تازغاندیک تحصیل کند چنانکه در صفت بیت و شتم از عجوب القلوب در ذکر [illegible] گوید که [illegible] باجاد نه
قونغارا ایچون تازغانغای [illegible] تازغانور [illegible] تحصیل کند علم [illegible] تازاغ بفتح زاء و ضم غین معجمه و سکون جیم ترکی روی
تازاق و قزاق [illegible] بمعنی بودها [illegible] چنانکه در [illegible] الابرار گوید شعر [illegible] تازاق [illegible]
چکاک ایدی [illegible] تام طایفه ایست که در [illegible] است [illegible] سیم [illegible]
از میان خود بیرون کند تازالاغ و تازالاق پرنده ایست کوچک [illegible] و بفارسی چکاوک گویند و کباب گوشت آن [illegible]
بول و موافق امراض [illegible] است تازی [illegible] بمعنی بو دلولیکوم توپولیت کوتاه دهن فراخ چنانکه گوید [illegible]
کوله [illegible] تازاینی تاغ او [illegible] طایفه ترکان [illegible]
با جسم اولرکتد و سپید اغلیند [illegible] پادشاهیست از نسل چنکیز که [illegible] سلطنت کرد [illegible] چنانکه
شب غازان نوینید شتم تا ملکیست از ممالک روس [illegible] چنانکه [illegible] تحصیل کردن
تازاجوتاز اجلیغ [illegible] بسکون زاء و فتح غین جیم بمعنی تحصیل و اکتساب بود تازاغاق [illegible] نام [illegible]
تازغان [illegible] که از چوب [illegible] برکیرند بالای آن گذارند [illegible] برهان [illegible]
و بمعنی کنده و کندن هم می آید و نیز امر است از تحصیل کردن چنانکه گذشت تازمه بسکون زاء و فتح میم ترکی [illegible] گویند
کندو تیشه [illegible] تازو ترکی روی بمعنی تحصیل [illegible] چنانکه [illegible] شعر [illegible]

قانوسین [illegible] ترکیل کرک نفسلغا تفهیمی قازوق بضم زا و سکون الف بمعنی باشد وکلیخ ترک را کویند چنانکه خسرو شیرین در وصف
خرگاه کوید شعر دوچیه اوچ بوینز هنوز خرگاه آیمنک ایچی کوماجی مرایله مانا قازوقسیمن صمدیکم قابلغان سپهر اونوکوای نی
جاقیلغان دوم ستارهٔ قطبیه را جدی نامند که عبارت از جدی باشد وآنرا قوزوق تازوق هم خوانند قازیند و بکسر زا وسکون نون وضم دال
ترکی رومی بمعنی ملزات بود که ازهم سوهان بریزد وآنرا بعربی براده وبفارسی سوفش کویند ونیز خراشه وتراشه که از دم تیشه نجاری او شا
آن ریخته شود که آنرا بعربی جکاکه نامند مع التیز المهمله من المشتقات قاسماق بروی آتش جستن و پریدن تیر بروی نخم وجراحت سکر
جون اشتقاق آن متنج ماید صیغه که مصدر انفعالی شد من الجوامد قسرغه بکسر سین وسکون را [illegible] ترکی رومی کردن باشد که آنرا
قصرغه هم کویند وبعربی اصفار خوانند قاساق [illegible] پرده بیم که بروی نخم جراحت ظاهر شود قسناق بسکون سین و [illegible]
نون بالف کشیده ترکی رومی چنبر بود وآن چوبست که بشکل بابر [illegible] کند قسناچی چنبرساز را کویند قاسنی بمعنی کاسنی
صمغ نباتیست برکش شبیه [illegible] وآنرا بعربی [illegible] بارزد نامند [illegible] عموم است قاسیغ وقاسیق
هیکاه را کویند که بعربی عبارت از خاصره باشد ونیز [illegible] مملکت [illegible] قاسیق نامند مع الشین المعجمه من المشتقات قاشیماق
بکسر شین بمعنی خارید [illegible] قاشیماق یعنی خاریدن وکنایه است [illegible] شدن قاشید وق خاریدیم قاشیر وقاشید [illegible]
[illegible] قاشیغان وقاشیرغان [illegible] قاشی وقاشیغیل مفرد مخاطب [illegible]
قاشیماغیل [illegible] مفرد مخاطب [illegible] قاشینکلار جمع مخاطب [illegible] قاشیمانکلار جمع مخاطب
[illegible] قاشی من [illegible] قاشیمان وقاشیمان [illegible] قاشیب قاشینان وقاشیمیش خاریده
خاریده [illegible] قاشیب [illegible] قاشیماس [illegible] خاریدن قاشیماس [illegible]
قاشید [illegible] باشد قاشی [illegible] آیا بخارم [illegible] قاشیمای یو بخارد
قاشیماق وقاشیغاندا [illegible] قاشیغلی برای خاریدن [illegible] چنانکه [illegible]
یکم [illegible] قاشیغلی [illegible] قاشیماچ [illegible] خاریدن قاشیغوچی خارنده قاشیغوچ
قاشیغوچ وقاشیغاچه [illegible] قاشیغوم [illegible] قاشیغونک [illegible] قاشیغوسید [illegible]
خارید [illegible] قاشیغای قاشیناقاشینون وقاشیدیک [illegible] قاشیدیک خاریدنم قاشیماق مع الثاء
بمعنی خاراندن وصیغ آن [illegible] اشتقاق [illegible] قاشلماق مع الکاف بمعنی خاریده شدن وصیغ آن [illegible] اشتقاق [illegible] قاشیماق
مع النون خودرا خاریدن وصیغ آن [illegible] اشتقاق [illegible] قاشاماق بفتح شین بالف کشیده وسکون نون بمعنی بولکردن [illegible]
اسب را کویند خصوصا قاش قرلماق کنایه است [illegible] شدن وظاهر شدن [illegible] من الجوامد قاش [illegible]
کویند چنانکه کوید شعر قاشینک [illegible] سیاه [illegible] اول نون [illegible]
[illegible] قاس را بسین مهمله ظاهر [illegible] لفظ ترکی [illegible] نموده وقاش قرلماق کنایه است از ظاهر شدن [illegible]
شام چنانکه مذکور شد دوم بمعنی برابر وحضور باشد چنانکه میر [illegible] کوید شعر قاشیدا [illegible]
ابماس [illegible] قاشاغو آلتی است [illegible] وآنرا قاشاو وقاشاق
هم کویند قاشانات بسکون نون [illegible] باشد الشاهد علیه شعر [illegible]
[illegible] قاشانک قاشاو بسکون واو وقاشاوج بضم واو وسکون جیم همان قاشاغو باشد که مذکور شد قاشقالدی

[illegible] که از کوشش بوی کل آید وازان [illegible] قاشقه بسکون شین وفتح قاف سیه [illegible]
باشد که [illegible] باشد دوم [illegible] که از آهن [illegible]
[illegible] قاشقه [illegible] نام شغلی است [illegible] میر [illegible]
قشی بسکون شین [illegible] ترکی رومی بمعنی خشم بود قاشوق معروفست شعر [illegible] قاشیق [illegible]
دیشام [illegible] قاشوق [illegible] وآنرا بفارسی کفچه نامند مع الغین المعجمه قغشلت بفتحتین ونون وسکون [illegible]
[illegible] مع الف
قضان [illegible] باشد که آنرا [illegible] هم کویند چنانکه [illegible] قیحوس خلج دیوانه بود وآنرا [illegible]
هم نامند چنانکه مذکور شد مع القاف من المشتقات قاقماق یعنی چیزی را بچیزی زدن وکوبیدن چنانکه کوید شعر [illegible]
[illegible] چرخ [illegible] قاقماق [illegible] قاقوق [illegible]
وقاقار بمعنی [illegible] مصدر هم می آید قاقا [illegible] قاقادی [illegible] چنانکه شاهد [illegible]
ابوالحسین [illegible] کوید [illegible] ابوسعید [illegible] قاقار [illegible] وقاقار [illegible]
قاقادی [illegible] کوبیدن وکوبیده وبمعنی مصدر هم می آیند قاق وقاقغیل مفرد مخاطب [illegible] الشاهد علی الثانی شعر قاقیل [illegible]
[illegible] قاقسار وقاقاغیل مفرد مخاطب [illegible] قاقینکلار [illegible]
جمع مخاطب [illegible] قاقانکلار جمع مخاطب [illegible] قاقار [illegible] الشاهد [illegible]
الثالث شعر [illegible] قاقادیم [illegible] قاقمانی قاقماق
[illegible] قاقیب قاقیبان قاقیش زده وکوبیده الشاهد علی الثانی شعر [illegible] قاقیبان [illegible]
یاقیبان [illegible] قاقیبان [illegible] قاقیشین زده وکوبیده [illegible] قاقیشانک زده وکوبیده
قاقیب [illegible] قاقاس [illegible] زدن وکوبیدن قاقماس [illegible] زننده وکوبنده
باشد [illegible] زننده وکوبنده باشد قاقا قاقا قاقا زده زده [illegible] مستعمل [illegible]
آیا [illegible] قاقماق [illegible] قاقغانی [illegible] قاقغالی برای زدن وکوبیدن
قاقمه وکوبیده قاقماچ چون [illegible] قاقغوچی زننده وکوبنده قاقغوچ وقاقغو
قاقماقچه قازدن وکوبیدن [illegible] قاقغونک [illegible] قاقغوسید [illegible]
زد وکوبید قاقغوبوق زدن وکوبیدن [illegible] قاقغای [illegible] قاقدیک [illegible] قاقدیک
زدم وکوبیدم [illegible] قاقیشماق بکسر قاف وسکون شین [illegible] وصیغ آن [illegible] اشتقاق [illegible]
بکسر قاف وسکون لام کوبیده شدن قاقیلغان وقاقیلغان [illegible] کوبیده شوند وکوبیده شد چنانکه خسرو شیرین در وصف
خرگاه کوید الشاهد علی الاول [illegible] الثانی شعر قازوقسیمن [illegible] قاقیلغان سپهر [illegible]
وبمعنی مصدر هم می آید وصیغ آن [illegible] اشتقاق [illegible] قاقنوماق [illegible] چنانکه کوید
شعر [illegible] قاقماق [illegible] وصیغ آن [illegible]
می یابد قاقشالماق خشک وقاق شدن [illegible] از خشکی هم ترکی قاقشاله [illegible] خشک قاق شده قاقشا [illegible]

خشك تاق بشود وتاقشالوهیجوع جل وستمره هتم می آید تاقشالقیلی تاقشالوغای تاقشالادی فحشك وتاق شونه وتاق شه الشاهد علی
الاول بالمعنی الثانی شعر قوچی وجسیم اوتوزدیك توبراق شیده تاقشالنان * آنگا اوتكاندا بجران كاروانی اهل اوجی نیاز
وتیز دملهان الطیر كوید شعر جسم ادا بر بیکاری تالملای بوتون * پاسو پلو چونكه تاقشالنان اوتون وبمعنی مصدر هم می آید
روی تاقشالفان از امر شرطی تاقشغالنان بتقدیم شین بر قاف خوانند وشرط بود لیكن اجرا آمره وتاقشقان هم باجنبی نوشته
مرهو لفظ اجزای وجملولست تاقشالیبی تاقشالیبا وتاقشالمیش تاق شی تاقشالماس تاق بشود تاقشالماسلیغ تاق شدن
تاقشالماس بی الحاق شونه باشد تاقشالادی بتر وتاقیشه باشد تاقشالا تاقشالا تاق شی شه وبدون تکرار هم مستعملست
تاقشالغلی برای تاق شدن وتاقتاق شه تاقشالغاج چون تاق شود وبعض شدن تاقشالغوچی تاق شونه تاقشالنوسیدگی باق
خواهد شد تاقشالغاه وتاقشالسی تاقشالسو تاقشالسو تاقشالدیك تاق شود تاقشالنوك وتاقشالوبرالیتا وشده وچنانكه
تاقالاماناغ بیناد فریاد كردن ناكیان بود ودروقت خشم كداشتن وصیغ آن موافق شرطی اشتقاق می یابد تاقرماناغ بجرقاف
وسكون رای مهمله ترك ربودی بمعنی فریاد كردن باشد تاقیماناغ بكسر قاف ترك روبی یعنی خشمناك شدن من الجوهر تاقد وبمعنی
اول بمعنی خشك باشد چنانكه در تاریخ الانبیا مذكور حضرت یوسف ویوشع علیهما السلام كوید كه تاق بالیغ ایدی خضر علیه السلام
بركا قوینا ولی بالیغ تیریلیب تالیبیب امرنیزوضه سالدی دوم آب نادانرا كویند كه در دشت جمع شده تالاب شود وبعماند قاقاس
بمعنی خارج راه وخارج سمت باشد چنانكه در تاریخ ناسری در وصف بشاهرکه نام محلی است مذكورست كه بشاهر برنیه یولدین
تاقاس یرق ده اوتوبلا مهرده ابلیرسا آن سیرقیلیم تاقالاغات مرحمرا كویند كه بسیار فریاد كند تاقرمه بكسر قاف وسكون رای
مهمله وفتح میم ترك روبی بمعنی آواز وفریاد بود تاقرداغ بترك روبی سنبه را كویند كه بریان كرده وخون آنرا كرفته باشند وآنرا الجنت
جنای چسنغ وبلبر سی چرده کویند تاقشالن وبمعنی طره اولك هم تاقرا كویند كه از غایت خشكی تركیده باشد الشاهد علیه شعر
ادب تاقسه جسیم اسون كه كلاه تاقالیماس كیم ایمرا وت سرواییك داجی بر تاقشالوتون * وآنرا كوینه تاقشاق نامند بمعنی حافظه
تاقشاق بترکی رومی هیمه تاق بود كه آنرا اجنابیه تاقشالكویند تاقلجم بكسر قاف ثانی وسكون لام ومیم وفتح جیم ترکی رومی شراره
آتش باشد تاقماج مانند خشك برانامند تاقتش بمعنی كوسپد نفت چنانكه كوید شعر بنی خودا ولتیوده او اوخشم وتلیزالیته باتیش
او لسمینا رتوقا اولوب توریجه كوزتانقیشیك * وحرارت شرکوپ جشم عبارت از چشمه نفت كه آنرا عرب عمر خوانند تامیقاتلیغ
بتركی رومی بمعنی خشمناك وبدخوی بود مع الكلم من المشتقات تالماقاغ ماندن وبمعنی نام طایفه ایست معروف چنانكه در ذیل جو امده
خواهد شد تاندوق ماندیم تالوبوق تالادی ماندد وتالوبمعنی فاعل ومصدر هم می آید تالقانو تالوبرقان وتالادور ماندد ما
وبمعنی مصدر هم می آیند تال وتالغیل مفرد مخاطب امر تاسا وتالماغیل مفرد مخاطب نهی تالینك وتالینكیز
تاشنحاخ جمع مخاطب بفضل لامانك تالمانكیز وتالمانكلار جمع مخاطب نهی تالامی وتالوبرین وتالادیكه وتالوبلیمام تالمك
تالماس بین بیمانم تالیبه تالیبان وتالمیش ماندو تالمیشین ماندو اشراتالیشانك ماندو تالیب تالیب توندیكماند ایم
تالماس بیمانند تالماسلیغ بماندن تالماس بولسلمانی باشد تالادورمیش بولغا بیمانده باشد تالا تالا ماندو ماند وبدون
تكرار هم مستعملست تالادی وتالایتین بمانم وبماند وبغلبه بیماند چنانكه شاه بیرتکی راعیا اول كوید شعر بیرتن جایبمانیوق
تالایین دینا آدین * خوی دین كونكلوما بیزیم بولایین دینا هرزة * وباسیغه مصدر تالاماق نیز اشتراك دارند یعنی بیرهم حنیم
بچیند وبچیوق وچیده ونیز طایفه سانگینت قرمه خودرا بلفظ تالادی امراز خیمه كند تالامیو آیا بمانم وبماند وبماند وآنا

بیرهم چینیم وچیند وچیوق تالمایو بمانند تالساق تالقاپزوتالقاپزو تالاجیلر تالاینك بمانم وتالالیعنی بیرهم چینیم تالغای
بلوهماندن وتلملوه تالغاج چون ماند وچلانی وبعض ماندن تالغوچی ماننده تالغوجه تالغوجه تالغانجه تالماندن وبعض ماندن
الشاهد علی الثالث شعر جوبیدامیك توكانما تالغاز ایل الخلیفه * چرخ دیز هم اونوچ آننا نك اكولیاز تالغاغیلی اشو
خواهم ماند تالغونك خواهی ماند تالغوسی خواهد ماند چنانكه در منشات محكومیت مكلم كوید شعر تالغوجی باقی بو
تابولغوسی انسانه سیمیاتالمكابی تالغولوق ماننده تالغاغ تالغه تالسعه تالعنی وتالدیك بمانند الشاهد علی الخامس شعر بیشك
بیرآیدین آیردیو ابتلاخه چرخ * تالدیك اوزآی چیره چیك بالخه چرخ * تالغودیك تالوبرلیك ماننده وچنانكه ماند الشاهد علی
الاول شعر یاریلیبیب عقل وهوش وجان وكونكلوم قوزغالیب * تن یاتیب كوزبولیجیك تالغه تالیپ تالغودیك تالغودیك تیزیكو تالونم
ماندن تالیناقغ بكسر لام وسكون نون وتالینماقغ مع التین وابرماندن یعنی بناء كرامومین تالینماس وتالیشماس وابرماندن
الشاهد علی الاول شعر تابم اولكا لیدین بولوتیز نیكلیغ هوالی بلیشلم * نیم صبحی ایدیعین اینكم تالینماس ادمدین * الشاهد علی الثانی
من كلطفی شعر سیفنك شیرزلیبینك جالدین تالیشماس شا چینك نیك كزولی ماندین تالیشماس وصیغ تالیناق بانون ولاریمانم
باشین موافق شوی اول اشتقاق می یابد تالاماناغ بفتح لام بالمكیشه بیرهم چیدن تالادی بیرهم چیدم تالایرو تالایدور
بچیند وتالادی بمعنی فاعل ومصدر هم می آید تالامان تالاغان تالاید ورغان بیرهم چیند بیرهم چید چنانكه شاه صبا بمعنی اول نی ساقی
بابری در وصف سیخا چه مذكورست كه تاشنی تالارلادیو تالاغان تاش شد او سیتیدین سوالار وبمعنی مصدر هم می آیند تالاو تالاغیل
مفرد مخاطب امر تالاسا وتالاماغیل مفرد مخاطب نهی تالادا وتالایكیز وتالایكلار جمع مخاطب امر تالامانك وتالامانكیز وتالامانكلار
جمع مخاطب نهی تالای میرم تالایرمین تالایدور میرم تالادیم بیرهم چینم الشاهد علی الثالث شعر دیبیم كونكلوم كاهر نیك
خد نیكینك سید صیبا اجسات تیغه دیدیم اوتونده یکم تالایدی دونی تالامان تالامانی سین بیرهم نی چینم تالادیم تالادیم تالاباش
بیرهم چید چنانكه در آغاز نظم ستی سكندری در صفحه نظامی خسرو كوید الشاهد علی الاول شعر اول اوتنه اونوینیك
دین تالاتی زمانه تاراجین ملكونی تالات تالامیشین بیرهم چید اشرتالاتالایشانك بیرهم چید تالاب پژو تالاب تورینا بیرهم چیده
تالاماس بیرهم نچیند تالاماسلیغ بیرهم بچیدن تالاماس بولسا بیرهم نچیند باشد تالاید ورمیش بولغا بیرهم چید باشد
تالایو تالای تالاپ بیرهم چید چید وبدون تکرار هم مستعملست تالای سو آیا بیرهم چینم وچیند وچیوق بالمصدر الملاق
اشتراك دارد یعنی آیا بمانم وبماند وبمانی تالامایو بیرهم چید تالاساق وتالاغاپزو تالاغای پژو تالاغونكالا لیلغعر هم چینیم وتا
بمعنی بالنیم هم آمده تالاغلی برای بیرهم چیدن وتلچیدن تالاغاج چون بیرهم چیند وچید وبعض چیدن تالاغوچی بیرهم
چیننده تالاغوچه تالاغوجه وتالاغانجه تا بیرهم چیدن وبعد از آن تالاغوسی دور بیرهم خواهم چید تالاغونك دور بیرهم خواهی
چید تالاغوسیدور بیرهم خواهد چید تالاغولوق بیرهم چیننده تالاغای تالاسعه تالاسی وتالادیك بیرهم چیند وتالامای
كاغذ ابریشم را كویند چنانكه مذكور شود تالاغودیك تورمین تالارتیلیب بیرهم چینه ظام تالایماقغ مع الت المصدریت
یعنی دیگری را چیدن بیرهم امر كردن وصیغ آن بدستور تاناقرشا اشتقاق می یابد تالاماناغ مع الكلم بیرهم چیده شدن
بالام اشتقاق می یابد تالقیماقغ بسكون لام وكسر قاف ثانی بمعنی برخاستن صوحیه تالقیماق كویند تالقیدوق برخاستیم تالقیدو
تالقیدو بیر نیمز الشاهد علی الاول شعر اشك اوتی تالقیونجیف مزاج جسیم آه دین * تندیل بجریكیدین آندا كمر بجرا امیزو شامان
وتالقیر بمعنی فاعل ومصدر هم می آید تالقیمان تالقیرغان تالقیدورغان برخیزنده وبرخاسته چنانكه سلطان حسین میرزا فرماید تالقوم

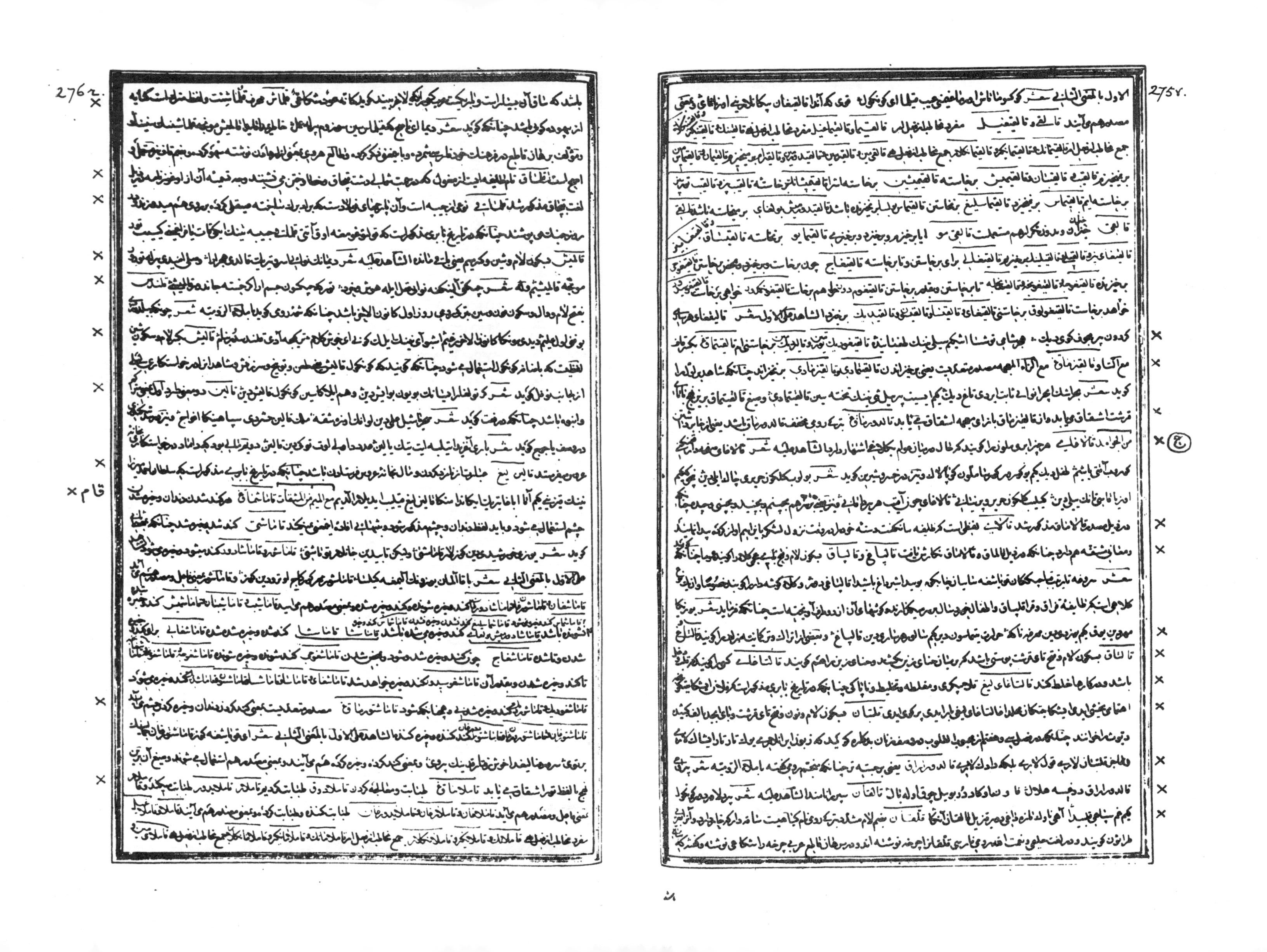

[illegible]

قام

[illegible]

تاملامیشین و تاملامیشمک مر لبنانبتمک تاملاشاننا مرتاملامانت لبنانبتمنیکم تاملامانمک لبنانبتمنکند تاملاشانسلیغ
لبنانبت کردن تاملامس بولسنا لبنانبت نکند تاباشد تایدوریش لبنانبت میکرد مناشد تاملایو و تاملامیی تاملامیی لبنانبت کنان ویزد
بکرار هم مستعملست تاملامیو ایا لبنانبتکنم و کنند و کنی تاملامانیو لبنانبت کرده تاملاماناقه تاملاملمرع تاملامیلیزمع تاملامکلم تاملامی
لبنانبت کنیم تاملامنیله برای لبنانبت کردن و تا لبنانبت کرده تاملامیلیج چون لبنانبت کردند و بجنس کردن تاملامیب لبنانبت کنند تاملامیبرد
تاملامیری تاملامیلیجه تا لبنانبت کردن و بقدر آن تاملامیدی لبنانبت خواهم کرد تاملامیکندور لبنانبت خواهی کرد تاملامیدی لبنانبت
خواهد کرد تاملامیزلوق لبنانبت کردنی تاملامانیو تاملامیلیو تاملامیون تاملامادیلت لبنانبت کنند تاملامیدیلت تاملامیلیک لبنانبت کردنیم
من الجواسد قام طبیب و معالج و حکیم و دانشمند را گویند یوچی بکسر جیم یکنوع از زیانهای معروف الشاهد علیه سعر کلدا
هریان آبکش خطا هرکیو قالیش نشان یوچی بکم توشوبتم اول تدچا الاداونوق و ازآن بعربی سوطو و لغت تعلیم سیاه و نربان سوی
مانند تمغا ق مکور میم وقتم غین معجمه با الف کشیده یکنوع کیا هیست شبیه به بوته نایچشان که بهم پیچیده و نحنیلو کور از آست
و هم سبکی آنرا در صحرا میغلطانند چنانکه گوید سعر کرچه تو باشتین بیصرش عالم بورنکا طام بصیرحو اتمعاق و بیکار نجستاندراتی
بوتاتوکه سعر آختر ایغ و یزید من ده و سیل بن عمر سیز خرد تاج بینکل ایلیت فرطید بن باداین معقما ق بیار اتی تاملامیشه یعنی
و مطالعه بود چنانکه در تاریخ رشیدی میفرماید که کتابی بیکم ارزبوشد ملازنان جل از جمله مطالعه و طلب الشدیاملکر
کرد و او خواند و تام را چیزی بدادند و بخانه فرستادند تاموق یعنی جمیع چنانکه در لشکر کشیدن امیر تیمور کوید سعر تیلب کلم
ملک سلطانلری تاموق چیل و کتور بکبان لاری ونیز در جنگ سکندر بامرولن مغرب زمین کوید سعر چاوتی لادا ولیدور اسیکه
تاموق سیل دیلیت چیه میفرمایید ای تامیش ییغ نیستار اکو یند مع النون من المشتقات تامنا ق بسکون نون بمعنی سیرشدن باشد ای
سیری که از اکل باشد استعمال میشود مثل سیراب شدن و سیرمعنی شدن چنانکه در خسرو شیرین گوید سعر بجه کونکل دیستما
تا یاما قنوبید و مان بو تاملرین کونکلی الملاق و سیری که از اکل باشد آنرا تویماق میگویند تامدوق سیرشدیم تاماقنا ناد و سیرمیشود تاماد
بالمصدر تامناق هم اشتراک طرح یعنی خوبی بیشود و بمعنی اصل مصدر هم می آید تامغان و تامانغان بمعنی تامادوقان سیرشنوه و سیرشده الشاهد علی
الاول سعر بیبنت کسبل سیرشکنو آتیرور قان دیلی ایمصبوتامدیلت بیملر اول لیلت تامنغان دیلت و بمعنی مصدر هم می آیند تامان
تامنیل مفرد مخاطب نفی امر تامیمنا و تامنا عیل مفرد مخاطب نفی ایه تامینک و تامینکز و تامینکلار جمع مخاطب نفی امر تامانک
تامانیکز و تامانکلار جمع مخاطب نفی ایه تامایمن و تامارین و تامادوغ و تامادیم سیرنیشوم و تامادوین و تامادیم یعنی سیرنیشوم هم باشد
تامان و تاماس هین سیرنیشوم الشاهد علی الاول سعر سیز کرلیلیت دیر ایشیتسلم ایلکیم آبحیات تامادوی لیان تایریلیت هین
آری بکولر ایلجان تاینس و تاییناتو تامیش سیرشده تامیشین سیرشده اش را تامیشانک سیرشده تایب بزه تایب تو بر سیر
سیرشده ام تاماس سیرنیشوم الشاهد علیه سعر لب لعلیت خیالی هیلر ابا غزیجه تان قیلدیلار جعت بو عدم چلاتامان ایکادیریک
و بکولی تامماس ونیز بمعنوقات سیرین کوید سعر ولا ایسیقو لیکه سا آبدین تاماس اویسیقو تیباسلمه دیکین اویلا تماس اویسیقو تامماسلیغ
سیرنشدن تاماس بولسا سیرنشونده باشد تامادیم سیرنشه سیرنیشن باشد تامانا تامانا سیرشده شدن و بوجنه تکرار هم مستعملست تاملامیو
آیا سیرشوم و شود و شوی و بامصدر تامناق هم اشتراک طرح یعنی خوبی شوم و شود و شوی تامنایو سیرشده تاماناق تامنالینیز تامنا
تامانبلک تامانالینک سیرشویم و تامانالی بمعنی خویی شویم هم باشد تامناج چنین سیرشد و شود و بحض شدن تامنوجی سیرشونده تامنوجه
تامنوبجه تامناعجه تا سیرشدن و بقدم آن الشاهد علی الثانی با المعنی الثانی سعر نوانی دلیلا کی محکو ابحاس کرلیجه حیات بخشن لبینک

نیم سیزی تامنوبجه تامنوم سیرخواهم شد تامنوبنک سیرخواهی شد تامنوجی سیرخواهد شد تامغا خوم سیرنخواهم شد
تامانمغونک سیرنخواهی شد چنانکه در سکندر نامه گوید سعر بجه سیر قتوبیتیو بزتامانمغونلند بکبلر خونمکه دراول نقیغ بکم الجلفونلد
تامانمغوجی سیرنخواهد شد تامنوبلوق سیرشدنی تامنغالی تامنوتاغنه تامنوبدی تامنوبغ سیرمیشود تامنوبدیلت تمریعو تامنیلیت سیرشده
و تامنولیت بین بالمصدر تامناق هم اشتراک طرح یعنی خونین شده ظلم تاماندماق مصدر متعدیست یعنی سیرکردن از قبیل بلیک کندی
کردن و صیغ آن بدستور المقدمه اشتقاق می یابد تامانماق بفتح نون بالف کشیده بمعنی خونین شدن باشد تامادوق خونین شدیم تاماد
تامادورس خونین میشود و تامار بالمصدر تاماغاق هم اشتراک طرح یعنی خونین میشود و بمعنی اصل مصدر هم می آید تامارغان تامارغان تامیدیلکان
خونین شونده و خونین شده و بمعنی مصدر هم می آیند تامسناد و تامساعیل مفرد مخاطب نفی امر تامساو تامساعیل مفرد مخاطب نفی ایه
تاماسنیلت تامانیکز و تامانکلار جمع مخاطب نفی امر تامانسانیکز و تامانکلار جمع مخاطب نفی ایه تامادیم تامارمیری تامادیتلار
تامادام خونین شیوم و تامادوین و تامادیم بمعنی خونین نیشوم هم باشد چنانکه گذشت تامانماس تامادیس هین خونین نیشوم تامانب
تامابار و تامامیش خونین شده چنانکه در خسرو شیرین گوید الشاهد علی الاول سعر تامابلدیه تامونیلیب ایامی ین دلفی اندوه تامی
تاملیبتین خونین شده اش را تامیسانک خونین شده تامانماس خونین نیشوم چنانکه گوید سعر چو معشقین سونکاک اولیدیم سینا
تامانماش فراق تاسوتیبیب جسم تاموانجفیه تاملماسلیغ خونین نشدن تامامس بولسا خونین نشونده باشد تابدیش بوجنه خونین شونده باشد
تامابوچانای تامای خونین شده شده و بدو نکرار هم مستعملست تامایو ایا خونین شوم و شود و شوی و بامصدر تاملاق هم مشترکست
یعنی آیا سیرشوم و شود و شوی تامنایو خونین شده تاماناسای تامانامبزمو تامانغای برزمو تامالیم تامالینک خونین شویم تامالی بمعنی بر شویم باشد
تامانالی برای خونین شدن و تامانغوچه تامانغاچ چون خونین شد و شود و بحض شدن تامانغوجی خونین شونده تامانغوچه
تامانغوچه تامانغانجه تا خونین شدن و بقدم خونین شدن تامغومدور خونین خواهم شد تامغونکدور خونین خواهی شد تامغوسیدور خونین
خواهد شد تامانغولوق خونین شدنی تامانغانچه تامانسموتاماسورعه تامادیلت خونین شده تامانغولیت تمرتیو تامادیلیت خونین شده ظلم
تامادیلت بالمصدر تاماغاق نیز اشتراک طرح چنانکه گذشت تامانماق مع النامصدر متعدیست یعنی خون آلود کردن تامانوجانا تامیدور
خون آلود میکند چنانکه در لیلی مجنون در وصف جنگ گوید الشاهد علی الاول سعر یا غیمکه کولکوبین امزاتورش دمراز الشتمیزی تاما
و باقی صیغ آن بترتیب تاماق تاناماق و فرشتا اشتقاق می یابد تامانتلاماق بفتح نون اول و لام و سکون تای قرشت و نون ظاهره بمعنی بر آمدن
تامانتلاندوق بر برآمدیم تامانتلادور برآمد تامانتلادادور برآمده و تامانتلاغان بمعنی اصل مصدر هم می آیند تامانتلاغان تامانتلاغانلار
بر آمده و بر برآمده و بمعنی مصدر هم می آیند تامانتلاغیل مفرد مخاطب نفی امر تامانتلاماعیل مفرد مخاطب نفی ایه
تامانتلاسنکز تامانتلاسنکلار جمع مخاطب نفی امر تامانتلاماسکلار جمع مخاطب نفی ایه تامانتلادیم تامانتلامادیم تامانتلادیمز برآمدیم
تامانتلادیمز برآمدیم تامانتلاماس تامانتلامادیم برآمدیم تامانتلادیب تامانتلامسا و تامانتلادیش برآمده تامانتلادیشین برآمده
تامانتلاسانک بر برآمده تامانتلاماس برنیامدیم تامانتلاماسلیغ بر نیامدن تامانتلاماس بولسا برنیامده باشد تامانتلادیریش بهمراه
بر آمده باشد تامانتلاتلامانلا برآمده برآمده و بدو نکرار هم مستعملست تامانتلادایو آیا برآیم و برآید و برآیی تامانتلادایو
بر بیامده تامانتلاسناق و تامانتلاسابزه تامانتلادایرهمو تامانتلاکلوتا تامانتلاکلیم تامانتلادنا بر برآمدیم تامانتلاغالی برای بر برآمدن و تا بر برآمده تامانتلاغاچ
چون بر برآمد و برآید و بحض بر آمدن تامانتلاغوجی بر برآینده تامانتلاغوچه تامانتلاغانچه تا بر برآمدن و بقدم بر برآمدن
تامانتلاغومدور بر برخواهم آمد تامانتلاغونکدور بر برخواهی آمد تامانتلاغوسیدور بر برخواهد آمد تامانتلاغولوق بر برآمدنی تامانتلاغانچه

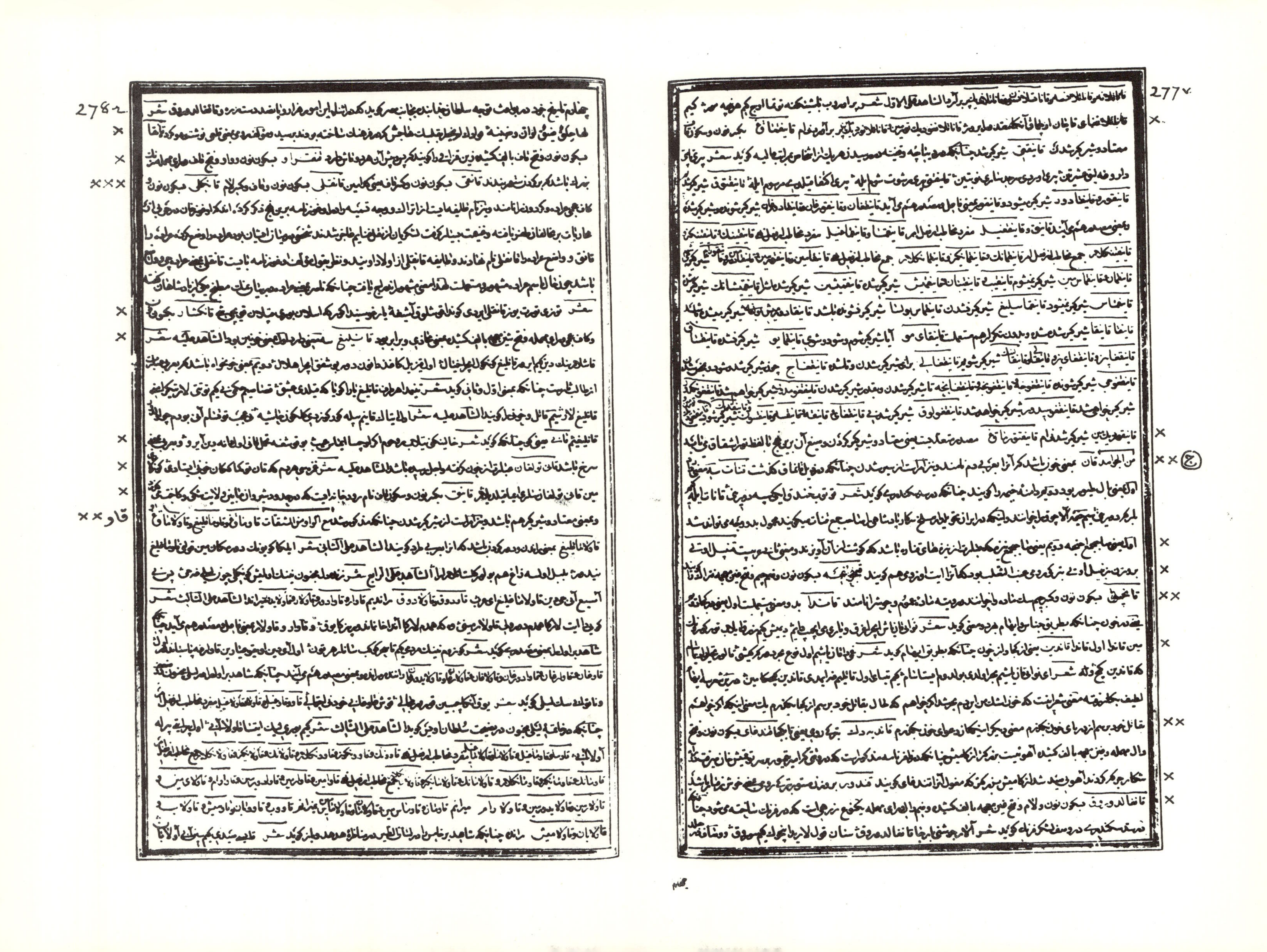

[illegible] الشاهد علی الاول شعر [illegible] بلشنکنه [illegible] ادبج کیم [illegible] کیم

× [illegible] تاپنان اوچاق آنکه [illegible] برآ [illegible] تاینغناق بکسر نون و سکون قاف

معتاد و شیر گیر شدن تاینغوق شیر گیر شده چنانکه [illegible] الیه گوید شعر پری [illegible]

دار [illegible] شیر گیر شد

تاینقور و تاینغادور شیر گیر میشود [illegible] مستعمل هم می آید تاینغان و [illegible] شیر گیر شونده و شیر گیر شده

بمعنی مصدر هم می آیند تاینوق و تاینغیل مفرد مخاطب [illegible] تاینقا و [illegible] مفرد مخاطب [illegible]

[illegible] جمع مخاطب [illegible] جمع مخاطب [illegible] شیر گیر

[illegible] شیر گیر میشوم [illegible] شیر گیر شده [illegible] شیر گیر

تاینغاس شیر گیر نمیشود [illegible] شیر گیر نشدن تاینغاس بولسا شیر گیر نشونده باشد [illegible] شیر گیر میشد

تاینغا تاینقا شیر گیر شده و بمعنی تکرار هم مستعملست تاینغای مو آیا شیر گیر شوم و شود و شوی [illegible] شیر گیر شده [illegible]

[illegible] شیر گیر شوم [illegible] شیر گیر شدن [illegible] چون شیر گیر شده [illegible]

[illegible] شیر گیر شونده [illegible] شیر گیر شدن [illegible] شیر گیر شدن [illegible] شیر گیر خواهد [illegible]

شیر گیر خواهی [illegible] شیر گیر خواهد شد [illegible] شیر گیر شده [illegible] شیر گیر شود [illegible]

× [illegible] شیر گیر [illegible] مصدر متعدی یعنی معتاد و شیر گیر کردن و سنغ آن [illegible] بالفظ [illegible] اشتقاق می یابد

×× (ج) من الجوامد قان بمعنی خون باشد که آنرا بعربی دم [illegible] چنانکه [illegible] گذشت [illegible]

[illegible] بود [illegible] چنانکه [illegible] گوید شعر [illegible]

[illegible] میتواند شد

× [illegible] باشد که [illegible]

× [illegible] گویند [illegible] بسکون نون و ضم جیم و فتح [illegible]

×× [illegible] بسکون نون و کسر جیم [illegible] مانند [illegible] بد و معنی [illegible]

[illegible] چنانکه [illegible] گوید شعر [illegible]

× [illegible] اول [illegible] چنانکه [illegible] گوید شعر [illegible]

که [illegible] شعرای نوائی [illegible]

لطیف [illegible] معنی شعر اینست که [illegible] اگر خواهم

×× [illegible] معنی دیگر اینکه [illegible] بسکون نون و فتح

دال مهمله و ضم جیم بالف کشیده آهو [illegible] چنانکه [illegible]

× شکار [illegible] آهو و صید [illegible] گویند [illegible]

× [illegible] بسکون نون و لام و فتح [illegible] بالف کشیده و ضم [illegible]

[illegible] گوید شعر [illegible]

چهارم [illegible] سلطان [illegible] گوید [illegible] شعر

× [illegible] نوشته [illegible]

× بسکون نون و فتح [illegible] بالف کشیده [illegible] گویند [illegible] بسکون نون و واو و فتح [illegible]

××× [illegible] باشد [illegible] بسکون نون و کسر [illegible] بسکون نون و [illegible] بسکون نون

[illegible] ذکر کرده [illegible]

[illegible]

[illegible] نامه [illegible]

باشد [illegible] چنانکه [illegible]

× شعر [illegible]

× [illegible] بالف کشیده [illegible] الشاهد علیه شعر

[illegible] باشد [illegible]

[illegible] چنانکه [illegible] گوید شعر [illegible]

[illegible] الشاهد علیه شعر [illegible]

× [illegible] چنانکه گوید شعر [illegible]

× [illegible] الشاهد علیه شعر [illegible]

× [illegible] بکسر نون و سکون [illegible]

قاو×× و بمعنی معتاد و شیر گیر هم باشد [illegible] شیر گیر شدن چنانکه [illegible]

[illegible] الشاهد علی الثانی شعر [illegible]

[illegible] الشاهد علی الرابع شعر [illegible]

[illegible] الشاهد علی الثالث شعر

[illegible]

[illegible] گوید شعر [illegible]

[illegible] چنانکه شاهد [illegible]

[illegible] گوید شعر [illegible]

چنانکه [illegible] سلطان [illegible] الشاهد علی الثالث شعر [illegible]

[illegible] جمع مخاطب [illegible]

[illegible]

[illegible]

[illegible] چنانکه شاهد [illegible] گوید شعر [illegible]

ونچو تاشلادب ململ تقالیبقلولابان تاوشین و تاولامیشین وانداش ایتاومیشانلت تای لامیشانلت ماندنه تاوماس و تاولاکامیش انقلوماتیغ
تاولاماس منحصر اندن تاوماس بولسالولا کاالتماس بولسالار اندن نلمستقلاده ویش تکان تاولامید ویش نکنیم انوه باشد تاواتا تاولامیو تاولای تاولای
رانده وانده و بدون تکرار هم مستعملست تاوای تاواین تاولای تاولاین برانم و براند و براند و رانده چنانچه کوید الشاهد علی الاول
شعر کونکول کهایق بیلیب تیغ مانیغ تاوای کرینه کیکسا یوزنی تاوه قیلیب و شاهد بر ثالث او معنی لیغنی درتاریخ الانبیا میکوید کرکا
علیه السلام کوید که ایل اداسیدین تاپتی والادر تاولای بلیب شهوره دیدیکیرا اول حضرتیغ شکایتنه بلودی تاوامو تاولامو
آیا برانم و براند و براند تاومایوده تاولامایو براند نلوساق تاوغلیز تلوغای تاولیتو تاوالینیت تاولاشاق و تاولاماپزی تاولاغاپ تاولا
تاولالیت برانیم تاولاغلی برای راندن و تلوغلیج و تاولاماج چون راندند براند و بجنس راندن تاوغوجی و تاولاغوجی رانده
تاوغوجیغ تاوغوجغ تاوغاجه تاولاغوجیه تاولاغوجه تاولاغاجه تا راندن و بفتح راندن تاولاغوسدوغی تاوغوسمیبنوا هم اندکی غوغای
تاولاغوتکلوس خواهد راندن تاوغوسیدور تاولاغوسیدور بخواهد راند تاوغولوق تاولاغولوق راندنی تاوغاغو تاوغاوسه تاوسوق
تاودیلت و تاولاغای و تاولاسلو تاولاسون و تاولادیلت براندن تاوغودیلت تورمین تاولادیلت مین و تاولاغودیلت قیه مین تاولاریدی
تاودوریغا تغ بکون واو و صفدر معنی تیلیب یعنی خولنج فرمودن تاودوردی یعنی خولنج فرمود شعر ای نواوایادکی تاودوری
آندین انکلاکیم کوسید اونکان کچه دین کوپ لغفان البلخینت وتاق صیغ آن بر بیغ بالفظ در اشتقاق می یابد تاودیلماغ بضم
مع الکلم ابهاشدن و صیغ آن بدستور بالام اشتقاق می یابد تاودرماغ بضم واو و مع الراء المهمله بمعنی بریان کردن باشد چنانچه در تبیان
مصوبات لنلوبکوید که اوت اثیو تاوصوناق بیل ایشی الوصناق تاودرد وق بریان کردیم تاودرور تلودر دور بریان میکند و تاودرور بمعنی احراق
هم می آید تاودوغان و تاودرغان تاودرادوغان بریان کننده و بریان کرده و بمعنی سوخته هم می آید تاودروغ تاودرغیل مفرد مخاطب امر تاودرنک
تاودرنکیل مفرد مخاطب امر تاودرونک و تاودرونکیز تاودرونکلار جمع مخاطب امر تاودرغای تاودرغایکه تاودرنکلار جمع مخاطب
امر تاودرلیبین و تاودرمین و تاودرادیریع و تاودرصارم بریان میکنم تلودر دان تلودرداشیمین بریان میکنم تاودرب و تاودرماتو تاودرمش بریان کرده
تاودرمیش بریان کرده اش تاودرمیشانند بریان کرده تاودرماس بریان نمیکند تاودرماسلیغ بریان نکردن تاودرماس بولسا بریان نکننده
تاودرندرمیش نوکنه بریان میکرده باشد تاودرا تاودرا بریان کنان و بدون تکرار هم مستعملست تاودرای مو آیا بریان کنم و کنند کی تاودرای
بریان نکرده تاودرباقی تاودرغایزو تاودرغای پزم تاودرنکیز تاودرلیدین بریان کنیم تاودرغی برای بریان کردن و تا بریان نکرده تاودرغلیج چون
بریان کرد و کند و بجنس کردن تاودرغوجی بریان کننده تاودرغوجه تاودرغوجه و تاودرغاجه تا بریان نکردن و بقدر بریان کردن تاودرغوسدوغی بریان
خواهم کرد تاودرغوسکید بریان خواهی کرد تاودرغوسیدور بریان خواهد کرد تاودرغولوق بریان کردنی تاودرغاغو تاودرسوتا تاودرسلوتاوسه تاودرنک
بریان کند و بی تاودرسون بریان مطلوبست چنانچه در ذیل جواد خواهد آمد تاودرغودیلت تورمین و تاودرغودیلت بریان کردهام تاودرماغ بکون
واو و ضم را و مع الجیم بریان شدن تاودرلو تاودرلادور بریان نمی شود الشاهد علی الثانی شعر اول اوت کهاوتلیغ پروانه
فن هولتونه تین کوروندلت که تاودرلادوشم ذاتی یانی پیله و تاق صیغ آن بدستور بالام اشتقاق می یابد تاودشماق بضم واو و ضم الشین
المعجمه بهم پیوستن تاودشوق بهم پیوستیم تاودشورو تاودشادور بهم می پیوندد و تاودشورمیش فاعل و مصدر هم می آید تاودشلو تاودشور
تاودشاد ان بهم پیوندنده و پیوسته و بمعنی مصدر هم می آید تاودشو تاودشغیل مفرد مخاطب امر الشاهد علی الاول شعر
دیماجر یوردین نوا وهم سیزلار نیاس بیرزمان ا ایتسا نلیکیم غم دیرنک بر لیغلای آینتک پیله تاودش تاودشماو تاودشماغیل مفرد مخاطب امر
تاودشونک تاودشونکیز و تاودشونکلار جمع مخاطب امر تاودشماغ تاودشمانکلار جمع مخاطب امر تاودشاین و تاودشورمین

تاودشادورمین و تاودشورام بهم می پیوندم تاودشماغ تاودشامن بهم می پیوندم تاودشوب و تاودشوبانو تاودشمیش بهم پیوسته تاودشمیش
بهم پیوسته اش تاودشمیشانلت بهم پیوسته تاودشوبنو تاودشوبنونه بهم پیوسته ایم تاودشماس بهم نمی پیوندد تاودشماسلیغ بهم
تاودشماس بولسا بهم نپیوندنده باشد تاودشادور میش نوکنه بهم می پیوسته باشد تاودشاتاودشا بهم پیوسته پیوسته و بدون تکرار
هم مستعملست تاودشای مو آیا بهم بپیوندم و بپیوندد و بپیوندی تاودشای پو بهم نپیوسته تاودشاقه تاودشغاپزو تاودشغای
تاودشانکیز تاودشاینیب بهم پیوندیم تاودشغالی برای بهم پیوستن و تا پیوسته تاودشغاج چون بهم پیوست و پیوندد و بجنس پیوستن
بهم پیوندنده تاودشوغوجه تاودشوغاجه تاودشغاجه تا بهم پیوستن و بقدر بهم پیوستن تاودشغوسدور بهم خواهم پیوست تاودشغوسکید بهم
پیوست تاودشغوسیدور بهم خواهد پیوست تاودشغولوق بهم پیوستنی تاودشاغو تاودشه و تاودشه تاودشوسون تاودشین بهم پیوندد
تاودشغودیلت تورمین تاودشوردیلت مین بهم پیوسته ام تاودشورماغ بضم واو و فتح شین معجمه و سکون راء مهمله مصدر متعدیست بهم پیوسته کردن
تاودشورغوچه تاودشورغاچه تاودشورماغ تا بهم پیوسته کردن چنانچه در مقطعات کوید الشاهد علی الاول شعر کیم که عالمدین
کرچه تابیاد نخوش اق اوشا الناسلیق قول تاودشورغوچه بولماق دیمش کیم آنینک حیقا ایکی سینمنا قولی و نیز بمعنی
کشت و تاق صیغ آن بر بنیاق بالفظ در اشتقاق می یابد تاودشاناغ و تاودشاماناغ بترکیب و بمعنی بند بکردن چنانچه شاعر
استنود کوید ملاحه الرتبیه شعر یارکی اوشمرمه تیکوه تاودشانور سودین کو شلوکی من الجوامد تاو بمعنی ناو چوب باشد
که از زیر بوستان برآید و از آن چوبی سازند که از جماق آنرا بکرد و بسر بیجا لعرو بفارسی پیچه کویند و در سال کند
طلسم آنش کشمیر کوید که شعر دیکیل خیبلاره کو نکل دیمیت بولدی قاش که آندین ایمان مطالعا شعله فاش یعنی کو ناسلک مثال لغت
که از آن مطالعا شعله فاش نیست و نو آن روی از نسخه یعنی لفظ غلط اخر بو یوخ بولد ریخ ... بالمنشی
یحیا معنی سنت چماق نوشته و یحیا خود منفصل نلفت بمعنی ناو چماق نوشته هم بود و چنانچه در شعر بو بیلدا شاهد آورده و نصیری هم
بمناسبت او این لغت مجهول لطمارکتاب او نقل نسخه خود نموده و بآن اکتفا نکرده خوبله احبای بیکو خسلا ایلیبین جمله خوانده
سبز هم ملیح مذکر کرده نیما الفاظ منصلی بی چهار حراءی ملت تاوات بجوفکاوالذات بمعنی بیان می باشد و دو حجت هتی کمر نسالرام هم کویند
تاواق آماچی بترکیب و معنی وعده باشد که آنرا بعربی مضماد کویند تاوشاق بکون واو و قاف و فتح شین معجمه بمعنی تاوخوز
بکون واو و نون و ضم نون معجمه بمعنی تفاب و معتماب کنند و اهم نامند چنانچه در صحیفه شیلو دو استان جهادیم کوید شعر
سحدیلم کیمه نی شناسیله بیوق شاهد لعل اضطرابی پله و نیز مصنف تاریخ الملوک در دیکر شعر کویند کرمی المش ابراهیم ترایی اندام کیمی تاوخونی
یا القوزه بتیکر بناه اما شوندی تاوخونجی تفاب کننده چنانچه در تاریخ الملوک در ذکر جراد و چوبینه کویند که جراد بیدن بقمه تلوخوتجی
بیلیرب اعزی پادشاهلیقنه اولتوردی تاولوج بکون واو و جیم و ضم لام احلت نقی بحکر صمینه آدمی بمسیر کند تاونوق
فروندن باشد که از زبین هم میرسند آن بیبار زلزله فیلچهادم بود تاووت بضم واو و سکون تای قرشت که روی کندم و نخود است بریان
آرد نموده بخورند و آنرا بعربی سویق خوانند تاووجی بضم واو و کسر جیم ترکی روی کندم و نخود بریان باشد تاوور بضم واو کوکنار
بمله بمعنی چپی و بمعنی آلت تاووراق مصنف قاوور باشد که در فوق منذ کور شد و بجاز اسور بیجواد کویند که دختر کان در طفلی سازند آنرا انا
کنند و بطلب حور و تمن نامند و نیز اشکال و تماثیل است که شبلی زان از چوب پرده ظاهر و پیدا نمایند الشاهد علیه شعر یمانلیزی کر لعبتما
ایره کرد و دون نغرمینکنفه بولعبت لار کرایل کو نکلی آکوبل آسنک تاووجاغی تاووجاچی شطرنج کویند چنانچه در مقاله جهارم از تبرک
الابرار در شیدت بنازی ظلت کوید شعر لعبه تاوجاغی کبیحیله مه ثم کمرکمنوبان جاجی بنیک مهوش تاوورداغ و تاووراق کوکی

279ر.

باشد که مصروض بیان کند چنانکه در تاریخ بابری مذکور است که آزوق ویغی وتاووداق ده نیمه کم خلقرا بیری یکلتو دیلادی
تاوپرسون بضم واو وسین مهمله وسکون رای مهمله ونون برلیوسعا گویند که تا ندرویدن هنوز سبز باشد شعر چو [illegible]
منکا قطع ایچینات تابیج هم ودمدینک اوستی تمنا یرآت یکم آغه تلمه سون پر اولوب بولسه تاتات طایر بولوبان ستکابین آلوسنکا با
دیز در وصف شکار قصر فرهاد گوید شعر پریب یافراغ نشان طوطی پر یکیدین شجر الوسرخت سیکریدین آنکادا قی تاوپرسون
آبکش دین مونکا هم تلچ شاخ خضو ترودین تاووسی بکسر جیم مهمله پیچ وغند وغنچه را مانند تاووماج بسکون رای مهمله و
جیم وفتح میم بالف کشیده گندم برشته واشال آن را خوانند چنانکه در لیلی مجنون در وصف [illegible] گوید شعر [illegible]
ترنابه سیدین [illegible] تاوحماج ونیز آنرا اجلی است از ولایات ماوراء النهر تاوون بضم واو وسکون رای [illegible] تاوز [illegible] بضم واو و کاف
زای معجمه وفتح ضین [illegible] که [illegible] گویند از دانه [illegible] جدا شود تاووق بضم واو وسکون الف شانه را گویند و [illegible]
روی هم با معنی [illegible] چنانکه در لغت [illegible] شانه [illegible] مذکور است که تاووق شانه [illegible] و نیز [illegible]
پنبه [illegible] که [illegible] تاپیا [illegible] و نون و فتح [illegible]
کشیدن [illegible] تاپیا [illegible] تاپیاندوق [illegible]
کشیده [illegible] تاپیا [illegible] تاپیادور [illegible] بیکو میکند و تاپیا [illegible] تاپیاغان و تاپیا [illegible] تاپیا [illegible]
بیکو کشیدن و بیکو کشیده [illegible] می آیند تاپیان و تاپیا [illegible] مفرد غائب [illegible] تاپیا [illegible] مفرد غائب [illegible]
تاپیا [illegible] تاپیا [illegible] جمع غائب [illegible] تاپیا [illegible] تاپیا [illegible] جمع غائب [illegible] تاپیا [illegible] تاپیا [illegible]
تاپیا [illegible] خوب بیکو میکشم تاپیا [illegible] تاپیا [illegible] خوب بیکو [illegible] تاپیا [illegible] تاپیا [illegible] خوب بیکو کشید [illegible]
بیکو کشیدن [illegible] تاپیا [illegible] خوب بیکو کشیدن تاپیا [illegible] تاپیا [illegible] خوب بیکو [illegible]
بیکو نکشیدن تاپیا [illegible] بیکو نکشیدن نباشد تاپیا [illegible] بیکو کشیده نباشد تاپیا نا تاپیا نا بیکو کشان [illegible]
[illegible] تاپیا نا [illegible] آیا بیکو [illegible] تاپیا [illegible] بیکو نکشیده تاپیا [illegible] تاپیا [illegible]
تاپیا [illegible] بیکو بکشیم تاپیا [illegible] برای بیکو کشیدن و تا بیکو کشیده تاپیا [illegible] چون خوب بیکو کشیده [illegible]
بیکو کشیدن تاپیا [illegible] تاپیا [illegible] خوب بیکو کشیدن [illegible] تاپیا [illegible] خوب بیکو [illegible] تاپیا [illegible]
بیکو خواهی کشید تاپیا [illegible] بیکو خواهد کشید تاپیا [illegible] بیکو کشیدنی تاپیا [illegible] تاپیا [illegible] تاپیا [illegible]
خوب بیکو بکشد تاپیا [illegible] خوب بیکو کشیده ام [illegible] تاپتما [illegible] بسکون یا و [illegible] تاپتوق
بکشیم تاپتور [illegible] تاپیادور [illegible] بمعنی [illegible] می آید چنانکه [illegible] گوید شعر [illegible]
تاپتور [illegible] تاپتیلدی باشد [illegible] تاپتیلی [illegible]
[illegible] تاپتار [illegible] تاپتار [illegible] تاپتیا [illegible] تاپتور [illegible] برکشنده و برکشته [illegible] می آیند تاپت
تاپتیل [illegible] مفرد غائب [illegible] شعر [illegible] تاپت [illegible]
تاپتما و تاپتما [illegible] مفرد غائب [illegible] تاپتیلنک و تاپتیلر و تاپتیکلار [illegible] جمع غائب [illegible] تاپتما [illegible] تاپتما [illegible]
جمع غائب [illegible] تاپتسا [illegible] تاپتور [illegible] تاپتادور [illegible] و تاپتور [illegible] الشاهد [illegible] شعر [illegible] تاپتور [illegible]
ابدی [illegible] تاپتما [illegible] تاپتیب و تاپتمسان و تاپتمش برکشته

280ر.

برکشته [illegible] تاپتما [illegible] برکشته تاپتیب [illegible] تاپتیب [illegible] برکشته [illegible] تاپتماس بمعنی [illegible] تاپتا [illegible] برنکشیده [illegible] تاپتماس بولسا
برنکوده باشد تاپتا [illegible] برمیکشیده باشد تاپتا تاپتا [illegible] برکشته [illegible] تاپتیای مو آیا برکشیدم
برکشید و برکشیدی [illegible] تاپتما بو برنکشته [illegible] تاپتیا [illegible] تاپتیا [illegible] تاپتیا [illegible] برای برکشتن و تا برکشته
تاپتا [illegible] چون برکشت و برکشید [illegible] برکشتی تاپتور [illegible] برکردمی [illegible] تاپتیا [illegible] تاپتیا [illegible] برکشتن [illegible]
[illegible] برکشت تاپتور [illegible] برکشت [illegible] تاپتولوق برکشتی تاپتیا [illegible] تاپتیا [illegible] تاپتیا [illegible] [illegible]
تاپتور [illegible] تاپتور [illegible] تاپتیا [illegible] تاپتار [illegible] [illegible] برکردانیدن چنانکه [illegible]
اولمیش [illegible] تاپتار [illegible] [illegible] اولش [illegible]
تاپتار [illegible] تاپتیا [illegible] تاپتار [illegible] تاپتار [illegible] [illegible] می آید تاپتار [illegible] تاپتار [illegible] تاپتار [illegible]
کردانند [illegible] می آیند تاپتار [illegible] تاپتار [illegible] تاپتار [illegible] مفرد غائب [illegible]
شعر تا [illegible] تاپتار [illegible] تاپتار [illegible] تاپتار [illegible] مفرد غائب [illegible]
[illegible] تاپتار [illegible] تاپتار [illegible] جمع غائب [illegible] تاپتار [illegible] تاپتار [illegible] جمع غائب [illegible] تاپتار [illegible]
تاپتار [illegible] تاپتار [illegible] تاپتار [illegible] برکردانیدن تاپتار [illegible] برکردانیدن
تاپتار [illegible] برکردانیده تاپتار [illegible] برنکردانند تاپتار [illegible] برنکردانیده باشد تاپتار [illegible]
باشد تاپتار [illegible] تاپتار [illegible] چنانکه گوید شعر [illegible] تاپتار [illegible]
[illegible] شعر [illegible] تاپتار [illegible]
تاپتار [illegible] برکردانم و برکرداند و برکردانی [illegible] الشاهد علی الاول [illegible] شعرا [illegible]
[illegible] تاپتار [illegible] آیا برکردانم و برکرداند و برکرداندی تاپتار [illegible] برنکردانیدن تاپتار [illegible] تاپتار [illegible]
[illegible] تاپتار [illegible] برای برکردانیدن و تا برکردانیدن تاپتار [illegible] چون برکردانید و برکرداند و [illegible] برکردانیدن تاپتار [illegible]
برکردانیدن تاپتار [illegible] تاپتار [illegible] برکردانیدن [illegible] برکردانیدن تاپتار [illegible] خواهم برکردانید تاپتار [illegible] خواهد برکرداند
تاپتار [illegible] خواهد برکردانید تاپتار [illegible] برکردانیدنی تاپتار [illegible] تاپتار [illegible] تاپتار [illegible] برکرداند تاپتار [illegible]
تاپتار [illegible] برکرداند [illegible] الشاهد علی الاول شعر [illegible]
[illegible] تاپتیشما [illegible] بسکون یا [illegible] تاپریلما [illegible]
یا ولام [illegible] برکشتن [illegible] تاپریلدوق [illegible] برکشتیم تاپریلور [illegible] تاپریلادور [illegible] الشاهد علی
الاول شعر [illegible] تاپریلور [illegible] تاپریلور [illegible] می آید چنانکه [illegible]
شعر [illegible] تاپریلور [illegible] تاپریلغان [illegible] تاپریلور [illegible]
[illegible] برکشته [illegible] می آیند تاپریلو [illegible] تاپریلغیل مفرد غائب [illegible] تاپریلسا [illegible] مفرد غائب [illegible]
تاپریلسنک و تاپریلسنکر [illegible] جمع غائب [illegible] تاپریلما [illegible] تاپریلمین و تاپریلورمین و تاپریلادورمین
تاپریلورام [illegible] تاپریلغان و تاپریلماس [illegible] تاپریلسا [illegible] تاپریلمش [illegible] تاپریلمیش [illegible]
برکشته [illegible] تاپریلغان [illegible] تاپریلیب [illegible] برکشته ایم تاپریلماس [illegible] تاپریلماس

280v.

بعقب برنگشت [illegible] بعقب برنگردنده باشد [illegible] بعقب برگشته باشد مثال [illegible] برگشته برگشته و بدون تکرار هم

مستعملست [illegible] آیا بعقب برگردم و برگردد و برگردی و با مصدر [illegible] هم اشتراک دارد یعنی بعقب بمانم و بمانند و بمانی [illegible]

بعقب برنگشته [illegible] بعقب برگردیم و نیز بعضی بعقب بمانیم [illegible] برای بعقب برگشتن و تا مصدر

مانده [illegible] چون برگشت و برگردد و بعضی برگشتن [illegible] بعقب برگردنده [illegible]

و بعد از آن [illegible] بعقب خواهم برگشت [illegible] بعقب خواهی برگشت [illegible] بعقب خواهد برگشت [illegible]

برگشتی [illegible] بعقب خواهد برگشت [illegible] بعقب برگشتیم [illegible]

لازم بعقب ماندن [illegible] بعقب مانده [illegible] فاعل و مصدر هم می آید [illegible]

[illegible] بعقب مانده و بعقب مانده و بمعنی مصدر هم می آید [illegible] مفرد غائب [illegible]

[illegible]

281r.

[illegible]

کمتی نامیدا که مرد شوریده وازرا قاشقا هم کویند قابدین بیغولرنکا چنانچه در ختایم الحجه در فرا ایام ماضی کویند که دیدیلر اچمیش
امامقه بیتکوردیدیم آنی قابدین از بیرین قابدین نام جدی هم میر تیمور ست و نیز نام نبیره اوکتای قاآنست که در عهد قبلای قاآن اکثر ممالک
ماوراء النهر را صاحب بود خانبالیغ بجیم و تحتانی سر آمد قابراق سنگ فسان را باشد که آنرا بیلاو هم کویند قایرو بضم را و بمعنی اعتباری
بکسر را بمعنی عقب باشد قایریای بکسر را و فتح تای والف کشیده لعظیم امرا و اکابر را خوانند که در خدمت سلاطین باشند و آن تالی نوین است
قایرچی بکسر را بمعنی مهیم ترکی رودی بمعنی مشفق و غمخوار بود قایی معنی کا بین چنانچه کوید شعر نوای قایغی ایرپله سینینک جمالی
بیانی قیلبونی سیکان جنسکلی وصفین قیلو که کمنک ایرسه کویا قایغو و قایقو بمعنی غم و اندوه باشد الشاهد علیه شعر دیلبین سیز
بجو که هیکیم سیوا ولتمه زاد پ قایغوسنکا یوقتور جزوین خود اولوبیمن اوشبوقایغودین قایغولوق قورش چند باشد که آنرا ابیغار نیز
بوتیلیه هم کویند تیغساق بفتح عین معجمه و قاف و نون با الف کشیده خاکینه بود که از تخم بخته بشود و آنرا بعربی عجه خوانند تیماق
پرده رقیقی بود که بر روی شیر بندد و آنرا بعربی جطاط در غوه و بفارسی چه کویند قیناشلیق صاحب جوشش قیناق بفتح نون
با الف کشیده بمعنی پرده اولنام طایفه ایست از اتراک قدیم ترکی دری چنکال در غان مبوا رح شکل جهار پهلو است جوشیدلیق که در ایم
و دهن زنان نوزاینده بهم میرسد قیناد و ق بفتح نون با الف کشیده و ضم واو بمعنی لیست که آب از آنجا جوشیده بر آید که دابرا هم لمنند تایین
بکون یا و نون برادر زن را کویند و تای آتا که کویند یعنی پدر زن و تایآنا یعنی مادر زن و آنرا بکسر یا و تایین هم خوانند قایو بضم یا
بمعنی کلام چنانچه کویند شعر قیله ایمدی آندا پکلب در هم تایواق که زخم فعله امر بوناک وله شعر نی جون ز کجبر تو سوز
و در داولودین پرم دشع تاسیش قایو پر کلسه دایکیم یار آب و تاب قایوق بضم یا و سکون واو ظرف خرد را کویند الشاهد علی الاول شعر
نرق می دین مینوسانی بوم یرکیم چرخ جویکی دم طناز ایسی اوزی قایوق در ویته تایق بکسر یا مد که در مینلرزند قاسبی بکسر یا بعنی
کلام و نیز نام طایفه ایست از اتراک که خود را از نسل تایی خان بن آی خان ولعض قبایل ترکمان رسیدانند و سلاطین آل عثمان از آن قبیله اند
بمعنی تسمه باشد و آن پوستیست که در از بیرند تایین بکسر یا همان تای بفتح ابطه زاد باشد که در فوق مذکور شد و نیز نام ولایتی است
خراسان باب القاف مع الباء الموحده مع البای المثناه و با ضم بابا ناچی برخاستن قوپی برخاست چنانچه در لیلی مجنون کوید شعر تعجیل اپله
لعت شنک کیم باغ ساری قیلوبیدین از ساهنک قوبار قوپادور برخیزد و قوپار بمعنی فاعل و مصدر هم می آید قوپغان و قوپارغان و قوپادورغان
برخیزنده و برخاسته الشاهد علی الاول بالمعنی الثانی شعر یقیلغان عشق اراعتیلغ قیلماغ سجادین که بو بیلماغ یبغدین کچه قوبغای
یوق دما الیجب و بمعنی مصدر هم می آید قوپ و قوپیل مفرد غائب الفعل امر الشاهد علی الثانی شعر کیلادیبنک منیدیم بیلاک
او شیخ ایسین هم پند اینیت قوپیل و دیر ایچرا ابوطلسین بیرون بدنام کیت قوپیا و قوپیا غیل مفرد غائب الفعل امر قوپوبلدنک قوپونکوز
قوپونکلار جمع غائب الفعل امر الشاهد علی الثانی شعر رهو الیغ اوقیرایلا قوتلیشب کیل امعربین اواجیل لا اخت قوپونکوز جهکیم
دیک قوپیا لیسقو قوپیا جز قوپیا خلار جمع غائب الفعل امر قوپارمین قوپارمین و قوپادورمین و قوپارام برخیزم قوپیارام قوپارمین برخیزم
قوپوپ قوپوبان قوپیش برخاسته قوپیشین برخاسته قوپیشانک برخاسته قوپیپ قوپیبیز قوپیپ توز برخاسته ایم قوپاس
برنخیزد قوپماس لیغ برنخاستن قوپاس بولسا برنخیزنده باشد قوپادورمیش و جه برخاسته بوده باشد قوپیا قوپیا خیزان خیزان و بعد
هم مستعمل قوپامیو آیا برخیزد و برخیزد و برخیزد قوپیا یو برخاسته قوپساق قوپاق بزه قوپغای بزه قوپاشیلنک برخیزد قوپاشیلنک برخیزد
برخواستن و بار بر خاسته قوپاج چون برخاسته برخیزد و بعضی برخاستن قوپوچی برخیزنده قوپیوچی قوپیو غقوچی برخیزنده تا برخاستن
و قصد برخاستن قوپیغو مدد برخواهم برخاست قوپقونکلار برخواهی برخاست قوپقوسیدور برخواهد برخاست قوپغولوق برخاستنی قوپغانی و قوپ

قوپیون قوپیدیلیک برخیزیم الشاهد علی الاول شعر جان نابیسغار نواوقوپقیانی نغزا وابرسیتیکلسون ناظر که بالشاهد علی الثانی
رستبزاد آنکه کم دیر خرابات اهلیم الیرایشا ایمتی ترتیب اینسون قوپیدیلیک انچاکه کا مسبوح اهل پاپ با مکلفلام هر طاق بهواته قوپقوسیلیک قوپارمین
قوپادیلیک برخاستیم قوپارتاق قوپارغالیغ بفتح یای بجی با الف کشیده مصدر متعدیست یعنی برخیزانیدن الشاهد علی الثانی شعر
که مطرب تالیغ کوی با تو تانساپو قویسه اوی قوپارغالیغ ابرو و شوار چیوپاوسیتنه قوپارغای برخیزانید چنانچه شاهد آن مذکور شد تا
مذکور شد و تلو سیمین رنج بفتح تای بجی را والف مهمله اشتقاقی نیابد قوپاتیاق بکون یای ابجد و فتح سین مهمله با الف کشیده بیز تیره قوپاتیرین
قوپادوق قواتیتیم قوپار قوپاتقوپاتیب نغارنده قوپاتیار برخیزند فاعل و مصدر هم می آید قوپاتیمان قوپاتیارتاپ قوپاتیابیم قوپاتیلیس و قوپاتیمه قو
مصدر هم می آید قوپاتیو قوپاتیغیل مفرد غائب الفعل امر الشاهد علی الاول شعر حیرحیبن اولدی نوای تاپیلتوف نیلم نی اسپهبد
سپیس نوا آه سنکو را قوپاتیو قوپاتیون قوپاتیلو قوپاتیاغیل مفرد غائب الفعل امر قوپاتیلار جمع غائب الفعل امر قوپاتیانکیز قوپاتیانکلار جمع غائب الفعل امر قوپاتیانکا
قوپاتیانکیزقوپاتیانکلار جمع غائب الفعل امر قوپاتیایین قوپاتیارمین قوپاتیاتدرمین قوپاتیادورمین قوپاتیارام میسوالیم قوپاتیامان قوپاتیاسان بمنوالم قوپا
قوپاتیلیو قوپاتیش نولغینه قوپاتیمیشین نولغینه قوپاتیمیشام قوپاتیپ قوپاتیپ بزد قوپاتیپ تور نولغینه ایم قوپاتیماس نمیتواند
قوپاتیماسلیغ نتوانستن قوپاتیماس بولسا نتواند نباشد قوپاتیپ بیدر بیش نتوانسته باشد قوپاتیا بیو قوپاتیای قوپاتیه توان توانا
و بعد بفتح هم مستعمل قوپاتیامو آیا بتواند و بتواند قوپاتیا نا بو نتوانسته قوپاتیاساق قوپاتیغای قوپاتیای
قوپاتیالی قوپاتیالیشیو ازیم قوپاتیا غلبه برای توانستن و توانسته قوپاتیاغاج چون توانست و بتواند بعضی توانستن قوپاتیاوچی توانا
قوپاتیغوچی قوپاتیغونچی قوپاتیاغالی نوانستن و بقصد توانستن قوپاتیغومدد خواهم توانست قوپاتیغونکدور خواهی توانست قوپاتیغوسیدور
خواهد توانست قوپاتیغولوق قوپاتیغولیغی قوپاتیاغای قوپاتیاسا قوپاتیابسا قوپاتیانکیز قوپاتیابیلیک توانستیم قوپاتیاغولیک توانستیم قوپاتیاوم
الجوامد قوپا سه معنی دارد اول بمعنی بر لیسه و تخم که کویند و از اتابا هم خوانند دویم نام علفیست که بنابیین و بهند و شارانداج است
سیم لغت قلیج نیز بوده که در چنانچه بوشد قوباج و قوباق نام ولایتیست از ترکستان که در حین که چینکیزخان ما النهر را بسخیر
تسخیر کرد آن ولایت را با ولجای کر داما آنکه او را بو صفر داشته بمحول ب آنجا بعضی داشته باشد قوباشلوق جاشتکاه بلند
بکون با و فتح غین معجمه و اب بنا بنا سرچنانچه در تاریخ الانبیا حضرت یوسف علیه السلام کوید که اول جاه باشید ایر کاروان قوشیا لقمه
قوبه سنا ایب قیز بیع دلبرا کویند چنانچه در سبک کندری در سراج کوید شعر بولی اوستیدا قوبه کیم سوناجیپ ساجلیدین
سیوق که ابوسلیچب قبلای بفتح با و لام با الف کشیده علم برادر بزرگ آن پادشاه خطاست که مقدار بر ابو بصیر بن غایت فسخ
و شاه در وصف او کفته شعرا لعمریدن طلا حب تا آنشا قبلای والجد بیک بن یاصری قوبار قوپ بضم با و سکون را بمعنی تری زوقبانی
بود که بچه بر زنان آن کار دنچنانچه کیش ار قوبصیر کویند قوبودجوق مصغر قوبیاسیت ترکی زوی قوقیباشد که آنرا بعربی حمه منهد
قوبوز بضم بای ابجد و سکون زا عجمه بنطل خوانند و آن مجمع ساز یست معروف چنانچه کوید شعر شانیای نولایجم روجا بیسناد
او قونغمه سیالا باشلا جلو کور دو که کافو بون ساز کا چغه جمشید است و نیز قبوض بی بضاعت کویند باملاه الرومیه شعر بیلدی مطرب کر
خال کو تو تورو قوبوزن بنها ساچکینی اینیغو زاچر دستور قوبوسف بضم با و عجمی و سکون زای مهمله و فتح حین مهمله تریک دوی نبایت براده
صمم جیدن که آنرا با خاجیه کلم کویند باب القاف مع التاء المثناه قوتورما فی باشتاع و فتحتین مع الراء المهمله بمعنی دیوانه شدن قوتورد دیوانه
قوتورتوب قوتوراد و ر دیوانه میشود و قوتورود بمعنی فاعل و مصدر هم می آید قوتورغان و قوتورمیش دیوانه قوتوردار بیماریست دیوانه شدن
مصدر هم می آید قوتور و قوتورغیل مفرد غائب الفعل امر قوتورسون مفرد غائب الفعل امر قوتورماو قوتورفونکیز قوتورونکر قوتورکونکیز جمع

[illegible]

ازغضبلر قوتورغانلق قوتورغانجه قوتورغانلکلاجمع غالبا ... قوتورابین ... قوتوراده ... تورودامی دیوانه میشوم قوتورمان
قوتورماس ... دیوانه نمیشوم قوتوروب ... قوتورمیش دیوانه شده قوتورمیشین دیوانه شده قوتورمیشانک دیوانه شده
قوتورماس دیوانه نمیشود قوتورغاسلیغ دیوانه شدن قوتورماس بولسا دیوانه نشوند باشد ... دیوانه میشد
قوتورا قوتول دیوانه شده ... قوتورایمو آیا دیوانه شوم ... قوتورمایو دیوانه شده قوتورساق
قوتورمانو قوتورغای ... دیوانه شدن ... قوتورغاج چون دیوانه شد ...
قوتورغوچی دیوانه شونده ... دیوانه شدن ... دیوانه خواهم شد

[illegible]

283v

بابری در وصف تیغ هند گوید کم تیغ نینک اولوغلوغ خسروی تا وجه بولغای یوسق قوتود بو توقدونا اهل درمه قوتوز بنیم تا
سخنانلای مجمه سک دیوانه داکهیند چنانکه گوید شعر تیلبه دور اکین قیمینک مثل ایره رواجب انکا شوندیغ یا قانکا بو قوالای
ابتیکم اول بولغای قوقوز وآن را قوده زیاد الجمید استعمال نمایند مع الجیم من المشتقات قوجاق باشباغ ضمه یعنی آغوش کشیدن و بغل
کردن چنانکه گوید شعر بیلی بولغوی کمرلرکه مسلمان جون شهادایره ش حرکنی قوجاق بوف اوینالی تالچان امکان ایرمس قوجلدوم بغل
کردم الشاهد علیه شعر قوشدا سرو کل دین ایسا ایب جنی قوجلدوم سرینی ایلا کیلا ای سرو کلرخ بو قوشوم تیمیره قوجلدوق بغل
کفتیم قوجا رمقوجاد ور بغل میکرد و قوجار بمعنی فاعل و مصدر هم می آید چنانکه بمعنی مصدری گوید شعر قوجار خسرو فقاله
قدینک دیک ایماش کو کیتور ایا نی باغبان قوجاقی بیله ونیز دوست سکندری در ملاقات سکندر با راهبند گوید شعر بانیب چون
قوجاردین بولوب کوینکلی خوش کیتور کانلادیغا ایلابان پیشکش قوجعان و قوجار غان و قوجاد ور غان بغل کیرنده و بغل کرفته و بمعنی مصدر هم
می آید چنانکه گوید الشاهد علی الاول شعر قیلیچ اوی بلینک قوجعان حاصل دین کوزونکا اتمرمی دورمیش کل قلای قوج و قوجغیل
مفرد مخاطب از فعل امر قوجا و قوجاغیل مفرد مخاطب از فعل امر قوجعان و قوجونکیز و قوجونکلار جمع مخاطب از فعل امر قوجامانک و قوجامانکیز و
قوجمانکلار جمع مخاطب از فعل امر قوجامین و قوجادمین و قوجادورمین و قوجادارم بغل میکرم قوجمان و قوجماس مین بغل نمیکرم قوجسام و قوجماسمین
قوجادورمین بغل بکیرم الشاهد علی الثانی شعر قوجغلین سیلن کر نیغرا ایله دیب بولدی غم تاتوان جسیم مطلا ایا کا ن لالا ب دلیت
قوجوب و قوجوبان و قوجمیش بغل کرفته چنانکه شاهد بر اول در دوست سکندری در ملاقات سکندر با راهبند گوید شعر بوتار براق
چیکیب شاه اکرام ایله قوجوب شاه فرایوهم کام ایله قوجمیش بغل کرفته اشک قوجمیشانک بغل کرفته قوجماس بغل نمیکرم قوجماسلیغ
بغل نکرفتن قوجماس بولسا بغل نکیرند باشد قوجادورمیش بولغای بغل میکرفته باشد قوجا قوجا بغل کرفته کرفته و بعدن تکرار هم
مستعملست قوجای مو آیا بغل بکیرم و بکیرد و بکیرد قوجا یو بغل نکرفته قوجساق قوجغاینز قوجغای بز و قوجا و قوجالینک بغل
بکیریم قوجغلی برای بغل کرفتن تا کرفته قوجماج چون بغل کرفت و بکیرد و بعض کرفتن قوجوجی بغل کیرنده قوجوچی و قوجونکیز و قوجغا
تا بغل کرفتن و بعد بغل کرفتن قوجوسدور بغل خواهم کرفت قوجوتکدور بغل خواهد کرفت قوجوسیده و تعبیر خواهد کرفت قوجو
بغل کرفتن قوجغای قوجه قوجبه قوجسون قوجدیک بغل بکرد قوجوبیک و قوجادیک قوجونکلیغ بغل کرفتنی و چنانکه گفته شود
الشاهد علی الثالث من خسرو شیرین شعر بوی وجسمین دیکلمان قوجونکلیغ ثری دیک جت لوغدین اوچغونکلیغ قوجوشماق
مع الثین با یکدیکر معانقه و بغل کیری کردن چنانکه در ملاقات سکندر با راهبند گوید شعر شه اعزاز ایله اجهند ایلادی قوجوشماق
بیله سر بلند ایلادی قوجوشوم بغل کیری کردم الشاهد علیه شعر قوجوشتوم سرو بیرله نوشته کیا بویان اول لحظه خوش نفار اکلکم
قوجوشوم قوجوشیلا امر است از بغل کیری کردن الشاهد علی الاول شعر ولادیکم بولغان آوارزنک یتیشمیش آلیسکا ثری چلیسیفه ایلیلیک سوزخود
الماس دین قوجوش قوجوشقوجی بغل کیری کننده چنانکه در خاتمه سبقه بیان در خواب دیدن خود گوید شعر شاه بیرله قوجوشقوجی بیرله
خولانه هم بلیبلیک ا وجی بیرله قویوبان چون کوره شونگلار محبوب توروبان بیکا سیکجی لار ههر خوب قوجوشقا یلارلار قوجوشه لارلار
قوجوشیلیک لانقل کیری کند الشاهد علی الاول شعر بوصوبت غه نالانی بجرد م اولفلیج اولوش کیم قوجوشقا یلاجرا الاییر یکا ناکاه او چرا
واقسیق برجمو العواق شواد ل بانقمام شین اشتقاقی پیدا بد قوجوشورماق مصدر متعدیست معانقه و بغل کیری فرمودن و صیغ آن بدستور
بالفظ نور اشتقاق می یابد من الجوامد قوجاق بمعنی آغوش باشد قوجچاد بسکون جیم و دای مهمله نقیح غین معجمه قوج را کویند اما از ان کوچ
یامنی کوچی چنانکه در مصطلح گوید شعر بای کوشه نو توب قدری خمیدین قوجقار ادولب و حکم مقد دین و نیز نهر لسان الطیر

284r

منزه دین نا پوق قویزی قوجقارلیق نیوهه بیتول سلکه طریق قوجه مرد پیر را نامند قوجه میشو بز که کوچی نو عی از کل است و آن بسیار شبیه
شبیه بعناب بیکی از عناب بیز کرلت قوجی بز که کوچی نوعی از تخت روان باشد که بالفا بکشند مع الخا قوجی بو سرابند انگور
مع الدال المهملة من المشتقات قودرماق باشباغ ضمه یعنی قو تهماق بمعنی دیوانه شدن باشد قود رغب و قودوغان قود بمعنی دیوانه شده چنانکه در
تاریخ الملوک در ذکر هرام بن یزدجرد گوید که بیر پیشه کیم بول تیر لغیند ا بولغای جو شلیغ سیل قودروب یامست بولوب و ناقی صیغ سوایش همان
که در ذیل مصدر قوتورماق مذکور شد لیکن حرف ابدال تبدیل یافته است من الجوامد قودا بفتح دال مهمله را گویند که دختر پسر هند و
که دختر میکیرند انرا نامند قودوق دو معنی دارد اول چاه را گویند دوم که خر بچه کوریی خر را خوانند چنانکه مثل است که قولان باشیغه
ایش توشسا قودوقیغه تا دا ناس یعنی بر سر که خر کار بیفتد بیچه خر کار میکند و انرا خود ولد هم نامند قودو نات بضم الدیوان
خشک مغز را گویند مع الراء المهملة من المشتقات قورماق باشباغ ضمه بمعنی استعمال می شود اول آراستن دوم نصب کردن و در کار اول ما ضیه
جله کوه زمین بکند مثل آنکه گویند مجلس قورماق یعنی مجلس آراستن و با قورماق یعنی چله کمان نصب کردن اما تنها می آید بمعنی بکند با
قابل آن مذکور شود چنانکه بمعنی دوم گوید شعر تلمر فلاحوردین بولک خان سرشته سیدین چله ولار اتیمش قاشینک یا سین نوا و قصد
کرا بیتا سا نانک قورماق قوردی آراست و نصب کرد چنانکه در لیلی مجنون در صرع سپی مجنون گوید بالمعنی الاول شعر جن لفیین خطیم قورد
اول خیلینی بزم ارا نوشوردی قورار و قوراد در می آراید و نصب میکند و قورار بمعنی فاعل و مصدر هم می آید قورغلو قوراغان و قورادرغان
آراینده و نصب کننده و آراسته و نصب کرده و بمعنی مصدر هم می آید چنانکه شاهد بر اول در تحفه آراستن در عنوان خسرو شیرین گوید که
همین با نو مهی لار ضر سد طلبین نظام ایتیب طوتآبی کوزلکا بزم سلطنت قورغلیه و قورغان با مجاز بمعنی حسن و جمال هم باشد قورماغان
قورغاید و غان آراسته نکرده و نصب نکرده الشاهد علی الاول و بالمعنی الثانی شعر قاشیدین کوز ناز جنگام یو قکر بو قوشی سپهر هیچ کیم
ایرماس جیا یاسین قورماغان قو بمعنی فاعل و مصدر منفی هم می آید قورد قورغیل مفرد مخاطب از فعل امر و قورغیلا ما هم دلدر کرده
جامد مذکور خواهد شد قورسانا و قورنا عیل مفرد مخاطب از فعل امر قورونک و قورونکیز و قورونکلار جمع مخاطب از فعل امر الغیر الشاذ
خشک شدن و قورو ق کردن چنانکه در مصدر قورو ماق مذکور خواهد شد قورماتک و قورمانکیز قورمانکلار جمع مخاطب از فعل امر
قورامین و قورارمین و قورادورمین و قوردادم می آرایم و نصب میکنم قورمان و قورماس مین نمی آرایم و نصب نمیکنم قورامین قورادورمین
می آراید و نصب میکند الشاهد علی الثالث بالمعنی الثانی شعر بیر باران که آنار چرخ معوس جبه دورش چه قاش یاسینی قصد بیغمه قورادور
آخر قوروبه قوروبان و قورمیش آراسته و نصب کرده الشاهد علی الاول بالمعنی الثانی شعر فی الاله دو منه ثالله کیم عزادین بوزلار فیه
کوله رصد لادن تازاین تاج اوستیدا قوروب تور و قوروب و قوروبان بمعنی خشک شده و قورو ق کرده هم باشد قورمیشین آراسته است
و نصب کرده ما شرا قورمیشانک آراسته و نصب کرده قورماس صیغه مفرد مخاطب از مضارع منفی قورماسلیغ نیارآستن و نصب نکردن
قورماس بولسا نیارایند نباشد و نصب نکند نباشد قورادورمیش بولغای می آراسته باشد و نصب میکرده باشد قورا قورا آراسته
و نصب کنان و بدون تکرار هم مستعملست قورغی مو آیا بیارایم و بیارایم آیا نصب کنم و کند وکی قورمایو نیاراسته و نصب
نکرده قورساق قورغای بز قورغای بز قورای قورالینک بیارایم و نصب کنیم قورغلی برای آراستن و نصب کردن چنانکه بمعنی اول گوید
شعر قاشی یاسین قورغلی ابل قصد یغمه بولمیش کیر پیش فه لیغ جن کیم توشلار اول نرکس جادو اوزه و نیز بمعنی تا آراسته و نصب کرده قورغلیغ
چون آراسته و بیارایند و چون نصب کرد و کند و بعض آراستن و نصب کردن قورغوجی آراینده و نصب کننده قورغوجه و قورغونچه قورغلیغه
تا آراستن و تا نصب کردن قورغوسیدور بخواهم آراست و نصب خواهم کرد قورغوتکدور بخواهد آراست و نصب خواهد کرد قورغوسیدور بخواهد

284v.

آلمت ونصب خواهد کرد قورغولوق آلماستی ونصب کردن قورغاوه قوره وقوربه وقوربسون وقوردیلک بنا راید ونصب کند قورغودیلک [illegible]

قورغودیلک مین آراسته ام ونصب کرده ام قوردورمنا ق متعدی بمعنی مصدر قورغاقات وصیغ آن بانضمام لفظ دور اشتقاق می یابد [illegible]

بضم میم الکلم بمعنی مرتب وآراسته شدن ونصب شدن چنانکه ضمیر ابدالی پیغمبر مانی آن را بعضی مرتب شد کوید با لاجاه الرتبه

شعر ... کلک نماشی ... ناوق عشق بیدا اولالیپ ... قورولمیش پیچق قورتولما ق مبکوز ... ولام ... تا [illegible]

وآنرا قورغلاق هم کویند چنانکه مذکور شد قورقولوب قورتولوبان نعوذ تولمیش خلاص شد چنانکه در خسرو شیرین در نامه [illegible]

شیرین بفرهاد کوید الشاهد علی الاول عشق ... کیما سلیک کالمبی ... آندین قورتولوب جان ... قوتولغمونی [illegible]

در این شعر قورتولوب خوانده وقورتولوب را بمعنوع کرده وشعر ... شاهد آمده سهو کرده لفظ اختراعیست ونا قص صیغ [illegible]

مع الراء المهمله اشتقاق می یابد قورشانا ق میکند ... دومعنی دارد اول بمعنی کرببستن باشد دوم بمعنی اخاله کردن [illegible]

تلاح استعمال شود قورشا دوق کربستیم واخاله کردیم قورشا بعقورشا بد ودر کربندید واخالهمی کند وقورشامق بمعنی حاصل مصدر هم [illegible]

قورشاغان وقورشارغان وقورشا یدورغان کربندنده وکربسته واخاله کننده واخاله کرده وبمعنی مصدر هم می آیند قورشاو قورشا [illegible]

مفرد مخاطب فعل امر قورشانا وقورشانا غیل مفرد مخاطب فعل نهی قورشانک قورشانکیز قورشانکلار جمع مخاطب فعل امر قورشا مانک

قورشانانکیز قورشانانکلار جمع مخاطب فعل نهی قورشای قورشار قورشایدور قورشادم کربندم واخاله میکنم قورشا [illegible]

کرمی بندم واخاله میکنم قورشابدی قورشاناپ وقورشامیش کربسته واخاله کرده قورشالیتین کربسته اش را واخاله کرده اش [illegible]

کربسته واخاله کرده قورشاناس صیغه مفرد مغایب از فعل مضارع منفی قورشالماسلیغ کرنبستن واخاله نکردن قورشاناس بولسا [illegible]

نبندد ونبلشد واخاله نکند باشد قورشا یدور بوغنه کرمی بسته باشد ودر دهان میکرفته باشد قورشایو وقورشای قورشای [illegible]

بسته کنان واخاله کنان وبدون تکرار هم مستعملست قورشایو آیا کربندم وبندم وبندی وایا اخاله کنم وکند قورشانایو

کرنبسته واخاله نکرد قورشانا قعقورشا غایزر قورشاغای بز قورشالیق قورشانیک کربندیم واخاله کنیم قورشاغلی برای کربستن وتا [illegible]

وبرای اخاله کردن وتا کرده قورشاغاج چون کربست وبند کرد وبعض کربستن وچون اخاله کرد وکند وبعض کردن قورشاغوچی کرسندی [illegible]

اخاله کننده قورشاغونچه قورشاغونچه وقورشاغانچه تا کربستن وتا اخاله کردن ودر مقام آن قورشاغونیدور کر خواهم بست واخاله خواهم کرد

قورشاغونکدر کر خواهی بست واخاله خواهی کرد وقورشاغوسیدور کر خواهد بست واخاله خواهد کرد قورشاغولوق کر بستن واخاله کردن [illegible]

قورشاغای وقورشا سه وقورشاغوی قورشاغوچه کربندد واخاله کند قورشاغودیلک نوبین وقورشاولیک کربستیم واخاله کردیم قورشاغا ق مع الکاف [illegible]

مصدر متعدی بمعنی کربسته ساختن واخاله فرمودن وصیغ آن بستور انای قورشالماق اشتقاق می یابد قورشالماق مع الکاف [illegible]

مع النون کربسته شدن واخاله شدن وصیغ آن بالام اشتقاق می یابد قورغادنماق بحذف دال وبفتح غین معجمه ودال المهمله ما کشیده

متحصن شدن قورغادادوق متحصن شدیم قورغادایعقورغادایدور متحصن میشود وقورغادار بمعنی حاصل مصدر هم می آید قورغاداغان [illegible]

قورغادارغان قورغادایدورغان متحصن شونده ومتحصن شده وبمعنی مصدر هم می آیند قورغادا وقورغاداغیل مفرد مخاطب فعل امر قورغاداما

قورغاداغیل مفرد مخاطب فعل نهی قورغادانک قورغادانکیز قورغادانکلار جمع مخاطب فعل امر قورغادامانک قورغادامانکیز قورغادامانکلار جمع مخاطب فعل نهی [illegible]

قورغادوبین وقورغادارمین وقورغادایدورمین وقورغادادم متحصن میشوم قورغادامان وقورغاداماسمین متحصن نمیشوم قورغاداب قورغاداپ وقورغاداپ [illegible]

متحصن شده چنانکه شاهد اول در تاریخ بابری مذکورست که برکه نینک ... الاردا قورغاداب ... قورغادابیشین

متحصن شده اش را قورغادابیشانک متحصن شده قورغاداناس متحصن نمیشود قورغاداماسلیغ متحصن نشدن قورغاداناس بولسا متحصن [illegible]

285r.

باشد قورغادایدورمیش بولغانا متحصن میشده باشد قورغادایو وقورغاداای قورغاداای متحصن کنان وبدون تکرار هم مستعملست قورغادایو

آیا متحصن شوم وشوند وشوی قورغادامانایو متحصن نشدی قورغاداناشاق وقورغاداغایز وقورغاداغای بز قورغادالیق قورغادالینک متحصن شویم [illegible]

برای متحصن شدن وتا متحصن شده قورغاداغاج چون متحصن شد وشود وبعض شدن قورغاداغوچی متحصن شونده قورغاداغونچه

قورغاداغونچه وقورغاداغانچه تا متحصن شدن ودر مقام متحصن شدن قورغاداغوسیدور متحصن خواهم شد قورغاداغونکدر متحصن خواهی شد

قورغاداغوسیدور متحصن خواهد شد قورغاداغای وقورغاداسه وقورغاداسون قورغاداغولوق متحصن شدنی قورغاداغای بز قورغادالیک متحصن شویم قورغادا

غودیلک نوبین وقورغادادیلک متحصن شدیم قورغاناق مع النون متعدی بمعنی رسیدن قورقونوق ترسیدن تسلیم شدن قورقادور ترسیدن [illegible]

وقورقادار بمعنی حاصل مصدر هم می آید قورقغان وقورقارغان وقورقایدورغان ترسنده وترسیده وبمعنی مصدر هم می آیند قورقو وقورقغیل

مفرد مخاطب فعل امر قورقما وقورقماغیل مفرد مخاطب فعل نهی قورقونک وقورقونکیز وقورقونکلار جمع مخاطب فعل امر قورقمانک وقورقمانکیز

قورقمانکلار جمع مخاطب فعل نهی قورقامین وقورقارمین وقورقایدورمین وقورقادم میترسم الشاهد علی الثالث شعر اول قوتلیغ ... [illegible]

... هر ساعت کیم ... ترسیده [illegible] قورقوب وقورقوپ وقورقوپ وقورقمیش ترسیده

قورقمیشین ترسیده اش را قورقیشانک ترسیده قورقماس نمیترسد قورقماسلیغ نترسیدن قورقماس بولسا نترسیده [illegible]

قورقادورمیش بولغانا ترسیده باشد قورقا قورقا ترسان ترسان وبدون تکرار هم مستعملست قورقایو آیا بترسم وبترسد [illegible]

نترسید قورقماناق وقورقغایز وقورقغای بز قورقالیق قورقالینک بترسیم قورقغالی برای ترسیدن وتا ترسیده قورقغاج چون ترسید وبترسد

وبعض ترسیدن قورقغوچی ترسنده وآنرا قورقاق هم کویند قورقغونچه وقورقغونچه وقورقغانچه تا ترسیدن ودر مقام ترسیدن قورقغوسیدور [illegible]

خواهم ترسید قورقغونکدر خواهی ترسید قورقغوسیدور خواهد ترسید قورقغولوق ترسیدنی قورقغای وقورقسه وقورقسون وقورقه وقورقه [illegible]

بترسد قورقغودیلک وقورقادیلک ترسیدیم وچنانکه ترسیده شود چنانکه در تاریخ بابری شاهد اول مذکورست کرتیلکا آلغیرضه

سیقغوسیز قورقغودیلک واقعه ایردی قورقغودیلک توبین وقورقادیلک مین ترسیده ام قورقوتماق مع الکاف مصدر متعدی است بمعنی

ترسانیدن وصیغ آن بدستور بانضمام تای قورشاتماق اشتقاق می یابد قورقوتماق مع الکاف باهم ترسیدن وصیغ آن بالمیش قورقیش اشتقاق [illegible]

قورونماق باشباع ضمه بمعنی خشک شدن وبلا اشباع بمعنی منع وحراست کردن بود قورودوق خشک شدیم ومنع وحراست کردیم

قورویدور خشک میشود ومنع وحراست میشود چنانکه شاهد بر اول معنی ثانی در تاریخ بابری مذکورست که ... [illegible]

اوچینک بجاملا ... کم قوریغانی ودر قوروق بمعنی حاصل مصدر هم می آید چنانکه در صحیفه سیاره بمعنی خشک شدن کوید شعر بولوب [illegible]

تا فلک تاندین ... ولی العلی ... کمر بازینک ... آیلی مجنون در وصف ضعف وناتوانی ... لیلی بمعنی منع وحراست کردن

کوید شعر ... قوروغان وقورودیغان ... خشک شونده وخشک شده [illegible]

علی الاول بالمعنی الثانی شعر ... قوروغان ... [illegible]

ونیز در صحیفه الابرار فرماید شعر صدف تاکهر آنما ... آنینک ... ایرور ... کهر دین ... ایرور اول صدف [illegible]

ایرور تینک اول وبر قوروغان کشف وبمعنی منع وحراست کننده وکرده نیز باشد وبمعنی مصدر هم می آیند قورو وقوروغیل مفرد [illegible]

از فعل امر قوروما وقوروماغیل مفرد مخاطب فعل نهی قورونک وقورونکیز وقورونکلار جمع مخاطب فعل امر ونیز ... آراستن ونصب کردن [illegible]

شدن وقوروق کردن چنانکه ... قورواق وقوروناق مذکور شد قورومانک وقورومانکیز وقورومانکلار جمع مخاطب فعل نهی قورویو [illegible]

قوروبین وقورویدورمین وقورودم خشک میشوم ومنع وحراست میکنم قوروماس خشک نمیشوم ومنع وحراست نمیکنم قوروب وقوروبان

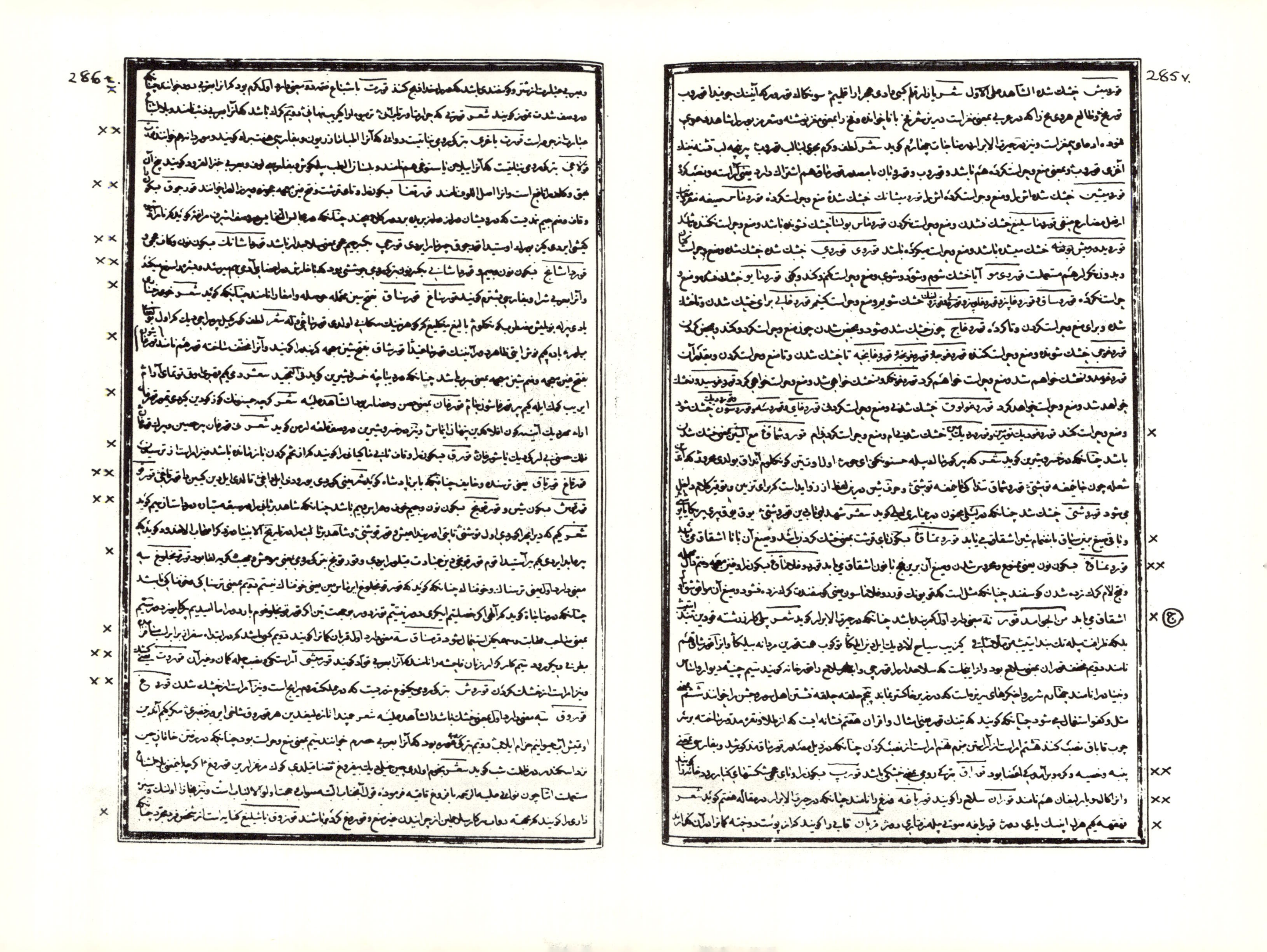

قوریش خشک شده الشاهد ملا الاول شعر یا ذلم قلم کبی وادی هجر ادا قلیم سونکالاد قورغو که آیینک جویندا قوروب
قورغوی ظالم هر ویغ زاکه در عربی بمعنی غزالست در این شعر غیر با ما خوانده و منع را بمعنی غریز نوشته و شعر بر موجب شاهد هم عیب
قوید اداهای بیغزالست و نیز در حیرة الابرار در مناجات چهارم گوید شعر لطف و کرم بجوی الباب قوروب پرنچه لب تشنه تینک
آغزی قوروب و بمعنی منع و حراست کرده هم باشد و قوروب و قوروبان با مصدر قورماق هم اشتراک دارد یعنی آراسته و نصب کرده
قوروییشن خشک شده اش یا و منع و حراست کرده اش یا قوروییشانک خشک شده منع و حراست کرده قورونما صیغه مضارع
از فعل مضارع منفی قورونما سلین خشک نشدن و منع و حراست نکردن قوروماس بولسا خشک نشونده باشد و منع و حراست نکننده باشد
قورویدورویش بوغه خشک میشده باشد و منع و حراست میکرده باشد قوروی قوروی خشک شدن خشک شده و منع و حراست کردن
دیدون تکرار هم مستعملست قوروی مو آیا خشک شوم و شوید و شوی و منع و حراست کنم و کنید و کنی قورونا بو خشک شده هم و منع و
حراست کرده قوروساق قوروغاینز و قوروغاینز و قورغالی و قورغولیک خشک شویم و منع و حراست کنیم قوروغالی برای خشک شدن و تا خشک
شده و برای منع و حراست کردن و تا کرده قوروغاج چون خشک شد و شود و بمحض شدن چون منع و حراست کرد و کند و بمحض کردن
قوروغوچی خشک شونده و منع و حراست کننده قوروغوچه قوروغوچه و قوروغاینچه تا خشک شدن و تا منع و حراست کردن و بمقدار آن
قوروغودور تخشک خواهم شد و منع و حراست خواهم کرد قوروغوسی تخشک خواهی شد و منع و حراست خواهی کرد قوروغوسیدور تخشک
خواهد شد و منع و حراست خواهد کرد قوروغولوق خشک شدنی و منع و حراست کردنی قوروغای و قوروسون قوروسون خشک شود
و منع و حراست کند قوروغودیک قوریین و قوروددیک خشک شدیم و منع و حراست کردیم قوروشماق مع الغیر بمعنی خشک شدن
باشد چنانچه در خسرو شیرین گوید شعر که بیر کوردا لدیله حسنونکنی ای جورت اولا وتیتین کونکلوم آنداق بولدی محروق که اند
شعله چون خاخیغه توتشق قوروشماق سکا که خاخیغه توتشق و حرف شین در این لفظ از زوایداست که برای تزیین و توقیر کلام داخل
میشود قوروشی خشک شد چنانچه در لیلی مجنون در مناجات لیلی گوید شعر شهد لبدا بین قوروشی یوق یوق قیری بر کیا یا یو
و باقی صیغ بر سیاق ماضمام شین اشتقاق میباید قوروتماق بکون تا قورت بمعنی خشک کردن باشد و صیغ آن با تا اشتقاق میباید
قوروتماق بکون نون یعنی ممنوع و محروس شدن و صیغ آن بر نهج با نون اشتقاق میباید قورود و فلحما آق بکون لام و فتح معجمه و تم و دال
و فتح لام کرک زده شدن گوسفند چنانچه مثل است که قوی بونک قورود طلحما سون یعنی گوسفند کرک زده [illegible] و صیغ آن بر وفق شوی
اشتقاق میباید من الجوامد قورن نه معنی دارد اول کمربند باشد چنانچه در حیرة الابرار گوید شعر بیلی کار زدشته قودین تبند
بلکه نظر افت بیله تن بندایتیب [illegible] کرنیب سیاح لار دیلی ایل دین الیکا توکوب هستم رین مردانه بیلیکا و از آن قورشاق هم
نامند دویم مخفف قوران بمعنی سلاح بود و ازاینجاست که سلاحدار را قورچی و انبار سلاح را قورخانه گویند سیم چینه دیوار و انبار
و بنیاد را نامند چهارم شهر و احنکرهای بیرونست که در غیر یخاکستر نماید پنجم حلقه حلقه نشستن اهل بیرو جشن را خوانند ششم
مثل و کفو و استعمال بیه شود چنانچه گویند که تینک قور یعنی مثال و اقران هفتم نشانه ایست که از طلا و نقره مدور ساخته بر سر
چوب قاباق نصب کند هشتم اراسته از آراستن بنیم هشتم اراسته نصب کردن چنانچه در ذیل مصدر قورناق مذکور شد و بفارسی یعنی
پنبه و خصیه و کرمو بر آمدگی اعضا بود قوراق بترکی دو معنی خشکی باشد قوروب بکون را و نای عجمی شکستهای کنار رود خانه را گویند
و از اکالحو یار ایغان هم نامند قوران سلاح را گویند قوربافه منع را نامند چنانچه در حیرة الابرار در مقاله هفتم گوید شعر
فقعم کیم هر ایشنک یاری دمش قوربافه موی چیله قارتای دمش قربان قابی را گویند که از پوست دوخته کمان را در آن نگاه دارند

و بعربی حنظل بیابان و گوسفندی باشد که صحرا را خراب کند قورت با شباع ضمه سه معنی دارد اول کرم بود که از ابریشم بی [illegible] دود خوانند چنانچه
در وصف شدت تموز گوید شعر قورتی که جیلارتا و رتلیلار توتی ترسوی اوراکی بیمایی دویم کرک باشد که آن را بعربی ذئب نامند و بلاد انساب
منار خزر چه است قورت باغری بترکی رومی نباتیست دوایی که آن را المیانا در یونانی و بفارسی هفت برادر گویند و مهر دار نرم خوانند
قولاچی بترکی رومی نباتیست که آن را ایلادن یا سوقی هم نامند و بلسان العطب پیلکوش و بفارسی لیه و بعربی خبز القرود گویند بیخ آن
حبق و کلف [illegible] است و آن را اصل الیوقی نامند قورقتا بکون قاف و تاء قرشت و فتح میم بمعنی جونه و صیغ الماخوانند قدجوق بکون
قاف و ضم جیم نمدیست که درویشان [illegible] بر بدن بندند چنانچه در مجالس النفایس در وصف اشرف مراغه گوید گر نامراد
کیشو ایرمکیز بیرله اوستیدا قدجوق جیرزار ایردی قورچپ بکسر جیم هم بمعنی لاجه دار باشد قوچاشانک بکون نون و کاف عجمی
قوراشاغ بکون نون و جیم و قوراشانی بکسر نون بترکی رومی جوشنی بود که با خار خارچه را اعضای آدمی هم پیوندد و بشره را سنج میکند
و آن را بعربی شرا و بفارسی پشترم گویند قورساغ قورساق بفتح سین مهمله حوصله و امغاق را نامند چنانچه گوید شعر خوبورخنا
یادی ییرله بولیش منظور بکه نکلوم بالیغ منکلیغ کرکو هر نینک سکانی اولدی قورساغی که شعر لطف که کیل پیرا جو جیلک کر اول یو
بیلمه باده کیم نوش ایتی ظاهر دور آنینک قورساغیدا قورشاق بفتح شین معجمه کمر را گویند و آن را مخفف شالخته قور هم نامند قورشا
بفتح میم بجیم و ضم شین معجمه بمعنی سر باشد چنانچه در دیباچه خسرو شیرین گوید در التحمید شعر دی کیم قورشا قیم توتمای آدام
ایر یب کنک ایله کیم بر قورغاشونجام قورغان بمعنی حصن و حصار بود الشاهد ملیه شعر کیم جیبی نینک کوزکودین کوهی تیموره قورغان
اراه مرده یک آینه کون املاک دین پنهان ایماس دیز در خسرو شیرین در وصف قلعه ارمن گوید شعر نی قورغان بر حصین و برج قورغا
فلک حسن بی لر [illegible] با شوقرغان قورق بکون را و قاف ثانی باکیانرا گویند که از چشم کردن باز داشته باشد و نیز ایراست از ترسیدن
قورقاغ قورقاق یعنی ترسنده و خایف چنانچه بابر پادشاه گوید شعر یعنی کبردی یوردنی ایلنی ما لدی ایل دین کیس [illegible] قورقاغی قورق
قورقوش بکون شین و قورقونج بکون نون و جیم خوف و هراس و بیم باشد چنانچه شاهد بر تلفظ اول صیغه مستانه در داستان بیم گوید
شعر کیم که دیرایم انکوری اول توتشق تاپتی امرسید لعیش و قورقوش و شاهد بر ثانی [illegible] تاریخ الانبیا در ذکر اصحاب الاخدود گوید که
بر جا بیرایدی کیم بر آستیدا توم قورقونج و بر عبادت میلوایدی و قورقونج بترکی رومی بمعنی موحش و مهیب که بیه لفظ قورقونچلوغ سه
معنی دارد اول یعنی ترسناک و خوفناک چنانچه گوید که قورقونچلوغ ایرماس مین یعنی خوفناک نیستم دویم بمعنی ترسناکی و خوفناکی باشد
چنانچه در مناجات گوید کم آلوی اکر خصلتیم ایکری ده [illegible] نیستم قورقونچلوغوم با [illegible] ما امیدیم [illegible] سیم
بمعنی صاحب مطابت و [illegible] استعمال شود قورساق سه معنی دارد اول قربان کمان را گویند دویم کویا [illegible] که در ابتدا سفر ازبر ابر [illegible] سیم
بطرف دیگر رود سیم کار که از زبان ماجشه را نامند که آن را بعربی فواد گویند قورشقی آراستگی و نصب چله کمان و غیر آن قوروت کیند
و نیز اراستن خشک کردن قوروش بترکی رومی بمعنی نمدیست که در ملک عجم رایج است و نیز آراستن خشک شدن قوروع
قوروق سه معنی دارد اول بمعنی خشک باشد الشاهد ملیه شعر چند اتا زلیفدین هر قوروق شاخی ایره خضری سکر کیم آندین
او تمیش آب حیوانیم حرام ایلاب دویم بترکی شدیده بود که آن را بعربی حرم خوانند سیم بمعنی منع و حراست بود چنانچه در متن خاقانی حسن
ندا سحکنده در ظلمات شب گوید شعر [illegible] جیلک بیغمبر [illegible] قصا قیلدی کوک مرغزار تین قوروغ [illegible]
مستعملست اما چون نوایی علیه الرحمه با قوروغ قافیه فرموده [illegible] و لو لالتناب است و نیز جانوا اولنک و سبز
زار را گویند که بجهت دعامیه [illegible] قوروق با شلیغ کنایه است از شخص فرد و مجرد چنانچه

مجالس النفایس در وصف سید جعفر نوربخش گفته که پادشاه سیلداپش بیلا آلتون تیلرغاق وایکی بوزخو طراشلیغ بامحمد الکیم
برقوروق باشلیغ بجرو کیشی ایردی وجه معاش ایچون مقتصیلدی قورونتای یعنی بود خانه خشک وبزنام مونولت که [illegible]
یکتفا دو کابل واقعست قورو قلوق بمعنی خشکی باشد قورولتای بضم را وسکون لام وتای جیمی وفتح تای قرشت بالف کشیده و
قوریلتای بکسر را لغت مغولی بمعنی مجمع عظیم بود که برای مشاوره وکنکاش انعقاد یابد چنانچه در ظفرنامه گوید شعر سانیا [illegible]
وقوریل جونه خان قورولتای [illegible] قیتره جلدا دالایغ وصاف در مکتوبی که از جانب سلطان احمد برلاس
شاه شده این عبارت مندرج است که جعلت هذه المملکة علینا واهدی عقیلتها الینا ما جمع عندنا فی قوریلتای المبارک و هو
المجمع الذی ینعقد فیه ندا را جمیع الاخوان والاولاد ومقدمی العساکر وزعماء الاجناد اکرچه وصاف در تواریخ چنگیزخانی
همه جا قوریلتای بکسر را ضبط کرده اما بضم را اصح و اوضح است قورون بمعنی وقت وهنگام بود و کچ قورون یعنی بی وقت
چنانچه گوید شعر سایه ثابت نشاطینک بولسانا نک یوقکیلم یرحث کچ قورون شاه اولسانا همان کیمسه کا بیلا خبج [illegible]
المحبه [illegible] شیخ ابو علی دقاق گوید که هر کون افشام قورون تامغه چقارا ایردی وکونش باتار چاغی [illegible] ایردی [illegible]
بو کون نیچوک ایردی نیک [illegible] نوشته که امرا [illegible] حفظ کن قوریها بری زن [illegible] دیوانه بستر اکوید الشاهد
شعر کونکاتا کوری خیالینک [illegible] آهیم [illegible] باغلامیش مین [illegible] کاندین آنکا [illegible]
سلطان محمود گوید شعر [illegible] کیب باغ وبستان [illegible] قوریا [illegible] بمعنی خراب وآباد
نوشته [illegible] شاهد آمده [illegible] خراب کرده گفته که بوزوغ قوریا یعنی خراب [illegible] قرتیق بفتح راو سکون یا
جلی [illegible] کلاه [illegible] آنکه [illegible] الشاهد علیه شعر [illegible] نازکلوکیدین کورتیق
[illegible] سلطان حسین میرزا فرماید شعر اولاشیل تونلوغ [illegible]
[illegible] قرتیق [illegible] من المشتقات قوزغالماق [illegible] بمعنی حرکت
باشد الشاهد علی الاول شعر [illegible] [illegible] قوزغالماق قوزغاتماق
قوزغالتوق [illegible] قوزغاتور وقوزغاتا [illegible] الشاهد علی الاول شعر کونکلونی [illegible] پریشان [illegible]
[illegible] قوزغالادبولور [illegible] الشاهد علی الثانی شعر [illegible]
قوزغایدورش [illegible] [illegible] مجبوب القلوب گوید [illegible]
قوزغاتقه وقوزغاد [illegible] بمعنی [illegible] الشاهد [illegible] مجبوب القلوب
[illegible] گوید که [illegible] قوزغاغان وقوزغالغان وقوزغایدورغان
قوزغاتغان [illegible] الشاهد علی الاول بالمعنی الاول شعر کونکلونا [illegible]
[illegible] قوزغاغان [illegible] قوزغاو وقوزغاغیل [illegible] مفرد بصیغة المبالغه
الشاهد علی الثالث شعر [illegible] آشفته [illegible] آفاق اولوسین قوزغات قوزغاتما
قوزغاتاغیل وقوزغاتماغیل [illegible] بصیغة المبالغه قوزغاتنک وقوزغاتکیز وقوزغاتکلار [illegible] قوزغاتینک [illegible]
جمع [illegible] قوزغاتماغیز [illegible] قوزغاتماغیز [illegible] جمع بصیغة المبالغه قوزغاتای
قوزغادسیم [illegible] قوزغالام [illegible] قوزغادسین [illegible] قوزغاتامن [illegible] قوزغاتامان

برمنتیم قوزغاب وقوزغابان وقوزغابیش وقوزغایتب وقوزغیلیبان وقوزغاغیش بمعنی الشاهد علی الاول [illegible]
قوزغالیب کونکل [illegible] چون [illegible] قوزغالیب قوزغابیش وقوزغاغیشیں بمعنی برخاستن [illegible]
قوزغالتماق بمعنی [illegible] قوزغاب [illegible] قوزغابیز [illegible] بمعنی [illegible] قوزغالماس [illegible]
قوزغالماسلیغ بمعنی برنخاستن قوزغالماس [illegible] قوزغالیدور [illegible] قوزغایدور [illegible] باشد قوزغایو
قوزغای قوزغاتا وقوزغاتا بمعنی [illegible] قوزغالایو وقوزغایمو آیا [illegible] قوزغامایو
قوزغامایو بمعنی [illegible] قوزغالیب [illegible] قوزغالیب [illegible] قوزغاتقا [illegible] قوزغانقای [illegible] قوزغانیلی
قوزغانیلیک بمعنی [illegible] قوزغالماق [illegible] قوزغاتاج قوزغاتاج [illegible]
[illegible] قوزغاغوچ [illegible] قوزغالغوچی [illegible] قوزغالغوچیه [illegible]
[illegible] قوزغالغوسی [illegible] قوزغالغوسی [illegible] خواهد [illegible] قوزغالغوسید
قوزغالغوسیدور [illegible] قوزغالغولوق وقوزغالغولوق [illegible] قوزغالغاسو [illegible] قوزغالغاسی [illegible] قوزغاتقای
قوزغانمو وقوزغاتقه وقوزغاتسون وقوزغاتدیلر [illegible] الشاهد علی الثانی شعر [illegible] قوزغاسه [illegible]
[illegible] قوزغالماق [illegible] قوزغالماق
بسکون الام و قوزغالیشماق بکسر اللام یعنی [illegible] شدن الشاهد علی الاول شعر [illegible]
قوزغالماق [illegible] یعنی مضطرب شدن نوشته
[illegible] قوزغالدی [illegible] الشاهد علی الثانی شعر جان وکونکول [illegible] کیلکاچ
[illegible] قوزغالیشتی [illegible] قوزغالغان وقوزغالدورغان وقوزغالیشقان وقوزغالیشورغان
قوزغالیشادورغان [illegible] الشاهد علی الاول المعنی الثانی شعر [illegible]
[illegible] قوزغالغان قوزغالماسیز [illegible] قوزغالیشاسیز [illegible] چنانچه در [illegible]
از جانب [illegible] خطاب [illegible] گوید الشاهد علی الثانی شعر [illegible] قوزغالماسیز [illegible]
قوزغالغودیک [illegible] قوزغالیشغو [illegible] الشاهد علی الاول المعنی الثانی شعر [illegible]
[illegible] عقل وهوش وجان وکونکلوم [illegible] قوزغالغودیک [illegible]
اشتقاق [illegible] قوز [illegible] ترکی [illegible]
[illegible] قوزالاق بفتح زا ولام بالف کشیده وسکون نون [illegible] قوزالیب [illegible]
[illegible] قوزغالاق [illegible] بکسر لام وسکون شین معجمه [illegible]
باشد چنانچه [illegible] گوید الشاهد علی الاول شعر [illegible] خیل [illegible] قوزغالان [illegible]
[illegible] گوید الشاهد علی الثانی شعر [illegible] قوزغالیش [illegible] قوزغون
بسکون [illegible] ونون وضم غین معجمه کلاغ سیاه [illegible] چنانچه [illegible] گوید شعر [illegible] قوزغون [illegible]
قوشی [illegible] وازاغونک هم گویند قوزغی [illegible] شعر [illegible] جیران [illegible]
کباب [illegible] مانند [illegible] فرزند [illegible] آدمی را هم گویند چنانچه از زبان فرهاد [illegible] خطاب [illegible] گوید شعر

287v

بو وحشی‌غه خطاب ایتیب‌سه قونده دیب بو سیکنی ساغینیب‌سه یا لغوزهم دیب بو تیکنی ساغینیب‌سه یا لغوز و دیبدیب قونده قولاغ اسم
جانوریست که از اجزای تیشه خوانند چنانکه میر لیلی و مجنون گوید شعر مرا ایستادی چو نعل فراقی دشت قونده و بولمه قونده قولاغ
و آن بری و جنبانیدن ... میباشد مسکن و غیشان صفراوی و جهت نفع خمار و تقویت جگر نافع است مع التین المعجمه من الثقات توسماق
بمعنی کردن باشد و صیغه آن موافق ثقل و الاستعمال ... یابد من الجواهد توسقون بترکی رومی قوشقو بمعنی پاردم بود توسوندی
بضم سین و سکون نون بترکی رومی بمعنی ... وغیشان باشد مع التاء المعجمه من المثلثات توسماق دو معنی دارد اول اموات ... شود
چنانکه از زبان شیرین در ... فرهاد گوید شعر کیمی قوشما مدام ... دیب ... دویم بمعنی همراه کردن و
آمیختن باشد الشاهد علیه شعر ... ایکی سین پیر پری کا قوشماق ایماس ... و بالمجاز بنام دواند
کنند قوشمادی نسود و همراه بکرد الشاهد علیه بالمعنی الثالث شعر ... کردون نولی کمهری نالم قوشماغی کوبلک
اهل بحث ... قوشا ... دود میستاید و همراه سیکند و قوشار بمعنی ناجل و مصدر هم می‌آید توشغان ... قوشا دورمان ...
نسود و همراه کنند و همراه کرد چنانکه شاهد براولها بمعنی همراه کنند گوید شعر عشق ... قوشغان
با غیر ... ناشیغه و بمعنی مصدر هم می‌آید چنانکه شاهد براول بمعنی همراه کن گوید شعر غم اوتی ...
تیلاهین خانیمه ... قوشنانک قوش ولیکن ... قوشمای ...
قوشمایل مفرد مخاطب ... چنانکه شاهد براول بمعنی همراه کن گوید شعر غم اوتی ... خانیمه قوشوك
قوشوغوهقوشوغلار جمع مخاطب ... قوشماغ قوشمابحر قوشماغلار جمع مخاطب ... قوشابین قوشار ... قوشا ... قوشالکیستایر
و همراه میکنم قوشمان ... نیستایم و همراه ... قوشوب قوشوباغ قوشمیش سود و همراه کرده چنانکه ... خسرو شیرین
از زبان فرهاد خطاب ... گوید الشاهد علی الاول المعنی الاول شعر قوشوب ... تایوا ...
الحیه ... ذکر شیخ ابو اللیث ... قوشوب ...
... المعنی الثانی شعر ... قوشوب باشلار
قوشمیشین ستوده ... و همراه کرده ... قوشمیشانک ستوده و همراه کرده قوشوبیز ... ستوده ایم و همراه کرده ایم قوشماس نمی‌ستاید
و همراه نمیکند قوشماسلیغ نستودن و همراه نکردن قوشماس ... ستایند ... باشد و همراه نکننده باشد قوشا ... میستوده باشد
و همراه میکرده باشد قوشا قوشا ستایش کنان و همراه کنان و بدون تکرار هم مستعملست قوشار قوشابین بستایم و بستاید و بستانید
ستوده و همراه کم و کند و کنی و کرده چنانکه شاهد براول بمعنی همراه کم ... شیرین ... فرهاد گوید شعر ...
ناهیم ... قوشای ... قوشا ... همراه قوشایمو آیا بستایم و بستاید و بستاند و آیا همراه کم و کند و کنی قوشمایو ستوده و همراه
قوشاق قوشغایز و قوشغاویز و قوشلو قوشالیك بستایم و همراه کنیم قوشغالی برای ستودن و ناستوده و برای همراه کردن و ناهمراه کرده قوشغاچ
چون بستاید و ستوده ... و چون همراه کرده ... کردن قوشقوچ ستاینده و همراه کننده قوشغوچه و قوشغوبخه و قوشغابچه
تا ستودن ... تا همراه کردن ... قوشغومدور ... خواهیم ستود ... همراه خواهیم کرد قوشغوسکرود خواهید ستود و همراه خواهید
کرد قوشغوسیدور خواهند ستود و همراه خواهند کرد قوشغولوق ستودن و همراه کردن قوشغای قوشه و قوشسه و قوشسون قوشسونلار ستاید
و همراه کند قوشغودیك ... ستونیدم و همراه کردنیدم قوشولماق بضم شین و سکون لام و قوشوشماق بضم شین اول کشتن
تان همراه شدن و آمیخته شدن الشاهد علی الاول شعر ... ایرکا بن عشق اهلی ... قوشولماق ...

288r

قودون آیرلمادی قوشولدی و قوشوشق همراه شد الشاهد علی الاول شعر قوشولدی گوز ... هم ایت کوتارم
بولدی قاان ... از زوج و بات ... صیغ بریغی ان قوشوشلاق ... قوشوشماق باشیر الشقاق ... قوشولور نافع و قوشوشتور ناقع
مصدر متعدیست بمعنی ... همراه ساختن و آمیخته کردن قوشولدرغوچ قوشوشتورغوچ همراه کننده و آمیخته کننده چنانکه
با ول ... محبوب القلوب گوید ... مقصود ... واسطه پیر ... قوشولدرغوچ
هم ... قیسیله ... اشقاق ... توشلاماق دو اتابه شدن و اسب ... بیدلرا کرفتن و آن لفظ ...
... ایمی سکیدی ... توشلاتاق توشلادی بیدلر کرفت توشلاجون توشلاید و در
بیدلیت ... توشلار ... توشلاغار توشلاغای ... بیدلر بکیرند و بیدلر کرفته و ...
هم می‌آید توشلاد و توشلاغیل مفرد غائب ... توشلاما و توشلادنا غیل مفرد ... توشلاغیل توشلاغیوز توشلا
جمع ... توشلاماندی توشلاغای ... توشلاغوسی ... توشلاغان ... بیدلر میکرد
توشلاسلو توشلاماس بیدلر ... توشلاغیب ... توشلاغیش بیدلر کرفته چنانکه شاهد براول ... الملوك گفته ذکر
ایچیش بابلیک گوید ... آنداغ ... توشلاغاچی ...
... توشلابین بیدلر کرفتن توشلاغیلیك
برکرفته توشلابیز و توشلاب توشیز بیدلر کرفته ایم توشلاماس بیدلر نکیرد توشلاماسلیغ بیدلر نکرفتن توشلاماز
بیدلر نکیرنده باشد توشلاید ... بیدلر میکرفته باشد توشلاو یوغ توشلای توشلایه بیدلر بکیرد ... بیدلر
هم مستعملست توشلایمو آیا بیدلر بکیرم و بکیرد و بکیری توشلامایو بیدلر نمیکرفته توشلاشاق توشلاغایز توشلاغای
توشلانک بیدلر بکیریم توشلاغالی برای بیدلر کرفتن و تا بر کرفته توشلاغاچ چون بیدلر کرفت و بکیرد و مجیز کرفتن توشلاغوچی
بیدلر بکیرنده توشلاغوچه توشلاغوبخه توشلاغوچاچی تا بیدلر کرفتن و بعد از آن توشلاغومدور بیدلر خواهیم کرفت توشلاغوسکروسیدور
خواهید کرفت توشلاغوسیدور بیدلر خواهید کرفت توشلاغولوق بیدلر کرفتن توشلاغای توشلاسه و توشلاسون و توشلاسون
بیدلر بکیرد توشلاغودیك ... توشلاغیب بیدلر کرفتم من الجواهد قوش چهار معنی دارد اول ... کویند دوم بمعنی جفت
بود چنانکه گوید شعر ... ایکیسینکا قوش ... جمع ... بالمجاز
را کویند ... الشاهد علیه شعر ... قوش ... ایکی ... قوش
در لسان الطیر ... گوید شعر ... قوش ... چهارم جفت کاو ... مانند
چنانکه ... محبوب القلوب ... دهقان گوید ... ایکی هم زور پهلوان ... سونوب ... روان بو
... الشاهد علیه شعر ... تیب طفل
اقسام قوش ... ایتکاندین ... شعر ... قوشی ... کل شیء ...
دوش ... بمعنی ... شاهد آورده ... قوش اتکی بفتح الف و سکون تای قرشت
... المبارز الطیب ... توشاق بفتح
بمعنی ... قوشانت ... و تای قرشت ... قوش ... فرستند
کمان ... کویند ... تاج ... قوش پچی ... کویند قوش ...

288

X

یعنی مکار و قحبه خانه چنانکه مجالس النفایس در وصف میر حسین علی جلایر گفته که قوشچی بواندی امیرلیقده و پروانچی بولدی قوشچی لیق

مار و اول نشان الصنایع یعنی آن مهرچوبی است عظیم بر کرشمه براق با دامهای شش صد یعنی وطولانی دو در جوف هریک دانه از دنده خوبی در دراز

شبیه بزبان گنجشک و مسکن یا لاجیم غلیظ و در بر چهلو و کمر و رحم نالند تقسیم نوعی از طعام باشد و آن چنانست که خمیر را مثل زبان مرغ ببرند

در روغن و شکر بپزند و بر روی طعام افشانند قوش غنچه یعنی مرغک چنانکه در ذیل جنون در وصف طعام گوید شعر هم قوش غنچه

چقور بر له پوچ هم بولور بلاچه قوشه محمد دش قوشوق یکچمچ تصغیرات در مضرت نوعی در منزل کلاه از آن در تصحیح لغت

آن گوید که قوشوقا رخو شتان اصولیدا شایع دمر واو لسود اعرابی ننگ توه سوار جمدی لابی منزه سلام دل مبیح محمد وقد

واقع بولور و آیینک اصلی بو نوع دم کیم سحر وه که اول الکی سحر به در مجمع دارغ فرهنه هم این مطالعه اوتیوجم حلیم آنچی ویتر

در حیرت الابرار در وصف سخن گوید شعر آنکلا یا بین سوزدا تو یوق بحریته تا بیتی تو یوق یلکه قوشوق بحرینه توشوقه تفسیر ای تو شوق

در این سطر توشوقا بالای قریش خوانده و شعر را بصواب شاهد آمرده سهو کرده است لفظ الجراحیت توشو تلوق ممزوج و آمیخته

بد و معنی بو عاملی چاشنکاه و اگر نه تقسیم بمعنی رخیت و طینت بود چنانکه در مقدمه سکندر به مراج داد ز سکندر به سواد کوک ستاره

بود فرماید شعر مینک خیلیمه کیلدی تمثلوق ضرا یکیم اول توشنه کیدی دیوا و لغای محیذا توسما ز بکوز شین مراد حامله ملیم الف

کشیده بر که روی صورت چوب که آنرا باحبلهای آهنین تعبیه کرده بهم پیوسته شالدان یدست بگیرند در دکان جلا را اینکه

شکار کنند توشون بکوزشین و کبر نون همسایه را گویند اشاهد علیه شعر تو ترکه جو جاحبن کمر لیرا سینک کاننا

دعک لدانا الدیلمه تو شونی اویبا قوم بمالکیم و لطایف هروی تو شونی را در مصرع اخیر از نسخه سقیمی توشنی خوانده و توشنی ایضا صحیح تصور کرده

چنانکه در ذیل جه کو لدا نا التشرع طاعه شد و نیز در ترجمه اربعین گوید شعر کیم کیر مومن توروسا جا نیدا ناخای کم امونی توق و توشی

بو لنلماج و همچنین در نسایم المحبة در ذکر عبد الرحمن اسفراینی فرماید که جو تو بولو دل وجه لا ربی آوج آوقج توشی لای جودکاسا

تو شون قوچ صبکی را مانند چنانکه در سبعه سیاره گوید شعر ولمنکا جو اختصار منسوب بر بن الی ایوش

بیهاوه وار دو نیشن کوبر نیکلیغ یمیش لار دهیلتی توشون یل جمعه هر یا بینینک شولیق توشه دوچ را گویند که صحرا لشان بهم رسد

ومعانی مشتغه هم حاری کند در ذیل معسر توشماق منذ کمه شد مع الطا قطاس کاو جویی بود که دم آنرا بر تزیین بر گذر ای سانچنی

حصب بند و منز گفته اند که گاو دشت کوههای ما بین ملک ختا و هندوستان میباشد و مؤلف برهان الماطع از لغت این روی نوشته که

همان قوتان بو دکه آنرا مرغ سقا نامند مع الغین المعجمه قوغ برضک بوع ترکی و مثل قرغاش بود قوغلاسه بکوغیندن فتح لام

و میم یعنی باتن خشک شده چنانکه در خاتمه محبوب القلوب گوید که تر تر بیحه الملک متماسا قوغلا مه او غیاث حرمیشم دهستی

الا لا له من المشتقات قولماق ح یعنی خواستن و طلب کردن باشد و معنی لفظ وجع و معنی در آنقدر داده اما عنقریب گفتن دویم از برای تکلم

دخترخواستن و بهویه معنی بهو کرده زیرا که همان بمعنی خواستن باشد لیم از انکه منه بود یا دختر یا غیر آن قولدوق خواستیم قولا دویم

بخواهد و قولار بمعنی فاعل مصدر هم می آید چنانکه بمعنی مصدر گوید شعر منغو بن چینقلی دیم نیتیب آخر لا بایت لای ان کیم

قولار منه منه عدوم لوق با غیورین نا نکرایت قولغان بمعنی لا جان بمعنی لا بدن زبان خواهنده و خواسته و بمعنی مصدر هم می آید قول و قولغیل

مفرد خاطب فعل امر قولغا ضافی ناجمه هم آمده چنانکه در ذیل جواسه منکه خواهد شد قولماو قولما غیل مفرد خاطب فعل نهی قولونک

قولونکیز و قولو نکلار جمع خاطب فعل امر قولمالیک قولماجز قولمانکلار جمع خاطب فعل نهی قولا ییرم قولا ییرمیز قولا ییرمیز قولادام

میخواهم قولمان و قولماس بمعنی نخواهم قولوب قولوران قولمیش خواسته چنانکه شاهد با بل اول در تاریخ الملوک گوید

کشتاسب قیصر نینک قیزی بیلا قولوب دعوا دین یانمدی قولمیش خواسته مشار الیه قولمیشانک خواسته قولوب به قولوب قوریت خواسته ام

قولماس نخواهد قولماسلیغ نخواستن قولماس بولسا نخواهنده باشد قولاعدوم یعنی آن بنای نخواهنده باشد قولا قولا خواهان بخواهان

و بدون تکرار هم مستعملست قولای قولایین بخواهم و بخواهد و بخواهی خواسته چنانکه در سبعه سیاره در حکایت فرخ شاه که

شاهد علی الاول المعنی الاول شعر شاه دیدی کی چشاه بولای خواجه سینک منهم فوج قولای و قولای بمعنی بخواهم نیز یا است شاهد

قولا یمو ایا بخواهم و بخواهد و بخواهی قولسا یو بخواسته قولسا و قولغای ز قولغای ز قولای قولانینک بخواهیم چنانکه در منهج علم

صحیح با نواز فرهاد گوید شاهد علی الرابع شعر اکو پونیتره مقتر آتین بولانیه ینتیبه کی بخیلیک منهمین قولابی قولمابی تا

خواستن و تاخواسته قولغاج چون خواست و بخواهد و بجز خواستن قولغوچی خواهنده قولغوچه قولغو غنچه قولغانچه تا خواستن

و بعد خواستن قولمدی خواهم خواست قولغوسید ای خواهی خواست قولغوکهای خواهند خواست قولغولوق خواستنی قولغات

قولغولنه و قولغولیغ یوق بولیت بخواهد قولغود بلت نورسی قولا ردیلت مین خواستوام قولداماغ دستگیری کردن قولدادوق دستگیری

کردیم قولداتور قولداید و دستگیری میکند و قولدار بمعنی فاعل و مصدر هم می آید قولدار بردی دستگیری میکرد چنانکه گوید شعر

قولدار ایردی سلف اول دم کیم نوایی بولسه مشت لطف ایتیب دم اهل اللهی سیکمرهنک قولدالیشغه قولدا مان و قولدامادی قولدایدی

دستگیری کننده و دستگیری کرده و بمعنی مصدر هم می آید قولداو قولداغیل مفرد مخاطب فعل امر شاهد علی الاول شعر زهر بازیدا هیکا

دهر چه قوبار بخاوید سوا لیتیب قولداپر اوفر کمیستا و ایمدی قولونگ قولداماو قولداماغیل مفرد مخاطب فعل نهی قولدانک و قولدانگیز

قولدانکلار جمع خاطب فعل امر چنانکه در سبعه سیاره گوید شاهد علی الثانی شعر کیم الیجا بیکی قولوم قولدانکیز سوز اللیسا ری

قولدانکیز قولدامانک قولدامانکیز قولدامانکلار جمع خاطب فعل نهی قولدایین قولداییز قولدای ییرم قولداییرمیز قولدارام دستگیری میکنم قولدا

قولدامس دستگیری نمیکنم قولدام قولدام قولدامیش دستگیری کرده قولدامیشین دستگیری کرده ماشیم قولدامیشانک دستگیری

کرده قولدایدی قولدالیب تورینز دستگیری کرده ایم قولداماس دستگیری نمیکند قولداماسلیغ دستگیری نکردن قولداماس بولسا

دستگیری نکرده باشد قولدایدور سیر تقه دستگیری میکرده باشد قولدایو قولدای قولدانای دستگیری کنان و بمعنی تکرار هم مستعملست

قولدایمو آیا دستگیری کنم و کند و کنی قولداسا یو دستگیری بکنم قولداسا تقو قولداغای و قولدا غای بز و قولدایلار دستگیری کنیم قولداغا

برای دستگیری کردن و تا کرده قولداماج چون دستگیری کرد و کند و بجز کردن قولداغوچی دستگیری کننده قولداغوچه قولداغونچه

قولداغانچه تا دستگیری کردن و بعد دستگیری کردن قولداغوسیدور دستگیری خواهم کرد قولداغوسیدور دستگیری خواهند کرد قولداغو

دستگیری خواهد کرد قولداغولوق دستگیری کردنی قولداغای قولداغای قولداغوچو و قولداولت دستگیری کند قولداغودیلت تورسی

قولداولدیلت مین دستگیری کرده ام قولداماغ مع الکاف صدر متعدی یعنی دستگیری نمودن قولداتیبه قولداتباو قولدا غیش دستگیر

زیرا که الشاهد علی الاول شعر دبرادایمس دست و ملزمان خویشدین او منجه بزم دین تلو لا دینق کمسو مراتب که قولدانیب یا ذیبع

بیرشیاق ملتمام نای قرشتا اشقاقی بابد قولداماق مع النون دستگیری یافتن و صنع آن بمستعملات اشتقاقی یا بد قولا ملاجتماق

بمعنی سرکوبی کردن چنانکه گوید شعر جو دردیدین قولاملاجتماق عجم سایه دم تکیه کا الشام شام قرت منعقد برد بو ارضه بولاه

سرکوبی کردیم قولاملاجتو و قولاملاجتاور سرکوبی میکند و قولاملاجتور بمعنی فاعل و مصدر هم می آید قولاملاجتغان و قولاملاجتوحاج و یصدا تنا

سرکوبی کننده و کرده و بمعنی مصدر هم می آید قولاملاجتاو قولاملاجتغیل مفرد مخاطب فعل امر قولاملاجتماو قولاملاجتما بلیم فیکا

فعل نهی قولاملاجتسانک و قولاملاجتکیز و قولاملاجتکلار جمع مخاطب فعل امر قولاملاجتمانک قولاملاجتمانکیز جمع مخاطب فعل نهی قولاملاجتاغای

290r.

289v.

10

تابعین ذوی ذو جسمو پرچ دین توکولدی غم اقرنا کیتی ارلمسند که مکحوله مالک باشد تونار ضد تونالر غال بمعنای املت
چنانچه در سبعه سیار در وصف صید امکی هارمر کو یلاشاهد علی الثانی شعر چون تونالر غال انه یتوا لجبر کا خلق برکیتی الار البلغ
برکا میتو لقمه دی تونالر غان را هم ازین شعر تمرغال بجلد فیم خوانده و شعر استکلف باین نحو موزون کرده که چونکه تمر غال انه تیوا ولجبر کا
تمرغال را بمعنی اخاله نوشته لفظ الفتراهیت تونا لاغ و تونا لاق بفتح میم و لام با الف کشیده شکل اخولته چنانچه در جنبل پستو شیم
از محبوب القلوب صرفه کرده قصته خان کوید که تیوه تونا الامین شا تاره آمدی دیکوچ مرکز سید اغی معتقد لاری آنی شاتقون آسر
بیکوجی قومبول بسکون میم و لام و نون یای ابجد بمعنی فوج و دسته باشد چنانچه در سد سکندری کوید شعر صف تورتدی قومبول ناکاکا
جو مه که بو قومبولی شر قایدی پری خرث و قونبول با نون هم باین معنی استعمال میشود و این لفظ عربی مترادف است چنانچه دو قومبولی
مع النون مذکور خواهد شد قوم با لیغی بترکی روی قاو تنقیص را کوینید قوم ال بترکی روی بمعنی ملک باشد چنانچه در شرح
قمراد سقال کوینید قومسی بسکون میم و کسر سین مهمله بترکی روی بمعنی خمان و مکار باشد قوملاغ و قوملاق ریکستان قومین پای
نامند چنانچه در سد سکندری در حالت نزع سکندر کوید شعر قومویه توشی تمسنده قوملا تقا و ذه تیلبیل ایچین آهنک قومرای
قوموریعه بضم میم و سکون رای مهمله بجلیتین و فتح عین معجمه سوچقه را کوینید مع النون من الملحقات قونماق بمعنی نشستن و منزل کردن باشد
قوندی نشست الشاهد علیه شعر برادکه قوندی کیچه امرکلیر دایاری آیینک کمنیدین اسیتو او چار نه بونی اخیلر بارآیینک قونار و قونا
می نشیند و قونلر بمعنی زمل و سفیدم هم می آید قونغان و قونار غان و قونادورغان نشسته و نشسته الشاهد علی الاول مع المعنی الثانی شعر
بر بو نوع جنون قوشلاری قونغان کیم صدش تاش کیم باقدیم مهر اول شمع سنکلاریکا و بمعنی نشسته هم می آید چنانچه شاهد برا ول علی با نه
کوید شعر تو لوغا ریلدی را اوچغدیم قونغا یا پوشتی چیبین نیک پرته دین برلی قونغان بیافلا با العقد قون قونغیل مفرد مخاطب
انهل ایر قونماو قونماغیل مفرد مخاطب المفعلیه قونونک و قونونکیز و قونونکلار جمع مخاطب المفعل ایر قونماننک و قونمانکیز و قونمانکلار
جمع مخاطب الفعلیه قونایین و قونالین و قونادورمین و قونماسمن بمعنی دارم مینشینم قونماد و قونماسمین نمینشینم قونوب و قونوبان و قونغونیش نشسته
و نشیتین نشسته اشرا قونغیشانک نشسته قونوبیز و قونوب توریز نشسته ایم قونماس بمی نشیند قونماسلیغ نشستن قونماس
نشستن باشد قونا قونا نشسته نشسته و بدون تکرار هم مستعملت قونای من آیا بنشینم بنشیند و بنشینی قونغایو نشسته
قونماق قونغایرم و قونغای پرد قونمالیقونا لینک برای نشستن و نا نشسته چنانچه در لسان الطیر فشان بیمرغ کوید
با المعنی الاول شعر آندایر نون قونغالی کا شانه یوق جسم قیلماقته سودا نه یوق قونغاج چونز نشست و نشیند بمجرد نشستن
قونقوجی نشیننده قونقوچه قونقوچه نعتا بچه تا نشستن و مقید نشستن قونقوسیدور نشواهم نشست قونقوسی کلدور خواهی نشست
قونقوسیدور خواهد نشست قونقولوق نشستنی قونغای و قونر قونسه و قونسونکوتومدیک بنشیند الشاهد علی الاول من سلطان حسین میرزا
شعر نقطه سویدا خال تیکوی اول البصیکونه اوزه یا آنکار او خشار کم قونغا شکر اوستیدا چیین قونغوسیدور قونار یک شوی اوزو
قونوشماق بضم نون و سکون شین معجمه با همنشستن و با هم منزل کردن و صیغ آن بصیغ او با مثنی اشتقاق می یابد قونغدورماق تشغید
نشاندن قونغدور بغی نشاند است الشاهد علیه من قصول با ملامحال رومیه شعر خالم تر لب جان پرور بحکم تلخلیک قونغدورد
که آتسه آنکا هیم قونقاتاغ بسکون نون و رای مهمله و فتح غین معجمه با الف کشیده مع الالف الامرغاکبدن و قونکار تاقیز با کاف عجمی
مستعملت قونغاردوق ازهاکندیم قونغلیهو قونغار ادور ازجا سیکند قونغار ابرمعنی ابولوم مسلم هم می آید قونغار غان قونغار
قونغار ادورکان ازجا کننده و ازجا کنده و بمعنی مسلم هم می آیند قونغار و قونغار غیل مفرد مخاطب المفعل ابر چنانچه در سلم کشید

الشاهد علی الثانی شعر قلیچ توکی بله مصیبتی جنیل شاب بر نچه لوز بهدین قونغار غیل قونغار غان مو قونغار غیل مفرد مخاطب
الفعلیه قونغار بیلک و قونغار بیکیز و قونغار بیکلار جمع مخاطب المفعل ایر قونغار مانک و قونغار مانکیز و قونغار مانکلار جمع مخاطب الفعلیه قونغار این
قونغار من و قونغار ادورمین و قونغار دورکان ازجا میکنم قونغار سان و قونغار ماس مین ازجا نمیکنم قونغار یب و قونغار یبان و قونغار غیش ازجا کنده
الشاهد علی الاول شعر عشق تیغی کونکولدا ایکیتیم با رجانینک میلی ایقالیس قونغار یب قونغار یبین ازجا کنده اشرا قونغار یشانک
ازجا کنده قونغار یبیز و قونغار یب توریبیز ازجا کنده ایم قونغار ماس ازجا نمیکند قونغار ماسلیغ ازجا نکندن قونغار ماس
ازجا نکندن باشد قونغار ادور بیش بنه ازجا سیکند باشد چنانچه در نسایم المحبه در ذکر شیخ ابوالحسن خرقانی کوید که آنی آسمان دین
پرتا یا بیلاک بیرله آنمیش بو لغایلار و سیلی ابیاد ادور بیش بو لغای بیکم با الارضی و سیفا جلال الارضی قونغار ادور بیش بو لغای و منه الارضی کنیا
قیلمادوریش بولغای و آنسیر دین تیرالی الماغای قونغار ار قونغار ار المجا کخان ازجا کخان و بدون تکرار هم مستعملت قونغار ایو ابا ازا
بکنم و بکند و بکنی قونغار غایو ازجا کنده قونغار یاق و قونغار غای پرد قونغار ایلیغی قونغار السالی ازجا بکنیم قونغار غالی برای ازجا کندن
و تا ازجا کندن قونغار غلج چون ازجا کند و بکند و بمجرد کندن قونغار غوچی ازجا کنده قونغار غوچه و قونغار غوچه تا ازجا
و بعید ازجا کندن قونغار غوسیدور ازجا خواهم کند قونغار غو سیکد ازجا خواهی کند قونغار غوسیدور ازجا خواهد کند قونغار غو
ازجا کندنی قونغار غای و قونغار سه و قونغار سون و قونغار دیلا ازجا بکند الشاهد علی الاول شعر قونغار غای ایلاینی بلفنا نهال
چنداسرو دیلک ایقسه امانت اول الملت قونغار غودیک قونغار غو و قونغار سون دیک ازجا کنده شدن و صیغ آن بصیغ
با لام اشتقاق می یابد من الجوامد قوناچین بفتح نون با الف کشیده و کسر جیم و سکون نون ثانی بی شاد یان و بناده کاو دو ساله را کوینید قوناش
قوناشیق با صطلاح ارباب حساب مقابله نتیجه و پروین باشد و آن چند کوکب است مجتمع کلانی و جمیع مقوطیست و جمیع شهر العتیاد انیکه
در رفع طالع می شود جمیع لحلاد نیست و از پیت مع قیر نوبت و جمیع مقرب مضمون طرلت دهم هوشا بکشنا بناه مقلند بکند و از آن کانیما
میکویند و از جونهما چون و قت حصاد است چون قوناش کوینید قوناغ و قوناق به معنی بود دل لحلحناه بحل خانه نعیم
مهمان باشد چنانچه در سد سکندری در عنوان داستان در ضیافت کردن خاقان مر خصر کوید که قوناغ ریکا قری بولوب واکر بیلا
کیم هر بیر اوز جوره خالیغه کیم اول لغاندین بوله تا پار لا لا رسیم و جبیه خانه و سرا و منزل اطعام مند قوناغلوق یعنی میهمانی
بفتح نون و غین معجمه و سکون لام خرج نزول باشد چنانچه در محبوب القلوب بعد وصف فتوحی کوید شعر قوناغنه ایکی قلیلا تونه
دو آت آریاسی جو طعمه قوشیقه هم قونان بفتح نون اول و سکون ثانی لب سه ساله را کوینید قونام بفتح نون و سکون میم
که از بدن انسان بر آید و آن برد و نوع است یکوح داشار بیمه دیکر نوع را قراچه خوانند قونبول لفظ عربی مترادف است بمعنی دسته
و فوج بوده چنانچه شاکر کفته شعر اولوس اول بر زبا بولا بولای مشغول بیقیلادی بیر بیر بکا قومبول قونبول و انرا قونبول هم کوینید
قونبولرا قونبول بتقدیم با و موحده و ضم تا منقوطه حبل نوشته و شعری بولس شاهد آورده و سهو کرده و در عربی بفتح فا و با معجمه صاحب
کفته القبیل الطایفه من الناس و من الحیل و با الفتح الرجل الغلیظ قونبلغ و قونداق بسکون نون و فتح قاف باشد که اطفال نونه را
بر آن بند و چوبی را هم کوینید که بطریق تو پچه تراشیده سیل فشک جل دعی آن کمان زنند قوندوز بسکون نون و ضم دال
مهمله سک آبی بود که پوست آن را بر کنار کلاه و پوستین دوزند و پوستین کنند و جندبید ستر خصیه آنست الشاهد علیه شعر شاد
آمیمدین اولسانت بو تحمل کونکا کیلتو ربوذ که آنرا الیق لیمیش بن مرتبی کولیمی قوندوز ونیز تام قلعه ایستار ملک بوخشان کیفتر آنشو
حو کهم کیره نوشته اند و سروری و جامع کتبا اللغات و صاحب ادات الفضلا جلیل زمهنک نیز کفته اند که بمعنی پوستین است کیبلا

بهشند سوکوکه ماعی نظیر است مهره تاقم وسنجاب کرلیم پوستین جنت ملک کیلیم خانه نوحیت که از پوست آنها پوستین کنند [illegible]

کمال آنرا [illegible]

خسته ساخت آبیست و در خانه با کویند قوندز رسته [illegible] مانند منغر بسکون نون وغین معجمه وضم غین معجمه اسبی بوده کرزیان

نابلیتر [illegible] چنانکه [illegible] در وصف عزاول ذکر کرده که او در هنوی کرده بود که اسب منغر [illegible] اولنلک بینلم ولسب الآرادی

الآلاغ الملاق کم والاراء استعمال [illegible] انبوه فیان فرو نکتلیم وینر [illegible] شاهزادکان چنکریحت که در عهد براق بوده منغز ولنلک

نام ملعنان و سیولیت که در حوالی زنجان واقعست وسلطانا و مجایتو در آنجا شهری کنید نیز بنا کرده از آن سلطانیه موسوم ساخت

تو نغرات بسکون نون وغین معجمه و تونکات بسکون نون وکاف عجمی نام قبیله ایست از اتراک که عجب نسبتی بر تمایل هر یکی دارند

الشاهد علیه شعر بیز تبالجی حسن و ناشاه سوی [illegible] ونبث سنکلابی سیله صندوالی کا تونغرات وتیات دسولغه

در این شعر تغرات بکسر تا وحذف نون خوانده و در حرف قاف مکتوبه ذکر کرده و شعر نیز بدو برا شاهد آمده سهو کرده تونغوز بسکون نون

مع الالماله وزای معجمه وضم غین معجمه خانوریست سیاه که آنرا بعربی جعل و خنفسا و بفارسی کو کردانک کویند تونکاف بسکون نون

وفتح کاف عجمی مع الاماله ترکیب رومی چرخ خشک باشد که لنبه و بند دارو ابلغت جغتای قوانق و بفارسی سبوسه کویند تونختی

بسکون نون و کاف عجمی و کسر شین معجمه بمعنی همسایه بود و آنرا قوشنی هم نامند تونوث بضم نون وسکون ثای معجمه بمعنی تردکند

باشد چنانکه در لسان الطیر کوید شعر چنجیان بستلیدام نوع توش چه کون تا پسا اوچوشا قنود تونوش وینز همسایه

شاه و بیوز باشد که آنرا تونوش و توناشو هم کویند چنانکه مذکور شود مع الواو من المشتقات تو وانماق بفتح واو وسکون نون

فخر کردن ومباهات باشد تو واندوق فخر کردیم تو وانیع تو وانادون فخر میکند و تو وانور بمعنی [illegible] هم می آید تو وانغای

تو وانور فخر تو وانادور فخر کننده و فخر کرده و بمعنی [illegible] هم می آید تو وانی تو وانغیل مفرد خطاب فعل امر الشاهد علی الاول شعر بیز تا

در ان مقرمین تو وانای چرخ دون خاقان معتبر سیله شمسه فرکادینیم و تو وان ترکه رومی کند معنی مستقبل هم باشد تو وانغیل غائب

مفرد خطاب فعل امر تو وانغیل تو وانیکز تو وانینکلار جمع خطاب فعل امر تو وانمانک تو وانماکنیز تو وانماکلار جمع خطاب فعل نهی

تو وانایین تو وانور تو وانادیم تو وانور فخر میکنم تو وانغیسه تو وانسا تو وانیش فخر کرده تو وانغیش فخر

کرده اند تو وانغیشانک فخر کرده تو وانیسه تو وانیب تو وانیسز فخر کرده ام تو وانماس فخر نمیکند تو وانماسلیغ فخر کردن تو وانماس بو

فخر نکننده باشد تو وانادور پیش جهت فخر میکرده باشد تو وانا تو وانا فخر کنان و بعضی تکرار هم مستعملست تو وانایمو آیا فخر کنم

و یکی تو وانمایو فخر نکرده تو وانساقعتو وانماینز تو وانغای تو وانا تو وانماسانک فخر نکنم چنانکه مذکور شد الشاهد [illegible]

حسن المعنویه بجتیین تو وانشاق یوق دیه بیله سابق تو وانشاق تو وانغالی برای فخر کردن و تا فخر کرده تو وانماج فخر کنم

تو وانغجور فخر خواهی کرد تو وانغوسیدور فخر خواهد کرد تو وانغولوق فخر کردن تو وانغای تو وانه و تو وانسه و تو وانسون تو وانان

فخر کند الشاهد علی الاول شعر آدم اول ساعت که جنتا بحر ملولادین کولمیش تو وانغای مسلم سین نازنین قصه تو وانغولیدور

توونودیلدین فخر کردیم تومنا قوق ترکه رومی کماشتن و آنرا قوتیاق هم کویند تورد ترکه رومی بمعنی سیکلر الشاهد علیه من فصولی

باملاته الرومیه شعر زلال لطف عدالتدن دکوندم بیانز بیهلو شاید ستندن اولنقطه ایکم تورلنز لا لا لا العدیری من الجوامد قو

نام مرغابیست که بر بطای نعطر دو از آن بالترکند و از ابفارسی حلبح کویند تو واق بفتح واو والف کشیده وسکون قاف ثلثه دلسه کوه زنا

تو وان ترکیه رومی جاذ باشد که نبوع سل در میان آن خانه کنند و عسل شان دهد و از اسری کو آم خوانند و ترا استران فخر کردن چنانکه

تو وانوق بفتح واو با الف کشیده وسکون نون وقاف جرلخ خشکی بود که از نه فرغ نمیرود و آنرا رومیه تو نکان کویند مع الیا من المشتقات تو یماق و تو یماغ

دو معنی دارد اول بمعنی کماشتن باشد و آنرا رومیه قوناق کویند دوم بمعنی آب الملاقی شود الشاهد علی الثانی با المعنی الاول شعر بوق

چو یکیل ای کوز خاک در او لای لاسیک سیم ایه چوک دخنه بولغان بیکار قوبیا اللیغ بیکن قویدی کماشت معنی قویان قوباد و دمیکه

و میریزد و قویار بمعنی فاعل و مصدر هم می آید و از اینجاست که مونوس اهل بحا آب تاپی میریزد و سوقیار میکویند قویان قو بارغان قوباد و عام

کمارده و کماشته و ریزنده و ریخته و بمعنی مصدر هم می آید قوی قوبضل و قوبنا کوبر مفرد خطاب فعل امر الشاهد علی الاول المعنی الثانی

شعر کرواکی دینا ایجان [illegible] بیکسان بو غریبه قویتر تولاجام او یناغی الشاهد علی الثانی بالمعنی الثانی

شعر ای ساقی [illegible] سلفر قوی [illegible] اول [illegible] ایله کوک قوینیل [illegible] الشاهد علی الثالث

المعنی جملایک باشین قویا الکاش [illegible] لای الملعینه باش قوبما و قوبناغیل مفرد خطاب فعل امر فو بونک قو بونکوز

قو یونکلار جمع خطاب فعل امر قو یمانک قو یماکیز قو یما نکلار جمع خطاب فعل نهی قو یابین و قو یاریم قو یادورم و قو یارم میکذارم و میریزم قویا

قو یامن میکذارم و میریزم قو یسانک و قو یسا بین قو بنلو بین بکذارم و بریزم الشاهد علی الاول المعنی الثانی شعر چونکه تورغ

اولدی بادینکدین نوای بیتر [illegible] قو یسانک جرعه تو فراغته الحبایی پاد قو یوب و قو یوبان و قو یمیش کماشته و ریخته قویمیشن

کماشته است و ریخته است قو یمیشانک کماشته و ریخته قو یوب بیز و قو یوب تو بهز کماشته ایم و ریخته ایم قو یماس نمیکذارد و نمیریزد

قو یماسلیغ نکماشتن و نریختن قو یماس بولسا نکذارنده باشد و نریزنده باشد قو یوب بولماس و قو یسا بولماس بمعنی توان کماشت و نتوان کرد

الشاهد علی الثانی با المعنی الثانی شعر ای نوای بیمار هم کم قدحی قوی تولادی نی آخر قو یسا خود بولماس قدح دین تملیقی قو یاتورین

بولغای میکماشته باشد و میریخته باشد قو یا قو یا کماشته کماشته و ریزان ریزان و بعضی تکرار هم مستعملست قو یاسو آیا

بکذارم و بکذارد و بکذاری و بریزم و بریزد و بریزی قو یماسا یو نکماشته و نریخته قو یسا قو و قو یغای بیز و قو یغای و قو یغای دور قو یا النک بکذاریم و بریزیم

قو یغالی برای کماشتن و تا کماشته و برای ریختن و تا ریخته قو یغاج چون کماشت و بکذارد و ریخت کماشتن مجهول نیت و بریزد و ریختن بعنی

چنانکه بمعنی ایش کوید شعر حیکاراو ن کونکلوم ایر شا المنتلغ سداد نیتانک سو قو یصلغ ایتمانک شعله قو یاذ قو یغوچی کماشته و ریزنده

قو یغو تورفو نعمجه قو یغاچه تا کماشتن و بعضی کماشتن و ریختن و بعضی ریختن قو یغوسیدور بخواهم کماشت و خواهم ریخت قو یغونکور خواهم

کماشت و خواهی ریخت الشاهد علیه با المعنی الاول شعر نوایی بیمه و صینا دا بسلیمان که قو یغوسیدور اچلغونلک معیلا قو یغو

خواهد کذشت و خواهد ریخت قو یغولوق کماشتنی و ریختنی قو یغاع قو یغو قو یسه قو یسون قو یدیک بکذارد و بریزد قو یغو دیک تو رمین

قو یلدیکلدین کماشتیم و ریختیم الشاهد علی الاول المعنی الاول شعر ای اجل قو یماکیم قو یلاخ بوزار نینک کوزی فرکم قو یغو دیک ممکن

ارمادی بر آنه یوزی قو یولماق کماشته شدن و ریخته شدن آب و صیغ آن بنام اشتقاق میابد قو یلماق تریزیر دفن کردن قو یلادور

دفن کردیم قو یلادم قو یلادیدور دفن میکند و قو یلادور بمعنی فاعل و مصدر هم می آید قو یلادور قو یلادورغان دفن کننده و دفن کرده و

بمعنی مصدر هم می آید قو یلادو قو یلاغیل مفرد خطاب فعل امر قو یلادو قو یلاغیل مفرد خطاب فعل نهی قو یلادیکز قو یلاکلار

جمع خطاب فعل امر قو یلاما نک قو یلاما کیز قو یلاما نکلار جمع خطاب فعل نهی قو یلایین قو یلادورمین و قو یلارام دفن میکنم قو یلا

قو یلادین دفن میکنیم قو یلاسانک قو یلادان قو یلامیش دفن کرده قو یلامیشن دفن کرده است قو یلامیشانک دفن کرده قو یلاغیم

قو یلاغیر دفن کرده ایم قو یلاماس دفن نمیکند قو یلاماسلیغ دفن نکردن قو یلاماس بولسا دفن نکننده باشد قو یلادیم قو یلادور

دفن میتوان کرد قو یلاتورغان بولغای دفن میکرده باشد قو یلا قو یلا دفن کنان و بعضی تکرار هم مستعملست قو یلایمو آیا دفن کنم

و یکی قو یلاماسا یو دفن نکرده قو یلاسا قو قو یلاغای بیز و قو یلاغای و قو یلاغای دور قو یلاغالی برای دفن کردن و تا دفن کرده

قو یلاغاج چون دفن کرد و کند دفن کرده قو یلاغوچی دفن کننده قو یلاغو سیدور قو یلاغوسیدور قو یلاغاچه تا دفن کردن و بعضی دفن کردن

292v

قولاچغو سدود دنن خواهم کرد قولاچغوزخکد نفوخوابی کرد قولاچغو سیلادوبر نرنجواهد کرد قولاچغو لوق دنن کرد بن قولاچقا قولاق
قولاچقو قولاچادلیك دنرکند قولاچغو دیك توسن قولاچغو دیك دنن کرد نلم قولاچغو نما فی مع الکاف المسدده تعدیت بمعنی فرزند
و بمعنی آن بدستور امانه تاکی قولشا شقاقی باید قولاچغو نما فی مع الکون بمعنی فرشدن و بمعنی الکی تا نوز اشقاقی باید من الجوامد قوی
کوسفند کمینه الشاهد علیه شعر [illegible] بیتشماسین [illegible] اولاد چین ایمیش کیم بولساکوب قصاب قوی [illegible] اولاد [illegible]
ارلستانرکاشتن و بمعنی چنانچه گذشت قوناش آفتاب باشد چنانچه کوید شعر [illegible] قارلاف [illegible]
قو باشغه تانك [illegible] بولسه [illegible] قوناق بفتح با والف کشیده و سکون [illegible] چنانچه [illegible]
بوشند و [illegible] آفته که بر کفای [illegible] قوباق بفتح نای والف کشیده
و سکون نون [illegible] انامند قوبانك بفتح نا و سکون نون و کاف فارسی قوباننقو بسکون نون و ضم [illegible] که چون [illegible]
انکشتان باتا [illegible] و آنرا بعربی [illegible] و بفارسی [illegible] و هندی [illegible] کویند چنانچه شاهد [illegible]
بابر [illegible] که [illegible] قوباق [illegible] قوبحی [illegible]
یا و کسر جیم [illegible] مراعی [illegible] و کویند [illegible] ار استاز کاشتن [illegible] کلام از مقوله [illegible]
می آمد چنانچه [illegible] بیم چنانچه [illegible] کوید شعر ای [illegible] قوبچی [illegible]
مراد [illegible] و نون خوانده [illegible] نوشته [illegible] کند [illegible]
قوبرغه قوبروق دو معنی دارد اول دم بود که آنرا بعربی ذنب کویند دوم نام ستاره سهیل باشد قوبرق قالالان ترکه [illegible]
که بوسته دم [illegible] آنرا بعربی [illegible] نامند قوی قوبی [illegible]
که سران خط [illegible] قوبن بسکون با و نون [illegible] کویند چنانچه کوید شعر [illegible]
کرچه صبا الملکی [illegible] آخشار [illegible] چنانچه در نامه لیلی خطاب بمجنون کوید شعر
ساس [illegible] ولیه شکر الحکیم [illegible] و آنرا قوبون بضم با هم خوانند قوبوق [illegible] کویند [illegible]
بود که تا آن [illegible] باشد قوبوم [illegible] که آنرا بعربی [illegible] کویند قوبوچی [illegible]
ضم با و سکون نون [illegible] باشد چنانچه [illegible] کوید شعر [illegible]
الغا قوبیدن [illegible] بمعنی آغوش بود [illegible] مستعمل چنانچه مذکور شد [illegible]
علیه شعر [illegible] لاله زار [illegible] قوبون [illegible] لاله زار [illegible]
لاله زار [illegible] قوبون [illegible] چنانچه [illegible] خسرو شیرین کوید شعر قوبون [illegible]
[illegible] قوبوچوب [illegible] که آنرا بعربی [illegible] خوانند قوبی بکسر با [illegible]
بود که آنرا بعربی [illegible] نامند الشاهد علیه شعر قوبی [illegible]
چاه را کویند قوبی [illegible] چنانچه [illegible] کوید شعر [illegible]
[illegible] قوپ [illegible] المذکور تحرف [illegible] مع الباء المثلثات قپا فی [illegible] چشمك [illegible] باشد که آنرا
بعربی [illegible] کویند [illegible] معنی [illegible] قپدوق چشمك [illegible]
[illegible] دور چشمك [illegible] چشمك [illegible] قپارغان [illegible]

293r

و آیند قپ و قپقیل مفرد فاعل المنفصل از قپماو قپماقیل مفرد فاعل المتصل [illegible] قپماقلار جمع فاعل المتصل
[illegible] جمع فاعل المنفصل [illegible] قپارام چشمك [illegible] قپماغین چشمك [illegible]
قپماقپمیش چشمك [illegible] چشمك [illegible] قپیب [illegible] چشمك [illegible]
چشمك [illegible] قپماسلیغ چشمك [illegible] قپا [illegible] قپا چشمك
[illegible] مستعمل قپاقو المچشمك [illegible] قپا بو چشمك [illegible] قپاق [illegible]
چشمك [illegible] قپماقلی [illegible] قپماچ چون چشمك [illegible] قپموجی چشمك [illegible]
[illegible] قپماقه [illegible] چشمك [illegible] چشمك [illegible] قپموکود چشمك [illegible]
چشمك [illegible] قپموق چشمك [illegible] قپماقپا [illegible] چشمك [illegible] چشمك [illegible]
ج
من الجوامد قپ قرزی بمعنی [illegible] مع الجیم من المشتقات قچیشما فی بکسر جیم و سکون [illegible] باشد قچیشوق
[illegible] قچیشما دور [illegible] شعر [illegible]
[illegible] قچیشما دورغان [illegible]
و بمعنی [illegible] قچیشما [illegible] قچیشماسلیغ [illegible]
[illegible] قچیشما قچیشما [illegible]
[illegible] مستعمل قچیشماقلی برای [illegible] قچیشماچ [illegible]
[illegible] قچیشماق [illegible]
کند الشاهد علی الثالث شعر [illegible] قچیشما [illegible]
[illegible] قچقلاتما فی [illegible]
و آنرا بعربی [illegible] کویند قچقلاتدوق [illegible] قچقلاتدور [illegible]
می آید قچقلاتقان [illegible] قچقلاتقو [illegible] مفرد فاعل المنفصل [illegible]
قچقلاتما [illegible] مفرد فاعل المتصل [illegible] جمع فاعل المنفصل [illegible] قچقلاتماقلار جمع
فاعل المنفصل [illegible] قچقلاتقام [illegible]
چنانچه [illegible] الشاهد علی الاول شعر [illegible] قچقلاتیب
قچقلاتقیش [illegible] قچقلاتقاس [illegible] قچقلاتماسلیغ [illegible]
قچقلاتمار [illegible] قچقلاتقو [illegible] مستعمل
قچقلاتمو آیا [illegible] قچقلاتقای [illegible] قچقلات [illegible]
برای [illegible] قچقلاتماچ چون [illegible] قچقلاتقوچی [illegible]
[illegible] قچقلاتقو [illegible] قچقلاتغا قچقلات
[illegible] قچیرما فی بکسر جیم [illegible] فریاد
کردن باشد قچیردوق فریاد [illegible] قچیرما [illegible] قچیردی [illegible]

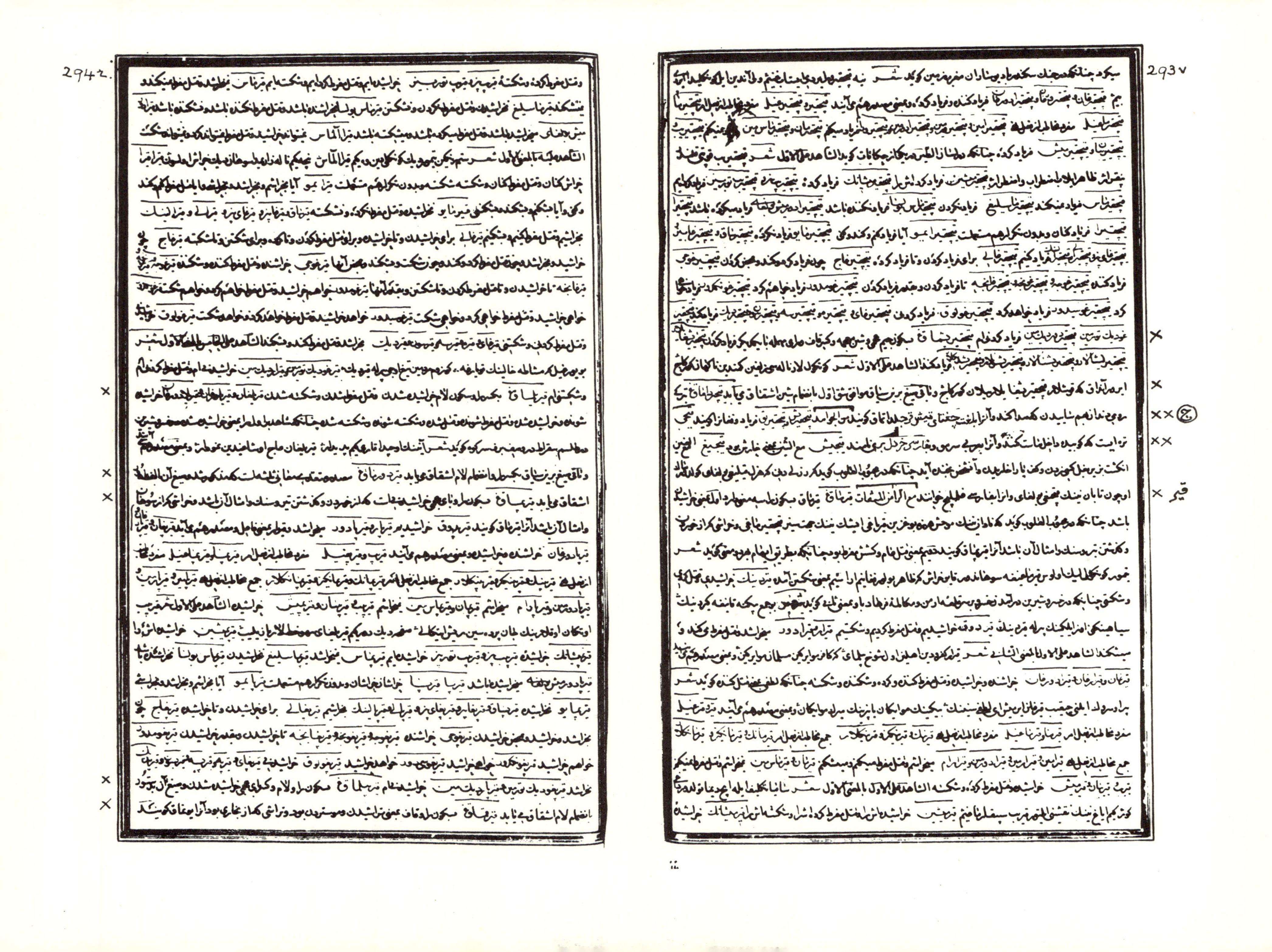

سیکرد چنانکه در جنگ سکندر با دیوداران منوچهر میں کوید شعر بنه بیچکیرماق بیلا بیچا ییتیشتیم ولی آندین ایلکه نکیلدا ایری
بیم بیچکیرغان و بیچکیرورتاو بیچکیرا یورغان فریاد کننده و فریاد کرده و بمعنی مصدر هم می آیند بیچکیر و بیچکیرمک جمع مفرد غائب المستقبل بیچکیرماس
بیچکیرماغیل مفرد غائب الماضی بیچکیرایین بیچکیرمیز و بیچکیرادور بیچکیر فریاد میکنم بیچکیرمان و بیچکیرماس مین عنیکم بیچکیریب
بیچکیرتا و بیچکیریش فریاد کرده چنانکه در لسان الطیر میکاز حکایات کوید الشاهد علی الاول شعر بیچکیریب قوپتی قیلدی
بیچکیرایش ظاهر ایلادی اضطراب و اضطرابی بیچکیریشین فریاد کرده اش را بیچکیریشانک فریاد کرد بیچکیرمادی بیچکیریب توریبین فریاد کنیم
بیچکیرماس فریاد میکند بیچکیرماسلیغ فریاد نکردن بیچکیرماس بولسا فریاد نکننده باشد بیچکیرادورغان فریاد میکرده باشد بیچکیر
بیچکیرا فریاد کنان و بدون تکرار هم مستعملست بیچکیرایمو آیا فریاد کنم و کند و کی بیچکیرمایو فریاد نکرده بیچکیراق و بیچکیرغایلیر
بیچکیرغای و بیچکیرکای بیچکیرکانیم فریاد کنیم بیچکیرغالی برای فریاد کردن و تا فریاد کرده بیچکیرغاج چون فریاد کرد و کند و بعضی کردن بیچکیرکوچی
فریاد کننده بیچکیرکوچی و بیچکیرغوچی بیچکیرغانچه تا فریاد کردن و بقدر فریاد کردن بیچکیرکوسیدور فریاد خواهم کرد بیچکیرکونمکدور فریاد خواهی
کرد بیچکیرکوسیدور فریاد خواهد کرد بیچکیرکولوک بیچکیرکوچی بیچکیرغای فریاد کردن بیچکیرمو بیچکیرسه بیچکیرکای بیچکیرسانک فریاد کنید بیچکیر
غودیک تورمین بیچکیرکودیک مین فریاد کردنم بیچکیرتماق بکسر بیم عجمی و تشدید و کسر قاف مادی بمعنی با یکدیگر فریاد کردن بیچکیرشماق
بیچکیرشالار و بیچکیرشتی و بیچکیرشتیلار بیچکیرشکاندا فریاد کنند الشاهد علی الاول شعر کونکول لار ناله سی یوزلانین کیندین نالهانکیز لاغ
ایرور آنداق که توشلاردا بیچکیرشتیا یلار یولدین کوکاج و نافع قسمع بیرینیسا قسما قی تو اول با انضمام شین اشتقاق می یابد بیچکیرماق ترک
مو و بینداء نهم شایدن که صدا کند و آنرا بلغت جغتای تیتیش ترجیلدا تماق کویند من الجوامد بیچکیریش و بیچکیریق فریاد و فغان کویند بیچکی
تره ایست که کوبیده داخل ماست کنند و آنرا بعربی سرمق و بفارسی خردل برگ کویند بیچکیش مع الثنیه بجیم خانه بود بیچکیغ مع الفین
انکشت زیر بغل کسی زدن و کف پا را خلیدن و آنرا خنده آید چنانکه در محبوب القلوب کوید کر دنیا دین کمی لیقیلیو لقای کولالماس
او چون تابان نینک محبوب لقای و آنرا بفارسی غلغلچ خوانند مع الراء المشددات قیرماق فتح قاف و سکون راء بمعنی خراشیدن و قتل منع میشد
باشد چنانکه در محبوب القلوب کوید که ناداننینک سرحد معنی نهوزین قیرماقی ایشک نینک جستیر بیچکیرماقی و خراش که از خوردن
و کرستن تیر و سنک و امثال آن باشد آنرا قیرماق کویند تحقیق بمعنی قتل عام و کشتن مفرط بود چنانکه مطلع توقیعام میر و میکوید شعر
جمهور کونکلی ایلی اولوس تیر قرابغیقه سو خاندین تا نو خراش کرظاهر بولسه قانیم ارا سینمعنی نکستن آمده تیرادی نینک خراشیدن قتل کردن
و شکوچ چنانکه در خسرو شیرین در آنجا که خسرو بسیتوقه ارمن و مکالمه فرهاد با و بمعنی ثانی کوید شعر بجسم بیکه تابیقه کیرد نیک
سیاهینکی امرایلکینک برله مردینک تیرد و قنه خراشیدیم و قتل مفرط کردیم و شکستیم قیرادیم قیرادور مینخراشد و قتل مفرط می کند و
میشکند الشاهد علی الاول والمعنی الثانی شعر قیرادکودین اهلین او لشو جمایی کر کافر بولیر کین مسلمان بولیر کین و بمعنی مستقبل هم می آید
قیرغان و قیرغانیم قیرادورغان خراشنده و خراشیده و قتل مفرط کننده و کرده و شکنند و شکسته چنانکه لطفی بمعنی قتل کننده کوید شعر
برادوس ول ابلینی چیقیب قیرغان ایرمیش ای لطفی سیفینینک بیکینک هوا یکان بایزینک میراد هوا یکان و بمعنی مصدر هم می آید قیرسا قیرسیل
مفرد غائب المستقبل امر قیرسا و قیرسا غیل مفرد غائب الماضی قیرسا قیرسا مزماس قیرسا جمع غائب المستقبل امر قیرسانک قیرسانکیز قیرسانکلار
جمع غائب الماضی قیرایین و قیرایمیز قیرادورمین و قیرادورمیز قیرادور قیرارمین میخراشم و قتل مفرط میکنم و میشکنم قیرماس مین نمیخراشم و قتل مفرط نمیکنم
قیریب قیریبان قیرمیش خراشیده و قتل مفرط کرده و شکسته الشاهد علی الاول بالمعنی الاول شعر سانیا نکلیفا بیله ایچید بیمار تولدوردم
کوز کیم ایاغ نینک نقشی المتم قیریب سیقیلغانیم قیرمیشین خراشیده اش را و قتل مفرط کرده اش را و شکسته اش را قیرمیشانک خراشیده

و قتل مفرط کرده و شکسته قیریپ بیریب قیرپ تورور مین خراشیدهام و قتل مفرط کرده ام و شکسته ام قیرماس نمیخراشد و قتل مفرط نمیکند و
نمیشکند قیرماسلیغ نخراشیدن و قتل مفرط کردن و شکستن قیرماس بولسا نخراشنده باشد و قتل مفرط نکننده باشد و نشکننده باشد قیراد
میش جغتای میخراشیده باشد و قتل مفرط میکرده باشد و میشکسته باشد قیرا آلماس نمیتواند خراشید و قتل مفرط نمیتواند کرد و نمیتواند شکست
الشاهد علیه بالمعنی الاول شعر سینم نیکین تیمورچیلیک کونکلیدین دیکیم قیرا آلماس غم تیغیکیم نالهزلیک سوهان دیلیکی خراش اولوشی قیرا قیرا
خراش کنان و قتل مفرط کنان و شکسته شکسته و بدون تکرار هم مستعملست قیرایمو آیا بخراشم و بخراشد و بخراشد یا یا قتل مفرط کنم کند
و کی و آیا بشکنم و بشکند و بشکنی قیرمایو نخراشیده و قتل مفرط نکرده و شکسته قیراق قیرغایبر قیرغای بیر قیرمالی و قیرا لیک
بخراشیم و قتل مفرط کنیم و بشکنیم قیرغالی برای خراشیدن و تا خراشیده و برای قتل مفرط کردن و تا کهه و برای شکستن و تا شکسته قیرغاج چون
خراشید و بخراشد و چون قتل مفرط کرد و کند و چون شکست و بشکند و بعضی آنها قیرغوچی خراشنده و قتل مفرط کننده و شکننده قیرغوسیدور قیرغای
قیرغانچه تا خراشیدن و تا قتل مفرط کردن و تا شکستن و بقدر آنها قیرغوسیدور نخواهم خراشید و قتل مفرط خواهم کرد و نخواهم شکست قیرغوسی
خواهی خراشید و قتل مفرط خواهی کرد و نخواهی شکست قیرغوسیدور خواهد خراشید و قتل مفرط خواهد کرد و نخواهد شکست قیرغولوق قیرغوچی
و قتل مفرط کردن و شکستن قیرغای قیرغایسیز قیرسانک قیرسانکیز قیرغودیک بخراشید و قتل مفرط کنید و بشکنید الشاهد علی الجامع المفصل الاول شعر
بو بیوفا صنم که مشاطه خالینک قیا بقیه کوزوم دین تیغ دور چیرایقه قیرغودیک تورور تو قیرارحیلیک مین خراشیده ام قتل مفرط کرده ام
و شکسته ام قیرلماق بکسر و سکون لام خراشیده شدن و قتل مفرط شدن و شکسته شدن قیرلغان و قیرلماق قیرلیلدی قیرلغاندا خراشیده
شونده و خراشیده شده و قتل مفرط شونده و قتل شده و شکسته شونده و شکسته شده چنانکه شاه مبارک طغرا بمعنی خراشیده شده و مخفی شده
در ملا سلم ستر الجده و صفه بر فسر کوه کوید شعر آیینه اوچیدا تارهکیم بیدیلدی قیرلیلغان ملح اوشاغیدین توطره و بمعنی مصدر هم
و نافع قسمع برین سا قی بجیم و انضمام لام اشتقاق می یابد قیرچماق بفتح صاد و سکون راء بمعنی ثلاث کلمه کمه بیع آن المظلم
اشتقاق می یابد قیرسماق بفتح سین و سکون راء و ثای بمعنی خراشیدن سهات که از خوردن و کدشتن تیر و سنک و امثال آن باشد و خراشی که از سوختن
و امثال آن باشد آنرا قیرماق کویند قیرسیدوق خراشیده م قیرسار قیرسادور خراشیده م قیرسادور میخراشد یعنی تقطیر بمعنی اصل و مستقبل هم می آید قیرسغان قیرسای
قیرسادورغان خراشنده و خراشیده و بمعنی مصدر هم می آید قیرسب و قیرسغیل مفرد غائب المستقبل امر قیرسسون قیرسپ قیرسغیل مفرد غائب
الماضی قیرسایین و قیرسایمیز قیرسادورمین قیرسار قیرسانک قیرسانکیز قیرسانکلار جمع غائب المستقبل قیرساین قیرسایلیک قیرسیدیم قیرسدی و قیرسدیب
قیرسادورمین و قیرسادوردام میخراشم قیرسادوریمی قیرسیدوم قیرسب خراشیده قیرسمیش الشاهد علی الاول شعر قیریب
اویکان اوقلاری نینک جان برده سین یوق ایش اینکالی صفحه دیک دهیکم قیرسیغان ای صفحه الاقران لیلی قیرسیشین خراشیده اش را
قیرسیشانک خراشیده قیرسیپ تورور قیرسیب تورور مین خراشیده ام قیرسماس نمیخراشد قیرسماسلیغ نخراشیدن قیرسماس بولسا نخراشنده با
قیرسادور میش بخراشیده باشد قیرسا قیرسا خراشان خراشان و بدون تکرار هم مستعملست قیرسایمو آیا بخراشم و بخراشد و بخراشی
قیرسمایو نخراشیده قیرساق قیرسغایبر قیرسغای بیز قیرسالیک قیرسالیک بخراشیم قیرسغالی برای خراشیدن و تا خراشیده قیرسغاج چون
بخراشد و بخراشید و بعضی خراشیدن قیرسغوچی خراشنده قیرسغوسیدور قیرسغوسیدور قیرسغانچه تا خراشیدن و بقدر خراشیدن قیرسغوسیدور
خواهم خراشید قیرسغوسیدور خواهی خراشید قیرسغوسیدور خواهد خراشید قیرسغولوق خراشیدن قیرسغای قیرسغای قیرسانک قیرسانکیز و قیرسانکلار
بخراشید قیرسغودیک تورور مین قیرسیب ایدیم مین بخراشیده نظام قیرسلماق بفتح سکون سین و لام و کسر لام مجهول خراشیده شدن و صیغ آن برهم بود
با انضمام لام اشتقاق می یابد قیرقماق بفتح سکون راء و قاف بمعنی تراشیدن و موستره بود و تراشی که از تجار بود آنرا یوغاق کویند

تیرموق تراشیدیم تیرقار و تیرقادور میتراشد و بقیاس بمعنی فاعل و مصدر هم آید چنانچه در دیلی عجوبت در جنك نوقل ابتیله ئیل
بمعنی مصدری کوکل صحبت ایتیك خیلیجی ایسناب ایلهلاکه ئی ناش تیرقادور بیچوك که پاکی تیرغان و تیرغار غان و تیرقادور غان تراشنده ورا
و بمعنی مصدر هم می‌آیند تیرق و تیرقیغیل مفرد غائب امر فصل امر تیرق و مفرد حال امر کوید تیرقسا و تیرقیغیل مفرد حاضر
فصل امر تیرقیلك تیرقینکر و تیرقینکلار جمع غائب فصل امر تیرقیالك و تیرقیالیکر و تیرقیالیکلار جمع غائب فصل امر تیرقاسین و تیرقاسین تیرقادور و تیرقای
میتراشم تیرقارم و تیرقادورمین بمیتراشم تیرقیسه تیرقسان و تیرقیش تراشیده تیرقیشین تراشیدن و تیرقیشالك تراشیدن و تیرقیب
تیرقیب تو بیین تراشیده ایم تیرقاس بمیتراشد تیرقاسلیغ تراشیدن تیرقاس بولسا تراشد و باشد تیرقادور میتراشیدند تا
تیرقا تیرقا تراشان تراشان و بدون تکرار هم مستعملت تیرقامو آیا بتراشم و بتراشد و بتراشی تیرقایو تراشیده تیرقان و تیرقای
تیرقای بیر و تیرقا تیرقالیك تراشیم تیرقالی برای تراشیدن و تا تراشیده تیرقاج چون تراشید و بتراشد و بعض تراشیدن تیرقای
تراشنده تیرقوچی تیرقوچی تیرقاجه تا تراشیدن و بقدر تراشیدن تیرقوچ مدور خواهم تراشید تیرقونکدور خواهد تراشید
خواهد تراشید تیرقوچوق تراشیدنی تیرقای تیرقور تیرقیسه تیرقیشوق تیرقیلک تراشد تیرقوچیک تیرقاچیک تیرقادین تراشیدنی ام
تیرقیلماق تراشیده شدن و صیغ آن بحذف باء انضمام لام اشتقاق می‌یابد تیرقیمناق مصدر متعدیست یعنی تراشانیدن چنانچه
در منشآت و مکتوبی که بسلطان بدیع الزمان نوشته کوید ارکان دولتینکیزنیك سقالین تیرقیماق نینك تمامی حینی اکر ملاحظه
میتلسا نیکز شاید تا بقای سین صیغ آن بدستور لفظ تیرقا اشتقاق می‌یابد تیرلاماق بکون طاء و فتح لام با الف کشیدن بگوه پچیدن
کوید دیکر معانی افاده این معنی میکند باید لفظ راه مذکور شود تیرلادی راه بگوه پچید تیرلاید و بگوه می‌پچید و
بمعنی فاعل و مصدر هم می‌آید تیرلاغان و تیرلاغان و تیرلایدورغان بکوه پچنده و پچیده و بمعنی مصدر هم می‌آیند تیرلاب تیرلابان تیرلاکالیش بگوه
پچیده چنانچه شاهد بر اول در تاریخ بابری مذکور است که بولغود تیرلاب و قشلاپ چقمان ایکاندر تیرلاماس بگوه نمی
تیرلاماسلیغ بگوه نپچیدن تیرلاماس بولسلیکی نپچیده نباشد تیرلایدور غان بگوه پچنده نباشد تیرلاغای تیرلاغسه بیلی
بگوه بپچید و نا قبض صیغ چون با بعض موافقت نداشت مذکور نشد تیرچیلداماق بکون طاء و لام و تای قرشت و کسر جیم و فتح دال
متعدیست یعنی دندان بهم سایید و آنرا رونتیه تیرچیلداتماق کویند لیکن شیطانه افاده معنی میکند باید لفظ دندان مذکور شود تیرچیلداتی دندان
بهم سایید تیرچیلداتورمن تیرچیلداتادور دندان بهم میسایید و تیرچیلداتمق بمعنی فاعل و مصدر هم می‌آید تیرچیلداتغان تیرچیلداتورغان و تیرچیلداتی
دندان بهم ساینده و بهم ساییده و بمعنی مصدر هم می‌آیند تیرچیلداتات و تیرچیلداتغیل مفرد غائب فصل امر تیرچیلداتمای تیرچیلداتماغیل
مفرد غائب فصل امر تیرچیلداتینك تیرچیلداتینکر و تیرچیلداتینکلار جمع غائب فصل امر تیرچیلداتاسین تیرچیلداتالیکر و تیرچیلداتالیکلار جمع غائب
فصل امر تیرچیلداتاسین تیرچیلداتورمن تیرچیلداتادور دندان بهم میسایم الشاهد علی الثانی بیت نوشته کوید که
با نیچه خندان بهمین او تروداشیك دین هر لحظه تیش تیرچیلداتور بین او تیقوداتی تیرچیلداتمان تیرچیلداتماس بین دندان بهم نمیسایم تیرچیلداتی
تیرچیلداتیسار تیرچیلداتیش دندان بهم سایید تیرچیلداتیشالك دندان بهم سایند تیرچیلداتیب تیرچیلداتیب تونکدور دندان بهم ساییده ام
تیرچیلداتماس دندان بهم نساید تیرچیلداتماسلیغ دندان بهم نساییدن تیرچیلداتماس بولسا دندان بهم نساییده باشد تیرچیلداتا
دندان بهم میساید باشد تیرچیلداتا تیرچیلداتا دندان بهم سایند کنان و بدون تکرار هم مستعملت تیرچیلداتایو آیا دندان بهم
سایم و ساید و سایی تیرچیلداتایو دندان بهم ساییده تیرچیلداتاق تیرچیلداتغلی تیرچیلداتای تیرچیلداتای بیر تیرچیلداتغالی دندان بهم
سایم تیرچیلداتغالی برای دندان بهم ساییدن و تا هم ساییده تیرچیلداتاج چون دندان بهم سایید و ساید تیرچیلداتوچی تیرچیلداتوچی

تیرچیلداتقانچه تا دندان بهم ساییدن و بقدر آن تیرچیلداتقوسی تیرچیلداتقودور دندان بهم خواهم ساید تیرچیلداتقونکدور دندان بهم خواهی
ساید تیرچیلداتقوسیدور دندان بهم خواهد ساید تیرچیلداتقولوق دندان بهم ساییدنی تیرچیلداتقای تیرچیلداتقیل تیرچیلداتقاییدی
تیرچیلداتقوسی تیرچیلداتقودین دندان بهم ساید تیرچیلداتقونلیك تیرچیلداتقوسی تیرچیلداتقودین دندان بهم ساییدنیام تیرچیلداتماق مصدر
لازم است یعنی دندان بهم ساییده شدن و صیغ آن بدستور لفظ اشتقاق می‌یابد تیرغاماق کماه جنس من الجوالیق هفت
معنی دارد اول ولایتی که در آنجا است چنانکه بابر پادشاه در جنك هزاره کوید شعر تاغنه جقتوق هزاره نی تا ولایت
تیرغاق و قولدا کیلیك کوی آی ولایت دویم اثر العکاشه ولایتی کنار کرده مقاماتی که عقبی قابل زمین ظاهر اثر العدم بنا با بقا برابر اخوانند
چهارم بمعنی موبه بود پنجم اثر است که خراشیدن ششم المسابقه منطوق کردن هفتم اثر است از شکستن و نظیر چیزی قسم کوینده
مسفول است سیاه و چسبنده که از درخت صنوبر حاصل شود و بر کشتی مالند تا آب بجوف کشتی نرود و بعضی از بعضی بیتا و نیز استعمال یابد شود
تیراغ و تیراق بمعنی کنار باشد الشاهد علی الاول شعر کرچه یوقتور لا له زار کشیمه تیراغ بیدا تیراغ دوده آمیم بیله قوی یاقیبو لطافتی
داغ الشاهد علی الثانی شعر شه با نیم نفیس کوی کج لار مقام ایتمیش نیا لیك لرات رولا دو صه دین کرچه سالار درخ دیلینیل
تیراغو بفتح طا معجم مبهم کدبه یی شنیم بوجود قران دیرمنجلاری اول معنی مواید باشد که زبان جبره بر کناره چنانچه کوید
موشیم کیم جهره دمینه ارانا ایتمیش جیان دمی تیرنینك موستحیلا اولد دو رضا جبقران و له شعر یوزد صید قران دور بر النجم
ایجوسید بن کددین تیر بجمعه مقیلدی قره ها له دویم بمعنی تمام و اکمال و رضا بجهد کمال بود الشاهد علیه شعر قران تیلدینک
نوا و نظم ارا کیم الصغات ایتماش بصورت یکین اورکا سوز کا حصر و صاحبقران هر کز و نیز بمعنی اول و دو بیر بطریق ایهام فرماید شعر
یوزی و صیقد انوله وامی المحتبس قران نظم سلبکی کا کیمه جکیش در صحیح قریلی دو بیر بجان قاتا تیرانات تعلوی باشد که از آن
استدلال بر شوکت و قوت سلاطین نمایند تیرا و بفتح راء و سکون واو و شنیم بر قسا باشد که آنرا مرج صنعتی کویند الشاهد علیه شعر
یوزدا و زده خوی کال اوتیو شینمی بیرتیلا ابیا ان شب ایله چوزیا قدی کاشینك او زده تیرا او دیر نیمه فرهاد و شیرین کوید شعر مقابل
اولیکا شرو حمدی تیرکلیك سبز بول و زده تیرا و دوی تیرتیق بکون صاد و تا و کسر بای عجمی خطه و بو شنق بود که برو مرکب
دوزنده یی ما نند تیرتیلیك بکون نون و کسر بای عجمی و دال مهمله بر ترکه روی زمین خانه بود که در وقت قطع از هم متفرق
شود تیرتیش بکون نون و شین و کسر بای قرشت در بعضی طرح ترک در شیه را کویند چنانچه کوید شعر نحل عیشیم قوشلار دی
عینك کیم مکانیدا تا المادی تیرتیش و له شعر اول کال حرمی کلش طاپر کیناه ایدیم نوعی قوشلار دیب حجر کر تا المادی تیرتیشیم و شیش
تا زغ و صید و امثال آن ما نند که هنوز بر ریشه باشد و چه تیر تراش بود که برای تخفیف بر بوستر زنند تیرتیکمن بجبرنا و کاف نام دکا
از توران قرغاول تمرمعلوم کویند الشاهد علیه شعر قرغاول تیرتاردا با لسوتقان کوبه حسب کوبندان المکاتب نظام بیچین
ایشلاسین لطفی تیرغو نام پرنده ایست شکاری از جنس باز اما از باز کوچک که آنرا باشه مانند تیرغیج بکون طا و جیم کسر ضمه
طعام بود که در زیر پیاله بیان شود تیرغیز بکون طا و زاء معجمه و کسر قاف نام طایفه ایست عظیم از اتراک که در جهت شمال سکونت
دارند و مساکن ایشان از مواضع صعبه است و در اوغوزنامه مذکور است که اوغوز خان جمله ولایت هرات دعوای بزرگی کرد ند
ایشان از مطلبه در غیر شاد ایشان عقب از جهت ئی بلز کشته چهار تن از ایشان تیرا مدند بر کرو چند و تیرغیز و نظام شدند تیرق عسکر
کویند و نیز نام اوی خواست از او نیک چه و طرار تراشیده هم باشد تیرق اباغ اسم جانوریست از حشرات الارض که از اطفال هم دارنا
و بعربیه مشط المیه مانند تیرقیلیغ بمعنی اوّل یشم جنس خوانند تیرقیس مع الراء المهملتین بیوقیه تیمه و تلندی بسبب غیچا نه

295v.

تایغ باری مذکورست که تیز قاتار الامر یکه دوبی معنی دشت بدشت تیز تیز را طعام جمله ورای ثانی منجه تولی عجایب الملکت گفته

که قلعه ایست عظیم بهر کوهی وسیع و مردم ... آن ناحیه بسیار اند و اهالی تیز تیز را آس کویند و لباس تیز تیزی از چیزهای مشهورست تیز تیز

[illegible]

296r.

[illegible]

296v.

شعر اتیش ویرامونی ناقیز یغیش قول برتی مطربا اولاو تو تیز ایچمالیککا آل اغز سنکه مد و ناقی صنع بر بر نا قیمو اوتی شو اول اشتاق ویاید

تیز چاناق بکسر زا وسکون نون بترکی ... کم شد ... [illegible] ... برآید

... [illegible] ... تیز الاغ بفتح زا و لام و سکون ... [illegible]

تیزاوق ... [illegible] ... تیزاوغلان ... [illegible] ... تیزغین ... [illegible]

چنانکه ... [illegible] ... بادشاه خوانیم کوید شعر ... [illegible]

... [illegible]

... [illegible] ... خوانند تیز تیغ ... [illegible]

اول ... [illegible] ... تیز یغ بکسر ... [illegible]

[illegible]

297r.

[illegible]

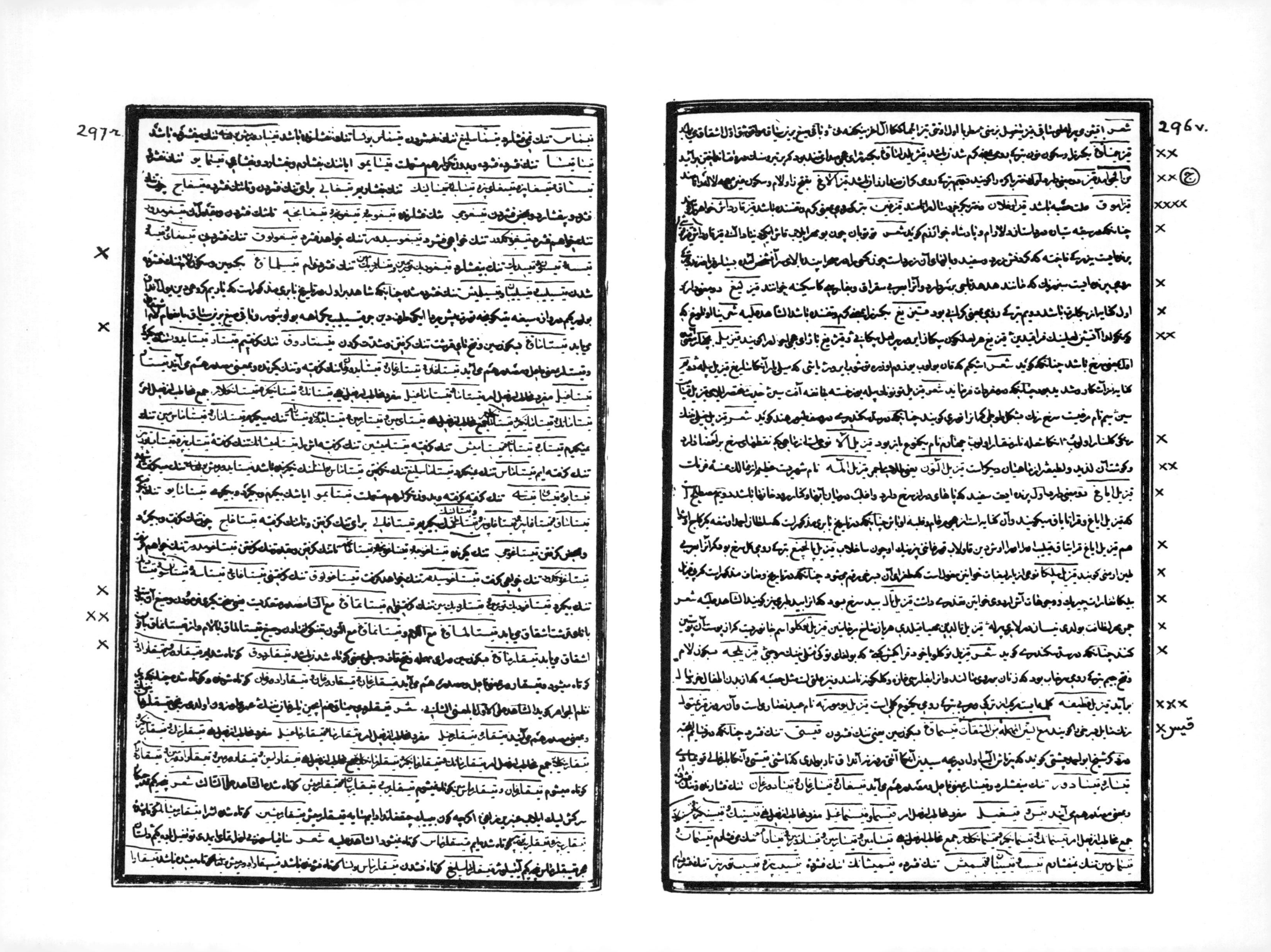

قیسقارا کوتاه شده و بدون تکرار هم مستعملست قیسقارا بو آیا کوتاه شوم شود شوی قیسقارغایبو کوتاه شده قیسقارغان

قیسقارغاینچه قیسقارغونچه قیسقارمای کوتاه شوید قیسقارغالی برای کوتاه شدن و تا کوتاه شدن قیسقارغاچ چون کوتاه شد و

و بعد از شدن قیسقارغوچی کوتاه شونده قیسقارغوجه قیسقارغونچه قیسقارغانچه تا کوتاه شدن و بمعنی کوتاه شدن قیسقارغوسیدور کوتاه خواهد

قیسقارغوسی کوتاه خواهد شد قیسقارغوسیدور کوتاه خواهد شد قیسقارغولوق کوتاه شدنی قیسقارغای قیسقاریب قیسقاریتون

قیسقارمیلیک کوتاه شوی قیسقارغودیک توریدور قیسقاریدیکمین کوتاه شدنی ام قیسقاماق بسکون سین و نون بترکی رومی بمعنی فشار

مصدر معدوده باشد من الجوامد قیساج بترکی رومی کلبتین باشد و آن ابزاریست که بدان دندان زکنند و آهنگران بآن آهن نیم گفته آنرا

میگیرند و کلبتین گویند قیراج نام [illegible] و آنرا اتراک مغول [illegible] خوانند قیسقنج بسکون سین و نون و جیم عجمی نام

بترکی رومی بمعنی [illegible] باشد و بمعنی خاصه نیز استعمال شود قیسیر جوانی که آبستن نباشد قیسقه کوتاه قیسیق بمعنی شدت بود

چنانچه در تاریخ بابری مذکورست که بیرون ولایت [illegible] قیسیق یوق ایدی مع الثاء المثلثه من المشتقات قیشلاماق قیشلاو

کردن یعنی زمستان را در مکان گرمسیر گذرانیدن قیشلادوق قیشلاق کردیم قیشلادیم قیشلادی [illegible] قیشلامیکید و قیشلار بمعنی حال و مستقبل

هم می آید چنانچه شاهد براول بمعنی مصدری در تاریخ بابری مذکورست که [illegible] آنرا قیشلامیز [illegible]

[illegible] قیشلاغان و قیشلارغان و قیشلایدورغان قیشلاق کننده و کرده چنانچه در تاریخ بابری مذکورست که ترکان [illegible]

قیشلاغان ایکاندور بمعنی قیشلامیش هم می آید قیشلاغو قیشلاغیل مفرد غائب امر قیشلاسون و قیشلاغیل مفرد مخاطب امر

قیشلانک و قیشلانکیز جمع مخاطب امر قیشلاغای و قیشلاغایلار جمع غائب [illegible] قیشلادیم قیشلادیمیز

قیشلار [illegible] قیشلامیکم قیشلاغان [illegible] قیشلادیم قیشلادیک قیشلادیلار قیشلاق کرده [illegible] قیشلادی

کرده اند [illegible] قیشلاق کرده قیشلاتیب [illegible] قیشلاغ کرده ام قیشلاغاس قیشلامیکیم [illegible] قیشلاق

نکردن قیشلاماس [illegible] قیشلاق نکننده باشد [illegible] قیشلاق [illegible] قیشلاق کنانیده

تکرار هم مستعملست قیشلا بو آیا قیشلاق کنم و کند [illegible] قیشلاماق [illegible]

قیشلاغلیک [illegible] قیشلاغالی برای قیشلاق کردن و تا کرده قیشلاغاچ چون قیشلاق کند و بعد از کردن قیشلاغوچی قیشلاق

کننده قیشلاغوجه [illegible] تا قیشلاق کردن و بمعنی [illegible] قیشلاق خواهم کرد [illegible]

قیشلاغوسیدور [illegible] قیشلاق خواهد کرد قیشلاغولوق [illegible] قیشلاق کرده [illegible]

قیشلادیلیمین قیشلاق کنندهام من الجوامد قیش سه ماه فصل زمستان و بطریقی سه ماه فصل را بهار باشد [illegible]

[illegible] ثانی [illegible] چنانچه [illegible] کوید [illegible]

[illegible] بولغای هرکون [illegible] کوید شعر [illegible]

[illegible] قیشلاق مکان گرمسیر باشد که در آنجا زمستان را بگذرانند [illegible]

زمستان [illegible] قیشیق بکسر شین و سکون [illegible] بمعنی کج [illegible] مع الفا قیف [illegible]

[illegible] مع القاف قیق [illegible] مع اللام من المشتقات قیلماق یعنی کردن قیلدوق کردیم قیلور قیلادور میکند و قیلور بمعنی حال [illegible]

هم می آید چنانچه در داستان [illegible] بمعنی کردن [illegible] شعر [illegible]

قیلورمن قیلغان قیلورغان قیلادورغان کننده و کرده چنانچه شاهد [illegible] در خاتمه [illegible]

قیلاچی [illegible] و در تاریخ الانبیا مذکورست که حضرت سلیمان علیه السلام [illegible]

که دیو [illegible] قیلادورغان [illegible] نیز بمعنی [illegible] می آید چنانچه شاهد [illegible]

[illegible] در وصف [illegible] کوید [illegible] قیلغوچی قیلادورغان [illegible]

الشاهد علی الثالث شعر [illegible] قیلیب [illegible] قیلور [illegible]

[illegible] قیلغیل مفرد مخاطب امر قیلسین [illegible]

قیلینکیز قیلینکلار جمع مخاطب امر [illegible] قیلغایلار جمع غائب [illegible]

[illegible] قیلادورمیز [illegible] الشاهد علی الاول شعر [illegible]

[illegible] قیلیشتین [illegible] قیلیشان [illegible]

[illegible] قیلماس [illegible] قیلماسلیغ نکردن [illegible] قیلا المماسه [illegible] الشاهد

شعر [illegible] قیلا المماسه [illegible] چنانچه کوید شعر

[illegible] قیلغان [illegible] باشد [illegible]

[illegible] قیلا قیلا [illegible] بدون تکرار هم مستعملست چنانچه در [illegible]

دارا [illegible] اسکندر کوید شعر [illegible]

[illegible] قیلادین [illegible]

[illegible] قیلماغای [illegible] چنانچه شاهد [illegible] مصرع [illegible] کوید شعر

[illegible] شعر [illegible]

[illegible] آیا [illegible] قیلغانیز [illegible]

[illegible] الشاهد علی الرابع شعر [illegible]

[illegible] کوید شعر [illegible]

[illegible] قیلغاچ چون کرد و کند و بعد از کردن قیلغوچی کننده قیلغوجه قیلغونچه قیلغانچه تا کردن و بمعنی کردن [illegible]

الثالث [illegible] شعر [illegible]

قیلا [illegible] الشاهد علی الثالث شعر قیلا [illegible]

[illegible] شعر [illegible]

خواهم کرد قیلغوسیدور [illegible] قیلغولوق کردنی [illegible] کوید شعر [illegible]

قیلغولوق [illegible] قیلغانی [illegible] الشاهد علی الخامس شعر [illegible]

[illegible] قیلغایلار [illegible] قیلمیش [illegible] الشاهد علی [illegible]

شعر [illegible] در خاتمه [illegible]

[illegible] قیلیشماق [illegible] مع [illegible] بمعنی [illegible] در خاتمه [illegible]

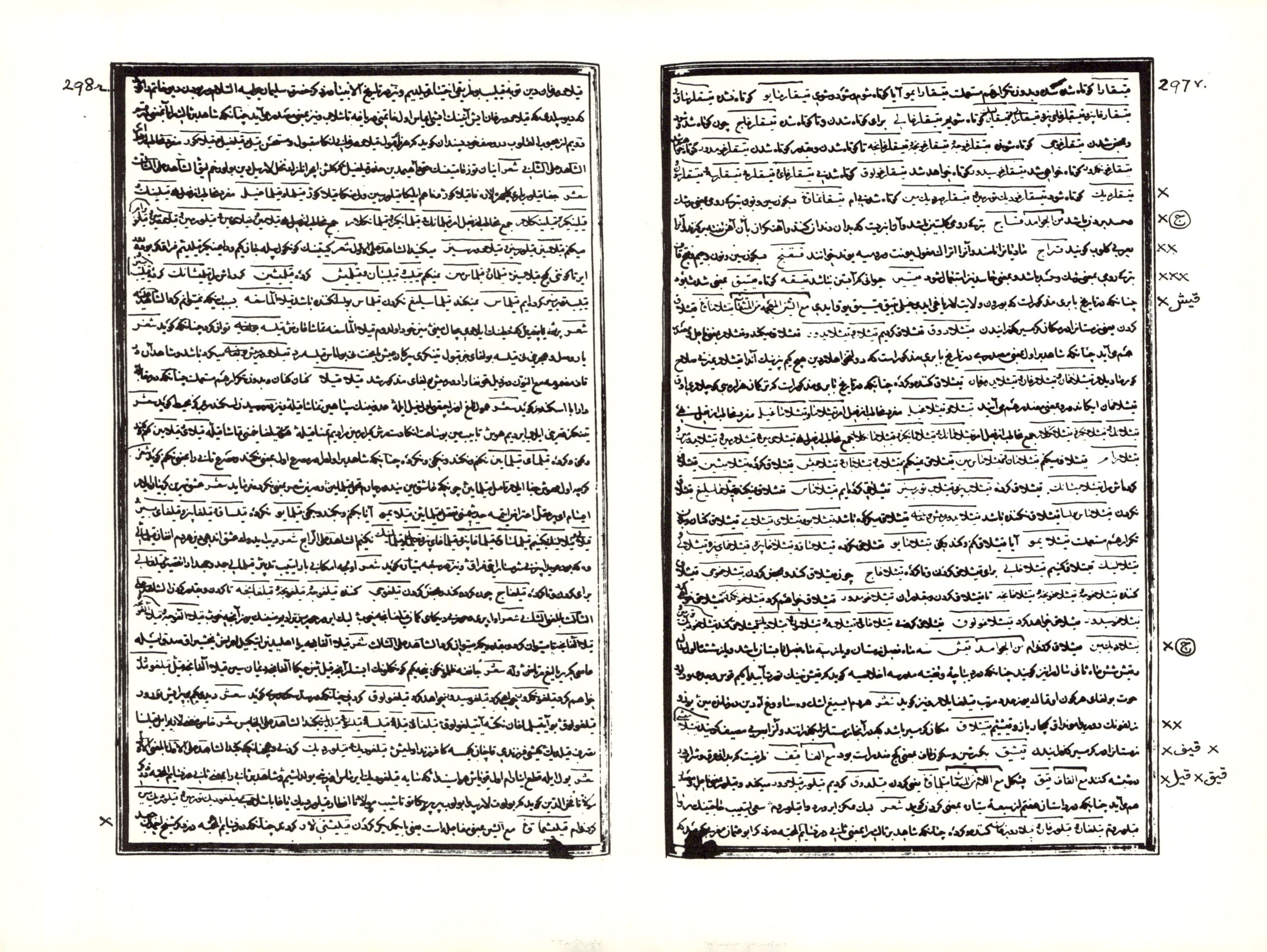

وشیخ سعید گوید که بولدا شیخ احمد آنکا بولوقیب ملاقات تیلیشتی لار تیلیشیب تیلیشیبان تیلیشمیش کرده چنانکه در لیلی مجنون در
وداع کردن لیلی مجنون گوید که کوبدا الشاهد علی الاول شعر بر بیر لارغینیک اوبوب ایاغینی تان تیلیشیب فراق داغینی وصیغ آن تانتر
اشتقاق می یابد تیلماق بکسر لام اول و سکون ثانی بمعنی تیلیماق بکسر لام و سکون نون خفیف کرده شدن تیلیلدی تیلیلادور تیلینور [illegible]
کرده میشود چنانکه شاهد بر اطلاق همین معنا گوید که آلمی چو زهرنی تیلیلدی سنکا قندیده تیلغوچیغه [illegible]
تیلیلدی و تیلینور بمعنی فاعل و مصدر هم می آید تیلیلغان تیلیلدی غان تیلیلادورغان تیلینغان تیلینورغان تیلیپ دوغان کرده شو و کرد
شد چنانکه شاهد بر بناء [illegible] قسم دویم از محبوب القلوب در باب گوید که استغفار بسیار تیلینا [illegible] استغفار [illegible]
تیلیلادی تیلیلادیک تیلیلادیلار تیلیلادیم تیلیلنیب تیلیلنیشی تیلیلنینکا تیلیلنیب تیلیلنیب و تیلیلنیسون و تیلیلنید لیت کرده شد الشاهد علی الاول
شعر حیات بولسا [illegible] نافات نغان که [illegible] ستود و [illegible] صیغ تیلماق بکسر لام و از تیلماق بلفون [illegible]
می یابد تیلدوروماق کنانیدن [illegible] الشاهد علی الثانی شعر اول [illegible]
اولدی نوا [illegible] صیغ [illegible] اشتقاق [illegible] تیزکدن
شمشیر و کارد [illegible] صیغ [illegible] موافق [illegible] اشتقاق می یابد من الجوامد مثل [illegible] چنانکه گوید شعر [illegible]
[illegible] چنانکه گذشت [illegible]
اول تیز کردن شمشیر گویند الشاهد علیه شعر [illegible]
بود که [illegible] آزار [illegible] چنانکه [illegible]
[illegible] گوید شعر [illegible]
[illegible] بسکون لام و [illegible] گویند [illegible]
[illegible] باشد و آنرا [illegible] چنانکه [illegible]
[illegible] چنانکه گوید شعر [illegible]
[illegible] کرده [illegible]
[illegible] محبوب القلوب [illegible] گوید که [illegible]
[illegible] الشاهد علیه شعر [illegible]
تیمنا ماق بسکون میم و نون و فتح شین [illegible] باشد و صیغ آن موافق [illegible] اشتقاق می یابد من الجوامد [illegible]
چشم احول باشد [illegible] چنانکه گوید شعر [illegible]
[illegible] شعر [illegible]
[illegible] باشد [illegible]
[illegible] بکسر جیم و سکون [illegible] آنرا [illegible] کرده [illegible] من [illegible] النون
المشتقات [illegible] بفتح نون بالف کشیده بمعنی [illegible] باشد [illegible]
[illegible] بمعنی فاعل و مصدر هم می آید [illegible] و بمعنی مصدر هم می آید [illegible]
مفرد غائب [illegible] جمع غائب [illegible]

جمع غائب [illegible]
شکنجه کرده الشاهد علی الاول شعر [illegible]
[illegible] شکنجه [illegible]
[illegible] شکنجه [illegible] باشد [illegible]
[illegible] شکنجه [illegible]
کردن [illegible] شکنجه [illegible]
کردن [illegible] شکنجه [illegible]
شکنجه کردن [illegible] چنانکه [illegible] گوید الشاهد علی الثانی شعر [illegible]
[illegible]
[illegible] بفتح نون و سکون لام [illegible] چنانکه گوید شعر [illegible]
[illegible] الشاهد علیه شعر [illegible]
[illegible] الشاهد علی الاول شعر [illegible]
[illegible] الشاهد علی الثانی شعر [illegible]
[illegible]
[illegible] الاول شعر [illegible]
[illegible] اشتقاق می یابد [illegible]
و [illegible] بمعنی فاعل و مصدر هم می آید [illegible] و بمعنی مصدر هم می آید [illegible]
[illegible]
[illegible]
[illegible]
[illegible]
[illegible]
[illegible]
[illegible]
[illegible] کردن [illegible]
[illegible] من الجوامد [illegible]
گوید شعر [illegible]
[illegible] شعر [illegible]
[illegible]

له شعر یا ردین آیرومی
وسمه بیرله قاشین اول

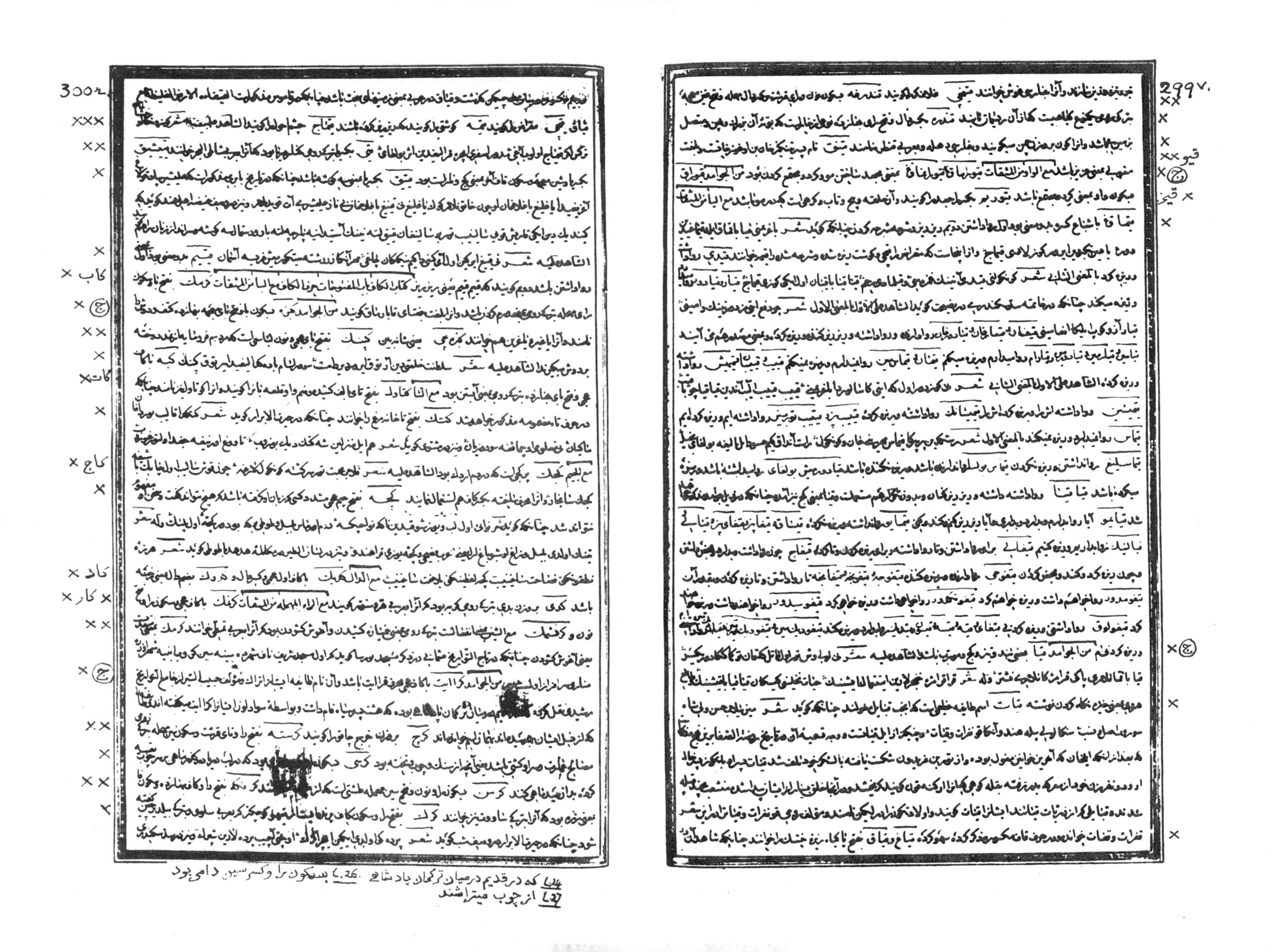

جمعیت و عذر نمایند و آنرا بفارسی خوش خوانند تیتغی قلاغه کله گویند تندرغه بکون نون و رای قرشت و کسر دال مهمله و فتح غین معجمه
ترکی مهره یکنوع کلاه است که از آن رهبانان بافند تندرم بکسر دال و فتح را و بمعنی تندرغه نوعیست از خار که بوته آن بزمین چسبیده متصل
بزمین باشد و از آن کون بعضی چیزها میگویند و بفارسی چوچه و بعربی قنطری نامند تیتوق نام پسر چنگیز خان بن اوغوز خان است و لغت
مغولیست بمعنی پز باشد مع الواو من المشتقات تیتوراما قاتیتوراما قاع بمعنی بجد ساختن و مهیا کردن و جمع کردن بود من الجوامد تیوراق
میگویند و بمعنی گرد و جمع باشد تیتوریم بجد گویند و آن حلقه پیچ و تاب و کر و لایت که در صوا باشد مع الیا من المشتقات
تیماقاق باشتباه کردن و بمعنی بود و اولکه روا داشتن ندیم دیدن و نوشته شرح کردن چنانکه گوید شعر باغ بیغیا باقاقالیغیماغید
معنی با میر بکجو ایمه کوز لاموی قیماج و از اینجاست که سرافراز مچی و گوشت ریزه شده و شرحه شده را قیمه خوانند تیدی روادا
و دریغ کرد بالمعنی الثانی شعر کونکولنی تیدی ... نینک ... تیماتیما باقینان اولالیگی کوزی قیماج قیماریفیا دور ...
دریغ میکند چنانکه در خاتمه ... بکند ... گوید الشاهد علی الاول المعنی الاول شعر جونغ ایق ... واسیق
تیاد آنرو کوپ بلکا انعامیق تیغماده تیماغان تیاد تیار ... ردواداشته و دریغ کنند ... بمعنی ... هم می آیند
تیاسیم تیلمیم تیادتیغیم ... رواداشتم و دریغ میکنم تیمام تیماسین روا ندارم ... تیبا تیمیش روادا
و دریغ کرد الشاهد علی الاول المعنی الثانی شعر ... اول ... تیب تیب ... تیماقیاچو تا
تیمیشین رواداشته ... تیبیانک رواداشته و دریغ کرده ... تیبسیز رواداشته ایم و دریغ کرده ایم
تیماس روا ندارد و دریغ نمیکند بالمعنی الاول شعر ... الیغه بولغای بجا
تیماسلیغ روا نداشتن و دریغ نکردن تیماس ... باشد ... بولغای ... باشد و دریغ
میکند باشد تیما قیتا رواداشته داشته و دریغ کرده ... چنانکه ... کوی
شد تیاتیمو آیا روا داشتم ... آیا دریغ کنم ... تیماتیمو ... تیناقه ... تیناب
تیالیند روا ندارد ... تیغمای ... روا داشتن و تا ... قیغاج ... روا داشت ... نرا
و چیزی دریغ کرد و کند و بخشش کردن متفوحی ... متفوجه ... تا روا داشتن و نا دریغ کردن ... آن
تیغومدور روا خواهم داشت و دریغ خواهم کرد تیغو ... روا خواهد داشت و دریغ خواهد کرد ... روا خواهد داشت
کرد تیغولوق رواداشتن و دریغ کردن ... تیغولیق ...
و دریغ کردن من الجوامد تیا بمعنی ... باشد الشاهد علیه شعر ... کماکان ...
تیا با تقا ... فراش ... قراقراش ... تیاقیا ... الیغ
هو یعنی خود نکاه کردن نوشته تیات اسم طایفه ... چنانکه گوید شعر ... ولی شاه
سور ... بنده و آنکه ... تیات ... ازالیقیات ... تاریخ ... الصفا ... فیع
که بعد از نکه ... که آخرین خوانین مغول بوده و از تیمورین فریدون ... شد تیات
اوده ... که بجهه ... کویند ... اسد ... قبله
شد ... تیات ... کویند ... الخلفوری ... تیات ... شعر
تیرات و تیشات خوانند ... تیاح و تیاق ... پاکجا ... خوانند چنانکه شاه ...

تیمیم ... کنشت و تیاق ... باشد ... تیغماده ... الارض ... تیم
تیاق تیمی ... تیمه کوشتوان کویند ... تیماج چرم ... کویند الشاهد ... شعر ...
ترکی ... تیماچ ... تیق ... ماند ... تیشوق
بکسیا و شین معجمه ... تیوق ... چنانکه در تاریخ ... تیمالیمه
آنرو ... یا فلیغ ... خاقان ... تیماکه ... یا فلیغ ... آن ... کویند که
کند یک ... تیمریسا ... بولورچ ... نرم
الشاهد علیه شعر ... آسمان تیم ... بود آنک
روا داشتن باشد ... کویند که ... کتاب الکاف باب المفتوحات حرف الکاف مع الباء من المشتقات کربلک ... با سکون
رای مهمله ... و از ... من الجوامد ... بسکون ... کف ... دو شد
آنرا ... خوانند ... کبسک ... نون ... ها
بدوش ... الشاهد علیه شعر ... توق کبک کبه نا
چی و فتح ... آیتن بود مع التا کتاول ... تا ... کویند ... چنانکه
در حرف ... خواهد شد کتک ... خوانند چنانکه در جریدة الابرار کوید شعر ... بوردا
تاکیان ... شعر ... او ...
مع الجیم کجک ... که ... الشاهد علیه شعر ... کشته ... کیا ... ولغا ... تا
کجک ... لجه ... چیم ... کوید مفهوم
نتواند شد چنانکه کوید شعر ... که ... اولبلیک ... شعر
... فراهند ... کوید شعر ...
... مع الدال الکدک ... ولعجمی و کسر ... مضبوط المعنی ...
باشد کدی ... مع الراء المهمله من المشتقات کرمک باکاف عجمی ...
نون و کرفیمک مع الیتب ... کشیدن و آغوش کشودن ... خوانند کرمک ...
یعنی آغوش کشودن چنانکه در تاج التواریخ ... سینه ... شمراورد
... من الجوامد کرا ... باکاف عجمی ... باشد و آن نام طایفه ... حبیب السیر ... جامع التواریخ
رشید ... ترکمان ... بوده که ... نام داشت و بواسطه ... کفته اند ...
که از قبل ایشان ... کرج ... چاقو را کویند کرسته ... راو تای قرشت و سکون سین مهمله ... بود
مصالح ... کربی ... بود ... جوب
کرده ... کرس ... بسکون را و نون و فتح سین مهمله ... کرنکه ... کفته
... بود که آنرا ... خوانند کرلک ... سلوچ ... سلید ...
شود چنانکه در جریدة الابرار ... کوید شعر ... پرده ... شعله ...

کل که در قدیم در میان ترکمان پادشاهی 26 بسکون را و کسر سین دامی بود
کل از چوب میتراشند

300v.

زنمایند شعر کرد خیل فه قرچنای [illegible] الاد چوقه [illegible] بو بیر [illegible] وبقار [illegible] المقدس [illegible]
سقف خانه را گویند کرکا بسکون را و فتح کاف ثانی بمعنی [illegible] چوب اطراف الاجوق باشد و چوبهای فوق آنرا اوق و [illegible]
کرکاو بسکون را و فتح واو و فتح کاف [illegible] شبیه [illegible] که در کوهستان باشد و گوشت آن [illegible] دارد کرمید بفتح را و کسر میم [illegible]
دال بترکی روغنی خشت پخته بود کرویه بفتح را و کسر یا بترکی روغنی [illegible] خوانند [illegible] مانند که
برای [illegible] و آنرا بعربی [illegible] گویند [illegible] کاروان قیران بترکی روغنی نام ستاره کاروان کش
بود که آنرا بعربی شعری و بفارسی [illegible] خوانند کرکه بفتح را و کاف [illegible] بترکی روغنی نوعی از [illegible] باشد و آن [illegible]
کرکی بسکون را و کسر کاف بترکی روغنی تیشه بود که بنایان [illegible] کار کنند مع الزاء المعجمه کرز باکاف عجمی [illegible]
گویند و آن [illegible] که دوسر آن باریک و میان آن [illegible] شعر [illegible]
و همه [illegible] و بفارسی [illegible] باشد [illegible] که از آهن یا چوب ساخته [illegible]
[illegible] کنند [illegible] و آنرا بترکی [illegible] و بعربی [illegible] گویند [illegible] بترکی [illegible]
[illegible] باشد چنانچه [illegible] شعر [illegible]
[illegible] باکاف عجمی و فتح زا [illegible]
چنانکه در [illegible]
[illegible] شعر [illegible]
[illegible]
لغات [illegible] باکاف عجمی و کسر لام [illegible] مع التاء المهمله [illegible]
[illegible]
[illegible] شعر [illegible]
[illegible]
[illegible] مع الشین المعجمه [illegible] مع الکاف [illegible]
[illegible]
خوانند [illegible] نام نباتیست که آنرا بعربی [illegible]
[illegible]
[illegible]
[illegible]
[illegible] بترکی روغنی [illegible]

301r.

[illegible] نوشته [illegible]
[illegible]
[illegible] باکاف عجمی و کسر لام و سکون نون و فتح جیم بترکی روغنی [illegible]
[illegible]
[illegible] کلینجک [illegible] بترکی روغنی
لاله کوهی بود که آنرا بعربی شقایق النعمان خوانند مع المیم کم باکاف عجمی بترکی روغنی [illegible] مولف برهان [illegible]
[illegible] نوشته [illegible]
[illegible] نوشته [illegible]
[illegible] بسکون میم و کاف [illegible]
[illegible] باکاف عجمی [illegible] باکاف عجمی و سکون را
و فتح تای قرشت [illegible] باکاف اول عجمی بترکی روغنی [illegible] که مثل گوشت نرم است و آنرا بعربی [illegible]
خوانند مع النون من المشتقات کندی را ناق باکاف عجمی و سکون نون و فتح دال [illegible]
[illegible]
[illegible]
[illegible]
[illegible]
[illegible]
[illegible]
[illegible]
[illegible]
[illegible]
[illegible]
[illegible] مع الکاف [illegible]
[illegible]
[illegible] باکاف عجمی و سکون نون [illegible] بترکی روغنی [illegible]
[illegible] شعر [illegible]
نون [illegible] بترکی روغنی [illegible] که از آن [illegible] و آنرا بعربی [illegible] و بفارسی [illegible] خوانند [illegible]
که از پوست [illegible] و آنرا بعربی [illegible] و بفارسی [illegible] بسکون نون [illegible]
[illegible] بفتح نون و کاف عجمی و سکون سین مهمله نام [illegible] بترکی روغنی [illegible]

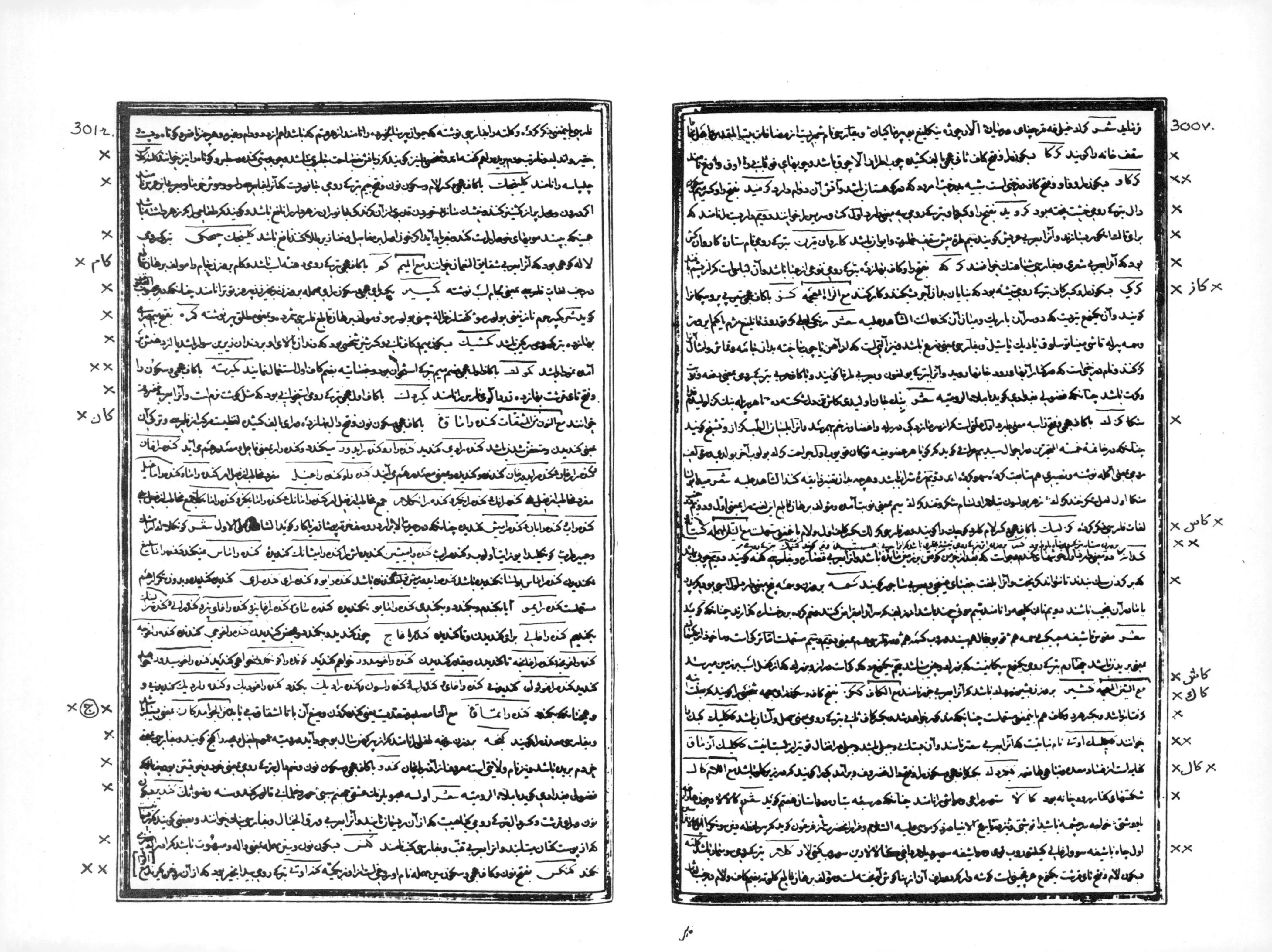

من المشتقات کاوشانالک با کاف عجمی و سکون واو و فتح شین معجمه بمعنی نشخوار کردن باشد و ترکی رومی بمعنی نرم و سست شدن هم استعمال شود

و صیغ آن بدستور مواقق شوثلثی اشتقاق می یابد کاولاماق بسکون واو بمعنی کاویدن باشد شعر اوتلار بنجه بن یکم کوزدم هم موشن کاویدی

هم آچیق تشمولی بعدیکم بو لوستور کاولاماق پراه یا روق کاولادوق کاویدیم کاولار و کاولایدور میکاود و کاولار بمعنی فاعل و مصدر هم

می آید کاولامان و کاولاعوان عکاولایدوان کاونده و کاویده و بمعنی مصدر هم می آید کاولا و کاولاغیل مفرد مخاطب فعل امر کاولاما و کاولاماغیل

مفرد مخاطب فعل نهی کاولانک و کاولانکز و کاولانکلار جمع مخاطب فعل امر کاولامانک و کاولامانکز و کاولامانکلار جمع مخاطب فعل نهی کاولای من

کاولادمین و کاولایدورمین و کاولادرام میکاوم کاولامان و کاولاماس مین نمیکاوم کاولاب و کاولابان و کاولامیش کاویده کاولامیشین

کاویده اش کاولامیشانک کاویدی کاولابتز و کاولاب تور بیز کاویده ایم کاولاماس نمیکاود کاولاماسلیغ نکاویدن کاولاماس بولسا

نکاویدن باشد کاولامیدور میش بو لغه سیکاویدن باشد کاولایو و کاولای کاولای کاوید کاویدن و بدون تکرار هم مستعملت کاولامو آیا بکاوم

و بکاود و بکاوی کاولامایو نکاوید کاولاسا و کاولاسانک کاولاغایمیز و کاولاجک کاولاتیلیق کاویر کاولاغلی برای کاویدن و تا کاویدن

کاولاغاچ چون کاوید و بکاود و بعض کاویدن کاولاغونچه کاولاغوجه کاولاغوجه و کاولاماغونچه تا کاویدن و بعد کاویدن کاولاغوسیدور

خواهم کاوید کاولاغوسیدور خواهی کاوید کاولاغوسیدور خواهد کاوید کاولاغولوق کاویدنی کاولاغاچ کاولاسه کاولاسونچه کاولادیلان بکاود

کاولاکودیلیبن کاولاکودیک تو تیر کاولاجلیک کاویده ام من الجوامد کاور کاورکا بضم واو و سکون را و فتح کاف کوسفند کلان را

خوانند چنانکه در فرهاد و شیرین در وصف پادشاه گوید شعر کورکا دیرانا یسغیر بوی بیچولدیکم مست بولغای نه دیوی کورک بسکون

واو و کاف ثانی و فتح رای مهمله بر وزن بلبلک ترکی رومی بمعنی لرزه و شکننده کوزنه بفتح واو و زای معجمه بمعانه ترکی رومی کوکنتر

الکلام بود که آنرا بعربی بقباق نامند کوزن بر وزن بوزن جانوریست که آنرا آهو گویند کوش بسکون واو و شین بمعنی نشخوار است

کوشک بسکون واو و کاف آخر و فتح شین معجمه ترکی رومی خانه بلند و ایوان را گویند مع البا من المشتقات کیمالک باشباع کسره بمعنی پوشیدن

پوشیدیر دیار کیادور بپوشد الشاهد علی الاول شعر تورتینک مختلف زحله کیم خاناتکیاد تورتینضر کیوف دوروکو یا کیم

کیاد و کیار بمعنی فاعل و مصدر هم می آید کیکار و کیکاکان و کیادکان پوشنده و پوشیده الشاهد علی الاول المعنی الثالث شعر خه

برام لار ایکیکان برنه سین تیزار اهلی بینک خوار کهربا ای که خلعت تو بنیه الوان سنکا و بمعنی مصدر هم می آید کی کیکیل مفرد

امر فعل کیما و کیماغیل مفرد مخاطب فعل نهی کیینک و کیینکز و کیینکلار جمع مخاطب فعل امر کیمانک و کیمانکز و کیمانکلار

جمع مخاطب فعل نهی دیامین کیادمین و کیاد ورمن کیار مین بپوشم کیمان کیماس مین نپوشم کییب کیبان کییمش پوشیده کیمیشین

پوشیده اش را کیمیشانک پوشیده کییب تور بیز پوشیده ایم کیماس نپوشد کیماسلیک نپوشیدن کیماس بولسا نپوشیدن

باشد کیمیش بولغه سی پوشیدن باشد کیا کیا پوشان پوشان و بدون تکرار هم مستعملت کیامو آیا بپوشم و بپوشد و بپوشی کیماپو

نپوشید کیسا که کیکایم کیکای بز کیکیلی و کیا لیک بپوشیم کیکلی برای پوشیدن و تا پوشیدن کیکاچ چون پوشید و بپوشد

و بعض پوشیدن کیکونچه کیکونچه کیکانچه تا پوشیدن و بعد پوشیدن کیکوسیدور خواهد پوشید کیکوسیدور

خواهی پوشید ~~کیکوسیدور خواهد پوشید~~ کیکولوک پوشیدنی چنانکه گوید شعر تغین کیکولوک اولسه یالانک تنیم خه

هوش حیرت تشبیهی لباس بر تنه جز کیکاکیه تکیه کیسونه کیدیلک پوشد الشاهد علی الخامس شعر اهل عیشی آلتون

اباغ ساغین ایچب کیدیلک حریرکیم سفال خرقه بستور و شلیه سنکا کیچو دیلدین کیچو دیلک تو بر بیلدیک پوشد تمام کیدورماک

مصدر متعدیست بمعنی پوشاندن کیدورکولک خواهی پوشانید الشاهد علیه شعر بهار خاطره سی سوچیزله کیدورکونک جون

بتو تعدیه حل و حال و نا قی و سنح بر بنج مواتی تنوا و الالفظ مصر اشتقاق مجاید کیسه لمنا المشع الالم پوشیده شدن و صیغ آن مجنود

بالام المشتقه تبعیه یا بد من الجوامد کیبر بسکون یا و راء مهمله و ضم با و جیم عجمی پیکان بزرانشکل است که مخصوص صید جوشانست

تیر بی را هم گویند که آن نوع پیکان تراشنه باشد چنانکه در صیغه بستان در وصف شکل بهرام گوید شعر چو نیمه سال الدولجی قوی

شکال کبر آیین بو خوز الاذی فی الجبال قاز اکمی و هم نامند و مولف فرهنگ جهانگیری و برهان قاطع کبر با کاف عجمی بمعنی پیکان تیر

نوشته کمبلی بر وزن طیلی هاون بزرگ را گویند کمیود هو فیکیر باشد که مند کومه شد چنانکه شاعر گوید شعر سوی کوری

کمپیر بی قاری مادی یاسین کیبن مانی ادیبه کوردی اما این کین بسکون یا و نون و کیبن بکسر یا و سکون نون بمعنی غضب شد هد

علی الاول شعر همیر او بین عقل و هوش و صبر و حس یاسین طوی ثمر الامع تصرتبرقع کیو دین پنهان اغیاش کیبنجه یعنی غضب

مقتایح للمولد مرد کو فتح زاد کو میکه تعبل الملای موقفه بلرهی و آندا هم کوچه تاوخون کیلیسه بتکرهانداتا شوندی باب

المضمومات حرف الکاف مع البا المثناه کو بربا بضم با و عجمی بمعنی کف کرده تاب و هر باشد کو بر بی کفن کو چنانکه گوید شعر دم

قدح ابجیل که پیلبه بو لماسا ماقط شیدن با بی اوره و نوب بقصبه که آنوخی کو بربی کو بر بوک کف کیر کو بردیکو بر کو

کف سیکند و کو بربر بمعنی فاعل و مصدر هم می آید کو برکان و کو برپرکان و کو بر ادرکان کف کننده و کف کرده و بمعنی مصدر هم می آید کو بو

کو بر کید مفرد مخاطب فعل امر کو بر نا و کو بر ناکید مفرد مخاطب نهی کو برند و کو بر بندو کو بر دیکو بر و نکلار جمع مخاطب فعل امر

کو بر نایکز و کو بر نانکلار جمع مخاطب نهی کو برامین و کو برمین و کو برادمین و کو بر مرام کف میکنم کو برمان و کو برماس مین کف

مینکم کو بروب و کو بروبان و کو بر میش کف کرده کو برمیشین کف کرد اش را کو برمیشانک کف کرده کو بر وبسیز و کو بر دوب تور کف

کرده ایم کو بر ماس کف میکند کو برماسلیک کف نکرده کو بر ماس بولسا کف نکنند باشد کو بر دو میش و بعضی کف میکرده باشد کو بو

کو برار کف کنان کف کنان و بدون تکرار هم مستعملت کو برامیو آیا کف کنم و کند و کنی کو بر مانیو کف نکرده کو بر ماسنکو بو

کو بولی امدو بو ارلنداز کف کنیم کو بر کاچه برای کف کردن و تا کف کرده کو بر کاچ چون کف کرده کند و بعض کردن کو بر کوچی کف کنند

کو برکه و کو بر کو غه و کو بر طغه تا کف کردن و بمعنی کف کردن و کو بر مسدود کف خواهم کرد کو بر کو نکو در کف خواهد کرد کو بر فوسیدو کف

خواهد کرد کو بر کو لوک کف کردنی کو بر کای و کو بر موکو بر سمو کو بر سو تیکو بر دیک کف کند کو بر کید یکمین و کو بر کید یک

کف کرده ام کو بر مسانک بسکون طا و تا و قرشت مصدر متعدیست و صیغ آن با تمام تای قرشت اشتقاق می یابد کو بو لمالک بسکر

و صیغ آن بدستور بالا ما اشتقاق می یابد من الجوامد کوب با بای عجمی بمعنی دار و اول بمعنی بسیار باشد و دوم خم را گویند چنانکه در معنی

حیرت الابرار بطریق ایهام گوید شعر ساقی آکیکیل تولا بجمانه تو تو غلط ایتیم تولا بجمانه آکوب کوب آلیبان سیبقاد اوکو

کو بلیپص هو دم ارنو مدین باراتی کو بجلک بسکون بای عجمی و کاف ثانی و فتح جیم عجمی چرخ چراه باشد و از استیکرالک نیز نامند

بسکون با و نون و کسر جیم و کو بجوک بضم جیم و کو بجوک مع الکاف بالشبه زین بوده کو بجوک با بای عجمی ترکی روغن کو چلدام

کو برالک یعنی بیشتر و زیادتر چنانکه گوید شعر چو تیغین کردی قانمه فرح بولدیب منکا افزون بیوک کیم سو فری

بو لماغ کو بر دلک بسکون بای عجمی و کاف و ضم رای مهمله پل را گویند که آنرا بعربی قنطره خوانند در حیرت الابرار شعر کو بر و دا او لوبا

تا حیات لیک خیالی که اول اولنای خیال کوبلت با کاف اول عجمی و فتح تای عربی بمعنی ناف باشد و با کاف عربی و بای عجمی

که کسه کوبلت ساز بنغ نام جانوریست ز دو کسی که از پوست پوستین میسازند کو پلک با کاف عربی و فتح بای عجمی و لام

شبیه پروانه اما بزرگتر از آن که نقشهای الوان در پر و بال دارد و در باغستانات می باشد الشاهد علیه شعر لباس الافتق

کبلدی براق که کوبیلر ارخه پروانه دیلنا و نجار کوبالث و باکاف عجمی و بای عربی نباتیست سفید بشکل پنجه تخم مرغ که مسکر باشد
و بی برلد و مناقش کوناه و جفنا و هلوا و مضارع و بغار جی تلج و ملبان الکلب فطر و کما .. کویند و بنات الرعد نیز خوانند و آن
ماکول و غیر ماکول میباشد و غیر ماکول آن در جاهای نمناک و تر خمهای و جوف درختان میروید و آن در ظلمه جیلست
کوبنک بفتح با و نون بلغت مغولی پنبه باشد که آنرا بعربی قطن کویند کوپوک بضم بای عجمی کفی که بر روی آب و مانند آن پیدا
شود و آنرا بعربی زبد کویند کوپوک طاشی سنکی روی نیز مانند کف دریاست و آن مانند سنکی بود سفید که بجوف بسیار دارد
و آنرا بفارسی پفک کویند و فیشنج و معرب ان فست کوبون بضم با و سکون نون بلغت مغولی پیمانه را نامند کوبه بفتح با بمعنی جهان
که آنرا بعربی عطف خوانند و مغولیه ختا و طایفه قلماق نیز کوبر کویند لیکن اتراک توران و خوارزم و پری و غفراوین خوانند
و این دو لفظ فارسی است و کوپر بای عجمی بر که روی کوشوله بود و بفارسی پشلغ و شیشه جام باشد کوبرجی نام محلی است از بها
ز اقتاع داغستان که شبکاه و لکز به لغت نما مطرح و نیز نام یکنوع شالیست آبی نیز جانانکه از چشم نامند و با متن آن مخصوص ماوراء نهر است
کوپنه باکاف عجمی و کسر بای عجمی خیزی باشد که در آنجا ماست ریخته بر هرزه و روغن بکیرند و آنرا با پیچ هم نامند کوپ با عجمی کنایه از شطر
انکور باشد که بصیر و پای المثل بنظام شود چنانچه کوید شعر کوشه بخانه دین کلشفه تا بطان یکم شکا کل العین نیز بی کل آنک
امنه کوپ تاقی جین و له شعر بیناء کردون شبستانیدا انجمن شمع ایمز شمع کون حق سوز تای ایمکوم اولسا نیز مو کوپ تا قی
مع التاء المثناة کوتماک بمعنی جرانیدن باشد چنانچه در لسان الطیر در مکالمه دختر ترسا با شیخ صنعان کوید شعر کونفو
اونه تومناغای سین ناتوان کیم تونکوز کوتماکقا بولغای سین روان و از اینجهت کوتماک با دال الاستعمال نامند کوتوک
کوتارم کوتار دو در بچراند چنانچه شاه میر لطفی در حالت جرانیدن شیخ صنعان کوید شعر کچه آتشکا اوتین جلالا یا نار بولدی
چون کوند و تونکوز لار نی کوتار و کوتلر بمعنی فاعل و مصدر هم می آید کوتکان و کوتارکان و کوتار دورکان چرانده و چرانیده بمعنی مسند
هم می آید کوت و کوتکیل مفرد مخاطبه بنفی امر کوتمه و کوتماکیل مفرد مخاطبه نفی امر کوتونک و کوتونکیز و کوتونکلار
جمع مخاطبه بنفی امر کوتمانک و کوتمانکیز و کوتمانکلار جمع مخاطبه بنفی امر کوتاین و کوتارین و کوتادورین و کوتادام بچرانم کوتقان کوتماس
بچرانم کوتوبم کوتوبان و کوتمیش چرانیده کوتمیشین چرانیده اشترا کوتمشانک چرانیده کوتوبیز و کوتوب تورمیز چرانیده ایم
کوتماس بچراند کوتماسلیک چرانیدن کوتماس بولسا بچرانیده باشد کوتادورور لفظی بچرانیده باشد کوتا کوتا چرانیده چرانیده
و بدون تکرار هم مستعملست کوتاعمو آیا بچرانم و بچراند بچرانی کوتماس بو چرانیده کوتسا ام و کوتکای بیز و کوتای و کوتکای نیک بچرانیم
کوتکالی برای چرانیدن و تا چرانیده چنانچه بمیر اول کوید شعر جون جبرایل یار ایدا بای بوقاریکاندا بمعجزه زنلیک که بولغای وحشی
جیلین کوتکالی چوپان بعون دیک کوتکاج چون چرانید و بچراند و پس چرانیدن کوتکوچی چراننده کوتکوچه و کوتکونچه و کوتکانچه
تا چرانیدن و بقصد چرانیدن کوتوسدور خواهم چرانید و کوتوسدورمو خواهد چرانید و کوتسادور خواهد چرانید کوتکولوک چرانیدنی
کوتکای و کوتکوسی و کوتکوچه بچراند چنانچه شاه میر لطفی در تاریخ الانبیاء در ذکر موسی علیه السلام کوید که مفعول آنلیغ تیرین
آتا آنادی بوشوکیله کیم سیکوز یل موسی شعیب علیهما السلام نینک قوینین کوتکای کوتکودیک هم کوتکودیلک تبریه هم کوتار چراند فی ام
کوتارغالک بفتح تا و سکون را و عین مهمله بمعنی برداشتن کوتاردوک برداشتیم کوتاردو کوتارادور و کوتارسیلار و کوتارغوچی بمعنی فاعل و مصدر هم
می آید کوتارکان و کوتاروکان و کوتارداکان برداشته و برداشته بمعنی مصدر هم می آید کوتار و کوتارغیل مفرد مخاطبه بالامر برداشتن
کوتارماغیل مفرد مخاطبه بنفی امر کوتارینک و کوتارینکیز و کوتارینکلار جمع مخاطبه بنفی امر کوتارمانک و کوتارمانکیز و کوتارمانکلار جمع مخاطبه

کوتارامین و کوتارادورمین و کوتاراتورمین و کوتارادوام برمیدارم کوتارمان و کوتارماس و کوتارسام برمیدارم کوتارماکامین و کوتارماکادورمین برمیدارم کوتارالماغای مین
نتوانم برداشت چنانکه در منتهی بلیجه و غنیه کوید کوتارغالی و چارچه قدم کوتارا الماغایمین کوتاریب کوتاریبان و کوتارمیش برداشته کوتارمیشین
برداشته ام اشترا کوتارمیشانک برداشته کوتارماس برنمیدارد کوتارماسلیک برنداشتن کوتارماس بولسا برنداشته باشد کوتارادورمیش تونکاهی برداشته
باشد کوتارا کوتارا برداشته برداشته و بدون تکرار هم مستعملست کوتاراعمو آیا بردارم و بردارد و بردارید کوتارغای بو بردارد و برداشته
کوتارسام و کوتارکای بیز و کوتارکای و کوتارکای نینک بردارم کوتارغالی برای برداشتن و تا برداشته کوتارکاچ چون برداشت و بردارد و پس برداشتن
چنانکه در منتخب اللطایف در صفت امیر خسرو کوید شعر بنجه قیاس شکاه کوتارکاچ علم ایلدی مسخر ملکت کیتی علم کوتارکوچی بردارنده و چنانچه
تسلیم الجنته منوچهر کا ابو سعید ابوالخیر کوید که خلیل علیه السلام کوتارکوچی لوا مولانا الروم که آنی سیزوم کوتارکای کوتارکوچه کوتارکونچه و کوتارکانچه
تا برداشتن و بقصد برداشتن کوتارکوم خواهم برداشت کوتارکونک خواهی برداشت چنانکه در فرهاد و شیرین کوید شعر جون منع ایل
ملجا اولک هرنه دانه اکوتار کونک جان و دانه کوتارکوچی خواهد برداشت کوتارکولوک برداشتنی کوتارکای کوتارسون کوتارسیه کوتاریسون و کوتارمای
بر طرح کوتارکودیلین و کوتارکودیلک توبیرمی کوتارادیر تور برداشتم من الجواهر کوتاول مرکبیست از کوت که بلغت هندی بمعنی قلعه است
و لفظ اول که بلغت ترکی در اول اکثر الفاظ افاده معنی فاعلیت میکند و معنی ترکیبی آن قلعه بان نشسته قراول که بمعنی دیده بان باشد کوتوال
مرکبست از کوت بمعنی قلعه و لفظ وال که بمعنی بانست در ظاهر معنی ترکیبی آن قلعه بان باشد چنانکه شحنه و الی بمعنی شحنه بان بود کوتل
بفتح تا و سکون لام اسب جنیبه را نامند و بفارسی کوه پستان خوانند کوتوروم بضم تا و را و مهمله شل زمین کیر که کویند که پای او از جنس
جلکنا مانده باشد کوتولدی بضم تا در معنی طرح او کاهیمه کنده کویند حوتم با سطلاح اتراک درم دفتر خانه پادشاهی باشد کوتی بمعنی تا
برکه دو معنی دارد بمعنی بوده مع الجیم من المثناة کوچماک با جیم بمعنی کوچ کردن کوچنولوک کوچ کردیو کوچار کوجاد و کوچ
کوچار بمعنی فاعل و مصدر هم می آید کوچکان و کوچارکان و کوچادورکان کوچ کننده و کوچ کرده چنانچه شاه میر لطفی در تاریخ الانبیا
در وصف بنی اسرائیل کوید که آقشام منزل نه تونکاندین سونکرا کوچکان منزل ایردی و بمعنی مصدر هم می آید کوچ و
کوچکیل مفرد مخاطبه بالامر کوچماو کوچماکیل مفرد مخاطبه بنفی امر کوچونک و کوچونکیز و کوچونکلار جمع مخاطبه بنفی امر کوچمانک
کوچمانکیز و کوچمانکلار جمع مخاطبه بنفی امر کوجامین و کوجادورمین و کوجاتورمین کوچ میکنم کوجمان و کوجماس مین کوچ نمیکنم کوچوب و کوچ
کوچمیش کوچ کرده کوچمیشین کوچ کرده ام کوچمیشانک کوچ کرده کوچماس کوچ نمیکند کوچماسلیک کوچ نکردن کوچماس بولسا کوچ نکرده باشد کوچادورمیش کوچ کرده باشد کوچا کوچا کوچ کنان و بدون تکرار هم مستعملست کوچاعمو
آیا کوچ کنم و کنید و کنی کوچای بو کوچ نکرده کوچسام کوچکای بیز و کوچکای و کوچکای نینک کوچ کنیم کوچکالی برای کوچ کردن و تا کوچ
کرده کوچکاچ چون کوچ کرد و کنید پس کوچ کردن کوچکوچی کوچ کننده کوچکوچه کوچکونچه و کوچکانچه تا کوچ کردن و بقصد کوچ کردن کوچکوم
کوچ خواهم کرد کوچکونک خواهی کرد کوچکوسی خواهد کرد کوچکولوک کوچ کردنی کوچکای کوچکای کوچکوسی کوچسون
کوچ کند کوچکودیلین و کوچکودیلک توبیرمی کوچادیر تور کوچ کرده ام کوچماک بضم جیم و سکون را و مهمله مصدر متعدی است بمعنی کوچانیدن
کوچورونک کوچانیدی الشاه علیه شعر کونکلوم بوزه لوب صبر و خرد ایلا هیلاهی رخت چون مالک بوزه دونک ایلینی
کوچوروک مزاق صیغ برین تاق بضم جیم مع الراء المهمله اشتقاقی باید کوچکانمالی بسکون جیم و نون و فتح کاف ثلاثی بمعنی نعره
کوچکاغورک نعره زدیم کوچکانور کوچکانادور نعره میکند و کوچکانکوچی بمعنی فاعل و مصدر هم می آید کوچکانکان کوچکانورکان کوچکانادورکان
نعره زننده و نعره زده و بمعنی مصدر هم می آید کوچکان کوچکانکیل مفرد مخاطبه بالامر کوچکانماکیل مفرد مخاطبه بنفی امر

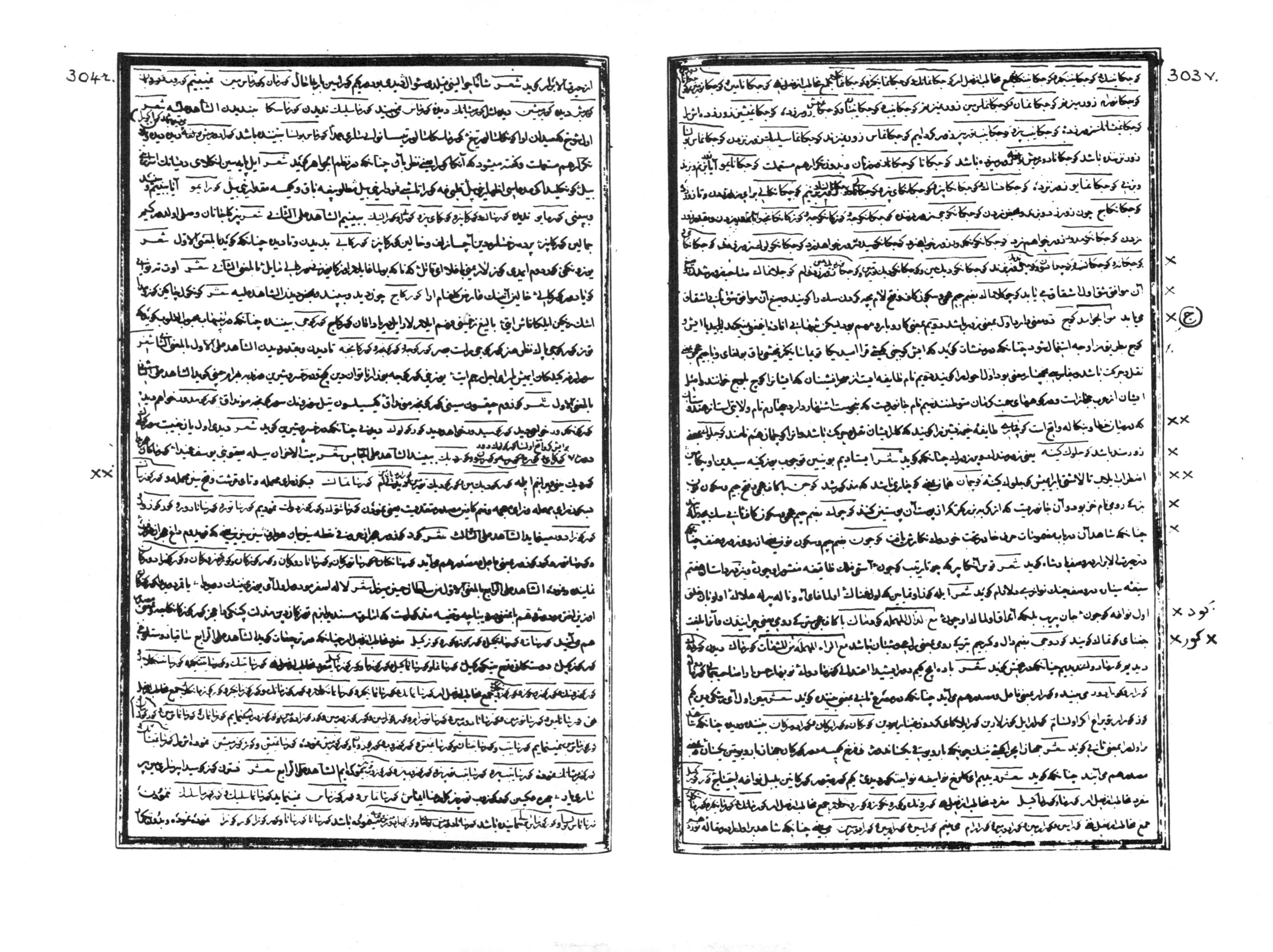

[illegible]

[illegible]

هم مستعملست کورساتاای و کورساتا نیز و کورکوزنا و کورن بنمایم و بنماید و بنمای و بنموده چنانچه بمعنی اول گوید لشاهد علی الاول شعر چهره
که لجانچا لدلریقین کورناتی عشق اهلیغه دعوی قیلماسان ایلکا امرکا تاکا لشاهد علی الرابع شعر نوایا سنکا بو سوز طشیمه
قدح کیتمه کیم خلولیغیه کورکوزکای پیر پر کورساتا یو و کورکوزا یو آیا بنمایم و بنماید و بنمای کورسلغایو و بنمایم و بنموده کورساتانک کورساتکا
کورساتکای نیز و کورساتلی و کورساتالیک و کورساتکو و کورکوزکای نیز و کورکوزلکو کورسالنجایم و کورساتکو و کورکوزکالی برای نمودن و
تا نمودن کورساتکلچ و کورکوزکاچ چون نمود و بنماید و بعض نمودن کورساتکوچی و کورکوزکوچی نماینده چنانچه شاه بدیع در تاریخ بابری
مذکورست که ابو سعید میرزانینک بوراغی بین خبری با رایگان ندهد بلکه بوراغی کورساتکوچی اوشول غدار ایکاندور شاه بدیع
در دیباچه نظم الجواهر گوید لکوفا کهنه و نخل جهان سیله سحر بطالت کد کوزکوچی کورساتکوچی کورساتکنه و کورکوزکونه
و کورکوزکوچی کورساتکا خه تا نمودن و بقدم نمودن کورساتکوچی و کورکوزکونه و کورکوزکو برای نمودن کورساتکای و کورساتکو کورساتقانه و کورساتقون و
کورساتالیک و کورکوزکای و کورساتکو و کورکوزکوچی و کورکوزلی بنماید کورساتکوچی و کورساتکو و کورکوزکوچی نمودنی و همچنانچه نما
چنانچه سید سکندری در وصف آینه ... گوید لشاهد علی الثالث بالمعنی الاخیر شعر یار و قهر یوزی چهره کورد کوز کوردیک
دیبای بریوزی نه دو کوز کوردیک کورونماک بضم الراء و سکون النون و میم مفتوحه مرئی و نمودار شدن کورونکان و کورونوکان و کورونادرکان نمودار شونده
و نمودار شده لشاهد علی الاول بالمعنی الثانی شعر ملرضیلغا مرافیدا کل جمال کورونکان ای پری یا متردد بنده لاصفه تا ترتیب
شد و سید لادو بمعنی سید هم می آیند کورونکاچ چون نمودار شد و نمود و بعض شدن چنانچه گوید شعر کیچه مرکوک
کورونکاچ مادیمه آییم کیلوری آیچو طالع بولدی مهر طالم آرایم کیلوری کورونکوچه و کورونکوچکا و کورونکاچه تا نمودار شدن و بقدم نمودار
شدن لشاهد علی الثالث بالمعنی الثانی شعر جان بیبیم ای ای باصفه شارایتای لیلطایر بلمولیمونی کورنکا کورونکانچه
بونساع و نالنه سیغ بری ساق بانور اشتقاق می یابد کورشمک بضم الراء الثانی بهمدیگر دیدن و ملاقات کردن چنانچه گوید شعر
کورشماکیمکا اگر بولسا ملتفت بولغای وصال طوی جنت بیله کیا هیم فه کورشور و کورشاد و ملاقات میکند و کورشور بمعنی فاعل
و مصدر هم می آید چنانچه بمعنی مصدر فرماید شعر یا بوسوی احتساب بکرای شاولیغ اشکی بخل ایله دلبر کورشماغا یو کورشکا
کورشکوچی و کورشکلی مفرد غائب المتصل کورشکانچه گوید لشاهد علی الثانی شعر کورشکیلی اریچی پیرله حریت
بیله ... مفرد باجراتیله و باقیسیغ برین فعل باشیغ بنا اشتقاق می یابد کورشمک بالکاف العجمی و فتح الراء الثانی بمعنی کشتی گرفتن باشد
کورشوکورشادور کشتی میگیرد و کورشور بمعنی فاعل و مصدر هم می آید کورشکان کورشکان کورشور کورشادورکان کشتی گیرنده و کشتی گرفته
و بمعنی مصدر هم می آیند کورشور کورشکوچی مفرد غائب المتصل کورشاتور کورشاتکوچی مفرد غائب المتصل کورشیسنکیز کورشکورسنکیز
کورشیسنکلار جمع غائب المتصل کورشاتمالک کورشاتمانکیز کورشاتقالار جمع غائب المتصل کورشاتور کورشاتمایمن کورشانادورمن کورشادورام
کشتی میگیرم کورشاتمان کورشاتمانس کشتی میگیریم کورشاتیسه کورشاتماسان و کورشاتمش کشتی گرفته کورشاتمیشمین کشتی گرفته ام کورشاتوری
کشتی گرفته کورشاتمیسه و کورشاتمشوبر کشتی گرفته ایم کورشاتماس کشتی میگیرم کورشاتماس کورشاتماسلیک کشتی نگرفتن کورشاتماس بولسا کشتی نگرفته باشد
کورشادوسون کشتی میگرفته باشد کورشاتا کورشاتا کشتی گرفته گرفته و بعضی تکرار هم مستعملست کورشاتا یو آیا کشتی گیرم و
بگیری کورشاتا یو کشتی نگرفته کورشاتالیک و کورشکانکای نیز و کورشکالی و کورشاتالیک کشتی گیرم کورشکالی برای کشتی گرفتن
و تا گرفته کورشکاچ چون کشتی گرفت و بگیرد و بعض گرفتن کورشکوچی کشتی گیرنده کورشکوچه کورشکونه و کورشکانچه تا کشتی گرفتن و
بقدم کشتی گرفتن کورشکوچه کشتی خواهم گرفت کورشکوسیده کشتی خواهد گرفت کورشکولوک کشتی گرفتنی است

کورشتورماک کورشتورمک و کورشتور ماک کشتی گیرانیدن کورشتورکان کورشتوروچی میرکورنک کورشتور ماک کشتی گرفتن کورشتورماک مضی
مستعمل چیست میبی بکشتی انداختن و سیغ الکی بر قیاس تا لفظ و اشتقاق می یابد کورکاماک بکسر الراء و تای حطی و فتح کاف و سکون حرف
مناسب حسن شدن کورکاییوک مناسب حسن شدیم کورکایورو کورکانادور مناسب حسن میشود و کورکایور بمعنی فاعل و مصدر هم
کورکایکان و کورکایکان و کورکایادورکان مناسب حسن شونده و مناسب حسن شده و بمعنی مصدر هم می آیند کورکای و کورکایچیل مفرد غائب المتصل
کورکایسا و کورکایساکیل مفرد غائب المتصل کورکایسلار و کورکایسنکلار جمع غائب المتصل کورکایمانک کورکایمانکیز و کورکایماسنکلار
جمع غائب المتصل جمع کورکایمن و کورکایورمین و کورکایادورمن مناسب حسن میشوم کورکایمان و کورکایمامن مناسب حسن میشوم کورکایب
کورکاییسان و کورکایمش مناسب حسن شده چنانچه میر سید سکندری در وصف پری گوید لشاهد علی الاول شعر بلشافان ساریغ انش
ایچرا با بیبی کان دلبر ... کورکایب و مولف گوید کورکایب تا تا ... بعضی نوشته سهو کرده کورکایمیشمین مناسب
حسن شده ام کورکایمیشمیز مناسب حسن شده کورکایسیز و کورکایب توریز مناسب حسن شده ایم کورکایماس مناسب حسن نیشود کورکایما
مناسب حسن شدن کورکایماس بولسا مناسب حسن نشده باشد کورکایدورکان مناسب حسن نیشده باشد کورکانا کورکانا مناسب حسن
شده و بدون تکرار هم مستعملست کورکایمو آیا مناسب حسن شوم و شوی کورکایکانیو مناسب حسن شونده کورکایالیک و کورکالی نیز
کورکایکالی و کورکالی کورکایا مناسب حسن شویم کورکایکالی برای مناسب حسن شدن و تا شدن کورکایکاچ چون مناسب حسن شد و شود
کورکایکوچی مناسب حسن شونده کورکایکوچه و کورکایکونه و کورکایکانچه تا مناسب حسن شدن و بقدم آن کورکایکومدور مناسب حسن خواهم شد
کورکایکوسیدور مناسب حسن خواهی شد کورکایکوسیدور مناسب حسن خواهد شد کورکایکولوک مناسب حسن شدنی کورکایکای و کورکایکاوی
کاینمو کورکایوتور و کورکایب مناسب حسن شود کورکایب توربن و کورکایب تورییک مناسب حسن شده نیام کوردکلا تماک بضم دال
سکون کاف و فتح لام شعله ور شدن آتش و ماننده آن دمیدن دم و غیم و صیغ آن موافق شق اول اشتقاق می یابد کورکولداماک و کورکولدا اشماک
بالکاف العجمی غرید نعره کشیدن شیر و امثال آن را گویند و صیغ کورکولداتماک موافق شق ثانی واز کورکولداشماک موافق شق اول اشتقاق می یابد
کورماک بفتح راء کورمه بمعنی پا رو کردن بیل پاروکوراش بالکاف الفارسی بمعنی کشتی باشد کوراشچی بمعنی کشتی گیر چنانچه
الحقه موکب پهلوان محمود پهلوان گوید که هند ملکی ... اوشا و پینک پیر کوراشچی بار ایدی پهلوانی آهینلا و جنیلا کان ایمیش کورکنک
بیله کوراشکاندا تفای کوبنز بضم با و ضم جیم و سکون نون اعجمی ... مرد نوخاسته را گویند و بعضی بضم
باشد چنانچه در قاموس سطور است الحمرز بالضم الخبیث معرب کبند و بمعنی مکار و خداع هم استعمال میشود و مولف برهان قاطع تو
کمخیا ... که از آن قماش ... کنید در نوت ... و ترکی بمعنی کاری و ... چنانچه شاه
در تفصیل کتاب ... لغات ... کوربیه بسکون اول و فتح ثانی ... بمعنی جامه اول ... گویند دوم ...
جانند کوردون بسکون اول و نون و ضم تای قرشت ترکمه ... الآن ... را مانند ترکی بالکاف العجمی و سکون ... و کسر جیم توله ... گویند
ونیز نام طایفه کرج باشد کوند روبینه جوانان نوخاسته را گویند و از آن ... خوانند و بفارسی ... آهن بود کورلت
و سکون کاف ... معوج ... را کویند ... استخوان شانه را خوانند ... سکون اول و کاف بعد بمعنی ... اوک
پشم ... که از ... موی ... و از لغت ... خوانند ... که از ... باشد و مولف برهان قاطع کورلک
باشد و بمعنی ... لغات ... بسکون ... حسن و جمال و نمود باشد چنانچه ... گوید
وصف پادشاه گوید شعر اولا ملکا که دشت ... ترک و عرب ... لاله کوکطا ... کورلک ...

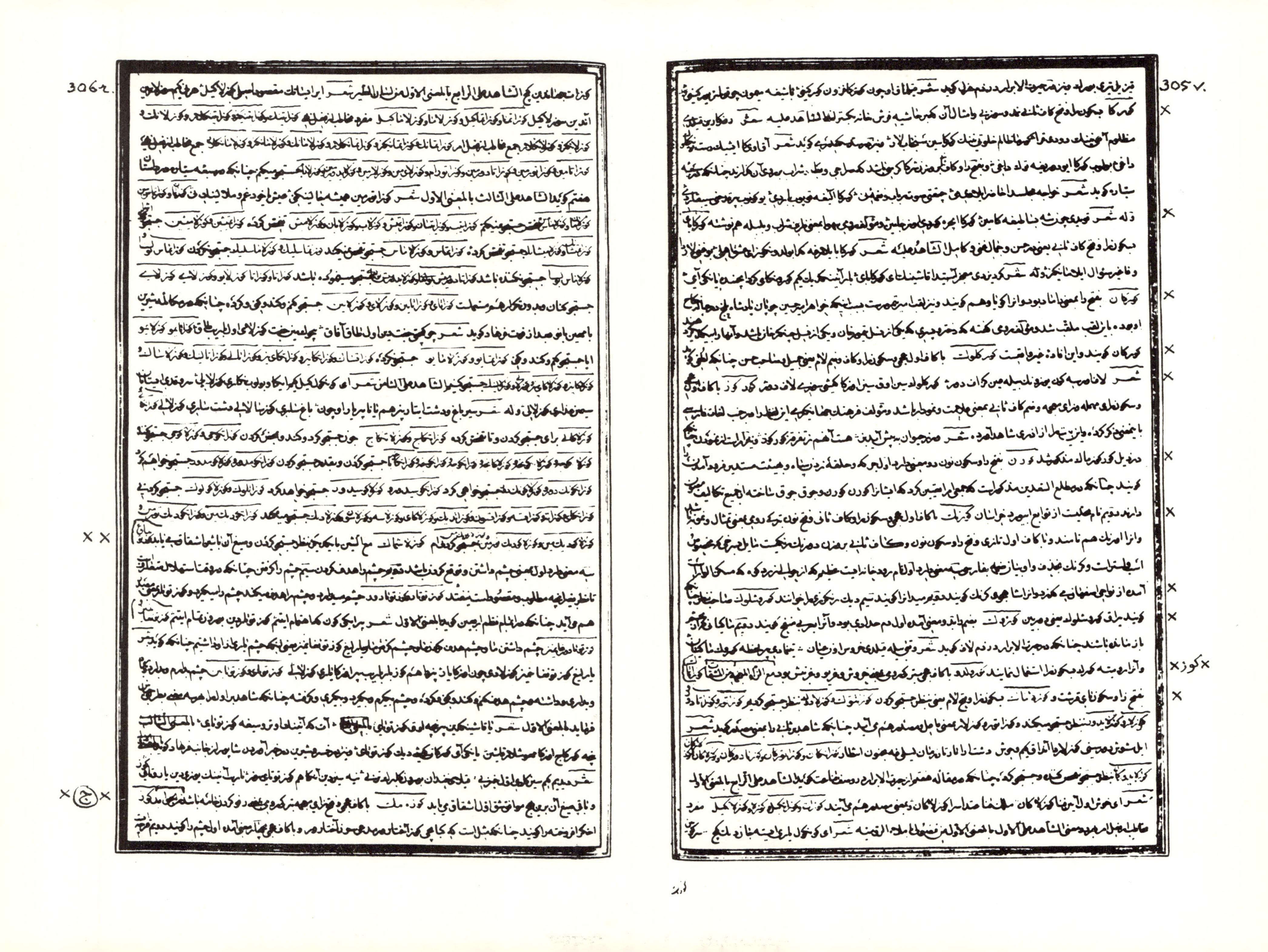

کوز

[illegible]

[illegible]

306v.

که از بدن بر آید چنانچه بمرود معنوی بطریق ایهام گوید شعر یا کوزلار دور لوب تنلار چو بولدی خیره اول بیر زمین مایشا بیلن مرهم ایکی

توکانلار نشکوی زمینك سیتم سه تا مفصل خونریز انا منداله شاهد علیه شعر یوق تفاوت عشق دشتی ظلمیدا ایسیغ تاووغ [illegible]

اوت ته سیر الیه دوا نینك دمی ایدو کوزنی و بیرنه خسرو شیرین و یوسف ملبدی کی گوید شعر بیلها و لاغر اوجی الیکیم کوزنی ساوو حلب

با فلاطون چشمه لار موز چها ام معنی چشمه بود چنانچه دولیغ تاری منکر کابلی تکرارست که کوزلار اوج تهرتای کیم ناد کور [illegible]

یکچید بیول لار نینك عبوری محل بود کوز کو باکاف عجمی آینه را گویند کوزل بفتح زا کاه و چاشالك سوخته و بسینه تر خوب [illegible]

و باکاف عجمی و بمعنوی طرد اول بمعنی خوب و ملیح باشد چنانچه ضیا گوید با ملك الزنیته شعر در هر ده همتا سنکا ولار دیبی [illegible]

واد کوزل چنخ و لیمن کبی خوبلیو یبغ دویم کیلدی داخواند کوز لولت باکاف عجمی بمعنی دارد اول کمند کرگس کهنا یعنی [illegible]

چنانچه لطفی گوید شعر ای اوج ملاحت او سیدا آی یوز لوله کلاز لطافت ارا زکس کهنالوك ثویم تبرکه دو معینك باشد [illegible]

با من بر چشم کلازند سیم دانه ایت سیاه و لغزیده که در بوطهای چشم بکار برند و کیا هیت که آن را بفارسی چشمك و بعربی اضراس الکلب

گویند تونسه باکاف عجمی و فتح زا و میم بهاز بمعنی تبرکه دو معنی بود باشد که بر خامه پلمور نیند کوز ولسا باکاف عجمی و میم زا و فتح نون و سکون

آخر از الآن نجاست الشاهد علیه شعر ای نوا اول سفر که نیش حنظل ایچون کوز ولماپیدار که هر پلیژ تکیلیش کوز لار ...

مع السین المهملة من المشتقات کوسماك فتر کردن چنانچه سلطان حسین بیرزا فرماید شعر ایت بانا حاجت تیرا کاسیکا خبر یوقلی کوسولت

بوشلیمك هم زمان لوك شوخ دین کوسما لغنیدهمت و سیغ آن موافق شود اول اشتقاق باید کوستیمك باکاف عجمی و سکون سین فتح تا

قرشت بترکه رومی بمعنی نمودن باشد من الجوامد کوسنا و کیکون و او و همنم حنظل گفته چنانچه گوید شعر فراق لمیدا تا دار و بیر کوکه

بوادی تاروننقلی میوه هوا نایلیکیتکیلدی کمنلو وارتکومینه کوسنا کو نامند کوستیلك بکوزهین فتح نا قرشت و یا ابجد ترکیده

یکجوع موشی لت که چشم ندارد کوستلك بکوزهین فتح تا قرشت بترکه رومی شکال و نابند کو ناهات که بپایت مخرزند کو سم فتح

سین بترکه رومی بزنجی باشد که بتاچش که منضدان نه روند و از ابلیغ جتای اورکه نامند و بعربی قاید و کلان جفار حرف خزنعلر گفته

مع الشین المعجمة کوشك بفتح شین و سکون کاف تازی بمعنی کوشك بفتح شین و لام شتربچه یکساله را خوانند و دو سال را ازا تو و هم سه سال را

تابلاق نامند مع الکاف من المشتقات کوکاریتماك با هر دو کاف عجمی و سکون را بمعاوره تا فوقانیت سمعیت دو معنی اول کردن و نیلی شدن

و سبز کردن دویم معنی کبود و کبود کردن باشد کوکاریتولت سبزکیم و کبود کردن کوکاریتدی کوکاریتاد و سبز میکند و کبود میکند کوکاریتبر معنی اول

و معنی دویم و آید چنانچه بمعنی سبز کردن گوید شعر کوکلیدا تبرکا عجت دشتی تیشکیم نایلمسی بیراه برلیغیم ددوجین کولیمیدا آی

الحمد کوکاریتاد و کاریتاد نا ... کبود کرده و سبز کرده و کبود کرده و معنی منصوم سیم آیند کوکاریتمک کا تیکیل مفرد غائب

مضارع کوکاریتیمادوکاریتایکل مفرد غائب مضارع کوکاریتیدیکه کوکاریتیکاری جمع غائب ماضی ار کوکاریتایك و کوکاریتیکرو کوکاریتیمادا

جمع غائب مضارع ده تر بر بر حرفکاریتیه بین حکوکاریتادی مرنتبه کوکاریتادام سبزمیکیم و کبود میکیم کوکاریتماس بین سبزمیکنم و کبود

میکنم کوکاریتیسه مطاریتیسان کوکاریتیس سبز کرده و کبود کرده الشاهد علی الاول المعنی الاول شعر ایماستمره بیوکلالاله

که ز اله تاشیدن کردون کوکاریتیسه ابیرین هر طرف ظلم ای اجیح تانی کوکاریتیس سبز کرده ای او کبود کرده ای کوکاریتانك سبز

و کبود کرده کوکاریتیه بهر تکوکاریتیه تیمر بر سبز کرده ایم و کبود کرده ایم کوکاریتیابا س سبز میکند و کبود میکند نه ... سبز کردن کوکاریتماس

نکردن کوکاریتماس بولسا سبز نکنند باشد و کبود نکنند باشد کوکاریتماس ... سبز میکند باشد و کبود میکند باشد کوکاریتا

کوکاریتا سبزکنان و کبود کنان و بمعنی کلا هم مستعملت کوکاریتیمو آیا سبز کنیم و کبود کنیم و کبود کنیم کوکاریتا بو سبز کرده

و کبود نکرده کوکاریتساله کوکاریتکایمنر و کوکاریتکای مرد کوکاریتماس ابد کوکاریتسالوك سبز نکنیم و کبود نکنیم کوکاریتکیلی برای سبز کردن و کبود کردن

و برای کبود کردن و نا کبود کرده کوکاریتکاچ چون سبز کند و کبود کند و چون کبود کند بعضی گفته اند کوکاریتوچی سبز کننده و کبود کننده کوکاریتکیه

کوکاریتکوچی کوکاریتکانیه تا سبز کردن و بعد از آن و تا کبود کردن و بعد از آن کوکاریتکودیدور سبز خواهد کرد و کبود خواهد کرد کوکاریتکولدی

سبز خواهم کرد و کبود خواهم کرد کوکاریتکیسیدور سبز خواهد کرد و کبود خواهد کرد کوکاریتکولولت سبز کرده و کبود کرده کوکاریتماکلک

کوکاریتماکلیکی کوکاریتیدور سبز کند و کبود کند کوکاریتکیسی ... و کوکاریتکیسی سبز کردنم و کبود کردنم کوکاریتکولوك [illegible]

باشد اول سبز شدن و سیدن چنانچه گوید شعر قازیاشیم بیلا بیقیلدی یاغو موندیغی تلیغی آنداتا نماسا بولمس کوکارماق [illegible]

متن بل تعدیم معنی کبود شدن باشد و سیغ آن موافق شود اول اشتقاق بی باید کوکارمالیکو کراتیم انت غوپیلوو غرو کشیدن و در شکم

آرا گویند کوکادی کوکراشی غرید کوکرادی کوکرایدی کوکراشور کوکراشادور سیغرید کوکراد و کوکراشور نقل مصدر

کوکراکان کوکراکان و کوکرایدکان و کوکراشکان کوکراشادور غرنده و غرنده و بمعنی مصدر هم آمده کوکراکیل و کوکراش

کوکراشکیل مفرد غائب ماضی کوکراماس کوکراماکیل و کوکراشماس کوکراشماکیل مفرد غائب مضارع کوکرالر و کوکرایکر و کوکراشیکر

کوکراشیسلر کوکراشیکر و کوکراشیکلار جمع غائب ماضی کوکرامایلر و کوکراماشیکلر و کوکراشماکلار و کوکراشماس

کوکراشماسلار جمع غائب مضارع کوکرایمن و کوکرایدیم کوکرادیم و کوکرام و کوکرایغا و کوکراشایمین و کوکراشورمین

شاخهرمن کوکراشودامن میغرم کوکرامان کوکرامامین و کوکراشمان و کوکراشماسین میغرم کوکراب و کوکراسان و کوکراشیش و

کوکراشیه کوکراشاسکوکرامیش غریوه الشاهد علی الاول شعر خلایماس که کوکاب تاغ اوزه هر طرف یوز الاغلیش که دود آه ولغا

فلك ظاقیه تیره خیرامیش الشاهد علی الرابع شعر جم خراینداتو کلیتین باشك لار تاریب غریوی تومان اوراق که یاغضا یلکر یولدی کوکراد

کوکرابشیم و کوکراشیشین غریوه اشلوکوکراسانلر کوکراشیماسان غریوه کوکراب تو بیرو کوکرابیرو کوکراشیب بیرو کوکراشیب تو بیری غریونه امیم

کوکراسا و کوکراشاس بیغوم کوکراماسلیك کوکراشماسلیك نغریده کوکراماس بولسا کوکراشماس بولسا نغریده باشد کوکرایدورمیش بولغاو کوکراشاد

میغرید باشد کوکرایمکوکرای کوکرای و کوکراشا کوکراشا غران غران و بدون تکرار هم مستعملت کوکرای و کوکراین و کوکراشای

کوکراشاین سبز و سبزی و سبزیه چنانچه شاهد بابا ایل بمعنی اول مرسکن خرمی گوید شعر یا غیرکیم سره که تلیتاعیلین چو

بولای کوکاریاو اوراق کیمیشین کوکرایمو آیا سبز و سبز و سبزیه کوکرالایو سبزیه کوکراشالیو کوکراکانیه کوکراکانیه کوکرای الیند

کوکراشانیه کوکراشکانیه و کوکراشکالیه کوکراشابیکه کوکراشابیك بغریه کوکراکالی و کوکراشکالی برای غریدن و تلغیدن کوکراکالیج کوکراکاچ

چون غرید و چون غرید کوکراکوجی غرنده کوکراکوجی کوکراکوجیه کوکراکاغیه کوکراشکوچیه و کوکراشکوچی

کوکراشکانیه تا غریدن و بعد از غریدن کوکراکوسیدور و کوکراشکوسیدور خواهم غرید کوکراکیلمیدور و کوکراشکولمیدور خواهد غرید کوکراکو

کوکراشکوسیدور خواهد غرید کوکراکولولت و کوکراشکولولت غرنیده کوکراکالیکه کوکراکاسیه کوکراسوله و کوکراشکالیکه کوکراشکا

کوکراشیه کوکراشیسو و کوکراشیسونه کوکراشیدیلك بغرید کوکراکیدیلسین کوکراکیدلیك تونین کوکرامسینمن کوکراشکا

کوکراشکولیدیورمین کوکراشکوبرمین غریده خواهم کوکراکالیاده بمعنی طرف اول غنیمای بیر ایمیلی زدلعو بتم دمین دیبیمسانا کوکراکیه

کوکلادورلدی هم دو خیم و کوك کردیم کوکلادرو کوکلامیلدور همه سبز شده و کوکلامیکند و کوکلادر بمعنی مصدر هم می آید کوکلاکان

کوکلادیکان کوکلاشیکان هم سبز شده و سبز شده و کوکلاد کنده و کوکلاد کرده و بمعنی مصدر هم می آید کوکلادی کوکلاکیل مفرد غائب ماضی

چنانچه شاهد ... شعر ... کوکلاد وبوز

اکوکلادیلکوکلادیلکیل مفرد غائب مضارع کوکلادیلوکوکلادیلکر کوکلادیکار جمع غائب ماضی کوکلادیلیسلر کوکلادیلکلار جمع غائب مضارع

کوس

کوش

کوك

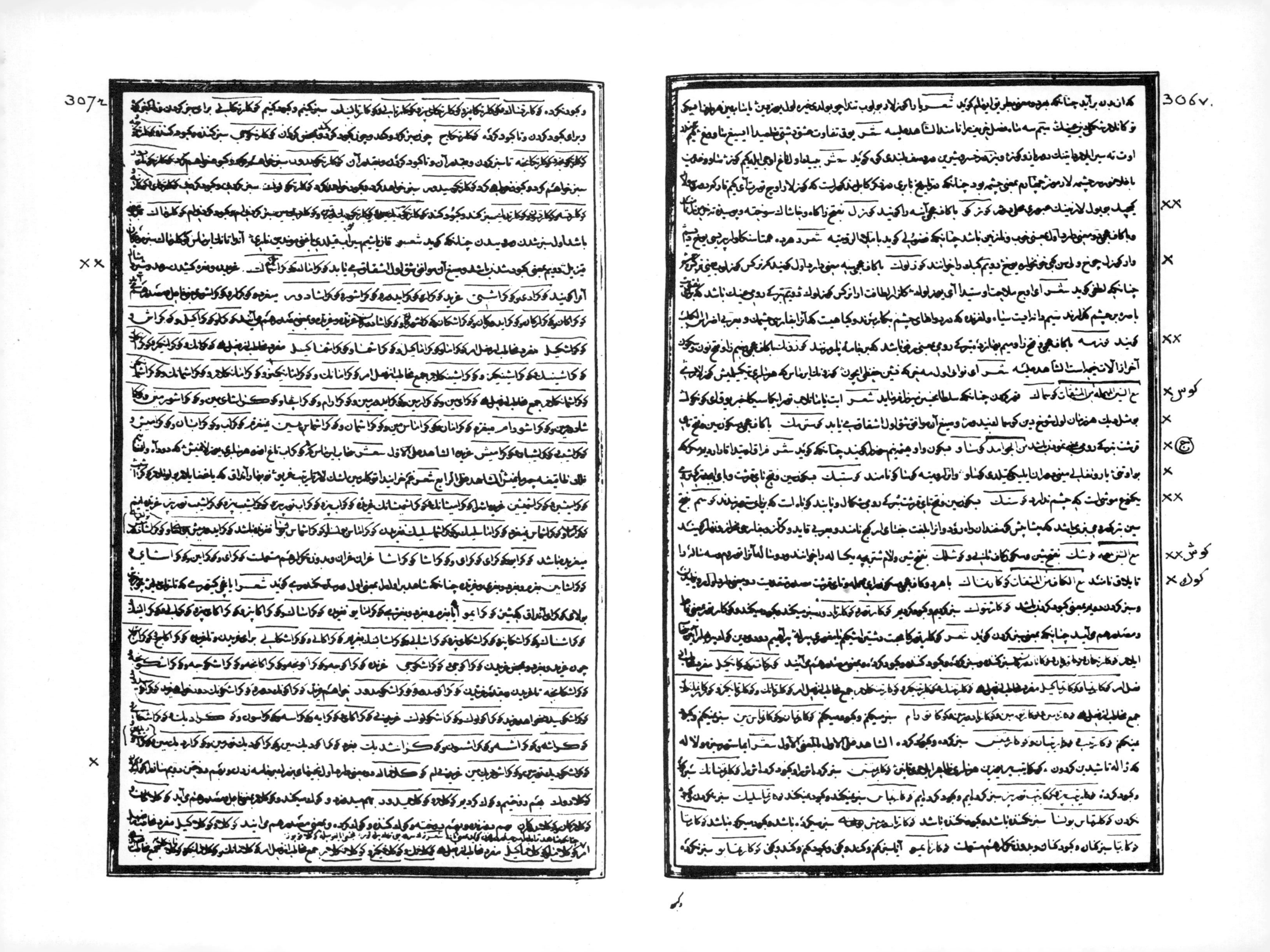

كوكلادى بين و كوكلادين و كوكلادم بهم ميدوزم و كوك ميكنم كوكلاغاى كوكلاغان بين بهم ميدوزم و كوك ميكنم كوكلاتور كوكلاتاى [illegible]

بهم دوخته و كوك كرده كوكلاشيين بهم دوخته و كوك كرده كوكلاتيم [illegible] بهم دوخته ايم و كوك كرده ايم كوكلاتا

بهم ميدوزد و كوك ميكند كوكلاغاسى ليك بهم دوختن و كوك كردن كوكلاغان بولسا بهم دوخته باشد و كوك كرده باشد كوكلاتقو

بولساى بهم ميدوخته باشد و كوك ميكرده باشد كوكلابدور كوكلادى كوكلاديى بهم دوختن و كوك كردن و بدوزيد [illegible] كوكلا

كوكلادين بهم بدوزم و بدوز و بدوزيد و دوخته و كوك كنم و كند و كن و كرده. چنانكه شاهد بر اول بمعنى بهم دوخته [illegible] يارب

چنين [illegible] كه [illegible] لطيفه [illegible] كوكلاى [illegible] كوكلاميو آيا بهم بدوزم و بدوز

و بدوزيد و آيا كوك كنم و كند و كن كوكلاغاى بهم ندوخته و كوك نكرده كوكلاغان [illegible] كوكلاتيلين

بهم بدوزيد و كوك كنيم كوكلاتالى براى بهم دوختن و تا دوخته و براى كوك كردن و تا كرده. كوكلاتاج چون بهم دوخت و بدوزيد

دوختن و [illegible] كوك كند [illegible] كردن كوكلاتوجى بهم دوزنده و كوك كننده كوكلاتكو [illegible] كوكلاتاغيتا بهم دوختن تا كوك

كردن و بقدر آن كوكلاتومدور بهم خواهم دوخت و كوك خواهم كرد كوكلاتوبدور بهم خواهد دوخت و كوك خواهد كرد كوكلاتوبيلدور

بهم خواهد دوخت و كوك خواهد كرد كوكلاتوك بهم دوختنى و كوك كردنى كوكلاتاغ [illegible] بهم بدوزد و كوك كند

كوكلاتودور [illegible] كوكلاتومينكيلم بهم دوختنيم و كوك كردنيم كوكلات مثالث مع النون [illegible] بهم دوختن و كوك [illegible]

[illegible] آن با تاى قرشت اشتقاق مى يابد كوكلات مثالث مع النون بمعنى انفعال است بمعنى بهم دوخته شدن و كوك شدن [illegible]

با نون اشتقاق مى يابد [illegible] كوك بمعنى آمده اول [illegible] باشد [illegible]

كويد شعر [illegible]

[illegible]

[illegible]

[illegible] كوك كردن نوشته و شعر [illegible] شاهد آورده [illegible] مسامحه كرده [illegible]

[illegible] كويند [illegible]

[illegible] چنانكه كويد شعر [illegible]

كوك [illegible] چنانكه شاهد آن [illegible]

شعر [illegible]

[illegible]

[illegible] بايد [illegible]

كوكانات بفتح كاف و نون [illegible] شبيه باشد كه [illegible]

[illegible] لغات [illegible] كوكان [illegible]

[illegible] چنانكه [illegible]

[illegible]

[illegible] شعر [illegible]

عريان كوكراكه [illegible] و آنرا كوس و كوكوس هم نامند و مولف [illegible] نوشته و [illegible] كرده [illegible]

[illegible] خوانند كوكچينليك بمعنى [illegible] باشد [illegible] كوكس سينه را نامند چنانكه [illegible]

[illegible] كويد شعر [illegible]

و آنرا كوكراك و كوكوس هم كويند و مولف رومى كوكس را در اين شعر كوكس خوانده و كوكرك را هم بمعنى سينه نوشته [illegible]

كوكسون بسكون كاف و نون و ضم شين معجمه بلغت مغولى بمعنى [illegible] كوك [illegible] بكاف عجمى [illegible] را نامند كوك كينه

[illegible] چنانكه كويد شعر [illegible] كوك كينه

كوك كوبانات [illegible] چنانكه [illegible] مجنون كويد شعر [illegible] كوك

[illegible] كوكلك بفتح كاف و سكون لام

بمعنى [illegible] باشد كوكلتاش [illegible] چنانكه [illegible] كويد شعر [illegible]

[illegible] كوكم با هر دو كاف عجمى و فتح [illegible] و سكون ميم [illegible]

شبيه [illegible] آنرا [illegible] هم نامند [illegible] كوكن بفتح كاف ثانى و سكون نون بلغت مغولى [illegible]

[illegible] بضم كاف و سكون [illegible]

[illegible] كوكوز بضم كاف و سكون زاى معجمه بمعنى [illegible] باشد [illegible] فرهنك [illegible]

[illegible] كوكوس بضم كاف و سكون سين مهمله سينه را كويند چنانكه [illegible] كويد شعر [illegible]

[illegible] چنانكه [illegible] كوكوم [illegible]

[illegible] باشد كوكوتول با هر دو كاف عجمى [illegible] كويند [illegible] شعر [illegible]

[illegible] مع الكاف [illegible] كولمك [illegible] بمعنى خنديدن كولدوك خنديدم [illegible]

[illegible] چنانكه [illegible] خندان كويد شعر [illegible]

باشد [illegible] كولكان [illegible] خنده و خنديده و بمعنى [illegible] هم مى آيد كول و كولكيل [illegible]

[illegible] چنانكه شاهد بر اول [illegible]

[illegible] نوشته و شعر [illegible] شاهد آورده [illegible] شعر [illegible]

[illegible]

جمع [illegible] كولا بين كولادين [illegible] خنديدم [illegible]

كولماس بين بخندم [illegible] خنديد [illegible]

خنديدم [illegible] بخندد [illegible] چنانكه كويد شعر [illegible]

[illegible] خنديده باشد كولا كولا خندمكان [illegible]

[illegible] چنانكه كويد شعر [illegible]

كولا [illegible] خنديدن و تا [illegible]

كولكاج چون خنديد و بخنديد و خنديدن كولكوچى خنده كولكوسه [illegible] خنديدن و بقدر آن كولكوم خواهم خنديد

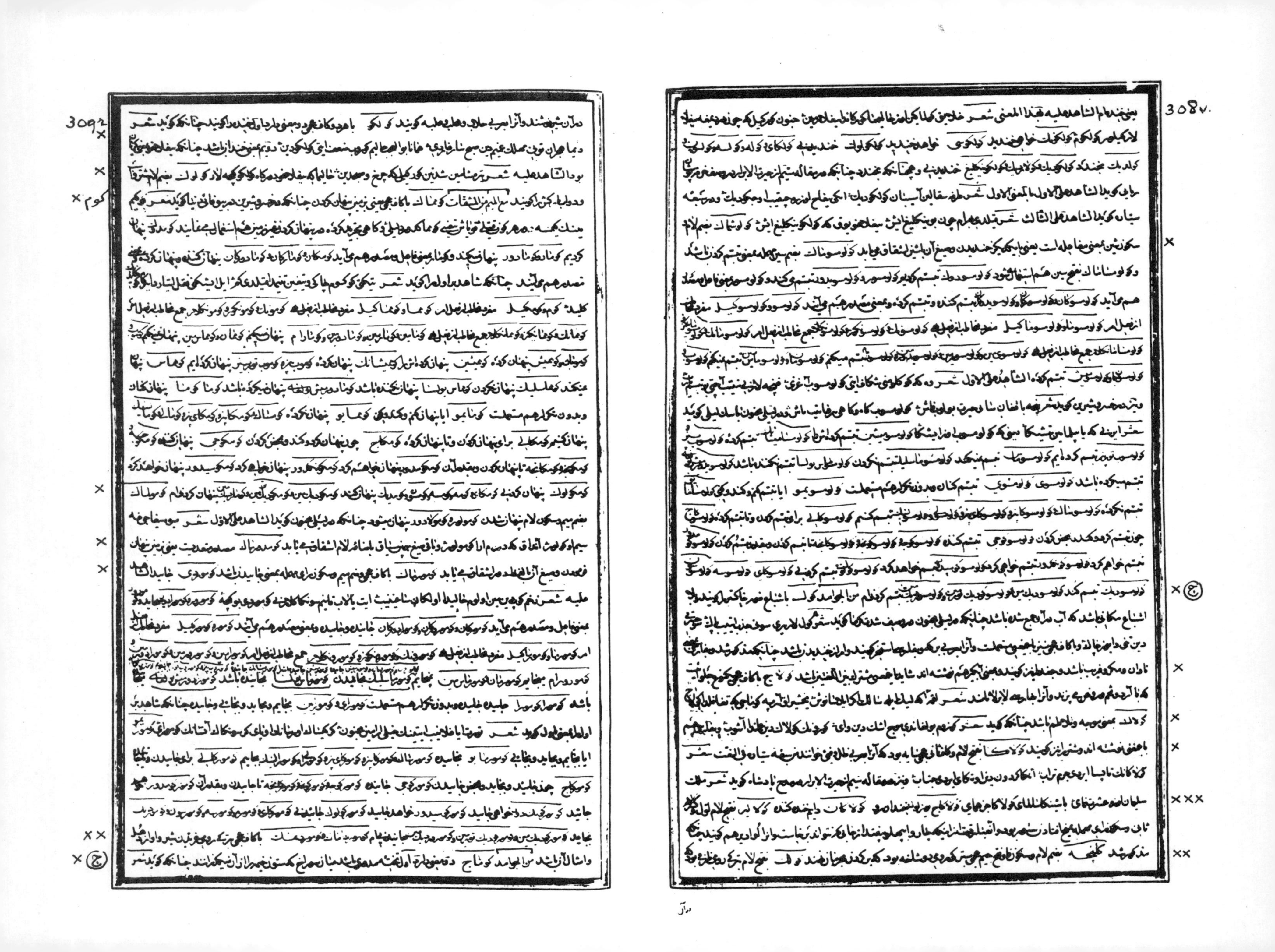

یعنی خندیدم الشاهد علیه بهذا المعنی شعر [illegible]

لاریکیلور کولکوم کولکیلت خواهد خندید کولکوی خواهم خندید کولکولوات خندیدنی کولکای کولمو [illegible]

کولدیلت بخندند کولکویلت [illegible] خندیدنی و همچنانکه بخندد چنانکه [illegible]

[illegible] الشاهد علی الاول بالمعنی الاول شعر [illegible] آسیان کولکودیلت [illegible]

سیانه کوبدا الشاهد علی الثالث شعر [illegible]

[illegible]

[illegible]

309v.

ظلمت بنک باکاهیفه کوماج اولمش قوناتر جوجه آنکا آهیم ستوندیك نعدی موندا ق کیم اولا شب توش دوبیم یکنوج نایت کر آزا پچیه
بشك کند چنانکه شاهد آن صوفی بل کولاج نکارش رفت و باید دو معنی سیاق نظر هم هنر مستهلت چنانکه ملا جامی علیه الرحمه کوید
بناز خشك کا مردی بچشم چو الماس بجو شنو شن کماج خشك نان کر تواش زوی کند دن بندانیم قم کو بچوت بسکون میم و نا و فتح میم
جو هیزم نیم سوخته باشد و آنرا کوشا و هم کویند کورول باکاف عجمی و سکون میم و ضم را مهمله باصطلاح رومیه تاج درویشی بود که
از نمد دوزند کومس بفتح میم و سکون سین مهمله ترکی دو جی خانه مرغ را نامند کومل بفتح میم بمعنی مرد وسطا و زبلند چنانکه
کوید شعر جان مکو نکول فراق مجو سید ایتی لار شیرین زبون و زارلقا ولمش کومک لار دیر ونیز در تاریخ الملوك در احوال سیف طغرل
کوید کرنوشین روان امداد قیلیب دمیا یولدین عرفه بساریب آتیننك کومک دیدی بیله سلکین آلدی و مولف روی بمعنی جهت ضمانت
نوشته و نظر و مزبور شاهد آمده سوو کده و با کاف عجمی بمعنی طرد اول شفت دهان باشد که آنرا بعربی [illegible] کویند
الشاهد علیه شعر کوبیدوم غم عشقیم نوحیان ایلا ماکیم دین [illegible] کوماکیم دین دوبیم کویند که کوله کوناك [illegible]
کبود محض در نیل مجنون موفات [illegible] کیدا صوی [illegible] باش کیم کولد کوناك [illegible] کومکوت با مرده کافه
کبود محض و آنرا کوناك هم کویند چنانکه [illegible] کومله بفتح میم و لام بغلمزده و کومه بترکی روی خانه کوچکت
که صیادان و مرغ کران از چوب و نی در صحرا برای خود بنا کنند و جای مرغان خانکی را هم کویند کومود بضم میم و سکون واو و دال مهمله [illegible]
کویند چنانکه در ترتیب هند و کوید شعر [illegible] ایلیب اسل آتین [illegible] نتیجه بولغای آنکا قایدا توشکوید
و آنرا کبود هم نامند کومونت باکاف عجمی و ضم میم بمعنی استخوان باشد چنانکه در تاریخ بابری در وصف کردن مذکور است [illegible]
آت ینك الیلیکی و کومونك بولور [illegible] بولور صومیه بفتح کاف اول [illegible] کومکولنمد [illegible]
چنانکه در انده هاکش فرهاد کوید شعر کومکولیدیر کانلیدیم شبه کون [illegible] کوبولدور [illegible]
بجزم ضم میم و دال و را مهملتین و سکون لام و کاف آخر ترکی روی سینه بند لب و شتر [illegible] آنرا بعربی [illegible] کوینده مع النون
ز المیقات کونکرانات بسکون و نون و کاف [illegible] کونکراندولك لند لند که
کونکراند و کونکرانادو لند لند [illegible] معنی فاعل و مصدر هم [illegible] لند لند که
و بمعنی مصدر هم می آید کونکران و کونکرانجك مفرد غائب [illegible] کونکرانال مفرد غائب [illegible] الشاهد علی الثانی شعر
لانم عشق اولدی هجران [illegible] عاشق کیمسه کا [illegible] کونکرانمایل کونکرایناك [illegible]
انفصال [illegible] کونکراناجو [illegible] جمع غائب [illegible] کونکراناس [illegible] کونکرانا
کونکرانات لند [illegible] کونکرایس [illegible] لند لند که چنانکه [illegible]
شعر کونکرایب [illegible] الشاهد علی الثانی شعر [illegible]
[illegible] کونکراینان [illegible] لند لند که [illegible] لند لند که [illegible]
لند لند که [illegible] کونکراناس [illegible] لند لند که [illegible] کونکرانا [illegible]
[illegible] باشد کونکرانا کونکرانا لند لند که [illegible] کونکرانا [illegible]
[illegible] کونکراناك [illegible] کونکرانکانی [illegible] لند لند کیم کونکرانکالی برای لند لند که [illegible]
لند لند که و کند [illegible] کونکرانکچه لند لند که [illegible] کونکرانکچه [illegible]

1.23 مجنون الحق کوید الشاهد علی الاول
1.24 حق امری توروز شکر ایله قیل کیم

310r

خواهم کرد کونکرانکو نکرو [illegible] کونکرانکولیك [illegible] لند کند [illegible] کونا مالك بفتح نون و لول
لند لند خواهد کرد کونکرانکو [illegible] لند لند خواهد کرد [illegible]
و سکون ثانی خشونت و مخلوط شدن و آن بحرف و امنا قلت کونا ند صرفنك [illegible] یعنی خشونت مخلوط [illegible]
بترکی روی بمعنی لب و هرزه زن و مطمع باشد کونیلمك باکاف عجمی و کسر نون اول و سکون ثانی و فتح لام ترکی روی بمعنی [illegible]
مزیدن من الجوامد کون باکاف عجمی بمعنی طرد اول آفتاب را کویند [illegible] نام او غوزخان بن قراخان بن [illegible]
که بعد از پدر مالك سلطنت شد و اصل کونخان خوانند و او رابع خوانین طبقه مغولیه بود و اکثر لقب و کنیت و نشان طوایف [illegible]
او موضوع شد و ایل و کون بطریق ترکی [illegible] بمعنی اعوان و انصار هم استعمال میشود و ایل [illegible] ذکر میشود اما کون [illegible]
و بفارسی [illegible] بود مثل کلکون [illegible] بولمش بلغت ترکی [illegible] پوست مدبوغ است که آنرا بفارسی چرم کویند کوناکوت
با مره کاف عجمی [illegible] چنانکه [illegible] بیان کوید شعر کوناکوز دین [illegible] کل چیزلاد توقیب [illegible]
بمعنی [illegible] باشد کونای باکاف عجمی [illegible] بخلاف توزای که [illegible] باشد کون باتار خانبغز [illegible] کویند
باکاف عجمی بترکی [illegible] باشد که آنرا از پوست [illegible] کون توغار خانبغز [illegible] نامند کون چیچکی بترکی روی کل [illegible] آنرا
شمس قمر و بفارسی کل آفتاب پرست کویند کوندالیك باکاف عجمی باصطلاح اتراك [illegible] باشد کوندلان بسکون [illegible]
و فتح دال مهمله و لام بمعنی [illegible] چنانکه در تاریخ بابری مذکور است [illegible] کوندلاندین [illegible]
[illegible] و مولف برهان قاطع نوشته که کندلان بفتح اول و ضم ثالث [illegible] باشد و بعضی از [illegible]
حرکات لفظ اشتباه نموده کوندوز بمعنی روز باشد کوندولك آفتابه و ابریق را خوانند و بفارسی [illegible] باشد [illegible]
[illegible] کوناسر کوکوش بفتح نون و سکون سین مهمله آفتاب را کویند چنانکه در حرف سین [illegible]
فرموده الشاهد علی الثانی شعر [illegible] شب [illegible] کوندخر [illegible] کیسه لار [illegible] وکوش
و شاهد برای [illegible] تاریخ الانبیا در فوت شدن [illegible] علیه السلام کوید [illegible]
[illegible] استعمال [illegible] چنانکه [illegible] کوید شعر [illegible]
[illegible] آدش [illegible] جهان [illegible]
کوناش هم کویند کون تولاشی بترکی [illegible] شبیه [illegible] آفتاب پرست [illegible]
با مره کاف عجمی و سکون [illegible] کونخلات [illegible] کویند کونخلا [illegible]
چنانکه کوید شعر [illegible]
[illegible] چنانکه [illegible] کوید [illegible]
[illegible] کونلوك باکاف عجمی و سکون نون و ضم لام ترکی روی [illegible] کویند
دویم بمعنی وظیفه و بومیه بود کونتاخار باکاف عجمی و فتح نون و قاف [illegible] خوانند کونی باکاف
[illegible] بترکی روی [illegible] کویند و از [illegible] نامند
کونلو بترکی روی [illegible] الواو مع المیقات کوا بمالك باکاف عجمی و فتح
واو و سکون نون [illegible] آن اشتقاق یافته
من الجوامد کواج بفتح واو و سکون [illegible] کوید شعر

آنان که [illegible] کوید [illegible] کونا [illegible]
على الاول شعر [illegible] الشاهد على [illegible] شعر [illegible]
[illegible] می‌آید [illegible] سخن [illegible]
الشاهد على الاول بالمعنى الثاني شعر [illegible] ممکن نبود [illegible]
[illegible] الشاهد على الثالث بالمعنى الاول شعر [illegible]
[illegible] مفروقا المنفصل الشاهد على الاول [illegible] شعر [illegible]
[illegible] مفروقا المنفصل [illegible] فالطالب المنفصل [illegible]
[illegible] الشاهد على الاول [illegible]
[illegible]
[illegible] باشد [illegible]
[illegible] آیا [illegible]
[illegible] چنانکه [illegible]
شعر [illegible]
[illegible] الشاهد على الاول شعر [illegible]
[illegible] الشاهد على الاول شعر [illegible]
[illegible]
[illegible] الشاهد على الثالث شعر [illegible]
[illegible] می‌آید [illegible]
[illegible] الشاهد على الاول بالمعنى الثاني شعر [illegible]
[illegible] چنانکه شاهد [illegible] شعر [illegible]
[illegible] الشاهد على الاول شعر [illegible]
[illegible]
[illegible] شاهد آمده [illegible]
[illegible] چنانکه [illegible]
[illegible] چنانکه [illegible]
[illegible] باشد [illegible]
[illegible] می‌آید [illegible]
[illegible] مفروقا المنفصل [illegible] الشاهد على الثاني شعر [illegible]
[illegible]

[illegible] جمع فالطالب [illegible] متصل [illegible]
[illegible] متصل [illegible] الشاهد على الاول شعر [illegible]
[illegible] متصل [illegible]
[illegible] متصل [illegible] باشد [illegible]
[illegible] متصل [illegible]
[illegible] متصل [illegible]
[illegible] متصل [illegible]
[illegible] متصل [illegible] من الجوامد [illegible]
[illegible] چنانکه [illegible]
[illegible] آن [illegible]
[illegible] چنانکه [illegible] شعر [illegible]
[illegible] شعر [illegible]
[illegible] شعر [illegible]
[illegible] المشتقات [illegible]
[illegible] می‌آید [illegible]
[illegible] مفروقا المنفصل [illegible]
مفروقا المنفصل [illegible] جمع فالطالب [illegible]
[illegible]
[illegible]
[illegible] باشد [illegible]
[illegible] باشد [illegible]
[illegible]
[illegible]
[illegible]
[illegible]
[illegible] من الجوامد [illegible] چنانکه [illegible]
شعر [illegible]
[illegible] شاهد آمده [illegible]

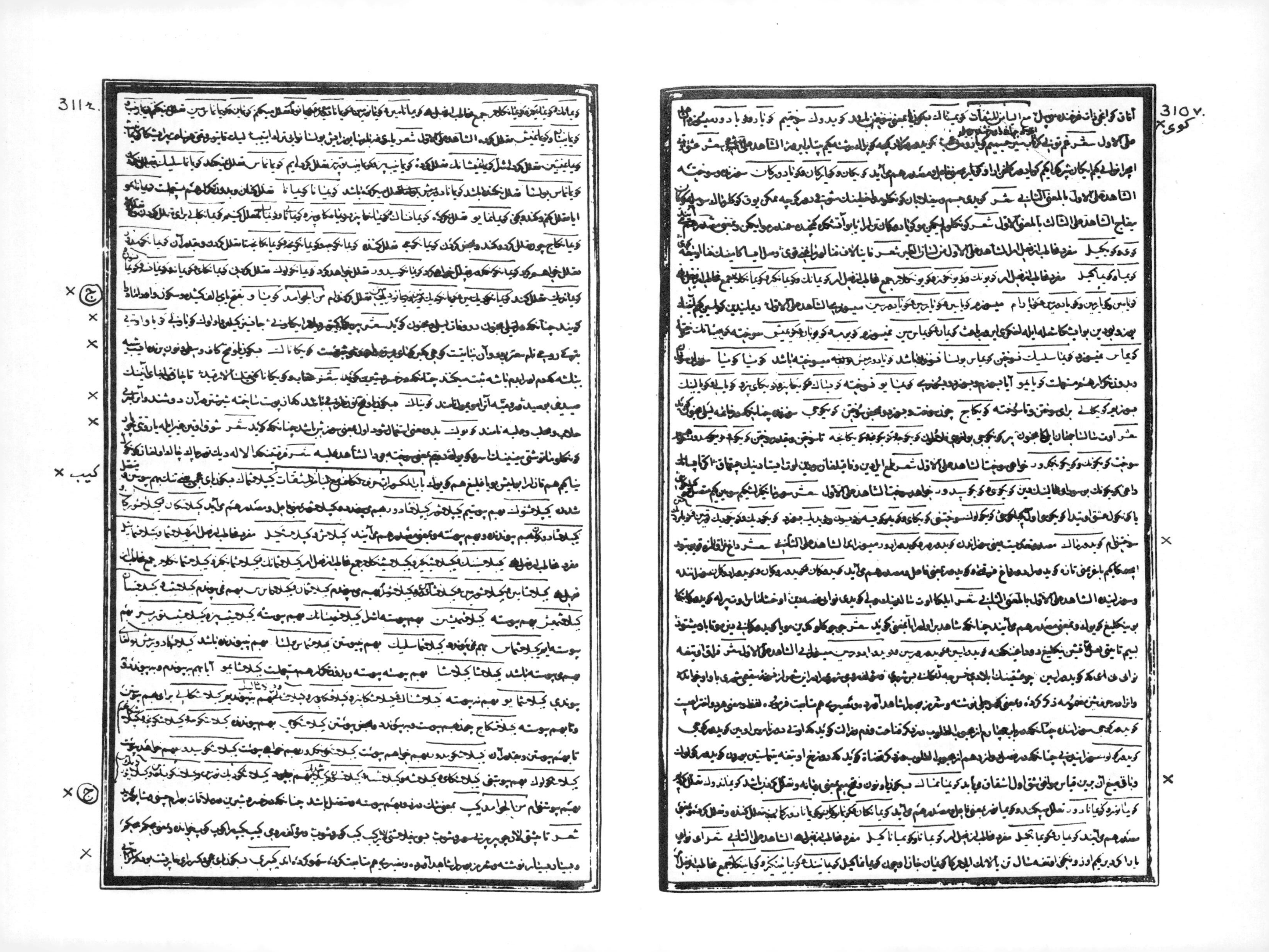

311v. کیت

نفذ کمند کپری تیکن یکنوع خار [illegible] بزرگ [illegible] نامند کیبو بمعنی ادات تشبیه است بمعنی مثل و مانند که
اواخر الفاظ واقع می‌شود الشاهد علیه شعر [illegible] کیماک
بمعنی رفتن کیتوک نعتیم کیتا رهکیتا دو [illegible] الشاهد علی الاول شعر [illegible] کیتار [illegible]
[illegible] کیتار بمعنی فاعل و مصدر نیز می‌آید [illegible] چنانکه [illegible]
مذکور خواهد شد کیتکا [illegible] و بمعنی [illegible] هم می‌آیند کیت و کیتکیل مفرد مخاطب امر [illegible]
[illegible] کیتما و کیتماکیل مفرد غائب امر فصل [illegible]
جمع غائب امر فصل [illegible] کیتا سین و کیتار [illegible] جمع غائب [illegible] کیتماس [illegible]
کیتیب و کیتیبان و کیتیمیش رفته [illegible] کیتیب [illegible] کیتماس [illegible]
رفتن کیتماس بولسا [illegible] باشد کیتا دو [illegible] باشد کیتا کیتا [illegible] مستعملت کیتا بو
آیا [illegible] کیتا بو رفته کیتسا [illegible] کیتکالی برای رفتن [illegible] کیتکاچ
[illegible] کیتکو [illegible]
خواهد رفت الشاهد علی الاول شعر [illegible]
کیتکوسی و کیتکوسی [illegible] کیتکولوک [illegible] کیتکودیک [illegible]
[illegible] الشاهد علی الاول شعر [illegible]
کیتارمک بفتح تا بمعنی بردن [illegible] کیتار [illegible]
علی الاول شعر [illegible]
گوید شعر [illegible]
[illegible] کیتار [illegible] هم می‌آیند [illegible]
[illegible] الشاهد علی الاول شعر [illegible]
کیتمالک بمعنی [illegible] می‌آید [illegible] شعر [illegible]
[illegible] کیتار [illegible]
جمع غائب [illegible] کیتار [illegible]
[illegible] کیتار [illegible] کیتار [illegible]
[illegible] کیتار [illegible] باشد کیتار [illegible] باشد [illegible]
مستعملت کیتار [illegible] کیتار [illegible]
برای بردن [illegible] کیتار [illegible]
کیتار [illegible] کیتار [illegible] چنانکه شاهد [illegible]
[illegible] شعر [illegible]
کیتار [illegible] کیتار [illegible]

312r. کیچ

وصیغ آن بر بنیق بانضمام تای قرشت اشتقاق می‌یابد کیتالماک بکسر را و سکون لام برده شدن و صیغ آن بدستور [illegible] اشتقاق می‌یابد
کیتورماک بضم تا بمعنی آوردن باشد کیتوروک آورده‌ایم کیتوردم [illegible] می‌آورد و کیتورمک بمعنی فاعل و مصدر هم می‌آید [illegible]
کیتورادور [illegible] آورده و بمعنی [illegible] هم می‌آیند کیتور و کیتورکیل مفرد مخاطب امر کیتورسا کیتورساکیل مفرد غائب
امر فصل [illegible] کیتورینک [illegible] جمع غائب [illegible] کیتوراین [illegible]
کیتوراین [illegible] آورد [illegible] کیتورماس [illegible] آورده کیتوریب [illegible] آورده [illegible]
[illegible] آورده‌ایم کیتورماس [illegible] باشد [illegible] آورده و بدون
[illegible] مستعملت کیتورابو آیا بیاورم [illegible] کیتوراک [illegible]
کیتوکالی برای آوردن و تا آورده کیتورکاچ [illegible] الشاهد علیه شعر [illegible]
[illegible] کیتورگوسی آورنده کیتورگو [illegible] تا آوردن و [illegible]
آورد کیتورکیلک [illegible] آورد [illegible] کیتورکای [illegible]
[illegible] کیتورتماک بضم تای اول و سکون را و تای ثانی مصدر متعدیست یعنی
[illegible] و صیغ آن بدستور بانضمام [illegible] اشتقاق می‌یابد [illegible] بضم تا و را [illegible] سکون لام [illegible] شدن
آن بر [illegible] اشتقاق می‌یابد [illegible] کیچماک بکسر [illegible] مع الجیم [illegible]
[illegible] گذاشتن و عبور کردن باشد [illegible] گذشتیم [illegible] و بمعنی فاعل و مصدر هم می‌آید [illegible]
[illegible] و بمعنی [illegible] هم می‌آیند کچ و کچکیل مفرد مخاطب امر الشاهد علی الاول [illegible]
[illegible] الشاهد علی الثانی شعر [illegible]
دولت باقی [illegible] کچسا و کچساکیل مفرد غائب امر [illegible] جمع
[illegible] جمع غائب امر فصل [illegible]
[illegible] گذشته [illegible] گذشته [illegible]
[illegible] باشد [illegible] گذشته
و بدون [illegible] مستعملت کچابو آیا بگذرم [illegible]
[illegible] برای گذشتن و تا گذشته کچکاچ [illegible]
تا گذشتن [illegible] خواهد گذشت [illegible]
[illegible] بضم جیم [illegible]
[illegible] الشاهد علی الاول شعر [illegible]
[illegible] شعر
[illegible] مع الراء المهمله اشتقاق می‌یابد [illegible]
مع [illegible] و صیغ آن بدستور [illegible] اشتقاق می‌یابد [illegible] کچ [illegible]
شعر [illegible]

خونیچ کوید که هر کیچه لوز آلق اون ایتو [illegible] ایدی بیر کیچه کچه کا [illegible] ایردیم [illegible] چنانچه کوید شعر [illegible]

داغی بولدی [illegible] آشفته [illegible] چنانچه [illegible]

کوید شعر [illegible]

عجب [illegible] خواند کچ قودون وقت شام [illegible] چنانچه کوید شعر [illegible]

کچ قودون [illegible] شعر [illegible]

مهمان [illegible] کچکا [illegible] چنانچه کوید شعر [illegible]

[illegible]

[illegible] چنانچه کوید [illegible]

[illegible]

[illegible]

[illegible]

[illegible]

313v

و فتح لام چرک آلوده شدن جامه و جراحت باشد کیرناشماق باکاف عجمی و سکون را و شین و فتح نون خمیازه کشیدن من الجوامد کیر بکاف
سیر بمعنی چرک و صبر بود چنانکه در نسایم المحبة [illegible] شیخ ابو الحسن [illegible] کوید که [illegible] کیردین آریغ [illegible] بولغای بین
کیرانک یعنی باید کیر اکلیک بمعنی [illegible] بود چنانکه کوید شعر [illegible]
کیر اکلیک [illegible] بولغای [illegible] کیرچ بکسرهای عجمی خشت را کویند شعر [illegible]
خشتی دین باشینکه [illegible] کیرپک بسکون را و کاف [illegible] و کسرهای عجمی [illegible] الشاهد علیه شعر [illegible]
بازار مین [illegible] خط [illegible] بسکون را و کاف [illegible] و فتح تای قرشت [illegible]
جلقوم باشد چنانکه در تاریخ بابری در وصف [illegible] قاللیمیت
کرج بفتح را و سکون جیم [illegible] رومی کج بود [illegible] مالند و آنرا [illegible] کویند کیرشان بفتح شین قرشت سفید باشد
زنان [illegible] کیرش بکسر را و سکون شین قرشت [illegible] کویند [illegible]
کوید شعر [illegible] بابکاف عجمی بمعنی [illegible]
بود چنانکه در تاریخ بابری [illegible] و بمعنی [illegible] مستعملست چنانکه کوید
[illegible] کیرمک بسکون را بمعنی کشتن
و سیر کردن باشد [illegible] و بمعنی فاعل و مصدر هم می آید [illegible]
و کردین و بمعنی مصدر هم می آیند کیر و کیرکیل مفرد مخاطب بفصل الاول الشاهد علی الاول شعر [illegible]
خواه [illegible] مفرد مخاطب بفصله [illegible] جمع مخاطب بفصل [illegible]
[illegible] جمع مخاطب بفصله [illegible] سیکرهم [illegible]
[illegible] کردیم [illegible] کردیده [illegible]
[illegible] نکردن باشد [illegible] سیکردیده باشد [illegible] بمعنی [illegible] مستعملست [illegible] آیا کیرکیم
و بکردد و بکردی [illegible] نکردیده [illegible] برای کردین و تاکردین کیرکاج
چون کند بد و بکردد و بعضی کشتن [illegible] تاکردیده [illegible] خواهم کردن
[illegible] خواهی کرد [illegible] خواهد کرد [illegible] الشاهد علی
الجناس [illegible]
کردید دام [illegible] مصدر متعدیست بمعنی [illegible]
الشاهد علی الاول بالمعنی الثانی شعر [illegible] شمر [illegible] مسلمانا [illegible]
کیرد و آنی [illegible] چنانکه بمعنی اول کوید شعر [illegible]
[illegible] بمعنی مصدر هم می آید [illegible] اشتقاق می یابد [illegible] بکسر کاف [illegible] الشین المعجمه [illegible]
سیر کردن و منع آن [illegible] اشتقاق می یابد [illegible] بسکون زا [illegible] مصدر متعدیست بمعنی پنهان کردن [illegible]
[illegible] پنهان کند [illegible] پنهان [illegible] بمعنی فاعل و مصدر هم می آید چنانکه [illegible]
بمعنی [illegible] کوید شعر [illegible]

314r

[illegible] پنهان کند [illegible] پنهان کرده و بمعنی مصدر هم می آید [illegible]
مفرد مخاطب بفصل الامر [illegible] مفرد مخاطب بفصله [illegible]
[illegible] جمع مخاطب بفصل الامر [illegible] جمع مخاطب بفصله
[illegible] پنهان کنیم [illegible]
[illegible] پنهان کنیم [illegible] پنهان کرده [illegible]
پنهان کرده [illegible] پنهان کرده [illegible] پنهان کرده ایم
[illegible] پنهان نکند [illegible] پنهان نکرده [illegible] پنهان نکرده باشد
[illegible] پنهان میکرده باشد [illegible] پنهان کنان و بدون تکرار هم
مستعملست [illegible] آیا پنهان کنم و کند و کنی [illegible] پنهان نکرده [illegible]
[illegible] پنهان نکنیم [illegible] برای پنهان کردن و تا پنهان
[illegible] چون پنهان کرد و کند و بعضی گفتن [illegible] پنهان کنند [illegible]
[illegible] تا پنهان کردن و بعد پنهان کردن [illegible] پنهان خواهم کرد [illegible]
[illegible] پنهان خواهی کرد [illegible] پنهان خواهد کرد [illegible] پنهان خواهیم کرد
[illegible] پنهان کردنی [illegible]
پنهان کننده [illegible] پنهان کردیم [illegible]
مع النون بمعنی مفاعله است یعنی باهم پنهان شدن و صیغ آن با شین اشتقاق می یابد [illegible] مع النون پنهان شدن و صیغ آن
با نون اشتقاق می یابد [illegible] بود که آنرا [illegible] کویند الشاهد علیه شعر [illegible]
[illegible] باکاف عجمی و فتح زا و سکون کاف
بمعنی [illegible] باشد و بالمجاز [illegible] کوید شعر [illegible] الشاهد علیه
[illegible] پاسبان و خارجی را نامند
[illegible] کوید شعر [illegible] بمعنی نوبت باشد [illegible] باکاف عجمی
پاسبان [illegible] بضم تای قرشت و واو و لام و سکون [illegible] خانه را خوانند [illegible] باشد
مع السین المهمله [illegible] بمعنی بریدن باشد [illegible] بمعنی فاعل و مصدر هم می آید چنانکه
بمعنی مصدر کوید شعر [illegible]
برنده و بریدن و بمعنی مصدر هم می آید [illegible] مفرد مخاطب بفصل الامر [illegible] مفرد مخاطب بفصله [illegible]
[illegible] جمع مخاطب بفصل الامر [illegible] جمع مخاطب بفصله [illegible]
[illegible] کیسه [illegible]
[illegible] باشد [illegible] بران و بدون تکرار
هم مستعملست [illegible] آیا [illegible]

الشاهد علیه بالمعنی الاول شعر لمعه سنونلوغینا برق چاقیلغان کبی کیم کویا کیسکالی الیکیدین ایتار خنجر قیلیچ کیسکاج چوپ
ببرد و بحص برید کیسکوچی برنده کیسکوچه و کیسکوچی و کیسکانچه تا ببرید و بقطع برید کیسکوسدور خواهم برید کیسکوبکور
خواهی برید کیسکوسیدور خواهد برید کیسکولوک بریدنی چنانچه در مقاله دهم از حیرة الابرار در عنوان سخن گوید کر لیکی کیسه
اکر زلف دیک چیرکه رحمینیدا بیر تونا ریکیم باشی کیسکولوک دور دور کیسکان و کیسه کیسون و کیسکالی برد کیسکیتاب
کیسکیدیک تونیمچینا ارا آن ببیده فام کیشتمالت بکسر سین مهمله مع الشین المعجمه بمعنی مقابله است یعنی با هم بریدن و قطعه قطعه
کردن کیسیتیب کیسیتینا و کیسیتمش با هم قطعه قطعه کرده الشاهد علی الاول شعر کونکلونی سو خلاص آیراق تالاشولاد
کیسپشیب که قالمادی معنی سپید نصیبی یرکندی ثوبا و قمیع بزن بکسر سین مهمله و انضمام شین معجمه اشتقاق می یابد کیسیلمالت
بکسر سین مهمله مع اللام بریده شدن کیسیلور کیسیلادور بریده می شود و کیسیلمک بمعنی فاعل و مصدر هم می آید چنانچه بمعنی
شعر کیم که الا الا صابلیه کونکلی کا ایتار پیوند تولا ... ایدین کیسیلور کا متراض و نامه ... اشتقاق می یابد
مصدر متعدیت یعنی بریدانیدن و صیغ آن بدستور لفظ تو ... اشتقاق می یابد کیسکولا تمالت بکسر سین و تلوی قرشت و ضم کاف
ثم لام مصدر متعدیت بمعنی ذبح فرمودن باشد کیسکولاتور ذبح فرمود کیسکولاتیب ذبح فرمود چنانچه گوید شعر
ایتیننک کونکلی کا ... خاص ... ناتوان ... کیسکولاتیب ... کیسکولاتور و کیسکولاتا ذبح ... فرماید و
بمعنی فاعل و مصدر هم می آید کیسکولاکان و کیسکولاکای و کیسکولاتا ذبح فرماینده و ذبح فرموده و بمعنی مصدر هم می آید کیسکولات
مفرد غائب ... کیسکولاتما ... مفرد غائب ... کیسکولاتسنک و کیسکولاتسنکز جمع غائب ...
کیسکولاتاند و کیسکولاتانکز و کیسکولاتما جمع غائب ... کیسکولاتاین و کیسکولاتای ... کیسکولاتورین و کیسکولاتادورین ذبح فرمایم
کیسکولاتمان و کیسکولاتمامن ذبح نفرمایم ... کیسکولاتسه و کیسکولاتسان ... ذبح فرموده کیسکولاتیشن ذبح فرموده ...
ذبح فرموده کیسکولاتیبتور و کیسکولاتیبتورتر ذبح فرموده ... کیسکولاتماس ذبح نفرماید کیسکولاتدیلار ذبح نفرموده ...
نفرماینده باشد کیسکولاتمادور ... کیسکولاتا کیسکولاتا ذبح کنان و بدون تکرار هم مستعمل کیسکولاتای
آیا ذبح نفرمایم و نفرماید ... کیسکولاتسا ... ذبح نفرموده کیسکولاتات و کیسکولاتکای ... کیسکولاتکانیز و کیسکولاتا
ذبح نفرمایم کیسکولاتکالی برای ذبح فرمودن ... ذبح فرموده ... کیسکولاتکیچ ... کیسکولاتوکیچ ...
کیسکولاتکیچه و کیسکولاتکیچه ... ذبح فرمودن ... کیسکولاتکودور ذبح خواهم فرمود کیسکولاتکودور ذبح خواهد
ذبح خواهد فرمود کیسکولاتکولوک ذبح فرمودنی کیسکولاتکای و کیسکولاتسه و کیسکولاتسون و کیسکولاتماید ذبح نفرماید
کیسکولاتکوبدیک ... کیسکولاتتی ... من الجوامد کیساک کلوخ را گویند الشاهد علیه شعر چنانچه گوید
بر کیساک ملمع بالاد ایتالد ... کلوخ کیسامان ... چنانچه گوید شعر ...
عشقینک ... آنی یوق ... بولادیله کیسانان اگرچه ... کیسکن ...
و نون و کسر کاف ... لاش ... کیسمه ... آن ...
دارد ... چنانچه گوید شعر ...
کیسمه ... کیسکان ... صفت ... چنانچه ...
کلاه اشتغال شود کیسوک ... الشاهد علیه شعر ... کیسلمون کیسوک بلفرغه

و نیز در حیرة الابرار در وصف جمله گوید شعر نقطه لار ایل بول ... کیسوله باشلاغ کیسیم بکسرتین
و سکون میم مقالهه و بولیدا گویند چنانچه در ... گوید شعر ولیکن ... اوا
ایش ایردی سلاح و ... اولکیم ... طالب ولفای ایردی ... کوزات
که ... کیسیم ... قیلیچ ...
مع الشین المعجمه من المشتقات کیشنامالت بکسر شین ... شیهه زدن اسب را گویند کیشنادی شیهه زد کیشنار کیشناید
شیهه میزند و کیشنار بمعنی فاعل و مصدر هم می آید چنانچه ... گوید شعر ...
... کیشناکان ... کیشنادیکان شیهه زننده و شیهه زده و بمعنی مصدر هم می آید کیشنا
کیشنابان و کیشنامیش شیهه زده کیشناماس شیهه نمیزند کیشنامالیک شیهه زدن کیشنار ... شیهه زننده باشد کیشنایدور
... شیهه زدن باشد کیشنا و کیشنای کیشنای شیهه زنان و بدون تکرار هم مستعمل کیشناکالی برای شیهه زدن
... کیشناکاج چون شیهه زد و زند ... کیشناکای ... کیشنالسه و کیشناسون و کیشنادلشیه
من الجوامد کیش ... گویند چنانچه گوید ... که کیش ... و آنرا ...
... ترکی ... سیم ... خصوصا ... نام جزء ...
نوعی از جامه باشد که از کتان بافند ... کیشان
زنجیر را گویند کیشو بکسرتین ... چنانچه گوید شعر ...
... گوید شعر ...
نشان ... گوید شعر ...
کیشیکا ... چنانچه در حیرة الابرار گوید شعر کیم ...
اما کیشی ... بمعنی ... چنانچه ... نوشته است گوید ...
کیشوق ... و ...
واسع ذکر کرده ... کیف ...
... چنانچه ... گوید شعر ...
اول ... مع الکاف من المشتقات کیکیرماک ... بمعنی آروغ زدن ... کوینده ...
آروغ زدیم کیکیردی ... آروغ میزند و کیکیر ... بمعنی فاعل و مصدر هم می آید ... آروغ زننده و
آروغ زده و بمعنی مصدر هم می آید کیکیرو کیکیر ... مفرد غائب ... کیکیرما ... مفرد غائب ...
کیکیر ... جمع غائب ... جمع غائب ... کیکیر ...
آروغ میزنم کیکیر ... آروغ میزند کیکیرتیب ... آروغ زده ... آروغ زده کیکیر ...
کیکیریب ... آروغ زدیم کیکیرماس ... آروغ میزند ... آروغ زدن کیکیرماس بولسا آروغ زننده باشد کیکیرادور
آروغ میزده باشد کیکیرا کیکیرا آروغ زنان و بدون تکرار هم مستعمل کیکیرا ... آیا آروغ زنیم و زند ...
آروغ زده کیکیرکای ... کیکیرکالی ... کیکیرالیک ... آروغ زنیم کیکیرکالی برای آروغ زدن ... آروغ زده کیکیرکاج

315v.

چون آروغ زد و بند و بمعنی زدن کیکر کوجی آروغ زننده کیکر کوجه و کیکر نوغر و کیکرکانجه تا آروغ زدن و بمقدار آن کیکر کو مدتا آروغ
خواهم زد کیکر یونکل و تا آروغ خواهی زد کیکر کوسید و تا آروغ خواهد زد کیکر کو بولت آروغ زدن کیکرکای و کیکره و کیکر تا
کیکر سون و کیکر ملنا آروغ بزند چنانکه شاهد ثالث اشاره خواهیم نمود از محبوب القلوب که ذکر خود حیدان کوید کر اکر ایلاسیدین کیکر تا
و کیکره لن مس
وکنودین لمز کابیل کیکر تا طموی یکیم برسید اغی خاصر لار اونین لپسند یکایلار کیکر کودلی مین و کیکر کودیلتو تا آروغ فدنام
من الجوامد کیکرت بکسر هر دو کاف عجمی و سکون رای مهمله و کاف آخر و فتح دال الفضوف و بر آمده که نای حلق بود کیکرتا بکسر هر دو
کاف عجمی و سکون رای مهمله و فتح میم بمعنی آروغ باشد که آنرا عربی جشا نامند مع الزاء المعجمه کیکین بکسر هر دو کاف و سکون رای معجمه
بمعنی تابوت بود چنانکه در فضل بیست و دویم از محبوب القلوب مذکور بمعنی و مطلب کوید که مغنی و ناسیر کیکو جیا سیزا بر سوبر تیلشاهدی دور
لمنا ز و سلاجیم کوستد ا مفسدی خانه بر انداز و بفتح هر دو کاف نیز مستعملست چنانکه دو کاف مفتوحه کذشت مع اللام لیقات کیلما
بمعنی آمدن باشد کیلدولت آمدیم کیلدوم کیلادور می آید و کیلور بمعنی عامل و مصدر هم می آید چنانکه بمعنی مصدری کوید
شعر کیلدی منکا جو یلی بیچکیتیم مثل توبره جون نظار قنا بولور کیلوری بولسا اتیل بیله و سیاق نیز خواستیت کر جون کیلورکی
بولسا تیل بیله تارقنا بولور یعنی جون آمدن نثر باشد با مو میتوان کشید و نیز بمعنی بعض کوید شعر کیلورنکا باشا دیم کونکلوم
اوبین باشا لور کلبه جو مهمان کیرکاخ کیلور ایردی و کیلا دور ایردی می آمد شاهد مثال اول شعر کیلادور ایردی چیپیم منتظر کونکلو
باندی او نوای نیکا جیسیم معنی تا دان او تروش کیلکا کیلورکان و کیلادور کان آینده و آمده چنانکه شاهد ثالث را بمعنی اول در شش
محبوب القلوب در وصف خوشکوی کوید که کونکولکا بیزم کیلادور کان بولسا آینینک سوزی جین تا یغمای و بمعنی مصدر هم می آید
چنانکه شاهد ثالث بمعنی آمدن در نسایم المحبه در ذکر خواجه عبد الرحمن کهواره کر مذکور است که کیت اهلی مولانا فخر الدین
که خواجه سینینک کیلادور کانی بیتکر جشنیدین خراسانه جو قصه کریب نود و نیز در تاریخ بابری مذکور است که خراسان دین کیلادور کان
جا بنوبتی با ریب قالین قوی کیلتور دیلار و کیلادور کان هم با بمعنی ذکر کرده چنانکه مستحکدی دو خواندن کوید
که خانا ز جین آینینک قویا شر بیک کیم خویلوغ سیله تیغ جمانکه ترتیب کیلادور کان نیز اشتیب و این نوع مخالف قیاس و موافق استعمالست
کیل کیلکیل مفرد مخاطب فضل امر چنانکه شاهد ثالث دعا مقالة سیزد هم از نثر الابرار در داستان ابو تعب خلف و هزه کوید
شعر کیم بولک اولوندور دی نفیسنیک کیمک بولسا که کیلکیل که آچوند در ایشیک کیلا کیلی کیل مفرد مخاطب فضل امر کیلینک
کیلینکز و کیلینکلار جمع مخاطب فضل امر کیلمانک و کیلمانکز و کیلمانکلار جمع مخاطب فضل نهی کیلای و کیلایم و کیلادور مین و
کیلورلم می آیم کیلمان و کیلماس مین نمی آیم کیلیب کیلیبان و کیلیش آمده کیلیشین آمدن را چنانکه در سبحه مکتوب در آمدن
موالی از جانب او هند کوید شعر سوزی هم ایتیب خیل درکه فنی شه آلیبه موفق کیلادور کیلیبش کیلیشانک آمدن کیلیب بیزو
کیلیب تو بیتی آمد ایم کیلماس نمی آید کیلماسلیک نیامدن کیلماس بولسا نیاید باشد کیلا در سرش و بمعنی آمدن باشد کیلا
آمده آمده و بعدین تکرار هم مستعملست کیلا یمو آیا بیایم و بیاید و بیایی کیلا بو بیا من چنانکه در خاتمه نثر الابرار در وصف الخوکه
مشو کیلا بو با بمعنه ز مان جان ملفانم این کیلاکان آمدن و نات کیلکا بیکا و کیلکا بیزو کیلکا بیزو کیلای و کیلکای بیایم کیلکای بیای
و تا آمده کیلکاج چون آمد و بیاید و بمحض آمدن کیلکو جی آینده کیلکو جه کیلکو نجه و کیلکانجه تا آمدن و بمقدار آمدن کیلکو دور
جو هم آمد کیلکو نکودور خواهم آمد کیلکو سیدور خواهد آمد کیلکو لوک آمدنی کیلکای و کیلکای کیلسه و کیلسون و کیلسون باید
کیلکو دیک کیلکو دیک کیلکو دیک تو بیتی کیلتو زونک فقا مهابتام کیلتورماک بمعنی آوردن باشد کیلتور دی آوردیم کیلتور ور کیلتور اده در محمدره

316r.

بمعنی فاعل و مصدر هم می آید کیلتورکان کیلتور کا و کیلتورور کان آورنده و آورده و بمعنی مصدر هم می آید کیلتور و کیلتورکیل
مفرد مخاطب فضل امر چنانکه شاهد ملک الاول شعر شاه و فنع آهیم در اولشانک یا ب محل کرز کا کیلتور بیز که آنی الحق ایتمش بیز بیکرا
و ندوز و مولف روی کیلتور را در این شعر بکسر کاف مفتوحه و میم مضمومه خوانده و نوشته که بمعنی بپوش و مخفی کن و شعر را بصیغه کند
و نصیری هم مناسبت کرده و لفظ و معنی هر دو خطا است شاهد ملک الثانی شعر بو که بیسه نقاش جونی نیسه حق یو انکلاکم
کامل نی کیلتور کیل بیمیش یغیبین کیلکانی قانیا رمیش کیلتور ما و کیلتور ما سیل مفرد مخاطب فضل نهی کیلتور و کیلتور کور
کیلتورونکلار جمع مخاطب فضل امر کیلتورمانک کیلتور مانکز و کیلتورمانکلار جمع مخاطب فضل نهی کیلتورامین و کیلتور ورمین و کیلتورادورمین و
کیلتور ورام می آورم کیلتوریان کیلتورماس من نمی آورم کیلتوریانان و کیلتور کاسیز و کیلتور کاوسین بیاورید شاهد ملک الثانی شعر
خضر وش خطی بیله چون جبینونک خندین سر کاسین بیزنی کندنی سوفه المنتب سوبن کیلتور کاسین کیلتوری و کیلتوریان و کیلتوریش
آورده کیلتوریشین آورده اش را کیلتوریشانک آورده کیلتوریب و کیلتوریب تو ربیر آورده ایم کیلتور ماس نمی آرد کیلتور ماسلیک نیاورد
کیلتور ماس بولسا نیاورده باشد کیلتور اورشتقه نیاورده باشد کیلتورا کیلتورا آورده آورده و بدون تکرار هم مستعمل کیلتور ایو
آیا بیاورم و بیاورد و بیاوری کیلتوربو بیاورم کیلتور انوکیلتور و کیلتور نیزکیلتور انی و کیلتور اینک بیاورم کیلتورکلی برای
آوردن و تا آورده کیلتورکاج چون آورد و بیاورد و بمحض آوردن کیلتورکوجی آورنده چنانکه در تنبیهات محبوب القلوب کوید که نالها
امانه لارادا ایتو کیلتورکوجی کیلتورکوجه کیلتورکونجه و کیلتورکانجه تا آوردن و بمقدار آوردن کیلتورکودور خواهم آورد کیلتورکودور
خواهی آورد کیلتورکوسیدور خواهد آورد کیلتورکولوک آوردنی کیلتورکای و کیلتورکای و کیلتورسه و کیلتورسون بیارد کیلتوردیک بیاورد بیرو
کیلتورکیلیت توبیتی و کیلتوریب تو بیتی آورده ایم کیلتور باتان سم تاری قول و سکون رای مهمله و نای ثانی مشدد متعدیست و صیغ آن بدستور
کیلتورماک جاری شده کیلتور نیز بعد از بیش مشهد آورده و لفظ ازکام اشتقاق یافته از الجوامد کیل
بامافزای قوشا شتاق میباید کیلتورشانک لفظ رابعیت که از لغتی غیر کلام علم صیغه مفرد مخاطب فضل امر و بمعنی مضامه
و اقع میشود چنانکه در داستان هفتم از سبعه سیاره کوید شعر شو حکیم المجنیک و تا اینکیل جد یار الجمل تو تصوفا این کیتکیل و نیز از
آمدن چنانکه در غزل کیلما لکنکشت کیلیش بمعنی آمدن بود چنانکه در خاتمه سبعه سیاره در وصف مظفر حسین میرزا کوید شعر
اول بس چهره ظالم از و هر ی بیتی سیلوسیل کیشی نی نو میوزی حوش کیلتین عروس را کوید چنانکه در محبوب جهانی کوید شعر کوب بزنیت
زیب ایتیب ایکانی کیلتور کیلین بیله کو باونی مع تیمی کیم بدو معنی باشد اول لطیف که منزله که در روابط مستعملست جنانکه
کوید شعر سنلونک توشا المحینک آسید از بی کیم کل بله مخبرشینینک آسید الام و علبه ناد و دیم حروف استفهام است بمعنی
و یک یمیسه بفتح میم و سین مهمله و سکون رای مهمله بمعنی نشین بود چنانکه در مکتوب هفتم از منشآت در وصف بهار کوید که مونداق وقت
یم هیچ وقت هیچ مونیدن ادب کیمیسه یادیدار و آنرا و بینه کیمسنه کوید کیمساسات بسکون میم و نون و فتح سین مهمله بالف کشیده و تای
کاراز امعصه بوزین میسازند چنانکه در محبوب الابرار در وصف اهلین کوید شعر و ملایمه فیه نوزات کیرالیشنا سانیغ ایم کیمات
که کیسمان دین آلتونیغ فرقایلکا کانی کیمسنه بفتح میم و نون و سکون سین مهمله ترکی و بمعنی شخص باشد کیمون بفتح الموحده کرا آنرا
هم نامند چنانکه در خسرو شیرین در وصف کرمه هم کوید شعر کیمو شام و دم آل احمد ملی شها با اول کیم دیت جنقفان علم پسل کیمیه
بفتح میم بمعنی جهاز شه سفینه مزهر قرار نامند الفا حمیه بشر آنکان دنیان جو ندا اول آنی کیمیرله سر لیتار با ملاول وموکیس ایل کیداد
چیمون را دو نیز در تنبیهات محبوب القلوب کوید کو او شا الهرانی حرمیه بولماس پیته تا یوه ن کمه بولماس بیع اتور تنبیهات کیتکا شاک
بامه و کاف عجمی و سکون نون و شین معجمه و فتح کاف ثانی مع الالفاله بمعنی مشوق کردن باشد کیتا شتوک مشوقی کردیم کیتا شتوق مشوق کرد

چنانکه در خسرو شیرین در صورت خاقان با اطبا گوید کینکاشیب توزوب جمع احبا بولوب خاضر بیکم بولغای اطبا کینکاشورد
کیناشادور مشورت میکند و کینکاشور بمعنی فاعل و مصدر هم می آید کینکاشکان و کینکاشورکان و کینکاشادورکان مشورت کننده و شده
کرده و بمعنی مصدر هم می آید کینکاش و کینکاشیکلا مفرد مخاطبه فعل امر و کینکاش بمعنی مشورت هم باشد کینکاشماق و کینکاشماک مذ
مخاطبه فعل نهی کینکاشینک و کینکاشینکیز و کینکاشینکلار جمع مخاطبه فعل امر کینکاشماینک و کینکاشمانکیز و کینکاشمانکلار جمع مخاطبه فعل نهی
کینکاشایین و کینکاشورمین و کینکاشادورمین و کینکاشغوم مشورت میکنم کینکاشمان و کینکاشماس مین مشورت نمیکنم کینکاشیب و کینکاشیبان و کینکاشیش
مشورت کرده الشاهد علی الاول شعر چوا لیتیبا ایکی طرفین ایلیشیب قیلا الغینکاز لیف مکر که قیلیمه پیرپر بیننک چاله کینکاش
کینکاشمین مشورت کرده ام ایشیکاشیمیشتانک مشورت کرده کینکاشیبسیز و کینکاشیب توریز مشورت کرده ایم کینکاشماس مشورت نکند
کینکاشماسلیک مشورت نکردن کینکاشماس بولسا مشورت نکند باشد کینکاشادورغان مشورت میکرده باشد کینکاشا کینکاشا
مشورت کنان و بدون تکرار هم مستعملست کینکاشا یمو آیا مشورت کنم و کند و کنی کینکاشمایو مشورت نکرده کینکاشانک
کینکاشغانم و کینکاشکایرم کینکاشلی و کینکاشالی مشورت کنیم کینکاشلی برای مشورت کردن و تا مشورت کرده کینکاشکاچ چون مشورت کرد و کند
و بعض کردن کینکاشوب مشورت کند کینکاشکوجه کینکاشکونجه و کینکاشکانچه تا مشورت کردن و بقدر آن کینکاشکوسیدور مشورت
خواهم کرد کینکاشکوسیدور مشورت خواهی کرد کینکاشکوسیدور مشورت خواهد کرد کینکاشکولوک مشورت کردنی کینکاشکای کینکاشه
کینکاشسو و کینکاشکون مشورت کند کینکاشکودیلار و کینکاشکودیک توریمین و کینکاشکور مشورت کرده ام کینکالماک بسکون نون
ولام و فتح کاف ثانی عجمی و کینکیشمانک بسکون نون و شین و کسر کاف ثانی عجمی وسیع و فراخ شدن و صیغ کینکالمانک بفتح کاف مع
اللام و صیغ کینکیشمانک بکسر کاف مع الشین موافق قانون اول اشتقاق می باید کینکالتماک بسکون نون و لام و تای قرشت و فتح کاف
وسکون و ضم تای قرشت مصدر متعدیست بمعنی فراخ کردن و صیغ آنها نیز بدستور موافق قانون اول اشتقاق می باید در سیما مذ کینکیت بسکون نون
و تای قرشت و کینکید مع الدال ده و قریه را گویند چنانکه در حیرة الابرار گوید الشاهد علی الاول شعر دخل ضعا عتیبیله الی
اچیعین مزرعه کینکت تیلیب الکه شهر کیننک بسکون نون و کاف آخر و کسر دال مهمله بمعنی ناف باشد لاادری هر قایش بین کینکو
ابنا سرهیکان بن لازم کل هر کیمک بیننک کینکید بین نافر تا ناراما س کینکات باهردو کاف عجمی و سکون نون و شین و فتح کاف ثانی بمعنی
مشورت بود الشاهد علیه شعر دیمایم پر بحش سمیز بیله نوای جانیق آسام اول بولغا بمو راضی بحش سمیز کانی کینکاش و نیز آنرا
از مشورت کردن چنانکه مذکور شد کیناداکین کیکنک بسکون نون بمعنی فراخ و وسیع باشد کیکینه با کاف عجمی و فتح نون خاطر زده
مرد فتنه در مقام تصغیر استعمال می شود چنانکه گوید شعر پر پچک یا شلیغ نگاری تا پیشام نلرلا کینه سیکریتور اونین
میداندرا جابک کینه بیرالوی میر نیهان کیوچماک با کاف عجمی و ضم واو و سکون رای مهمله بمعنی داخل کردن بود کیوچوری داخل کرد
الشاهد علیه شعر تاراج ایتیبان دین و تاقیب یونیمه منتار بو نیچال ایغ کهنا رجناپیغه کیوچوری و نیز در حیرة الابرار گوید شعر
جونکه قویا شریلشین اباغ بولدی مهر کا کیوچوردی آن هر کون سپهر یو بوردردونلت داخل کردی چنانکه گوید شعر پر کیوچالدولمانا
بیله ای خسته نولئی عشق اجلی ار اسیدا بانکو سیم کیوچوردونک بیوچورو ر کا نیکو و ار ادور کا داخل میکند چنانکه در تاریخ نا بیمنه کوهر سکوز
بیهم ایکار لا دیوز بیکا تمام نا بیکو فراغ کیوچوروی کا لا دو کیوچورمو بمعنی فاعل و مصدر هم می آید کیوچورکان و کیوچوروکان نوکیوچورادورکان داخل کنند
و داخل کرده و بمعنی مصدر هم می آیند کیوچور و کیوچورکیل مفرد مخاطبه فعل امر کیوچورماو کیوچورماکیل مفرد مخاطبه فعل نهی چنانکه سا
راولطاء در نیهان محبوب القلوب گوید کیوچوراماندورکان دوست ناوبه کیوچورکا کیوچور ولماتیکوچور و تنکو تره کیوچورانکلار جمع مخاطبه فعل امر

کیوچورمانک و کیوچورمانکیز و کیوچورمانکلار جمع مخاطبه فعل نهی کیوچورامین و کیوچوره مین و کیوچوره دورمین و کیوچورغوم داخل میکنم کیوچورماسمین و کیوچوری
داخل نمیکنم کیوچوروب و کیوچوروبان و کیوچوروبیش داخل کرده کیوچوروبتین داخل کرده ام کیوچوروبتانک داخل کرده کیوچوروبیس
داخل نمیکند کیوچورماسلیک داخل نکردن کیوچورماس بولسا داخل نکند باشد کیوچورادورغان داخل میکرده باشد کیوچوره
کیوچوره داخل کنان و بدون تکرار هم مستعملست کیوچوره یمو آیا داخل کنم و کند و کنی کیوچورمایو داخل نکرده کیوچورکانک و کیوچورکانیم
کیوچورکانیم و کیوچورکایرم و کیوچورالینک داخل کنیم کیوچورکالی برای داخل کردن و تا داخل کرده کیوچورکاچ چون داخل کرد و کند و بعض کردن
کیوچورکوچ داخل کنند کیوچورکونچه و کیوچورکونچه و کیوچورکانچه تا داخل کردن و بقدر داخل کردن کیوچورکوسیدور داخل خواهم کرد کیوچورکوسیدور
داخل خواهی کرد کیوچورکوسیدور داخل خواهد کرد کیوچورکولوک داخل کردنی کیوچورکایلار و کیوچورکایلار کیوچورسالار و کیوچورسونلار و کیوچورسونلار
داخل کنند الشاهد علی الثالث شعر بو اوت که میندا تورور در دوزخ ایمرا ملجای خلق کیوچورسالار دیسو آتش بیرله محشر ارا کیوچورکون
کیوچوردیک تورمین و کیوچوردیک تورمین داخل کرده ام من البحر الی المد کیوی با کاف عجمی بروزن نیوه ترکی رومی طاهر نیست که بر کاغذ و پشمینه ما
و آن ابریشم قت گویند و بغا ریبی نوعی از کشتی با یاقر از اسکر رومی آن از بر پیمان دعوی بلد و ته آنرا التشه سلزند مع کینا کیمه بکیزیا کوک
رای مهمله بمعنی قصب باشد چنانکه مسیح سمکدوی در دنیم باوقبیبی با پهلوان مغربی گوید شعر کمی بو ناچیب اولکیمه دین سیب کم
بلشیفه میکن میتکوبوب و نیز در خسرو شیرین در صورت شیرین گوید شعر که چون صوش اولا دی ایم اکر یب چت ایشیک لازمی کیمیب
ایلانبان رست و آنرا کیمیز هم گویند کیمی بکیلا و سین مهمله ترکی رومی پشار و نیز پوشاک و لباس بود کیمیک آهو را گویند الشاهد علیه
لاله کوز عین مرا رایش کور کا ریلیک اول نوع کیم لاله زار او سیدا هر ان آغنا لیش بولغا یکیک کیمیم دو معنی دارد اول بمعنی پیشانی
بود چنانکه در حیرة الابرار گوید شعر امیر سپهر دیش کیمی چله شاش خواه ریلیل آن کر طیلسانی دوم نیز دانشمند کیمین بمعنی عقب
باشد چنانکه گوید شعر کیلکلاج اول یوز آلیمه تا لورقرا قامو کیمین شا یه توشکا نرات کیمین خورشید بولغا ایلکا جیکیو کیمی
بضم یا و نون و سکون کاف ثانی و فتح لام بمعنی لباس پوشی بود و نوروز مغولیه را هم گویند چنانکه در تاریخ وصاف مذکور است کر بجون
انبا ل ایلخان مشتری طالع را آنجو در زمان نوروز مغول که آنرا کیونوکلا میشی گویند ده رسید جز خامس بغیر معنی ربیع کتاب اللام باب الکاف
حرف تلام مع الالف لاد در چغتای بمقام استعمال می شود اول بمعنی ای و امثوی بی آید چنانکه گوید شعر یار در دیم سوزا بن کونکلو سی
صرنوز قیلدی لا جانیم آشوبی که قیلما ایدین ازوز سیلدی لا و نیز در صفه سیاره گوید شعر امیر نی اولتوریا شام اولا رمین لا کیمکا
توشتی جهان اراسیله بلا دوم بمعنی نمیمه صوت در آخر کلمات در می آید الشاهد علیه شعر قطر خوبلوغ فار زسنک دم قیس نون ملیحه لالی
لطف طبع ابیات نظمیں دم سکون فیلدی لا سیم محذف لاله نعمه دردی و کل باشد که در ته ظرف دم خشنده وار ابری روبکو بید چنانکه در
سکمکده ب موصف شتن دوات فرماید شعر دو اینم که آیینی و کانکمر هما ناکه بو بچا عذ لا سین آمینک سلابیه قیلور دی قربین آسینک
تا میوانده مرطوب سو آنکا سوا ضیدا نا مغان دم لایحو آنکا معنی شراییت که هما نا دو قت شستن لا ینره هنگام سلابه کردن سیا مثقوبه
چکانیدن مرطوب آب با آن بجای آب سواد ریا آن چکیده و قرامی لا سین اطعاین شرکلمه و احد فرم کرده موبعض تا س بعضی ار دیشه در بیت نوشته
کرد لفظ دمعوم و انتزامیت بها دیم بعضی از کلمات نجا بده را خواسته ایم که بیج ملفه تکلم کنند مثل لا اچاق بمعنی زیج کردن نو
کردن و تا شلاچاق بمعنی انداختن و سلتن و دوزن بوز لا ناک بمعنی نگاه کردن و تیشلاماق بمعنی بدندان گرفتن و امثال آنها لا چین شاهین
که آنرا بعربی صقر نامند و نیز نام قبیله ایست از تراک و مرتبه کو بخت را گویند لاچین قایا ترکی رومی کو بخت بو دهو تا و کوهی نامند
کنار قطعه مراد مرتبه آن واقع است خصوصا لا ث تر صیحه را خوانند الشاهد علیه شعر خلق دینی رامی نیک سفاقی

317v.

یاقوت زنکی کیمیا توشکان نوروز لعلینک هلاکی لاشیئه و بمعنی سه مهی بادره اول تغارت و تاراج بود ندیم ضایع و فرومایه را گویند
سیم بمعنی چیز کم و اندک نیز باشد لاغ لاغ از توابع است یعنی زبان بزبان چنانکه گوید شعر نی خس کیم اوتولمادین یا ترلاغ لاغ
ن حاجت نیه تویماق اول اوت فه باغ و آنرا لاولاو هم گویند و بفارسی لاغ بمعنی بازی و هزل و ظرافت بود لاغ و لاق حرفیست
که در آخر بعضی کلمات واقع شده افاده معنی کثرت و انبوهی مینماید مثل قومدلاق یعنی ریکستان و تاولاق یعنی مکان بسیار لاو لاو [illegible]
لاغ لاغ است یعنی زبان به زبان چنانکه گوید شعر توش توشیدین [illegible] سوالیغ اوتی لاولاو [illegible]
لاب یا نیم دین ایل و بفارسی خاک سفیدی باشد که خانها [illegible] بدود سیاه شده باشد بدان سفید کنند و بمعنی لابه هم می آید مع الباء لبنا
لاف بروزن قنا بلغت مغولی بمعنی مرشد باشد لباشاق بلغت مغولی تغار را گویند مع الفاء لفادن بفتح فا و دال الف کشیده [illegible]
لاق نون ترکی رومی [illegible] نیم برشت بود مع القاف لوق مع القاف ترکی رومی [illegible] باشد و آنرا شالوق هم گویند و نیز چنبه بود که منقش شده با[illegible]
لان و بفارسی بمعنی [illegible] مع النون لنجک بسکون نون و جیم و فتح کاف [illegible] باشد که آنرا [illegible]
گویند لنکر بسکون نون و [illegible] و فتح کاف [illegible] بمعنی آمده اول آهنی بود [illegible] سنکی که [illegible] بکشتی است چون خواهند که کشتی را
از رفتار باز دارند آنرا بدریا اندازند و در این معنی با فارسی مشترکست و آنرا بعربی انجر گویند دوم مکانی [illegible] اولیا را نامند عموماً و محل
معروف از ولایت جام توابع هرات که مزار شیخ احمد [illegible] جامی در آنجا واقعست خصوصاً سیم مکانی را گویند که هر روز در آنجا المقام [illegible]
کنند چنانکه در مجالس النفایس در وصف مولانا [illegible] گوید که آبدان و [illegible] در [illegible] لنکری [illegible]
لای و بفارسی بمعنی [illegible] بود و [illegible] گویند که در مکر و حیله در [illegible] داشته باشد و [illegible] مع الیاء [illegible]
لایلاماق بمعنی اندود کردن و [illegible] لایلادی [illegible] لایلایدور اندود میکند و لایلاغ بمعنی فاعل و [illegible] هم می آید لایلاغان
لایلاغمان [illegible] اندود کننده و اندود کرده و بمعنی [illegible] هم می آید لایلاتو لایلاتیل [illegible] اندود کن لایلاتیلار [illegible] اندود کن
لایلاتیلار [illegible] اندود کرده چنانکه در تاریخ [illegible] گوید [illegible]
کلمه دا [illegible] آشلیغ [illegible] لایلاغ [illegible] اندود کرده لایلایمو آیا اندود
کم و کند و [illegible] لایلاغامو آیا اندود کند لایلاتاق و لایلاغان [illegible] اندود کنیم لایلاغالی برای اندود کردن و تا
کرده لایلادی [illegible] برای [illegible] اندود تواند کرد [illegible] چون اندود کرد و کند و [illegible] کردن لایلاتوچی اندود کننده
لایلاتو [illegible] اندود کردن و [illegible] لایلاغوم اندود [illegible] کرد لایلاتوچی اندود [illegible]
کرد لایلاماق و لایلاتماق [illegible] اندود [illegible] لایلاتماسدین [illegible] اندود کردنست لایلاشماق مع التاء [illegible]
بمعنی اندود فرمودن و صیغ آن [illegible] شقاق می باید لایلانماق مع النون بمعنی اندود شدن و صیغ آن [illegible] می باید
ج مراجعه لایبیت بکسر یا و سکون نون ترکی رومی [illegible] تشبیه است چنانکه گویند [illegible] یعنی مانند [illegible]
لو و [illegible] مثل [illegible] لوپاک [illegible] شبیه [illegible] که آنرا بفارسی [illegible] گویند
لوج بمعنی برهنه و عریان بود و بفارسی [illegible] که آنرا لوچ [illegible] گویند لوچه بفتح جیم [illegible] خوانند و [illegible]
دولانه نامند لودوس باصطلاح اتراک [illegible] که میانه جنوب و مغرب [illegible] ترکی رومی [illegible] که آنرا بفارسی
[illegible] گویند لوق و لوق و لوک اگرچه در معنی [illegible] اما در استعمال [illegible] چنانکه [illegible]
[illegible] مثل [illegible] بمعنی [illegible]

318r.

دوم بمنزله یای مصدریت مثل چوقلوق بمعنی بسیاری و تیزلوک بمعنی [illegible] سیم بمعنی [illegible] مثل یورولوق بمعنی [illegible]
بمعنی [illegible] نوک [illegible] بمعنی [illegible] مثل لوغ و لوق [illegible] شد به معنی [illegible] اول [illegible] گویند چنانکه [illegible]
دروصف [illegible] گوید شعر [illegible] دوم ترکی رومی [illegible] و آن مانند [illegible]
که بدان دسته کارد و شمشیر [illegible] و آنرا بفارسی [illegible] گویند سیم نوعی [illegible] باشد [illegible]
و حقیر نوشته و بلغت اهل بیستان بمعنی [illegible] بود و آن گیاهیست که [illegible] و نیز کسی را گویند که [illegible]
لی و [illegible] هم گویند که [illegible] تا قروت شود لوی بلغت مغولی [illegible] باشد و [illegible] هم گویند و نیز نام [illegible]
ترکی [illegible] لیق و لیک [illegible] باشد چنانکه معانی ثلثه آنها مذیل لوغ و لوق [illegible]
و این الفاظ مکسور اللام [illegible] معانی ثلثه [illegible] در آخر [illegible] مضارع [illegible] آنرا بمعنی [illegible]
الماسلیغ [illegible] و [illegible] یعنی [illegible] مثل [illegible] کیمکلیک
ماج بمعنی [illegible] لیمان [illegible] ترکی رومی [illegible] که در آنجا کشتی [illegible] کتاب المیم باب [illegible] مع الجیم ماج
بوسه را گویند [illegible] شعر [illegible] چون [illegible]
مات هم [illegible] مع التاء مات [illegible] و آنرا [illegible] خوانند [illegible] بفتح تای [illegible]
ماش [illegible] مع الثاء [illegible]
بسکون لام اول [illegible] شبیه و مانند چنانکه گوید شعر [illegible]
[illegible] شعر [illegible]
ماخ چنانکه گوید شعر [illegible] مع الخاء ماخ بمعنی
بوسه باشد [illegible] شعر [illegible]
ماد خای با الف کشیده و کسر نون و سکون کاف [illegible] بود که [illegible] مع الدال المهمله [illegible]
مار [illegible] گویند مع الراء المهمله [illegible] ماریماق [illegible] فریاد کردن [illegible] ماریدی فریاد کرد ماریغای [illegible] فریاد کند
و ماری بمعنی فاعل [illegible] هم می آید [illegible] فریاد کننده و فریاد کرده و بمعنی [illegible] هم می آید [illegible]
ماریمش فریاد کرده [illegible] فریاد نمیکند [illegible] فریاد کنان [illegible] مستعملست [illegible] برای فریاد نکردن
فریاد نکرده [illegible] چون فریاد کرد و کند و [illegible] کردن [illegible] فریاد کننده [illegible] فریاد کردن و [illegible]
[illegible] فریاد کند [illegible] فریاد کرد [illegible] فریاد کند و [illegible]
ج بذکر آنها [illegible] من الجوامد [illegible] گویند [illegible] بسکون را و نون و کسر [illegible] ترکی رومی [illegible]
که آنرا بعربی [illegible] نامند [illegible] بسکون را و نون و فتح کاف [illegible] گویند [illegible] بفتح را و سکون نون [illegible]
چنانکه در سد سکندری گوید شعر [illegible]
سنان گوید شعر کیمیا [illegible] بفتح را و سکون لام ترکی رومی [illegible]
[illegible] خوانند [illegible] بفتح را و جیم و سکون لام [illegible] ترکی رومی [illegible] باشد و آن سفید و سیاه [illegible] نوع سفید
[illegible] و [illegible] کبوتر شبیه است [illegible] نوع آن [illegible] لفظ مغولیست [illegible]

1.15 در اشتباه

318v

کمد دهجنات و تیراندازی و امثال آن چون بر حریف غالب کردند امروی خنثالد دست افشانده بر میگویند مع زاء معجمه مسئ بردن
خرمنده بود و آن دانهای کردات که از گوشت مغز پوست میآید مع تای مثلثه مسکه روغن نانه و اکویند مع شین معجمه ماشاب
بفتح شین با الف کشیده و سکون بای ابجد شال و ششخش نامسند الثانی هد علیه شعر تیرکما با نقان کردولاردین مکرمع الحمیش اوزلکی
چرکین محترلعدین ابرباك ماشاب لاردیع الفان من المشتقات مانقا مانوغ بسکون نون و فتح تای با الف کشیده بمعنی تعریف کردن مانقار
مانقا بعود تعریف میکند و مانقا و بمعنی فاعل و مصدر هم می آید مانقانای تعریف میتواند کرد مانقاغان و مانقاغانو مانقا بیدر ما
تعریف کننده و تعریف کرده و بمعنی مصدر هم می آیند مانقانا و مانقامیلو مانقای کور تعریف کن مانقا سا و مانقاماغل تعریف مکن مانقاما
مانقاغاسی و مانقاغای سن تعریف کنی الشاهد علی الاول شعر ولعطا ایلا حیبنیکل ایلیك نیمیکم کوزمینیش مانقاسانك خاشاکرمن
رطل کران دین کیمکامین مانقاب و مانقابان و مانقامیش تعریف کرده مانقامیشانك تعریف کرده مانقاغا میو آیا تعریف کند مانقانا
مانقاغاپزم مانقاغای پزم مانقانیل مانقانیل تعریف کنیم مانقاغالی برای تعریف کردن و تا تعریف کرده مانقاغاج چون تعریف کرد و کند
و بعض کردن مانقانوجی تعریف کننده مانقانوجه و مانقانوجه مانقاغانجه تا تعریف کردن و بعد از آن مانقاغوم تعریف خواهم کرد
مانقاغونك تعریف خواهی کرد توانائی تعریف خواهد داشت مانقانوجی تعریف خواهد کرد مانقاغاج مانقانیلما مانقاسون و مانقانیك
تعریف کند مانقانوریك توم مانقاغاسیدیك تعریف نکرده است من الجوامد مانقا بمعنی تعریف و تحسین باشد مغره بفتح ثاء
و رای مهمله بهمانزده بترکی روبی آلتی است از نهال چیغ که بجهد شود و بگردد مع الکاف منك بفتح کاف و سکون نون آهوئیست که از کام
بترکیز چنانکه در ظفرنامه مذکوراست که وقتی که امیر تیمور بر سر توقتمش خان میرفت در راه شکار جرگه کردند آهوئی سید شد آنگاه
بشکل که مغول از آن خاوی دشتستان منك کویند مع که باکاف اول مشدد و ثلثه مکسور از نجیکه تهران کوشلو را کویند مع اللام
ملش بفتح لام و سکون شین معجمه نام طایفه ایست از اتراك الشاهد علیه شعر اعبراب بیکل ایل ترخان ایله برلاسیدی کیم پرکیلدی کو
حالا ناش اول بفتح ملش بمعنی خوش نما را هم کویند چنانکه کوید شعر سرونانیم قاشیدا کیلدی نوایی او بی ملش کیم صورت
جلوه او هم آن ملش لفظ عربیست در ذیل خاتمه کتاب مذکور خواهد شد مع المیم ماموغ ماموغ پنبه را کویند الشاهد علیه
شعر آغاز تبعشق باشیمغه نان بولمیش نا بیغ چرم ماموغ ایرابیمغه چرماغان بیکلیغ کیمنی ... مع النون مانوغ بسکون
نون فروبردن نان و امثال آن بآب و غیره است و اشباه آن مانا بمعنا نادر بسبب و مانا بمعنی فاعل و مصدر هم می آید مانا غان و مانانیك
ماناد رخان فروبرنده و فروبرده و بمعنی مصدر هم می آیند مانابعنا خیلام مانانا کور فروبر مانا لونا ماغل فرومبر مانانك معنا نغاش
مانتقاق فروبری مانیب ... مانیساد مانمیش فروبرده مانیشانك فروبرده ساغاس فرومبرچنانکه کوید شعر که الا ... کوین
فرو خوا مانات ابرانا جه دعوت ... کانوتشاد فرونان باده ... مانامانی بمعنی فاعل و مصدر هم می آید مانا غامیو آیا فروبرد
مانیاقو مانقاپزم مانقای پزم مانانك مانانیك فروبرم مانقالی برای فروبردن و تا فروبرده مانقاج چون فروبرد و بعض بردن
مانقوجی فروبرنده مانقوجه مانقوجه مانقاغنجه تا فروبردن و بعد از آن فروبردن مانقوم فروخواهم برد مانقونك فروخواهی برد
مانقوسی فروخواهد برد مانقای مانالو مانیلونا نونی مانارغه ... مانا غوریك تو ... بلیغ فروبرد است ما ند و ماخ مصدر
و صنیع آن بمعنی ربا لفظ ... بابدنا نکاغ بسکون نون و کاف عجمی قدم گذاشتن ماتکار ماتکاد قدم بیکلا و ماتکبان
ماتکاغان ماتکادر ... قدم کذارنده و قدم گذاشته و بمعنی مصدر هم می آیند ماتکیم ماتکیلو ماتکاکور قدم بگذار الشاهد علی الاول شعر
قطع قبلغو صد بادشوی را یورمعیك الا نك تاتالعه ... قدم بر نجا جای مالك و مالك کو ستفه ... ناله راهم کویند

جنکو

319r

چنانکه مغول بجواسد خواهد آمد ماتکما و ماتکما حبل قدم مکذار ماتکسانك ماتکماسین ماتکمای بن قدم بکذاری ماتکب
ماتکیان و ماتکیش قدم کذاشته ماتکیشانك قدم کذاشته ماتکا میو آیا قدم بکذارد ماتکاق ماتکا پزم و ماتکای پزم ماتکما
قدم بکذاریم ماتکماله برای قدم کذاشتن و تا قدم کذاشته ماتکاج چون قدم کذاشت و بکذارد و بعض کذاشتن ماتکوجی قدم کذارنده
ماتکوجه و ماتکوجه و ماتکاغانجه تا قدم کذاشتن و بعد از آن ماتکوم قدم خواهم کذاشت ماتکونك قدم خواهی کذاشت
ماتکوسی قدم خواهد کذاشت ماتکای ماتکالو ماتکلو ماتکیما ماتکقدم بکذارد ماتکا غوریك توم ماتکاسیدیك توم قدم نکذاشته
ماتکورماتوغ مصدر متعدیست بمعنی برفتار آوردن ماتکوروب ماتکورتاغ ماتکقیش برفتار آورده چنانکه در حبیب الابرار
در رزم حسین اصفهانی کوید شعر قرا ایله کافر ... حمله قیلار بیری ... تاتی کیلکان ... یورو
کبك خرامین ... ماتکماق بالفظ ... اول اشتقاق می یابد ماتکراماق بسکون نون و کاف عجمی و فتح
رای مهمله ناله کردن کاو و کوسفند و امثال آن را کویند و از افغان مونکراماق خوانند ماتکرادی ناله کرد ماتکرایدی ناله می کند
و ماتکرا بمعنی فاعل و مصدر هم می آید ماتکراغان و ماتکراغان و ماتکرایدرکان ناله کننده و ناله کرده و بمعنی مصدر هم می آیند ماتکرا ماتکراب
ماتکراسیش ناله کرده چنانکه در خسرو شیرین مصراع کویلا الشاهد علی الاول شعر حمل ماتکراب ... باش کیمولناق
ایچیندقربان ... ماتکراسانك ناله میکند ماتکرا یورما ماتکرای ماتکرایسا ... ماتکراهم مستعملست ماتکراغالی برای ناله
و تا ناله کرده ماتکراغاج چون ناله کرد و کند و بعض کردن ماتکرغوجی ناله کننده ماتکراغوجه و ماتکراغانجه تا ناله کردن و
آن ماتکراغای و ماتکراسا و ماتکراسون و ماتکرادیك ناله کند ماتکراغودیك ماتکرارلیلسا ناله کرده و چنانکه کند چون مانع مسح
مطابقت نداشت بذکر آنها مبادرت نشد من الجوامد منتر بسکون نون و رای مهمله و فتح تای قرشت ترکی روبی بمانعیغ بود و آن
نباتیست معطر و چیزی که میوه بی نظر و کما منخوانند سنداغان بسکون نون و فتح دال مهمله و غین معجمه کویند چنانکه در تاریخ
بابریه مذکور است که توب ... سنداغان سپله ... منطل بعضی ... باشد که از آنها
سنرس خوانند سنقلای بسکون نون و قاف و لام با الف کشیده بمعنی پیشانی باشد که از ما نکلیمی نیز کویند و مقدمه الجیش را هم ناسکای
کوسکاکه بمعنی فضای سرابست بالطاز چند اول ... خوانند نانك بعضی بانك کوسفند ... ناله را کویند ... قدم کذاشتن چنانکه
در فیل ماتکاق کذشت ... ماتکست بسکون نون و کاف عجمی و تای قرشت و کسر شین معجمه اسم طایفه ایست از اتراك
ماتکلای بسکون نون و کاف عجمی و تای حطی و فتح لام با الف کشیده بمعنی پیشانی باشد الشاهد علیه شعر ... چین که ... ماتکلای
نینیك ... منکل بسکون نون و لام و فتح کاف عجمی ترکی روبی خال بود منکوش بسکون نون و شین معجمه و ضم کاف
عجمی ترکی روبی ... باشد که آنرا ... کویند ماتکیش بسکون نون و کسر کاف عجمی مع لاما الف بمعنی ... و قدم کذاشتن
چنانکه ... کوید شعر ... یوق یوق ... آمت سانه ... بمعنی ...
باشد که ... منوار ... نامند ... خانه بود مع الواو ماد ... روزنکار ...
کویند ماوی ... بود چنانکه ... شعر ... سیاه کوید شعر ... نیلفروش
لباس ... مع الیا مای ... بسکون یا و قاف و ضم رای مهمله ... ناسد
بع ... باشد الشاهد علیه شعر ...
سین بسکون یا و نون و سین ...

کمه‌ر بوسیم کونا از بخار زمین تولید یابد دویم بمعنی بوسه باشد که از عربی بقبله نامند چنانچه گوید شعر لبینک دین اینا تی
جانیم جیان بیلماس مین کیم بو کونج بو ناصدی یه بو جات بولیکین و له شعر تیر کوز و بیطا مقسینک یوزنی تا چوبناق نی ایدی
مبل قیلماس خود اولوک کیمسه دین آلماقنه موچلک موچلکا بفتح جیم عجمی و کاف عجمی با الف کشیده و سکون لام و شیئه و محصول گویند که
در عهود دیوانی دشت شود موجنه بفتح جیم و نون ستر ادام و مزد یا گو داشال الزا نامند موچه بفتح جیم عجمی یعنی شغل و عمل بوانی
مع الراء المهمله مر بعضی در تیر که ردیمی رزنک بیلی ولاجوردی باشد بلغت مغولی بمعنی راه وطریق آسمن رجار آقاجی درختکو کی
که از انیاعنب الدب گویند و آنرا زوبناده باشد از آن بعد تامی و شاخهای آن زبیلوبنایل بزمین بچیزی و نجار باشد مرغاول بکون
راو لام و فتح غین معجمه و ضم واو اسم بهادری است از لشکر براق پادشاه ترکستان که بدلاوری مشهور بود چنانچه پور بهای جامی گوید
شعر مرغاول فراق تو در ملک صبر کرده با لشکر براق بغارت برابری موری بلغت کاشغری حوض باشد و نیز نام ولایتی است
از ترکستان و بفارسی ناوه که از آب دلوله سفالین بود که در مر آب گذارند و نوعی از بافته سر پیمانی و مر ظاهری نه که زنان بردوشکند
مع الزاء المعجمه موز یخ بود که آنرا بعربی جمد نامند الشاه علیه شعر لعلی دین چونیکه تکلدا المار آب حیات شادیغ لعیم
اولوبا فلاحنا موجب نبات مع السین المهمله موسون بلغت مغولی یخ باشد که آنرا جغتایه موز گویند مع الشین المعجمه موش
یخ خانه را خوانند و بفارسی ها نوعی است معروف که آنرا بعربی فاره نامند موشک بفتح شین تیر بخش بود و آن لولر از کافذ خانه
بسیار و طیر کرده چون تیر هند هوا رود چنانچه مسیح بکمری در افاز داستان اسکندر گوید شعر اگرچه ایمه موشکن آتماق
ایشی بولوت ساخوفین امرنای آلماس کیشی و آنرا موبه فشک گویند موشمله بضم میم و سکون شین و فتح لام ترکی رومی میوه ایست
جنگلی که از اهل طبرستان و دیلمان از کیل خوانند موشوک بضم شین که به بود که از عربی هر و سنور نامند چنانچه در قسم سیم
از صوب المقلوب گوید که موشوک کاهیابتکو بهر آفت تصریح لصاد موسلو ق بکون ضاد تیرکه رومی میوه بمعنی طبر و آوند
باشد که آنرا بعربی یخ گویند دویم شیر بچه که از سر و برنج ساخته در آب انبار ها و در خزینه حمام نصب کنند چون بر حیثیتها از آن
بر آید مع الغین المعجمه موغول اسم پسر النجه خان بن کیوک خان است و از اطبقه دو نفر سلطنت کرده اولین ایشان مغول خان و
بعد ایشان ایلخانست چنانچه کیفیت احوال ایشان در ذیل لغت تاتار بعربیاتی مشروحه ذکر یافت موغولچین بیشهی و مغلها
و کنایه است از سفید فام چنانچه در قصیده سعدیه گوید که کوز تینک خوی هندوی سیاهی و یوز تینک نه کیچکا تیره چیکی دین فارغ
و شام تینک مشکوی سیاه چهره لاری و صبح تینک مغولچین چاچکولری ترکتان بچین این مع اللام مول بعضی مغول بمعنی
حرامزاده باشد که آن را بعربی هجبن گویند و نوایی علیه الرحمه در حیرت الابرار فرموده که شعر که تا ایتنک آیی چیچک آلدی بولونی
قول مونچا ضایم آنکا بملک بولوب ومؤلفه وهی تو لقصد این شعر مول خوانده و مول را بعضی تیاس بمعنی محتاج نوشته وضبطهم بیاک
کرده سهو کرده اند و مول بفارسی بمعنی بودن و درنگ کردن در کارها و بازایستادن باشد و معشوق تقرن و ملنزو خرداهم گویند
و بهمی ضکوت و ضبطی رقت و بهای چیزها باشد مولدور بکون لام و ضم دال مهمله و ضم با المهمله ترکی بود که از عربی
بره نامند من سلحکنده بی شعر دم بوق که بهر کمینک دستا چپ شغالیا بیکم برکامولدور کا چپ مولون بضم لام و سکون
نون معجمه ترکی رومی بمعنی خشب با بولواست مع النون مونکاتیماق بکون نون و یای حطی و فتح کاف عجمی بمعنی بوق و غمناک
مونکایدی غمناک شد چنانچه گوید شعر مونکایدی کونکلوم آینینک دیک کر نغمه سیدین که ایلکا کونکل تا اتا را آشکار
مفطام بین مونکایدی و مونکایادور غمناک میشود و مونکایو بمعنی فاعل و مصدر هم می آید مونکا تقاو موجاریدن مونکمغانتا

شویدو و غمناک شد و بمعنی مصدر هم می آید مونکای و مونکایغیل و مونکا یادور امرست از غمناک شدن مونکایما و مونکایماغیل نفی
از غمناک شدن مونکایسانکز مونکایغاسین و مونکایغای مین غمناک شوی مونکایغای و مونکایبان و مونکامیش غمناک شده ماضی
الثانی شعر قوروب تاشیندا محب لا یخشیعو ویبن هم هم مونکاییان بو زولو بغاطر پریشانیم مونکامیشتا غمناک شدن مونکاینابو
آیا غمناک شود مونکایساق و مونکایغای برز و مونکایغای برز مونکالیم و مونکایالیق غمناک شویم مونکایغای برای غمناک شدن و تا غمناک شدن آن
مونکاتقاج چون غمناک شد مونکایوت و محض شدن مونکاینوچی غمناک شونده مونکاینوچه و مونکاینوچی مونکایغای تا غمناک شده بود
مونکاینوم غمناک خواهم داشت مونکاینونک غمناک خواهی شد مونکاینوری غمناک خواهد شد مونکایغای و مونکایلو مونکایسلو مونکایلو
مونکاندیلیک غمناک شوند مونکایماغوچیلیک تورمونکاسیدین تود غمناک شدن است مونکرامات قق بکون نون و کاف عجمی و فتح رای مهمله و
مونکراشماق باشین معجمه و مونکراماق بایای حطی و مونکرلماق بکون نون و رای مهمله وضم کاف عجمی و فتح غین معجمه ناله کردن
گویند و از حیوان ناخوش آواز نامند چنانچه بمد که پرشد مونکرام مونکراید و مونکراشور و مونکراشادور و مونکرابور و مونکر یادور و مونکرکد
مونکرغاید ناله میکند مونکرلدیمونکراشمرمونکرابورمونکرغای بمعنی فاعل و مصدر هم می آید مونکرامان و مونکرامان و مونکرایدیمان و
مونکراشغان و مونکراشورغان و مونکراشادرغان و مونکرابغان و مونکرابورغان و مونکرابادرغان و مونکر غاغان و مونکرغای درغان ناله کنده
و ناله کرده و بمعنی مصدر هم می آید مونکرامونکرلیغیل و مونکرای و مونکرای و مونکراشقیل و مونکراتو و مونکرغیل و مونکرابغیل و مونکرماکود
مونکرغای مونکر غیل و مونکرماغیل نا له مکن مونکرماو مونکراشماو مونکراشماغیل و مونکرابماو مونکرابماغیل و مونکرغاماو مونکرغاماغیل
ناله مکن مونکراسانکز مونکراغاسین مونکراغای مین مونکراشغاسین و مونکراشالم و مونکراشغای مین و مونکرایسانکز و مونکرابغلیغی و مونکرغای
مونکرغایسانکز مونکرغاسین مونکرغای مین ناله کنی مونکرام مونکرابان مونکرابغای مونکراشیم مونکراشیم مونکراشیمش مونکراغیمش و مونکرامت
مونکرامش و مونکراشیم و مونکرابان و مونکرغامش ناله زاری کرده چنانچه شاه عبید اولیا در تهلیل مجنون در مکالمه مجنون با آهو
گوید شعر بنکا بغیم ایله آشکاراد مونکرامیس مونکو رآیت چیدا را الشاه علی الرابع شعر کیمسه یلری پرلاه خوشتو غم دیشیبه ونکای
یا تمنا کاهی چهر باشیب ولتمرشا کاهی وانداشیب الشاه علی السابع شعر بو کمیم عهد و وایلیعی مرتو بهی خانیمه مونکرایب بیکی لیم گیم دین
اوت تو تاشیب خانیمه وله شعر تیلمو رهیمین مونکرایب او لیبوغا ده متصل هم آندین مدخا تیمنه نظر بولغامو دیبل الشاه علی الثانی
من لطائف تعیین میرزا شعر هجر دستیدا مونکروا قلیش ایری خسته جان کیم او تعریفه توانیم کلدی مو مونکرایشالم مونکراشماتنو
مونکرولیشاتک ناله کرد مونکرامو و مونکراشغابو و مونکرابو و مونکرو جاجا تمو آیا ناله کند مونکراساق و مونکرامبر و مونکرغای
مونکرالیم و مونکرالیک و مونکراشغا فه و مونکراشغابرز و مونکراشلی و مونکراشغای مونکراشالیک و مونکرابسا قه و مونکر بیابرز و مونکر
غای برز و مونکرابالی و مونکرابالیک و مونکرغاساق و مونکرغابرز و مونکرغابالی و مونکرغالیک ناله کنیم مونکراغالی
مونکراشغالی مونکرابغالی و مونکرغالی برای ناله کردن و تا ناله کرده مونکرامغاج و مونکراشغاج و مونکرابغاج و مونکرغاماج چون ناله کرده و کنده و
کردن مونکرانوچی و مونکراشنوچی و مونکرابنوچی مونکرنوچی ناله کنند مونکراغوچه و مونکرابغوچه و مونکراشغوچه مونکر اشغوچه
مونکراشغایه مونکرابغوچه مونکرابغوچه مونکر غاچه و مونکرابا چه و مونکرابا چه و مونکربا غوچه تا ناله کرده و تقیضه ناله کنان مونکرغوچه مونکراشغوچه مونکرابغوچه
مونکرغایوم ناله خواهم کرد مونکرغوک مونکراشغوک مونکرابغوک و مونکرغاموک ناله خواهی کرد مونکرغوسی و مونکراشغوسی و مونکرابغوسی
مونکرغاغوسی ناله خواهد کرد مونکراماسی مونکراسا و مونکراسون و مونکرادیت و مونکراشغاسه و مونکراشاو مونکرانسون و مونکراشدیت و مونکرغا
مونکراماو مونکراپسا و مونکرابسون و مونکرابدیت و مونکرغاسا و مونکرغاغای و مونکرغاسون و مونکرغابادیت ناله کنند

320v

مونکلاشماق بسکون نون وکاف عجمی وشین معجمه وفتح لام با هم غم دل گفتن مونکلاشور مونکلاشا تا غم دل میگوید مونکلاشور یعنی با هم و
هم می آید مونکلاشمان مونکلاشوران مونکلاشا دو غم دل گوینده و گفته و بمعنی مصدر هم می آید مونکلاشور مونکلاشمیل مونکلاشوا از
غم دل گفتن مونکلاشیم مونکلاشیمیل نمی خواست از غم دل گفتن مونکلاشسانک مونکلاشماسین مونکلاشقای تا غم دل گوید مونکلاشیش مونکلاش
مونکلاشمیش غم دل گفته چنانکه در مقاله هشتم از حیرة الابرار در باب وفا گوید الشاهد علی الاول شعر بولسا زمان غم بیز ان
مونکلاشیب تدین ... چاره نیز در خسرو شیرین گوید شعر ایکاولان مونکلاشیب ... تیشه کا نی ... دین
بیلدی مونکلاشمیشلدین غم دل گفته مونکلاشقا غیو آیا غم دل گوید مونکلاشساق و مونکلاشقا یار مونکلاشقای تا غم دل گویم مونکلاشقا
برای غم دل گفتن و تا گفته مونکلاشقاج چون غم دل گفته گوید مونکلاشوچی غم دل گوینده مونکلاشوچه مونکلاشوم
مونکلاشقاعه تا غم دل گفتن و بعد از آن مونکلاشوم غم دل خواهد گفت مونکلاشقای و مونکلاشسا و مونکلاشسا و مونکلاشتک
غم دل گوید مونکلاشما فودیک ... غم دل گفتنی است من الجوامد مونا بفتح نون ... اشاره باشد یعنی اینست الشاهد
شعر ایت لارینک ... کونکلی ... مونا که ... آغزیدا برابر کونکول مونجا و مونجه بسکون نون وفتح جیم
بمعنی انبه چنانکه ... شعر مونجه آنکه ... توشمیش ... ابدی
ابدی مونجا آت مونداه در اینجا مودا می یعنی در اینجا ... الشاهد ... شعر دیما بولماغدا ... میشر
بین اندامین ... مونداقی خوب مونداقین در اینجا ... مونداق بدو معنی استعمال میشود اول بمعنی اینچنین چنانکه گوید شعر
جرخ ... نیشک ... دم ... مونداق ... ایووقت و موندا قدا یعنی در اینوقت چنانکه
در لیلی مجنون گوید شعر موندا قدا ایکی ... و نیز مجنون در وفات پدر خود گوید شعر کم
تا ... مونداقدا ... بولمای یعنی با شنکلماغه ... و بسکون نون وضم
دال ... سیخی است که سر آن تیز و شکل نیزه کوچک است ... و همچنین سیخی است که ...
بدال ... شعر ... مونداق ... که هندو ...
وله شعر ... و نیز مجنون در وصف ترکان فرماید
شعر دیما ... مونداق ... و
طایع ... مونکلما ... معنی ... مونکلا ...
رفتار ... مونک بسکون نون وکاف عجمی بمعنی درد و غم باشد چنانکه در خسرو شیرین در وفات فرهاد
گوید شعر مونک ... نایب ... مونک ... آیت ... داغی ...
مونکغه ... مجنون ... لیلی مجنون گوید شعر ایل ... یعنی ...
و زبان ... و آن ... مونکا بسکون نون
وفتح کاف عجمی مع الامالة بمعنی این ... مونکان ... موکلوم ... معلوم ...
چنانکه بمعنی معلوم فرماید شعر ... مونکلوم ... لاله ...
شام گوید شعر ... مونکلوم ... اوله ... اولغو ...
مونکوی ... مونکلوم ... بسکون نون و ضم کاف عجمی بمعنی طول العمر

321r

و دایم و همیشه باشد و نیز نام پادشاهیست که چنگیز ... سکندر او را ... و همچنین نام پسر ... چنگیز ... که خطا ...
بوده و امرا او را مونکوقاآن گویند مونکوز بسکون نون ... وضم کاف عجمی مع الامالة شاخ حیوانات را گویند چنانکه ... بوده
در وصف ... گوید شعر ... ناقه ... مونکوز ... آن ...
هم گویند مونکوش ... که در کلیله و دمنه ترکی در حکایت ... موش ... کریاد ... خواجه ...
بر ... مونوغان ... مونوملک اسم اشارت چنانکه گوید مونوک ... موو
نواینک ... بلبل نوای ... که مونکلا ... مونونک ... موو حرف استفهام است
و ... چنانکه ... شعر ... سوز ... موی
با ... بسکون با و لام وضم میم ... باشد و آن ... تشبیه ... که دم ... میت
با ... که ... آنها ... و ...
در مقاله ... میش
و ... میغ
که ... میو
و بسکون نون ... بسکون لام وقاف ... میراء
در ... و ... میناو و ... میل
بمعنی ... الشاهد علی الاول ... شعر او ... من
مینکان ... و بمعنی مصدر هم می آید ... و مینکا ...
سینا و سیناکیل ... سیناش ... سیناش ... سینماش ...
شد سیناسیدا ... میناب ...
وشوی چنانکه ... الشاهد علی الاول ... شعر ...
سینکا ... سینکاچ ...
شد ... سینکوم ...
سینکوش ... سینکای ... سینکار ...
سنددیل ... مصدر ... سینکیشمال بسکون نون وشین وکسر
بمعنی ... و صیغ آن موافق ... بسکون نون وکاف عجمی وفتح ...
سینکانک بمعنی شبیه و مانند ... و صیغ آن موافق ... اشتقاق ... مع الثنا
مصدر ... تشبیه و مانند کردن سینکانی تشبیه ... شعر کیم ... سینکی ...
اصل ... و ... اشتقاق ... سینکاماک مع الشین ... یعنی ... شبیه
شدن و صیغ آن ... اشتقاق ... من الجوامد ... آخر الفاظ ...
میکدم مین ... الشاهد علی الاول شعر مین ... سین ...

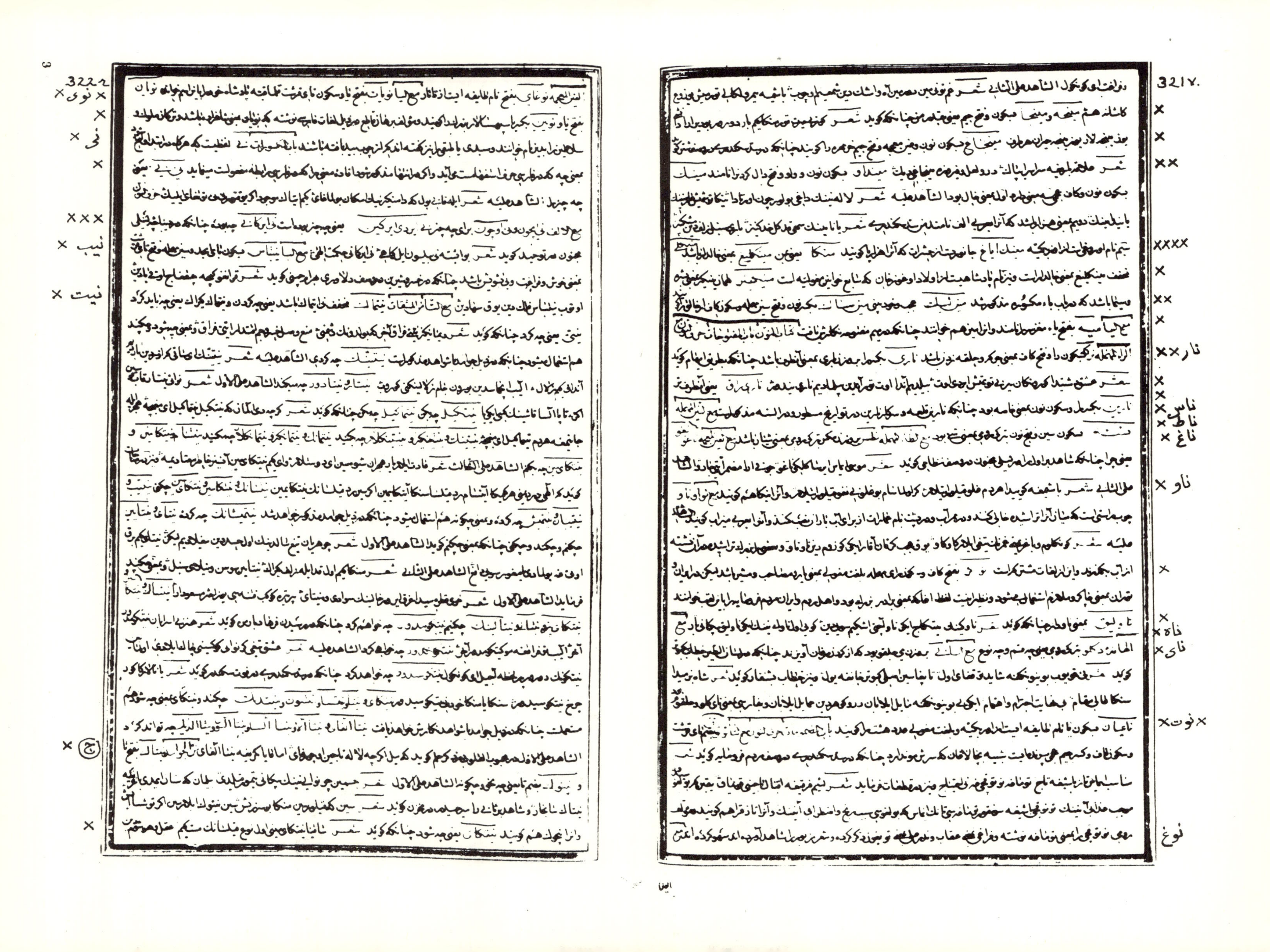

321v.

دو افتادی کونکول الشاهد علی الثانی شعر [illegible]

کاشانه هم ... بسکون و فتح جیم ... چنانچه کوید شعر [illegible]

... مینجاغ بسکون نون وغین معجمه وفتح جیم ... چنانچه ... [illegible]

شعر ... بسکون نون و واو وفتح دال کردن ... [illegible]

بسکون نون و کاف ... الشاهد علیه شعر [illegible]

[illegible]

[illegible]

نار ×× — ناس × — ناط × — ناغ × — ناو × — ناه × — نای × — نوت × — نوغ

322r.

نوی × — نی × — نیب × — نیت × — (ج)

[illegible]

نشان بلکیم اثرهم بولماسا وله شعر نوای ایلاجدی شبغره دا یلیغ تینکای که بیسا بر کچه باشیغه ماه شبکردیم نیتی
به معنی آمده لولعنی چه شود چنانچه کوید شعر نیتی جیبی که آشنا الاریبن ثریه هم آنکا آشنا قیلینکیز وله شعر خیلی اخاندا بیدادی
سوزی انغاندا بیدلحوث اوزی هم نیتی ده ایکماد بولسا برزمان سیدا دوتیم یعنی چکند چنانچه در تاریخ الانبیا آمده که الیاس و الیسع
کوید ساعی الیاس چو الیسع ن والحاتی تحت ین آنکا انوار نبوت سینی که اول قاچیا پل ملاحت دین کچتی اولکینکان دیک بوداغی کیمه
نیتی سیم یعنی چه کرد چنانچه با شاهد مذیل مصدر نیتاالمرقوم شد نیتیب و نیتیسان بدین معنی مستعملت اول یعنی چه نحو و چکونه
الشاهد علی الاول شعر وه نیتیب مشلطه فی آلیدا که کاپین که یاد عکسی ین غیرت قیلورمین ایلکیدا کوزکو کوروب الشاهد
علی الثانی شعر جمال حسن نی نوای نیتیسان تا شورفای ایلکه زیاچ چوق ابروکا وزی قیلغای انغماض دوتیم یعنی چه کرده چنانچه
مذیل نیتماک مرتب یافت مع الجیم من المشتقات نیتوکان شمات یعنی چه نحو کردن نیتو کلا شتی چه نحو کرد نیتوکلاشتوت چه نحو کنیم نیتوکرکیم
نیتوکلا ناد ور چه نحو میکند نیتوکلا شکیل چه نحو بکن نیتوکلا شماکیل چه نحو بکن نیتوکلا شسام نیتوکلا شکامین و نیتوکلا شماکان نیتوکچه نحو کنم
نیتوکلا شسا ملنع نیتوکلا شکامین و نیتوکلا نیچه نیتوکی الشاهد علی الثالث شعر ای نوای عشق صحراسیدا لخود قویدونک قدم تا نیتوکلا شکا
سین اول با نالینی یوق وادی پله نیتوکلا شیب نیتوکلا شماو نیتوکلا شمش چه نحو کرده نیتوکلا شماتا چه نحو کرده نیتوکلا شاو نیتوکلا شسا
چه نحو کنم و کند و کجی دکرده نیتوکلا شسا نیتوکلا شکا پر و نیتوکلا شکای برم نیتوکلا شسا نیچه نحو کنیم نیتوکلا شومد نیچه نحو خواهم کرد نیتوکلا
چه نحو خواهی کرد نیتوکلا شوسیده چه نحو خواهد کرد نیتوکلا شکای نیتوکلا شسا و نیتوکلا شتی و نیتوکلا چه نحو کند من خوامد نیتوت
بنم جیم عجمی یعنی چکونه و چه نحو چنانچه کوید شعر آفینه بر له مذ و تاش کمزونک زهد و صفه قویا سلا ذ نیتوک قیلغای کیشی پریش
که بولغای بوقد دماغ نیچه بفتح جیم یعنی چه قدر و چند الشاهد علیه شعر فراقینک ابچینده ایچرا نیچه سیلاب فغان چیکتیم
نیم تیلمادینک هیچ و با جیم عجمی یعنی چند تا چنانچه کوید شعر ایساده جسم ایوی بر بهزن او قونکین دوا کیم نا لمادی رضات
برای کیم نچه روزن بولمادی مع الدال ینیدین یعنی از چه جهت چنانچه کوید شعر نقطه خالینک نیدین شیرین لبینک اوق
نقطه جوز آسیداده هر قاید ایکیم یا زمیسا اب مع السین المهمله نیس بکرمین یعنی چه چیز الشاهد علیه شعر نیسی اولغینک نم
دین از توق ایماس حلو ایلاجه هروی هونا مغیه خندلیسو مع الکاف نکندکه بفتح کاف عجمی و دال بهانه زده و سکون نون ثانی ترکی
دمی بجیه سود که نیکاطان بهانه و لباس نغبه طمزیند نیکا بفتح کاف عجمی یعنی جستبه و چرا الشاهد علیه شعر نیکا
کوردکوزدی سا و ونماه و سایغ خسارجیغ که ضافی مرده بیر سیرچ یک اماس بیمار دیغ مع اللام من المشتقات نیلاکا مصنف ابلحای
باشد یعنی چه کردن نیلادیم چه کردم نیلادی آلدیم چه توانستم کرد چنانچه کوید شعر مینی که هجر ابلیما عجز ایلاجی آلدیم
کیم زهب ذاه زبکا هجر ابتسا نیلاکامین نیلاد کی چه کردیم نیلاد نیلاعدوب چه میکند و نیلای یعنی چه انداز استعمال می شود
چنانچه با شاهد مذیل خواهد ملکه بر خواهد شد نیلاکیل چه بکن نیلاکیل چه بکن نیلاشام نیلاکامیم نیلاکای چه کنم
چنانچه شاهد بلی مذیل نیلاغی الدیم مذکور شد نیلابیرچ نیلادی بیرچه میکنی نیلایی اورنیغ نیلای ا دوبن چه میشود کرد
الشاهد علی الاول شعر ایساما عجین که شاکرین نیکیسا الیکا شکر قیلمای نیلایی اورهین قضانی بازغموب نیلاب
نیلاتیاو نیلاعیش چه کرده نیلاعیاتک چه کرده نیلاعیلادین چکنم و کند و کی دکرده نیلاعیساک نیلاتابز و نیلاتکای بر نیلای
چکنم نیلاکو صد در چه خواهم کرد نیلاکو چه خواهی کرد الشاهد علیه شعر ای نوای تولار آخر بی جون تیمانه نیلاکولدنک
دو مر بونفس سیکوددین باری چه سب نیلاکوسی نیچه خواهد کرد نیلاکای نیلاعیلینک و کی نیلادیک چه کند الشاهد علی الثالث

کاز ایله مرداساه مین نیلاغوبن لولکیسه کیم دیرادا لعل روان دین خام مهلالامالی تا از من بحو مدنیلاد ر چه الشاهد علیه شعر
با رهی قاصد بولدی شام وکیلما دی لب ندین جواب تا نخنه صبر نیلای اونکای دیدنی خواب غه ونیز یعنی چه میکند چنانچه کذشت مع المیم
نیمه بفتح میم و بنمره بفتح میم و سین مهمله و سکون رای مهمله بمعنی چیز بود که آنرا بر چیزی کویند الشاهد علی الاول شعر
دنیانک آکه بولای مدین امر و نیمه کی هیچ سلماتیک که غفلت تورنیا طویدل امزنی بر نیمه سیلانک و له بر کیمه یالشیلیغ اوچون
بولمیش اولوغ نیمه ایشیم که چه عشقی دادی نیغله قویاس یعنی آتش وشاهد بر ثانی ادرشات کوید که اول سواد ظلمتی دین آب حیات
نلانلی کیما سا ابردی و لی اوت فه خبر بره تیکین برکای نیم لفظ نیم باشد که بمیم ضمیر متکلم وجه اضافه شده یعنی چیز من چنانچه
کوید شعر دیمایکم عشقین نهان تو تصیل حیی عریانغه کیم تنغوز خمین یوق نیم با فلاحه یا شورباغه هکم مع النون نینانت بفتح
نون ثانی و سکون کاف موحد حیثیم داکوید چنانچه کوید شعر تیکان نشانی موکلا یک کهند اده داخوذ بیتشکلاج اغا
کوزنعم تالدی یا بیتیب بیناکیم ولترا سپا لقمه خوانند و هر دو لغت بفتح اول نیز مستعملت نینلک بسکون نون ثانی و کاف عجمی
داکه مرفار بیچ رابطه مفعولت استعمال میشود چنانچه کوید عشقیم آرتار خطی ظاهر بولغای خانانه نینک شمع دودی شعله سین
افزون قیلور پروانه نینک نیغی یعنی چه چیز الشاهد علیه شعر ای نوائی شام غم دین آیرد بو تقوی صبح وصل آتی ابریکن
قاده مرنی نیزنک ایتسا لمرات نی نیمه یعنی چه چیز چنانچه در مهتیم ترمحبوب القلوب کوید که جاهل لیغیدین سیطا منانیغ اوقیه
نیمه با راول که اوزین بیکانکای مع الواو نیو چو بتحکون واو مخفف ناوچون نباشد یعنی چرا و برای چه چیز چنانچه کوید شعر
پیرهیکا با شاهر بن پیوسته نیوچون قویدیلار غشه انکیزی کینه و البکی ماش لرکتاب الواو با مفتوحا مع الخا بعضی
لغیت که هم مرهکا تاسف و حسرت و هم صمقلم انظاش طیبت کفته می شود الشاهد علیه شعر جا لظالم ایچون لولدعنات آی
قلره جو پایچی غار صنو خط اولیا الدینلعاییکین واخ و بطرتوقزاوجه نیز مستعملت چنانچه کویند واخ واخ مع الرا امر ساتیح ترکمانی
بجنوع تعنیویت که بخوانند مع الها واه بمعنی واخ باشد که مذکور شد چنانچه در نعت کوید شعر سنینک عشقینک
ایکی عالم اراسی دوربر جیب قضه فاشقلیغ انکا کرچه مدا ابر غاسی وه قا ابر هم مستور واخ بطریق زاوجه استعمال میشود چنانچه کوید
وه وه با بر غمنو تام خرمها و جلا لغرطلیت که تنها نی مستقل معنی نیست نهایت مراخوا الغلی عکوام میشود افاده معنی ملت میکند مثل
فراوان معنی نکهبان و نیا ولا معنی ازینه مع الواو د و وه بعمر زن کوی نوعه برجی باشد که سلن و شغال طمثال آن کند چنانچه
شیرین دیوان طلسم مرمین کوید شعر شغالی با ریتپان اضغان اندوه حیک یکرکان کیشی نینک خالیغه دوه مع الرا ویر معنی
شعر ویرانه دا صحت اولسا اندوه جغد ایلا ایکان باشینک اوزه دوه با کوزبیمی اوا و میرحر مهمله ویرسی بفتح و کسر
مهمله بمعنی که دو معنایست مع شیر سلف و سلم باشد مع الشین المعجمه و شنه بسکون شین و فتح نون هاخلرده بترکی دوه با اکو بالبود
کتاب الها با باب المفتوحا من الها مع الباء هاوی کمیدای بجی برکرو بمعنی جله هیچ بود مع الرا من المشتقات هارنا و بسکون را
بمعنی خسته و مانده شدن چنانچه کوید شعر بیکسه قونک خالبلیش تیلبه لاله دبلک ای ری بوتمور هر یون که سخا ایلنک پر له
سن لاب هلیقاتیم هارونیک خسته شدی چنانچه شاهد آن در ذیل هویدین مذکور خواهد شد هاردوق خسته شدیم
هارا هارا نچسته میشود الشاهد علی الثانی شعر کیماد یکی عشق بحرا بینکیل لدانکه بو یولدا امر لولیعو کوی تا شلاکماسا هارما
معنیش معلم بمعنی اجل و مقدار هم می آید چنانچه در صحبه نیسان معرا ستان هفتم بمعنی مصادر کوید شعر کامالا دیو زماناه
باودشو خوابه بر چشمه باشیدا تو شتی ما رزار و هالدی هان و هار دوران خسته شوند خسته شدن چنانچه در صحبه نیسان در سبع

323v.

[illegible]

هارمق [illegible] خسته شدن هارتماق [illegible] خسته شدن هارتانك [illegible] هارغاسین [illegible] خسته شوی [illegible]

هاریاتق [illegible] خسته شده چنانکه [illegible] خسرو شیرین [illegible] کوید الشاهد على الاول شعر [illegible]

[illegible]

هارالمنك خسته شوید هارغالی برای خسته شدن هارغاچ چون خسته شد و شود و مجهول شدن هارغوچی خسته شونده

هارغوچه و هارغوچه هارغاغنه تا خسته شده و بقدر آن هارغوم خسته بخواهم شد هارغونك خسته خواهید شد هارغوچی

خسته خواهد شد [illegible] خسته شود [illegible]

[illegible]

324r

[illegible]

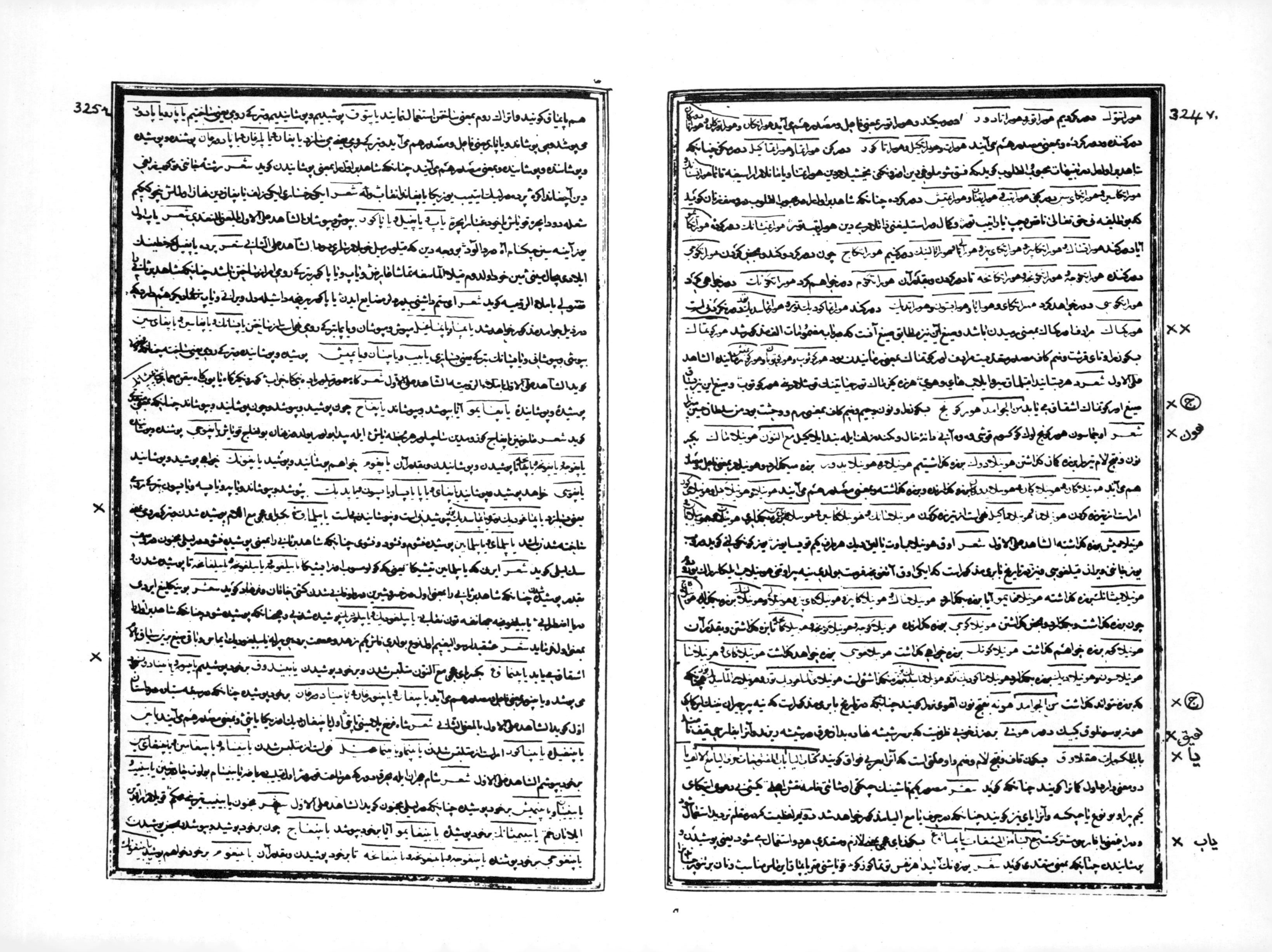

هورلتول دم کردیم هورلتو و هورلتادور ادم میکند و هورلتور بمعنی فاعل و مصدر هم می آید هورلتکان و هورلتوکلی و هورلتا [illegible]
دم کننده و دم کرده و بمعنی مصدر هم می آیند هورلت و هورلتکیل و هورلتا کور دم کن هورلتماق و هورلتا کیل دم کن چنانچه
شاه عبد اللطیف در تنبیهات محبوب القلوب گوید که فوق شوملو فیدین اوزونکی [illegible] هورلتا و یا نالا [illegible] تا هورلتا [illegible]
هورلتکاسی و هورلتکای سر دم کن هورلتیب و هورلتماق و هورلتیش دم کرده چنانچه شاه عبد اللطیف در محبوب القلوب در وصف زنان گوید
[illegible] حق تعالی [illegible] استیلیغنی [illegible] دین هورلتیب [illegible] هورلتیشانک دم کرده هورلتکا
آیا دم کند هورلتسانک و هورلتکایز و هورلتکای بیز و هورلتماسو هورلتالیلیک دم کنیم هورلتکاج چون دم کرد و کند و بمعنی کردن هورلتکوچی
دم کننده هورلتوچه و هورلتکوچه و هورلتکاغه تا دم کردن و بمقدار آن هورلتکوم دم خواهم کرد هورلتکونک دم خواهی کرد
هورلتکوسی دم خواهد کرد هورلتکای و هورلتا و هورلتتون و هورلتدیلیک دم کند هورلتماکو دیلیک تورو هورلتماس بلیک دم نکردنی لیک
هورکمالک مرادف هورکمالک بمعنی رمیدن باشد و صیغ آن نیز مطابق صیغ آنست که مذکور شد با مضمومات الفصل [illegible] هورکوتمالک xx
بکون لام و تای قرشت و ضم کاف مصدر متعدی است مرادف هورکوتمالک بمعنی رمانیدن بود هورکوتوب و هورکوتوب رمانیده الشاهد
علی الاول شعر [illegible] هر کوتوب [illegible] هورکوتوب و صیغ این نیز [illegible]
صیغ امر کوتمالک اشتقاق می یابد من الجامد هورکوچ بکون لام و نون و جیم و ضم کاف بمعنی مرم و وحشت بود من سلطان حسین میرزا × (ج)
شعر اوچماسون هورکونج لوق کوکسوم قوشی [illegible] مانند خال و کند [illegible] ایله بند [illegible] مع النون هونیلامالک بکسر × هون
نون و فتح لام و تای تا بمعنی کاشتن هونیلادوک بمعنی کاشتیم هونیلادو هونیلادی [illegible] بمعنی میکاشت و هونیلادی [illegible]
هم می آید هونیلاکان و هونیلادور [illegible] بمعنی کاشته و بمعنی مصدر هم می آید هونیلاتو هونیلادی
[illegible] کردن هونیلاغیل [illegible] هونیلاکاش [illegible] هونیلاکاسیز [illegible] هونیلاغی [illegible]
هونیلامیش بمعنی کاشته الشاهد علی الاول شعر اوق هونیلادی بوت [illegible] قویسا [illegible] کوز [illegible] کویل [illegible]
[illegible] تاریخ نا بری مذکور است که ایکی اوق آتمق بمعنی فرصت بولدی سیه پر اوتی هونیلادی [illegible]
هونیلایشانک بمعنی کاشته هونیلاغا [illegible] آیا بمعنی بکارد هونیلاسانک و هونیلاکایز و هونیلاکای [illegible] هونیلاماسون بمعنی بکارید [illegible]
چون بمعنی کاشت و بکارد و بمعنی کاشتن هونیلاکوچی بمعنی کارنده هونیلاکوچه و هونیلاغوچه [illegible] تا بمعنی کاشتن و بمقدار آن
هونیلاکوم بمعنی خواهم کاشت هونیلاکونک بمعنی خواهی کاشت هونیلاکوسی بمعنی خواهد کاشت هونیلاکای و هونیلاسا
هونیلاسون و هونیلادیلیک بمعنی بکارد و هونیلاماکو دیلیک [illegible] هونیلامای [illegible] هونیلاماسلیک [illegible] چنانچه
که بمعنی نتواند کاشت من الجامد هونه بفتح نون آهوی نر گویند چنانچه در تاریخ بابری مذکور است که [illegible] × (ج)
هونه بوسونلوق کییک دو هونه بمعنی نخوبی ظرفیت که بمعنی [illegible] بدان [illegible] تا [illegible] × هیق
باب الکلمات هقلاوق بکون قاف و فتح لام و ضم واو ملول است که آنرا بعربی فواق گویند کتاب الیا باب المفتوحات حروف الیا مع الالف × یا
دو معنی دارد اول کاف گویند چنانچه گوید شعر مصحف کیم [illegible] حق [illegible] ثانی [illegible] کینی [illegible] تکای
[illegible] نوع یاجیکه و آنرا یای [illegible] گویند چنانچه در حرف یا مع الیا [illegible] خواهد شد [illegible] لفظ [illegible] استعمال
و در [illegible] کتب مع النون المفتوحات یاپماق بکون یای حطی [illegible] لازم و متعدی هر دو استعمال می شود یعنی پوشیدن × یاب
پوشانیدن چنانچه بمعنی متعدی گوید شعر [illegible] توتماکو [illegible] یاپا [illegible] مناسب دنان [illegible]

هم یاپماق گویند و اتراک روم بمعنی ساختن استعمال نمایند یاپتوق پوشیدیم و پوشانیدیم و ترکی رومی بمعنی ساختیم یاپا یا یاپادور
می پوشید می پوشاند و یاپار بمعنی فاعل و مصدر هم می آید و ترکی رومی بمعنی می سازد یا یاپغان یا یاپغان یا یاپدوران پوشنده و پوشیده
و پوشاننده و پوشانیده و بمعنی مصدر هم می آیند چنانچه شاه عبد اللطیف بمعنی پوشانیدن گوید شعر [illegible]
دین [illegible] بریتیب [illegible] یاپغانی نقاب [illegible] شعر ایکی [illegible] زلف یاپغان [illegible]
[illegible] یاپیپ یاپیپ یا یاکور [illegible] الشاهد علی الاول بالمعنی المتعدی شعر یاپیپ
[illegible] آینه [illegible] الشاهد علی الثانی شعر [illegible] یاپیپ [illegible]
[illegible] یا پوریا [illegible] ساختن باشد چنانچه شاه عبد [illegible]
[illegible] الرومیه گوید شعر ای [illegible] یا [illegible]
در ذیل جوامد مذکور خواهد شد یاپما و یاپمایغیل بپوش و بپوشان و یا پما ترکی رومی [illegible] ساختن یاپسانک [illegible] یاپغای [illegible]
بپوشی و بپوشانی و یا پسانک ترکی بمعنی بسازی یاپیب و یاپسان و یاپمیش پوشیده و پوشانیده و ترکی رومی بمعنی [illegible]
گوید الشاهد علی الاول [illegible] الرومیه الشاهد علی الاول شعر [illegible] ساختن [illegible]
پوشید و پوشانید یاپغای بمو آیا بپوشد و بپوشاند یاپغاج چون بپوشید و بپوشد و چون بپوشانید و بپوشاند چنانچه بمعنی [illegible]
گوید شعر [illegible] یاپغوچی پوشنده و پوشاننده
یاپغوچه یاپغوچه و یاپغالی تا پوشیدن و پوشانیدن و بمقدار آن یاپغوم خواهم پوشانید و پوشید یاپغونک خواهی پوشید و پوشانید
یاپغوسی خواهد پوشید و پوشانید یاپمای و یاپا و یاپسا و یاپسون و یاپدیلیک بپوشد و بپوشاند و یاپمیه و یاپسون [illegible]
بمعنی [illegible] یاپماغوسیلیک [illegible] یاپماسلیک [illegible] پوشیده نهانست یاپیلماق بکسر بای حطی مع الکاف [illegible] پوشیده شدن [illegible] ×
ساخته شدن [illegible] یاپیلمای یاپیلمایین پوشیده شوم و شود و شوی چنانچه شاه عبد [illegible] بمعنی پوشیده شوم [illegible] مجنون [illegible]
[illegible] گوید شعر [illegible] یاپیلمایین [illegible] یاپیلغوچی یاپیلغوچه یاپیلماغه تا پوشیده شدن
[illegible] چنانچه شاه عبد [illegible] بمعنی [illegible] شدن [illegible] گوید شعر [illegible]
[illegible] یاپیلغوچه [illegible] یاپیلغوچی [illegible] چنانچه [illegible] شاه عبد [illegible]
[illegible] شعر [illegible] ×
اشتقاق می یابد یاپینماق بکسر بای حطی مع النون [illegible] و بر خود پوشیدن یاپیندوق [illegible] یاپینورمن [illegible]
می پوشد و یاپینور بمعنی فاعل و مصدر هم می آید یاپینغان [illegible] یاپینادورغان [illegible] پوشیده چنانچه [illegible]
اول گوید الشاهد علی الاول بالمعنی الثانی شعر [illegible] یاپینغان [illegible] و بمعنی مصدر هم می آیند یاپ
یاپینغیل یاپیناکور [illegible] یاپینسانک و یاپینغای [illegible]
بر خود بپوشم الشاهد علی الاول شعر [illegible] یاپینسام [illegible] یاپینیب
یاپیناو یاپینمیش بر خود پوشیده چنانچه [illegible] مجنون گوید الشاهد علی الاول شعر مجنون یاپینیب [illegible]
[illegible] یاپینمیشانک بر خود پوشید یاپینغای بمو آیا بر خود بپوشد یاپینغاج چون بر خود پوشید و بپوشد [illegible] پوشیدن
یاپینغوچی بر خود پوشنده یاپینغوچه و یاپینغوچه و یاپینغالی تا بر خود پوشیدن و بمقدار آن یاپینغوم بر خود خواهم پوشید یاپینغونک

بر خود خواهد پوشید یاپنتوسی بر خود خواهد پوشید یاپنقای یاپینا کا پینسا کا پینسون کا پینک بر خود پوشد یاپیما خوبیلیک تورد

یاپنیلمدیلیک تورد بر خود نپوشید نخواست یاپوشماق بفتح بای عجمی بمعنی چسپیدن و یاپشماق بکسر بای عجمی نیز مستعملست یاپوشوق چسپیده

یاپشتوم یاپوشادور بچسپد و یاپوشمو یاپشادم معنی فاعل و مصدر هم می آید یاپوشغان و یاپوشغاریخ یاپوشادورغان چسپنده و چسپیده

الشاهد علی الاول و المعنی الثانی شعر ضعفیم [illegible] تا یاتغان دیلک تور [illegible] هر تاتان کورماننک یاپوشغان کوینیکینک

دیوار ایدا [illegible] و بمعنی مصدر هم می آیند و یاپوشغان بمعنی سرچشم هم باشد چنانکه در ذیل جواهر مذکور شود یاپوش و یاپوشیل و یاپوشاکو

یاپشو و یاپشقلیخ یاپشاکورا [illegible] چسپیدن یاپوشما و یاپوشماغیل و یاپشماغیل [illegible] چسپیدن یاپوشدیلیک یاپوشکور یاپو

یاپشینک و یاپشینکور و یاپشینکلار جمع غایب [illegible] الشاهد علی الرابع شعر [illegible] الآلای دینا

ایاغ لیک کوز [illegible] یاپشینک یاپوشسالک یاپوشغا [illegible] یاپوشغلو بچسپی یاپوشوسه یاپوشوبان و یاپوشمش چسپیده الشاهد

علی الثالث شعر [illegible] یاپوشمش یاپوشماسلیک چسپیده

یاپوشغایمو آیا بچسپد یاپوشغالی برای چسپیدن و تا چسپیده الشاهد علیه بالمعنی الاول شعر زخمیم [illegible]

[illegible] چنانکه [illegible] یاپوشغلی [illegible] یاپوشغاچ چون چسپید بچسپید و بمحض چسپیدن یاپوشغوچ چسپنده

یاپوشغوچه و یاپوشغوچه و یاپوشغانچه تا چسپیدن و بقدر چسپیدن یاپوشغوم خواهم چسپید یاپوشغولک خواهی چسپید

یاپوشغوسی خواهد چسپید یاپوشالغوسی توانم چسپید یاپوشغای و [illegible] یاپوشمالیق بچسپید یاپوشماغولیک

یاپوشلمدیلیک تورد بچسپید نخواست یاپشماق بکسر بای عجمی چسپیدن و بضم نیز مستعملست چنانکه مذکور شد یاپوشلماق بفتح

عجمی و شین [illegible] و یاپشلماق بکسر یا و شین بمعنی چسپیده شدن و صیغ آنها بر صیغ بضم یا و بکسر آن هر دو قسم اشتقاق می یابد

مصدر متعدیست بمعنی چسپانیدن و صیغ آن با لفظ [illegible] اشتقاق [illegible] یاپشتورماق بسکون شین و ضم تا [illegible]

چسپانیده شدن و بضم نیز مستعملست یاپشتورولدی چسپانیده شد الشاهد علیه شعر یا شیم [illegible] عشقدا [illegible]

[illegible] یاپشتورولدی [illegible] و باقی صیغ بر سیاق [illegible] اشتقاق می یابد [illegible] مر آنرا کویند [illegible]

[illegible] و نابود باشد و با تای عجمی ترکی لفظ زاید نیست که از برای مبالغه [illegible] بعضی الفاظ واقع می شود مثل یاپ یاشیل یعنی سبز

[illegible] و یاپ یاپی یعنی [illegible] و نیز آراسته پوشیدن [illegible] و بمعنی [illegible] اول آراسته [illegible] دوم کوینده [illegible]

آهسته [illegible] الاستعمال [illegible] یاما برمزن [illegible] که بدان [illegible]

بناد دهند و آنرا [illegible] کویند یاپاغ و یاپاق بفتح بای عجمی [illegible] که [illegible] روی چشم [illegible]

که آنرا [illegible] خوانند یاپالاق بفتح تای عجمی و لام [illegible] که [illegible]

کوینده [illegible] یاپان برمزن [illegible] که [illegible] آن [illegible]

چنانکه کوید شعر [illegible]

الابرار [illegible] حضرت سلیمان علیه السلام کوید شعر [illegible] یاپان [illegible]

بفتح یا و سکون نون و کسر [illegible] روی [illegible] یاپان [illegible]

[illegible] که آنرا [illegible] کویند [illegible] یاپانه بفتح بای [illegible]

کشیده و نون [illegible] چنانکه یاپانه [illegible] یاپار بفتح بای عجمی

سکون

سکون رای مهمله و فتح صین [illegible] اولی [illegible] کویند چنانکه [illegible] الابرار کوید الشاهد علی [illegible] نام [illegible] آی خان [illegible]

و نیز بمعنی پوشد و می پوشاند [illegible] روی [illegible] هرچه [illegible] یاپراغ و یاپراق بسکون بای عجمی

رای [illegible] کشیده و یاپرغاغ و یاپرغاق بضم بای عجمی و سکون رای مهمله و فتح [illegible] کویند چنانکه [illegible]

کوید الشاهد علی الاول و الثانی شعر [illegible] یاپراغ [illegible]

یاپراغ [illegible] و آنرا یاپراغ و یاپراق [illegible] یاپرغان [illegible] شعر یاپرغان

بانون خوانده [illegible] یاپرغان [illegible] یاپو [illegible] یاپوچی [illegible] کویند یاپوشغا

سرچشم [illegible] چسپیده [illegible] چنانکه [illegible] کذشت یاپوخ و یاپوق [illegible]

پوشیده باشد الشاهد علی الثانی شعر کرچه [illegible] یاپوق [illegible]

[illegible] یاپوق [illegible]

احمد کوید [illegible] یاپوق [illegible] تاریخ بابری [illegible]

[illegible] کوید که [illegible] یاپوق [illegible] پوشش [illegible] کویند [illegible]

چیزی پوشد عموما چنانکه [illegible] کوید الشاهد علی الاول شعر [illegible]

نوشته [illegible] یاپوچی [illegible] چنانکه در تاریخ بابری [illegible]

مذکورست که [illegible] یاپوچی [illegible] یاپچ بکسر بای عجمی [illegible] خوانند یاپچی

[illegible] کویند یاپنجی بکسر بای عجمی و سکون نون و کسر جیم اسم جنس است [illegible] از برای [illegible]

و آنرا [illegible] سیاه [illegible] کویند چنانکه سلطان [illegible]

[illegible] کویند که [illegible] و امثال آن

[illegible] یاتماق بمعنی خوابیدن باشد یاتوق خوابیدیم [illegible] الشاهد علی الاول شعر

[illegible] بمعنی فاعل و مصدر هم می آید [illegible]

خوابیده بود چنانکه [illegible] کوید شعر [illegible] یاتغان [illegible]

[illegible] خوابیده الشاهد علی الاول [illegible] الثانی شعر [illegible]

[illegible] می آیند یاتسا [illegible] یاتاکور [illegible] خوابیدن [illegible] باشد یاتماماغیل [illegible]

[illegible] خوابیدن [illegible] خوابیده [illegible] خوابید [illegible] آیا بخوابید

یاتقاچ چون خوابید و بخوابد و بمحض خوابیدن یاتقوچی خوابنده یاتقوچه [illegible] تا خوابیدن و بقدر خوابیدن [illegible]

علی الثانی بالمعنی الاول شعر [illegible] یاتقوم خواهم خوابید

یاتقولک خواهی خوابید یاتقوسی خواهد خوابید [illegible] نخوابیده است

یاتقوزماق بسکون تای [illegible] و ضم [illegible] مصدر متعدیست یعنی خوابانیدن یاتقوزدیلار خوابانیدند چنانکه [illegible]

کوید شعر یاتقوزدیلار [illegible] خوابانند و [illegible]

هم می آید [illegible] خوابانیده [illegible] یاتقوزغان [illegible] چنانکه

بیلی مجنون صوحبتیدا لیلی کویدا لشاهد علی الاول شعر چون روح ایله روح تاپتی پیوند پر بهلدا یاتقور ایکی فرزند یاتقورلیقا یاتقو
بخوابان یاتقورمانک یاتقورغایمیز یاتقورمادی بخوابانید یاتقوروبمیا یاتقوروبان و یاتقورمیش بخوابانیده یاتقورمایانک خوابانیدن یاتقورغایمو آیا
بخواباند یاتقورغاج چون بخوابانید و بخواباند و بعضی خوابانیدن یاتقورغوجه یاتقورغوچی خوابانیدن یاتقورغوسی خوابانید
وبقصد خوابانیدن یاتقورغوم خواهم خوابانید یاتقورغونک خواهی خوابانید یاتقورغوسی خواهد خوابانید یاتقورغای یاتقو
یاتقورسا یاتقورسون یاتقورمیلی بخواباند یاتقورغودیک تو هم یاتقورسا هدیک تو نیز خوابانید خواست یاتیشما ق غ بجکت مع البئین
خوابانیدن بصیغ آن موافق شق اول اشتقاق می یابد یاتلاماق بیگانه و دور کردن یاتلادوق بیگانه کردیم یاتلادی
بیگند و یاتلامق بمعنی فاعل و مصدر هم می آید یاتلاغان یاتلادیغان بیگانه کشتن و بیگانه کرده و بمعنی مصدر هم می آید یاتلادی
بیگانه کن چنانکه در بهین منظوم فرماید الشاهد علی الاول شعر اول کیم ... کونکلونکا ... یاتلاغ چونکه
مومن ... یاتلاغ یاتلاماق ... بیگانه کردن یاتلاغان یاتلاشماق
بیگانه کی ... یاتلاغان یاتلامیش بیگانه کرده یاتلاغایمو آیا بیگانه کند ... بمعنی بیگانه
واجنبی بود الشاهد علیه شعر ... وطن ...
ونیز استراحت از خواب کردن یاتاغ و یاتاق خوابگاه را گویند چنانکه در احوال مجنون ... لیلی گوید شعر ...
... یاتقدین یا ایله کوک ... یاتقدین ... الرغینه شعر ...
یاتوق منزل ویرانه ... هم استعمال میشود ...
برهان قاطع ... یاتاغان بفتح تا و ... وسکون نون ...
که بر کمر بندند ونیز بمعنی ... یاتی ... بسکون تا و کسر ... باشد
ساخته ... یاتیلیغ ... چنانکه ... گوید شعر ...
با ... الشاهد ... گوید شعر ...
... یاتوغان ...
گویند چنانکه در ... نامه فرماید شعر ... یاتوغان ...
خطاب بمطرب گوید شعر ... یاتوغانچی نوازنده
ساز چنانکه در ساقی نامه گوید شعر یاتوغانچی ... یاتوق ...
که از ... الشاهد علیه شعر ...
ومولف ... یاتیش بجزم تا وسکون شین ...
باشد چنانکه ... گوید ... یاتیش ...
بکدلکاندین ... نیز بمعنی استحسان ... چنانکه
دوازدهم ... گوید شعر ...
این نوبت ... خوب ...
صفت ... الشاهد ... یاداناق بمعنی ...

وناتوان باشد یاداماق ناتوان شدیم یاداماق ناتوان میشود چنانکه مجنون از زبان لیلی خطاب بمجنون گوید
الشاهد علی الاول شعر عشقیم اسیدا یادامایکن ... و یاداماق بمعنی فاعل و مصدر هم می آید یاداغان و یادانغا
یادایدرغان ناتوان شونده وناتوان شده و بمعنی مصدر هم می آید یاداغان ... ناتوان شدن یاداناماق
از ناتوان شدن یادامادی ... ناتوان نشوم الشاهد علی الاول شعر ... یادادی
بیقنا ... یاداماس ... یاداغای ناتوان شوی چنانکه شاهد ... گوید
... ناتوان شد چنانکه
مجنون گوید الشاهد علی الاول شعر ... ناتوان شده یاداغایمو آیا
ناتوان شود ... یاداغاچ چون ناتوان شد ... یاداغوچی ناتوان
یاداغوجه ... یاداغوم ناتوان خواهم شد یاداغونک ناتوان خواهی شد یاداغونک ناتوا
خواهی شد ... ناتوان توانی شد یاداغوسی ناتوان خواهد شد ... یاداسا و یاداسون
یادادیک ناتوان شود ... ناتوان تواند شد ... ناتوان شدی
... ناتوان نتواند شد یاداغماق ... بمعنی ضعیف و ناتوان کردن
ناتوان کرد چنانکه ... یادمق بمعنی
باشد چنانکه گوید شعر ...
... چنانکه ...
... الشاهد علی الاول شعر ...
... الشاهد علی الثانی ... شعر ...
گویند ... شعر ... یاداغ بمعنی
باشد ... گوید شعر ...
... یارادیم ...
... الشاهد علی الاول ... شعر ...
... یارادیم ...
الشاهد ... شعر ...
... یاراغان ... یاراتماق ...
... یارینک ... یارادین ...
... یاراغایمو آیا ... یاراغاج چون ...
... یاراغوچی ... یاراغوم ...
... یاراغونک ...
... الشاهد علی الاول شعر ... یاراغودیک

دهرمین یارلغوریلیک تورما یارلناسلیک تونشکا منتواست یارلماق قخ مصدر متعدیست یعنی شکافانیدن و صیغ آن موافق شق اول
با مضافه لفظ حرف اشتقاق می‌یابد یارلماق قخ پند دادن موافق و سلنر کلماتر فتادن و شایسته شدن و یارلماق با نون ظهار بمعنی هم
مستعملست یارادوق پند شنیدیم یارار یارایدور پند میشود و یارار بمعنی شایسته هم باشد چنانکه مذکور شد و بمعنی حاصل و
مصدر هم می‌آید یارلغان یارلوغان و یارایدورغان پند شنونده و پند شنوده و بمعنی مصدر هم می‌آید یارلو یارلغاع یارای کود پند بین شود
الشاهد علی الاول شعر مینی بین ویر یا لناس کونکلوم آنینک قتلی اوچون کوز فراقیدا پر ایشیمکا یارای قرانکی یارلغانلیار ایکانلیک
پند بده شو یارلیمیع یارلدیمیع یارلایدور یارلارام پند دهیم الشاهد علی الثالث شعر مینی بیدل سنکا جان اوسانماق
برله یارایدورمین بلی مین طفلنی مبرله یارلغادایدورمین و یارارمین و یارارام بمعنی شکافم هم استعمال میشود یارلاتلیک و یارلغا
یارلغای مین پند شوی یارلایم یارلاباع یارلامیش پند شد چنانکه خسرو شیرین در صفت کوید الشاهد علی الاول شعر یولیدا الیکرین
لاره عصا اورودوریک مایرها ولتوری کالی بوعلا اودوریک یارامیشانلک پند شده یارلاماس پند نمیشود و بمعنی حاصل مصدر نیز هم
می‌آید چنانکه بمعنی ناپند و ناموافق کوید شعر آیتسام ای شیخ بونیکا قلیغ ایتینک مین دیر یارلانار قاچیپ ایتکر مهر نیدور
یارلای یارلاین پند شوم و شود و شوی چنانکه شاهد برای اول و بمعنی اول کوید شعر خدمتو ته مادیول بیش بیرله یارلایکم کیماش
نیز لیک دین اوزکا مین یوزی قرادین اوزکا ایش ولکه بر سکندری شعر بعجم کراجلار ت پهرسین یارلای کیملاوابکم هرنیشنکا
و نیز با مصدر یارلماق موافقت دارد یعنی شکافم و شکافند و شکافی یارلغایمو آیا پند شود یارلغاج چون پند شد و شود بعض
شدن یارلغوچی پند شونده یارلغوچه یارلغونچه و یارلغاغنچه تا پند شدن و بقدر آن یارلغوم پند خوام شد یارلغونک پند خواهی
شد یارلغوسی پند خواهد شد یارلغای یارلنساغا یارلسون یارلدیک پند شوی یارلغوریلیک تورتما یارلناسلیک پند ناشدنیست
یارلماق قخ بفتح را مع النون مرادف یارلماق بمعنی پند شدن یارلناشی یارلغای یانا و یارلغنلو یارلنسون یارلنیلک پند شود الشاهد علی الاول
شعر فرقنطن کراشی ایلا نوم کونکول دین جقاردیم میدیم که سنینک خاطرنکه یارلنغای سنکا آنچه اوت سالدی هرنیکیم طبع کرای
حیات اولتا آندین اوسانماق و باقی صیغ بر سیاق بانضمام نون اشتقاق می‌یابد یارلشماق قخ مع الشین معنی منافات است یعنی صلح
و سازکار شدن و بالمجاز بمعنی برازنده شدن هم استعمال میشود یارلشتی سازکار و برازنده شد چنانکه خسرو شیرین در کلمه
زال مکالمه با فرهاد کوید الاول المعنی الاول شعر صبن با نوسیلی خسرو یارلشتی خصوصیت لار اچاره من لیکتشی بالمعنی الثانی شعر خسرو
اصولومی دین کل لار اولغان کل اونده و فطن لار تکلیغ یارلشتی یارلشور و یارلشادور سازکار و برازنده میشود و بیاید بمعنی حاصل مصدر
هم می‌آید یارلشغان یارلشوچی یارلشادورغان سازکار و برازنده شونده و شده و بمعنی مصدر هم می‌آید یارلشوع یارلشمیش و یارلشاکو یارلشماق
سازکار شدن و برازنده شدن یارلشماق شماعیل فواستلار بمعنی یارلشماین و یارلشورمین یارلشادیمان سازکار و برازنده میشوم
یارلشسانکیم یارلشماین یارلشتیلر سازکار و برازنده شد الشاهد علی الاول بالمعنی الاول شعر نوا حکبه یادی بیله تان یوتتی جان تنی
قیساییل کر بو شرت انکا چیدا یارلشیب تور بالمعنی الثانی شعر ولی و تلوم جهره کا زیبنده خلعت قیا یارلشیب توره سکر خلعت قاول
یونرلعنی دین اوت توتا شیب تورما یارلشقایمو آیا سازکار و برازنده شود یارلشاج چون سازکار و برازنده شد و شود بعض شدن
یارلشغوچی سازکار و برازنده شونده یارلشغوچه یارلشغونچه و یارلشقاغنچه تا سازکار و برازنده شدن و بقدر آن یارلشغوم سازکار
و برازنده خوام شد یارلشغونک سازکار و برازنده خواهی شد یارلشغوسی سازکار و برازنده خواهد شد یارلشغای یارلشسا و یارلشسون یا
یارلشسون و یارلشدیک سازکار و برازنده شود یارلشغوریلیک تورتما یارلشماسلیک تورور سازکار نشدن نیست و برازنده نشدنیست یارومای قخ

بضم را و یارونماق قخ بضم را مع الشین بمعنی روشن شدن و جلا یافتن یاشنا الشاهد علی الاول شعر یارومای بیتار ایکانلیک
اول آریت کونکلوم بیکی ای نوائی کوزوما یوممایکیشی کیم کونکلی آریب یارودی یاروتی روشن شد چنانکه در لیلی مجنون در مکالمه
مجنون با لیلی کوید الشاهد علی الثالث شعر کیم اوتلاریدین جهانی یاروتی خرمن لاریکا یو شعله توشتی یارودوق یاروشوق
روشن شدیم یارودی یارودور روشن شود و یاروشادور روشن میتواند شد الشاهد علی الاول شعر شه صدقا اهل دین شعل است
یارودی مهرنیلیکیم صبح انفاسی چلوطلعت آنکا و یارور و یاروشور بمعنی حاصل مصدر هم می‌آید یاروغان و یاروغان و یارویدورغان و
یاروتغان یاروتوغان و یاروشادورغان روشن شونده و روشن شده الشاهد علی الاول بالمعنی الثانی شعر ساچینکا زرفشان چهره لیک
ضلالت شامیدا هریان تجلی شعله دین یاروغان شمع هدایت تور و بمعنی مصدر هم می‌آید یارودوع یاروغاع یاروکو و یاروت
یاروشغیل و یاروتشا کور روشن شود چنانکه در لیلی مجنون از زبان مجنون خطاب آتش کوی لیلی کوید الشاهد علی الاول شعر آی
کوزومنکا ایکی مقل اولسون میمنت باری هجر و صندل اولسون دایم بو طریق و شیوه نی توتقم یارودوم جهانی یاروت و یارولماز
شکافتن هم باشد چنانکه با شاهد هم ذیل یاردماق هم قوم شد یارودماو یارومایالیک یارومایلاغ روشن شوی یارونانک یاروفغا
یارونغای مین و یارومشانک و یاروشغای مین روشن شوی یاروتیه یاروغان و یاروتمیش و یاروتوبه یاروتقای و یاروتمیش تکن
شد چنانکه در مجنون مطبوع کوید الشاهد علی الاول فی النعت شعر فا یتینکا تنمیب تیمنش ایکی فرقی ظا رضینک یاروب یاروب یلی کیم
وله شعر سبز خط دین یاروب نظارضینک مرآت ده کیم کوکا بو نوع کیم یوپیش حالا خر نکار ایلیه یاروتمیشانک یاروتیمانک روشن شدن
یاروتغایمو یاروشغایمو آیا روشن شود یاروفلیج و یاروشماج چون روشن شد و شود چنانکه در داستان جهانی از بسفه سیاه کوید الشاهد
علی الاول شعر یاروفاج تانک سپهر خاموریک تاچی تون هندوی جرلا دیک یاروغوچی روشن شونده یاروغوچه یاروغونچه و یاروغاغنچه
یاروشغوچه یاروشغونچه یاروشغاغنچه تا روشن شدن و بقدر آن یاروغوم یاروشغوم روشن خوام شد یاروغونک یاروشغونک روشن خواهی شد
یاروغوسی یاروشغوسی روشن خواهد شد یاروغای یاروشغای یاروسون و یاروسون یارودیک یاروشسا یاروندیک روشن شود الشاهد
علی الاول شعر بتون شامینک فیض بیهچین دیبانیکیم یاروغای توتقیل ابرل تکلیغ که تونغای کوشه بحراب جمع یاروغوریلیک تورما یارونا
روشن نشدنیست یاروتماق قخ و یاروتشورماق قخ بضم الصدر متعدیست بمعنی روشن کردن یاروتود و یاروتادور و یاروتوروب یاروشتور
روشن میکند الشاهد علی الاول شعر بعزی کونزنی یاروتولیک توباش خنجر مقلوی سلهای اولکیم کوزی بالیکم کونکا یوق خبست آنکا
یاروتماق روتعامل یاروتولیم یاروشتورکی روشن کن چنانکه شاهد او معنی لا مصدر یارومای مذکور شد و باقی صیغ بر سیاق موافق شق اول
اشتقاق می‌یابد یاراتیلماق قخ بفتح را و کسر تای فوقانیه و سکون لام بمعنی آفریده شدن یاراتیلدی آفریده شد یاراتیلور و یاراتیلادور
آفریده میشود و یاراتیلیش بمعنی حاصل مصدر هم می‌آید یاراتیلغان یاراتیلوغان و یاراتیلادورغان آفریده شونده و آفریده شده چنانکه
شاهد با لطف بمعنی ثانی در توحید کوید شعر نی کرظلوقا لیکا یاراتیلغان سن یاراتغان آلا یاراتیلغان بمعنی مصدر هم می‌آید
یاراتیلوع یاراتیلغاع یاراتیلاقو یاراتیلماق آفریده شدن یاراتیلغای یاراتیلسا و یاراتیلسون یاراتیلدیک آفریده شود
یاراتیلغایمو آیا آفریده شود یاراتیلغاج چون آفریده شد و شود و بعض شدن یاراتیلغوچی آفریده شونده یاراتیلغوچه یاراتیلغونچه
و یاراتیلغاغنچه تا آفریده شدن و بقدر آن یاراتیلغوم آفریده خواهم شد یاراتیلغونک آفریده خواهی شد یاراتیلغوسی آفریده خواهد شد
یاراتیلغای یاراتیلسا و یاراتیلسون آفریده شود یاراتیلغوریلیک تورما یاراتیلماسلیک آفرین نشدنیست یاراتماق قخ آفریدن چنانکه شاهد اول

بمعنی حاصل بمصدر اطباق مذکور شد وباقی صیغ بر سیاق موافق اول اشتقاق می‌باید یارغلامیشی تغ آماده و موبلق کردن

یارغلامق آماده کردیم یارغلاق ونا یارغلادی آماده میکند یارغلامق بمعنی فاعل مصدر هم می‌آید یارغلامق یارغلامه

آماده کنند وآماده کننده بمعنی مصدر هم می‌آید یارغلامق یارغلامق یارغلامق آماده کردن یارغلامق یارغلامق

از آماده کردن یارغلامق یارغلامق یارغلامق آماده کن یارغلامق یارغلامق آماده کرده یارغلامق

کرده یارغلامغایو آیا آماده کرد یارغلامغاج چون آماده کرده کند یارغلامق آماده کننده یارغلامق

یارغلامغانچه تا آماده کردن وبمعنی آن یارغلامغوم آماده خواهم کرد یارغلامغونک آماده خواهی کرد یارغلامغوسی آماده

خواهد کرد یارغلامغای لا ریغا یارغلامسا لا ریغا یارغلامق آماده کنند چنانکه مرقوله مجنون کوید الشاهد علی

الثالث شعر ... کوکلک ...

یارغلامق ... آماده کردن ... مع الکاف ...

اشتقاق می‌باید یارغلامشما تغ ... یارلیغامق تغ ...

وتع ... یارلیغامق ... بمعنی فاعل ومصدر هم

یارلیغامق ... یارلیغاماق ... آمرزیدن ... بمعنی مصدر هم می‌آید یارلیغامق ... چنانکه

اول ... کوید ...

یارلیغا ... یارلیغامق ... چنانکه ... کوید الشاهد علی

الاول شعر ... یارلیغاماق ... آمرزیدن چنانکه

امام ... لسان الطیر کوید شعر ... آمرزیدن

یارلیغاماس ... بمعنی فاعل ومصدر هم می‌آید ... آیا ... چون آمرزید ...

یارلیغاغوسی آمرزیدن ... تا آمرزید ... یارلیغاغوم ... آمرزید ...

یارلیغاغوسی خواهد آمرزید ...

مع النون ... مع السین المهمله ... یارماق ... بالازمین ...

یارمامق ... یارماق ... بمعنی فاعل ... هم می‌آید ... یارمامق ...

یارماشمان ... بالازمین ... بمعنی مصدر هم می‌آید ... بالازمین

یارماماق ... بالازمین ... یارماشماق ...

بالاربعه ... یارماشمش ... چنانکه ...

... هندوستان کوید شعر ... آنکه ...

... الشاهد علی الرابع شعر ...

اولمنغ ... یارماشماق ...

جون ... یارماشموق ...

... یارماشموق ...

یارماشمای ... یارماشقای ... الاربعه ... یارماشمای ... یارماشمیان ...

... اسبطلیمق ... یارشیمای ... اسبطلیمق ... دور اسبطلیمق ...

فاعل ومصدر هم می‌آید ... یارشیمق ... اسبطلیمق ... وبمعنی مصدر هم می‌آید ...

مفرد ... یارشیماق ... مفرد ... یارشیمق ...

اسبطلیمق الشاهد علی الاول شعر ... یارشیب ...

اسبطلیمق ... اسبغلیمق ... بمعنی فاعل ومصدر هم می‌آید ... آیا اسبطلیمق ... چون اسبطلیمق ...

وبمعنی ... یارشیقوسی اسبطلیمق ... تا اسبطلیمق وبمعنی آن یارشیقوم اسبطلیمق یارشیقونک

اسبطلیمق یارشیقوسی اسبطلیمق ... اسب ... یارشیقوسی ...

اسب ... بعضی ... چنانکه ... شعر ای ...

... یارماق ...

... یاراشیق ...

... الشاهد علی الاول شعر ...

... شعر ...

... بمعنی ... یاراغ ... یاراقی ...

... الشاهد علی الاول شعر ...

... چنانکه ... کوید الشاهد علی ... شعر

... یاراغ ...

یاراقسز ... یارلیغ ... کوید شعر ...

... شعر ...

... کوید شعر ...

... یارلیغ ... کرد ...

... یارلیغ ... آنرا ... خوانند ... یارلیغ ...

... الشاهد علی الاول شعر ...

... یارلیغ ...

... لسان الطیر کوید شعر ...

... کوید شعر ...

... الشاهد علیه شعر ...

... شعر ...

البدها یارغو یارغوچ بمعنی کلمنده باشد و همین نسبت میوه را نیز خوانند یارغوماق آسیاب بود که آنرا بدست گردانند لاشاهد علیه
هضم اشیا میکردن هم اینکه مزن اشیای ناشکسته را و چون قیلدی چرخ اخضرینا ملای دوکونی یارغوجاق یارقانات نام شپرک بود که آنرا مرغ
خفاش گویند و آن مخفف یارغاغ قانات باشد بمعنی بال پوست یارپاغی قصیر مقل را خوانند یارپیغ دو معنی دارد اول رقم و فرمان پادشاه
ترک را خوانند و بمعنی طغرای رقم هم مستعمل است چنانچه گوید مصرع یوزیغه کلمه ساری نینک طرحی کوره طغرا دیک یوزیدیلی کیل الالیغ
امزم آل تمغا دهر و نیز کشوری شاعر در مجموعة الغرائب نیز گوید مصرع روانی بخشدا دیرا که دیر شه خانی جمودی بر سلطانا
کشد یارلیغ الجانبی دویم بمعنی یاری باشد چنانچه گوید مصرع کهی ایلیب بیضا الم کهی بو دم کور کوزیبا ریلیغا بیر
دیوان خود بمعنی اول و ثانی بطریق تجنیس گوید که اولا آستان سلطان قول لاجی نینک بو قول بیله یارلیغ قیلسا اول دم سلطان صاحبقران
صاحبقرانی دین یارلیغ نشانی بیتیلگای یارلیغا بسکون را و کسر لام و فتح غین معجمه با الف کشیده بمعنی آمرزش و رحمت بود یارلیغان مع النون
شکستهای کنار ... را گویند یارماق بضم میم و صحیح ... چنانچه گوید مصرع باغ ایرا سنکا ساچی کل آلتون قیزیل یاراق شه
باشیغه آلتا قیلیم ایل آلتون قیزیل یاراق و بمعنی شکافتن هم باشد چنانچه در ذیل اشتقاقات گذشت یارمه بسکون را و فتح میم طعامی که در آسیا
نیم شکسته در غوی نرم شود و آنرا بعربی جریش گویند یارجه بفتح میم و جیم ترکی ردیف همه ... بود یاروغ و یاروق بضم راء
آمده اول بمعنی روشن و نورانی بود لاشاهد علیه مصرع چاپتی اوتی قیلدی الماس تیغ تونیغه یاروق سحاب سیکل الکاس نوکلاجین مسالق
دویم شکاف را گویند چنانچه جوهری گوید مصرع بو یاریغلوق قاسیدا ولدی ایلیه ... تابان که دشت ... یاروق
یاروق و بطریق ایهام گوید بمعنی مصرع چالدی کونکلوم ... کونکلی ... تاپتی شکست ده بو توتون ... یاروق شه سند ...
یارقلیغ ... چنانچه شاهد آن در ذیل یاروق مذکور شد یارماق بضم را و ... و فتح میم و سکون ...
چنانچه گوید مصرع ... توکیب اشک ... یارماغیم ... چندان تاپتیم یاره ... بضم ...
و ... لاشاهد علیه مصرع کوکونی ... قیلدی ... لبینک ... مرلین ... تیز ... آنرا یا
هم خوانند و بمعنی چهار معنی دارد اول ... دویم ... از ادویه ... که ... بود
... سیم بمعنی توانایی بود چهارم بمعنی ... باشد یاره تا ... سنکت شبیه ... که از ... و آنرا
... و ... گویند ... و ... چنانچه ...
... یاری بمعنی اول بمعنی نصف ... و آنرا یاریم هم خوانند دویم ... باشد و نیز ...
... گویند یارش بمعنی ... چنانچه ... گوید مصرع ... کونکلی ...
آلتیدا ... یاریم بمعنی نصف بود یارموق بسکون میم بمعنی ... چنانچه شاهد ... گوید
مصرع یارموق ... یاریق بمعنی ... باشد چنانچه ...
گوید مصرع ... یا بیلدی ...
یاریتیق بمعنی ... یارلیغ ... چنانچه گوید مصرع ... کونکلی ...
دلکش ... یاردیم ... و شروع کردن ... یاردیم نوشتم و خطا کردم
و کشودم و شروع کردم چنانچه بمعنی ثانی ... گوید مصرع ... یاردیم ... آچیغ ...
... یاریلاتدیم یارماتو

و خطا نکرد و نکشود و قطع نکرد و شروع نکرد چنانچه بطریق تجنیس گوید بالمعنی الثانی شعر ... یاناغی ... بالمعنی الرابع ...
... یازدی ... بالمعنی الاول ... یازاریغا یازادور ... خطا
میکند و میکشاید و شروع میکند الشاهد علی الاول والمعنی الاول شعر یازار ... جهاراطلم ... آینیک ...
... و بمعنی ثانی ... یاریغ یاری مذکور است که ... و یاریلیغ ... و یازی ...
هم می آید یازغان و یازار یازغان نوشته و خطا کرده و کشاینده و کشوده و شروع کننده و شروع کرده
شاهد اول ... نوشته و کشوده بطریق ایهام گوید شعر ... یازماق ... یازغان
... یازغیل ... یازماغ ...
یازغای ... بنویسد و خطا کند و بکشاید و شروع کند چنانچه شاعر بطریق تجنیس گوید الشاهد علی الرابع شعر ...
... بالمعنی الرابع ... یازسین ... بالمعنی الاول ... یازیب
یازیب و یازیپ ... نوشته و خطا کرده و کشوده و شروع کرده چنانچه شاهد ... بمعنی اول گوید شعر ...
... یازیشتی ...
... شاهد ...
... نوشته و خطا کرده و کشوده و شروع کرده ... صیغه ...
... یازایین ... بنویسم و خطا کنم و بکشایم و شروع کنم چنانچه شاهد ... گوید مصرع ...
... یازغوچی ... یازغوچ ...
و خطا کننده و کشاینده و شروع کننده چنانچه ... گوید ... مصرع ...
... یازغوچه ... یازغانچه ... نوشتن و خطا کردن و کشودن و شروع کردن و ...
یازغوم ... خواهم نوشت و خطا خواهم کرد و خواهم کشود و شروع خواهم کرد یازغول صیغه ... یازغوی صیغه ...
یازغای یازاقای ... بنویسد و خطا کند و بکشاید و شروع کند الشاهد علی الاول والمعنی الثالث مصرع حیات ...
... شاهد ... خسرو شیرین ... کشودن ...
... یازیلماق ...
کشاده ... یازیلماق ... شد اول نوشته شدن ...
شدن ... کشوده شدن ... شروع شدن یازیلادی نوشته شد و خطا شد و کشوده شد و شروع شد چنانچه بمعنی ثالث گوید
شعر ... یازیلماغای ... نوشته نشود و ...
... و ... و کشوده نشود ... و شروع نشود ... چنانچه بمعنی نوشته شده و کشوده شده ...
شعر ... یازیلماید ... یازیلمیش ... و بمعنی کشوده شده گوید شعر
... یازیلغان ... یازیلغان ... نوشته شونده و نوشته
و خطا شونده و کشوده شونده و شروع شونده چنانچه شاهد اول ... نوشته شده گوید ...
... یازیلغان ... آیت رحمت بوده ... یازیلغوچی ...

330v

نوشته میشوید و خطا میشوید و کشوده میشوید و شروع می شوید الشاهد علی الاول المعنی الاول شعر کونکول افغانی [illegible]
سین بیله نیتیب یاشورای بو نفع کیم بولدوزه تان یاشرایله یازلمیش یازیلغای [illegible] یازیلدیلیک نوشته
و خطا شود و کشوده شود و شروع شود الشاهد علی الاول المعنی الرابع من مترادفاته شعر بو نوع کیم [illegible]
محمود بولوب مین مشکل کم [illegible] بو [illegible] شلغر بولوب [illegible] نوشته و خطا شده
و کشوده شده و شروع شده الشاهد علی الاول المعنی الرابع شعر [illegible]
بیله یازیلغوسی [illegible] و نیز بمعنی همچنانکه نوشته شود و خطا شود و کشوده شود و شروع شود [illegible]
لازم اشتقاق می یابد یازغورماق [illegible] مقصر ساختن و [illegible] داده و [illegible]
بسبب گناه یازغوردن مقصر ساختیم یازغوردی یازغوردی مقصر ساخت [illegible] معنی حاصل مصدر هم می آید یازغورغان و
یازغورغان یازغورغوچی مقصر سازنده و ساخته و بمعنی صیغه هم می آید یازغورغوم یازغوراکور [illegible] الشاهد
علی الاول شعر [illegible] یازغوردی [illegible]
[illegible] جمع [illegible]
الشاهد علی الاول شعر [illegible] یازغوردی [illegible] یازغورغامین و
یازغورغامین مقصر ساختم الشاهد علی الاول شعر [illegible]
[illegible] مقصر ساخته یازغورماس مقصر [illegible]
و مصدر هم می آید یازغوراین یازغورای مقصر ساختم [illegible] چنانکه شاهد [illegible]
اول بری [illegible] یازغورلق یازغورغامو آیا مقصر [illegible]
چون مقصر ساخت [illegible] ساختن یازغورمک مقصر سازند یازغورغوچه یازغورغاغه تا مقصر ساختن [illegible]
یازغورغوم مقصر خواهم ساخت یازغوریک مقصر خواهی ساخت یازغورغوسی مقصر خواهد ساخت یازغورغای [illegible]
یازغورغونه یازغورمات مقصر [illegible] یازغورمادیک [illegible] مقصر ساختوت من الجوامد [illegible] شتماه [illegible]
و [illegible] الشاهد علیه شعر [illegible]
[illegible] وله شعر [illegible]
و بمعنی [illegible] نیز استعمال می شود چنانکه گوید شعر [illegible]
[illegible] وله شعر [illegible]
و نیز از [illegible] نوشتن و خطا کردن و کشودن و شروع کردن چنانکه [illegible] یازر [illegible]
و نیز نام [illegible]
[illegible]
و خطا سیکند و سیکشاید و شروع سیکند چنانکه [illegible] یازوق [illegible] الشاهد
شعر ای که [illegible] یازوق وله شعر
[illegible] یازوق [illegible]

331r

و ضمیر [illegible] یازیم [illegible] و آن کنایه از [illegible] باشد یازی دشت [illegible]
نامیده چنانکه گوید شعر [illegible] من الاشتقاق یاسانماق
آراستن و ساختن یاساد [illegible] یاساریدور [illegible] چنانکه شاهد [illegible] شعر نرکس آکور
اولسا باده [illegible] یاسادور [illegible]
علی الاول شعر [illegible] یاساغان یاساغان یاسایدورغان ساخته
و ساخته و بمعنی مصدر هم می آید یاسالوا یاساغیل یاسای کور [illegible] الشاهد علی الاول شعر [illegible]
آیینک [illegible] یاسا [illegible] یاسانماق [illegible]
یاسانک [illegible] الشاهد علی الثانی شعر [illegible]
یاسانک [illegible] خواند و یاسانک [illegible] نوشته اند چنانکه [illegible]
یاسانمانک یاسانماغ [illegible] یاساماس [illegible] ساخته الشاهد
علی الاول شعر [illegible] الشاهد علی الثانی من
حروف الابرار شعر [illegible]
مصدر هم می آید [illegible] چنانکه [illegible]
گوید الشاهد علی الاول شعر [illegible]
الشاهد علی الثانی شعر [illegible] ساختن [illegible]
چون ساخت [illegible] ساختن [illegible] خواهم ساخت
[illegible] خواهد ساخت [illegible] الشاهد علی الثانی شعر [illegible]
[illegible] یاسامق [illegible]
[illegible] چنانکه گوید شعر [illegible] یاساماق [illegible]
[illegible] چنانکه شاهد [illegible] گوید شعر [illegible]
[illegible] مع اللام و یاساماق مع النون [illegible]
شده [illegible] چنانکه شاهد [illegible] گوید [illegible]
[illegible] الشاهد علی الثالث شعر [illegible]
[illegible]
و ساخته شد الشاهد علی الثانی بالمعنی الاول شعر [illegible]
یاساغلغ [illegible] یاساناج [illegible] چنانکه [illegible] الشاهد علی الاول [illegible] یاساد
[illegible] مشغول [illegible] مشغول [illegible] یاساماق [illegible]
یاسا ماق [illegible] یاساماق [illegible] بمعنی حاصل مصدر هم می آید یاساد
[illegible] چنانکه شاهد [illegible] گوید [illegible]

دفتر ۱

یاستاغان و یاستاغول و یاستایغوغا تکیه و تکیه دهنده و تکیه داده و بمعنی مصدر هم می آیند یاستاغا یاستاغیل و یاستای کود تکیه مید[ه] شاهد

علی الثانی بیت ای نوائی عیدا بولسانك كل الیغ پرله منت ناش قوبار بولسانك سفالینکنی باشینکغه یاستاغیل یاستلماغ یاستاماغ

تکیه مده یاستانك و یاستاماسون و یاستاغای یعنی تکیه مده یعنی یاستابه و یاستابان و یاستایش تکیه داده الشاهد علی الثانی

بیت مین بیم قیلماق هوس ایتینك قولدین منکا کوسیدا بیر یاتسام الیکینی باشیمغه یاستابان الشاهد علی الثالث بیت قوتی نوائی

عزیز کوسیدا اول تاشنی کاه آنی باشیغه کاه باشین آنکا یاستلمیش یاستایشالك تکیه داده یاستاناس تکیه میدهد بمعنی حال و مصدر نیز

هم می آید یاستاغایو آلتکیه بدهد یاستاناق و یاستاغاینر و یاستاناینر و یاستاسلی و یاستانینك تکیه بدهیم یاستاغلی برای تکیه

دادن و تا تکیه داده یاستاغاج چون تکیه داده و بدهد و بعضی گفته اند یاستاغوجی تکیه دهنده یاستاغوچه و یاستاغوبجه یاستاغچه

تا تکیه دادن و بمعنی آن یاستاغوم تکیه خواهم داد یاستاغونك تکیه خواهی داد یاستاغوبی تکیه خواهد داد یاستاغای

یاستاناتا یاستاسون و یاستادیك تکیه بدهد یاستاناغودیك نیز و یاستاماسیك تو تکیه ندادی و نداست یاستاماق مع النون x

تکیه کردن و فراهی بعضی لغتکان نوشته سهو کرده یاستامادیم تکیه نکردم چنانکه گوید بیت سلطنت کوردیم خیالی مهر دین

ایی لاد چون نامیغا نیرسی نینك یکم پوچین یاستاغادیم یاستانوم یاستانادو تکیه میکند الشاهد علی الاول بیت ای خوش الحکم

باشینینك آستیدا دم طلب قیلی کیم نوائی تکیه لاد لمیغا ضیاعیکن یاستانوش یاستانوش بمعنی حال و مصدر هم می آید یاستلیب یاستا

یاستاغیش تکیه کرده الشاهد علی الاول شعر مست بولسام آستانینك بیر منکا باش قویغلی نوصلیم کیم تکیه قیلغاین تیز بیتکی

یاستاییب و تا قصیح بر نیاق با نضمام نون لشقاق می آید یاستماق بترکه ریعی کار اشکستن چنانکه در تاریخ آل عثمان در جنبك مین کوید x

که مطهر نیك امر دوبی یاسماق و مکا کاسلانینك قوتبی کاغذ یاسماق بیتنه کلدی وینز کوید که او قمی آتوب کمانی یاسدی و طلب

یامادهم نوینسد من لجواسد یاب بعضی ناس بمعنی عزا و ماتم باشد چنانکه در داستان هفتم سبعه سیاره در خال لالالام کوید شعر x ج

بو کش کیم لباسیم الی جمیز خلعت موت و یاسیم الیجمیز یاسا بفتح سین بالف کشیده و یاساق مع القاف بمعنی سیاست و نسق و ترتیب xx

سلطنتی باشد چنانکه شاهد بنا بر اسکندری در آغاز کتاب کوید بیت معانی بنا معنی جهان ملکی بیت نی جهان ملکی دین لا مکان

ملکی بیت یاساق پرله بیتکمیزایس فوج فوج که وقتون چریك نی حصین و قوفا مج بیچاره رایس معول برا لعهر کناهی بیکوع تضا می قریب

و بفرمان و الحکم فی القصاص جبوه انسان متضمن سیاست و انسان امر ملکی میباشد و مجازا بمعنی قصاص هم استعمال میشود چنانکه

حیرة الابرار کوید شعر توشی سیناهی پرچین یانچلی شاه قیاسی دین انان تاپغلی مینزه تاریخ بابر بعضی کولیت کر قالغودین کیم انواع

قسه لا انتظام هو لوب یادی قیاسغه بیتکوردی دیم کیمی کوه فرمان باشد چنانکه کوید دینا متکش بیفه فرمانکش دینز ضمان مجلد

مر او لمار تاریخ خود کوید که براق با مقتضا دعا سعد ادار مشغول شده نخت یاساقی بود که هیچ آفرید باسباب اختیار نشیند مشاهد

کوید که سکه او غول لهار حکم شده بود که باشکوه تیر بین همه باشند و نیز عدد یاساقچان و توا رد حیوتات و مولف برهان قاطع

نوشته که یاساق ترکی به ماتم را کوینده اشتباه کرده یاس بمعنی ماتم باشد و یاساق نیز بمعنی لغات ظاهرا نکرکرده بمعنی شربت منقولان شته

یاساقینی دو معنوله ماند بمعنی سپاهی باشد چنانکه در صفت ایشان از جمیع قلوب درزد که لشکریان کوید که کرد یا بلیغ و کان قر لجیریان بلوغ x

و ماجع خلیفه شرك دویم بمعنی ملحق و ملحق سیاست باشد چنانکه در تهانات کوید که اکر پادشاه یاساقلیغ دور ایشنینك الکا

بار هیچ حمایت ضه یاساقلیغ دور یا ساقی سپاهی مانند چنانکه کوید شعر سالماقاوت برلاس و نخان هاری تیکیم تیزی x

و یکان جمع پیله بر فیاق کوید عوننده له شعر ای نوائی پر فیاق و شغه آلماقین خراب کیم لونوغش بر حمان ترخان الیله بولاتی تیت

x یاسال صفحه کوینداالشاهد علیه شعر ای که مژکان دین یاسال توز دونك کونکول لا تو صید بغه کوز یوسوب آچقونی اوشبو خیلنی توقتاغای

و که من سد سکندری شعر یاسال لفی میلادی آیدالاق آراسته که بیر توزچین سری نوخواسته دار ایاسا و هم خوانند نیز آراسته ساخته شد

xx و نقار سرتا جی باشد انعام عین که در مرقع شیرت بر سر شد یاسا میشی بمعنی نظم و ترتیب و سلطنتی و ملکی باشد یاساغاق سکوتو

xx و قاف و فتح جیم شخص خود را طلا کوید که برای نظم صفوف و طرد و منع سپاه نیز در صف امرای باب دولت باشد الشاهد علیه شعر

(بالای سطر:) چنانکه در تهنهات کوید که یاساغاق تیره بر ایلاس یاسا و مع الواو هم باشد یاساول چوبدار را کوید

xx دره و غم توزیمیش یا ولی یك کونکول غا کاوله تو یاسانامنه کیلسا هوش صبر خیلی ایچکاری یاساغاق تکیه کاه یاستو قیسکوت سین

و تاء و ضم تاء قرشت متکا و بالش را نامند الشاهد علیه من صنوتی ملاحه آثر و بیته شعر اولوسیلارالغزونی آستانك واشه هر دم

xx اکرچه دمد صریاستوقدان اکر ایلك ساین و ایموق بیکوزین و ضم میم مدور را کوینده یاسوت بلغه مفول بمعنی استخوان باشد

x یایی بکسرتین بمعنی من و مریض بود و هنکام خفتن را نیز خوانند و اصل آن یاتبی بوده تا را بالمقابله ثقیل نعرغذی تکرده یاسی بیتکو

بیاش x مع الشین المعجمه من المشتقات یاشلماغ بفتح شین بالف کشیده یعنی زینت و زینت کردن یاشاد و قتی زینت کوییم یاشاریعا یاشاید و

زینت میکند و بمعنی حال و مصدر هم می آید چنانکه بمعنی زینت کنده کوید شعر کال دین فی که لوتی تینا یا رضان کرکوه

یاشاد کیرایرا الطفال چرکه سیکا شیوخ معنی عجیب نظم غلط اندلرات سیاق شعر چنیزا است که کوپ یاشار شیوخ الطفال چرکر سیکا

کیرایر یاشاغان و یاشاغان و یاشاید وغان زینت کننده و زینت کرده و بمعنی مصدر هم می آید چنانکه شاهد اقلام بمعنی پری

دانشمندان کوید شعر یاشاغان ساوی طرف اجرا باییت کتان دیك پچه ادیکیب کم کاییت یاشاما یاشاغیل و یاشا تو مرحیت کرالشاد

علی الاول شعر الطفا المطری الارضه دینانك یکم امروز یاشا کیم طبعهاس حیان تیلپا نینزه کاچین یکیت یاشاما یاشلماغیلماز نیت بیکن

یاشانك و یاشاغاسین و یاشاغلمر تحسیکی یاشابه یاشانایا و یاشاسیز زینت کرده یاشامیشالك زینت کرده یاشاناس زینت میتواند کرد

و بمعنی حال و مصدر هم می آید یاشاغایو آلیزینت کند یاشاغاج چون زینت کرد و کند و محض کردن یاشاغوجی زینت کننده یاشاغوچه

یاشاغونر یاشاماغینا زینت کردن و بمعنی آن یاشاغوم زینت خواهم کرد یاشاغونك زینت خواهی کرد یاشاغوسی زینت خواهد کرد

x یاشاغای و یاشاسا یاشاسون یاشادیك زینت کند یاشاغودیك تو و یاشاما سلیك زینت نکرده است یاشاماق مع التاء زینت نمودن

x و طویل العمر یافتن و سیغ آن بجستوی یا تای قرشت اشتقاق نیابد یاشارماق مع الراء المهمله بمعنی اشك ریختن و اشك آلوده شدن چشم

باشد و صرایم معنی لفظ چشم باید منذکر شود و بمعنی غمناك شدن هم استعمال میشود یاشاری اشك آلوده شد یاشلدی و یاشا دادو یاشلی

میریزد و اشك آلوده میشود و یاشارور بمعنی حال و مصدر هم می آید چنانکه بمعنی حال کوید شعر بعه آلمای کوز یاشیم بیتکوریشار

ای غنیم فر خوصن ایر صلیشار بصرکور کاشاماق توتیا یاشاغلا و یاشار و غار و یاشارادوغان اشك ریزنده و اشك آلوده و بمعنی مصدر هم

می آید یاشار یاشارغیل و یاشارا کود اشك آلود شو یاشارما یاشارماغیل اشك آلوده مشو یاشارمانك یاشارماسین و یاشارغای عین

اشك آلوده شوید یاشارسه و یلیمهان و یاشاریش اشك آلوده شده یاشار میشالك اشك آلوده شده یاشارناس اشك آلوده میشود بمعنی

حال و مصدر معنی هم می آید یاشارغایو آلا اشك آلوده شود یاشارغاج چون اشك آلوده شود و محض شدن یاشارغوجی اشك

آلوده شونده یاشارغوچه و یاشارغوبجه و یاشارغلغچه تا اشك آلوده شدن و بمعنی آن یاشارغوم اشك آلوده خواهم شد یاشارغونك اشك آلوده

خواهی شد یاشارغوسی اشك آلوده خواهد شد یاشارغای و یاشارای و یاشارسا یاشارسون و یاشاردیك اشك آلوده شود الشاهد علی الاول

بیت کوز کالج اول الطاف صوی مفالحی بین توشو بمفر یعنی جوش ایلایکیم کال دین یاشلغایی کوز تیزیق بولغلج دماغ یاشارغاغوندلك تو و

x یاشارماسیك یماشك آلوده نشده است یاشاماق مع ضمکونرای مهمله و کاف قرشت مصدر متعدی بیت بمعنی اشك آلوده کردن چشم و نمناك

ساختن و صیغ آن بر قیاس انتقام تا اشتقاق می‌یابد یاشورماق بفتح یا و ضم شین مع الرای المهمله پنهان کردن یاشوردی یعنی پنهان کردیم یاشوردور
یاشوردورکه [illegible] پنهان میکند الشاهد علی الاول شعر کونکلوم [illegible] اوینامانقا توز یاشوردور
کل خندان ارا [illegible] یاشور بمعنی فاعل و مصدر هم می‌آید یاشورغان یاشورادورغان پنهان کند و پنهان کرده و بمعنی مصدر
هم می‌آید یاشوردیلار [illegible] یاشورطین [illegible] پنهان [illegible] یاشوروبان [illegible] پنهان کرده یاشورمایین پنهان کرده
یاشورماس پنهان نمیکند و بمعنی فاعل و مصدر منفی هم می‌آید یاشورغایمو آیا پنهان کند یاشورغاچ چون پنهان کرد و کند [illegible]
چنانکه در صفحه سیاه [illegible] گوید شعر [illegible] یاشورغاچ [illegible] یاشورغونچه
یاشورغانچه تا پنهان کردن و بقدر آن یاشورغوم پنهان خواهم کرد چنانکه گوید شعر جاندا یاشورغوم [illegible]
نامه سین [illegible] یاشورغونک پنهان خواهی کرد یاشورغوسی پنهان خواهد کرد یاشورغه
[illegible] پنهان کند [illegible] پنهان کردن و جمع آنکه پنهان کند الشاهد علی الاول
بالمعنی الاول شعر ای کونکول [illegible] یاشورونماق مع النون
پنهان شدن چنانکه گوید شعر ای خط [illegible] تاشیدا [illegible]
یاشورنغان [illegible] پنهان شده الشاهد علی الاول والمعنی الثانی شعر خط [illegible]
مو یاشونغان [illegible] اشتقاق می‌یابد من الجوامد یاش
بمعنی [illegible] چنانکه [illegible] گوید شعر [illegible] یاشیم [illegible]
[illegible] وله شعر [illegible] یاشیم [illegible]
[illegible] یاشیم [illegible] الشاهد علیه شعر [illegible]
[illegible] بالمعنی الاول شعر [illegible] یاشیم
بالمعنی الثانیه [illegible] یاشیم [illegible] بالمعنی الثالث [illegible] یاشیم
[illegible] استعمال [illegible] شعر [illegible]
[illegible] یاشاد [illegible] یاشاد [illegible] چنانکه
گوید شعر [illegible] یاشلیغ بمعنی [illegible]
[illegible] شعر [illegible] یاشلیغ و نیز گویند که
کچیک یاشلیغ بمعنی خرد سال [illegible] یاشلیغ [illegible] چنانکه گوید شعر [illegible] یاشلیغ [illegible]
[illegible] یاشماق بسکون شین [illegible]
[illegible] یاشورون بضم شین و رای مهمله و سکون نون بمعنی [illegible] پنهان بود الشاهد علیه شعر [illegible]
[illegible] یاشیق بکسر شین بمعنی [illegible]
یاشیل [illegible] یاشیل [illegible] یاشیمتول [illegible] یاشین بکسر شین و
نون بمعنی برق [illegible] شعر [illegible]
[illegible] الشاهد علی الثانی شعر [illegible]

دانه دار

دانه [illegible] یاغاچ [illegible]
[illegible] الشاهد علی الاول والمعنی الثانی شعر [illegible]
[illegible] یاغ [illegible]
[illegible] بمعنی فاعل و مصدر منفی هم می‌آید [illegible] یاغماچ [illegible]
[illegible] الشاهد علی الثانی شعر
[illegible]
[illegible] شعر [illegible]
[illegible] یاندی [illegible]
[illegible] چنانکه [illegible] گوید شعر [illegible]
[illegible] الشاهد علیه المعنی الثانی شعر [illegible]
[illegible]
چنانکه [illegible] گوید شعر [illegible] اشتقاق می‌یابد
یاغیقماق بفتح [illegible] یاغیقتی [illegible] یاغیقدی چنانکه در تاریخ الملوک [illegible] گوید
[illegible] بمعنی فاعل و مصدر هم می‌آید [illegible]
[illegible] بمعنی مصدر هم می‌آید چنانکه [illegible] در تاریخ [illegible]
[illegible]
[illegible] بمعنی فاعل و مصدر منفی هم می‌آید [illegible]
آیا [illegible] چون [illegible] شده [illegible]
[illegible]
[illegible] گویند [illegible] چنانکه [illegible]
[illegible] گوید شعر [illegible]
[illegible] گویند یاغچا [illegible]
[illegible] یاغدو بمعنی [illegible]
گوید شعر [illegible]
الشاهد علیه شعر [illegible] گویند [illegible]
[illegible] یاغریق [illegible]
یاغرین بسکون غین و نون و کسر رای مهمله شانه [illegible] چنانکه [illegible]
[illegible] گویند یاغرنچی [illegible]
[illegible] که اول [illegible]

333v.

الكت بناء علامات نكشتير بر تربنا انداختارا یافلاحیتی کویند ونیز صفحه که سوء اکمال طوحله بنای علم آرند می کویند که توزغ

یافلاحیتی کویند غلباء و توسی نام بزرگ است یافلنع و یافلیق بمعنی چوب مرغن آلود بود چنانکه کوید شعر لاغر اولا [illegible]

تاثیر ضایع ایتسانانک هیچ نیمه یالقاستور [illegible] یافلیق یاغمور بترکی روی بمعنی باز [illegible] یامغور را

یاغی دشمن را خوانند یاغیر بکسر غین وسکون [illegible] که نشانه بود چنانکه در تاریخ الانبیاء درج که عزیر علیه السلام را

زنده شدن [illegible] یاغیر [illegible] هم نامند و یاغیر الجاز جراحت

نیز کویند که موضع [illegible] نشانه [illegible] چنانکه کویند یاغیر اولوپتور یعنی [illegible] آن مجروح شده است یاغیز بکسر غین

بترکی روی بمعنی چهره [illegible] سیاه باشد و بصفت توضیحی کویند [illegible] یعنی سیاه چرده و مجاز اسب سیاه را هم نامند

[illegible] باشد یاغیش یعنی [illegible] یاغین [illegible] شعر [illegible] یاغین [illegible]

[illegible] یافراغ و یافراق [illegible] الشاهد علی الاول شعر [illegible]

[illegible] الشاهد علی الثانی شعر باغ [illegible]

[illegible] یافراق [illegible] هم خوانند چنانکه مذکور [illegible]

[illegible] یاقاق [illegible] چنانکه کوید شعر [illegible]

[illegible] یاقاق [illegible] چنانکه [illegible] کوید شعر [illegible]

[illegible] سیاق [illegible] یاقاق [illegible]

[illegible] یاموق [illegible]

[illegible] چنانکه [illegible]

[illegible] کوید شعر [illegible]

[illegible] چنانکه [illegible] کوید شعر [illegible]

[illegible] چنانکه [illegible] کوید شعر [illegible]

[illegible] چنانکه [illegible] کوید شعر [illegible]

[illegible] الشاهد علی الاول [illegible] الثالث شعر [illegible]

[illegible] چنانکه [illegible] کوید شعر [illegible]

[illegible] کوید شعر [illegible]

یاقای

334r

یاقاج یاقاین صیغه [illegible] چنانکه [illegible] کوید شعر [illegible]

[illegible] یاقا یاقا [illegible]

[illegible] کویند [illegible]

[illegible] چنانکه [illegible]

شعر [illegible] کوید شعر [illegible]

[illegible] یاقاج [illegible]

[illegible]

[illegible]

[illegible] شاهد [illegible]

[illegible] کوید که [illegible]

[illegible] تاریخ [illegible]

[illegible] چنانکه [illegible]

[illegible]

[illegible] شدن [illegible] شدن [illegible]

[illegible] الشاهد علی الثالث بالمعنی الاول شعر [illegible]

[illegible] چنانکه [illegible]

[illegible] کوید [illegible]

[illegible] چنانکه [illegible] کوید شعر [illegible]

[illegible] کوید شعر [illegible]

[illegible] کوید شعر [illegible]

[illegible] الصلح [illegible]

[illegible] الصلح [illegible]

[illegible] الصلح [illegible]

[illegible] الصلح کرده [illegible] الصلح [illegible]

[illegible] الصلح [illegible]

[illegible] الصلح کنده [illegible] الصلح [illegible]

[illegible] الصلح [illegible] الصلح [illegible]

[illegible] چنانکه [illegible]

[illegible]

334 v.

فاعل و مصدر هم می آید یاتالاغاغه یا تالارغاغه یاتالابدمز کیبنار کیده و کرده، و بمعنی مصدر هم می آید یاتالاما یاتالاغیل یاتالاکی

کیبنان کیر کن یاتالاقتناو یاتالاقماغیل کیبنان کیر کن [illegible] یاتالاقماسین یاتالاقماس کیبنان کیر کن [illegible]

کیبنان کیر کرده یاتالامیشانك کیبنان کیر کرده یاتالاماس کیبنان کیر نمیکند و بمعنی فاعل و مصدر منفی هم می آید یاتالاغایو [illegible]

تواند کرد یاتالاغلج چون کیبنان کیر کرد و کند و بعض کردن یاتالاغوجی کیبنان کیر کند یاتالاغوجه یاتالاغانجه تا کیبنا

کیر کردن و بمقدار آن یاتالاغوم کیبنان کیر خواهم کرد یاتالاغونك کیبنان کیر خواهی کرد یاتالاغوسی کیبنان کیر خواهد کرد

یاتالاغای یاتالاسانا یاتالاسونجه [illegible] کیبنان کرد نباست یاتالاشماق مع الشین [illegible]

مقابله است یعنی یکدیگر را کیبنا کیر کردن و صیغ آن بر نحو الخمسه [illegible] اشتقاق می یابد یاقیناشماق بسکون نون و شین و فتح لام

نزدیک شدن یاقیناشتوق نزدیک شدیم [illegible] نزدیک می شود و [illegible] بمعنی فاعل و مصدر هم می آید [illegible]

[illegible] نزدیک شونده و شده و بمعنی مصدر هم می آید [illegible] نزدیک شو [illegible]

نزدیک شو [illegible] نزدیک شوی [illegible] نزدیک شد [illegible]

نزدیک شدن [illegible] نزدیک شود و بمعنی فاعل و مصدر منفی هم می آید [illegible] نزدیک شود [illegible] چون نزدیک شد

و شود و بمجرد شدن [illegible] نزدیک شونده [illegible] تا نزدیک شدن و بمقدار آن [illegible]

نزدیک خواهم شد [illegible] نزدیک خواهی شد [illegible] نزدیک خواهد شد [illegible]

[illegible] نزدیک شود [illegible] نزدیک [illegible] مصدر متعدیست بمعنی نزدیک

کردن [illegible] نزدیک کرد چنانکه گوید شعر [illegible]

و [illegible] بالفظ [illegible] اشتقاق [illegible] سمت و جانب را گویند چنانکه [illegible]

[illegible] چنانکه [illegible]

[illegible] چنانکه [illegible] گوید شعر [illegible]

[illegible] شعر [illegible]

[illegible] گوید شعر [illegible]

و [illegible] چنانکه [illegible]

[illegible] گویند چنانکه [illegible] گوید شعر [illegible]

[illegible]

[illegible] من الصفات [illegible]

[illegible] و بمعنی فاعل و مصدر هم می آید [illegible]

[illegible] و بمعنی فاعل و مصدر هم می آید چنانکه شاهد [illegible]

[illegible] گوید [illegible]

[illegible]

[illegible] الشاهد على [illegible]

335 v.

[illegible]

[illegible] الشاهد على المعنى الاول شعر [illegible]

[illegible] الشاهد على المعنى الاول في المصرع الثاني شعر [illegible]

[illegible] المعنى الثاني في المصرع الثاني [illegible]

[illegible] و بمعنی فاعل و مصدر منفی هم می آید [illegible]

[illegible]

[illegible] خواهم [illegible] خواهی [illegible] خواهد [illegible]

[illegible]

[illegible] چنانکه [illegible] گوید شعر [illegible]

[illegible]

[illegible] برهنه کردن [illegible]

[illegible]

و بمعنی فاعل و مصدر هم می آید [illegible] برهنه کرده

و بمعنی مصدر هم می آید [illegible]

[illegible]

[illegible] چنانکه [illegible] گوید الشاهد على الرابع شعر [illegible]

[illegible]

[illegible] برهنه کرد چنانکه [illegible]

[illegible] گوید الشاهد على الاول شعر [illegible]

[illegible] الشاهد على الرابع شعر [illegible]

[illegible] برهنه کرده [illegible] و بمعنی فاعل و مصدر منفی هم می آید [illegible]

برهنه کند [illegible] برهنه کند چنانکه شاهد [illegible]

[illegible] برهنه کردن و بمقدار آن [illegible]

[illegible] برهنه خواهم کرد [illegible] برهنه خواهی کرد [illegible] برهنه خواهد کرد [illegible]

[illegible] برهنه کند [illegible]

[illegible] مصدر متعدیست بمعنی برهنه

[illegible]

[illegible] برهنه [illegible] چنانکه شاهد [illegible]

که [illegible] اشتقاق می یابد [illegible]

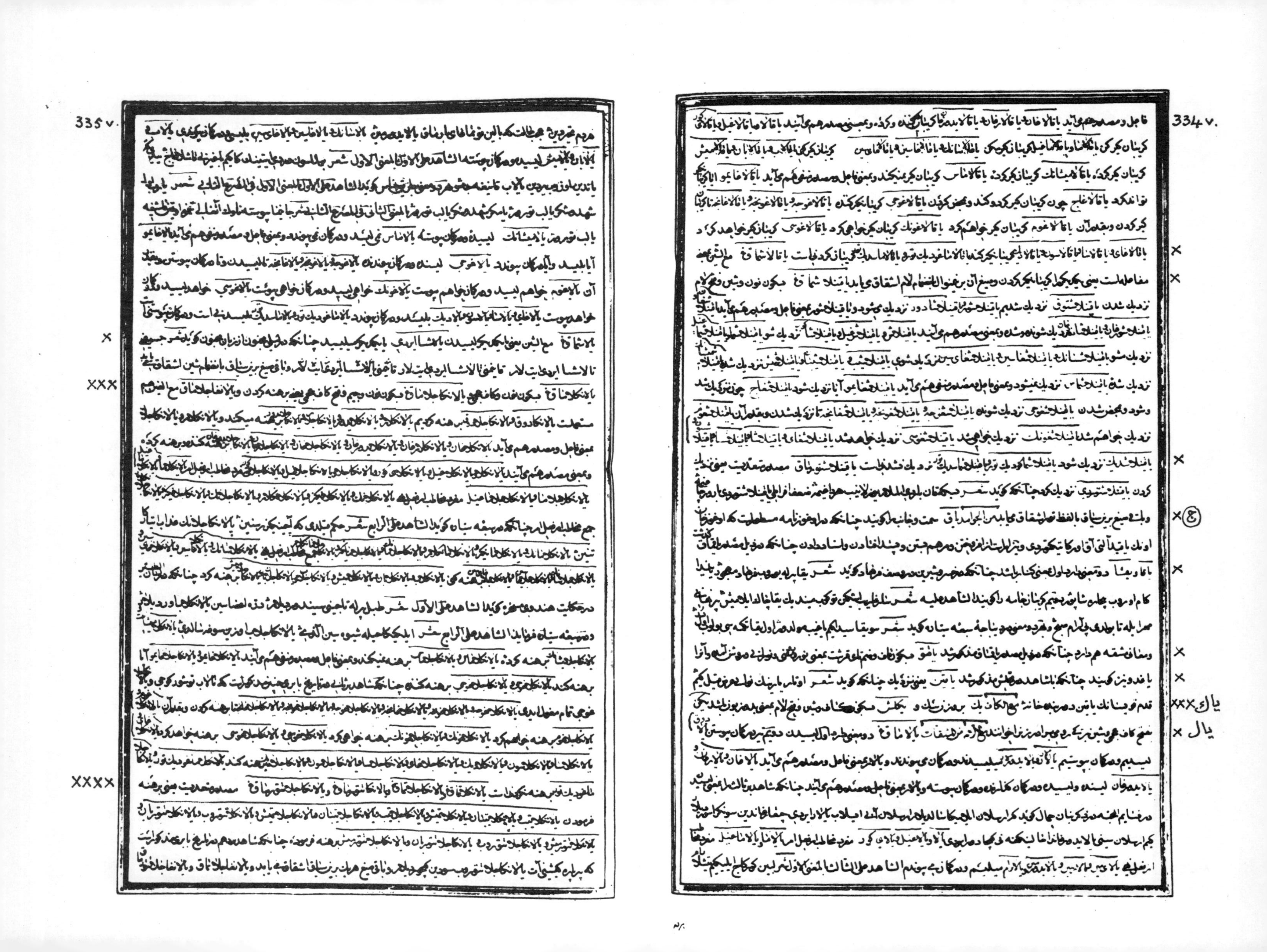

335v

بافتن جمه هم مستعملت وصیغ آنها نیز یافتن اشتقاق می‌باید یا انبلوما فی عجز کردن چنانکه گوید شعر [illegible]
[illegible] یا البارد و قی عجز کردیم یا البارو [illegible]
[illegible] می‌آید [illegible] عجز کننده و عجز کننده [illegible]
یا البارا کو عجز کنا الشاهد علی الثلثی شعر [illegible]
[illegible] عجز کرده [illegible]
عجز نکند و [illegible] می‌آید یا البارد یا البادره عجز کنان چنانکه گوید شعر [illegible]
[illegible] یا البارخاج چون
عجز کند و [illegible] عجز کردن [illegible]
یا البارغونك عجز خواهی کرد [illegible]
یا الباردونك [illegible] الشاهد علی الاول شعر [illegible]
یا البلر غودیك [illegible] مع الکون برهنه شدن وصیغ آنها [illegible]
[illegible]

336r

[illegible]

و.

یالانغاج مع الغین و یالانکاج مع الکاف الفارسی یعنی برهنه و عریان باشد چنانکه شاهد اول لعل صفا نه [illegible] حیرت الابرار میرسد
کم کوید شعر یایاز آنکا سفو یکیم اولاچ ایماس بیر و آنکا توزیکیم یالانغلیچ ایماس و نیز شیخ علی کوید شعر صرصر یانیبان چمن [illegible]
بستان ایلین ایلیچی یالانغاج الشاهد علی الکاف شعر تماشا قبان داغلاغی پر مرجی بیرله تاموغین تیلبه [illegible] چا یانین [illegible]
اولغای یالانکاج و آنرا یالانک هم کویند یالانک بسکون نون و کاف عجمی دو معنی دارد اول بمعنی برهنه و عریان بود چنانکه کوید شعر
عشق مرکشته سی بیز یغمه خاجت کرک بوینه ملبس موقوبون نینک اناغی بولسا یالانک دویم قماش و متاع نادوخته را کویند
چنانکه [illegible] کمینه را فرماید شعر ایکی یوز کام دیکلاجی و تون بیرتیب یالانک تون آلاریغانیه
اوت بیرتیب یالاو بسکون واو بمعنی آمد اولغی بیر سر خلیت که بر کلاه خود میچسپند و شقه بیرق و علم را کویند الشاهد علیه شعر
[illegible] اول [illegible] یالاو [illegible] یالاولاو [illegible] کوید شعر [illegible]
یالاو دلپذیر [illegible] یالاوز [illegible] شعر یالاوز [illegible]
[illegible] چنانکه در باب تا مفتوحه [illegible] لغت تاماغ کورشد دوییم بمعنی شعله باشد چنانکه خسرو شیرین کوید شعر [illegible]
[illegible] یالپاق بسکون لام و قاف و فتح بای عجمی بمعنی [illegible]
و آنرا یاپانک هم نامند یالتاغلیغ ترکیبی [illegible] یالچی بسکون لام و ضم جیم [illegible]
[illegible] یالدوز [illegible]
یالدیراوق [illegible] یالدیراق [illegible] نام ستاره سهیل باشد یالدیراش
بکسر دال و یای [illegible] دمیغ را کویند چنانکه کوید شعر [illegible]
جان بولسا [illegible] کتاب [illegible] دمیغ کوینه الشاهد علی
الثانی شعر [illegible] یالغوز تنها
یالغوزون یعنی [illegible] چنانکه [illegible] شعر [illegible] یالغوزون [illegible] قطع
طریق [illegible] یالقین [illegible]
یا [illegible] یلماس [illegible] چنانکه [illegible]
یاجنج کوید شعر [illegible]
یالمان آنکا [illegible] یلن بفتح لام و سکون نون [illegible] که بر سر چادر [illegible]
[illegible]
[illegible] یالین بکسر لام و سکون نون [illegible] الشاهد علیه شعر [illegible]
[illegible] کوید شعر [illegible]
[illegible]
نوشته [illegible]
سک و آشنا [illegible] چنانکه شاهدان [illegible] یالین لیغ [illegible] چنانکه
[illegible] خسرو شیرین کوید شعر [illegible]

اول

اولغالین لیغ کوینه نی اوق یالین راق افروخته تر و مشتعل تر یالینک بکسر لام و فتح [illegible] بمعنی برهنه مجازا باشد چنانکه در خاتمه
حیرت الابرار کوید شعر [illegible] نبشتهجات متعدد [illegible]
مرقوم بوند یالینک لیغ برهنکی چنانکه در ملقاات کوید [illegible] یالینک [illegible]
[illegible] یالینچوق بکسر لام و سکون نون و فتح جیم ترکی بمعنی عریان بود یالینکاکات بکسر لام و سکون نون و کاف عجمی و
فتح قاف ترکی [illegible] المیم من المشتقات یاما یاماق بفتح هر دو میم بمعنی پینه [illegible] یام
چنانکه در عنوان خاتمه حیرت الابرار کوید [illegible]
[illegible] شعر [illegible]
[illegible]
[illegible]
الشاهد علی الکاف شعر [illegible]
[illegible]
پینه [illegible]
پینه [illegible]
پینه خواهد کرد [illegible]
[illegible] الشاهد علی الثانی [illegible]
شعر [illegible] اشتقاق [illegible]
مع اللام پینه و وصله شدن [illegible] اشتقاق [illegible]
[illegible]
[illegible]
[illegible]
[illegible] چنانکه شاهد [illegible]
[illegible]
[illegible]
[illegible]
[illegible]
[illegible]
[illegible]
[illegible] یاساق [illegible] ج
از حیرت الابرار [illegible] کوید شعر [illegible]

337v

نشاء بین جابرا پاره یا مالغ که کشان و منقوص وصف اهل هنر فرمایند شعر آغ یا مالغ ایکیندا لوکولی خوزمنی خوشراق آنکا سیم و طلا دین

متر کوری سیمعنی بدو اول اشتر بد واکویند که از پوست و تلاطین یممزید دیم خرم از ینکچوی کرامند که سفت فلاج میباشد سیم

خدمتکار از نرم لی خوانند که در کارخانجات خدمت میکنند بیلجا طلیغ یا ماطلیغ بپنه دا بیچنانچه گوید شعر دیبان کل ینده

سیده دور بویین باغلیغ کمال دوه دور تون هر این یا ماطلیغ یامان بمعنی بد و زبون است شاهد علیه شعر دیب یا بینک آلنوم

نوایی کونکلی انکلیج امتا دینک بخشیده الماق بیان الاری کونکلینی موندا ف بودور و بلغت مغولی بر بود که از امیر بمعنی گویند

یانالیغ بکسر و زبون عمیدی بسکون میم و ضم دال بلغت جغتای و عیدک بجر دال و سکون کاف ترکیه رومی بمعنی ها را است یا منور

مار از نامند چنانچه گوید شعر تیرلجان هینک جسیم فتیله دی بیر کاپت ده که یامنور کره تصفیق هینک و یراتق یا مجی لفظیست ترکی

انطربی و ترک ضا بطانیها گویند که موصل از الذبر او چاپاران بسته شود مع النون من المشتقات ایما ق ع دو معنی دارد اول کوختن

دویم برکشتن یاند و ق سوختیم و برکشتیم یانار و یانادور میسوزد و بر میکردد الشاهد علی الثانی بالمعنی کل اول شعر اول امانت

شمعی دین موندا ق که جسیم یانه دور هر برا و چون غم شیشانیدا پر پروانه دور فیز هست بکنجیده مقابله دار با اسکندر بمعنی

برگشتن گوید شعر بو بیدین یانار نینک خود امکانی یوق نیز دالیشام خینه صانی یوق و یانار بمعنی فاعل و مصدر هم می آید یانغان

یانار غان یانا دور غان سوزنده و سوخته و بر کرده و برگشته چنانچه شاهد بر ثانی را بمعنی اول در خیام المجیه مرزد که ابونصر سراج گوید که

پرفیش بیمی وقتی خوش بولدی یانا دور غان اوت اچیدا تینکری تعالی حضرت عبیدالله و یوز یکا اوت دین آسیب تیمادی و بمعنی مصدر

هم می آید یان میا نیل و بیانا کور مفرد خطاب از فصل امر و دو معنی یا زیغیه حصه و طلب هم باشد چنانچه بمعنی سترا دو مصرع اول

دو معنی اول را در مصرع ثانی بطریق ایهام فرماید شعر ای نوایی عشق ابرماس ایردی اول یان با ر لفنک چو زلیب ا و زینک قیلدینک تماشا

بمعنی ثانی و شاهد بر ثانی را نیز هر دو معنی هم ایهام گوید شعر ار ده ها لا عشق و شوق ا کبرا دین دور زبون اوت قو نلیب تیمور بولادی

ایمرا یانیل اوکونکول یامنا یما ضیل مفرد خطاب از فصل ایمر و دو معنی یا نیلغه یا نینکر و یا نینکلارهم خطاب از فصل امرا شاهد علی الاول و

المعنی الثانی شعر نوا ی عشق وا دی سیغه کیردی خطرلیغ بولدر ای احباب یا نینک یا نمانک یا نمانکر یا نانکلارهم خطاب از فصل نیر

یاغانالغ یاغا سین و یاغا ی بین بسوز ید بر کردی یاینغ یا نیبان و یا نیش سوخته و برکشته الشاهد علی الاول بالمعنی الثانی شعر

امعدین که حقیق گرینا کی ممکن ایماس یانیب یاش دیک که کوزکا کرماس کر چه الاشفاری یانمیشانک سوخته و برکشته یاغاس عیوده

و برنگردد چنانچه بمعنی ثانی گوید شعر آتینک دیک تیلیبه کونکلوم اول پری کو سیکا یانمیش کر کرنیه لا ایرا حیکا کوکلی یم

یاغاس و بمعنی فاعل و مصدر نفی هم می آید یانا آلماس نمیتواند سوخت و نمیتواند برکشت چنانچه خسرو شیرین بمعنی برکردی گوید المعنی الثانی

شعر غرض کیم مکر و حیله برله ملزی یانا آلماس یک لیک کوینار یانه یانه سوزانیده جمع کنان و بدون یکر لا هم مستعملست چنانچه

شاهد اول را هر دو معنی بطریق ایهام گوید شعر عشق امیدی کیمی پر تا لا کویوب بولسا خلاص جو نسیه یا تیغا نانیل اشغله شبیه

یانه کوی و یانه و یانار بمعنی ایضا و دیکر هم مستعملست چنانچه بمعنی سوزان و بمعنی دیکر بطریق ایهام در نامه فرستادن فرهاد بجانب

شیرین گوید شعر بیت شاه هزن سیلدی یکا نه لونی هر دا تی ابرا مالدی یانه یا نقامیو آیا بسوزد و آیا بر گردد یانغاج چون

سوخت و بسوز د و چون برکشت و برکردد و بعضی آن یانغوجی سوزنده و برکرد نده یانغوجه یانغوجغه یانغانجه تا سوختن و تا برکشتن چنانچه

هر دو معنی بطریق ایهام فرماید الشاهد علی الثانی شعر دو سنلار وصل اوتین ایستلکا نولیی بلمیش ناش یاتلانک بوصدیشی آتینک

یانغوجه قیز بمعنی تقدیم سوختن و تقدیم برکشتن یانغومدی نمیخواهم سوخت و نمیخواهم برکشت یانغومک کدرنه خواهی برکشت و نخواهی سوخت

خوش ده

338r

یانغوسیدور نمیخواهد سوخت و نمیخواهد برکشت یا المعنی الثانی شعر ای نوایی ملا مردم اول مخلر یار او چون تم جمله یانغوسیدور انکا لوحوردی

کیلکوسی یانغای یانار و یانسا و یانسون و یاندیک بسوزد و بر کردد چنانچه شاهد بر اول را بمعنی ثانی در منم خواهی نی یاز فرهاد گوید شعر

ایشینک منیدا یونچه دیمک آوتغانلی فی یزدین تینکری دین اکینکه یانغای یانغوسیدور یانماس نه قو خوتولست و بر نکشتی ست یانغیل

مصدر متعدیست دو معنی دارد اول سوزانیدن دویم برکردانیدن یاندوردوک سوزانیدیک و بر کردانیدیک چنانچه بمعنی ثانی گوید شعر

بیلریخی ایستای نوایی بلمیش ایردی ایمر یوق سیلمادیم آیی نوایی نون برله یاندوردونک بلیریب یاندور یاندوردیل بسوزان و بر کردان چنانچه

شاهد اول را هر دو معنی بسبیل ایهام گوید شعر شوقی و تیغه یانمانغه امزین اودی نوایی تاوعینک کیل علطاف ایلاجان اوز ایلیله

حن یاندورا الشاهد علی الثانی بالمعنی الثانی شعر یارغیلای همدم هرلانی کونکلوم ایمیش یانغیل آتی استدعا الیحیب یاندوردیل کیکا

بولسا دی پنهانی یاندوروریک یاندوریک سوزانیدی و بر کردانیدی الشاهد علی الاول بالمعنی الثانی شعر میش تیمین پیل تفحیث کیم

ایرور یم اوشبو دم چرخ ایرنلس فوت بولغان وقت فی یاندور غوریک نیز بمعنی همچنانچه بسوزاند و بر گرداند و باقی صیغ بر بنیاق الفعلی

اشتقاق می یابد یانجماق ع بسکون نون و جیم بمعنی نرم کردن یانجدوق نرم کردیم یانجادیم یانجادی نرم میکند و یانجار بمعنی فاعل

منفی هم می آید یانجاندار یانجاغان یانجادور غان نرم کننده و نرم کرده و بمعنی مصدر هم می آیند یانجیا یانجیل و یانجاکور نرم کن یانجا

یانجاغیل نرم مکن یانجانانک یانجانسین و یانجای نرم کنی یانجیب یانجبان یانجیش نرم کرده چنانچه شاهد بر اول امیر خسرو شیرین

در وصف کشتی گوید شعر او جی کو لعثیری و هوتینی سلجیث توپی برکا و منا هی سینی یانجیث یانجیشانک نرم کرده یانجا یمو آیا نرم کند

یانجغانج چون نرم کرد و کند و بعضی کردن یانجغوجی نرم کننده یانجغوجه یانجغوجغه یانجغانجه تا نرم کردن و تقدیم آن یانجغوم نرم نکنم

کردیا یانجغونک نرم خواهی کرد یانجغوجی نرم خواهد کرد یانجغای یانجاما یانجاسا یانجغون و یانجیدیل نرم کند و یانجای آلت نرم کردن

هم کویند یانجاغودیک تورد یانجماسدیک نرم نکردنداست یانجدیماق ع مصدر متعدیست بمعنی نرم فرمودن و صیغ آن بالفظ در اشتقاق

یانجلماق ع نرم شدن و صیغ آن بکسر جیم بالالام اشتقاق می یابد یانداشماق ع بسکون نون و شین معجمه و فتح دال الحمد و شرکت هم پهلو شدن

یانداشتوق هم پهلو شدیم یانداشور یانداشادور هم پهلو میشود و یانداشور بمعنی فاعل و مصدر هم می آید یانداشغان یانداشورغان و یانداشادور

هم پهلو شونده و هم پهلو شده الشاهد علی الاول بالمعنی الثانی شعر منغایلیغ حسن بسلیکو کان بو غولام صیانین انکا

یانداشغان تو کانلار نینک شبیهی تارا و بمعنی مصدر هم می آیند یانداش و یانداشغیل یانداشاکور هم پهلو شو یانداشما یانداشما

هم پهلو مشو یانداشانک یانداشغای و یانداشغیل هم پهلو شوی یانداشیب یانداشیبان یانداشمیش هم پهلو شده الشاهد علی الاول شعر

سکر نالیغ کونکول لاد قوشلاغی وصل ایلاشیب او چکان تو نونکا انکه کیم یاقوت احمر دین قطار ایتینک یانداشمیشانک هم پهلو شده یانداشغا

آیام پهلو شود یانداشغاج چون هم پهلو شد و شود و بعضی شدن یانداشغوجی هم پهلو شونده یانداشغوجه یانداشغوجغه و یانداشغا

تا هم پهلو شدن و تقدیم آن یانداشغوم هم پهلو خواهم شد یانداشغونک هم پهلو خواهی شد یانداشغوسی هم پهلو خواهد شد یانداشغا

یانداشغای یانداشسا یانداشسون یانداشدیک هم پهلو شود چنانچه شاهد بر اول امیر خسرو شیرین در احوال فرهاد گوید شعر ولی یانما

ایدی بو ایشکا جاتی که یانداشغای بلور و سنک خاره و بمعنی کفر و یانداشغا و لعلی را شعر یانداشای یانا و قیز سنجوا نن و نوشته

که بمعنی نزد امر مقتن باشد و شعر بصورت شاهد آمده لفظ مذکور دو اخبار است یانداشما غودیک توریا یانداشماسلیک هم پهلو نشدن

یانداشتور ماق ع مصدر متعدیست یعنی پهلو هم کذاشتن یانداشتور یانداشتورایلار و یانداشتورغا لا ر یانداشتور یانداشتوریا

پهلو هم بگذارید چنانچه شاهد بر اثبات قطعا نگوید شعر طا قیم ن کر لار صیقی یانداشتوریلار نی بوانتین بجیر ا قیغا

ن اوکیدین یانان و باقی صیغ برین سیاق ما انفظ تغرا اشتقاق می یابد یانکماق بسکون نون و کاف عجمی دیهو و غلط انداختن و صحیح
کردن یانکیوق بغلط انداختیم یانکارها یانکادور بغلط می اندازد و یانکار بمعنی حاصل مصدر هم می آید یانکشان و یانکار و یانکامد
بغلط انداززن و بغلط انداخته و معنی مصدر هم می آیند یانلغه یانکیل و یانکاکو بمفرد حال المبنی بر اصل امر یانکماو یانکماغیل مفرد
غائب بنفل بهه یانکانانک و یانکلیمن و یانکمای بغلط بیندازی یانکچه یانکیان و یانکمش بغلط انداخته یانکیشانک بغلط اندا
یانکمامو آیا بغلط بیندازد یانکماج چون بغلط انداخت و اندازد و بمعنی انداختن یانکوجی بغلط اندازنده یانکوجه و یانکوچه
یانکماغه تا بغلط انداختن و بمقدم آن یانکوم بغلط خواهم انداخت یانکونک بغلط خواهی انداخت یانکوسی بغلط خواهد
انداخت یانکمای و یانکما یانکای یانکودی یانکمای بغلط بیندازی الشاهد علی الثالث شعر یانکا دبر ایچرا مینی حیرت بینا مانلار بغیچه
بیم تو ره بو کادکه وضعیف ایکیم حیران ایلماس یانکیلغوبان تو و یانکلساید غلط نکرده است یانکیتماق بسکون نون و قاف و فتح
و کسر کاف عجمی مع الاماله خبر بغلط کردن یانکیتماق یانکیتماق بغلط بینکند الشاهد علی الاول شعر فراق شامی یانکیتماس او قونک
کونکول بولیغ که بادبه اول شایع میکانی دین چراغ سیله و باقی صیغ برین نهج بکاف عجمی با ای قرشت موافق و اشتقاق می یابد
یانکیلماق مع الاعم خود غلط کردن یانکیلدیم غلط کردم چنانکه کوید شعر توحید نکته سیدا خوش اولدی سیز شرح
شرح قیلدیم آنی یانکیلدیم یانکیلدی یانکیلسانک یانکیلیش غلط کرده الشاهد علی الاول شعر هرکیشی قیلکیم ایلدار اولدین
ربنکین که بر هم یانکیلب سوزان سوز جیران یافته آن یانکیلماس غلط نکند چنانکه کوید شعر کوی یاری هرکه کرم ایتسا
نوایی اوشمین اوچه چیغ که اول بولیغ یانکیلماس یانکیلماسانک و یانکیلماغاسین و یانکیلماغایسین غلط نکنی الشاهد علی الثا
شعر دنیا لار لیلی مو آرتو قحس را اوا اول پری کرچه مجنون سین کرانک یانکیلماغای سین ای کونکول و باقی صیغ برین سیاق بالام
اشتقاق می یابد یانکشاماق بسکون نون و کاف عجمی و فتح شین معجمه بمعنی بسیار حرف زدن چنانکه در شبهات حوبیا الغلوب در وصف
حلم کوید کر حق کوی قوش نینک تیکین سیله ذکر آیتیوری تالشیدا تار لو غلیچ نینک جی داول یانکشاماغی حالت کیلتوروب یانکشادوق
بسیار حرف زدیم یانکشادی یانکشاید بسیار حرف زد و یانکشار بمعنی حاصل مصدر هم می آید یانکشاغان و یانکشارغان و یانکشاید
بسیار حرف زننده و بسیار حرف زده و معنی مصدر هم می آیند یانکشا یانکشاغیل و یانکشاکو مفرد حال المبنی بر اصل امر یانکشلا یانکشانا
مفرد غائب بنفل بهه یانکشانانک و یانکشاغاسین یانکشاغای سین بسیار حرف زنی یانکشاب یانکشایان یانکشامیش بسیار حرف زده
یانکشیشانک بسیار حرف زنده یانکشامو آیا بسیار حرف زند یانکشاماج چون بسیار حرف زد و بمعنی زدن یانکشاغوجی بسیار حرف زننده
یانکشاغوجه یانکشاغونه تا بسیار حرف زدن و بمقدم آن یانکشاغوم بسیار حرف خواهم زد یانکشاغونک بسیار حرف
خواهی زد یانکشاغای یانکشاغای یانکشاماغای یانکشاماغای یانکشامینار حرف زند یانکشاسیده یانکسیار حرف زن نبی یانقولانما
تر کرده می بمعنی سیاه کردن باشد یانکیلاماق بسکون نون و کاف عجمی و کسر سین مهمله تر کردن و بی کوشش العضا تحلید کردن این المدینا
بمعنی آمد او لحیت و جانب را می بیند چنانکه کوید شعر منعمدین قدیم الف بولدی الکی لام ایکی دالف هر یانیمیز خلوی کرد
جمکر لاالعین دویم طلنا بمعنی پهلو و جنب استعمال شود چنانکه جر و معنی بطریق ایهام فرماید شعر جون نوایی جانیغه مرهم ایرور
بیکا لرهیک کاش یا قسام جمی اوقونک یا یغیه اولتوروب وینرا آرایش از سوختن و بر کشش چنانکه دو بولایغا ق تعذکور شد بغلط
بمعنی طرد المهد یا نرا کویند دویم مرکب طراط و انه باشد و ازینجاست که اسب طراز زبان و بناده و اتنادی یانیغوانلیم سو فیه
آنچه در عالم غیب مشاهده می شود نان می کویند یا نسا به معنی باشد او لا بمعنی نیز باشد کره نظر جی مقام تکرار و ستعملت وانرا بعری

ایضا کویند قدیم بمعنی یکی و صحیح یکسو معنی برابر باشد چنانکه در بیت سکندری در صفت سکندر را بنا میر شکوید شعر خوانی اولسا یانیدا
یانا لار کیچی او خولنا عید آنالار کیو آنرا یانه ضیه و صنا هم خواننده چنانکه نمیبه معراج قدیم بهر دو معنی کوید شعر ای خوانی یانک او لور بید
دین بولسام خاص حرم قیلدیم کیم نیه بولمای بینا فرسنباق و یانا بمعنی سوزان در جمع کمان هم باشد چنانکه مذکور شد یانا ق بکسر
نون و فتح تای قرشت بروزن چاولاق خارشتر را کویند یانجا ق بسکون نون و فتح جیم با الف کشیده جوش بوست که بر تحمل و اطلس ناکو
در روز جنک بر دو پهلوی اسب ببندند و کیم آنست که بر اسب افکنند چنانکه در عجائب الغرائب در وصف الاسناق کوید کر تیکه مشتو
کیمیش آلیغ مقرینید ادیب تور شعر تغوی ایرور ما لیند آکه ایکی یانجاق بولوب ایکی فنالیغ یانجای بسکون نون و جیم و فتح
میم با الف کشیده آلتی است که بدان چیزها را نرم کنند و نیز بمعنی نرم کند یانجوق بسکون نون و قاف و ضم جیم کیسه و چیبی را کویند که
در پهلوی قبا از زیر بدوخته شود یا نغو بسکون نون و فتح غاف انست که جون صرکی و کیب با آواز بلند چیزی کویند همان صدا بجواب شنود
و آنرا عربی صدا و بفارسی پژواک نامند و با صطلاح رومیه ا لحواق و سوختن سرا و حرارت باشد و در هر دو معنی یا خونا زبانا ق بمعنی برکشتن
و سوختن باشد یانغی بسکون نون و کسر غین معجمه بمعنی هر تازه چنانکه کوید شعر اول صنم قدی نینک سرو یغیه کی تکلوم بولکای
باغ آئیین کل لار آنکا هر یانغی قا تلیغ تازه داغ یانک بر وزن بانک بمعنی نو و تلمو باشد چنانکه در خامه سیحه سیاره کوید شعر
آینما او جیمیش ایرو آلماة آنینک یانک بلشدین ایلار یحیک ساز و آنرا یانکی هم کویند و مفرد حاضر المبنی بر اصل امر مصدر یانکلاق هم باشد بمعنی بیلاد
بیفکن چنانکه کذشت یانکا بسکون نون و فتح کاف عجمی بستر که روی جانب و جهت بود یانکا جیغ بکسر جیم در صف که باشد یانکا
بمعنی آنطرف یانکاق و یانکاق بسکون نون و فتح کاف عجمی مع الاماله در معنی چار و اول بمعنی جهره در خسار بود و چنانکه در سبزا مطلع
شعر لبینک نار یانکاغی اوزوه تا پارچه صر یانک یوق اکیه جو هر طیتو آنی اصل بیتی قدیم جز نمل کویند چنانکه در صنعت سکندری
در وصف لشام کوید شعر سیمنلیغ اوروه کی بولسا یلجیه نینک یانکاغ کوما یتکا مزنی لو خوبلار اوشان یانکاغ فیرقه تلیغ لاله دره در صف نار کیل کرکه
که بنچی کیکم یانکاغ نینک تا شیدا کولده بوسق بولور نارکیل نینک تاشیدا هم کوک پوستی باد بنیا کان بفتح نون اول و کلف عجمی با الف کشیده و سکون
نون آخر کرکه کر ما را کویند یانکلاو بسکون نون و کاف عجمی و کسر لام بمعنی مثل و مانند بود چنانکه کوید شعر یانکلاو کو نکلوم وصل اتی ام
قیلوله تیکم شد کیلورین یانکی بو کیکان بلبوفه آن الرابیه و تیره لیلی بمعنی تابد شعر شاخ طوبی معنم قیلیبکل لاسیم امنی یانکلاو آکمید کل
ینکلیغ بسکون نون و کاف عجمی و کسر لام بمعنی مثل و مانند بود چنانکه کوید شعر قلمو نینک خورشید و لعل نینک خود دین تمثال ایسر
ذره و قطره ینکلیغ لعل نینک لعنو خیال الیوحش یانکی بسکون نون و کسر کاف عجمی بمعنی نو و تلمو باشد الشاهد علیه شعر جان بر وحه
هر یان یکیم یانکی تو کانلاه وحش قیلیم ضعفلان تیغ کان محضر بولیکین آیا و آنرا یانک هم کویند چنانکه بالشاهد بهر فوق نکاره یانف و لعل قلعه
در مثال در صفیه که آنرا یانکی قلعه نامند یانکیش بسکون نون و شین معجمه و کسر کاف عجمی تر کردن بمعنی سهو و غلط بود یانکیلماج بسکون نون
و لام و نای قرشت و جیم و کسر کاف عجمی و فتح میم با الف کشیده لغز را کویند و نیز جیزی باشد که معنی آن مفهوم نباشد و غلط اندازد یا نلی قورت
ترکیه و تمام خانه چه که آنرا عربی ضبح و بفارسی کفتار نامند یان و یانه همان بینا و یانا باشد که در فوق مذکور شد و آن درهم معنی
اول تیز و ایضا تیم یکی نیم غیرا لشاهد علی الاول با المعنی الثانی شعر لب لعلینک غرا و خشا ما نی یوق بیته در ازه و صل یانینه الشا
علی الاول بالمعنی الاول فی المصرع الاول و علی الثانی بالمعنی الثانی فی المصرع الثانی شعر دیلبین دیوا مزه بیکو نکلونک سینه مبر یانه تو یش تن
کان قیلیا که عالم اجرا سین دیک یانه بولغای الشاهد علی الثانی بالمعنی الثانی شعر زاهدا هنکین تو لیه هر غیچه لعیکم آزاپانا دیر شهر
معنی یانه مهمله آن خبرهم و یانه بمعنی سوزان و جمع کمان هم باشد جی بفارسی بدو معنی آمده اول بمعنی بو جمکه از آن در حرکت مساز ایرد انکم

دیم طاوغلار نلسند مع الواو من المشتقات باواشماق بفتح واو با الف کشیده یعنی حلیم و بردبار شدن باواشتوق بردبار شدیم

باواشورم باواشمادو بردبار بودیم معنی حاصل مصدر هم می آید باواشغان باواشادم باواشا بردبار شدند و بردبار

معنی مصدر هم می آید باواشیم باواشغیل باواشاکور مفرد مخاطب امر باواشماو باواشماغیل مفرد مخاطب باواشمانک باواشنا

باواشغای بین بردبار شویم باواشیب باواشیبان باواشیش بردبار شدن الشاهد علی الاول شعر کونکلیم اسرو توسن ایردی نزهد

آبنی داکم کیل کم عشقینک بردبار بولدی باواشغا یمو آیا بردبار شود باواشغاج چون بردبار شد و شود

و محض شدن باواشغوچی بردبار شونده باواشغوچیا باواشغاغه تا بردبار شدن و بمعنی آن باواشغوم بردبار خواهم شد

باواشغونک بردبار خواهد شد باواشغای باواشلو باواشسا و باواشسون و باواشدیلک بردبار شود باواشماغو دیک

بردبار شد نخست باوشماق و باوشماق مع التبن یعنی نزدیک شدن چنانکه شاهد براولان در فوت فرهاد و مجنون گوید

ودام کوید شعر بولو باطل نوع اطرامید اسانکه کیم ... باوودی ... باوشتی ... نزدیک شدند چنانکه

شاهد ... در حیرة الابرار کوید شعر شیخ ... باووشتی ... باوودی باوودو

باووشادو نزدیک میشود الشاهد علی الاول لالامی شعر کیم کرشمه ... جهان آرای دین دوست قرین کرا الماس

دشمن ... دین و شاهد ثانی ... خسرو و شیرین کوید شعر ... باووشور جان ... باوق

و باووشور بمعنی حاصل مصدر هم می آید باووقان و باوودرغان و باووشغان و باووشورغان و باووشادرغان

نزدیک شونده ... بمعنی مصدر هم می آیند باوونک و باوونکوز باوونکلار و باووشونک و باووشونکوز و باووشونکلار

نزدیک شوید باووماتک و باوومانکوز و باووشمانک و باووشمانکوز نزدیک مشوید الشاهد علی الاول شعر

نازنین ... باوومانک ... باووصانک ... باووغای بین ... باووشسا

باووشغایین ... نزدیک شویم باووب باووبان ... باووشوب و باووشوبان و باووشمیش نزدیک شده

چنانکه شاهد ... در مناجات کوید ... باووتاس باووشماس

نزدیک نمیشود الشاهد علی الاول شعر ... باووغای

باووشغایلار نزدیک شود باووغوچی باووشغوچی نزدیک شونده باووغوچیغه و باووغاغه و باووشغوچیغه باووشغاغه

نا نزدیک شدن و بمعنی آن باووغوم و باووشغوم نزدیک خواهم شد باووغونک و باووشغونک نزدیک خواهی شد باووغوسی باووشغوسی

نزدیک خواهد شد باووغای و باووسا و باووسون و باووشسا و باووشسون و باووشدیلک

نزدیک شود باوو مساغو دیک ... باووشمساغو دیک ... نزدیک شدنی است ...

باووشماغو دیک باووشا آلماس ... نزدیک نتواند شد الشاهد علی الثانی شعر ... لکیم ...

نزدیک ... باووماق و باووشتوماق ... یعنی نزدیک کردن باووتون و باووتوز

باووتونکلار نزدیک کنید الشاهد علی الاول شعر ... کیم باووتوق

باووتوب ... باووتساو ... نزدیک نتوان کرد چنانکه در خسرو و شیرین ... کوید شعر

که حضرت ... باووتیلاش ... باووتیلاش نزدیک کردن الشاهد علی الاول

شعر ... باووتماق ... اغتنام ناي

قرشت واو باووشتورماق ... موافقت والاشتقاق بحاید باووماک بضم واو و سکون تا و فتح کاف فضیلت دادن و ... ساختن

و برکزیدن باووختن و امثال آن ... باووتکار ... برکزیدیم باووتکار و باووتکاید ... برکزید

میکرداند الشاهد علی الاول شعر فراقینک ... باووتکارکیم ... باووتکا

بمعنی حاصل مصدر هم می آید باووتکان ... باووتکاریان ... برکزینده چنانکه در تاریخ بابری در وصف سلطان احمد

میرزا بمعنی ... خواجه ... باووتکان ... بمعنی مصدر هم می آیند باووتکوبا باووتکیل

باووتکل ... مفرد مخاطب ... باووتکان ... مفرد مخاطب ... باووتکای ... باووتکالوق کردانی باووتکا

باووتکاباش و باووتکاباش ... برکزیدن چنانکه شاهد ... کوید ... باووتکاب ... باووتکای

خالات دین ... نیز در تاریخ بابری در وصف سلطان احمد ... حضرت خواجه ...

فادت ... باووتکاب ... باووتکا یمو آیا برکزیده باووتکاج چون برکزیدند ... باووتکاکوچی

باووتکاکوچیغه ... برکزیده ... برکردانند ... باووتکاکوم ... برکزیده ... باووتکا

خواهد برکرداند باووتکای ... باووتکاسون ... دیک ... باووتکاماس ... برکرداند

باولاماق بسکون واو و فتح لام و ضمن الرابع و مطیع ساختن باولادوق مطیع ساختیم باولادو ... مطیع ساختند ... باولاد

بمعنی حاصل و مصدر هم می آید باولاغان ... باولادرغان ... مطیع سازنده و ساختنده و بمعنی مصدر هم می آیند باولاو

باولاکور مفرد مخاطب ... باولاماغیل مفرد مخاطب ... باولاغایبین ... مطیع سازیم باولا

باولاب ... باولامیش مطیع ساخته باولامیشان مطیع ساخته باولاغا یمو آیا مطیع سازد باولاغاج چون مطیع ساخت

باولاغوچی مطیع سازنده باولاغوچیغه ... باولاغاغه ... مطیع ساختن و بمعنی آن باولاغوم مطیع خواهم ساخت باولاغونک

مطیع خواهی ساخت باولاغوسی مطیع خواهد ساخت باولاغای ... باولاسا ... باولاسون ... مطیع ... باولاماغو دیک ...

مطیع ساختنی است ... باوش بمعنی ... حلیم باشد چنانکه کوید شعر ...

... باشد و آن حلقه

بود ... باوچی بسکون واو و کسر جیم ...

که از برای ... باشد باوری بسکون واو و کسر راء ... باوشان

واو و نون ... چنانکه ... کوید شعر ...

... باشد ...

... باوغان بسکون واو و نون و فتح غین معجمه با الف کشیده ...

... چنانکه ... کوید شعر ... باوقان

باولاق بسکون واو و قاف و فتح لام ... دشمن ... نوشته باوو

بضم واو ... باشد باووز بضم واو و سکون زاء ... چنانکه ... کوید

در مناجات کوید شعر ... شعر

... باووغ و باووق بضم و بمعنی نزدیک باشد ... نقع

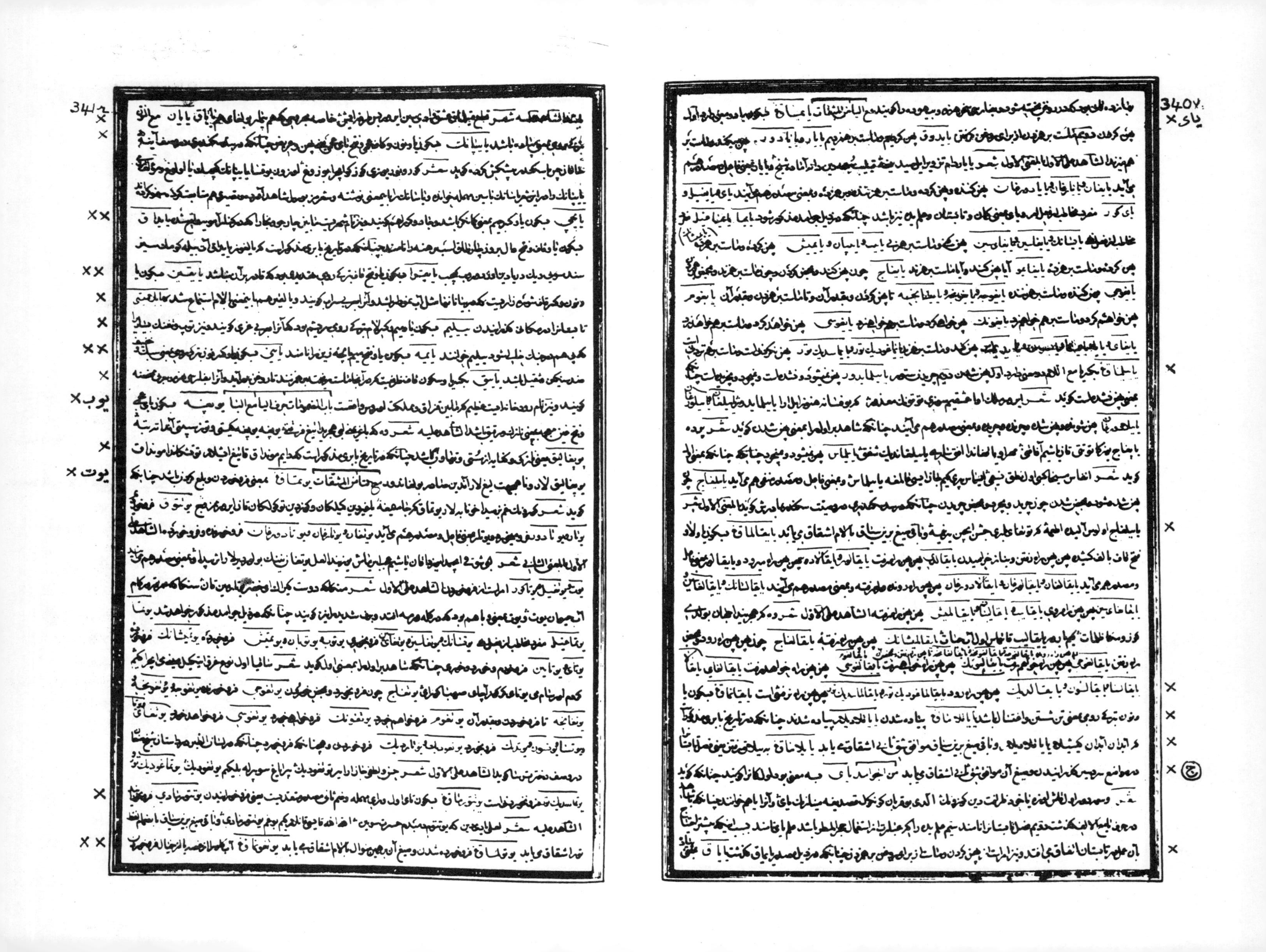

[illegible]

[illegible]

وصیغ آن با نون اشتقاق یابد یوتالماق منع تا وسکون لام سفر کردن یوتالدوک سفر کردیم یوتالو معو تالاجون سفر کنند یوتالید
معنی فاعل مستعمل می آید یوتالکای یوتالکان یوتالادوکان سفر کننده سفر کرده و معنی مصدر هم می آید چنانکه شاهد اول
در تاریخ بابری معنی مصدری مذکور است که آنشام ...
یوتالغو یوتالغیل و یوتالای کور سفر کن و یوتالغوسی سفر هم باشد یوتالماغای یوتالماجیل مفرد مخاطب یوتالسانک یوتالکای
یوتالکای مین سفر کنم یوتالیب یوتالیبان و یوتالمیش سفر کرده یوتالمیشانک فرمودند یوتالماس سفر نکند و معنی ...
منفی هم می آید یوتالکایمو ایا سفر کند یوتالکاج چون سفر کرد و بعضی گفته اند یوتالکوجی سفر کننده یوتالکوجه و یوتالکونچه
تا سفر کردن و مقدار آن یوتالکوم سفر خواهم کرد یوتالکونک سفر خواهی کرد یوتالکوسی سفر خواهد کرد یوتالکای یوتالا
یوتالسامو یوتالسون یوتالدیلک سفر کند یوتالماکودیک یوتالماسدیک تور سفر نکردند ...
...

...

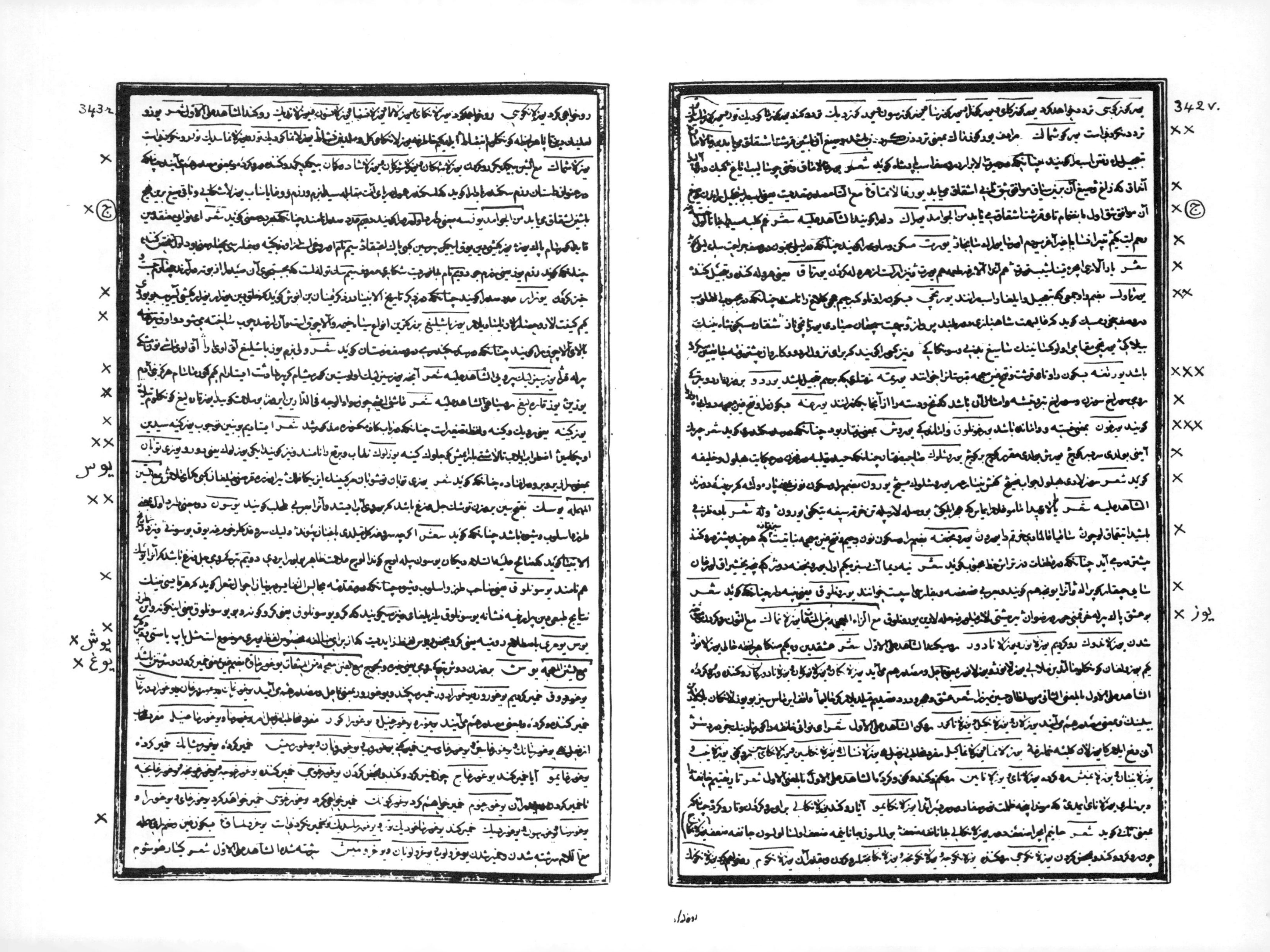

342v.

بیرکوزکوچی تردد خواهد کرد بیرکوز کلوی بیرکوز کتال بیرکوز [illegible] کوزسون [illegible] کوزدیلک قدمکند [illegible]

تردد نکرد خواست بیرکوشمالک مرادف بیرکوزماک بمعنی تردد کردن [illegible] قریشتا اشتقاق می‌یابد [illegible]

تحصیل نقش اسب کویند چنانچه در محبوب القلوب در وصف اسب [illegible] کوید شعر [illegible]

اتفاق که [illegible] آن [illegible] موافق [illegible] اشتقاق می‌یابد یورغالاماق مع الکاف [illegible]

آن موافق [illegible] تا قریشتا اشتقاق می‌یابد من الجوامد [illegible] الشاهد علیه شعر [illegible]

[illegible] یورت مسکن و ماوی را کویند چنانچه در لیلی و مجنون در صفت [illegible]

شعر [illegible] یورتاق [illegible] و تحصیل کند

[illegible] و ایلغار و اسب را نند یورتچی [illegible] چنانچه در محبوب القلوب

در وصف [illegible] کوید [illegible] شاهباز [illegible] صیادی [illegible] شقار [illegible]

[illegible] کویند که [illegible] سونکاکه [illegible]

باشد یورتمه بسکون راو تای قرشت و فتح [illegible] یورتمه [illegible] تحصیل باشد یوردو [illegible]

[illegible] باشد که [illegible] از آنجا [illegible] یورغه [illegible]

کویند یورغون بمعنی خسته و ماندگی باشد یورغونلوق [illegible] یوروش بمعنی رفتار بود چنانچه [illegible] کوید شعر [illegible]

[illegible] بیلوک [illegible] چنانچه [illegible] در حکایت بهلول و خلیفه

کوید شعر [illegible] بهلول [illegible] یوروشلوک [illegible] یوروت بضم [illegible] بسکون [illegible]

الشاهد علیه شعر [illegible] تیکی یوروت و له شعر [illegible]

[illegible] یوریمه بضم [illegible] بسکون نون و [illegible] که [illegible]

[illegible] آید چنانچه [illegible] کوید شعر [illegible]

[illegible] بیرغانلوق [illegible] چنانچه کوید شعر

[illegible] مع الزاء [illegible] مع النون [illegible]

شدن [illegible] الشاهد علی الاول شعر [illegible]

[illegible] آید [illegible]

الشاهد علی الاول المعنی الثانی [illegible] شعر [illegible]

[illegible] آید [illegible] الشاهد علی الاول شعر [illegible]

[illegible]

[illegible] الشاهد علی الاول [illegible] شعر [illegible]

[illegible] کوید شعر [illegible]

[illegible]

343r

روخواهی کرد یوزلانکوچی [illegible] روکند الشاهد علی الاول شعر [illegible]

[illegible]

یوزلانشماک مع الشین [illegible]

[illegible]

[illegible] اشتقاق می‌یابد من الجوامد [illegible] چنانچه [illegible] کوید شعر [illegible]

[illegible]

چنانچه کوید [illegible]

[illegible] یوزار [illegible] کویند چنانچه در تاریخ الانبیا در ذکر قینان بن انوش کوید [illegible]

[illegible] یوزباشلیغ [illegible]

[illegible] کویند چنانچه [illegible] کوید شعر [illegible] یوزباشلیغ [illegible]

[illegible] الشاهد علیه شعر [illegible]

[illegible] الشاهد علیه شعر [illegible]

یوزکینه [illegible] چنانچه [illegible] شعر [illegible]

[illegible] یوزلوک [illegible] یوزی تومان

[illegible] چنانچه کوید شعر [illegible]

[illegible] یوسک [illegible] کویند یوسون [illegible]

[illegible] باشد چنانچه کوید شعر [illegible]

[illegible] یوسون [illegible]

[illegible] یوسونلوق [illegible] چنانچه [illegible] کوید [illegible]

[illegible] یوسونلوق [illegible]

یوس یومری [illegible]

مع الشین المعجمه یوش [illegible]

[illegible] یوغان [illegible]

[illegible]

[illegible]

[illegible]

[illegible]

[illegible]

[illegible] الشاهد علی الاول شعر [illegible]

تاپخان ایلاچین اولیب قبری دیوارینی مکریکیم و یوقولوب تقری لاینی دین دیرنینک دانه و باقی صیغ برین سیاق بالالام اشتقاق

می یابد من الجوامد بوقانی یوخون خضم و سطبر چنانچه شاهد براولمی حبیه تلیبه در هجو کوید شعر کیم نامو غمی سیت

و بیو دوی یقان یوزجی آتو قوبی نی کرال تو قوقانی یوغروش بمعنی رشت و خمیر و بد یوغری اول نام بیناباب نیت نابین بیل النیغ

و خانبالیغ مع القاف بن المثقات یوقماق مکوب تاف بمعنی سرایت کردن یوقتی سرایت کرد چنانچه خسرو شیرین در مکالمه فرهاد

با نال مکاره کوید شعر مکر ارضد الری بولدی ظلم کیم یوقتی کونکلونکا آیینک غباری یوقار و یوقادور سرایت میکند

الشاهد علی الاول شعر یوقار یا تانلیغ آنکا کیم کرایا نان ایل الکو موراد ایلیک امرهان تمیلوم ایلیبی قرار دکه شعر کیم اهل

یوقار مین دیر جنون حالیمغه باغ کیم خرد اهلی اولوس نینک باعث سوداسی میش یوقنان و یوقار غان و یوقادوغان سرایت کننده و کرده

مصدر هم می آیند یوق و یوقتی و یوقا کور امراستان سرایت کردن و یوق بمعنی لا و نفی هم باشد یوقتلو و یوقاغیل هم لواستار

کردن یوقسانک و یوقسانین و یوقسای مین سرایت کنی یوقوب و یوقوبان و یوقتیش سرایت کرده الشاهد علی الثالث شعر زلبی

بینک جولجه پرله توب اول کوی عار اکریمیش که آفیش برکا یوقتی تامغه هر بیاعی قاز آنداز یوقتیش انک سرایت کرده یوقسا یمو آلماز

کند یوقماج چون سرایت کند و بحض کردن یوقتوبی سرایت کنده یوقتوجه و یوقتوبجه و یوقماغچه تا سرایت کردن و مقدار آن

یوقتوم سرایت خواهم کرد یوقتونک سرایت خواهی کرد یوقتوسی سرایت خواهد کرد یوقتای و یوقتایو و یوقسایو قسونی یوقدیک

سرایت کند و یوقسا بمعنی جامد دلرد که مصدر جوامد که خواهد شد یوقتودیک و یوقطودیک سرایت کردن و همچنانچه کنداشت

علی الاول المعنی الاول شعر باشیم چاپقان اول چابک باشینکا سلجغیل ای کوز کیم اولمحودین یوقار مین قارد یوقتودیک بولسام لیکن

سیاق شیرعینایت که قان یوقار دیک بولسا اول محودین قراکین یوقار مین یوقتلدیک توم یوقتماسیدیک تور سرایت خواهد نبات یوقتمان

بفتم تاف مع اللام سرایت کرده شدن و صیغ آن برین سیاق بالالام اشتقاق می یابد یوقلاماق دو معنی دارد اول تفحص کردن چنانچه کوید

شعر مشکل ایش توراو بدا برغاپیب هرم یوقلاماق لیک بحالت یوقلاغان دین سونکرا ایستاب یاناناق دویم کم نا پدید کردن

یوقلادوق تفحص کردیم و کم ناپدید کردیم یوقلادیم یوقلادور تفحص میکند و کم ناپدید میکند و یوقلادی بمعنی فاعل و مصدر هم می آیند

چنانچه بمعنی تفحص کننده کوید شعر نی عجب سیل الاحتام یوقلوقه مرهم ای کونکول کیم یوق اولسام یوقتور و ر یوقلادیکیم مرای

یوقلامان و یوقلاغان و یوقلایدورغان تفحص کننده و کرده و کم کننده و کرده و بمعنی مصدر هم می آیند یوقلا و یوقلاغیل و یوقلای کور مفرد

خاطبه فعل امر یوقلاما یوقلاماغیل مفرد خاطبه فعل نهی یوقلاسانک و یوقلاسای مین تفحص کنی و کم کنی یوقلاب و یوقلا

یوقلامیش تفحص کرده و کم کرده الشاهد علی الثالث المعنی الثانی شعر ایم اشیکین توکاتانک آ تغوجه مین دیلک سیر یوقلامیش

اول هم مکربیم مالمکره بیشی یوقلاسینا نتفحص کرده و کم کرده یوقلاغا یمو آیا تفحص کند و آیا کم کند یوقلاغاج چون تفحص کند

و بعض کردن یوقلاغوجی تفحص کننده و کم کننده یوقلاغوجه و یوقلاغونچه و یوقلاغانچه تا تفحص کردن و تا کم کردن و مقدار آن یوقلاغوم

تفحص خواهم کرد و کم خواهم کرد یوقلاغونک تفحص خواهی کرد و کم خواهی کرد یوقلاغوسی تفحص خواهد کرد و کم خواهد کرد

یوقلاغای و یوقلای و یوقلاسون و یوقلادیک تفحص کند و کم کند الشاهد علی الاول المعنی الاول شعر خاطریم ویرانلیغین سیلکای یراقلیغ

اول که مصلحت پرلوبی یوقلاغای ویرانیدا یوقلانماقولیک و یوقلانماق اسدیک تفحص کرد نخواست یوقلانماق مع النامه صیغه

بمعنی تفحص فرمودن و صیغ آن مستوریا ای قرینه اشتقاق می یابد یوقالماق نیست و معدوم شدن یوقالتماق مبکون اللام بامستقیم

بمعنی نیست و معدوم کردن من الجوامد یوق بمعنی نه باشد که آنرا بعربی لا کویند چنانچه کوید شعر یار دیرای یوق کونکول ملکی تور دور

سلطان یوق ملکه کیم سلطانی یوقتر جسمی و تیریکیم جانی یوق یوقتا بفتح بمعنی نازک بود و بالمجاز بچکوش ان شکافت که آنرا

نازک کرده بمروی نلج بیزند یوقتلی یوقتلاری بالانوق صله کنند الشاهد علی الاول شعر تانکلا باپاس پوسته تلشلار ظلم نینک

اوستیدا کیم پایی بپوسته مصحف دین یوتبار الاری یوقتلاری یوقتاینلو یوقتاسلو یوقسا بمعنی بوداملک معنی باکه آزادات توبیکی

استعمال شود دیم معنی ساند بسیم که معنی الاول کونر چنانچه شاهد برثانی بمعنی اول کوید شعر سلجوق دم اول کوزلام اخلاق هندی آ

نقطه دور جار خرا عینیوق ایسا جادو آستیدا الشاهد علی الثالث بالمعنی الاول شعر صعبا جشل ریشین توایه بابینینک خاخینی

یوقسا بویسا ایکلیک ناحیر آبیم دیزکیار الشاهد علی الثالث بالمعنی الثانی من خسرو شیرین شعر اکر بلقیس ملق یوقسا حلیر پیکی

خود ملانی قیلسا دیم الشاهد علی الثالث بالمعنی الثالث شعر خوش مین اشک ایجرا کیم عشقینک تنیمنی ایمرامیش یوقسا اوت

کیم کور دیکیم خاشاک ارا پنهان ایرور و یوقسا بمعنی سرایت کند هم باشد چنانچه کوید بیل یوقماق که ذش یوقتولغوقینه مفتوح

چنین اکویند یوقسول لوغ و یوقسوزلوغ و یوقسیزلیغ افلاس و بی چیزی چنانچه شاهد برثانی دارد در خالیم المحبه در فکر عادت شی کوید کر یوقتور

لوقمه صیدین عیال نینک بورونچالی کین آلیب بازار غه المیکان لبیمش کمر سانیب سیکولوک کیلتو رکای و نیز در دیباچه و قفیه ملک

کوید کر یوقتوز لوق شرابین قریداق کوتوب بیلدا جدی دیک پیش اهیکونزو الفانی حیف پیلکا لکاجه و شاهد بر تانله در نسبه

مجمع الفلوب کوید کر بیلدار لیغ لطف و کریمای بولنای بوقتیز لیغدا انکا بارجا ایل دریکام بولنای یوقتولوق بمعنی نیست چنانچه در فرهاد

خسرو شیرین کوید شعر او تومدا یوق تیر کیلیک مصری طالب توینیم یوقتولوق بیناسانی سرایب و نیز در دیباچه وقفیه کوید شعر عدم شا

یوقتولوق خلوتینده ایدی اینحکمیک اوبیقو مستولی ایردی آدم که آبین جینانه کمر ما سرا یردی توشیکا یل یوقا یردی آیدانو ثم یوقوش جکو

شین جهه جانب بلندی و فراز کوه و کریوه را نامند مع الکاف بن المثقات یوکلاماق بار کردن یوکلادوک بار کردیم یوکلادی و یوکلای

بار میکند و بمعنی فاعل و مصدر هم می آید یوکلاکان و یوکلاغان و یوکلاکیدورکان بار کننده و بار کرده و بمعنی مصدر هم می آیند یوکلا و یوکلای

یوکلای کور مفرد خاطبه فعل امر یوکلاما یوکلاماغیل مفرد خاطبه فعل نهی یوکلاسانک و یوکلاسای مین بارکنی یوکلاب و یوکلاب

یوکلامیش بار کرده الشاهد علی الاول شعر فراق ایجرا الف دیک قدیمغه خم ناغیتی یوکلاب اُحُد آستیدا قوی الینتا جسم ناتواننی یوکلادی

بار کرده ؟ یوکلاغایمو آیا بار کند یوکلاغاج چون بار کرد و کند و بعض کردن یوکلاغوجی بار کننده یوکلاغوجه و یوکلاغونچه و یوکلاغانچه تا بار

کردن و مقدار آن یوکلاغوم بار خواهم کرد یوکلاغونک بار خواهی کرد یوکلاغوسی بار خواهد کرد یوکلاغای و یوکلاسون و یوکلاسون

یوکلادیک بار کند چنانچه شاهد بر اطلاق در محبوب القلوب کوید کر خیر سیز غوغا طینین بیز حجاب و جمل سیز عالم دابه کر یوکلاکا یلدور آنکا

یوکلاغای دیک تونه یوکلاتماسدیک تیار نکرد نخواست یوکلاتماق مع التا مصدر متعدیست بمعنی بار فرمودن و صیغ آن مستوریا ای

قرینه اشتقاق می یابد یوکلانماق با هم بار کردن و صیغ آن باشین اشتقاق می یابد یوکلانماق مع النون بار شدن یوکلانکان و یوکلانغان

یوکلانادوکان بار شونده و بار شده و بمعنی مصدر هم می آید چنانچه شاهد بر اولش در فصل پنجم قسم از محبوب القلوب در وصف نوکرها

حلم بمک کوید کر ایرا نامحودین ملامت کناه و جرم فه یکلا یوکلانکان دین سونکرا ایستی یا امر لادو و باقی صیغ آن با نون اشتقاق

یوکورماک بضم کاف فارسی بمعنی دویدن یوکوردی دوید یوکوردی دوید یوکورادور میدود و یوکورودور بمعنی فاعل و مصدر هم می آید یوکو

یوکوریکان و یوکورکان دونده و دویده و بمعنی مصدر هم می آیند یوکور و یوکورکیل و یوکورکای کور مفرد خاطبه فعل امر یوکورما یوکورماغیل مفرد

خاطبه فعل نهی یوکورسانک و یوکورسای مین بدوی یوکوروب و یوکوروبان و یوکوریب دویده یوکورکان دویده و یوکورکایمو

آیا بدود یوکورکاج چون دوید و بدود و بحض دویدن یوکورکوجی دونده یوکورکوجه و یوکورکونچه تا دویدن و مقدار آن

344v.

بوکودکو مر خواهم دوید و یکره کونک خواهی دوید چنانکه در خسرو شیرین در مکالمهٔ صبا با حکیم تا فرهاد گوید شعر
چوکوز کو سرینی انکلاب بوکودکونکث کموب کوز کینه کودکونک هم کودکونک یوکره کوچی خواهد دوید یوکوکای ور کوزل و
یکره سالکم [illegible] کودیلک جمیعا الشاهد علی الاول شعر کوز یاشیم ولایه دوان اولنر کوز خادو کوروب طفل یکلیغ کیم سرکای
هوا و هو کوروب بو کمرنا کودیلک تورو یوکوز یاسدیلک تو تدیغ حالت یوکوز تالک بعنی کافیجی سکوز ماه [illegible] وتای فرشته مثل
شعکیت بعنی دوانیدن یوکوز تامین [illegible] الشاهد علی الثالث شعر عشق جمشید ا
بوکودتودمین قوینا کورا آهدیث [illegible] بوطرفرنی مجنون جیرات تاپلدوز یوکودتوبه یوکوز تهان [illegible] دوانیدن چنانکه شاهد
اوکرا معنی تان در خسرو شیرین در مصراع گوید شعر چیکیم انده های کنج مقصود یوکودتوبا یلدابان بوبیغی تابوتغیز [illegible]
سنکر اشوغ فرهاد گوید شعر بابی چون سالیبتین [illegible] یوکوز توب تله قلامت سالری یوکوز تکا [illegible] یوکوز سالا
یوکوز [illegible] یوکوتیه کلام بدوانند چنانکه شاهد اولرا معنی ثانی در فصل پیت و منتم از محبوب القلوب جون کراصل صنعت گوید
اتیش تانک هدین آقشام فحه جمال شد صنعت سازو هنر المولی فنون پرداز شعر ایلدابان بوطرفنی وندوش که پرالیکا یوکوز [illegible]
وتاق صیغ بزن یاق با تای فرشته اشتقاق می یابد یوکوتکالک با یکدیکر دویدن و صیغ آن باشین اشتقاق می یابد یوکوتالد یعنی کاف و
نون زانو بزمین زدن از برای تعظیم و حصول مرادات که چون بخدمت سلاطین روند در مقام سلام زانو بزمین زده تسلیمات کنند و نیز
ارباب حاجت زانو نشسته عرض مطلب نمایند و این عمل را اتراک یوکونماک کویند و عراقیان با بوس نامند چنانکه در تاریخ بابری مذکور
آمدن دولت خان [illegible] مذکور است که یوکوتماک انا خیر قیلدی [illegible] یوکوندو [illegible] و بالمجاز معنی
کردن هم می آید یوکوندی زانو بزمین زد و عرض کرد چنانکه در لیلی مجنون در عروسی مجنون و نصحت نوفل گوید المصراع الاول شعر
چو یسمر کیلین کیوی اشوندیم توتیرکا کو یا دکو یوکوندی و بیزیم سلکندری در شکری که ایندن خانانز چی گوید شعر حابین
ایتیب شه سالی یکتی لارث [illegible] دولت ارکان عرض اتی لارث چو عرض اولدی خاقان یوکوندی جوان یوکوندی نیه خسرو نوجوان یوکوزود
[illegible] یوکونادور زانو بزمین میزند و یوکوندی معنی حاصل مصدر هم می آید یوکونکان [illegible] یوکونادمکان زانو بزمین زننده و نیز معنی
مصدر هم می آید یوکون و یوکونکلی یوکونادور مفرد خاطب التفضل امر یوکوغا [illegible] یوکونماسل مفرد خاطب النفضل یوکوناماسو یوکونکلی
یوکونکالیین زانو بزمین زدم و عرض کردم چنانکه شاهد بزاك معنی اول در تاریخ بابری مذکور است که مقرتدی افت ابیکیم او معنی کاج
یوکانکان بوکونو یوکونوبان [illegible] زانو بزمین زده چنانکه شاهد بر او لطف در خاتمهٔ حیرة الابرار گوید شعر شاقلاب
شطیخلنا دونوث الیمه توتغوکو نیب باده نوث یوکونتیلک زانو بزمین زده یوکونکایمو آیا بزمین زند یوکونکاج چو نقل نوبتی
زده میزند و چون عرض کند چنانکه در سد سکندری گوید شعر یوکونکاج تیلا جیشاه مرورنی اوزایتیکالم دلم [illegible] یوکونکوچی
زانو بزمین زننده یوکونکوچی یوکونکوده یوکونکاغه تا زانو بزمین زدن و مقدار آن یوکونکوم زانو بزمین خواهم زد یوکونکولک زانو
بزمین خواهی زد یوکونکوچی زانو بزمین خواهد زد یوکونکای یوکونکا یوکو [illegible] یوکونکونون یوکونکولیک زانو بزمین زنید و [illegible]
زانو بزمین زد [illegible] یوکوندورماک مصدر متعدیست زانو نشانیدن از برای تعظیم و تعلیم و امثال آن معنی عرض کنانیدن هم آید یوکوندورد
زانو نشانید و عرض کنانید چنانکه در سد سکندری معنی ثانی در عرض شکر خاقان چین گوید شعر آلیب یوکوندوراق سیوندی
دیلی شه الیدا توتو یوکونیو چیلیغی و تاتی صیغ بزن یاق با ما اشتقاق می یابد یوکوندورمالک زانو نشانیده شد یوکوندوز
ایدی زانو نشانیده شده بود چنانکه در تاریخ بابری مذکور است که اکثرا ایچکیلاری کیم تونوبت کالدابسلا لیک کا یوکوندورولوب

345r.

بوقامچنانلار نینک کینی جبه قاوشونچی آیچدوق و تاقی صیغ بزن یاق با لام اشتقاق می یابد من الجوامد یوک بار شتر و نحو ما را گویند ویقال
آهو باشد با الای تیمرهند دوکشته بار اترا آرتوپند بیرکوج بر امر کوچک تیز [illegible] چنانکه این یلدم بنهند را گویند یوکو دوش
یعنی دویدن یوکورک منا صبیدر و یوکباک می گون هرچه کاف و فتح سین بمعنی میوه بلند در تعجب آنرا او کنا العم [illegible] چنانکه
یوکوک منم سین بمعنی بزرگ و می انکشو انهخیال می باشد یوکوش بمعنی نیلی باشد چنانکه فضولی ضبطی گوید ایاک ارتونیه
توکوبی جام می دستنی تمنا سین حق طلب دین یوکوش الارتوکوب خالمدی قتغا پیمیکدنک دوت در صحبت اهل جنسان کوش سمت
چنانکه در حسن دیباچه اقام ترکیبات یلما قع یکون لام بمعنی کند تحو و پر بود که آنرا بعربی تفنگ گویند چنانکه خواجه خسرو شیرین
در صف سفید یعنی مجالس گوید شعر آنی اضطالتسیکت بیلماقی عید شافال یلماق قدر لعل ناعیدا و کند بلبل دلو نماق کوک
زمین را قاق ناقد و کند آن بیخ و مصیبت و اشیا آنرا انجا دیو بیماق حقیقت نیز رانکوا نند یلدوق موکنیم یولانعو لاد نیک کندیکلی
بمعنی حاصل مصدر هم می آید و ترکیبو هم کنا دوبمک بمعرت [illegible] زنند یلغان هو لاغان دو یلادو رغان موکنرم و کنز دو بمعنی مصدر هم
می آید یوکبوقیل ویو لاکو ن امیشلار کدن دو بمعنی هم باشد و این مرحبت پیماو یماقیل مفرد خطاب النفضل هم
یوکسانک یو تفاسین یعنی یلغای سین موهکی یولوبه بولوبان هو یلمش کنت الشاهد علی الاول شعر یولوب پنهان توشیک
یه بیکانین بیغیب یوکلمش اوقونک سینغا لهرین کیا بانا یلغان او چون ناوک یولمش الت موکنه یولغایمو آیا موکنیلغا
چون موبکند و معنی کندن یولغوچی موکننده یولغوجه یولغوغه بولغانجه تا موکندن و مقدار آن یولغوم میخواهم کند
یولغونک میخواهی کند یولغوچی میخواهد کند یولغای یولادیولغای یولاوبوسنا ویونونون یولدیک میکند یلمادیک تورم سلاسیک
مونکند نیست یولدورماق مصدر متعدیست و صیغ آن با لفظ عمل اشتقاق می یابد یولوغماق مع النون میوکند شدن و صیغ آن
با نون اشتقاق می یابد یولاماق بمعنی لام مع الکاف بمعنی راه طی دادن یولاتوق راه دادیم یولاتوبعیولاتادو رله سیدهند ویولاتور یعنی
تا حاصل مصدر هم می آید یولاتغان ویولاترغان یولاتا دورغان راه دهنده و راه داده و بمعنی مصدر هم می آید یولاتعو یولاتغیل و یولاتاکو
مفرد خاطب النفضل امر یولاتما ویولاتماغیل مفرد خاطب النفضل هه یولاتسانک ویولاتغایسین و یولاتغایسین راه بدهی یولاتیب ویولاتیبان یولاتیش
راه داده یولاتیشانک راه داده یولاتغایمو آیا راه بدهی یولاتقاج چون راه دهد و چون راه داده یولاتغوچی راه دهنده
یولاتغوجه یولاتغوغه ویولاتغانجه تا راه دادن و مقدار آن یولاتغوم راه خواهم داد یولاتغونک راه خواهی داد یولاتغوچی راه خواهد داد
یولاتغای و یولاتغایلار یولاتاسون یولاتادیک راه میدهد چنانکه مولانا هاشم در محبوب القلوب در توجیهکر گوید که دنیا و آخرت سفاهت
عرض قیلسالار رسید یقالدور آتین جلوه [illegible] لار سالک اول یا نظر اوقیس آتما غایش دکونکلیکا آخرتینک ره فتولیس مطلقا یولاتماغای
یولاتمادیک یولاتما سدیک نیاز ندارد [illegible] یولداماق راه نمائی کردن و پیراهن یولدادوق راهنمائی کردیم یولدا و یولدایدیک
راهنمائی میکند و یولداغوچی راهنما و بمعنی مصدر هم می آید یولدا غان ویولداغا ن و یولدا یدور غان راهنمائی کننده کرده و بمعنی مصدر هم
می آید یولدا غیل یولدا مغیل مفرد خاطب النفضل امر الشاهد علی الاول من حیرة الابرار فی النعت شعر المخضوعان لطف برله قولنی توت
دالیاو نجاتیغه بولدا یولوم یولدا سلو یولدا ماغیل مفرد خاطب النفضل یولداسانک یولداغایسین یولداغایسین راهنمائی کنی یولدا
یولدایانی مویونیلش راهنمائی کرده الشاهد علی الاول من حیرة الابرار فی المعراج شعر رقاص دل آنکه بقبول یولداب یایدی کیلکان سا
آنی یولداب یولدایشانک راهنمائی کرده یولداغایمو آیا راهنمائی کند یولداقاج چون راهنمائی کند و چون راهنمائی کرد یولدغوچی
راهنمائی کننده یولداغوجه یولداغوغه ویولداغانجه تا راهنمائی کردن و مقدار آن یولداغوم راهنمائی خواهم کرد یولداغونک راهنمائی

خواهی کرد یولداغوی واهنکاری خواهد کرد یولداغلو یولداشلیغی یولداشون یولداشلیك واهمکاری کنده ییلداشلو دیك قدیم یولداشلیك
راهنمائی نکرده خواست یولوقماق بمعنی دچار شدن ناشدن الشاهد علیه شعر جهان کوزنی هرنشه کمجانانغه یولوقمیلای
مشقوق کرا اولوك جانغه یولوقی یولوقدی یولوقادور دچار میشود یولوقوبمعنی فاعل مصدر هم می آید یولوقمان ویولوقغان
یولوقادورغان دچار شونده دچار شده بمعنی مصدر هم می آید یولوقیولو نسبی یولوقا کرد المطلب از کند یولوقون موی
کنده هم باشد چنانکه مذکور خواهد شد یولوقتلو یولوقماعیل مفرد خطاب فاعل یولوقمانك یولوقماس یولوقمای
دچار شوی یولوقوب یولوقوبان یولوقمیش دچار شده یولوقمیشنلك دچار شدن یولوقماغیمو آیا دچار شود یولوقماج چون دچار شد
وشود وبعضی شدن یولوقی دچار شونده یولوقونچه یولوقونچه یولوقمانچه تا دچار شدن ووقت دچار شدن چنانکه
درسیدن فرهاد شاپور بارمنیه کوید الشاهد علی الثانی ما المعنی الاول شعر تملشا ایلادیو یولسون خوانینك یولوقونچه
طلب قیلغانی مقامینك یولوقغوم دچار خواهم شد یولوقغونك دچار خواهی شد یولوقغوسی دچار خواهد شد یولوقمای ویولوقمای
ونقیض یولوقمای دچار شود یولوقغودیك تقدیر یولوقماسدیك توبولوقمشدنی است یولوقوق یولوقماق بضم لام والف مع السین بیکر
دچار شدن یولوقوشتی لار بهم دچار شدند چنانکه در فصل ششم از محبوب القلوب در حکایت کم شدن کوه تلخ خسرو کوید
که چون در طلب ایلکا یادوشتی لار داملخلوقنی باشلاب جیقغانی کیشیکا یولوقوشتی لار یولاق بریناق باشین اشتقاق می یابد
من الحوامد یول بمعنی راه وطریق بود ومابجای راه سلوك را کویند ونیز امر است از کذن موی چنانکه کذشت یولاد بفتح لام وسکون
دال مهمله ترکیست روسی مصالح تیغ وافسانه وامراکویند ونیز بمعنی موی میکند وبمعنی موکنده وموکند نیز هم می آید چنانکه مذکور شد
یولاوچ بفتح لام بالف کشیده وضم واو وسکون جیم مشهورست اهنا ... شبها نامند یولبارس جانوریست درنده از شیر ویلنك بزرکتر
برنك شیر ومخططات وسیلهای ... خوانند وارال بیلریه باشد وبعضی از نسخ ... بابا سریا ...
ومعنی سیر ذکر کرده سهوکرده یولجی بمعنی راهرو ومسافر باشد چنانکه در مقاله دهم از سیر الاخیار ... کوید شعر
یولچه توز یولچیغه مقصد ... توشاپراق ... خاتم ... داکوید شعر
خاتم طی کوردکر بوخلی سیلة یولچی ... شعر ... غلط یکجا ...
مفهومه ذکر کرده ویکجا ... یکجا یا وجه ... بمعنی ...
ودر ... جامی شعر ... یوچین ... اوهم ...
استشهاد ... ومعنی ... نیز نوشته ... ووجه اشتقاق ایشان
که هریك ... نسخه ...
سقیم غلط خوانده وبعضی ... نوشته اند ویولداش بمعنی رفیق وهمراه چنانکه کوید شعر قالدی ... یولداش ...
عشق یولینه ... یولداش ... کویند ... که ...
وادوسادر ... است یولدوز توزتی برکوکسکم ... کویند ... وسلوك چنانکه
... کوید شعر توشتی ... یولیغی ... طریق ...
که ... کویند ... است یولغون توزغی ... چوب ...
کرمانج ... تام ... ولایت خوارزم ... واقع ...

یوم

موکند کویند چنانکه ... شعر یاتابکلاریکم ... ولولوق ... بولوق
ونیز امر است از بخیل شدن چنانکه ... یولوم ... یولی بکسر لام بمعنی راه چنانکه ...
یلقوس کوید شعر کوروندی ... دیوانه ... کاشانه وکویند که پر ... الشاهد علیه شعر
کونکلدین بولماس ... هرنچه کیم ... بلا ... چنانکه ...
مذکور شود مع المیم من المشتقات یوماق بهم نهادن چشم ودهن را کویند ولی لفظ خصوص پوشیدن چشم ودهن استعمال شود
وبا چشم یا دهن ... کوید شعر قدح ... آغزینك ... کوزی ...
نوایغه ... بهم نهاد یومار ویومادور بهم می نهد ویوماق بمعنی فاعل مصدر هم می آید یوماغان ویوماغان ...
بهم نهاد ... یوماکودا از ... بهم نهادن چشم ... الشاهد علی الاول
شعر ای نوای ... تیلیل ... یوماغیل مفرد خطاب
یومسانك یومغاین یومغای ... یوموب یوموبان یومیش بهم نهاده یومیشانك بهم نهاده یومای یومایین
الشاهد علی الثانی المعنی الاول شعر ... کوزنی ... یومار ...
آیا بهم نهد یومغاچ چون بهم نهد ... یومغونچه یومغوچه تا چشم بهم نهادن
بمعنی آن چنانکه شاهد ... مصرع کوید شعر ... آچیب ...
بلیهث یومغوم بهم خواهم نهاد یومغونك بهم خواهی نهاد یومغوسی بهم خواهد نهاد یومای ...
یوماخودیك ... بهم نهادن است یوماشماق بضم میم مع اللام بهم نهاده شدن چشم ودهن یوشلماس بهم نهاده
میشود چنانکه کوید ... شعر ...
هم می آید ... اشتقاق ... یومالاماق بفتح میم ولام بالف کشیده وسکون ... مصدر ...
غلطانیدن یومالاتوق غلطانیدیم یومالاتور یومالاتادور میغلطانند ویومالاتقوچی بمعنی فاعل ومصدر هم می آید یومالاتغان
یومالاتدورغان غلطاننده وبمعنی مصدر هم می آید یومالات یومالاتغیل یومالاتاکو مفرد خطاب یومالاتمای
مفرد خطاب ... یومالاتسانك یومالاتماس ... یومالاتیب یومالاتیبان یومالاتمیش غلطانیده چنانکه
... ونکر کرده ... کشیکا ... یومالاتیب ...
غلطانیده یومالاتغایمو آیا بغلطاند یومالاتغاج چون غلطاند ... یومالاتغوچی غلطاننده یومالاتقوچه یومالاتقونچه
یومالاتغانچه تا غلطانیدن ... یومالاتغوم ... غلطانید یومالاتغوسی ...
یومالاتاخودیك ... یومالاماق مع النون ... یومالانماق غلطان شدن چنانکه
... تیکسچه ... یومالاناکیلدی ...
... اشتقاق می یابد یوشاماق یعنی نرم شدن ... اللام ... می آید ...
یوموشادوق نرم شدیم یوموشادور نرم میشود یوموشاغان ... بمعنی فاعل مصدر هم می آید یوموشاغان ...
یوموشایدورغان نرم شونده ونرم شده بمعنی مصدر هم می آید یوموشا یوموشاغیل ... مفرد خطاب ... یوموشاماغیل
مفرد خطاب ... یوموشامای یوموشامیش نرم شده یوموشامیشلك نرم شدن

یوشاغامو آیا نرم شود یوشاغاج چون نرم شد وشود ومجس شدن یوشاغوجی نرم شونده یوشاغوجه ویوشاغوجه ویوشاغانه
تا نرم شده وبعد از آن یوشاغوم نرم خواهم شد یوشاغونك نرم خواهی شد یوشاغوسی نرم خواهد شد یوشاغای ویوشاسا
یوشاسون ویوشادیك نرم شود الشاهد علی الاول شعر بر کوزلاحیم دین اوشول بد مهر کونکلی یوشاغای نجکیم فولاد
ایمه طاینغ تاپاراوت تین کلدی الشاهد علی الثانی شعر کونکلی دین ترلالس محبت جوهرین میلماق قطع هرنجه کیم یوشاناپر بولسه
پولاد املادی یوشاناخودیك تورو یوشالماسیلیترم نشد نرم است یوشاتماق مع التا مصدر متعدیست یعنی نرم کردن یوشاتیش
نرم کرده چنانکه در خسرو وشیرین کوید شعر دلدار تو توب کوزدا وجیدین یاش کرخاراکی نچوك یوشاتمیش الماس وباقی صیغ
آن بانضمام تای قرشت اشتقاق می یابد یوموریماك بضم میم وسکون رای مهمله یعنی خراب کردن وبعضی یومورماك بجیم نیز مستعمل ودر صیغ
همین تا مدام معانست یوموردی خراب کرد الشاهد علیه شعر هجری دین تو فراغ بولدیم کویا الشکیم سوینی باشیما چرخ کهن
طامتین یوموردی بوکچه یوموروروی یومورادور خراب میکند ویومورمق یعنی فاعل ومصدر هم می آید یومورکان ویومورغوچی یومورادیدر
خراب کننده وخراب کرده چنانکه شاهد بر اولار معنی ثانی در سکندرنامه در وصف فیلقوس کوید شعر کوروندی بیله
اوزره ویرانه یومورکان فلك ظلم کاشانه ومعنی مصدر هم می آید یومورو ویومورکیل یومورای سفرد خطاب فصل الله یومورسا یاکید
مفرد خطاب فصل الله یومورمانك یومورکاسیجا یومورکای بین خرابکنی یومورو یومورمای ویومورمیش خراب کرده یومورمیشانك خراب
کرده یومورکایمو آیا خراب کند یومورکاج چون خراب کرد وکند وخراب کردن یومورکوجی خراب کننده یومورکوجه ویومورکانجه
تا خراب کردن وبعد از آن یومورکوم خراب خواهم کرد یومورکونك خراب خواهی کرد یومورکوسی خراب خواهد کرد یومورکای ویومورسا
یومورسون ویومورودیك خراب کند یومورماکودیك تو یعنی یومورماسدیك تو خراب نکردی است یومرو لما لسعکون میم ولام وضم رای
مهمله ویومرو وشمزات مع الثین یعنی خراب شدن ونکیا نیز مستعملست یومرولدی خراب شد چنانکه شاهد
اوکلار در صفت شاه در وصف کارکاه خرابه کوید شعر ایله یومرولدی بیرکه یوزمینك خیل فیلدیلار بربیلی سو قرتیغه
میل ودیناقی صیغ بدستور از یمرولماك بالام ولنز یومرولماك باشین اشتقاق می یابد وبجکیا نیز استعمال نشوند من الجوامد یوناق کلنج
رخ را کوینند وبمعنی شستن هم باشد چنانکه در حرف یا مع الواو مذکور خواهد شد یوناداق غلطك باشد وآن چوبی باشد که
سبلغ نمرك که آنرا پاینه موافقه کنند وهر چیز مدور را کویند که بشکل کوی غلطان باشد یوراان موش را کویند چنانکه در
سکندرنامه در خطاب پادشاه کشیر یا بکنمه صد لادافو نکران کوید شعر که کرفته یتسا املاکدین میلوم بر یورای بیلکه
فنون پرله بیمرلفی شیرباتی کونبره صلاحیدا بیرپاساه یوراغجی مرغ موش کیمر ناسند یوران تاذیق نام نوعی از موش بزرکیست
ودر مدد یوروف مثت یوروقینه یعنی شستن وغنیه لقلیست که در مقام تصغیر استعمال نشود چنانکه کوید شعر
یوزا وباركا قوینادی بیلکین دیدیم باریلی وباقی تاشلاجان یوروقینه میلاری کونیلی کولبکینه یورولکو یعنی خراب ویران یوشاق
نرم یوشاقلیغ نرمی الشاهد علیه شعر کردیسانك تاتیغ بلاحنه تا الماقای بین جوغ دین طالم اجلی پرله یوشالمیش بیله قمیلمیش لقماغ
یومورتقه بضم میم وسکون راء وتای قرشت وقاف مضموم بیضه را کویند چنانکه در تاریخ الملوك در وصف تاج خسرو پرویز کوید که مینك
کومیله مکللی ایدیکیم هر بیر چونچه تی یومورتقه سیچه یوموف چشم ودهن بر هم نهاده را کویند مع النون من المشتقات
یونماق مع النون تراشید نجوب ولنا الآنرا کویند وتراشیدن هم وچشم وامثال آنرا مرقان نامند یوندوق میتراتیم یوناد قوناددور
میتراشید دیونه یعنی فاعل ومصدر هم می آید یونقان ویونارغان ویوناد ورغان تراشنده وتراشیده ومعنی مصدر هم می آید یونقوچیل

یونکور ویونماغین
امراست از تراشیدن ویون بمعنی یو وشامان وآلستکی هم باشد چنانکه مذکور خواهد شد یونغا ویونغاچیل فعل ملازم تراشیدن یونغان
یونغاچین تراشیم الشاهد علی الاول شعر عشق طونی بیزنشان تا الغاندین ایل حاجانیم آلکوذی یوقسا کیماس تیغ ایله یوغسلم نشان کوپرالعتالغیر یونوب
یونوبان ویونغیش تراشیده یونغانك تراشیدی یونغایمو آیا بتراشد یونغاج چون تراشید وبعد تراشید ونجس تراشیدن یونغوچی تراشنده
یونغوجه ویونغوچه ویونغانجه تا تراشیده وبعد از آن یونغوم خواهم تراشید یونغونك خواهی تراشید یونغوسی خواهد تراشید یونغای
یونالا ویونغاسالار ویونغونالدی وبیدیر کلکه تراشند الشاهد علی الاول شعر تا یوقوش کیم قلم ییکیچونی الوزره ایرمه تن صنعفیدین قوشدیك
کمیولغا یلدی حلاح الوزره یونغاخودیك تورو یونغاسیلیترتیشد نیست یوندورماق مصدر متعدیست یعنی تراشانیدن وصیغ آن بانضمام الفظ
در اشتقاق می یابد یونولماق بضم نون مع الکم یعنی تراشیده شدن وصیغ آن بالالام اشتقاق می یابد من الجوامد یونت دشمن ودد
اوکده را کویند وحیم بمعنی امان وآلستکی بود ونیز امراست از تراشیدن چنانکه کذشت ودر لغت بیعنی عند ونمدزین بوملس وطلوس وسرایك و
کویند ونیز نام سبخانه است یونت مادیان را کویند ونیز نام سالیست از سال های ترکی یونت قوینی ترکی وی نام پرنده ایست کوچك که آنرا
بعربی صنعوه نامند یونغه علوفات سبز خاری که باسب دهند وآنرا یونجه هم کویند چنانکه مذکور شد یونغه ترکی دی آنرا
بود کما زهم تیشه درزان نجاران درزد یونلت بسکون نون وکاف عجمی سر طیور وچشم حیوانات را کویند چنانکه در لیلی ومجنون در وصف بلبل
سپاه کوید شعر اوت ۲ بونکی شمیم التحیت آنفلاج اوتوبان تو هزفالدین ونیز صیغه مفرد خطاب است از فصل یونیماق چنانکه
باشاهد در حرف یا مع الواو مذکور مصدر یوناق مذکور خواهد شد یونکول بسکون نون مع الالف الموضع کاف عجمی بمعنی سبك باشد وآنرا
سنکیل هم کویند یونه بفتح نون تکلموی مزین بود وآنرا توقصم هم خوانند مع الواو یوما قع بالاشباع یعنی شستن چنانکه کوید شعر
محابح که خلق کا هین یوماشه ابرکتی یا غار جلدا ایماس نیده وبلر سنان الحوط وکلاه نیز را هم کویند چنانکه مذکور جامد حرف یا مع الیم کذ
یوددوق شستیم یورو یویدور میشوید الشاهد علی الاول شعر دم دهر بیغه نی سیلیکاه چون یوراشکیم صفحه نی اول مسلفر سار کاوی
یکیم رقم فیلسام پیتك ونیز بمعنی فاعل ومصدر هم می آید چنانکه شاهد آن لفرشته سکندری بمعنی صدری در باب الهم مفتوحه مذکور باشد
یومذکور شد یوبایوری یوغیو یدوراری میشست چنانکه شاهد بر اولار در خسرو شیرین در سوکواری شیرین کوید شعر سر شکی تا لخی یونسا
دین آلماشی هما تا کیم یودایری تا بیله تان یوغان ویوغان تونیه یوغان شوینده وشسته چنانکه شاهد بر اولار بمعنی اول کوید شعر
یو قی شفق ظلم ملیضه خالیب یری یسم آرین یوغان بحر اشکیم محو جین کولالدامیش یو ویوخیل ویوی کود امراست از شستن الشاهد علی
الثانی شعر مکحل اینساکونکول لیشه سیون هر نیغم تو ایا بکیل یوخیل تیح زلال ایله یوماکو یوناغیل نهی است از شستن یونك و
یوکوز ویو یخلوس جمیع خطاب فصل امر الشاهد علی الاول شعر باده پرله یونك تو ایغیحما مرتبه هلاطه با غلاجیکر احتیاب اصحاب تحل برکت تا کیم
الشاهد علی الثالث شعر جومستا طلعوم ادیلب بیله یونکوز بنیم تا نیکنك اوشا لغان فشیم بیلیکا رشته نا لدی یونك بمعنی یوغوشم
هم باشد چنانکه مذکور جوامد حرف یا مع النون مذکور شد یونانك ویوما نیکدو یوما نکلار جمع خطاب فصل امر یوغیبن ویوریب و
یویغورین میشوید چنانکه شاهد برثانی در صفة الکبیر لحجه الابرار در نعت امامان کوید یوغیبن ایلیك تا نینکا یعنی که بن قصد
ایتلین جانینکا یعنی که تو یوسانك ویوغاسین ویوغای بین بشوید تو ویوبان ویومیش شسته چنانکه کوید الشاهد علی الاول
شعر تولسا جانك نوای دیر ایرابی پرله یوپ باشی نیناك خم کمر بهر خسته مزاریغ بلاجین یومیشانك شسته یوی یوبین بشویم و
وبشوی وشسته ویوی لعل زهیبت وتا بعد کردن هم باشد چنانکه مذکور صدر یو یماق کذشته یوبای ویومایین نشوم ونشوید ونشوی وشسته
چنانکه شاهد بر اولار بمعنی اول کوید شعر دم ایتیب حالیغه با قشا کوزیا شیغه سیبز فهده یوماینکیز کیسن لوا دم عشق طایماندین بیلیك

بوغامو آیا بشوید بوسنا که بوغابزه بوغای بزه بوله بوتینک بشوید الشاهد على الرابع شعر اعنواول ایلسانک بولماق بوغیتینک
لوحلوک می جوین کیلتمرکیم آنی خیرنفشیدین بیله بوغلبی براوشتن وتاشته بوغاج چوزشت وشوید وبجنبشتن بوغوچ
شوید بوغوجه وبوغوبجه وبوغایخه مالشتن وبمعنی آن بوغوم خواهشت بوغونلک خواهشت بوغوچی خواهدشت
بوغاغ بولا بوسنا وبوسون وبوزدیک بشوید الشاهد على الاول شعر نوایلسکرادیبار که بنی بوزدین بوغایدات وحسرت بیله
توکولسا یاشیم وشاهد بغلس داد وتوجه که بوغاده دوشتن نانی بقاش نقوش را کوید شعر چیکیب توسحی ایتیب جیلاو بیناد بوغلیک
بلشتین ایاغ تغفاد ونقاش بوتلفودیک توحد بغلیک تشولست بوحدم تاغ مصدر متعدیست بمعنی شولیدن وبمعنی آن بمعنی ابتما
منظ دمر اشتقاق می یابد بوروملاتغ بضم واو ومع الکلم بسنی شته شدن وبمعنی آن بوزماق بضم واو مع الکلم موافق تو اول الشقا
می یابد بوالاخفاق بغیو والاعتاق بمعنی طلاندن باشد وآنرا بوسالاتاق هم کویند چنانچه بالصیغ در حروف یا مع المیم مذکور شد وصیغ
اینها هم بمعان سابق اشتقاق یافته مبدلیم آن واو داخل میشود من الجوامد بوا بمعنی اشیانه طیور بود که آنرا سبه کرد
حشو ومعرض کویند چنانچه ضوبلی کوید یا به الزینه شعر دیمالک بجنونلار قاشوکیم بلشند قوش بوادوعیش بنم قاشق کم
سیل اشیکو بابشید آشیوروعش فنزلیم طایفه ایسا زارلک بوداق بفتح واو ولام بالف کشیده بترکی روی جنی کلو لمه کوی ...
بودوسفه بضم واو وسکون بین مهمله وفتح غین معجمه منسل بودن کویند بودوش بضم واو وسکون شین معجمه تمام بود که از ابطال ...
وخامه نامند بوعد ودر بضم واو ودال مهمله وسکون نون سن که ...

جوبیم وچیدعم کرده باشد بوبیدوق ... بوکیم بو بایعقو بیادور ... سنده هم می آید بوبیسغا ... بوایغان ...
... جوکنده وجوکرده وبمعنی مصدر هم می آید ... مفهم مخاطب ... بوبیماو بوبیما حیل مفرد مخاطب ...
بوبیسانک جوبیغلسین جوبیغای ... بوبوب ... جوکرده بوبیسانک جوکرده بوبیامو آیا جوکند بوبیاج چون جو
کرد وکنده جوکن کوغه بوبغوچی جوکننده بوبغوجه بوبغوبجه وبوبیغایخه ما جوکرده وبمعنی آن بوبغوم جوخواهم کرد بوبغونک جو
که بوبغوچی جوخواهد کرد بوبیغای جوبیا جوبیاولدین وبوبیدیک جوکند نیست خواهد کند بوبیامودیک ... بوبیغا ...
جو مصدر معدم شدن بوبولمی جوشد چنانچه مخمرشیرین ... الشاد شیرین جوشاکوید شعر وجودینی ...
کونکول نیننک هم وجدیکین ... بوبیلغای جو بولا ... وچمعدم شد چنانچه شاهد ... الاعلی

الابرار کوید شعر خامه بیلیم ... اولوب ... نامه بوبتصدین هم اولوب ... تو شماره ... وا ... آیلدی ...
قراوثا ... صیغ بوبیسانک بالام اشتقاق می یابد ... حروف ... الکتاب من المثات بیسار نانک بمعنی فرستادن باشد بیسارلدی ...
بیساردو بیسارا دور میفرستد وبیسارو ... مستقبل هم می آید چنانچه بمعنی ... کوید شعر ...
... اولدیان ایلوف ... بیسار ... کاقیلاحین قطع حیات ... بیسارکان و بیسارا دوکان فرستاده شد و فرستاده الشاهد على الاول
بالمعنی الثانی شعر ... بیسارکان تارایم ... بمعنی مصدر هم می آید بیسار...
بیسارا کو بفرست بیسارما مفرست بیسارانک ... بیسارکاین وبیسارکایمن بفرستم بیسارایب وبیسارایان وبیسارمیش فرستاده
فرستاده بیسارکا بو آیا بفرستد بیساراج چون بفرستد ... بفرستادن بیسارکوچی فرستادنده بیسارکوجه وبیسارکوبجه وبیساراکا
...فرستادن ... بیسارکم خواهم فرستاد بیسارکوسی خواهد فرستاد بیسارکوسی خواهد فرستاد بیسارکای و بیسارا ایمبار
بیساجون وبیساروبیک بفرستد بیساراکودیک ... فرستادیست ... من الجوامد بیب ... بیکو یای ... که ... کویند بیساد ...

نامند بیلیک بیکو نای ... بود که ... ... باشد مع التابع للشغات بیمالک بیکو نادر ... بمعنی ... لوکوبیدن
بیدن کشیدن وبوبه ... اناطال استعمال نمایند بیتولک ... کشیدیم ... وبسابودن ...
بیدن کشد ... هم می آید ... بیسا اکر ... ادود ... کشید
الشاهد على الاول المعنی الاول شعر ... الشاهد ... اعلام ... الفان ...
بیتاکان ... کشیده ... بمعنی مصدر هم می آید بیتیکیل وبیتاکود ... کشید
چنانچه ... الشاهد على الاول المعنی الثانی شعر ... منیب ...
بیت بنیا ... اوال ... بیتکولکیل بنا وبنیا کیسل مفرد مخاطب ...
بیتنانک ... بیتکاسین ... بیتنیان وبیتمیش ... کشیده چنانچه شاهد ...
نابی ... کند ... شعر ... ایلکیدا ...
توتی جست روان بولدی ... بیتیمشانک ... کشید بیتکابو آیا ...
وآیابیک بکشد بیتاله ... بیتاکاین ... الشاهد على الرابع المعنی الاول ...
بجر بو نوع اولسا ... بیتکاج ... بکشد ...
... بیتکوجه بیتکوبجه بیتکایخه ... کشیدن ... بیتکوم خواهم ...
بکشد بیتکونک خواهد کشید بیتکوسی ... خواهد کشید بیتکای ... بیتکودیک ...
بیسد ... بکشد بیتکودیک ... چنانچه ... شاهد على الثانی المعنی
شعر ای کونکول ... داولفاق ... بیتماک ...
وبید ... بیتماک ... بیتکان ... الشاهد على الاول
بالمعنی الثالث شعر دوران ایلیدین ... بر آنینک کینه ...
... چنانچه ... الابرار کوید الشاهد على الثانی شعر ...
بیل ... بیتکاج ... چنانچه ... کوید شعر ...
... بیتکولک ... الشاهد علیه شعر ...
بیتکوی ... بیتیلدی ... بیتلماک ...
چنانچه تاریخ الملوک ... انوشیروان ... بیتیلدی ...
... ذکر کرده ... بیتیلکان بیتیلوکان ...
چنانچه شاهد ... الشاهی ...
چان کیب وبمعنی مصدر هم می آید بیتیلیب بیتیلیان وبیتیلیش ... الشاهد على الاول شعر ...
آنت بیتیلیب ... بیتیلیب ... الشاهد على الثالث شعر ...
سالدی ... صیغ بوبیسانک بالام اشتقاق می یابد بیتوریاک ... بیتکوریاک ...
... بیتوکان ... بیتکوکان ... بیتکورکان ...

بیتکوتا دوکان و بیتشتوکان و بیتشتوریورکان و بیتشتورادورکان   بیتاننده مرحانیده بمعنی مصدر هم می آید چنانکه شاهد بر
رابع را معنی مصدری کوید شعر جانیما بیتکیم بیکا ولی لعل بعدان آشا فرح البکا بیتکوکان ش لبیک لعلکون صهبا فرح بیتور بیتوکیل
بیتن اکور و بیتور و بیتکوکیل و بیتکوراکور و بیتکورته بیتکوتکیل و بیتکوراکور و بیتشتور و بیتشتورکیل و بیتشتوراکور را استلزم بیتنکه
چنانکه در خسرو شیرین در وصف نظامی و خسرو کوید الشاهد علی الثانی شعر نوا برقه دا بیتوکنت بیتورکیل بوالیکی پلین توت
بیتکوکیل الشاهد علی السادس شعر جانی جانانغه بولای تا چیقتی لیغ بیتکول کوکلیم بیلبلی بیتورای و بیتوراین و بیتکورای و
بیتکولین و بیتکوتای و بیتکولاین و بیتشتورای و بیتشتولاین برنام و بیتانده بیتانه مرحانیده چنانکه شاهد بیتا در عامی ولدم آنند
سدسکندری کوید شعر سفانه سپاهی خان ملکی دین فخان ملکی دین لا امکان و ملکیدین یاشلیق بیلا بیتکوتا این فوج فوج کیتیتو
چرلب فو حسین نوا بیتورکوچی و بیتکورکوچی و بیتشتورکوچی   بیتانده چنانکه شاهد بر ثالث را در فصل مضمم از محبوب القلوب
در ترک فساق کوید که دولت خه بیتکورکوچی تینکری هم الفوج هم برکوچی تینکریه بیتور کوریلک بیتور بیردیلک بیتور برتکلیغ بیتکورکو
بیتور ور دیلک و بیتکور برتکلیغ و بیتکوردتکودیلک و بیتکودتوردیلک و بیتکوتور برتکلیغ و بیتشتورکودیلک و بیتشتوروردیلک و بیتشتورور تکلیغ
بیتانیدنی و بیتانیدنهاست الشاهد علی الرابع بالمعنی الثانی شعر قیلیدم یتا کیلتوردور موتکلوغ باشیمه بیتور لادی فوجیاملام
جانانه ضمیر بیتکورکودیلک اوفنعین باردنا الشاهد علی السادس بالمعنی الاول شعر کونکلوم بیتلبادی لطا آیفورای یوزکیم مزیه
بیتکورور برتکلیغ دمعدد کردن بمعنی خواهیه وتاق صیغ ربیع موافق شق اول اشتقاق بیابد من الجواهر بتاد بمعنی جرد کا چنانکه کا
شعر کونکولدا غلظم بیلا بقیلما بیتیا احداث چیقیلمینک اشبو بیتلر قبیلما فیلیا احداث نیز بیتوبکه چنانکه شنوی مهر و مینی کوید
بامئلاء الرومیه شعر دییم نیرا بیتجم جنالیم و بیتا ولدیغم دیبیعکه بیتجم بینک تا اثرلیک ذاتی بیر بیتوبیدک بی کسنده بمعنی باطل و
اینده بمعنی هم استعمال میشود چنانکه مدوبل بیتیماک کمشت بیتاک بیتم تاسیجنیبیتغ کویند که طال صرالنه بیلنه مشهور است و مستعمل
بیتمی مدوصفت کویند بعضی بیتیمی مبتلا بیتی آتا کنایه است از آبا علیه چنانکه مدح صفت کوید شعر جنون بیتری وقتی کینک
خورشید خاک مکینک کوک مصدا اطفل بیتینک بیتی آلمو قوتوتا بیتی او بیتی هفت پا چنانکه کوید شعر خلخیتیغ اکیتیو کوکا
چقمونکمه دو بیتیکه بیتی المونیه بیتوبیدلیکی آوا بیتیلان بکسر تا بمعنی انعقاد باشد بیتیکان بکسر تا و فتح کاف عجمی و نون نام
ستاره بنات النعش و جره و آنرا هفت برادران نیز خوانند مع الکاف العجمیه و النون المشتقات بیتمالک بیکور بیتمالیک کروبی بمعنی جنیبت کشیدن
و جانه کشیدن بود چنانکه منه ازده روعمر که بیت خود در بیان جنیبت کوید کمبیله باشاهلرا و کنده بیتدیم بیز ازالحنیم و کلم
نذر بن کویند که بیدا بینک لولون بمعنی جانه کشته مرده بیتیدن ترکمان سیکند چنانکه مدرل بیجا ام ارکیلیه دیته نجه که ده کوید که
اختیارم قبضه تصرفه غوده ظهر ترکا بیتانیمیر بیتشیرلرابه بیدر مع الجوابید بیدلیک اسیح جنیبت بود مع فتح نون بیتیلیق بیتیکوکی
نام ستاره بنات النعش باشد مع الراء المهمله بیرتماق بیرما ناق بمعنی شکافتن باشد که با سیغ مدح مع الواحد کو به کیتی چنانکه [illegible]
از محبوب القلوب بحرف کویه حقایق کوید که دهقان که دانه ساچار بیرجاق بیله بذق بولیق اتجار بیر ابریزو بیر جدوریز میشکاتیم چنانکه شا
برآول لعل مرحسن و شیرین از زبان شیرین خطاب به فرهاد کوید شعر که کرتاغ و کوی دود بیرلیمیز قرا تفرانیه کیمنانک هم کیکلر بیز بیربیب و
بیربیار و بیربیش شکافته چنانکه شاهد بیر اول را صحیفه بیانه دواستان جم وقصه جم بهار کوید شعر خصم غنیک کیمیسی تو بکا
قریحه تیغ المه خمه نینک توبیمیز بیر غای و بیر بیرساخ بیرسون و بیرلمک بشکافد الشاهد علی المجلس شعر قوبولیتیغی کو فتوح شکا
بیرولک فراتیه لایام ازلسه کیدیلک و بالفتح میم تکه صبحیم بیامق که دمعوقه جیم است استعفاقیا فیه بهینیا یا بمعصوم کهنه تبدیل یا

بیرتماق بیکون تاء و تاء قرشت مفتوح بیرتوق در بیتیم بیرتا بیرتادون   بیرتاد و بیرتا بمعنی فاعل و مصدر هم می آید بیرتغان و
بیرتلغان بیرتادورغان بیلرتکند و بیرتو کرده و بمعنی مصدر هم می آید بیرتیقیل و بیرتا کور اما استلزام کردن چنانکه شاهد
ثانی را مطلع از آغاز نظم سبعه سیاره کوید شعر مشرق بیرتقیل جامه اوچین بیرآ بیرتا فقفه آیدا خامه اوچین بیرتا و بیرتا عیل موخذ
خاطر بیرتقیل بیرتیتانک بیرتغاسین و بیرتغاییین باعث بیرتقیه بیرتینان و بیرتیش صیغه بیرتیشانک صیغه بیرتغا عیو آلیتیه
بیرتقاج چون صیغه بسیار و بمعنی مبهدک بیرتغوجی صیغه بیرتغوچی بیرتغو خدو بیرتغانچه تا صیغه مستقبل آن بیرتغوم خواهم
درید بیرتغونک خواهیم درید بیرتغوسی خواهد درید بیرتغای و بیرتا فیرتقا بیرتدیلک بیرتغوسی عادیک تور بیرتماسدیک تور
ندیدن و نیست بیرتیشماق بکسر تاء مع الثاء بمعنی مقابله است جنک کردن و باهم درید بیرتیشی تور بکد بکر ادریدند و باهم درید
چنانکه کوید شعر بوعشقیک پیرله خونتوجدو ونضوان تیرتیشیق لاد تیلو فصله لادیر یهر فلوق و تاق صیغ بیرتیشماق باشیدن اشتقاق
می آید بیرتیلماق بکسر تاء مع الکاف صیغه شدن و صیغ آن با الام اشتقاق می آید بیرلاماق بالاشباع بیکون تاء و فتح لام با الف کشیده
خواندن بکه کردن بیرلاماک بلا اشباع بجا کردن بیرلادی خواند که بکه کرد و بجا کرد بیرلادیم که بید و د خواندیم که بکه کردیم بجا بیرلا
فاعل و مصدر هم می آید بیرلاغان و بیرلاغان و بیرلاییدورغان خوانند که و بکه کند و بمعنی مصدر هم می آید بیرلاماک و بیرلاکان و بیرلامیدیم
جا کنده و بجا کنده و بمعنی مصدر هم می آید بیرلاو بیرلای کور صیغه مطلب بیرلاتاک بیرلا عیل بخوان بیرلاکیل
جا کن بیرلاما صیغه مطلب بیرلاماعیل بخوان بیرلامکیل جا مکن بیرلاسانک بخوانی جا کنی بیرلاغاسین و بیرلاغایسین
بخوانی بیرلاکاسین و بیرلاکایسین جا کنی بیرلاج بیرلابان بیرلابش خوانده و جا کرده بیرلاینانک خوانده و جا کرده بیرلاغایو آیا بخواند
بیرلاکایو آیا جا کند بیرلاغاج چون بخواند بیرلاکاج چون جا کند بیرلاغوچی خواننده چنانکه
جنانم از محبوب القلوب که نظایر خوان بیله بیرلاکوچی جا کنده بیرلاغوچی
بیرلاغانچه تا بخواند بیرلاغوم خواهم خواند بیرلاکوم جا خواهم کرد بیرلاغو
خواهی خواند بیرلاغونک جا خواهی کرد بیرلاغوسی خواهد خواند بیرلاغای بخواند بیرلاکای جا کند بیرلاسا
بخوانیم و بیرلادیک بخواندیم و جا کندیم بیرلاماغودیک بیرلاماسدیک تور نخواندیم و جا نکردیم
بیرلاشماق مع الثاء بیرلاشماق بمعنی موافقت با اشتقاق
[illegible]
شعر [illegible]
[illegible]
مع الیاء [illegible] بیرآزوق [illegible] شعر [illegible]
[illegible] بیراق [illegible]
شعر [illegible]
چنانکه [illegible] شعر [illegible]
[illegible]
هم [illegible] بیرتاج [illegible] بیرتوق [illegible]

بکشادیم بمعنی نه باشد برقانی مجب لغت دو معنی دارد اول خون که عیش و دویم خون زمین را نامند باصطلاح کنایه از استاد چیزی که بر زمین نهد
ضایع شود چنانچه مصداق آن در خیرة الابرار در وصف میخوار ... گوید شعر [illegible]
اوزده توکنالسینیکی قرا و فراغ لوزه ناز ... [illegible] ... لعل ... بمعنی جمع تعلیمه کند
محتسب ... شرابخوار کار فرموده گوید که محتسبنینک توککان ... برقانی بولیتور ... [illegible]
برقوی بمعنی بر زمین باشد الشاهد علیه شعر دیشام ... [illegible]
شبر معیار کم برکوک ... که آنرا بفارسی ... گویند برلیک برین یعنی خابجا ... چنانچه ... گوید
... خاقانی چین گوید شعر ... [illegible] ... نوایی علیه الرحمه فرموده که شعر
طالبیم نینک ... [illegible]
خوانده ... [illegible] ... چنانچه ... گوید شعر
باسلماج ... [illegible] ... بزنه ... [illegible]
وفتح نون ... [illegible] ... کوچیم بینی کوچماک
... [illegible] ... گوید شعر ... [illegible]
... [illegible] ... کشاینده و گشوده ... [illegible]
... [illegible] ... الشاهد علی المعنی الاول شعر ... [illegible]
... [illegible] ... گشوده الشاهد علی المعنی الثانی شعر ... [illegible]
... [illegible]
... [illegible] ... چنانچه ... گوید شعر ... [illegible]
... [illegible]
... [illegible]
... [illegible] ... کشاینده ... [illegible]
... [illegible] ... خواهد گشود ... [illegible]
... [illegible]
... المعنی الثانیه شعر ... [illegible]
... [illegible] ... کشوده شده الشاهد علی المعنی الاول شعر
... [illegible]
... [illegible] ... مع النون ... [illegible]
... [illegible] ... جمع کردن ... جمع کردیم ... [illegible]
جمع کننده جمع ... [illegible]
... [illegible] ... جمع کرده ... جمع کرده ... آیا جمع کند ...

بوغ

چون جمع کرد و کند و جمع کردن ... جمع کننده ... تا جمع کردن ... [illegible]
کرد ... جمع خواهی کرد ... جمع خواهد کرد ... [illegible] ... جمع کنان الشاهد علی الاول
شعر ... [illegible]
جمع نکردنی ... [illegible] ... جمع ... [illegible]
الشاهد علی الاول المعنی الثانی شعر ... [illegible]
هم می آید ... [illegible] ... جمع شدن ... [illegible]
... [illegible] ... چنانچه شاهد ... [illegible]
... [illegible]
... [illegible] ... هم می آید ... [illegible]
و گرد کرده چنانچه شاهد ... گوید شعر ... [illegible]
... [illegible] ... هم می آید چنانچه شاهد ... شعر ... [illegible]
... [illegible]
... [illegible]
... [illegible] ... چنانچه شاهد ... گوید ... [illegible]
... [illegible] ... الشاهد علی المعنی الاول شعر ... [illegible]
... [illegible] ... گوید شعر ... [illegible]
... [illegible] ... الشاهد علی المعنی الاول شعر ... [illegible]
... [illegible]
... [illegible] ... چنانچه ... [illegible]
... [illegible] ... چنانچه ... [illegible]
... [illegible] ... الشاهد علی الاول شعر ... [illegible]
... [illegible]
مع الثاء ... [illegible]
... [illegible]
... [illegible] ... هم می آید ... [illegible]
... [illegible] ... هم می آید ... [illegible]
... [illegible] ... الشاهد علی
الاول شعر ... [illegible]
... [illegible]

350v.

سیغلا سیغتور سیغلامسینا خه تا کریه ناك شدن وبقطعمان آن سیغلا سیغتور کریه ناك خواهم شد سیغلا سیغتونك کریه ناك خواهد شد
سیغلا سیغتوق کریه ناك خواهد شد سیغلامسینغای سیغلامینا سیغلامسینا سیغلا مسینتو سیغلا مسیند یك کریه ناك شود
سیغلا سینا غودیك نه سیغلا مسیما کریه ناك شدنی است من الجوامد سیغلیج دو معنی دارد اول چیزی که بیندازند شاهد علیه شعر قوینك
چندا کوروب ماجبان کورمین کوزیکا ایلسا ایما کراکوزایکا سیغلاج دویم بمعنی حلقه تا ماسند چنانچه بدو معنی مقاله نوز بهم گوخت
الا برلغه در وصف هرات کوید شعر صحنی ایوز کل چیقلیب هر سیغلیج هر کلی نینك عطری غالیب بر سیغلیج سیغلاغو بمعنی بود واکر
بمعنی کریه است چنانچه کوید شعر خسته کونکلم ادرتا نوری یاسیوا جانیم بار دور سیغلاغوم کیلور کوکلار جهندا نیم بار دور دویم بمعنی
کران بود الشاهد علیه شعر بیز وشامین شدتین کورکیل کوچوخ وصبوحیتی خالیه که سیغلا ختوی دو رکاه کولکو کچه لار سیغناق بمعنی
جمعیت چنانچه صنایع بابری مذکور است که سلطان حسین میرزا دولت تیمور بیك امیرخه اولتوزخان لولوغ پادشاه سیغنا قیلیب بمعنی
بمعنی کریه باشد چنانچه کوید شعر تا بیقوچیغ بیتیم بیزین کرکیلماس ایدی کمرد بجز بیتایم تمام سیغلا حرین وله شعر کلاب
چو لعلینك وایل الملکی بین یا اله الی بیغوچ ما تیرا اماکیم دیر یونکا کلام برادر شایبت یبغینت بکسر غین وسکون نون فیح وکروه انبوه را کویند
یبغینت بکسر غین وسکون نون وتای قرشت جانور ریست سیاه وخطوط دارد قوی جثه که آنرا میل بند حواله ما فاتحا یا بمعنی نوشته
مع الفتوحات المنهیات بیقماق دو معنی دارد اول بر زمین انکندن دویم بمعنی خراب کردن بود بیقتوق بر زمین انکندیم خراب کردیم
بیقا بیقسا اود بر زمین بیفکند وخراب میکند بیقلار بمعنی ناصل مصدر هم می آید بیقمان بیقارغان بیقادورغان بر زمین انکنده وانکند
وخراب کنده وخراب کرده وبمعنی مصدر هم می آید بیقتیق بیقماق بیقا کو مفرد مخاطب از فعل امر بیقما بیقماس نیز مفرد مخاطب بیقسا
بیقماین بیقماق بیقتی وخراب کنی بیقسه بیقیشان بیقیش انکنده وخراب کرده بیقمیشان انکنده وخراب کنه بیقمایمو آیا بیقند
وخراب کند بیقماج چون بیقند مجهول انکندن وخراب کند ومجهول کردن بیقتوقچی انکنده وخراب کنده بیقتومچی بیقتوقچی بیقماس
تا انکندن وبمعنی آن تا خراب کردن وبمعنی آن بیقتوم خواهم انکند خراب خواهم کرد بیقتونك خواهد انکند خراب خواهد کرد بیقتوق
خواهد انکند خراب خواهد کرد بیقماق بیقلیقما بیقسون وبیقدیك بیقتکند خراب کند الشاهد علی الاول المعنی الثانی شعر نخچلیکم
بیقتای ایل صبری بنا سین کیمیدا کیم اوبولماق کاشکی وچشم خونباریم مینینك بیقتودیك دیر بیقلای یلن تور انکندن ولیت خراب کردن است
الشاهد علی الاول المعنی الثانی شعر اوبیقماق تازا آمیم دین یقیقیل کیم مو کونك کوب کمن سیکر تیغر بیقتودیك قوصور تم تمام غولیك توبیقماق
بیقتکندن دست وخراب کردن است بیقتورماق مصدر متعدی بمعنی انداز انایند وخراب فرمودن وصیغ آن بالفظ تیر اشتقاق میاید بیقیلماق
بمعنی افتادن خراب شدن بیقیلدی افتاد وخراب شد چنانچه در بیان فصول در وصف جنون بمعنی اول کوید شعر بچکر بیقیلدی قوچی یانه ارولیق
که ایدی آنکا بهانه بیقیلسا بیقیلمیش بیقیلار کور امرست بمعنی افتادن الشاهد علی الاول المعنی الاول شعر ای نوای قوتوقوزا عیقه کوب توکتونك
سیقلت کیتلادی بولسانك نمام آتدا اوقا بیدی بیقیلغ بیقیلاد بیقیلاد افتان افتان ومعنی تکرار هم با بمعنی مستعمل چنانچه در وصف جنون کوید
شعر تجحونه بیقلادو کوبا بیق خاک غوینه بیتی جو بتی کونی وباقی صیغ بیغ سیاق بیقلماق الضم لام اشتقاق میابد من الجوامد بیقاق بضم اول وسکون ثانی
بمعنی ویران باشد بیقیقیقوی بمعنی افتاده و ویران شده الشاهد علیه شعر کلیم ایو این ملك بیقیقانی بیقیل اولکاندوی کیم ایمینی یوق بیقیلقو کامدی
ایولاندا وله شعر هر امید امنع لسکه کاملانت ناشادی غی فرتابیه کوب بیقیلقونکلیه اجزار را بیقیلماخون بیقتلمه ویران شده
مع الکاف المنهیات بیکرنانك بکاف وسکون رای مهمله بمعنی ناخوش آمدن وآنرا بیکرقیناك هم کویند بیکرید ولتا خوش آمدیم بیکرید بیکراکا
ناخوش آمد وبیکرو بمعنی ناصل مصدر هم می آید بیکرادو کان ناخوش آینده وناخوش آمد وبمعنی مصدر هم می آید بیکرو

351r.

بیکرکیل بیکراکو بیکرو مفرد مخاطب از فعل امر بیکرماکو بیکرماس نیز مفرد مخاطب بیکرماینك بیکرکاسین وبیکرکاسین ناخوش شود
بیکرسه بیکرسه بیکریوش بیکرمیش ناخوش آمده بیکرمیشانك ناخوش آمده بیکرکایمو آیا ناخوش باشد بیکرکاج چون ناخوش باشد بیکرکلی
بیکرکوچی ناخوش آینده بیکرکوچی بیکرکونچه بیکرکانچه تا ناخوش آمدن وبمعنی آن بیکرکوم ناخوش خواهم آمد بیکرکونك
ناخوش خواهد آمد بیکرکوسی ناخوش خواهد آمد بیکرکای بیکرکای بیکرکانی بیکرسون وبیکرکودیك ناخوش باید الشاهد علیه شعر
قانوندین اول آتی خه کونکلوم بمعنی کرچه اول خه کمرنا سیکرکودیك بیکرکار کونکلیك تیز وبیکرکار خاطر تا خوش بود بدانست سیکرنانك بکاف
ونون فتح رای مهمله هم بیکرنانك بمعنی ناخوش آمدن باشد وصیغ آن بر بیکرماق بفتح رای مهمله مع النون اشتقاق میاید من الجوامد بیکلیك
بمعنی بیدور بود وناخوش باشد چنانچه کوید شعر بو بلا حیرت دعا دور کیم نوایی دیوانه تیق اوشول آی چیقیب کونکلوم حسن آنکا ابراغ ایتا
بیکن بفتح کاف عجمی وسکون نون همشیره زاده را کویند بیکولوك بمعنی ملوك خودیدن چنانچه صاحب سکندری کوید شعر بیکولوك نوز
حداوشاها دین دعا و حمد لوشانیم کیم الآدین ودم چوغا لیا مع اتامذ که هم خواهد شد بیکیت بکاف عجمی جوان را کویند الشاهد علیه
شعر کونکلوم الدیم بری بیکولر ملك سیما بیکیت کیم نکادم دامونداق یولماس سیاه بیکیت لیك جوان بیکیمه بکسر کاف وسکون رای مهمله
وفتح میم وبعده بیت باشد بیکن بکسر کاف عجمی وسکون نون بترکی روی بمعنی خوب ومرغوب بود بیکیز بیکیز بمعنی خوب مع اللام من المستقبلات
بسکون لام پویه کردن مرادف رفتن بتعجیل وعوید بطریق هروله باشد چنانچه کوید شعر حرم وصلین تیلا حرین پویه اصرما ناری
شالات قدم آهسته میکیا ملحق بسك اول بیلا کیا اتا الفتاعیب سیلماق بترکی روی بمعنی تر بسیلدی سیلدی پویه زد چنانچه کوید
جنیدی کوید بابلاد ما الرومیه شعر عشق العوادین سلم ایلدی کوبدون سکا موجیکم سیلدی بوکو رعیه بیتدی بمعنی سیلکا بکبج
روی بمعنی تر بسیلدی سیلیدوك پویه زدیم لا ادری مخبر کیم سیلدعك بو کم دیولات تا یما دوق قرب وصال زانوی نوسید لیغه اولتوکو
تا جان میز وبترکی روی یعنی ترسیلیم سیلادی سیلادی پویه زنه وسیلاد بعینه تا صل مصدر هم می آید وبترکی روی یعنی بیلکان
بیلاکان بیلادور کیکویه زنند وپویه زده وبمعنی مصدر هم می آید سیل سیلکیل وسیلاکور امراست از پویه زدن وسیل بترکی روی بیلمه باید
هم باشد ومعانی لها مذه آن دو زیل الجوامد مذکور خواهد شد بیلما وبیلماکیل نفی است از پویه زدن وسیلما بترکی روی نفی از پویه
هم باشد بیلما نامع بیلکاسین سیلکای بیر پویه زدن بیلیقع بیلینا بیلیش پویه زده الشاهد علی الاول شعر فراقیدا شید
اینکان کونکل ایلیب چیقا آلماس آنینك بورادی لولا هورهیقوی مواب کان وبترکی روی بمعنی ترسیده سیلیشانك پویه زده بیلکایمو آیا
پویه بزند سیلکاج چون پویه زد وبزند سیلکودی پویه زننده سیلکوچی پویه زنده سیلکو بیلکودی سیلکانچه تا پویه زدن وبمعنی آن سیلکوم
پویه خواهم زد سیلکونك پویه خواهی زد سیلکوسی پویه خواهد زد سیلکای بیلای بیلسا بیلسون بیلدا پویه زند چنانچه شاعر روی
در وصف اسب کفته الشاهد علی الثالث با ملاد الرومیه شعر سیله آتی خه تشبه ایدوك تنزیقی که صبه که سیلیه مینك بیل سیله
وسیلیه وسیلسون بترکی روی یعنی پر سد بیلما کو دیان توریت بیلمادیك تو پویه زد خواست بیلدو نانك مصدر متعدی بمعنی دوانیدن وتعجیل
دوان ساختن باشد وبو سیلدورمیش دوانیده ساخته چنانچه حمید قلندر در مخزن در مقام خاتم کوید الشاهد علی الاول
سیلکوچی جانه سینی سیلدورمیش بر هر جبر لیقوی ناندا شتور یوب بترکیرو بمعنی ترسانیده باشد سیلدرماك بفتح لام بمعنی ترسانیدن چنانچه
تنبیها تحبوب القلوب در قرب سلاطین کوید که الا ارضه تقرب سیلادنگانکا او زقیلیغه الاتقین سیلاکاه که بیلاده دوك ترسانیدیم بیلادی
بیلدوخاند سیلادی بمعنی ناصل مصدر هم می آید سیلاکان سیلاکان بیلادورکان ترسانند وترسانیده وبمعنی مصدر هم می آید وسیلاکا
مسرع دو پویه زن هم باشد سیلاد سیلادکیل وسیلادکور مفرد مخاطب از فعل امر سیلاتا سیلاتا نیز مفرد مخاطب بیلادسانك

یلپکاسین یلپکای بین بمعنی جنبانیدن یلپاب یلپابان یلپامیش بجنبانیم چنانکه شاهد اول در [illegible]
مثل کوید شعر [illegible] تیغین یلپاب [illegible] ستولف [illegible] شعر بابای [illegible]
حرفها [illegible] نوشته و بمعنی [illegible] بر داشته ذکر کرده و شعر [illegible] شاهد آورده و نصیری هم متابعت کرده هر دو سهو کرده اند
یلپامیشانک بجنبانیم یلپاکایمو آیا بجنبانید یلپاکاج چون بجنباند و بجنبانیدن یلپاکوچی جنباننده یلپاکوجه
یلپاکوچی یلپکانچه تا بجنبانیدن و بمعنی آن یلپاکوم خواهم جنبانید یلپاکونک خواهد جنبانید یلپاکوسی خواهد
جنبانید یلپاکای یلپاسا یلپاسون یلپادرین بجنبانید یلپاماکدین [illegible] بجنبانیدنی است یلپیماک بکسر کلام
و کسر یا عجمی باد زدن و هر چه جنبانیدن باشد یلپید دوک باد زدیم یلپیر و یلپیدور باد میزند و یلپیر بمعنی فاعل و مصدر هم می آید
یلپیکان یلپیر [illegible] باد زننده و باد زده و بمعنی مصدر هم می آید یلپی و یلپی بیا و یلپی بود امر است از باد زدن الشاهد
علی الاول شعر [illegible] کلشنه [illegible] هم آن یلپی و هم [illegible] ناشیفته تاج یلپیما و یلپیما کیل [illegible]
یلپیناک [illegible] یلپکای باد بزنی یلپیب یلپیبان و یلپیمیش باد زده یلپوی یلپیبین باد بزنم و بزند و بزنی یلپیکایمو
آیا باد بزند یلپیب [illegible] یلپیکای [illegible] یلپکالی برای باد زدن و تا باد زده یلپکاج چون باد بزند و بجر
زدن یلپکوچی باد زننده یلپکوچه یلپکونچه یلپیکانچه تا باد زدن و بمعنی آن یلپکوم باد خواهم زد یلپکونک باد خواهی زد
یلپکوسی باد خواهد زد یلپکای یلپیسا یلپیسون یلپیدیک باد بزنید یلپیما [illegible] یلپیماسلیک باد نزدنی است یلپاماک بکسر
لام اول و نون و فتح لام ثانی بمعنی باد کردن و متورم شدن چنانکه کوید شعر [illegible] بیک بکیم
یلپاز دیک بو وادی [illegible] چندین لاز یلپاند وک باد کردیم یلپانور یلپاناد و باد میکند و یلپانور بمعنی فاعل و مصدر هم
می آید یلپانکان یلپانور [illegible] باد کننده و باد کرده و بمعنی مصدر هم می آید یلپان یلپانکیل و یلپان [illegible]
امر است یلپان [illegible] یلپانمای [illegible] یلپانب یلپانیبان و یلپانمیش
باد کرده یلپانمیشانک باد کرده یلپانکایمو آیا باد کند یلپانکاج چون باد کند و بجر کردن یلپانکوچی باد کننده یلپانکوچه
یلپانکانچه تا باد کردن و بمعنی آن یلپانکوم باد خواهم کرد یلپانکونک باد خواهی کرد یلپانکوسی باد خواهد کرد یلپانکای یلپانسا یلپانسون
یلپانیک یلپانکیل باد کند یلپانما [illegible] یلپانماسلیک باد نکردنی است یلپیتماک مصدر متعدیست بمعنی چیزی را باد کردن و صیغ آن بر منهج
یلپیماک [illegible] بمعنی باد باشد [illegible] پوز زدن و [illegible] ترسیدن
چنانکه در ذیل [illegible] یلپاق مذکور شد یلپاق بفتح لام [illegible] بالاپوش [illegible] کوتاه را کویند چنانکه کوید
شعر [illegible] یلپاک [illegible] باقلجاکی [illegible]
[illegible] بولدی [illegible] یلپاک لیک بالاپوش را چنانکه
[illegible] یلپان [illegible] نیز نام [illegible]
[illegible] نام نباتیست [illegible]
[illegible] و آن را بعربی [illegible] کویند یلپان بالمعنی [illegible]
یلپاناج [illegible] یلپانک بکون نون و کاف [illegible] کویند چنانکه در تاریخ [illegible]
[illegible] یلپاک و با یاق بالاکوچله [illegible]

و دست و پا [illegible] کوتاه [illegible] الش کوتاهست و آن جانور را تا [illegible] کند و آن را [illegible]
یلپاز [illegible] بزرکی [illegible] کویند [illegible]
و کبیر و کبیر آن را شجرة التنین کویند [illegible] و آن را اصل [illegible] خوانند یلپاز [illegible]
[illegible] چنانکه شاهد [illegible] شعر
[illegible] چنانکه [illegible]
شعر [illegible] کویند [illegible]
[illegible] چنانکه کوید شعر [illegible]
استعمال شود یلپق [illegible] چنانکه کوید [illegible] الشاهد علیه شعر [illegible]
[illegible] چنانکه [illegible]
شد یلپکا بفتح کاف [illegible] یلپکان باد بازکنی بود که آن را بعربی [illegible] شعر [illegible]
[illegible] چنانکه [illegible]
[illegible] یلپکو بضم کاف عجمی [illegible]
یلپکن [illegible] چنانکه [illegible]
[illegible] چنانکه شاهد [illegible] کوید شعر [illegible]
[illegible] یلپا یا [illegible]
[illegible] چنانکه [illegible]
[illegible] الشاهد علیه شعر [illegible]
[illegible] مع [illegible]
خواب شد چنانکه [illegible] الشاهد علی الثانی شعر [illegible]
[illegible] خواب [illegible] الشاهد علی الرابع شعر [illegible]
[illegible] و بمعنی مصدر هم می آید [illegible]
علی الثانی [illegible] شعر [illegible]
[illegible] الشاهد علی الثالث بالمعنی الاول شعر [illegible]
[illegible] خواب شدنی است [illegible]
الشاهد علی الثالث شعر [illegible]
[illegible] اشتقاق [illegible] کویند [illegible]
هم باشد [illegible] هم [illegible]
بود [illegible] اسم نباتیست [illegible] کویند [illegible]
شبیه [illegible] و آن را [illegible]

مع النون من المشتقات ینکماك بکون نون وکاف عجمی یعنی مغلوب کردن و مبهوت کردن ینکدوك مغلوب کردیم ینکای و ینکاید
مغلوب کند الشاهد علی الاول شعر زمانه اهلیغه کیم اویوتیلیغ ساتیش ینکارم آخر الامر زمانه نینك اوینی و ینکای یعنی
تامل و مصادر هم می آید ینکماك ینکاران و ینکاکان مغلوب کننده و مغلوب کرده و بمعنی مصادر هم می آید ینکیك و ینکیکلی ینکاکود
یعنی مغلوب کن و ینیك بمعنی آستین هم باشد چنانکه در بدیعی فرماید شعر حسن یوسف تول ینیك دین چهار زنبر پیچ اعتقاد
فانینك ینیك و مجنین خسرو شیرین کوید شعر کیم زمانه بوغم خیلیغ ینیك که این سخن قول راشاه و کرا ایستنك تنجیم مخاطب آ
انفعال مصادر ینکاك یعنی بخرید چنانکه در ذیل جاء الدین نکارش خواهد یافت ینکا و ینکا کیل یعنی مغلوب کن ینکانك و ینکاکا
ینکاوین مغلوب کن ینکیج ینکیان و ینکیمش مغلوب کرده چنانکه شاهد بر اول در سد سکندری کوید شعر بو حالت دا
حیرت ینکیب شاهینی نیا اول سهروك دانش اکاهی قیبزیر لیلی مجنون در حال مجنون کوید شعر هر لحظه ینکیب نی تفتکراز ما
ایتیب مستتر و مؤلف وی ینکیب را صیغه شعر ینکیب را نای قرشت خوانده و بعض را بی معنی کرده از حیرت نوشته و شعر زیر را شاهد آورده و
نصیری هم متابعت کرده سهو کرده اند لفظ و معنی هر دو اختراعیست ینکیشالك مغلوب کرده ینککا ایو آیا مغلوب کند ینکیکاج
چون مغلوب کرد و کند و بعض کردن ینککوی مغلوب کننده ینککوچه و ینککوخه و ینککانجه تا مغلوب کردن و بقدر آن ینککو
مغلوب خواهیم کرد ینککونك مغلوب خواهی کرد ینککوسی مغلوب خواهد کرد ینککای و ینکاقینکیا تیمنکون و ینکیکلیك
مغلوب کند الشاهد علی الثالث شعر ینکا دیر ایدی ایمحیرت نینا ملنای بغتیه کیم دو بود بیکار که و نصیحتکیم حیران ینماس ینککای
ینکماسدیك تا مغلوب نکرده است ینکماك بکون نون و کسر کاف عجمی مع الالام یعنی مغلوب شده باشد و صیغ آن بر نسق بالا م
اشتقاق می یابد من الجوامد ینك بکون نون و کاف عجمی آستین بود و نیز امر است از مغلوب کردن چنانکه شاهد هر دو در ذیل مصادر ینکماك
کذشت و بمعنی بخرید هم باشد چنانکه در ذیل مصادر یال مذکور خواهد شد ینکه بکون نون و فتح کاف عجمی زینت که عروس را ارایش کرده
بحجله برده بداماد میسپارند ینکلاک بکون نون و کاف عجمی و فتح لام با الف کشیده یعنی تبانرو محو چنانکه فضولی کوید شعر
کونکول کوب یار اینکلاج تن بولور جان سینکا دین او الفتنی تکرار اینکلاج و بفتح تا نیز مستعملست ینکی بکون نون و کسر کاف عجمی نو و تازه
ینکیچری بترکیب و بمعنی ترکیبی آن لشکر جدید باشد و کروهی اند که در رسم در مدار شاهان پادشاهی شمرده می شوند و صاحب اوجاق و رسم و
طریقت و مشهور بهتدیب و کثرت و قوتاند ینکیل بکون نون مع الاماله و لام و کسر کاف عجمی یعنی سبك و خفیف باشد الشاهد علیه
شعر نوایی نینکا املاك نفع بولمیش اکر غیم بیا یاس مزه که سیدا ینکیل و نیز امر است از مغلوب شدن ینوتماك بضم واو و
سکون تای قرشت تغیر دادن و برکردانیدن و باو و تماك بفتح یا نیز مستعملست و صیغ آن بحسب صیغی که در ذیل متفرقه مع الواو مذکور شد
اشتقاق می یابد و نای مفتوحه بکو و تبدیل بی یابدع الیاس المشتقات یماك بمعنی خوردن باشد و نیز مهموم الجمه را کویند بیدوك خورده
بی اندوق توانستیم خورد بیرو بید ... میخورد الشاهد علی الاول شعر خرابی لا امیدا هر ناکان زنی که نویر خونع جلو کر اوکتا
تندیعیله تا دوق وشاهد بر ثانی متابع بابری در صفت دخت که اهل مملکت که خوردادن بوشاقراق کوشتجار آنی سید ملاك و نیز بمعنی
تامل و مصادر هم می آید چنانکه بمعنی مصدریه کوید شعر می تولا الحب نوایی فضه تو تونك اول اهل نیم ایچماسنام برکا ارزیاس بوهر دون
دینکیز و نیز امر است از شکافتن باشد و با بمعنی ملخوم ... است یسیا بو ... یسیا بودور ... میتوان شد چنانکه شاهد بر ثانی
متابع بابری در وصف ... که بخشی ... بیکا ... برکان و سید ... بخوره خورده
الشاهد علی الاول المعنی الثانی شعر نیم بیکان کونکلوم توشین تونمالغه کو یا صغیمدا قطعه مخطبیه ...

مصادر هم می آیند و بیدورکان یعنی خورانده و خوراننده و خورانیدن هم استعمال میشود و با بمعنی خوناز مصدر بیدیمه خالداستی و
بیکل بیکوبی کودر اولست از خوردن الشاهد علی الثانی شعر بیکل ارب حیاتینك ... کیم می لطلینك دیکاوکلا
بنکا برخوردار لیغ ... کیل ... امر است از خوردن بینك و بینکز و بیکلار یعنی بخورید الشاهد علی الثانی شعر عشق ...
چرا ...
بخوری بیب ... خوری الشاهد علی الا... [illegible] ... باغ ...
تولادب ... خوری بی وبسین بخوریم و بخورد و بخوری می خورد ... چنانکه شاهد ... کوید
که دیری که ... آیا بخورد ... بخوریم چنانکه شاهد ...
در سد سکندری ... شعر ... شاهد ...
المحبه ... کوید که روزی ... چون خورد و بخورد بعض خوردن بیکو
خورده چنانکه در ذیل ... محبوب القلوب کوید که شاهد ... بیکوچه بیکونه و ...
تا خوردن و بقدر آن بیکوم خواهم خورد بیکونك خواهی خورد بیکوسی خواهد خورد بیکای ... بخورد الشاهد علی
الرابع شعر نوایی ... اول ...
بیکودیك ... بیدیك ... خورد و ... چنانکه خورده شود و شاهد بر اول در تاریخ بابری مذکور است ...
تا سفر بیکودیك ... بیدیر ... بخورد ... مصدر ...
بیدیلار ... خوراننده ... چنانکه شاهد بر اول ... شعر شاه ...
طمع ... بیدیرکان ... می آیند و بیدیرکان ... خوراننده و خوردن ... چنانکه در ذیل
جاء الدین نکارش یافت ... چنانکه ... محبوب القلوب ... کوید که روزی ...
هم و باقی صیغ بر نسق بالا ... یتماك ... یسیلدی خورده شد
چنانکه در ... شعر ... آتش ... باقی صیغ بر
نسق بالا اشتقاق می یابد من الجوامد یر آزوق یعنی آزوقه خوردنی ... کنایه است از چیزی که بر زمین ریخته شود و ناشل چیزی
ریخته که بهیچ ... شود ... یعنی چیز خوردنی و شواهد هر سه لغت ... مع الراء المهمله نکارش یافت

تذییل در بیان لغات عربی و فارسی و کنایاتی که در کتب منظومه و محبوب القلوب حضرت نوایی استعمال شده و اکثر
از آنها در کتب لغت و فرهنگها مذکور است اما چون در اشعار نوایی وارد و اثبات معنی آنها محتاج بشاهدات لهذا شاهد هر یک ...
بجهة ... الاطناب بدون قید شواهد بیان معنی آنها بحروف لا الف آب آتش رنك کنایه است از شراب آباد ...
خوش و نیکو ... خانه ... آباد ان معمور و خوب و خوش ... در ... اصطلاح است آبدان خوب و خوش و
شانه ... آب ... آبکش ... آبجون آبنوس ... آبجینه شیشه آبنوس درختی باشد ...
بوی خوش ... کنایه است از ... آذر بفتح ذال ...
فتح ... مفصل ... آذر ... راست ... و نوعی ... و نام ... و مطلق ...
از ... و ... نام ... حضرت ابراهیم علیه السلام ... آذرم حیا و شرم ...

و مرحمت و غم و اندوه و صدا و انصاف و ظاهر و آشکار و صلاحیت و هستی و غضب و تعصب و کنایه از بخاری [illegible] داشتن
و پاس خاطر نگاه داشتن و نام دختر خسرو پرویز هم هست آشان مکاه آشام [illegible] اول بتجرع و آشامیدن دویم [illegible]
سیم نام ولایتی است ما بین مشرق و شمال [illegible] چهارم آب [illegible] و [illegible] طبقه [illegible] و سقف خانه بود چنانکه مذکور شد آغاز
آیین بالکاف [illegible] آیین [illegible] آغشته [illegible] آماج خاک [illegible] که بر آن نشانه گذاشته تیر [illegible]
کنند و آنی که [illegible] آمو مخفف آموی است [illegible] که از حوالی بلخ و بخارا میگذرد آن [illegible]
و متصل [illegible] که [illegible] اشاره است آواز صدا آوازه شهرت آهار [illegible]
آنچه [illegible] آهنگ قصد [illegible] آینه فولادی که [illegible] جنگ بر [illegible] بندند [illegible]
مذکور [illegible] داشت [illegible] لغات ترکی هم مذکور شد آیان ظاهر [illegible] چنانکه [illegible]
سقس [illegible] آیین زینت و آرایش [illegible] ابابیل [illegible]
مانند ابا [illegible] بالمد [illegible] چنانکه [illegible] گوید شعر [illegible]
میان [illegible] ابرا بالکسر [illegible] ابرش [illegible] اسبی که بر اندام او [illegible] سفید باشد ابرص
مبروص ابرق بالکسر [illegible] ابلق [illegible] سیاه و سفید [illegible] ابواب [illegible]
و دروغ [illegible] شعر [illegible]
اثنینیت بالکسر [illegible] اجرام اجسام اجنبی بیگانه [illegible] بالکسر [illegible] احد [illegible]
[illegible] مجاز اجداد [illegible] چنانکه [illegible]
[illegible] گوید شعر [illegible] لفظ احداث که [illegible] اصطلاح [illegible]
[illegible] بالکسر [illegible] اجناس [illegible] اولاد [illegible]
دو چند اخلاص بالکسر [illegible] ادویه [illegible] ادوات [illegible] ادوار جمع دور [illegible]
موسیقی [illegible] گویند ادهم سیاه و اسب سیاه ادیب [illegible] ادیم پوست [illegible] ارجمند [illegible]
نام ولایتی است [illegible] ارزال جمع رذل [illegible] نام رودخانه ایست معروف [illegible]
از حوالی تفلیس [illegible] نام [illegible] آن افلاطون بوده [illegible] نام کتاب [illegible] شعبه [illegible]
چنانکه در حرف [illegible] مذکور خواهد شد ارم بالکسر باغ شداد و نام شخصی که [illegible] ارمن [illegible]
از [illegible] که مسکن [illegible] بوده ازاره بالکسر [illegible] پایین دیوار [illegible] اژدها [illegible]
بالکسر [illegible] بالکسر کنایه است از [illegible] اسب معروف و نام [illegible] از آلات شطرنج اسباق جمع سبق [illegible]
استغراق بالکسر [illegible] صوفیه مستغرق [illegible] استفاده [illegible]
[illegible] بالکسر [illegible] چنانکه [illegible] گوید [illegible]
[illegible] اسماع بالکسر شنوانیدن اشترک بالضم [illegible] اشتلم بالضم [illegible] اشک آب چشم [illegible] و نام [illegible]
هرات که اشکانیان منسوب باویند اشکانیان طبقه [illegible] اشهب [illegible] سفید [illegible]
اصبع بالکسر انگشت اصم [illegible] بالکسر [illegible] اطلاق [illegible]

نشانها و نمانا [illegible] اشیا [illegible] العرب بادیه نشین اعجوبه بالضم آنچه عجب و شگفت آید [illegible] حرکات کلمه [illegible]
از [illegible] باشد اعراب عرب بادیه نشین اعراض جمع عرض [illegible] چنانکه [illegible] و شعرهای [illegible]
[illegible] خلق حضرت خیر البشر علیه السلام اغلال بالکسر [illegible] اعمی کور اغلال جمع غل [illegible]
[illegible] افراط بالکسر [illegible] افروغ [illegible] افسانه [illegible]
حکایت و داستان افسون مکر و افسون و حیله [illegible] خوانند
افکار [illegible] افیون تریاک اقاله بالکسر [illegible] اقامت بالکسر [illegible] اقصی [illegible]
[illegible] اقطاب جمع قطب [illegible] اصطلاح صوفیه [illegible]
از اولیا اقطار جمع قطر [illegible] اطراف [illegible] ولایت [illegible]
زمین اکحال بالکسر [illegible] اکسیر بالکسر کیمیا اکمه نابینای [illegible]
[illegible] الهاهه [illegible] چنانکه [illegible] گوید [illegible]
جمع [illegible] البرز نام کوهی است [illegible] بالکسر [illegible]
[illegible] ام الکتاب بالضم [illegible] امثال [illegible]
و بالمجاز [illegible] املا بالکسر [illegible] بالضم نام خواهر [illegible] علیها السلام [illegible] بالضم
[illegible] انابت بالکسر [illegible] انبار [illegible] که بیکجا جمع کرده باشند و نام [illegible]
و بمعنی [illegible] باشد [illegible] که [illegible] کرده باشند [illegible] نام [illegible]
[illegible] انجام بالکسر [illegible] انجم جمع نجم [illegible] انداز بالکسر [illegible]
چنانکه گوید شعر [illegible] اندام شکل و شمایل [illegible]
[illegible] اندام داشتن [illegible] انس [illegible] انکار بالکسر [illegible]
انکاف جمع [illegible] منع کردن [illegible] انهی بالکسر [illegible] انها باشد [illegible]
[illegible] اوباش طایفه [illegible] اوتاد [illegible] باصطلاح صوفیه [illegible] اولیاء [illegible]
اوج بلندی اوجه بالضم [illegible] نام ولایتی [illegible] اورنگ تخت [illegible]
و نام شخصی که عاشق [illegible] بوده و نام [illegible] که از اعراب [illegible] گویند اوحد [illegible] بالضم [illegible] اویس بالضم نام [illegible]
اهتزاز بالکسر جنبیدن اهرمن اهرمن دیو و شیطان ایاز نام غلامی که معشوق محمود غزنوی بوده [illegible] بالکسر [illegible]
بود [illegible] ایضاح بالکسر [illegible] ایمن بکسر الهمزه [illegible] ایماض بالکسر [illegible]
اینک بکسر الهمزه و فتح نون [illegible] حرف [illegible] الباء العربیه [illegible] شهری است مشهور [illegible]
و الحال [illegible] خراب [illegible] که [illegible] عجوس بوده اند [illegible]
نام ولایتی معروف از توابع هرات [illegible] آنجا مشهور است [illegible] اول [illegible] دویم [illegible]
سیم [illegible] چهارم [illegible] پنجم [illegible] چنانکه گویند [illegible] بارو بار [illegible]
[illegible] که [illegible] هشتم [illegible] و هم [illegible] نازه [illegible] دو [illegible]

ب

354v

حلوانان و حیوانات دیکر بیز هم معنی نموده و کناه بنیلر چنکرده هم انباری کر بجهت قوه زراعت و زمین بریزند پانزدهم منزل که مطربان
نوازند شانزدهم آرد بیغ وانزه که بجهت بعضی مهیا کرده باشند هفدهم نام دهی است از ولایت طوس هیجدهم آنچه بانو فنون هر کراز
نفند نوزدهم آنچه نویسندکان نویسند بیستم هر چیز که آنرا لغو زند بیت و یکم شاخ را کویند بیست و دوم تکلیف مالا یطاق باشد بار بد
بضم با و ثانی و فتح آن نام مطرب خسرو پرویز است بارقه بفتح فجش بابه بروزن خار و اسب مرکب و نوبت و جمله بعد یواطلبه و شعر بمعنی
دوست هم باشد چنانچه کویند فلاحی بابه و بمعنی حق و شان نیز بود چنا[...] شیده در بابه فلان باذکون بازکونه وارونه با
چیزی که نمو کتر است باغ جهان آرا باغ زاغان باغ سفید باغ کل افشان باغ نو نام باغهاست معروف که در هرات می باشد
بربهان جبه جامه ایست که رستم روز جنک میپوشیده و بعضی کویند که از پوست اکوان دیو بوده و بعضی کفته اند که جانوریست که دشمن
شیر است و ابر رستم هر که جامه ازین کشته پوست او جبه ساخت و بیبان و بیر نیز هم کفته اند بت آزری آزر نام حضرت ابراهیم
است که بت تراش بوده باعتبار زینت و بصناعت بت تراشان محبوب را چون خواهند که بخوبی و استادی وصف کنند باو نسبت دهند بخ شاخ
کنایه است از کف دست بخی بجل بکسر با و خا جلال کردن بخیرات دریاهای کوچک بختی بضم با شتر بخت النصر بکون ضاد
بخت النصر بفتح صاد بخت نصر باشد چنانچه شاهد برادلطاهر لسان الطیر کوید شعر یا که بخت النصر قبیله عظیم و یکی یا که نوشیروان
عدل او لدی قریش و شاهد بر ثانی او صبح سکندری در ذکر طبقه دوم ملوک فرماید شعر یقین دین آنکا ایترولدی بعیش کرلشکرکش
بولدی بخت النصر بحرد جو هسند بخش بروزن خش حصه مهند بخورات آنچه بآتش دود کنند بددود وداع بدملعت
کنایه است از جا و دلی که جواهر بجوید و مهارت باشد بدیع عجیب بدل نظیر و مانند بربط ساز چنک بزلهت نوشته حواله
و شبینه شمعی را کویند چنانچه میلی مجنون در وصف لیلی کوید شعر بوق ایکی سلجی تونیکا غایت منی ایکی لیلی بی نهایت آندین
بولوب آتی جلوه آرای آنداق که برات وقدر اراآق برجیس بروزن ادریس ستاره مشتری برسرب بفوق و برتری و فایق و برتر و علاوه
برغند جشن و عیش را کویند که بسبب نزدیک شدن ماه رمضان در آخرهای شعبان کنند و آنرا کلوخ انداز آن کویند برطاس نام ولایتی
از ترکستان برک بلد رخت و ساز و نوا و سامان و اسباب برکستوان جبه خامه ایست که در جنک پوشند و بر اسب پوشانند برکی
عبا مجتت از نمد سبز منسوب برلعل بر که بکسرا ول جای ایستادن آب برنا بمعنی جوان باشد و صاحب برهان قاطع بمعنی جانام نوشته
که بر دست بندند و بزعم مولف آنست که برنا را که در عربی بمعنی حناست برنا خوانده و در فرهنک داخل کرده از پیش برده اند بجز الطلعت جانانه
بربخینه الآن عزیزی که از میغ سازند بزعم بت پرستی و پرستش بت پرستان بزید قاصد بزه بفتح بزه کناه و خطا و جرم و حیف
و مسکین و نامراد بس کافی و بسیار و کویند که بسکی بمعنی موقوف کن بسا چه بسیار بساط آنچه بکسترانند و از اصطلاحات بازی
شطرنج هم هست بستان افروز نام کلیست سرخ رنک که آنرا تاج خروس نیز کویند بسط پهن کردن و کستردن و مجازا بمعنی خوشحالی هم
مستعملست بسمل بکسر با و میم مذبوح و وجه تسمیه آنست که در وقت ذبح بسم الله میکویند بسی بسیار بسیط پهن و خالص خنده کند
و نام بحریست از شعر بشر بکسر با نام زاهدیست مشهور که از ابشر حافی کویند بط امردی و صراحی شراب بطحا زمین هموار که در آن سنگریزها
باشد و نام موضعی معروف در حجاز بطوش کند ضد سریع بقل تره خضر بقم بفتح قاف مخفف بقم باشد و آن درختی است که بدان سرخ رنک
میکنند
بقیع نام قبرستانیست معروف در مدینه طیبه بلارک تیر و شمشیر بلال نام غلام حضرت رسول علیه السلام که موذن آنحضرت و حبشی بود بلبله
کوزه لوله دار و صدا و آواز صراحی بلقیس نام ملکه سبا که بعقد حضرت سلیمان علیه السلام درآمد بم فروضد بمت و نام قصبه ایست
از توابع کرمان و زیر و بم اوج و حضیض و نغمه را کویند بنات انکشتان بنکاه بروزن کراه منزل و مسکن و جایی که اشیا در آنجا نهند

355r

بوذرد نام یکی از خطبای معروف بوقبیس بضم قاف نام کوهیست معروف در حجاز بوقلمون نوعی از دیبای رومی است که هر لحظه برنکی نماید
و بآن نسبت شخص متلون المزاج و امور متغیر الاوضاع را هم بالمجاز بوقلمون توصیف کنند و نیز نام مرغیست بوالعلا نام یکی از خطبای
معروف بولهب یعنی ملازم النار و نام عم حضرت رسول علیه السلام که کافر بوده بوالهوس یعنی ملازم الهوس چنانچه کویند بولهب یعنی
ملازم النار و فرهنک جهانکیری این لفظ را بالهوس تحریر و لو و الف ذکر کرده و نوشته که بلغت اهل هند بمعنی بسیار باشد و معنی ترکیبی
بسیار هوس باشد و صاحب برهان قاطع نیز متابعت نموده اکرچه بل تنها بمعنی بسیار باشد اما هوس لفظیست عربی و ترکیب آن با لفظ هندی
انسب از آنست که با هندی و ترکی ترکیب یابد بوم جغد و زمین هکو جنه و غیب بهرام نام پادشاهیست معروف که از اجرام کور کشید
و ستاره مریخ بهرام چوبین نام سپه سالار است که سردار لشکر هرمز بن نوشیروان بوده و بسبب آنکه لاغر و خشک اندام بوده او را چوبین میکفتند
میکفتند بهمن بروزن مخزن نام اردشیر که پسر اسفندیار است و نام ماه دوم از زمستان و تخمهای برفی و نام پرده ایست از موسیقی و نام کیاهی است
و نام کوهیست بسیار بلند و نام قلعه ایست در حوالی اردبیل و نام چشمه ایست در جرجان و نام قلعه ایست در هندوستان بجیم چونه
سیاته نام شهر و مقامی از موسیقی بیرلت بی هم صحبت سامان بیت الحزن بفتح حا خانه غم خانه بیت الصنم بفتح لام بتخانه
بیجاده کهربا بیخواسته طلب و ناخواسته بیحال ناتوان و شکسته حال و بطلوع بمعنی تیز زبان هم استعمال شده چنانچه میرعلیشیر کوید شعر
کونکلوم کی کلبکون بحال اولدی چون جیبین مقتادن بیلهسون بحال بحال لای کونکول آغر بیکل بیداد ظلم و ستم و نام شهریست در ترکستان
بیجار اول نام شهریست از ممالک هند و بفتح اول در عربی بمعنی خرما باشد بیدق پیاده شطرنج بیرنک نقش اول که نقاشان برای امتیاز
بدون رنگ بر کاغذ کشند بیرنکی باصطلاح صوفیه تجرد و بی تعلقی بیضا آفتاب بیکران بی نهایت بین بین متوسط میان الجنبه
پاداش جزا و مزد پاده کله کاو و خر و چوب بستن و چراکاه پارسا زاهد و پرهیزکار پازند نام کتابیست در آیین آتش پرستی که منسوب بزند است
و بعضی کفته اند که ترجمه و تفسیر زند است پاره چوبی دراز بود که بر سر کاوآهن بندند تا زمین را شیار کند پاس حراست و کشیک و پهرا
از شب پاسخ بضم سین جواب پاک اساس کنایه است از صاحب عفت و پرهیزکار پاکی تمامی و طهارت و تیغ دلاکی پالا صاف کننده پالرد
بروزن آمرد کوشش و سعی پایه زینه که از آن بالا روند و مقدم و منزلت پخته پنبه بروزن پنبه پالعکده و با ابجد بغلط چوب بمعنی داد
اول کوسفند سه ساله را کویند دوم چیزی که پوست آنرا کنده باشند و مولف برهان قاطع پخته بمعنی پنبه را با بای ابجد نوشته خش
بروزن خش کفته شده و پس پذیرفتار باذالبجه قبول کننده پرتاب بمد از انداختن پرچم دو معنی دارد اول کیسو نوعی از کاو کوهی با
که آنرا خرغاو کویند دوم کاکل بوده باجانداشته را کویند که از علم آویزند و مولف برهان
قاطع نوشته که چیزی باشد سیاه و سرخ که بر کردن علم و نیزه بندند پرنده نام تنکیه که نقاشان در چهره سازی و غیر آن بمویی کرده زنند
و اسم مصدر پرپوشدن و جلا دادن صیقل کردن و آراستن و ساختن و برانکیختن و فارغ کشتن باشد پرستار غمخوار پرغار پرزم طیلسان که له
لحت و پاره پرکار بیرنشا بجلوه زاده است از رخت و بطریق تجرید بمعنی پرنده استعمال شده چنانچه در سنکلاخ فرهاد کوید شعر
هول کون او قحلیرخانه پکاوش صیا فیلدی خارا ایجره بیزاو پرکند قطعه و پاره پرمکس جنسی از جامه ابریشمی است که آن را کوجهر
فولاد جوهردار نیز پرمکی کویند پرند بافته ایست ابریشمی بسیار نازک و بی نشان منقش و زین [...] وش و ستاره پروین و تیغ شمشیر و مسن ابیت نام
که آنرا بترکی پوپر کویند پرنیان بافته ای [...] نقش پرداخته و منسوب بادشاهان و جانوریست معروف که خوش آشیانه برچراغ زند پروز
منطوق و منسوب کرکه و ارتفع خسرو و نام ستاره پروین و مخفف پرویز باشد یعنی آن دیز پرویزن آلتی است که بدان آرد بیزند و منکوی اشال
صاف کند پروین ستاره کوچکانست که یکجا جمع است و از اهل عرب ثریا کویند و نام منزلیست از منازل بیست و هشتکانه قمر پریخوان افسون کر

وکوکه تیغ‌جی کرده باشد بر سر تیغ بزه و جستجو و تفحص [illegible] پشیز بعضی تیز قلس کیچیک [illegible] که آنرا [illegible] کویند
پشیز • قلس [illegible] کوچک و قلس [illegible] که از برنج و امثال آن [illegible]
و پولی که از طلا و نقره صورت کرده بر سینه بندند اسب و امثال آن [illegible] بدان [illegible]
کیمه لاف [illegible] بلپوش [illegible] پوشش بود [illegible] و آن [illegible]
بطریق [illegible] پوشند شعر [illegible] کویا بلپوش [illegible]
پلنکنه نوعی از پوششی است که از پوستین [illegible] پوشند [illegible]
پوده • [illegible] و چوب پوسیده [illegible] کویند [illegible] پول قلس [illegible]
پیلوی بعضی [illegible] شعر [illegible]
و چیزی را کویند که [illegible] بعضی [illegible] پیشان [illegible]
تا صد پیل فیل و نام آلتی است از آلات شطرنج پیل بالا [illegible] پیلپایه ستونی که سقف بر آن [illegible] تاب
طاقت و توانایی و تابش و پیچ و خم تاپالت [illegible] تابدان بعضی [illegible]
و کاغذ چسبانیده باشند [illegible] تاج خروس [illegible] کویند تاراجیت [illegible]
و بافته چنانکه [illegible] کوید شعر [illegible]
[illegible] تال [illegible] و امثال آن [illegible]
از برنج که [illegible] هندوستان [illegible] هندوستان که از [illegible]
کویند تاول [illegible] معنی ظاهر [illegible] تبع [illegible] اتباع و پیروان تجدد نو شدن تجرد آزاد شدن
تجرید قطع علایق کردن تجزی جزو جزو کردن تجلی ظاهر شدن و جلوه کردن تجمیل آراستن و نیکو ساختن تجویف میانه را خالی
کردن [illegible] تحریر نوشتن و آزاد کردن و خط [illegible] که بر دور کتابت طلا و نقشها کشند تحریر [illegible]
تحلیل [illegible] کردن تحمیق [illegible] تخلخل [illegible] تخلیص [illegible] کردن
و خالص کردن [illegible] کوید شعر [illegible]
[illegible] تدوین کتب تالیف کردن و دیوان شعر ترتیب دادن [illegible]
ترانه باصطلاح اهل نغمه تصنیفی است که [illegible] باشد [illegible] ترصیع [illegible]
[illegible] شعر [illegible] ترجیع
تردامن فاسق [illegible] ترسا [illegible] ترسناک [illegible] ترصیع [illegible]
کلام [illegible] ترکیب [illegible] ترنم [illegible] تریاق [illegible] تزویر
فریب دادن تسلسل [illegible] تشحید تیز کردن تشریف خلعت [illegible] تشهیر [illegible]
[illegible]
[illegible] شعر [illegible] تضعیف دو برابر کردن
تطبیق مطابق ساختن تعادل باهم برابر [illegible] تعبیه [illegible] پنهان کردن تعریض [illegible] تعزیر [illegible]

ت

[illegible] کردن تعفین بدبو کردن تعمیق [illegible] کردن تعمیم [illegible] کردن تعوید مع الدال [illegible] چنانکه [illegible]
و تشدید [illegible] شعر [illegible]
[illegible] تفحص [illegible] تفت [illegible] و التهاب [illegible] پرتو و روشنی [illegible]
و تکرار [illegible] تفریح [illegible] تفسیر [illegible] تقریب [illegible] کردن [illegible]
[illegible] تکاپوی [illegible] تکسیر شکستن و باصطلاح [illegible]
نقاشان [illegible] تلالا [illegible]
[illegible] تلخ [illegible] باشد [illegible]
تلخیص مختصر کردن و نام کتابیست در علم بیان تلمیذ شاکرد [illegible]
[illegible] تلقین تفهیم تمثال [illegible]
[illegible] تنبل [illegible]
[illegible] که آنرا [illegible] هند [illegible] کویند [illegible]
هندوستان تنصیف دو نیم کردن تنقل نقل خوردن [illegible]
[illegible] تنقیص کم کردن تنگ [illegible]
و نام [illegible] ترکستان [illegible]
مانند جوشن و پوستین [illegible]
چرخ آسیا [illegible]
توانان [illegible] توزیع [illegible] تقسیم [illegible] کردن [illegible]
و تیز کردن [illegible] و نام ولایت [illegible] ته [illegible]
[illegible]
[illegible] و نام ستاره [illegible]
[illegible] ثریا نام ستاره پروین [illegible] الجیم [illegible] جادو [illegible]
[illegible] و نام ولایت [illegible] خراسان
[illegible] از ولایت سند جام جم و جام جمشید جام شراب جام جهان نما [illegible] که از آنجا استخراج [illegible]
جام [illegible] جانا جان [illegible]
جانان چنانکه کوید شعر [illegible]
جاوید همیشه [illegible] و نام [illegible]
بالفتح بخت [illegible]
[illegible] جراد [illegible] جرده اسب [illegible]
بالضم کناه [illegible] جره [illegible]

ث ج

ل.٢١ ستاری

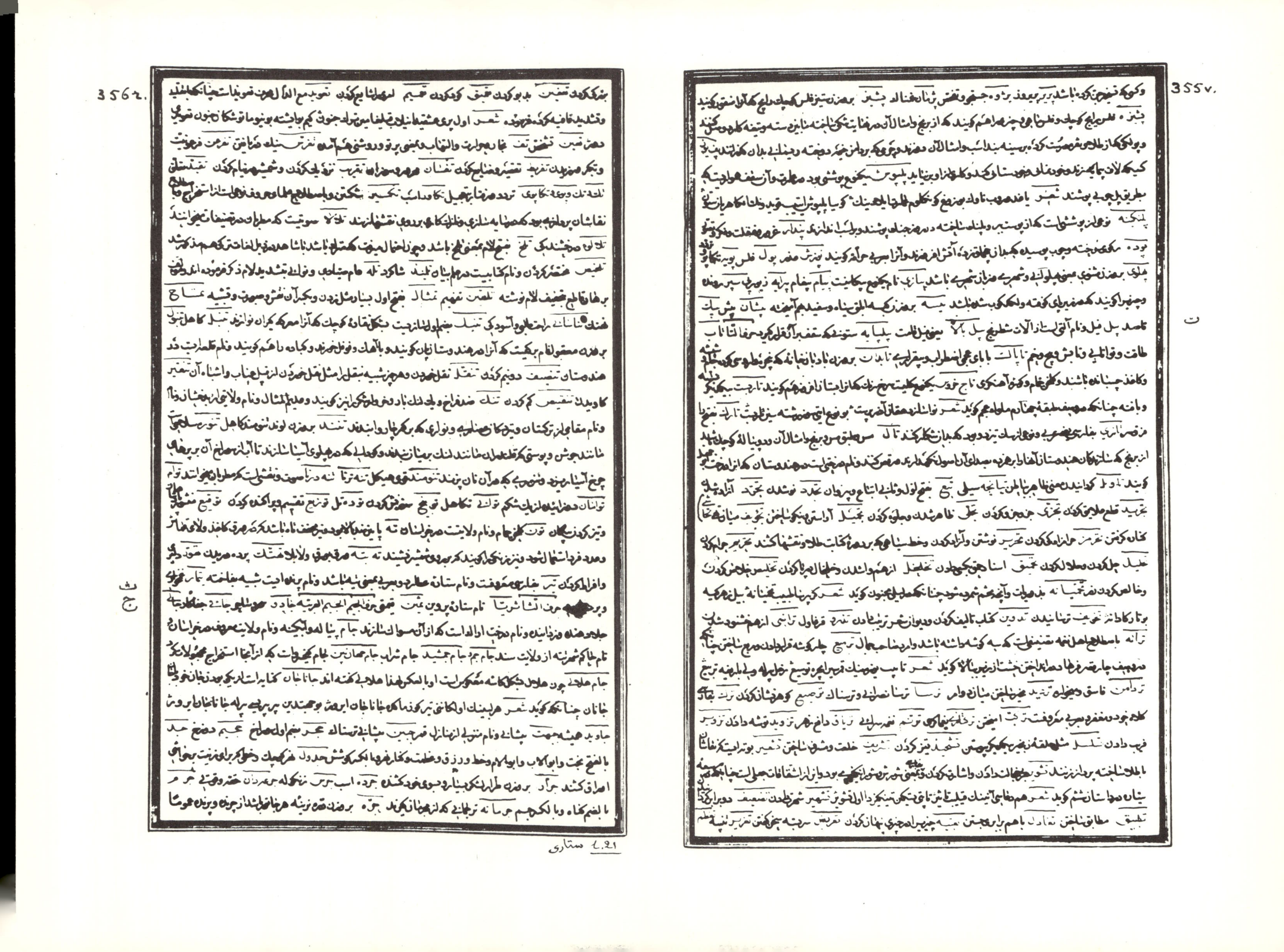

356v.

و زینه بانرا گویند خصوصا و بعضی ابریشمینه را گویند اعم از آنکه نر باشد یا ماده و بعضی کوچک هر چیز را گویند و بعضی شالع و علیق جابد
و جابك هم هست و نام سازیست مانند شش تو اما از آن کوچك تر است و نام قریه ایست از توابع شیراز جمجمه ... و ... و شبها و غیره
کوچك المنداران جزایر بیشهای سواحل هوای هوما و نام ولایتی که در سواحل دریا واقع است خصوصا جزر لا یتجزی با صطلاح حکما
جوهریست که قابل قسمت نباشد جزع بالفتح و الکسر نام یکنوع سنگیست مخطط سیاه و سفید شبیه بچشم و نیز کنایه است
از چشم چنانکه گوید شعر او لعل صبح عقیق و لعل سیراب جز ضمیر این ... جبه تیرهان که از ابلق رخش گویند
جعفری نوعی از طلا باشد چنانکه در غزلیات گفته جحت یاجوج و ماجوج گوید شعر نیه تا الغلاج ایچ کورنجی ... بولد که باذ
سیلان دم محول دشنام اول که باذ ایمه ... واقی جعفری بولیب هر ... جنات ماست جف القلم
اشاره است بحدیث جف القلم بما هو کاین یعنی خشکید قلم با بچه شدنی بود جل بالضم و الفتح پوشش دواب جلا بالفتح ترك
وطن کردن و با لکسر زدودن و روشن جلب برهزن زلف ... که ... ماه ... باشد و بعضی شهرت هم استعمال
میشود چنانکه گویند شعر لذت تا یار اول شیخ جوجوك جانیم ... ولنانکی ... منت جل
سنجهای کوچکست که بر اطراف دایره نصب کنند جلا ... ظهور آثار جمالیت ظهور آثار لطف جمال بالفتح شکل نکو
و با لکسر شتران ... جمیل نیکو و مطلب جمال جناب ... آستان در ... کردن جاده ... بیغ
اول ... بغا ... وکیل ... دامنه زین و تسمه رکاب و شرط وکردی ... جناحین دو بال و دو بازو جنایت
گناه کردن جندره ... بروی خط کنه کشیدن و ... کنده و ناتراشیده عموما و چوبی که
بجمه ... پوشیدنی تراشند خصوصا و انچه بدان صوف و شال و جامهای دیگر ... کنند جنیبت اسب کوتل
جوامع الکلم قرآن مجید و کلامی کثیر المعانی و قلیل الالفاظ ... چنانکه در ...
دیدن جهون ... کبوتر بچه گوید شعر ... کبوتر ... چو ... چیغ
ایلجی ... مضطرب ... و از افسانه از اجوان گویند جوجرس حقه ... و ... قرجه ... گویند
که ... جوق فوج و گروه جوکی طایفه ریاضت کش ... هند وان را گویند ... جول
جونکانت جوخه مخفف جولاهه است ... کنایه است ... چنانکه ...
الابرار ... گوید شعر ... نام ... هرات
جمهر ... جیب بالفتح ... جیحون نام رود خانه ایست که ... کنند و آنرا آمویه هم
گویند جیغ فریاد جیفه جسم ... بالجیم ... منتکانی بود که بر اطراف ... چارتاب نوعی از جامه
درشت و بد قماش بود که انرا چار پود هم گویند چارگاه نام مقامیست که از موسیقی چنانکه گوید شعر بدن ...
... چارگاهی ایت خارج نوا ... چاشتگاه ... هنگام چاشت ... هنگامی که
آفتاب بلند شده بر آفاق عالم مسلط شده باشد چنانکه در حیرة الابرار گوید شعر ... سلطانی ... چاشتگاه ...
سلطان ... خیل و سپاه چرخ اطلس فلك الاعظم چرخ شعله ... که از آهن از ... ساخته ...
... چرکس نام طایفه ایست معروف که در ... داغستان می نشینند چست ... و چالاك ... نام
سازیست که مطربان نوازند و نام ... از موسیقی ... چغانه ... گویند ... اول و ثانی

11

357r

کوهی که برای ایذای مردم افشاری ... و دفع کند ... و منشور ... مصاحب ... و ...
شکستن چیزی و شتہ ... چاپ ... که ... گویند ... بعضی ... باشد ... نام ...
کجنك که ... گویند و نام ... موسیقی چکل ... نام شهریست از ترکستان ... گویند
چله ... کمان ... کوشه ... چلیپا صلیب ... که آنرا ...
... حضرت عیسی علیه السلام ... و آن بدین شکل است X و نصاری آنرا ...
برای ... و کنایه از ... چنبر ... چنك نام سازیست ...
چمن ... ح ... حاجب ... حاشا ...
و انکار ... حافظ ... خال ... حالت ... کنایه است ...
چنانکه ... گوید شعر ... و له
چون ... آلت ...
... حال ... کنایه ...
... چنانکه ... گوید شعر ...
... حبیب ... حج ...
... حجاز ... مقامی ... از موسیقی ... حج ...
... حجله ... گوید
... حرم ...
... حرف ... تخمین ...
... احیاط ... حسام شمشیر حسان ...
حسینی ... نام مقامیست از موسیقی ... چشم ...
... حصیر ... جامه ...
حشیش ... حلقه ... کمال ...
... حلقه ... چنانکه ...
... جلوه ...
... حمل ... بغداد ... کبوتر حمل ...
... حنا ... خنظل ...
حیلان ... چنانکه ... گوید شعر ...
حیلات ... خ ...
باشد ...
... خاد ... خاده ...

نانند موف خار ابهم کنایه است از اسب بچه نوزاد خار خار خلجان خاطر خار خسک نام گیاهیست سه پهلو و نیز پاره‌های آهن را گویند
که بدان شکل ساخته به سر راه خصم اندازند و از ابر بی حسک گویند خار کاو و خار پرکاو سنگ تراش خاشه مصحف خاشاک باشد
[illegible] خاک [illegible] که آن را در آماج خانه بر فشانند اندازند و نیز هر چیز منسوب به خاک را
گویند خال معروف و نیز دانه‌ایست که در چشم پیدا شود [illegible] ابر بی باران و برق
[illegible] خام [illegible] خام خوانند و
شراب [illegible] جامه قلم [illegible] خاور مشرق خاوران نام ولایتی
از خراسان که [illegible] داخل آن ولایت [illegible] خانقاه [illegible] خانقاه قدس کنایه است [illegible]
[illegible] خاوند مخفف خداوند است یعنی صاحب [illegible] خبط آشفتگی [illegible] خبتن [illegible]
[illegible] مسعود خنگ اسب چنانکه در لیلی مجنون گوید شعر [illegible]
[illegible] خدنگ نام درختیست صلب که از چوب آن خانه زین و تیر و نیزه سازند [illegible]
[illegible] پادشاه [illegible] خراب مست لایعقل [illegible] خرابات شرابخانه و قمارخانه و امثال آن خراز [illegible]
[illegible] خراس [illegible] خرده [illegible]
[illegible] گویند خرده دان [illegible]
[illegible] خریطه ظرفیست از پوست و غیر آن که چیزها در آن نهند خز نام جانوریست که
[illegible] پوست آن پوستین دوزند خزف سفال [illegible] خسروچین کنایه است از آفتاب [illegible]
[illegible] خس خانه خانه‌ایست که [illegible] تا هوا را خنک کند [illegible]
[illegible] خشت [illegible] خشتخانه [illegible]
[illegible] و آن نیزه کوچکیست که [illegible]
[illegible]
[illegible] خشخاش لشکر مکمل با سلاح چنانکه در لیلی مجنون گوید شعر [illegible]
[illegible] خضرا سبز و آسمان [illegible]
[illegible] بالضم [illegible] چنانکه در لیلی مجنون گوید شعر [illegible]
[illegible] خط جام [illegible]
[illegible] خطه [illegible]
[illegible] خفقان [illegible] خلف
[illegible] خلاب [illegible] خلخ [illegible]

شعر [illegible] خلیدن [illegible] خماد [illegible]
شراب و بالکسر [illegible] خمول [illegible] خنج [illegible]
و عیش و طرب و ناز و کرشمه خنک [illegible] هر چیز [illegible] گویند [illegible]
[illegible] چنانکه [illegible] شعر [illegible]
[illegible] مؤلف برهان قاطع [illegible] خواب
خوکوش کنایه است از [illegible] آلت تناسل [illegible]
باشد خوازه [illegible] و امثال آن کنند و آفرین و خواهش خوانق جمع خانقاه خودکامه
[illegible] خورنق [illegible] که نعمان بن امرء القیس [illegible] خیر باد کنایه است
از وداع خوی عرق [illegible] عادت و خصلت خیال خام فکر بیهوده خیزران [illegible] چوبیست هندی [illegible]
[illegible] خیل [illegible] خیلخانه [illegible]
چنانکه در لیلی مجنون گوید شعر [illegible]
گوید شعر [illegible] مؤلف برهان قاطع [illegible]
د [illegible] حرف الدال داج [illegible]
[illegible] دارا نام پادشاهیست معروف [illegible]
هم گویند [illegible] دارو [illegible] و امثال آن را هم گویند
داس آلت [illegible] نام گیاهیست [illegible]
گویند [illegible] داغ معروف [illegible] آن را هم داغ گویند [illegible]
[illegible] شعر [illegible]
[illegible] معروف [illegible]
[illegible] دام معروف است [illegible] شطرنج [illegible]
[illegible] را هم گویند داور پادشاه [illegible]
دبابه [illegible] آلات قلعه گیریست [illegible] دبستان
مکتب [illegible] دجله نام رود بغداد [illegible]
[illegible] بالضم [illegible]
[illegible] شکاف [illegible]
باشد [illegible] شعر [illegible]
[illegible]
گویند [illegible]
[illegible]

358v.

درے زبان دری قدیم کبک را هم دری گویند یعنی منسوب بقوم دریغ حیف وافسوس وحسرت کنایه از دمدمه دژم بالثانی
بمعنی دم اندوهگین وچیار وافسرده دستان جمع دستان یعنی افسانه وحکایت دستانسرا قصه خوان وافسانه گوی دستاویز
وسیله وبهانه دست پیچ بهانه دستور بالضم وزیر وقاعده مهم وکتابی که در او قوانین امری نوشته باشند ورخصت واجازت دیکچه
که برهوی کشتی وبرچپ ... نام کتابیست بحروف هر لغت دغل بر وزن زحل نام زنیست دغا با زحیله مکر دغل حیله و
ناراست وپشه بر وزن دفت ... بمعنی ایاره است دقیق آرد ونبات دلال ناز وکرشمه دلاله زنی که دلق بر وزن حلق
پاره دلق دلزاله الفضال ... چنانکه گوید شعر ... تا ...
پر فرسیله دلیل ... بر وزن ... کمان وفریاد کنان ... دم کیر
نفس کیر دمن بکحل ... دموع قطرات اشک چشم ... باشد دنکسه
وآشفته دماغ دنکا ... خود برای ... دواج روپوش ... دوده
سیاهی که ... شراب ... دوستکانی ... دختر رز
توام چنانکه ... شعر ... دم
باشه ... دی بالفتح ماه دیم
وبالکسر ... دیبا جامه ... دیباچه
دیوانه ... کنایه از ... دیولاخ
دیوستان ... ذباب مگس ... ذرایر جمع ذری
است یعنی آنچه پاشیده شود چنانکه ... شعر ...
ذقن زنخدان ذل بالضم خواری ذنب ... ذوذوابه ...
شود ذوذنب ... ذو النون نام ... است که
بمصر ... ذهاب ... حرف ... راح ریحانی شراب خوشبوی راد کریم
وشجاع ... راستان جمع ... شعر ...
ای ویران ... راه ...
... رای ... پادشاه هندوستان ... رباب ... ربیع بالفتح منزل
... بالضم ... رتبه ... رجه ... رخ
بدان ... رحل ... روکن ...
ساخته ... راح ... که ...
از آلات شطرنج ... رخ ...
... رز ...
در ... علیه السلام گوید ... رسن ...
رستخیز ... رشته ... علیه السلام ...

359r.

از آن الیه ... رسیدن ... رطل ... بن ... کنایه از ...
مانند او ... رقص ... که ... رقم ...
باشکوه ... رکاب ... ده هشت ... گویند چنانکه ...
اسب ... رکیب ... رنگ ...
قسمت ... صبح وجان ... وسوی ... چیله ...
ونظافت ... روح ... رسیم ...
ورشیز ... خانه ...
ساخته باشند ... استعمال ... روح ... علیه السلام روح ...
روح ... روح روان جان ... نام ... روده هشت
روسی ... نام پهلوان ... روی ... باشد روی تن ...
وآن ... روی ... کنایه از ... رهبان جمع راهب یعنی ترسنده ...
... رهنورد ... کنایه از ... ریاح ... ریش ...
ومال واسباب ... زاج ... تلیستان وتوابع که از
... زاد ... زاغ ...
... کمان ... کنایه از ... کمان گویند ... جوهریست ...
سیاه ... زبانه ... شعله ... زجاج ... شیشه ...
زحل ... بالضم ... آلات شطرنج ... چنانکه ...
کافر ... زردشت نام حکیمی ... آتش پرستی ...
ابراهیم علیه السلام است ... زرق ... کنایه از آفتاب ... زرد نام ...
که آن را ... زره حلقه ... حلقه را هم گویند ...
... شعر ...
المبابت که ... نام ولایتیست ... زریر ...
وآن را ... گویند ونام ... باشد ... کنایه از آفتاب ... شود ...
معروف که ... زلال ... آب صاف ...
ضم ... زمان وقت ... زمانه ...
... زمرد ... کنایه از ... سبز معروف چنانکه گوید شعر ...
هم ... زنخ زنخدان ... زنخ ... کنایه از ...
علیه شعر ...
زنگ ... آینه ... آفتاب ... زنگبار ... نام ولایتیست معروف ...

359v.

زنگی شب: زنگ کنایه است از هندوستان. زنجبیل [illegible] که در مقام تحذیر گفته می شود. زور بمعنی مکر
و دروغ و نام شهریست در نواحی همدان و بمعنی قوت و توانائی. زورق کشتی. زولانه بالضم بمعنی زنجیر پای مجرمان که بندند. جله
کمان و آفرین. زه چشم کنایه است از نگاه خشم آمیز. زیبق سیماب. زیج رصدیست که منجمان بندند. زیر بمعنی بم و بمعنی [illegible]
و [illegible] اوج و حضیض. [illegible] نغمه را گویند. [illegible] ژاله تگرگ و قطره شبنم. ژرف عمیق. ژنده پاره. ژولیده موی
و پریشان و [illegible] سار نام پرنده ایست سیاه رنگ که خالهای سفید دارد. [illegible] العرش
و عنبر [illegible] و نام شهریست [illegible] ساعی شتابنده و [illegible] و قاصد پیاده را هم گویند
باصطلاح صوفیه راهرو راه طریقت [illegible] سایر سیر کننده [illegible] و هم سایر [illegible] مقام کنایه است از حضرت جبرئیل
سایل گدا و جاری. سپاس [illegible] جمع لشکر سپاه [illegible] سپاهان شهر اصفهان و مقامیست از موسیقی. سبحه بالضم تسبیح. سپری تمام
آخر و شکل [illegible] هم گویند و آنرا [illegible] ترنج مانند. سبز [illegible] سبزخنگ اسب کبود. سبع بضم با
[illegible] سبع مثانی سوره [illegible] سبعه سیاره هفت کوکب معروف که آنرا سیارات گویند و نیز نام مثنویست که نوائی علیه الرحمه [illegible]
[illegible] منظوم نموده. سبلت بفتح اول و ثانی بروت. سپنج [illegible] سپندان اسپند باشد که آنرا [illegible] حرمل گویند. سپوخ
فرشتگان. سپهبد بضم [illegible] سپید [illegible] سپیده [illegible] سپیدی [illegible] که زنان بروی مالند. سبیل
راه [illegible] سبیل الله. ستر پرده. سترون زن عقیم نازاینده. ستوه ملول [illegible] سجاده
جای نماز. سخت کوش [illegible] سخره بالضم شخصی که [illegible] سخط غضب و خشم. سدره [illegible]
در بهشت. سراب [illegible] سراج چراغ. سراج [illegible] کتاب [illegible]
صوفیست و ملقب بطاووس الفقرا [illegible] الشاهد علیه [illegible]
آنکه [illegible] سراغوج [illegible] که زنان ترک [illegible]
بر کمر بندند [illegible] سرخوش [illegible] سرداشت [illegible] سرهنگ [illegible]
[illegible] سروش فرشته [illegible] پنهان
و آشکار. سروناز [illegible] سرو سهی [illegible] از موسیقی. سره [illegible]
و برگزیده [illegible] سطح [illegible] مکان کنایه است
از [illegible] سفال بالفتح [illegible] جمع سفله [illegible] کوزه و سبو [illegible]
آن که از گل پخته باشند و بضم هم آمده و مولف برهان قاطع بمعنی ریزه و شکسته کوزه و سبو و امثال آن نوشته. سفت
بروزن زفت سوراخ سوزن و ثقبه که در جواهر کنند. سفله بالکسر [illegible] سفینه کشتی و مجموعه نظم و نثر و نام یکی
از صور [illegible] فلکیات. سقرلات [illegible] پشمینه ایست [illegible] سقسین نام ولایتیست [illegible] شمال
سقط [illegible] سقلاب نام ولایتی
ممالک شمالی. سقیفه صفه [illegible] سقیفه بنی ساعده. سگال اندیشه و اندیشیدن. سکاکی [illegible] نام فاضلیست
معروف که [illegible] کرده بود. سکر مستی و باصطلاح صوفیه [illegible] شوق باشد. [illegible]
[illegible] سلاح [illegible] سپاهی و مستعد قتال [illegible] مقدمة الجیش [illegible] نام قلعه ایست

ش ر

س

360r.

در حوالی کوهستان [illegible] که بانی آن دیوی بوده. سلاجل [illegible] شوشتر را هم گویند. سلب
ربودن [illegible] سلسبیل نام نهریست در بهشت. سلطانیه [illegible] سلم بفتحتین
نام درختیست [illegible] سلمی [illegible] محبوبه و نام قبیله ایست از عرب [illegible]
گفت [illegible] خطاب [illegible]
که شعرای عرب در مقام [illegible] سلیم سالم [illegible] سماع خواندن [illegible] سمع بالفتح
قوه سامعه و بالکسر [illegible] سنباده سنگیست که
بدان [illegible] تیز کنند [illegible] سنج [illegible]
[illegible] سنمار بسکون نون [illegible] نام بناییست
رومی که برای نعمان بن المنذر [illegible] قصر [illegible] نعمان [illegible] از بام قصر بزیر انداخته هلاک کرد و از [illegible]
جزای سنمار [illegible] سنین [illegible] سواد [illegible] شهر و سیاهی [illegible]
سواد [illegible] گویند. سودای خام خیال باطل [illegible] سوره بالفتح [illegible]
و بالضم [illegible] نام شهریست [illegible] سوسن [illegible] سوسن آزاد [illegible] کنایه است از [illegible] سوگ
ماتم. سوگوار ماتم زده. سومنات نام بتخانه ایست [illegible] گجرات بوده. سها نام ستاره ایست [illegible]
الشاهد علیه شعر [illegible]
تیر [illegible]
گویند [illegible] سهیل نام ستاره ایست یمانی [illegible]
سیاح [illegible] سیاره [illegible]
سیب. سیحان صاحب برهان قاطع نوشته که رودخانه ایست [illegible] ماوراء النهر [illegible] صاحب کنز اللغه گفته
که نام رودخانه ایست در هندوستان [illegible] مولف گوید که [illegible]
از هندوستان [illegible] سیر و سلوک باصطلاح صوفیه طی مقامات و مراحل تصوف. سیفور [illegible]
بافته [illegible] سیم ناب نقره خالص. سیه تاب آلت فولادی را گویند که بدو زنجیرها ساخته باشند. سیما
علامت [illegible] سیه کار کنایه است از [illegible] سیه گلیم کنایه است از بدبخت و سیه [illegible]
کنایه از فاجر و ظالم [illegible] شادروان [illegible] پیش ایوان ملوک کشند [illegible]
[illegible] شارع راه واضح [illegible] شارک پرنده ایست سیاه [illegible] مانند طوطی سخن
کند. شاغل صاحب شغل. شافی دوائی [illegible] شافعی [illegible] مذاهب اربعه
شامت نحوست. شاه جوگی [illegible]
میرزا [illegible] که آنرا شاه جوگی گویند [illegible]
این شعر [illegible] شعر [illegible]
تو [illegible] شاه جوگی [illegible] شاهد [illegible] معشوق [illegible] کنایه است [illegible]

ش

ضایع روزگار 1.22

360v.

و دو رقیبان شاهراه ... شابه ... خالص شباب جوانی شبان چوپان ... شب
نام یکنوع جامه ایست شبپر ... شبدیز نام اسب خسرو پرویز شبرنگ نام اسب سیاوخش و نام ...
زنان مایل بزردی و نام سنگی است سیاه که آنرا شبه گویند شبلی نام زاهد معروف شبنم یکنوع نازک ایست ...
و نیز شبه ایست که شبها بر روی سبزه نشیند چنانکه ... گوید شعر ...
گر تو شاه شبنم ... شتا زمستانی شتر بعضی ... قماد ... شحنه
امیر بلد ... شحنه ... عنبر ... امیر المؤمنین علیه السلام ... شد بالفتح ...
ابتدای نغمه و آهنگ باشد ... آنچه ... ابریشم ... آویزند شراک بند نعلین
شرب نوشیدن و کنایه است از شراب ... شربتی ... لطیف چنانکه ... القلوب
در فکر ... کنایه ... باشد شرزه خشمناک
و صاحب قوة ... شرق مشرق و آفتاب ... شرجی ... شست دام صیادی و ... و انگشت ابهام ...
شاز و تاری ... ششمان بضم اول ... نقاشان ... نقشها
زنند چنانکه ... گوید شعر ... ششقان ... چشم
از ... گوید شعر ... شستر یکنوع آلتی از
آهنین ... شفا بالکسر ... زرین ...
کتاب الشفا ... شعبده ... گویند ... شعب ... شغناک ...
شق ... شکافته ... هرچیزی
هرچیزی هر گاه شکافته شود و بالمجاز ... گویند ... باشد
شکال بند ... شکر ... شکرف ...
و حشم شکیب صبر ... شکیل ... شتم ... شمال دست چپ و نسیم
شمایل ... شم ... و ایستاده ...
خطا ... و شاهد ...
نیم ... گوید شعر ... نخبه ... اول ... شمع ...
شمع خاوری کنایه است از آفتاب و محبوب شمع طراز کنایه از محبوب شمسه ... آفتاب ... شمط
بعضی ... شموس بالفتح ... و بالضم جمع شمس ... آفتاب ... شمیا
مخفف شامیانه باشد ... شمیم بوی ... شنعت ... شنگ شوخ و ظریف و شیرین حرکات ...
باشد ... شنیع ... شو ... آمیختن ... جامه ...
نکوشه ... شوخ ... شوخابه آب چشم ... نخجیر ...
بسته شود ... واشباه آن ... بالنزع ... شهرزاد پادشاه ... شهر ... شهمار
نام مقامیست در موسیقی شنیاد ... گفتار ... آن ...

361r.

از ... الغذا ... شود ... الشاه ... شعر
... گوید شعر ...
... الشاه ...
... بالفتح ... شید بالفتح ...
... روشن و نام ... شیفته مفتون ... شیمه ... شین ...
... صاعقه برق ... صبا باد ... صباغ ...
از ... صبوح ... صبیح ... چنانکه ... گوید
شعر ... صراحی ... شعر ...
چشم ... صرصر ...
... صرف بالکسر ... صفر ...
... گوید شعر ...
... صلا ... باشد
صلابه ... صوامع ... صومعه ...
... صورت ...
... چنانکه ... گوید شعر ...
یکنوع ... صنوبر نام درختیست معروف ... صهبا شراب
صهیب بالضم ... صیرفی ...
گویند ... ضیافت ... گوید شعر ...
... چنانکه ...
کنایه است ... طاق ...
طارم ... طاس ...
از آسمان طارم ... طاق ... چنانکه
گوید شعر ... طالع ...
یکنوع ... طبع ... کنایه است ...
... طبیب ... طرب ...
طراز نام شهریست ... ولایت ...
... طره ...
نام ولایتیست ... طرف ...
بالطرف ... طرفه ...

361 v.

عجب الفزا العین بالفتح یعنی چشم [illegible] تلمن مزید جنک ونیز طمرا آنچه عنوان فرمان پادشاهان نویسند خخیل
نام شخصی [illegible] که تا خوانند [illegible] شیخ والجلیل کویند طلاییه [illegible] لشکر لمنان [illegible]
[illegible] طوبی نام درختی است در بهشت و بمعنی خوش حال باشد طوب [illegible] طوبی و نوبت [illegible] کردند
چنانکه کوید شعر [illegible] با لیلی و مجنون [illegible] جستن و سر هم
استعمال کنند طومار کنایه است از کریه [illegible] باشد چنانکه در لیلی مجنون
مرد و کوید شعر [illegible] لیلب بالکسر [illegible] خوشبوی
نام [illegible] و خوشطبعی [illegible] حرف لغا
ظرافت خوشطبعی [illegible] انسان [illegible] حروف العین
کنند عاج استخوان پیل [illegible] عالم صغری [illegible] عالم کبری جهان عامه [illegible]
آنچه [illegible] مشهور [illegible] موسیقی [illegible]
سبب تعجب شود عجوز [illegible] و آسمان و آفتاب [illegible] و ولایت [illegible]
و شتر و روباه [illegible] و کشتی [illegible]
[illegible] آفتاب [illegible]
[illegible] و [illegible] و طریق [illegible]
[illegible] نام ولایتی است در ساحل بحرین [illegible] شبیه و نظیر عراق [illegible]
[illegible] معروف [illegible] موسیقی [illegible]
عزازیل شیطان عزیمت آهنک [illegible] عس [illegible]
عشر بالفتح ده [illegible] عشق [illegible] عشقه باشد [illegible]
[illegible] شعر [illegible] عشیات [illegible]
عفریت دیو عفن [illegible] عقبه [illegible] عقل کل [illegible]
و [illegible] علیه و آله [illegible] عقل [illegible] کنایه است [illegible]
[illegible] چنانکه کوید شعر [illegible] دیوانه [illegible]
[illegible] کوید شعر [illegible]
[illegible] باشد [illegible]
[illegible] عمل و [illegible]
عناصر خاک و باد و آب و آتش [illegible] اصل آن [illegible]
[illegible]
[illegible] عنوان ابتدا [illegible] عوان متوسط [illegible] عود [illegible]
معروف [illegible] خواهند [illegible] نام [illegible] چشم [illegible]

362 r.

عین زر و چشم و چشمه و آفتاب و [illegible] حقیقت و [illegible] [illegible] غاب بیشه
[illegible] [illegible] [illegible] غضب کشتی
و نام [illegible] غدوات [illegible] غرام [illegible]
شدید و عشق [illegible] تاوان غرش [illegible] چنانکه کوید شعر [illegible]
[illegible] چنانکه حکیم اسدی کفته
شعر [illegible]
[illegible] باشد [illegible]
غریدن [illegible] کتاب [illegible]
هر چیز [illegible] غزال آهو [illegible] آهو [illegible]
غزالی [illegible] باشد غزو جهاد کردن [illegible]
[illegible] هندوستان [illegible] بعضی [illegible]
و حضرت [illegible] چنانکه شاعر [illegible]
غش بیهوشی و بیهوش شدن [illegible] غلغل آواز [illegible] غلو [illegible]
[illegible] چنانکه کوید شعر [illegible]
[illegible] غنا [illegible]
[illegible] غنج بالفتح کرشمه کردن [illegible] غود [illegible]
[illegible] فال [illegible]
[illegible] چنانکه
کوید شعر [illegible] فانوس [illegible]
[illegible] فراش بالفتح [illegible]
[illegible] فراغ [illegible]
[illegible] فرجه بالضم [illegible] فرخ [illegible]
[illegible] فرزانه [illegible]
[illegible] دوات [illegible]
[illegible] فرهنک [illegible] فرس [illegible]
[illegible] کویند فریق کروه فش [illegible]
جامه [illegible] فص [illegible]
[illegible] فضیل برمکی [illegible] چنانکه کوید شعر
[illegible] فضیل [illegible]

362v.

ق

پادشاهان چین را گویند قنطر معرب قنطره یعنی جسر چنانکه گوید شعر [illegible] نوای عشقنی [illegible]
اول شعر [illegible] ششم نقطه ... باشد و قطعا [illegible] شده [illegible]
مجروح [illegible] جمع قلم [illegible] و نام کتابیست چنانکه گوید شعر نوای [illegible] باب و فا [illegible] کو ضوء [illegible]
کو خصوص [illegible] قلاچ [illegible] قلماسنک و آن معروفست قلزات معدنیات [illegible] قلق [illegible] قلوری نام [illegible]
در مجلس شعر [illegible] قولابولسون قلوری [illegible] اولسون قله [illegible]
که از حیوانات قانون [illegible] را گویند [illegible] علم موسیقی قوله [illegible] قهرست تفصیل فصول
و ابواب کتاب که در ابتدا تالیف [illegible] کتاب [illegible] قاف [illegible] کنایه از آسمان [illegible]
آسمانی فیلسوف استاد یگانه فیلقوس بر وزن [illegible] نام پادشاه روم [illegible] قادر انداز
کسی را گویند که در انداختن تیر [illegible] باشد [illegible] قارن نام سرهنگی [illegible]
معلم فرهاد بوده و نیز نام پهلوانیست معروف قارون نام شخصی [illegible] علیه السلام [illegible] و نام دولتی
آنرا اوج گویند قاروره شیشه [illegible] قال [illegible]
انداخته خانها [illegible] قافیه در علم عروض [illegible] قالب [illegible]
قالب خشت و گلوله و امثال آن [illegible] قامت [illegible] قد [illegible]
باشد چنانکه در لیلی مجنون [illegible] کتاب گوید شعر [illegible] قاید پیشوا و دلیل [illegible]
نام پادشاهیست معروف [illegible] قدرانداز یعنی انداز [illegible] تیرانداز [illegible]
انداز هم گویند چنانکه [illegible] فرشتگان قرابه [illegible] چنانکه نظامی گفته شعر [illegible]
شکسته بسنگ قرابه را [illegible] تسبیح [illegible] با اصطلاح [illegible]
ساخته میشود [illegible] قرص [illegible]
[illegible] قرص [illegible] قرص آفتاب [illegible] قرص کافور [illegible]
کمان برای [illegible] ترتیب [illegible] اعظم آن [illegible] قرطاس [illegible]
شعر [illegible] قرن مدت سی سال و شاخ حیوانات [illegible]
گویند [illegible] جمع قرحه [illegible] قسام قسمت کننده قسم [illegible] قصاب معروفست [illegible]
[illegible] قصب [illegible] قطار بالکسر جمع قطر [illegible]
[illegible] قفس [illegible] قطر [illegible]
[illegible] خوشبو [illegible] قطیف نام [illegible] قفس [illegible]
[illegible] قفل [illegible]
چنانکه [illegible] قلاب بالفتح قلب کننده
و بالضم [illegible] قلاش [illegible] قلب [illegible]
[illegible] قلتبان [illegible] قلزم نام دریای [illegible] قله کوه قمص [illegible] قندیل شیشه

کهواده

363r.

ک

که در آن [illegible] قوا [illegible] قواس کمانگر قوس قزح [illegible]
[illegible] قیرمان [illegible] قیصر [illegible]
قیروان [illegible]
معروف [illegible] کاخ [illegible]
[illegible] کاسه [illegible] کاریز [illegible]
نام کلی [illegible] چنانکه [illegible] گوید شعر [illegible] کاسه [illegible]
[illegible] کاشکی [illegible] کاشی منسوب [illegible] گویند [illegible]
[illegible] کاشی [illegible] کاشان [illegible]
کالا [illegible] کام خواهش و تمنا کاو [illegible] کاوش [illegible]
[illegible] کبر [illegible] کبوتر [illegible]
[illegible] کت [illegible] تخت [illegible] خواب کنند [illegible]
خوانند کتابه نوشتن [illegible] کتاره تیغ هندی [illegible]
[illegible] کتم [illegible] کتان [illegible] کتون [illegible]
گویند چنانکه گوید شعر [illegible] کثافت ضد لطافت [illegible]
[illegible] کحل [illegible] کحل [illegible]
[illegible] کد [illegible]
[illegible] کرامت [illegible] کرام جمع کریم [illegible]
[illegible] گوید شعر [illegible]
[illegible] کرخ [illegible]
و آن [illegible] چنانکه گوید شعر [illegible]
[illegible] باشد کرک [illegible] چنانکه [illegible] گوید شعر [illegible]
[illegible] کروی یعنی شکل کره [illegible] چنانکه گوید شعر [illegible]
[illegible] کریاس [illegible]
[illegible] کسری لقب نوشیروان [illegible] کسروی منسوب بکسری کسوف گرفتن آفتاب [illegible]
[illegible] کش [illegible]
[illegible] کشاف [illegible] کشف [illegible]
[illegible] کعبتین [illegible]
[illegible] کفچه [illegible]

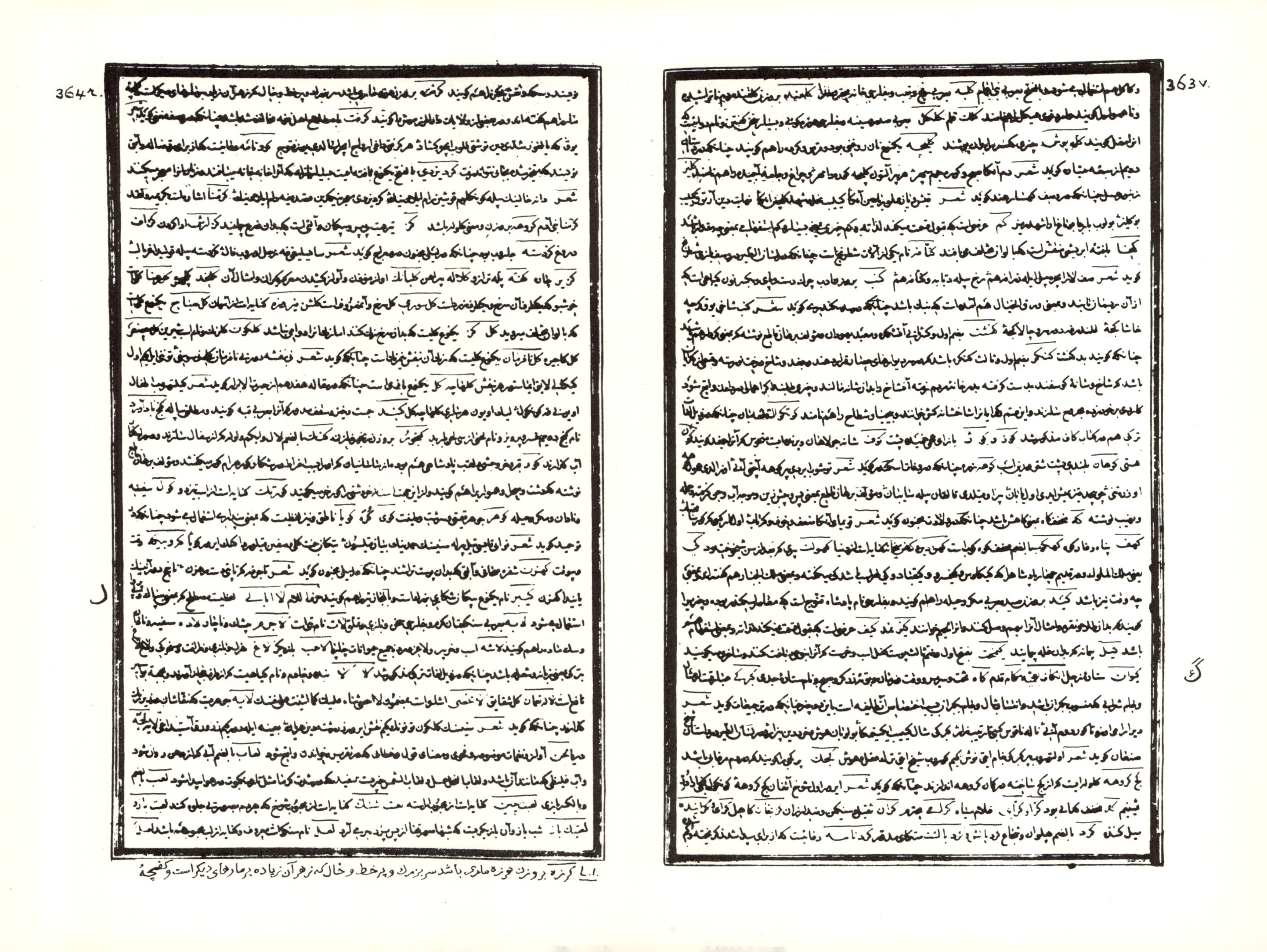

گ

ل

لغا گرزه بروزن حوزه ماری باشد سر بزرگ و پرخط و خال که زهر آن زیاده بر مارهای دیگر است و کفچه

[illegible] لعل سیراب [illegible] کنایه است از لب محبوب لعل رمانی یکنوع لعل است که [illegible]
[illegible] کنایه است [illegible] لطیفه [illegible] الطاف بمعنی جامع باشد که [illegible] عبارت
[illegible] جمع لطیفه بود لفائف [illegible] لکن شمعدان و طشت کوچک که در آن دست شویند
لمعه [illegible] لوث [illegible] لوح بالفتح صفحه و تخته چوب و استخوان نوشته شدن و درخشیدن و
شدن [illegible] و بالضم شدت [illegible] لوحه بالفتح تام پرنده ایست بر [illegible]
شبیه [illegible] چنانکه [illegible] گوید شعر [illegible] زیبای
[illegible] باشد لوخ [illegible]
[illegible] و منسوب به [illegible]
باشد [illegible] لیف
[illegible]
[illegible] مات [illegible] مغلوب شدن [illegible]
ماش [illegible] شعر [illegible]
[illegible] ماغ
[illegible] جسم [illegible]
[illegible] هشت
[illegible] ماغ [illegible]
[illegible] مالک [illegible]
[illegible] ماوی
[illegible] شعر [illegible]
[illegible] کنعان [illegible] یوسف علیه السلام
[illegible] آبخوشکوار [illegible]
[illegible]
[illegible] آنرا [illegible]
هم گویند [illegible] میوه دهنده [illegible] مجاز [illegible] حقیقت آنرا باشد و بالمجاز ضد حقیقت بود
مجال [illegible] دیوانگان مجدول [illegible] مجذوب باصطلاح صوفیه گویا [illegible] جذبه عشق حقیقی
[illegible] باشد مجرور کشیده شده و باصطلاح [illegible] آتشدان [illegible] مجنن دیوانه کننده
مجوز [illegible] تجویز کرده شده [illegible] محارب حرب کننده محاسن نیکوئیها [illegible]
[illegible] حکایت کردن [illegible] بفتح اول [illegible] حیله کردن [illegible]
[illegible] گویند محرق سوخته شده [illegible] نوشته شده

۱.۱ جان پرور و لعل سیراب و لعل گوهریار کنایه است از لب محبوب لعل رمانی

[illegible] محرق سوزاننده محروق سوخته شده [illegible] جمع [illegible]
[illegible] و آسیا [illegible] که بآن [illegible]
[illegible] باشد [illegible] بالفتح [illegible] مخلوط آمیخته [illegible]
[illegible] شراب [illegible] بالفتح
[illegible] شعر [illegible]
[illegible] نام [illegible]
[illegible] چنانکه [illegible] گوید شعر [illegible]
[illegible]
کننده [illegible] مدیح مدح [illegible] و ستایش [illegible] گویند
[illegible] بالفتح [illegible]
[illegible] و بالضم [illegible] و نام [illegible]
[illegible] مرحبا لفظیست [illegible] و تحسین گفته شود [illegible]
[illegible]
[illegible] پرستان [illegible]
[illegible]
[illegible] نام [illegible] چنانکه گوید شعر [illegible]
[illegible]
[illegible] گویند مرق [illegible] مرقع [illegible]
گویند [illegible] نام ولایتیست [illegible] خراسان [illegible]
[illegible] طعام [illegible] زعفران آمیخته [illegible]
و نام کتابیست [illegible]
[illegible] مستدل [illegible]
[illegible] مستغرق [illegible]
[illegible] مسقوط [illegible] مسلوک [illegible]
[illegible] مسموم زهرناک [illegible] بالفتح جمع [illegible] کننده
[illegible] و نام [illegible] مشرب [illegible]
آشنا باشد [illegible] مشرف [illegible] بالفتح [illegible]
[illegible] مشکوة [illegible] و نام کتابیست مشموم [illegible] و نام شهریست معروف
از ولایت [illegible] مصاف بالفتح [illegible] و بالضم

۱.۱ آزاد شده محرق سوزاننده محروق سوخته شده محسوس دریافته شده محفل مجمع محلول
حل شده محن جمع محنت محور ۱.۲ تیرچرخ ۱.۳ باریکتر از جانب پایانی باشد

صفالاهل مصابیح [illegible] مجنفا حق [illegible] حضرت رسول صلی الله علیه وآله [illegible] امیر [illegible]
شمع مصقل بالکما آلت [illegible] مضاف افزوده شده منجنیق [illegible] آمده مضراب آلتی که بدان [illegible]
منجلا بیت شد مضمر پنهان شده مضیق تنگ [illegible] طبقه طبقه و هر که گم شده و نوعی از بافته ابریشمی [illegible]
مطبوع مقبول مطری تازه شده و [illegible] معطر از [illegible] پریشان شده چنانکه گوید شعر [illegible]
[illegible] مشکل [illegible] مطرا و آن مقبول طبع [illegible] لغات و اصل آن [illegible]
[illegible] حروف [illegible] قلب بنا [illegible] چنانکه [illegible] دست [illegible] گفته [illegible]
معترض [illegible] مانند [illegible] که از [illegible] برآمده [illegible] گویند [illegible]
[illegible] نامه [illegible] مطلع [illegible] گوشه نشین منصب [illegible]
مقنعه [illegible] اندازند [illegible] معدل [illegible] آماده [illegible] دایره [illegible]
که چون آفتاب محاذات آن دایره [illegible] شب [illegible] شود [illegible] معطوف بازگردانیده شده معلوم معلومست
و باصطلاح صوفیه [illegible] مفتاح کلید و نام
کتابیست در علم معانی بیان مفتش تفتیش کننده مفتون شیفته [illegible] از [illegible]
[illegible] مقالات [illegible] باصطلاحات صوفیه مراحل سیر و سلوک و باصطلاح [illegible]
نغمه نواهای موسیقی [illegible] قطعه [illegible] نون مقنعه که زنان بر سر اندازند و [illegible]
نون بر وزن [illegible] چنانکه [illegible] مقنع گویند [illegible] شکل کمان [illegible]
مقتی [illegible] پنهان شده [illegible] شده [illegible] محل [illegible] مکمن محل اختفا
[illegible] از [illegible] مکان گرفته و استوار [illegible] صاحب منزلت باشد [illegible]
[illegible] ملاحظه [illegible] کننده [illegible]
[illegible] چنانکه گوید شعر [illegible]
[illegible] صورت [illegible]
[illegible] ملتمس [illegible] بیمار شود [illegible] نام
[illegible] منبع محل برآمدن آب منجمد افسرده [illegible]
منجنیق آلتیست که بدان سنگ [illegible] قلعه اندازند [illegible]
[illegible] موافق [illegible] قانونیه [illegible]
[illegible] منطقة البروج گویند منعقد بسته شده [illegible]
[illegible] چنانکه گوید شعر [illegible]
[illegible] شیشه [illegible] شعله [illegible] منقل [illegible] منقله [illegible] نوشته [illegible]
و حکایت باشد منکسف آفتاب گرفته شده [illegible] منوم خواب آورنده [illegible]
[illegible] موازی مساوی و برابر [illegible] معادن و نبات و حیوان [illegible]

۶. گفته اند کما فی قوله تعالی

[illegible] پستان [illegible] والست [illegible]
[illegible] گوید که [illegible] شبیه [illegible]
[illegible]
[illegible] آن [illegible] باشد [illegible]
[illegible] چنانکه [illegible]
[illegible] موسیقار [illegible] معروف [illegible]
[illegible] و از آن [illegible]
[illegible] باشد [illegible]
چنانکه [illegible] پیچ [illegible]
[illegible]
[illegible] که [illegible]
[illegible] گویند [illegible]
[illegible] کشتی [illegible]
[illegible] گویند [illegible]
[illegible] چنانکه گوید شعر [illegible]
[illegible] باشد [illegible]
[illegible] آبگینه شیشه الوان [illegible]
[illegible] پیدا آید [illegible]
[illegible] شیشه [illegible]
[illegible]
[illegible] ناکام [illegible]
[illegible]
[illegible] صاحب [illegible]
[illegible]
[illegible] گویند [illegible]
[illegible] گویند [illegible]
[illegible] گویند [illegible]
[illegible] شعر [illegible]

۱. کوچک که در اطراف اردو بجهت محارست ۳. و بعضی گویند ۴. که سعوه است
۵. موشک تیر تحش بود

366v.

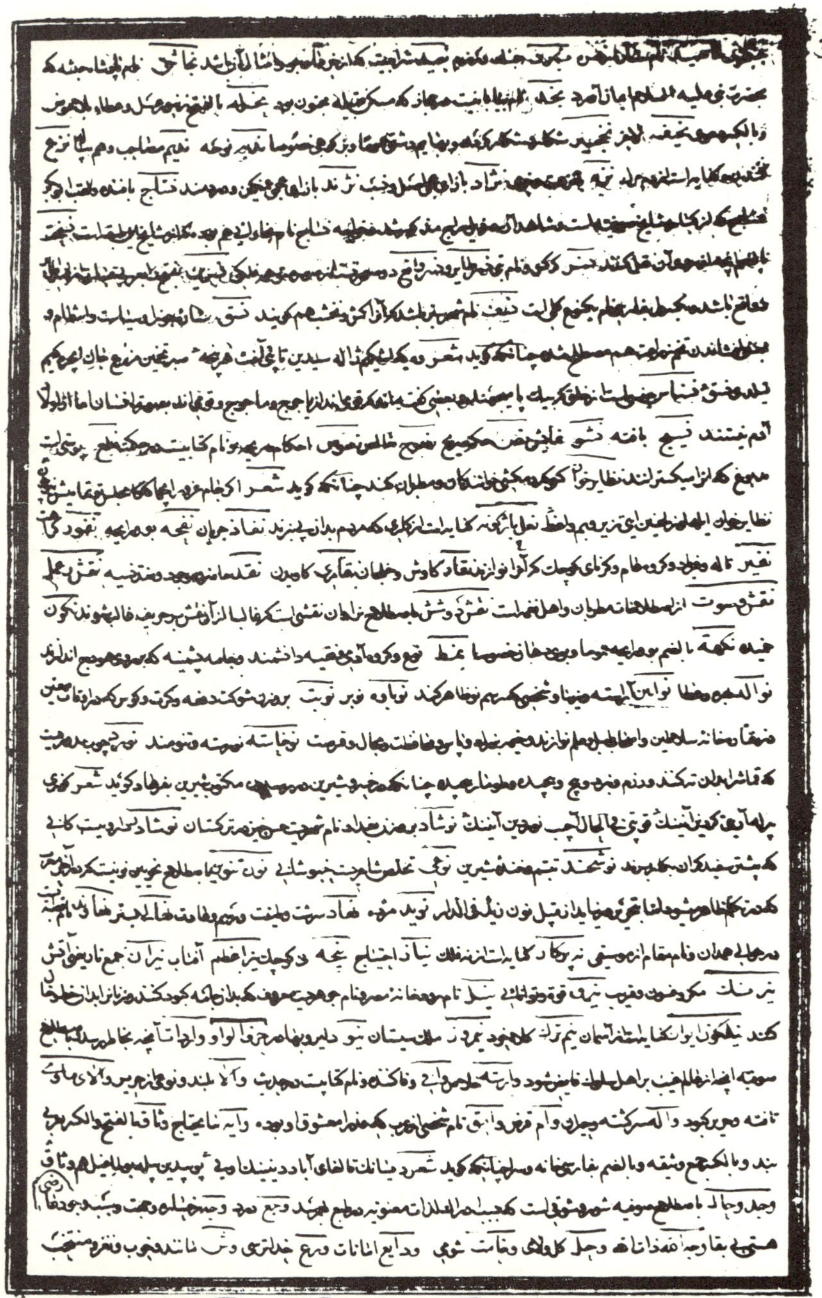

[illegible]

۱.۱ جنگجوی ناهید نام ستاره زهره نبرد جنگ و رزم نبید ۱.۴ نزه با نزهت و خرمی

۱.۵ نساج که از کبار مشایخ صوفیه است و شاهد آن در ذیل سراج

367r

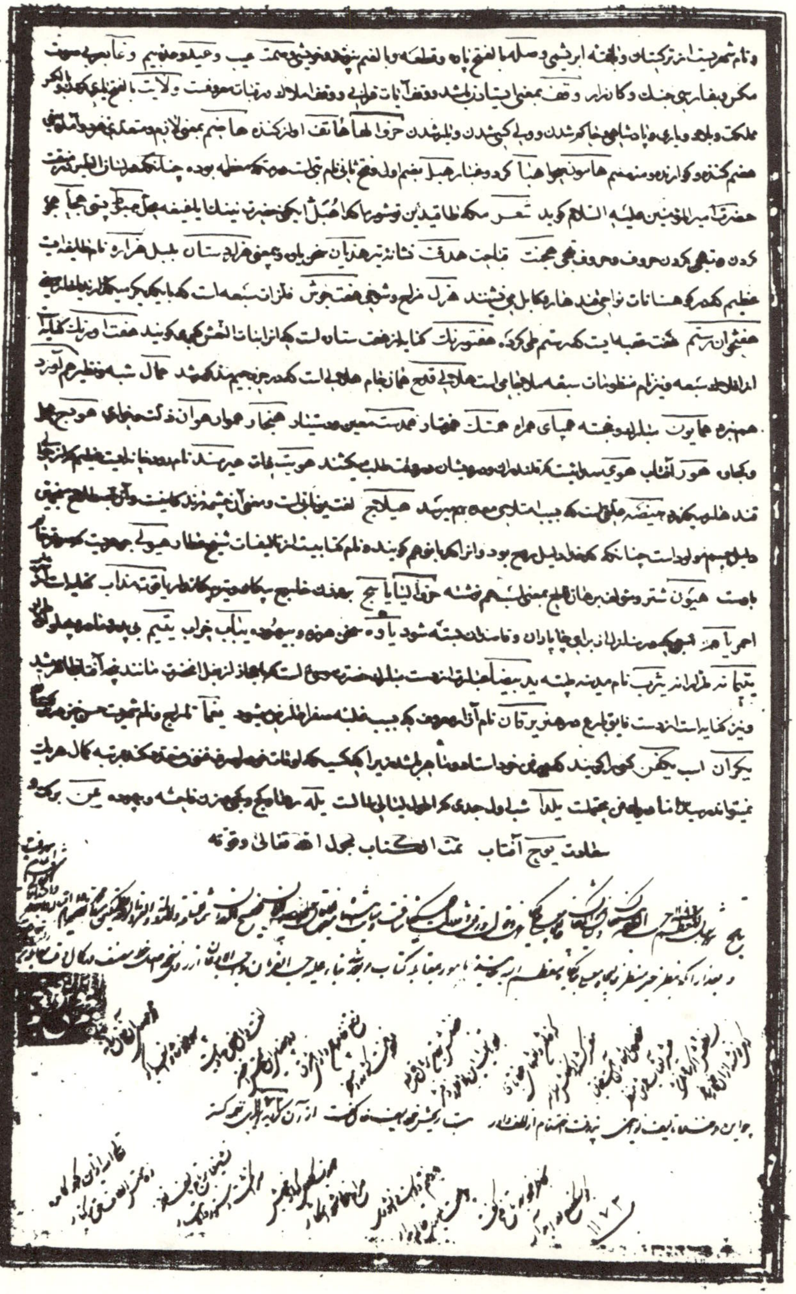

[illegible]

خلعت بوج آفتاب تمت الکتاب بحمد الله تعالی و توفیقه

[illegible]